# Reviewer's Guide for

# Addison-Wesley Mathematics

## Book 6

The large numbers — 1, 2 for example — identify eight of the major features of Addison-Wesley Mathematics. Turn to the pages listed below each number to make reviewing easy.

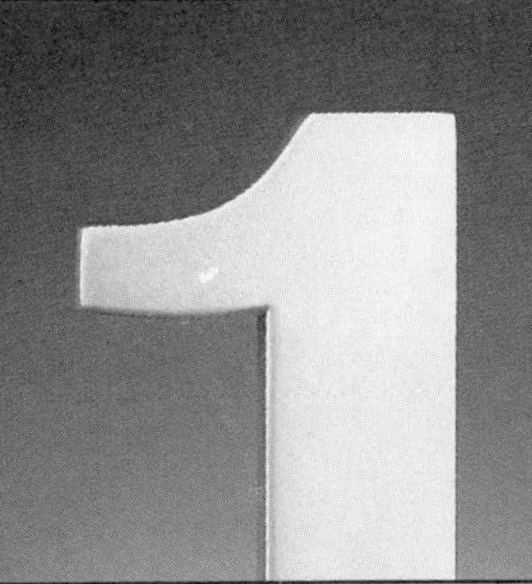

**Traditional mathematics applied to the challenges of today**

See pages:
T4-T5
137
104-105

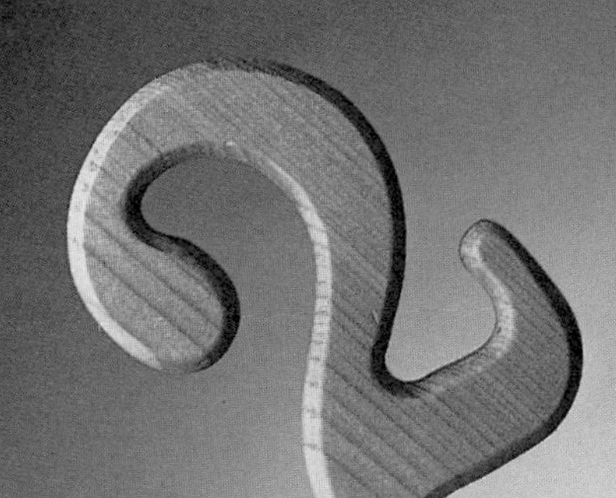

**Solid skills development with measurable results**

See pages:
T6-T7 140-141
58-59 158-159

**Problem solving for the decision-makers of the future**

See pages:
T8-T9 100
8-9 314
35

**Daily teaching support when you need it**

See pages:
T10-T11 120-121
62-63 154-155

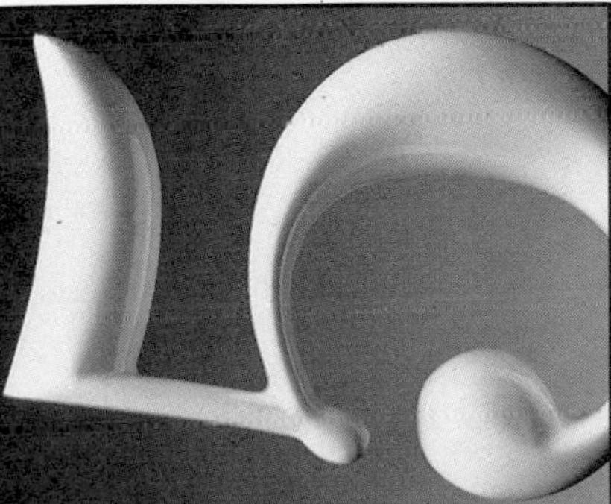

**Resources to meet the challenge of every classroom**

See pages:
T12-T13 277A
53B-53C 426-427

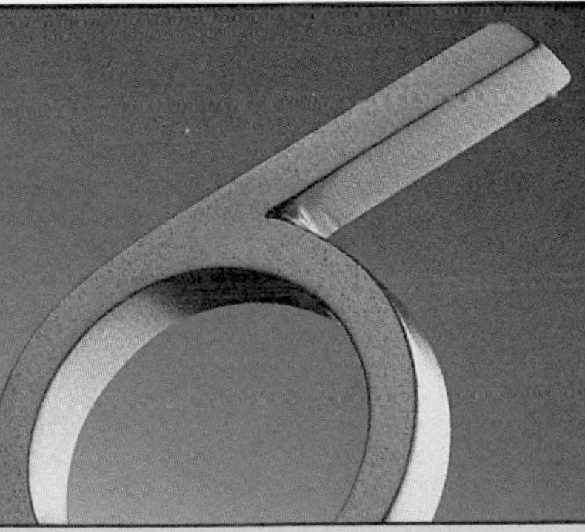

**Planning and assessment for simplified management**

See pages:
T14-T15
133-136

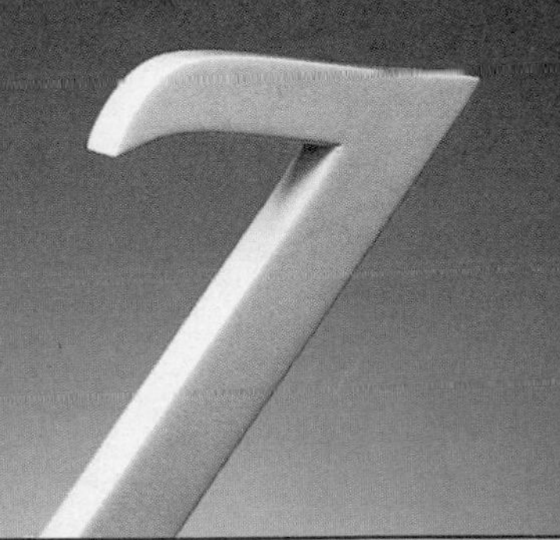

**A flexible teaching package that promotes success**

See pages:
T16-T17
225D-225E

**A team of math professionals you can trust**

See pages:
T18-T19

# Addison-Wesley Mathematics K-8 Components

Each one unique and totally integrated
into a complete program

Student Books
Teacher's Editions
Teacher's Resource Books
Practice, Reteaching, Enrichment
- Workbooks
- Duplicator Masters
- Blackline Masters

Cumulative Record Cards K-8
Kindergarten Big Book
Manipulative Kits
Computer Management System
Instructional Software
Answer Booklets
Spanish Editions

and the Addison-Wesley family
of fine mathematics supplements
and teaching source books.


ISBN 0-201-24602-3 DEFGHIJKL-VH-8987654

# Addison-Wesley Mathematics

# Teacher's Edition Book 6

**Robert E. Eicholz** **Phares G. O'Daffer** **Charles R. Fleenor**

Randall I. Charles Sharon Young Carne S. Barnett

## Contents

Addison-Wesley Publishing Company

Menlo Park, California Reading, Massachusetts London Amsterdam Don Mills, Ontario Sydney

# Traditional mathematics . . .

Solid math principles remain the core of professional mathematics instruction. Addison-Wesley puts these basic principles in a format that is clear and easy to follow. But we also recognize that students must go

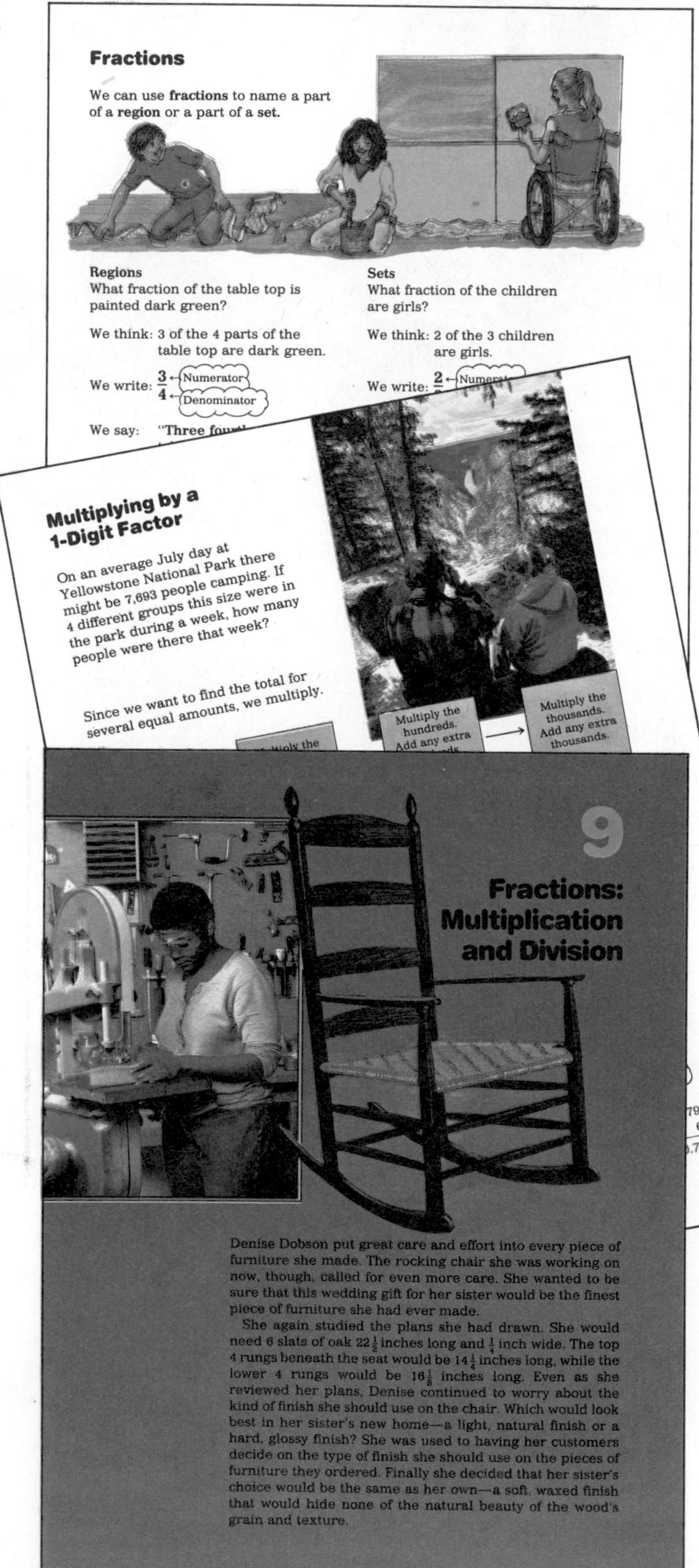

**Fractions**

We can use **fractions** to name a part of a **region** or a part of a **set.**

**Regions**
What fraction of the table top is painted dark green?

We think: 3 of the 4 parts of the table top are dark green.

We write: $\frac{3}{4}$ ←Numerator ←Denominator

We say: "Three fou

**Sets**
What fraction of the children are girls?

We think: 2 of the 3 children are girls.

We write: 2 ←Numera

**Multiplying by a 1-Digit Factor**

On an average July day at Yellowstone National Park there might be 7,693 people camping. If 4 different groups this size were in the park during a week, how many people were there that week?

Since we want to find the total for several equal amounts, we multiply.

Multiply the hundreds. Add any extra

Multiply the thousands. Add any extra thousands.

**9**

**Fractions: Multiplication and Division**

Denise Dobson put great care and effort into every piece of furniture she made. The rocking chair she was working on now, though, called for even more care. She wanted to be sure that this wedding gift for her sister would be the finest piece of furniture she had ever made.

She again studied the plans she had drawn. She would need 6 slats of oak $22\frac{1}{2}$ inches long and $\frac{1}{4}$ inch wide. The top 4 rungs beneath the seat would be $14\frac{1}{4}$ inches long, while the lower 4 rungs would be $16\frac{1}{8}$ inches long. Even as she reviewed her plans, Denise continued to worry about the kind of finish she should use on the chair. Which would look best in her sister's new home—a light, natural finish or a hard, glossy finish? She was used to having her customers decide on the type of finish she should use on the pieces of furniture they ordered. Finally she decided that her sister's choice would be the same as her own—a soft, waxed finish that would hide none of the natural beauty of the wood's grain and texture.

## Program Overview

The major reason for studying mathematics is to learn how to solve problems. To become effective problem solvers students need to understand *concepts,* know *basic facts,* efficiently use *computational skills,* and select and apply appropriate *problem-solving strategies.* To implement this philosophy Addison-Wesley Mathematics provides a balanced program in each of these areas.

### Understanding Concepts

To ensure real understanding of mathematical concepts, teachers are encouraged to use manipulative materials or pictorial models with students whenever appropriate. Understanding of concepts is emphasized through a variety of problem-solving experiences.

### Learning Skills

To develop a solid foundation in basic facts and skills students follow an instructional sequence of (1) involvement with *models,* (2) understanding the *fact* or *procedure,* (3) extensive *practice,* and (4) *application* of the skill to problem-solving situations. Mental mathematics and estimation skills are carefully developed and sequenced.

### Solving Problems

In Addison-Wesley Mathematics, problem solving is realistic. Students have opportunities to collect data from many different sources and to solve a wide variety of problems. Inherent in the Addison-Wesley Mathematics philosophy is the belief that a student's attitude toward problem solving is extremely important. By choosing problems which come from the real world, by providing understandable techniques for solving problems, and by encouraging students to share their problem solutions with others, positive attitudes are developed and success in problem solving is ensured.

# . . . applied to the challenges of today

*beyond* basic skills in order to solve problems in a complex, technological era. It's the successful combination of the traditional and the modern that makes Addison-Wesley *the* math text for today.

**What reviewers and users say about Addison–Wesley Mathematics.**

- **A complete program**—a balanced development of concepts, facts, computational skills, and problem solving. It is well sequenced. The pace through topics is unhurried, yet all the content is covered.
- **A helpful program**—exceptional opportunities for review and reteaching based on student needs. It provides real help in teaching problem solving. The teachable approach to facts and skills makes learning easy for students.
- **A natural program**—the art and photographs are humanized and interesting to students. Applied problems allow students to make decisions in natural, everyday settings. Problem themes are related to careers and integrated with other subject areas. Students are encouraged to become actively involved with physical models.
- **A sensible program**—solid mathematics for today's needs and for the future. Addison–Wesley Mathematics includes a technology strand, with ample opportunities for students to learn about and use calculators and computers. Calculator exercises are interspersed throughout the program. The development of computer literacy begins with readiness lessons in flowcharting and builds to actual programming in BASIC and logo languages.

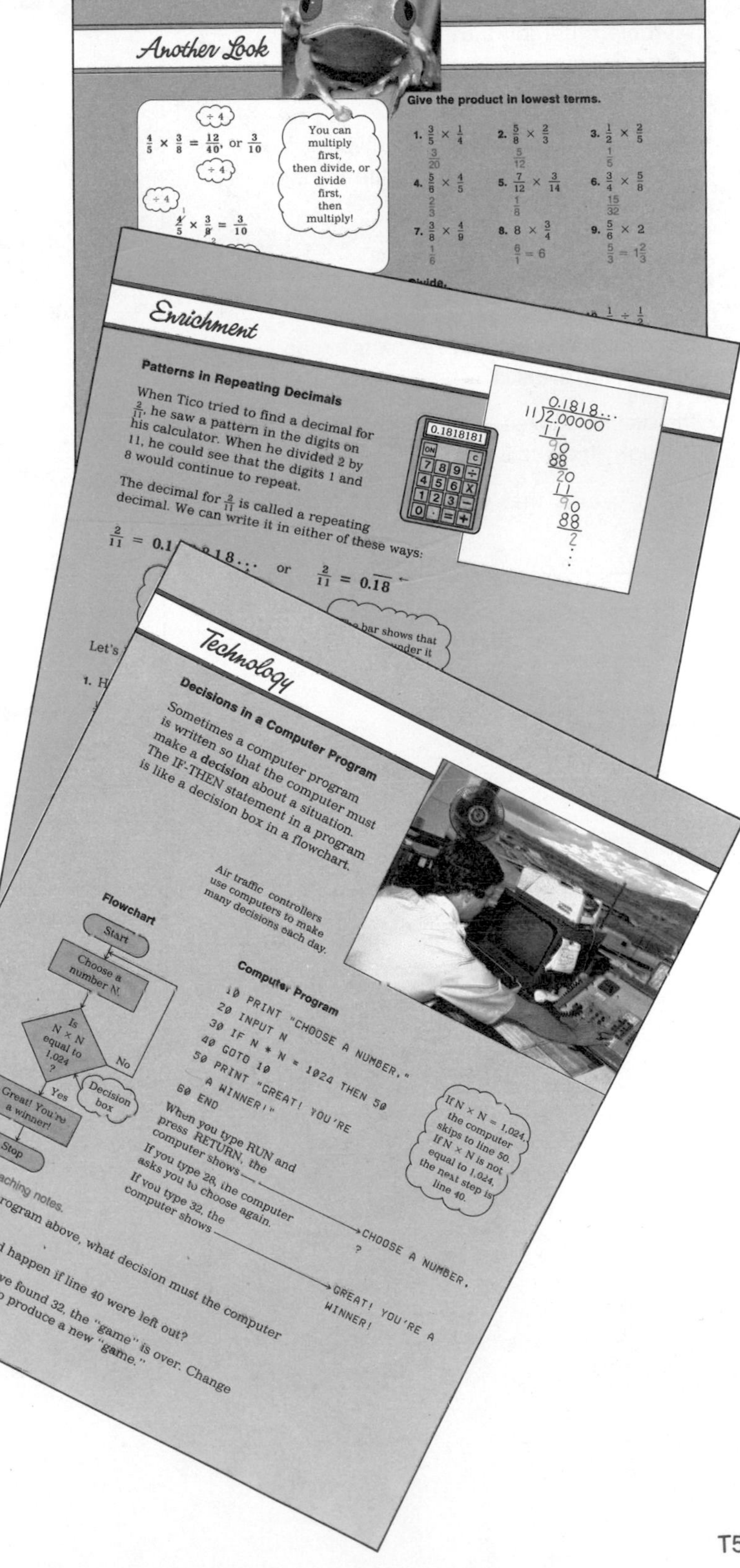

# Solid skills development . . .

Through the years, Addison–Wesley has continued to refine its presentation of basic math skills. This new program provides a clear, consistent format for teaching the skills that effectively build your students'

## Motivation

- A problem that sets the theme for the lesson and provides a real-life application of the skill to be taught
- Appealing illustrations that involve students' imaginations and bring life and lightness to the page

## Development

- Concept statement that suggests a reason for learning the skill
- Instruction boxes that guide students through algorithms
- Think clouds that verbalize the thought process
- Functional color that clarifies development

## Examples

Variations of the skill that cover special cases

## Diagnosis

An **informal assessment** that enables the teacher to evaluate students' grasp of the skill before assigning the exercises

### Subtracting Whole Numbers

A recent record for distance traveled in a large hot-air balloon was 611 km. The record for a small hot-air balloon was 369 km. How much farther did the large balloon travel?

Since we want to compare the distances, we subtract.

Subtract the ones. Trade if necessary. → Subtract the tens. Trade if necessary. → Subtract the hundreds.

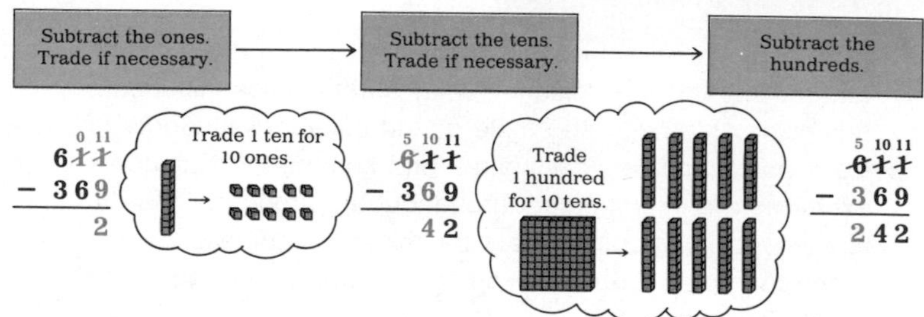


$\begin{array}{r} 611 \\ -\ 369 \\ \hline 2 \end{array}$ $\begin{array}{r} 611 \\ -\ 369 \\ \hline 42 \end{array}$ $\begin{array}{r} 611 \\ -\ 369 \\ \hline 242 \end{array}$

The large balloon traveled 242 km farther.

**Other Examples**

$\begin{array}{r} 835 \\ -\ 796 \\ \hline 39 \end{array}$ $\begin{array}{r} 6{,}421 \\ -\ 975 \\ \hline 5{,}446 \end{array}$ $\begin{array}{r} 75{,}364 \\ -\ 34{,}780 \\ \hline 40{,}584 \end{array}$ $\begin{array}{r} \$63.25 \\ -\ 24.69 \\ \hline \$38.56 \end{array}$

To subtract money, subtract as with whole numbers. Then write the answer as dollars and cents.

**Warm Up** Subtract. Check by adding.

1. 847 − 269
2. 653 − 576
3. 8,637 − 789
4. 83,216 − 29,457
5. $37.75 − 19.98

40

proficiency *and* understanding. And, at all levels, motivating illustrations actively involve your students in the learning process.

Subtract.

1. 527 − 188
2. 963 − 879
3. 7,432 − 865
4. 8,276 − 5,498
5. 6,213 − 5,654
6. 4,136 − 1,874
7. 7,238 − 6,450
8. 16,342 − 9,237
9. 27,641 − 19,506
10. 56,375 − 37,588
11. 87,465 − 59,387
12. 93,274 − 8,680
13. $9.75 − 3.98
14. $18.25 − 7.56
15. $256.45 − 97.75

16. 742 − 578
17. 9,534 − 806
18. 7,316 − 4,857
19. 17,386 − 9,419
20. 78,211 − 65,879
21. $56.32 − $38.49

22. Estimate, then find the difference of 7,219 and 3,899.

23. Estimate, then find how many more 925 is than 478.

24. The record altitude (height above sea level) for an AX-2 balloon was 3,477 m. The record for an AX-3 balloon was 4,642 m. How much greater was the second record?

25. Make up the missing information and solve the problem. A recent record distance for a helium balloon was 3,339 km. By how much did Tim's balloon flight miss the record?

26. **DATA BANK** How much greater is the altitude for an AX-10 balloon than for an AX-7 balloon? than for an AX-3 balloon? (See Data Bank, page 409.)

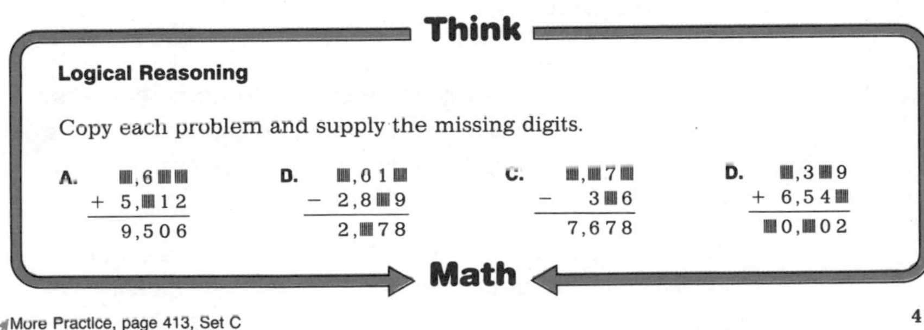

**Think Math**

**Logical Reasoning**

Copy each problem and supply the missing digits.

A. ■,6■■ + 5,■12 = 9,506

D. ■,01■ − 2,8■9 = 2,■78

C. ■,■7■ − 3■6 = 7,678

D. ■,3■9 + 6,54■ = ■0,■02

More Practice, page 413, Set C



60 sets of practice exercises in the appendix of the student book.

## Practice

- Ample exercises to reinforce learning
- Horizontal and vertical format
- Skillkeepers to help students maintain skills taught previously

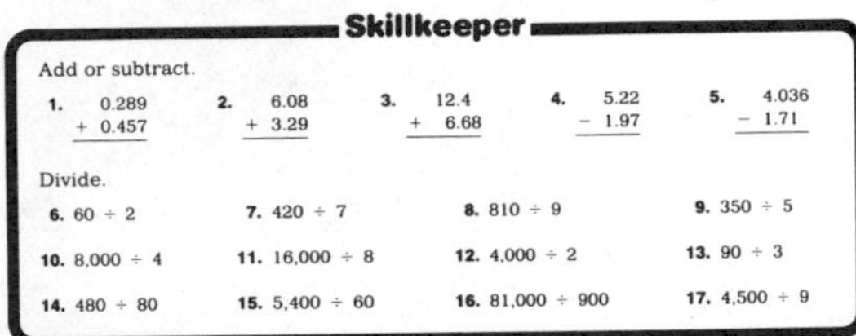

**Skillkeeper**

Add or subtract.

1. 0.289 + 0.457
2. 6.08 + 3.29
3. 12.4 + 6.68
4. 5.22 − 1.97
5. 4.036 − 1.71

Divide.

6. 60 ÷ 2
7. 420 ÷ 7
8. 810 ÷ 9
9. 350 ÷ 5
10. 8,000 ÷ 4
11. 16,000 ÷ 8
12. 4,000 ÷ 2
13. 90 ÷ 3
14. 480 ÷ 80
15. 5,400 ÷ 60
16. 81,000 ÷ 900
17. 4,500 ÷ 9

## Application

- Problems that carry through the theme of the page
- Data Hunts in which data is gathered either firsthand or from a variety of sources outside the book

30. **DATA HUNT** Suppose you have $\frac{1}{4}$ of a **score** of nickels and $\frac{2}{3}$ of a **gross** of dimes. How much money do you have? (Use a dictionary if necessary.)

- Data Banks in which data is found in the appendix of the student book

38. **DATA BANK** The model of one of the world's largest passenger ships is 22 feet long. The actual ship is 45 times that length. What is the name of the ship? (See Data Bank, page 408.)

- Calculator exercises in which students apply the skills they've learned to the calculator

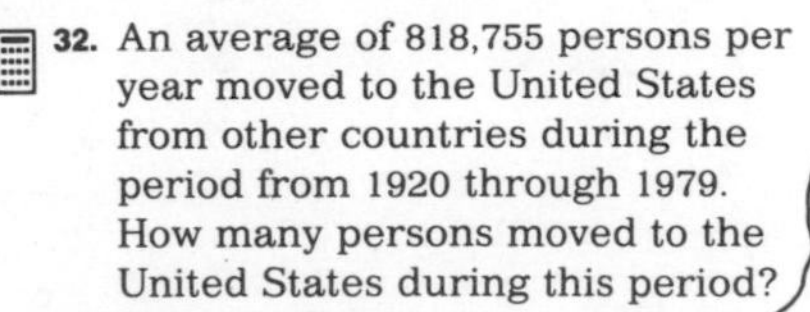

32. An average of 818,755 persons per year moved to the United States from other countries during the period from 1920 through 1979. How many persons moved to the United States during this period?

## Extension

Starred problems and Think Math activities challenge students to extend their skills

★ 7. A plane left St. Louis at 3:15 p.m. Central Standard Time. It arrived in Los Angeles at 6:10 p.m. Central Standard Time. How long did the flight take? What was the Pacific Standard Time when the plane arrived in Los Angeles?

# Problem solving . . .

In Addison–Wesley Mathematics, students become actively involved in problem solving through a variety of real-life situations. The problems encourage students to be decision-makers and apply the techniques they learn

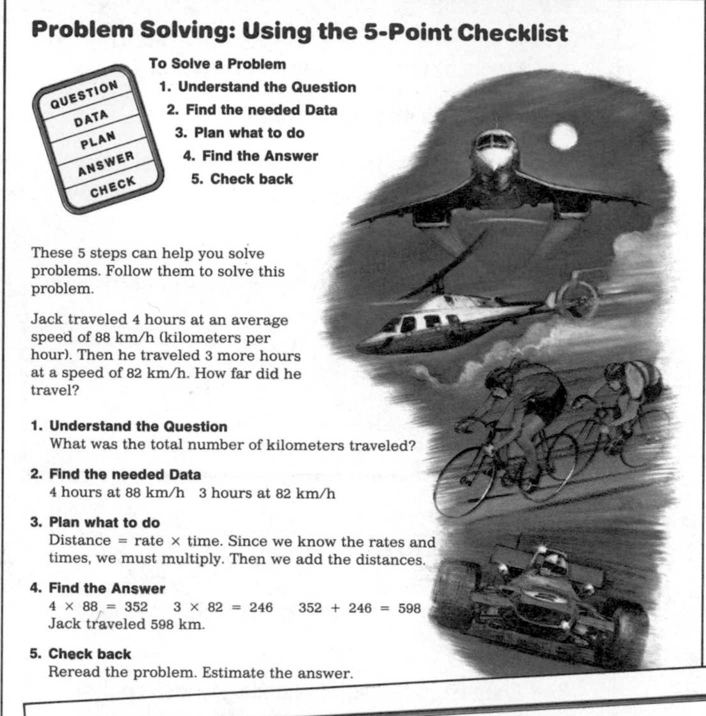

### Problem Solving: Using the 5-Point Checklist

**To Solve a Problem**

1. **Understand the Question**
2. **Find the needed Data**
3. **Plan what to do**
4. **Find the Answer**
5. **Check back**



These 5 steps can help you solve problems. Follow them to solve this problem.

Jack traveled 4 hours at an average speed of 88 km/h (kilometers per hour). Then he traveled 3 more hours at a speed of 82 km/h. How far did he travel?

1. **Understand the Question**
   What was the total number of kilometers traveled?
2. **Find the needed Data**
   4 hours at 88 km/h 3 hours at 82 km/h
3. **Plan what to do**
   Distance = rate × time. Since we know the rates and times, we must multiply. Then we add the distances.
4. **Find the Answer**
   4 × 88 = 352 3 × 82 = 246 352 + 246 = 598
   Jack traveled 598 km.
5. **Check back**
   Reread the problem. Estimate the answer.

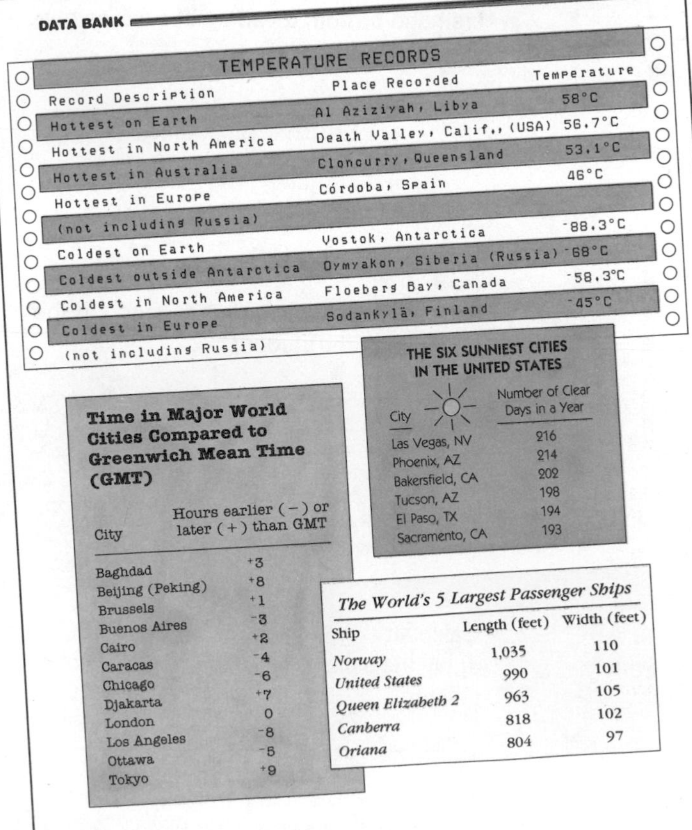

**DATA BANK**

**TEMPERATURE RECORDS**

| Record Description | Place Recorded | Temperature |
|---|---|---|
| Hottest on Earth | Al Aziziyah, Libya | 58°C |
| Hottest in North America | Death Valley, Calif., (USA) | 56.7°C |
| Hottest in Australia | Cloncurry, Queensland | 53.1°C |
| Hottest in Europe (not including Russia) | Córdoba, Spain | 46°C |
| Coldest on Earth | Vostok, Antarctica | -88.3°C |
| Coldest outside Antarctica | Oymyakon, Siberia (Russia) | -68°C |
| Coldest in North America | Floeberg Bay, Canada | -58.3°C |
| Coldest in Europe (not including Russia) | Sodankylä, Finland | -45°C |

**THE SIX SUNNIEST CITIES IN THE UNITED STATES**

| City | Number of Clear Days in a Year |
|---|---|
| Las Vegas, NV | 216 |
| Phoenix, AZ | 214 |
| Bakersfield, CA | 202 |
| Tucson, AZ | 198 |
| El Paso, TX | 194 |
| Sacramento, CA | 193 |

**Time in Major World Cities Compared to Greenwich Mean Time (GMT)**

| City | Hours earlier (−) or later (+) than GMT |
|---|---|
| Baghdad | +3 |
| Beijing (Peking) | +8 |
| Brussels | +1 |
| Buenos Aires | -3 |
| Cairo | +2 |
| Caracas | -4 |
| Chicago | -6 |
| Djakarta | +7 |
| London | 0 |
| Los Angeles | -8 |
| Ottawa | -5 |
| Tokyo | +9 |

*The World's 5 Largest Passenger Ships*

| Ship | Length (feet) | Width (feet) |
|---|---|---|
| *Norway* | 1,035 | 110 |
| *United States* | 990 | 101 |
| *Queen Elizabeth 2* | 963 | 105 |
| *Canberra* | 818 | 102 |
| *Oriana* | 804 | 97 |

408

## Problem Solving in Addison–Wesley Mathematics

The foundation of Addison–Wesley Mathematics is a carefully structured and sequenced problem-solving strand. It provides both motivational content and ample opportunity for students to participate in a wide range of problem-solving experiences.

Clear organization and specific instructions for solving problems give the very best help possible for teachers as they work with students in this important task. Strategies and techniques are carefully presented and developed.

### The 5-Point Checklist

Throughout the program, sequential instruction in problem solving is based on the following 5-Point Checklist.

**5-Point Checklist**

1. Understand the *question.*
2. Find the needed *data.*
3. *Plan* what to do.
4. Find the *answer.*
5. *Check back.*

Selected problem-solving lessons focus on one step in this checklist while others focus on all five steps. In these lessons, students are given real help in using important ideas under each point of the checklist.

- *Understand the Question*— In the early grades short sentence problems and pictures help students focus on the question. In later grades data or an equation may be given and students are asked to formulate an appropriate question. In all cases, the reading level of the word problems has been analyzed carefully to ensure that it is appropriate for the students at a given grade level.
- *Find the Needed Data*— In addition to the problem-solving lessons which focus on finding data from tables, pictures, advertisements, menus, and so on, other important experiences with data are provided throughout Addison–Wesley Mathematics. Data Bank problems require students to go beyond the text page to collect the needed data from a reference source in the

# . . . for the decision-makers of the future

to their own lives. The clear, efficient organization of the problem-solving program is sequentially consistent from chapter to chapter and from book to book.

Appendix of the textbook. Data Hunt problems encourage students to go outside the textbook to find the needed data from other reference sources or from an experiment conducted by the students.

Integrated into the program are problems with too much data, problems without enough data, and problems in which students must supply data by completing a table, making an organized list, or by other means.

- *Plan What to Do*— Problem-solving lessons which involve using a strategy such as Choose the Operations, Guess and Check, Draw a Picture, or Make a Table, help students learn to plan an approach to solving a problem. A clear understanding of the operations of addition, subtraction, multiplication, and division provides a foundation for the planning phase of problem solving. Problems solved by using one or more operations are given considerable emphasis as students develop their problem solving skills.
- *Find the Answer*— The main reason to develop computational skills is to be able to use them in solving problems. In Addison-Wesley Mathematics, each skill lesson is motivated by a word problem which can be solved using the skill developed in that lesson. After the particular computational skill has been developed and practiced, the students again solve a word problem which involves recognizing and performing the appropriate operation.
- *Check Back*— Selected lessons provide techniques for checking computational procedures and exercises to develop estimation skills. Students are also encouraged to reread the original problem to decide whether or not the answer makes sense.

## Problem Solving Strategies

The Addison-Wesley problem-solving program gives considerable attention to the important task of solving nonroutine problems (often called process problems) which are not readily solvable using one or more of the basic operations. After a strategy is developed in a given chapter, "Try This" problems in subsequent chapters give students an opportunity to practice using that strategy. Detailed help, including hints, questions to ask students, problem solutions, and an extension problem, is provided in the Teacher's Edition.

## Applied Problem Solving

In each Applied Problem Solving lesson, students are asked to make a decision about a real-life situation given specific information to consider. These special lessons require students to bring together the computational and problem-solving skills they have been learning throughout the program.

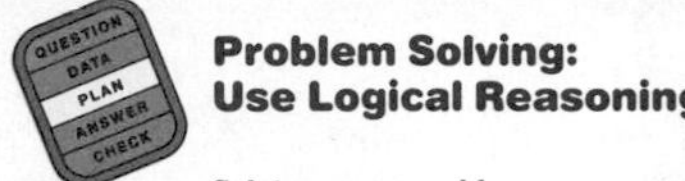


**Problem Solving: Use Logical Reasoning**

Solving some problems involves more than simply deciding whether to add, subtract, multiply, or divide. To solve such problems, we may use a strategy called

**Use Logical Reasoning**

A chart can help you keep a record of what you know. It can help you reason logically.

First, I'll write what I know in a chart.

| | Soccer | Tennis | Bowling | Softball |
|---|---|---|---|---|
| Carla | | no | | |
| José | | | yes | |
| Fran | | | | no |
| Ron | no | | | no |

Then I'll use what I know to find more information.

| | Soccer | Tennis | Bowling | Softball |
|---|---|---|---|---|
| Carla | | no | no | |
| José | | no | yes | |
| Fran | yes | no | no | no |
| Ron | no | yes | no | no |

**Try This** Carla, José, Fran, and Ron each have different favorite sports: soccer, tennis, bowling, and softball. The favorite sport of Carla's best friend in the group is tennis. Fran and Ron do not like softball. José's favorite sport is bowling. Ron used to like soccer but no longer does. Which sport is Carla's favorite?

Solve.

1. Four turtles—Lightning, Swifty, Flash, and Rocket—came in first, second, third, and fourth (not in that order) in a race. Lightning was second and Swifty was not fourth. If Flash was third, where did Rocket finish? fourth
2. Beverly, Ralph, and Ginny each

**Applied Problem Solving**

Suppose you are reseeding a lawn with bluegrass. You need to decide how many boxes of grass seed to buy.

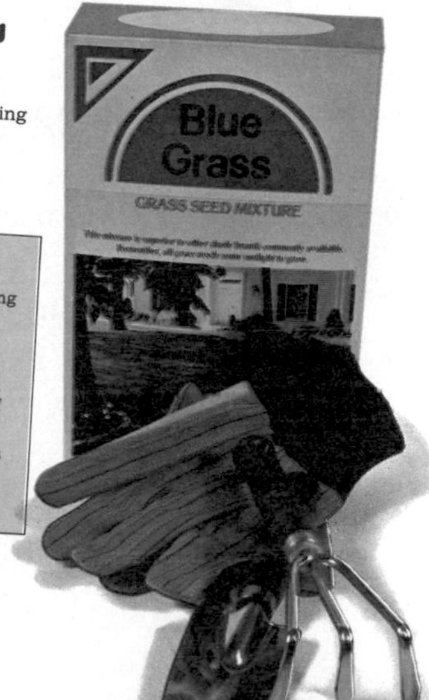


**Some Things to Consider**

- The house takes up an area 19 m long and 13 m wide on a lot that is 36 m long and 34 m wide.
- For a light cover of grass, you need 1 kg of seed for every 100 m² of lawn. For a heavy cover, you need 1.5 kg of seed for every 100 m² of lawn.
- You can buy grass seed only in boxes of 2 kg of seed per box.
- A box of grass seed costs $10.95.

**Some Questions to Answer**

1. What is the area of the lot? 1,224 m²
2. What is the area covered by the house? 247 m²
3. What is the area of the lawn? 977 m²
4. How many kilograms of seed do you need for a light cover of grass? for a heavy cover of grass? 9.77 kg; 14.7 kg
5. How many boxes of seed do you need for a light cover of grass? for a heavy cover? 5 (4.9); 8 (7.35)

**What Is Your Decision?**

How many boxes of seed will you buy?
Answers will vary.

360

# Daily teaching support . . .

We know that every teacher has an individual style. The organization of the Teacher's Edition makes it quick and easy to locate everything your style demands

## Starting the lesson

*Quick Review*—An optional daily skill maintenance program.

*Ideas for Getting Started*—Exciting manipulative activities that introduce or prepare students for the content of the lesson.

## Teaching the lesson

All the essentials for teaching the page tinted in yellow for easy access

Clear concise notes that make math easy to teach

Specific questions and step-by-step explanations to lead students through the concepts presented

---

112
**Division**

**Quick Review** Students say, then write, the number indicated by each phrase.
4 hundreds 400   3 tens, 2 ones 32   7 hundreds, 2 tens, 9 ones 729   5 tens 50
3 hundreds, 1 one 301   1 thousand, 4 hundreds 1,400   4 tens, 8 ones 48
8 hundreds, 3 ones 803   7 tens, 7 ones 77   2 hundreds, 1 ten 210

**Lesson Focus** To divide by a 2-digit number to find 2- or 3-digit quotients

**Suggested Materials** Play money

### Ideas for Getting Started

Tell students the following story: Three students found an envelope containing $81, which they turned over to the police. After a time, when the owner could not be found, they were given the money to divide equally among themselves.

Have an envelope with play money or slips of paper representing $81. Ask a volunteer to show how to divide the money. Suggest that the larger bills be divided first. Then have students work in small groups or individually to divide up these amounts: $56 among 2 students; $72 among 3 students; $92 among 4 students; and $80 among 5 students. Emphasize the idea of first dividing the tens, trading a ten for 10 ones, and then dividing the ones.

### Using Page 112

**Motivational Problem** Read the problem at the top of the page. "What question is asked about Ken's 'Swim for Charity'?" (How much did each of the 3 charities receive?) "What data is given in the problem?" (He earned $75 to divide among the 3 charities.) Elicit from students that we can use division as the plan to find the answer to this problem.

**Lesson Development** Have three students divide the 7 tens and 5 ones. As students complete the task, write the corresponding numerical procedure on the chalkboard as shown in the text. Point out that the 75 represents the total amount of money, the divisor 3 is the number of charities to share the money. The first quotient figure, 2, is the number of $10 bills each charity gets. The number subtracted, 6, is the total number of $10 bills shared; the difference, 1, is the number of extra $10 bills. In the second step, students should understand that the extra ten is traded for 10 ones and combined with the 5 ones to produce 15. The second quotient figure represents the number of $1 bills each gets when the 15 $1-bills are divided among the 3 people. The 15 being subtracted represents the total number of bills shared and the 0 shows that there are no extra $1 bills left over. The quotient, 25, shows that each charity received $25.

**Other Examples** Use the money model if necessary to work through these examples. Encourage students to think about the model if they have difficulty.

**Warm Up** As students complete these exercises, be alert for basic fact errors. Caution students to be particularly careful with exercises 3 and 5 in which there are not enough hundreds and they must start the dividing in the tens place.

### 1-Digit Divisors

Ken earned $75 in a "Swim for Charity." He divided it equally among 3 charities. How much did each charity receive?

Since the money is shared equally, we divide.

Decide where to start. → 3)75
3 < 7 Divide the tens.
Start with 7 [$10 bill]s. 5 [$1 bill]s.

Dividing Tens
- Divide
- Multiply
- Subtract
- Compare

2
3)75
6
1

Divide the 7 tens.
Each gets 2 1 extra.

Trade 1 [$10 bill] for 10 [$1 bill]s.

Dividing Ones
- Bring Down
- Divide
- Multiply
- Subtract
- Compare

25
3)75
6↓
15
15
0

Divide the 15 ones.
Each gets 5 0 extra.

Each gets 2 [$10 bill]s, 5 [$1 bill]s.

Check: 25 × 3 = 75
Each charity received $25.

**Other Examples**

163 R3
4)655
4
25
24
15
12
3 (Remainder)

Check: 163 × 4 = 652; 652 + 3 = 655

Not enough hundreds. Start with the tens.

46
6)276
24
36
36
0

61 R1
5)306
30
06
5
1

**Warm Up** Divide. Check by multiplying.

1. 2)49 (24 R1)
2. 3)87 (29)
3. 6)199 (33 R1)
4. 8)985 (123 R1)
5. 7)359 (51 R2)

112

### Follow Up

**Reteaching**

Use an example such as 4)128 to review the division algorithm. "Can the hundreds be shared among 4 people?" (The answer is no, so the hundred is exchanged for 10 tens and combined with the 2 tens to make 12 tens.) "Can 12 tens be shared among 4 people?" (Yes, the ones can be shared equally.) Then show these steps in the algorithm.

- 4)128 Is 4 < 1? The hundreds cannot be shared, so we consider the tens.
- 4)128 Is 4 < 12? Yes, we can divide in the tens place.
- 4)128 Is 4 < 8? Yes, we can divide the ones equally.

**Enrichment**

Write the following problems on the chalkboard. Challenge students to fill in the missing numbers.

459
6)2754
24
35
30
54
54
0

352 R4
7)2468
21
36
35
18
14
4

552 R4
5)2764
25
26
25
14
10
4

# . . . when you need it

for lesson support. The lesson plan is reliably consistent so you can readily choose whatever is necessary for your class.

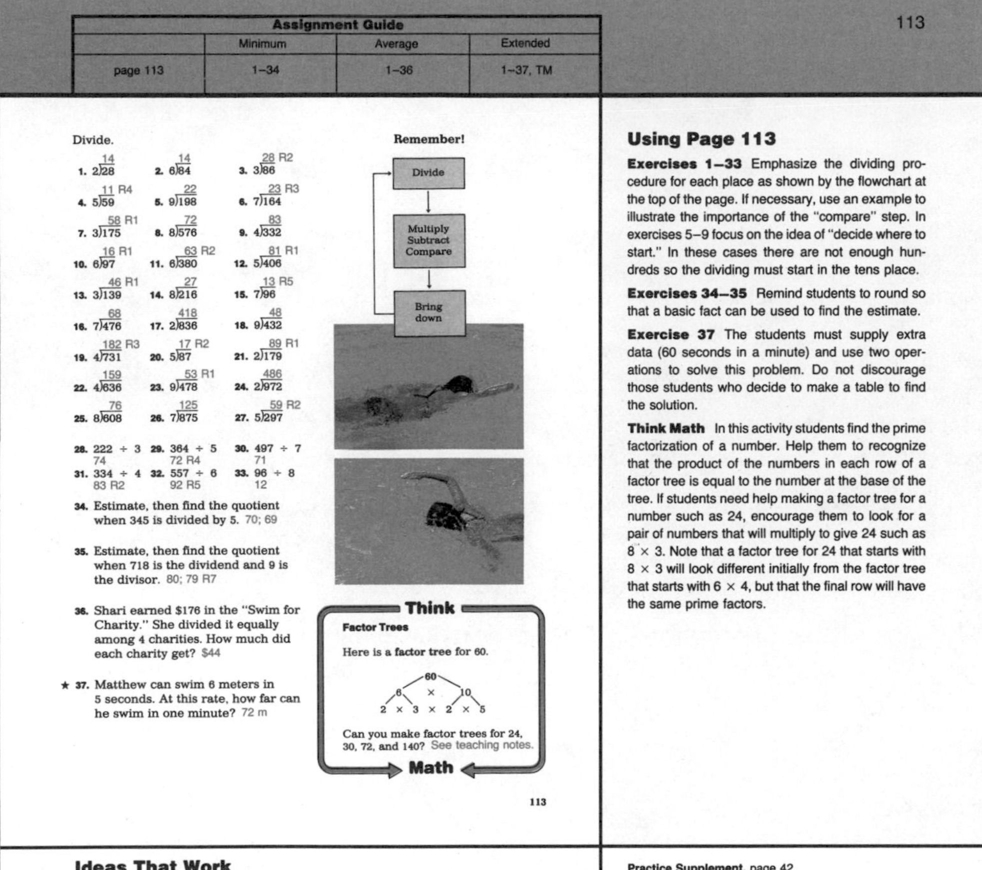

| Assignment Guide | Minimum | Average | Extended |
|---|---|---|---|
| page 113 | 1–34 | 1–36 | 1–37, TM |

113

Divide.

1. 2)28 14
2. 6)84 14
3. 3)86 28 R2
4. 5)59 11 R4
5. 9)198 22
6. 7)164 23 R3
7. 3)175 58 R1
8. 8)576 72
9. 4)332 83
10. 6)97 16 R1
11. 6)380 63 R2
12. 5)406 81 R1
13. 3)139 46 R1
14. 8)216 27
15. 7)96 13 R5
16. 7)476 68
17. 2)836 418
18. 9)432 48
19. 4)731 182 R3
20. 5)87 17 R2
21. 2)179 89 R1
22. 4)636 159
23. 9)478 53 R1
24. 2)972 486
25. 8)608 76
26. 7)875 125
27. 5)297 59 R2
28. 222 ÷ 3 74
29. 364 ÷ 5 72 R4
30. 497 ÷ 7 71
31. 334 ÷ 4 83 R2
32. 557 ÷ 6 92 R5
33. 96 ÷ 8 12
34. Estimate, then find the quotient when 345 is divided by 5. 70; 69
35. Estimate, then find the quotient when 718 is the dividend and 9 is the divisor. 80; 79 R7
36. Shari earned $176 in the "Swim for Charity." She divided it equally among 4 charities. How much did each charity get? $44
★ 37. Matthew can swim 6 meters in 5 seconds. At this rate, how far can he swim in one minute? 72 m

Remember!

Divide → Multiply Subtract Compare → Bring down

Think

Factor Trees

Here is a factor tree for 60.

60 → 6 × 10 → 2 × 3 × 2 × 5

Can you make factor trees for 24, 30, 72, and 140? See teaching notes.

Math

113

**Using Page 113**

**Exercises 1–33** Emphasize the dividing procedure for each place as shown by the flowchart at the top of the page. If necessary, use an example to illustrate the importance of the "compare" step. In exercises 5–9 focus on the idea of "decide where to start." In these cases there are not enough hundreds so the dividing must start in the tens place.

**Exercises 34–35** Remind students to round so that a basic fact can be used to find the estimate.

**Exercise 37** The students must supply extra data (60 seconds in a minute) and use two operations to solve this problem. Do not discourage those students who decide to make a table to find the solution.

**Think Math** In this activity students find the prime factorization of a number. Help them to recognize that the product of the numbers in each row of a factor tree is equal to the number at the base of the tree. If students need help making a factor tree for a number such as 24, encourage them to look for a pair of numbers that will multiply to give 24 such as 8 × 3. Note that a factor tree for 24 that starts with 8 × 3 will look different initially from the factor tree that starts with 6 × 4, but that the final row will have the same prime factors.

**Ideas That Work**

**Special Education**

Allow students to work in groups of five to check their work in this activity. Each student in a group should select one step in the chart and take turns with other members of the group talking through, *step by step*, the calculation of the problems.

| 1. Divide |
|---|
| 2. Multiply |
| 3. Subtract |
| 4. Compare |
| 5. Bring Down |

If a student in the group has reasoning or memory difficulties, let that student have first choice in selecting a step to be described. For example, the student might feel more comfortable with the subtraction step, and may prefer to describe the subtraction calculation each time. After observing other students discuss their steps, the student might feel confident enough to select a different step to describe.

As follow-up, write several incomplete division examples on the chalkboard, and challenge the groups to finish these problems. If time allows, group sessions could be used as practice periods.

**Practice Supplement**, page 42

1-Digit Divisors

## Assigning the exercises

*Assignment Guide* for individualization in three ability groups

Teaching notes that alert teachers to special difficulties students may encounter

## Meeting individual needs

### Follow Up

*Reteaching* activity—Another way to teach the concept or skill presented in the lesson—for students who demonstrate misunderstanding

*Enrichment* activity—To broaden or extend the skills and concept taught in the lesson

*Reteaching, Enrichment, Practice* Supplements

- pages reproduced for informed planning
- overprinted answers
- available as workbooks, blackline masters, and duplicator masters

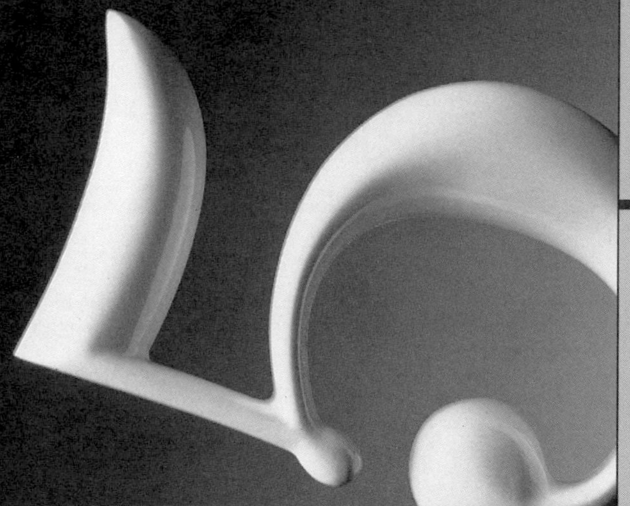

# Resources to meet . . .

There are more special features and practical ideas in the Teacher's Edition than any teacher can use. Designed to allow you to find quickly exactly what your needs demand, it frees your valuable time for

## Teaching Tips

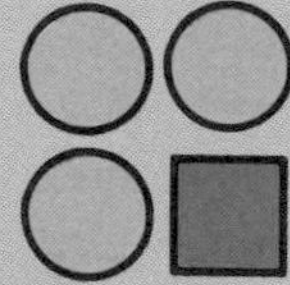

### Error Analysis

Student errors often fall into predictable patterns that have been observed over and over in classrooms. Once the diagnosis of an error has been made and the cause understood, a program of remediation can be carried out. If the error pattern is caught in its early stages, the errors can be remediated before the pattern is internalized. The Error Analysis section anticipates likely errors related to the content of each chapter and provides the tools to affect change. Two discussions are provided for each error pattern:

- **Diagnosis**
- **Remediation**

### Problem Solving

Tips for teaching problem solving contain a large number of classroom-tested techniques for teaching problem solving. The topics selected for this section address five questions teachers ask when building a problem-solving program:

1) How will I provide a classroom environment conducive to problem solving?
2) How can I develop problem-solving skills?
3) What can I do to guide students' work while they solve problems?
4) How can I meet individual needs?
5) How will I evaluate students' problem-solving performance and attitudes?

## Background Information

### Chapter Overview

Easy to find, understandable information for teaching each key skill or concept
(See page 1A.)

- **Objectives**
- **Summary**
- **Mathematical Background**
- **Vocabulary**

### Just for Teachers

Interesting facts and information related to the history of mathematics, economics, and current educational theories
(See page 76.)

### Technology for Teachers

A guide to understanding and teaching the basics of calculator and computer technology
(See page 318.)

# . . . the challenge of every classroom

working with students. Whatever your classroom needs, it's the problem solver—The Addison–Wesley Teacher's Edition.

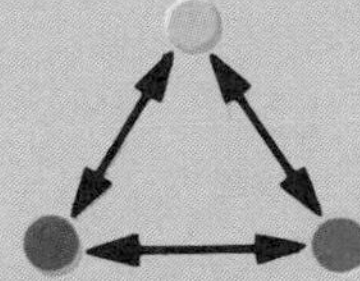

### Special Education

This section highlights the special needs of physically-impaired, learning-disabled, mentally-retarded, or behaviorally-disordered learners. These students often lack the information-processing skills of the regular K-8 students and require supplementary activities and special teaching approaches.

The guidelines for working with special students are organized around the triangle model. The corners of this triangle suggest the various levels of abstraction students need in learning mathematics. Specific sides of the triangle may require special emphasis. For example, if a student has verbal and writing deficiencies, the instruction might emphasize the pattern shown on the left below. For the student possessing strong visual and speaking skills, but poor written communication skills, the instructional program might attempt an approach like that shown in the model on the right below.

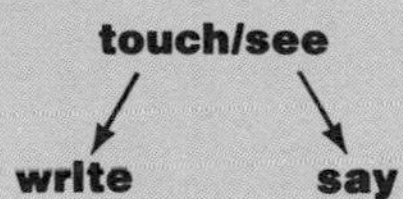


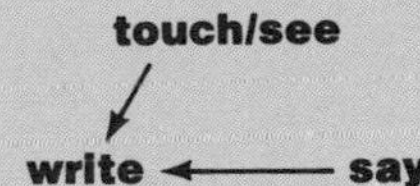

### Subject Integration

The themes of the problems in the student book have been carefully selected from a cross section of the curriculum areas in order to provide an integration of mathematics with other subject areas. A list of the themes from the content areas, and from the areas of career and consumer awareness, gives teachers the opportunity to make mathematics part of the total curriculum.

- **Science**
- **Social Studies**
- **Health**
- **Fine Arts**
- **Language Arts**
- **Physical Education**
- **Consumer Awareness**
- **Career Awareness**

## Activity Ideas

### Ideas That Work

Practical suggestions for chalkboard activities, manipulative ideas, extensions, and ways to use the calculator in the classroom
(See page 35.)

- **Chalk It Up**
- **Math for the Gifted**
- **Special Education**
- **Calculator Bonus**

### Activities That Count

A bank of activity ideas and long-range projects adaptable to a variety of skills and appropriate for all ability levels
(See page 193F.)

- **Math Lab**
- **Game**
- **Project**

### Quick Review

A 2-minute activity to review and maintain basic skills, intended for use at the beginning of each lesson.
(See page 64.)

# Planning and assessment . . .

Only you can accurately evaluate students' progress and diagnose their needs. Addison–Wesley's new program offers a complete range of testing options and an organized class

## A comprehensive guide for planning each chapter

| Teaching Chapter 1 | | | | Meeting Individual Needs | | | | | |
|---|---|---|---|---|---|---|---|---|---|
| Objectives | Chapter Content | Pages | TRB Test Items | Lesson Assignments | | | Follow Up | | |
| | | | | Minimum | Average | Extended | Reteaching | Enrichment | Practice |
| | Chapter Opener | 1 | | | | | | | |
| **1.1** Recall basic addition, subtraction, multiplication, and division facts and solve equations using basic facts. | Addition and Subtraction | 2–3 | 1–21 | 1–40 | 1–42 | 1–42, TM | SE5 Ch 1 RS 1 | ES 1 | MP 411 PS 1 |
| | Multiplication | 4–5 | | 1–22 | 1–24 | 1–24, TM | SE5 Ch 1 RS 2 | ES 2 | MP 411 PS 2 |
| | Division | 6–7 | | 1–35 | 1–38 | 1–38, TM | SE5 Ch 1 RS 3 | ES 3 | MP 411 PS 3 |
| | Practice the Facts | 10 | | 1–46 | 1–54 | 1–54 | | | |
| **1.2** Use parentheses | | | | | | | | | |

**Supplements to fill every need keyed to specific lessons**

**Clear, concise objectives**

**Test items correlated to objectives and lessons**

**Distinct Assignment Guides for 3 ability groups**

**References to previous student book for reteaching or readiness**

**Approximately 900 additional exercises in the appendix of the student book**

## Built-in review and individualization at the end of each chapter of the student book

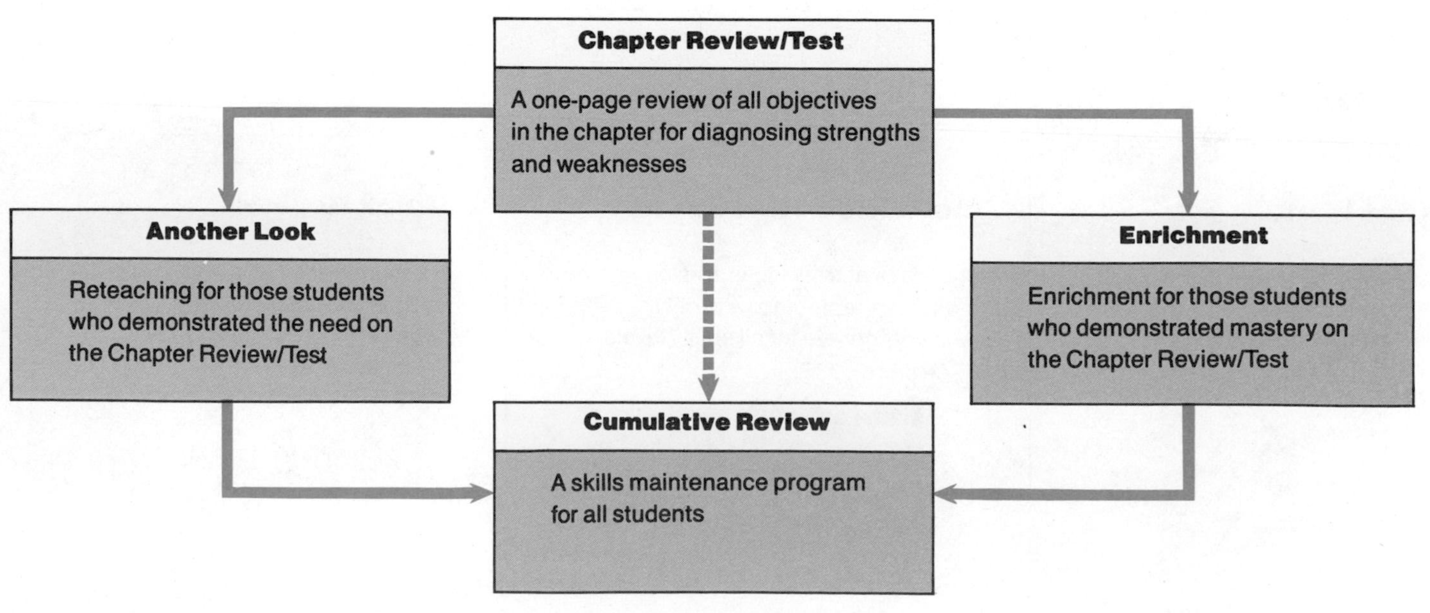

Chapter Review/Test
A one-page review of all objectives in the chapter for diagnosing strengths and weaknesses
Another Look
Reteaching for those students who demonstrated the need on the Chapter Review/Test
Enrichment
Enrichment for those students who demonstrated mastery on the Chapter Review/Test
Cumulative Review
A skills maintenance program for all students

management plan that can help you measure student achievements and direct remedial activities. Efficient management produces lesson-by-lesson accountability.

## Fully cross-referenced assessment options

Criterion-referenced chapter tests in two forms:

- Multiple-choice
- Free-response

The items have a one-to-one correspondence in terms of the level of difficulty so you can use them as a pre- and post-test.

Plus, these extra testing materials:

- Basic-Facts Test
- Mid-Year Test
- End-of-Year Test
- Grading Aid
- Answer Sheet

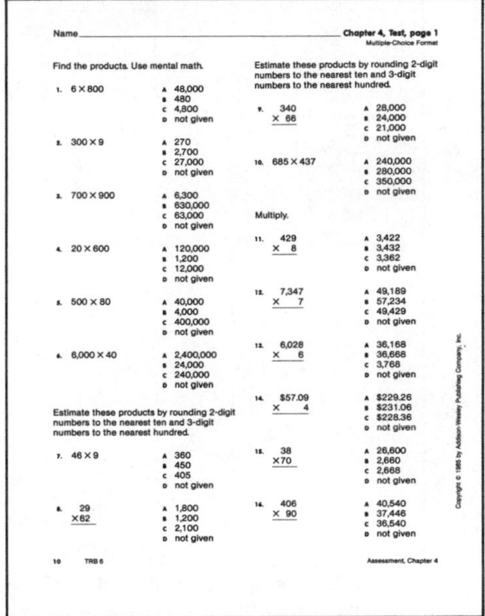

Name ______________________ **Chapter 4, Test, page 1**
Multiple-Choice Format

Find the products. Use mental math.

1. 6 × 800 — A 48,000 B 480 C 4,800 D not given
2. 300 × 9 — A 270 B 2,700 C 27,000 D not given
3. 700 × 900 — A 6,300 B 630,000 C 63,000 D not given
4. 20 × 600 — A 120,000 B 1,200 C 12,000 D not given
5. 500 × 80 — A 40,000 B 4,000 C 400,000 D not given
6. 6,000 × 40 — A 2,400,000 B 24,000 C 240,000 D not given

Estimate these products by rounding 2-digit numbers to the nearest ten and 3-digit numbers to the nearest hundred.

7. 46 × 9 — A 360 B 450 C 405 D not given
8. 29 × 62 — A 1,800 B 1,200 C 2,100 D not given

Estimate these products by rounding 2-digit numbers to the nearest ten and 3-digit numbers to the nearest hundred.

9. 340 × 66 — A 28,000 B 24,000 C 21,000 D not given
10. 685 × 437 — A 240,000 B 280,000 C 350,000 D not given

Multiply.

11. 429 × 8 — A 3,422 B 3,432 C 3,362 D not given
12. 7,347 × 7 — A 49,189 B 57,234 C 49,429 D not given
13. 6,028 × 6 — A 36,168 B 36,668 C 3,768 D not given
14. $57.09 × 4 — A $229.26 B $231.06 C $228.36 D not given
15. 38 × 70 — A 26,600 B 2,660 C 2,668 D not given
16. 406 × 90 — A 40,540 B 37,446 C 36,540 D not given

Copyright © 1985 by Addison-Wesley Publishing Company, Inc.

10 TRB 6 Assessment, Chapter 4

**Multiple-Choice Tests**

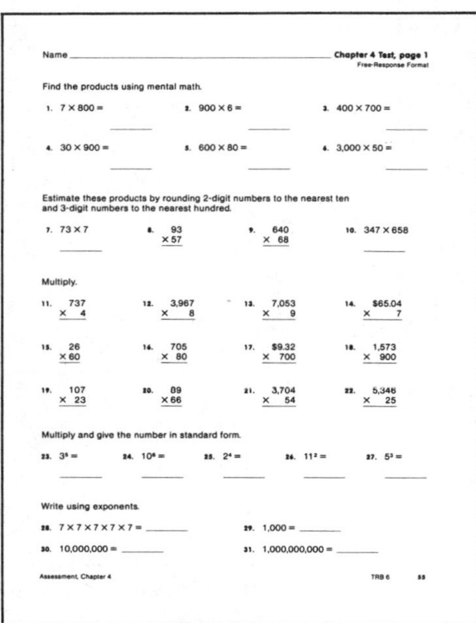

Name ______________________ **Chapter 4 Test, page 1**
Free-Response Format

Find the products using mental math.

1. 7 × 800 = ____
2. 900 × 6 = ____
3. 400 × 700 = ____
4. 30 × 900 = ____
5. 600 × 80 = ____
6. 3,000 × 50 = ____

Estimate these products by rounding 2-digit numbers to the nearest ten and 3-digit numbers to the nearest hundred.

7. 73 × 7 ____
8. 93 × 57
9. 640 × 68
10. 347 × 658 ____

Multiply.

11. 737 × 4
12. 3,967 × 8
13. 7,053 × 9
14. $65.04 × 7
15. 26 × 60
16. 705 × 80
17. $9.32 × 700
18. 1,573 × 900
19. 107 × 23
20. 89 × 66
21. 3,704 × 54
22. 5,346 × 25

Multiply and give the number in standard form.

23. $3^5$ = ____
24. $10^6$ = ____
25. $2^4$ = ____
26. $11^2$ = ____
27. $5^3$ = ____

Write using exponents.

28. 7 × 7 × 7 × 7 × 7 = ____
29. 1,000 = ____
30. 10,000,000 = ____
31. 1,000,000,000 = ____

Assessment, Chapter 4 TRB 6 55

**Free-Response Tests**

## Forms to record test scores and assignments

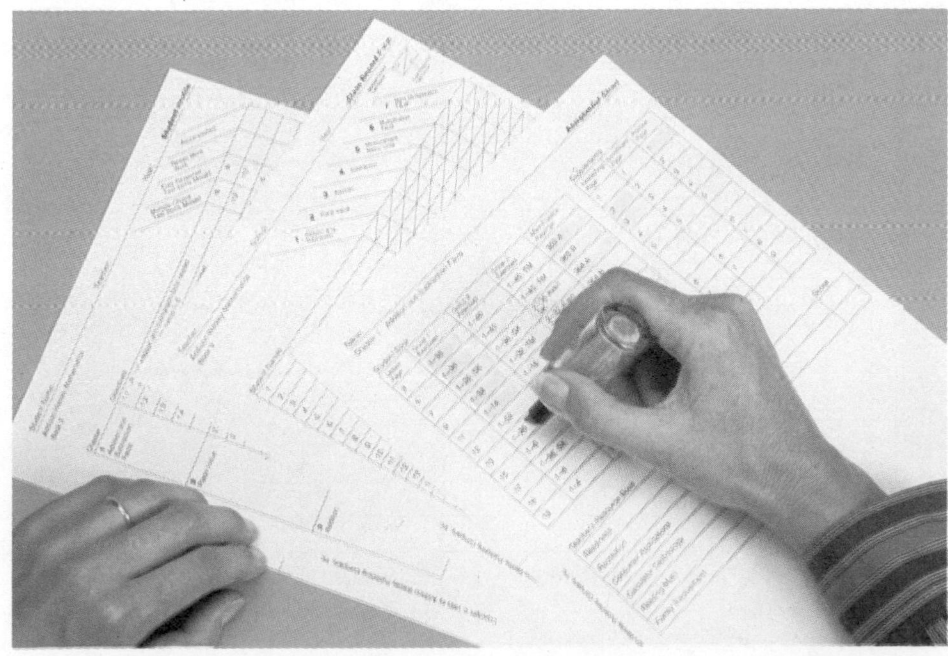

# A flexible teaching package . . .

The very concept of a Teacher's Resource Book to supplement the math program was created by Addison–Wesley. Our new program has an expanded TRB that includes more sections, more features, and

### Readiness

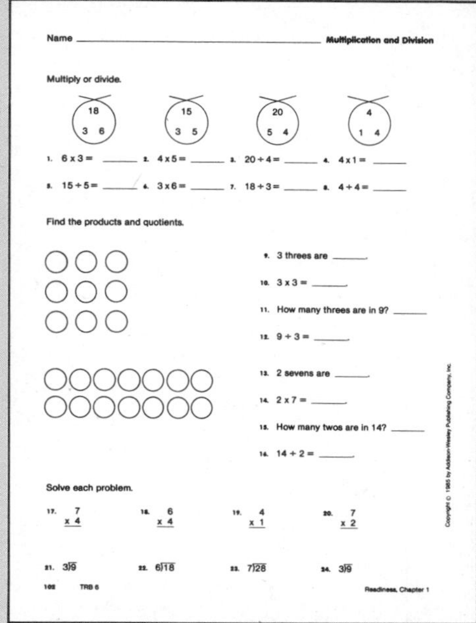

Name ______ **Multiplication and Division**

Multiply or divide.

18 / 3 6    15 / 3 5    20 / 5 4    4 / 1 4

1. 6 x 3 = ____ 2. 4 x 5 = ____ 3. 20 ÷ 4 = ____ 4. 4 x 1 = ____
5. 15 ÷ 5 = ____ 6. 3 x 6 = ____ 7. 18 ÷ 3 = ____ 8. 4 ÷ 4 = ____

Find the products and quotients.

9. 3 threes are ____.
10. 3 x 3 = ____.
11. How many threes are in 9? ____
12. 9 ÷ 3 = ____.
13. 2 sevens are ____.
14. 2 x 7 = ____.
15. How many twos are in 14? ____
16. 14 ÷ 2 = ____.

Solve each problem.

17. 7 x 4    18. 6 x 4    19. 4 x 1    20. 7 x 2

21. 3)9    22. 6)18    23. 7)28    24. 3)9



102 TRB 6 Readiness, Chapter 1

Prepares students for the chapter lessons by presenting and reviewing prerequisite skills and concepts

### Activities That Count

Name ______ **Division Drop**

| Bonus! Add 2 points. | 36 | 5.88 | 134 | 17.77 |
|---|---|---|---|---|
| 162 | 100 | 97.36 | 25 | Sorry! Lose 5 points. |
| 38.03 | 40.9 | 862 | 500 | 7.9 |
| 400 | 73.6 | 0.210 | Bonus! Add 5 points. | 931.2 |
| 589 | Sorry! Lose 2 points. | 173 | 12.22 | 10 |
| 32.5 | 182 | 60.8 | 12.65 | 4.983 |



140 TRB 6 Activities That Count, Chapter 6

Supports math labs, games, and projects described in the Teacher's Edition

### Recreation

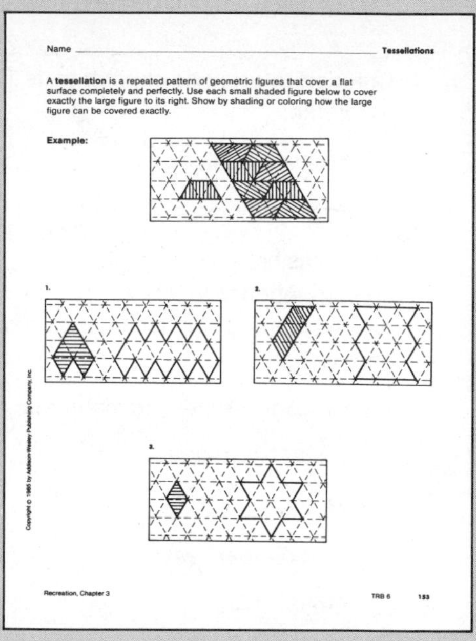

Name ______ **Tessellations**

A **tessellation** is a repeated pattern of geometric figures that cover a flat surface completely and perfectly. Use each small shaded figure below to cover exactly the large figure to its right. Show by shading or coloring how the large figure can be covered exactly.

**Example:**

1.    2.    3.



Recreation, Chapter 3 TRB 6 153

Presents interesting, creative ways of working with numbers, math concepts, and special topics

### Calculator Technology

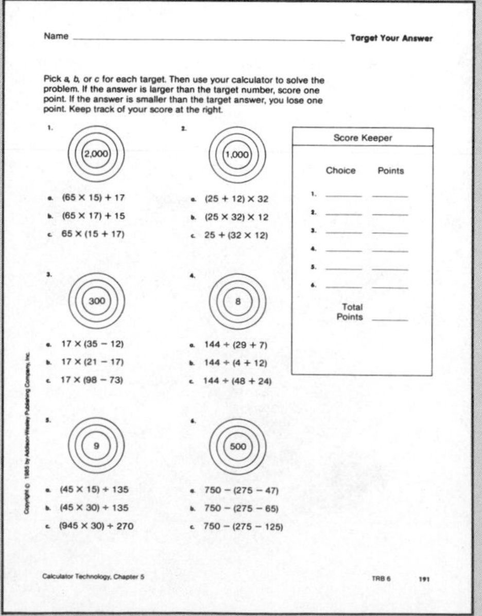

Name ______ **Target Your Answer**

Pick *a*, *b*, or *c* for each target. Then use your calculator to solve the problem. If the answer is larger than the target number, score one point. If the answer is smaller than the target answer, you lose one point. Keep track of your score at the right.

1. 2,000
   a. (65 × 15) + 17
   b. (65 × 17) + 15
   c. 65 × (15 + 17)

2. 1,000
   a. (25 + 12) × 32
   b. (25 × 32) × 12
   c. 25 + (32 × 12)

3. 300
   a. 17 × (35 − 12)
   b. 17 × (21 − 17)
   c. 17 × (98 − 73)

4. 8
   a. 144 ÷ (29 + 7)
   b. 144 ÷ (4 + 12)
   c. 144 ÷ (48 + 24)

5. 9
   a. (45 × 15) ÷ 135
   b. (45 × 30) ÷ 135
   c. (945 × 30) ÷ 270

6. 500
   a. 750 − (275 − 47)
   b. 750 − (275 − 65)
   c. 750 − (275 − 125)

Score Keeper

| | Choice | Points |
|---|---|---|
| 1. | ____ | ____ |
| 2. | ____ | ____ |
| 3. | ____ | ____ |
| 4. | ____ | ____ |
| 5. | ____ | ____ |
| 6. | ____ | ____ |
| Total Points | | ____ |



Calculator Technology, Chapter 5 TRB 6 191

Helps students become comfortable using calculators

### Computer Technology

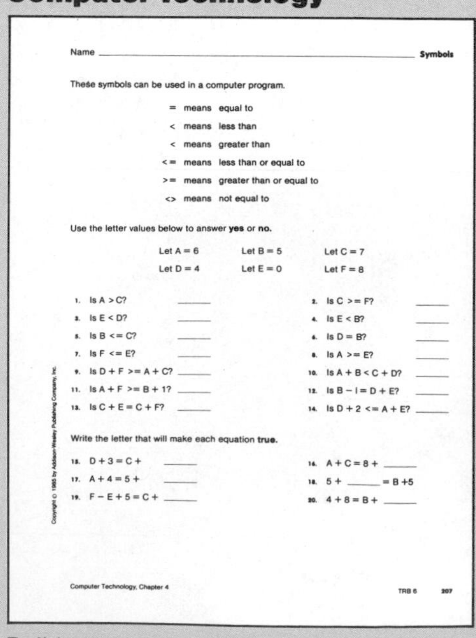

Name ______ **Symbols**

These symbols can be used in a computer program.

= means equal to
< means less than
< means greater than
<= means less than or equal to
>= means greater than or equal to
<> means not equal to

Use the letter values below to answer **yes** or **no**.

Let A = 6   Let B = 5   Let C = 7
Let D = 4   Let E = 0   Let F = 8

1. Is A > C? ____ 2. Is C >= F? ____
3. Is E < D? ____ 4. Is E < B? ____
5. Is B <= C? ____ 6. Is D = B? ____
7. Is F <= E? ____ 8. Is A >= E? ____
9. Is D + F >= A + C? ____ 10. Is A + B < C + D? ____
11. Is A + F >= B + 1? ____ 12. Is B − I = D + E? ____
13. Is C + E = C + F? ____ 14. Is D + 2 <= A + E? ____

Write the letter that will make each equation **true**.

15. D + 3 = C + ____ 16. A + C = 8 + ____
17. A + 4 = 5 + ____ 18. 5 + ____ = B + 5
19. F − E + 5 = C + ____ 20. 4 + 8 = B + ____



Computer Technology, Chapter 4 TRB 6 207

Builds on computer literacy skills introduced in the student book

# . . . that promotes success

more teaching aids than ever. This unique, convenient collection of additional materials is completely correlated to the Teacher's Edition. It's designed to encourage students to become successful, independent learners.

### Reading Math

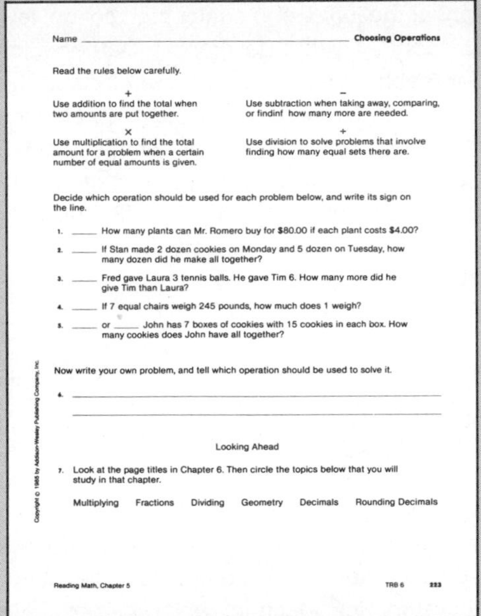

Name ______________ **Choosing Operations**

Read the rules below carefully.

+ Use addition to find the total when two amounts are put together.

− Use subtraction when taking away, comparing, or findinf how many more are needed.

× Use multiplication to find the total amount for a problem when a certain number of equal amounts is given.

+ Use division to solve problems that involve finding how many equal sets there are.

Decide which operation should be used for each problem below, and write its sign on the line.

1. _____ How many plants can Mr. Romero buy for $80.00 if each plant costs $4.00?
2. _____ If Stan made 2 dozen cookies on Monday and 5 dozen on Tuesday, how many dozen did he make all together?
3. _____ Fred gave Laura 3 tennis balls. He gave Tim 6. How many more did he give Tim than Laura?
4. _____ If 7 equal chairs weigh 245 pounds, how much does 1 weigh?
5. _____ or _____ John has 7 boxes of cookies with 15 cookies in each box. How many cookies does John have all together?

Now write your own problem, and tell which operation should be used to solve it.

6. ______________________________

Looking Ahead

7. Look at the page titles in Chapter 6. Then circle the topics below that you will study in that chapter.

Multiplying Fractions Dividing Geometry Decimals Rounding Decimals





Involves vocabulary, study skills, and reading comprehension in the content area of mathematics

### Consumer Applications

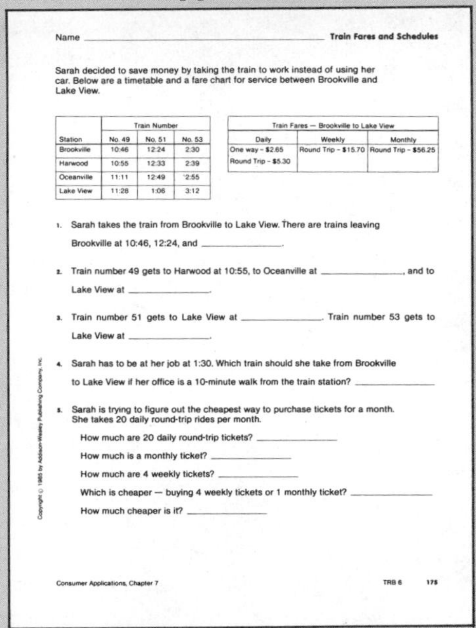

Name ______________ **Train Fares and Schedules**

Sarah decided to save money by taking the train to work instead of using her car. Below are a timetable and a fare chart for service between Brookville and Lake View.

| Station | Train Number No. 49 | No. 51 | No. 53 |
|---|---|---|---|
| Brookville | 10:46 | 12:24 | 2:30 |
| Harwood | 10:55 | 12:33 | 2:39 |
| Oceanville | 11:11 | 12:49 | 2:55 |
| Lake View | 11:28 | 1:06 | 3:12 |

| Train Fares — Brookville to Lake View Daily | Weekly | Monthly |
|---|---|---|
| One way - $2.65<br>Round Trip - $5.30 | Round Trip - $15.70 | Round Trip - $56.25 |

1. Sarah takes the train from Brookville to Lake View. There are trains leaving Brookville at 10:46, 12:24, and ______________.
2. Train number 49 gets to Harwood at 10:55, to Oceanville at ______________, and to Lake View at ______________.
3. Train number 51 gets to Lake View at ______________. Train number 53 gets to Lake View at ______________.
4. Sarah has to be at her job at 1:30. Which train should she take from Brookville to Lake View if her office is a 10-minute walk from the train station? ______________
5. Sarah is trying to figure out the cheapest way to purchase tickets for a month. She takes 20 daily round-trip rides per month.

   How much are 20 daily round-trip tickets? ______________

   How much is a monthly ticket? ______________

   How much are 4 weekly tickets? ______________

   Which is cheaper — buying 4 weekly tickets or 1 monthly ticket? ______________

   How much cheaper is it? ______________





Provides practice with real-life consumer skills such as banking, comparative shopping, taxes, unit pricing, and budgets

### Family Involvement

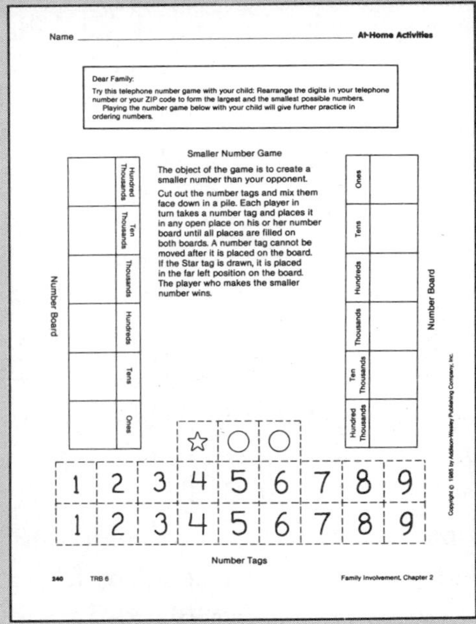

Name ______________ **At-Home Activities**

Dear Family:

Try this telephone number game with your child: Rearrange the digits in your telephone number or your ZIP code to form the largest and the smallest possible numbers.

Playing the number game below with your child will give further practice in ordering numbers.

Smaller Number Game

The object of the game is to create a smaller number than your opponent.

Cut out the number tags and mix them face down in a pile. Each player in turn takes a number tag and places it in any open place on his or her number board until all places are filled on both boards. A number tag cannot be moved after it is placed on the board. If the Star tag is drawn, it is placed in the far left position on the board. The player who makes the smaller number wins.







Acquaints parents with the mathematics their children are studying and supports interaction between parents and children

### Assessment

- Multiple-Choice Tests
- Free-Response Tests
- Basic-Facts Tests
- Mid-Year Test
- End-of-Year Test

### Record Keeping

- Class Record Form
- Student Profile
- Assignment Charts

And, a bulletin board bonus on each TRB divider

### Teaching Aids

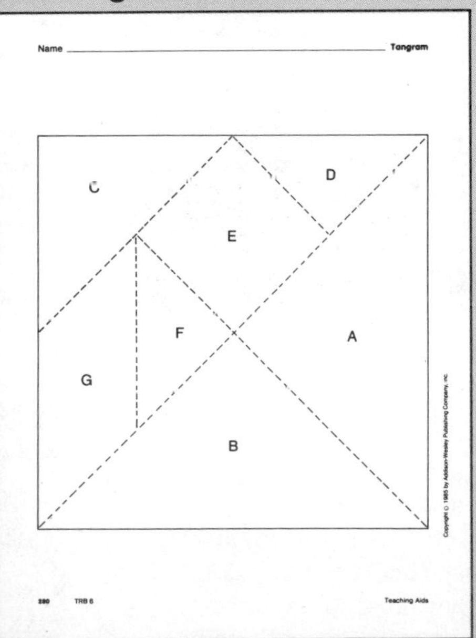

Name ______________ **Tangram**







Provides resources for hands-on learning experiences

# A team of math professionals .

The authors and consultants bring a broad range of teaching experience and contemporary mathematical application to this new program. Their experiences will save you

"The program provides students with the solid mathematical background and skills that will enable them to face the consumer, technological, and scientific challenges of the future."

**Robert E. Eicholz**
He has taught at the junior and senior high school levels and has spent 25 years developing mathematics textbooks for teachers and students. He directed the writing team of the Greater Cleveland Mathematics Program K-3, and coauthored *Elementary School Mathematics, Investigating School Mathematics,* and *Mathematics in Our World.* He is often called upon to speak at in-service programs and workshops for mathematics teachers throughout the country.

"Your students will experience a variety of problem situations with an emphasis on real-world applications. Skills are carefully developed so that students will build the repertoire of strategies necessary for creative problem solving."

**Phares G. O'Daffer**
With teaching experiences at elementary through high school levels, he is now engaged in pre-service and in-service education of elementary mathematics teachers at Illinois State University. He has coordinated the development of a comprehensive mathematics laboratory for teachers and students. He coauthored *Elementary School Mathematics, Investigating School Mathematics,* and *Mathematics in Our World* as well as many other textbooks and journal articles.

"We focus on understanding and careful skill development, with ample practice immediately and at carefully-spaced intervals. Your students will learn mental math and estimation skills that will help them compute quickly, accurately, and properly."

**Charles R. Fleenor**
His teaching experiences include working with students at the elementary through high school levels. He has conducted many in-service programs for mathematics teachers at all grade levels. The past 15 years he has devoted to developing and writing elementary and junior high school mathematics textbooks including the previous Addison-Wesley series *Investigating School Mathematics* and *Mathematics in Our World.*

## Consultants

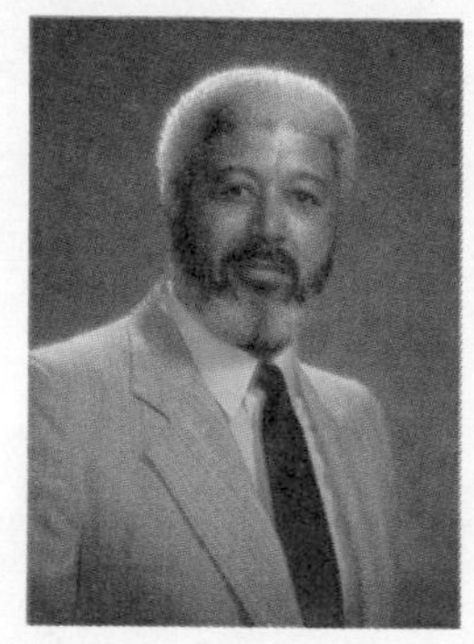

**Martin L. Johnson**
With teaching experience at elementary, middle school, and secondary levels, he has published many articles and books on diagnostic and prescriptive mathematics. He teaches mathematics education courses at the University of Maryland.

**Carol A. Thornton**
After 10 years as an elementary and high school math teacher, she joined the staff of Illinois State University. She has authored many publications relating to mathematics for handicapped or underachieving students.

time and make your teaching efficient. With Addison–Wesley Mathematics, you have a distinguished group of colleagues with you in the classroom.

**Randall I. Charles**
He has teaching experience at all levels including five years as an elementary and junior high school mathematics supervisor. For several years, he was involved in federally-funded problem solving projects for Indiana University and for the West Virginia Department of Education. While at Illinois State University, he has presented in-service programs and authored several publications on the subject of problem solving.

"We give you a flexible teaching package that allows you to teach, test, and manage with ease. You will have the information and materials to select your teaching style to assure success for you and your students."

**Sharon Young**
Formerly an elementary school teacher in California and New Jersey, she now teaches pre-service and in-service education courses at Louisiana State University. She previously taught mathematics education courses at the University of Colorado and West Virginia University. She has conducted numerous in-service programs and workshops in the United States, Canada, and Europe.

"We provide opportunities to reinforce, reteach, or enrich each lesson. Teaching tips on error analysis, problem solving, and special education allow you to meet all students' needs."

**Carne S. Barnett**
Her classroom experience includes several years of teaching at the elementary, junior high, and secondary levels. She now instructs and supervises teacher candidates in the Elementary and Secondary Education Departments at the University of California at Berkeley. She is the author of several mathematics education publications.

"Your students will learn to understand the power of calculators and computers. They will be able to read and write simple programs."

**John A. Dossey**
His teaching background includes experience as a K-12 mathematics coordinator. Now at Illinois State University, he has published many articles and, with Carol Thornton and others, co-authored *Teaching Mathematics to Children with Special Needs.*

**Betty C. Lee**
As a mathematics demonstration teacher and city-wide teacher consultant, she has planned and conducted in-service mathematics workshops, trained teachers, and developed enrichment materials for the Detroit Board of Education.

## Computer Advisors

**Bobby Goodson**
Sunnyvale, CA

**Barbara Peck**
New Haven, CT

**Connie Beaudry**
West Haven, CT

# Scope and Sequence

| Book 5 | Book 6 | Book 7 |
|---|---|---|
| **Adding Whole Numbers** | | |
| Basic facts, 2-3, 7, 22, 26, 48, 74<br>Missing addends, 3<br>Addition properties, 6<br>Mental addition, 50-51<br>Estimating sums, 50-51, 67*<br>Adding 2- through 5-digit numbers, 52-55, 72, 102, 160<br>Column addition, 56-57, 72, 102, 160 | Basic facts, 2-3, 10, 15,* 18, 22, 52, 78<br>Missing addends, 2-3<br>Addition properties, 3<br>Mental addition, 32-33. 39<br>Estimating sums, 32-33<br>Adding whole numbers, 36-37, 50, 52, 78, 106, 136<br>Column addition, 38-39 | Adding whole numbers, 9,* 12-13, 26, 30, 35,* 133<br>Estimating sums, 10-11<br>Column addition, 12-13, 30, 35*<br>Mental addition, 13*<br>Missing addends, 43<br>Addition properties, 370 |
| **Subtracting Whole Numbers** | | |
| Basic facts, 4-5, 7, 22, 26, 48, 74<br>Subtraction properties, 6<br>Checking subtraction, 6-7, 62<br>Mental subtraction, 60-61<br>Estimating differences, 60-61, 67*<br>Subtracting 2- through 5-digit numbers, 62-67, 72, 102, 160<br>Subtracting across a zero, 66-67 | Basic facts, 2-3, 10, 15,* 18, 22, 52, 78<br>Checking subtraction, 2<br>Subtraction properties, 3<br>Mental subtraction, 32-33<br>Estimating differences, 32-33<br>Subtracting whole numbers, 40-43, 50, 52, 78, 136<br>Subtracting across a zero, 42-43 | Subtracting whole numbers, 9,* 14-15, 26, 30, 35*<br>Estimating differences, 10-11<br>Mental subtraction, 15* |
| **Multiplying Whole Numbers** | | |
| Basic facts, 10, 13, 22, 26, 35,* 48, 74, 104-105, 117*<br>Multiples, 10<br>Missing factors, 11*<br>Multiplication properties, 12<br>Mental multiplication, 104-108, 128, 141,* 175,* 218<br>Estimating products, 108-109, 111,* 163*<br>Multiplying by a 1-, 2-, or 3-digit factor, 110-113, 116-117, 120-122, 128, 160, 167,* 175,* 195,* 218<br>Multiplying by multiples of 10 and 100, 114-115, 117,* 122, 128, 141,* 160, 195*<br>Multiplying three numbers, 122<br>Lattice multiplication, 129 | Basic facts, 4-5, 10, 15,* 18, 22, 52, 78<br>Multiplication properties, 5, 80<br>Missing factors, 5<br>Multiples, 14<br>Mental multiplication, 80-81, 102, 115,* 192<br>Estimating products, 82-83, 87,* 95, 97<br>Multiplying whole numbers, 84-89, 94-97, 102, 136, 192<br>Exponential notation, 92-93, 115,*<br>Multiplying three numbers, 96,* 97*<br>Russian peasant multiplication, 103 | Multiplication properties, 56<br>Mental multiplication, 57, 73,* 84, 114, 175*<br>Estimating products, 58-59, 86, 114, 277*<br>Multiplying whole numbers, 15, 19,* 39,* 60-63, 73, 84, 86, 114, 134<br>Exponential notation, 66-67, 84, 86, 114, 134, 175*<br>Napier's Rods, 85 |
| **Dividing Whole Numbers** | | |
| Basic facts, 16-18, 22, 26, 48, 74, 117,* 175*<br>Division properties, 18<br>Mental division, 132-133, 162-163, 175,* 184, 218<br>Estimating quotients, 134-135, 147*<br>Dividing by a 1-digit number: 1-, 2-, 3-, and 4-digit quotients, 136, 137-144, 146-147, 158, 167,* 186, 248, 270<br>short division, 150-151<br>Remainders, 136, 149<br>Zero in the quotient, 144, 174-175<br>Average, 152, 158<br>Dividing by multiples of 10, 164-165, 179, 184, 195<br>Dividing by a 2-digit number: 1-, 2-, and 3-digit quotients, 166-169, 172-175, 179, 184, 195* | Basic facts, 6-7, 10, 15,* 18, 22, 52, 78, 95*<br>Division properties, 7<br>Mental division, 108-109<br>Estimating quotients, 110-111, 115*<br>Dividing by a 1-digit number, 112-117, 134, 143,* 166, 173,* 224<br>Remainders, 112, 118<br>Zero in the quotient, 114, 128<br>Average, 118-119, 134<br>Dividing by multiples of 10, 120-121, 143,* 173,* 224<br>Dividing by a 2-digit number, 122-124, 126-128, 134, 143,* 166, 173,* 224<br>Dividing by a 3-digit number, 129, 143 | Mental division, 70, 84, 86, 91,* 134<br>Estimating quotients, 71, 277*<br>Dividing whole numbers, 19,* 39,* 72-76, 84, 86, 91,* 134 |
| **Integers** | | |
| | Positive and negative, 366-367, 382, 389*<br>Adding, 368-371, 374-375, 382, 389,* 406<br>Subtracting, 372-375, 382, 389,* 406<br>Equations, 372-373, 382-383<br>Comparing and ordering, 376, 379,* 382, 389,* 406<br>Integer coordinates, 378-379 | Positive and negative, 368-369, 390, 412<br>Comparing and ordering, 368-369, 390, 412<br>Integer properties, 370-371<br>Adding, 372-375, 377,* 383,* 390, 412<br>Subtracting, 376-377, 383,* 390, 412<br>Multiplying, 380-381, 390, 395,* 412<br>Dividing, 382-383, 390, 395,* 412<br>Integer coordinates, 384-385 |

**Note:** Red type indicates that a topic is being introduced for the first time. The page numbers labeled with a * indicate references in Skillkeeper or Think Math activities.

# Scope and Sequence

## Rounding and Estimation

| Book 5 | Book 6 | Book 7 |
|---|---|---|
| Rounding whole numbers and money, 40-41, 46, 50-51, 57*, 74, 102, 130<br>Rounding decimals, 84-85, 91*, 98, 186<br>Estimating<br>amounts, 36<br>sums and differences with whole numbers and decimals, 50-51, 60-61, 67*, 86-87, 89*, 163*<br>on a number line, 77*<br>products, 108-109, 111*, 163*<br>quotients, 134-135, 147*, 163*<br>time, 115*<br>measurement, 192-193, 205, 206, 247, 392-393, 398, 400<br>with fractions, 231, 252, 317<br>ratio, 369* | Rounding, 30-31, 50, 60-61, 78, 106, 136, 150-151, 166, 325*<br>Estimating<br>sums and differences, 32-34, 62-63, 68, 255*<br>products and quotients, 82-83, 87*, 95, 97, 110 138-139, 145*, 146, 149*, 157*, 159*, 160*, 241<br>measurement, 171, 178, 180, 182, 191, 292, 396, 398<br>time, 185*, 283*<br>with graphs, 323*<br>area, 355* | Rounding, 8-9, 30, 38-39, 52, 54, 86, 118-119<br>Estimating<br>sums and differences, 10-11, 26, 30, 44-45, 54, 86<br>products and quotients, 58-59, 71, 86, 90-91, 100-101, 110, 114, 128-129, 132, 134, 162, 192, 222, 277<br>with fractions, 204<br>percent, 299<br>measurement, 249, 335* |

## Fractions

| Book 5 | Book 6 | Book 7 |
|---|---|---|
| Parts of regions or sets, 220-221<br>Equivalent fractions, 222-223, 228, 237*, 246, 353<br>Cross products, 223, 229<br>Lowest-terms fractions, 226-227, 237*<br>Comparing and ordering, 228-229, 237*, 246, 270<br>Improper fractions and mixed numbers, 234-235, 253, 257, 291*<br>Least common denominator, 236-237<br>Adding and subtracting fractions and mixed numbers<br>like denominators, 232-233, 246, 250-251, 254-255, 268, 270, 300, 305*, 320, 325*, 342<br>unlike denominators, 238-241, 246, 250-251, 254-255, 258-263, 268, 270, 291*, 300, 305*, 320, 325*, 342<br>Estimating with, 231, 252, 317<br>Finding a fraction of a whole number, 302-303<br>Multiplying fractions and mixed numbers, 304-305, 308-309, 316, 327*, 386<br>Dividing fractions, 312-313<br>Fractions and decimals, 331* | Parts of regions or sets, 194-195<br>Equivalent and lowest-terms fractions, 196-197, 199, 220, 243*, 250, 267, 287*, 298, 320<br>Improper fractions and mixed numbers, 200-201<br>Comparing and ordering fractions and mixed numbers, 202, 209*, 213*, 241*<br>Least common denominator, 207, 220<br>Adding and subtracting fractions and mixed numbers<br>like denominators, 204-205, 216, 220, 229*<br>unlike denominators, 208-216, 220, 250, 298<br>Estimating with, 206, 245<br>Cross products, 213<br>Finding a fraction of a whole number, 226-227, 248, 276, 281*, 320<br>Multiplying and dividing fractions and mixed numbers, 228-233, 239-243, 248, 276, 281*, 287*, 320<br>Reciprocals, 228-229, 231<br>Mental multiplication, 233*<br>Fractions and decimals, 236-238, 248, 276, 320 | Fractions, 194-195, 197*, 211*<br>Equivalent lowest-terms fractions, 196-199, 209*, 220, 246, 274, 292<br>Improper fractions and mixed numbers, 200-201, 209*, 220, 246, 292<br>Comparing and ordering fractions and mixed numbers, 202-203, 220, 246, 278-279, 290, 292<br>Cross products, 203*<br>Estimating fractions, 204<br>Least common denominator, 206, 208<br>Adding and subtracting fractions and mixed numbers, 206-215, 220, 229*, 230, 233*, 246, 292<br>Finding a fraction of a whole number, 224-225, 235<br>Multiplying and dividing fractions and mixed numbers, 226-230, 232-237, 244, 253*, 274, 320<br>Reciprocals, 231, 274<br>Fractions and decimals, 238-241, 244-245, 274, 320 |

## Decimals

| Book 5 | Book 6 | Book 7 |
|---|---|---|
| Decimal place value through thousandths, 76-81, 98, 186<br>Decimals and money, 79*, 92<br>Comparing and ordering, 82-83, 91*, 98, 130, 186<br>Rounding, 84-85, 91*, 98, 186, 313*<br>Mental addition and subtraction, 86-87<br>Estimating sums and differences, 86-87, 89*<br>Adding, 88-89, 98, 113*, 130, 186, 205*, 345*<br>Subtracting, 90-91, 98, 113*, 130, 186, 205*<br>Estimating products and quotients, 322-323, 340, 366<br>Multiplying, 324-327, 340, 347*, 366, 375*<br>working with zeros, 326-327<br>Dividing by a whole number, 330-333, 340, 366, 375*<br>working with zeros, 332-333<br>Mental multiplication and division, 336-337<br>Multiplying and dividing by multiples of 10, 336-337, 340, 347* | Decimal place value through hundred-thousandths, 54-57, 76, 87*, 106, 166<br>Comparing and ordering, 58-59, 76, 87*, 106, 136<br>Rounding, 60-61, 76, 106, 150-151, 166<br>Estimating sums and differences, 62-63, 68<br>Adding, 64-65, 67*, 76, 95*, 106, 159*, 166<br>Subtracting, 66-67, 76, 95*, 106, 159*, 166<br>Estimating products and quotients, 138-139, 145, 146, 149*, 157*, 160*<br>Multiplying, 140-145, 159*, 160, 164, 183*, 192, 250, 309*, 337*<br>Mental multiplication and division, 144-145, 152-153, 159*, 164, 174, 175, 192, 250<br>Whole number divisors, 148-151, 153, 160, 173*, 183*, 192, 205*, 250<br>Decimal divisors, 156-160, 164, 173*, 183*, 192, 205*<br>Fractions and decimals, 236-238, 248, 276, 320<br>Mixed decimals, 238, 304-305<br>Repeating decimals, 249 | Decimal place value through millionths, 32-35, 52, 54, 109*<br>Comparing and ordering, 36-37, 52, 54, 86, 240-241<br>Rounding, 38-39, 52, 54, 86, 118-119<br>Adding, 40-41, 43*, 52, 54, 61*, 86<br>Subtracting, 42-43, 52, 54, 61*, 86<br>Estimating sums and differences, 44-45, 54, 86<br>Multiplying, 88-89, 92-95, 110, 114, 151*, 162, 192<br>Estimating products, 90-91, 100-101, 110, 114, 162, 192<br>Zeros in products, 94-95<br>Mental multiplication, 98-99, 103*, 110, 119*, 192<br>Whole number divisors, 116-117, 132, 134, 162, 167*, 222<br>Mental division, 120, 125*, 132, 134, 222<br>Decimal divisors, 124-125, 132, 134, 162, 167*, 222<br>Estimating quotients, 128-129, 132, 134, 162, 222<br>Repeating and terminating decimals, 240-241 |

**Note:** Red type indicates that a topic is being introduced for the first time. The page numbers labeled with a * indicate references in Skillkeeper or Think Math activities.

# Scope and Sequence

| Book 5 | Book 6 | Book 7 |
|---|---|---|
| **Numbers and Numeration** | | |
| Whole number place value through hundred billions, 28-35, 46, 74, 102, 130<br>Expanded notation, 30-34<br>Roman numerals, 37, 389*<br>Egyptian numerals, 39*<br>Comparing and ordering<br>whole numbers, 38-39, 43, 46, 57*, 74<br>decimals, 82-83, 91*, 98, 102, 130, 186<br>fractions, 228-229, 237*, 246<br>Number line, 40, 228, 234<br>Decimal place value through thousandths, 76-81, 98, 186<br>Integers, 207*<br>Number patterns, 5*, 15*, 17*, 51*, 65*, 105*, 122*, 239*, 251*, 263*, 279*, 309*, 341* | Whole number place value through hundred billions, 24-27, 43*, 50, 59, 78, 136<br>Expanded notation, 24-27<br>Comparing and ordering<br>whole numbers, 28-29, 50, 78<br>decimals, 58-59, 76, 87*, 106, 136, 166<br>fractions and mixed numbers, 202, 209, 213<br>integers, 376, 379*, 382, 389*, 406<br>Roman numerals, 47<br>Decimal place value through hundred-thousandths, 54-57, 76, 87*, 106, 166<br>Exponential notation, 92-93, 115*<br>Scientific notation, 403<br>Number patterns, 5*, 77, 85, 123*, 153*, 160*, 211*, 249, 279*, 317, 329*, 371*, 383 | Whole number place value through hundred trillions, 4-5, 139*<br>Comparing and ordering<br>whole numbers, 6-7, 26, 30<br>decimals, 36-37, 52, 54, 86, 240-241<br>fractions, 202-203, 220, 246, 278-279, 290, 292<br>integers, 369, 390, 412<br>Ancient numeration systems, 2-3<br>Decimal place value through millionths, 32-35, 52, 54, 139*<br>Other bases, 55, 339<br>Exponential notation, 66-67, 84, 86, 114, 134, 175*<br>Scientific notation, 102-103, 110, 114, 162, 192<br>Number patterns, 7*, 117*, 169*, 239*, 375* |
| **Ratio, Proportion, and Percent** | | |
| Ratio, 328, 368-371, 384<br>Estimating ratios, 369*<br>Equal ratios, 370, 372-373, 384, 393*, 408<br>Cross products, 373<br>Ratio and percent, 374-375, 384<br>Percents, decimals, and fractions, 376-378<br>Percent of a number, 380-381, 405<br>Equations, 372-373, 393* | Ratio, 278-279, 296, 303*, 320, 364<br>Equal ratios, 280-281, 296, 303*, 320<br>Cross products, 280-281<br>Solving proportions, 282-283, 296, 309*, 320<br>Using proportions, 284-285, 288-292<br>Pi, 297<br>Ratio and percent, 300-301, 316<br>Percent, decimals, and fractions, 301-306, 316, 325*, 344, 384<br>Percent of a number, 308-312, 316, 326*, 327*, 337*, 344, 349*, 384 | Ratio and rate, 276-277, 285*, 290<br>Equal ratios, cross products, 278-279, 290, 366<br>Solving proportions, 280-281, 286, 290, 366<br>Golden ratio, 291<br>Ratio and percent, 294-295, 307*<br>Percent, decimals, and fractions, 296-298, 300-301, 307*, 311*, 318, 325*, 342, 392<br>Estimating percents, 299<br>Percent of a number, 302-304, 307*, 308-309, 318, 342, 392<br>Percent one number is of another, 306-309, 318-319, 325*, 342, 392<br>Finding a number when the percent is known, 310-311, 318, 392<br>Proportion and percent, 314-315<br>Percent of change, 319 |
| **Number Properties and Number Theory** | | |
| Order and grouping properties, 6, 12<br>One and zero properties, 6, 12, 18<br>Multiplication-addition property, 12, 311<br>Even and odd numbers, 11*<br>Order of operations, 19<br>Palindromes, 55*<br>Divisibility, 149*<br>Prime numbers, 159<br>Positive and negative integers, 207*<br>Square root, 215<br>Greatest common factor, 224<br>Least common multiple, 236 | Order and grouping properties, 3, 5, 80<br>One and zero properties, 3, 5, 7<br>Multiplication-addition property, 5<br>Order of operations, 11, 65*<br>Even and odd numbers, 14, 165<br>Factors, 15, 113*<br>Prime and composite numbers, 117*, 165<br>Divisibility, 135<br>Perfect numbers, 165<br>Greatest common factor, 198-199<br>Least common multiple, 207<br>Square and triangular numbers, 29*, 221<br>Square root, 351 | Properties of addition and multiplication, 56, 370<br>Square and triangular numbers, 11*, 67<br>Fibonacci numbers, 27<br>Palindromic numbers, 65<br>Order of operations, 75<br>Casting out nines, 111<br>Factors, 164-165, 181*, 188<br>Divisibility, 166-167, 382*<br>Prime and composite numbers, 168-169, 181*, 188<br>Prime factorization, 170-171, 174-175, 181*, 188, 199*, 222, 274<br>Greatest common factor, 172-173, 188, 189, 198, 199*, 222, 274<br>Abundant numbers, 167*<br>Least common multiple, 174-175, 188, 274 |
| **Pre-Algebra** | | |
|  |  | Writing and evaluating expressions, 176-177, 188<br>Addition, subtraction, multiplication, and division equations, 178-181, 188, 222, 274, 279*<br>Using and writing equations, 182-185<br>Graphing equations, 386-387<br>Using formulas, 81, 252, 256, 260, 304-305, 322, 324, 328, 330, 338, 398-399 |

**Note:** Red type indicates that a topic is being introduced for the first time. The page numbers labeled with a * indicate references in Skillkeeper or Think Math activities.

# Scope and Sequence

| Book 5 | Book 6 | Book 7 |
|---|---|---|
| **Graphing, Probability, and Statistics** | | |
| Reading and making tally charts, 42<br>Coordinate graphing, 292-293, 299, 365<br>Bar graphs, 344-347, 356-357, 364, 386<br>Pictographs, 344-345, 348-349, 364, 408<br>Circle graphs, 344-345, 350-351, 364, 408<br>Line graphs, 344-345, 352-353, 355, 364, 408<br>Making a bar graph, a pictograph, a circle graph, a line graph 354-355<br>Probability, 358-361<br>Prediction, 361,* 405 | Coordinate graphing, 268-269, 287, 378-379<br>Bar graphs, 98, 322-323, 330-331, 342, 364<br>estimating with, 323*<br>double bar graphs, 333<br>Line graphs, 98, 328-329, 331<br>Circle graphs, 307, 326-327, 342<br>Pictographs, 324-325<br>Making graphs, 323, 325, 327, 329<br>Evaluating graphs, 330-331<br>Mean, 151, 332, 342, 357,* 364<br>Median and mode, 334<br>Probability, prediction, and expected numbers 336-339, 342, 364 | Equally likely outcomes, 344-345, 364<br>Chance and probability, 346-347, 350-351, 353,* 364-365, 392<br>Ordered pairs in probability, 348-351, 364<br>Prediction, 349*<br>Frequency, range, and mode, 352-353, 364, 392<br>Mean and median, 354-355, 364, 373,* 392<br>Bar graphs, 201*<br>double bar graphs, 299, 356, 360<br>histograms, 356, 360<br>Circle graphs, 299, 359, 361, 364<br>Line segment graphs, 357, 361, 378<br>Pictographs, 358, 392<br>Making graphs, 356, 357, 358, 359<br>Coordinate graphing, 385-387<br>Graphing equations, 386-387 |
| **Geometry** | | |
| Points, lines, and segments, 272-273, 298<br>Lines: parallel, intersecting, and perpendicular, 272-273, 298<br>Rays and right, acute, and obtuse angles, 274-275, 280-281, 298, 320, 366<br>Measuring and drawing angles, 276-277, 320<br>Triangles: equilateral, isosceles, and scalene 278-279, 298, 320, 366<br>Quadrilaterals, 280-281, 298, 366<br>Other polygons, 282, 298<br>Circles: center, radius, diameter, 284-285, 298<br>Congruent figures, 286-287, 366<br>Similar figures, 288-289, 366<br>Lines of symmetry, 290-291<br>Prism, sphere, cylinder, cone, pyramid, 294<br>Face, edge, vertex, 294<br>Constructing star polygons, 23<br>Shape perception, 85,* 227,* 275,* 287*<br>Space perception, 99, 121,* 143,* 233* | Points, lines, segments, rays, and angles, 252-253<br>Measuring and drawing angles, 254-255<br>Perpendicular and parallel lines, 256-257<br>Triangles: equilateral, isosceles, scalene, acute, right, obtuse, 258-259, 274, 298, 344<br>Quadrilaterals, 260-261, 274<br>Other polygons, 262, 274, 298, 344<br>Circles: center, radius, diameter, chord, central angle, 263, 274, 298, 344<br>$\pi$ 297<br>Congruent figures, 264-265, 268, 274<br>Lines of symmetry, 266-267, 274<br>Graphing congruent and similar figures, 268-269<br>Drawings and constructions, 255-257, 263, 275<br>Prism, sphere, cylinder, cone, pyramid, 270-271<br>Similar figures, 286-287<br>Translations, 343<br>Space perception, 19, 265,* 271,* 331,* 387*<br>Shape perception, 93,* 157,* 195,* 227,* 305* | Basic geometric figures, 136-137, 192, 246<br>Angles: acute, right, obtuse, straight, complementary, supplementary, 138-139, 160, 192, 246<br>Triangles, 140-141, 160, 192, 246<br>Quadrilaterals, 142-143, 160, 246<br>Other polygons, 144-145, 192<br>Circles: center, radius, diameter, chord, central angle, arc, 146-147, 160, 192, 246, 322-325, 329,* 331*<br>Congruent figures, 148-149<br>Lines of symmetry, 150-151<br>Polyhedrons, 156-157, 161<br>Constructions<br>perpendicular and parallel lines, 152-153<br>segment and angle bisectors, 154-155<br>Similar figures, 284-285, 290<br>Cross sections, 334-335<br>Shape perception, 143,* 145,* 149,* 155,* 157,* 213,* 257*<br>Space perception, 161, 315* |
| **Technology** | | |
| Calculator<br>using a calculator, 24-25<br>place value, 33*<br>adding and subtracting, 53,* 57,* 61,* 89* 133*<br>multiplying, 113,* 115,* 117,* 121,* 122,* 169,* 215, 223,* 229,* 327*<br>dividing, 133,* 139,* 141,* 151,* 191*<br>square root, 215<br>Computer<br>inputs, rules, and outputs, 73<br>variables in programs, 318-319<br>flowcharts, 100-101<br>using programs, 216-217<br>computer drawings (Logo), 406-407 | Calculator<br>using a calculator, 20-21, 383<br>multiplying, 27,* 85,* 95,* 97, 145,* 317, 383<br>adding, 39,* 65,* 383<br>dividing, 117,* 123,* 129,* 139,* 151,* 153,* 157,* 160,* 305*<br>combining operations, 283,* 317, 355*<br>Computer<br>binary digits, 51<br>giving input, 104-105<br>flowcharts, 104-105, 222-223<br>decisions in programs, 222-223<br>using strings in programs, 318-319<br>computer drawings (Logo), 404-405 | Calculator<br>combining operations, 15,* 227,* 353,* 361<br>using a calculator, 28-29, 77,* 373*<br>dividing, 189,<br>exponents, 67,* 103*<br>percent, 303,* 307,* 311,* 319<br>Computer<br>binary place value, 53<br>computer operations, 75*<br>flowcharts and computer programs, 112-113<br>inputs in computer programs, 190-191<br>computer decisions, 272-273<br>loops in computer programs, 340-341<br>computer drawings (Logo), 410-411 |

**Note:** Red type indicates that a topic is being introduced for the first time. The page numbers labeled with a * indicate references in Skillkeeper or Think Math activities.

# Scope and Sequence

## Time and Money

### Book 5

**Time**

Estimating, 115*
Units of time, 208, 261*
Elapsed time, 209
Time zones, 210
Calendar, 211

**Money**

Place value, 29*, 79*
Rounding, 50-51
Adding and subtracting, 14, 54-55, 57, 62-63, 67, 72*, 86, 89, 90-96, 102, 130, 160, 205*
Estimating sums and differences, 50-51, 60-61, 67*, 68, 86-87
Mixed practice, 69, 124-125, 171, 180, 256, 264-265, 329, 334, 338, 357, 379
Making change, 92-93
Tax, 125, 329, 411
Multiplying and dividing, 110-113, 137-138, 139*, 142, 148-149, 176-177, 179, 195*, 270, 330-331
Unit prices, 176-177, 334, 382

### Book 6

**Time**

Units of time, 184
Adding and subtracting, 185, 190, 205*
Estimating, 185, 283*
Time zones, 186
Elapsed time, 187

**Money**

Mixed practice, 12, 46, 71-73, 146, 203, 310, 312
Rounding, 30-31, 150-151
Estimating sums and differences, 32-33, 62, 68-69, 255
Adding, 31*, 36-39, 50, 52, 64-65, 127*, 159
Subtracting, 31*, 40-43, 50, 66-67, 122*, 136, 159
Making change, 70
Multiplying, 84-85, 127*, 141-143, 145
Dividing, 114-117, 126-127, 143*, 148-151, 153, 161
Estimating products and quotients, 138-139, 146
Unit price, 161
Simple interest, 310-311, 314
Discount price, 312

### Book 7

**Time**

Adding and subtracting units of time, 18-19, 30
Time zones, 48-49

**Money**

Adding, 40-41, 54, 61*, 297*
Subtracting, 42-43, 54, 61*
Estimating
 sums and differences, 44-45, 54, 86
 products and quotients, 58-59, 90-91, 100-101, 128-129
Mixed practice, 47, 68-69, 96-97, 104-105, 218, 316, 404-405
Multiplying, 93-95, 122-123
Dividing, 118-119
Simple interest, 304-305
Discount and sale price, 312-313
Sales tax, 94-95

## Measurement

### Book 5

Length
 m, cm, km, mm, 188-195, 214, 225*, 248, 277*, 300, 337
 in., ft, yd, mi, 303*, 388-390, 404, 408
Perimeter
 metric units, 196-197, 214, 225*, 248, 300
 customary units, 391
Area
 $cm^2$, $m^2$, 198-199, 214, 225*, 248, 300
 $in.^2$, $ft^2$, $yd^2$, 394
Volume
 $cm^3$, $m^3$, 200-201, 214, 255*, 248, 300, 408
 $in.^3$, $ft^3$, 395
Capacity
 L, mL, kL, 202-203, 214, 248, 300, 337
 fl oz, c, pt, qt, gal, 303*, 396-397, 404, 408
Weight
 g, kg, 204-205, 214, 300, 337
 oz, lb, T, 303*, 398-399, 404, 408
Temperature
 Celsius, 206-207
 Fahrenheit, 400
Estimating
 length, 192-193, 392-393
 weight, 205, 398
 temperature, 206, 400
 area, 247
Scale drawing, 335
Changing metric units, 337

### Book 6

Length
 mm, cm, m, dm, dam, hm, km, 168-177, 190, 197*, 224, 276, 328*
 in., ft, yd, mi, 386-389, 399, 402, 406
 computing with customary units, 390
Capacity
 L, mL, kL, 178-179, 190, 224, 276
 fl oz, c, pt, qt, gal, 394-395, 402, 406
Weight
 g, mg, kg, 121*, 180-181, 190, 224, 329*
 oz, lb, T, 396-397, 399, 402, 406
Temperature
 Celsius, 182-183, 190
 Fahrenheit, 398, 402
Volume
 $cm^3$, $m^3$, 358-359, 367, 373*, 384
 $ft^3$, $yd^3$, 393
Changing metric units, 172-175, 178-180, 190
Scale drawing, 290-292
Perimeter, 346-347, 367, 384, 392, 406
Circumference, 348-349, 384, 406
Area
 of a rectangle, 350-351, 360, 367, 369*, 392, 406
 of a triangle, 352, 367, 384
 of a parallelogram, 352*
 of a circle, 354-355, 367, 369*, 384
 on a geoboard, 368
Surface area, 356-357, 367, 393
Estimating, 171, 178, 180, 182, 191, 355*, 359, 391, 396, 398

### Book 7

Length
 mm, cm, dm, m, dam hm, km, 248-251, 261*, 270, 292, 320, 342
 in., ft, yd, mi, 394-395, 403*, 408, 412
Perimeter, 252-253, 255, 270, 292, 320, 342
Area
 rectangles and parallelograms, 254-255, 270, 320, 396-397, 408, 412
 triangles and trapezoids, 256-257, 270, 292, 301*, 342
 circles, 324-327, 329*, 331*, 338, 366, 396-397, 408
Surface area
 rectangular prisms, 258-259, 320
 cylinders, 328-329, 338, 366
Volume
 prisms, 260-261, 270, 292, 301*, 342, 347*, 398-399, 408
 cylinders, 330-331, 335*, 338, 366, 398-399, 408, 412
 displacement, 271
Capacity
 L, mL, kL, 262-263, 270, 342
 fl oz, c, pt, qt, gal, 400-401, 408, 412
Weight
 mg, g, kg, t, 264-265, 320
 oz, lb, T, 402, 408, 412
Temperature
 Celsius, 266-267
 Fahrenheit, 403, 408, 412
Scale drawings, 286
Circumference, 322-323, 326-327, 331*, 338, 366
Estimating, 249, 335*

**Note:** Red type indicates that a topic is being introduced for the first time. The page numbers labeled with a * indicate references in Skillkeeper or Think Math activities.

## Problem Solving/ Applications

### Book 5

Use the checklist, 8-9, 118-119
Understand the question, 14, 171
question formulation, 14#5-12; 55#25; 69#8; 91#25; 107#34; 111#24; 133#31; 141#30; 163#38; 169#32; 251#28; 283#7; 327#28; 1, 27, 49, 75, 103, 131, 161, 187, 219, 249,271, 301, 321, 343, 367, 387
Find the data
graph, 42, 94, 153, 356
menu, 124-125
table, 42, 59, 95, 153, 180, 371
advertisement, 264-265, 334
catalog, 329
calendar, 211
recipe, 310
blueprint, 335
picture, 283
other sources, 15, 42-43, 94-95, 242-243, 335
missing and extra data, 43, 94-95; 9#1, 2; 14#3; 57#21; 63#27; 115#29; 117#26; 133#30; 145#4; 239#28; 241#28; 255#24; 305#22; 309#30; **DB** 43, 63, 65, 89, 109, 125, 153, 175, 189, 259, 307, 333, 334, 353, 391; **DH** 36, 42, 68, 93, 107, 111, 167, 189, 261, 310, 329, 355, 391, 394, 395, 401
Plan what to do (Strategies)
Choose the operations, 20, 154-155; **TT** 42, 43, 68, 95, 123, 171, 311, 334, 356
Guess and check, 44; **TM** 7, 273, 303, 349; **TT** 58, 59, 69, 93, 125, 155, 181, 231, 256, 295, 310, 329, 335, 357, 394, 399
Use logical reasoning, 47, 156, 269; **TM** 3, 31, 53, 63, 107, 111, 139, 173, 259, 289, 333, 345; **TT** 170, 180, 203, 371, 381, 397
Draw a picture, 70, 197; **TT** 87, 243, 307, 391,395
Make a list, 126; **TT** 135, 145, 178, 211
Find a pattern, 244, 341; **TM** 5, 17, 51, 55, 65, 105, 122, 149, 239, 251, 263, 279, 313, 323; **TT** 252, 265, 283
Make a table, 96; **TT** 109, 119, 153, 328
Work backward, 182; **TT** 197, 199, 209, 379, 401
Solve a simpler problem, 212; **TT** 230
Answer and check back, 36, 58, 68, 87, 109, 135, 170, 178, 209, 231, 252, 311
Practice and application, 69, 123, 145, 101, 199, 203, 230, 256, 266, 295, 296, 314, 306-307, 328, 338, 357, 362, 379, 381, 382, 391, 394, 395, 397, 399, 401, 402
Multiple-step problems, 9#7-9; 20#1, 2; 21#44; 25#3-5; 42#6; 58#3, 4; 68#1, 4, 5, 7; 69#2-4, 6, 7; 70#1, 2; 71#25, 26; 74#14; 87#4, 6, 8; 93#4, 6-9; 94#2, 3; 95#13; 109#5, 7; 119#1-5; 123#2-8; 124#2, 3, 5; 125#7-9, 12; 127#29; 135#7, 8; 147#27; 155#5-7; 157#36; 160#14; 165#28; 171#1-6; 180#2-4; 182#1, 2; 197#1, 2, 4, 6, 7; 199#4-6, 8; 203#5; 230#1, 5; 243#9; 263#20; 266#3; 279#14; 283#5; 295#4, 5; 296#1; 297#21; 307#6; 310#6; 314#1, 2; 327#29; 329#1-3; 334#1-5; 338#1; 356#7; 357#6, 7; 362#1; 379#1, 2, 5-7; 381#6, 7; 382#1; 394#2, 3, 6; 395#4, 6; 397#4; 399#7; 401#1, 3, 5; 402#3, 4

### Book 6

Use the checklist, 8-9, 90-91
Understand the question, 12
question formulation, 12#1-8; 37#30; 39#16; 85#31; 115#35; 143#33; 205#33; 209#31; 231#38; 243#37; 1, 23, 53, 79, 107, 137, 167, 193, 225, 251, 277, 299, 321, 345, 365, 385
Find the data
graph, 44, 98, 154, 333
table, 119, 155
advertisement, 312
map, 130
catalog, 203
plan sheet, 234-235
picture, 291, 347, 392-393
reference book, 155, 176-177
other sources, 13, 35, 72-73, 154-155, 284-285, 374-375
missing and extra data, 35; 41#25; 125#5, 6; 141#26; 149#35; 154#3; 159#30; 229#41; **DB** 35, 41, 61, 67, 89, 119, 141, 183, 233, 241, 291, 309, 325, 359, 377, 397; **DH** 69, 83, 98, 119, 127, 146, 155, 215, 233, 281, 285, 289, 307, 311, 349, 351, 359, 393, 397, 398, 399
Plan what to do (Strategies)
Choose the operations, 16, 131, 217; **TT** 34, 35, 44, 45, 46, 69, 99, 131, 187, 245, 311, 359, 377, 393
Guess and check, 48; **TT** 63, 71, 73, 98, 130, 155, 181, 291, 307, 347, 397; **TM** 11, 25, 27, 39, 67, 97, 141, 185, 231, 367
Use logical reasoning, 162; **TT** 177, 179, 244, 395; **TM** 3, 33, 37, 41, 59, 89, 121, 139, 149, 209, 215, 289, 379
Draw a picture, 74; **TT** 83, 91, 125, 293, 313
Make a list, 132; **TT** 146, 147, 203
Find a pattern, 77, 221, 246, 249, 317, 383; **TT** 333, 375, 399; **TM** 5, 29, 85, 123, 153, 160, 211, 279, 329, 371
Make a table, 100; **TT** 111, 119, 161, 217, 285, 335, 351
Work backward, 188; **TT** 206, 312
Solve a simpler problem, 218; **TT** 235
Answer and check back, 34, 46, 63, 69, 83, 111, 146, 161, 187, 206, 245, 307, 310-311, 355,399
Practice and application, 45, 71, 99, 125, 147, 179, 181, 244, 272, 293, 294, 313, 314, 335, 340, 351, 360, 377, 380, 395, 397, 400
Multiple-step problems, 9#4, 8; 16#1, 2; 17#45; 21#7, 8; 34#7, 8; 45#6; 46#2, 5; 49#28; 67#31; 69#3, 8; 71#3, 6-9; 72#4; 73#6, 9; 83#6; 91#6, 8; 98#6; 99#5, 8; 101#38; 111#2, 7; 119#2; 125#7; 130#3, 5; 131#5-7; 146#6; 147#5-7; 154#1, 2, 4; 161#3, 6, 7; 163#36; 179#8; 188#1, 2; 217#4-8; 227#28-30; 229#40; 231#37; 234#4; 235#6; 244#6; 245#7; 247#48; 293#2; 309#34; 312#1-5; 313#6, 7; 314#3; 329#1; 335#4, 5, 8; 340#2-5; 347#3-7; 351#3-5; 355#11; 357#7, 8; 359#4-9; 361#11-13; 377#9; 380#3; 392#5, 6, 8; 393#10, 11, 14, 16, 17; 395#3, 6, 7; 397#2-5; 399#5, 6; 401#28

### Book 7

Use the checklist, 16-17, 282-283
Understand the question, 20
question formulation, 41#39; 207#28; 303#44; 329#19; 347#21; 1, 31, 55, 87, 115, 135, 163, 193, 223, 247, 275, 293, 321, 343, 367, 393
Find the data
graph, 360-361, 378
table, 96-97, 105, 122-123, 205, 236-237, 265, 355
advertisement, 47
map, 48-49, 286
missing and extra data, 23; 63#48; 129#14; 277#29; 297#35; 311#31; 373#41; 377#40; 403#10; **DB** 23, 37, 39, 75, 103, 117, 199, 213, 237, 267, 283, 287, 301, 355, 395; **DH** 7, 19, 33, 45, 47, 57, 59, 119, 127, 157, 185, 207, 235, 237, 251, 261, 279, 297, 315, 329, 347, 387, 395
Plan what to do (Strategies)
Choose the operations, 78-79, 218; **TT** 237, 255, 327, 361, 379
Guess and check, 24; **TT** 47, 49, 81, 101, 105, 107, 123, 127, 265, 355, 401, 405; **TM** 93, 233, 281, 297, 329, 377, 399
Use logical reasoning, 242; **TT** 259, 286, 287, 309, 351; **TM** 19, 43, 99, 179, 213, 215, 371,385
Draw a picture, 108; **TT** 121, 217, 333, 378
Make a list, 50; **TT** 69, 79, 305
Find a pattern, 27, 82; **TT** 97; **TM** 7, 11, 65, 117, 169, 175, 239, 381
Make a table, 186; **TT** 205, 263
Work backward, 130; **TT** 185, 267, 283
Solve a simpler problem, 158; **TT** 183
Using equations and formulas, 81, 182-185, 305
Answer and check back, 21, 101, 126-127, 287, 404-405
Practice and application, 68-69, 106-107, 121, 217, 255, 259, 263, 267, 268, 288, 308-309, 316, 326-327, 332-333, 336, 350-351, 362, 379, 388, 401, 406
Multiple-step problems, 13#25; 21#3, 4; 41#37; 45#31; 47#3-5, 7; 51#29; 59#37-38; 61#32; 63#48; 65#29; 68#1, 6; 69#8, 10-12; 72#10; 75#27; 77#28; 78#3; 91#31; 95#37; 96#10; 97#7; 101#6-7, 105#8; 109#28, 29, 31; 119#35; 121#3, 8; 123#6, 8, 9; 125#34; 205#6, 9, 11; 211#27; 215#26; 217#4, 5, 7; 225#34; 229#30; 231#20; 233#29; 236#8, 6; 237#9, 11, 15; 253#14, 15; 259#2, 4-8; 261#14; 263#4, 5, 9-12; 265#4, 9; 267#6-7; 283#3, 5, 6, 9, 10; 286#5, 6; 287#2; 295#27; 297#34, 35; 303#42; 305#2, 4-7, 9; 307#22; 309#7, 11, 13; 323#20; 325#17; 326#2, 3; 327#9, 11, 12; 331#7, 8; 333#4, 7-9; 361#19, 20; 375#31; 378#5; 379#1, 3, 7; 395#18; 397#11, 12; 401#5, 12; 402#19, 20; 405#11, 12

**TM** Think Math
**TT** Try This
**DB** Data Bank
**DH** Data Hunt

**Note:** Red type indicates that a topic is being introduced for the first time. The page numbers labeled with a * indicate references in Skillkeeper or Think Math activities.

# Objectives for Book 6

**Chapter 1 Basic Facts**

1.1 Recall basic addition, subtraction, multiplication, and division facts and solve equations using basic facts.
1.2 Use parentheses to determine the order of operations.
1.3 Use basic facts to find multiples and factors of a given number.
1.4 Solve word problems using the 5-Point Checklist and cumulative computational skills.

**Chapter 2 Addition and Subtraction**

2.1 Read, write, compare, and order whole numbers.
2.2 Round whole numbers and estimate their sums and differences.
2.3 Add and subtract whole numbers up to 5 digits.
2.4 Read and write Roman numerals.
2.5 Solve word problems using the 5-Point Checklist and cumulative computational skills.

**Chapter 3 Decimals: Addition and Subtraction**

3.1 Read, write, compare, and order decimals.
3.2 Round decimals and estimate their sums and differences.
3.3 Add and subtract decimals.
3.4 Solve word problems using the 5-Point Checklist and cumulative computational skills.

**Chapter 4 Multiplication**

4.1 Use multiplication facts to find and estimate products.
4.2 Multiply by 1- and 2-digit factors.
4.3 Write exponents to show factors and powers of ten, and write standard numbers for numbers written in expanded notation.
4.4 Multiply by a 3-digit factor.
4.5 Solve word problems using the 5-Point Checklist and cumulative computational skills.

**Chapter 5 Division**

5.1 Use division facts to find and estimate quotients.
5.2 Divide by 1-digit divisors.
5.3 Find the average of a list of numbers.
5.4 Divide by 2- and 3-digit divisors.
5.5 Solve word problems using the 5-Point Checklist and cumulative computational skills.

**Chapter 6 Decimals: Multiplication and Division**

6.1 Round decimals and estimate their products and quotients.
6.2 Find products when one or both factors are decimals.
6.3 Find quotients of decimals divided by a whole number.
6.4 Find quotients of decimals divided by another decimal.
6.5 Solve word problems using the 5-Point Checklist and cumulative computational skills.

**Chapter 7 Measurement**

7.1 Express units of length in equivalent metric units using meters, centimeters, millimeters, and kilometers.
7.2 Choose appropriate metric units of capacity and express in larger or smaller units.
7.3 Choose appropriate metric units of weight and express in larger or smaller units.
7.4 Estimate and measure temperatures using degrees Celsius.
7.5 Express time in larger or smaller units and add and subtract units of time.
7.6 Solve word problems using the 5-Point Checklist and cumulative computational skills.

**Chapter 8 Fractions: Addition and Subtraction**

8.1 Find equivalent and lowest-terms fractions.
8.2 Compare and order fractions and mixed numbers.
8.3 Find sums and differences of fractions and mixed numbers with common denominators.
8.4 Find sums and differences of fractions and mixed numbers with unlike denominators.
8.5 Solve word problems using the 5-Point Checklist and cumulative computational skills.

**Chapter 9 Fractions: Multiplication and Division**

9.1 Find the product of fractions or of mixed numbers.
9.2 Find decimal and fraction equivalents.
9.3 Find the quotient of fractions or of mixed numbers.
9.4 Solve word problems using the 5-Point Checklist and cumulative computational skills.

**Chapter 10 Geometry**

10.1 Identify and write symbols for basic geometric figures.
10.2 Identify, classify, and draw angles according to their measure.
10.3 Identify and draw parallel and perpendicular lines.
10.4 Identify and classify polygons according to the measure of their angles, length of their sides, and number of sides.
10.5 Identify and write symbols for a chord, diameter, radius, and central angle.
10.6 Identify pairs of congruent and symmetric figures and lines of symmetry; use coordinates to graph congruent and symmetric figures.
10.7 Identify basic space figures and count their faces, vertices, and edges.

**Chapter 11 Ratio and Proportion**

11.1 Write a ratio as a fraction and use cross products to determine if the two ratios are equal.
11.2 Write and solve proportions.
11.3 Use proportions to solve problems involving similar figures or scale drawings.
11.4 Use proportions to estimate distances on a map.
11.5 Solve word problems using the 5-Point Checklist and cumulative computational skills.

**Chapter 12 Percent**

12.1 Write comparisons as ratios, fractions, decimals, and percents.
12.2 Find a percent of a number
12.3 Solve word problems using the 5-Point Checklist and cumulative computational skills.

**Chapter 13 Graphing and Probability**

13.1 Read and interpret graphs.
13.2 Find the mean, median, and the mode for a set of data.
13.3 Identify possible outcomes and predict the probability of a given event.
13.4 Solve word problems using the 5-Point Checklist and cumulative computational skills.

**Chapter 14 Perimeter, Area, and Volume**

14.1 Find the perimeter of a region.
14.2 Find the circumference of a circle.
14.3. Find the area of a rectangle or a triangle.
14.4 Find the area of a circle.
14.5 Find the surface area or volume of a box.
14.6 Solve word problems using the 5-Point Checklist and cumulative computational skills.

**Chapter 15 Integers**

15.1 Find sums and differences of two integers.
15.2 Compare two integers using the inequality symbols $>$ or $<$ .
15.3 Give integer coordinates of points in a coordinate plane.
15.4 Solve word problems using the 5-Point Checklist and cumulative computational skills.

**Chapter 16 Measurement: Customary Units**

16.1 Find and use appropriate units of length involving inches, feet, yards, and miles.
16.2 Find and use appropriate units of capacity involving tablespoons, ounces, cups, pints, quarts, and gallons.
16.3 Choose appropriate units to measure weight.
16.4 Estimate and measure temperatures using degrees Fahrenheit.
16.5 Solve word problems using the 5-Point Checklist and cumulative computational skills.

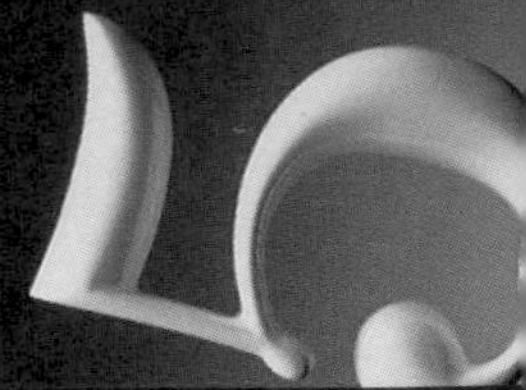

*The Overview is a great one-stop reference source for new teachers, substitutes, or teacher aides.*

## Objectives

- **1.1** Recall basic addition, subtraction, multiplication, and division facts, and solve equations using basic facts.
- **1.2** Use parentheses to determine the order of operations.
- **1.3** Use basic facts to find multiples and factors of a given number.
- **1.4** Solve word problems using the 5-Point Checklist and cumulative computational skills.

## Summary

In this chapter students review the meaning of the operations of addition, subtraction, multiplication, and division and practice the basic facts for these operations. The properties for the operations are presented and practical uses of these properties are suggested. The role of parentheses when these operations are combined is explored. Students then learn to use basic facts to find multiples and factors of given numbers. Throughout the chapter, students apply their understanding of the operations and knowledge of basic facts to solve word problems. A 5-Point Checklist is introduced as a guide in solving problems.

## Mathematical Background

**Addition and Subtraction** To help students understand the basic operations of addition and subtraction, emphasize the idea of addition as the combining of two sets of objects to find the total number. Provide students with experiences to illustrate the "take away," "compare," and "find how many more are needed" interpretations of subtraction. An understanding of the relationship between addition and subtraction helps students find and remember subtraction facts. Place-value models and fact families can be used to illustrate this relationship.

Part Part

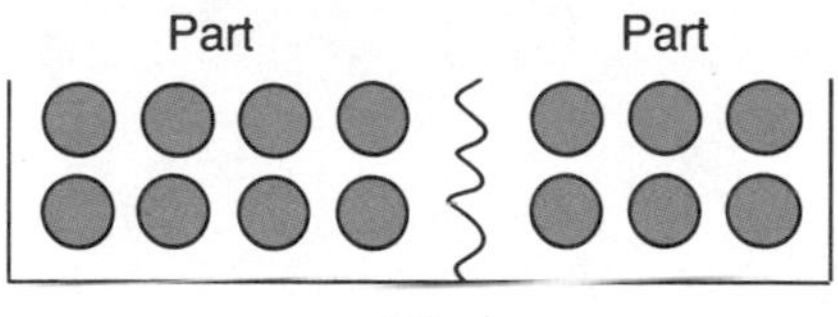

Whole

| Addend | Addend |
|---|---|
| 8 | 6 |
| Sum 14 | |

Fact Family

Students should be aware that two parts make up the whole and that if we start with a whole and take away one of the parts, we are left with the other part. Numbers representing the parts are called addends; the whole is called the sum. Emphasize the idea that subtraction is finding one addend when the other addend and the sum are known.

**Multiplication and Division** Emphasis on real-world situations in which students find the total amount for a number of equal amounts will prepare students for solving multiplication problems. To help students to understand division, present situations in which a total number of objects are given and have students find (a) how many sets of a given size can be formed; or (b) how many objects are in each of the given number of same-size sets.

As students write multiplication and division facts, emphasize the idea of factors and a product. In the illustration below, the first factor tells how many equal sets; the second factor tells how many in each of these sets. This points out the relationship between addition and multiplication. To emphasize the relationship between division and multiplication, remind students about fact families involving two factors and a product. In multiplication students see two factors and give the product; in division they see the product and one factor and are asked to give the other factor. This relationship between the two operations should be continually emphasized.

Factor Factor Product

$3 \times 4 = 12$

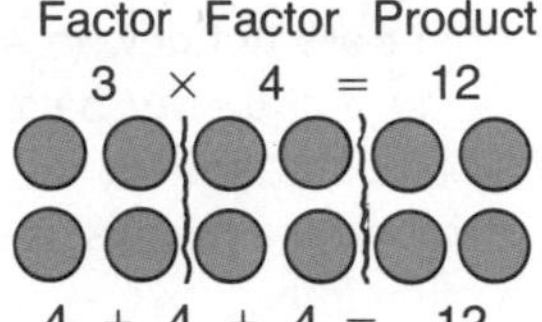

$4 + 4 + 4 = 12$

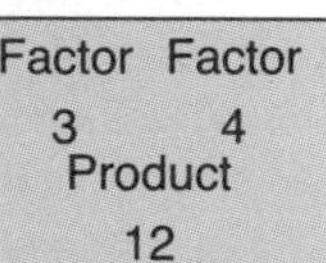


Fact Family

**Properties** An understanding of the 0 property for addition, the 1 property for multiplication, the commutative property, and the distributive property reduces the number of facts students must memorize. For example, students who understand the commutative property realize that when they know the fact $3 \times 4 = 12$ they also know the fact $4 \times 3 = 12$. The multiplication-addition (distributive) property can be used to find facts and to make computations involving larger factors.

$3 \times 4$ $3 \times 5$

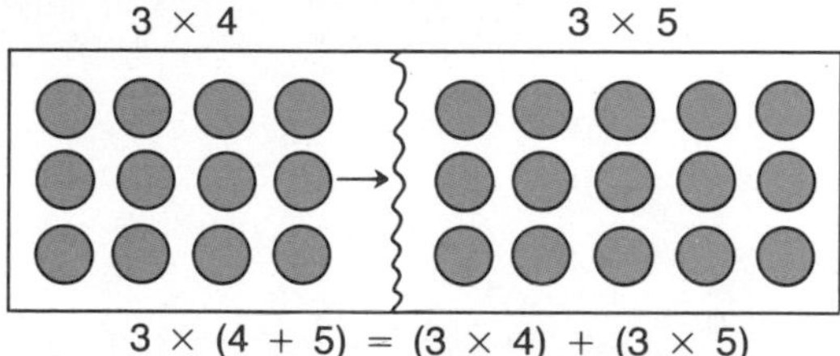

$3 \times (4 + 5) = (3 \times 4) + (3 \times 5)$

**Problem Solving** The 5-Point Checklist is introduced on page 8 as a guide to problem solving. The checklist is not a set of "rules" or an algorithm to solve every problem; it is suggested as a general approach to problem solving. Throughout the text, the focus will be on one or more of these five steps—question, data, plan, answer, and check—as important elements in attempting to solve a problem. Each problem-solving lesson will highlight some aspect of the checklist. In Chapter 1, following the introduction of the 5-Point Checklist on page 8, the first two points of the checklist—understanding the question (page 12), and using data from an information sheet (page 13)—are emphasized.

Chapters 1 through 9 each introduce a new strategy to help solve problems. The nine strategies include Choose the Operations, Guess and Check, Draw a Picture, Make a Table, Make an Organized List, Use Logical Reasoning, Work Backward, Solve a Simpler Problem, and Find a Pattern. The first strategy, Choose the Operations, is introduced on page 15. Chapters 10 and 11 focus on practicing the strategies. In Chapters 12 through 16, students apply the strategies in practical, real-world situations.

### Vocabulary

| | | |
|---|---|---|
| addend | divisor | even number |
| sum | dividend | odd number |
| difference | quotient | order property |
| factor | multiple | grouping property |
| product | zero property | multiplication-addition property |

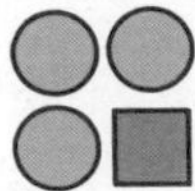

## Error Analysis

This introductory chapter reviews the basic whole number operations of addition, subtraction, multiplication, and division. Students are encouraged to focus on relationships that exist between addition and subtraction, and between multiplication and division.

Factors and multiples are reviewed as multiplication and division are taught. These concepts are used as problem-solving situations are presented. Students are encouraged to use the meaning of the operations as they decide which operation to use.

Although the concepts in this chapter are not new to students, there is still a potential for error. Some of the error patterns that occur with the content of this chapter reflect a lack of knowledge of basic facts or a misunderstanding of the meaning of the operations. Following are some problem areas often found.

- Inadequate or incorrect knowledge of the role of zero in addition, subtraction, multiplication, and especially division facts. Computation such as $0 \div 8$ and $8 \div 0$ are often interchanged and computed, although division by zero is not allowed.
- The relationship between addition and subtraction and between multiplication and division is often misunderstood and misapplied when deciding which operation is needed in problem-solving situations. These relationships should be constantly reviewed.

## Problem Solving

**Using the 5-Point Checklist**

Throughout the Addison-Wesley math program, a 5-step plan is presented in the text as a guide for solving problems. The five steps are: 1) Understand the *Question,* 2) Find the needed *Data,* 3) *Plan* what to do, 4) Find the *Answer,* 5) *Check* back. This plan is intended to guide a student's thinking by drawing attention to the key actions that need to be taken and the key decision that must be made when solving problems. Successful problem solving is not guaranteed by the use of this plan. It provides a useful framework for attacking problems and for discussing problems and their solutions. You should also recognize the cyclic nature of the plan. For example, if students are nearing the answer but reach an impasse, encourage them to return to an earlier step in order to continue their work toward a solution.

Many teachers find it helpful to make a bulletin-board display using the checklist theme. Then students can refer to this guide in solving problems on their own. Or, the bulletin-board display can be used as the focal point of a class discussion of a problem. Here is a sample bulletin-board display.

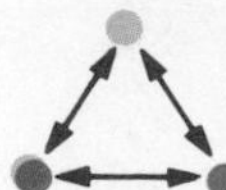

## Special Education

Many students with learning difficulties do not spontaneously use efficient or organized strategies that would enable them to learn and retain basic facts as reviewed in this chapter. To help students master these basic concepts, introduce them to learning techniques that will make fact mastery possible. Ideas like the following will help achieve the mastery necessary for success with computation, estimation, problem solving, and other application topics.

### Establishing a Baseline

Start by determining which facts students know well. The basic facts tests (TRB pp. 89–92) may help with this evaluation. Then, for each student, create a blackout list for each operation on which all known facts are blackened.

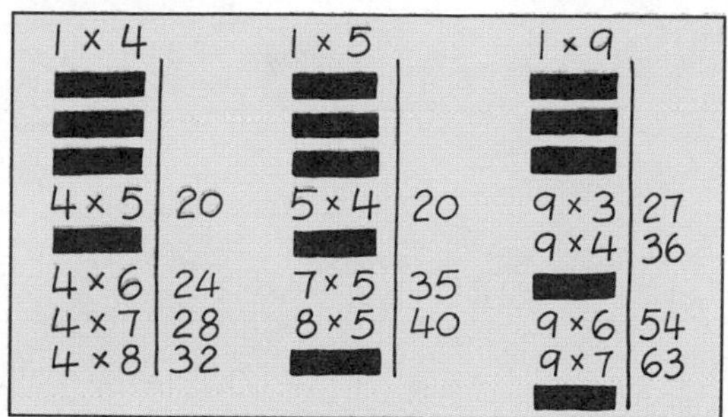


### Giving Help for Harder Facts

Require students to memorize several unknown facts each week and then cross these from the list as well. Be sure students have mastered one group of addition facts before trying to memorize related subtraction facts. Similarly, students will find it easier to use multiplication to find division facts.

### Using Pictures, Patterns, and Groups of 10

Visual cues may help some students. For example, present a picture for each *double,* such as an egg carton to illustrate 6 + 6. Then use similar pictures for near doubles and related subtraction facts.

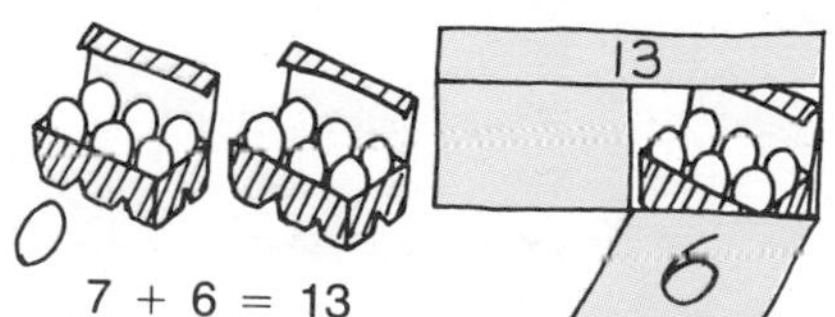


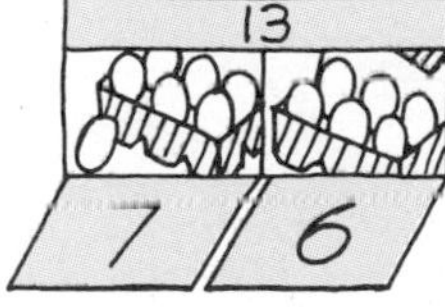


fold down card

Suggest that students add or subtract through 10 if this is helpful. For example, 8 + 5 = 10 + 3, or 13. In subtraction students would count up from the known part to reach the total. Let them use a "0" finger if it helps.

$$\begin{array}{r}13\\-\ 8\\\hline\end{array}\qquad\begin{array}{r}1\\-\ 8\\\hline\end{array}\qquad\begin{array}{r}13\\-\ 8\\\hline\end{array}\qquad\begin{array}{r}13\\-\ 8\\\hline 5\end{array}$$

Think 2    Think 2 + 3

Encourage students to look for patterns in the addition and subtraction facts for 9.

### Using Visual Cues and Strategies

If multiplication or division 9s are troublesome, help students look for patterns or allow them to use fingers to count.

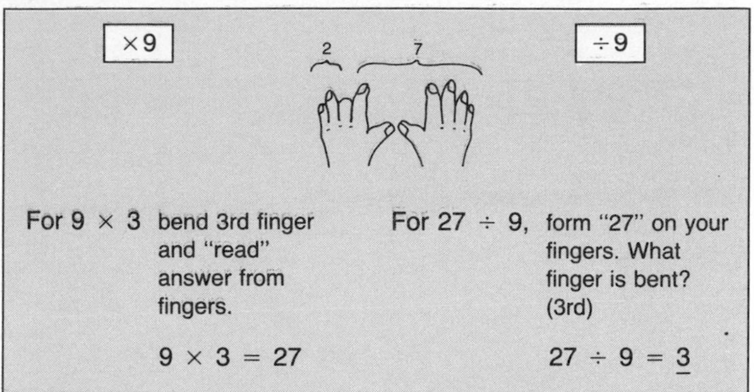

×9
2
7
÷9
For 9 × 3 bend 3rd finger and "read" answer from fingers.
9 × 3 = 27
For 27 ÷ 9, form "27" on your fingers. What finger is bent? (3rd)
27 ÷ 9 = 3


Help students select easier, known facts to help with harder multiplication facts. For example, 9 × 4 = 36, so 8 × 4 = 32 (4 less). 5 × 8 = 40, so 6 × 8 = 48 (another 8). 2 × 7 = 14, so 4 × 7 = 28 (twice as much). Provide exercises and activities in which students match division to related multiplication facts.

Help students to "think multiplication" to find division answers. Provide exercises and activities in which students match or write division and related multiplication facts.

Provide special help for "0" facts. Have students draw pictures for given facts. Let students sort out facts with 0 answers for all operations from others.

## Subject Integration

Subject matter related to other areas of the curriculum has been integrated into the following lessons. This provides an opportunity to highlight the interaction between mathematics and other subjects.

**Fine Arts** Stamp collecting, page 2; visiting the amusement park, pages 8–9

**Consumer Awareness** Buying batteries, page 14

**Career Awareness** Physical therapist, page 1; part-time jobs, page 12; making pottery, page 16

# Management Guide

| Teaching Chapter 1 | | | | Meeting Individual Needs | | | | | |
|---|---|---|---|---|---|---|---|---|---|
| | | | | Lesson Assignments | | | Follow Up | | |
| Objectives | Chapter Content | Pages | TRB Test Items | Minimum | Average | Extended | Reteaching | Enrichment | Practice |
| | Chapter Opener | 1 | | | | | | | |
| **1.1** Recall basic addition, subtraction, multiplication, and division facts and solve equations using basic facts. | Addition and Subtraction | 2–3 | 1–21 | 1–40 | 1–42 | 1–42, TM | SE5 Ch 1<br>RS 1 | ES 1 | MP 411<br>PS 1 |
| | Multiplication | 4–5 | | 1–22 | 1–24 | 1–24, TM | SE5 Ch 1<br>RS 2 | ES 2 | MP 411<br>PS 2 |
| | Division | 6–7 | | 1–35 | 1–38 | 1–38, TM | SE5 Ch 1<br>RS 3 | ES 3 | MP 411<br>PS 3 |
| | Practice the Facts | 10 | | 1–46 | 1–54 | 1–54 | | | |
| **1.2** Use parentheses to determine the order of operations. | Combining Operations | 11 | 22–27 | 1–21 | 1–28 | 1–30, TM | SE5 Ch 1<br>RS 5 | ES 5 | MP 411<br>PS 5 |
| **1.3** Use basic facts to find multiples and factors of a given number. | Using Basic Facts: Finding Multiples | 14 | 28–31 | 1–8 | 1–9 | 1–10 | | | |
| | Using Basic Facts: Finding Factors | 15 | 32–35 | 1–15, SK | 1–18, SK | 1–21, SK | RS 6 | ES 6 | PS 7 |
| **1.4** Solve word problems using the 5-Point Checklist and cumulative computational skills. | Problem Solving: The 5-Point Checklist | 8–9 | 36–40 | 1–6 | 1–7 | 1–8 | RS 4 | ES 4 | PS 4 |
| | Problem Solving: Understanding the Question | 12 | | 1–6 | 1–7 | 1–8 | | | |
| | Problem Solving: Using Data from an Information Sheet | 13 | | 1–8 | 1–9 | 1–10 | | | PS 6 |
| | Problem Solving: Choose the Operations | 16 | | | | | | | |
| | Chapter Review-Test | 17 | | | | | | | |
| | Another Look/Enrichment | 18–19 | | | | | | | |
| | Technology | 20–21 | | | | | | | |
| | Cumulative Review | 22 | | | | | | | |

**SE5** Student Edition, Book 5
**RS** Reteaching Supplement
**ES** Enrichment Supplement
**PS** Practice Supplement
**MP** More Practice
**TM** Think Math
**SK** Skillkeeper
**TRB** Teacher's Resource Book

# Teacher's Resource Book

## Masters for Use

**. . . before Chapter 1**

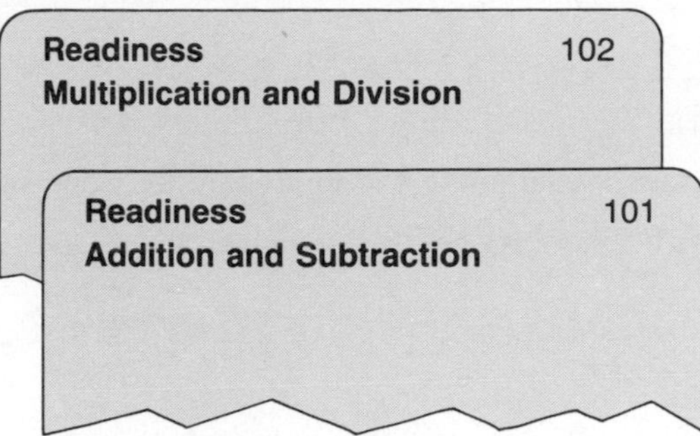


**. . . during Chapter 1**

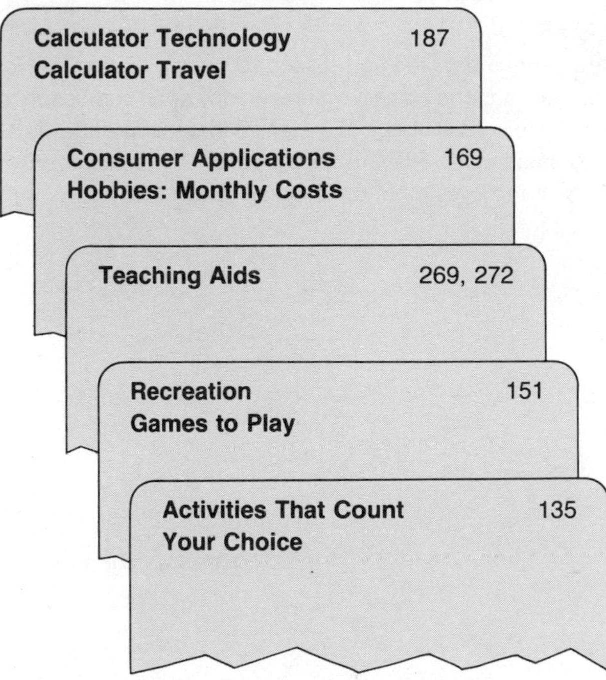


**. . . after Chapter 1**

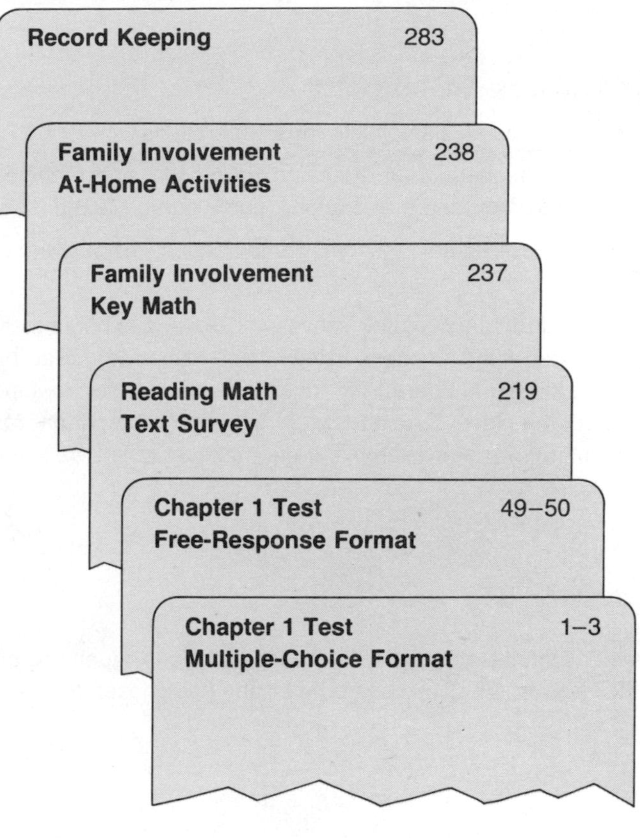


## Supplements

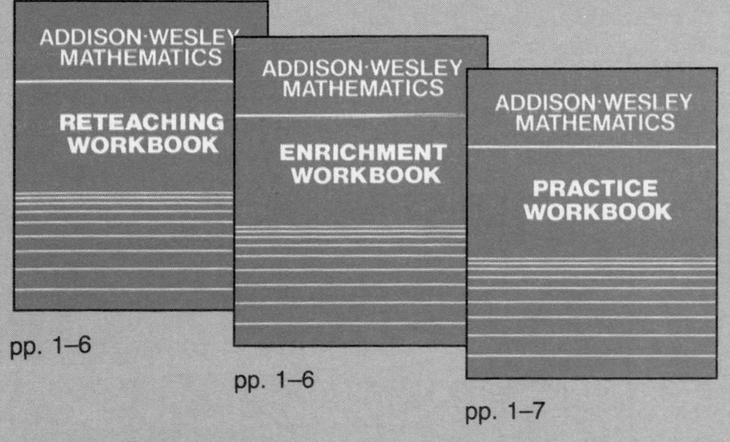


pp. 1–6

pp. 1–6

pp. 1–7

## Other Addison-Wesley Resources

### Books and Kits

*The Mad Minute* pp. 1–110, 121–145, 151–170

*Dice and Dots* Game 7

*The Arithmetic Primer* pp. 3–7, 21–25, 39–42, 66–68

*Baseball, A Game of Numbers* pp. 72–78

*Problem-Solving Experiences in Mathematics, Grade 6,* Problems 3, 4, 5, 6, 12, 14, 16, 19, 20

### Technology

*Computer Math Activities* Volumes 1–5

*Computer Math Games* Volumes 1–4, 6

# Activities That Count

Activities That Count are designed for use throughout this chapter and subsequent chapters. Before beginning Chapter 1, you may wish to review these activities and select the ones you consider appropriate for your class.

## **Your Choice** Game

**Purpose** To practice basic facts for all operations

**Materials** 3 number cubes: 2 labeled 1 through 6 and 1 labeled 4 through 9, colored pencils or crayons, game board (TRB p. 135)

**Preparation** Reproduce the TRB game board for each group of players.

**Activity** In turn each player tosses all three number cubes. Player first looks at the numbers on the number cubes as well as the numbers on the game board. After deciding on a number from the game board, the player then adds, subtracts, multiplies, or divides the numbers shown. For example, if the numbers rolled are

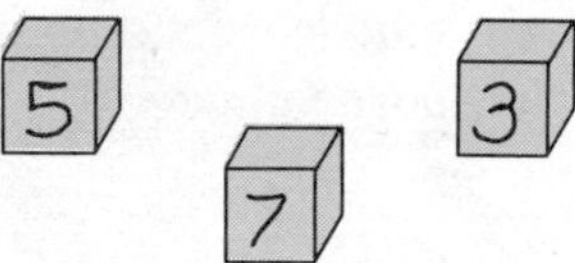


the player might make any of the following equations depending on which number on the game board he or she has chosen to color.

$$(7 - 5) \times 3 = 6$$
$$7 + 3 + 5 = 15$$
$$(7 + 3) \div 5 = 2$$
$$(7 + 3) \times 5 = 50$$

The player colors the square that contains the resulting number and scores one point. A player who cannot name an open number on the board must pass. When each player has passed three times, the game is over and the player with the most points wins.

## **Facto** Game

**Purpose** To review division facts and to prepare for work with factors

**Materials** Number cards labeled 1 through 9 (TRB p. 279), inch graph paper (TRB p. 269), markers

**Preparation** Make a game board by numbering the graph paper squares consecutively from 10 through 73, or use the game board from Your Choice game (TRB p. 135).

**Activity** Cards are mixed and placed facedown. In turn, players draw a number card and place a marker on any open number on the game board that is divisible by (a factor of) that number. Cards are mixed before each turn. Players take turns until one player covers five spaces in a row, column, or diagonal to win the game.

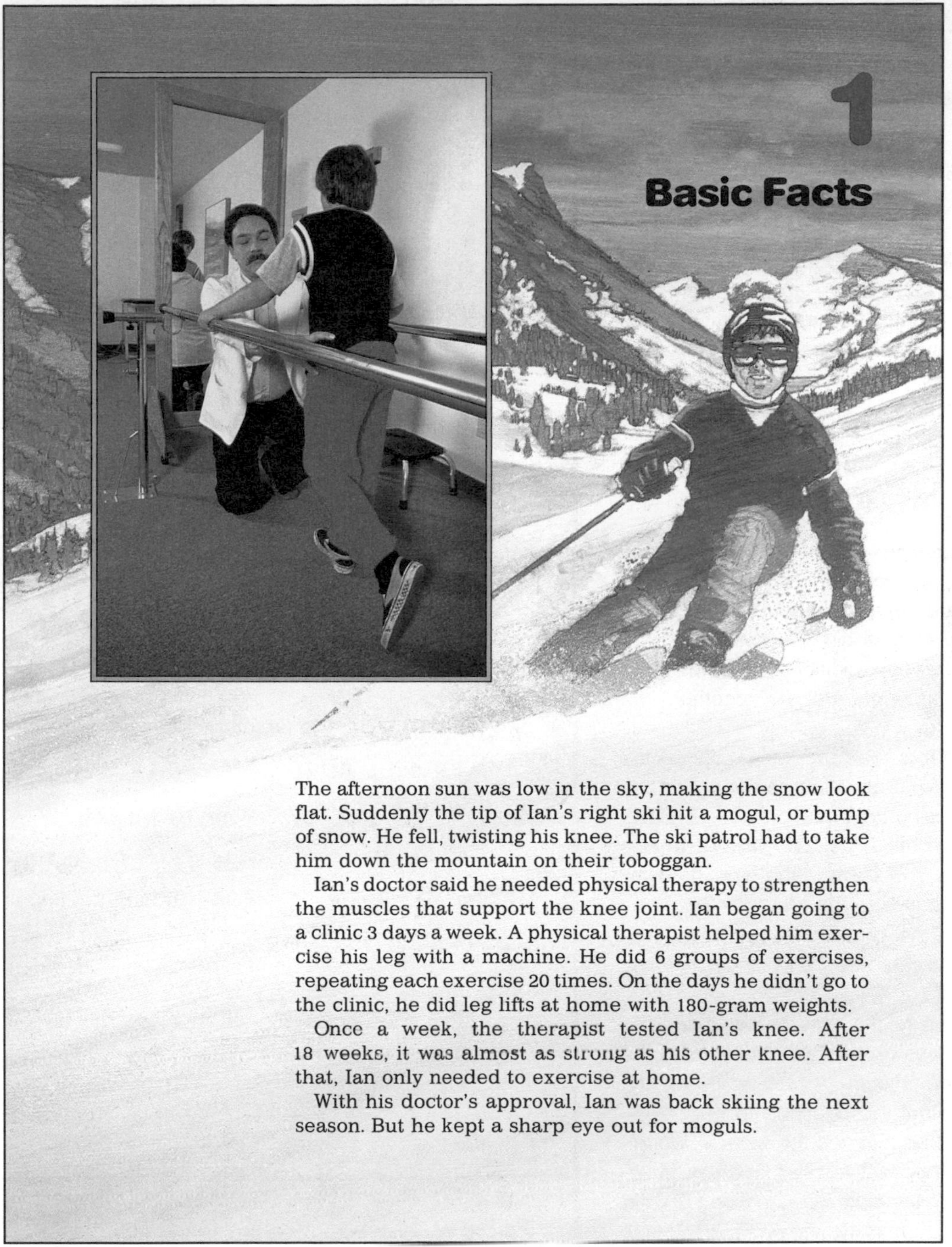

1
Basic Facts
The afternoon sun was low in the sky, making the snow look flat. Suddenly the tip of Ian's right ski hit a mogul, or bump of snow. He fell, twisting his knee. The ski patrol had to take him down the mountain on their toboggan.
Ian's doctor said he needed physical therapy to strengthen the muscles that support the knee joint. Ian began going to a clinic 3 days a week. A physical therapist helped him exercise his leg with a machine. He did 6 groups of exercises, repeating each exercise 20 times. On the days he didn't go to the clinic, he did leg lifts at home with 180-gram weights.
Once a week, the therapist tested Ian's knee. After 18 weeks, it was almost as strong as his other knee. After that, Ian only needed to exercise at home.
With his doctor's approval, Ian was back skiing the next season. But he kept a sharp eye out for moguls.


## Introducing the Chapter

**Discussion** Before students open their books, explain that the first chapter reviews the basic facts for addition, subtraction, multiplication, and division. Then introduce a discussion of careers in health care. Ask questions such as, "What people besides nurses and doctors might be involved in helping you after an accident or a long illness?" Point out that in many cases a specially trained person called a *physical therapist* actually gives the treatments that a doctor prescribes to help a patient recover from such injuries as pulled muscles or fractured bones. After students have had time to read the story and enjoy the art, give them an opportunity to create word problems based on the story. As you teach the chapter, you may wish to refer back to this page and discuss the questions below.

## Follow-Up Questions

**After Page 3** A physical therapist gave treatments to 12 patients in the morning. She gave treatments to 5 fewer patients in the afternoon. How many patients did she give treatments in the afternoon? (7)

**After Page 5** Ian received physical therapy treatments 3 times each week for 8 weeks. How many treatments did he receive? (24)

**After Page 7** Ian spent a total of 30 minutes a day doing 6 different kinds of leg exercises. If he spent the same amount of time on each exercise, how many minutes did he spend on each kind of exercise? (5 min)

# Addition and Subtraction

**Quick Review** Students give sums and differences aloud as quickly as possible.

| | | | | | | | |
|---|---|---|---|---|---|---|---|
| 6 + 3 | 10 − 3 | 8 − 2 | 4 + 5 | 11 − 2 | 2 + 8 | 9 − 6 | 4 + 8 |
| 12 − 4 | 6 + 5 | 7 + 3 | 13 − 7 | 17 − 8 | 9 + 7 | 7 + 5 | 16 − 9 |
| 8 + 6 | 18 − 9 | 8 + 7 | 9 + 9 | 15 − 6 | 4 + 9 | 14 − 8 | 12 − 9 |

**Lesson Focus** To review addition and subtraction meanings, facts, and properties

## Ideas for Getting Started

Write the following equations on the chalkboard: 8 + 7 = 15, 15 − 7 = 8. "What is meant by addition? By subtraction?" Select volunteers to use counting objects to demonstrate the meaning of these two operations to the class. After this brief review, ask students to make up a problem that could be solved using this addition fact and one that could be solved using the subtraction fact. Emphasize the meaning of the operations as you briefly discuss these problems. Use the counting objects to model the problems students have written.

## Using Page 2

**Lesson Development** Have students read the information in the first column under the picture. "What question are we asked about Megan's boat trip?" (How many whales did she see during the trip?) "Why should we use addition to solve the problem?" (When two amounts are "put together," we use addition.)

Then have students read the information in the second column. "What question can you ask that can be answered using the equation 16 − 7 = 9?" A possible question might be: Eric saw 16 whales altogether. He saw 7 of them in the morning. How many whales did he see in the afternoon?

As you discuss the questions, emphasize the terms "take-away," "compare," and "find how many more are needed."

To emphasize the relationship between addition and subtraction, focus on the two equations in the middle of the page. Picture a fact family on the chalkboard to highlight this relationship.

Be sure students understand the terms *addends* and *sum.* Show other fact families and ask questions such as, "If the two addends are 8 and 6, what is the sum?" "If the sum is 17 and one addend is 9, what is the other addend?" "Can you use these addends and sums to write two addition facts and two subtraction facts?"

**Warm Up** As students give these answers aloud, look for those who have difficulty recalling the facts quickly. There may be students who continue to use counting strategies and who need help in memorizing the facts.

## Addition and Subtraction

We use **addition** to find the total when two amounts have been **put together.**

We use **subtraction** when **taking away, comparing,** or finding **how many more are needed.**

Megan went on a boat trip to watch the whales migrating north for the summer. She saw 9 adult whales and 7 very young whales. How many whales did she see during their trip?

During an all-day boat trip Eric saw 16 whales. He saw 7 of them in the morning. Can you make up a question about this data that can be answered using the subtraction equation below?

Since 9 (Addend) + 7 (Addend) = 16 (Sum), then 16 (Sum) − 7 (Addend) = 9 (Addend) ← Difference

**Warm Up** Add or subtract. Check your subtraction by adding.

1. $6 + 4 = n$ 10
2. $7 + 5 = n$ 12
3. $8 + 3 = n$ 11
4. $9 + 4 = n$ 13
5. $9 + 6 = n$ 15
6. $8 + 7 = n$ 15
7. $7 + 6 = n$ 13
8. $5 + 8 = n$ 13
9. $10 - 6 = n$ 4 (? + 6 = 10)
10. $12 - 7 = n$ 5
11. $13 - 4 = n$ 9
12. $14 - 6 = n$ 8
13. $11 - 7 = n$ 4
14. $15 - 9 = n$ 6
15. $15 - 7 = n$ 8
16. $16 - 8 = n$ 8
17. 6 + 8 = 14
18. 4 + 7 = 11
19. 9 + 7 = 16
20. 8 + 8 = 16
21. 5 + 9 = 14
22. 17 − 9 = 8
23. 16 − 7 = 9
24. 15 − 6 = 9
25. 18 − 9 = 9
26. 13 − 5 = 8



## Follow Up

### Reteaching

Write a basic fact such as 7 + 8 = 15 and ask for the two related subtraction facts: 15 − 7 = 8 and 15 − 8 = 7. Review several other facts in this way. Lead a discussion on the meaning of addition and subtraction. Focus attention on the relationship between addition and subtraction. Also, use the appropriate facts to emphasize

- the role of zero in addition and subtraction,
- the order property of addition, and
- the grouping property of addition.

### Enrichment

Write the following scrambled number names on the chalkboard. Let students unscramble the words, and then scramble their own math words to challenge classmates.

| | |
|---|---|
| nifftee fifteen | ozre zero |
| eno one | owt two |
| welvet twelve | ixs six |
| ofur four | vief five |
| eelnve eleven | veens seven |
| enni nine | ether three |
| githe eight | ent ten |
| newtty twenty | uhndder hundred |

| Assignment Guide | | | |
|---|---|---|---|
| | Minimum | Average | Extended |
| page 3 | 1–40 | 1–42 | 1–42, TM |

Find the sums and differences below. These properties of addition may help.

**0 Property**
When one addend is 0, the sum is the other addend.

**Order Property**
When the order of addends is changed, the sum is the same.

**Grouping Property**
When the grouping of addends is changed, the sum is the same.

| 1. | 2. | 3. | 4. | 5. | 6. | 7. |
|---|---|---|---|---|---|---|
| 8<br>+ 0<br>8 | 0<br>+ 9<br>9 | 7<br>+ 3<br>10 | 3<br>+ 7<br>10 | 9<br>+ 4<br>13 | 4<br>+ 9<br>13 | 0<br>+ 0<br>0 |

A number subtracted from itself is 0.

Subtracting 0 doesn't change a number.

| 8. | 9. | 10. | 11. |
|---|---|---|---|
| 9<br>− 9<br>0 | 7<br>− 7<br>0 | 0<br>− 0<br>0 | 6<br>− 0<br>6 |

| 12. | 13. | 14. | 15. | 16. | 17. | 18. |
|---|---|---|---|---|---|---|
| 9<br>+ 2<br>11 | 2<br>+ 9<br>11 | 8<br>− 0<br>8 | 7<br>+ 4<br>11 | 18<br>− 9<br>9 | 14<br>− 7<br>7 | 8<br>+ 8<br>16 |

| 19. | 20. | 21. | 22. | 23. | 24. | 25. |
|---|---|---|---|---|---|---|
| 5<br>4<br>+ 6<br>15 | 6<br>4<br>+ 5<br>15 | 8<br>6<br>+ 3<br>17 | 9<br>3<br>+ 7<br>19 | 6<br>8<br>+ 4<br>18 | 5<br>7<br>+ 6<br>18 | 8<br>3<br>+ 8<br>19 |

**26.** 9 + 7 16 **27.** 6 + 5 11 **28.** 0 + 4 4 **29.** 7 + 7 14 **30.** 6 + 8 14

**31.** 17 − 8 9 **32.** 16 − 9 7 **33.** 15 − 6 9 **34.** 14 − 8 6 **35.** 13 − 8 5

**36.** What is the sum of 9 and 8? 17

**37.** What is 7 more than 8? 15

**38.** What is the difference of 15 and 6? 9

**39.** What is 9 less than 13? 4

**40.** An adult gray whale was 12 meters long. Her calf was 4 meters long. How much longer was the adult whale? 8 meters

★ Find the number for $n$.

**41.** $n + 5 = 12$ 7 **42.** $n - 4 = 9$ 13

**Think**

**Logical Reasoning**

Copy this figure and write the digits 1, 2, 3, 4, 5, 6, 7, 8, 9 in the circles so that the sum on each side of the triangle is the same.

9 7 5 6 1 2 3 4 8 +

Sample solution is shown.

**Math**

More Practice, page 411, Set A



## Using Page 3

**Lesson Development** Call students' attention to the basic properties for addition on this page. If students have difficulty understanding the order property, make dot cards showing basic facts. For example, [•••••|•••] In one position the card shows 5 + 3; when rotated 180° it shows 3 + 5.

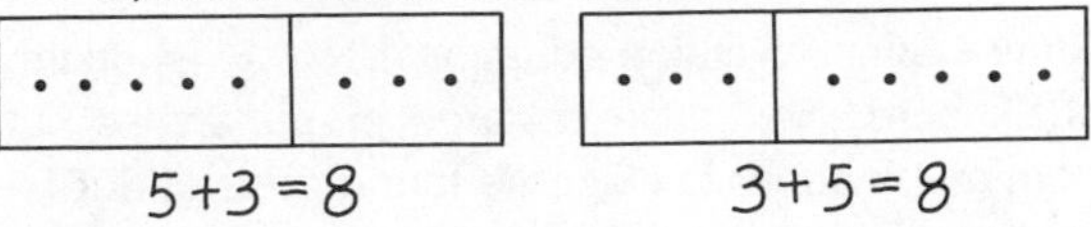


Discuss the idea that people sometimes check addition with three addends by adding from the top and then adding again from the bottom. Be sure students understand that the grouping property helps them know that the sum should be the same no matter which pair of addends are added first.

**Exercises 1–40** As students complete these exercises, help them focus on the role of the basic properties. In exercises 19–25, be sure students understand that the order property allows them to add either the first two or the last two addends first.

**Exercises 41–42** Do not attempt to teach rules for solving equations at this time. Encourage students to think about the basic addition and subtraction facts.

**Think Math** Encourage students to draw triangles like the one shown and try some numbers in the circle to see what happens. They will quickly draw some conclusions that there must be a balance of large and small numbers on each side of the triangle. As students continue to make trials, encourage them to use reasoning to decide upon a systematic way to find the answer.

**More Practice,** page 411, Set A

**Reteaching Supplement,** page 1

Name ______ To follow text page 3

**Addition and Subtraction**

HELPERS
A "Count on" if one number is a 3, 2, or 1.
9 + 3 = 12 (9, 10, 11, 12)
B Use the "doubles" for facts close to a double.
5 + 6 = 11 (Since 5 + 5 = 10, 5 + 6 is 1 more.)
6 + 8 = 14 (Since 6 + 6 = 12, 6 + 8 is 2 more.)
C "Make a 10" if one number is a 9.
9 + 5 = 14 (Since 10 + 5 = 15, 9 + 5 is 1 less.)

Use the Helpers as needed to find the sums.

1. 3 + 5 8 2. 6 + 3 9 3. 2 + 7 9 4. 8 + 1 9
5. 8 + 2 10 6. 5 + 4 9 7. 6 + 4 10 8. 9 + 4 13 9. 9 + 5 14

10. 7 + 9 = 16 11. 5 + 6 = 11 12. 7 + 5 = 12 13. 8 + 9 = 17

Find the differences.

14. 7 − 3 4 (4 + 3 = 7) 15. 9 − 2 7 16. 12 − 7 5 17. 14 − 6 8 18. 10 − 5 5
19. 17 − 9 8 20. 16 − 7 9 21. 11 − 7 4 22. 8 − 8 0 23. 15 − 9 6

24. 11 − 6 = 5 25. 10 − 4 = 6 26. 18 − 9 = 9 27. 16 − 7 = 9

Add.

28. 9 6 + 3 18 (9 + 6 = 15, 15 + 3 = 18) 29. 6 2 + 5 13 30. 8 8 + 3 19 31. 2 9 + 7 18

**Enrichment Supplement,** page 1

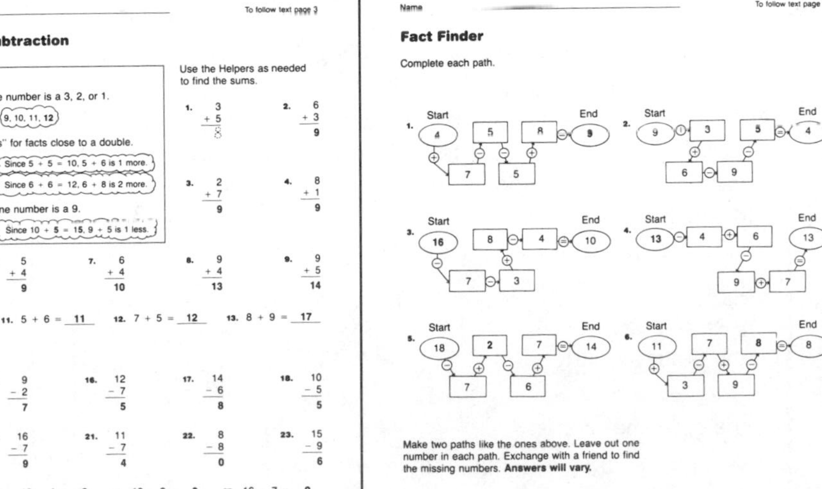

Name ______ To follow text page 3

**Fact Finder**

Complete each path.



Make two paths like the ones above. Leave out one number in each path. Exchange with a friend to find the missing numbers. **Answers will vary.**

7. Start End 8. Start End

**Practice Supplement,** page 1

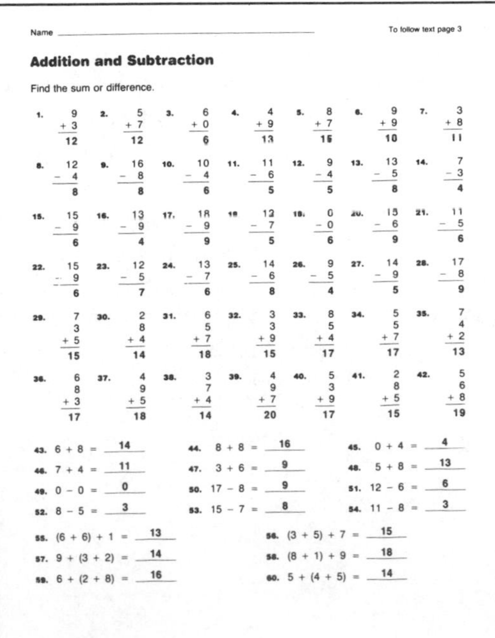

Name ______ To follow text page 3

**Addition and Subtraction**

Find the sum or difference.

1. 9 + 3 12 2. 5 + 7 12 3. 6 + 0 6 4. 4 + 9 13 5. 8 + 7 15 6. 9 + 9 10 7. 3 + 8 11
8. 12 − 4 8 9. 16 − 8 8 10. 10 − 4 6 11. 11 − 6 5 12. 9 − 4 5 13. 13 − 5 8 14. 7 − 3 4
15. 15 − 9 6 16. 13 − 9 4 17. 18 − 9 9 18. 12 − 7 5 19. 0 − 0 6 20. 15 − 6 9 21. 11 − 5 6
22. 15 − 9 6 23. 12 − 5 7 24. 13 − 7 6 25. 14 − 6 8 26. 9 − 5 4 27. 14 − 9 5 28. 17 − 8 9
29. 7 3 + 5 15 30. 2 8 + 4 14 31. 6 5 + 7 18 32. 3 3 + 9 15 33. 8 5 + 4 17 34. 5 5 + 7 17 35. 7 4 + 2 13
36. 6 8 + 3 17 37. 4 9 + 5 18 38. 3 7 + 4 14 39. 4 9 + 7 20 40. 5 3 + 9 17 41. 2 8 + 5 15 42. 5 6 + 8 19

43. 6 + 8 = 14 44. 8 + 8 = 16 45. 0 + 4 = 4
46. 7 + 4 = 11 47. 3 + 6 = 9 48. 5 + 8 = 13
49. 0 − 0 = 0 50. 17 − 8 = 9 51. 12 − 6 = 6
52. 8 − 5 = 3 53. 15 − 7 = 8 54. 11 − 8 = 3

55. (6 + 6) + 1 = 13 56. (3 + 5) + 7 = 15
57. 9 + (3 + 2) = 14 58. (8 + 1) + 9 = 18
59. 6 + (2 + 8) = 16 60. 5 + (4 + 5) = 14

# Multiplication

**Quick Review** Have students give these products aloud as quickly as possible.

| | | | | | | | |
|---|---|---|---|---|---|---|---|
| 3 × 4 | 2 × 8 | 6 × 3 | 5 × 4 | 6 × 4 | 5 × 5 | 3 × 7 | 7 × 4 |
| 6 × 5 | 5 × 7 | 9 × 3 | 1 × 6 | 6 × 6 | 7 × 6 | 9 × 5 | 8 × 7 |
| 4 × 8 | 8 × 0 | 6 × 9 | 8 × 9 | 4 × 9 | 7 × 7 | 9 × 1 | 3 × 5 |

**Lesson Focus** To review multiplication facts and properties

**Suggested Materials** Graph paper (TRB p. 271)

## Ideas for Getting Started

Write the multiplication equation 4 × 6 = 24 on the chalkboard. Next, use squares or rectangles cut from graph paper to illustrate four groups of 6. Discuss the meaning of multiplication as shown by the models.

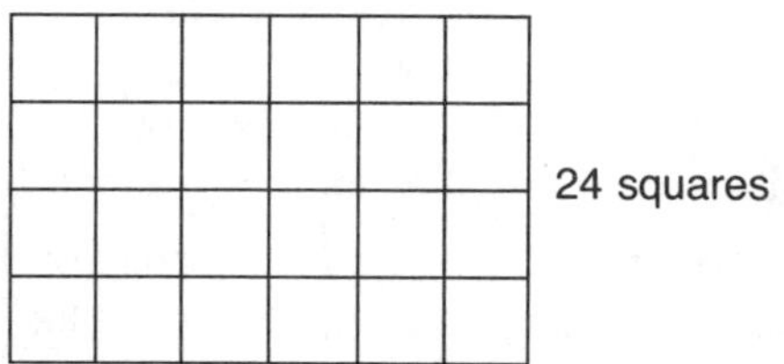

24 squares

4 rows, 6 squares in each row.
4 × 6 = 24

Then have students cut graph paper to show multiplication for 3 × 4, 5 × 3, 4 × 5, 4 × 7, and 6 × 6.

## Using Page 4

**Motivational Problem** Have students read the problem at the top of the page. "What question is asked about Jeff's video game tapes?" (How much money did he receive for his tapes?) "What data do we need to answer the question?" (number of tapes sold, amount received for each) "Why should we multiply to solve the problem?" (To find the total amount for a certain number of equal amounts, we multiply.)

**Lesson Development** Focus on the equation showing multiplication as repeated addition and emphasize the idea that we can multiply two factors to find a product. For further emphasis give students other multiplication equations to write as repeated addition.

Remind students that the 0 property and the 1 property of multiplication reduce the number of multiplication facts that must be memorized. Point out that the order property reduces the number of facts to be memorized almost by one-half.

**Warm Up** As students give these products, look for those who have not memorized the facts and who may be using time-consuming techniques. Work with these students to help them memorize the facts for immediate recall.

## Multiplication

We use **multiplication** to find the **total amount** for a problem when a **certain number** of equal **amounts** are given.

**Problem**

Jeff sold 7 used video game tapes for $9 each. How much money did he receive?

7 × 9 = 63 Jeff received $63.

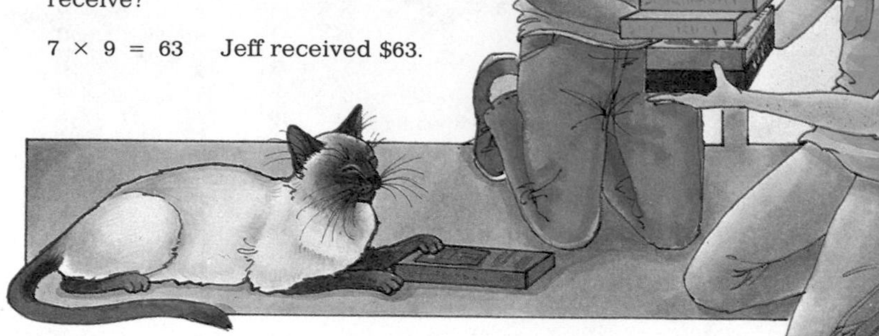

Multiplication by whole numbers other than 0 or 1 can be thought of as a shortcut for adding equal addends.

Since 9 + 9 + 9 + 9 + 9 + 9 + 9 = 63, then **7** (Factor) × **9** (Factor) = **63** (Product)

**Warm Up** Find the products.

1. 2 × 4 = *n* 8
2. 2 × 3 = *n* 6
3. 2 × 5 = *n* 10
4. 2 × 6 = *n* 12
5. 5 × 2 = *n* 10
6. 5 × 3 = *n* 15
7. 5 × 4 = *n* 20
8. 5 × 6 = *n* 30
9. 9 × 2 = *n* 18
10. 9 × 3 = *n* 27
11. 9 × 4 = *n* 36
12. 9 × 5 = *n* 45
13. 4 × 4 = *n* 16
14. 5 × 5 = *n* 25
15. 6 × 6 = *n* 36
16. 7 × 7 = *n* 49
17. 8 × 8 = 64
18. 9 × 9 = 81
19. 6 × 9 = 54
20. 9 × 7 = 63
21. 9 × 8 = 72
22. 5 × 7 = 35
23. 5 × 8 = 40
24. 2 × 7 = 14
25. 2 × 8 = 16
26. 2 × 9 = 18

4

## Follow Up

### Reteaching

Generate a discussion to review the meaning of multiplication. Use models or arrays to show multiplication as repeated addition. Then use basic facts to illustrate the multiplication properties. For example:

$0 \times n = 0$ and $1 \times n = n$
0 and 1 properties

$a \times b = b \times a$
the order property

$(a \times b) \times c = a \times (b \times c)$
the grouping property

$(a \times n) + (b \times n) = (a + b) \times n$
the multiplication-addition (distributive) property

### Enrichment

Have students find the rule that has been applied to the number pairs in the first column to get the answers in the second column. Tell students to use the rule to complete the tables.

| Rule: a × b + 2 | |
|---|---|
| 4,6 | 26 |
| 4,3 | 14 |
| 6,2 | 14 |
| 8,4 | 34 |
| 5,7 | 37 |

| Rule: a × b − 1 | |
|---|---|
| 5,8 | 39 |
| 9,1 | 8 |
| 3,9 | 26 |
| 6,8 | 47 |
| 7,6 | 41 |

| Assignment Guide | | | |
|---|---|---|---|
| | Minimum | Average | Extended |
| page 5 | 1–22 | 1–24 | 1–24, TM |

Find the products below. These properties of multiplication may help.

**0 and 1 Properties**
When either factor is 0, the product is 0. When either factor is 1, the product is the other factor.

**Order Property**
When the order of the factors is changed, the product is the same.

**Grouping Property**
When the grouping of three factors is changed, the product is the same.

| 1. | 2. | 3. | 4. | 5. | 6. | 7. |
|---|---|---|---|---|---|---|
| $5 \times 0$ = 0 | $0 \times 6$ = 0 | $8 \times 1$ = 8 | $1 \times 8$ = 8 | $3 \times 4$ = 12 | $4 \times 3$ = 12 | $3 \times 9$ = 27 |

| 8. | 9. | 10. | 11. | 12. | 13. | 14. |
|---|---|---|---|---|---|---|
| $9 \times 3$ = 27 | $4 \times 8$ = 32 | $8 \times 4$ = 32 | $3 \times 7$ = 21 | $7 \times 3$ = 21 | $6 \times 5$ = 30 | $5 \times 6$ = 30 |

**15.** $(4 \times 2) \times 3$ 24 **16.** $4 \times (2 \times 3)$ 24 **17.** $(4 \times 3) \times 2$ 24

**Multiplication–Addition Property**
When two products have a common factor, you can add to find another product of the same factor.

Find the first two products. Then add to find the third.

**18.** $8 \times 5$ = 40, $8 \times 2$ = 16 → $8 \times 7$ = 56

**19.** $4 \times 5$ = 20, $4 \times 3$ = 12 → $4 \times 8$ = 32

**20.** What is the product of 7 times 4? 28

**21.** One factor is 8. The other factor is 6. What is the product? 48

**22.** Mary bought 8 used video tapes for $8 each. How much did she pay for them? $64

★ Give the number for $n$.

**23.** $n \times 9 = 45$ 5 **24.** $8 \times n = 56$ 7

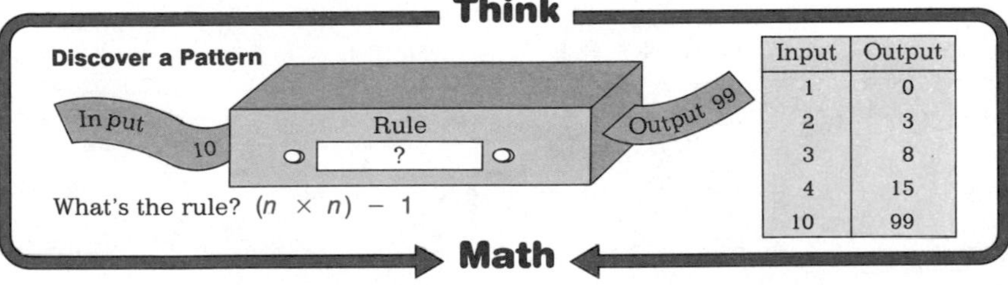


What's the rule? $(n \times n) - 1$

More Practice, page 411, Set B



## Using Page 5

**Exercises 1–14** As students complete these facts ask them to be alert for examples of the order property, the 0 property, and the 1 property.

**Exercises 15–17** Use these exercises to focus on the grouping property of multiplication.

**Exercises 18–19** These exercises illustrate the multiplication-addition property.

**Exercises 20–22** The verbal descriptions in these problems will help students prepare for later problem-solving experiences.

**Exercises 23–24** Encourage students to solve these exercises by thinking about multiplication facts. It is not necessary to teach rules for solving equations at this time.

**Think Math** Some students may discover that the output numbers increase by 3, 5, 7, and so on. Praise them for this discovery, but indicate that their goal should be to find a rule that can be applied to the input number to produce the output number. A good hint would be, "If you multiply the input number by itself how close do you come to the output number?"

**More Practice,** page 411, set B

**Reteaching Supplement,** page 2

Name ______ To follow text page 5

**Multiplication**

HELPERS
A Multiplying by 2 is the same as doubling the number. $2 \times 4 = 8$ (since 4 + 4 = 8)
B Add to find facts that are near doubles. $8 \times 7 = 56$ (Since 7 × 7 = 49, 8 × 7 is 7 more.)
C If one factor is a 5, the product ends in a 0 or 5. (5 × 6 = 30, 7 × 5 = 35)

Use the Helpers to find the products.

1. $6 \times 2$ = 12 2. $0 \times 5$ = 0 3. $5 \times 4$ = 20 4. $4 \times 3$ = 12

5. $5 \times 6$ = 30 6. $6 \times 6$ = 36 7. $6 \times 7$ = 42 8. $8 \times 8$ = 64 9. $8 \times 9$ = 72

10. $4 \times 4$ = 16 11. $9 \times 5$ = 45 12. $9 \times 2$ = 18 13. $3 \times 5$ = 15

Use smaller facts to help find larger products. $8 \times 6$ = ? (6 = 4 + 2) $8 \times 4$ = 32 and $8 \times 2$ = 16; $8 \times 6$ = 48 ← (32 + 16)

Find the products.

14. $6 \times 4$ = 24 15. $7 \times 5$ = 35 16. $9 \times 6$ = 54 17. $8 \times 4$ = 32 18. $7 \times 6$ = 42

19. $5 \times 5$ = 25 20. $8 \times 6$ = 48 21. $7 \times 7$ = 49 22. $4 \times 9$ = 36 23. $9 \times 3$ = 27

24. $7 \times 8$ = 56 25. $5 \times 8$ = 40 26. $6 \times 6$ = 36 27. $7 \times 7$ = 49

**Enrichment Supplement,** page 2

Name ______ To follow text page 5

**Hidden Numbers**

Here are four cards for each of the numbers 0 through 9. Decide which cards should go in each box to make the equations true. Write the numbers. The cards on the top and bottom equations in each box should match. You will not use all of the cards.

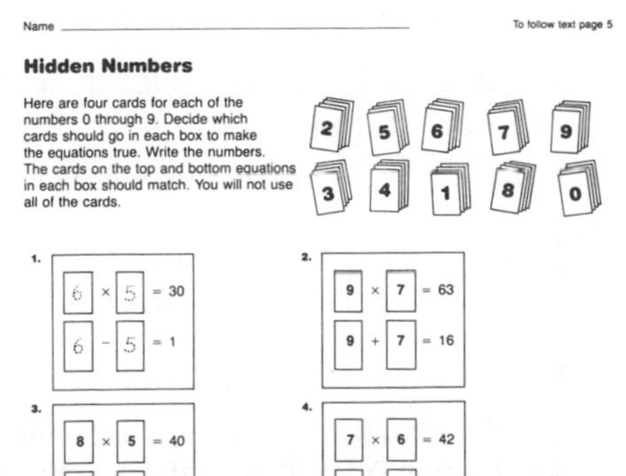


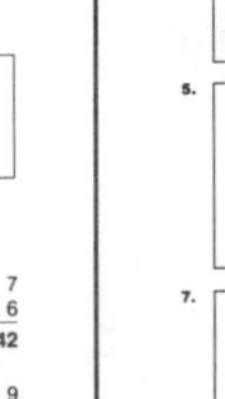


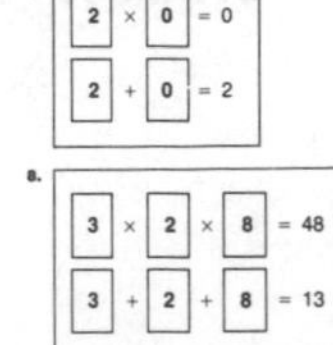


**Practice Supplement,** page 2

Name ______ To follow text page 5

**Multiplication**

Find the products.

1. $8 \times 5$ = 40 2. $6 \times 6$ = 36 3. $2 \times 5$ = 10 4. $8 \times 9$ = 72 5. $5 \times 7$ = 35 6. $4 \times 6$ = 24 7. $7 \times 9$ = 63

8. $6 \times 8$ = 48 9. $9 \times 2$ = 18 10. $7 \times 3$ = 21 11. $5 \times 5$ = 25 12. $8 \times 4$ = 32 13. $5 \times 6$ = 30 14. $3 \times 4$ = 12

15. $4 \times 0$ = 0 16. $6 \times 7$ = 42 17. $4 \times 4$ = 16 18. $3 \times 9$ = 27 19. $0 \times 7$ = 0 20. $8 \times 8$ = 64 21. $3 \times 1$ = 3

22. $4 \times 7$ = 28 23. $9 \times 9$ = 81 24. $3 \times 6$ = 18 25. $7 \times 8$ = 56 26. $4 \times 2$ = 8 27. $3 \times 5$ = 15 28. $9 \times 4$ = 36

29. $8 \times 3$ = 24 30. $5 \times 4$ = 20 31. $9 \times 6$ = 54 32. $7 \times 2$ = 14 33. $8 \times 6$ = 48 34. $9 \times 3$ = 27 35. $5 \times 8$ = 40

36. $9 \times 9$ = 81 37. $7 \times 7$ = 49 38. $3 \times 3$ = 9 39. $6 \times 0$ = 0 40. $7 \times 4$ = 28 41. $6 \times 9$ = 54 42. $7 \times 6$ = 42

43. $7 \times 5$ = 35 44. $4 \times 5$ = 20 45. $8 \times 3$ = 24 46. $5 \times 9$ = 45 47. $9 \times 7$ = 63 48. $4 \times 9$ = 36 49. $0 \times 7$ = 0

50. $3 \times 8$ = 24 51. $5 \times 4$ = 20 52. $9 \times 9$ = 81

53. $0 \times 0$ = 0 54. $7 \times 7$ = 49 55. $2 \times 6$ = 12

56. $6 \times 9$ = 54 57. $8 \times 0$ = 0 58. $1 \times 9$ = 9

59. $3 \times 3$ = 9 60. $5 \times 1$ = 5 61. $8 \times 2$ = 16

62. $(3 \times 2) \times 5$ = 30 63. $3 \times (2 \times 5)$ = 30

64. $3 \times (3 \times 2)$ = 18 65. $(3 \times 3) \times 2$ = 18

66. $8 \times (4 \times 2)$ = 64 67. $(2 \times 2) \times 9$ = 36

# Division

**Quick Review** Students give these quotients aloud as quickly as possible.

| | | | | | |
|---|---|---|---|---|---|
| 24 ÷ 8 | 16 ÷ 2 | 18 ÷ 9 | 27 ÷ 3 | 45 ÷ 9 | 18 ÷ 2 |
| 32 ÷ 4 | 35 ÷ 7 | 42 ÷ 6 | 48 ÷ 8 | 36 ÷ 4 | 64 ÷ 8 |
| 49 ÷ 7 | 54 ÷ 9 | 63 ÷ 7 | 72 ÷ 8 | 81 ÷ 9 | 36 ÷ 6 |

**Lesson Focus** To review division facts and properties

**Suggested Materials** Graph paper (TRB p. 271)

## Ideas for Getting Started

Write 24 ÷ 6 on the chalkboard. Then cut a 6 × 4 rectangle from the graph paper. Show students the rectangle and ask: "There are 24 squares with 6 in each row. How many rows?" Then turn the rectangle 90° and say, "There are 24 squares. There are 6 rows. How many in each row?" If needed, cut out other rectangles and ask similar questions.

## Using Page 6

**Motivational Problem** Have students read problem 1 at the top of the page. "What question is asked about the boxes of paint?" (How many boxes did Jonita use?) "What data is needed to answer the question?" (How many tubes of paint in all? How many tubes in each box?) "Why should we use division to solve this problem?" Point out that division can be used to solve problems that involve finding the number of equal sets. Write "How many sets?" on the chalkboard.

Then read problem 2. "What question is asked in this problem?" (How many brushes did Carl put in each box?) "What data is needed to answer the question?" (the number of brushes and the number of boxes) "What operation could we use to solve this problem?" (We use division to solve problems that involve finding out how many are in each equal set.) Write "How many in each set?" on the chalkboard.

**Lesson Development** Call students' attention to the multiplication and division equations in the middle of the page. Emphasize the relationship between multiplication and division by reminding students that in multiplication we know two factors and find the product; in division we know the product and one factor and find the other factor.

After reviewing the terms *factor* and *product*, write "32 divided by 8 equal 4" on the chalkboard. Help students identify the divisor, the dividend, and the quotient for the division equation. Be sure students understand that 8 and 4 are factors and 32 can be called the product.

**Warm Up** As students respond with these quotients, try to determine the techniques they are using to find the quotients. Students who take an extra long time to give a specific fact may need help in memorizing or in quickly recalling the facts.

## Division

We use **division** to solve problems that involve finding **how many equal sets there are.**

**Problem 1**
Jonita had 56 tubes of paint.
She put 8 tubes in each box.
How many boxes did she use?

**56 ÷ 8 = 7**

Jonita used 7 boxes.

We also use division for problems that involve finding **how many are in each equal set.**

**Problem 2**
Carl put 56 brushes in 8 boxes.
He put the same number in each. How many brushes did he put in each box?

**56 ÷ 8 = 7**

Carl put 7 brushes in each box.

Division is related to multiplication as shown below.

Since 7 (Factor) × 8 (Factor) = 56 (Product), then 56 (Product, Dividend) ÷ 8 (Factor, Divisor) = 7 (Factor) ← Quotient

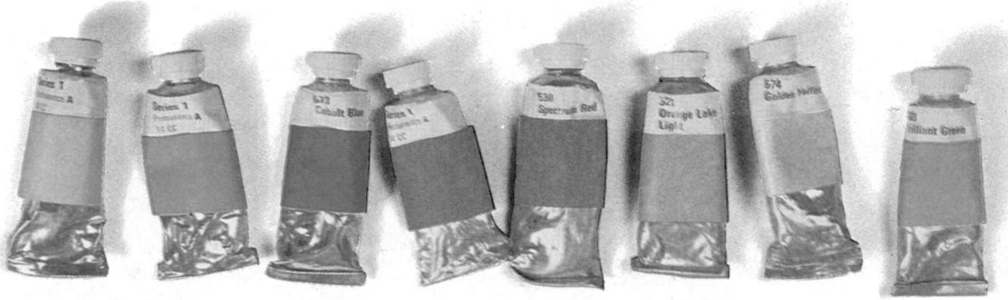

**Warm Up** Find the quotients. Check by multiplying.

(? × 3 = 24)

| | | | |
|---|---|---|---|
| **1.** 24 ÷ 3 = *n* 8 | **2.** 12 ÷ 2 = *n* 6 | **3.** 15 ÷ 5 = *n* 3 | **4.** 18 ÷ 3 = *n* 6 |
| **5.** 20 ÷ 4 = *n* 5 | **6.** 24 ÷ 6 = *n* 4 | **7.** 27 ÷ 3 = *n* 9 | **8.** 32 ÷ 8 = *n* 4 |
| **9.** 35 ÷ 7 = *n* 5 | **10.** 36 ÷ 6 = *n* 6 | **11.** 30 ÷ 5 = *n* 6 | **12.** 40 ÷ 8 = *n* 5 |
| **13.** 42 ÷ 6 = *n* 7 | **14.** 45 ÷ 9 = *n* 5 | **15.** 48 ÷ 6 = *n* 8 | **16.** 54 ÷ 9 = *n* 6 |

| | | | | |
|---|---|---|---|---|
| **17.** $8\overline{)64}$ 8 | **18.** $3\overline{)24}$ 8 | **19.** $9\overline{)72}$ 8 | **20.** $6\overline{)54}$ 9 | **21.** $7\overline{)56}$ 8 |
| **22.** $7\overline{)49}$ 7 | **23.** $5\overline{)25}$ 5 | **24.** $4\overline{)16}$ 4 | **25.** $8\overline{)32}$ 4 | **26.** $7\overline{)63}$ 9 |



## Follow Up

### Reteaching

Discuss the relationship of division to multiplication and how students can use multiplication facts to find division facts. Use several basic facts as examples. Then focus attention on rules and properties that apply to the division operation. Review the role of 1 in division: $n \div 1 = n$ and $n \div n = 1$; and the role of zero in division: $0 \div n = 0$ and we *never* divide by zero. Take time to practice basic facts of division, noting any facts that appear to cause students difficulty.

### Enrichment

Have students play "Division Concentration." Have available sets of index cards that include division equations with the corresponding quotients. Direct students to mix the cards and place facedown in a row. Players take turns turning over any two cards at a time. The player may keep the two cards if one card is a division equation and the other card is the correct quotient. The player with the most cards at the end of the game is the winner.

| Assignment Guide | | | |
|---|---|---|---|
| | Minimum | Average | Extended |
| page 7 | 1–35 | 1–38 | 1–38, TM |

Divide. Check by multiplying.

Any number divided by 1 is that number.

1. $1\overline{)6}$ 6
2. $1\overline{)8}$ 8
3. $1\overline{)1}$ 1
4. $1\overline{)0}$ 0

Any nonzero number divided by itself is 1.

5. $7\overline{)7}$ 1
6. $9\overline{)9}$ 1
7. $1\overline{)1}$ 1
8. $6\overline{)6}$ 1

0 divided by another number is 0.

9. $5\overline{)0}$ 0
10. $8\overline{)0}$ 0
11. $9\overline{)0}$ 0
12. $7\overline{)0}$ 0

Remember: WE NEVER DIVIDE BY 0.

| | |
|---|---|
| $0\overline{)6}$ ? Check: ? × 0 = 6 No solution! | $0\overline{)0}$ ? Check: ? × 0 = 0 Too many solutions! |

13. $3\overline{)27}$ 9
14. $5\overline{)30}$ 6
15. $7\overline{)49}$ 7
16. $6\overline{)48}$ 8
17. $9\overline{)63}$ 7
18. $8\overline{)24}$ 3
19. $5\overline{)45}$ 9
20. $7\overline{)56}$ 8
21. $8\overline{)64}$ 8
22. $8\overline{)72}$ 9
23. 20 ÷ 4 5
24. 21 ÷ 3 7
25. 6 ÷ 1 6
26. 8 ÷ 8 1
27. 54 ÷ 6 9
28. 56 ÷ 7 8
29. 0 ÷ 4 0
30. 54 ÷ 9 6
31. 42 ÷ 6 7
32. 36 ÷ 4 9
33. What is 63 divided by 7? 9
34. What is the quotient when the divisor is 7 and the dividend is 42? 6
35. At the art store, Alejandro had 42 prints of famous paintings. He put 6 prints in each bin. How many bins did he use? 7

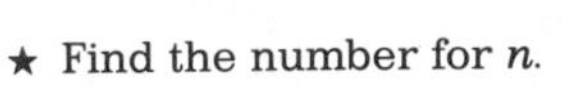

★ Find the number for $n$.

36. $n \div 6 = 9$ 54
37. $72 \div n = 8$ 9
38. $45 \div n = 9$ 5

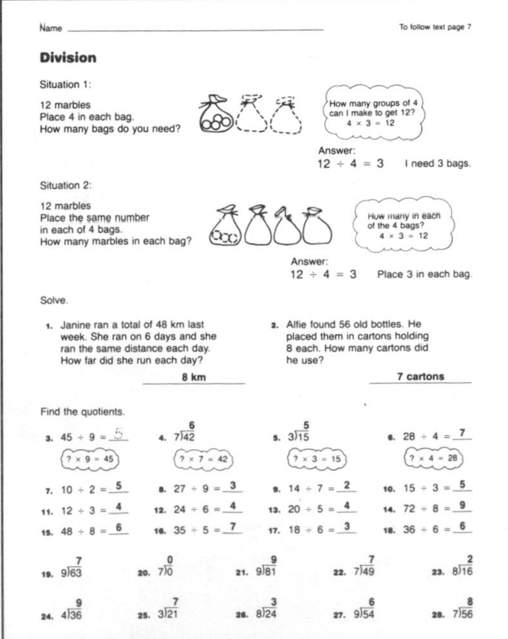

## Think

**A Game of Nim!**

Play this game with a friend. Place 15 markers in 3 rows as shown.

**Rules**

1. Two players take turns.
2. In turn, a player picks up one or more markers from one row only.
3. Whoever has to pick up the last marker loses the game.

## Math

More Practice, page 411, Set C



## Using Page 7

**Lesson Development** Point out that division can be checked by using multiplication. "How do you know that 8 divided by 1 is 8?" (Because 8 × 1 = 8.) "How do you know that 6 divided by 6 is 1?" (Because 1 × 6 = 6.) "How do you know that 0 divided by 5 is 0?" (Because 0 × 5 = 0.)

Emphasize the idea that *we never divide by 0.* Because there is no number that can be multiplied by 0 to get 6, there is no answer for 6 divided by 0. Because any number would multiply by 0 to give 0, there is no single answer for 0 divided by 0. For these reasons we agree that we never divide by 0.

**Exercises 4, 9–12, 29** Note that these exercises involve dividing 0 by a number and each has the answer 0. Be sure students do not confuse these with an attempt to divide a number by 0.

**Exercises 33–34** These verbal experiences with division will help students solve word problems involving division.

**Exercises 36–38** Encourage students to solve these problems by thinking about basic division facts.

**Think Math** As students play the game of Nim, help them discover that the first player can win by picking all but one of the counters in a given row. Encourage students to use different numbers of counters and look for different strategies as they play the game.

**More Practice,** page 411, Set C

**Reteaching Supplement,** page 3

Name ____________ To follow text page 7

**Division**

Situation 1:

12 marbles
Place 4 in each bag.
How many bags do you need?

How many groups of 4 can I make to get 12? 4 × 3 = 12

Answer:
12 ÷ 4 = 3 I need 3 bags.

Situation 2:

12 marbles
Place the same number in each of 4 bags.
How many marbles in each bag?

How many in each of the 4 bags? 4 × 3 = 12

Answer:
12 ÷ 4 = 3 Place 3 in each bag.

Solve.

1. Janine ran a total of 48 km last week. She ran on 6 days and she ran the same distance each day. How far did she run each day? **8 km**
2. Alfie found 56 old bottles. He placed them in cartons holding 8 each. How many cartons did he use? **7 cartons**

Find the quotients.

3. 45 ÷ 9 = 5 (? × 9 = 45)
4. $7\overline{)42}$ 6 (? × 7 = 42)
5. $3\overline{)15}$ 5 (? × 3 = 15)
6. 28 ÷ 4 = 7 (? × 4 = 28)
7. 10 ÷ 2 = 5
8. 27 ÷ 9 = 3
9. 14 ÷ 7 = 2
10. 15 ÷ 3 = 5
11. 12 ÷ 3 = 4
12. 24 ÷ 6 = 4
13. 20 ÷ 5 = 4
14. 72 ÷ 8 = 9
15. 48 ÷ 8 = 6
16. 35 ÷ 5 = 7
17. 18 ÷ 6 = 3
18. 36 ÷ 6 = 6
19. $9\overline{)63}$ 7
20. $7\overline{)0}$ 0
21. $9\overline{)81}$ 9
22. $7\overline{)49}$ 7
23. $8\overline{)16}$ 2
24. $4\overline{)36}$ 9
25. $3\overline{)21}$ 7
26. $8\overline{)24}$ 3
27. $9\overline{)54}$ 6
28. $7\overline{)56}$ 8

**Enrichment Supplement,** page 3

Name ____________ To follow text page 7

**It's Divisible**

Color in the squares below that have numbers that are divisible by 6, 7, or 9.

| | | | | | | | | | |
|---|---|---|---|---|---|---|---|---|---|
| 19 | 56 | 2 | 17 | 60 | 15 | 87 | 81 | 41 | 53 |
| 32 | 48 | 13 | 55 | 35 | 29 | 5 | 42 | 23 | 16 |
| 73 | 45 | 22 | 43 | 63 | 44 | 8 | 18 | 44 | 34 |
| 8 | 7 | 50 | 31 | 30 | 19 | 25 | 36 | 26 | 64 |
| 80 | 14 | 42 | 0 | 0 | 40 | 61 | 42 | 62 | 50 |
| 52 | 28 | 6 | 21 | 60 | 29 | 32 | 54 | 15 | 37 |
| 29 | 36 | 43 | 41 | 54 | 59 | 47 | 49 | 43 | 53 |
| 76 | 56 | 23 | 80 | 72 | 39 | 20 | 70 | 52 | 65 |
| 41 | 24 | 38 | 20 | 42 | 37 | 34 | 48 | 40 | 31 |
| 59 | 12 | 11 | 17 | 27 | 33 | 57 | 9 | 50 | 32 |

Make a two-letter word design of your own on the grid below. Write numbers that are divisible by 3, 5, and 8 in the squares that will form the design. Write other numbers in the remaining squares. Then trade with a friend and color in each other's design. **Designs will vary.**

**Practice Supplement,** page 3

Name ____________ To follow text page 7

**Division**

Divide. Check by multiplying.

1. 40 ÷ 8 = 5
2. 54 ÷ 6 = 9
3. 16 ÷ 2 = 8
4. 27 ÷ 9 = 3
5. 35 ÷ 5 = 7
6. 64 ÷ 8 = 8
7. 32 ÷ 4 = 8
8. 18 ÷ 2 = 9
9. 48 ÷ 6 = 8
10. 0 ÷ 3 = 0
11. 49 ÷ 7 = 7
12. 54 ÷ 9 = 6
13. 81 ÷ 9 = 9
14. 25 ÷ 5 = 5
15. 42 ÷ 6 = 7
16. 24 ÷ 3 = 8
17. 45 ÷ 9 = 5
18. 63 ÷ 7 = 9
19. 45 ÷ 9 = 5
20. 36 ÷ 6 = 6
21. 30 ÷ 5 = 6
22. 56 ÷ 8 = 7
23. 72 ÷ 9 = 8
24. 12 ÷ 4 = 3
25. 18 ÷ 9 = 2
26. 36 ÷ 4 = 9
27. 16 ÷ 4 = 4
28. 42 ÷ 7 = 6
29. 21 ÷ 7 = 3
30. 15 ÷ 3 = 5
31. 20 ÷ 4 = 5
32. 18 ÷ 6 = 3
33. 28 ÷ 7 = 4
34. 32 ÷ 8 = 4
35. 24 ÷ 6 = 4
36. 40 ÷ 5 = 8
37. $3\overline{)27}$ 9
38. $5\overline{)40}$ 8
39. $7\overline{)28}$ 4
40. $9\overline{)36}$ 4
41. $6\overline{)0}$ 0
42. $8\overline{)48}$ 6
43. $7\overline{)35}$ 5
44. $8\overline{)72}$ 9
45. $6\overline{)36}$ 6
46. $7\overline{)56}$ 8
47. $4\overline{)20}$ 5
48. $3\overline{)21}$ 7
49. $9\overline{)63}$ 7
50. $4\overline{)28}$ 7
51. $2\overline{)0}$ 0
52. $8\overline{)32}$ 4
53. $4\overline{)4}$ 1
54. $7\overline{)42}$ 6
55. $8\overline{)56}$ 7
56. $5\overline{)45}$ 9
57. $3\overline{)12}$ 4
58. $6\overline{)30}$ 5
59. $9\overline{)72}$ 8
60. $4\overline{)16}$ 4
61. $7\overline{)21}$ 3
62. $9\overline{)18}$ 2
63. $5\overline{)20}$ 4
64. $4\overline{)36}$ 9
65. $5\overline{)30}$ 6
66. $8\overline{)24}$ 3

# Applications

**Quick Review** Students give these basic facts aloud as quickly as possible.

5 + 8 7 − 6 12 − 8 6 × 9 48 ÷ 8 5 × 5 7 + 9
15 − 6 9 + 0 11 − 8 4 + 9 9 + 8 72 ÷ 8
14 − 8 6 × 7 36 ÷ 4 32 ÷ 8 5 × 4 42 ÷ 7

**Lesson Focus** To use the 5-Point Checklist and basic facts to solve word problems

## Ideas for Getting Started

Give the problem below to the class. For each problem work with students to answer the following questions.

1. What *question* is asked in the problem?
2. What *data* is needed so that the problem can be solved?
3. Which operation would you *plan* to use to solve the problem?

Bill earned money for a trip to the amusement park. The first day he earned ____ dollars. The next day he earned 2 dollars more than the first day. What were his total earnings?

Jeff took 13 rollercoaster rides. Tim took ____ rides. How many more rides did Jeff take than Tim?

There were 16 people in Mary's group. ____ of them arrived for a meeting. How many people were still to come?

Tickets cost ____ dollars each. There were 9 people in one group. How much did they pay for their tickets?

## Using Page 8

**Lesson Development** Ask a volunteer to read the 5-Point Checklist. Tell students that this checklist does not give "rules" for solving problems. Rather, it gives five important things to think about as they work toward the solution to a problem.

Help students follow the steps of the checklist used to solve the problem in the text. Discuss steps 1 through 5 emphasizing question, data, plan, answer, and check. Tell students that after they check to see if they performed the operation correctly, they should reread the problem to see if the answer seems reasonable.

As students solve problems 1 and 2 at the bottom of the page, point out that all necessary data has been included in the problems. Tell students that there will be times when they have to go to other sources to find the needed data. Also, in some problems there may be more data than is needed.

Tell students that the plan for solving these problems involves choosing the operations of addition, subtraction, multiplication, or division. Tell students that they will learn how to solve many different kinds of problems throughout the year.

## Problem Solving: The 5-Point Checklist

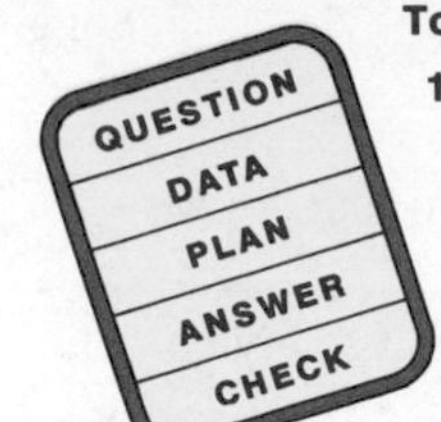


**To Solve a Problem**

1. **Understand the Question**
2. **Find the needed Data**
3. **Plan what to do**
4. **Find the Answer**
5. **Check back**

These five steps can help you solve problems. Follow them to solve this problem.

Neil and 8 friends went to an amusement park. Tickets cost $8 each. How much did the group pay?

**1. Understand the Question**
What was the total cost of the tickets?

**2. Find the needed Data**
There were 9 persons (Neil and 8 friends) who bought tickets. The tickets cost $8 each.

**3. Plan what to do**
Since we want the total for 9 equal amounts, we multiply.

**4. Find the Answer**
9 × 8 = 72 Neil and his friends paid $72 for tickets.

**5. Check back**
Read the problem again. The answer 72 seems reasonable.

Solve. Use the 5-Point Checklist.

1. Eddie went on 6 rides an hour for 5 hours. How many rides did he take? 30
2. Jenny rode 14 rides in the first 3 hours. Nan rode 6 less than this. How many rides did Nan take? 8

8

## Follow Up

### Reteaching

Carefully read through each step of the 5-Step Checklist with students and help them apply the five steps in the checklist. Present students with word problems that can be solved by using one of the basic addition, subtraction, multiplication, or division facts. Emphasize the importance of checking back to see if the answer is reasonable.

### Enrichment

Ask students to make up word problems that can be solved using basic addition, subtraction, or multiplication, or division facts. When they have completed their problems, have them exchange with classmates and solve each others' word problems.

| Assignment Guide | | | |
|---|---|---|---|
| | Minimum | Average | Extended |
| page 9 | 1–6 | 1–7 | 1–8 |

Solve.

1. Marie stayed at the amusement park for 15 hours during 2 days. She stayed 7 hours the first day. How many hours did she stay the second day? 8

2. Todd spent $8 to get into the park, $4 for gifts, and $6 for food. What was the total amount Todd spent? $18

3. A rollercoaster ride lasts only 7 minutes. During the first hour, Sam took 6 rides. How many minutes did Sam spend on the roller coaster the first hour? 42 minutes

4. Tim thought he would see more people he knew at the park than Jay would. Tim saw 5 people he knew the first day and 4 people the second. How many did Jay see if he saw 6 more than Tim? 15

5. On one trip 24 people rode the Runaway Rails Train. There were 4 people on each car. How many cars did the train have? 6

6. The Giant Caterpillar ride has 9 rows of seats. Each row has seats for 6 people. How many people can the ride carry? 54

7. Miranda and her sister together spent $16 for food and gifts at the park. Her sister spent $9 of that amount. How much did Miranda spend? $7

★ 8. Each car of the Log Splash ride holds 9 people. An average of 8 cars are filled every 5 minutes. How many people ride the Log Splash in 10 minutes? 144



## Using Page 9

**Exercise 4** Caution students to read this problem carefully. Only addition is needed to solve the problem, even though the word clues may suggest subtraction to some students.

**Exercise 8** This problem goes slightly beyond the basic facts. Students might multiply 9 × 8 to find the number of persons riding each 5 minutes and then double 72 to find the number riding during a 10-minute period. Or they might determine that there are 16 cars filled in 10 minutes and multiply that number by 9, the number of people in each car.

*The 5-Point Checklist gives students a practical guide for solving problems of all types.*

### Reteaching Supplement, page 4

Name ______ To follow text page 9

**Problem Solving: The 5-Point Checklist**

Study how the 5-point Checklist is used to solve the problem.

Vicki collected (48) twelve-ounce bottles. She placed them in cartons that held (6) each. How many cartons did she use?

1. Understand the Question. *Underline it.*
2. Find the needed Data. *Ring it.*
3. Plan what to do. *Find the action.* → ". . . placed them in cartons that held 6 each." (Divide to find this answer.)
4. Find the Answer. *Choose the operation.* → 48 ÷ 6 = 8 She used 8 cartons.
5. Check back. *Compare the facts.* → 8 × 6 = 48 8 is correct.

Solve. Use the 5-Point Checklist.

1. Steph found (8) bottles. She was paid (5¢) for each bottle. How much was she paid? **40¢**
2. Last week, Juan found (6) bottles on Monday and (8) bottles on Tuesday. How many bottles did Juan find on the two days? **14**
3. Jean collected (5¢) for each 12-ounce bottle and (8¢) for each 16-ounce bottle. How much more did she collect for each large bottle? **3¢**
4. Arnold found (7) bottles. Kiki found (16) bottles. How many more bottles did Kiki find than Arnold? **9**
5. Jimmy was paid (60¢) for returning 3 bottles. He spent (35¢) for an eraser. How much money did he have left to spend? **25¢**
6. Kara placed (56) bottles into (7) boxes. Each box had the same number of bottles. How many bottles did she place in each box? **8**

4

### Enrichment Supplement, page 4

Name ______ To follow text page 9

**It's a Fact**

To solve each of the problems below, you need to know one fact that is not stated. Write the fact. Then solve the problem.

1. Dori said that it was 1 week and 4 days until her birthday. How many days was it until her birthday?
   Fact: 7days = 1 week
   Answer: 11
2. Ben wanted to buy a yogurt bar for 41¢. He gave the clerk 2 quarters. How much change should he get back?
   Fact: **quarter = 25¢**
   Answer: **9¢**
3. My birthday was 3 months ago. How many months must I wait until my next birthday?
   Fact: **1 year = 12 months**
   Answer: **9**
4. Maria is buying dinner rolls. She can buy a package of 1 dozen for 87¢ or 2 packages of 6 for 45¢ per package. Which is the better bargain?
   Fact: **dozen = 12**
   Answer: **dozen for 87¢**
5. One side of a square is 6 cm long. What is the total distance around the square?
   Fact: **A square has 4 equal sides.**
   Answer: **24 cm**
6. If the temperature is 5°C and dropping, how many more degrees must it drop in order for water to freeze?
   Fact: **Water freezes at 0°C.**
   Answer: **5°C**
7. Jennifer repairs skis. She has 5 pairs in her shop to be fixed. She has already repaired 3 of the skis. How many skis are left to fix?
   Fact: **pair = 2**
   Answer: **7**
8. Arnie put all new tires on 9 cars in one day. How many tires in all did he put on?
   Fact: **Each car has 4 wheels.**
   Answer: **36**

4 Problem Solving: The 5-Point Checklist

### Practice Supplement, page 4

Name ______ To follow text page 9

**Problem Solving: The 5-Point Checklist**

Use these five steps to help you solve the problems.

5-POINT CHECKLIST
1. Understand the Question.
2. Find the needed Data.
3. Plan what to do.
4. Find the Answer.
5. Check back.

Solve.

1. Sally and 6 friends went to the circus. Tickets cost $7 each. How much did they pay for tickets? **$49**
2. There were 15 lions. If 3 lions shared each cage, how many cages were there? **5**
3. Isabelle bought a ticket for $7, a hat for $2, and spent $5 on food. How much did she spend in all? **$14**
4. 20 horses were lined up in rows of 4. How many rows were there? **5**
5. There were 17 elephants in the parade. 8 elephants had riders. How many elephants did not have riders? **9**
6. Leo spent $17 at the circus. Ben spent $8 less. How much did Ben spend? **$9**
7. Frank bought sandwiches for himself and 3 friends. Each sandwich cost $3. How much did Frank spend? **$12**
8. 6 clowns each had 8 balloons. How many balloons did they have in all? **48**

4

# Operations

**Quick Review** As oral drill, students give both multiplication facts for each number pair. Example: **7 × 3** 7 × 3 = 21; 3 × 7 = 21

4,3 9,5 8,3 6,7 9,6 7,5 4,8 8,9 5,6
3,4 8,6 4,6 2,8 7,8 9,1 3,9 5,4

**Lesson Focus** To practice the basic facts; to use parentheses to determine the order of operations

## Ideas for Getting Started

To begin this lesson, review with students the meanings of the four operations. Elicit from students the terms discussed involving each operation: addend, sum, difference, factor, product, quotient. Ask volunteers to make up word problems that can be solved by the four operations.

## Using Page 10

**Lesson Development** Tell students that this page will help them show how well they have mastered the basic facts. Observe as students complete the exercises to see how quickly and easily they are able to respond with answers. Students who take an extra long time may need extra help in memorizing or recalling the facts.

**Exercises 1–26** These exercises are grouped and clearly labeled according to the operation.

**Exercises 27–46** Caution students to be alert for the sign indicating the required operation.

**Exercises 47–54** Remind students to think about basic facts as they solve these problems.

## Practice the Facts

Add.

1. 6 + 5 = 11
2. 7 + 6 = 13
3. 8 + 5 = 13
4. 9 + 4 = 13
5. 8 + 7 = 15
6. 9 + 8 = 17
7. 6 + 9 = 15

Subtract.

8. 17 − 8 = 9
9. 13 − 7 = 6
10. 14 − 6 = 8
11. 15 − 9 = 6
12. 16 − 8 = 8
13. 14 − 7 = 7
14. 13 − 8 = 5

Multiply.

15. 9 × 6 = 54
16. 8 × 7 = 56
17. 9 × 9 = 81
18. 8 × 9 = 72
19. 9 × 7 = 63
20. 8 × 6 = 48
21. 6 × 7 = 42

Divide.

22. 7)42 6
23. 9)54 6
24. 7)56 8
25. 5)45 9
26. 6)54 9

Add, subtract, multiply, or divide.

27. 8 + 6 14
28. 9 × 3 27
29. 17 − 8 9
30. 36 ÷ 4 9
31. 8 × 7 56
32. 15 − 6 9
33. 9 + 8 17
34. 36 ÷ 9 4
35. 49 ÷ 7 7
36. 4 × 9 36
37. 13 − 5 8
38. 7 + 4 11
39. 8 × 3 24
40. 9 + 7 16
41. 63 ÷ 9 7
42. 45 ÷ 5 9
43. 7 + 5 12
44. 14 − 9 5
45. 6 × 8 48
46. 4 × 7 28

★ Give the number for $n$.

47. $6 + n = 14$ 8
48. $8 \times n = 32$ 4
49. $13 - n = 8$ 5
50. $24 \div n = 4$ 6
51. $n + 8 = 17$ 9
52. $n \times 9 = 54$ 6
53. $n - 6 = 9$ 15
54. $n \div 5 = 9$ 45

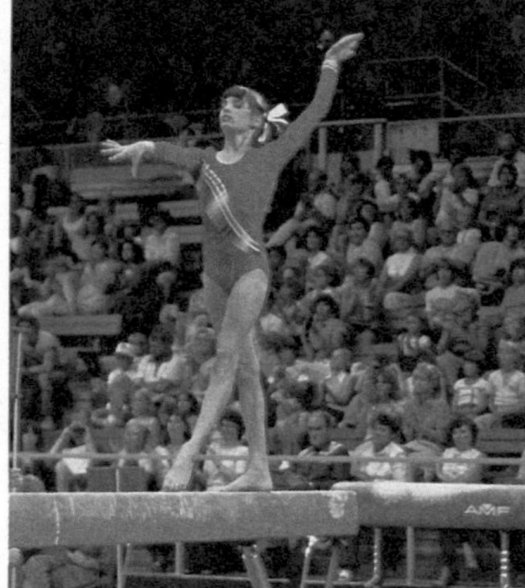



## Follow Up

### Reteaching

Provide practice with models, games, calculators, and other motivating techniques. Use these practice activities for both diagnostic and achievement purposes. For students who have difficulty with specific facts, provide review of the basic meanings of the operations for addition, subtraction, multiplication, and division.

### Enrichment

Provide students with a worksheet as shown below. Have students find the rule that has been applied to the number pairs in the first column to get the answers in the second column and then complete the worksheet.

| Rule: a + b − 2 | |
|---|---|
| 5,4 | 7 |
| 6,0 | 4 |
| 9,2 | 9 |
| 3,3 | 4 |
| 7,4 | 9 |

| Rule: a × b + 4 | |
|---|---|
| 3,6 | 22 |
| 2,5 | 14 |
| 4,1 | 8 |
| 8,5 | 44 |
| 1,7 | 11 |

| Assignment Guide | | | |
|---|---|---|---|
| | Minimum | Average | Extended |
| page 10 | 1–46 | 1–54 | 1–54 |
| page 11 | 1–21 | 1–28 | 1–30, TM |

## Combining Operations

Bart and Felicia were asked to find 36 ÷ 6 + 3. Their work for this problem shows that the placement of the parentheses makes a difference in the answer. It is important to use parentheses to tell which operation to do first when combining operations.

(36÷6)+3
6+3
9
Bart

36÷(6+3)
36÷9
4
Felicia

Do the operations in the order shown by the parentheses. Give the answer.

1. (9 + 7) − 8 8
2. (6 × 4) ÷ 8 3
3. (42 ÷ 7) + 9 15
4. 6 + (13 − 4) 15
5. 7 × (5 + 4) 63
6. 7 × (4 × 2) 56
7. (48 ÷ 6) − 8 0
8. 4 × (15 − 6) 36
9. (5 + 2) × 4 28
10. 81 ÷ (9 × 1) 9
11. (54 ÷ 9) + 8 14
12. 7 × (6 − 6) 0
13. (3 + 4) × 8 56
14. 3 × (6 + 2) 24
15. (72 ÷ 8) − 5 4
16. (42 ÷ 6) + 7 14
17. (9 × 8) ÷ 9 8
18. (16 ÷ 4) − (24 ÷ 6) 0
19. 8 + (20 ÷ 5) − 6 6
20. (3 × 2) + (4 × 2) 14
21. (15 + 6) ÷ (9 − 2) 3

Copy and put in parentheses to show which operation has been done first.

22. 3 × 2 + 5 = 21
3 × (2 + 5) = 21
23. 6 × 4 − 3 = 6
6 × (4 − 3) = 6
24. 5 + 2 × 4 = 28
(5 + 2) × 4 = 28
25. 4 + 4 ÷ 2 = 6
4 + (4 ÷ 2) = 6
26. 12 ÷ 6 + 8 = 10
(12 ÷ 6) + 8 = 10
27. 9 + 9 ÷ 3 = 6
(9 + 9) ÷ 3 = 6
28. 12 − 4 × 3 = 0
12 − (4 × 3) = 0
★ 29. 8 + 7 ÷ 9 − 4 = 3
(8 + 7) ÷ (9 − 4) = 3
★ 30. 16 ÷ 4 + 4 × 2 = 4
16 ÷ (4 + 4) × 2 = 4

### Think Math

**Guess and Check**

Write the equations using the signs +, −, ×, ÷ and parentheses ( ) as needed so that as many as possible of the equations will be correct. Which one cannot be written so that it is correct?

Sample answers are shown.

(4 − 4) × 4 = 0
4 4 4 = 1 Not possible
(4 + 4) ÷ 4 = 2
4 − (4 ÷ 4) = 3
(4 + 4) − 4 = 4
(4 ÷ 4) + 4 = 5

More Practice, page 411, Set D



## Using Page 11

**Lesson Development** Discuss the two problems at the top of the page. Point out that the grouping property for addition and for multiplication tells us that the placement of the parentheses does not make any difference when adding or multiplying three numbers. However, the placement of parentheses does make a difference when combining different operations.

**Exercises 1–21** As students complete these problems, emphasize that the parentheses tell which operation to do first. Note that all the exercises involve basic facts.

**Exercises 22–28** After students have completed these exercises, ask them to put the parentheses in a different place and tell what each answer would be.

**Exercises 29–30** In these starred exercises students must place two sets of parentheses in each equation.

**Think Math** In this exercise students use parentheses, operation signs, and multiples of 4 to make equations that equal a given number.

**More Practice,** page 411, Set D

**Reteaching Supplement,** page 5

Name ______ To follow text page 11

**Combining Operations**

Example 1: (42 ÷ 7) + 5 → 6 + 5 → 11
Do the operation in parentheses first. Then do the other operation.

Example 2: (12 ÷ 4) + (16 ÷ 8) → 3 + 2 → 5
Do the operations in both parentheses first. Then do the other operation.

Solve. Show your work.

1. (8 + 5) − 4 → 13 − 4 → 9
2. 3 + (6 × 3) ← Finish. → 3 + 18 → 21
3. (2 + 5) × (3 + 6) → 7 × 9 → 63
4. (42 ÷ 6) + 3 → 7 + 3 → 10
5. (5 ÷ 5) × 9 → 1 × 9 → 9
6. 7 + (12 − 8) → 7 + 4 → 11

Solve.

7. 4 × (11 − 7) = 16
8. (7 + 1) × 8 = 64
9. 72 ÷ (9 − 1) = 9
10. (56 ÷ 8) + 8 = 15
11. 7 × (9 − 9) = 0
12. (6 + 7) − 9 = 4
13. (4 + 7) × 0 = 0
14. (64 ÷ 8) − 5 = 3
15. (7 × 6) ÷ 7 = 6
16. (12 ÷ 6) + (15 ÷ 5) = 5
17. (4 × 3) ÷ (7 − 1) = 2
18. (4 × 2) + (3 × 3) = 17
19. (8 × 3) − (12 − 2) = 14
20. (7 × 0) + (0 × 7) = 0
21. (7 + 1) + (6 + 2) = 16

**Enrichment Supplement,** page 5

Name ______ To follow text page 11

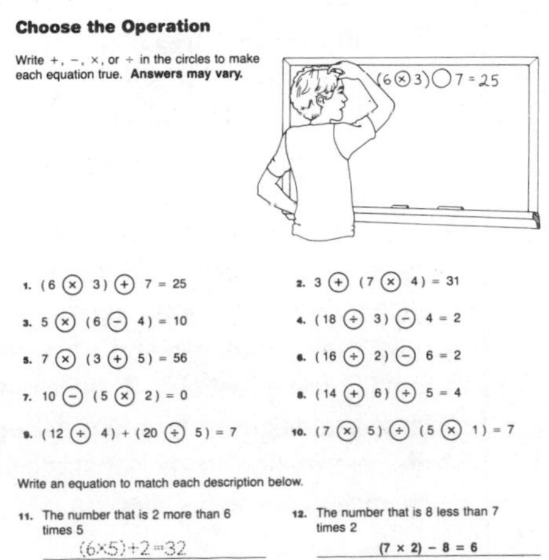

**Choose the Operation**

Write +, −, ×, or ÷ in the circles to make each equation true. **Answers may vary.**



1. (6 ⊗ 3) ⊕ 7 = 25
2. 3 ⊕ (7 ⊗ 4) = 31
3. 5 ⊗ (6 ⊖ 4) = 10
4. (18 (÷) 3) ⊖ 4 = 2
5. 7 ⊗ (3 ⊕ 5) = 56
6. (16 (÷) 2) ⊖ 6 = 2
7. 10 ⊖ (5 ⊗ 2) = 0
8. (14 ⊕ 6) (÷) 5 = 4
9. (12 (÷) 4) + (20 (÷) 5) = 7
10. (7 ⊗ 5) (÷) (5 ⊗ 1) = 7

Write an equation to match each description below.

11. The number that is 2 more than 6 times 5
(6×5)+2=32
12. The number that is 8 less than 7 times 2
(7 × 2) − 8 = 6
13. The number that is 3 times the difference of 12 and 8
(12 − 8) × 3 = 12
14. The number that is 5 more than the quotient of 45 divided by 9
(45 ÷ 9) + 5 = 10
15. The number that is 2 less than the product of 9 times 8
(9 × 8) − 2 = 70
16. The number that is 7 more than twice the quotient of 54 divided by 6
2 × (54 ÷ 6) + 7 = 25

**Practice Supplement,** page 5

Name ______ To follow text page 11

**Combining Operations**

Do the operations in the order shown by the parentheses. Write the answer.

1. (6 + 5) − 3 = 8
2. (3 × 4) ÷ 2 = 6
3. (56 ÷ 7) + 5 = 13
4. 6 × (3 × 2) = 36
5. 8 × (3 + 4) = 56
6. 5 + (15 − 9) = 11
7. (01 ÷ 9) − 4 = 5
8. 3 × (12 − 3) = 27
9. (7 + 1) × 5 = 40
10. 3 × (4 − 4) = 0
11. (36 ÷ 6) + 6 = 12
12. 48 ÷ (2 × 4) = 6
13. (6 + 2) × 5 = 40
14. 5 × (3 + 3) = 30
15. (64 ÷ 8) × 2 = 16
16. (16 ÷ 4) + 9 = 13
17. (6 × 3) ÷ 9 = 2
18. 7 + (54 ÷ 9) = 13
19. 8 − (21 ÷ 7) = 5
20. (6 − 6) + 4 = 4
21. 54 ÷ (12 − 3) = 6
22. (35 ÷ 7) × 5 = 25
23. 3 + (13 − 5) = 11
24. (49 ÷ 7) + 6 = 13
25. 4 × (21 ÷ 7) = 12
26. (72 ÷ 8) × 5 = 45
27. (3 + 3) × (3 ÷ 3) = 6
28. (2 + 5) + (4 + 3) = 14
29. (28 ÷ 4) + (15 − 7) = 15
30. 17 − (56 ÷ 7) + 2 = 11
31. (15 ÷ 5) + (24 ÷ 3) = 11
32. (8 − 3) × (15 − 6) = 45
33. (36 ÷ 6) × (54 ÷ 9) = 36
34. (4 × 3) − (4 × 2) = 4
35. 8 − (12 ÷ 4) + 7 = 12
36. (6 − 4) × (45 ÷ 5) = 18

# Applications

**Quick Review** Use these basic facts for oral drill. Students use the appropriate inverse operation to check their answers.

6 + 5 3 + 8 9 + 7 7 + 4 8 + 7 7 + 6 8 + 9

8 × 6 9 × 5 4 × 8 6 × 3 7 × 9 5 × 6

**Lesson Focus** To understand the question and use basic facts to solve word problems; to use data from an information sheet to solve word problems

## Ideas for Getting Started

Write the 5-Point Checklist on the chalkboard and call students' attention to the first step "Understand the *question.*" Emphasize the importance of understanding the question in solving problems. Give a list of data such as:

- Mary works 5 hours per day.
- Tim earns 4 dollars per hour.
- A store is open 6 days a week, 8 hours a day.

Then generate a discussion in which students ask questions that can be answered using the given data.

## Using Page 12

**Lesson Development** Read the example data at the top of the page. "What question could be asked about this information?" (How much did Nell receive?) "What data in the problem is needed to answer this question?" (7 cars washed, $6 per car) Use the 5-Point Checklist to help find and check the solution. Emphasize the importance of using a complete sentence to give the answer.

**Exercises 1–8** Read through the directions for each problem. Make sure students understand the three parts to each question. Tell them that the data in each exercise suggests questions that could be answered by one of the four operations.

Possible answers:

1. **How much did Eric earn for mowing 1 lawn?**
   **24 ÷ 3 = 8**
   **Eric earned $8 for mowing 1 lawn.**
2. **How much money did Peggy have left?**
   **12 − 3 = 9**
   **Peggy had $9 left.**
3. **How much does John earn in 7 days (a week)?**
   **7 × 8 = 56**
   **John earns $56 in 7 days (a week).**
4. **How much more did Theresa earn than Tim?**
   **16 − 9 = 7**
   **Theresa earned $7 more than Tim.**
5. **How many hours will Jan need to work on Saturday?**
   **15 − 6 = 9**
   **Jan will need to work 9 hours on Saturday.**
6. **How many hours did Tom work?**
   **36 ÷ 4 = 9**
   **Tom worked 9 hours to earn $36.**
7. **How much did Carlos earn in those three days?**
   **5 + 8 + 9 = 22**
   **Carlos earned $22 in three days.**
8. **What was the total amount Dana earned?**
   **(3 × 4) + (2 × 5) = 12 + 10 = $22**
   **Dana earned $22 altogether.**

## Problem Solving: Understanding the Question

To solve a problem, you must first **understand the question.**

For each set of data below, complete the following activities:

A Write a question.

B Solve the problem.

C Write a short sentence that answers the question.

See teaching notes.

Example:

DATA: Nell washed cars to earn money. She washed 7 cars. She received $6 for each car.

A Question: How much did Nell earn?

B Solution: 7 × 6 = 42

C Sentence: Nell earned $42 by washing cars.

1. DATA: Eric mows lawns on weekends. He earned $24 for mowing 3 lawns.
2. DATA: Peggy earned $12 for painting a fence. She paid her little sister $3 for helping her.
3. DATA: John earns $8 a day from his paper route. He delivers papers 7 days a week.
4. DATA: Theresa earned $16 by babysitting. Tim earned $9 by babysitting.
5. DATA: Jan agreed to work a total of 15 hours on Friday and Saturday. She worked 6 hours on Friday.
6. DATA: Tom was paid $4 an hour for delivering ads. He earned $36.
7. DATA: Carlos worked as a golf caddy. He earned $5 on Monday, $8 on Tuesday, and $9 on Wednesday.
8. ★ DATA: Dana worked 3 hours at $4 an hour and 2 more hours at $5 an hour.



## Follow Up

### Reteaching

Put the following headings on the chalkboard: Question, Data, Plan, Answer, Check. Generate a discussion to review the 5-Point Checklist, with an emphasis on understanding the question. Ask each student to make up a word problem suggesting addition, subtraction, multiplication, or division. Have volunteers read their problems and have the class identify the questions. Then as the problems are discussed, record the appropriate information to demonstrate how the checklist can help solve the problem.

### Enrichment

Challenge students to use the 5-Point Checklist to help them solve the following word problem: Ed worked 5 hours at $4 an hour on Saturday. He earned $8 more on Monday. On Tuesday, he bought 4 records for $6 each. He already had 24 records. How much money did Ed have after he bought the records? ($4)

| Assignment Guide | | | |
|---|---|---|---|
| | Minimum | Average | Extended |
| page 12 | 1–6 | 1–7 | 1–8 |
| page 13 | 1–8 | 1–9 | 1–10 |

## Problem Solving: Using Data from an Information Sheet

Sometimes you must search for data needed to solve a problem. Use data from this sheet as needed to solve these problems.

**Ring-a-Peg Game Direction Sheet**

**Rules:** Players must stand the same distance from the board. Each player throws 6 rings. The player with the highest score wins.

| Zone | Points |
|---|---|
| Gold (Bull's eye) | 9 |
| Red | 7 |
| Blue | 5 |
| Green | 3 |
| White | 1 |
| Outside White | 0 |

1. How many more points do you get for a bull's eye than for a ring in the green zone? 6
2. Todd threw 6 rings onto pegs in the red zone. What was his score? 42
3. What is the highest number of points you can get with two rings that hit pegs in different zones? 16
4. Sheila played the game 3 times. How many rings did she throw in all? 18
5. Paul threw a total of 30 rings one afternoon. How many times did he play the game? 5
6. The first time Allison played, she scored 8 points. The second time, she scored 17 points. How many more points did she score the second time? 9
7. Darrell made 21 points with rings in the red zone. How many rings did he get in the red zone? 3
8. Brenda threw 4 rings onto pegs in the green zone. Her other 2 rings fell outside the white zone. What was her score? 12
9. Jeff threw 3 rings. He got 1 in the gold zone, 1 in the red zone, and 1 in the white zone. What was the total number of points from the 3 rings? 17
10. ★ What would be your score if you threw 6 rings and hit a peg in each zone, with 1 ring falling outside the white zone? 25



## Using Page 13

**Lesson Development** Refer again to the 5-Point Checklist on the chalkboard. Point out that often we must search for data needed to solve a problem. Sometimes data is provided on an information sheet. Read and discuss the rules for scoring the Ring-a-Peg game shown on the Direction Sheet.

**Exercises 1–10** Be sure students understand that the data needed to solve these exercises can be found in the Direction Sheet at the top of the page. Note that exercise 8 contains data that is not needed to solve the problem. In exercise 9 students must find the sum of three addends. In exercise 10 students add up the five odd numbers, 1, 3, 5, 7, and 9 to arrive at a sum of 25.

## Ideas that Work

### Chalk It Up

To give students practice in recalling the basic facts quickly, let them play "Catch a Fact."

One player is chosen to call out a basic fact, for example 5 × 7. At the same time he or she throws a bean bag or chalkboard eraser to a player chosen to give the answer. A third player tries to write the answer on the chalkboard before the player with the bean bag can answer. The player who responds with the correct answer first is the one who calls out the basic fact for the next round.

**Practice Supplement,** page 6

Name ______________________ To follow text page 12

**Problem Solving: Understanding the Question**

For each set of data below, complete the following activities:

A Write a question.
B Solve the problem.
C Write a short sentence that answers the question.

1. DATA: Susie worked a total of 13 hours on Thursday and Friday. She worked 7 hours on Thursday.

   **Answers will vary.**

2. DATA: Barbara earns $4 an hour walking dogs. She earned $32.
3. DATA: Phil earns $8 a week cleaning houses. He worked 7 weeks.
4. DATA: Alex earned $8 selling flowers. Emmy earned $16 selling flowers.
5. DATA: Brad worked for 9 hours at $5 an hour.
6. DATA: Betty earned $15 raking leaves. She paid Jane $6 for helping her.

# Number Theory

**Quick Review** Students skip count around the room. Students count first by twos, then fives, then tens.

**Lesson Focus** To use basic facts to find multiples; to use basic facts to find factors

## Ideas for Getting Started

Ask students to think of things that are usually considered in sets of 2, 3, 4, 5, 6, 7, 8, and 9 (examples: 2 gloves; 3 tennis balls in a can; 4 persons in a quartet; 5 pennies in a nickel; 6 cans of juice in a carton; 7 days in a week; 8 crayons in a small box; 9 players on a baseball team). Choose one of the examples for each number and write multiples of that number on the chalkboard. For example, "There are 5 pennies in one nickel. How many pennies are in 2 nickels? 3 nickels?" and so on. Write, "5, 10, 15, 20, 25, 30, 35, 40, 45" on the chalkboard.

## Using Page 14

**Lesson Development** Direct students' attention to the picture and question at the top of the page. As students give the numbers of batteries that can be purchased, list these multiples of 4 on the chalkboard. Help students see that these multiples can be produced by counting by 4 or by using multiplication facts with 4 as a factor. Show a multiplication table on the chalkboard and ask volunteers to fill in the rows that correspond with the multiples of the numbers indicated.

| | x | 0 | 1 | 2 | 3 | 4 | 5 | 6 | 7 | 8 | 9 |
|---|---|---|---|---|---|---|---|---|---|---|---|
| | 2 | | | | | | | | | | |
| | 3 | | | | | | | | | | |
| multiples of 4 | 4 | 0 | 4 | 8 | 12 | 16 | 20 | 24 | 28 | 32 | 36 |
| | 5 | | | | | | | | | | |
| | 6 | | | | | | | | | | |
| | 7 | | | | | | | | | | |
| | 8 | | | | | | | | | | |
| | 9 | | | | | | | | | | |

**Exercises 1–8** Encourage students to think about the multiplication table if they have difficulty with these exercises.

**Exercises 9 and 10** Note that exercise 9 contains the idea of least common multiple in a certain set of numbers.

**Answers**

1. 0, 3, 6, 9, 12, 15, 18, 21, 24, 27
2. 0, 5, 10, 15, 20, 25, 30, 35, 40, 45
3. 0, 6, 12, 18, 24, 30, 36, 42, 48, 54
4. 0, 7, 14, 21, 28, 35, 42, 49, 56, 63
5. 0, 8, 16, 24, 32, 40, 48, 56, 64, 72
6. 0, 9, 18, 27, 36, 45, 54, 63, 72, 81

## Using Basic Facts: Finding Multiples

Batteries are often sold in packages of 4. What are some of the different numbers of batteries you can buy when they are sold 4 to a package?

To show some different numbers of batteries that can be bought, we can list some **multiples** of 4.

Any number that is a product of 4 and another whole number is a multiple of 4!

| | 0 × 4 | 1 × 4 | 2 × 4 | 3 × 4 | 4 × 4 | 5 × 4 | 6 × 4 | 7 × 4 | 8 × 4 | 9 × 4 |
|---|---|---|---|---|---|---|---|---|---|---|
| **Some multiples of 4:** | 0, | 4, | 8, | 12, | 16, | 20, | 24, | 28, | 32, | 36 |

You could buy any number of batteries that is a multiple of 4 (0, 4, 8, 12, . . . ).

Write ten multiples of each number, starting with 0. See teaching notes.

**1.** 3 **2.** 5 **3.** 6 **4.** 7 **5.** 8 **6.** 9

**7.** The multiples of 2 are called **even numbers.** Write 10 even numbers, starting with 0.
0, 2, 4, 6, 8, 10, 12, 14, 16, 18

**8.** Numbers that are 1 more than a multiple of 2 are called **odd numbers.** Write 10 odd numbers, starting with 1.
1, 3, 5, 7, 9, 11, 13, 15, 17, 19

★ Find the Mystery Number.

**9.** This Mystery Number is the smallest number that is a multiple of 6 and also a multiple of 8.
24

**10.** This Mystery Number is the largest number less than 50 that is a multiple of 9 and a multiple of 6.
36

14

## Follow Up

### Reteaching

Review the meaning of multiplication of whole numbers. Then have students fill in the column for the number 5 in a practice table. Begin with 0 × 5, then 1 × 5, 2 × 5, and so on. When the column is completed, call attention to the set of products, 0, 5, 10, 15, 20, 25, . . . , 45. Emphasize that each number is called a *multiple* of 5. Using the table, help students generate multiples of other whole numbers.

### Enrichment

Give students the following squares to complete. Elicit from students that they are called magic squares because the sum of the three numbers in every row, column, and diagonal is the same.

| | | |
|---|---|---|
| 5 | 8 | 5 |
| 6 | 6 | 6 |
| 7 | 4 | 7 |

| | | |
|---|---|---|
| 6 | 9 | 6 |
| 7 | 7 | 7 |
| 8 | 5 | 8 |

| | | |
|---|---|---|
| 8 | 9 | 4 |
| 3 | 7 | 11 |
| 10 | 5 | 6 |

| | | |
|---|---|---|
| 4 | 8 | 9 |
| 12 | 7 | 2 |
| 5 | 6 | 10 |

| Assignment Guide | | | |
|---|---|---|---|
| | Minimum | Average | Extended |
| page 14 | 1–8 | 1–9 | 1–10 |
| page 15 | 1–15, SK | 1–18, SK | 1–21, SK |

## Using Basic Facts: Finding Factors

To find the factors of 12, Jolene wrote these "product 12" equations. (There are 3 more if you change the order of the factors.)

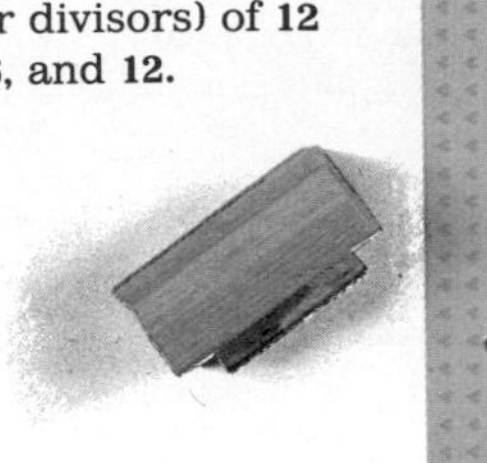

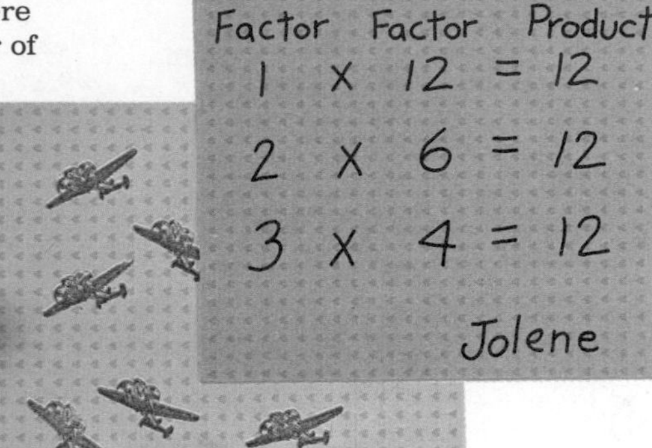


The **factors** (or divisors) of **12** are **1, 2, 3, 4, 6,** and **12.**

Copy and complete the equations. Then list all the factors of the product.

**1.** $1 \times n = 18$ 18
$2 \times n = 18$ 9
$3 \times n = 18$ 6
1, 2, 3, 6, 9, 18

**2.** $1 \times n = 14$ 14
$2 \times n = 14$ 7
1, 2, 7, 14

**3.** $1 \times n = 20$ 20
$2 \times n = 20$ 10
$4 \times n = 20$ 5
$5 \times n = 20$ 4
1, 2, 4, 5, 10, 20

List all the factors of each number. See teaching notes.

**4.** 10 **5.** 15 **6.** 21 **7.** 13 **8.** 16 **9.** 5

**10.** 8 **11.** 7 **12.** 17 **13.** 4 **14.** 27 **15.** 9

**16.** 25 **17.** 6 **18.** 22 ★ **19.** 28 ★ **20.** 24 ★ **21.** 36

### Skillkeeper

Solve.

**1.** $16 - 9 = n$ 7 **2.** $6 + 7 = n$ 13 **3.** $12 \div 3 = n$ 4 **4.** $7 \times 5 = n$ 35

**5.** $32 \div 8 = n$ 4 **6.** $18 - 9 = n$ 9 **7.** $6 \times 9 = n$ 54 **8.** $9 + 8 = n$ 17

**9.** $15 - 7 = n$ 8 **10.** $45 \div 5 = n$ 9 **11.** $9 + 5 = n$ 14 **12.** $7 \times 6 = n$ 42



## Using Page 15

**Lesson Development** Have students consider the "product 12" equations shown at the top of the page. Ask students if there are any other "product 12" equations involving other factors that could be written. (No, factors could be written in different orders, but no other factors are possible.)

Point out that the factors of 12 can also be called divisors of 12. Emphasize that any number that can be multiplied by another whole number to give the product 12 is called a factor of 12.

**Exercises 1–3** Have students find the missing factors by thinking about multiplication facts or the 1 property. If necessary, ask: "Are there any other pairs of factors that multiply to give the number?"

**Exercises 4–21** Except for starred exercises 19, 20, and 21, all of these numbers can be factored using the one property or the basic facts. Pay particular attention to exercises such as 7, 9, 11, and 12 in which the number has exactly two factors.

**Skillkeeper** This skillkeeper reviews the basic addition, subtraction, multiplication, and division facts.

**Answers**

4. 1, 2, 5, 10
5. 1, 3, 5, 15
6. 1, 3, 7, 21
7. 1, 13
8. 1, 2, 4, 8, 16
9. 1, 5
10. 1, 2, 4, 8
11. 1, 7
12. 1, 17
13. 1, 2, 4
14. 1, 3, 9, 27
15. 1, 3, 9
16. 1, 5, 25
17. 1, 2, 3, 6
18. 1, 2, 11, 22
19. 1, 2, 4, 7, 14, 28
20. 1, 2, 3, 4, 6, 8, 12, 24
21. 1, 2, 3, 4, 6, 9, 12, 18, 36

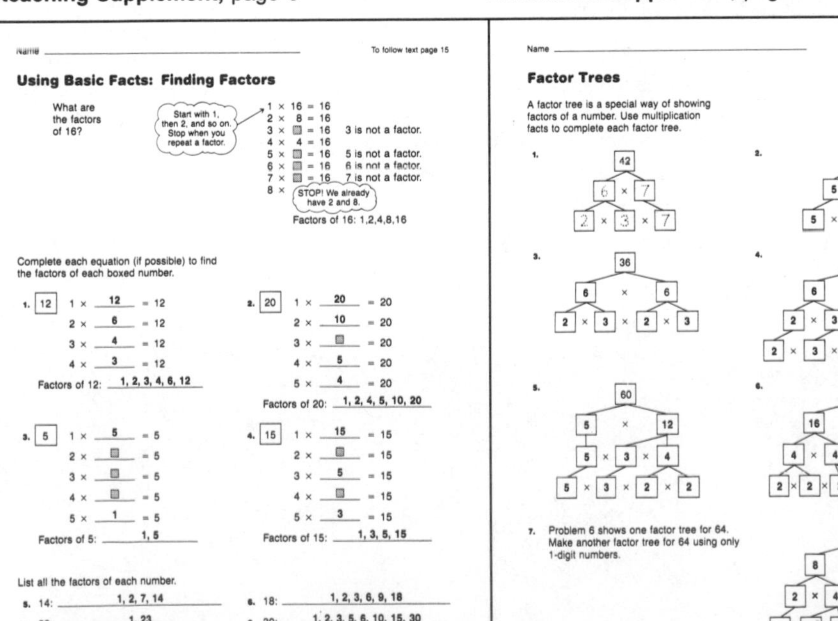

**Reteaching Supplement,** page 6

Name ______ To follow text page 15

**Using Basic Facts: Finding Factors**

What are the factors of 16?

Start with 1, then 2, and so on. Stop when you repeat a factor.

1 × 16 = 16
2 × 8 = 16
3 × ▢ = 16 3 is not a factor.
4 × 4 = 16
5 × ▢ = 16 5 is not a factor.
6 × ▢ = 16 6 is not a factor.
7 × ▢ = 16 7 is not a factor.
8 × STOP! We already have 2 and 8.

Factors of 16: 1,2,4,8,16

Complete each equation (if possible) to find the factors of each boxed number.

1. [12] 1 × 12 = 12; 2 × 6 = 12; 3 × 4 = 12; 4 × 3 = 12
Factors of 12: 1, 2, 3, 4, 6, 12

2. [20] 1 × 20 = 20; 2 × 10 = 20; 3 × ▢ = 20; 4 × 5 = 20; 5 × 4 = 20
Factors of 20: 1, 2, 4, 5, 10, 20

3. [5] 1 × 5 = 5; 2 × ▢ = 5; 3 × ▢ = 5; 4 × ▢ = 5; 5 × 1 = 5
Factors of 5: 1, 5

4. [15] 1 × 15 = 15; 2 × ▢ = 15; 3 × 5 = 15; 4 × ▢ = 15; 5 × 3 = 15
Factors of 15: 1, 3, 5, 15

List all the factors of each number.

5. 14: 1, 2, 7, 14
6. 18: 1, 2, 3, 6, 9, 18
7. 23: 1, 23
8. 30: 1, 2, 3, 5, 6, 10, 15, 30

**Enrichment Supplement,** page 6

Name ______ To follow text page 15

**Factor Trees**

A factor tree is a special way of showing factors of a number. Use multiplication facts to complete each factor tree.

1. 42 → 6 × 7 → 2 × 3 × 7
2. 30 → 5 × 6 → 5 × 2 × 3
3. 36 → 6 × 6 → 2 × 3 × 2 × 3
4. 48 → 6 × 8 → 2 × 3 × 2 × 4 → 2 × 3 × 2 × 2 × 2
5. 60 → 5 × 12 → 5 × 3 × 4 → 5 × 3 × 2 × 2
6. 64 → 16 × 4 → 4 × 4 × 2 × 2 → 2 × 2 × 2 × 2 × 2 × 2
7. Problem 6 shows one factor tree for 64. Make another factor tree for 64 using only 1-digit numbers.
64 → 8 × 8 → 2 × 4 × 2 × 4 → 2 × 2 × 2 × 2 × 2 × 2

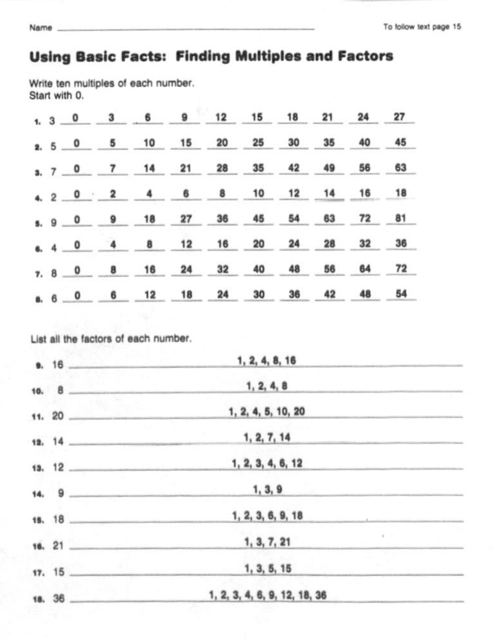

**Practice Supplement,** page 7

Name ______ To follow text page 15

**Using Basic Facts: Finding Multiples and Factors**

Write ten multiples of each number.
Start with 0.

1. 3: 0, 3, 6, 9, 12, 15, 18, 21, 24, 27
2. 5: 0, 5, 10, 15, 20, 25, 30, 35, 40, 45
3. 7: 0, 7, 14, 21, 28, 35, 42, 49, 56, 63
4. 2: 0, 2, 4, 6, 8, 10, 12, 14, 16, 18
5. 9: 0, 9, 18, 27, 36, 45, 54, 63, 72, 81
6. 4: 0, 4, 8, 12, 16, 20, 24, 28, 32, 36
7. 8: 0, 8, 16, 24, 32, 40, 48, 56, 64, 72
8. 6: 0, 6, 12, 18, 24, 30, 36, 42, 48, 54

List all the factors of each number.

9. 16: 1, 2, 4, 8, 16
10. 8: 1, 2, 4, 8
11. 20: 1, 2, 4, 5, 10, 20
12. 14: 1, 2, 7, 14
13. 12: 1, 2, 3, 4, 6, 12
14. 9: 1, 3, 9
15. 18: 1, 2, 3, 6, 9, 18
16. 21: 1, 3, 7, 21
17. 15: 1, 3, 5, 15
18. 36: 1, 2, 3, 4, 6, 9, 12, 18, 36

**Lesson Focus** To choose the operations as a strategy for solving nonroutine word problems

## Ideas for Getting Started

Tell the class that today's lesson introduces the strategy for solving problems called Choose the Operations. Explain that a strategy is a kind of plan. As a long-term project, begin to develop a problem-solving bulletin board. As you teach each of the nine strategies presented in Book 6, add the name of the newly-introduced strategy to the bulletin board. Students can then refer to the bulletin board to help them think of a strategy to complete a Try This problem.

## Using Page 16

**Motivational Problem** Have students read the Try This problem. "What question is asked in the problem?" (How many vases could Tina make in the 5-day week and three extra days?) "What information is needed to answer this question?" (the number of vases made in a 5-day week) Tell students that some problems can be solved by choosing a single operation, other problems may need two or more operations. Tell students that as they plan to solve the problem they must decide which operations to use.

**Lesson Development** Review the meaning of the four operations shown in the display boxes in the middle of the page. Have students read the Try This problem and ask them to suggest which operation they could use to solve it. Then read through each of the think clouds that show how to solve the problem. Have students check the answer by asking, "Have the computations been done correctly?" (yes) "Does it seem reasonable that Tina would make 56 vases in one 5-day week and 3 extra days?" (Yes. She can make 35 vases in one 5-day week. The 3-day week is more than half of another 5-day week. 56 vases seems about right.)

**Exercises 1–2** Remind students to refer to the 5-Point Checklist as needed to help them with each problem. Emphasize the need to read the problem carefully and to understand the question.

QUESTION
DATA
PLAN
ANSWER
CHECK

## Problem Solving: Choose the Operations

Some problems can be solved by choosing a single operation (+, −, ×, ÷). For other problems, you may need to use more than one operation. A problem-solving strategy that might help you is called

**Choose the Operations**

**Try This** Tina found that she could make 35 pottery vases in a 5-day week. At this rate, how many vases could she make in a 5-day week and 3 days?

Think about when to use each operation. What does the problem involve?

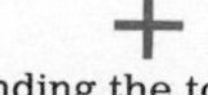

- Finding the total after putting together?

−

- Taking away?
- Comparing?
- Finding how many more are needed?

×

- Finding the total for a number of same-size sets?

- Finding the number of same-size sets?
- Finding the number in each same-size set?

Since I want to know the number of vases Tina can make each day, I divide.

$35 \div 5 = 7$
Tina can make 7 vases each day.

Since I want to find the total for 7 vases a day for 3 days, I multiply.

$7 \times 3 = 21$
In 3 days, Tina can make 21 vases.

Since I want to put together two numbers of vases, I add.

$35 + 21 = 56$
Tina can make 56 vases in a 5-day week and 3 days.

Solve.

1. Waldo bought 9 vases for $27 and sold them for $7 each. How much total profit did he make? $36
2. Beth received $54 for 9 hours work. Erin received $36 for the same number of hours. How much more did Beth make per hour than Erin? $2



## Strategy Test Item

**Optional Problem** If you wish to assess students' ability to apply the strategy called Choose the Operations introduced in this chapter, provide them with the problem below.

Alice has $42 to spend. She wants to buy 5 records that cost $7 each. How much money will she have left?

**Solution** Alice will have $7 left. $42 − (5 × $7) = $7

## Chapter Review-Test

Add, subtract, multiply, or divide.

1. 9 + 7 = 16
2. 13 − 6 = 7
3. 9 × 7 = 63
4. 8 + 0 = 8
5. 7 × 1 = 7
6. 9 − 9 = 0
7. $8\overline{)56}$ 7
8. 8 + 5 13
9. 4 × 9 36
10. 48 ÷ 6 8
11. 16 − 7 9
12. 7 × 3 21
13. 8 − 8 0
14. 8 × 8 64
15. 6 × 0 0
16. 4 ÷ 4 1
17. 7 × 5 35
18. 5 × 7 35
19. 9 + 6 15
20. 6 + 9 15
21. $6\overline{)42}$ 7
22. 8 + 5 + 4 17
23. (54 ÷ 9) + 8 14
24. (3 × 2) × 4 24
25. 3 × (2 × 4) 24
26. 8 + (12 − 7) 13
27. (6 × 6) ÷ 9 4
28. (3 × 3) + (18 ÷ 6) 12
29. (4 + 3) × 7 49
30. (2 × 9) − (27 ÷ 3) 9
31. Give the first five multiples of 4. 0, 4, 8, 12, 16
32. Give the first five multiples of 7. 0, 7, 14, 21, 28
33. List all the factors of 12. 1, 2, 3, 4, 6, 12
34. List all the factors of 18. 1, 2, 3, 6, 9, 18

Solve.

35. 9 + 5 = $n$ 14
36. 8 + 4 = $n$ 12
37. 15 − 9 = $n$ 6
38. 7 + $n$ = 11 4
39. 18 − $n$ = 9 9
40. 8 × $n$ = 48 6
41. $n$ ÷ 4 = 7 28
42. $n$ × 5 = 35 7
43. 21 ÷ 7 = $n$ 3

Solve.

44. Gary washed windows 9 hours to make money for a two-day trip to the amusement park. He received $5 an hour. How much did he earn? $45
45. In a target game you get 9 points for a bull's eye, 7 for a red, 5 for a blue, 3 for a black, and 1 for a white. Cindy scored 2 blacks and 1 bull's eye. How many points did she get? 15

17

## Using Page 17

The exercises in the Chapter Review/Test emphasize the major concepts and skills presented in this chapter. These exercises may be used as a review assignment or as a test, depending upon your needs.

**Item Analysis** The table below correlates the Chapter Review/Test items with objectives and with the student text pages on which the concepts or skills were taught.

| Items | Objectives | Related text pages |
|---|---|---|
| 1–21, 35–43 | 1.1 | 1–7, 10 |
| 22–30 | 1.2 | 11 |
| 31–34 | 1.3 | 14–15 |
| 44–45 | 1.4 | 8–9, 12–13 |

## Assessment Options

If you use the Chapter Review-Test as a review assignment, you may wish to use the multiple-choice test or the free-response test to evaluate mastery of the chapter objectives. The items on these tests have a one-to-one correspondence in terms of content and level of difficulty. A correlation of test items to objectives and student text pages is provided in the Management Guide for Chapter 1.

**Multiple-Choice Test,** TRB pages 1–3

**Free-Response Test,** TRB pages 49–50

## TRB Options

The following blackline masters are available for use with this chapter. If you have not already assigned these materials, you may wish to use them to close the chapter.

**Recreation,** TRB page 151

**Consumer Applications,** TRB page 169

**Calculator Technology,** TRB page 187

**Reading Math,** TRB page 219

**Family Involvement,** TRB page 237–238

# Reteaching

## Using Page 18

The exercises on this page are intended for those students who experienced difficulty with the Chapter Review/Test on page 17. Should students require reteaching of these key concepts and skills, please refer to the teaching notes below. Otherwise, the Another Look exercises can be assigned as independent work, with students using the accompanying sample problems and hints as guides.

**Exercises 1–19** These skills were originally taught on pages 2–3. As you discuss the first box, focus on the basic properties for addition, including the order principle and the grouping principle. Thinking about the dots on dominoes can help students see that changing the order of the addends does not change the sum. Be sure students understand that when zero is added to a number, the sum is the number.

If students have difficulty thinking about subtraction in terms of knowing the sum and one addend and finding the other addend, use objects to discuss the concept of part-part-whole. Help students see that in addition we put two parts of a set together to make the whole set. In subtraction we start with the whole set, take away one of the parts, and are left with the other part. Tell students that when we speak about sets we use parts and wholes; when we speak about numbers we use addends and sums. Continue to talk about subtraction as finding the missing addend.

**Exercises 20–32** This skill was originally taught on pages 4–5. As you discuss the idea in the multiplication example box, encourage students to memorize the multiplication facts. Emphasize how an understanding of the order property reduces the number of facts they need to memorize. Also emphasize the 0 and 1 properties of multiplication. For students who still have difficulty remembering certain facts, have them make a fact card containing these facts. Allow them to use the fact cards, and as they learn to recall a given fact it can be removed from the set.

**Exercises 33–44** This skill was originally taught on pages 6–7. As students focus their attention on the last display box, emphasize the idea that in multiplication there are two factors and a product; in division there is the product (dividend) and one factor (divisor) and they must find the other factor. Make sure students understand the difference between dividing zero by a number, as in exercise 35, and attempting to divide a number by 0, which is not possible. To emphasize the idea of dividing to find the missing factor, have students check these exercises using multiplication.

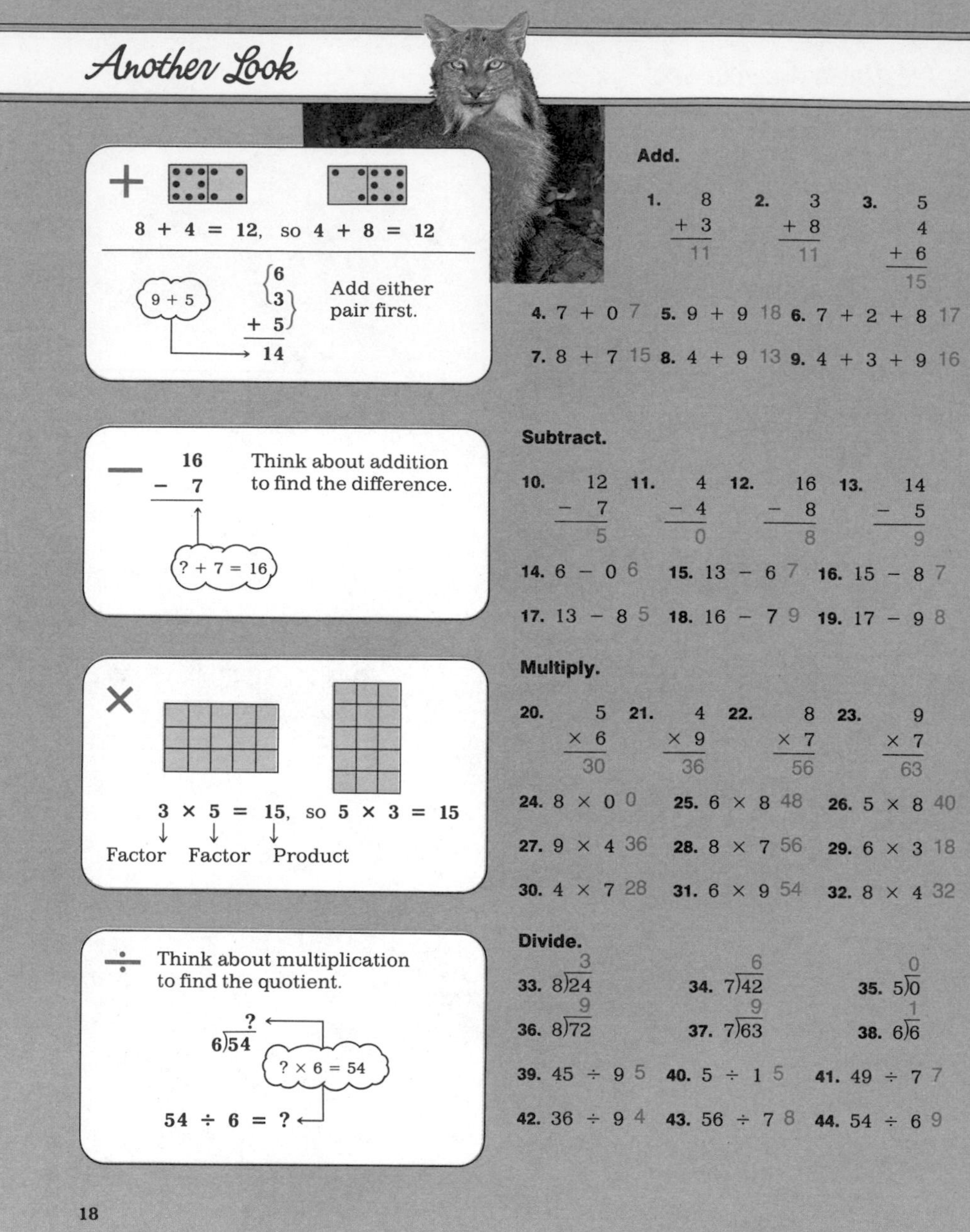


## Just For Teachers

### History of Math

The philosophy of mathematics instruction until the mid nineteenth century was that mathematics was first and foremost a discipline of the mind. However, practical needs fostered by the Industrial Revolution required a new educational approach. Society required better-skilled workers, and students required better academic preparation in both elementary and secondary schools.

In the late 1800s, the educational community began several important steps to facilitate improvements. The first formal methods textbook for elementary mathematics teachers, *The Philosophy of Arithmetic* by Edward Brooks, appeared in 1880. In 1890, the National Education Association appointed the Committee of Ten on Secondary School Studies to emphasize the need to address instructional goals. These trends intensified educational change in the twentieth century. Teacher training and methods instruction assumed greater importance, and more professional organizations and publications devoted to improving mathematics instruction were developed. Of particular importance, however, was the impact of two relatively new movements—psychological research into the nature of learning and standardized testing.

Psychologist Edward L. Thorndike, whose "Connectionist Theory" drew upon

## Enrichment

**Space Perception**

Each of the twelve figures below is made with five squares. They are called **pentominoes.** Figure G can be folded on the dotted lines to make an open-top box as shown.

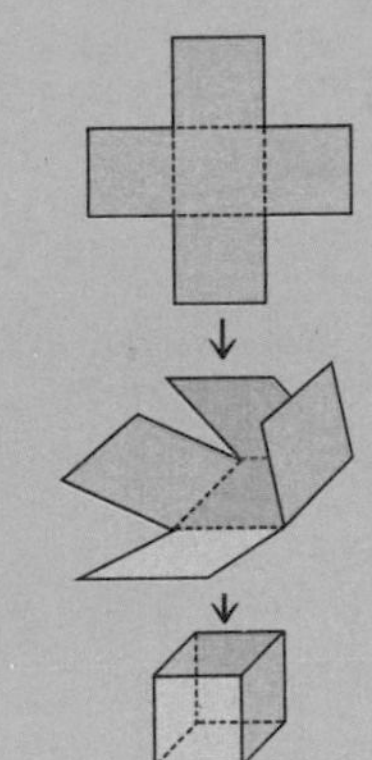

1. Which other pentominoes can be folded to make an open-top box? A, B, D, E, F, I, J
2. A hexomino is made of 6 squares. Show on graph paper 5 hexominoes that can be folded to make a closed box. See teaching notes.

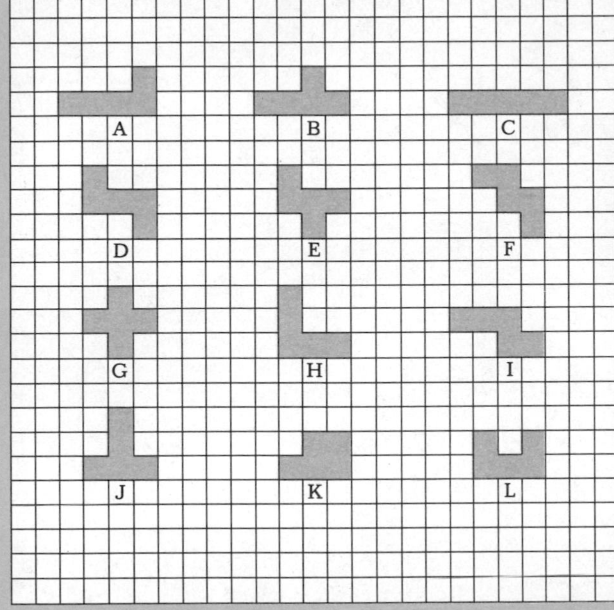




stimulus-response psychology, believed that learning mathematics involved the formation of bonds, built largely through practice. Thorndike included in his 1923 book *The Psychology of Algebra* a criticism of current mathematics instruction which resulted in studies that questioned the applicability of mathematics to everyday life. Standardized tests could provide data on just how well—or how poorly—students mastered basic, utilitarian arithmetic. New research stimulated new philosophies of instruction and new theories on the nature of learning.

The "Gestalt Theory," based on the ideas of European psychologists, included two important new provisions in its summary of the learning process: subconscious work on a problem and sudden insight into its solution.

Since World War II, educational psychologists have concluded that neither the Connectionist nor the Gestalt theory adequately explains the entire learning process and have modified these theories. B. F. Skinner, Robert Gagné, and Patrick Suppes formed variations of the bonding-formation behavioral theory. The cognitive-oriented Gestalt theory, on the other hand, has been modified by the research of Jean Piaget, Jerome Bruner, and Kenneth Lovell.

## Using Page 19

This page is intended for those students who successfully completed the Chapter Review/Test on page 17. You may wish to assign this page as independent work while you use Another Look exercises to reteach the basic concepts and skills of the chapter. Or you may decide that all students would benefit from exposure to this Enrichment activity.

**Lesson Development** Focus on the picture that shows how Figure G is folded to make an open top box. "Can Figure B be folded to form an open top box?" (yes) "Can Figure H be folded to make an open top box?" (no) If possible, have large models of figures B and H so that students who have difficulty visualizing these ideas can see the folding process.

**Exercise 1** Have students make decisions on the remaining figures. After they have decided about each figure, have them cut models from large-grid graph paper to verify any decisions about which they are not sure.

**Exercise 2** As a preliminary to this exercise have students make as many hexominoes as possible on graph paper. There are 35 possible hexominoes. The 11 shown here can be folded to make a closed box. Encourage students to find as many of these as possible.

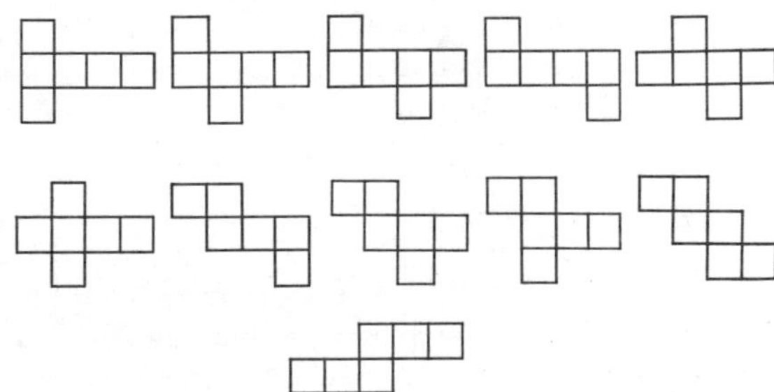

Also encourage students to form generalizations about those figures that can be made into boxes and those that cannot. For example, hexominoes with 5 squares in a row cannot be made into a box. Nor can one with 4 squares that form another square.

# Technology

**Lesson Focus** To review how a calculator works and to use the calculator to solve problems

## Ideas for Getting Started

Select four students to "play" calculator at the board. One student will be "Display." The second student will be "Number Storage." The third student will be "Arithmetic Operator." The fourth student will calculate results.

Draw a rectangle on the chalkboard to represent a calculator display. Make a circle at one side for number storage. On the other side make a circle for storing the arithmetic operator. Explain that a calculator has electronic parts for storing one piece of information at a time. "Number storage" holds only one number, for example. Tell students they will "act out" the problem, 23 + 34, like a calculator. Give the following directions:

Enter [23]. ("Display" writes 23 in the calculator rectangle.)

Enter [+]. ("Number Storage" writes 23 in that circle. "Arithmetic Operator" writes + in his or her circle.)

Enter [34]. ("Display" erases 23 and writes 34.)

Enter [=]. (The student calculating results uses number storage, the arithmetic operator, and the display. He/she performs the addition. "Display" erases 34. "Number Storage" writes 34. "Display" writes the result, 57.)

## Using Page 20

**Lesson Development** Have students follow the calculator model in the middle of the page showing 486 + 735. Emphasize that calculators usually store only one result at a time.

Let students sketch a picture of the three mountains in the example on page 21 to help them understand the problem. Point out the intermediate products that must be recorded on paper.

Before assigning the exercises on page 21, remind students to clear their calculators after each problem. They can also use the calculators to check each answer.

*Technology*

**Using a Calculator**

A calculator is a tool that can help us solve problems. We must carefully enter the correct numbers and arithmetic operations on the calculator because it does only what we tell it to do.

**How the Calculator Works**

A calculator has the ability to "remember," or store, numbers for future use. For example, when a number is entered and an operation key such as [+] is pushed, the calculator stores the number and "remembers" that it is to add that number to the next number entered. Also, the sum of two numbers can be stored and later added to another number. The memory ability of a calculator helps it do computations quickly and accurately.

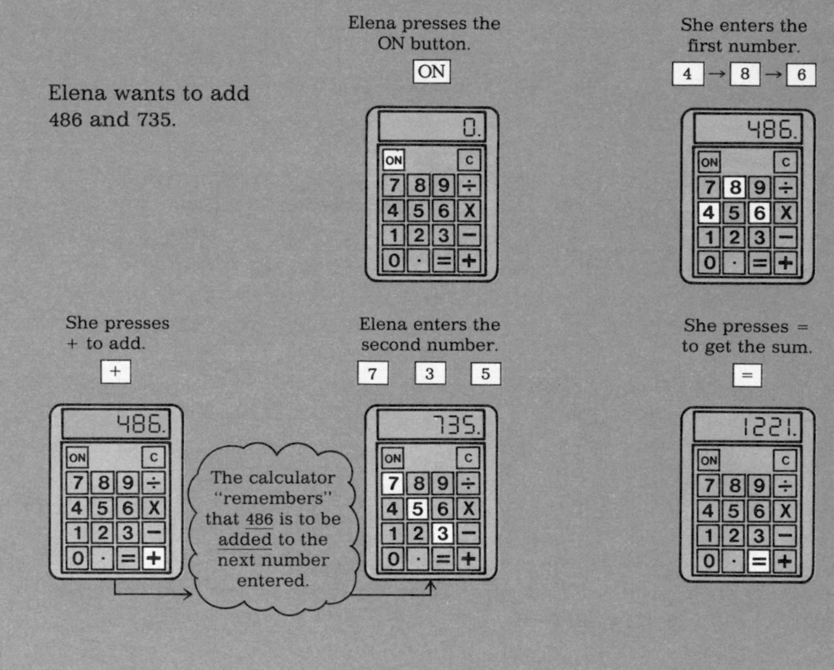


20

## Technology for Teachers

Technological tools such as calculators and computers become easier to use when you develop a model in your mind that explains and predicts results. Thinking of a calculator as a complicated network of electric circuits does not improve how we use the machine. It is more effective to think of a calculator as a set of boxes for holding numbers and having rules about how those boxes are affected by various keys. A calculator with keys for parentheses and memory, for example, stores more intermediate results than a calculator without those keys. A left parenthesis key tells the calculator to store the result so far and to begin calculating a new result until a right parenthesis appears. Then the new result becomes the next number in the calculation.

**Example**
One summer Nils, a mountain climber, climbed the Matterhorn 6 times, the Eiger 4 times, and Dufour Peak 9 times. Use a calculator to find the total number of meters Nils climbed that summer.

| Mountain | Height (m) |
|---|---|
| Matterhorn | 4,478 |
| Eiger | 3,970 |
| Dufour Peak | 4,634 |

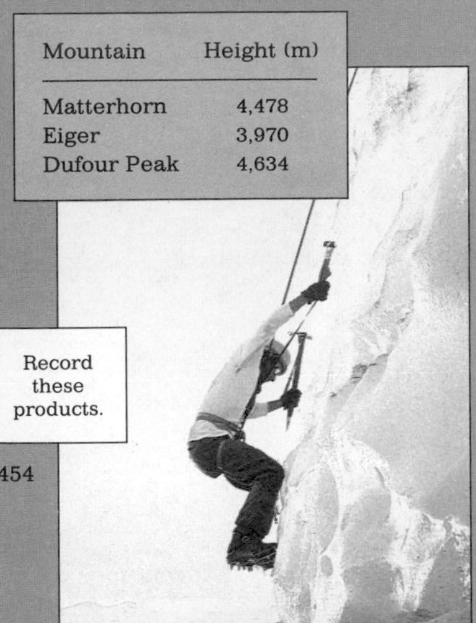

First, multiply to find how many meters Nils climbed on each mountain.

| | | | | |
|---|---|---|---|---|
| Matterhorn | 4478 × 6 | = | 26868 | ← Record these products. |
| Eiger | 3970 × 4 | = | 15880 | ← |
| Dufour Peak | 4634 × 9 | = | 41706 | ← |

Then add: 26868 + 15880 + 41706 = 84454

Nils climbed a total of 84,454 m.

Use a calculator to help solve these problems. Check your answers to see if they are reasonable.

1. 2,910 + 1,479 + 409 + 675 = *n*
   *n* = 5,473
2. (75 × 8) + (59 × 4) + (98 × 9) = *n*
   *n* = 1,718
3. (4,096 − 8) − 256 = *n* *n* = 3,832
4. (795 + 3,685 − 1,020) − 5 = *n*
   *n* = 3,455
5. (391 ÷ 17) + (48 × 29) = *n*
   *n* = 1,415
6. Gretchen climbed 1,306 m the first day. The second day she climbed 948 m. How much farther did she climb the first day than she climbed the second day? 358 m
7. For their hiking trip Duffy's family needed to buy 4 backpacks, 4 sleeping bags, and a first aid kit. The backpacks cost $18 each, the sleeping bags cost $47 each, and the first aid kit cost $9. What was the total cost? $269
8. In June a ranger took 23 groups of visitors on hikes. There were 18 in each group. In July she took 38 groups on hikes, with 14 in each group. How many more did she take in one month than in the other? 118 more in July



## Using Page 21

**Exercises 1–5** Students should think about what numbers are stored in their calculators as they work the problems. In exercise 2 they must record the results of each multiplication before they add.

**Exercises 6 –8** Suggest that students draw pictures for these exercises to help plan the solutions.

## Using Page 22

The exercises on this page provide practice for maintaining cumulative skills. The emphasis in this Cumulative Review is on basic facts (Chapter 1) and problem solving (Chapter 1).

**Item Analysis** The table below correlates the Cumulative Review items with objectives and with the student book pages on which the concepts or skills were taught.

| Items | Objectives | Related Text Pages |
|---|---|---|
| 1–12 | 1.1 | 1–7, 10 |
| 13–14 | 1.4 | 8–9, 12–13 |

## *Cumulative Review*

Add.

1. $\begin{array}{r} 3 \\ +\ 7 \\ \hline \end{array}$
   A 9
   (B) 10
   C 15
   D not given

2. 5 + 4
   A 6
   (B) 9
   C 10
   D not given

3. $\begin{array}{r} 3 \\ 0 \\ +\ 9 \\ \hline \end{array}$
   A 0
   B 10
   C 11
   (D) not given

Subtract.

4. $\begin{array}{r} 16 \\ -\ 8 \\ \hline \end{array}$
   A 9
   (B) 8
   C 4
   D not given

5. $\begin{array}{r} 17 \\ -\ 9 \\ \hline \end{array}$
   A 5
   (B) 8
   C 7
   D not given

6. 15 − 8
   A 9
   B 6
   (C) 7
   D not given

Multiply.

7. $\begin{array}{r} 5 \\ \times\ 0 \\ \hline \end{array}$
   A 50
   B 10
   C 5
   (D) not given

8. $\begin{array}{r} 7 \\ \times\ 7 \\ \hline \end{array}$
   A 7
   B 70
   (C) 49
   D not given

9. 4 × 9
   A 24
   B 32
   (C) 36
   D not given

Divide.

10. 72 ÷ 9
   A 6
   (B) 8
   C 9
   D not given

11. $8\overline{)40}$
   A 8
   B 10
   C 4
   (D) not given

12. $7\overline{)56}$
   A 5
   B 7
   (C) 8
   D not given

13. Sue has 32 large stamps to put in her album. Each page will hold 8 stamps. How many pages will she fill?
   A 2  (B) 4
   C 9  D not given

14. Tomás worked 2 hours at his father's store on Thursday. He worked 3 hours on Friday and 6 hours on Saturday. How many hours did he work in all?
   A 10  B 9
   (C) 11  D not given

## Objectives

**2.1** Read, write, compare, and order whole numbers.
**2.2** Round whole numbers and estimate their sums and differences.
**2.3** Add and subtract whole numbers up to 5 digits.
**2.4** Read and write Roman numerals.
**2.5** Solve word problems using the 5-Point Checklist and cumulative computational skills.

## Summary

In this chapter students review and extend the ideas of place value, estimation, and addition and subtraction. An understanding of place value provides the basis for comparing, ordering, and rounding whole numbers. Rounding skills are then used to estimate sums and differences. These estimates are used to check the reasonableness of calculated answers. As students review and sharpen their addition and subtraction skills, emphasis is placed on column addition and on more difficult addition and subtraction problems, such as subtraction problems involving zero. A lesson about Roman numerals is included.

Technically, a *number* is a quantitative idea, and a *numeral* is a symbol used to represent this idea. To avoid confusion, however, we have used the word *number* throughout the text. When we say, "write the number," we mean "write the symbol that represents the number." Because of long-standing tradition, we will continue to use *Roman numerals* to describe the symbols for numbers used by the early Romans.

## Mathematical Background

**Place Value** Our system of place value, based on grouping by tens, provides a means of representing every number using the digits, 0, 1, 2, 3, 4, 5, 6, 7, 8, or 9. By agreement a digit can represent ones, tens, hundreds, thousands, and so on, depending upon the position it occupies in the number. Each block of three digits in a number is called a *period.* In this chapter students work with the following periods starting at the right: ones, thousands, millions, and billions. As indicated in the diagram below, patterns of ones, tens, and hundreds repeat in each period, with a comma used to separate periods.

| Periods → | BILLIONS | | | MILLIONS | | | THOUSANDS | | | ONES | | |
|---|---|---|---|---|---|---|---|---|---|---|---|---|
| Place Values → | hundred billions | ten billions | one billions | hundred millions | ten millions | one millions | hundred thousands | ten thousands | one thousands | hundreds | tens | ones |
| Number in Standard form → | 1 | 5 | 0, | 4 | 7 | 2, | 2 | 9 | 6, | 7 | 8 | 3 |

Models or money can be useful in helping students review and extend the basic ideas of place value. It is helpful for students to translate from the model, the number, and the verbal description. It is also useful for students to write a number in expanded form as shown below to illustrate grouping by tens and the additive characteristics of our system of place value.

$$2{,}314 = 2{,}000 + 300 + 10 + 4$$

Standard form    Expanded form

**Comparing, Ordering, and Rounding** The greater of two whole numbers is always to the right on the number line. Students' counting skills often help make this idea clear. A technique for comparing two larger numbers involves checking the digits in each place, starting at the left. A set of numbers is ordered by listing them from greatest to least or from least to greatest. We do this by comparing the numbers two at a time and inserting numbers in the list in the appropriate places.

The number line is also a useful tool for helping students understand the process of rounding numbers. Rounding skills are particularly important because they form the basis for estimation techniques.

**Estimating** To estimate, students must first be able to round numbers to the nearest ten, hundred, thousand, and so on. Second, they must be able to find sums or differences involving these "rounded numbers." (It is helpful if students can add or subtract the "rounded numbers" without using pencil and paper.)

> Estimating (+ or −)
> - Round to the desired place.
> - Find the sum or difference of the "rounded number."

**Adding and Subtracting** The important concepts underlying the process of addition and subtraction are place value, basic facts, and trading from ones to tens, tens to hundreds, hundreds to thousands, and vice versa. Models can help students understand the trades necessary in adding and subtracting. For example, the model below shows that 2 hundreds can be thought of as 20 tens. In the problem, one of these tens is traded for 10 ones so that 9 ones can be subtracted. This leaves 19 tens or 1 hundred and 9 tens. The subtraction can now be completed.

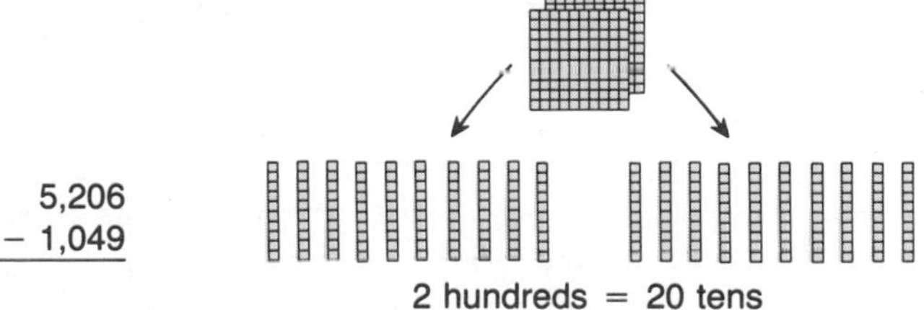


2 hundreds = 20 tens

**Problem Solving** In this chapter students gain further experience using the 5-Point Checklist introduced on page 8. Problem-solving activities include using estimation (page 34), using a data bank (page 35), using data from a bar graph (page 44), problem-solving practice, and using a calculator (page 46). On pages 48–49 students learn a new strategy for solving nonroutine problems called Guess and Check.

**Vocabulary**

| | | |
|---|---|---|
| period | compare | data |
| standard form | order | data bank |
| expanded form | round | deposit slip |

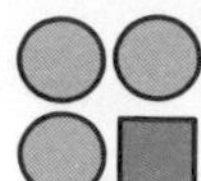

## Error Analysis

This chapter begins with a review of place-value ideas, including reading and writing numbers through billions. Some facility with large numbers is necessary as students develop a concept of a 5- to 10-digit number and then use these numbers in comparing and ordering situations. To help students feel comfortable with these larger numbers, the use of a calculator is sometimes suggested.

Computational work involving whole number addition and subtraction will reflect a student's knowledge of basic facts and of place-value concepts. The idea of regrouping or trading is a basic idea in our place-value system. A misunderstanding of this relationship is reflected in the errors made in computational work. Search the error patterns below to determine if the error is related to lack of mastery of basic facts, faulty understanding of place value, or lack of knowledge of the procedural steps to follow.

**Error Pattern 1**

| 563 | 974 | $9.76 |
|---|---|---|
| + 437 | + 38 | + 4.89 |
| 9,910 | 91,012 | $1,315.15 |

**Diagnosis** The student has written the sum of each basic fact in the answer starting from left to right and indicates no awareness of place value. The error is based on insufficient understanding of place value with no apparent attempt to regroup ones to tens or tens to hundreds.

**Remediation** The most basic work with place value and trading is needed. Use models and manipulatives to review the "trading-rules" of 10 for 1 and 1 for 10. Then relate this to the algorithm form. As an example is presented, represent it with a model. For example, to add 326 + 475, first represent both numbers with place-value models. Then as you add, show the corresponding trades. Because the error indicates a lack of understanding about when to trade, make sure to highlight this step in the example.

**Error Pattern 2**

| 27,362 | 5,278 | $256.44 |
|---|---|---|
| − 18,937 | − 3,694 | − 97.75 |
| 11,635 | 2,424 | $241.31 |

**Diagnosis** The student interprets subtraction as "subtract the smaller from the larger" regardless of whether this is subtracting the part from the total or the total from the part. This error indicates a faulty understanding of the meaning of subtraction as well as incorrect knowledge of how to work through the algorithm.

**Remediation** Start with simple examples that can be illustrated with word problems. For example: Jack had 16 stamps. He sold 8 to a friend. How many did he have left?

Analyze the situation using a part-part-total explanation to arrive at the following algorithm to be solved.

16 → Total
− 8 → Known part
□ → Unknown part

Next discuss the order in which the algorithm is processed. That is, the known part is subtracted from the total. Model with manipulatives to show the trading needed to carry out the subtraction. Refer back to the examples on which the errors were made and work through each algorithm correctly.

**Error Pattern 3**

| 508 | 736 | 323 |
|---|---|---|
| − 169 | − 148 | − 184 |
| 249 | 498 | 39 |

**Diagnosis** The student has taken "2" from the hundreds place to give more units in the tens place and in the ones place. The computation is correct, but an incomplete understanding of the trading process is indicated.

**Remediation** Use place-value materials to model these numbers: 20, 22, 120, 102, 122. Use the following questioning sequence to discuss each number. "Read the number. How many ones? How many tens? How many hundreds?" As you discuss each number, show it in expanded notation on the chalkboard. Then use a simple problem such as 102 − 22 to illustrate subtracting ones and tens.

## Problem Solving

### Developing a Positive Classroom Atmosphere

There are four essential ingredients to a successful problem-solving program: 1) The content of the program must be appropriate for the students; 2) the problem-solving program must be part of a sound instructional program in all other basic skill areas of mathematics (computational skills, estimation, measurement, and so on); 3) students must have ample opportunity to participate in problem-solving experiences; and 4) the teacher's actions must promote a positive classroom atmosphere related to problem solving.

A successful problem-solving program must have all of the above characteristics. Assistance with the first three is provided by the text. The importance of the teacher in developing a classroom atmosphere that is conducive to problem solving cannot be overemphasized.

There are two ways in which your actions affect the classroom atmosphere. First, your attitude about problem solving will influence your students' attitudes about problem solving. If you demonstrate that problem solving is important, exciting, and fun, most students will develop a similar attitude. Here are some things you can do to promote positive problem-solving attitudes among your students.

- Be enthusiastic about problem solving.
- Encourage students to contribute problems from their personal experiences.
- Personalize problems whenever possible; use students' names in problems, for example.
- Provide the appropriate amount and type of assistance to avoid excessive frustration.

Second, your comments about problem solving communicate to students the types of behaviors you consider to be desirable related to problem solving. Here are some things you can do to promote desirable problem-solving behavior.

- Recognize and reinforce willingness and perseverance.
- Reward risk takers.
- Encourage students to play hunches.
- Accept unusual solutions.
- Praise students for getting correct solutions but emphasize the selection and use of problem-solving strategies.
- Emphasize persistence rather than speed.

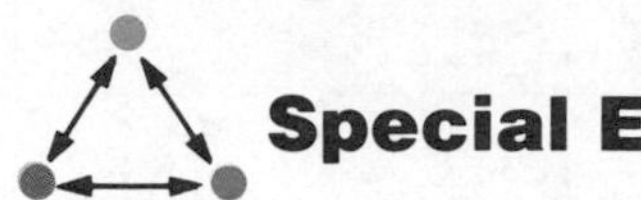

## Special Education

In this chapter students review place value, numeration, and addition and subtraction of whole numbers. Ideas for helping the special-needs students in your class with these skills are presented below. As you become more aware of the particular learning needs of your students, choose from the following material those ideas you consider appropriate for your class.

### Using Visual and Kinesthetic Guidance

As students review reading and writing larger numbers, help them realize that because they can read and write 1-, 2-, and 3-digit numbers, they can quickly learn to read larger numbers. A number expander made of laminated tagboard may help.

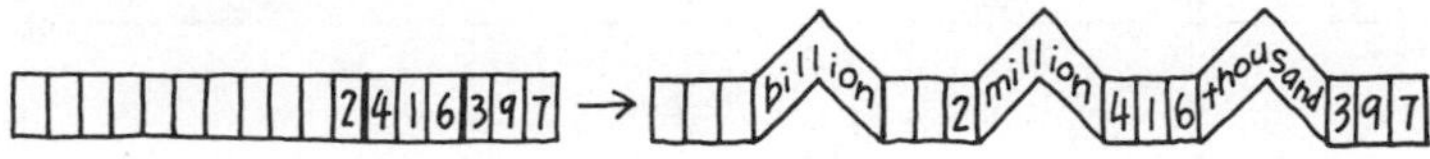


Students open the pleated card at each comma to read the name of the period. Let students write in the "billion," "million," and "thousand" labels before beginning. If necessary, a black-out card can be used to gradually reveal numbers.

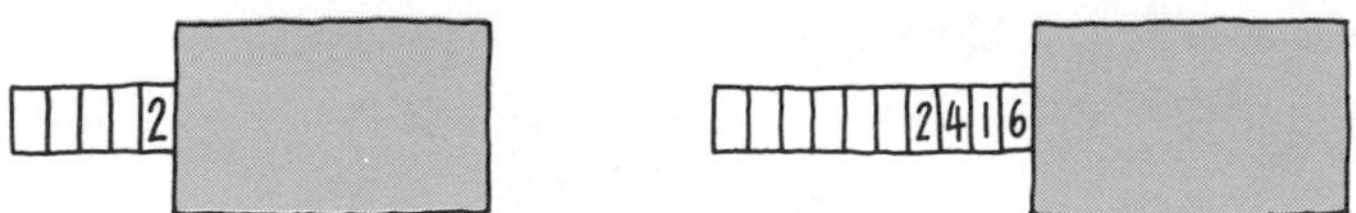


### Using Color as Cues

Because color perceptions develop early, keep colored chalk available to highlight important points and help students focus on patterns. Color underscoring, for example, can draw attention to the recurring "ones, tens, hundreds" pattern within each period of a larger number. Students could be asked to circle the tens place and the hundreds place of the chart on page 26 each with a distinct color.

When comparing two numbers, students should align vertically digits having the same place value and color underscored digits in the first place where the digits are different. Some students will have difficulty discriminating between the inequality symbols. Post the symbols on cards (two different colors) and use a verbal or visual reminder such as "the small end points to the number that means less."

Often the familiar traffic colors can be used effectively. For example, use green for "*start* working here." Use color as in the illustration to help students follow the instruction boxes on page 30 for rounding a number. Let students underline the digit in the place to be rounded, then mark the digit to its right green. "We *start* here to make the decision. If the digit we have circled is $<5$, keep the underlined digit; if it is $\geq 5$, make the circled digit 1 greater. Make all digits to the right of the underlined digit zeros."

9 , ⑥ 4 5

### Using Finger Tracing

Students with memory and perception difficulties could be encouraged to finger trace:

- the digit that initiates the decision for rounding numbers.
- the first *un*like digits of a pair when comparing or ordering numbers.
- the $<$ and $>$ symbols, to trigger recognition.
- the operation sign in written exercises like those on page 49, which contains both addition and subtraction problems, to focus attention on the procedure to be carried out.

### Crossing Out Tens

If students are still struggling with column addition, allow them to use the following "cross out" technique. As shown, they add down a column until a 2-digit sum is reached ($4 + 8 = 12$). The last digit, 8, is crossed out to represent 10 (of the 12). The student mentally retains the 2 and adds it to 9, and then repeats the cross-out procedure. When a column is added, the number of cross-outs is the number carried. If students reverse digits or have trouble remembering, they can write each digit that is retained, as in the second part of the figure.

```
   2           2
  674         674
  398         398 2
+ 409       + 409 1
-----       -----
    1           1
```

## Subject Integration

Subject matter related to other areas of the curriculum has been integrated into the following lessons. This provides an opportunity to highlight the interaction between mathematics and other subjects.

**Fine Arts** Cave art, pages 36–37; diamond cutting, page 45

**Science** Flight, page 24; bathyscaph, pages 30–31; balloon travel, pages 40–41

**Social Studies** Canoe trips, pages 38–39; average elevations, page 44

**Consumer Awareness** Using electricity, page 34; checking accounts, page 46

**Career Awareness** Owning a restaurant, pages 32–33

**Physical Education** Sports safety, pages 42–43

# Management Guide

| Teaching Chapter 2 | | | | Meeting Individual Needs | | | | | |
|---|---|---|---|---|---|---|---|---|---|
| Objectives | Chapter Content | Pages | TRB Test Items | Lesson Assignments | | | Follow Up | | |
| | | | | Minimum | Average | Extended | Reteaching | Enrichment | Practice |
| | Chapter Opener | 23 | | | | | | | |
| 2.1 Read, write, compare, and order whole numbers. | Place Value: Thousands | 24–25 | 1–8 | 1–27 | 1–28 | 1–28, TM | SE5 Ch 2 | | PS 8 |
| | Millions and Billions | 26–27 | | 1–21 | 1–22 | 1–22, TM | SE4 Ch 2 RS 7 | ES 7 | PS 9 |
| | Comparing and Ordering | 28–29 | 9–11 | 1–21 | 1–26 | 1–26, TM | SE5 Ch 2 RS 8 | ES 8 | MP 412 PS 10 |
| 2.2 Round whole numbers and estimate their sums and differences. | Rounding | 30–31 | 12–15 | 1–37, SK | 1–37, SK | 1–39, SK | SE5 Ch 2 RS 9 | ES 9 | MP 412 PS 11 |
| | Estimating Sums and Differences: Mental Math | 32–33 | 16–19 | 1–20 | 1–25 | 1–25, TM | | | MP 412 PS 12 |
| 2.3 Add and subtract whole numbers up to 5 digits. | Adding Whole Numbers | 36–37 | 20–36 | 1–29 | 1–30 | 1–30, TM | SE5 Ch 3 RS 10 | ES 10 | MP 413 PS 14 |
| | Column Addition | 38–39 | | 1–17, TM | 1–17, TM | 1–18, TM | SE5 Ch 3 | | MP 413 PS 15 |
| | Subtracting Whole Numbers | 40–41 | | 1–24 | 1–25 | 1–26, TM | SE5 Ch 3 RS 11 | ES 11 | MP 413 PS 16 |
| | Subtracting with Zeros | 42–43 | | 1–24, SK | 1–24, SK | 1–25, SK | SE5 Ch 3 RS 12 | ES 12 | MP 414 PS 17 |
| 2.4 Read and write Roman numerals. | Roman Numerals | 47 | 37–40 | 1–10 | 1–11 | 1–12 | SE5 Ch 2 | | |
| 2.5 Solve word problems using the 5-Point Checklist and cumulative computational skills. | Problem Solving: Using Estimation | 34 | 41–45 | 1–6 | 1–7 | 1–8 | | | PS 13 |
| | Problem Solving: Using Data from a Data Bank | 35 | | 1–6 | 1–7 | 1–8 | | | |
| | Problem Solving: Using Data from a Bar Graph | 44 | | 1–5 | 1–6 | 1–7 | | | PS 18 |
| | Problem Solving: Practice | 45 | | 1–4 | 1–5 | 1–6 | | | |
| | Problem Solving: Using a Calculator | 46 | | 1–3 | 1–4 | 1–5 | RS 13 | ES 13 | PS 19 |
| | Problem Solving: Guess and Check | 48 | | | | | | | |
| | Chapter Review-Test | 49 | | | | | | | |
| | Another Look/Enrichment | 50–51 | | | | | | | |
| | Cumulative Review | 52 | | | | | | | |

**SE5** Student Edition, Book 5
**RS** Reteaching Supplement
**ES** Enrichment Supplement
**PS** Practice Supplement
**MP** More Practice
**TM** Think Math
**SK** Skillkeeper
**TRB** Teacher's Resource Book

# Teacher's Resource Book

## Masters for Use

**. . . before Chapter 2**

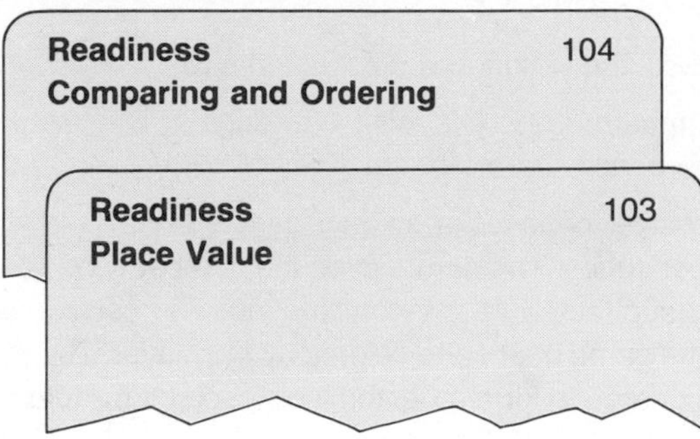


**. . . during Chapter 2**

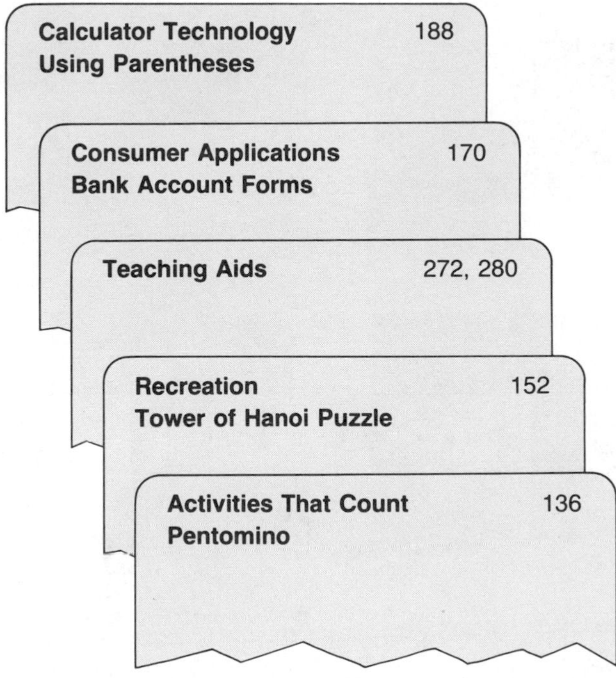

Calculator Technology 188
Using Parentheses
Consumer Applications 170
Bank Account Forms
Teaching Aids 272, 280
Recreation 152
Tower of Hanoi Puzzle
Activities That Count 136
Pentomino


**. . . after Chapter 2**

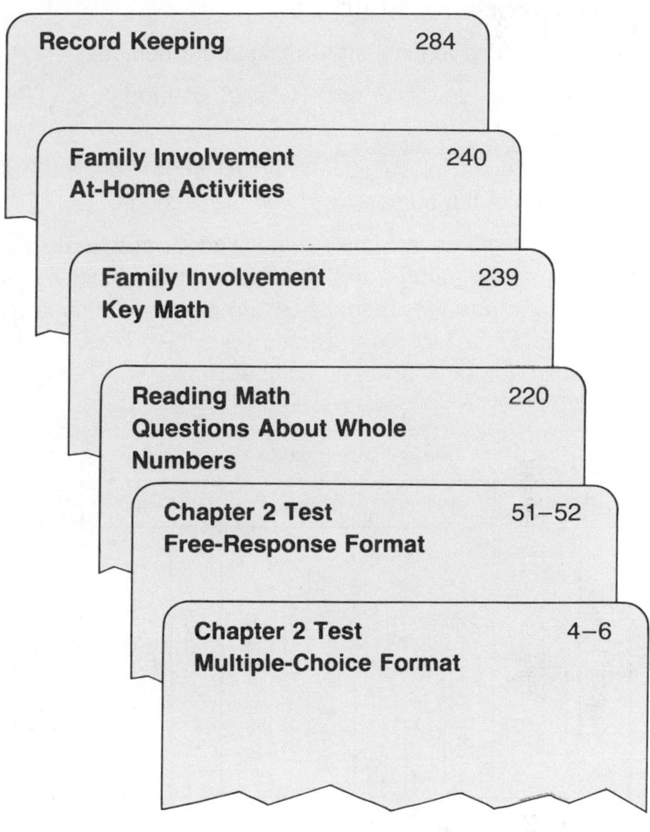


## Supplements

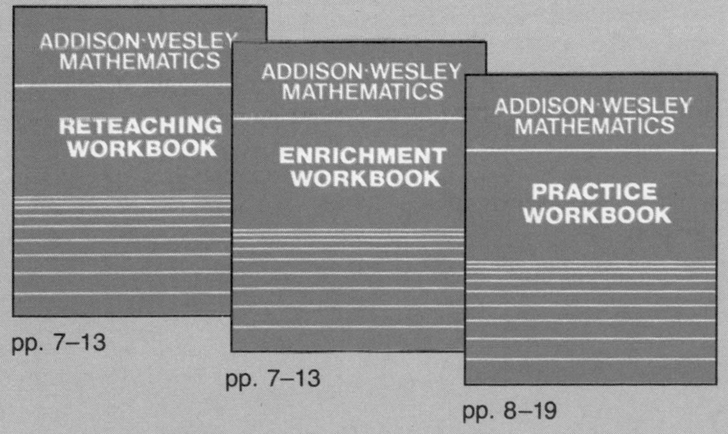


pp. 7–13

pp. 7–13

pp. 8–19

## Other Addison-Wesley Resources

### Books and Kits

*Skillseekers 1* (+) Lessons 1–10; (−) Lessons 1–12

*The Arithmetic Primer* pp. 8–19, 25–37, 298–299

*Arithmetic Skill Cards* pp. D 1–2

*Baseball, A Game of Numbers* pp. 2–3, 23–27, 103

*Problem Solving Experiences in Mathematics,* Grade 6
Problems 2, 4, 5, 13, 18, 23, 32, 33, 37, 39, 40, 42, 53, 68, 72, 73, 75, 79, 80, 83, 87, 99, 100, 103, 107, 108, 109, 110, 113, 114, 115, 123, 127, 129, 133, 134, 135, 145, 150

### Technology

*Computer Math Activities* Volumes 1–5

*Computer Math Games* Volumes 1, 2, 4, 6

# Activities That Count

Activities That Count are designed for use throughout this chapter and subsequent chapters. Before beginning Chapter 2, you may wish to review these activities and select the ones you consider appropriate for your class.

## **What-a-Number** Math Lab

**Purpose** To practice reading and writing larger numbers

**Materials** Number cards: 2 each labeled 0 through 9 (TRB p. 279); tagboard

**Preparation** Make a place-value chart as shown below, and duplicate two sets of the number cards on the tagboard.

**Activity** Number cards are mixed and placed facedown in a stack. Working with a partner, a student takes 12 number cards from the stack and arranges them below the place-value chart as illustrated. Student then records and reads aloud the number name. Students check each other's written number words.

| Place-Value Periods | | | | | | | | | | | |
|---|---|---|---|---|---|---|---|---|---|---|---|
| Billions | | | Millions | | | Thousands | | | Ones | | |
| hundred billions | ten billions | billions | hundred millions | ten millions | millions | hundred thousands | ten thousands | thousands | hundreds | tens | ones |
| 1 | 2 | 3 | 4 | 5 | 6 | 7 | 8 | 9 | 0 | 1 | 2 |

## **Large Numbers** Project

**Purpose** To practice place-value skills

**Materials** Encyclopedia, place-value chart

**Activity** Students select a favorite city that they have visited or would like to visit. Each student then finds statistics about their city—population, area, elevation, and so on. Information about each city could be mounted on tagboard or colored paper so that the sizes of the numbers can be compared. The place-value chart can be used as an aid in reading the larger numbers, if necessary.

## **Pentomino** Game

**Purpose** To practice addition and subtraction skills

**Materials** 4 number cubes: 2 labeled 0 through 6, 2 labeled 4 through 9; colored pencils; game board (TRB p. 136)

**Activity** Each player chooses a colored pencil. In turn players toss all four number cubes. The numbers on the number cubes can then be added or subtracted in any combination. The correct answer is found on the game board and colored by the player. The first player to color 5 squares to form a pentomino (5 adjacent squares) wins the game.

Possible pentomino shapes:

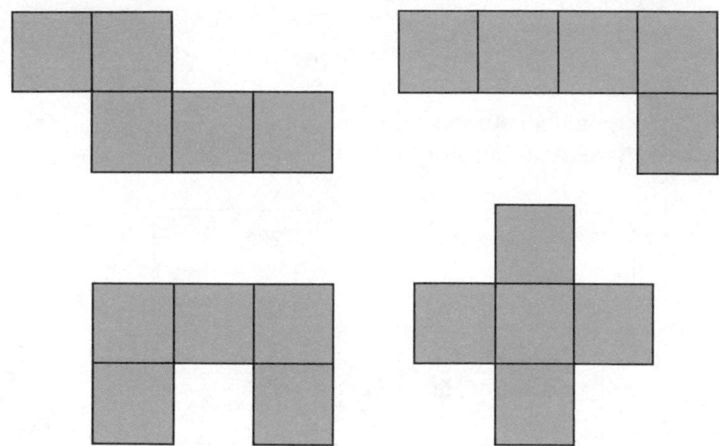

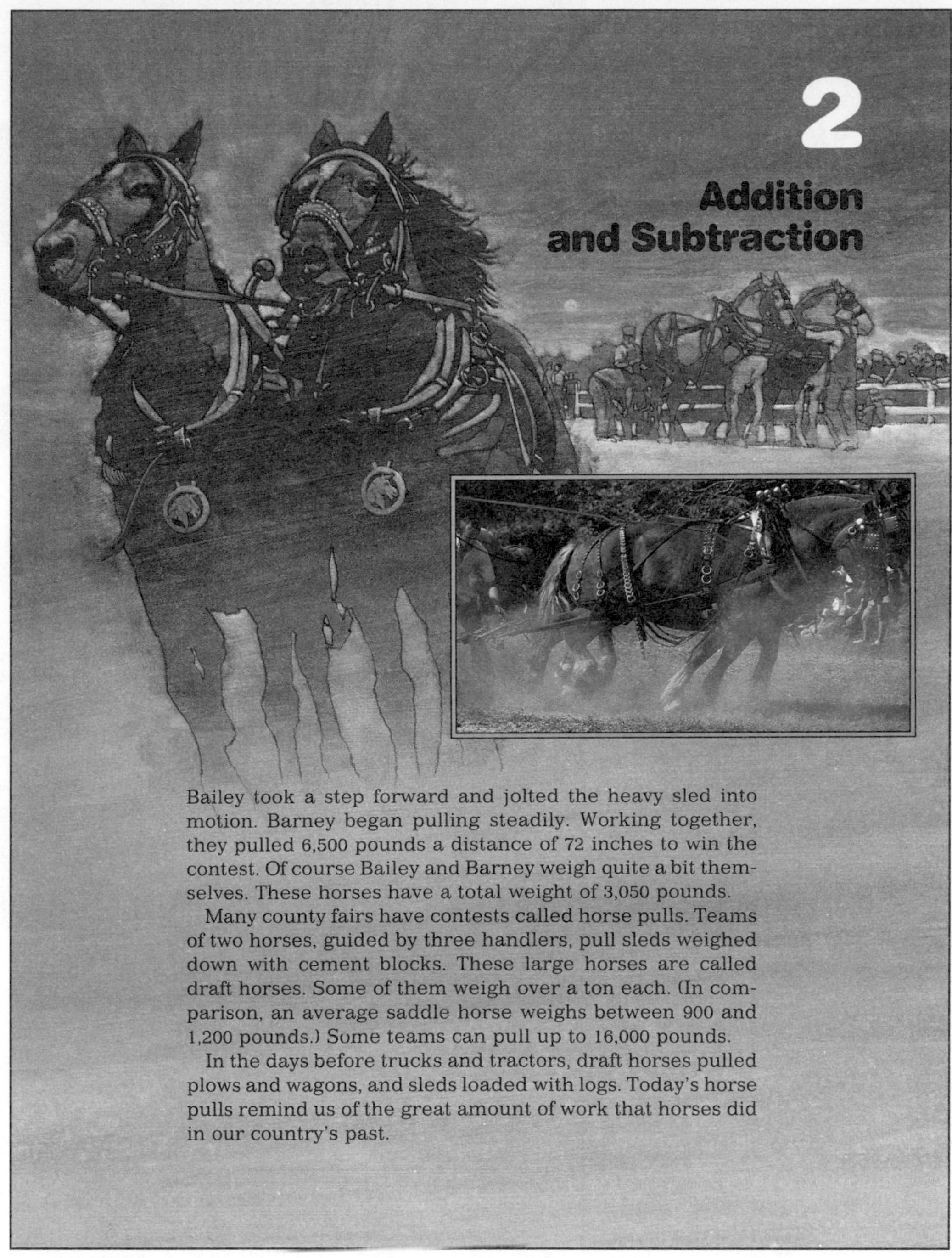

2
Addition and Subtraction
Bailey took a step forward and jolted the heavy sled into motion. Barney began pulling steadily. Working together, they pulled 6,500 pounds a distance of 72 inches to win the contest. Of course Bailey and Barney weigh quite a bit themselves. These horses have a total weight of 3,050 pounds.
Many county fairs have contests called horse pulls. Teams of two horses, guided by three handlers, pull sleds weighed down with cement blocks. These large horses are called draft horses. Some of them weigh over a ton each. (In comparison, an average saddle horse weighs between 900 and 1,200 pounds.) Some teams can pull up to 16,000 pounds.
In the days before trucks and tractors, draft horses pulled plows and wagons, and sleds loaded with logs. Today's horse pulls remind us of the great amount of work that horses did in our country's past.


## Introducing the Chapter

**Discussion** After explaining to students that Chapter 2 deals with place value as well as the addition and subtraction algorithms, lead a brief discussion of the roles played by horses in today's world. Make sure students understand that although in our highly mechanized nation horses are used primarily in recreational activities, in some other countries horses still are used extensively for pulling plows and doing other valuable work on farms. Give students time to read the story and examine the illustration. Then allow time for discussion and encourage students to suggest questions that could be asked about the data given. As you teach the chapter, you may wish to refer back to this page and discuss the problems below. Review the content of the story briefly before posing the problems.

## Follow-Up Questions

**After Page 25** How much did Bailey and Barney weigh together? Write the weight in words. (three thousand, fifty pounds)

**After Page 29** In five horse–pull contests, a champion team of draft horses pulled these weights: 11,050 pounds; 9,900 pounds; 10,600 pounds; 11,500 pounds; 10,090 pounds. List the numbers in order from greatest to least. (11,500; 11,050; 10,600; 10,090; 9,900)

**After Page 37** One draft horse weighs 1,457 pounds. Another weighs 1,682 pounds. What is their combined weight? (3,139 pounds)

**After Page 41** Two draft horses have a combined weight of 2,946 pounds. One of the two weighs 1,479 pounds. How much does the other horse weigh? (1,467)

**Quick Review** Students give the standard numbers for the following expanded numbers.

2 tens 20 4 hundreds 400 8 tens 80 5 ones 5 1 ten 6 ones 16
8 tens 0 ones 80 1 hundred 7 ones 107 2 hundreds 1 ten 9 ones 219

**Lesson Focus** To read and write numbers up to 6-digits in standard and expanded form

**Suggested Materials** Place-value materials

## Ideas for Getting Started

Review the values of the place-value models. Then write a number such as 473 on the chalkboard. Ask a volunteer to show this number with the place-value materials. Then display or ask students to show 3 hundreds, 4 tens, and 7 ones. "What number does this represent?" (347) Have students translate back and forth between verbal descriptions, the model, and the written symbol. If models for thousands are available, include 4-digit numbers such as 5,281. A place-value chart or Number Reader like the one shown below could also be helpful.

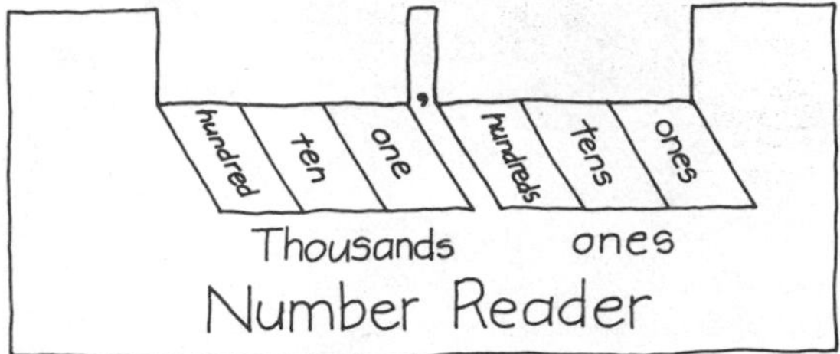


## Using Page 24

**Lesson Development** After reading aloud the information about the flights at the top of the page, discuss these historical events and the importance of using numbers accurately. Remind students that the symbols 0, 1, 2, 3, 4, 5, 6, 7, 8, and 9 are called digits. "How many digits are used to show the distance Earhart flew?" (4) "How many digits are used to show the distance Armstrong and Aldrin traveled?" (6) "What digits are needed to show any number?" (Any number can be written using a combination of the ten digits 0 through 9.)

Discuss the meaning of a period in a number. "What digits are in the ones period of the number shown in standard form?" (2, 8 and 4) "What digits are in the thousands period of the number?" (3, 7 and 6) Point out that in the ones period the digits represent *hundreds, tens,* and *ones.* In the thousands period the digits represent *hundred* thousands, *ten* thousands, and *one* thousands. Have students read the expression for the number written in expanded form and relate each addend in the expression to a place value in the number shown above it.

**Warm Up** If students have difficulty giving the place value for the red digit, refer back to place-value models that deal with ones, tens, hundreds, and thousands.

## Place Value: Thousands

**Two Famous Trips**

- May 21, 1932 Amelia Earhart landed in Ireland after the first solo flight by a woman across the Atlantic Ocean. A **3,241**-km trip!
- July 20, 1969 Neil Armstrong and Edwin Aldrin, Jr., made the first landing on the moon after a flight to our nearest neighbor in space. A **376,284**-km trip!

You can think about the number for Earhart's trip as shown below.

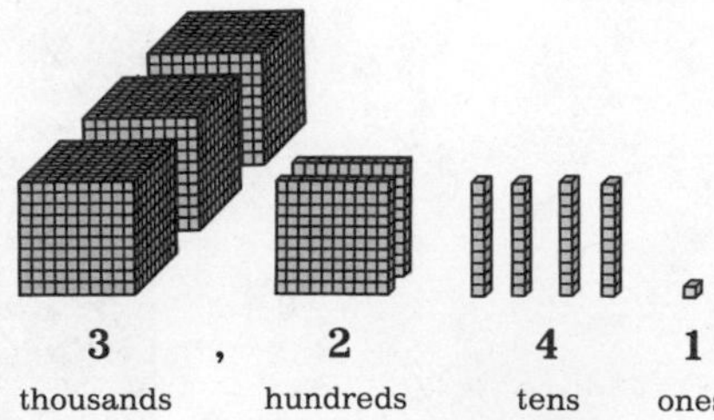


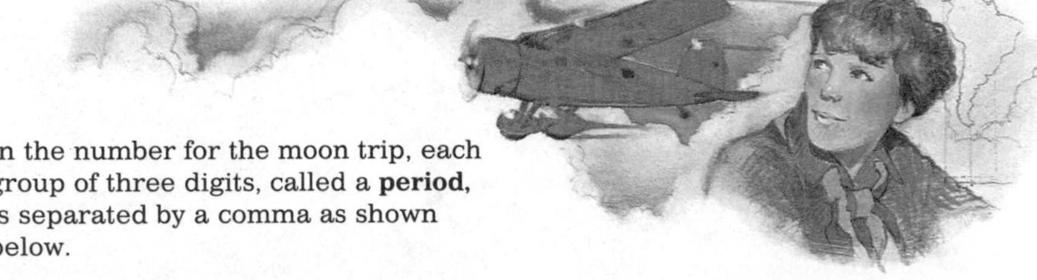

In the number for the moon trip, each group of three digits, called a **period,** is separated by a comma as shown below.

| | Thousands Period | | | | Ones Period | | ← Periods |
|---|---|---|---|---|---|---|---|
| We write, in **standard form:** → | 3 | 7 | 6 | , | 2 | 8 | 4 |
| | hundred thousands | ten thousands | thousands | | hundreds | tens | ones ← Place Values |

We read: "three hundred seventy-six thousand, two hundred eighty-four"

We can write, in **expanded form:**

$$300{,}000 + 70{,}000 + 6{,}000 + 200 + 80 + 4$$

**Warm Up** Read each number. Give the place value of the red digit.

| | | | |
|---|---|---|---|
| **1.** 3,574 7 tens | **2.** 6,384 6 thousands | **3.** 3,596 5 hundreds | **4.** 23,329 3 thousands |
| **5.** 45,204 4 ones | **6.** 72,521 7 ten thousands | **7.** 425 2 tens | **8.** 197,600 1 hundred thousand |
| **9.** 647,938 4 ten thousands | **10.** 502,749 2 thousands | **11.** 86,074 0 hundreds | **12.** 986,240 9 hundred thousands |



## Follow Up

### Reteaching

Show a period chart on the chalkboard. Make sure students understand the value of each position in the chart. If possible, use different colored chalk for each period. Write a number such as 267,835 on the chalkboard. Then write each digit in its proper place in the chart as you ask questions such as "How many tens?" "How many thousands?" "How many hundred thousands?" and so on. Ask one volunteer to write the number in expanded notation, and a second to read the number aloud.

### Enrichment

Have students use the clues to write the missing numbers:

1. My tens name is three. My thousands name is two times my tens. I have no hundreds or ones. Who am I? 6030
2. I name a four-digit number. The number of my thousands is greater than my tens by four. My tens are two times the number of my ones. Hundreds have I none. I can be named by two different numbers. Who are we? 8,042 or 6,021
3. My name is one less than a million. Who am I? 999,999

| Assignment Guide | | | |
|---|---|---|---|
| | Minimum | Average | Extended |
| page 25 | 1–27 | 1–28 | 1–28, TM |

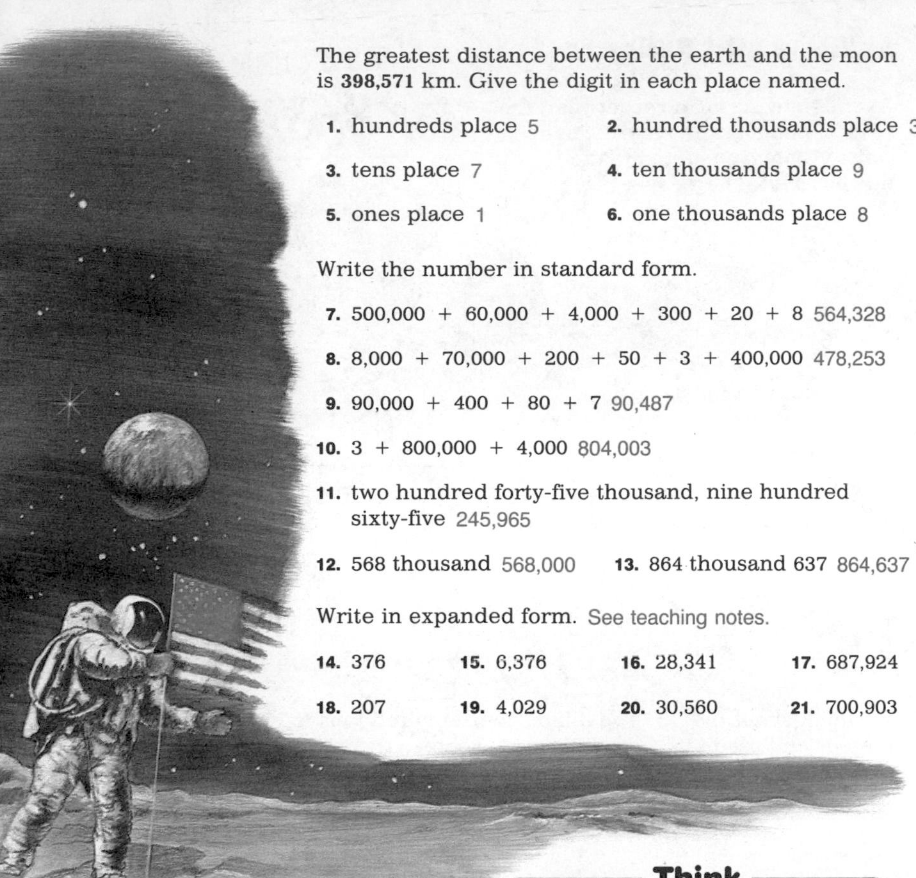

The greatest distance between the earth and the moon is **398,571** km. Give the digit in each place named.

1. hundreds place 5
2. hundred thousands place 3
3. tens place 7
4. ten thousands place 9
5. ones place 1
6. one thousands place 8

Write the number in standard form.

7. 500,000 + 60,000 + 4,000 + 300 + 20 + 8 564,328
8. 8,000 + 70,000 + 200 + 50 + 3 + 400,000 478,253
9. 90,000 + 400 + 80 + 7 90,487
10. 3 + 800,000 + 4,000 804,003
11. two hundred forty-five thousand, nine hundred sixty-five 245,965
12. 568 thousand 568,000
13. 864 thousand 637 864,637

Write in expanded form. See teaching notes.

| | | | |
|---|---|---|---|
| **14.** 376 | **15.** 6,376 | **16.** 28,341 | **17.** 687,924 |
| **18.** 207 | **19.** 4,029 | **20.** 30,560 | **21.** 700,903 |

Write in words. See teaching notes.

| | | |
|---|---|---|
| **22.** 247 | **23.** 5,620 | **24.** 12,306 |
| **25.** 34,029 | **26.** 86,492 | **27.** 374,982 |

★ **28.** Write the largest number and the smallest number that use the digits 0 through 6 exactly once.
largest: 6,543,210
smallest: 1,023,456

**Think**

**Place Value—Guess and Check**

Find the largest 6-digit number in which

- the thousands period contains three different odd digits with sum 21

and

- the ones period contains three different even digits with sum 18. 975,864

**Math**



## Using Page 25

**Exercises 1–6** As students complete these exercises, allow them to use a place-value chart if necessary.

**Exercises 7–13** Have students read some of these expressions aloud. If each addend can be read correctly, it is easier for students to write the number in standard form. Note that in exercises 8 and 10 the addends are not ordered according to place value.

**Exercises 22–27** Students may need additional help in writing these numbers in words. Be especially attentive to any difficulties they might have with zeros in exercises 23, 24, and 25.

**Think Math** Encourage students to list the important information needed to solve the problem (6 digit number, 3 *odd* digits in the thousands period with sum 21, 3 *even* digits in the hundreds period with sum 18). Suggest that they use Guess and Check to find the digits in each of the periods.

**Answers**

14. 300 + 70 + 6
15. 6,000 + 300 + 70 + 6
16. 20,000 + 8,000 + 300 + 40 + 1
17. 600,000 + 80,000 + 7,000 + 900 + 20 + 4
18. 200 + 7
19. 4,000 + 20 + 9
20. 30,000 + 500 + 60
21. 700,000 + 900 + 3
22. two hundred forty-seven
23. five thousand, six hundred twenty
24. twelve thousand, three hundred six
25. thirty-four thousand, twenty-nine
26. eighty-six thousand, four hundred ninety-two
27. three hundred seventy-four thousand, nine hundred eighty-two

## Ideas That Work

### Math for the Gifted

Challenge students with the following number pattern activity:

- Write each of the numbers from 1 through 25 as the sum of 2 or more consecutive numbers. (For example: 3 + 4 = 7 or 4 + 5 + 6 = 15 or 9 + 1 = 10, and so on.)
- How many different ways can you find to write each number?
- Can you extend this idea to numbers up through 50?

**Practice Supplement,** page 8

Name ______________________ To follow text page 25

**Place Value: Thousands**

Use the number 586,372. Which digit is in the place named?

1. hundreds place 3
2. hundred thousands place 5
3. tens place 7
4. ten thousands place 8
5. ones place 2
6. thousands place 6

Write the number in standard form.

7. 700,000 + 30,000 + 2,000 + 100 + 40 + 6 732,146
8. ·,000 + 80,000 + 400 + 20 + 8 89,428
9. 20,000 + 600 + 90 + 1 20,691
10. 5 + 7,000 + 900,000 907,005
11. seven hundred fifty-six thousand 756,000
12. 384 thousand 384,000
13. 921 thousand 444 921,444

Write in expanded form.

14. 265 200 + 60 + 5
15. 1,624 1,000 + 600 + 20 + 4
16. 63,496 60,000 + 3,000 + 400 + 90 + 6
17. 482,195 400,000 + 80,000 + 2,000 + 100 + 90 + 5
18. 800,206 800,000 + 200 + 6
19. 50,270 50,000 + 200 + 70
20. 9,388 9,000 + 300 + 80 + 8

# Numeration

**Quick Review** Students give the numbers for these number names.
twenty-two forty sixteen zero eight ninety-three eighty-eight
two hundred six fifty-six nine hundred ninety-nine five hundred fifteen

**Lesson Focus** To read and write numbers through billions

**Suggested Materials** Place-value chart

## Ideas for Getting Started

Ask students to guess how long a million seconds would be. (11½ 24-hour days) "How long is a billion seconds?" (about 34 years) "How many sixth-grade classes each containing 30 students would weigh about a million pounds?" (400) "How many classes would weigh 1 billion pounds?" (400,000) Use these questions to help give students a feel for the size of 1 million and 1 billion. Then draw this place value chart on the chalkboard.

| Thousands | | | Ones | | |
|---|---|---|---|---|---|
| H | T | O | H | T | O |
| | | | | | |

Review the periods and the place values, and extend the chart to include the millions and billions periods. Emphasize the role of hundreds, tens, and ones in each period.

| Billions | | | Millions | | | Thousands | | | Ones | | |
|---|---|---|---|---|---|---|---|---|---|---|---|
| H | T | O | H | T | O | H | T | O | H | T | O |
| | | | | | | | | | | | |

## Using Page 26

**Lesson Development** After the class has read the information about phonograph record sales, discuss some "million dollar records." Emphasize the need for larger numbers to describe the number of records sold. Call students' attention to the number in the display box. "What digits are in the ones period?" (6, 8, 0) "The thousands period?" (5, 1, 7) Point out that the digits 4, 3 and 9 are in the millions period and that there is one digit in the billions period. Refer to the chart shown on the page and discuss the place values within the millions and billions periods. Have students give the digits in the number for each of these places. Help students write the number using expanded form. Give students another number, such as 236,573,981,437, and have them describe each period, name the place value for each digit, and read the number. Be sure they understand that the word "and" is not used when reading large numbers.

**Warm Up** Some students may need to be reminded of the right-to-left orientation when moving from the ones period to the thousands, the millions, and the billions periods. Also, if necessary, review the role of hundreds, tens, and ones within each period. In exercises 7–18 have students identify digits other than the ones asked for in the text. Then name a period and ask students to give the digit in that place.

## Millions and Billions

At one time during a recent year, the sales of phonograph records in the United States amounted to the number shown here.

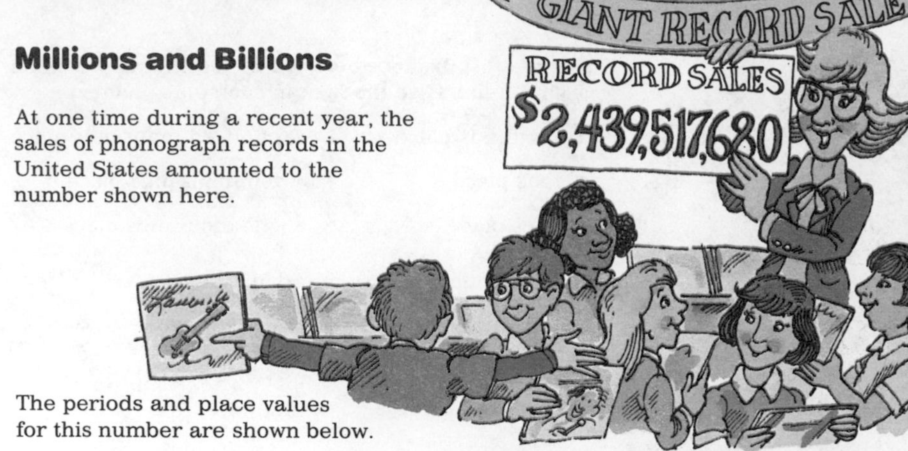


The periods and place values for this number are shown below.

| Periods | Billions | | | Millions | | | Thousands | | | Ones | | |
|---|---|---|---|---|---|---|---|---|---|---|---|---|
| Place Values | hundred billions | ten billions | billions | hundred millions | ten millions | millions | hundred thousands | ten thousands | thousands | hundreds | tens | ones |
| | | | 2, | 4 | 3 | 9, | 5 | 1 | 7, | 6 | 8 | 0 |

We think about the periods and read: "two **billion**, four hundred thirty-nine **million**, five hundred seventeen **thousand**, six hundred eighty"

**Warm Up** Give the digits in the period named. Then read each number.

1. 467,398,275 (thousands) 398
2. 367,248,204 (millions) 367
3. 86,240,302,617 (billions) 86
4. 9,460,300,480 (ones) 480
5. 68,943,287,400 (millions) 943
6. 975,837,246,781 (billions) 975

Read each number. Then give the place value of the red digit.

7. 59,876,476 — 6 ones
8. 864,327,413 — 7 thousands
9. 362,470,198 — 2 millions
10. 5,468,294,300 — 5 billions
11. 42,385,297 — 9 tens
12. 3,576,284 — 7 ten thousands
13. 57,936,485,800 — 3 ten millions
14. 684,362,943,702 — 8 ten billions
15. 1,743,849 — 8 hundreds
16. 59,241,708 — 2 hundred thousands
17. 165,376,240 — 1 hundred million
18. 463,807,620,700 — 4 hundred billion

26

## Follow Up

### Reteaching

Review how numbers are read by the period names. For instance, 2,437,821 is read "*two million,* four hundred thirty-seven *thousand,* eight hundred twenty-one." Emphasize the italicized words as the names for the periods. After a discussion of how to read such numbers, find examples from newspapers, almanacs, and other sources and have students read these numbers to become comfortable with the larger numbers.

### Enrichment

Have students collect large numbers cut from newspapers or magazines. Let students use these numbers to form a collage of "Millions and Billions." The collage can be displayed or used as a bulletin board.

| Assignment Guide | | | |
|---|---|---|---|
| | Minimum | Average | Extended |
| page 27 | 1–21 | 1–22 | 1–22, TM |

Write the digits in the period named.

1. 86,342,975 (thousands) 342
2. 3,649,380,263 (billions) 3
3. 857,832,467 (ones) 467
4. 59,462,384,000 (millions) 462
5. 657,923,406 (thousands) 923
6. 50,386,000,465 (millions) 386

Use the number shown for 8-track tape sales. Which digit is in the place named?

7. ten millions 8
8. thousands 0
9. hundred thousands 3
10. ten thousands 2
11. hundred millions 6
12. millions 4

Write the number that has these digits in the periods shown.

13. billions: 376; thousands: 724; ones: 325; millions: 423
376,423,724,325
14. thousands: 204; billions: 217; millions: 749; ones: 200
217,749,204,200
15. ones: 461; millions: 613; thousands: 209; billions: 24
24,613,209,461

Write in standard form.

16. 5,000,000 + 300,000 + 80,000 + 4,000 + 600 + 2
5,384,602
17. 3,000,000,000 + 400,000,000 + 70,000,000 + 1,000,000
3,471,000,000
18. Three billion, seven hundred six million, five hundred forty thousand
3,706,540,000
19. 836 billion 836,000,000,000
20. 792 million 792,000,000
21. How many zeros are in the number one thousand? one million? one billion? 3; 6; 9

★ 22. Write the largest number and the smallest number that use the digits 0 through 9 exactly once.
largest: 9,876,543,210;
smallest: 1,023,456,789

**Think**

**Use a Calculator**

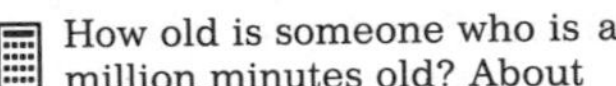

How old is someone who is a million minutes old? About

**A** 2 months? **B** 2 years?

**C** 20 years? **D** 200 years?

about 2 years old

Guess first. Then check using your calculator.

**Math**



## Using Page 27

**Exercises 1–6** To work with individual students, point to one of these exercises and identify three digits in a period. Ask the student to name the period from which the digits were selected.

**Exercises 13–15** Note that the periods have been rearranged so that students must write the number in the correct order.

**Exercises 16–20** It is helpful to have students read aloud the expressions in exercises such as 16 and 17 before writing the number.

**Think Math** Tell students that they are to guess one of the four answers—A, B, C, or D—before they begin to calculate the answer. If possible, work with the group to make a small chart showing the frequency of guesses in each category. Then have students work together in small groups using a calculator to find the exact answer.

**Reteaching Supplement,** page 7

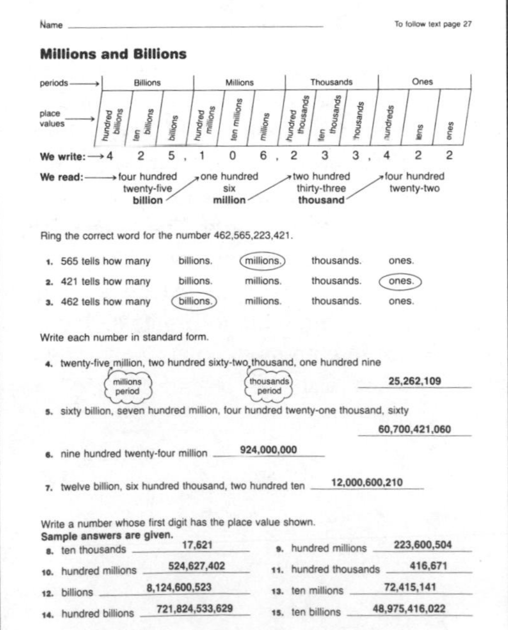

Name ______ To follow text page 27

**Millions and Billions**

| periods → | Billions | | | Millions | | | Thousands | | | Ones | | |
|---|---|---|---|---|---|---|---|---|---|---|---|---|
| place values → | hundred billions | ten billions | billions | hundred millions | ten millions | millions | hundred thousands | ten thousands | thousands | hundreds | tens | ones |
| We write: → | 4 | 2 | 5, | 1 | 0 | 6, | 2 | 3 | 3, | 4 | 2 | 2 |

We read: → four hundred twenty-five **billion** → one hundred six **million** → two hundred thirty-three **thousand** → four hundred twenty-two

Ring the correct word for the number 462,565,223,421.

1. 565 tells how many billions. (millions.) thousands. ones.
2. 421 tells how many billions. millions. thousands. (ones.)
3. 462 tells how many (billions.) millions. thousands. ones.

Write each number in standard form.

4. twenty-five million, two hundred sixty-two thousand, one hundred nine 25,262,109
(millions period) (thousands period)
5. sixty billion, seven hundred million, four hundred twenty-one thousand, sixty 60,700,421,060
6. nine hundred twenty-four million 924,000,000
7. twelve billion, six hundred thousand, two hundred ten 12,000,600,210

Write a number whose first digit has the place value shown.
**Sample answers are given.**

8. ten thousands 17,621
9. hundred millions 223,600,504
10. hundred millions 524,627,402
11. hundred thousands 416,671
12. billions 8,124,600,523
13. ten millions 72,415,141
14. hundred billions 721,824,533,629
15. ten billions 48,975,416,022

**Enrichment Supplement,** page 7

Name ______ To follow text page 25

**A Crossnumber Puzzle**

| | [1]2 | 0 | [2]9 | [3]9 | [4]7 | 0 | [5]4 | |
|---|---|---|---|---|---|---|---|---|
| [6]9 | 9 | | [7]6 | 4 | 4 | | [8]3 | [9]3 |
| 9 | | [10]1 | 2 | 6 | 7 | [11]6 | | 3 |
| [12]9 | [13]6 | 1 | | 8 | | [14]3 | [15]8 | 3 |
| [16]9 | 6 | 2 | 0 | | [17]3 | 0 | 0 | 3 |
| [18]9 | 7 | 1 | | [19]4 | | [20]4 | 8 | 3 |
| 9 | | [21]1 | [22]3 | 0 | [23]1 | 6 | | 3 |
| [24]9 | [25]7 | | [26]5 | 2 | 0 | | [27]1 | 3 |
| | [28]4 | 5 | 7 | 1 | 6 | 0 | 2 | |

**Across**

1. two million, ninety-nine thousand, seven hundred four
6. the largest two-digit number
7. 6 hundreds, 4 tens, and 4 ones
8. both digits the same
10. 12,000 + 600 + 70 + 6
12. one less than 2 down
14. 300 + 80 + 3
16. ten times 2 down
17. This number reads the same forward and backward.
18. 10 more than 12 across
20. one hundred more than 14 across
21. 13,000 + 300 + 10 + 6
24. 9 tens and 7 ones
26. 5 hundreds and 2 tens
27. an "unlucky" number
28. four million, five hundred seventy-one thousand, six hundred two

**Down**

1. one less than 30
2. 900 + 60 + 2
3. 9,000 + 400 + 60 + 8
4. jet airplane number
5. 4 tens and 3 ones
6. one less than ten million
9. This number is one third as large as 6 down.
10. This number reads the same forward and backward.
11. sixty-three thousand, forty-six
13. 600 + 60 + 7
15. This number reads the same forward, backward, or upside down.
19. 4,000 + 300 + 20 + 1
22. 300 + 50 + 7
23. upside down it is 901
25. halfway between 71 and 77
27. an even dozen

**Practice Supplement,** page 9

Name ______ To follow text page 27

**Millions and Billions**

Write the digits in the period named.

1. 74,638,249 thousands 638
2. 1,243,756,891 billions 1
3. 646,215,938 ones 938
4. 69,287,416,000 millions 287
5. 985,361,208 thousands 361
6. 82,916,400,200 millions 916

Use the number 578,439,261,805. Which digit is in the place named?

7. thousands 1
8. ten millions 3
9. hundred billions 5
10. ones 5
11. ten thousands 6
12. hundred millions 4
13. billions 8
14. hundreds 8

Write the number that has these digits in the periods shown.

15. billions: 742; millions: 638; ones: 400; thousands: 214 742,638,214,400
16. millions: 200; thousands: 521; billions: 43; ones: 406 43,200,521,406
17. ones: 891; billions: 86; millions: 588; thousands: 600 86,588,600,891

Write in standard form.

18. 9,000,000 + 400,000 + 90,000 + 2,000 + 700 9,492,700
19. 5,000,000,000 + 60,000 + 100,000,000 + 200 5,100,060,200
20. 20,000,000 + 100,000,000 + 50,000 + 6,000 120,056,000
21. seven billion, three hundred two million, five thousand, seven 7,302,005,007
22. ninety billion, eighty million, twenty thousand, fifty 90,080,020,050

**Quick Review** Use the number pairs below as oral drill. Students name the larger of the two numbers.

28, 88 14, 41 33, 22 76, 67 11, 101 61, 61 89, 98 88, 89
20, 22 39, 40 42, 24 65, 56 20, 19 13, 33 404, 440

**Lesson Focus** To compare and order whole numbers

**Suggested Materials** Spinner labeled 0 through 9

## Ideas for Getting Started

Have each student draw a grid of five squares like the one shown below.

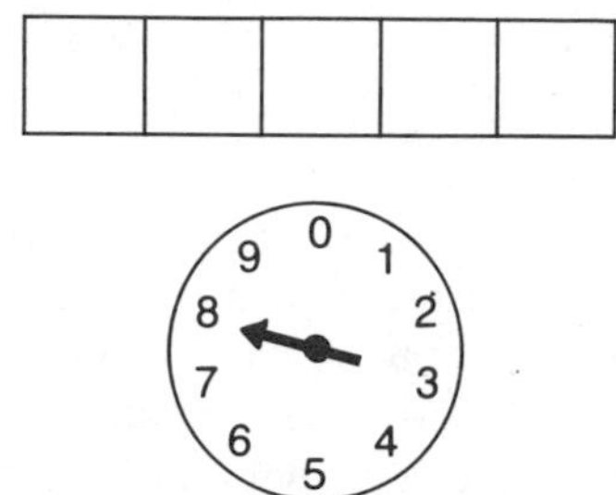

Then spin a spinner as shown or draw slips of paper labeled 0 through 9. Have each student write the resulting digit in any one of the five squares. The object of the game is to produce the greatest whole number. After selecting the five digits ask students to decide who has formed the largest whole number. Encourage students to discuss their method of deciding which number is greater.

## Using Page 28

**Lesson Development** Have students read the problem and the list of stadiums. Discuss sports that are played in the stadiums and ask students to tell about any of the stadiums they may have visited. "Which of the listed stadiums holds the least number of people?" (Soldier Field, Chicago) "Which stadium holds the greatest number of people?" (Texas Stadium, Dallas)

Ask students to think about counting and try to decide which of the two numbers being compared would be counted first. Students might find it helpful to think about counting to compare two numbers. "If you start with one number and count on, do you come to the other number? If so, the second number is larger."

Write the two numbers on the chalkboard and use the procedure described in the instruction boxes to decide which of the two numbers is greater. Be sure students know which symbol means "greater than" and which means "less than."

Review the term "order." Help students compare numbers two at a time to rank the numbers from greatest to least. Point out that it is useful to rank the tens place first: if the digits there are the same, look at each successive place, moving to the right.

**Warm Up** Check to be sure students are starting to compare at the left rather than the right. Let them use a number line to aid in making the comparison.

## Comparing and Ordering

Which stadium holds the greater number of people, Schaefer Stadium or Candlestick Park?

We **compare** two numbers by deciding which is greater.

**Stadium Capacities**

| Stadium | Capacity |
|---|---|
| Soldier Field, Chicago | 58,064 |
| Candlestick Park, San Francisco | 61,246 |
| Atlanta-Fulton Stadium, Atlanta | 60,489 |
| Texas Stadium, Dallas | 65,101 |
| Schaefer Stadium, Foxboro, Mass. | 61,297 |
| Memorial Stadium, Baltimore | 60,020 |

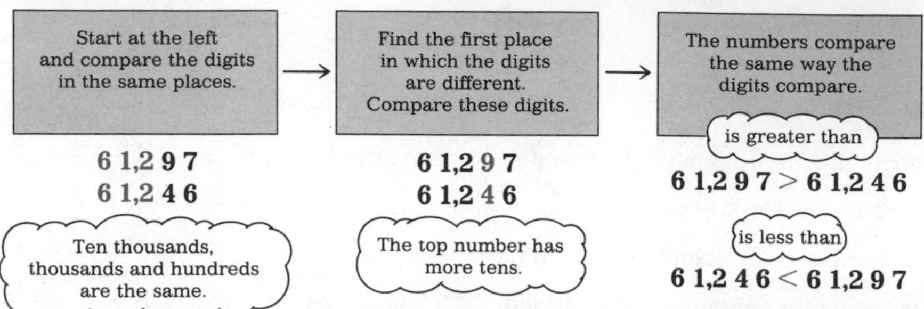

Start at the left and compare the digits in the same places.
Find the first place in which the digits are different. Compare these digits.
The numbers compare the same way the digits compare.
is greater than
61,297
61,246
61,297
61,246
61,297 > 61,246
Ten thousands, thousands and hundreds are the same.
The top number has more tens.
is less than
61,246 < 61,297


Schaefer stadium holds the greater number of people.

We **order** numbers by listing them from least to greatest or from greatest to least. We do this by comparing them two at a time.

65,101 ← greatest
61,297
61,246
60,489
60,020
58,064 ← least

**Warm Up** Which stadium capacity is greater? Use greater than (>) to compare the numbers.

1. Oakland-Alameda Stadium: 54,615
   San Diego Stadium: 52,552
   54,615 > 52,552
2. R. F. Kennedy Stadium, Washington, D.C.: 55,031
   Milwaukee County Stadium: 55,958
   55,958 > 55,031
3. Lambeau Field, Green Bay: 56,267
   Riverfront Stadium, Cincinnati: 56,200 56,267 > 56,200
4. Order the stadium capacities in exercises 1 through 3 from least to greatest. 52,552; 54,615; 55,031; 55,958; 56,200; 56,267



## Follow Up

### Reteaching

Write the numbers 36 and 39 on the chalkboard so that the ones place and the tens place are aligned. Then ask: "Do both have the same number of digits? If not, the one with the greater number of digits is larger. If both have the same number of digits, begin with the digit at the left. Find the place where the digits are different. Compare these digits. Since 9 > 6, then 39 > 36." Help students use the steps above to compare these numbers: 5,432 and 432; 83,761 and 82,699.

### Enrichment

Have students make a set of digit cards from index cards—five cards each for the digits 0 through 9. Two players draw six cards and arrange them in the order in which they were drawn. Players then read their numbers. The player with the smaller number scores a point. The two numbers are then placed in a pocket chart from least to greatest. The player scoring the most points wins. The game could also be played for the greater number.

| Assignment Guide | | | |
|---|---|---|---|
| | Minimum | Average | Extended |
| page 29 | 1–21 | 1–26 | 1–26, TM |

Write > (greater than) , < (less than), or = for each ●.

1. 973 ● 898 >
2. 7,436 ● 7,440 <
3. 1,000 ● 999 >
4. 10,000 ● 99,999 <
5. 78,604 ● 78,640 <
6. 863,426 ● 86,526 >
7. 9,743,800 ● 9,743,008 >
8. 65,000 ● 64,999 >
9. 784,946 ● 946,784 <
10. 1,010,000 ● 1,001,100 >
11. 475 thousand ● 475,000 =
12. 42 million ● 23 billion <
13. 800,000 ● 8 million <
14. 764 billion ● 698 billion >

Use > or < to compare the top number with the bottom number.

15. 946,627 > 938,576
16. 95,606 > 95,599
17. 3,467,936,800 < 3,468,107,400
18. 367,432,567 > 367,432,498

19. Which holds more people, Yankee Stadium or Tiger Stadium?
Tiger Stadium
20. Order the capacities of these baseball parks by listing them from the greatest to least.
56,581; 54,220; 54,208; 50,230; 50,101

| Baseball Park | Capacity |
|---|---|
| Tiger Stadium, Detroit | 54,220 |
| Three Rivers Stadium, Pittsburgh | 50,230 |
| Yankee Stadium, New York | 54,208 |
| Busch Memorial Stadium, St. Louis | 50,101 |
| Veterans Stadium, Philadelphia | 56,581 |

Order from least to greatest.

21. 7,983; 7,979; 7,899; 7,958
7,899; 7,958; 7,979; 7,983
22. 57,384; 57,099; 57,401
57,099; 57,384; 57,401
23. 5,396,238; 5,396,229; 5,401,107; 5,396,199
5,396,199; 5,396,229; 5,396,238; 5,401,107

Write the number that is

24. 1,000 less than 37,398. 36,398
25. 1,000,000 more than 18,365,421.
19,365,421
26. 100,000 less than 367,548,219.
367,448,219

**Think Math**

**Discovering Patterns**

These dots should help you see why 3, 6, and 10 are sometimes called triangular numbers.

3 6 10

Give the next 5 triangular numbers.
15, 21, 28, 36, 45

More Practice, page 412, Set A



## Using Page 29

**Exercises 1–14** In exercises 3 and 8, be alert for students who allow the nines to overshadow other considerations when comparing the two numbers. Note that in exercise 5 and 7 the digits are the same but the order is different.

**Exercises 24–26** If students understand place value, these exercises will be quite easy. In exercise 25, for example, the students read 1 million and simply add to the digit in the millions place. In exercise 26 the students subtract 1 from the digit in the hundred thousands place.

**Think Math** Help students discover that the dots are arranged so that there is one dot in the top row, two dots in the second row, three dots in the third row, four dots in the fourth row, and so on. This will make it easy for them to draw the next triangle in the sequence. A table like the one shown below would also be helpful.

| Triangle | Number of dots |
|---|---|
| 1st | 3 |
| 2nd | 6 |
| 3rd | 10 |
| 4th | 15 |
| ⋮ | ⋮ |

(differences: 3, 4, 5)

Encourage students to look for a pattern and extend the table without actually counting the dots in all the triangles.

More Practice, page 412, Set A

**Reteaching Supplement,** page 8

**Enrichment Supplement,** page 8

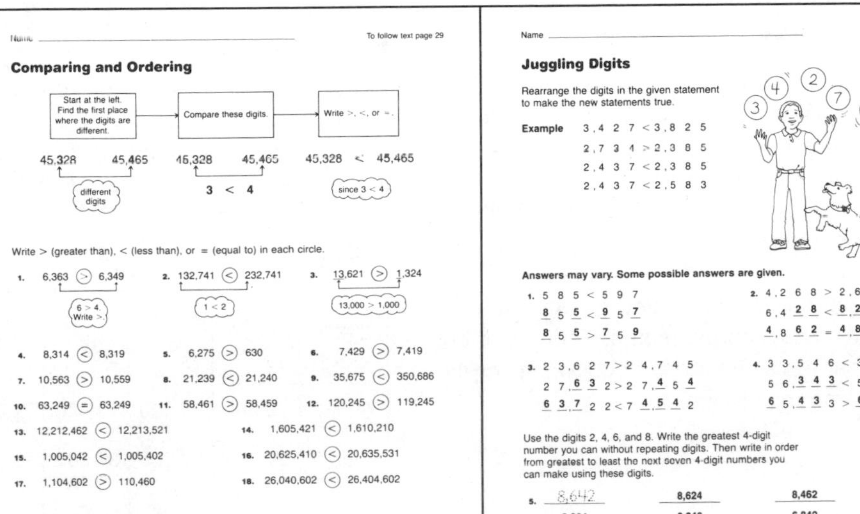

Name ______ To follow text page 29

**Comparing and Ordering**

Start at the left. Find the first place where the digits are different. → Compare these digits. → Write >, <, or =.

45,328 45,465 (different digits) 45,328 45,465 3 < 4 45,328 < 45,465 (since 3 < 4)

Write > (greater than), < (less than), or = (equal to) in each circle.

1. 6,363 (>) 6,349 (6 > 4. Write >.)
2. 132,741 (<) 232,741 (1 < 2)
3. 13,621 (>) 1,324 (13,000 > 1,000)
4. 8,314 (<) 8,319
5. 6,275 (>) 630
6. 7,429 (>) 7,419
7. 10,563 (>) 10,559
8. 21,239 (<) 21,240
9. 35,675 (<) 350,686
10. 63,249 (=) 63,249
11. 58,461 (>) 58,459
12. 120,245 (>) 119,245
13. 12,212,462 (<) 12,213,521
14. 1,605,421 (<) 1,610,210
15. 1,005,042 (<) 1,005,402
16. 20,625,410 (<) 20,635,531
17. 1,104,602 (>) 110,460
18. 26,040,602 (<) 26,404,602

Write in order from least to greatest.

19. 575; 874; 821 — 575 821 874
20. 1,623; 1,459; 1,470 — 1,459 1,470 1,623
21. 135,321; 13,512; 1,351,120 — 13,512 135,321 1,351,120

Name ______ To follow text page 29

**Juggling Digits**

Rearrange the digits in the given statement to make the new statements true.

**Example** 3,4 2 7 < 3,8 2 5
2,7 3 4 > 2,3 8 5
2,4 3 7 < 2,3 8 5
2,4 3 7 < 2,5 8 3

**Answers may vary. Some possible answers are given.**

1. 5 8 5 < 5 9 7
8 5 5 < 9 5 7
8 5 5 > 7 5 9

2. 4,2 6 8 > 2,6 8 4
6,4 2 8 < 8,2 4 6
4,8 6 2 = 4,8 6 2

3. 2 3,6 2 7 > 2 4,7 4 5
2 7,6 3 2 > 2 7,4 5 4
6 3,7 2 2 < 7 4,5 4 2

4. 3 3,5 4 6 < 3 3,6 4 5
5 6,3 4 3 < 5 6,4 3 3
6 5,4 3 3 > 6 5,3 4 3

Use the digits 2, 4, 6, and 8. Write the greatest 4-digit number you can without repeating digits. Then write in order from greatest to least the next seven 4-digit numbers you can make using these digits.

5. 8,642 8,624 8,462 8,426
8,264 8,246 6,842 6,824

Use the digits 2, 4, 4, and 6. Write in order from greatest to least all of the 4-digit numbers you can make without repeating digits. Hint: the two 4s are used in each number.

6. 6,442 6,424 6,244 4,642 4,624
4,462 4,426 2,644 2,464 2,446

**Practice Supplement,** page 10

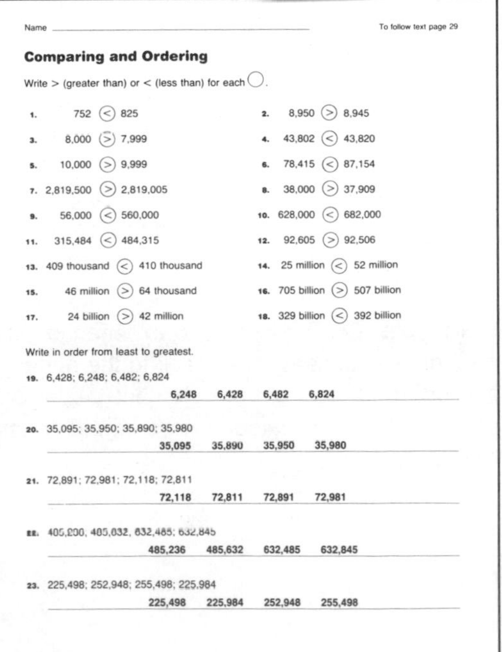

Name ______ To follow text page 29

**Comparing and Ordering**

Write > (greater than) or < (less than) for each ◯.

1. 752 (<) 825
2. 8,950 (>) 8,945
3. 8,000 (>) 7,999
4. 43,802 (<) 43,820
5. 10,000 (>) 9,999
6. 78,415 (<) 87,154
7. 2,819,500 (>) 2,819,005
8. 38,000 (>) 37,909
9. 56,000 (<) 560,000
10. 628,000 (<) 682,000
11. 315,484 (<) 484,315
12. 92,605 (>) 92,506
13. 409 thousand (<) 410 thousand
14. 25 million (<) 52 million
15. 46 million (>) 64 thousand
16. 705 billion (>) 507 billion
17. 24 billion (>) 42 million
18. 329 billion (<) 392 billion

Write in order from least to greatest.

19. 6,428; 6,248; 6,482; 6,824
6,248 6,428 6,482 6,824
20. 35,095; 35,950; 35,890; 35,980
35,095 35,890 35,950 35,980
21. 72,891; 72,981; 72,118; 72,811
72,118 72,811 72,891 72,981
22. 485,236; 485,632; 632,485; 632,845
485,236 485,632 632,485 632,845
23. 225,498; 252,948; 255,498; 225,984
225,498 225,984 252,948 255,498

# Estimation

**Quick Review** Students give answers aloud for these basic facts.

6 + 5  9 − 7  4 + 3  8 + 6  7 × 5  5 × 9  27 ÷ 3  48 ÷ 6  42 ÷ 6
8 − 0  9 + 5  12 − 8  7 × 9  40 ÷ 8  32 ÷ 4  6 + 9  14 − 8

**Lesson Focus** To round whole numbers to the nearest ten, hundred, thousand, ten thousand, and nearest dollar

**Suggested Materials** Laminated number line or a number line on the chalkboard

## Ideas for Getting Started

Mark a number such as 376 on a laminated number line or on a chalkboard number line.

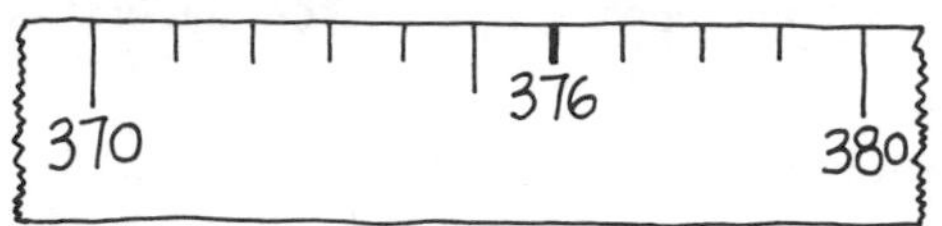


"Is 376 closer to 370 or 380?" Point out that 375 is the midpoint between 370 and 380, and because 376 is to the right of 375, it is closer to 380. Then have students count by hundreds (100, 200, 300, 400, and so on). "Between what two hundreds is the number 376?" (between 300 and 400) Mark the number line as shown. "Which hundred is 376 closest to?" (400)

## Using Page 30

**Lesson Development** Read aloud the problem at the top of the page. Ask a volunteer to read the number that tells the depth that the bathyscaph went. "Is this number closer to 31,000 or 32,000?" Have students look at the number line at the top of the page to verify their ideas that the number 31,829 is closer to 32,000.

Then tell students that there is a useful shortcut to help quickly round any number to any place. Write 9,645 on the chalkboard and follow the steps given in the instruction boxes on the page. Emphasize the importance of the digit in the place to which you want to round and the importance of the digit that is one place to its right. Be sure students understand that if the digit is 5, it will be rounded up.

**Other Examples** Note that in the second example there is a 5 to the right of the place to be rounded. In the first example be sure students round according to directions rather than using sequential rounding. That is, some students may want to round to the nearest ten (9,650) and then round to the nearest hundred (9,700).

**Warm Up** For students who experience difficulty with these exercises, refer back to the number line and use it to illustrate the shortcut taught on this page. Be alert to students who round by simply "dropping digits."

## Rounding

A bathyscaph went to a depth of 31,829 ft. This is greater than the height of the world's highest mountain! What is this number of feet rounded to the nearest thousand?

The number line helps us understand how to round numbers.

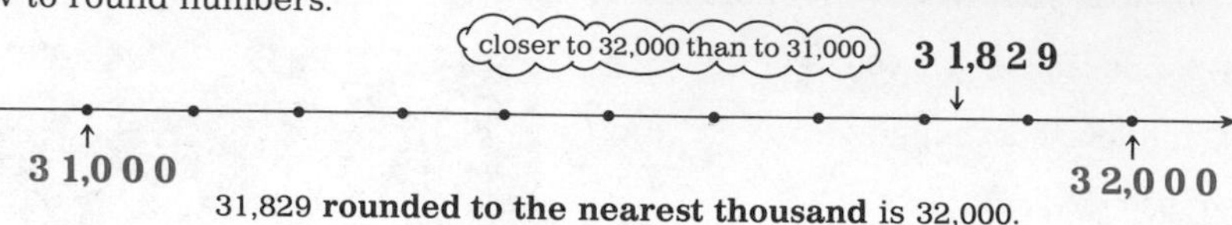


31,829 **rounded to the nearest thousand** is 32,000.

We can round a number to any desired place as shown below.

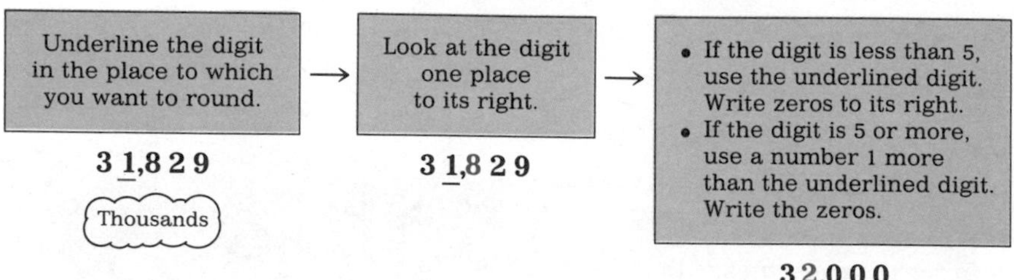


**Other Examples**

9,645 rounded to the **nearest hundred** is 9,600.

9,645 rounded to the **nearest ten** is 9,650.

74,962 rounded to the **nearest ten thousand** is 70,000.

$8.65 rounded to the **nearest dollar** is $9.

**Warm Up** Round to the place indicated.

1. 683 (nearest ten) 680
2. 7,285 (nearest hundred) 7,300
3. 34,725 (nearest thousand) 35,000
4. $4.55 (nearest dollar) $5
5. 86,398 (nearest thousand) 86,000
6. 9,453 (nearest hundred) 9,500
7. $19.75 (nearest dollar) $20
8. 8,366 (nearest ten) 8,370
9. 85,382 (nearest ten thousand) 90,000

30

## Follow Up

**Reteaching**

Write a number such as 536,826 on the chalkboard. Discuss how to round to the nearest ten. (Look at the digit to the right of the tens place. If the digit is 5 or more, increase the tens digit by one. Write zeros to its right. If the digit is less than 5, use that digit and write zeros to its right.) Use several examples to work through this rounding procedure. Then point out that the same steps apply whatever the place rounded to.

**Enrichment**

Write several numbers on the chalkboard. Have students complete a chart such as the one below in which each number is rounded as specified on the chart. For example: 74,362; 87,875

| Number | Rounded to the Nearest | | | |
|---|---|---|---|---|
| | ten thousand | thousand | hundred | ten |
| 74,362 | 70,000 | 74,000 | 74,400 | 74,360 |
| 87,875 | 90,000 | 88,000 | 87,900 | 87,880 |

| Assignment Guide | | | |
|---|---|---|---|
| | Minimum | Average | Extended |
| page 31 | 1–37, SK | 1–37, SK | 1–39, SK |

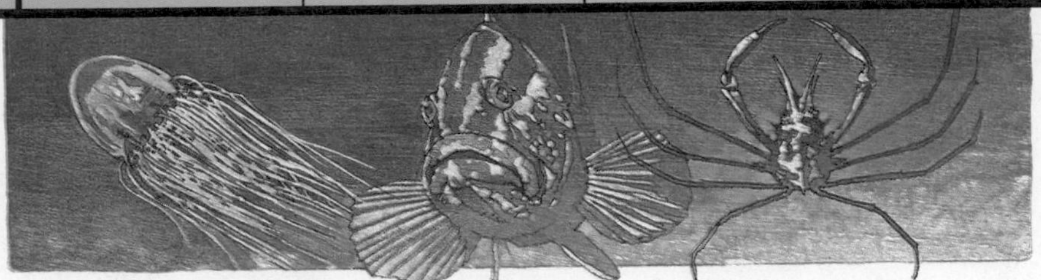

Round to the nearest ten. Then round to the nearest hundred.

1. 764 — 760; 800
2. 495 — 500; 500
3. 976 — 980; 1,000
4. 8,652 — 8,650; 8,700
5. 9,374 — 9,370; 9,400
6. 15,643 — 15,640; 15,600
7. 27,386 — 27,390; 27,400
8. 607 — 610; 600
9. 9,338 — 9,340; 9,300
10. 10,655 — 10,660; 10,700

Round to the nearest thousand.

11. 4,374 — 4,000
12. 9,568 — 10,000
13. 10,246 — 10,000
14. 24,872 — 25,000
15. 37,594 — 38,000
16. 7,249 — 7,000
17. 18,076 — 18,000
18. 79,423 — 79,000
19. 236,472 — 236,000
20. 178,537 — 179,000

Round to the nearest ten thousand.

21. 74,652 — 70,000
22. 36,478 — 40,000
23. 35,350 — 40,000
24. 140,985 — 140,000
25. 68,370 — 70,000
26. 15,863 — 20,000
27. 267,840 — 270,000
28. 345,659 — 350,000
29. 229,780 — 230,000
30. 369,010 — 370,000

Round to the nearest dollar.

31. \$3.45 — \$3
32. \$5.69 — \$6
33. \$9.51 — \$10
34. \$12.19 — \$12
35. \$36.79 — \$37

36. Round 763,984 to the nearest hundred thousand. 800,000

37. Round 34,579,643 to the nearest million. 35,000,000

★ 38. Give 4 numbers that give 16,000 when rounded to the nearest thousand. Answers will vary. Any numbers from 15,500 through 16,499 are correct.

★ 39. A newspaper headline reported, "BATHYSCAPH REACHES A DEPTH OF 36,000 FEET." If this number has been rounded to the nearest thousand, what are the smallest and largest possibilities for the actual depth? 35,500; 36,499

**Skillkeeper**

Add or subtract.

1. 50 + 70 = 120
2. 90 − 60 = 30
3. \$70 − 20 = \$50
4. 800 + 400 = 1,200
5. 1,500 − 600 = 900
6. \$9,000 + 7,000 = \$16,000

More Practice, page 412, Set B



## Using Page 31

**Exercises 1–10** Be sure students round each number to the nearest ten, and then go back to the original number to round to the nearest hundred. Discourage students from doing sequential rounding here.

**Exercises 11–30** If necessary, go back to the number line to help students who are having difficulty with the rounding process.

**Exercises 31–35** Students usually find it easy to round to the nearest dollar. They can look at the number of cents to decide whether or not the amount is over 50. In other words, they can look at the first digit after the decimal point to complete the rounding.

**Exercises 36–37** Note that these exercises extend the rounding process to larger numbers.

**Exercises 38–39** Exercise 38 involves a type of guess and check. The students can choose a number, round it, and get additional information about the characteristics of the number desired. This exercise should help students complete exercise 39.

**Skillkeeper** These skills were originally taught in Chapter 3 of Book 5.

**More Practice,** page 412, Set B

**Reteaching Supplement,** page 9

Name ____________ To follow text page 31

**Rounding**

What is 2,375 rounded to the nearest hundred?

Is the tens digit 5 or more? → No → Keep the hundreds digit the same. / Yes → Add 1 to the hundreds digit. → Replace all digits to the right of the hundreds place with zeros.

2,375 2,4 ▢▢ 2,400

2,375 rounded to the nearest **thousand** is **2,000.** (Check here. 3 < 5 Keep the digit the same.)

2,375 rounded to the nearest **ten** is **2,380.** (Check here. 5 = 5 Add 1 to the tens digit.)

Round each number to the nearest hundred. (Check here.)

1. 3,266 3,300
2. 1,828 1,800
3. 23,746 23,700
4. 69,513 69,500
5. 983 1,000
6. 5,227 5,200

Round each number to the nearest thousand. (Check here.)

7. 26,671 27,000
8. 42,395 42,000
9. 77,766 78,000
10. 48,211 48,000
11. 1,763 2,000
12. 2,994 3,000

Round each number to the nearest ten. (Check here.)

13. 268 270
14. 5,409 5,410
15. 776 780
16. 1,245 1,250
17. 59 60
18. 5,555 5,560

**Enrichment Supplement,** page 9

Name ____________ To follow text page 31

**Round About**

We often round numbers to a certain number of **significant digits.**

**Example** 242,746 rounded to two significant digits is 240,000. 5,849,213 rounded to three significant digits is 5,850,000.

Round each number to **two** significant digits.

1. 742,966 740,000
2. 58,929 59,000

Round each number to **three** significant digits.

3. 972,471 972,000
4. 1,258,746 1,260,000

5. Rank these metropolitan areas in order of population from greatest to least. Then round each number to **two** significant digits.

Tokyo, Japan Pop. 11,696,373 | Buenos Aires, Argentina Pop. 9,910,000 | Mexico City, Mexico Pop. 13,993,866 | New York City, U.S.A. Pop. 16,478,769 | Los Angeles, U.S.A. Pop. 10,606,665

| Metropolitan Area | Rounded Population |
|---|---|
| **New York City** | 16,000,000 |
| **Mexico City** | 14,000,000 |
| **Tokyo** | 12,000,000 |
| **Los Angeles** | 11,000,000 |
| **Buenos Aires** | 10,000,000 |

6. Rank the Canadian provinces by their size from greatest to least. Then round the area of each province to **two** significant digits.

| Province | Area ($km^2$) | Rank | Rounded Area |
|---|---|---|---|
| Newfoundland | 404,519 | 9 | 400,000 |
| Prince Edward Island | 5,655 | 12 | 5,700 |
| Nova Scotia | 55,490 | 11 | 55,000 |
| New Brunswick | 73,436 | 10 | 73,000 |
| Quebec | 1,540,687 | 2 | 1,500,000 |
| Ontario | 1,068,587 | 3 | 1,100,000 |
| Manitoba | 650,090 | 7 | 650,000 |
| Saskatchewan | 651,903 | 6 | 650,000 |
| Alberta | 661,188 | 5 | 660,000 |
| British Columbia | 949,600 | 4 | 950,000 |
| Yukon Territory | 536,326 | 8 | 540,000 |
| Northwest Territories | 3,379,698 | 1 | 3,400,000 |

**Practice Supplement,** page 11

Name ____________ To follow text page 31

**Rounding**

Round these numbers.

| | | To the nearest ten | To the nearest hundred |
|---|---|---|---|
| 1. | 540 | 550 | 500 |
| 2. | 809 | 810 | 800 |
| 3. | 912 | 910 | 900 |
| 4. | 4,381 | 4,380 | 4,400 |
| 5. | 6,168 | 6,170 | 6,200 |
| 6. | 14,247 | 14,250 | 14,200 |
| 7. | 26,593 | 26,600 | 26,600 |
| 8. | 50,462 | 50,460 | 50,500 |

| | | To the nearest thousand | To the nearest ten thousand |
|---|---|---|---|
| 9. | 16,482 | 16,000 | 20,000 |
| 10. | 32,719 | 33,000 | 30,000 |
| 11. | 65,488 | 65,000 | 70,000 |
| 12. | 91,611 | 92,000 | 90,000 |
| 13. | 348,217 | 348,000 | 350,000 |
| 14. | 795,663 | 796,000 | 800,000 |
| 15. | 292,814 | 293,000 | 290,000 |

Round to the nearest dollar.

16. \$8.24 \$8
17. \$3.66 \$4
18. \$7.51 \$8
19. \$16.62 \$17
20. \$23.19 \$23
21. \$87.88 \$88

# Estimation

**Quick Review** Students write answers only for these exercises.

| 40 | 180 | 100 | 10 | 80 | 40 | 480 ÷ 6 | 30 × 5 |
|---|---|---|---|---|---|---|---|
| + 80 | − 90 | − 50 | + 70 | × 3 | × 4 | 20 × 4 | 100 ÷ 2 |

**Lesson Focus** To use mental math to estimate sums and differences

**Suggested Materials** Calculator

## Ideas for Getting Started

Write the numbers 695 and 216 on the chalkboard. Tell students that you want their help in finding the total. Enter 6,955 and 216 in your calculator for a sum of 7,171. Write this sum on the chalkboard. Allow time for students to notice that the sum is not correct. (Students may have estimated or have realized that because both numbers on the chalkboard are less than 1,000, their sum could not be larger than 2,000.) Point out that it is a common mistake to push a key twice. In this case, when 695 was entered, the last digit was pushed twice and the number entered was 6,955 instead of 695. Tell students that estimation and mental math are valuable skills in checking to see if a calculated answer is reasonable.

## Using Page 32

**Lesson Development** Have students look at the pictures and read the statements at the top of the page. "Without calculating, can you decide whether Mr. Gonzales has enough chairs to seat 150 customers?" (Students might suggest that because he had about 50 chairs in one room and about 70 in another, he could seat only about 120 people.) Point out that in many situations an estimated answer is all that is needed. Also emphasize the idea that if a calculator is used, it is wise to check the reasonableness of answers.

Remind students that estimation consists of the following steps:
1) Round the numbers to the desired place.
2) Find a special sum or difference.
Work through each of the examples on the page. Point out that in the first example the numbers were rounded to the nearest ten; in the second, to the nearest hundred. Tell students that we usually round to a place so that estimation can be done by using basic facts.

**Other Examples** Point out that the estimation in the first example could be in response to the following problem: Profit for November, $3,456; profit for December, $9,765; about how much more profit for December? The second example might be: Steak costs $8.95; lobster costs $12.25. About how much more is lobster?

**Warm Up** Be alert for students who round by simply dropping the last digits. Also look for errors that involve appropriate rounding procedures but basic fact errors in finding the special sums or differences.

## Estimating Sums and Differences: Mental Math

Mr. Gonzales owns a restaurant. He uses a calculator to find the answers to questions such as these. He makes estimates to see if the calculated answers are reasonable.

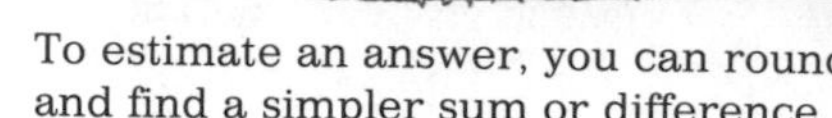

Took in $318 at lunch. Took in $589 at dinner. About how much?
48 chairs in one area. 72 chairs in another. About how many?


To estimate an answer, you can round and find a simpler sum or difference.

Round to the nearest ten.

| | |
|---|---|
| 48 → | 50 |
| + 72 → | + 70 |
| Estimate: | 120 |

About 120 chairs

Round to the nearest hundred.

| | |
|---|---|
| $318 → | $300 |
| + 589 → | + 600 |
| Estimate: | $900 |

About $900

**Other Examples**

Round to the nearest thousand.

| | |
|---|---|
| $9,765 → | 10,000 |
| − 3,456 → | − 3,000 |
| Estimate: | 7,000 |

Round to the nearest dollar.

| | |
|---|---|
| $12.25 → | $12 |
| − 8.95 → | − 9 |
| Estimate: | $ 3 |

**Warm Up** Estimate the sums or differences.

Round to the nearest ten: **1.** 87 + 55 150 **2.** 123 − 47 70

Round to the nearest hundred: **3.** 389 + 841 1,200 **4.** 1,276 − 653 600

Round to the nearest thousand: **5.** 8,638 + 9,299 18,000 **6.** 15,386 − 6,899 8,000

Round to the nearest dollar: **7.** $9.27 + $5.89 $15 **8.** $13.53 − $8.39 $6

32

## Follow Up

### Reteaching

Remind students that an ability to estimate answers helps to determine how reasonable a calculated answer is. We round the numbers to make the problem simpler. Review with students the process, using the following steps.

1. Read the problem carefully.
2. Round to the specified place.
3. Find the estimated answer.
4. Find the exact answer and compare with the estimate.

### Enrichment

Have students plan a dinner from a menu. The planned meal should be itemized and costs should be listed. Let students estimate the cost for one person and then for four people ordering the same food. Rounding should be to the nearest dollar. The exact cost can then be computed using the calculator.

| Assignment Guide | | | |
|---|---|---|---|
| | Minimum | Average | |
| page 33 | 1–20 | 1–25 | 1–25, TM |

Estimate by rounding to the nearest ten.

1. 94 + 46 = 140
2. 78 + 45 = 130
3. 123 − 58 = 60
4. 86 + 75 170
5. 134 − 69 60

Estimate by rounding to the nearest hundred.

6. 456 + 809 = 1,300
7. 875 − 299 = 600
8. 1,358 + 367 = 1,800
9. 1,423 − 777 600
10. 647 + 869 1,500

Estimate by rounding to the nearest thousand.

11. 15,562 − 9,274 = 7,000
12. 8,436 + 8,597 = 17,000
13. 11,906 − 5,888 = 6,000
14. 5,323 + 4,576 10,000
15. 13,099 − 3,644 9,000

Estimate by rounding to the nearest dollar.

16. $6.75 + 8.23 = $15.00
17. $15.39 − 8.89 = $ 6.00
18. $13.64 − 7.99 = $ 6.00
19. $9.27 + $8.65 $18.00
20. $16.72 − $8.54 $8.00

Estimate. Decide how to round.

21. 7,653 − 3,999 4,000
22. 4,432 + 6,579 11,000
23. 56,342 − 28,476 30,000

24. Advertising costs for a restaurant were $376 in May and $857 in June. Estimate the difference in those costs. $500

25. Restaurant income was as follows: January, $4,436; February, $4,737; March, $7,526. Estimate the total income. $17,000

**Think**

**Logical Reasoning**

Start with 20 counters. Two players take turns and each may pick up 1, 2, or 3 counters. The player who picks up the last counter loses the game.

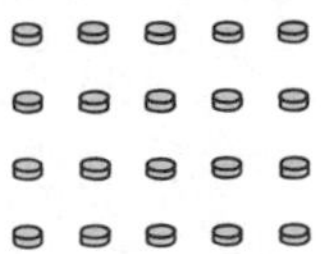

Try the game! Can you always win if you start first?
See teaching notes.

**Math**

More Practice, page 412, Set C



## Using Page 33

**Exercises 1–20** Allow students to complete these estimates mentally if possible. Some students may need to write down the special sums or products.

**Exercises 21–23** Encourage students to decide how to round so that they can use a basic fact to estimate the sums or differences for these exercises. For example, in exercise 23 a student should think, "60,000 minus 30,000 is 30,000." If the student decided to round to the nearest thousand, the estimate would be more difficult to do mentally.

**Exercises 24–25** Caution students to read these problems carefully. Note that essentially the same decisions are required as for exercises 21–23. Exercise 25 involves estimating the sum of three numbers.

**Think Math** Students may need to play this game several times before they can develop a strategy. A key discovery for students is that when there are five counters left, the person forced to make the first pick loses. Similarly, when there are ten or fifteen counters left, the person forced to make the first pick loses. Thus what happens when the first five counters are picked up is very important.

**More Practice,** page 412, Set C

## Ideas That Work

### Special Education

To reinforce rounding skills, let students work in pairs to play "Estimation War." Students will need 24 cards marked with 2, 3, or 4-digit addition exercises, and an answer key, keyed with estimated sums. Players take turns being dealer. Cards are mixed and all are dealt out to players. Players stack their cards facedown in a pile. To begin play, students turn over their top card, mentally round each addend to the nearest ten (hundred or thousand), and tell the estimated sum. The player with the greatest accurate estimate captures both cards. Play continues in this manner, with ties being resolved in traditional "War" fashion. If necessary, players can refer to the answer sheet to settle differences. The first player to capture all the cards is the winner.

**Practice Supplement,** page 12

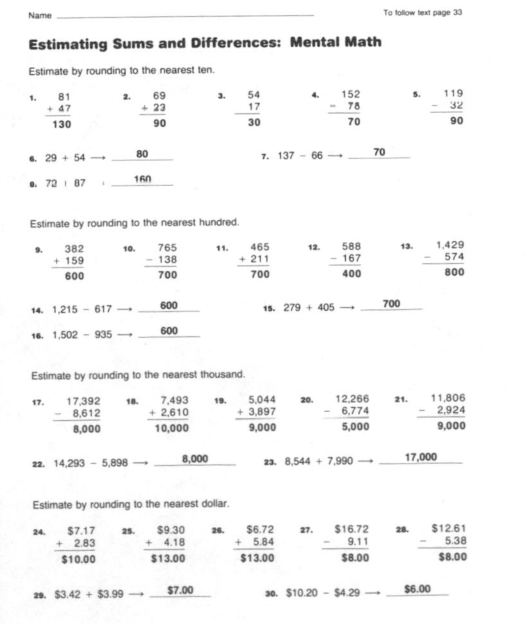

Name ______________ To follow text page 33

**Estimating Sums and Differences: Mental Math**

Estimate by rounding to the nearest ten.

1. 81 + 47 = 130
2. 69 + 23 = 90
3. 54 17 = 30
4. 152 − 78 = 70
5. 119 − 32 = 90
6. 29 + 54 → 80
7. 137 − 66 → 70
8. 72 + 87 → 160

Estimate by rounding to the nearest hundred.

9. 382 + 159 = 600
10. 765 − 138 = 700
11. 465 + 211 = 700
12. 588 − 167 = 400
13. 1,429 − 574 = 800
14. 1,215 − 617 → 600
15. 279 + 405 → 700
16. 1,502 − 935 → 600

Estimate by rounding to the nearest thousand.

17. 17,392 − 8,612 = 8,000
18. 7,493 + 2,610 = 10,000
19. 5,044 + 3,897 = 9,000
20. 12,266 − 6,774 = 5,000
21. 11,806 − 2,924 = 9,000
22. 14,293 − 5,898 → 8,000
23. 8,544 + 7,990 → 17,000

Estimate by rounding to the nearest dollar.

24. $7.17 + 2.83 = $10.00
25. $9.30 + 4.18 = $13.00
26. $6.72 + 5.84 = $13.00
27. $16.72 − 9.11 = $8.00
28. $12.61 − 5.38 = $8.00
29. $3.42 + $3.99 → $7.00
30. $10.20 − $4.29 → $6.00

# Applications

**Quick Review** Students give these sums and differences orally.

| 500 | 700 | 300 | 8,000 | 13,000 | 180 | 300 + 600 + 800 = |
|---|---|---|---|---|---|---|
| + 300 | − 400 | + 600 | + 7,000 | − 5,000 | − 90 | 200 + 400 + 400 = |

**Lesson Focus** To use estimation to solve word problems involving addition and subtraction skills; to use data from a Data Bank to solve word problems

## Ideas for Getting Started

Display the 5-Point Checklist presented on page 8 in Chapter 1. Remind students to look for the question, decide what data is needed, plan a solution, find the answer, and then check back to see if the answer seems reasonable. Present a problem such as, "Kim's family used 987 kilowatt hours one month and 919 kilowatt hours the next. About how many kilowatt hours less than 2,000 did they use during the two months?" As you help students work through the problem, emphasize the role of estimation in planning the answer and in deciding if the answer seems reasonable.

## Using Page 34

**Lesson Development** Read and discuss the meaning of a kilowatt-hour given at the top of the page. Specific information such as the number of kilowatt-hours that a household might use during a month might be researched by students.

Be sure students understand the directions for the problems on this page. Then help students work through the first problem. "What question is asked in the problem?" (How many more kilowatt-hours are used for the air conditioner than for the water heater?) "What important data is needed?" (The air conditioner uses 805 kWh; the water heater, 578 kWh.) "What operation can be used to *compare* the number of kilowatt-hours used?" (subtraction) "About how much is 805 minus 578?" (200) "What is the exact answer?" (227) "Does the answer seem reasonable?" (yes)

**Try This** A possible strategy, Choose the Operations, was introduced on page 16.

**Discussion** "What are we asked to find out about the number of kilowatt-hours used?" (How much does the third 300 kWh cost?) "What information do we know about the costs of kilowatt-hours?" (The first 300 kWh cost $11.89, the second 300 kWh cost $17.89; total cost for 900 kWh, $56.67.) "In planning the solution what do we need to know about the first 600 kWh?" (the total cost, $29.78) "How can we use this information to find the cost of the third 300 kWh?" (Subtract from $56.67.)

**Solution** The cost of the third 300 kWh of electricity is $26.89.

## Problem Solving: Using Estimation

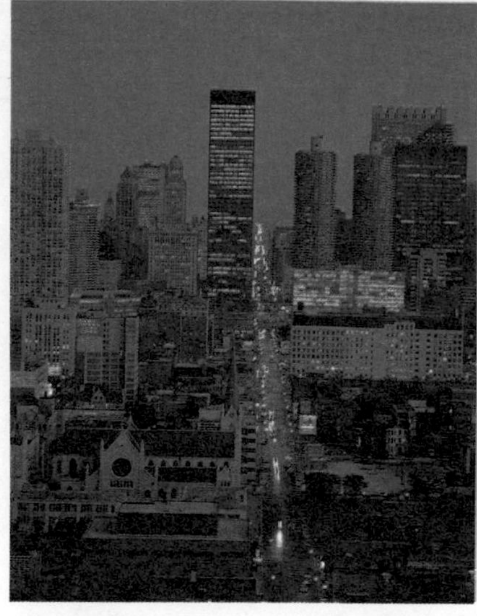

The amount of electricity we use is measured in kilowatt-hours (kWh). A kilowatt-hour is the amount of electrical power needed to light ten 100-watt bulbs for 1 hour.

Estimate the answer. Then find the exact answer. Compare the exact answer with the estimated answer to see whether the answer seems reasonable.

1. An air conditioner uses 805 kWh per month. A water heater uses 578 kWh. About how many more kilowatt-hours does the air conditioner use than the water heater? 200 kWh; 227 kWh
2. A color TV uses 395 kWh in a year. A black and white TV uses 109 kWh. How many kilowatt-hours do the two TV sets use in a year? 500 kWh; 504 kWh
3. A water heater uses 578 kWh per month, a refrigerator uses 141 kWh, and a clothes dryer uses 96 kWh. About how many kilowatt-hours is this per month altogether? 800 kWh; 815 kWh
4. A space heater uses 6,936 kWh per year. An air conditioner uses 9,660 kWh. About how many more kilowatt-hours does the air conditioner use than the heater? 3,000 kWh; 2,724 kWh
5. In a year, two television sets used 595 kWh of electricity. Electric lights used double this amount. About how many kilowatt-hours did the lights use? 1,200 kWh; 1,190 kWh
6. For one month electricity costs are $3.68 for lights, $1.07 for a color TV, and $7.98 for a space heater. About how much do all three cost together? $13.00; $12.73
7. The Pecks' electric bill for May was $14.79. The bill for June was $3.29 less than for May. The July bill was $4.82 more than the June bill. How much was the July bill? $17.00; $16.32
8. **Try This** The first 300 kWh of electricity cost $11.89. The second 300 kWh cost $17.89. The total cost for 900 kWh was $56.67. What did the third 300 kWh cost? Hint: Choose the operations. $26.89

34

## Follow Up

### Reteaching

Provide students with numbers to round to the nearest ten, hundred, and thousand. Review the rules for rounding on page 30. Then help students apply the rules to estimate to the nearest million in the following problem: A national park in Oregon has 82,536,826 acres. A park in Arizona has 5,873,265 acres. About how many acres in both parks? (about 89,000,000 acres)

82,536,826 → 83,000,000
5,873,265 → + 6,000,000
89,000,000

### Enrichment

Have the students use estimation to solve the problem below. Round to the nearest thousand.

If 80 characters are written across the monitor of a microcomputer and 60 lines are printed on each page from the printer, about how many characters will be printed on a page? **About 5,000** About how many pages of paper will 32,000 characters cover? **About 6 pages**

| Assignment Guide | | | |
|---|---|---|---|
| | Minimum | Average | Extended |
| page 34 | 1–6 | 1–7 | 1–8 |
| page 35 | 1–6 | 1–7 | 1–8 |

## Problem Solving: Using a Data Bank

A **data bank** is any source of information or **data.**

A microcomputer (or larger computer) can store large amounts of data on disks. When specific data is needed, the computer searches for it and a printer prints it on paper. Data stored in a computer can be passed to another computer over the telephone. This makes it possible for people all over the world to use data stored in a central library, or data bank.

Starting on page 407, a **Data Bank** has been printed for your use. Use it to find the data needed to solve the problems below and other Data Bank problems throughout the book.

1. Estimate how much longer the L1011 is than the 737. 20 m
2. Estimate how much greater the usual gross weight of the 747 is than that of the 707. 200,000 kg
3. Estimate the total number of passengers carried when a DC8, a DC9, and a DC10 leave on a trip. 600
4. Order the maximum lengths of all the transport planes listed in the Data Bank from the shortest to the longest. 27, 38, 41, 44, 46, 54, 56, 71
5. Order the 6 fastest plane speeds from greatest to least. Include each different speed only once. 1,030; 1,006; 982; 966; 943; 927
6. Estimate how much faster the maximum speed of the L1011 is than the speed of a plane that flies 695 km/h. 300 km/h
7. Order the gross weights of all the planes listed in the Data Bank from the heaviest plane to the lightest plane. 332,490 kg, 259,460 kg, 211,380 kg, 142,880 kg, 117,030 kg, 77,110 kg, 54,890 kg, 50,350 kg
8. **Try This** There were 398 men, women, and children on a 747. There were two times as many women as there were men. There were 103 men. Estimate the number of children. 100



## Using Page 35

**Lesson Development** Have a student read aloud the information at the top of the page. A classroom demonstration of software that includes sets of data would be useful. Tell students that there are data banks in a variety of different fields of study. For example, one data bank might provide articles from selected major newspapers and magazines. Another contains articles from medical journals. Still another might contain legal files from federal court decisions. Have students turn to the Data Bank on page 407 and look for the data needed to solve the problems on this page.

**Try This** A possible strategy, Choose the Operations, was introduced on page 16.

**Discussion** Have students tell in their own words what is being asked. (About how many of the group are children?) "How many men were there?" (about 100) "How many women?" (two times the number of men, or about 200) "About how many people altogether?" (400) "In planning the solution, what do we need to know about the number of men and women?" (the total number of men and women, or about 300) "How can we use this information to find the number of children?" (400 − 300)

**Solution** There are about 100 children. There are about 100 men and about 2 times 100, or 200, women. Thus there are 400 − (200 + 100) or about 100 children.

*The Data Bank—a unique Addison-Wesley feature—helps students learn to use sources of data.*

## Ideas That Work

### Calculator Bonus

Let students play the calculator game "How Close?" to practice estimation and mental math. Provide students with cards labeled 1 through 50. A second set of ten "key cards" is labeled in multiples of 5—from 55 to 100. One card from the stack of key cards is turned over in the center of the playing area to show the key number for that round.

To begin play, each player is dealt five cards from the set of consecutively numbered cards. Then players select any three of their five cards, attempting to select three numbers with a sum closest to the key number. Players make their selections by estimating or by mental addition. After making their selections, players place their cards on the playing surface for all to see. Calculators are then used to check the sums. Player having the sum closest to the key number is the winner.

**Practice Supplement,** page 13

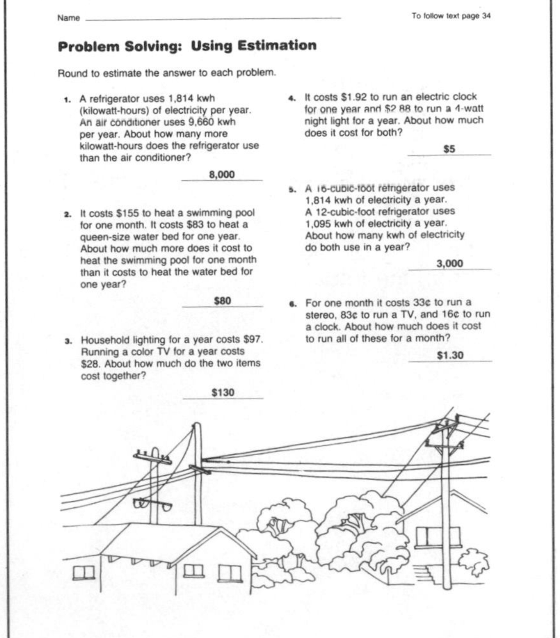

Name ______________________ To follow text page 34

**Problem Solving: Using Estimation**

Round to estimate the answer to each problem.

1. A refrigerator uses 1,814 kwh (kilowatt-hours) of electricity per year. An air conditioner uses 9,660 kwh per year. About how many more kilowatt-hours does the refrigerator use than the air conditioner? **8,000**
2. It costs $155 to heat a swimming pool for one month. It costs $83 to heat a queen-size water bed for one year. About how much more does it cost to heat the swimming pool for one month than it costs to heat the water bed for one year? **$80**
3. Household lighting for a year costs $97. Running a color TV for a year costs $28. About how much do the two items cost together? **$130**
4. It costs $1.92 to run an electric clock for one year and $2.88 to run a 4-watt night light for a year. About how much does it cost for both? **$5**
5. A 16-cubic-foot refrigerator uses 1,814 kwh of electricity a year. A 12-cubic-foot refrigerator uses 1,095 kwh of electricity a year. About how many kwh of electricity do both use in a year? **3,000**
6. For one month it costs 33¢ to run a stereo, 83¢ to run a TV, and 16¢ to run a clock. About how much does it cost to run all of these for a month? **$1.30**

# Addition

**Quick Review** Students write answers only for these addends.

12 + 3  10 + 4  16 + 2  18 + 4  22 + 6  4 + 10  25 + 5
19 + 1  32 + 2  30 + 4  13 + 3  12 + 1  28 + 0

**Lesson Focus** To find the sum of two addends

## Ideas for Getting Started

Tell students that a number like 12,321 is called a palindrome. That is, it reads the same backward or forward. Then write the following information on the chalkboard.

```
   567 ← start
+  765 ← reverse
  1332 ← sum
+ 2331 ← reverse
  3663   Palindrome
```

Help students find the palindrome for the following numbers: 314, 647, 86.

## Using Page 36

**Motivational Problem** Have students read the problem at the top of the page. "What question is asked about the cave art?" (How many deer, bison, and horses were in the sample?) "What data is needed to solve the problem?" (275 deer or bison and 189 horses) "What do we do to find the total number of animal drawings?" (add)

**Lesson Development** On the chalkboard work through adding the numbers 275 and 189. If necessary, use place-value models to describe the trading procedures. Write the answer to the problem, using a complete sentence beside the algorithm. Tell students to refer to the instruction boxes on the page as a reference if they need a reminder of the algorithm steps. Remind students that we can add 4- and 5-digit numbers just as we add 3-digit numbers except that sometimes we need to trade 10 hundreds for 1 thousand and 10 thousands for 1 ten-thousand.

**Other Examples** Point out the trades from hundreds to a thousand and from thousands to a ten thousand in the first and second examples. If necessary, give additional exercises like the second example in which students must correctly align the numbers. Note in the fourth example that students are instructed to add as with whole numbers. The decimal point can then be added to show dollars and cents.

**Warm Up** If students are having trouble aligning digits correctly, encourage them to write their problems on graph paper. Also, errors sometimes occur because students neglect to add in the digit that resulted from the trade.

## Adding Whole Numbers

The different kinds of animals drawn on the walls of caves in Europe were counted. In one sample, there were 275 deer or bison and 189 horses. How many of these kinds of animals were there?

Since we want to find the combined number of animals, we add.

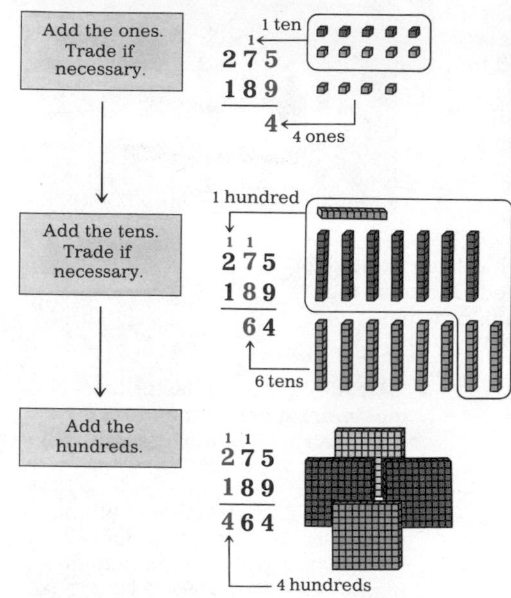


There were 464 of the animals in the sample.

**Other Examples**

```
  1 1       1 1 1        1   1         1 1 1
  864       9,684       56,384       $16.79
+ 759     +   919     + 95,430     +   3.43
1,623      10,603      151,814       $20.22
```

To add money, add as with whole numbers. Then write the answer as dollars and cents.

**Warm Up** Add.

```
1.  369    2.  974    3.  3,468    4.  27,397    5.  $15.26
  + 423      +  38      + 2,769      + 59,876      +  27.98
    792      1,012        6,237        87,273        $43.24
```

36

## Follow Up

### Reteaching

Review with students the idea of trading 10 ones for 1 ten in addition. Illustrate with two 2-digit numbers such as 26 + 37. If an abacus is available, use it to show this addition. Then show an example where no trading is necessary. Extend the review to show a 3- or 4-digit number. Point out that the trading process is the same as with the 2-digit numbers. If possible, use the abacus to illustrate this trading in larger problems.

### Enrichment

Supply students with the following problems. Have them write the missing digits in the blank spaces.

```
1.   3937      2.   5746
       86            237
      109             63
   + 4385         + 8128
    8,517         14,174

3.   53737     4.    347
     71059          8524
      7006            17
   +    69        +  735
   131,871         9,623
```

| Assignment Guide | | | |
|---|---|---|---|
| | Minimum | Average | Extended |
| page 37 | 1–29 | 1–30 | 1–30, TM |

Add.

| 1. | 2. | 3. | 4. | 5. |
|---|---|---|---|---|
| 864<br>+ 119<br>983 | 368<br>+ 576<br>944 | 965<br>+ 847<br>1,812 | 759<br>+ 86<br>845 | 8,468<br>+ 970<br>9,438 |

| 6. | 7. | 8. | 9. | 10. |
|---|---|---|---|---|
| 5,436<br>+ 2,849<br>8,285 | 7,652<br>+ 5,896<br>13,548 | 9,786<br>+ 4,528<br>14,314 | 9,657<br>+ 879<br>10,536 | 16,756<br>+ 8,439<br>25,195 |

| 11. | 12. | 13. | 14. | 15. |
|---|---|---|---|---|
| 18,765<br>+ 3,479<br>22,244 | 24,621<br>+ 36,569<br>61,190 | 38,570<br>+ 46,238<br>84,808 | 79,684<br>+ 86,598<br>166,282 | 98,729<br>+ 67,365<br>166,094 |

| 16. | 17. | 18. | 19. | 20. |
|---|---|---|---|---|
| $7.59<br>+ 3.86<br>$11.45 | $25.68<br>+ 13.49<br>$39.17 | $54.95<br>+ 39.89<br>$94.84 | $327.58<br>+ 269.29<br>$596.87 | $896.69<br>+ 436.74<br>$1,333.43 |

**21.** 754 + 398 1,152 **22.** 6,874 + 876 7,750 **23.** 9,863 + 7,476 17,339

**24.** 25,937 + 9,836 35,773 **25.** 34,943 + 26,875 61,818 **26.** 59,086 + 74,397 133,483

**27.** What is the sum of 6,743 and 8,635? Estimate to check your answer. 15,378

**28.** What is 879 more than 654? Estimate to check your answer. 1,533

**29.** An art historian took 9,678 photos of cave art in Europe. She took 6,395 photos of cave art in Africa. How many photos did she take in all? 16,073

**30.** Write a question that can be answered using the data below. Then solve the problem.

A collection of cave art had 978 pictures of elephants and 567 pictures of rhinoceroses.
See teaching notes.

**Think Math**

**Logical Reasoning**

Every row, column, and diagonal of a MAGIC SQUARE has the same "magic sum."

| 152 | 157 | 156 |
|---|---|---|
| 159 | 155 | 151 |
| 154 | 153 | 158 |

Draw a grid like this and complete a magic square using the numbers 151 through 159. What is the "magic sum?" 465

More Practice, page 413, Set A

## Using Page 37

**Exercises 1–26** Have students use a graph paper grid if they have difficulty aligning digits. Be alert for any difficulties students might have with problems involving larger numbers or amounts of money.

**Exercises 27–28** In each of these exercises students must decide how to round when estimating. In exercise 27 they should round to the nearest thousand, in exercise 28 to the nearest hundred.

**Exercises 29–30** Note in exercise 30 that students are asked to read the data given and write a question that can be answered using that data. This activity emphasizes the importance of understanding the question when the question is given. A possible question might be: How many pictures were there altogether?

**Think Math** Review the idea that every row, column, and diagonal of a Magic Square has the same sum. "What is the sum for this Magic Square?" By adding along the diagonal we can find the magic sum, 465. Help students see that they can find the middle number in the left hand column by adding the two numbers shown and subtracting from 465. They can find the middle number in the bottom row by adding the two numbers shown and subtracting from 465. In a similar manner they can find the number in the other diagonal and the number in the top row and right hand column. As a follow-up, have students subtract 78 from each number in the completed Magic Square. "Is this new square also a Magic Square?" (Yes)

**More Practice,** page 413, Set A

**Reteaching Supplement,** page 10

Name ______ To follow text page 37

**Adding Whole Numbers**

Add the ones. Trade if necessary. → Add the tens. Trade if necessary. → Add the hundreds. Trade if necessary. → Add the thousands.

| | | | |
|---|---|---|---|
| 4,228<br>+ 8,914<br>2 (8 + 4 = 12, Trade.) | 4,228<br>+ 8,914<br>42 (1 + 2 + 1 = 4, No trade!) | 4,228<br>+ 8,914<br>142 (2 + 9 = 11, Trade.) | 4,228<br>+ 8,914<br>13,142 |

Find the sums.

| 1. | 2. | 3. |
|---|---|---|
| 3,685<br>+ 9,421<br>13,106 | 2,364<br>679<br>+ 4,204<br>7,247 (Finish. 4 + 9 = 13, 13 + 4 = 17 Trade.) | $47.26<br>+ 28.36<br>$75.62 (Add. Then write as dollars and cents.) |

| 4. | 5. | 6. | 7. | 8. |
|---|---|---|---|---|
| 627<br>+ 298<br>925 | 126<br>+ 322<br>448 | 128<br>+ 137<br>265 | 508<br>+ 176<br>684 | 2,747<br>+ 5,869<br>8,616 |

| 9. | 10. | 11. | 12. | 13. |
|---|---|---|---|---|
| 1,664<br>+ 2,375<br>4,039 | 7,764<br>+ 568<br>8,332 | 56,387<br>+ 27,759<br>84,146 | 81,094<br>+ 6,646<br>87,740 | 60,673<br>+ 29,339<br>90,012 |

| 14. | 15. | 16. | 17. |
|---|---|---|---|
| $29.64<br>83.92<br>56.07<br>+ 62.49<br>$232.12 | $ 50.93<br>8.62<br>72.54<br>+ 123.45<br>$255.54 | $ 0.56<br>12.79<br>124.89<br>+ 4.74<br>$142.98 | $2,325.24<br>675.08<br>55.24<br>+ 3,262.45<br>$6,318.01 |

| 18. 2,345 + 62,109 | 19. $4,285.40 + $128.69 + $75.02 | 20. 26,424 + 5,264 + 67,495 |
|---|---|---|
| 2,345<br>+ 62,109<br>64,454 | $4,285.40<br>128.69<br>+ 75.02<br>$4,489.11 | 26,424<br>5,264<br>+ 67,495<br>99,183 |

**Enrichment Supplement,** page 10

Name ______ To follow text page 37

**Number Palindromes**

Numbers such as 181, 2,112, and 72,527 read the same forward and backward. They are called **number palindromes.** Study the example to see how to get a palindrome by reversing digits and adding.

| **Example** | | |
|---|---|---|
| | Starting with any number. | 438 |
| | Reverse it. | + 834 |
| | Find the sum. | 1,272 |
| | Reverse it. | + 2,721 |
| | The sum is a palindrome. | 3,993 |

Find the palindromes for each of the following numbers. Some will require several reversals.

| 1. | 2. | 3. | 4. |
|---|---|---|---|
| 871<br>+ 178<br>1,049<br>+ 9,401<br>10,450<br>+ 05,401<br>15,851 | 2,743<br>+ 3,472<br>6,215<br>+ 5,126<br>11,341<br>+ 14,311<br>25,652 | 69<br>+ 96<br>165<br>+ 561<br>726<br>+ 627<br>1,353<br>+ 3,531<br>4,884 | 78<br>+ 87<br>165<br>+ 561<br>726<br>+ 627<br>1,353<br>+ 3,531<br>4,884 |

| 5. | 6. | 7. | 8. |
|---|---|---|---|
| 581<br>+ 185<br>766<br>+ 667<br>1,433<br>+ 3,341<br>4,774 | 987<br>+ 789<br>1,776<br>+ 6,771<br>8,547<br>+ 7,458<br>16,005<br>+ 50,061<br>66,066 | 6,523<br>+ 3,256<br>9,779 | 5,187<br>+ 7,815<br>13,002<br>+ 20,031<br>33,033 |

**9.** Choose a number of your own. See if you can find a palindrome for it. Be careful, not all numbers will form palindromes. **Answers will vary.**

**Practice Supplement,** page 14

Name ______ To follow text page 37

**Adding Whole Numbers**

Add.

| 1. | 2. | 3. | 4. | 5. |
|---|---|---|---|---|
| 586<br>+ 127<br>713 | 75<br>+ 585<br>660 | 409<br>+ 682<br>1,091 | 166<br>+ 82<br>248 | 493<br>+ 134<br>627 |

| 6. | 7. | 8. | 9. | 10. |
|---|---|---|---|---|
| 6,808<br>+ 438<br>7,246 | 5,395<br>+ 105<br>5,500 | 2,519<br>+ 5,949<br>8,468 | 3,989<br>+ 1,484<br>5,473 | 6,417<br>+ 1,145<br>7,562 |

| 11. | 12. | 13. | 14. | 15. |
|---|---|---|---|---|
| 5,655<br>+ 2,179<br>7,834 | 8,625<br>+ 391<br>9,016 | 7,644<br>+ 3,115<br>10,759 | 5,773<br>+ 2,165<br>7,938 | 5,026<br>+ 755<br>5,781 |

| 16. | 17. | 18. | 19. | 20. |
|---|---|---|---|---|
| 48,406<br>+ 5,968<br>54,374 | 71,633<br>+ 2,491<br>74,124 | 80,015<br>+ 23,647<br>103,662 | 41,832<br>+ 16,009<br>57,841 | 51,224<br>+ 30,620<br>81,844 |

| 21. | 22. | 23. | 24. | 25. |
|---|---|---|---|---|
| $8.75<br>+ 2.90<br>$11.65 | $3.54<br>+ 6.88<br>$10.42 | $7.77<br>+ 8.91<br>$16.68 | $28.75<br>+ 4.66<br>$33.41 | $33.09<br>+ 14.85<br>$47.94 |

| 26. | 27. | 28. | 29. | 30. |
|---|---|---|---|---|
| $16.89<br>+ 25.05<br>$41.94 | $169.95<br>+ 32.50<br>$202.45 | $248.68<br>+ 193.13<br>$441.81 | $404.04<br>+ 271.38<br>$675.42 | $853.07<br>+ 206.49<br>$1,059.56 |

| 31. 791 + 847 | 32. 1,768 + 834 | 33. 5,400 + 897 | 34. $7.94 + $1.42 |
|---|---|---|---|
| 791<br>+ 847<br>1,638 | 1,768<br>+ 834<br>2,602 | 5,400<br>+ 897<br>6,297 | $7.94<br>+ 1.42<br>$9.36 |

| 35. 631 + 87 | 36. 5,642 + 79 | 37. $18.63 + $7.19 | 38. $14.19 + $8.13 |
|---|---|---|---|
| 631<br>+ 87<br>718 | 5,642<br>+ 79<br>5,721 | $18.63<br>+ 7.19<br>$25.82 | $14.19<br>+ 8.13<br>$22.32 |

# Addition

**Quick Review** Students give these sums orally.

6 + 9 + 4  8 + 2 + 7  5 + 3 + 4  7 + 0 + 9  3 + 9 + 1  6 + 0 + 9
7 + 4 + 2  4 + 3 + 8  8 + 1 + 6  5 + 8 + 0  2 + 8 + 4

**Lesson Focus** To find sums of three or more addends

**Suggested Materials** Number cards labeled 0 through 9 (TRB p. 279)

## Ideas for Getting Started

Call out a number such as 36. Then hold up one of the number cards, for example 8, and have students mentally add that number to 36 and give the sum aloud. Use several different starting numbers, and have students add numbers from the number cards. This type of mental arithmetic requires the use of skills that students will need in column addition.

## Using Page 38

**Motivational Problem** After students read the problem at the top of the page, encourage them to share stories about any canoe trips they may have taken. "What questions do we want to answer about Hal's canoe trip?" (How far did the group travel?) Have students describe the data given that will help solve the problem. "How could this data be used to find the total distance the group traveled?" (Add the numbers.)

**Lesson Development** Work through the problem with students, discussing each step. First, add the ones, starting from top to bottom. Emphasize that 20 ones can be traded for 2 tens. Then discuss hints for adding ones, such as looking for combinations that make 10 and adding from bottom to top to check your work. Next add the tens. Emphasize that the 2 resulting from the trading must also be added with the tens. Then, add the hundreds. Emphasize that the digits must be aligned correctly so that it is clear in which place the digits belong. Use a complete sentence to write the answer to the problem.

**Other Examples** As you discuss each example, note that in the second and third examples digits resulting from trades are greater than 1. The students who have become accustomed to adding only two addends need to adjust to this situation and remember to add these numbers as they add in each of the different places.

**Warm Up** Be alert for situations described above in which students assume that the digit resulting from a trade will be 1. Encourage students to check their work by adding from bottom to top as well as from top to bottom.

## Column Addition

Hal went on a 4-week canoe trip in Canada. His group traveled these distances on different lakes and rivers:

Trout Lake—97 km
Otter Lake—164 km
Contact Lake—26 km
Churchill River—285 km

How far did the group travel? Since we want to find the total distance traveled, we add.

Add the ones. Trade if necessary. → Add the tens. Trade if necessary. → Add the hundreds.

| Add the ones. | Add the tens. | Add the hundreds. |
|---|---|---|
| ²97 (7 + 4 = 11) | ²97 | ²97 |
| 164 (11 + 6 = 17) | ²164 | ²164 |
| 26 (17 + 5 = 22) | 26 | 26 |
| 285 | 285 | 285 |
| 2 | 72 | 572 |

The group traveled 572 km.

**Other Examples**

| | | | |
|---|---|---|---|
| 5 | ¹¹674 | ²³²7,437 | ²²²²³ $ 8,650.79 |
| 9 | 398 | 8,396 | 3,596.38 |
| 7 | + 407 | ²480 | 474.67 |
| + 6 | 1,479 | + 16,789 | + 15,968.49 |
| 27 | | 33,102 | $28,690.33 |

**Warm Up** Add.

| 1. | 2. | 3. | 4. | 5. |
|---|---|---|---|---|
| 276 | 5,963 | 18,365 | 78,349 | $9,346.38 |
| 89 | 286 | 744 | 63,258 | 647.89 |
| + 147 | 4,932 | 7,638 | 91,340 | 521.70 |
| 512 | + 694 | + 24,502 | + 67,536 | + 6,487.39 |
| | 11,875 | 51,249 | 300,483 | $17,003.36 |

38

## Follow Up

### Reteaching

Encourage students to try "adding by endings." To add by endings, students hold the tens digit in mind and add the ones digits. If the sum is ≥ 10, the answer will be in the next tens decade. For instance in 14 + 6, since 6 + 4 = 10, the answer will be in the decade 20–29.

since 7 + 7 = 14
17 + 7 = 24

since 6 + 4 = 10
6 + 24 = 30

| | | |
|---|---|---|
| 6 | | 6 |
| 7 | 24 | 7 |
| 8 | 17 | 8 |
| + 9 | | + 9 |
| | | 30 |

### Enrichment

Have students find the missing numbers below.

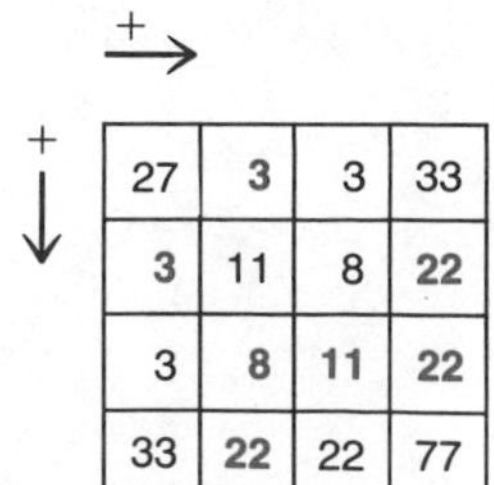

| 27 | 3 | 3 | 33 |
|---|---|---|---|
| 3 | 11 | 8 | 22 |
| 3 | 8 | 11 | 22 |
| 33 | 22 | 22 | 77 |

| Assignment Guide | Minimum | Average | Extended |
|---|---|---|---|
| page 39 | 1–17, TM | 1–17, TM | 1–18, TM |

Add.

| 1. | | 2. | | 3. | | 4. | | 5. | |
|---|---|---|---|---|---|---|---|---|---|
| | 674 | | 576 | | 5,643 | | 17,863 | | $236.59 |
| | 39 | | 380 | | 796 | | 9,748 | | 87.65 |
| | + 897 | | + 998 | | + 8,321 | | + 3,675 | | + 479.23 |
| | 1,610 | | 1,954 | | 14,760 | | 31,286 | | $803.47 |

| 6. | | 7. | | 8. | | 9. | | 10. | |
|---|---|---|---|---|---|---|---|---|---|
| | 9,863 | | 28,648 | | 96,700 | | 75,309 | | $375.75 |
| | 469 | | 7,379 | | 68,488 | | 64,752 | | 463.23 |
| | 527 | | 15,648 | | 34,599 | | 37,867 | | 550.88 |
| | + 8,436 | | + 32,571 | | + 67,347 | | + 59,346 | | + 795.69 |
| | 19,295 | | 84,246 | | 267,134 | | 237,274 | | $2,185.55 |

11. 23,468 + 847 + 9,635 33,950

12. 65,479 + 5,638 + 978 + 747 72,842

13. 68,666 + 7,435 + 8,627 84,728

14. 43,999 + 27,364 + 9,765 81,128

15. Estimate, then find the sum of 7,246, 8,907, and 3,549. 20,000; 19,702

16. Make up a story problem about this map of 3 lakes. Solve. Answers will vary.

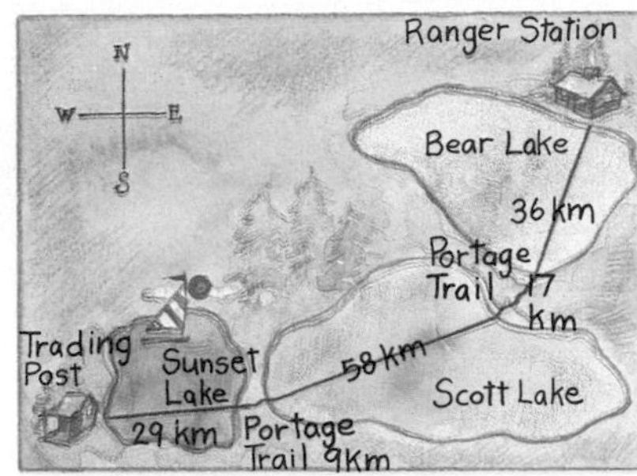


17. Linda's group took these canoe trips: Hale Lake—119 km; Hunter Bay—57 km; Hidden Lake—96 km; Lynx Lake—9 km; Otter Lake—274 km. How far did the group travel? 555 km

18. Is the total area of the five Great Lakes more than or less than 275,000 km² (square kilometers)? Estimate first. Then find the exact answer. Compare it with your estimate. less than; 245,222 km²

| Areas of the Great Lakes (km²) | |
|---|---|
| Superior 82,414 | Huron 59,596 |
| Michigan 58,016 | Erie 25,719 |
| Ontario 19,477 | |

**Think Math**

**Mental Math**

If the letter A = $1, B = $2, C = $3, . . . , Z = $26, what is the "value" of a name?

| S | U | S | A | N |
|---|---|---|---|---|
| $19 | $21 | $19 | $1 | $14 |

"Susan" has a value of $74. List the letter values. Use mental math to find the value of your name.

Can you find some names worth $100 or more? See teaching notes.

More Practice, page 413, Set B



## Using Page 39

**Exercises 1–10** Observe students as they work these problems. Be alert for errors caused by difficulty with mental arithmetic as columns are added or for errors resulting from misalignment of digits. Encourage students who have alignment problems to use a graph paper grid to show their work.

**Exercises 11–14** It is particularly important that students align digits correctly when writing these problems. You may also wish to suggest that "rough estimates" be made to decide if their answer seems reasonable.

**Exercise 15** In this exercise rounding to the nearest thousand would be most helpful in estimating the sum. Note that two answers are required here: an estimated sum and an exact sum.

**Exercise 16** In this exercise students are asked to study the map given and make up a story problem about the situation. A sample problem might be: Marie's group made a trip from the trading post to the ranger station. How many miles did they travel?

**Exercise 18** Be sure students understand that they are to estimate first, then find the answer on a calculator and compare it with the estimate.

**Think Math** This activity is a good vehicle for estimation, mental mathematics, and the use of a guess-and-check strategy. As a follow-up for this activity, ask students to find the value of the following words: sum, addend, difference, compare.

**More Practice,** page 413, Set B

## Ideas That Work

### Special Education

The game "Roll em" can help students practice place-value concepts and comparison skills. Each student in turn rolls the number cube (labeled 0, 2, 4, 5, 8, and 9) four times. The first roll is for the number of ones; the second roll, the number of tens; the third roll, the number of hundreds; and the fourth roll, the number of thousands. Student then selects pieces from place-value materials to model each of the four numbers. The student with the set of blocks representing the largest number is the winner.

After students have had some practice in playing the game, have them write out the number they have represented with their place-value materials.

**Practice Supplement,** page 15

Name ______________________ To follow text page 39

**Column Addition**

Add.

| 1. | | 2. | | 3. | | 4. | | 5. | |
|---|---|---|---|---|---|---|---|---|---|
| | 935 | | 371 | | 2,457 | | 12,963 | | 3,856 |
| | 68 | | 279 | | 383 | | 758 | | 9,635 |
| | + 402 | | + 727 | | + 78 | | + 5,605 | | + 6,709 |
| | **1,405** | | **1,377** | | **2,918** | | **19,326** | | **20,200** |

| 6. | | 7. | | 8. | | 9. | | 10. | |
|---|---|---|---|---|---|---|---|---|---|
| | 635 | | 3,700 | | 732 | | 7,623 | | 4,276 |
| | 27 | | 894 | | 568 | | 507 | | 4,000 |
| | 568 | | 787 | | 8 | | 832 | | 3,887 |
| | + 40 | | + 63 | | + 47 | | + 567 | | + 5,965 |
| | **1,270** | | **5,444** | | **1,355** | | **9,609** | | **18,128** |

| 11. | | 12. | | 13. | | 14. | | 15. | |
|---|---|---|---|---|---|---|---|---|---|
| | $3.83 | | $5.17 | | $17.00 | | $15.62 | | $488.50 |
| | 6.27 | | 2.35 | | 3.60 | | 3.87 | | 217.17 |
| | + 4.81 | | + 4.40 | | + 4.85 | | + 25.38 | | + 362.24 |
| | **$14.91** | | **$11.92** | | **$25.45** | | **$44.87** | | **$1,067.91** |

| 16. | | 17. | | 18. | | 19. | | 20. | |
|---|---|---|---|---|---|---|---|---|---|
| | 18,981 | | 24,479 | | 63,521 | | $575.98 | | $493.21 |
| | 2,747 | | 83,024 | | 10,409 | | 202.60 | | 685.82 |
| | 25,636 | | 1,695 | | 36,824 | | 391.27 | | 403.13 |
| | + 54,257 | | + 44,921 | | + 19,338 | | + 89.74 | | + 902.06 |
| | **101,621** | | **154,119** | | **130,092** | | **$1,259.59** | | **$2,484.22** |

21. 206 + 380 + 974

**206**
**380**
**+ 974**
**1,560**

22. 27,643 + 208 + 13,461

**27,643**
**208**
**+ 13,461**
**41,312**

23. 538 + 66 + 89,401

**538**
**66**
**+ 89,401**
**90,005**

24. $15.07 + $7.19 + $4.29

**$15.07**
**7.19**
**+ 4.29**
**$26.55**

# Subtraction

**Quick Review** Students write the numbers that make these number sentences true.
3 × (4 × 3) = (3 × 4) × [3]  [7] × (2 × 3) = (7 × 2) × 3  3 + [1] = 2 + 2
([5] × 2) + (6 × [1]) = 10 + 6  10 − 2 = [5] + 3  ([8] × 5) = (20 × 2)

**Lesson Focus** To find differences of whole numbers

## Ideas for Getting Started

To assess students' understanding of the subtraction algorithm, provide the activity below.

```
   563    Start with a 3-digit
 − 365    number. Reverse the
   198    digits and subtract
 + 891    the smaller number
  1089    from the larger.
          Reverse again, and add.
```

Ask for three volunteers to try this with other 3-digit numbers. "What did you discover?" (The answer is always 1,089.)

## Using Page 40

**Motivational Problem** After students have read the problem at the top of the page, have them tell what question is asked about the balloons. (How much farther did the large balloon travel?) "What is the record distance for the large balloon?" (611 km) "The small balloon?" (369 km) "What operation could we use to find how much farther the large balloon traveled?" (subtract)

**Lesson Development** Write 611 − 369 on the chalkboard in algorithm form. Work through each step as shown by the instruction boxes on the page. Emphasize the importance of writing accurately the numbers resulting from the trades; carelessly written numbers can cause errors in the subtraction. Be sure students understand that it is not always necessary to trade when subtracting. Have a volunteer write the answer to the problem in a complete sentence. Suggest that students refer back to the instruction boxes if they have difficulty with the subtraction algorithm.

**Other Examples** Note that the first example involves zero difference in the hundreds place. In the second example there is no number to subtract in the thousands place. The third example involves subtracting zero in the ones place. In the fourth example remind students that to subtract money, subtract as with whole numbers and then write the answer as dollars and cents.

**Warm Up** Be alert for errors involving basic subtraction facts, subtracting the smaller digit from the larger digit regardless of whether it is in the top number or the bottom number, and difficulties involved in trading.

## Subtracting Whole Numbers

A recent record for distance traveled in a large hot-air balloon was 611 km. The record for a small hot-air balloon was 369 km. How much farther did the large balloon travel?

Since we want to compare the distances, we subtract.

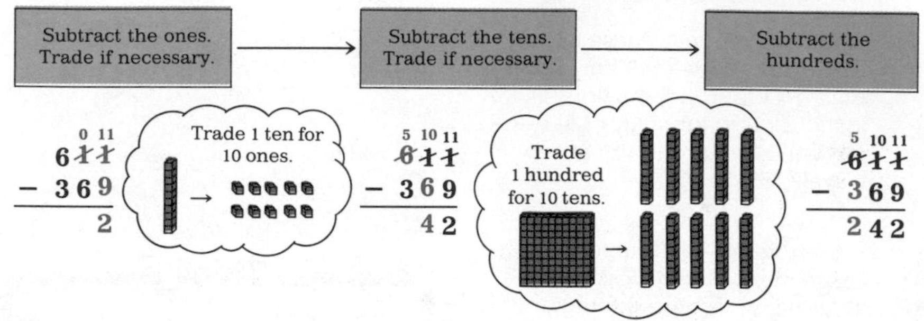


The large balloon traveled 242 km farther.

**Other Examples**

```
  7 12 15     5 13 11 11      4 12 16      5 12 11 15
  8 3 5       6,4 2 1       7 5,3 6 4     $6 3.2 5
− 7 9 6     −   9 7 5     − 3 4,7 8 0   −   2 4.6 9
    3 9       5,4 4 6       4 0,5 8 4     $3 8.5 6
```

To subtract money, subtract as with whole numbers. Then write the answer as dollars and cents.

**Warm Up** Subtract. Check by adding.

```
1.   847    2.   653    3.  8,637    4.  83,216    5.  $37.75
   − 269       − 576        − 789      − 29,457       − 19.98
     578          77        7,848        53,759        $17.77
```



## Follow Up

### Reteaching

Use the abacus to show subtraction of a 2-digit number such as 63 − 49. Focus on why a trade must be made (we cannot subtract 9 ones from 3 ones). Emphasize the trading of 1 ten for 10 ones, and remind students of how they traded 10 ones for 1 ten in the adding process. Work through the algorithm step by step. Ask students to describe what happens after trading for ones. (Subtract the 9 ones, then subtract the 4 tens from the remaining 5 tens.)

### Enrichment

Major League Attendance

| | National (NL) | American (AL) |
|---|---|---|
| Game 1 | 12,699 | 20,116 |
| Game 2 | 19,739 | 27,264 |
| Game 3 | 9,432 | 7,349 |

Have students use the table above to answer the following questions.

1. In the National League (NL) how many more fans attended Game 2 than Game 3? **10,307**
2. How many more fans attended AL Game 1 than NL Game 1? **7,417**
3. Which league had the greater attendance for its 3 games? **AL:54,729**

| Assignment Guide | Minimum | Average | Extended |
|---|---|---|---|
| page 41 | 1–24 | 1–25 | 1–26, TM |

Subtract.

1. 527 − 188 339
2. 963 − 879 84
3. 7,432 − 865 6,567
4. 8,276 − 5,498 2,778
5. 6,213 − 5,654 559
6. 4,136 − 1,874 2,262
7. 7,238 − 6,450 788
8. 16,342 − 9,237 7,105
9. 27,641 − 19,506 8,135
10. 56,375 − 37,588 18,787
11. 87,465 − 59,387 28,078
12. 93,274 − 8,680 84,594
13. \$9.75 − 3.98 \$5.77
14. \$18.25 − 7.56 \$10.69
15. \$256.45 − 97.75 \$158.70
16. 742 − 578 164
17. 9,534 − 806 8,728
18. 7,316 − 4,857 2,459
19. 17,386 − 9,419 7,967
20. 78,211 − 65,879 12,332
21. \$56.32 − \$38.49 \$17.83
22. Estimate, then find the difference of 7,219 and 3,899. 3,000; 3,320
23. Estimate, then find how many more 925 is than 478. 400; 447
24. The record altitude (height above sea level) for an AX-2 balloon was 3,477 m. The record for an AX-3 balloon was 4,642 m. How much greater was the second record? 1,165 m
25. Make up the missing information and solve the problem. A recent record distance for a helium balloon was 3,339 km. By how much did Tim's balloon flight miss the record? Answers will vary.

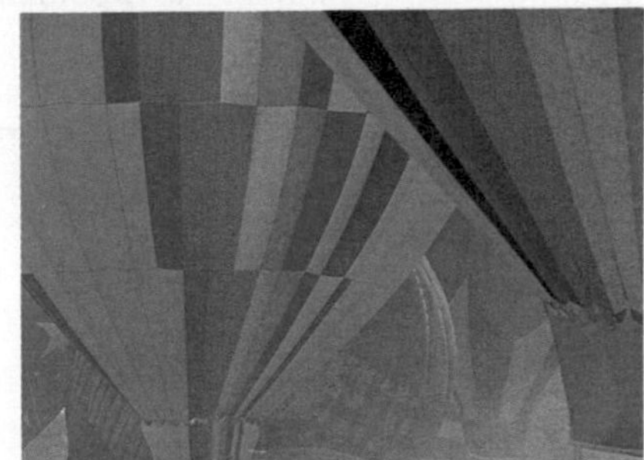

26. **DATA BANK** How much greater is the altitude for an AX-10 balloon than for an AX-7 balloon? than for an AX-3 balloon? (See Data Bank, page 409.) 4,929 m; 11,573 m

**Think** — **Logical Reasoning**

Copy each problem and supply the missing digits.

A.
3 94
■,6■■
\+ 5,■12 8
9,506

B.
5 7
■,61■
− 2,8■9 3
2,■78 7

C.
8 0 4
■,■7■
− 3■6 9
7,678

D.
4 5
■,3■9
\+ 6,54■ 3
■0,■02
1 9

**Math**

More Practice, page 413, Set C



## Using Page 41

**Exercises 1–21** Make sure that students align the digits correctly when they copy exercises 3, 8, 12, 14, 15, 17, and 19. Also be sure that students are not making errors involving zeros in exercises 7, 9, 12, and 17.

**Exercises 22–23** Caution students to think carefully about the correct choices for the place to which they estimate in these exercises.

**Exercise 25** In this exercise students are asked to supply missing information—the distance of Tim's balloon flight.

**Data Bank** Remind students of the discussion of the Data Bank on page 35. Have them read the Data Bank problem and decide what data is needed. Encourage them to search the Data Bank in the back of the book for this information.

**Think Math** Encourage students to select a digit for a missing place, try it, and then change it if it does not work. Students often find the problems difficult because they are reluctant to try a digit. A guess-and-check strategy is useful for beginning to think about the problems. Note in exercise A that the digit resulting from a trade influences the digit in the hundreds place. In exercise B the result of a trade must be considered in the tens place and in the hundreds place. Some students may use the idea of addition as a way of checking subtraction to find some of the missing digits in exercises B and C. Suggest that students make up other missing digit problems of their own.

**More Practice,** page 413, Set C

**Reteaching Supplement,** page 11

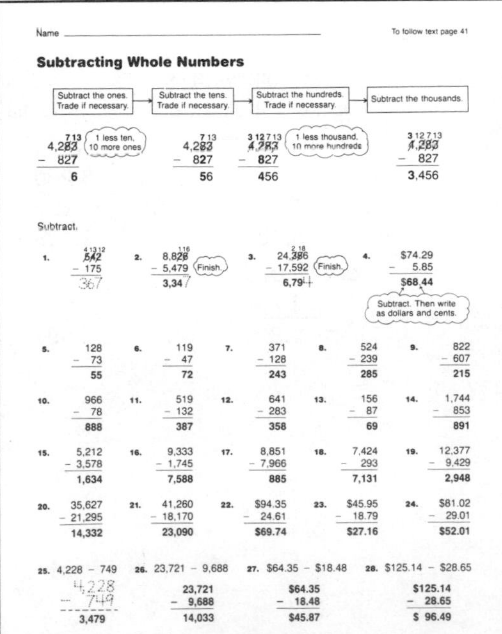

Name ______ To follow text page 41

**Subtracting Whole Numbers**

Subtract the ones. Trade if necessary. → Subtract the tens. Trade if necessary. → Subtract the hundreds. Trade if necessary. → Subtract the thousands.

4,283 − 827 = 6 (1 less ten, 10 more ones) → 56 → 456 (1 less thousand, 10 more hundreds) → 3,456

Subtract.

1. 542 − 175 367
2. 8,826 − 5,479 3,347 (Finish.)
3. 24,386 − 17,592 6,794 (Finish.)
4. \$74.29 − 5.85 \$68.44 (Subtract. Then write as dollars and cents.)
5. 128 − 73 55
6. 119 − 47 72
7. 371 − 128 243
8. 524 − 239 285
9. 822 − 607 215
10. 966 − 78 888
11. 519 − 132 387
12. 641 − 283 358
13. 156 − 87 69
14. 1,744 − 853 891
15. 5,212 − 3,578 1,634
16. 9,333 − 1,745 7,588
17. 8,851 − 7,966 885
18. 7,424 − 293 7,131
19. 12,377 − 9,429 2,948
20. 35,627 − 21,295 14,332
21. 41,260 − 18,170 23,090
22. \$94.35 − 24.61 \$69.74
23. \$45.95 − 18.79 \$27.16
24. \$81.02 − 29.01 \$52.01
25. 4,228 − 749 3,479
26. 23,721 − 9,688 14,033
27. \$64.35 − \$18.48 \$45.87
28. \$125.14 − \$28.65 \$ 96.49

**Enrichment Supplement,** page 11

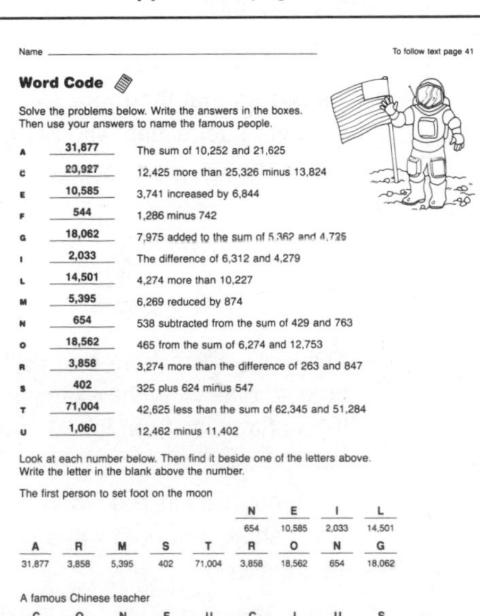

Name ______ To follow text page 41

**Word Code**

Solve the problems below. Write the answers in the boxes. Then use your answers to name the famous people.

| | | |
|---|---|---|
| A | 31,877 | The sum of 10,252 and 21,625 |
| C | 23,927 | 12,425 more than 25,326 minus 13,824 |
| E | 10,585 | 3,741 increased by 6,844 |
| F | 544 | 1,286 minus 742 |
| G | 18,062 | 7,975 added to the sum of 5,362 and 4,725 |
| I | 2,033 | The difference of 6,312 and 4,279 |
| L | 14,501 | 4,274 more than 10,227 |
| M | 5,395 | 6,269 reduced by 874 |
| N | 654 | 538 subtracted from the sum of 429 and 763 |
| O | 18,562 | 465 from the sum of 6,274 and 12,753 |
| R | 3,858 | 3,274 more than the difference of 263 and 847 |
| S | 402 | 325 plus 624 minus 547 |
| T | 71,004 | 42,625 less than the sum of 62,345 and 51,284 |
| U | 1,060 | 12,462 minus 11,402 |

Look at each number below. Then find it beside one of the letters above. Write the letter in the blank above the number.

The first person to set foot on the moon

N E I L
654 10,585 2,033 14,501

A R M S T R O N G
31,877 3,858 5,395 402 71,004 3,858 18,562 654 18,062

A famous Chinese teacher

C O N F U C I U S
23,927 18,562 654 544 1,060 23,927 2,033 1,060 402

**Practice Supplement,** page 16

Name ______ To follow text page 41

**Subtracting Whole Numbers**

Subtract.

1. 732 − 568 164
2. 431 − 255 176
3. 643 − 376 267
4. 832 − 567 265
5. 756 − 548 208
6. 3,678 − 989 2,689
7. 8,632 − 747 7,885
8. 7,219 − 3,957 3,262
9. 9,756 − 6,382 3,374
10. 5,428 − 3,077 2,351
11. 46,788 − 9,759 37,029
12. 83,121 − 4,783 78,338
13. 92,164 − 33,912 58,252
14. 87,474 − 21,686 65,788
15. 25,279 − 20,562 4,717
16. \$3.56 − 1.34 \$2.22
17. \$2.75 − 1.26 \$1.49
18. \$3.47 − 2.18 \$1.29
19. \$5.63 − 3.28 \$2.35
20. \$17.41 − 4.35 \$13.06
21. \$29.34 − 6.88 \$22.46
22. \$75.28 − 31.66 \$43.62
23. \$228.94 − 37.69 \$191.25
24. \$147.37 − 19.99 \$127.38
25. \$472.85 − 257.03 \$215.82
26. 16,824 − 9,743 7,081
27. 17,624 − 8,715 8,909
28. 8,154 − 6,107 2,047
29. 9,203 − 7,151 2,052
30. 18,707 − 7,659 11,048
31. 634 − 291 343
32. 5,329 − 777 4,552
33. \$46.23 − \$12.69 \$33.54
34. \$89.60 − \$17.81 \$71.79
35. \$23.68 − \$11.29 \$12.39
36. \$407.21 − \$213.07 \$194.14
37. 641 − 259 382
38. 1,719 − 806 913

# Subtraction

**Quick Review** Students write the symbols (>, <, =) that will make these number sentences true.

6 + 2 (=) 4 + 4   10 − 1 (<) 8 + 2   9 + 0 (>) 5 + 3   8 + 1 (=) 6 + 3
3 + 3 (=) 6 − 0   9 + 2 (<) 8 + 4   7 − 2 (<) 9 − 3

**Lesson Focus** To find differences involving one or more zeros

**Suggested Materials** Place-value materials

## Ideas for Getting Started

Use place-value models to illustrate that 3 hundreds can be thought of as 30 tens. Ask questions such as, "5 hundreds, how many tens? 2 hundreds, how many tens? 7 hundreds, how many tens?" Have students use models to practice making the trades as discussed. Write a number, for example 302, on the chalkboard. Tell students to think of the 3 hundreds and the 0 tens as 30 tens. They could record the following result of trading one of these tens.

```
2 9 12
3 0 2
```

Have students show the result of trading a ten for each of these numbers: 403, 605, 507, 804.

## Using Page 42

**Motivational Problem** Have students read the information at the top of the page and discuss the importance of following safety rules in sports activities. "What is the question asked about baseball and soccer?" (How many more injuries in baseball than in soccer?) "Where can we get the data needed to answer this question?" (from the table; baseball, 9,807; soccer, 4,158) "What operation can we use to find the difference between these two numbers?" (subtraction)

**Lesson Development** On the chalkboard write the problem 9,807 − 4,158 in algorithm form. Work through each step of the procedure as shown in the instruction boxes. Emphasize that when trading a ten, the 80 tens are marked out to show that 79 tens are left. Emphasize careful recording of the results of these trades. Have students use addition to check the result of their subtraction. Suggest that students refer to the instruction boxes for future help if they have difficulty with the subtraction algorithm.

**Other Examples** Note in the first example that there are two zeros and that 1 ten is traded leaving 69 tens. In the second example it is not necessary to trade 1 ten for 10 ones, but it is necessary to trade 1 hundred for 10 tens. In example 3 note that the idea that 5,000 is 500 tens is used.

**Warm Up** Be alert for trading errors in these exercises and for students who subtract zeros in the top number from the corresponding digit in the bottom number.

## Subtracting with Zeros

If we follow the safety rules in our sports activities, we can have fun with fewer accidents!

How many more injuries per 100,000 participants were there in baseball than in soccer?

**Sports Injuries**
(per one hundred thousand participants in a recent year)

| | |
|---|---|
| Baseball—9,807 | Soccer—4,158 |
| Football—9,587 | Snow Skiing—1,101 |
| Ice Hockey—8,082 | Ice Skating—505 |
| Basketball—5,383 | Tennis—429 |

Since we want to compare the two numbers, we subtract.

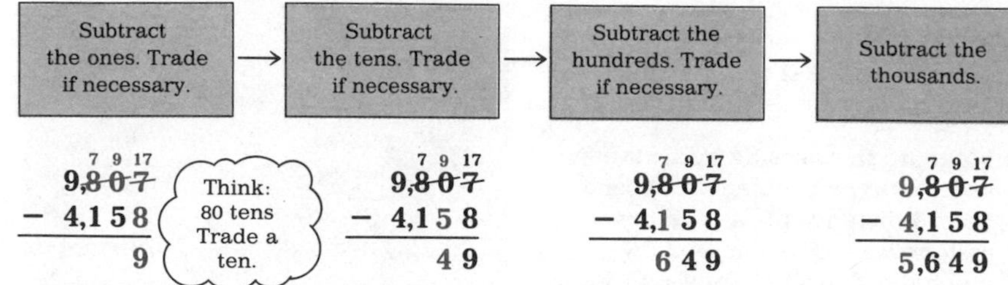


There were 5,649 more injuries per 100,000 participants in baseball than in soccer.

**Other Examples**

```
  69 10       6 15 10      4 9 9 12     5 9 9 9 10
  700         7,605        5,002        60,000
− 356       − 2,972      − 2,684     − 46,521
  344         4,633        2,318       13,479
```

**Warm Up** Subtract. Check by adding.

1. 508 − 169 = 339
2. 900 − 367 = 533
3. 7,065 − 3,897 = 3,168
4. 8,007 − 3,669 = 4,338
5. 36,000 − 17,386 = 18,614

42

## Follow Up

### Reteaching

Tell students that there are two ways to think about subtracting with zeros.

1. Think of trading as necessary at each place.

```
     9  9
  7 10 10 16
  8, 0  0  6
− 2, 2  5  9
```

2. Think of trading from one of the total number of tens. In the example above, think of trading 1 ten for 10 ones leaving 799 tens.

Go through each procedure with students to show that both ways produce a correct answer.

### Enrichment

Write the following problems on the chalkboard. Challenge students to fill in the missing numbers.

1. 9,004 − 5,012 = 3,992
2. 6,200 − 3,892 = 2,308
3. 4,030 − 1,734 = 2,296
4. 8,000 − 2,907 = 5,093

| Assignment Guide | Minimum | Average | Extended |
|---|---|---|---|
| page 43 | 1–24, SK | 1–24, SK | 1–25, SK |

Subtract.

| | | | | |
|---|---|---|---|---|
| 1. 702 − 256 = 446 | 2. 600 − 176 = 424 | 3. 5,303 − 2,748 = 2,555 | 4. 4,704 − 2,381 = 2,323 | 5. 3,024 − 867 = 2,157 |
| 6. 6,004 − 5,789 = 215 | 7. 8,000 − 4,237 = 3,763 | 8. 4,009 − 2,765 = 1,244 | 9. 2,900 − 1,435 = 1,465 | 10. 26,082 − 7,395 = 18,687 |
| 11. 98,004 − 67,385 = 30,619 | 12. 80,000 − 36,594 = 43,406 | 13. $10.05 − 3.69 = $ 6.36 | 14. $30.00 − 17.49 = $12.51 | 15. $40.27 − 23.79 = $16.48 |

16. 608 − 79 529 17. 900 − 462 438 18. 5,036 − 2,178 2,858

19. 6,805 − 3,677 3,128 20. 7,004 − 5,666 1,338 21. 42,000 − 36,784 5,216

22. Estimate, then find the difference of 6,002 and 3,976. 2,000; 2,026

23. Estimate, then find how many more 16,201 is than 8,898. 7,000; 7,303

Use the table on page 42 for problems 24 and 25.

24. How many more injuries per 100,000 participants were there in ice hockey than in basketball? 2,699

25. How much more or less is the number of injuries in basketball and soccer combined than in football? 46 less

## Skillkeeper

Give the place value of each red digit.

1. 35,278 5 thousands
2. 420,356 2 ten thousands
3. 634,219 1 ten
4. 75,341,892 5 millions

Write the standard number.

5. 30,000 + 6,000 + 500 + 10 + 9 36,519
6. 200,000 + 9,000 + 300 + 40 + 1 209,341
7. 5,000,000,000 + 2,000,000 + 8,000 + 700 + 8 5,002,008,708

More Practice, page 414, Set A



## Using Page 43

**Exercises 1–21** Encourage students to use graph or grid paper to align the digits in exercises 5, 10, 13 and 16 if necessary. Note in exercises 4 and 8 that no trade is needed from tens to ones. Thus these exercises must be worked differently from the problems preceding them. Alert students to this difference.

**Exercises 22–23** Observe students' work to be sure that they make the right decision in rounding the numbers.

**Exercises 24–25** Note that these exercises use information from the table on page 42. In exercise 25 in order to decide whether the number is more or less, students must first add the number of injuries for basketball and soccer and then subtract from the number of injuries for football.

**Skillkeeper** This skillkeeper reviews skills taught in the beginning of this chapter.

**More Practice,** page 414, Set A

**Reteaching Supplement,** page 12

Name ______ To follow text page 43

### Subtracting with Zeros

Subtract the ones. Trade if necessary. → Subtract the tens. Trade if necessary. → Subtract the hundreds.

804 − 268 = 6 (80 tens and 4 ones is the same as 79 tens and 14 ones.) → 36 → 536

Subtract.

1. 8,002 − 7,426 = 576 (800 tens and 2 ones is the same as 799 tens and 12 ones.)
2. 5,046 − 2,273 = 2,773 (50 hundreds and 4 tens is the same as 49 hundreds and 14 tens.) Finish.
3. 300 − 146 = 154 Finish.

| | | | | |
|---|---|---|---|---|
| 4. 107 − 33 = 74 | 5. 420 − 138 = 282 | 6. 704 − 138 = 566 | 7. 620 − 79 = 541 | 8. 600 − 235 = 365 |
| 9. 800 − 176 = 624 | 10. 408 − 192 = 216 | 11. 801 − 99 = 702 | 12. 320 − 185 = 135 | 13. 2,630 − 1,829 = 801 |
| 14. 4,026 − 1,819 = 2,207 | 15. 5,004 − 2,692 = 2,312 | 16. 3,001 − 1,848 = 1,153 | 17. 5,000 − 2,774 = 2,226 | 18. 79,081 − 36,426 = 42,655 |
| 19. 70,200 − 21,798 = 48,402 | 20. 81,004 − 6,275 = 74,729 | 21. 90,000 − 56,843 = 33,157 | 22. $86.05 − 9.79 = $76.26 | 23. $100.45 − 28.84 = $ 71.61 |

24. 5,020 − 4,648 = 372 25. 20,400 − 8,925 = 11,475 26. $60.50 − $14.95 = $45.55

**Enrichment Supplement,** page 12

Name ______ To follow text page 43

### You Must Be Mistaken!

Pretend that you are a math teacher. Someone has made some errors on this quiz. Find each error and rewrite the problem so that it is correct.

1. 509 − 273 = 236
2. 400 − 207 = 103; corrected: 400 − 207 = 193
3. 628 − 494 = 134
4. 800 − 294 = 516; corrected: 800 − 294 = 506
5. 5,300 − 2,654 = 2,656; corrected: 5,300 − 2,654 = 2,646
6. 25,046 − 8,628 = 16,418
7. 7,000 − 2,674 = 4,426; corrected: 7,000 − 2,674 = 4,326
8. 5,019 − 4,723 = 296
9. 13,207 − 11,639 = 1,578; corrected: 13,207 − 11,639 = 1,568
10. 60,624 − 5,932 = 54,692
11. 40,024 − 2,641 = 38,483; corrected: 40,024 − 2,641 = 37,383
12. $28.27 − 14.95 = $13.32
13. $30.45 − 12.64 = $18.81; corrected: $30.45 − 12.64 = $17.81
14. $70.05 − 26.49 = $44.56; corrected: $70.05 − 26.49 = $43.56

Score Number correct: 7 Number incorrect: 9

**Practice Supplement,** page 17

Name ______ To follow text page 43

### Subtracting with Zeros

Subtract.

| | | | | |
|---|---|---|---|---|
| 1. 604 − 278 = 326 | 2. 708 − [illegible] = 389 | 3. 901 − 140 = 761 | 4. 800 − 131 = 669 | 5. 600 − 518 = 82 |
| 6. 2,504 − 385 = 2,119 | 7. 7,204 − 3,417 = 3,787 | 8. 8,001 − 3,274 = 4,727 | 9. 5,003 − 1,274 = 3,729 | 10. 8,040 − 4,238 = [illegible] |
| 11. 7,000 − 6,481 = 519 | 12. 9,000 − 1,240 = 7,760 | 13. 47,003 − 5,212 = 41,791 | 14. 35,000 − 8,465 = 26,535 | 15. 60,000 − 17,400 = 42,600 |
| 16. $5.02 − 3.16 = $1.86 | 17. $8.08 − 4.50 = $3.58 | 18. $7.00 − 2.17 = $4.83 | 19. $5.00 − 1.68 = $3.32 | 20. $9.00 − 2.75 = $6.25 |
| 21. $10.08 − 8.94 = $1.14 | 22. $30.20 − 16.65 = $13.55 | 23. $50.00 − 25.25 = $24.75 | 24. $40.04 − 13.97 = $26.07 | 25. $80.00 − 77.40 = $2.60 |
| 26. 1,600 − 541 = 1,059 | 27. 1,807 − 909 = 898 | 28. 2,100 − 796 = 1,304 | 29. 1,802 − 812 = 990 | 30. 2,704 − 926 = 1,778 |

31. 400 − 156 = 244 32. 3,070 − 499 = 2,571 33. 12,000 − 6,315 = 5,685 34. $181.09 − $67.24 = $113.85

35. 340 − 181 = 159 36. 5,001 − 320 = 4,681 37. 6,002 − 890 = 5,112 38. 2,201 − 809 = 1,392

# Applications

**Quick Review** Use these basic facts for oral drill. Students use the appropriate subtraction fact to check their answers.

6 + 5   3 + 9   8 + 2   7 + 3   7 + 5   6 + 4   8 + 6   8 + 8
5 + 9   4 + 8   2 + 9   6 + 6   9 + 8   6 + 7   2 + 7

**Lesson Focus** To solve word problems using data from a bar graph; to practice solving word problems involving all operations

## Ideas for Getting Started

Write the names of 4 subjects on small cards and tape them to the front of a desk or table. Then have students place their books above the card that represents their favorite subject. Draw a bar graph on the chalkboard to show students' data. Point out parts of the graph, such as title, number scale, and labels.

## Using Page 44

**Lesson Development** Tell students that a bar graph is a special way to show data, and that we can use the data from the bar graph on this page to solve the problems. Review the parts of a bar graph. Point out that the value of each bar is given by the number written above the bar. Caution students to check their work carefully and reread the problem to make sure that their answer makes sense.

**Try This** A possible strategy, Choose the Operations, was introduced on page 16.

**Discussion** "What are we asked to find out about Mt. Whitney?" (How much higher is it than the average elevation?) "What do we know about the average elevation?" (It is 970 m above Death Valley.) "What is the elevation of Death Valley?" (86 meters *below* sea level.) "How high is Mt. Whitney?" (From the graph we see that Mt. Whitney is 4,418 meters high.) In planning a solution what must we find first?" (We need to find the average elevation of California by subtracting the elevation of Death Valley below sea level from 970.) "How can we compare the height of Mt. Whitney to that of the average sea level?" (subtract)

**Solution** Mt. Whitney is 3,534 m higher than the average elevation. 970 − 86 = 884; 4,418 − 884 = 3,534.

**Extension** Death Valley is 86 meters below sea level. The highest spot in Los Angeles, California, is 1,635 m above Death Valley. The highest spot in San Francisco, California, is 282 above sea level. How much higher is the highest altitude in Los Angeles than the highest altitude in San Francisco? (1,267 m)

QUESTION DATA PLAN ANSWER CHECK

## Problem Solving: Using Data from a Bar Graph

Use data from this bar graph to solve the problems below.

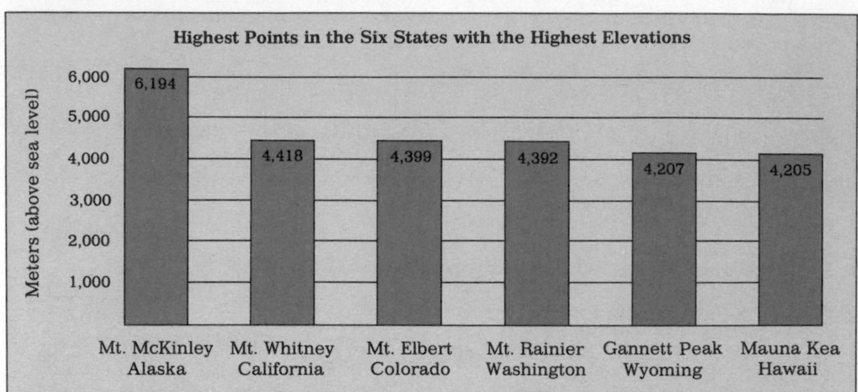


1. The average elevation in Colorado is 2,073 m. How much higher than the average is Mt. Elbert? 2,326 m
2. The average elevation in Alaska is 579 m. How much greater is the height of Mt. McKinley than the average? 5,615 m
3. The average elevation in the state of Washington is 5 hundred m. Is the height of Mt. Rainier more or less than 9 times the average elevation? less (9 × 5 hundred = 45 hundred)
4. The lowest place in Wyoming is the Belle Fourche River. It is 3,262 m lower than Gannett Peak. What is the elevation of the lowest place? 945 m
5. If you add the height of Mt. Elbert to the height of Mt. Whitney, you are still 31 m short of the height of Mt. Everest, the world's tallest mountain. How tall is Mt. Everest? 8,848 m
6. Beaverdam Creek, the lowest place in Utah, has an elevation of 609 m. The average elevation in Utah is 1,250 m higher than this. The highest point, King's Peak, is 2,264 m higher than the average. How high is King's Peak? 4,123 m
7. **Try This** The lowest place in California, Death Valley, is 86 m below sea level. The average elevation in California is 970 m above Death Valley. How much higher is Mt. Whitney than the average elevation? 3,534 m

44

## Follow Up

### Reteaching

Have available bar graphs taken from newspapers or magazines illustrating a variety of topics. Call students' attention to the following features of a graph:

- What is the title of the graph?
- What data is given?
- What is the scale of measurement?
- What are the units of measurement?

Discuss the sample graphs using the above questions. Encourage students to suggest questions that could be answered from the data in the graphs.

### Enrichment

Have students use information in the graph below to write questions for their classmates to solve.

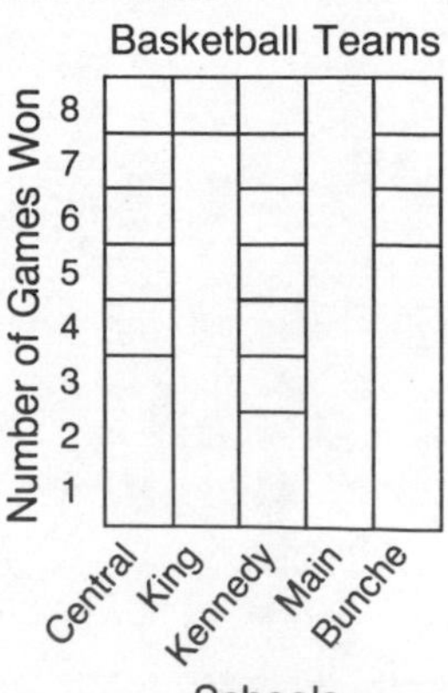

| Assignment Guide | | | |
|---|---|---|---|
| | Minimum | Average | Extended |
| page 44 | 1–5 | 1–6 | 1–7 |
| page 45 | 1–4 | 1–5 | 1–6 |

## Problem Solving: Practice

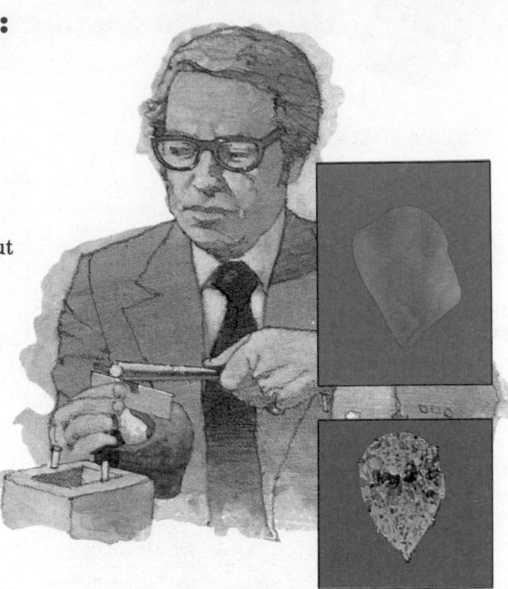

Diamond cutting is a very time-consuming process. Every step must be done with great care. The cutter must decide the best way to cut the stone to make the gem as nearly perfect as possible. The weights of diamonds and other precious stones are given in units called carats. Before it was cut, the world's largest rough diamond, the *Cullinan* diamond, weighed 3,106 carats.

Solve these problems about diamonds.

1. The *Excelsior* diamond was the world's second-largest rough diamond. It weighed 995 carats. How much less was its weight than that of the 3,106 carat *Cullinan*?
   2,111 carats
2. Two other famous uncut diamonds were the *Star of Sierra Leone,* which weighed 968 carats, and the *Great Mogul,* which weighed 787 carats. What is the total weight for these two diamonds? 1,755 carats
3. A good half-carat diamond might cost $600. What would the diamonds for a bracelet containing 8 of these cost? $4,800
4. The *Excelsior* diamond was discovered in South Africa in 1893. How many years ago was this?
   Answers will vary. (If present year is 1985, answer is 92 years.)
5. What is the total weight of these famous uncut diamonds? 2,690 carats

   | | |
   |---|---|
   | *Presidente Vargus* ....... | 727 carats |
   | *Jonker* .................. | 726 carats |
   | *Light of Peace*........... | 435 carats |
   | *Ice Queen*................ | 427 carats |
   | *Red Cross*................ | 375 carats |

6. **Try This** A cutter started with an uncut stone that weighed 726 carats. The cutter got 8 gems from it. The largest of these was 128 carats and the smallest was 9 carats. How many carats of the rough diamond were lost in the cutting if the other gems averaged 60 carats each?
   229 carats



## Using Page 45

**Lesson Development** Have students read the paragraph at the top of the page. Students might also be interested in these facts.

- A diamond is 90 times as hard as the second hardest substance on earth—corundum.
- The carat used for measuring diamonds is 200 mg. That is, it takes 5 carats to make one gram. (The weight of the *Cullinan* diamond in grams is 621 grams.)

Review the 5-Point checklist at the top of the page. Remind students to use these steps as a guide in solving the problems.

**Try This** A possible strategy, Choose the Operations, was introduced on page 16.

**Discussion** "What was the total weight of the uncut stone?" (726 carats) "How many gems were cut from it?" (8) "Were the gems all the same size?" (No, the largest was 128 carats; the smallest was 9 carats; the others averaged 60 carats each.) "What information must we find before we can answer the question?" (the total weight of the eight gems.) "What operation can we use to find the difference?" (subtraction)

**Solution** There were 229 carats of the rough diamond lost. The weight of uncut stone (726) minus the combined weights of the gems (497) equal 229.

**Extension** Suppose a cutter started with a 435 carat gem and got 6 stones from it; the largest was 75 carats, the smallest was 25 carats. What is the combined weight of the remaining stones if 146 carats of rough diamond were lost in the cutting? (189 carats)

## Ideas That Work

### Math for the Gifted

Have students list the letters for the clues that fit the given numbers. Then use some of those letters to form a word.

**B** It is a multiple of 3.
**C** It is a multiple of 4.
**D** It is a multiple of 5.
**E** It is less than 20.
**O** It is greater than 20.
**P** It is not a multiple of 10.
**R** It is not a multiple of 4.
**T** It is a factor of 100.
**U** It is less than 10.

1. The number is 15.
   Letters: B, D, E, P, R
   Word: Answers will vary.
2. The number is 4.
   Letters: C, E, P, T, U
   Word: ______
3. The number is 25.
   Letters: D, O, P, R, T
   Word: ______
4. The number is 50.
   Letters: D, O, R
   Word: ______

**Practice Supplement,** page 18

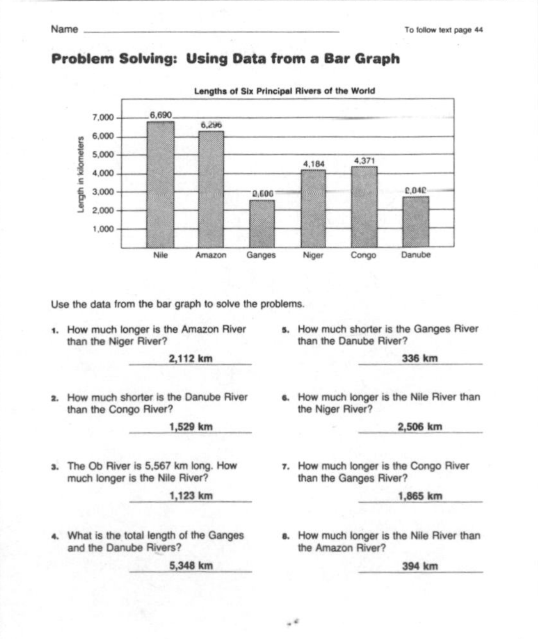

Name ______ To follow text page 44

**Problem Solving: Using Data from a Bar Graph**



Use the data from the bar graph to solve the problems.

1. How much longer is the Amazon River than the Niger River? 2,112 km
2. How much shorter is the Danube River than the Congo River? 1,529 km
3. The Ob River is 5,567 km long. How much longer is the Nile River? 1,123 km
4. What is the total length of the Ganges and the Danube Rivers? 5,348 km
5. How much shorter is the Ganges River than the Danube River? 336 km
6. How much longer is the Nile River than the Niger River? 2,506 km
7. How much longer is the Congo River than the Ganges River? 1,865 km
8. How much longer is the Nile River than the Amazon River? 394 km

# Applications

**Quick Review** Use these basic facts for oral drill. Students use the appropriate division fact to check their answers.

6 × 6  7 × 5  8 × 9  6 × 8  5 × 8  5 × 5  4 × 7  6 × 9  3 × 7
8 × 3  9 × 4  5 × 6  9 × 1  3 × 9  4 × 5  8 × 4  6 × 7

**Lesson Focus** To use a calculator to solve word problems involving a checking account; to read and write Roman numerals

## Ideas for Getting Started

Conduct a brief discussion about the nature and use of a checking account. Discuss with students what is meant by the three categories on a deposit slip. Then ask students to find the following totals:

**currency:** 3 twenties, 4 tens, 6 fives, and 12 ones
**coins:** 8 quarters, 7 dimes, 4 nickels, and 7 pennies
**checks:** $43.67 and $15.35, and $4.72

## Using Page 46

**Lesson Development** Direct students' attention to the deposit slip and checkbook record. Work through the checkbook record to be sure students understand how the totals were determined. Then assign the problems at the bottom of the page.

**Try This** A possible strategy, Choose the Operations, was introduced on page 16.

**Discussion** "What is the question asked about Mr. Rich's checking account balance?" (How large a check can he write to keep a balance no less than $1,000?) "What was the original amount in the account?" ($5,362) "How much were the checks that were written?" ($864.73, $1,167.39) "How much was deposited in the account?" ($1,729.58) "In planning the solution what number must we find first?" (the amount in the account after the two checks were written and the deposit made) "How can we find the answer to the question? (Find out how much greater this amount is than $1,000.)

**Solution** A check can be written for $4,059.46.
$5,362 − 864.73 + 1,729.58
− 1,167.39 = $5,059.46
$5,059.46 − 1,000 = $4,059.46

**Extension** Mr. Jones started with $3,024 in his account. He deposited $946.59 and wrote two checks for a total of $85.95. He deposited enough to make his final balance $6,000. What was the amount of his last deposit? ($2,115.36)

## Problem Solving: Using a Calculator

You can open a checking account by depositing money in a bank or a savings and loan company. You fill out a **deposit slip** when you put money in your account. After you write a check, you record the amount of the check in a checkbook record.

| DEPOSIT SLIP | | |
|---|---|---|
| List Checks by Bank Number | Dollars | Cents |
| Currency | 96 | 00 |
| Coin | 4 | 75 |
| Checks | 467 | 98 |
| | | |
| Total Deposit | 568 | 73 |

Study these examples. Then use a calculator to solve the problems below.

Checkbook Record

| Check number | Date | Description of transaction | Payment | Deposit | Balance |
|---|---|---|---|---|---|
| | 2/15 | | | 1,000.00 | 1,000.00 |
| 101 | 2/20 | Dr. Ruth Hauser | 50.00 | | 950.00 |
| 102 | 2/22 | Genuine Insurance Co. | 325.00 | | 625.00 |
| 103 | 2/26 | Corner Grocery | 47.87 | | 577.13 |
| | 2/27 | Deposit | | 100.00 | 677.13 |

1. Jean filled out a deposit slip with these amounts: Currency, $156.87; Coin, $4.96; Checks, $387.49. What was the total amount deposited? $549.32
2. A banker received a deposit slip with this information: Currency $5,976.58; Checks $3,748.98; Total $10,765.25. The amount of coins was blotted out. What was the amount of coins? $1,039.69
3. Mr. Gilmore had a balance of $3,675.54 in his account. What was his new balance after a deposit of $2,988.97? $6,664.51
4. Ms. Wilmont had a balance of $6,273.08 in her account. What was her new balance after she wrote a check for $3,495.79? $2,777.29
5. **Try This** Mr. Rich started with a balance of $5,362. He wrote a check for $864.73, deposited $1,729.58, and wrote another check for $1,167.39. What is the largest check he can write next if he wants to keep a balance of no less than $1,000? $4,059.46



## Follow Up

### Reteaching

Bring in catalogs from a department store or discount store. Form groups of four students each and give each group a catalog and a calculator. Tell students that they are going to fill out an order from the catalogs. Ask them to select one item from the catalog for each person in the group, then write the name and price of each item and use the calculator to find the total for their group. Give students a few minutes, and then have each group give their total in dollars and cents.

### Enrichment

Write the following problems on the chalkboard. Have students write each Roman numeral value in standard number form and then solve each problem. Tell students to show the answer in both Roman and standard numerals.

1. LX + DCLIII = **DCCXIII**
   **60 + 653 = 713**
2. MCDX − CMXVI = **CDXCIV**
   **1,410 − 916 = 494**
3. DXX × III = **MDLX**
   **520 × 3 = 1,560**
4. DCCCII ÷ II = **CDI**
   **802 ÷ 2 = 401**

| Assignment Guide | | | |
|---|---|---|---|
| | Minimum | Average | Extended |
| page 46 | 1–3 | 1–4 | 1–5 |
| page 47 | 1–10 | 1–11 | 1–12 |

## Roman Numerals

**Roman numerals** use alphabet letters to name numbers. They were developed by the Romans many centuries ago and are still sometimes used today. The values of the basic symbols are added or subtracted to show all numbers.

| | | | | | | | |
|---|---|---|---|---|---|---|---|
| **Basic Symbols** | I<br>1 | V<br>5 | X<br>10 | L<br>50 | C<br>100 | D<br>500 | M<br>1,000 |
| **Using Addition** | II<br>2 | XX<br>20 | CC<br>200 | MM<br>2,000 | VI<br>6 | LX<br>60 | DC<br>600 |
| **Using Subtraction** | (5 − 1)<br>IV<br>4 | IX<br>9 | XL<br>40 | XC<br>90 | CD<br>400 | CM<br>900 | |

**Subtract** when a letter with a smaller value is to the left of a letter with a larger value.

A bar over a basic symbol multiplies its value by 1,000.
Example: $\overline{\text{V}}$ = 5,000
Study these other examples.

L X IX → 50 + 10 + 9 = 69

M CM LXXX IV → 1,000 + 900 + 80 + 4 = 1,984

$\overline{\text{X}}$ DC XL → 10,000 + 600 + 40 = 10,640

Write as a Roman numeral.

**1.** 49 XLIX **2.** 194 CXCIV **3.** 747 DCCXLVII **4.** 1,776 MDCCLXXVI **5.** 2,001 MMI **6.** 5,836 $\overline{\text{V}}$DCCCXXXVI

Write as a standard number.

**7.** XXIX 29 **8.** CCXCV 295 **9.** MCDXCII 1,492 **10.** $\overline{\text{V}}$CCCXLV 5,345

**11.** Write your age and the current year using Roman numerals.
Answers will vary.

★ **12.** The date 1888 uses 13 letters as a Roman numeral. Can you write it?
MDCCCLXXXVIII



## Using Page 47

**Lesson Development** Generate a discussion to point out situations in which Roman numerals are used today. (clocks, reference books, building inscription, legal documents, movie dates, and so on.) Review the basic symbols: I, V, X, L, C, D, and M. Write these symbols on the chalkboard and give the value for each. Then tell students that other numbers can be shown by adding or subtracting these basic symbols. Write the numerals for 1 through 10 and explain the role of addition and subtraction.

Have students look at the symbols using addition given on the page and discuss each. Then have them look at the symbols using subtraction and discuss these. Emphasize that we subtract when a letter with a smaller value is to the left of the letter with the larger value.

Work through each of the examples to make sure students understand how these Roman numerals are written.

**Reteaching Supplement,** page 13

Name ______ To follow text page 46

**Problem Solving: Using a Calculator**

| Check Number | Date | Description of Transaction | Payment | Deposit | Balance 00.00 |
|---|---|---|---|---|---|
| — | 3/14 | Deposit | | 800.00 | 800.00 |
| 274 | 3/16 | Joe's Car Repair | 47.00 | | 753.00 |
| — | 3/16 | Deposit | | 14.75 | 767.75 |

Push 8 0 0 on the calculator to record the initial balance.

Push − 4 7 = to subtract the amount for this check and find the new balance.

Push + 1 4 . 7 5 = to add the deposit and find the new balance.

When we write a check, we subtract (−) to find the new balance.

When we make a deposit, we add (+) to find the new balance.

Use a calculator to complete each checkbook page. If you do not make an error, you should end with the last balance shown.

**1.**

| Check Number | Date | Description of Transaction | Payment | Deposit | Balance 750.00 |
|---|---|---|---|---|---|
| | 10/1 | | | 250.00 | **1,000.00** |
| | 10/4 | Deposit | | 740.50 | **1,740.50** |
| 102 | 10/4 | Food Mart | 67.95 | | **1,672.55** |
| 103 | 10/8 | Reliance Auto | 150.00 | | 1,522.55 |

**2.**

| Check Number | Date | Description of Transaction | Payment | Deposit | Balance 285.50 |
|---|---|---|---|---|---|
| | 12/10 | | | 200.00 | **485.50** |
| 165 | 12/15 | Zippy Cleaners | 28.00 | | **457.50** |
| 166 | 12/16 | Dental Clinic | 165.00 | | **292.50** |
| | 12/20 | Deposit | | 110.20 | **402.70** |
| 167 | 12/22 | Central Electric | 55.30 | | 347.40 |

**Enrichment Supplement,** page 13

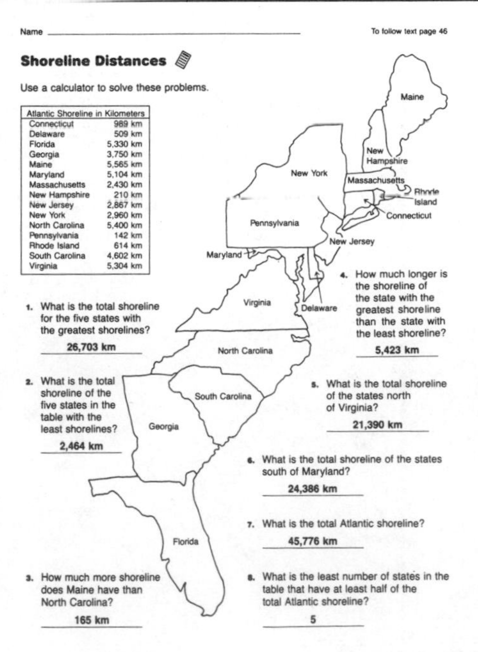

Name ______ To follow text page 46

**Shoreline Distances**

Use a calculator to solve these problems.

| Atlantic Shoreline in Kilometers | |
|---|---|
| Connecticut | 989 km |
| Delaware | 509 km |
| Florida | 5,330 km |
| Georgia | 3,750 km |
| Maine | 5,565 km |
| Maryland | 5,104 km |
| Massachusetts | 2,430 km |
| New Hampshire | 210 km |
| New Jersey | 2,867 km |
| New York | 2,960 km |
| North Carolina | 5,400 km |
| Pennsylvania | 142 km |
| Rhode Island | 614 km |
| South Carolina | 4,602 km |
| Virginia | 5,304 km |



1. What is the total shoreline for the five states with the greatest shorelines? **26,703 km**
2. What is the total shoreline of the five states in the table with the least shorelines? **2,464 km**
3. How much more shoreline does Maine have than North Carolina? **165 km**
4. How much longer is the shoreline of the state with the greatest shoreline than the state with the least shoreline? **5,423 km**
5. What is the total shoreline of the states north of Virginia? **21,390 km**
6. What is the total shoreline of the states south of Maryland? **24,386 km**
7. What is the total Atlantic shoreline? **45,776 km**
8. What is the least number of states in the table that have at least half of the total Atlantic shoreline? **5**

**Practice Supplement,** page 19

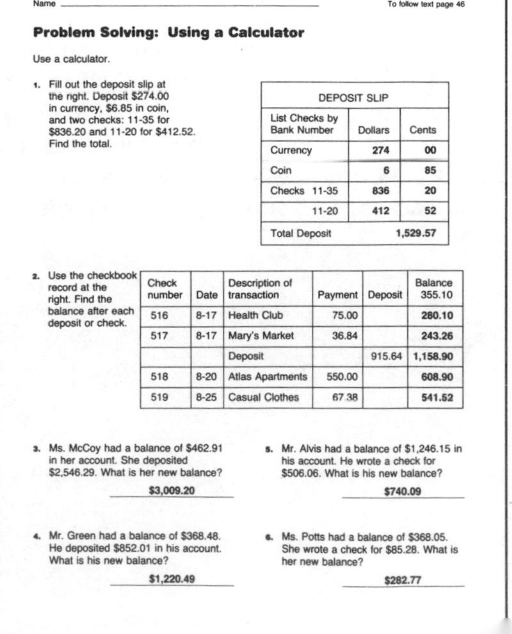

Name ______ To follow text page 46

**Problem Solving: Using a Calculator**

Use a calculator.

1. Fill out the deposit slip at the right. Deposit $274.00 in currency, $6.85 in coin, and two checks: 11-35 for $836.20 and 11-20 for $412.52. Find the total.

| DEPOSIT SLIP | | |
|---|---|---|
| List Checks by Bank Number | Dollars | Cents |
| Currency | **274** | **00** |
| Coin | **6** | **85** |
| Checks 11-35 | **836** | **20** |
| 11-20 | **412** | **52** |
| Total Deposit | **1,529.57** | |

2. Use the checkbook record at the right. Find the balance after each deposit or check.

| Check number | Date | Description of transaction | Payment | Deposit | Balance 355.10 |
|---|---|---|---|---|---|
| 516 | 8-17 | Health Club | 75.00 | | **280.10** |
| 517 | 8-17 | Mary's Market | 36.84 | | **243.26** |
| | | Deposit | | 915.64 | **1,158.90** |
| 518 | 8-20 | Atlas Apartments | 550.00 | | **608.90** |
| 519 | 8-25 | Casual Clothes | 67.38 | | **541.52** |

3. Ms. McCoy had a balance of $462.91 in her account. She deposited $2,546.29. What is her new balance? **$3,009.20**
4. Mr. Green had a balance of $368.48. He deposited $852.01 in his account. What is his new balance? **$1,220.49**
5. Mr. Alvis had a balance of $1,246.15 in his account. He wrote a check for $506.06. What is his new balance? **$740.09**
6. Ms. Potts had a balance of $368.05. She wrote a check for $85.28. What is her new balance? **$282.77**

**Lesson Focus** To use guess and check as a strategy for solving nonroutine word problems

## Ideas for Getting Started

Give students an oral question such as: I'm thinking of a number. If you add it to itself and subtract 7 you get 39. What is my number?" Encourage students to guess a number and then check their guesses. For example, if a student guessed 15, he or she would find that 15 + 15 − 7 = 23. Since this is smaller than 39, the student would have to make a larger guess. Emphasize the importance of making the initial guess regardless of how far off the guess might prove to be.

## Using Page 48

**Motivational Problem** Have students read the Try This problem at the top of the page and ask them to state the question in their own words. "How many tickets did Nancy buy?" (10) "How much money did she spend?" ($78) "She bought two kinds of tickets. How much did they cost?" ($9 and $5) Emphasize that it is difficult to decide which operations to use to solve a problem such as this. Suggest the Guess and Check strategy and add the strategy Guess and Check to the bulletin board or poster in your classroom.

**Lesson Development** Work through the solution shown on the page. "If you guess 6 main floor tickets, how would you find the number of balcony tickets?" (Subtract 6 from 10) Explain how to find the total cost of these tickets. (6 × $9 plus 4 × $5 would be $54 + $20, or a total of $74). "Was the guess too large or too small?" (too small) "What would happen if you guessed 5 balcony tickets?" (That would mean 5 main floor tickets, or 5 × $9 plus 5 × $5 = $70. Still too small.) Explain what happens when you guess 7 main floor tickets. (This would mean 3 balcony tickets; the total amount would be 7 × $9 plus 3 × $5, or $78.)

**Exercises 1–2** For each of these problems encourage students to use the Guess and Check strategy. Emphasize the importance of "making a guess—any guess" to get started. If students have difficulty, remind them of the 5-Point Checklist and suggest that they look for the question, list the important data, use Guess and Check as the plan, and check back to make sure the answer is reasonable.

QUESTION DATA PLAN ANSWER CHECK

## Problem Solving: Guess and Check

To solve a problem like this, you must do more than just decide whether to add, subtract, multiply, or divide. A problem-solving **strategy** which will help you is called

**Guess and Check**

**Try This** Nancy spent $78 for 10 tickets to a play. The main floor seats cost $9 and the balcony seats cost $5. How many of each kind did she buy?

Solve.

1. A test had 10 questions worth 3 points and 10 worth 5 points. Scott had 15 correct answers and a total score of 57 points. How many questions of each kind did he answer correctly? 9 worth 3 points each and 6 worth 5 points

2. Paula is 6 years old. Her Uncle Steve is 4 times as old. How old will Paula be when she is half as old as her uncle? 18

48

## Strategy Test Item

**Optional Problem** If you wish to assess students' ability to apply the strategy called Guess and Check introduced in this chapter, provide them with the problem below.

> Suppose a rabbit ate 32 carrots in 4 days. If it ate 2 more carrots each day than the day before, how many carrots did it eat each day?

**Solution** The rabbit ate 5 carrots the first day, 7 the second day, 9 the third day, and 11 the fourth day for a total of 32 carrots.

## Chapter Review-Test

Give the digits of this number in the place or period named. 4, 3 6 8, 5 9 7, 1 0 2

1. millions place 8
2. ten thousands place 9
3. hundreds place 1
4. billions place 4
5. millions period 368
6. thousands period 597
7. Write in standard form: 40,000 + 200 + 8,000 + 9 + 30. 48,239
8. Write in expanded form: 5,674. 5,000 + 600 + 70 + 4

Write >, <, or = for each ●.

9. 8,888 ● 999 >
10. 9,999 ● 10,000 <
11. 378,296 ● 378,902 <

Estimate. Round as indicated.

12. Nearest ten: 63 + 89 = 150
13. Nearest hundred: 705 − 296 = 400
14. Nearest thousand: 8,016 + 6,786 = 15,000
15. Nearest dollar: $12.89 − 5.24 = $ 8.00

Add or subtract.

16. 6,734 + 2,597 = 9,381
17. 15,365 − 9,407 = 5,958
18. 603 − 286 = 317
19. 65,384 + 9,768 + 23,602 = 98,754
20. 36,748 + 899 + 3,407 = 41,054
21. $57.34 + 26.59 = $83.93
22. 8,003 − 4,657 = 3,346
23. $186.42 − 97.68 = $ 88.74
24. 964 + 83,795 + 6,948 91,707
25. Write 454 as a Roman numeral. CDLIV
26. Write MLXVI as a standard number. 1,066

Solve.

27. A 747 flies from San Francisco to Chicago and from there to New York. It is 2,990 km from San Francisco to Chicago, and 1,147 km from Chicago to New York. How far does the plane travel? 4,137 km
28. Mrs. Blake has a balance of $3,106 in a checking account. Then she writes a check for $967, makes a deposit of $489, and writes another check for $2,627. How much does she have left in her account? $1

49

## Assessment Options

If you use the Chapter Review/Test as a review assignment, you may wish to use the multiple-choice test or the free-response test to evaluate mastery of the chapter objectives. The items on these tests have a one-to-one correspondence in terms of content and level of difficulty. A correlation of test items to objectives and student text pages is provided in the Management Guide for Chapter 2.

**Multiple-Choice Test,** TRB pages 4–6

**Free-Response Test,** TRB pages 51–52

## TRB Options

The following blackline masters are available for use with this chapter. If you have not already assigned these materials, you may wish to use them to close the chapter.

**Recreation,** TRB page 152

**Consumer Applications,** TRB page 170

**Calculator Technology,** TRB page 188

**Reading Math,** TRB page 220

**Family Involvement,** TRB pages 239–240

## Using Page 49

The exercises in the Chapter Review/Test emphasize the major concepts and skills presented in this chapter. These exercises may be used as a review assignment or as a test, depending upon your needs.

**Item Analysis** The table below correlates the Chapter Review/Test items with objectives and with the student text pages on which the concepts or skills were taught.

| Items | Objectives | Related text pages |
|---|---|---|
| 1–11 | 2.1 | 24–29 |
| 12–15 | 2.2 | 30–33 |
| 16–24 | 2.3 | 36–43 |
| 25–26 | 2.4 | 47 |
| 27–28 | 2.5 | 34–35, 44–46 |

# Reteaching

## Using Page 50

The exercises on this page are intended for those students who experienced difficulty with the Chapter Review/Test on page 49. Should students require reteaching of these key concepts and skills, please refer to the teaching notes below. Otherwise, the Another Look exercises can be assigned as independent work, with students using the accompanying sample problems and hints as guides.

**Exercises 1–8** The concept of place value was originally taught on pages 24–27. Have students examine the place-value chart showing periods and place values. Remind them that hundreds, tens, and ones repeat in each period. "At which digit do we start for the ones place?" (digit to the right) "For the number in exercise 3, start at the right and give the place-value names."

**Exercises 9–12** This skill was originally taught on pages 28–29. Focus on the two numbers to be compared in the chart to the left. "Do we start on the left or on the right when comparing two numbers?" (on the left) "What is the first place in which the digits are different?" (the hundreds place) "How could you write a statement describing how the numbers compare?" (84,965 > 84,895 or 84,895 < 84,965)

**Exercises 13–17** This skill was originally taught on pages 30–31. Direct students' attention to the display box on the left. "Suppose we want to round 6,754 to the nearest hundred. What digit is in the place to which we want to round?" (7) "What digit is in the place to the right of 7?" (5) "Is 5 less than 5?" (no) "Should we round up or down?" (up) "How do we write the rounded number?" (6,800)

**Exercises 18–23** These skills were originally taught on pages 36–37 and 40–43. Call students' attention to the problems in the display box to the left. Remind students that when we add amounts of money, we can think about pennies and add as with whole numbers.

Have students read the second problem and the think cloud. "4 thousands is how many tens?" (400) "If I start with 400 tens and trade 1 ten for 10 ones, how many tens do I have left?" (399) "How many ones?" (10) Emphasize that we mark out the 400 and write 399 above it, and then complete the subtraction.

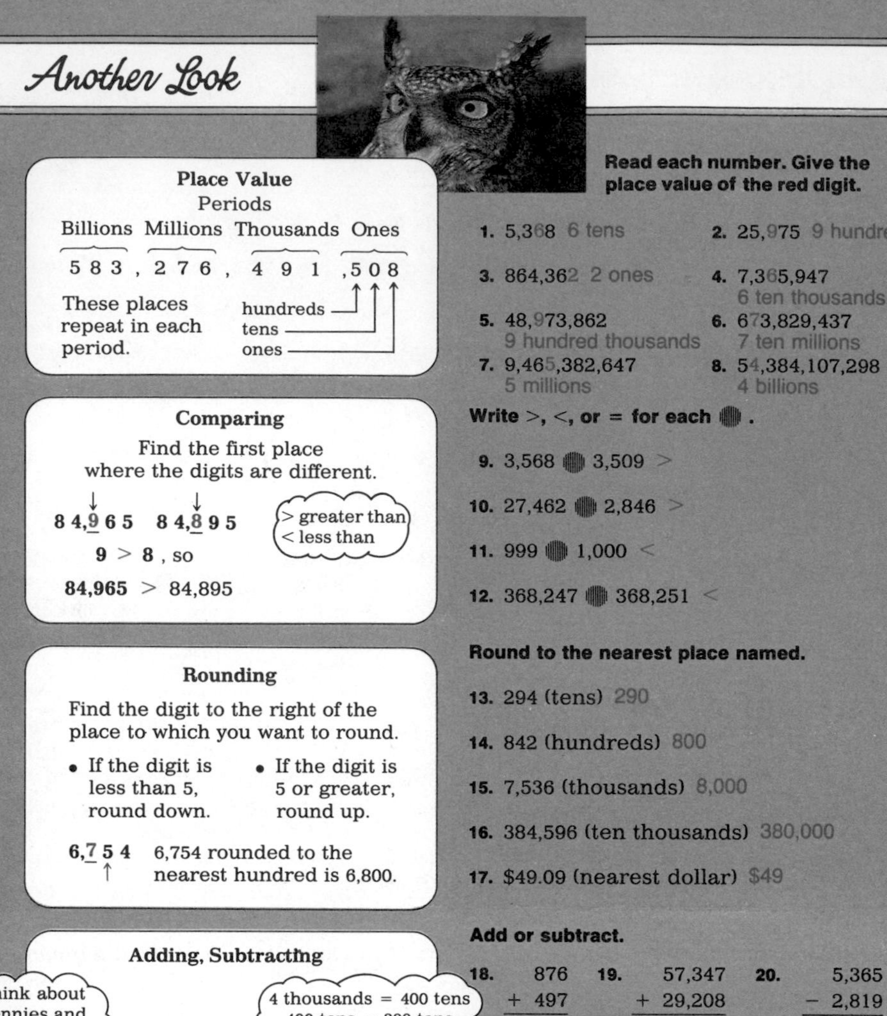

Another Look

**Place Value**
Periods
Billions Millions Thousands Ones
5 8 3 , 2 7 6 , 4 9 1 , 5 0 8
These places repeat in each period. — hundreds, tens, ones

**Comparing**
Find the first place where the digits are different.
8 4,9 6 5  8 4,8 9 5
9 > 8, so
84,965 > 84,895
> greater than
< less than

**Rounding**
Find the digit to the right of the place to which you want to round.
- If the digit is less than 5, round down.
- If the digit is 5 or greater, round up.

6,7 5 4  6,754 rounded to the nearest hundred is 6,800.

**Adding, Subtracting**
Think about pennies and add as with whole numbers.
3,9 4 5 ¢ + 2,4 1 9 ¢
Write the answer in dollars and cents.
$ 3 9.4 5 + 2 4.1 9 = $ 6 3.6 4
4 thousands = 400 tens
400 tens = 399 tens and 10 ones
4,0 0 3 − 1,8 4 7 = 2,1 5 6

**Read each number. Give the place value of the red digit.**

1. 5,368 6 tens
2. 25,975 9 hundreds
3. 864,362 2 ones
4. 7,365,947 6 ten thousands
5. 48,973,862 9 hundred thousands
6. 673,829,437 7 ten millions
7. 9,465,382,647 5 millions
8. 54,384,107,298 4 billions

**Write >, <, or = for each ●.**

9. 3,568 ● 3,509 >
10. 27,462 ● 2,846 >
11. 999 ● 1,000 <
12. 368,247 ● 368,251 <

**Round to the nearest place named.**

13. 294 (tens) 290
14. 842 (hundreds) 800
15. 7,536 (thousands) 8,000
16. 384,596 (ten thousands) 380,000
17. $49.09 (nearest dollar) $49

**Add or subtract.**

18. 876 + 497 = 1,373
19. 57,347 + 29,208 = 86,555
20. 5,365 − 2,819 = 2,546
21. 8,002 − 5,496 = 2,506
22. $25.75 + 19.95 = $45.70
23. $36.50 − 19.98 = $16.52

50

## Just for Teachers

### Language of Math

One of the simplest mathematical aids to counting and calculating is the abacus. The abacus got its name from the Greek word *abax,* meaning counting frame. Different types in varying degrees of sophistication have been used over the centuries by most of the world's civilizations.

The abacus evolved from the practice of scratching number symbols on a board covered with dust or sand. Quantities could then be temporarily recorded or basic calculation performed. This "dustboard" eventually was replaced by a table ruled with vertical lines. Loose markers were placed on the lines to represent numbers. This concept was further refined by the use of grooved tables with beads and the familiar wooden frame holding vertical rods and a horizontal crossbar separating sets of moveable beads.

The abacus was a common calculating aid to the Romans. Cicero (106-43 B.C.), the statesman and orator, and the poet Horace (65-8 B.C.), mention three different forms of abaci in their writings: the "dustboard" abacus, the ruled table with counters, and the grooved table with beads. The Romans used stone pebbles called *calculi* for their counters, giving rise to the word "calculate." Abaci were common in Europe until 1500.

## Enrichment

**Computer Literacy**

Modern computers use these ideas to remember and work with numbers:

A switch **on** can represent 1.

A switch **off** can represent 0.

The numbers 0 and 1 are called **binary digits** or **bits.**

For example, if we group by twos instead of by our usual tens and use place value, a panel of lights can show a number.

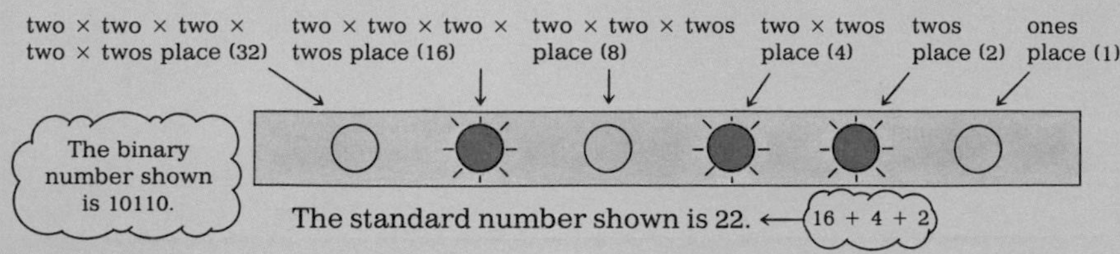


What standard number is shown by each panel of lights?

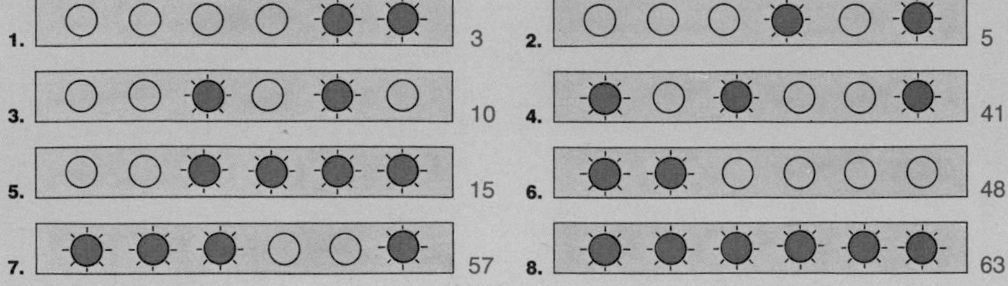


Can you draw a panel of lights to show these numbers?

**9.** 4 **10.** 9 **11.** 17 **12.** 26 ★ **13.** 100

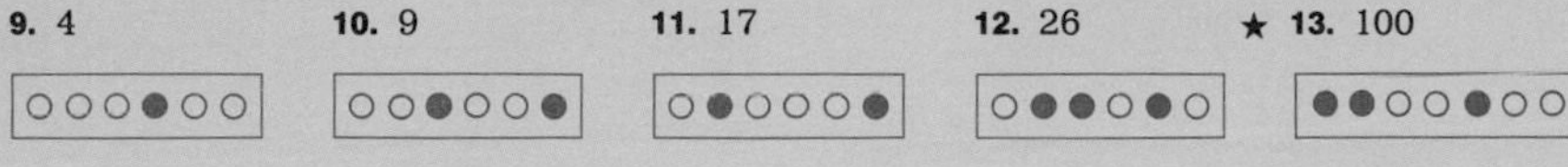



In the Orient, however, the abacus became a lasting fixture. As early as the twelfth century, the Chinese were using a wooden-framed abacus divided by vertical rods and a horizontal crossbar. On each rod were strung seven beads—two five-unit beads on the upper section, and five one-unit beads on each lower section. Each rod represented a specific place value, and the appropriate number of beads were moved up or down to the crossbar to denote a number or carry out an operation. The abacus, known in Japan as the *soroban,* evolved into a slightly different form. On each vertical rod, five (or sometimes six) beads were strung: one five-unit bead above the crossbar and four (or sometimes five) one-unit beads below the crossbar. Because the soroban uses the minimum number of beads necessary to express any number, the process of carrying out an arithmetical operation is streamlined.

## Using Page 51

This page is intended for those students who successfully completed the Chapter Review/Test on page 49. You may wish to assign this page as independent work while you use Another Look exercises to reteach the basic concepts and skills of the chapter. Or, you may decide that all students would benefit from exposure to this Enrichment activity.

**Lesson Development** Have students read the information at the top of the page. Make sure students understand that a computer switch **on** can represent 1, and a computer switch **off** can represent 0. Point out that because computers operate with electricity, it is easy to open or shut a circuit to represent these digits.

Remind students that in base ten the places start with ones, then tens, then 10 tens or 100, then 10 ten tens or 1,000, and so on. This system is selected because we have 10 digits, 0 through 9. Tell students that when two digits, 0 and 1, are used the system is based on twos rather than tens. In this system, the first place is ones, the second place is twos, the third place is 2 twos, the fourth place is 2 two twos, and so on.

Refer to the illustration on the page in which the places are shown. Explain that the term *bit* is derived from the two words binary and digit. Help students interpret this binary number and write the standard number it equals.

Refer students to exercise 5. "The first light on is in the ones place. What standard number does it represent?" (1) "The second light on is in the twos place. What standard number does it represent?" (2) "The third light on is in the two twos place. What standard number does it represent?" (4) "The fourth light on is in the 2 two twos place. What standard number does it represent?" (8) "What is the total of the standard numbers shown by the lights?" (8 + 4 + 2 + 1, or 15) The panel of lights show the binary number 1111, which is equal to the standard number 15.

## Using Page 52

The exercises on this page provide practice for maintaining cumulative skills. The emphasis in this Cumulative Review is on basic facts (Chapter 1), place value (Chapter 2), addition and subtraction of whole numbers (Chapter 2), and problem solving (Chapter 2).

**Item Analysis** The table below correlates the Cumulative Review items with objectives and with the student book pages on which the concepts or skills were taught.

| Items | Objectives | Related Text Pages |
|---|---|---|
| 1–4 | 1.1 | 1–7, 10 |
| 5–6 | 2.1 | 24–29 |
| 7–11 | 2.3 | 36–43 |
| 12–13 | 2.5 | 34–35, 44–46 |

## *Cumulative Review*

Add or subtract.

1. 7 + 9
   A 15  B 17  (C) 16  D not given

2. 13 − 5
   A 9  B 6  C 7  (D) not given

Multiply or divide.

3. 9)54
   A 7  (B) 6  C 60  D not given

4. 8 × 6
   (A) 48  B 56  C 42  D not given

Give the standard numeral.

5. nine hundred fifteen thousand, two hundred thirty-one
   A 915,031  (B) 915,231
   C 900,151  D not given

6. 3,000,000 + 70,000 + 6,000 + 800 + 50 + 3
   A 3,706,853
   B 3,760,853
   (C) 3,076,853
   D not given

Add or subtract.

7. 32 − 9
   A 41  (B) 23  C 33  D not given

8. 57 + 83
   A 130  B 134  (C) 140  D not given

9. 417 − 198
   (A) 219  B 319  C 229  D not given

10. $27.50 + 46.98
    A $63.48  B $74.38  C $73.42  (D) not given

11. $40.15 − 9.87
    A $30.32  (B) $30.28  C $30.38  D not given

12. Irina bought a new bike horn that cost $3.79 and a new seat cushion that cost $6.55. What was the cost for both items?
    (A) $10.34  B $9.24
    C $9.34  D not given

13. Pat jogged 4 km each day for 7 days. How many kilometers was that in all?
    A 11  B 24
    (C) 28  D not given

# Decimals: Addition and Subtraction



## Objectives

**3.1** Read, write, compare, and order decimals.

**3.2** Round decimals and estimate their sums and differences.

**3.3** Add and subtract decimals.

**3.4** Solve word problems using the 5-Point Checklist and cumulative computational skills.

## Summary

This chapter introduces the meaning of a decimal by building upon students' understanding of factors. Students are taught the concept of a decimal and how to read and write decimals through hundred thousandths. Then students are asked to compare, order, and round decimals. The skills for rounding decimals are then extended to include estimation of sums and differences in both computational and problem-solving settings. Addition and subtraction of decimals—with and without trading—are introduced next, followed by further estimation and problem-solving opportunities. A lesson on making change comes near the end of the chapter, followed by three problem-solving lessons involving the addition and subtraction of decimals.

## Mathematical Background

**Understanding Decimals** A decimal is a number that describes a fractional part of a unit and tells us that the unit is divided into *n* same-size smaller pieces when each smaller piece is "one-*n*th" of the entire unit. This idea, obviously, is consistent with students' understanding of fractions. The unit is divided into smaller units and the number of smaller units is a power of 10 (10, 100, 1,000, etc.). And because decimals deal with fractional units in multiples of 10, decimals can be written as an extension of our whole number place-value system.

The chart below shows how whole number place values can be extended to include the decimal place values to provide a complete system for writing numbers greater and less than 1 and how the whole-number and decimal place-value names are "symmetric" with respect to the *ones* place. This property often helps students remember the correct place-value names for the decimal part. The relationship between the whole-number and place-value names also helps students with reading and writing decimals.

Whole Number and Decimal Place Value Names

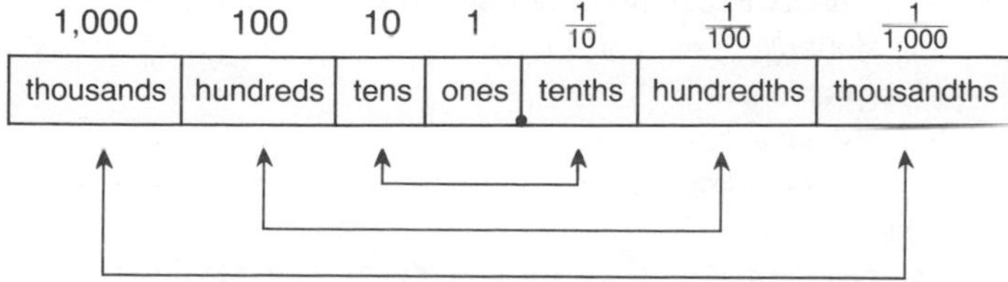


Consider, for example, the decimal 42.24351. Students learn that the whole-number part is read first, followed by the word "and," then the name for the decimal part. The decimal part is named by first reading the decimal part as a whole number ("twenty-four thousand three hundred fifty-one") and then adding the place-value name for the last digit on the right ("ten thousandths").

A common way to introduce students to reading and writing decimals is to build on an understanding of fractions. In particular, students are initially taught that $\frac{1}{10}$ and 0.1 both name "one tenth" of a unit. Similarly, students can conceptualize the decimal 0.001 by thinking of a unit divided into 1,000 smaller units where each smaller unit is one thousandth of the whole unit. Illustrating 0.001 with a model is difficult. For this reason, it is important that a student's understanding of the concept of a decimal be well established by working with tenths and hundredths. Then they can generalize this understanding to decimals of any size.

A number line, another model that can be used to introduce decimal concepts, shows how a unit (the segment 0 to 1) is divided into 10 smaller same-size units. The picture below shows an example illustrating tenths for 0 through 2.

0.2 0.4 0.6 0.8 0.2 0.4 0.6 0.8
0 0.1 0.3 0.5 0.7 0.9 1 0.1 0.3 0.5 0.7 0.9 2

Another model that can be used to introduce decimals is the meter stick. The meter stick is analogous to the number line model where ones, tenths, hundreds, and thousandths can be seen on the stick. The meter stick is particularly useful since thousandths can be shown.

The fourth model that can be used to explain decimals is money. The relationship between and among the monetary units is familiar to most students. For example, most students know that there are 10 dimes in $1, 10 pennies in 1 dime, and 100 pennies in $1. Furthermore, most students are familiar with reading and writing money using dollar and cent notation involving decimals (e.g. $4.37). This familiarity with money makes it a particularly useful model for teaching decimals.

**Addition and Subtraction of Decimals** The algorithms for adding and subtracting decimals are the same as those for whole numbers—with one exception. When adding and subtracting decimals, students must be careful to align the decimal points before starting the algorithm. This skill is particularly relevant when students must copy problems.

It is important that instruction include activities that show the reasonableness of the steps *related to decimals.* One effective way to communicate this to students is through the use of a money model. The lessons in this chapter illustrate how the money model can be used to show the reasonableness of the steps in the addition and subtraction algorithms for decimals.

**Problem Solving** In this chapter two problem-solving lessons—pages 63 and 69—focus on the answer as students are asked to use rounding and estimation involving decimals. In the problem-solving lesson called Using Data from a Tour Book on page 72, the emphasis is on finding the needed data. In a practice lesson on page 71, students choose the correct operations to solve problems involving decimals. The problem-solving strategy introduced on page 74 in this chapter is called Draw a Picture.

### Vocabulary

| | | |
|---|---|---|
| decimal | hundredths | ten thousandths |
| tenths | thousandths | hundred thousandths |

Here's a complete in-service guide—each section written by experts—for solving special classroom problems.

## Error Analysis

In this chapter the concepts of decimal place value and the operations of addition and subtraction with decimals are presented. Decimals through hundred thousandths are discussed. Activities such as rounding and estimating with decimals are designed to help develop skill at applying these important ideas to real-world situations.

Errors usually occur when students begin to add and subtract decimals. Many of these errors are the result of the same misconceptions as the errors in adding and subtracting whole numbers. Nevertheless, the decimal point and the idea of fractional parts introduce new potential for errors. In considering the error patterns below, try to determine why the error was made and look for other similar errors.

**Error Pattern 1**

| | | |
|---|---|---|
| 32.63 | 87.96 | 37.564 |
| + 8.7 | + 36.34 | + 8.32 |
| 41.40 | 124.30 | 45.886 |

**Diagnosis** The student has attempted to add "ragged decimals" but does not understand the process. In the first example, the student has added 3 + 7 instead of beginning with 3 + 0. If there are the same number of digits in both addends, the student adds correctly but errs when asked to add decimals of different place value.

**Remediation** Show an example of addition of whole numbers, such as 543 + 269 written in algorithm form. Point out that in this example digits are aligned so that ones are added to ones, tens to tens, and so on. Then explain that in decimal addition, digits representing the same place value are added together. Set up the example again and align as shown below.

| | | | | | |
|---|---|---|---|---|---|
| | 3 | 2 | . | 6 | 3 |
| + | | 8 | . | 7 | |

→ Then add.

Caution students to add the numbers in similar columns, that is, hundredths to hundredths, tenths to tenths, units to units, and so on. Remind students that 0.7 and 0.70 represent the same value. Use place-value models to show that 7 tenths is the same number of squares as 70 hundredths.

**Error Pattern 2**

| | | | |
|---|---|---|---|
| 0.8 | 8.7 | 265.3 | 7.5 |
| − 0.32 | − 3.46 | − 121.44 | − 6.83 |
| 0.52 | 5.36 | 143.94 | 0.73 |

**Diagnosis** The student has difficulty when there is no corresponding digit to subtract from in the minuend. If a digit is not shown, the student simply brings down the digit. For example, in the problem 7.5 − 6.83 the student has written the 3, then subtracts the remaining digits.

**Remediation** Review the different ways to write the same decimal, stressing that a decimal such as 0.5 can be written as 0.50, 0.500, 0.5000, and so on. Then show that a number such as 7.5, which is "seven and five tenths" may be written as 7.50, "seven and fifty hundredths." Show the original problem and rewrite 7.5 as 7.50. Then work through the algorithm with students. Use addition to check your answer, and compare with the incorrect answer.

## Problem Solving

### Helping Students Understand Problems

In teaching problem solving, one of the most critical moments is when a student says, "I don't know what to do." Because of a need to say something, we often respond with "Try again," or we tell the student exactly how to proceed to find the answer. In both cases, we have not taken a very positive step toward improving the student's ability to understand that problem in particular, or math problems in general.

There are many factors that influence the degree to which a student understands math problems. Among these are the student's abilities in the areas of reading, memory, and logical thinking, the number of problem-solving experiences the student has had, and the degree to which the student experiences anxiety to perform well. If a student has difficulty with a given problem, there are several techniques you can introduce to facilitate understanding.

One of the most powerful ways to help a student understand a problem is to give hints by asking leading questions that focus the student's attention on important data in the problem, the question to be answered, and possible ways to solve the problem. The teaching notes for the Try This problems in this problem-solving program exemplify this approach. Below is a sample problem and four questions or hints to help students understand it.

> Six children came to a birthday party. Each child shook hands one time with each other. How many handshakes were exchanged?

**Discussion:** "How many people came to the party?" (6) "What were the children doing?" (shaking hands) "If Bill would shake Mary's hand, would he shake her hand again?" (no) "If Bill shakes Mary's hand, is that one handshake or two?" (one)

Here are some other ideas for helping students improve their ability to understand math problems:

- Have students explain the problem in their own words.
- Remind students of a similar problem.
- Help students replace larger numbers with smaller numbers.
- Have students use a colored marker to highlight important phrases and data.
- Tell students to list the data needed to solve the problem.
- Help students draw a picture or use objects to show the action in the problem.
- Help students act out the problem.
- Remove the numbers from the problem and discuss the action in the problem.

Discuss key words as potential key words—that is, for a particular problem, discuss whether a key word suggests the correct operation or whether it is misleading. (Note: Do *not* teach students to rely on key words.)

Improving a student's ability to understand problems is a task not easily or quickly accomplished. However, it is something that can be achieved through hard work by student and teacher over a period of time.

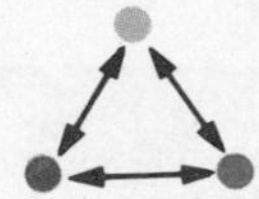

## Special Education

The particular skills of reading, writing, ordering, adding, and subtracting decimals are the main focal points in this chapter. The importance of these topics for daily living requires that the special-needs student master these skills to the highest level possible. The following suggestions provide some ideas for methods and activities to ease your work with students experiencing difficulty in mathematics.

### Using "Think, Write, and Read"

Getting students to model decimal numbers, read them, and write them is a sizeable task. With the special-needs student this task is even more difficult because of learning and communication problems. Thus, it is important that they are provided with a solid base from which to represent and deal with decimal numbers.

To help students build decimal skills, use an activity called "Triple Threat."

In this activity, 28 cards of the types shown above can be divided between two students of equal ability. Students then take turns asking their partner to "write" the decimal whose model or name is shown and then check it against the other side of the card; "read" the name of the decimal whose model or number is shown and then check it against the verbal operations shown; or "model" the decimal whose number or name is given on the card and check it against the model shown. The word at the top of each side of the card tells students the directions to give their partner. The response is checked against the information provided below.

This activity will help students learn to make the transitions between models and verbal and written representatives of decimal numbers.

### Developing Decimal Reading Skills

Students who have difficulty in reading decimal numbers aloud should consider the number of decimal places present in the number. Comparing the number of decimal places with the number of zeros behind a 1 in the base 10 representation helps students read a decimal. For example, in the decimal 0.23, there are two decimal places. Thus, we think of 100—two zeros—and immediately know we have hundredths. Thus, the decimal is read "twenty-three hundredths."

A look at 0.7 shows one decimal place. Students think 10, and determine that the number is seven tenths. The decimal 0.103 has three decimal places. They think 1,000, thus one hundred three thousandths.

### Using Paper Guides to Round Decimals

The rounding of decimals to a specified place can be helped with the use of a paper guide to direct attention to the relevant information. In the illustration below, a paper guide is used to round 0.276 to the nearest tenth and then to the nearest hundredth. The steps required are identifying the place we are rounding in, covering all digits to the right, exposing the next digit to the right, determining whether or not the next digit is greater than 5, and writing the final answer.

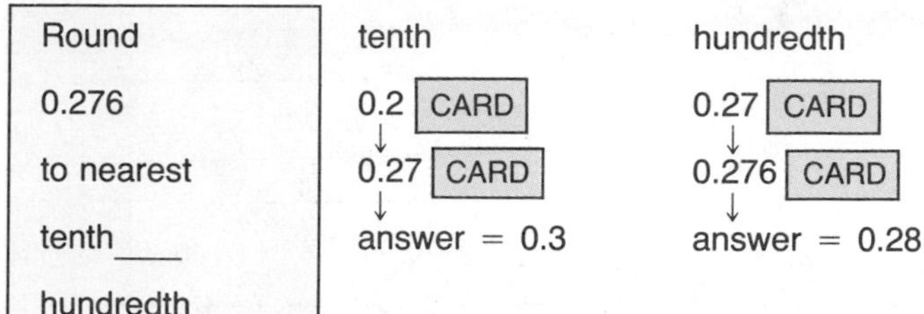


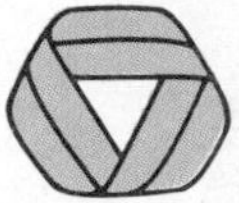

## Subject Integration

Subject matter related to other areas of the curriculum has been integrated into the following lessons. This provides an opportunity to highlight the interaction between mathematics and other subjects.

**Social Studies** Stamp collecting, page 54

**Consumer Awareness** Gas consumption, page 57; buying lunches, pages 68–69; making change, pages 70–71

**Career Awareness** Welder, pages 58–59

**Science** Geothermal energy, page 53; our solar system, pages 62–63; human body elements, pages 64–65

**Physical Education** Athletic arenas, pages 66–67

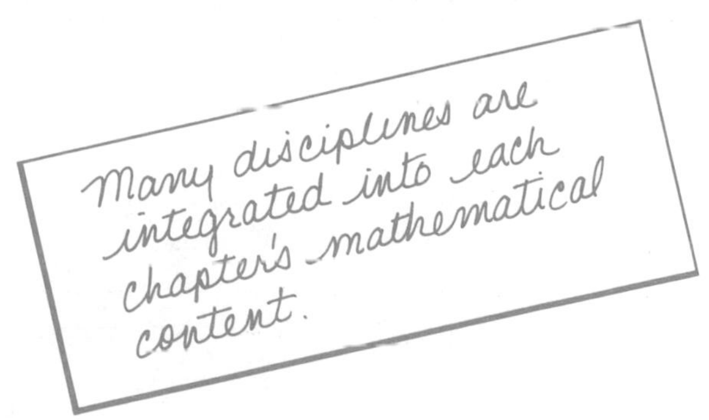

Many disciplines are integrated into each chapter's mathematical content.

# Management Guide

| Teaching Chapter 3 | | | | Meeting Individual Needs | | | | | |
|---|---|---|---|---|---|---|---|---|---|
| Objectives | Chapter Content | Pages | TRB Test Items | Lesson Assignments | | | Follow Up | | |
| | | | | Minimum | Average | Extended | Reteaching | Enrichment | Practice |
| | Chapter Opener | 53 | | | | | | | |
| **3.1** Read, write, compare, and order decimals. | Decimal Place Value: Tenths and Hundredths | 54–55 | 1–7 | 1–28 | 1–28 | 1–28, TM | SE5 Ch 4 | | PS 20 |
| | Thousandths | 56 | | 1–10, 16–20, 26–29 | 1–29 | 1–29 odd | SE5 Ch 4 | | |
| | Place Value through Hundred Thousandths | 57 | | 1–8, 13–16, 21–24 | 1–24 | 2–24 even | RS 14 | ES 14 | PS 21 |
| | Comparing and Ordering Decimals | 58–59 | 8–10 | 1–10, 25–27 | 1–28 | 13–28, TM | SE5 Ch 4<br>RS 15 | ES 15 | MP 414<br>PS 22 |
| **3.2** Round decimals and estimate their sums and differences. | Rounding Decimals | 60–61 | 11–13 | 1–37, SK | 1–39, SK | 2–40 even, SK | SE5 Ch 4<br>RS 16 | ES 16 | MP 414<br>PS 23 |
| | Estimating Sums and Differences | 62 | 14–17 | 1–11 | 1–13 | 1–15 | SE5 Ch 4 | | PS 24 |
| **3.3** Add and subtract decimals. | Adding with Decimals | 64–65 | 18–21 | 1–30 | 1–31 | 1–29 odd, 30–31 | SE5 Ch 4<br>RS 17 | ES 17 | MP 415<br>PS 25 |
| | Subtracting with Decimals | 66–67 | 22–25 | 1–30 | 1–32 | 2–20 even, 21–32, TM | SE5 Ch 4<br>RS 18 | ES 18 | MP 415<br>PS 26 |
| | More Estimating Sums and Differences | 68 | 26–28 | 1–10 | 1–10 | 1–10 | SE5 Ch 4 | | PS 27 |
| | Money: Making Change | 70 | 29–30 | 1–8 | 1–8 | 1–8 | SE5 Ch 4 | | PS 28 |
| **3.4** Solve word problems using the 5-Point Checklist and cumulative computational skills. | Problem Solving: Using Estimation | 63 | 31–35 | 1–5 | 1–7 | 1–8 | | | |
| | Problem Solving: Using Estimation | 69 | | 1–7 | 1–8 | 1–9 | RS 19 | ES 19 | |
| | Problem Solving: Practice | 71 | | 1–7 | 1–8 | 1–9 | | | |
| | Problem Solving: Using Data from a Tour Book | 72–73 | | 1–9 | 1–10 | 1–11 | | | PS 29 |
| | Problem Solving: Draw a Picture | 74 | | | | | | | |
| | Chapter Review-Test | 75 | | | | | | | |
| | Another Look/Enrichment | 76–77 | | | | | | | |
| | Cumulative Review | 78 | | | | | | | |

**SE5** Student Edition, Book 5
**RS** Reteaching Supplement
**ES** Enrichment Supplement
**PS** Practice Supplement
**MP** More Practice
**TM** Think Math
**SK** Skillkeeper
**TRB** Teacher's Resource Book

# Teacher's Resource Book

## Masters for Use

**. . . before Chapter 3**

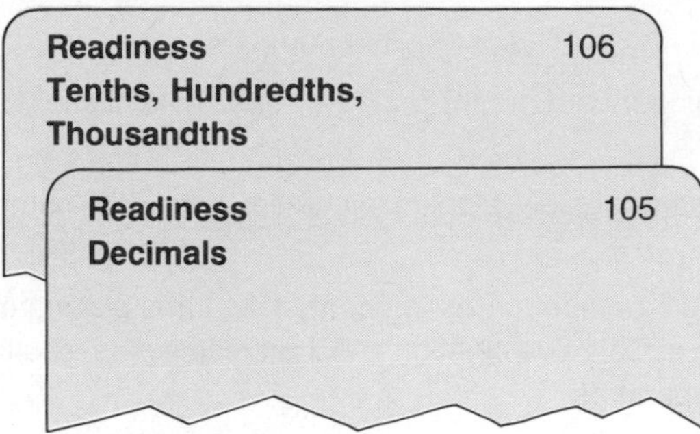


**. . . during Chapter 3**

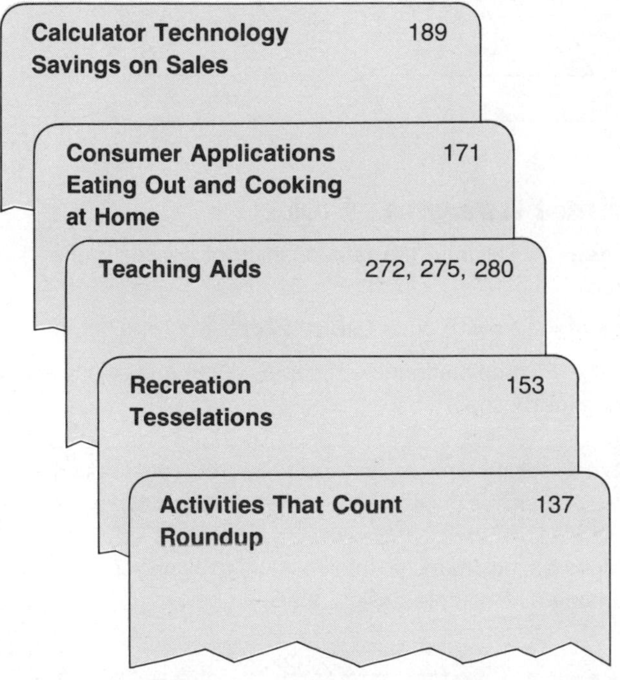


**. . . after Chapter 3**

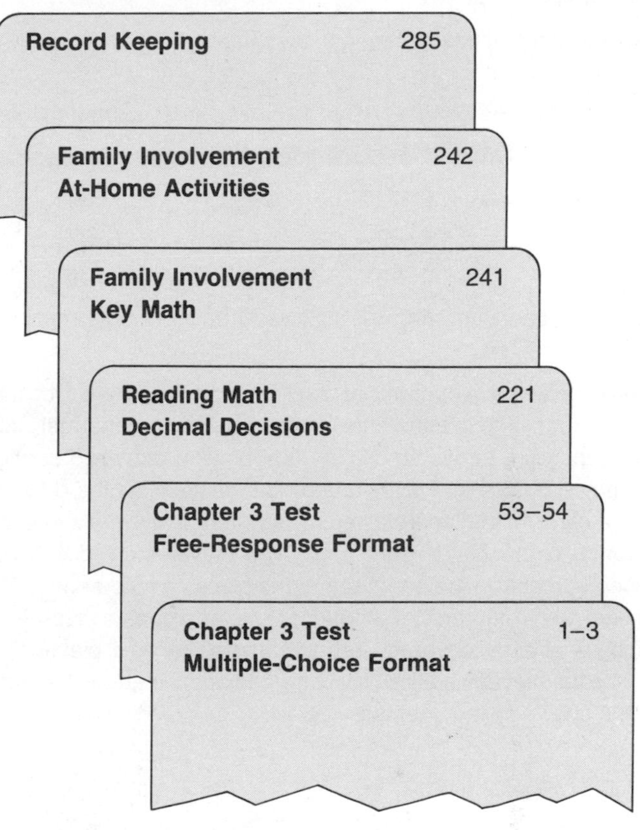


## Supplements

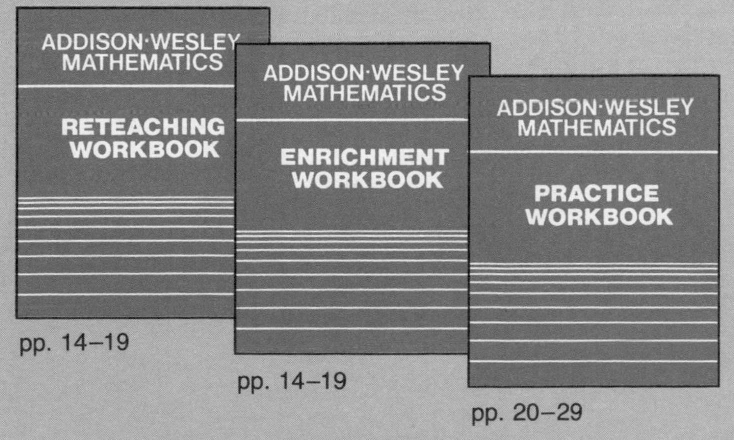


pp. 14–19

pp. 14–19

pp. 20–29

## Other Addison-Wesley Resources

### Books and Kits

*Skillseekers 3* ⊕ Lessons 1–3; ⊖ Lessons 4–6

*The Arithmetic Primer* pp. 206–213, 218–220, 222–231 270–272, 301–302

*Arithmetic Skill Cards* pp. D 1–2

*Baseball, A Game of Numbers* pp. 2–3, 23–27, 103

*Problem Solving Experiences in Mathematics,* Grade 6 Problems 9, 10, 17, 28, 38, 44, 45, 48, 62, 63, 78, 85, 92, 93, 97, 110, 133, 134, 142, 143, 148, 150

### Technology

*Computer Math Activities* Volumes 1–5

*Computer Math Games* Volumes 1, 2, 4, 6

# Activities That Count

Activities That Count are designed for use throughout this chapter and subsequent chapters. Before beginning Chapter 3, you may wish to review these activities and select the ones you consider appropriate for your class.

## **Roundup** Game

**Purpose** To practice rounding to the nearest tenth, hundredth, or whole number

**Materials** Game board (TRB p. 137); 24 cards; colored markers

**Preparation** Label 12 decimal-number cards as follows:

| | | | |
|---|---|---|---|
| 0.896 | 1.274 | 1.469 | 1.5345 |
| 0.725 | 1.6729 | 3.478 | 1.997 |
| 2.838 | 1.168 | 1.459 | 1.236 |

Label 12 place-value cards as follows: 4 each—whole numbers, tenths, hundredths.

**Activity** Each player chooses a set of colored markers. Decimal-number cards and place-value cards are mixed separately and placed facedown in two stacks. In turn, players draw two cards—one from each stack. Player rounds the decimal on the decimal-number card to the nearest tenth, hundredth, or whole number according to the place-value card. The player then locates the rounded number on the gameboard and places a marker on it. The cards are then returned to the bottom of the appropriate stack. If the number is already covered, turn passes to the next player. The winner is the player who first marks four adjacent triangular spaces, such as shown in the examples below.

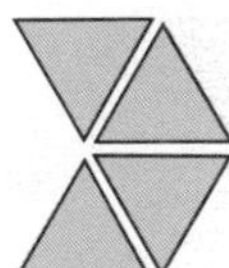

## **Place-Value Pals** Math Lab

**Purpose** To practice reading decimal numbers

**Materials** Number cards (TRB p. 279), tagboard or file folder

**Preparation** On the tagboard or file folder, make a chart similar to the example shown below. Duplicate one set of the TRB number cards.

**Activity** Using 6 number cards, students take turns placing one card below each place-value position and then reading the resulting number to their partners.

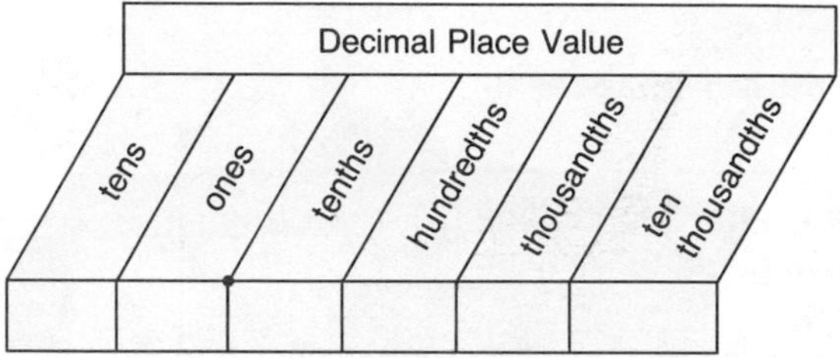


## **Decimal Designs** Project

**Purpose** To illustrate the relationships of decimal parts to one hundred

**Materials** 10 by 10 grid (TRB p. 274)

**Activity** Provide students with copies of the grids along with the following instructions:

> Make and color 6 designs using the hundred-square grids. Label each design with a decimal that names the parts that are colored.

Designs can be organized into booklets or displayed on a decimal bulletin board. A sample design is shown below.

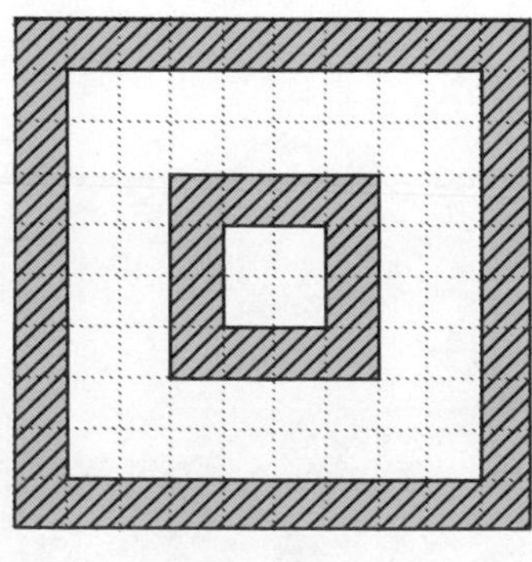

0.48
forty-eight hundredths

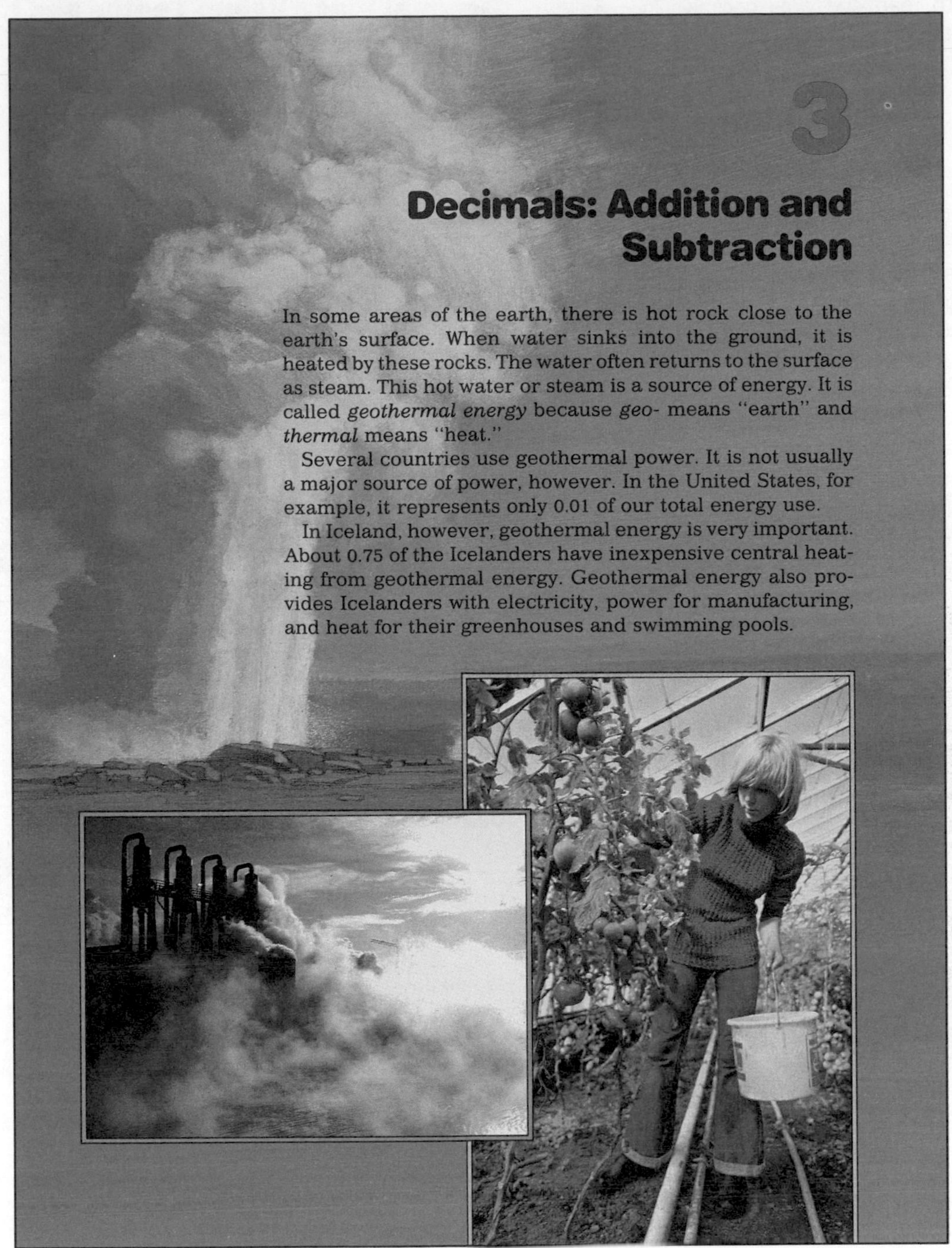
3

## Decimals: Addition and Subtraction

In some areas of the earth, there is hot rock close to the earth's surface. When water sinks into the ground, it is heated by these rocks. The water often returns to the surface as steam. This hot water or steam is a source of energy. It is called *geothermal energy* because *geo-* means "earth" and *thermal* means "heat."

Several countries use geothermal power. It is not usually a major source of power, however. In the United States, for example, it represents only 0.01 of our total energy use.

In Iceland, however, geothermal energy is very important. About 0.75 of the Icelanders have inexpensive central heating from geothermal energy. Geothermal energy also provides Icelanders with electricity, power for manufacturing, and heat for their greenhouses and swimming pools.

## Introducing the Chapter

**Discussion** Before asking students to open their books, point out that in Chapter 3 they will be studying decimal place value and the addition and subtraction algorithms for decimals. Then encourage a brief discussion of less-developed sources of energy, such as tidal, solar, wind, and geothermal. Explain that geothermal energy plays an especially important role in countries such as Iceland that have meager supplies of oil, coal, and other traditional energy sources. After allowing students ample time to read the story and enjoy the art, suggest that they try to make up some questions based on the facts given in the story. As you teach the chapter, you may wish to refer back to this page and pose the questions suggested below. Briefly review the story theme before asking the questions.

## Follow-Up Questions

**After Page 55** Geothermal energy provides heating for the homes of about 0.75 of all Icelanders. Write this decimal in words. (seventy-five hundredths)

**After Page 57** On the island of Hawaii a well 1.920 km deep has been drilled to produce geothermal energy. Write the word name for this decimal. (one and nine hundred twenty thousandths) What digit in this decimal is in the hundredths place? (2)

**After Page 60** Scientists estimate that the geothermal energy in the top 3.2 km of the earth's crust could supply the people of the United States with all their energy needs for the next 50 years if that energy source could be fully developed. What is 3.2 rounded to the nearest whole number? (3)

# Decimals

**Quick Review** Students skip count by twos to 20, by fives to 50, and by tens to 100. Then they skip count backward by twos, fives, and tens from 20, 50, and 100, respectively.

**Lesson Focus** To read and write decimals in tenths and hundredths

**Suggested Materials** 10 by 10 grids (TRB p. 274)

## Ideas for Getting Started

Tell students that each 10 by 10 square on the graph paper represents 1 unit. Elicit from students that there are 10 squares in each column and have them shade 2 columns of ten-squares on one of their grids. "How many columns of ten squares are in 1 unit?" (10) "If there are 10 columns in one unit, we can say that each column is one-tenth of the unit." "How many tenths have you shaded?" Write $\frac{2}{10}$ on the chalkboard. Now tell students that another way to write this is as a *decimal* or 0.2.

"How many small squares are in 1 unit?" (100) Then have students shade 4 more of the small squares in the next column. "How many small squares are now shaded? (24) Show students that we can show this as a fraction, $\frac{24}{100}$, or as a decimal 0.24. Write the word names for these two decimals on the chalkboard.

## Using Page 54

**Lesson Development** Have students read the paragraph about Carla and Vince and their stamp collection. "What questions are we asked about the stamp collection?" (How can Carla and Vince use fractions and decimals to tell how many pages of stamps they filled?)

Have students read the information about Carla's collection. Point out that "1 whole sheet is filled." "How many small squares (or stamps) fill 1 sheet?" (100) "How many squares on the second sheet are filled?" (47) Read through the statements that tell how to read and write the fraction, the decimal, and the word name for the picture. "In Vince's collection, how many squares are filled?" (70) "How many rows of 10 is that?" (7) "How many rows make up 1 sheet?" (10) Elicit from students that each row represents one tenth of the sheet. Have students read the information that tells how to read and write a fraction, decimal, and the word name for the picture. Emphasize that 0.7 = 0.70 and that the 0 on the right need not be written.

**Other Examples** Discuss the two examples at the bottom of the page with the class. For the first example, point out how a 0 is written to the *left* of the decimal point to show 0 whole units. For the second example, ask students to think of another way to write the decimal 2.3. (2.30, or two and thirty hundredths)

## Decimal Place Value: Tenths and Hundredths

Carla and Vince started stamp collections. Carla has filled 1 whole page and part of another page. Vince has filled less than 1 whole page. How can they use fractions and decimals to tell the number of pages they have filled?

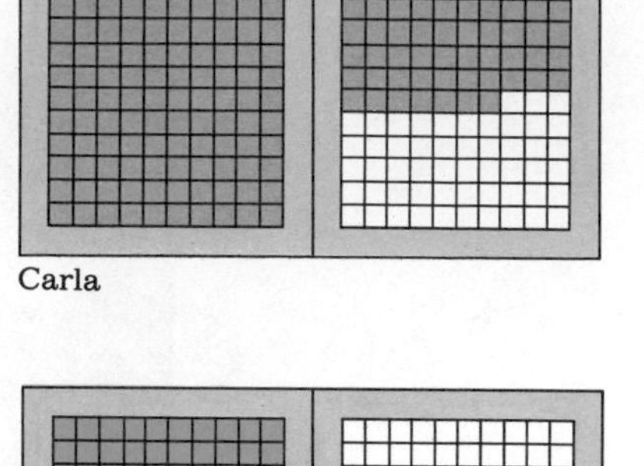
1 whole sheet is filled
47 out of 100 spaces are filled.
Carla

**Using a fraction** **Using a decimal**

$$1\frac{47}{100} = 1.47$$

**We read:** "one and forty-seven **hundredths**"

Carla can say she filled 1.47 pages.

**Using a fraction** **Using a decimal**

$$\frac{7}{10} = 0.7$$

or

$$\frac{70}{100} = 0.70$$

$\frac{70}{100} = \frac{7}{10}$ or $0.70 = 0.7$

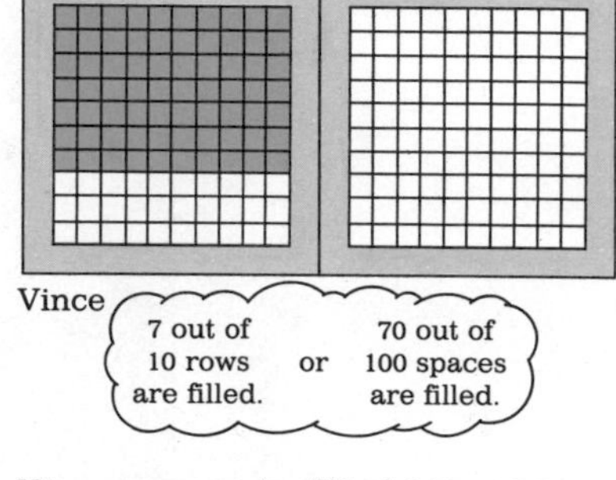
Vince
7 out of 10 rows are filled.
or
70 out of 100 spaces are filled.

**We read:** "seven **tenths**" or "seventy **hundredths**"

Vince can say he filled 0.7 or 0.70 pages.

**Other Examples**

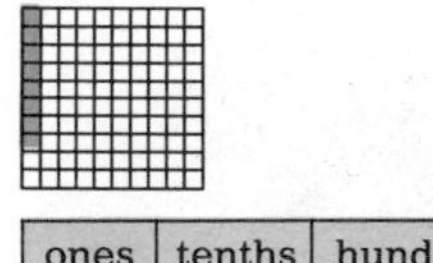

| | ones | tenths | hundredths |
|---|---|---|---|
| **We think:** | 0 | 0 | 8 |

**We write:** 0.08

**We read:** "eight hundredths"

| | ones | tenths | hundredths |
|---|---|---|---|
| **We think:** | 2 | 3 | |

**We write:** 2.3

**We read:** "two and three tenths"

54

## Follow Up

### Reteaching

On an overhead projector show a 10 by 10 grid (TRB p. 274). Remind students that there are 100 small squares and that each small square is one-hundredth of the grid. As you shade parts of the grid, name the value of the shaded parts. Then give students copies of the grids and ask them to show various amounts such as one tenth, four tenths, six hundredths, fifteen hundredths, and so on. Make sure students understand the relationship between tenths and hundredths.

### Enrichment

Provide students with four sets of different-colored cards labeled 0 through 9 (TRB p. 279). Each color represents a place value—ones, tens, tenths, or hundredths. Cards are mixed and placed in stacks according to color. Players take turns drawing four cards, one of each color and reading the number represented by the cards drawn. If the cards are read correctly, player draws another four cards and wins a second turn. If the number is not read correctly, player loses the turn and turn passes to the other player. The round ends when all of the cards have been used.

| Assignment Guide | | | |
|---|---|---|---|
| | Minimum | Average | Extended |
| page 55 | 1–28 | 1–28 | 1–28, TM |

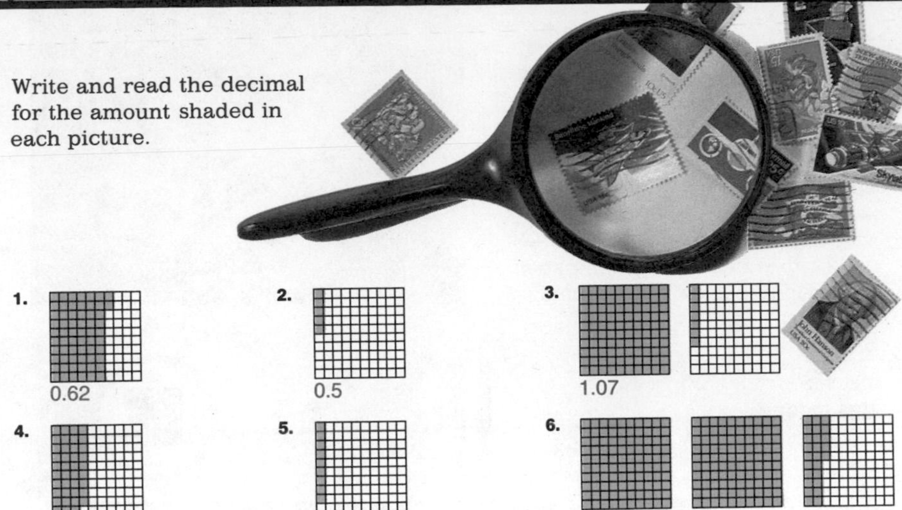

Write and read the decimal for the amount shaded in each picture.

1. 0.62
2. 0.5
3. 1.07
4. 0.39
5. 0.09
6. 2.25

Write the place value for each red digit.

7. 16.1 — 1 tenth
8. 0.49 — 9 hundredths
9. 12.15 — 2 ones
10. 8.08 — 0 tenths
11. 23.44 — 2 tens
12. 0.02 — 2 hundredths
13. 0.60 — 6 tenths
14. 4.25 — 5 hundredths

Write the decimal.

15. thirty-two hundredths — 0.32
16. five and two tenths — 5.2
17. seven hundredths — 0.07
18. one and fifty hundredths — 1.50
19. nine tenths — 0.9
20. twelve and twelve hundredths — 12.12

Write the word name for each decimal.

21. 0.4 — four tenths
22. 0.63 — sixty-three hundredths
23. 1.25 — one and twenty-five hundredths
24. 0.05 — five hundredths
25. 2.10 — two and ten hundredths
26. 0.58 — fifty-eight hundredths
27. 1.07 — one and seven hundredths
28. 5.3 — five and three tenths

**Think Math**

**A Line Segment Puzzle**

Draw 4 straight line segments to pass through all 9 dots. Each segment must be connected to an endpoint of at least one other segment.

55

## Using Page 55

**Exercises 1–6** Be sure students write a zero to the left of the decimal point in exercises 1, 2, 4, and 5.

**Exercises 7–28** Notice in exercise 16 that because the word name is given in tenths the correct answer is 5.2, not 5.20. For exercises 21–28, be sure students include the "th" at the end of the word name to indicate the decimal place value.

**Think Math** This is a famous puzzle problem that some students may have already seen. The puzzle is difficult for many because they incorrectly assume that the line segments cannot go beyond the imaginary square. If a hint is necessary, tell students that the line segments can extend beyond the dots.

**Skillkeeper** These skills were originally taught in Chapter 2.

## Ideas That Work

### Special Education

Have students practice reading decimals by using a list of 10 decimals and a tape recorder. Students write the names of these decimals. After the decimals have been written out correctly, students can insert the accompanying tape and listen to the oral form of the decimal names.

1.2 One and two tenths
0.37 Thirty seven hundredths
4.38 Four and thirty-eight hundredths

Then use class relays based on writing out the numbers after hearing the verbal names, writing out the verbal names in words upon seeing the decimal, and so on. Each person on the team must get the item correct for the team to progress.

**Practice Supplement,** page 20

Name ______ To follow text page 55

**Decimal Place Value: Tenths and Hundredths**

Use the decimal 25.37. Write the place value of each digit.

1. 5 ones
2. 3 tenths
3. 7 hundredths

Use the decimal 6.98. Write the place value of each digit.

4. 8 hundredths
5. 6 ones
6. 9 tenths

Write the decimal.

7. six tenths — 0.6
8. one and forty-five hundredths — 1.45
9. two and two hundredths — 2.02
10. twenty-eight and nine tenths — 28.9
11. fifty-six and eighty-eight hundredths — 56.88
12. seventy-one and one hundredth — 71.01
13. fifteen hundredths — 0.15
14. three hundred and three hundredths — 300.03
15. ten and 5 tenths — 10.5
16. eighty-nine and eighty-nine hundredths — 89.89

Write the word name for each decimal.

17. 0.7 — seven tenths
18. 12.8 — twelve and eight tenths
19. 0.56 — fifty-six hundredths
20. 0.03 — three hundredths
21. 4.29 — four and twenty-nine hundredths
22. 16.05 — sixteen and five hundredths

# Decimals

**Quick Review** Have students give the meaning of each underlined digit.

| | | | |
|---|---|---|---|
| 101 0 tens | 1,400 4 hundreds | 9,002 9 thousands | 2,428 8 ones |
| 5,602 5 thousands | 26 6 ones | 127 1 hundred | 4,986 9 hundreds |
| 922 2 tens | 286 8 tens | 21,137 2 ten thousands | |

**Lesson Focus** To read and write decimals through hundred-thousandths

**Suggested Materials** Graph paper (TRB p. 271)

## Ideas for Getting Started

Use centimeter graph paper to review tenths and hundredths. Have students outline a 10 by 10 square on their graph paper. "How many squares are in each row?" (10) "How many rows are in the square?" (10) "How many small squares are in the entire square?" (100) Next write 0.2 on the chalkboard. Tell students to shade two tenths on their graph paper. Then discuss that each row is $\frac{1}{10}$ of the whole unit so "2 tenths" is shaded. Then write 0.24 and have the students shade the additional squares to show this. Discuss that each small square is $\frac{1}{100}$ of the unit so "24 hundredths" is shaded.

To introduce the idea of thousandths of the unit, ask: "If we made 10 smaller regions in each small square, how many of these small regions would we have in the entire square (or unit)?" ($100 \times 10 = 1{,}000$). "What part of the whole unit would each small region represent?" Write $\frac{1}{1{,}000} = 0.001$ on the chalkboard.

## Using Page 56

**Lesson Development** Have students read the information about the micrometer at the top of the page. Write 0.243 on the chalkboard. Discuss the place value of each digit and how to read the decimal. Point out that to read the decimal, we look to the decimal place value of the digit farthest to the right (3). Then we read the digits as with whole numbers (two hundred forty-three) and then say the place value of the last digit (thousandths).

**Exercises 1–29** If necessary, lead students through one or two exercises in each group. When discussing the exercises, be sure to emphasize the leading zero before the decimal point. Also, discuss decimals such as exercise 10 where 0.050 could be written as 0.05.

Answers

16. three hundred twenty-three thousandths
17. forty-one thousandths
18. one and twenty-one hundredths
19. one and two hundred ten thousandths
20. eight and sixty-two hundredths
21. twelve and six-hundred two thousandths
22. one and three thousandths
23. thirty-seven thousandths
24. fourteen and two hundred six thousandths
25. thirty-two and two hundred seventy-five thousandths

## Thousandths

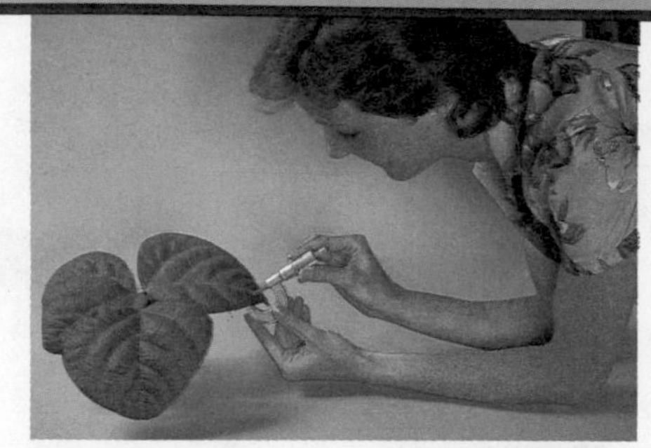

A **micrometer** is a tool that can be used to measure objects very accurately. For example, with a metric micrometer, Rhonda found that the thickness of a leaf was 0.243 cm. We can use graph paper as a model to show this decimal.

**We see** this model:

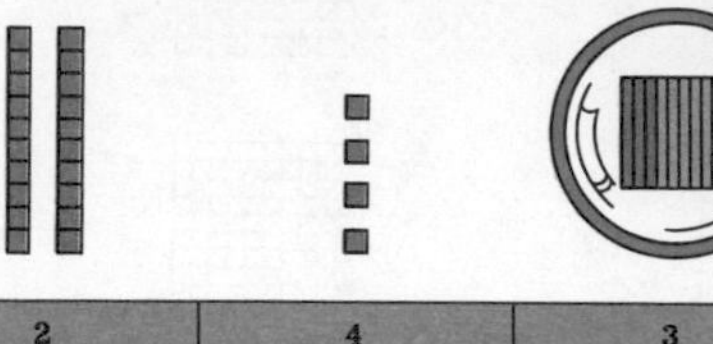

**We think:**

| 0 | 2 | 4 | 3 |
|---|---|---|---|
| ones | tenths | hundredths | thousandths |

**We write:** 0.243

**We read:** "two hundred forty-three **thousandths**"

Read each decimal. Give the place value of each red digit.

| | | | | |
|---|---|---|---|---|
| **1.** 4.286<br>8 hundredths | **2.** 0.753<br>3 thousandths | **3.** 0.042<br>0 tenths | **4.** 1.54<br>4 hundredths | **5.** 7.008<br>7 ones |
| **6.** 25.34<br>3 tenths | **7.** 4.622<br>2 thousandths | **8.** 18.531<br>1 thousandth | **9.** 0.427<br>2 hundredths | **10.** 0.050<br>0 thousandths |
| **11.** 120.04<br>2 tens | **12.** 63.556<br>3 ones | **13.** 4.205<br>0 hundredths | **14.** 0.886<br>8 hundredths | **15.** 132.247<br>7 thousandths |

Write the word name for each decimal. See teaching notes.

| | | | | |
|---|---|---|---|---|
| **16.** 0.323 | **17.** 0.041 | **18.** 1.21 | **19.** 1.210 | **20.** 8.62 |
| **21.** 12.602 | **22.** 1.003 | **23.** 0.037 | **24.** 14.206 | **25.** 32.275 |

Write the decimal.

**26.** four hundred twenty-five thousandths
0.425

**27.** one and one hundred eight thousandths
1.108

**28.** thirty-nine thousands
0.039

**29.** two hundred and five thousandths
200.005



## Follow Up

### Reteaching

Review several decimals up through the thousandths and discuss how such numbers are written. For example, 8.437. First analyze the decimal in terms of place value.

| 8 | 4 | 3 | 7 |
|---|---|---|---|
| ones | tenths | hundredths | thousandths |

Ask: "What digit is in the hundredths place?" Read "eight and four hundred thirty-seven thousandths." Use several numbers, giving students practice in identifying the place-value of the digits and in reading the decimals aloud.

### Enrichment

Have students look through magazines and newspapers to find examples in which decimals are used. The examples can be cut out and mounted on colored paper and then used as a bulletin board display. Challenge students to read their decimal examples as well as those of their classmates.

| Assignment Guide | | | |
|---|---|---|---|
| | Minimum | Average | Extended |
| page 56 | 1–10, 16–20, 26–29 | 1–29 | 1–29 odd |
| page 57 | 1–8, 13–16, 21–24 | 1–24 | 2–24 even |

## Place Value Through Hundred-Thousandths

Ms. Reilly uses her home computer to calculate and record the average amount of gas used in her home each day. The screen shows the daily average use for the three coldest months. What was the average number of therms (units of heat) used per day in January?

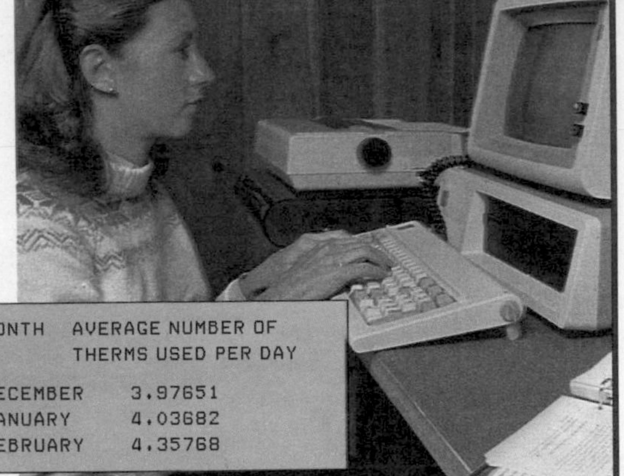

| MONTH | AVERAGE NUMBER OF THERMS USED PER DAY |
|---|---|
| DECEMBER | 3.97651 |
| JANUARY | 4.03682 |
| FEBRUARY | 4.35768 |

**We think:**

| 4 | 0 | 3 | 6 | 8 | 2 |
|---|---|---|---|---|---|
| ones | tenths | hundredths | thousandths | ten-thousandths | hundred-thousandths |

**We write:** 4.03682

**We read:** "four and three thousand, six hundred eighty-two **hundred-thousandths**"

The average number of therms used per day in January was 4.03682.

Read each decimal. Give the place value of the red digit.

1. 6.205 0 hundredths
2. 0.72364 7 tenths
3. 15.3834 8 hundredths
4. 9.45002 2 hundred-thousandths
5. 9.2 9 ones
6. 126.365 2 tens
7. 18.006 6 thousandths
8. 0.99999 9 hundred-thousandths
9. 4.50 0 hundredths
10. 0.61 6 tenths
11. 0.46290 9 ten-thousandths
12. 14.02105 1 thousandth

Write the word name for each decimal. See teaching notes.

13. 0.4256
14. 1.2005
15. 0.00645
16. 14.02
17. 6.007
18. 8.45
19. 12.0054
20. 0.32624

Write the decimal.

21. nine hundred forty-five thousandths 0.945
22. five and fifteen ten-thousandths 5.0015
23. two hundred six hundred-thousandths 0.00206
24. twelve thousand, four hundred twenty-four hundred-housandths 0.12424



## Using Page 57

**Motivational Problem** Have students read the problem at the top of the page. "What are we asked to find out about Ms. Reilly's gas usage?" Make sure students understand that the data for Ms. Reilly's gas usage was recorded in her home. Then point out that to answer the question, we need to read and write the decimal that shows the number of therms used in January.

**Lesson Development** Tell students that in this lesson they will learn to read and write decimals to decimal places smaller than the thousandths. Point out the place-value names for the 8 and 2 indicated on the chart. Then ask students to imagine dividing each of the thousandths into ten regions. This would give 10,000 small regions and each would be ten thousandth of the unit. (Write $\frac{1}{10{,}000}$ on the chalkboard.) Next, tell students that if we divided each of these into 10 smaller regions, there would be 100,000 small regions in the unit and each would be a hundred-thousandth of the unit. (Write $\frac{1}{100{,}000}$ on the chalkboard.) Discuss how to write and read the decimals shown. Emphasize how to read the decimal part as with whole numbers and then read the decimal place value of the last digit on the right.

**Exercises 1–24** If necessary, work through the exercises in each set to check for students' understanding.

Answers for exercises 13–20

13. four thousand, two hundred fifty-six ten-thousandths
14. one and two thousand five ten-thousandths
15. six hundred forty-five hundred-thousandths
16. fourteen and two hundredths
17. six and seven thousandths
18. eight and forty-five hundredths
19. twelve and fifty-four ten-thousandths
20. thirty-two thousand, six hundred twenty four hundred-thousandths

### Reteaching Supplement, page 14

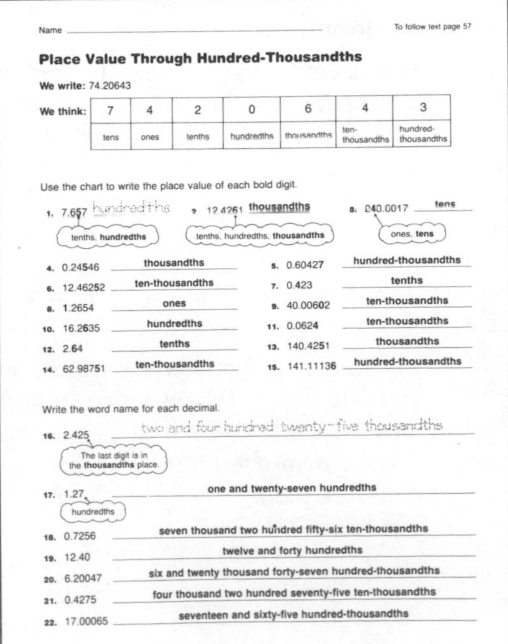

Name ______ To follow text page 57

**Place Value Through Hundred-Thousandths**

**We write:** 74.20643

**We think:**

| 7 | 4 | 2 | 0 | 6 | 4 | 3 |
|---|---|---|---|---|---|---|
| tens | ones | tenths | hundredths | thousandths | ten-thousandths | hundred-thousandths |

Use the chart to write the place value of each bold digit.

1. 7.657 hundredths (tenths, **hundredths**)
2. 12.4261 thousandths (tenths, hundredths, **thousandths**)
3. 040.0017 tens (ones, **tens**)
4. 0.24546 thousandths
5. 0.60427 hundred-thousandths
6. 12.46252 ten-thousandths
7. 0.423 tenths
8. 1.2654 ones
9. 40.00602 ten-thousandths
10. 16.2635 hundredths
11. 0.0624 ten-thousandths
12. 2.64 tenths
13. 140.4251 thousandths
14. 62.98751 ten-thousandths
15. 141.11136 hundred-thousandths

Write the word name for each decimal.

16. 2.425 two and four hundred twenty-five thousandths (The last digit is in the **thousandths** place.)
17. 1.27 one and twenty-seven hundredths (hundredths)
18. 0.7256 seven thousand two hundred fifty-six ten-thousandths
19. 12.40 twelve and forty hundredths
20. 6.20047 six and twenty thousand forty-seven hundred-thousandths
21. 0.4275 four thousand two hundred seventy-five ten-thousandths
22. 17.00065 seventeen and sixty-five hundred-thousandths

### Enrichment Supplement, page 14

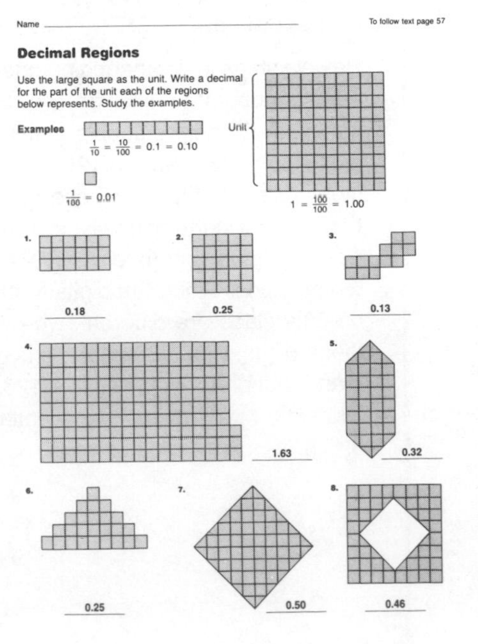

Name ______ To follow text page 57

**Decimal Regions**

Use the large square as the unit. Write a decimal for the part of the unit each of the regions below represents. Study the examples.

**Examples** $\frac{1}{10} = \frac{10}{100} = 0.1 = 0.10$

$\frac{1}{100} = 0.01$

Unit $1 = \frac{100}{100} = 1.00$

1. 0.18
2. 0.25
3. 0.13
4. 1.63
5. 0.32
6. 0.25
7. 0.50
8. 0.46

### Practice Supplement, page 21

Name ______ To follow text page 57

**Place Value Through Hundred-Thousandths**

Write the place value of the underlined digit.

1. 7.209 thousandths
2. 2.3857 tenths
3. 9.5084 ten-thousandths
4. 1.039 hundredths
5. 0.12347 hundred-thousandths
6. 0.1415 thousandths
7. 12.6472 hundredths
8. 25.19836 hundred-thousandths
9. 84.01623 ten-thousandths
10. 162.158 thousandths

Write the decimal.

11. five hundred seventeen thousandths 0.517
12. three thousand one hundred seven ten-thousandths 0.3107
13. sixty-eight hundred-thousandths 0.00068
14. two hundred two ten-thousandths 0.0202
15. five and nine thousandths 5.009
16. six hundred six hundred-thousandths 0.00606

Write the word name for each decimal.

17. 0.0001 one ten-thousandth
18. 0.014 fourteen thousandths
19. 0.00025 twenty-five hundred-thousandths
20. 8.205 eight and two hundred five thousandths
21. 1.00008 one and eight hundred-thousandths
22. 0.0603 six hundred three ten-thousandths

# Decimals

**Quick Review** Have students write the numbers below in order, from least to greatest.

9 1,600 7 606 6 601 10 6,601 2 61 1 16
8 1,006 5 166 11 10,006 3 66 4 106

**Lesson Focus** To compare decimals using the inequality symbols (> and <); to order decimals from greatest to least and from least to greatest

**Suggested Materials** Graph paper (TRB p. 271)

## Ideas for Getting Started

Give each student sheets of graph paper. Write 0.36 and 0.32 on the chalkboard. Have students mark 10 by 10 square, on their papers. Have half of the class shade 0.36 of their squares and the other half shade 0.32. Have students compare their graphs to decide which of the two decimals is greater. Remind students how to write the inequality symbols. Then elicit from students that we can say 0.36 is greater than 0.32 and write 0.36 > 0.32, or we can say that 0.32 is less than 0.36 and write 0.32 < 0.36.

## Using Page 58

**Motivational Problem** Have students read the paragraph at the top of the page. "What are we asked to find out about the steel bars cut by the welder?" (Is piece 1 longer or shorter than piece 2?) Then explain to students that the data needed is in the chart at the right of the paragraph. Have them read the decimals for the five pieces of steel bars.

**Lesson Development** Read the instruction boxes and relate each step to the work shown below the box. Emphasize that there are two correct ways to write a comparison of these decimals.

Discuss with students how the lengths must be compared two at a time to order the decimals. If necessary, write the lengths on the chalkboard and lead students through a comparison of each pair of lengths to arrive at the order shown.

**Warm Up** In exercises 3, 5, 6, and 7 students may find it helpful to annex a 0 to the right of the last digit. For example, to compare 0.5 and 0.62, have students rewrite 0.5 as 0.50.

## Comparing and Ordering Decimals

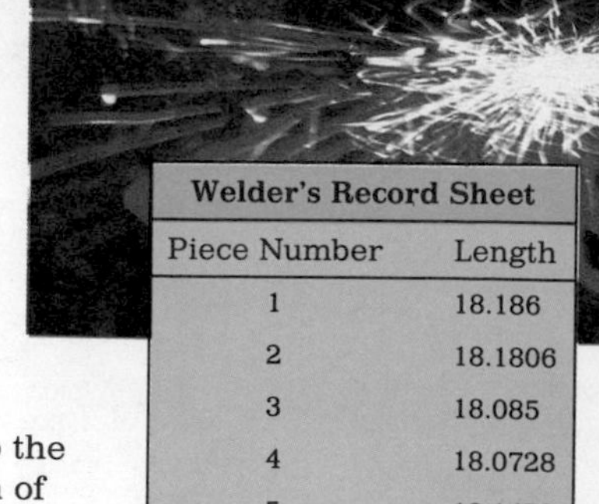

A welder is cutting pieces of steel bars to a length as close as possible to 18.125 in. (inches). The welder has cut five pieces. Is piece 1 longer or shorter than piece 2?

**Welder's Record Sheet**

| Piece Number | Length |
|---|---|
| 1 | 18.186 |
| 2 | 18.1806 |
| 3 | 18.085 |
| 4 | 18.0728 |
| 5 | 18.1472 |

**Compare** the length of piece 1 to the length of piece 2 to decide which of the two pieces has the greater length.

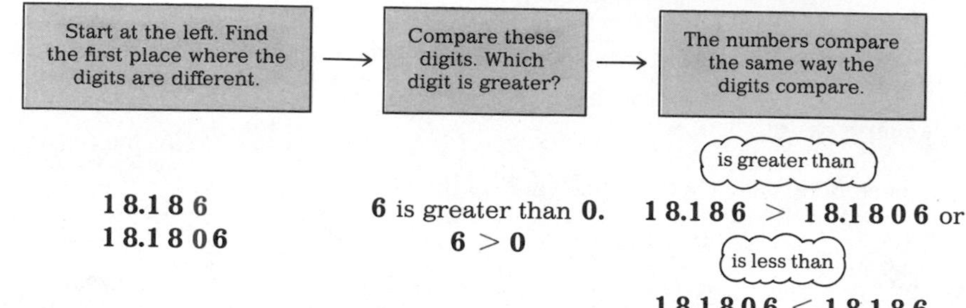

Start at the left. Find the first place where the digits are different.
Compare these digits. Which digit is greater?
The numbers compare the same way the digits compare.
is greater than
18.186
18.1806
6 is greater than 0.
6 > 0
18.186 > 18.1806 or
is less than
18.1806 < 18.186


The length of piece 1 is greater than the length of piece 2.

**Order** the lengths of the pieces by listing them from greatest to least. Do this by comparing them two at a time.

18.186 ← greatest
18.1806
18.1472
18.085
18.0728 ← least

**Warm Up** Write >, <, or = for each ●.

1. 6.5 ● 6.2 >
2. 26.4 ● 27.4 <
3. 0.5 ● 0.62 <
4. 423 ● 420 >
5. 0.052 ● 0.0520 =
6. 6.07353 ● 6.074 <
7. 0.009 ● 0.02 <
8. 10.01 ● 100.1 <

58

## Follow Up

### Reteaching

Review steps in comparing numbers. Remind students to line up the decimal points. Then help students compare the decimals 8.137 and 8.126 with these steps: Start at the left. Since both numbers have 8 in the ones place, look at the next digit. Both numbers have 1 in the tenths place. Since the digits in the hundredths place are different, we compare these digits. Since 3 hundreds is greater than 2 hundredths, 8.137 > 8.126. Have students read "8.137 is greater than 8.126."

### Enrichment

Let students work in pairs to play the decimal comparison game below. Make cards with each of the following division problems:

1 ÷ 2, 1 ÷ 3, 1 ÷ 4, 1 ÷ 5, 1 ÷ 6, 2 ÷ 3, 2 ÷ 5, 2 ÷ 7, 2 ÷ 9, 3 ÷ 4, 3 ÷ 5, 3 ÷ 7, 3 ÷ 8, 4 ÷ 5, 4 ÷ 7, 4 ÷ 9, 5 ÷ 7, 5 ÷ 8, 5 ÷ 9, 6 ÷ 7, 6 ÷ 8, 6 ÷ 9

Each player in turn draws two cards and guesses which division (using a calculator) will result in the larger decimal. Players earn one point for each correct guess. A score of ten points completes one round.

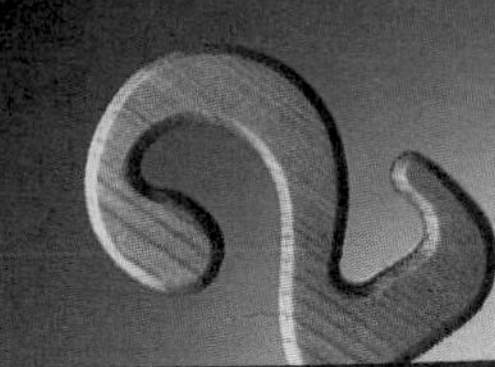

| Assignment Guide | | | |
|---|---|---|---|
| | Minimum | Average | Extended |
| page 59 | 1–10, 25–27 | 1–28 | 13–28, TM |

Write, >, <, or = for each ●

1. 7.8 ● 7.7 >
2. 0.67 ● 0.68 <
3. 0.742 ● 7.40 <
4. 50.3 ● 5.30 >
5. 9.32 ● 9.3 >
6. 832 ● 840 <
7. 16.2 ● 6.2 >
8. 0.006 ● 0.0060 =
9. 0.1 ● 0.01 >
10. 0.977 ● 0.978 <
11. 3.0740 ● 3.047 >
12. 9.500 ● 9.6 <
13. 0.76 ● 0.8 <
14. 14.050 ● 14.05 =
15. 0.503 ● 0.508 <
16. 4.7 ● 4.6999 >
17. 2.0234 ● 2.0243 <
18. 0.00006 ● 0.0006 <
19. 12.0640 ● 1.064 >
20. 63.95 ● 63.81 >
21. 40.2 ● 40.02 >
22. 0.7502 ● 0.752 <
23. 165.25 ● 165.3 <
24. 400.5 ● 40.55 >

25. Order the numbers from greatest to least.

| Drill Sizes | | |
|---|---|---|
| Drill number | | Hole size (in inches) |
| 1 | 0.594 | 0.531 |
| 2 | 0.578 | 0.422 |
| 3 | 0.531 | 0.484 |
| 4 | 0.484 | 0.594 |
| 5 | 0.422 | 0.578 |

26. Order the numbers from least to greatest.

| Electrical Wires for Cars | | |
|---|---|---|
| Wire number | | Diameter (in inches) |
| 1 | 0.007 | 0.01 |
| 2 | 0.0089 | 0.0126 |
| 3 | 0.01 | 0.007 |
| 4 | 0.0126 | 0.0179 |
| 5 | 0.0179 | 0.0089 |

27. Which of the five lengths of pieces shown in the table on page 58 were less than 18.125 in.? 18.085; 18.0728

28. A welder cut a steel rod that measured 12.5043 in. The needed length was 12.543 in. Was the piece cut longer or shorter than the needed length? shorter

**Think**

**Logical Reasoning**

Use all of the digits 5, 1, 6, 2, 0, and 4 to write these numbers. Use each digit only once.

1. the largest number less than 1 0.65421
2. the smallest number less than 1 0.12456
3. the largest number between 5 and 6 5.64210

**Math**

More Practice, page 414, Set B



## Using Page 59

**Exercises 1–28** Notice that exercises 25 and 26 ask the students to order 5 decimals.

**Think Math** This activity will test students' understanding of decimal place value as well as comparing and ordering of decimals. Students may need a hint that the zero can be used as a place holder to the left of the decimal point.

*Think Math activities provide interesting extensions of the lesson content.*

**More Practice,** page 414, Set B

### Reteaching Supplement, page 15

Name ________ To follow text page 59

**Comparing and Ordering Decimals**

Start at the left. Find the first place where the numbers are different. → Compare these digits. Which is greater? → The numbers compare the same way the digits compare.

21.6032 21.6029 (These are different.) | 3 is greater than 2, 3 > 2 | 21.6032 > 21.6029 (since 3 > 2)

Write > (greater than), < (less than), or = (equal to) in each circle.

1. 0.742 (<) 0.75 (4 < 5)
2. 4.6009 (<) 4.609 (0 < 9)
3. 11.2546 (>) 1.2546 (11 > 1)
4. 0.24736 (>) 0.24536
5. 1.060 (=) 1.06
6. 10.00745 (<) 10.0075
7. 1.74 (>) 1.739
8. 16.0256 (<) 16.0358
9. 40.075 (<) 40.75
10. 68.070 (=) 68.07
11. 0.26753 (<) 0.26755
12. 136.64 (>) 136.639
13. 0.20065 (<) 0.20605
14. 10.0279 (>) 0.100279
15. 75.8604 (<) 75.86114

Write in order from greatest to least.

16. 1.0102, 1.102, 0.10102, 1.1012 **1.102, 1.1012, 1.0102, 0.10102**
17. 0.7539, 0.754, 0.753, 0.759 **0.759, 0.754, 0.7539, 0.753**
18. 12.427, 12.0427, 12.4273, 12.00427 **12.4273, 12.427, 12.0427, 12.00427**
19. 0.00602, 0.0062, 0.0620, 0.00600 **0.0620, 0.0062, 0.00602, 0.00600**
20. 64.25, 64.205, 64.025, 64.245 **64.25, 64.245, 64.205, 64.025**

### Enrichment Supplement, page 15

Name ________ To follow text page 59

**In Between**

Using all of the digits given, write decimal numbers to make each statement true. Use each digit only once in each number. **Some answers may vary.**

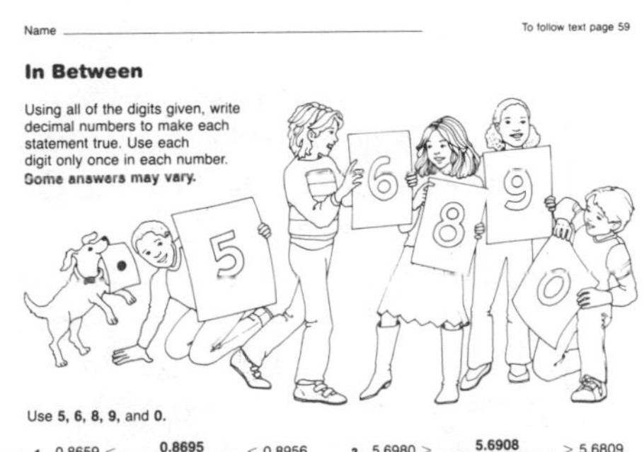


Use **5, 6, 8, 9,** and **0.**

1. 0.8659 < **0.8695** < 0.8956
2. 5.6980 > **5.6908** > 5.6809
3. 68.509 < **68.590** < 68.950
4. 8.6950 > **8.6905** > 8.6095

Use **1, 2, 3, 4,** and **0.**

5. 0.2341 < **0.2413** < 0.2431
6. 3.0124 < **3.1024** < 3.1042
7. 4.1023 > **4.0321** > 4.0312
8. 14.023 < **14.032** < 14.203

Use **6, 7, 8, 9,** and **0.**

9. 67.980 > **67.908** > 67.890
10. 8.7690 > **8.7609** > 8.7069
11. 98.607 < **98.670** < 98.760
12. 0.6789 < **0.6798** < 0.6879

Now take the numbers you wrote in 1 through 9 above and write them in order. Start with the greatest number.

13. 98.670
14. **67.908**
15. **8.7609**
16. **8.6905**
17. **5.6908**
18. **4.0321**
19. **3.1024**
20. **0.8695**
21. **0.2413**

### Practice Supplement, page 22

Name ________ To follow text page 59

**Comparing and Ordering Decimals**

Write >, <, or = for each ○

1. 6.5 (>) 6.4
2. 0.93 (<) 0.94
3. 6.3 (=) 6.30
4. 0.864 (>) 8.60
5. 9.02 (<) 9.20
6. 7.51 (>) 7.5
7. 6.18 (<) 6.20
8. 12.6 (>) 2.6
9. 0.008 (=) 0.0080
10. 0.3 (>) 0.03
11. 0.867 (<) 0.868
12. 6.0830 (>) 6.038
13. 2.400 (<) 2.5
14. 0.52 (<) 0.6
15. 11.060 (=) 11.06
16. 0.204 (<) 0.209
17. 5.2 (>) 5.1999
18. 3.0465 (<) 3.0645
19. 20.6 (<) 20.66
20. 1.1406 (<) 1.146
21. 20.06 (<) 20.66
22. 1.1406 (<) 1.146
23. 8.062 (>) 8.026
24. 14.602 (<) 14.62
25. 0.777 (>) 0.0777
26. 83.2 (>) 83
27. 6.419 (<) 6.42
28. 0.003 (<) 0.030
29. 7.2 (=) 7.20
30. 45.3 (>) 45.28

Order the numbers from greatest to least.

31. 0.684, 0.532, 0.584, 0.632, 0.588 **0.684, 0.632, 0.588, 0.584, 0.532**
32. 0.03, 0.0359, 0.001, 0.0412, 0.0019 **0.0412, 0.0359, 0.03, 0.0019, 0.001**
33. 0.304, 0.400, 0.430, 0.380, 0.404 **0.430, 0.404, 0.400, 0.380, 0.304**

# Decimals

**Quick Review** As an oral drill, students round each 2-digit number to the nearest ten and each 3-digit number to the nearest hundred.

86 11 985 250 77 25 649 547
44 18 109 482 339 91 27

**Lesson Focus** To round decimals to the nearest whole number, tenth, or hundredth

## Ideas for Getting Started

To review rounding of whole numbers, draw this number line on the chalkboard.

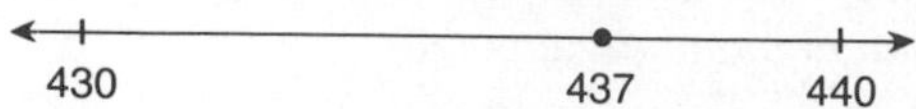


Ask students to round 437 to the nearest ten. Students should recognize that because 7 is greater than 5, they should round up to 440. Then point out on the number line that 437 is closer to 440 than to 430. Now draw this number line on the chalkboard.

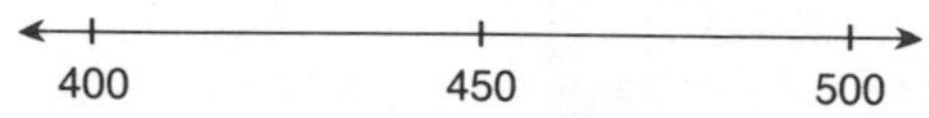


"Is 437 closer to 400 or 500?" Point out the location of 437 on the number line so students can see that it is closer to 400. "What is 437 rounded to the nearest hundred?" Discuss the rounding procedure pointing out that 3 is less than 5 so they "rounded down" to 400.

## Using Page 60

**Lesson Development** Ask students to read the paragraph about the bowling pin. "What are we asked to find out about the bowling pin?" (What is the diameter of the neck of the bowling pin rounded to the nearest tenth of a centimeter?) Ask a volunteer to read the various dimensions of the bowling pin and to identify the measurement of the neck.

As you discuss each instruction box, elicit from students that the procedure for rounding decimals is the same as that for whole numbers. After discussing the steps for rounding, discuss how the number line in the think cloud shows that 4.564 is closer to 4.6 than to 4.5.

**Other Examples** As you discuss each of these examples, point out that the steps for rounding are the same regardless of the place to which you want to round. If necessary, sketch number lines on the chalkboard to work through each of these examples. For the second example, remind students that we "round up" when the last digit is 5.

**Warm Up** If necessary, encourage students to make a mark below the digit in the decimal place to which they are to round. Make sure students understand the rounding steps before assigning the exercises on the next page.

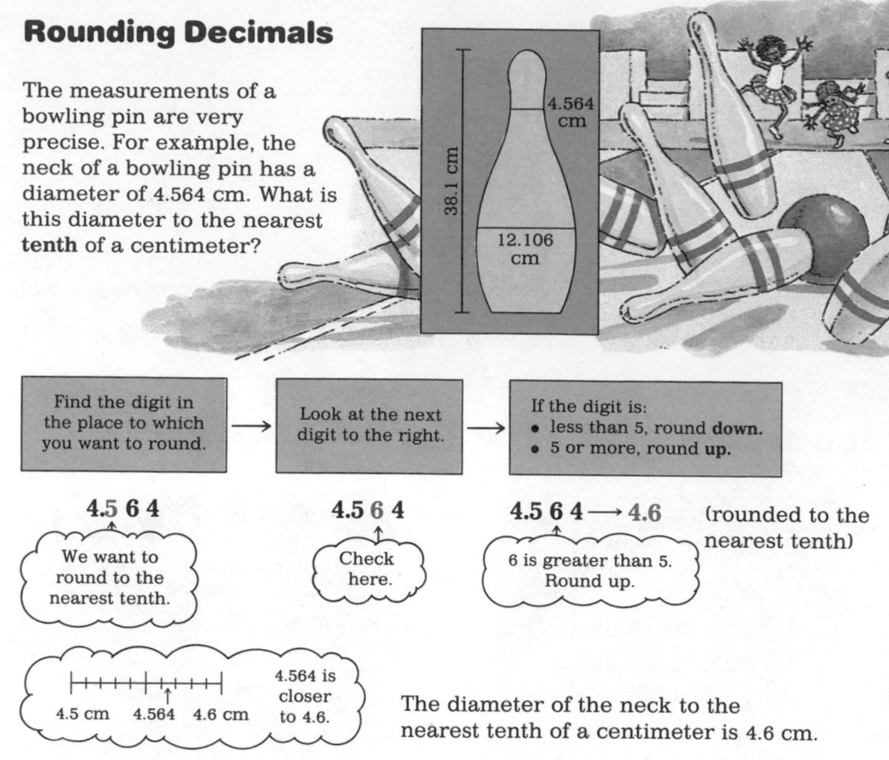

## Rounding Decimals

The measurements of a bowling pin are very precise. For example, the neck of a bowling pin has a diameter of 4.564 cm. What is this diameter to the nearest **tenth** of a centimeter?



Find the digit in the place to which you want to round. → Look at the next digit to the right. → If the digit is:
- less than 5, round **down.**
- 5 or more, round **up.**

**4.5 6 4** — We want to round to the nearest tenth.

**4.5 6 4** — Check here.

**4.5 6 4 → 4.6** (rounded to the nearest tenth) — 6 is greater than 5. Round up.

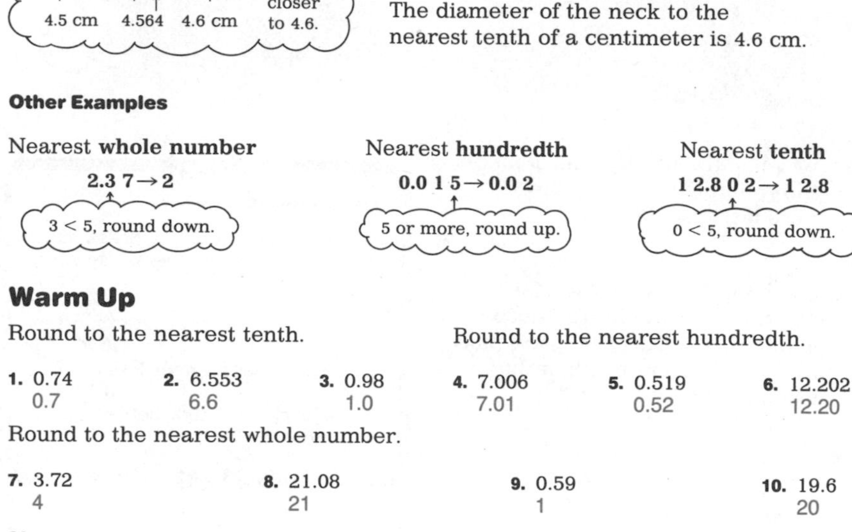


The diameter of the neck to the nearest tenth of a centimeter is 4.6 cm.

**Other Examples**

Nearest **whole number**
**2.3 7 → 2**
3 < 5, round down.

Nearest **hundredth**
**0.0 1 5 → 0.0 2**
5 or more, round up.

Nearest **tenth**
**1 2.8 0 2 → 1 2.8**
0 < 5, round down.

**Warm Up**

Round to the nearest tenth.

**1.** 0.74 (0.7) **2.** 6.553 (6.6) **3.** 0.98 (1.0)

Round to the nearest hundredth.

**4.** 7.006 (7.01) **5.** 0.519 (0.52) **6.** 12.2021 (12.20)

Round to the nearest whole number.

**7.** 3.72 (4) **8.** 21.08 (21) **9.** 0.59 (1) **10.** 19.6 (20)

60

## Follow Up

### Reteaching

Review rounding decimals to a specified place. For example, round 3.486 to the nearest tenth. First, find the digit in the place to which you want to round (tenth). Look at the next digit to the right (hundredth). If that digit is 5 or more, drop the digit and replace by zero and increase the tenth digit by one. If the hundredth digit is less than 5, drop the digit and replace by zero but do not increase the tenth digit. So 3.486 rounded to the nearest tenth is 3.500.

### Enrichment

Have students use reference books such as *The World Almanac, Book of Facts,* or *Guinness Book of Records* to locate information such as:

- Rainfall records for a state or city.
- Orbital velocity of planets in kilometers per second.
- Speed records for power boats or aircraft.

Let students show the decimal numbers as given in the reference source and then present the same information rounded to the nearest whole number, tenth, or hundredth.

| Assignment Guide | | | |
|---|---|---|---|
| | Minimum | Average | Extended |
| page 61 | 1–37, SK | 1–39, SK | 2–40 even, SK |

Round to the nearest tenth.

**1.** 2.67 2.7 **2.** 7.319 7.3 **3.** 0.884 0.9 **4.** 48.42 48.4

**5.** 365.55 365.6 **6.** 0.093 0.1 **7.** 1.89 1.9 **8.** 32.462 32.5

**9.** 4.95 5.0 **10.** 0.504 0.5 **11.** 12.85 12.9 **12.** 49.96 50.0

Round to the nearest hundredth.

**13.** 5.478 5.48 **14.** 2.828 2.83 **15.** 0.258 0.26 **16.** 0.048 0.05

**17.** 14.172 14.17 **18.** 165.642 165.64 **19.** 7.445 7.45 **20.** 18.066 18.07

**21.** 0.514 0.51 **22.** 64.064 64.06 **23.** 2.996 3.00 **24.** 3.502 3.50

Round to the nearest whole number.

**25.** 8.27 8 **26.** 42.81 43 **27.** 69.866 70 **28.** 2.845 3

**29.** 54.2 54 **30.** 10.904 11 **31.** 76.05 76 **32.** 146.49 146

**33.** 0.705 1 **34.** 9.824 10 **35.** 8.083 8 **36.** 12.457 12

**37.** What is the height of the bowling pin shown on page 60 to the nearest whole centimeter? 38 cm

**38.** The diameter of a bowling pin at its widest point is 12.106 cm. What is this measurement to the nearest hundredth of a centimeter? 12.11 cm

**39.** What is the diameter of a bowling pin at its narrowest point, to the nearest hundredth of a centimeter? (See page 60.) 4.56 cm

**40.** **DATA BANK** What is the length of a bowling alley lane to the nearest meter? (See the Data Bank, page 410.) 19 m

## Skillkeeper

Give the place value of each red digit.

1. 3,549 — 5 hundreds
2. 27,830 — 2 ten thousands
3. 216,349 — 6 thousands
4. 5,391,672 — 5 millions
5. 736,294 — 9 tens
6. 86,792 — 2 ones
7. 94,026,153 — 9 ten millions
8. 864,301 — 8 hundred thousands

More Practice, page 414, Set C



## Using Page 61

**Exercises 1–36** Remind students to be alert to the place value they are asked to round to.

**Exercises 37–39** Students use information from the illustration of the bowling pin on page 60 to complete these exercises.

**Data Bank** Here students must select the relevant data from the table in the back of the book and then round to the nearest whole number.

**Skillkeeper** These skills were originally taught in Chapter 2.

**More Practice,** page 414, Set C

**Reteaching Supplement,** page 16

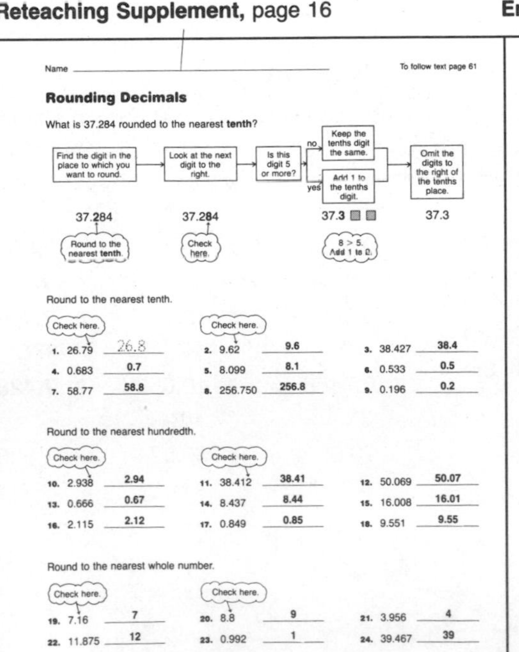

Name ______ To follow text page 61

**Rounding Decimals**

What is 37.284 rounded to the nearest **tenth**?

Find the digit in the place to which you want to round. → Look at the next digit to the right. → Is this digit 5 or more? → no: Keep the tenths digit the same. / yes: Add 1 to the tenths digit. → Omit the digits to the right of the tenths place.

37.284 (Round to the nearest **tenth**.) 37.284 (Check here.) 37.3 ▢ ▢ (8 > 5. Add 1 to 2.) 37.3

Round to the nearest tenth.

1. 26.79 26.8 2. 9.62 9.6 3. 38.427 38.4
4. 0.683 0.7 5. 8.099 8.1 6. 0.533 0.5
7. 58.77 58.8 8. 256.750 256.8 9. 0.196 0.2

Round to the nearest hundredth.

10. 2.938 2.94 11. 38.412 38.41 12. 50.069 50.07
13. 0.666 0.67 14. 8.437 8.44 15. 16.008 16.01
16. 2.115 2.12 17. 0.849 0.85 18. 9.551 9.55

Round to the nearest whole number.

19. 7.16 7 20. 8.8 9 21. 3.956 4
22. 11.875 12 23. 0.992 1 24. 39.467 39

**Enrichment Supplement,** page 16

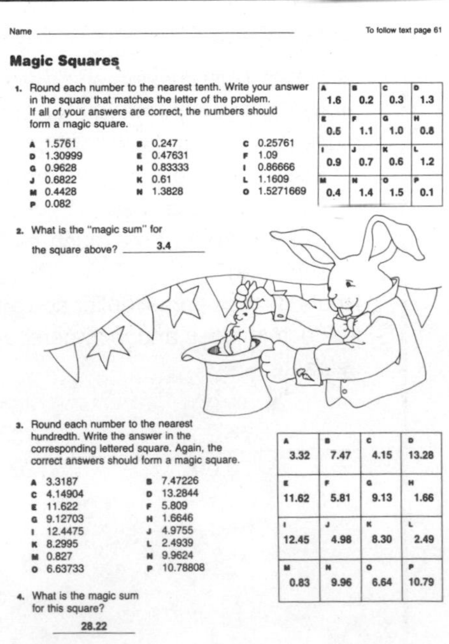

Name ______ To follow text page 61

**Magic Squares**

1. Round each number to the nearest tenth. Write your answer in the square that matches the letter of the problem. If all of your answers are correct, the numbers should form a magic square.

A 1.5761 B 0.247 C 0.25761
D 1.30999 E 0.47631 F 1.09
G 0.9628 H 0.83333 I 0.86666
J 0.6822 K 0.61 L 1.1609
M 0.4428 N 1.3828 O 1.5271669
P 0.082

| A 1.6 | B 0.2 | C 0.3 | D 1.3 |
|---|---|---|---|
| E 0.5 | F 1.1 | G 1.0 | H 0.8 |
| I 0.9 | J 0.7 | K 0.6 | L 1.2 |
| M 0.4 | N 1.4 | O 1.5 | P 0.1 |

2. What is the "magic sum" for the square above? 3.4

3. Round each number to the nearest hundredth. Write the answer in the corresponding lettered square. Again, the correct answers should form a magic square.

A 3.3187 B 7.47226
C 4.14904 D 13.2844
E 11.622 F 5.809
G 9.12703 H 1.6646
I 12.4475 J 4.9755
K 8.2995 L 2.4939
M 0.827 N 9.9624
O 6.63733 P 10.78808

| A 3.32 | B 7.47 | C 4.15 | D 13.28 |
|---|---|---|---|
| E 11.62 | F 5.81 | G 9.13 | H 1.66 |
| I 12.45 | J 4.98 | K 8.30 | L 2.49 |
| M 0.83 | N 9.96 | O 6.64 | P 10.79 |

4. What is the magic sum for this square? 28.22

**Practice Supplement,** page 23

Name ______ To follow text page 61

**Rounding Decimals**

Round to the nearest tenth.

1. 57.16 57.2 2. 17.75 17.8 3. 3.489 3.5
4. 47.854 47.9 5. 706.38 706.4 6. 3.089 3.1
7. 55.55 55.6 8. 7.13 7.1 9. 3.84 3.8
10. 51.455 51.5 11. 23.578 23.6 12. 42.89 42.9
13. 83.83 83.8 14. 6.18 6.2 15. 45.98 46.0

Round to the nearest hundredth.

16. 4.468 4.47 17. 3.761 3.76 18. 3.721 3.72
19. 51.708 51.71 20. 78.674 78.67 21. 3.499 3.50
22. 14.075 14.08 23. 115.066 115.07 24. 645.008 645.01
25. 2.108 2.11 26. 38.891 38.89 27. 346.788 346.79
28. 75.084 75.08 29. 148.245 148.25 30. 84.253 84.25

Round to the nearest whole number.

31. 68.347 68 32. 7.689 8 33. 50.9 51
34. 49.579 50 35. 99.17 99 36. 89.07 89
37. 36.087 36 38. 0.638 1 39. 51.508 52
40. 70.5 71 41. 39.59 40 42. 79.189 79
43. 42.91 43 44. 106.091 106 45. 38.83 39

# Estimation

*No materials are required for the Quick Review.*

**Quick Review** Students copy these addition problems, aligning the numbers vertically, and find the sums.

32 + 18 50   106 + 213 319   92 + 225 317   46 + 39 85   209 + 750 959
19 + 82 101   445 + 823 1,268   16 + 847 863   86 + 24 110

**Lesson Focus** To estimate decimal sums and differences; to use estimation to solve word problems

## Ideas for Getting Started

Review the rules for rounding. Then review rounding decimals to the nearest whole number. Write 14.758 on the chalkboard. Ask: "What is this number rounded to the nearest whole number?" Draw a number line on the chalkboard to show that 14.758 is closer to 15 than 14.

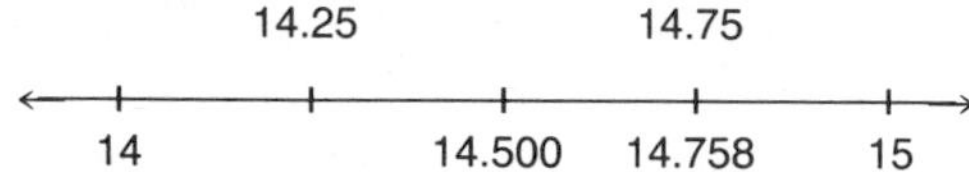


Write these decimals on the chalkboard and have students round each to the nearest whole number.

7.24    10.498    25.5    16.078

## Using Page 62

**Motivational Problem** Read the problem at the top of the page. "What are we asked to find out about Jupiter and Saturn?" (about how many years more than Jupiter it takes Saturn to revolve around the sun) Point out that the word "estimate" tells us we do not want to find the exact answer. "What data are we given in the problem?"(It takes Jupiter 11.862 years; it takes Saturn 29.458 years.) Then discuss that subtraction is the operation needed to find the answer because we are comparing two numbers.

**Lesson Development** Read the sentence that explains how to estimate the difference between these two decimals. Discuss how each number is rounded to the nearest whole number. Then ask students to read the sentence that gives the answer to the problem.

**Other Examples** In the first example, students should recognize that the technique for estimating sums is the same as that for estimating differences and that the number of addends does not change the process. The second example shows how to apply the same procedure when dollars and cents are involved.

**Exercises 1–15** Alert students to the fact that both sums and differences are estimated in these exercises.

## Estimating Sums and Differences

The planet Jupiter takes 11.862 years to revolve around the sun one time. Saturn takes 29.458 years. Estimate how many more years it takes Saturn to revolve around the sun.

Since we want to compare the times, we subtract.

To **estimate** the difference, round each number to the **nearest whole number** and subtract.

```
  29.458 →    29
- 11.862 →  - 12
              17 ← estimate
```

It takes Saturn about 17 more years to revolve around the sun than it takes Jupiter to revolve around the sun.

**Other Examples**

Round to the **nearest whole number** to estimate the sum.

```
   7.026 →     7
  12.8   →    13
+  4.54  →  +  5
              25 ← estimate
```

Round to the **nearest dollar** to estimate the difference.

```
  $42.85 →   $43
- 30.34  →  - 30
             $13 ← estimate
```

Estimate each sum or difference by rounding to the nearest whole number.

1. 7.63 + 4.71 — 13
2. 9.055 − 4.41 — 5
3. 12.4 − 10.66 — 1
4. $19.52 + 4.89 — $25
5. 23.328 − 19.720 — 3
6. $42.79 − 23.19 — $20
7. 0.72 + 4.53 — 6
8. 64.23 − 19.59 — 44
9. $139.52 + 29.61 — $170
10. 24.66 − 14.22 — 11
11. 9.215 + 8.804 + 7.521 — 26
12. 4.623 + 19.55 + 20.46 — 45
13. 8.47 + 6.3 + 39.5 — 54
14. $60.45 + 41.95 + 9.88 — $112
15. $124.50 + 59.95 + 100.40 — $285

62

## Follow Up

### Reteaching

Generate a discussion about when estimation skills might be useful. Work with students to solve the following problem:

Sally wants to buy a record changer for $46.32 and a set of speakers for $73.82. About how much money will she need?

Round to the nearest dollar and add. Find the actual cost and compare with the estimate.

```
  $ 46.00      $ 46.32
+   74.00    +   73.82
  $120.00      $120.14
```

### Enrichment

Write the twelve decimal numbers below on the chalkboard. Have students round each number to the nearest whole number.

1. 2.375 — 3
2. 6.84 — 7
3. 72.043 — 72
4. 9.566 — 10
5. 18.7 — 19
6. 276.9 — 277
7. 0.7466 — 1
8. 10.059 — 10
9. 7.428 — 7
10. 20.0077 — 20
11. 60.974 — 61
12. 1.828 — 2

| Assignment Guide | | | |
| --- | --- | --- | --- |
| | Minimum | Average | Extended |
| page 62 | 1–11 | 1–13 | 1–15 |
| page 63 | 1–5 | 1–7 | 1–8 |

## Problem Solving: Using Estimation

Estimate the answers by rounding to the nearest whole number.

1. It takes Venus 84.013 years to revolve around the sun. It takes Neptune 164.794 years. About how much longer does it take Neptune to revolve around the sun? 81 years

2. One day on Earth is 23.933 hours. One day on Jupiter is 9.833 hours. About how much longer is a day on Earth? 14 hours

3. A person who weighs 67.5 kg on Earth would weigh 10.8 kg on the moon. About how much less would the person weigh on the moon? 57 kg

4. It takes Mars 1.888 years to revolve around the sun once. About how many years would it take Mars to revolve around the sun 5 times? 10 years

5. A round-trip flight by rocket to Saturn could take 12.2 years. A round-trip flight to Mars could take 1.41 years. About how much longer is the round-trip flight to Saturn? 11 years

6. One year on Earth is 365.26 days. One year on Mercury is 87.97 days. About how much shorter is one year on Mercury than on Earth? 277 days

7. An object on Jupiter weighs 2.6 times as much as on Earth. About how much would a 2.25 kg math book weigh on Jupiter? 6 kg

8. **Try This** A rocket traveled 1,400 km in 7 minutes. If it flew 50 km more each minute than the minute before, how many kilometers did it travel during each minute of the flight? Hint: Guess and check. 1st minute, 50 km; 2nd, 100 km; 3rd, 150 km; 4th, 200 km; 5th, 250 km; 6th, 300 km; 7th, 350 km



## Using Page 63

**Lesson Development** Have students read the directions at the top of the page. Point out the problem-solving checklist in the logo and remind students that they are not asked to find *exact* answers to these problems, but rather, estimates. After students complete the exercises, discuss each problem using the 5-Point Checklist as a guide.

**Try This** A possible strategy, Guess and Check, was taught on page 48.

**Discussion** "What do you want to find out about the rocket?" (how many kilometers the rocket traveled each minute of the flight) "How far did the rocket travel altogether?" (1,400 km) "How long did it take to fly that distance?" (7 min) "What do we know about the distance the rocket flew each minute?" (50 km more than the minute before) "If you guessed 20 km for the first minute how far would the rocket have flown in 7 minutes?" (20 + 70 + 120 + 170 + 220 + 270 + 320 = 1,190 km) "Should your next guess be more or less than 20 km?" (more)

**Solution** In 7 minutes the rocket flew 1,400 km. 50 + 100 + 150 + 200 + 250 + 300 + 350 = 1,400

**Extension** Suppose another rocket traveled 620 km in 5 minutes, doubling the number of kilometers it flew each minute. How many kilometers did the rocket fly each minute? (620 km)

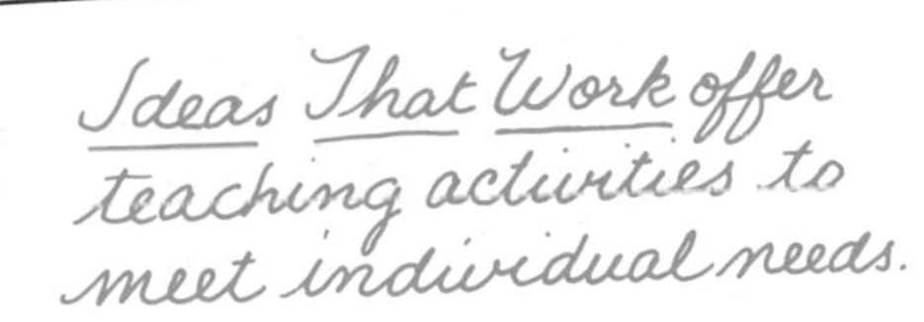

Ideas That Work offer teaching activities to meet individual needs.


## Ideas That Work

### Chalk It Up

Have students write a different decimal on each of 5 index cards. Collect the cards, mix, and place facedown in a stack. Students draw two cards from the stack and follow these directions that have been written on the chalkboard.

- Write an expression that tells which decimal is greater.
- Write an expression that tells which decimal is least.
- Estimate the sum of the decimals.
- Find the exact sum of the decimals.
- How does your estimated sum compare with the exact sum?

**Practice Supplement,** page 24

Name ______________________ To follow text page 62

**Estimating Sums and Differences**

Estimate each sum or difference by rounding to the nearest whole number.

| | Exercise | Estimate | Answer |
| --- | --- | --- | --- |
| 1. | 8.21 + 3.96 | 8 + 4 | 12 |
| 2. | 5.75 + 2.04 | 6 + 2 | 8 |
| 3. | 6.014 + 0.725 | 6 + 4 | 10 |
| 4. | 17.4 + 10.33 | 17 + 10 | 27 |
| 5. | $15.52 + 3.49 | $16 + 3 | $19 |
| 6. | 9.67 − 3.81 | 10 − 4 | 6 |
| 7. | 5.038 − 4.21 | 5 4 | 1 |
| 8. | 11.2 9.07 | 11 − 10 | 1 |
| 9. | 55.702 − 51.420 | 56 − 51 | 5 |
| 10. | $23.84 − 7.91 | $24 − 8 | $16 |
| 11. | 87.43 + 80.40 | 87 + 80 | 167 |
| 12. | 0.88 + 9.40 | 1 + 9 | 10 |
| 13. | 59.24 + 61.29 | 59 + 61 | 120 |
| 14. | 95.52 + 22.14 | 96 + 22 | 118 |
| 15. | $256.11 + 29.93 | $256 + 30 | $286 |
| 16. | 69.05 − 19.55 | 69 − 20 | 49 |
| 17. | 0.71 − 0.63 | 1 − 1 | 0 |
| 18. | 52.74 − 13.14 | 53 − 13 | 40 |
| 19. | 46.83 − 20.91 | 47 − 21 | 26 |
| 20. | $84.37 − 79.66 | $84 − 80 | $ 4 |
| 21. | 2.107 3.954 + 6.024 | 2 4 + 6 | 12 |
| 22. | 3.916 12.45 + 70.88 | 4 12 + 71 | 87 |
| 23. | $39.51 26.97 + 9.94 | $40 27 + 10 | $77 |

# Decimals: Addition

**Quick Review** Students write the numbers that make the number sentences true.

4 × 10 = [5] × 8 | 6 + 3 = [5] + 4 | 36 ÷ 6 = [1] × 6
25 − [5] = 15 + 5 | 36 ÷ 9 = [4] × 9 | (8 × 9) × 1 = 8 × (9 × [1])

**Lesson Focus** To add decimals with and without trading

**Suggested Materials** Play money (dollars, dimes, and pennies)

## Ideas for Getting Started

Write $4.27 + 2.18 on the chalkboard in algorithm form. Ask for two volunteers to show how to model $4.27 and $2.18 with the play money. Remind students that when adding decimals we start adding at the right just as with whole numbers. Have students first combine pennies (hundredths) and, if necessary, trade 10 pennies for 1 dime. After students complete this step with the play money, show the resulting digits on the chalkboard. Point out that we record the trade just with whole numbers. Next, have students combine the dimes (tenths) making sure to include the extra dime from the trade. Record this sum on the chalkboard. Then have students combine dollar bills and record the sum on the chalkboard. Call students' attention to the sum in the algorithm as you add the decimal point to indicate dollars and cents.

## Using Page 64

**Motivational Problem** Ask students to read the problem at the top of the page. "What do we want to know about the elements in the human body?" (How many kilograms of carbon and oxygen are in the human body?) Point out that the data needed to solve this problem is found in the table. Elicit from students that addition is the operation needed to find the total.

**Lesson Development** Discuss the boxes that show how to find the solution to the problem. Emphasize that addition begins with the place value farthest to the right and that decimals are added just like whole numbers. Make sure students understand that 12 tenths is one and 2 tenths. If necessary, use centimeter graph paper or play money to show this trade. Then have a volunteer read the complete sentence that gives the answer.

**Other Examples** In the third example, point out that zero can be annexed to help align digits for the addition.

**Warm Up** Observe as students work through these exercises before assigning the exercises on the next page.

## Adding with Decimals

The table shows the weights of the elements that make up an average human body. Carbon and oxygen make up the greatest part of the weight. How many kilograms of carbon and oxygen are in the average human body?

**Elements in the Human Body** (in kilograms)

| | | | | | | | |
|---|---|---|---|---|---|---|---|
| calcium | 1.27 | sulphur | 0.11 | nitrogen | 2.09 | iron | 0.46 |
| fluorine | 0.01 | carbon | 14.33 | potassium | 0.15 | oxygen | 41.91 |
| magnesium | 0.02 | hydrogen | 6.62 | chlorine | 0.51 | sodium | 0.05 |
| | | | | | | phosphorus | 0.64 |

Since we want the total, we add.

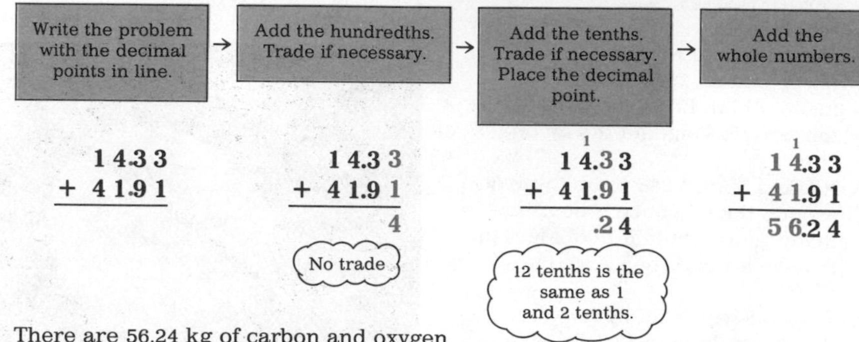

Write the problem with the decimal points in line. → Add the hundredths. Trade if necessary. → Add the tenths. Trade if necessary. Place the decimal point. → Add the whole numbers.

$$\begin{array}{r} 14.33 \\ +\ 41.91 \\ \hline \end{array} \qquad \begin{array}{r} 14.33 \\ +\ 41.91 \\ \hline 4 \end{array} \qquad \begin{array}{r} \scriptstyle 1 \\ 14.33 \\ +\ 41.91 \\ \hline .24 \end{array} \qquad \begin{array}{r} \scriptstyle 1 \\ 14.33 \\ +\ 41.91 \\ \hline 56.24 \end{array}$$

No trade

12 tenths is the same as 1 and 2 tenths.

There are 56.24 kg of carbon and oxygen in the average human body.

**Other Examples**

$$\begin{array}{r} 14.75 \\ +\ 12.88 \\ \hline 27.63 \end{array} \qquad \begin{array}{r} 0.0039 \\ +\ 0.0087 \\ \hline 0.0126 \end{array} \qquad \begin{array}{r} 24.72 \\ +\ \ 8.634 \\ \hline 33.354 \end{array} \qquad \begin{array}{r} 7.419 \\ 0.25 \\ +\ 1.8264 \\ \hline 9.4954 \end{array}$$

24.72 is the same as 24.720.

**Warm Up** Find the sum.

1. 4.0054 + 6.0239 = 10.0293
2. 0.68 + 0.4 = 1.08
3. 63.852 + 24.188 = 88.040
4. $19.85 + 4.72 = $24.57
5. $10.04 + 9.80 + 24.58 = $44.42

64

## Follow Up

### Reteaching

Have students use place-value models to show that 10 thousandths can be traded for 1 hundredth $\left(\frac{10}{1{,}000} = \frac{1}{100}\right)$, 10 hundredths can be traded for 1 tenth $\left(\frac{10}{100} = \frac{1}{10}\right)$, and 10 tenths can be traded for 1 unit $\left(\frac{10}{10} = 1\right)$. Then have students show these trades in the addition of decimals. For example, 42.387 + 3.493. Have students line up the decimal points and start adding in the thousandths' place. As students add in each place, have them point out where the trading takes place.

$$\begin{array}{r} 42.387 \\ 3.493 \\ \hline 45.880 \end{array}$$

### Enrichment

Ask students if they can pay each amount with the money shown in the box below the column. Have them try to decide by estimating. Then have students use a calculator to find the exact totals and the amount of change they would receive.

| 1. | 2. | 3. |
|---|---|---|
| $3.54 | $12.98 | $14.45 |
| 4.89 | 5.37 | 25.69 |
| 3.16 | 15.25 | 45.08 |
| 6.49 | 14.85 | 16.39 |
| $18.08 | $48.45 | $101.61 |
| $20 | $50 | $100 |
| **yes: $1.92** | **yes: $1.55** | **no** |

| Assignment Guide | Minimum | Average | Extended |
|---|---|---|---|
| page 65 | 1–30 | 1–31 | 1–29 odd, 30–31 |

Add.

| | | Answer |
|---|---|---|
| 1. | 4.7 + 8.6 | 13.3 |
| 2. | 0.55 + 0.78 | 1.33 |
| 3. | 47.5 + 26.4 | 73.9 |
| 4. | 6.472 + 1.131 | 7.603 |
| 5. | 0.082 + 0.69 | 0.772 |
| 6. | 622.8 + 67.3 | 690.1 |
| 7. | 0.045 + 0.264 | 0.309 |
| 8. | 61.0 + 9.71 | 70.71 |
| 9. | 172.61 + 148.94 | 321.55 |
| 10. | 3.472 + 2.5188 | 5.9908 |
| 11. | 0.4263 + 0.6178 | 1.0441 |
| 12. | 80.06 + 14.67 | 94.73 |
| 13. | 4.2572 + 0.628 | 4.8852 |
| 14. | 0.52 + 0.6897 | 1.2097 |
| 15. | 12.5265 + 24.6982 | 37.2247 |
| 16. | 4.251, 5.324, + 6.786 | 16.361 |
| 17. | 0.2621, 0.545, + 0.8259 | 1.633 |
| 18. | \$ 6.75, 12.64, + 9.49 | \$28.88 |
| 19. | \$ 4.45, 8.70, + 14.85 | \$28.00 |
| 20. | \$26.95, 48.49, + 14.78 | \$90.22 |

21. 6.234 + 0.567
6.801

22. 0.472 + 0.6598
1.1318

23. 12.62 + 26.074
38.694

24. 0.624+ 0.7539
1.3779

25. 4.6826 + 0.5827
5.2653

26. 14.623 + 29.6666
44.2896

27. 0.245 + 0.68 + 0.2987
1.2237

28. \$14.75 + \$12.08 + \$9.75
\$36.58

29. \$28.15 + \$16.95
\$45.10

30. How many kilograms of a typical person's weight is made up of hydrogen and nitrogen? See page 64.
8.71 kg

31. Find the total weight of the human body elements shown in the chart on page 64. 68.17 kg

## Skillkeeper

Solve.

1. 3 + 6 + 2 = *n* 11
2. 5 + 4 + 5 = *n* 14
3. 7 + 2 + 5 = *n* 14
4. (6 + 2) × 3 = *n* 24
5. 6 + (2 × 3) = *n* 12
6. (8 − 3) × 2 = *n* 10
7. (8 − (3 × 2) = *n* 2
8. (16 ÷ 4) × 2 = *n* 8
9. 16 ÷ (4 × 2) = *n* 2

More Practice, page 415, Set A



## Using Page 65

**Exercises 21–29** Remind students to align the decimal points carefully as they copy these exercises.

**Exercises 30–31** Refer students to the table on page 64 for the data needed to work these exercises. Suggest that students use the calculator to find the sum of all thirteen decimals.

**Skillkeeper** These skills were originally taught in Chapter 1.

**More Practice,** page 415, Set A

**Reteaching Supplement,** page 17

Name ______________________ To follow text page 65

### Adding with Decimals

Write the problem with the decimal points in line. → Add the hundredths. Trade if necessary. → Add the tenths. Trade if necessary. → Add the whole numbers.

42.78 + 19.56 → 4 (Trade.) → .34 (Write the decimal point.) → 62.34

Add.

1. 0.0046 + 0.0987 = 0.1033
2. 1.628 + 6.427 = 8.055 (Finish.)
3. \$62.75 + 29.85 = \$92.60 (Add. Then write as dollars and cents.)

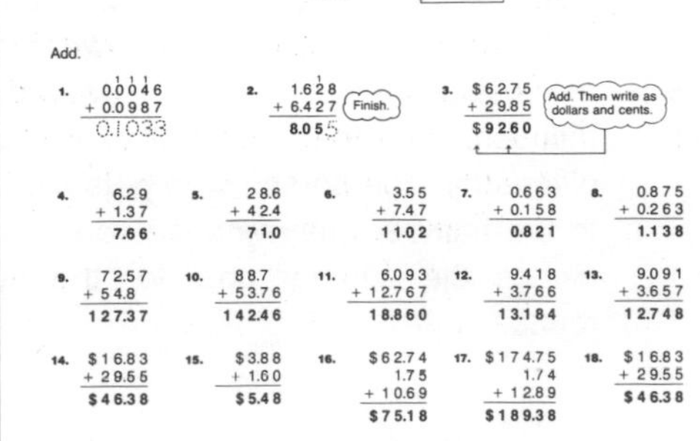

4. 6.29 + 1.37 = 7.66
5. 28.6 + 42.4 = 71.0
6. 3.55 + 7.47 = 11.02
7. 0.663 + 0.158 = 0.821
8. 0.875 + 0.263 = 1.138
9. 72.57 + 54.8 = 127.37
10. 88.7 + 53.76 = 142.46
11. 6.093 + 12.767 = 18.860
12. 9.418 + 3.766 = 13.184
13. 9.091 + 3.657 = 12.748
14. \$16.83 + 29.55 = \$46.38
15. \$3.88 + 1.60 = \$5.48
16. \$62.74 + 1.75 + 10.69 = \$75.18
17. \$174.75 + 1.74 + 12.89 = \$189.38
18. \$16.83 + 29.55 = \$46.38
19. 0.0764 + 0.12 + 0.0098 = 0.2062
20. \$62.75 + \$0.69 + \$146.42 = \$209.86

**Enrichment Supplement,** page 17

Name ______________________ To follow text page 65

### Ink Spots

Some ink was spilled on each problem. Rewrite each problem showing all the numbers.

1. 12.46 + 27.29 = 39.75
2. 0.0764 + 0.0856 = 0.1620
3. 16.28 + 8.795 = 25.075
4. 70.08 + 50.08 = 120.16
5. 0.4059 + 2.0087 = 2.4146
6. 5.088 + 9.74 = 14.828
7. \$28.49 + 35.85 = \$64.34
8. \$107.42 + 85.95 = \$193.37
9. 0.064 + 1.0257 + 0.03 + 2.646 = 3.7657
10. 25.2 + 6.746 + 8.29 + 7.488 = 47.724

**Practice Supplement,** page 25

Name ______________________ To follow text page 65

### Adding With Decimals

Add.

1. 6.8 + 7.9 = 14.7
2. 8.74 + 0.97 = 9.71
3. 5.934 + 0.685 = 6.619
4. 5.63 + 6.07 = 12.60
5. 87.9 + 37.9 = 125.8
6. 0.58 + 0.27 = 0.85
7. 470.69 + 160.66 = 631.35
8. 0.248 + 0.385 = 0.633
9. 513.21 + 310.56 = 823.77
10. 54.13 + 7.95 = 62.08
11. 2.60 + 71.84 + 3.70 = 78.14
12. 6.538 + 14.842 + 3.901 = 25.281
13. 0.140 + 0.385 + 0.671 = 1.196
14. 2.84 + 3.67 + 0.81 = 7.32
15. 7.67 + 3.54 + 14.08 = 25.29
16. 3.982 + 7.106 + 2.560 = 13.648
17. 0.1148 + 0.926 + 0.3174 = 1.3582
18. \$4.98 + 15.56 + 7.43 = \$27.97
19. \$0.92 + 5.64 + 73.08 = \$79.64
20. \$17.08 + 16.91 + 44.90 = \$78.89
21. 238.72 + 65.3 + 7.84 = 311.86
22. 56.43 + 179.6 + 4.98 = 241.01
23. 24.8 + 69.83 + 754.9 = 849.53
24. 38.64 + 9.586 = 48.226
25. 2.368 + 0.471 + 3.26 = 6.099
26. 0.47 + 0.463 + 3.27 = 4.203

# Decimals: Subtraction

**Quick Review** Students tell whether a trade is necessary, then subtract.

| 206 | 673 | 27 | 122 | 413 | 828 | 15 |
|---|---|---|---|---|---|---|
| − 105 no | − 608 yes | − 18 yes | − 114 yes | − 410 no | − 636 yes | − 9 yes |
| 101 | 65 | 9 | 8 | 3 | 192 | 6 |

**Lesson Focus** To subtract decimals with and without trading

**Suggested Materials** Play money (dollars, dimes, pennies)

## Ideas for Getting Started

Use the play money to show subtracting with decimals. Write this problem on the chalkboard.

$$\begin{array}{r} \$3.20 \\ -\ 1.45 \\ \hline \end{array}$$

Have a student show $3.20 using dollar bills, dimes, and pennies (0 pennies). Remind students to start subtracting at the right with the hundredths (pennies). Elicit from students that in order to subtract 5 pennies from 0 pennies they must trade 1 dime for 10 pennies. Have students show the trade with the play money and record the trade on the chalkboard. Then have a student take away the 5 pennies and record the subtraction on the chalkboard. "Can we subtract the tenths (dimes)?" Students should recognize they cannot subtract 4 dimes from 1 dime, so they need to trade $1 for 10 dimes. Have students subtract the tenths and record the subtraction on the chalkboard. Students subtract the whole number (dollars) and record the results.

## Using Page 66

**Motivational Problem** Read the problem at the top of the page. "What are we asked to find out about the basketball court?" (How much greater is the length of the basketball court than the width?) "What data do you need in order to find the answer?" (width of the court—16.65 m and the length—31.30 m) Help students understand that subtraction is the operation to use because we want to compare the two lengths.

**Lesson Development** Discuss each box and work through the computations shown. Point out that each step in this example involves a trade. Emphasize the units that are traded in each step. For example, in the first step point out that trading 1 *tenth* gives 10 more *hundredths.*

**Other Examples** Point out how a zero can be annexed in example 2 to keep the digits aligned. In the third example, help students think of 8.00 as 800 hundredths.

## Subtracting with Decimals

A college basketball court is 16.65 m wide and 31.30 m long. How much greater is the length of the court than the width?

Since we want to compare the length and the width, we subtract.

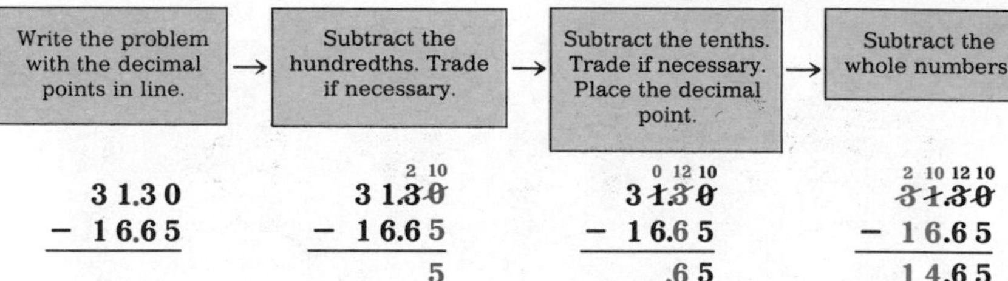


| 31.30 | 31.30 (2 10) | 31.30 (0 12 10) | 31.30 (2 10 12 10) |
|---|---|---|---|
| − 16.65 | − 16.65 | − 16.65 | − 16.65 |
| | 5 | .65 | 14.65 |

The length is 14.65 m greater than the width.

**Other Examples**

| 0.73 (6 13) | 7.5 → | 7.50 (4 10) | 8.000 (7 9 9 10) | $12.04 (1 9 14) |
|---|---|---|---|---|
| − 0.36 | − 4.26 | − 4.26 | − 3.824 | − 6.59 |
| 0.37 | | 3.24 | 4.176 | $5.45 |

**Warm Up** Subtract.

| 1. | 2. | 3. | 4. | 5. |
|---|---|---|---|---|
| 18.43 | 7.5 | 0.806 | 265.3 | $1.00 |
| − 7.26 | − 6.8 | − 0.448 | − 121.44 | − 0.63 |
| 11.17 | 0.7 | 0.358 | 143.86 | $0.37 |

66

## Follow Up

**Reteaching**

Use graph paper (TRB p. 271) to model 0.85 − 0.36. Show the algorithm on the chalkboard. Align the decimal points and then subtract as in whole number subtraction. Focus on trading and use the graph paper models to emphasize how this is carried out. Ask students to suggest other examples to be illustrated with the graph paper models.

**Enrichment**

Provide students with two sets of number cards labeled 0 through 9 (TRB p. 279). Before each game, a player names the number goal. Players in turn then draw 6 cards each from the pile of number cards, which have been placed facedown. Players position their cards to form two 3-digit numbers, and then subtract to find the difference. The person who gets closest to the number goal wins the round and names the number goal for the next round.

| Assignment Guide | | | |
|---|---|---|---|
| | Minimum | Average | Extended |
| page 67 | 1–30 | 1–32 | 2–20 even, 21–32, TM |

Subtract.

1. 9.2 − 2.6 = 6.6
2. 0.61 − 0.17 = 0.44
3. 4.63 − 3.55 = 1.08
4. 0.518 − 0.245 = 0.273
5. 7.546 − 2.485 = 5.061
6. 0.73 − 0.42 = 0.31
7. 2.585 − 2.499 = 0.086
8. 0.7655 − 0.4645 = 0.301
9. 1.42 − 1.265 = 0.155
10. 4.7642 − 1.5887 = 3.1755
11. 12.76 − 4.854 = 7.906
12. 8.6523 − 4.516 = 4.1363
13. 0.62 − 0.5203 = 0.0997
14. 21.5628 − 19.4731 = 2.0897
15. 42.05 − 25.05 = 17.0
16. $4.85 − 2.32 = $2.53
17. $0.83 − 0.29 = $0.54
18. $42.35 − 21.48 = $20.87
19. $60.05 − 21.48 = $38.57
20. $185.44 − 97.85 = $87.59

21. 18.33 − 6.47 11.86
22. 0.983 − 0.494 0.489
23. 42.1 − 35.42 6.68
24. 0.725 − 0.68 0.045
25. 0.2634 − 0.1725 0.0909
26. 17.24 − 5.0086 12.2314
27. $1.75 − $0.49 $1.26
28. $14.48 − $12.95 $1.53
29. $40.00 − $13.43 $26.57

30. A tennis court is 10.97 m wide and 23.77 m long. How much greater is the length than the width? 12.80 m

31. A men's soccer field is 119.88 m long. A women's soccer field is 19.98 m shorter. Both fields are 68.05 m wide. How much greater is the length of the women's field than the width of the women's field? 31.85 m

32. **DATA BANK** How much greater is the length of a bowling alley lane than the width of a bowling alley lane? (See Data Bank, page 410.) 18.11 m

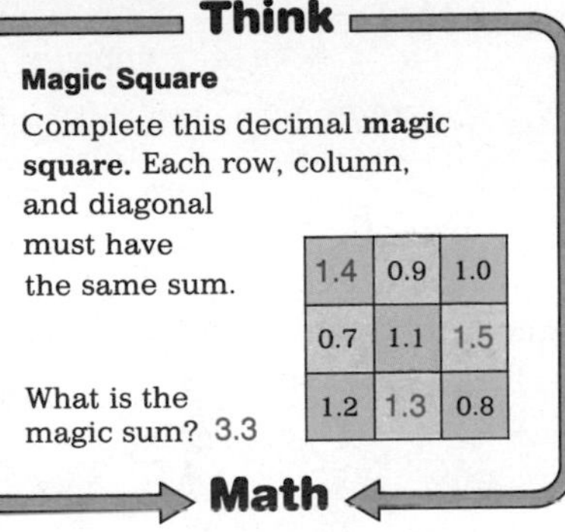

**Think Math**

**Magic Square**

Complete this decimal **magic square.** Each row, column, and diagonal must have the same sum.

| | | |
|---|---|---|
| 1.4 | 0.9 | 1.0 |
| 0.7 | 1.1 | 1.5 |
| 1.2 | 1.3 | 0.8 |

What is the magic sum? 3.3

More Practice, page 415, Set B



## Using Page 67

**Exercises 1–31** As you assign these exercises, remind students to annex zeros if necessary. In exercises 21–29 caution students to be careful to write the exercises with the decimal points aligned properly.

**Data Bank** Remind students that they must refer to the back of the book to select the data needed to solve this problem.

**Think Math** The solution to this magic square involves both addition and subtraction. Encourage students to guess and then test their guesses by finding the magic sum.

**More Practice,** page 415, Set B

**Reteaching Supplement,** page 18

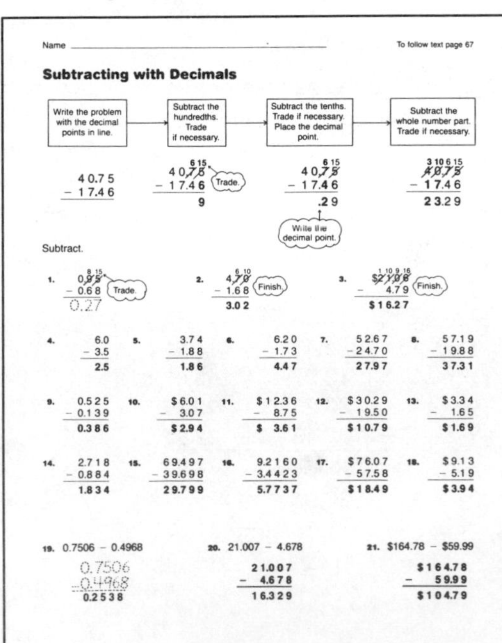

Name ______ To follow text page 67

**Subtracting with Decimals**

Write the problem with the decimal points in line. → Subtract the hundredths. Trade if necessary. → Subtract the tenths. Trade if necessary. Place the decimal point. → Subtract the whole number part. Trade if necessary.

40.75 − 17.46 → 9 (Trade.) → .29 (Write the decimal point.) → 23.29

Subtract.

1. 0.95 − 0.68 = 0.27 (Trade.)
2. 4.70 − 1.68 = 3.02 (Finish.)
3. $21.06 − 4.79 = $16.27 (Finish.)
4. 6.0 − 3.5 = 2.5
5. 3.74 − 1.88 = 1.86
6. 6.20 − 1.73 = 4.47
7. 52.67 − 24.70 = 27.97
8. 57.19 − 19.88 = 37.31
9. 0.525 − 0.139 = 0.386
10. $6.01 − 3.07 = $2.94
11. $12.36 − 8.75 = $3.61
12. $30.29 − 19.50 = $10.79
13. $3.34 − 1.65 = $1.69
14. 2.718 − 0.884 = 1.834
15. 69.497 − 39.698 = 29.799
16. 9.2160 − 3.4423 = 5.7737
17. $76.07 − 57.58 = $18.49
18. $9.13 − 5.19 = $3.94
19. 0.7506 − 0.4968 = 0.2538
20. 21.007 − 4.678 = 16.329
21. $164.78 − $59.99 = $104.79

**Enrichment Supplement,** page 18

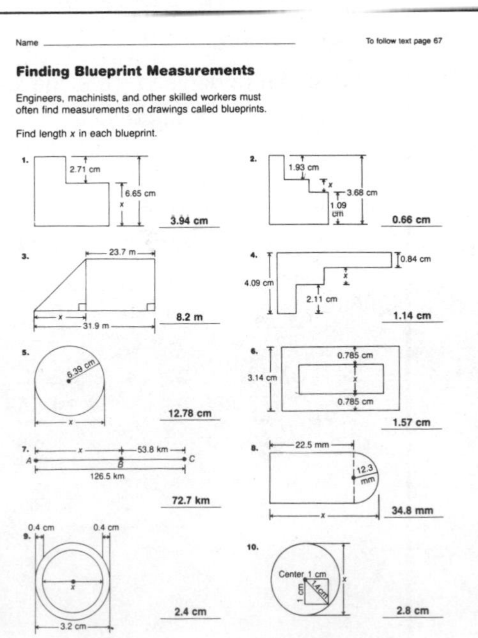

Name ______ To follow text page 67

**Finding Blueprint Measurements**

Engineers, machinists, and other skilled workers must often find measurements on drawings called blueprints.

Find length $x$ in each blueprint.

1. 2.71 cm, 6.65 cm, $x$ — 3.94 cm
2. 1.93 cm, $x$, 3.68 cm, 1.09 cm — 0.66 cm
3. 23.7 m, $x$, 31.9 m — 8.2 m
4. 0.84 cm, 4.09 cm, $x$, 2.11 cm — 1.14 cm
5. 6.39 cm, $x$ — 12.78 cm
6. 0.785 cm, 3.14 cm, $x$, 0.785 cm — 1.57 cm
7. A, B, C; $x$, 53.8 km, 126.5 km — 72.7 km
8. 22.5 mm, 12.3 mm, $x$ — 34.8 mm
9. 0.4 cm, 0.4 cm, $x$, 3.2 cm — 2.4 cm
10. Center, 1 cm, 1 cm, 1.4 cm, $x$ — 2.8 cm

**Practice Supplement,** page 26

Name ______ To follow text page 67

**Subtracting With Decimals**

Subtract.

1. 1.47 − 0.70 = 0.68
2. 9.71 − 0.97 = 8.74
3. 6.61 − 0.68 = 5.93
4. 6.8 − 3.9 = 2.9
5. 4.5 − 0.8 = 3.7
6. 0.85 − 0.27 = 0.58
7. 1.3586 − 0.6657 = 0.6929
8. 0.638 − 0.385 = 0.253
9. 13.21 − 10.56 = 2.65
10. 54.13 − 7.95 = 46.18
11. $5.25 − 3.87 = $1.38
12. $0.85 − 0.68 = $0.17
13. $51.04 − 22.63 = $28.41
14. $70.00 − 16.95 = $53.05
15. $143.79 − 88.81 = $ 54.98
16. 26.85 − 15.97 = 10.88
17. 71.35 − 4.66 = 66.69
18. 63.6336 − 17.3854 = 46.2482
19. 73.21 − 56.56 = 16.65
20. 54.135 − 27.950 = 26.185
21. 134.21 − 79.85 = 54.36
22. 66.4538 − 58.4705 = 7.9833
23. 32.900 − 7.853 = 25.047
24. 49.3907 − 6.8585 = 42.5322
25. 96.48 − 73.85 = 22.63
26. 432.56 − 58.98 = 373.58
27. 703.60 − 52.98 = 650.62
28. $77.32 − 8.70 = $68.62
29. 986.05 − 77.84 = 908.21
30. $95.41 − $8.72 = $86.69
31. 649.74 − 32.05 = 617.69

# Estimation

**Quick Review** As an oral drill, students round each amount to the nearest dollar.

| | | | | | |
|---|---|---|---|---|---|
| $11.17 | $9.52 | $48.55 | $13.80 | $36.49 | $2.09 |
| $4.72 | $6.50 | $42.58 | $1.45 | $29.90 | |
| $31.38 | $75.68 | $2.49 | $31.51 | $18.80 | $5.95 |

**Lesson Focus** To estimate sums and differences by rounding to the nearest ten cents or to the nearest ten dollars

## Ideas for Getting Started

Write $24.48 on the chalkboard. Tell students we want to round that amount to the nearest tenth. Elicit from students the steps for rounding. Help them recall that they need to look at the digit in the hundredths place since they want to round to the tenths. Point out that they would round up ($24.50) because 8 is greater than 5. Then ask what $24.48 would be rounded to the nearest whole number. This time students should recognize that they must look at the digit in the ones place and since it is less than 5, they should round down (24). If necessary, omit the dollar sign and find each number on the number line to show the closest tenth and whole number.

## Using Page 68

**Lesson Development** Read the paragraph at the top of the page. "What do we want to find out about Dorian's lunch?" (Does she have enough money for the food she wants for lunch?) "Which data from the menu do we need to solve this problem?" (amount of egg sandwich, soup, and milk) Then discuss that we can use estimation to find the answer. Read the sentence telling students to round to the nearest ten cents or tenth of a dollar. Discuss how each number was rounded and how the total estimate was found. Have students read the complete sentence that gives the answer to the problem. Emphasize that $1.30 is an *estimate* of the cost of Dorian's lunch.

**Other Examples** In the first example, make sure students understand that the only digit they need to examine to round to the nearest ten dollars is the digit in the ones' place—the numbers to the right of the decimal point do not affect the rounding process. Point out that when the number is rounded to the nearest ten, the addition problem becomes the sum of a basic fact. The second problem involves subtraction by rounding to tenths. This estimate also can be thought of as a basic fact.

**Exercises 1–5** In these exercises students practice rounding to the nearest ten cents.

**Exercises 6–10** In these exercises students estimate sums and differences by rounding to the nearest ten dollars.

## More Estimating Sums and Differences

Dorian has $1.50 to spend for lunch. She wants to have an egg sandwich, soup, and milk. Estimate whether she has enough money to pay for the items she wants.

Lunch Specials
Soup of the Day...... $0.38
Cheese Sandwich .... 0.42
Tuna Sandwich....... 0.79
Egg Sandwich........ 0.65
Green Salad.......... 0.48
Milk.................. 0.24
Fruit Juice .......... 0.37


Since we want to find the total cost, we add.

To **estimate** the sum, round each number **to the nearest ten cents** (**tenth** of a dollar) and add.

| | | |
|---|---|---|
| $0.38 → | $0.40 | |
| 0.65 → | 0.70 | |
| + 0.24 → | + 0.20 | |
| | $1.30 | ← estimate |

Since $1.50 is more than $1.30, Dorian has enough money to pay for the items she wants.

**Other Examples**

Estimate the sum by rounding to the nearest **ten dollars.**

| | | |
|---|---|---|
| $44.75 → | $40 | |
| + 28.20 → | + 30 | |
| | $70 | ← estimate |

Estimate the difference by rounding to the nearest **ten cents.**

| | | |
|---|---|---|
| $1.49 → | $1.50 | |
| − 0.62 → | − 0.60 | |
| | $0.90 | ← estimate |

Estimate by rounding to the nearest ten cents.

| 1. | 2. | 3. | 4. | 5. |
|---|---|---|---|---|
| $0.46 | $0.75 | $1.19 | $0.72 | $1.47 |
| + 0.62 | − 0.39 | − 0.52 | 0.88 | 2.14 |
| $1.10 | $0.40 | $0.70 | + 0.16 | + 1.25 |
| | | | $1.80 | $4.90 |

Estimate by rounding to the nearest ten dollars.

| 6. | 7. | 8. | 9. | 10. |
|---|---|---|---|---|
| $17.35 | $53.95 | $78.50 | $40.50 | $57.25 |
| + 62.60 | − 29.95 | − 43.15 | 18.75 | 22.95 |
| $80 | $20 | $40 | + 31.40 | + 68.90 |
| | | | $90 | $150 |



## Follow Up

### Reteaching

Work with students to round the following decimals to the nearest whole number and add or subtract the estimated numbers. Then help students find the exact answer to selected problems and compare with their estimated answer.

| | | | | | |
|---|---|---|---|---|---|
| 1. | 23.95 | 24 | 2. | $1.86 | $2 |
| | + 1.06 | + 1 | | − 0.75 | − 1 |
| | 25.01 | 25 | | 1.11 | 1 |
| 3. | 37.43 | 37 | 4. | $2.13 | $2 |
| | − 23.77 | − 24 | | + 4.55 | + 5 |
| | 13.66 | 13 | | $6.68 | $7 |

### Enrichment

Write the sample problems below on the chalkboard. Have students estimate each sum or difference by rounding to the nearest ten cents. Then let them use calculators to check their estimates.

| | | |
|---|---|---|
| 1. | $18.25 | $18.30 |
| | + 7.10 | + 7.10 |
| | $25.35 | $25.40 |
| 2. | $ 4.47 | $ 4.50 |
| | 12.97 | 13.00 |
| | 20.23 | 20.20 |
| | + 32.48 | + 32.50 |
| | $70.15 | $70.20 |
| 3. | $25.91 | $25.90 |
| | − 11.64 | − 11.60 |
| | $14.27 | $14.30 |

## Assignment Guide

| | Minimum | Average | Extended |
|---|---|---|---|
| page 68 | 1–10 | 1–10 | 1–10 |
| page 69 | 1–7 | 1–8 | 1–9 |

## Problem Solving: Using Estimation

For problems 1–4, estimate by rounding to the nearest ten cents. Use the list of prices on page 68.

1. About how much more does a tuna sandwich cost than a cheese sandwich? about $0.40

2. Maury had a tuna sandwich, green salad, and milk for lunch. About how much did his lunch cost? about $1.50

3. Val had soup, a cheese sandwich, and fruit juice for lunch. Roberto had a tuna sandwich, green salad, and milk. About how much more or how much less did Val's lunch cost than Roberto's? Val's lunch cost about $0.30 less.

4. Harriet's lunch cost $1.17. Luann's lunch cost $1.51. About how much more did Luann's lunch cost than Harriet's lunch? about $0.30

For problems 5 and 6, estimate by rounding to the nearest ten dollars.

5. The lunch room took in $93.45 on Thursday and $68.72 on Friday. About how much more did the lunch room take in on Thursday than on Friday? about $20

6. On Tuesday lunch room sales were $37.50 greater than on Monday. On Monday the sales totaled $62.75. About how much did the sales total on Tuesday? about $100

7. **DATA HUNT** About how much would a bowl of soup, a salad, and a container of milk cost in your school's lunch room? Estimate the total by rounding the cost of each item to the nearest ten cents. Answers will vary.

8. **Try This** Clark and Lee each had a Hot Plate Special. The Specials cost $1.50 each. Clark also had a glass of lemonade that cost $0.35. Lee had a glass of juice that cost $0.45. Clark paid for both lunches with a $10 bill. How much change should Clark have received? $6.20



## Using Page 69

**Exercises 1–4** Read the directions at the top of the page with students and make sure they understand they are to round to the nearest ten cents. Point out that they are to use data from page 68 as necessary.

**Exercises 5–6** Be sure students understand that in these exercises they are to round to the nearest ten dollars.

**Data Hunt** If you prefer, substitute other items depending on the selection of items in your school's lunch room.

**Try This** A possible strategy, Choose the Operations, was taught on page 16.

**Discussion** "What are we trying to find out about the cost of the lunches?" (How much change did Clark receive?) "What did Clark and Lee eat?" (Both had Hot Plate Specials. Clark had lemonade; Lee had juice.) "How much did each Hot Plate Special cost?" ($1.50) "How much did the two drinks cost?" ($0.80) "What was the total cost for the lunches?" ($3.80) "How can we find the amount of change Clark received?" (Subtract the cost of the lunches from the amount of money paid.)

**Solution** Clark should have received $6.20 change.

**Extension** Arnold bought 3 items from the lunch specials shown on page 68 and spent $1.51. What did he buy? (tuna sandwich, green salad, milk)

### Reteaching Supplement, page 19

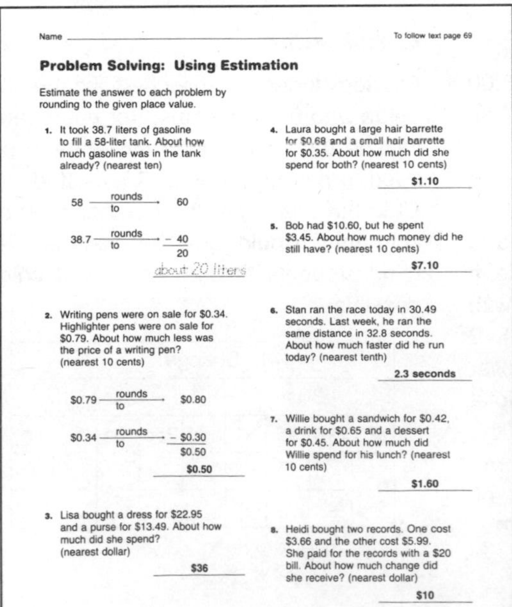

Name ____________ To follow text page 69

**Problem Solving: Using Estimation**

Estimate the answer to each problem by rounding to the given place value.

1. It took 38.7 liters of gasoline to fill a 58-liter tank. About how much gasoline was in the tank already? (nearest ten)

   58 rounds to 60
   38.7 rounds to − 40
   20
   about 20 liters

2. Writing pens were on sale for $0.34. Highlighter pens were on sale for $0.79. About how much less was the price of a writing pen? (nearest 10 cents)

   $0.79 rounds to $0.80
   $0.34 rounds to − $0.30
   $0.50
   $0.50

3. Lisa bought a dress for $22.95 and a purse for $13.49. About how much did she spend? (nearest dollar) $36

4. Laura bought a large hair barrette for $0.68 and a small hair barrette for $0.35. About how much did she spend for both? (nearest 10 cents) $1.10

5. Bob had $10.60, but he spent $3.45. About how much money did he still have? (nearest 10 cents) $7.10

6. Stan ran the race today in 30.49 seconds. Last week, he ran the same distance in 32.8 seconds. About how much faster did he run today? (nearest tenth) 2.3 seconds

7. Willie bought a sandwich for $0.42, a drink for $0.65 and a dessert for $0.45. About how much did Willie spend for his lunch? (nearest 10 cents) $1.60

8. Heidi bought two records. One cost $3.66 and the other cost $5.99. She paid for the records with a $20 bill. About how much change did she receive? (nearest dollar) $10

### Enrichment Supplement, page 19

Name ____________ To follow text page 69

**Grocery Store Check**

Here are some grocery store receipts. Some of the totals are incorrect. Use estimation to find which are incorrect. Then find the correct totals. The corrected sum of all the receipts should be the amount shown below as the total food budget.

1. $4.75, 0.69, 1.25, 0.49, 2.75, 1.40, 0.99; Total $15.42 — Estimate: about $12 — $12.32

2. $ 0.49, 21.79, 4.20, 0.79, 2.09; Total $29.36 — Estimate: about $29 — ______

3. $ 2.25, 1.78, 4.59, 0.99, 1.10, 5.29, 7.95, 0.55; Total $20.40 — Estimate: about $24 — $24.50

4. $ 6.45, 0.25, 7.25, 4.02, 0.75, 0.69, 1.79, 4.62; Total $25.82 — Estimate: about $26 — ______

TOTAL FOOD BUDGET = $92.00

Use estimation to make up two receipts. Each receipt should have five items and the estimated total should be close to the one given. **Answers will vary.**

5. $ ______ Estimated total: $17 Exact total: ______ Difference: ______

6. $ ______ Estimated total: $32 Exact total: ______ Difference: ______

### Practice Supplement, page 27

Name ____________ To follow text page 68

**More Estimating Sums and Differences**

Estimate by rounding to the nearest ten cents.

1. $0.83 + 0.67 = $1.50
2. $0.16 + 0.39 = $0.60
3. $3.18 + 0.77 = $4.00
4. $1.52 + 0.26 = $1.80
5. $2.57 + 0.17 = $2.80
6. $0.95 − 0.42 = $0.60
7. $0.43 − 0.21 = $0.20
8. $1.68 − 0.94 = $0.80
9. $1.32 − 0.66 = $0.70
10. $1.23 0.91 = $0.30
11. $0.44 + 0.38 + 0.62 = $1.40
12. $0.11 + 0.72 + 0.17 = $1.00
13. $0.52 + 0.42 + 0.48 = $1.40
14. $1.73 + 0.62 + 0.33 = $2.60
15. $0.57 + 0.22 + 1.48 = $2.30

Estimate by rounding to the nearest ten dollars.

16. $16.45 + 32.88 = $50.00
17. $94.12 + 62.35 = $150.00
18. $40.76 + 18.94 = $60.00
19. $73.18 + 90.14 = $160.00
20. $99.25 + 21.47 = $120.00
21. $62.95 − 43.70 = $20.00
22. $44.88 − 16.11 = $20.00
23. $94.57 − 81.62 = $10.00
24. $76.92 − 66.28 = $10.00
25. $85.03 − 22.19 = $70.00
26. $17.44 + 28.12 + 35.59 = $90.00
27. $15.90 + 41.46 + 34.07 = $90.00
28. $55.29 + 79.68 + 30.80 = $170.00
29. $88.41 + 51.32 + 24.49 = $160.00
30. $33.24 + 49.70 + 41.32 = $120.00
31. $52.25 − 16.71 = $30.00
32. $78.20 − 28.70 = $50.00
33. $55.00 − 15.00 = $40.00
34. $78.15 − 22.78 = $60.00
35. $95.00 − 72.00 = $30.00

# Money

**Quick Review** Students give two or more addends that will give each sum
$12 $70 $8 $14 $22 $62 $19
$17 $35 $81 $54 $28 $9

**Lesson Focus** To find change by counting money; to solve word problems involving decimals

**Suggested Materials** Play money ($5 bill, $1 bills, quarters, dimes, nickels, and pennies)

## Ideas for Getting Started

To introduce this lesson, give students practice counting by the various increments as suggested by the value of the coins. For example, have students count first by ones, then by fives, by tens, by twenty-five, and by fifty. After counting by these values, have students count first by ones to a given number, and from that number to 100 by another number.

## Using Page 70

**Motivational Problem** Ask students to read the problem at the top of the page. "What is the question we are asked in the problem?" (How much change should Aaron give the customer?) "What data do you need to find the answer?" (amount of purchase; amount of money the customer gave Aaron)

**Lesson Development** Read and discuss how Aaron counted to find the correct amount of change. Be sure to point out that when giving change, we should try to use the fewest possible number of bills and coins. Have a volunteer read the statement that tells how subtraction can be used to find the amount of change.

**Exercises 1–8** Before assigning these exercises, read through the directions with the students. If necessary, allow students to use the play money to count the change in these exercises.

## Money: Making Change

Aaron works in a bookstore. A customer bought a backpack for $6.70 and gave Aaron a $10 bill. How much change should Aaron give the customer?

Aaron starts with the cost of the backpack and counts out coins and bills to bring the total to $10.

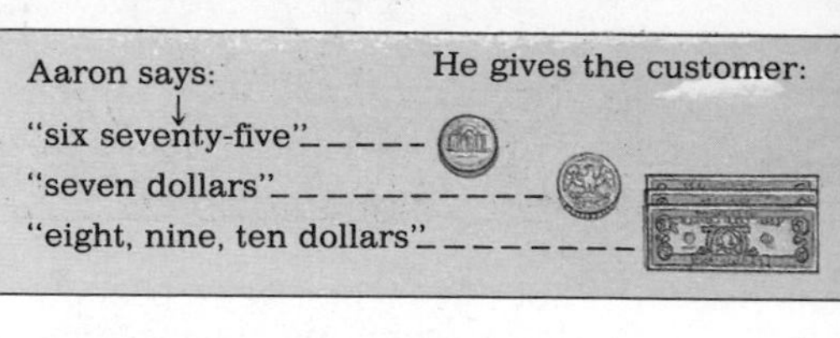

Aaron says:
He gives the customer:
"six seventy-five"
"seven dollars"
"eight, nine, ten dollars"


Count the coins and bills Aaron gave the customer to find the total amount of change.

Then check by subtracting.

$$\begin{array}{r} \$\,10.00 \\ -\;\;6.70 \\ \hline \$\;\;3.30 \end{array}$$

Aaron should give the customer $3.30 change.

List in order each coin or bill you would count out as change. Use the fewest possible coins and bills.

1. Cost $0.65. Customer paid with $1.00. 1 dime, 1 quarter
2. Cost $1.25. Customer paid with $2.00. 1 quarter, 1 half dollar
3. Cost $1.83. Customer paid with $5.00. 2 pennies, 1 nickel, 1 dime, 3 $1 bills
4. Cost $2.40. Customer paid with $5.00. 1 dime, 1 half dollar, 2 $1 bills
5. Cost $3.95. Customer paid with $10.00. Nickel, 1 $1 bill, 1 $5 bill
6. Cost $11.45. Customer paid with $15. 1 nickel, 1 half dollar, 3 $1 bills
7. Cost $14.75. Customer paid with two $10 bills. 1 quarter, 1 $5 bill
8. Cost $22.18. Customer paid with $50. 2 pennies, 1 nickel, 1 quarter, 1 half dollar, 2 $1 bills, 1 $5 bill, 1 $20 bill

70

## Follow Up

### Reteaching

Have available items "priced" from $5.00 and $10.00. Each student is to "buy" an item and pay for it with a ten-dollar bill of play money. Students take turns playing storekeeper and making change. Students begin with the cost of the item and count forward to $10.00. For example, if an item costs $7.27, students start with $7.27, count out 3 pennies ($7.30), 2 dimes ($7.50), 2 quarters or 1 half-dollar ($8.00), and 2 one-dollar bills to total $10.00. For each "purchase," show the subtraction problem in algorithm form. Students then state the amount of change as a complete sentence: "The change should be $2.73."

### Enrichment

Provide students with a chart like the one below and a list of items. For each item, include the cost of the item and the bill used to pay for the item. Have students fill in the chart with the number of each coin they would give in change. Remind students to use the fewest coins possible.

| Change | | | | | | | | |
|---|---|---|---|---|---|---|---|---|
| Bills | | | | Coins | | | | |
| $20 | $10 | $5 | $1 | 50¢ | 25¢ | 10¢ | 5¢ | 1¢ |
| | | | | | | | | |
| | | | | | | | | |

| Assignment Guide | | | |
|---|---|---|---|
| | Minimum | Average | Extended |
| page 70 | 1–8 | 1–8 | 1–8 |
| page 71 | 1–7 | 1–8 | 1–9 |

## Problem Solving: Practice

Solve.

1. A pad of notebook paper was on sale for $0.85. It regularly costs $1.39. How much do you save if you buy the paper on sale? $0.54

2. Maria worked in the bookstore 24.25 hours last week. This week she worked 30.5 hours. How many more hours did she work this week than last week? 6.25 hours

3. Mazi bought a school T-shirt for $3.95 and gym shorts for $1.50. How much change should she get if she paid with a $10 bill? $4.55

4. Eduardo bought a pen for $0.65, an eraser for $0.45, and colored pencils for $1.09. How much did he spend altogether? $2.19

5. Wes bought a photo album for $2.35. How much change should he get from a $5 bill? $2.65

6. Pete bought 3 felt-tip pens for $2 each and a calendar for $1.75. How much did he spend altogether? $7.75

7. Stephanie wants to buy a book bag for $4.95 and a school flag for $3.50. So far, she has saved $6 from her allowance. How much more does she need to buy the book bag and flag? $2.45

8. Heather saves $4 each week from her allowance. She wants to buy a school jacket that costs $24.59. She has been saving for 4 weeks. How much more does she need to save to buy the jacket? $8.59

9. **Try This** Pencils were on sale for 20¢. Pens were on sale for 30¢. Steve bought a total of 11 pens and pencils and spent $2.80. How many items of each kind did he buy? Hint: Guess and check. 5 pencils, 6 pens

## Using Page 71

**Lesson Development** Tell students that the purpose of this lesson is to practice solving word problems. Remind them of the 5-Point Checklist. Encourage students to ask themselves questions suggested by each part of the checklist. For example, "What am I asked to find in this problem?"

**Exercises 1–8** Note that exercises 3, 6, 7, and 8 require two operations to find the answer.

**Try This** A possible strategy, Guess and Check, was taught on page 48.

**Discussion** "What do we want to find out about the pens and pencils?" (How many of each did Steve buy?) "How many pens and pencils were bought altogether?" (11) "How much does a pencil cost?" (20¢) "A pen?" (30¢) "How much was spent altogether?" ($2.80) "Could you guess how many of each he bought and then check your guess? Could he have bought 5 of each?" (No, he bought a total of 11 items.) "What would be some possible combinations of pens and pencils?" (4 pencils, 7 pens; 6 pencils, 5 pens, etc.) "Does 4 pencils and 7 pens check?" (No) "Try another guess."

**Solution** (5 × 20¢) + (6 × 30¢) = $2.80 Steve bought 5 pencils and 6 pens.

**Extension** Mary bought some pencils and pens at the same sale and spent $2.00. How many of each kind could she have bought? (1 pencil, 6 pens; 4 pencils, 4 pens; 7 pencils, 2 pens)

## Ideas That Work

### Calculator Bonus

Have students bring newspaper advertisements that show items they might like to buy. Working in pairs, students exchange advertisements. One student states the amount of money given to make the "purchase." The second student counts out the amount due as change. Students use calculators to check their answers.

**Practice Supplement,** page 28

Name ______________________ To follow text page 71

**Money: Making Change**

List in order each coin or bill you would count out as change.
Use the fewest possible coins and bills.

1. Cost $0.87. Customer paid with $1.00. **3 pennies, 1 dime**
2. Cost $3.80. Customer paid with $5.00. **2 dimes, 1 dollar**
3. Cost $1.19. Customer paid with $2.00. **1 penny, 1 nickel, 1 quarter, 1 half-dollar**
4. Cost $4.62. Customer paid with $10.00. **3 pennies, 1 dime, 1 quarter, 1 $5 bill**
5. Cost $1.60. Customer paid with $5.00. **1 nickel, 1 dime, 1 quarter, 3 $1 bills**
6. Cost $16.49. Customer paid with $20.00. **1 penny, 1 half-dollar, 3 $1 bills**
7. Cost $12.70. Customer paid with $15.00. **1 nickel, 1 quarter 2 $1 bills**
8. Cost $17.68. Customer paid with $20.00. **2 pennies, 1 nickel, 1 quarter, 2 $1 bills**
9. Cost $8.14. Customer paid with $20.00. **1 penny, 1 dime, 1 quarter 1 half dollar, 1 $1 bill, 1 $10 bill**
10. Cost $21.26. Customer paid with $50.00. **4 pennies, 2 dimes, 1 half-dollar, 3 $1 bills, 1 $5 bill, 1 $20 bill**

Solve.

11. Mark bought 3 tapes at $7.98 each. He paid with a $50 bill. How much change did he receive? **$26.06**
12. Wendy bought 2 notebooks at $1.59 each and a pad of paper for $0.79. How much did she spend in all? **$3.97**

# Applications

**Quick Review** Students tell which is the smallest bill they would use to pay each amount—$1, $5, $10, $20, $50, or $100.

$1.80 $92.00 $10.05 $12.50 $25.00 $20.00
$0.75 $7.85 $55.00 $9.38 $86.50

**Lesson Focus** To use data from tour book to solve word problems

**Suggested Materials** Tour book

## Ideas for Getting Started

If possible have available tour books of various kinds that show hotel rates. Give students an opportunity to examine the books to see the options available.

## Using Page 72

**Lesson Development** Read the introductory paragraph at the top of the page. Ask several questions to make sure students understand how to read the table. For example, "How much does a standard double room cost at Grandview?" "What is the charge for one extra person over 6 years old at Moontick?" "Which has a room that costs $67.50?"

**Exercises 1–4** Read through these problems with students before assigning as independent work. Make sure students understand that they must find the needed data in the tour book table.

## Problem Solving: Using Data from a Tour Book

Amanda works in a travel agency. She uses a tour book to find the cost of rooms in hotels. Use data from Amanda's tour book table to solve the problems below.

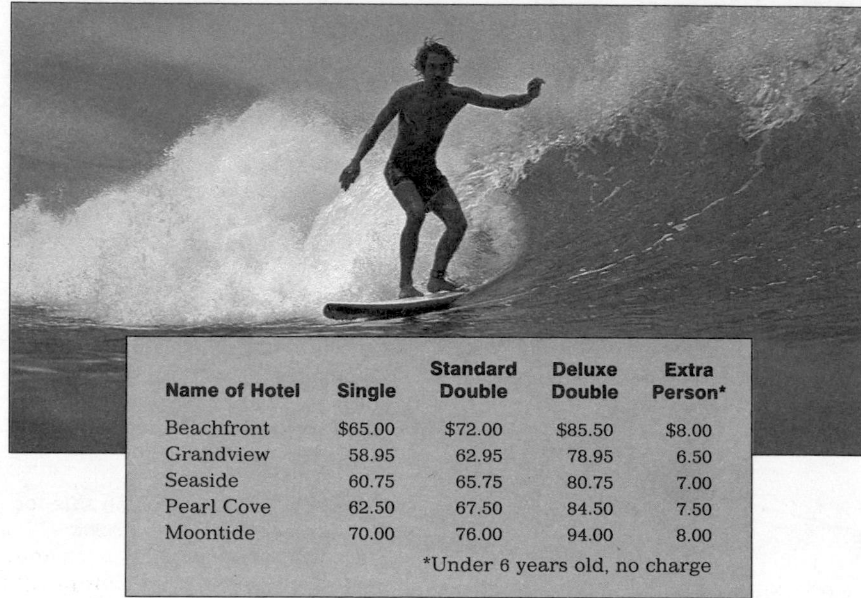

| Name of Hotel | Single | Standard Double | Deluxe Double | Extra Person* |
|---|---|---|---|---|
| Beachfront | $65.00 | $72.00 | $85.50 | $8.00 |
| Grandview | 58.95 | 62.95 | 78.95 | 6.50 |
| Seaside | 60.75 | 65.75 | 80.75 | 7.00 |
| Pearl Cove | 62.50 | 67.50 | 84.50 | 7.50 |
| Moontide | 70.00 | 76.00 | 94.00 | 8.00 |

*Under 6 years old, no charge

1. How much greater is the rate for a deluxe double than for a standard double room at the Seaside? $15.00

2. Tax on a single room for one night at the Grandview is $2.36. What is the cost of the room for one night including the tax? $61.31

3. How much less is the rate for a deluxe double at the Seaside than at the Moontide? $13.25

4. The Beachfront offered a special rate of $125 for two nights for a standard double. How much less is this than two nights at the usual rate? $19.00

72

## Follow Up

### Reteaching

Have copies of the travel section from several newspapers available for students to examine. Ask students to find examples of travel costs such as airfare, hotel, and food costs. Help students use this data to generate word problems. Then encourage students to use the 5-Point Checklist as they solve the problems.

### Enrichment

Challenge students to use the 5-Point Checklist to help them solve the following problem: In planning his vacation, Tom first bought a round-trip bus ticket. He then had $225 left. He expected to spend about $10 a day for meals. He planned to be gone 5 days. In which of the motels below could he not afford to stay?

| | |
|---|---|
| Royal Eagle | $ 22.75 |
| Town Home | 19.50 |
| Acreridge | 37.95 |
| Rolling Meadows | 35.50 |

**Acreridge or Rolling Meadow**

| Assignment Guide | | | |
|---|---|---|---|
| | Minimum | Average | Extended |
| pages 72–73 | 1–9 | 1–10 | 1–11 |

5. What is the rate for a standard double with 1 extra person at the Pearl Cove? $75.00

6. What is the cost per night of a deluxe double with 2 extra persons at the Beachfront? $101.50

7. A salesperson took a single room at the Pearl Cove for one night and stayed in a single at the Seaside the next night. What was the total cost of the rooms for both nights? $123.25

8. Mr. and Mrs. Ito have two children. One child is 2 years old, the other is 7. What is the cost of a standard double room for this family at the Moontide? $84.00

9. Which costs less at the Grandview—a deluxe double room or a standard double with 1 extra person? How much less? standard double with 1 extra person; $9.50 less

10. Last month, Mr. and Mrs. Randall spent one night in each hotel listed on page 72. They always had a deluxe double room. Estimate their total cost for rooms by rounding each rate to the nearest ten dollars. $420

11. **Try This** A person who cleans rooms at the Grandview found 58¢ under a bed. Altogether, there were 9 coins, and none of the coins was a half dollar or a quarter. What coins did the person find? 5 dimes, 1 nickel, 3 pennies



## Using Page 73

**Exercises 5–10** Remind students that they will need to refer to the table on page 72 for data needed to solve these problems.

**Try This** A possible strategy, Guess and Check, was taught on page 48.

**Discussion** "What are we trying to find out about the coins?" (How many of each kind were found?) "How many coins were found?" (9) "What type of coins were not found?" (half dollar, quarter) "What are the possibilities for the coins that were found?" (dimes, nickels, pennies) "What is the least number of pennies the person might have found?" (3) "Could you guess what coins were found and then check your guess?"

**Solution** The person found 5 dimes, 1 nickel, and 3 pennies.

**Extension** Suppose the person found 33¢ with 8 coins. What coins were found? (1 dime, 4 nickels, 3 pennies)

## Ideas That Work

### Math for the Gifted

Have students choose objects from mail order catalogs and fill out order forms completely. Then have students "spend" as near as they can to $100 from the mail order catalog with a minimum purchase of 6 items. Students carefully add and subtract as they go along and then use estimating and rounding skills.

**Practice Supplement,** page 29

Name ____________ To follow text page 73

**Problem Solving: Using Data from a Tour Book**

| Hotel | Single | Double | Extra Person |
|---|---|---|---|
| Sandcastle | $55.00 | $65.00 | $6.00 |
| Sun Towers | $60.00 | $65.00 | $4.50 |
| Beachcomber | $52.50 | $62.50 | $7.50 |
| Surf | $78.75 | $85.00 | $6.00 |

The data above are from a tour book.
Use the data to solve each problem.

1. How much less is the rate for a double at the Beachcomber than at the Surf? **$22.50**

2. What is the cost of a double with one extra person at the Sun Towers? **$69.50**

3. How much less is the rate for a single at the Beachcomber than at the Sun Towers? **$7.50**

4. Sun Towers offered a special rate of $100 for two nights for a double. How much less is this than two nights at the usual rate? **$30.00**

5. If a single person spends one night at Sandcastle and one night at the Surf, what will be the total cost for the two nights? **$133.75**

6. What is the rate for a double with one person extra at the Beachcomber? **$70.00**

7. Which costs more at the Surf—a single with one extra person or a double? How much more? **double $0.25**

8. If tax on a single room at Sandcastle is $3.30, what is the total cost of the room for one night? **$58.30**

**Lesson Focus** To draw a picture as a strategy for solving nonroutine word problems

## Ideas for Getting Started

Write this problem on the chalkboard.

Tanya had 4 bags for marbles with 5 marbles in each bag. How many marbles did she have?

Have students draw a picture, rather than multiplying to find the answer. Students will probably draw pictures like this:

Discuss how the pictures were used to solve this problem. Elicit from students that in this case a picture was not really necessary. Then explain that in some instances drawing a picture can help us to understand the problem better and may even suggest a particular solution plan.

## Using Page 74

**Motivational Problem** Read the Try This problem at the top of the page. "What are we trying to find out about this race?" (Who came in second?) "How many boys were in the race?" (5) "Who came in first? (Len) "Last?" (Jerry) "Now read the introductory paragraph telling about the strategy Draw a Picture."

**Lesson Development** Discuss each of the three steps shown in the illustrations. Make sure that students understand that one picture, not three, was made to help solve this problem. The second and third pictures emphasize how we must return to the original problem statement to get data needed to solve the problem.

**Exercise 1** This exercise is very similar to the Try This problem. A picture like this will give the solution.

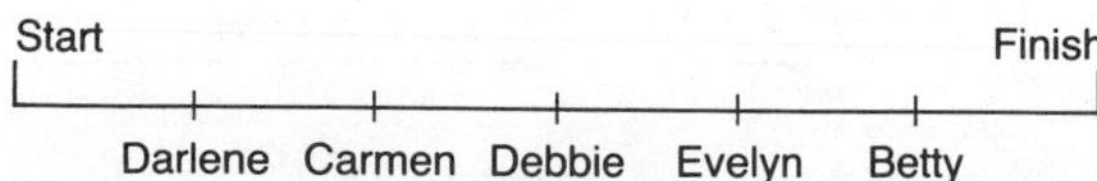


**Exercise 2** Students might incorrectly decide that 9 cuts are needed to get 9 pieces. Drawing a picture shows that only 8 cuts are needed. If a hint is necessary, ask: "How many cuts are needed to get 2 pieces? (1) "3 pieces?" (2) This should help students see that the number of pieces is 1 more than number of cuts.

## Problem Solving: Draw a Picture

When you are trying to solve a problem, it is often very helpful to

**Draw a Picture**

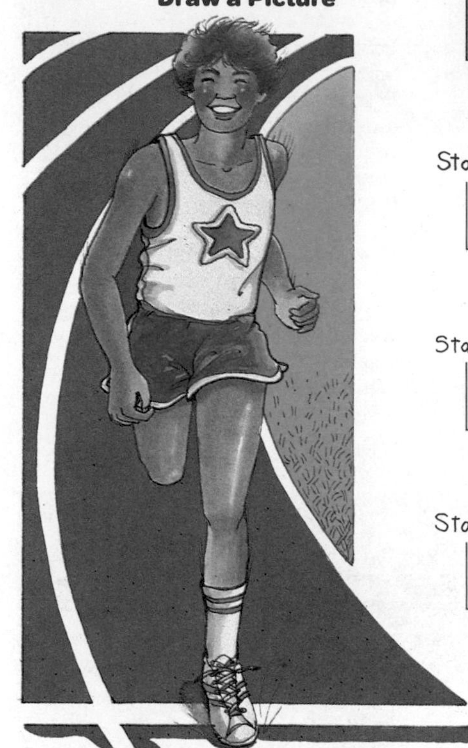

**Try This** Five boys ran in a 100-m dash. Len came in first. Jerry came in last. If Phil was ahead of Nico and Fred was just behind Nico, who came in second?

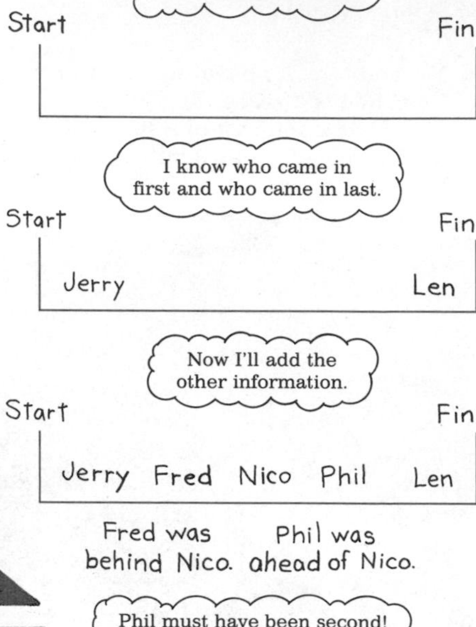


1. Five girls ran in a 100-m dash. Debbie finished ahead of Carmen, and Carmen was not last. Betty finished far ahead of Carmen, and Evelyn finished just behind Betty. If Darlene finished last, which girl finished next to last? Carmen

2. Derek has a ribbon 180 cm long. He wants to cut the ribbon into pieces 20 cm long. How many cuts will he have to make? 8

74

## Strategy Test Item

**Optional Problem** If you wish to assess students' ability to apply the strategy called Draw a Picture introduced in this chapter, provide them with the problem below.

> Dale had a kite string 24 m long. He cut it into 8 pieces that were each 3 m long. How many cuts did he make?

**Solution** Dale made 7 cuts in the kite string.

## Chapter Review-Test

Write the place value of the red digit.

1. 2.45 4 tenths
2. 0.673 3 thousandths
3. 41.05 4 tens
4. 1.0057 7 ten thousandths
5. 26.709 0 hundredths

Write the word name for each decimal.

6. 0.246 two hundred forty-six thousandths
7. 5.00732 five and seven hundred thirty-two hundred thousandths
8. 18.0502 eighteen and five hundred two ten thousandths

Write >, <, or = for each ●.

9. 4.20 ● 4.2 =
10. 12.705 ● 12.715 <
11. 0.96 ● 0.096 >
12. 1.40 ● 11.40 <
13. 82.4 ● 8.24 >
14. 0.5213 ● 0.5321 <

15. Write in order from greatest to least. 2.640 2.099 2.85 2.605 2.5
2.85, 2.640, 2.605, 2.5, 2.099

Round each number to the place given.

16. 25.43 (tenths) 25.4
17. 0.545 (hundredths) 0.55
18. 14.61 (whole number) 15

19. Estimate the sum by rounding to the nearest tenth. 4.02 + 12.58 + 1.98 = 18.6

20. Estimate the difference by rounding to the nearest dollar. $29.48 − 14.65 = $14

Add.

21. 0.527 + 0.822 = 1.349
22. 1.4905 + 6.070 = 7.5605
23. 12.06 + 18.7 + 4.99 = 35.75
24. 64.203 + 9.74 + 8.7 = 82.643
25. $62.95 + 49.95 = $112.90

Subtract.

26. 17.64 − 9.86 = 7.78
27. 0.402 − 0.186 = 0.216
28. 96.4 − 14.55 = 81.85
29. 126.424 − 86.63 = 39.794
30. $124.85 − 64.90 = $ 59.95

Solve.

31. Juanita ran the 100-m race in 16.5 seconds. Sharon ran the same race in 14.35 seconds. How much faster did Sharon run the race than Juanita? 2.15 seconds

32. Maury's ticket for the movie cost $3.25. He bought a cup of juice for $0.75 and a bag of peanuts for $0.85. How much money did Maury spend? $4.85



## Assessment Options

If you use the Chapter Review/Test as a review assignment, you may wish to use the multiple-choice test or the free-response test to evaluate mastery of the chapter objectives. The items on these tests have a one-to-one correspondence in terms of content and level of difficulty. A correlation of test items to objectives and student text pages is provided in the Management Guide for Chapter 3. Note that items 26–28 are derived from a lesson for which no minimum assignment was suggested in the Assignment Guide.

**Multiple-Choice Test,** TRB pages 7–9

**Free-Response Test,** TRB pages 53–54

## TRB Options

The following blackline masters are available for use with this chapter. If you have not already assigned these materials, you may wish to use them to close the chapter.

**Recreation,** TRB page 153

**Consumer Applications,** TRB page 171

**Calculator Technology,** TRB page 189

**Reading Math,** TRB page 221

**Family Involvement,** TRB pages 241–242

## Using Page 75

The exercises in the Chapter Review/Test emphasize the major concepts and skills presented in this chapter. These exercises may be used as a review assignment or as a test, depending upon your needs.

**Item Analysis** The table below correlates the Chapter Review/Test items with objectives and with the student text pages on which the concepts or skills were taught. Note that items 19 and 20 are derived from a lesson for which no minimum assignment was suggested in the Assignment Guide. Only those students who were assigned this lesson should be expected to complete the corresponding Chapter Review/Test items.

| Items | Objectives | Related text pages |
|---|---|---|
| 1–15 | 3.1 | 54–59 |
| 16–20 | 3.2 | 60–62 |
| 21–30 | 3.3 | 64–68, 70 |
| 31–32 | 3.4 | 63, 69, 71–73 |

# Reteaching

## Using Page 76

The exercises on this page are intended for those students who experienced difficulty with the Chapter Review/Test on page 75. Should students require reteaching of these key concepts and skills, please refer to the teaching notes below. Otherwise, the Another Look exercises can be assigned as independent work, with students using the accompanying sample problems and hints as guides.

**Exercises 1–9** Decimal place value was originally taught on pages 54–57. Use the place-value chart and the number 4.20164 to review decimal place value and how to read a decimal. If necessary, use dollars, dimes, and pennies to show the relationships among ones, tenths, and hundredths. For reading decimals, emphasize that the decimal part is read by saying the digits as with whole numbers (twenty thousand one hundred sixty-four) and then saying the decimal place value of the digit farthest to the right (hundred thousandths).

**Exercises 10–17** Comparing and ordering decimals was originally taught on pages 58–59. First read the rule shown in the box. Then relate the rule to the example given. Students should also be reminded that a zero can be annexed to the decimal part to help compare decimals (see, for example, exercise 13).

**Exercises 18–26** This skill was originally taught on pages 60–61. The example shows the three key steps in rounding decimals: (a) Find the decimal place to which you want to round; (b) look at the next digit to the right; and (c) round up if that digit is 5 or greater, round down if that digit is less than 5. A number line can be useful to show the reasonableness of these steps for rounding decimals. Relating the rounding of decimals to the rounding of whole numbers may also help some students.

**Exercise 27–32** These skills were originally taught on pages 64–67. Have students read the rule. Then discuss each example. If writing the decimal point seems to cause confusion, have students first add and subtract as with whole numbers, and then add the decimal point. Play money can also be used to help students understand trading.

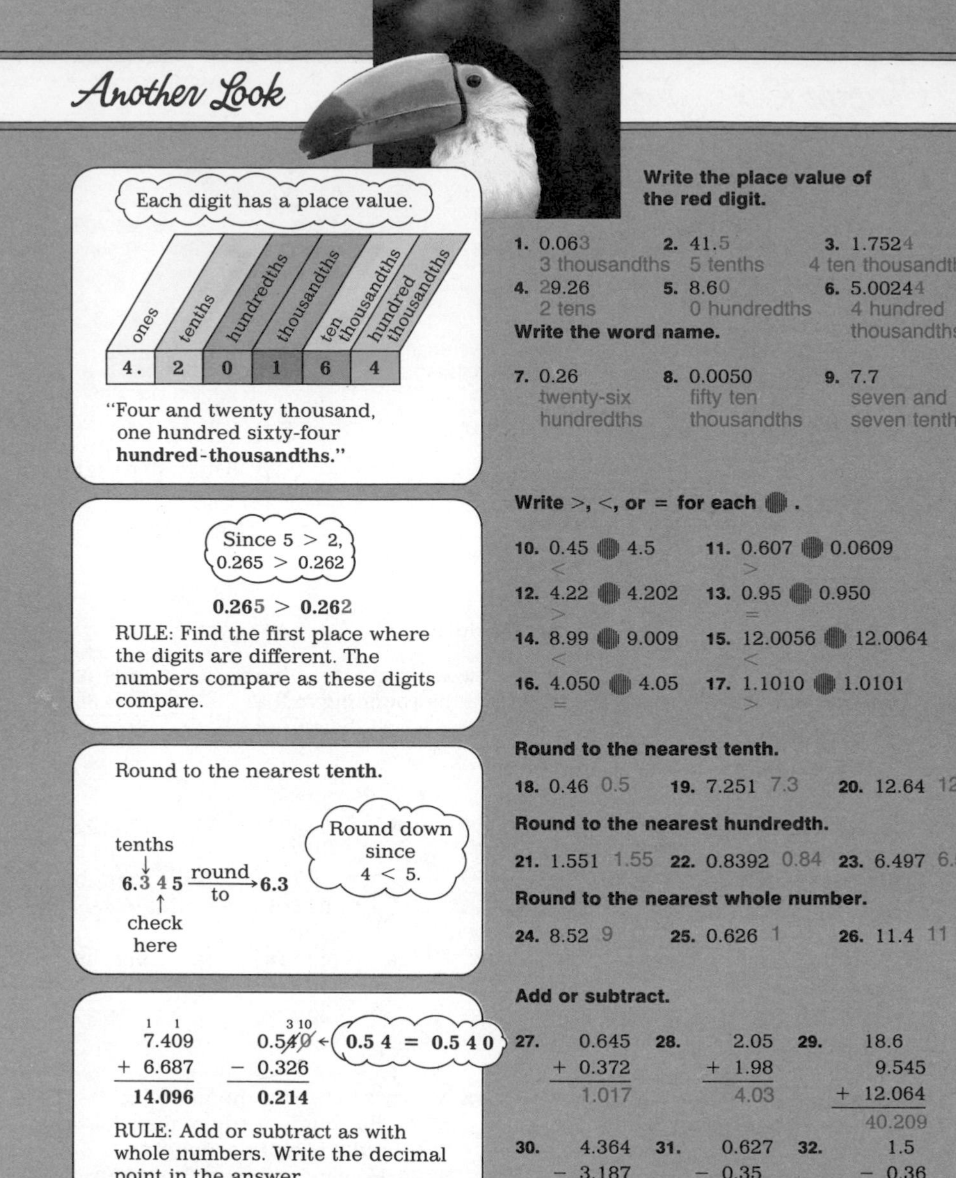

*Another Look*

Each digit has a place value.

| ones | tenths | hundredths | thousandths | ten thousandths | hundred thousandths |
|---|---|---|---|---|---|
| 4. | 2 | 0 | 1 | 6 | 4 |

"Four and twenty thousand, one hundred sixty-four **hundred-thousandths.**"

Since 5 > 2, 0.265 > 0.262

**0.265 > 0.262**

RULE: Find the first place where the digits are different. The numbers compare as these digits compare.

Round to the nearest **tenth.**

tenths ↓ 6.3 4 5 round to → 6.3 ↑ check here

Round down since 4 < 5.

7.409 + 6.687 = **14.096**

0.540 − 0.326 = **0.214**

0.5 4 = 0.5 4 0

RULE: Add or subtract as with whole numbers. Write the decimal point in the answer.

**Write the place value of the red digit.**

**1.** 0.063 3 thousandths **2.** 41.5 5 tenths **3.** 1.7524 4 ten thousandths
**4.** 29.26 2 tens **5.** 8.60 0 hundredths **6.** 5.00244 4 hundred thousandths

**Write the word name.**

**7.** 0.26 twenty-six hundredths **8.** 0.0050 fifty ten thousandths **9.** 7.7 seven and seven tenths

**Write >, <, or = for each ●.**

**10.** 0.45 ● 4.5 < **11.** 0.607 ● 0.0609 >
**12.** 4.22 ● 4.202 > **13.** 0.95 ● 0.950 =
**14.** 8.99 ● 9.009 < **15.** 12.0056 ● 12.0064 <
**16.** 4.050 ● 4.05 = **17.** 1.1010 ● 1.0101 >

**Round to the nearest tenth.**

**18.** 0.46 0.5 **19.** 7.251 7.3 **20.** 12.64 12.6

**Round to the nearest hundredth.**

**21.** 1.551 1.55 **22.** 0.8392 0.84 **23.** 6.497 6.50

**Round to the nearest whole number.**

**24.** 8.52 9 **25.** 0.626 1 **26.** 11.4 11

**Add or subtract.**

**27.** 0.645 + 0.372 = 1.017 **28.** 2.05 + 1.98 = 4.03 **29.** 18.6 + 9.545 + 12.064 = 40.209
**30.** 4.364 − 3.187 = 1.177 **31.** 0.627 − 0.35 = 0.277 **32.** 1.5 − 0.36 = 1.14

76

## Just for Teachers

### Language of Math

The decimal numeration system spread very slowly from India and the Middle East to Europe. In India by A.D. 400, it was used by Arabic mathematicians such as al Khowarismi during the ninth century and translated into western languages as early as the twelfth century by Catholic monks in Moorish-occupied Spain. The "new numbers," however, still had to undergo a period of fine-tuning that lasted several centuries. Standardized numeric and operative symbols, efficient algorithms for performing operations, and decimal fractions developed during the Middle Ages largely out of commercial use and proved its superiority over the old ways. During this period of evolution, the abacus remained a common aid to calculation.

In contrast to the familiar "counting frame" with beads strung on vertical rods, a popular abacus of Medieval Europe was a table ruled with horizontal place-value lines. These lines were spaced such that counters could be placed *on* the lines to represent ones, tens, hundreds, thousands, and so on, or *between* the lines to represent fives, fifties, five hundreds, and so on, to express a particular number. The thousands line was marked with an X as a visual aid to accurate positioning.

## *Enrichment*

**Patterns with Networks**

A truck driver needs to deliver packages in every town shown on the map. Can the driver travel over each road only once and visit every town?

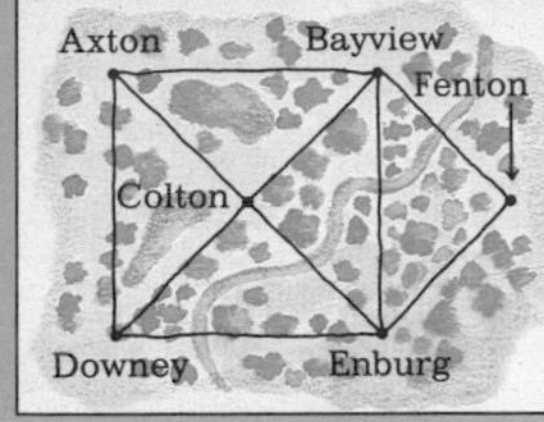


This problem can be reworded as, "Can you copy the segments of this figure without lifting your pencil from your paper and without retracing any line?"

Points *A, B, C, D, E,* and *F* are called **vertices.** An **odd vertex** is a point where an odd number of lines meet. Whether or not a figure can be traced without lifting your pencil or retracing a line depends upon how many odd vertices it has.

Odd vertex (3 paths) — *A*
Even vertex (4 paths) — *B*
*C*
*F* — Even vertex (2 paths)
*D* — Odd vertex
*E* — Even vertex

Copy the table below and give the number of odd vertices in each figure. Find out which figures you can draw without lifting your pencil or retracing any path. Then fill in the rest of the table. Do you see any pattern? See teaching notes.

| **Figure** | | | | | |
|---|---|---|---|---|---|
| **Number of Odd Vertices** | 2 | 4 | 2 | 4 | 2 |
| **Can It Be Copied?** | Yes | No | Yes | No | Yes |

Now draw two figures—one you can copy and one that you cannot copy using the rules given above. Do they follow the same pattern as the other figures?



## Using Page 77

This page is intended for those students who successfully completed the Chapter Review/Test on page 75. You may wish to assign this page as independent work while you use Another Look exercises to reteach the basic concepts and skills of the chapter. Or, you may decide that all students would benefit from exposure to this Enrichment activity.

**Lesson Development** The pattern students should observe in the table is that networks with more than 2 odd vertices are not traceable. To help students draw the figures, suggest that they begin their tracing at an odd vertex. For the example at the top, one sequence that works is D-E-F-B-E-C-A-D-C-B-A.

The "counting table," as it was called in England, was further divided into vertical columns. Each column accommodated one number, represented by counters on the appropriate lines and spaces. A calculation proceeded horizontally with the result indicated by the counters in the last column on the right.

Similar in principle to the Japanese *soroban,* the provision for five-unit values in the horizontal spaces minimized the number of counters needed to express any number. That is, five counters on a line could be replaced by one counter in the next higher space, and two counters in a space could be replaced by one counter on the next higher line.

## Using Page 78

The exercises on this page provide practice for maintaining cumulative skills. The emphasis in this Cumulative Review is on basic facts (Chapter 1), place value and rounding (Chapter 2), addition and subtraction of whole numbers (Chapter 2), and problem solving (Chapter 2).

**Item Analysis** The table below correlates the Cumulative Review items with objectives and with the student book pages on which the concepts or skills were taught.

| Items | Objectives | Related text pages |
|---|---|---|
| 1–5 | 1.1 | 1–7, 10 |
| 6–8 | 2.1 | 24–29 |
| 9 | 2.2 | 30–33 |
| 10–12 | 2.3 | 36–43 |
| 13–14 | 2.5 | 34–35, 44–46 |

## *Cumulative Review*

Add, subtract, multiply, or divide. Watch the signs.

1. 13 − 8
   A 4
   (B) 5
   C 21
   D not given

2. 9 + 7
   A 48
   B 17
   (C) 16
   D not given

3. 7 × 8
   A 48
   B 15
   C 78
   (D) not given

4. 6 × 9
   (A) 54
   B 63
   C 15
   D not given

5. $8\overline{)72}$
   A 8
   (B) 9
   C 12
   D not given

6. Give the digits in the millions period: 123,456,789,101
   A 123 (B) 456
   C 789 D not given

7. What is the place value of 8 in 1,268,374?
   A ten thousands
   B hundreds
   (C) thousands
   D not given

8. Which symbol (>, <, or =) goes in the ●?
   57,389 ● 57,839
   A > (B) < C =

9. Round 62,184 to the nearest thousand.
   A 60,000 B 62,200
   C 63,000 (D) not given

Add or subtract.

10. 738 + 295
    A 923
    B 443
    (C) 1,033
    D not given

11. 6,243 − 1,706
    A 5,547
    (B) 4,537
    C 7,949
    D not given

12. 14,331 + 62,284
    A 76,515
    B 63,516
    C 47,953
    (D) not given

13. One stereo costs $549. Another costs $638. What is the difference in price?
    A $1,187 (B) $89
    C $99 D not given

14. A shirt costs $24.89. A sweater costs $46.68. What is the cost of both items?
    (A) $71.57 B $70.47
    C $21.79 D not given

## Objectives

**4.1** Use multiplication facts to find and estimate products.
**4.2** Multiply by 1- and 2-digit factors.
**4.3** Write exponents to show factors and powers of ten; write standard numbers for numbers in expanded notation.
**4.4** Multiply by a 3-digit number.
**4.5** Solve word problems using the 5-Point Checklist and cumulative computational skills.

## Summary

In this chapter students review and use the basic multiplication facts to multiply larger numbers, including multiples of 10, 100, and 1,000. They review and use the rounding process to estimate the products of two whole numbers. The skill of multiplying a whole number by a single digit number is extended to larger numbers. This skill is then used to help students sharpen skills in multiplying by 2- and 3-digit numbers.

Exponents are introduced as an efficient way to represent numbers. Word problems that apply the multiplication algorithm as well as algorithms studied in earlier chapters are included. Multiplication in money notation is used throughout the chapter. In one lesson students use a calculator to extend their estimation skills.

## Mathematical Background

**Multiplying Multiples of 10, 100, and 1,000** In order to estimate and to understand the partial products in the multiplication algorithm, students must be able to find products such as 6 × 10, 6 × 100, 6 × 1,000, 6 × 30, 6 × 300, 6 × 3,000, 60 × 30, 600 × 300, 6,000 × 30. It is helpful if they can find these products mentally. This shortcut uses a basic fact and counting the number of zeros in each factor. Before they use the shortcut, students should understand why the shortcut works. In the illustration below, place-value blocks show the procedure for finding 3 × 50.

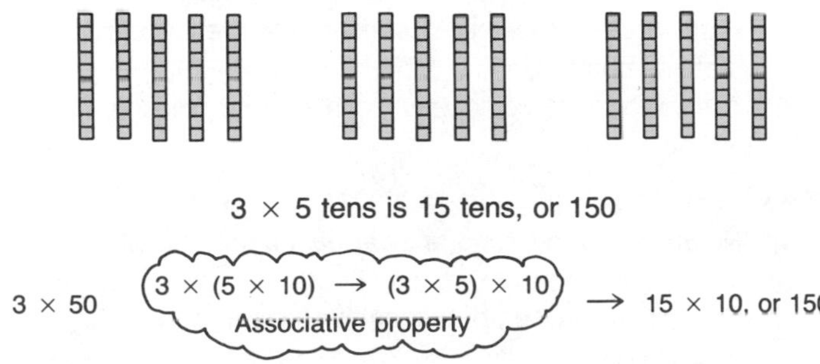


**Estimation** Students should recognize that estimation is a very practical skill in everyday situations when only an approximate answer is required. As a skill it involves two important components. First, the ability to round whole numbers to the nearest ten, hundred, thousand, and so on. Second, the ability to find products involving multiples of ones, hundreds, and thousands, and so on.

**Multiplication** A number of important ideas must be understood before students can clearly understand the multiplication algorithm. Although the primary goal is to develop an efficient procedure for finding a product, a reasonable emphasis on understanding will take the process beyond the "bag of tricks" phase and will help students to understand *why* they do what they do. An understanding of the following is necessary in the multiplication algorithm:

- a knowledge of the multiplication facts
- an understanding of place value
- an understanding of the idea of trading
- the ability to multiply and then add mentally [e.g., (6 × 4) + 2]
- an understanding of the distributive property
- a knowledge of addition facts
- a knowledge of the addition algorithm

At earlier grades, students may have used place-value blocks to model simple problems such as 3 × 124. Money can also provide a useful model for smaller products. However, for larger products such as 34 × 286, place-value models become quite laborious. In these instances, it is important that students understand how the distributive property allows us to think of any multiplication problem as a combination of single-digit problems and then use this skill for multiplying by a single digit in finding larger products.

The experiences with multiplying money in this chapter provide readiness for multiplying decimals in Chapter 6. At this stage students find the products as if working with whole numbers. To decide where to put the decimal point, students round the amounts of money to the nearest dollar and estimate the product using the estimated dollars to locate the decimal point.

**Exponents** An exponent is a special notation used to represent a product in which a given factor is repeated. The exponent tells how many times the number, called the base, is used as a factor.

For numbers written in scientific notation, powers of 10 are important. The models below show the first three powers of 10 and suggest reasons for the names commonly associated with these powers. Students can see that $10^1 = 10$, $10^2 = 100$, $10^3 = 1{,}000$, $10^4 = 10{,}000$. Note that the exponent tells the number of zeros that follow the 1.

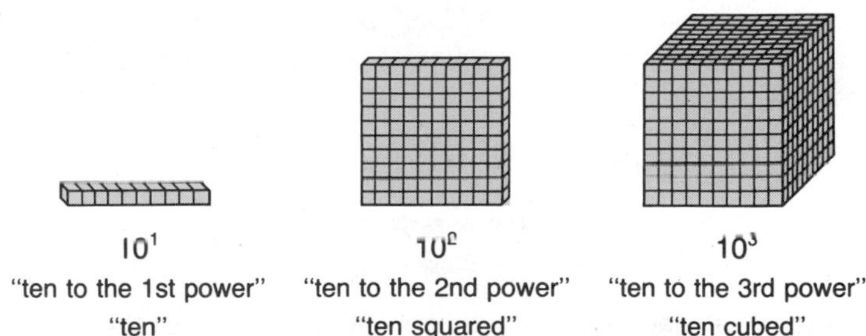

| $10^1$ | $10^2$ | $10^3$ |
|---|---|---|
| "ten to the 1st power" | "ten to the 2nd power" | "ten to the 3rd power" |
| "ten" | "ten squared" | "ten cubed" |

**Problem Solving** The 5-Point Checklist for solving problems is reviewed again in this chapter. While the checklist does not provide "rules" for solving a problem, it can help students organize their thinking when confronted with a problem. Encourage them to use each part of the checklist as a guide when solving a problem. Specific problem-solving experiences in this chapter include: Using Estimation, page 83; Using the 5-Point Checklist, pages 90–91; and Using Data from a Graph, page 98. Following problem-solving practice, page 99, a new strategy called Make a Table is introduced on page 100.

**Vocabulary**

exponent base powers of 10

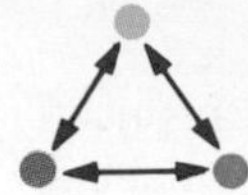

## Error Analysis

This chapter provides a review of whole number multiplication extending through 3-digit factors. The basic material in the chapter should be familiar to students, which means the teacher should focus on helping students to sharpen and extend these skills. The concept of exponents is probably new material for most students. Errors at this level may reflect long standing misconceptions, or misapplications of a recently taught concept or procedure. A few common errors are given below.

**Error Pattern 1**

| | | | | |
|---|---|---|---|---|
| 32 | 436 | 8,721 | 672 | 156 |
| × 20 | × 300 | × 2,000 | × 400 | × 30 |
| 640 | 13,080 | 164,420 | 25,880 | 4,680 |

**Diagnosis** The student has difficulty with multiplication when a zero occurs in one factor. When the factor is a multiple of 10, the student calculates correctly; however, when multiplying by a multiple of 100 or 1,000, the student places only one zero in the answer and multiplies.

**Remediation** Work through a step-by-step explanation of the multiplication algorithm for multiples of 10, 100, and 1,000. Multiply with an example such as 20 × 32, and show all partial products. Point out that a multiple of 10 will always have a zero in the ones place. Next show an example such as 300 × 436. Again put in all partial products.

| | | | |
|---|---|---|---|
| 30 | | 436 | |
| × 20 | | × 300 | |
| 00 | (0 × 32) | 000 | (0 × 436) |
| 640 | (20 × 32) | 000 | (0 × 436) |
| 640 | | 1308 | (3 × 436) |
| | | 130,800 | |

Call attention to the answer with the zeros in the ones and tens place. Elicit from students the "rule" for adding zeros. Then have students write the appropriate number of zeros before they begin to multiply.

**Error Pattern 2**

$10^2 = 2 \times 10$ $\quad 10^3 = 3 \times 10$ $\quad 10^6 = 6 \times 10$

$6^3 = 3 \times 6$ $\quad 10^8 = 8 \times 10$

**Diagnosis** The student has misunderstood the meaning of an exponent and interprets the exponent as a factor, using this idea to write a multiplication sentence.

**Remediation** Remind students that the exponent tells how many times the base is used as a factor—the exponent itself is not a factor. Use the chart and examples below to review these ideas.

| Number | Factors | Base | Exponent | Exponential form | Read |
|---|---|---|---|---|---|
| 10 | 1 × 10 | 10 | 1 | $10^1$ | Ten to the 1st power |
| 100 | 10 × 10 | 10 | 2 | $10^2$ | Ten squared, ten to the 2nd power |
| 8 | 2 × 2 × 2 | 2 | 3 | $2^3$ | Two cubed, two to the 3rd power |
| 9 | 3 × 3 | 3 | 2 | $3^2$ | Three squared, three to the 2nd power |

## Problem Solving

### Evaluating Problem-Solving Performance—Part 1

As problem-solving experiences play a greater role in your mathematics program, the evaluation of these experiences becomes more important. The best way to evaluate problem-solving performance is through a one-to-one interview either while the student is solving a problem or immediately after the problem is solved. Unfortunately, this type of interview takes more time than is available to most teachers.

There are, however, two evaluation techniques that do not require much time: 1) analyzing a student's written work, and 2) observing while a student solves problems in a whole-class setting. When used jointly, these techniques can provide valuable information about each student's problem-solving performance. A scheme for analyzing a student's written work and a sample problem are given below. Guidelines for observing students are presented in Chapter 7 (page 167B).

**A Scoring Scheme for Written Work**

Understanding the problem

- **0** – Complete misinterpretation of the problem
- **1** – Misinterpretation of part of the problem
- **2** – Complete understanding of the problem

Choosing and implementing a solution strategy

- **0** – No attempt or a totally inappropriate strategy
- **1** – Partly-correct strategy based on interpreting part of the problem correctly
- **2** – A strategy that could lead to a correct solution if used without error

Answering the problem

- **0** – No answer or a wrong answer based on an inappropriate solution strategy
- **1** – Copying error, computational error, partial answer for a problem with multiple answers, or an answer labeled incorrectly
- **2** – Correct solution

A well is 10 meters deep. A frog climbs up 5 meters during the day but slips back 4 meters during the night. If the frog starts at the bottom of the well, how many days does it take the frog to reach the top?

According to the scoring scheme, the following examples of solutions to the problem might be scored as shown below:

Student A

Solution:
5 meters
− 4 meters
1 meter gained each day

It takes 10 days for the frog to reach the top.

Score: 1, 1, 0

Student B

Solution:
5 meters each day
10 meters in all

It takes 2 days for the frog to reach the top.

Score: 1, 0, 0

Student C

Solution:
5 meters
− 4 meters
1 meter gained each day

It takes 6 days for the frog to reach the top.

Score: 2, 2, 2

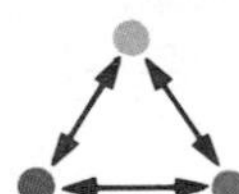

## Special Education

The suggestions of this section will help you plan multiplication activities for the special-needs students in your class. Many of the ideas involve learning approaches that can be incorporated in regular class lessons. Others focus on individualized ways to meet some of the more common difficulties that students may have.

### Using Visual/Kinesthetic Cues

Encourage students to color, underscore, or finger trace digits that are keys to the patterns illustrated on pages 80 and 81. This can help students "see," orally describe, and then retain the idea being presented. In follow-up exrcises, it may be necessary to allow students to write the problems (as shown in the illustration below) before giving the estimated product. As students become more confident, they will be able to think rather than write factors they use to find an estimated product.

| Given | Student writes |
|---|---|
| 279 × 2 | 300 × 2 |

### Building Prerequisite Learning

Use smaller numbers and base 10 blocks or visuals to review multiplication of whole numbers with the special-needs students in your class. This review will correct misconceptions and help insure retention of correct procedures. As you review multiplication with a 1-digit factor, allow students actually to combine and trade place-value materials *step by step* as they complete several written problems.

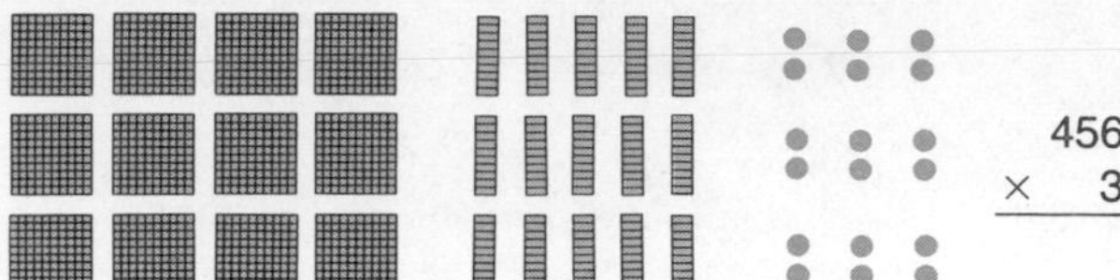

$$\begin{array}{r} 456 \\ \times \quad 3 \\ \hline \end{array}$$

### Looking Ahead

When students are multiplying by a 1-digit factor, have them cross out each digit as they use it. This will help avoid confusion with 2-digit factors when two or more traded digits are visually present.

### Using Visual/Verbal Input

When introducing multiplication involving 2-digit factors, allow students to use graph paper to illustrate the multiplication of selected problems. Focus on the shift from multiplication to addition within the algorithm. Elicit from students that they *add* the results of the two smaller multiplications to find the total, in this case 23 × 21.

| | | |
|---|---|---|
| | | 21 |
| | | × 23 |
| 3 rows of 21 | → | 63 |
| 20 rows of 21 | → | + 420 |
| | | 483 |

### Using Visual Help for Zeros

Exercises such as the one shown below cause problems for many students. Because one of the factors is a multiple of 100, the product will end in two zeros. In this example, however, a third zero must also appear because the product of 5 × 4 ends in zero also. For some students, underscoring as shown may help. Students can then proceed with 5 × 724 in the multiplication, and will be less likely to omit the third zero.

$$\begin{array}{r} 724 \\ \times\ 5\underline{00} \\ \hline \underline{00} \end{array}$$

Middle zeros in a factor can also cause difficulty. Before beginning, students could underscore each of the digits (605 in this example) as they verbally remind themselves: "First multiply the ones, then the tens, then the hundreds." Then, as students carry out the multiplication, the underscore serves as a visual reminder not to omit the multiplication involving the zero.

$$\begin{array}{r} \underline{6}\underline{0}\underline{5} \\ \times\ \ 26 \\ \hline \end{array}$$

## Subject Integration

Subject matter related to other areas of the curriculum has been integrated into the following lessons. This provides an opportunity to highlight the interaction between mathematics and other subjects.

**Consumer Awareness** Radio advertising, page 79

**Social Studies** Yellowstone Park, pages 84–85; population, pages 86–87; *Titanic*, pages 88–89; speed records, pages 90–91; new citizens, pages 94–95

**Science** Pulse rates, page 98; human body facts, page 99

# Management Guide

| Teaching Chapter 4 | | | | Meeting Individual Needs | | | | | |
|---|---|---|---|---|---|---|---|---|---|
| | | | | Lesson Assignments | | | Follow Up | | |
| Objectives | Chapter Content | Pages | TRB Test Items | Minimum | Average | Extended | Reteaching | Enrichment | Practice |
| | Chapter Opener | 79 | | | | | | | |
| **4.1** Use multiplication facts to find and estimate products. | Using Multiplication Facts: Mental Math | 80 | 1–6 | 1–20 | 1–20 | 1–20 | SE5 Ch 5 RS 20 | ES 20 | PS 30 |
| | Special Products: Mental Math | 81 | | 1–20 | 1–20 | 1–20 | SE5 Ch 5 | | |
| | Estimating Products | 82 | 7–10 | 1–22 | 1–25 | 1–25 | SE5 Ch 5 | | PS 31 |
| **4.2** Multiply by 1- and 2-digit factors. | Multiplying by a 1-Digit Number | 84–85 | 11–14 | 1–27, 30 | 1–31 | 11–32, TM | SE5 Ch 5 RS 22 | ES 22 | MP 415 PS 32 |
| | Multiplying by Multiples of 10, 100, and 1,000 | 86–87 | 15–18 | 1–23, 30, 32, SK | 1–32, SK | 11–33, SK | SE5 Ch 5 | | PS 33 |
| | Multiplying by a 2-Digit Factor | 88–89 | 19–22 | 1–24, 34–37 | 1–37 | 11–38, TM | SE5 Ch 5 RS 23 | ES 23 | MP 416 PS 34 |
| **4.3** Write exponents to show factors and powers of ten; write standard numbers for numbers written in expanded notation. | Exponents | 92–93 | 27–35 | 1–44 | 1–48 | 1–49 odd, TM | RS 24 | ES 24 | PS 36 |
| **4.4** Multiply by a 3-digit number. | Multiplying by a 3-Digit Factor | 94–95 | 23–26 | 1–27 30–31, SK | 1–31, SK | 1–32, SK | SE5 Ch 5 RS 25 | ES 25 | MP 416 PS 37 |
| | Multiplying: Practice | 96 | | 1–18, 25–30, 34 | 1–34 | 1–38 | | | PS 38 |
| | Calculator-Estimation Exercises | 97 | | 1–13, 17–18 | 1–20 | 6–20, TM | | | |
| **4.5** Solve word problems using the 5-Point Checklist and cumulative computational skills. | Problem Solving: Using Estimation | 83 | 36–40 | 1–6 | 1–7 | 1–8 | RS 21 | ES 21 | |
| | Problem Solving: Using the 5-Point Checklist | 90–91 | | 1–2 1–6 | 1–2 1–7 | 1–2 1–8 | | | PS 35 |
| | Problem Solving: Using Data from a Graph | 98 | | 1–6 | 1–7 | 1–9 | | | |
| | Problem Solving: Practice | 99 | | 1–6 | 1–7 | 1–8 | | | PS 39 |
| | Problem Solving: Make a Table | 100 | | | | | | | |
| | Chapter Review-Test | 101 | | | | | | | |
| | Another Look/Enrichment | 102–103 | | | | | | | |
| | Technology | 104–105 | | | | | | | |
| | Cumulative Review | 106 | | | | | | | |

**SE5** Student Edition, Book 5
**RS** Reteaching Supplement
**ES** Enrichment Supplement
**PS** Practice Supplement
**MP** More Practice
**TM** Think Math
**SK** Skillkeeper
**TRB** Teacher's Resource Book

# Teacher's Resource Book

## Masters for Use

**. . . before Chapter 4**

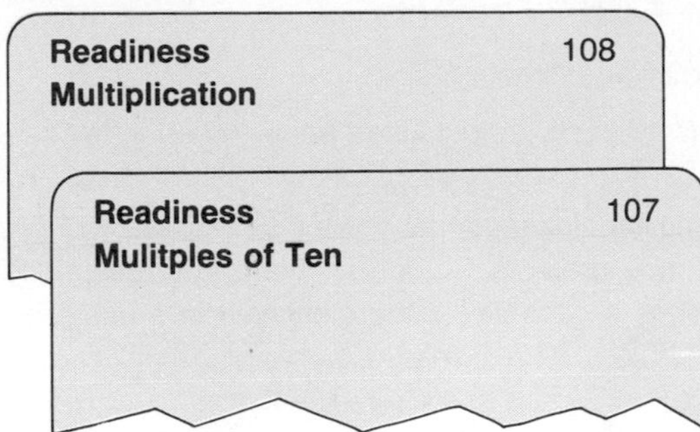


**. . . during Chapter 4**

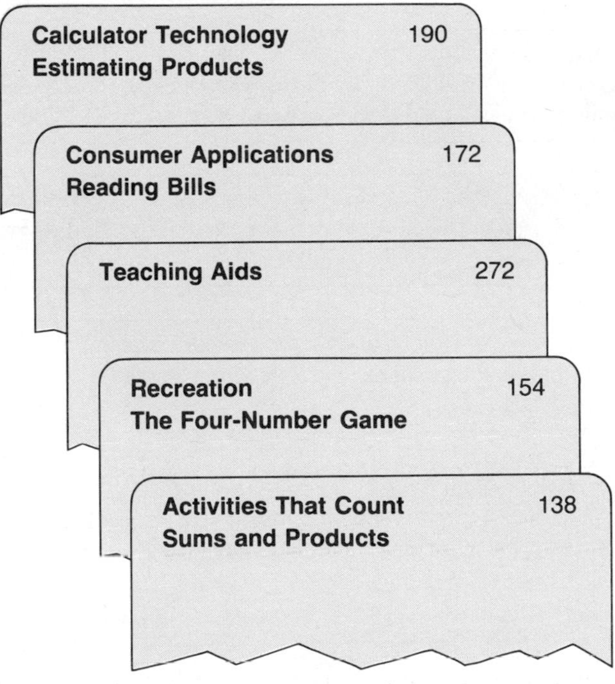

Calculator Technology 190
Estimating Products
Consumer Applications 172
Reading Bills
Teaching Aids 272
Recreation 154
The Four-Number Game
Activities That Count 138
Sums and Products


**. . . after Chapter 4**

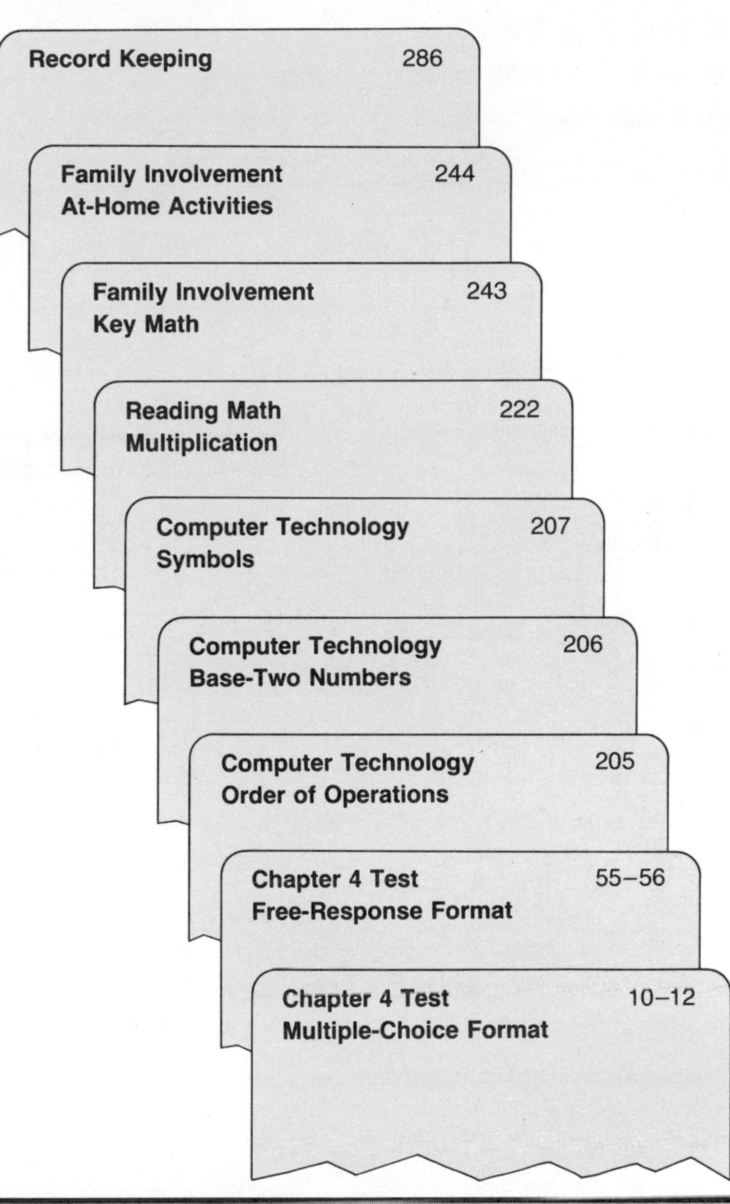

Record Keeping 286
Family Involvement 244
At-Home Activities
Family Involvement 243
Key Math
Reading Math 222
Multiplication
Computer Technology 207
Symbols
Computer Technology 206
Base-Two Numbers
Computer Technology 205
Order of Operations
Chapter 4 Test 55–56
Free-Response Format
Chapter 4 Test 10–12
Multiple-Choice Format


## Supplements

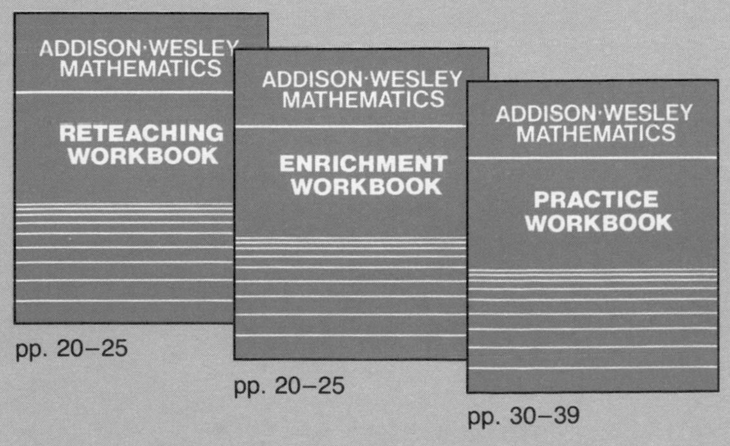


pp. 20–25

pp. 20–25

pp. 30–39

## Other Addison-Wesley Resources

### Books and Kits

*Skillseekers 2* ⊗ Lessons 1–12

*The Arithmetic Primer* pp. 43–58

*Arithmetic Skill Cards* pp. W 5–6

*Baseball, A Game of Numbers* pp. 17–22

*Problem Solving Experiences in Mathematics,* Grade 6
Problems 3, 12, 19, 20, 22, 23, 33, 43, 54, 55, 58, 67, 73, 77, 80, 83, 88, 89, 90, 95, 98, 102, 103, 104, 109, 118, 123, 124, 125, 132, 140, 144

### Technology

*Computer Math Activities* Volumes 1–5

*Computer Math Games* Volumes 1–4, 6

# Activities That Count

Activities That Count are designed for use throughout this chapter and subsequent chapters. Before beginning Chapter 4, you may wish to review these activities and select the ones you consider appropriate for your class.

## Name the Total Game

**Purpose** To practice multiplication skills

**Materials** Index cards, number cube labeled 4 through 9

**Preparation** Label 30 cards with the numbers shown below.

| 0 | 1 | 2 | 3 | 4 |
|---|---|---|---|---|
| 5 | 6 | 7 | 8 | 9 |

| 0 | 10 | 20 | 30 | 40 |
|---|---|---|---|---|
| 50 | 60 | 70 | 80 | 90 |

| 0 | 100 | 200 | 300 | 400 |
|---|---|---|---|---|
| 500 | 600 | 700 | 800 | 900 |

**Activity** Mix the cards in each set and place facedown in separate stacks. Players draw one card from each stack and roll the number cube. The value of each number card is then multiplied by the number rolled on the number cube, and the products are added together. Example:

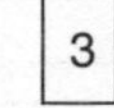

$$\begin{array}{lcr} 7 \times 3 & = & 21 \\ 7 \times 60 & = & 420 \\ 7 \times 200 & = & 1{,}400 \\ \hline \text{Total} & = & 1{,}841 \end{array}$$

Player with the highest total after a given number of rounds is the winner.

## Sums and Products Math Lab

**Purpose** To review finding sums and products

**Preparation** Duplicate the worksheet (TRB p. 138), and have available for students. Prepare one copy of the worksheet as an answer key.

**Activity** Direct students to work independently to fill in the blanks, or have them work with a partner to check each other's answers. Challenge students to use the last box on the worksheet to create their own sums and products for their classmates to complete.

## Estimation Fun Projects

**Purpose** To practice estimation skills

**Preparation** Write each project listed below on an index card.

**Activity** Working in pairs, students choose an estimation project. After completing their projects, students write a brief description, including illustrations if possible, to be displayed in a designated area.

- How many boxes 1 m on each edge could be stacked in your classroom? Make an estimate. Measure to check your estimate. How close was your estimate?

- Estimate how much water would be lost in one year from a dripping faucet. Plan and carry out an experiment to check your estimate. How close was your estimate?

- Guess the number of pages in an encyclopedia. Guess the number of words on one page of the encyclopedia. Check your guesses. Were your guesses good ones?

- Estimate the total weight of everyone in your class. Then add the correct weights to check your estimate. How close was your estimate?

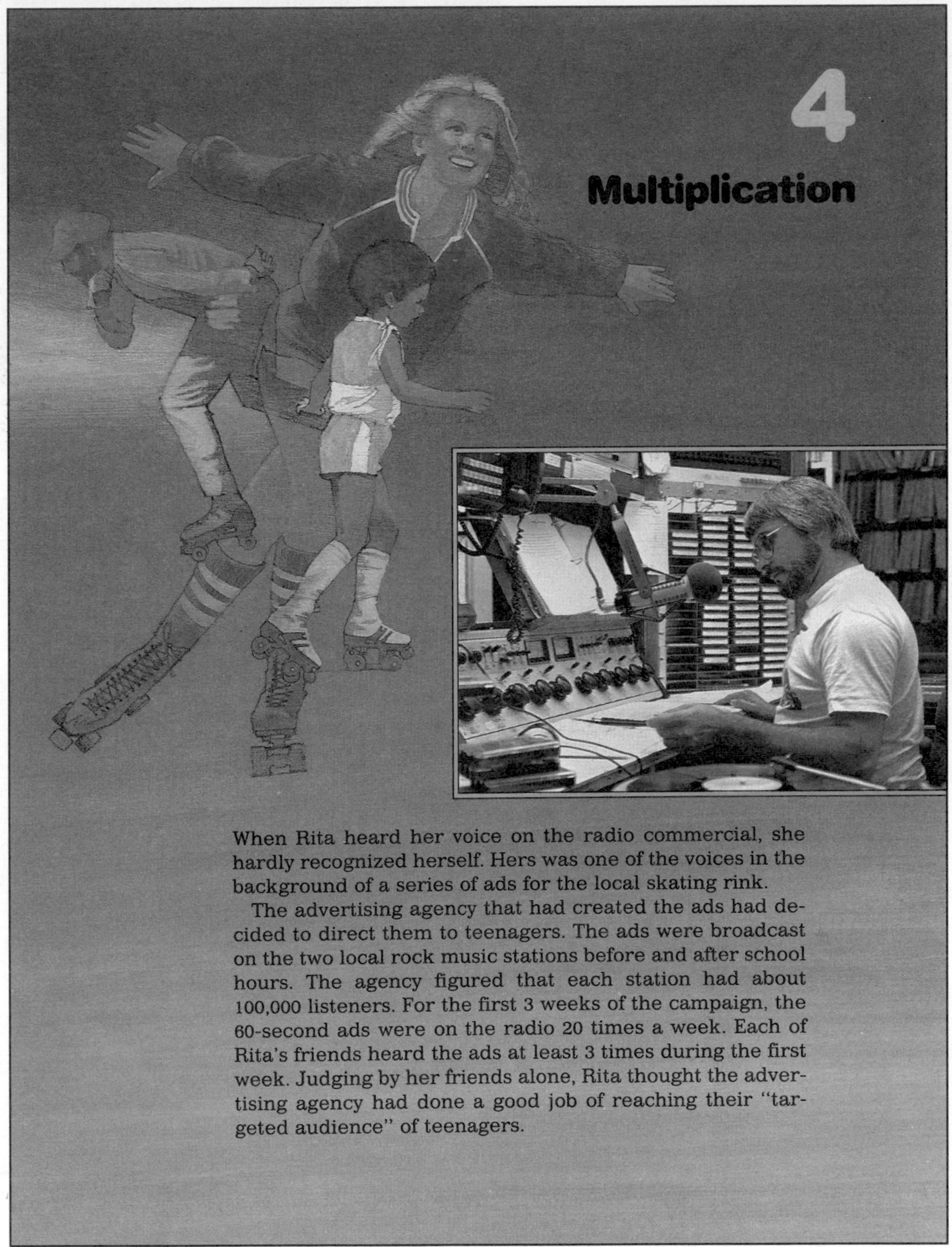


When Rita heard her voice on the radio commercial, she hardly recognized herself. Hers was one of the voices in the background of a series of ads for the local skating rink.

The advertising agency that had created the ads had decided to direct them to teenagers. The ads were broadcast on the two local rock music stations before and after school hours. The agency figured that each station had about 100,000 listeners. For the first 3 weeks of the campaign, the 60-second ads were on the radio 20 times a week. Each of Rita's friends heard the ads at least 3 times during the first week. Judging by her friends alone, Rita thought the advertising agency had done a good job of reaching their "targeted audience" of teenagers.

## Introducing the Chapter

**Discussion** Explain that in this chapter students will review and extend their skills in multiplying whole numbers. Then briefly discuss radio advertising. You might ask students whether commercials have ever influenced their choices of products or services. After students have read the story and examined the art, encourage them to create questions based on the data in the story. As you teach the chapter, you may wish to refer to this page and to pose the questions suggested below.

## Follow-Up Questions

**After Page 81** A radio station broadcast a 30-second ad for a chain of pizza parlors 80 times during one month. How many seconds was the ad broadcast during the month? (2,400 seconds)

**After Page 85** During the 4 weeks of a special advertising campaign, a department store's sales increased an average of $3,750 per week. What was the total sales increase for the 4-week period? ($15,000)

**After Page 87** A radio station broadcasts 90 minutes of commercials during each broadcast day. If the station broadcasts every day of the year (365 days), how many minutes of commercials does it broadcast in a year? (32,850 minutes)

# Multiplication

**Quick Review** As an oral drill, students say the names of these numbers.

116 4,000 982 174 3,122 605 550 489 705
5,640 8,072 633 209 808 9,900 399 226
5,083 1,201 6,009 293 770 4,000 639 818 2,019

**Lesson Focus** To use mental math and multiplication facts to find products that are multiples of 10, 100, or 1,000

**Suggested Materials** Place-value models

## Ideas for Getting Started

Use place-value models for tens, hundreds, and thousands to help students write a list of products such as the following:

| | | |
|---|---|---|
| $2 \times 10 = 20$ | $2 \times 100 = 200$ | $2 \times 1{,}000 = 2{,}000$ |
| $3 \times 10 = 30$ | $3 \times 100 = 300$ | $3 \times 1{,}000 = 3{,}000$ |
| $4 \times 10 = 40$ | $4 \times 100 = 400$ | $4 \times 1{,}000 = 4{,}000$ |
| ⋮ | ⋮ | ⋮ |

Encourage students to focus on the zeros in the factor and then the zeros in the product. Ask students to use these patterns to generalize a rule for multiplying a number by 10 (annex 1 zero), multiplying a number by 100 (annex 2 zeros), and multiplying a number by 1,000 (annex 3 zeros).

## Using Page 80

**Motivational Problem** Have students read the problem at the top of the page. "What do we want to find out about the attendance at the theater?" (the total number of people attending 3 shows) "What data are we given in the problem?" (The theater holds 500 people when full.) "What operation should we use to solve the problem?" (We multiply the number of people who attended each show by the number of shows.)

**Lesson Development** Direct students' attention to the equation which shows how the multiplication fact $3 \times 5$ is used to find a larger product. Point out the use of the grouping property in the think cloud. "How many hundreds in 500?" (5) "How many hundreds in three groups of 500?" (15) Use place-value models to show 3 groups of 500 as 15 hundreds. Use language such as, "Since $3 \times 5$ is 15, $3 \times 500$ is 1,500." Discuss other similar equations in this way and write the corresponding equation on the chalkboard referring back to the example $3 \times 500$. Ask students to check the reasonableness of the answer by rereading the problem at the top of the page.

**Other Examples** As you work through these examples, emphasize the idea that they are to be completed using mental math. Note that in the first example the basic fact ends in zero. In the third example the order of factors has been reversed; the first factor is a multiple of 1,000.

**Exercises 1–20** The first four exercises focus on the pattern of zeros using various multiples of 10. As students do these exercises mentally, be alert for basic fact errors or for students who have not formulated the rules for annexing zeros.

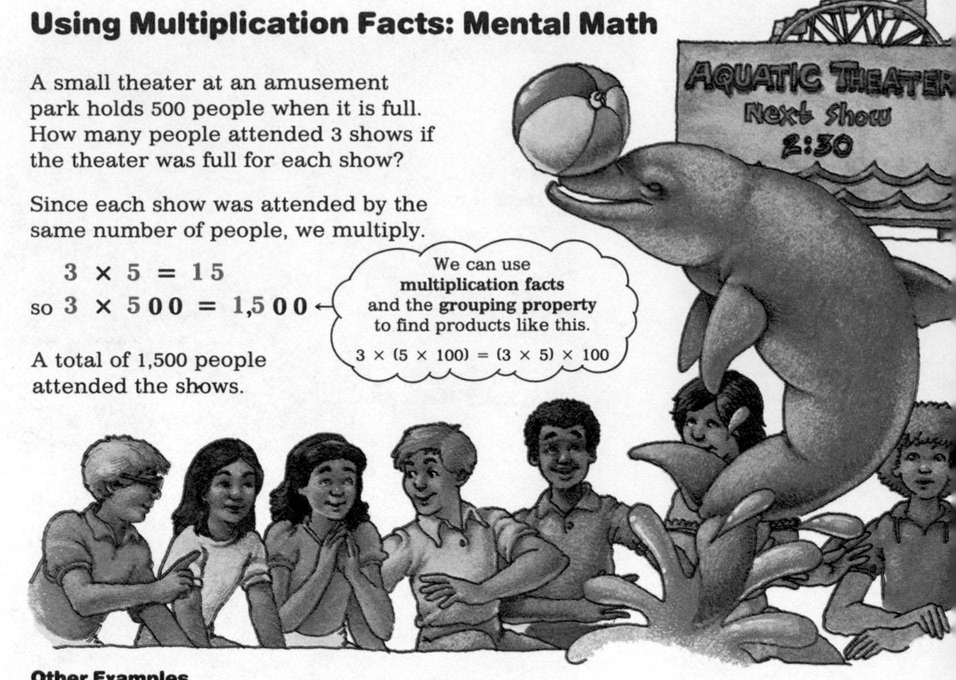


## Using Multiplication Facts: Mental Math

A small theater at an amusement park holds 500 people when it is full. How many people attended 3 shows if the theater was full for each show?

Since each show was attended by the same number of people, we multiply.

$3 \times 5 = 15$

so $3 \times 500 = 1{,}500$

We can use **multiplication facts** and the **grouping property** to find products like this.

$3 \times (5 \times 100) = (3 \times 5) \times 100$

A total of 1,500 people attended the shows.

**Other Examples**

| | | |
|---|---|---|
| $6 \times 5 = 30$ | $8 \times 1 = 8$ | $9 \times 7 = 63$ |
| so $6 \times 50 = 300$ | so $8 \times 100 = 800$ | so $9{,}000 \times 7 = 63{,}000$ |

Find the products using mental math.
Use pencils for answers only.

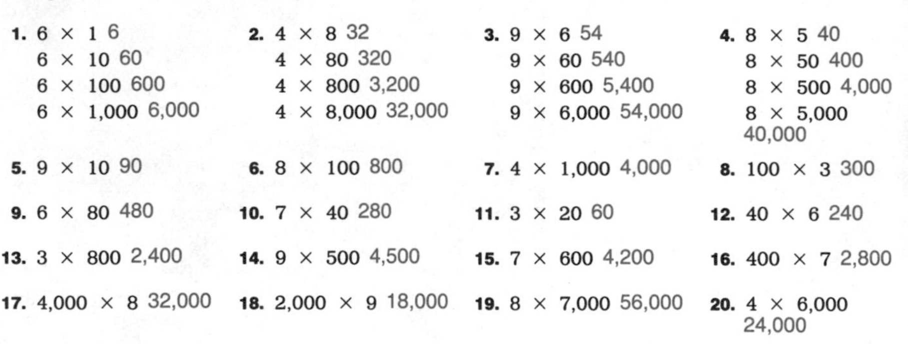

| | | | |
|---|---|---|---|
| **1.** $6 \times 1$ 6 | **2.** $4 \times 8$ 32 | **3.** $9 \times 6$ 54 | **4.** $8 \times 5$ 40 |
| $6 \times 10$ 60 | $4 \times 80$ 320 | $9 \times 60$ 540 | $8 \times 50$ 400 |
| $6 \times 100$ 600 | $4 \times 800$ 3,200 | $9 \times 600$ 5,400 | $8 \times 500$ 4,000 |
| $6 \times 1{,}000$ 6,000 | $4 \times 8{,}000$ 32,000 | $9 \times 6{,}000$ 54,000 | $8 \times 5{,}000$ 40,000 |
| **5.** $9 \times 10$ 90 | **6.** $8 \times 100$ 800 | **7.** $4 \times 1{,}000$ 4,000 | **8.** $100 \times 3$ 300 |
| **9.** $6 \times 80$ 480 | **10.** $7 \times 40$ 280 | **11.** $3 \times 20$ 60 | **12.** $40 \times 6$ 240 |
| **13.** $3 \times 800$ 2,400 | **14.** $9 \times 500$ 4,500 | **15.** $7 \times 600$ 4,200 | **16.** $400 \times 7$ 2,800 |
| **17.** $4{,}000 \times 8$ 32,000 | **18.** $2{,}000 \times 9$ 18,000 | **19.** $8 \times 7{,}000$ 56,000 | **20.** $4 \times 6{,}000$ 24,000 |



## Follow Up

### Reteaching

Have students use the "if-then" strategy to review multiplication. For example: If $5 \times 5 = 25$, then $6 \times 5 = 30$. $(6 \times 5) = (5 \times 5) + (1 \times 5) = 25 + 5 = 30$. Then extend this idea to examples such as "if $3 \times 1 = 3$, then $3 \times 10 = 30$," and "if $3 \times 1 = 3$, then $3 \times 100 = 300$." Or, "if $3 \times 6 = 18$, then $3 \times 60 = 180$," and "if $3 \times 6 = 18$, then $3 \times 600 = 1{,}800$." Emphasize the relationships noted in these statements and have students try to find answers without paper and pencil by applying the relationships.

### Enrichment

Use shadings on graph paper (TRB 271) to present another illustration of the grouping property.

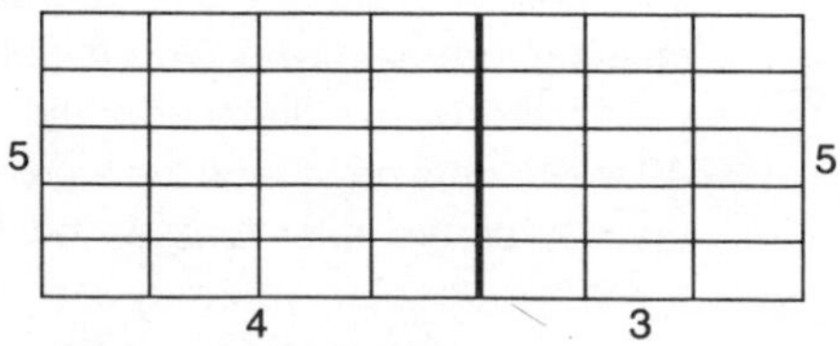


$$5 \times 7 = 5(4 + 3) = (5 \times 4) + (5 \times 3)$$
$$= 20 + 15$$
$$= 35$$

A bulletin board might be made from several of these.

| Assignment Guide | | | |
|---|---|---|---|
| | Minimum | Average | Extended |
| page 80 | 1–20 | 1–20 | 1–20 |
| page 81 | 1–20 | 1–20 | 1–20 |

## Special Products: Mental Math

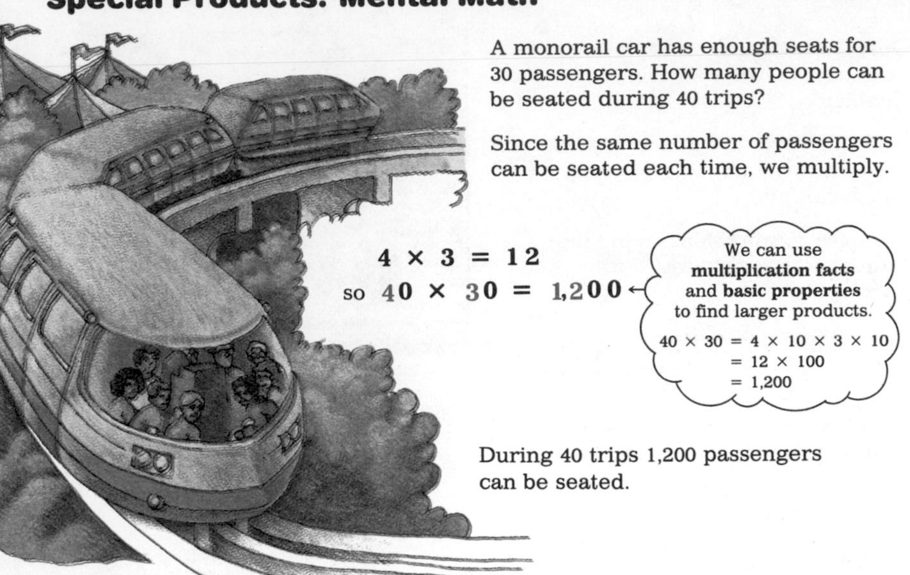

A monorail car has enough seats for 30 passengers. How many people can be seated during 40 trips?

Since the same number of passengers can be seated each time, we multiply.

4 × 3 = 12
so 40 × 30 = 1,200

We can use **multiplication facts** and **basic properties** to find larger products.
40 × 30 = 4 × 10 × 3 × 10
= 12 × 100
= 1,200

During 40 trips 1,200 passengers can be seated.

**Other Examples**

8 × 5 = 40
so 80 × 50 = 4,000

9 × 6 = 54
so 90 × 600 = 54,000
and 90 × 6,000 = 540,000

8 × 3 = 24
so 800 × 300 = 240,000

Find the products using mental math.

1. 7 × 4 28
   70 × 4 280
   70 × 40 2,800
   70 × 400 28,000
   70 × 4,000 280,000
   700 × 400 280,000
2. 6 × 8 48
   6 × 80 480
   60 × 80 4,800
   60 × 800 48,000
   60 × 8,000 480,000
   600 × 800 480,000
3. 9 × 8 72
   90 × 8 720
   90 × 80 7,200
   900 × 80 72,000
   9,000 × 80 720,000
   900 × 800 720,000
4. 5 × 6
   5 × 60
   50 × 60
   50 × 600
   50 × 6,000
   500 × 600
   See teaching notes.
5. 10 × 10 100
6. 100 × 10 1,000
7. 10 × 1,000 10,000
8. 100 × 100 10,000
9. 90 × 40 3,600
10. 30 × 70 2,100
11. 60 × 30 1,800
12. 80 × 60 4,800
13. 40 × 600 24,000
14. 800 × 40 32,000
15. 4,000 × 20 80,000
16. 500 × 200 100,000
17. 600 × 700 420,000
18. 4,000 × 90 360,000
19. 5,000 × 40 200,000
20. 600 × 600 360,000



## Using Page 81

**Motivational Problem** Have students read the problem at the top of the page. "What do we want to find out about the monorail car?" (How many people can be seated on the car during 40 trips?) "What data are we given in the problem?" (One car seats 30 passengers on each trip.) "Could we use multiplication to solve the problem?" Focus on the idea that since we are given the number of passengers on each trip and a certain number of trips, we use multiplication.

**Lesson Development** Call students' attention to the equation that shows how the multiplication fact 4 × 3 = 12 is used to find a larger product. Focus on the think cloud and point out that 40 is 4 tens and 30 is 3 tens. Since we can rearrange factors in any order when we multiply, 4 × 10 × 3 × 10 is 12 × 100, or 1,200. Use this idea to show the products for other similar equations. Then ask students to check the reasonableness of the answer by rereading the problem at the top of the page.

**Other Examples** Note that the first example involves a basic fact that ends in zero. This means there will be 3 zeros in the product rather than 2.

**Exercises 1–20** As students complete these exercises, emphasize how the products relate to the basic facts. Give special attention to exercise 4 in which the basic fact ends in a zero. Be alert for multiplication fact errors and continue to help students understand that the total number of zeros to be annexed in the product is the number of zeros in the factors.

**Answers to exercise 4**
30; 300; 3,000; 30,000; 300,000; 300,000

### Reteaching Supplement, page 20

Name ______ To follow text page 80

**Using Multiplication Facts: Mental Math**

Study the examples.

Count the number of zeros in the factors and the number of zeros in the product.

| | | |
|---|---|---|
| 8 × 1 = 8 | 6 × 7 = 42 | 3 × 5 = 15 |
| 8 × 10 = 80 | 6 × 70 = 420 | 3 × 50 = 150 |
| 8 × 100 = 800 | 6 × 700 = 4,200 | 30 × 50 = 1,500 |
| 8 × 1,000 = 8,000 | 6 × 7,000 = 42,000 | 30 × 500 = 15,000 |

Write the products.

1. 5 × 5 = 25 so 5 × 50 = 250 (1 zero, so →1 zero)
2. 7 × 8 = 56 so 70 × 80 = 5,600 (2 zeros) (Finish.)
3. 5 × 8 = 40 so 5 × 8,000 = 40,000 (3 zeros) (An extra zero!) (Finish.)
4. 12 × 10 = 120
5. 23 × 100 = 2,300
6. 7 × 1,000 = 7,000
7. 10 × 10 = 100
8. 50 × 500 = 25,000
9. 7 × 10 = 70
10. 40 × 100 = 4,000
11. 10 × 1,000 = 10,000
12. 50 × 20 = 1,000
13. 20 × 30 = 600
14. 7 × 20 = 140
15. 9 × 40 = 360
16. 30 × 60 = 1,800
17. 800 × 70 = 56,000
18. 5 × 50 = 250
19. 90 × 600 = 54,000
20. 60 × 500 = 30,000
21. 40 × 2,000 = 80,000
22. 40 × 400 = 16,000
23. 9 × 500 = 4,500
24. 80 × 4,000 = 320,000
25. 7,000 × 300 = 2,100,000
26. 800 × 500 = 400,000
27. 60 × 6,000 = 360,000
28. 400 × 300 = 120,000
29. 500 × 7,000 = 3,500,000
30. 600 × 20 = 12,000
31. 3,000 × 3,000 = 9,000,000
32. 700 × 7,000 = 4,900,000

### Enrichment Supplement, page 20

Name ______ To follow text page 80

**Flow Chart Operations**

Write +, −, ×, or ÷ in the boxes to make the given output number true. Study the example.

**Example**

(16 ÷ 4 = 4) (4 + 3 = 7)

| | Input | Step 1 | Step 2 | Step 3 | Output |
|---|---|---|---|---|---|
| Example | 16 | ÷ 4 | + 3 | | 7 |
| 1. | 16 | − 4 | ÷ 3 | | 4 |
| 2. | 9 | × 2 | ÷ 6 | | 3 |
| 3. | 4 | ÷ 4 | + 1 | | 2 |
| 4. | 4 | + 4 | − 1 | | 7 |
| 5. | 4 | × 40 | − 10 | × 20 | 3,000 |
| 6. | 10 | × 10 | × 10 | × 10 | 10,000 |
| 7. | 10 | + 10 | + 10 | × 20 | 600 |
| 8. | 8 | × 30 | − 40 | × 90 | 18,000 |
| 9. | 7 | + 3 | × 40 | × 80 | 32,000 |
| 10. | 60 | − 20 | × 40 | − 600 | 1,000 |

### Practice Supplement, page 30

Name ______ To follow text page 81

**Using Multiplication Facts: Mental Math**

Find the products using mental math.

1. 3 × 2 = 6
   3 × 20 = 60
   3 × 200 = 600
   3 × 2,000 = 6,000
2. 8 × 7 = 56
   8 × 70 = 560
   8 × 700 = 5,600
   8 × 7,000 = 56,000
3. 5 × 10 = 50
4. 9 × 100 = 900
5. 6 × 1,000 = 6,000
6. 100 × 4 = 400
7. 9 × 90 = 810
8. 3 × 500 = 1,500
9. 50 × 5 = 250
10. 8 × 4,000 = 32,000
11. 7 × 600 = 4,200
12. 6 × 400 = 2,400
13. 3,000 × 4 = 12,000
14. 4 × 40 = 160
15. 700 × 3 = 2,100
16. 6,000 × 6 = 36,000
17. 4 × 4 = 16
    40 × 4 = 160
    40 × 40 = 1,600
    40 × 400 = 16,000
    40 × 4,000 = 160,000
    400 × 400 = 160,000
18. 9 × 7 = 63
    9 × 70 = 630
    90 × 70 = 6,300
    90 × 700 = 63,000
    90 × 7,000 = 630,000
    900 × 700 = 630,000
19. 10 × 80 = 800
20. 100 × 80 = 8,000
21. 10 × 8,000 = 80,000
22. 100 × 800 = 80,000
23. 70 × 70 = 4,900
24. 20 × 50 = 1,000
25. 30 × 400 = 12,000
26. 600 × 90 = 54,000
27. 4,000 × 60 = 240,000
28. 600 × 900 = 540,000
29. 2,000 × 80 = 160,000
30. 500 × 900 = 450,000

# Estimation

**Quick Review** As an oral drill, students skip count by twos to 24, by fives to 60, and by tens to 120. Then students skip count backward by twos, fives, and tens. Have one student begin, and as you point to another student, he or she should continue the count.

**Lesson Focus** To estimate whole number products by rounding to the nearest ten and to the nearest hundred

## Ideas for Getting Started

Give numbers, such as 52, 78, 45, 64, and have students repeat each number rounded to the nearest ten. Then give numbers such as 653, 497, 236, 350, and so on, and have students round to the nearest hundred. Then conduct a brief oral review of special products such as 30 × 70, 40 × 600, 9 × 80, and so on.

## Using Page 82

**Motivational Problem** Have students read the problem at the top of the page. "What do we want to find out about the small car?" (Will $20 be enough to fill the gas tank?) "What data are we given in the problem?" (cost of gasoline, the number of liters the gas tank contains) "Does the problem ask for an exact answer or an estimate?" (Only an estimate is required.) "Why should we use multiplication to solve the problem?" (To find the total cost for a number of liters at a given cost for each liter, we can multiply.)

**Lesson Development** Call students' attention to the solution to the problem shown on the page. Point out that to estimate a product we first round the number to the nearest ten, hundred, and so on, and then find a special product. Have students read the complete sentence that gives the answer to the question.

**Exercises 1–15** Be sure students understand that 2-digit numbers should be rounded to the nearest ten, and 3-digit numbers rounded to the nearest hundred. Pay particular attention to exercises 1, 4, and 9 as examples of the different types of estimation involved. If you wish, have students use a calculator to find the answers for these problems and compare them with the estimates.

**Exercises 16–25** These exercises require the same kinds of estimation skills but are presented in algorithm format rather than in the horizontal format used in earlier exercises.

## Estimating Products

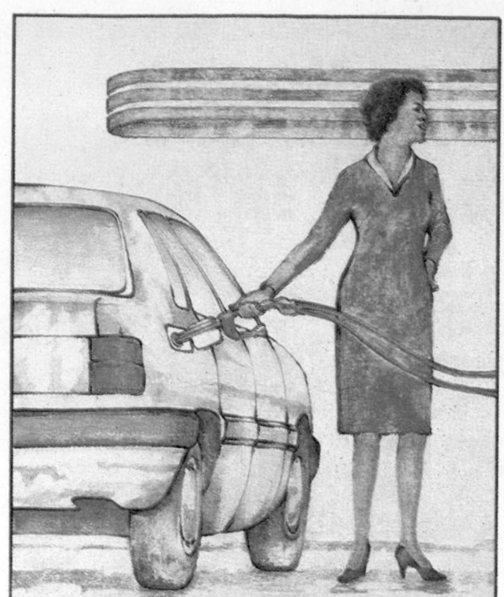

An estimated answer is often all that is needed to solve an everyday problem.

Gasoline costs 39¢ a liter. Will $20 be enough to fill a 49-liter gas tank on a small car?

To solve this problem, round the numbers to the nearest ten.

```
  49   →    50
× 39¢  →  × 40¢
          2,000¢, or $20.00
```

Since each number was rounded up, $20 is enough to fill the tank.

**Other Examples**

7 × 814 ↓ 7 × 800 = 5,600

25 × 319 ↓ ↓ 30 × 300 = 9,000

462 × 536 ↓ ↓ 500 × 500 = 250,000

Estimate these products by rounding 2-digit numbers to the nearest ten and 3-digit numbers to the nearest hundred.

**1.** 6 × 72 (6 × 70) 420
**2.** 4 × 98 400
**3.** 8 × 53 400
**4.** 5 × 894 (5 × 900) 4,500
**5.** 3 × 456 1,500

**6.** 7 × 634 4,200
**7.** 2 × 279 600
**8.** 9 × 852 8,100
**9.** 29 × 74 2,100
**10.** 38 × 43 1,600

**11.** 39 × 71 2,800
**12.** 19 × 389 8,000
**13.** 82 × 415 32,000
**14.** 68 × 720 49,000
**15.** 316 × 493 150,000

**16.** 75 × 46 = 4,000
**17.** 92 × 78 = 7,200
**18.** 47 × 23 = 1,000
**19.** 76 × 37 = 3,200
**20.** 97 × 64 = 6,000

**21.** 783 × 45 = 40,000
**22.** 507 × 49 = 25,000
**23.** 378 × 57 = 24,000
**24.** 741 × 986 = 700,000
**25.** 823 × 456 = 400,000

82

## Follow Up

### Reteaching

Discuss briefly the usefulness of estimating an answer. Then show the following word problem and solution as a review of the ideas of rounding and estimation: Joan has 76 cases of books, each weighing 18 kilograms. About how many kilograms of books does she have?

- Round each number to the nearest ten and multiply to find an estimate. (80 × 20 = 1,600)
- Determine the actual weight and compare with the estimate. 76 × 18 = 1,368.

### Enrichment

Have students estimate the products by rounding to the nearest ten to complete the multiplication wheel.

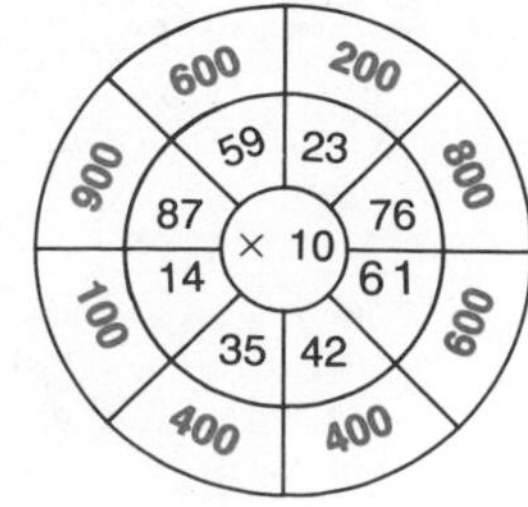

| Assignment Guide | | | |
|---|---|---|---|
| | Minimum | Average | Extended |
| page 82 | 1–22 | 1–25 | 1–25 |
| page 83 | 1–6 | 1–7 | 1–8 |

## Problem Solving: Using Estimation

Estimate the answers to these problems.

1. A family bought a new television set by paying $24 a month for 36 months. About what was the total amount paid? about $800

2. A service club wants to raise $150,000 to give to local charities. Has the goal been reached when 519 people have given an average of $305 each?
yes (500 × 300 = 150,000)

3. A bag of grass seed will cover an area of 425 $m^2$ (square meters). A yard has an area of 1,568 $m^2$. Will 4 bags of seed be enough to cover it?
yes (4 × 400 = 1,600)

4. A savings account pays interest daily. About how many days of interest will be paid on money left in the account for 5 years?
about 2,000 days

5. You can buy 3 records for $5.98. Is this a better price than $2.45 for one record? yes

6. The highway distance from Chicago to St. Louis is 465 km. If you leave Chicago at 8 a.m. and drive at an average speed of 78 km/h, can you reach St. Louis by 1:00 p.m.?
no (5 × 80 = 400)

7. **DATA HUNT** About how many breaths do you take in an hour? Count the number you take in a minute. Then estimate the number for an hour. Answers will vary.

8. **Try This** In an auto race, Auto number 67 finished 1 second ahead of Auto 34. Auto 34 was not the last place auto. Auto 25 finished 7 seconds ahead of Auto 46, which finished 3 seconds behind Auto 67. Auto 67 finished 7 seconds behind Auto 50. What was the finishing order of the autos? Hint: Draw a picture.
1st, 50; 2nd, 25; 3rd, 67; 4th, 34; 5th, 46

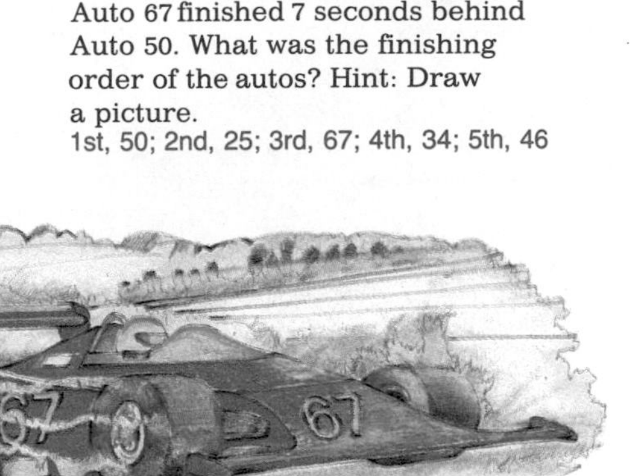


83

## Using Page 83

**Lesson Development** Have students estimate the answers to these problems. Review with them the rules for rounding 2- and 3-digit numbers.

**Exercises 1–6** Note that exercises 1–4 and 6 involve estimating products of whole numbers. In exercise 5 students round to the nearest dollar and then divide.

**Data Hunt** This exercise provides an opportunity for students to collect the data needed. If possible, have a watch or clock with a second hand available for timing one minute.

**Try This** A possible strategy, Draw a Picture, was taught on page 74.

**Discussion** "What are you asked to find in the problem?" (In what order did the autos finish the race?) "Which autos finished behind Auto 67?" (Autos 34 and 46) "Which auto finished ahead of Auto 67?" (Auto 50 and Auto 25) "Is there an operation you could use to solve this problem?" (no) Could you draw a picture to show the order in which the autos finished?"

**Solution** Auto 50 was first, followed by Autos 25, 67, 34, and 46. The order of the autos is shown in the picture below.

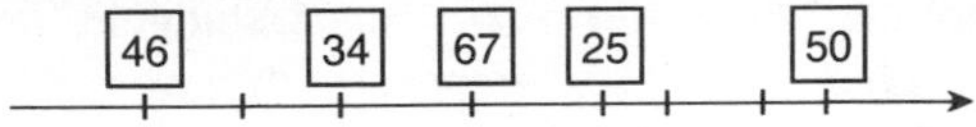


### Reteaching Supplement, page 21

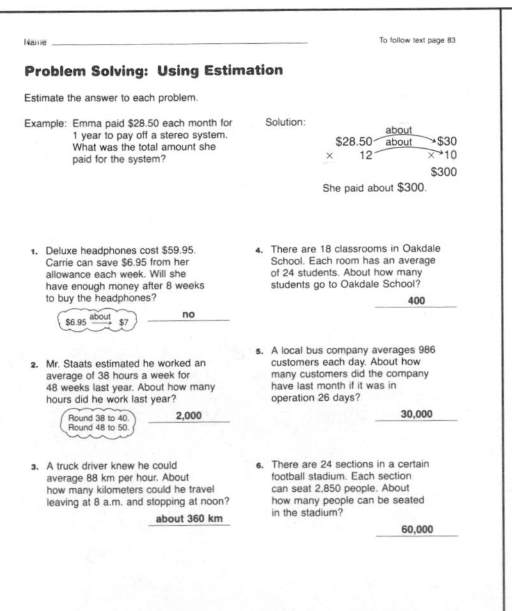

Name ______ To follow text page 83

**Problem Solving: Using Estimation**

Estimate the answer to each problem.

Example: Emma paid $28.50 each month for 1 year to pay off a stereo system. What was the total amount she paid for the system?

Solution: $28.50 about → $30; × 12 about → × 10; $300
She paid about $300.

1. Deluxe headphones cost $59.95. Carrie can save $6.95 from her allowance each week. Will she have enough money after 8 weeks to buy the headphones? ($6.95 about → $7) **no**

2. Mr. Staats estimated he worked an average of 38 hours a week for 48 weeks last year. About how many hours did he work last year? (Round 38 to 40. Round 48 to 50.) **2,000**

3. A truck driver knew he could average 88 km per hour. About how many kilometers could he travel leaving at 8 a.m. and stopping at noon? **about 360 km**

4. There are 18 classrooms in Oakdale School. Each room has an average of 24 students. About how many students go to Oakdale School? **400**

5. A local bus company averages 986 customers each day. About how many customers did the company have last month if it was in operation 26 days? **30,000**

6. There are 24 sections in a certain football stadium. Each section can seat 2,850 people. About how many people can be seated in the stadium? **60,000**

### Enrichment Supplement, page 21

Name ______ To follow text page 83

**Wrap It Up**

Luisa wanted to cover the school suggestion box with some colored paper. She had a roll of paper 200 cm long and 60 cm wide.

Luisa made a drawing of the box flattened out to help her decide how to cut the paper.

Top; Suggestion Box; End; Front; 45 cm; 30 cm; 54 cm

Give the measurement for each letter on the drawing.

1. A **30 cm**
2. B **45 cm**
3. C **30 cm**
4. D **45 cm**
5. E **45 cm**
6. X **150 cm**
7. Y **54 cm**
8. Z **144 cm**

Back; End; Top; End; Front; Bottom; A; B; C; D; E; X; Y; Z

Solve each of the problems below.

9. Luisa wanted to cut one piece of paper to cover all of the box except the two ends. How long and wide should this piece be? **150 cm × 54 cm**

10. After the piece in problem 9 is cut off the roll of paper, how long is the piece remaining on the roll? **50 cm**

11. Is there enough paper remaining on the roll to cover the two ends of the box? **yes**

12. Make a drawing to show how the remaining piece could be used to cover both ends. Put all measurements on the drawing.

60 cm; 30 cm; 50 cm; 45 cm; Each end is 30 cm × 45 cm.; Cut here.; Cut here.

### Practice Supplement, page 31

Name ______ To follow text page 82

**Estimating Products**

Estimate these products by rounding 2-digit numbers to the nearest ten and 3-digit numbers to the nearest hundred.

1. 8 × 93 **720**
2. 4 × 78 **320**
3. 5 × 31 **150**
4. 7 × 07 **490**
5. 27 × 3 **90**
6. 6 × 88 **540**
7. 2 × 481 **1,000**
8. 3 × 922 **2,700**
9. 4 × 428 **1,600**
10. 865 × 4 **3,600**
11. 790 × 6 **4,800**
12. 258 × 3 **900**
13. 583 × 5 **3,000**
14. 658 × 6 **4,200**
15. 842 × 3 **2,400**
16. 82 × 47 **4,000**
17. 68 × 58 **4,200**
18. 91 × 89 **8,100**
19. 56 × 42 **2,400**
20. 63 × 32 **1,800**
21. 52 × 87 **4,500**
22. 63 × 48 **3,000**
23. 21 × 85 **1,800**
24. 48 × 51 **2,500**
25. 81 × 68 **5,600**
26. 795 × 81 **64,000**
27. 666 × 38 **28,000**
28. 532 × 41 **20,000**
29. 75 × 25 **2,400**
30. 37 × 27 **1,200**
31. 562 × 562 **360,000**
32. 444 × 185 **80,000**
33. 667 × 815 **560,000**
34. 712 × 474 **350,000**
35. 818 × 376 **320,000**
36. 846 × 48 **40,000**
37. 369 × 118 **40,000**
38. 942 × 28 **27,000**
39. 284 × 284 **90,000**
40. 448 × 44 **16,000**
41. 488 × 23 **10,000**
42. 267 × 426 **120,000**
43. 694 × 65 **49,000**
44. 382 × 468 **200,000**
45. 814 × 628 **480,000**

# Multiplication

**Quick Review** As an oral activity, students give the meaning of the underlined digit in each number below.

1,390 9 tens | 23 3 ones | 2,106 1 hundred | 478 4 hundreds
12,233 1 ten thousand | 3,004 3 thousands | 2,349 9 ones

**Lesson Focus** To find products of 1-digit factors times 2-, 3-, 4- and 5-digit factors

## Ideas for Getting Started

Write a 4-digit number such as 5,723 on the chalkboard. Ask students to express this number using expanded notation. Then have students multiply each of the parts of the number by 4. (4 × 3, 4 × 70, 4 × 200, 4 × 5,000) Emphasize the role of the distributive principle in finding and adding the partial products.

## Using Page 84

**Motivational Problem** Ask students to read the problem at the top of the page. "What do we want to find out about the number of people camping in Yellowstone?" (How many people were in the park during an average July week?) "What data do we need to solve the problem?" (number of people in each group, number of groups) "Why should we plan to use multiplication to solve the problem?" Elicit from students that since there are 4 groups with the same number in each group, we can use multiplication to find a given number of same-size groups.

**Lesson Development** Help students work through each step and emphasize that we first multiply ones, then tens, then hundreds, then thousands, and so on. Tell students that this process is continued as long as necessary, depending upon the number of places in the largest factor. Put the following chart on the chalkboard and review the procedure.

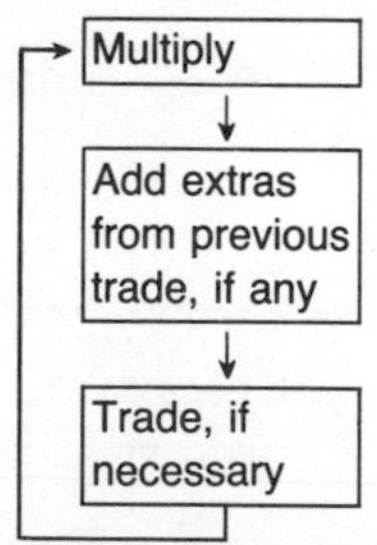


Have students read the sentence that gives the answer to the problem. Suggest that students round to the nearest thousand, estimate the product, and then reread the original problem to check if the answer seems reasonable.

**Other Examples** Note that in example 3 several trades must be made; be sure to emphasize the procedure discussed in the display box. In the last example remind students about the technique for multiplying using money notation: Multiply as with whole numbers, then use estimation to decide where to place the decimal point.

**Warm Up** Be alert for students who add the extras from a previous trade before multiplying.

## Multiplying by a 1-Digit Factor

On an average July day at Yellowstone National Park there might be 7,693 people camping. If 4 different groups this size were in the park during a week, how many people were there that week?

Since we want to find the total for several equal amounts, we multiply.

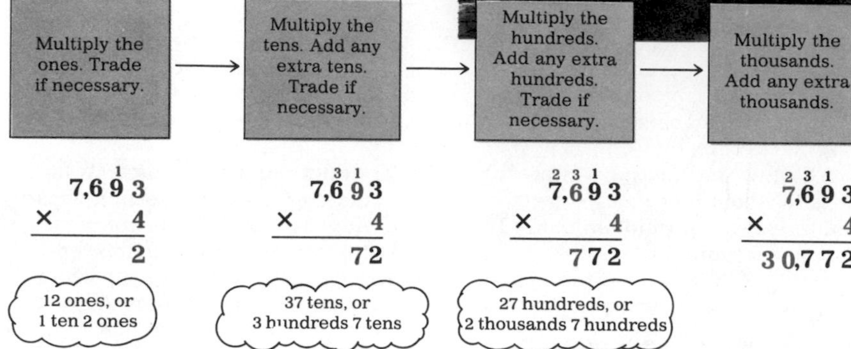

Multiply the ones. Trade if necessary.
Multiply the tens. Add any extra tens. Trade if necessary.
Multiply the hundreds. Add any extra hundreds. Trade if necessary.
Multiply the thousands. Add any extra thousands.
7,693 × 4 = 2
7,693 × 4 = 72
7,693 × 4 = 772
7,693 × 4 = 30,772
12 ones, or 1 ten 2 ones
37 tens, or 3 hundreds 7 tens
27 hundreds, or 2 thousands 7 hundreds

There were 30,772 campers.

**Other Examples**

| 890 × 7 | 9,076 × 5 | 38,974 × 6 | $58.76 × 4 |
|---|---|---|---|
| 6,230 | 45,380 | 233,844 | $235.04 |

Multiply as with whole numbers. Estimate to help you write the answer in dollars and cents.

About 4 × $60, or $240

**Warm Up** Multiply.

1. 787 × 9 = 7,083
2. 3,498 × 7 = 24,486
3. 5,036 × 8 = 40,288
4. 49,658 × 4 = 198,632
5. $61.79 × 6 = $370.74

84

## Follow Up

### Reteaching

Work through each algorithm below. Then show the shortened form, making sure students understand the related steps.

1) 36 × 3
18 (3 × 6)
90 (3 × 30)
108

Shortened form: 36 × 3 = 108

2) 865 × 4
20 (4 × 5)
240 (4 × 60)
3200 (4 × 800)
3,460

Shortened form: 865 × 4 = 3,460

### Enrichment

Write the following problems on the chalkboard. Have students estimate the products and then find the exact product using a calculator. Students then determine if their estimates were reasonable.

| 213 × 4 | 467 × 8 | 3,276 × 6 | 7,225 × 5 |
|---|---|---|---|
| 852 | 3,736 | 19,656 | 36,125 |
| 14,835 × 6 | 78,265 × 9 | 95,362 × 3 | 3,555 × 9 |
| 89,010 | 704,385 | 286,086 | 31,995 |

| Assignment Guide | Minimum | Average | Extended |
|---|---|---|---|
| page 85 | 1-27, 30 | 1-31 | 11-32, TM |

Multiply.

| | | | | |
|---|---|---|---|---|
| 1. 87<br>× 3<br>261 | 2. 62<br>× 5<br>310 | 3. 86<br>× 8<br>688 | 4. 75<br>× 7<br>525 | 5. 86<br>× 4<br>344 |
| 6. 678<br>× 7<br>4,746 | 7. 394<br>× 5<br>1,970 | 8. 275<br>× 6<br>1,650 | 9. 607<br>× 8<br>4,856 | 10. 1,980<br>× 2<br>3,960 |
| 11. 6,038<br>× 9<br>54,342 | 12. 7,954<br>× 3<br>23,862 | 13. 5,009<br>× 4<br>20,036 | 14. 32,947<br>× 8<br>263,576 | 15. 27,306<br>× 7<br>191,142 |
| 16. 19,417<br>× 5<br>97,085 | 17. 68,506<br>× 2<br>137,012 | 18. $9.65<br>× 6<br>$57.90 | 19. $31.98<br>× 3<br>$95.94 | 20. $49.23<br>× 4<br>$196.92 |

21. 6 × 417 2,502

22. 5 × 947 4,735

23. 9 × 3,208 28,872

24. 8,628 × 4 34,512

25. 6,305 × 7 44,135

26. 8 × 37,946 303,568

27. What is the product when the factors are 7 and 364? 2,548

28. Estimate, then calculate the product: 6 × 792. 4,800; 4,752

29. Estimate, then calculate the product: 3,975 times 8. 32,000; 31,800

30. Each of the 7,693 campers at Yellowstone on an average day creates about 3 kg of trash. About how many kilograms of trash is this in all? 23,079

31. Make up a story problem about Yellowstone National Park that can be solved with this number sentence:
875 × 5 = 2,375
Answers will vary.

32. Each visitor to Yellowstone costs the National Park Service an average of $2.74. In a recent year 2,487,084 people visited the park. What was the cost to the Park Service that year? $6,814,610.16

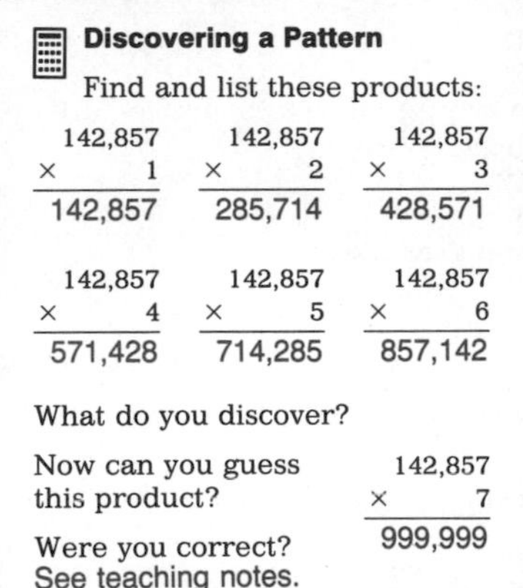

**Think Math**

**Discovering a Pattern**

Find and list these products:

| | | |
|---|---|---|
| 142,857<br>× 1<br>142,857 | 142,857<br>× 2<br>285,714 | 142,857<br>× 3<br>428,571 |
| 142,857<br>× 4<br>571,428 | 142,857<br>× 5<br>714,285 | 142,857<br>× 6<br>857,142 |

What do you discover?

Now can you guess this product? 142,857 × 7 999,999

Were you correct? See teaching notes.

More Practice, page 415, Set C



## Using Page 85

**Exercises 1–27** Check students' work carefully to be sure they understand the multiplying procedure. Pay particular attention to exercises 9, 10, 11, 13, 15, 17, 23, and 25 to see if students understand how to deal with zeros in one of the factors.

**Exercises 28–29** Encourage students to make a decision regarding the appropriate place to which each number is rounded (in exercise 28, to the hundred; in exercise 29, to the nearest thousand).

**Exercises 30–32** Have students read exercise 30 carefully and estimate to see if their answer makes sense. In exercise 31 students may need to invent hypothetical data. A possible problem might be, "If an average of 875 people watched Old Faithful during a one-hour period, how many people would watch Old Faithful during a five-hour period?" or "If a bear ate 875 kilograms of feed in a week, how many kilograms of feed would 5 bears eat in a week?"

**Think Math** In this activity students look for numerical patterns. In this case, the pattern might be visualized by a circular array of the digits in the number. Any of the 6 products given can be read by starting with the first digit of the product and reading around the circle. For example, the product for 142,857 × 4 can be read by starting at 5 and reading clockwise around the circular array of numbers.

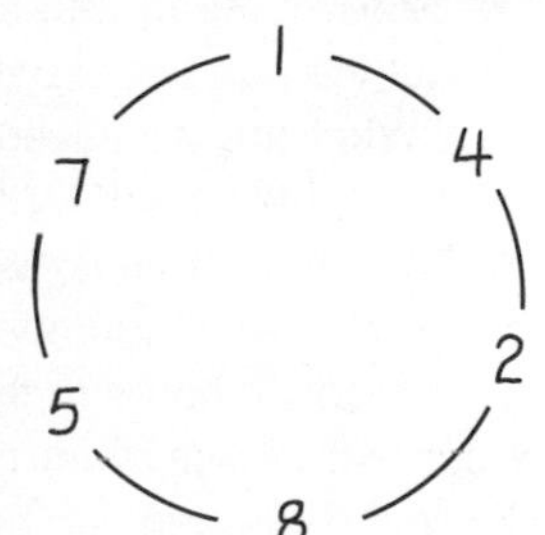


**More Practice,** page 415, Set C

**Reteaching Supplement,** page 22

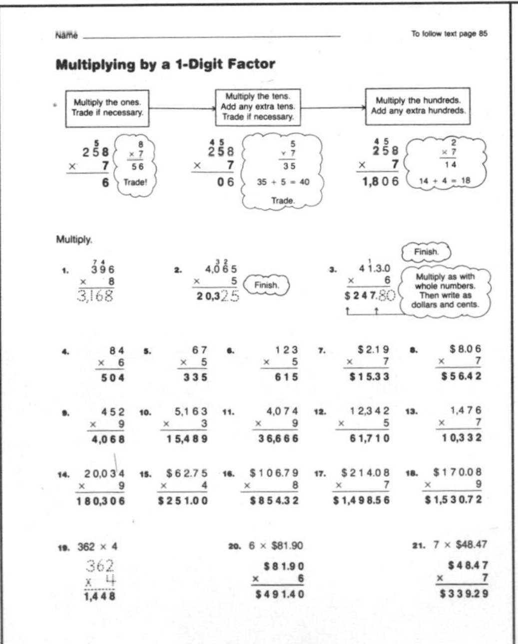

Name ______ To follow text page 85

**Multiplying by a 1-Digit Factor**

Multiply the ones. Trade if necessary. → Multiply the tens. Add any extra tens. Trade if necessary. → Multiply the hundreds. Add any extra hundreds.

258 × 7 = 6 (8 × 7 = 56 Trade!) → 258 × 7 = 06 (5 × 7 = 35; 35 + 5 = 40 Trade.) → 258 × 7 = 1,806 (2 × 7 = 14; 14 + 4 = 18)

Multiply.

1. 396 × 8 = 3,168
2. 4,065 × 5 = 20,325 (Finish.)
3. $41.30 × 6 = $247.80 (Finish. Multiply as with whole numbers. Then write as dollars and cents.)
4. 84 × 6 = 504
5. 67 × 5 = 335
6. 123 × 5 = 615
7. $2.19 × 7 = $15.33
8. $8.06 × 7 = $56.42
9. 452 × 9 = 4,068
10. 5,163 × 3 = 15,489
11. 4,074 × 9 = 36,666
12. 12,342 × 5 = 61,710
13. 1,476 × 7 = 10,332
14. 20,034 × 9 = 180,306
15. $62.75 × 4 = $251.00
16. $106.79 × 8 = $854.32
17. $214.08 × 7 = $1,498.56
18. $170.08 × 9 = $1,530.72
19. 362 × 4 — 362 × 4 = 1,448
20. 6 × $81.90 — $81.90 × 6 = $491.40
21. 7 × $48.47 — $48.47 × 7 = $339.29

**Enrichment Supplement,** page 22

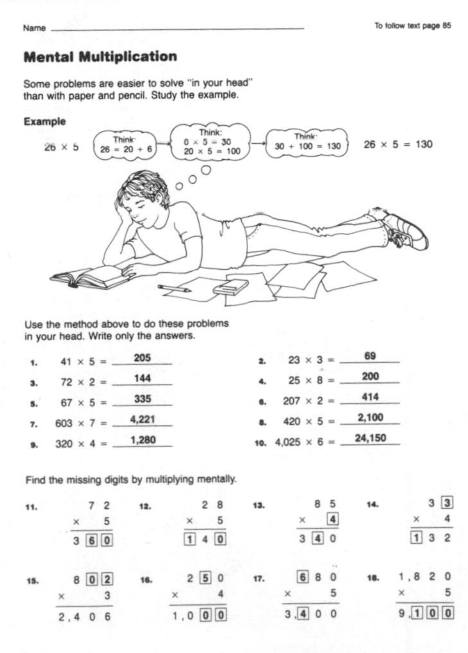

Name ______ To follow text page 85

**Mental Multiplication**

Some problems are easier to solve "in your head" than with paper and pencil. Study the example.

**Example**

26 × 5 → Think: 26 = 20 + 6 → Think: 6 × 5 = 30, 20 × 5 = 100 → Think: 30 + 100 = 130 → 26 × 5 = 130

Use the method above to do these problems in your head. Write only the answers.

1. 41 × 5 = 205
2. 23 × 3 = 69
3. 72 × 2 = 144
4. 25 × 8 = 200
5. 67 × 5 = 335
6. 207 × 2 = 414
7. 603 × 7 = 4,221
8. 420 × 5 = 2,100
9. 320 × 4 = 1,280
10. 4,025 × 6 = 24,150

Find the missing digits by multiplying mentally.

11. 72 × 5 = 3[6][0]
12. 28 × 5 = [1]4[0]
13. 85 × [4] = 3[4]0
14. 3[3] × 4 = [1]32
15. 8[0][2] × 3 = 2,406
16. 2[5]0 × 4 = 1,0[0][0]
17. [6]80 × 5 = 3,[4]00
18. 1,820 × 5 = 9,[1][0][0]

**Practice Supplement,** page 32

Name ______ To follow text page 85

**Multiplying by a 1-Digit Factor**

Multiply.

| | | | | |
|---|---|---|---|---|
| 1. 23<br>× 3<br>69 | 2. 34<br>× 4<br>136 | 3. 72<br>× 5<br>360 | 4. 45<br>× 6<br>270 | 5. 66<br>× 7<br>462 |
| 6. 155<br>× 7<br>1,085 | 7. 348<br>× 6<br>2,088 | 8. 283<br>× 9<br>2,547 | 9. 862<br>× 5<br>4,310 | 10. 407<br>× 7<br>2,849 |
| 11. 138<br>× 4<br>552 | 12. 482<br>× 6<br>2,892 | 13. 507<br>× 6<br>3,042 | 14. 961<br>× 8<br>7,688 | 15. 384<br>× 9<br>3,456 |

| | | | |
|---|---|---|---|
| 16. 3,350<br>× 3<br>10,050 | 17. 6,340<br>× 4<br>25,360 | 18. 5,907<br>× 9<br>53,163 | 19. 9,025<br>× 8<br>72,200 |
| 20. 2,040<br>× 6<br>12,240 | 21. 8,076<br>× 2<br>16,152 | 22. 5,006<br>× 7<br>35,042 | 23. 6,090<br>× 8<br>48,720 |
| 24. 63,204<br>× 2<br>126,408 | 25. 40,026<br>× 4<br>160,104 | 26. 19,008<br>× 3<br>57,024 | 27. 42,116<br>× 5<br>210,580 |
| 28. $24.61<br>× 3<br>$73.83 | 29. $31.50<br>× 5<br>$157.50 | 30. $40.75<br>× 4<br>$163.00 | 31. $89.72<br>× 4<br>$358.88 |

# Multiplication

**Quick Review** Students write each of these standard numbers in expanded form.

| 218 | 40 | 39 | 500 | 90 | 43 | 68 | 290 | 66 | 289 |
|---|---|---|---|---|---|---|---|---|---|
| 134 | 55 | 17 | 70 | 2,000 | 4,508 | 397 | 520 | 1,677 | |

**Lesson Focus** To find a product of a multiple of 10, 100, or 1,000 times a 2-, 3-, or 4-digit number

**Suggested Materials** Calculators

## Ideas for Getting Started

Write pairs of problems like the following on the chalkboard.

| 367 × 4 | 367 × 40 | 429 × 3 | 429 × 300 |
|---|---|---|---|
| 6,734 × 6 | 6,734 × 6,000 | | |

Have students use calculators to find the answers to the problems. Ask for volunteers to write the answers on the chalkboard. Ask questions like the following for the first pair of problems. "40 is how many times 4?" (10) "The answer to the second problem is how many times the first answer?" (10) For the second pair of problems ask: "300 is how many times 3?" (100) "The answer to the second problem is how many times the first answer?" (100) Ask these questions for other similar examples. Then, as you give students the answer to the first problem, see if they can mentally find the second answer in the pair of problems.

## Using Page 86

**Motivational Problem** Read with students the two paragraphs about the number of babies born in the United States. "What are we asked to find out about the number of babies born?" (the average number of babies born in February) "What data is needed to solve the problem?" (number of babies born in February; number of hours in the month of February) "How can we decide what operation to use? (Since we know the average number of babies born every hour and we know the number of hours in the month, we multiply.)

**Lesson Development** Direct students' attention to the instruction boxes. Ask for a volunteer to review the zero property. (Any number times zero is zero.) Point out that in the ones place, 0 × 672 is 0 and in the tens place 0 tens × 672 is 0. Finally, move to the third instruction box and point out that 4 × 672 is 2,688. Have students read the sentence that states the answer to the problem. Have students check the answer by rounding and estimating the product to see if the answer seems reasonable.

**Other Examples** Note that in the third example there is a zero in the basic fact which means that there will be three zeros in the product.

**Warm Up** As students complete these exercises, encourage them to use the shortcut for determining the number of zeros in the product.

## Multiplying by Multiples of 10, 100, and 1,000

Did you know that an average of about 400 babies are born every hour in the United States?

There are 672 hours in the month of February (except in a leap year). How many babies, on the average, are born in February?

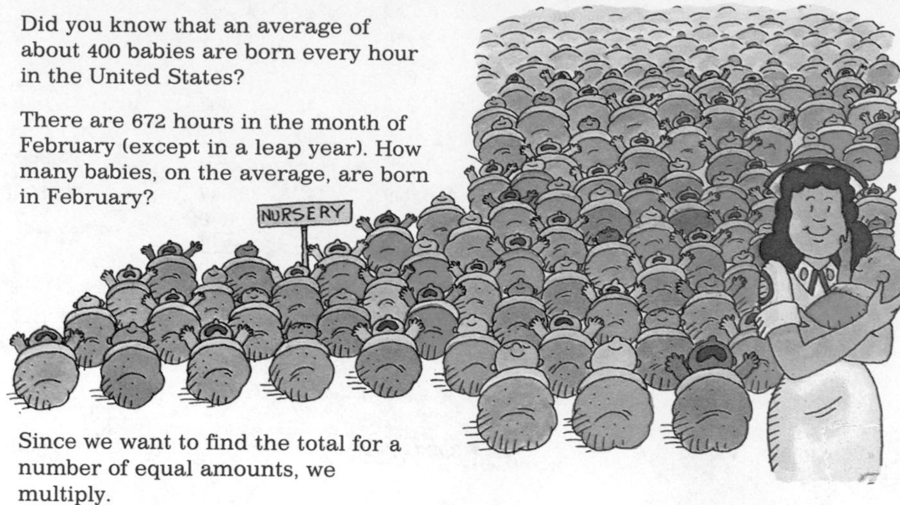
NURSERY

Since we want to find the total for a number of equal amounts, we multiply.

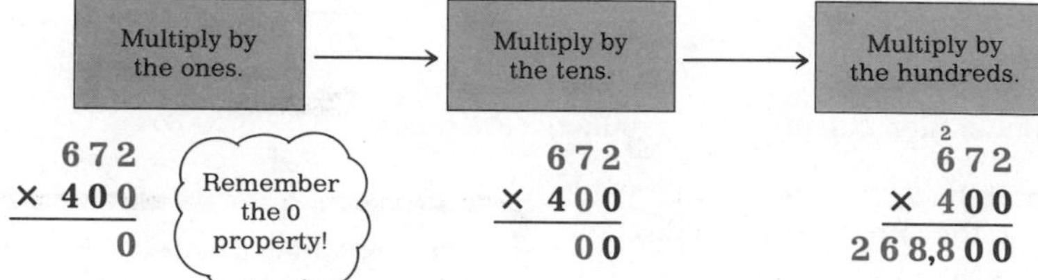
Multiply by the ones.
Multiply by the tens.
Multiply by the hundreds.

| 672 × 400 = 0 | Remember the 0 property! | 672 × 400 = 00 | 672 × 400 = 268,800 |
|---|---|---|---|

An average of 268,800 babies are born during February.

**Other Examples**

| 56 × 70 | 156 × 30 | 704 × 500 | 4,375 × 300 | 3,246 × 2,000 |
|---|---|---|---|---|
| 3,920 | 4,680 | 352,000 | 1,312,500 | 6,492,000 |

**Shortcut:** Just write the zeros in the product and multiply by the other number.

### Warm Up Multiply.

| 1. | 2. | 3. | 4. | 5. |
|---|---|---|---|---|
| 83 × 50 | 237 × 20 | 876 × 300 | 3,582 × 600 | 4,158 × 4,000 |
| 4,150 | 4,740 | 262,800 | 2,149,200 | 16,632,000 |

86

## Follow Up

### Reteaching

Write several zero facts on the chalkboard and review the zero property that states that multiplication by 0 results in 0. Then use examples such as 0 × 4, 0 × 42, and 0 × 437 to show that no matter what the other factor is, 0 × $n$ = 0. Use examples such as 10 × 42 to work through the multiplication algorithm.

```
  42              42
× 10            × 10
  00 (0 × 42)    420
 420 (10 × 42)
 420
```

### Enrichment

Provide students with the following table to complete.

1 meter (m) = 100 centimeters (cm)
1 meter = 10 decimeters (dm)
1 meter = 1,000 millimeter (mm)

| m | 2 | 4 | 5 | 7 | 14 |
|---|---|---|---|---|---|
| dm | 20 | 40 | 50 | 70 | 140 |
| cm | 200 | 400 | 500 | 700 | 1,400 |
| mm | 2,000 | 4,000 | 5,000 | 7,000 | 14,000 |

| Assignment Guide | Minimum | Average | Extended |
|---|---|---|---|
| page 87 | 1–23, 30, 32, SK | 1–32, SK | 11–33, SK |

Multiply.

1. 38 × 20 = 760
2. 79 × 40 = 3,160
3. 94 × 30 = 2,820
4. 78 × 50 = 3,900
5. 39 × 80 = 3,120
6. 504 × 40 = 20,160
7. 716 × 30 = 21,480
8. 638 × 60 = 38,280
9. 840 × 70 = 58,800
10. 496 × 90 = 44,640
11. 1,906 × 70 = 133,420
12. 4,387 × 40 = 175,480
13. 9,052 × 60 = 543,120
14. $8.98 × 40 = $359.20
15. 437 × 100 = 43,700
16. 803 × 500 = 401,500
17. $7.48 × 600 = $4,488.00
18. 1,654 × 800 = 1,323,200
19. 8,754 × 3,000 = 26,262,000
20. 9,540 × 6,000 = 57,240,000
21. 10 × 89 890
22. 10 × 563 5,630
23. 9,345 × 10 93,450
24. 59 × 40 2,360
25. 84 × 70 5,880
26. 365 × 60 21,900
27. 743 × 500 371,500
28. 400 × 608 243,200
29. 2,000 × 9,571 19,142,000
30. Estimate, then find 517 multiplied by 400. 200,000; 206,800
31. Estimate, then find the product if the factors are 800 and 2,987. 2,400,000; 2,389,600
32. There are 744 hours in the month of May. How many babies are born in May if the average number born each hour is 400? 297,600
33. It is estimated that the world's population increases at the rate of about 140 people each minute. About how much does the world's population increase in an hour? 8,400

## Skillkeeper

Write the place value of each red digit.

1. 0.37 7 hundredths
2. 1.0008 8 ten-thousandths
3. 3.95 9 tenths
4. 0.02146 6 hundred-thousandths
5. 6.051 1 thousandth
6. 0.47 4 tenths
7. 6.32 2 hundredths
8. 0.0143 3 ten-thousandths

Write >, <, or = for each ●.

9. 0.309 ● 0.039 >
10. 6.88 ● 6.808 >
11. 0.47 ● 0.470 =
12. 0.92 ● 9.2 <
13. 7.070 ● 7.07 =
14. 3.05 ● 3.5 <



## Using Page 87

**Exercises 1–29** Pay particular attention to exercises 9 and 20 because of problems students might have with additional zeros. Note that exercises 14 and 17 require students to multiply using money notation. Other problems that might cause difficulty because of zeros in the second factor are exercises 6, 11, 13, 16, and 28.

**Exercises 30–31** Encourage students to choose the place to which they will round in the estimation process. Note the term "multiplied by" in exercise 30 and the use of "product, factors" in exercise 31.

**Exercises 32–33** In exercise 32 students must supply the number of minutes in an hour to calculate the world's hourly population increase.

**Skillkeeper** This skill was originally taught in Chapter 3.

## Ideas That Work

### Calculator Bonus

To practice multiplication, have students work in pairs to play "In Order." Use a game mat as shown for each player, two number cubes labeled 0 through 5 and two labeled 4 through 9, a laminated game path as shown, and a calculator. In turn, players roll the number cubes, using the resulting numbers to fill in the game mat boxes to form a multiplication problem. At "GO" players work their problems. Players may then write their product on the game path or pass. Player 1 fills spaces to the RIGHT of start; player 2 to the LEFT. Space 1 must be filled first, then space 2, and so on in order. For player 1, each recorded product must be greater than 999, and products must *increase* from one space to the next. For player 2, the opposite holds—all products must be less than 999 and must *decrease* as they are recorded. If necessary, players can use a calculator to check answers. A round ends when a player reaches WIN. Player winning most rounds when time is called is the winner.

GameMat

WIN ⑤ ④ ③ ② ① START 999 ① ② ③ ④ ⑤ WIN

### Practice Supplement, page 33

Name ______ To follow text page 87

**Multiplying by Multiples of 10, 100, and 1,000**

Multiply.

1. 46 × 60 = 2,760
2. 29 × 80 = 2,320
3. 86 × 50 = 4,300
4. 94 × 90 = 8,460
5. 358 × 40 = 14,320
6. 449 × 30 = 13,470
7. 726 × 20 = 14,520
8. 189 × 70 = 13,230
9. 2,864 × 60 = 171,840
10. 3,902 × 20 = 78,040
11. 5,561 × 40 = 222,440
12. 7,280 × 30 = 218,400
13. 906 × 400 = 362,400
14. 241 × 800 = 192,800
15. 387 × 700 = 270,900
16. 642 × 500 = 321,000
17. 1,127 × 900 = 1,014,300
18. 3,469 × 300 = 1,040,700
19. 5,334 × 600 = 3,200,400
20. 7,020 × 200 = 1,404,000
21. 6,183 × 3,000 = 18,549,000
22. 8,205 × 8,000 = 65,640,000
23. 4,377 × 4,000 = 17,508,000
24. 4,670 × 5,000 = 23,350,000
25. 4,703 × 5,000 = 23,515,000
26. 3,852 × 7,000 = 26,964,000
27. 7,179 × 2,000 = 14,358,000
28. 5,809 × 9,000 = 52,281,000

# Multiplication

**Quick Review** Provide an oral drill of these addition and multiplication facts.

8 × 7 9 + 5 4 × 6 7 + 8 9 + 9 5 + 8 3 × 9 7 + 9
6 × 5 4 + 8 4 + 9 6 × 3 4 × 7 9 × 9 7 × 7
2 + 9 6 + 8 5 × 5 7 + 5 8 × 8 5 × 3 3 + 8 8 + 2

**Lesson Focus** To find the product of a whole number multiplied by a 2-digit factor

## Ideas for Getting Started

Write the following on the chalkboard.

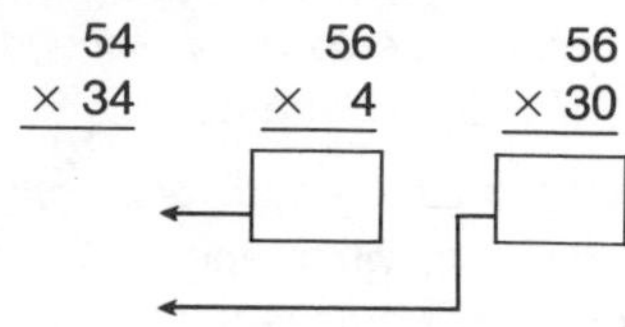


Have a volunteer find the first partial product, 4 × 56, and write it in the appropriate place. Then have another volunteer find the second partial product, 30 × 56, and write it below the first partial product. Have a third volunteer find the sum of these two partial products. Emphasize that because of the multiplication-addition property, 34 × 56 is the sum of 4 × 56 and 30 × 56.

## Using Page 88

**Motivational Problem** Have students read the paragraph about the *Titanic*. "What question are we asked about the *Titanic* ?" (How long was it?) "Using the idea of a scale model, what data do we need to find the *Titanic*'s length?" (length of the scale model, how many times larger the *Titanic* was) "Why is multiplication the operation to use to solve the problem?" (We want to find the total for an amount—the length of the model—repeated several times.) To help students understand this comparison, explain that the actual ship would be as long as 16 models laid end to end.

**Lesson Development** Help students find the answer by working through the steps shown in the instruction boxes. Point out that we can find the product of 16 × 55 by first finding the product 6 × 55, then finding the product 10 × 55 and adding the partial products. Call attention to the think clouds that show the use of the multiplication-addition property to multiply by the parts of 16 to find the partial products. As you describe this process, write 16 × 55 is (6 × 55) + (10 × 55).

Ask a volunteer to read the sentence that tells the answer to the problem. Encourage students to estimate the product and then reread the problem to see if the answer makes sense.

**Other Examples** As you work through these examples with students, remind them of the shortcut described in the think cloud. Point out that if they always place the right-hand digit of the product below the digit they are multiplying by, they can omit the 0. Have students draw vertical lines or use graph paper to help focus on this idea. Make sure students understand how to multiply the zero in one of the factors in example 2.

## Multiplying by a 2-Digit Factor

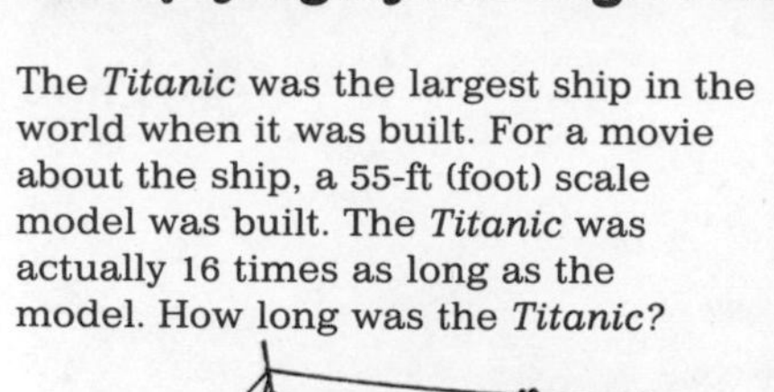

The *Titanic* was the largest ship in the world when it was built. For a movie about the ship, a 55-ft (foot) scale model was built. The *Titanic* was actually 16 times as long as the model. How long was the *Titanic*?

Since we want to find the total for the same amount repeated several times, we multiply.

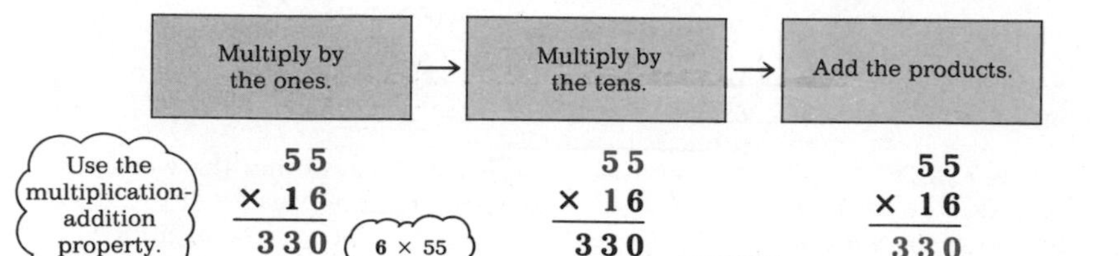


The *Titanic* was 880 ft (feet) long.

**Other Examples**

| 95 × 37 | 507 × 46 | 2,314 × 67 |
|---|---|---|
| 665 | 3042 | 16198 |
| 2850 | 2028 | 13884 |
| 3,515 | 23,322 | 155,038 |

Shortcut: Leave out the zero! Be sure to line up the products below the digit you're multiplying by!

**Warm Up** Multiply.

1. 86 × 29 = 2,494
2. 174 × 68 = 11,832
3. 309 × 45 = 13,905
4. 986 × 87 = 85,782
5. 3,528 × 23 = 81,144



## Follow Up

### Reteaching

To review the multiplication algorithm, work through sequences a, b, and c to find the product of 22 × 36

a)
```
  36
× 22
  12 (2 × 6)
  60 (2 × 30)
 120 (20 × 6)
 600 (20 × 30)
```

b)
```
  36
× 22
  72 (2 × 36)
 720 (20 × 36)
```

c)
```
  36
× 22
  72
 720
 792
```

### Enrichment

Challenge students to "cast out nines" to check their multiplication computation.

- Add the digits of each factor. Add the digits of each sum until you get a single digit. If the single digit is 9 (or if the digits total 9), cast it out to get 0.

57 → 5 + 7 = 12 → 1 + 2 = 3

392 → 3 + ~~9~~ + 2 = 5

```
  392  →    5
×  57  →  × 3
 2744      15 → 6
 1960
22,344 →    6
```

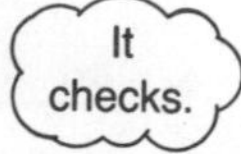

| Assignment Guide | Minimum | Average | Extended |
|---|---|---|---|
| page 89 | 1–24, 34–37 | 1–37 | 11–38, TM |

Multiply.

| | | | | |
|---|---|---|---|---|
| 1. 52 × 23 = 1,196 | 2. 48 × 16 = 768 | 3. 79 × 20 = 1,580 | 4. 88 × 55 = 4,840 | 5. 96 × 74 = 7,104 |
| 6. 132 × 46 = 6,072 | 7. 263 × 21 = 5,523 | 8. 374 × 65 = 24,310 | 9. 507 × 34 = 17,238 | 10. 747 × 26 = 19,422 |
| 11. 999 × 44 = 43,956 | 12. 850 × 37 = 31,450 | 13. 900 × 56 = 50,400 | 14. 1,537 × 28 = 43,036 | 15. 3,605 × 18 = 64,890 |
| 16. 4,032 × 71 = 286,272 | 17. 8,743 × 54 = 472,122 | 18. 9,400 × 78 = 733,200 | 19. $57.36 × 24 = $1,376.64 | 20. $19.95 × 12 = $239.40 |

| | | | |
|---|---|---|---|
| 21. 74 × 25<br>1,850 | 22. 48 × 14<br>672 | 23. 86 × 32<br>2,752 | 24. 71 × 68<br>4,828 |
| 25. 27 × 205<br>5,535 | 26. 315 × 41<br>12,915 | 27. 590 × 62<br>36,580 | 28. 54 × 618<br>33,372 |
| 29. 1,370 × 69<br>94,530 | 30. 83 × 2,431<br>201,773 | 31. 1,572 × 68<br>106,896 | 32. 5,046 × 29<br>146,334 |

33. What is the product when 426 is multiplied by 33? 14,058

34. If one factor is 59 and the other factor is 3,107 what is the product? 183,313

35. First estimate, then find the product: 379 times 42. 16,000; 15,918

36. First estimate, then find the result of multiplying 79 by 53. 4,000; 4,187

37. Suppose a full-size ship is 28 times the length of a scale model that will be used in a movie. If the model is 12 ft long, how long is the actual ship? 336 ft

38. **DATA BANK** The model of one of the world's largest passenger ships is 22 feet long. The actual ship is 45 times that length. What is the name of the ship? (See Data Bank, page 408.) *United States*

**Think Math**

**Logical Reasoning**

Copy and give the missing digits for each multiplication example.

```
     9 3 2              4 3
  ×    ■■ 61      ×   ■■ 28
    ■■■ 932          ■■■ 344
  ■■■■■ 55920        ■■■ 860
  5 6,■■■            ■■■4
      852            1,20
```

More Practice, page 416, Set A



## Using Page 89

**Exercises 1–32** Check students' work to be sure they understand the multiplying procedure and are correctly using the shortcut method. Encourage students to use grid paper to align digits when needed. Be especially alert for errors as students re-write exercises 21–32 in vertical notation.

**Exercises 33–37** Note in exercise 35 that the students must round 379 to the nearest hundred and 42 to the nearest ten to complete the estimate.

**Data Bank** This problem involves using information from a table in a different way. Note that the length of the ship is found in the exercise, and then this length is found in the table in order to answer the question.

**Think Math** Encourage students who have difficulty with the first problem to use estimation to help them find the first digit in the missing factor. (900 × 6 = 54,000) Then focus on the ones digit in this missing factor. "Can it be 2 or more?" (No. The first partial product is a 3-digit number, so the only possible digit for the ones place is 1.)

For the second problem give students the following hint: "In the missing factor, the ones digit must multiply 3 to give a product ending in 4. What number would do this?" (3 × 8 = 24) "What is the largest possible digit for the tens digit in the missing factor?" (2; 3 × 42 would require four digits in the second partial product) Caution students to think carefully about the missing digits in these problems.

More Practice, page 416, Set A

**Reteaching Supplement,** page 23

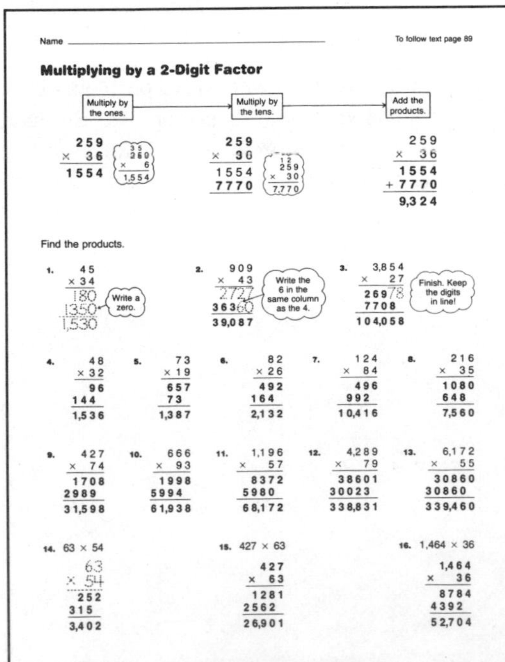

Name ______ To follow text page 89

**Multiplying by a 2-Digit Factor**

Multiply by the ones. → Multiply by the tens. → Add the products.

259 × 36: 1554 (259 × 6 = 1,554); 7770 (259 × 30 = 7,770); 1554 + 7770 = 9,324

Find the products.

1. 45 × 34: 180, 1350 — 1,530 (Write a zero.)
2. 909 × 43: 2727, 36360 — 39,087 (Write the 6 in the same column as the 4.)
3. 3,854 × 27: 26978, 7708 — 104,058 (Finish. Keep the digits in line!)
4. 48 × 32: 96, 144 — 1,536
5. 73 × 19: 657, 73 — 1,387
6. 82 × 26: 492, 164 — 2,132
7. 124 × 84: 496, 992 — 10,416
8. 216 × 35: 1080, 648 — 7,560
9. 427 × 74: 1708, 2989 — 31,598
10. 666 × 93: 1998, 5994 — 61,938
11. 1,196 × 57: 8372, 5980 — 68,172
12. 4,289 × 79: 38601, 30023 — 338,831
13. 6,172 × 55: 30860, 30860 — 339,460
14. 63 × 54: 252, 315 — 3,402
15. 427 × 63: 1281, 2562 — 26,901
16. 1,464 × 36: 8784, 4392 — 52,704

**Enrichment Supplement,** page 23

Name ______ To follow text page 89

**Some Number Patterns**

Find the first three products. Then predict the next three products. Multiply to check your predictions.

1. 12,345,679 × 9 = 111,111,111
2. 12,345,679 × 18: 98765432, 12345679 — 222,222,222
3. 12,345,679 × 27: 86419753, 24691358 — 333,333,333
4. Predicted product: 444,444,444 — 12,345,679 × 36: 74074074, 37037037 — 444,444,444
5. Predicted product: 555,555,555 — 12,345,679 × 45: 61728395, 49382716 — 555,555,555
6. Predicted product: 666,666,666 — 12,345,679 × 54: 49382716, 61728395 — 666,666,666

Now do problems 7 through 12 in the same way.

7. 99 × 45: 495, 396 — 4,455
8. 999 × 45: 4995, 3996 — 44,955
9. 9,999 × 45: 49995, 39996 — 449,955
10. Predicted product: 4,499,955 — 99,999 × 45: 499995, 399996 — 4,499,955
11. Predicted product: 44,999,955 — 999,999 × 45: 4999995, 3999996 — 44,999,955
12. Predicted product: 449,999,955 — 9,999,999 × 45: 49999995, 39999996 — 449,999,955

**Practice Supplement,** page 34

Name ______ To follow text page 89

**Multiplying by a 2-Digit Factor**

Multiply.

1. 75 × 38: 600, 2250 — 2,850
2. 36 × 47: 252, 1440 — 1,692
3. 64 × 57: 448, 3200 — 3,648
4. 47 × 33: 141, 1410 — 1,551
5. 83 × 57: 581, 4150 — 4,731
6. 69 × 48: 552, 2760 — 3,312
7. 21 × 35: 105, 630 — 735
8. 75 × 69: 675, 4500 — 5,175
9. 468 × 72: 936, 32760 — 33,696
10. 307 × 64: 1228, 18420 — 19,648
11. 481 × 98: 3848, 43290 — 47,138
12. 306 × 45: 1530, 12240 — 13,770
13. 3,761 × 56: 22566, 188050 — 210,616
14. 2,007 × 38: 16056, 60210 — 76,266
15. 3,060 × 73: 9180, 214200 — 223,380
16. 5,600 × 94: 22400, 504000 — 526,400
17. $29.46 × 19: 26514, 29460 — $559.74
18. $81.12 × 47: 56784, 324480 — $3,812.64
19. $41.83 × 55: 20915, 209150 — $2,300.65
20. $64.95 × 33: 19485, 194850 — $2,143.35

# Applications

**Quick Review** Students write the answers to these two-step equations.

$(7 \times 6) + (5 \times 4)$ 62 $(12 \times 6) - (8 - 6)$ 70 $(25 \times 2) + 13$ 63
$(4 \times 6) + (64 \div 8)$ 32 $(16 \times 2) - (6 \times 3)$ 14 $83 - (9 \times 4)$ 47

**Lesson Focus** To use the 5-Point Checklist to help solve word problems

## Ideas for Getting Started

Write this word problem on the chalkboard.

> Tim rode on a train for ____ hours at a speed of ____ kilometers per hour. Then he traveled ____ more kilometers at a slower speed.

Read through the problem with students. Discuss what questions could be asked about this story. (One possible question would be, "How far did Tim travel?" or, "How much farther did Tim travel at the faster speed?") Next, suggest numbers for the missing data. (A reference book might be used to find an appropriate speed for a train. Some students may know the train speeds from their own experience.) Then elicit from students a plan to solve the problem. Be sure students understand that the problems in this lesson are solved by using one or more of the operations. Refer to the last two steps in the checklist and remind students that it is important to write out the answer completely and then to check back to make sure that the answer makes sense.

## Using Page 90

**Lesson Development** Read through the 5-Point Checklist at the top of the page. Remind students that the checklist does not give specific "rules" for solving a problem. Rather, it gives five important things to think about as they work toward the solution of a problem. Point out how the checklist helped solve the problem about Tim's train ride. Discuss each step of the checklist and bring out the idea of Question, Data, Plan, Answer, and Check. Remind students that it is important to see that they have calculated correctly, but also it is important to read the original problem to see if an answer seems reasonable.

**Exercises 1–2** Help students solve these problems using the five steps of the Checklist as a guide.

## Problem Solving: Using the 5-Point Checklist

QUESTION
DATA
PLAN
ANSWER
CHECK

**To Solve a Problem**

1. **Understand the Question**
2. **Find the needed Data**
3. **Plan what to do**
4. **Find the Answer**
5. **Check back**

These 5 steps can help you solve problems. Follow them to solve this problem.

Jack traveled 4 hours at an average speed of 88 km/h (kilometers per hour). Then he traveled 3 more hours at a speed of 82 km/h. How far did he travel?

1. **Understand the Question**
   What was the total number of kilometers traveled?

2. **Find the needed Data**
   4 hours at 88 km/h  3 hours at 82 km/h
3. **Plan what to do**
   Distance = rate × time. Since we know the rates and times, we must multiply. Then we add the distances.
4. **Find the Answer**
   $4 \times 88 = 352$  $3 \times 82 = 246$  $352 + 246 = 598$
   Jack traveled 598 km.
5. **Check back**
   Reread the problem. Estimate the answer.
   $4 \times 90 = 360$, $3 \times 80 = 240$, and $360 + 240 = 600$, so 598 km seems reasonable.

Solve. Use the 5-Point Checklist.

1. A bicycle rider averaged 24 km/h for 8 hours. How far did she travel? 192 km
2. The average speed of the winning car in a 4-hour race was 249 km/h. How far did the car travel? 996 km

90

## Follow Up

### Reteaching

Have students use the items below to make up multiplication problems. Ask students to explain why their problems are multiplication problems. After students have explained their questions, work with them to use the 5-Point checklist to solve each problem.

Model Shop

| Race Car | Space Ship | Log Cabin |
| --- | --- | --- |
| \$4.75 | \$10.36 | \$2.49 |

### Enrichment

Have students write word problems to be exchanged with a classmate. Students should provide the solution for their own problems, applying the 5-Point Checklist before sharing with classmates.

| Assignment Guide | | | |
|---|---|---|---|
| | Minimum | Average | Extended |
| page 90 | 1–2 | 1–2 | 1–2 |
| page 91 | 1–6 | 1–7 | 1–8 |

Solve.

1. A high-speed train in France travels 380 km/h. If a train could travel across the United States at this speed, could it cover the 4,885 km distance from New York to San Francisco in 13 hours? yes

2. The record speed for a space vehicle is 68 times as fast as the record speed for a jet plane. The fastest jet plane flew 3,529 km/h. What is the record space vehicle speed? 239,972 km/h

3. The record speed for a car is 1,001 km/h. The record speed for a power boat is 219 km/h. How many more kilometers per hour is the record auto speed than the record power boat speed? 782 km/h

4. Light travels about 300 thousand km/s (kilometers per second). If it takes 311 seconds for the light from a sunspot flare-up to travel to the earth and be seen, about how far is it from the earth to the sun? 93,300 thousand km

5. Sound travels 1,460 m/s (meters per second) in sea water. It takes sound waves 7 seconds to reach the bottom of a deep part of the Pacific Ocean. How deep is it? 10,220 m

6. Sound travels 331 m/s through the air. The sound of a foghorn reached a fishing boat in 6 seconds. The sound reached an oil tanker in 14 seconds. How much farther away from the foghorn was the oil tanker than the fishing boat? 2,648 m

7. As passengers on Spaceship Earth, we travel around the sun at a speed of 107,211 km/h. How far do we travel during a 24-hour day? 2,573,064 km

8. **Try This** The highway distance from Boston to Cleveland is 1,028 km. A car leaves Boston averaging 88 km/h at the same time a car leaves Cleveland averaging 77 km/h. How far apart will the cars be when they have traveled toward each other for 6 hours? Hint: Draw a picture. 38 km



## Using Page 91

**Exercises 1–7** In exercise 1 students must multiply and then compare two numbers. Exercise 6 can be solved by subtracting 6 from 14 and multiplying the result by 331. However, some students might multiply 331 by 6, multiply 331 by 14, and then subtract. Be sure to point out the most efficient solution. In exercise 7 students use calculators to find the distance the earth travels in its orbit about the sun.

**Try This** A possible strategy, Draw a Picture, was taught on page 74.

**Discussion** "What is the question we want to answer in this problem?" (How far apart will the cars be after 6 hours of travel?) "What data is given?" (distance between the cars; the speed the cars are traveling; hours the cars travel) Suggest that a good plan might be to draw a picture.

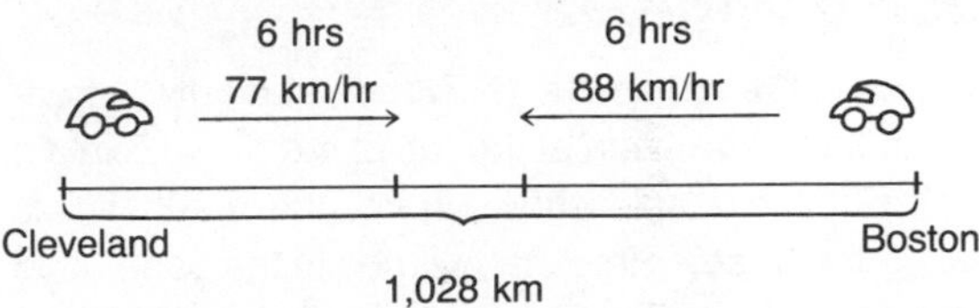


"How far will the first car travel in 6 hours?" (462 km) "How far will the second car travel in 6 hours?" (528 km) "What is the total distance traveled by both cars?" (990 km) "How can we find out how far apart the cars are?" (Subtract the distance the cars have traveled from the total distance between Cleveland and Boston.)

**Solution** The cars will be 38 km apart after 6 hours of travel.

## Ideas That Work

### Special Education

Students form groups of five and select a word problem from the text. Each student in a group should select *one* of the steps in the 5-Point Checklist and tell others what they thought or did at that step for the problem their group chose.

| 1. Question |
|---|
| 2. Data |
| 3. Plan |
| 4. Answer |
| 5. Check |

If a student with abstract reasoning, reading or memory difficulty is in a group, let that student make the first selection. The goal here is to build in as many success experiences as possible for that student in order to promote better attitudes towards problem solving. In other words, reinforce what these students can do best. As they become more confident by hearing others speak, they can take turns along with others in selecting from the checklist the step to be done.

If time allows, have practice periods during which students use input from others in the group to refine their descriptions before presenting them to the class.

**Practice Supplement,** page 35

Name ____________ To follow text page 91

**Problem Solving: Using the 5-Point Checklist**

Use the 5-Point Checklist to solve these problems.

To Solve a Problem
1. Understand the Question.
2. Find the needed Data.
3. Plan what to do.
4. Find the Answer.
5. Check back.

1. Sound travels at 1,460 m/s (meters per second) in sea water. How far does a sound travel in 6 s? **8,760 m**

2. Sound travels 331 m/s through air. If a person hears thunder from a storm in 5 s, how far away is the storm? **1,655 m**

3. A car is averaging 88 km/h. How far does it travel in 12 h? **1,056 km**

4. The record speed for a YF-12A Jet is 3,312 km/h. The record speed for a Douglas D-558 is 1,041 km/h. How many more kilometers per hour is the record jet speed? **2,271 km/h**

5. A train is traveling at a speed of 104 km/h. If it does not stop, how far will it travel in 17 h? **1,768 km**

6. A car traveled at 85 km/h for 3 h and 82 km/h for 2 h. How far did it travel in all? **419 km**

7. Betty traveled 664 km on a trip, and she averaged 83 km/h. How many hours did she travel? **8 h**

8. If Sam averages 83 km/h on a trip, will he be able to drive 950 km in 12 h? **Yes**

# Number Theory

**Quick Review** Students write the total value of each group of coins.

| | | |
|---|---|---|
| 3 quarters \$0.75 | 2 dimes, 2 pennies \$0.22 | 1 nickel, 1 dime \$0.15 |
| 4 nickels, 1 penny \$0.21 | 3 nickels \$0.15 | 2 nickels, 1 dime \$0.20 |
| 1 quarter, 3 pennies \$0.28 | 4 dimes, 1 nickel \$0.45 | 2 quarters \$0.50 |

**Lesson Focus** To express numbers as exponents or as powers of ten

**Suggested Materials** Place-value models for tens, hundreds, and thousands

## Ideas for Getting Started

Show students a ten-strip and ask: "How many singles in this block?" (10) Then show the hundreds square. "Why do you think this is sometimes called 10 squared?" (It is a square with 10 rows of 10.) "How many singles in the square?" ($10 \times 10$, or 100) Then show the thousands cube. "Why do you think this is sometimes called 10 cubed?" (It is a cube with 10 layers of the hundred squares.) "How many singles in this cube?" ($10 \times 10 \times 10$, or 1,000)

## Using Page 92

**Lesson Development** Direct students' attention to the information at the top of the page. Explain that in the example shown here, the number 5 is called the base. "How many times is the base used as a factor?" (3) Point out that the exponent is the small raised number and is used to tell how many times the base is used as a factor. In other words, $5^3$ is a short way to represent $5 \times 5 \times 5$. Use language such as "5 to the third power" or "5 cubed." Refer to the illustration and point out that the ten strip contains 10 singles and is written $10^1$. It is read "10 to the first power." Since the square with 100 units has 10 rows of 10, or $10 \times 10$, it can be thought of as having $10^2$ units. Since it is squares, it suggests the language "10 squared."

Discuss the thousand unit block in the same way. Because it has 10 layers of 10 tens, or $10 \times 10 \times 10$, it is written as $10^3$. Since it is a cube, it suggests the term "10 cubed."

**Other Examples** In the first example, ask, "What is the base?" (3) "What is the exponent?" (2) "What does the exponent represent?" (the number of times the base is used as a factor) Discuss the other examples by asking similar questions.

**Warm Up** Emphasize that exponents are used only when all the factors are the same. Be sure students understand that the repeated number is the base and that the number of factors is the exponent. Refer back to the first paragraph if necessary. In exercise 9 when the power is given, students should see that the exponent tells how many times the base is used as a factor.

## Exponents

Sometimes a number is used as a factor several times. An **exponent** tells how many times the number, called the **base**, is used as a factor.

3 factors — Exponent

$5 \times 5 \times 5 = 5^3$ ← Base

"5 to the third power" or "5 cubed"

Here are some **powers of ten:**

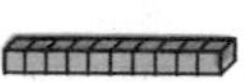

$10^1 = 10$

"ten to the first power" or "ten"

$10^2 = 10 \times 10 = 100$

"ten to the second power" or "ten squared"

$10^3 = 10 \times 10 \times 10 = 1{,}000$

"ten to the third power" or "ten cubed"

The exponent also tells how many zeros when 10 is the base.

**Other Examples**

$3^2 = 3 \times 3 = 9$

$8^4 = 8 \times 8 \times 8 \times 8 = 4{,}096$

$10^5 = 10 \times 10 \times 10 \times 10 \times 10 = 100{,}000$

$4 \times 4 \times 4 = 4^3$

$6 \times 6 \times 6 \times 6 \times 6 = 6^5$

$100 \times 100 = 100^2$

**Warm Up** Write the exponent.

1. $2 \times 2 \times 2 \times 2 \times 2 = 2^{■}$ 5
2. $10 \times 10 \times 10 \times 10 = 10^{■}$ 4
3. $5 \times 5 \times 5 \times 5 \times 5 \times 5 = 5^{■}$ 6
4. $7 \times 7 \times 7 \times 7 = 7^{■}$ 4

Write the base and the exponent.

5. $3 \times 3 \times 3 \times 3 \times 3$ $3^5$
6. $10 \times 10 \times 10 \times 10 \times 10 \times 10 \times 10$ $10^7$
7. $12 \times 12 \times 12$ $12^3$
8. $4 \times 4 \times 4 \times 4 \times 4 \times 4$ $4^6$
9. Multiply to find a number in standard form for $7^5$. 16,807

92

## Follow Up

### Reteaching

Begin a review of the concept of factors using examples from basic multiplication facts. Then look at the "doubles" from the set of basic facts, $2 \times 2$, $3 \times 3$, $4 \times 4$, for example. Point out that in these facts, the same factor is used twice, and we can write this as $2 \times 2 = 2^2$, $3 \times 3 = 3^2$, $4 \times 4 = 4^2$. Now apply this idea to examples such as $10 \times 10 = 10^2$, $10 \times 10 \times 10 = 10^3$, $10 \times 10 \times 10 \times 10 = 10^4$. Remind students that the exponent tells how many times the base is used as a factor.

### Enrichment

Challenge students to match Column A with Column B.

| | Column A | Column B |
|---|---|---|
| E | 1. $2^3$ | A. 16 |
| A | 2. $4^2$ | B. 32 |
| I | 3. $3\times3\times3\times3\times3$ | C. 729 |
| G | 4. $15^2$ | D. 64 |
| D | 5. $8^2$ | E. 8 |
| F | 6. $10^4$ | F. 10,000 |
| B | 7. $2^5$ | G. 225 |
| C | 8. $9\times9\times9$ | H. 4 |
| H | 9. $4^1$ | I. 243 |
| K | 10. $3^3$ | J. 625 |
| J | 11. $5^4$ | K. 27 |
| L | 12. $12^2$ | L. 144 |

| Assignment Guide | | | |
|---|---|---|---|
| | Minimum | Average | Extended |
| page 93 | 1–44 | 1–48 | 1–49 odd, TM |

Write using an exponent.

1. $3 \times 3 \times 3$ $3^3$
2. $7 \times 7 \times 7 \times 7 \times 7 \times 7$ $7^6$
3. $10 \times 10 \times 10 \times 10 \times 10$ $10^5$
4. $4 \times 4 \times 4 \times 4$ $4^4$
5. $9 \times 9 \times 9 \times 9 \times 9$ $9^5$
6. $5 \times 5 \times 5 \times 5 \times 5 \times 5 \times 5$ $5^7$

Write as a product of factors. Example: $4^3 = 4 \times 4 \times 4$ See teaching notes.

7. $2^4$ 8. $4^2$ 9. $5^3$ 10. $10^1$ 11. $6^5$ 12. $3^4$ 13. $10^2$

14. $10^3$ 15. $8^5$ 16. $15^2$ 17. $100^3$ 18. $7^6$ 19. $12^4$ 20. $6^2$

Multiply to find the number in standard form.

21. $2^3$ 8
22. $5^2$ 25
23. $6^2$ 36
24. $3^3$ 27
25. $10^4$ 10,000
26. $4^5$ 1,024
27. $10^3$ 1,000
28. $10^9$ 1,000,000,000
29. $8^5$ 32,768
30. $7^6$ 117,649
31. $9^4$ 6,561
32. $10^7$ 10,000,000
33. $12^3$ 1,728
34. $9^2$ 81

Use exponents to write each as a power of 10.

35. 100 $10^2$
36. 10,000 $10^4$
37. 1,000,000 $10^6$
38. 1,000 $10^3$
39. 100,000 $10^5$
40. 1,000,000,000 $10^9$
41. 100,000,000 $10^8$
42. 10 $10^1$

Solve the equations.

43. $7 \times 10^2 = n$ 700
44. $4 \times 10^6 = n$ 4,000,000
45. $5 \times 10^3 = n$ 5,000
46. $3 \times 10^4 = n$ 30,000
47. $10^{100}$ is called a googol. How many zeros would it have in standard form? 100

Write the numbers in exercises 48 and 49 in expanded form. Use exponents for powers of 10. Example: $345 = 3 \times 10^2 + 4 \times 10^1 + 5$

48. 4,279 $4 \times 10^3 + 2 \times 10^2 + 7 \times 10^1 + 9$

★ 49. 6,387,425 $6 \times 10^6 + 3 \times 10^5 + 8 \times 10^4 + 7 \times 10^3 + 4 \times 10^2 + 2 \times 10^1 + 5$

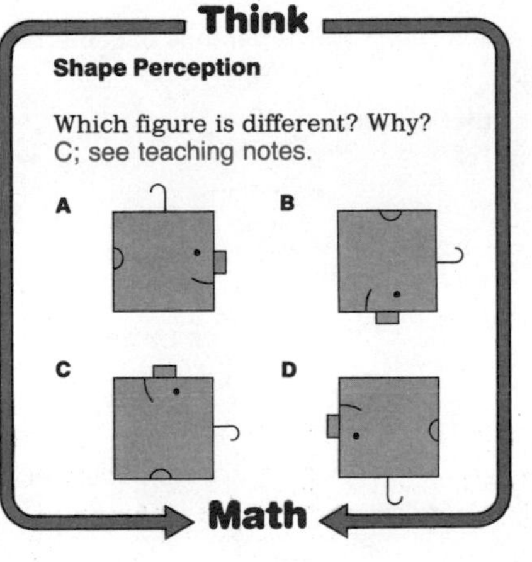


**Shape Perception**

Which figure is different? Why?
C; see teaching notes.



## Using Page 93

**Exercises 1–6** These exercises involve counting the number of times the base is used as a factor and writing the product using exponent notation.

**Exercises 7–20** Be sure that students understand that they are just to interpret the power and write each number as a product of factors.

**Answers**

7. $2 \times 2 \times 2 \times 2$ 8. $4 \times 4$ 9. $5 \times 5 \times 5$ 10. 10 11. $6 \times 6 \times 6 \times 6 \times 6$ 12. $3 \times 3 \times 3 \times 3$ 13. $10 \times 10$ 14. $10 \times 10 \times 10$ 15. $8 \times 8 \times 8 \times 8 \times 8$ 16. $15 \times 15$ 17. $100 \times 100 \times 100$ 18. $7 \times 7 \times 7 \times 7 \times 7 \times 7$ 19. $12 \times 12 \times 12 \times 12$ 20. $6 \times 6$

**Exercises 21–34** In these exercises students multiply to find the number in standard form. Make sure that students are not interpreting $6^2$, for example, as $6 \times 2$.

**Exercises 35–42** Students might find the answers to these exercises by multiplying enough tens to get the number given. Emphasize the relationship between the exponent and the number of zeros.

**Exercises 43–49** Students have already written standard numbers as numbers in expanded form in Chapter 2. These exercises extend this activity by asking students to write numbers such as 300 as $3 \times 10^2$.

**Think Math** Students must look at these figures carefully to decide what the difference is. Note that figure B can be produced by rotating figure A 90°. Figure D can be produced by rotating the figure another 90°. Figure C can be produced from figure B by flipping about a horizontal line. Figure C can also be produced from figures A and D by flipping and rotating.

**Reteaching Supplement,** page 24

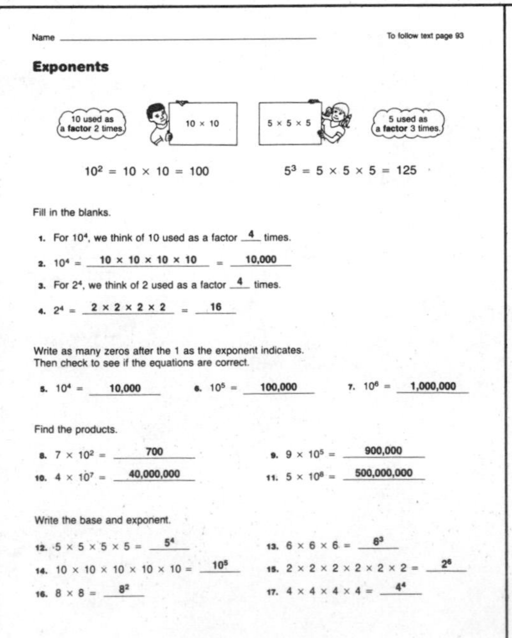


Name ______ To follow text page 93

**Exponents**

$10^2 = 10 \times 10 = 100$ $5^3 = 5 \times 5 \times 5 = 125$

Fill in the blanks.

1. For $10^4$, we think of 10 used as a factor 4 times.
2. $10^4$ = $10 \times 10 \times 10 \times 10$ = 10,000
3. For $2^4$, we think of 2 used as a factor 4 times.
4. $2^4$ = $2 \times 2 \times 2 \times 2$ = 16

Write as many zeros after the 1 as the exponent indicates. Then check to see if the equations are correct.

5. $10^4$ = 10,000 6. $10^5$ = 100,000 7. $10^6$ = 1,000,000

Find the products.

8. $7 \times 10^2$ = 700
9. $9 \times 10^5$ = 900,000
10. $4 \times 10^7$ = 40,000,000
11. $5 \times 10^8$ = 500,000,000

Write the base and exponent.

12. $5 \times 5 \times 5 \times 5$ = $5^4$
13. $6 \times 6 \times 6$ = $6^3$
14. $10 \times 10 \times 10 \times 10 \times 10$ = $10^5$
15. $2 \times 2 \times 2 \times 2 \times 2 \times 2$ = $2^6$
16. $8 \times 8$ = $8^2$
17. $4 \times 4 \times 4 \times 4$ = $4^4$

**Enrichment Supplement,** page 24

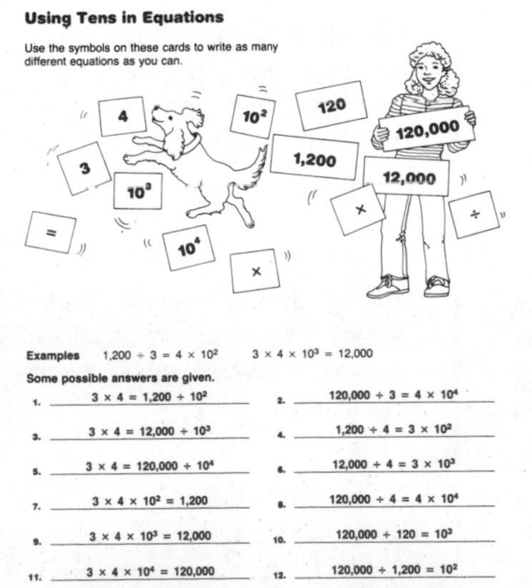


Name ______ To follow text page 93

**Using Tens in Equations**

Use the symbols on these cards to write as many different equations as you can.

**Examples** $1{,}200 \div 3 = 4 \times 10^2$ $3 \times 4 \times 10^3 = 12{,}000$

**Some possible answers are given.**

1. $3 \times 4 = 1{,}200 \div 10^2$
2. $120{,}000 \div 3 = 4 \times 10^4$
3. $3 \times 4 = 12{,}000 \div 10^3$
4. $1{,}200 \div 4 = 3 \times 10^2$
5. $3 \times 4 = 120{,}000 \div 10^4$
6. $12{,}000 \div 4 = 3 \times 10^3$
7. $3 \times 4 \times 10^2 = 1{,}200$
8. $120{,}000 \div 4 = 4 \times 10^4$
9. $3 \times 4 \times 10^3 = 12{,}000$
10. $120{,}000 \div 120 = 10^3$
11. $3 \times 4 \times 10^4 = 120{,}000$
12. $120{,}000 \div 1{,}200 = 10^2$
13. $1{,}200 \div 3 = 4 \times 10^2$
14. $12{,}000 \div 120 = 10^2$
15. $12{,}000 \div 3 = 4 \times 10^3$
16. $120 \times 10^2 = 12{,}000$

**Practice Supplement,** page 36

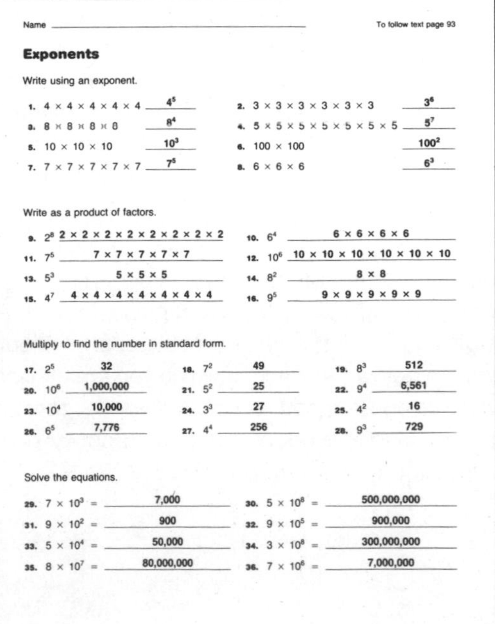

Name ______ To follow text page 93

**Exponents**

Write using an exponent.

1. $4 \times 4 \times 4 \times 4 \times 4$ $4^5$
2. $3 \times 3 \times 3 \times 3 \times 3 \times 3$ $3^6$
3. $8 \times 8 \times 8 \times 8$ $8^4$
4. $5 \times 5 \times 5 \times 5 \times 5 \times 5 \times 5$ $5^7$
5. $10 \times 10 \times 10$ $10^3$
6. $100 \times 100$ $100^2$
7. $7 \times 7 \times 7 \times 7 \times 7$ $7^5$
8. $6 \times 6 \times 6$ $6^3$

Write as a product of factors.

9. $2^8$ $2 \times 2 \times 2 \times 2 \times 2 \times 2 \times 2 \times 2$
10. $6^4$ $6 \times 6 \times 6 \times 6$
11. $7^5$ $7 \times 7 \times 7 \times 7 \times 7$
12. $10^6$ $10 \times 10 \times 10 \times 10 \times 10 \times 10$
13. $5^3$ $5 \times 5 \times 5$
14. $8^2$ $8 \times 8$
15. $4^7$ $4 \times 4 \times 4 \times 4 \times 4 \times 4 \times 4$
16. $9^5$ $9 \times 9 \times 9 \times 9 \times 9$

Multiply to find the number in standard form.

17. $2^5$ 32
18. $7^2$ 49
19. $8^3$ 512
20. $10^6$ 1,000,000
21. $5^2$ 25
22. $9^4$ 6,561
23. $10^4$ 10,000
24. $3^3$ 27
25. $4^2$ 16
26. $6^5$ 7,776
27. $4^4$ 256
28. $9^3$ 729

Solve the equations.

29. $7 \times 10^3$ = 7,000
30. $5 \times 10^8$ = 500,000,000
31. $9 \times 10^2$ = 900
32. $9 \times 10^5$ = 900,000
33. $5 \times 10^4$ = 50,000
34. $3 \times 10^8$ = 300,000,000
35. $8 \times 10^7$ = 80,000,000
36. $7 \times 10^6$ = 7,000,000

# Multiplication

**Quick Review** As an oral drill, students supply the missing number in each multiplication fact below.

| | | |
|---|---|---|
| 340 = 34 × ___ | 2,000 = 2 × ___ | 700 = 7 × ___ |
| 3,200 = 32 × ___ | 210 = 21 × ___ | 4,570 = 457 × ___ |

**Lesson Focus** To multiply a whole number by a 3-digit factor

**Suggested Materials** Spinner or slips of paper labeled 0 through 9.

## Ideas for Getting Started

To review multiplying a 3-digit number by a 2-digit number, let students play "Greatest Product." Have students draw a grid as shown below.

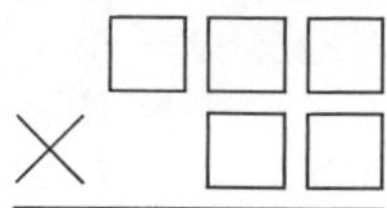

Five numbers are called by spinning the spinner or drawing a number slip. As each number is called, students write it in any of the unfilled squares on their grids. The object is to place the number so that the two factors created will produce the greatest product. Play the game several times, giving students opportunities to practice multiplying and to devise strategies for the most appropriate placement of the numbers.

## Using Page 94

**Motivational Problem** Read and discuss the problem at the top of the page. "What question are we asked about the new citizens?" (How many persons become new citizens in a year?) "What data is needed to solve the problem?" (the average number of new citizens each day and the number of days in a year) "What operation would you use to solve the problem?" (To find the total of a number of equal amounts, we multiply.)

**Lesson Development** Work through each step in the instruction boxes with students. Review the idea that 365 × 438 is (5 × 438) + (60 × 438) + (300 × 438). Tell students that each time we multiply in a given place, we find a partial product. The multiplication-addition property assures us that we can find the total product by adding these partial products. Have students read the complete sentence that tells the answer to the problem. Encourage them to check the product by rounding each of the factors to the nearest hundred and estimating to find the answer. Ask a volunteer to reread the problem to see if this answer seems reasonable.

**Other Examples** In these exercises, emphasize that 1 zero in the second partial product can be omitted, 2 zeros in the third partial product can be omitted, and so on. Also emphasize that the first digit that is written in a partial product should be written below the place in which you are multiplying. Note in the second example that the zero in the second partial product cannot be dropped because it was the result of multiplying 6 × 5.

## Multiplying by a 3-Digit Factor

An average of 438 persons per day from other countries become new United States citizens. At this rate how many persons become new citizens each year (365 days)?

Since we want to find the total for a number of equal amounts, we multiply.

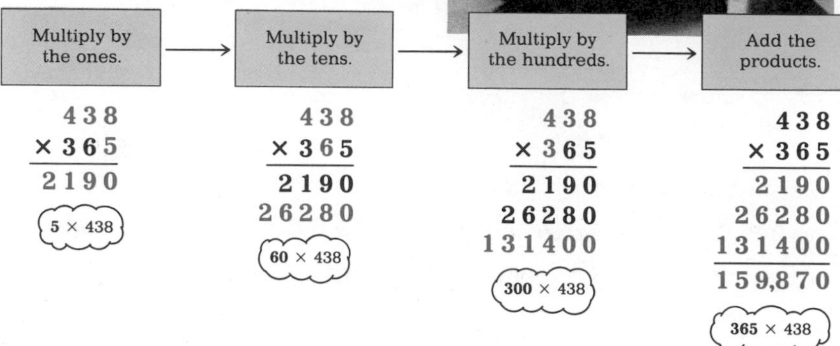


Each year 159,870 persons become new citizens.

**Other Examples**

```
   739            826        947       3,459
 × 403          × 250      × 800     ×   638
  2217          41300     757,600     27672
295600          1652                 10377
297,817        206,500               20754
                                    2,206,842
```

You can leave out these zeros!

**Warm Up** Multiply.

1. 547 × 326 = 178,322
2. 867 × 504 = 436,968
3. 976 × 340 = 331,840
4. 639 × 700 = 447,300
5. 6,432 × 758 = 4,875,456

94

## Follow Up

### Reteaching

Write an example such as 326 × 439 on the chalkboard. Encourage students to describe how to work through this example. Write specific steps such as:

1) Multiply the ones.
2) Multiply the tens.
3) Multiply the hundreds.

Then go through the multiplication. If necessary, help students recall simpler examples. Answers may be checked with a calculator.

### Enrichment

Have students identify the two factors that give each missing partial product. Then ask them to give the partial products and the total product.

```
   246       507
 × 378     × 349
  1968      4563
 17220     20280
 73800    152100
 92,988   176,943
```

| Assignment Guide | Minimum | Average | Extended |
|---|---|---|---|
| page 95 | 1–27, 30–31, SK | 1–31, SK | 1–32, SK |

Multiply.

1. 308 × 231 = 71,148
2. 530 × 604 = 320,120
3. 412 × 320 = 131,840
4. 253 × 800 = 202,400
5. 605 × 712 = 430,760
6. 432 × 351 = 151,632
7. 621 × 536 = 332,856
8. 784 × 197 = 154,448
9. 676 × 340 = 229,840
10. 943 × 507 = 478,101
11. 888 × 236 = 209,568
12. 750 × 423 = 317,250
13. 571 × 199 = 113,629
14. 806 × 430 = 346,580
15. 579 × 386 = 223,494
16. 1,763 × 847 = 1,493,261
17. 2,806 × 953 = 2,674,118
18. 5,764 × 678 = 3,907,992
19. 9,048 × 369 = 3,338,712
20. 7,005 × 378 = 2,647,890

21. 874 × 123 107,502
22. 436 × 827 360,572
23. 308 × 107 32,956
24. 5,416 × 841 4,554,856
25. 904 × 376 339,904
26. 8,764 × 895 7,843,780

27. What is the result when 555 is multiplied by 333? 184,815

28. If one factor is 121 and the other factor is 212, what is the product? 25,652

29. First estimate, then find the product when the factors are 379 and 618. 240,000; 234,222

30. First estimate, then find 2,986 multiplied by 428. 1,200,000; 1,278,008

31. An average of 501 persons a day move to the United States from Asia. How many persons would come from Asia in one year (365 days)? 182,865

32. An average of 818,755 persons per year moved to the United States from other countries during the period from 1920 through 1979. How many persons moved to the United States during this period? 48,306,545

## Skillkeeper

Add or subtract.

1. 0.289 + 0.457 = 0.746
2. 6.08 + 3.29 = 9.37
3. 12.4 + 6.68 = 19.08
4. 5.22 − 1.97 = 3.25
5. 4.036 − 1.71 = 2.326

Divide.

6. 60 ÷ 2 30
7. 420 ÷ 7 60
8. 810 ÷ 9 90
9. 350 ÷ 5 70
10. 8,000 ÷ 4 2,000
11. 16,000 ÷ 8 2,000
12. 4,000 ÷ 2 2,000
13. 90 ÷ 3 30
14. 480 ÷ 80 6
15. 5,400 ÷ 60 90
16. 81,000 ÷ 900 90
17. 4,500 ÷ 9 500

More Practice, page 416, Set B



## Using Page 95

**Exercises 1–28** Be sure students understand the process for multiplying by a 3-digit factor. Observe their work and be alert for problems involving multiplying by a factor that contains a zero. Also, check students' work in exercises 5, 6, 7, 12, 17, and 20 carefully since these exercises involve basic facts 2 × 5, 5 × 6, or 5 × 8 with products ending in zero.

**Exercises 29–30** Encourage students to select the appropriate places to round and find the estimates mentally. Note in exercise 29 that both numbers should be rounded to the nearest hundred. In exercise 30 the first number should be rounded to the nearest thousand while the second number is rounded to the nearest hundred.

**Exercise 32** This exercise involves two steps. The student must subtract to find the number of years from 1920 through 1979, and then multiply the average number of persons who moved to the United States. Because of the large numbers involved, this is a good calculator exercise.

**Skillkeeper** These skills were originally taught in Chapters 3 and 5.

**More Practice,** page 416, Set B

**Reteaching Supplement,** page 25

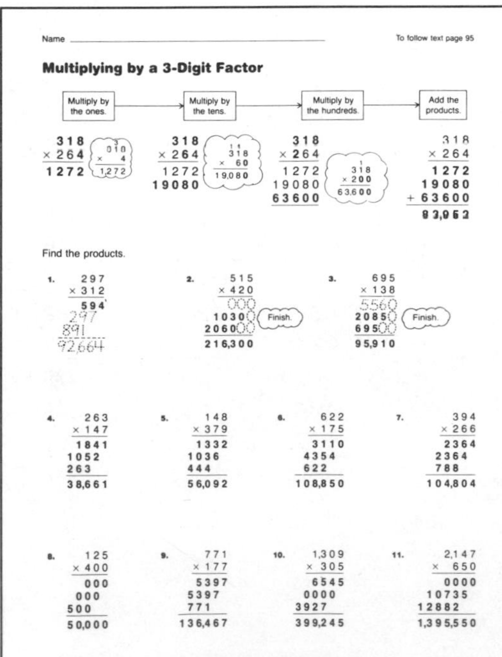

Name ______ To follow text page 95

### Multiplying by a 3-Digit Factor

Multiply by the ones. → Multiply by the tens. → Multiply by the hundreds. → Add the products.

318 × 264: 318 × 4 = 1,272; 318 × 60 = 19,080; 318 × 200 = 63,600; 1272 + 19080 + 63600 = 83,952

Find the products.

1. 297 × 312 — Partial products: 594, 297, 891 — 92,664
2. 515 × 420 — Partial products: 000, 10300, 206000 — Finish. — 216,300
3. 695 × 138 — Partial products: 5560, 20850, 69500 — Finish. — 95,910
4. 263 × 147 — Partial products: 1841, 1052, 263 — 38,661
5. 148 × 379 — Partial products: 1332, 1036, 444 — 56,092
6. 622 × 175 — Partial products: 3110, 4354, 622 — 108,850
7. 394 × 266 — Partial products: 2364, 2364, 788 — 104,804
8. 125 × 400 — Partial products: 000, 000, 500 — 50,000
9. 771 × 177 — Partial products: 5397, 5397, 771 — 136,467
10. 1,309 × 305 — Partial products: 6545, 0000, 3927 — 399,245
11. 2,147 × 650 — Partial products: 0000, 10735, 12882 — 1,395,550

**Enrichment Supplement,** page 25

Name ______ To follow text page 95

### Calculator Capers

Work each problem with a calculator. Turn the calculator upside down to read the words. If you do not have a calculator, print your answer in calculator numerals. Turn your paper upside down to read the words.

Calculator numerals: 0123456789
Upside down calculator numerals: 0I2EhS9L86
Letters: OIZEhSgLBG

1. What are golfers, gophers, and oil companies all concerned about? (937 × 567) − 477, 575 — 53704
2. Which cow was the dictator of the herd? (499 × 527) + (395 × 133) — 315508
3. What caused the snake to give up acting as a career? 14 × 29 × 1,319 — 535514
4. What did the stove make the teakettle do? (3,554 × 6) ÷ 3 — 7108
5. What do you get if you charge many things that you buy? 19,236,708 + 13,774,967 + 24,707,243 — 57718918
6. What did the three little pigs become when they grew up? (863 × 974) + 5,064,356 — 5904918

**Practice Supplement,** page 37

Name ______ To follow text page 95

### Multiplying by a 3-Digit Factor

Multiply.

1. 643 × 556 — Partial products: 3858, 32150, 321500 — 357,508
2. 824 × 538 — Partial products: 6592, 24720, 412000 — 443,312
3. 739 × 625 — Partial products: 3695, 14780, 443400 — 461,875
4. 433 × 836 — Partial products: 2598, 12990, 346400 — 361,988
5. 685 × 374 — Partial products: 2740, 47950, 205500 — 256,190
6. 985 × 706 — Partial products: 5910, 689500 — 695,410
7. 308 × 475 — Partial products: 1540, 21560, 123200 — 146,300
8. 761 × 233 — Partial products: 2283, 22830, 152200 — 177,313
9. 708 × 473 — Partial products: 2124, 49560, 283200 — 334,884
10. 369 × 319 — Partial products: 3321, 3690, 110700 — 117,711
11. 289 × 476 — Partial products: 1734, 20230, 115600 — 137,564
12. 179 × 385 — Partial products: 895, 14320, 53700 — 68,915
13. 8,261 × 385 — Partial products: 41305, 660880, 2478300 — 3,180,485
14. 4,006 × 159 — Partial products: 36054, 200300, 400600 — 636,954
15. 3,894 × 207 — Partial products: 27258, 778800 — 806,058
16. 6,555 × 873 — Partial products: 19665, 458850, 5244000 — 5,722,515
17. 7,492 × 307 — Partial products: 52444, 2247600 — 2,300,044
18. 5,050 × 515 — Partial products: 25250, 50500, 2525000 — 2,600,750
19. 2,681 × 794 — Partial products: 10724, 241290, 1876700 — 2,128,714
20. 9,148 × 109 — Partial products: 82332, 914800 — 997,132

**Quick Review** Students tell whether each equation is true. For each equation that is not true, students change some element to make it true.

$2 \times 8 = 8 \times 2$ T

$2 + 6 = 6 \times 2$ F

$3 + 3 + 2 = 3 + 2 + 3$ T

$2 \times 10 \times 5 = 5 \times 2 \times 10$ T

**Lesson Focus** To practice finding products involving 1-, 2-, and 3-digit factors; to use a calculator and estimation to find products

**Suggested Materials** Spinner or slips of paper labeled 0 through 9

## Ideas for Getting Started

Have students make a grid as shown below and play "Greatest Product" or "Smallest Product" described in Ideas for Getting Started, page 94.

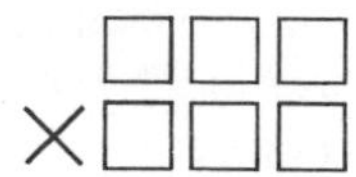

## Using Page 96

**Lesson Development** Write a problem such as $43 \times 27 \times 345$ on the chalkboard. Ask for volunteers to work through the problem and find the product. Allow the student to choose which two numbers to multiply first. For example, you could find $42 \times 27$ and multiply the result by 345. Or, the student could multiply 345 by 27 and then multiply the result by 43. As you discuss this, ask students for a third possibility for finding the product. ($345 \times 43$; the result times 27)

Review any areas of difficulty students might have in multiplying by 1-digit, 2-digit or 3-digit numbers before assigning these exercises.

**Exercises 1–24** Observe students' work and give help with any difficulties involving zero, placement of the partial products, or numbers carried over after a trade. On any of the exercises on this page you may wish to have students use a calculator to check their answers.

**Exercises 25–33** Note that these exercises involve finding the product of 3 or 4 factors. Caution students to copy the problems correctly. Encourage them to use lined paper if necessary.

**Exercise 34** Since $37 \times 91 \times 3 = 10{,}101$, the student's age multiplied by this product will result in a product in which the student's age repeats 3 times. For example, if the age is 12, the resulting answer would be 121,212.

**Exercises 35–38** For these more challenging exercises, write the instruction boxes shown on page 84 on the chalkboard and help students to continue the multiplying process. Note that calculators can be used to check exercises 35 and 36; however, many calculators have a read-out display of only 8 digits and cannot be used to check the 9-digit products in exercises 37 and 38.

## Multiplying: Practice

Find the products.

| | | |
|---|---|---|
| 1. 96 × 4 = 384 | 2. 347 × 8 = 2,776 | 3. 609 × 6 = 3,654 |
| 4. 1,735 × 5 = 8,675 | 5. 38,964 × 7 = 272,748 | 6. 174 × 80 = 13,920 |
| 7. 78 × 49 = 3,822 | 8. 36 × 27 = 972 | 9. 503 × 26 = 13,078 |
| 10. 479 × 87 = 41,673 | 11. 560 × 74 = 41,440 | 12. 906 × 80 = 72,480 |
| 13. 700 × 59 = 41,300 | 14. 1,364 × 28 = 38,192 | 15. 5,789 × 54 = 312,606 |
| 16. 627 × 123 = 77,121 | 17. 484 × 251 = 121,484 | 18. 645 × 230 = 148,350 |
| 19. 729 × 407 = 296,703 | 20. 868 × 474 = 411,432 | 21. 979 × 777 = 760,683 |
| 22. 806 × 485 = 390,910 | 23. 1,364 × 274 = 373,736 | 24. 3,547 × 676 = 2,397,772 |

25. $6 \times 8 \times 9$ 432
26. $7 \times 7 \times 7$ 343
27. $5 \times 4 \times 8 \times 6$ 960
28. $24 \times 61 \times 13$ 19,032
29. $56 \times 21 \times 43$ 50,568
30. $79 \times 46 \times 58$ 210,772
31. $9 \times 6 \times 8 \times 674$ 291,168
32. $27 \times 3 \times 826$ 66,906
33. $56 \times 57 \times 428$ 1,366,176
34. Find this product: (your age) $\times 37 \times 91 \times 3$
Try this using a different age. Digits in "age" repeat 3 times.

★ Try finding these larger products.

| | | | |
|---|---|---|---|
| 35. 5,738 × 4,659 = 26,733,342 | 36. 2,084 × 8,136 = 16,955,424 | 37. 64,968 × 4,387 = 285,014,616 | 38. 89,477 × 5,638 = 504,471,326 |

96

## Follow Up

### Reteaching

Use the exercises below to determine any difficulties students may be having with the concepts and skills in this chapter. If possible, let students use calculators to check their answers.

| | |
|---|---|
| 1. 654 × 7 = 4,578 | 2. 1,727 × 32 = 55,264 |
| 3. 926 × 43 = 39,818 | 4. 1,405 × 28 = 39,340 |
| 5. 800 × 57 = 45,600 | 6. 2,006 × 18 = 36,108 |

### Enrichment

Write the following problems on the chalkboard. Have students check their answers by division—product divided by factor equals factor.

| | | |
|---|---|---|
| 64 × 3 = 192 | 234 × 7 = 1,638 | 4,816 × 6 = 28,896 |
| 58 × 24 = 1,392 | 243 × 57 = 13,851 | 82 × 95 = 7,790 |
| 246 × 370 = 91,020 | 619 × 237 = 146,703 | 348 × 267 = 92,916 |

| Assignment Guide | Minimum | Average | Extended |
|---|---|---|---|
| page 96 | 1–18, 25–30, 34 | 1–34 | 1–38 |
| page 97 | 1–13, 17–18 | 1–20 | 6–20, TM |

## Calculator-Estimation Exercises

Estimate the product by rounding to the nearest hundred. Use a calculator to find the actual product and how much it differs from your estimate.

1. 587 × 216 = 126,792
2. 394 × 879 = 346,326
3. 506 × 729 = 368,874
4. 850 × 423 = 359,550
5. 742 × 653 = 484,526
6. 883 × 224 = 197,792
7. 426 × 787 = 335,262
8. 609 × 350 = 213,150
9. 979 × 236 = 231,044
10. 765 × 389 = 297,585

Choose a factor from each list to complete the multiplication problems so that they have the given products. Use as few multiplications as possible.

| Factor A | Factor B |
|---|---|
| 198 | 356 |
| 845 | 297 |
| 737 | 679 |
| 509 | 865 |
| 286 | 548 |
| 424 | 617 |

11. Factor A × Factor B = 151,173 (509 × 297)
12. Factor A × Factor B = 300,820 (845 × 356)
13. Factor A × Factor B = 122,166 (198 × 617)
14. Factor A × Factor B = 287,896 (424 × 679)
15. Factor A × Factor B = 637,505 (737 × 865)
16. Factor A × Factor B = 156,728 (286 × 548)

Use estimation and a calculator to find which three of the four factors given can be used to give the product. Use as few multiplications as possible.

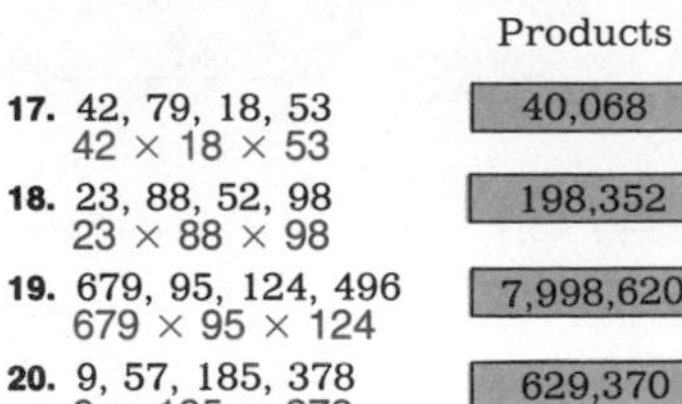

| | Products |
|---|---|
| 17. 42, 79, 18, 53 (42 × 18 × 53) | 40,068 |
| 18. 23, 88, 52, 98 (23 × 88 × 98) | 198,352 |
| 19. 679, 95, 124, 496 (679 × 95 × 124) | 7,998,620 |
| 20. 9, 57, 185, 378 (9 × 185 × 378) | 629,370 |

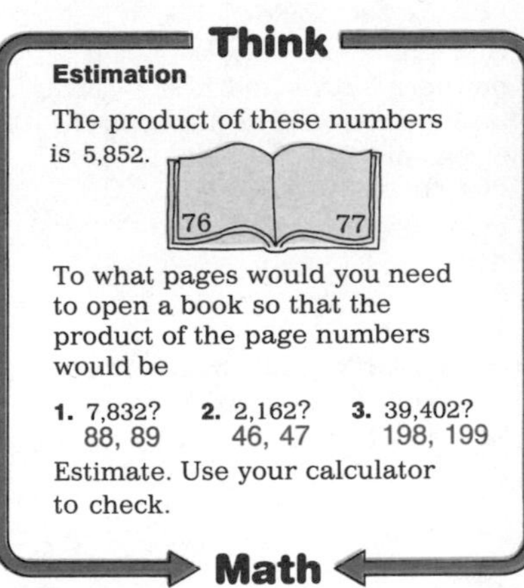

**Think Math**

**Estimation**

The product of these numbers is 5,852.



To what pages would you need to open a book so that the product of the page numbers would be

1. 7,832? (88, 89)
2. 2,162? (46, 47)
3. 39,402? (198, 199)

Estimate. Use your calculator to check.



## Using Page 97

**Lesson Development** Discuss the directions for each part of these estimation exercises and work an example of each type. As you work example 1 ask: "What is 587 rounded to the nearest hundred?" (600) "What is 216 rounded to the nearest hundred?" (200) "What is the estimated product?" (600 × 200 or 120,000) "Do you think this product would be more or less than the actual product?" Have students use the calculator to find the exact answer and determine how much it differs from the estimate.

In the next group of exercises, work exercise 11 as an example. "What factors from the table do you think would produce a product 151,173?" Remind students to use as few actual multiplications as possible. In table A possibilities are 509, 286; in table B, 297, 548. If a hint is needed, suggest that students look for factors that produce a product ending in 3.

In working exercise 17, ask students to round the numbers to the nearest ten. "What is the estimated product of 42, 79, and 18?" (40 × 80 × 20 or 64,000) "Is this product too large or too small?" (too large) "How could you reduce its size?" (Substitute 53 for 79.) "What is this estimated product?" (40 × 20 × 50 or 40,000)

**Think Math** Encourage students to use estimation and a guess-and-check strategy with as few calculations as possible. For exercise 1, for example, students might think, 80 × 80 is 6,400—too small. 90 × 90 is 8,100—too large. It is between 80 and 90." Then suggest that they determine whether it is closer to 80 or 90. Encourage students to use last digits to help them find the page numbers.

## Ideas That Work

### Calculator Activity

Have students play "Estimation Path." Players take turns choosing any two of these numbers.

11 35 56 78 91
23 44 67 89

Players multiply the chosen numbers with a calculator, find the answer on the gameboard, and mark the answer with a counter. The goal is to get a path of answers across the gameboard.

**Game Board**

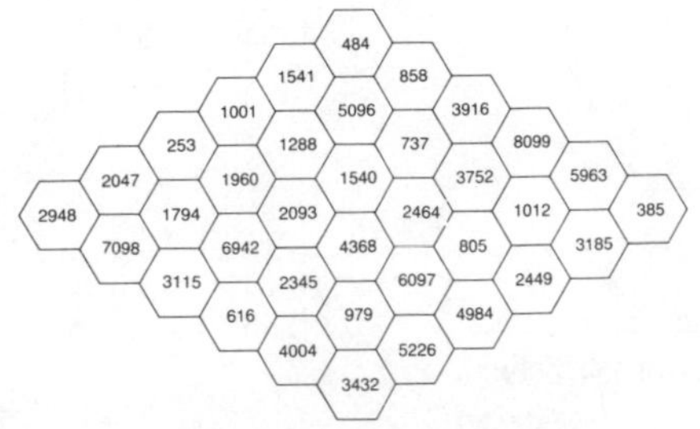



**Practice Supplement**, page 38

Name ____________ To follow text page 96

**Multiplying: Practice**

Find the products.

1. 248 × 3 = 744
2. 706 × 9 = 6,354
3. 5,230 × 4 = 20,920
4. 2,527 × 7 = 17,089
5. 27 × 68: 216; 1620; 1,836
6. 43 × 81: 43; 3440; 3,483
7. 77 × 63: 231; 4620; 4,851
8. 56 × 34: 224; 1680; 1,904
9. 281 × 16: 1686; 2810; 4,496
10. 756 × 24: 3024; 15120; 18,144
11. 2,546 × 93: 7638; 229140; 236,778
12. 8,621 × 48: 68968; 344840; 413,808
13. 803 × 479: 7227; 56210; 321200; 384,637
14. 640 × 384: 2560; 51200; 192000; 245,760
15. 769 × 734: 3076; 23070; 538300; 564,446
16. 4,630 × 227: 32410; 92600; 926000; 1,051,010
17. 583 × 717: 4081; 5830; 408100; 418,011
18. 392 × 408: 3136; 156800; 159,936
19. 927 × 814: 3708; 9270; 741600; 754,578
20. 2,072 × 864: 8288; 124320; 1657600; 1,790,208
21. 5 × 4 × 8 = 160
22. 9 × 3 × 2 × 5 = 270
23. 42 × 28 × 36 = 42,336
24. 51 × 7 × 308 = 109,956

# Applications

**Quick Review** As an oral drill, students give the standard numbers for the expanded numbers below.

300 + 2 **302** 400 + 6 + 50 **456** 1,000 + 60 + 9 **1,069** 40 + 8 **48**
40 + 200 **240** 5,000 + 800 + 90 + 2 **5,892** 600 + 2,000 **2,600**

**Lesson Focus** To use data from a graph to solve word problems; to practice solving word problems

**Suggested Materials** Stopwatch

## Ideas for Getting Started

Ask for a volunteer to show students how to count the pulse rate using the wrist, the temple, or the neck. Have one student time while the volunteer counts his or her pulse rate. Suggest that students work in small groups to make and solve word problems using the pulse information collected.

## Using Page 98

**Lesson Development** Read and discuss the bar graph at the top of the page. Be sure students understand the labeling on the graph. Then have students look at the line graph. "What information does this graph give us?" (pulse rates for children) "What does the horizontal scale tell?" (the age of the children) "What does the vertical scale tell?" (the pulse rate) Be sure students understand how to use this graph to find the needed information.

**Exercise 6** Note that this problem can be solved by subtracting the newborn baby's heart rate from a 6-year-old's heart rate and multiplying by 15, or by finding the newborn baby's heart rate for a 15-minute period and subtracting it from a 6-year-old's heart rate for a 15-minute period.

**Data Hunt** If a clock with a second hand is available, students could watch the second hand as they count their pulse. If necessary, ask students to count the pulse while you time a one-minute period with the stop watch.

**Try This** A possible strategy, Guess and Check, was taught on page 48.

**Discussion** "What do we want to find out about Joe's pulse rate?" (his pulse rate before exercise and after exrcise) "What data are we given in the problem?" (The difference between the two pulse rates is 47; the sum of the rates is 183.) Point out that this is a problem where we cannot compute the numbers directly to find the answer. "What strategy might we use?" (We could guess some pulse rates and check to see how close our guess is.) "Suppose we guess the rate 50 before exercise, what would be the rate after exercise?" (97) "What is the sum of these two rates?" (147) "Was that guess too large or too small?" (too small) Have students suggest another number to try.

**Solution** Joe's pulse rate before exercise is 68; after exercise it is 115. 68 + 115 = 183.

## Problem Solving: Using Data from a Graph

**A Look at Pulse Rates**

Solve.

1. A sprinter in excellent health might have a pulse rate of 58 beats per minute. How much less is this than the rate for the average man? 16 beats less
2. What is the average pulse rate per **hour** for girls? 5,100 beats per hour
3. A woman's pulse rate after jogging was 46 beats per minute greater than before jogging. What would that rate be for the average woman? 123 beats per minute
4. The pulse rate for a normal mouse is about 6 times the rate for a boy. What is the mouse's pulse rate? 492 beats per minute
5. By how much does a child's pulse rate decrease from birth to age 10? 48 beats per minute
6. How many more times does a newborn baby's heart beat during a 15-minute period than does a 6 year-old child's heart? 600 times
7. Find how many times the average man's heart beats in a year (365 days). 38,894,400
8. **DATA HUNT** How many times does your heart beat during a 24-hour day? (Count for 1 minute, then calculate.) Answers will vary.

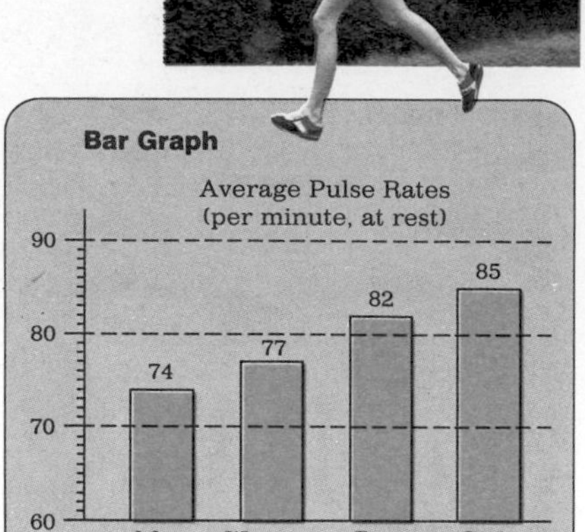


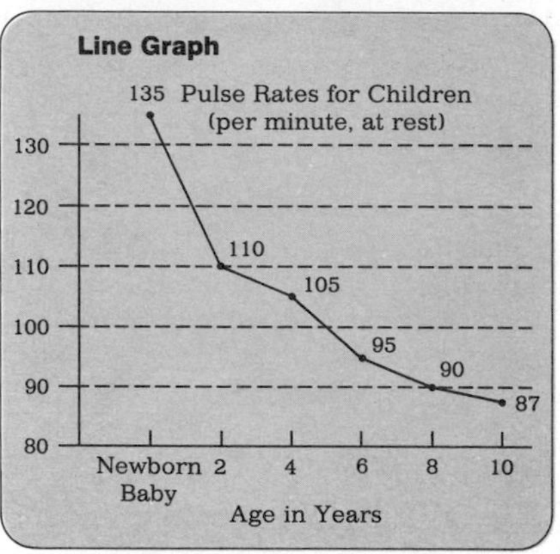


9. **Try This** The difference between Joe's pulse rate before exercise and his rate after exercise is 47. The sum of the two rates is 183. What are the two rates? 68, 115

98

## Follow Up

**Reteaching**

Ask students to look at the graph below. Then help them create problems from the given data. Elicit from students how they can use the 5-Point Checklist to help them solve the problems.

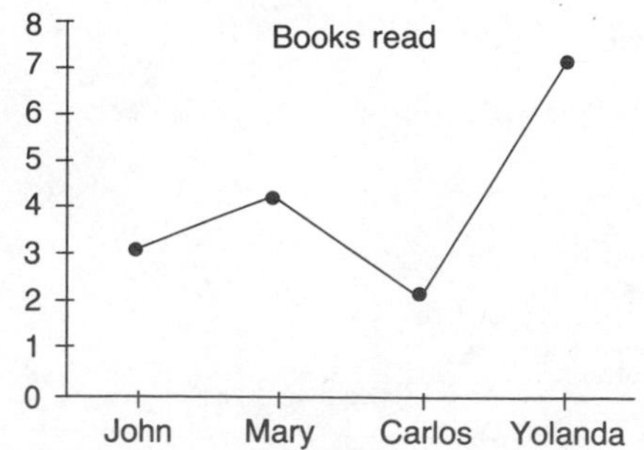


**Enrichment**

Have students find graphs in the newspaper or magazines. Let them cut out and glue the graphs to their papers. Students then write questions that pertain to the graphs and answer them. Students might enjoy making their own graphs rather than finding them in newspapers or magazines. The papers can be exchanged by classmates for solution.

| Assignment Guide | | | |
|---|---|---|---|
| | Minimum | Average | Extended |
| page 98 | 1–6 | 1–7 | 1–9 |
| page 99 | 1–6 | 1–7 | 1–8 |

## Problem Solving: Practice

**Human Body Facts**

Solve.

1. An adult usually has 8 incisor teeth, 4 canines, 8 premolars, and 12 molars. How many teeth does an adult have? 32
2. A person's total body weight is about 6 times the weight of the person's skin. If a person weighs 54 kg, about how much does the person's skin weigh? 9 kg
3. A baby is born with about 350 bones. As the baby grows, some of the bones grow together to form larger bones. An adult has 206 bones. How many more bones does a baby have than an adult? 144
4. Every extra kilogram of fat a person carries requires about 708 more kilometers of capillaries. If someone is 4 kg overweight, how many extra kilometers of capillaries are required? 2,832 km
5. The eyes of an average person blink 25 times per minute. How many blinks is this per day? per year? 36,000; 13,140,000
6. A person may take 25 breaths per minute while working and 18 breaths per minute while resting. At this rate, how many more breaths per hour are taken while working than while resting? 420 breaths per hour
7. A person's heart pumps about 5 L of blood every minute. How many liters is this per day? 7,200
8. **Try This** A person's hair grows about 15 cm each year. A child's hair was 31 cm long on her fourth birthday. She cut off 5 cm of hair on her fifth birthday and 7 cm on her seventh birthday. How long was her hair on her ninth birthday? 94 cm

## Using Page 99

**Lesson Development** Tell students that these problems involve a variety of operations and that some are multiple-step problems. Remind them that the 5-Point Checklist helps them think about the question, the data, developing a plan, and checking the answer to see that it makes sense.

**Exercises 1–7** Caution students to read the problems carefully, and remind them of the situations in which we use division. Note that exercise 5 requires that students supply the number of minutes in an hour, the number of hours in a day, and the number of days in a year. Problem 6 can be solved by subtracting 18 from 25 and multiplying by 60, or by multiplying both 25 and 18 by 60 and finding the difference. Ask students to decide which of these methods would be simpler.

**Try This** A possible strategy, Choose the Operations, was taught on page 16.

**Discussion** "What do we want to find out about the child's hair?" (How long was her hair on her ninth birthday?) "What data is given in the problem?" (hair grows about 15 cm a year, length of hair on fourth birthday, amount of hair cut off) "If the child had had no hair cut off, how would you find the length of her hair on her ninth birthday?" ($5 \times 15 + 31 = 106$.) "How can you find the length of her hair?" Subtract the amount cut off from the total length.

**Solution** The child's hair was 94 cm long on her ninth birthday. $106 - (5 + 7) = 94$

**Extension** Suppose the child continued the pattern by cutting off 9 cm on her ninth birthday, 11 cm on her eleventh birthday, and so on. How long would her hair be on her thirteenth birthday after she cut off the expected amount? (122 cm)

## Ideas That Work

### Chalk It Up

Write the following problems on the chalkboard and have pairs of students team up to find estimates and the actual products.

1. $8 \times 978$ 8000 / 7824
2. $4 \times 896$ 3600 / 3584
3. $3 \times 183$ 600 / 549
4. $4 \times 503$ 2000 / 2012
5. $7 \times 575$ 4200 / 4025
6. $8 \times 913$ 7200 / 7304
7. $2 \times 893$ 1800 / 1786
8. $241 \times 7$ 1400 / 1687
9. $542 \times 6$ 3000 / 3252
10. $649 \times 7$ 4200 / 4543
11. $517 \times 7$ 3500 / 3619
12. $133 \times 9$ 900 / 1197
13. $658 \times 7$ 4900 / 4606
14. $921 \times 4$ 3600 / 3684
15. $21 \times 86$ 1800 / 1806
16. $34 \times 18$ 600 / 612
17. $58 \times 42$ 2400 / 2436
18. $46 \times 74$ 3500 / 3404

**Practice Supplement,** page 39

Name ______________________ To follow text page 99

**Problem Solving: Practice**

Solve.

1. Jan's little brother is 64 cm tall. Her dad is 3 times as tall. How tall is Jan's dad? **192 cm**
2. It is 648 km from San Francisco to Los Angeles. The distance from Chicago to Seattle is almost 5 times as far. About what is the distance from Chicago to Seattle? **3,240 km**
3. A baby rhinoceros has a mass of 88 kg. An automobile has a mass 21 times as much. What is the mass of an automobile? **1,848 kg**
4. John just began collecting rocks and now has 64. Bill has 22 times as many. How many rocks does Bill have? **1,408**
5. On a trip Mike's father drove 88 km/h. How far did he drive in 48 hours? **4,224 km**
6. It is 1,289 km from St. Louis to Houston. The distance from Los Angeles to Boston is almost 4 times as far. About what is the distance from Los Angeles to Boston? **5,156 km**
7. Mary collects stamps. Each page of her album holds 34 stamps. If she has 96 pages filled, how many stamps does she have? **3,264**
8. An airplane flies 909 km/h. How many kilometers does it fly in 23 hours? **20,907 km**
9. If there were 365 days in each year, how many days would there be in 73 years? **26,645**
10. In a football stadium there are 78 rows of seats and 646 seats in each row. How many seats are in the stadium? **50,388**

**Lesson Focus** To make a table as a strategy for solving nonroutine word problems.

## Ideas for Getting Started

Tell students that one fifth-grade class has music 3 out of 5 days each week and art the other days. "Can you complete a table to show this information?" Write the following table on the chalkboard.

| Music | 3 | | | | | | |
|---|---|---|---|---|---|---|---|
| Art | | | | | | | |
| Total | 5 | | | | | | |

"What shall we put in the column beside the word "art"?" (2) "If we wanted to consider a total of 10 days, what numbers would we write in the table?" Help students complete eight columns of the table. Then ask other questions using data from the table.

## Using Page 100

**Motivational Problem** Read the Try This problem at the top of the page. "What do we want to find out about the paper deliveries?" (the number of papers each carrier delivers) "What data do we need in order to answer the question?" (40 papers; Julie delivers 2 out of 5; Ben, the others) "If Julie delivers 2 out of 5 papers, how many of the 5 does Ben deliver?" (3) Point out that this is a problem that may not be solved easily with the operations. Students might suggest the use of a table.

**Lesson Development** Direct students' attention to the first paragraph where Make a Table is named. If you have a problem-solving bulletin board, add Make a Table. Work through the example on the page, showing how this strategy is used to solve the Try This problem. As you focus on the table, point out that we want to look at the column of the table in which the total is 40. We can see that Julie has delivered 16 papers. "How many papers has Ben delivered?" (24)

Have students read the complete answer to the problem and then reread the original problem to see if the answer makes sense. As you discuss the solutions, be sure students understand how to use a table to solve the problems.

*These special lessons introduce strategies for solving word problems. The strategies are then practiced in Try This problems in Problem Solving lessons throughout the book.*

QUESTION
DATA
PLAN
ANSWER
CHECK

## Problem Solving: Make a Table

To solve a problem like this it sometimes helps to put the data in a table. This problem solving strategy is called

**Make a Table**

**Try This** Julie delivers 2 out of every 5 papers on a paper route. Her older brother, Ben, delivers the others. There are 40 customers on the route. How many papers does each carrier deliver?

I'll use the data in the problem and make a table.
I'll complete as much of the table as needed to solve the problem.

| Julie | 2 | | | | | | | |
|---|---|---|---|---|---|---|---|---|
| Ben | | | | | | | | |
| Total | 5 | | | | | | | |

Label ↑ carefully. ↑ Data from the problem

Answers to the problem ↓

| Julie | 2 | 4 | 6 | 8 | 10 | 12 | 14 | 16 |
|---|---|---|---|---|---|---|---|---|
| Ben | | | | | | | | 24 |
| Total | 5 | 10 | 15 | 20 | 25 | 30 | 35 | 40 |

Data from the problem ↑

Julie delivers 16 papers and Ben delivers 24.

Solve.

1. One out of evey 3 seats on a small bus is empty. If 14 passengers are on the bus, how many empty seats are there? 7

2. The body of a tropical fish is twice as long as its tail. The total length of the fish is 24 cm. How long is the fish's tail? 8 cm

100

## Strategy Test Item

**Optional Problem** If you wish to assess students' ability to apply the strategy called Make a Table introduced in this chapter, ask them to solve the problem below.

> The cabin attendant told the pilot that 2 out of every 3 seats on a plane were filled. There were 18 passengers on the plane. How many seats were there on the airplane?

**Solution:** There were 27 seats on the airplane and 9 were empty.

| Seats filled | 2 | 4 | 6 | 8 | 10 | 12 | 14 | 16 | 18 |
|---|---|---|---|---|---|---|---|---|---|
| Seats empty | | | | | | | | | 9 |
| Total seats | 3 | 6 | 9 | 12 | 15 | 18 | 21 | 24 | 27 |

## Chapter Review-Test

Multiply.

1. 8 × 600 4,800
2. 40 × 9 360
3. 6,000 × 5 30,000
4. 6 × 100 600
5. 20 × 80 1,600
6. 10 × 700 7,000
7. 600 × 900 540,000
8. 8,000 × 50 400,000

Estimate the products. Round 2-digit numbers to the nearest ten and 3-digit numbers to the nearest hundred.

9. 4 × 389 1,600
10. 61 × 38 2,400
11. 74 × 652 49,000
12. 813 × 496 400,000

Multiply.

13. 426 × 5 = 2,130
14. 5,943 × 6 = 35,658
15. 63,078 × 9 = 567,702
16. 83 × 20 = 1,660
17. 564 × 40 = 22,560
18. 396 × 500 = 198,000
19. 94 × 36 = 3,384
20. 97 × 48 = 4,656
21. 368 × 24 = 8,832
22. 6,439 × 67 = 431,413

Multiply and give the number in standard form.

23. $2^3$ 8
24. $3^2$ 9
25. $5^4$ 625
26. $10^3$ 1,000
27. $7^5$ 16,807
28. $10^6$ 1,000,000

Write using exponents.

29. 2 × 2 × 2 × 2 × 2 × 2 $2^6$
30. 10,000 $10^4$
31. 10,000,000 $10^7$

Multiply.

32. 508 × 345 = 175,260
33. 295 × 406 = 119,770
34. 386 × 124 = 47,864
35. 809 × 341 = 275,869
36. 4,102 × 506 = 2,075,612

Solve.

37. A spacecraft in orbit around the earth might travel 28,163 km/h. How far would it travel in 8 hours? 225,304 km

38. Dale's pulse rate at rest is 76 beats per minute. During fast jogging, his rate is 123 beats per minute. How many more times does Dale's heart beat during a 25-minute jog than during 25 minutes at rest? 1,175 times

101

## Using Page 101

The exercises in the Chapter Review/Test emphasize the major concepts and skills presented in this chapter. These exercises may be used as a review assignment or as a test, depending upon your needs.

**Item Analysis** The table below correlates the Chapter Review/Test items with objectives and with the student text pages on which the concepts or skills were taught. Note that items 23–31 are derived from a lesson for which no minimum assignment was suggested in the Assignment Guide. Only those students who were assigned this lesson should be expected to complete the corresponding Chapter Review/Test items.

| Items | Objectives | Related text pages |
|---|---|---|
| 1–21 | 4.1 | 80–82 |
| 13–22 | 4.2 | 84–88 |
| 23–31 | 4.3 | 92–93 |
| 32–36 | 4.4 | 94–97 |
| 37–38 | 4.5 | 83, 90–91, 98–99 |

## Assessment Options

If you use the Chapter Review/Test as a review assignment, you may wish to use the multiple-choice test or the free-response test to evaluate mastery of the chapter objectives. The items on these tests have a one-to-one correspondence in terms of content and level of difficulty. A correlation of test items to objectives and student text pages is provided in the Management Guide for Chapter 4. Note that items 26–31 are derived from a lesson from which no minimum assignment was suggested in the Assignment Guide.

**Multiple-Choice Test,** TRB pages 10–12

**Free-Response Test,** TRB pages 55–56

## TRB Options

The following blackline masters are available for use with this chapter. If you have not already assigned these materials, you may wish to use them to close the chapter.

**Recreation,** TRB page 154.

**Consumer Applications,** TRB page 172.

**Calculator Technology,** TRB page 190.

**Computer Technology,** TRB pages 205–207.

**Reading Math,** TRB page 222.

**Family Involvement,** TRB pages 243–244.

## Using Page 102

The exercises on this page are intended for those students who experienced difficulty with the Chapter Review/Test on page 101. Should students require reteaching of these key concepts and skills, please refer to the teaching notes below. Otherwise, the Another Look exercises can be assigned as independent work with students using the accompanying sample problems and hints as guides.

**Exercises 1–12** This skill was originally taught on pages 80–81. Focus students' attention on the first review box at the top of the page. Work through the examples in sequence and emphasize that we can use basic facts to find the special products. Remind students about the rules for annexing the same number of zeros in the answer as there are in the factors. If necessary, give additional practice with problems such as 5 × 40, 8 × 500, and 6 × 5,000 in which extra zeros are involved.

**Exercises 13–22** This skill was originally taught on page 82. Help students work through the first two examples. Point out that the think clouds tell that 2-digit numbers are rounded to the nearest ten and 3-digit number are rounded to the nearest hundred. Then call students' attention to the third example where they must round both a 2-digit and a 3-digit number.

**Exercises 23–31** This skill was originally taught on pages 84–89, and 94–95. Direct students' attention to the third review box. Review the idea that to multiply by a 1-digit number we multiply first the ones, then the tens, and then the hundreds. Be sure students understand how to make the appropriate trades, how to deal with the number produced by the trade, and where to write the digits in the partial products.

### Another Look

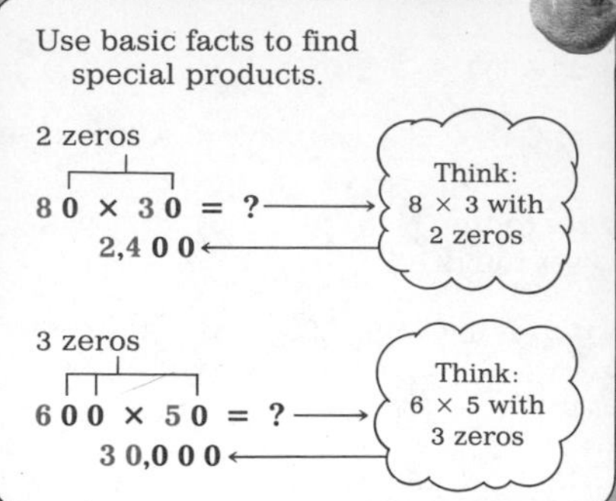
Use basic facts to find special products.
2 zeros
80 × 30 = ?
2,400
Think: 8 × 3 with 2 zeros
3 zeros
600 × 50 = ?
30,000
Think: 6 × 5 with 3 zeros

**Multiply.**

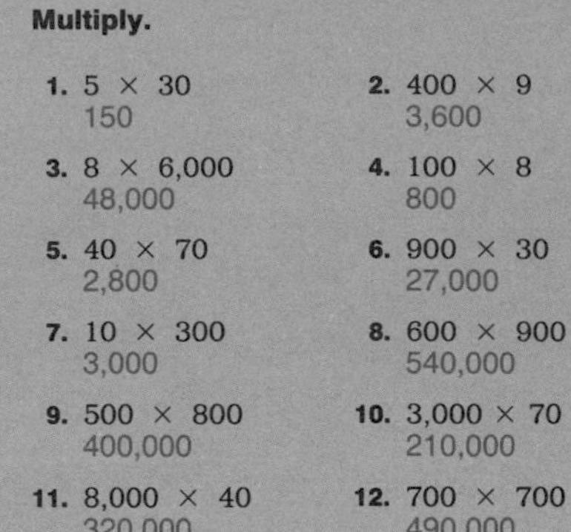

| | | | |
|---|---|---|---|
| **1.** 5 × 30 | 150 | **2.** 400 × 9 | 3,600 |
| **3.** 8 × 6,000 | 48,000 | **4.** 100 × 8 | 800 |
| **5.** 40 × 70 | 2,800 | **6.** 900 × 30 | 27,000 |
| **7.** 10 × 300 | 3,000 | **8.** 600 × 900 | 540,000 |
| **9.** 500 × 800 | 400,000 | **10.** 3,000 × 70 | 210,000 |
| **11.** 8,000 × 40 | 320,000 | **12.** 700 × 700 | 490,000 |

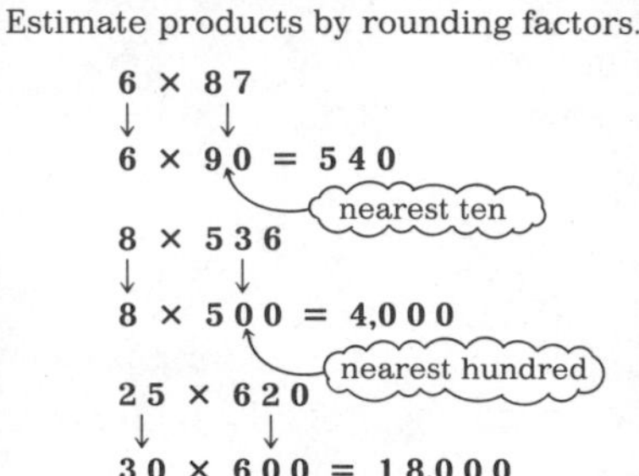
Estimate products by rounding factors.
6 × 87
6 × 90 = 540
nearest ten
8 × 536
8 × 500 = 4,000
nearest hundred
25 × 620
30 × 600 = 18,000

**Estimate the product by rounding to the nearest ten or the nearest hundred.**

| | | | |
|---|---|---|---|
| **13.** 4 × 68 | 280 | **14.** 37 × 42 | 1,600 |
| **15.** 6 × 382 | 2,400 | **16.** 93 × 8 | 720 |
| **17.** 56 × 72 | 4,200 | **18.** 34 × 875 | 27,000 |
| **19.** 8 × 379 | 3,200 | **20.** 68 × 23 | 1,400 |
| **21.** 41 × 526 | 20,000 | **22.** 619 × 88 | 54,000 |

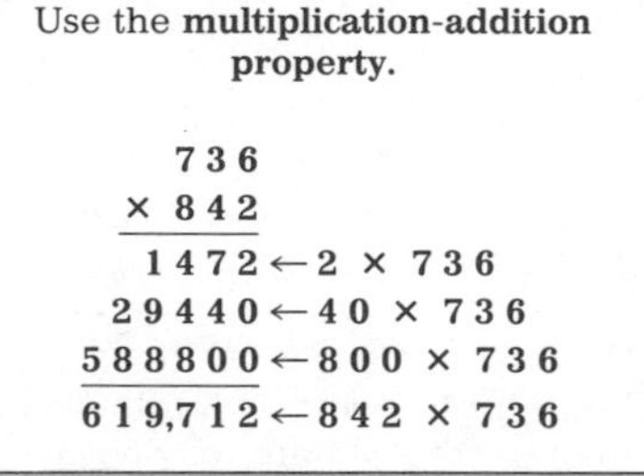
Use the multiplication-addition property.
736
× 842
1472 ← 2 × 736
29440 ← 40 × 736
588800 ← 800 × 736
619,712 ← 842 × 736

**Find the products.**

| | | |
|---|---|---|
| **23** 176 × 8 = 1,408 | **24.** 4,365 × 9 = 39,285 | **25.** 57,384 × 6 = 344,304 |
| **26.** 73 × 28 = 2,044 | **27.** 547 × 56 = 30,632 | **28.** 3,459 × 38 = 131,442 |
| **29.** 924 × 186 = 171,864 | **30.** 708 × 567 = 401,436 | **31.** 4,836 × 941 = 4,550,676 |

102

## Just for Teachers

### Language of Math

*Algorithms*—rules for carrying out the basic arithmetic operations on paper—were developed to eliminate the need for mechanical aids to computation. The term *algorithm* was derived from the name of the ninth century Arabic mathematician al Khowarismi, the early proponent of the Hindu numeration system.

One of the earliest books written in English on the decimal system and its various operations was *The Craft of Nombrygne,* about 1300. Less than two centuries later, a book published in Treviso, Italy, recommended a method for multiplication, which proved very popular. Called *gelosia* or lattice multiplication, the method involved the use of a diagram that simplified the multiplication of multi-digit factors.

In 1617, the Scottish mathematician John Napier published the method he had devised for simplifying the operation of multiplication, *Rabdologia.* Drawing on the principle of lattice multiplication, "Napier's Bones," as the system became known, consisted of a set of rods showing in a vertical format the products of each numeral and the numbers 1 through 9. An eleventh rod was used as an index. Napier's Bones eliminated the need to draw and fill in the lattice diagram.

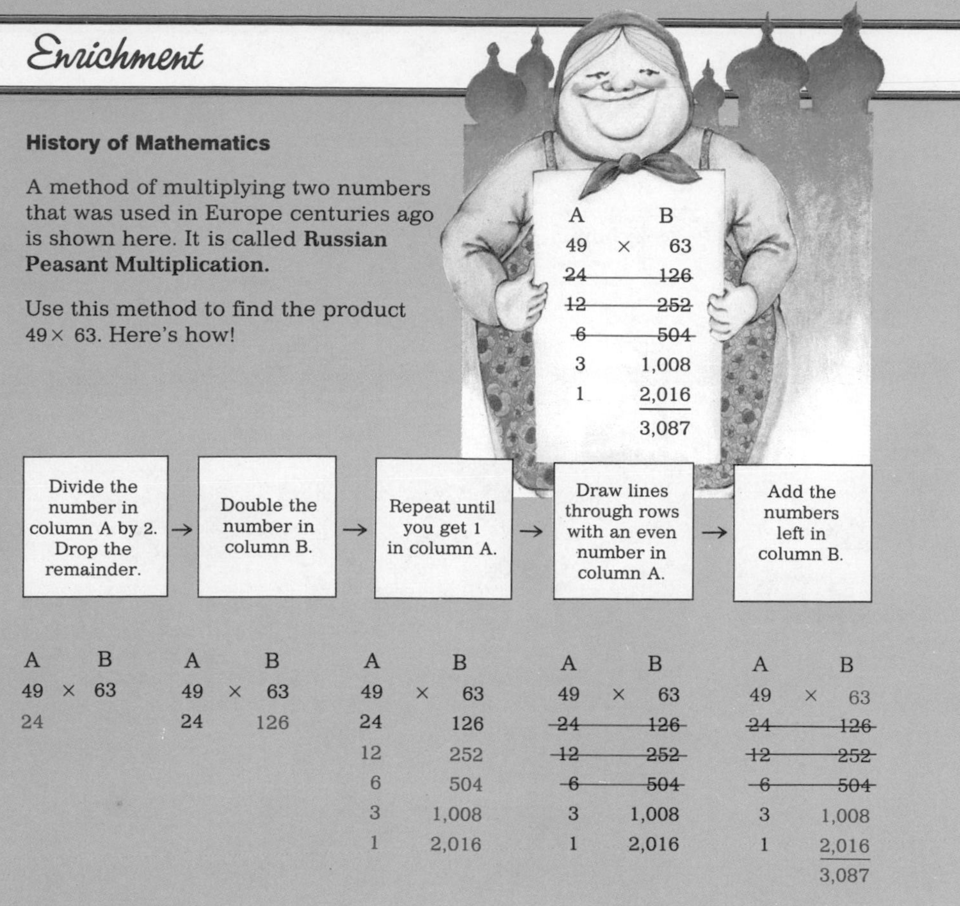

## Enrichment

**History of Mathematics**

A method of multiplying two numbers that was used in Europe centuries ago is shown here. It is called **Russian Peasant Multiplication.**

Use this method to find the product 49 × 63. Here's how!

| A | | B |
|---|---|---|
| 49 | × | 63 |
| ~~24~~ | | ~~126~~ |
| ~~12~~ | | ~~252~~ |
| ~~6~~ | | ~~504~~ |
| 3 | | 1,008 |
| 1 | | 2,016 |
| | | 3,087 |

Divide the number in column A by 2. Drop the remainder. → Double the number in column B. → Repeat until you get 1 in column A. → Draw lines through rows with an even number in column A. → Add the numbers left in column B.

| A | | B |
|---|---|---|
| 49 | × | 63 |
| 24 | | |

| A | | B |
|---|---|---|
| 49 | × | 63 |
| 24 | | 126 |

| A | | B |
|---|---|---|
| 49 | × | 63 |
| 24 | | 126 |
| 12 | | 252 |
| 6 | | 504 |
| 3 | | 1,008 |
| 1 | | 2,016 |

| A | | B |
|---|---|---|
| 49 | × | 63 |
| ~~24~~ | | ~~126~~ |
| ~~12~~ | | ~~252~~ |
| ~~6~~ | | ~~504~~ |
| 3 | | 1,008 |
| 1 | | 2,016 |

| A | | B |
|---|---|---|
| 49 | × | 63 |
| ~~24~~ | | ~~126~~ |
| ~~12~~ | | ~~252~~ |
| ~~6~~ | | ~~504~~ |
| 3 | | 1,008 |
| 1 | | 2,016 |
| | | 3,087 |

The product of 49 × 63 is 3,087.

Use Russian Peasant Multiplication to find these products. Check by multiplying the usual way.

**1.** 12 × 42 504 **2.** 23 × 35 805 **3.** 37 × 53 1,961 **4.** 43 × 71 3,053

**5.** 54 × 73 3,942 **6.** 18 × 49 882 **7.** 36 × 67 2,412 **8.** 78 × 96 7,488

**9.** 101 × 101 10,201 **10.** 365 × 42 15,330 **11.** 627 × 143 89,661 **12.** 546 × 695 379,470



To find the product of 37 × 564, for example, the rods for 3 and 7 were selected and placed side by side in that order next to the index. The products of 5 × 37, 6 × 37, and 4 × 37 were determined by reading horizontally from the index. The partial products were aligned according to correct place value and then added.

## Using Page 103

This page is intended for those students who successfully completed the Chapter Review/Test on page 101. You may wish to assign this page as independent work while you use Another Look exercises to reteach the basic concepts and skills of the chapter. Or, you may decide that all students would benefit from exposure to this Enrichment activity.

**Lesson Development** Explain that Russian Peasant Multiplication was one of the very first methods used to find the product of two numbers. Tell students that the method might be described as "halving and doubling." Then let them try to discover how the method works. "What product do we want to find?" (49 × 63) "What was the first step?" (In column A the number was divided in half, the remainder omitted; in column B the number was doubled.) "What happens in the third row?" (In column A the number was divided in half; in column B the number was doubled.) "Which rows were marked out?" (rows with an even number in column A) "How was the final product determined?" (by adding the numbers in column B not marked out) Read through the instruction boxes to be sure students understand the procedure. Encourage them to try to find out why the method works. If a hint is needed, point out that the numbers in the right-hand column are 1 × 63, 2 × 63, 4 × 63, 8 × 63, 16 × 63, 32 × 63. If the even multiples of 63 are marked out, the multiples left are 1, 16, and 32 × 63, or a total of 49 × 63.

**Lesson Focus** To use, adapt, or write simple computer programs involving INPUT statements

## Ideas for Getting Started

Have students try the following:

1. Enter the number for the month of your birth (January = 1, February = 2, and so on).
2. Multiply by 4.
3. Add 13.
4. Multiply by 25.
5. Add your age.
6. Subtract the number of days in a year (365).
7. Add 40.

"What number do you see in the answer?" (The student's birth month number and age should appear.) "What INPUT did you give?" (birth month number, age) Generate a discussion in which you emphasize that INPUT is information that a person types into the computer in response to a question.

## Using Page 104

**Lesson Development** Ask a volunteer to go to the chalkboard and follow the directions given in the flowchart as you read each step. Then discuss how the computer program instructs the computer to carry out the procedure in the flowchart. Review the use of PRINT, LET, and symbol (/), and the use of quotes. If a demonstration computer is available, type in the program and verify the RUN.

Then tell students that the word INPUT is a special command that causes the computer to show a blinking curser and a question mark as a signal for the operator to type in some data. For example, in the computer program in the middle of the page, the computer will ask: "How tall are you (in cm)?" Line 2Ø—INPUT H—signals the operator to type in data that tells the computer the value for H.

Discuss each step of the program for guessing weight, and then try it on a demonstration computer if possible. Have students answer the question at the bottom of the page and comment on the accuracy of the computer's guesses.

*Technology lessons are optional. They require no special teacher expertise.*

## *Technology*

### Giving Input to a Computer

A set of instructions for a computer is often developed first in flowchart form. Then it is typed into the computer as a computer program. A simple example is given below.

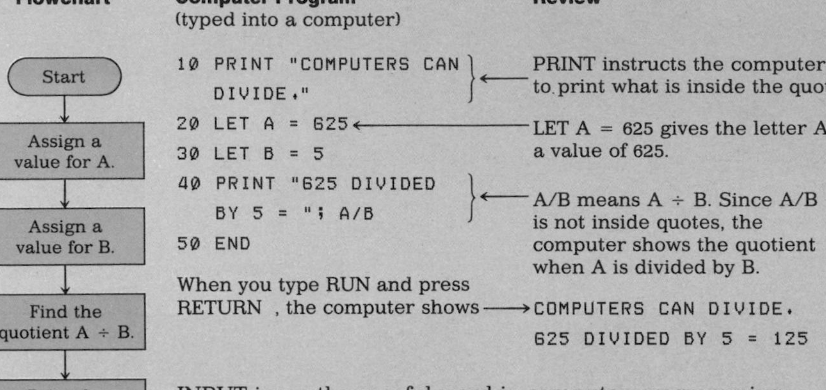
Flowchart
Start
Assign a value for A.
Assign a value for B.
Find the quotient A ÷ B.
Print the quotient statement.
Stop

**Computer Program** (typed into a computer)

```
1Ø PRINT "COMPUTERS CAN
   DIVIDE."
2Ø LET A = 625
3Ø LET B = 5
4Ø PRINT "625 DIVIDED
   BY 5 = "; A/B
5Ø END
```

**Review**

PRINT instructs the computer to print what is inside the quotes.

LET A = 625 gives the letter A a value of 625.

A/B means A ÷ B. Since A/B is not inside quotes, the computer shows the quotient when A is divided by B.

When you type RUN and press RETURN, the computer shows

```
COMPUTERS CAN DIVIDE.
625 DIVIDED BY 5 = 125
```

INPUT is another useful word in computer programming. It allows you to respond to a computer question by typing in data. Study the example below.

**Computer Program**

```
1Ø PRINT "HOW TALL ARE YOU (IN CM)?"
2Ø INPUT H
3Ø PRINT "I GUESS YOUR WEIGHT (IN KG)"
4Ø PRINT "TO BE "; (4 * H-39Ø)/5
5Ø END
```

When you type RUN and press RETURN, the computer shows

```
HOW TALL ARE YOU (IN CM)?
?
```

(This signals you to type in a number for H.)

If you type 144 and press RETURN, the computer shows

```
I GUESS YOUR WEIGHT (IN KG)
TO BE 37.2
```

In the program above, what would be the computer's final statement if you type in 150? if you type in 138? 42; 32.4

## Technology for Teachers

Computers need simple step-by-step instructions to accomplish even the most routine task. Each computer project must be broken down into small modules, and instructions or programs must be developed in a logical sequence to accomplish each module.

A flowchart is often the technique that is used to lay out complex computer applications. A systems analyst, meeting with everyone involved in planning a project, must consider every step needed to reach a specified goal. After receiving the requirements, the available data, and the desired outcomes, the analyst determines the sequence of steps that will accomplish the task. One small step or detail overlooked can affect the outcome of the project.

When satisfied with the plan, the analyst turns it over to the computer programmer, and the programmer works out the specific instructions to the computer.

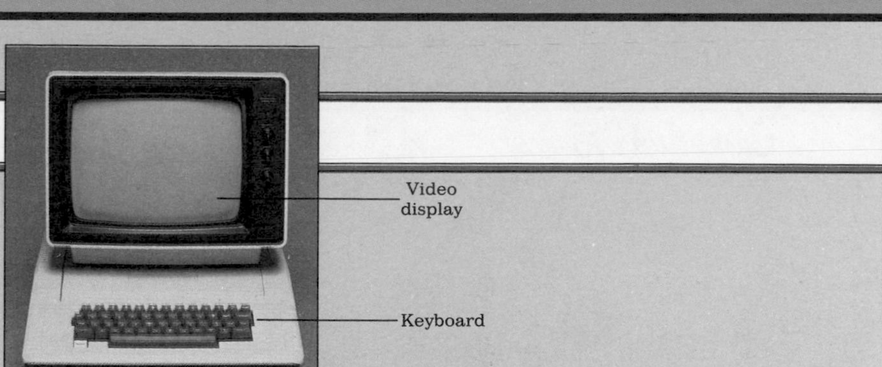


Give a RUN for each program. Choose your own INPUT numbers.
Answers will vary.

1.
```
10 PRINT "GIVE THE LENGTH OF"
20 PRINT "A SIDE OF A SQUARE."
30 INPUT S
40 PRINT "THE SQUARE'S AREA
   IS "; S * S
50 END
```

2.
```
10 PRINT "CHOOSE A NUMBER."
20 INPUT N
30 PRINT "WE SAY THAT"
40 PRINT N; " SQUARED IS ";
   N * N
50 END
```

3.
```
10 PRINT "GIVE THE LENGTH OF"
20 PRINT "THE SIDE OF A CUBE."
30 INPUT S
40 PRINT "THE CUBE'S VOLUME
   IS "; S * S * S
50 END
```

4.
```
10 PRINT "CHOOSE A NUMBER."
20 INPUT N
30 PRINT "WE SAY THAT"
40 PRINT N; " CUBED IS ";
   N * N * N
50 END
```

5.
```
10 PRINT "NUMBER OF LETTERS
   IN FIRST NAME?"
20 INPUT F
30 PRINT "NUMBER OF LETTERS
   IN LAST NAME?"
40 INPUT L
50 PRINT "YOUR LUCKY NUMBER
   IS "; F * L
60 END
```

6.
```
10 PRINT "TO THE NEAREST TENTH"
20 PRINT "HOW MANY CM LONG IS"
30 PRINT "YOUR MIDDLE FINGER?"
40 INPUT M
50 PRINT "I GUESS YOUR HEIGHT"
60 PRINT "IN CM TO BE "; 20 * M
70 END
```

7. Use INPUT to write a computer program that will find the product of any two numbers the program's user chooses.

8. Write a program that will find the area of any rectangle the program's user chooses.



## Using Page 105

**Exercises 1–6** Note that exercises 1 and 2 suggest that the area of the square is the origin of the expression "*n* squared." Exercises 3 and 4 suggest that the volume of a cube is the origin of the expression "*n* cubed." In exercise 6, let each student compare his or her actual height in centimeters with the computer's guess by finding the difference of the two heights.

**Exercises 7–8** Allow for variations in the steps students choose for these programs. Point out that more than one step can be written in a given line of the program.

Calculator and computer skills and awareness are developed as a fully-integrated strand.

On larger or more complex jobs there may be a systems designer who lays out the initial design with the systems analyst. A systems programmer then takes the plan developed by the analyst and writes the guidelines for the overall program. The programmer develops the complete set of instructions needed by the computer. When the program is nearly complete it goes to the coder, who fills in the necessary procedures and directions. A coding or data clerk then enters the instructions into the computer.

## Using Page 106

The exercises on this page provide practice for maintaining cumulative skills. The emphasis in this Cumulative Review is on place value and addition and subtraction of whole numbers (Chapter 2), place value and addition and subtraction of decimals (Chapter 3), and problem solving (Chapter 3).

**Item Analysis** The table below correlates the Cumulative Review items with objectives and with the student book pages on which the concepts or skills were taught.

| Items | Objectives | Related text pages |
|---|---|---|
| 1–3 | 2.1 | 24–29 |
| 4 | 2.3 | 30–33 |
| 5 | 2.2 | 36–43 |
| 6–9 | 3.1 | 54–59 |
| 10 | 3.2 | 60–62 |
| 11–12 | 3.3 | 64–68, 70 |
| 13–14 | 3.4 | 63, 69, 71–73 |

## *Cumulative Review*

1. What is the place value of the 4 in the number 234,601?
   A 4 hundreds (B) 4 thousands
   C 4 ten thousands D not given

2. What is the place value of the 6 in the number 826,471,395?
   A 6 ten thousands B 6 bilions
   C 6 thousands (D) not given

Which symbol (>, <, or =) goes in each ● ?

3. 36,209 ● 36,029
   A < (B) > C =

4. 417,298 ● 471,289
   (A) < B > C =

Add or subtract.

5. 6,785 + 2,619
   A 4,166
   B 8,394
   (C) 9,404
   D not given

6. 2,308 − 194
   A 2,214
   (B) 2,114
   C 1,402
   D not given

7. What is the place value of the 5 in the number 2.3651?
   A 5 hundredths (B) 5 thousandths
   C 5 tenths D not given

8. What is the place value of the 3 in the number 0.0362?
   A 3 tenths B 3 thousandths
   (C) 3 hundredths D not given

Which symbol (>, <, or =) goes in each ● ?

9. 0.38 ● 3.8
   (A) < B > C =

10. 0.72 ● 0.720
    A < B > (C) =

Add or subtract.

11. 9.02 − 5.34
    (A) 3.68
    B 4.78
    C 4.36
    D not given

12. 5.1 + 2.56 + 1.4
    A 8.07
    B 8.61
    C 8.06
    (D) not given

13. Barbara drove 378 km one week and 504 km the next week. How many kilometers did she drive in the two weeks?
    (A) 882 km B 126 km
    C 927 km D not given

14. Andy bought a record for $7.29. How much change did he receive from a $10 bill?
    A $17.29 (B) $2.71
    C $3.81 D not given

## Objectives

**5.1** Use division facts to find and estimate quotients.
**5.2** Divide by 1-digit divisors.
**5.3** Find the average of a list of numbers.
**5.4** Divide by 2- and 3-digit divisors.
**5.5** Solve word problems using the 5-Point Checklist and cumulative computational skills.

## Summary

In this chapter students use the division facts to find quotients involving multiples of 10, 100, 1,000, and so on. This skill and the rounding skill learned earlier is used to estimate quotients. The procedures for dividing by 1-digit divisors, including short division, are modeled and reviewed. Finding averages, a special application of these dividing procedures, is reviewed and extended. Students then follow a carefully developed sequence for dividing by 2-digit divisors, starting with dividing by multiples of 10 and ending with special problems involving quotients with zeros. Working with 3-digit divisors with emphasis on use of the calculator is included. Estimation, dividing money, and problem solving is integrated throughout the chapter.

## Mathematical Background

**Special Quotients and Estimation** To solve problems in which an exact answer is not required, students need to find special quotients mentally involving multiples of 10. They can find these special quotients by looking for the missing factor. If students discover a shortcut, allow them to use it. The idea behind the shortcut is expressed by the equations below. It is not advisable to attempt to explain this to most students at this time.

$$\overset{P}{3{,}200} \div \overset{F}{40} = \overset{F}{80}, \text{ since } \overset{F}{80} \times \overset{F}{40} = \overset{P}{3{,}200}$$

$$3{,}200 \div 40 \; (32 \times 100) \div (4 \times 10) \longrightarrow (32 \div 4) \times (100 \div 10) \longrightarrow 80$$

Only selected divisions can be estimated directly using basic facts. For example, if the problem above were 3,265 ÷ 39, the special quotient after rounding would be 3,300 ÷ 40. To estimate this quickly, students must recognize the basic fact 32 ÷ 4 that is closest to the quotient 33 ÷ 4.

**Division** As students review the division process for 1-digit divisors, a money model is used. If students have sufficient initial experience with this model, they can refer to it when they have difficulty remembering a particular step in the division process. At first, students are given hundreds, tens, and ones and asked to divide these equally among a given number of people. They then proceed from experiences with the model to the related algorithm. The following diagram is used to show dividing in each place.

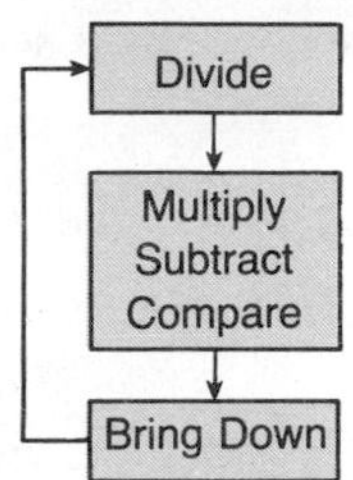


Several things should be noted about the division instruction in this chapter.

**1.** The direction, "Decide where to start," is used because in some problems such as 164 ÷ 7 students must observe that the hundreds cannot be divided. Thus the decision to start by dividing tens is an important one.

**2.** The lesson on dividing by multiples of 10, pages 120 and 121, is readiness for dividing by 2-digit divisors. Note that in dividing by a 2-digit divisor such as 432 ÷ 72 we mentally round the divisor 72 to 70 and estimate the quotient as if the divisor is a multiple of 10.

**3.** To help students avoid problems with zeros in the quotient, emphasize that "Every time you bring down a digit you must divide." Specifically, if the number of tens (or hundreds or thousands) is less than the divisor, the quotient digit in that place is always zero and must be written.

**4.** In division we can think of any division problem as a series of simpler problems with a 1-digit quotient. For a problem such as 9,752 ÷ 46, we first do a division problem with a single-digit quotient by dividing in the tens place. Finally, we do a third problem with a single-digit quotient by dividing in the ones place.

**5.** When dividing money, students can think of the number of dollars and cents as pennies and divide just as with whole numbers. Estimation can then be used to help decide how to write the quotient using dollar and cent notation.

**Problem Solving** The logo for the 5-Point checklist appears on every problem-solving page in the chapter to emphasize the key ideas from the checklist. One or more key aspects of problem solving is emphasized in each lesson. For example, on page 111 estimation is used to check if the answer is reasonable. Page 125 is a practice lesson in which students are encouraged to employ all steps of the 5-Point Checklist. On page 130 students must use data from a map to solve the problems given. Students focus on the plan on page 131 to decide what operations are needed. And, on page 132 a new strategy for solving nonroutine problems, Make an Organized List, is presented.

**Vocabulary**

| | | |
|---|---|---|
| quotient | division | |
| average | remainder | dividend |

# Teaching Tips

## Error Analysis

This chapter reviews and extends the operation of division of whole numbers. Because the division algorithm also involves addition, subtraction, and multiplication, a lack of knowledge in any of these operations will result in difficulty in carrying out the algorithm correctly. Many errors that are made reflect problems with these operations as well as a lack of conceptual knowledge of the meaning of division.

**Error Pattern 1**

```
  142      145      121      128
6)67     5)59     3)37     4)47
  6        5        3        4
  —        —        —        —
   7        9        7        7
```

**Diagnosis** The student has begun the division algorithm correctly but runs into difficulty when dividing the ones digit. At this point, the student has multiplied the ones digit times the divisor and then has written that product in the quotient. The student understands that multiplication is a part of the division algorithm but does not understand where or when to multiply.

**Remediation** Model an example problem such as 67 ÷ 6 with place-value materials. Discuss each step, pointing out what each step means in the sequence below.

a) "Can we share (divide) the tens?" If possible, do so, and record.

```
  1
6)67
  6
  —
```

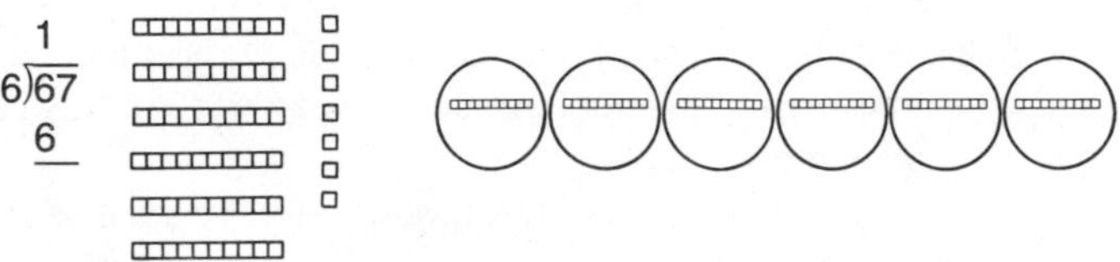

b) "Can we share (or divide) the ones?" This is shown by "bringing down" the ones. "Can seven be divided by 6?" Then do so and record.

```
  1
6)67
  6
  —
  7
```

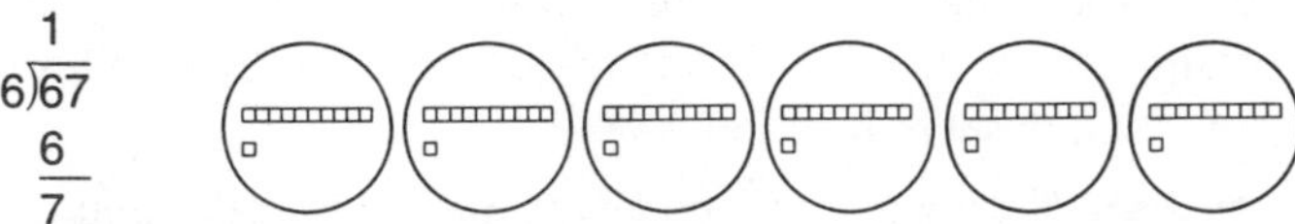

c) "Name the amount now in each collection." (1 ten, 1 one, with 1 one left over.)

d) Then use the algorithm to show the process step by step.

```
            1                          1
6)67      6)67    6 ÷ 6 = 1          6)67   Bring down
            6     1 × 6 = 6            6    the ones
            —     6 − 6 = 0            —
            0                          07

 11                          11
6)67     7 ÷ 6 = 1          6)67
  6      1 × 6 = 6            6
  —      7 − 6 = 1            —
  07                          7
   6                          6
   —                          —
   1                          1          67 ÷ 6 = 11R1
```

Work through several examples in this manner, discussing each step of the algorithm.

**Error Pattern 2**

```
  124      581      562      481
6)76     8)465    7)394    9)377
  6        40       35       36
  —        —        —        —
  16       65       44       17
  12       64       42        9
  —        —        —        —
   4        1        2        8
```

**Diagnosis** The student does not know how to complete the division algorithm and has used the remainder as a quotient digit instead of indicating a remainder.

**Remediation** Review the division algorithm with a discussion of the remainder—what the remainder represents and how a remainder is shown in the quotient. In an example such as 6)76, work through the algorithm to explain when to stop dividing: When the remaining ones are less than the divisor, the process is completed, and the "left over" ones are shown in the quotient as the remainder. Remind students that the remainder represents an amount that cannot be shared or divided. Then have students check the accuracy of the quotient by multiplying the divisor times the quotient plus the remainder. Have them use this method to evaluate the answers given in the problems shown above.

## Problem Solving

### Using Hints to Help Develop Solution Strategies

You may be able to recall a time in math class when you were working on a problem, got stuck, asked for help, and were given a hint. Often, the hint was just what was needed to get you started toward finding a solution. Sometimes, however, the hint was of absolutely no help. It may have actually been confusing since it suggested an approach different from the idea you had for solving the problem.

Giving hints is a necessary part of teaching problem solving. Because each student reacts differently to a hint, selecting appropriate hints and deciding when to use them are two of the most difficult tasks in teaching problem solving. There are no rules or signals from the students that will assure you of the right hint to use or the right time to use it. The best way to improve one's skills in selecting and using hints is through experience teaching problem solving. Following are a few guidelines to help decide when to use a hint.

- The student's work on a particular problem is based on a misconception or misunderstanding.
- The student is ignoring or overlooking important information.
- The student has thought of a good strategy but needs your help to use it effectively.
- It seems appropriate to suggest that the student give more serious thought to using one or more strategies.
- You feel that the student will become frustrated unless you give some assistance.

There are three general categories of hints: 1) hints to help students understand a problem, 2) hints to help students develop a solution strategy, and 3) hints to help students accurately carry out or evaluate a particular strategy.

In the Teaching Tips for problem solving in Chapter 3 a problem is presented with examples of discussion questions and hints to help students understand the problem. Here is the same problem with examples of hints to help students develop a solution strategy.

> Six children came to a birthday party. Each child shook hands one time with every other child. How many handshakes were exchanged?

**Discussion** "Write the names of 6 children and show with whom the first child would shake hands." Or "Draw a picture of 6 children. Show who would shake hands." Or, "If you were the first child, with how many people would you shake hands?"

Discussion questions are provided in the Teacher's Edition for each nonroutine problem; however, hints to help students accurately carry out a particular solution strategy cannot be identified prior to the lesson. As you observe and question students while they solve problems, your comments must be related to the particular way the student is solving the problem. Studying the example hints for understanding and for developing a solution strategy will help you decide on the appropriate hints as needed when you are working with the students.

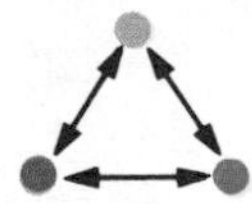

## Special Education

Long division is difficult for most students and is especially hard for those with learning difficulties. Because the process can be long and involved, there are great demands on a student's retention and sequencing abilities. Inadequate mastery of basic facts and difficulty aligning numbers during computation are also common problems that hamper success. Suggestions for handling common difficulties experienced by special students follow.

### Using a "Middle Step"

Special students may at first need some form of paper and pencil support as a middle step to success with the mental math of pages 108–109. For problems like those shown, for example, students might at first be allowed to underscore what they round to highlight the basic fact that will help determine a quotient digit. Later, as students become more confident, they will independently drop this step and carry out the calculation mentally.

| Given | Child writes |
|---|---|
| 7)205 | 7)210 (7 and 21 underscored) |

### Resequencing to Facilitate Transfer

For special-needs students it might be better to delay the introduction of short division until the end of the chapter. This will make it easier for students to apply their understanding of long division involving 1-digit divisors.

### Using Oral/Visual Guidance

The sharing language used on page 112 provides important oral guidance for introducing and helping special-needs students "make sense" of the long division procedure. Once introduced, this language can be applied throughout the chapter as work is extended to division with 2-digit divisors.

As you discuss the examples on page 112, the basic steps for long division can be charted as shown. These steps can be posted for future reference or written on a personal file card for ready access by students. One mnemonic for helping those with memory or reasoning difficulties is: Dad: Mother: Sister likes a Cat: Brother (likes a Dog). You and your students may be able to suggest another.

| |
|---|
| 1. Divide |
| 2. Multiply |
| 3. Subtract |
| 4. Compare |
| 5. Bring Down |

### Applying Verbal/Visual Cues

Before asking students to find the quotient digits, suggest that they determine where the digits will occur. Systematically uncovering and marking digits as shown below often helps. Marking the digits helps to align them and visually reminds students when a middle or terminal zero in a quotient is omitted.

4)1,932    4)1,    4)1,9    4)1,932

In the example above, there are not enough thousands to share with four people, but there are enough hundreds. So sharing (dividing) begins with the hundreds.

### Using the One-Step

For students with memory or reasoning difficulties, it often is necessary to build mastery one step at a time: (1) rounding the divisor; (2) multiplying "sideways;" (3) determining whether a quotient digit is too large or too small; and (4) multiplying or estimating to check an answer.

## Subject Integration

Subject matter related to other areas of the curriculum has been integrated into the following lessons. This provides an opportunity to highlight the interaction between mathematics and other subjects.

**Consumer Awareness** Advertising, pages 116–117

**Social Studies** Calendars, page 107; Colorado River, pages 120–121; Model-T Ford, pages 124–125; Travel distances, pages 114–115, 130

**Fine Arts** School band, page 126–127; making stained glass, pages 122–123

**Career Awareness** Horse care, pages 108–109

# Management Guide

| Teaching Chapter 5 | | | | Meeting Individual Needs | | | | | |
|---|---|---|---|---|---|---|---|---|---|
| | | | | Lesson Assignments | | | Follow Up | | |
| Objectives | Chapter Content | Pages | TRB Test Items | Minimum | Average | Extended | Reteaching | Enrichment | Practice |
| | Chapter Opener | 107 | | | | | | | |
| 5.1 Use division facts to find and estimate quotients. | Using Division Facts: Mental Math | 108 | 1–6 | 1–20 | 1–20 | 1–20 | SE5 Ch 6 | | |
| | Special Quotients: Mental Math | 109 | | 1–20 | 1–20 | 1–20 | SE5 Ch 6<br>RS 26 | ES 26 | PS 40 |
| | Estimating Quotients | 110 | | 1–24 | 1–24 | 9–24 | SE5 Ch 6 | | MP 416<br>PS 41 |
| 5.2 Divide by 1-digit divisors. | 1-Digit Divisors | 112–113 | 7–9 | 1–34 | 1–36 | 1–37, TM | SE5 Ch 6 | | PS 42 |
| | 1-Digit Divisors: Larger Quotients | 114–115 | 10–11 | 1–34, SK | 1–35, SK | 11–35, SK | SE5 Ch 6<br>RS 27 | ES 27 | MP 417<br>PS 43 |
| | Short Division | 116–117 | 12–13 | 1–37 | 1–38 | 2–38 even, TM | SE5 Ch 6<br>RS 28 | ES 28 | PS 44 |
| 5.3 Find the average of a list of numbers. | Finding Averages | 118 | 14–15 | 1–7 | 1–7 | 1–7 | SE5 Ch 6 | | PS 45 |
| 5.4 Divide by 2- and 3-digit divisors. | Dividing by Multiples of 10 | 120–121 | 16–17 | 1–30, 34–36 | 1–37 | 1–37 odd, TM | SE5 Ch 7<br>RS 30 | ES 30 | PS 46 |
| | 2-Digit Divisors: 1-Digit Quotients | 122–123 | 18–19 | 1–40 | 1–41 | 11–42, TM | SE5 Ch 7 | | MP 417<br>PS 47 |
| | 2-Digit Divisors: Changing Estimates | 124 | 20–21 | 1–22 | 1–22 | 1–22 | SE5 Ch 7 | | MP 417<br>PS 48 |
| | 2-Digit Divisors: Larger Quotients | 126–127 | 22–23 | 1–17, 24–29, SK | 1–30, SK | 2–30 even, SK | SE5 Ch 7<br>RS 31 | ES 31 | MP 417<br>PS 49 |
| | Zeros in the Quotient | 128 | 24 | 1–17 | 1–17 | 1–17 | SE5 Ch 7 | | MP 418 |
| | 3-Digit Divisors | 129 | 25 | 1–8, 17–19 | 1–19 | 8–19, TM | SE5 Ch 7<br>RS 32 | ES 32 | MP 418<br>PS 50 |
| 5.5 Solve word problems using the 5-Point Checklist and cumulative computational skills. | Problem Solving: Using Estimation | 111 | 26–30 | 1–6 | 1–7 | 1–8 | | | |
| | Problem Solving: Using Data from Tables | 119 | | 1–7 | 1–9 | 1–10 | RS 29 | ES 29 | |
| | Problem Solving: Practice | 125 | | 1–6 | 1–7 | 1–8, TM | | | |
| | Problem Solving: Using Data from a Map | 130 | | 1–5 | 1–6 | 1–7 | | | |
| | Problem Solving: Understanding the Operations | 131 | | 1–5 | 1–6 | 1–7 | | | PS 51 |
| | Problem Solving: Make an Organized List | 132 | | | | | | | |
| | Chapter Review-Test | 133 | | | | | | | |
| | Another Look/Enrichment | 134–135 | | | | | | | |
| | Cumulative Review | 136 | | | | | | | |

**SE5** Student Edition, Book 5
**RS** Reteaching Supplement
**ES** Enrichment Supplement
**PS** Practice Supplement
**MP** More Practice
**TM** Think Math
**SK** Skillkeeper
**TRB** Teacher's Resource Book

## Masters for Use

**. . . before Chapter 5**

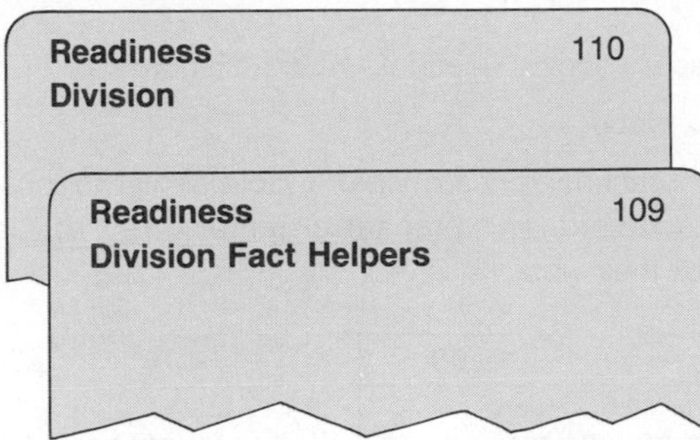


**. . . during Chapter 5**

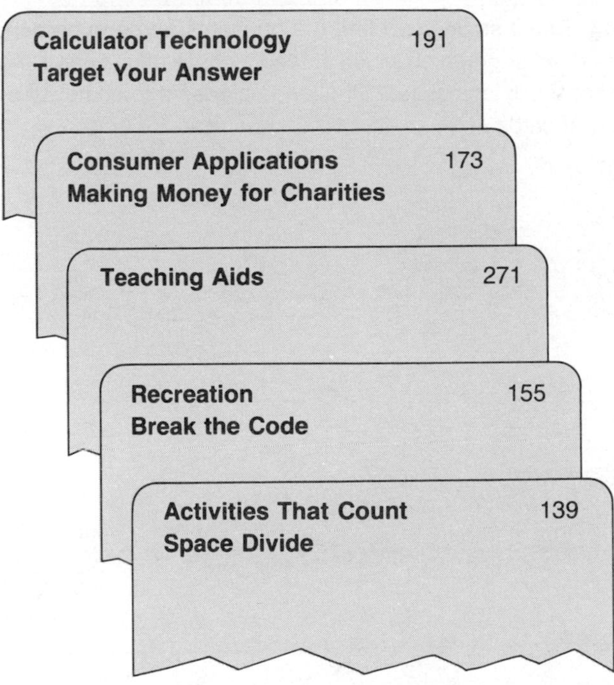

Calculator Technology 191
Target Your Answer
Consumer Applications 173
Making Money for Charities
Teaching Aids 271
Recreation 155
Break the Code
Activities That Count 139
Space Divide


**. . . after Chapter 5**

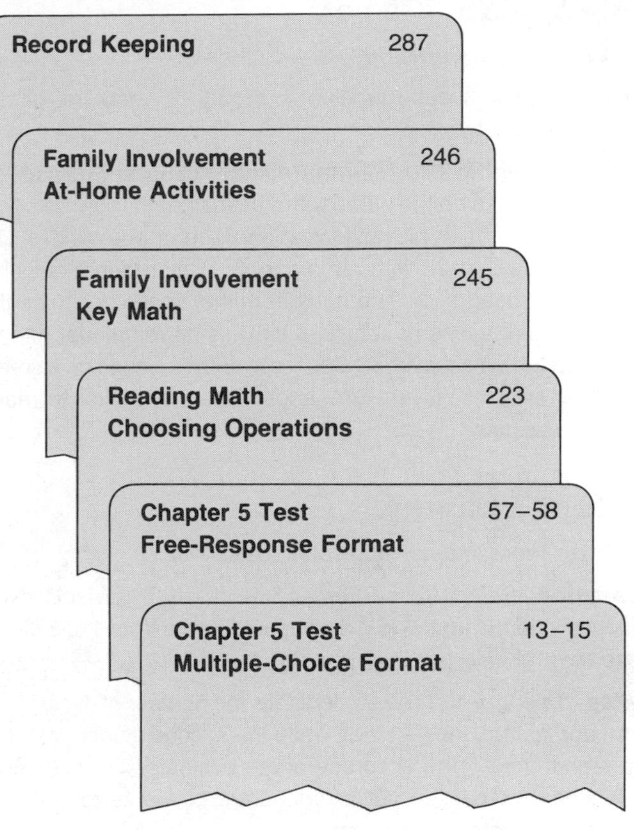


## Supplements

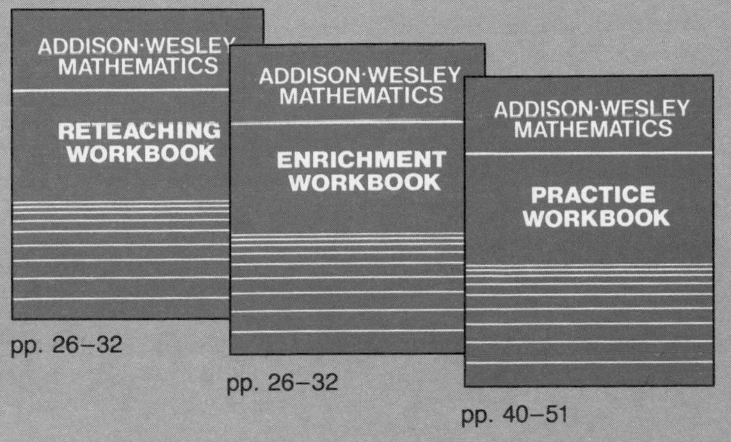


pp. 26–32

pp. 26–32

pp. 40–51

## Other Addison-Wesley Resources

### Books and Kits

*Skillseekers 2* (÷) Lessons 1–12
*The Arithmetic Primer* pp. 68–84
*Arithmetic Skill Cards* pp. W 7–10, 13
*Baseball, A Game of Numbers* pp. 112–117
*Problem Solving Experiences in Mathematics,* Grade 6
Problems 3, 8, 14, 15, 18, 22, 27, 43, 49, 50, 52, 58, 82, 83, 84, 100, 105, 108, 112, 113, 118, 119, 122, 130, 137

### Technology

*Computer Math Activities* Volumes 1–5
*Computer Math Games* Volumes 1, 2

# Activities That Count

Activities That Count are designed for use throughout this chapter and subsequent chapters. Before beginning Chapter 5, you may wish to review these activities and select the ones you consider appropriate for your class.

## Space Divide Game

**Purpose** To review dividing with 1-digit divisors

**Materials** Number cube labeled 4 through 9, markers, gameboard (TRB p. 139)

**Activity** Players in turn toss the number cube and divide the number in the space on the gameboard by the number on the cube. For example, if the first player tosses an 8, he or she divides 179 by 8 for an answer of 22 with remainder 3. Player then moves his or her marker ahead by 3. The number in that space becomes the dividend for the player's next turn. If there is no remainder, player gets an extra turn. If a player divides incorrectly, or lands on a space occupied by another player, turn is lost. The first player to reach Finish is the winner.

## Quotient Estimate Game

**Materials** Work sheets, stopwatch, calculator

**Preparation** Select from Chapter 5 a variety of division exercises with dividends from 3 to 6 digits and divisors from 1 to 3 digits. Prepare several different work sheets.

**Activity** Taking turns, one student tells the number of digits in the quotient and names the first digit while the second student records the time and checks the accuracy of the estimate with the calculator. A time limit can be set to encourage students to estimate rather than compute the quotient.

For example:

| | |
|---|---|
| $6\overline{)2,769}$ | There are 3 digits in the quotient. The first digit is 4. |
| $36\overline{)85,729}$ | There are 4 digits in the quotient. The first digit is 2. |

Students might also score points for staying within the time limit and for the accuracy of their estimates.

## Quotient Quiz Math Lab

**Purpose** To practice finding quotients with 2-digit divisors

**Materials** Index cards

**Preparation** On each index card write a table similar to those below. Number each card, and prepare an answer key so that students can check their work.

| ÷ 81 | |
|---|---|
| 5,402 | |
| 3,365 | |
| 2,461 | |
| 6,791 | |

| ÷ 68 | |
|---|---|
| 6,401 | |
| 5,926 | |
| 4,824 | |
| 2,187 | |

| ÷ 76 | |
|---|---|
| 2,401 | |
| 1,604 | |
| 4,408 | |
| 5,183 | |

**Activity** Direct students to find the quotients for each dividend. Display a chart or graph on which students check off the cards they have successfully completed. Challenge students to complete the entire set of cards.

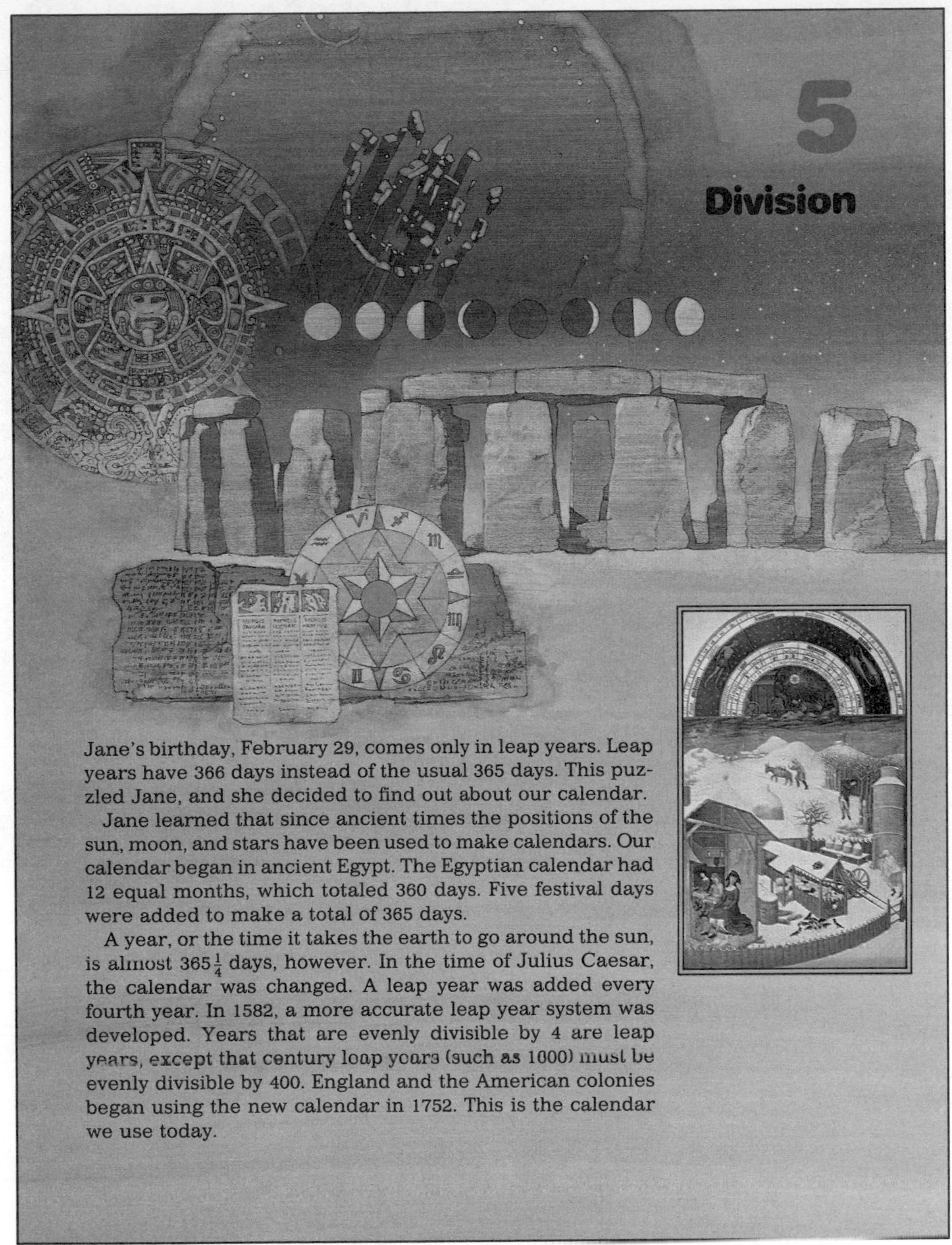

# 5 Division

Jane's birthday, February 29, comes only in leap years. Leap years have 366 days instead of the usual 365 days. This puzzled Jane, and she decided to find out about our calendar.

Jane learned that since ancient times the positions of the sun, moon, and stars have been used to make calendars. Our calendar began in ancient Egypt. The Egyptian calendar had 12 equal months, which totaled 360 days. Five festival days were added to make a total of 365 days.

A year, or the time it takes the earth to go around the sun, is almost $365\frac{1}{4}$ days, however. In the time of Julius Caesar, the calendar was changed. A leap year was added every fourth year. In 1582, a more accurate leap year system was developed. Years that are evenly divisible by 4 are leap years, except that century leap years (such as 1000) must be evenly divisible by 400. England and the American colonies began using the new calendar in 1752. This is the calendar we use today.

## Introducing the Chapter

**Discussion** Introduce this chapter by explaining to students that these lessons will give them an opportunity to review and expand their skills in dividing whole numbers. Then encourage students to discuss the calendars we use today—wall calendars, desk calendars, wallet-size calendars, and so on. Then allow time for students to read the story and enjoy the art, which depicts several of the devices used by our forebears for measuring or recording the passage of time (the ruins at Stonehenge, the Aztec calendar, the phases of the moon, Babylonian and Roman calendars, the zodiac, and the Book of Hours). This would be a good opportunity for students to make up questions based on the data in the story. As you teach the chapter, you may wish to refer again to this page and pose the questions suggested below.

## Follow-Up Questions

**After Page 111** When Megan asked her grandfather how old he was, he replied, "At my last birthday I was 3,120 weeks old." About how many years old was he? (60 years old)

**After Page 113** Glen's teacher told the class that there were just 115 more school days before vacation. If there are 5 school days in a week, how many weeks were left before vacation? (23)

**After Page 121** Sid's sister complained, "I'm exhausted! I haven't had any sleep for 960 minutes." How many hours was that? (16 hours)

**After Page 123** Columbus's first voyage across the Atlantic Ocean took about 864 hours. About how many days did the voyage take? (36 days)

# Division

**Quick Review** Students work the following problems as mental math.

10 × 52   11 × 10   6 × 100   42 × 100   10 × 10   62 × 100
860 × 10   100 × 40   68 × 10   403 × 100   55 × 10
4 × 100   10 × 88   100 × 67   10 × 3   100 × 8   57 × 10

**Lesson Focus** To use mental math to find quotients involving basic facts; to use mental math to find multiples of 10, 100, and 1,000

**Suggested Materials** Flashcards for division facts

## Ideas for Getting Started

Conduct a review of basic division facts using flashcards. Encourage students to give the answers as quickly as possible. Remind them that they can find a quotient such as 56 ÷ 7 by thinking about the number that multiplies by 7 to give 56. Then give the answer for a division fact and ask students to name a division fact for that number.

## Using Page 108

**Motivational Problem** Have students read the problem about horses. "What does the question ask us to find out about a horse at Buckaroo Ranch?" (How much water does each horse drink a day?) "What data are we given that would help us find the answer?" (the number of horses and the total amount of water the horses drink) "How do you know that division should be used to find the answer?" (320 L of water are used; each of the 8 horses gets the same amount.) Emphasize that when we want to find the size of one of eight equal amounts we divide.

**Lesson Development** Call students' attention to the equation that shows that the division fact 32 ÷ 8 = 4 can be used to find the quotient for 320 ÷ 8. Point out the multiplication check and be sure students understand that they can find these quotients by thinking about the missing factor. Write another equation such as 420 ÷ 6 on the chalkboard. "What basic fact is involved?" (42 ÷ 6 = 7) "What do we know about 420 ÷ 6?" (The answer is 70.) "How could we check?" (70 × 6 = 420) Emphasize that these quotients can be found by using the basic fact and then annexing the correct number of zeros.

**Other Examples** Ask students to think of multiplication to find the answer to these examples and to check each one. Be sure students understand that in the second example only three zeros are annexed to the quotient. The third example uses the standard notation for division.

**Exercises 1–20** In these exercises, focus on the patterns as larger dividends are used. As an answer is given, ask students to give the check using multiplication.

## Using Division Facts: Mental Math

The 8 horses on the Buckaroo Ranch drink a total of about 320 L of water each day. About how much water is this for each horse?

Since we want to find the size of 1 of 8 equal amounts, we divide.

32 ÷ 8 = 4
so 320 ÷ 8 = 40

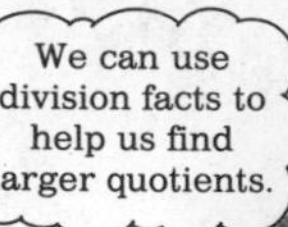

We can use division facts to help us find larger quotients.


**Check:** 40 × 8 = 320, so the answer is correct.

Each horse drinks about 40 L of water.

**Other Examples**

48 ÷ 6 = 8
so 4,800 ÷ 6 = 800

40 ÷ 5 = 8
so 40,000 ÷ 5 = 8,000

$9\overline{)63}$ = 7, so $9\overline{)630}$ = 70

Find the quotients. Use pencils for answers only.

1. 32 ÷ 4 8
 320 ÷ 4 80
 3,200 ÷ 4 800
 32,000 ÷ 4 8,000
2. 72 ÷ 9 8
 720 ÷ 9 80
 7,200 ÷ 9 800
 72,000 ÷ 9 8,000
3. 42 ÷ 6 7
 420 ÷ 6 70
 4,200 ÷ 6 700
 42,000 ÷ 6 7,000
4. 30 ÷ 5 6
 300 ÷ 5 60
 3,000 ÷ 5 600
 30,000 ÷ 5 6,000
5. 210 ÷ 7 30
6. 180 ÷ 3 60
7. 560 ÷ 7 80
8. 2,700 ÷ 9 300
9. 4,800 ÷ 8 600
10. 45,000 ÷ 5 9,000
11. 4,000 ÷ 8 500
12. 8,100 ÷ 9 900
13. 3,600 ÷ 4 900
14. 140 ÷ 2 70
15. 54,000 ÷ 6 9,000
16. 3,500 ÷ 5 700
17. $6\overline{)300}$ 50
18. $4\overline{)3,600}$ 900
19. $3\overline{)15,000}$ 5,000
20. $8\overline{)64,000}$ 8,000

108

## Follow Up

### Reteaching

After reviewing basic division facts, set up examples to allow students to focus on patterns. For example, 12 ÷ 6 = 2; 120 ÷ 6 = 20; 1,200 ÷ 6 = 200; 12,000 ÷ 6 = 2,000, and so on. Arrange this information in a chart so that patterns may be seen.

8 ÷ 4 = 2
80 ÷ 4 = 20
800 ÷ 4 = 200
8,000 ÷ 4 = 2,000

Check by multiplying 2,000 × 4 = 8,000, and so on. Help students do these types of examples mentally.

### Enrichment

Provide students with the equations below.

240 ÷ 80 = **3**
2,400 ÷ 800 = **3**
2,400 ÷ 30 = **80**
240,000 ÷ 300 = **800**
24,000 ÷ 300 = **80**
240 ÷ 3 = **80**
240,000 ÷ 30 = **8,000**

Have students find the products.

$(3 \times 10^1) \times (8 \times 10^1) = 24 \times 10^2 =$ **2,400**

$(3 \times 10^2) \times (8 \times 10^2) = 24 \times 10^4 =$ **240,000**

$(3 \times 10^1) \times (8 \times 10^3) =$ **$24 \times 10^4 = 240,000$**

| Assignment Guide | | | |
|---|---|---|---|
| | Minimum | Average | Extended |
| page 108 | 1–20 | 1–20 | 1–20 |
| page 109 | 1–20 | 1–20 | 1–20 |

## Special Quotients: Mental Math

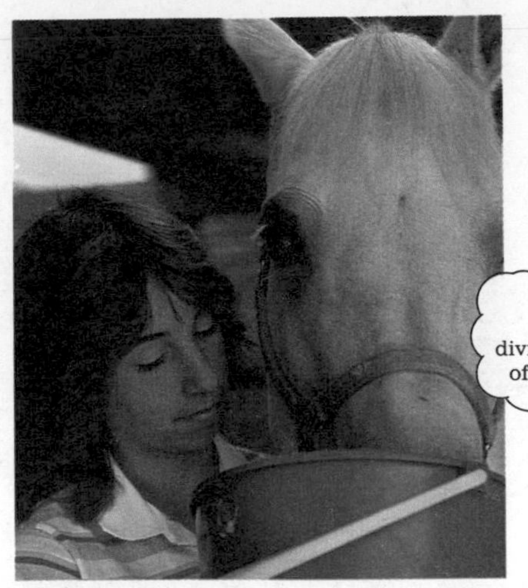

Sara feeds her horse 1 kg of grain for every 90 kg the horse weighs. If the horse weighs 540 kg, how much grain does it get?

Since we want to find the number of same-size amounts in the total, we divide.

Division facts also help us divide with multiples of 10, 100, or 1,000.

54 ÷ 9 = 6
so 540 ÷ 90 = 6

**Check:** 6 × 90 = 540, so the answer is correct.

The horse gets 6 kg of grain.

**Other Examples**

36 ÷ 4 = 9
so 3,600 ÷ 40 = 90

30 ÷ 6 = 5
so 30,000 ÷ 60 = 500

9 ÷ 1 = 9
so 900 ÷ 10 = 90

$8\overline{)56}$ = 7
so $800\overline{)5{,}600}$ = 7

Find the quotients. Use pencils for answers only.

1. 35 ÷ 7 5
   350 ÷ 70 5
   3,500 ÷ 70 50
   35,000 ÷ 70 500
2. 45 ÷ 9 5
   450 ÷ 90 5
   4,500 ÷ 90 50
   45,000 ÷ 90 500
3. 72 ÷ 8 9
   720 ÷ 80 9
   7,200 ÷ 80 90
   72,000 ÷ 80 900
4. 40 ÷ 8 5
   4,000 ÷ 800 5
   40,000 ÷ 800 50
   400,000 ÷ 800 500
5. 420 ÷ 70 6
6. 540 ÷ 60 9
7. 3,600 ÷ 40 90
8. 6,300 ÷ 90 70
9. 18,000 ÷ 60 300
10. 27,000 ÷ 30 900
11. 210 ÷ 70 3
12. 2,800 ÷ 40 70
13. 24,000 ÷ 40 600
14. 5,600 ÷ 800 7
15. 4,500 ÷ 500 9
16. 72,000 ÷ 900 80
17. $60\overline{)360}$ 6
18. $50\overline{)2{,}000}$ 40
19. $80\overline{)48{,}000}$ 600
20. $90\overline{)6{,}300}$ 70



## Using Page 109

**Motivational Problem** Read the problem at the top of the page about Sara's horse. "What are we asked about the horse's feed?" (How many kilograms of feed does the horse get?) "What data is given in the problem?" (The horse gets 1 kg for every 90 kg of weight; Sara's horse weighs 540 kg.) "Why should we use division to find the problem?" (We want to find out how many 90-kg weights are in 540 kg.) Emphasize that since we want to find the number of same-size amounts in the total, we divide.

**Lesson Development** Call students' attention to the equation that shows how the multiplication fact 54 ÷ 9 is used to find a quotient when the dividend and divisor are multiples of 10. Emphasize how the check statement can be used to find this quotient. Have students read the complete sentence giving the answer and then reread the problem to see if the answer given makes sense.

**Other Examples** Encourage students to look for the basic fact that can be used to find each larger quotient. Emphasize that the number of extra zeros in the divisor subtracted from the number of extra zeros in the dividend will give the correct number of zeros that should be annexed to the quotient.

**Exercises 1–20** In exercises 1 through 4, point out that the dividend increases by a multiple of ten each time. Encourage students to observe the resulting pattern of quotients and to check quotients by mental multiplication.

**Reteaching Supplement,** page 26

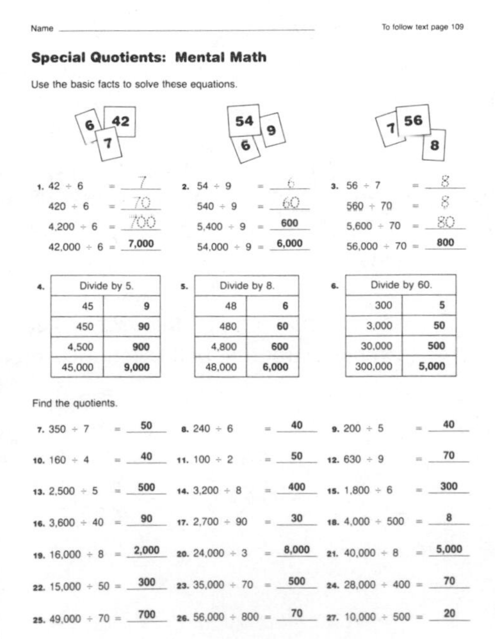

Name ______ To follow text page 109

**Special Quotients: Mental Math**

Use the basic facts to solve these equations.

1. 42 ÷ 6 = 7
   420 ÷ 6 = 70
   4,200 ÷ 6 = 700
   42,000 ÷ 6 = 7,000
2. 54 ÷ 9 = 6
   540 ÷ 9 = 60
   5,400 ÷ 9 = 600
   54,000 ÷ 9 = 6,000
3. 56 ÷ 7 = 8
   560 ÷ 70 = 8
   5,600 ÷ 70 = 80
   56,000 ÷ 70 = 800

4.

| Divide by 5. | |
|---|---|
| 45 | 9 |
| 450 | 90 |
| 4,500 | 900 |
| 45,000 | 9,000 |

5.

| Divide by 8. | |
|---|---|
| 48 | 6 |
| 480 | 60 |
| 4,800 | 600 |
| 48,000 | 6,000 |

6.

| Divide by 60. | |
|---|---|
| 300 | 5 |
| 3,000 | 50 |
| 30,000 | 500 |
| 300,000 | 5,000 |

Find the quotients.

7. 350 ÷ 7 = 50
8. 240 ÷ 6 = 40
9. 200 ÷ 5 = 40
10. 160 ÷ 4 = 40
11. 100 ÷ 2 = 50
12. 630 ÷ 9 = 70
13. 2,500 ÷ 5 = 500
14. 3,200 ÷ 8 = 400
15. 1,800 ÷ 6 = 300
16. 3,600 ÷ 40 = 90
17. 2,700 ÷ 90 = 30
18. 4,000 ÷ 500 = 8
19. 16,000 ÷ 8 = 2,000
20. 24,000 ÷ 3 = 8,000
21. 40,000 ÷ 8 = 5,000
22. 15,000 ÷ 50 = 300
23. 35,000 ÷ 70 = 500
24. 28,000 ÷ 400 = 70
25. 49,000 ÷ 70 = 700
26. 56,000 ÷ 800 = 70
27. 10,000 ÷ 500 = 20

**Enrichment Supplement,** page 26

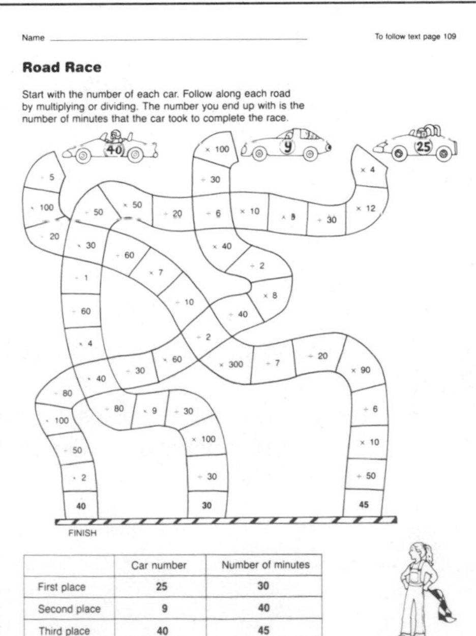

Name ______ To follow text page 109

**Road Race**

Start with the number of each car. Follow along each road by multiplying or dividing. The number you end up with is the number of minutes that the car took to complete the race.



| | Car number | Number of minutes |
|---|---|---|
| First place | 25 | 30 |
| Second place | 9 | 40 |
| Third place | 40 | 45 |

**Practice Supplement,** page 40

Name ______ To follow text page 109

**Using Division Facts: Mental Math**

Find the quotients.

1. 80 ÷ 2 = 40
2. 3,600 ÷ 6 = 600
3. 2,000 ÷ 4 = 500
4. 1,800 ÷ 6 = 300
5. 6,300 ÷ 7 = 900
6. 3,200 ÷ 8 = 400
7. 300 ÷ 5 = 60
8. 1,200 ÷ 6 = 200
9. 12,000 ÷ 3 = 4,000
10. 4,500 ÷ 50 = 90
11. 2,500 ÷ 500 = 5
12. 4,900 ÷ 70 = 70
13. 4,000 ÷ 4 = 1,000
14. 540 ÷ 6 = 90
15. 4,000 ÷ 5 = 800
16. 35,000 ÷ 7 = 5,000
17. 810 ÷ 9 = 90
18. 1,200 ÷ 4 = 300
19. 240 ÷ 30 = 8
20. 5,600 ÷ 700 = 8
21. 7,200 ÷ 90 = 80
22. 4,200 ÷ 7 = 600
23. 4,800 ÷ 6 = 800
24. 3,200 ÷ 4 = 800
25. 48,000 ÷ 8 = 6,000
26. 140 ÷ 2 = 70
27. 10,000 ÷ 5 = 2,000
28. 2,400 ÷ 6 = 400
29. 1,800 ÷ 2 = 900
30. 2,700 ÷ 9 = 300
31. 15,000 ÷ 3 = 5,000
32. 640 ÷ 8 = 80
33. 1,500 ÷ 5 = 300
34. 27,000 ÷ 30 = 900
35. 600 ÷ 300 = 2
36. 40,000 ÷ 800 = 50
37. 8,000 ÷ 4 = 2,000
38. 210 ÷ 7 = 30
39. 14,000 ÷ 7 = 2,000
40. 28,000 ÷ 4 = 7,000

# Estimation

**Quick Review** Provide the following oral drill of division facts.

9)81 4)28 3)27 9)36 8)64 8)48 6)54 3)18 2)16 6)24 7)56 5)35 5)45
7)63 8)72 9)18 4)16 6)30 7)21 5)20

**Lesson Focus** To use estimation to check calculator answers; to use estimation to check answers in problem solving

## Ideas for Getting Started

Review rounding to the nearest ten and the nearest hundred by writing numbers on cards as shown below.

| Front | Back |
|---|---|
| 634 people nearest 10 | 630 people |

To the nearest ten: 417 race cars, 358 days, 27 students, 724 kilometers.
To the nearest hundred: 4,496 packages, 2,784 points, 8,236 dollars, 6,350 automobiles.
Review the procedure: "Round down if the digit to the right of the desired place is less than 5. Round up if the digit is 5 or greater."

## Using Page 110

**Motivational Problem** Have students read the problem at the top of the page. "What question do we want to answer about Rex's trip?" (How many kilometers per liter of gasoline did they travel?) "What is the data given?" (kilometers traveled; liters of gasoline used) Help students see that to find the number of kilometers per liter they can use division. Conduct a brief discussion of the use of calculators in solving problems such as this. Also discuss possible errors that could be made when using the calculator and emphasize the need to estimate the answer in order to see if the calculated answer seems reasonable.

**Lesson Development** Write the problem on the chalkboard and help students complete the estimation process. Emphasize the idea that they must first *round* the numbers so that a basic fact can be used. Then they must *find a special quotient* involving the basic fact. Have students focus on the answer shown in the calculator display. By multiplying that number times 72, they can see that instead of the number 629, the number 329 was entered (the 3 button was right below the 6 button on the calculator).

**Exercises 1–24** Be sure students understand the directions for these exercises. The numbers in each case must be rounded so that a basic fact can be used. Note that exercises 1–16 involve rounding the dividend and sometimes the divisor to the nearest ten. In exercises 17 through 20 both the dividend and the divisor must be rounded to the nearest ten. In exercises 21 through 24 both the dividend and the divisor must be rounded to the nearest hundred.

## Estimating Quotients

Using a calculator can often help us solve problems. Sometimes, though, the answer shown on the calculator may be wrong because we did not push the proper keys or because the battery is weak. We can use estimation to see if the answer on the calculator seems reasonable.

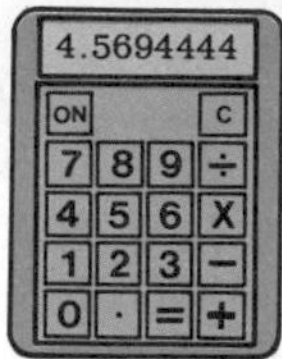


Rex's family drove 629 km on 72 liters of gasoline. How many kilometers did they travel for each liter of gasoline?

To check the calculator answer, round the numbers to the nearest ten and divide.

$$629 \div 72$$
$$\downarrow \quad \downarrow$$
$$630 \div 70 = 9$$

The estimate is 9 km per liter. The answer on the calculator is not reasonable.

Estimate these quotients.
Round so that you can use a basic fact.

| | | | |
|---|---|---|---|
| **1.** 124 ÷ 3 40 | **2.** 420 ÷ 6 70 | **3.** 163 ÷ 2 80 | **4.** 205 ÷ 7 30 |
| **5.** 302 ÷ 5 60 | **6.** 354 ÷ 7 50 | **7.** 634 ÷ 9 70 | **8.** 362 ÷ 4 90 |
| **9.** 176 ÷ 18 9 | **10.** 237 ÷ 38 6 | **11.** 158 ÷ 44 4 | **12.** 324 ÷ 77 4 |
| **13.** 23)119 6 | **14.** 45)354 7 | **15.** 61)423 7 | **16.** 86)719 8 |
| **17.** 94)2,740 30 | **18.** 19)1,750 90 | **19.** 36)3,240 80 | **20.** 49)3,950 80 |
| **21.** 217)1,240 6 | **22.** 598)4,186 7 | **23.** 306)1,530 5 | **24.** 787)6,396 8 |



More Practice, page 416, Set C

## Follow Up

### Reteaching

Show how to use rounding to estimate a quotient. For example: 635 ÷ 82. First, round the divisor and the dividend to the nearest ten, or 640 ÷ 80. Next estimate how many 80s there are in 640. Show this as

$$80\overline{)640}\ \ 8$$

So 8 is an estimate for the division equation 635 ÷ 82.

Try additional examples focusing on how to use estimation to determine the quotient.

### Enrichment

Have students locate information showing the prices of various kinds of merchandise. Encourage students to look for ads which involve pricing of several of a given item at one rate—3 for $1.98 or 8 for $2.00, for example. Let students estimate the cost per item in each ad. Then have students find the actual cost using their calculators. In this way, students can compare their estimates with the actual costs.

| Assignment Guide | | | |
|---|---|---|---|
| | Minimum | Average | Extended |
| page 110 | 1–24 | 1–24 | 9–24 |
| page 111 | 1–6 | 1–7 | 1–8 |

## Problem Solving: Using Estimation

Give your estimate for the answer to each problem. Write **R** (Reasonable) or **NR** (Not Reasonable) for the answer given.

1. A record store sold $3,451 worth of record albums during a special sale. At $7 per album, how many records were sold?
   Answer: 493 500, R

2. How much farther would you travel during an 8-hour trip at 79 km/h (kilometers per hour) than during a 7-hour trip at 89 km/h?
   Answer: 100 km 10 km, NR

6. A tennis ball manufacturer put 3 balls in each of 897 cans during a 2-hour period. How many balls were put in cans?
   Answer: 300 2,700, NR

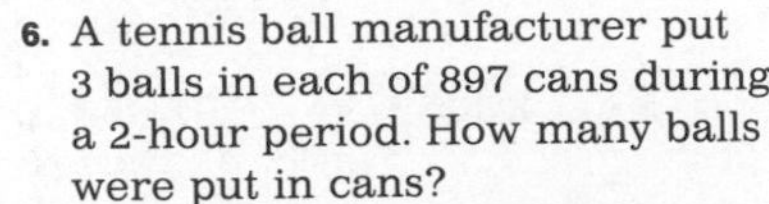

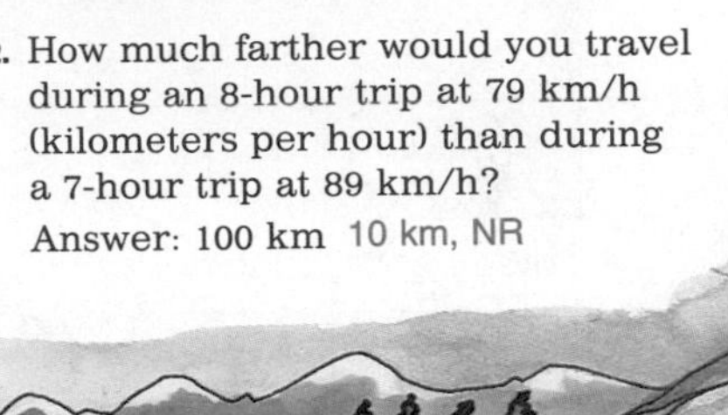

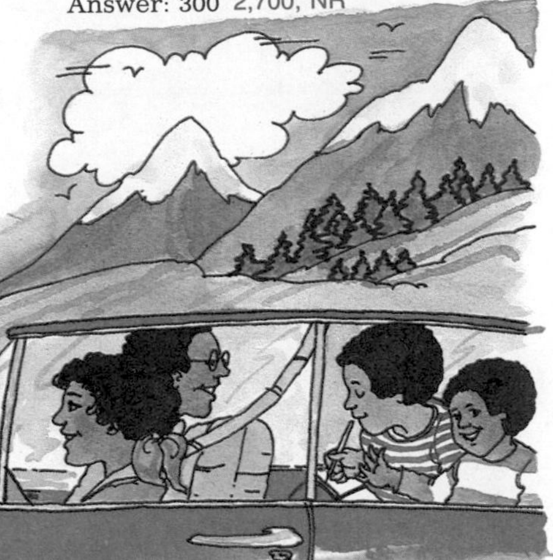

3. A pro basketball player made 2,365 points in 80 games. How many points did he average per game?
   Answer: 29.6 30, R

4. A clerk earned $245 for 48 hours' work. How much did the clerk earn per hour?
   Answer: $5.10 $5, R

5. How many egg cartons that hold 1 dozen eggs each are needed to hold 612 eggs?
   Answer: 61 60, R

7. A full school bus holds 43 children. If 119 children from one school and 162 from another are to be taken on a field trip, how many buses are needed?
   Answer: 7 7, R

8. **Try This** Nick spends twice as much time practicing basketball as practicing his horn. One week his total practice time was 24 hours. How many hours did he practice his horn? Hint: Make a table.
   8 hours

111

## Using Page 111

**Lesson Development** Remind students that estimating to find an approximate answer will help decide if a calculated answer is reasonable. If necessary, help students focus on rounding so that the estimate can be made using a basic fact.

**Exercises 1–7** Note that the answers to exercises 2 and 6 are definitely not reasonable. Also note that exercises 6 and 7 involve more than one operation.

**Try This** A possible strategy, Make a Table, was taught on page 100.

**Discussion** "What are we asked to find about Nick's practice time?" (how many hours he practiced his horn) "How does his basketball time compare with his horn practice time?" (twice as long) "What was his total practice time in one week?" (24) "If Nick practiced his horn 1 hour, how many hours would he have practiced basketball?" (2) "If he practiced his horn 2 hours, how many hours would he have practiced basketball?" (4)

**Solution** Nick practiced his horn 8 hours during the week.

| Horn practice (hrs) | 1 | 2 | 3 | 4 | 5 | 6 | 7 | 8 |
|---|---|---|---|---|---|---|---|---|
| Basketball practice (hrs) | 2 | 4 | 6 | 8 | 10 | 12 | 14 | 16 |
| Total practice time | 3 | 6 | 9 | 12 | 15 | 18 | 21 | 24 |

**More Practice,** page 416, Set C

## Ideas That Work

### Special Education

Use one or more of the following ideas to help students who are experiencing difficulty with the work on these pages.

- Suggest that students finger trace or mark the smaller problem within each division step to help determine a quotient digit.

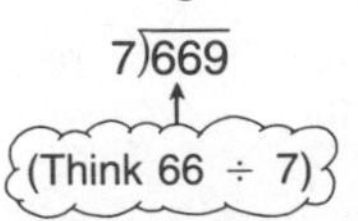


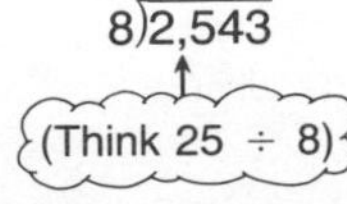


- Provide problem triples as illustrated below, in which the number being divided is the same each time and the divisors are similar.

21)6,931  22)6,931  23)6,931

In these exercises only the first problem is challenging. The others provide practical drill.

- Because division computation can seem complex, it might be helpful to simplify the process by eliminating decision points for some students. Rather than teaching these students to round some divisors up and to round others down, it may be best to suggest that they *always round down.* Then, when a quotient digit must be changed, the direction of change will *always* be the same: "too large, so make it less."

**Practice Supplement,** page 41

Name ______________________  To follow text page 110

**Estimating Quotients**

Estimate these quotients. Round so that you can use a basic fact.

1. 717 ÷ 9 __80__  2. 349 ÷ 7 __50__  3. 639 ÷ 8 __80__
4. 723 ÷ 8 __90__  5. 488 ÷ 7 __70__  6. 253 ÷ 5 __50__
7. 627 ÷ 7 __90__  8. 94 ÷ 3 __30__  9. 62 ÷ 6 __10__
10. 123 ÷ 2 __60__  11. 158 ÷ 4 __40__  12. 446 ÷ 5 __90__
13. 250 ÷ 48 __5__  14. 402 ÷ 82 __5__  15. 279 ÷ 67 __4__
16. 421 ÷ 59 __7__  17. 539 ÷ 87 __6__  18. 240 ÷ 79 __3__

19. 4)358 (90)  20. 6)418 (70)  21. 3)209 (70)  22. 5)148 (30)
23. 7)561 (80)  24. 9)716 (80)  25. 8)323 (40)  26. 4)277 (70)
27. 92)450 (5)  28. 85)268 (3)  29. 79)479 (6)  30. 28)273 (9)
31. 68)210 (3)  32. 59)299 (5)  33. 69)419 (6)  34. 57)244 (4)
35. 491)2,490 (5)  36. 623)4,814 (8)  37. 899)6,278 (7)  38. 444)3,641 (9)
39. 588)3,624 (6)  40. 885)3,579 (4)  41. 596)5,421 (9)  42. 783)5,566 (7)
43. 423)1,870 (5)  44. 48)3,484 (70)  45. 28)2,680 (90)  46. 39)3,612 (90)

# Division

**Quick Review** Students say, then write, the number indicated by each phrase.
4 hundreds 400 3 tens, 2 ones 32 7 hundreds, 2 tens, 9 ones 729 5 tens 50
3 hundreds, 1 one 301 1 thousand, 4 hundreds 1,400 4 tens, 8 ones 48
8 hundreds, 3 ones 803 7 tens, 7 ones 77 2 hundreds, 1 ten 210

**Lesson Focus** To divide by a 2-digit number to find 2- or 3-digit quotients

**Suggested Materials** Play money

## Ideas for Getting Started

Tell students the following story: Three students found an envelope containing $81, which they turned over to the police. After a time, when the owner could not be found, they were given the money to divide equally among themselves.

Have an envelope with play money or slips of paper representing $81. Ask a volunteer to show how to divide the money. Suggest that the larger bills be divided first. Then have students work in small groups or individually to divide up these amounts: $56 among 2 students; $72 among 3 students; $92 among 4 students; and $80 among 5 students. Emphasize the idea of first dividing the tens, trading a ten for 10 ones, and then dividing the ones.

## Using Page 112

**Motivational Problem** Read the problem at the top of the page. "What question is asked about Ken's 'Swim for Charity'?" (How much did each of the 3 charities receive?) "What data is given in the problem?" (He earned $75 to divide among the 3 charities.) Elicit from students that we can use division as the plan to find the answer to this problem.

**Lesson Development** Have three students divide the 7 tens and 5 ones. As students complete the task, write the corresponding numerical procedure on the chalkboard as shown in the text. Point out that the 75 represents the total amount of money, the divisor 3 is the number of charities to share the money. The first quotient figure, 2, is the number of $10 bills each charity gets. The number subtracted, 6, is the total number of $10 bills shared; the difference, 1, is the number of extra $10 bills. In the second step, students should understand that the extra ten is traded for 10 ones and combined with the 5 ones to produce 15. The second quotient figure represents the number of $1 bills each gets when the 15 $1-bills are divided among the 3 people. The 15 being subtracted represents the total number of bills shared and the 0 shows that there are no extra $1 bills left over. The quotient, 25, shows that each charity received $25.

**Other Examples** Use the money model if necessary to work through these examples. Encourage students to think about the model if they have difficulty.

**Warm Up** As students complete these exercises, be alert for basic fact errors. Caution students to be particularly careful with exercises 3 and 5 in which there are not enough hundreds and they must start the dividing in the tens place.

## 1-Digit Divisors

Ken earned $75 in a "Swim for Charity." He divided it equally among 3 charities. How much did each charity receive?

Since the money is shared equally, we divide.

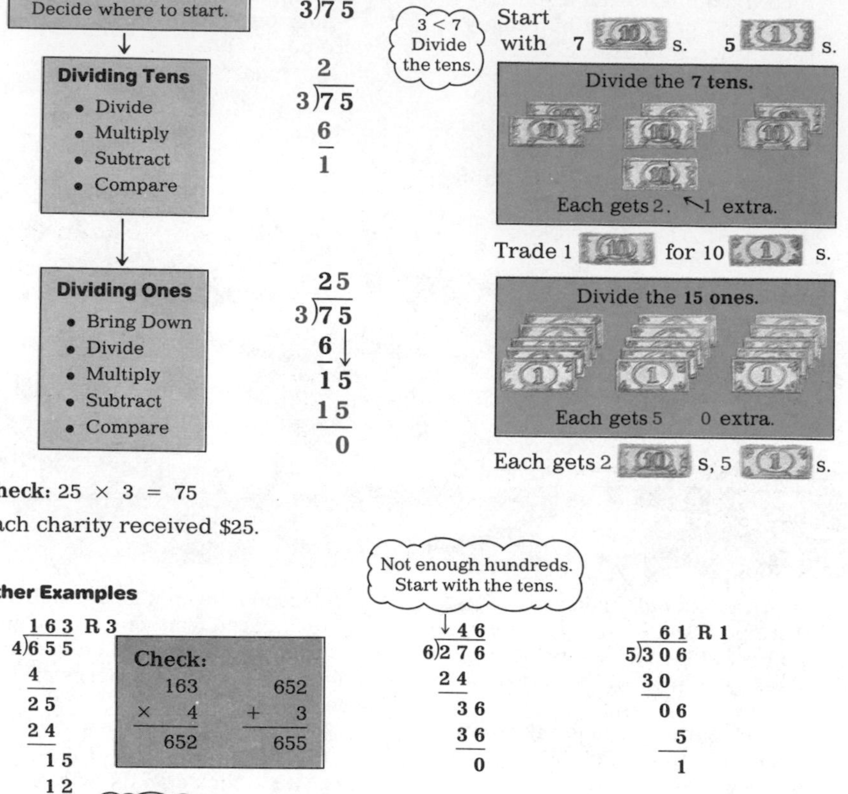


Check: 25 × 3 = 75

Each charity received $25.

**Warm Up** Divide. Check by multiplying.

1. 2)49 24 R1
2. 3)87 29
3. 6)199 33 R1
4. 8)985 123 R1
5. 7)359 51 R2

112

## Follow Up

### Reteaching

Use an example such as 4)128 to review the division algorithm. "Can the hundreds be shared among 4 people?" (The answer is no, so the hundred is exchanged for 10 tens and combined with the 2 tens to make 12 tens.) "Can 12 tens be shared among 4 people?" (Yes, the ones can be shared equally.) Then show these steps in the algorithm.

- 4)128 Is 4 < 1? The hundreds cannot be shared, so we consider the tens.
- 4)128 Is 4 < 12? Yes, we can divide in the tens place.
- 4)128 Is 4 < 8? Yes, we can divide the ones equally.

### Enrichment

Write the following problems on the chalkboard. Challenge students to fill in the missing numbers.

| 459 | 352 R4 | 552 R4 |
|---|---|---|
| 6)2754 | 7)2468 | 5)2764 |
| 24 | 21 | 25 |
| 35 | 36 | 26 |
| 30 | 35 | 25 |
| 54 | 18 | 14 |
| 54 | 14 | 10 |
| 0 | 4 | 4 |

| Assignment Guide | | | |
|---|---|---|---|
| | Minimum | Average | Extended |
| page 113 | 1–34 | 1–36 | 1–37, TM |

Divide.

1. 2)28 14
2. 6)84 14
3. 3)86 28 R2
4. 5)59 11 R4
5. 9)198 22
6. 7)164 23 R3
7. 3)175 58 R1
8. 8)576 72
9. 4)332 83
10. 6)97 16 R1
11. 6)380 63 R2
12. 5)406 81 R1
13. 3)139 46 R1
14. 8)216 27
15. 7)96 13 R5
16. 7)476 68
17. 2)836 418
18. 9)432 48
19. 4)731 182 R3
20. 5)87 17 R2
21. 2)179 89 R1
22. 4)636 159
23. 9)478 53 R1
24. 2)972 486
25. 8)608 76
26. 7)875 125
27. 5)297 59 R2
28. 222 ÷ 3 74
29. 364 ÷ 5 72 R4
30. 497 ÷ 7 71
31. 334 ÷ 4 83 R2
32. 557 ÷ 6 92 R5
33. 96 ÷ 8 12
34. Estimate, then find the quotient when 345 is divided by 5. 70; 69
35. Estimate, then find the quotient when 718 is the dividend and 9 is the divisor. 80; 79 R7
36. Shari earned $176 in the "Swim for Charity." She divided it equally among 4 charities. How much did each charity get? $44

★ 37. Matthew can swim 6 meters in 5 seconds. At this rate, how far can he swim in one minute? 72 m

**Remember!**

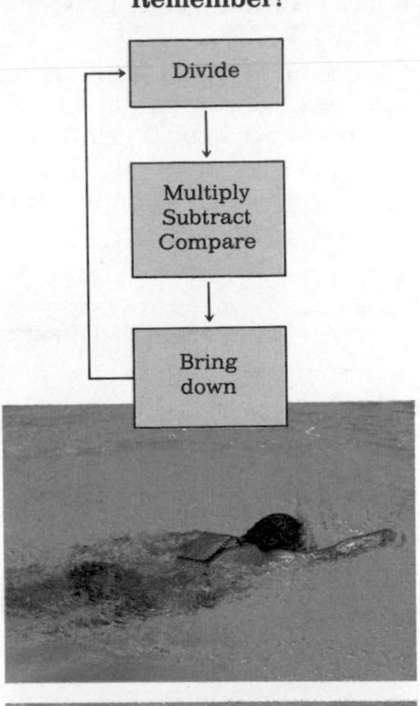

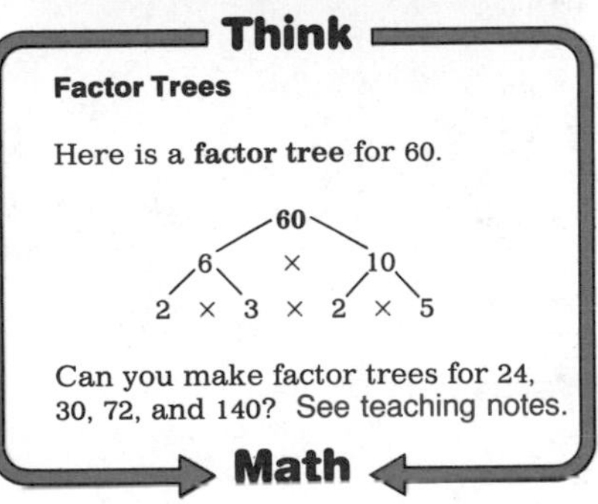

Think
Factor Trees
Here is a factor tree for 60.
60
6 × 10
2 × 3 × 2 × 5
Can you make factor trees for 24, 30, 72, and 140? See teaching notes.
Math




## Using Page 113

**Exercises 1–33** Emphasize the dividing procedure for each place as shown by the flowchart at the top of the page. If necessary, use an example to illustrate the importance of the "compare" step. In exercises 5–9 focus on the idea of "decide where to start." In these cases there are not enough hundreds so the dividing must start in the tens place.

**Exercises 34–35** Remind students to round so that a basic fact can be used to find the estimate.

**Exercise 37** The students must supply extra data (60 seconds in a minute) and use two operations to solve this problem. Do not discourage those students who decide to make a table to find the solution.

**Think Math** In this activity students find the prime factorization of a number. Help them to recognize that the product of the numbers in each row of a factor tree is equal to the number at the base of the tree. If students need help making a factor tree for a number such as 24, encourage them to look for a pair of numbers that will multiply to give 24 such as 8 × 3. Note that a factor tree for 24 that starts with 8 × 3 will look different initially from the factor tree that starts with 6 × 4, but that the final row will have the same prime factors.

Factors of 24: 3 × 2 × 2 × 2
Factors of 30: 3 × 2 × 5
Factors of 72: 3 × 3 × 2 × 2 × 2
Factors of 140: 2 × 7 × 2 × 5

## Ideas That Work

### Special Education

Allow students to work in groups of five to check their work in this activity. Each student in a group should select one step in the chart and take turns with other members of the group talking through, *step by step,* the calculation of the problems.

| 1. Divide |
|---|
| 2. Multiply |
| 3. Subtract |
| 4. Compare |
| 5. Bring Down |

If a student in the group has reasoning or memory difficulties, let that student have first choice in selecting a step to be described. For example, the student might feel more comfortable with the subtraction step, and may prefer to describe the subtraction calculation each time. After observing other students discuss their steps, the student might feel confident enough to select a different step to describe.

As follow-up, write several incomplete division examples on the chalkboard, and challenge the groups to finish these problems. If time allows, group sessions could be used as practice periods.

**Practice Supplement,** page 42

Name ______________________ To follow text page 113

**1-Digit Divisors**

Divide.

1. 7)84 12
2. 3)94 31 R1
3. 5)60 12
4. 8)91 11 R3
5. 8)734 91 R6
6. 4)296 74
7. 5)386 77 R1
8. 9)487 54 R1
9. 2)371 185 R1
10. 5)821 164 R1
11. 3)993 331
12. 4)706 176 R2
13. 8)569 71 R1
14. 5)865 173
15. 5)77 15 R2
16. 3)707 235 R2

**Quick Review** Students each give an example of a problem that can be solved using one of the operations.

**Lesson Focus** To divide by a 1-digit number to find up to 4-digit quotients

## Ideas for Getting Started

Write the flowchart from page 113 on the chalkboard. Use it to illustrate the steps of the division process by working the following examples: 4)148, 3)288, 5)435. As students consider the first example ask: "Can you divide in the hundreds place?" (No, there are not enough hundreds to divide by 4.) Emphasize that in each case students must decide where to start. The flowchart then describes the process used to divide in each place. Review each step as you complete the example problems.

## Using Page 114

**Motivational Problem** Read the problem at the top of the page. "What question are we asked about the trip from Hawaii to Los Angeles?" (What was the speed per hour?) "What information do we need to solve this problem?" (the distance and the number of hours of the flight) As you discuss the plan, emphasize that to find kilometers per hour suggests that we use the division operation.

**Lesson Development** Write the division exercise on the chalkboard. Point out that to decide where to start we first look at the thousands place. Because there are not enough thousands, we think of 42 hundreds and divide 42 by 7. Ask students to refer to the flowchart to divide the hundreds.

Emphasize that to divide the tens we bring down and use the same process as in dividing hundreds. Emphasize that every time we bring down a digit, we divide and write a digit (sometimes 0) in the quotient. Then emphasize that this same process is used after bringing down to divide in the ones place. Have a volunteer give the answer to the problem using a complete sentence and then check the division using multiplication.

**Other Examples** In the first example call attention to the need to write the zero in the ones place when dividing ones. Continue to emphasize the dividing process described as you work the second example with a 4-digit quotient. In the third example, encourage students to think about pennies and divide as for whole numbers. Since the dividend is $65 and the divisor 7, the quotient must be about $9. Point out that the decimal point in the quotient is always written directly above the decimal point in the dividend.

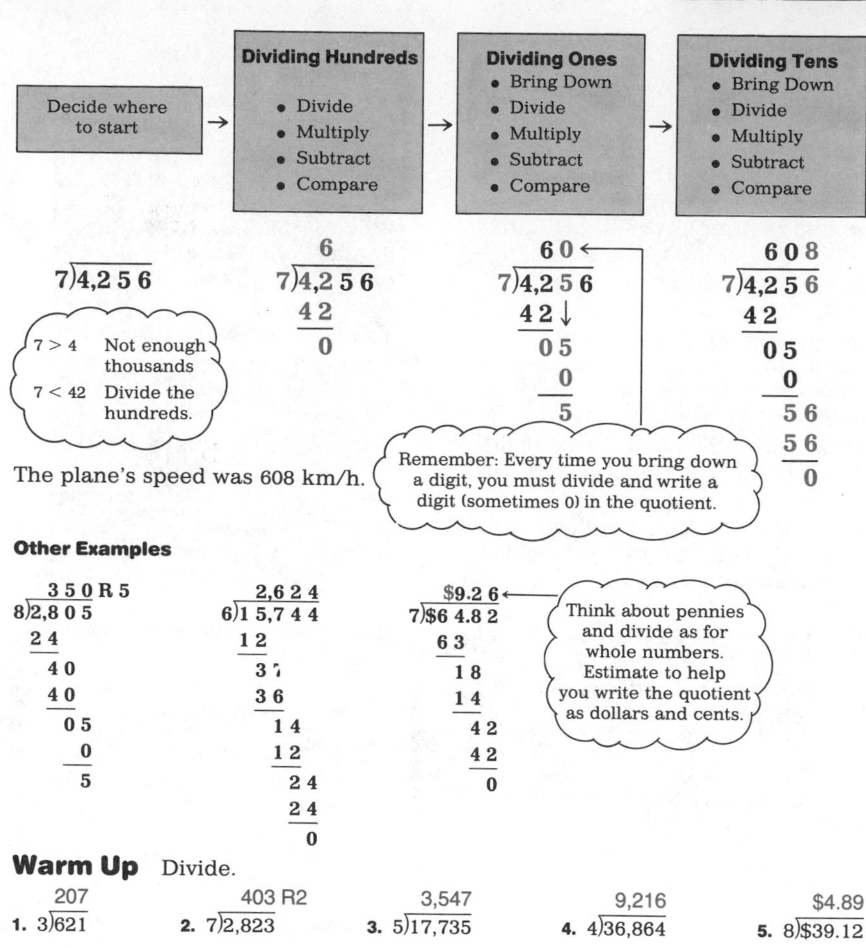

## 1-Digit Divisors: Larger Quotients

On a trip from Honolulu, Hawaii, to Los Angeles, California, a plane traveled 4,256 km in 7 hours. What was its speed in kilometers per hour (km/h)?

Since we want to find the number of kilometers traveled per hour, we divide.

Decide where to start → **Dividing Hundreds** • Divide • Multiply • Subtract • Compare → **Dividing Ones** • Bring Down • Divide • Multiply • Subtract • Compare → **Dividing Tens** • Bring Down • Divide • Multiply • Subtract • Compare

7)4,2 5 6

7 > 4 Not enough thousands
7 < 42 Divide the hundreds.

```
     6
7)4,2 5 6
  4 2
    0
```

```
     6 0
7)4,2 5 6
  4 2↓
    0 5
      0
      5
```

```
     6 0 8
7)4,2 5 6
  4 2
    0 5
      0
      5 6
      5 6
        0
```

Remember: Every time you bring down a digit, you must divide and write a digit (sometimes 0) in the quotient.

The plane's speed was 608 km/h.

**Other Examples**

```
   3 5 0 R 5
8)2,8 0 5
  2 4
    4 0
    4 0
      0 5
        0
        5
```

```
   2,6 2 4
6)1 5,7 4 4
  1 2
    3 7
    3 6
      1 4
      1 2
        2 4
        2 4
          0
```

```
   $9.2 6
7)$6 4.8 2
   6 3
     1 8
     1 4
       4 2
       4 2
         0
```

Think about pennies and divide as for whole numbers. Estimate to help you write the quotient as dollars and cents.

**Warm Up** Divide.

1. 3)621 (207)
2. 7)2,823 (403 R2)
3. 5)17,735 (3,547)
4. 4)36,864 (9,216)
5. 8)$39.12 ($4.89)

114

## Follow Up

### Reteaching

Work through an algorithm using place-value models. Illustrate as you go through each step. For example: 3)5,261. Show 5,261 with place-value models. As you divide, show each step in the algorithm. "Can you share 5 among 3 groups?" (yes) "How many will each group receive?" (1, with 2 left over) Continue until the example is completed. Discuss such points as why and when to multiply, why and when to subtract, and the meaning of a remainder. Using another example, ask for volunteers to work through the algorithm.

### Enrichment

Let students cut out pictures from the newspapers and paste them on colored paper. For each picture, challenge students to create a related division problem and attach it to the colored paper. Several of these can be used as a bulletin board.

| Assignment Guide | | | |
|---|---|---|---|
| | Minimum | Average | Extended |
| page 115 | 1–34, SK | 1–35, SK | 11–35, SK |

Divide and check.

1. 3)547 182 R1
2. 6)278 46 R2
3. 7)963 137 R4
4. 2)587 293 R1
5. 4)689 172 R1
6. 9)3,476 386 R2
7. 8)1,920 240
8. 5)4,115 823
9. 3)607 202 R1
10. 6)1,218 203
11. 2)1,876 938
12. 4)2,836 709
13. 7)4,760 680
14. 5)2,076 415 R1
15. 9)4,996 555 R1
16. 8)9,872 1,234
17. 6)27,366 4,561
18. 2)19,712 9,856
19. 4)25,548 6,387
20. 3)9,072 3,024
21. 6)19,248 3,208
22. 5)22,510 4,502
23. 7)45,500 6,500
24. 8)$57.84 $7.23
25. 9)$6.66 $0.74

26. 804 ÷ 3 268
27. 3,604 ÷ 4 901
28. 2,880 ÷ 6 480
29. 30,065 ÷ 5 6,013
30. $36.00 ÷ 8 $4.50
31. $14.68 ÷ 4 $3.67

32. Estimate, then find the quotient when 4,242 is divided by 7. 600; 606

33. Estimate, then find the quotient when the dividend is 2,760 and the divisor is 4. 700; 690

34. A plane flew 3,520 km from San Francisco, California, to Cleveland, Ohio, in 4 hours. What was the rate of speed? 880 km/h

35. Make up a question involving this data. Solve the problem. On 5 flights a plane carried a total of 2,145 passengers. See teaching notes.

## Skillkeeper

Multiply.

1. 7 × 40 280
2. 600 × 8 4,800
3. 5 × 2,000 10,000
4. 100 × 3 300
5. 50 × 90 4,500
6. 300 × 40 12,000
7. 10 × 700 7,000
8. 800 × 800 640,000

Write each number in standard form.

9. $3^3$ 27
10. $10^4$ 10,000
11. $8^3$ 512
12. $2^4$ 16
13. $10^6$ 1,000,000
14. $4^5$ 1,024

More Practice, page 417, Set A



## Using Page 115

**Exercises 1–31** Continue to emphasize the idea of "decide where to start" and the process for dividing in each place. Caution students to be alert for the exercises that have zeros in the quotients.

**Exercises 32–33** In both exercises the dividend must be rounded to the nearest hundred in order to estimate using a basic fact.

**Exercise 35** This exercise helps students focus on the question. A possible question might be: "About how many passengers are carried on each flight?"

**Skillkeeper** These skills were originally taught in Chapter 4.

**More Practice,** page 117, Set A

**Reteaching Supplement,** page 27

Name ________ To follow text page 115

### 1-Digit Divisors: Larger Quotients

Decide where to start. → Divide the hundreds. → Divide the tens. → Divide the ones.

4)2,943 — 4 is less than 29. Divide hundreds.

4)2,943 → 7; 28 (4 × 7); 1 — Subtract and compare. 1 < 4

4)2,943 → 73; 14, 12 (4 × 3); 2 — Subtract and compare. 2 < 4

4)2,943 → 735 R3; 23, 20 (4 × 5); 3 — Subtract and compare. 3 < 4

Divide — Multiply, Subtract, Compare — Bring Down

Divide.

1. 7)247 35 R2
2. 7)3,220 460 — Write the 0 in the quotient.
3. 3)$14.25 $4.75 — Divide as with whole numbers. Write the quotient as dollars and cents.
4. 7)5,863 837 R4
5. 4)$12.16 $3.04
6. 6)3,579 596 R3
7. 8)$60.32 $7.54
8. 4,736 ÷ 8 592
9. $53.70 ÷ 6 $8.95
10. $42.15 ÷ 5 $8.43

**Enrichment Supplement,** page 27

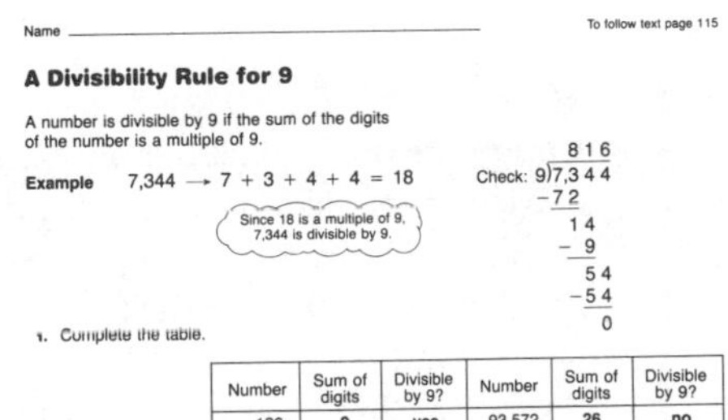

Name ________ To follow text page 115

### A Divisibility Rule for 9

A number is divisible by 9 if the sum of the digits of the number is a multiple of 9.

**Example** 7,344 → 7 + 3 + 4 + 4 = 18 — Since 18 is a multiple of 9, 7,344 is divisible by 9.

Check: 9)7,344 = 816; −72, 14, −9, 54, −54, 0

1. Complete the table.

| Number | Sum of digits | Divisible by 9? | Number | Sum of digits | Divisible by 9? |
|---|---|---|---|---|---|
| 126 | 9 | yes | 93,572 | 26 | no |
| 747 | 18 | yes | 81,933 | 24 | no |
| 3,996 | 27 | yes | 70,002 | 9 | yes |
| 8,138 | 20 | no | 51,643 | 19 | no |
| 5,778 | 27 | yes | 22,221 | 9 | yes |
| 17,532 | 18 | yes | 234,567 | 27 | yes |
| 64,281 | 21 | no | 568,944 | 36 | yes |

**Answers will vary.**

2. What year were you born? ____ Is the number for that year divisible by 9? ____
3. Is the present year number divisible by 9? ____
4. What is the next year that will be divisible by 9? ____
5. Write any number that uses all ten digits, 0 through 9, exactly once. ____ Is the number divisible by 9? yes
6. Write another number using all ten digits. Is it divisible by 9? yes
7. What can you conclude about all such numbers? They are all divisible by 9.

**Practice Supplement,** page 43

Name ________ To follow text page 115

### 1-Digit Divisors: Larger Quotients

Divide.

1. 7)862 123 R1
2. 3)195 65
3. 6)918 153
4. 2)664 332
5. 4)3,386 846 R2
6. 5)2,416 483 R1
7. 7)4,791 684 R3
8. 8)4,610 576 R2
9. 5)2,368 473 R3
10. 9)6,588 732
11. 6)3,840 640
12. 9)7,568 840 R8
13. 8)26,747 3,343 R3
14. 5)$72.95 $14.59
15. 3)$213.78 $71.26
16. 2)$47.88 $23.94

# Division

**Quick Review** As an oral drill, students round 2-digit numbers to the nearest ten and 3-digit numbers to the nearest hundred.

25 38 789 550 48 91 350 449
44 908 756 281 87 55 95

**Lesson Focus** To use short division to find quotients with a 1-digit divisor

## Ideas for Getting Started

Provide practice in which students give quotients and remainders orally for problems such as the ones below:

| | |
|---|---|
| $6\overline{)28}$ (4, remainder 4) | $4\overline{)9}$ (2, remainder 1) |
| $6\overline{)45}$ (7, remainder 3) | $9\overline{)17}$ (1, remainder 8) |
| $8\overline{)37}$ (4, remainder 5) | $6\overline{)38}$ (6, remainder 2) |
| $5\overline{)23}$ (4, remainder 3) | $9\overline{)65}$ (7, remainder 2) |

These mental exercises provide readiness for the type of mental computations needed to complete the short division process.

## Using Page 116

**Motivational Problem** Have students read the paragraph at the top of the page. "What question are we asked about the advertising time on radio?" (What was the cost per minute?) "How much did the company pay for 6 minutes?" ($2,850) Point out that this type of comparison suggests that we could plan to use division to find the answer.

**Lesson Development** Write the problem on the chalkboard and work through the procedure shown in the instruction boxes. Emphasize that we must decide where to start. Since there are not enough thousands, we begin by dividing the hundreds. In the hundreds place we think, "28 divided by 6, quotient 4, remainder 4." Be sure students understand that the remainder tells how many extra hundreds to be traded for tens. Then divide in the tens place. In the tens place we think, "45 divided by 6, quotient 7, remainder 3." The 3 tells how many extra tens which must be traded for ones. Finally, divide in the ones place. Have students check the short division problem by multiplying 6 × 475. Then have them reread the question and estimate to see if the answer, 475, seems reasonable.

**Other Examples** In the first example note the zero in the dividend. In the second example there is no remainder when 56 is divided by 7, and since there are not enough tens to divide there is a middle zero in the quotient. Point out that the procedure for finding larger quotients is simply an extension of the procedure used for finding 2- and 3-digit quotients. In the last example, encourage students to divide as with whole numbers and place the decimal point for dollars and cents.

**Warm Up** Be alert for students who have difficulty performing short division with a remainder. Also give special attention to problems with zeros in the quotient such as exercises 3, 4, 5, and 7.

## Short Division

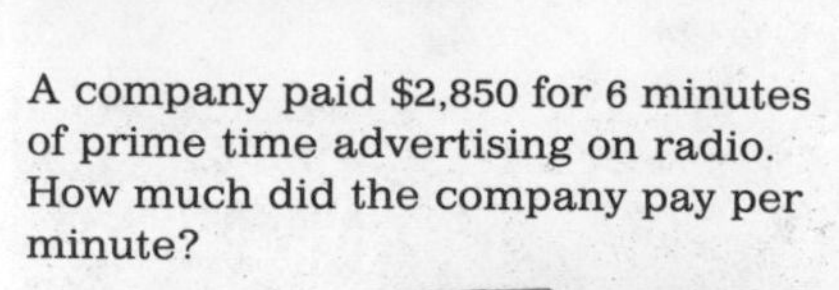

A company paid $2,850 for 6 minutes of prime time advertising on radio. How much did the company pay per minute?

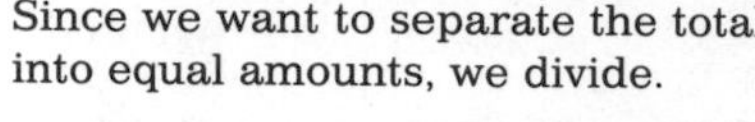

Since we want to separate the total into equal amounts, we divide.

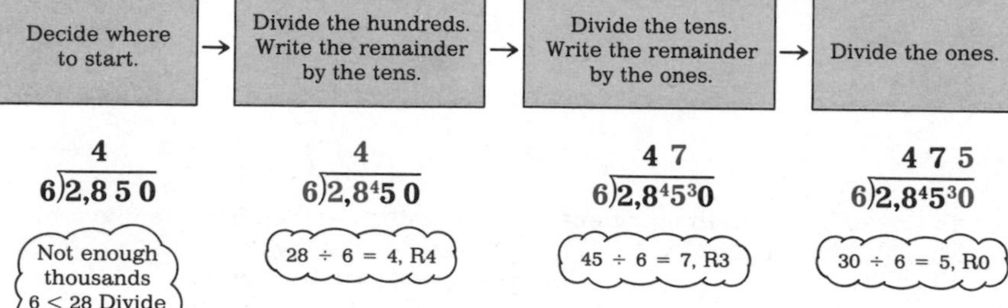

| Decide where to start. → | Divide the hundreds. Write the remainder by the tens. → | Divide the tens. Write the remainder by the ones. → | Divide the ones. |
|---|---|---|---|
| $\frac{\;4}{6\overline{)2{,}850}}$ | $\frac{\;4}{6\overline{)2{,}8^450}}$ | $\frac{\;47}{6\overline{)2{,}8^45^30}}$ | $\frac{\;475}{6\overline{)2{,}8^45^30}}$ |
| Not enough thousands $6 < 28$ Divide the hundreds. | $28 \div 6 = 4$, R4 | $45 \div 6 = 7$, R3 | $30 \div 6 = 5$, R0 |

The company paid $475 per minute for the advertising.

**Other Examples**

| | | | |
|---|---|---|---|
| 269 | 806 | 4,594 R 4 | $4.73 |
| $3\overline{)8^20^27}$ | $7\overline{)5{,}642}$ | $6\overline{)27^35^56^28}$ | $8\overline{)\$37^58^24}$ |

**Warm Up** Divide. Use short division.

1. $2\overline{)576}$ (288)
2. $5\overline{)2{,}307}$ (461 R2)
3. $6\overline{)1{,}830}$ (305)
4. $9\overline{)7{,}836}$ (870 R6)
5. $3\overline{)2{,}408}$ (802 R2)
6. $7\overline{)16{,}563}$ (2,366 R1)
7. $8\overline{)24{,}076}$ (3,009 R4)
8. $4\overline{)65{,}384}$ (16,346)
9. $7\overline{)\$9.73}$ ($1.39)
10. $6\overline{)\$136.26}$ ($22.71)



## Follow Up

### Reteaching

Review with students the meaning of "short division." Remind them that "long division" refers to the fact that the division process is shown at every step. Short division requires that students keep each step in mind while dividing. Use an example such as $3\overline{)47}$. Help students think 4 ÷ 3 = 1 with remainder 1. The remainder 1 from the tens place is mentally placed with the 7 in the ones place: $3\overline{)4^17}$. Then the ones are divided: 17 ÷ 3 = 5. When the ones are subtracted (17 − 15), there is a remainder 2.

$$\frac{15 \quad R2}{3\overline{)4^17}}$$

### Enrichment

Let students work the problems, match the remainders with the corresponding letter, then unscramble the message.

| | | |
|---|---|---|
| 802 R2 | 1,939 R4 | 918 R5 |
| $3\overline{)2{,}408}$ | $5\overline{)9{,}669}$ | $8\overline{)7{,}349}$ |
| 1,175 R7 | 647 R1 | 1,139 R3 |
| $8\overline{)9{,}407}$ | $2\overline{)1{,}295}$ | $7\overline{)7{,}976}$ |
| 803 R6 | 109 R8 | 1,701 |
| $8\overline{)6{,}430}$ | $9\overline{)989}$ | $5\overline{)8{,}505}$ |

| 1 | 2 | 8 | 4 | 7 |
|---|---|---|---|---|
| G | R | O | A | K |

| 5 | 6 | 0 | 3 |
|---|---|---|---|
| T | E | W | R |

GREAT WORK

| Assignment Guide | | | |
|---|---|---|---|
| | Minimum | Average | Extended |
| page 117 | 1–37 | 1–38 | 2–38 even, TM |

Divide and check. Use short division.

1. 4)172 **43**
2. 3)483 **161**
3. 6)867 **144 R3**
4. 3)832 **277 R1**
5. 5)945 **189**
6. 2)8,765 **4,382 R1**
7. 9)1,927 **214 R1**
8. 7)2,520 **360**
9. 3)2,953 **984 R1**
10. 5)3,105 **621**
11. 7)25,494 **3,642**
12. 9)28,890 **3,210**
13. 2)13,178 **6,589**
14. 4)24,136 **6,034**
15. 6)31,224 **5,204**
16. 8)92,146 **11,518 R2**
17. 3)57,183 **19,061**
18. 2)46,872 **23,436**
19. 4)73,946 **18,486 R2**
20. 5)28,970 **5,794**
21. 7)71,848 **10,264**
22. 6)$8.46 **$1.41**
23. 9)$74.70 **$8.30**
24. 8)$146.56 **$18.32**
25. 6)$98.70 **$16.45**

26. 1,876 ÷ 7 **268**
27. 3,745 ÷ 9 **416 R1**
28. 42,324 ÷ 5 **8,464 R4**
29. 2,432 ÷ 4 **608**
30. 32,364 ÷ 6 **5,394**
31. 45,382 ÷ 8 **5,672 R6**
32. 71,057 ÷ 7 **10,151**
33. 18,054 ÷ 9 **2,006**
34. 20,721 ÷ 3 **6,907**

35. Estimate, then find 23,574 divided by 6. **4,000; 3,929**

36. Estimate, then find the quotient if the dividend is 8,865 and the divisor is 3. **3,000; 2,955**

37. The advertising cost for 4 minutes of radio time was $2,032. What was the cost per minute? **$508 per minute**

38. In a recent year, the record charge for television advertising was about $250,000 per minute. At this rate, about how many minutes could be bought with $1,550,000? **6 min**

### Think Math

**Prime Numbers**

A **prime number** is a number that has exactly two factors, the number itself and 1. Other whole numbers (except 0 and 1) are **composite.**

- 7 is a prime number, since it is the product of the two factors 1 and 7 and no others.
- 6 is a composite number, since it is the product of 3 and 2 as well as 1 and 6.

Can you list the prime numbers up to 50? **See teaching notes.**



## Using Page 117

**Exercises 1–34** Be alert for special problems with zero as related to the short division process in these exercises. Also observe students' work with exercises involving 5-digit quotients.

**Exercises 35–36** Each of the dividends in these exercises must be rounded to the nearest thousand in order to estimate using a basic fact. Encourage students to compare the estimate with the actual answer.

**Exercise 38** Have students use calculators with 8-digit displays to find this answer. To extend the problem, have students time the commercials during a favorite program and calculate the cost at the rate given.

**Think Math** This activity provides an opportunity to define and emphasize the idea of prime and composite numbers. For students who have completed the factor tree Think Math on page 113, describe prime numbers as numbers with factor trees which contain only the number itself and 1. Composite numbers can be also shown as a rectangular array of dots; prime numbers cannot.

●●●●<br>●●●● → 8 is composite

●●●●●●● → 7 is prime

The prime numbers less than 50 are 2, 3, 5, 7, 11, 13, 17, 19, 23, 29, 31, 37, 41, 43, and 47.

**Reteaching Supplement,** page 28

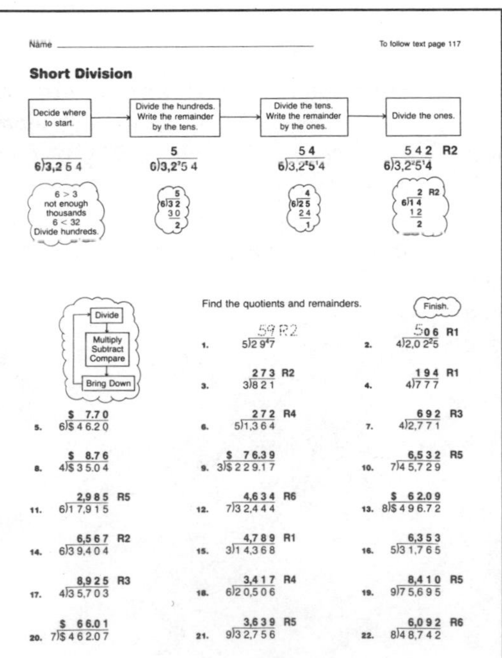

Name ______ To follow text page 117

**Short Division**

Decide where to start. → Divide the hundreds. Write the remainder by the tens. → Divide the tens. Write the remainder by the ones. → Divide the ones.

6)3,254 → 5 → 54 → 542 R2

6 > 3 not enough thousands; 6 < 32 Divide hundreds.

Divide → Multiply, Subtract, Compare → Bring Down

Find the quotients and remainders. Finish.

1. 5)297 **59 R2**
2. 4)2,025 **506 R1**
3. 3)821 **273 R2**
4. 4)777 **194 R1**
5. 6)$46.20 **$7.70**
6. 5)1,364 **272 R4**
7. 4)2,771 **692 R3**
8. 4)$35.04 **$8.76**
9. 3)$229.17 **$76.39**
10. 7)45,729 **6,532 R5**
11. 6)17,915 **2,985 R5**
12. 7)32,444 **4,634 R6**
13. 8)$496.72 **$62.09**
14. 6)39,404 **6,567 R2**
15. 3)14,368 **4,789 R1**
16. 5)31,765 **6,353**
17. 4)35,703 **8,925 R3**
18. 6)20,506 **3,417 R4**
19. 9)75,695 **8,410 R5**
20. 7)$462.07 **$66.01**
21. 9)32,756 **3,639 R5**
22. 8)48,742 **6,092 R6**

**Enrichment Supplement,** page 28

Name ______ To follow text page 117

**A Division Race**

Use long division to solve problems 1 through 6. Write all your work. Find the total amount of time you need to solve these problems. Record your time.

1. 4)212 **53** (20, 12, 12, 0)
2. 5)9,870 **1,974** (5, 48, 45, 37, 35, 20, 20, 0)
3. 9)20,090 **3,210** (27, 18, 18, 09, 9, 00, 0, 0)
4. 3)37,706 **12,568 R2** (3, 7, 6, 17, 15, 20, 18, 26, 24, 2)
5. 8)38,800 **4,850** (32, 68, 64, 40, 40, 00, 0, 0)
6. 7)37,996 **5,428** (35, 29, 28, 19, 14, 56, 56, 0)

Time: ______

Use short division to solve these problems. Record your time.

7. 4)272 **68**
8. 5)8,625 **1,725**
9. 9)31,275 **3,475**
10. 3)39,812 **13,270 R2**
11. 8)34,880 **4,360**
12. 7)34,545 **4,935**

Time: ______

Difference in times: ______

13. What can you conclude about short division? **It is faster than long division.**

**Practice Supplement,** page 44

Name ______ To follow text page 117

**Short Division**

Divide. Use short division.

1. 5)235 **47**
2. 4)562 **140 R2**
3. 3)946 **315 R1**
4. 7)602 **86**
5. 9)4,627 **514 R1**
6. 6)3,589 **598 R1**
7. 4)2,281 **570 R1**
8. 8)6,513 **814 R1**
9. 4)3,014 **753 R2**
10. 5)2,947 **589 R2**
11. 6)2,618 **436 R2**
12. 7)2,692 **384 R4**
13. 8)35,468 **4,433 R4**
14. 3)29,477 **9,825 R2**
15. 4)29,030 **7,257 R2**
16. 7)86,395 **12,342 R1**
17. 5)78,755 **15,751**
18. 6)91,666 **15,277 R4**
19. 3)$7.53 **$2.51**
20. 2)$77.94 **$38.97**
21. 4)$266.64 **$66.66**
22. 8)$78.40 **$9.80**
23. 9)$158.58 **$17.62**
24. 7)$452.34 **$64.62**
25. 5)58,473 **11,694 R3**
26. 6)48,590 **8,098 R2**
27. 4)81,654 **20,413 R2**

**Quick Review** Students give orally the missing number in each division fact.

25 ÷ 5 = □   42 ÷ □ = 7   12 ÷ 3 = □   □ ÷ 9 = 4   81 ÷ □ = 9
□ ÷ 9 = 6   14 ÷ □ = 2   56 ÷ 8 = □   □ ÷ 5 = 4
72 ÷ □ = 9   49 ÷ □ = 7   □ ÷ 9 = 5   28 ÷ □ = 7   60 ÷ □ = 6

**Lesson Focus** To find the average of a set of numbers; to use data from tables to solve word problems

## Ideas for Getting Started

Write the following numbers on the chalkboard: 93, 88, 76, 95, 83. "Which of the following numbers would you choose as the best possibility for the average of the five numbers (no computation please): 99, 85, or 52?" Why did you decide not to choose 52. (It is smaller than any of the numbers.) "Why did you choose 85?" (It is the best representative for the numbers.) Write a problem such as ___ + ___ + ___ + ___ = 32 on the chalkboard. Ask students to write a different number in each blank so that the sum will equal 32. Encourage as many different solutions as possible. Then ask students to write the same number in each blank so that the sum will equal 32. Tell them that this number is a representative number of any four numbers with the sum 32 and is called the average of these four numbers.

## Using Page 118

**Motivational Problem** Have students read the problem at the top of the page. "What question are we asked about Nina's test scores?" (What is her average score?) "Where can we get the data we need to answer this question?" (from the graph) Elicit ideas from students on how to find the average of the five test scores.

**Lesson Development** Have students read the instruction boxes that tell how to find the average of a set of numbers. Work through the example on the chalkboard as students follow the instruction boxes. "What is the sum of the test scores?" (460) "How many test scores are there?" (5) "What is 460 ÷ 5?" (92) Have students check the answer to the division by multiplying 5 × 92. Then have them read the sentence that gives the answer to the question.

**Other Examples** Note that in this example when the test score total is divided, there is a remainder. Point out that because the remainder is closer to 0 than to the divisor 4, the average to the nearest whole number is the quotient. However, if the remainder had been 2 or more, the average to the nearest whole number would have been 87.

**Exercises 1–7** If possible, have students guess the average of one or two of the numbers before they calculate the exact average. Be alert for difficulties in deciding how to round the answer to the nearest whole number.

## Finding Averages

The graph shows Nina's scores on 5 mathematics tests. What is her average score?

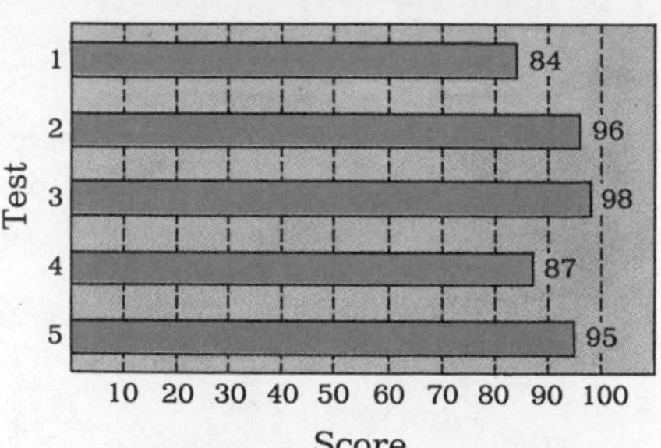


To find the average of a set of numbers, we add the numbers and divide the sum by the number of addends.

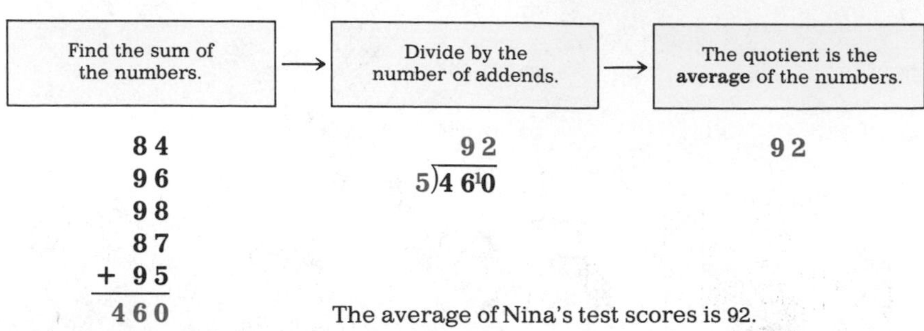

Find the sum of the numbers.
Divide by the number of addends.
The quotient is the average of the numbers.
84
96
98
87
+ 95
460
92
5)4 6¹0
92


The average of Nina's test scores is 92.

**Other Examples**

Find the average of these test scores.

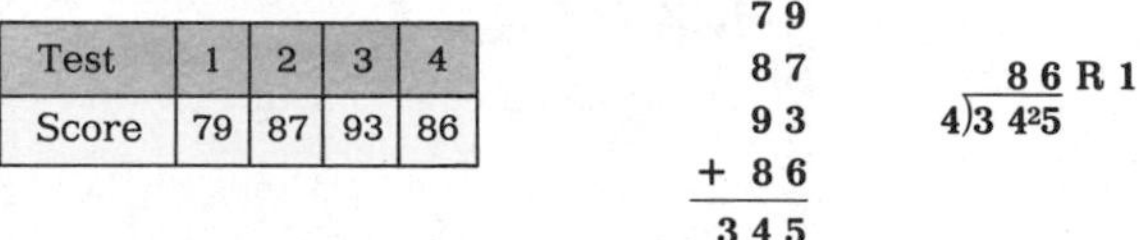

| Test | 1 | 2 | 3 | 4 |
|---|---|---|---|---|
| Score | 79 | 87 | 93 | 86 |

79
87
93
+ 86
345

86 R 1
4)3 4²5

The remainder, 1, is closer to 0 than to the divisor, 4, so the average, to the nearest whole number, is 86.

Find the average of these test scores, to the nearest whole number.

**1.** 76, 84, 96, 80 84   **2.** 98, 91, 86, 92 92   **3.** 99, 89, 83 90

**4.** 67, 74, 86, 92, 95 83   **5.** 71, 75, 86, 94, 82, 74 80

**6.** 92, 88, 96, 98, 99, 100 96   **7.** 74, 86, 91, 82, 79 82



## Follow Up

### Reteaching

Discuss what is meant by an average. Suggest some nonmathematical applications of this concept, such as an "average car," " an average person," and so on, to bring out that the term refers to a representative idea. Then define the concept of arithmetic average and demonstrate with examples how a representative number is found. Help students to generalize the rule shown below.

$$\text{Average} = \frac{\text{sum of addends}}{\text{number of addends}}$$

### Enrichment

Have students find articles from the sports section of the local newspaper and compute the average number of points scored per player in a given game or the average number of points scored by a player or a team per game or per season.

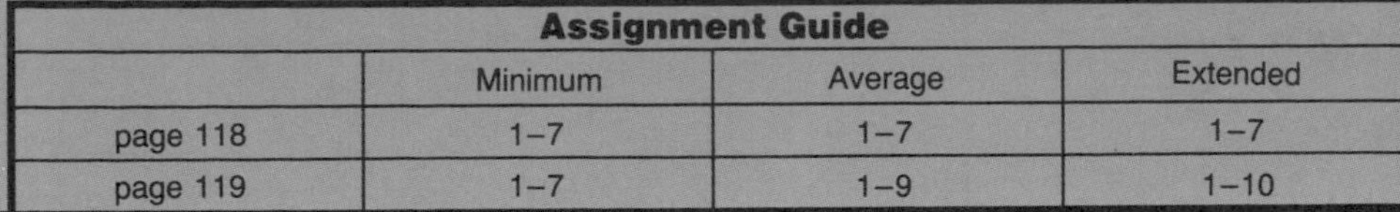

| Assignment Guide | | | |
|---|---|---|---|
| | Minimum | Average | Extended |
| page 118 | 1–7 | 1–7 | 1–7 |
| page 119 | 1–7 | 1–9 | 1–10 |

## Problem Solving: Using Data from Tables

Solve.

| Jorge's Bowling Scores | |
|---|---|
| Game | Score |
| 1 | 174 |
| 2 | 190 |
| 3 | 158 |

1. What is Jorge's average bowling score for the 3 games? 174
2. How much higher is Jorge's highest bowling score than his average? 16
3. What is the average height of the students? the average weight? 149 cm; 39 kg
4. What is the difference between the average height of the girls and the average height of the boys? 6 cm
5. By how much does the average weight of the children in the table differ from the average weight of 37 kg for children their age? 2 kg more

| Name | Height (cm) | Weight (kg) |
|---|---|---|
| Doug | 149 | 40 |
| Carol | 148 | 38 |
| Bret | 143 | 35 |
| Ann | 152 | 42 |
| Art | 145 | 37 |
| Joan | 155 | 39 |

6. What is the average speed for the race car on the 4 time trials? 307 km/h
7. By how much does the average time trial speed differ from the time trial record speed of 325 km/h? 18 km/h less

| Time Trial | Race Car Speed (km/h) |
|---|---|
| 1 | 314 |
| 2 | 295 |
| 3 | 318 |
| 4 | 301 |

8. **DATA BANK** To the nearest whole number, what is the average number of clear days per year in the six sunniest cities in the United States? (See Data Bank, page 408.) 203
9. **DATA HUNT** Suppose you write the names of the students in your class on slips of paper and put them in a hat. Then you draw 5 names. What is the average height of those students in centimeters? Guess first, then find out. Answers will vary.
10. **Try This** During a 30-day month there were 2 rainy days for every 3 clear days. How many of the days were clear? Hint: Make a table. 18



## Using Page 119

**Lesson Development** If necessary, read the problems with students and discuss the sources of data before students are assigned the exercises.

**Exercises 1–5** Note that exercise 2 relies on the answer from exercise 1 as well as information in the table. Note also that exercises 4 and 5 use information calculated in exercise 3.

**Data Bank** This Data Bank refers students to the back of the book for the necessary information about the six sunniest U.S. cities.

**Data Hunt** In this activity students have an opportunity to collect their own data for the solution of a problem.

**Try This** A possible strategy, Make a Table, was taught on page 100.

**Discussion** "What question are we asked about the 30-day month?" (How many of the days were clear?) "How many days in the month?" (30) "How many clear days were there?" (3 clear for every 2 rainy days) "If there were 4 rainy days, how many clear days?" (6) "How can a table be used to help find the solution to the problem?"

**Solution** For the 30-day month, there were 18 clear days.

| Rainy days | 2 | 4 | 6 | 8 | 10 | 12 |
|---|---|---|---|---|---|---|
| Clear days | 3 | 6 | 9 | 12 | 15 | 18 |
| Total | 5 | 10 | 15 | 20 | 25 | 30 |

**Reteaching Supplement,** page 29

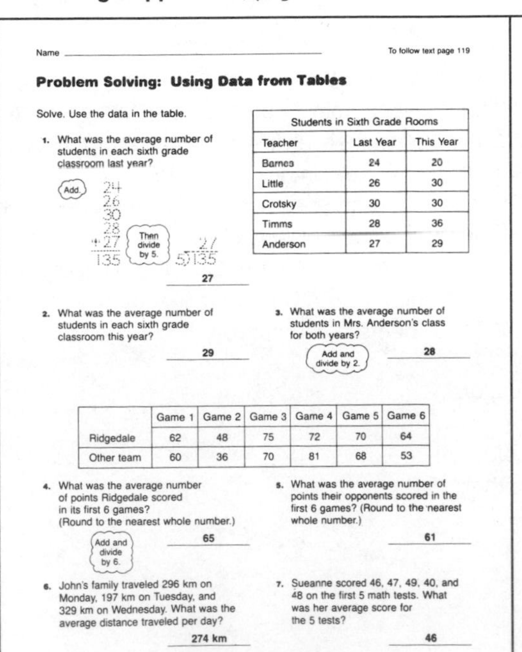

Name ______ To follow text page 119

**Problem Solving: Using Data from Tables**

Solve. Use the data in the table.

| Students in Sixth Grade Rooms | | |
|---|---|---|
| Teacher | Last Year | This Year |
| Barnes | 24 | 20 |
| Little | 26 | 30 |
| Crotsky | 30 | 30 |
| Timms | 28 | 36 |
| Anderson | 27 | 29 |

1. What was the average number of students in each sixth grade classroom last year?
   Add. 24, 26, 30, 28, + 27 = 135. Then divide by 5. 5)135 = 27
   27
2. What was the average number of students in each sixth grade classroom this year? 29
3. What was the average number of students in Mrs. Anderson's class for both years? Add and divide by 2. 28

| | Game 1 | Game 2 | Game 3 | Game 4 | Game 5 | Game 6 |
|---|---|---|---|---|---|---|
| Ridgedale | 62 | 48 | 75 | 72 | 70 | 64 |
| Other team | 60 | 36 | 70 | 81 | 68 | 53 |

4. What was the average number of points Ridgedale scored in its first 6 games? (Round to the nearest whole number.) Add and divide by 6. 65
5. What was the average number of points their opponents scored in the first 6 games? (Round to the nearest whole number.) 61
6. John's family traveled 296 km on Monday, 197 km on Tuesday, and 329 km on Wednesday. What was the average distance traveled per day? 274 km
7. Sueanne scored 46, 47, 49, 40, and 48 on the first 5 math tests. What was her average score for the 5 tests? 46

**Enrichment Supplement,** page 29

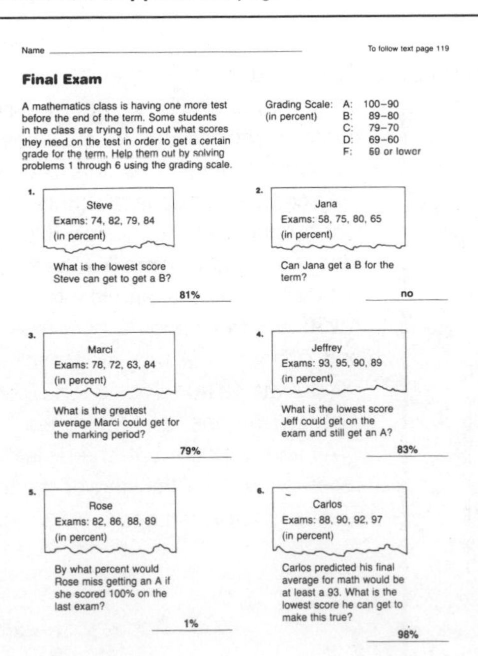

Name ______ To follow text page 119

**Final Exam**

A mathematics class is having one more test before the end of the term. Some students in the class are trying to find out what scores they need on the test in order to get a certain grade for the term. Help them out by solving problems 1 through 6 using the grading scale.

Grading Scale: (in percent)
A: 100–90
B: 89–80
C: 79–70
D: 69–60
F: 59 or lower

1. Steve — Exams: 74, 82, 79, 84 (in percent)
   What is the lowest score Steve can get to get a B? 81%
2. Jana — Exams: 58, 75, 80, 65 (in percent)
   Can Jana get a B for the term? no
3. Marci — Exams: 78, 72, 63, 84 (in percent)
   What is the greatest average Marci could get for the marking period? 79%
4. Jeffrey — Exams: 93, 95, 90, 89 (in percent)
   What is the lowest score Jeff could get on the exam and still get an A? 83%
5. Rose — Exams: 82, 86, 88, 89 (in percent)
   By what percent would Rose miss getting an A if she scored 100% on the last exam? 1%
6. Carlos — Exams: 88, 90, 92, 97 (in percent)
   Carlos predicted his final average for math would be at least a 93. What is the lowest score he can get to make this true? 98%

**Practice Supplement,** page 45

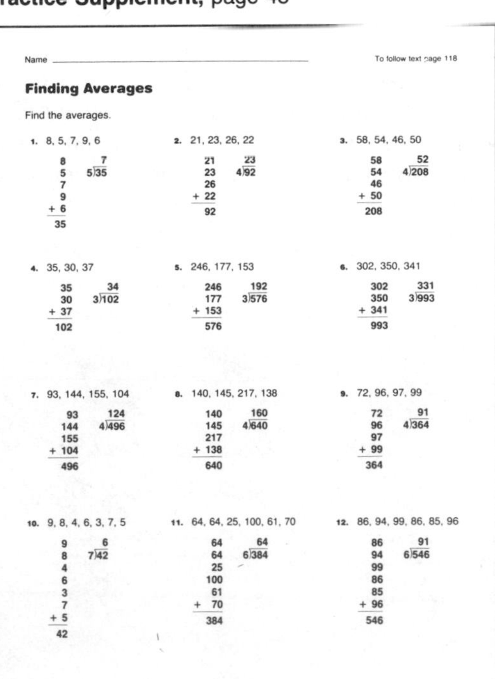

Name ______ To follow text page 118

**Finding Averages**

Find the averages.

1. 8, 5, 7, 9, 6 — 8 + 5 + 7 + 9 + 6 = 35; 5)35 = 7
2. 21, 23, 26, 22 — 21 + 23 + 26 + 22 = 92; 4)92 = 23
3. 58, 54, 46, 50 — 58 + 54 + 46 + 50 = 208; 4)208 = 52
4. 35, 30, 37 — 35 + 30 + 37 = 102; 3)102 = 34
5. 246, 177, 153 — 246 + 177 + 153 = 576; 3)576 = 192
6. 302, 350, 341 — 302 + 350 + 341 = 993; 3)993 = 331
7. 93, 144, 155, 104 — 93 + 144 + 155 + 104 = 496; 4)496 = 124
8. 140, 145, 217, 138 — 140 + 145 + 217 + 138 = 640; 4)640 = 160
9. 72, 96, 97, 99 — 72 + 96 + 97 + 99 = 364; 4)364 = 91
10. 9, 8, 4, 6, 3, 7, 5 — 9 + 8 + 4 + 6 + 3 + 7 + 5 = 42; 7)42 = 6
11. 64, 64, 25, 100, 61, 70 — 64 + 64 + 25 + 100 + 61 + 70 = 384; 6)384 = 64
12. 86, 94, 99, 86, 85, 96 — 86 + 94 + 99 + 86 + 85 + 96 = 546; 6)546 = 91

# Division

**Quick Review** Students tell whether a trade is necessary, then subtract.

| 54 | 70 | 48 | 92 | 45 | 206 | 114 | 38 | 84 | 50 |
|---|---|---|---|---|---|---|---|---|---|
| − 6 | − 30 | − 46 | − 77 | − 26 | − 50 | − 101 | − 9 | − 60 | − 20 |
| yes 48 | no 40 | no 2 | yes 15 | yes 19 | yes 156 | no 13 | yes 29 | no 24 | no 30 |

**Lesson Focus** To divide by 2-digit multiples of 10

## Ideas for Getting Started

Write the following on the chalkboard.

| 60 Multiplier and Divider | | | | | | | | | |
|---|---|---|---|---|---|---|---|---|---|
| 1 | 2 | 3 | 4 | 5 | 6 | 7 | 8 | 9 | 10 |
| 60 + | 60 + | 60 + | 60 + | 60 + | 60 + | 60 + | 60 + | 60 + | 60 |
| 60 | 120 | 180 | 240 | 300 | 360 | 420 | 480 | 540 | 600 |

Then have students make and use the Multiplier and Divider to estimate quotients such as 60)195, 60)256, 60)478, 60)536, 60)439. Next ask students to make a 70 Multiplier and Divider and use it to estimate quotients such as 70)153, 70)294, 70)510, 70)361. Then have students make other multipliers and dividers, or provide oral practice with quotients such as 60)240, 30)240, 50)250, 80)320, 90)360.

## Using Page 120

**Motivational Problem** "What question are we asked about the raft trip?" (How many days will the trip take?) "What data are we given in the problem?" (total trip, 362 km; average 30 km per day) In discussing the plan for solving the problem, point out that we want to find the number of 30-kilometer trips in a 362-kilometer trip. Since we want to find out how many equal amounts in the total, we use division.

**Lesson Development** Work through the example problem on the chalkboard. Remind students that we divide with a 2-digit divisor much the same way as with a 1-digit divisor. In this case we divide the hundreds, then the tens, then the ones. In each place the dividing process is the same. In "deciding where to start," point out that since there are not enough hundreds, we start by dividing the tens. Emphasize the *divide, multiply, subtract,* and *compare* process.

**Other Examples** Note in the first exercise that there are not enough hundreds or tens to divide. The quotient is found by dividing ones. The second example requires that students complete the dividing process in the hundreds, tens, and the ones place. Note the role of the zero in the quotient in the third example.

**Warm Up** Be alert for confusion between these exercises and similar exercises with 1-digit divisors. Emphasize the importance of deciding where to start.

*Manipulative activities are suggested in Ideas for Getting Started.*

## Dividing by Multiples of 10

A guidebook suggests that you can average 30 km a day on a 362-km raft trip on the Colorado River through the Grand Canyon. About how many days will the trip take?

Since we want to find how many equal amounts in the total, we divide.

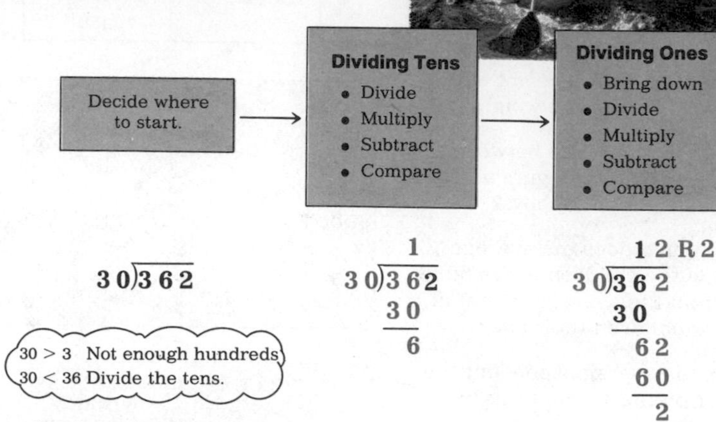


The raft trip will take about 12 days.

**Other Examples**

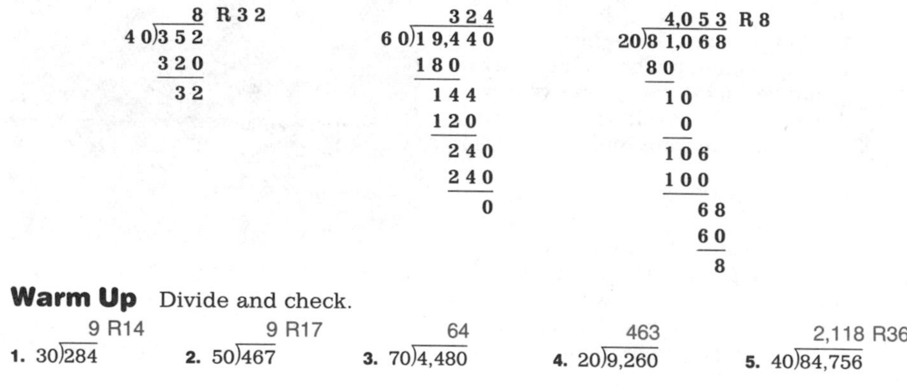


**Warm Up** Divide and check.

1. 30)284 (9 R14)
2. 50)467 (9 R17)
3. 70)4,480 (64)
4. 20)9,260 (463)
5. 40)84,756 (2,118 R36)

120

## Follow Up

### Reteaching

Point out to students that the division process here is similar to that in estimating quotients; all divisors are multiples of ten. Remind students that this means that they can use basic facts to find the special products and quotients. Review the idea that we can name numbers in different ways. For example, the number 4,230 is 4 thousands 2 hundreds 3 tens and 0 ones. We can also think of this number as 42 hundreds 3 tens 0 ones, or 423 tens 0 ones, or 4,230 ones.

As you work through the division algorithm, show how thinking of these other number names is important.

### Enrichment

Have students find lengths (arm span, door height, and so on) in centimeters and then divide by 10 to find the equivalent decimeter measure.

In another activity, have students find the sum of arm spans for 20 or 30 students, and then find the average arm span by dividing by the number of students in the survey.

| Assignment Guide | | | |
|---|---|---|---|
| | Minimum | Average | Extended |
| page 121 | 1–30, 34–36 | 1–37 | 1–37 odd, TM |

Divide and check.

1. 20)174 — 8 R14
2. 60)252 — 4 R12
3. 40)362 — 9 R2
4. 30)291 — 9 R21
5. 70)572 — 8 R12
6. 50)1,226 — 24 R26
7. 80)4,560 — 57
8. 40)2,743 — 68 R23
9. 30)2,520 — 84
10. 90)5,895 — 65 R45
11. 20)1,560 — 78
12. 60)4,182 — 69 R42
13. 50)4,199 — 83 R49
14. 70)2,600 — 37 R10
15. 80)7,492 — 93 R52
16. 90)28,260 — 314
17. 20)13,140 — 657
18. 40)12,200 — 305
19. 60)43,858 — 730 R58
20. 80)53,298 — 666 R18
21. 30)15,600 — 520
22. 50)106,700 — 2,134
23. 70)434,280 — 6,204
24. 90)128,250 — 1,425
25. 40)241,697 — 6,042 R17
26. 60)308,765 — 5,146 R5
27. 80)250,240 — 3,128

28. 565 ÷ 60 — 9 R25
29. 337 ÷ 40 — 8 R17
30. 2,856 ÷ 70 — 40 R56
31. 50,960 ÷ 80 — 637
32. 20,700 ÷ 30 — 690
33. 474,390 ÷ 90 — 5,271

34. Estimate, then find the quotient: 1,756 divided by 60. 30; 29 R16

35. Estimate, then find the quotient if the dividend is 2,439 and the divisor is 80. 30; 30 R39

36. A motor boat can average 50 km a day on the 362-km river trip through the Grand Canyon. About how many days will the trip take? about 7 days (7 R12)

37. If there were 30 people on the boat trip described on page 120 and 60 dozen eggs were eaten, how many eggs per person per day were eaten? 2

**Think**

**Logical Reasoning**

On the scale the large blocks weigh the same. Each small block weighs 1 g (gram). What is the weight of each large block?
124 g

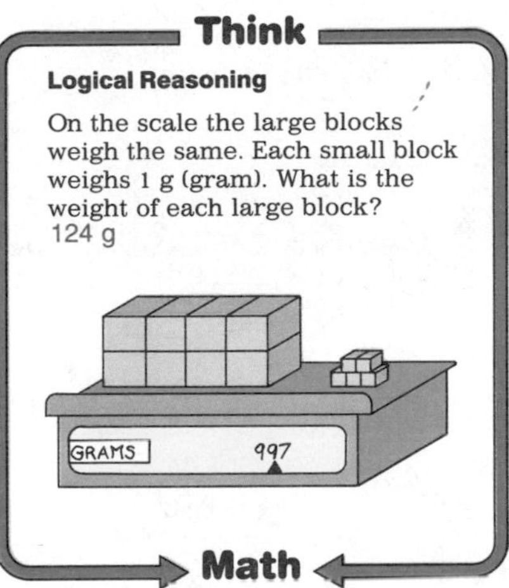

**Math**



## Using Page 121

**Exercises 1–33** Before assigning these exercises, review "deciding where to start." In exercise 12 elicit from students that there are not enough thousands and not enough hundreds to divide, so the dividing process must begin with tens. If necessary, encourage students to draw a light line under the digit in the tens place. This will remind them that the first quotient digit should be written in the tens place.

**Exercises 34–35** The dividends in each of these exercises should be rounded to the nearest hundred in order to estimate using a basic fact. Encourage students to compare the estimate with the calculated answer.

**Exercise 37** Note that students must get data from the problem on page 120 in order to solve this problem. Students also need to know that there are 12 eggs in a dozen. Caution them to think through this problem carefully.

**Think Math** This problem provides an opportunity for students to think logically about a situation involving weights of different size blocks. As hints to help students get started, ask: "What is the weight of each small block?" (1 gram) "If the small blocks were taken off the scale, what weight would the scale show for the 8 large blocks?" (997 − 5, or 992) Students should be able to complete the exercise with this information.

*Activities or worksheets are available for follow up based on individual needs for reteaching, enrichment, or practice.*

### Reteaching Supplement, page 30

Name ________________ To follow text page 121

**Dividing by Multiples of 10**

Decide where to start. → Divide the hundreds. → Divide the tens. → Divide the ones.

40)5,360 — 40 > 5, not enough thousands; 40 < 53, Divide hundreds.

40)5,360: 1 (4)5); 40 (40 × 1); 13 — Subtract and compare. 13 < 40

40)5,360: 13; 40; Bring down. 136; 3 (4)13); 120 Multiply.; 16 Subtract and compare.

40)5,360: 134; 40; 136; 120; 160 Divide.; 160 Multiply.; 0 Subtract and compare.

Divide.

1. 30)3,362 — 112 R2
2. 20)4,754 — 237 R14 (Finish dividing.)
3. 50)41,332 — 826 R32 (Finish dividing.)
4. 60)3,755 — 62 R35
5. 20)888 — 44 R8
6. 90)3,066 — 34 R6
7. 40)1,443 — 36 R3
8. 29,636 ÷ 40 — 740 R36
9. 66,364 ÷ 80 — 829 R44
10. 6,500 ÷ 20 — 325

### Enrichment Supplement, page 30

Name ________________ To follow text page 121

**Lost and Found**

Write the missing digits.

1. 40)960 — 24
2. 50)18,324 — 366 R24
3. 60)35,240 — 587 R20
4. 20)7,793 — 389 R13
5. 70)117,892 — 1,684 R12
6. 90)280,090 — 3,112 R10

### Practice Supplement, page 46

Name ________________ To follow text page 121

**Dividing by Multiples of 10**

Divide.

1. 50)163 — 3 R13
2. 90)377 — 4 R17
3. 60)598 — 9 R58
4. 80)183 — 2 R23
5. 20)1,915 — 95 R15
6. 40)2,593 — 64 R33
7. 70)3,257 — 46 R37
8. 50)4,378 — 87 R28
9. 80)6,143 — 76 R63
10. 90)4,699 — 52 R19
11. 60)5,005 — 83 R25
12. 40)3,152 — 78 R32
13. 60)11,052 — 184 R12
14. 90)48,786 — 542 R6
15. 70)38,112 — 544 R32
16. 40)366,240 — 9,156
17. 80)434,561 — 5,432 R1
18. 60)409,635 — 6,827 R15

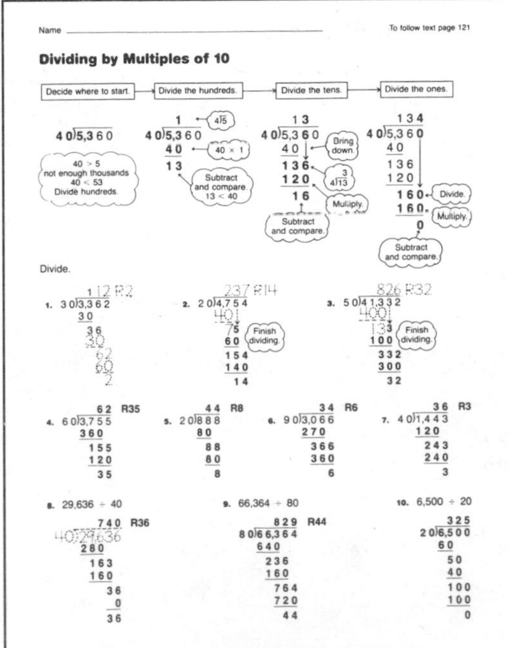

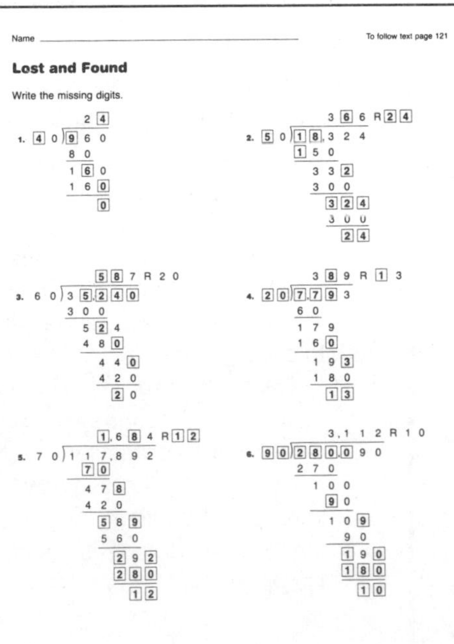

**Quick Review** Provide the following review of multiplication facts.

7 × 8 4 × 9 5 × 6 2 × 8 7 × 4 3 × 6 9 × 4
7 × 2 8 × 5 6 × 9 4 × 6 7 × 9 3 × 8
8 × 4 5 × 9 6 × 6 8 × 3 6 × 8 9 × 9 2 × 6

**Lesson Focus** To divide by a 2-digit divisor to find a 1-digit quotient

## Ideas for Getting Started

Write the following on the chalkboard.

| 73 × 2 = 146 | 73 × 3 = 219 | 73 × 4 = 292 | 73 × 5 = 365 |
|---|---|---|---|
| 73 × 6 = 438 | 73 × 7 = 511 | 73 × 8 = 584 | 73 × 9 = 657 |

Then have students use the chart to find quotients such as the following: 73)365, 73)300, 73)595, 73)524, 73)462, 73)230, 73)164, 73)663. After students have found these quotients, discuss how the quotient could have been estimated by rounding the divisor to the nearest multiple of 10.

## Using Page 122

**Motivational Problem** "What are we asked to find about Marguerite's hobby?" (how many stained glass pictures she sold) "What data is given in the problem?" (total earnings, $432; each picture, $72) As you discuss the plan for solving the problem, point out that since we want to find how many $72 pictures could be purchased for $432, we can divide.

**Lesson Development** As you work through the problem, pay particular attention to the decision about where to start. Since there are not enough hundreds or tens, we start by dividing 432 ones. Emphasize that we can estimate the quotient by first rounding the divisor, 72, to 70. Since six 70s are 420 and seven 70s are over 432, we can try 6 as the quotient.

Remind students that they could also look at the first digit, 7, and the first two digits of the dividend, 43. Since 43 ÷ 7 is 6, we use this as our estimated quotient.

Have students reread the problem to see if the answer seems reasonable. Then ask a volunteer to read the sentence that gives the answer.

**Other Examples** Note in the third example that the divisor is 45. In this case, students round to 50 and estimate the quotient.

**Warm Up** Note that in each of these cases the rounded divisor provides the correct quotient. Be alert for errors in rounding the divisor and estimating the quotient.

## 2-Digit Divisors: 1-Digit Quotients

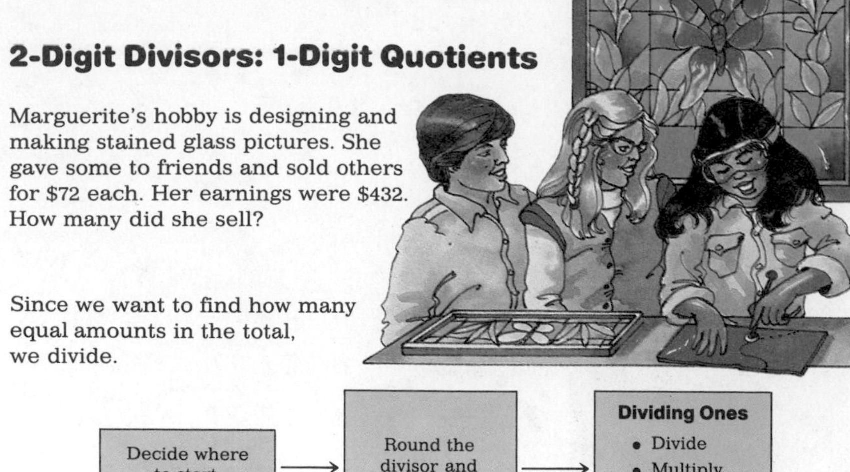

Marguerite's hobby is designing and making stained glass pictures. She gave some to friends and sold others for $72 each. Her earnings were $432. How many did she sell?

Since we want to find how many equal amounts in the total, we divide.

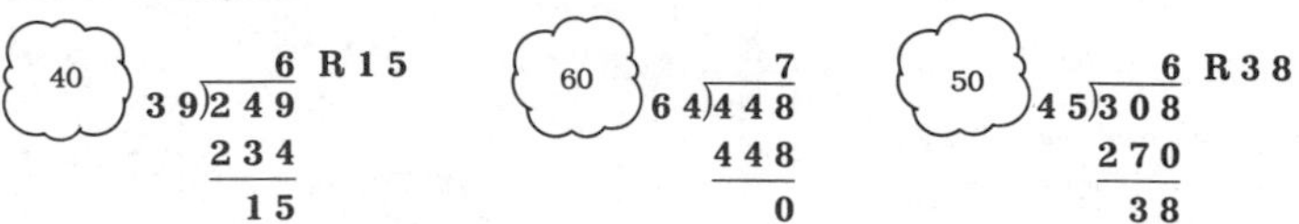


72)432

Not enough hundreds
Not enough tens
72 < 432 Divide the ones.

about 70
72)432

72)432 = 6
432
0

Marguerite sold 6 pictures.

**Other Examples**

(40) 39)249 = 6 R15; 234; 15

(60) 64)448 = 7; 448; 0

(50) 45)308 = 6 R38; 270; 38

**Warm Up** Divide and check.

1. 21)175 8 R7
2. 49)267 5 R22
3. 52)312 6
4. 78)578 7 R32
5. 33)231 7
6. 87)579 6 R57
7. 64)348 5 R28
8. 36)281 7 R29
9. 35)241 6 R31
10. 53)424 8

122

## Follow Up

### Reteaching

To help students understand 2-digit division, review the following ideas:

- Decide where to start. For example, in 32)465, we compare the divisor and the first digit of the dividend. Is 32 < 4? Since the answer is no, we consider the next digit. Is 32 < 46? The answer is yes, so we can begin to divide.
- Estimate to find the first quotient figure. This means we round the divisor to the nearest ten. Emphasize that this number is used only to determine a trial quotient. After that, only the original divisor is used in the algorithm.

### Enrichment

Write problems similar to the ones below on the chalkboard. Have students solve each problem and then write each problem and quotient in Roman numerals.

| | |
|---|---|
| 20)157 = 7 R17 | XX)CLVII = VII RXVII |
| 31)279 = 9 | XXXI)CCLXXIX = IX |
| 78)298 = 3 R64 | LXXVIII)CCXCVIII = III RLXIV |

| Assignment Guide | | | |
|---|---|---|---|
| | Minimum | Average | Extended |
| page 123 | 1–40 | 1–41 | 11–42, TM |

Divide and check.

| | | | | |
|---|---|---|---|---|
| 1. 42)252 6 | 2. 67)217 3 R16 | 3. 38)284 7 R18 | 4. 23)138 6 | 5. 41)205 5 |
| 6. 75)328 4 R28 | 7. 83)664 8 | 8. 56)360 6 R24 | 9. 34)238 7 | 10. 62)558 9 |
| 11. 29)223 7 R20 | 12. 48)150 3 R6 | 13. 72)360 5 | 14. 91)648 7 R11 | 15. 55)262 4 R42 |
| 16. 84)504 6 | 17. 42)378 9 | 18. 38)296 7 R30 | 19. 71)497 7 | 20. 67)443 6 R41 |
| 21. 53)425 8 R1 | 22. 44)396 9 | 23. 29)205 7 R2 | 24. 76)532 7 | 25. 94)567 6 R3 |

| | | | |
|---|---|---|---|
| 26. 164 ÷ 18 9 R2 | 27. 448 ÷ 56 8 | 28. 337 ÷ 42 8 R1 | 29. 439 ÷ 73 6 R1 |
| 30. 123 ÷ 37 3 R12 | 31. 496 ÷ 62 8 | 32. 360 ÷ 51 7 R3 | 33. 362 ÷ 48 7 R26 |
| 34. 286 ÷ 65 4 R26 | 35. 744 ÷ 93 8 | 36. 558 ÷ 62 9 | 37. 504 ÷ 84 6 |

38. Estimate, then find 328 divided by 82. 4

39. Estimate, then find the quotient when the divisor is 49 and the dividend is 354. 7; 7 R11

40. Marguerite uses $26 worth of supplies to make 1 "picture." How many "pictures" can she make for $234? 9

41. Marguerite sold some large stained glass pictures for an average of $94 each. Her earnings fell $30 short of $500. How many pictures did she sell? 5

★ 42. The largest stained glass window in the world has 2,448 panels. Suppose it is rectangular in shape and has the same number of panels in each row. Give four different possible numbers of rows and numbers of panels in each row it might have. Sample answers: 144 × 17, 51 × 48, 102 × 24, 34 × 72 ($2{,}448 = 2^4 \cdot 3^2 \cdot 17$)

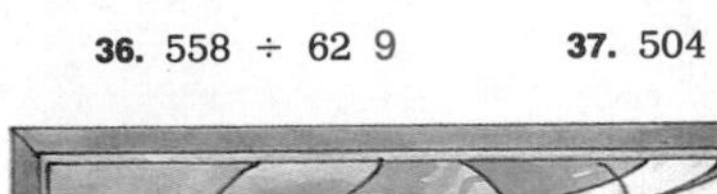

**Think**

**Discovering Some Patterns**

1. Use short division to find this quotient:

   9)11,111,111,010 — 1,234,567,890

   What patterns do you see? See teaching notes.

2. Divide 427,427 by 7. Divide the first quotient by 11, then divide the second quotient by 13. What is the result? Does this work for any number like 427,427? See teaching notes.

**Math**

More Practice, page 417, Set B



## Using Page 123

**Exercises 1–37** In exercises 6, 15, and 34, be sure students round up to the next multiple of 10 before they estimate the quotient. In exercises in which the divisor is rounded up, be sure students who use the shortcut for estimating the quotient use the first digit of the estimated divisor rather than the first digit of the divisor.

**Exercises 38–39** In these exercises both the dividend and the divisor must be rounded to the nearest ten in order to estimate using a basic fact.

**Exercise 41** Note that this exercise involves subtraction and division.

**Exercise 42** Encourage students to use their calculators to find factors of 2,448. Note that smaller factors include 2, 4, 8, 16, 3, 9, and 17.

**Think Math** This activity provides opportunities for students to observe numerical patterns. In the first exercise they might notice that the quotient uses the digits in order from 1 through 9 followed by a 0. Ask students if they can find a division problem that would produce these same digits in reverse order. (9)8888888889)

In exercise 2 students should find that the answer is 427. This works for any number that has a block of three repeating digits. After students have tried several examples, help them see that this is true because 7 × 11 × 13 = 1,001; 1,001 times any 3-digit number equals a number with two blocks of digits identical to the original number.

**More Practice,** page 417, Set B

## Ideas That Work

### Special Education

To review dividing with 1-digit divisors, let students practice distributing or sharing play money. The following procedure can help reinforce students' understanding of the division process.

**Teacher:** Look at the problem. What is the greatest number of tens each will get? Think *down* to the nearest basic fact to help.

**Student:** 6

**Teacher:** If we give 6 to each of 4 people, that is 24 tens with 1 ten left over. Let's use the money to check.

**Student:** (Gives 6 tens to each and sees the 1 ten left over.)

Students should be encouraged to use basic facts to solve larger division problems, to use the language of sharing, and to use the play money to check their thinking.

**Practice Supplement,** page 47

Name ______________________ To follow text page 123

**2-Digit Divisors: 1-Digit Quotients**

Divide.

| | | | |
|---|---|---|---|
| 1. 23)183 7 R22; 161; 22 | 2. 42)370 8 R34; 336; 34 | 3. 76)434 5 R54; 380; 54 | 4. 55)372 6 R42; 330; 42 |
| 5. 37)317 8 R21; 296; 21 | 6. 54)414 7 R36; 378; 36 | 7. 68)393 5 R33; 340; 53 | 8. 46)356 7 R34; 322; 34 |
| 9. 84)602 7 R14; 588; 14 | 10. 52)116 2 R12; 104; 12 | 11. 67)254 3 R53; 201; 53 | 12. 48)177 3 R33; 144; 33 |
| 13. 73)490 6 R52; 438; 52 | 14. 92)775 8 R39; 736; 39 | 15. 81)548 6 R62; 486; 62 | 16. 55)470 8 R30; 440; 30 |
| 17. 63)592 9 R25; 567; 25 | 18. 39)106 2 R28; 78; 28 | 19. 78)321 4 R9; 312; 9 | 20. 41)367 8 R39; 328; 39 |

**Quick Review** Students round 2-digit numbers to the nearest ten and 3-digit numbers to the nearest hundred and then estimate answers.

| | | | |
|---|---|---|---|
| 16 + 12 + 28 60 | 236 − 98 100 | 92 × 12 900 | 45 + 80 + 22 150 |
| 17 + 42 60 | 233 − 140 100 | 13 × 28 300 | 109 × 423 40,000 |

**Lesson Focus** To change estimated quotients of 2-digit divisors

## Ideas for Getting Started

Write the following exercises on the chalkboard. Check ✓ the quotients that are incorrect.

a) ✓ 34)167 quotient 5  b) ✓ 27)173 quotient 5  c) 39)284 quotient 7  d) 45)353 quotient 7

e) ✓ 54)351 quotient 7  f) ✓ 75)379 quotient 4  g) 43)259 quotient 6  h) ✓ 44)259 quotient 6

After students have completed the exercises, discuss each of the answers. Elicit from students that an estimated quotient may be too large or too small. In such cases the quotient would have to be revised.

## Using Page 124

**Lesson Development** Have students read the information in the three paragraphs at the top of the page. Then ask students to focus their attention on Les's problem. "How did Les know his estimated quotient was too small?" (He found the remainder greater than the divisor when comparing.) Have students check Les's revised quotient (and remainder) by multiplying and adding. Then have students consider Eve's problem. "How did Eve know her estimated quotient was too large?" (When she multiplied the quotient by the divisor, the answer was larger than the dividend.) Have students check Eve's revised quotient (and remainder) by multiplying and adding. Have students write the answer to each problem using a complete sentence, and then check to see if their answers are reasonable.

Call students' attention to the reminder about the steps for the dividing process. Without completing the division, discuss several exercises having students decide where to start and explain their decisions.

**Exercises 1–22** Point out that in each of these exercises the dividing starts in the ones place.

## 2-Digit Divisors: Changing Estimates

In the early 1900s the most popular car in America was the Model T Ford. Les and Eve solved these problems about the Model T.

The Model T could travel 340 km at a speed of 56 km/h on one tank of gas. How long would the trip take?

Les

(about 60)
56)340 quotient 5
−280
60
→ 56)340 quotient 6 R4
336
4

Les's first estimated quotient was too small. How did he know it must be larger?

A factory assembly line could turn out 1 Model T every 93 minutes. At this rate how many cars could the line turn out in a 450-minute shift?

Eve

(about 90)
93)450 quotient 5
−465
→ 93)450 quotient 4 R78
372
78

Eve's first estimated quotient was too large. How did she know it must be smaller?

Divide. Watch for estimates that need to be changed.

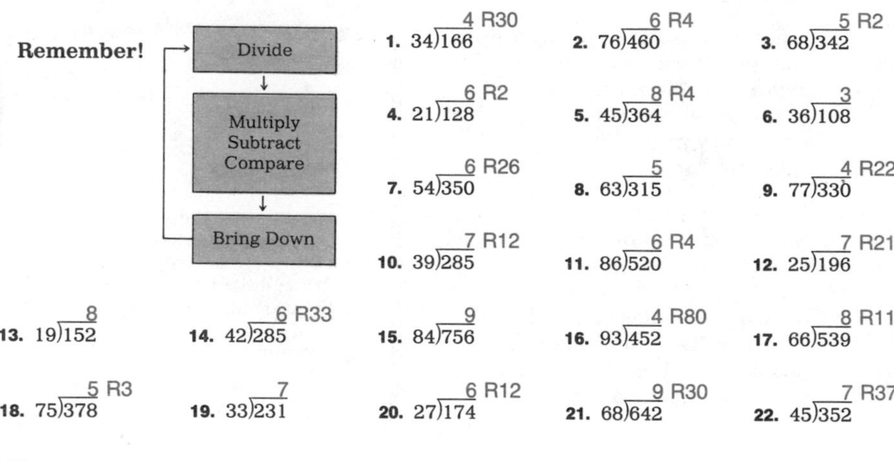


1. 34)166 4 R30  2. 76)460 6 R4  3. 68)342 5 R2
4. 21)128 6 R2  5. 45)364 8 R4  6. 36)108 3
7. 54)350 6 R26  8. 63)315 5  9. 77)330 4 R22
10. 39)285 7 R12  11. 86)520 6 R4  12. 25)196 7 R21
13. 19)152 8  14. 42)285 6 R33  15. 84)756 9  16. 93)452 4 R80  17. 66)539 8 R11
18. 75)378 5 R3  19. 33)231 7  20. 27)174 6 R12  21. 68)642 9 R30  22. 45)352 7 R37



More Practice, page 417, Set C

## Follow Up

### Reteaching

Use the example and steps below to focus on making an estimate and then changing the estimate if necessary.

First try 9 as an estimate of the number of multiples of 30 contained in 275.

(30) 32)275 quotient 9
288 → 288 > 275

9 is too large. Try 8.

(30) 32)275 quotient 8
256
19 → 19 < 32.

8 is the largest multiple of 32 we can use.

### Enrichment

Have students bring to school mail catalogs or newspaper advertisements that show the prices of quantities of a given merchandise—for example, 3 packages of note paper for $1.98 or 5 batteries for $3.49. Have students write word problems to be shared with classmates. Ask students to estimate the cost per item and then find the actual cost per item to check their estimates.

| Assignment Guide | | | |
|---|---|---|---|
| | Minimum | Average | Extended |
| page 124 | 1–22 | 1–22 | 1–22 |
| page 125 | 1–6 | 1–7 | 1–8, TM |

## Problem Solving: Practice

Solve.

1. A Model T cost $850 in 1908. In 1984, a low-cost compact car cost $6,125. How much greater was the cost of the 1984 car? $5,275

2. A Model T went 504 km on 56 L of gasoline. How many kilometers did it go on 1 liter? 9 km

3. In 1904 a steering wheel was first used instead of a steering stick. 47 years later power steering was first used. In what year was that? 1951

4. An auto company in 1903 made a total of 850 cars in 6 months. About how many was this per month? about 141 (141 R4)

5. In 1900 about 42 hundred cars were built. 50 years later 1,909 times as many were built. How many hundreds was that? 80,178 hundred

6. Henry Ford set a record in 1904 when his racing car, the Arrow, reached a speed of 147.2 km/h. About 75 years after that a rocket-powered car reached a speed 874.56 km/h faster than the Arrow's record. What was the speed of the rocket-powered car? 1,021.76 km/h

7. In 1914 a worker in an automobile factory earned $5.04 for 8 hours' work. Some automobile factory workers today earn $96 for 8 hours' work. How much more per hour does today's worker earn? $11.37

8. **Try This** In an antique car tour Felipe started at the park and drove 20 km west, 15 km north, 55 km east, and 70 km south. If all roads run north and south or east and west only, what is the shortest route Felipe can take to return to the park? Give the direction and distances he must travel. Hint: Draw a picture. 35 km west, 55 km north



## Using Page 125

**Lesson Development** Briefly review the 5-Point Checklist—question, data, plan, answer, check—by referring to the logo in the upper left-hand corner of the page. Encourage students to use this checklist as a guide to solving the problems. Alert them to the fact that the problems involve a variety of operations.

**Exercises 1–7** Note that in exercises 1, 4, 5, 6, and 7 dates are given which are not needed in the calculation of the problems. In exercise 3 the date given is used in the calculation. Note that exercise 7 involves two divisions and a subtraction of decimals.

**Try This** A possible strategy, Draw a Picture, was taught on page 74.

**Discussion** "What question do we want to answer about Felipe's car tour?" (What is his shortest route to the park?) "Which direction did Felipe drive first?" (20 km west) "Next?" (15 km north, 55 km east, and 70 km south) "What information could you get if you drew a picture of Felipe's travels?" (his location with regard to his starting place—the park)

**Solution** The shortest route Felipe can take to return to the park is 55 km north and 35 km west.

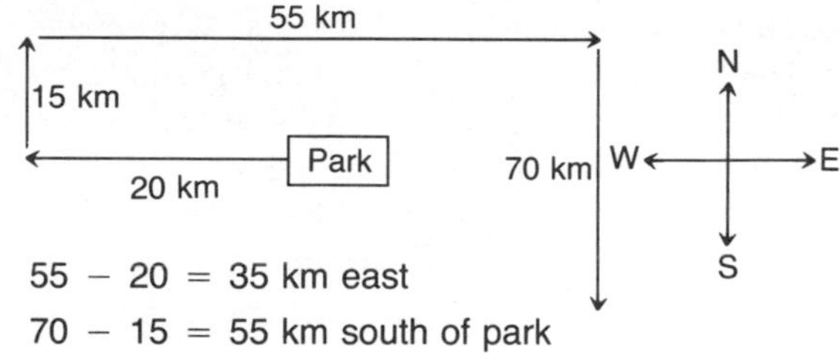


55 − 20 = 35 km east

70 − 15 = 55 km south of park

**More Practice,** page 417, Set C

## Ideas That Work

### Special Education

Slower and learning disabled students may need special help changing estimates. One approach involves breaking instruction into smaller steps:

Step 1: Recognize when a quotient digit is too large. Present a worksheet of partially completed problems as shown below. Instruct students to tell whether the quotient figure is too large or just right. The sharing language will help students decide.

```
     6          5
65)340     93)450
   336        465
```

☐ too large  ☐ just right      ☐ too large  ☐ just right

Step 2: When a quotient digit is too large, make it "right." When the worksheet (above) is checked, return it and ask students how to correct the problems for which the quotient digit was too large.

Steps 3 and 4: Repeat the above steps and focus on examples where the quotient digit was too small.

Step 5: Successfully handle both types of problems. When students have mastered each of the above steps, present a mix of problems similar to those in the lesson on page 124.

**Practice Supplement,** page 48

Name ____________  To follow text page 124

**2-Digit Divisors: Changing Estimates**

Divide.

1. 74)529 = 7 R11 (518, 11)
2. 42)198 = 4 R30 (168, 30)
3. 63)250 = 3 R61 (189, 61)
4. 81)542 = 6 R56 (486, 56)
5. 36)198 = 5 R18 (180, 18)
6. 89)365 = 4 R9 (356, 9)
7. 44)416 = 9 R20 (396, 20)
8. 92)708 = 7 R64 (644, 64)
9. 61)582 = 9 R33 (549, 33)
10. 77)309 = 4 R1 (308, 1)
11. 23)115 = 5 (115, 0)
12. 66)391 = 5 R61 (330, 61)
13. 47)377 = 8 R1 (376, 1)
14. 52)470 = 9 R2 (468, 2)
15. 34)263 = 7 R25 (238, 25)
16. 86)711 = 8 R23 (688, 23)
17. 37)305 = 8 R9 (296, 9)
18. 68)429 = 6 R21 (408, 21)
19. 72)660 = 9 R12 (648, 12)
20. 58)333 = 5 R43 (290, 43)

**Quick Review** Students copy the quotients below, adding dollar signs, decimal points, and zeros where necessary.
$12.00 ÷ 3 = 400 $30.00 ÷ 5 = 600 $81.00 ÷ 9 = 900 $0.18 ÷ 6 = 3
$49.00 ÷ 7 = 700 $0.32 ÷ 4 = 8 $5.15 ÷ 5 = 103

**Lesson Focus** To divide by 2-digit numbers to find larger quotients

## Ideas for Getting Started

Write the division process shown in the chart on page 124 on the chalkboard. Then review the process as you work through these problems with 1-digit quotients: 32)97, 39)173, 65)365, 71)497, 68)296. Ask students to describe each step as they work an example. "What important steps are not included in the chart?" (deciding where to start, estimating the quotient) Discuss these steps as you review the division process.

## Using Page 126

**Motivational Problem** Ask a volunteer to read the problem at the top of the page. "What is the question asked about the band's trip?" (What was the cost for each band member?) "What data from the problem is needed to answer the question?" (total cost, $6,578; number of band members, 46) As you discuss the plan for solving the problem, ask students why they could divide to find the answer. (Since the cost for each member is the same, we could divide to separate the total into equal parts.)

**Lesson Development** Point out to students that division problems with larger quotients are completed by solving a series of simpler problems like the ones reviewed in the Getting Started activity. Discuss the decision regarding where to start. Then complete the dividing process in the hundreds, tens, and ones place. In each place, discuss the shortcut procedure used for estimating the quotient. Then work through each step of the sample problem. Have students check the quotient by multiplying.

Point out that this long division was completed by doing the following three simpler problems: to divide hundreds, 46)65; to divide tens, 46)197; and to divide ones, 46)138. Emphasize that every long division problem can be broken down into two or more simpler divisions with 1-digit quotients. Ask a volunteer to read the complete sentence that gives the answer to the problem.

**Other Examples** In the first example the estimated quotient digits are correct and the answer is a 2-digit number. The second example involves dividing in the thousands place as well as hundreds, tens, and ones. Note that the third example involves money notation.

**Warm Up** Be alert for difficulties in (a) deciding where to start, (b) estimating quotient digits, (c) carrying out the dividing process, (d) basic fact errors, and (e) errors in the multiplication or subtraction algorithms.

## 2-Digit Divisors: Larger Quotients

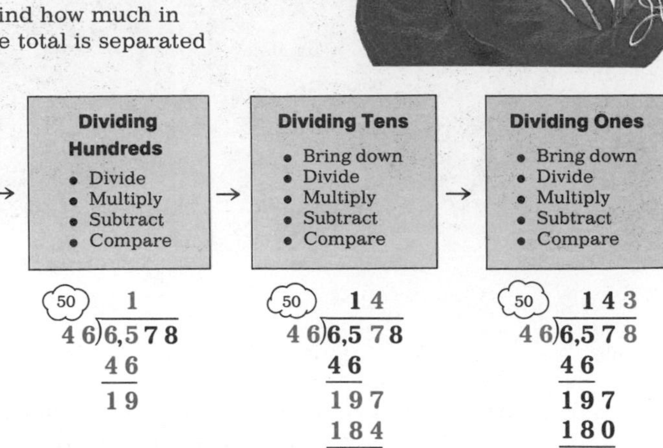

A trip for the 46 members of the school marching band cost a total of $6,578. What was the cost per band member?

Since we want to find how much in each part when the total is separated equally, we divide.

| Decide where to start. | → | **Dividing Hundreds** • Divide • Multiply • Subtract • Compare | → | **Dividing Tens** • Bring down • Divide • Multiply • Subtract • Compare | → | **Dividing Ones** • Bring down • Divide • Multiply • Subtract • Compare |
|---|---|---|---|---|---|---|

```
46)6,578        (50)   1          (50)   14         (50)   143
                   46)6,578          46)6,578          46)6,578
                      46                46                46
                      19                197               197
                                        184               180
                                         13                138
                                                           138
                                                             0
```

Not enough thousands 46 < 65 Divide the hundreds.

The cost per band member was $143.

**Other Examples**

```
    21 R5           2,317             $3.95
23)488          37)85,729         45)$177.75
   46              74                 135
    28             117                 427
    23             111                 405
     5              62                 225
                    37                 225
                   259                   0
                   259
                     0
```

**Warm Up** Divide.

1. 34)782 — 23
2. 68)9,658 — 142 R2
3. 75)94,725 — 1,263
4. 29)7,016 — 241 R27
5. 46)$114.54 — $2.49



## Follow Up

**Reteaching**

Review how the division process is carried out in this example: 37)4683. Emphasize 1) deciding where to start, 2) rounding the divisor to form an estimate, 3) order of division, 4) changing estimates, 5) placing the remainders in the quotients. Work through the example, focusing on the position of each digit in the quotient. Then ask students to explain each step of the procedure in their own words.

**Enrichment**

Give students problems similar to the one below. Ask them to find the factors for the partial products as they subtract in the process of division.

```
37)1,184
     370     10 × 37
     814
     370     10 × 37
     444
     370     10 × 37
      74
      74      2 × 37
       0
```

1,184 ÷ 37 = 32

| Assignment Guide | | | |
|---|---|---|---|
| | Minimum | Average | Extended |
| page 127 | 1–17, 24–29, SK | 1–30, SK | 2–30 even, SK |

Divide and check.

1. 43)2,322 54
2. 68)1,564 23
3. 54)918 17
4. 27)1,975 73 R4
5. 31)2,666 86
6. 78)11,076 142
7. 85)27,540 324
8. 46)9,752 212
9. 92)37,998 413 R2
10. 57)19,762 346 R40
11. 36)14,796 411
12. 62)58,967 951 R5
13. 25)2,495 99 R20
14. 77)6,622 86
15. 86)10,234 119
16. 91)112,294 1,234
17. 37)78,218 2,114
18. 55)200,475 3,645
19. 49)$316.05 $6.45
20. 28)$691.32 $24.69

21. 1,836 ÷ 27 68
22. 2,700 ÷ 58 46 R32
23. 7,875 ÷ 35 225
24. 48,269 ÷ 79 611
25. 28,967 ÷ 83 349
26. 2,660 ÷ 66 40 R20

27. Estimate, then find the quotient: 3,967 divided by 48. 80; 82 R31

28. Estimate, then find the result of dividing 64,276 by 79. 800; 813 R49

29. New uniforms for the school band cost a total of $5,167.50 for 65 students. What was the cost of each uniform? $79.50

30. **DATA HUNT** If a band instrument of your choice was to be paid for in 12 monthly installments (no interest), how much would each monthly payment be? Answers will vary.

## Skillkeeper

Add or subtract.

1. $3.14 + 5.27 = $8.41
2. $7.12 − 3.56 = $3.56
3. $8.75 + 6.49 = $15.24
4. $26.60 − 13.78 = $12.82
5. $38.98 + 17.42 = $56.40

Find the products.

6. $2.42 × 8 = $19.36
7. $69.22 × 4 = $276.88
8. $2.03 × 47 = $95.41
9. $36.51 × 12 = $438.12
10. $4.28 × 317 = $1,356.76

More Practice, page 417, Set D



## Using Page 127

**Exercises 1–26** If necessary, have students use graph paper as an aid in keeping the digits aligned. Select several problems for students to check by using a calculator.

**Exercises 27–28** For these exercises the dividend is rounded to the nearest thousand and the divisor to the nearest ten so that the estimate can be made using a basic fact. Encourage students to compare their estimated answers with their calculated answers.

**Data Hunt** This exercise provides students with an opportunity to collect data outside the textbook. Suggest that students contact selected music stores to determine prices of instruments. As an alternative, students might look in the classified section of the newspaper to see what a used band instrument might cost. A third alternative would be to ask students to discuss prices of instruments with the music teacher in their school.

**Skillkeeper** These skills were originally taught in Chapter 2 and Chapter 4.

**More Practice,** page 417, Set D

**Reteaching Supplement,** page 31

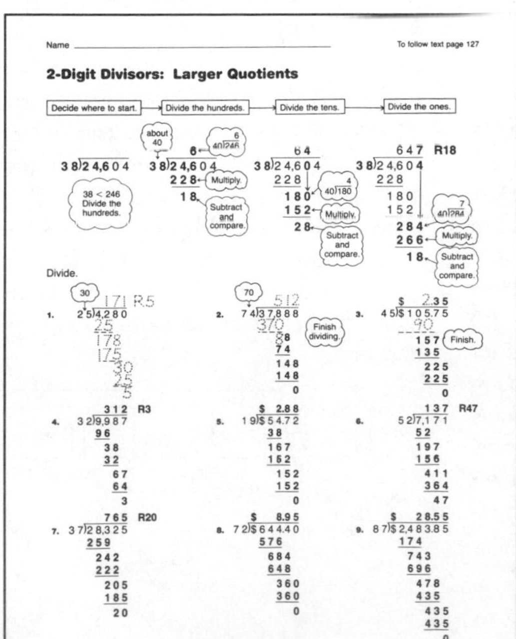

Name ______ To follow text page 127

**2-Digit Divisors: Larger Quotients**

Decide where to start. → Divide the hundreds. → Divide the tens. → Divide the ones.

38)24,604 — 38 < 246 Divide the hundreds.

about 40; 40)246 = 6. 38)24,604: 6; 228 Multiply. 18 Subtract and compare.

64: 228; 180; 40)180 = 4; 152 Multiply. 28 Subtract and compare.

647 R18: 228; 180; 152; 284; 40)284 = 7; 266 Multiply. 18 Subtract and compare.

Divide.

1. 25)4,280 171 R5
2. 74)37,888 512 Finish dividing.
3. 45)$105.75 $2.35 Finish.
4. 32)9,987 312 R3
5. 19)$54.72 $2.88
6. 52)7,171 137 R47
7. 37)28,325 765 R20
8. 72)$644.40 $8.95
9. 87)$2,483.85 $28.55

**Enrichment Supplement,** page 31

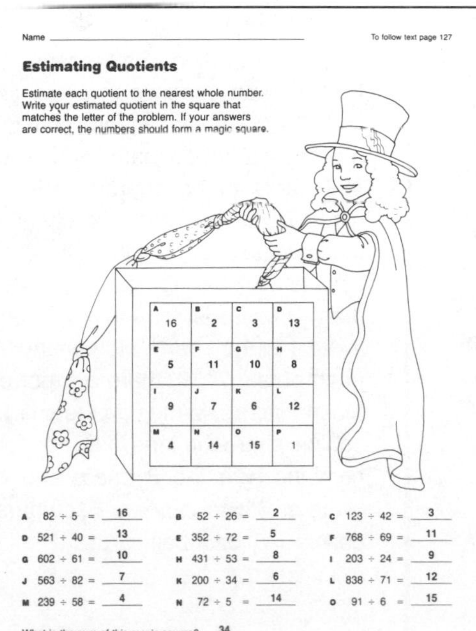

Name ______ To follow text page 127

**Estimating Quotients**

Estimate each quotient to the nearest whole number. Write your estimated quotient in the square that matches the letter of the problem. If your answers are correct, the numbers should form a magic square.

| A 16 | B 2 | C 3 | D 13 |
|---|---|---|---|
| E 5 | F 11 | G 10 | H 8 |
| I 9 | J 7 | K 6 | L 12 |
| M 4 | N 14 | O 15 | P 1 |

A 82 ÷ 5 = 16
B 52 ÷ 26 = 2
C 123 ÷ 42 = 3
D 521 ÷ 40 = 13
E 352 ÷ 72 = 5
F 768 ÷ 69 = 11
G 602 ÷ 61 = 10
H 431 ÷ 53 = 8
I 203 ÷ 24 = 9
J 563 ÷ 82 = 7
K 200 ÷ 34 = 6
L 838 ÷ 71 = 12
M 239 ÷ 58 = 4
N 72 ÷ 5 = 14
O 91 ÷ 6 = 15

What is the sum of this magic square? 34

**Practice Supplement,** page 49

Name ______ To follow text page 127

**2-Digit Divisors: Larger Quotients**

Divide.

1. 54)4,106 76 R2
2. 29)1,775 61 R6
3. 32)2,820 88 R4
4. 81)3,766 46 R40
5. 98)6,200 63 R26
6. 66)2,310 35
7. 53)3,803 71 R40
8. 45)4,369 97 R4
9. 45)17,010 378
10. 76)45,380 597 R8
11. 54)37,102 687 R4
12. 82)44,875 547 R21
13. 68)$880.60 $12.95
14. 35)$894.25 $25.55
15. 77)$863.94 $11.22
16. 56)$514.08 $9.18

**Quick Review** Students copy the products below, adding dollar signs and decimal points.

5 × $4.00 = 2000 6 × $6.00 = 3600 2 × $7.00 = 1400 3 × $4.00 = 1200
4 × $7.00 = 2800 9 × $5.00 = 4500 7 × $7.00 = 4900 9 × $8.00 = 7200

**Lesson Focus** To divide by 2-digit numbers to find quotients, some of which contain zeros; to divide by 3-digit numbers

## Ideas for Getting Started

Let students play "Division Relay" described below.

1. Divide the class into groups of 5. If there are extra students, have them substitute in a team after each round.
2. Provide a piece of chalk and an eraser for each team.
3. Name members of each team to be the divider, the multiplier, the subtracter, the comparer, and the bring-downer.
4. Have teams line up at an assigned place at the chalkboard.
5. Present a division exercise with a 1-digit divisor.
6. At the signal the divider begins and completes his or her step, then moves to the back of the line. Each person on the team completes his or her designated step.
7. The team that first completes the problem correctly wins.

Do the relay several times, changing team positions so that each student has a chance to do each step.

## Using Page 128

**Lesson Development** Direct students' attention to the division problem at the top of the page. "What mistake did Lisa make in the problem?" (She did not divide when she brought down the 8 in the tens place.) Have students read the reminder: Every time you bring down a digit you must divide and write a digit (sometimes 0) in the quotient. Work Lisa's problem correctly on the chalkboard and demonstrate the dividing process when the 8 in the tens place has been brought down. Have students check both of Lisa's problems to verify that a mistake was made in the first exercise and that the second one is correct.

**Other Examples** Note that the first example has a quotient zero in the ones place. It is tempting for students to discontinue the dividing process after they have found the quotient digit, 7, in the tens place. Point out that it is important to divide in the ones place and write a digit, 0 if necessary, in the quotient. The third example contains two zeros in the quotient. Stress that every time you bring down a digit you must divide and write a digit (sometimes 0) in the quotient.

**Exercises 1–17** Be alert for errors involving zeros in the quotient. Continue to emphasize that we must divide in each place. Have students check several exercises with a calculator to determine if they have completed the dividing correctly.

## Zeros in the Quotient

After Lisa worked an exercise incorrectly, her teacher asked her to show it on graph paper and correct her mistake.

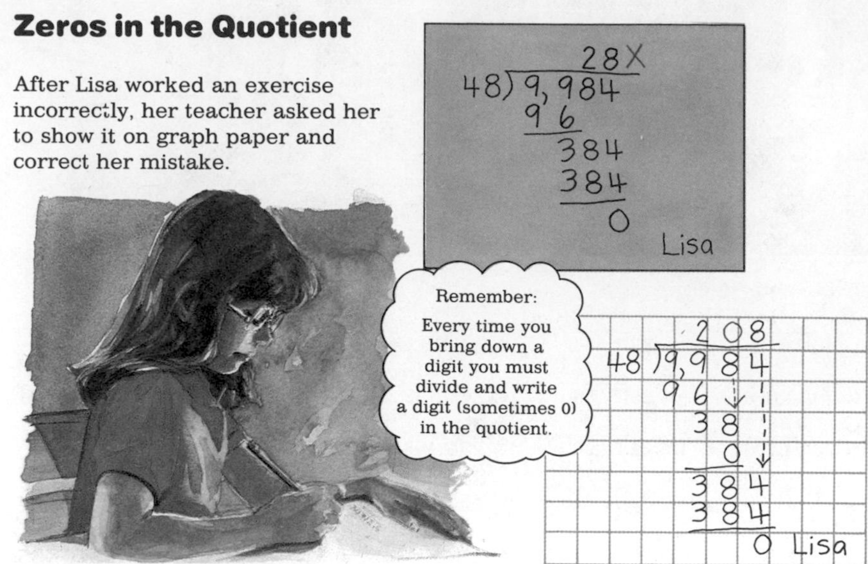


Remember:
Every time you bring down a digit you must divide and write a digit (sometimes 0) in the quotient.

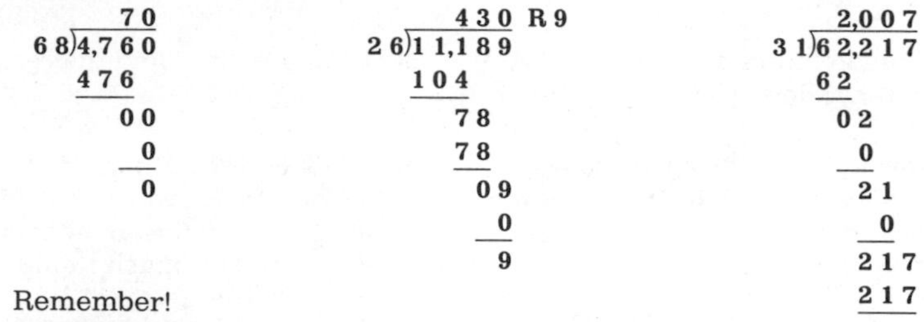


**Other Examples**

```
     70           430 R9          2,007
68)4,760      26)11,189       31)62,217
   476           104             62
    00            78              02
     0            78               0
     0            09               21
                   0                0
                   9              217
                                  217
                                    0
```

Remember!

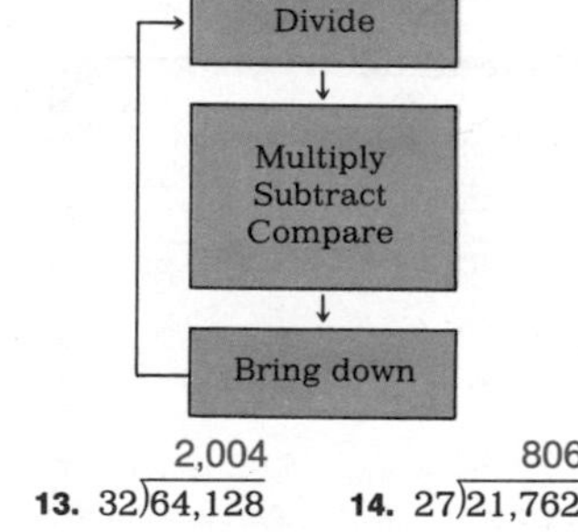


Divide.

| | | |
|---|---|---|
| **1.** 43)2,580 → 60 | **2.** 67)6,045 → 90 R15 | **3.** 53)3,551 → 67 |
| **4.** 89)9,970 → 112 R2 | **5.** 74)7,548 → 102 | **6.** 26)6,240 → 240 |
| **7.** 38)9,984 → 262 R28 | **8.** 22)8,866 → 403 | **9.** 19)6,097 → 320 R17 |
| **10.** 91)7,957 → 87 R40 | **11.** 75)8,175 → 109 | **12.** 46)9,245 → 200 R45 |
| **13.** 32)64,128 → 2,004 | **14.** 27)21,762 → 806 | **15.** 34)21,270 → 625 R20 |
| **16.** 53)34,450 → 650 | **17.** 74)37,000 → 500 | |



More Practice, page 418, Set A

## Follow Up

### Reteaching

To review dividing with zeros in the quotient, use an example in a real-life context. For example: 4 friends plan to divide a collection of baseball cards. There are 428 cards to be shared equally. How many cards will each receive? Use a place-value chart and the following questions to work through the algorithm. "How many hundreds for each person?" (1) Write 1 in the chart. "How many tens for each person?" (0, there are not enough tens to share.) Write 0 in the chart. "How can we share the tens?" (Trade for ones, combine with the 8 ones, and divide.) Write a "7" in the chart. Each person receives 107 baseball cards.

### Enrichment

Write target quotients on the chalkboard. Have one person call out six digits from 0 through 9. Each student fills in the squares as the digits are called out (see illustration below). A calculator can be used to check the answers. For example, if the target quotient is 3,000, students place the six digits so that they reach a quotient as close as possible to the target quotient.

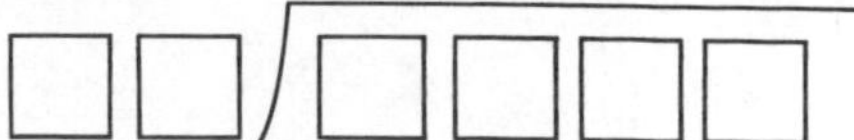

| Assignment Guide | | | |
|---|---|---|---|
| | Minimum | Average | Extended |
| page 128 | 1–17 | 1–17 | 1–17 |
| page 129 | 1–8, 17–19 | 1–19 | 8–19, TM |

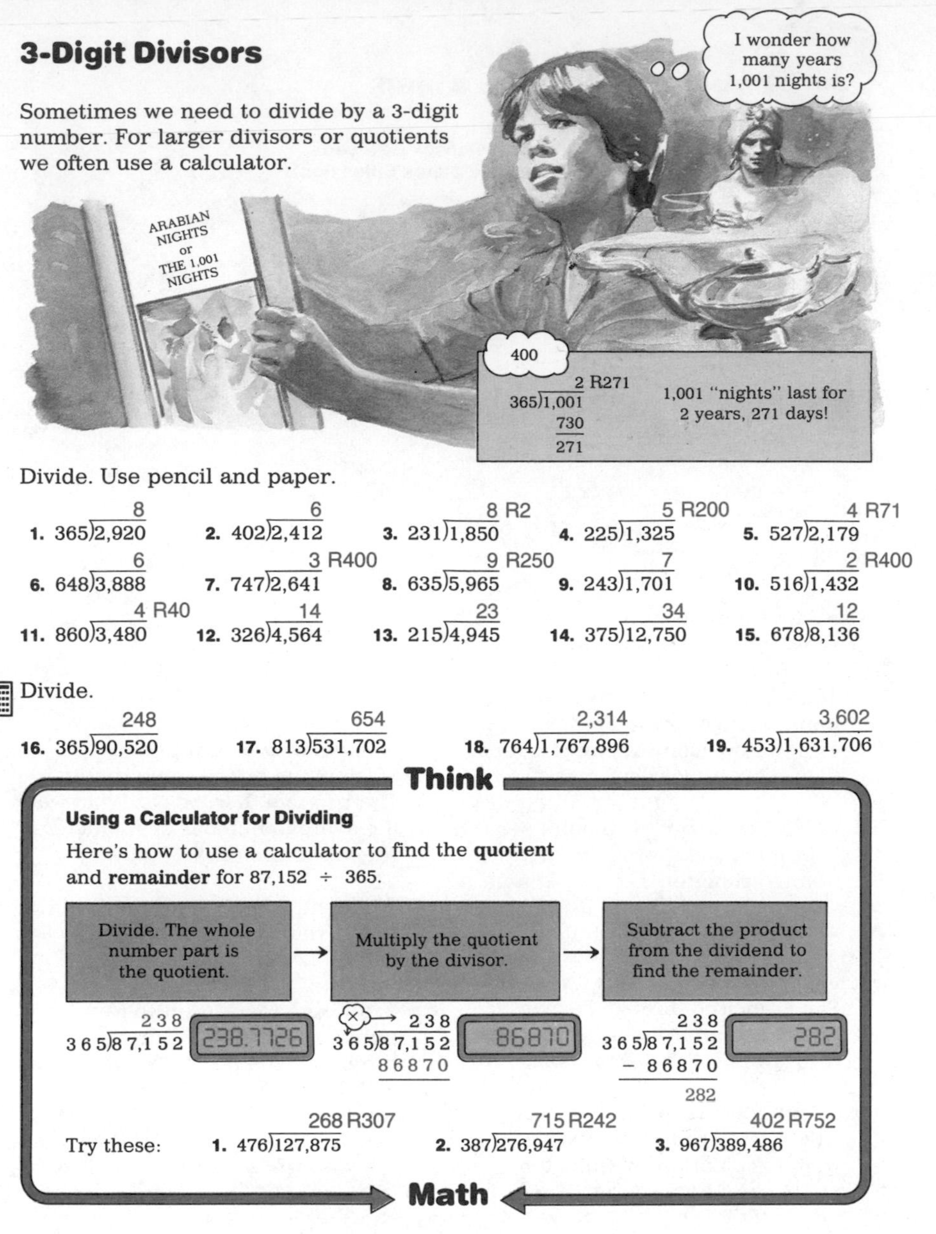

## 3-Digit Divisors

Sometimes we need to divide by a 3-digit number. For larger divisors or quotients we often use a calculator.

I wonder how many years 1,001 nights is?
ARABIAN NIGHTS or THE 1,001 NIGHTS
400
365)1,001 = 2 R271
730
271
1,001 "nights" last for 2 years, 271 days!



Divide. Use pencil and paper.

1. 365)2,920 — 8
2. 402)2,412 — 6
3. 231)1,850 — 8 R2
4. 225)1,325 — 5 R200
5. 527)2,179 — 4 R71
6. 648)3,888 — 6
7. 747)2,641 — 3 R400
8. 635)5,965 — 9 R250
9. 243)1,701 — 7
10. 516)1,432 — 2 R400
11. 860)3,480 — 4 R40
12. 326)4,564 — 14
13. 215)4,945 — 23
14. 375)12,750 — 34
15. 678)8,136 — 12

Divide.

16. 365)90,520 — 248
17. 813)531,702 — 654
18. 764)1,767,896 — 2,314
19. 453)1,631,706 — 3,602

**Think Math**

**Using a Calculator for Dividing**

Here's how to use a calculator to find the **quotient** and **remainder** for 87,152 ÷ 365.

Divide. The whole number part is the quotient. → Multiply the quotient by the divisor. → Subtract the product from the dividend to find the remainder.

365)87,152 = 238 [238.7726] → 238 × 365 = 86870 [86870] → 87,152 − 86870 = 282 [282]

Try these:

1. 476)127,875 — 268 R307
2. 387)276,947 — 715 R242
3. 967)389,486 — 402 R752

More Practice, page 418, Set B



## Using Page 129

**Lesson Development** Direct students' attention to the picture of the *Arabian Nights* book. "How could we answer the question about how many years are represented by 1,001 nights?" (We could divide 1,001 by 365.) Work through the procedure for finding this quotient on the chalkboard. Point out that there are not enough thousands, hundreds, or tens, so we begin dividing in the ones place. Help students estimate the quotient by rounding the divisor 365 to 400. Complete the dividing and ask a volunteer to use multiplication to check the answer.

**Exercises 1–11** Note that the quotient in each of these exercises is 1 digit. Encourage students to round each divisor to the nearest hundred and use the shortcut to estimate the quotient.

**Exercises 12–19** Students should be able to work through these exercises using only pencil and paper. Allow students to use calculators to check the answers if possible.

**Think Math** Explain that a calculator usually gives a remainder to a division problem as a decimal. In this activity students learn how to use a calculator to find both the quotient and remainder. Be sure students are aware that in the first step, the whole number part is the quotient and the decimal part represents the remainder. In the second step, students should recall that in division the quotient is multiplied by the divisor to give the number that is subtracted from the dividend. This multiplication can be done on the calculator because we know the quotient, 238. Finally, in the third step, by subtracting we can find the whole number remainder.

**More Practice,** page 418, Set A
**More Practice,** page 418, Set B

**Reteaching Supplement,** page 32

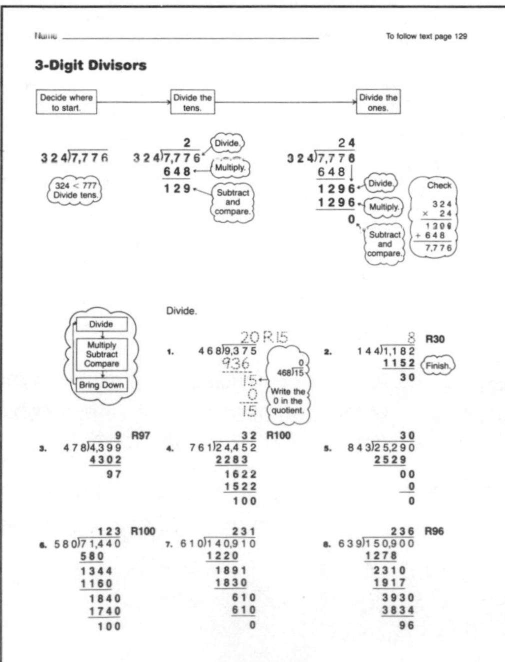

Name ______ To follow text page 129

### 3-Digit Divisors

Decide where to start. → Divide the tens. → Divide the ones.

324)7,776 (324 < 777 Divide tens.) — 2 (Divide.), 648 (Multiply.), 129 (Subtract and compare.) — 24, 648, 1296 (Divide.), 1296 (Multiply.), 0 (Subtract and compare.) — Check: 324 × 24 = 1296 + 648 = 7,776

Divide / Multiply / Subtract / Compare / Bring Down

Divide.

1. 468)9,375 — 20 R15 (936, 15, 0, 15; 468 > 15, Write the 0 in the quotient.)
2. 144)1,182 — 8 R30 (1152, 30; Finish.)
3. 478)4,399 — 9 R97 (4302, 97)
4. 761)24,452 — 32 R100 (2283, 1622, 1522, 100)
5. 843)25,290 — 30 (2529, 00, 0, 0)
6. 580)71,440 — 123 R100 (580, 1344, 1160, 1840, 1740, 100)
7. 610)140,910 — 231 (1220, 1891, 1830, 610, 610, 0)
8. 639)150,900 — 236 R96 (1278, 2310, 1917, 3930, 3834, 96)

**Enrichment Supplement,** page 32

Name ______ To follow text page 129

### Calculator Division

Play this number line game.

Rules:

- Pick nine different pairs of numbers from the board. Try to pick numbers that will give a quotient that is on a high-scoring number line. You can use a number more than once.
- On your calculator, divide each pair of numbers. Always divide the larger number by the smaller number.
- Write each quotient on the correct number line below.
- Keep track of your points. Play until the nine number pairs have been used. **Answers will vary.**

| | | |
|---|---|---|
| 8 | 24 | 32 |
| 96 | 128 | 150 |
| 250 | 450 | 799 |
| 1,875 | 2,379 | 2,416 |
| 2,875 | 4,770 | 9,432 |
| 12,500 | 16,000 | 28,000 |

0 — Score 1 point — 1

1 — Score 2 points — 10

10 — Score 3 points — 100

100 — Score 0 points

**Awards:**

Champion: 24 or more points
2nd place: 23 to 20 points
3rd place: 19 to 14 points
Try again: less than 14 points

**Practice Supplement,** page 50

Name ______ To follow text page 129

### 3-Digit Divisors

Divide.

1. 462)3,764 — 8 R68 (3696, 68)
2. 784)3,186 — 4 R50 (3136, 50)
3. 270)1,430 — 5 R89 (1350, 89)
4. 520)4,463 — 8 R303 (4160, 303)
5. 671)1,954 — 2 R612 (1342, 612)
6. 333)2,671 — 8 R7 (2664, 7)
7. 415)6,374 — 15 R149 (415, 2224, 2075, 149)
8. 712)9,403 — 13 R147 (712, 2283, 2136, 147)
9. 602)8,135 — 13 R309 (602, 2115, 1806, 309)
10. 588)7,787 — 13 R143 (588, 1907, 1764, 143)
11. 843)62,170 — 73 R631 (5901, 3160, 2529, 631)
12. 376)24,995 — 66 R179 (2256, 2435, 2256, 179)

**Quick Review** Students divide each number by the three numbers in parentheses, giving the three answers as quickly as possible.

| | | | | |
|---|---|---|---|---|
| 6 (3, 2, 1) | 12 (2, 4, 6) | 36 (9, 6, 4) | 45 (9, 1, 5) | 8 (4, 8, 2) |
| 16 (4, 8, 2) | 28 (7, 1, 4) | 24 (3, 4, 8) | 18 (3, 9, 2) | 10 (2, 10, 5) |

**Lesson Focus** To use data from a map to solve word problems; to choose the operations to solve word problems

## Ideas for Getting Started

Call students' attention to the logo at the top left-hand corner of pages 130 and 131. Have students review the steps in the 5-Point Checklist. Emphasize that the checklist should not be thought of as a set of "rules," but rather as a guide to help them solve problems.

## Using Page 130

**Lesson Development** Direct students' attention to the map showing distances between some U.S. cities. Point out that the numbers beside the lines between two cities give the road distance in kilometers between these cities. "How could you find the distance from San Francisco to New York City?" (Add the distance from San Francisco to Chicago to the distance from Chicago to New York City) Make sure students understand that they will need to select data from the map to solve the problems on this page.

**Exercise 4** This exercise requires that students divide a 4-digit number by a 3-digit number. Calculator might be used here to check computations.

**Exercise 6** This exercise at first appears to be difficult, but after the distance of two round trips between Chicago and St. Louis is calculated, it is obvious that the distance from Los Angeles to Denver (1,889 km) is closest to that amount.

**Try This** A possible strategy, Guess and Check, was taught on page 48.

**Discussion** "What are we asked to find out about Mark's trip?" (What cities did he travel through?) "Where did Mark start?" (Los Angeles) "What was his final destination?" (New York) "How many cities did he drive through on the way?" (two) "What was his total trip?" (5,560 km) "Could Mark have driven through Denver and Chicago to New York City?" (No, the total number of kilometers for this trip is 4,930, less than 5,560) "What other trip might Mark have taken?" (Los Angeles through Dallas and Atlanta to New York City?) "Why is this not the trip Mark took?" (The number of kilometers is still less than 5,560.) "What other cities could Mark have driven through?"

**Solution** Mark drove from Los Angeles to San Francisco to Chicago to New York. The distance is as follows: 649 + 3,560 + 1,351. This total is 5,560 km.

## Problem Solving: Using Data from a Map

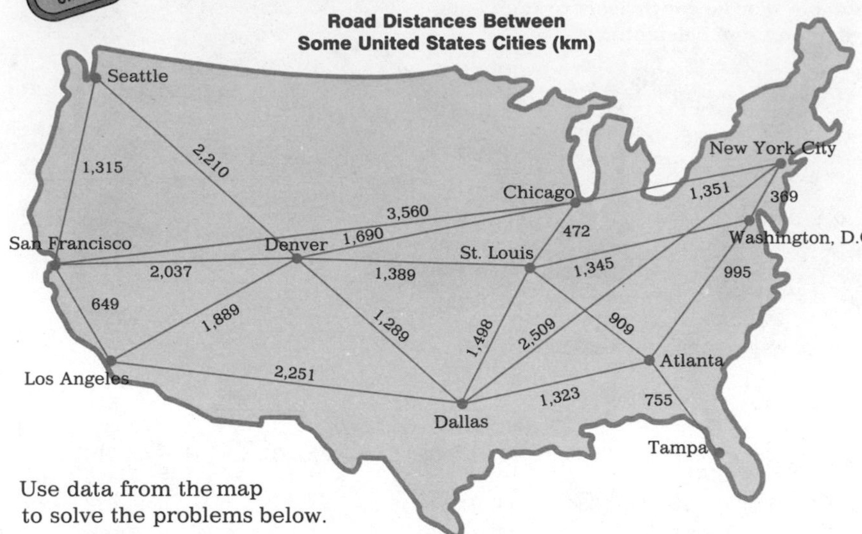


Use data from the map to solve the problems below.

1. Stuart's family wants to drive direct from Chicago to San Francisco in 4 days. How many kilometers must they average per day? 890 km
2. About how many kilometers per hour must you average to drive from Washington, D.C., to Atlanta, Georgia, in 12 hours? about 83 km/h (82 R11)
3. Find how much farther it is from San Francisco through Denver to St. Louis than from San Francisco through Los Angeles to Dallas. 526 km
4. About how many times as far is it from Los Angeles to Denver as it is from New York to Washington, D.C.? about 5 times as far (5 R44)
5. Clea Jenkins drove to Tampa from Washington, D.C., by way of Atlanta, and returned to Washington by the same route. The trip took her 7 days. What was the average number of kilometers she drove each day? 500 km
6. What one trip is closest in distance to two round trips between Chicago and St. Louis? Los Angeles to Denver
7. **Try This** Mark went to New York from Los Angeles. He drove through two other cities on the way. He traveled a total of 5,560 km. Describe his trip. Hint: Guess and check. Los Angeles to San Francisco to Chicago to New York



## Follow Up

### Reteaching

Have available a map of your state or province. Select cities students know, and let students help determine different attributes to discuss. For example:

- Distances between cities
- Population
- Altitude
- Location of cities in relation to each other (N/S/E/W).

Challenge students to make up word problems focusing on one or more of these attributes. For problems involving large numbers, encourage students to use a calculator.

### Enrichment

Write and solve an equation for each of the following problems.

1. When 9 is subtracted from a certain number, the difference is 12. What is the number? Let $x$ = the number. (21)
2. Twelve times a certain number is 132. What is the number? Let $k$ = the number. (11)
3. A number divided by 4 is 36. What is the number? Let $r$ = the number. (544)
4. The sum of 37 and a number is 278. What is the number? Let $y$ = the number. (241)

| Assignment Guide | | | |
|---|---|---|---|
| | Minimum | Average | Extended |
| page 130 | 1–5 | 1–6 | 1–7 |
| page 131 | 1–5 | 1–6 | 1–7 |

## Problem Solving: Understanding the Operations

Here is a review of the four basic operations.

| | |
|---|---|
| **Add** + • **Put together** How many in all? | **Multiply** × • **Put together a number of same-size sets** How many in all? |
| **Subtract** — • **Take away** How many are left? • **Compare** How many more or less than? • **Missing amount** How many more are needed? | **Divide** ÷ • **Put the same number into a given number of sets** How many in each set? • **Put into sets of a given size** How many sets? |

Tell which operation or operations you would use to solve the problems below if the numbers were given.

1. Oakdale School has ■ students. Hoose School has ■. How many more students does Oakdale have than Hoose? subtract
2. Brigham School took ■ bus loads of students on a field trip. A total of ■ students went on the trip. About how many students rode on each bus? divide
3. The ■ band members from Glenn School joined the ■ band members from Field School for a concert. How many members were in the combined band? add
4. At Sugar Creek School there are an average of ■ students per class. There are ■ classes. How many students are in the school? multiply
5. All but ■ of the ■ middle grade children at Fairview School played on a soccer team. Each team had ■ players. How many teams were there? subtract, divide
6. Sande sold ■ student tickets to the school play at $■ each and ■ adult tickets at $■ each. How much were her total sales? multiply, add
7. **Try This** Bent School has an average of 28 students per class. It has 20 classes. The numbers of students in Stevenson, Washington, and Centennial Schools are 614, 555, and 598. How much greater is the average number of students in these three schools than the number of students in Bent School? 29



## Using Page 131

**Lesson Development** As you review and discuss the four operations displayed at the top of the page, ask students to make up problems that are solved using the interpretations of the operations.

Then point out that the numbers are missing from the problems on this page. Tell students they are to read the problem, think about the four operations described above, and tell which operation or operations would be used to solve the problem if numbers had been given.

**Try This** A possible strategy, Choose the Operations, was taught on page 16.

**Discussion** "What question are we asked about the schools?" (How much greater is the average number of students in Stevenson, Washington, and Centennial Schools than the total number of students in Bent School?) "What is the average number of students in each class at Bent School?" (28) "How many classes at Bent School?" (20) "What is the total number of students at Bent School?" (560) "How many students in Stevenson, Washington, and Centennial Schools?" (614, 555, 598) "What is the average number of students in these three schools?" (589) "Can you use this information to answer the question?"

**Solution** The average number of students in the three schools is 29 more than the total number of students in Bent School.

**Extension** Last year, Bent School had an average of 26 students in each of 23 classes. Stevenson had 614 students, Washington had 2 more than this and Centennial had 2 more than Washington. How much greater was this average than Bent's average? (18)

## Ideas That Work

### Math for the Gifted

Prepare 20 division equations and write the divisor, dividend, and quotient for each equation on index cards, one per card. The 20 sets of three cards are mixed. Seven cards are dealt to each player. The remaining cards are placed facedown in a pile. One card is turned over to start the discard pile. Players take turns drawing one card from the draw pile or the discard pile and then putting one card faceup in the discard pile.

The object of the game is to collect sets of three cards that form a division equation such as 360, 4, and 90. As players collect these sets, they place them faceup on the playing surface. The winner is the first player to put down all his or her cards or the player who has collected the most sets of division equations when the draw cards are gone.

**Practice Supplement,** page 51

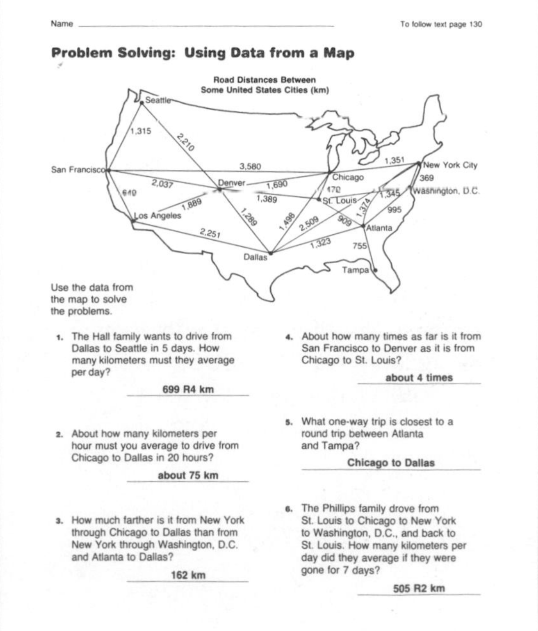

Name ______ To follow text page 130

**Problem Solving: Using Data from a Map**



Use the data from the map to solve the problems.

1. The Hall family wants to drive from Dallas to Seattle in 5 days. How many kilometers must they average per day? **699 R4 km**
2. About how many kilometers per hour must you average to drive from Chicago to Dallas in 20 hours? **about 75 km**
3. How much farther is it from New York through Chicago to Dallas than from New York through Washington, D.C. and Atlanta to Dallas? **162 km**
4. About how many times as far is it from San Francisco to Denver as it is from Chicago to St. Louis? **about 4 times**
5. What one-way trip is closest to a round trip between Atlanta and Tampa? **Chicago to Dallas**
6. The Phillips family drove from St. Louis to Chicago to New York to Washington, D.C., and back to St. Louis. How many kilometers per day did they average if they were gone for 7 days? **505 R2 km**

**Lesson Focus** To make an organized list as a strategy to solve nonroutine word problems

## Ideas for Getting Started

Show the number of license plates that can be made using the digits 2, 3, and 4. On any license plate no digit may be used more than once. Start with the digit 2 and list all the possible numbers. Then start with the digit 3 and list all the possible numbers. Finally, start with the digit 4 and list all the possible numbers. (234, 243, 324, 342, 423, 432) Point out that this can be called an organized list because an organized approach (starting with 2, then 3, and so on) was used.

## Using Page 132

**Motivational Problem** Have students read the Try This problem. "What question is asked about the playoff?" (How many matches must be played so that each person plays every other person just once?) "How many players are there?" (5). Tell students that in this lesson they will learn a strategy called Make an Organized List that will help them plan a solution for this problem. If you have a problem-solving bulletin board, this would be an appropriate time to include this strategy.

**Lesson Development** Tell students that A will stand for Al, B for Bob, C for Connie, D for Debra, and E for Earl. Using these letters, work with students to make an organized list of all possible player combinations. "Suppose we start with A. What players can A play with?" (AB, AC, AD, AE) "Next let's list the players B could play with. Remember that B has already played with A." (BC, BD, BE) "What other players can C play with? Remember that C has already played with B and A." (CD, CE) "Since D has already played with A, B, and C, what other player can D play with?" (DE) "How many matches have we listed above?" (4 + 3 + 2 + 1, or 10 matches) Have students recheck the list to be sure no pairings have been left out. Then have them reread the problem to see if this answer seems reasonable.

**Exercise 1** If necessary, help students get started making an organized list for this problem. Note that there are three different types of shorts and four different types of shirts, or a total of 3 × 4 or 12 different outfits.

**Exercise 2** This exercise is different from the exercises above in that the order of the letters are involved. Note that if we start with A there are 6 possible orders: ABCD, ABDC, ACBD, ACDB, ADBC, ADCB. With each of the other letters there are 6 similar orders, making a total of 4 × 6 or 24 different orders.

## Problem Solving: Make an Organized List

To solve some problems, it helps to write all the possibilities for the situation in a certain order. This problem-solving strategy is called

**Make an Organized List**

**Try This** Al, Bob, Connie, Debra, and Earl are having playoff matches to decide who plays number 1, number 2, and so forth, on a tennis team. How many matches must they play so that each person plays every other person just once?

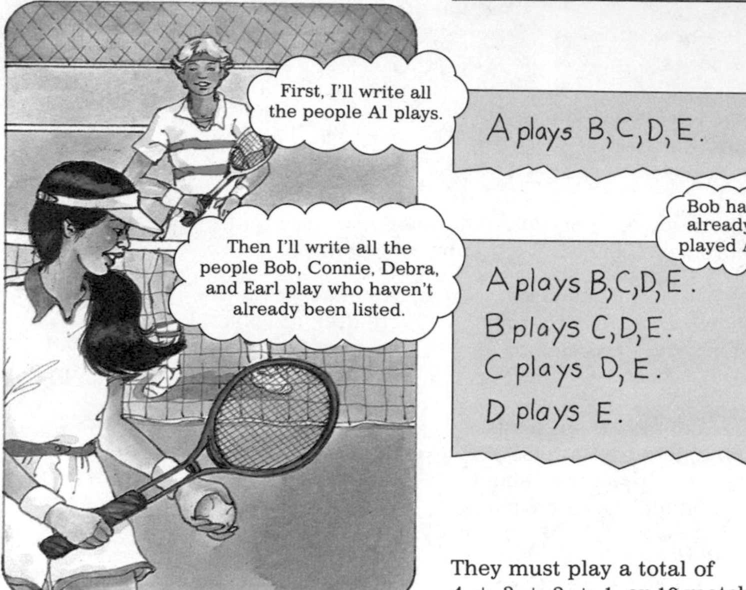


A plays B, C, D, E. 4

Bob has already played Al.

A plays B, C, D, E. 4
B plays C, D, E. 3
C plays D, E. 2
D plays E. 1

They must play a total of 4 + 3 + 2 + 1, or 10 matches.

Solve.

1. Shelly has white, tan, and gray shorts. She has brown, red, blue, and green shirts. How many different outfits can she wear? 12

2. How many different playing orders are possible for 4 players on a tennis team? (If the players are Angie, Brigid, Curtis, and Dano, one order is A, B, C, D. Another is B, D, A, C.) 24

132

## Strategy Test Item

**Optional Problem** If you wish to assess students' ability to apply the strategy called Make an Organized List introduced in this chapter, provide them with the problem below.

> There are 6 students in Mary's class who want to take a ride on a "bicycle built for two." How many rides must they take so that each person rides with every other person just once?

**Solution** The 6 students must take 15 rides. (5 + 4 + 3 + 2 + 1)

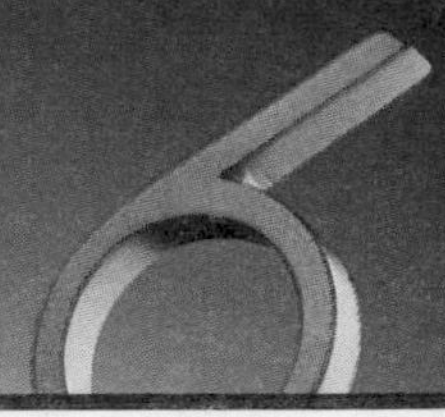

## *Chapter Review-Test*

Find the quotients mentally. Write only the answer.

**1.** 360 ÷ 9 40 **2.** 4,200 ÷ 60 70 **3.** 5,600 ÷ 800 7 **4.** 4,000 ÷ 8 500 **5.** 3,200 ÷ 10 320

**6.** 810 ÷ 90 9 **7.** 3,500 ÷ 7 500 **8.** 4,800 ÷ 80 60 **9.** 5,400 ÷ 6 900 **10.** 6,300 ÷ 70 90

Estimate the quotients. Round so that you can use basic facts.

**11.** 538 ÷ 6 90 **12.** 324 ÷ 8 40 **13.** 447 ÷ 5 90 **14.** 719 ÷ 92 8 **15.** 6,295 ÷ 71 90

Divide.

**16.** 4)344 86 **17.** 6)2,838 473 **18.** 5)2,010 402 **19.** 3)10,843 3,614 R1 **20.** 8)71,739 8,967 R3

**21.** 6)5,148 858 **22.** 9)4,617 513 **23.** 7)8,192 1,170 R2 **24.** 5)3,840 768 **25.** 4)27,386 6,846 R2

Find the average of these sets of numbers to the nearest whole number.

**26.** 318, 459, 296 358 **27.** 75, 63, 82, 94, 71 77

**28.** 11, 8, 14, 9, 12, 18 12 **29.** 516, 497, 501, 528, 476 504

Divide.

**30.** 30)1,455 48 R15 **31.** 70)25,270 361 **32.** 41)287 7 **33.** 59)374 6 R20 **34.** 34)1,923 56 R19

**35.** 78)5,400 69 R18 **36.** 92)$345.00 $3.75 **37.** 67)$75.04 $1.12 **38.** 185)840 4 R100 **39.** 342)3,078 9

Solve.

**40.** During a vacation trip Akim and his family drove 1,106 km in 14 hours. What was the average distance they traveled in an hour? 79 km

**41.** The total cost of Tracy's trombone was $345.80. She paid for it with 52 weekly payments. How much did she pay each week? $6.65

133

## Using Page 133

The exercises in the Chapter Review/Test emphasize the major concepts and skills presented in this chapter. These exercises may be used as a review assignment or as a test, depending upon your needs.

**Item Analysis** The table below correlates the Chapter Review/Test items with objectives and with the student text pages on which the concepts or skills were taught.

| Items | Objectives | Related text pages |
|---|---|---|
| 1–15 | 5.1 | 108–110 |
| 16–25 | 5.2 | 111–117 |
| 26–29 | 5.3 | 118 |
| 30–39 | 5.4 | 119–124, 126–129 |
| 40–41 | 5.5 | 111, 119, 125, 130–131 |

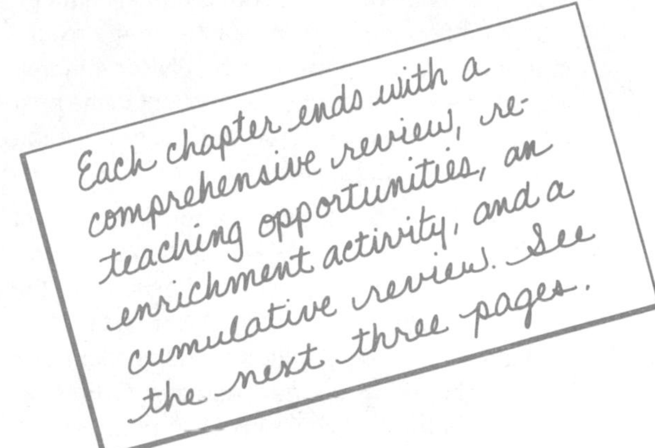

Each chapter ends with a comprehensive review, re-teaching opportunities, an enrichment activity, and a cumulative review. See the next three pages.


## Assessment Options

If you use the Chapter Review/Test as a review assignment, you may wish to use the multiple-choice test or the free-response test to evaluate mastery of the chapter objectives. The items on these tests have a one-to-one correspondence in terms of content and level of difficulty. A correlation of test items to objectives and student text pages is provided in the Management Guide for Chapter 5.

**Multiple-Choice Test,** TRB pages 13–15

**Free-Response Test,** TRB pages 57–58

## TRB Options

The following blackline masters are available for use with this chapter. If you have not already assigned these materials, you may wish to use them to close the chapter.

**Recreation,** TRB page 155

**Consumer Applications,** TRB page 173

**Calculator Technology,** TRB page 191

**Reading Math,** TRB page 223

**Family Involvement,** TRB pages 245–246

# Reteaching

## Using Page 134

The exercises on this page are intended for those students who experienced difficulty with the Chapter Review/Test on page 133. Should students require reteaching of these concepts and skills, please refer to the teaching notes below. Otherwise, the Another Look exercises can be assigned as independent work with students using the accompanying sample problems and hints as guides.

**Exercises 1–10** This skill was originally taught on pages 112–117. Review the steps in the dividing process as you work through a sample problem with students. Give particular emphasis to the idea that they must first decide where to start. Use lined or graph paper, if necessary, to help students focus on the different places. Have students check each problem by multiplying the quotient times the divisor and adding the remainder.

**Exercises 11–15** This skill was originally taught on page 118. Refer to the middle example box and emphasize that there are two steps necessary for finding the average of a list of numbers. First, find the sum of the numbers. Second, divide the sum by the number of addends. Point out that in the example the remainder 3 is closer to the divisor 4 than it is to 0. Thus we would round the quotient to the next whole number. This would be the average of the numbers to the nearest whole number.

**Exercises 16–25** This skill was originally taught on pages 122–128. Review with students the procedure for rounding the divisor and estimating the first quotient digit. Point out that when the 1 is brought down, 0 must be written as the quotient digit before bringing down the next number, 5. Emphasize the importance of checking each problem.

*Students who need reteaching can take another look at the chapter content while the others work on an enrichment activity.*

## *Another Look*

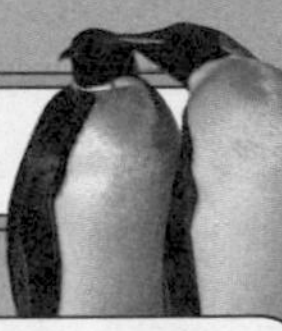

After you **decide where to start**, use these steps to divide in each place.

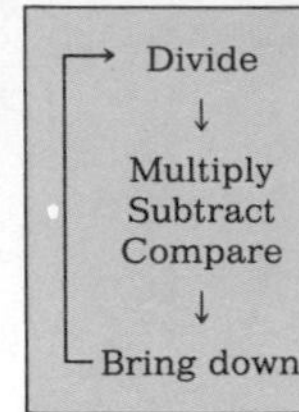


**Divide and check.**

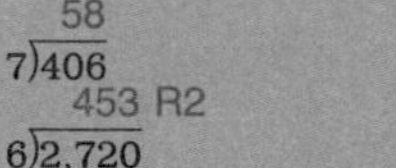

1. 7)406 58
2. 2)194 97
3. 6)2,720 453 R2
4. 5)3,123 624 R3
5. 8)50,808 6,351
6. 4)774 193 R2
7. 9)56,957 6,328 R5
8. 3)9,162 3,054
9. 9)2,947 327 R4
10. 8)20,917 2,614 R5

To find the **average** of a list of numbers: 21, 33, 29, 36

1. Find the sum.
2. Divide the sum by the number of addends.

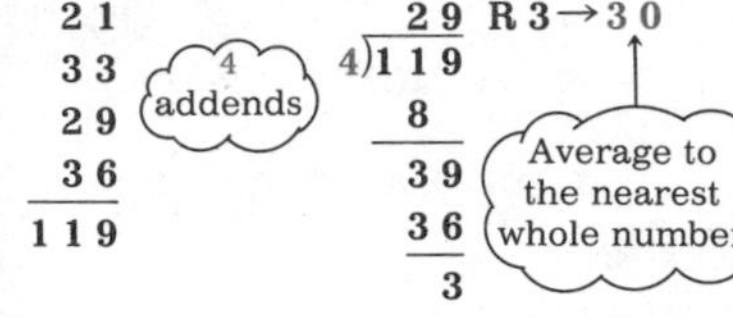


**Find the average of each set of numbers to the nearest whole number.**

11. 15, 19, 11, 22 17
12. 68, 79, 56, 74, 83 72
13. 311, 514, 476, 343, 417 412
14. 48, 53, 39, 45, 58, 61 51
15. 254, 351, 277, 316, 335 307

Round the divisor to estimate the quotient.

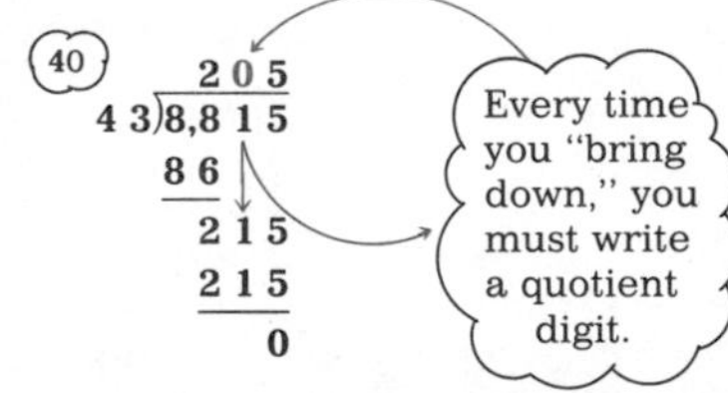


**Divide and check.**

16. 32)256 8
17. 76)685 9 R1
18. 59)1,593 27
19. 43)2,686 62 R20
20. 64)12,992 203
21. 25)21,000 840
22. 87)127,281 1,463
23. 94)192,324 2,046
24. 27)2,200 81 R13
25. 89)12,575 141 R26



## Just for Teachers

### Women in Math

Mary Fairfax Somerville was born in Scotland during the Industrial Revolution. The only daughter of an admiral in the Scottish navy, Mary developed an early interest in nature, animals, and the physical world. Though Mary's formal education was brief and apparently unpleasant, in her early teens she became fascinated with the study of algebra through puzzles that appeared in a ladies' magazine. Eager to learn more, she went to considerable lengths to obtain textbooks on algebra and geometry, which she studied with an intensity that alarmed her parents. Although discouraged by popular attitudes that suggested that women should not attempt rigorous academic subjects, Mary succeeded in teaching herself mathematics while at the same time continuing traditional feminine activities such as sewing, dancing, and painting.

Mary Somerville had a long and successful professional career. Nevertheless, she had to overcome the considerable prejudices of her day. Her first husband did not believe women capable of serious accomplishment. Mary had to put aside her academic interests during this marriage. Even more overt discrimination, such as being barred from an observatory because she was a woman, did not deter her from her chosen career. Later, most of her professional correspondence was carried on through

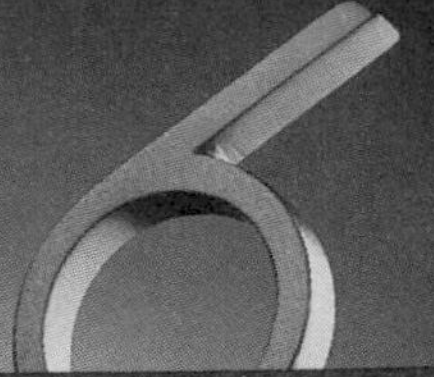

## Enrichment

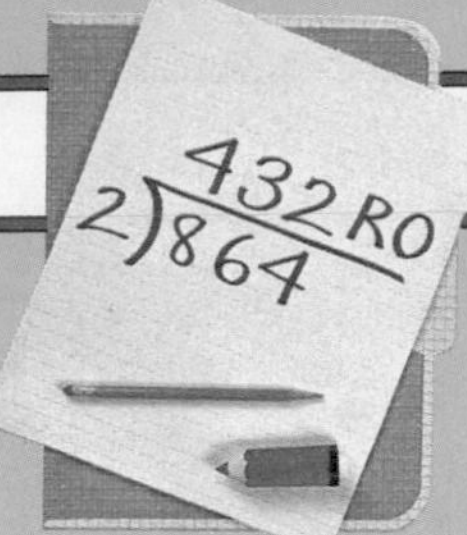

432 R0
2)864

**Number Relationships**

We say 864 is **divisible by** 2 because the remainder is 0 when 864 is divided by 2. Here are some easy-to-use **divisibility tests.**

- A number is divisible by **2** if its last digit is 0, 2, 4, 6, or 8.
- A number is divisible by **5** if its last digit is 0 or 5.

I just look at the last digit!

**9,43<u>6</u>** is divisible by 2.
**87,96<u>5</u>** is divisible by 5.

- A number is divisible by **3** if the sum of its digits is divisible by 3.
- A number is divisible by **9** if the sum of its digits is divisible by 9.

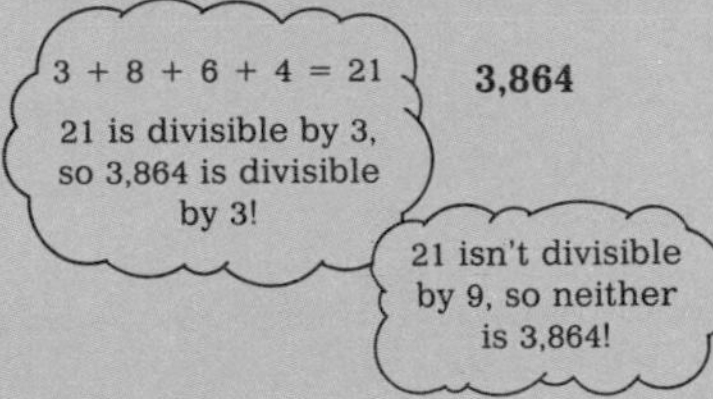

3 + 8 + 6 + 4 = 21
21 is divisible by 3, so 3,864 is divisible by 3!
21 isn't divisible by 9, so neither is 3,864!

**3,864**

- A number is divisible by **4** if twice its tens digit plus its ones digit is divisible by 4.

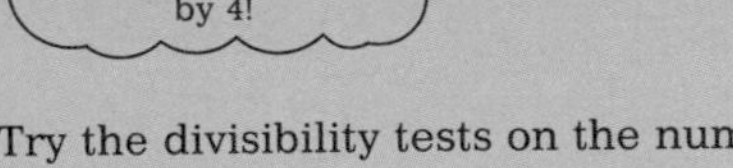

(2 × 5) + 6 = 16
16 is divisible by 4, so 4,756 is divisible by 4!

**4,756**

- A number is divisible by **6** if it is divisible by 2 and by 3.

This number is divisible by 2 and by 3, so it is divisible by 6!

**3,282**

Try the divisibility tests on the numbers below. Give the number or numbers (2, 3, 4, 5, 6, 9) each is divisible by.

**1.** 570
2, 3, 5, 6
**2.** 2,684
2, 4
**3.** 7,926
2, 3, 6
**4.** 417
3
**5.** 1,260
2, 3, 4, 5, 6, 9
**6.** 2,340
2, 3, 4, 5, 6, 9
**7.** 56,879
none
**8.** 492,657
3
**9.** 246,904
2, 4
**10.** 1,376,844
2, 3, 4, 6

## Using Page 135

This page is intended for those students who successfully completed the Chapter Review/Test on page 133. You may wish to assign this page as independent work while you use Another Look exercises to reteach the basic concepts and skills of the chapter. Or, you may decide that all students would benefit from exposure to this Enrichment activity.

**Lesson Development** Tell students that it is often helpful to find out whether a larger number is divisible by a smaller number. Explain that this means that when the larger number is divided by the smaller number the remainder is 0. Tell students that this activity gives some special tests to help them decide if numbers are divisible by 2, 3, 4, 5, 6, and 9. Ask a volunteer to tell without looking at the page how they would decide if a number is divisible by 2. (If the last digit is even, the number is divisible by 2.) "How could we decide if the number is divisible by 5?" (The number is divisible by 5 if the last digit is 0 or 5.) Explain each of the other divisibility tests by using an example for each. Work as many examples as needed to help students understand the divisibility tests.

To extend the lesson, ask students to develop additional exercises like these to give to their classmates. Caution them to be sure that they can give the solution to any exercise they make up.

*Use these pages immediately after the Chapter Review or save them for review or enrichment later.*

her second husband—incoming letters were almost invariably addressed to Mr. Somerville, even when her correspondents knew Mary to be the scholar.

In 1827 Mary Somerville began work on the project that established her professionally. *Mechanics and the Heavens,* a text on higher mathematics and astronomy, explained the physical laws of the universe to the non-scientist. The book was enormously popular. In 1835, the Royal Astronomical Society recognized her contribution and elected her and Caroline Herschel as its first women members. She continued to write about mathematics and science and to compile the latest discoveries into popular, easily understood texts, such as *Connection of the Physical Sciences and Physical Geography.* She wrote her final work, *Molecular and Microscopic Science,* summarizing developments in chemistry and physics when she was 89 years old.

## Using Page 136

The exercises on this page provide practice for maintaining cumulative skills. The emphasis in this Cumulative Review is on whole number place value (Chapter 2), addition and subtraction of whole numers (Chapter 2), decimal place value (Chapter 3), multiplication of whole numbers (Chapter 4), and problem solving (Chapter 4).

**Item Analysis** The table below correlates the Cumulative Review items with objectives and with the student book pages on which the concepts or skills were taught.

| Items | Objective | Related text pages |
|---|---|---|
| 1–2 | 2.1 | 24–29 |
| 3 | 2.2 | 30–33 |
| 4–6 | 2.3 | 36–43 |
| 7–8 | 3.1 | 54–59 |
| 9–11 | 4.2 | 84–88 |
| 12 | 4.4 | 94–97 |
| 13–14 | 4.5 | 83, 90–91, 98–99 |

## *Cumulative Review*

1. What is the place value of 9 in 294,362?
   Ⓐ 9 ten thousands B 9 thousands
   C 9 ten millions D not given

2. Which symbol (>, <, or =) goes in the ● ?
   637,218 ● 607,218
   A < Ⓑ > C =

3. Round 429,375 to the nearest hundred.
   A 430,000 B 429,000
   Ⓒ 429,400 D not given

Add or subtract.

4. 646 + 389
   A 257 B 925 Ⓒ 1,035 D not given

5. 7,000 − 434
   A 6,676 Ⓑ 6,566 C 7,434 D not given

6. \$42.75 − 18.83
   A \$61.58 Ⓑ \$23.92 C \$34.92 D not given

7. What is the place value of 8 in 3.581?
   A 8 tenths Ⓑ 8 hundredths
   C 8 thousandths D not given

8. Which symbol (>, <, or =) goes in the ● ?
   1.101 ● 1.011
   Ⓐ > B < C =

Multiply.

9. 461 × 8
   A 3,288 B 3,598 C 3,678 Ⓓ not given

10. 3,785 × 6
    A 2,271 B 21,610 Ⓒ 22,710 D not given

11. 71 × 24
    Ⓐ 1,704 B 1,724 C 2,471 D not given

12. 322 × 265
    Ⓐ 85,330 B 85,930 C 8,533 D not given

13. A jacket cost \$44.80. How much change would you receive from \$50.00?
    A \$45.52 B \$5.52
    C \$39.80 Ⓓ not given

14. There are 48 cans in a case. How many cans are there in 24 cases?
    Ⓐ 1,152 B 2,016
    C 484 D not given

# Decimals: Multiplication and Division

## Objectives

**6.1** Round decimals and estimate their products and quotients.
**6.2** Find products when one or both factors are decimals.
**6.3** Find quotients of decimals divided by a whole number.
**6.4** Find quotients of decimals divided by another decimal.
**6.5** Solve word problems using the 5-Point Checklist and cumulative computational skills.

## Summary

In this chapter students use basic multiplication and division facts to estimate decimal products and quotients. Such estimation is helpful in solving practical problems in which a high degree of accuracy is not needed and in helping students understand the procedure for placing decimal points. Students also find products of decimals, including those in which extra zeros are needed to have the correct number of decimal places. Emphasis is also placed on mental multiplication and division of decimals by 10, 100 and 1,000.

The division skills for whole numbers developed in Chapter 5 are used to help students divide a decimal by a whole number and a decimal by a decimal. Students learn to divide a whole number by a larger whole number, and then round the decimal quotient. These skills for multiplying and dividing decimals are then applied throughout the chapter to solve word problems.

## Mathematical Background

**Estimating with Decimals** Difficulties in estimating with decimals arise from two sources. First, the product or the quotient cannot always be found by referring to a basic fact after the numbers are rounded. Second, students must make careful decisions regarding the place to which to round. For example, when estimating 273.5 ÷ 2.8, the numbers should be rounded so that a basic fact can be used to find the estimated quotient. Thus, 273.5 would be rounded to the nearest ten and 2.8 would be rounded to the nearest whole number.

Models can be used to demonstrate the technique for placing the decimal point in the product for a decimal multiplication and to help students find the shortcut: Add the number of places in the factors to find the number of places in the product. A basic understanding of multiplication of fractions can also be used to explain how to determine the number of places in the product.

$$0.4 \times 0.32 = 0.128$$

$$\downarrow \quad \downarrow \quad \downarrow$$

$$\frac{4}{10} \times \frac{32}{100} = \frac{128}{1{,}000}$$

(tenths) (hundredths) (thousandths)

1 place × 2 place = 3 place

Students can estimate products to see that the rule for placing decimal points makes sense.

$$\begin{array}{r} 5.36 \\ \times\ 3.87 \\ \hline 20.7432 \end{array} \begin{array}{c} \rightarrow \\ \rightarrow \\ \\ \end{array} \begin{array}{r} 5 \\ \times\ 4 \\ \hline 20 \end{array}$$

The product of the rounded numbers is 20, so we know that the product of the decimals is approximately 20 and we place the decimal point accordingly. Notice that a 2-place decimal times a 2-place decimal gives a 4-place decimal product.

In finding the product of three hundredths times two hundredths, extra zeros must be written before placing the decimal point. It is important that students understand why this is necessary and how to find these types of products.

**Special Decimal Products and Quotients** Students should recognize a shortcut for mentally finding products of 10, 100, and 1,000: To multiply by 10, move the decimal point one place to the right; to multiply by 100, move the decimal point to the right two places; and for 1,000, move the decimal point to the right three places. A similar rule applies for division except that the decimal point is moved to the left.

**Dividing Decimals** Students should understand that decimal division is essentially the same as whole number division but with a decimal point placed in the quotient directly above the decimal point in the dividend. To divide a decimal such as 38.32 by 4, we first divide the whole number part, then we divide the decimal part. Students can use this skill to find all decimal quotients. To find 38.32 divided by 0.4, both the divisor and dividend are multiplied by 10 to find an equivalent problem with the whole number divisor 4. To help sudents understand this procedure, use whole number quotients and fractions illustrated below.

Multiplying the divisor and dividend by the same number does not change the quotient.

- Whole Numbers $6\overline{)24}$ with quotient 4; $60\overline{)240}$ with quotient 4
- Fractions $2 = \frac{2}{1} = \frac{2 \times 10}{1 \times 10} = \frac{20}{10}$
- Decimals $0.5\overline{)2.5}$ with quotient 5; $5\overline{)25}$ with quotient 5

Emphasize that the number needed to multiply both the dividend and the divisor is the number that must be used to produce a whole number divisor. In the example 1.6308 ÷ 0.027 both the dividend and divisor should be multiplied by 1,000 so that the divisor for the equivalent problem will be 27.

As with whole number division, watch for students who have special problems with zeros. Be alert for situations where students must write an extra zero in the dividend to complete the dividing.

**Problem Solving** Five problem-solving experiences are presented in this chapter. On page 146, students choose the best estimate and then find the exact answer. This is followed by a problem-solving practice lesson (page 147). In a lesson, Using Data from Several Sources, pages 17–18, students find the needed data to solve the problems. On page 161, students use a calculator to find unit prices. The problem-solving strategy in this chapter, Use Logical Reasoning, is introduced on page 162.

**Vocabulary**

decimal place power of 10 unit price

## Error Analysis

The content of this chapter requires the integration of many of the skills and concepts presented earlier. An understanding of place value, whole number multiplication and division skills, as well as rounding and estimating skills are all needed in work with multiplication and division of decimals. The errors that are made might reflect inadequate prerequisite skills or a lack of basic computational skills.

### Error Pattern 1

$$\begin{array}{r} 6.3 \\ \times\ 0.5 \\ \hline 31.5 \end{array} \qquad \begin{array}{r} 9.7 \\ \times\ 0.5 \\ \hline 48.5 \end{array} \qquad \begin{array}{r} 1.6 \\ \times\ 0.9 \\ \hline 14.4 \end{array} \qquad \begin{array}{r} 13.2 \\ \times\ 0.7 \\ \hline 92.4 \end{array}$$

**Diagnosis** The student has multiplied and placed the decimal point as with addition or subtraction. The student did not count the proper decimal places, which indicates a lack of understanding of decimal place-value.

**Remediation** Review multiplication of common fractions such as $\frac{1}{3} \times \frac{1}{2} = \frac{1}{6}$. Then use fractions with 10 and multiples of 10 as denominators. As these fractions are multiplied, focus on the denominator of the resulting fraction, for example $\frac{1}{10} \times \frac{2}{10} = \frac{2}{100}$. Point out tenths times tenths equal hundredths. Remind students that the product, $\frac{2}{100}$, can be written as 0.02. Elicit from students that 6.3 × 0.5 can also be interpreted as $6\frac{3}{10} \times \frac{5}{10}$. Since we know that tenths times tenths equal hundredths, we multiply and place the decimal point to show hundredths. After working through several problems, help students generalize the rule: (1) count the number of decimal places in both factors, and (2) write the decimal point to show the number of decimal places.

### Error Pattern 2

$$\begin{array}{r} 5.6 \\ \times\ 0.9 \\ \hline 50.4 \end{array} \qquad \begin{array}{r} 3.24 \\ \times\ 0.06 \\ \hline 1.944 \end{array} \qquad \begin{array}{r} 5.22 \\ \times\ 0.16 \\ \hline 8.352 \end{array} \qquad \begin{array}{r} 3.40 \\ \times\ 0.26 \\ \hline 8.840 \end{array}$$

**Diagnosis** The student has completed the multiplication algorithm correctly, but has incorrectly placed the decimal point in each answer. There seems to be confusion about where to begin counting for the right number of decimal places.

**Remediation** Set up a chart such as shown below.

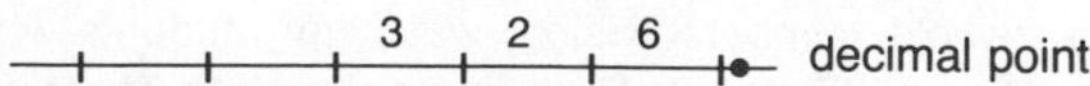


Point out that when whole numbers such as 326 are shown in a place-value chart, the decimal point is always to the right of the ones digit. To count the decimal places in an answer, we do not count the place the point is already in but count as we move to the right or to the left. A good verbal explanation integrated with illustrations should be helpful in remediating this error pattern.

### Error Pattern 3

10 × 3.4 = 0.34     100 × 5.32 = 0.0532
100 × 365.1 = 3.651     10 × 856.7 = 85.67

**Diagnosis** The student is confused about the rules for multiplication and division by 10 and multiples of 10.

**Remediation** Review with students the rule for moving the decimal point. Then provide several examples and carry out the multiplication algorithm. For example,

$$\begin{array}{r} 3.4 \\ \times\ 10 \\ \hline 340 \end{array}$$

Have students count the number of decimal places in the algorithm and place the decimal point in the correct place.

Organize a chart to record the answers for a variety of problems.

$$\begin{aligned} 10 \times 3.4 &= 34.0 \\ 100 \times 3.4 &= 340.0 \\ 1{,}000 \times 3.4 &= 3{,}400.0 \end{aligned}$$

Emphasize that the decimal point moves to the right the same number of places as zeros in the multiplier. Suggest that students round and estimate answers as a check of their work. For example, students can see that 3.4 rounded to 3 and multiplied by 10 is 30. An answer of 0.34 (less than 1) is obviously not reasonable.

## Problem Solving

### Helping Students Check Back

Question, Data, Plan, Answer, Check—each of these steps is very important in the problem-solving process. Many students have difficulty understanding problems and in selecting and carrying out solution strategies. Because of this, there is a tendency to emphasize the first four of these stages during instruction and to play down the importance of checking back. No problem-solving session is complete, however, unless the check back stage is included.

The purpose of the check back stage of problem solving is for students to evaluate their work on a particular problem. To help students check back, there are four teaching techniques you can use.

- Have students check whether all the relevant information was used. Two common errors made by elementary school students are 1) forgetting to use a necessary piece of data, and 2) neglecting a certain condition stated in the problem. Students who have committed these types of errors will often detect their error when they are asked to check back.
- Have students check the reasonableness of their answers. Students should be required to estimate the answers to problems whenever possible. Estimating answers and comparing estimates to exact answers verifies whether correct solution strategies (for example, the correct operation) were selected and whether computational work was performed with reasonable accuracy.
- Have students check their computations. Students should always be required to check for and, if necessary, correct any computational errors.
- Have students write their answers in complete sentences. This action encourages the student to relate the numerical part of a solution to the story setting. Also, it helps students determine whether they have indeed answered the question asked in the problem.

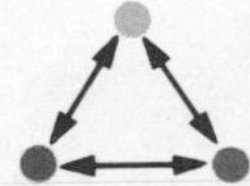

## Special Education

At the practical level students can multiply or divide money amounts without really thinking "decimals." The extent to which special students should be involved in this chapter, then, is dependent upon the severity of the disability and on personal vocational goals. Students who are mainstreamed should be able to follow the basic presentation of each lesson and carry out at least the minimum assignment. Ideas like the following will be necessary to assist some of these students as they work to master the basic concepts and skills of this chapter.

### Writing A Middle Step

As pointed out in the previous chapter, some students at first will need to write a middle step when giving an estimated answer. As students become more confident of the process, they will be able to carry out the calculations mentally and drop the intermediate step.

| Given | Student rounds and writes |
|---|---|
| 7.58<br>× 3.24 | 8<br>× 3 |

### Practicing One Step

This chapter contains several lessons in which special students, particularly those with memory or reasoning difficulties, should be allowed to practice each of the steps of a computational procedure before attempting to complete it start to finish.

Multiplying Decimals Let students who are confident with whole number multiplication practice placing the decimal point in the product. For example, for the lesson on page 140 (before the Warm Up), provide exercises like the one shown in which students carry out this one step. After they have mastered the skill of placing the decimal point in products, assign the Warm Up exercises.

Dividing Decimals For the lesson on page 148, provide exercises in which students place just the decimal point in otherwise complete divisions.

Rounding Decimal Quotients After introducing the lesson on page 150 (before the Warm Up), assign exercises which require students to annex as many zeros as are necessary to carry out the rounding. Students do not begin to divide until this first step is checked.

Decimal Divisors For problems like the one shown below, provide special practice to show the decimal shift and the extra zero(s) in the dividend.

$$0.03\overline{)6.1}$$

### Using Kinesthetic Cues to Mental Math

Some special-needs students, particularly those with auditory and memory difficulties, might find it helpful to finger trace the *one* zero in 10 and the *one* decimal point shift to emphasize the pattern for multiplying by 10. Similar finger movements can be used to highlight the patterns for other multiplications and division by powers of 10.

$$10 \times 29.95 = \underline{\quad}$$

### Providing Oral Guidance

If students understand why they process numbers the way they do during computation, they will remember procedures longer and make fewer procedural errors. For special students, this point is especially important. In decimal division, the language of sharing will help clarify major points for these students.

For problems like $0.3\overline{)6.9}$, it is necessary to establish the need to modify the problem. "It doesn't make sense to share *part* of a person." A calculator check shows that for an equivalent problem with a whole number divisor $3\overline{)69}$ gives the same answer. Making the change makes it easier to think about the numbers as we divide or "share" tens, ones, and so on.

Explain why we multiply both divisor and dividend by the same power of 10. Again the sharing idea can help minimize errors made in this part of the division. "A rich man shared the $24 in his pocket with 12 people. Each got $2. The next day 10 times as many people awaited him hoping to get $2 a piece. Hearing this, the rich man put 10 times as much money in his pocket so that each person would get $2." What we do to the divisor, we must do to the dividend, too.

$$12\overline{)24}^{\,2} \qquad 120\overline{)240}^{\,2}$$

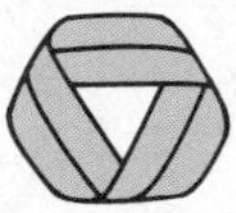

## Subject Integration

Subject matter related to other areas of the curriculum has been integrated into the following lessons. This provides an opportunity to highlight the interaction between mathematics and other subjects.

**Science** Measuring gold plating, pages 142–143; man-powered flight, page 147; average weights, pages 152–153; checking reaction times, pages 154–155

**Career Awareness** Careers at sea, page 137; jewelry store owner, page 144

**Consumer Awareness** Comparing prices, page 146; comparing cameras, pages 158–159; finding unit prices, page 161

**Physical Education** Olympic records, pages 148–149; basketball scores, pages 150–151

**Social Studies** Famous buildings, pages 156–157

# Management Guide

| Teaching Chapter 6 | | | | Meeting Individual Needs | | | | | |
|---|---|---|---|---|---|---|---|---|---|
| **Objectives** | **Chapter Content** | **Pages** | **TRB Test Items** | **Lesson Assignments** | | | **Follow Up** | | |
| | | | | Minimum | Average | Extended | Reteaching | Enrichment | Practice |
| | Chapter Opener | 137 | | | | | | | |
| **6.1** Round decimals and estimate their products and quotients. | Estimating Decimal Products and Quotients | 138–139 | 1–4 | 1–36 | 1–37 | 1–37, TM | SE5 Ch 13 | | MP 418<br>PS 52 |
| **6.2** Find products when one or both factors are decimals. | Multiplying Decimals | 140–141 | 5–7 | 1–25 | 1–27 | 1–27, TM | SE5 Ch 13<br>RS 33 | ES 33 | MP 419<br>PS 53 |
| | More Multiplying Decimals | 142–143 | | 1–32, SK | 1–33, SK | 1–33, SK | SE5 Ch 13<br>RS 34 | ES 34 | MP 419<br>PS 54 |
| | Multiplying Decimals by 10, 100, and 1,000: Mental Math | 144 | 8–9 | 1–20 | 1–20 | 1–20 | SE5 Ch 13 | | MP 419<br>PS 55 |
| | Multiplying Decimals: Practice | 145 | | 1–37 | 1–38 | 11–38, TM | SE5 Ch 13 | | |
| **6.3** Find quotients of decimals divided by a whole number. | Dividing Decimals by a Whole Number | 148–149 | 10–11 | 1–34 | 1–35 | 11–35, TM | SE5 Ch 13<br>RS 36 | ES 36 | MP 420<br>PS 57 |
| | Rounding Decimal Quotients | 150–151 | 14–15 | 1–27 | 1–29 | 6–29, TM | RS 37 | ES 37 | MP 420<br>PS 58 |
| | Dividing Decimals by 10, 100, and 1,000: Mental Math | 152 | 12–13 | 1–16 | 1–16 | 1–16 | SE5 Ch 13 | | MP 420 |
| | Dividing Decimals: Practice | 153 | | 1–32 | 1–33, TM | 9–33, TM | SE5 Ch 13 | | PS 59 |
| **6.4** Find quotients of decimals divided by another decimal. | Dividing by a Decimal | 156–157 | 16–18 | 1–39 | 1–40 | 1–40, TM | RS 38 | ES 38 | MP 421<br>PS 61 |
| | More Dividing by a Decimal | 158–159 | 19–20 | 1–29, SK | 1–30, SK | 1–30, SK | RS 39 | ES 39 | MP 421<br>PS 62 |
| | Decimals: Mixed Practice | 160 | | 1–25 | 1–26 | 1–26, TM | | | PS 63 |
| **6.5** Solve word problems using the 5-Point Checklist and cumulative computational skills. | Problem Solving: Using Estimation | 146 | 21–25 | 1–6 | 1–7 | 1–8 | RS 35 | ES 35 | |
| | Problem Solving: Practice | 147 | | 1–6 | 1–7 | 1–8 | | | PS 56 |
| | Problem Solving: Using Data from Several Sources | 154–155 | | 1–9 | 1–10 | 1–11 | | | PS 60 |
| | Problem Solving: Using a Calculator | 161 | | 1–6 | 1–7 | 1–8 | | | |
| | Problem Solving: Use Logical Reasoning | 162 | | | | | | | |
| | Chapter Review-Test | 163 | | | | | | | |
| | Another Look/Enrichment | 164–165 | | | | | | | |
| | Cumulative Review | 166 | | | | | | | |

**SE5** Student Edition, Book 5
**RS** Reteaching Supplement
**ES** Enrichment Supplement
**PS** Practice Supplement
**MP** More Practice
**TM** Think Math
**SK** Skillkeeper
**TRB** Teacher's Resource Book

## Masters for Use

**. . . before Chapter 6**

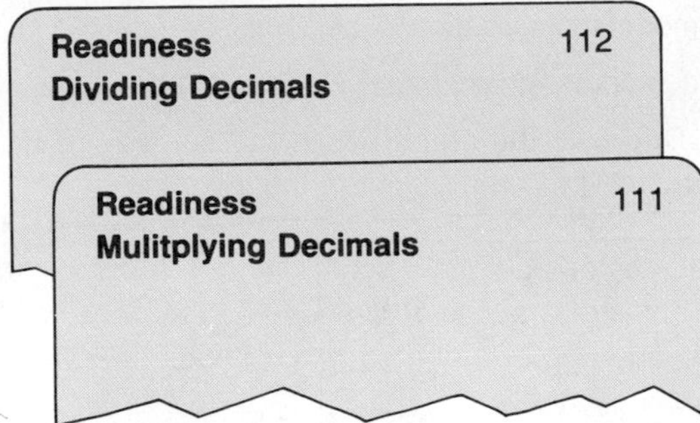


**. . . during Chapter 6**

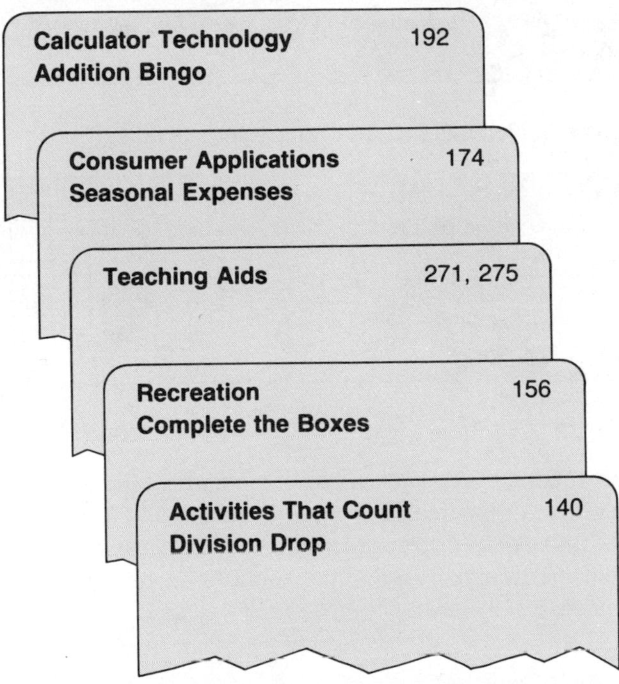

Calculator Technology 192
Addition Bingo
Consumer Applications 174
Seasonal Expenses
Teaching Aids 271, 275
Recreation 156
Complete the Boxes
Activities That Count 140
Division Drop


**. . . after Chapter 6**

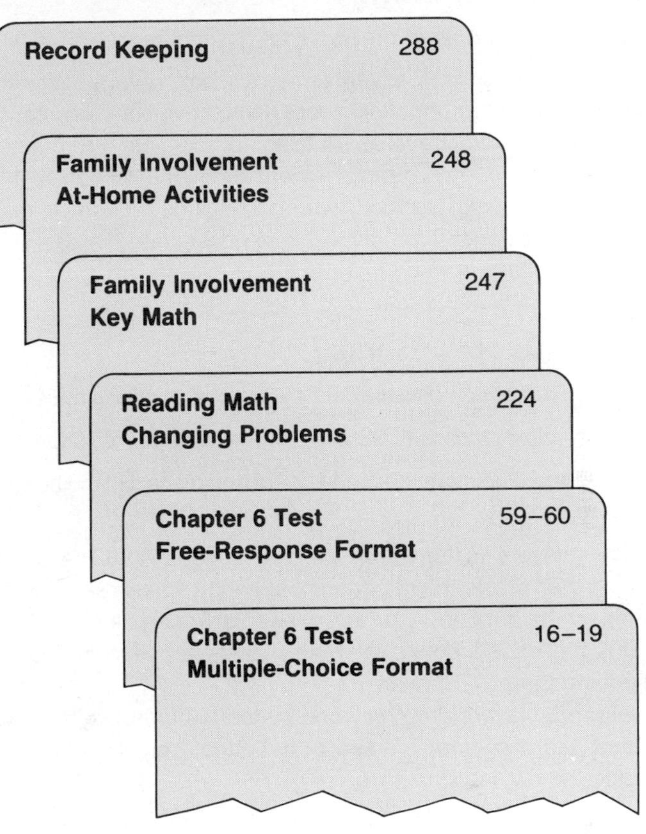

Record Keeping 288
Family Involvement 248
At-Home Activities
Family Involvement 247
Key Math
Reading Math 224
Changing Problems
Chapter 6 Test 59–60
Free-Response Format
Chapter 6 Test 16–19
Multiple-Choice Format


## Supplements

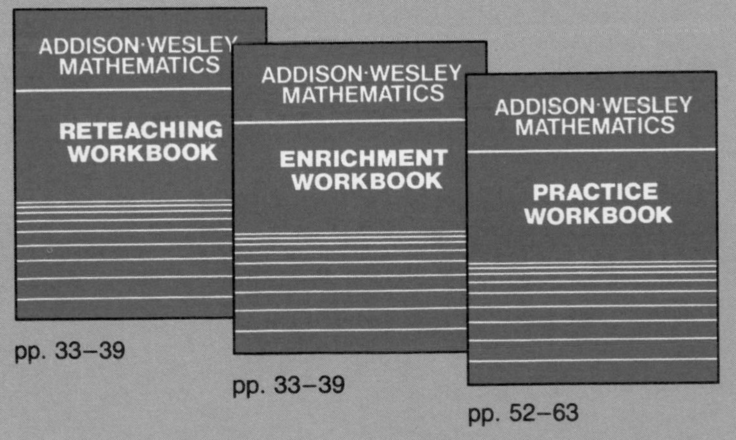


pp. 33–39

pp. 33–39

pp. 52–63

## Other Addison-Wesley Resources

**Books and Kits**

*Skillseekers 3* ⊗ Lessons 7–11; ⊕ Lessons 12–18
*Dice and Dots* Game 2
*The Arithmetic Primer* pp. 231–240, 273–274
*Arithmetic Skill Cards* pp. D 3–6
*Baseball, A Game of Numbers* pp. 28–36, 53–58, 98–102
*Problem Solving Experiences in Mathematics,* Grade 6
Problems 7, 8, 28, 34, 35, 38, 47, 48, 53, 63, 70, 74, 93, 94, 105, 114, 133, 147, 148, 149

**Technology**

*Computer Math Activities* Volumes 1–5
*Computer Math Games* Volumes 1, 2, 6

# Activities That Count

Activities That Count are designed for use throughout this chapter and subsequent chapters. Before beginning Chapter 6, you may wish to review these activities and select the ones you consider appropriate for your class.

## Decimals and Money Project

**Purpose** To create word problems for decimal numbers

**Activity** Students find advertisements from several different sources and select information about items of special interest to them—sporting goods, records, clothing, for example. From these advertisements students generate word problems related to the cost of particular items. Instruct students to include answers to their problems. Projects can be available in designated areas and shared by the class.

## Division Drop Game

**Purpose** To practice division and multiplication of decimals

**Materials** Game board (TRB p. 140), 2 small buttons, shoe box

**Preparation** Duplicate the game board and place it in the bottom of the shoe box

**Activity** Players in turn drop the two buttons onto the game board and then divide the larger number by the smaller number as indicated by the buttons. A correct answer is worth one point. If an answer is challenged, both player and challenger use multiplication to determine the correct answer.

If preferred, players drop only one button to determine the dividend and use a spinner marked with 1- and 2-digit numbers to determine the divisor.

## Grid Multiplication Math Lab

**Purpose** To model multiplication of decimals

**Materials** Index cards, graph paper (TRB p. 270)

**Preparation** Duplicate the graph paper and cut it in 10 by 10 squares. Prepare activity cards similar to the following:

1. Shade 3 tenths of the square lightly.
2. Shade 7 tenths of 3 tenths of the square heavily.
3. How many hundredths of the square is shaded heavily?
4. $0.3 \times 0.7 =$ ___?___

---

1. Shade 6 tenths of the square lightly.
2. Shade 4 tenths of 6 tenths of the square heavily.
3. How many hundredths of the square is shaded heavily?
4. $0.6 \times 0.4 =$ ___?___

---

Prepare the following as an example for students.

| Front | Back |
|---|---|
| 1. Shade 3 tenths of the square lightly.<br>2. Shade 4 tenths of 3 tenths of the square heavily.<br>3. How many hundredths of the square is shaded heavily?<br>4. $0.3 \times 0.4 =$ ___?___ | 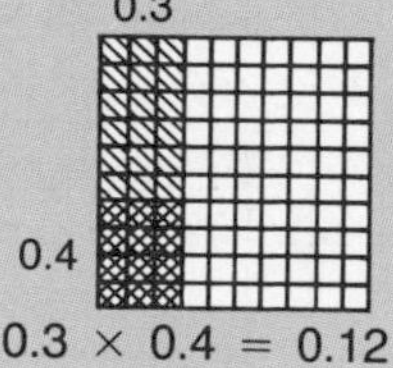<br>$0.3 \times 0.4 = 0.12$ |

**Activity** Let students choose one or more activity cards and then illustrate the decimal multiplication as directed on the cards. The decimal grids can be displayed on a decimal bulletin board. Encourage students to make up decimal cards to exchange with their classmates.

Realistic art and story themes put the mathematics into meaningful and relevant settings.

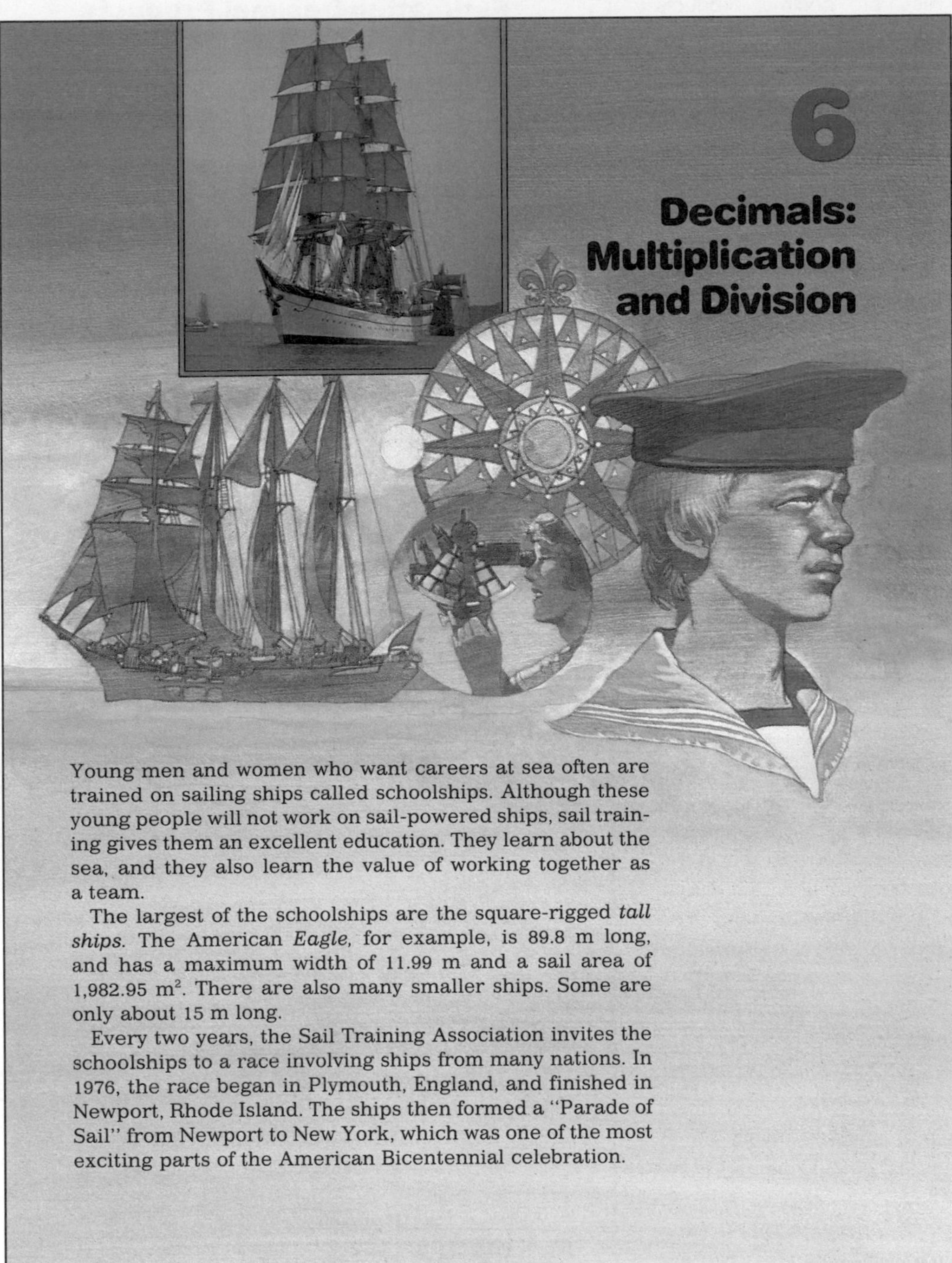


Young men and women who want careers at sea often are trained on sailing ships called schoolships. Although these young people will not work on sail-powered ships, sail training gives them an excellent education. They learn about the sea, and they also learn the value of working together as a team.

The largest of the schoolships are the square-rigged *tall ships.* The American *Eagle,* for example, is 89.8 m long, and has a maximum width of 11.99 m and a sail area of 1,982.95 $m^2$. There are also many smaller ships. Some are only about 15 m long.

Every two years, the Sail Training Association invites the schoolships to a race involving ships from many nations. In 1976, the race began in Plymouth, England, and finished in Newport, Rhode Island. The ships then formed a "Parade of Sail" from Newport to New York, which was one of the most exciting parts of the American Bicentennial celebration.

## Introducing the Chapter

**Discussion** Before introducing the first lesson, explain to students that in this chapter they will have an opportunity to strengthen their skills in multiplying and dividing with decimals. Then lead a brief discussion of ships and sailing, perhaps including a consideration of the advantages and disadvantages of sailing vessels compared to motor-powered ships. After giving students time to read the story and enjoy the art, encourage them to create some questions based on the data in the story. As you teach the chapter, you may wish to refer back to this page and pose the problems suggested below.

## Follow-Up Questions

**After Page 139** Round so that you can use a basic fact and estimate the area of a rectangular sail that is 9.4 m long and 6.83 m wide. Remember: Area = length × width. (63 $m^2$)

**After Page 141** Marcus is building a model sailboat that has a maximum width of 10.5 cm. Its length is 7.5 times as great as its maximum width. What is the boat's length? (78.75 cm)

**After Page 149** A fast sailboat traveled 128.35 km in 5 h. What was the boat's average speed in kilometers per hour? (25.67 km/h)

**After Page 157** A large rectangular sail has an area of 77.7 $m^2$. The sail's width is 8.4 m. What is the length of the sail? (9.25 m)

# Estimation

**Quick Review** Students give the meaning of each underlined digit.
1.23 1 one .09 9 hundredths 33.28 2 tenths 298.55 9 tens 14.09 0 tenths
4.55 5 hundredths 220.7 2 hundreds 73.87 8 tenths 210.6 0 ones
43.33 3 hundredths 3.75 7 tenths 19.38 8 hundredths 147.8 4 tens 11.31 1 ten

**Lesson Focus** To estimate decimal products and quotients by rounding to basic facts

## Ideas for Getting Started

Review the rules for rounding decimals to the nearest whole number: If the tenths digit is 5 or more, round up; if it is less than 5, round down. Ask students to round the following decimals to the nearest whole number: 8.32, 9.5, 6.375, 8.678, 13.052, 3.499. Then ask students to round these numbers to the nearest ten: 246.38, 367.92, 435.04, 694.59. Finally ask students to round these numbers to the nearest hundred: 543.64, 250.97, 178.632, 864.9. Remind students that in rounding to the nearest ten or hundred, they ignore the decimal part.

## Using Page 138

**Lesson Development** Tell students that it is easy to push the wrong button when using a calculator and that calculators sometimes make errors when the batteries are weak. For these reasons, it is important to estimate mentally the answer to a calculation to see if the calculator answer is reasonable. Direct students' attention to the first display on the page. Point out that since 8.56 rounds to 9 and 6.25 rounds to 6, the estimated answer is 54. The answer shown on the calculator seems reasonable.

As you discuss the estimation procedure in the second display box, point out that when the divisor is rounded to 4, we can see that the dividend must be rounded to 280 in order to use a basic fact to estimate.

In the third display box the divisor is rounded to 5 and the dividend is rounded to the nearest hundred, that is, 400. Note in this case the calculated answer does not seem reasonable.

**Warm Up** In exercise 3 students might round each decimal to the nearest whole number. If so, they will be faced with finding the product 7 × 56. Since this does not involve a basic fact, they must round 56 to the nearest ten or 60. Then they can use 6 × 7 to estimate the answer. Be alert for rounding errors, basic fact multiplication and division errors, and for difficulties finding special products or quotients.

## Estimating Decimal Products and Quotients

Rick used a calculator to solve some decimal multiplication and division problems. Then he checked to see if the calculator answers were reasonable. To do this, he rounded the numbers so that he could estimate using a basic fact.

| $8.56 \times 6.25$ | $3.9\overline{)282.75}$ | $412.88 \div 5.2$ |
|---|---|---|
| 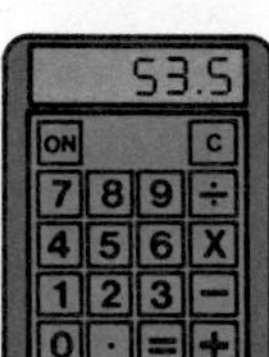  | 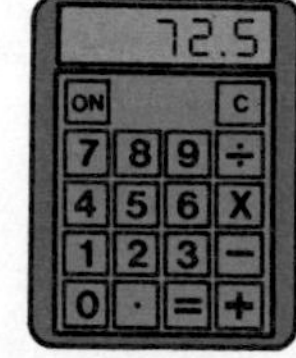  | 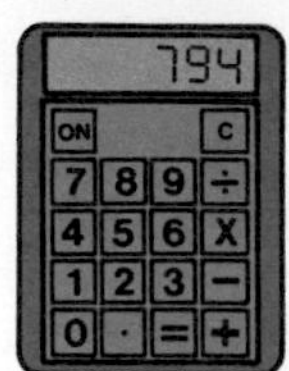  |
| Round to the **nearest whole number.** | Round the divisor to the **nearest whole number.** Round the dividend to the **nearest ten.** | Round the divisor to the **nearest whole number.** Round the dividend to the **nearest hundred.** |
| 8.56 → 9; × 6.25 → × 6; 54 | $3.9\overline{)282.75} \longrightarrow 4\overline{)280}$ = 70 | 412.88 ÷ 5.2 → 400 ÷ 5 = 80 |
| The calculator answer seems reasonable. | The calculator answer seems reasonable. | The calculator answer does not seem reasonable. |

**Warm Up** Estimate by rounding so that you can use a basic fact.

1. 7.58 × 3.24 24
2. 4.736 × 8.5 45
3. 56.287 × 7.3 420
4. 89.76 × 38.2 3,600
5. $787.53 × 6 $4,800
6. $2.8\overline{)273.5}$ 100
7. $7.4\overline{)62.96}$ 9
8. $5\overline{)\$379.86}$ $80
9. $6.9\overline{)35.68}$ 5
10. $3\overline{)11.777}$ 4

138

## Follow Up

### Reteaching

Remind students that is important to determine the place to which to round. Have them look at the examples below and explain why each was rounded as it was.

a) 4.37 × 2.65 → 4 × 3 = 12 — Round to nearest whole number so basic facts can be used.

b) 26.7 × 3.9 → 30 × 4 = 120 — Round one factor to nearest ten, other to nearest whole number so that a multiple of 10 can be used.

### Enrichment

Have students complete the decimal estimation table by rounding each factor to the nearest whole number. The students can check the estimates for closeness to the actual product by using the calculator.

| Estimate | | | | | | |
|---|---|---|---|---|---|---|
| × | 2.3 | 3.3 | 9.1 | 8.7 | 5.4 | 6.2 |
| 1.2 | 2 | 3 | 9 | 9 | 5 | 6 |
| 3.6 | 8 | 12 | 36 | 36 | 20 | 24 |
| 5.8 | 12 | 18 | 54 | 54 | 30 | 36 |
| 7.3 | 14 | 21 | 63 | 63 | 35 | 42 |
| 8.6 | 18 | 27 | 81 | 81 | 45 | 54 |
| 4.5 | 10 | 15 | 45 | 45 | 25 | 30 |

| Assignment Guide | | | |
|---|---|---|---|
| | Minimum | Average | Extended |
| page 139 | 1–36 | 1–37 | 1–37, TM |

Estimate the products by rounding so that you can use a basic fact.

1. 3.7 × 8.3 — 32
2. 6.47 × 7.19 — 42
3. 8.96 × 4 — 36
4. 5.94 × 8.36 — 48
5. 9.08 × 6.89 — 63
6. $48.36 × 5 — $250
7. 71.794 × 8.6 — 630
8. 67.46 × 39.28 — 2,800
9. 319.38 × 86.759 — 27,000
10. $809.36 × 6.2 — $4,800
11. 7.4 × 3.826 28
12. 9.324 × 6.7 63
13. 57.8 × 9.15 540
14. 6.45 × 8.591 54
15. 68.9 × 7.38 490
16. $486.25 × 7.75 $4,000
17. 66.57 × 23.69 1,400
18. 398.6 × 27.43 12,000
19. 687.4 × 719.6 490,000

Estimate the quotients by rounding so that you can use a basic fact.

20. 4)283.64 — 70
21. 6)478.34 — 80
22. 8)724.62 — 90
23. 3)$265.98 — $90
24. 3.2)14.862 — 5
25. 7.6)322.47 — 40
26. 5.8)355.93 — 60
27. 9.1)$536.71 — $60
28. 55.982 ÷ 7.8 7
29. 483.7 ÷ 6.3 80
30. 34.967 ÷ 4.7 7
31. 53.84 ÷ 9.25 6
32. 719.6 ÷ 8.35 90
33. 397.2 ÷ 49.6 8
34. 357.28 ÷ 3.5 90
35. 299.76 ÷ 5.2 60
36. 634.73 ÷ 8.9 70

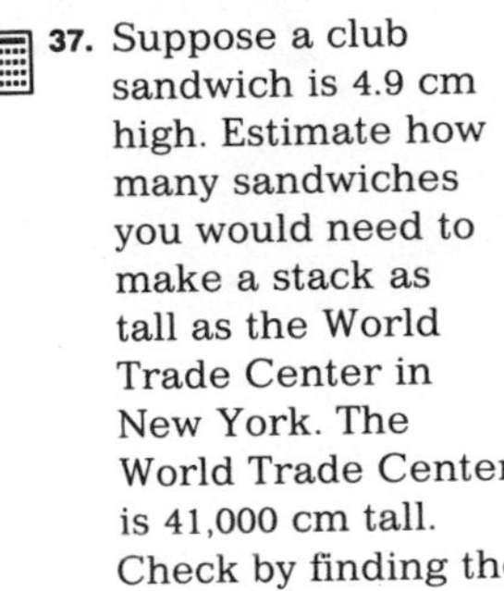

37. Suppose a club sandwich is 4.9 cm high. Estimate how many sandwiches you would need to make a stack as tall as the World Trade Center in New York. The World Trade Center is 41,000 cm tall. Check by finding the exact answer. about 8,000; 8,367.3469

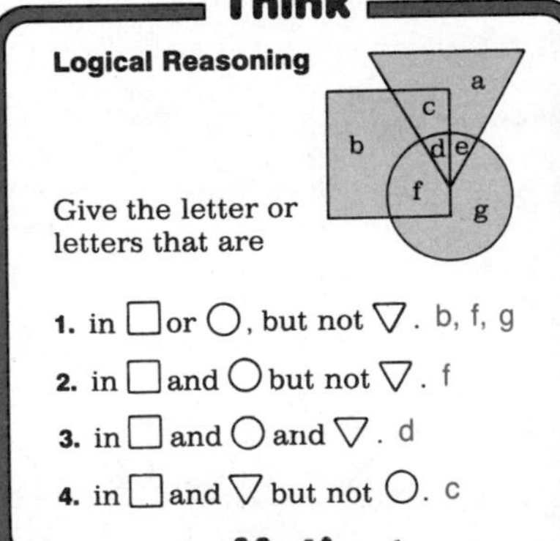

**Think Math**

**Logical Reasoning**



Give the letter or letters that are

1. in □ or ○, but not ▽. b, f, g
2. in □ and ○ but not ▽. f
3. in □ and ○ and ▽. d
4. in □ and ▽ but not ○. c



More Practice, page 418, Set C

## Using Page 139

**Exercises 1–19** Note that in exercises 1–5 students must round each decimal to the nearest whole number. However, in exercises 6–8 at least one of the factors must be rounded to the nearest ten. In exercises 9 and 10 one of the factors must be rounded to the nearest hundred. Exercises 11–19 provide a variety of practice exercises. If necessary, discuss briefly with students about deciding how to round numbers.

**Exercises 20–36** In exercises 20–23 only the dividend needs to be rounded to the nearest ten. In exrcises 24–27 the divisor must be rounded to the nearest whole number and the dividend rounded so that a basic fact can be used. Exercises 28–36 provide a variety of practice exercises.

**Exercise 37** In this exercise students use their calculators to check estimated answers. Note that to estimate they will need to round 41,100 to 40,000 and 4.9 to 5.

**Think Math** This activity provides students an opportunity to use logical connectives such as "and," "or," "not," "but," "both" to make decisions about the elements of intersecting sets. In exercise 1 be sure students are aware that the letters b, f, g are "in the square or in the circle" since each of these letters are in one or the other or both of the figures. In exercise 2 be sure the students are aware that the letter f is in "both the square and the circle" because it is in the intersection of these two figures. After students have chosen their answers for these four questions, discuss their answers and ask students to explain their choices.

**More Practice,** page 418, Set C

## Ideas That Work

### Chalk It Up

Draw a figure like the one below on the chalkboard. Choose a multiplier and write it in the center of the circles. Have students round decimals to the nearest whole number, multiply by the number in the center, and write the product on the line outside the circle.

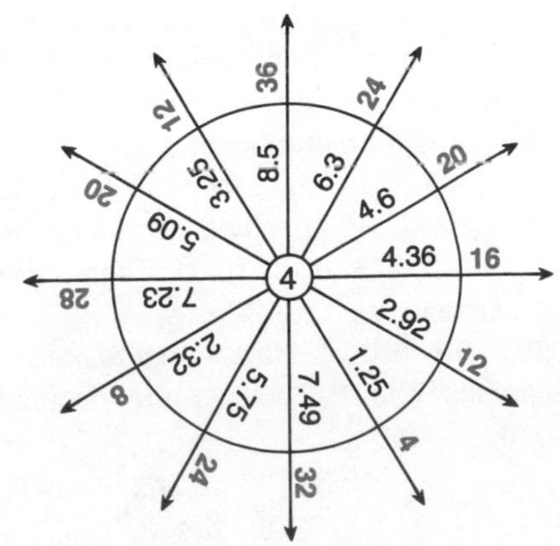



**Practice Supplement,** page 52

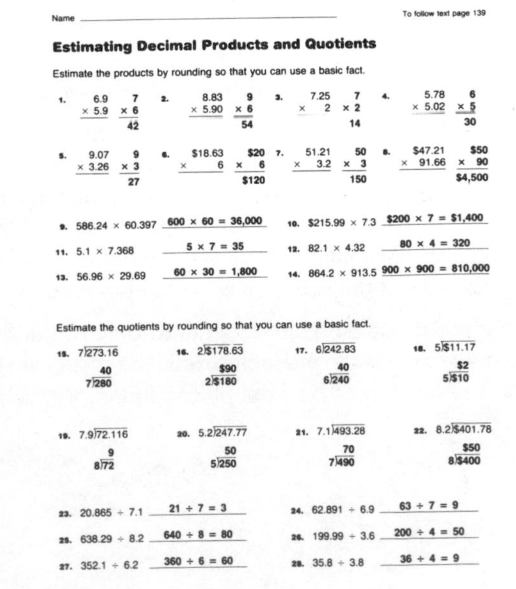

Name ______________________ To follow text page 139

**Estimating Decimal Products and Quotients**

Estimate the products by rounding so that you can use a basic fact.

1. 6.9 × 5.9 — 7 × 6 = 42
2. 8.83 × 5.90 — 9 × 6 = 54
3. 7.25 × 2 — 7 × 2 = 14
4. 5.78 × 5.02 — 6 × 5 = 30
5. 9.07 × 3.26 — 9 × 3 = 27
6. $18.63 × 6 — $20 × 6 = $120
7. 51.21 × 3.2 — 50 × 3 = 150
8. $47.21 × 91.66 — $50 × 90 = $4,500
9. 586.24 × 60.397 — 600 × 60 = 36,000
10. $215.99 × 7.3 — $200 × 7 = $1,400
11. 5.1 × 7.368 — 5 × 7 = 35
12. 82.1 × 4.32 — 80 × 4 = 320
13. 56.96 × 29.69 — 60 × 30 = 1,800
14. 864.2 × 913.5 — 900 × 900 = 810,000

Estimate the quotients by rounding so that you can use a basic fact.

15. 7)273.16 — 7)280 = 40
16. 2)$178.63 — 2)$180 = $90
17. 6)242.83 — 6)240 = 40
18. 5)$11.17 — 5)$10 = $2
19. 7.9)72.116 — 8)72 = 9
20. 5.2)247.77 — 5)250 = 50
21. 7.1)493.28 — 7)490 = 70
22. 8.2)$401.78 — 8)$400 = $50
23. 20.865 ÷ 7.1 — 21 ÷ 7 = 3
24. 62.891 ÷ 6.9 — 63 ÷ 7 = 9
25. 638.29 ÷ 8.2 — 640 ÷ 8 = 80
26. 199.99 ÷ 3.6 — 200 ÷ 4 = 50
27. 352.1 ÷ 6.2 — 360 ÷ 6 = 60
28. 35.8 ÷ 3.8 — 36 ÷ 4 = 9

# Decimals: Multiplication

**Quick Review** Students give the number that makes each expression true.

4 × 7 = □ □ × 8 = 56 6 × □ = 30 2 × 9 = □ 8 × □ = 64
3 × □ = 18 □ × 6 = 24 9 × 8 = □ 3 × □ = 9
5 × 9 = □ □ × 7 = 63 8 × □ = 64 4 × 8 = □ 7 × □ = 35

**Lesson Focus** To find products of up to 4-place decimals

**Suggested Materials** 10 by 10 grids (TRB p. 274)

## Ideas for Getting Started

Provide students with a 10 by 10 grid. Tell them that this square is one unit on a side and then show a rectangle that is 0.8 × 0.6 of a unit. Have them shade the 0.8 × 0.6 rectangle. "How can you show the area of the shaded rectangle?" (L × W = 0.8 × 0.6 = 0.48) Verify that the shaded rectangle contains 48 of the small squares. Discuss this model as it relates to multiplying a 1-place decimal times a 1-place decimal to find a 2-place decimal.

## Using Page 140

**Motivational Problem** Have students read the problem at the top of the page." What question are we asked in this problem?" (How far apart are the rails on a real railroad?) "Why should we plan to use multiplication as the operation to solve the problem?" (We can multiply to find the number of same-size units on the model for each meter on the real railroad.)

**Lesson Development** Work through the multiplication problem on the chalkboard as with whole numbers. After you have multiplied 9 × 16, ask students where they think the decimal point should be placed in the answer and have them give reasons for their decision. Then direct students' attention to the square grids. "What decimal shows the amount of the two grids in the lighter shade?" (1.6) "What part of the 1.6 shaded area is the darker shade?" (0.9 of it) "What is the area of the darker region?" (0.9 × 1.6) "How many of the 200 squares are in the darker shade?" (144, or 1 whole square and 0.44 of another) Point out that in this problem a 1-place decimal multiplied by a 1-place decimal produced a 2-place decimal. Elicit from students that since 0.9 is just less than 1, then 1.6 × 0.9 should be just less than 1.6; the answer 1.44 seems reasonable. Then have students read the complete sentence that gives the answer to the question.

**Other Examples** Work through the other examples using estimation to help decide where to place the decimal point. When you have completed all three examples, remind students that the sum of the number of decimal places in the factors is equal to the number of decimal places in the product.

**Warm Up** Be alert for students who think that the number of places in the factors must be multiplied to find the number of decimal places in the product.

## Multiplying Decimals

The inside distance between the rails on some model railroads is about 1.6 cm. If we use the scale given below, about how far apart are the rails on a real railroad?

Scale: 1 cm on the model is about 0.9 m on a real railroad.

Since each centimeter on the model stands for the same actual distance, we multiply.

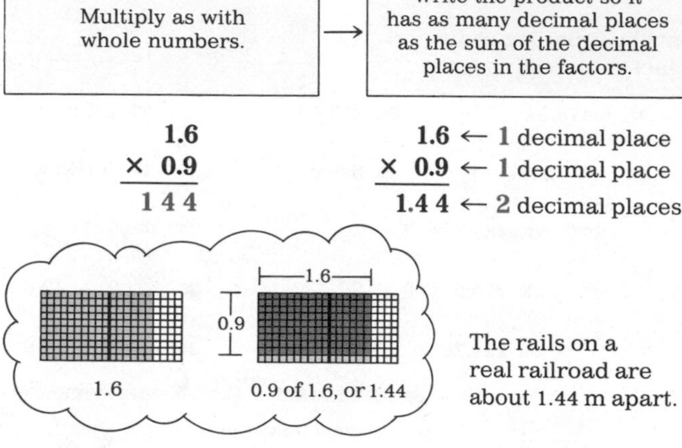

| Multiply as with whole numbers. | → | Write the product so it has as many decimal places as the sum of the decimal places in the factors. |
|---|---|---|

```
  1.6              1.6  ← 1 decimal place
× 0.9            × 0.9  ← 1 decimal place
  144              1.44 ← 2 decimal places
```

1.6 | 0.9 | 1.6 | 0.9 of 1.6, or 1.44

The rails on a real railroad are about 1.44 m apart.

**Other Examples**

```
  9.43 ← 2 decimal places      0.276 ← 3 places       1.32 ← 2 places
×  0.6 ← 1 decimal place     ×     3 ← 0 places     × 0.87 ← 2 places
 5.658 ← 3 decimal places      0.828 ← 3 places        924
                                                      1056
                                                    1.1484 ← 4 places
```

**Warm Up** Multiply.

```
1.  4.27     2.  1.374     3.  2.41     4.  9.4     5.   46.75
  ×  0.7       ×     6       × 0.68       × 6.8        ×  8.68
   2.989         8.244       1.6388       63.92       405.7900
```

140

## Follow Up

### Reteaching

Review multiplication of the fractions $\frac{1}{10} \times \frac{1}{10} = \frac{1}{100}$. Then review decimal place value and how decimal numbers are related to fractions. For example: $0.1 = \frac{1}{10}$ is read one tenth; $0.01 = \frac{1}{100}$ is read one hundredth. Elicit from students that $\frac{1}{10} \times \frac{1}{10} = \frac{1}{100}$ could be written as decimals: 0.1 × 0.1 = 0.01. Then show an example such as $\frac{3}{10} \times \frac{7}{10} = \frac{21}{100}$ and 0.3 × 0.7 = 0.21. Help students generalize the rule for placing the decimal point.

### Enrichment

Provide students with problems like the one below and have them find the missing digits and insert the decimal point in the top factor.

```
   3^76
 ×  3.9
   3384
  11280
 14.664
```

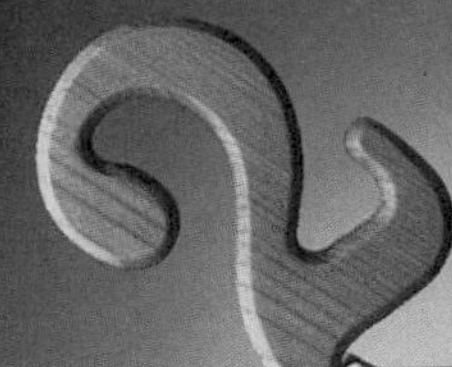

## Assignment Guide

| | Minimum | Average | Extended |
|---|---|---|---|
| page 141 | 1–25 | 1–27 | 1–27, TM |

Multiply.

1. 3.4 × 0.6 = 2.04
2. 2.8 × 5.9 = 16.52
3. 0.35 × 6 = 2.10
4. 4.28 × 9 = 38.52
5. 26.5 × 0.46 = 12.190
6. 1.765 × 8 = 14.120
7. 3.46 × 2.9 = 10.034
8. 2.78 × 4.6 = 12.788
9. 437.9 × 26.4 = 11,560.56
10. $7.23 × 4.5 = $32.535
11. 0.58 × 8.41 = 4.8778
12. 9.67 × 4.5 = 43.515
13. 2.75 × 1.89 = 5.1975
14. 6.461 × 28 = 180.908
15. $9.45 × 0.9 = $8.505
16. 6.8 × 3.2 21.76
17. 9.7 × 0.56 5.432
18. 4.75 × 0.9 4.275
19. 5.62 × 3.84 21.5808
20. 0.763 × 9.4 7.1722
21. 8.98 × 4.36 39.1528

22. Estimate, then find the product of the factors 6.8 and 4.2 28; 28.56
23. Estimate, then find 38.67 multiplied by 72.46. 2,800; 2,802.0282
24. A scale model caboose is 12.2 cm long. Each centimeter on the model is exactly 0.87 m on the actual caboose. How long is the actual caboose? 10.614 m
25. Model railroad track sections 23 cm long cost $2.75 each. What will be the cost for a 299-cm section of track? $35.75
26. Some needed data is missing from the problem below. Make up the needed data and solve the problem.

    A six-car model train is 73.2 cm long. How long is the actual train? Data and answers will vary.
27. **DATA BANK** Give the actual lengths of these train cars: box car, auto-loader, tank car, passenger car. (See Data Bank, page 407.) box car, 12.702 m; auto-loader, 15.486 m; tank car, 7.917 m; passenger car, 15.225 m

**Think Math**

**Guess and Check**

$a + b = 0.9$

$a \times b = 0.18$

Can you find a decimal for $a$ and a decimal for $b$ so that their sum is 0.9 and their product is 0.18? $a = 0.6$, $b = 0.3$

More Practice, page 419, Set A



## Using Page 141

**Exercises 1–21** Remind students that they are to find the products as if they were working with whole numbers and then use the addition rule to place the decimal point. Note that most of the problems have 2- and 3-place decimals as answers. In exercises 11, 13, and 19–21, the products are 4-place decimals. If necessary, have students tell how many places are in each factor and how many places in the product before they work the exercises.

**Data Bank** Remind students that they must find the appropriate data in the Data Bank in the back of the book and then use it to find the actual lengths of the train cars.

**Think Math** This activity provides students with an opportunity to use the Guess and Check strategy. Point out that the two numbers chosen must satisfy both conditions; that is, the sum must be 0.9, the product must be 0.18. Encourage students to pick any pair of decimals, find the sum and product, then refine their guesses.

*A full page of practice, problem solving, and extension exercises allows for individualized assignments.*

*Over 2,000 additional exercises are located in the appendix of each student book.*

**More Practice,** page 419, Set A

### Reteaching Supplement, page 33

Name ____________ To follow text page 141

**Multiplying Decimals**

Find the product: 35.4 × 0.06

Multiply as with whole numbers. → Write the decimal point in the product.

354 × 6 = 2124

35.4 ← 1 decimal place
× 0.06 ← 2 decimal places
2.124 ← 3 decimal places

The number of decimal places in the product equals the sum of the number of decimal places in each factor.

Find the products.

1. 6.7 × 3.5: 335, 201, 23.45 (2 decimal places)
2. 8.09 × 57: 5663, 4045, 461.13 (2 decimal places)
3. 12.5 × 0.74: 500, 875, 9.250
4. 9.4 × 2.7: 658, 188, 25.38
5. 12.8 × 3.5: 640, 384, 44.80
6. 5.12 × 7.6: 3072, 3584, 38.912
7. 9.12 × 6.8: 7296, 5472, 62.016
8. 127.8 × 9.4: 5112, 11502, 1,201.32
9. 62.9 × 12.5: 3145, 1258, 629, 786.25
10. 1.01 × 379: 909, 707, 303, 382.79
11. 0.928 × 45.6: 5568, 4640, 3712, 42.3168
12. 7.4 × 6.25 (Write the biggest factor on top.) 6.25 × 7.4: 2500, 4375, 46.250
13. 2.31 × 1.7: 1617, 231, 3.927
14. 6.4 × 146: 146 × 6.4: 584, 876, 934.4

### Enrichment Supplement, page 33

Name ____________ To follow text page 141

**A Decimal Product Riddle**

Write the product in each of the problems below. Then use your answers to solve the riddle.

- A 1.64 × 0.96 = 1.5744
- C 2.98 × 0.083 = 0.24734
- E 1.31 × 0.79 = 1.0349
- H 1.96 × 0.67 = 1.3132
- L 1.38 × 0.34 = 0.4692
- N 2.53 × 0.43 = 1.0879
- O 5.04 × 0.19 = 0.9576
- R 9.57 × 0.87 = 8.3259
- S 1.27 × 0.537 = 0.68199
- T 0.654 × 2.11 = 1.37994
- W 3.41 × 0.448 = 1.52768



Look at each number below. Then find it as a product in one of the problems above. Write the letter of the problem in the blank above the number.

What is the difference between a watchmaker and a jailer?

| O | N | E | S | E | L | L | S |
|---|---|---|---|---|---|---|---|
| 0.9576 | 1.0879 | 1.0349 | 0.68199 | 1.0349 | 0.4692 | 0.4692 | 0.68199 |

| W | A | T | C | H | E | S |
|---|---|---|---|---|---|---|
| 1.52768 | 1.5744 | 1.37994 | 0.24734 | 1.3132 | 1.0349 | 0.68199 |

| T | H | E | O | T | H | E | R |
|---|---|---|---|---|---|---|---|
| 1.37994 | 1.3132 | 1.0349 | 0.9576 | 1.37994 | 1.3132 | 1.0349 | 8.3259 |

| W | A | T | C | H | E | S |
|---|---|---|---|---|---|---|
| 1.52768 | 1.5744 | 1.37994 | 0.24734 | 1.3132 | 1.0349 | 0.68199 |

| C | E | L | L | S |
|---|---|---|---|---|
| 0.24734 | 1.0349 | 0.4692 | 0.4692 | 0.68199 |

### Practice Supplement, page 53

Name ____________ To follow text page 141

**Multiplying Decimals**

Multiply.

1. 32.6 × 5 = 163.0
2. 4.38 × 7 = 30.66
3. 7.39 × 0.6 = 4.434
4. 53.7 × 0.9 = 48.33
5. 64.2 × 0.7 = 44.94
6. 79.65 × 0.3 = 23.895
7. 6.38 × 0.9 = 5.742
8. 5.96 × 6 = 35.76
9. 8.35 × 6 = 50.10
10. 47.6 × 0.7 = 33.32
11. 0.73 × 42: 146, 2920, 30.66
12. 0.37 × 68: 296, 2220, 25.16
13. 5.6 × 8.3: 168, 4480, 46.48
14. 0.85 × 2.8: 680, 1700, 2.380
15. 0.69 × 0.54: 276, 3450, 0.3726
16. 0.47 × 5.8: 376, 2350, 2.726
17. 8.4 × 3.9: 756, 2520, 32.76
18. 6.5 × 0.72: 130, 4550, 4.680
19. 0.58 × 0.43: 174, 2320, 0.2494
20. 0.75 × 0.82: 150, 6000, 0.6150
21. 8.42 × 73: 2526, 58940, 614.66
22. 7.58 × 48: 6064, 30320, 363.84
23. 53.7 × 6.9: 4833, 32220, 370.53
24. 4.86 × 3.7: 3402, 14580, 17.982
25. 6.45 × 7.6: 3870, 45150, 49.020
26. 6.93 × 5.4: 2772, 34650, 37.422
27. 0.584 × 8.7: 4088, 46720, 5.0808
28. 0.952 × 3.6: 5712, 28560, 3.4272
29. 0.875 × 5.6: 5250, 43750, 4.9000
30. 0.736 × 8.5: 3680, 58880, 6.2560

# Decimals: Multiplication

**Quick Review** Students use these multiplication problems for oral drill.

24 × 10   100 × 8   10 × 68   2 × 1,000   3 × 100   10 × 9
17 × 100   10 × 8   63 × 1,000   6 × 100   1,000 × 7
19 × 10   4 × 1,000   10 × 77   100 × 59   60 × 100   10 × 26

**Lesson Focus** To find products of decimals where annexing zeros is necessary.

## Ideas for Getting Started

To review decimal place value, put the chart below on the chalkboard.

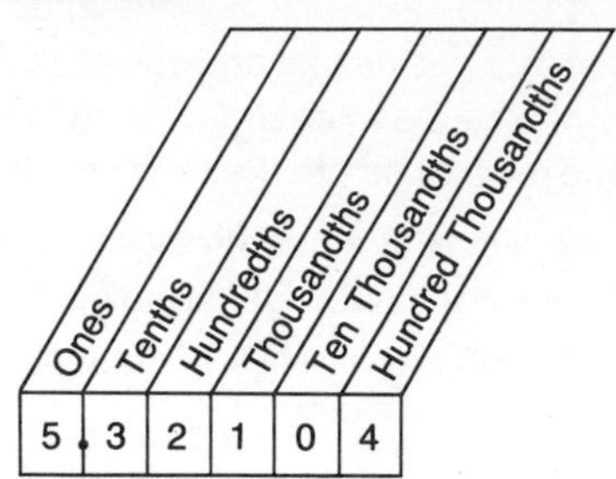


"What digit is in the ten thousandths place?" (0) "the hundred thousandths place?" (4) "the tenths place?" (3) Write another decimal such as 16.05342. "The 4 is in what place?" (ten thousandths) "The 0 is in what place?" (tenths) Then have students write a 3-place decimal, a 4-place decimal, and a 5-place decimal.

## Using Page 142

**Motivational Problem** Have students read the problem at the top of the page. "What are we asked to find out about the protective coating on the space vehicle?" (How thick is the gold layer?) "What data will help answer the question?" (The gold layer is 675 times as thick as 0.000009.) Elicit from students that since we want to find the thickness of a layer that is 675 *times* as thick as the thin layer, we multiply.

**Lesson Development** Work through the decimal multiplication problem on the chalkboard. "How many decimal places in the first factor?" (0) "How many decimal places in the second factor?" (6) "How many decimal places should be in the product?" (0 + 6 or 6) Point out that in order to have a 6-place decimal product, we must annex 2 zeros to the left digit of the product before placing the decimal point. Have students reread the original problem and decide if the answer seems reasonable. Then have them round the answer 0.006075 to the nearest thousandth. (0.006)

**Other Examples** Note that in the first example only one zero was annexed to the product before writing the decimal point. In the second example three zeros were needed. Remind students again of the rule that the sum of the number of decimal places in the two factors is the number of decimal places required for the product. In the last example note that the answer is rounded to the nearest cent.

**Warm Up** Be sure students are correctly using the rule for placing the decimal point and be sure they annex the zeros to the left of the initial product rather than to the right.

## More Multiplying Decimals

Gold can be hammered into leaves with a thickness of only 0.000009 cm (9 millionths of a centimeter). A gold layer about 675 times this thick has been used as a protective coating on the outside of space vehicles. How thick is this layer?

Since we want to find the total of several equal amounts, we multiply.

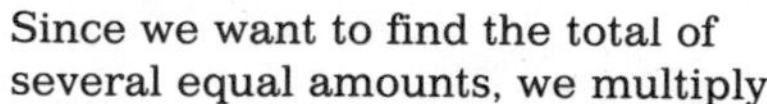

```
      675 ← 0 places
× 0.000009 ← 6 places
  0.006075 ← 6 places
```

Write as many extra zeros as are needed to show the correct number of places in the product.

The gold layer is 0.006075 cm thick.

**Other Examples**

| 0.08 × 0.4 | 0.03 × 0.02 | 435 × 0.0002 | $0.73 × 0.05 |
|---|---|---|---|
| 0.032 | 0.0006 | 0.0870 | $0.0365 or $0.04 (rounded to the nearest cent) |

**Warm Up** Multiply. Write extra zeros in the product as needed.

1. 0.06 × 0.3 = 0.018
2. 0.04 × 0.02 = 0.0008
3. 57 × 0.003 = 0.171
4. 590 × 0.0001 = 0.0590
5. $0.59 × 0.06 = 0.0354
6. 2.05 × 0.02 = 0.0410
7. 0.006 × 0.05 = 0.00030
8. 2.3 × 0.004 = 0.0092
9. 8.1 × 0.06 = 0.486
10. $0.47 × 0.03 = $0.0141



## Follow Up

### Reteaching

As a review for this lesson, help students practice reading up to 5-place decimals. Put a list of decimals on the chalkboard. Have students read through the numbers disregarding the decimal points. For example, "six thousand three hundred twenty-nine." Observe that the last digit is in the hundred thousandths place. Tell students to add that to the number name: "six thousand three hundred twenty-nine hundred thousandths." Let students practice reading 4- and 5-place decimals. Then have students write the number name for each decimal.

### Enrichment

Have students decode the message by matching the value of each letter with the appropriate answer below.

| | |
|---|---|
| E = 8.6 × 0.7 6.02 | D = 0.4 × 2.1 8.4 |
| N = 0.06 = 0.2 0.012 | I = 0.3 × 0.2 0.06 |
| F = 15.6 × 0.35 5.46 | C = 3.4 × 0.2 0.68 |
| M = 0.1 × 0.2 0.02 | S = 30 × 0.2 6 |
| R = 0.27 × 0.4 0.108 | A = 1.5 × 0.3 0.45 |
| U = 1,537 × 0.6 922.2 | L = 1.2 × 0.2 0.24 |

| D | E | C | I | M | A | L | S |
|---|---|---|---|---|---|---|---|
| 8.4 | 6.02 | 0.68 | 0.06 | 0.02 | 0.45 | 0.24 | 6 |

| A | R | E | | F | U | N ! |
|---|---|---|---|---|---|---|
| 0.45 | 0.108 | 6.02 | | 5.46 | 922.2 | 0.012 |

## Assignment Guide

| | Minimum | Average | Extended |
|---|---|---|---|
| page 143 | 1–32, SK | 1–33, SK | 1–33, SK |

Multiply.

1. 4.3 × 5.7 = 24.51
2. 0.05 × 0.09 = 0.0045
3. 3.2 × 0.004 = 0.0128
4. 5.765 × 8.6 = 49.5790
5. 4.8 × 0.0005 = 0.00240
6. 1.3 × 0.04 = 0.052
7. 6.375 × 0.02 = 0.12750
8. 0.009 × 4.3 = 0.0387
9. 5.67 × 2.98 = 16.8966
10. $5.77 × 0.05 = $0.2885
11. 7.38 × 0.06 = 0.4428
12. 0.76 × 0.003 = 0.00228
13. 50 × 0.8 = 40.0
14. 0.015 × 2.6 = 0.0390
15. $46.06 × 0.06 = $2.7636
16. 0.0012 × 4.6 = 0.00552
17. 179 × 0.01 = 1.79
18. 67.86 × 0.0003 = 0.020358
19. $9.65 × 0.15 = $1.4475
20. 0.080 × 0.005 = 0.000400

21. 4.3 × 0.007 0.0301
22. 5.7 × 0.18 1.026
23. 3.04 × 0.016 0.04864
24. 0.09 × 0.015 0.00135
25. 4.86 × 9.573 46.52478
26. 0.0054 × 0.025 0.0001350
27. 0.075 × $3.45 $0.25875
28. 1.34 × 5.062 6.78308
29. 0.105 × $9.67 $1.01535

30. What is the product when 0.016 is multiplied by 0.025? 0.000400

31. Estimate, then find the product of the factors 3.87 and 19.605. 80; 75.87135

32. The thickest gold plating on the outside of some spacecraft is 0.006 cm thick. The thinnest plating is only 0.2 times that thick. What is the thickness of the thinnest gold plating? 0.0012 cm

33. Write a question about this data and solve the problem. Certain parts of an astronaut's helmet must be coated with 3 layers of gold film. Each layer is 0.0012 cm thick. Answers will vary.

### Skillkeeper

Divide.

1. 6)540 — 90
2. 8)496 — 62
3. 5)254 — 50 R4
4. 7)875 — 125
5. 3)726 — 242
6. 9)819 — 91
7. 6)4,270 — 711 R4
8. 5)26,385 — 5,277
9. 40)1,757 — 43 R37
10. 70)18,760 — 268
11. 43)3,827 — 89
12. 55)$70.40 — $1.28
13. 125)6,275 — 50 R25
14. 36)2,052 — 57
15. 230)5,750 — 25
16. 65)$81.25 — $1.25

More Practice, page 419, Set B



## Using Page 143

**Exercises 1–32** Note that there are exercises that need to have zeros annexed in the product and others that do not. Remind students again of the rule for finding a number of decimal places in the product and of the importance of annexing the appropriate number of zeros to the left of the initial product.

**Exercise 33** This problem asks students to supply a question that can be answered using the data given. One possible question might be: "What is the total thickness of gold film on the astronaut's helmet?"

**Skillkeeper** This skill was originally taught in Chapter 5.

**More Practice,** page 419, Set B

**Reteaching Supplement,** page 34

Name ______________ To follow text page 143

**More Multiplying Decimals**

Sometimes you must place zeros in the product in order to have the correct number of decimal places.

4.32 ← 2-place decimal
× 0.02 ← 2-place decimal
864 ← This product must be a 4-place decimal.
0.0864 ← Correct product
(Write an extra 0.)

Find the products.

1. 0.2 × 0.4 = 0.08 (2 decimal places in the product.) (Write a 0.)
2. 0.12 × 0.5 = 0.060 (3 decimal places in the product.) (Write the correct product.)
3. 0.006 × 0.09 = 0.00054 (Write 0s to have 5 decimal places in the product.)
4. 1.09 × 0.07 = 0.0763
5. 0.18 × 0.3 = 0.054
6. 0.026 × 0.009 = 0.000234
7. 3.2 × 0.08 = 0.256
8. 0.23 × 0.15: 115, 23; 0.0345
9. 0.471 × 0.016: 2826, 471; 0.007536
10. 0.018 × 0.73: 54, 126; 0.01314
11. 0.981 × 0.065: 4905, 5886; 0.063765
12. 3.35 × 0.02 = 0.0670
13. 6.8 × 0.007 = 0.0476
14. 7.039 × 0.005 = 0.035195
15. 0.555 × 0.003 = 0.001665
16. 0.062 × 0.087: 434, 496; 0.005394
17. 0.418 × 0.025: 2090, 836; 0.010450
18. 0.061 × 0.032: 122, 183; 0.001952
19. 0.75 × 0.041: 75, 300; 0.03075

**Enrichment Supplement,** page 34

Name ______________ To follow text page 143

**Flow Charts and Equations**

Study the equation, its flow chart, and the **inverse flow chart.** Then find the output number $n$. This is the solution for the equation.

1. Equation: $(n \div 0.02) + 4.235 = 8.205$
   Flow chart: n → ÷ 0.02 → + 4.235 → 8.205
   Inverse flow chart: 8.205 → − 4.235 → × 0.02 → n
   $n =$ 0.0794

Complete the inverse flow chart and find the number for $n$ in the equation.

2. Equation: $(n \div 0.043) - 0.04 = 0.07$
   Flow chart: n → ÷ 0.043 → − 0.04 → 0.07
   Inverse flow chart: 0.07 → + 0.04 → × 0.043 → n
   $n =$ 0.00473

Complete the flow charts and find the number for $n$.

3. Equation: $(n + 0.046) \div 0.002 = 26.5$
   Flow chart: n → + 0.046 → ÷ 0.002 → 26.5
   Inverse flow chart: 26.5 → × 0.002 → − 0.046 → n
   $n =$ 0.007

4. Equation: $(n \div 5) \div 0.0125 = 400$
   Flow chart: n → ÷ 5 → ÷ 0.0125 → 400
   Inverse flow chart: 400 → × 0.0125 → × 5 → n
   $n =$ 25

Solve this equation by making an inverse flow chart.

5. Equation: $(n + 0.07427) \div 0.073 = 4.06$
   Inverse flow chart: 4.06 → × 0.073 → − 0.07427 → n
   $n =$ 0.22211

6. Equation: $(n \div 0.01) \times 1{,}000 = 1{,}000{,}000$
   Inverse flow chart: 1,000,000 → ÷ 1,000 → × 0.01 → n
   $n =$ 10

**Practice Supplement,** page 54

Name ______________ To follow text page 143

**More Multiplying Decimals**

Multiply.

1. 0.36 × 0.0004 = 0.000144
2. 0.17 × 0.36: 102, 510; 0.0612
3. 0.85 × 0.46: 510, 3400; 0.3910
4. 0.012 × 0.38: 96, 360; 0.00456
5. 0.786 × 0.34: 3144, 23580; 0.26724
6. 0.386 × 0.15: 1930, 3860; 0.05790
7. 0.014 × 0.6 = 0.0084
8. 0.08 × 0.7 = 0.476
9. 3.8 × 0.08 = 0.304
10. 0.207 × 0.6 = 0.1242
11. 0.086 × 0.08 = 0.00688
12. 0.056 × 0.03 = 0.00168
13. 0.568 × 0.09 = 0.05112
14. 0.003 × 0.36: 18, 90; 0.00108
15. 0.009 × 2.7: 63, 180; 0.0243
16. 0.0034 × 0.27: 238, 680; 0.000918
17. 3.56 × 0.92: 712, 32040; 3.2752
18. 0.103 × 4.8: 824, 4120; 0.4944
19. 0.893 × 0.053: 2679, 44650; 0.047329
20. 0.069 × 0.056: 414, 3450; 0.003864
21. 0.065 × .048: 520, 2600; 0.003120
22. 53.7 × 0.068: 4296, 32220; 3.6516
23. 0.348 × 7.4: 1392, 24360; 2.5752
24. 0.0038 × 0.6 = 0.00228

# Decimals: Multiplication

**Quick Review** Students tell the amount of money represented by each set of coins.

6 dimes 5 pennies **$0.65** 1 quarter 2 dimes **$0.45** 2 quarters **$0.50**
8 pennies 4 nickels **$0.28** 1 quarter 1 penny **$0.26** 1 nickel 5 dimes **$0.55**

**Lesson Focus** To use mental math to multiply decimals by 10, 100, 1,000; to practice finding decimal products

**Suggested Materials** Calculators

## Ideas for Getting Started

Have students write the following problems on their papers and find the answers using their calculators.

| | |
|---|---|
| $4.365 \times 10 =$ | $0.0632 \times 10 =$ |
| $4.365 \times 100 =$ | $0.0632 \times 100 =$ |
| $4.365 \times 1{,}000 =$ | $0.0632 \times 1{,}000 =$ |

"What do you observe about each set of answers?" (The numbers in the answers are the same; the decimal point is in a different location.) "How did multiplying by 10 affect the decimal point?" (The decimal point moved one place to the right.) "Try other numbers on your calculator. Does multiplying by 10 always affect the decimal point in this way?" (Yes, multiplying by 10 always moves the decimal point one place to the right.) "How does multiplying by 100 affect the decimal point?" (moves the decimal point two places to the right) "Multiplying by 1,000?" (three places to the right) Have students multiply other decimals by 10, 100, and 1,000 on the calculator to see if these patterns continue.

## Using Page 144

**Motivational Problem** Have students read the problem at the top of the page. Focus on the questions asked and be sure students can express the questions in their own words. "What data do we need in order to answer each question?" (The cost of one watch, the number of watches sold) Point out that since each watch costs the same amount and we want to find the total amount for a given number of watches, we can multiply.

**Lesson Development** Direct students' attention to the pictures of the calculators on the page. If students have calculators available let them verify that $10 \times 29.95$ is 299.5. Then have them estimate this product to see if the calculated answer is reasonable. Do this for the displays for 100 and 1,000. Emphasize the value of estimating to check an answer.

**Exercises 1–20** These exercises are designed to be completed by students mentally. Be sure they understand that they are to use the shortcut rules given in the boxes to find these products. Errors can result from confusion about the right and left orientation as it relates to multiplication or division in using the shortcut. Help students see that in multiplying, the number gets bigger; thus the decimal point would be moved to the right. In dividing, the number gets smaller; thus the decimal point would be moved to the left.

## Multiplying Decimals by 10, 100, and 1,000: Mental Math

The owner of a jewelry store sells a very popular digital watch for $29.95. What will the store's total amount of sales be for 10 watches? 100 watches? 1,000 watches? Are these calculator answers reasonable?

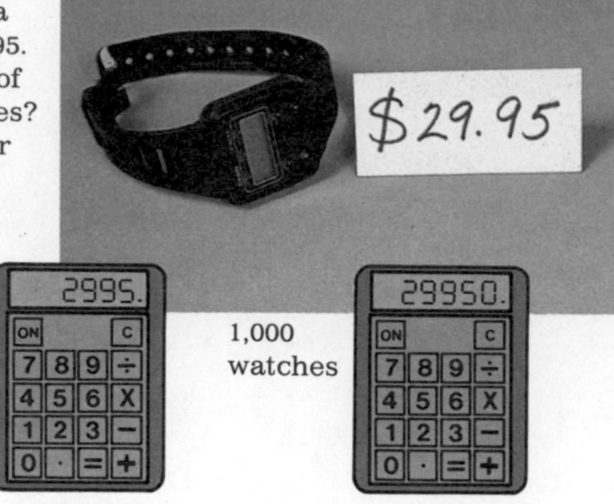


10 watches — calculator display: 299.5

$10 \times 29.95$ → $10 \times 30 = 300$

The calculator answer seems reasonable.

To multiply by 10, move the decimal point 1 place right. 29.9.5

100 watches — calculator display: 2995.

$100 \times 29.95$ → $100 \times 30 = 3{,}000$

The calculator answer seems reasonable.

To multiply by 100, move the decimal point 2 places right. 29.95.

1,000 watches — calculator display: 29950.

$1{,}000 \times 29.95$ → $1{,}000 \times 30 = 30{,}000$

The calculator answer seems reasonable.

To multiply by 1,000 move the decimal point 3 places right. 29.950.

Multiply. Write only the answers.

1. $3.54 \times 10$ 35.4
2. $4.8 \times 10$ 48
3. $0.65 \times 10$ 6.5
4. $10 \times 7.372$ 73.72
5. $10 \times 0.8$ 8
6. $2.74 \times 100$ 274
7. $0.68 \times 100$ 68
8. $1.765 \times 100$ 176.5
9. $54.8 \times 100$ 5,480
10. $100 \times 0.9$ 90
11. $4.376 \times 1{,}000$ 4,376
12. $7.28 \times 1{,}000$ 7,280
13. $0.762 \times 1{,}000$ 762
14. $1{,}000 \times 0.81$ 810
15. $1{,}000 \times 6.7$ 6,700
16. $2.7 \times 100$ 270
17. $0.64 \times 1{,}000$ 640
18. $9.2 \times 10$ 92
19. $28.4 \times 1{,}000$ 28,400
20. $676 \times 100$ 67,600



More Practice, page 419, Set C

## Follow Up

### Reteaching

Review with students multiplication of whole numbers by 10, 100, and 1,000. Then show several decimals multiplied by 10, 100, and 1,000. For example:

$$10 \times 3.5 = 35.0$$
$$100 \times 3.5 = 350.0$$
$$1{,}000 \times 3.5 = 3{,}500.0$$

Encourage students to state a generalization about the decimal point. (Multiplying by 10 moves the decimal point 1 place to the right; multiplying by 100 moves the decimal point 2 places to the right; multiplying by 1,000 moves the decimal point 3 places to the right.)

### Enrichment

Have students fill in the products in the multiplication chart below.

| X | 0.1 | 0.01 | 0.001 |
|---|---|---|---|
| 3.5 | **0.35** | **0.035** | **0.0035** |
| 6.27 | **0.627** | **0.0627** | **0.00627** |
| 4.087 | **0.4087** | **0.04087** | **0.004087** |
| 0.76 | **0.076** | **0.0076** | **0.00076** |

| Assignment Guide | | | |
|---|---|---|---|
| | Minimum | Average | Extended |
| page 144 | 1–20 | 1–20 | 1–20 |
| page 145 | 1–37 | 1–38 | 11–38, TM |

## Multiplying Decimals: Practice

Multiply.

1. 9.7 × 6.8 = 65.96
2. 57 × 3.6 = 205.2
3. 4.076 × 2.9 = 11.8204
4. 7.25 × 3.46 = 25.0850
5. 8.76 × 100 = 876
6. 0.075 × 4.9 = 0.3675
7. 0.096 × 0.003 = 0.000288
8. 4.56 × 7.3 = 33.288
9. 7.042 × 10 = 70.42
10. 6.432 × 0.003 = 0.019296
11. 8.6 × 0.0004 = 0.00344
12. 9.47 × 0.68 = 6.4396
13. 9.674 × 1,000 = 9,674
14. 3.75 × 0.08 = 0.3000
15. 0.792 × 1.46 = 1.15632
16. 3.4 × 100 = 340
17. 7.214 × 29.6 = 213.5344
18. $37.58 × 0.07 = $2.6306
19. $4.57 × 0.20 = $0.9140
20. $35.64 × 0.25 = $8.9100

21. 4.75 × 3.2 15.20
22. 8.67 × 100 867
23. 3.047 × 9.2 28.0324
24. 1,000 × 0.46 460
25. 29.07 × 8.6 250.002
26. 10 × 9.472 94.72
27. 543 × 0.86 466.98
28. 100 × 0.7 70
29. 9.72 × 1,000 9,720
30. Estimate, then find the product when 8.743 is multiplied by 6.075. 54; 53.113725
31. Estimate, then find the product of the factors 286.38 and 75.2. 24,000; 21,535.776

Multiply. Write only the answers.

32. 2.65 × 10 26.5
33. 10 × 0.73 7.3
34. 100 × 2.8 280
35. 0.62 × 100 62
36. 0.571 × 1,000 571
37. 1,000 × 5.4 5,400

38. Solve these equations. Then write the equation that would come next in each list.

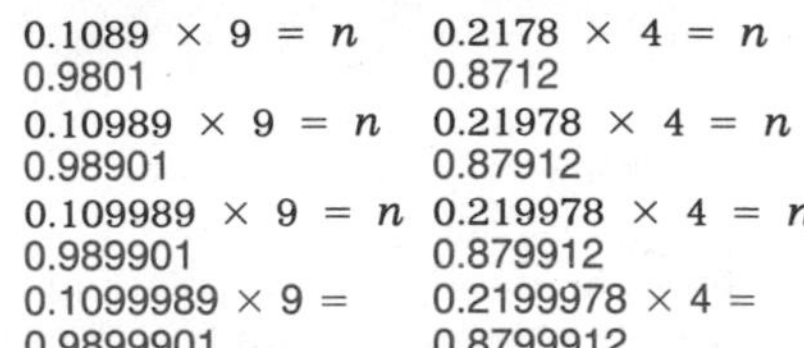

0.1089 × 9 = $n$ 0.9801 | 0.2178 × 4 = $n$ 0.8712
0.10989 × 9 = $n$ 0.98901 | 0.21978 × 4 = $n$ 0.87912
0.109989 × 9 = $n$ 0.989901 | 0.219978 × 4 = $n$ 0.879912
0.1099989 × 9 = 0.9899901 | 0.2199978 × 4 = 0.8799912

**Think**

**Greatest-Product Game**

Put slips of paper containing the digits 0 through 9 in a hat.

Draw boxes like this on your paper. As a digit is drawn from the hat, write it in a square of your choice. Then find the product. Greatest product wins!

**Math**



## Using Page 145

**Lesson Development** Review the procedure for finding decimal products and placing the decimal point in the answer. Work an example to review how to annex zeros in the product.

**Exercise 1–29** Discourage students from using the multiplication algorithm to find these products. In exercises 7, 10, and 11 be sure that students have correctly annexed the necessary number of zeros.

**Exercises 30–31** In exercise 30 the numbers need to be rounded to the nearest whole number to use a basic fact in the estimation. In exercise 31 the first factor is rounded to the nearest hundred, the second to the nearest ten.

**Exercise 38** Students should observe a pattern in the first three problems. In the first answer there is no 9 following the "98." In the second answer there is one 9. In the third answer there are two 9s following the "98." Recognizing this pattern, students should write 0.9899901 (three 9s following the "98") for the next equation in the list.

**Think Math** In this activity students devise strategies for placing the digits so that the product will be the largest possible. This employs the ideas of whole number and decimal place value. If necessary, give these hints: If you draw a 9, where would be the best place to write it? (in the tens place of the top factor) If you draw a 0, where would be the best place for it? (the ones place of the second factor)

**More Practice,** page 419, Set C

## Ideas That Work

### Special Education

To give students practice placing the decimal point in the product, let them work in pairs to play "Challenge."

Prepare several game mats with multiplication problems completed except for the decimal point in the product.

Players in turn point to a problem and challenge their partner to tell where the decimal point should be placed in the product. If a player gives a correct response, the player can cover the problem with a game chip. If a wrong answer is given, the opponent can claim the square by giving the correct answer. If necessary, use a calculator or answer key to check answers. When all squares are covered, the player with most chips on the board wins the round. Each round is played with a different game mat.

**Practice Supplement,** page 55

Name ______ To follow text page 144

**Multiplying Decimals by 10, 100, and 1,000: Mental Math**

Multiply.

1. 10 × 0.54 = 5.4
2. 3.2 × 10 = 32
3. 0.764 × 10 = 7.64
4. 36.48 × 10 = 364.8
5. 10 × 0.076 = 0.76
6. 10 × 75.3 = 753
7. 43.7 × 100 = 4,370
8. 0.762 × 100 = 76.2
9. 5.93 × 100 = 593
10. 0.065 × 100 = 6.5
11. 10 × 0.007 = 0.07
12. 100 × 3.965 = 396.5
13. 10 × 0.9 = 9
14. 100 × 436.5 = 43,650
15. 0.8643 × 1,000 = 864.3
16. 100 × 0.069 = 6.9
17. 3.468 × 100 = 346.8
18. 10 × 1.059 = 10.59
19. 0.7 × 1,000 = 700
20. 97.64 × 10 = 976.4
21. 100 × 432.7 = 43,270
22. 85.42 × 100 = 8,542
23. 0.0135 × 1,000 = 13.5
24. 7.643 × 10 = 76.43
25. 0.3210 × 100 = 32.10
26. 100 × 5.43 = 543
27. 26.7 × 100 = 2,670
28. 10 × 0.0043 = 0.043
29. 7.326 × 100 = 732.6
30. 0.0436 × 100 = 4.36
31. 9.530 × 100 = 953.0
32. 1.765 × 10 = 17.65
33. 0.0407 × 100 = 4.07
34. 0.6803 × 100 = 68.03
35. 57.6 × 100 = 5,760
36. 1.5 × 10 = 15
37. 0.5 × 100 = 50
38. 7.3821 × 1,000 = 7,382.1
39. 0.0432 × 1,000 = 43.2
40. 1,000 × 0.604 = 604

# Applications

**Quick Review** Students round 2-digit numbers to the nearest ten and 3-digit numbers to the nearest hundred.

223 49 52 650 877 36 29 14 11
215 444 87 64 92 109 81 45

**Lesson Focus** To use estimation to check the reasonableness of an answer; to solve word problems involving all operations

## Ideas for Getting Started

Ask students to estimate answers to the following questions: "You can get 3 records for $5.98. Is this a better price than $2.45 for 1 record? About how much for 3 records?" ($6) "About how much would this be per record?" ($2) "Which price is better?" (3 records for $5.98) Emphasize the usefulness of estimation in making simple decisions and in checking to see if an answer seems reasonable. Then use the logo at the top of the page to review briefly the 5-Point Checklist. Remind students to use the checklist as a guide to help solve problems and not as a set of rules.

## Using Page 146

**Lesson Development** Be sure students understand that in solving the problem they are to first choose the best estimate. Then they are to find the exact answer. If necessary, complete the first problem with students. Point out that these problems are about the costs of services that are part of our daily lives.

**Exercises 5–6** Note that these exercises are multiple-step problems.

**Data Hunt** This activity provides students with an opportunity to collect data about the cost of running ads in a local newspaper. If necessary, have students form committees to work together to call the newspaper to collect this information.

**Try This** A possible strategy, Make an Organized List, was taught on page 132.

**Discussion** "What are we trying to find out about the telephone number area codes?" (How many codes are possible with the given restrictions?) "How many digits do the codes have?" (3) "What are the restrictions on the three digits?" (The first digit is 4; the other two digits must be less than 4.) "If the first digit of a code is 4, what are the possibilities for the second digit?" (3, 2, 1, or 0) "How can you decide how many numbers there would be?" (Make an organized list.)

**Solution** The following organized list shows that there are 16 possible area code numbers:

| | | | |
|---|---|---|---|
| 433 | 423 | 413 | 403 |
| 432 | 422 | 412 | 402 |
| 431 | 421 | 411 | 401 |
| 430 | 420 | 410 | 400 |

**Extension** How many 3-digit number area codes can there be if the first digit is 5 and the other 2 digits are less than 5 and no digit may be repeated in any one area code? (20)

## Problem Solving: Using Estimation

What is the cost? First choose the best estimate. Then find the exact answer.

**Auto Repair**

1. A car repair ratesbook lists 2.5 hours as the time needed for a tuneup of an 8-cylinder auto. Suppose the hourly labor charge is $24.75. What is the total cost?
   **A** under $75 **B** about $90
   **C** over $90 A; $61.875

**Electricity**

2. A color TV set might use 540 kWh (kilowatt-hours) of electricity per year. If electricity costs 3.05¢ for 1 kWh, what is the yearly cost?
   **A** under $15 **B** over $18
   **C** between $15 and $18 C; $16.47

**Heat**

3. It might take 119 million B.T.U.s (British thermal units) of natural gas to heat a house for 1 year. A million B.T.U.s might cost $3.94. What would be the total yearly cost?
   **A** about $40 **B** about $400
   **C** about $4,000 B; $468.86

**Water**

4. Water might cost $0.48 for 1,000 L. A family might use 50,000 L in one month. What would that amount of water cost?
   **A** about $2.50 **B** about $25
   **C** about $250 B; $24

**Want Ad**

5. A 4-line ad that runs for 6 days in a newspaper might cost $1.93 per line per day. What would the total cost be?
   **A** less than $50 **B** more than $60
   **C** between $50 and $60 A; $46.32

**Telephone**

6. A weekday telephone call from San Francisco to New York City might cost $2.95 for the first 3 minutes and $0.41 for each additional minute. How much would a 24-minute call cost?
   **A** about $17 **B** about $15
   **C** about $11 C; 11.56

7. **DATA HUNT** How much more would it cost to run an ad like this in your local paper for 7 days than for 3 days? Answers will vary.

> Used mini bike. Good condition. 5 hp. Good tires. Only $125

8. **Try This** How many 3-digit telephone number area codes can there be if the first digit is 4 and the other two digits are less than 4? Hint: Make an organized list. 16; see teaching notes.

146

## Follow Up

### Reteaching

Provide problems based on data from a sale advertisement or have students generate their own problems. Emphasize how estimation can be used to make a reasonable first guess about an answer. Be alert for students who have difficulties with the following prerequisite skills for this activity.

- Knowledge of decimal place value
- Estimation and rounding skills
- Understanding of the meaning of the operations

### Enrichment

Tell students to pretend that they have $250.00 to spend on clothing. Have them list the items that they would like to buy. Have them estimate to the nearest half-dollar or dollar the total cost of the items to see if they have enough money to purchase the desired items. Then have them find the exact cost by using a calculator.

| Assignment Guide | | | |
|---|---|---|---|
| | Minimum | Average | Extended |
| page 146 | 1–6 | 1–7 | 1–8 |
| page 147 | 1–6 | 1–7 | 1–8 |

## Problem Solving: Practice

**Kremer Prize—50,000 British Pounds**

This prize was offered for the first completely man-powered flight of a heavier-than-air machine over a set course around two towers a half-mile apart. The plane had to cross both the start line and finish line at least 10 feet above the ground.

The Kremer Prize was won in 1977 by Dr. Paul MacCready of Pasadena, California, when Bryan Allen pedaled MacCready's plane, the *Gossamer Condor,* around the course and maintained the required height.

Solve.

1. When MacCready won the prize, a British pound was worth $1.90 American dollars. How much was the Kremer Prize worth in dollars at that time? $95,000
2. The prize was first offered in 1959. It was won in 1977. How many years after it was first offered was the prize won? 18 years
3. If the Kremer prize money was given out in equal monthly payments for 1 year, how large would each payment be (to the nearest pound)? 4,167 pounds
4. The wingspan of the *Gossamer Condor* is 96 feet. The greatest wingspan on record was 224 feet more than this. How many feet was the greatest wingspan? 320 feet
5. The *Gossamer Condor* made 430 flights in 10 months. What was the average number of flights it made each week? (Use 30 days per month and 7 days per week, and round to the nearest whole number.) 10
6. The plane covered the course in 6 minutes 23 seconds. Its speed was 0.003 miles per second. How long was the course (to the nearest hundredth of a mile)? 1.15 miles
7. In 1979 Bryan Allen pedaled another MacCready plane across the English Channel in 2 hours 40 minutes. How many seconds did the flight last? 9,600 seconds
8. **Try This** How many possible orders are there for four test planes to take off one at a time from an airfield? Hint: Make an organized list. 24; see teaching notes.



## Using Page 147

**Lesson Development** Have students read the information about the Kremer Prize at the top of the page. Briefly review the 5-Point Checklist before assigning the problems.

**Try This** A possible strategy, Make an Organized List, was taught on page 132.

**Discussion** "What question are we asked about the four test planes?" (How many possible orders are there for take-off?) "What data are we given in the problem?" (There are 4 planes; they take off one at a time.) "If Plane 1 takes off first, what planes could be second to take off?" (Plane 2, Plane 3, or Plane 4) "If Plane 1 takes off first and Plane 2 takes off second, what are the possibilities?" (2 and 4 or 4 and 2) "If Plane 1 takes off first and Plane 4 takes off second, what are the possibilities?" (2 and 3 or 3 and 2) "Can you use this information to decide how many possible orders there are for take off?" (There are six possibilities when Plane 1 takes off first, so there would be six possibilities for each of the other planes.)

**Solution** There are 24 possible orders in which the planes can take off.

| | | | |
|---|---|---|---|
| 1,2,3,4 | 2,1,3,4 | 3,1,2,4 | 4,1,2,3 |
| 1,2,4,3 | 2,1,4,3 | 3,1,4,2 | 4,1,3,2 |
| 1,3,2,4 | 2,3,1,4 | 3,2,1,4 | 4,2,1,3 |
| 1,3,4,2 | 2,3,4,1 | 3,2,4,1 | 4,2,3,1 |
| 1,4,2,3 | 2,4,1,3 | 3,4,2,1 | 4,3,1,2 |
| 1,4,3,2 | 2,4,3,1 | 3,4,1,2 | 4,3,2,1 |

**Extension** How many possible orders are there for three test planes to land one at a time? (6)

**Reteaching Supplement,** page 35

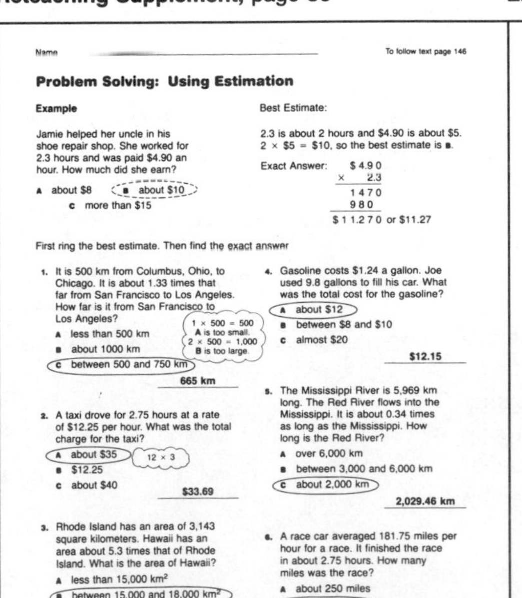

Name ____________ To follow text page 146

**Problem Solving: Using Estimation**

**Example**

Jamie helped her uncle in his shoe repair shop. She worked for 2.3 hours and was paid $4.90 an hour. How much did she earn?

A about $8 B about $10 C more than $15

Best Estimate:

2.3 is about 2 hours and $4.90 is about $5. 2 × $5 = $10, so the best estimate is B.

Exact Answer: $4.90 × 2.3 = 1470 + 980 = $11.270 or $11.27

First ring the best estimate. Then find the exact answer

1. It is 500 km from Columbus, Ohio, to Chicago. It is about 1.33 times that far from San Francisco to Los Angeles. How far is it from San Francisco to Los Angeles?
   A less than 500 km
   B about 1000 km
   C between 500 and 750 km
   (1 × 500 = 500 A is too small. 2 × 500 = 1,000 B is too large.)
   665 km
2. A taxi drove for 2.75 hours at a rate of $12.25 per hour. What was the total charge for the taxi?
   A about $35 (12 × 3)
   B $12.25
   C about $40
   $33.69
3. Rhode Island has an area of 3,143 square kilometers. Hawaii has an area about 5.3 times that of Rhode Island. What is the area of Hawaii?
   A less than 15,000 km²
   B between 15,000 and 18,000 km²
   C about 20,000 km²
   16,657.9 km²
4. Gasoline costs $1.24 a gallon. Joe used 9.8 gallons to fill his car. What was the total cost for the gasoline?
   A about $12
   B between $8 and $10
   C almost $20
   $12.15
5. The Mississippi River is 5,969 km long. The Red River flows into the Mississippi. It is about 0.34 times as long as the Mississippi. How long is the Red River?
   A over 6,000 km
   B between 3,000 and 6,000 km
   C about 2,000 km
   2,029.46 km
6. A race car averaged 181.75 miles per hour for a race. It finished the race in about 2.75 hours. How many miles was the race?
   A about 250 miles
   B about 500 miles
   C almost 600 miles
   499.8 miles

**Enrichment Supplement,** page 35

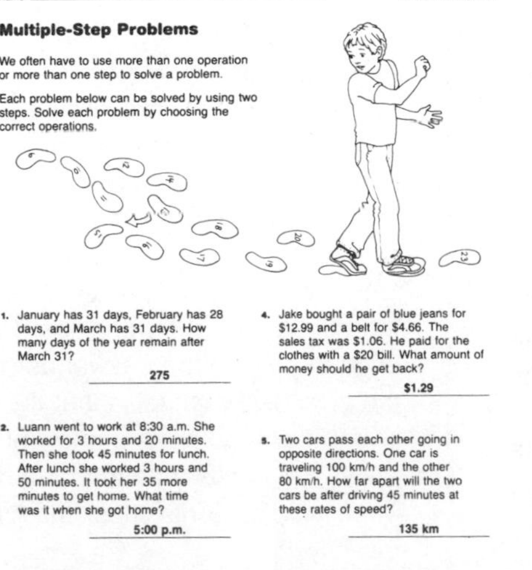

Name ____________ To follow text page 146

**Multiple-Step Problems**

We often have to use more than one operation or more than one step to solve a problem.

Each problem below can be solved by using two steps. Solve each problem by choosing the correct operations.

1. January has 31 days, February has 28 days, and March has 31 days. How many days of the year remain after March 31? 275
2. Luann went to work at 8:30 a.m. She worked for 3 hours and 20 minutes. Then she took 45 minutes for lunch. After lunch she worked 3 hours and 50 minutes. It took her 35 more minutes to get home. What time was it when she got home? 5:00 p.m.
3. Lenny says, "If I could triple the amount of money I now have and then earn $12.40 more, I would have exactly $100.00." How much money does Lenny have now? $29.20
4. Jake bought a pair of blue jeans for $12.99 and a belt for $4.66. The sales tax was $1.06. He paid for the clothes with a $20 bill. What amount of money should he get back? $1.29
5. Two cars pass each other going in opposite directions. One car is traveling 100 km/h and the other 80 km/h. How far apart will the two cars be after driving 45 minutes at these rates of speed? 135 km
6. Maxine hiked to the top of a small mountain in 4 hours and 20 minutes. She hiked down the mountain in just half that time. How long did it take Maxine to hike up and down the mountain? 6 h 30 min

**Practice Supplement,** page 56

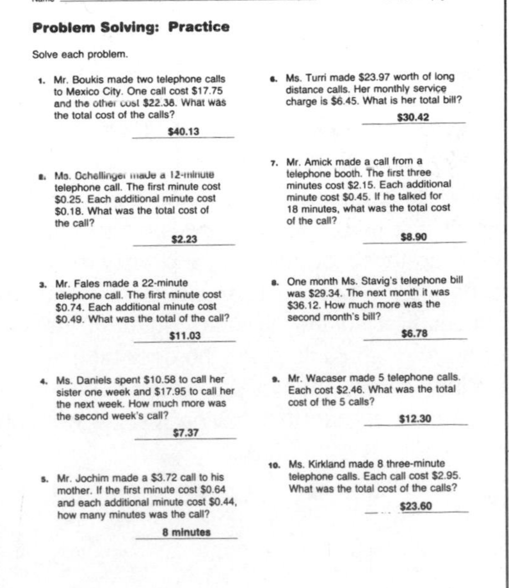

Name ____________ To follow text page 147

**Problem Solving: Practice**

Solve each problem.

1. Mr. Boukis made two telephone calls to Mexico City. One call cost $17.75 and the other cost $22.38. What was the total cost of the calls? $40.13
2. Ms. Schellinger made a 12-minute telephone call. The first minute cost $0.25. Each additional minute cost $0.18. What was the total cost of the call? $2.23
3. Mr. Fales made a 22-minute telephone call. The first minute cost $0.74. Each additional minute cost $0.49. What was the total of the call? $11.03
4. Ms. Daniels spent $10.58 to call her sister one week and $17.95 to call her the next week. How much more was the second week's call? $7.37
5. Mr. Jochim made a $3.72 call to his mother. If the first minute cost $0.64 and each additional minute cost $0.44, how many minutes was the call? 8 minutes
6. Ms. Turri made $23.97 worth of long distance calls. Her monthly service charge is $6.45. What is her total bill? $30.42
7. Mr. Amick made a call from a telephone booth. The first three minutes cost $2.15. Each additional minute cost $0.45. If he talked for 18 minutes, what was the total cost of the call? $8.90
8. One month Ms. Stavig's telephone bill was $29.34. The next month it was $36.12. How much more was the second month's bill? $6.78
9. Mr. Wacaser made 5 telephone calls. Each cost $2.46. What was the total cost of the 5 calls? $12.30
10. Ms. Kirkland made 8 three-minute telephone calls. Each call cost $2.95. What was the total cost of the calls? $23.60

# Decimals: Division

**Quick Review** Students respond orally with these division facts.

10 ÷ 5  8 ÷ 4  16 ÷ 8  72 ÷ 9  56 ÷ 7  45 ÷ 5
42 ÷ 7  27 ÷ 3  15 ÷ 5  24 ÷ 6  18 ÷ 2
54 ÷ 6  64 ÷ 8  81 ÷ 9  30 ÷ 5  63 ÷ 9  48 ÷ 8

**Lesson Focus** To find the quotient of a decimal divided by a whole number

**Suggested Materials** Play money

## Ideas for Getting Started

Have available $10 bills, $1 bills, dimes, and pennies in play money. "How many dimes are in a dollar?" (10) "What part of a dollar is a dime?" (one tenth) "How many pennies are in a dollar?" (100) "What part of a dollar is a penny?" (one hundredth) Emphasize that we can use money as a model for a decimal. "What money would we use to show the decimal 38.32?" (three $10 bills, eight $1 bills, 3 dimes, and 2 pennies) "Suppose you wanted to divide this money among 4 persons. How could you do it?" Help students demonstrate the following procedure: First divide the whole $38. Since we cannot divide the tens, we would trade them for ones and divide among the 4 people. Each person would get 9 ones and there would be 2 ones left over. Since we cannot divide the 2 ones we would exchange them for dimes and divide. Each person would get 5 dimes with 3 left over. Then we trade the 3 dimes for pennies and divide. Each person would get 8 pennies. Thus each person would receive 9 ones, 5 dimes, and 8 pennies or $9.58.

## Using Page 148

**Motivational Problem** Have students read the problem at the top of the page. "What question is asked about the Olympic team relay?" (What was the average time for 100 meters?) Point out that the team runs a 400-m relay in 38.32 seconds. Since we want to find the average time for 100 m, we use division.

**Lesson Development** Work through the problem on the chalkboard. Relate each division stage to the money model used to divide $38.32 among 4 students. Be sure students understand that since 2 ones cannot be divided, they are traded for 20 tenths making a total of 23 tenths. In dividing hundredths, point out that 3 tenths cannot be divided, and because each tenth is 10 one hundredths, the 3 tenths can be traded for 30 hundredths for a total of 32 hundredths. Ask a volunteer to check the division by multiplying. Then have students read the answer in a complete sentence.

**Other Examples** Refer to the money model to explain the first example if necessary. Emphasize the importance of checking the answer by multiplying. In the second example there is no whole number part so the dividing begins in the tenths place. After students place the decimal point in the quotient directly above the decimal point in the dividend, they can then divide just as with whole numbers.

## Dividing a Decimal by a Whole Number

An Olympic team ran the 400-m relay in 38.32 s (seconds). Each of the team members ran 100 m. What was the average time for 100 m?

Since we want to find the average, we divide.

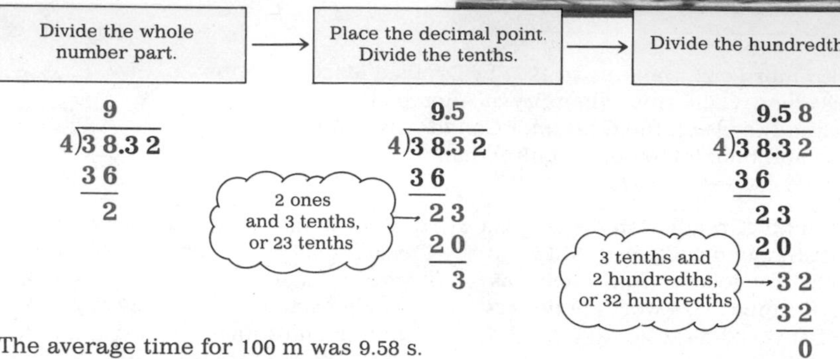

Divide the whole number part.
Place the decimal point. Divide the tenths.
Divide the hundredths.
9
4)38.32
36
2
9.5
4)38.32
36
23
20
3
2 ones and 3 tenths, or 23 tenths
9.58
4)38.32
36
23
20
32
32
0
3 tenths and 2 hundredths, or 32 hundredths


The average time for 100 m was 9.58 s.

**Other Examples**

```
    7.12
8)56.96
  56
   09
    8
    16
    16
     0
```

Check
7.12
× 8
56.96

```
   0.292
3)0.876
   6
   27
   27
    06
     6
     0
```

```
      0.504
26)13.104
   130
     10
      0
     104
     104
       0
```

**Warm Up** Divide. Check your answers.

1. 4)25.92 (6.48)
2. 7)2.555 (0.365)
3. 5)1.535 (0.307)
4. 8)49.04 (6.13)
5. 32)$45.76 ($1.43)
6. 6)20.58 (3.43)
7. 9)5.166 (0.574)
8. 13)$59.93 ($4.61)
9. 62)22.196 (0.358)
10. 54)144.72 (2.68)



## Follow Up

### Reteaching

Review whole number division and point out that the division algorithm is basically the same for decimal division. The only difference is in the placement of the decimal point. Use a money model as an illustration: If 3 children share $6.96 equally, how much will each child receive?

Show that the dollars are divided, then the dimes, and then pennies. Place the decimal point in the answer as you finish the division. Emphasize that the decimal point is placed in the quotient directly above the decimal point in the dividend. Then have students check the answer by multiplying.

### Enrichment

Provide students with the following problems. Remind them to continue to divide until the remainder is zero.

6)75.0 (12.5)  8)76.0 (9.5)  5)41.0 (8.2)
30)39.0 (1.3)  12)27.00 (2.25)  25)64.00 (2.56)
128)1.0000000 (0.0078125)  640)1.0000000 (0.0015625)

| Assignment Guide | | | |
|---|---|---|---|
| | Minimum | Average | Extended |
| page 149 | 1–34 | 1–35 | 11–35, TM |

Divide. Check your answers.

1. 2)7.24 3.62
2. 4)31.76 7.94
3. 3)17.52 5.84
4. 5)30.15 6.03
5. 7)63.84 9.12
6. 6)2.898 0.483
7. 8)8.344 1.043
8. 9)0.5733 0.0637
9. 4)93.04 23.26
10. 3)168.6 56.2
11. 2)19.6 9.8
12. 7)17.738 2.534
13. 5)1.835 0.367
14. 8)288.24 36.03
15. 6)340.2 56.7
16. 19)28.5 1.5
17. 24)59.28 2.47
18. 43)165.55 3.85
19. 26)244.4 9.4
20. 35)819.7 23.42
21. 37)9.361 0.253
22. 85)158.95 1.87
23. 73)$33.58 $0.46
24. 3)$50.25 $16.75
25. 24)$245.28 $10.22
26. 61.38 ÷ 9 6.82
27. 9.506 ÷ 7 1.358
28. 68.8 ÷ 8 8.6
29. 4.737 ÷ 3 1.579
30. 4.842 ÷ 6 0.807
31. 193.15 ÷ 5 38.63
32. Estimate, then find the quotient when 8.763 is divided by 3. 3; 2.921
33. Estimate, then find 362.16 divided by 9. 40; 40.24
34. The time for one woman in the Olympic 800-m run was 114.96 s. What was the average time for each 100 m of this race? 14.37 s

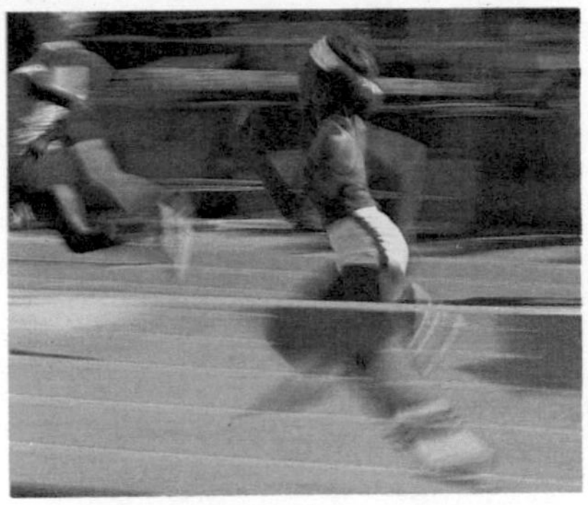

35. Tell what data is not needed in this problem. Then solve.
The U.S. women's speed skating record time for 500 m is 42.76 s. For 1,500 m it is 140.85 s. What is the average time for 100 m of the 500-m race?
Time for 1,500-m race; 8.552 s

**Think Math**

**Logical Reasoning**

How many moves do you need to move the four coins (dime, penny, nickel, quarter) to square C?

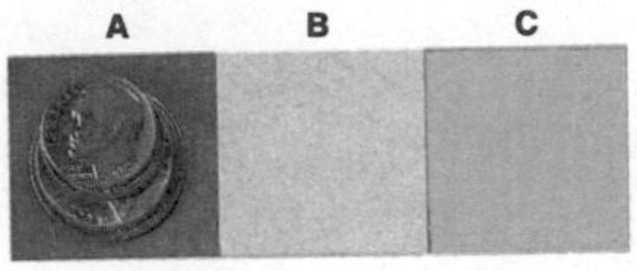


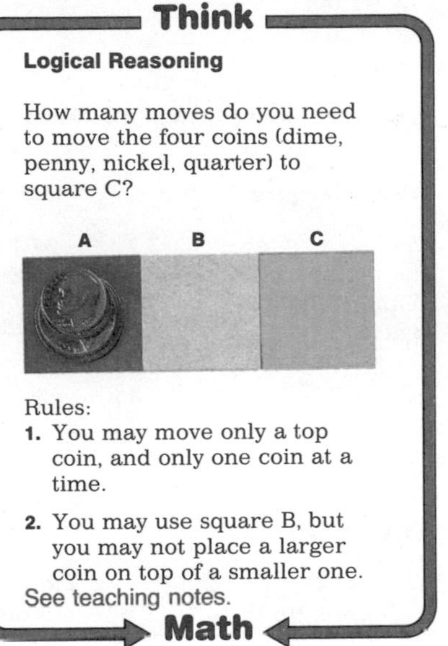

Rules:
1. You may move only a top coin, and only one coin at a time.
2. You may use square B, but you may not place a larger coin on top of a smaller one.

See teaching notes.

More Practice, page 420, Set A



## Using Page 149

**Exercises 1–31** Note in exercises 8, 13, 21, 23, and 30 that it is necessary to write a zero in the ones place in the quotient.

**Exercises 32–33** In exercise 32 the first number is rounded to the nearest whole number so that the estimation can be made. In exercise 33 the first number is rounded to the nearest ten.

**Exercise 35** In this exercise some unneeded data is given. Encourage students to read the problem carefully to choose the necessary data.

**Think Math** Be sure students understand the rules for moving the coins and encourage them to experiment. Note that if a student begins by placing the dime in square B and the penny in square C, the dime, penny, and nickel can be placed in square B in 7 moves and at the 8th move the quarter will be on square C.

Starting 2 Moves

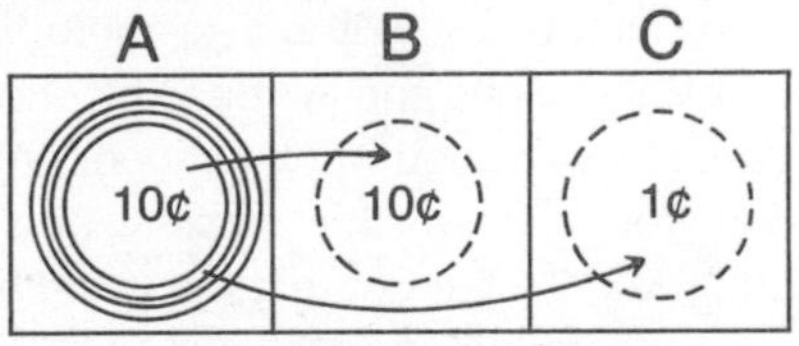


First 2 moves

The first two moves after this are shown below.

First 2 moves after quarter is in square C

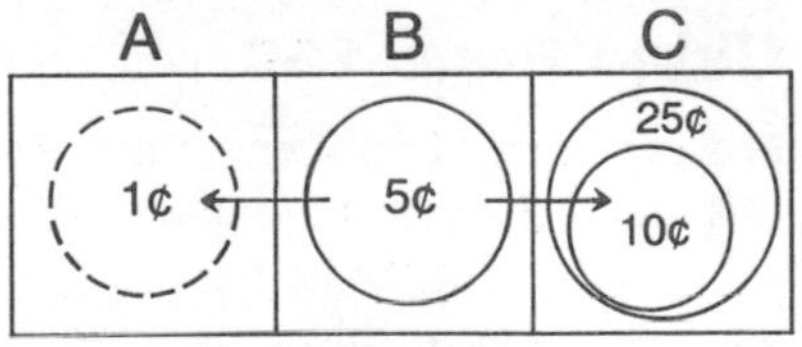


In 5 more moves—a total of 15 moves—the coins can be placed in order on top of the quarter. At first students may take considerably more than 15 moves. Encourage them to keep trying to solve the puzzle in 15 moves.

**More Practice,** page 420, Set A

**Reteaching Supplement,** page 36

Name ______ To follow text page 149

**Dividing a Decimal by a Whole Number**

Divide as with whole numbers. → Place the decimal point directly above the decimal point in the dividend. → Write the quotient.

42)26.46 63; 252, 126, 126, 0 — 42)26.46 .63 — 42)26.46 0.63; Check: 42 × 0.63 = 126 + 252 = 26.46

Divide and check your answer.

1. 5)3.5 0.7
2. 8)6.48 0.81 Finish dividing.
3. 4)1.08 0.27 Finish.
4. 18)94.14 5.23
5. 3)70.8 23.6
6. 6)1.944 0.324
7. 5)20.35 4.07
8. 186.11 ÷ 37 5.03
9. 783.75 ÷ 95 8.25
10. 4,819.8 ÷ 87 55.4

**Enrichment Supplement,** page 36

Name ______ To follow text page 149

**Missing Digits**

Write the missing digits in the boxes.

1. 8)210.2 27.4
2. 26)85.28 3.28
3. 45)3,280.5 72.9
4. 72)55.008 0.764
5. 37)2,412.4 65.2
6. 48)9,374.4 195.3

**Practice Supplement,** page 57

Name ______ To follow text page 149

**Dividing a Decimal by a Whole Number**

Divide.

1. 7)164.5 23.5
2. 5)39.15 7.83
3. 4)2.632 0.658
4. 8)34.88 4.36
5. 3)1.953 0.651
6. 8)19.68 2.46
7. 7)21.28 3.04
8. 5)2.365 0.473
9. 6)6.72 1.12
10. 4)0.1288 0.0322
11. 8)35.92 4.49
12. 2)0.994 0.497
13. 6)322.2 53.7
14. 9)6.1299 0.6811
15. 3)277.56 92.52
16. 7)60.48 8.64

# Decimals: Division

**Quick Review** Students write answers only to these division problems.
2 ÷ 10 30 ÷ 10 140 ÷ 10 33 ÷ 11 140 ÷ 1 80 ÷ 10
450 ÷ 10 3,000 ÷ 1,000 120 ÷ 10 600 ÷ 200 2,400 ÷ 60
4,900 ÷ 700 42 ÷ 2 600 ÷ 100 800 ÷ 100 1,000 ÷ 1,000 600 ÷ 60

**Lesson Focus** To divide and round decimal quotients to the nearest tenth, hundredth, or thousandth

## Ideas for Getting Started

To review place value for decimals, write the following chart on the chalkboard.

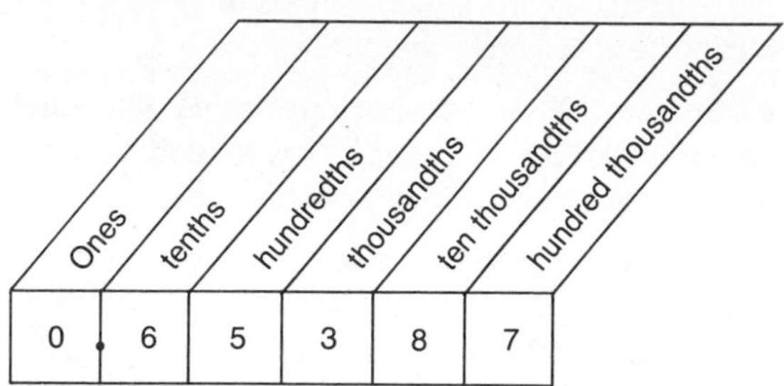


Then review the procedure for rounding decimals: Find the place to which you want to round. Look at the next digit; if it is less than 5, drop it and the remaining digits. If it is 5 or more, drop it and the remaining digits and increase by one the digit in the place to which you want to round. "What is the number rounded to the nearest ten thousandth?" (0.6539) "To the nearest thousandth?" (0.654) "To the nearest hundredth?" (0.65) "To the nearest tenth?" (0.7)

## Using Page 150

**Motivational Problem** Have students read the problem at the top of the page. "What question are we asked about Tina's basketball game?" ("What was her shooting average?") "What data do we need to answer this question?" (total number of shots, 13; the number of goals scored, 7) Point out that because division is a form of comparison, we can divide to compare 7 to 13.

**Lesson Development** As you work through the problem, emphasize the need to write additional zeros following the decimal point to complete the dividing. Remind students that we want to find the average to the nearest thousandth. Point out that to do this we must divide in one more place beyond the thousandths so that we can round to the nearest thousandth. Complete the dividing to the nearest hundred thousandth. Then use the ideas for rounding decimals that were reviewed in the Getting Started activity.

Point out that a shooting average of 0.538 means that a person has made slightly over half of their shots. Have students reread the original problem to see if this answer seems reasonable.

**Other Examples** Note that decimals that involve money as in the first example are usually rounded to the nearest cent or hundredth. Emphasize again the need to write extra zeros so that the dividing can be completed. In the second example, be sure students understand that since the decimal is to be rounded to the nearest tenth, they must divide through hundredths.

## Rounding Decimal Quotients

In a 4-H Club basketball game Tina scored goals on 7 of the 13 shots she took. What was her shooting average?

To find a basketball shooting average, we divide the number of baskets made by the number of shots taken and give the answer to the nearest thousandth.

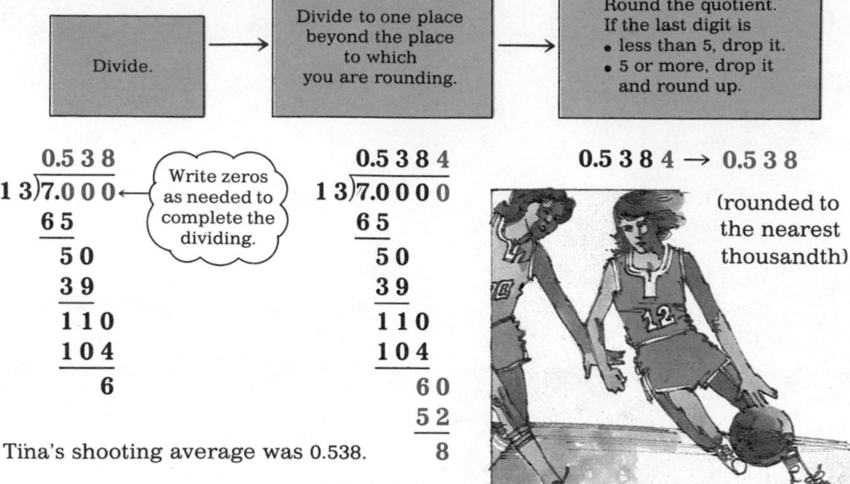


Tina's shooting average was 0.538.

**Other Examples**

Find \$3 ÷ 8 to the nearest cent (hundredth of a dollar).

```
   $0.3 7 5 → $0.3 8 (nearest cent or hundredth)
8)$3.0 0 0
   2 4
     6 0
     5 6
       4 0
       4 0
         0
```

Find 10.3 ÷ 7 to the nearest tenth.

```
   1.4 7 → 1.5 (nearest tenth)
7)1 0.3 0
   7
   3 3
   2 8
     5 0
     4 9
       1
```

### Warm Up

1. Find 24 ÷ 9 to the nearest tenth. 2.7
2. Find \$25.43 ÷ 7 to the nearest cent. \$3.63
3. Find 8 ÷ 17 to the nearest thousandth. 0.471

150

## Follow Up

### Reteaching

Review the following procedure for rounding:

- Determine the place to which you wish to round.
- If the digit to the right is 5 or more, drop it and round up.
- If the digit is less than 5, drop it and do not increase the digit to be rounded.

Point out that if a quotient is to be rounded to two places, for example, division must be carried to 3 places. Review with students how zeros can be added to complete the division process.

### Enrichment

Provide students with a chart like the one below. Have students find each quotient and then round the quotients to the nearest tenth, hundredth, or thousandth as indicated.

| Find the quotient | Round to: tenths | hundredths | thousandths |
|---|---|---|---|
| \$10.00 ÷ 8 | | | |
| 20.145 ÷ 3 | | | |

## Assignment Guide

| | Minimum | Average | Extended |
|---|---|---|---|
| page 151 | 1–27 | 1–29 | 6–29, TM |

Find the quotients. Round to the nearest tenth.

1. 3)11 3.7
2. 7)5 0.7
3. 9)4 0.4
4. 6)13 2.2
5. 8)3 0.4
6. 14)7.34 0.5
7. 18)6.45 0.4
8. 25)3 0.1
9. 27)96 3.6
10. 43)287 6.7

Find the quotients. Round to the nearest hundredth or cent.

11. 6)5 0.83
12. 6)31 5.17
13. 7)5 0.71
14. 19)6 0.32
15. 28)87.2 3.11
16. 8)$10.06 $1.26
17. 3)$19.06 $6.35
18. 7)$3.94 $0.56
19. 25)$64.75 $2.59
20. 36)$38.93 $1.08

Find the averages in this table. Round to the nearest thousandth.

| | Player | Goals | Shots Taken | Average |
|---|---|---|---|---|
| 0.455 21. | Sally | 5 | 11 | ■ |
| 0.471 22. | Arnold | 8 | 17 | ■ |
| 0.524 23. | Glenna | 11 | 21 | ■ |
| 0.316 24. | Wing | 6 | 19 | ■ |
| 0.429 25. | Orlando | 3 | 7 | ■ |
| 0.429 26. | Roger | 9 | 21 | ■ |

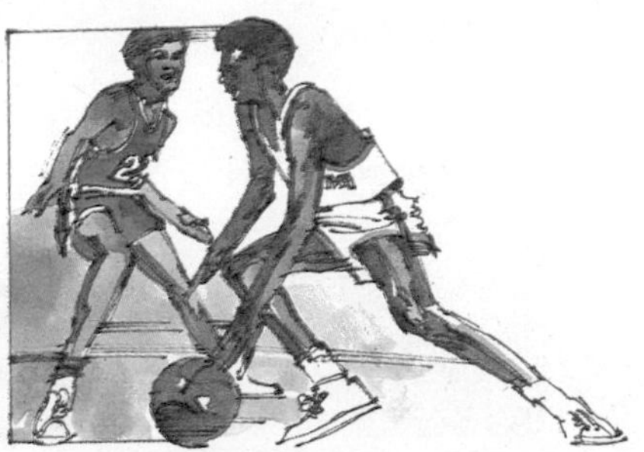

27. Rebecca's team won 9 out of 13 games. What was the team's "winning average" rounded to the nearest thousandth? Hint: winning average = games won ÷ games played. 0.692

28. Chris missed on the first 9 shots he took, but he scored goals on his next 5 shots. What was his shooting average then? 0.357

29. Aram scored goals on 108 of the 235 shots he took during the season. Brendan scored on 111 of 251 shots taken. Find their averages to the nearest thousandth. How much greater is the higher average?
Aram's 0.460 average is 0.018 higher than Brendan's 0.442 average.

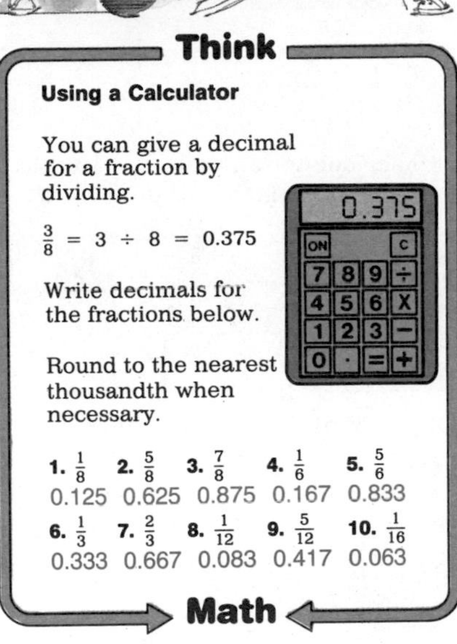

**Think**

**Using a Calculator**

You can give a decimal for a fraction by dividing.

$\frac{3}{8} = 3 \div 8 = 0.375$

Write decimals for the fractions below.

Round to the nearest thousandth when necessary.

1. $\frac{1}{8}$ 0.125 2. $\frac{5}{8}$ 0.625 3. $\frac{7}{8}$ 0.875 4. $\frac{1}{6}$ 0.167 5. $\frac{5}{6}$ 0.833

6. $\frac{1}{3}$ 0.333 7. $\frac{2}{3}$ 0.667 8. $\frac{1}{12}$ 0.083 9. $\frac{5}{12}$ 0.417 10. $\frac{1}{16}$ 0.063

**Math**



More Practice, page 420, Set B



## Using Page 151

**Exercises 1–10** Note that several of these exercises involve dividing a whole number by a larger whole number. Since students are asked to round to the nearest tenth, they must divide in the hundredths place.

**Exercises 11–20** In each of these exercises students must divide in the thousandths place so they can round to the nearest hundredth or cent.

**Exercise 28** Note that students must first add 9 and 5 to find the total number of shots taken and then divide 5 by 14.

**Exercise 29** This exercise illustrates the power of the calculator. A division process that would be quite lengthy using pencil and paper can be completed very quickly. Emphasize the importance of looking at the calculator display and finding the place to which to round. The number following this place gives the clues needed to complete the rounding process.

**Think Math** This activity gives students an opportunity to use a calculator to find a decimal for a fraction. Point out that this is also an easy way to compare two fractions. For example, ask: "Which is larger, five eighths or two thirds?" (Two thirds, because 0.667 is greater than 0.625.) "Which is greater, seven eighths or five sixths?" (Seven eighths, because 0.875 is greater than 0.833.)

**More Practice,** page 420, Set B

**Reteaching Supplement,** page 37

Name ____________ To follow text page 151

**Rounding Decimal Quotients**

Find the quotient to one place beyond the place to which you are rounding. → Round the quotient. If the last digit is
- less than 5, drop it.
- 5 or more, drop it and round up.

12)3.20 = 0.26 (To find a quotient to the nearest tenth, divide to the hundredths place.)

0.26 → 0.3 (6 > 5 Round up.)

Divide and round to the nearest tenth.

1. 6)50.00 8.33 → 8.3
2. 8)23.00 2.87 → 2.9 (Finish.)
3. 6)7.41 1.23 → 1.2 (Finish.)
4. 9)4.20 0.46 → 0.5
5. 7)6.60 0.94 → 0.9
6. 28)6.66 0.23 → 0.2

Divide and round to the nearest hundredth.

7. 3)19.000 6.333 → 6.33 (Find the quotient to the thousandths place.)
8. 6)20.000 3.333 → 3.33
9. 12)77.000 6.416 → 6.42

**Enrichment Supplement,** page 37

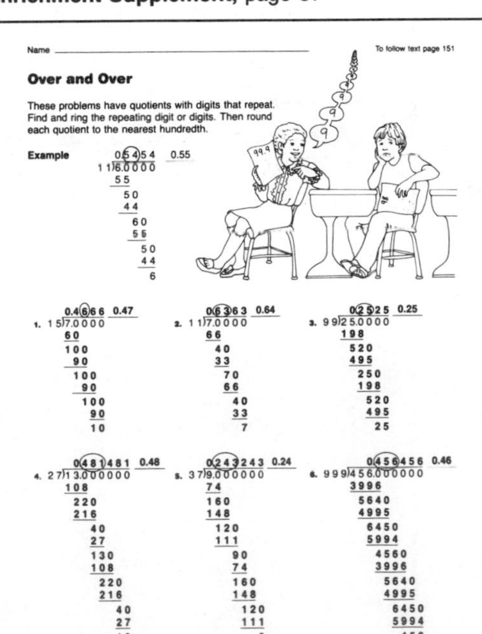

Name ____________ To follow text page 151

**Over and Over**

These problems have quotients with digits that repeat. Find and ring the repeating digit or digits. Then round each quotient to the nearest hundredth.

**Example** 11)6.0000 0.5454 0.55

1. 15)7.0000 0.4666 0.47
2. 11)7.0000 0.6363 0.64
3. 99)25.0000 0.2525 0.25
4. 27)13.000000 0.481481 0.48
5. 37)9.000000 0.243243 0.24
6. 999)456.000000 0.456456 0.46

**Practice Supplement,** page 58

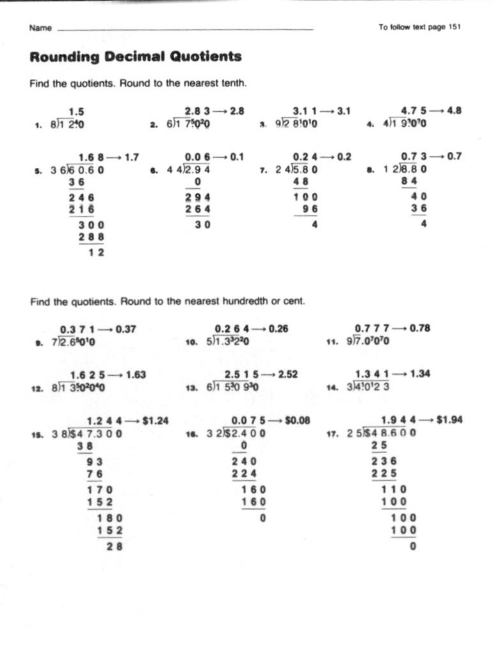

Name ____________ To follow text page 151

**Rounding Decimal Quotients**

Find the quotients. Round to the nearest tenth.

1. 8)12.0 1.5
2. 6)17.00 2.83 → 2.8
3. 9)28.00 3.11 → 3.1
4. 4)19.00 4.75 → 4.8
5. 36)60.60 1.68 → 1.7
6. 44)2.94 0.06 → 0.1
7. 24)5.80 0.24 → 0.2
8. 12)8.80 0.73 → 0.7

Find the quotients. Round to the nearest hundredth or cent.

9. 7)2.600 0.371 → 0.37
10. 5)1.320 0.264 → 0.26
11. 9)7.000 0.777 → 0.78
12. 8)13.000 1.625 → 1.63
13. 6)15.090 2.515 → 2.52
14. 3)4.023 1.341 → 1.34
15. 38)$47.300 1.244 → $1.24
16. 32)$2.400 0.075 → $0.08
17. 25)$48.600 1.944 → $1.94

# Decimals: Division

**Quick Review** As an oral drill, students name each number that can be divided evenly by 7 and give the quotients. Repeat with 8 and 9.

56 64 32 27 72 81 24 49 64 54
14 28 40 80 21 45 63 35 18

**Lesson Focus** To use mental math to find the quotient of a decimal divided by 10, 100, or 1,000

**Suggested Materials** Calculators

## Ideas for Getting Started

Have students write the following problems on their papers and find the answers using their calculators.

| | |
|---|---|
| 5.32 ÷ 10 = | 436.25 ÷ 10 = |
| 5.23 ÷ 100 = | 436.25 ÷ 100 = |
| 5.23 ÷ 1,000 = | 436.25 ÷ 1,000 = |

"What do you observe about each set of answers?" (The numbers are the same; the decimal point is in a different place.) "How did dividing by 10 affect the decimal point?" (The decimal point moved one place to the left.) "Try other numbers on your calculator. Does dividing by 10 always affect the decimal point in this way?" (Yes, dividing by 10 always moves the decimal point one place to the left.) "How does dividing by 100 affect the decimal point?" (moves the decimal point two places to the left) "Dividing by 1,000?" (three places to the left) Have students use their calculators to see if these patterns continue.

## Using Page 152

**Lesson Development** Emphasize that we are using the weight of the pilot whale to find the average weight of a man, a dog, and a guinea pig. We are told that the pilot whale weighed 734.83 kg, and that this is ten times an average man's weight. Dividing the weight of the pilot whale by 10 will tell us the average man's weight. Similarly, dividing the weight of the pilot whale by 100 gives the dog's weight, and by 1,000 gives the guinea pig's weight. Point out that these divisions can be done mentally.

Have students focus on the first calculator display. "How has dividing 734.83 by 10 affected the decimal point? (It has moved one place to the left.) Have students estimate 734.83 ÷ 10 to verify that the calculated answer seems reasonable. Then have students look at the second calculator display. "How has dividing 734.83 by 100 affected the decimal point?" (It has moved two places to the left.) Show students why this answer seems reasonable. "How has dividing 734.83 by 1,000 affected the decimal point?" (It has moved three places to the left.) Help students generalize that since 10 has one zero, we move the decimal point one place to the *left* when dividing by 10; and since 1,000 has three zeros, we move the decimal point three places to the left when dividing by 1,000.

**Exercises 1–16** Use these exercises as a mental math activity. Be sure students understand that when multiplying, the decimal point is moved to the right and when dividing, the decimal point is moved to the left.

## Dividing Decimals by 10, 100, and 1,000: Mental Math

A pilot whale weighed 734.83 kg. This is 10 times an average man's weight, 100 times a small dog's weight, and 1,000 times a guinea pig's weight. To find these weights, we divide. Are these calculator answers reasonable?

Man's Weight = Whale's Weight ÷ 10

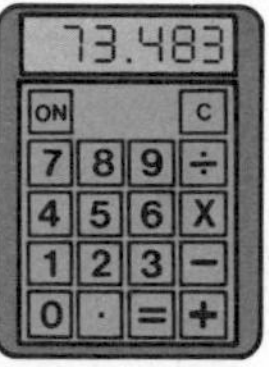


734.83 ÷ 10
↓
700 ÷ 10 = 70

The calculator answer seems reasonable.

To divide by 10, move the decimal point 1 place left.

73.4.83

Dog's Weight = Whale's Weight ÷ 100

734.83 ÷ 100
↓
700 ÷ 100 = 7

The calculator answer seems reasonable.

To divide by 100, move the decimal point 2 places left.

7.34.83

Guinea Pig's Weight = Whale's Weight ÷ 1,000

734.83 ÷ 1,000
↓
700 ÷ 1,000 = 0.7

The calculator answer seems reasonable.

To divide by 1,000, move the decimal point 3 places left.

.734.83

Divide. Write only the answers.

| | | | |
|---|---|---|---|
| **1.** 9.6 ÷ 10<br>0.96 | **2.** 27.54 ÷ 10<br>2.754 | **3.** 0.7 ÷ 10<br>0.07 | **4.** 75 ÷ 10<br>7.5 |
| **5.** 34.2 ÷ 100<br>0.342 | **6.** 8.7 ÷ 100<br>0.087 | **7.** 536.5 ÷ 100<br>5.365 | **8.** 278 ÷ 100<br>2.78 |
| **9.** 496.4 ÷ 1,000<br>0.4964 | **10.** 387.25 ÷ 1,000<br>0.38725 | **11.** 86.3 ÷ 1,000<br>0.0863 | **12.** 0.9 ÷ 1,000<br>0.0009 |
| **13.** 68.3 ÷ 100<br>0.683 | **14.** 29.74 ÷ 10<br>2.974 | **15.** 456.8 ÷ 1,000<br>0.4568 | **16.** 9.4 ÷ 100<br>0.094 |



More Practice, page 420, Set C

## Follow Up

### Reteaching

As you work through the example below, call attention to where the decimal point was placed and how a zero was added to complete the division.

```
   0.83
10)8.30
   8 0
     30
     30
      0
```

Then show how the quotients below compare to the one above. Ask a volunteer to describe the relationships observed.

8.3 ÷ 100 = 0.083
8.3 ÷ 1,000 = 0.0083

### Enrichment

Ask students to apply the rules for dividing or multiplying by 10, 100, or 1,000 as they work the exercises below.

```
    3.76        0.376        37.6
10)37.6     10)3.76      10)376

   3.76        0.376        37.6
 ×   10      ×    10      ×   10
   37.6         3.76         376

     42.86      0.04286        4.286
100)4286    100)4.286     100)428.6

   42.86       0.04286       4.286
 ×   100     ×     100     ×   100
   4,286       4.28600     428.600
                 or           or
                4.286        428.6
```

| Assignment Guide | | | |
|---|---|---|---|
| | Minimum | Average | Extended |
| page 152 | 1–16 | 1–16 | 1–16 |
| page 153 | 1–32 | 1–33, TM | 9–33, TM |

## Dividing Decimals: Practice

Divide.

| | | | |
|---|---|---|---|
| **1.** 4)11.48  2.87 | **2.** 6)45.924  7.654 | **3.** 3)187.41  62.47 | **4.** 5)1.545  0.309 |
| **5.** 8)3.824  0.478 | **6.** 2)130.94  65.47 | **7.** 9)0.783  0.087 | **8.** 7)258.3  36.9 |
| **9.** 3)2.067  0.689 | **10.** 5)219.35  43.87 | **11.** 7)5.439  0.777 | **12.** 9)62.01  6.89 |
| **13.** 42)68.46  1.63 | **14.** 64)37.568  0.587 | **15.** 36)11.088  0.308 | **16.** 18)46.44  2.58 |
| **17.** 57)780.9  13.7 | **18.** 86)398.18  4.63 | **19.** 74)9.102  0.123 | **20.** 95)$605.15  $6.37 |

**21.** 31.23 ÷ 9  3.47  **22.** $56.70 ÷ 10  $5.67  **23.** $29.28 ÷ 8  $3.66

**24.** 562.8 ÷ 1,000  0.5628  **25.** $747 ÷ 100  $7.47  **26.** $3.50 ÷ 5  $0.70

Divide. Round to the nearest hundredth or cent.

**27.** 8)5  0.63  **28.** 23)67  2.91  **29.** 9)$32.10  $3.57  **30.** 35)$170.21  $4.86

**31.** Estimate, then find 63.63 divided by 8. 8; 7.95

**32.** Estimate, then find the quotient when the dividend is 144.69 and the divisor is 23. 7; 6.291

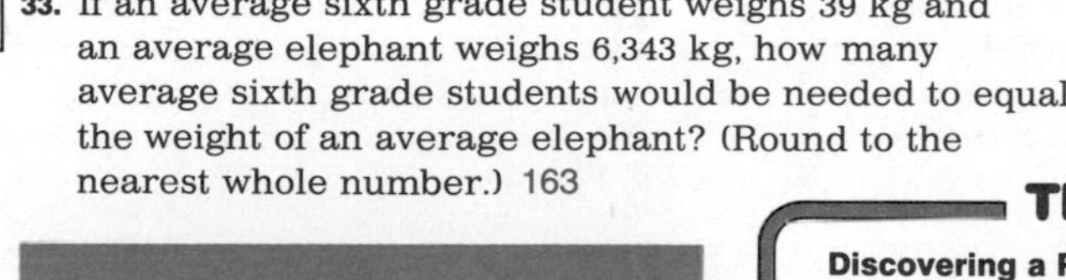

**33.** If an average sixth grade student weighs 39 kg and an average elephant weighs 6,343 kg, how many average sixth grade students would be needed to equal the weight of an average elephant? (Round to the nearest whole number.) 163

**Think Math**

**Discovering a Pattern**

Here is a magic square. The sum in each row, column, and diagonal is the same. If you divide each number by 10 (or by 100), is it still a magic square? Yes, see teaching notes.

| | | |
|---|---|---|
| 36 | 31 | 38 |
| 37 | 35 | 33 |
| 32 | 39 | 34 |



## Using Page 153

**Lesson Development** Work one or two examples to help students review the dividing process. Be sure they can estimate the first quotient digit and proceed with the dividing process.

**Exercises 27–32** In exercises 27–30 students must divide in the thousandths place so that the answer can be rounded to the nearest hundredth. In exercise 31 the first number is rounded to the nearest whole number, and in exercise 32 both the dividend and the divisor are rounded to the nearest ten.

**Exercise 33** Even though this problem can be done with pencil and paper, it is a good situation to help students understand the speed with which the calculator can help them solve problems.

**Think Math** This activity provides an opportunity for students to discover some properties of magic squares. At the same time, they practice dividing a number by 10 or 100 and adding decimals. Note that the sum of the numbers in each row in the magic square is 105. This is also the sum of the numbers in each column and in each diagonal. When each of the numbers in the magic square is divided by 10, the magic number is 10.5, and the sum of each row, column, or diagonal is this number. When the numbers are divided by 100, the magic number is 1.05 and the sum of each row, column, and diagonal is this number. Students should generalize that when all of the numbers in a magic square are divided by the same number, the resulting array is still a magic square.

## Ideas That Work

### Chalk It Up

Write the table below on the chalkboard and give students these instructions: Each line of the table below shows a multiplication or division problem, three answer choices, and an estimate. For a hint to the correct answer, carry out the estimation shown in the last column.

| | Calculate | Answer Choices | | | Estimate |
|---|---|---|---|---|---|
| | | a. | b. | c. | |
| 1. | 4.05 × 4.2 | 0.1701 | 17.01 | 1.701 | 4 × 4 |
| 2. | 0.78 × 33 | 0.2745 | 257.4 | 25.74 | 0.8 × 30 |
| 3. | 6.3 × 5.1 | 32.13 | 3.213 | 0.3213 | 6 × 5 |
| 4. | 23.8 ÷ 0.28 | 0.085 | 8.5 | 85 | 24 ÷ 0.3 |
| 5. | 19.245 ÷ 0.05 | 38.49 | 3.849 | 384.9 | 20 ÷ 0.05 |
| 6. | 6.4 ÷ 0.32 | 0.2 | 200 | 20.0 | 6 ÷ 0.3 |

**Practice Supplement,** page 59

Name ______________________  To follow text page 153

**Dividing Decimals: Practice**

Divide.

| | | | |
|---|---|---|---|
| **1.** 3)11.25  3.75 | **2.** 8)36.288  4.536 | **3.** 6)44.514  7.419 | **4.** 5)13.35  2.67 |
| **5.** 9)5.076  0.564 | **6.** 4)297.88  74.47 | **7.** 2)1.972  0.986 | **8.** 3)186.93  62.31 |
| **9.** 7)2.884  0.412 | **10.** 5)261.10  52.22 | **11.** 8)30.16  3.77 | **12.** 6)82.2  13.7 |
| **13.** 68)4.488  0.066 | **14.** 73)4.161  0.057 | **15.** 49)23.275  0.475 | **16.** 56)115.92  2.07 |

**Quick Review** Students give the sums orally.

| 0.14 | 0.06 | 0.20 | 3.98 | 12.48 | 0.2 | 0.09 | 6.03 | 0.25 |
|---|---|---|---|---|---|---|---|---|
| + 0.12 | + 0.92 | + 0.45 | + 0.02 | + 8.50 | + 5.7 | + 0.88 | + 4.98 | + 0.75 |
| 0.26 | 0.98 | 0.65 | 4.00 | 20.98 | 5.9 | 0.97 | 11.01 | 1.00 |

**Lesson Focus** To use data from several sources to solve word problems

**Suggested Materials** Meter sticks

## Ideas for Getting Started

Have students work in pairs to check their reaction time as described in the first example on the page. That is, have one person hold a meter stick while a partner is ready to catch the meter stick as quickly as possible. Have students determine how far the stick fell before the person caught it. Then show students how to calculate the reaction time in seconds by (a) multiplying the fall distance by 4, (b) adding 90, (c) dividing the result by 1,000. Encourage students to compare reaction times and then attempt to improve their reaction times.

## Using Page 154

**Lesson Development** Point out that some of these problems have more data than needed. For other problems, however, data must be sought in the data source beside the problem. Emphasize the importance of data in solving a problem and the various data sources that are available. If necessary, discuss the reaction experiments and reaction data shown in the data source before students work the problems.

**Exercise 2** Note that students must find the distance the stick fell by subtracting 16 from 31 before they can use the procedure given to find the reaction time.

**Exercise 3** In this exercise, the information about Rosaura's second try is not needed to solve the problem.

**Exercise 4** To solve this problem students must do two addition and one subtraction operation.

*Many sources of data—pictures, graphs, tables, menus—are explored as opportunities for problem solving.*

QUESTION DATA PLAN ANSWER CHECK

## Problem Solving: Using Data from Several Sources

Solve these problems about reaction times. For some of these problems more than the needed data is given. For other problems you must find needed data in the data source shown beside the problem.

1. The stick had fallen 18 cm when Michael caught it. What was his reaction time (in seconds)? 0.162 s

2. The stick fell from the 16 cm mark to the 31 cm mark before Janine caught it. What was her reaction time? 0.15 s

3. On her first try Rosaura's reaction time was 0.65 s (seconds). On the second try it was 0.58 s. Her best time was equal to the time for her first try divided by 2. What was her best time? 0.325 s

**Data Source:**
An Experiment

1. Hold a meter stick. Have someone be ready to catch it as quickly as possible.
2. Drop the meter stick. How far did it fall before it was caught?

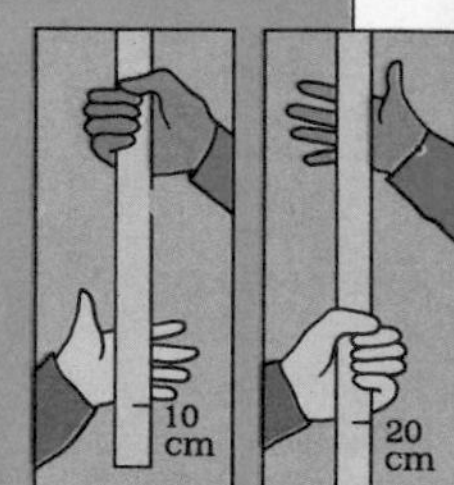


A person's approximate reaction time (in seconds) can be found as follows:
1. Multiply the fall distance by 4.
2. Add 90.
3. Divide by 1,000.

4. The total stopping distance is the sum of the reaction distance and the braking distance. How much greater is the total stopping distance at 100 km/h than at 80 km/h? 31.79 m

5. If use of a medicine caused a person's reaction distance to be 1.25 as great as the average reaction distance, what would be the reaction distance at 100 km/h? 26.0625 m

**Data Source:** A graph from a driver's book

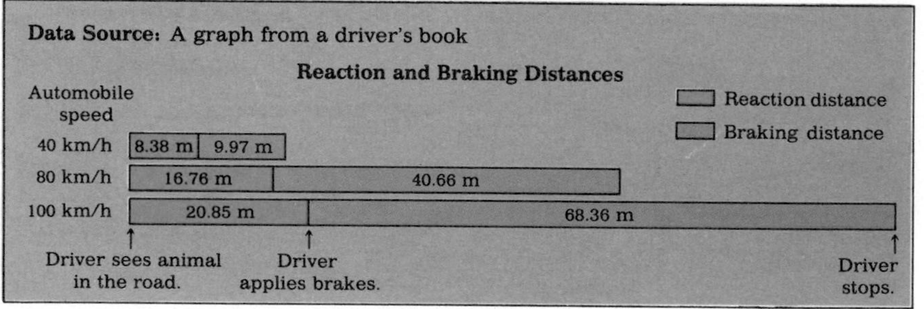


154

## Follow Up

### Reteaching

To help students recognize the need to analyze problems carefully, present a variety of problems, including those with unneeded information. For example: John and Sally cut lawns on Saturday to earn extra money. They earned a total of $5.60. Larry also cuts lawns and earned $8.50. Suppose the movies cost $2.75 per person. Did John and Sally earn enough to go to the movies? As students use the 5-Point Checklist to help solve the problem, encourage them to focus on the information needed in the solution.

### Enrichment

Have students find data on a given topic and then use the data source to write questions and chart the information for another student to interpret. Some topics might be: popular records, sports scores, rain or snowfall increases or decreases, gains in test scores, and so on.

| Assignment Guide | | | |
|---|---|---|---|
| | Minimum | Average | Extended |
| pages 154–155 | 1–9 | 1–10 | 1–11 |



6. Margie's best reaction time on the tone-light test was at the break between "Excellent" and "Good." Her first time was 4 times as great as her best time. What was her first time? 0.2 s

7. Matt's times, in order, were 0.24, 0.18, 0.15, 0.16, 0.12, 0.09. What was his average time for his first 5 tries? 0.17 s

**Data Source:**
A science museum display

As the tone sounds, tiny bulbs begin to light up in order from bottom to top. The goal is to push the button as fast as possible when you hear the tone to stop the "climbing light" as quickly as possible.

| Seconds | |
|---|---|
| 0.25 | Poor |
| 0.20 | Average |
| 0.15 | Good |
| 0.10 | |
| 0.05 | Excellent |
| 0 | |

8. At what age range is the clapping hands reaction time the shortest? 30–39

9. What is the average reaction time for all ages? (Round to the nearest thousandth.) 0.385 s

10. **DATA HUNT** What is the difference between your shortest and longest reaction times in the stick-catching experiment on page 154? Answers will vary.

11. **Try This** Terry's slowest reaction time in the tone-light test above was 3 times her fastest time. The difference in the times was 0.12 s. What was her fastest time? 0.06 s

**Data Source:**
A table from a reference book

Time needed to clap hands together from a distance of 80 cm when a light flashes

| Age | Average Reaction Time (seconds) |
|---|---|
| 6–8 | 0.466 |
| 9–13 | 0.411 |
| 14–19 | 0.344 |
| 20–29 | 0.344 |
| 30–39 | 0.335 |
| 40–49 | 0.357 |
| 50–59 | 0.391 |
| 60+ | 0.431 |



## Using Page 155

**Lesson Development** Discuss the reaction experiment described in the science museum display. Be sure students understand that at the sound of the tone, tiny bulbs in a vertical column light up in order from bottom to top. The quicker a person pushes the button after the tone sounds, the quicker the lighting of the bulbs is stopped.

**Data Hunt** This exercise requires that students use the data they collected in the experiment on page 154. If necessary, have students try to answer the question based on five trials.

**Try This** A possible strategy, Guess and Check, was taught on page 48.

**Discussion** "What do we want to find out about Terry's reaction time in the tone-light test?" (What was her fastest time?) "How much greater was Terry's slowest reaction time than her fastest reaction time?" (three times greater) "What was the difference in the two times?" (0.12 seconds) "If Terry's fastest reaction time was 0.15 seconds, what would her slowest reaction time be?" (0.45 seconds) "What would be the difference between these two times?" (0.3 seconds) "What fastest reaction time might be closer to the correct answer?" (Answers will vary.)

**Solution** Terry's fastest reaction time is 0.06 seconds. Her slowest reaction time, three times as fast, would be 0.18 s.

*Try This teaching notes give real help in reviewing strategies.*

## Ideas That Work

### Chalk It Up

Write the problems below on the chalkboard and instruct students to place a decimal point in each product to make the equation true. Note that in some problems students must write one or more zeros before placing the decimal point.

1. 2.4 × 0.37 = 888
2. 0.6 × 0.04 = 24
3. 5.1 × 6.3 = 3213
4. 0.03 × 0.04 = 12
5. 8.01 × 2 = 1602
6. 0.08 × 0.001 = 8
7. 4.83 × 0.61 = 29463
8. 0.025 × 0.5 = 125
9. 2.007 × 0.5 = 10035
10. 36.18 × 2.507 = 9070326

**Practice Supplement,** page 60

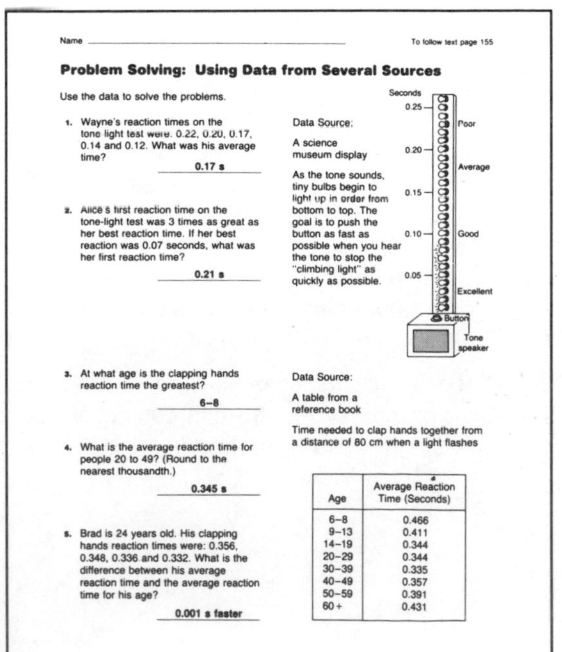

Name ______ To follow text page 155

**Problem Solving: Using Data from Several Sources**

Use the data to solve the problems.

1. Wayne's reaction times on the tone light test were: 0.22, 0.20, 0.17, 0.14 and 0.12. What was his average time? **0.17 s**

2. Alice's first reaction time on the tone-light test was 3 times as great as her best reaction time. If her best reaction was 0.07 seconds, what was her first reaction time? **0.21 s**

3. At what age is the clapping hands reaction time the greatest? **6–8**

4. What is the average reaction time for people 20 to 49? (Round to the nearest thousandth.) **0.345 s**

5. Brad is 24 years old. His clapping hands reaction times were: 0.356, 0.348, 0.336 and 0.332. What is the difference between his average reaction time and the average reaction time for his age? **0.001 s faster**

Data Source:

A science museum display

As the tone sounds, tiny bulbs begin to light up in order from bottom to top. The goal is to push the button as fast as possible when you hear the tone to stop the "climbing light" as quickly as possible.



Data Source:

A table from a reference book

Time needed to clap hands together from a distance of 80 cm when a light flashes

| Age | Average Reaction Time (Seconds) |
|---|---|
| 6–8 | 0.466 |
| 9–13 | 0.411 |
| 14–19 | 0.344 |
| 20–29 | 0.344 |
| 30–39 | 0.335 |
| 40–49 | 0.357 |
| 50–59 | 0.391 |
| 60+ | 0.431 |

# Decimals: Division

**Quick Review** Students write the decimal as the number is read aloud.

0.002 1.6 16.67 7.08 100.2 8.33 0.255 0.09
34.589 0.24 4.56 8.125 90.01 55.2 10.5
0.98 0.6 0.368 2.283 183.25 44.9 39.003 0.89

**Lesson Focus** To find the quotient of a decimal divided by a decimal

## Ideas for Getting Started

Write 8)24 on the chalkboard. "What is the quotient?" (3) If you multiply the dividend and the divisor by 10, what problem do you have?" (80)240) "Now what is the quotient?" (3) "If you multiply the divisor and the dividend by 100, what problem do you have?" (800)2,400) "Now what is the quotient?" (3) "What statement can you make about this situation?" (Multiplying the dividend and the divisor by the same number does not change the quotient.) Use other examples to convince students that this statement is true.

## Using Page 156

**Motivational Problem** Have students read the problem at the top of the page. If any students in the class have been to the Skydeck of the Sears Tower, encourage them to share their experiences. "What question are we asked about the Skydeck of the Sears Tower?" (How many seconds does it take to get from the ground floor to the Skydeck?) "What data is needed to answer this question?" (distance the tower is above the ground; meters per second the elevator travels) As you discuss the plan for solving the problem, help students see that we can divide the total number of meters by the meters per second to find the number of seconds.

**Lesson Development** Emphasize that we can multiply the dividend and the divisor by the same number and not change the quotient. "What number can we use to multiply the divisor so that we have a whole number divisor?" (10) "If we multiply both the dividend and the divisor by 10, what will the problem be?) (4,127.5 ÷ 65) Point out that if the divisor is a whole number, the division problem is like those they have worked earlier. Have students complete the division and then multiply to check the answer. Reread the original problem and estimate to see if the answer, 63.5 seconds, makes sense. Ask a volunteer to write the answer to the problem using a complete sentence.

**Other Examples** Note that the first example involves multiplying the dividend and the divisor by 10. In the second example, the dividend and the divisor have been multiplied by 100. In the third example note that the dividend and the divisor are multiplied by 1,000. Also note that the quotient contains a middle zero.

**Warm Up** Watch for students who multiply the divisor by a multiple of 10, 100, or 1,000 but neglect to multiply the dividend by that same multiple.

## Dividing by a Decimal

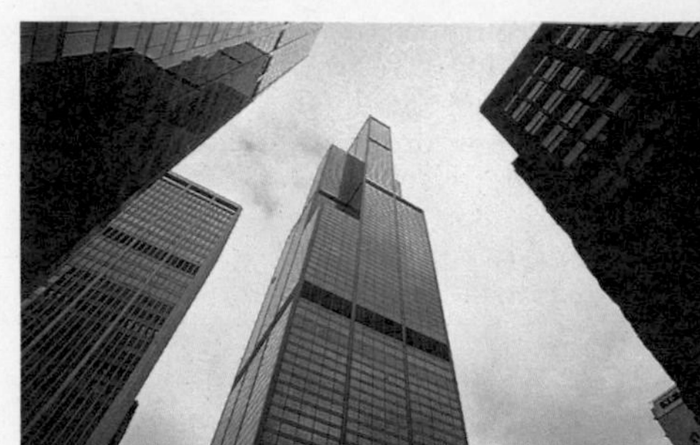

The Skydeck of the Sears Tower in Chicago is 412.75 m above the ground. If the elevator from the ground floor to the Skydeck travels 6.5 m/s (meters per second), how many seconds does it take to get to the Skydeck?

Since we want to find how many one-second distances are in the total, we divide.

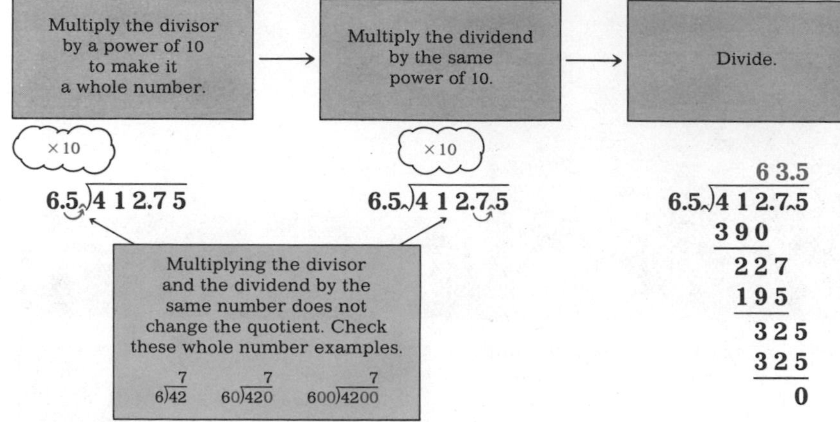

Multiply the divisor by a power of 10 to make it a whole number.
Multiply the dividend by the same power of 10.
Divide.
×10
6.5)4 1 2.7 5
×10
6.5)4 1 2.7 5
63.5
6.5)4 1 2.7 5
3 9 0
2 2 7
1 9 5
3 2 5
3 2 5
0
Multiplying the divisor and the dividend by the same number does not change the quotient. Check these whole number examples.
7
6)42
7
60)420
7
600)4200


It takes 63.5 s to get to the Skydeck.

**Other Examples**

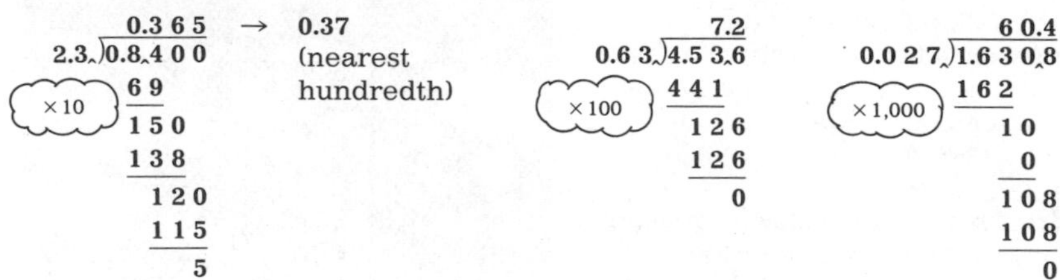


**Warm Up** Divide. Round to the nearest hundredth when necessary.

1. 4.3)201.24 (46.8)
2. 0.7)6.65 (9.5)
3. 0.54)4.433 (8.21)
4. 0.038)3.0666 (80.7)



## Follow Up

### Reteaching

Help students recall that multiplying both divisor and dividend by the same value did not affect the quotient. For example, 12 ÷ 6 = 2, and 120 ÷ 60 = 2. Use this idea to explain the algorithm to use when dividing by a decimal. In the example below, both the divisor and the dividend were multiplied by 10 to change the problem to a whole number division. Elicit from students how the divisor was changed to a whole number and why it could be done.

3.1)36.7

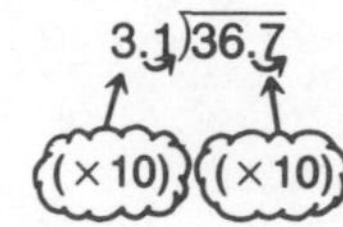


### Enrichment

Prepare 20 index cards with decimal numbers as shown below. Tape a playing square made from a large sheet of paper on the floor. Have players stand a specified distance from the playing square and toss a bean bag on the playing square. To score a point, players accurately divide the number on the square by the decimal on a drawn index card. The calculator can be used to check answers.

| 0.8 | 0.05 | 3 |
|---|---|---|
| 0.06 | 18 | 24 |
| 0.002 | 0.64 | 9 |

Playing Square

| 0.2 |
|---|

Index card

| Assignment Guide | Minimum | Average | Extended |
|---|---|---|---|
| page 157 | 1–39 | 1–40 | 1–40, TM |

Divide. Round to the nearest hundredth when necessary.

1. 3.4)12.92 3.8
2. 0.8)26.08 32.6
3. 0.67)3.643 5.44
4. 0.03)0.294 9.8
5. 7.4)1.5244 0.21
6. 0.62)2.914 4.7
7. 0.7)3.682 5.26
8. 0.08)5.072 63.4
9. 9.5)0.8265 0.09
10. 0.6)0.576 0.96
11. 0.09)34.283 380.92
12. 0.87)7.221 8.3
13. 5.8)3.828 0.66
14. 0.36)2.1312 5.92
15. 0.4)0.487 1.22
16. 0.05)0.4515 9.03
17. 0.068)0.5848 8.6
18. 0.018)0.0162 0.9
19. 0.007)0.0868 12.4
20. 0.046)3.0084 65.4
21. 0.37)2.143 5.79
22. 0.09)0.9562 10.62
23. 0.26)0.5743 2.21
24. 0.058)0.0796 1.37
25. 1.44 ÷ 0.45 3.2
26. 0.3904 ÷ 0.061 6.4
27. 0.72 ÷ 0.96 0.75
28. 2.16 ÷ 0.52 4.15
29. 81.5 ÷ 0.41 198.78
30. 0.5318 ÷ 0.49 1.09
31. 1.692 ÷ 4.7 0.36
32. 25.16 ÷ 6.8 3.7
33. 10.71 ÷ 0.7 15.3
34. 4.7742 ÷ 0.73 6.54
35. 1.984 ÷ 0.08 24.8
36. 0.8178 ÷ 0.094 8.7
37. Estimate, then find the quotient when 63.96 is divided by 7.8. 8; 8.2
38. Estimate, then find the quotient when the dividend is 23.94 and the divisor is 3.7. 6; 6.47
39. How long would it take an elevator traveling 7.5 m/s to travel the 327.25 m between the ground and the Sky Pod at the top of the CN Tower in Toronto? 43.63 s
40. Mt. Everest is 8,840 m high. If you could ride an elevator traveling 6.5 m/s to the top, how many minutes would the trip take? 22.67 min

**Think Math**

**Shape Perception**

Trace 4 copies of this shape. Show how to divide it into these numbers of pieces having the same size and shape:

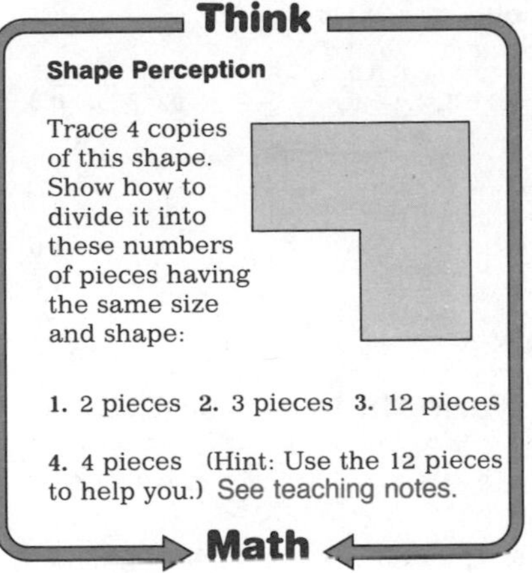

1. 2 pieces 2. 3 pieces 3. 12 pieces
4. 4 pieces (Hint: Use the 12 pieces to help you.) See teaching notes.

More Practice, page 421, Set A



## Using Page 157

**Exercises 1–36** In exercises 1–16 the dividend and the divisor are multiplied by either 10 or 100 to produce whole number divisors with the same quotient as the original problem. In exercises 17–24, the dividend and divisor must be multiplied by 1,000. Exercises 25–36 are mixed practice exercises.

**Exercises 37–38** The numbers must be rounded to the nearest whole number in order to use a basic fact to complete the estimation. In exercise 38 note that students review the meaning of the terms "dividend" and "divisor."

**Exercise 40** This problem can be solved using pencil and paper calculations; however, it provides an excellent opportunity to illustrate the power and speed of a calculator in performing the operations.

**Think Math** This activity provides an opportunity to think about how shapes fit together. Encourage students to try to draw the indicated divisions. The solutions to the four parts are shown below.

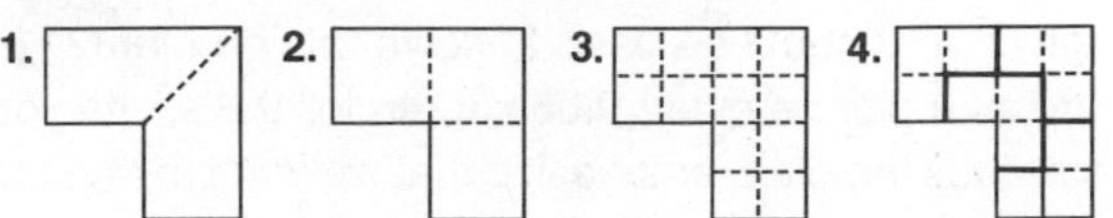


**Reteaching Supplement**, page 38

Name ______ To follow text page 157

**Dividing by a Decimal**

Multiply the divisor by a power of ten that will make it a whole number. → Multiply the dividend by the same number. → Divide as with whole numbers. Place the decimal point above its new position in the dividend.

0.43)1.5996 → 0.43)1.59.96 → 0.43)1.59.96 3.72

Divide.

1. 0.6)2.04 3.4
2. 0.14)5.04 36
3. 3.8)1.634 0.43
4. 6.4)13.44 2.1
5. 0.07)16.52 236
6. 0.54)0.3888 0.72
7. 0.72)3.456 4.8
8. 0.02)0.0132 0.66
9. 1.3)129.87 99.9
10. 4.7)22.654 4.82
11. 2.9)18.038 6.22

**Enrichment Supplement**, page 38

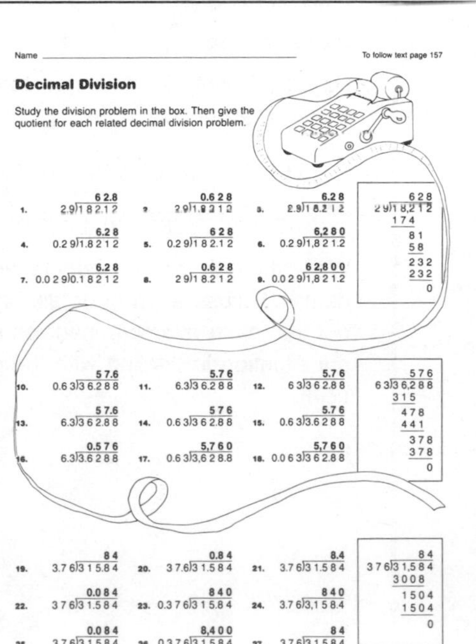

**Practice Supplement**, page 61

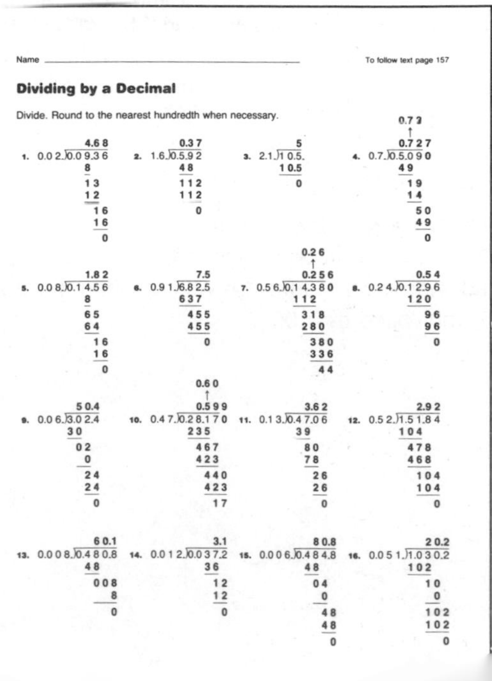

# Decimals: Division

**Quick Review** Students round these decimals to the nearest tenth.

| | | | | | | |
|---|---|---|---|---|---|---|
| 0.06 | 1.22 | 0.098 | 34.25 | 0.58 | 0.029 | 4.67 |
| 9.004 | 0.12 | 100.25 | 32.77 | 18.05 | 0.072 | 0.35 |
| 0.76 | 16.73 | 3,506.345 | 0.309 | 0.336 | 0.75 | 96.85 |

**Lesson Focus** To find the quotient of a decimal divided by a decimal when an additional zero is needed

## Ideas for Getting Started

As an oral review have students give the product of each decimal below times 10, 100, or 1,000.

0.009 0.015 0.75 0.06

0.04 0.007 0.534

Then have a brief review of the procedure for dividing with a decimal divisor. Use the following problem as an example: 4.768 × 0.74. Ask students to round the answer to the nearest hundredth.

## Using Page 158

**Motivational Problem** Ask students to read the paragraph at the top of the page. "What question is asked about the motor-driven camera?" (How many pictures did it take in 9.6 s?) "What data is given that could be used to solve this problem?" (It takes a picture every 0.06s; it ran for 9.6 s.) As you discuss the plan, emphasize that we want to find out how many 0.06-second time periods there are in a total of 9.6 s. To do this we can divide 9.6 by 0.06.

**Lesson Development** "What number must we use to multiply the divisor so that it will be a whole number?" (100) "What number must we use to multiply the dividend so that the quotient will remain the same as the original problem?" (100) Point out that it is necessary to write another zero in order to show the product of the dividend times 100. Emphasize that this happens in many of the decimal division problems in this lesson.

Complete the dividing and ask a volunteer to multiply to check the answer. Then read the original problem to see if the answer makes sense.

**Other Examples** Note that in the first example two additional zeros must be written when the dividend and the divisor are multiplied by 1,000. In the second example two zeros must be written in order to complete the dividing process. Note in the third example that when the dividend and the divisor are multiplied by 100, a 3-digit divisor is produced. Students should have little difficulty dividing by a 3-digit divisor in this case.

**Warm Up** Look for errors when students fail to write the extra zeros needed. In exercise 2, three additional zeros must be written when the dividend is multiplied by 1,000.

## More Dividing by a Decimal

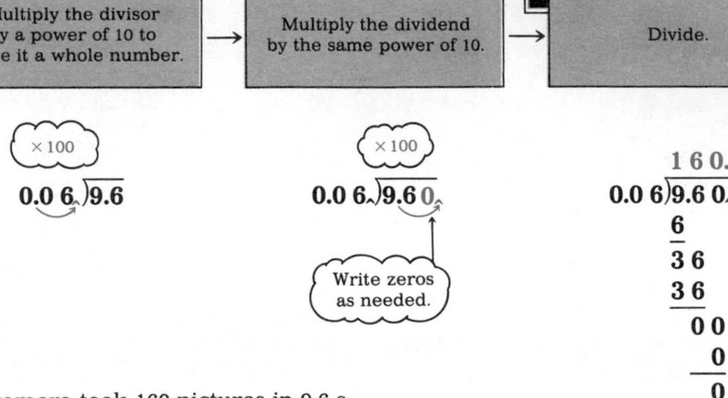

A motor-driven camera can take a picture every 0.06 second. While taking some action pictures, a photographer let the camera run for 9.6 seconds. How many pictures did it take?

Since we want to find the number of equal time periods in the total, we divide.

Multiply the divisor by a power of 10 to make it a whole number. → Multiply the dividend by the same power of 10. → Divide.

× 100: 0.0 6)9.6

× 100: 0.0 6)9.6 0 (Write zeros as needed.)

160.
0.0 6)9.6 0
6
36
36
00
0
0

The camera took 160 pictures in 9.6 s.

**Other Examples**

800.
0.0 0 3)2.4 0 0
24
0

62.5
0.0 8)5.0 0.0
48
20
16
40
40
0

2.
3.0 5)6.1 0
610
0

**Warm Up** Divide. Write zeros in the quotient as needed.

1. 0.04)8 (200)
2. 0.007)56 (8,000)
3. 0.015)0.75 (50)
4. 3.25)13 (4)
5. 0.75)31.5 (42)
6. 0.009)0.72 (80)
7. 4.5)153 (34)
8. 0.12)78 (650)

158

## Follow Up

### Reteaching

Use the examples below to review division by a decimal.

3.6)4.5 0.36)13.2 0.36)132

0.002)6,528 0.002)3,005

Work through each example with students. Discuss each in detail, and point out that each example involves a different situation in dealing with the decimal point.

### Enrichment

Have students find the missing digits in the decimal division problems below. Challenge students to create similar problems to share with their classmates.

2.6
3.4)8.8 4
68
204
204
0

3.57
0.6)2.1 4 2
18
34
30
42
42
0

| Assignment Guide | | | |
|---|---|---|---|
| | Minimum | Average | Extended |
| page 159 | 1–29, SK | 1–30, SK | 1–30, SK |

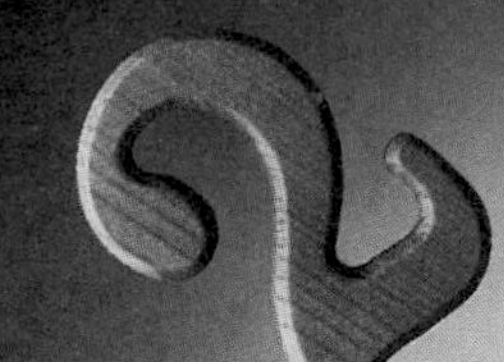

Divide. Check by multiplying.

1. 0.04)1.6 40
2. 0.007)14.7 2,100
3. 3.2)96 30
4. 0.82)12.3 15
5. 4.3)258 60
6. 3.6)18 5
7. 0.08)18.4 230
8. 0.009)27 3,000
9. 0.17)68 400
10. 8.6)1.204 0.14
11. 0.016)0.48 30
12. 0.027)1.62 60
13. 0.7)224 320
14. 0.003)5.1 1,700
15. 3.1)108.5 35
16. 0.75)6 8
17. 8.7)261 30
18. 0.08)0.0072 0.09
19. 0.008)0.0248 3.1
20. 0.83)58.1 70
21. 42 ÷ 0.06 700
22. 12 ÷ 0.005 2,400
23. 296 ÷ 3.7 80
24. 51 ÷ 0.3 170
25. 32.2 ÷ 0.46 70
26. 10.08 ÷ 0.084 120
27. Estimate, then find the result when 242 is divided by 5.5. 40; 44
28. Estimate, then find the quotient when the dividend is 99 and the divisor is 4.5. 20; 22
29. A motor-driven camera takes a picture every 0.06 s. How many pictures can it take during the 4.8 s it takes for an egg to hatch? 80
30. Tell what data is not needed. Then solve the problem. Don's camera takes 1 picture every 0.05 s. He took pictures for 3 s. A picture costs $0.85. How many pictures did Don take? Not needed: cost; 60 pictures

### Skillkeeper

Add or subtract.

1. 3.9 + 6.5 = 10.4
2. 11.4 − 5.8 = 5.6
3. $32.74 + 18.36 = $51.10
4. $50.70 − 16.85 = $33.85
5. 6.087 + 7.938 = 14.025

Multiply.

6. 67 × 10 670
7. 93 × 100 9,300
8. 6.4 × 10 64
9. 0.8 × 100 80
10. 5.32 × 1,000 5,320
11. 100 × 2.7 270
12. 0.54 × 1,000 540
13. 1,000 × 0.7 700

More Practice, page 421, Set B



## Using Page 159

**Exercises 1–26** Note that several of these exercises require that additional zeros be written. Also note that in most of these exercises the answer is a whole number rather than a decimal. Observe students' work carefully on these problems and be alert for errors associated with the dividing process and dividing by decimals.

**Exercises 27–28** In exercise 27 the first number must be rounded to the nearest ten, and the second is rounded to the nearest whole number. Encourage students to compare their estimates with the exact answer. In exercise 28 the dividend must be rounded to the nearest ten, while the divisor is rounded to the nearest whole number.

**Exercise 30** This problem includes data that is not needed in the solution of the problem. Caution students to read problems carefully and to pay close attention to the data actually needed to solve the problem.

**Skillkeeper** These skills were originally taught in Chapters 2 and 4.

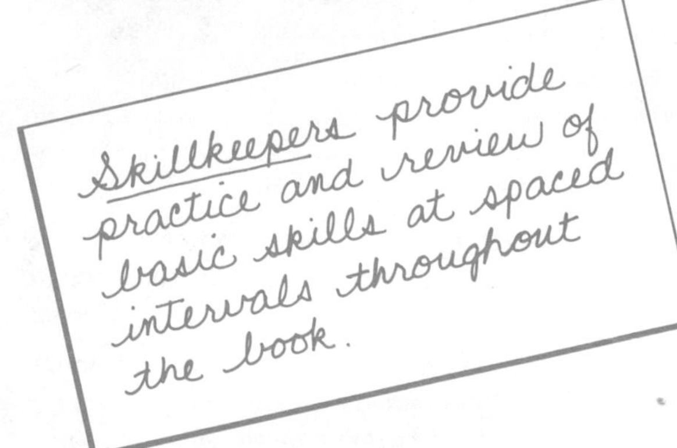

Skillkeepers provide
practice and review of
basic skills at spaced
intervals throughout
the book.


**Reteaching Supplement,** page 39

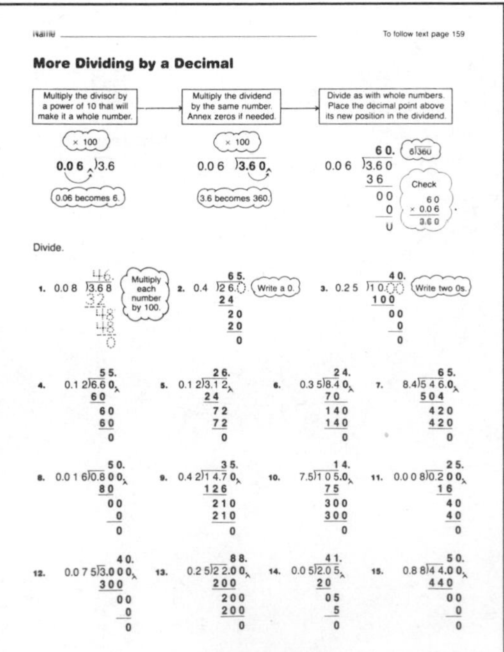

Name ______ To follow text page 159

**More Dividing by a Decimal**

Multiply the divisor by a power of 10 that will make it a whole number. → Multiply the dividend by the same number. Annex zeros if needed. → Divide as with whole numbers. Place the decimal point above its new position in the dividend.

× 100 — 0.06)3.6 — 0.06 becomes 6.
× 100 — 0.06)3.60 — 3.6 becomes 360.
0.06)3.60 = 60. (6)360) Check: 60 × 0.06 = 3.60

Divide.

1. 0.08)3.68 46. (Multiply each number by 100.)
2. 0.4)26.0 65. (Write a 0.)
3. 0.25)10.00 40. (Write two 0s.)
4. 0.12)6.60 55.
5. 0.12)3.12 26.
6. 0.35)8.40 24.
7. 8.4)546.0 65.
8. 0.016)0.800 50.
9. 0.42)14.70 35.
10. 7.5)105.0 14.
11. 0.008)0.200 25.
12. 0.075)3.000 40.
13. 0.25)22.00 88.
14. 0.05)2.05 41.
15. 0.88)44.00 50.

**Enrichment Supplement,** page 39

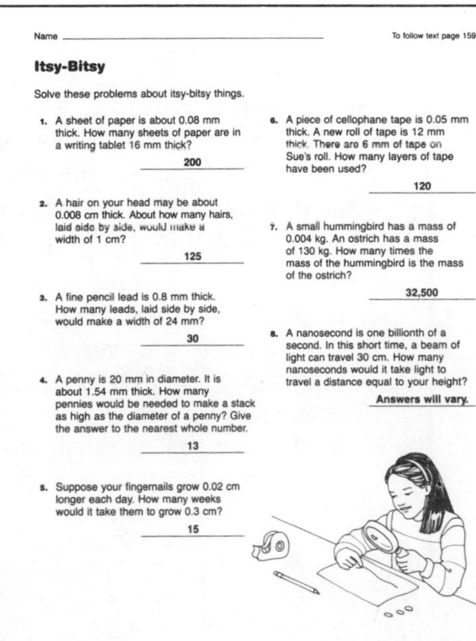

Name ______ To follow text page 159

**Itsy-Bitsy**

Solve these problems about itsy-bitsy things.

1. A sheet of paper is about 0.08 mm thick. How many sheets of paper are in a writing tablet 16 mm thick? 200
2. A hair on your head may be about 0.008 cm thick. About how many hairs, laid side by side, would make a width of 1 cm? 125
3. A fine pencil lead is 0.8 mm thick. How many leads, laid side by side, would make a width of 24 mm? 30
4. A penny is 20 mm in diameter. It is about 1.54 mm thick. How many pennies would be needed to make a stack as high as the diameter of a penny? Give the answer to the nearest whole number. 13
5. Suppose your fingernails grow 0.02 cm longer each day. How many weeks would it take them to grow 0.3 cm? 15
6. A piece of cellophane tape is 0.05 mm thick. A new roll of tape is 12 mm thick. There are 6 mm of tape on Sue's roll. How many layers of tape have been used? 120
7. A small hummingbird has a mass of 0.004 kg. An ostrich has a mass of 130 kg. How many times the mass of the hummingbird is the mass of the ostrich? 32,500
8. A nanosecond is one billionth of a second. In this short time, a beam of light can travel 30 cm. How many nanoseconds would it take light to travel a distance equal to your height? Answers will vary.

**Practice Supplement,** page 62

Name ______ To follow text page 159

**More Dividing by a Decimal**

Divide.

1. 0.04)13.60 340
2. 0.0006)4.860 810
3. 1.4)770.0 550
4. 0.8)40.0 50
5. 0.24)16.80 70
6. 0.04)36.00 900
7. 0.13)481.00 3,700
8. 0.006)0.420 70
9. 0.03)0.93 31
10. 7.2)25.92 3.6
11. 0.007)3.920 560
12. 0.21)588.00 2,800
13. 0.09)7.20 80
14. 1.6)5.12 3.2
15. 0.045)4.050 90

**Quick Review** Students work these problems on paper and use inverse operations to check their answers.

63 × 8 504   26 × 81 2,106   12 × 16 192   208 × 47 9,776   37 × 14 518

17)153 9   3)540 180   7)812 116   96)3840 40   42)714 17   28)1540 55

**Lesson Focus** To practice finding decimal products and quotients; to use a calculator to solve word problems

## Ideas for Getting Started

Duplicate the two grids shown below and let students play Greatest Product and Greatest Quotient Game described in the Think Math on page 145. Use a spinner or draw numbers from a hat or box to produce the digits. Students write the digits in the grids and then divide or multiply the decimals to decide the winner for each round. Play several rounds to review the material in this chapter. As a change of pace, have students play smallest product or smallest quotient.

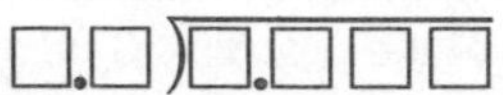

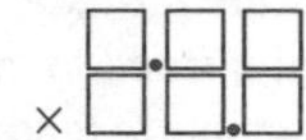

## Using Page 160

**Lesson Development** Work through examples as necessary to review decimal multiplication or division ideas that students are finding difficult.

**Exercise 9** In this exercise it is important that students decide where to start dividing. Check to be sure that they include the necessary zero following the decimal point in the quotient.

**Exercise 19** Be sure students understand that to place the decimal point correctly in this problem, they must annex zeros to make a 5-place decimal.

**Exercises 24–25** In these exercises both numbers must be rounded to the nearest whole number in order to estimate using a basic fact.

**Exercise 26** Note that this calculator problem is a multiple-step problem: two divisions and a subtraction are required.

**Think Math** This activity provides students with an opportunity to search for a pattern in a code and then decode a message. Students will discover that the lines that enclose the dots designate the category of letters and the dots within these lines indicate the location of the letters. The diagram shown below illustrates this.

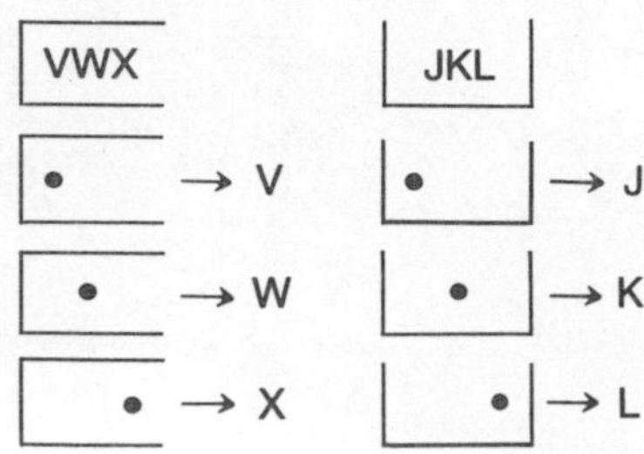


## Decimals: Mixed Practice

Multiply.

1. 7.8 × 0.3 = 2.34
2. 9.6 × 8.5 = 81.60
3. 7.59 × 3.84 = 29.1456
4. 0.057 × 35 = 1.995
5. 19.46 × 0.008 = 0.15568

Divide.

6. 7)25.2   3.6
7. 6)2.52   0.42
8. 4)15   3.75
9. 22)0.550   0.025
10. 12)1.80   0.15
11. 3.5)176.05   50.3
12. 0.84)63   75
13. 0.007)3.5   500

Multiply or divide.

14. 5.92 ÷ 8 0.74
15. 3.46 × 7 24.22
16. 0.546 ÷ 6 0.091
17. 8.75 × 4.02 35.1750
18. 0.378 ÷ 6.3 0.06
19. 9.47 × 0.005 0.04735

Divide. Round to the nearest tenth.

20. 7 ÷ 4 1.8
21. 5.2 ÷ 6 0.9

Divide. Round to the nearest hundredth.

22. 13 ÷ 8 1.63
23. 2.75 ÷ 76 0.04

24. Estimate, then find the quotient: 63.911 divided by 7.9. 8; 8.09

25. Estimate, then find the product: 9.97 times 6.08. 60; 60.6176

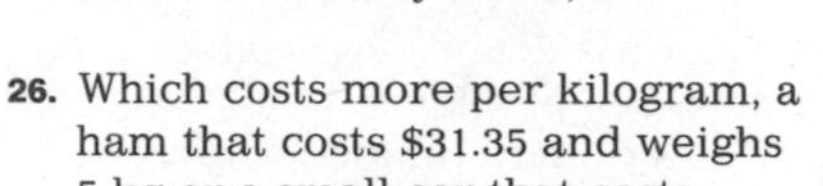

26. Which costs more per kilogram, a ham that costs $31.35 and weighs 5 kg or a small car that costs $6,492 and weighs 1,200 kg?
The ham costs $0.86 more per kilogram.

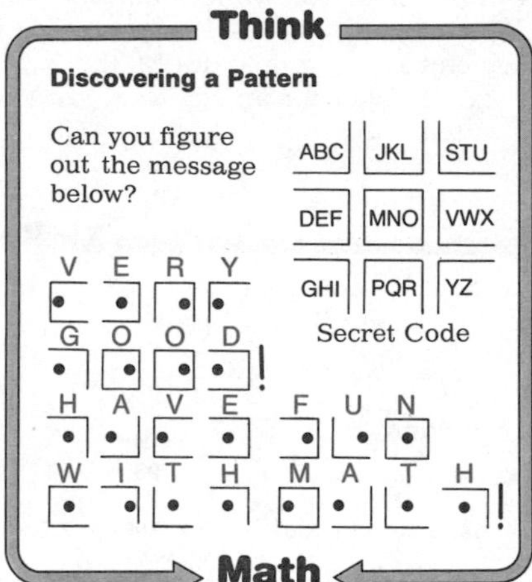

Think
Discovering a Pattern
Can you figure out the message below?
ABC JKL STU
DEF MNO VWX
GHI PQR YZ
Secret Code
VERY
GOOD!
HAVE FUN
WITH MATH!
Math




## Follow Up

### Reteaching

As students review multiplying and dividing decimals, check to make sure that they understand the concepts and are able to carry out the procedures. If further practice is indicated, present students with some of the following practice situations.

- small group or team games
- board games, allowing ample time where computation is required
- chalkboard practice
- number puzzles, allowing use of a calculator

### Enrichment

Have each student write multiplication or division word problems in which decimals are used. Let them exchange problems and solve each other's problems with a calculator.

| Assignment Guide | | | |
|---|---|---|---|
| | Minimum | Average | Extended |
| page 160 | 1–25 | 1–26 | 1–26, TM |
| page 161 | 1–6 | 1–7 | 1–8 |

## Problem Solving: Using a Calculator

Use a calculator to find **unit prices** and solve these problems. Round each calculated figure to the nearest cent.

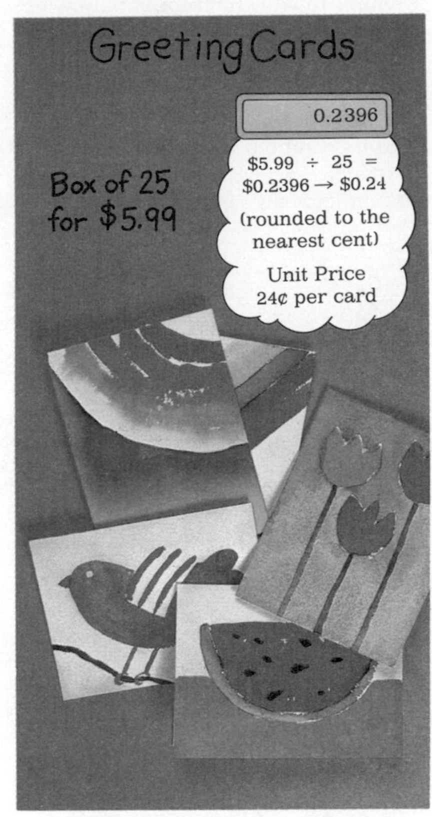

1. A box of 16 friendship cards sells for $3.60. What is the price per card? $0.23 per card
2. When you buy a package of 3 bars of soap for $1.49, you get an extra bar free. What is your cost per bar? $0.37 per bar
3. The total cost of having a magazine sent to you each week for 52 weeks is $44.75. How much more or less is this cost per copy than the newsstand cost of $1.25 per copy? $0.39 per copy
4. Which charge for developing 35-mm film is cheaper, 36 pictures for $6.49 or 24 pictures for $3.88? 24 for $3.88 is $0.02 per picture cheaper.
5. A dozen large eggs cost $0.98. A dozen medium eggs cost $0.89. How much more per egg do the larger eggs cost? $0.01 per egg
6. A sports store buys baseballs from the manufacturer for $467 a gross (144). If the store sells each ball for $4.72 how much greater is their selling price than their cost for each ball? $1.48 per ball
7. A set of 6 books on gardening costs $41.25. A single copy of each book, bought separately, costs $8.25. How much less is the cost per copy if you buy the set? $1.37 per copy
8. **Try This** For every $800 worth of goods sold, a store owner has expenses of $700. What would the owner's profit (sales minus expenses) be for sales totaling $4,000? $500



## Using Page 161

**Lesson Development** Review the 5-Point Checklist in the logo at the top of the page. Tell students that they are to use a calculator to find the answers to these problems. Discuss the idea of unit prices. Using examples, help students see that to find the price of one item they can divide the price by the number of items. Then focus on the illustration at the top of the page and work through the example. Point out that the answers are rounded to the nearest hundredth or cent.

**Try This** A possible strategy Make a Table, was taught on page 100.

**Discussion** "What question are we asked to answer about the store owner's sales?" (What would be the owner's profit if sales totaled $4,000?) "What data tells about the store owner's expenses compared to his total sales?" (For every $800 worth of sales, his expenses are $700.) "If his sales were $1,600, what would his expenses be?" ($1,400) "In this case what would his profit be?" ($1,600 − $1,400 or $200) Could we make a table to find the answer?"

**Solution** The following table shows that for sales totaling $4,000, the owner's profit is $500.

| | | | | |
|---|---|---|---|---|
| Sales | $800 | $2,400 | $3,200 | $4,000 |
| Expenses | $700 | $2,100 | $2,800 | $3,500 |
| Profit | $100 | $300 | $400 | $500 |

## Ideas That Work

### Special Education

To reinforce the idea of placing the decimal point in the quotient, let students play "Speedway" in groups of two or three.

Prepare several game mats with division problems completed except for the decimal point in the quotient. Provide a washable marker or grease pencil for each player.

| SPEEDWAY | | | |
|---|---|---|---|
| 3)13.104 → 504 | 4)38.32 → 958 | 3)0.876 → 292 | 8)56.96 → 712 |

Each player selects a game mat and places it facedown. At the signal "GO," players turn the mats over and place the missing decimal points in the quotients.

The first player to complete the quotients correctly, wins the round. A calculator or answer key can be used to check answers as needed. To play another round, players exchange mats.

### Practice Supplement, page 63

Name ______________________ To follow text page 160

**Decimals: Mixed Practice**

Multiply.

1. 64.8 × 3 = 194.4
2. 6.43 × 7 = 45.01
3. 86.27 × 0.3 = 25.881
4. 33.3 × 0.5 = 16.65
5. 0.82 × 0.17: 574, 82, 0.1394
6. 4.9 × 3.4: 196, 147, 16.66
7. 5.07 × 1.8: 4056, 507, 9.126
8. 0.552 × 2.3: 1656, 1104, 1.2696
9. 0.19 × 0.0003 = 0.000057
10. 0.1214 × 2.4: 4856, 2428, 0.29136
11. 0.075 × 0.66: 450, 450, 0.04950
12. 0.044 × 0.093: 132, 396, 0.004092

Divide.

13. 5)26.5 = 5.3
14. 6)21.0 = 3.5
15. 3)2.76 = 0.92
16. 8)14.08 = 1.76
17. 42)66.78 = 1.59: 42, 247, 210, 378, 378, 0
18. 39)1.56 = 0.04: 156, 0
19. 61)268.4 = 4.4: 244, 244, 244, 0
20. 72)40.032 = 0.556: 360, 403, 360, 432, 432, 0
21. 0.04)0.3568 = 8.92: 032, 36, 36, 08, 8, 0
22. 1.3)1.118 = 0.86: 104, 78, 78, 0
23. 0.009)0.0081 = 0.9: 81, 0
24. 0.45)85.50 = 190.: 45, 405, 405, 00

**Lesson Focus** To use logical reasoning as a strategy to solve nonroutine word problems

## Ideas for Getting Started

Ask students one or more of the following riddles. Use the riddles to emphasize the importance of reading problems carefully.

- Some months have 30 days, some 31; how many have 28? (all of them)
- A farmer has 17 cows. All but 6 died. How many does the farmer have left. (6)
- Take 2 apples from 3 apples and what do you have? (You have 2 apples.)
- Divide 30 by one half. What's the answer? (60)
- How much dirt can we remove from a hole that is 3 m deep, 2 m wide, and 10 m long? (You cannot take dirt from a hole.)
- If you went to bed at 8 P.M. and set the alarm for 9 in the morning, how many hours of sleep would you get? (One hour; the alarm would go off at 9 P.M.)

## Using Page 162

**Motivational Problem** Encourage students to read the Try This problem carefully. "What question is asked about the favorite sports?" (Which sport is Carla's favorite?) Emphasize that it is important to read carefully to understand all of the data given in the problem and to reread if necessary. "How many people are involved?" (4) "What are the favorite sports?" (soccer, tennis, bowling, softball) "What do we know about the people's favorite sports?" (Each has a different favorite sport.)

**Lesson Development** On the chalkboard draw a chart like the one shown, omitting the "yes's" and "no's." Work with students to fill in the chart. "Can Carla's favorite sport be tennis?" (No, her best friend's favorite is tennis.) Mark "no" in the chart in the tennis column in Carla's row. "Can softball be the favorite sport of Fran or Ron?" (No, they do not like softball.) Mark a "no" in the appropriate boxes. "What is José's favorite sport?" (bowling) Mark "yes" in José's row in the bowling column. "Can Ron's favorite sport be soccer?" (No, Ron does not like soccer anymore.) Mark a "no" in Ron's row in the soccer column. "Can you fill in any of the other columns from what you know so far?" Continue helping students draw conclusions from the chart until they can answer the question in the problem.

**Exercises 1–2** Help students set up tables and give appropriate hints as students record the information from the problem.

QUESTION / DATA / PLAN / ANSWER / CHECK

## Problem Solving: Use Logical Reasoning

Solving some problems involves more than simply deciding whether to add, subtract, multiply, or divide. To solve such problems, we may use a strategy called

**Use Logical Reasoning**

A chart can help you keep a record of what you know. It can help you reason logically.

First, I'll write what I know in a chart.

| | Soccer | Tennis | Bowling | Softball |
|---|---|---|---|---|
| Carla | | no | | |
| José | | | yes | |
| Fran | | | | no |
| Ron | no | | | no |

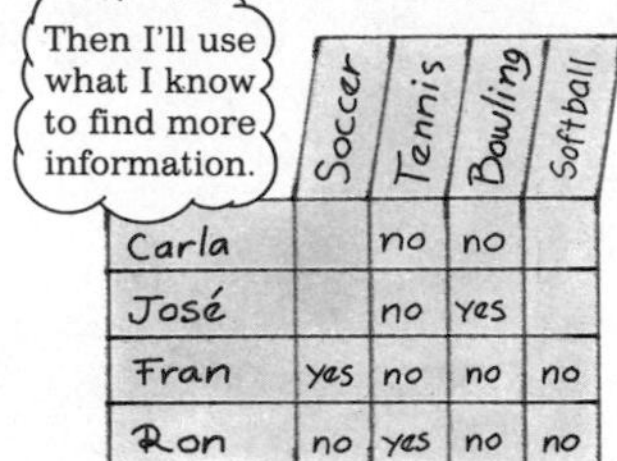

Then I'll use what I know to find more information.

| | Soccer | Tennis | Bowling | Softball |
|---|---|---|---|---|
| Carla | | no | no | |
| José | | no | yes | |
| Fran | yes | no | no | no |
| Ron | no | yes | no | no |

Hmm . . . Now I know that Carla likes softball!

| | Soccer | Tennis | Bowling | Softball |
|---|---|---|---|---|
| Carla | | no | no | yes |
| Jose | | no | yes | |
| Fran | yes | no | no | no |
| Ron | no | yes | no | no |

**Try This** Carla, José, Fran, and Ron each have different favorite sports: soccer, tennis, bowling, and softball. The favorite sport of Carla's best friend in the group is tennis. Fran and Ron do not like softball. José's favorite sport is bowling. Ron used to like soccer but no longer does. Which sport is Carla's favorite?

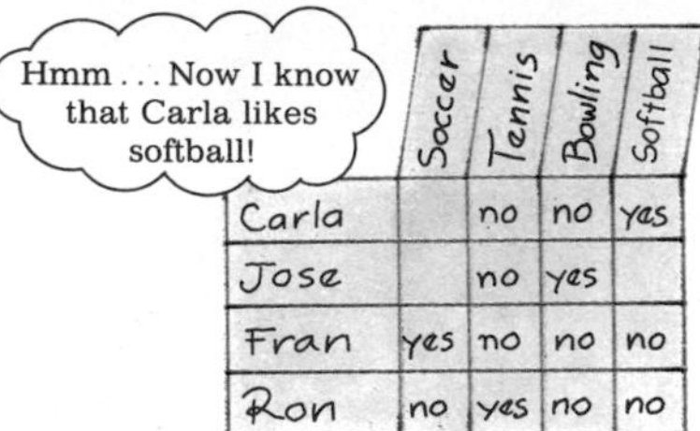

Solve.

1. Four turtles—Lightning, Swifty, Flash, and Rocket—came in first, second, third, and fourth (not in that order) in a race. Lightning was second and Swifty was not fourth. If Flash was third, where did Rocket finish? fourth

2. Beverly, Ralph, and Ginny each wore a blue, red, or green T-shirt with Benton, Ridgeville, or Georgetown on it. No two shirts had the same color or school name. No person's shirt had a color or school name with the same first letter as the person's name. Ginny wore a blue Ridgeville shirt. What shirts did Beverly and Ralph wear?
Beverly: red Georgetown; Ralph: green Benton

162

## Strategy Test Item

**Optional Problem** If you wish to assess students' ability to apply the strategy called Logical Reasoning introduced in this chapter, provide them with the problem below.

> Lewis, Mary, Chuck, and Mickey love music. One loves rock and roll. One loves jazz. One loves country-western, and one loves classical music. Lewis's best friend loves country-western. Chuck and Mickey never really liked jazz. Mary loves rock and roll. Mickey did love classical music but does not anymore. Which type of music does each person love?

**Solution** Mary loves rock and roll; Lewis loves jazz; Mickey loves country western; and Chuck loves classical music.

## Chapter Review-Test

Estimate the product or quotient by rounding so that you can use a basic fact.

1. 6.3 × 7.8 — 48
2. 5.91 × 3.2 — 18
3. 9.43 × 7.59 — 72
4. 5)39.6 — 8
5. 7.47)63.26 — 9

Multiply.

6. 7.6 × 2.8 — 21.28
7. 8.5 × 0.7 — 5.95
8. 28.3 × 7 — 198.1
9. 0.64 × 9 — 5.76
10. 5.03 × 2.75 — 13.8325
11. 0.14 × 0.6 — 0.084
12. 0.0041 × 0.02 — 0.000082
13. 0.0012 × 13 — 0.0156
14. 76.3 × 1.07 — 81.641
15. 8.63 × 0.009 — 0.07767
16. 3.56 × 10 35.6
17. 0.472 × 100 47.2
18. 5.743 × 1,000 5,743

Divide. Check by multiplying.

19. 5)12.80 — 2.56
20. 8)25.6 — 3.2
21. 37)155.03 — 4.19
22. 23)16.1 — 0.7

Divide. Round the quotient to the place named.

23. 1.6 ÷ 3 (nearest tenth) 0.5
24. 2 ÷ 7 (nearest hundredth) 0.29
25. 32.3 ÷ 97 (nearest thousandth) 0.333
26. $2.47 ÷ 9 (nearest cent) $0.27

Divide.

27. 4.7 ÷ 10 0.47
28. 56.3 ÷ 100 0.563
29. 2.78 ÷ 100 0.0278
30. 748 ÷ 1,000 0.748
31. 3.4)20.4 — 6
32. 0.03)0.174 — 5.8
33. 0.009)0.72 — 80
34. 0.34)18.7 — 55

Solve.

35. One of the first land speed records was 63.15 km/h. A more recent record is 15.86 times as fast. How fast is the more recent record? 1,001.5590 km/h
36. Which is a better buy, 4 batteries in a package for $2.88 or 2 batteries in a package for $1.38? What is the difference in the price per battery? 2 batteries for $1.38 is $0.03 per battery cheaper.



## Using Page 163

The exercises in the Chapter Review-Test emphasize the major concepts and skills presented in this chapter. These exercises may be used as a review assignment or as a test, depending on your needs.

**Item Analysis** The table below correlates the Chapter Review-Test items with objectives and with the student text pages on which the concepts or skills were taught.

| Items | Objectives | Related text pages |
|---|---|---|
| 6.1 | 1–5 | 138–139 |
| 6.2 | 6–18 | 140–145 |
| 6.3 | 19–30 | 148–153 |
| 6.4 | 31–34 | 156–160 |
| 6.5 | 35–36 | 146–147, 154–155, 161 |

## Assessment Options

If you use the Chapter Review-Test as a review assignment, you may wish to use the multiple-choice test or the free-response test to evaluate mastery of the chapter objectives. The items on these tests have a one-to-one correspondence in terms of content and level of difficulty. A correlation of test items to objectives and student text pages is provided in the Management Guide for Chapter 6.

**Multiple-Choice Test,** TRB pages 16–17

**Free-Response Test,** TRB pages 59–60

## TRB Options

The following blackline masters are available for use with this chapter. If you have not already assigned these materials, you may wish to use them to close the chapter.

**Recreation,** TRB page 156

**Consumer Applications,** TRB page 174

**Calculator Technology,** TRB page 192

**Reading Math,** TRB page 224

**Family Involvement,** TRB pages 247–248

## Using Page 164

The exercises on this page are intended for those students who experienced difficulty with the chapter review test on page 163. Should students require reteaching of these concepts and skills please refer to the teaching notes below. Otherwise Another Look exercises can be assigned as independent work with students using the accompanying sample problems and hints as guides.

**Exercises 1–10** These skills were originally taught on pages 144 and 152. Tell students that the first box at the top left gives rules for multiplying or dividing decimals by 10, 100, and 1,000. Write a decimal such as 3.4572 on the chalkboard and move the decimal point as described to multiply the decimal by 10, 100, and 1,000. Then write another decimal such as 723.56 and move the decimal point as described to divide by 10, 100, and 1,000.

**Exercises 11–16** This skill was originally taught on pages 140–143. Work through the example in the second box. Have students multiply as with whole numbers. Then point out that the first decimal is a 2-place decimal; the second decimal a 1-place decimal. Review the rule that the number of decimals in the product is the sum of the places in the two factors. Verify this by rounding each of the factors to the nearest whole number and multiplying to see that the answer should be close to 24.

**Exercises 17–24** This skill was originally taught on pages 156–159. Work through the example in the bottom left box. Remind students that the goal is to redefine the division problem so that it has the same quotient as the original problem but a divisor that is a whole number. Review the idea that we can do this by multiplying both the dividend and the divisor by 10, 100, or 1,000. After students complete the dividing process, have them multiply to check their answers.

## *Another Look*

| To multiply by | move the decimal point |
|---|---|
| 10 | 1 place right. |
| 100 | 2 places right. |
| 1,000 | 3 places right. |

| To divide by | move the decimal point |
|---|---|
| 10 | 1 place left. |
| 100 | 2 places left. |
| 1,000 | 3 places left. |

**Find the product or quotient.**

1. 3.46 × 100 — 346
2. 4.89 ÷ 10 — 0.489
3. 8.347 × 1,000 — 8,347
4. 100 × 0.46 — 46
5. 93.3 ÷ 1,000 — 0.0933
6. 0.472 × 1,000 — 472
7. 0.56 × 10 — 5.6
8. 9.42 × 100 — 942
9. 43.8 ÷ 1,000 — 0.0438
10. 6.9 × 100 — 690

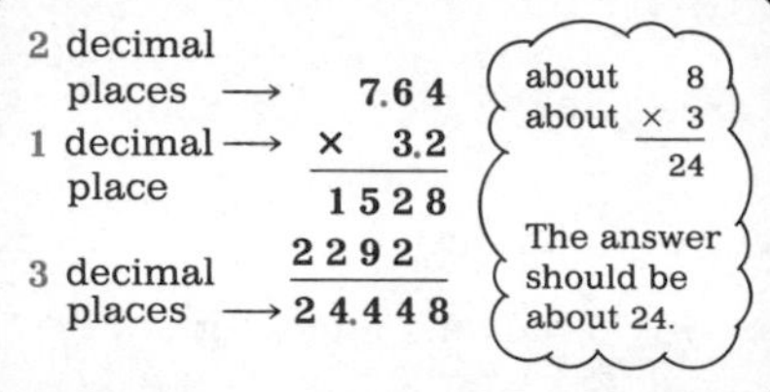


**Multiply.**

11. 2.9 × 0.6 — 1.74
12. 3.8 × 0.06 — 0.228
13. 7.5 × 3.8 — 28.50
14. 2.76 × 0.08 — 0.2208
15. 0.478 × 0.016 — 0.007648
16. 24.95 × 423 — 10,553.85

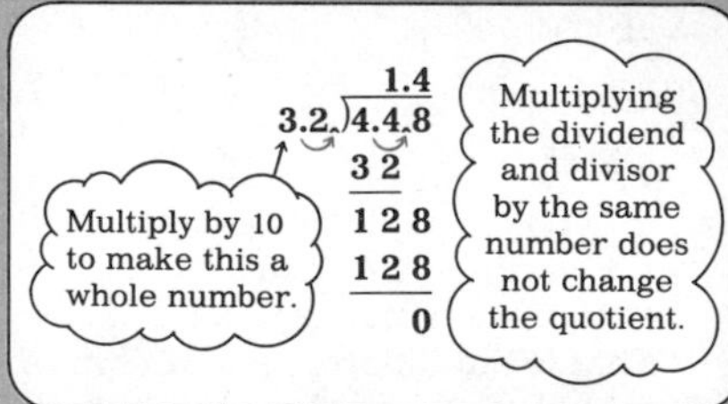


**Divide. Check by multiplying.**

17. 8)25.6 — 3.2
18. 4)260.4 — 65.1
19. 7)4.28 — 0.61
20. 4.8)14.4 — 3
21. 0.6)2.1 — 3.5
22. 0.59)0.7729 — 1.31
23. 0.07)0.0406 — 0.58
24. 0.014)0.9436 — 67.4



## Just for Teachers

### Math Language

In antiquity, numbers were often used in operations which to our modern definition were not arithmetical in nature. Our word *arithmetic* comes from the Greek *arithmetike,* and in ancient times this branch of knowledge included much supersitition as well as precision. The Pythagorean Brotherhood in the sixth century B.C. believed that both numbers and geometric shapes were endowed with certain powers and qualities. Mathematical historians believe the Brotherhood may have been influenced by the Asian number lore that trade brought to the Mediterranean. However, historians are not in agreement as to the date of this early Chinese treatise, which classified odd numbers as male and even numbers as female. *The Book of Permutations,* for example, provided possibly the first example of a Magic Square, a 3 by 3 or 4 by 4 layout of numbers in which all rows, horizontal, vertical, and diagonal, total the same number. In addition, qualities such as reason, justice, and potency were associated with certain numbers. Other numbers, and various shapes, were thought to hold the secrets of perfection, fire, love, and health. There were perfect numbers and amicable numbers, as well.

When the Greeks and the Hebrews devised numeric systems using letters of their alphabets to stand for various numbers, another superstitious practice began, *gematria.* Gematria was the process of adding up the values of the letters in a name or a word.

## Enrichment

**Number Relationships**

The table shows the numbers 1 through 100. Read the descriptions of the special kinds of numbers and answer the questions below.

| 1 | 2 | 3 | 4 | 5 | 6 | 7 | 8 | 9 | 10 |
|---|---|---|---|---|---|---|---|---|---|
| 11 | 12 | 13 | 14 | 15 | 16 | 17 | 18 | 19 | 20 |
| 21 | 22 | 23 | 24 | 25 | 26 | 27 | 28 | 29 | 30 |
| 31 | 32 | 33 | 34 | 35 | 36 | 37 | 38 | 39 | 40 |
| 41 | 42 | 43 | 44 | 45 | 46 | 47 | 48 | 49 | 50 |
| 51 | 52 | 53 | 54 | 55 | 56 | 57 | 58 | 59 | 60 |
| 61 | 62 | 63 | 64 | 65 | 66 | 67 | 68 | 69 | 70 |
| 71 | 72 | 73 | 74 | 75 | 76 | 77 | 78 | 79 | 80 |
| 81 | 82 | 83 | 84 | 85 | 86 | 87 | 88 | 89 | 90 |
| 91 | 92 | 93 | 94 | 95 | 96 | 97 | 98 | 99 | 100 |

A **prime number** has exactly 2 different factors—the number itself and 1. All other whole numbers (except 0 and 1) are **composite.**

An **even** number is a multiple of 2. An **odd** number is 1 more or 1 less than an even number.

A **twin prime** is one of a pair of prime numbers whose difference is 2 (like 17 or 19).

A prime number that produces another prime number when its digits are reversed (like 13) is sometimes called **a reversal prime.**

If all the factors of a number (except the number itself) add up to the number, the number is called **perfect**.

1. How many even numbers are in the table? How many odd numbers? 50; 50
2. How many prime numbers are in the table? How many composite? 25; 74
3. How many reversal primes can you find? List them. 8 (13, 17, 31, 37, 71, 73, 79, 97)
4. How many even primes are there? 1 (2)
5. How many pairs of twin primes can you find? List them. 8 (3,5; 5,7; 11,13; 17,19; 29,31; 41,43; 59,61; 71,73)
6. There are only 2 perfect numbers in the table. One is less than 10. The other is between 25 and 30. Can you find them? 6; 28



## Using Page 165

This page is intended for those students who successfully completed the chapter review test on page 163. You may wish to assign this page as independent work while you use Another Look exercises to reteach the basic concepts and skills of the chapter. Or, you may decide that all students would benefit from exposure to this Enrichment activity.

**Lesson Development** Call students' attention to the table of numbers at the top of the page. Consider in turn each of the definitions given and ask students to give examples of the numbers described. Make sure students understand these concepts before assigning the exercises.

**Exercise 1** Students will immediately recognize that every other number is even. They may also recognize that the columns of numbers alternate odd and even.

**Exercise 4** Ask students why there are no even primes other than 2. (Any other even prime would be divisible by 2. A prime number has exactly two different factors—the number itself and 1.)

**Exercise 6** Point out that the next perfect number is 496, then 8,128. They might also be interested to know that all known perfect numbers are even. If there is an odd perfect number, mathematicians know that it is greater than $10^{25}$. To extend this lesson, discuss deficient numbers (numbers in which the sum of its factors, except the number itself, add up to less than the number) and abundant numbers (numbers in which the sum of its factors, except the number itself, add up to more than the number).

Good and bad omens, political and religious implications, the fortunes of an individual or a people were divined from the particular number value which resulted. For example, the letters of the name Achilles added up to 1,276, and those in the name Hector only 1,225. To the Greeks, this was positive evidence of the superiority of the Greek hero over the Trojan hero.

# Review

## Using Page 166

The exercises on this page provide practice for maintaining cumulative skills. The emphasis in this Cumulative Review is on decimal place value (Chapter 3), addition and subtraction of decimals (Chapter 3), division of whole numbers (Chapter 5), and problem solving (Chapter 5).

**Item Analysis** The table below correlates the Cumulative Review items with objectives and with the student book pages on which the concepts or skills were taught.

| Items | Objectives | Related text pages |
|---|---|---|
| 1–2 | 3.1 | 54–59 |
| 3 | 3.2 | 60–62 |
| 4–8 | 3.3 | 64–68, 70 |
| 9–10 | 5.2 | 112–117 |
| 11–12 | 5.4 | 120–124, 126–129 |
| 13–14 | 5.5 | 111, 119, 125, 130–131 |

## *Cumulative Review*

1. What is the place value of 5 in 27,361.752?
   A 5 tens  B 5 tenths
   (C) 5 hundredths  D not given

2. Which symbol (>, <, or =) goes in the ● ?
   7.468 ● 7.668
   A >  (B) <  C =

3. Round 5.782 to the nearest tenth.
   A 5.7  B 5.79
   C 6  (D) not given

Add, subtract, or divide. Watch the signs.

4. 3.45 + 6.29
   (A) 9.74
   B 97.4
   C 974
   D not given

5. 5.266 − 4.197
   A 9.463
   B 1.299
   (C) 1.069
   D not given

6. 56.905 + 47.098
   A 93.993
   (B) 104.003
   C 103.903
   D not given

7. 7.013 + 8.99
   (A) 16.003
   B 15.903
   C 90.613
   D not given

8. 0.942 − 0.16
   (A) 0.782
   B 0.926
   C 0.958
   D not given

9. 7)328
   A 46
   B 47
   C 46 R2
   (D) not given

10. 4)2,224
    A 456
    (B) 556
    C 565
    D not given

11. 15)375
    (A) 25
    B 15
    C 31
    D not given

12. 23)4,762
    A 206 R22
    B 207 R9
    C 207
    (D) not given

13. Jeff has 7.9 m of wire fence. If he needs 12 m of fence, how much more does he need?
    (A) 4.1  B 4.9
    C 3.9  D not given

14. A fruit packer has 3,060 apples. If 36 apples are put in each box, how many boxes are needed?
    A 100  (B) 85
    C 60  D not given

## Objectives

**7.1** Express units of length in equivalent metric units using meters, centimeters, millimeters, and kilometers.

**7.2** Choose appropriate metric units of capacity and express in larger or smaller units.

**7.3** Choose appropriate metric units of weight and express in larger or smaller units.

**7.4** Estimate and measure temperatures using degrees Celsius.

**7.5** Express time in larger or smaller units, and add and subtract units of time.

**7.6** Solve word problems using the 5-Point Checklist and cumulative computational skills.

## Summary

In this chapter students review and extend their understanding of the basic metric units for measuring length, capacity, weight, and temperature. They learn techniques for changing from one metric unit to another by multiplying or by dividing. Throughout the chapter they practice using decimals to represent these measures. A study of the measurement of time includes clocks, calendars, and time zones. Units of time are added and subtracted, and the concepts of earlier and later are developed.

An important aspect of the chapter is the role of estimation in helping students get a feel for the size of units. Throughout the chapter students solve problems involving metric measurements.

## Mathematical Background

**Length** Most of the nations of the world use the standard system of measurement called the Système International (SI). The units of length in the metric system that are commonly used are shown in the table below.

| Unit | Relation to Basic Unit |
|---|---|
| Kilometer (km)* | 1,000 meters |
| Hectometer (hm) | 100 meters |
| Dekameter (dam) | 10 meters |
| Meter (m)* | Basic Unit |
| Decimeter (dm) | 0.1 meter |
| Centimeter (cm)* | 0.01 meter |
| Millimeter (mm)* | 0.001 meter |

The asterisks show the units most often used in our non-scientific society and the ones given greatest emphasis in this chapter. The prefixes of each length unit have been underlined. In the metric system the prefixes indicating a certain multiple of the basic units are used for all of the units of measure.

It is often useful to be able to express a measurement given in one unit as another unit. In the table below, students can see the relationships between the units in the metric system.

| km | hm | dam | m | dm | cm | mm |
|---|---|---|---|---|---|---|
| | 2 | 3 | 8. | 6 | 5 | 2 |
| | 2 | 3 | 8 | 6 | 5. | 2 |

Each metric unit shown is 10 times the length of the unit to its right, illustrating how well the metric units work with the decimal system. Note in the table shown, the top number gives a measurement in meters because the decimal point on the bar is to the right of the meter. The bottom number gives the same measurement in centimeters because the decimal point has been moved on the bar to the right of the centimeter unit. By moving the decimal point in a chart like this, any metric unit shown in the table can be converted to any other metric unit in the table. The movement of the decimal point essentially amounts to multiplying or dividing a number by 10 or by a multiple of 10.

**Capacity and Weight** The basic unit of capacity (liter) is the amount of water held in an open-top cube 1 decimeter on a side. Since it takes 1,000 cubic centimeters to fill a 1-dm cube, the capacity of a 1-cm cube is one thousandth of a liter, or 1 milliliter.

The *mass* of an object is the same whether it is on the earth or on the moon, since it will balance with the standard unit in both places. The *weight* of an object, however, changes depending on where the object is located. An object on the earth might pull a spring scale down to 36, while the same object on the moon would pull the spring scale down to only 6. The difference between mass and weight is important for scientific purposes, but it does not significantly affect practical everyday measurement on earth. Throughout this program we will use the term *weight* when discussing the basic metric units of gram and kilogram.

**Temperature and Time** The metric unit for measuring temperature is the degree Celsius (°C). Water freezes at 0°C and boils at 100°C. Normal room temperature is around 20°C and normal body temperature is around 37°C. Students can develop skills in estimating temperatures by thinking in terms of categories rather than exact temperatures. For example, is hot soup (a) over 100°, (b) between 50° and 100°, between 0° and 50°, or below 0°? Broad estimations such as these can help students develop an understanding of the Celsius unit.

Note that the standard units of time are the same in both the English and metric systems. Students at this level use an understanding of these units to combine or subtract times and learn to trade for larger or smaller units when performing these operations.

**Problem Solving** Most of the problem-solving lessons in this chapter are applications of the basic ideas of measurement. Units of length are the focus on pages 176–177, Using Data from a Reference Book. On page 179, students use the idea of capacity to solve problems. On page 181, students solve problems involving weight. On page 187 students use mental math to determine times that are earlier or later than a given time. The problem-solving strategy in this chapter, Work Backward, is introduced on page 188.

### Vocabulary

| | | |
|---|---|---|
| meter | hectometer | gram |
| decimeter | dekameter | milligram |
| centimeter | liter | kilogram |
| millimeter | milliliter | degree Celsius |
| kilometer | kiloliter | |

## Error Analysis

In Chapter 7 students review and extend the study of the measurement in metric units. Much of the computation found in the chapter involves the use of decimals, since the units of the metric system are related by multiples of 10. Changing from one unit to another thus involves multiplying or dividing decimals. Because decimal work involves an understanding of place value, this skill is also important for success in the study of metric measurement.

**Error Pattern 1**

5 mm = <u>50</u> cm 12 dm = <u>120</u> m
18 dam = <u>180</u> km 13 cm = <u>130</u> dm

**Diagnosis** The student has multiplied to change a smaller unit to a larger one. The student seems to realize the relationship of the metric system to the base-10, or decimal system, but has not yet mastered the relative sizes of the units.

**Remediation** Use a meter stick or centimeter ruler to review the size of each unit. Display a chart such as the one shown below to reinforce the progression of the units.

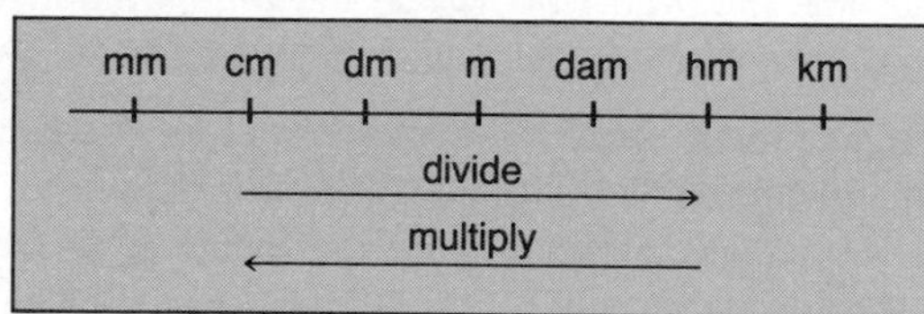


Next use play money—pennies, dimes, and dollars—to focus on the process of changing from smaller units to larger units and vice versa. Emphasize that if pennies are grouped into dimes, there will be fewer dimes than pennies, and thus to find the number of larger units, we would divide, not multiply. In relating this idea to millimeters and centimeters, emphasize that because the centimeter is a larger unit, there would be fewer centimeters than millimeters. Stress that in going from a smaller unit to a larger unit, we would divide; in going from a larger unit to a smaller unit, we multiply.

**Error Pattern 2**

```
  3 h 35 min            8 h  4 min                9 m 40 s
+ 6 h 50 min          + 9 h 32 min              - 6 m 47 s
  9 h 50 min = 14 h    17 h 36 min = 20 h 3 min   2 m 33 s
```

**Diagnosis** In adding and subtracting units of time, the student has traded groups of ten instead of groups of 60. The student has confused addition and subtraction of whole numbers with addition and subtraction of units of time.

**Remediation** Briefly remind students of the process involved in trading groups of ones, tens, hundreds, and so on. Then discuss the basic units of time—hour, minute, and second. Use questions such as: "How many hours in 120 minutes? How many seconds in 5 minutes?" and so on. Relate the addition and subtraction of whole numbers to the addition and subtraction of units of time. Work through the examples above, and point out the units that are being traded in each case.

## Problem Solving

### Evaluating Problem-Solving Performance—Part 2

A complete and accurate evaluation of students' problem-solving performances cannot be achieved if evaluation techniques are limited to the point system described in the Teaching Tips for Chapter 4. Many of the goals in teaching problem solving involve students' attitudes toward problem solving and their methods of understanding problems, choosing and implementing solution strategies, and checking solutions. Goals like these cannot be accurately assessed only by examining students' written work for problems.

While students are involved in solving problems, observe and question them about their work. Informal evaluative comments can be made directly to them at that time, or observations can be recorded and shared later, at a parent or child conference, for example. Here is a checklist that can be used to summarize and report your observations.

**Problem-Solving Observation Checklist**

Name ______________________ Date __________

| | Always | Sometimes | Never |
|---|---|---|---|
| shows a willingness to try | ____ | ____ | ____ |
| demonstrates self-confidence | ____ | ____ | ____ |
| approaches problems systematically (question–data–plan–answer–check) | ____ | ____ | ____ |
| selects appropriate solution strategies | ____ | ____ | ____ |
| tries different strategies when stuck | ____ | ____ | ____ |

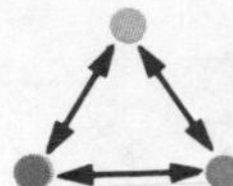

## Special Education

In this chapter, students are given an opportunity to practice earlier measurement skills, while extending skills in estimation, changing metric units, and problem solving. The materials in this chapter and the related classroom activities provide the special-needs student with daily living skills in measurement.

### Using a Metric Place-Value Chart

The introduction and development of the names and values of the metric unit prefixes is aided by having a chart, as shown below, at the front of the room. The chart can help students learn the metric units, and the appropriate conversions between the units.

| kilo- | hecto- | deka- | base unit | deci- | centi- | milli- |
|---|---|---|---|---|---|---|
| 1,000 | 100 | 10 | 1 | 0.1 | 0.01 | 0.001 |
| | | | | | | |

### Using Mental Estimation

Have students close their eyes and think of objects having specific dimensions. Have estimating contests where students observe but do not touch objects, and then suggest the appropriate measures. These activities can be accompanied by activities in which students guess, write their estimates, and then measure to find the actual measure.

### Converting Metric Measures

The place-value chart discussed above can be used to convert from one metric measurement to another as follows:

- The given measurement is placed on the chart with the decimal point on the bar at the right of the appropriate box.
- The metric unit the measurement is to be converted to is then determined and the place-value position of the new metric unit is located on the chart. In the example in the chart below, 34.1 cm is to be changed to millimeters.
- The decimal point is moved to the bar at the right of the appropriate place-value box.
- The measurement in the new unit is read from the box using the new unit name and the new decimal point position. In the chart, the measurement is 341 mm.

| | km | hm | dam | meter | dm | cm | mm |
|---|---|---|---|---|---|---|---|
| 34.1 cm | | | | | 3 | 4 • | 1 |

↓

| | km | hm | dam | meter | dm | cm | mm |
|---|---|---|---|---|---|---|---|
| 341 mm | | | | | 3 | 4 | 1 • |

This procedure works because each of the units is 10 times greater than the one to the right and $\frac{1}{10}$ of the unit to the left. Moving the decimal point from left to right multiplies the value by 10 for each box and divides the value by 10 for each box in going from right to left. This approach, combined with the estimation of whether the answer should be larger or smaller, can help the special-needs student with conversions of metric measurement.

### Operating With Time

The development of skills in adding and subtracting units of time can be difficult for the special student. The work done with operations in base-10 may cause problems as students learn to deal in minutes, hours, and days, or units of 60 or 24. These difficulties can be overcome by the use of clock faces for trading as shown below. One day can be traded for two 12-hour clock faces. One hour can be traded for 60 minutes. The use of these materials, just as with base-10 blocks for whole number operations, can help students make the transition to computing in these units.

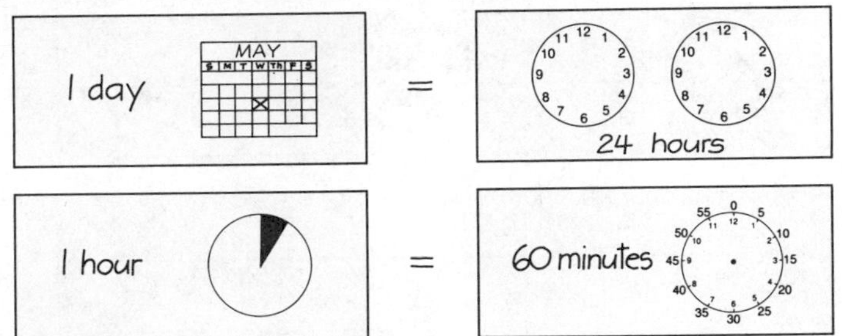

## Subject Integration

Subject matter related to other areas of the curriculum has been integrated into the following lessons. This provides an opportunity to highlight the interaction between mathematics and other subjects.

**Fine Arts** Building a birdhouse, pages 174–175

**Science** Tide pools, page 168; measurement records, pages 176–177

**Consumer Awareness** Comparing quantities, page 181

# Management Guide

| Teaching Chapter 7 | | | | Meeting Individual Needs | | | | | |
|---|---|---|---|---|---|---|---|---|---|
| **Objectives** | **Chapter Content** | **Pages** | **TRB Test Items** | **Lesson Assignments** | | | **Follow Up** | | |
| | | | | Minimum | Average | Extended | Reteaching | Enrichment | Practice |
| | Chapter Opener | 167 | | | | | | | |
| **7.1** Express units of length in equivalent metric units using meters, centimeters, millimeters, and kilometers. | Length: Metric Units | 168–169 | 1–16, 20–21 | 1–31 | 1–32 | 1–32, TM | SE5 Ch 8 | | PS 64 |
| | More About Length | 170 | | 1–13 | 1–14 | 1–14 | SE5 Ch 8 | | PS 65 |
| | Estimating with Metric Units | 171 | | 1–8 | 1–9 | 1–9 | SE5 Ch 8 | | |
| | Metric Units and Decimals | 172–173 | | 1–23 | 1–24 | 1–24 | RS 40 | ES 40 | PS 66 |
| | Changing Metric Units by Multiplying | 174 | | 1–15 | 1–15 | 1–15 | | | |
| | Changing Metric Units by Dividing | 175 | | 1–15 | 1–15 | 1–15 | RS 41 | ES 41 | PS 67 |
| **7.2** Choose appropriate metric units of capacity and express in larger or smaller units. | Volume and Capacity | 178 | 17, 19 22–23 | 1–14 | 1–14 | 1–14 | SE5 Ch 8 RS 42 | ES 42 | PS 69 |
| **7.3** Choose appropriate metric units of weight and express in larger or smaller units. | Weight | 180 | 18, 24–25 | 1–19 | 1–19 | 1–21 | SE5 Ch 8 | | PS 70 |
| **7.4** Estimate and measure temperatures using degrees Celsius. | Temperature | 182–183 | 26–28 | 1–14 / 1–7, SK | 1–14 / 1–8, SK | 1–14 / 1–9, SK | SE5 Ch 8 RS 43 | ES 43 | PS 71 |
| **7.5** Express time in larger or smaller units, and add and subtract units of time. | Time: Basic Units | 184 | 29–32 | 1–15 | 1–15 | 1–15 | | | |
| | Adding and Subtracting Time | 185 | 33–35 | 1–12 | 1–12 | 1–12, TM | RS 44 | ES 44 | PS 72 |
| | Time Zones | 186 | | | 1–6 | 1–7 | | | PS 73 |
| **7.6** Solve word problems using the 5-Point Checklist and cumulative computational skills. | Problem Solving: Using Data from a Record Book | 176–177 | 36–40 | 1–8 | 1–9 | 1–10 | | | PS 68 |
| | Problem Solving: Practice (capacity) | 179 | | 1–8 | 1–9 | 1–10 | | | |
| | Problem Solving: Practice (weight) | 181 | | 1–7 | 1–8 | 1–9 | | | |
| | Problem Solving: Using Mental Math | 187 | | 1–6 | 1–7 | 1–8 | | | |
| | Problem Solving: Work Backward | 188 | | | | | | | |
| | Chapter Review-Test | 189 | | | | | | | |
| | Another Look/Enrichment | 190–191 | | | | | | | |
| | Cumulative Review | 192 | | | | | | | |

**SE5** Student Edition, Book 5
**RS** Reteaching Supplement
**ES** Enrichment Supplement
**PS** Practice Supplement
**TM** Think Math
**SK** Skillkeeper
**TRB** Teacher's Resource Book

## Masters for Use

**. . . before Chapter 7**

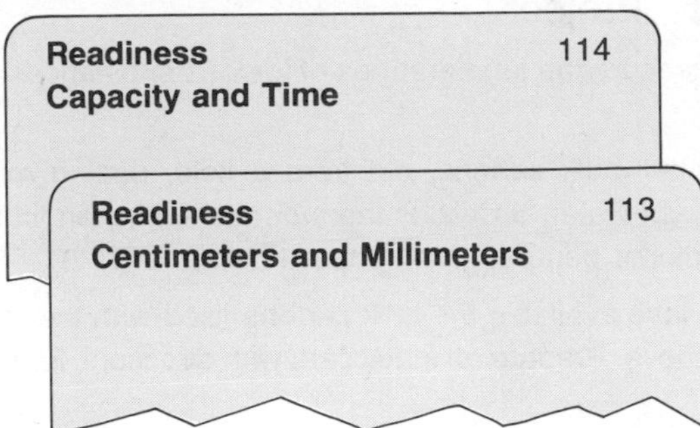


**. . . during Chapter 7**

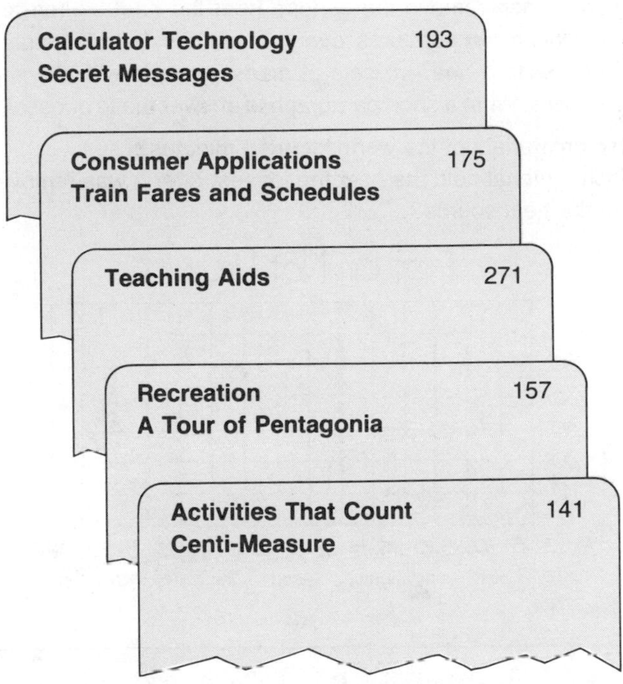


**. . . after Chapter 7**

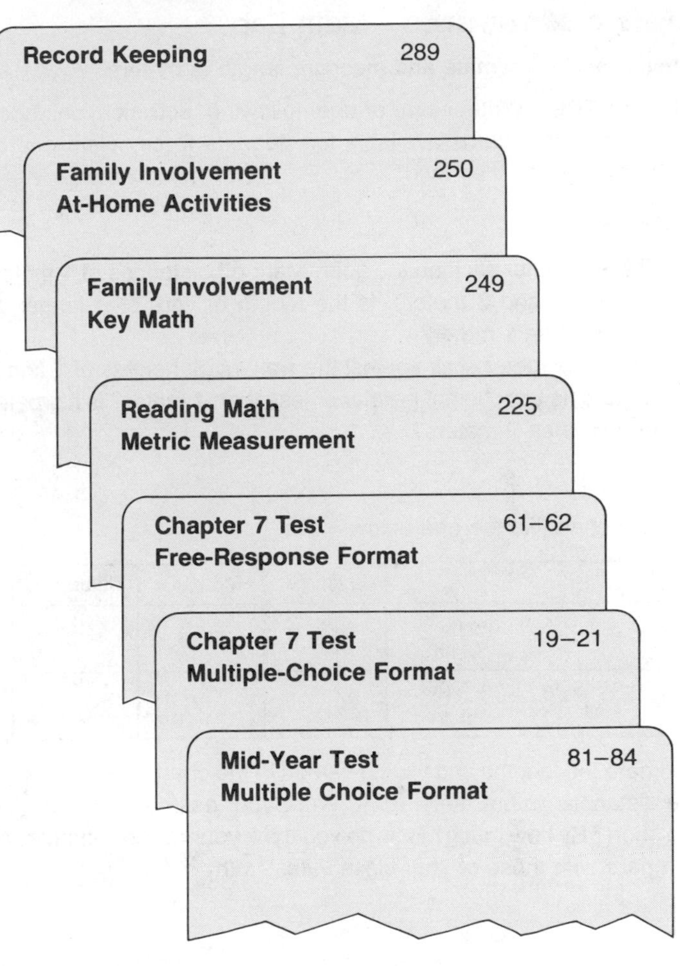


## Supplements

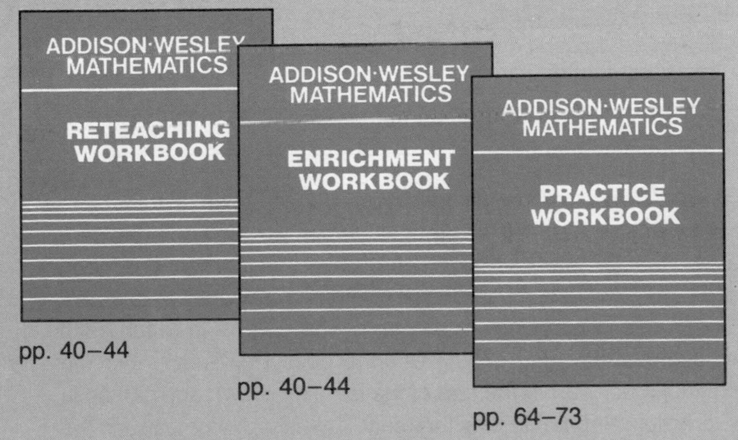


pp. 40–44

pp. 40–44

pp. 64–73

## Other Addison-Wesley Resources

### Books and Kits

*The Metric System* pp. 2–30, 50, 54–65, 76–86

*The Arithmetic Primer* pp. 277–280

*Problem Solving Experiences in Mathematics,* Grade 6
Problems 22, 24, 25, 28, 33, 57, 59, 60, 75, 99, 108, 115, 117, 118, 120, 129, 138

### Technology

*Computer Math Activities* Volume 1

# Activities That Count

Activities That Count are designed for use throughout this chapter and subsequent chapters. Before beginning Chapter 7, you may wish to review these activities and select the ones you consider appropriate for your class.

## Metric Measures Math Lab

**Purpose** To estimate and measure length in meters

**Preparation** Write each of the following activities on index cards. Have the cards available for students to complete one or both activities on their own.

### Activity 1

- Place a meter stick on the floor. Mark off distances of 1 meter, 2 meters, and 3 meters. Is the length of your step longer or shorter than 1 meter?
- Place the meter stick against the wall. Mark heights of 1 and 2 meters. Is your height greater or less than 1 meter? Is it greater or less than 2 meters?

### Activity 2

Make a chart like the one below.

| | | Estimate | Measure | Difference |
|---|---|---|---|---|
| Classroom | Length<br>Width | | | |
| School Hall | Length<br>Width | | | |

Estimate the lengths and widths named in the chart. Then measure the distances with a meter stick. Were your estimates too long or too short? By how much? How do you think your measurements will compare with those of your classmates? Why?

## Hot or Not Project

**Purpose** To measure the temperatures of various substances in degrees Celsius.

**Materials** 5 small milk cartons, dirt from a field, potting mix, sand, tap water, salt water, 5 Celsius thermometers, kitchen timer or stop watch, colored pencils, graph paper (TRB p. 271)

**Preparation** Have available the milk cartons filled with the five materials listed above. Prepare an index card with directions for the activity.

**Activity** Place a thermometer in each carton, and place the cartons in the sun (or under a heat lamp) for 15 minutes. Check the temperatures every 5 minutes for 15 minutes and record the results on a graph. Then remove the cartons from the heat source and again check the temperatures every 5 minutes for 15 minutes. Show the results of the two sets of measurements with different colored pencils. Write a short paragraph to answer these questions:

- Which material got the warmest in 15 minutes?
- Which material held the heat the longest after it was removed from the heat source?

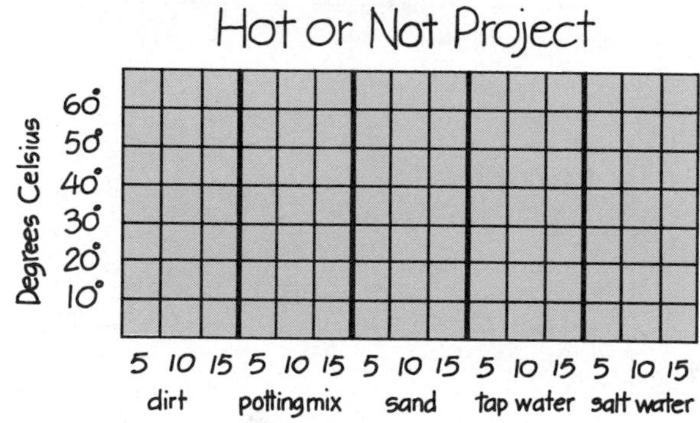


## Centi-Measure Game

**Purpose** To estimate and measure length in centimeters

**Materials** Game sheet (TRB p. 141), index cards, centimeter rulers

**Preparation** Write each of the following activities on a separate index card.

> Use the measure of the length of your little finger for your next line segment.

> Use the measure of the length of the pencil you are using to draw your line segment.

> Use the measure of the width of this card to draw your line segment.

> Find the card with the longest measure in the pile and use that length to draw your line segment.

> Use the measure of the width of your thumb at its widest point to draw your line segment.

> Estimate the length you will need to reach the next Centi-Measure body segment. Tell it to another player and then draw that line segment.

**Activity** The cards are mixed and placed facedown. In turn, players draw a card, read it to the other players, and then return the card to the bottom of the deck. Players then draw the segment described by the card. The first segment must begin at the end of the gnome's baton aiming toward body segment 1. The goal is to reach each body segment in order, ending with the head (5). Successive line segments must start at the end of the last line drawn and can go in any direction. Segments may intersect. The first player to reach the Centi-Measure's head wins the game.

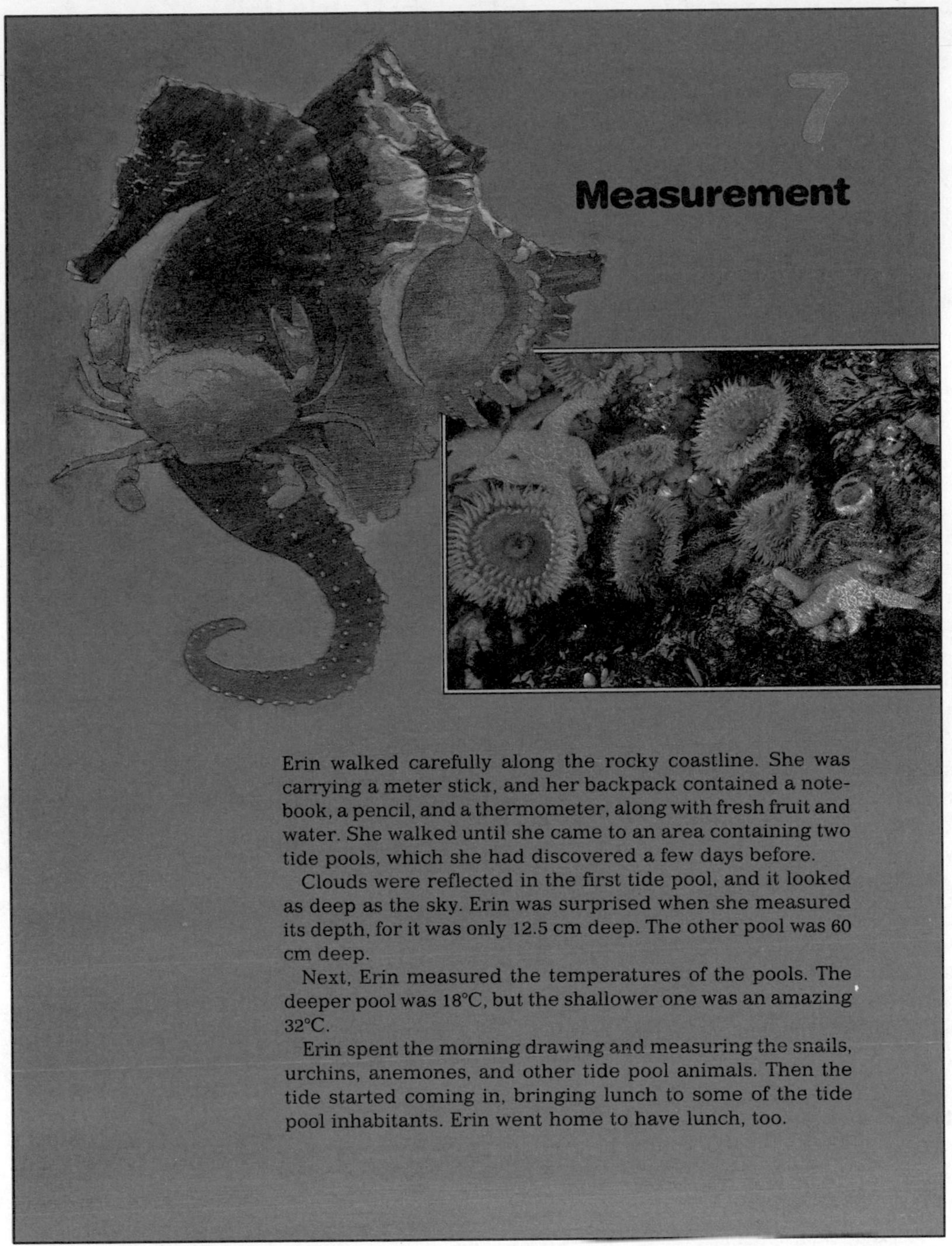

7
Measurement
Erin walked carefully along the rocky coastline. She was carrying a meter stick, and her backpack contained a notebook, a pencil, and a thermometer, along with fresh fruit and water. She walked until she came to an area containing two tide pools, which she had discovered a few days before.
Clouds were reflected in the first tide pool, and it looked as deep as the sky. Erin was surprised when she measured its depth, for it was only 12.5 cm deep. The other pool was 60 cm deep.
Next, Erin measured the temperatures of the pools. The deeper pool was 18°C, but the shallower one was an amazing 32°C.
Erin spent the morning drawing and measuring the snails, urchins, anemones, and other tide pool animals. Then the tide started coming in, bringing lunch to some of the tide pool inhabitants. Erin went home to have lunch, too.


## Introducing the Chapter

**Discussion** Explain that in this chapter students will review and extend their ability to work with metric units of measure. Initiate a discussion of marine animal life, especially the many kinds of sea creatures found in the shallow waters along the seashore. Some students may wish to tell about experiences they have had collecting shells and driftwood. After giving students an opportunity to enjoy the story and illustrations, encourage them to make up some questions related to the data in the story. As you teach the chapter, you may wish to refer to this page and ask the questions below.

## Follow-Up Questions

**After page 169** Eric found that a tide pool he was studying was 30 cm deep. What was the pool's depth in millimeters? (300 mm)

**After Page 173** Cindy has a sand dollar that has a diameter of 95 mm. What is the diameter in centimeters? (9.5 cm)

**After Page 179** Kevin estimated that there were about 2.4 kL of sea water in a tide pool he explored. How many liters of sea water was that? (2,400 L)

**After Page 180** Elena found a large conch shell that weighed 475 g. What was the shell's weight in kilograms? (0.475 kg)

**After Page 185** Russ spent 3 h 25 min on the beach in the morning. That afternoon he spent 1 h 45 min on the beach. How much time did Russ spend on the beach that day? (5 h 10 min)

# Measurement

**Quick Review** As an oral drill, students give the numbers that are ten more and ten less than these numbers.

205 59 1,000 330 105 1985 2001 42 101 99 56
6,008 455 196 12 486 693 5,088 400 37 1,100

**Lesson Focus** To express measurement in appropriate unit of length using the meter, decimeter, centimeter, and millimeter

**Suggested Materials** Meter stick

## Ideas for Getting Started

Tell students that a person's height might be given as 19, 54, 8, or 172, depending upon the unit used. Height would be 19 hands, 54 paperclips, or 8 spans, using the units pictured below.

1 "hand"

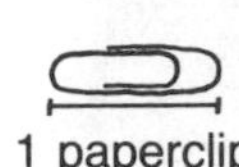
1 paperclip

1 span

Have students measure the tops of their desks using the hand unit. Then tell the class that in order to communicate effectively with other people about units of measure, we have agreed to use standard units. A person's height might be 172 using a standard unit called a centimeter. Show the meter stick and point out that a meter is 100 centimeters long.

## Using Page 168

**Lesson Development** Have students read the information in the three display boxes on this page. Show students the meter stick and point out the decimeter unit. "How many decimeters in a meter?" (10) "What part of a meter is a decimeter?" $\left(\frac{1}{10}\right)$ Emphasize that the prefix *deci* means one tenth, and decimeter means one tenth of a meter. Point out the centimeter marks on the meter stick. "How many centimeters in a decimeter?" (10) "How many centimeters in a meter?" (100) "What part of a meter is a decimeter?" $\left(\frac{1}{100}\right)$ Tell students that the prefix *centi* means one hundredth, so centimeter means one hundredth of a meter. Point out the millimeter marks on the meter stick. "How many millimeters in a centimeter?" (10) "How many millimeters in a meter?" (1,000) "What part of a meter is a millimeter?" $\left(\frac{1}{1{,}000}\right)$ Tell students that the prefix *milli* means one thousandth, so millimeter means one thousandth of a meter.

**Warm Up** Use these exercises as oral practice. If students have difficulty, encourage them to refer back to the display boxes.

## Length: Metric Units

The **meter (m)** is the basic metric unit of length.

The **decimeter (dm)** is one tenth of a meter.
10 dm = 1 m

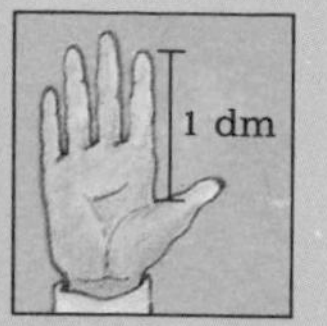


**deci-** means **one tenth.**

The **centimeter (cm)** is one hundredth of a meter.
100 cm = 1 m
10 cm = 1 dm

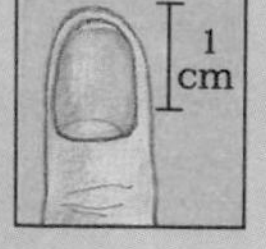


**centi-** means **one hundredth.**

The **millimeter (mm)** is one thousandth of a meter.
1,000 mm = 1 m
100 mm = 1 dm
10 mm = 1 cm

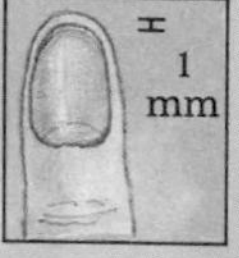


**milli-** means **one thousandth.**

← dm
← cm
← mm

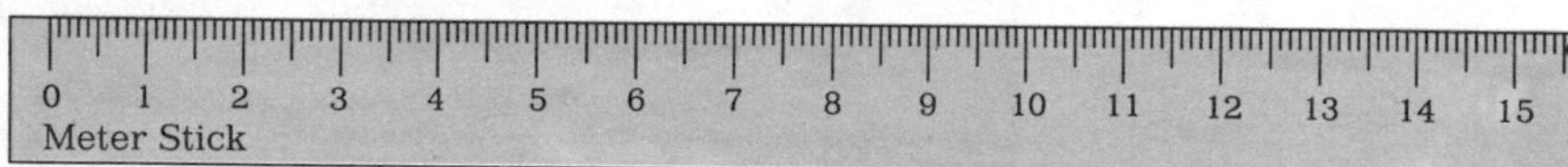


**Warm Up** Give the number for each ■.

1. A meter is ■ centimeters long. 100
2. A meter is ■ millimeters long. 1,000
3. A meter is ■ decimeters long. 10
4. A decimeter is ■ centimeters long. 10
5. A decimeter is ■ millimeters long. 100
6. A centimeter is ■ millimeters long. 10

168

## Follow Up

### Reteaching

Encourage activities that will help students become familiar with metric units of length. Challenge them to measure familiar classroom objects in meters, decimeters, centimeters, and millimeters. Then discuss some of the objects that might have been chosen, such as:

- A meter is about the distance from the floor to the doorknob.
- A decimeter is about the length of a short pencil.
- A centimeter is about the width of a piece of chalk.
- A millimeter is about the width of the mark made by a pencil point.

### Enrichment

Let students work in groups of two or three. Have them measure various things around the room, record their findings, and then compare their measurements with those of other groups.

| Assignment Guide | | | |
|---|---|---|---|
| | Minimum | Average | Extended |
| page 169 | 1–31 | 1–32 | 1–32, TM |

Choose the best measure.

1. length of a pencil 19 cm
   19 mm 19 cm 19 dm
2. length of a housefly 9 mm
   9 mm 9 cm 9 m
3. height of a child 12 dm
   12 cm 12 dm 12 m
4. height of a flag pole 9 m
   9 cm 9 dm 9 m
5. height of the Statue of Liberty 93 m
   93 m 93 dm 93 cm
6. length of a small paper clip 28 mm
   28 m 28 cm 28 mm
7. thickness of a writing tablet 6 mm
   6 cm 6 m 6 mm
8. length of a basketball court 26 m
   26 dm 26 m 26 cm

Which unit (**m**, **cm**, or **mm**) would you use to measure

9. the width of your book? cm
10. the length of a soccer field? m
11. the height of a tree? m
12. the thickness of a quarter? mm
13. the length of a dollar bill? cm
14. the length of your shoe? cm
15. the height of a mountain? m
16. the width of a shoelace? mm

Give the number for each ■.

17. 1 m = ■ cm 100
18. 1 m = ■ dm 10
19. 1 m = ■ mm 1,000
20. 1 dm = ■ mm 100
21. 1 cm = ■ mm 10
22. ■ cm = 1 dm 10
23. ■ mm = 1 m 1,000
24. ■ dm = 1 m 10
25. 1,000 mm = ■ m 1

Give the missing unit.

26. 10 ? = 1 dm cm
27. 10 ? = 1 m dm
28. 100 ? = 1 m cm
29. 1 dm = 100 ? mm
30. 1 m = 10 ? dm
31. 1,000 ? = 1 m mm
32. Name an object you would measure using each of these units: m, cm, and mm. Answers will vary.

**Think**

**Metric Prefixes**

Suppose metric prefixes (deci-, centi-, and milli-) were used for time.

How many minutes would there be in

1. a deciday? 144 minutes
2. a centiday? 14.4 minutes
3. a milliday? 1.44 minutes

**Math**



## Using Page 169

**Exercises 1–8** Have students decide on the answers to these exercises by thinking about the relative length of each unit.

**Exercises 9–16** In these exercises students are asked to select the most useful unit for measuring the objects or distances named. If necessary, point out that we would not ordinarily measure the width of a book in millimeters because the number would be too large. We would not measure the width of the book in meters because the book is less than one meter. Thus, the centimeter would be the best unit of measurement.

**Exercises 17–25** These exercises use information presented on page 168. If possible, have students complete these exercises without looking at the boxes. Review the meanings of *deci-*, *centi*, and *milli-* to remind students how the units relate to the meter.

**Exercises 26–31** In these exercises students supply the unit rather than the number and must think about how the three units relate to each other.

**Think Math** In this activity students demonstrate their understanding of the metric prefixes by using the terms in a different context. Since a day contains 24 times 60, or 1,440 minutes, a deciday would be one tenth of a day and would contain 144 minutes. A centiday would be one hundredth of a day and would contain 1,440 ÷ 100 or 14.4 minutes. A milliday would be one thousandth of a day and would contain 1,440 ÷ 1,000 or 1.44 minutes. Tell students that there have been serious suggestions over the years that we measure time using these prefixes.

## Ideas That Work

### Chalk It Up

Have students give the best metric unit for measuring the following lengths:

a) shoe cm b) paper clip mm
c) table height dm d) ship m
e) notebook paper cm f) fence m
g) width of a computer cm
h) height of a tree m
i) distance from San Francisco to Los Angeles km

**Practice Supplement**, page 64

Name ______________ To follow text page 169

**Length: Metric Units**

Which unit (**m, cm, or mm**) would you use to measure each of the following?

1. the length of a building m
2. the width of a paper clip mm
3. the width of your finger mm
4. the length of a pen cm
5. the length of a swimming pool m
6. the height of a telephone pole m
7. the thickness of a dime mm
8. the height of a waterfall m
9. the length of a fork cm
10. the distance around a basketball cm
11. the length of a football field m
12. the wing span of a moth mm

Write the missing number.

13. 1 m = 1,000 mm
14. 10 cm = 1 dm
15. 10 dm = 1 m
16. 1 dm = 100 mm
17. 1 m = 100 cm
18. 10 mm = 1 cm
19. 1,000 mm = 1 m
20. 1 m = 10 dm
21. 100 cm = 1 m
22. 1 dm = 10 cm

Write the missing unit.

23. 100 mm = 1 dm
24. 1,000 mm = 1 m
25. 1 m = 100 cm
26. 10 cm = 1 dm
27. 10 mm = 1 cm
28. 1 dm = 100 mm
29. 1 m = 10 dm
30. 1 dm = 10 cm
31. 100 cm = 1 m
32. 10 mm = 1 cm

# Measurement

**Quick Review** Student write these numbers as they are read aloud.

7,642 0.004 892 1,003 0.545 43.24 18.5 0.568
0.125 0.7 56,874 0.072 0.408 4,007 11.111
66.67 14,280 0.667 0.314 0.87 305.5 6.002 0.98

**Lesson Focus** To express measurement in appropriate units of length using the kilometer and related units; to estimate with metric units

**Suggested Materials** Stopwatch, meter stick

## Ideas for Getting Started

Mark off a 10-meter course in your classroom. The course might go along one side of the room and across the end of the room, for example. Use a stopwatch to determine the time it takes a student to walk 10 meters. On the chalkboard, record the time for several students and find the average of these times. "Suppose you could walk 10 meters in 6 seconds. How long would it take you to walk 100 meters?" (60 seconds or one minute) "How long would it take you to walk 1,000 meters?" (10 minutes) Tell students that 1,000 meters is a distance we call one kilometer. It takes about 10 minutes to walk one kilometer.

## Using Page 170

**Lesson Development** Have students read the information about the kilometer in the display at the top of the page. Tell them that if their steps were one meter in length, it would take 1,000 steps to walk one kilometer. Point out that *kilo* means 1,000, so kilometer means 1,000 meters. Be sure students understand the relationship between the units of length given in the table on the upper right corner of the page. Emphasize that the units used most often for everyday measurement are the centimeter, meter, and kilometer. Point out that *deka* means 10, so that dekameter is 10 meters. *Hecto* means 100 so, a hectometer is 100 meters.

**Exercises 1–4** These exercises are designed to help students make gross differentiations between the centimeter, meter, and kilometer units. In exercise 1 note that it would be foolish to think about a jogger running 5 centimeters. Even a 5-meter jog would be short. In each case ask students to think about the length of the unit and determine which measurement is reasonable.

**Exercises 5–13** Note that exercises 5 and 7 can be completed by looking at the table. The remaining exercises can be completed by reasoning about the units shown in the table.

**Exercise 14** If students have difficulty with this exercise, encourage them to refer back to exercises 1–4. Generate a group discussion of the selections students have made.

## More About Length

The **kilometer (km)** unit is one thousand meters. It is used to measure longer distances.
**1 km = 1,000 m**

It takes 1,000 one-meter steps to walk 1 km.

It takes about 10 minutes to walk 1 km.

It takes about 3.5 minutes to ride a bike 1 km.

Kilo means one thousand.

| Metric Units of Length | |
|---|---|
| millimeter (mm) | 0.001 m |
| *centimeter (cm) | 0.01 m |
| decimeter (dm) | 0.1 m |
| *meter (m) | 1 m |
| dekameter (dam) | 10 m |
| hectometer (hm) | 100 m |
| *kilometer (km) | 1,000 m |

*The units used most often in everyday life are the centimeter, meter, and kilometer.

Choose the best measure.

1. Distance a jogger runs 5 km
   5 cm 5 m 5 km
2. Length of a city block 100 m
   100 cm 100 m 100 km
3. Height at which a plane flies 9,000 m
   9,000 cm 9,000 m 9,000 km
4. Height of a basketball player 200 cm
   200 cm 200 m 200 km

Give the number for each ■.

5. 1 km = ■ m 1,000
6. 4 km = ■ m 4,000
7. 1,000 m = ■ km 1
8. 4,000 m = ■ km 4
9. 1 km = ■ hm 10
10. 1 km = ■ dam 100
11. 1 hm = ■ dam 10
12. 9 km = ■ m 9,000
13. 12,000 m = ■ km 12
14. Name something you would measure using each of these units: cm, m, km.
    Answers will vary.

170

## Follow Up

### Reteaching

Use a device such as a trundle wheel to help students develop a feel for measures that are larger than a meter. Ask students to measure:

a) length of a hallway
b) distance around the playground
c) distance around a football field

Tell students to count the meters as each measurement is taken, and help them compare the various distances.

### Enrichment

Provide students with a table similar to the one below. Have students complete the table. For some students the columns for dam, hm, and km might be omitted.

Metric Units of Length

| mm | cm | dm | m | dam | hm | km |
|---|---|---|---|---|---|---|
| | 400 | 40 | 4 | 0.4 | 0.04 | |
| | | | 1 | | | |
| | | | 6 | | | |
| | | | 5 | | | |
| | | | 7 | | | |

| Assignment Guide | | | |
|---|---|---|---|
| | Minimum | Average | Extended |
| page 170 | 1–13 | 1–14 | 1–14 |
| page 171 | 1–8 | 1–9 | 1–9 |

## Estimating with Metric Units

First estimate. Then measure. Answers will vary.

1. Your estimate: ▪ cm
   Actual measure: ▪ cm 3 cm
   (to the nearest centimeter)

2. Your estimate: ▪ mm
   Actual measure: ▪ mm 70 mm
   (to the nearest millimeter)

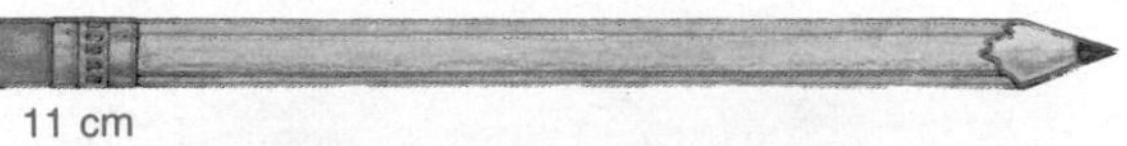

3. Your estimate: ▪ cm
   Actual measure: ▪ cm
   (to the nearest centimeter) 11 cm

4. Your armspan
   Your estimate: ▪ cm
   Actual measure: ▪ cm
   (to the nearest centimeter)

5. Your height
   Your estimate: ▪ m, ▪ cm
   Actual measure: ▪ m, ▪ cm
   (to the nearest centimeter)

6. Width of your desk top
   Your estimate: ▪ cm, ▪ mm
   Actual measure: ▪ cm, ▪ mm
   (to the nearest millimeter)

7. Length of your normal step
   Your estimate: ▪ m, ▪ cm
   Actual measure: ▪ m, ▪ cm
   (to the nearest centimeter)

8. Length of your classroom
   Your estimate: ▪ m
   Actual measure: ▪ m
   (to the nearest meter)

★ 9. Estimate and mark off a distance of 10 m. (You may want to count steps or tiles.) Measure to see how many centimeters you were from the actual measure.



## Using Page 171

**Lesson Development** Select one object such as a piece of chalk whose width can be measured in millimeters, another object such as the mathematics textbook whose length can be measured in centimeters, and a third object or distance such as the length of the chalkboard that can be measured in meters. Measure the length of these objects beforehand; then conduct an estimation experiment in which the students record their estimates of the length of the objects. After all estimates have been recorded, determine which estimate is closest to the actual measure. Tell students that they will have an opportunity to sharpen their estimation skills through the activities on this page.

**Exercises 1–3** In these exercises, students estimate the length of the picture on the page; then they find the actual measure to the nearest centimeter or millimeter. Remind students that when an object measures between 3 cm and 4 cm, for example, but is closer to 4 cm, its length to the nearest centimeter is 4.

**Exercises 5–7** Note that 2 units are used for each estimate and measure in these exercises. This means a more accurate measure of the object.

**Exercise 9** In this starred exercise students estimate a distance of 10 meters or 1 hectometer.

## Ideas That Work

### Special Education

Let students make an air distance map of their state scaled in kilometers. Students can be given a map with the cities marked with a scale and the distances between the cities. They can then draw in straight lines for the air routes and mark the distances in kilometers along the routes.

Generate a variety of questions about the map for students to answer. The questions might focus on which town is closest by air to a second town; what the distance is from one town to a second with a stop enroute at a third town; and other related questions.

**Practice Supplement,** page 65

Name ______ To follow text page 170

**More About Length**

Which unit (**cm, m, or km**) would you use to measure each of the following?

1. the distance between cities km
2. the length of a garden m
3. the distance to the moon km
4. the length of a toothbrush cm
5. the length of a frog's jump cm
6. the length of your school m
7. the distance a biker rides km
8. the diameter of a record cm
9. the height of a chimney m
10. the length of a highway km
11. the length of a flashlight cm
12. the distance jogged in 2 minutes m
13. the length of a day's hike km
14. the height at which a bird flies m
15. the width of a table cm
16. the length of a cruise ship m

Write the missing number.

17. 1,000 m = 1 km
18. 1 dam = 10 m
19. 1 hm = 100 m
20. 100 cm = 1 m
21. 60 m = 6 dam
22. 3 km = 3,000 m
23. 4 km = 4,000 m
24. 9 m = 900 cm
25. 6,000 m = 6 km
26. 800 m = 8 hm
27. 700 cm = 7 m
28. 5 km = 5,000 m
29. 2 m = 200 cm
30. 9,000 m = 9 km
31. 3 dam = 30 m
32. 7 hm = 700 m

# Measurement

**Quick Review** Provide the following as an oral drill.

10 × 60   11 × 100   9 × 100   1,000 × 23   415 × 100   76 × 100
1,000 × 67   42 × 10   549 × 100   300 × 100   566 × 1,000
1,000 × 550   12 × 100   56 × 10   620 × 10   100 × 877   178 × 100

**Lesson Focus** To use decimals to express measurements and relationships involving metric units

**Suggested Materials** Meter stick

## Ideas for Getting Started

As you display a meter stick, remind students that the meter is the basic metric unit of length. "How many decimeters are in one meter?" (10) "What numbers could we use to show that relationship?" $\left(\frac{1}{10}\text{ or } 0.1\right)$ "How many centimeters are in one meter?" (100) "How could we show that relationship?" $\left(\frac{1}{100}\text{ or } 0.01\right)$ "How many millimeters are in one meter?" (1,000) "What numbers could we use to show this relationship?" $\left(\frac{1}{1{,}000}\text{ or } 0.001\right)$ Remind students that fractions and decimals can be used to show comparisons. Then elicit from students that the prefixes of these metric units tell us what multiple of 10 the unit of length is being compared with.

## Using Page 172

**Lesson Development** Direct students' attention to illustrations of meter sticks on the page and discuss the relationships shown. Have students point out these units on a meter stick or centimeter ruler. Be sure they understand why one decimeter is 0.1 meter, one centimeter is 0.01 meter, and one millimeter is 0.001 meter. Relate these ideas to the metric prefixes of *deci, centi,* and *milli.* Review the idea that there are 1,000 meters in 1 kilometer, so 1 meter is 0.001 of a kilometer.

**Warm Up** Encourage students to give the missing numbers without looking at the information on the page. If they have difficulty, have them refer to the meter stick or to the explanation above. Be sure students understand the basic relationships between these units.

## Metric Units and Decimals

We can use decimals to compare metric units.

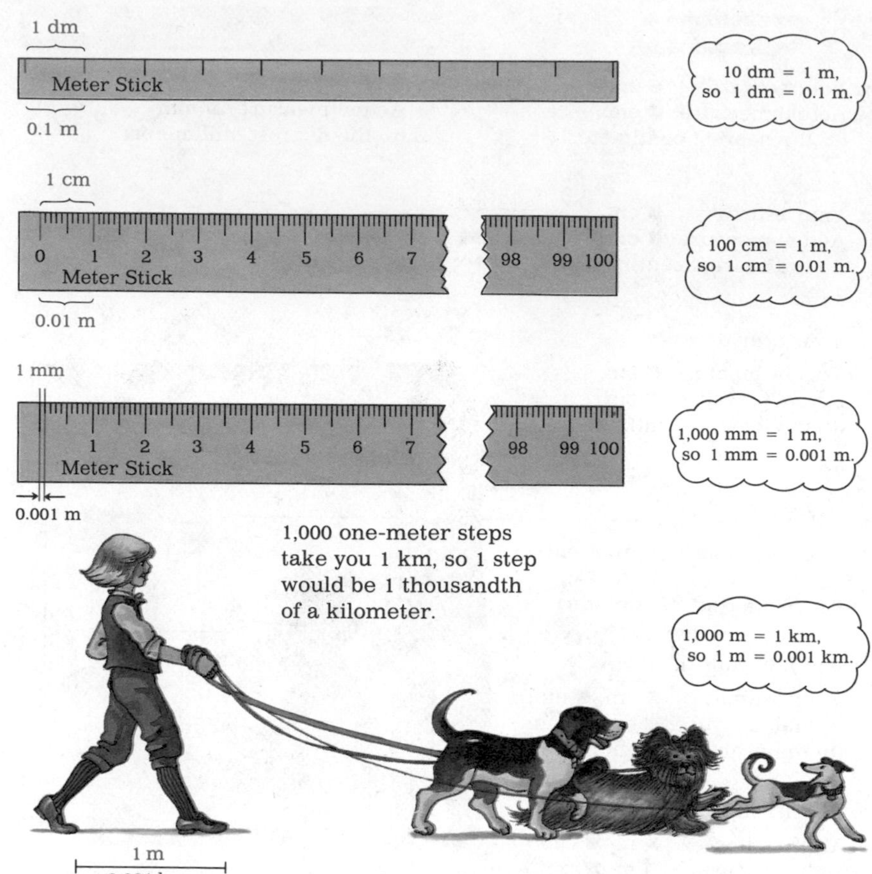


**Warm Up** Give the missing numbers or units.

1. 1 cm = ■ m 0.01
2. 1 m = ■ km 0.001
3. 1 mm = ■ m 0.001
4. 1 dm = ■ m 0.1
5. 1 cm = ■ dm 0.1
6. 1 mm = ■ cm 0.1
7. 1 ■ = 0.01 m cm
8. 1 ■ = 0.001 m mm
9. 1 mm = 0 01 ■ dm

172

## Follow Up

### Reteaching

Relate the metric system and metric units with the decimal system by showing a place-value chart like the one below.

| thousands | hundreds | tens | ones | tenths | hundredths | thousandths |
|---|---|---|---|---|---|---|
| km | hm | dam | m | dm | cm | mm |
|  |  |  | 3 | 2 | 7 |  |

Then choose a measure such as 3.27 m. Using the chart, point out that 3.27 could also be thought of as 32.7 dm or 327 cm, for example. Work through several examples to reinforce the relationships between these units.

### Enrichment

Have students make a metric flower by measuring metric petals and making a circle which has a metric radius. The shapes are then cut out and glued together.

In a similar activity students can make award ribbons by attaching metrically measured ribbons of construction paper to their metric flowers.

| Assignment Guide | Minimum | Average | Extended |
|---|---|---|---|
| page 173 | 1–23, SK | 1–24, SK | 1–24, SK |

Since both the place-value system and the metric system are based on 10, we can use decimals to show measurements that fall between whole numbers of units.

A small flower garden is 2 m 54 cm or 2.54 m long.

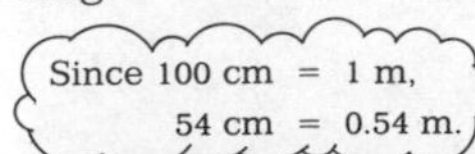


A hole-digger can dig holes 9 cm 5 mm or 9.5 cm deep.

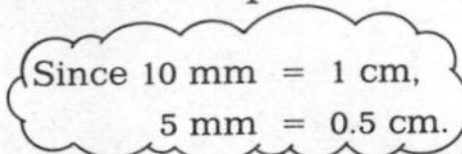


A walk from home to the garden store is 3 km 725 m or 3.725 km.

Since 1,000 m = 1 km,
725 m = 0.725 km.

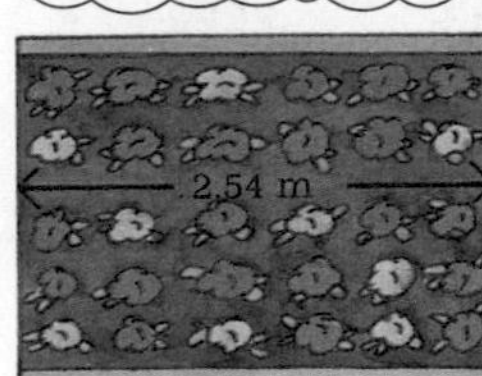


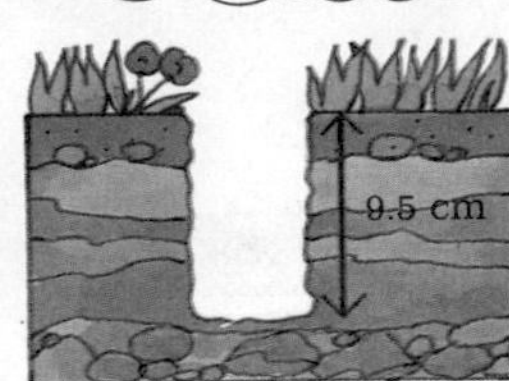


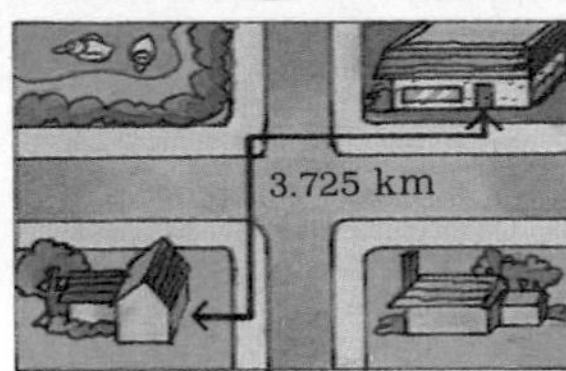


Give the decimal for each ■.

1. 5 m 23 cm = ■ m 5.23
2. 8 cm 3 mm = ■ cm 8.3
3. 2 km 465 m = ■ km 2.465
4. 9 mm = ■ cm 0.9
5. 4 km 983 m = ■ km 4.983
6. 6 m 87 cm = ■ m 6.87
7. 43 cm = ■ m 0.43
8. 9 m 4 cm = ■ m 9.04
9. 1 km 86 m = ■ km 1.086
10. 3 m 7 dm = ■ m 3.7
11. 6 m 72 cm = ■ m 6.72
12. 6 m 9 dm = ■ m 6.9
13. 3 km 100 m = ■ km 3.1 or 3.100
14. 8 m 50 cm = ■ cm 8.50
15. 4 dm 9 cm = ■ m 0.49
16. 3.76 m = ■ m ■ cm 3; 76
17. 3.7 dm = ■ dm ■ cm 3; 7
18. 2.375 km = ■ km ■ m 2; 375
19. 4.6 m = ■ m ■ cm 4; 60
20. 9.4 cm = ■ cm ■ mm 9; 4
21. 1.128 km = ■ km ■ m 1; 128
22. 4.23 m = ■ m ■ cm 4; 23
23. 8.9 cm = ■ cm ■ mm 8; 9

★24. 3.086 km = ■ m ■ cm 3,000; 8,600

## Skillkeeper

Divide.

1. 5)43 — 8 R3
2. 9)68 — 7 R5
3. 7)96 — 13 R5
4. 6)126 — 21
5. 8)3,410 — 426 R2
6. 20)89 — 4 R9
7. 32)384 — 12
8. 27)1,325 — 49 R2
9. 52)4,529 — 87 R5
10. 76)16,654 — 219 R10



## Using Page 173

**Lesson Development** Before assigning these exercises, have students read each of the examples at the top of the page. Point out that because metric units are based on 10, we can use decimals to show measurements that are between units. For example, in the second example, the depth of the hole can be shown using both centimeter and millimeter units.

**Exercises 1–15** Note that in each of these exercises, a measurement has been given using two units. Students must think about the meaning of the units and write the measurement as a single unit using a decimal. In exercise 15, students must recognize that 4 dm is 0.4 of a meter and 9 cm is 0.09 of a meter, so 4 dm, 9 cm is 0.49m.

**Exercises 16–23** These exercises are the reverse of exercises 1–15. Students are given the single unit expressed as a decimal and then express the measurement as two units.

**Exercise 24** Students must recognize that 3 km is 3,000 m, and 0.086 of a kilometer is 86 m or 8,600 cm. Thus the answers are 3,000 m and 8,600 cm.

**Skillkeeper** These skills were originally taught in Chapter 5.

### Reteaching Supplement, page 40

Name ______________ To follow text page 173

**Metric Units and Decimals**

1 millimeter → | 1 decimeter | 0 1 2 3 4 5 6 7 8 9 10 Centimeters

The **meter** (m) is the basic unit of length. **Kilometers** are used for measuring large distances. **Millimeters** and **centimeters** are used for measuring the lengths of small objects.

| Units of Length | | |
|---|---|---|
| Unit | Meaning | Symbol |
| millimeter | 0.001 meter | mm |
| centimeter | 0.01 meter | cm |
| decimeter | 0.1 meter | dm |
| meter | 1 meter | m |
| dekameter | 10 meters | dam |
| hectometer | 100 meters | hm |
| kilometer | 1,000 meters | km |

Use the rules and table to help you complete each item.

1. 1 m = 10 dm
2. 1 m = 100 cm
3. 1 m = 1,000 mm
4. 1 dm = 0.1 m
5. 1 cm = 0.01 m
6. 1 mm = 0.001 m
7. 1,000 m = 1 km
8. 1 km = 10 hm
9. 1 dam = 10 m

Write the correct symbol (**cm**, **m**, or **km**) for each blank.

10. Jane's hand was about 7 cm wide.
11. Fred's little finger was about 1 cm wide.
12. The door was about 2 m tall.
13. Diane's height was 165 cm
14. Mary drove her car 68 km in an hour.
15. The room was about 10 m long.
16. A robin is about 20 cm long.

### Enrichment Supplement, page 40

Name ______________ To follow text page 173

**Metric Word Search**

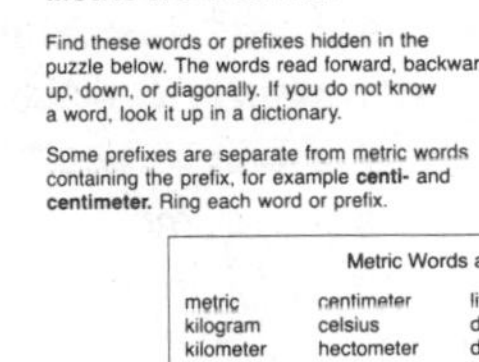

Find these words or prefixes hidden in the puzzle below. The words read forward, backward, up, down, or diagonally. If you do not know a word, look it up in a dictionary.

Some prefixes are separate from metric words containing the prefix, for example **centi-** and **centimeter.** Ring each word or prefix.

| Metric Words and Prefixes | | | | |
|---|---|---|---|---|
| metric | centimeter | liter | kilo | joule |
| kilogram | celsius | deka- | centi- | watt |
| kilometer | hectometer | deci- | milli- | mega- |
| milliliter | gram | hectare | nano- | pico- |

| | | | | | | | | | |
|---|---|---|---|---|---|---|---|---|---|
| M | A | R | G | O | L | I | K | R | R |
| G | I | T | N | E | C | A | G | E | M |
| R | O | L | L | I | W | A | T | T | C |
| A | K | I | L | O | M | E | T | E | R |
| M | I | L | L | I | M | E | L | M | P |
| E | L | N | C | I | L | S | L | O | I |
| T | O | E | T | U | I | I | N | T | C |
| R | D | N | O | U | T | A | T | C | O |
| I | E | J | S | E | N | A | K | E | D |
| C | L | E | R | A | T | C | E | H | R |

### Practice Supplement, page 66

Name ______________ To follow text page 173

**Metric Units and Decimals**

Write the missing units.

1. 1 mm = 0.1 cm
2. 1 mm = 0.001 m
3. 1 cm = 10 mm
4. 1 cm = 0.01 m
5. 1 m = 0.001 km
6. 1 dm = 0.1 m
7. 1,000 mm = 1 m
8. 1 m = 10 dm
9. 1,000 m = 1 km
10. 1 cm = 0.1 dm

Write the missing numbers.

11. 4 km 312 m = 4.312 km
12. 5 cm 3 mm = 5.3 cm
13. 7 m 14 cm = 7.14 m
14. 8 mm = 0.8 cm
15. 9 km 605 m = 9.605 km
16. 3 m 15 cm = 3.15 m
17. 2 km 25 m = 2.025 km
18. 6 m 6 cm = 6.06 m
19. 51 cm = 0.51 m
20. 1 m 5 dm = 1.5 m
21. 4 m 65 cm = 4.65 m
22. 3 m 7 dm = 3.7 m
23. 5 m 70 cm = 570 cm
24. 9 km 200 m = 9.2 km
25. 2.59 m = 2 m 59 cm
26. 6.3 cm = 6 cm 3 mm
27. 5.821 km = 5 km 821 m
28. 4.1 cm = 4 cm 1 mm
29. 4.396 km = 4 km 396 m
30. 7.484 km = 7 km 484 m
31. 9.25 m = 9 m 25 cm
32. 8.3 dm = 8 dm 3 cm
33. 1.6 m = 1 m 60 cm
34. 2.017 km = 2 km 17 m

**Quick Review** Students write the symbol (>, <, =) that makes each number sentence true.

| | | |
|---|---|---|
| 6 × 8 [=] 40 + 8 | 65 − 15 [>] 15 + 5 | 17 + 4 [=] 4 + 17 |
| 18 + 3 [=] 7 × 3 | 49 ÷ 7 [<] 8 × 1 | 100 ÷ 2 [<] 75 |

**Lesson Focus** To change a measurement to another metric unit by multiplying; to change a measurement to another metric unit by dividing

## Ideas for Getting Started

Draw the chart below on the chalkboard, but without the numbers. Tell students that this chart can help them convert from one metric unit of length to another.

| km | hm | dam | m | dm | cm | mm |
|---|---|---|---|---|---|---|
| | 1 | 6 | 4. | 2 | 1 | |
| | 1 | 6 | 4 | 2 | 1. | |
| | | | | | | |
| | | | | | | |

Review the relationships between the units in the table. Then write 164.21 in the chart with the decimal point on the separation bar to the right of the meter column, and read the number in meters. Move the decimal point to the right of the centimeter column and have students read the answer in centimeters. (16,421 cm) Emphasize that moving the decimal point one column to the right is equivalent to multiplying the number by 10; moving one column to the left is equivalent to dividing the number by 10.

## Using Page 174

**Lesson Development** Read the introductory paragraph. Tell students that we want to give the 3.8 centimeter width in millimeters. That is, we want to change the measurement from centimeters to millimeters. Emphasize that this is changing from a larger unit to a smaller unit. "If we know something is 3 m long, would it be a larger or smaller number of centimeters?" (larger, since the centimeter is a smaller unit) "If we know that a distance is so many kilometers, will it be a greater or smaller number of meters?" (a greater number of meters, since the meter is a smaller unit)

Be sure students understand that because each centimeter is equal to 10 millimeters, we must multiply the centimeter measurements by 10 to find the number of millimeters. In the table with the names of the units, we can see that the millimeter box is to the right of the centimeter box. This means we must multiply centimeters by 10 or move the decimal point one place to the right to find the number of millimeters.

**Other Examples** Point out that the table helps to decide whether to multiply by 10, 100, or 1,000, depending on how far apart in the table the units are.

**Exercises 1–15** Encourage students to draw a table like the one shown with the first example to use with exercises 1–4, 6–9, and 11–16. Have students use a table as shown with the last example with exercises 5 and 10. Emphasize that to change each unit to a smaller unit, we must multiply.

## Changing Metric Units by Multiplying

Yasmin built a birdhouse with an entrance just 3.8 cm wide so that birds larger than bluebirds cannot get into it. What is this width in millimeters?

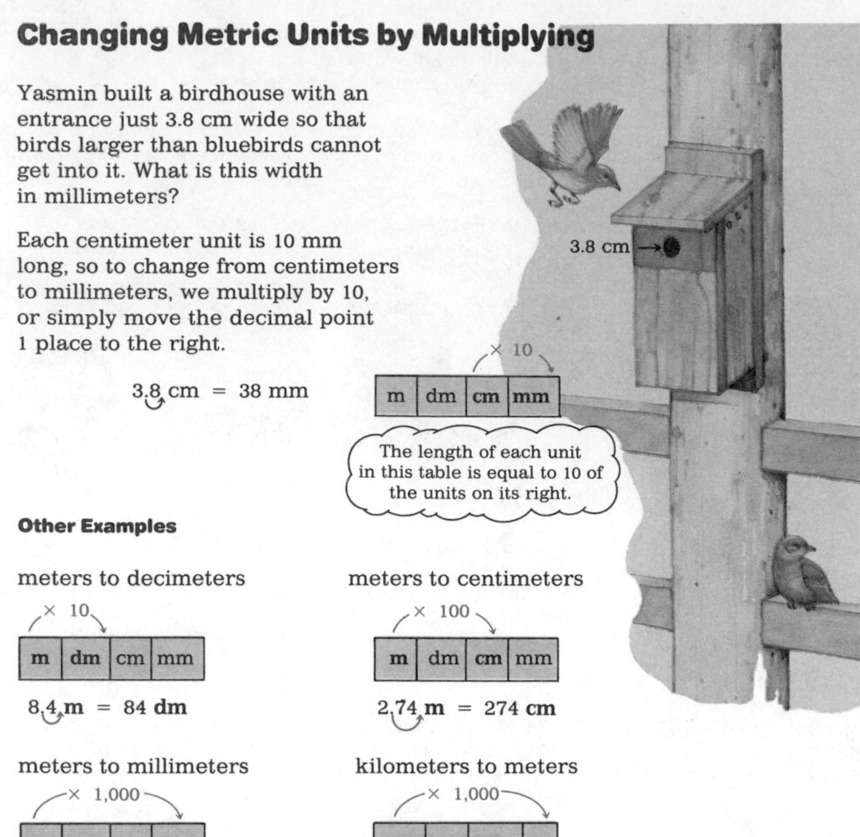


Each centimeter unit is 10 mm long, so to change from centimeters to millimeters, we multiply by 10, or simply move the decimal point 1 place to the right.

3.8 cm = 38 mm

× 10

| m | dm | cm | mm |
|---|---|---|---|

The length of each unit in this table is equal to 10 of the units on its right.

**Other Examples**

meters to decimeters

× 10

| m | dm | cm | mm |
|---|---|---|---|

8.4 m = 84 dm

meters to centimeters

× 100

| m | dm | cm | mm |
|---|---|---|---|

2.74 m = 274 cm

meters to millimeters

× 1,000

| m | dm | cm | mm |
|---|---|---|---|

9.367 m = 9,367 mm

kilometers to meters

× 1,000

| km | hm | dam | m |
|---|---|---|---|

5.465 km = 5,465 m

Give the number for each changed unit.

1. 3.6 m = ■ dm
36
2. 3.64 m = ■ dm
36.4
3. 3.64 m = ■ cm
364
4. 3.642 m = ■ mm
3,642
5. 5.876 km = ■ m
5,876
6. 4.3 m = ■ dm
43
7. 9.68 m = ■ cm
968
8. 2.75 m = ■ mm
2,750
9. 0.86 m = ■ cm
86
10. 7.8 km = ■ m
7,800
11. 4.9 dm = ■ cm
49
12. 8.04 m = ■ cm
804
13. 4.65 dm = ■ mm
465
14. 12.2 m = ■ cm
1,220
15. 8.4 cm = ■ mm
84

174

## Follow Up

### Reteaching

Draw on the chalkboard the "stairstep" shown below and use it to discuss the relationships of one unit to another. For example, which is larger, mm or cm? Focus on the fact that a given measure can be expressed as a smaller unit by multiplying by a multiple of 10. For example, 5 m may also be thought of as 500 cm or 5,000 mm.

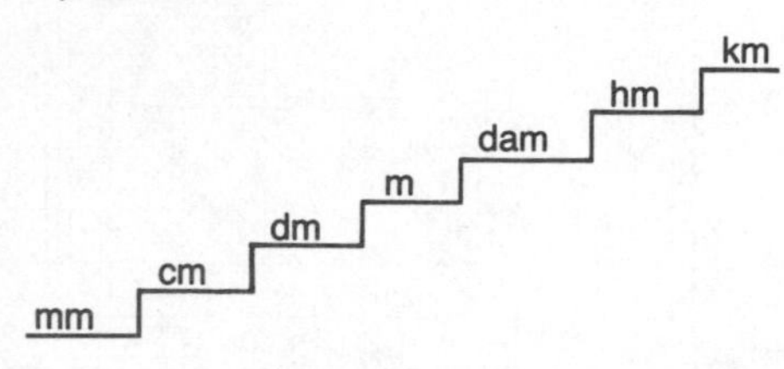


### Enrichment

Provide students with a metric recipe and tell them that the recipe must be multiplied by 10 in order to serve the number of people coming to a party. Have students indicate how much of each ingredient will be needed when the recipe has been multiplied by 10.

| | Assignment Guide | | |
|---|---|---|---|
| | Minimum | Average | Extended |
| page 174 | 1–15 | 1–15 | 1–15 |
| page 175 | 1–15 | 1–15 | 1–15 |



## Changing Metric Units by Dividing

The diameter of the entrance to a bird house for a purple martin should be 57 mm across. What is this measure in centimeters?

It takes 10 mm to make 1 cm, so to change from millimeters to centimeters we divide by 10, or simply move the decimal point 1 place to the left.

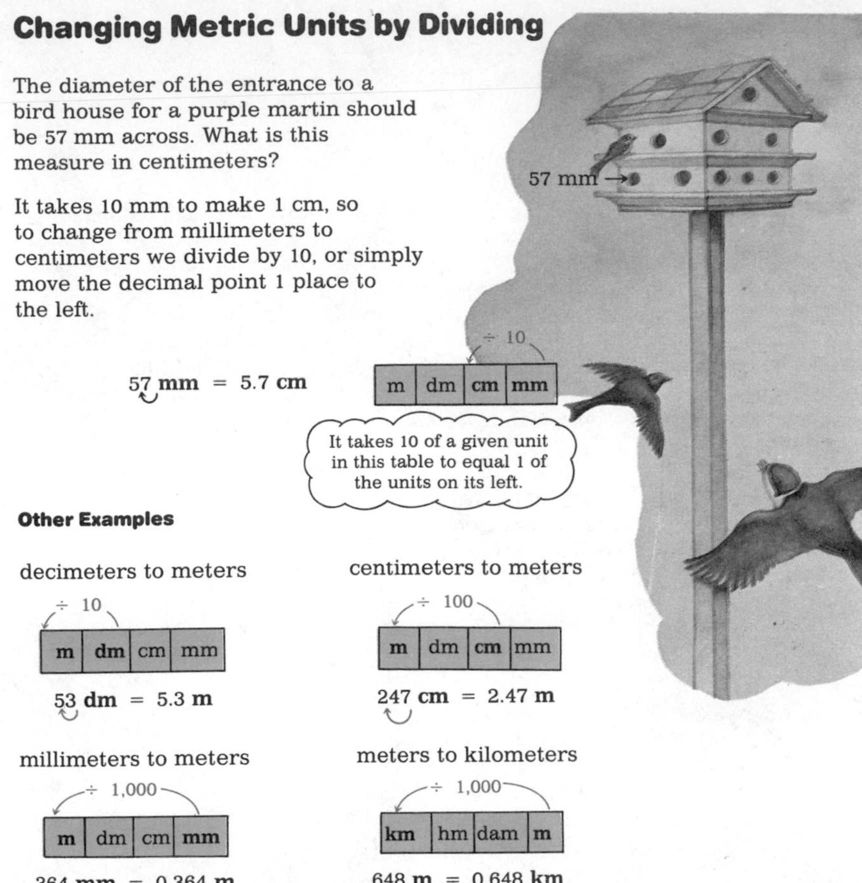


57 mm = 5.7 cm

÷ 10

| m | dm | cm | mm |
|---|---|---|---|

It takes 10 of a given unit in this table to equal 1 of the units on its left.

**Other Examples**

decimeters to meters

÷ 10

| m | dm | cm | mm |
|---|---|---|---|

53 dm = 5.3 m

centimeters to meters

÷ 100

| m | dm | cm | mm |
|---|---|---|---|

247 cm = 2.47 m

millimeters to meters

÷ 1,000

| m | dm | cm | mm |
|---|---|---|---|

364 mm = 0.364 m

meters to kilometers

÷ 1,000

| km | hm | dam | m |
|---|---|---|---|

648 m = 0.648 km

Give the number for each changed unit.

1. 68 dm = ■ m
6.8
2. 369 cm = ■ m
3.69
3. 867 m = ■ km
0.867
4. 743 mm = ■ m
0.743
5. 147 dm = ■ m
14.7
6. 48 cm = ■ m
0.48
7. 98 m = ■ km
0.098
8. 56 mm = ■ m
0.056
9. 47 mm = ■ dm
0.47
10. 376 cm = ■ m
3.76
11. 1,264 m = ■ km
1.264
12. 9,467 mm = ■ m
9.467
13. 2,876 m = ■ km
2.876
14. 157 dm = ■ m
15.7
15. 137 mm = ■ dm
1.37



## Using Page 175

**Lesson Development** Tell students that in this lesson we want to change smaller units to larger units. "If the height of a door is given in centimeters, would the measurement in meters be a larger or smaller number?" (a smaller number) "If the height of a mountain is given in meters, would the measurement be a larger or smaller number of kilometers?" (a smaller number) Emphasize that because there are 10 millimeters in one centimeter, then 57 millimeters would be 57 ÷ 10 or 5.7 centimeters. Point out the table and help students understand that since the centimeter unit is one box to the left of the millimeter unit, we must divide by 10 to change from millimeters to centimeters. In other words, we can move the decimal point one place to the left.

**Other Examples** Help students to understand the relationship between these examples, and remind them of the table on page 174, which helped them change to smaller units by multiplying.

**Exercises 1–15** Have students use the table in the first example to help them complete exercises 1–6, 8–10, 12, 14–15. The table in the last example will help them with exercises 7, 11, and 13. Note that there are no examples exactly like exercises 9 and 15. In these exercises, since the decimeter unit is two boxes to the left of the millimeter unit, we move the decimal point two places to the left to change millimeters to decimeters.

**Reteaching Supplement,** page 41

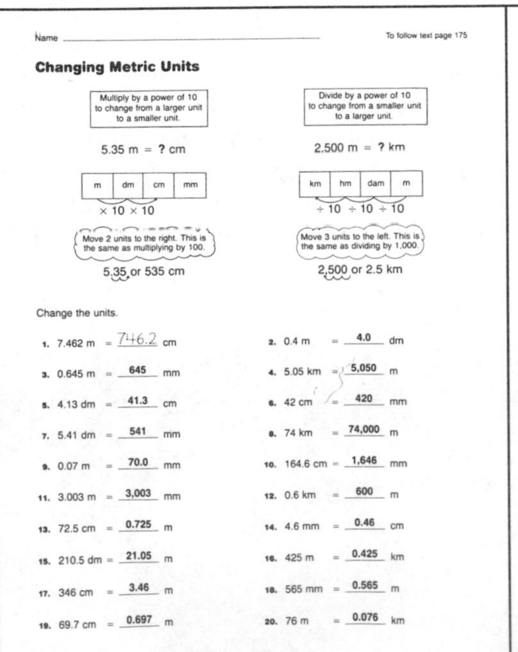

Name ____________ To follow text page 175

**Changing Metric Units**

Multiply by a power of 10 to change from a larger unit to a smaller unit.

5.35 m = ? cm

| m | dm | cm | mm |
|---|---|---|---|

× 10 × 10

Move 2 units to the right. This is the same as multiplying by 100.

5.35 or 535 cm

Divide by a power of 10 to change from a smaller unit to a larger unit.

2.500 m = ? km

| km | hm | dam | m |
|---|---|---|---|

÷ 10 ÷ 10 ÷ 10

Move 3 units to the left. This is the same as dividing by 1,000.

2,500 or 2.5 km

Change the units.

1. 7.462 m = 746.2 cm
2. 0.4 m = 4.0 dm
3. 0.645 m = 645 mm
4. 5.05 km = 5,050 m
5. 4.13 dm = 41.3 cm
6. 42 cm = 420 mm
7. 5.41 dm = 541 mm
8. 74 km = 74,000 m
9. 0.07 m = 70.0 mm
10. 164.6 cm = 1,646 mm
11. 3.003 m = 3,003 mm
12. 0.6 km = 600 m
13. 72.5 cm = 0.725 m
14. 4.6 mm = 0.46 cm
15. 210.5 dm = 21.05 m
16. 425 m = 0.425 km
17. 346 cm = 3.46 m
18. 565 mm = 0.565 m
19. 69.7 cm = 0.697 m
20. 76 m = 0.076 km

**Enrichment Supplement,** page 41

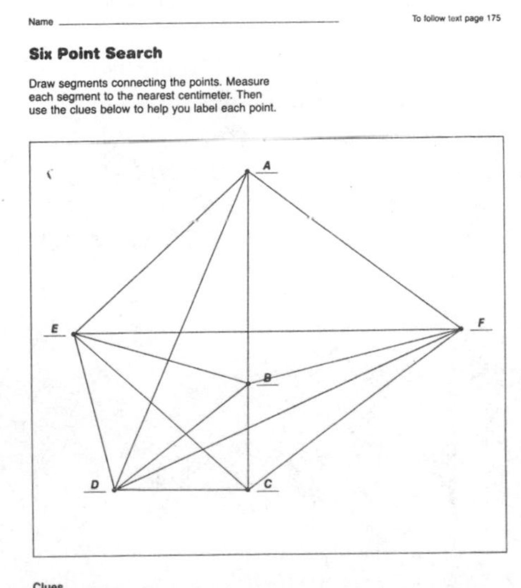

Name ____________ To follow text page 175

**Six Point Search**

Draw segments connecting the points. Measure each segment to the nearest centimeter. Then use the clues below to help you label each point.



Clues

1. A and B are 0.08 m apart.
2. A and D are 130 mm apart.
3. The length of $\overline{DC}$ is 0.5 dm.
4. F is 0.0001 km from both A and C.
5. A and C are 120 mm apart.
6. E is 0.06 m from D and 0.9 dm from A.

**Practice Supplement,** page 67

Name ____________ To follow text page 175

**Changing Metric Units**

Write the missing number.

1. 5.4 m = 54 dm
2. 2.59 m = 25.9 dm
3. 7.27 m = 727 cm
4. 8.436 m = 8,436 mm
5. 5.309 km = 5,309 m
6. 2.3 m = 23 dm
7. 4.13 m = 413 cm
8. 5.44 m = 5,440 mm
9. 0.61 m = 61 cm
10. 6.6 km = 6,600 m
11. 3.7 dm = 37 cm
12. 9.01 m = 901 cm
13. 7.24 dm = 724 mm
14. 2.5 m = 250 cm
15. 4.9 cm = 49 mm
16. 6.115 dm = 611.5 mm
17. 5.043 m = 5,043 mm
18. 7.9 m = 79 dm
19. 54 dm = 5.4 m
20. 781 cm = 7.81 m
21. 394 m = 0.394 km
22. 173 mm = 0.173 m
23. 267 dm = 26.7 m
24. 92 cm = 0.92 m
25. 43 m = 0.043 km
26. 71 mm = 0.071 m
27. 65 mm = 0.65 dm
28. 516 cm = 5.16 m
29. 3,214 m = 3.214 km
30. 1,673 mm = 1.673 m
31. 4,848 m = 4.848 km
32. 456 dm = 45.6 m
33. 803 mm = 8.03 dm
34. 36 mm = 3.6 cm

# Applications

**Quick Review** Students halve and double each number below as an oral drill.

20 12 100 50 52 18 90 1,000
10 200 250 60 24 22 202
40 500 6 16 106 44 400 5,000

**Lesson Focus** To use data from a reference book to solve word problems

## Ideas for Getting Started

Review the 5-Point Checklist by referring to the logo in the upper left-hand corner of the page. Point out that the checklist is not meant to be a set of rules for solving problems but rather a guide that suggests some important things to think about. Because this lesson focuses on data from a reference book, have students use interesting data from the *Guinness Book of World Records* to generate word problems of their own.

## Using Page 176

**Lesson Development** Point out that the data needed to solve many of these problems can be found in the items from a reference book that are shown on the page. Tell students that in many cases they will need to change measurement units in order to solve the problems. If necessary, read through and discuss the problems before assigning independent work.

**Exercise 1** In this exercise the units must be changed in order to make a comparison. In this case 0.3 m can be changed to 30 cm. Or, 38 cm could be changed to 0.38 m. Note that the difference in this case would be expressed as 0.08 m.

**Exercise 3** Caution students to read this problem carefully and note that there are three questions to be answered.

## Problem Solving: Using Data from a Reference Book

Solve. Change units when necessary.

1. The diameter of a long-playing phonograph record is about 0.3 m. About how much larger is the diameter of a squid's eye than the diameter of the record? about 8 cm

2. The diameter of a human's eye is about 0.05 times the diameter of a giant squid's eye. About how many millimeters is this? about 19 mm

3. If the clam grows the same amount every year, how long will it be when it is 50 years old? 25 years old? How long will it take for the clam to grow to be 1 cm long? 4 mm; 2 mm; 125 yr

4. A recent men's world record for a long jump is 8.90 m. How many meters longer is that men's record than the frog's jump? 3.55 m

5. The longest wingspan of any airplane was about 26.85 times as long as the wingspan of the wandering albatross. About how many meters was the airplane's wingspan? about 93.975 m

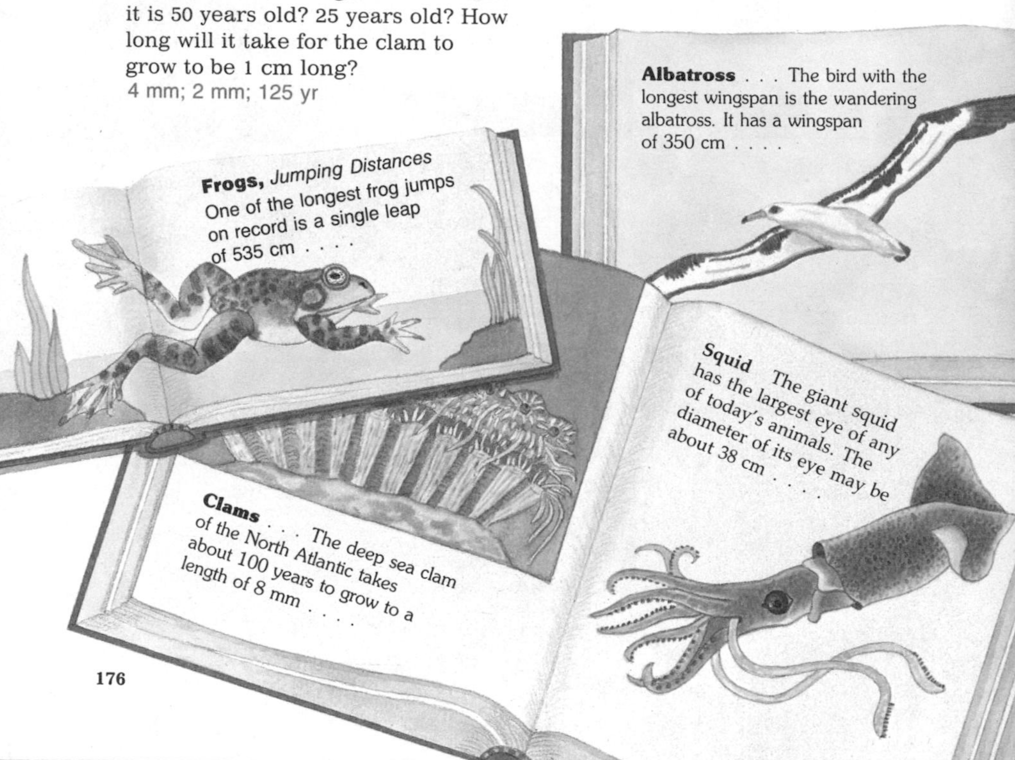

Albatross . . . The bird with the longest wingspan is the wandering albatross. It has a wingspan of 350 cm . . . .
Frogs, Jumping Distances
One of the longest frog jumps on record is a single leap of 535 cm . . . .
Squid The giant squid has the largest eye of any of today's animals. The diameter of its eye may be about 38 cm . . . .
Clams . . . The deep sea clam of the North Atlantic takes about 100 years to grow to a length of 8 mm . . . .
176


## Follow Up

### Reteaching

Look in an almanac or reference book for information about sports events and use the data to create word problems involving metric units of length. Discuss each of the problems, and help students apply the 5-Point Checklist as a guide in solving the problem.

### Enrichment

Have students compare the physical education records for their grade and a grade above or below. Comparisons can be made for 60 meter run, broad jump, shuttle run, and so on. Have students generate word problems that use data from the two classes for each event.

| Assignment Guide | | | |
|---|---|---|---|
| | Minimum | Average | Extended |
| pages 176–177 | 1–8 | 1–9 | 1–10 |

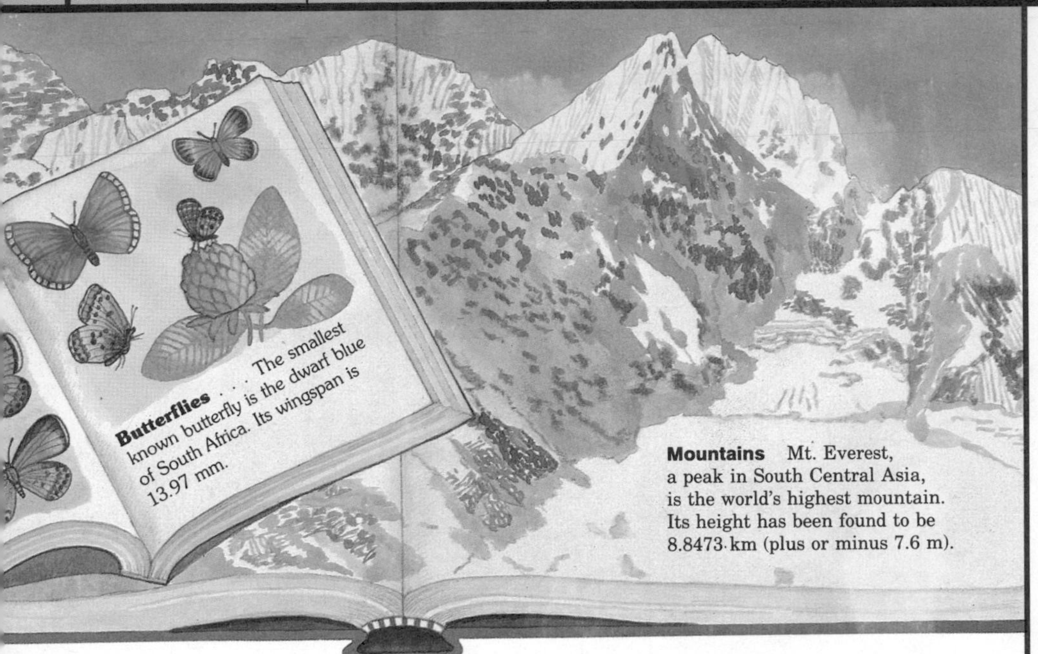

Butterflies . . . The smallest known butterfly is the dwarf blue of South Africa. Its wingspan is 13.97 mm.
Mountains Mt. Everest, a peak in South Central Asia, is the world's highest mountain. Its height has been found to be 8.8473 km (plus or minus 7.6 m).


6. What are the upper and the lower limits for the height of Mt. Everest (in meters)?
upper, 8,854.9 m; lower, 8,839.7 m

7. The deepest known part of any ocean is the Marianas Trench, 10,912 m deep. How much greater is this depth than the height of Mt. Everest (8.8473 km) in meters? 2,064.7 m

8. The giant swallowtail butterfly is one of the largest butterflies found in North America. The giant swallowtail's wingspan may be as great as 13 cm. How many millimeters greater is this wingspan than the wingspan of the smallest known butterfly? 116.03 mm

9. The world's largest butterfly is the Queen Alexandra birdwing of New Guinea. Its wingspan is about 20 times that of the smallest butterfly. About how many centimeters is the wingspan of the largest butterfly?
about 27.94 cm

10. **Try This** Bill Brown, Cindy Cole, Denise Downs, and Ed Evans are editors of a book of facts. One is the sports editor, one the science editor, one the geography editor, and one the politics editor. The sports editor is a woman who rides to work with Cindy Cole. Neither Bill Brown nor Cindy Cole has any interest in geography. Cindy Cole is the science editor's cousin. Which job does each person have?
sports—Denise Downs; science—Bill Brown; geography—Ed Evans; politics—Cindy Cole



## Using Page 177

**Exercises 6–9** Caution students to read these problems carefully in order to determine when it is necessary to change units.

**Try This** A possible strategy, Use Logical Reasoning, was taught on page 162.

**Discussion** "What question are we asked about the editors?" (Which job does each editor have?) "How many editors are there?" (4) "How many different kinds of jobs are there?" (4) "What do we know about the sports editor?" (It is a woman; it is not Cindy; it must be Denise.) "What do we know about the science editor?" (It is not Cindy.) "What further conclusions can we draw from this information?" Help students make a chart to show the data.

**Solution** The following chart shows that Denise is the sports editor; Bill is the science editor; Ed is the geography editor; and Cindy is the politics editor.

| | sports | science | geography | politics |
|---|---|---|---|---|
| Bill | no | yes | no | no |
| Cindy | no | no | no | yes |
| Denise | yes | no | no | no |
| Ed | no | no | yes | no |

## Ideas That Work

### Math for thc Gifted

Give students the following directions for a challenging measurement activity: Stand in front of a large mirror (76–100 cm high) with its center approximately at eye level. Hold a meter stick just in front of your face with the middle of the stick at eye level. Move toward and away from the mirror. Does your moving change the amount of stick you can see? Can you formulate a general rule to connect the length of the stick that can be seen with the height of the mirror? Make a diagram to show what is happening.

**Practice Supplement,** page 68

Name ____________ To follow text page 177

**Problem Solving: Using Data from a Reference Book**

Solve. Change units when necessary.

1. How many millimeters longer is the carrion beetle than the black carrion beetle?
**5.1 mm**

**Beetles.** A carrion beetle is 1.78 cm long. A black carrion beetle is 1.27 cm long.

2. The wingspan of an American Cooper is 2.5 times its body length. How long is the wingspan?
**25 mm**

**Butterflies.** The body of an American Cooper is 10 mm long.

3. The kidneys are about how many centimeters longer than they are wide?
**6 cm**

**Kidneys.** Your two kidneys filter the blood. Each kidney is about 11 cm long and 50 mm wide.

4. The lowest point in Vermont is 1,309 m lower than the highest point. What is the elevation of the lowest point?
**29 m**

**Vermont.** Mount Mansfield, 1,338 m high, is the highest point in Vermont.

5. What is the difference in the heights of the two volcanoes?
**2,411 m**

**Volcanoes of Ecuador.** Cotopaxi is 5,896 m high. Reventador is 3,485 m high.

**Quick Review** Students write the symbols (>, <, =) that make each decimal statement true.

0.8 (>) 0.08 2.6 (<) 6.2 9.9 (=) 9.90 0.245 (<) 2.045
2.03 (<) 3.02 12.36 (<) 21.63 3.45 (>) 3.38

**Lesson Focus** To express measurement in appropriate units of capacity; to solve word problems involving metric units of capacity

**Suggested Materials** Box 10 cm on a side; centimeter place-value materials, including a unit cube and a thousand-unit cube

## Ideas for Getting Started

Hold up the unit cube and the thousand-unit cube. "The unit cube is one centimeter on a side. How many centimeters long is the large cube." (10) "How many decimeters is this?" (1) Tell students that the large cube is a decimeter cube. "How many unit cubes in one layer of the large cube?" (A layer is 10 unit cubes by 10 unit cubes, so there are 100 cubes in each layer.) "How many layers in the large cube?" (10) "How many small unit cubes in the large cube?" (10 × 10 × 10, or 1,000.) Emphasize that the large cube is a cubic decimeter and has a volume of 1,000 of the unit centimeter cubes. Then tell students that a box that is 1 dm on each side (the same size as the large cube) will hold exactly one liter. A very small box the size of the unit cube will hold 0.001 of the amount held by the large cube or one millimeter.

## Using Page 178

**Lesson Development** Direct students' attention to the paragraph at the top of the page. Emphasize that volume is measured by counting the number of cubic units that the container will hold. Read the display boxes at the top of the page that describe the basic units of capacity. Use models when possible to give students better understanding of the size of the liter and the milliliter units and the relationships between these units.

**Exercises 1–6** These estimation exercises are designed to help students develop a feel for relative sizes of the liter, kiloliter, and milliliter units. After students have completed the exercises, ask them to explain the reasons for their choices.

**Exercises 7–14** In exercise 7, because a kiloliter is 1,000 times a liter, the number of kiloliters must be multiplied by 1,000 to find the number of liters. In exercise 8, the number of liters must be multiplied by 1,000 to find the number of milliliters. In exercise 13, since a liter is 0.001 of a kiloliter, the number of liters is divided by 1,000 to find the number of kiloliters. In exercise 12, the number of milliliters is divided by 1,000 to find the number of liters.

## Volume and Capacity

The **volume** of a container is the number of cubic units of space it encloses. Metric units of volume are usually used for very accurate, scientific measurements.

The units of **capacity** are used in everyday measurements to describe how much a container will hold.

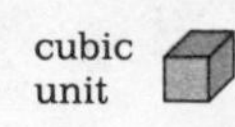


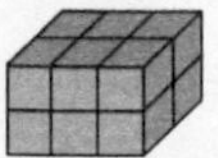


The **liter** (L) is the basic unit of capacity.

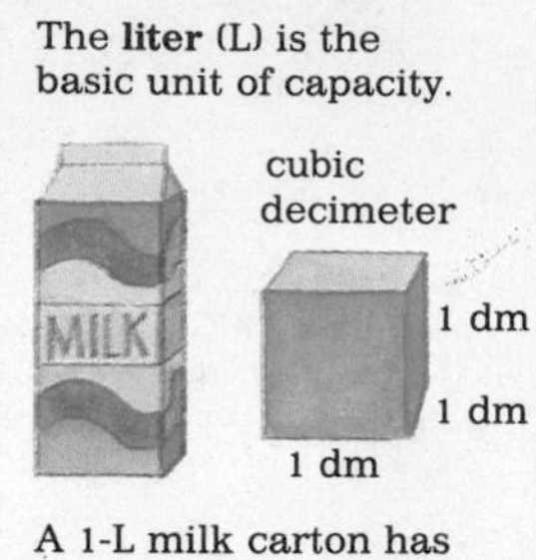


A 1-L milk carton has a volume of 1 cubic decimeter (dm³).

A **milliliter** (mL) is one thousandth of a liter.

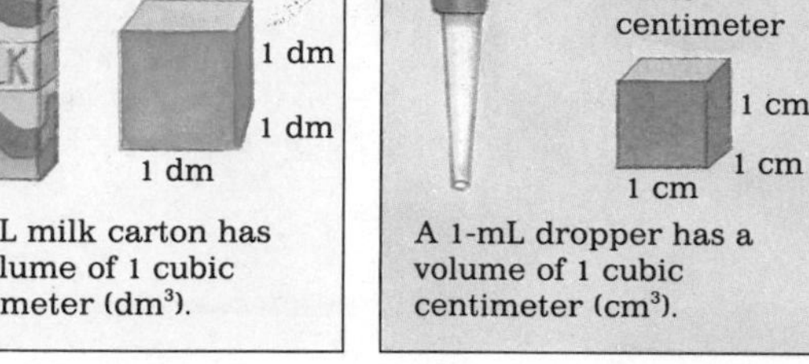


A 1-mL dropper has a volume of 1 cubic centimeter (cm³).

A **kiloliter** (kL) is one thousand liters.

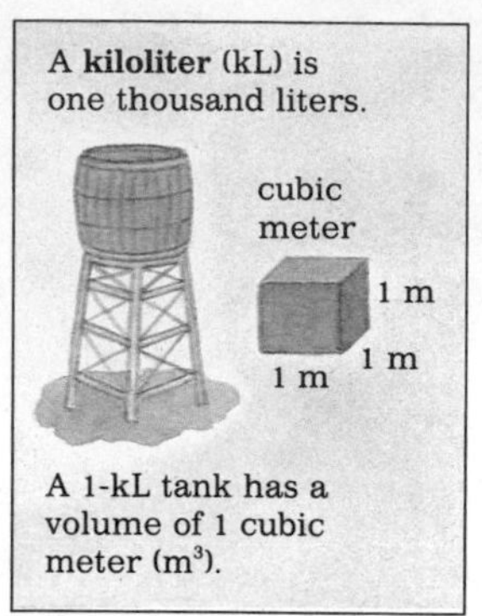


A 1-kL tank has a volume of 1 cubic meter (m³).

1,000 mL = 1 L 1 mL = 0.001 L 1,000 L = 1 kL 1 L = 0.001 kL

Choose the best estimate for the capacity of each container.

**1.** can of juice 825 mL

825 mL 825 L 825 kL

**2.** tablespoon 15 mL

15 mL 15 L 15 kL

**3.** bathtub 225 L

225 mL 225 L 225 kL

**4.** city water storage tank
2,000 mL 2,000 L 2,000 kL
2,000 kL

**5.** goldfish tank
40 mL 40L 40kL
40 L

**6.** small can of soup 200 mL
200 mL 200 L 200 kL

Give the number for each changed unit.

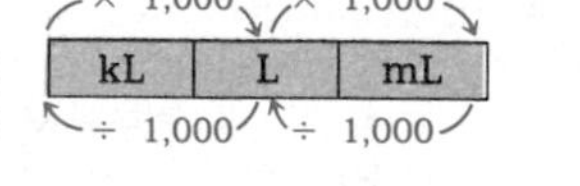


**7.** 3 kL = ■ L 3,000
**8.** 7 L = ■ mL 7,000
**9.** 0.250 kL = ■ L 250
**10.** 0.750 L = ■ mL 750
**11.** 1,435 L = ■ kL 1.435
**12.** 2,374 mL = ■ L 2.374
**13.** 476 L = ■ kL 0.476
**14.** 375 mL = ■ L 0.375

178

## Follow Up

### Reteaching

Help students develop an understanding of units of capacity through measurement activities such as the following:

- Determine the capacity of a teaspoon. (5 mL)
- Find a 250 mL cup.
- Find the capacity of a large milk or soda container.
- Estimate the capacity of a child's wading pool. (225 L)

Point out that metric units of capacity compare to each other in much the same way as metric units of length.

### Enrichment

Have students draw models to illustrate capacity. They can then exchange their work to compare the capacity of other students' models.

| Assignment Guide | Minimum | Average | Extended |
|---|---|---|---|
| page 178 | 1–14 | 1–14 | 1–14 |
| page 179 | 1–8 | 1–9 | 1–10 |

## Problem Solving: Practice (Capacity)

Solve.

1. How many cups with a capacity of 250 mL can you fill from a 1-L bottle of milk? 4 cups

2. How many 5-mL teaspoons does it take to fill a 250-mL cup? 50 teaspoons

3. About how many tablespoons with a capacity of 15 mL can you fill from a 250-mL cup? (Round to the nearest whole number.) about 17 tablespoons

4. A pitcher has 2 L of juice in it. How many 200-mL glasses can you fill with this amount of juice? 10 glasses

5. A bottle of apple juice contains 1.5 L of juice. How many milliliters is this? 1,500 mL

6. The tank on a truck used to ship milk holds 15 kL of milk. How many 1-L bottles can be filled with this milk? 15,000 bottles

7. A large water cooler holds 16 L of water. About how many water coolers does it take to hold 1 kL of water? (Round to the nearest whole number.) about 63

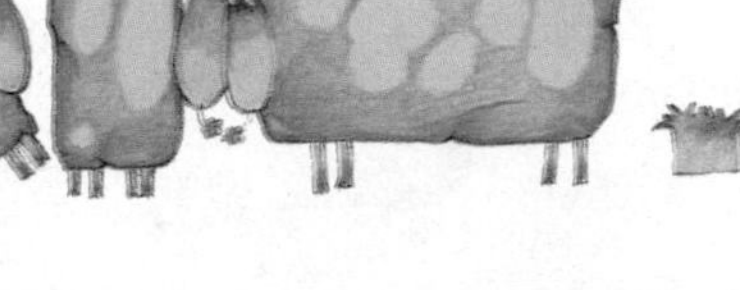

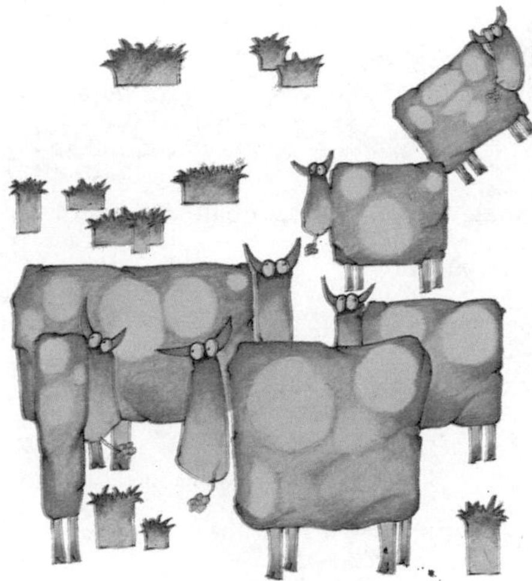

8. A large bottle holds 3.785 L of juice. How many milliliters does it hold? 3,785 mL

9. A can of frozen grape juice has a capacity of 177 mL. How much more or less than a liter of liquid do you have after you add 3 cans of water to the juice? 292 mL less

10. **Try This** Suppose you have these pails. There are no markings on either pail. How can you use the pails to get 4 L of water in the larger pail? See teaching notes.

3 L 8 L

179

## Using Page 179

**Lesson Development** Briefly review the checklist in the logo at the top of the page. Tell students that in these exercises we can apply all five steps in the checklist to help solve problems that use a variety of operations. Students will also use their knowledge of the relationship between milliliters and liters to solve the problems.

**Exercises 1–9** Remind students to read the problems carefully. If necessary, suggest that they refer back to the table on page 178 to remind them of the relationship between these units.

**Try This** A possible strategy, Use Logical Reasoning, was taught on page 162.

**Discussion** "What question is asked about the two pails?" (How can you use them to get 4 liters of water in the larger pail?") "What do you know about the pails?" (There are no markings on either pail.) "Can you measure 4 L by pouring from the larger into the smaller?" (No, after filling the 8-L pail and pouring it into the 3-L pail, there would be 5 L left in the larger pail.) "What if you filled and poured the 3-L pail as many times as possible into the 8-liter pail?" (The 8-L pail could be filled with 1 L left over in the 3-L pail.) "How can this help you solve the problem?"

**Solution** To get 4 L of water in the larger pail, use these steps: Fill and pour the 3-L pail into the 8-L pail until the 8-L pail is full. There will be 1 L left in the 3-L pail. Empty the 8-L pail, and pour the 1 L left in the 3-L pail into the 8-L pail. Fill the 3-L pail and pour it into the 8-L pail to make a total of 4 L in the 8-L pail.

**Reteaching Supplement,** page 42

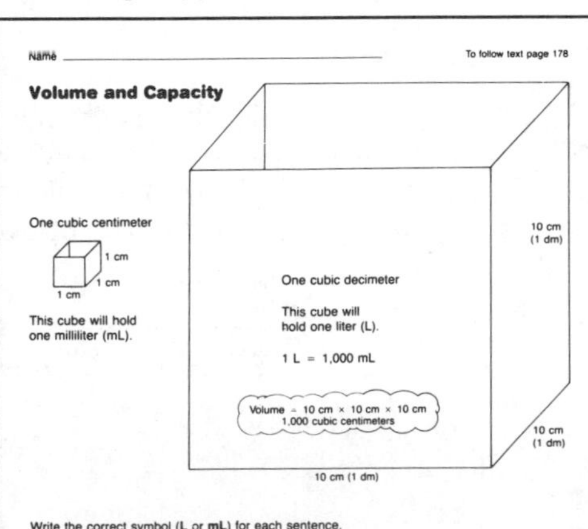

Name ______ To follow text page 178

**Volume and Capacity**

One cubic centimeter

1 cm 1 cm 1 cm

This cube will hold one milliliter (mL).

One cubic decimeter

This cube will hold one liter (L).

1 L = 1,000 mL

Volume = 10 cm × 10 cm × 10 cm
1,000 cubic centimeters

10 cm (1 dm) 10 cm (1 dm) 10 cm (1 dm)

Write the correct symbol (**L** or **mL**) for each sentence.

1. A teacup will hold about 250 __mL__ .
2. Linda bought 40 __L__ of gasoline for her car.
3. The Williams family uses about 15 __L__ of milk each week.
4. A soft drink can holds about 450 __mL__ .
5. Each person needs to drink about 2 __L__ of water each day.
6. An elephant needs to drink about 100 __L__ of water a day.
7. Jack bought a 100- __mL__ tube of toothpaste.
8. There were 1.89 __L__ of ice cream in each carton.
9. Joe put 5 __mL__ of cream in his coffee.
10. The goldfish aquarium held 40 __L__ of water.

**Enrichment Supplement,** page 42

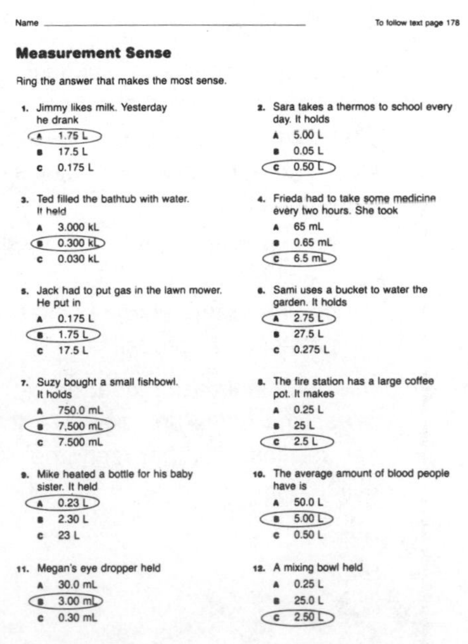

Name ______ To follow text page 178

**Measurement Sense**

Ring the answer that makes the most sense.

1. Jimmy likes milk. Yesterday he drank
   A 1.75 L (ringed)
   B 17.5 L
   C 0.175 L
2. Sara takes a thermos to school every day. It holds
   A 5.00 L
   B 0.05 L
   C 0.50 L (ringed)
3. Ted filled the bathtub with water. It held
   A 3.000 kL
   B 0.300 kL (ringed)
   C 0.030 kL
4. Frieda had to take some medicine every two hours. She took
   A 65 mL
   B 0.65 mL
   C 6.5 mL (ringed)
5. Jack had to put gas in the lawn mower. He put in
   A 0.175 L
   B 1.75 L (ringed)
   C 17.5 L
6. Sami uses a bucket to water the garden. It holds
   A 2.75 L (ringed)
   B 27.5 L
   C 0.275 L
7. Suzy bought a small fishbowl. It holds
   A 750.0 mL
   B 7,500 mL (ringed)
   C 7.500 mL
8. The fire station has a large coffee pot. It makes
   A 0.25 L
   B 25 L
   C 2.5 L (ringed)
9. Mike heated a bottle for his baby sister. It held
   A 0.23 L (ringed)
   B 2.30 L
   C 23 L
10. The average amount of blood people have is
    A 50.0 L
    B 5.00 L (ringed)
    C 0.50 L
11. Megan's eye dropper held
    A 30.0 mL
    B 3.00 mL (ringed)
    C 0.30 mL
12. A mixing bowl held
    A 0.25 L
    B 25.0 L
    C 2.50 L (ringed)

**Practice Supplement,** page 69

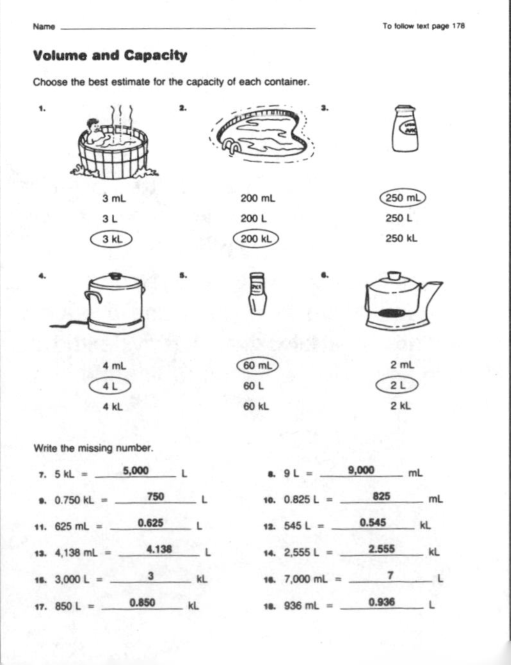

Name ______ To follow text page 178

**Volume and Capacity**

Choose the best estimate for the capacity of each container.

1. 3 mL / 3 L / 3 kL (ringed)
2. 200 mL / 200 L / 200 kL (ringed)
3. 250 mL (ringed) / 250 L / 250 kL
4. 4 mL / 4 L (ringed) / 4 kL
5. 60 mL (ringed) / 60 L / 60 kL
6. 2 mL / 2 L (ringed) / 2 kL

Write the missing number.

7. 5 kL = __5,000__ L
8. 9 L = __9,000__ mL
9. 0.750 kL = __750__ L
10. 0.825 L = __825__ mL
11. 625 mL = __0.625__ L
12. 545 L = __0.545__ kL
13. 4,138 mL = __4.138__ L
14. 2,555 L = __2.555__ kL
15. 3,000 L = __3__ kL
16. 7,000 mL = __7__ L
17. 850 L = __0.850__ kL
18. 936 mL = __0.936__ L

**Quick Review** Students use the appropriate units to express answers to these problems.

5 × 6 cm  8)$40.00  6 × 3 cm  90 L × 10  32 mL × 2  $2.00 ÷ 10
12 mL × 2  8 × 9 km  4 × 7 m  $6.00 × 7  8 L × 5

**Lesson Focus** To express measurement in appropriate unis of weight; to solve word problems involving metric units of weight

**Suggested Materials** 1-kg weights or objects weighing 1 kilogram

## Ideas for Getting Started

Pass around a 1-kg weight or object to give students a sense of this metric unit. Tell students that 1 mL of water weighs about 1 gram and that the gram is one thousandth of a kilogram. Write the names for these unis on the chalkboard.

## Using Page 180

**Lesson Development** Direct students' attention to the display boxes at the top of the page. Point out that the gram is the basic metric unit of weight. Call attention to the illustrated objects that weigh about a gram. Tell students that a dry tea bag weighs about two grams and that a dime weighs about two grams. Then point out that 1 mL of water weighs one gram. Discuss the milligram and be sure students understand that this unit is used to measure very small amounts accurately. Finally, discuss the kilogram. Be sure to emphasize the relationships between the milligram, gram, and kilogram.

**Exercises 1–9** These exercises provide students with an opportunity to make gross decisions regarding the units of weight. Since the gram and the milligram are such small units, many of the comparisons should be easy for students to make. It would be clear, for example, that a bowling ball would have to be 7 kilograms. After students have completed these exercises, let them discuss the choices they made for the estimates.

**Exercises 10–19** Direct students' attention to the table that shows the kilogram, gram, and milligram units. Point out that since a kilogram is 1,000 grams, and a gram is 1,000 milligrams, it is possible to multiply or divide by 1,000 to change from one unit to an adjacent unit. For example, in exercise 10, we can multiply the number of kilograms by 1,000 to find the number of grams. In exercise 14, we can divide the number of grams by 1,000 to find the number of kilograms.

**Exercises 20–21** These starred exercises are more challenging. In exercise 20, since a kilogram is 1,000 grams and a gram is 1,000 miligrams, 1 kg is 1,000,000 mg. In exercise 21, since the milligram is one thousandth of a gram and a gram is one thousandth of a kilogram, we divide the number of milligrams by one million to find the number of kilograms.

## Weight

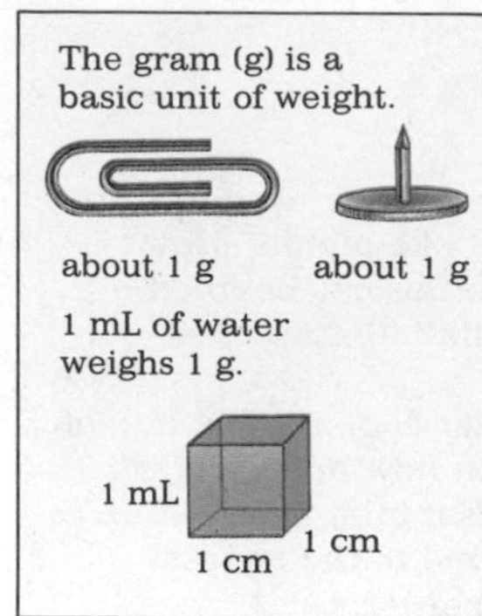

The gram (g) is a basic unit of weight.
about 1 g
about 1 g
1 mL of water weighs 1 g.
1 mL
1 cm
1 cm


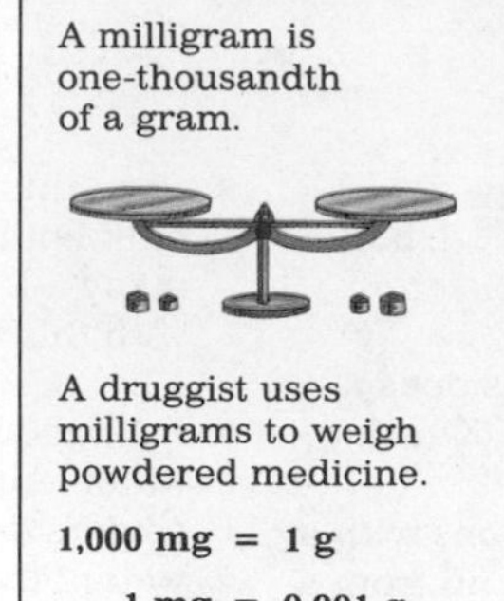

A milligram is one-thousandth of a gram.
A druggist uses milligrams to weigh powdered medicine.
1,000 mg = 1 g
1 mg = 0.001 g


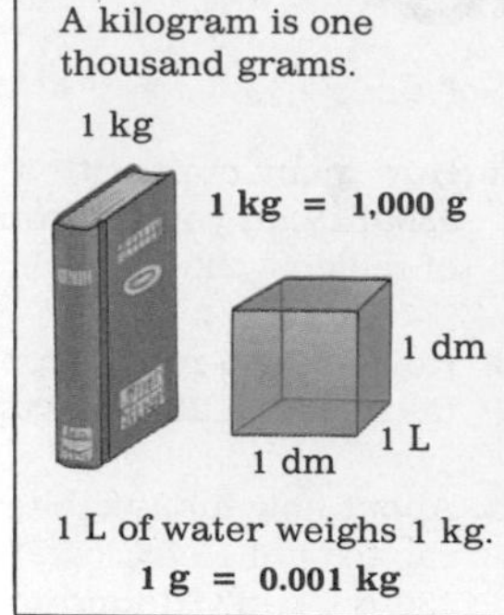

A kilogram is one thousand grams.
1 kg
1 kg = 1,000 g
1 dm
1 dm
1 L
1 L of water weighs 1 kg.
1 g = 0.001 kg


Choose the best estimate of the weight.

1. A bowling ball 7 kg
   7 mg  7 g  7 kg
2. A nickel 5 g
   5 mg  5 g  5 kg
3. A drop of water 50 mg
   50 mg  50 g  50 kg
4. A baseball bat 1 kg
   1 mg  1 g  1 kg
5. A large man 90 kg
   90 mg  90 g  90 kg
6. A ballpoint pen 15 g
   15 mg  15 g  15 kg
7. A horse 500 kg
   500 mg  500 g  500 kg
8. A pin 125 mg
   125 mg  125 g  125 kg
9. A bicycle 12 kg
   12 mg  12 g  12 kg

Give the number for each changed unit.

Think about this table.

| kg | g | mg |
|---|---|---|

(× 1,000 from kg to g and from g to mg; ÷ 1,000 from mg to g and from g to kg)

10. 5 kg = ■ g 5,000
11. 12 g = ■ mg 12,000
12. 0.250 kg = ■ g 250
13. 0.500 g = ■ mg 500
14. 8,346 g = ■ kg 8.346
15. 1,765 mg = ■ g 1.765
16. 425 mg = ■ g 0.425
17. 750 g = ■ kg 0.750
18. 56 kg = ■ g 56,000
19. 1.3 g = ■ mg 1,300
★ 20. 1 kg = ■ mg 1,000,000
★ 21. 4,000,000 mg = ■ kg 4

180

## Follow Up

### Reteaching

Challenge students to suggest objects that weigh one gram and one kilogram. Then use balance scales to check the weights of the suggested objects. Some possible items are:

- one gram: a vitamin pill, a credit card, a dollar, two paper clips
- one kilogram: a large book, bag of 5 potatoes, a baseball bat

Use the "staircase" idea shown in the reteaching notes on page 174 to show the relationships between the various units.

### Enrichment

Have students estimate the weight of several items. Then let them check the actual measure and record the information on a chart such as the one below.

| Metric Units | | |
|---|---|---|
| Item | Estimated | Actual |
| button | | |
| paper clip | | |
| pencil | | |
| book | | |

| Assignment Guide | | | |
|---|---|---|---|
| | Minimum | Average | Extended |
| page 180 | 1–19 | 1–19 | 1–21 |
| page 181 | 1–7 | 1–8 | 1–9 |

## Problem Solving: Practice (Weight)

Solve.

1. The powdered cocoa in a box weighs 120 g and makes 24 cups of cocoa. How many grams of cocoa are needed for each cup? 5 g
2. A package of crackers weighs 539 g. There are 36 crackers in the box. What is the weight of each cracker to the nearest gram? 15 g
3. How many pieces of sausage that weigh 250 g each can be cut from a large piece that weighs 1 kg? 4 pieces
4. A baking potato weighs 245 g. How many kilograms does a bag of 6 potatoes weigh? 1.47 kg
5. There are 250 mg of sodium in each 30-g serving of a certain cereal. How much would a serving of the cereal that contains 1 g of sodium weigh? 120 g
6. A raisin weighs about 500 mg. If there are 28 raisins in a box, what is the total weight of the raisins in grams? 14 g
7. A family-size package of ground beef weighs 2.486 kg. If each hamburger patty made from the beef weighs 113 g, how many patties can be made? 22 patties
8. A giant box of washing powder weighs 3.2 kg. It takes 60 g of the powder to wash a load of dishes. How many loads of dishes can be washed with a box of the powder? (Round to the nearest whole number.) 53 loads
9. **Try This** An apple and a banana together weigh 417 g. The apple weighs 73 g less than the banana. How much does each piece of fruit weigh? banana, 245 g; apple, 172 g

## Using Page 181

**Lesson Development** Briefly review the 5-Point Checklist in the logo at the top of the page. Explain that these problems involve a variety of operations and that the information involving units of weight will be useful in solving the problems.

**Exercises 1–8** Caution students to read the problems carefully. If necessary, read through each problem and discuss the changes in units of weight that need to be made. In exercise 8 students are to round answers to the nearest whole number.

**Try This** A possible strategy, Guess and Check, was taught on page 48.

**Discussion** "What is the question we are asked about the fruit?" (How much does each piece of fruit weigh?) "What is the weight of the apple and banana together?" (417 g) "Which piece of fruit weighs more?" (the banana) "How much more does the banana weigh?" (17 g more than the apple) "If you guess that the banana weighs 185 g, what would the apple weigh?" (185 − 73 or 122 g) "Was this guess too large or too small?" (Too small; total weight would be only 307 g.) "Can you revise your guess so that your answer will be closer?"

**Solution** The banana weighs 245 g; the apple weighs 172 g. These two weights satisfy the conditions stated in the problem.

**Extension** Suppose a pear and a peach together weigh 432 g. The peach weighs 56 g less than the pear. How much does each piece of fruit weigh? (The pear weighs 244 g; the peach, 188 g.)

## Ideas That Work

### Special Education

An interesting activity for students is to estimate and measure their lung capacities in liters.

Use a large glass jar filled with water and marked in liters down one side as shown in the illustration. (Determine capacity marks by pouring in liters of water and marking the appropriate levels, upside down, on a piece of tape on the side of the jar.) The jar, filled with water, is then placed upside down on a wire rack in a basin of water as shown, and a rubber tube is inserted in the neck of the jar.

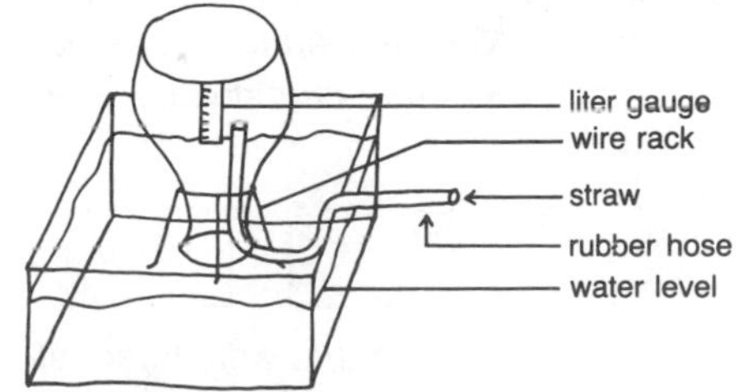


Students make and record an estimate of the capacity of their lungs. Then they insert a plastic straw into the rubber hose and blow air from their lungs into the jar. The amount of water displaced shows the capacity of their lungs in liters.

**Practice Supplement,** page 70

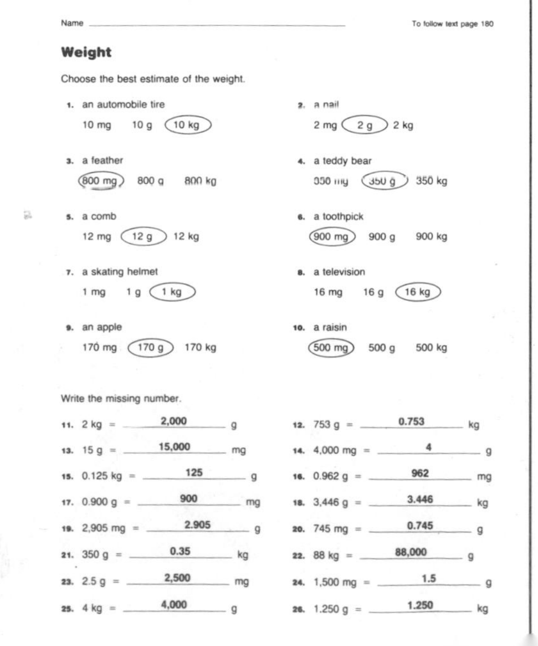

Name ______________________ To follow text page 180

**Weight**

Choose the best estimate of the weight.

1. an automobile tire
   10 mg 10 g (10 kg)
2. a nail
   2 mg (2 g) 2 kg
3. a feather
   (800 mg) 800 g 800 kg
4. a teddy bear
   350 mg (350 g) 350 kg
5. a comb
   12 mg (12 g) 12 kg
6. a toothpick
   (900 mg) 900 g 900 kg
7. a skating helmet
   1 mg 1 g (1 kg)
8. a television
   16 mg 16 g (16 kg)
9. an apple
   170 mg (170 g) 170 kg
10. a raisin
    (500 mg) 500 g 500 kg

Write the missing number.

11. 2 kg = 2,000 g
12. 753 g = 0.753 kg
13. 15 g = 15,000 mg
14. 4,000 mg = 4 g
15. 0.125 kg = 125 g
16. 0.962 g = 962 mg
17. 0.900 g = 900 mg
18. 3,446 g = 3.446 kg
19. 2,905 mg = 2.905 g
20. 745 mg = 0.745 g
21. 350 g = 0.35 kg
22. 88 kg = 88,000 g
23. 2.5 g = 2,500 mg
24. 1,500 mg = 1.5 g
25. 4 kg = 4,000 g
26. 1.250 g = 1.250 kg

**Quick Review** Students express answers in the appropriate units.

12 mL + 3 mL  4 km − 3 km  15 m + 15 m  $40.00 + $50.00  50 L − 40 L
200 mL + 50 mL  $45.00 − $25.00  6 L + 82 L  1,500 km + 500 km
36 cm − 16 cm  16 m + 3 m  $60.00 − $2.00  12 m − 2 m  50 km − 25 km

**Lesson Focus** To read and estimate temperatures in degrees Celsius

**Suggested Materials** Celsius thermometer

## Ideas for Getting Started

Put these statements on the chalkboard: Water freezes at 0°C. Normal body temperature is 37°C. Normal room temperature is about 20°C. Then ask students to estimate other temperatures, such as the temperature of a cold drink, the temperature of hot tap water, the temperature near a light bulb, or the temperature when the thermometer is held in a closed hand. After students have made their estimates, use a thermometer to determine the actual temperatures. Activities such as these will help students develop a feel for the Celsius unit.

## Using Page 182

**Lesson Development** Direct students' attention to the name and symbol of the basic metric unit of temperature, the degree Celsius. Then focus on the thermometer shown on the left. "At what temperature does water freeze?" (0°C) "At what temperature does water boil?" (100°C) "What is normal body temperature?" (37°C)

**Exercises 1–6** Be sure students understand the directions for these exercises. Emphasize that they may need to use a process of elimination. For example, since frozen yogurt would be colder than cold water, the letter indicating the temperature would be at the lowest point on the thermometer. Have students make their best guesses to complete these exercises. Then discuss each exercise and write the appropriate temperatures on the chalkboad. Remind students that because the temperature for frozen yogurt is below zero, we use a minus sign, ⁻12 for example, to show this.

**Exercises 7–14** If students have difficulty with these exercises, suggest that they refer back to exercises 1–6.

## Temperature

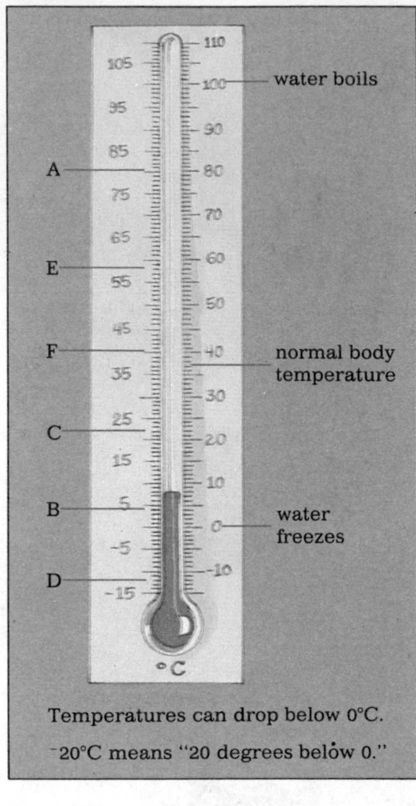


Temperatures can drop below 0°C.

⁻20°C means "20 degrees below 0."

The **degree Celsius** (°C) is the basic unit of temperature.

Give the letter for the temperature on the thermometer that best fits each condition or object pictured below.

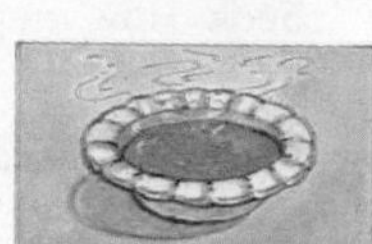
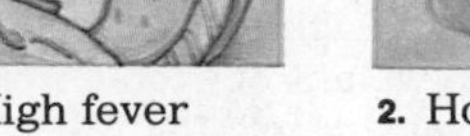

1. High fever F
2. Hot soup A

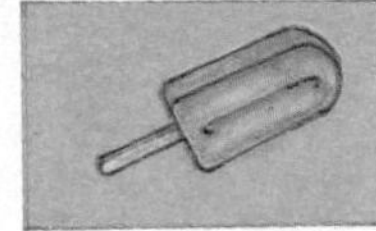

3. Frozen yogurt D
4. Cold water B

5. Comfortable room temperature C
6. Hottest air temperature recorded on earth E

Choose the best temperature estimate.

7. Hot drink 81°C  
   18°C  81°C
8. Crushed ice 0°C  
   0°C  30°C
9. Drinking water 12°C  
   12°C  92°C
10. Hot oven 190°C  
    40°C  190°C
11. Inside a refrigerator 4°C  
    4°C  40°C
12. Snowy day ⁻5°C  
    ⁻5°C  25°C
13. Your classroom 20°C  
    2°C  20°C
14. Hot bath 45°C  
    45°C  95°C

182

## Follow Up

### Reteaching

Let students play a game called "What's My Temp?" Write temperatures between 0°C and 100°C on three index cards as shown:

On the back of the cards write three different clues, such as "At my temperature you should turn on the heat." Only one clue is accurate. Let three students each pretend to be 17°C. After the clues are read, the class votes for the person believed to have the correct clue, and the "real 17°C" is asked to step forward.

### Enrichment

Have students bring in weather forecasts for a week. Let them compile data on high and low temperatures and show the data on a graph. Students then calculate the average high and low temperature for the week.

| | Assignment Guide | | |
|---|---|---|---|
| | Minimum | Average | Extended |
| page 182 | 1–14 | 1–14 | 1–14 |
| page 183 | 1–7, SK | 1–8, SK | 1–9, SK |

Read and write the temperature shown on each thermometer.

1.
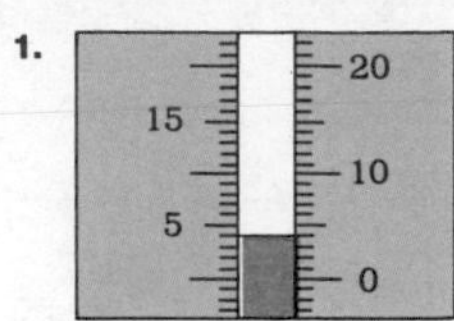


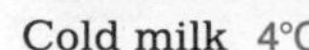
Cold milk 4°C

2.
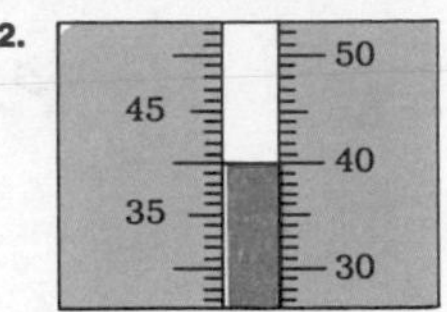

Very warm day 40°C

3.
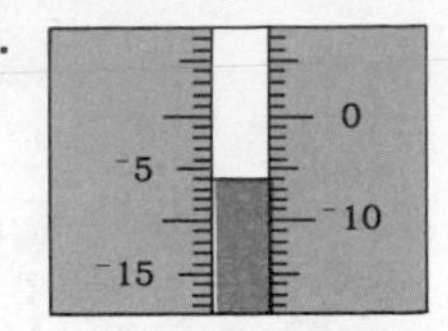

Inside a freezer ⁻6°C

4.
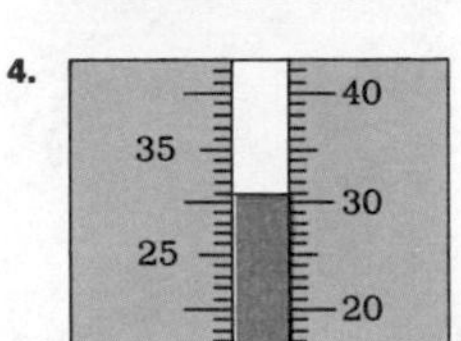

Butter melts 31°C

5.
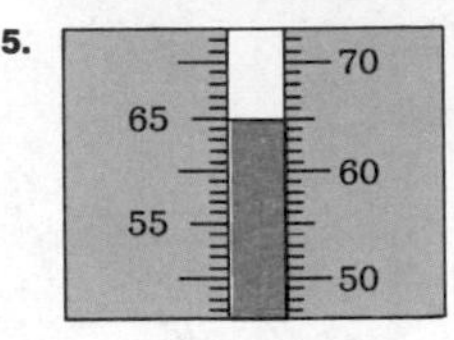

Broiled steak 65°C

6.
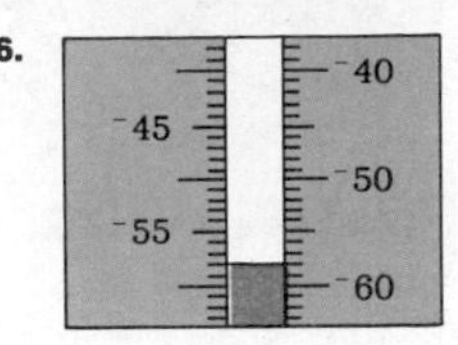

Record cold day ⁻58°C

7. This temperature graph shows a normal temperature for each season in San Antonio, Texas. What is the average of these temperatures? 20.5°C

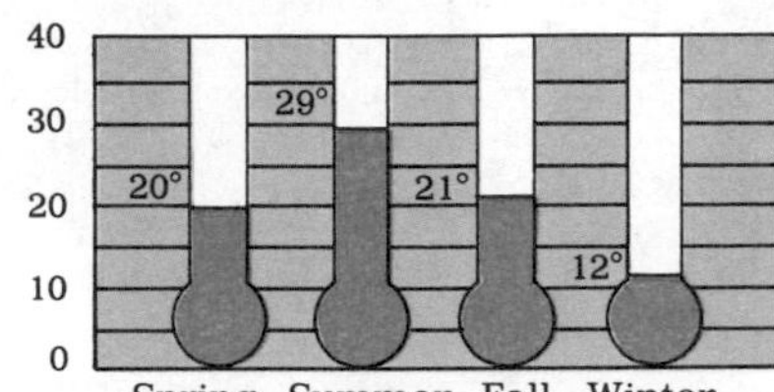


8. The temperature at which water boils changes with the altitude (height above sea level). At sea level water boils at 100°C. At the top of Mt. Everest water boils at a temperature only 0.71 times as great. By how many degrees do these two temperatures differ? 29°C

9. **DATA BANK** How many degrees would the world's record cold temperature have to rise to reach the record high temperature? (See Data Bank, page 408.) 146.3°C

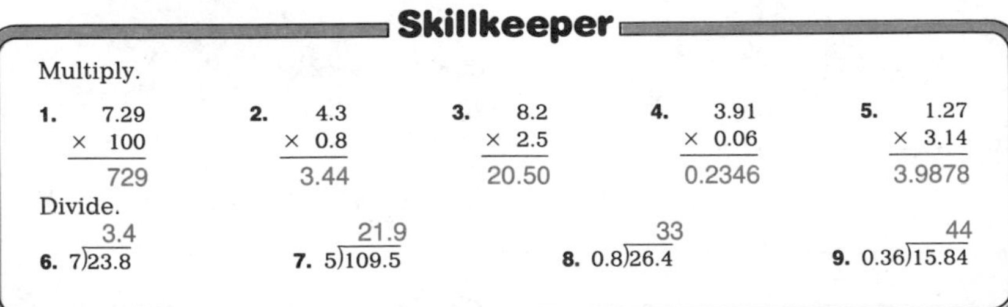

**Skillkeeper**

Multiply.

1. 7.29 × 100 = 729
2. 4.3 × 0.8 = 3.44
3. 8.2 × 2.5 = 20.50
4. 3.91 × 0.06 = 0.2346
5. 1.27 × 3.14 = 3.9878

Divide.

6. 7)23.8 — 3.4
7. 5)109.5 — 21.9
8. 0.8)26.4 — 33
9. 0.36)15.84 — 44



## Using Page 183

**Lesson Development** Discuss the first exercise with the students. "How many spaces are there from 0 to 5 on the scale?" (5) "What is the value of each space?" (1) "How many spaces up from 0 is the red liquid in the thermometer?" (4) "What is the temperature in degrees Celsius?" (4 degrees Celsius) Call attention to the temperature below zero in exercise 3. Be sure students understand that each mark on the scale represents one degree Celsius. Elicit that the reading for this thermometer is ⁻6°C.

**Exercises 1–6** After students have completed these exercises, discuss the answers and correct any misunderstanding in reading the thermometers.

**Exercise 8** Note that in this exercise students must first multiply 0.71 by 100 and then subtract 71° from 100°.

**Data Bank** This Data Bank provides an opportunity for students to search beyond the text page for important data needed to solve the problem. If necessary, suggest that students draw a rough sketch of a thermometer to show the two extreme temperatures. Students should see that the temperature would have to rise 88.3 degrees to reach zero, and then rise 58 degrees more to reach the record high temperature. Thus they would add 88.3 + 58 to find the total number of degrees.

**Skillkeeper** This skill was originally taught in Chapter 6.

**Reteaching Supplement,** page 43

Name ______ To follow text page 183

**Temperature**

Use the thermometer to find the best estimate of temperature for each item below.

−20 −10 0 10 20 30 40 50 60 70 80 90 100 110
−15 −5 5 15 25 35 45 55 65 75 85 95 105

degree Celsius (°C) — water freezes — comfortable room temperature — normal body temperature — water boils

Ring the best estimate.

1. a snow storm — A 5°C (ringed), B 20°C, C 32°C (Room temperature is around 20°C, so it must be less than 20°.)
2. a day at the beach — A 5°C, B 20°C, C 32°C (ringed) (Normal body temperature is between 35°C and 40°C.)
3. cold juice — A −5°C, B 5°C (ringed), C 15°C (Water freezes at 0°C.)
4. ocean temperature — A 0°C, B 15°C (ringed), C 40° C
5. the North Pole — A −20°C (ringed), B 0°C, C 20°C
6. a car's hot engine — A 9°C, B 30°C, C 90°C (ringed)
7. warm water — A 15°C, B 33°C, C 78°C (ringed)
8. air-conditioned store — A 20°C (ringed), B 40°C, C 60°C
9. hot slice of pizza — A 35°C, B 40°C, C 80°C (ringed)
10. Florida in July — A 16°C, B 20°C, C 36°C (ringed)
11. a dog's temperature — A 35°C (ringed), B ⁻60°C, C 80°C
12. a hot iron — A 20°C, B 40°C, C 90°C (ringed)

**Enrichment Supplement,** page 43

Name ______ To follow text page 183

**Melting Points**

The melting point of any substance is that temperature at which the solid begins to change to a liquid when heat is added.

Below is a table showing the melting points of a number of substances.

| Substance | Temperature | Substance | Temperature |
|---|---|---|---|
| copper | 1,083.4°C | silver | 961.93°C |
| gold | 1,064.43°C | tin | 231.9°C |
| lead | 327.5°C | water | 0°C |
| mercury | ⁻38.87°C | zinc | 419.58°C |

Solve using data from the table.

1. Which substance has the lowest melting point? **mercury**
2. Which has the highest melting point? **copper**
3. Which substances are liquid at normal room temperature? **mercury and water**
4. How many degrees difference are there between the melting points of copper and gold? **18.97°C**
5. How many degrees difference are there between the melting points of gold and silver? **102.5°C**
6. Write the substances in order of melting points from highest to lowest. **copper, gold, silver, zinc, lead, tin, water, mercury**
7. How many degrees difference are there between the melting points of mercury and water? **38.87°C**

Between water and copper? **1,083.4°C**

Between mercury and copper? **1,122.27°C**

**Practice Supplement,** page 71

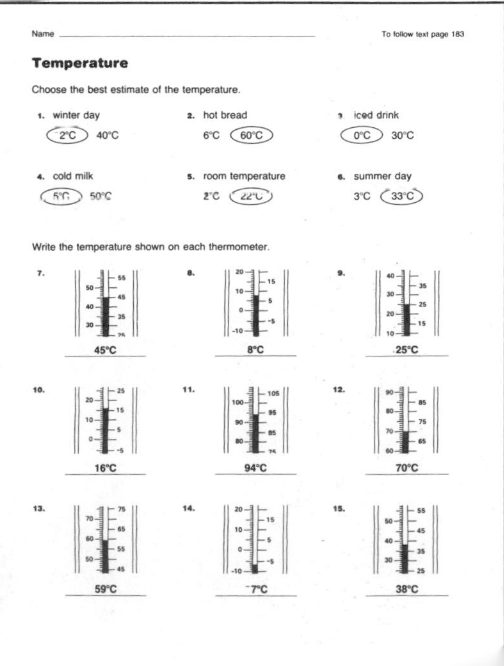

Name ______ To follow text page 183

**Temperature**

Choose the best estimate of the temperature.

1. winter day — ⁻2°C (ringed) 40°C
2. hot bread — 6°C 60°C (ringed)
3. iced drink — 0°C (ringed) 30°C
4. cold milk — 5°C (ringed) 50°C
5. room temperature — 2°C 22°C (ringed)
6. summer day — 3°C 33°C (ringed)

Write the temperature shown on each thermometer.

7. 45°C
8. 8°C
9. 25°C
10. 16°C
11. 94°C
12. 70°C
13. 59°C
14. ⁻7°C
15. 38°C

# Time

**Quick Review** Students skip count by twos and fives to 100, then by tens, twenty-fives, and fifties to 500.

**Lesson Focus** To express time in larger and smaller units; to add and subtract units of time

## Ideas for Getting Started

Generate a discussion to review that there are 60 seconds in a minute, 60 minutes in an hour, and 24 hours in a day. Then ask students if they recall the number of days in each of the months. Help them remember this rhyme:

Thirty days hath September
April, June and November,
And just for fun,
all the rest have 31, except February.
February alone doesn't hold the line.
For three years it has 28,
and in the fourth year, 29.

## Using Page 184

**Lesson Development** Call students' attention to the display at the top of the page. Review the relationships between seconds, minutes, hours, and days. Be sure students understand the use of a.m. and p.m. Point out that when it is exactly 12 noon or 12 midnight, it is neither a.m. nor p.m. Then focus on the second box and discuss the relationship between days, weeks, months, years, and centuries. Then work through the examples with students. Point out that in Example A, we multiply by 7 because there are 7 days in 1 week. In Example B, because there are 60 minutes in an hour, we divide by 60.

**Exercises 1–15** In some of these exercises, students must multiply to change a larger unit to a smaller one. In others they must divide to change a smaller unit to a larger one. Be sure students understand why they are performing these operations. Note that in exercises 10–12, two operations—multiplication and addition—are needed. If students have difficulty with these exercises, encourage them to refer to the tables that show the relationship between the units.

## Time: Basic Units

Here are some commonly used devices and units for measuring time.

Hours between midnight and noon are **a.m.** Hours between noon and midnight are **p.m.**

| | | |
|---|---|---|
| 60 seconds (s) | = | 1 minute (min) |
| 60 minutes | = | 1 hour (h) |
| 24 hours (h) | = | 1 day (d) |

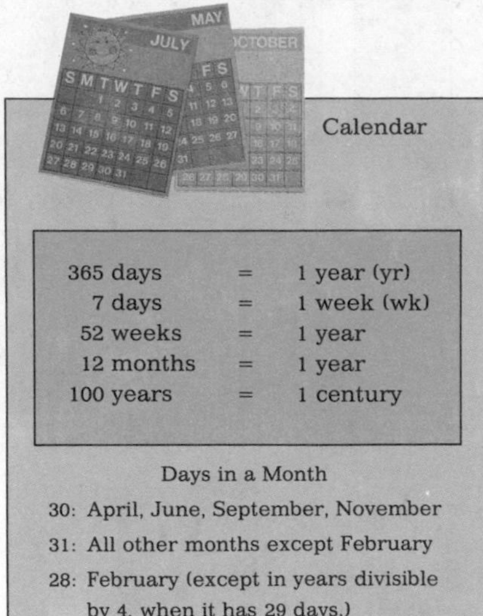


| | | |
|---|---|---|
| 365 days | = | 1 year (yr) |
| 7 days | = | 1 week (wk) |
| 52 weeks | = | 1 year |
| 12 months | = | 1 year |
| 100 years | = | 1 century |

Days in a Month

30: April, June, September, November
31: All other months except February
28: February (except in years divisible by 4, when it has 29 days.)

We can change from one time unit to another as shown in the examples below.

**Example A:**
Jenny was on vacation for 3 wk 4 d. How many days was this?

3 wk = 3 × 7, or 21 d
21 + 4 = 25

Answer: 25 d

**Example B:**
Byron recorded music for 135 min. How many hours and minutes was this?

135 ÷ 60 = 2 R15

Answer: 2 h 15 min

Give the missing numbers.

1. 5 h = ■ min 300
2. 4 min = ■ s 240
3. 6 wk = ■ d 42
4. 4 yr = ■ mo 48
5. 3 yr = ■ d 1,095
6. 5 yr = ■ wk 260
7. 20 centuries = ■ yr 2,000
8. 180 min = ■ h 3
9. 240 s = ■ min 4
10. 6 min 24 s = ■ s 384
11. 5 h 25 min = ■ min 325
12. 3 d 8 h = ■ h 80
13. 65 mo ■ yr ■ mo 5; 5
14. 85 h = ■ d ■ h 3; 13
15. 340 min = ■ h ■ min 5; 40



## Follow Up

### Reteaching

Review the various units of time discussed in this lesson. Encourage students to share their ideas about the need for some means of telling time or measuring elapsed time. Suggest that students prepare brief reports on various timekeeping systems—for example, that used by the Mayans of Central America. Then provide examples of different time units and have students change weeks to days, years to weeks, hours to minutes, and minutes to seconds.

### Enrichment

Tell students that Jay and Jane work for different hourly pay rates. Then have students compute the number of hours each person worked and how much pay each earned for that week.

| Jay ($3.45 per hour) | | |
|---|---|---|
| Mon. | Tues. | Wed. |
| 7:30–12:30 | 8:00–4:00 | 9:00–5:00 |

**21 h; $72.45**

| Jane B ($4.50 per hour) | | |
|---|---|---|
| Thu. | Fri. | Sat. |
| 9:00–5:00 | 12:00–8:00 | 9:00–3:00 |

**22 h; $99.00**

| | Assignment Guide | | |
|---|---|---|---|
| | Minimum | Average | Extended |
| page 184 | 1–15 | 1–15 | 1–15 |
| page 185 | 1–12 | 1–12 | 1–12 TM |

## Adding and Subtracting Time

Juan worked at the hospital 3 h 25 min in the morning and 2 h 45 min in the afternoon.

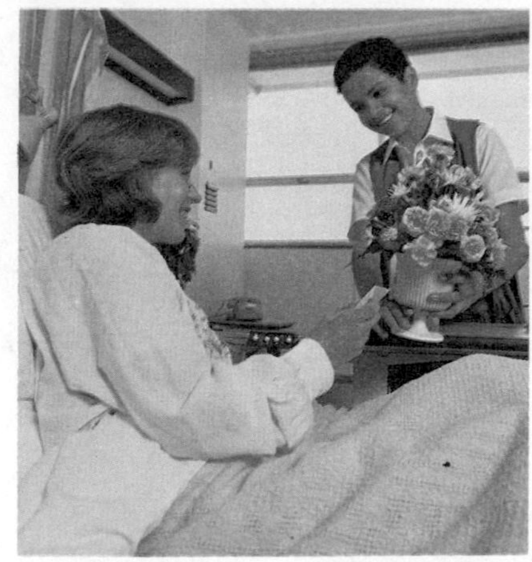

**A.** How long did Juan work that day?

3 h 25 min
+ 2 h 45 min
5 h 70 min

(more than 1 h: 70 min = 1 h 10 min)

or 6 h 10 min

Juan worked 6 h 10 min.

**B.** How much longer did Juan work in the morning than in the afternoon?

3 h 25 min
− 2 h 45 min

(We must trade 1 h for 60 min.)

2 h 85 min
~~3 h 25 min~~
− 2 h 45 min
0 h 40 min

Juan worked 40 min longer in the morning.

Add or subtract.

1. 3 h 45 min + 4 h 30 min — 8 h 15 min
2. 4 h 55 min + 2 h 35 min — 7 h 30 min
3. 5 h 37 min + 16 h 23 min — 22 h
4. 3 min 25 s + 2 min 44 s — 6 min 9 s
5. 4 min 29 s + 8 min 46 s — 13 min 15 s
6. 9 min 55 s + 6 min 42 s — 16 min 37 s
7. 8 h 20 min − 3 h 45 min — 4 h 35 min
8. 12 h 10 min − 7 h 50 min — 4 h 20 min
9. 8 h 4 min − 2 h 19 min — 5 h 45 min
10. 6 min 15 s − 4 min 45 s — 1 min 30 s
11. 9 min 12 s − 3 min 20 s — 5 min 52 s
12. 12 min 24 s − 7 min 56 s — 4 min 28 s

### Think Math

**Estimation**

Guess which answer is greatest and which is smallest. Calculate to check your guesses! See teaching notes.

**A.** 1 h = ■ s — 3,600

**B.** 1 yr = ■ h — 8,760

**C.** 1 wk = ■ min — 10,080



## Using Page 185

**Lesson Development** Read the paragraph at the top of the page. Then have students read question A and B. Briefly discuss the data needed to answer the questions. "How long did Juan work in the morning?" (3 hours 25 minutes) "How long did he work in the afternoon?" (2 hours 45 minutes) Point out that in the first question we want to find the total hours Juan worked during the day, so we use addition. In question B, we will use subtraction to make a comparison.

In working through the first example, help students see that the sum is 5 h and 70 min. Because 70 minutes is more than one hour, we trade 60 minutes for one hour and write the answer as 6 h 10 min. Have students reread the problem to be sure this answer makes sense.

In example B students should observe that we must trade in order to subtract minutes; thus we rewrite 3 h 25 min as 2 h 85 min. Again have students reread the problem to make sure that the answer 40 minutes makes sense.

**Exercises 1–12** These exercises are similar to the examples and should cause little difficulty. Remind students that there are 60 seconds in one minute. Point out that they must use this relationship to add and subtract minutes and seconds just as with hours and minutes.

**Think Math** In this activity students are to make guesses and not actually perform the operations. Encourage students to use the relationships given in the table to calculate each answer in order to check their estimates.

### Reteaching Supplement, page 44

Name ____________ To follow text page 185

**Adding and Subtracting Time**

Samantha started jogging at 1:45 p.m. She jogged for 2 hours and 20 minutes. What time did she stop jogging?

(1 hour = 60 minutes)

We should add to find the time.

1 h 45 min + 2 h 20 min = 3 h 65 min → (65 min − 60 min = 5 min → 1 h) → (65 min = 1 h 5 min) → 3 hr + 1 hr 5 min = 4 hr 5 min

Samantha stopped jogging at 4:05 p.m.

Add or subtract.

1. 7 min 15 s − 5 min 45 s → (1 less minute, 60 more seconds) 6 min 75 s − 5 min 45 s = 1 min 30 s
2. 4 h 12 min − 1 h 40 min → (12 + 60) (1 less hour, 60 more minutes) 3 h 72 min − 1 h 40 min = **2 h 32 min**
3. 7 h 35 min + 2 h 35 min — **10 h 10 min**
4. 10 min 52 s + 4 min 45 s — **15 min 37 s**
5. 3 h 60 min − 2 h 35 min — **1 h 25 min**
6. 5 h 10 min − 1 h 50 min — **3 h 20 min**
7. 4 h 30 min + 6 h 45 min — **11 h 15 min**
8. 12 min 40 s + 22 min 18 s — **34 min 58 s**
9. 10 min 7 s − 9 min 45 s — **0 min 22 s**
10. 10 h 40 min + 7 h 15 min — **17 h 55 min**
11. 12 h 30 min − 11 h 45 min — **45 min**
12. 7 min 41 s − 2 min 55 s — **4 min 46 s**
13. 19 min 50 s + 27 min 38 s — **47 min 28 s**
14. 14 h 28 min + 16 h 32 min — **31 h**

### Enrichment Supplement, page 44

Name ____________ To follow text page 185

**Time Clock**

Below is a work and wage summary sheet for the Roberts Box Company. Some of the numbers have been omitted. Use the information below to complete the chart.

- Each employee gets $\frac{1}{2}$ hour each day for lunch and is not paid for that time.
- If an employee works longer than 8 hours, he or she gets paid twice the hourly wage for the overtime.

Complete the chart.

| Name | Time in | Time out | Total hours | Hourly wage | Total wage |
|---|---|---|---|---|---|
| J. Robinson | 8:00 a.m. | 4:30 p.m. | 8 | **$4.25** | $34.00 |
| J. Peck | 7:30 a.m. | 4:00 p.m. | **8** | $4.50 | **$36.00** |
| L. Petrosky | 8:00 a.m. | 4:00 p.m. | **7.5** | **$5.30** | $39.75 |
| F. Innerst | **9:00 a.m.** | 3:00 p.m. | **5.5** | $4.80 | $26.40 |
| C. Anderson | 9:00 a.m. | 4:30 p.m. | **7** | $4.95 | **$34.65** |
| M. Randolph | 7:00 a.m. | **5:30 p.m.** | 10 | $4.50 | **$54.00** |

### Practice Supplement, page 72

Name ____________ To follow text page 185

**Time**

Write the missing number.

1. 3 h = **180** min
2. 5 min = **300** s
3. 4 wk = **28** d
4. 6 yr = **72** mo
5. 2 yr = **730** d
6. 3 yr = **156** wk
7. 8 centuries = **800** yr
8. 360 s = **6** min
9. 240 min = **4** h
10. 35 d = **5** wk
11. 72 h = **3** d
12. 24 mo = **2** yr
13. 2 h 15 min = **135** min
14. 5 min 10 s = **310** s
15. 52 mo = **4** yr **4** mo
16. 1 d 15 h = **39** h
17. 320 min = **5** h **20** min
18. 62 h = **2** d **14** h

Add or subtract.

19. 2 h 35 min + 5 h 30 min — **8 h 5 min**
20. 1 h 45 min + 3 h 50 min — **5 h 35 min**
21. 7 h 14 min + 2 h 55 min — **10 h 9 min**
22. 4 min 10 s + 3 min 52 s — **8 min 2 s**
23. 2 min 49 s + 1 min 22 s — **4 min 11 s**
24. 3 min 58 s + 5 min 58 s — **9 min 56 s**
25. 10 h 40 min − 5 h 15 min — **5 h 25 min**
26. 8 h 10 min − 3 h 45 min — **4 h 25 min**
27. 5 h 2 min − 1 h 17 min — **3 h 45 min**
28. 9 min 20 s − 4 min 40 s — **4 min 40 s**
29. 7 min 7 s − 2 min 30 s — **4 min 37 s**
30. 12 min 30 s − 6 min 55 s — **5 min 35 s**

# Time

**Quick Review** As each phrase is read aloud, students write the time in digital notation.

half past two 2:30 six minutes to eight 7:54 a quarter past ten 10:15
twelve minutes to one 12:48 seven thirty 7:30 twenty minutes to six 5:40

**Lesson Focus** To compare times in different time zones; to use mental math to solve word problems involving time

**Suggested Materials** Tennis ball, flashlight

## Ideas for Getting Started

To help students see how it can be daylight in one time zone while it is still dark in another time zone, use the following model.

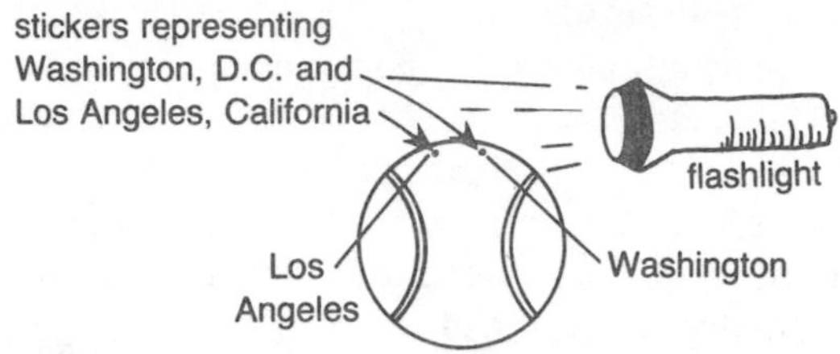


As you place stickers in the appropriate locations on the tennis ball, tell students that one sticker represents Los Angeles, California, in the Pacific time zone and the other sticker represents Washington, D.C., in the Eastern time zone. Tell students that the flashlight represents the sun. Then rotate the tennis ball so that only the sticker representing Washington is in the light of the flashlight. Continue to turn the tennis ball until the stick representing Los Angeles is also in the light of the flashlight. Discuss the fact that because of the rotation of the earth, the sun shines in the east before it shines in the west.

## Using Page 186

**Lesson Development** Direct students' attention to the information at the top of the page. Point out that although there are many different time zones around the world, we will be concerned with only the time zones that relate to the United States. As students look at the time zone map, have them name various time zones and a city in each of the zones. Then name a city and have students tell the time zone the city is in. Remind students that moving east to west across the United States, the time is one hour earlier in each time zone.

**Exercises 1–6** These exercises can be completed by observing the hour differences between various time zones on the map.

**Exercise 7** In this exercise, students can change 10 a.m. Chicago time to 8 a.m. Seattle time and add 4 hours to get 12 noon Seattle time; or they can add 4 hours to 10 a.m., getting 2 o'clock Chicago time, and subtract 2 hours to get 12 noon Seattle time.

## Time Zones

The world is divided into 24 different time zones. Because of the earth's shape and rotation, the sun may appear in a city in one time zone while it is still dark in a city in another zone. Here are the six time zones in the United States.

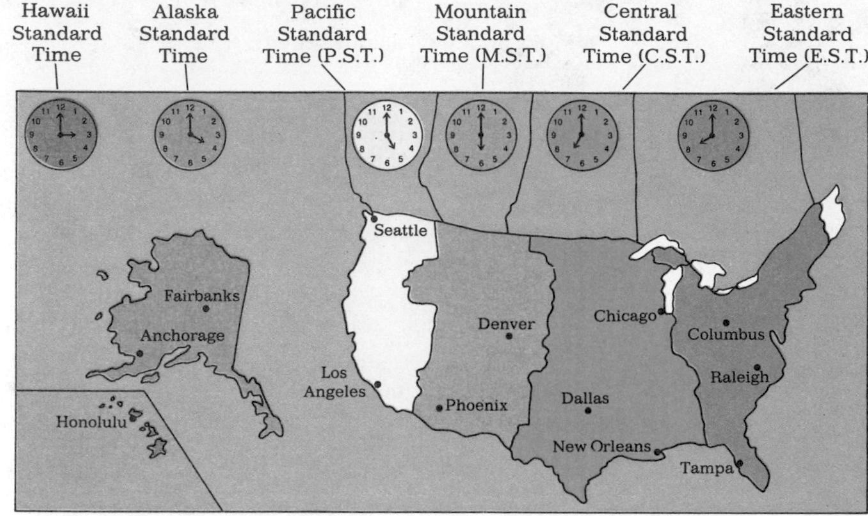


Give the missing times. Use the map above.

1. When it is 9:00 p.m. Eastern time, it is __?__ Central time and __?__ Pacific time. 8 p.m.; 6 p.m.
2. When it is 6:00 p.m. Hawaii time, it is __?__ Mountain time. 9 p.m.
3. The voting polls close in Fairbanks at 6:00 p.m. At that time it is __?__ in Columbus and __?__ in Phoenix. 10 p.m.; 8 p.m.
4. When Kirk made a phone call to Raleigh, it was 7:00 p.m. Denver time. The Raleigh time was __?__. 9 p.m.
5. When it is 12:00 midnight in New Orleans, it is __?__ in Anchorage and __?__ in Tampa. 9 p.m.; 1 a.m.
6. The World Series game begins at 5:00 p.m. in Los Angeles. To watch it in Dallas, turn on your TV at __?__. 7 p.m.
7. A flight from Chicago to Seattle takes 4 h. If a plane leaves at 10:00 a.m. Chicago time, it arrives at __?__ Seattle time. 12 noon

186

## Follow Up

### Reteaching

Use these activities to review the idea of time zones.

- Show a map of the time zones. Then demonstrate with a globe and flashlight how the sun shines in the east before it reaches the west.
- Students check the different times that special programs are televised across the country. They can then use a time zone map to explain why there are differences in times.
- Find an airline schedule in which a flight leaves, for example, at 7:52 a.m. and arrives at its destination at 7:55 a.m. Discuss how this could happen.

### Enrichment

Have students locate and name other cities in each of the time zones. (Refer to student text page 186). Students can then use a clock face above each time zone to indicate a simultaneous time in all zones. Students should keep their work in folders for future reference.

| Assignment Guide | | | |
|---|---|---|---|
| | Minimum | Average | Extended |
| page 186 | | 1–6 | 1–7 |
| page 187 | 1–6 | 1–7 | 1–8 |

## Problem Solving: Using Mental Math

Do these without pencil and paper whenever possible.

**Example:** A soccer match started at 1:30 p.m. and ended 2 h 35 min later. When did the match end?

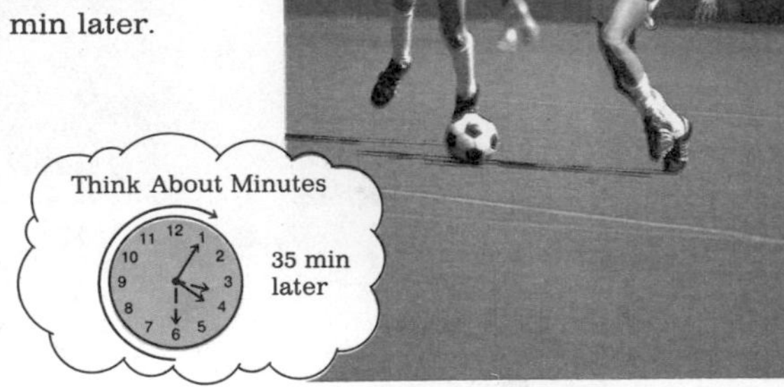


The soccer match was over at 4:05 p.m.

1. Roger's music lesson will begin at 8:00 a.m. He wants to get up 1 h and 15 min earlier than this. What time should he get up? 6:45 a.m.

   Think: 1 hour earlier than 8:00 is what time?
   15 minutes earlier than this is what time?

2. Lila's family left home at 12:15 p.m. At 2:30 p.m. they arrived at the beach. How long did the trip take? 2 h 15 min

   Think: 12:15 to 2:15 is how many hours?
   2:15 to 2:30 is how many minutes?

3. A school baseball game started at 2:15 p.m. and finished 2 h 40 min later. At what time was it over? 4:55 p.m.
4. Jim started work at 1:30 p.m. Tad started work 1 h 20 min earlier. When did Tad start work? 12:10 p.m.
5. Marie planned to finish her project at 4:30 p.m., but actually finished 2 h 45 min earlier. When was that? 1:45 p.m.
6. School starts at 8:30 a.m. and ends at 3:15 p.m. How long is this? 6 h 45 min
7. ★ A plane left St. Louis at 3:15 p.m. Central Standard Time. It arrived in Los Angeles at 6:10 p.m. Central Standard Time. How long did the flight take? What was the Pacific Standard Time when the plane arrived in Los Angeles? 2 h 55 min; 4:10 p.m.
8. **Try This** Mike's time card for two days at work looked like this:

| MONDAY | | TUESDAY | |
|---|---|---|---|
| IN | 8:05 a.m. | IN | 7:50 a.m. |
| OUT | 11:45 a.m. | OUT | 12:15 p.m. |
| IN | 12:54 p.m. | IN | 1:05 p.m. |
| OUT | 4:47 p.m. | OUT | 4:56 p.m. |

How much longer did Mike work on Tuesday than on Monday? 43 min



## Using Page 187

**Lesson Development** Remind students to complete the problems on this page without pencil and paper whenever possible. Work through the example, pointing out that the match started at 1:30; two hours later would be 3:30; 35 minutes later would be 4:05. Tell students that first we deal with the number of hours and then the number of minutes that have elapsed. If necessary, work through the first exercise with students.

**Exercises 4– 5** If needed, allow students to use a demonstration clock to help them visualize these situations.

**Exercise 7** In this two-step problem, students determine how long the flight took, and then refer to the time zone map on page 186 to find the Pacific Standard Time.

**Try This** A possible strategy, Choose the Operations, was taught on page 16.

**Discussion** "What question are we asked about Mike's work record?" (How much longer did he work on Tuesday than on Monday?) "How can we use the data on Mike's time card to find out how long he worked?" (Find hours worked each morning, hours worked each afternoon, then total hours for each day.) "What operation could we use to compare the hours for the two days?"

**Solution** Mike worked 43 min longer on Tuesday than on Monday. On Monday he worked a total of 7 h 33 min; on Tuesday, 8 h 16 min.

**Extension** Leona goes to work at 7:55 each morning, checks out at 11:45 for lunch, checks back in at 12:55, and checks out in the evening at 4:45. How many hours does she work in a five-day week? (38 hours 20 minutes)

## Ideas That Work

### Special Education

An activity to help students learn to estimate temperature is the construction of a "Temperature Line." This is a paper model of the Celsius thermometer on which various temperatures of significance to students can be indicated.

Appropriate temperatures to enter on the thermometer include local record high and low temperatures, the average local temperature for each month of the year, and the temperatures associated with favorite outdoor activities, such as swimming, football, and ice skating.

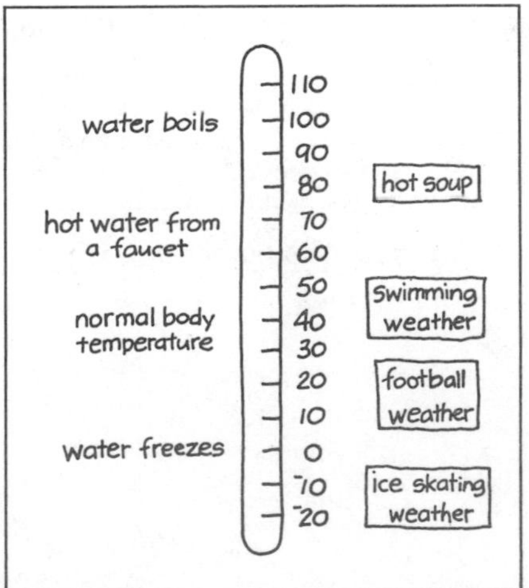


**Practice Supplement,** page 73

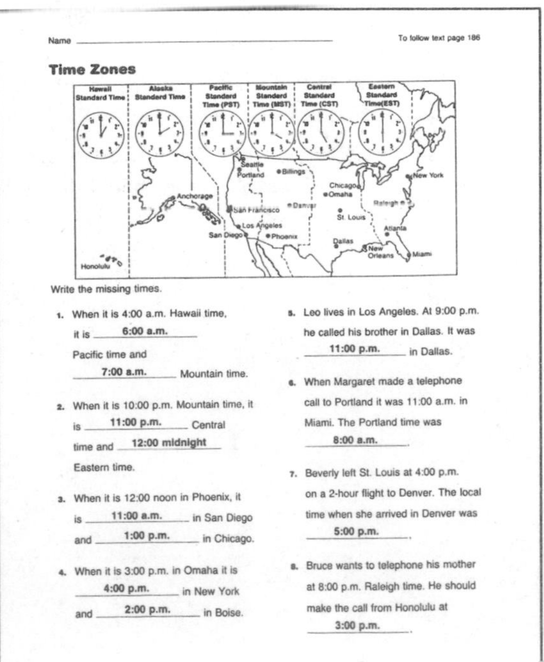

Name ______________ To follow text page 186

**Time Zones**



Write the missing times.

1. When it is 4:00 a.m. Hawaii time, it is 6:00 a.m. Pacific time and 7:00 a.m. Mountain time.
2. When it is 10:00 p.m. Mountain time, it is 11:00 p.m. Central time and 12:00 midnight Eastern time.
3. When it is 12:00 noon in Phoenix, it is 11:00 a.m. in San Diego and 1:00 p.m. in Chicago.
4. When it is 3:00 p.m. in Omaha it is 4:00 p.m. in New York and 2:00 p.m. in Boise.
5. Leo lives in Los Angeles. At 9:00 p.m. he called his brother in Dallas. It was 11:00 p.m. in Dallas.
6. When Margaret made a telephone call to Portland it was 11:00 a.m. in Miami. The Portland time was 8:00 a.m.
7. Beverly left St. Louis at 4:00 p.m. on a 2-hour flight to Denver. The local time when she arrived in Denver was 5:00 p.m.
8. Bruce wants to telephone his mother at 8:00 p.m. Raleigh time. He should make the call from Honolulu at 3:00 p.m.

**Lesson Focus** To work backward as a strategy for solving nonroutine word problems

## Ideas for Getting Started

Use the following questions to review the idea of inverse operations and the procedure for working backward.

- I started with a number, added 5 and got 15. How can I get back to the number? (subtract 5; the number was 10)
- I started with a number and subtracted 7. The answer was 12. How can I get back to the number? (add 7; the number was 19)
- I started with a number and multiplied by 4. The result was 36. How can I get back to the number? (divide by 4; the number was 9)
- I started with a number and divided by 9. The result was 5. How can I get back to the number? (multiply by 9; the number was 45)

## Using Page 188

**Motivational Problem** Have students read the Try This problem at the top of the page. "What question are we asked about the stock?" (What was the price of the stock on January 1?) "How did the price on June 1 compare to the price on January 1?" (It was $8 higher.) "How did the December price compare to the June price?" (It was twice as great.) "What was the price on December 1?" ($46 per share) As you discuss the plan for solving the problem, point out that these problems can be solved by using the strategy called Work Backward.

**Lesson Development** Help students make a flowchart to show the data in this problem. Then work with students to make a reverse flowchart. Focus on the inverse operations, and help students see that we started with a number, added 8, and multiplied by 2 to arrive at the result, 46. To get back to the number, we start with 46. divide by 2, and subtract 8.

Have students reread the Try This problem and check to see if the January price of $15 is correct. Ask a volunteer to state the answer to the Try This problem, using a complete sentence.

**Exercises 1–2** Encourage students to make flowcharts and reverse flowcharts for each problem.

## Problem Solving: Work Backward

Problems that give data about the final result of a series of operations can be solved most easily by using a strategy called

**Work Backward**

It often helps to think about a **flowchart** and a **reverse flowchart** to solve the problem.

**Try This** Nan checked the price of a share of stock on the New York Stock Exchange on January 1. On June 1 its price was $8 higher. By December its price was twice as great as on June 1. The price on December 1 was $46 a share. What was the price on January 1?

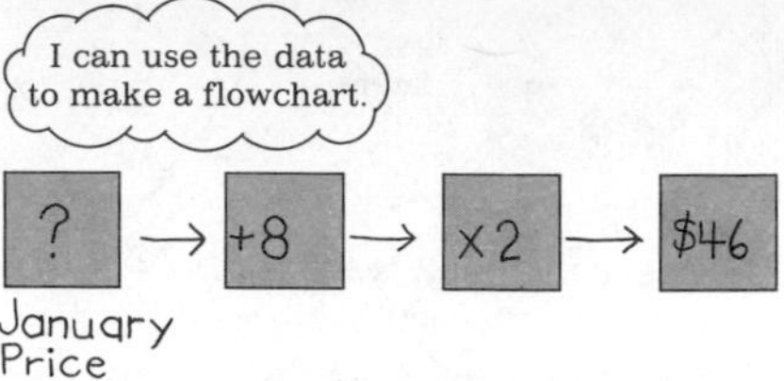


Addition and subtraction are inverse operations.

Multiplication and division are inverse operations.

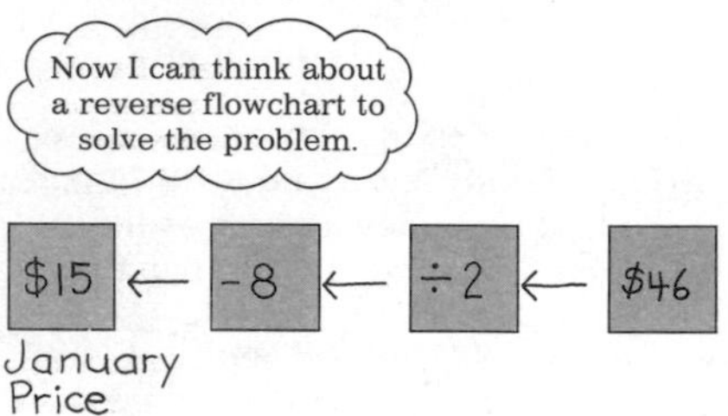


The stock was worth $15 on January 1.

Solve.

1. Janet had some tulip bulbs. She gave 8 to her mother and equally divided the ones that were left among herself and 2 friends. Her final share was 12 bulbs. How many did she have at the beginning? 44

2. Bill bought a belt for $5.75 and a pair of pants that cost 4 times as much as the belt. Then he had $4.24 left. How much money did he have before he bought the belt and pants? $32.99



## Strategy Test Item

**Optional Problem** If you wish to assess students' ability to apply the strategy called Work Backward introduced in this chapter, provide them with the problem below.

> When Jane received her paycheck she spent $6.75 of it on a record and twice that much on a book. Then she had $9.75. How much was her paycheck?

**Solution** Jane's paycheck was $30.00. $9.75 + (2 × $6.75) + $6.75 = $30.00.

## Chapter Review-Test

Give the missing units or ... bers.

1. 100 cm = 1 ? — m
2. 1 dm = 10... — mm
3. 1,000 m = 1 ?
4. 1 ? = 10 dm — m
5. 1 m = ■ mm — 1,000
6. 1 dm = ■ cm — 10
7. 1 c... — 10 ...m
8. 1 km = ■ m — 1,000
9. Estimate the length of this segment in centimeters. (Use a decimal if you wish.) Then measure the actual length. Estimates will vary; actual length, 9.4 cm.

Write decimals for these measurements. Use a single unit.

10. 4 m 8 dm — 4.8 m
11. 6 m 46 cm — 6.46 m
12. 12 cm 7 mm — 12.7 cm
13. 9 dm 5 cm — 9.5 dm

Give the missing numbers.

14. 4 m = ■ dm — 40
15. 8 m = ■ cm — 800
16. 2.6 cm = ■ mm — 26
17. 6 km = ■ m — 6,000
18. 400 m = ■ km — 0.4
19. 279 cm = ■ m — 2.79
20. 2 kL = ■ L — 2,000
21. 3L = ■ mL — 3,000

Choose the best estimate for each.

22. Capacity 250 mL

250 mL 250 L 250 kL

23. Weight 150 g

150 mg 150 g 150 kg

24. Temperature 80°C

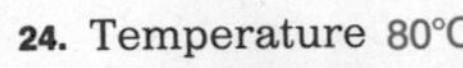

⁻8°C 8°C 80°C

Give the missing numbers.

25. 4 h = ■ min — 240
26. 5 min = ■ s — 300
27. 3 yr = ■ mo — 36
28. 6 wk = ■ d — 42

Solve.

29. Jeff worked 8 h 45 min on Monday and 6 h 53 min on Tuesday. How many hours was this in all? How much longer did he work on Monday than on Tuesday? 15 h 38 min; 1 h 52 min
30. A parking meter showed 2 h 15 min of time left when Mindy parked by it. Her watch showed 3:05 p.m. At what time did the meter need more coins? 5:20 p.m.

189

## Using Page 189

The exercises in the Chapter Review-Test emphasize the major concepts and skills presented in this chapter. These exercises may be used as a review assignment or as a test, depending upon your needs.

**Item Analysis** The table below correlates the Chapter Review-Test items with objectives and with the student text pages on which the concepts or skills were taught.

| Items | Objectives | Related text pages |
|---|---|---|
| 2... | 7.1 | |
| 23 | | 170–175 |
| 24 | 7.4 | 178 |
| 25–28 | 7.5 | 180 |
| 29–30 | 7.6 | 176–177, 17... |

## Assessment Options

If you use the Chapter Review-Test as a review assignment, you may wish to use the multiple-choice test or the free-response test to evaluate mastery of the chapter objectives. The items on these tests have a one-to-one correspondence in terms of content and level of difficulty. A correlation of test items to objectives and student text pages is provided in the Management Guide for Chapter 7.

**Multiple-Choice Test,** TRB pages 19–21

**Free-Response Test,** TRB pages 61–62

**Mid-Year Test,** TRB pages 81–84

## TRB Options

The following blackline masters are available for use with this chapter. If you have not already assigned these materials, you may wish to use them to close the chapter.

**Recreation,** TRB page 157

**Consumer Applications,** TRB page 175

**Calculator Technology,** TRB page 193

**Reading Math,** TRB page 225

**Family Involvement,** TRB page 249–250

## Using Page 190

The exercises on this page are intended for those students who experienced difficulty with the Chapter Review-Test on page 189. Should students require reteaching of these key concepts and skills, please refer to the teaching notes below. Otherwise, the Another Look exercises can be assigned as independent work with students using the accompanying sample problems and hints as guides.

**Exercises 1–10** The skill involving these relationships was originally taught on pages 168–17? Use the example box at the top of the page ... illus- the relationships between these ... length. Use a meter stick or ... was originally taught trate the measurem... ...us on the second example ...nts that to change a larger unit to **Exercise**..., we multiply. Show how the table ...change 5.36 m to 536 cm. Then remind students that to change a smaller unit to a larger unit, we divide. Show how the table helps change 58 mm to 5.8 cm.

**Exercises 22–30** These relationships were originally taught on pages 178–183. Refer to the display that illustrates the unit relationships for capacity, weight, and temperature. If necessary, demonstrate these units using containers, scales, or thermometers. Again emphasize the idea that to change a larger unit to a smaller unit, we multiply; to change a smaller unit to a larger unit, we divide.

**Exercises 31–34** This skill was originally taught on page 185. As you work through these examples with students, remind them that when adding minutes and hours, we trade 60 minutes for an hour when necessary. Also, when adding minutes and seconds, we trade 60 seconds for a minute when necessary.

Answers for exercises 1–10

| 1. cm | 2. mm | 3. m | 4. km | 5. km |
|---|---|---|---|---|
| 6. m | 7. cm | 8. cm | 9. km | 10. m |

## Another Look

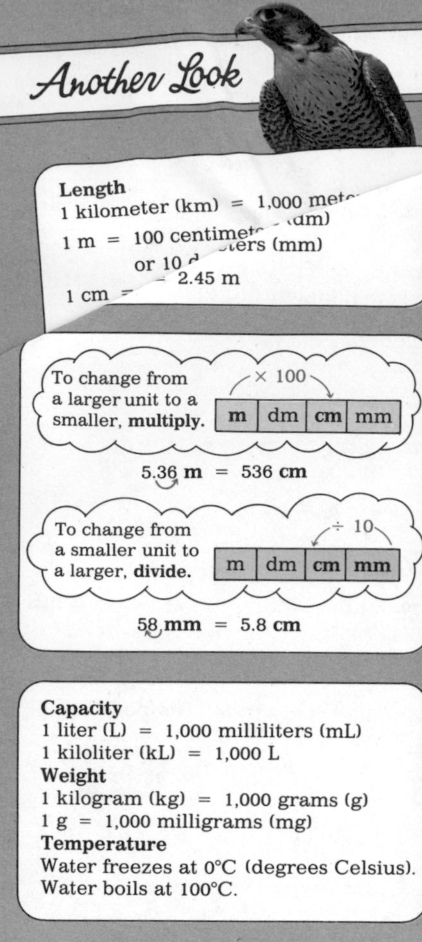
Length
1 kilometer (km) = 1,000 mete...
1 m = 100 centimet... ...(dm)
...ters (mm)
or 10 d...
... 2.45 m
1 cm = ...
To change from a larger unit to a smaller, multiply.
× 100
m dm cm mm
5.36 m = 536 cm
To change from a smaller unit to a larger, divide.
÷ 10
m dm cm mm
58 mm = 5.8 cm
Capacity
1 liter (L) = 1,000 milliliters (mL)
1 kiloliter (kL) = 1,000 L
Weight
1 kilogram (kg) = 1,000 grams (g)
1 g = 1,000 milligrams (mg)
Temperature
Water freezes at 0°C (degrees Celsius).
Water boils at 100°C.

Giv... ...ssing units. See teaching notes.

1. 1 mm = 0.1 ?
2. 1 cm = 10 ?
3. 1 cm = 0.01 ?
4. 1,000 m = 1 ?
5. 1 m = 0.001 ?
6. 10 dm = 1 ?
7. 1 dm = 10 ?
8. 1 m = 100 ?
9. 8 km 435 m = 8.435 ?
10. 5 m 3 dm = 5.3 ?

**Give the missing numbers.**

11. 1 m = ■ cm 100
12. 1,000 m = ■ km 1
13. 1 cm = ■ mm 10
14. 1 dm = ■ cm 10
15. 1 m = ■ km 0.001
16. 1 dm = ■ m 0.1
17. 8 m = ■ cm 800
18. 12 cm = ■ mm 120
19. 5.46 m = ■ cm 546
20. 384 mm = ■ cm 38.4
21. 1,386 m = ■ km 1.386

**Give the missing units.**

22. 1,000 mL = 1 ■ L
23. 1,000 mg = 1 ■ g
24. 1,000 L = 1 ■ kL
25. 1,000 g = 1 ■ kg
26. Hot day temperature: 38 ■ °C

**Give the missing numbers.**

27. 3 L = ■ mL 3,000
28. 2,000 L = ■ kL 2
29. 1 kg = ■ g 1,000
30. 1 g = ■ mg 1,000

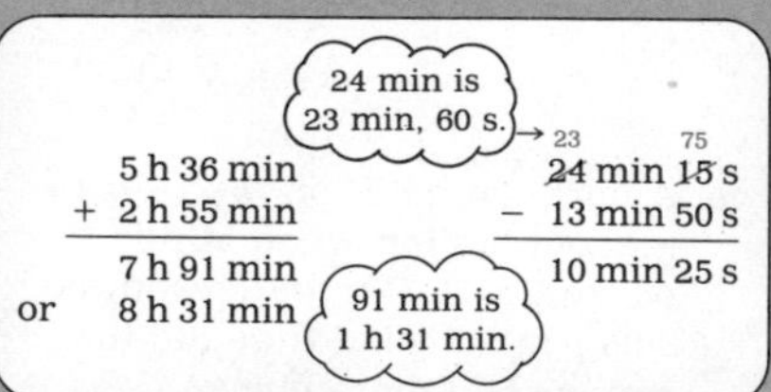
24 min is 23 min, 60 s.
5 h 36 min
+ 2 h 55 min
7 h 91 min
or 8 h 31 min
91 min is 1 h 31 min.
23 75
24 min 15 s
− 13 min 50 s
10 min 25 s

**Add or subtract.**

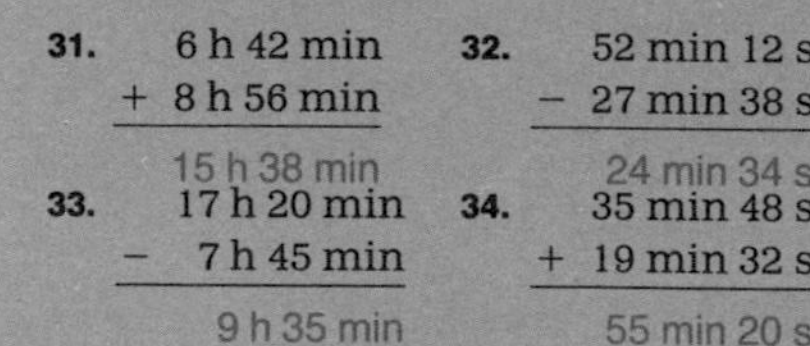

31. 6 h 42 min + 8 h 56 min = 15 h 38 min
32. 52 min 12 s − 27 min 38 s = 24 min 34 s
33. 17 h 20 min − 7 h 45 min = 9 h 35 min
34. 35 min 48 s + 19 min 32 s = 55 min 20 s

190

## Just for Teachers

### History of Math—the Metric System

In 1670, Gabriel Mouton, vicar of St. Paul's Church in Lyon, France, proposed that the arc of one minute of longitude serve as the linear standard with smaller units derived decimally. Mouton's proposal was discussed in 1790 by the French National Assembly. The National Assembly instructed the French Academy of Science to study the idea. Two months later the Academy recommended that the meter be established as the standard unit of length and defined as one ten-millionth of the distance from the North Pole to the Equator measured on the meridian which passed through Paris; and that a new standard weight unit be set according to the weight of a cubic meter of water. In June of 1799, the metric system, which defined units of length, area, volume, and weight, was established according to its motto "for all people, for all time."

In the nineteenth and early twentieth centuries, use of the metric system spread to countries throughout the world, with the notable exceptions of Great Britain and the United States. At the same time, vast increases in scientific and technical knowledge required certain new units of measurement and more accurate definitions and standards of the original units.

## Enrichment

**Estimating Size**

Estimate your "size" for each item in the table. Record your estimate. Then measure and record the actual "size." Find the difference between your estimate and the measure. Then find the sum of these differences. The smallest sum wins!

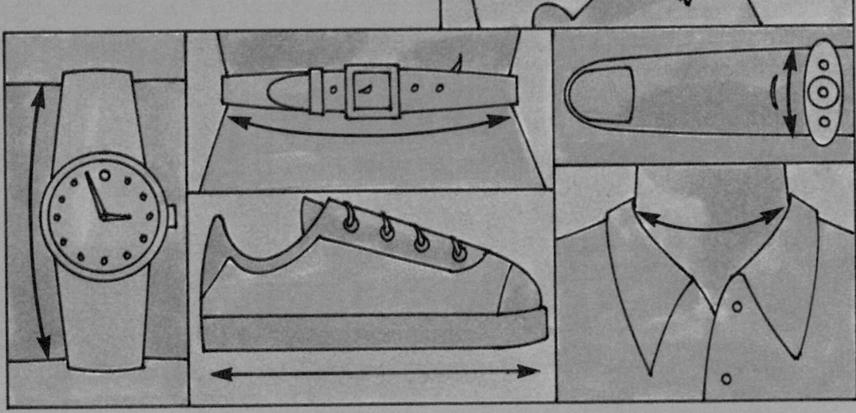

| Size | Estimate | Actual measurement | Difference between estimate and actual measure |
|---|---|---|---|
| Ring size | ■ cm | ■ cm | ■ cm |
| Wristwatch size | ■ cm | ■ cm | ■ cm |
| Hat size | ■ cm | ■ cm | ■ cm |
| Collar size | ■ cm | ■ cm | ■ cm |
| Belt size | ■ cm | ■ cm | ■ cm |
| Shoe size | ■ cm | ■ cm | ■ cm |
| | | Sum of differences = | ■ cm |



In 1960 the 11th General Conference on Weights and Measures met in Paris to discuss and revise the old metric system in light of modern measurement needs and applications. The Conference adopted the International System of Units, or Système International (SI). SI includes six base units; length—meter; mass—kilogram; time—second; electric current—ampere; thermodynamic temperature—degree Kelvin (from which Celsius degrees are derived); and light intensity—candela. With the exception of the kilogram, all SI base units are defined in terms of unvarying scientific phenomena, such as wavelengths of light and cycles of radiation.

## Using Page 191

This page is intended for those students who successfully completed the Chapter Review-Test on page 189. You may wish to assign this page as independent work while you use Another Look exercises to reteach the basic concepts and skills of the chapter. Or, you may decide that all students would benefit from exposure to this Enrichment activity.

**Lesson Development** Have students look at their centimeter rulers and suggest objects that measure about one centimeter (the diameter of a head of a thumbtack, the width of a piece of chalk). Tell students that they are to use the centimeter unit to estimate the sizes indicated. Then they are to measure to find the actual size and compute the difference. The best score is the smallest sum of these differences. Suggest that they use a piece of string to do the actual measurements. The string can be marked and then measured with a centimeter ruler. Point out that estimates and actual measures can be given using decimals. For example, a wrist size might measure 15.4 cm. When students have completed the activity, discuss the results and encourage them to try to improve their estimating ability.

## Using Page 192

The exercises on this page provide practice for maintaining cumulative skills. The emphasis in this Cumulative Review is on multiplication of whole numbers (Chapter 4), multiplication and division of decimals (Chapter 6), and problem solving (Chapter 6).

**Item Analysis** The table below correlates the Cumulative Review items with objectives and with the student book pages on which the concepts or skills were taught.

| Items | Objectives | Related text pages |
|---|---|---|
| 1 | 4.1 | 80–82 |
| 2–3 | 4.2 | 84–88 |
| 4–5 | 4.3 | 92–93 |
| 6–9 | 6.2 | 140–145 |
| 10–11 | 6.3 | 148–153 |
| 12 | 6.4 | 156–160 |
| 13–14 | 6.5 | 146–147, 154–155, 161 |

## *Cumulative Review*

Multiply or divide.

1. 7 × 60
   A 42
   (B) 420
   C 4,200
   D not given

2. 436 × 9
   A 39.24
   B 392.4
   C 39,240
   (D) not given

3. 215 × 67
   (A) 14,405
   B 16,340
   C 16,817
   D not given

4. 505 × 505
   A 25,525
   B 25,502
   C 25,505
   (D) not given

5. 500 × 500
   (A) 250,000
   B 25,000
   C 2,500
   D not given

6. 5.72 × 100
   A 0.572
   B 57.2
   (C) 572
   D not given

7. 0.333 × 1,000
   A 3.33
   B 33.3
   (C) 333
   D not given

8. 9.8 × 0.2
   (A) 1.96
   B 19.6
   C 196
   D not given

9. 5.7 × 0.07
   A 0.0399
   (B) 0.399
   C 3.99
   D not given

10. $7\overline{)1.19}$
   A 1.7
   (B) 0.17
   C 0.017
   D not given

11. 52.6 ÷ 100
   A 526
   B 5.26
   (C) 0.526
   D not given

12. $3.1\overline{)27.9}$
   (A) 9
   B 0.9
   C 9.9
   D not given

13. Marcia put 36 stamps on each of 28 pages. How many stamps did she use?
   A 1,800 B 1,080
   (C) 1,008 D not given

14. Each of 12 students needs 2.9 m of cloth for a costume. How many meters of cloth are needed in all?
   A 348 m (B) 34.8 m
   C 3.48 m D not given

# Fractions: Addition and Subtraction

## Objectives

**8.1** Find equivalent and lowest-terms fractions.
**8.2** Compare and order fractions and mixed numbers.
**8.3** Find sums and differences of fractions and mixed numbers with common denominators.
**8.4** Find sums and differences of fractions and mixed numbers with unlike denominators.
**8.5** Solve word problems using the 5-Point Checklist and cumulative computational skills.

## Summary

The chapter begins with a review of the meaning of a fraction. The four lessons that follow develop students' understanding of fractions and teach particular skills needed for computation with fractions. First, the concept of equivalent fractions is developed, and techniques for finding equivalent fractions are presented. Next the greatest common factor (GFC) is taught followed by techniques for writing fractions in lowest terms. After changing improper fractions to mixed numbers and mixed numbers to improper fractions, students learn to compare and order fractions and mixed numbers. Then they add and subtract fractions and mixed numbers with common denominators. Following a lesson on how to find the least common denominator, students add and subtract fractions and mixed numbers with unlike denominators. Four problem-solving lessons provide students with opportunities to apply fraction concepts in practical situations.

## Mathematical Background

**Understanding Fractions** There are two common interpretations of a fraction. The first is as a unit subdivided into equal-sized parts. The region and number-line models shown below are examples of this interpretation.

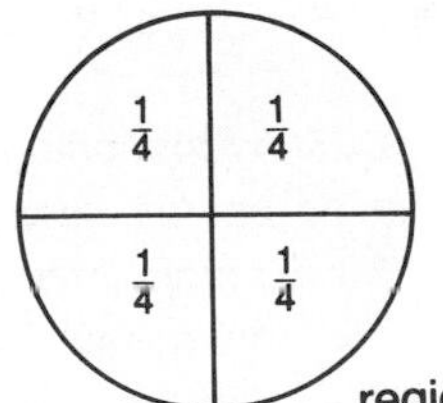

region

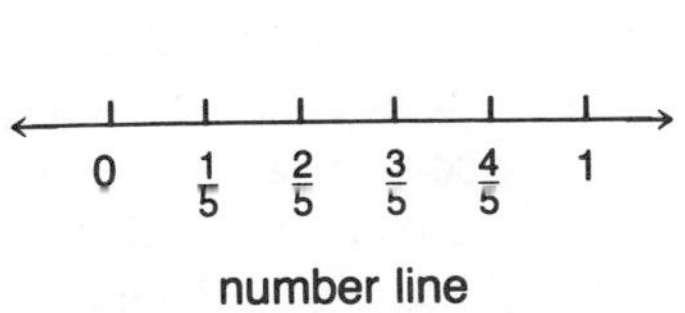

number line

The second interpretation is as a set subdivided into equal-sized groups.

$\frac{1}{4}$ of the balls is shaded.

The region and set models are the most common fraction models students encounter in the real world. Therefore, these models are used to review the meaning of a fraction. For both models, students must recognize what represents the whole unit or 1 unit. For the region model, the entire region represents 1 unit, and for the set model, the total set represents 1 unit.

Understanding fractions involves more than just relating a fraction to a region or set model. It also involves recognizing and finding different names for a fraction—equivalent fractions or fractions in lowest terms—and determining the relative size of fractions—comparing and ordering fractions.

**Adding and Subtracting Fractions and Mixed Numbers** Before students can become proficient in adding and subtracting fractions and mixed numbers with unlike denominators, they must develop the ability to compute fractions and mixed numbers with like denominators and to find the least common denominators of two or more fractions. Both the region and number-line models below are useful for showing the reasonableness of adding and subtracting with common denominators.

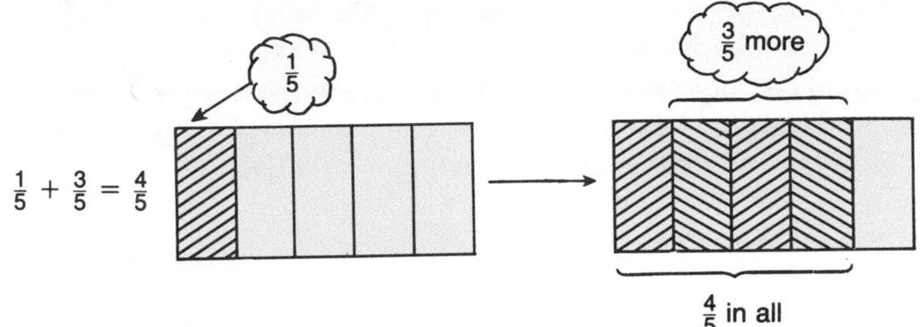


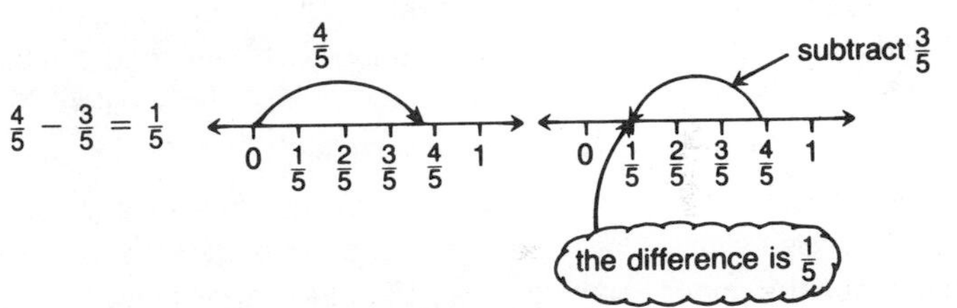


Writing two or more fractions as equivalent fractions with the least common denominator (LCM) requires that students first find the least common multiple and then find equivalent fractions. Students then must find equivalent factors with the LCM as the denominator.

There are two general approaches for the algorithms for adding and subtracting mixed numbers. Following is the solution for $8\frac{1}{3} - 4\frac{1}{2}$ using each approach.

**A.**
$$\begin{array}{rcrcr} 8\frac{1}{3} & = & \frac{25}{3} & = & \frac{50}{6} \\ -\ 4\frac{1}{2} & = & -\ \frac{9}{2} & = & -\ \frac{27}{6} \\ \hline & & & & \frac{23}{6} = 3\frac{5}{6} \end{array}$$

**B.**
$$\begin{array}{rcrcr} 8\frac{1}{3} & = & 8\frac{2}{6} & = & 7\frac{8}{6} \\ -\ 4\frac{1}{2} & = & 4\frac{3}{6} & = & 4\frac{3}{6} \\ \hline & & & & 3\frac{5}{6} \end{array}$$

Most teachers find approach B more desirable because the computational demands are not as great. Approach A has the advantage of not requiring students to rename $8\frac{2}{6}$ as $7\frac{8}{6}$; however, most students have little difficulty in learning this technique. In both approaches, fractions are renamed as equivalent fractions with the LCM and then the fractions are subtracted.

**Problem Solving** Each of the four problem-solving lessons in this chapter stresses one aspect of the 5-point Checklist. On page 203, Using Data from a Catalog, the activity focuses on finding the data; in Using Estimation on page 206, students first find estimated answers then exact answers to problems involving fractions. On page 217, the emphasis is on choosing the appropriate operation as a plan for solving problems. The new problem-solving strategy, Solve a Simpler Problem, is taught on page 218.

**Vocabulary**

| | | |
|---|---|---|
| numerator | greatest common factor | mixed number |
| denominator | lowest-terms fraction | improper fraction |
| equivalent fractions | least common multiple | |

## Error Analysis

This chapter reviews basic information on fraction concepts and extends the operations of addition and subtraction of fractions. The concepts that most often cause difficulty include ordering of fractions, generating equivalent fractions, finding least common denominators, and writing fractions in lowest terms. A solid understanding of whole number multiplication and division is also necessary as students deal with the content of this chapter. Student errors can be due to a lack of prerequisite knowledge, a lack of knowledge of how to carry out the algorithms, or basic computational errors. Some common errors are discussed below.

### Error Pattern 1

$\frac{1}{2} = \frac{2}{4} = \frac{4}{6} = \frac{6}{8}$ $\frac{1}{4} = \frac{2}{8} = \frac{4}{12} = \frac{6}{16}$ $\frac{1}{3} = \frac{2}{6} = \frac{4}{9}$

**Diagnosis** To generate equivalent fractions, the student has added a value to both numerator and denominator instead of multiplying both numerator and denominator by the same value. The student is obviously confused about equivalent fractions.

**Remediation** Use models to illustrate the idea of equivalent fractions. Use a piece of paper cut into a rectangle and folded in half. Open the paper and color one half of the paper with a crayon. Write $\frac{1}{2}$ to emphasize that one half of the paper is colored. Fold the paper again so that the paper is folded in fourths. Open the paper so that students see that $\frac{2}{4}$ are colored; thus $\frac{1}{2} = \frac{2}{4}$. Fold the paper again to show that $\frac{1}{2} = \frac{2}{4} = \frac{4}{8}$. As you discuss these relationships, point out how equivalent fractions can be generated. For example, $\frac{1 \times \boxed{2}}{2 \times \boxed{2}} = \frac{2}{4}$ and $\frac{2 \times \boxed{2}}{4 \times \boxed{2}} = \frac{4}{8}$.

### Error Pattern 2

$1\frac{3}{4} = \frac{12}{4}$ $2\frac{1}{6} = \frac{12}{6}$ $5\frac{5}{8} = \frac{200}{8}$ $6\frac{2}{3} = \frac{36}{3}$

**Diagnosis** The student has tried to change mixed numbers to improper fractions but is confused about the correct procedure. The student has correctly multiplied the denominator times the whole number amount, but then incorrectly multiplies rather than adds the fractional part.

**Remediation** Review with students what a mixed number represents—a number of units plus a fractional part. Discuss how the whole number can also be written as a fraction. For example, $1\frac{3}{4} = \frac{4}{4} + \frac{3}{4} = \frac{7}{4}$ and $2\frac{1}{6} = \frac{6}{6} + \frac{6}{6} + \frac{1}{6} = \frac{13}{6}$.

### Error Pattern 3

$$\begin{array}{r} 3\frac{1}{5} = \frac{3}{15} \\ +\ 4\frac{2}{3} = \frac{10}{15} \\ \hline \frac{13}{15} \end{array} \qquad \begin{array}{r} 2\frac{1}{4} = \frac{3}{12} \\ 3\frac{1}{2} = \frac{6}{12} \\ +\ 5\frac{5}{6} = \frac{10}{12} \\ \hline \frac{19}{12} = 1\frac{7}{12} \end{array}$$

**Diagnosis** In finding a common denominator for these mixed numbers, the student has failed to include the whole number amount. Thus, when adding mixed numbers, the student has added only the fractional part and has omitted the whole number.

**Remediation** Review the algorithm, reminding students that both units and fractions are to be added. If possible, show regions to represent the mixed numbers. Next combine the whole number amounts then the fraction parts, and indicate each amount separately on the chalkboard. Using the first problem as an example, point out that since the whole number amount is 7, the correct total sum must be greater than 7.

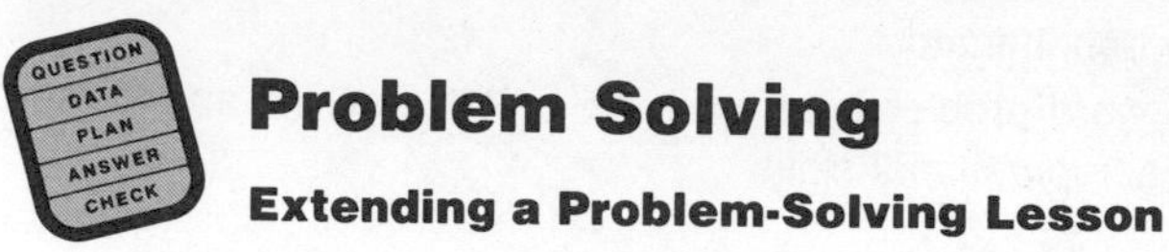


## Problem Solving

### Extending a Problem-Solving Lesson

In the 5-Point Checklist, "checking back" is the final stage in solving a particular problem. It is important that problem solving does not end with the solution to a particular problem. Extend the problem-solving experience by helping students generalize what they did on a particular problem to what they know in general about problem solving. Here are four teaching actions you can use to extend your problem-solving lessons.

- *Show two solution strategies for a problem whenever possible.* Many students have the misconception that there is only one way to solve every math problem. Showing more than one solution strategy for a problem helps change this misconception. Also, when possible, show variations in the use of a particular solution strategy. For example, two students may both have used an organized list to solve a problem but may have organized their lists in different ways. Showing variations in the way a particular strategy is used to solve a given problem expands students' knowledge about the use of that strategy.
- *Name the strategy or strategies used.* The primary reason for having students name the problem-solving strategies is to make them aware of the techniques they have learned for solving problems. When students are aware of the strategies in their repertoire, they are better able to suggest possible solution strategies for a particular problem. Naming the solution strategy reinforces that the method the student used is an accepted problem-solving technique.
- *Relate the problem to similar problems.* Many students have difficulty recognizing problems that can be solved using the same solution strategy. Some students, for example, may think that two problems can be solved using the same solution strategy if both problems have the same setting—for example, if both are about cows—regardless of other characteristics of the problems. Discussing problems similar to the original one illustrates how a particular problem-solving strategy can be used in a variety of settings. Relating a problem to similar ones shows that problem-solving strategies are not problem specific.
- *Discuss or solve extensions of the problem.* Problem extensions may have the same setting as the original problem but differ in certain characteristics such as the size of the numbers or the conditions of the problem. Presenting problems that involve changes in problem characteristics helps students understand that certain conditions in a problem may affect the way one goes about finding the solution. Extensions may also have the effect of encouraging students to generalize using a particular solution strategy in situations similar to the original problem.

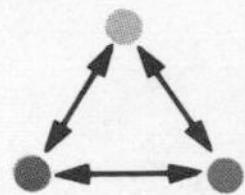

## Special Education

This chapter deals with basic concepts and skills involving addition and subtraction of fractions. The following teaching tips can help your special-needs students master these ideas.

### Using a Visual, Hands-On Approach

When reviewing the procedure for converting improper fractions and mixed numbers, use bars and pieces to help students visualize what is happening.

$\frac{9}{4} \longrightarrow$ 

How many bars can be filled?
How many pieces are left? (1 of the fourths)
So $\frac{9}{4} = 2\frac{1}{4}$.

The denominator, 4, tells the number of pieces that fill one bar, so we can divide to find the number of bars that are filled. Students who have difficulties with visual perception or memory might benefit from color coding, as illustrated, during this part of the discussion.

$$\frac{9}{4} \longrightarrow 4\overline{)9}^{\,2\text{ R }1} = \boxed{2}\,\frac{1}{4} = 2\frac{1}{4}$$

A similar approach, in which whole bars are traded for pieces, can be used to establish the "multiply and add" procedure for converting mixed numbers to improper fractions.

### Developing Visual and Verbal Reinforcement

Students with memory and reasoning difficulties will profit from the use of pictures to develop the idea that we multiply or divide both numerator and denominator by the same factor.

(a) Complete. Shade to check.

(b) Complete. Shade to check.

(c) Complete.

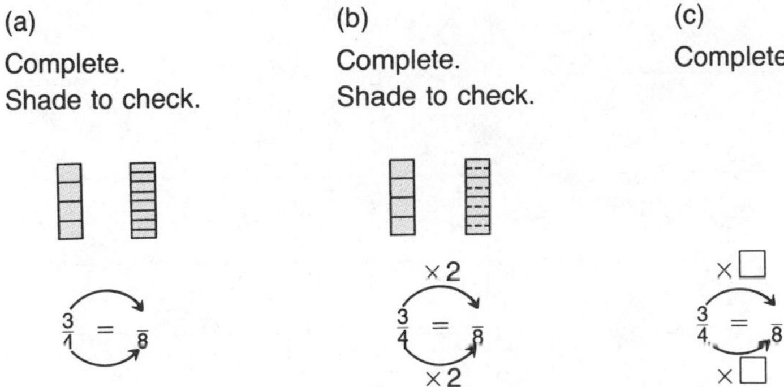


Then give each student a set of laminated multiple strips—one each for numbers 1 through 9. Show students how to form a fraction strip by placing two multiple strips on top of each other. Use these fraction strips to check exercises such as those illustrated above. Have students (1) circle the pair of equivalent fractions that are pictured; (2) describe the multiplication that relates the two fractions; and (3) then write the equivalent pair. This activity can also be used as an introduction to finding lowest-terms fractions. Ask students to explain what must be done to both numerator and denominator of $\frac{6}{8}$ to find its equivalent on the fraction strip.

### Providing Small Steps

As a further help for students with learning difficulties, break instruction into small steps by providing exercises as shown **(a)** before assigning the practice sets **(b)**. If students still have difficulty, suggest that they refer to the numbers 2 through 9 written on an index card or a wall chart and ask themselves: "Is 2 the greatest number that divides both numerator and denominator? Is 3? Is 4? . . . ."

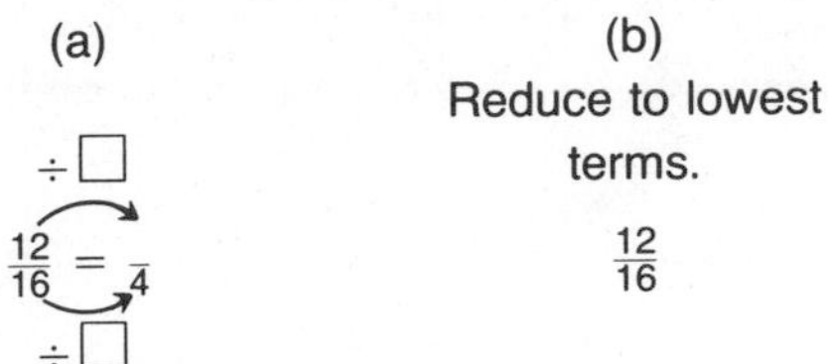


### Translating to Words

Having students write out several problems as shown below will help them to avoid the tendency to add both numerator and denominator of a fraction.

(a)

$$\begin{array}{r} 1\frac{3}{8} \\ +\ 2\frac{3}{8} \\ \hline 3\frac{6}{8} \end{array}$$

(b)

$$\begin{array}{r} 1\frac{3}{8} \\ +\ 2\frac{3}{8} \\ \hline \end{array} \longrightarrow \begin{array}{r} \text{1 and 3 eighths} \\ +\ \text{2 and 3 eighths} \\ \hline \text{3 and 6 eighths} \end{array} = 3\frac{6}{8} \text{ or } 3\frac{3}{4}$$

### Finger Tracing

In this chapter there are several computation exercises in which both addition and subtraction problems are presented. Some special-needs students may need to finger trace the sign as a reminder to carry out the correct operation before they begin to compute.

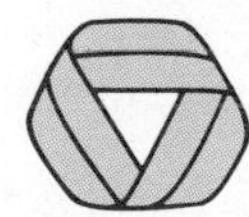

## Subject Integration

Subject matter related to other areas of the curriculum has been integrated into the following lessons. This provides an opportunity to highlight the interaction between mathematics and other subjects.

**Consumer Awareness** Buying clocks, page 203; using tape recorders, pages 214–215; buying hardware items, page 217.
**Science** Calorie counting, pages 208–209
**Career Awareness** Carpentry, pages 212–213
**Fine Arts** Music camp, page 193

# Management Guide

| Teaching Chapter 8 | | | | Meeting Individual Needs | | | | | |
|---|---|---|---|---|---|---|---|---|---|
| Objectives | Chapter Content | Pages | TRB Test Items | Lesson Assignments | | | Follow Up | | |
| | | | | Minimum | Average | Extended | Reteaching | Enrichment | Practice |
| | Chapter Opener | 193 | | | | | | | |
| **8.1** Find equivalent and lowest-terms fractions. | Fractions | 194–195 | 1–2 | 1–19 | 1–19 | 4–10, 15–21, TM | SE5 Ch 9 | | PS 74 |
| | Equivalent Fractions | 196–197 | 3–5 | 1–31, SK | 1–33, SK | 2–30 even, 31–33, SK | SE5 Ch 9<br>RS 45 | ES 45 | PS 75 |
| | Greatest Common Factor | 198 | | 1–18 | 1–18 | 1–18 | SE5 Ch 9 | | |
| | Lowest-Terms Fractions | 199 | 6–9 | 1–24 | 1–24 | 1–24 | SE5 Ch 9<br>RS 46 | ES 46 | MP 422<br>PS 76 |
| **8.2** Compare and order fractions and mixed numbers. | Improper Fractions to Mixed Numbers | 200 | 10–13 | 1–24 | 1–24 | 1–24 | SE5 Ch 9 | | MP 422 |
| | Mixed Numbers to Improper Fractions | 201 | | 1–24 | 1–24 | 1–25 | SE5 Ch 9<br>RS 47 | ES 47 | MP 422<br>PS 77 |
| | Comparing and Ordering Fractions | 202 | 14–17 | 1–16 | 1–18 | 1–19 | SE5 Ch 9<br>RS 48 | ES 48 | MP 422<br>PS 78 |
| **8.3** Find sums and differences of fractions and mixed numbers with common denominators. | Adding and Subtracting Fractions: Common Denominators | 204–205 | 18–21 | 1–32, SK | 1–32, SK | 1–31 odd, 32–33, SK | SE5 Ch 9 | | MP 423<br>PS 79 |
| **8.4** Find sums and differences of fractions and mixed numbers with unlike denominators. | Least Common Multiple (Denominator) | 207 | 22–23 | 1–10 | 1–15 | 1–15 | SE5 Ch 9 | | MP 423<br>PS 80 |
| | Adding and Subtracting Fractions: Unlike Denominators | 208–209 | 24–27 | 1–29 | 1–30 | 1–28 even, 29–30 TM | SE5 Ch 9<br>RS 49 | ES 49 | MP 423<br>PS 81 |
| | Adding Mixed Numbers: Unlike Denominators | 210–211 | 28–31 | 1–20 | 1–20 | 1–21, TM | SE5 Ch 10 | | MP 424<br>PS 82 |
| | Subtracting Mixed Numbers: Unlike Denominators | 212–213 | 32–35 | 1–24 | 1–25 | 1–25, TM | SE5 Ch 10<br>RS 50 | ES 50 | MP 424<br>PS 83 |
| | More Subtracting Mixed Numbers | 214–215 | | 1–24 | 1–25 | 1–21 odd, 23–25, TM | SE5 Ch 10 | | MP 424<br>PS 84 |
| | Adding and Subtracting Fractions: Practice | 216 | | 1–30 | 1–42 | 2–42 even | | | PS 85 |
| **8.5** Solve word problems using the 5-Point Checklist and cumulative computational skills. | Problem Solving: Using Data from a Catalog | 203 | 36–40 | 1–6 | 1–7 | 1–8 | | | |
| | Problem Solving: Using Estimation | 206 | | 1–4 | 1–5 | 1–6 | | | |
| | Problem Solving: Choosing the Operations | 217 | | 1–7 | 1–8 | 1–9 | RS 51 | ES 51 | |
| | Problem Solving: Solve a Simpler Problem | 218 | | | | | | | |
| | Chapter Review-Test | 219 | | | | | | | |
| | Another Look/Enrichment | 220–221 | | | | | | | |
| | Technology | 222–223 | | | | | | | |
| | Cumulative Review | 224 | | | | | | | |

**SE5** Student Edition, Book 5
**RS** Reteaching Supplement
**ES** Enrichment Supplement
**PS** Practice Supplement
**MP** More Practice
**TM** Think Math
**SK** Skillkeeper
**TRB** Teacher's Resource Book

# Teacher's Resource Book

## Masters for Use

**. . . before Chapter 8**

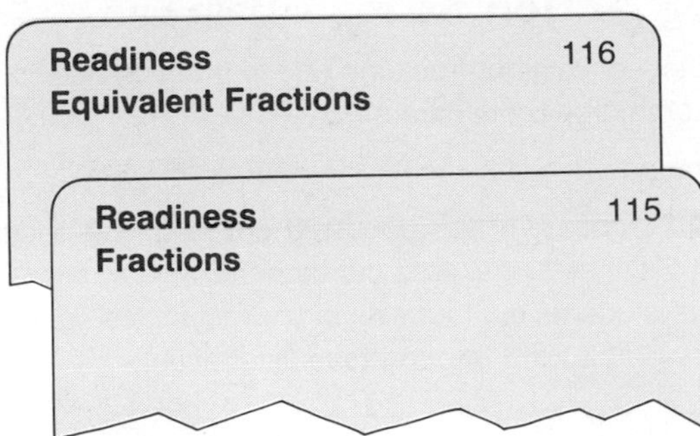


**. . . during Chapter 8**

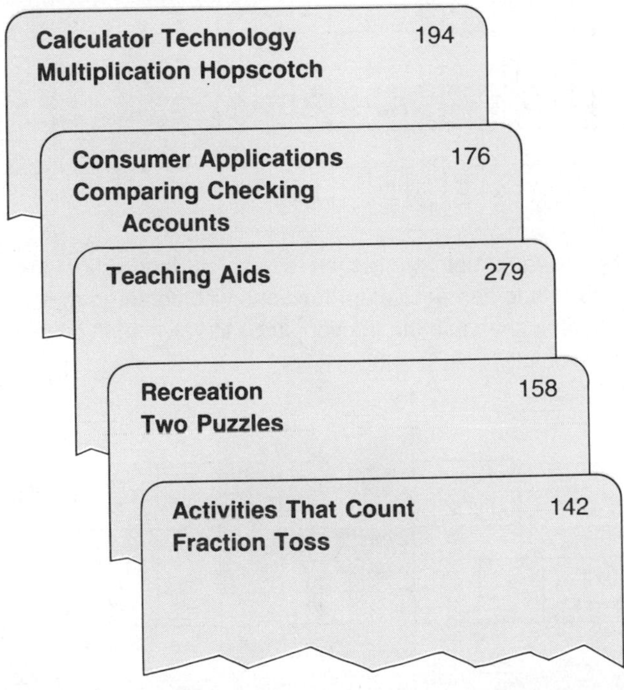


**. . . after Chapter 8**

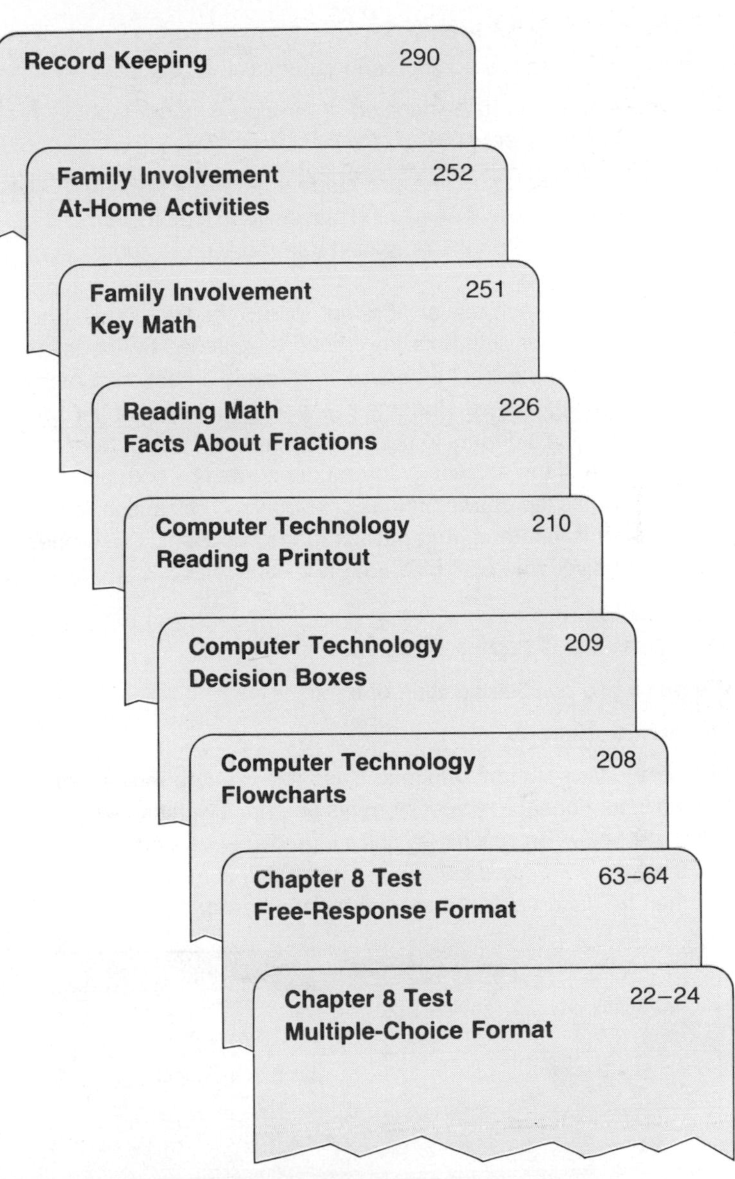


## Supplements

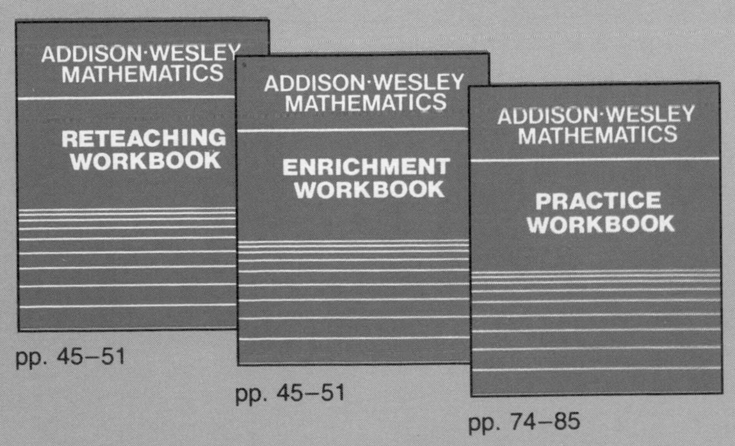


pp. 45–51

pp. 45–51

pp. 74–85

## Other Addison-Wesley Resources

### Books and Kits

*The Mad Minute* pp. 111–120, 146–150, 171–175

*The Arithmetic Primer* pp. 97–102, 114–129, 132–135, 139–165, 300–301

*Arithmetic Skill Cards* pp. W 11–12; F 1–8

*Problem Solving Experiences in Mathematics,* Grade 6 Problems 128, 138

### Technology

*Computer Math Activities* Volumes 2, 4, 5

*Computer Math Games* Volumes 1, 3, 6

# Activities That Count

Activities That Count are designed for use throughout this chapter and subsequent chapters. Before beginning Chapter 8, you may wish to review these activities and select the ones you consider appropriate for your class.

## Fraction Toss Game

**Purpose** To practice addition and subtraction of fractions

**Materials** Number cube labeled 1 through 6, cube labeled A through F, game sheet (TRB p. 142)

**Activity** Before play begins, one student writes a fraction in six of the twelve fraction cells. The second player fills in the other six cells. Next, players decide on the operation rule (addition or subtraction) for that round.

To begin play, each player at a turn tosses the two cubes. The player then adds or subtracts the fractions indicated by the letter and number on the cubes. If necessary, provide a fraction number line (TRB p. 278) to help students determine the larger of the two fractions. Remind students to subtract the smaller fraction from the larger fraction. If the answer is correct, as agreed by both players, the player writes the answer in the corresponding cell and initials it. If the answer is incorrect, turn passes to the opponent. The winner is the first player who can initial four adjacent cells.

## Double or Triple Recipe Project

**Purpose** To practice addition of fractions

**Materials** Recipes

**Activity** Each student brings to class one or more recipes for a favorite food. For each recipe, students prepare a worksheet similar to the one below, on which they show ingredients needed to double and triple the suggested servings of their original recipes. Recipes can then be displayed on a special bulletin board.

| Gingerbread | | |
|---|---|---|
| Double (16 servings) | Triple (24 servings) | 8 Servings |
| | | 1 tablespoon vinegar<br>$\frac{3}{4}$ cup milk<br>2 cups flour<br>$\frac{1}{4}$ teaspoon soda<br>2 teaspoons baking powder<br>$\frac{1}{2}$ teaspoon salt<br>$1\frac{1}{2}$ teaspoons ground ginger<br>1 teaspoon ground cinnamon<br>$\frac{1}{4}$ teaspoon ground cloves<br>$\frac{1}{3}$ cup shortening<br>$\frac{1}{2}$ cup sugar<br>1 egg<br>$\frac{3}{4}$ cup molasses |

## Equivalent Fraction Strips Math Lab

**Purpose** To review equivalent fractions and to practice addition of fractions with common denominators

**Materials** Tagboard

**Preparation** Cut tagboard strips about 25 cm long and 5 cm wide. Mark off ten 2-cm sections. Also cut tagboard rectangles 20 cm by 10 cm. Have students cut four slits in the rectangles so that the fraction strips will just slide through (see illustration).

| One half | $\frac{1}{2}$ | $\frac{2}{4}$ | $\frac{3}{6}$ | $\frac{4}{8}$ | $\frac{5}{10}$ | $\frac{6}{12}$ | $\frac{7}{14}$ | $\frac{8}{16}$ | $\frac{9}{18}$ | $\frac{10}{20}$ |
|---|---|---|---|---|---|---|---|---|---|---|

| Three fourths | $\frac{3}{4}$ | $\frac{6}{8}$ | $\frac{9}{12}$ | $\frac{12}{16}$ | $\frac{15}{20}$ | $\frac{18}{24}$ | $\frac{21}{28}$ | $\frac{24}{32}$ | $\frac{27}{36}$ | $\frac{30}{40}$ |
|---|---|---|---|---|---|---|---|---|---|---|

| Four fifths | $\frac{4}{5}$ | $\frac{8}{10}$ | $\frac{12}{15}$ | $\frac{16}{20}$ | $\frac{20}{25}$ | $\frac{24}{30}$ | $\frac{28}{35}$ | $\frac{32}{40}$ | $\frac{36}{45}$ | $\frac{40}{50}$ |
|---|---|---|---|---|---|---|---|---|---|---|

| Two thirds | $\frac{2}{3}$ | $\frac{4}{6}$ | $\frac{6}{9}$ | $\frac{8}{12}$ | $\frac{10}{15}$ | $\frac{12}{18}$ | $\frac{14}{21}$ | $\frac{16}{24}$ | $\frac{18}{27}$ | $\frac{20}{30}$ |
|---|---|---|---|---|---|---|---|---|---|---|

**Activity** Using a pair of fraction strips, students slide them through the slits to find equivalent fractions with common denominators. Students then use the fraction strips to solve addition problems. For example, $\frac{4}{5} + \frac{2}{3} = \frac{22}{15}$.

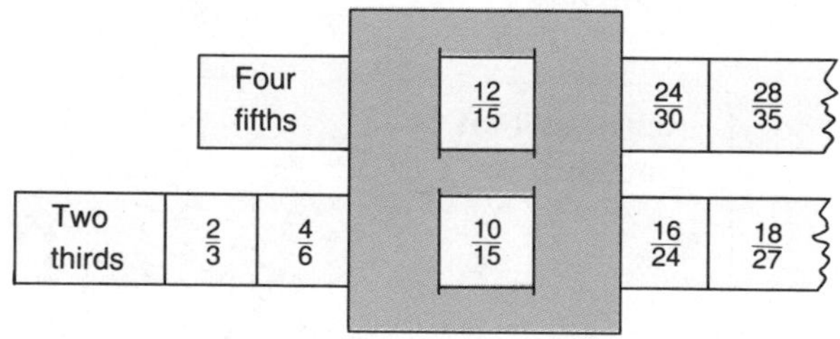

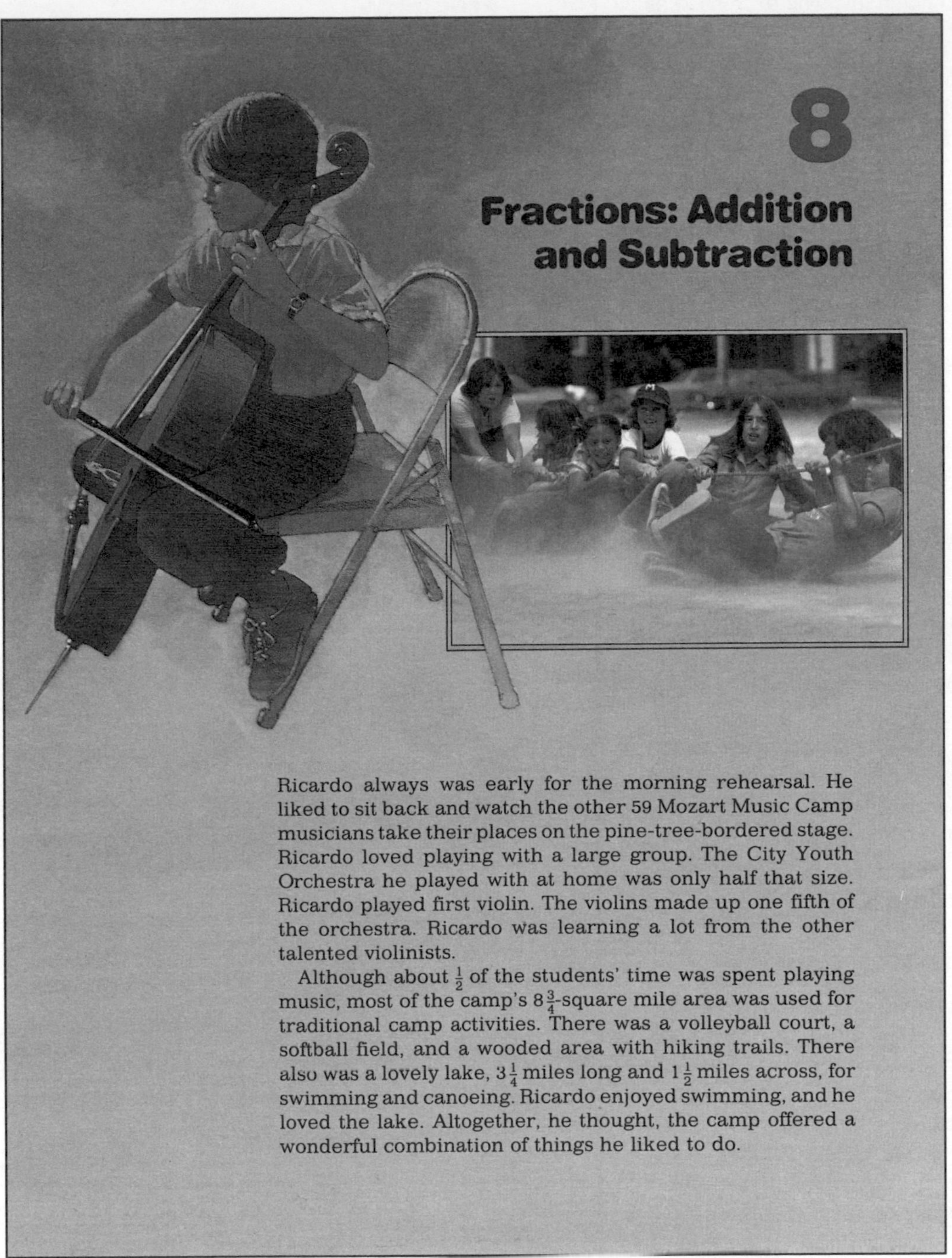

# 8
## Fractions: Addition and Subtraction

Ricardo always was early for the morning rehearsal. He liked to sit back and watch the other 59 Mozart Music Camp musicians take their places on the pine-tree-bordered stage. Ricardo loved playing with a large group. The City Youth Orchestra he played with at home was only half that size. Ricardo played first violin. The violins made up one fifth of the orchestra. Ricardo was learning a lot from the other talented violinists.

Although about $\frac{1}{2}$ of the students' time was spent playing music, most of the camp's $8\frac{3}{4}$-square mile area was used for traditional camp activities. There was a volleyball court, a softball field, and a wooded area with hiking trails. There also was a lovely lake, $3\frac{1}{4}$ miles long and $1\frac{1}{2}$ miles across, for swimming and canoeing. Ricardo enjoyed swimming, and he loved the lake. Altogether, he thought, the camp offered a wonderful combination of things he liked to do.

## Introducing the Chapter

**Discussion** After explaining to students that in this chapter they will review and strengthen their skills in working with fractions, encourage students to discuss any experiences they may have had at summer camp. Try to elicit the idea that many camps offer special educational as well as recreational programs. Then give students time to read the story and enjoy the art. Afterward, allow time for them to suggest some questions pertinent to the data in the story. As you teach the chapter, you may wish to refer back to this page and pose the problems presented below.

## Follow-Up Questions

**After Page 195** Mozart Music Camp has 15 counselors. 11 of the counselors play a musical instrument. What fraction of the counselors play a musical instrument? $\left(\frac{11}{15}\right)$

**After Page 199** 50 of the 80 students at Camp Harmony are girls. What is the lowest-terms fraction for $\frac{50}{80}$? $\left(\frac{5}{8}\right)$

**After Page 209** In the afternoon $\frac{1}{2}$ the students at camp go swimming, $\frac{2}{5}$ play softball, and $\frac{1}{10}$ play tennis. How much greater is the fraction of students who go swimming than the fraction of students who play softball? $\left(\frac{1}{10}\right)$

**After Page 211** Each day Ricardo spends $1\frac{3}{4}$ hours playing the violin by himself. He spends $1\frac{1}{2}$ hours practicing with the student orchestra. How many hours is this in all? $\left(3\frac{1}{4}\text{ hours}\right)$

# Fractions

**Quick Review** Students add $<$, $>$, or $=$ to make each statement true.

$3 + 12 < 17$ $45 \div 9 = 5$ $100 \times 100 = 10{,}000$ $80 \div 20 < 6$

$16 \div 8 < 4$ $9 \times 9 > 80$ $14 \div 7 = 2$ $75 \div 3 < 50$

$800 + 200 < 1{,}100$ $6 \times 7 > 35$ $30 + 30 + 30 < 100$

**Lesson Focus** To name fractions expressed as parts of regions and parts of sets

**Suggested Materials** Paper for folding

## Ideas for Getting Started

Give each student a sheet of paper. Have students fold the paper in half and then in half again. When opened, the paper should look like this.

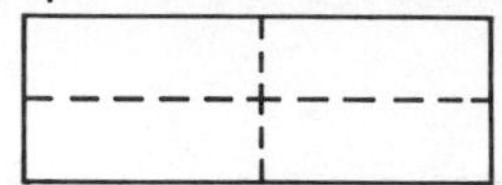

Have students draw along the lines of the folds. "How many pieces of paper do you have?" (1) "We can say that it is 1 unit. Into how many smaller regions did you fold the unit?" (4) "Is each region the same size?" (yes) Then have students shade 1 of the 4 regions. "We can use a *fraction* to tell the part of the paper that is shaded." Write $\frac{1}{4}$ on the chalkboard. Explain that the 4 tells us the unit is divided into 4 same-size regions and the 1 tells us that 1 of the regions is shaded. Ask students what fraction tells which part is not shaded. $\left(\frac{3}{4}\right)$ Then name the numerator and the denominator as you write these terms on the chalkboard.

Use 3 pencils and 1 pen to illustrate the idea of a fraction of a set. "How many of these objects are pens? We can also use a fraction to tell us what part of this total group is pens." Write $\frac{1}{4}$ on the chalkboard. Explain that the 4 tells the total number of objects and the 1 tells that there is 1 pen.

## Using Page 194

**Lesson Development** Have students read the introductory sentence at the top of the page. Discuss the idea of regions, pointing out the two regions on the table top and emphasizing that they are the same size. Next discuss the *sets.* Emphasize that the denominator shows the total number of children, or the *whole* group. Refer back to the region model and discuss what the *whole* was there—the table represents the whole or 1 *unit.* Have students identify the numerator and the denominator in both the region and the set.

**Other Examples** In these examples, the checkerboard is a region model and the Ping Pong paddles are a set model. Make sure students understand how to read the fractional name for each.

## Fractions

We can use **fractions** to name a part of a **region** or a part of a **set.**

**Regions**
What fraction of the table top is painted dark green?

We think: 3 of the 4 parts of the table top are dark green.

We write: $\frac{3}{4}$ ← Numerator (3), Denominator (4)

We say: "**Three fourths** of the table is dark green."

**Sets**
What fraction of the children are girls?

We think: 2 of the 3 children are girls.

We write: $\frac{2}{3}$ ← Numerator (2), Denominator (3)

We say: "**Two thirds** of the children are girls."

**Other Examples**

32 squares out of 64 squares are red.
$\frac{32}{64}$ of the checkerboard is red.

2 out of 5 paddles are green.
$\frac{2}{5}$ of the paddles are green.

**Warm Up** Write the fraction for each picture.

1. ■ of the balls are footballs. $\frac{2}{3}$
2. ■ of the starter's flag is shaded blue. $\frac{2}{4}$
3.  ■ of the bowling pins are still standing. $\frac{3}{10}$



## Follow Up

### Reteaching

Review the idea of fractions as parts of regions and parts of sets, using models if possible. Discuss the meaning of the numerator and the denominator. To illustrate parts of regions, use a circle divided into 8 equal parts. As you shade each part, refer to it as an eighth and emphasize that $\frac{8}{8}$ equals the whole unit.

To illustrate parts of sets, use 4 red checkers and 2 white checkers. Elicit from students that the set consists of 6 objects. Thus, the white checkers represent $\frac{2}{6}$ of the set, and the red checkers, $\frac{4}{6}$ of the set.

### Enrichment

Have students cut flower petals from colored paper and arrange them so that they show fractional parts. Glue the petals to newsprint to create flowered placemats. The placemats can be laminated.

| Assignment Guide | | | |
|---|---|---|---|
| | Minimum | Average | Extended |
| page 195 | 1–19 | 1–19 | 4–10, 15–21, TM |

Write the fraction for each picture.

1. 
■ of the tennis balls are orange. $\frac{2}{6}$

2. 
■ of the sports blanket is blue. $\frac{5}{9}$

3. 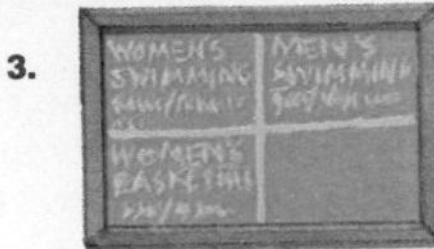
■ of the schedule board is filled. $\frac{3}{4}$

4. ■ of the circle is yellow. $\frac{3}{8}$

5. 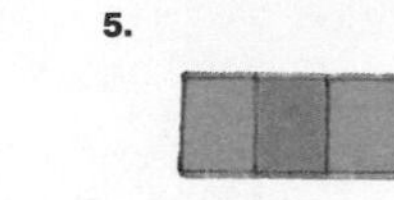
■ of the strip is green. $\frac{2}{3}$

6. 
■ of the stars are blue. $\frac{2}{7}$

Write the fraction.

7. two fifths $\frac{2}{5}$
8. four sixths $\frac{4}{6}$
9. one third $\frac{1}{3}$
10. seven tenths $\frac{7}{10}$
11. one half $\frac{1}{2}$
12. three eighths $\frac{3}{8}$

Write the word name for each fraction.

13. $\frac{2}{3}$ two thirds
14. $\frac{1}{10}$ one tenth
15. $\frac{3}{4}$ three fourths
16. $\frac{5}{8}$ five eighths
17. $\frac{5}{6}$ five sixths
18. $\frac{4}{5}$ four fifths

19. Which region has $\frac{1}{4}$ shaded? B **A.** **B.** **C.** **D.**

★ 20. Draw a circle and shade $\frac{3}{4}$ of it. Construction

★ 21. Draw a rectangle and shade $\frac{1}{3}$ of it. Construction

**Think Math**

**Shape Perception**

A cube has 6 faces. Study the outlined regions.

Which ones could be folded on the dotted lines to form a cube?
B, C, D, E, G

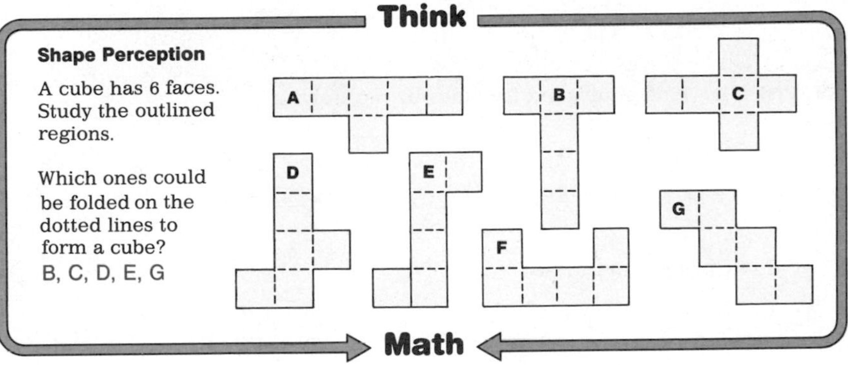




## Using Page 195

**Exercises 1–6** Remind students that they should first find how many parts are in the whole or 1 unit.

**Exercises 7–19** Exercises 7–18 provide practice translating between the symbols and the word names for fractions. Exercise 19 reinforces the idea of same-sized regions.

**Exercises 20–21** Both of these starred exercises ask students to construct region models for fractions.

**Think Math** If necessary, provide students with graph paper so that they can fold the shapes to verify which ones are cubes.

## Ideas That Work

### Calculator Bonus

Have students find the missing numerator or denominator.

a) $\frac{5}{17} = \frac{105}{357}$

b) $\frac{26}{27} = \frac{546}{567}$

c) $\frac{6}{11} = \frac{60}{110}$

d) $\frac{23}{41} = \frac{644}{1148}$

**Practice Supplement,** page 74

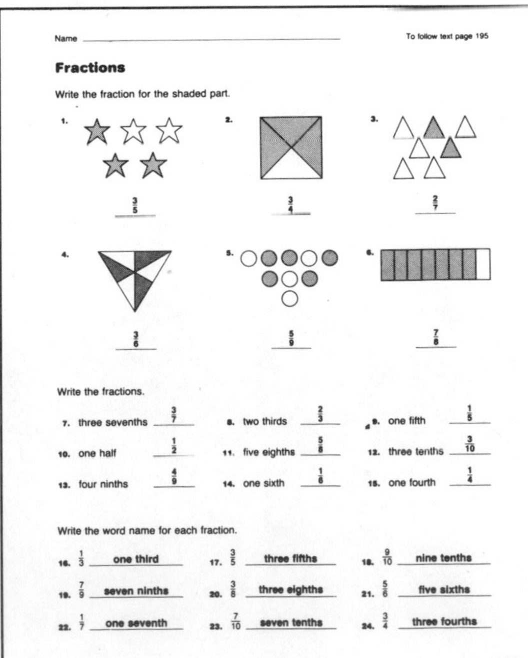
Name ____________ To follow text page 195

**Fractions**

Write the fraction for the shaded part.

1. $\frac{3}{5}$
2. $\frac{3}{4}$
3. $\frac{2}{7}$
4. $\frac{3}{6}$
5. $\frac{5}{9}$
6. $\frac{7}{8}$

Write the fractions.

7. three sevenths $\frac{3}{7}$
8. two thirds $\frac{2}{3}$
9. one fifth $\frac{1}{5}$
10. one half $\frac{1}{2}$
11. five eighths $\frac{5}{8}$
12. three tenths $\frac{3}{10}$
13. four ninths $\frac{4}{9}$
14. one sixth $\frac{1}{6}$
15. one fourth $\frac{1}{4}$

Write the word name for each fraction.

16. $\frac{1}{3}$ one third
17. $\frac{3}{5}$ three fifths
18. $\frac{9}{10}$ nine tenths
19. $\frac{7}{9}$ seven ninths
20. $\frac{3}{8}$ three eighths
21. $\frac{5}{6}$ five sixths
22. $\frac{1}{7}$ one seventh
23. $\frac{7}{10}$ seven tenths
24. $\frac{3}{4}$ three fourths

**Quick Review** Students use multiplication facts to find the sums below. Note that the first addend is a multiple of the second.

42 + 6 56 + 8 12 + 6 81 + 9 63 + 9 64 + 8 27 + 9
28 + 7 36 + 4 56 + 7 49 + 7 54 + 6 48 + 6

**Lesson Focus** To find equivalent fractions

**Suggested Materials** Paper for folding

## Ideas for Getting Started

Have each student fold a piece of paper into two parts, open it, and shade one half. Write $\frac{1}{2}$ on the chalkboard. Then have students refold the paper into two parts. Have students open it and discuss what they see. The two foldings should show this.

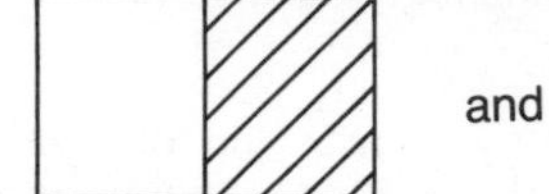 and 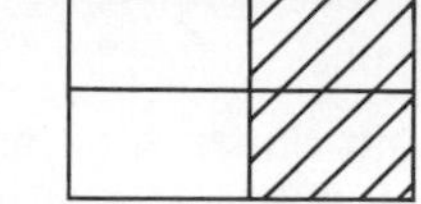

Identify the fraction shown by the second fold as $\frac{2}{4}$ and write $\frac{1}{2} = \frac{2}{4}$ on the chalkboard. Tell students that these fractions are *equivalent*.

## Using Page 196

**Lesson Development** Ask students to read the paragraph at the top of the page. "What question are we asked?" (What fraction describes the part of the candles that are red?) Direct students' attention to the picture and have them identify the number of red candles and the total number of candles. Then discuss the fact that 2 out of 6 candles are red, or 1 out of 3 pairs have red candles. Discuss how both of these descriptions tell what part of the total set or group of candles is red. Then have students read the definition of equivalent fractions in the display box.

Ask a volunteer to read the paragraph that explains how to find equivalent fractions. Point out that in this example the numerator and denominator were both multiplied by 2.

**Other Examples** Identify the number in each example that was used to multiply the numerator and denominator. Emphasize that the two fractions in each example are equivalent.

**Warm Up** If necessary suggest that students use the method shown in exercises 1–4 to help them with exercises 5–8.

## Equivalent Fractions

Lupe bought some candles. Some of them were yellow and some were red. What fraction describes the part of the candles that were red?

2 out of 6 candles are red.
$\frac{2}{6}$ of the candles are red.

OR

1 out of 3 pairs have red candles.
$\frac{1}{3}$ of the candles are red.

$\frac{2}{6}$ and $\frac{1}{3}$ are **equivalent fractions.**

$$\frac{2}{6} = \frac{1}{3}$$

Two fractions that name the same part of a set or the same part of a region are **equivalent fractions.**

We can multiply to find equivalent fractions. Multiply the numerator and denominator by the same number (not zero).

$$\frac{1}{3} \xrightarrow{1 \times 2 \,/\, 3 \times 2} \frac{2}{6}$$

**Other Examples**

$$\frac{2}{5} \xrightarrow{\times 2} \frac{4}{10} \qquad \frac{3}{4} \xrightarrow{\times 5} \frac{15}{20} \qquad \frac{1}{6} \xrightarrow{\times 6} \frac{6}{36}$$

**Warm Up** Find equivalent fractions by multiplying.

1. $\frac{1}{2} \xrightarrow{\times 4} \frac{■}{■}$ 4/8
2. $\frac{3}{5} \xrightarrow{\times 3} \frac{■}{■}$ 9/15
3. $\frac{3}{8} \xrightarrow{\times 2} \frac{■}{■}$ 6/16
4. $\frac{2}{3} \xrightarrow{\times 3} \frac{■}{■}$ 6/9

Find the missing numerators.

5. $\frac{1}{3} = \frac{■}{12}$ 4
6. $\frac{5}{6} = \frac{■}{18}$ 15
7. $\frac{3}{10} = \frac{■}{50}$ 15
8. $\frac{1}{4} = \frac{■}{12}$ 3



## Follow Up

### Reteaching

Discuss the idea that 1 can be named in many ways as a fraction. For example, $\frac{2}{2}$, $\frac{3}{3}$, $\frac{4}{4}$, and so on, all represent 1. Help students recall the 1 property which says that when either factor is 1, the product is the other factor. Thus, we can write $\frac{1}{2} \times \frac{2}{2}$ or $\frac{1 \times 2}{2 \times 2} = \frac{2}{4}$, $\frac{1 \times 3}{2 \times 3} = \frac{3}{6}$, and so on and know that the product is still equal to $\frac{1}{2}$.

### Enrichment

Have students use a $8\frac{1}{2}'' \times 11''$ sheet of unruled paper and fold or measure it to show fractional parts. Have students color a fractional part of the unruled paper, glue it to newsprint or colored paper, and then write equivalent fractions around the illustration. For example:

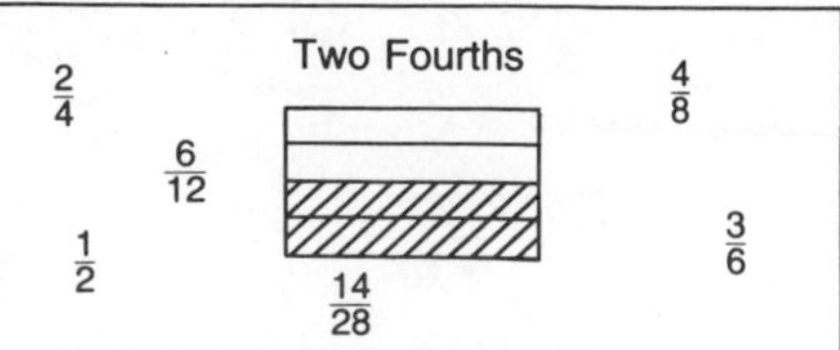

| Assignment Guide | | | |
|---|---|---|---|
| | Minimum | Average | Extended |
| page 197 | 1–31, SK | 1–33, SK | 2–30 even, 31–33, SK |

Write two equivalent fractions for the red part.

1. 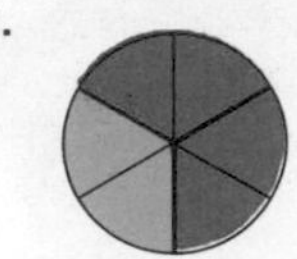 $\frac{2}{3} = \frac{4}{6}$

2. 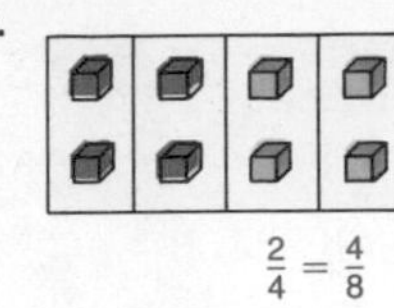 $\frac{2}{4} = \frac{4}{8}$

3. 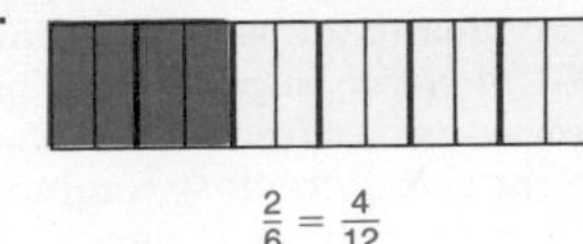 $\frac{2}{6} = \frac{4}{12}$

Write an equivalent fraction.

4. $\frac{1}{5}$ (× 4, × 4) = $\frac{\blacksquare}{\blacksquare}$ $\frac{4}{20}$
5. $\frac{7}{10}$ (× 3, × 3) = $\frac{\blacksquare}{\blacksquare}$ $\frac{21}{30}$
6. $\frac{5}{8}$ (× 5, × 5) = $\frac{\blacksquare}{\blacksquare}$ $\frac{25}{40}$
7. $\frac{1}{6}$ (× 3, × 3) = $\frac{\blacksquare}{\blacksquare}$ $\frac{3}{18}$

Find the missing numerator or denominator.

8. $\frac{2}{5} = \frac{\blacksquare}{20}$ 8
9. $\frac{3}{10} = \frac{\blacksquare}{100}$ 30
10. $\frac{2}{2} = \frac{\blacksquare}{8}$ 8
11. $\frac{3}{4} = \frac{\blacksquare}{32}$ 24
12. $\frac{5}{12} = \frac{\blacksquare}{48}$ 20
13. $\frac{3}{8} = \frac{\blacksquare}{24}$ 9
14. $\frac{1}{2} = \frac{\blacksquare}{100}$ 50
15. $\frac{1}{4} = \frac{\blacksquare}{16}$ 4
16. $\frac{9}{10} = \frac{\blacksquare}{80}$ 72
17. $\frac{4}{7} = \frac{\blacksquare}{21}$ 12
18. $\frac{5}{6} = \frac{25}{\blacksquare}$ 30
19. $\frac{2}{3} = \frac{40}{\blacksquare}$ 60
20. $\frac{7}{8} = \frac{28}{\blacksquare}$ 32
21. $\frac{5}{8} = \frac{60}{\blacksquare}$ 96
22. $\frac{3}{5} = \frac{27}{\blacksquare}$ 45

Write one fraction equivalent to the given fraction. Answers will vary. Sample answers are given.

23. $\frac{4}{5}$ $\frac{8}{10}$
24. $\frac{7}{8}$ $\frac{14}{16}$
25. $\frac{7}{12}$ $\frac{14}{24}$
26. $\frac{3}{8}$ $\frac{6}{16}$
27. $\frac{5}{6}$ $\frac{10}{12}$
28. $\frac{3}{4}$ $\frac{6}{8}$
29. $\frac{1}{10}$ $\frac{2}{20}$
30. $\frac{5}{12}$ $\frac{10}{24}$

Write the next three equivalent fractions.

31. $\frac{1}{5}, \frac{2}{10}, \frac{3}{15}, \frac{\blacksquare}{\blacksquare}, \frac{\blacksquare}{\blacksquare}, \frac{\blacksquare}{\blacksquare}$ $\frac{4}{20}, \frac{5}{25}, \frac{6}{30}$
32. $\frac{3}{8}, \frac{6}{16}, \frac{9}{24}, \frac{\blacksquare}{\blacksquare}, \frac{\blacksquare}{\blacksquare}, \frac{\blacksquare}{\blacksquare}$ $\frac{12}{32}, \frac{15}{40}, \frac{18}{48}$
33. $\frac{2}{7}, \frac{4}{14}, \frac{6}{21}, \frac{\blacksquare}{\blacksquare}, \frac{\blacksquare}{\blacksquare}, \frac{\blacksquare}{\blacksquare}$ $\frac{8}{28}, \frac{10}{35}, \frac{12}{42}$

## Skillkeeper

Give the missing units.

1. 1 m = 100 ? cm
2. 1,000 mm = 1 ? m
3. 1 dm = 10 ? cm
4. 1 ? = 1,000 m km
5. 1 kg = 1,000 ? g
6. 1,000 mL = 1 ? L

Give the missing numbers.

7. 2 dm = ■ cm 20
8. 1 kL = ■ L 1,000
9. 500 cm = ■ m 5
10. 5 kg = ■ g 5,000
11. 4 km = ■ m 4,000
12. 3,000 mm = ■ m 3
13. 1 m = ■ km 0.001
14. 50 cm = ■ m 0.5
15. 7 mm = ■ cm 0.7

More Practice, page 421, Set C



## Using Page 197

**Exercises 1–30** These exercises help students progress from concrete situations using pictures to the point where they find equivalent fractions as well as missing numerators and denominators.

**Exercises 31–33** Students should recognize that these sequences of equivalent fractions are found by multiplying the original fraction (both numerator and denominator) by 4, 5, and 6. For example,

$$\frac{1}{5} = \frac{4}{20} \quad (\times 4 \text{ numerator and denominator})$$

**Skillkeeper** This skillkeeper reviews material originally taught in Chapter 7.

**More Practice,** page 421, Set C

**Reteaching Supplement,** page 45

Name ____________ To follow text page 197

**Equivalent Fractions**

To find **equivalent fractions** Multiply the numerator and the denominator by the same number.

**Examples**

$\frac{2}{3} = \frac{8}{12}$ (2 × 4, 3 × 4) Multiply by **4**.
$\frac{3}{4} = \frac{9}{12}$ (3 × 3, 4 × 3) Multiply by **3**.
$\frac{1}{6} = \frac{5}{30}$ (1 × 5, 6 × 5) Multiply by **5**.

Write the missing numerator or denominator.

1. $\frac{3}{4} = \frac{12}{16}$ Multiply by 4.
2. $\frac{3}{3} = \frac{15}{15}$ Multiply by 5.
3. $\frac{1}{3} = \frac{2}{6}$ Multiply by 2.
4. $\frac{3}{5} = \frac{9}{15}$
5. $\frac{3}{4} = \frac{15}{20}$
6. $\frac{3}{8} = \frac{9}{24}$
7. $\frac{2}{3} = \frac{18}{27}$
8. $\frac{1}{2} = \frac{6}{12}$
9. $\frac{5}{1} = \frac{15}{3}$
10. $\frac{3}{5} = \frac{15}{25}$
11. $\frac{6}{10} = \frac{30}{50}$
12. $\frac{7}{9} = \frac{28}{36}$
13. $\frac{1}{2} = \frac{8}{16}$
14. $\frac{2}{5} = \frac{4}{10}$
15. $\frac{1}{3} = \frac{3}{9}$
16. $\frac{0}{4} = \frac{0}{8}$
17. $\frac{6}{6} = \frac{1}{1}$
18. $\frac{4}{5} = \frac{12}{15}$
19. $\frac{5}{3} = \frac{15}{9}$
20. $\frac{4}{6} = \frac{12}{18}$
21. $\frac{3}{20} = \frac{15}{100}$
22. $\frac{3}{12} = \frac{1}{4}$
23. $\frac{7}{8} = \frac{21}{24}$
24. $\frac{5}{6} = \frac{30}{36}$
25. $\frac{1}{12} = \frac{5}{60}$
26. $\frac{3}{9} = \frac{9}{27}$
27. $\frac{2}{4} = \frac{10}{20}$

**Enrichment Supplement,** page 45

Name ____________ To follow text page 197

**Fraction Stars**

Find pairs of equivalent fractions. Draw straight lines to connect the pairs. Use the dots to guide you. If you pair all the fractions correctly, you should see three 5-pointed stars formed by the lines. Shade them.

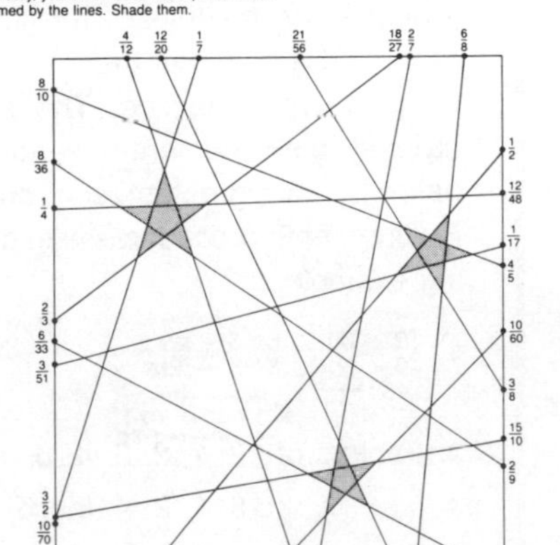

**Practice Supplement,** page 75

Name ____________ To follow text page 197

**Equivalent Fractions**

Write two equivalent fractions for the shaded part.

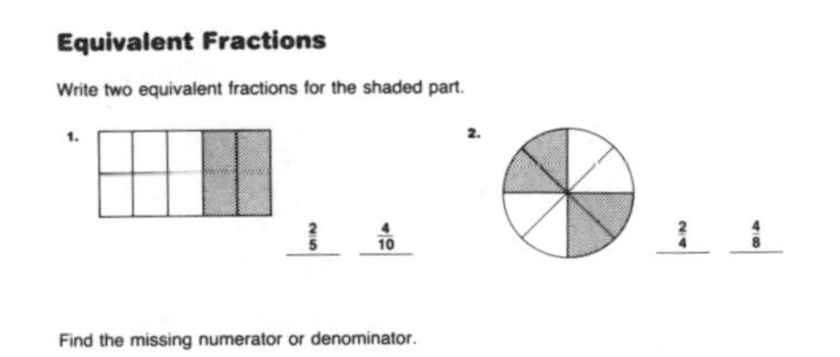

1. $\frac{2}{5}$ $\frac{4}{10}$
2. $\frac{2}{4}$ $\frac{4}{8}$

Find the missing numerator or denominator.

3. $\frac{1}{2} = \frac{6}{12}$
4. $\frac{1}{2} = \frac{21}{42}$
5. $\frac{1}{5} = \frac{2}{10}$
6. $\frac{4}{25} = \frac{16}{100}$
7. $\frac{2}{5} = \frac{4}{10}$
8. $\frac{1}{3} = \frac{15}{45}$
9. $\frac{9}{10} = \frac{36}{40}$
10. $\frac{3}{10} = \frac{9}{30}$
11. $\frac{20}{50} = \frac{40}{100}$
12. $\frac{1}{2} = \frac{50}{100}$
13. $\frac{7}{3} = \frac{35}{15}$
14. $\frac{2}{3} = \frac{12}{18}$
15. $\frac{4}{5} = \frac{16}{20}$
16. $\frac{9}{10} = \frac{27}{30}$
17. $\frac{9}{10} = \frac{90}{100}$
18. $\frac{2}{3} = \frac{20}{30}$
19. $\frac{5}{6} = \frac{25}{30}$
20. $\frac{1}{4} = \frac{7}{28}$
21. $\frac{3}{10} = \frac{18}{60}$
22. $\frac{5}{8} = \frac{30}{48}$
23. $\frac{3}{2} = \frac{27}{18}$
24. $\frac{7}{25} = \frac{28}{100}$
25. $\frac{3}{10} = \frac{15}{50}$
26. $\frac{8}{4} = \frac{64}{32}$

Write the next three equivalent fractions.

27. $\frac{1}{2}, \frac{2}{4}, \frac{3}{6}$, $\frac{4}{8}$, $\frac{5}{10}$, $\frac{6}{12}$
28. $\frac{5}{6}, \frac{10}{12}, \frac{15}{18}$, $\frac{20}{24}$, $\frac{25}{30}$, $\frac{30}{36}$
29. $\frac{2}{3}, \frac{4}{6}, \frac{6}{9}$, $\frac{8}{12}$, $\frac{10}{15}$, $\frac{12}{18}$
30. $\frac{4}{7}, \frac{8}{14}, \frac{12}{21}$, $\frac{16}{28}$, $\frac{20}{35}$, $\frac{24}{42}$

**Quick Review** As an oral drill, students give the quotient of each listed number divided by the number in parentheses.

63, 49, 21, 14, 56 (7) 36, 42, 54, 48, 30 (6) 24, 18, 9, 27, 15 (3)
81, 27, 36, 18, 45 (9) 56, 32, 72, 24, 48 (8) 36, 12, 20, 28, 40 (4)

**Lesson Focus** To find the greatest common factor for a pair of numbers; to write fractions in lowest terms

## Ideas for Getting Started

Write the number 12 on the chalkboard. If necessary, use 2 × 6 = 12 to explain that 2 and 6 are factors of 12. Then write the factors of 12 on the chalkboard: 1, 2, 3, 4, 6, 12. Be sure students recognize that 1 and 12 are factors of 12. Then write the factors of 20 on the chalkboard: 1, 2, 4, 5, 10, 20. "What factors are common to both 12 and 20?" (1, 2, 4) Then point out that 4 is the greatest common factor.

## Using Page 198

**Lesson Development** Have students read the paragraph at the top of the page about finding greatest common factors. Then discuss each instruction box and the examples of 24 and 36. Next call students' attention to the shortcut and discuss why it is a shortcut. Students should see that any factor greater than the smaller of the two numbers cannot be a *common* factor.

**Other Examples** Point out that for 9 and 13, 1 is the only common factor, and thus the greatest one.

**Exercises 1–18** Read through the direction line with students before assigning these exercises.

## Greatest Common Factor

The idea of the **greatest common factor (GCF)** of two numbers will help you find lowest-terms fractions in the next lesson. What is the greatest common factor of the numerator and denominator of $\frac{24}{36}$?

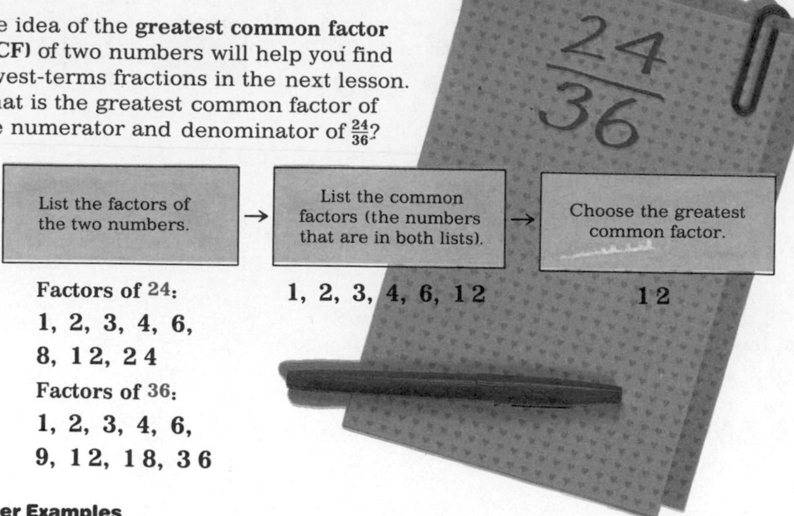


List the factors of the two numbers. → List the common factors (the numbers that are in both lists). → Choose the greatest common factor.

Factors of 24: 1, 2, 3, 4, 6, 8, 12, 24
Factors of 36: 1, 2, 3, 4, 6, 9, 12, 18, 36

1, 2, 3, 4, 6, 12

12

**Other Examples**

16→1, 2, 4, 8, 16
24→1, 2, 3, 4, 6, 8, 12
Common factors: 1, 2, 4, 8
Greatest common factor: 8

9→1, 3, 9
13→1, 13
Common factor: 1
Greatest common factor: 1

Find the greatest common factor for 24 and 36.

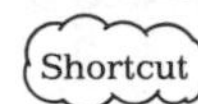


**A** List only the factors of the smaller number. 24: 1, 2, 3, 4, 6, 8, 12, 24

**B** List those that are also factors of the other number (36). 1, 2, 3, 4, 6, 12

**C** The largest is the greatest common factor. 12

Find the greatest common factor for each pair of numbers.

| | | | | | |
|---|---|---|---|---|---|
| 1. 8, 24 — 8 | 2. 3, 12 — 3 | 3. 15, 25 — 5 | 4. 4, 8 — 4 | 5. 7, 20 — 1 | 6. 12, 54 — 6 |
| 7. 18, 30 — 6 | 8. 20, 50 — 10 | 9. 6, 7 — 1 | 10. 18, 38 — 2 | 11. 12, 36 — 12 | 12. 9, 32 — 1 |
| 13. 42, 36 — 6 | 14. 100, 50 — 50 | 15. 15, 45 — 15 | 16. 14, 63 — 7 | 17. 21, 60 — 3 | 18. 45, 72 — 9 |



More Practice, page 421, Set D

## Follow Up

### Reteaching

Explain to students that there are two procedures that can be used to find lowest-terms fractions. The first is successive dividing until there are no common factors remaining. The second is dividing both numerator and denominator by the greatest common factor. Illustrate both procedures with the following example.

1. $\frac{12 \div 2}{16 \div 2} = \frac{6}{8}$, $\frac{6 \div 2}{8 \div 2} = \frac{3}{4}$ (a name for 1)

2. Factors of 12: 1, 2, 3, 4, 6, 12
16: 1, 2, 4, 8, 16

The greatest common factor of 12 and 16 is 4. $\frac{12 \div 4}{16 \div 4} = \frac{3}{4}$

### Enrichment

Have students find the greatest common factor for each spoke in the wheel below.

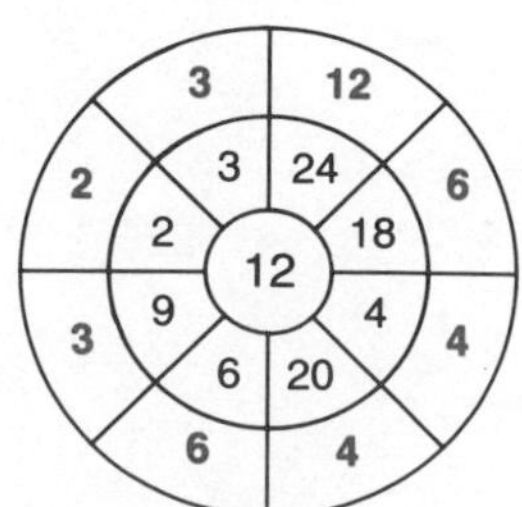

| Assignment Guide | | | |
|---|---|---|---|
| | Minimum | Average | Extended |
| page 198 | 1–18 | 1–18 | 1–18 |
| page 199 | 1–24 | 1–24 | 1–24 |

## Lowest-Terms Fractions

In Lettie's class, 6 out of 24 students, or $\frac{6}{24}$ of the class, are in the tumbling club. To show this number more simply, we write $\frac{6}{24}$ as a **lowest-terms fraction.**

A fraction is in **lowest terms** when the greatest common factor of the numerator and denominator is 1.

Divide the numerator and the denominator by any common factor and continue to divide until you find the lowest-terms fraction.

$$\frac{6 \div 2}{24 \div 2} = \frac{3}{12} \rightarrow \frac{3 \div 3}{12 \div 3} = \frac{1}{4}$$

OR

Divide the numerator and the denominator by the **greatest common factor** (GCF) to find the lowest-terms fraction.

$$\frac{6 \div 6}{24 \div 6} = \frac{1}{4}$$

1 is the only common factor of 1 and 4.

6 is the GCF.

**Other Examples**

$\frac{4}{6}$: $4 \div 2 \rightarrow 2$, $6 \div 2 \rightarrow 3$: $\frac{4}{6} = \frac{2}{3}$

$\frac{8}{36}$: $8 \div 4 \rightarrow 2$, $36 \div 4 \rightarrow 9$: $\frac{8}{36} = \frac{2}{9}$

$\frac{50}{100}$: $50 \div 50 \rightarrow 1$, $100 \div 50 \rightarrow 2$: $\frac{50}{100} = \frac{1}{2}$

Reduce to lowest terms.

1. $\frac{25}{50}$ — $\frac{1}{2}$
2. $\frac{27}{30}$ — $\frac{9}{10}$
3. $\frac{6}{9}$ — $\frac{2}{3}$
4. $\frac{7}{35}$ — $\frac{1}{5}$
5. $\frac{6}{30}$ — $\frac{1}{5}$
6. $\frac{8}{24}$ — $\frac{1}{3}$
7. $\frac{5}{20}$ — $\frac{1}{4}$
8. $\frac{8}{16}$ — $\frac{1}{2}$
9. $\frac{20}{25}$ — $\frac{4}{5}$
10. $\frac{4}{28}$ — $\frac{1}{7}$
11. $\frac{6}{18}$ — $\frac{1}{3}$
12. $\frac{18}{24}$ — $\frac{3}{4}$
13. $\frac{30}{100}$ — $\frac{3}{10}$
14. $\frac{18}{27}$ — $\frac{2}{3}$
15. $\frac{30}{60}$ — $\frac{1}{2}$
16. $\frac{70}{100}$ — $\frac{7}{10}$
17. $\frac{16}{24}$ — $\frac{2}{3}$
18. $\frac{16}{40}$ — $\frac{2}{5}$
19. $\frac{24}{30}$ — $\frac{4}{5}$
20. $\frac{45}{60}$ — $\frac{3}{4}$
21. $\frac{32}{40}$ — $\frac{4}{5}$
22. $\frac{80}{100}$ — $\frac{4}{5}$
23. $\frac{30}{36}$ — $\frac{5}{6}$
24. $\frac{24}{36}$ — $\frac{2}{3}$

More Practice, page 422, Set A



## Using Page 199

**Lesson Development** Read and discuss the paragraph at the top of the page. Be sure students understand that there are 24 students in all and that 6 of the 24 students are in the tumbling club. Read the definition of *lowest terms* and then explain the two methods for writing the fraction in lowest terms. Point out to students that instead of dividing by 2 first, they could have divided by 3. Also point out that dividing by the greatest common factor we can write a lowest-terms fraction in one step.

**Other Examples** Point out in the third example that the GCF is one of the terms of the fraction.

**More Practice,** page 421, Set D

**More Practice,** page 422, Set A

### **Reteaching Supplement,** page 46

Name ______________ To follow text page 199

**Lowest-Terms Fractions**

Write $\frac{6}{18}$ as a lowest-terms fraction.

Divide the numerator and denominator by the same common factor. (Try 3.) $\frac{6 \div 3}{18 \div 3} = \frac{2}{6}$ → Can you divide the numerator and denominator again by a common factor (other than 1)? no → The fraction is in lowest terms. yes → Divide. Yes, **2** is a factor of 2 and 6. $\frac{2 \div 2}{6 \div 2} = \frac{1}{3}$ → Keep dividing until the only common factor is 1. $\frac{1}{3}$ is in lowest terms.

Examples:

A $\frac{6}{12} = \frac{6 \div 2}{12 \div 2} = \frac{3}{6} \rightarrow \frac{3 \div 3}{6 \div 3} = \frac{1}{2}$ (Try 2.) (Try 3.) lowest-terms fraction

B $\frac{15}{24} = \frac{15 \div 3}{24 \div 3} = \frac{5}{8}$ (Try 3.) lowest-terms fraction

Write the lowest-terms fractions.

1. $\frac{16}{24} = \frac{16 \div 8}{24 \div 8} = \frac{2}{3}$
2. $\frac{25}{40} = \frac{25 \div 5}{40 \div 5} = \frac{5}{8}$
3. $\frac{12}{20} = \frac{12 \div 4}{20 \div 4} = \frac{3}{5}$
4. $\frac{40}{50} = \frac{40 \div 10}{50 \div 10} = \frac{4}{5}$

Find the lowest-terms fraction for each.

5. $\frac{6}{10} = \frac{3}{5}$
6. $\frac{15}{25} = \frac{3}{5}$
7. $\frac{4}{16} = \frac{1}{4}$
8. $\frac{14}{16} = \frac{7}{8}$
9. $\frac{5}{10} = \frac{1}{2}$
10. $\frac{10}{12} = \frac{5}{6}$
11. $\frac{14}{21} = \frac{2}{3}$
12. $\frac{9}{15} = \frac{3}{5}$
13. $\frac{9}{27} = \frac{1}{3}$
14. $\frac{16}{40} = \frac{2}{5}$
15. $\frac{4}{10} = \frac{2}{5}$
16. $\frac{6}{8} = \frac{3}{4}$
17. $\frac{12}{16} = \frac{3}{4}$
18. $\frac{18}{27} = \frac{2}{3}$
19. $\frac{2}{20} = \frac{1}{10}$
20. $\frac{9}{30} = \frac{3}{10}$
21. $\frac{80}{100} = \frac{4}{5}$
22. $\frac{30}{60} = \frac{1}{2}$
23. $\frac{2}{12} = \frac{1}{6}$
24. $\frac{8}{12} = \frac{2}{3}$
25. $\frac{14}{20} = \frac{7}{10}$
26. $\frac{15}{20} = \frac{3}{4}$
27. $\frac{12}{72} = \frac{1}{6}$
28. $\frac{14}{49} = \frac{2}{7}$
29. $\frac{50}{75} = \frac{2}{3}$
30. $\frac{8}{20} = \frac{2}{5}$
31. $\frac{10}{25} = \frac{2}{5}$
32. $\frac{21}{56} = \frac{3}{8}$

### **Enrichment Supplement,** page 46

Name ______________ To follow text page 199

**Relatively Prime**

Two numbers are **relatively prime** if their greatest common factor (GCF) is 1.

Use the numbers at the right to answer questions 1 through 6 below.

9 28 24 15 12 11 14 8 25 21

1. Which numbers are relatively prime to 4? **9, 15, 21, 11, 25**
2. Which numbers are relatively prime to 6? **25, 11**
3. Which numbers are relatively prime to 7? **all but 14, 21, 28**
4. Find two pairs of numbers that have a GCF of 4. **8 and 12, 24 and 28**
5. Find two pairs of numbers that have a GCF of 7. **21 and 28, 14 and 21**
6. Which pair of numbers has the largest GCF? **12 and 24**

Now answer these questions about other numbers that are relatively prime.

7. Which of the numbers 2 through 20 are relatively prime to 12? **5, 7, 11, 13, 17, 19**
8. Which of the numbers 2 through 20 are relatively prime to 13? **all**
9. Can two even numbers be relatively prime? **no**
10. Can two odd numbers be relatively prime? **yes**

### **Practice Supplement,** page 76

Name ______________ To follow text page 199

**Greatest Common Factor and Lowest-Terms Fractions**

Find the greatest common factor for each pair of numbers.

1. 4 and 6 **2**
2. 8 and 12 **4**
3. 7 and 35 **7**
4. 6 and 9 **3**
5. 3 and 5 **1**
6. 18 and 4 **2**
7. 12 and 18 **6**
8. 8 and 20 **4**
9. 36 and 54 **18**
10. 21 and 56 **7**
11. 9 and 12 **3**
12. 45 and 60 **15**

Write each fraction in lowest terms.

13. $\frac{6}{12} = \frac{1}{2}$
14. $\frac{2}{10} = \frac{1}{5}$
15. $\frac{5}{50} = \frac{1}{10}$
16. $\frac{12}{30} = \frac{2}{5}$
17. $\frac{4}{20} = \frac{1}{5}$
18. $\frac{21}{28} = \frac{3}{4}$
19. $\frac{18}{30} = \frac{3}{5}$
20. $\frac{16}{20} = \frac{4}{5}$
21. $\frac{16}{24} = \frac{2}{3}$
22. $\frac{15}{20} = \frac{3}{4}$
23. $\frac{15}{18} = \frac{5}{6}$
24. $\frac{30}{100} = \frac{3}{10}$
25. $\frac{40}{50} = \frac{4}{5}$
26. $\frac{27}{30} = \frac{9}{10}$
27. $\frac{18}{20} = \frac{9}{10}$
28. $\frac{42}{63} = \frac{2}{3}$
29. $\frac{25}{30} = \frac{5}{6}$
30. $\frac{7}{28} = \frac{1}{4}$
31. $\frac{18}{60} = \frac{3}{10}$
32. $\frac{32}{40} = \frac{4}{5}$
33. $\frac{27}{18} = \frac{3}{2}$
34. $\frac{20}{100} = \frac{1}{5}$
35. $\frac{15}{50} = \frac{3}{10}$
36. $\frac{12}{15} = \frac{4}{5}$

**Quick Review** Students divide each number in half, then in fourths.

| | | | | | | | | |
|---|---|---|---|---|---|---|---|---|
| 24 | 32 | 4 | 20 | 100 | 44 | 80 | 60 | 12 |
| 120 | 16 | 28 | 200 | 1,000 | 36 | 40 | 48 | |
| 64 | 84 | 8 | 400 | 88 | 72 | 4,000 | 300 | 440 |

**Lesson Focus** To write improper fractions as mixed numbers; to write mixed numbers as improper fractions

**Suggested Materials** Paper for folding

## Ideas for Getting Started

Give each student two sheets of paper. Have students fold each sheet in fourths (4 same-sized parts). "What fraction of the whole unit is each part?" $\left(\frac{1}{4}\right)$ Write $\frac{1}{4}$ on the chalkboard. Now have students shade *all* parts of one sheet and 1 part on the second sheet. "How many fourths have you shaded altogether?" (5) Write $\frac{5}{4}$ on the chalkboard. Tell students that $\frac{5}{4}$ is called an *improper fraction* because the numerator is greater than the denominator. Then remind students that they shaded 1 whole unit and $\frac{1}{4}$ of the other unit, or one and one fourth. Write $1\frac{1}{4}$ on the chalkboard. Identify this as a *mixed number* and point out that $1\frac{1}{4}$ and $\frac{5}{4}$ both name the same number.

## Using Page 200

**Lesson Development** Read the question at the top of the page and have students read the next paragraph. Be sure they understand that the unit, or 1, in this instance is the case of apple juice and that each jug is $\frac{1}{4}$ of a case. Remind students that an improper fraction is one in which the numerator is greater than the denominator. A mixed number is one with both a whole number and a fraction. Emphasize that $\frac{9}{4}$ can be written $4\overline{)9}$. Then work through each instruction box to change the improper fraction $\frac{9}{4}$ to the mixed number $2\frac{1}{4}$.

**Other Examples** In second example, note that there is no fractional part after dividing. In the last example, point out that the fractional part should be written in lowest terms.

**Exercises 1–24** Read through the direction line with students, and remind them to write the fractional part in lowest terms when necessary.

## Improper Fractions to Mixed Numbers

If we have 9 jugs of apple juice, how many cases of juice do we have?

Each jug is $\frac{1}{4}$ of a case, so there are $\frac{9}{4}$ cases of juice. We can also say there are $2\frac{1}{4}$ cases of juice. $\frac{9}{4}$ is an **improper fraction.** $2\frac{1}{4}$ is a **mixed number.**

We can use the idea that $\frac{9}{4}$ means $9 \div 4$ to write $\frac{9}{4}$ as a mixed number.

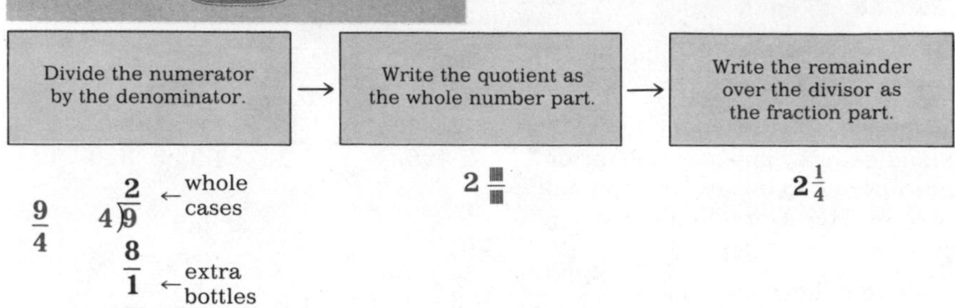


We have $2\frac{1}{4}$ cases of juice.

**Other Examples**

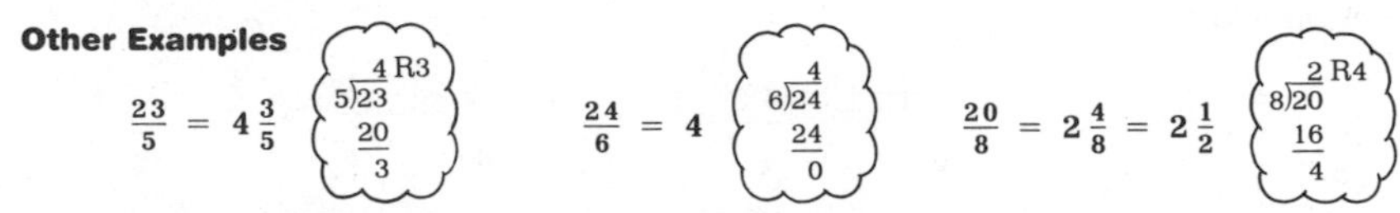

$\frac{23}{5} = 4\frac{3}{5}$ ($5\overline{)23}$ = 4 R3; 20; 3)

$\frac{24}{6} = 4$ ($6\overline{)24}$ = 4; 24; 0)

$\frac{20}{8} = 2\frac{4}{8} = 2\frac{1}{2}$ ($8\overline{)20}$ = 2 R4; 16; 4)

Write each improper fraction as a mixed number or whole number.

1. $\frac{27}{5}$ $5\frac{2}{5}$
2. $\frac{9}{2}$ $4\frac{1}{2}$
3. $\frac{15}{4}$ $3\frac{3}{4}$
4. $\frac{23}{10}$ $2\frac{3}{10}$
5. $\frac{32}{8}$ 4
6. $\frac{7}{3}$ $2\frac{1}{3}$
7. $\frac{43}{8}$ $5\frac{3}{8}$
8. $\frac{19}{10}$ $1\frac{9}{10}$
9. $\frac{7}{4}$ $1\frac{3}{4}$
10. $\frac{19}{6}$ $3\frac{1}{6}$
11. $\frac{32}{3}$ $10\frac{2}{3}$
12. $\frac{29}{5}$ $5\frac{4}{5}$
13. $\frac{73}{2}$ $36\frac{1}{2}$
14. $\frac{51}{3}$ 17
15. $\frac{59}{12}$ $4\frac{11}{12}$
16. $\frac{17}{2}$ $8\frac{1}{2}$
17. $\frac{127}{8}$ $15\frac{7}{8}$
18. $\frac{54}{6}$ 9
19. $\frac{719}{100}$ $7\frac{19}{100}$
20. $\frac{84}{20}$ $4\frac{4}{20} = 4\frac{1}{5}$
21. $\frac{200}{25}$ 8
22. $\frac{130}{40}$ $3\frac{10}{40} = 3\frac{1}{4}$
23. $\frac{150}{50}$ 3
24. $\frac{28}{10}$ $2\frac{8}{10} = 2\frac{4}{5}$



More Practice, page 422, Set B

## Follow Up

### Reteaching

Set up a number line marked as shown below. Elicit from students that the number line is marked into fourths.

0 1 2 3 4

Then name the number of fourths represented by counting from zero: there are 16 fourths, or $\frac{16}{4}$. Ask a volunteer to tell how many units are in the 16 fourths. Help students see that if we start at zero we have $\frac{1}{4}, \frac{2}{4}, \frac{3}{4}, \frac{4}{4}, \frac{5}{4}$, and so on. Because $\frac{4}{4} = 1$, every group of $\frac{4}{4}$ can be renamed as 1. We can also find the units by dividing: $16 \div 4 = 4$.

### Enrichment

Label 10 cards with improper fractions. Label another 10 cards with the mixed number equivalents of the fractions. Mix the cards and place facedown. Each player takes turns turning over two cards. If the improper fraction matches the mixed number, the player keeps both cards. If not, the player returns the cards to the original position. The player who has the most cards when the board is cleared wins.

| | Assignment Guide | | |
|---|---|---|---|
| | Minimum | Average | Extended |
| page 200 | 1–24 | 1–24 | 1–24 |
| page 201 | 1–24 | 1–24 | 1–24 |

## Mixed Numbers to Improper Fractions

How many orange halves can you get from $5\frac{1}{2}$ oranges?

The picture shows 5 whole oranges and $\frac{1}{2}$ of an orange or $5\frac{1}{2}$ oranges. Each whole orange has 2 halves ($\frac{2}{2}$) so we can also say there are $\frac{11}{2}$ oranges.

We can use this method to write $5\frac{1}{2}$ as an improper fraction.

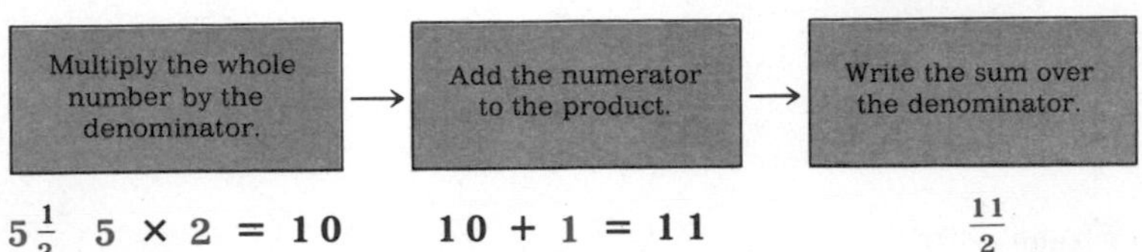
Multiply the whole number by the denominator.
Add the numerator to the product.
Write the sum over the denominator.

$5\frac{1}{2}$ $\quad 5 \times 2 = 10 \quad\quad 10 + 1 = 11 \quad\quad \frac{11}{2}$

**Other Examples**

$3\frac{2}{5} = \frac{17}{5}$ $\quad\quad 6\frac{1}{2} = \frac{13}{2}$ $\quad\quad 4\frac{3}{4} = \frac{19}{4}$

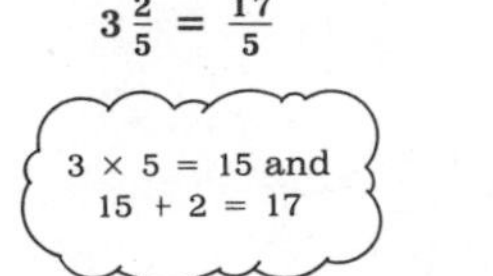
3 × 5 = 15 and
15 + 2 = 17

6 × 2 = 12 and
12 + 1 = 13

4 × 4 = 16 and
16 + 3 = 19

Write each mixed number as an improper fraction.

| | | | | | |
|---|---|---|---|---|---|
| 1. $1\frac{3}{4}$ $\frac{7}{4}$ | 2. $2\frac{1}{10}$ $\frac{21}{10}$ | 3. $4\frac{1}{2}$ $\frac{9}{2}$ | 4. $5\frac{1}{3}$ $\frac{16}{3}$ | 5. $4\frac{1}{4}$ $\frac{17}{4}$ | 6. $3\frac{1}{6}$ $\frac{19}{6}$ |
| 7. $2\frac{3}{5}$ $\frac{13}{5}$ | 8. $6\frac{3}{10}$ $\frac{63}{10}$ | 9. $3\frac{1}{7}$ $\frac{22}{7}$ | 10. $4\frac{3}{8}$ $\frac{35}{8}$ | 11. $4\frac{9}{10}$ $\frac{49}{40}$ | 12. $2\frac{5}{8}$ $\frac{21}{8}$ |
| 13. $6\frac{2}{3}$ $\frac{20}{3}$ | 14. $5\frac{5}{8}$ $\frac{45}{8}$ | 15. $4\frac{3}{50}$ $\frac{203}{50}$ | 16. $9\frac{1}{6}$ $\frac{55}{6}$ | 17. $10\frac{1}{8}$ $\frac{81}{8}$ | 18. $4\frac{1}{12}$ $\frac{49}{12}$ |
| 19. $14\frac{1}{2}$ $\frac{29}{2}$ | 20. $8\frac{4}{5}$ $\frac{44}{5}$ | 21. $6\frac{17}{100}$ $\frac{617}{100}$ | 22. $9\frac{9}{10}$ $\frac{99}{10}$ | 23. $12\frac{4}{5}$ $\frac{64}{5}$ | 24. $7\frac{5}{6}$ $\frac{47}{6}$ |

More Practice, page 422, Set C

## Using Page 201

**Lesson Development** Read the question at the top of the page. Then have students read the next paragraph. Call attention to the picture of the oranges showing that $5\frac{1}{2}$ is the same as $\frac{11}{2}$. Read and discuss each instruction box explaining how to change the mixed number $5\frac{1}{2}$ to the improper fraction $\frac{11}{2}$.

**Other Examples** Work each of these examples to make sure students understand the procedure.

**Exercises 1–24** Read the direction line with students. Suggest that they refer back to the examples as a reminder if necessary.

**More Practice,** page 422, Set B

**More Practice,** page 422, Set C

**Reteaching Supplement,** page 47

Name ______________________ To follow text page 201

**Improper Fractions and Mixed Numbers**

PART A: Changing an improper fraction to a mixed number.

Divide the numerator by the denominator. → Write the quotient as the whole number part. → Write the remainder over the divisor as the fraction part.

$\frac{23}{5}$ $\quad 5\overline{)23}$ → 4 (quotient); 20; 3 (remainder); 5 (divisor) $\quad 4\frac{\square}{\square} \quad\quad 4\frac{3}{5}$

Write a mixed numeral for each improper fraction.

| | | | |
|---|---|---|---|
| 1. $\frac{15}{4} = 3\frac{3}{4}$ | 2. $\frac{17}{3} = 5\frac{2}{3}$ | 3. $\frac{11}{2} = 5\frac{1}{2}$ | 4. $\frac{25}{8} = 3\frac{1}{8}$ |
| 5. $\frac{5}{3} = 1\frac{2}{3}$ | 6. $\frac{21}{5} = 4\frac{1}{5}$ | 7. $\frac{108}{10} = 10\frac{4}{5}$ | 8. $\frac{55}{8} = 6\frac{7}{8}$ |
| 9. $\frac{27}{6} = 4\frac{1}{2}$ | 10. $\frac{19}{2} = 9\frac{1}{2}$ | 11. $\frac{33}{10} = 3\frac{3}{10}$ | 12. $\frac{42}{5} = 8\frac{2}{5}$ |
| 13. $\frac{27}{4} = 6\frac{3}{4}$ | 14. $\frac{99}{10} = 9\frac{9}{10}$ | 15. $\frac{43}{8} = 5\frac{3}{8}$ | 16. $\frac{13}{3} = 4\frac{1}{3}$ |

PART B: Changing a mixed number to an improper fraction.

Multiply the whole number by the denominator. → Add the numerator to the product. → Write the sum over the denominator.

$4\frac{2}{3} \rightarrow 4 \times 3 = 12$ (whole number, denominator) $\quad 4\frac{2}{3}$ (numerator) $12 + 2 = 14 \quad\quad \frac{14}{3}$

Write an improper fraction for each mixed number.

| | | | |
|---|---|---|---|
| 1. $1\frac{5}{8} = \frac{13}{8}$ | 2. $2\frac{1}{2} = \frac{5}{2}$ | 3. $3\frac{1}{4} = \frac{13}{4}$ | 4. $4\frac{2}{5} = \frac{22}{5}$ |
| 5. $6\frac{1}{3} = \frac{19}{3}$ | 6. $1\frac{3}{10} = \frac{13}{10}$ | 7. $7\frac{1}{2} = \frac{15}{2}$ | 8. $4\frac{5}{8} = \frac{37}{8}$ |
| 9. $1\frac{1}{10} = \frac{11}{10}$ | 10. $2\frac{4}{5} = \frac{14}{5}$ | 11. $5\frac{2}{5} = \frac{27}{5}$ | 12. $10\frac{1}{2} = \frac{21}{2}$ |
| 13. $1\frac{2}{3} = \frac{5}{3}$ | 14. $3\frac{7}{8} = \frac{31}{8}$ | 15. $9\frac{1}{3} = \frac{28}{3}$ | 16. $5\frac{7}{10} = \frac{57}{10}$ |

**Enrichment Supplement,** page 47

Name ______________________ To follow text page 201

**Mixed Number Change**

1. Suppose that you had these cards.

2 3 5 7 8 11

Using two of the cards, you could form an improper fraction. $\frac{5}{3}$

Write as many other improper fractions as possible from these cards using only two of them at a time. **Order may vary.**

$\frac{3}{2}$ $\frac{5}{2}$ $\frac{7}{2}$ $\frac{8}{2}$ $\frac{11}{2}$ $\frac{5}{3}$ $\frac{7}{3}$ $\frac{8}{3}$ $\frac{11}{3}$ $\frac{7}{5}$ $\frac{8}{5}$ $\frac{11}{5}$ $\frac{8}{7}$ $\frac{11}{7}$ $\frac{11}{8}$

2. Write a mixed number or a whole number for each of your improper fractions. **Order may vary.** $1\frac{1}{2}, 2\frac{1}{2}, 3\frac{1}{2}, 4, 5\frac{1}{2}, 1\frac{2}{3},$ $2\frac{1}{3}, 2\frac{2}{3}, 3\frac{2}{3}, 1\frac{2}{5}, 1\frac{3}{5}, 2\frac{1}{5}, 1\frac{1}{7}, 1\frac{4}{7}, 1\frac{3}{8}$

3. Write six different mixed numbers using only three of the cards above at a time. (Remember, the fraction part of the mixed number must be less than 1.) **Answers will vary.**

4. Write an improper fraction for each of your mixed numbers. **Answers will vary.**

5. Study the pattern. Then give the missing numbers in each row.

1 1 2 3 5 8 13 21 34 55

$\frac{1}{1}$ $\frac{2}{1}$ $\frac{3}{2}$ $\frac{5}{3}$ $\frac{8}{5}$ $\frac{13}{8}$ $\frac{21}{13}$ $\frac{34}{21}$ $\frac{55}{34}$

1 2 $1\frac{1}{2}$ $1\frac{2}{3}$ $1\frac{3}{5}$ $1\frac{5}{8}$ $1\frac{8}{13}$ $1\frac{13}{21}$ $1\frac{21}{34}$

**Practice Supplement,** page 77

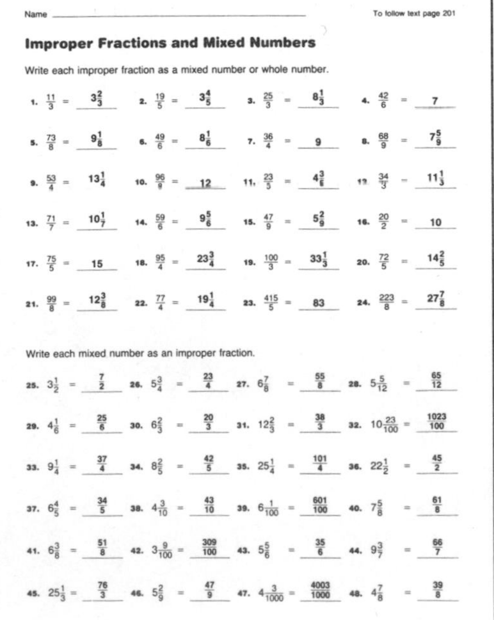

Name ______________________ To follow text page 201

**Improper Fractions and Mixed Numbers**

Write each improper fraction as a mixed number or whole number.

| | | | |
|---|---|---|---|
| 1. $\frac{11}{3} = 3\frac{2}{3}$ | 2. $\frac{19}{5} = 3\frac{4}{5}$ | 3. $\frac{25}{3} = 8\frac{1}{3}$ | 4. $\frac{42}{6} = 7$ |
| 5. $\frac{73}{8} = 9\frac{1}{8}$ | 6. $\frac{49}{6} = 8\frac{1}{6}$ | 7. $\frac{36}{4} = 9$ | 8. $\frac{68}{9} = 7\frac{5}{9}$ |
| 9. $\frac{53}{4} = 13\frac{1}{4}$ | 10. $\frac{96}{9} = 12$ | 11. $\frac{23}{5} = 4\frac{3}{5}$ | 12. $\frac{34}{3} = 11\frac{1}{3}$ |
| 13. $\frac{71}{7} = 10\frac{1}{7}$ | 14. $\frac{59}{6} = 9\frac{5}{6}$ | 15. $\frac{47}{9} = 5\frac{2}{9}$ | 16. $\frac{20}{2} = 10$ |
| 17. $\frac{75}{5} = 15$ | 18. $\frac{95}{4} = 23\frac{3}{4}$ | 19. $\frac{100}{3} = 33\frac{1}{3}$ | 20. $\frac{72}{5} = 14\frac{2}{5}$ |
| 21. $\frac{99}{8} = 12\frac{3}{8}$ | 22. $\frac{77}{4} = 19\frac{1}{4}$ | 23. $\frac{415}{5} = 83$ | 24. $\frac{223}{8} = 27\frac{7}{8}$ |

Write each mixed number as an improper fraction.

| | | | |
|---|---|---|---|
| 25. $3\frac{1}{2} = \frac{7}{2}$ | 26. $5\frac{3}{4} = \frac{23}{4}$ | 27. $6\frac{7}{8} = \frac{55}{8}$ | 28. $5\frac{5}{12} = \frac{65}{12}$ |
| 29. $4\frac{1}{6} = \frac{25}{6}$ | 30. $6\frac{2}{3} = \frac{20}{3}$ | 31. $12\frac{2}{3} = \frac{38}{3}$ | 32. $10\frac{23}{100} = \frac{1023}{100}$ |
| 33. $9\frac{1}{4} = \frac{37}{4}$ | 34. $8\frac{2}{5} = \frac{42}{5}$ | 35. $25\frac{1}{4} = \frac{101}{4}$ | 36. $22\frac{1}{2} = \frac{45}{2}$ |
| 37. $6\frac{4}{5} = \frac{34}{5}$ | 38. $4\frac{3}{10} = \frac{43}{10}$ | 39. $6\frac{1}{100} = \frac{601}{100}$ | 40. $7\frac{5}{8} = \frac{61}{8}$ |
| 41. $6\frac{3}{8} = \frac{51}{8}$ | 42. $3\frac{9}{100} = \frac{309}{100}$ | 43. $5\frac{5}{6} = \frac{35}{6}$ | 44. $9\frac{3}{7} = \frac{66}{7}$ |
| 45. $25\frac{1}{3} = \frac{76}{3}$ | 46. $5\frac{2}{9} = \frac{47}{9}$ | 47. $4\frac{3}{1000} = \frac{4003}{1000}$ | 48. $4\frac{7}{8} = \frac{39}{8}$ |

# Fractions

**Quick Review** Students add to check each answer then correct as needed.

| | | | | |
|---|---|---|---|---|
| 312 | 4,002 | 35,678 | 5,239 | 900 |
| − 216 | − 2,998 | − 22,808 | − 5,190 | − 874 |
| 106 **96** | 1,004 | 11,870 **12,870** | 149 **49** | 26 |

**Lesson Focus** To compare and order fractions and mixed numbers; to use data from a catalog to solve word problems

**Suggested Materials** Fraction number line

## Ideas for Getting Started

Use the TRB fraction number line, or draw two number lines on the chalkboard and mark one in fifths and the other in thirds. Be sure the 0 and 1 marks are in line vertically with each other as shown.

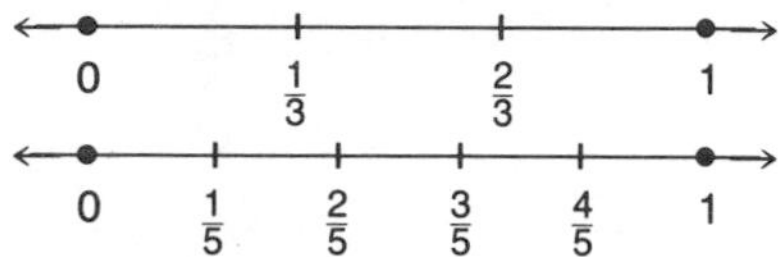


Let students compare fractions using the number lines. For example, have students tell which is greater for these pairs: $\frac{2}{3}$ and $\frac{4}{5}$; $\frac{1}{3}$ and $\frac{3}{5}$; $\frac{1}{3}$ and $\frac{1}{5}$; $\frac{2}{5}$ and $\frac{2}{3}$. Point out that using a number line to compare fractions is not practical in most situations. Tell students that the text shows another way to compare fractions.

## Using Page 202

**Motivational Problem** Have students read the paragraph at the top of the page. "What question is asked about these distances in Craig and Inez's neighborhood?" (Which is closer to school, the library or the fire station?) Point out how the data can be found in the chart.

**Lesson Development** Work through each instruction box and the demonstration problem. In the second step, explain that 20 is the least common multiple for 10 and 4. If necessary, discuss the numbers that were multiplied to find the equivalent fractions.

**Other Examples** The first example involves mixed numbers. Students should recognize that if the whole number parts are different, the mixed numbers can be compared just as whole numbers compare. The second example is similar to the demonstration problem.

**Exercises 16–19** For these exercises students compare numbers two at a time to order in much the same way they compared whole numbers. In exercise 16, students should understand that when the numerators are the same, the smaller the denominator is, the larger the fraction will be.

## Comparing and Ordering Fractions and Mixed Numbers

Craig and Inez made a map of the neighborhood around their school. They also made a table showing the distance from the school to several important places. Which is closer to the school, the library or the fire station?

| School to | police station | library | park | fire station |
|---|---|---|---|---|
| Miles | $3\frac{1}{2}$ | $\frac{3}{10}$ | $3\frac{1}{10}$ | $\frac{3}{4}$ |

Look at the denominators. → Write equivalent fractions with a common denominator. → Compare the numerators. → The fractions compare the same way the numerators compare.

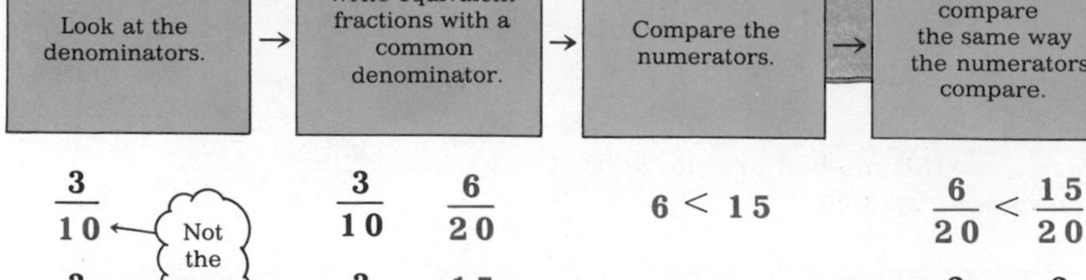

$\frac{3}{10}$, $\frac{3}{4}$ — Not the same

$\frac{3}{10} = \frac{6}{20}$ $\quad$ $\frac{3}{4} = \frac{15}{20}$

$6 < 15$

$\frac{6}{20} < \frac{15}{20}$ so $\frac{3}{10} < \frac{3}{4}$

The library is closer to the school.

**Other Examples**

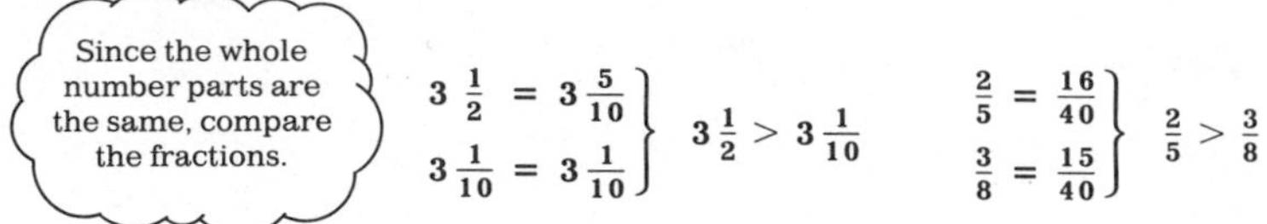

Since the whole number parts are the same, compare the fractions.

$3\frac{1}{2} = 3\frac{5}{10}$, $3\frac{1}{10} = 3\frac{1}{10}$; $3\frac{1}{2} > 3\frac{1}{10}$

$\frac{2}{5} = \frac{16}{40}$, $\frac{3}{8} = \frac{15}{40}$; $\frac{2}{5} > \frac{3}{8}$

Write >, <, or = for each ●.

1. $\frac{1}{4}$ ● $\frac{1}{5}$ **>**
2. $\frac{7}{8}$ ● $\frac{2}{3}$ **>**
3. $\frac{5}{8}$ ● $\frac{3}{4}$ **<**
4. $\frac{4}{5}$ ● $\frac{3}{4}$ **>**
5. $\frac{4}{6}$ ● $\frac{8}{12}$ **=**
6. $\frac{7}{10}$ ● $\frac{3}{4}$ **<**
7. $\frac{9}{16}$ ● $\frac{7}{8}$ **<**
8. $\frac{3}{10}$ ● $\frac{1}{4}$ **>**
9. $4\frac{1}{6}$ ● $4\frac{2}{3}$ **<**
10. $5\frac{1}{8}$ ● $4\frac{2}{7}$ **>**
11. $2\frac{5}{8}$ ● $2\frac{1}{2}$ **>**
12. $9\frac{1}{8}$ ● $9\frac{1}{6}$ **<**
13. $7\frac{3}{10}$ ● $8\frac{3}{10}$ **<**
14. $12\frac{1}{2}$ ● $12\frac{3}{8}$ **>**
15. $1\frac{3}{10}$ ● $1\frac{30}{100}$ **=**

Compare the fractions or mixed numbers two at a time. Then list them in order from least to greatest.

16. $\frac{1}{3}, \frac{1}{4}, \frac{2}{5}$ — $\frac{1}{4}, \frac{1}{3}, \frac{2}{5}$
17. $5\frac{3}{4}, 6\frac{2}{3}, 5\frac{5}{12}$ — $5\frac{5}{12}, 5\frac{3}{4}, 6\frac{2}{3}$
18. $1\frac{5}{6}, \frac{5}{8}, 1\frac{1}{3}, 2\frac{1}{4}$ — $\frac{5}{8}, 1\frac{1}{3}, 1\frac{5}{6}, 2\frac{1}{4}$
19. $4\frac{1}{2}, 4\frac{1}{3}, 4, 3\frac{4}{5}, 3$ — $3, 3\frac{4}{5}, 4, 4\frac{1}{3}, 4\frac{1}{2}$



More Practice, page 422, Set D

## Follow Up

### Reteaching

Discuss how to determine which is more, two sixths or five sixths. On the chalkboard, show the fractions using regions.

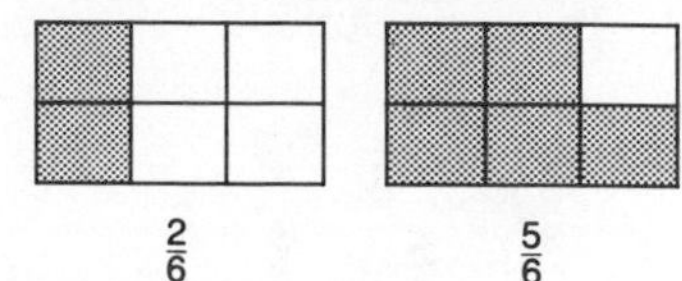


Elicit from students that if the denominator is the same, the two fractions can be compared by looking at the numerators. Next compare $\frac{3}{4}$ and $\frac{5}{6}$. Point out that before a comparison can be made, the fractions must have the same denominator. For example: $\frac{3}{4} = \frac{9}{12}$ and $\frac{5}{6} = \frac{10}{12}$.

### Enrichment

Have students fold strips of paper into fourths, fifths, and other fractional parts. Let students use the strips as learning aids to compare fractions and/or to make a bulletin board. For example:

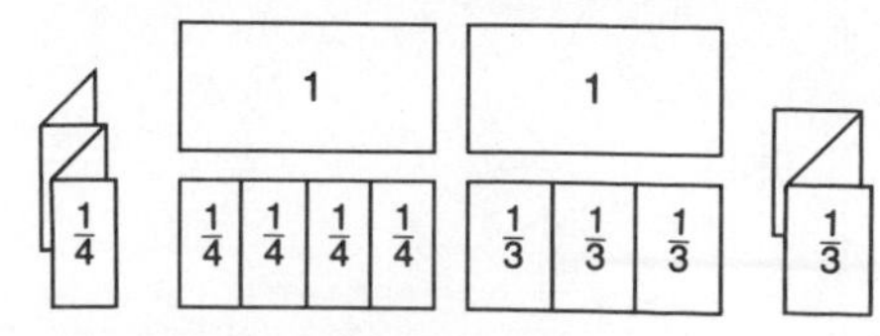


By placing the thirds below the fourths, students can see that $\frac{2}{3} < \frac{3}{4}$.

| Assignment Guide | Minimum | Average | Extended |
|---|---|---|---|
| page 202 | 1–16 | 1–18 | 1–19 |
| page 203 | 1–6 | 1–7 | 1–8 |

## Problem Solving: Using Data from a Catalog

QUESTION / DATA / PLAN / ANSWER / CHECK

A store offers special prices on items ordered from their catalog. Use the catalog data shown below to solve the problems.

| Clock | Size | Weight | Regular price | Special price |
|---|---|---|---|---|
| Butcher-block quartz | $11\frac{1}{2}'' \times 11\frac{1}{2}''$ | $4\frac{1}{2}$ lb | \$31.40 | \$19.90 |
| Desktop digital | $9\frac{1}{2}'' \times 2\frac{1}{4}''$ | $3\frac{1}{3}$ lb | \$21.99 | \$12.99 |
| Cuckoo clock | $9\frac{7}{8}'' \times 7\frac{5}{8}''$ | $3\frac{1}{2}$ lb | \$61.95 | \$44.70 |
| Kitchen quartz | $8\frac{1}{2}'' \times 15\frac{1}{2}''$ | 15 lb | \$28.95 | \$19.90 |
| Round wall clock | 14″ diameter | $6\frac{3}{4}$ lb | \$39.95 | \$24.90 |
| World-time quartz | $7\frac{1}{4}'' \times 9\frac{3}{4}''$ | $4\frac{1}{4}$ lb | \$76.50 | \$49.94 |
| Electric alarm | $5\frac{3}{4}'' \times 4\frac{2}{4}''$ | 1 lb | \$16.95 | \$11.89 |

Solve.

1. There is a space on a kitchen wall that measures $9'' \times 15\frac{3}{8}''$. Will a kitchen quartz clock fit in that wall space? no
2. What is the difference in the regular prices of the most expensive clock and the least expensive clock? \$59.55
3. The mailing charge for a clock is \$0.50 per pound. Will it cost more to mail a butcher-block quartz clock or a world-time quartz clock? Butcher-block will cost \$0.12 more.
4. The butcher-block clock and the world-time clock can be mailed in boxes that are the same weight. When the clocks are boxed for mailing which will be heavier? The butcher-block clock
5. How much would it cost to mail a kitchen quartz clock, if the mailing charge is \$0.50 per pound? \$7.50
6. A girl bought two electric alarm clocks at the special price. What was the total cost for the clocks not including tax or mailing cost? \$23.78
7. **DATA BANK** What would be the cost, including sales tax but not mailing charge, of 2 round wall clocks bought at the regular price? (See Data Bank, page 409.) \$83.90
8. **Try This** An antique dealer wanted to display 2 of his 5 antique clocks in the store window. How many different choices did the dealer have for the pair of clocks? Hint: Make an organized list. 10



## Using Page 203

**Lesson Development** Review the 5-Point Checklist, noting that this lesson focuses on using data from a catalog. Ask several questions to be sure students understand how to read the catalog page. For example: "What is the size of the world-time quartz clock?" "Which clock costs \$61.95?" "Which clock weighs between 6 and 7 pounds?"

**Exercises 1–6** Note that each of these problems requires data from the catalog but applies various skills and operations.

**Data Bank** Remind students that they can find the needed sales tax information in the back of the book.

**Try This** A possible strategy, Make an Organized List, was taught on page 132.

**Discussion** "What are we trying to find out about the clocks?" (the number of choices for the pairs of clocks) "How many clocks did the dealer have to choose from?" (5) "How many were to be displayed at one time?" (2) "If we labeled the clocks A through E, would pair AB be the same as pair BA?" (yes)

**Solution** There are 10 different choices for the pairs of clocks.

| | | | |
|---|---|---|---|
| AB | BC | CD | DE |
| AC | BD | CE | |
| AD | BE | | |
| AE | | | |

**Extension** Suppose the dealer wanted to display 3 of the 5 clocks. How many different choices would the dealer have? (10)

**More Practice,** page 422, Set D

**Reteaching Supplement,** page 48

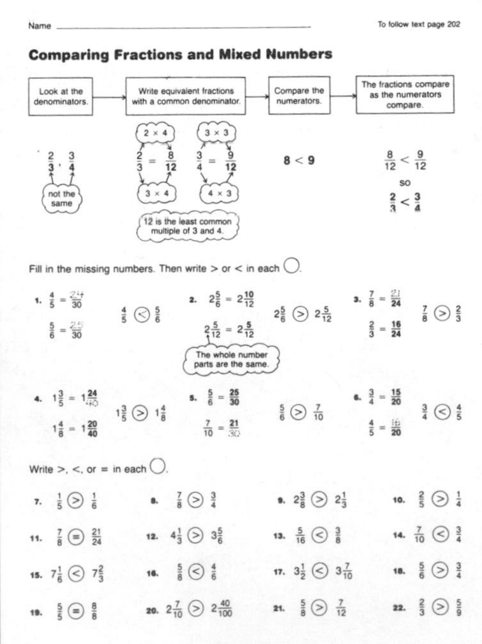
Name ______ To follow text page 202

**Comparing Fractions and Mixed Numbers**



$\frac{2}{3}, \frac{3}{4}$   $\frac{2}{3} = \frac{8}{12}$   $\frac{3}{4} = \frac{9}{12}$   $8 < 9$   $\frac{8}{12} < \frac{9}{12}$ so $\frac{2}{3} < \frac{3}{4}$

Fill in the missing numbers. Then write > or < in each ◯.

1. $\frac{4}{5} = \frac{24}{30}$, $\frac{5}{6} = \frac{25}{30}$; $\frac{4}{5} < \frac{5}{6}$
2. $2\frac{5}{6} = 2\frac{10}{12}$, $2\frac{5}{12} = 2\frac{5}{12}$; $2\frac{5}{6} > 2\frac{5}{12}$ (The whole number parts are the same.)
3. $\frac{7}{8} = \frac{21}{24}$, $\frac{2}{3} = \frac{16}{24}$; $\frac{7}{8} > \frac{2}{3}$
4. $1\frac{3}{5} = 1\frac{24}{40}$, $1\frac{4}{8} = 1\frac{20}{40}$; $1\frac{3}{5} > 1\frac{4}{8}$
5. $\frac{5}{6} = \frac{25}{30}$, $\frac{7}{10} = \frac{21}{30}$; $\frac{5}{6} > \frac{7}{10}$
6. $\frac{3}{4} = \frac{15}{20}$, $\frac{4}{5} = \frac{16}{20}$; $\frac{3}{4} < \frac{4}{5}$

Write >, <, or = in each ◯.

7. $\frac{1}{5} > \frac{1}{6}$
8. $\frac{7}{8} > \frac{3}{4}$
9. $2\frac{3}{8} > 2\frac{1}{3}$
10. $\frac{2}{5} > \frac{1}{4}$
11. $\frac{7}{8} = \frac{21}{24}$
12. $4\frac{1}{3} > 3\frac{5}{6}$
13. $\frac{5}{16} < \frac{3}{8}$
14. $\frac{7}{10} < \frac{3}{4}$
15. $7\frac{1}{6} < 7\frac{2}{3}$
16. $\frac{5}{8} < \frac{4}{6}$
17. $3\frac{1}{2} < 3\frac{7}{10}$
18. $\frac{5}{6} > \frac{3}{4}$
19. $\frac{5}{5} = \frac{8}{8}$
20. $2\frac{7}{10} > 2\frac{40}{100}$
21. $\frac{5}{8} > \frac{7}{12}$
22. $\frac{2}{3} > \frac{5}{9}$

**Enrichment Supplement,** page 48

Name ______ To follow text page 202

**More or Less**

Write >, <, or = in the ◯ to make the statement true. Then ring the letter under the symbol you selected. Use your answers to solve the riddle.

| | > | < | = |
|---|---|---|---|
| 1. $\frac{7}{8} > \frac{4}{5}$ | (T) | I | B |
| 2. $4\frac{1}{3} = 4\frac{8}{24}$ | N | E | (O) |
| 3. $2\frac{1}{4} < 2\frac{3}{10}$ | T | (C) | S |
| 4. $3\frac{5}{8} < 3\frac{5}{6}$ | E | (U) | H |
| 5. $5\frac{3}{4} > 5\frac{2}{3}$ | (T) | E | R |
| 6. $6\frac{5}{6} > 6\frac{5}{8}$ | (D) | T | A |
| 7. $4 = 3\frac{5}{5}$ | A | T | (O) |
| 8. $12\frac{7}{12} < 12\frac{5}{8}$ | E | (W) | R |
| 9. $14\frac{3}{8} > 12\frac{3}{8}$ | (N) | S | T |

Look at each number below. Find that problem number above. In the blank, write the letter you ringed for that problem number.

Why did the saw go on a diet?

T (1) O (2)   C (3) U (4) T (5)   D (6) O (7) W (8) N (9)

**Practice Supplement,** page 78

Name ______ To follow text page 202

**Comparing and Ordering Fractions and Mixed Numbers**

Write >, <, or = for each ◯.

1. $\frac{2}{9} < \frac{3}{4}$
2. $\frac{6}{8} = \frac{9}{12}$
3. $\frac{7}{10} > \frac{13}{26}$
4. $\frac{4}{9} > \frac{8}{27}$
5. $\frac{5}{6} < \frac{7}{8}$
6. $\frac{4}{5} < \frac{7}{8}$
7. $\frac{2}{16} < \frac{1}{6}$
8. $\frac{4}{10} = \frac{2}{5}$
9. $\frac{1}{2} > \frac{5}{12}$
10. $\frac{2}{3} > \frac{3}{8}$
11. $\frac{17}{100} < \frac{3}{10}$
12. $\frac{1}{3} < \frac{2}{5}$
13. $\frac{5}{6} = \frac{10}{12}$
14. $\frac{7}{8} > \frac{1}{2}$
15. $\frac{11}{12} > \frac{17}{24}$
16. $1\frac{7}{10} < 1\frac{5}{6}$
17. $9\frac{6}{7} > 9\frac{2}{3}$
18. $3\frac{3}{5} > 3\frac{2}{7}$
19. $1\frac{12}{16} = 1\frac{9}{12}$
20. $4\frac{3}{8} > 4\frac{2}{6}$
21. $5\frac{7}{10} < 5\frac{7}{8}$

List the fractions in order from least to greatest.

22. $\frac{4}{9}, \frac{3}{4}, \frac{5}{6}$   $\frac{4}{9}, \frac{3}{4}, \frac{5}{6}$
23. $\frac{7}{8}, \frac{9}{10}, \frac{5}{6}$   $\frac{5}{6}, \frac{7}{8}, \frac{9}{10}$
24. $\frac{11}{12}, 1\frac{3}{8}, 1\frac{5}{9}$   $\frac{11}{12}, 1\frac{3}{8}, 1\frac{5}{9}$
25. $4\frac{1}{2}, 4\frac{2}{3}, 4\frac{5}{8}$   $4\frac{1}{2}, 4\frac{5}{8}, 4\frac{2}{3}$

# Fractions

**Quick Review** Students use multiplication to check each answer and correct as needed.

$67\overline{)3{,}314}$ = 42 | $19\overline{)361}$ = 18 19 | $15\overline{)315}$ = 22 21 | $39\overline{)2{,}886}$ = 75 74 | $85\overline{)4{,}760}$ = 56

**Lesson Focus** To add and subtract fractions and mixed numbers with common denominators

**Suggested Materials** Paper for folding

## Ideas for Getting Started

Give each student two sheets of paper. Ask students to fold each piece into fourths and shade three of the fourths on one of the sheets. Write $\frac{3}{4} + \frac{3}{4}$ on the chalkboard. "We want to find the sum of $\frac{3}{4}$ and $\frac{3}{4}$. Now shade another $\frac{3}{4}$. If you need to, use your second sheet. When students complete the shading, their papers should look like this.

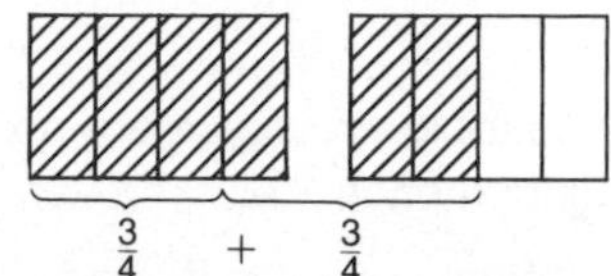


Have students count to verify that $\frac{3}{4} + \frac{3}{4} = \frac{6}{4}$. Students can also see this is the same as $1\frac{2}{4}$, or $1\frac{1}{2}$.

Then write $\frac{4}{5} - \frac{3}{5}$ on the chalkboard. Use a number line to show the subtraction.

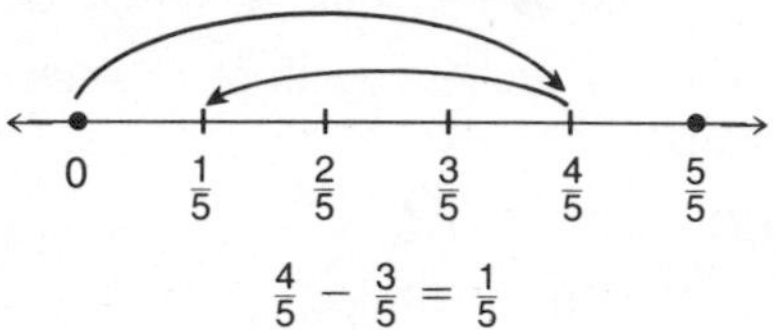


$$\frac{4}{5} - \frac{3}{5} = \frac{1}{5}$$

## Using Page 204

**Motivational Problem** Read the problem at the top of the page. "What are we trying to find out about the stadium?" (How many sections of seats did students paint?) "What data do we need to find the answer?" (number of sections painted red; number of sections painted blue) Point out that the problem gives the data. "Why is addition the operation needed to find the answer?" (We want to find the total number of sections painted.)

**Lesson Development** Read each instruction box and work through the problem. Point out to students that they are adding two *mixed numbers* and that the correct procedure is to first add the fractions and then the whole numbers. Ask a volunteer to complete the sentence that states the answer to the problem.

**Other Examples** Point out that two of the examples were reduced to lowest terms and that one of the examples was renamed from an improper fraction to a mixed number.

**Warm Up** Caution students to watch for the operation signs. Exercises 1, 3, and 5 involve addition, and exercises 2, 4, and 6 involve subtraction.

## Adding and Subtracting Fractions and Mixed Numbers: Common Denominators

The Boosters Club at Kirby School volunteered to paint four sections of seats in the local soccer stadium. The first week the club members painted $1\frac{1}{5}$ sections red and $1\frac{3}{5}$ sections blue. How many of the sections did they paint the first week?

Since we want to find the total number of sections painted, we add.

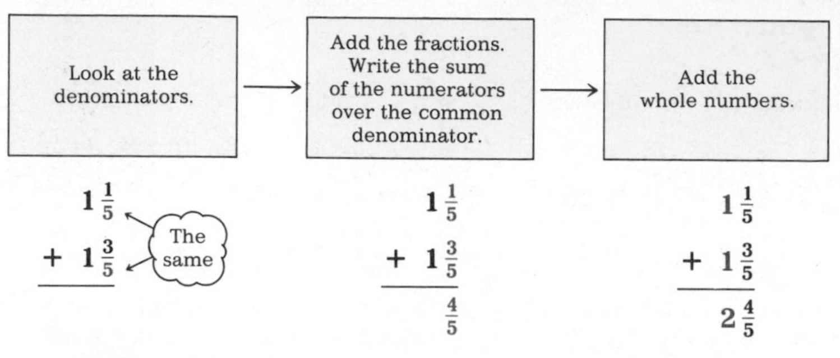

Look at the denominators.
Add the fractions. Write the sum of the numerators over the common denominator.
Add the whole numbers.
The same


$1\frac{1}{5} + 1\frac{3}{5}$ → $\frac{4}{5}$ → $2\frac{4}{5}$

The club members painted $2\frac{4}{5}$ sections of the stadium the first week.

**Other Examples**

$\frac{2}{3} - \frac{1}{3} = \frac{1}{3}$ $\quad$ $\frac{1}{8} + \frac{3}{8} = \frac{4}{8} = \frac{1}{2}$ $\quad$ $\frac{5}{6} + \frac{2}{6} = \frac{7}{6} = 1\frac{1}{6}$ $\quad$ $8\frac{1}{4} + 3\frac{1}{4} = 11\frac{2}{4} = 11\frac{1}{2}$ $\quad$ $10\frac{7}{10} - \frac{4}{10} = 10\frac{3}{10}$

**Warm Up** Add or subtract.

1. $\frac{4}{8} + \frac{1}{8}$ $\quad \frac{5}{8}$
2. $\frac{6}{9} - \frac{4}{9}$ $\quad \frac{2}{9}$
3. $\frac{4}{7} + \frac{1}{7}$ $\quad \frac{5}{7}$
4. $\frac{7}{12} - \frac{5}{12}$ $\quad \frac{2}{12} = \frac{1}{6}$
5. $3\frac{1}{5} + 1\frac{2}{5}$ $\quad 4\frac{3}{5}$
6. $4\frac{3}{8} - 2\frac{1}{8}$ $\quad 2\frac{2}{8} = 2\frac{1}{4}$



## Follow Up

### Reteaching

Review briefly with students equivalent fractions, mixed numbers, improper fractions, and how to compare fractions. Then use unit regions to show $\frac{1}{4} + \frac{1}{4}$. Show the algorithm as you work through the procedure with models.

$\frac{1}{4} + \frac{1}{4}$ $\quad$ $\frac{1}{4} + \frac{1}{4} = \frac{2}{4}$ $\quad$ $\frac{1}{4} + \frac{1}{4} = \frac{2}{4} = \frac{1}{2}$

Add the fractions | Reduce to lowest terms

Then use a similar procedure to demonstrate subtraction of fractions.

### Enrichment

Show students a quick way to check addition of fractions that have a numerator of 1. For example:

$$\frac{1}{5} + \frac{1}{3} = \frac{8}{15}$$

Have students add the denominators to get the numerator for the sum, and multiply the denominators to get the denominator for the sum. Have them use the quick method to check the problems below:

(1) $\frac{1}{2} + \frac{1}{4}$ $\quad$ (2) $\frac{1}{6} + \frac{1}{5}$ $\quad$ (3) $\frac{1}{9} + \frac{1}{7}$

| Assignment Guide | | | |
|---|---|---|---|
| | Minimum | Average | Extended |
| page 205 | 1–32, SK | 1–32, SK | 1–31 odd, 32–33, SK |

Add or subtract.

1. $\frac{7}{10} - \frac{2}{10}$ — $\frac{5}{10} = \frac{1}{2}$
2. $\frac{3}{4} + \frac{3}{4}$ — $\frac{6}{4} = 1\frac{1}{2}$
3. $\frac{9}{8} - \frac{2}{8}$ — $\frac{7}{8}$
4. $\frac{3}{16} + \frac{5}{16}$ — $\frac{8}{16} = \frac{1}{2}$
5. $\frac{1}{6} + \frac{5}{6}$ — $\frac{6}{6} = 1$
6. $\frac{11}{12} - \frac{5}{12}$ — $\frac{6}{12} = \frac{1}{2}$
7. $\frac{9}{10} - \frac{7}{10}$ — $\frac{2}{10} = \frac{1}{5}$
8. $\frac{5}{6} - \frac{4}{6}$ — $\frac{1}{6}$
9. $\frac{1}{2} + \frac{1}{2}$ — $\frac{2}{2} = 1$
10. $\frac{3}{5} + \frac{4}{5}$ — $\frac{7}{5} = 1\frac{2}{5}$
11. $\frac{8}{5} - \frac{4}{5}$ — $\frac{4}{5}$
12. $\frac{7}{8} + \frac{5}{8}$ — $\frac{12}{8} = 1\frac{1}{2}$
13. $\frac{2}{5} + \frac{2}{5}$ — $\frac{4}{5}$
14. $\frac{3}{8} + \frac{7}{8}$ — $\frac{10}{8} = 1\frac{1}{4}$
15. $\frac{7}{8} - \frac{4}{8}$ — $\frac{3}{8}$
16. $\frac{4}{6} - \frac{1}{6}$ — $\frac{3}{6} = \frac{1}{2}$
17. $10\frac{3}{10} + 3$ — $13\frac{3}{10}$
18. $9\frac{4}{5} - 3\frac{1}{5}$ — $6\frac{3}{5}$
19. $8\frac{7}{12} - 8\frac{5}{12}$ — $\frac{2}{12} = \frac{1}{6}$
20. $7\frac{5}{6} - 5\frac{2}{6}$ — $2\frac{3}{6} = 2\frac{1}{2}$
21. $21\frac{1}{4} + 14$ — $35\frac{1}{4}$
22. $19\frac{7}{8} - 12\frac{7}{8}$ — $7$
23. $42\frac{5}{10} + 28\frac{3}{10}$ — $70\frac{8}{10} = 70\frac{4}{5}$
24. $16\frac{1}{12} + 37\frac{7}{12}$ — $53\frac{8}{12} = 53\frac{2}{3}$
25. $\frac{19}{20} - \frac{11}{20}$ — $\frac{8}{20} = \frac{2}{5}$
26. $\frac{14}{24} + \frac{8}{24}$ — $\frac{22}{24} = \frac{11}{12}$
27. $2\frac{1}{8} + 8\frac{4}{8}$ — $10\frac{5}{8}$
28. $18\frac{1}{5} + 29\frac{3}{5}$ — $47\frac{4}{5}$
29. $9\frac{5}{6} - 5\frac{1}{6}$ — $4\frac{4}{6} = 4\frac{2}{3}$
30. Find the sum of $6\frac{1}{6}$ and $3\frac{3}{6}$. $9\frac{4}{6} = 9\frac{2}{3}$
31. How much greater is $9\frac{7}{8}$ than $\frac{5}{8}$? $9\frac{2}{8} = 9\frac{1}{4}$

32. The club members used $42\frac{3}{4}$ cans of blue paint and $35\frac{1}{4}$ cans of red paint to paint the stadium. How much more blue paint than red paint did they use? $7\frac{2}{4} = 7\frac{1}{2}$ cans

33. Write a question you could answer using the data in this story. Then find the answer to your question.

Joanne earns \$6 an hour painting on weekends. She worked $3\frac{1}{2}$ h on Saturday and $4\frac{1}{2}$ h on Sunday.
See teaching notes.

**Skillkeeper**

Add or subtract.

1. 5 h 21 min + 3 h 44 min — 9 h 5 min
2. 7 min 28 s + 3 min 40 s — 11 min 8 s
3. 8 h 9 min − 4 h 20 min — 3 h 49 min
4. 28 min 35 s − 19 min 38 s — 8 min 57 s

Divide.

5. $8\overline{)5.000}$ — 0.625
6. $4\overline{)3.00}$ — 0.75
7. $5\overline{)2.00}$ — 0.40
8. $2\overline{)7.0}$ — 3.5

More Practice, page 423, Set A



## Using Page 205

**Exercises 1–29** Caution students to watch the operation signs as they work these exercises.

**Exercises 30–31** These exercises use language that suggests addition and subtraction.

**Exercise 33** In this exercise students formulate a question that can be answered using data in the story. A possible question might be: How many hours did Joanne work on Saturday and Sunday?

**Skillkeeper** These skills were originally taught in Chapters 6 and 7.

**More Practice,** page 423, Set A

## Ideas That Work

### Special Education

To provide students with practice finding equivalent fractions, let them play "Draw and Match" in pairs. The following materials are needed: a game mat as shown; Deck A cards: $\frac{1}{2}, \frac{1}{3}, \frac{2}{3}, \frac{1}{4}, \frac{3}{4}, \frac{1}{6}, \frac{5}{6}$; Deck B cards: $\frac{2}{4}, \frac{3}{6}, \frac{4}{6}, \frac{2}{8}, \frac{4}{8}, \frac{6}{8}, \frac{3}{9}, \frac{5}{10}, \frac{2}{12}, \frac{3}{12}, \frac{4}{12}, \frac{6}{12}, \frac{8}{12}, \frac{9}{12}, \frac{10}{12}$; 6 chips per player (2 different colors); and an answer key.

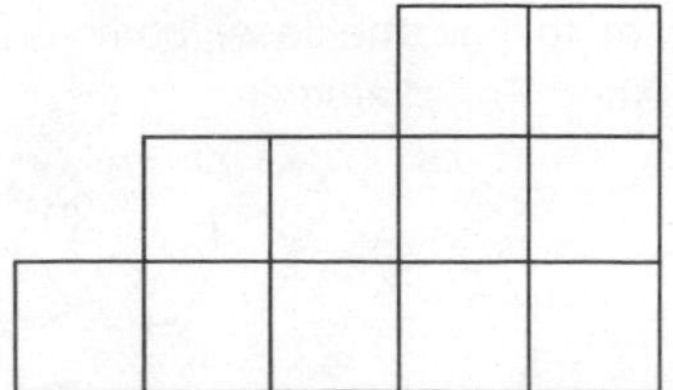

Deck B cards are mixed and 11 of these cards are placed in the spaces on the game mat. Taking turns, students draw a card from Deck A and look for an equivalent fraction on the game mat. If an unclaimed equivalent fraction is found, the player tells the factor used to multiply the numerator and denominator of the Deck A fraction. If player's response is correct, the space is covered with one of the player's chips, and the player earns one point. If no player gets three in a row before all spaces are claimed, the game is a draw and no points are awarded. The winner is the player with the most points at the end of the playing period.

**Practice Supplement,** page 79

Name ______________________ To follow text page 205

**Adding and Subtracting Fractions and Mixed Numbers: Common Denominators**

Add or subtract.

1. $\frac{2}{3} + \frac{1}{3}$ — $\frac{3}{3} = 1$
2. $\frac{3}{8} + \frac{1}{8}$ — $\frac{4}{8} = \frac{1}{2}$
3. $\frac{3}{10} + \frac{1}{10}$ — $\frac{4}{10} = \frac{2}{5}$
4. $\frac{1}{4} + \frac{3}{4}$ — $\frac{4}{4} = 1$
5. $\frac{2}{3} + \frac{2}{3}$ — $\frac{4}{3} = 1\frac{1}{3}$
6. $\frac{7}{8} - \frac{5}{8}$ — $\frac{2}{8} = \frac{1}{4}$
7. $\frac{4}{5} - \frac{2}{5}$ — $\frac{2}{5}$
8. $\frac{9}{10} - \frac{3}{10}$ — $\frac{6}{10} = \frac{3}{5}$
9. $\frac{5}{6} - \frac{3}{6}$ — $\frac{2}{6} = \frac{1}{3}$
10. $\frac{5}{6} - \frac{1}{6}$ — $\frac{4}{6} = \frac{2}{3}$
11. $\frac{9}{10} - \frac{1}{10}$ — $\frac{8}{10} = \frac{4}{5}$
12. $\frac{2}{3} - \frac{2}{3}$ — $0$
13. $\frac{3}{8} + \frac{3}{8}$ — $\frac{6}{8} = \frac{3}{4}$
14. $\frac{7}{12} - \frac{5}{12}$ — $\frac{2}{12} = \frac{1}{6}$
15. $\frac{3}{6} + \frac{1}{6}$ — $\frac{4}{6} = \frac{2}{3}$
16. $15\frac{4}{5} + 6\frac{1}{5}$ — $21\frac{5}{5} = 22$
17. $9\frac{1}{8} + 3\frac{5}{8}$ — $12\frac{6}{8} = 12\frac{3}{4}$
18. $7\frac{7}{10} - 5\frac{3}{10}$ — $2\frac{4}{10} = 2\frac{2}{5}$
19. $2\frac{15}{16} - 2\frac{7}{16}$ — $\frac{8}{16} = \frac{1}{2}$
20. $14\frac{9}{10} - 8\frac{5}{10}$ — $6\frac{4}{10} = 6\frac{2}{5}$
21. $12\frac{3}{5} + 4\frac{1}{5}$ — $16\frac{4}{5}$
22. $5\frac{1}{8} + 9\frac{7}{8}$ — $14\frac{8}{8} = 15$
23. $3\frac{7}{10} + 7\frac{3}{10}$ — $10\frac{10}{10} = 11$
24. $8\frac{7}{5} - 2\frac{2}{5}$ — $6\frac{5}{5} = 7$
25. $1\frac{6}{7} - 1\frac{3}{7}$ — $\frac{3}{7}$

# Applications

**Quick Review** Students practice reading these numbers aloud.

$14\frac{1}{4}$ $27\frac{5}{11}$ $4\frac{1}{2}$ $13\frac{1}{3}$ $119\frac{8}{15}$ $\frac{7}{12}$ $6\frac{5}{8}$

$202\frac{11}{16}$ $8\frac{2}{3}$ $\frac{14}{15}$ $5\frac{5}{12}$ $84\frac{4}{7}$ $62\frac{3}{4}$

**Lesson Focus** To solve word problems involving estimation of fractions; to find the least common multiple of two fractions

## Ideas for Getting Started

Ask students to draw a number line from 0 to 6, and then mark each segment into fifths. Have students place a dot at $3\frac{4}{5}$ and ask: "Is $3\frac{4}{5}$ closer to 3 or to 4?" (4) Use several examples such as $1\frac{1}{5}$, $\frac{2}{5}$, and $4\frac{2}{5}$ and ask an appropriate question. Then ask "Is $3\frac{1}{2}$ closer to 3 or 4?" Students should recognize that $\frac{1}{2}$ is exactly mid-point between the two numbers. Remind students of the rule for rounding whole numbers that end in 5.

## Using Page 206

**Lesson Development** Review the 5-Point Checklist at the top of the page, and point out that this lesson focuses on using estimation to find the answer. Have students read the introductory paragraph about Eileen Owen's buses. Then read and discuss the rules for rounding fractional numbers. If necessary, draw a number line to illustrate the two examples. Then work through the example problems. Point out that in this case the estimate is greater than the exact answer, but emphasize that this will not always happen.

**Exercise 1–5** Before assigning the problems, read through the directions to make sure students understand that they are to estimate the answer and then find the exact answer for each problem.

**Try This** A possible strategy, Work Backward, was taught on page 188.

**Discussion** "What are we trying to find out about the bus? (How many people were on the bus when Rose got on?) "How many got *off* the bus at the last stop?" (12) "If there were 12 on the bus and 3 of those got on at the previous stop, how could we find how many were on the bus before those 3 got on?" (Subtract) "If 2 got off, how could we reverse that step?" (Add) "What operation could we apply to reverse the addition of the 4 people who got on at the next stop after Rose?" (Subtract) Remind students that Rose is still included in the number of people in the bus.

**Solution** There were 6 people on the bus when Rose got on. $(12 - 3) + 2 - 4 - 1 = 6$

**Extension** The next day Rose counted the number of boys and the number of girls on the bus. The total number on the bus was 20, and there were more girls than boys. The product of the number of boys and the number of girls was 96. How many boys and how many girls were on the bus? (12 girls, 8 boys)

## Problem Solving: Using Estimation

Eileen Owen owns a fleet of school buses. Solve these problems about her buses.

**Rules for Rounding Mixed Numbers**

- **Round down** if the fraction part is less than $\frac{1}{2}$. $2\frac{1}{3} \rightarrow 2$
- **Round up** if the fraction part is greater than or equal to $\frac{1}{2}$. $2\frac{2}{3} \rightarrow 3$

First **estimate** the answer by rounding each mixed number to the nearest whole number. Then find the **exact** answer. (Remember the rules for rounding mixed numbers!)

| Example | Estimate | Exact | |
|---|---|---|---|
| Bus route A is $9\frac{7}{10}$ miles. Bus route B is $7\frac{1}{10}$ miles. How much longer is route A than route B? | $9\frac{7}{10}$ is about 10. $7\frac{1}{10}$ is about 7. $10 - 7 = 3$, so route A is about 3 miles longer. | $9\frac{7}{10} - 7\frac{1}{10} = 2\frac{6}{10} = 2\frac{3}{5}$ | Route A is $2\frac{3}{5}$ miles longer. |

1. Bus 26 travels $5\frac{3}{4}$ miles on its morning route and $8\frac{3}{4}$ miles on its afternoon route. What is the total distance Bus 26 travels? 15 miles; $13\frac{6}{4} = 14\frac{1}{2}$ miles
2. In April Bus 16 traveled an average of $5\frac{1}{5}$ miles on each gallon of gasoline. In May Bus 16 traveled an average of $7\frac{4}{5}$ miles per gallon. How much did the average number of miles per gallon increase from April to May? 3 miles per gallon; $2\frac{3}{5}$ miles per gallon
3. Bus 17 has an oil leak. On Monday the bus needed $2\frac{1}{4}$ quarts of oil. On Tuesday it needed $3\frac{3}{4}$ quarts of oil. What was the total amount of oil Bus 17 needed on those two days? 6 quarts; $5\frac{4}{4} = 6$ quarts
4. On the highway Bus 13 averages $9\frac{7}{10}$ miles per gallon of gas. In the city the average is only $5\frac{3}{10}$ miles per gallon. How many more miles per gallon is the highway than the city average? 5 miles; $4\frac{4}{10} = 4\frac{2}{5}$ miles
5. Bus 17 needed $34\frac{9}{10}$ gallons of gas to be filled last week. This week it only needed $25\frac{3}{10}$ gallons. How much less gasoline did it need this week? 10 gallons; $9\frac{6}{10} = 9\frac{3}{5}$ gallons
6. **Try This** When Rose got on the bus there were already some people on it. At the next stop, 4 people got on. At the next stop, 2 people got off and 3 got on. At the last stop, all 12 people who were still on the bus, including Rose, got off. How many people were on the bus when Rose got on? Hint: Work backward. 6

206

## Follow Up

### Reteaching

Elicit from students that in rounding fractions we follow the same rules as with whole numbers or decimals, and that we always round to a whole number. For example, $5\frac{4}{5}$ would be rounded to 6; $5\frac{1}{5}$ would be rounded to 5. Remind students to round up if the fraction part is greater than or equal to $\frac{1}{2}$. Work with students to round the following fractions: $1\frac{1}{4}$, $24\frac{2}{3}$, $3\frac{1}{5}$, $6\frac{9}{10}$, $8\frac{1}{8}$.

### Enrichment

Have students make prime factor trees for denominators of pairs of fractions with unlike denominators. Then draw a Venn diagram for the two denominators. Place any prime factors common to both denominators in the intersection of the circles; place the other prime factors in the nonintersecting portions of the appropriate circles. Multiply all the factors in the diagram to find the least common denominator. For example:

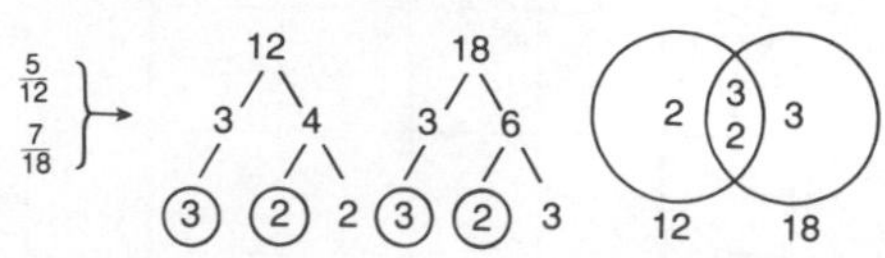


$2 \times 3 \times 2 \times 3 = 36$

| Assignment Guide | | | |
|---|---|---|---|
| | Minimum | Average | Extended |
| page 206 | 1–4 | 1–5 | 1–6 |
| page 207 | 1–10 | 1–15 | 1–15 |



## Least Common Multiple (Denominator)

To add fractions with unlike denominators, we must first rewrite the fractions with a **common denominator.**

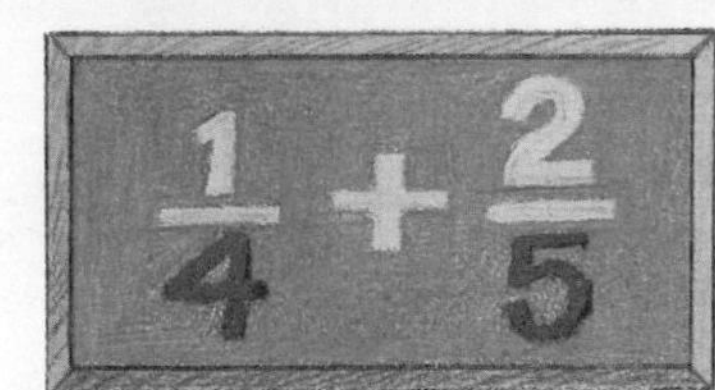


The **least common denominator** of two or more fractions is the **least common multiple** of the denominators.

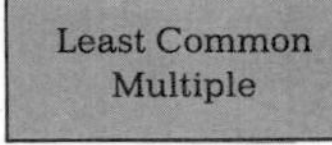


What is the least common multiple of 4 and 5?

**A.** List some multiples of each number. (Do not include zero.)

**4 → 4, 8, 12, 16, 20, 24, 28**
**5 → 5, 10, 15, 20**

**B.** **20** is the least common multiple of **4** and **5.**

Least Common Denominator

What is the least common denominator of $\frac{1}{4}$ and $\frac{2}{5}$?

**A.** Find the least common multiple of the denominators.

**20** is the least common multiple.

**B.** **20** is the least common denominator for the fractions $\frac{1}{4}$ and $\frac{2}{5}$.

**Other Examples**

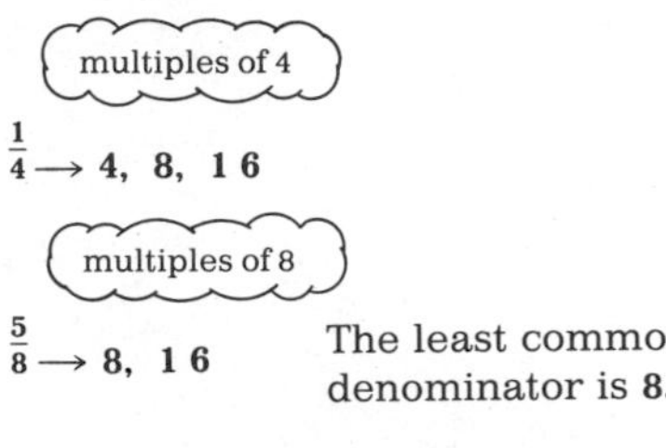


$\frac{1}{4}$ → **4, 8, 16**

$\frac{5}{8}$ → **8, 16**

The least common denominator is **8.**

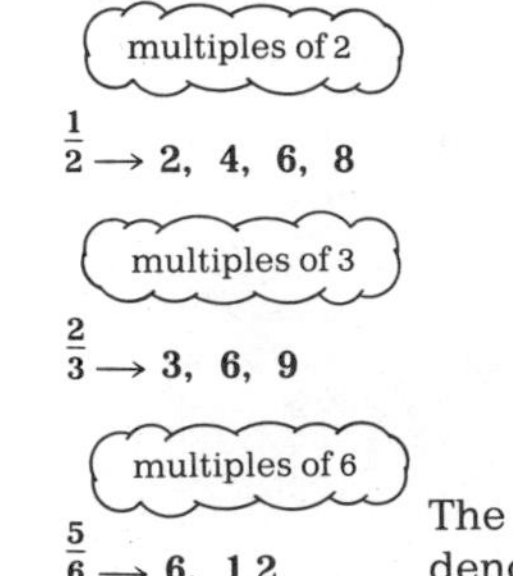


$\frac{1}{2}$ → **2, 4, 6, 8**

$\frac{2}{3}$ → **3, 6, 9**

$\frac{5}{6}$ → **6, 12**

The least common denominator is **6.**

Find the least common denominator of these fractions.

**1.** $\frac{1}{2}, \frac{3}{4}$ 4 **2.** $\frac{2}{3}, \frac{1}{6}$ 6 **3.** $\frac{1}{3}, \frac{1}{2}$ 6 **4.** $\frac{2}{5}, \frac{7}{10}$ 10 **5.** $\frac{5}{16}, \frac{3}{8}, \frac{3}{4}$ 16

**6.** $\frac{3}{9}, \frac{2}{3}$ 9 **7.** $\frac{4}{5}, \frac{5}{6}$ 30 **8.** $\frac{1}{3}, \frac{2}{5}$ 15 **9.** $\frac{3}{4}, \frac{2}{3}$ 12 **10.** $\frac{1}{8}, \frac{1}{3}, \frac{1}{2}$ 24

**11.** $\frac{2}{9}, \frac{5}{8}$ 72 **12.** $\frac{3}{20}, \frac{1}{3}$ 60 **13.** $\frac{5}{10}, \frac{1}{3}$ 30 **14.** $\frac{4}{10}, \frac{5}{8}$ 40 **15.** $\frac{5}{12}, \frac{4}{5}, \frac{5}{6}$ 60

More Practice, page 423, Set B



## Using Page 207

**Lesson Development** Ask students to read the two paragraphs at the top of the page. Then direct students' attention to steps A and B for finding the *least common multiple*. Then have them read the steps for finding the *least common denominator.* Tell students that in order to add and subtract fractions with unlike denominators, they will need to find the least common multiples.

Point out that in the case of $\frac{1}{4}$ and $\frac{2}{5}$, the least common multiple (denominator) was the product of the two numbers. Caution students that although the product of two numbers will always be a common multiple, it is not always the least common multiple.

**Other Examples** Note that in the second example the least common multiple is found for three fractions.

**More Practice,** page 423, Set B

## Ideas That Work

### Special Education

Students work in groups of 2 or 3 to play "Rank-O." Use a score sheet as shown below for each player, 36 number cards (one proper fraction with denominator 2, 3, 4, 6, or 12 on each card).

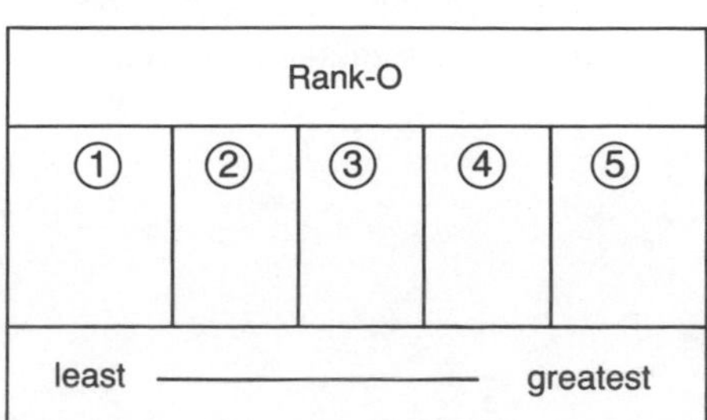


To begin play, mix the cards and deal three to each player. Players in turn select two of the cards and place the third in a discard pile. At "GO," players either add the two fractions or subtract the smaller from the larger. Correct answers are written on one space of the score sheet. Because the goal is to rank answers from least to greatest, it may be necessary at times for a player to pass and not record an answer. The first player to rank correctly five answers wins the round.

**Practice Supplement,** page 80

Name ____________ To follow text page 207

**Least Common Multiple (Denominator)**

Complete.

1. List the first six nonzero multiples of 4. **4, 8, 12, 16, 20, 24**
2. List the first six nonzero multiples of 6. **6, 12, 18, 24, 30, 36**
3. List the first two nonzero common multiples of 4 and 6. **12, 24**
4. What is the least common multiple of 4 and 6? **12**

List the first six nonzero multiples of each number.
Then give the least common multiple of each pair of numbers.

5. 2 **2, 4, 6, 8, 10, 12**
5 **5, 10, 15, 20, 25, 30**
**10**

6. 14 **14, 28, 42, 56, 70, 84**
21 **21, 42, 63, 84, 105, 126**
**42**

7. 9 **9, 18, 27, 36, 45, 54**
12 **12, 24, 36, 48, 60, 72**
**36**

8. 24 **24, 48, 72, 96, 120, 144**
18 **18, 36, 54, 72, 90, 108**
**72**

9. 15 **15, 30, 45, 60, 75, 90**
20 **20, 40, 60, 80, 100, 120**
**60**

10. 10 **10, 20, 30, 40, 50, 60**
12 **12, 24, 36, 48, 60, 72**
**60**

Find the least common denominator of each set of fractions.

11. $\frac{3}{8}, \frac{1}{6}$ **24** 12. $\frac{2}{3}, \frac{1}{4}$ **12** 13. $\frac{1}{12}, \frac{3}{4}$ **12**

14. $\frac{2}{9}, \frac{3}{4}$ **36** 15. $\frac{3}{5}, \frac{1}{8}$ **40** 16. $\frac{1}{6}, \frac{2}{3}$ **6**

17. $\frac{1}{6}, \frac{1}{4}, \frac{1}{2}$ **12** 18. $\frac{2}{7}, \frac{1}{7}, \frac{3}{14}$ **14** 19. $\frac{5}{8}, \frac{1}{3}, \frac{5}{6}$ **24**

80

**Quick Review** Students write these fractions as they are read aloud.

$200\frac{2}{5}$ $\frac{5}{7}$ $\frac{7}{12}$ $8\frac{11}{12}$ $14\frac{2}{7}$ $6\frac{3}{4}$ $34\frac{5}{6}$

$\frac{67}{100}$ $\frac{13}{32}$ $8\frac{3}{10}$ $2\frac{10}{11}$ $28\frac{1}{6}$ $1\frac{2}{7}$

**Lesson Focus** To add and subtract fractions with unlike denominators

## Ideas for Getting Started

To review finding equivalent fractions, write $\frac{2}{3}$ and the number 15 on the chalkboard. Tell students that we want to find a fraction equivalent to $\frac{2}{3}$ with a denominator of 15. Then ask a volunteer to name the number that was used to find the denominator 15 (5). Ask a second student to name the number that could be used to find the numerator (5). Then have students write these fractions on their papers: $\frac{1}{2}, \frac{3}{4}, \frac{1}{3}, \frac{4}{5}$. Challenge students to name an equivalent fraction for each fraction. Have students exchange papers to check each other's work.

## Using Page 208

**Motivational Problem** Read the problem at the top of the page. "What we are trying to find out about the calorie portions?" (How much greater is the fraction of a cup of corn than the fraction of a cup of lima beans?) "Where can we find the data needed to solve the problem?" (in the chart) "Why is subtraction the operation we should use to find the solution?" (We want to compare the two fractions.)

**Lesson Development** Read and discuss each instruction box. Point out that 12 is the least common *multiple* for 3 and 4, and it is the least common denominator for the fractions $\frac{3}{4}$ and $\frac{2}{3}$. Review how the equivalent fractions were found and point out that the fractions now have common denominators. After students have observed the subtraction process, have them read the sentence that states the answer to the problem.

**Other Examples** Point out in the first example that the process for finding the common denominator is the same for addition. The first two examples illustrate the need to rename the sum from an improper fraction to a mixed number.

**Warm Up** Caution students to watch the operation signs for addition or subtraction. Also, remind students to rename the fractions when necessary.

## Adding and Subtracting Fractions: Unlike Denominators

| 100-Calorie Portions of Foods | |
|---|---|
| canned apricots | $\frac{1}{2}$ cup |
| fresh orange juice | $\frac{9}{10}$ cup |
| canned peaches | $\frac{3}{5}$ cup |
| lima beans | $\frac{2}{3}$ cup |
| canned corn | $\frac{3}{4}$ cup |

The chart shows 100-calorie portions of selected foods. How much greater is the fraction of a cup of corn than the fraction of a cup of lima beans?

Since we want to compare two amounts, we subtract.

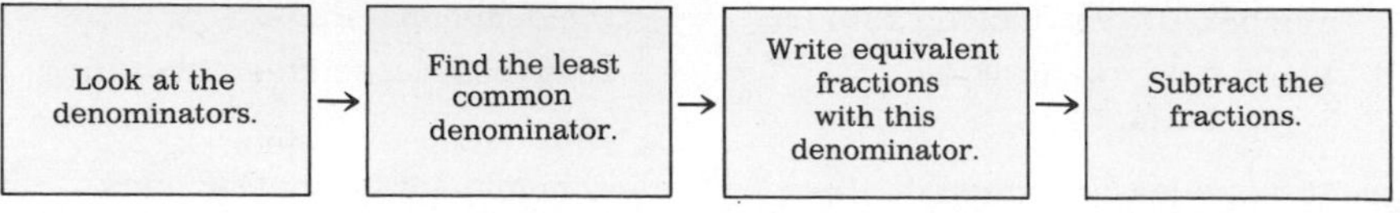
Look at the denominators.
Find the least common denominator.
Write equivalent fractions with this denominator.
Subtract the fractions.

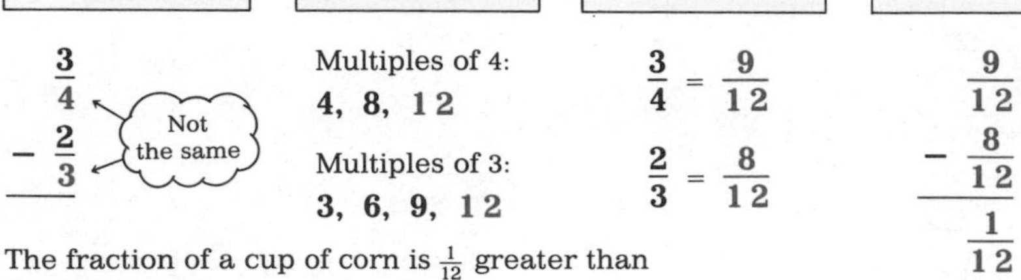
3/4
− 2/3
Not the same
Multiples of 4:
4, 8, 12
Multiples of 3:
3, 6, 9, 12
3/4 = 9/12
2/3 = 8/12
9/12
− 8/12
1/12

The fraction of a cup of corn is $\frac{1}{12}$ greater than the fraction of a cup of lima beans.

**Other Examples**

$\frac{3}{8} = \frac{3}{8}$, $+\frac{3}{4} = \frac{6}{8}$, $\frac{9}{8} = 1\frac{1}{8}$

$\frac{3}{5} = \frac{18}{30}$, $+\frac{5}{6} = \frac{25}{30}$, $\frac{43}{30} = 1\frac{13}{30}$

$\frac{5}{6} = \frac{5}{6}$, $-\frac{1}{2} = \frac{3}{6}$, $\frac{2}{6} = \frac{1}{3}$

$\frac{4}{5} = \frac{8}{10}$, $-\frac{1}{2} = \frac{5}{10}$, $\frac{3}{10}$

**Warm Up** Add or subtract.

1. $\frac{1}{2} + \frac{3}{4}$ — $1\frac{1}{4}$
2. $\frac{1}{2} + \frac{1}{3}$ — $\frac{5}{6}$
3. $\frac{4}{5} - \frac{7}{10}$ — $\frac{1}{10}$
4. $\frac{5}{6} + \frac{3}{4}$ — $\frac{19}{12} = 1\frac{7}{12}$
5. $\frac{6}{9} - \frac{2}{3}$ — 0
6. $\frac{2}{3} - \frac{1}{4}$ — $\frac{5}{12}$

## Follow Up

### Reteaching

Remind students that in order to add or subtract fractions with unlike denominators we must change them to equivalent fractions with like denominators. Review the following steps that can be used:

- Generate multiples of each denominator, then choose the least common denominator. If this method is used, the answer often will be in lowest terms.
- Multiply unlike denominators together to get a common denominator. In this case, the answer will most likely need to be reduced to lowest terms.

### Enrichment

Have students solve the following riddle:

We are two mixed numbers who have a sum of 5. The difference between us is 2. Who are we? $3\frac{1}{2}$ and $1\frac{1}{2}$

Challenge students to create fraction riddles for their classmates to solve.

| Assignment Guide | | | |
|---|---|---|---|
| | Minimum | Average | Extended |
| page 209 | 1–29 | 1–30 | 1–28 even, 29–31, TM |

Add.

1. $\frac{3}{10} + \frac{2}{5}$   $\frac{7}{10}$
2. $\frac{4}{5} + \frac{1}{2}$   $\frac{13}{10} = 1\frac{3}{10}$
3. $\frac{2}{3} + \frac{1}{2}$   $\frac{7}{6} = 1\frac{1}{6}$
4. $\frac{5}{6} + \frac{1}{3}$   $\frac{7}{6} = 1\frac{1}{6}$
5. $\frac{3}{4} + \frac{3}{8}$   $\frac{9}{8} = 1\frac{1}{8}$
6. $\frac{1}{3} + \frac{1}{4}$   $\frac{7}{12}$
7. $\frac{3}{8} + \frac{5}{8}$   $\frac{8}{8} = 1$
8. $\frac{17}{100} + \frac{3}{10}$   $\frac{47}{100}$
9. $\frac{4}{5} + \frac{3}{4}$   $1\frac{11}{20}$
10. $\frac{13}{16} + \frac{1}{2}$   $1\frac{5}{16}$
11. $\frac{3}{5} + \frac{2}{3}$   $\frac{19}{15} = 1\frac{4}{15}$
12. $\frac{1}{6} + \frac{7}{12}$   $\frac{9}{12} = \frac{3}{4}$

Subtract.

13. $\frac{9}{10} - \frac{3}{5}$   $\frac{3}{10}$
14. $\frac{5}{3} - \frac{1}{2}$   $\frac{7}{6} = 1\frac{1}{6}$
15. $\frac{4}{5} - \frac{1}{6}$   $\frac{19}{30}$
16. $\frac{3}{2} - \frac{1}{4}$   $\frac{5}{4} = 1\frac{1}{4}$
17. $\frac{3}{4} - \frac{3}{8}$   $\frac{3}{8}$
18. $\frac{2}{3} - \frac{1}{4}$   $\frac{5}{12}$
19. $\frac{5}{8} - \frac{1}{3}$   $\frac{7}{24}$
20. $\frac{73}{100} - \frac{7}{10}$   $\frac{3}{100}$
21. $\frac{7}{3} - \frac{1}{4}$   $\frac{25}{12} = 2\frac{1}{12}$
22. $\frac{11}{12} - \frac{2}{3}$   $\frac{3}{12} = \frac{1}{4}$
23. $\frac{3}{5} - \frac{1}{3}$   $\frac{4}{15}$
24. $\frac{7}{8} - \frac{1}{4}$   $\frac{5}{8}$

Add.

25. $\frac{1}{2} + \frac{1}{3} + \frac{1}{4}$   $1\frac{1}{12}$
26. $\frac{3}{4} + \frac{1}{2} + \frac{3}{8}$   $\frac{13}{8} = 1\frac{5}{8}$
27. $\frac{1}{4} + \frac{3}{8} + \frac{3}{4}$   $\frac{11}{8} = 1\frac{3}{8}$
28. $\frac{3}{4} + \frac{1}{6} + \frac{1}{3}$   $\frac{15}{12} = 1\frac{1}{4}$

Use the chart on page 208 for problems 29 and 30.

29. How much greater is the 100-calorie portion of orange juice than the 100-calorie portion of peaches? $\frac{3}{10}$ cup

30. The class made a fruit dessert by mixing 100-calorie portions of canned apricots and canned peaches. How many cups of fruit were in the dessert? $\frac{11}{10} = 1\frac{1}{10}$ cups

31. Write a question that could be answered using the data given below. Then find the answer.

Irene cooked $\frac{2}{3}$ cup of oatmeal, $\frac{1}{2}$ cup of rice, and $\frac{1}{4}$ cup of granola. Answers will vary.

**Think Math**

**Logical Reasoning**

Use the numbers 1, 2, or 6 for each ■ to make each statement true.

1. $\frac{■}{■} < \frac{■}{■}$   $\frac{1}{5}\ \frac{1}{6}$
2. $■\frac{■}{■} > 4\frac{1}{5}$   $6\frac{1}{2}$
3. $\frac{■}{■} = \frac{■}{■}$   $\frac{1}{3}\ \frac{2}{6}$
4. $■\frac{■}{■} = 4\frac{2}{3} - 2\frac{1}{2}$   $2\frac{1}{6}$

More Practice, page 423, Set C



## Using Page 209

**Exercises 1–28** Remind students to rename the fractions when necessary.

**Exercises 29–30** Students must refer to the chart on page 208 for data needed to solve these exercises.

**Exercise 31** In this exercise, students use the data provided to write questions involving fractions. A possible question might be: How much more oatmeal than rice did Irene cook?

**Think Math** This activity challenges students' understanding of the relative size of fractions and mixed numbers. In exercise 4, students should reason that the whole number part has to be 2, because 2 is being subtracted from 4.

**More Practice,** page 423, Set C

**Reteaching Supplement,** page 49

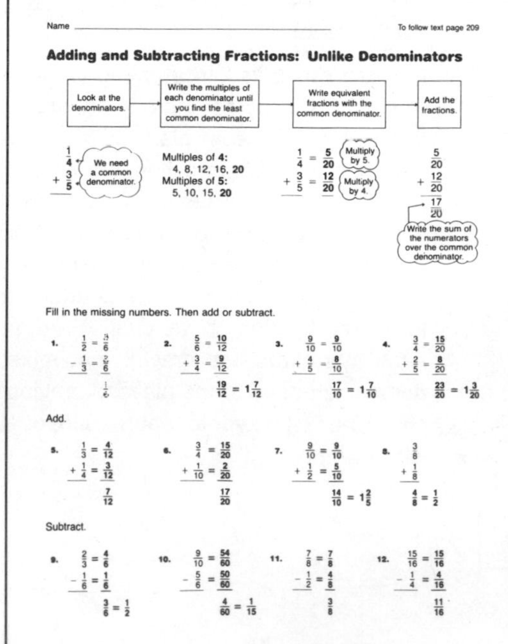

Name ______ To follow text page 209

**Adding and Subtracting Fractions: Unlike Denominators**

Look at the denominators. → Write the multiples of each denominator until you find the least common denominator. → Write equivalent fractions with the common denominator. → Add the fractions.

Multiples of 4: 4, 8, 12, 16, 20
Multiples of 5: 5, 10, 15, 20

Fill in the missing numbers. Then add or subtract.

Add.

Subtract.

**Enrichment Supplement,** page 49

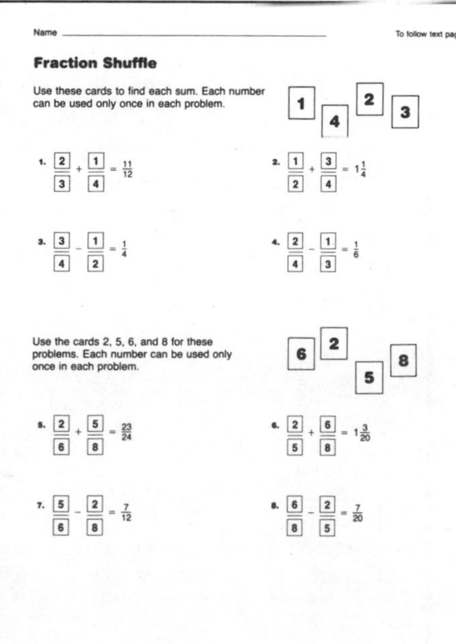

Name ______ To follow text page 209

**Fraction Shuffle**

Use these cards to find each sum. Each number can be used only once in each problem.

Use the cards 2, 5, 6, and 8 for these problems. Each number can be used only once in each problem.

**Practice Supplement,** page 81

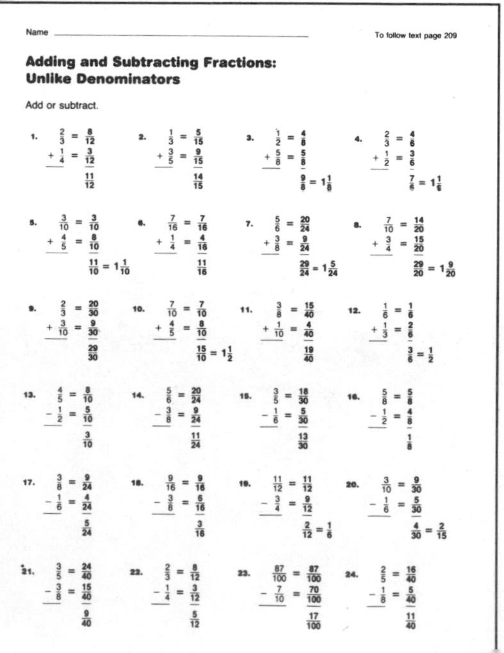

Name ______ To follow text page 209

**Adding and Subtracting Fractions: Unlike Denominators**

Add or subtract.

**Quick Review** Students give the numbers that make each expression true.

$2 \times 3 = 3 \times \boxed{2}$ $6 + 4 = 7 + \boxed{3}$ $55 - 5 = 2 \times \boxed{25}$

$18 - 3 = 3 \times \boxed{5}$ $30 + 50 = (3 \times 10) + (5 \times \boxed{10})$

$4 > 2 \times \boxed{1}$ $50 + 40 = 60 + \boxed{30}$ $(3 + 4) + 6 = \boxed{3} + (4 + 6)$

**Lesson Focus** To add mixed numbers with unlike denominators

## Ideas for Getting Started

Write these improper fractions on the chalkboard: $\frac{7}{4}$ and $\frac{12}{10}$. Ask two students to show their work as they rename each fraction as a mixed number. If necessary, draw rectangles to show that

$$\tfrac{7}{4} = 1\tfrac{3}{4} \text{ and } \tfrac{12}{10} = 1\tfrac{2}{10} = 1\tfrac{1}{5}.$$

Below each of these, write the following.

$$2\tfrac{7}{4} = \qquad 5\tfrac{12}{10} =$$

"How can we rename these fractions?" Show that $2\frac{7}{4} = 2 + \frac{7}{4} = 2 + 1\frac{3}{4} = 3\frac{3}{4}$ and relate this process to the fractions above. Show the same relationships for $5\frac{12}{10}$.

## Using Page 210

**Motivational Problem** Ask a volunteer to read the paragraph at the top of the page. "What do we want to know about the roadbed?" (What was the total number of miles of roadbed leveled in two days?) "What data do we need in order to solve the problem?" (miles leveled each day) "Why is addition the operation needed to find the solution?" (To find a total amount, we add.)

**Lesson Development** Work through the sample problem as explained by each instruction box. Elicit from students that 10 is the least common multiple for 5 and 10 in step 2. Discuss the renaming of the mixed number as shown in the think cloud. Then ask a volunteer to read the complete sentence that gives the answer to the problem.

**Other Examples** Point out in the third example that the process does not change when three mixed numbers are involved.

**Warm Up** Note that in exercise 3 the fraction is named as a whole number not a mixed number.

## Adding Mixed Numbers: Unlike Denominators

The highway department was building a road. The first day they leveled $2\frac{4}{5}$ miles of roadbed. The second day they leveled $2\frac{7}{10}$ miles of roadbed. What was the total number of miles of roadbed leveled in the first two days?

Since we want to find the total distance, we add.

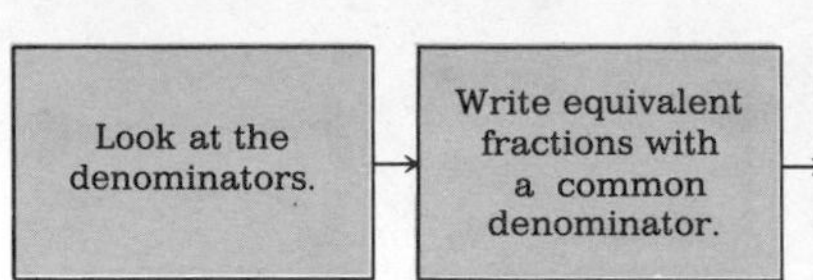

Look at the denominators. → Write equivalent fractions with a common denominator. → Add the fractions. → Add the whole numbers.

$2\frac{4}{5}$ + $2\frac{7}{10}$ (Not the same)

$2\frac{4}{5} = 2\frac{8}{10}$, $+ 2\frac{7}{10} = 2\frac{7}{10}$

$2\frac{8}{10} + 2\frac{7}{10}$ → $\frac{15}{10}$

$2\frac{8}{10} + 2\frac{7}{10}$ → $4\frac{15}{10} = 5\frac{5}{10} = 5\frac{1}{2}$

($4 + \frac{15}{10}$ or $4 + 1\frac{5}{10}$)

A total of $5\frac{1}{2}$ miles of roadbed were leveled in the first two days.

**Other Examples**

$1\frac{1}{2} = 1\frac{3}{6}$, $+ 4\frac{2}{3} = 4\frac{4}{6}$ → $5\frac{7}{6} = 6\frac{1}{6}$

$6\frac{7}{8} + 3\frac{7}{8}$ → $9\frac{14}{8} = 10\frac{6}{8} = 10\frac{3}{4}$

$2\frac{1}{4} = 2\frac{3}{12}$, $3\frac{1}{2} = 3\frac{6}{12}$, $+ 1\frac{5}{6} = 1\frac{10}{12}$ → $6\frac{19}{12} = 7\frac{7}{12}$

**Warm Up** Add.

1. $2\frac{1}{2} + 4\frac{3}{4}$ → $6\frac{5}{4} = 7\frac{1}{4}$
2. $7\frac{9}{10} + 4\frac{1}{2}$ → $11\frac{14}{10} = 12\frac{2}{5}$
3. $6\frac{2}{5} + 4\frac{3}{5}$ → $10\frac{5}{5} = 11$
4. $2\frac{2}{3} + 12\frac{1}{2}$ → $14\frac{7}{6} = 15\frac{1}{6}$
5. $6\frac{1}{3} + 9\frac{1}{2} + 2\frac{5}{6}$ → $17\frac{10}{6} = 18\frac{2}{3}$



## Follow Up

### Reteaching

To help students understand how to add mixed numbers with unlike denominators, use models to illustrate each step in the algorithm. For example:

a) $1\frac{2}{3} =$ ○ ◔
$+ 2\frac{5}{6} =$ ○ ○ ◔

Find the common denominator.

b) $1\frac{4}{6} =$ ○ ◔
$+ 2\frac{5}{6} =$ ○ ○ ◔

$3\frac{9}{6} = 4\frac{3}{6} = 4\frac{1}{2}$

Add the fraction parts. Add the whole numbers. Reduce to lowest terms.

### Enrichment

Prepare two sets of cards—one set of whole number cards and one set of fraction cards. To begin play, write on the chalkboard a mixed fraction, for example $1\frac{1}{4}$. Players in turn draw one card from the whole number set and one card from the fraction set. They use the two cards to form a mixed number, which is added to the mixed fraction on the chalkboard. As each two cards are drawn, that mixed number is added to the player's previous sum. The first player to reach a sum of 10 is the winner.

| Assignment Guide | | | |
|---|---|---|---|
| | Minimum | Average | Extended |
| page 211 | 1–19 | 1–20 | 1–21, TM |

Find the sums.

1. $2\frac{3}{8} + 4\frac{3}{4}$ — $6\frac{9}{8} = 7\frac{1}{8}$
2. $3\frac{3}{4} + 5\frac{1}{2}$ — $8\frac{5}{4} = 9\frac{1}{4}$
3. $7\frac{1}{4} + 2\frac{1}{6}$ — $9\frac{5}{12}$
4. $6\frac{3}{5} + 5\frac{4}{5}$ — $11\frac{7}{5} = 12\frac{2}{5}$
5. $4\frac{7}{8} + 1\frac{1}{2}$ — $5\frac{11}{8} = 6\frac{3}{8}$
6. $6\frac{5}{8} + 7\frac{3}{4}$ — $13\frac{11}{8} = 14\frac{3}{8}$
7. $9\frac{7}{10} + 11\frac{3}{10}$ — $20\frac{10}{10} = 21$
8. $3\frac{5}{6} + 8\frac{1}{2}$ — $11\frac{8}{6} = 12\frac{1}{3}$
9. $61\frac{1}{2} + 91\frac{1}{8}$ — $152\frac{5}{8}$
10. $46\frac{7}{10} + 23\frac{1}{2}$ — $69\frac{12}{10} = 70\frac{1}{5}$
11. $3\frac{1}{2}$, $7\frac{1}{4}$, $+ 6\frac{1}{8}$ — $16\frac{7}{8}$
12. $7\frac{1}{2}$, $9\frac{1}{3}$, $+ 6\frac{1}{4}$ — $22\frac{13}{12} = 23\frac{1}{12}$
13. $19\frac{4}{5}$, $26\frac{1}{10}$, $+ 35\frac{1}{4}$ — $80\frac{23}{20} = 81\frac{3}{20}$
14. $14\frac{1}{4}$, $12\frac{3}{8}$, $+ 16\frac{1}{2}$ — $42\frac{9}{8} = 43\frac{1}{8}$
15. $22\frac{5}{6}$, $9\frac{1}{2}$, $+ 11\frac{2}{3}$ — $42\frac{12}{6} = 44$
16. $15\frac{7}{8} + 22\frac{5}{6}$ — $37\frac{41}{24} = 38\frac{17}{24}$
17. $4\frac{1}{6} + 2\frac{1}{3} + 8\frac{2}{3}$ — $14\frac{7}{6} = 15\frac{1}{6}$
18. $16\frac{1}{4} + 7\frac{1}{5} + 9\frac{7}{10}$ — $32\frac{23}{20} = 33\frac{3}{20}$

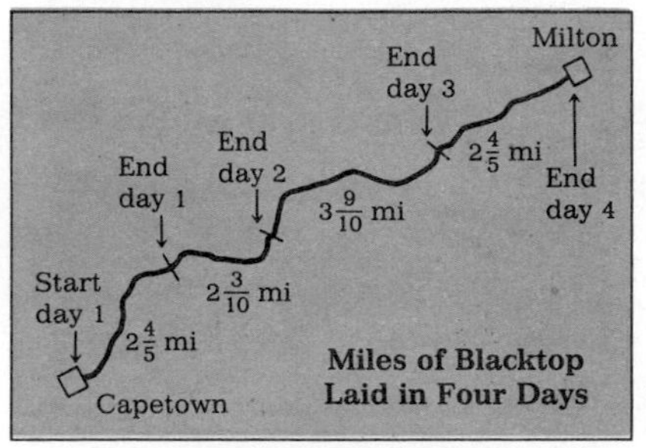


Use the map for problems 19–21.

19. How many miles of blacktop were laid altogether on days 1 and 2? $4\frac{11}{10} = 5\frac{1}{10}$ mi
20. How many miles of blacktop were laid altogether on days 3 and 4? $5\frac{17}{10} = 6\frac{7}{10}$ mi
★ 21. What is the total length of the new road? $10\frac{18}{10} = 11\frac{4}{5}$ mi

## Think Math

**Patterns and Fractions**

Find the pattern and write the missing fractions or mixed numbers. Be sure the last number fits your pattern.

1. $0, \frac{2}{3}, \frac{4}{3}, \frac{6}{3}$, ?, ?, ?, ?, $\frac{16}{3}$ — $\frac{8}{3}, \frac{10}{3}, \frac{12}{3}, \frac{14}{3}$
2. $2\frac{4}{5}, 4\frac{1}{5}, 5\frac{3}{5}$, ?, ?, ?, ?, $12\frac{3}{5}$ — $7, 8\frac{2}{5}, 9\frac{4}{5}, 11\frac{1}{5}$
3. $12, 10\frac{1}{2}, 9, 7\frac{1}{2}$, ?, ?, ?, ?, 0 — $6, 4\frac{1}{2}, 3, 1\frac{1}{2}$

More Practice, page 424, Set A



## Using Page 211

**Exercises 19–20** Students refer to the map to find the data needed to solve these exercises.

**Exercise 21** This exercise may be more challenging for students because it requires the addition of four mixed numbers.

**Think Math** Each pattern is determined by finding the differences between adjacent numbers. The pattern in exercise 1 should be seen readily. In exercise 2, each number increases by $1\frac{2}{5}$; and, in exercise 3, each number decreases by $1\frac{1}{2}$ going from left to right.

**More Practice,** page 424, Set A

## Ideas That Work

### Special Education

Students with learning difficulties have a better chance to feel successful when they are learning one step at a time. The "One Step" idea helps students focus on small parts of problems which, taken separately, they can handle. This approach minimizes difficulty with typical trouble spots such as renaming in subtraction of fractions.

Many special-needs students will confuse whole or decimal subtraction with that involving fractions and make the mistake illustrated in (a). A helpful activity is one in which students trade a whole in each instance for the appropriate number of fractional parts. In follow-up exercises students would carry out just the renaming step, as in (b). After this step is checked, students complete the problems.

8 more eighths, that's 9 eighths.

(a) $7\frac{1}{2} - 6\frac{7}{8}$ = $\overset{6}{\not 7}\frac{14}{8} - 6\frac{7}{8}$ = $\frac{7}{8}$

(b) $13\frac{1}{8} - 8\frac{7}{8}$ = $12\frac{9}{8} - 8\frac{7}{8}$

**Practice Supplement,** page 82

Name ______________________ To follow text page 211

**Adding Mixed Numbers: Unlike Denominators**

Find the sums.

1. $3\frac{1}{2} = 3\frac{2}{4}$; $+ 5\frac{1}{4} = 5\frac{1}{4}$; $8\frac{3}{4}$
2. $7\frac{5}{8} = 7\frac{5}{8}$; $+ 4\frac{3}{4} = 4\frac{6}{8}$; $11\frac{11}{8} = 12\frac{3}{8}$
3. $2\frac{1}{3} = 2\frac{4}{12}$; $+ 5\frac{3}{4} = 5\frac{9}{12}$; $7\frac{13}{12} = 8\frac{1}{12}$
4. $16\frac{3}{4} = 16\frac{15}{20}$; $+ 2\frac{1}{5} = 2\frac{4}{20}$; $18\frac{19}{20}$
5. $9\frac{2}{3} = 9\frac{4}{6}$; $+ 7\frac{1}{2} = 7\frac{3}{6}$; $16\frac{7}{6} = 17\frac{1}{6}$
6. $8\frac{4}{5} = 8\frac{16}{20}$; $+ 1\frac{3}{4} = 1\frac{15}{20}$; $9\frac{31}{20} = 10\frac{11}{20}$
7. $4\frac{7}{8} = 4\frac{21}{24}$; $+ 3\frac{1}{3} = 3\frac{8}{24}$; $7\frac{29}{24} = 8\frac{5}{24}$
8. $27\frac{3}{8} = 27\frac{6}{16}$; $+ 16\frac{9}{16} = 16\frac{9}{16}$; $43\frac{15}{16}$
9. $18\frac{3}{4} = 18\frac{15}{20}$; $+ 1\frac{3}{10} = 1\frac{6}{20}$; $19\frac{21}{20} = 20\frac{1}{20}$
10. $6\frac{8}{15} = 6\frac{8}{15}$; $+ 3\frac{4}{5} = 3\frac{12}{15}$; $9\frac{20}{15} = 10\frac{1}{3}$
11. $84\frac{3}{4} = 84\frac{9}{12}$; $+ 17\frac{2}{3} = 17\frac{8}{12}$; $101\frac{17}{12} = 102\frac{5}{12}$
12. $237\frac{1}{10} = 237\frac{1}{10}$; $+ 166\frac{4}{5} = 166\frac{8}{10}$; $403\frac{9}{10}$
13. $8\frac{1}{4} = 8\frac{4}{16}$; $\frac{7}{16} = \frac{7}{16}$; $+ 1\frac{5}{8} = 1\frac{10}{16}$; $9\frac{21}{16} = 10\frac{5}{16}$
14. $6\frac{7}{12} = 6\frac{7}{12}$; $4\frac{3}{4} = 4\frac{9}{12}$; $+ 1\frac{2}{3} = 1\frac{8}{12}$; $11\frac{24}{12} = 13$
15. $1\frac{2}{3} = 1\frac{4}{6}$; $2\frac{1}{6} = 2\frac{1}{6}$; $+ 4\frac{1}{2} = 4\frac{3}{6}$; $7\frac{8}{6} = 8\frac{1}{3}$
16. $5\frac{1}{10} = 5\frac{1}{10}$; $3\frac{1}{2} = 3\frac{5}{10}$; $+ 8\frac{2}{5} = 8\frac{4}{10}$; $16\frac{10}{10} = 17$
17. $83\frac{5}{12} = 83\frac{5}{12}$; $27\frac{1}{3} = 27\frac{4}{12}$; $+ 66\frac{3}{4} = 66\frac{9}{12}$; $176\frac{18}{12} = 177\frac{1}{2}$
18. $50\frac{1}{4} = 50\frac{9}{36}$; $82\frac{1}{6} = 82\frac{6}{36}$; $+ 9\frac{2}{9} = 9\frac{8}{36}$; $141\frac{23}{36}$

**Quick Review** Students name orally the numerator or denominator that makes each fraction equal to $\frac{1}{2}$.

$\frac{7}{\square}$ $\frac{\square}{8}$ $\frac{50}{\square}$ $\frac{\square}{6}$ $\frac{\square}{60}$ $\frac{8}{\square}$ $\frac{\square}{20}$

**Lesson Focus** To subtract mixed numbers with unlike denominators

## Ideas for Getting Started

Write this problem on the chalkboard and discuss each step as you work toward the solution.

$$\begin{array}{r} \frac{5}{6} = \frac{10}{12} \\ -\frac{1}{4} = \frac{3}{12} \\ \hline \frac{7}{12} \end{array}$$

Review how to write equivalent fractions with the least common denominator. Point out that with common denominators, the problem is in a form where we can more easily find the solution.

## Using Page 212

**Motivational Problem** Ask a volunteer to read the paragraph at the top of the page. "What are we trying to find out about the wood siding?" (How much greater is the width of the siding than the exposed surface?) If necessary, generate a discussion to help students understand the expression "exposed surface." "What data do we need to find the answer?" (width of siding and width of exposed surface) "Why is subtraction the operation needed?" (To compare two amounts, we subtract.)

**Lesson Development** Discuss each step shown by the instruction boxes. Point out how the procedure, as with addition, changes the problem into one we can more easily solve—subtraction of mixed numbers with common denominators. Then have students read the sentence that gives the answer in a complete sentence.

**Other Examples** In the first example, the fraction in the answer should be reduced to lowest terms. In both the second and third examples, there is one number that is not a mixed number.

**Warm Up** Caution students to be alert for fractions that must be reduced to lowest terms.

## Subtracting Mixed Numbers: Unlike Denominators

The Carlsons are putting new wood siding on their house. The width of siding that is not covered by overlapping siding is called the **exposed surface.** The Carlsons are using siding with a total width of $3\frac{3}{4}$ in. and an exposed surface of $2\frac{1}{2}$ in. How much greater is the total width than the exposed surface?

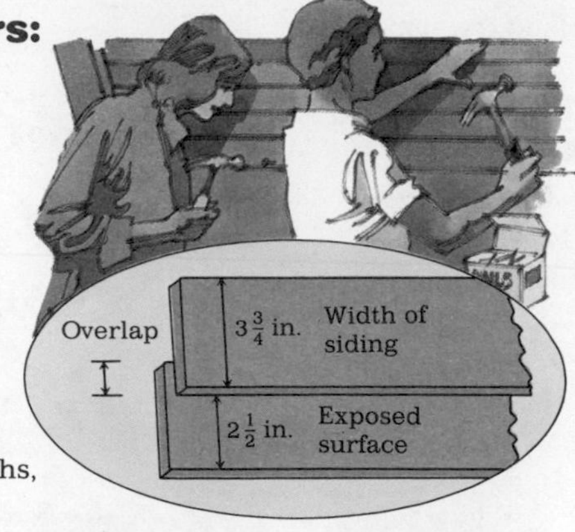
Overlap
$3\frac{3}{4}$ in.
Width of siding
$2\frac{1}{2}$ in.
Exposed surface

Since we want to compare the two widths, we subtract.

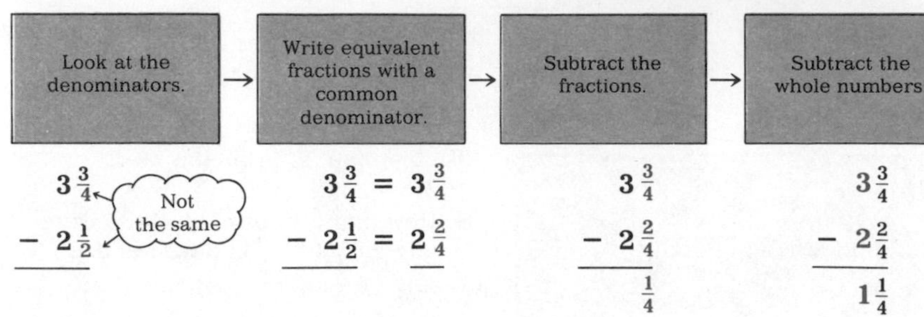
Look at the denominators.
Write equivalent fractions with a common denominator.
Subtract the fractions.
Subtract the whole numbers.

$$\begin{array}{r} 3\frac{3}{4} \\ -\ 2\frac{1}{2} \\ \hline \end{array} \quad \text{Not the same} \qquad \begin{array}{r} 3\frac{3}{4} = 3\frac{3}{4} \\ -\ 2\frac{1}{2} = 2\frac{2}{4} \\ \hline \end{array} \qquad \begin{array}{r} 3\frac{3}{4} \\ -\ 2\frac{2}{4} \\ \hline \frac{1}{4} \end{array} \qquad \begin{array}{r} 3\frac{3}{4} \\ -\ 2\frac{2}{4} \\ \hline 1\frac{1}{4} \end{array}$$

The total width is $1\frac{1}{4}$ in. greater than the exposed surface.

**Other Examples**

$$\begin{array}{r} 12\frac{2}{3} = 12\frac{4}{6} \\ -\ 4\frac{1}{6} = 4\frac{1}{6} \\ \hline 8\frac{3}{6} = 8\frac{1}{2} \end{array} \qquad \begin{array}{r} 7\frac{5}{8} \\ -\ 4 \\ \hline 3\frac{5}{8} \end{array} \qquad \begin{array}{r} 2\frac{4}{5} = 2\frac{24}{30} \\ -\ \frac{1}{6} = \frac{5}{30} \\ \hline 2\frac{19}{30} \end{array}$$

**Warm Up** Subtract.

1. $7\frac{1}{2} - 5\frac{1}{4} = 2\frac{1}{4}$
2. $16\frac{1}{2} - 8\frac{4}{9} = 8\frac{1}{18}$
3. $14\frac{5}{8} - 10 = 4\frac{5}{8}$
4. $8\frac{2}{3} - 1\frac{1}{2} = 7\frac{1}{6}$
5. $10\frac{1}{2} - \frac{1}{5} = 10\frac{3}{10}$

212

## Follow Up

### Reteaching

Remind students that the steps to be followed in subtraction of fractions are similar to those in addition.

1. Check to see if denominators are the same.
2. If not, find the least common denominator. Then rewrite both fractions as equivalent fractions with that denominator.
3. Subtract the fraction parts, then the whole number parts.

Use several examples to demonstrate each step in the process.

### Enrichment

Provide students with a recipe and have them double all of the ingredients in the recipe. Then have them write the recipe listing the new quantities and noting the number of servings in the doubled recipe.

| Assignment Guide | | | |
|---|---|---|---|
| | Minimum | Average | Extended |
| page 213 | 1–24 | 1–25 | 1–25, TM |

Subtract.

1. $5\frac{7}{10} - 2\frac{3}{5}$ $3\frac{1}{10}$
2. $6\frac{1}{2} - 5\frac{1}{3}$ $1\frac{1}{6}$
3. $9\frac{5}{9} - 7\frac{2}{9}$ $2\frac{3}{9} = 2\frac{1}{3}$
4. $4\frac{1}{3} - 4\frac{2}{9}$ $\frac{1}{9}$
5. $7\frac{7}{8} - 3\frac{1}{4}$ $4\frac{5}{8}$
6. $8\frac{3}{4} - \frac{1}{5}$ $8\frac{11}{20}$
7. $3\frac{7}{10} - 1\frac{1}{5}$ $2\frac{5}{10} = 2\frac{1}{2}$
8. $21\frac{1}{2} - 3\frac{1}{8}$ $18\frac{3}{8}$
9. $14\frac{4}{5} - 6$ $8\frac{4}{5}$
10. $13\frac{2}{3} - 4\frac{2}{5}$ $9\frac{4}{15}$
11. $7\frac{5}{6} - 4\frac{1}{6}$ $3\frac{4}{6} = 3\frac{2}{3}$
12. $45\frac{5}{6} - 33\frac{1}{4}$ $12\frac{7}{12}$
13. $12\frac{3}{5} - 10\frac{1}{10}$ $2\frac{5}{10} = 2\frac{1}{2}$
14. $67\frac{7}{10} - 45\frac{45}{100}$ $22\frac{25}{100} = 22\frac{1}{4}$
15. $38\frac{5}{9} - 20\frac{1}{6}$ $18\frac{7}{18}$
16. $9\frac{2}{3} - 7\frac{1}{12}$ $2\frac{7}{12}$
17. $4\frac{3}{4} - 2\frac{3}{8}$ $2\frac{3}{8}$
18. $9\frac{5}{6} - 6\frac{3}{8}$ $3\frac{11}{24}$
19. $7\frac{1}{2} - 3\frac{5}{12}$ $4\frac{1}{12}$
20. $5\frac{5}{8} - 3\frac{1}{2}$ $2\frac{1}{8}$
21. $2\frac{5}{7} - \frac{2}{5}$ $2\frac{11}{35}$
22. $56\frac{2}{3} - 8\frac{1}{5}$ $48\frac{7}{15}$
23. $27\frac{11}{15} - 9\frac{2}{5}$ $18\frac{5}{15} = 18\frac{1}{3}$

24. The suggested amount of exposed surface for a certain kind of siding is $4\frac{3}{4}$ in. When the carpenter finished putting on the siding, it had $\frac{3}{8}$ in. less exposed surface than that. How much of the siding was exposed? $4\frac{3}{8}$ in.

25. The suggested amount of overlap for a certain siding is $1\frac{1}{2}$ in. A carpenter decided to overlap by only $1\frac{1}{8}$ in. How much greater is the suggested overlap than the amount actually used? $\frac{3}{8}$ in.

**Think Math**

**Fraction Comparison with Cross Products**

We can compare fractions by comparing their **cross products.**

First cross product ⟶ (4)(7) ⟶ 5 × 7 = 35

Second cross product ⟶ (5)(9) ⟶ 4 × 9 = 36

$\frac{4}{5} > \frac{7}{9}$

Since the first cross product is greater, the first fraction is greater than the second fraction.

Which fraction in each pair is greater?

1. $\frac{11}{12}, \frac{15}{16}$ $\frac{15}{16}$
2. $\frac{14}{25}, \frac{5}{12}$ $\frac{14}{25}$
3. $\frac{162}{220}, \frac{215}{300}$ $\frac{162}{220}$
4. $\frac{200}{325}, \frac{300}{475}$ $\frac{300}{475}$

More Practice, page 424, Set B



## Using Page 213

**Exercises 1–25** Remind students that finding the least common denominator will make the computation process simpler.

**Think Math** This activity introduces students to another way to compare fractions. Students might find it helpful to record their products as shown below to help them recall which fraction is greater.

first cross product ⟶ 36 > 35 ⟵ second cross product

(4)(7) / (5)(9)

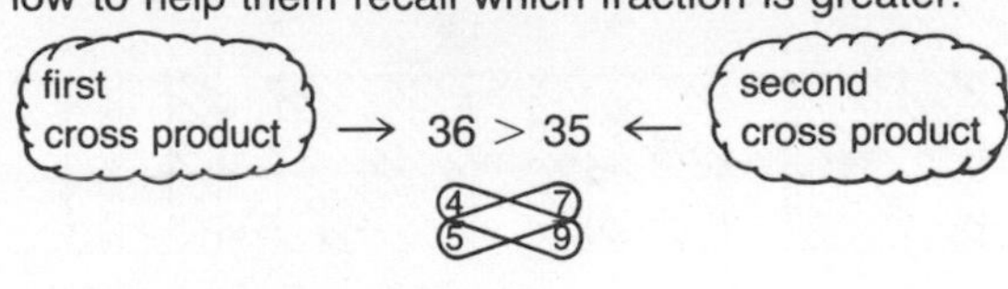

$36 > 35$ so $\frac{4}{5} > \frac{7}{9}$

**More Practice,** page 424, Set B

**Reteaching Supplement,** page 50

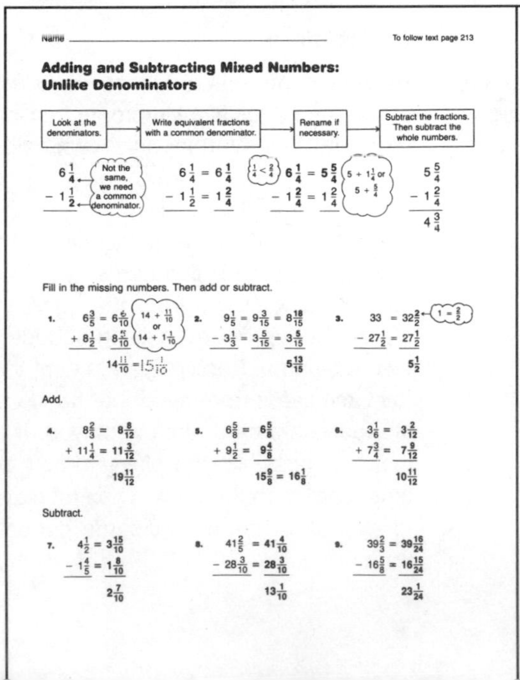
Name ______ To follow text page 213

**Adding and Subtracting Mixed Numbers: Unlike Denominators**

Look at the denominators. → Write equivalent fractions with a common denominator. → Rename if necessary. → Subtract the fractions. Then subtract the whole numbers.

$6\frac{1}{4} - 1\frac{1}{2}$ (Not the same, we need a common denominator.) $6\frac{1}{4} = 6\frac{1}{4}$, $-1\frac{1}{2} = 1\frac{2}{4}$ ($\frac{1}{4} < \frac{2}{4}$) $6\frac{1}{4} = 5\frac{5}{4}$, $-1\frac{2}{4} = 1\frac{2}{4}$ ($5 + 1\frac{1}{4}$ or $5 + \frac{5}{4}$) $5\frac{5}{4} - 1\frac{2}{4} = 4\frac{3}{4}$

Fill in the missing numbers. Then add or subtract.

1. $6\frac{3}{5} = 6\frac{6}{10}$, $+ 8\frac{1}{2} = 8\frac{5}{10}$; $14\frac{11}{10} = 15\frac{1}{10}$ ($14 + \frac{11}{10}$ or $14 + 1\frac{1}{10}$)
2. $9\frac{1}{5} = 9\frac{3}{15} = 8\frac{18}{15}$, $- 3\frac{1}{3} = 3\frac{5}{15} = 3\frac{5}{15}$; $5\frac{13}{15}$
3. $33 = 32\frac{2}{2}$ ($1 = \frac{2}{2}$), $- 27\frac{1}{2} = 27\frac{1}{2}$; $5\frac{1}{2}$

Add.

4. $8\frac{2}{3} = 8\frac{8}{12}$, $+ 11\frac{1}{4} = 11\frac{3}{12}$; $19\frac{11}{12}$
5. $6\frac{5}{8} = 6\frac{5}{8}$, $+ 9\frac{1}{2} = 9\frac{4}{8}$; $15\frac{9}{8} = 16\frac{1}{8}$
6. $3\frac{1}{6} = 3\frac{2}{12}$, $+ 7\frac{3}{4} = 7\frac{9}{12}$; $10\frac{11}{12}$

Subtract.

7. $4\frac{1}{2} = 3\frac{15}{10}$, $- 1\frac{4}{5} = 1\frac{8}{10}$; $2\frac{7}{10}$
8. $41\frac{2}{5} = 41\frac{4}{10}$, $- 28\frac{3}{10} = 28\frac{3}{10}$; $13\frac{1}{10}$
9. $39\frac{2}{3} = 39\frac{16}{24}$, $- 16\frac{5}{8} = 16\frac{15}{24}$; $23\frac{1}{24}$

**Enrichment Supplement,** page 50

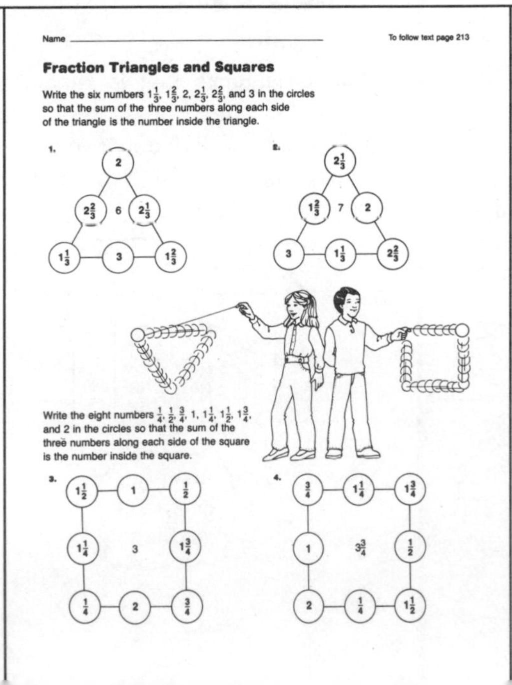
Name ______ To follow text page 213

**Fraction Triangles and Squares**

Write the six numbers $1\frac{1}{3}$, $1\frac{2}{3}$, 2, $2\frac{1}{3}$, $2\frac{2}{3}$, and 3 in the circles so that the sum of the three numbers along each side of the triangle is the number inside the triangle.


1.
2
$2\frac{2}{3}$ 6 $2\frac{1}{3}$
$1\frac{1}{3}$ 3 $1\frac{2}{3}$
2.
$2\frac{1}{3}$
$1\frac{2}{3}$ 7 2
3 $1\frac{1}{3}$ $2\frac{2}{3}$


Write the eight numbers $\frac{1}{4}$, $\frac{1}{2}$, $\frac{3}{4}$, 1, $1\frac{1}{4}$, $1\frac{1}{2}$, $1\frac{3}{4}$, and 2 in the circles so that the sum of the three numbers along each side of the square is the number inside the square.


3.
$1\frac{1}{2}$ 1 $\frac{1}{2}$
$1\frac{1}{4}$ 3 $1\frac{3}{4}$
$\frac{1}{4}$ 2 $\frac{3}{4}$
4.
$\frac{3}{4}$ $1\frac{1}{4}$ $1\frac{3}{4}$
1 $3\frac{3}{4}$ $\frac{1}{2}$
2 $\frac{1}{4}$ $1\frac{1}{2}$


**Practice Supplement,** page 83

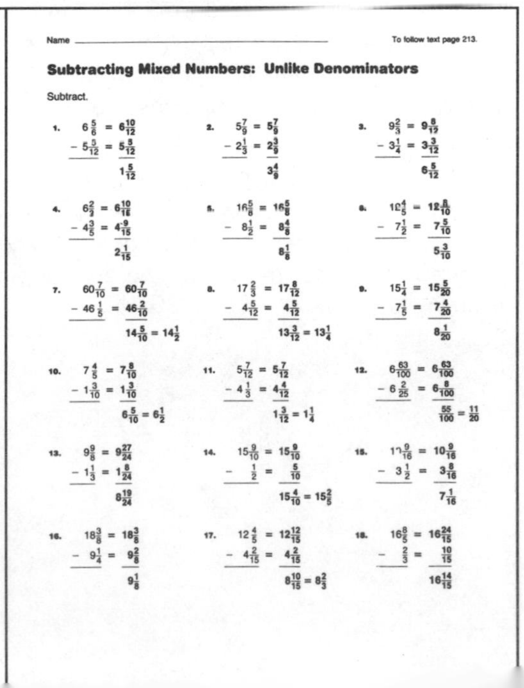
Name ______ To follow text page 213.

**Subtracting Mixed Numbers: Unlike Denominators**

Subtract.

1. $6\frac{5}{6} = 6\frac{10}{12}$, $- 5\frac{5}{12} = 5\frac{5}{12}$; $1\frac{5}{12}$
2. $5\frac{7}{9} = 5\frac{7}{9}$, $- 2\frac{1}{3} = 2\frac{3}{9}$; $3\frac{4}{9}$
3. $9\frac{2}{3} = 9\frac{8}{12}$, $- 3\frac{1}{4} = 3\frac{3}{12}$; $6\frac{5}{12}$
4. $6\frac{2}{3} = 6\frac{10}{15}$, $- 4\frac{3}{5} = 4\frac{9}{15}$; $2\frac{1}{15}$
5. $16\frac{5}{8} = 16\frac{5}{8}$, $- 8\frac{1}{2} = 8\frac{4}{8}$; $8\frac{1}{8}$
6. $12\frac{4}{5} = 12\frac{8}{10}$, $- 7\frac{1}{2} = 7\frac{5}{10}$; $5\frac{3}{10}$
7. $60\frac{7}{10} = 60\frac{7}{10}$, $- 46\frac{1}{5} = 46\frac{2}{10}$; $14\frac{5}{10} = 14\frac{1}{2}$
8. $17\frac{2}{3} = 17\frac{8}{12}$, $- 4\frac{5}{12} = 4\frac{5}{12}$; $13\frac{3}{12} = 13\frac{1}{4}$
9. $15\frac{1}{4} = 15\frac{5}{20}$, $- 7\frac{1}{5} = 7\frac{4}{20}$; $8\frac{1}{20}$
10. $7\frac{4}{5} = 7\frac{8}{10}$, $- 1\frac{3}{10} = 1\frac{3}{10}$; $6\frac{5}{10} = 6\frac{1}{2}$
11. $5\frac{7}{12} = 5\frac{7}{12}$, $- 4\frac{1}{3} = 4\frac{4}{12}$; $1\frac{3}{12} = 1\frac{1}{4}$
12. $6\frac{63}{100} = 6\frac{63}{100}$, $- 6\frac{2}{25} = 6\frac{8}{100}$; $\frac{55}{100} = \frac{11}{20}$
13. $9\frac{9}{8} = 9\frac{27}{24}$, $- 1\frac{1}{3} = 1\frac{8}{24}$; $8\frac{19}{24}$
14. $15\frac{9}{10} = 15\frac{9}{10}$, $- \frac{1}{2} = \frac{5}{10}$; $15\frac{4}{10} = 15\frac{2}{5}$
15. $10\frac{9}{16} = 10\frac{9}{16}$, $- 3\frac{1}{2} = 3\frac{8}{16}$; $7\frac{1}{16}$
16. $18\frac{3}{8} = 18\frac{3}{8}$, $- 9\frac{1}{4} = 9\frac{2}{8}$; $9\frac{1}{8}$
17. $12\frac{4}{5} = 12\frac{12}{15}$, $- 4\frac{2}{15} = 4\frac{2}{15}$; $8\frac{10}{15} = 8\frac{2}{3}$
18. $16\frac{8}{5} = 16\frac{24}{15}$, $- \frac{2}{3} = \frac{10}{15}$; $16\frac{14}{15}$

**Quick Review** Students write these fractions and mixed numbers in order, from smallest to largest.

$\frac{1}{4}$ 1 $\quad$ $\frac{11}{12}$ 4 $\quad$ $1\frac{1}{2}$ 5 $\quad$ $1\frac{3}{4}$ 6 $\quad$ $\frac{1}{2}$ 3 $\quad$ $\frac{3}{8}$ 2

**Lesson Focus** To subtract mixed numbers with unlike denominators

**Suggested Materials** Paper for folding

## Ideas for Getting Started

Have two students use paper to model the mixed number $3\frac{1}{4}$. Their models should look like this:

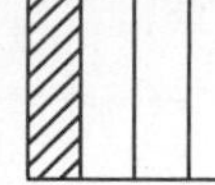

Draw a picture of the model above, label each region, and write $3\frac{1}{4}$ on the chalkboard. Then have students fold one of the whole sheets into fourths and label each section. Students should now see the model below on their papers and on the chalkboard.

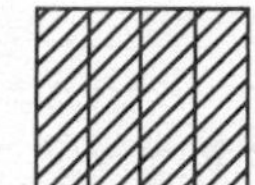
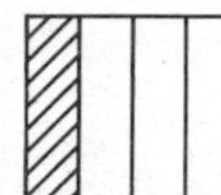

"Did the amount of shaded space change when you folded and renamed this mixed number?" (no) Elicit from students that the paper and chalkboard models show that $3\frac{1}{4}$ is the same as $2\frac{5}{4}$.

## Using Page 214

**Motivational Problem** Have students read the paragraph at the top of the page. "What do we want to find out about tape recorder speeds?" (What is the difference between the two speeds?) Discuss what data we need to solve the problem. "Why is subtraction the operation needed to find the answer?" (When we want to compare two amounts, we subtract.)

**Lesson Development** In discussing each instruction box, pay particular attention to the third step where students must rename the mixed number. If necessary, draw rectangles on the chalkboard to model the renaming process. Ask students to read the answer in a complete sentence.

**Other Examples** In the second example, note that the whole number 5 was renamed as thirds because the denominator of the fraction in the mixed number was thirds. The last example shows the three steps required to find the answer when renaming is needed.

## More Subtracting Mixed Numbers

The speed of a tape recorder is measured in inches per second (ips). Two of the most common speeds for a reel-to-reel recorder are $7\frac{1}{2}$ ips and $3\frac{3}{4}$ ips. What is the difference in the two speeds?

Since we want to compare the two speeds, we should subtract.

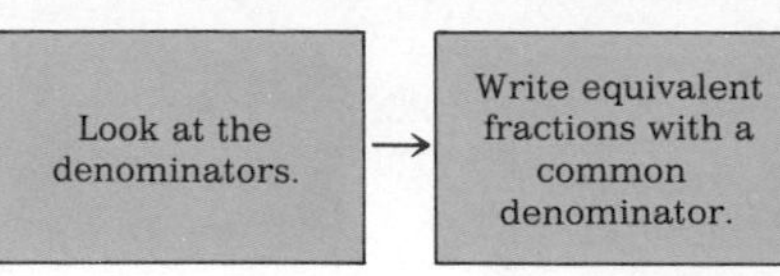


Subtract the whole numbers.

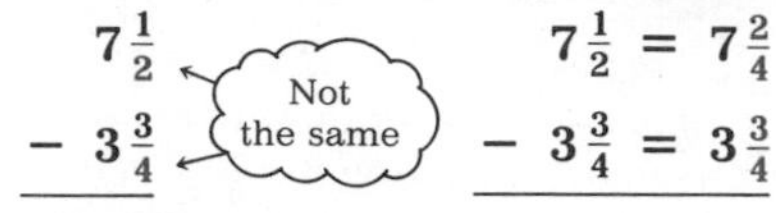


$$7\frac{1}{2} - 3\frac{3}{4}$$

$$7\frac{1}{2} = 7\frac{2}{4} \qquad -3\frac{3}{4} = 3\frac{3}{4}$$

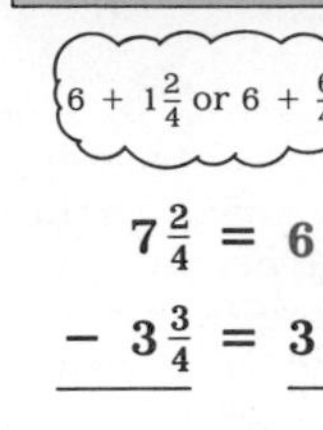


$$7\frac{2}{4} = 6\frac{6}{4} \qquad -3\frac{3}{4} = 3\frac{3}{4} \qquad \frac{3}{4}$$

$$6\frac{6}{4} - 3\frac{3}{4} = 3\frac{3}{4}$$

The difference in the two recording speeds is $3\frac{3}{4}$ ips.

**Other Examples**

$$9\frac{1}{6} = 8\frac{7}{6} \qquad -4\frac{5}{6} = 4\frac{5}{6} \qquad 4\frac{2}{6} = 4\frac{1}{3}$$

$$5 = 4\frac{3}{3} \qquad -3\frac{1}{3} = 3\frac{1}{3} \qquad 1\frac{2}{3}$$

$$8\frac{1}{3} = 8\frac{2}{6} = 7\frac{8}{6} \qquad -4\frac{1}{2} = 4\frac{3}{6} = 4\frac{3}{6} \qquad 3\frac{5}{6}$$

**Warm Up** Subtract.

1. $4\frac{1}{3} - 1\frac{5}{6}$ $\quad 2\frac{3}{6} = 2\frac{1}{2}$
2. $9\frac{3}{5} - 3\frac{7}{10}$ $\quad 5\frac{9}{10}$
3. $14\frac{3}{4} - 5\frac{3}{8}$ $\quad 9\frac{3}{8}$
4. $12 - 4\frac{1}{6}$ $\quad 7\frac{5}{6}$
5. $26\frac{1}{6} - 9\frac{7}{12}$ $\quad 16\frac{7}{12}$

214

## Follow Up

### Reteaching

Remind students that in renaming for subtraction of fractions, the renaming is determined by the denominator. Work through several examples, to focus on this renaming step.

$$16\frac{7}{21} = 15 + \frac{21}{21} + \frac{7}{21} = 15\frac{28}{21}$$

$$16\frac{1}{3} - 6\frac{3}{7} = 16\frac{7}{21} - 6\frac{9}{21} = 15\frac{28}{21} - 6\frac{9}{21}$$

Write as equivalent fractions.

### Enrichment

Have students make domino cards with at least four equivalent improper fractions for each whole number as shown below.

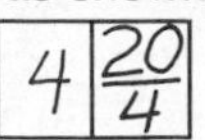


Place the shuffled deck facedown and have players draw five cards each. Another card is drawn from the deck and placed faceup on the playing surface to start the game. Each player, in turn, tries to match cards from his or her hand with an equivalent card already played. If no match is possible, the player draws another card from the deck. The first player to play all of his or her cards correctly wins.

| Assignment Guide | Minimum | Average | Extended |
|---|---|---|---|
| page 215 | 1–24 | 1–25 | 1–21 odd, 23–25, TM |

Subtract.

1. $7\frac{1}{5} - 4\frac{5}{10}$ $2\frac{7}{10}$
2. $6\frac{1}{4} - 3\frac{3}{4}$ $2\frac{2}{4} = 2\frac{1}{2}$
3. $12\frac{1}{2} - 3\frac{3}{4}$ $8\frac{3}{4}$
4. $8 - 5\frac{3}{4}$ $2\frac{1}{4}$
5. $9\frac{3}{4} - 2\frac{7}{8}$ $6\frac{7}{8}$
6. $7\frac{1}{4} - 6\frac{5}{6}$ $\frac{5}{12}$
7. $8\frac{1}{8} - 1\frac{3}{4}$ $6\frac{3}{8}$
8. $12\frac{3}{5} - 7\frac{9}{10}$ $4\frac{7}{10}$
9. $24\frac{5}{8} - 8\frac{1}{2}$ $16\frac{1}{8}$
10. $15\frac{5}{12} - 11\frac{7}{12}$ $3\frac{10}{12} = 3\frac{5}{6}$
11. $14 - 9\frac{7}{10}$ $4\frac{3}{10}$
12. $4\frac{7}{10} - 2\frac{11}{15}$ $1\frac{29}{30}$
13. $6\frac{2}{3} - 1\frac{7}{12}$ $5\frac{1}{12}$
14. $8\frac{7}{9} - 5\frac{5}{6}$ $2\frac{17}{18}$
15. $13\frac{1}{5} - 4\frac{7}{10}$ $8\frac{5}{10} = 8\frac{1}{2}$
16. $79\frac{23}{100} - 64\frac{7}{10}$ $14\frac{53}{100}$
17. $49\frac{1}{2} - 26\frac{3}{5}$ $22\frac{9}{10}$
18. $78\frac{3}{4} - 69\frac{7}{8}$ $8\frac{7}{8}$
19. $67\frac{1}{2} - 18\frac{1}{4}$ $49\frac{1}{4}$
20. $34\frac{1}{8} - 11\frac{3}{4}$ $23\frac{3}{8}$

21. Subtract $9\frac{4}{5}$ from $27\frac{7}{10}$. $17\frac{9}{10}$

22. How much greater is $83\frac{2}{3}$ than $15\frac{3}{4}$? $67\frac{11}{12}$

23. Tape cartridges play at only one speed, $3\frac{3}{4}$ ips. Cassettes also play at only one speed, $1\frac{7}{8}$ ips. What is the difference in these speeds? $1\frac{7}{8}$ ips

24. The usual maximum speed for a reel-to-reel recorder is $7\frac{1}{2}$ ips. The usual minimum speed is $5\frac{5}{8}$ ips less than the maximum. What is the usual minimum speed for reel-to-reel recorders? $1\frac{7}{8}$ ips

25. **DATA HUNT** Record turntables usually have three speeds at which they can be played. Find the difference between the fastest and the slowest. See teaching notes.

**Think**

**Logical Reasoning**

How many different ways can 4 postage stamps be attached to each other on at least one edge? Draw a picture to show each way. See teaching notes.

**Math**

More Practice, page 424, Set C



## Using Page 215

**Exercises 1–24** As you assign these exercises remind students to give their answers as lowest-terms fractions. Note in exercises 21 and 22 the language that suggests subtraction.

**Data Hunt** The typical record turntable speeds are 78, 45, and $33\frac{1}{3}$. Therefore, students should find the difference between 78 and $33\frac{1}{3}$.

**Think Math** There are 12 possible ways the stamps can be attached as directed. One way to organize a list of answers is to find all possibilities with a given number of stamps arranged vertically.

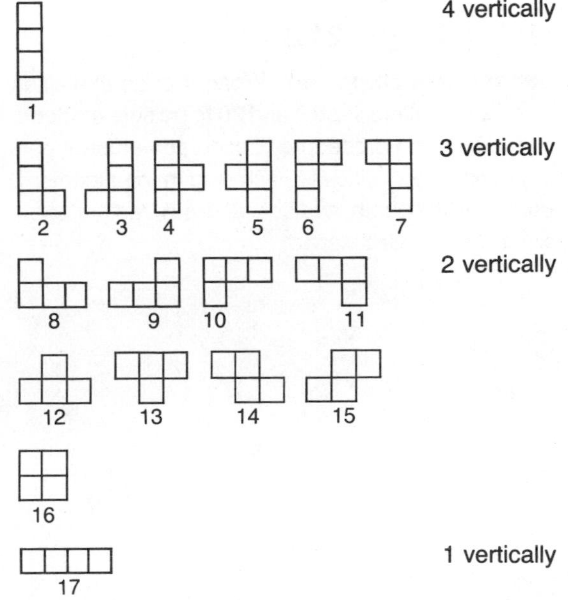


**More Practice,** page 424, Set C

## Ideas That Work

### Special Education

Let students team with a partner to play "Three Out." Players will need a game mat; number cubes (labeled A, B, C, A, B, C and 1, 2, 3, 1, 2, 3); 36 problem cards sized to fit the game mat, answer key, and 6 chips per player.

| | Three Out | | |
|---|---|---|---|
| | A | B | C |
| 1 | | | |
| 2 | | | |
| 3 | | | |

$8\frac{2}{3} - 1\frac{1}{2}$

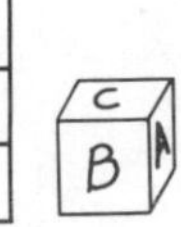

Cards are mixed and 9 are placed faceup on the game mat. In turn, each player tosses the cubes, finds the matching game mat problem and copies it. At "GO," all players subtract and those with a correct answer claim that space with a chip. If necessary, the answer key can be used to check. The first player to claim three spaces in a row—down, across, or diagonally—earns one point. If no player gets three in a row, the round is called a draw and no points are awarded. To play another round, mix the cards and play again. The winner is the player with most points at the end of the playing period.

**Practice Supplement,** page 84

Name ______________________ To follow text page 215

**More Subtracting Mixed Numbers**

Subtract.

1. $15\frac{1}{5} = 15\frac{2}{10} = 14\frac{12}{10}$; $-8\frac{1}{2} = 8\frac{5}{10} = 8\frac{5}{10}$; $6\frac{7}{10}$
2. $11\frac{3}{5} = 11\frac{18}{30} = 10\frac{48}{30}$; $-8\frac{5}{6} = 8\frac{25}{30} = 8\frac{25}{30}$; $2\frac{23}{30}$
3. $8\frac{1}{8} = 8\frac{1}{8} = 7\frac{9}{8}$; $-3\frac{1}{4} = 3\frac{2}{8} = 3\frac{2}{8}$; $4\frac{7}{8}$
4. $72\frac{3}{4}$; $-19$; $53\frac{3}{4}$
5. $43\frac{3}{4} = 43\frac{9}{12} = 42\frac{21}{12}$; $-26\frac{5}{6} = 26\frac{10}{12} = 26\frac{10}{12}$; $16\frac{11}{12}$
6. $65\frac{1}{3} = 64\frac{4}{3}$; $-14\frac{2}{3} = 14\frac{2}{3}$; $50\frac{2}{3}$
7. $23\frac{1}{6} = 23\frac{1}{6} = 22\frac{7}{6}$; $-7\frac{1}{3} = 7\frac{2}{6} = 7\frac{2}{6}$; $15\frac{5}{6}$
8. $28 = 27\frac{5}{5}$; $-17\frac{1}{5} = 17\frac{1}{5}$; $10\frac{4}{5}$
9. $33\frac{1}{3} = 33\frac{4}{12} = 32\frac{16}{12}$; $-17\frac{3}{4} = 17\frac{9}{12} = 17\frac{9}{12}$; $15\frac{7}{12}$
10. $71\frac{21}{100} = 71\frac{21}{100} = 70\frac{121}{100}$; $-17\frac{7}{10} = 17\frac{70}{100} = 17\frac{70}{100}$; $53\frac{51}{100}$
11. $40 = 39\frac{3}{3}$; $-16\frac{2}{3} = 16\frac{2}{3}$; $23\frac{1}{3}$
12. $3\frac{3}{8} = 2\frac{11}{8}$; $-2\frac{7}{8} = 2\frac{7}{8}$; $\frac{4}{8} = \frac{1}{2}$
13. $12\frac{1}{4} = 12\frac{5}{20} = 11\frac{25}{20}$; $-3\frac{7}{10} = 3\frac{14}{20} = 3\frac{14}{20}$; $8\frac{11}{20}$
14. $91\frac{7}{9} = 91\frac{14}{18} = 90\frac{32}{18}$; $-86\frac{5}{6} = 86\frac{15}{18} = 86\frac{15}{18}$; $4\frac{17}{18}$
15. $80\frac{1}{6} = 80\frac{4}{24} = 79\frac{28}{24}$; $-34\frac{5}{8} = 34\frac{15}{24} = 34\frac{15}{24}$; $45\frac{13}{24}$
16. $14\frac{5}{6} = 14\frac{15}{18}$; $-8\frac{7}{9} = 8\frac{14}{18}$; $6\frac{1}{18}$
17. $39\frac{3}{5} = 39\frac{6}{10}$; $-15\frac{1}{2} = 15\frac{5}{10}$; $24\frac{1}{10}$
18. $22 = 21\frac{10}{10}$; $-16\frac{7}{10} = 16\frac{7}{10}$; $5\frac{3}{10}$

# Fractions

**Quick Review** Students tell what is the largest remainder possible for each problem.

| Problem | Answer |
|---|---|
| 62)388 | 61 |
| 809)1,256 | 808 |
| 4)10,244 | 3 |
| 16)456 | 15 |
| 5)90,332 | 4 |
| 233)876 | 232 |

**Lesson Focus** To practice addition and subtraction of fractions; to tell the operation needed to solve word problems

## Ideas for Getting Started

Review with students several simple fraction exercises before assigning this lesson. For example, work through the addition of two fractions with common denominators. Then ask a volunteer to demonstrate how to find the difference between two mixed numbers with common denominators. When students seem confident with this procedure, continue with sample addition and subtraction exercises with unlike denominators.

## Using Page 216

**Lesson Development** Work through exercises 1 and 2 and exercises 19 and 20 to be sure students understand the procedure. Encourage student participation as you discuss each step in the algorithm. Point out that both addition and subtraction exercises are included here.

## Adding and Subtracting Fractions: Practice

Add or subtract. Give answers in lowest terms.

1. $\frac{1}{3} + \frac{1}{3}$ → $\frac{2}{3}$
2. $\frac{4}{5} - \frac{2}{5}$ → $\frac{2}{5}$
3. $\frac{1}{4} + \frac{1}{2}$ → $\frac{3}{4}$
4. $\frac{1}{3} + \frac{1}{6}$ → $\frac{3}{6} = \frac{1}{2}$
5. $\frac{5}{8} + \frac{1}{4}$ → $\frac{7}{8}$
6. $\frac{11}{12} - \frac{5}{6}$ → $\frac{1}{12}$
7. $\frac{3}{4} - \frac{1}{3}$ → $\frac{5}{12}$
8. $\frac{2}{3} + \frac{5}{6}$ → $\frac{9}{6} = 1\frac{1}{2}$
9. $\frac{1}{4} + \frac{1}{6}$ → $\frac{5}{12}$
10. $\frac{4}{5} - \frac{2}{3}$ → $\frac{2}{15}$
11. $\frac{3}{8} + \frac{3}{4}$ → $\frac{9}{8} = 1\frac{1}{8}$
12. $\frac{2}{3} - \frac{1}{6}$ → $\frac{3}{6} = \frac{1}{2}$
13. $\frac{5}{6} + \frac{1}{4}$ → $\frac{13}{12} = 1\frac{1}{12}$
14. $\frac{5}{16} + \frac{7}{8}$ → $\frac{19}{16} = 1\frac{3}{16}$
15. $\frac{2}{3} - \frac{1}{4}$ → $\frac{5}{12}$
16. $\frac{1}{4} - \frac{1}{5}$ → $\frac{1}{20}$
17. $\frac{6}{7} + \frac{2}{3}$ → $\frac{32}{21} = 1\frac{11}{21}$
18. $\frac{1}{3} - \frac{1}{8}$ → $\frac{5}{24}$
19. $2\frac{1}{4} + 5\frac{1}{4}$ → $7\frac{2}{4} = 7\frac{1}{2}$
20. $7\frac{3}{8} - 5$ → $2\frac{3}{8}$
21. $3\frac{4}{5} + 5\frac{1}{5}$ → $8\frac{5}{5} = 9$
22. $4\frac{1}{2} + 6$ → $10\frac{1}{2}$
23. $10\frac{5}{6} - 5\frac{1}{3}$ → $5\frac{3}{6} = 5\frac{1}{2}$
24. $16\frac{3}{4} - 9\frac{1}{3}$ → $7\frac{5}{12}$
25. $13\frac{5}{6} - 8\frac{3}{4}$ → $5\frac{1}{12}$
26. $9\frac{1}{8} + 7\frac{3}{4}$ → $16\frac{7}{8}$
27. $15\frac{1}{2} - 6\frac{1}{3}$ → $9\frac{1}{6}$
28. $12\frac{1}{4} - 5\frac{3}{4}$ → $6\frac{2}{4} = 6\frac{1}{2}$
29. $7\frac{3}{8} + 6\frac{7}{8}$ → $13\frac{10}{8} = 14\frac{1}{4}$
30. $14\frac{1}{2} + 4\frac{5}{6}$ → $18\frac{8}{6} = 19\frac{1}{3}$
31. $8\frac{2}{5} + 5\frac{2}{3}$ → $13\frac{16}{15} = 14\frac{1}{5}$
32. $16 - 7\frac{3}{8}$ → $8\frac{5}{8}$
33. $27\frac{1}{8} - 14\frac{3}{4}$ → $12\frac{3}{8}$
34. $17\frac{7}{8} + 12\frac{1}{2}$ → $29\frac{11}{8} = 30\frac{3}{8}$
35. $23\frac{1}{4} + 8\frac{5}{6}$ → $31\frac{13}{12} = 32\frac{1}{12}$
36. $32\frac{2}{5} - 19\frac{2}{3}$ → $12\frac{11}{15}$
37. $46\frac{5}{6} - 26\frac{11}{12}$ → $19\frac{11}{12}$
38. $51\frac{3}{8} - 38\frac{2}{3}$ → $12\frac{17}{24}$
39. $60\frac{7}{12} + 29\frac{5}{8}$ → $89\frac{29}{24} = 90\frac{5}{24}$
40. $40\frac{1}{2} - 17\frac{9}{16}$ → $22\frac{15}{16}$
41. $19\frac{4}{5} + 18\frac{1}{3}$ → $37\frac{17}{15} = 38\frac{2}{15}$
42. $24\frac{7}{10} + 35\frac{3}{4}$ → $59\frac{29}{20} = 60\frac{9}{20}$



## Follow Up

### Reteaching

Review the idea that a mixed number can be shown as the sum of a whole number and a fraction $\left(2\frac{1}{4} = 2 + \frac{1}{4}\right)$. Next show how $2\frac{1}{4} + 3\frac{1}{4}$ can be found by using the above fact and the associative and commutative properties for addition:

$$\begin{aligned} 2\tfrac{1}{4} + 3\tfrac{1}{4} &= \left(2 + \tfrac{1}{4}\right) + \left(3 + \tfrac{1}{4}\right) \\ &= (2 + 3) + \left(\tfrac{1}{4} + \tfrac{1}{4}\right) \\ &= 5 + \tfrac{2}{4} \\ &= 5\tfrac{1}{2} \end{aligned}$$

Then write the problem in vertical form and show how the sum can be found by adding fraction to fraction and whole number to whole number.

### Enrichment

Challenge students to take away one toothpick and then change the position of three others to spell a word of affection.

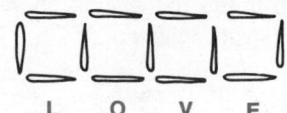

L O V E

| Assignment Guide | | | |
|---|---|---|---|
| | Minimum | Average | Extended |
| page 216 | 1–30 | 1–42 | 2–42 even |
| page 217 | 1–7 | 1–8 | 1–9 |

QUESTION / DATA / PLAN / ANSWER / CHECK

## Problem Solving: Choosing the Operations

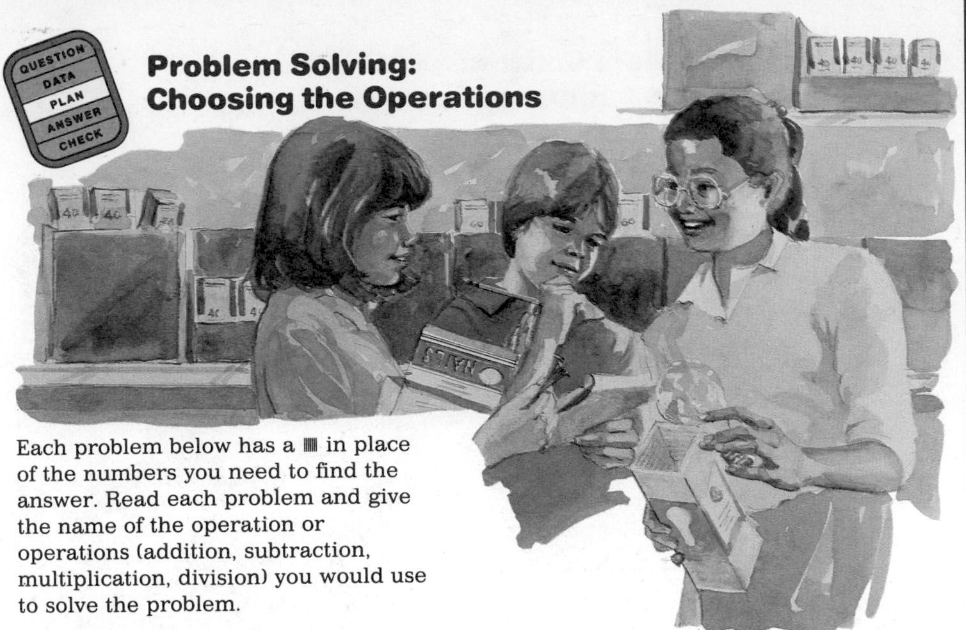

Each problem below has a ■ in place of the numbers you need to find the answer. Read each problem and give the name of the operation or operations (addition, subtraction, multiplication, division) you would use to solve the problem.

1. A 500-ft length of rope costs $■. A 1,200-ft length of the same rope costs $■. How much more does the 1,200-ft length cost? subtraction
2. A 2-pound box of nails costs $■. What is the cost of ■ boxes? multiplication
3. A spool of electrical wire has ■ ft of wire on it. How many ■-ft pieces can be cut from one spool? division
4. A jigsaw blade costs $■. A drill bit costs $■. How much would you pay if you bought ■ jigsaw blades and ■ drill bits? multiplication, addition
5. A painter bought ■ gallons of paint. Each gallon regularly costs $■, but there was $■ off the regular price for each gallon. What was the total cost for the ■ gallons? subtraction, multiplication
6. Plywood was on sale for $■. The regular price is $■ more. How much money do you save buying ■ pieces of plywood on sale? subtraction, multiplication
7. A bag of cement costs $■. A bag of grass seed costs $■. What is the total cost for ■ bags of cement and ■ bags of grass seed? multiplication, addition
8. A boy bought two rolls of tape and a paint brush. The total cost was $■. If a roll of tape costs $■ what was the cost of the paint brush? multiplication, subtraction
9. **Try This** Out of every 5 light bulbs in a carton 1 bulb was broken. There were 20 bulbs in the carton that were not broken. How many bulbs were broken? Hint: Make a table. 5



## Using Page 217

**Lesson Development** Have students read the introductory paragraph. Point out that the problems in this lesson have ■ rather than the numbers needed to find the answer. Caution students to read the problems and to think carefully about which operation is needed to find a solution. Be sure students focus on the action in the problem rather than on a key word or phrase.

**Exercises 1–8** After students have completed these exercises, have them explain their selections for each problem.

**Try This** A possible strategy, Make a Table, was taught on page 100.

**Discussion** "What question are we trying to answer about the light bulbs?" (How many bulbs were broken?) "What do we know about the bulbs in the carton?" (There were 20 bulbs that were not broken.) "What do we know about the bulbs that were broken?" (For every 5 light bulbs in a carton, 1 was broken.) "If 1 out of every 5 was broken, how many out of every 5 were not broken?" (4) "If 1 of 5 was broken, how many would be broken out of 10?" (2)

**Solution** There were 5 broken bulbs in the carton.

| broken bulbs | not broken | total |
|---|---|---|
| 1 | 4 | 5 |
| 2 | 8 | 10 |
| 3 | 12 | 15 |
| 4 | 16 | 20 |
| 5 | 20 | 25 |

### Reteaching Supplement, page 51

Name ______ To follow text page 217

**Problem Solving: Choosing the Operations**

The action in the story tells which operation or operations you need to find the answer.

+ *Addition* Put together or combine groups to find a total.

− *Subtraction* Take away, compare, or find how many more are needed.

× *Multiplication* Find the total when you have several same-size groups.

÷ *Division* Find the number of same-size sets when you know the total, or find the number in each same-size set.

Write +, −, ×, or ÷ in each answer space.

1. Kip hiked ■ km on Saturday and ■ km on Sunday. How many more kilometers did he hike on Saturday? (Compare the two distances.) −
2. Each day Kimberly rides her horse ■ km. Last week she rode her horse on ■ days. How many kilometers did she ride last week? (Find the total for several same-size groups.) ×
3. The Carson family drove ■ km on their vacation. They were gone for ■ days and they drove about the same number of kilometers each day. About how many kilometers did they drive each day? ÷
4. Kara's goal was to collect ■ aluminum cans. She has collected ■ cans. How many more cans does she need to meet her goal? −
5. A "45-rpm" record costs ■. Marcie bought ■ records for her mother's birthday. What was the total cost for the records? ×
6. There are ■ students in York School. Buses took all of the students to a park. If each bus holds ■ students, how many buses were needed to take all of the students? ÷

### Enrichment Supplement, page 51

Name ______ To follow text page 217

**Working Between Limits**

Some problems do not have one exact answer. Instead, any number within a **range**—the smallest possible number to the greatest possible number—is correct. Study the example.

**Example** 24 students plan to go on a field trip in cars. Each car must carry at least 3 students but no more than 5 students. What is the least number of cars needed? What is the greatest number of cars needed?

$24 \div 5 = 4\frac{4}{5}$ If each car carried 5 students, 5 cars would be needed.

$24 \div 3 = 8$ If each car carried 3 students, 8 cars would be needed.

5 to 8 cars are needed. (The range is 5–8.)

Answer the questions in each of the problems below to find the answer range.

1. Anne can read between 200 and 300 words a minute. What is the shortest time it would take her to read a magazine story of 12,000 words? What is the longest time? 40 min – 60 min
2. Brenda has a 9:00 a.m. flight to San Francisco. She estimates that it will take her from 30 to 50 minutes to get to the airport from her house. She also wants to check in $\frac{1}{2}$ hour ahead of her flight time. What are the earliest and latest times she should leave her house? 7:40 a.m. – 8:00 a.m.
3. A machinist must drill a hole 2.530 cm in diameter in a metal block. The hole can be no more than 0.006 cm larger or smaller than this. What are the smallest and the largest diameters allowed? 2.524 cm – 2.536 cm
4. Bill read that a boy his age usually grows from 4.3 cm to 9.4 cm in height in a year. Bill is now 148.8 cm tall. What is the shortest height Bill is likely to be in a year? What is the greatest height he is likely to be? 153.1 cm – 158.2 cm
5. Julio is buying fruit punch for a party. The punch costs 85¢ for a 1-L carton. Julio wants to spend between $10 and $12 for the punch. What are the least and the greatest number of liters of punch he can buy? 12 L – 14 L
6. A baseball game usually lasts between 2 and 4 hours. A Sunday doubleheader (2 games) begins at 1:00 p.m. There is a $\frac{1}{2}$ hour break between games. What is the earliest time both games could end? What is the latest time? 5:30 p.m. – 9:30 p.m.

### Practice Supplement, page 85

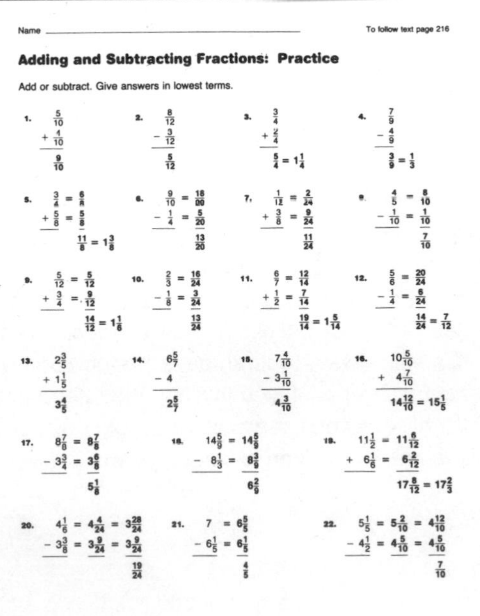

Name ______ To follow text page 216

**Adding and Subtracting Fractions: Practice**

Add or subtract. Give answers in lowest terms.

1. $\frac{5}{10} + \frac{4}{10} = \frac{9}{10}$
2. $\frac{8}{12} - \frac{3}{12} = \frac{5}{12}$
3. $\frac{3}{4} + \frac{2}{4} = \frac{5}{4} = 1\frac{1}{4}$
4. $\frac{7}{9} - \frac{4}{9} = \frac{3}{9} = \frac{1}{3}$
5. $\frac{3}{4} = \frac{6}{8}$; $+\frac{5}{8} = \frac{5}{8}$; $\frac{11}{8} = 1\frac{3}{8}$
6. $\frac{9}{10} = \frac{18}{20}$; $-\frac{1}{4} = \frac{5}{20}$; $\frac{13}{20}$
7. $\frac{1}{12} = \frac{2}{24}$; $+\frac{3}{8} = \frac{9}{24}$; $\frac{11}{24}$
8. $\frac{4}{5} = \frac{8}{10}$; $-\frac{1}{10} = \frac{1}{10}$; $\frac{7}{10}$
9. $\frac{5}{12} = \frac{5}{12}$; $+\frac{3}{4} = \frac{9}{12}$; $\frac{14}{12} = 1\frac{1}{6}$
10. $\frac{2}{3} = \frac{16}{24}$; $-\frac{1}{8} = \frac{3}{24}$; $\frac{13}{24}$
11. $\frac{6}{7} = \frac{12}{14}$; $+\frac{1}{2} = \frac{7}{14}$; $\frac{19}{14} = 1\frac{5}{14}$
12. $\frac{5}{6} = \frac{20}{24}$; $-\frac{1}{4} = \frac{6}{24}$; $\frac{14}{24} = \frac{7}{12}$
13. $2\frac{3}{5} + 1\frac{1}{5} = 3\frac{4}{5}$
14. $6\frac{5}{7} - 4 = 2\frac{5}{7}$
15. $7\frac{4}{10} - 3\frac{1}{10} = 4\frac{3}{10}$
16. $10\frac{5}{10} + 4\frac{7}{10} = 14\frac{12}{10} = 15\frac{1}{5}$
17. $8\frac{7}{8} = 8\frac{7}{8}$; $-3\frac{3}{4} = 3\frac{6}{8}$; $5\frac{1}{8}$
18. $14\frac{5}{9} = 14\frac{5}{9}$; $-8\frac{1}{3} = 8\frac{3}{9}$; $6\frac{2}{9}$
19. $11\frac{1}{2} = 11\frac{6}{12}$; $+6\frac{1}{6} = 6\frac{2}{12}$; $17\frac{8}{12} = 17\frac{2}{3}$
20. $4\frac{1}{6} = 4\frac{4}{24} = 3\frac{28}{24}$; $-3\frac{3}{8} = 3\frac{9}{24} = 3\frac{9}{24}$; $\frac{19}{24}$
21. $7 = 6\frac{5}{5}$; $-6\frac{1}{5} = 6\frac{1}{5}$; $\frac{4}{5}$
22. $5\frac{1}{5} = 5\frac{2}{10} = 4\frac{12}{10}$; $-4\frac{1}{2} = 4\frac{5}{10} = 4\frac{5}{10}$; $\frac{7}{10}$

**Lesson Focus** To solve a simpler problem as a strategy for solving nonroutine word problems

## Ideas for Getting Started

Write the following problem on the chalkboard.

The gas company had to lay $24\frac{3}{4}$ miles of pipe. They have already laid $12\frac{1}{2}$ miles of pipe. How much more pipe do they have to lay?

Ask students what *plan* they should use to find the answer. Discuss that subtraction is the correct operation to compare the two lengths. Then erase the mixed numbers and replace them with 10 and 5. "Now which operation should you use to find the answer?" Students should see that subtraction is still the operation needed. Use this example to point out that sometimes a simpler problem can be used to solve a more difficult one.

## Using Page 218

**Motivational Problem** Ask students to read the Try This problem. "What are we trying to find out about the tennis tournament?" (How many matches are needed?) "How many people are in the tournament?" (20) "How long does each person play?" (until he or she loses) Elicit from students that choosing one of the operations would not be an adequate plan for solving this problem. Tell them that an appropriate strategy for solving this problem is to solve a simpler problem.

**Lesson Development** Have students read the paragraph that explains this strategy. Then call students' attention to the first think cloud. Point out that in this example we started by finding the number of matches for 3 people. "Could we start with 2 people?" (yes) Show that 1 match would be needed if 2 people were in the tournament. To help students see the pattern, organize the information in a table.

| number of players | number of games needed |
|---|---|
| 2 | 1 |
| 3 | 2 |
| 4 | 3 |
| . | . |
| . | . |
| . | . |

**Exercises 1–2** For both of these exercises students can substitute any numbers for the ones given. For exercise 1, if there were 2 boys and 2 girls, there would be 2 × 2, or 4 handshakes. If there were 3 girls and 3 boys, there would be 3 × 3, or 9 handshakes. For exercise 2, the third sock pulled out must be either blue or black, so three socks will always guarantee a match. Some students may get confused thinking they need to have a pair of socks of a particular color, but point out that this is not a condition of the problem.

### Problem Solving: Solve a Simpler Problem

When a problem has large numbers, you can sometimes find out how to solve it by solving the same problem but with smaller numbers. This strategy is called

**Solve a Simpler Problem**

**Try This** There are 20 people in a table tennis tournament. Two people play in each match. Each person plays until she or he loses. How many matches are needed to find a tournament champion?

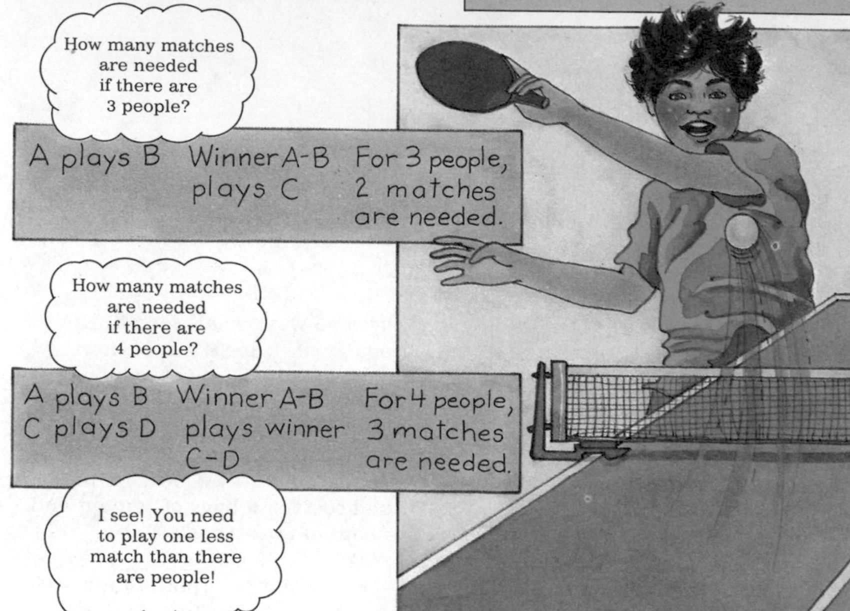

How many matches are needed if there are 3 people?
A plays B
Winner A-B plays C
For 3 people, 2 matches are needed.
How many matches are needed if there are 4 people?
A plays B
C plays D
Winner A-B plays winner C-D
For 4 people, 3 matches are needed.
I see! You need to play one less match than there are people!


You need 19 matches to find a champion.

Solve.

1. There were 10 girls and 10 boys at a party. Each girl shook hands with each boy one time. How many handshakes were there? 100

2. Carlton Careless had 12 black socks and 18 blue socks mixed together in a dresser drawer. How many socks would he have to pull out of the drawer to be sure that he got a pair that matched? 3

218

## Strategy Test Item

**Optional Problem** If you wish to assess students' ability to apply the strategy called Solve a Simpler Problem introduced in this chapter, provide them with the problem below.

> Eight people have entered a chess tournament. Each person is scheduled to play every other person once. How many games are scheduled for the tournament? (Hint: How many games if only two persons play? Three persons?)

**Solution** For 6 people 28 games will need to be scheduled.

## Chapter Review-Test

Write a fraction for each ■.

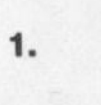
1. 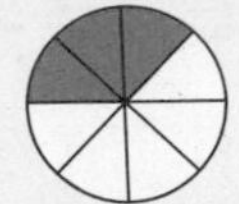
■ of the circle is red. $\frac{3}{8}$

2. 
■ of the stars are red. $\frac{4}{5}$

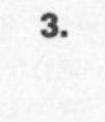
3. 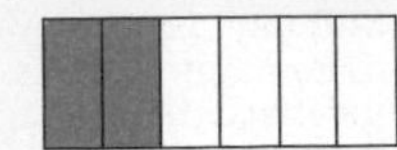
■ of the strip is red. $\frac{2}{6}$

Find the missing numerator or denominator.

4. $\frac{2}{3} = \frac{■}{12}$ 8
5. $\frac{5}{8} = \frac{■}{24}$ 15
6. $\frac{1}{4} = \frac{3}{■}$ 12
7. $\frac{2}{3} = \frac{■}{9}$ 6
8. $\frac{4}{5} = \frac{12}{■}$ 15

Give the next two equivalent fractions.

9. $\frac{1}{3}, \frac{■}{■}, \frac{■}{■}$ $\frac{2}{6}, \frac{3}{9}$
10. $\frac{1}{5}, \frac{■}{■}, \frac{■}{■}$ $\frac{2}{10}, \frac{3}{15}$
11. $\frac{3}{4}, \frac{■}{■}, \frac{■}{■}$ $\frac{6}{8}, \frac{9}{12}$
12. $\frac{1}{6}, \frac{■}{■}, \frac{■}{■}$ $\frac{2}{12}, \frac{3}{18}$
13. $\frac{3}{8}, \frac{■}{■}, \frac{■}{■}$ $\frac{6}{16}, \frac{9}{24}$

Reduce each fraction to lowest terms.

14. $\frac{6}{8}$ $\frac{3}{4}$
15. $\frac{8}{12}$ $\frac{2}{3}$
16. $\frac{8}{16}$ $\frac{1}{2}$
17. $\frac{3}{9}$ $\frac{1}{3}$
18. $\frac{4}{10}$ $\frac{2}{5}$
19. $\frac{9}{12}$ $\frac{3}{4}$
20. $\frac{5}{50}$ $\frac{1}{10}$

Write >, <, or = for each ●.

21. $\frac{4}{5}$ ● $\frac{4}{7}$ >
22. $\frac{5}{8}$ ● $\frac{7}{16}$ >
23. $\frac{2}{6}$ ● $\frac{7}{21}$ =
24. $\frac{8}{15}$ ● $\frac{3}{5}$ <
25. $\frac{7}{8}$ ● $\frac{13}{16}$ >

Add or subtract. Give answers in lowest terms.

26. $\frac{3}{8} + \frac{3}{8}$ — $\frac{6}{8} = \frac{3}{4}$
27. $\frac{5}{6} - \frac{1}{6}$ — $\frac{4}{6} = \frac{2}{3}$
28. $\frac{7}{8} - \frac{5}{8}$ — $\frac{2}{8} = \frac{1}{4}$
29. $1\frac{1}{5} + 3\frac{2}{5}$ — $4\frac{3}{5}$
30. $11\frac{7}{12} - 3\frac{5}{12}$ — $8\frac{2}{12} = 8\frac{1}{6}$
31. $4\frac{1}{6} + 3\frac{5}{6}$ — $7\frac{6}{6} = 8$
32. $\frac{7}{8} - \frac{1}{2}$ — $\frac{3}{8}$
33. $\frac{4}{5} + \frac{3}{10}$ — $\frac{11}{10} = 1\frac{1}{10}$
34. $6\frac{3}{4} - 2\frac{1}{3}$ — $4\frac{5}{12}$
35. $12\frac{3}{8} - 9\frac{3}{4}$ — $2\frac{5}{8}$
36. $7\frac{1}{4} + 2\frac{5}{6}$ — $9\frac{13}{12} = 10\frac{1}{12}$
37. $16\frac{2}{3} - 5\frac{8}{9}$ — $10\frac{7}{9}$

Solve.

38. Marlene worked $12\frac{1}{2}$ h last week. This week she worked $15\frac{1}{4}$ h. How many hours in all did Marlene work in the last two weeks? $27\frac{3}{4}$ h

39. Marlene received 20 cases of juice on Monday. By the end of the week only $2\frac{1}{2}$ cases were left. How many cases of juice were used? $17\frac{1}{2}$ cases



## Using Page 219

The exercises in the Chapter Review-Test emphasize the major concepts and skills presented in this chapter. These exercises may be used as a review assignment or as a test, depending upon your needs.

**Item Analysis** The table below correlates the Chapter Review-Test items with objectives and with the student text pages on which the concepts or skills were taught.

| Items | Objectives | Related Text Pages |
|---|---|---|
| 1–20 | 8.1 | 194–199 |
| 21–25 | 8.2 | 200–202 |
| 26–31 | 8.3 | 204–205 |
| 32–37 | 8.4 | 208–215 |
| 38–39 | 8.5 | 203, 206, 216–217 |

## Assessment Options

If you use the Chapter Review-Test as a review assignment, you may wish to use the multiple-choice test or the free-response test to evaluate mastery of the chapter objectives. The items on these tests have a one-to-one correspondence in terms of content and level of difficulty. A correlation of test items to objectives and student text pages is provided in the Management Guide for Chapter 8.

**Multiple-Choice Test,** TRB pages 22–23

**Free-Response Test,** TRB page 63–64

## TRB Options

The following blackline masters are available for use with this chapter. If you have not already assigned these materials, you may wish to use them to close the chapter.

**Recreation,** TRB page 158

**Consumer Applications,** TRB page 176

**Calculator Technology,** TRB page 194

**Computer Technology,** TRB pages 208–210

**Reading Math,** TRB page 226

**Family Involvement,** TRB page 251–252

# Reteaching

## Using Page 220

The exercises on this page are intended for those students who experienced difficulty with the Chapter Review-Test on page 219. Should students require reteaching of these key concepts and skills, please refer to the teaching notes below. Otherwise, the Another Look exercises can be assigned as independent work with students using the accompanying sample problems and hints as guides.

**Exercises 1–9** This skill was originally taught on page 196. Draw students' attention to the boxes in the example that show that both the numerator and the denominator are multiplied by the same number. If necessary, show the multiplication like this.

$$\frac{1}{2} \times \frac{3}{3} = \frac{1 \times 3}{2 \times 3} = \frac{3}{6}$$

(same as 1)

Then help students generate a sequence of equivalent fractions, for example, $\frac{1}{2} = \frac{2}{4} = \frac{3}{6} = \frac{4}{8}$. Elicit from students what number is multiplied with the numerator and denominator to give each equivalent fraction.

**Exercises 10–17** This skill was originally taught on pages 198–199. Remind students that the most efficient way to reduce a fraction to lowest-terms is to divide the numerator and denominator by the greatest common factor. However, if finding the GCF is difficult for them, encourage students to use the "repeated division" approach shown in the example. Students should recognize that it does not matter which of the multiples they use first for the division; that is, they could solve the example by first dividing by 3 and then by 2.

**Exercises 18–25** This skill was originally taught on pages 208–209. Because the most difficult step in this process is finding the least common multiple (denominator), focus attention on the steps for finding the least common denominator in the sample problem.

**Exercises 26–31** These skills were originally taught on pages 210–213. Discuss the examples shown, focusing on the renaming of the mixed numbers. If necessary, draw rectangles to illustrate the renaming of $4\frac{2}{6}$ as shown in the example.

### *Another Look*

**Multiply** the numerator and denominator by the same number (not zero) to find an **equivalent fraction.**

$$\frac{1}{2} \xrightarrow{\times 3} \frac{3}{6} \qquad \frac{3}{5} \xrightarrow{\times 4} \frac{12}{20}$$

**Divide** the numerator and denominator by common factors to get a fraction in **lowest terms.**

$$\frac{6}{18} \longrightarrow \frac{6 \div 2}{18 \div 2} = \frac{3}{9} \longrightarrow \frac{3 \div 3}{9 \div 3} = \frac{1}{3}$$

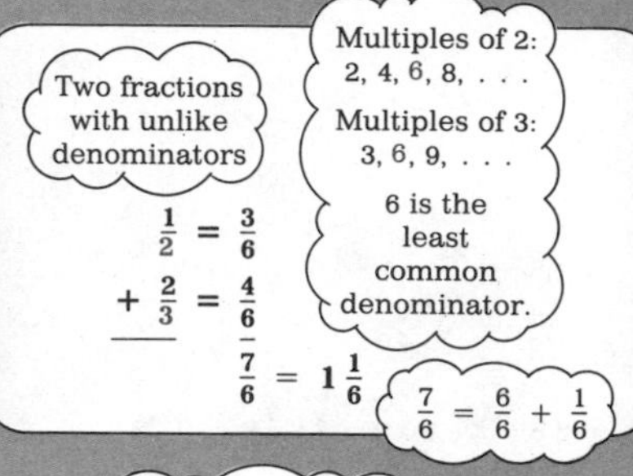

Two fractions with unlike denominators
Multiples of 2: 2, 4, 6, 8, . . .
Multiples of 3: 3, 6, 9, . . .
6 is the least common denominator.

$$\frac{1}{2} = \frac{3}{6}$$
$$+\frac{2}{3} = \frac{4}{6}$$
$$\frac{7}{6} = 1\frac{1}{6} \qquad \left(\frac{7}{6} = \frac{6}{6} + \frac{1}{6}\right)$$

Rename: $4\frac{2}{6} = 3 + 1 + \frac{2}{6} = 3 + \frac{6}{6} + \frac{2}{6}$

$$4\frac{1}{3} = 4\frac{2}{6} = 3\frac{8}{6}$$
$$-\,1\frac{1}{2} = 1\frac{3}{6} = 1\frac{3}{6}$$
$$2\frac{5}{6}$$

$$7\frac{7}{8}$$
$$+\,4\frac{5}{8}$$
$$11\frac{12}{8} = 12\frac{4}{8} = 12\frac{1}{2} \qquad \left(11 + 1\frac{4}{8}\right)$$

**Find the missing numerator or denominator.**

1. $\frac{1}{3} = \frac{■}{12}$ 4
2. $\frac{3}{8} = \frac{■}{24}$ 9
3. $\frac{7}{10} = \frac{■}{100}$ 70
4. $\frac{5}{6} = \frac{30}{■}$ 36
5. $\frac{3}{4} = \frac{15}{■}$ 20
6. $\frac{2}{3} = \frac{■}{6}$ 4

**Give the next two equivalent fractions.**

7. $\frac{1}{2}, \frac{■}{■}, \frac{■}{■}$ $\frac{2}{4}, \frac{3}{6}$
8. $\frac{1}{3}, \frac{■}{■}, \frac{■}{■}$ $\frac{2}{6}, \frac{3}{9}$
9. $\frac{3}{4}, \frac{■}{■}, \frac{■}{■}$ $\frac{6}{8}, \frac{9}{12}$

**Reduce each fraction to lowest terms.**

10. $\frac{3}{12}$ $\frac{1}{4}$
11. $\frac{6}{8}$ $\frac{3}{4}$
12. $\frac{8}{24}$ $\frac{1}{3}$
13. $\frac{9}{27}$ $\frac{1}{3}$
14. $\frac{12}{24}$ $\frac{1}{2}$
15. $\frac{10}{12}$ $\frac{5}{6}$
16. $\frac{20}{100}$ $\frac{1}{5}$
17. $\frac{35}{70}$ $\frac{1}{2}$

**Add or subtract.**

18. $\frac{3}{4} + \frac{3}{4}$ — $\frac{6}{4} = 1\frac{1}{2}$
19. $\frac{1}{2} + \frac{3}{8}$ — $\frac{7}{8}$
20. $\frac{3}{5} + \frac{7}{10}$ — $\frac{13}{10} = 1\frac{3}{10}$
21. $\frac{1}{6} + \frac{5}{9}$ — $\frac{13}{18}$
22. $\frac{3}{8} - \frac{1}{4}$ — $\frac{1}{8}$
23. $\frac{5}{6} - \frac{1}{4}$ — $\frac{7}{12}$
24. $\frac{1}{2} - \frac{1}{5}$ — $\frac{3}{10}$
25. $\frac{5}{6} - \frac{3}{8}$ — $\frac{11}{24}$

**Add or subtract.**

26. $9\frac{3}{5} + 6\frac{4}{5}$ — $15\frac{7}{5} = 16\frac{2}{5}$
27. $10\frac{2}{3} + 8\frac{5}{6}$ — $18\frac{9}{6} = 19\frac{1}{2}$
28. $20\frac{4}{5} + 32\frac{3}{4}$ — $52\frac{31}{20} = 53\frac{11}{20}$
29. $5\frac{3}{4} - 2\frac{5}{8}$ — $3\frac{1}{8}$
30. $14\frac{1}{3} - 5\frac{5}{6}$ — $8\frac{3}{6} = 8\frac{1}{2}$
31. $64\frac{1}{4} - 45\frac{5}{7}$ — $18\frac{15}{28}$

## Just for Teachers

### Ancient Egyptian Methods of Computation

The Rhind Papyrus, named after the Scottish scholar A. Henry Rhind, is a collection of examples illustrating the rules for mathematical calculations followed by the ancient Egyptians. The compilation of these examples is generally credited to a scribe known as Ahmes, who is believed to have completed the papyrus about 1650 B.C. Much of what we know about Egyptian methods of computation has come from the Rhind Papyrus.

The Egyptians approached mathematics with an interest in practical applications rather than theoretical explanations. To them, the important thing was a formula that worked in a given situation, regardless of why it worked. Most of their calculations used only addition and subtraction. However, Egyptian mathematicians recognized the theoretical fact that any number could be expressed as the sum of numbers from the series 1, 2, 4, 8, 16, . . . $2^n$. They used this concept in their method of multiplication. A similar method, based on doubling and redoubling, was used to solve division problems.

Most of the ancient Egyptians worked with fractions also involving addition. Except for one special fraction, $\frac{2}{3}$, the ancient Egyptians used only unit fractions—fractions having a numerator of 1. All other fractions were expressed as the sum of unit fractions. Thus, for example, the fraction $\frac{3}{8}$ might have been expressed as $\frac{1}{4} + \frac{1}{10} + \frac{1}{40}$. How the

## Enrichment

### An Odd-Number Sequence

The L-shapes below show the first three odd numbers. Look for a pattern in these shapes.

1. Use graph paper to draw shapes for the next two odd numbers.

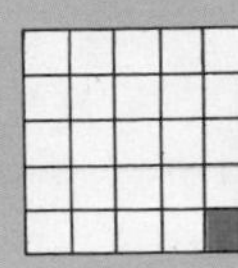
1

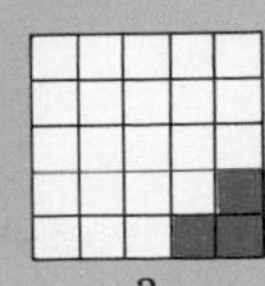
3

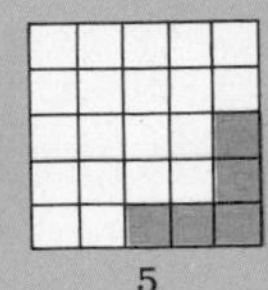
5

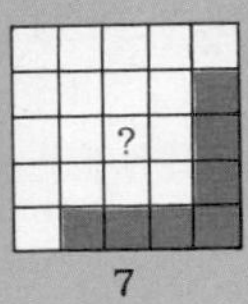

7

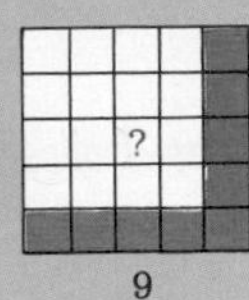

9

If we fit the L-shapes together as shown below we get increasingly large square shapes. This shows that **the sums of successive odd numbers are successive square numbers.** (These are sometimes called "perfect squares.")

2. Use graph paper to show the next square number.

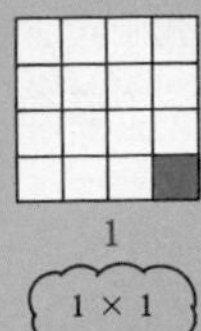
1
1 × 1

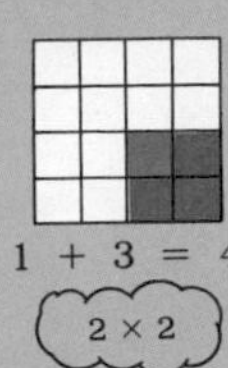
1 + 3 = 4
2 × 2

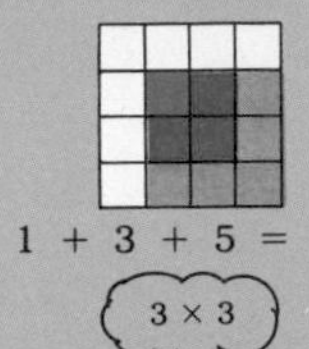
1 + 3 + 5 = 9
3 × 3

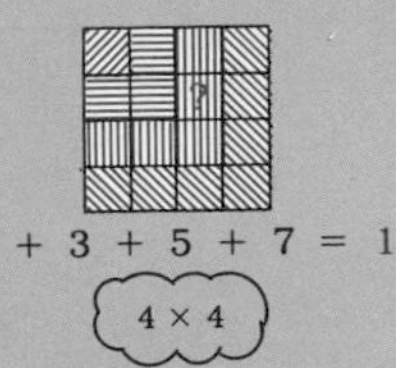

1 + 3 + 5 + 7 = 16
4 × 4

3. Use the pattern you see above. Copy and complete this table.

| Odd Number Sum | Number of Odd-Number Addends | Product | Square Number |
|---|---|---|---|
| 1 + 3 + 5 + 7 | 4 | 4 × 4 | 16 |
| 1 + 3 + 5 + 7 + 9 | ? 5 | ? 5×5 | 25 |
| 1 ? + . . . + 13 | ? 7 | 7 × 7 | 49 |
| 1 ? + . . . + 17 | 9 | ? 9×9 | 81 |
| 1 ? + . . . + 19 | ? 10 | ? 10 × 10 | 100 |

4. How can you find the sum for **any** number of successive odd number addends? The sum is equal to the square of the number of addends.

221

## Using Page 221

This page is intended for those students who successfully completed the Chapter Review-Test on page 219. You may wish to assign this page as independent work while you use the Another Look exercises to reteach the basic concepts and skills of the chapter. Or, you may decide that all students would benefit from exposure to this Enrichment activity.

**Lesson Development** Have students read the introductory information and the directions for exercise 1 at the top of the page. After students have completed the exercise, ask them to read through the paragraph explaining perfect squares. Encourage students to use the illustrations in exercise 2 to help them as they complete the table in exercise 3.

Egyptians derived unit fractions appears to be related to their concept of ratio. In the Rhind Papyrus, for example, the ratio 2:43 is broken down to $\frac{1}{42} + \frac{1}{86} + \frac{1}{129} + \frac{1}{301}$. Why this particular set of unit fractions was chosen is not clear, since the ratio could be expressed as the sum of other sets of unit fractions, including the obvious $\frac{1}{43} + \frac{1}{43}$. None of the rules for fractions given in the Rhind Papyrus applied to all cases, and each Egyptian mathematician seems to have worked from his own secret rules. Consequently, no general rule for handling fractions was formulated.

**Lesson Focus** To analyze, use, and adapt simple computer programs that involve the IF-THEN decision command

## Ideas for Getting Started

Ask students to give examples of situations where the words "if-then" are used. Possible suggestions might be:

<u>If</u> Leo gets above 93 on the test, <u>then</u> he will get an A.

<u>If</u> I wash the car, <u>then</u> I will be paid $5.

<u>If</u> you are going to be late, <u>then</u> give me a call.

Discuss "if-then" situations and emphasize that each situation involves a decision. That is, when the "if" part is true, one thing happens. When the "if" part is false, another thing may happen.

## Using Page 222

**Lesson Development** Have a student go to the chalkboard and follow the instructions in the flowchart as you read them. Emphasize the decision involved when deciding if the number squared is 1,024. Then read through the computer program and compare it with the flowchart. Pay particular attention to line 3Ø. "If N X N is equal to 1,024, what line of the program shows next?" (line 5Ø) "If N X N is not 1,024, what line shows next?" (line 4Ø)

**Exercises 1–3** Read through and discuss these questions with students. If possible, allow them to run the program and modify it to involve numbers other than 1,024.

**Answers**

**1. The computer decides whether the number you choose for N makes the statement N X N = 1024 true.**
**2. The computer would show "GREAT! YOU'RE A WINNER!" no matter what number you chose for N.**
**3. Answers will vary.**

*Technology*

**Decisions in a Computer Program**

Sometimes a computer program is written so that the computer must make a **decision** about a situation. The IF-THEN statement in a program is like a decision box in a flowchart.

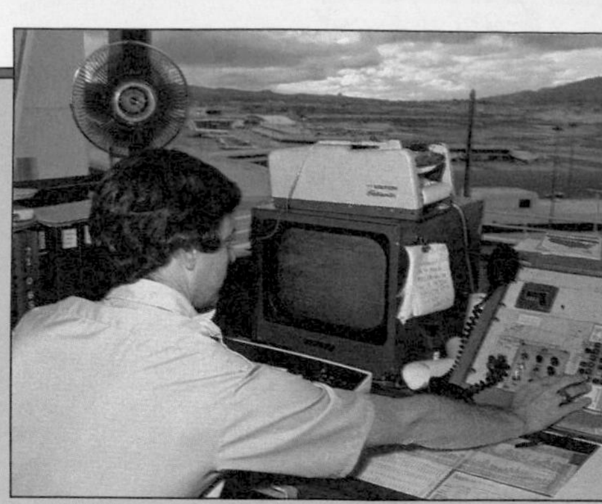

Air traffic controllers use computers to make many decisions each day.

**Flowchart**

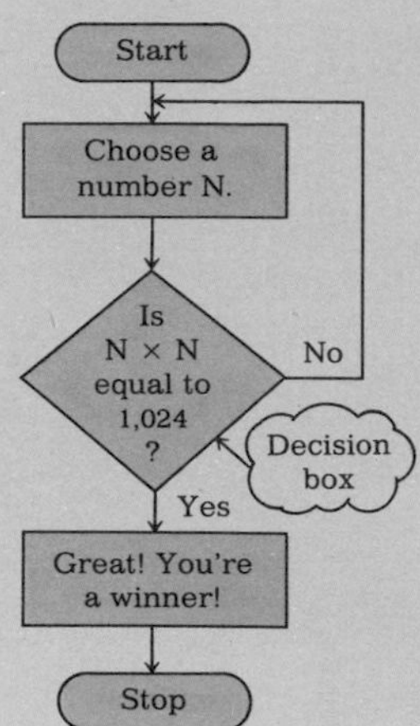
Start
Choose a number N.
Is N × N equal to 1,024 ?
No
Yes
Decision box
Great! You're a winner!
Stop

**Computer Program**

```
10 PRINT "CHOOSE A NUMBER."
20 INPUT N
30 IF N * N = 1024 THEN 50
40 GOTO 10
50 PRINT "GREAT! YOU'RE
   A WINNER!"
60 END
```

If N × N = 1,024, the computer skips to line 50. If N × N is not equal to 1,024, the next step is line 40.

When you type RUN and press RETURN, the computer shows → CHOOSE A NUMBER.
?

If you type 28, the computer asks you to choose again.

If you type 32, the computer shows → GREAT! YOU'RE A WINNER!

See teaching notes.

1. In the program above, what decision must the computer make?
2. What would happen if line 40 were left out?
3. When you have found 32, the "game" is over. Change the program to produce a new "game."

## Technology for Teachers

To communicate with a computer you must be able to use a language that the computer understands. BASIC is one of the most common languages used on microcomputers. It is an acronym for Beginners All purpose Symbolic Instructional Code. This is a computer language that utilizes English words to represent the most common routines the computer is asked to execute. For example, the word PRINT represents the entire set of instructions that are necessary for the computer to display a specific set of symbols on the screen. Even a single punctuation mark may represent a complete routine. A comma can be used to instruct the computer to leave a long space and place numbers or letters in predetermined columns on the screen, while a semicolon instructs the computer to leave no space at all and continue printing at that place.

A computer needs very specific instructions to complete any task. The computer cannot understand misspelled words or misplaced punctuation marks. One of the side benefits of learning a language like BASIC is that students learn very quickly the need for precision in writing and entering their information or instructions into the computer.

Answer the questions about each flowchart program. See teaching notes.

**Flowchart**

Start

Ask for age. Call it A.

Is A less than 12? — Yes → You're in Group A.

No → You're in Group B.

Stop

**Computer Program**

```
10 PRINT "WHAT IS YOUR AGE?"
20 INPUT A
30 IF A < 12 THEN 60
40 PRINT "YOU'RE IN GROUP B."
50 GOTO 70
60 PRINT "YOU'RE IN GROUP A."
70 END
```

1. What line in the program relates to the flowchart decision box?
2. What is the RUN (output) for your age?
3. Jim is 9 years old. He typed the program. What was the run?

**Flowchart**

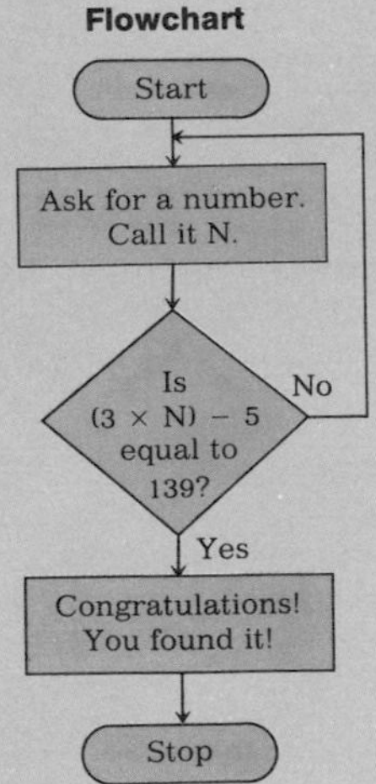
Start
Ask for a number.
Call it N.
Is
(3 × N) − 5
equal to
139?
No
Yes
Congratulations!
You found it!
Stop

**Computer Program**

```
10 PRINT "CHOOSE A NUMBER."
20 INPUT N
30 IF (3 * N) - 5 = 139 THEN 50
40 GOTO 10
50 PRINT "CONGRATULATIONS!
   YOU FOUND IT!"
60 END
```

4. What decision must the computer make?
5. What happens if you choose the wrong number?
6. What is the correct number? What is the RUN if you choose this number?

The BASIC language has many "dialects" which vary from one type of equipment to another. These variations are most apt to be found in the way graphics are handled on the screen and in special functions and formatting commands.

## Using Page 223

**Exercises 1–3** Direct students' attention to the flowchart at the top of the page and go through it one box at a time. Discuss the decision involved and relate it to the "if-then" command in the computer program (line 30). "Which box is the decision box?" (the diamond-shaped box)

**Exercises 4–6** Be sure students understand that the computer must decide whether (3 × N) − 5 equals 139. Use an example to show how the computer returns to the first line of the program when the wrong number is chosen. To improve students' chances of finding the correct number within a reasonable time, you might suggest that they limit their choices to numbers from 1 through 50.

**Answers**

**1. line 30**

**2. For students less than 12 the RUN is**
**WHAT IS YOUR AGE?**
**? (student's age)**
**YOU'RE IN GROUP A.**
**For students 12 or older the RUN is**
**WHAT IS YOUR AGE?**
**? (student's age)**
**YOU'RE IN GROUP B.**

**3. WHAT IS YOUR AGE?**
**? 9**
**YOU'RE IN GROUP A.**

**4. The computer decides whether the number you chose makes the statement (3 × N) − 5 = 139 true.**

**5. The computer returns to the first line of the program.**

**6. 48; the RUN is**
**CHOOSE A NUMBER.**
**? 48**
**CONGRATULATIONS! YOU FOUND IT!**

## Using Page 224

The exercises on this page provide practice for maintaining cumulative skills. The emphasis in this Cumulative Review is on division of whole numbers (Chapter 5), measurement in metric units (Chapter 7), and problem solving (Chapter 5).

**Item Analysis** The table below correlates the Cumulative Review items with objectives and with the student book pages on which the concepts or skills were taught.

| Items | Objectives | Related text pages |
|---|---|---|
| 1–2 | 5.2 | 112–117 |
| 3–4 | 5.4 | 120–124, 126–129 |
| 5–7 | 7.1 | 170–175 |
| 8 | 7.2 | 178 |
| 9 | 7.3 | 180 |
| 10–12 | 7.5 | 184–186 |
| 13–14 | 5.5 | 176–177, 179, 181 |

## *Cumulative Review*

Add, subtract, or divide.

1. 9)685
   A 76
   Ⓑ 76 R1
   C 76 R8
   D not given

2. 8)18,240
   A 228
   B 2,228
   Ⓒ 2,280
   D not given

3. 27)1,323
   A 4.9
   Ⓑ 49
   C 490
   D not given

4. 30)137,010
   A 4,765
   Ⓑ 4,567
   C 4,657
   D not given

Give the missing units.

5. 8 m = 800 ?
   A dm  Ⓑ cm
   C mm  D not given

6. 476 mm = 0.476 ?
   A cm  B dm
   Ⓒ m  D not given

7. 10 km = 10,000 ?
   Ⓐ m  B dm
   C cm  D not given

Give the missing numbers.

8. 3 L = ■ kL
   A 0.3  B 30
   C 0.03  Ⓓ not given

9. 2 kg = ■ g
   A 20  B 200
   Ⓒ 2,000  D not given

10. 5 h 32 min + 2 h 15 min
    Ⓐ 7 h 47 min
    B 5 h 47 min
    C 3 h 17 min
    D not given

11. 51 min 12 s − 22 min 20 s
    A 73 min 32 s
    B 28 min 52 s
    Ⓒ 28 min 52 s
    D not given

12. 5 min 12 s + 3 min 15 s
    A 9 min 57 s
    B 8 min 47 s
    C 2 min 27 s
    Ⓓ not given

13. 416 people are going on a bus trip. If each bus can carry 52 people, how many buses are needed?
    A 7  Ⓑ 8
    C 9  D not given

14. If a plane can carry 188 people, how many planes are needed for 1,620 people?
    A 12  Ⓑ 9
    C 8  D not given

# Fractions: Multiplication and Division

## Objectives

**9.1** Find the product of fractions or of mixed numbers.
**9.2** Find decimal and fraction equivalents.
**9.3** Find the quotient of fractions or of mixed numbers.
**9.4** Solve word problems using the 5-Point Checklist and cumulative computational skills.

## Summary

In this chapter students use models to understand how to find a fraction of a number. They then learn to multiply fractions, to use a shortcut for multiplying fractions, and to multiply mixed numbers. The idea of the reciprocal of a number is used in the development of these concepts. Division of fractions is explained using models, followed by the algorithm for dividing fractions and mixed numbers. Students learn to write decimals as fractions and fractions as decimals. Throughout the chapter students apply the procedures for multiplying and dividing fractions to solve problems. Estimation involving mixed numbers is also emphasized.

## Mathematical Background

**Multiplying Fractions and Mixed Numbers** To help students understand the procedure for multiplying fractions, a model involving area is often used. One such model is described below.

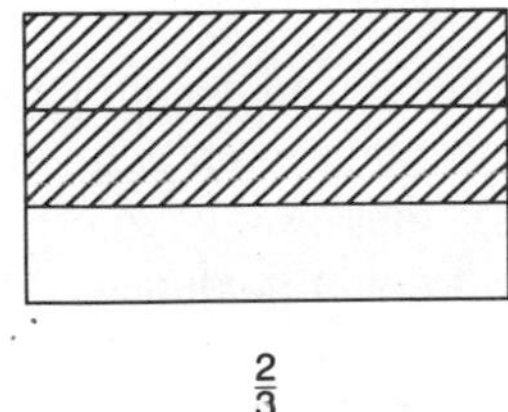

$\frac{2}{3}$

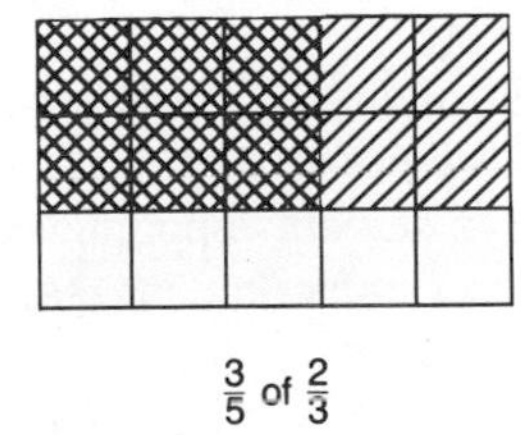

$\frac{3}{5}$ of $\frac{2}{3}$

First, we shade $\frac{2}{3}$ of a rectangle. Then we crosshatch $\frac{3}{5}$ of this $\frac{2}{3}$. We observe that 6 of the 15 parts of the rectangle are both crosshatched and shaded. This suggests that $\frac{3}{5} \times \frac{2}{3} = \frac{6}{15}$, or $\frac{2}{5}$. Through examples of this kind students discover that to find the product of two fractions first we multiply the numerators and then we multiply the denominators. Models can also be used effectively after students have learned the procedure for multiplying fractions.

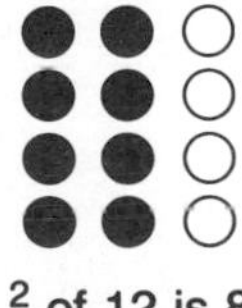

$\frac{2}{3}$ of 12 is 8

$$\frac{2}{3} \times 12 = \frac{2}{3} \times \frac{12}{1} = 8$$

It is helpful to review the procedure for writing a mixed number as an improper fraction before developing multiplication of improper fractions. This procedure provides the prerequisite skills students need in order to find products involving improper fractions. The following example shows the procedure and the skills involved.

$$4\frac{2}{3} \times 2\frac{3}{4}$$

1. change to improper fractions

$$\frac{\overset{7}{\cancel{14}}}{3} \times \frac{11}{\underset{2}{\cancel{4}}} = \frac{77}{6}, \text{ or } 12\frac{5}{6}$$

2. multiply

3. change to a mixed number

**Dividing Fractions and Mixed Numbers** The models on pages 240 and 242 show how situations in the physical world can be used to prepare students for dividing fractions. As students progress from the physical models to a procedure for dividing fractions, the following explanation can be used.

Multiply the Dividend and Divisor by the Same Number.

$$\frac{\frac{3}{4}}{\frac{2}{3}} = \frac{\frac{3}{4} \times \frac{3}{2}}{\frac{2}{3} \times \frac{3}{2}} = \frac{\frac{3}{4} \times \frac{3}{2}}{1} = \frac{3}{4} \times \frac{3}{2} = \frac{9}{8} \text{ or } 1\frac{1}{8}$$

**Remember:** Multiplying the dividend and divisor by the same number does not change the quotient.

The example shows that multiplying the dividend and divisor by the same number does not change the quotient. The idea of the reciprocal of a number must be developed so that the appropriate number can be chosen in this situation. For example, $\frac{3}{2}$ is the reciprocal of $\frac{2}{3}$, because $\frac{2}{3} \times \frac{3}{2} = 1$.

**Fractions and Decimals** Students are often asked to write decimals as fractions. When the decimal is 0.375, for example, they simply read the decimal "three hundred seventy-five thousandths," write the fraction $\frac{375}{1{,}000}$, and then reduce that fraction to $\frac{3}{8}$.

When students are asked to write a fraction as a decimal, the usual procedure is to divide the numerator of the fraction by the denominator. We can use the relationship between multiplication and division to show that this procedure is correct. For example, because $\frac{5}{8} \times 8 = 5$, we know that $5 \div 8 = \frac{5}{8}$ and of course, $\frac{5}{8} = 5 \div 8$. Thus we can divide (or use a calculator to divide) and find that $\frac{5}{8} = 0.625$. Students should be aware that sometimes a mixed decimal is used; instead of writing 0.625 we write $0.62\frac{1}{2}$.

**Problem Solving** Measurements in metric units are easily expressed with decimals, while measurements in customary units often use fractions. For this reason customary units are used in the measurement problems in this chapter. If you wish to provide introductory or review work with customary units, refer to Chapter 16.

There is continued emphasis on the 5-Point Checklist as students complete the problems in this chapter. Problem-solving lessons include: Using Data from a Plan Sheet, pages 234–235; Problem-Solving Practice, page 244; and Using Estimation, page 245. On page 246, a new strategy, Find a Pattern, is introduced.

**Vocabulary**

reciprocal mixed decimal

## Error Analysis

In this chapter the emphasis is on multiplication and division of fractions. Students also learn to translate decimals to fractions and fractions to decimals. Because of the numerous prerequisite skills required with this content, numerous errors can occur.

**Error Pattern 1**

$\frac{1}{3} \times 18 = \frac{1}{54}$ $\quad \frac{3}{4} \times 16 = \frac{3}{64}$ $\quad \frac{4}{5} \times 25 = \frac{4}{125}$

**Diagnosis** In multiplying a fraction times a whole number, the student has multiplied the whole number by the denominator of the fraction instead of the numerator.

**Remediation** There could be several different sources for this kind of error. One possibility is that the student has been taught the shortcut and recalls that the denominator is somehow involved. Review the idea that 18 can be written as $\frac{18}{1}$. Have students verify this by pointing out that $\frac{18}{1}$ reduced to lowest terms ($18 \div 1$) is 18. Repeat this demonstration with other whole numbers. Then work the equation above using the improper fraction $\frac{18}{1}$ instead of the whole number.

**Error Pattern 2**

$3\frac{1}{2} \times 2\frac{1}{5} = 6\frac{1}{10}$ $\quad 3\frac{3}{4} \times 2\frac{2}{3} = 6\frac{6}{12}$ $\quad 2\frac{2}{5} \times 6\frac{1}{3} = 12\frac{2}{15}$

**Diagnosis** To multiply mixed numbers, the student has multiplied the whole numbers, then multiplied the fractions.

**Remediation** First, review changing a mixed number to an improper fraction. Then work through each step to multiply the improper fractions. For example, to multiply $3\frac{1}{2} \times 4\frac{2}{3}$, first change each mixed number to an improper fraction and multiply. Thus, $\frac{7}{2} \times \frac{14}{3} = \frac{98}{6}$. If possible, use manipulatives to illustrate changing mixed numbers to improper fractions. Suggest that students check the reasonableness of their answers by rounding to the nearest whole number and multiplying.

**Error Pattern 3**

$\frac{3}{4} \div \frac{3}{5} = \frac{4}{3} \times \frac{3}{5} = \frac{12}{15}$ $\quad \frac{3}{8} \div \frac{4}{3} = \frac{8}{3} \times \frac{4}{3} = \frac{32}{9}$

$\frac{4}{1} \div \frac{1}{8} = \frac{1}{4} \times \frac{1}{8} = \frac{1}{32}$ $\quad \frac{7}{8} \div \frac{7}{8} = \frac{8}{7} \times \frac{7}{8} = \frac{56}{56}$

**Diagnosis** In these examples, the student has used the reciprocal of the dividend instead of the divisor.

**Remediation** Focus on the relationship of multiplication to division with the emphasis on reciprocals. Begin with an example from whole number multiplication such as $3 \times 4 = 12$.

| factor | × | factor | = | product |
|---|---|---|---|---|
| 3 | × | 4 | = | 12 |

and

| product | ÷ | factor | = | factor |
|---|---|---|---|---|
| 12 | ÷ | 4 | = | 3 |

Hence, a division example such as $\frac{1}{2} \div \frac{3}{4} = n$ may be written as a multiplication sentence $n \times \frac{3}{4} = \frac{1}{2}$. Using the reciprocal idea, $n \times \frac{3}{4} \times \left(\frac{4}{3}\right) = \frac{1}{2} \times \frac{4}{3}$ and $n \times 1 = \frac{1}{2} \times \frac{4}{3}$, so $n = \frac{1}{2} \times \frac{4}{3}$. Point out that in this multiplication sentence, the reciprocal of $\frac{3}{4}$ was used.

## Problem Solving

### Helping Students Read Mathematics Problems

A student's reading ability obviously has some influence on whether a student becomes a successful problem solver. At the most basic level, a student must be able to recognize words and associate meaning with them. At a higher level, a student must be able to combine words into sentences and give meaning to the sentences. Research suggests, however, that the ability to read each word and sentence in a problem, and even the ability to explain the meaning of each sentence, does *not* guarantee that a student will *understand* a problem sufficiently to select and implement an appropriate solution strategy. The teaching-tips discussion in Chapter 3, provides a list of ideas for helping students understand math problems. The ideas listed below for improving students' reading skills will also increase their skills in understanding problems. Experience in both the area of reading math problems and the area of understanding math problems may be necessary for your students.

- Make a bulletin board display of words that have special meanings in mathematics. Examples:

| | | |
|---|---|---|
| place value | difference | perimeter |
| sum | divisor | area |
| addend | meter | face |

- Have students write sentences illustrating the different meanings of a word. Example:

  Johnny's *face* is red.
  The *face* of a cube is square.

- Have students rewrite number words as numerals. Example: Have students write two hundred twenty-five as 225.
- Give students opportunities to write their own word problems. See Chapter 11 for teaching tips to help students formulate problems.
- Have students first read problems silently, then slowly reread the problems aloud.
- Have students substitute nouns for pronouns if the action in the problem is confusing.
- Have a mathematics dictionary available to students.

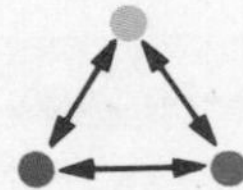

## Special Education

This chapter reviews and extends previous work with fraction multiplication and division. The following ideas focus on ways to provide important visual, verbal, and manipulative guidance to special students.

**Providing Visual and Kinesthetic Guidance**

To help students picture multiplications such as $\frac{2}{3} \times 24$, provide a sheet of clear plastic for them to place over page 226 (Finding a Fraction of a Whole Number). Then, for each example presented, have students partition the whole into equal parts and shade or mark the required part.

Students can also finger trace the movement of the minute hand around a clock (the whole), then retrace in two movements the *two* half-hour parts.

$\frac{1}{2}$ of 60 is 30

$\frac{1}{2} \times 60 = 30$

**Using Multi-Sensory Follow-Through**

Give students paper models or worksheet pictures of geometric shapes and instruct them to shade $\frac{1}{3} \times 6$, $\frac{3}{4} \times 12$, and so on. Let students *say* and *write* number sentences that describe the shaded parts. This activity can be used later for examples such as $\frac{2}{3} \times \frac{3}{4}$, $\frac{7}{10} \times \frac{5}{6}$, and so on.

**Looking for Patterns**

As students work on the shading activity above, ask them to keep a list of problems and answers. Then ask if they can see a pattern in what the numbers do. (The same answers can be found by multiplying numerators and multiplying denominators.) Test this pattern on other problems before turning to the summary of this idea on page 228.

**Resequencing the Lessons**

For special-needs students, it may be better to cover the complete procedure for multiplying two fractions, *including* multiplication of mixed numbers, *before* introducing the shortcut on page 230.

**Using a Simpler Approach**

After the shortcut for finding the product in lowest terms is introduced, the approach below may be helpful to some students. Here, the visual field is simplified by writing the problem as one fraction.

$$\frac{6}{7} \times \frac{21}{12} = \frac{6 \times 21}{7 \times 12}$$

**Using a Verbal, Hands-on Approach**

Introduce an equation such as $6 \div \frac{1}{3} = 18$ as an example. Tell students that there are 6 granola bars. If $\frac{1}{3}$ of a bar is eaten in every bite, how many bites does it take to finish all 6 bars? (18) Provide colored paper "granola bars" marked into thirds, fourths, and sixths. Invite students to cut out the bites and tell the total number of bites needed to eat all bars for problems such as $\frac{2}{3} \div \frac{1}{6}$, $\frac{1}{2} \div \frac{1}{4}$, and so on. Then show how the same result is obtained (without the models) when multiplying by the reciprocal of the divisor.

**Using the One Step**

The errors shown below are typical of those made by students with learning difficulties. Teachers can anticipate these as possible trouble spots and minimize the frequency with which they occur. One approach is to break instruction into small segments and provide specific practice on isolated steps. Students might, for example, carry out the first step of each problem. This would require changing mixed numbers to improper fractions (a); and writing the multiplication sentence containing the reciprocal of the divisor (b). In each case, after the *one step* is checked, the problem can then be completed.

**(a)**

$1\frac{1}{3} \times 2\frac{1}{2} = 2\frac{1}{6}$

**(b)**

$\frac{3}{4} \div \frac{2}{3} =$

$\frac{4}{3} \times \frac{2}{3} = \frac{8}{9}$

## Subject Integration

Subject matter related to other areas of the curriculum has been integrated into the following lessons. This provides an opportunity to highlight the interaction between mathematics and other subjects.

**Career Awareness** Making Furniture, page 225

**Social Studies** Coin collection, page 226–227; Pacific Ocean, page 237; geography, page 238

**Science** Space facts, page 232

# Management Guide

| Teaching Chapter 9 | | | | Meeting Individual Needs | | | | | |
|---|---|---|---|---|---|---|---|---|---|
| Objectives | Chapter Content | Pages | TRB Test Items | Lesson Assignments | | | Follow Up | | |
| | | | | Minimum | Average | Extended | Reteaching | Enrichment | Practice |
| | Chapter Opener | 225 | | | | | | | |
| **9.1** Find the product of fractions or of mixed numbers. | Finding a Fraction of a Whole Number | 226–227 | 1–4 | 1–28 | 1–29, TM | 1–30, TM | SE5 Ch 12 | | PS 86 |
| | Multiplying Fractions | 228–229 | 5–8 | 1–39 | 1–40 | 1–41 | SE5 Ch 12 RS 52 | ES 52 | PS 87 |
| | Multiplying Fractions: A Short Cut | 230–231 | 9–12 | 1–36 | 1–46 | 11–46, TM | RS 53 | ES 53 | MP 425 PS 88 |
| | Multiplying Mixed Numbers | 232–233 | | 1– 29 | 1–31 | 2–32 even, TM | SE5 Ch 12 RS 54 | ES 54 | MP 425 PS 89 |
| **9.2** Find decimal and fraction equivalents. | From Decimals to Fractions | 236 | 13–16 | 1–26 | 1–26 | 1–26 | | | MP 425 |
| | From Fractions to Decimals | 237 | 17–20 | 1–18 | 1–18 | 1–18 | RS 55 | ES 55 | MP 425 PS 91 |
| | Writing Fractions as Mixed Decimals | 238 | | 1–18 | 1–18 | 1–18 | | | |
| **9.3** Find the quotient of fractions or of mixed numbers. | Getting Ready to Divide Fractions | 239 | 21–22 | 1–8 | 1–8 | 1–8 | SE5 Ch 12 | | PS 92 |
| | Dividing Fractions | 240–241 | 23–26 | 1–31 | 1–33 | 11–33, TM | SE5 Ch 12 RS 56 | ES 56 | MP 426 PS 93 |
| | Dividing with Mixed Numbers | 242–243 | 27–30 | 1–36, SK | 1–37, SK | 1–37, SK | SE5 Ch 12 RS 57 | ES 57 | MP 426 PS 94 |
| **9.4** Solve word problems using the 5-Point Checklist and cumulative computational skills. | Problem Solving: Using Data from a Plan Sheet | 234–235 | 31–35 | 1–8 | 1–9 | 1–10 | | | PS 90 |
| | Problem Solving: Practice | 244 | | 1–5 | 1–6 | 1–7 | | | PS 95 |
| | Problem Solving: Using Estimation | 245 | | 1–6 | 1–7 | 1–8 | RS 58 | ES 58 | |
| | Problem Solving: Find a Pattern | 246 | | | | | | | |
| | Chapter Review-Test | 247 | | | | | | | |
| | Another Look/Enrichment | 248–249 | | | | | | | |
| | Cumulative Review | 250 | | | | | | | |

**SE5** Student Edition, Book 5
**RS** Reteaching Supplement
**ES** Enrichment Supplement
**PS** Practice Supplement
**MP** More Practice
**TM** Think Math
**SK** Skillkeeper
**TRB** Teacher's Resource Book

*For each chapter, the objectives, lessons, assignments, test items, and follow up options are organized and cross-referenced in the management guide.*

*In Addison-Wesley Mathematics, all of the supplemental materials are unique. Each is designed to fill an individual classroom need.*



# Teacher's Resource Book



## Masters for Use

**. . . before Chapter 9**

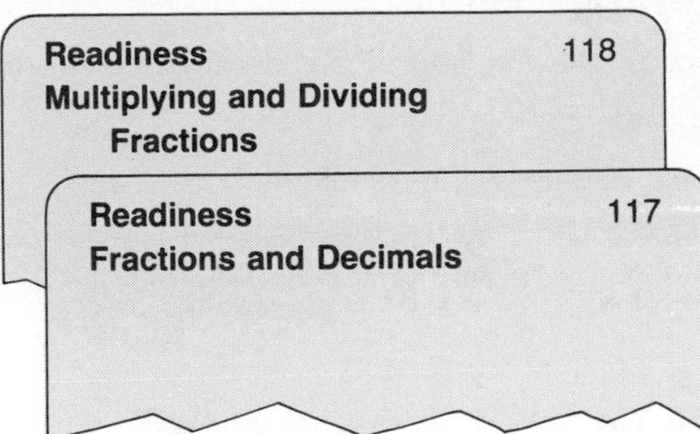


**. . . during Chapter 8**

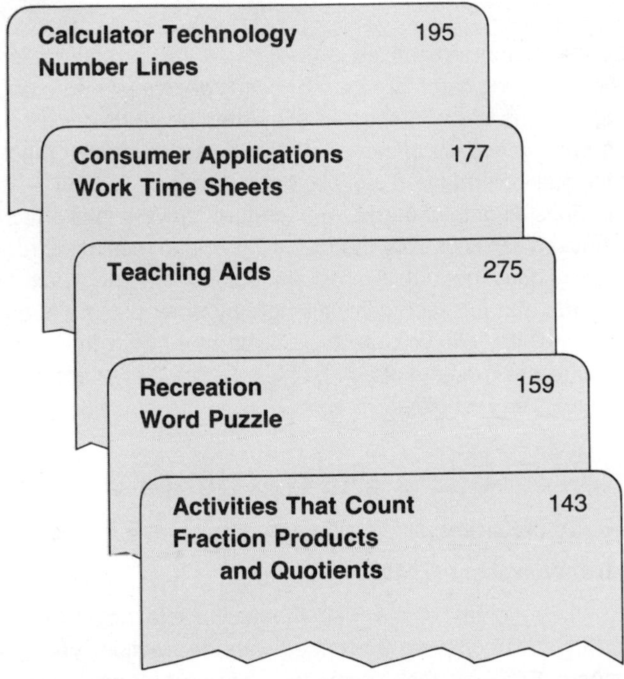

Calculator Technology 195
Number Lines
Consumer Applications 177
Work Time Sheets
Teaching Aids 275
Recreation 159
Word Puzzle
Activities That Count 143
Fraction Products and Quotients


**. . . after Chapter 9**

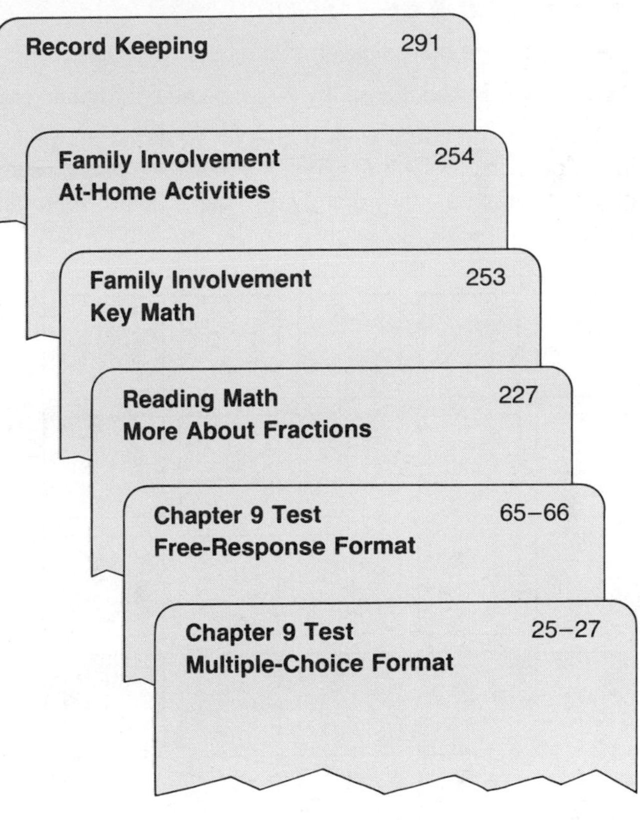

Record Keeping 291
Family Involvement 254
At-Home Activities
Family Involvement 253
Key Math
Reading Math 227
More About Fractions
Chapter 9 Test 65–66
Free-Response Format
Chapter 9 Test 25–27
Multiple-Choice Format


## Supplements

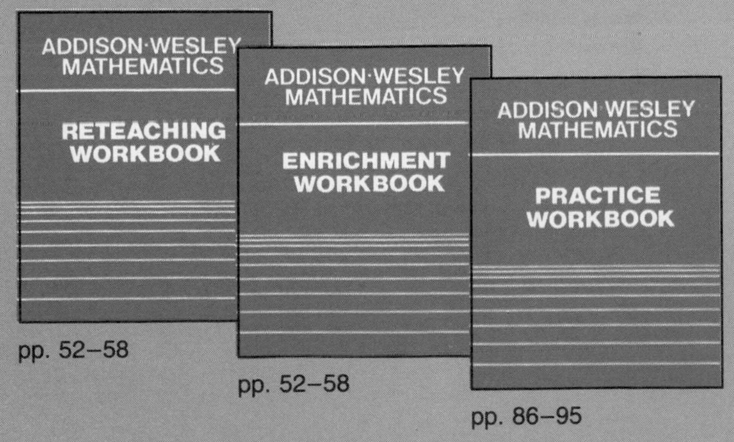


pp. 52–58

pp. 52–58

pp. 86–95

## Other Addison-Wesley Resources

### Books and Kits

*The Arithmetic Primer* pp. 135, 167–168, 171–181, 187–199, 216–217, 221–222

*Arithmetic Skill Cards* pp. F 9–12, D 7, 9

*Baseball, A Game of Numbers* pp. 64–71

*Problem Solving Experiences in Mathematics,* Grade 6 Problems 29, 30, 64, 65, 89, 104, 123, 125, 128, 138, 144

### Technology

*Computer Math Activities* Volume 4

*Computer Math Games* Volume 1

# Activities That Count

Activities That Count are designed for use throughout this chapter and subsequent chapters. Before beginning Chapter 9, you may wish to review these activities and select the ones you consider appropriate for your class.

## Mul-di Tic Tac Toe Game

**Purpose** To practice multiplication and division of fractions

**Materials** 40 cards about 5 cm by 7 cm; game board; markers

**Preparation** On the cards write problems similar to the multiplication and division problems in Chapter 9 (see examples below). Use tagboard to prepare a 5 by 5 array as a game board; each cell of the array should be slightly larger than the problem cards.

| | | | | |
|---|---|---|---|---|
| $\frac{1}{6} \times 18$ | $\frac{3}{5} \div \frac{2}{3}$ | $5 \div 9$ | $\frac{5}{9} \div \frac{1}{3}$ | $\frac{5}{8} \times \frac{2}{3}$ |
| $\frac{4}{3} \times 9$ | $3 \times \frac{2}{3}$ | $\frac{3}{8} \div \frac{5}{4}$ | $\frac{1}{2} \times \frac{1}{3}$ | $2 \div 8$ |
| $\frac{3}{10} \times 50$ | $2 \times \frac{1}{3}$ | $\frac{2}{3} \times \frac{1}{3}$ | $\frac{1}{4} \times \frac{1}{5}$ | $\frac{3}{4} \div \frac{5}{6}$ |
| $4 \times 6\frac{1}{4}$ | $2\frac{1}{8} \times 1\frac{3}{5}$ | $\frac{7}{5} \times \frac{3}{8}$ | $10 \times \frac{3}{5}$ | $4\frac{1}{3} \div 1\frac{2}{3}$ |
| $6 \div \frac{1}{6}$ | $\frac{7}{8} \div 2\frac{1}{4}$ | $\frac{5}{8} \div \frac{5}{8}$ | $9 \div \frac{1}{2}$ | $5\frac{1}{2} \div \frac{1}{8}$ |

**Activity** Cards are mixed, and one is placed in each of the 25 cells on the game board. In turn, players choose a card and solve the problem on it. For a correct answer, players keep the card and mark the cell with a marker. When an answer is incorrect, the card is replaced by one from the pile of unused cards. The first player to solve correctly 5 problems in a row, column, or diagonal wins.

## Fraction Rummy Game

**Purpose** To practice matching fraction and decimal equivalents

**Materials** Index cards

**Preparation** Label 50 index cards as follows:

| | | | |
|---|---|---|---|
| $\frac{1}{2}, \frac{2}{4}, \frac{5}{10}$, 0.5 | $\frac{1}{5}$, 0.2 | $\frac{1}{8}$, 0.125 | $\frac{1}{10}$, 0.1 |
| $\frac{1}{3}, \frac{2}{6}, \frac{4}{12}$, $0.33\frac{1}{3}$ | $\frac{2}{5}$, 0.4 | $\frac{3}{8}$, 0.375 | $\frac{3}{10}$, 0.3 |
| $\frac{2}{3}, \frac{4}{6}, \frac{8}{12}$, $0.66\frac{2}{3}$ | $\frac{3}{5}$, 0.6 | $\frac{5}{8}$, 0.625 | $\frac{7}{10}$, 0.7 |
| $\frac{1}{4}, \frac{2}{8}, \frac{3}{12}$, 0.25 | $\frac{4}{5}$, 0.8 | $\frac{7}{8}$, 0.875 | $\frac{9}{10}$, 0.9 |
| $\frac{3}{4}, \frac{6}{8}, \frac{9}{12}$, 0.75 | $\frac{1}{6}$, $0.16\frac{2}{3}$ | | $\frac{1}{12}$, $0.08\frac{1}{3}$ |
| | $\frac{5}{6}$, $0.83\frac{1}{3}$ | | |

**Activity** The cards are mixed and each player is dealt seven cards. The remaining cards are placed facedown in a pile, with one card placed faceup to start a discard pile. After the cards are dealt, all players who have pairs of cards naming the same number place them on the playing surface. Then players in turn try to "go out"—to match into pairs all of their cards. At each turn, players take a card from the unused cards or from the discard pile, and must discard a card except if they go out. Points are scored for each pair of matched cards and for each card still held by other players at the end of a round. If a player collects 4 cards that name the same number (there are 5 such sets: $\frac{1}{2}, \frac{1}{3}, \frac{2}{3}, \frac{1}{4}, \frac{3}{4}$), the player scores a 5-point bonus. The first player to collect 50 points wins the game.

## Fraction Products and Quotients Math Lab

**Purpose** To practice multiplication and division of fractions

**Materials** Worksheet (TRB p. 143)

**Activity** Have copies of the worksheet available for students. Challenge them to complete the tables with the fraction products and quotients. Students then check their answers or work with a partner to check each other's papers.

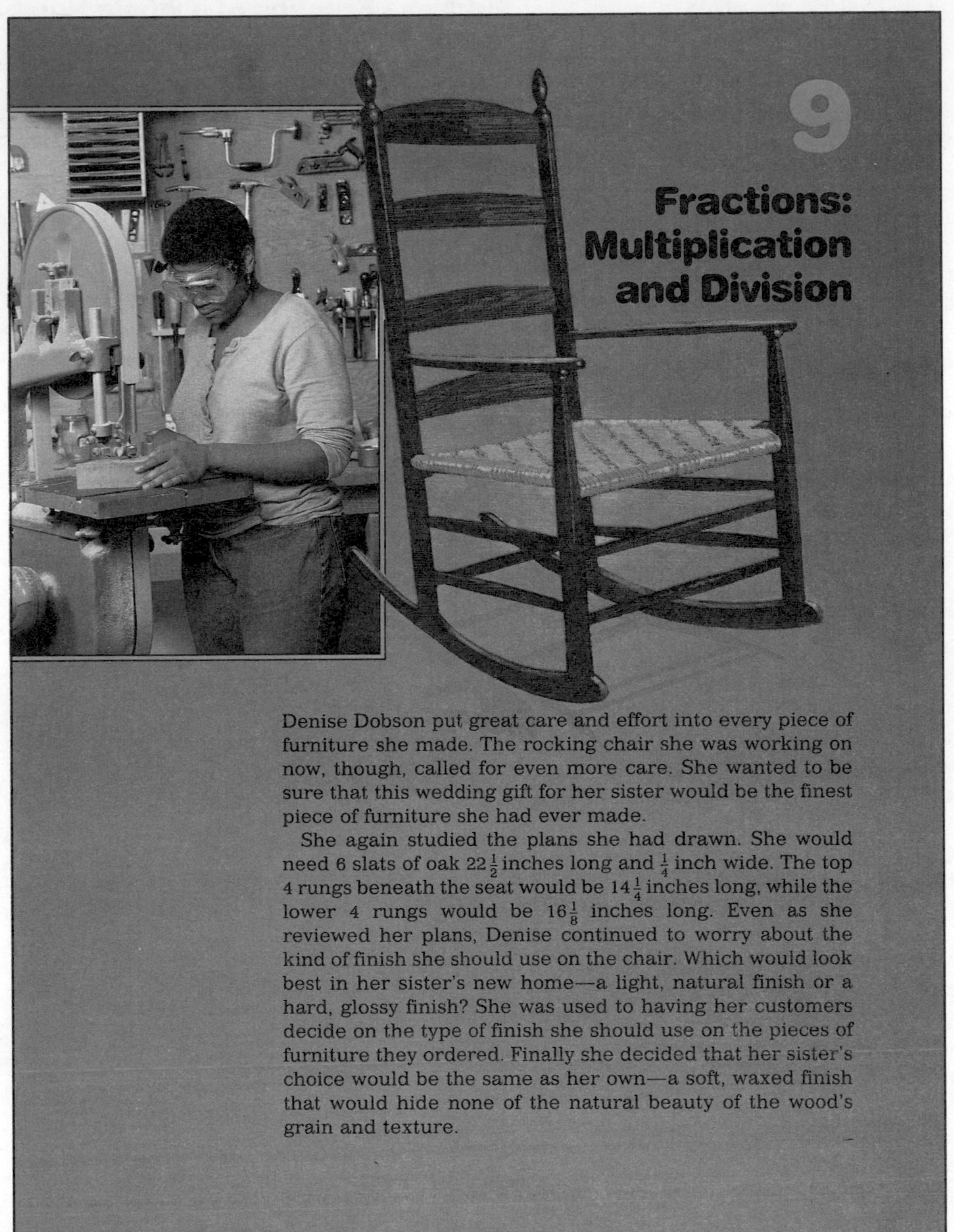

9
Fractions:
Multiplication
and Division
Denise Dobson put great care and effort into every piece of furniture she made. The rocking chair she was working on now, though, called for even more care. She wanted to be sure that this wedding gift for her sister would be the finest piece of furniture she had ever made.
She again studied the plans she had drawn. She would need 6 slats of oak $22\frac{1}{2}$ inches long and $\frac{1}{4}$ inch wide. The top 4 rungs beneath the seat would be $14\frac{1}{4}$ inches long, while the lower 4 rungs would be $16\frac{1}{8}$ inches long. Even as she reviewed her plans, Denise continued to worry about the kind of finish she should use on the chair. Which would look best in her sister's new home—a light, natural finish or a hard, glossy finish? She was used to having her customers decide on the type of finish she should use on the pieces of furniture they ordered. Finally she decided that her sister's choice would be the same as her own—a soft, waxed finish that would hide none of the natural beauty of the wood's grain and texture.


## Introducing the Chapter

**Discussion** Explain to students that in this chapter they will learn more about multiplying and dividing with fractions. Then encourage students to discuss any experiences they, their friends, or their relatives may have had in woodworking or other handicrafts. You might want to note that many schools offer classes in woodworking (often called "shop"). Give students an opportunity to read the story and examine the art. Then ask them to create questions based on the data in the story. You may want to refer to this page as you teach the chapter, and pose the problems suggested below.

## Follow-Up Questions

**After Page 227** Julio bought a case of 24 squares of wood tiling. He used $\frac{3}{4}$ of the case. How many squares did he use? (18)

**After Page 231** Margaret had $\frac{7}{8}$ of a can of oak stain. She used $\frac{1}{2}$ of that amount to stain a bookcase. What fraction of a can did she use for the bookcase? $\left(\frac{7}{16}\text{ of a can}\right)$

**After Page 237** Jared needed $1\frac{5}{8}$ yards of canvas to make a hammock. What is the decimal for $1\frac{5}{8}$? (1.625)

**After Page 243** Leslie Ann wants to cut a board that is $6\frac{3}{4}$ feet long into 9 pieces of the same length. How long will each piece be? $\left(\frac{3}{4}\text{ foot}\right)$

# Fractions

**Quick Review** As an oral drill, students give these quotients as quickly as possible.

12 ÷ 3 16 ÷ 4 72 ÷ 9 56 ÷ 8 15 ÷ 3 20 ÷ 5 45 ÷ 9
80 ÷ 8 24 ÷ 2 63 ÷ 7 27 ÷ 9 48 ÷ 8 54 ÷ 6

**Lesson Focus** To find a fraction of a whole number

**Suggested Materials** Egg carton, counters

## Ideas for Getting Started

Tell students that there is a counter in each of the sections of an egg carton. "Suppose you take half of the counters. How many will you take?" (6) "Suppose I give someone $\frac{1}{3}$ of the counters. How many is this?" (4) "If $\frac{1}{4}$ of the objects are removed, how many is this?" (3)

If students have difficulty with these questions, show them how to divide the egg carton into halves, thirds, and fourths in order to decide how many counters would be selected for $\frac{1}{2}$, $\frac{1}{3}$ and $\frac{1}{4}$. "How many objects would I give you if I give you $\frac{1}{6}$ of the counters?" (2) Ask for volunteers to show that $\frac{1}{6}$ of 12 is 2.

## Using Page 226

**Motivational Problem** As you read and discuss the problem at the top of the page with students, have them state the question in their own words. (How many of the dimes are Liberty Heads?) Then have them describe the data needed to solve the problem. (There are 24 dimes; $\frac{1}{3}$ of the dimes are Liberty Head dimes.) Ask students how they could use the available data to find the answer to the problem. (Since $\frac{1}{3}$ of the dimes are Liberty Heads, we must find $\frac{1}{3}$ of 24.)

**Lesson Development** Focus attention on the 24 dimes in Janet's collection. Remind students that to find out how many dimes are in $\frac{1}{3}$, we divide the 24 dimes into three parts. There are 8 dimes in each of these parts. Emphasize the idea that to find $\frac{1}{3}$ of 24 we divide 24 by 3.

Then look at the second part of the example. Help students see that we can find $\frac{2}{3}$ of the total amount by doubling $\frac{1}{3}$. Illustrate this using the picture of the 24 dimes.

**Other Examples** Review the units given in each of these examples as necessary. If students are not familiar with foot and inch units, show a foot ruler and demonstrate the meaning of each unit on the chalkboard.

**Warm Up** Students should have little difficulty with the exercises that involve a unit fraction such as $\frac{1}{2}$, $\frac{1}{3}$, $\frac{1}{4}$, and so on. Observe students' work in exercises 2, 4, 7, 8, 11, and 12 to make sure that they first divide by the denominator of the fraction and then multiply by the numerator. Use phrases such as "$\frac{4}{5}$ of a number is four times $\frac{1}{5}$ of a number."

## Finding a Fraction of a Whole Number

Each page of Janet's coin collection book holds 24 dimes. On one full page $\frac{1}{3}$ of the dimes are Liberty Heads. How many are Liberty Heads?

$\frac{1}{3}$ **of 24 is 8.**

We write: $\frac{1}{3} \times 24 = 8$ ← To find $\frac{1}{3}$ of a number, divide the number by 3.

8 of the 24 dimes are Liberty Head dimes.

The remaining $\frac{2}{3}$ of the dimes on the page in Janet's book are Roosevelt dimes. How many are Roosevelt dimes?

$\frac{2}{3}$ **of 24 is 16.** We write: $\frac{2}{3} \times 24 = 16$ ← To find $\frac{2}{3}$ of a number, divide by 3 and multiply the result by 2.

16 of the dimes are Roosevelt dimes.

**Other Examples**

| 1 hour = 60 minutes | 1 dozen = 12 | 1 foot = 12 inches |
|---|---|---|
| $\frac{1}{2}$ of 60 is 30. | $\frac{3}{4}$ of 12 is 9. | $\frac{1}{4}$ of 12 is 3. |
| $\frac{1}{2} \times 60 = 30$ | $\frac{3}{4} \times 12 = 9$ | $\frac{1}{4} \times 12 = 3$ |

**Warm Up** Find the fraction of the number.

1. $\frac{1}{3} \times 18$ 6
2. $\frac{2}{3} \times 18$ 12
3. $\frac{1}{4} \times 24$ 6
4. $\frac{3}{4} \times 24$ 18
5. $\frac{1}{2} \times 10$ 5
6. $\frac{1}{5} \times 25$ 5
7. $\frac{3}{5} \times 25$ 15
8. $\frac{4}{5} \times 25$ 20
9. $\frac{1}{2} \times 16$ 8
10. $\frac{1}{4} \times 16$ 4
11. $\frac{3}{10} \times 50$ 15
12. $\frac{7}{8} \times 24$ 21



## Follow Up

### Reteaching

Illustrate for students the algorithm for finding a fraction of a whole number by representing the whole number with models and showing how to find a fractional part. For instance, to find $\frac{3}{4}$ of 12, begin by grouping 12 models in 4 sets to show that $\frac{1}{4}$ of 12 is 3. Then put the groups together to demonstrate first that $\frac{2}{4}$ of 12 is 6 and then that $\frac{3}{4}$ of 12 is 9. Using this approach can help students understand why in fraction multiplication, unlike whole number multiplication, the product of two fractions is smaller than either factor.

### Enrichment

Instruct students to fold an unruled $8\frac{1}{2}''$ by 11″ paper in half three times in the length and width. The result will be an 8 by 8 array. Then have students use this model to identify the following:

- the product of the array **64**
- $\frac{1}{2}$ of 64 **32**
- $\frac{1}{4}$ of 64 **16**
- $\frac{1}{8}$ of 64 **8**
- $\frac{1}{16}$ of 64 **4**
- $\frac{1}{32}$ of 64 **2**
- $\frac{1}{64}$ of 64 **1**
- $\frac{3}{4}$ of 64 **48**

| Assignment Guide | Minimum | Average | Extended |
|---|---|---|---|
| page 227 | 1–28 | 1–29, TM | 1–30, TM |

Find the fraction of the number.

1.

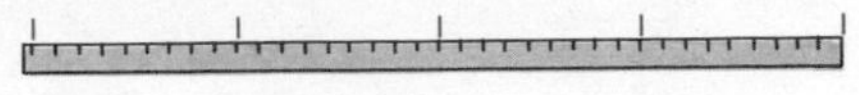

yardstick

1 yard = 36 inches

$\frac{1}{4} \times 36 = ■$ 9

2.

1 qt 1 qt 1 qt 1 qt 1 gallon

4 qt (quarts) = 1 gallon

$\frac{3}{4} \times 4 = ■$ 3

**3.** $\frac{1}{2} \times 20$ 10 **4.** $\frac{3}{4} \times 36$ 27 **5.** $\frac{1}{3} \times 12$ 4 **6.** $\frac{2}{3} \times 9$ 6

**7.** $\frac{1}{8} \times 32$ 4 **8.** $\frac{3}{8} \times 32$ 12 **9.** $\frac{1}{10} \times 40$ 4 **10.** $\frac{2}{5} \times 25$ 10

**11.** $\frac{3}{10} \times 60$ 18 **12.** $\frac{1}{7} \times 28$ 4 **13.** $\frac{5}{6} \times 30$ 25 **14.** $\frac{4}{5} \times 40$ 32

**15.** $\frac{7}{8} \times 24$ 21 **16.** $\frac{1}{4} \times 100$ 25 **17.** $\frac{1}{5} \times 100$ 20 **18.** $\frac{5}{8} \times 40$ 25

**19.** $\frac{2}{3} \times 12$ 8 **20.** $\frac{5}{6} \times 18$ 15 **21.** $\frac{1}{6} \times 18$ 3 **22.** $\frac{9}{10} \times 50$ 45

**23.** $\frac{1}{3} \times 27$ 9 **24.** $\frac{7}{10} \times 100$ 70 **25.** $\frac{2}{7} \times 35$ 10 **26.** $\frac{3}{5} \times 100$ 60

**27.** On one page of a coin collection book $\frac{3}{8}$ of the 24 coins are Indian Head pennies. How many Indian Head pennies are on the page? 9

**28.** Jeremy's coin collection book has spaces for 24 coins on each of its 8 pages. The book is $\frac{5}{6}$ full. How many coins are in Jeremy's book? 160

**29.** Denise has a coin book for nickels with spaces for 30 nickels on each of its 8 pages. She also has a book for dimes. It has spaces for 36 dimes on each of 6 pages. Her nickel book is $\frac{5}{8}$ full and her dime book is $\frac{3}{4}$ full. Does Denise have more nickels or more dimes? How many more? 12 more dimes

**30.** **DATA HUNT** Suppose you have $\frac{1}{4}$ of a **score** of nickels and $\frac{2}{3}$ of a **gross** of dimes. How much money do you have? (Use a dictionary if necessary.) $9.85

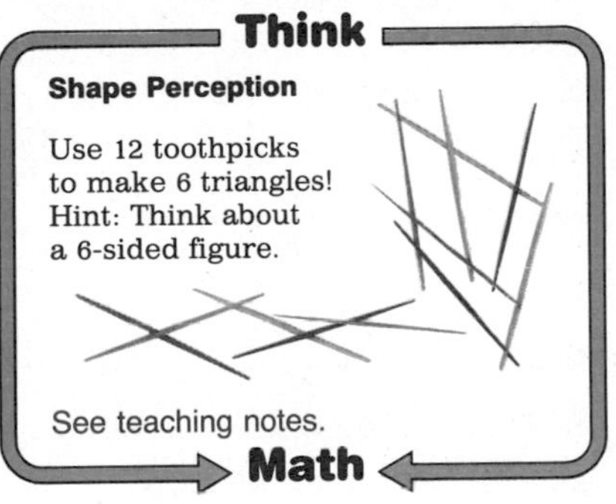

Think
Shape Perception
Use 12 toothpicks to make 6 triangles! Hint: Think about a 6-sided figure.
See teaching notes.
Math




## Using Page 227

**Exercises 1–26** Introduce the yard, inch, quart, and gallon units. For more detailed information on these units, see Chapter 16. If students have difficulty with these exercises, refer back to sets of objects and review the procedure of partitioning the sets and counting the objects in each new set.

**Exercises 27–29** These exercises are a direct application of the procedure practiced in exercises 1–26.

**Data Hunt** For this exercise students may need to go to an outside source to find the meaning of terms in the problem in order to determine what numbers to use in solving it.

**Think Math** Encourage students to experiment with placement of the toothpicks. Some students may place them as shown below and find that they need one more toothpick. Give hints, as necessary, to help break out of this pattern.

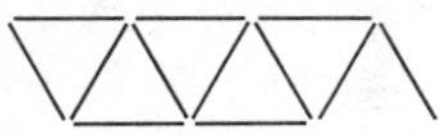

The correct placement is shown below.

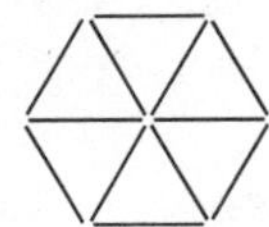

## Ideas That Work

### Chalk It Up

Have students complete this puzzle by adding and subtracting mixed numbers.

| | | | | |
|---|---|---|---|---|
| 1. 6 | $\frac{5}{6}$ | | 2. 7 | $\frac{1}{4}$ |
| $\frac{1}{2}$ | | 3. 7 | $\frac{11}{24}$ | |
| | 4. 4 | $\frac{2}{9}$ | | 5. 1 |
| 6. 7 | $\frac{7}{30}$ | | 7. 7 | 0 |
| $\frac{19}{30}$ | | 8. 1 | 4 | $\frac{1}{36}$ |

**Across**

1. $4\frac{1}{3} + 2\frac{1}{2}$
2. $10\frac{3}{4} - 3\frac{1}{2}$
3. $12\frac{7}{8} - 5\frac{5}{12}$
4. $2\frac{2}{3} + 1\frac{5}{9}$
6. $15\frac{9}{10} - 8\frac{2}{3}$
7. $43\frac{2}{5} + 26\frac{3}{5}$
8. $14\frac{5}{12} - \frac{7}{18}$

**Down**

1. $8\frac{3}{5} - 2\frac{1}{10}$
2. $18\frac{5}{6} - 11\frac{3}{8}$
3. $2\frac{1}{3} + 4\frac{8}{9}$
4. $3\frac{1}{15} + 1\frac{1}{6}$
5. $6\frac{1}{4} + 3\frac{7}{9}$
6. $3\frac{3}{10} + 4\frac{1}{3}$
7. $34\frac{1}{8} + 39\frac{7}{8}$

**Practice Supplement,** page 86

Name ______________________ To follow text page 227

**Finding a Fraction of a Whole Number**

Find the fraction of the number.

| | | |
|---|---|---|
| 1. $\frac{3}{4} \times 20 =$ 15 | 2. $\frac{1}{2} \times 26 =$ 13 | 3. $\frac{2}{5} \times 10 =$ 4 |
| 4. $\frac{1}{3} \times 18 =$ 6 | 5. $\frac{5}{6} \times 24 =$ 20 | 6. $\frac{1}{7} \times 14 =$ 2 |
| 7. $\frac{3}{8} \times 32 =$ 12 | 8. $\frac{2}{3} \times 18 =$ 12 | 9. $\frac{5}{9} \times 27 =$ 15 |
| 10. $\frac{1}{4} \times 16 =$ 4 | 11. $\frac{2}{9} \times 45 =$ 10 | 12. $\frac{1}{5} \times 100 =$ 20 |
| 13. $\frac{4}{7} \times 28 =$ 16 | 14. $\frac{1}{8} \times 64 =$ 8 | 15. $\frac{1}{2} \times 44 =$ 22 |
| 16. $\frac{1}{10} \times 80 =$ 8 | 17. $\frac{3}{5} \times 30 =$ 18 | 18. $\frac{1}{6} \times 42 =$ 7 |
| 19. $\frac{7}{8} \times 24 =$ 21 | 20. $\frac{3}{4} \times 100 =$ 75 | 21. $\frac{5}{7} \times 35 =$ 25 |
| 22. $\frac{4}{5} \times 20 =$ 16 | 23. $\frac{2}{7} \times 21 =$ 6 | 24. $\frac{1}{4} \times 28 =$ 7 |
| 25. $\frac{2}{3} \times 66 =$ 44 | 26. $\frac{1}{9} \times 36 =$ 4 | 27. $\frac{3}{7} \times 42 =$ 18 |
| 28. $\frac{5}{8} \times 80 =$ 50 | 29. $\frac{1}{2} \times 100 =$ 50 | 30. $\frac{4}{9} \times 54 =$ 24 |
| 31. $\frac{5}{6} \times 18 =$ 15 | 32. $\frac{6}{7} \times 49 =$ 42 | 33. $\frac{7}{10} \times 90 =$ 63 |
| 34. $\frac{5}{9} \times 36 =$ 20 | 35. $\frac{3}{8} \times 72 =$ 27 | 36. $\frac{2}{5} \times 35 =$ 14 |

# Fractions: Multiplication

**Quick Review** As an oral drill, students give these products as quickly as possible.

$4 \times 3$ $7 \times 8$ $4 \times 9$ $6 \times 6$ $8 \times 5$ $7 \times 9$ $3 \times 5$ $8 \times 6$
$7 \times 7$ $9 \times 6$ $6 \times 8$ $7 \times 6$ $9 \times 7$ $8 \times 8$ $6 \times 9$
$7 \times 3$ $9 \times 8$ $5 \times 9$ $4 \times 8$ $3 \times 6$ $5 \times 7$ $4 \times 7$

**Lesson Focus** To multiply two fractions

**Suggested Materials** Paper for folding

## Ideas for Getting Started

Have students fold a piece of paper twice so that it is divided vertically into fourths. "How many parts are marked?" (4) Focus on one of the parts and ask: "What part of the paper is this?" $\left(\frac{1}{4}\right)$ Then have students fold the paper in half horizontally. Ask them to shade $\frac{1}{2}$ of $\frac{1}{4}$ as you write "$\frac{1}{2}$ of $\frac{1}{4}$" on the chalkboard. Below this write $\frac{1}{2} \times \frac{1}{4}$. Then have students count the number of parts shaded and compare this with the number of parts in all. Complete the equation $\frac{1}{2} \times \frac{1}{4} = \frac{1}{8}$.

## Using Page 228

**Motivational Problem** Read the information at the top of the page with students. Relate each statement to the picture below. "What question are we asked about the carrot cake?" (How much of the whole cake did Jeff's sister get?) Be sure students understand that we want to know how much of the original whole cake Jeff's sister got. "How can we find the amount?" (Either count the parts or find the product of $\frac{1}{2} \times \frac{3}{4}$.)

**Lesson Development** Point out that there are 3 of the original 8 parts left. Thus Jeff's sister received $\frac{3}{8}$ of the cake. Tell students that the answer could be found by multiplying $\frac{1}{2} \times \frac{3}{4}$. Write this problem on the chalkboard and work through the process described by the instruction boxes. Be sure students understand that the example with the cake suggests the same procedure as the rules described for multiplying fractions.

**Other Examples** As you work through the other examples, encourage students to help you reduce fractions to lowest terms or write improper fractions as mixed numbers whenever possible. Point out that $12 \times \frac{2}{3}$ is the same as $\frac{2}{3} \times 12$. Review the procedure students used on pages 226 and 227. Then tell them that 12 can be written as $\frac{12}{1}$ and the product can be found using the rules described above.

Give special emphasis to the example explaining that two numbers whose product is 1 are *reciprocals* of each other. Have students give the reciprocal of $\frac{2}{3}$, $\frac{7}{4}$, 2, $\frac{1}{3}$, and 1.

**Warm Up** Errors with these problems might be caused by difficulties with basic facts or by confusion with addition. Be alert for students who may write the fractions with a common denominator or confuse the multiplication process with the addition process.

## Multiplying Fractions

Jeff found $\frac{3}{4}$ of a whole carrot cake on the table.

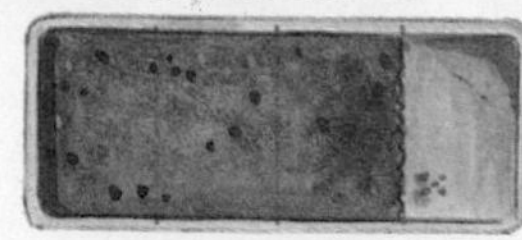

He saved $\frac{1}{2}$ of it for his sister.

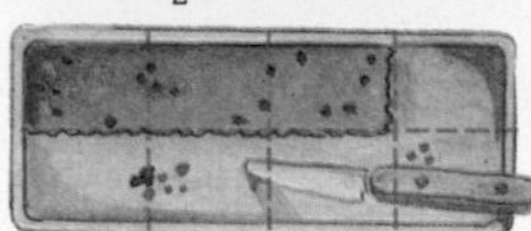

How much of the whole cake did Jeff's sister get?

The picture shows that $\frac{1}{2}$ of $\frac{3}{4}$ of the cake is $\frac{3}{8}$ of the whole cake. This suggests the following way to multiply two fractions.

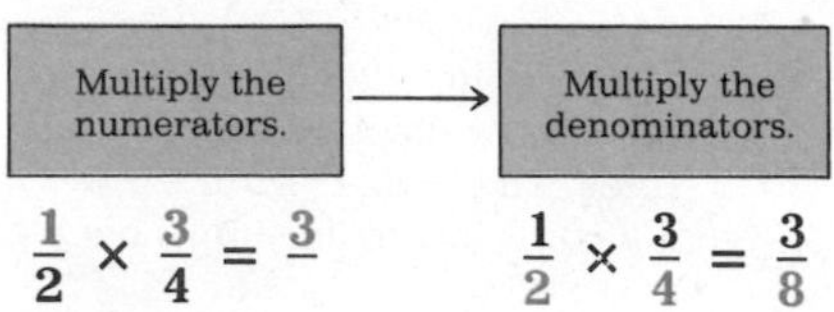


$$\frac{1}{2} \times \frac{3}{4} = \frac{3}{\phantom{8}} \qquad \frac{1}{2} \times \frac{3}{4} = \frac{3}{8}$$

Jeff's sister received $\frac{3}{8}$ of the whole cake.

**Other Examples**

$\frac{2}{3} \times \frac{7}{4} = \frac{14}{12} = 1\frac{2}{12} = 1\frac{1}{6}$ $\quad 12 \times \frac{2}{3} = \frac{12}{1} \times \frac{2}{3} = \frac{24}{3} = 8$ $\quad \frac{3}{5} \times \frac{5}{3} = \frac{15}{15} = 1$

Two numbers whose product is 1 are **reciprocals** of each other.

**Warm Up** Multiply.

1. $\frac{1}{2} \times \frac{1}{3}$ $\frac{1}{6}$
2. $\frac{2}{5} \times \frac{2}{3}$ $\frac{4}{15}$
3. $\frac{3}{4} \times \frac{5}{3}$ $\frac{15}{12} = 1\frac{1}{4}$
4. $\frac{5}{8} \times \frac{8}{5}$ $\frac{40}{40} = 1$
5. $\frac{4}{5} \times \frac{1}{4}$ $\frac{4}{20} = \frac{1}{5}$
6. $12 \times \frac{2}{3}$ $\frac{24}{3} = 8$
7. $3 \times \frac{1}{3}$ $\frac{3}{3} = 1$
8. $\frac{9}{10} \times \frac{3}{10}$ $\frac{27}{100}$
9. $\frac{4}{3} \times 9$ $\frac{36}{3} = 12$
10. $3 \times \frac{2}{3}$ $\frac{6}{3} = 2$
11. Which of exercises 1–10 show numbers that are reciprocals of each other? 4, 7

228

## Follow Up

### Reteaching

Draw a unit region and divide it horizontally into thirds. Then shade 2 of the thirds. Next divide the unit region vertically into fourths and shade 3 of the fourths.

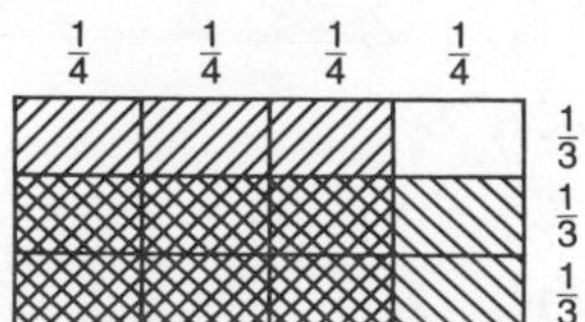


Count the number of equal parts the unit region is partitioned into and determine the number of parts that are shaded twice. Since there are 12 parts and 6 are shaded twice, $\frac{3}{4} \times \frac{2}{3} = \frac{6}{12}$ or $\frac{1}{2}$.

### Enrichment

Write several multiplication equations on the chalkboard. Have students use graph paper to illustrate the whole unit according to the fractional parts being multiplied. For example: $\frac{1}{2} \times \frac{1}{3}$.

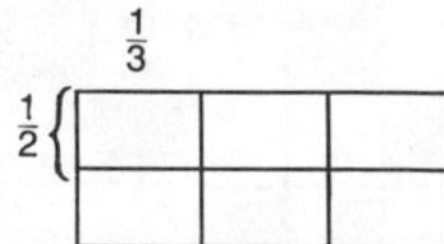


The students can then shade the product of $\frac{1}{2} \times \frac{1}{3}$ $\left(\frac{1}{6}\right)$ with colored pencils.

| Assignment Guide | | | |
|---|---|---|---|
| | Minimum | Average | Extended |
| page 229 | 1–39 | 1–40 | 1–41 |



Multiply. Reduce to lowest terms.

1. $\frac{2}{5} \times \frac{1}{3}$ $\frac{2}{15}$
2. $\frac{1}{2} \times \frac{1}{4}$ $\frac{1}{8}$
3. $\frac{3}{4} \times \frac{7}{8}$ $\frac{21}{32}$
4. $\frac{2}{3} \times 9$ 6
5. $\frac{5}{6} \times \frac{2}{3}$ $\frac{5}{9}$
6. $\frac{2}{3} \times 36$ 24
7. $\frac{2}{3} \times \frac{3}{5}$ $\frac{2}{5}$
8. $\frac{7}{4} \times \frac{3}{2}$ $2\frac{5}{8}$
9. $\frac{4}{5} \times \frac{5}{4}$ 1
10. $\frac{3}{4} \times \frac{1}{3}$ $\frac{1}{4}$
11. $4 \times \frac{3}{5}$ $2\frac{2}{5}$
12. $\frac{3}{5} \times \frac{7}{10}$ $\frac{21}{50}$
13. $\frac{3}{4} \times 32$ 24
14. $\frac{3}{8} \times \frac{4}{5}$ $\frac{3}{10}$
15. $\frac{1}{6} \times \frac{6}{7}$ $\frac{1}{7}$
16. $\frac{1}{10} \times \frac{9}{10}$ $\frac{9}{100}$
17. $\frac{7}{3} \times \frac{1}{2}$ $1\frac{1}{6}$
18. $\frac{1}{4} \times 48$ 12
19. $\frac{4}{3} \times \frac{5}{2}$ $3\frac{1}{3}$
20. $20 \times \frac{2}{5}$ 8
21. $\frac{3}{8} \times \frac{8}{3}$ 1
22. $\frac{5}{6} \times \frac{3}{4}$ $\frac{5}{8}$
23. $\frac{5}{8} \times \frac{2}{3}$ $\frac{5}{12}$
24. $6 \times \frac{1}{6}$ 1
25. $\frac{7}{8} \times 4$ $3\frac{1}{2}$
26. $\frac{2}{5} \times \frac{3}{4}$ $\frac{3}{10}$
27. $\frac{5}{8} \times 4$ $2\frac{1}{2}$
28. $\frac{1}{3} \times \frac{3}{5}$ $\frac{1}{5}$
29. $6 \times \frac{2}{3}$ 4
30. $\frac{5}{6} \times \frac{3}{10}$ $\frac{1}{4}$
31. Which of exercises 1–30 show numbers that are reciprocals of each other? 9, 21, 24

Give the reciprocal of each number.

32. $\frac{2}{3}$ $\frac{3}{2}$
33. $\frac{1}{2}$ 2
34. 4 $\frac{1}{4}$
35. $\frac{7}{5}$ $\frac{5}{7}$
36. 5 $\frac{1}{5}$
37. $\frac{3}{4}$ $\frac{4}{3}$
38. 8 $\frac{1}{8}$

39. Vicky's recipe called for $\frac{3}{4}$ cup of flour. How much flour should she use to make $\frac{1}{2}$ of the recipe? $\frac{3}{8}$ cup

40. Chano worked in the bakery 7 hours Friday and $\frac{3}{5}$ that long Saturday. How many hours did he work in all? $11\frac{1}{5}$ h

41. Tell what data in this problem is not needed. Then solve.
Whole wheat bread takes $\frac{2}{3}$ hour to bake. It takes gingerbread $\frac{3}{4}$ as long. Blueberry muffins take $\frac{5}{8}$ as long. How long does it take gingerbread to bake?
Time it takes to bake blueberry muffins; $\frac{1}{2}$ h

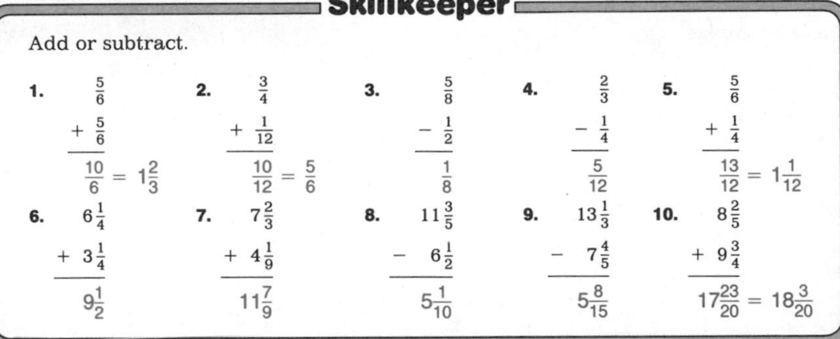

**Skillkeeper**

Add or subtract.

1. $\frac{5}{6} + \frac{5}{6} = \frac{10}{6} = 1\frac{2}{3}$
2. $\frac{3}{4} + \frac{1}{12} = \frac{10}{12} = \frac{5}{6}$
3. $\frac{5}{8} - \frac{1}{2} = \frac{1}{8}$
4. $\frac{2}{3} - \frac{1}{4} = \frac{5}{12}$
5. $\frac{5}{6} + \frac{1}{4} = \frac{13}{12} = 1\frac{1}{12}$
6. $6\frac{1}{4} + 3\frac{1}{4} = 9\frac{1}{2}$
7. $7\frac{2}{3} + 4\frac{1}{9} = 11\frac{7}{9}$
8. $11\frac{3}{5} - 6\frac{1}{2} = 5\frac{1}{10}$
9. $13\frac{1}{3} - 7\frac{4}{5} = 5\frac{8}{15}$
10. $8\frac{2}{5} + 9\frac{3}{4} = 17\frac{23}{20} = 18\frac{3}{20}$



## Using Page 229

**Exercises 1–30** Exercises such as 4, 6 and 24 allow students to use either procedure they have learned to find the products. Be sure they understand that in exercise 4, 9 can be written as $\frac{9}{1}$ so that numerators can be multiplied by numerators and denominators can be multiplied by denominators. Remind students to reduce all products to lowest terms.

**Exercises 31–38** Remind students that reciprocals are numbers whose product is 1. Students may think of finding the reciprocal of a number as "interchanging the numerator and denominator of the number." Regardless of the procedure used, have students verify that any number times its reciprocal gives the product 1.

**Exercise 41** Note that this exercise requires students to identify data that is not needed to solve the problem. Point out that often in everyday problem-solving experiences, needed data must be selected from a collection of data.

**Skillkeeper** These skills were originally taught in Chapter 8.

**Reteaching Supplement,** page 52

Name ________ To follow text page 229

**Multiplying Fractions**

Multiply the numerators. → Multiply the denominators.

5 × 3 = 15

$\frac{5}{8} \times \frac{3}{4} = \frac{15}{\ }$ $\frac{5}{8} \times \frac{3}{4} = \frac{15}{32}$

8 × 4 = 32

Multiply. Reduce to lowest terms.

Reduce to lowest terms.

1. $\frac{1}{5} \times \frac{2}{3} = \frac{2}{15}$ (5 × 3)
2. $\frac{3}{8} \times 16 = \frac{3}{8} \times \frac{16}{1} = \frac{48}{8} =$ 6
3. $\frac{2}{3} \times \frac{1}{4} = \frac{2}{12} = \frac{1}{6}$
4. $\frac{3}{8} \times \frac{1}{2} = \frac{3}{16}$
5. $\frac{3}{5} \times 15 = \frac{45}{5} = 9$
6. $\frac{3}{10} \times \frac{1}{2} = \frac{3}{20}$
7. $\frac{3}{4} \times \frac{3}{4} = \frac{9}{16}$
8. $\frac{2}{9} \times \frac{3}{4} = \frac{6}{36} = \frac{1}{6}$
9. $\frac{4}{3} \times \frac{3}{2} = \frac{12}{6} = 2$
10. $\frac{7}{10} \times 20 = \frac{140}{10} = 14$
11. $\frac{4}{5} \times \frac{5}{6} = \frac{20}{30} = \frac{2}{3}$
12. $\frac{5}{8} \times \frac{5}{2} = \frac{25}{16} = 1\frac{9}{16}$
13. $24 \times \frac{5}{6} = \frac{120}{6} = 20$
14. $\frac{5}{8} \times \frac{8}{5} = \frac{40}{40} = 1$
15. $\frac{9}{10} \times \frac{2}{3} = \frac{18}{30} = \frac{3}{5}$
16. $\frac{1}{6} \times \frac{1}{4} = \frac{1}{24}$
17. $\frac{12}{3} \times \frac{1}{2} = \frac{12}{6} = 2$
18. $\frac{1}{4} \times \frac{8}{3} = \frac{8}{12} = \frac{2}{3}$
19. $\frac{7}{10} \times \frac{10}{1} = \frac{70}{10} = 7$
20. $\frac{2}{5} \times \frac{5}{8} = \frac{10}{40} = \frac{1}{4}$
21. $\frac{1}{6} \times 36 = \frac{36}{6} = 6$
22. $\frac{9}{10} \times \frac{1}{3} = \frac{9}{30} = \frac{3}{10}$
23. $\frac{3}{5} \times \frac{4}{3} = \frac{12}{15} = \frac{4}{5}$
24. $\frac{1}{2} \times \frac{1}{2} = \frac{1}{4}$
25. $\frac{3}{10} \times \frac{2}{3} = \frac{6}{30} = \frac{1}{5}$
26. $\frac{5}{4} \times \frac{2}{5} = \frac{10}{20} = \frac{1}{2}$
27. $30 \times \frac{2}{3} = \frac{60}{3} = 20$
28. $\frac{10}{3} \times \frac{3}{5} = \frac{30}{15} = 2$
29. $\frac{7}{4} \times \frac{3}{7} = \frac{21}{28} = \frac{3}{4}$
30. $\frac{1}{2} \times \frac{4}{5} = \frac{4}{10} = \frac{2}{5}$
31. $\frac{1}{3} \times \frac{3}{4} = \frac{3}{12} = \frac{1}{4}$
32. $\frac{3}{5} \times \frac{5}{9} = \frac{15}{45} = \frac{1}{3}$

**Enrichment Supplement,** page 52

Name ________ To follow text page 229

**Fraction Pairs**

Use the numbers 1 through 8 to write two fractions with the given product and sum. You can use each digit as many times as you need.

1 2 3 4 5 6 7 8

1. Product: $\frac{6}{49}$ Sum: $\frac{5}{7}$ — $\frac{2}{7}$ and $\frac{3}{7}$
2. Product: $\frac{3}{32}$ Sum: $\frac{5}{8}$ — $\frac{1}{4}$ and $\frac{3}{8}$
3. Product: $\frac{1}{5}$ Sum: $\frac{9}{10}$ — $\frac{1}{2}$ and $\frac{2}{5}$
4. Product: $\frac{1}{9}$ Sum: $\frac{5}{6}$ — $\frac{2}{3}$ and $\frac{1}{6}$
5. Product: $\frac{1}{6}$ Sum: $\frac{11}{12}$ — $\frac{2}{3}$ and $\frac{1}{4}$
6. Product: $\frac{1}{16}$ Sum: $\frac{13}{24}$ — $\frac{3}{8}$ and $\frac{1}{6}$
7. Product: $\frac{4}{35}$ Sum: $\frac{27}{35}$ — $\frac{4}{7}$ and $\frac{1}{5}$
8. Product: $\frac{1}{10}$ Sum: $\frac{13}{20}$ — $\frac{2}{5}$ and $\frac{1}{4}$

**Practice Supplement,** page 87

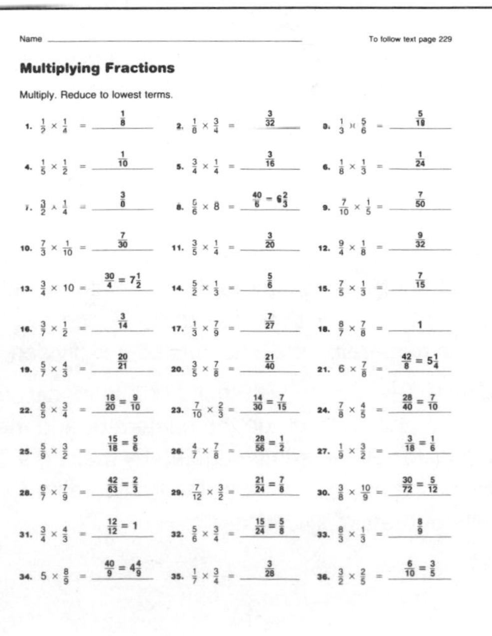

Name ________ To follow text page 229

**Multiplying Fractions**

Multiply. Reduce to lowest terms.

1. $\frac{1}{2} \times \frac{1}{4} = \frac{1}{8}$
2. $\frac{1}{8} \times \frac{3}{4} = \frac{3}{32}$
3. $\frac{1}{3} \times \frac{5}{6} = \frac{5}{18}$
4. $\frac{1}{5} \times \frac{1}{2} = \frac{1}{10}$
5. $\frac{3}{4} \times \frac{1}{4} = \frac{3}{16}$
6. $\frac{1}{8} \times \frac{1}{3} = \frac{1}{24}$
7. $\frac{3}{2} \times \frac{1}{4} = \frac{3}{8}$
8. $\frac{5}{6} \times 8 = \frac{40}{6} = 6\frac{2}{3}$
9. $\frac{7}{10} \times \frac{1}{5} = \frac{7}{50}$
10. $\frac{7}{3} \times \frac{1}{10} = \frac{7}{30}$
11. $\frac{3}{5} \times \frac{1}{4} = \frac{3}{20}$
12. $\frac{9}{4} \times \frac{1}{8} = \frac{9}{32}$
13. $\frac{3}{4} \times 10 = \frac{30}{4} = 7\frac{1}{2}$
14. $\frac{5}{2} \times \frac{1}{3} = \frac{5}{6}$
15. $\frac{7}{5} \times \frac{1}{3} = \frac{7}{15}$
16. $\frac{3}{7} \times \frac{1}{2} = \frac{3}{14}$
17. $\frac{1}{3} \times \frac{7}{9} = \frac{7}{27}$
18. $\frac{8}{7} \times \frac{7}{8} = 1$
19. $\frac{5}{7} \times \frac{4}{3} = \frac{20}{21}$
20. $\frac{3}{5} \times \frac{7}{8} = \frac{21}{40}$
21. $6 \times \frac{7}{8} = \frac{42}{8} = 5\frac{1}{4}$
22. $\frac{6}{5} \times \frac{3}{4} = \frac{18}{20} = \frac{9}{10}$
23. $\frac{7}{10} \times \frac{2}{3} = \frac{14}{30} = \frac{7}{15}$
24. $\frac{7}{8} \times \frac{4}{5} = \frac{28}{40} = \frac{7}{10}$
25. $\frac{5}{9} \times \frac{3}{2} = \frac{15}{18} = \frac{5}{6}$
26. $\frac{4}{7} \times \frac{7}{8} = \frac{28}{56} = \frac{1}{2}$
27. $\frac{1}{9} \times \frac{3}{2} = \frac{3}{18} = \frac{1}{6}$
28. $\frac{6}{7} \times \frac{7}{9} = \frac{42}{63} = \frac{2}{3}$
29. $\frac{7}{12} \times \frac{3}{2} = \frac{21}{24} = \frac{7}{8}$
30. $\frac{3}{8} \times \frac{10}{9} = \frac{30}{72} = \frac{5}{12}$
31. $\frac{3}{4} \times \frac{4}{3} = \frac{12}{12} = 1$
32. $\frac{5}{6} \times \frac{3}{4} = \frac{15}{24} = \frac{5}{8}$
33. $\frac{8}{3} \times \frac{1}{3} = \frac{8}{9}$
34. $5 \times \frac{8}{9} = \frac{40}{9} = 4\frac{4}{9}$
35. $\frac{1}{7} \times \frac{3}{4} = \frac{3}{28}$
36. $\frac{3}{2} \times \frac{2}{5} = \frac{6}{10} = \frac{3}{5}$

# Fractions: Multiplication

**Quick Review** Students name the whole number that each fraction equals.

$\frac{15}{3}$ $\frac{8}{4}$ $\frac{35}{7}$ $\frac{7}{1}$ $\frac{16}{8}$ $\frac{18}{3}$ $\frac{6}{1}$ $\frac{90}{10}$ $\frac{45}{9}$ $\frac{36}{4}$ $\frac{21}{3}$ $\frac{56}{8}$

**Lesson Focus** To use a shortcut to multiply two fractions

## Ideas for Getting Started

Give students pairs of problems like the following.

| | | | |
|---|---|---|---|
| $\frac{2}{3} \times \frac{6}{7}$ | $\frac{3}{5} \times \frac{4}{9}$ | $\frac{5}{8} \times \frac{7}{10}$ | $\frac{3}{5} \times \frac{10}{7}$ |
| $\frac{6}{3} \times \frac{2}{7}$ | $\frac{4}{5} \times \frac{3}{9}$ | $\frac{7}{8} \times \frac{5}{10}$ | $\frac{10}{5} \times \frac{3}{7}$ |

Have students find each of the products in lowest terms. They will probably notice that the products are the same for each pair of problems. "Why is this true?" (The problems are the same except that the numerators and denominators have been reversed. Because of the commutative principle, the product is not altered by reversing the numerators.) Then point out that after this reversal, one of the pairs of fractions could have been reduced to minimize the complexity of the multiplication.

## Using Page 230

**Motivational Problem** Have students read the problem at the top of the page. "What question do we want to answer about Jan's ribbon?" (How much ribbon was cut off?) "What data do we have about the ribbon Jan had at the beginning?" (She had $\frac{7}{8}$ of a yard of ribbon.) "What part of this ribbon did she cut off?" $\left(\frac{4}{5}\text{ of it}\right)$ "How can we use this information to find the part of the yard that Jan cut?" $\left(\text{We must multiply to find } \frac{4}{5} \text{ of } \frac{7}{8}.\right)$

**Lesson Development** Write the problem $\frac{4}{5} \times \frac{7}{8}$ on the chalkboard twice. Tell students that there are two ways to solve this problem. Work the problem by multiplying numerators and denominators and reducing the resulting fraction as shown in the first display box. Point out that with this method after the fractions are multiplied, the numerator and denominator of the product are divided by 4 to find the lowest-terms fraction.

Then work through the shortcut shown in the second display box. Explain that this shortcut is based on the idea that $\frac{4}{5} \times \frac{7}{8}$ is the same as $\frac{7}{5} \times \frac{4}{8}$. Put the solution on the chalkboard in the same way as it is shown, dividing 4 by 4, 8 by 4, and then multiplying to find the fraction $\frac{7}{10}$. Be sure students observe that since the factors are smaller when multiplying with the shortcut, the solution to the problem is simpler. Have students read the complete sentence that gives the answer to the original story problem.

**Other Examples** Work through these examples giving special attention to the example in which a numerator and a denominator is divided by 2 and then a numerator and a denominator is divided by 3.

**Warm Up** Errors with these problems can result from forgetting to divide the numerator and the denominator by the same number, by making a basic division error, or by inaccurately recording the results of the simplifications.

## Multiplying Fractions: A Shortcut

Jan had $\frac{7}{8}$ of a yard of ribbon. She cut off $\frac{4}{5}$ of it. How much ribbon was cut off? Here are two ways to find the product.

We can multiply the fractions and then divide the numerator and the denominator by 4.

OR

**Shortcut**

We can divide a numerator and a denominator by 4 and then multiply the fractions.

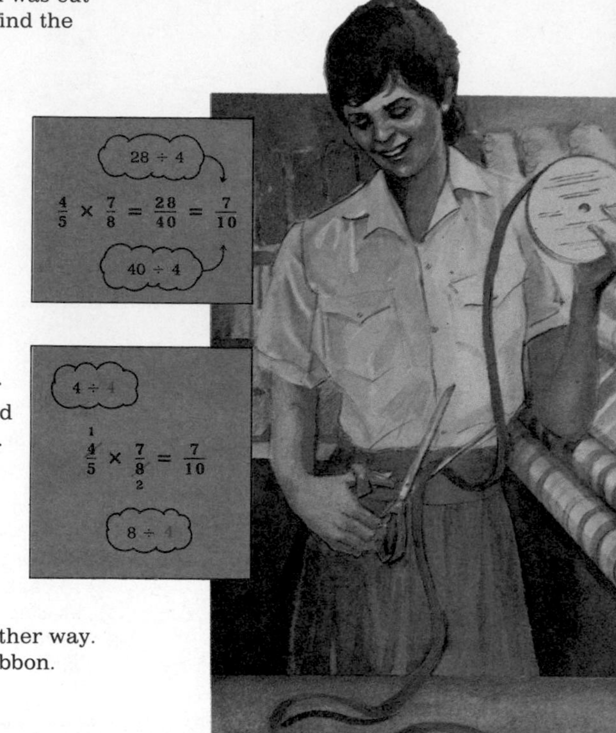

28 ÷ 4
$\frac{4}{5} \times \frac{7}{8} = \frac{28}{40} = \frac{7}{10}$
40 ÷ 4
4 ÷ 4
$\frac{\not{4}^{1}}{5} \times \frac{7}{\not{8}_{2}} = \frac{7}{10}$
8 ÷ 4


The product is the same either way. Jan cut off $\frac{7}{10}$ of a yard of ribbon.

**Other Examples**

$\frac{\not{2}^{1}}{\not{3}_{1}} \times \frac{\not{9}^{3}}{\not{4}_{2}} = \frac{3}{2}$ (Here we use the shortcut twice!)

$\frac{3}{\not{4}_{1}} \times \not{24}^{6} = 18$

**Warm Up** Find the products. Use the shortcut when possible.

1. $\frac{2}{3} \times \frac{5}{8}$ $\frac{5}{12}$
2. $\frac{3}{5} \times \frac{7}{12}$ $\frac{7}{20}$
3. $\frac{3}{8} \times \frac{4}{9}$ $\frac{1}{6}$
4. $\frac{3}{4} \times \frac{5}{6}$ $\frac{5}{8}$
5. $\frac{5}{9} \times \frac{3}{10}$ $\frac{1}{6}$
6. $\frac{5}{8} \times \frac{4}{15}$ $\frac{1}{6}$
7. $\frac{7}{10} \times 80$ 56
8. $\frac{8}{5} \times \frac{9}{12}$ $1\frac{1}{5}$
9. $\frac{3}{5} \times 20$ 12
10. $\frac{3}{8} \times \frac{8}{9}$ $\frac{1}{3}$



## Follow Up

### Reteaching

Point out to students that when multiplying fractions, we divide numerators and denominators by common factors *after* multiplying to reduce the product to lowest terms. To use the shortcut, we similarly divide numerators and denominators by common factors, but do so *before* multiplying. Demonstrate the similarity by multiplying $\frac{3}{4} \times \frac{2}{3}$ two ways. To illustrate the shortcut, divide numerators and denominators by 2 and 3.

### Enrichment

Write problems similar to the one below on the chalkboard. Have students indicate the greatest common factor for the numerator and denominator and use division to complete the operation. For example:

$$\frac{5}{8} \times \frac{4}{15} \rightarrow \frac{\not{5}^{1}}{8} \times \frac{4}{\not{15}_{3}} \rightarrow \frac{1}{\not{8}_{2}} \times \frac{\not{4}^{1}}{3} \rightarrow \frac{1}{2} \times \frac{1}{3} = \frac{1}{6}$$

(1) The greatest common factor for 5 and 15 is 5—divide by 5.

(2) The greatest common factor for 4 and 8 is 4—divide by 4.

| Assignment Guide | | | |
|---|---|---|---|
| | Minimum | Average | Extended |
| page 231 | 1–36 | 1–46 | 11–46, TM |

Find the product in lowest terms. Use the shortcut when possible.

1. $\frac{3}{4} \times \frac{4}{5}$ $\frac{3}{5}$
2. $\frac{3}{5} \times \frac{5}{6}$ $\frac{1}{2}$
3. $\frac{4}{3} \times \frac{3}{4}$ 1
4. $\frac{1}{2} \times 10$ 5
5. $\frac{5}{12} \times \frac{9}{10}$ $\frac{3}{8}$
6. $\frac{5}{6} \times \frac{12}{25}$ $\frac{2}{5}$
7. $\frac{5}{9} \times \frac{3}{8}$ $\frac{5}{24}$
8. $\frac{8}{9} \times \frac{21}{12}$ $1\frac{5}{9}$
9. $\frac{8}{3} \times \frac{7}{24}$ $\frac{7}{9}$
10. $6 \times \frac{2}{3}$ 4
11. $\frac{1}{3} \times 15$ 5
12. $\frac{7}{5} \times \frac{5}{14}$ $\frac{1}{2}$
13. $\frac{2}{3} \times 27$ 18
14. $\frac{3}{4} \times \frac{8}{9}$ $\frac{2}{3}$
15. $28 \times \frac{3}{7}$ 12
16. $\frac{3}{5} \times \frac{5}{12}$ $\frac{1}{4}$
17. $\frac{5}{6} \times \frac{18}{25}$ $\frac{3}{5}$
18. $\frac{4}{3} \times \frac{3}{8}$ $\frac{1}{2}$
19. $\frac{2}{3} \times 18$ 12
20. $\frac{7}{10} \times 5$ $\frac{7}{2} = 3\frac{1}{2}$
21. $\frac{6}{5} \times \frac{5}{14}$ $\frac{3}{7}$
22. $\frac{7}{6} \times \frac{6}{21}$ $\frac{1}{3}$
23. $\frac{1}{6} \times \frac{9}{4}$ $\frac{3}{8}$
24. $\frac{5}{8} \times \frac{8}{15}$ $\frac{1}{3}$
25. $\frac{5}{16} \times \frac{4}{15}$ $\frac{1}{12}$
26. $24 \times \frac{3}{8}$ 9
27. $\frac{3}{8} \times \frac{8}{3}$ 1
28. $6 \times \frac{1}{6}$ 1
29. $100 \times \frac{7}{10}$ 70
30. $\frac{5}{9} \times 27$ 15
31. $\frac{5}{8} \times 16$ 10
32. $\frac{5}{12} \times \frac{7}{10}$ $\frac{7}{24}$
33. $21 \times \frac{2}{3}$ 14
34. $\frac{5}{33} \times 11$ $\frac{5}{3} = 1\frac{2}{3}$
35. $\frac{6}{11} \times \frac{33}{42}$ $\frac{3}{7}$

36. Janella used $\frac{1}{3}$ of a piece of ribbon that was $\frac{3}{4}$ yd long. What part of a yard of ribbon was the piece that she used? $\frac{1}{4}$ yd

37. Kerry bought 18 yd of blue ribbon and 10 yd of silver ribbon to wrap some presents. She used $\frac{5}{6}$ of the blue ribbon and $\frac{2}{3}$ of the silver ribbon. What was the total number of yards of ribbon not used? $6\frac{1}{3}$ yd

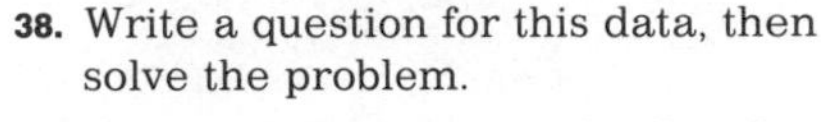

38. Write a question for this data, then solve the problem.

Ted needed 24 pieces of ribbon for party decorations. Each piece had to be $\frac{3}{4}$ yd long. Answers will vary.

★ Find the reciprocal by finding the number for $n$.

39. $\frac{2}{3} \times n = 1$ $\frac{3}{2}$
40. $n \times \frac{5}{6} = 1$ $\frac{6}{5}$
41. $4 \times n = 1$ $\frac{1}{4}$
42. $\frac{4}{5} \times n = 1$ $\frac{5}{4}$
43. $n \times \frac{1}{3} = 1$ 3
44. $n \times 5 = 1$ $\frac{1}{5}$
45. $\frac{7}{4} \times n = 1$ $\frac{4}{7}$
46. $n \times \frac{8}{7} = 1$ $\frac{7}{8}$

**Think**

**Guess and Check**

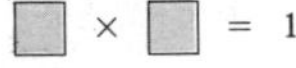

$\square \times \square = 1$

Two numbers are reciprocals of each other. One of them is 4 times as large as the other. What are the two numbers? 2, $\frac{1}{2}$

**Math**

More Practice, page 425, Set A



## Using Page 231

**Exercises 1–35** Note that problems such as exercise 13 can be solved by writing the whole number as an improper fraction. In this case a numerator and a denominator may be divided by 3 to simplify the multiplication. In problems such as exercise 2, remind students that both the numerator and denominator can be divided by 5, resulting in 1 in both the numerator and denominator. Note also in exercises 3, 27 and 28, that when a number is multiplied by its reciprocal, the result is 1.

**Exercise 38** In this exercise students are asked to read the data given and suggest a question that could be solved using the data. A possible question for this data might be: "How many yards of ribbon will Ted need?"

**Exercises 39–46** These exercises provide students with additional practice in dealing with the reciprocal of a number as well as readiness for division of fractional numbers. Students may recognize that the missing number can be found by reversing the numerator and the denominator of the fraction in the other factor.

**Think Math** This activity provides students with an opportunity to use the Guess and Check strategy to solve a numerical problem. Encourage students to guess a number, to find its reciprocal, then to test to see if one of the two numbers produced is 4 times as large as the other. Encourage them to revise their guess, if necessary, and try again.

**More Practice,** page 425, Set A

**Reteaching Supplement,** page 53

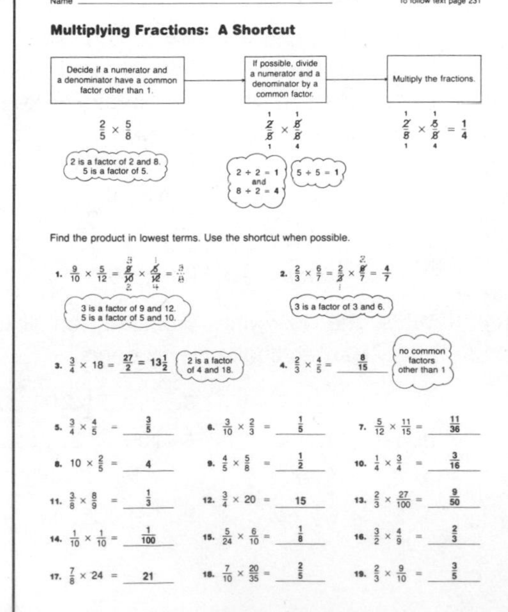

Name ________ To follow text page 231

**Multiplying Fractions: A Shortcut**

Decide if a numerator and a denominator have a common factor other than 1. → If possible, divide a numerator and a denominator by a common factor. → Multiply the fractions.

$\frac{2}{5} \times \frac{5}{8}$ — 2 is a factor of 2 and 8. 5 is a factor of 5.

$2 \div 2 = 1$ and $8 \div 2 = 4$; $5 \div 5 = 1$

$\frac{1}{4}$

Find the product in lowest terms. Use the shortcut when possible.

1. $\frac{9}{10} \times \frac{5}{12} = \frac{3}{8}$ — 3 is a factor of 9 and 12. 5 is a factor of 5 and 10.
2. $\frac{2}{3} \times \frac{6}{7} = \frac{4}{7}$ — 3 is a factor of 3 and 6.
3. $\frac{3}{4} \times 18 = \frac{27}{2} = 13\frac{1}{2}$ — 2 is a factor of 4 and 18.
4. $\frac{2}{3} \times \frac{4}{5} =$ $\frac{8}{15}$ — no common factors other than 1
5. $\frac{3}{4} \times \frac{4}{5} =$ $\frac{3}{5}$
6. $\frac{3}{10} \times \frac{2}{3} =$ $\frac{1}{5}$
7. $\frac{5}{12} \times \frac{11}{15} =$ $\frac{11}{36}$
8. $10 \times \frac{2}{5} =$ 4
9. $\frac{4}{5} \times \frac{5}{8} =$ $\frac{1}{2}$
10. $\frac{1}{4} \times \frac{3}{4} =$ $\frac{3}{16}$
11. $\frac{3}{8} \times \frac{8}{9} =$ $\frac{1}{3}$
12. $\frac{3}{4} \times 20 =$ 15
13. $\frac{2}{3} \times \frac{27}{100} =$ $\frac{9}{50}$
14. $\frac{1}{10} \times \frac{1}{10} =$ $\frac{1}{100}$
15. $\frac{5}{24} \times \frac{6}{10} =$ $\frac{1}{8}$
16. $\frac{3}{2} \times \frac{4}{9} =$ $\frac{2}{3}$
17. $\frac{7}{8} \times 24 =$ 21
18. $\frac{7}{10} \times \frac{20}{35} =$ $\frac{2}{5}$
19. $\frac{2}{3} \times \frac{9}{10} =$ $\frac{3}{5}$

**Enrichment Supplement,** page 53

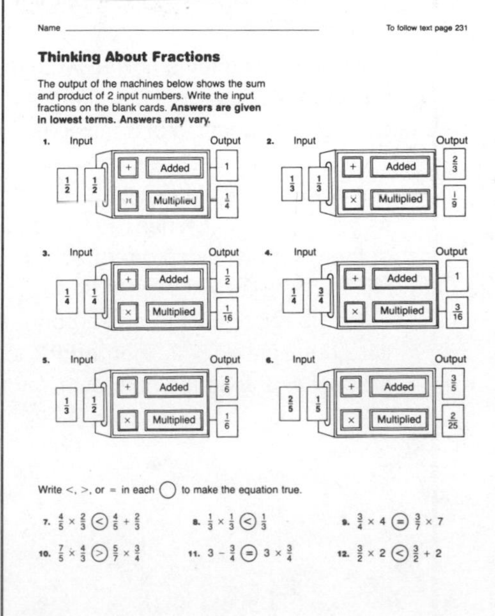

Name ________ To follow text page 231

**Thinking About Fractions**

The output of the machines below shows the sum and product of 2 input numbers. Write the input fractions on the blank cards. **Answers are given in lowest terms. Answers may vary.**

1. Input $\frac{1}{2}$, $\frac{1}{2}$ — Added: 1; Multiplied: $\frac{1}{4}$ (Output)
2. Input $\frac{1}{3}$, $\frac{1}{3}$ — Added: $\frac{2}{3}$; Multiplied: $\frac{1}{9}$ (Output)
3. Input $\frac{1}{4}$, $\frac{1}{4}$ — Added: $\frac{1}{2}$; Multiplied: $\frac{1}{16}$ (Output)
4. Input $\frac{1}{4}$, $\frac{3}{4}$ — Added: 1; Multiplied: $\frac{3}{16}$ (Output)
5. Input $\frac{1}{3}$, $\frac{1}{2}$ — Added: $\frac{5}{6}$; Multiplied: $\frac{1}{6}$ (Output)
6. Input $\frac{2}{5}$, $\frac{1}{5}$ — Added: $\frac{3}{5}$; Multiplied: $\frac{2}{25}$ (Output)

Write <, >, or = in each ◯ to make the equation true.

7. $\frac{4}{5} \times \frac{2}{3} < \frac{4}{5} + \frac{2}{3}$
8. $\frac{1}{3} \times \frac{1}{3} < \frac{1}{3}$
9. $\frac{3}{4} \times 4 = \frac{3}{7} \times 7$
10. $\frac{7}{5} \times \frac{4}{3} > \frac{5}{7} \times \frac{3}{4}$
11. $3 - \frac{3}{4} = 3 \times \frac{3}{4}$
12. $\frac{3}{2} \times 2 < \frac{3}{2} + 2$

**Practice Supplement,** page 88

Name ________ To follow text page 231

**Multiplying Fractions: A Shortcut**

Find the products in lowest terms. Use the shortcut when possible.

1. $\frac{3}{4} \times \frac{2}{3} =$ $\frac{1}{2}$
2. $\frac{7}{8} \times \frac{4}{5} =$ $\frac{7}{10}$
3. $\frac{2}{9} \times \frac{3}{8} =$ $\frac{1}{12}$
4. $\frac{5}{6} \times \frac{2}{7} =$ $\frac{5}{21}$
5. $\frac{8}{9} \times \frac{3}{4} =$ $\frac{2}{3}$
6. $\frac{5}{8} \times \frac{2}{5} =$ $\frac{1}{4}$
7. $\frac{4}{9} \times 18 =$ 8
8. $\frac{3}{7} \times \frac{7}{9} =$ $\frac{1}{3}$
9. $\frac{8}{7} \times \frac{7}{8} =$ 1
10. $\frac{3}{10} \times \frac{5}{6} =$ $\frac{1}{4}$
11. $\frac{10}{9} \times \frac{3}{5} =$ $\frac{2}{3}$
12. $16 \times \frac{5}{8} =$ 10
13. $\frac{7}{6} \times \frac{3}{14} =$ $\frac{1}{4}$
14. $\frac{5}{9} \times \frac{2}{5} =$ $\frac{2}{9}$
15. $\frac{5}{16} \times \frac{4}{5} =$ $\frac{1}{4}$
16. $20 \times \frac{1}{8} =$ $2\frac{1}{2}$
17. $\frac{2}{3} \times \frac{15}{4} =$ $2\frac{1}{2}$
18. $\frac{1}{2} \times 9 =$ $4\frac{1}{2}$
19. $\frac{3}{4} \times \frac{5}{12} =$ $\frac{5}{16}$
20. $\frac{4}{9} \times \frac{3}{8} =$ $\frac{1}{6}$
21. $\frac{4}{5} \times \frac{10}{12} =$ $\frac{2}{3}$
22. $\frac{1}{3} \times \frac{9}{16} =$ $\frac{3}{16}$
23. $\frac{3}{5} \times \frac{15}{6} =$ $1\frac{1}{2}$
24. $2 \times \frac{7}{4} =$ $3\frac{1}{2}$
25. $\frac{12}{7} \times \frac{7}{8} =$ $1\frac{1}{2}$
26. $100 \times \frac{3}{10} =$ 30
27. $\frac{2}{5} \times \frac{5}{2} =$ 1
28. $11 \times \frac{1}{11} =$ 1
29. $\frac{9}{25} \times \frac{5}{3} =$ $\frac{3}{5}$
30. $\frac{9}{10} \times \frac{2}{3} =$ $\frac{3}{5}$
31. $\frac{5}{7} \times 21 =$ 15
32. $\frac{6}{7} \times \frac{21}{36} =$ $\frac{1}{2}$
33. $\frac{5}{9} \times \frac{3}{10} =$ $\frac{1}{6}$
34. $\frac{15}{16} \times \frac{4}{5} =$ $\frac{3}{4}$
35. $\frac{5}{7} \times \frac{14}{3} =$ $3\frac{1}{3}$
36. $\frac{4}{9} \times \frac{18}{8} =$ 1

# Fractions: Multiplication

**Quick Review** Students write each improper fraction as a mixed number.

$\frac{24}{7}$ $3\frac{3}{7}$ $\frac{23}{5}$ $4\frac{3}{5}$ $\frac{13}{6}$ $2\frac{1}{6}$ $\frac{16}{3}$ $5\frac{1}{3}$ $\frac{20}{13}$ $1\frac{7}{13}$ $\frac{33}{4}$ $8\frac{1}{4}$ $\frac{53}{10}$ $5\frac{3}{10}$ $\frac{17}{2}$ $8\frac{1}{2}$ $\frac{9}{7}$ $1\frac{2}{7}$

**Lesson Focus** To find the product of two mixed numbers

## Ideas for Getting Started

Conduct a brief review in which students write a mixed number as an improper fraction. Give students the following: $2\frac{1}{2}\left(\frac{5}{2}\right)$, $3\frac{2}{3}\left(\frac{11}{3}\right)$, $3\frac{3}{4}\left(\frac{15}{4}\right)$, $2\frac{4}{5}\left(\frac{14}{5}\right)$, $4\frac{3}{8}\left(\frac{35}{8}\right)$, $3\frac{1}{3}\left(\frac{10}{3}\right)$, $1\frac{3}{4}\left(\frac{7}{4}\right)$. Then briefly review the procedure for reducing fractions to lowest terms.

## Using Page 232

**Motivational Problem** Read the problem at the top of the page. "What question are we asked about Dennis's high jump?" (How high could he jump on the planet Mars?) "What data will we need to answer this question?" (How high can he jump on Earth? How many times as high can he jump on Mars?) Point out that some of the data needed to solve this problem is found in the Space Fact box. Elicit from students that since we know that a person can jump $2\frac{1}{2}$ times as high on Mars as on Earth, we can multiply the height of the Earth jump by $2\frac{1}{2}$ to find the height of the Mars jump.

**Lesson Development** Direct students' attention to the instruction boxes on the page. As you work the problem on the chalkboard, encourage students to change mentally the improper fraction to a mixed number and write the multiplication problem with improper fractions below the original problem. Review the process for renaming the fraction $\frac{55}{6}$ as the mixed number $9\frac{1}{6}$. Then have students state the answer to the problem using a complete sentence. Have them reread the original problem and estimate to see if the answer seems reasonable. Point out that one foot equals 12 inches, so $\frac{1}{6}$ foot is $\frac{1}{6}$ of 12, or 2 inches. A jump of 9 feet 2 inches on Mars seems reasonable.

**Other Examples** In the first example, be sure students divide a numerator and denominator by 5 and a numerator and denominator by 2 to simplify the multiplication. Also remind them that $\frac{21}{2}$ must be renamed as a mixed number. In the second example, review the idea that 6 may be written as $\frac{6}{1}$. In this case students should recognize that both numerator and denominator are divisible by 2. Caution students to pay close attention to the renaming process.

**Warm Up** As students complete these problems, be alert for difficulties in rewriting a mixed number as an improper fraction. Also watch for students who are still having difficulty using the shortcut for multiplying two fractions. Be sure students are completing the process by renaming an improper fraction as a mixed number when necessary.

## Multiplying Mixed Numbers

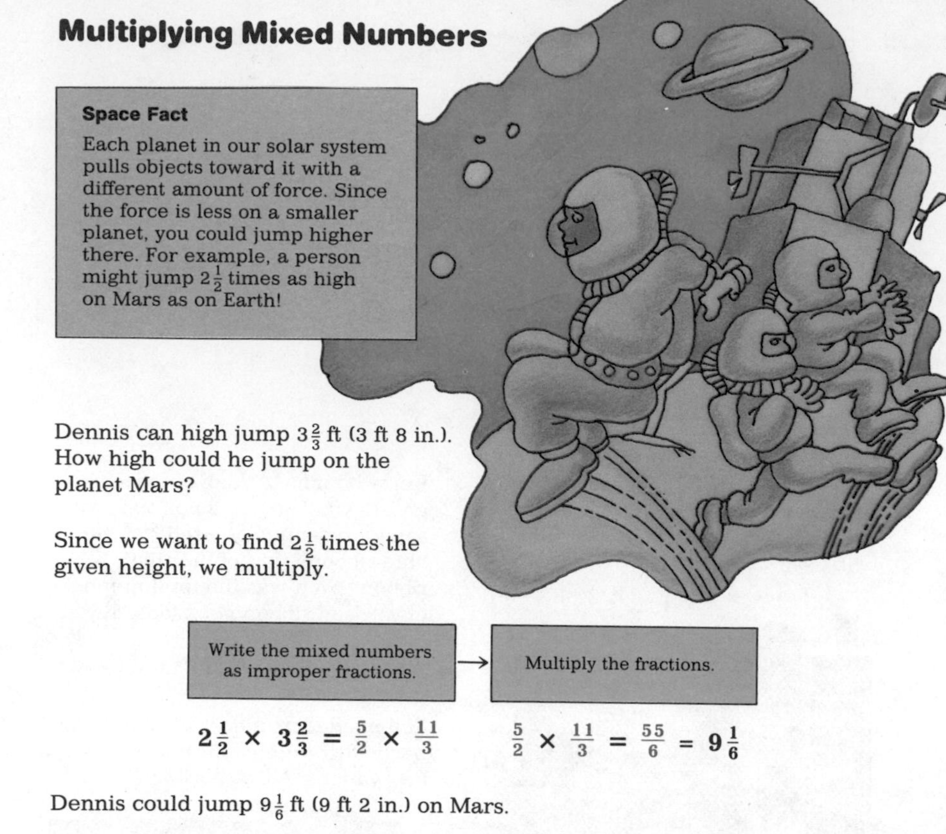

**Space Fact**

Each planet in our solar system pulls objects toward it with a different amount of force. Since the force is less on a smaller planet, you could jump higher there. For example, a person might jump $2\frac{1}{2}$ times as high on Mars as on Earth!

Dennis can high jump $3\frac{2}{3}$ ft (3 ft 8 in.). How high could he jump on the planet Mars?

Since we want to find $2\frac{1}{2}$ times the given height, we multiply.

Write the mixed numbers as improper fractions. → Multiply the fractions.

$$2\frac{1}{2} \times 3\frac{2}{3} = \frac{5}{2} \times \frac{11}{3} \qquad \frac{5}{2} \times \frac{11}{3} = \frac{55}{6} = 9\frac{1}{6}$$

Dennis could jump $9\frac{1}{6}$ ft (9 ft 2 in.) on Mars.

**Other Examples**

$$3\frac{3}{4} \times 2\frac{4}{5} = \frac{\overset{3}{\cancel{15}}}{\underset{2}{\cancel{4}}} \times \frac{\overset{7}{\cancel{14}}}{\underset{1}{\cancel{5}}} = \frac{21}{2} = 10\frac{1}{2} \qquad 6 \times 4\frac{3}{8} = \frac{\overset{3}{\cancel{6}}}{1} \times \frac{35}{\underset{4}{\cancel{8}}} = \frac{105}{4} = 26\frac{1}{4}$$

**Warm Up** Multiply. Use the shortcut when possible.

1. $1\frac{1}{3} \times 2\frac{1}{2}$ $\frac{10}{3} = 3\frac{1}{3}$
2. $2\frac{1}{5} \times 1\frac{1}{4}$ $\frac{11}{4} = 2\frac{3}{4}$
3. $3\frac{1}{2} \times \frac{1}{2}$ $\frac{7}{4} = 1\frac{3}{4}$
4. $9 \times 1\frac{2}{3}$ $\frac{15}{1} = 15$
5. $3\frac{3}{4} \times 2\frac{2}{3}$ $\frac{10}{1} = 10$
6. $1\frac{3}{8} \times 2\frac{1}{3}$ $\frac{77}{24} = 3\frac{5}{24}$
7. $8 \times 4\frac{3}{4}$ $\frac{38}{1} = 38$
8. $2\frac{2}{5} \times 6\frac{1}{2}$ $15\frac{3}{5}$
9. $2\frac{1}{10} \times 5$ $\frac{21}{2} = 10\frac{1}{2}$
10. $\frac{3}{4} \times 16$ $\frac{12}{1} = 12$
11. $\frac{3}{4} \times 2\frac{5}{8}$ $\frac{63}{32} = 1\frac{31}{32}$
12. $4\frac{1}{2} \times 3\frac{1}{3}$ $\frac{15}{1} = 15$

232

## Follow Up

### Reteaching

Review with students how to write mixed numbers as improper fractions by discussing the meaning of a mixed number. That is, $2\frac{3}{4}$ means $2 + \frac{3}{4}$, or $1 + 1 + \frac{3}{4}$. But since $1 = \frac{4}{4}$ we can write $1 + 1 + \frac{3}{4}$ as $\frac{4}{4} + \frac{4}{4} + \frac{3}{4}$, or $\frac{11}{4}$. Then remind students of their work with improper fractions and mixed numbers in Chapter 8. Ask a volunteer to change $2\frac{3}{4}$ to an improper fraction. (Multiply $4 \times 2$, then add 3 to the product and write the sum over 4.)

### Enrichment

The method shown below can be used to help students develop mental calculation skills when multiplying certain mixed numbers by whole numbers.

$3\frac{1}{4} \times 12$

$$\begin{aligned} 3 \times 12 &= 36 \\ \tfrac{1}{4} \times 12 &= \underline{\phantom{0}3} \\ &\phantom{=}\ 39 \end{aligned}$$

Thus $3\frac{1}{4} \times 12 = 39$

Write the following problems on the chalkboard to challenge students.

1. $10 \times 4\frac{1}{5}$ **42**
2. $12 \times 1\frac{1}{6}$ **14**
3. $6 \times 4\frac{1}{2}$ **27**
4. $20 \times 6\frac{1}{5}$ **124**
5. $9 \times 2\frac{1}{3}$ **21**
6. $100 \times 2\frac{1}{10}$ **210**
7. $4 \times 7\frac{1}{2}$ **30**
8. $16 \times 2\frac{1}{8}$ **34**

| Assignment Guide | | | |
|---|---|---|---|
| | Minimum | Average | Extended |
| page 233 | 1–29 | 1–31 | 2–32 even, TM |

Find the product in lowest terms.

1. $2\frac{2}{3} \times 1\frac{1}{4}$ $3\frac{1}{3}$
2. $1\frac{3}{5} \times \frac{3}{5}$ $\frac{24}{25}$
3. $1\frac{1}{2} \times 2\frac{2}{3}$ 4
4. $2\frac{1}{4} \times 5\frac{1}{3}$ 12
5. $1\frac{3}{4} \times 1\frac{1}{2}$ $2\frac{5}{8}$
6. $2\frac{2}{5} \times 4\frac{5}{6}$ $11\frac{3}{5}$
7. $6 \times 3\frac{3}{4}$ $22\frac{1}{2}$
8. $4\frac{5}{6} \times 3\frac{3}{4}$ $18\frac{1}{8}$
9. $\frac{9}{10} \times 3\frac{1}{3}$ 3
10. $2\frac{1}{4} \times 20$ 45
11. $2\frac{3}{4} \times 1\frac{1}{10}$ $3\frac{1}{40}$
12. $4\frac{1}{3} \times 5\frac{1}{2}$ $23\frac{5}{6}$
13. $15 \times 4\frac{1}{6}$ $62\frac{1}{2}$
14. $3\frac{1}{4} \times 2\frac{2}{3}$ $8\frac{2}{3}$
15. $\frac{4}{5} \times 3\frac{3}{8}$ $2\frac{7}{10}$
16. $\frac{3}{4} \times 16$ 12
17. $15 \times 3\frac{1}{10}$ $46\frac{1}{2}$
18. $4 \times 5\frac{3}{8}$ $21\frac{1}{2}$
19. $3\frac{1}{5} \times 4\frac{2}{3}$ $14\frac{14}{15}$
20. $3\frac{1}{4} \times 3\frac{1}{4}$ $10\frac{9}{16}$
21. $18 \times 2\frac{2}{3}$ 48
22. $3\frac{1}{7} \times 2\frac{1}{2}$ $7\frac{6}{7}$

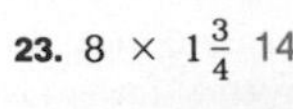

23. $8 \times 1\frac{3}{4}$ 14
24. $1\frac{7}{10} \times 2\frac{3}{10}$ $3\frac{91}{100}$

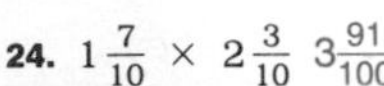

25. $5\frac{1}{3} \times 3\frac{3}{4}$ 20
26. $6\frac{1}{4} \times 2\frac{2}{5}$ 15
27. What is the product when 9 is multiplied by $4\frac{1}{3}$? 39
28. Give the product of the factors $3\frac{3}{5}$ and $2\frac{1}{2}$. 9
29. The world's record for the high jump in a recent year was about $7\frac{3}{4}$ ft. On Mars this jump would be $2\frac{1}{2}$ times as high. How high would that be? $19\frac{3}{8}$ ft
30. Suppose you can high jump $4\frac{1}{6}$ ft (4 ft 2 in.) on Earth. You could jump only $\frac{5}{6}$ as high on Saturn. How high would that be? $3\frac{17}{36}$ ft
31. You could jump $6\frac{1}{4}$ times as high on the moon as on Earth. Jack can jump $5\frac{7}{12}$ ft high on Earth. How high could he jump on the moon? Estimate which of these answers is reasonable. B

    **A** $7\frac{3}{20}$ ft **B** 35 ft **C** 30 ft **D** $3\frac{1}{2}$ ft

32. **DATA HUNT** Find the latest women's and men's world records for the high jump. How high would each of these jumps be on Mars? Answers will vary.

## Think

**Mental Math**

You can use the multiplication-addition property (page 5) to multiply mixed numbers mentally.

$4 \times 3\frac{1}{2}$

$4 \times 3 = 12$
$4 \times \frac{1}{2} = 2$
so $4 \times 3\frac{1}{2} = 14$

Try these!

1. $6 \times 2\frac{1}{3}$ 14
2. $9 \times 5\frac{1}{3}$ 48
3. $20 \times 2\frac{1}{4}$ 45
4. $12 \times 2\frac{2}{3}$ 32
5. $24 \times 2\frac{3}{4}$ 66
6. $15 \times 3\frac{4}{5}$ 57

## Math

More Practice, page 425, Set B



## Using Page 233

**Exercises 1–26** Note in exercise 2 that only one of the fractions needs to be rewritten as an improper fraction. Note also that exercise 10 is a special case in which one of the factors is a whole number that can be written as an improper fraction, $\frac{20}{1}$. In selected exercises encourage students to round the mixed numbers to the nearest whole number and estimate to see if the calculated product is reasonable.

**Exercise 31** This exercise emphasizes the importance of checking the reasonableness of an answer. In this case students round $6\frac{1}{4}$ to 6, $5\frac{3}{5}$ to 6. Since 6 × 6 = 36, answer B seems reasonable.

**Data Hunt** This activity encourages students to search for data outside the book. The high jump records might be found in a recent *Almanac, Book of Facts* or *Guinness Book of World Records.*

**Think Math** This activity provides students with an opportunity to find mentally the products of a whole number and a mixed number by "multiplying in parts." Students should already be familiar with the procedure for mentally multiplying. To be sure they complete the problems without using pencil and paper, have students work this type of problem with a partner.

**More Practice,** page 425, Set B

**Reteaching Supplement,** page 54

Name ______ To follow text page 233

### Multiplying Mixed Numbers

Write the mixed numbers as improper fractions. → Multiply the fractions.

$2\frac{2}{3} \times 1\frac{3}{4} = \frac{8}{3} \times \frac{7}{4}$ ($2\frac{2}{3} = \frac{8}{3}$, $1\frac{3}{4} = \frac{7}{4}$) $\frac{8}{3} \times \frac{7}{4} = \frac{14}{3} = 4\frac{2}{3}$ (Rename.)

Write an improper fraction for each mixed number or whole number. Then find the product in lowest terms.

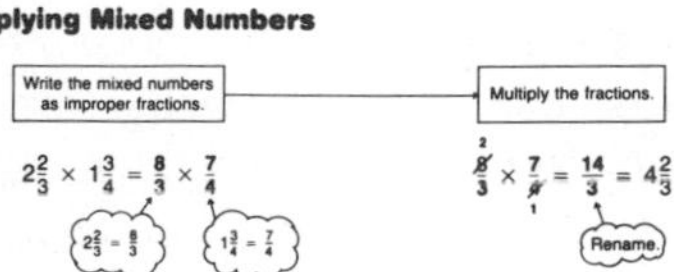

1. $1\frac{1}{3} \times 2\frac{1}{2}$: $\frac{4}{3} \times \frac{5}{2} = \frac{10}{3} = 3\frac{1}{3}$
2. $\frac{4}{5} \times 2\frac{2}{3}$: $\frac{4}{5} \times \frac{8}{3} = \frac{32}{15} = 2\frac{2}{15}$
3. $3\frac{1}{2} \times 5\frac{2}{5}$: $\frac{7}{2} \times \frac{27}{5} = \frac{189}{10} = 18\frac{9}{10}$
4. $5\frac{1}{2} \times 1\frac{3}{4}$: $\frac{11}{2} \times \frac{7}{4} = \frac{77}{8} = 9\frac{5}{8}$
5. $4 \times 3\frac{1}{4}$: $\frac{4}{1} \times \frac{13}{4} = \frac{13}{1} = 13$
6. $4\frac{1}{2} \times 5\frac{2}{3}$: $\frac{9}{2} \times \frac{17}{3} = \frac{51}{2} = 25\frac{1}{2}$

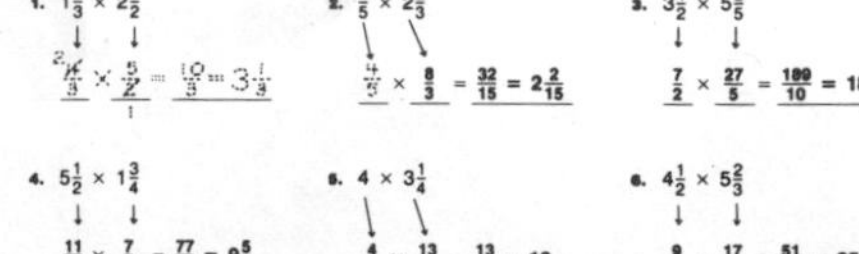

Find the product in lowest terms.

7. $13\frac{1}{2} \times 8\frac{1}{3} = \frac{27}{2} \times \frac{25}{3} = \frac{225}{2} = 112\frac{1}{2}$
8. $12 \times 4\frac{2}{3} = \frac{12}{1} \times \frac{14}{3} = \frac{56}{1} = 56$
9. $10 \times 1\frac{1}{10} = \frac{100}{10} \times \frac{11}{10} = \frac{1100}{100} = 11$
10. $10\frac{1}{4} \times 2\frac{4}{5} = \frac{41}{4} \times \frac{14}{5} = \frac{287}{10} = 28\frac{7}{10}$
11. $4\frac{9}{10} \times 36 = \frac{49}{10} \times \frac{36}{1} = \frac{882}{5} = 176\frac{2}{5}$
12. $15 \times \frac{4}{5} = \frac{15}{1} \times \frac{4}{5} = \frac{12}{1} = 12$
13. $1\frac{2}{3} \times 6 = \frac{5}{3} \times \frac{6}{1} = \frac{10}{1} = 10$
14. $\frac{3}{4} \times 12\frac{1}{2} = \frac{3}{4} \times \frac{25}{2} = \frac{75}{8} = 9\frac{3}{8}$
15. $2\frac{3}{4} \times 2 = \frac{11}{4} \times \frac{2}{1} = \frac{11}{2} = 5\frac{1}{2}$
16. $3\frac{1}{5} \times 20 = \frac{16}{5} \times \frac{20}{1} = \frac{64}{1} = 64$
17. $4\frac{3}{8} \times 8 = \frac{35}{8} \times \frac{8}{1} = \frac{35}{1} = 35$
18. $9\frac{7}{10} \times \frac{2}{3} = \frac{97}{10} \times \frac{2}{3} = \frac{97}{15} = 6\frac{7}{15}$

**Enrichment Supplement,** page 54

Name ______ To follow text page 233

### Fraction Number Trees

Write the missing fraction, whole number, or mixed number.

1. $\frac{1}{10}$ = $\frac{3}{4}$ × $\frac{2}{15}$; $\frac{1}{2}$ × $\frac{3}{2}$ × $\frac{2}{5}$ × $\frac{1}{3}$
2. $\frac{3}{100}$ = $\frac{1}{10}$ × $\frac{3}{10}$; $\frac{1}{5}$ × $\frac{1}{2}$ × $\frac{3}{5}$ × $\frac{1}{2}$
3. $4\frac{1}{8}$ = $1\frac{1}{2}$ × $\frac{55}{20}$; 3 × $\frac{1}{2}$ × $1\frac{1}{4}$ × $2\frac{1}{5}$
4. $3\frac{6}{7}$ = 9 × $\frac{3}{7}$; 5 × $1\frac{4}{5}$ × 3 × $\frac{1}{7}$

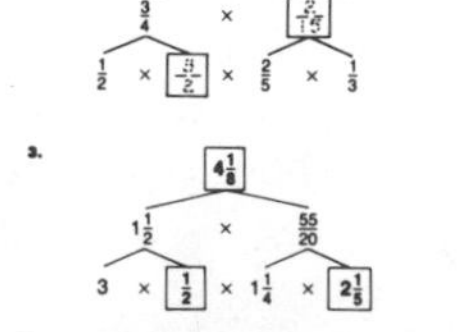

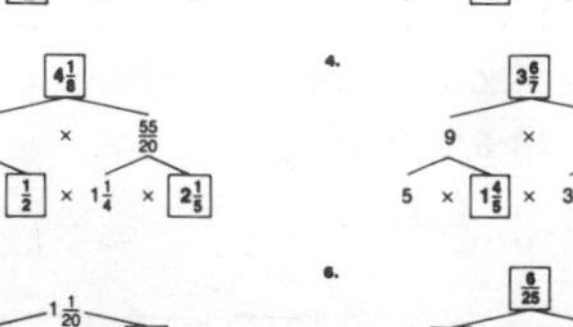

5. $1\frac{1}{20}$ = $\frac{7}{15}$ × $\frac{9}{4}$; $\frac{1}{5}$ × $2\frac{1}{3}$ × $4\frac{1}{2}$ × $\frac{1}{2}$
6. $\frac{6}{25}$ = 6 × $\frac{1}{25}$; 2 × 3 × $\frac{1}{5}$ × $\frac{1}{5}$
7. $\frac{24}{35}$ = 24 × $\frac{1}{35}$; 8 × 3 × $\frac{1}{5}$ × $\frac{1}{7}$
8. $\frac{49}{100}$ = 49 × $\frac{1}{100}$; 7 × 7 × $\frac{1}{10}$ × $\frac{1}{10}$
9. Make your own fraction number tree for $\frac{25}{64}$.

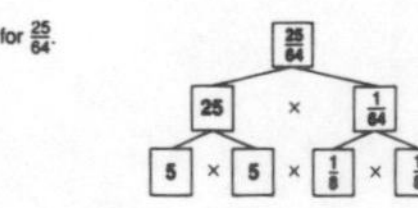

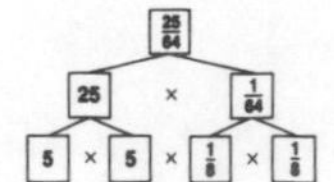

$\frac{25}{64}$ = 25 × $\frac{1}{64}$; 5 × 5 × $\frac{1}{8}$ × $\frac{1}{8}$

**Practice Supplement,** page 89

Name ______ To follow text page 233

### Multiplying Mixed Numbers

Find the product in lowest terms.

1. $20 \times 3\frac{2}{5}$ = 68
2. $\frac{2}{3} \times 18$ = 12
3. $4\frac{3}{5} \times \frac{5}{6}$ = $3\frac{5}{6}$
4. $15 \times \frac{3}{10}$ = $4\frac{1}{2}$
5. $3\frac{6}{7} \times \frac{7}{6}$ = $4\frac{1}{2}$
6. $9 \times 2\frac{2}{3}$ = 24
7. $1\frac{5}{9} \times 2\frac{3}{8}$ = $3\frac{25}{36}$
8. $1\frac{3}{4} \times 2\frac{4}{5}$ = $4\frac{9}{10}$
9. $21 \times \frac{5}{6}$ = $17\frac{1}{2}$
10. $5\frac{1}{2} \times \frac{4}{9}$ = $2\frac{4}{9}$
11. $\frac{3}{7} \times 1\frac{14}{15}$ = $\frac{29}{35}$
12. $\frac{5}{18} \times 12$ = $3\frac{1}{3}$
13. $\frac{21}{10} \times 2\frac{4}{9}$ = $5\frac{2}{15}$
14. $9\frac{3}{4} \times \frac{3}{5}$ = $5\frac{17}{20}$
15. $\frac{2}{5} \times 3\frac{3}{5}$ = $1\frac{11}{25}$
16. $2\frac{5}{9} \times \frac{4}{5}$ = $2\frac{2}{45}$
17. $\frac{9}{16} \times 5\frac{1}{3}$ = 3
18. $2\frac{3}{7} \times 4\frac{2}{3}$ = $11\frac{1}{3}$
19. $1\frac{5}{6} \times 12\frac{3}{4}$ = $23\frac{3}{8}$
20. $3\frac{3}{5} \times 1\frac{2}{3}$ = 6
21. $1\frac{1}{4} \times 6\frac{2}{3}$ = $8\frac{1}{3}$
22. $5\frac{2}{3} \times 1\frac{2}{7}$ = $7\frac{2}{7}$
23. $6 \times 1\frac{3}{4}$ = $10\frac{1}{2}$
24. $2\frac{1}{4} \times 3\frac{1}{3}$ = $7\frac{1}{2}$
25. $3\frac{2}{3} \times 1\frac{4}{11}$ = 5
26. $\frac{5}{9} \times 3\frac{3}{10}$ = $1\frac{5}{6}$
27. $2\frac{3}{8} \times 4$ = $9\frac{1}{2}$
28. $1\frac{5}{8} \times \frac{4}{5}$ = $1\frac{3}{10}$
29. $2\frac{1}{4} \times 5\frac{1}{3}$ = 12
30. $2\frac{2}{5} \times \frac{3}{4}$ = $1\frac{4}{5}$

**Quick Review** Students name the decimal that each group of coins represents.

| | | |
|---|---|---|
| 3 pennies **0.03** | 2 quarters **0.50** | 5 dimes **0.50** |
| 3 quarters **0.75** | 8 dimes **0.80** | 1 half dollar **0.50** |
| 19 pennies **0.19** | 4 dimes, 5 pennies **0.45** | 1 quarter **0.25** |

**Lesson Focus** To use data from a plan sheet to solve word problems

## Ideas for Getting Started

Bring to class pieces of 1 by 6 board and 2 by 4 board. Show students the boards and say that these are two common board sizes. Point out that one is called a 2 by 4 and the other is called a 1 by 6. Tell students that these names are derived from the approximate dimensions of the boards. Explain that as the boards are cut and processed, the dimensions are reduced. Then ask volunteers to measure the width and height of the 2 by 4 board. (These measurements should be approximately $3\frac{1}{2}$ inches by $1\frac{5}{8}$ inches.) Then have another student measure the width and height of the 1 by 6 board. (These measurements should be approximately $5\frac{1}{2}$ inches by $\frac{3}{4}$ inch.) Point out that it is important to know the exact measurements of the boards when involved in a building project.

## Using Page 234

**Lesson Development** Encourage a brief discussion about any building experiences students have had. Elicit from them the value of using accurate plans in any building project. Tell students that they will need to use data from the plan sheets to solve these problems. If necessary, read and discuss each problem before assigning independent work.

**Exercise 1** Be sure students understand that the width of the floor will be the combined width of the 18 1 by 6 boards. Draw a picture like the one below to clarify this situation, if needed.

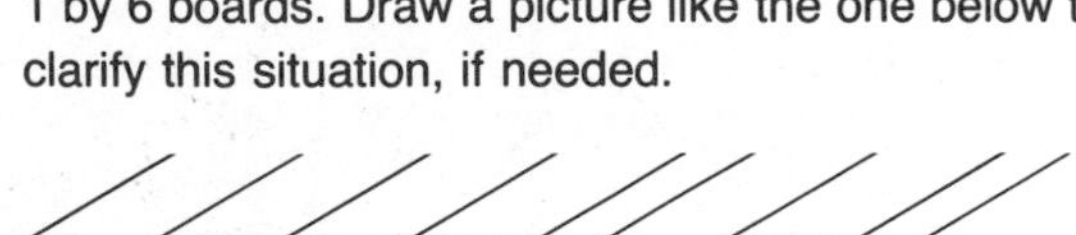

18 1 by 6 boards

**Exercise 2** Use the answer from exercise 1 to help students understand why the boards must be $8\frac{1}{4}$ ft long to make the floor square. (The width of the floor is 99 in.; this is 8 ft. 3 in. or $8\frac{1}{4}$ ft. Thus the length of each of the 18 boards must be $8\frac{1}{4}$ ft.)

**Exercise 3** Note that students must use the answer from exercise 2 to calculate the answer to this problem.

**Exercise 4** Emphasize the importance of getting the thickness of the 1 by 6 board from Plan Sheet A.

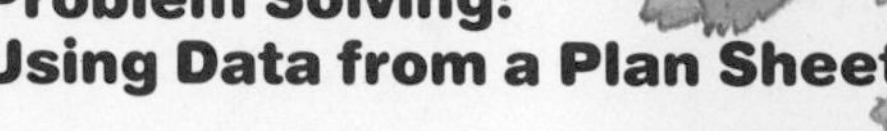


## Problem Solving: Using Data from a Plan Sheet

Kay and Scott's parents agreed to help them build a tree house. They used a plan they found in a magazine. Here are some problems they needed to solve. Use the data from the drawings as needed to solve the problems.

1. They used 18 of the 1 by 6 boards side by side to make the floor. How many inches wide was the floor? 99 in.
2. The 1 by 6 boards must be $8\frac{1}{4}$ ft long to make the floor a square. How many total feet of board will actually be needed if 18 boards are used? $148\frac{1}{2}$ ft
3. The 1 by 6 boards cost \$0.29 per foot of length. If there were no waste, what would be the cost for the floor? (Use the answer from problem 2.) \$43.07
4. What size nail should you use if you want to nail three 1 by 6 boards together as shown and have the nail go $\frac{1}{2}$ in. into the third board? 6 penny nail

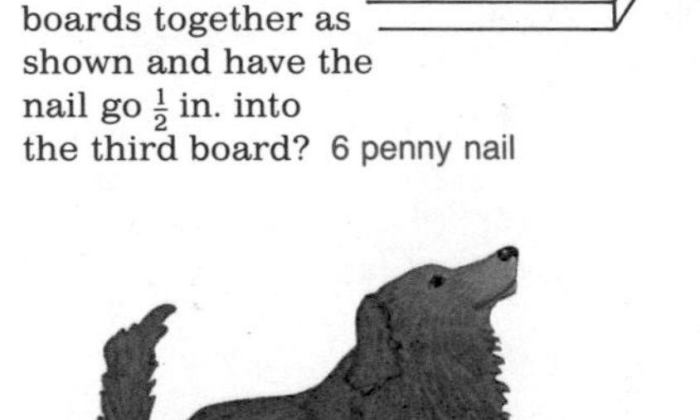

**Plan Sheet A**

Use 1 by 6 boards for the floor.

Note that 1 by 6 boards have the dimensions shown.

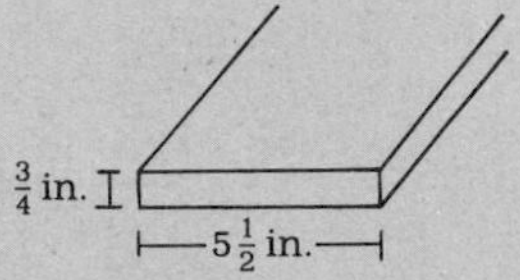


These boards are available in 6, 8, 10, 12, 14, 16, 18, and 20 foot lengths.

**Information About Nails**

With each 1 "penny" increase, the length of the nail increases $\frac{1}{4}$ in.

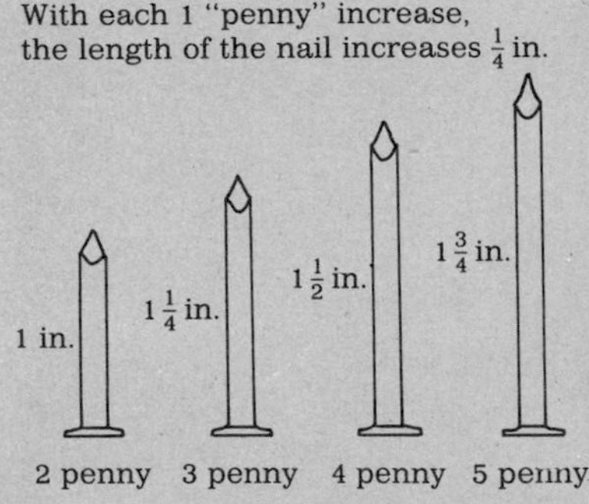


## Follow Up

### Reteaching

Draw a figure like the one below on the chalkboard. Ask students to suggest possible problems based on the drawing and then help them to solve their problems by using the 5-Point Checklist. For example, discuss with them how to find the height of the wall.

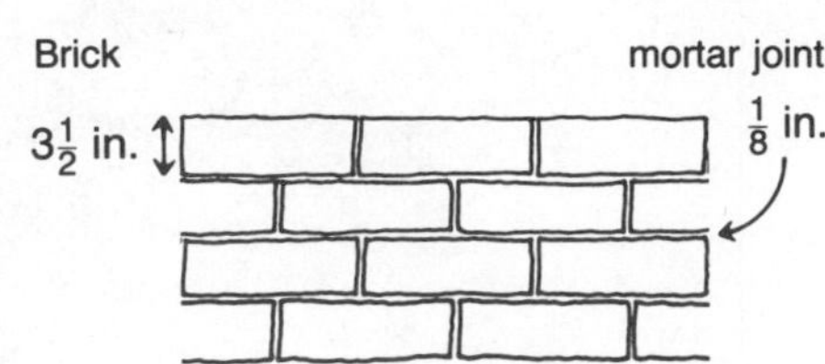


### Enrichment

Have students solve the puzzle below: You can use a balance scale to weigh any item that weighs $\frac{1}{2}$, 1, $1\frac{1}{2}$, and so on up to 20 pounds. You have only four weights. What are they?
**$\frac{1}{2}$ lb, $1\frac{1}{2}$ lb, $4\frac{1}{2}$ lb, $13\frac{1}{2}$ lb**

| Assignment Guide | | | |
|---|---|---|---|
| | Minimum | Average | Extended |
| pages 234–235 | 1–8 | 1–9 | 1–10 |



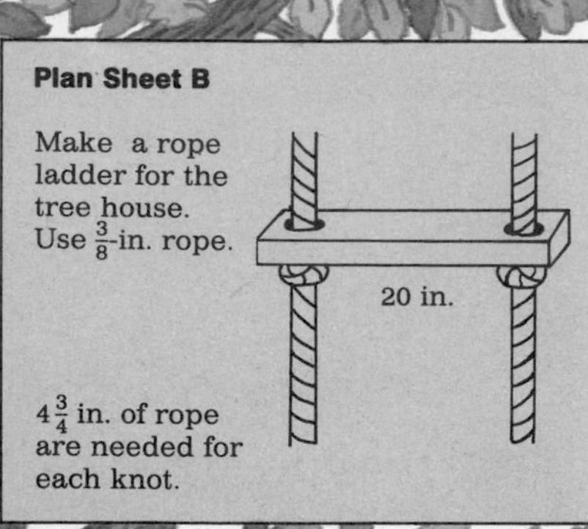

**Plan Sheet B**

Make a rope ladder for the tree house. Use $\frac{3}{8}$-in. rope.

20 in.

$4\frac{3}{4}$ in. of rope are needed for each knot.

5. They will need to tie 20 knots to make the rope ladder. How many extra inches of rope must they include for the knots? 95 in.

6. To make the ladder, ten 2 by 2 boards, each 20 in. long, are needed. How many inches of these boards do they need? How many feet? (1 foot = 12 inches. Round to the nearest foot.) If these boards cost 13.7¢ per foot, what would the total cost for ladder boards? 200 in.; 17 ft; $2.329 or $2.33

**Plan Sheet C**

Use three 2 by 4 boards for each side of a low wall around the tree house. Note that 2 by 4 boards have the dimensions shown:

$1\frac{5}{8}$ in.

$3\frac{1}{2}$ in.

7. How high would a wall made with three 2 by 4 boards be? $10\frac{1}{2}$ in.

8. How high is a stack of four 2 by 4 boards? $6\frac{1}{2}$ in.

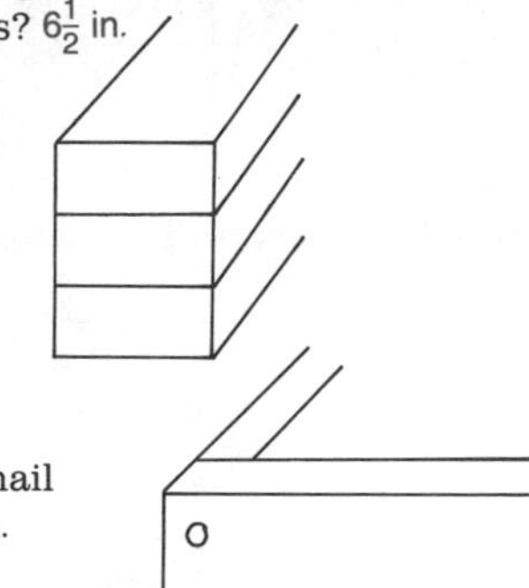

9. How long a nail should you use if you want to nail 2 by 4 boards like this and have the nail go $\frac{3}{4}$ in. into the second board? $2\frac{3}{8}$ in.

10. **Try This** Scott wanted to cut a long board into 20 pieces. How many cuts are needed to do this? Hint: Solve a simpler problem. 19



## Using Page 235

**Exercise 5** Information from Plan Sheet B must be used to determine how many inches of rope are needed for each of the 20 knots.

**Exercise 6** This problem contains data not needed for the solution; the fact that the boards are 2 by 2 boards is not used. Note that this problem asks three separate questions.

**Try This** A possible strategy, Solve a Simpler Problem, was taught on page 218.

**Discussion** "What question is asked in the problem?" (How many cuts are needed to cut a board into 20 pieces?) "Could you solve a simpler problem to find out how many cuts are needed? For example, how many pieces of board would you have after two cuts?" (3 pieces) "After three cuts?" (4 pieces)

**Solution** It will take 19 cuts to form 20 pieces. By solving a simpler problem, we can see that since 2 cuts form 3 pieces, 3 cuts form 4 pieces, 4 cuts form 5 pieces, and so on.

**Extension** Ted made 15 cuts on a long board. How many pieces of board did he have? (16)

## Ideas That Work

### Special Education

Students can practice multiplying fractions by playing "Cover Up." Provide students with 36 cards, each having a multiplication problem with fractions written on it and a game mat as shown below with 36 squares, each with an answer to a problem card written in it.

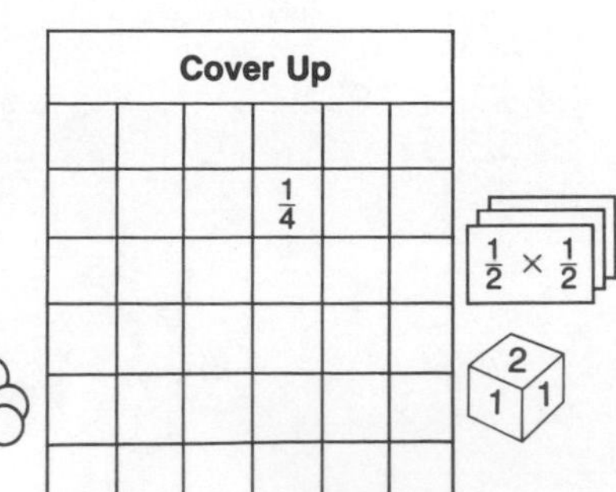


Each player begins with 15 chips of one color. Mix the cards and place them in a pile facedown. Each player rolls a number cube labeled with the numbers 1 and 2 and draws 1 or 2 cards as indicated by the number cube. Players use a colored chip to cover the answer to their problem(s) on the board. The first player to cover four spaces in a row wins the round. If neither player gets four in a row and all spaces are covered, the one with the most chips on the board wins.

**Practice Supplement,** page 90

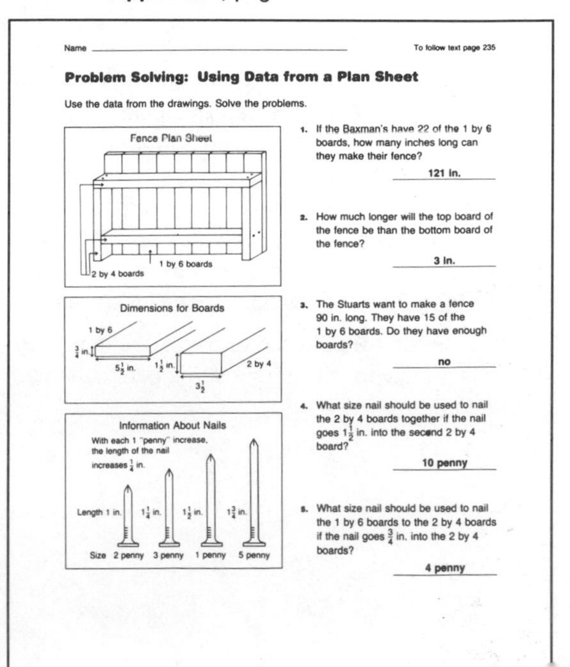

Name ______________________ To follow text page 235

**Problem Solving: Using Data from a Plan Sheet**

Use the data from the drawings. Solve the problems.



1. If the Baxman's have 22 of the 1 by 6 boards, how many inches long can they make their fence? **121 in.**

2. How much longer will the top board of the fence be than the bottom board of the fence? **3 in.**

3. The Stuarts want to make a fence 90 in. long. They have 15 of the 1 by 6 boards. Do they have enough boards? **no**

4. What size nail should be used to nail the 2 by 4 boards together if the nail goes $1\frac{1}{2}$ in. into the second 2 by 4 board? **10 penny**

5. What size nail should be used to nail the 1 by 6 boards to the 2 by 4 boards if the nail goes $\frac{3}{4}$ in. into the 2 by 4 boards? **4 penny**

**Quick Review** Students read these decimals aloud.

| | | | | | | |
|---|---|---|---|---|---|---|
| 0.004 | 5.98 | 0.2 | 0.667 | 0.09 | 9.5 | 0.905 |
| | 0.954 | 4.8 | 8.42 | 2.23 | 0.3297 | |
| 0.33 | 0.06 | 0.112 | 0.321 | 0.92 | 3.088 | 0.16 |

**Lesson Focus** To write a lowest-terms fraction or mixed number for a decimal; to write a decimal for a fraction

**Suggested Materials** 10 by 10 grids (TRB p. 274), colored pencils

## Ideas for Getting Started

Give students 10 by 10 grids and have them draw lines to make four equal parts as shown below. Have students shade one of the four equal parts.

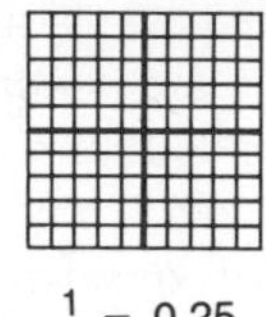

$\frac{1}{4} = 0.25$

"How many of the small squares out of 100 have been shaded?" (25) "What decimal tells the part of the square that has been shaded?" (0.25) "What fraction tells the part of the square that has been shaded?" $\left(\frac{1}{4}\right)$ Be sure students understand how the picture shows that $0.25 = \frac{25}{100} = \frac{1}{4}$.

## Using Page 236

**Lesson Development** Have students read the paragraph about the part of the Earth's surface covered by land. Explain that it is often desirable to find a lowest-terms fraction for a decimal. Also point out that since 0.25 means 25 hundredths, this decimal can be written as the fraction $\frac{25}{100}$. This fraction can then be reduced to $\frac{1}{4}$.

**Other Examples** Note in the first example, since 0.4 means four tenths, we can write 0.4 as the fraction $\frac{4}{10}$. This fraction can then be reduced to $\frac{2}{5}$, so $0.4 = \frac{2}{5}$. In the second example 0.35 means 35 hundredths and can be written as the fraction $\frac{35}{100}$. The lowest-terms fraction is $\frac{7}{20}$, so $0.35 = \frac{7}{20}$. In the third example, the decimal part can be shown to be $\frac{1}{8}$, thus $4.125 = 4\frac{1}{8}$.

**Exercises 1–20** Have students read these decimals aloud before writing the lowest-terms fraction or mixed number. For selected examples such as "three and four tenths," have students write the corresponding mixed number or fraction on the chalkboard. In this case, $3\frac{4}{10}$. Note that exercise 20 involves ten thousandths and requires special attention. It is important in these exercises to encourage students to reduce the fractions to the lowest terms.

**Exercises 21–26** In these exercises everyday situations are given to illustrate some common uses of fractions.

## From Decimals to Fractions

A little more than 0.25 of the Earth's surface is land. What is the lowest-terms fraction for this decimal?

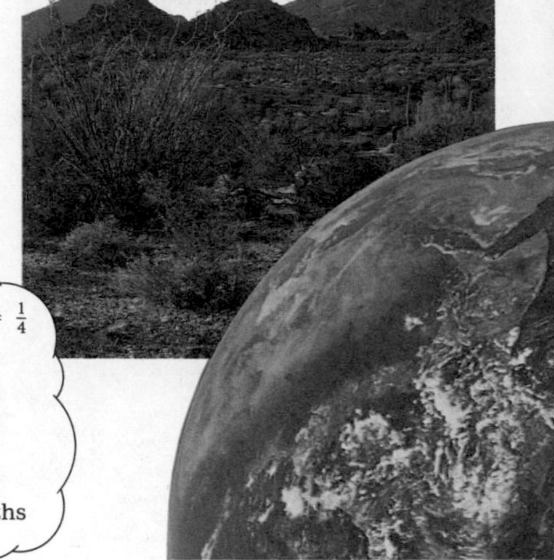

To find a fraction for a decimal, decide if the decimal is in **tenths, hundredths,** or **thousandths,** and write it as a fraction. Then reduce the fraction if necessary.

**25 hundredths**

$$0.25 = \frac{25}{100} = \frac{1}{4}$$

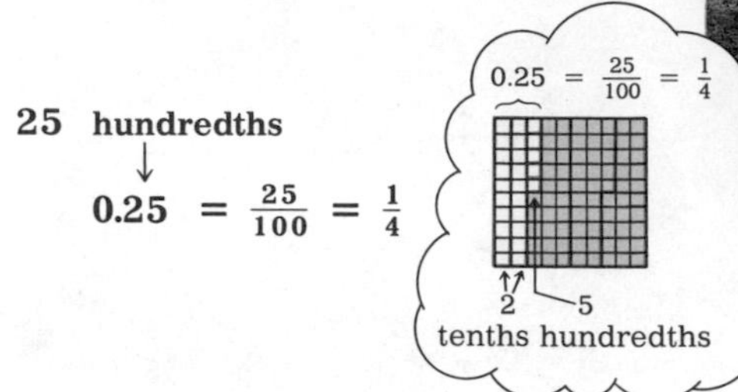


The lowest-terms fraction for the decimal 0.25 is $\frac{1}{4}$.

**Other Examples**

$0.4 = \frac{4}{10} = \frac{2}{5}$ $\quad$ $0.375 = \frac{375}{1{,}000} = \frac{3}{8}$ $\quad$ $4.125 = 4\frac{125}{1{,}000} = 4\frac{1}{8}$

Write the lowest-terms fraction or mixed number for each decimal.

**1.** 0.75 $\frac{3}{4}$ **2.** 3.4 $3\frac{2}{5}$ **3.** 6.25 $6\frac{1}{4}$ **4.** 0.45 $\frac{9}{20}$ **5.** 0.50 $\frac{1}{2}$

**6.** 0.10 $\frac{1}{10}$ **7.** 0.125 $\frac{1}{8}$ **8.** 1.875 $1\frac{7}{8}$ **9.** 0.375 $\frac{3}{8}$ **10.** 0.005 $\frac{1}{200}$

**11.** 0.7 $\frac{7}{10}$ **12.** 9.75 $9\frac{3}{4}$ **13.** 0.625 $\frac{5}{8}$ **14.** 0.04 $\frac{1}{25}$ **15.** 3.45 $3\frac{9}{20}$

**16.** 0.050 $\frac{1}{20}$ **17.** 2.025 $2\frac{1}{40}$ **18.** 1.01 $1\frac{1}{100}$ **19.** 4.02 $4\frac{1}{50}$ **20.** 0.0625 $\frac{1}{16}$

**21.** 0.80 of a granola bar $\frac{4}{5}$ **22.** 0.625 of a cup $\frac{5}{8}$ **23.** 3.25 hours $3\frac{1}{4}$

**24.** 2.75 pizzas $2\frac{3}{4}$ **25.** 2.5 laps on a track $2\frac{1}{2}$ **26.** 0.25 of a dollar $\frac{1}{4}$



More Practice, page 425, Set C

## Follow Up

### Reteaching

List several decimal numbers on the chalkboard and have students read them aloud. Students should pay special attention to what they say for the part of the number that follows the decimal point. For example, 323.6 is read "three hundred twenty-three and *six tenths*." Then ask them if they can think of another way to write that part of the number. For example, six tenths can be written as a fraction as $\frac{6}{10}$. Thus 323.6 can be written $323\frac{6}{10}$.

### Enrichment

Provide students with models of various decimals such as the one shown below. Then challenge students to draw models and give several other fractional equivalents for each decimal. For example:

Model:

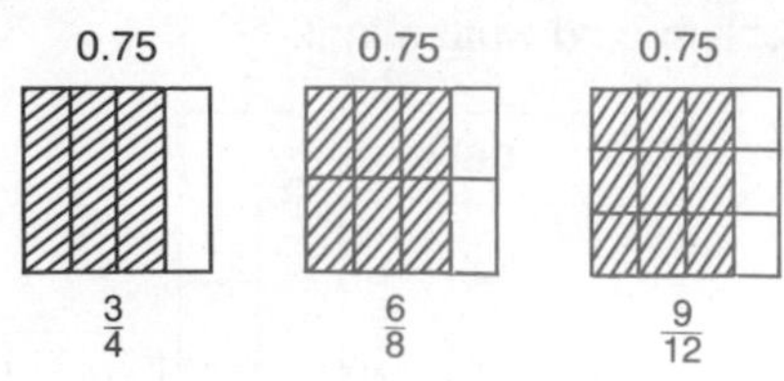

| Assignment Guide | | | |
|---|---|---|---|
| | Minimum | Average | Extended |
| page 236 | 1–26 | 1–26 | 1–26 |
| page 237 | 1–18 | 1–18 | 1–18 |

## From Fractions to Decimals

The Pacific Ocean covers almost $\frac{3}{8}$ of the Earth's surface. What is the decimal for this fraction?

To find a decimal for a given fraction, we can divide the numerator by the denominator.

$$\begin{array}{r} 0.375 \\ 8\overline{)3.000} \\ \underline{24\phantom{00}} \\ 60\phantom{0} \\ \underline{56\phantom{0}} \\ 40 \\ \underline{40} \\ 0 \end{array}$$

F P F
$\frac{3}{8} = 3 \div 8$
because
F F P
$\frac{3}{8} \times 8 = 3$
So we can divide 3 by 8 to find a decimal for $\frac{3}{8}$.

The decimal for the fraction $\frac{3}{8}$ is 0.375.

### Other Examples

$\frac{4}{10} = 0.4$

$\frac{27}{100} = 0.27$

We don't have to divide to find these!

$\frac{3}{4} \rightarrow \begin{array}{r} 0.75 \\ 4\overline{)3.0} \\ \underline{28} \\ 20 \\ \underline{20} \\ 0 \end{array} \rightarrow 0.75$

$\frac{8}{5} \rightarrow \begin{array}{r} 1.6 \\ 5\overline{)8.0} \\ \underline{5\phantom{0}} \\ 30 \\ \underline{30} \\ 0 \end{array} \rightarrow 1.6$

Write a decimal for each fraction.

**1.** $\frac{1}{2}$ 0.5 **2.** $\frac{2}{5}$ 0.4 **3.** $\frac{5}{10}$ 0.5 **4.** $\frac{5}{8}$ 0.625 **5.** $\frac{1}{4}$ 0.25 **6.** $\frac{16}{100}$ 0.16

**7.** $\frac{7}{5}$ 1.4 **8.** $\frac{3}{16}$ 0.1875 **9.** $\frac{4}{5}$ 0.8 **10.** $\frac{5}{4}$ 1.25 **11.** $\frac{1}{8}$ 0.125 **12.** $\frac{7}{20}$ 0.35

**13.** $\frac{12}{10}$ 1.2 **14.** $\frac{11}{8}$ 1.375 **15.** $\frac{5}{100}$ 0.05 **16.** $\frac{7}{8}$ 0.875 **17.** $\frac{3}{20}$ 0.15 **18.** $\frac{3}{2}$ 1.5

More Practice, page 425, Set D



## Using Page 237

**Lesson Development** Have students read the paragraph that tells the fraction of the Earth's surface covered by the Pacific Ocean. Point out that it is sometimes useful to show a fraction as a decimal. "In the equation $24 \div 4 = 6$, which numbers are the factors and which is the product?" (The factors are 4 and 6; the product is 24.) Then write $\frac{3}{8} = 3 \div 8$ on the chalkboard. "Which is the product and which are the factors?" (The product is 3; the factors are $\frac{3}{8}$ and 8.) Write F and P above the appropriate numbers. "How can you show that this equation is true?" $\left(\frac{3}{8} \times 8 = 3\right)$ Use the idea of the two factors and the product to help students see that a decimal for a fraction can be found by dividing the numerator by the denominator. Work through this division on the chalkboard. Ask students to read the sentence that tells that the Pacific Ocean covers almost 0.375 of the Earth's surface.

**Other Examples** In the first example, point out that when the denominator of a fraction is 10, 100, 1,000 and so on, the decimal can be written directly without dividing.

**Exercises 1–18** Pay particular attention to exercise 8, where the division must be carried out to four places and the decimal is given in ten-thousandths. Note that in exercise 15, the 5 is written in the hundredths place and zeros must be added to produce the decimal 0.05. Also note that exercises 3, 6, 13 and 15 can be done mentally, since the denominators are multiples of 10. Encourage students to complete mentally as many of the exercises as possible.

**More Practice,** page 425, Set C

**More Practice,** page 425, Set D

### Reteaching Supplement, page 55

Name ______ To follow text page 237

**From Decimals to Fractions and From Fractions to Decimals**

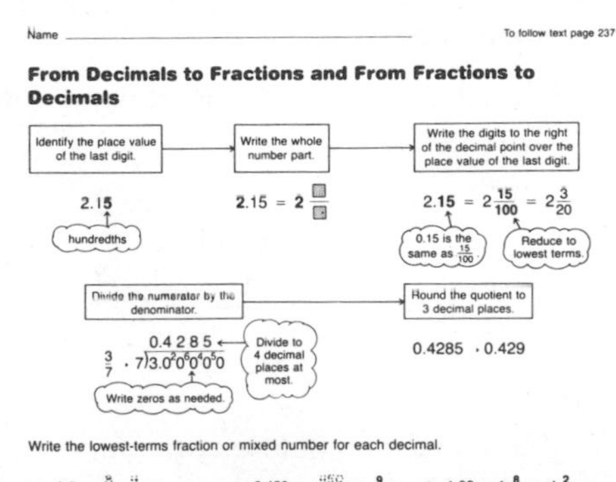

Identify the place value of the last digit. → Write the whole number part. → Write the digits to the right of the decimal point over the place value of the last digit.

2.15 (hundredths)

$2.15 = 2\frac{\square}{\square}$

$2.15 = 2\frac{15}{100} = 2\frac{3}{20}$ (0.15 is the same as $\frac{15}{100}$.) (Reduce to lowest terms.)

Divide the numerator by the denominator. → Round the quotient to 3 decimal places.

$\frac{3}{7}$ · $7\overline{)3.00000}$ = 0.4285 (Write zeros as needed.) (Divide to 4 decimal places at most.)

0.4285 · 0.429

Write the lowest-terms fraction or mixed number for each decimal.

1. $0.8 = \frac{8}{10} = \frac{4}{5}$ (tenths)
2. $0.450 = \frac{450}{1000} = \frac{9}{20}$ (thousandths)
3. $1.08 = 1\frac{8}{100} = 1\frac{2}{25}$ (hundredths)
4. $0.24 = \frac{24}{100} = \frac{6}{25}$
5. $0.5 = \frac{5}{10} = \frac{1}{2}$
6. $0.30 = \frac{30}{100} = \frac{3}{10}$
7. $0.225 = \frac{225}{1000} = \frac{9}{40}$
8. $0.75 = \frac{75}{100} = \frac{3}{4}$
9. $1.75 = 1\frac{75}{100} = 1\frac{3}{4}$
10. $0.005 = \frac{5}{1000} = \frac{1}{200}$
11. $5.64 = 5\frac{64}{100} = 5\frac{16}{25}$
12. $6.875 = 6\frac{875}{1000} = 6\frac{7}{8}$

Write a decimal for each fraction. Round to 3 decimal places.

13. $\frac{9}{40}$ · $40\overline{)9.000}$ = 0.225 · 0.225
14. $\frac{3}{10}$ · $10\overline{)3.0}$ = 0.3 · 0.3
15. $\frac{11}{20}$ · $20\overline{)11.00}$ = 0.55 · 0.55
16. $\frac{7}{8}$ · $8\overline{)7.000}$ = 0.875 · 0.875
17. $\frac{4}{7}$ · $7\overline{)4.0000}$ = 0.5714 · 0.571
18. $2\frac{5}{12}$ · $12\overline{)29.0000}$ = 2.4166 · 2.417

### Enrichment Supplement, page 55

Name ______ To follow text page 237

**A Fraction–Decimal Riddle**

Write each fraction as a decimal or write each decimal as a fraction. Then use your answers to solve the riddle.

A $\frac{1}{2}$ = 0.5 D $\frac{3}{8}$ = 0.375 E 0.70 = $\frac{7}{10}$

F $\frac{3}{20}$ = 0.15 G $\frac{7}{4}$ = 1.75 H 0.75 = $\frac{3}{4}$

I 2.625 = $2\frac{5}{8}$ N $\frac{5}{8}$ = 0.625 O $\frac{5}{16}$ = 0.3125

S 0.5625 = $\frac{9}{16}$ T $\frac{7}{8}$ = 0.875 U 0.125 = $\frac{1}{8}$

W $\frac{4}{25}$ = 0.16 Y $\frac{5}{4}$ = 1.25

Look at each number below. Then find it in one of the problems above. Write the letter of the problem in the blank above the number.

What do you feed a 200-kg gorilla?

Y O U F E E D
1.25 0.3125 $\frac{1}{8}$ 0.15 $\frac{7}{10}$ $\frac{7}{10}$ 0.375

I T A N Y T H I N G
$2\frac{5}{8}$ 0.875 0.5 0.625 1.25 0.875 $\frac{3}{4}$ $2\frac{5}{8}$ 0.625 1.75

I T W A N T S
$2\frac{5}{8}$ 0.875 0.16 0.5 0.625 0.875 $\frac{9}{16}$

### Practice Supplement, page 91

Name ______ To follow text page 237

**Fractions and Decimals**

Write the lowest-terms fraction or mixed number for each decimal.

1. 0.25 = $\frac{1}{4}$ 2. 3.5 = $3\frac{1}{2}$ 3. 0.85 = $\frac{17}{20}$
4. 0.8 = $\frac{4}{5}$ 5. 0.625 = $\frac{5}{8}$ 6. 1.04 = $1\frac{1}{25}$
7. 3.015 = $3\frac{3}{200}$ 8. 0.22 = $\frac{11}{50}$ 9. 2.375 = $2\frac{3}{8}$
10. 5.35 = $5\frac{7}{20}$ 11. 2.03 = $2\frac{3}{100}$ 12. 0.9 = $\frac{9}{10}$
13. 0.455 = $\frac{91}{200}$ 14. 6.75 = $6\frac{3}{4}$ 15. 1.12 = $1\frac{3}{25}$
16. 4.875 = $4\frac{7}{8}$ 17. 0.28 = $\frac{7}{25}$ 18. 1.55 = $1\frac{11}{20}$

Write a decimal for each fraction.

19. $\frac{4}{5}$ = 0.8 20. $\frac{3}{25}$ = 0.12 21. $\frac{19}{20}$ = 0.95
22. $\frac{14}{50}$ = 0.28 23. $\frac{23}{25}$ = 0.92 24. $\frac{2}{20}$ = 0.1
25. $\frac{9}{8}$ = 1.125 26. $\frac{45}{12}$ = 3.75 27. $\frac{9}{50}$ = 0.18
28. $\frac{9}{16}$ = 0.5625 29. $\frac{14}{8}$ = 1.75 30. $\frac{9}{4}$ = 2.25
31. $\frac{13}{8}$ = 1.625 32. $\frac{37}{50}$ = 0.74 33. $\frac{17}{25}$ = 0.68

**Quick Review** Students round 3-place decimals to the nearest hundredth and 2-place decimals to the nearest tenth.

0.009 0.34 0.605 0.475 0.06 0.14 0.074
0.65 0.29 0.404 0.387 0.56 0.335

**Lesson Focus** To write a mixed decimal for a given fraction; to use models to prepare for dividing fractions

## Ideas for Getting Started

On the chalkboard make a chart like the following. Work with students to give the decimals for the fractions shown.

| Fraction | $\frac{1}{2}$ | $\frac{1}{3}$ | $\frac{1}{4}$ | $\frac{1}{5}$ | $\frac{1}{8}$ | $\frac{2}{3}$ | $\frac{2}{5}$ | $\frac{3}{4}$ | $\frac{3}{5}$ |
|---|---|---|---|---|---|---|---|---|---|
| Decimal | | | | | | | | | |

First, include only those decimals that come out even to two or three places. $\left(\frac{1}{2} = 0.5; \frac{1}{4} = 0.25; \frac{1}{5} = 0.2; \frac{1}{8} = 0.125; \frac{2}{5} = 0.4; \frac{3}{4} = 0.75; \frac{3}{5} = 0.6\right)$ Then begin the dividing process to find a decimal for $\frac{1}{3}$. Help students see that this dividing process can be continued indefinitely with threes repeating in each place of the quotient. Explain that in this lesson, we will learn ways to write decimals for fractions when the division does not come out even.

## Using Page 238

**Lesson Development** Read and discuss the information about the areas of Africa and Asia at the top of the page. Then discuss the procedure for writing a mixed decimal for the fraction $\frac{2}{3}$. Show the dividing process on the chalkboard. After you have divided in the hundredths place, call attention to the remainder 2 and the divisor 3. Point out that we can compare the remainder to the divisor to find a fractional part of one hundredth and write a mixed decimal $0.66\frac{2}{3}$. Also show students that the dividing can be continued indefinitely with sixes repeating in the quotient. Or, we can divide to three places and round to the nearest hundredth. Thus, the decimal 0.67 is a close approximation to the fraction $\frac{2}{3}$. Ask a volunteer to read the sentence that tells that the area of Africa is about $0.66\frac{2}{3}$ or 0.67 of the area of Asia.

**Other Examples** In each of these examples, be sure students reduce the fractional part of the mixed decimal to the lowest terms. Also show students how the dividing could be continued to the thousandths place, and the decimal rounded to the nearest hundredth. Remind students to annex zeros in the dividend as needed to complete the dividing.

**Exercises 1–12** Observe students as they find the mixed decimals for these fractions. Be sure they annex zeros to complete the dividing process to the number of places desired. Note that exercises 5 and 9 involve improper fractions and thus produce decimals greater than one.

**Exercises 13–18** Remind students that they must carry the dividing to the thousandths place in order to round to the nearest hundredth.

## Writing Fractions as Mixed Decimals

The area of Africa is about $\frac{2}{3}$ the area of Asia.

What decimal can be used for this fraction?

You can find a **mixed decimal** for $\frac{2}{3}$ by dividing to two places and writing a fraction using the remainder and the divisor.

$0.66\frac{2}{3}$: $3\overline{)2.00}$, $-18$, $20$, $-18$, $2$

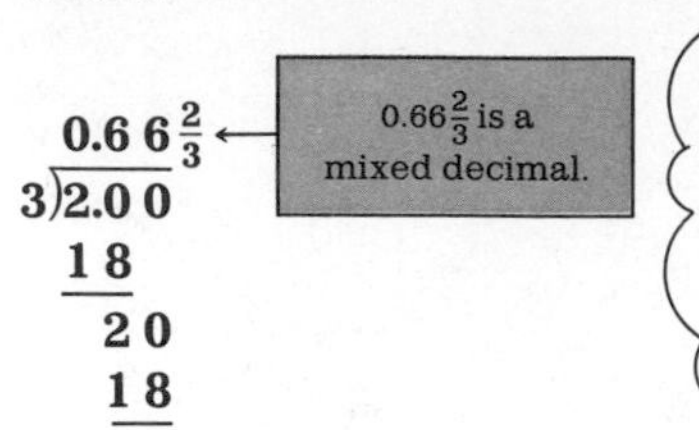
$0.66\frac{2}{3}$ is a mixed decimal.

We can get a decimal that's close by dividing to three places and rounding to two places.

$3\overline{)2.000} = 0.666$ or 0.67

The area of Africa is about $0.66\frac{2}{3}$ or 0.67 of the area of Asia.

**Other Examples**

$\frac{5}{6} \rightarrow 6\overline{)5.00}$ = 0.83 (48, 20, 18, 2) $\rightarrow 0.83\frac{2}{6}$ or $0.83\frac{1}{3}$

$\frac{9}{8} \rightarrow 8\overline{)9.00}$ = 1.12 (8, 10, 8, 20, 16, 4) $\rightarrow 1.12\frac{4}{8}$ or $1.12\frac{1}{2}$

Write a mixed decimal for each fraction.

**1.** $\frac{1}{8}$ $0.12\frac{1}{2}$ **2.** $\frac{5}{6}$ $0.83\frac{1}{3}$ **3.** $\frac{1}{3}$ $0.33\frac{1}{3}$ **4.** $\frac{5}{8}$ $0.62\frac{1}{2}$ **5.** $\frac{5}{3}$ $1.66\frac{2}{3}$ **6.** $\frac{7}{16}$ $0.43\frac{3}{4}$

**7.** $\frac{1}{6}$ $0.16\frac{2}{3}$ **8.** $\frac{7}{12}$ $0.58\frac{1}{3}$ **9.** $\frac{7}{6}$ $1.16\frac{2}{3}$ **10.** $\frac{5}{16}$ $0.31\frac{1}{4}$ **11.** $\frac{5}{9}$ $0.55\frac{5}{9}$ **12.** $\frac{4}{15}$ $0.26\frac{2}{3}$

Write a decimal rounded to the nearest hundredth for each fraction.

**13.** $\frac{7}{8}$ 0.88 **14.** $\frac{7}{3}$ 2.33 **15.** $\frac{11}{6}$ 1.83 **16.** $\frac{5}{16}$ 0.31 **17.** $\frac{3}{8}$ 0.38 **18.** $\frac{5}{12}$ 0.42

238

## Follow Up

### Reteaching

Ask for student volunteers to write mixed decimals on the chalkboard as you say the numbers aloud. Here are some examples to get started.

- thirty-six and one half hundredths $\left(0.36\frac{1}{2}\right)$
- sixty-six and two thirds hundredths $\left(0.66\frac{2}{3}\right)$
- thirty-seven and one fifth hundredths $\left(0.37\frac{1}{5}\right)$
- one and forty-two and one fourth hundredths $\left(1.42\frac{1}{4}\right)$

### Enrichment

Provide students with copies of the game sheet below.

$$\frac{\square}{\square} \div \frac{\square}{\square} = n$$

Set a goal for $n$ before each game. Draw 4-digit cards made from index cards on which are written the digits 1 through 9. Have students fill in the squares with the four numbers which are drawn. The person closest to the goal wins.

| Assignment Guide | | | |
|---|---|---|---|
| | Minimum | Average | Extended |
| page 238 | 1–18 | 1–18 | 1–18 |
| page 239 | 1–8 | 1–8 | 1–8 |

## Getting Ready to Divide Fractions

The exercises below will help you get ready to divide fractions. Use the pictures to answer the questions.

By counting, we see there are six $\frac{1}{2}$s in 3 oranges.

We count the number of $\frac{1}{4}$ pieces in the $\frac{5}{2}$ pizzas!


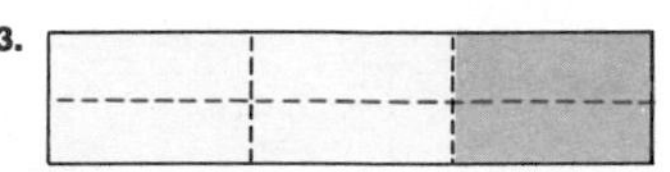

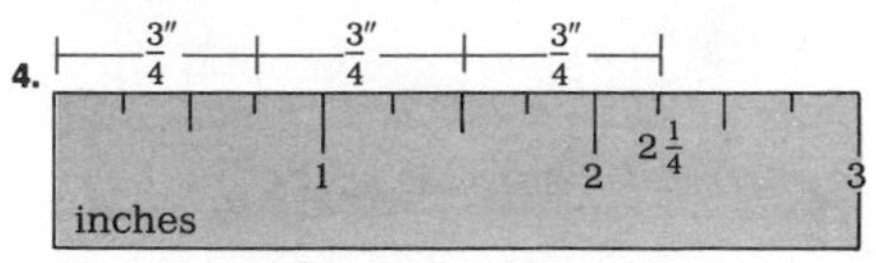

1. How many $\frac{1}{2}$s are in 3? 6

2. How many $\frac{1}{4}$s are in $\frac{5}{2}$? 10

3. 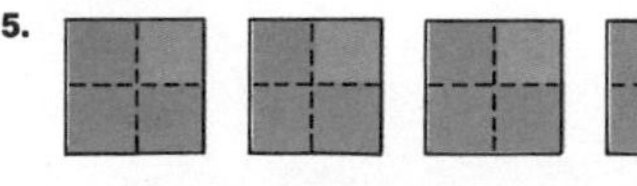

   How many $\frac{1}{6}$s are in $\frac{2}{3}$? 4

4. $\frac{3''}{4}$ $\frac{3''}{4}$ $\frac{3''}{4}$ — 1 2 $2\frac{1}{4}$ 3 inches

   How many $\frac{3}{4}$s are in $2\frac{1}{4}$? 3

5. How many $\frac{3}{4}$s are in $3\frac{3}{4}$? 5

6. 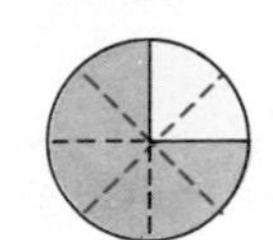

   How many $\frac{1}{8}$s are in $\frac{3}{4}$? 6

Use the pictures to help you solve the equations. Check each division by multiplying.

7. 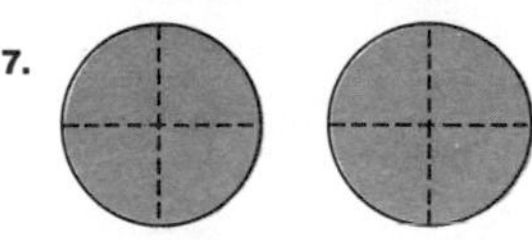

   How many $\frac{1}{4}$s are in 2?

   $2 \div \frac{1}{4} = n$ $n = 8$

8. 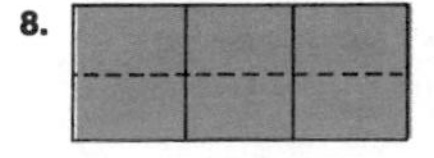 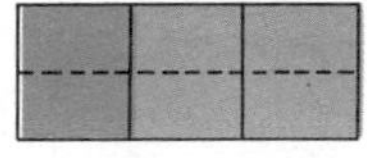

   How many $\frac{1}{6}$s are in $\frac{4}{3}$?

   $\frac{4}{3} \div \frac{1}{6} = n$ $n = 8$



## Using Page 239

**Lesson Development** Have students focus on the illustrations on this page. Work through exercises 1 and 2 and have students refer to the pictures to count the number of parts involved. After students have completed the remaining exercises, discuss each one, focusing on the idea of dividing. Do not introduce the rule for dividing fractions at this time; rather, focus on the models as an aid to understanding the division process.

**Exercise 4** Note that this exercise uses the ruler as a device for determining the number of $\frac{3}{4}$s in $2\frac{1}{4}$. Ask students other fraction questions involving the ruler, such as: "How many $\frac{1}{2}$s in $2\frac{1}{2}$? How many $\frac{1}{4}$s in $3\frac{1}{4}$?" and so on.

**Exercises 7–8** Point out that these exercises show a division equation, and ask students to use each model to help solve the equation. Note in exercise 7 that 2 is the quotient, $\frac{1}{4}$ is the factor, and we want to find the missing factor. Answers can be checked using multiplication of fractions.

## Ideas That Work

### Math for the Gifted

Decimals for fractions with denominators of 7, $\frac{1}{7}, \frac{2}{7}, \frac{3}{7}, \ldots, \frac{6}{7}$, have repeating, cyclic patterns which can be illustrated using a dial like the one below.

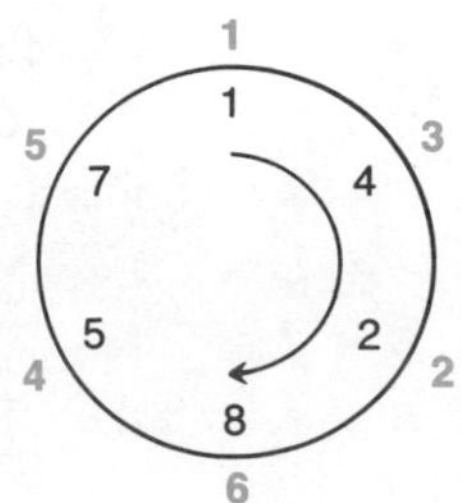


To use the dial to find the repeating decimals for fractions whose denominators are 7, follow these steps.

- Locate the numerator on the outside ring.
- Start with the digit beside the numerator inside the dial. Read the digits in clockwise order around the dial.

$\frac{1}{7} = 0.142857\ldots$ $\frac{4}{7} = 0.571428\ldots$
$\frac{2}{7} = 0.285714\ldots$ $\frac{5}{7} = 0.714285\ldots$
$\frac{3}{7} = 0.428571\ldots$ $\frac{6}{7} = 0.857142\ldots$

**Practice Supplement,** page 92

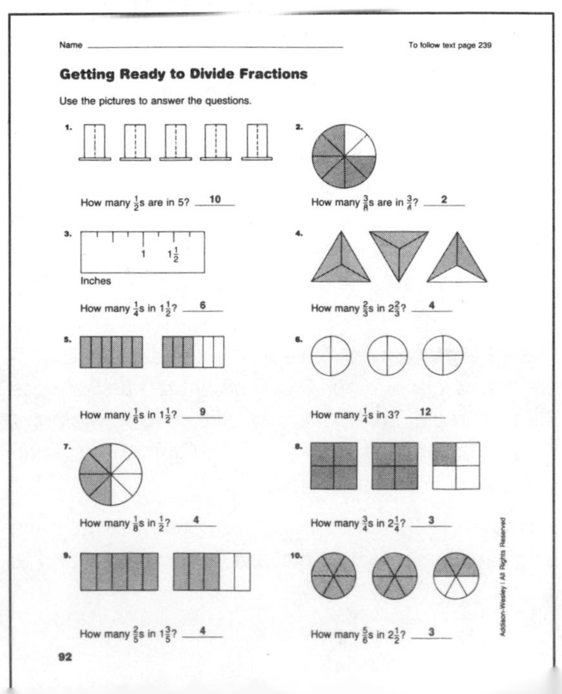
Name ________ To follow text page 239

**Getting Ready to Divide Fractions**

Use the pictures to answer the questions.

1. How many $\frac{1}{2}$s are in 5? 10
2. How many $\frac{3}{8}$s are in $\frac{3}{4}$? 2
3. (1, $1\frac{1}{2}$, Inches) How many $\frac{1}{4}$s in $1\frac{1}{2}$? 6
4. How many $\frac{2}{3}$s in $2\frac{2}{3}$? 4
5. How many $\frac{1}{6}$s in $1\frac{1}{2}$? 9
6. How many $\frac{1}{4}$s in 3? 12
7. How many $\frac{1}{8}$s in $\frac{1}{2}$? 4
8. How many $\frac{3}{4}$s in $2\frac{1}{4}$? 3
9. How many $\frac{2}{5}$s in $1\frac{3}{5}$? 4
10. How many $\frac{5}{6}$s in $2\frac{1}{2}$? 3

92

# Fractions: Division

**Quick Review** Students supply the missing numbers to make equivalent fractions.

$\frac{50}{100} = \frac{1}{\square}$ $\frac{\square}{6} = \frac{1}{3}$ $\frac{7}{\square} = \frac{1}{4}$ $\frac{1}{4} = \frac{\square}{20}$ $\frac{\square}{21} = \frac{1}{3}$ $\frac{\square}{8} = \frac{2}{16}$

$\frac{14}{\square} = \frac{28}{40}$ $\frac{1}{2} = \frac{\square}{18}$ $\frac{1}{3} = \frac{3}{\square}$ $\frac{1}{2} = \frac{5}{\square}$ $\frac{2}{\square} = \frac{1}{4}$

**Lesson Focus** To find the quotient of two fractions

## Ideas for Getting Started

Refer to the problems on page 239. For each problem, write a division equation on the chalkboard as follows and have students give the quotient.

1. $\frac{5}{2} \div \frac{1}{4} = n$ 2. $3 \div \frac{1}{2} = n$
3. $\frac{2}{3} \div \frac{1}{6} = n$ 4. $2\frac{1}{4} \div \frac{3}{4} = n$
5. $3\frac{3}{4} \div \frac{3}{4} = n$ 6. $\frac{3}{4} \div \frac{1}{8} = n$
7. $2 \div \frac{1}{4} = n$ 8. $\frac{4}{3} \div \frac{1}{6} = n$

Below each of those equations write the following:

(a) $\frac{5}{2} \times \frac{4}{1} = n$ (b) $3 \times \frac{2}{1} = n$
(c) $\frac{2}{3} \times \frac{6}{1} = n$ (d) $2\frac{1}{4} \times \frac{4}{3} = n$
(e) $3\frac{3}{4} \times \frac{4}{3} = n$ (f) $\frac{3}{4} \times \frac{8}{1} = n$
(g) $2 \times \frac{4}{1} = n$ (h) $\frac{4}{3} \times \frac{6}{1} = n$

"What do you notice about these pairs of equations?" (The answers are the same in each pair.) "The first number in the second equation is the same as the first number in the first equation. What can you say to describe the second numbers in each equation?" (They are reciprocals of each other.)

## Using Page 240

**Motivational Problem** Have students read the problem at the top of the page. "What question are we asked about the map?" (How many miles is it from Clinton to Farmer City?) "What data is given in the problem?" ($\frac{1}{4}$ in. on the map equals one mi on the road; $\frac{7}{8}$ in. on the map from Clinton to Farmer City.) Elicit from students that we want to find out how many $\frac{1}{4}$-in. segments are in a $\frac{7}{8}$-in. segment.

**Lesson Development** Direct students' attention to the instruction boxes. Point out that the answer to the division problem $\frac{7}{8} \div \frac{1}{4}$ is the same as the answer to the multiplication problem $\frac{7}{8} \times \frac{4}{1}$. Write $\frac{7}{8} \times \frac{4}{1}$ on the chalkboard and have students find the product. Use their suggestions to rename $\frac{7}{2}$ as $3\frac{1}{2}$. "How can we check to see if this is the correct answer to the division equation?" (We can multiply this quotient by the divisor $\frac{1}{4}$.) Have students complete the multiplication to show that $3\frac{1}{2} \times \frac{1}{4} = \frac{7}{8}$. Be sure students understand that we can find the quotient of two fractions by multiplying the dividend by the reciprocal of the divisor.

**Other Examples** Note that in the second example the whole number 6 can be written as $\frac{6}{1}$. In the third example, the quotient involves two whole numbers. After each is written as a fraction, the dividing process can be completed.

**Warm Up** Be alert for errors where students have used the reciprocal of the dividend rather than the divisor.

## Dividing Fractions

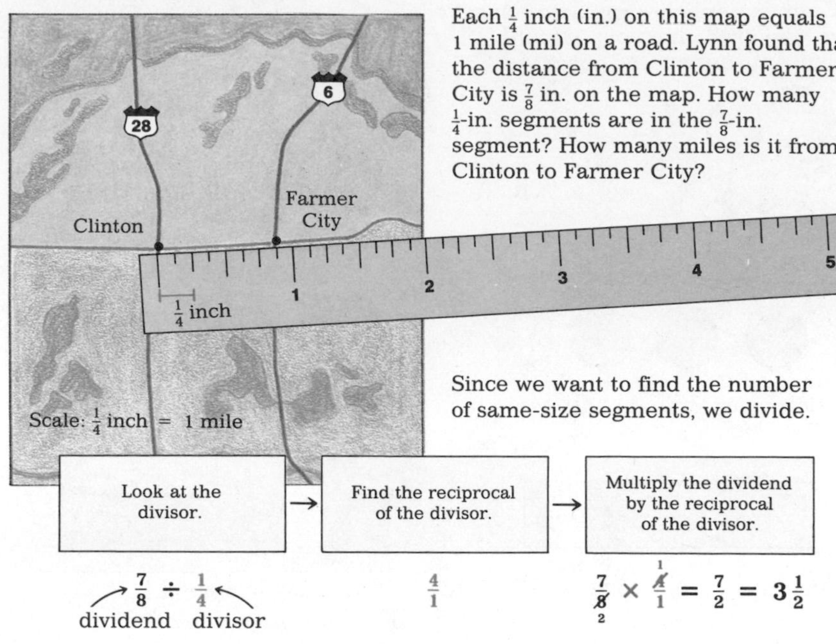


Each $\frac{1}{4}$ inch (in.) on this map equals 1 mile (mi) on a road. Lynn found that the distance from Clinton to Farmer City is $\frac{7}{8}$ in. on the map. How many $\frac{1}{4}$-in. segments are in the $\frac{7}{8}$-in. segment? How many miles is it from Clinton to Farmer City?

Since we want to find the number of same-size segments, we divide.

Look at the divisor. → Find the reciprocal of the divisor. → Multiply the dividend by the reciprocal of the divisor.

$\frac{7}{8} \div \frac{1}{4}$ (dividend, divisor) $\qquad \frac{4}{1} \qquad \frac{7}{\not{8}_2} \times \frac{\not{4}^1}{1} = \frac{7}{2} = 3\frac{1}{2}$

There are $3\frac{1}{2}$ of the $\frac{1}{4}$-in. segments in the $\frac{7}{8}$-in. segment, so it is $3\frac{1}{2}$ mi from Clinton to Farmer City.

**Other Examples**

$\frac{3}{5} \div \frac{2}{3} = \frac{3}{5} \times \frac{3}{2} = \frac{9}{10}$ $\qquad 6 \div \frac{3}{4} = \frac{\not{6}^2}{1} \times \frac{4}{\not{3}_1} = 8$ $\qquad 6 \div 9 = \frac{\not{6}^2}{1} \times \frac{1}{\not{9}_3} = \frac{2}{3}$

Check: $\frac{\not{9}^3}{\not{10}_5} \times \frac{\not{2}^1}{\not{3}_1} = \frac{3}{5}$

**Warm Up** Find the quotients. Check by multiplying.

1. $\frac{2}{3} \div \frac{1}{4}$ $\frac{8}{3} = 2\frac{2}{3}$ 2. $\frac{1}{2} \div \frac{2}{5}$ $\frac{5}{4} = 1\frac{1}{4}$ 3. $\frac{3}{4} \div \frac{1}{10}$ $\frac{15}{2} = 7\frac{1}{2}$ 4. $4 \div \frac{3}{8}$ $\frac{32}{3} = 10\frac{2}{3}$ 5. $\frac{2}{5} \div \frac{1}{2}$ $\frac{4}{5}$
6. $\frac{2}{3} \div 5$ $\frac{2}{15}$ 7. $3 \div 5$ $\frac{3}{5}$ 8. $\frac{9}{10} \div \frac{1}{5}$ $\frac{9}{2} = 4\frac{1}{2}$ 9. $\frac{5}{6} \div \frac{2}{3}$ $\frac{5}{4} = 1\frac{1}{4}$ 10. $\frac{3}{4} \div \frac{7}{8}$ $\frac{6}{7}$

240

## Follow Up

### Reteaching

Demonstrate to students that dividing by a number and multiplying by its reciprocal gives the same result. First use simple division problems without fractions and then show that the same is true for dividing fractions.

| | |
|---|---|
| $12 \div 2 = 6$ | $12 \times \frac{1}{2} = 6$ |
| $6 \div 3 = 2$ | $6 \times \frac{1}{3} = 2$ |
| $3 \div 3 = 1$ | $3 \times \frac{1}{3} = 1$ |
| $4 \div 2 = 2$ | $4 \times \frac{1}{2} = 2$ |
| $1 \div \frac{1}{2} = 2$ | $1 \times 2 = 2$ |
| $\frac{1}{2} \div \frac{1}{4} = 2$ | $\frac{1}{2} \times \frac{4}{1} = 2$ |

### Enrichment

Have students complete the following exercises. Emphasize that given the same dividend, the smaller the divisor the greater the quotient.

| | | |
|---|---|---|
| $24 \div 4$ 6 | $6 \div 12$ $\frac{1}{2}$ | $1 \div 1{,}000$ $\frac{1}{1{,}000}$ |
| $24 \div 3$ 8 | $6 \div 6$ 1 | $1 \div 100$ $\frac{1}{100}$ |
| $24 \div 2$ 12 | $6 \div 3$ 2 | $1 \div 10$ $\frac{1}{10}$ |
| $24 \div 1$ 24 | $6 \div 1$ 6 | $1 \div 1$ 1 |
| $24 \div \frac{1}{2}$ 48 | $6 \div \frac{1}{3}$ 18 | $1 \div \frac{1}{10}$ 10 |
| $24 \div \frac{1}{3}$ 72 | $6 \div \frac{1}{6}$ 36 | $1 \div \frac{1}{100}$ 100 |
| $24 \div \frac{1}{4}$ 96 | $6 \div \frac{1}{12}$ 72 | $1 \div \frac{1}{1{,}000}$ 1,000 |

| Assignment Guide | Minimum | Average | Extended |
|---|---|---|---|
| page 241 | 1–31 | 1–33 | 11–33, TM |

Find the quotients. Check by multiplying.

1. $\frac{1}{2} \div \frac{4}{5}$ $\frac{5}{8}$
2. $\frac{3}{4} \div \frac{3}{5}$ $\frac{5}{4} = 1\frac{1}{4}$
3. $\frac{2}{3} \div \frac{3}{4}$ $\frac{8}{9}$
4. $\frac{1}{2} \div \frac{1}{4}$ $\frac{2}{1} = 2$
5. $\frac{7}{8} \div \frac{7}{8}$ $\frac{1}{1} = 1$
6. $5 \div \frac{2}{5}$ $\frac{25}{2} = 12\frac{1}{2}$
7. $\frac{5}{6} \div 10$ $\frac{1}{12}$
8. $3 \div 8$ $\frac{3}{8}$
9. $\frac{1}{2} \div \frac{5}{8}$ $\frac{4}{5}$
10. $\frac{9}{14} \div \frac{3}{7}$ $\frac{3}{2} = 1\frac{1}{2}$
11. $\frac{7}{8} \div \frac{3}{4}$ $\frac{7}{6} = 1\frac{1}{6}$
12. $\frac{1}{3} \div \frac{2}{3}$ $\frac{1}{2}$
13. $\frac{3}{10} \div \frac{3}{4}$ $\frac{2}{5}$
14. $\frac{4}{5} \div \frac{2}{3}$ $\frac{6}{5} = 1\frac{1}{5}$
15. $\frac{1}{2} \div \frac{7}{10}$ $\frac{5}{7}$
16. $7 \div \frac{2}{3}$ $\frac{21}{2} = 10\frac{1}{2}$
17. $\frac{9}{10} \div 3$ $\frac{3}{10}$
18. $4 \div 12$ $\frac{1}{3}$
19. $\frac{1}{10} \div \frac{3}{10}$ $\frac{1}{3}$
20. $\frac{3}{5} \div \frac{2}{3}$ $\frac{9}{10}$
21. $\frac{3}{8} \div \frac{3}{4}$ $\frac{1}{2}$
22. $\frac{2}{5} \div \frac{3}{2}$ $\frac{4}{15}$
23. $\frac{5}{6} \div \frac{2}{3}$ $\frac{5}{4} = 1\frac{1}{4}$
24. $\frac{3}{8} \div \frac{4}{3}$ $\frac{9}{32}$
25. $4 \div \frac{1}{8}$ $\frac{32}{1} = 32$
26. $8 \div \frac{2}{5}$ $\frac{20}{1} = 20$
27. $\frac{5}{8} \div \frac{1}{3}$ $\frac{15}{8} = 1\frac{7}{8}$
28. $\frac{4}{5} \div \frac{1}{6}$ $\frac{24}{5} = 4\frac{4}{5}$
29. $\frac{5}{2} \div \frac{3}{4}$ $\frac{10}{3} = 3\frac{1}{3}$
30. $\frac{5}{12} \div \frac{1}{6}$ $\frac{5}{2} = 2\frac{1}{2}$

31. Each $\frac{1}{2}$ in. on a certain map represents a mile on the road. It is $\frac{3}{4}$ in. between two cities on the map. How many miles is it between the two cities? $1\frac{1}{2}$ mi

32. Use the data given on the map to find the actual distance from Perry to Milton. $4\frac{1}{2}$ mi

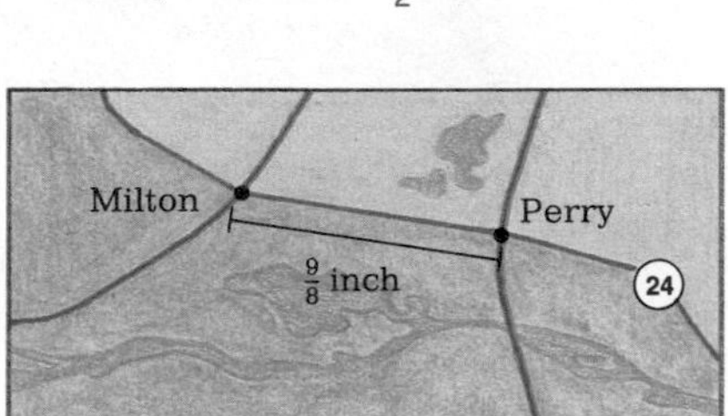


33. **DATA BANK** How many miles farther is it from Orlando to Ocala than it is from Sanford to DeLand? (See page 409.) 45 mi

**Think**

**Understanding Fractions**

You can find a fraction between any two fractions by finding the average of those fractions. Find a fraction between $\frac{2}{3}$ and $\frac{3}{4}$ by dividing the sum of these fractions by 2. Use the symbol < to show that your fraction is greater than $\frac{2}{3}$ but less than $\frac{3}{4}$.

$\frac{17}{24}$, $\frac{16}{24} < \frac{17}{24} < \frac{18}{24}$

0 $\frac{2}{3}$ $\frac{3}{4}$ 1

**Math**

More Practice, page 426, Set A



## Using Page 241

**Exercises 1–30** Give special attention to exercises such as 6, 7, and 8 which involve whole numbers. Note in exercise 5 that students should be able to give the answer immediately, because any number divided by itself is 1. Observe students' work to be sure they are finding the reciprocal of the divisor and not the dividend. Be sure they are completing the multiplication process correctly, and encourage them to go back to the original division problem to check their answers.

**Exercise 32** Note that this exercise requires students to use the information from the map to find the distance between the two cities. In this case $\frac{1}{4}$ in. on the map equals 10 mi on the road. Be sure students understand that to find how many $\frac{1}{4}$-in. segments are in a $\frac{9}{8}$-in. segment, they divide.

**Data Bank** This exercise gives students an opportunity to seek data in the special reference section in the back of the book. Be sure students know how to use the distances on the map to find the distances between the cities.

**Think Math** This activity asks students to think about points for numbers on the number line. Explain that between *any two* fractions on the number line, there is another fraction. Be sure they understand the procedure for adding the two fractions and dividing by 2 to find this fraction. Note that when the fractions are written using the denominator 24, it is easy to see that the fraction produced by the procedure is between $\frac{2}{3}$ and $\frac{3}{4}$. Extend this activity by challenging students to find a fraction between $\frac{3}{7}$ and $\frac{4}{9}$, and between $\frac{5}{8}$ and $\frac{2}{3}$.

**More Practice,** page 426, Set A

**Reteaching Supplement,** page 56

Name ______ To follow text page 241

**Dividing Fractions**

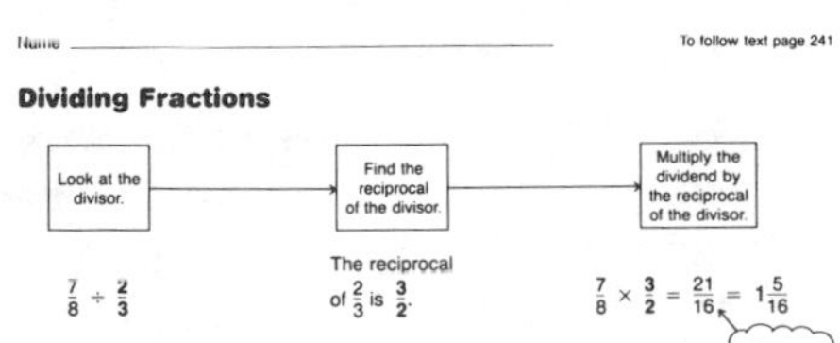


$\frac{7}{8} \div \frac{2}{3}$ The reciprocal of $\frac{2}{3}$ is $\frac{3}{2}$. $\frac{7}{8} \times \frac{3}{2} = \frac{21}{16} = 1\frac{5}{16}$ Rename.

Find the quotients. Write each division problem as a multiplication problem.

1. $\frac{6}{7} \div \frac{2}{3} = \frac{6}{7} \times \frac{3}{2} =$ $\frac{9}{7} = 1\frac{2}{7}$
2. $10 \div \frac{1}{2} = \frac{10}{1} \times \frac{2}{1} =$ 20
3. $\frac{1}{2} \div \frac{1}{3} = \frac{1}{2} \times \frac{3}{1} =$ $\frac{3}{2} = 1\frac{1}{2}$
4. $\frac{3}{7} \div 3 = \frac{3}{7} \times \frac{1}{3} =$ $\frac{1}{7}$
5. $\frac{2}{5} \div \frac{1}{4} = \frac{2}{5} \times \frac{4}{1} =$ $\frac{8}{5} = 1\frac{3}{5}$
6. $\frac{3}{5} \div \frac{2}{3} = \frac{3}{5} \times \frac{3}{2} =$ $\frac{9}{10}$
7. $\frac{5}{9} \div \frac{1}{2} = \frac{5}{9} \times \frac{2}{1} =$ $\frac{10}{9} = 1\frac{1}{9}$
8. $\frac{5}{18} \div \frac{5}{18} = \frac{5}{18} \times \frac{18}{5} =$ 1

Find the quotients.

9. $\frac{3}{4} \div \frac{5}{6} =$ $\frac{3}{4} \times \frac{6}{5} = \frac{9}{10}$
10. $\frac{2}{3} \div 8 =$ $\frac{2}{3} \times \frac{1}{8} = \frac{1}{12}$
11. $4 \div \frac{2}{3} =$ $\frac{4}{1} \times \frac{3}{2} = \frac{6}{1} = 6$
12. $\frac{1}{2} \div 6 =$ $\frac{1}{2} \times \frac{1}{6} = \frac{1}{12}$
13. $\frac{6}{7} \div \frac{1}{2} =$ $\frac{6}{7} \times \frac{2}{1} = \frac{12}{7} = 1\frac{5}{7}$
14. $\frac{9}{10} \div 3 =$ $\frac{9}{10} \times \frac{1}{3} = \frac{3}{10}$
15. $\frac{7}{10} \div \frac{4}{5} =$ $\frac{7}{10} \times \frac{5}{4} = \frac{7}{8}$
16. $\frac{3}{8} \div \frac{1}{2} =$ $\frac{3}{8} \times \frac{2}{1} = \frac{3}{4}$
17. $\frac{1}{2} \div \frac{1}{4} =$ $\frac{1}{2} \times \frac{4}{1} = \frac{2}{1} = 2$
18. $\frac{1}{3} \div \frac{4}{9} =$ $\frac{1}{3} \times \frac{9}{4} = \frac{3}{4}$
19. $\frac{7}{10} \div \frac{2}{5} =$ $\frac{7}{10} \times \frac{5}{2} = \frac{7}{4} = 1\frac{3}{4}$
20. $\frac{2}{3} \div \frac{2}{5} =$ $\frac{2}{3} \times \frac{5}{2} = 1\frac{2}{3}$

**Enrichment Supplement,** page 56

Name ______ To follow text page 241

**Reciprocals**

1. Connect the points for each fraction and its reciprocal.

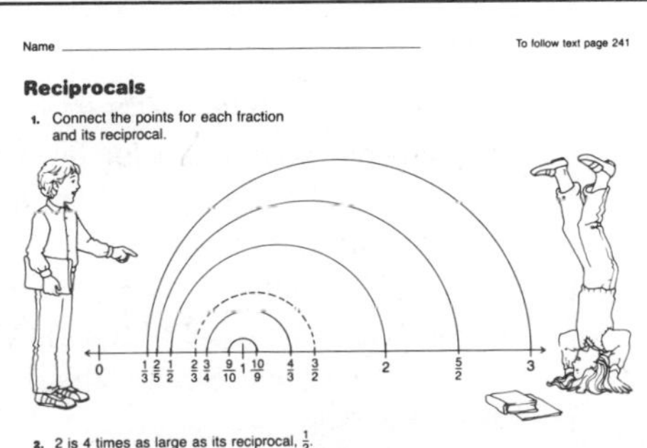


2. 2 is 4 times as large as its reciprocal, $\frac{1}{2}$.

   $4 \times \frac{1}{2} = 2$

   What number is 9 times as large as its reciprocal? 3
3. What number is 25 times its reciprocal? 5
4. How many times larger is 10 than its reciprocal? 100
5. What is the only number that is equal to its reciprocal? 1
6. List the reciprocals of 2, 3, and 6. $\frac{1}{2}$ $\frac{1}{3}$ $\frac{1}{6}$
7. Find the sum of the reciprocals of 2, 3, and 6. 1
8. Write the reciprocals of 2, 4, 7, 14, and 28. $\frac{1}{2}$ $\frac{1}{4}$ $\frac{1}{7}$ $\frac{1}{14}$ $\frac{1}{28}$
9. Find the sum of the reciprocals of 2, 4, 7, 14, and 28. 1

**Practice Supplement,** page 93

Name ______ To follow text page 241

**Dividing Fractions**

Find the quotients.

1. $\frac{1}{4} \div \frac{2}{3} =$ $\frac{3}{8}$
2. $\frac{1}{2} \div \frac{5}{8} =$ $\frac{4}{5}$
3. $\frac{1}{4} \div \frac{1}{2} =$ $\frac{1}{2}$
4. $\frac{1}{3} \div \frac{2}{5} =$ $\frac{5}{6}$
5. $5 \div \frac{1}{2} =$ 10
6. $\frac{3}{7} \div \frac{3}{4} =$ $\frac{4}{7}$
7. $\frac{5}{8} \div \frac{2}{3} =$ $\frac{15}{16}$
8. $\frac{5}{6} \div \frac{5}{8} =$ $1\frac{1}{3}$
9. $\frac{4}{5} \div \frac{5}{6} =$ $\frac{24}{25}$
10. $\frac{3}{5} \div \frac{1}{10} =$ 6
11. $\frac{5}{6} \div \frac{2}{3} =$ $1\frac{1}{4}$
12. $\frac{3}{4} \div \frac{1}{3} =$ $\frac{9}{4} = 2\frac{1}{4}$
13. $\frac{1}{2} \div \frac{1}{3} =$ $\frac{3}{2} = 1\frac{1}{2}$
14. $\frac{3}{4} \div \frac{5}{6} =$ $\frac{9}{10}$
15. $\frac{1}{5} \div 3 =$ $\frac{1}{15}$
16. $\frac{5}{6} \div \frac{5}{6} =$ 1
17. $2 \div \frac{3}{5} =$ $\frac{10}{3} = 3\frac{1}{3}$
18. $\frac{2}{5} \div \frac{4}{7} =$ $\frac{7}{10}$
19. $\frac{7}{8} \div \frac{5}{3} =$ $\frac{21}{40}$
20. $\frac{2}{3} \div \frac{1}{4} =$ $\frac{8}{3} = 2\frac{2}{3}$
21. $\frac{5}{7} \div \frac{1}{2} =$ $\frac{10}{7} = 1\frac{3}{7}$
22. $\frac{4}{5} \div \frac{5}{8} =$ $\frac{32}{25} = 1\frac{7}{25}$
23. $\frac{1}{3} \div \frac{4}{5} =$ $\frac{5}{12}$
24. $\frac{5}{9} \div \frac{1}{2} =$ $\frac{10}{9} = 1\frac{1}{9}$
25. $\frac{4}{9} \div \frac{1}{3} =$ $\frac{4}{3} = 1\frac{1}{3}$
26. $\frac{3}{5} \div 3 =$ $\frac{1}{5}$
27. $\frac{9}{10} \div \frac{3}{5} =$ $\frac{3}{2} = 1\frac{1}{2}$
28. $3 \div \frac{3}{7} =$ 7
29. $\frac{2}{3} \div \frac{3}{2} =$ $\frac{4}{9}$
30. $\frac{4}{5} \div \frac{4}{5} =$ 1

# Fractions: Division

**Quick Review** Students give quotients and remainders orally.

4)9 5)12 2)5 2)11 6)25 10)49 3)5 2)7
6)11 10)19 7)16 6)15 5)37 10)63

**Lesson Focus** To find quotients involving mixed numbers

## Ideas for Getting Started

Briefly review the process for writing an improper fraction for a given mixed number. Put the following mixed numbers on the chalkboard and have students give the improper fraction.

$1\frac{2}{3}$, $6\frac{3}{8}$, $2\frac{1}{2}$, $3\frac{1}{4}$, $5\frac{3}{8}$, $1\frac{5}{6}$, $4\frac{5}{8}$, $3\frac{1}{2}$, $3\frac{2}{3}$.

## Using Page 242

**Motivational Problem** Read the problem at the top of the page with students. Have them describe the situation in their own words. "What question are we asked about the ceramic tiles?" (How many are needed in each row?) "What data in the problem will help us answer this question?" (The tiles are $4\frac{1}{4}$ in. wide; the wall space is $27\frac{5}{8}$ in. wide.) As you discuss the plan for solving this problem, help students see that they must find how many $4\frac{1}{4}$-in. segments there are in a $27\frac{5}{8}$-in. segment. Emphasize that we divide to find how many $4\frac{1}{4}$s there are in $27\frac{5}{8}$.

**Lesson Development** Write the division problem involving mixed numbers on the chalkboard. Remind students of the process for changing a mixed number to an improper fraction and then write $27\frac{5}{8}$ as $\frac{221}{8}$. Have students perform the division by finding the product of the dividend and the reciprocal of the divisor. Point out that 17 will divide evenly into 221. Then go back to the original problem and multiply the answer times the divisor to check that the quotient is correct. Ask a volunteer to estimate to see if the answer $6\frac{1}{2}$ seems reasonable. Finally, have students give the answer to the question in a complete sentence.

**Other Examples** Note that in the first example the dividend is a mixed number and the divisor is an ordinary fraction. In the second example the dividend is a whole number and the divisor is a mixed number. In the third example after the dividend is changed to an improper fraction, the multiplication shortcut can be used to find the quotient.

**Warm Up** Be alert for errors in changing mixed numbers to improper fractions. Also check to see if students are multiplying the dividend by the reciprocal of the divisor. Be alert for any fact errors when completing the dividing process, and be sure students rename improper fraction answers as mixed numbers.

## Dividing with Mixed Numbers

Gwen Strothers is putting new tiles around her kitchen sink. She needs to glue $4\frac{1}{4}$-in. square ceramic tiles on a wall $27\frac{5}{8}$ in. wide. How many tiles will Ms. Strothers need to glue in each row across the wall?

Since we want to find how many same-size tiles, we divide.

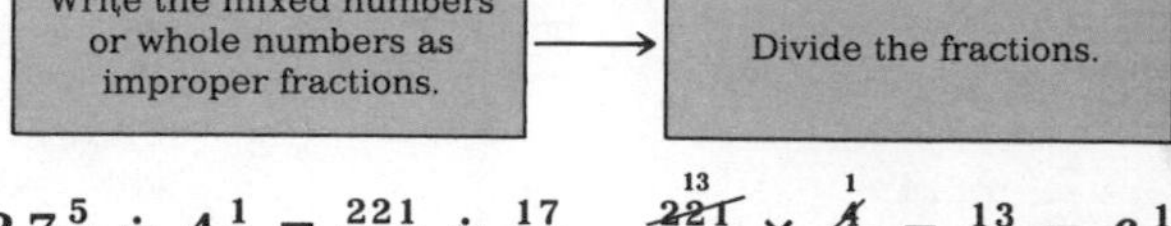


$$27\frac{5}{8} \div 4\frac{1}{4} = \frac{221}{8} \div \frac{17}{4} \quad \frac{\overset{13}{\cancel{221}}}{\underset{2}{\cancel{8}}} \times \frac{\overset{1}{\cancel{4}}}{\underset{1}{\cancel{17}}} = \frac{13}{2} = 6\frac{1}{2}$$

Ms. Strothers will need to glue $6\frac{1}{2}$ tiles in each row across the wall.

**Other Examples**

$$2\frac{2}{3} \div \frac{3}{4} = \frac{8}{3} \div \frac{3}{4} = \frac{8}{3} \times \frac{4}{3} = \frac{32}{9} = 3\frac{5}{9}$$

$$8 \div 3\frac{1}{5} = \frac{8}{1} \div \frac{16}{5} = \frac{\overset{1}{\cancel{8}}}{1} \times \frac{5}{\underset{2}{\cancel{16}}} = \frac{5}{2} = 2\frac{1}{2}$$

$$6\frac{3}{8} \div \frac{3}{4} = \frac{51}{8} \div \frac{3}{4} = \frac{\overset{17}{\cancel{51}}}{\underset{2}{\cancel{8}}} \times \frac{\overset{1}{\cancel{4}}}{\underset{1}{\cancel{3}}} = \frac{17}{2} = 8\frac{1}{2}$$

**Warm Up** Divide.

1. $2\frac{1}{2} \div 1\frac{1}{3}$   $\frac{15}{8} = 1\frac{7}{8}$
2. $3\frac{1}{4} \div \frac{3}{8}$   $\frac{26}{3} = 8\frac{2}{3}$
3. $\frac{4}{5} \div 4\frac{3}{4}$   $\frac{16}{95}$
4. $5\frac{3}{8} \div 2\frac{1}{2}$   $\frac{43}{20} = 2\frac{3}{20}$
5. $1\frac{5}{6} \div 2\frac{1}{3}$   $\frac{11}{14}$
6. $9 \div 1\frac{1}{2}$   $\frac{6}{1} = 6$
7. $4\frac{5}{8} \div 6$   $\frac{37}{48}$
8. $\frac{9}{10} \div 1\frac{1}{4}$   $\frac{18}{25}$
9. $3\frac{1}{2} \div 2\frac{1}{4}$   $\frac{14}{9} = 1\frac{5}{9}$
10. $8 \div 3\frac{1}{5}$   $\frac{5}{2} = 2\frac{1}{2}$



## Follow Up

### Reteaching

Have students compare these lists to see that the only new step for dividing with mixed numbers is to write the mixed numbers as improper fractions.

Dividing Fractions
1. Find the reciprocal of the divisor.
2. Multiply the dividend by the reciprocal of the divisor.

Dividing Mixed Numbers
1. Write mixed numbers as improper fractions.
2. Find the reciprocal of the divisor.
3. Multiply the dividend by the reciprocal of the divisor.

### Enrichment

Write several fractions on the chalkboard and have students find the decimal equivalents by dividing the numerator by the denominator on a calculator. Use these sample problems.

1. $\frac{3}{4} = 0.75$
2. $\frac{1}{2} = 0.5$ or $0.50$
3. $\frac{1}{8} = 0.125$
4. $\frac{2}{5} = 0.4$ or $0.40$

| Assignment Guide | | | |
|---|---|---|---|
| | Minimum | Average | Extended |
| page 243 | 1–36, SK | 1–37, SK | 1–37, SK |

Divide and check.

1. $1\frac{3}{8} \div 4\frac{1}{3}$ $\frac{33}{104}$
2. $3\frac{2}{3} \div 2$ $\frac{11}{6} = 1\frac{5}{6}$
3. $5\frac{1}{4} \div 2\frac{1}{2}$ $\frac{21}{10} = 2\frac{1}{10}$
4. $4 \div 1\frac{1}{3}$ $\frac{3}{1} = 3$
5. $3\frac{1}{2} \div 2\frac{1}{3}$ $\frac{3}{2} = 1\frac{1}{2}$
6. $8 \div 3\frac{1}{5}$ $\frac{5}{2} = 2\frac{1}{2}$
7. $8\frac{1}{3} \div 1\frac{1}{6}$ $\frac{50}{7} = 7\frac{1}{7}$
8. $7 \div 1\frac{1}{7}$ $\frac{49}{8} = 6\frac{1}{8}$
9. $\frac{1}{6} \div 3\frac{1}{2}$ $\frac{1}{21}$
10. $\frac{5}{6} \div 1\frac{2}{3}$ $\frac{1}{2}$
11. $2\frac{2}{3} \div 1\frac{1}{4}$ $\frac{32}{15} = 2\frac{2}{15}$
12. $10 \div 1\frac{1}{4}$ $\frac{8}{1} = 8$
13. $4\frac{3}{5} \div 2\frac{1}{5}$ $\frac{23}{11} = 2\frac{1}{11}$
14. $8 \div 3\frac{1}{4}$ $\frac{32}{13} = 2\frac{6}{13}$
15. $3\frac{3}{8} \div 2\frac{1}{4}$ $\frac{3}{2} = 1\frac{1}{2}$
16. $2\frac{3}{8} \div 4$ $\frac{19}{32}$
17. $6\frac{1}{4} \div 1\frac{1}{8}$ $\frac{50}{9} = 5\frac{5}{9}$
18. $2\frac{1}{10} \div 1\frac{1}{5}$ $\frac{7}{4} = 1\frac{3}{4}$
19. $3\frac{1}{3} \div 1\frac{2}{3}$ $\frac{2}{1} = 2$
20. $4 \div 1\frac{2}{5}$ $\frac{20}{7} = 2\frac{6}{7}$
21. $6\frac{1}{2} \div 1\frac{1}{4}$ $\frac{26}{5} = 5\frac{1}{5}$
22. $4\frac{1}{2} \div 2\frac{7}{10}$ $\frac{5}{3} = 1\frac{2}{3}$
23. $7\frac{1}{4} \div 3$ $\frac{29}{12} = 2\frac{5}{12}$
24. $1\frac{3}{10} \div 2\frac{4}{5}$ $\frac{13}{28}$
25. $3\frac{2}{3} \div 2\frac{1}{6}$ $\frac{22}{13} = 1\frac{9}{13}$
26. $\frac{5}{8} \div 4\frac{1}{4}$ $\frac{5}{34}$
27. $2\frac{4}{5} \div \frac{7}{8}$ $\frac{16}{5} = 3\frac{1}{5}$
28. $\frac{9}{5} \div 2\frac{1}{3}$ $\frac{27}{35}$
29. $6\frac{1}{2} \div 4$ $\frac{13}{8} = 1\frac{5}{8}$
30. $2\frac{1}{8} \div 3\frac{3}{4}$ $\frac{17}{30}$

Round each mixed number to the nearest whole number and estimate the quotient.

31. $35\frac{3}{4} \div 8\frac{7}{8}$ 4
32. $16\frac{2}{5} \div 3\frac{7}{8}$ 4
33. $12\frac{1}{6} \div 5\frac{2}{3}$ 2
34. $23\frac{4}{5} \div 5\frac{3}{4}$ 4
35. $17\frac{5}{8} \div 3\frac{4}{9}$ 6

36. The tiled area around a sink is $25\frac{1}{2}$ inches high. How many $4\frac{1}{4}$-inch tiles high is this? 6

37. Write a question for this data. Then solve the problem. A stack of tiles was $11\frac{1}{4}$ inches high. Each tile was $\frac{5}{16}$ inch thick. Answers will vary.

**Skillkeeper**

Give the missing numbers.

1. $\frac{1}{4} = \frac{■}{16}$ 4
2. $\frac{2}{5} = \frac{10}{■}$ 25
3. $\frac{2}{3} = \frac{■}{24}$ 16
4. $\frac{5}{9} = \frac{15}{■}$ 27
5. $\frac{3}{4} = \frac{12}{■}$ 16
6. $\frac{5}{6} = \frac{15}{■}$ 18
7. $\frac{1}{2} = \frac{■}{16}$ 8
8. $\frac{3}{8} = \frac{12}{■}$ 32
9. $\frac{4}{7} = \frac{■}{35}$ 20
10. $\frac{3}{10} = \frac{■}{60}$ 18

Reduce each fraction to lowest terms.

11. $\frac{4}{10}$ $\frac{2}{5}$
12. $\frac{16}{48}$ $\frac{1}{3}$
13. $\frac{15}{30}$ $\frac{1}{2}$
14. $\frac{6}{21}$ $\frac{2}{7}$
15. $\frac{12}{20}$ $\frac{3}{5}$
16. $\frac{10}{12}$ $\frac{5}{6}$
17. $\frac{50}{100}$ $\frac{1}{2}$
18. $\frac{18}{42}$ $\frac{3}{7}$
19. $\frac{4}{12}$ $\frac{1}{3}$
20. $\frac{9}{15}$ $\frac{3}{5}$
21. $\frac{27}{30}$ $\frac{9}{10}$
22. $\frac{24}{36}$ $\frac{2}{3}$

More Practice, page 426, Set B



## Using Page 243

**Exercises 1–30** There are a considerable number of operations involved in working each of these problems, giving many opportunities for computational errors. Observe students' work carefully to differentiate between procedural and computational errors.

**Exercises 31–35** Students should have little difficulty rounding these mixed numbers to the nearest whole number. Be sure they understand that if the fraction part is $\frac{1}{2}$ or greater, the fraction is rounded up; if the fraction part is less than $\frac{1}{2}$, the fraction is rounded down.

**Exercise 37** In this problem students must read the data carefully and write a question that can be answered using the given data. A possible question might be: "How many tiles were in the stack?" Ask students to solve and then check their answers.

**Skillkeeper** These skills were originally taught in Chapter 8.

**More Practice,** page 426, Set B

**Reteaching Supplement,** page 57

Name ______ To follow text page 243

**Dividing with Mixed Numbers**

Write mixed numbers or whole numbers as improper fractions. → Divide the fractions.

$4\frac{1}{4} \div 1\frac{2}{3} = \frac{17}{4} \div \frac{5}{3}$ $\frac{17}{4} \div \frac{5}{3} = \frac{17}{4} \times \frac{3}{5} = \frac{51}{20} = 2\frac{11}{20}$

Multiply by the reciprocal of $\frac{5}{3}$. $20\overline{)51}$ 2, −40, 11

Divide. Write a mixed number or lowest-terms fraction for each quotient.

1. $1\frac{1}{4} \div \frac{1}{5}$ → $\frac{5}{4} \div \frac{1}{5} = \frac{5}{4} \times \frac{5}{1} = \frac{25}{4} = 6\frac{1}{4}$
2. $4\frac{1}{2} \div \frac{2}{3}$ → $\frac{9}{2} \div \frac{2}{3} = \frac{9}{2} \times \frac{3}{2} = \frac{27}{4} = 6\frac{3}{4}$
3. $2\frac{3}{4} \div 1\frac{1}{2}$ → $\frac{11}{4} \div \frac{3}{2} = \frac{11}{4} \times \frac{2}{3} = \frac{11}{6}$
4. $\frac{9}{10} \div 1\frac{1}{2}$ → $\frac{9}{10} \div \frac{3}{2} = \frac{9}{10} \times \frac{2}{3} = \frac{3}{5}$
5. $3\frac{2}{3} \div 1\frac{1}{3} = \frac{11}{3} \div \frac{4}{3} = \frac{11}{3} \times \frac{3}{4} = 2\frac{3}{4}$
6. $6\frac{1}{3} \div 2\frac{1}{2} = \frac{19}{3} \div \frac{5}{2} = \frac{19}{3} \times \frac{2}{5} = 2\frac{8}{15}$
7. $1\frac{7}{10} \div \frac{2}{5} = \frac{17}{10} \div \frac{2}{5} = \frac{17}{10} \times \frac{5}{2} = 4\frac{1}{4}$
8. $8\frac{3}{4} \div \frac{2}{3} = \frac{35}{4} \div \frac{2}{3} = \frac{35}{4} \times \frac{3}{2} = 13\frac{1}{8}$
9. $10 \div 2\frac{1}{4} = \frac{10}{1} \div \frac{9}{4} = \frac{10}{1} \times \frac{4}{9} = 4\frac{4}{9}$
10. $6 \div 1\frac{2}{3} = \frac{6}{1} \div \frac{5}{3} = \frac{6}{1} \times \frac{3}{5} = 3\frac{3}{5}$
11. $5\frac{3}{8} \div 2\frac{1}{2} = \frac{43}{8} \div \frac{5}{2} = \frac{43}{8} \times \frac{2}{5} = 2\frac{3}{20}$
12. $12 \div 2\frac{2}{5} = \frac{12}{1} \div \frac{12}{5} = \frac{12}{1} \times \frac{5}{12} = 5$
13. $10 \div 3\frac{1}{3} = \frac{10}{1} \div \frac{10}{3} = \frac{10}{1} \times \frac{3}{10} = 3$
14. $1\frac{2}{3} \div 1\frac{1}{2} = \frac{5}{3} \div \frac{3}{2} = \frac{5}{3} \times \frac{2}{3} = 1\frac{1}{9}$
15. $17\frac{1}{2} \div 3\frac{3}{4} = \frac{35}{2} \div \frac{15}{4} = \frac{35}{2} \times \frac{4}{15} = 4\frac{2}{3}$
16. $16 \div 2\frac{2}{3} = \frac{16}{1} \div \frac{8}{3} = \frac{16}{1} \times \frac{3}{8} = 6$

**Enrichment Supplement,** page 57

Name ______ To follow text page 243

**Continued Fractions**

$\frac{1}{\frac{2}{3}}$ means $1 \div \frac{2}{3}$. $\frac{1}{\frac{2}{3}}$ can be simplified to $\frac{3}{2}$ because $1 \div \frac{2}{3} = 1 \times \frac{3}{2} = \frac{3}{2}$.

Simplify each of the following fractions.

1. $\frac{1}{\frac{5}{4}} = \frac{4}{5}$
2. $\frac{1}{\frac{1}{2}} = 2$
3. $\frac{1}{\frac{5}{3}} = \frac{3}{5}$
4. $\frac{1}{\frac{1}{8}} = 8$
5. $\frac{1}{\frac{7}{3}} = \frac{3}{7}$
6. $\frac{1}{\frac{10}{7}} = \frac{7}{10}$

Write each fraction as a simple fraction. $\frac{1}{3 + \frac{1}{4}} = 1 \div 3\frac{1}{4} = 1 \times \frac{4}{13} = \frac{4}{13}$

7. $\frac{1}{1 + \frac{1}{3}} = \frac{3}{4}$
8. $\frac{1}{2 + \frac{1}{2}} = \frac{2}{5}$
9. $\frac{1}{3 + \frac{1}{5}} = \frac{5}{16}$
10. $\frac{1}{1 + \frac{1}{2}} = \frac{2}{3}$
11. $\frac{1}{2 + \frac{1}{4}} = \frac{4}{9}$
12. $\frac{1}{1 + \frac{1}{7}} = \frac{7}{8}$

An expression such as $1 + \frac{1}{1 + \frac{1}{1 + \frac{1}{2}}}$ is called a **continued fraction.**

To simplify such an expression, begin at the lower right corner of the expression and "work your way back up."

$$1 + \frac{1}{1 + \frac{1}{1 + \frac{1}{2}}} = 1 + \frac{1}{1 + \frac{1}{\frac{3}{2}}} = 1 + \frac{1}{1 + \frac{2}{3}} = 1 + \frac{1}{\frac{5}{3}} = 1 + \frac{3}{5} = \frac{8}{5} = 1\frac{3}{5}.$$

Simplify these continued fractions.

13. $1 + \frac{1}{1 + \frac{1}{3}} = 1\frac{3}{4}$
14. $1 + \frac{1}{2 + \frac{1}{2}} = 1\frac{2}{5}$

**Practice Supplement,** page 94

Name ______ To follow text page 243

**Dividing with Mixed Numbers**

Divide.

1. $1\frac{3}{5} \div 2\frac{1}{2} = \frac{16}{25}$
2. $3\frac{1}{3} \div 5 = \frac{2}{3}$
3. $8 \div 2\frac{2}{3} = 3$
4. $2\frac{1}{3} \div 4\frac{1}{5} = \frac{5}{9}$
5. $\frac{7}{8} \div 1\frac{1}{2} = \frac{7}{12}$
6. $\frac{5}{9} \div 2\frac{1}{6} = \frac{10}{39}$
7. $10 \div 2\frac{1}{2} = 4$
8. $3\frac{1}{4} \div \frac{3}{8} = 8\frac{2}{3}$
9. $7\frac{1}{2} \div 1\frac{1}{4} = 6$
10. $2\frac{3}{4} \div \frac{1}{2} = 5\frac{1}{2}$
11. $4\frac{1}{2} \div \frac{1}{2} = 9$
12. $2\frac{3}{5} \div 1\frac{5}{8} = 1\frac{3}{5}$
13. $2\frac{2}{3} \div 2\frac{2}{5} = 1\frac{1}{9}$
14. $1\frac{3}{7} \div 2\frac{2}{3} = \frac{15}{28}$
15. $3\frac{1}{5} \div \frac{1}{4} = 12\frac{4}{5}$
16. $5\frac{1}{3} \div 4 = 1\frac{1}{3}$
17. $4 \div 1\frac{1}{7} = 3\frac{1}{2}$
18. $2\frac{5}{8} \div 7 = \frac{3}{8}$
19. $6\frac{3}{4} \div \frac{3}{4} = 9$
20. $7\frac{2}{5} \div 1\frac{1}{5} = 6\frac{1}{6}$
21. $6\frac{1}{2} \div 3\frac{7}{12} = 1\frac{35}{43}$
22. $4\frac{1}{3} \div \frac{2}{3} = 6\frac{1}{2}$
23. $2\frac{1}{3} \div \frac{5}{20} = 9\frac{1}{3}$
24. $2\frac{5}{6} \div \frac{3}{10} = 9\frac{4}{9}$
25. $4\frac{1}{8} \div 1\frac{4}{7} = 2\frac{5}{8}$
26. $1\frac{5}{9} \div 1\frac{3}{4} = \frac{8}{9}$
27. $3\frac{3}{5} \div 9 = \frac{2}{5}$
28. $6 \div 1\frac{3}{4} = 3\frac{3}{7}$
29. $3\frac{1}{3} \div \frac{1}{6} = 20$
30. $3\frac{3}{4} \div 1\frac{2}{3} = 2\frac{1}{4}$

# Applications

**Quick Review** Students write these decimals in order from least to greatest.
0.25 3 0.7 7 0.5 6 0.01 1 0.2 2 0.9 11 0.75 8
0.8 10 0.3 4 0.4 5 0.79 9 1.0 12 1.5 13

**Lesson Focus** To practice solving word problems involving a variety of operations; to use estimation to see if the answers to word problems seem reasonable

## Ideas for Getting Started

Write the following problem on the chalkboard:

Jean worked in a flower shop ___ hours a day for ___ days. Her salary was ___ dollars per hour. She earned a total of ___ dollars.

Without giving specific numbers, ask questions to elicit from students the operations they would choose to answer certain questions. If necessary, supply numbers for some of the blanks and ask students to use the operations needed to find the answers.

## Using Page 244

**Lesson Development** Briefly review the 5-Point Checklist for solving problems by referring to the logo at the top of the page. Remind students again that the checklist does not give rules for solving word problems; rather, it suggests important things to consider in solving problems.

Work through the problem in exercise 1 with students. Point out that the problem involves both fractions and decimals. Tell students that the problem can be solved using decimals or using fractions. Give students the option of choosing fractions or decimals for the problems on the page.

**Try This** A possible strategy, Use Logical Reasoning, was taught on page 162.

**Discussion** "What question is asked about the plant food pellets?" (How can Mr. James find the heavier pellet in just two weighings on the balance scale?) "How many pellets are there?" (6) "Are they all the same weight?" (No, one is heavier than the others.) "If three of the pellets are placed on each side of the balance, how can you find out about the heavier pellet?" (The group that contains the heavier pellet will make the balance go down.) "How could you find the heavier pellet in the group of three?"

**Solution** First put three pellets on each side of the balance scale. The heavier pellet is on the side that goes down. Next, choose two of the three pellets from the group containing the heavier pellet and put one on each side of the balance. If the scale remains balanced, the third pellet is the heavier. If one side goes down, that side contains the heavier pellet.

An alternative solution would be to put two pellets on each side of the balance scale. If neither side goes down, the heavier pellet is in the third group of pellets. If one side goes down, that side contains the heavier pellet. Then put one of the two pellets from the group that contains the heavier pellet on each side to determine the heavier pellet.

## Problem Solving: Practice

Mr. James owns a flower shop. Here are some problems he needs to solve.

Solve.

1. During summer vacation, Kim works in the flower shop $5\frac{1}{2}$ h each day. Her salary is \$3.50 an hour. How much does she earn each day? \$19.25

Change the fraction to a decimal and find 5.5 × \$3.50. OR Change the decimal to a fraction and find $5\frac{1}{2} \times 3\frac{1}{2}$.

2. Suzy needs $3\frac{1}{2}$ yd of rope to make a hanger for a plant. How many plants can she hang with 56 yd of rope? 16
3. If a $2\frac{1}{2}$-lb bag of plant soil costs \$1.75, how much does the soil cost per pound? \$0.70
4. Mr. James pays about $\frac{7}{8}$ of his total income for expenses. The rest is profit. His income for one month was \$6,640. What was his profit? \$830
5. When mixed with water, $\frac{1}{2}$ teaspoon of a special plant food mixture makes $1\frac{1}{2}$ quarts of plant food. How many teaspoons are needed to make 6 quarts of plant food? 2 teaspoons
6. Gina's regular pay is \$4.00 per hour. She earns one and one-half times her regular hourly pay if she works overtime. One week she worked $2\frac{1}{2}$ hours overtime each evening for 6 days. How much did she earn for overtime work that week? \$90
7. **Try This** Mr. James has 6 plant food pellets that look exactly alike, but one is heavier than the others. How can he be sure to find the heavier pellet in just two weighings on the balance scale? See teaching notes.

244

## Follow Up

### Reteaching

Review with students the ways in which factors and products relate to multiplication and division.

In multiplication, we know the factors and want to find the product. One factor represents the number of parts; the other factor represents the number in each part; and the product represents the total number.

In division, we know the product and one factor and want to find the other factor. The factor we have may name either the number in each part *or* the number of parts.

### Enrichment

Have students find the fraction named by the Roman numerals below.

1. $\frac{\text{IX}}{\text{CCCV}}$ $\frac{9}{305}$
2. $\frac{\text{L}}{\text{XC}}$ $\frac{50}{90}$
3. $\frac{\text{IV}}{\text{IX}}$ $\frac{4}{9}$
4. $\frac{\text{XXX}}{\text{LXII}}$ $\frac{30}{62}$

| Assignment Guide | | | |
|---|---|---|---|
| | Minimum | Average | Extended |
| page 244 | 1–5 | 1–6 | 1–7 |
| page 245 | 1–6 | 1–7 | 1–8 |

QUESTION / DATA / PLAN / ANSWER / CHECK

## Problem Solving: Using Estimation

First estimate the answer for problems 1 through 7. Then find the exact answer and compare it with the estimate to see whether it is reasonable.

**Review**

**To round a mixed number to the nearestwhole number:**

- When the fraction part is less than $\frac{1}{2}$, round down.
- When the fraction part is equal to or greater than $\frac{1}{2}$, round up.

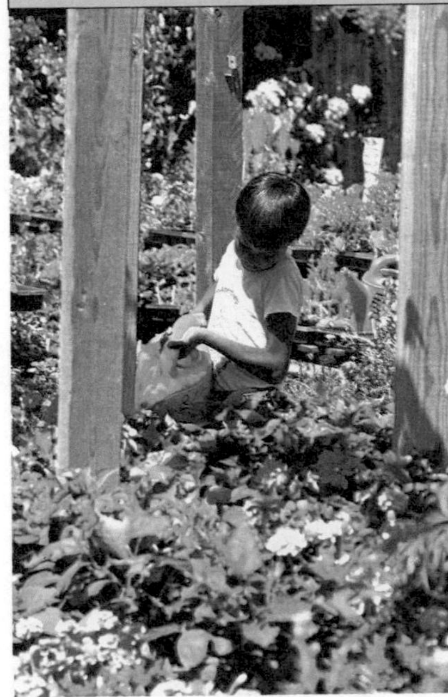

1. Chad helps in his mother's plant store for $3\frac{3}{4}$ h (hours) 5 days a week. How many hours does he work each week? 20 h; $18\frac{3}{4}$ h
2. A juice glass holds $5\frac{7}{8}$ oz (ounces). How many glasses can you fill from a pitcher containing 48 oz of juice? 8 glasses; $8\frac{8}{47}$ glasses
3. A faucet leaks 1 qt (quart) of water every $\frac{3}{4}$ h. How many quarts will it leak in $3\frac{3}{4}$ h? 4 qt; 5 qt
4. Nan drove 252 miles in $4\frac{2}{3}$ h. What was her average speed in miles per hour? 50 mph; 54 mph
5. Roland spends $\frac{7}{8}$ of an hour giving a tennis lesson. About how many lessons can he give in 7 hours? 7 lessons; 8 lessons
6. A recipe calls for $1\frac{3}{4}$ cups of flour. Kip wants to make $2\frac{1}{2}$ times as much as the recipe. How many cups of flour must he use? 6 cups; $4\frac{3}{8}$ cups
7. It takes $2\frac{7}{8}$ yd (yards) of fabric to make a dress and $\frac{3}{4}$ yd to make a jacket. How many yards of fabric are needed for 3 dress-and-jacket outfits? 12 yd; $10\frac{7}{8}$ yd
8. **Try This** Jenny lived half her life in New York and one third of her life in Los Angeles. Then she moved to Chicago. If she has lived in Chicago for 4 years, how old is she now? 24



## Using Page 245

**Lesson Development** Review the procedure for rounding a mixed number. Elicit from students the importance of estimation to check if a calculated answer is reasonable. Be sure students understand that for each problem they are to estimate the answer and then find the exact answer. Next they compare their estimates with the exact answer to see if the calculated answer is reasonable.

**Try This** A possible strategy, Choose the Operations, was taught on page 16.

**Discussion** "What question are we asked about Jenny?" (How old is she?) "What part of Jenny's life was spent in New York?" (one half) "What part was spent in Los Angeles?" (one third) "What length of time did she live in Chicago?" (4 years) "Can you find what part of Jenny's life was spent in New York and Los Angeles together?" $\left(\frac{1}{2} + \frac{1}{3}\text{, or } \frac{5}{6}\text{, of her life}\right)$ "What fraction of her life has she spent in Chicago?" $\left(\frac{1}{6}\right)$ "If one sixth of Jenny's life is 4 years, how can you find how old she is now?" (Multiply 4 by 6.)

**Solution** Jenny is now 24 years old. Jenny lived one half of her life in New York and one third in Los Angeles, or a total of $\frac{5}{6}$ of her life. This means she lived $\frac{1}{6}$ of her life in Chicago. We know she lived in Chicago 4 years. Thus, $4 \times \frac{6}{1} = 24$.

**Extension** Suppose Jenny lived one fourth of her life in New York, five eighths of her life in Los Angeles, and had lived in Chicago for 6 years. How old would she be? (48 years old)

**Reteaching Supplement,** page 58

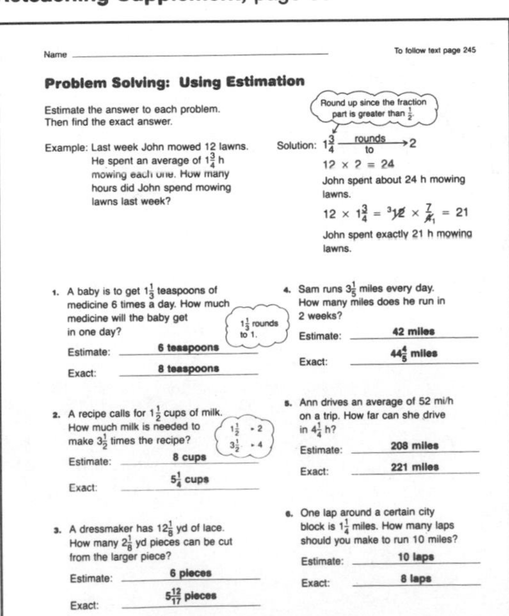

Name ______ To follow text page 245

**Problem Solving: Using Estimation**

Estimate the answer to each problem. Then find the exact answer.

Example: Last week John mowed 12 lawns. He spent an average of $1\frac{3}{4}$ h mowing each one. How many hours did John spend mowing lawns last week?

Round up since the fraction part is greater than $\frac{1}{2}$.

Solution: $1\frac{3}{4} \xrightarrow{\text{rounds to}} 2$

$12 \times 2 = 24$

John spent about 24 h mowing lawns.

$12 \times 1\frac{3}{4} = {}^{3}\cancel{12} \times \frac{7}{\cancel{4}_1} = 21$

John spent exactly 21 h mowing lawns.

1. A baby is to get $1\frac{1}{3}$ teaspoons of medicine 6 times a day. How much medicine will the baby get in one day? ($1\frac{1}{3}$ rounds to 1.)
   Estimate: **6 teaspoons**
   Exact: **8 teaspoons**
2. A recipe calls for $1\frac{1}{2}$ cups of milk. How much milk is needed to make $3\frac{1}{2}$ times the recipe? ($1\frac{1}{2} \to 2$, $3\frac{1}{2} \to 4$)
   Estimate: **8 cups**
   Exact: **$5\frac{1}{4}$ cups**
3. A dressmaker has $12\frac{1}{8}$ yd of lace. How many $2\frac{1}{8}$ yd pieces can be cut from the larger piece?
   Estimate: **6 pieces**
   Exact: **$5\frac{12}{17}$ pieces**
4. Sam runs $3\frac{1}{5}$ miles every day. How many miles does he run in 2 weeks?
   Estimate: **42 miles**
   Exact: **$44\frac{4}{5}$ miles**
5. Ann drives an average of 52 mi/h on a trip. How far can she drive in $4\frac{1}{4}$ h?
   Estimate: **208 miles**
   Exact: **221 miles**
6. One lap around a certain city block is $1\frac{1}{4}$ miles. How many laps should you make to run 10 miles?
   Estimate: **10 laps**
   Exact: **8 laps**

**Enrichment Supplement,** page 58

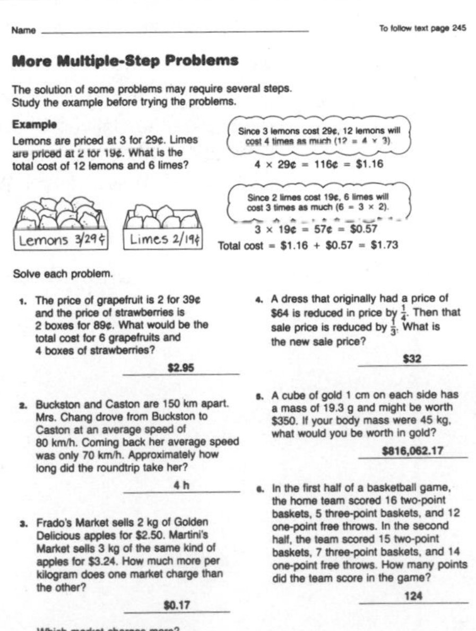

Name ______ To follow text page 245

**More Multiple-Step Problems**

The solution of some problems may require several steps. Study the example before trying the problems.

**Example**

Lemons are priced at 3 for 29¢. Limes are priced at 2 for 19¢. What is the total cost of 12 lemons and 6 limes?

Lemons 3/29¢ Limes 2/19¢

Since 3 lemons cost 29¢, 12 lemons will cost 4 times as much (12 = 4 × 3).

4 × 29¢ = 116¢ = $1.16

Since 2 limes cost 19¢, 6 limes will cost 3 times as much (6 = 3 × 2).

3 × 19¢ = 57¢ = $0.57

Total cost = $1.16 + $0.57 = $1.73

Solve each problem.

1. The price of grapefruit is 2 for 39¢ and the price of strawberries is 2 boxes for 89¢. What would be the total cost for 6 grapefruits and 4 boxes of strawberries? **$2.95**
2. Buckston and Caston are 150 km apart. Mrs. Chang drove from Buckston to Caston at an average speed of 80 km/h. Coming back her average speed was only 70 km/h. Approximately how long did the roundtrip take her? **4 h**
3. Frado's Market sells 2 kg of Golden Delicious apples for $2.50. Martini's Market sells 3 kg of the same kind of apples for $3.24. How much more per kilogram does one market charge than the other? **$0.17**
   Which market charges more? **Frado's**
4. A dress that originally had a price of $64 is reduced in price by $\frac{1}{4}$. Then that sale price is reduced by $\frac{1}{3}$. What is the new sale price? **$32**
5. A cube of gold 1 cm on each side has a mass of 19.3 g and might be worth $350. If your body mass were 45 kg, what would you be worth in gold? **$816,062.17**
6. In the first half of a basketball game, the home team scored 16 two-point baskets, 5 three-point baskets, and 12 one-point free throws. In the second half, the team scored 15 two-point baskets, 7 three-point baskets, and 14 one-point free throws. How many points did the team score in the game? **124**

**Practice Supplement,** page 95

Name ______ To follow text page 245

**Problem Solving: Practice**

Solve each problem.

1. Jane Adams drove for 36 minutes. She averaged $\frac{3}{4}$ mile per minute. How many miles did she drive? **27 miles**
2. $1\frac{1}{4}$ yd of terry cloth are needed to make a towel. How many towels can be made from $7\frac{1}{2}$ yd of terry cloth? **6**
3. A tape measures 18 in. long. How many pieces $1\frac{1}{2}$ in. long can be cut from it? **12**
4. One day Will worked for $7\frac{1}{2}$ h. He was paid $4.50 an hour. How much did he earn that day? **$33.75**
5. A 10-lb bag of potatoes costs $1.30. How much do the potatoes cost per pound? **$0.13**
6. Jo's science book is $\frac{3}{4}$ in. thick. How much room on the shelf will 28 science books take up? **21 in.**
7. There is a total of $63\frac{1}{3}$ pounds of potatoes in 8 bags. About how many pounds are in each bag? **$7\frac{11}{12}$ lb**
8. Juan had to walk 15 miles on a camping trip. He walked $2\frac{1}{2}$ miles per hour. How long did it take him? **6 h**
9. Sally bought $3\frac{3}{4}$ yd of cloth. The cloth costs $4.80 a yard. How much did she pay for the cloth? **$18**
10. A recipe calls for $\frac{5}{8}$ cup of nuts. If Mike is making 4 times the recipe, how many cups of nuts does he need? **$2\frac{1}{2}$ c**

**Lesson Focus** To find a pattern as a strategy for solving nonroutine word problems

## Ideas for Getting Started

Write the first few numbers of each of the following patterns on the chalkboard and ask students to give numbers that continue the pattern.

1, 3, 5, 7, 9 (11, 13,15, 17, 19)
2, 4, 6, 8, 10 (12, 14, 16, 18, 20)
1, 2, 4, 8, 16, (32, 64, 128, 256, 512)
1, 3, 6, 10, 15 (21, 28, 36, 45, 55)

Discuss each of these patterns and emphasize the importance of searching for a pattern in solving problems.

## Using Page 246

**Motivational Problem** Have students read the Try This problem at the top of the page. "What question are we asked about Jane's salary?" (Which salary plan would be best?) Discuss the data needed to answer this question. "How long will the job last?" (16 days) "How much would Jane make under plan A?" ($20 a day) "What would Jane's salary be with plan B?" (1¢ the first day, 2¢ the second day, and so on.) As students plan how to solve this problem, point out that a useful strategy in solving problems such as these is to look for a pattern.

**Lesson Development** Suggest that making a table would help us see a pattern for plan B. Point out that it is important to label the table and list enough information to solve the problem. "Do you see a pattern in the table?" If students do not recognize the pattern, use these hints: "How many twos must you multiply to find the pay for the second day?" (1) "How many times must 2 be used as a factor to get the pay for the third day?" (2) "How many times must 2 be used as a factor to get the pay for the fourth day?" (3) As you ask these questions, write the following on the chalkboard.

| Day | Number of times 2 is used as a factor | |
|---|---|---|
| 2 | 2 | (*1* factor) |
| 3 | 2 × 2 | (*2* factors) |
| 4 | 2 × 2 × 2 | (*3* factors) |
| 5 | 2 × 2 × 2 × 2 | (*4* factors) |

"If 2 is used as a factor twice, 2 times for 3 days, 3 times for 4 days, 4 times for 5 days; how many times will 2 be used as a factor for 16 days?" (15 times) Help students find Jane's salary under plan A (20 × 16 or 320) and her salary under plan B (2 × 2 × 2 × 2 × 2 × 2 × 2 × 2 × 2 × 2 × 2 × 2 × 2 × 2 × 2 or $327.68). Have students reread the original problem and decide which of the plans they think Jane would choose.

QUESTION
DATA
PLAN
ANSWER
CHECK

## Problem Solving: Find a Pattern

To solve this problem, first try the strategy Make a Table. Then it might help to use a strategy called

**Find a Pattern**

**Try This** Jane's uncle offered her a choice of two salary plans for a job that would last 16 days.

PLAN A: $20 a day for each of the 16 days.

PLAN B: 1¢ the first day, 2¢ the second, 4¢ the third, 8¢ the fourth, and so on.

Jane found what her salary would be for the sixteenth day under plan B and made her choice. Which plan do you think she chose?

First I'll make a table. I'll label it carefully and list the pay for the first 5 days.

Plan B

| Day | Pay |
|---|---|
| 1 | 1¢ |
| 2 | 2¢ |
| 3 | 4¢ = 2 × 2 |
| 4 | 8¢ = 2 × 2 × 2 |
| 5 | 16¢ = 2 × 2 × 2 × 2 |

Now I'll look for a pattern. Aha! I use 2 as a factor one less time than the number of days.

| Day | Pay |
|---|---|
| 1 | 1¢ |
| 2 | 2¢ |
| 3 | 4¢ = 2 × 2 (two factors) |
| 4 | 8¢ = 2 × 2 × 2 (three factors) |
| 5 | 16¢ = 2 × 2 × 2 × 2 (four factors) |

Under plan B Jane's salary just for day 16 would be
2 × 2 × 2 × 2 × 2 × 2 × 2 × 2 × 2 × 2 × 2 × 2 × 2 × 2 × 2
or $327.68. Jane probably chose plan B, since her total plan A salary would be only $320.

Solve.

1. Suppose you catch 1 fish the first day and 2 more fish each day than the day before. How many fish will you catch during a 12-day vacation? 144 fish
2. Each of 8 friends rides a Ferris wheel once with everyone else in the group (2 friends to a seat). How many rides do they take altogether? 28 rides

246

## Strategy Test Item

**Optional Problem** If you wish to assess students' ability to apply the strategy called Find a Pattern introduced in this chapter, provide them with the problem below.

> A mailcarrier delivered 1 letter to the first house on a route, 3 letters to the second house, 5 letters to the third house, and so on. If the pattern continues, how many letters would the carrier deliver to the first 10 houses?

**Solution** The mailcarrier would deliver 100 letters in all to the ten houses.

## *Chapter Review-Test*

Give the product in lowest terms.

**1.** $\frac{1}{3} \times 12$ 4 **2.** $\frac{3}{5} \times \frac{1}{4}$ $\frac{3}{20}$ **3.** $\frac{5}{6} \times \frac{3}{10}$ $\frac{1}{4}$ **4.** $100 \times \frac{4}{5}$ 80 **5.** $\frac{5}{8} \times \frac{3}{5}$ $\frac{3}{8}$

**6.** $\frac{8}{3} \times \frac{9}{16}$ $1\frac{1}{2}$ **7.** $2\frac{1}{3} \times 5\frac{3}{4}$ $13\frac{5}{12}$ **8.** $8 \times 3\frac{1}{4}$ 26 **9.** $4\frac{7}{10} \times 5$ $23\frac{1}{2}$ **10.** $3\frac{1}{3} \times 2\frac{7}{10}$ 9

Write a lowest-terms fraction for each decimal.

**11.** 0.375 $\frac{3}{8}$ **12.** 0.5 $\frac{1}{2}$ **13.** 0.25 $\frac{1}{4}$ **14.** 0.125 $\frac{1}{8}$ **15.** 0.35 $\frac{7}{20}$ **16.** 0.60 $\frac{3}{5}$

**17.** 0.75 $\frac{3}{4}$ **18.** 0.625 $\frac{5}{8}$ **19.** 0.9 $\frac{9}{10}$ **20.** 0.875 $\frac{7}{8}$ **21.** 0.4 $\frac{2}{5}$ **22.** 0.99 $\frac{99}{100}$

Write as a decimal.

**23.** $\frac{7}{10}$ 0.7 **24.** $\frac{3}{4}$ 0.75 **25.** $\frac{2}{5}$ 0.4 **26.** $\frac{3}{8}$ 0.375 **27.** $\frac{7}{20}$ 0.35 **28.** $\frac{4}{25}$ 0.16

**29.** $\frac{9}{20}$ 0.45 **30.** $\frac{3}{10}$ 0.3 **31.** $\frac{5}{16}$ 0.3125 **32.** $\frac{3}{20}$ 0.15 **33.** $\frac{1}{10}$ 0.1 **34.** $\frac{9}{100}$ 0.09

**35.** Write $\frac{9}{24}$ as a mixed decimal. $0.37\frac{1}{2}$ **36.** Write $\frac{30}{45}$ as a mixed decimal. $0.66\frac{2}{3}$

Give the quotient in lowest terms. Check by multiplying.

**37.** $4 \div \frac{1}{3}$ 12 **38.** $\frac{3}{4} \div \frac{2}{3}$ $1\frac{1}{8}$ **39.** $8 \div \frac{3}{4}$ $10\frac{2}{3}$ **40.** $6 \div 8$ $\frac{3}{4}$ **41.** $\frac{5}{6} \div 3\frac{1}{3}$ $\frac{1}{4}$

**42.** $\frac{3}{8} \div \frac{5}{4}$ $\frac{3}{10}$ **43.** $3\frac{2}{3} \div \frac{5}{6}$ $4\frac{2}{5}$ **44.** $12 \div 3\frac{1}{4}$ $3\frac{9}{13}$ **45.** $2\frac{3}{4} \div 3\frac{2}{3}$ $\frac{3}{4}$ **46.** $3\frac{1}{2} \div 2\frac{1}{6}$ $1\frac{8}{13}$

Solve.

**47.** Earl bought a $34\frac{1}{2}$-oz bottle of grape juice. He poured all of the juice into some glasses that hold $5\frac{3}{4}$ oz each. How many glasses was he able to fill? 6

**48.** For one side of a rope ladder, you need to end up with a 182-in. length of rope that includes 8 knots. If each knot uses up $4\frac{3}{4}$ in. of rope and adds $1\frac{1}{2}$ in. to the length of the rope, how much rope do you need to use? 208 in.



## Using Page 247

The exercises in the Chapter Review-Test emphasize the major concepts and skills presented in this chapter. These exercises may be used as a review assignment or as a test, depending upon your needs.

**Item Analysis** The table below correlates the Chapter Review-Test items with objectives and with the student text pages on which the concepts or skills were taught.

| Items | Objectives | Related text pages |
|---|---|---|
| 1–10 | 9.1 | 226–233 |
| 11–36 | 9.2 | 236–238 |
| 37–46 | 9.3 | 239–243 |
| 47–48 | 9.4 | 234–235, 244–245 |

## Assessment Options

If you use the Chapter Review-Test as a review assignment, you may wish to use the multiple-choice test or the free-response test to evaluate mastery of the chapter objectives. The items on these tests have a one-to-one correspondence in terms of content and level of difficulty. A correlation of test items to objectives and student text pages is provided in the Management Guide for Chapter 9.

**Multiple-Choice Test,** TRB pages 25–26

**Free-Response Test,** TRB pages 65–66

## TRB Options

The following blackline masters are available for use with this chapter. If you have not already assigned these materials, you may wish to use them to close the chapter.

**Recreation,** TRB page 159

**Consumer Applications,** TRB page 177

**Calculator Technology,** TRB page 195

**Reading Math,** TRB page 227

**Family Involvement,** TRB pages 253–254

# Reteaching

## Using Page 248

The exercises on this page are intended for those students who experienced difficulty with the Chapter Review-Test on page 247. Should students require reteaching of these key concepts and skills, please refer to the teaching notes below. Otherwise the Another Look exercises can be assigned as independent work with students using the accompanying sample problems and hints as guides.

**Exercises 1–9** Direct students' attention to the display box at the left. Remind them of the rule for multiplying fractions. That is, multiply the numerators, multiply the denominators, and reduce the resulting fraction to lowest terms. Stress the shortcut procedure in which a numerator and a denominator may be divided by the same number before multiplying. Also remind students that a whole number can be written as a fraction with denominator 1.

**Exercises 10–15** Refer to the display box at the left. Remind students that dividing by a fraction is done by multiplying by the reciprocal of the fraction. It is important to check by multiplying to see if the answer is the quotient of the two fractions.

**Exercises 16–24** Using the example in the display box, review the procedure for changing a mixed number to an improper fraction. Be sure students understand that before multiplying or dividing, they should write mixed numbers as improper fractions. Remind students to rewrite the answer in lowest terms.

**Exercises 25–32** Direct students' attention to the display box. Remind students that since 0.75 is read as seventy-five hundredths, they can write 0.75 as the fraction $\frac{75}{100}$. Help them reduce this fraction to lowest terms. As you work the second example, emphasize that a fraction such as $\frac{5}{8}$ can be thought of as $5 \div 8$. Work through the division problem and review the procedures for writing the answer as a mixed decimal, a three-place decimal, or as a decimal rounded to the nearest hundredth.

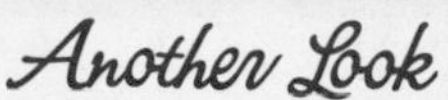


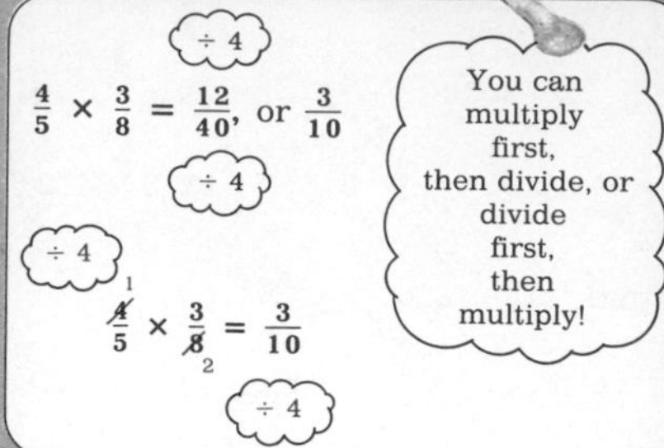


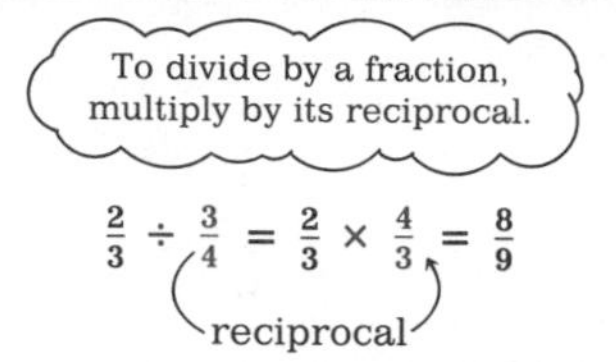


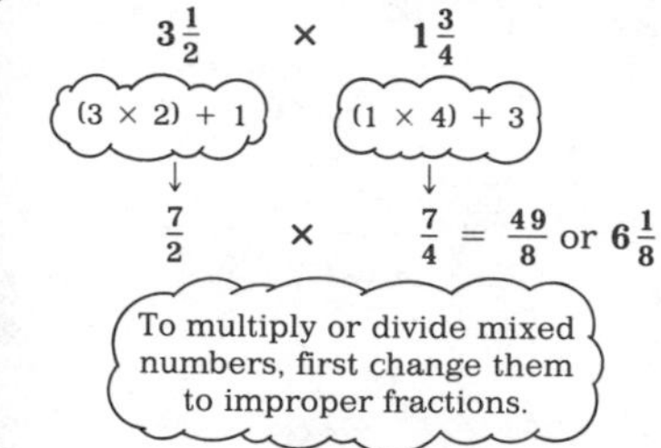


Think about place value to write a decimal as a fraction.

$0.75 = \frac{75}{100} = \frac{3}{4}$

To write a fraction as a decimal or mixed decimal, divide.

$\frac{5}{8} \rightarrow 8\overline{)5.000}$ = 0.625 → 0.625 or $0.62\frac{1}{2}$

**Give the product in lowest terms.**

1. $\frac{3}{5} \times \frac{1}{4}$ $\frac{3}{20}$
2. $\frac{5}{8} \times \frac{2}{3}$ $\frac{5}{12}$
3. $\frac{1}{2} \times \frac{2}{5}$ $\frac{1}{5}$
4. $\frac{5}{6} \times \frac{4}{5}$ $\frac{2}{3}$
5. $\frac{7}{12} \times \frac{3}{14}$ $\frac{1}{8}$
6. $\frac{3}{4} \times \frac{5}{8}$ $\frac{15}{32}$
7. $\frac{3}{8} \times \frac{4}{9}$ $\frac{1}{6}$
8. $8 \times \frac{3}{4}$ $\frac{6}{1} = 6$
9. $\frac{5}{6} \times 2$ $\frac{5}{3} = 1\frac{2}{3}$

**Divide.**

10. $\frac{1}{4} \div \frac{2}{3}$ $\frac{3}{8}$
11. $\frac{3}{4} \div \frac{5}{8}$ $\frac{6}{5} = 1\frac{1}{5}$
12. $\frac{1}{6} \div \frac{1}{2}$ $\frac{1}{3}$
13. $\frac{5}{6} \div \frac{1}{5}$ $\frac{25}{6} = 4\frac{1}{6}$
14. $\frac{3}{5} \div \frac{3}{8}$ $\frac{8}{5} = 1\frac{3}{5}$
15. $4 \div \frac{2}{5}$ $\frac{10}{1} = 10$

**Multiply or divide.**

16. $2\frac{4}{5} \times 1\frac{1}{3}$ $\frac{56}{15} = 3\frac{11}{15}$
17. $5\frac{3}{8} \times \frac{3}{4}$ $\frac{129}{32} = 4\frac{1}{32}$
18. $2\frac{1}{6} \div \frac{1}{2}$ $\frac{13}{3} = 4\frac{1}{3}$
19. $3\frac{1}{2} \div \frac{3}{4}$ $\frac{14}{3} = 4\frac{2}{3}$
20. $5\frac{2}{3} \div 1\frac{5}{6}$ $\frac{34}{11} = 3\frac{1}{11}$
21. $2\frac{2}{3} \times \frac{3}{8}$ $\frac{1}{1} = 1$
22. $6 \times 3\frac{2}{3}$ $\frac{22}{1} = 22$
23. $12\frac{1}{2} \div 1\frac{1}{4}$ $\frac{10}{1} = 10$
24. $4\frac{2}{5} \times 2\frac{1}{2}$ $\frac{11}{1} = 11$

**Write a fraction in lowest terms.**

25. 0.3 $\frac{3}{10}$
26. 0.85 $\frac{17}{20}$
27. 0.625 $\frac{5}{8}$
28. 0.02 $\frac{1}{50}$

**Write a decimal.**

29. $\frac{3}{4}$ 0.75
30. $\frac{3}{5}$ 0.6
31. $\frac{7}{8}$ 0.875
32. $\frac{6}{15}$ 0.4



## Just for Teachers

### Math Anxiety: The Language of Mathematics.

There are many aspects of mathematics that may create math anxiety in students. One area that may prove troublesome is in the language of mathematics. Teachers of mathematics realize that the language of mathematics is quite precise. Students may not realize that words may have such precise meanings. There are words used in daily life which have different meanings in mathematics. As a result, ambiguity may result when the everyday meaning of a word conflicts with its mathematical meaning.

The simple preposition "of" is used in a wide variety of ways in everyday language. In mathematics students learn that it is a key word that may mean the operation of multiplication. Thus $\frac{1}{2}$ of $\frac{3}{4}$ means $\frac{1}{2}$ times $\frac{3}{4}$. Compounding the problem is the fact that many students learn, from work with whole numbers, that the product of two numbers is larger than either of the factors. But $\frac{1}{2} \times \frac{3}{4} = \frac{3}{8}$, and $\frac{3}{8}$ is less than either $\frac{1}{2}$ or $\frac{3}{4}$. Similarly, students learn that when dividing whole numbers the quotient is always smaller than the dividend. But when $\frac{3}{4}$ is divided by $\frac{1}{2}$ the quotient, $1\frac{1}{2}$, is larger than the dividend, $\frac{3}{4}$.

How can anxieties related to such experiences described above be alleviated? The use of mathematical words should be carefully explained to students and the differences between their everyday use and use in mathematics made clear. Help students

# Enrichment

### Patterns in Repeating Decimals

When Tico tried to find a decimal for $\frac{2}{11}$, he saw a pattern in the digits on his calculator. When he divided 2 by 11, he could see that the digits 1 and 8 would continue to repeat.

0.1818181

$$\begin{array}{r} 0.1818\ldots \\ 11\overline{)2.00000} \\ \underline{11} \\ 90 \\ \underline{88} \\ 20 \\ \underline{11} \\ 90 \\ \underline{88} \\ 2 \\ \vdots \end{array}$$

The decimal for $\frac{2}{11}$ is called a repeating decimal. We can write it in either of these ways:

$\frac{2}{11} = 0.181818\ldots$ or $\frac{2}{11} = 0.\overline{18}$

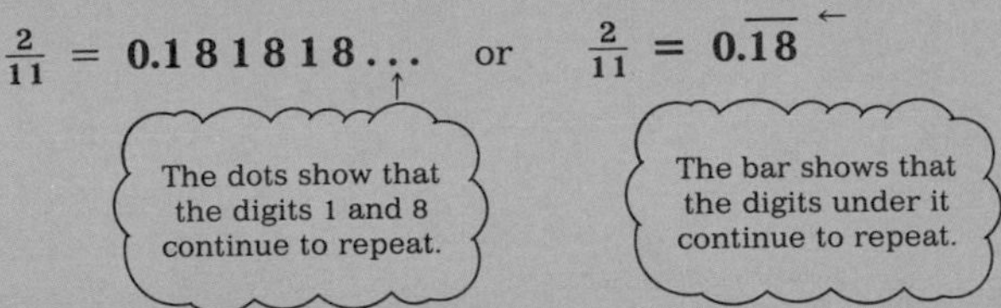
The dots show that the digits 1 and 8 continue to repeat.
The bar shows that the digits under it continue to repeat.

Let's look at some patterns of repeating decimals.

1. Here is the repeating decimal for $\frac{1}{3}$.

   $\frac{1}{3} = 0.333\ldots = 0.\overline{3}$

   Give the repeating decimal for $\frac{2}{3}$ without calculating.

   Use a calculator, if you wish, to find repeating decimals for $\frac{1}{6}$, $\frac{5}{6}$, and $\frac{1}{12}$.

   $0.\overline{6}$, $0.1\overline{6}$, $0.8\overline{3}$, $0.08\overline{3}$

2. Check these repeating decimals by dividing.

   $\frac{1}{11} = 0.\overline{09}$ $\frac{2}{11} = 0.\overline{18}$ $\frac{3}{11} = 0.\overline{27}$

   Can you give repeating decimals for the fractions $\frac{4}{11}$ through $\frac{10}{11}$ without calculating?

   $0.\overline{36}$, $0.\overline{45}$, $0.\overline{54}$, $0.\overline{63}$, $0.\overline{72}$, $0.\overline{81}$, $0.\overline{90}$

3. Check these repeating decimals by dividing.

   $\frac{4}{99} = 0.\overline{04}$ $\frac{12}{99} = 0.\overline{12}$ $\frac{23}{99} = 0.\overline{23}$

   Can you give the fractions for these repeating decimals?

   $0.\overline{08}$, $0.\overline{47}$, $0.\overline{65}$, $0.\overline{98}$ $\frac{8}{99}$, $\frac{47}{99}$, $\frac{65}{99}$, $\frac{98}{99}$

4. Check these repeating decimals by dividing.

   $\frac{5}{999} = 0.\overline{005}$ $\frac{76}{999} = 0.\overline{076}$ $\frac{345}{999} = 0.\overline{345}$

   Can you give fractions for these repeating decimals?

   $0.\overline{008}$, $0.\overline{083}$, $0.\overline{694}$, $0.\overline{996}$, $0.\overline{444}$

   $\frac{8}{999}$, $\frac{83}{999}$, $\frac{694}{999}$, $\frac{996}{999}$, $\frac{444}{999}$

249

use the language of mathematics correctly when discussing mathematics. Make good use of concrete materials to illustrate mathematical ideas. For example, use a pie chart to show the meaning of $\frac{1}{2}$ of $\frac{3}{4}$. Use a $\frac{1}{2}$-cup measure to illustrate $\frac{3}{4}$ divided by $\frac{1}{2}$ to show how many times $\frac{1}{2}$ is contained in $\frac{3}{4}$.

Many cases of math anxiety can be prevented or overcome by using good teaching techniques that help students understand the concepts of mathematics. Be alert for those situations that can cause math anxiety and work with students in understanding and encouraging ways.

## Using Page 249

This page is intended for those students who successfully completed the Chapter Review-Test on page 247. You may wish to assign this page as independent work while you use Another Look exercises to reteach the basic concepts and skills of the chapter. Or, you may decide that all students would benefit from exposure to this Enrichment activity.

**Lesson Development** Direct students' attention to the fraction $\frac{2}{11}$. Have them divide 2 by 11 on their calculators and observe that the digits (1,8) repeat in the display. Then work through the division process in which 2 is divided by 11. "When we divide 2 by 11 to find the first quotient digit, what is the remainder after the subtraction." (9) "When we divide to find the second quotient digit, what is the remainder after the subtraction?" (2) "Do you see a pattern in the remainders?" (9 and 2 continue to repeat in that order.) "Do you think there would ever be another remainder other than 9 or 2?" (No, these same numbers are involved each time.) Point out that since the remainders 9 and 2 alternate, the quotient will repeat 1,8; 1,8; 1,8 and so on. Then call students' attention to the use of the three dots after the 8 or the bar over the repeating digits used to indicate a repeating decimal.

**Exercise 1** In this exercise students could reason that if the repeating decimal for $\frac{1}{3}$ is 0.333. . . , then the repeating decimal for $\frac{2}{3}$ would be twice as much or 0.666. . . .

**Exercise 2** Students might observe that because the repeating decimal for $\frac{1}{11}$ is $0.\overline{09}$, then the decimal for $\frac{2}{11}$ would be $0.\overline{18}$, and the decimal for $\frac{4}{11}$ would be twice that, or $0.\overline{36}$. They might also observe that the repeating parts are multiples of 9 and conclude that the repeating decimal for $\frac{10}{11}$ would be $0.\overline{90}$.

**Exercises 3–4** Encourage students to look for patterns in these repeating decimals. Many students will quickly observe that when the denominator is 99, the repeating part of the decimal is the same as the numerator; when the denominator is 999, the repeating part of the decimal is the same as the numerator written as thousandths.

# Review

## Using Page 250

The exercises on this page provide practice for maintaining cumulative skills. The emphasis in this Cumulative Review is on multiplication and division of decimals (Chapter 6), addition and subtraction of decimals (Chapter 8), and problem-solving (Chapter 8).

**Item Analysis** The table below correlates the Cumulative Review items with objectives and with the student book pages on which the concepts or skills were taught.

| Items | Objectives | Related text pages |
|---|---|---|
| 1–3 | 6.2 | 140–145 |
| 4–5 | 6.3 | 148–153 |
| 6–8 | 8.1 | 194–199 |
| 9–12 | 8.4 | 207–215 |
| 13–14 | 8.5 | 203, 206, 216–217 |

## *Cumulative Review*

Multiply or divide.

1. 12.483 × 100
   Ⓐ 1,248.3 **B** 124.83 **C** 0.12483 **D** not given

2. 1.8 × 0.09
   Ⓐ 0.162 **B** 0.972 **C** 1.89 **D** not given

3. 4.3 × 4.3
   **A** 184.9 **B** 1.849 **C** 12.09 Ⓓ not given

4. 34.8 ÷ 100
   **A** 3,480 **B** 348 **C** 3.48 Ⓓ not given

5. $4\overline{)9.64}$
   **A** 241 Ⓑ 2.41 **C** 1.94 **D** not given

6. What is the missing numerator?
   $\frac{5}{8} = \frac{■}{40}$
   Ⓐ 25 **B** 36 **C** 32 **D** not given

7. What is the missing denominator?
   $\frac{5}{9} = \frac{20}{■}$
   **A** 45 Ⓑ 36 **C** 18 **D** not given

8. Reduce $\frac{18}{48}$ to lowest terms.
   **A** $\frac{2}{5}$ **B** $\frac{1}{3}$ Ⓒ $\frac{3}{8}$ **D** not given

Add or subtract.

9. $\frac{2}{5} + \frac{3}{10}$
   **A** $\frac{1}{10}$ **B** $\frac{5}{10}$ Ⓒ $\frac{7}{10}$ **D** not given

10. $\frac{8}{9} - \frac{1}{3}$
    **A** $\frac{2}{3}$ Ⓑ $\frac{5}{9}$ **C** $\frac{7}{9}$ **D** not given

11. $6\frac{1}{2} + 2\frac{1}{3}$
    Ⓐ $8\frac{5}{6}$ **B** $9\frac{1}{6}$ **C** $4\frac{1}{6}$ **D** not given

12. $9\frac{1}{4} - 3\frac{1}{2}$
    **A** $12\frac{3}{4}$ **B** $6\frac{3}{4}$ **C** $5\frac{1}{4}$ Ⓓ not given

13. A recipe calls for $\frac{1}{4}$ cup of milk and $\frac{1}{2}$ cup of water. What is the total amount of liquid?
    **A** $\frac{1}{4}$ cup **B** $\frac{1}{8}$ cup Ⓒ $\frac{3}{4}$ cup **D** not given

14. A rope 10.5 m long is cut into 7 pieces of equal length. How long is each piece?
    **A** 15 m Ⓑ 1.5 m **C** 7 m **D** not given

## Objectives

**10.1** Identify and write symbols for basic geometric figures.
**10.2** Identify, classify, and draw angles according to their measure.
**10.3** Identify and draw parallel and perpendicular lines.
**10.4** Identify and classify polygons according to the measure of their angles, length of their sides, and number of sides.
**10.5** Identify and write symbols for a chord, diameter, radius, and central angle.
**10.6** Identify pairs of congruent and symmetric figures and lines of symmetry; use coordinates to graph congruent and symmetric figures.
**10.7** Identify basic space figures and count their faces, vertices, and edges.

## Summary

In this chapter students first identify objects in the real world that suggest basic geometric figures and relationships such as points, lines, segments, rays, and angles. Students use protractors to measure and draw right, acute, and obtuse angles, and they also generalize that the sum of the angles of a triangle is 180°. Techniques are given to help students draw perpendicular and parallel lines. After this basic introduction, students classify triangles and quadrilaterals according to sides, angles, and lines of symmetry. The basic ideas of polygons and circles are also developed.

Students learn to recognize congruent and symmetric figures and to graph geometric figures using coordinates. Space figures are discussed, and students count faces, edges, and vertices of prisms and pyramids.

## Mathematical Background

**Basic Figures and Relationships** Students should recognize that basic figures such as points, lines, segments, rays, angles, and polygons of all types are suggested by ordinary objects that they see every day. Note the way the ideas are presented on page 252. First *we see* a physical object and abstract common characteristics from the object. Then *we think* about an idea to which we may attach a word and *we write* a symbol for the abstracted concept. These three stages of concept learning are emphasized with each new geometric idea. The basic figures are discussed as well as the relationships between these figures.

**Measuring Angles** The measurement of angles is similar to the measurement of segments. When measuring segments we may use a unit of length called a centimeter; when measuring angles we often use a unit of angle called a degree. To measure an angle, we use a device called a protractor that lays several angle units alongside each other so that they can be easily counted.

When measuring a segment we lay the ruler alongside the segment and find the number of units; when measuring angles we lay the protractor so that we can count the number of units it takes to fill up the interior of the angles. It is important that students learn to use the protractor to measure angles that are placed in a variety of positions.

**Classifying Polygons** Polygons are usually classified in terms of certain characteristics of angles, sides, or lines of symmetry. For example, we classify triangles as equilateral, isosceles, or scalene. An equilateral triangle has all three sides congruent, all three angles congruent, and exactly three lines of symmetry. An isosceles triangle has two sides congruent, two angles congruent, and one line of symmetry. A scalene triangle has no sides congruent, no angles congruent, and no lines of symmetry.

In a similar manner we classify quadrilaterals. A parallelogram has two pairs of sides that are both congruent and parallel. It may have no lines of symmetry. A rectangle is a parallelogram with four right angles. It has two lines of symmetry. A square is a special type of rectangle. It has four congruent sides and four lines of symmetry. A rhombus is a special type of parallelogram. It has four congruent sides. It also has two lines of symmetry. A trapezoid is not a parallelogram. It has only one pair of parallel sides. Sometimes a trapezoid, called an isosceles trapezoid, has a pair of congruent sides. This type of trapezoid has one line of symmetry.

**Graphing Figures** The discovery of analytic geometry (sometimes called coordinate geometry) was important in the development of mathematics because it allowed a "marriage" of geometry and numbers. As shown in the diagram, two perpendicular rays (number "lines") are drawn. Then an ordered pair of numbers called coordinates can be used to locate a point, for example, the point (3, 2). Note that the ordered pair (3, 2) can be described as "to the right 3, and up 2."

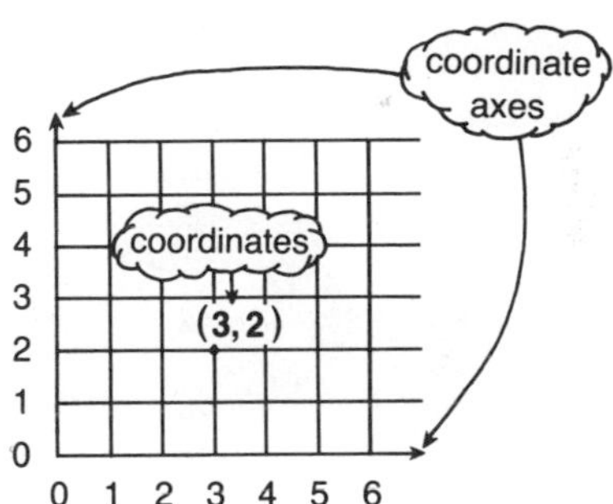


**Vocabulary**

point
line
segment
ray
angle
protractor
degree
right angle
acute angle
obtuse angle
perpendicular
parallel
scalene
isosceles
equilateral
acute triangle
right triangle
obtuse triangle
quadrilateral
parallelogram
square
trapezoid
rhombus
rectangle
polygon
pentagon
hexagon
octagon
decagon
circle
chord
diameter
radius
central angle
congruent
symmetric
coordinates
polyhedron
vertices
faces
edges
triangular prism
cube
rectangular prism
triangular pyramid
square pyramid
pentagonal pyramid
hexagonal prism
cylinder
cone
sphere

## Error Analysis

In this chapter basic geometric concepts are discussed. Students learn to identify geometric figures and to recognize the relationships that exist among these figures. Because the computation required in this chapter is minimal, errors in computation should be few. Most errors will be the result of misunderstanding of definitions or confusion about the relationships that exist among and between the various geometric elements. In each instance, the first step in error analysis is to make a careful diagnosis of the misunderstandings. This suggests more than a simple check of students' papers to determine whether answers are correct or incorrect. Encourage students to discuss the procedures or methods used to solve the problem. Students might also demonstrate their knowledge by constructing various geometric figures with three-dimensional materials. Projects or field trips can help to enrich students' basic geometric knowledge and understanding. As the first step for each concept, it would be helpful to introduce each idea with an activity that requires experimentation or construction.

## Problem Solving

### Working with Small Groups

Many teachers find that using small groups can be a valuable way to organize the classroom for teaching problem solving. One of the most important things a teacher of problem solving can do is to move around the room observing and questioning students while they solve problems. If there are 25 students in a class, it is difficult to give much attention to any one student. When small groups are formed, most teachers find it easier to monitor and assess their students' problem-solving performance.

In addition to helping in the management of instruction, there are other benefits of using small groups. Students who have not had much experience with problem solving may have considerable problem-solving anxiety. The use of small groups is one way to reduce the pressure on the individual student. In problem-solving groups, progress and success on a problem are the responsibility of the group, not the individual. Another benefit of small-group instruction is in eliciting behaviors that promote the improvement of problem-solving performance. For example, students are often required to justify their ideas, evaluate the ideas of others, and deal with contradictions. Here are other guidelines for using small groups.

- Limit the group size to 3 or 4 students.
- Accept a higher noise level in the classroom.
- Do not interrupt a group that is working well. If a group appears to be floundering, however, ask a student to tell what the group is discussing or which part of the problem is giving difficulty.
- Ask discussion questions, rather than telling a group what to do.
- Try different grouping patterns—homogeneous, heterogeneous, teacher-selected, student-selected, for example—to find what works best for your students.

When small groups are used, it is important to keep every student involved in the problem-solving task. Here are some ideas.

- Identify a group captain for the day. This person is responsible for explaining the group's work that day.
- Identify a *recorder* to write all of the group's work.
- Require that students ask for your help only when everyone in the group has the same question.
- Require that everyone in the group agree on one answer.
- Question students who appear not to be involved in the group's work. Try to determine whether the students do not understand the problem or whether they are not participating.

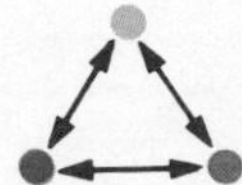

## Special Education

This chapter deals with the development of several central concepts in geometry, while strengthening concepts studied at earlier levels.

### Solidifying Students' Geometric Concepts

The development of students' concepts of various geometric ideas can be directed by helping students differentiate between examples and non-examples of a given concept. This can be done for the ideas of line, line segment, ray, angle, and polygon by putting several different examples of each concept on index cards and then having students sort the cards into sets of like geometric objects. Students can then play a game in which the object is to match a shape card with a card with the written symbol for that shape. Some examples of these cards are shown below. To vary this exercise, have students place the cards in rows and play a game of geometry concentration.

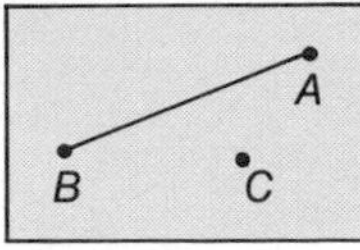


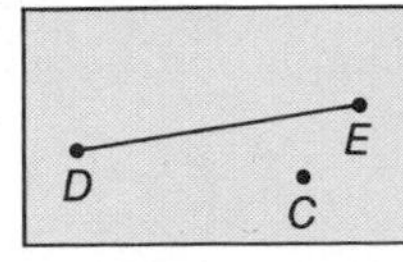


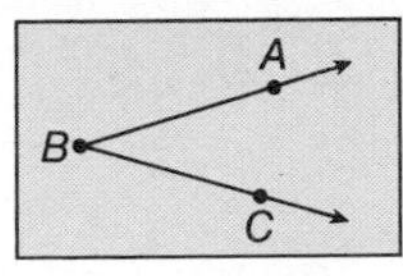


Segment
*AB*

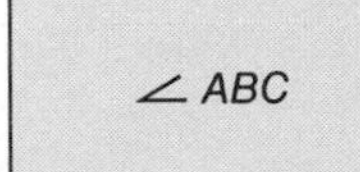


### Showing Real-World Geometry

The development of geometric concepts can be aided by having students walk about the school and list the various places in the school environment where these ideas can be seen. If possible, use a camera to make slides of the community with the concepts visible in the pictures. These slides can then be shown in the classroom, and the various shapes can be identified and discussed.

### Building Quadrilaterals

Give students a collection of cardboard strips and brass fasteners and have them make different types of quadrilaterals from the various strips. Examples are shown in the illustration below.

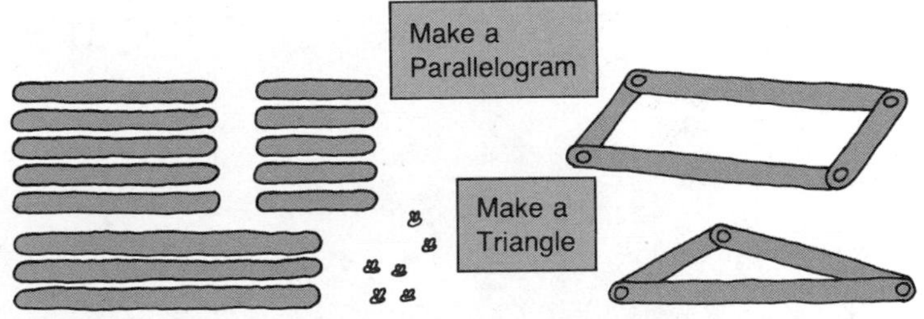


### Developing Orientation and Comparison Skills

The study of congruent, similar, and symmetric figures requires that students make judgments on the orientation and relative sizes of various objects. One step in this process is to recognize a figure after it has been slid, turned, or flipped about a fixed line or point. If students have trouble in doing these things, let them use tracing paper to carry out these actions. This is especially useful in determining congruency. Another approach is to model these activities with transparencies on the overhead projector. Give students hints about steps in checking to see if two figures are congruent. Then give hints on lining up the corresponding parts on similar and symmetric figures. For similar figures, note the placement of sides having the same relative sizes or the matching of corresponding angles. Point out that the angle size remains the same in similar figures, only the lengths of the sides possibly change.

## Subject Integration

Subject matter related to other areas of the curriculum has been integrated into the following lessons. This provides an opportunity to highlight the interaction between mathematics and other subjects.

**Social Studies** Coats of arms, page 251

# Management Guide

| Teaching Chapter 10 | | | | Meeting Individual Needs | | | | | |
|---|---|---|---|---|---|---|---|---|---|
| | | | | Lesson Assignments | | | Follow Up | | |
| Objectives | Chapter Content | Pages | TRB Test Items | Minimum | Average | Extended | Reteaching | Enrichment | Practice |
| | Chapter Opener | 251 | | | | | | | |
| **10.1** Identify and write symbols for basic geometric figures. | Basic Geometric Figures | 252–253 | 1–4 | 1–16 | 1–16, TM | 1–17, TM | | | PS 96 |
| **10.2** Identify, classify, and draw angles according to their measure. | Measuring Angles | 254 | 5–6 | 1–5 | 1–5 | 1–5 | SE5 Ch 11<br>RS 59 | ES 59 | |
| | Drawing Angles | 255 | | 1–12, SK | 1–12, SK | 1–13, SK | SE5 Ch 11 | | PS 97 |
| **10.3** Identify and draw parallel and perpendicular lines. | Perpendicular Lines | 256 | 7 | 1–3 | 1–3 | 1–4 | SE5 Ch 11 | | |
| | Parallel Lines | 257 | 8 | 1–3 | 1–4 | 1–4 | SE5 Ch 11<br>RS 60 | ES 60 | PS 98 |
| **10.4** Identify and classify polygons according to the measure of their angles, length of their sides, and number of sides. | Triangles | 258–259 | 9–11 | 1–11 | 1–11 | 1–13, TM | SE5 Ch 11 | | PS 99 |
| | Quadrilaterals | 260–261 | 12–14 | 1–9 | 1–9, TM | 1–9, TM | SE5 Ch 11<br>RS 61 | ES 61 | PS 100 |
| | Other Polygons | 262 | 15–17 | 1–10 | 1–10 | 1–11 | SE5 Ch 11 | | |
| **10.5** Identify and write symbols for a chord, diameter, radius, and central angle. | Circles | 263 | 18–20 | 1–10 | 1–10 | 1–11 | SE5 Ch 11 | | PS 101 |
| **10.6** Identify pairs of congruent and similar figures and lines of symmetry in figures; use coordinates to graph congruent, similar, and symmetric figures. | Congruent Figures | 264–265 | 21 | 1–6 | 1–6, TM | 1–6, TM | SE5 Ch 11<br>RS 62 | ES 62 | PS 102 |
| | Symmetric Figures | 266–267 | 22 | 1–6 / 1–7, SK | 1–6 / 1–8, SK | 1–6 / 1–9, SK | SE5 Ch 11<br>RS 63 | ES 63 | PS 103 |
| | Graphing Geometric Figures | 268–269 | 23–25 | 1–12 | 1–12, TM | 1–12, TM | SE5 Ch 11<br>RS 64 | ES 64 | PS 104 |
| **10.7** Identify basic space figures and count their faces, vertices, and edges. | Space Figures | 270–271 | 26–31 | 1–5 / 1–10 | 1–5 / 1–10 | 1–5 / 1–10, TM | SE5 Ch 11 | | PS 105 |
| | Problem Solving: Using the Strategies | 272 | | | | | | | |
| | Chapter Review-Test | 273 | | | | | | | |
| | Another Look/Enrichment | 274–275 | | | | | | | |
| | Cumulative Review | 276 | | | | | | | |

**SE5** Student Edition, Book 5
**RS** Reteaching Supplement
**ES** Enrichment Supplement
**PS** Practice Supplement
**MP** More Practice
**TM** Think Math
**SK** Skillkeeper
**TRB** Teacher's Resource Book

## Masters for Use

**. . . before Chapter 10**

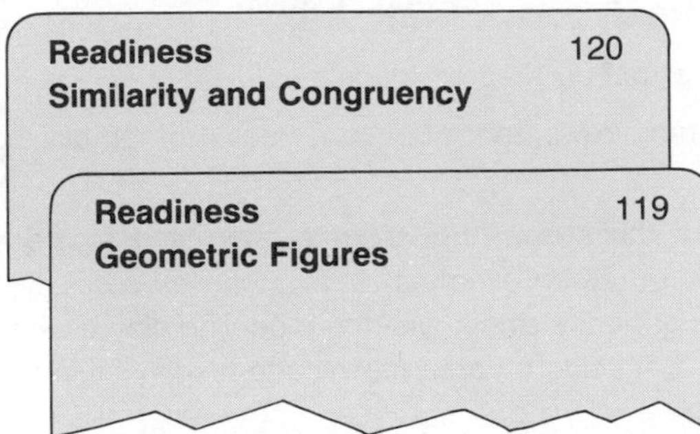


**. . . during Chapter 10**

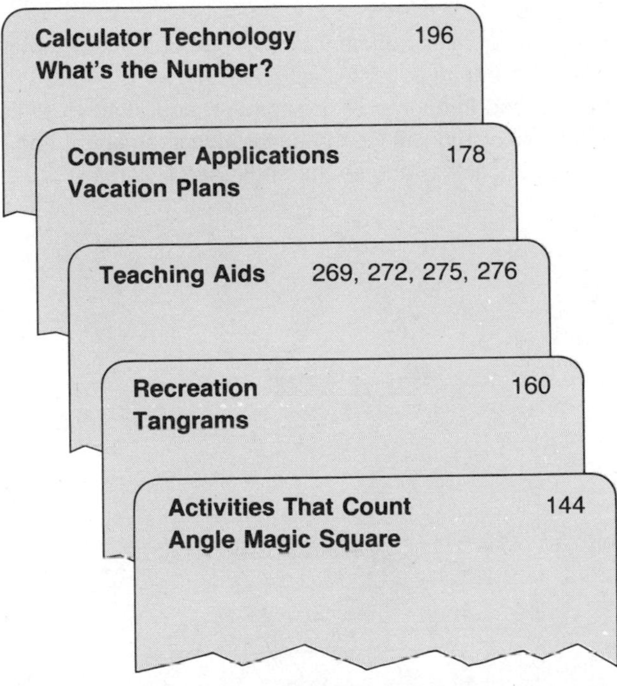


**. . . after Chapter 10**

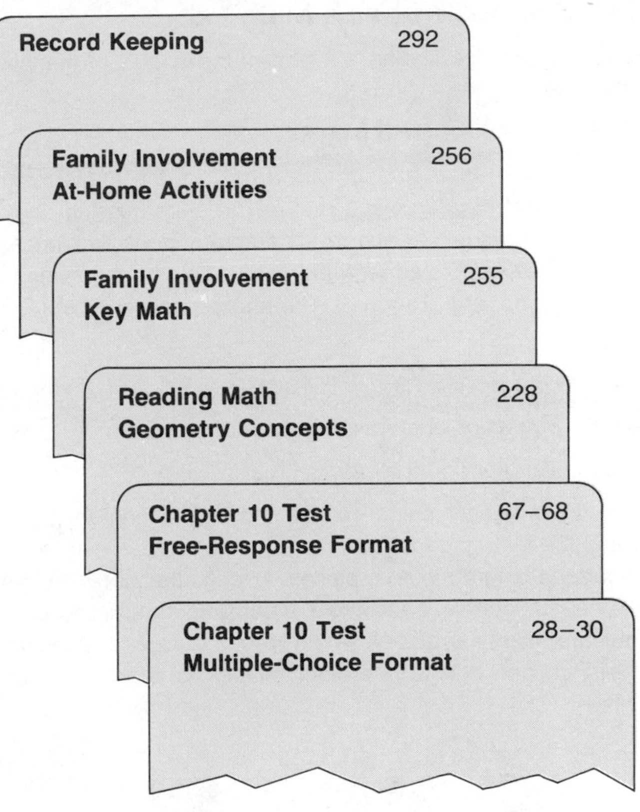


## Supplements

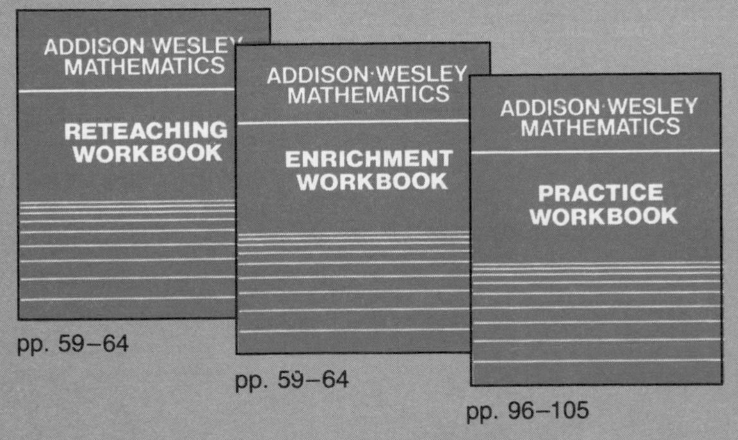

ADDISON WESLEY MATHEMATICS
RETEACHING WORKBOOK
pp. 59–64
ADDISON·WESLEY MATHEMATICS
ENRICHMENT WORKBOOK
pp. 59–64
ADDISON·WESLEY MATHEMATICS
PRACTICE WORKBOOK
pp. 96–105


## Other Addison-Wesley Resources

**Books and Kits**

*Dice and Dots* Game 1–4, 6–8, 10

*Problem-Solving Experiences in Mathematics, Grade 6,* Problems 29, 30, 64, 65, 89, 104, 125, 144

**Technology**

*Computer Math Activities* Volumes 2, 3, 5

*Computer Math Games* Volume 1

# Activities That Count

Activities That Count are designed for use throughout this chapter and subsequent chapters. Before beginning Chapter 10, you may wish to review these activities and select the ones you consider appropriate for your class.

## Angle Magic Square Math Lab

**Purpose** To practice finding the sum of the angles of triangles and quadrilaterals

**Materials** Worksheet (TRB p. 144)

**Activity** Provide each student with a copy of the angle magic square worksheet. Students find and record each missing angle. Then they find the sum of each row, column, and the two longest diagonals. If their work is correct, the sum should be the same for every row, column, and diagonal. (The angle magic sum is 340.)

## Tangram Teasers Project

**Purpose** To practice and extend geometric concepts

**Materials** Tangram puzzle pieces (TRB p. 280)

**Activity** Provide each student with a copy of the tangram puzzle pieces and the following instructions:

Cut apart the tangram puzzle pieces. Arrange the pieces to form these four quadrilaterals: a rectangle, a parallelogram, a trapezoid, and a square. Can you use all seven pieces to form a rhombus? Now make up and outline five other shapes to share with your classmates.

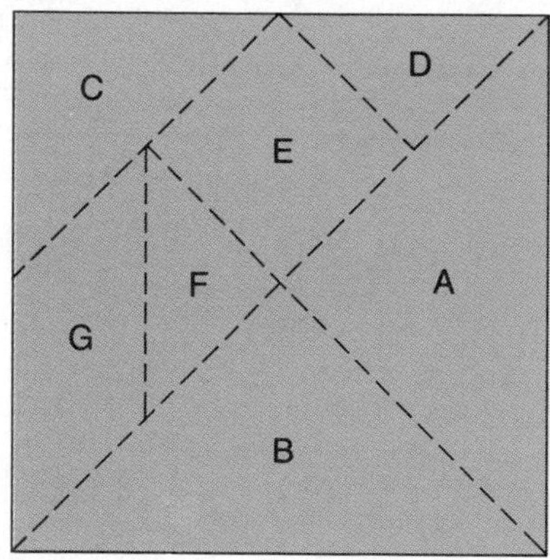


## Straw Polyhedrons Math Lab

**Purpose** To construct polyhedron models

**Materials** Colored straws, modeling clay, heavy thread or pipe cleaners

**Preparation** Cut the straws into 8-cm segments. Prepare a completed polyhedron as an example. Straws can be connected with pipe cleaners or heavy string, with the modeling clay used to bond the vertices. Set aside an area in which to display students' polyhedrons.

**Activity** Provide students with the following instructions.

1. String three segments together. Arrange the segments into a triangle and tie the ends of the thread to hold the triangular shape (see illustration A).
2. String a fourth and fifth segment to one side of the first triangle to form a double triangle (see illustration B).
3. Insert the thread through a sixth segment, and attach it to the double triangle by running the thread through segments 1 and 4. Pull the figure together and tie the ends (see illustration C).

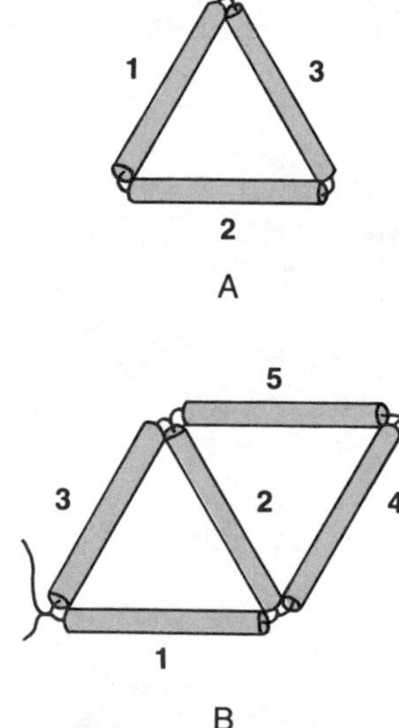


A

B

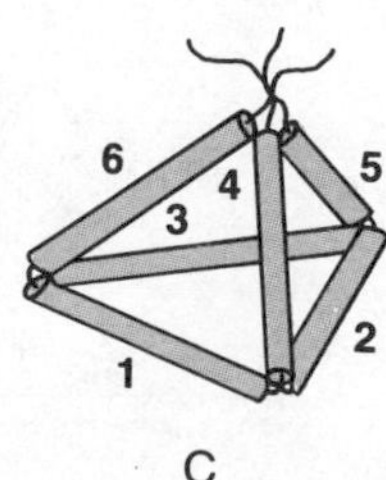


C

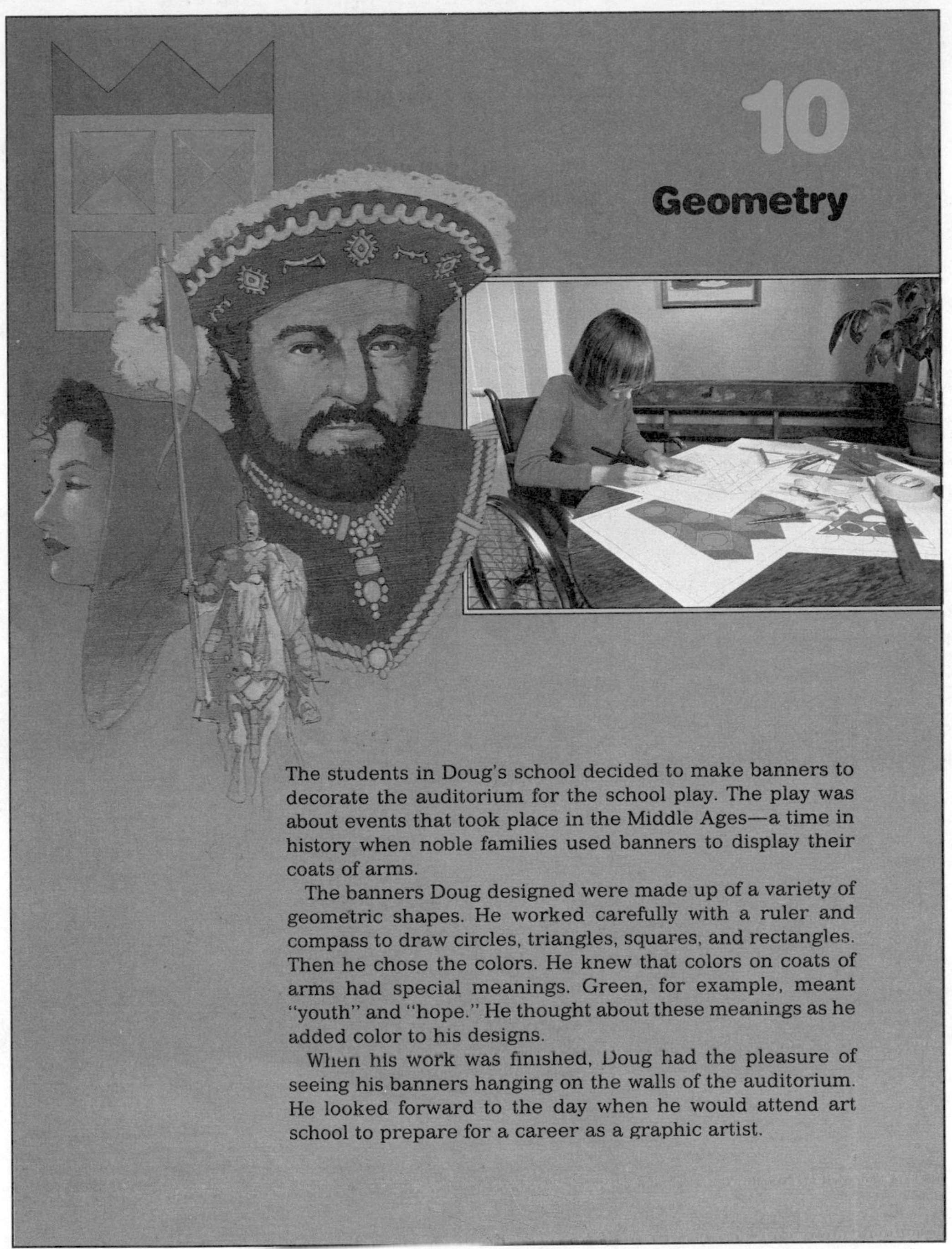

10
Geometry
The students in Doug's school decided to make banners to decorate the auditorium for the school play. The play was about events that took place in the Middle Ages—a time in history when noble families used banners to display their coats of arms.
The banners Doug designed were made up of a variety of geometric shapes. He worked carefully with a ruler and compass to draw circles, triangles, squares, and rectangles. Then he chose the colors. He knew that colors on coats of arms had special meanings. Green, for example, meant "youth" and "hope." He thought about these meanings as he added color to his designs.
When his work was finished, Doug had the pleasure of seeing his banners hanging on the walls of the auditorium. He looked forward to the day when he would attend art school to prepare for a career as a graphic artist.


## Introducing the Chapter

**Discussion** Tell students that in this chapter they will review and broaden their understanding of some important geometric concepts. Lead a brief discussion about the use of coats of arms in the past and in modern times. Point out that the types of symbols used on coats of arms of individuals and families in medieval times are frequently used today in the flags and official seals of states and nations. Give students an opportunity to read the story and enjoy the art. As you teach the chapter, you may wish to refer to this page and pose the questions suggested below.

## Follow-Up Questions

**After Page 254** What kind of angle—right, acute, or obtuse—is an angle whose measure is 120°? 90°? 65°? (obtuse, right, acute)

**After Page 256** What kind of lines intersect at right angles? (perpendicular lines)

**After Page 259** If the measures of two of the angles of an isosceles triangle are 75°, what is the measure of the third angle? (30°)

**After Page 263** What is the radius of a circle whose diameter is 300 mm? (150 mm)

**After Page 271** If a space figure has 6 faces and 6 vertices, how many edges does it have? (10)

# Geometry

**Quick Review** Provide an oral drill using the problems below.

| | | | | | |
|---|---|---|---|---|---|
| 60 + 60 | 120 + 30 | 90 − 60 | 2 × 90 | 180 ÷ 60 | 40 × 2 |
| 3 × 60 | 90 + 50 | 30 + 60 | 360 ÷ 90 | 2 × 180 | |
| 270 ÷ 90 | 90 − 30 | 180 − 60 | 360 ÷ 6 | 150 ÷ 3 | 6 × 90 |

**Lesson Focus** To identify and name points, lines, line segments, rays, and angles

**Suggested Materials** Pictures from magazines to illustrate the geometric ideas discussed in this lesson

## Ideas for Getting Started

Draw figures of points, lines, line segments, rays, and angles on the chalkboard. Have students look for examples of these geometric ideas in the magazine pictures.

## Using Page 252

**Lesson Development** Discuss each of the pictures shown on the page. Point out that a point shows only location. Emphasize that a line extends indefinitely in both directions. Note that a line can be named by any two points on it or by a lower case letter. Remind students that a line segment has two endpoints and can be thought of as a part of a line. Emphasize that a ray has one endpoint and extends indefinitely in one direction. A ray is always named by giving the endpoint first. Finally, point out that an angle is formed by two rays with a common endpoint. Discuss the different ways to name angles.

## Basic Geometric Figures

Many real world objects suggest important geometric ideas and figures.

| We see | We think | We write |
|---|---|---|
| Pin tip | a **point** | $P$ |
| Center line of a road | a **line** | $\ell$ or $\overleftrightarrow{AB}$ |
| File cabinet edge | a **line segment** (with **endpoints** $C$ and $D$) | $\overline{CD}$ |
| Penlight beam | a **ray** (with **endpoint** $E$) | $\overrightarrow{EF}$ |
| Clock hands | an **angle** (with **vertex** $S$ and **sides** $\overrightarrow{SR}$ and $\overrightarrow{ST}$) | $\angle RST$ or $\angle TSR$ or $\angle S$ |

252

## Follow Up

### Reteaching

Use the overhead projector to review points, lines, line segments, rays, and angles. Include the appropriate notation. Then have students look around the classroom to find examples of each of the geometric ideas discussed. The floor, ceiling, walls, and furniture all contain examples of points, lines, and so on.

### Enrichment

Draw six line segments to form a six pointed star. Then challenge students to label all of the geometric ideas they can find in the star.

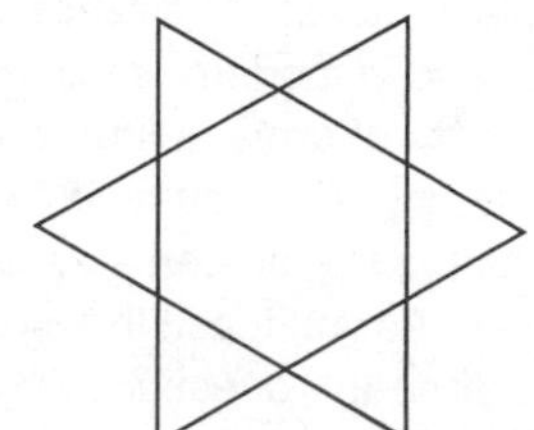

| Assignment Guide | | | |
|---|---|---|---|
| | Minimum | Average | Extended |
| page 253 | 1–16 | 1–16, TM | 1–17, TM |

Write the name and symbol for each figure.

1. 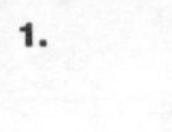 point, Q

2. 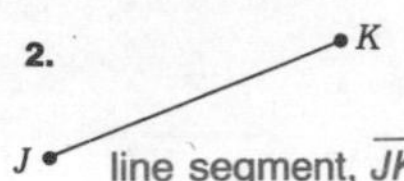 line segment, $\overline{JK}$

3. 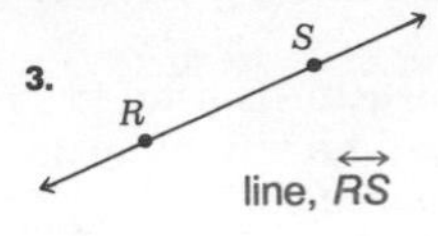 line, $\overleftrightarrow{RS}$

4. 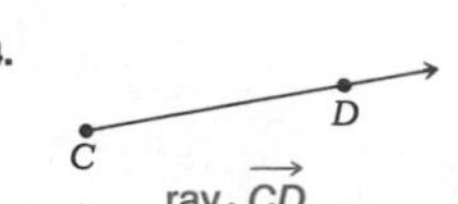 ray, $\overrightarrow{CD}$

5. 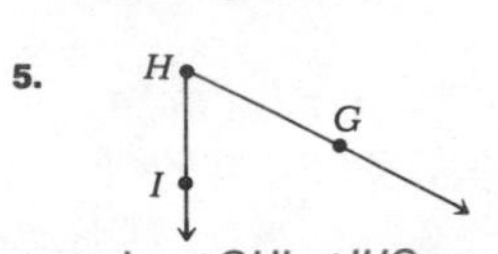 angle; ∠GHI, ∠IHG, or ∠H

6. 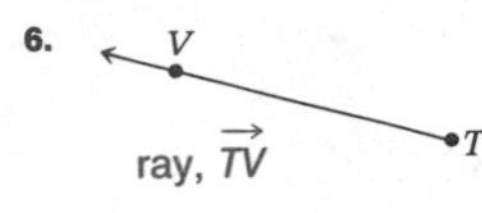 ray, $\overrightarrow{TV}$

Draw a picture for each symbol. See teaching notes.

7. $\overline{DE}$ 8. ∠EFG 9. point G 10. $\overrightarrow{BC}$ 11. $\overleftrightarrow{MN}$

12. Name 6 different line segments in this figure. $\overline{ED}$, $\overline{DF}$, $\overline{FE}$, $\overline{EC}$, $\overline{DC}$, $\overline{FC}$

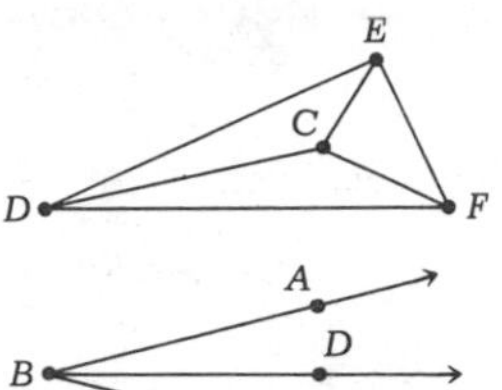

13. Name 3 different rays in this figure. $\overrightarrow{BA}$, $\overrightarrow{BD}$, $\overrightarrow{BC}$

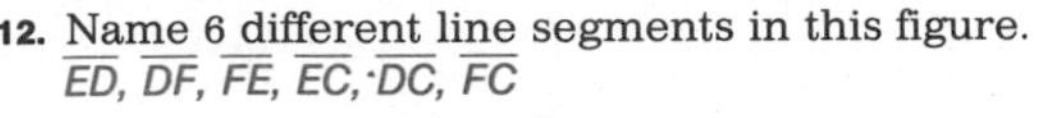

14. Name 3 different angles in this figure. ∠ABC, ∠DBC, ∠ABD

15. Name 2 different rays in this figure. $\overrightarrow{YX}$, $\overrightarrow{XY}$

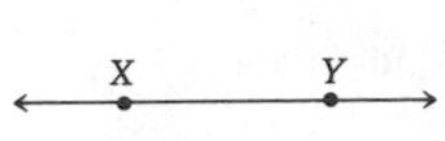

16. Give 3 different names for this angle. ∠TSR, ∠RST, ∠S

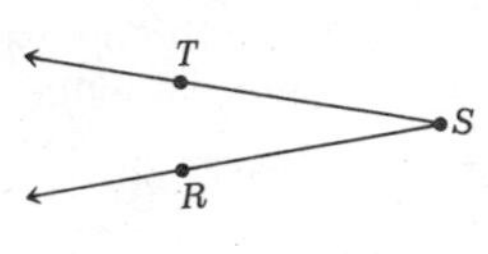

★ 17. Name 10 different line segments in this figure. $\overline{AB}$, $\overline{AC}$, $\overline{AD}$, $\overline{AE}$, $\overline{BC}$, $\overline{BD}$, $\overline{BE}$, $\overline{CD}$, $\overline{CE}$, $\overline{DE}$

## Think Math

**Optical Illusions**

A Tall Hat!

Which segment, $\overline{AB}$ or $\overline{CD}$, do you think is longer? Or are they the same length?

First estimate. Then check by measuring to the nearest millimeter. $\overline{AB}$ is longer.



## Using Page 253

**Exercises 1–6** Be alert for the following errors: (a) confusing a line with a line segment, (b) naming a ray by a point on the line rather than with the endpoint (note exercise 6), (c) failing to put the name of the vertex in the middle when naming an angle.

**Exercises 7–11** Student constructions should show the following figures:

7. 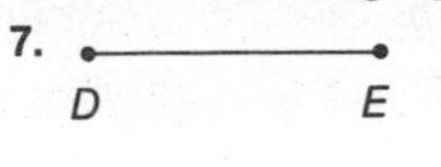

8. 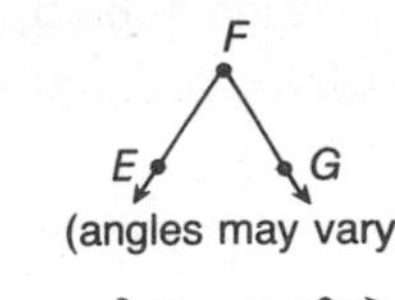 (angles may vary)

9. • G

10. B C

11. 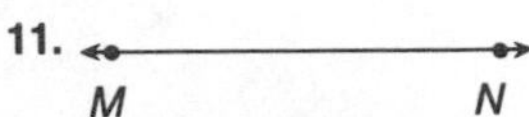

**Exercises 12–16** In exercise 14 some students may focus on ∠ABD and ∠DBC and overlook ∠ABC. Help them see that any two rays from a common endpoint form an angle.

**Exercise 17** Encourage students to be systematic in naming the 10 different line segments. That is, start with A and name each possible segment with A as an endpoint, and so on. Be sure students understand that $\overline{AB}$ is the same as $\overline{BA}$.

**Think Math** Students should attempt to estimate the answer before measuring. Help students see that such judgments cannot always be made solely on the appearance of a figure.

## Ideas That Work

### Special Education

Have students complete the puzzle below.

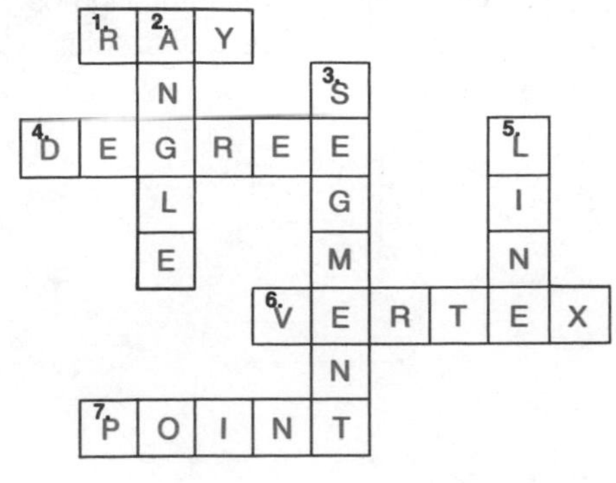


**Across**

1. A part of a line, having only one end point.
4. A unit of angle measure.
6. The point that the two rays of an angle have in common.
7. A single, exact location, often represented by a dot.

**Down**

2. Two rays from a single point.
3. A straight path from one point to another.
5. A straight path that is endless in both directions.

**Practice Supplement**, page 96

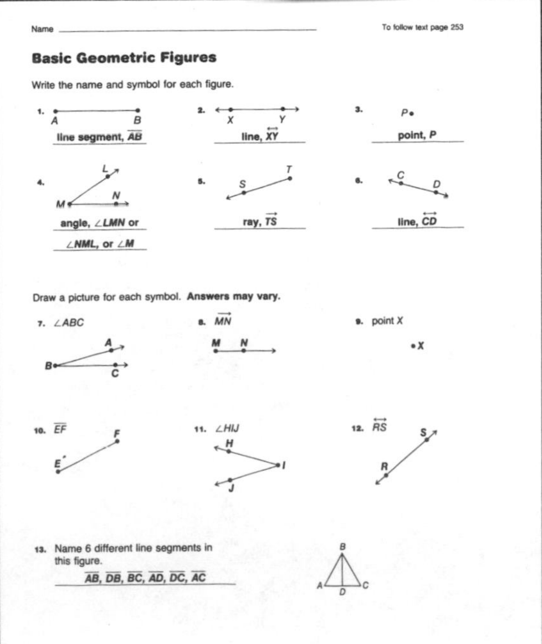
Name ______ To follow text page 253

**Basic Geometric Figures**

Write the name and symbol for each figure.

1. line segment, $\overline{AB}$ 2. line, $\overleftrightarrow{XY}$ 3. point, P

4. angle, ∠LMN or ∠NML, or ∠M 5. ray, $\overrightarrow{TS}$ 6. line, $\overleftrightarrow{CD}$

Draw a picture for each symbol. Answers may vary.

7. ∠ABC 8. $\overrightarrow{MN}$ 9. point X

10. $\overline{EF}$ 11. ∠HIJ 12. $\overrightarrow{RS}$

13. Name 6 different line segments in this figure. $\overline{AB}$, $\overline{DB}$, $\overline{BC}$, $\overline{AD}$, $\overline{DC}$, $\overline{AC}$

**Quick Review** Students skip count by threes to 30, by sixes to 60, by nines to 90, and by twelves to 120. Then they count from the end points backward.

**Lesson Focus** To measure and draw angles using a protractor

**Suggested Materials** Protractor, demonstration clock, string, tacks

## Ideas for Getting Started

Tack a string on the bulletin board as shown below to demonstrate 1° angle. Use 200 cm of string and separate the ends by 1.75 cm. Discuss with students that a circle can be divided into 360 angles of 1° each.

1° 100 cm I 1.75 cm

## Using Page 254

**Lesson Development** Have students read aloud the three-step procedure for measuring angles. Then demonstrate the procedure with a chalkboard protractor, emphasizing the three steps. Note that on some protractors the arrow is given along the bottom edge rather than as shown in the figure. Students should practice measuring angles positioned upside down, sideways, and so on.

Direct students to the clock faces shown on the page. Show more of these types of angles with a demonstration clock. "What kind of angle is shown when it is 4:00?" (obtuse angle) "What kind of angle is shown when it is 10:00?" (acute angle) "What kind of angle is shown when it is 9:00?" (right angle), and so on. Then reverse this procedure and have students give a time when the hands of the clock show a right angle; an acute angle; an obtuse angle.

**Exercises 1–5** These exercises provide realistic situations in which angles are used. Have students first estimate the number of degrees in these angles and then measure the angles to check. As they measure, be sure that students have mastered the procedure for measuring angles.

## Measuring Angles

A **protractor** is used for measuring angles. The unit of angle measure is the **degree** (°).

1°

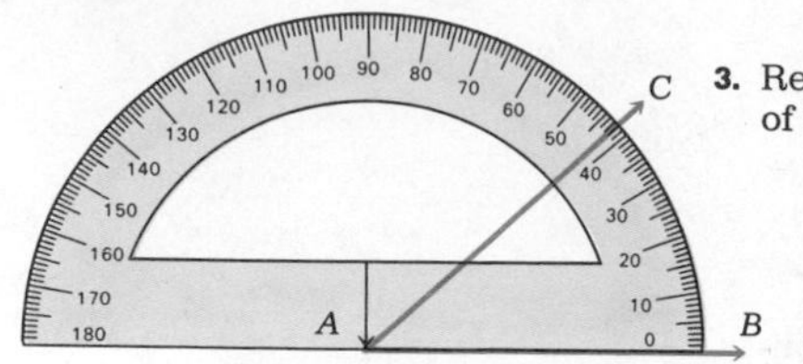


3. Read the measure of the angle.

2. Place the zero edge on one side of the angle.

1. Place the arrow on the vertex of the angle.

The measure of $\angle BAC$ is 42°.

Angles are named by their measures.

**Right angle**

**Acute angle**

**Obtuse angle**

First estimate the measure of each angle. Then measure to check your estimate. Is the angle **right**, **acute**, or **obtuse?** Estimates will vary.

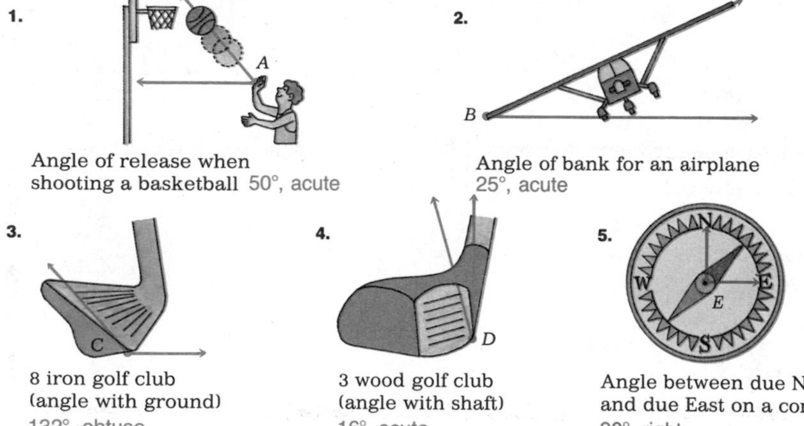

1. Angle of release when shooting a basketball 50°, acute

2. Angle of bank for an airplane 25°, acute

3. 8 iron golf club (angle with ground) 132°, obtuse

4. 3 wood golf club (angle with shaft) 16°, acute

5. Angle between due North and due East on a compass 90°, right



## Follow Up

### Reteaching

Use a demonstration geoboard or dot arrays (TRB p. 272) to show movement of a ray around a point. Start with two rubber bands in the same position. Then rotate one band. Describe each band as a ray and point out that an angle is formed as one ray is rotated. Explain that the distance between the bands may be measured with a unit called a "degree." Then show how angles are measured with a protractor, and discuss proper notation for angles.

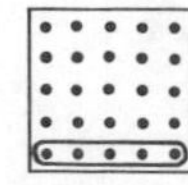
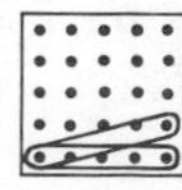
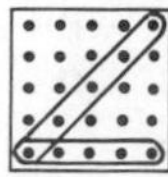

### Enrichment

Fasten two tagboard strips together with a paper fastener. Have students adjust the angles to a given number of degrees. The angles can be measured with a protractor.

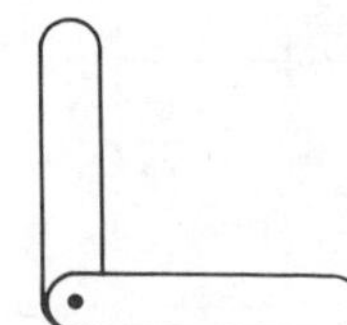

| Assignment Guide | | | |
|---|---|---|---|
| | Minimum | Average | Extended |
| page 254 | 1–5 | 1–5 | 1–5 |
| page 255 | 1–12, SK | 1–12, SK | 1–13, SK |

## Drawing Angles

Follow the steps below to draw $\angle ABC$ with measure 25°.

**Step 1**
Draw $\overrightarrow{AB}$.

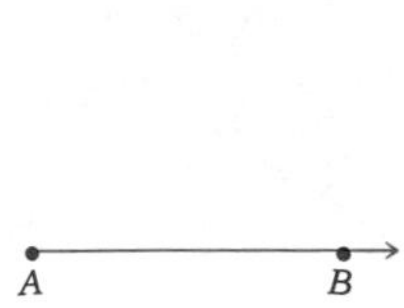


**Step 2**
Place the protractor arrow on $A$ and mark point $C$ at 25°.

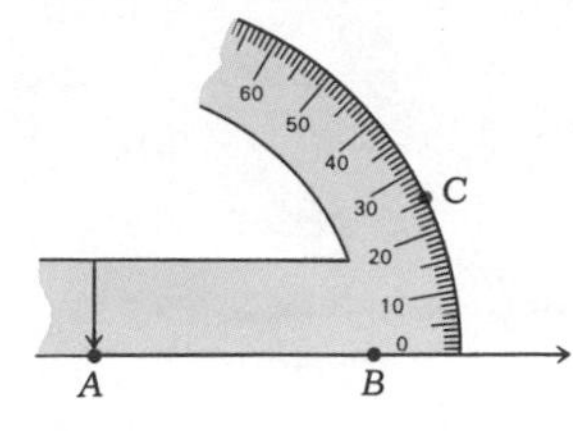


**Step 3**
Remove the protractor and draw $\overrightarrow{AC}$.

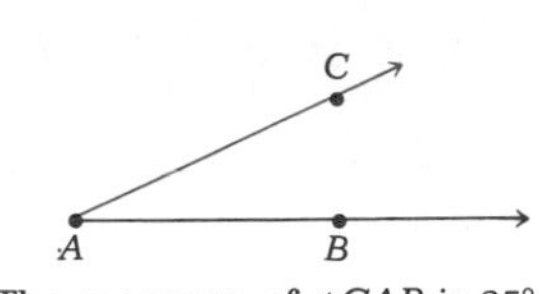


The measure of $\angle CAB$ is 25°.

Draw angles with the following measures. student construction

**1.** 35° **2.** 50° **3.** 95° **4.** 120° **5.** 145° **6.** 175°

Draw angles (without using a protractor) which you estimate to have the measures given below. Then measure each angle to check your estimate. student construction

**7.** 20° **8.** 45° **9.** 80° **10.** 110° **11.** 150° **12.** 170°

★ **13.** The measure of $\angle B$ is twice the measure of $\angle A$. The sum of the measures of $\angle A$ and $\angle B$ is 90°. Draw $\angle A$ and $\angle B$. student construction ($m\angle A = 30°$, $m\angle B = 60°$)

### Skillkeeper

Estimate the sum or difference by rounding to the nearest hundred.

**1.** 672 + 415 = 1,100
**2.** 358 + 240 = 600
**3.** 792 − 483 = 300
**4.** 919 − 174 = 700
**5.** 638 + 768 = 1,400

Estimate the sum or difference by rounding to the nearest dollar.

**6.** \$8.43 + 6.72 = \$15
**7.** \$15.88 − 2.17 = \$14
**8.** \$9.75 − 3.58 = \$6
**9.** \$7.29 + 8.80 = \$16
**10.** \$17.62 − 12.70 = \$5



## Using Page 255

**Lesson Development** Using a demonstration protractor, demonstrate on the chalkboard the procedure for drawing an angle. Point out that this is similar to the procedure for measuring angles.

**Exercises 1–6** These exercises provide practice in drawing angles given a certain measure. Be sure students have placed the protractor correctly and have completed the drawings correctly.

**Exercises 7–12** These estimation exercises help students get a feel for the size of the degree. Encourage students to base their estimates on 45°, 90°, 135°, and 180° angles.

**Exercise 13** If students have difficulty with this exercise, suggest that they use a guess and check strategy to find the measure of the two angles.

**Skillkeeper** These skills were originally taught in Chapters 2 and 3.

**Reteaching Supplement,** page 59

Name ________ To follow text page 254

**Measuring Angles**

3. Read the measure of the angle. 135°

To measure this angle: 1. Place the arrow on the vertex of the angle. 2. Place the zero edge on one side of the angle.

Write the measure of each angle.

1. 70° 2. 115°

First estimate the measure of each angle. Then measure to check your estimate.

3. Estimate: ____ Exact: 50°
4. Place the zero edge on this side. Estimate: ____ Exact: 118°

**Enrichment Supplement,** page 59

Name ________ To follow text page 254

**What's the Angle?**

1. Angle $AOB$ is one angle on the geoboard that has ray $OA$ as a side. Draw all the other angles that use ray $OA$ as one side. Each ray should start at $O$ and contain at least one other point of the geoboard. There are eleven angles other than $\angle AOB$.

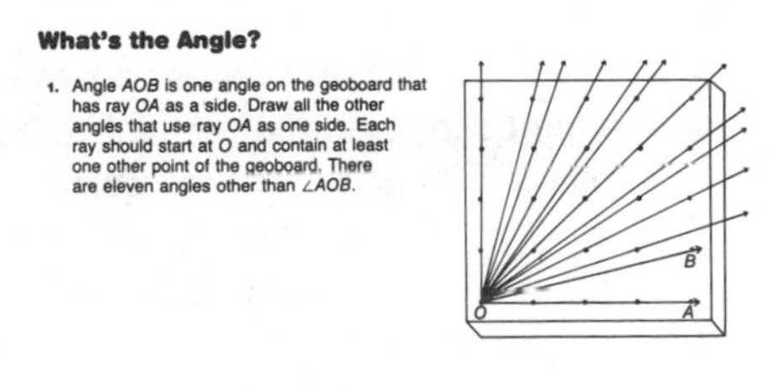

2. Estimate the measure of each angle in the figures below. Then use a protractor to check your estimate. The sum of your measurements should equal the given total. **Estimates will vary.**

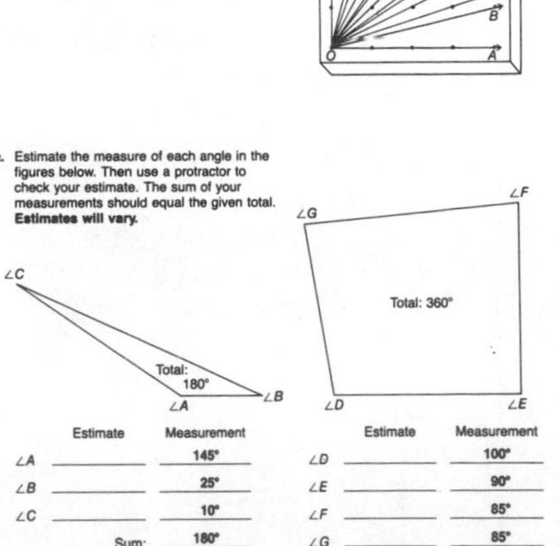

| | Estimate | Measurement |
|---|---|---|
| $\angle A$ | | 145° |
| $\angle B$ | | 25° |
| $\angle C$ | | 10° |
| Sum: | | 180° |

| | Estimate | Measurement |
|---|---|---|
| $\angle D$ | | 100° |
| $\angle E$ | | 90° |
| $\angle F$ | | 85° |
| $\angle G$ | | 85° |
| Sum: | | 360° |

**Practice Supplement,** page 97

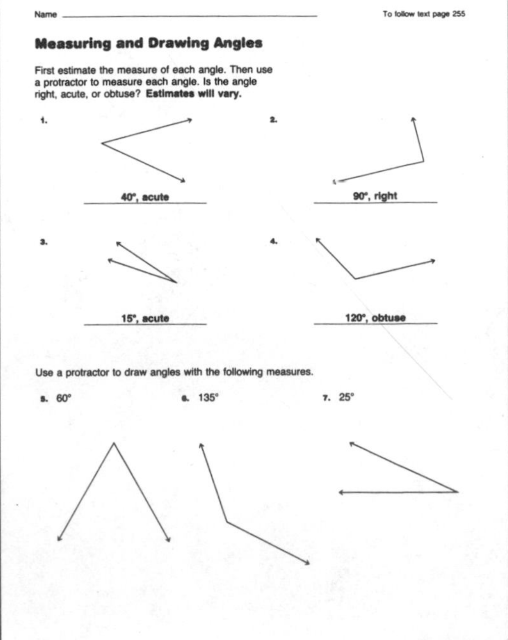
Name ________ To follow text page 255

**Measuring and Drawing Angles**

First estimate the measure of each angle. Then use a protractor to measure each angle. Is the angle right, acute, or obtuse? **Estimates will vary.**

1. 40°, acute
2. 90°, right
3. 15°, acute
4. 120°, obtuse

Use a protractor to draw angles with the following measures.

5. 60° 6. 135° 7. 25°

**Quick Review** Students give the numbers that will make each equation true.

| | |
|---|---|
| $60 + (45 + 45) = (45 + \boxed{60}) + 45$ | $(2 \times 45) \times 10 = (10 \times 2) \times \boxed{45}$ |
| $30 \times (3 \times 2) = 2 \times (3 \times \boxed{30})$ | $180 + (45 + 90) = (180 + 90) + \boxed{45}$ |
| $45 \times (2 \times 2) = (2 \times \boxed{45}) \times 2$ | $(270 + 30) + 60 = 30 + (270 + \boxed{60})$ |

**Lesson Focus** To draw perpendicular lines; to draw parallel lines

**Suggested Materials** Paper for folding

## Ideas for Getting Started

Have students fold a piece of paper once and crease it, then fold it again so that the edge of the first fold falls on itself. When they unfold the paper they will see a pair of perpendicular lines. Point out that these lines form 90° angles. Ask students to give examples of real-world situations that suggest perpendicular lines. (city intersection, a window frame, the lines in a building, and so on)

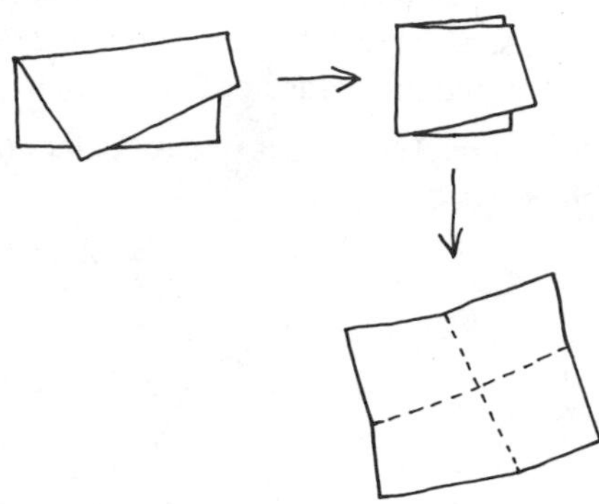

## Using Page 256

**Lesson Development** Direct students' attention to the top of the page, emphasizing the progression from seeing a situation in the physical world, thinking about a geometric idea, and writing a symbol to express it. Point out that when two lines are perpendicular, each of the four angles formed has a measure of 90°. Call attention to the symbol for perpendicular lines.

As you demonstrate the protractor method for drawing perpendicular lines, encourage students to use what they learned in the previous lesson to coach you on how to proceed. Point out that the second method does not require measurement. As you demonstrate this method, students can use compass and ruler to follow along.

**Exercises 1–3** Exercises 1 and 2 provide practice in the methods described above. In exercise 3, if students cannot readily give the measures of the angles, they can trace the figure, extend the sides, and measure each angle.

**Exercise 4** In this exercise students are asked to construct the midpoint of a line segment. Note that the construction is very similar to method 2 described above.

## Perpendicular Lines

| We see | We think | We write |
|---|---|---|
| An intersection of two streets | **Perpendicular lines** (lines that intersect at right angles) | $\ell \perp m$ (We say: "Line $\ell$ is perpendicular to line $m$.") |

Here are two ways to draw perpendicular lines.

**Method 1: Using a Protractor**

Draw a line $\ell$. Mark points $P$ and $Q$.

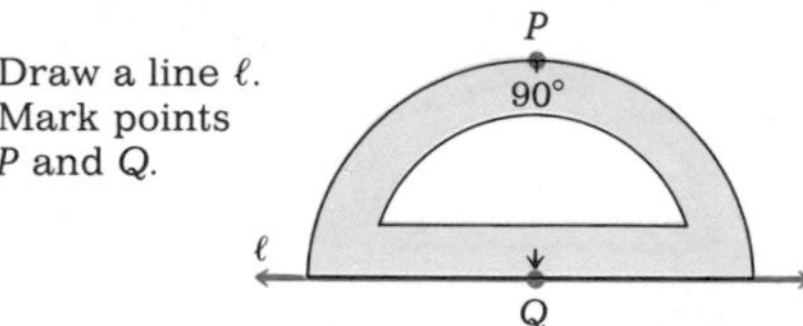


Draw line $m$ through $P$ and $Q$. $m \perp \ell$

**Method 2: Using a Compass and Ruler**

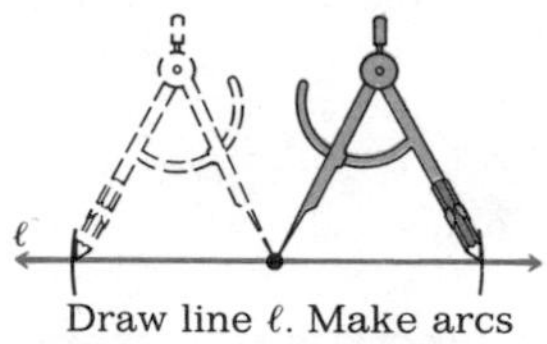


Draw line $\ell$. Make arcs with your compass.

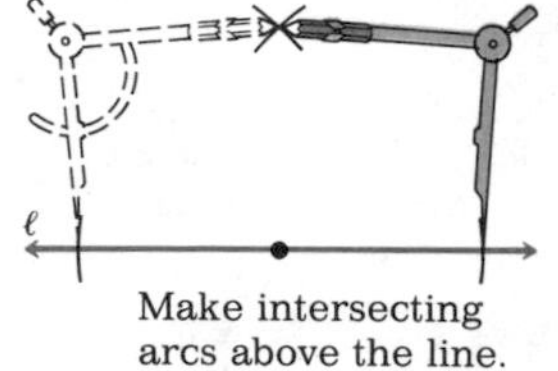


Make intersecting arcs above the line.

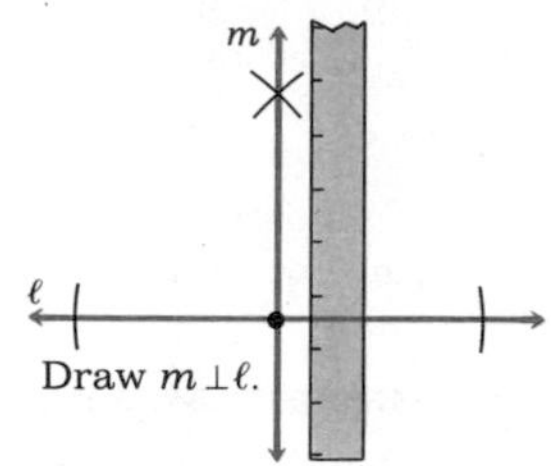


Draw $m \perp \ell$.

1. Use method 1 to draw a pair of perpendicular lines. student construction
2. Use method 2 to draw a pair of perpendicular lines. student construction
3. Line $r$ is perpendicular to line $s$. The angles formed are named by the numerals. Give the measure of $\angle 1$, $\angle 2$, $\angle 3$, and $\angle 4$. 90°

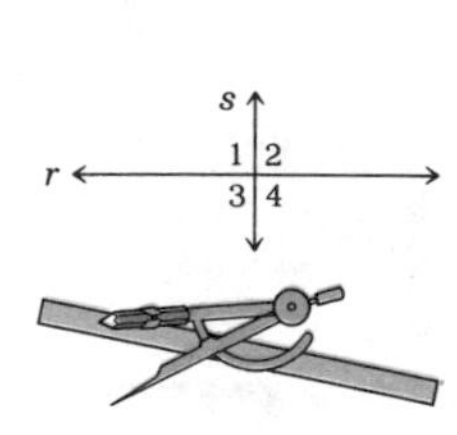


★ 4. Draw a segment $AB$. Without measuring, draw a line that goes through a point midway between $A$ and $B$. student construction



## Follow Up

### Reteaching

Have students find real-world examples of perpendicular and parallel lines. Help them distinguish between perpendicular lines and lines that simply intersect. Then discuss the defining characteristics of perpendicular and parallel lines and review the proper notation ($\ell \perp k$ or $\overleftrightarrow{AB} \perp \overleftrightarrow{CD}$) and ($m \parallel n$ or $\overleftrightarrow{WX} \parallel \overleftrightarrow{YZ}$).

### Enrichment

Have students draw two parallel lines, using both sides of the ruler as a guide. Then challenge students to use their compasses to draw a line perpendicular to the parallel lines.

| Assignment Guide | | | |
|---|---|---|---|
| | Minimum | Average | Extended |
| page 256 | 1–3 | 1–3 | 1–4 |
| page 257 | 1–3 | 1–4 | 1–4 |

## Parallel Lines

| We see | We think | We write |
|---|---|---|
|  Railroad tracks | **Parallel lines** (lines that do not intersect) | $\ell \parallel m$ (We say: "Line $\ell$ is parallel to line $m$.") |

Here are two ways to draw parallel lines.

**Method 1: Using a Ruler**

Draw a line on each side of your ruler.

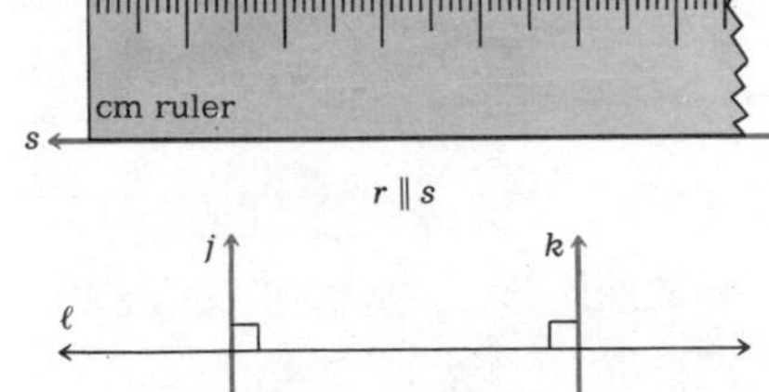


$r \parallel s$

**Method 2: Using Perpendicular Lines**

Draw line $\ell$. Then use a protractor or compass and ruler to draw 2 other lines, each perpendicular to $\ell$.

j k ℓ
perpendicular to line $\ell$
$j \parallel k$

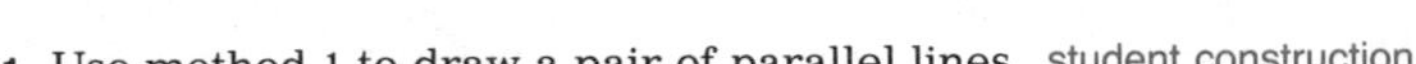

1. Use method 1 to draw a pair of parallel lines. student construction
2. Use method 2 to draw a pair of parallel lines with a protractor. student construction
3. Use method 2 to draw a pair of parallel lines with a compass and ruler. student construction
4. In this figure, $k \parallel \ell$. The angles formed are named by the numerals. Which angles do you think have the same measure?
   $\angle 1 \cong \angle 4 \cong \angle 5 \cong \angle 8$, $\angle 2 \cong \angle 3 \cong \angle 6 \cong \angle 7$

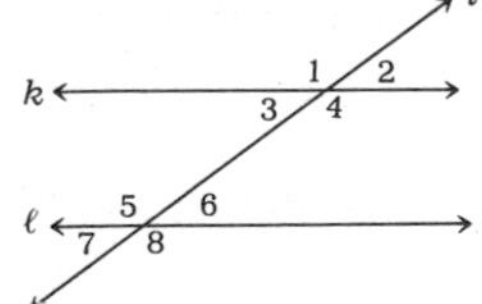




## Using Page 257

**Lesson Development** Discuss with students the information at the top of the page, again emphasizing that we see a situation in the real world, think about a geometric idea, and write a symbol to describe the idea. Ask students to identify other situations that suggest parallel lines. Possibilities from the classroom include the top and bottom edges of the chalkboard and lines along the sides of a door.

Next ask students to suggest ways of drawing parallel lines. After presenting method 1, ask them, "What is the disadvantage of this method?" (You can only draw parallel lines that are the width of your ruler apart.) Then discuss method 2. Note that this method uses the procedure for drawing perpendicular lines that students learned on the preceding page. In fact, the method is based on the idea that two lines perpendicular to the same line are parallel.

**Exercises 1–4** Note that exercise 3 requires students to complete the construction of parallel lines using a compass and a ruler. Some students may need help tying these ideas together. In exercise 4, if students do not intuitively identify angles such as $\angle 3$ and $\angle 2$ as having the same measure, encourage them to trace the figure, extend the lines, and measure the angles.

**Reteaching Supplement,** page 60

Name ______ To follow text page 257

**Perpendicular Lines and Parallel Lines**

**Perpendicular lines** meet to form 90° angles. Lines *l* and *m* are perpendicular. To draw perpendicular lines, use a protractor to draw a 90° angle.

**We write:** $l \perp m$

**Parallel lines** are lines that do not intersect. Lines *a* and *b* are parallel. To draw parallel lines, use a protractor to draw two lines perpendicular to the same line.

**We write:** $a \parallel b$

1. Use a protractor to draw a line perpendicular to line *t*.
2. Use a protractor to draw a line parallel to line v.

Write True (T) or False (F) for each statement. Then measure with a protractor to check your answers.

3. $q \parallel p$ F
4. $n \perp p$ T
5. $p \perp m$ T
6. $m \parallel n$ T

**Enrichment Supplement,** page 60

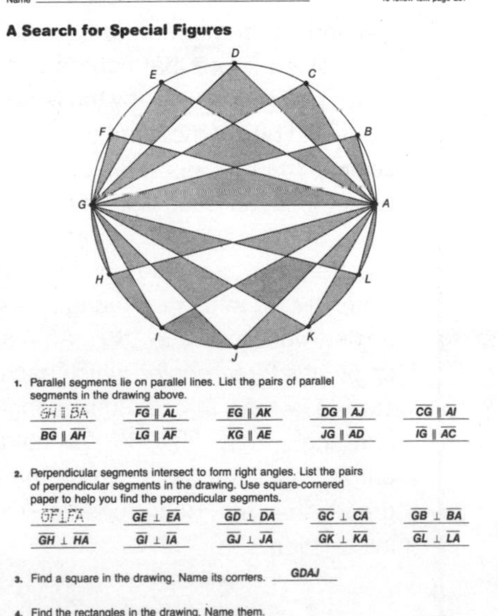
Name ______ To follow text page 257

**A Search for Special Figures**

1. Parallel segments lie on parallel lines. List the pairs of parallel segments in the drawing above.
   $\overline{GH} \parallel \overline{BA}$, $\overline{FG} \parallel \overline{AL}$, $\overline{EG} \parallel \overline{AK}$, $\overline{DG} \parallel \overline{AJ}$, $\overline{CG} \parallel \overline{AI}$, $\overline{BG} \parallel \overline{AH}$, $\overline{LG} \parallel \overline{AF}$, $\overline{KG} \parallel \overline{AE}$, $\overline{JG} \parallel \overline{AD}$, $\overline{IG} \parallel \overline{AC}$
2. Perpendicular segments intersect to form right angles. List the pairs of perpendicular segments in the drawing. Use square-cornered paper to help you find the perpendicular segments.
   $\overline{GF} \perp \overline{FA}$, $\overline{GE} \perp \overline{EA}$, $\overline{GD} \perp \overline{DA}$, $\overline{GC} \perp \overline{CA}$, $\overline{GB} \perp \overline{BA}$, $\overline{GH} \perp \overline{HA}$, $\overline{GI} \perp \overline{IA}$, $\overline{GJ} \perp \overline{JA}$, $\overline{GK} \perp \overline{KA}$, $\overline{GL} \perp \overline{LA}$
3. Find a square in the drawing. Name its corners. GDAJ
4. Find the rectangles in the drawing. Name them.
   GBAH GFAL GKAE GDAJ GCAI

**Practice Supplement,** page 98

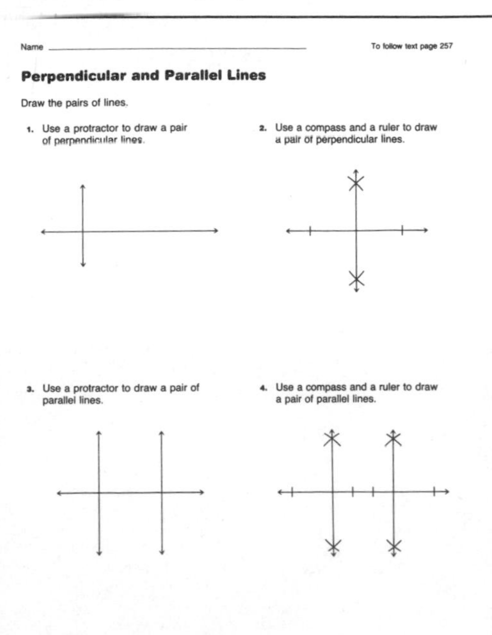
Name ______ To follow text page 257

**Perpendicular and Parallel Lines**

Draw the pairs of lines.

1. Use a protractor to draw a pair of perpendicular lines.
2. Use a compass and a ruler to draw a pair of perpendicular lines.
3. Use a protractor to draw a pair of parallel lines.
4. Use a compass and a ruler to draw a pair of parallel lines.

**Quick Review** Students write >, <, or = to make each statement true.

45 + 45 (=) 80 + 10   180 ÷ 90 (=) 90 ÷ 45   180 × 2 (=) 90 × 4
30 + 45 (>) 15 + 55   60 ÷ 30 (<) 45 ÷ 15   180 + 60 (>) 120 + 45
90 + 270 (<) 330 + 45   15 × 3 (=) 9 × 5

**Lesson Focus** To classify a triangle according to the lengths of its sides or the measures of its angles

**Suggested Materials** Colored paper

## Ideas for Getting Started

Pin three different shaped scalene triangles, three different shaped isosceles triangles, and three different sized equilateral triangles on the bulletin board. Be sure some of these triangles are acute, right, and obtuse. Help students to identify three different types of triangles among the shapes. Give hints as you work to enable students to classify the triangles according to the lengths of their sides: (a) all three sides have different lengths (scalene), (b) exactly two sides have the same length (isosceles), and (c) all three sides have the same length (equilateral). Then help students to group the triangles according to the size of the angles.

## Using Page 258

**Lesson Development** Draw a triangle on the chalkboard and define what is meant by the *sides* and *angles* of the triangle. Then focus first on the characteristics of scalene, isosceles, and equilateral triangles. Second, discuss the characteristics of acute, right, and obtuse triangles. Be sure students understand these characteristics. If you used the Getting Started activity, remind students how these characteristics were used to put the triangles in groups. Emphasize that in the first classification triangles were separated according to the length of their sides; in the second classification the triangles were separated according to the measure of their angles.

Direct students' attention to the display at the bottom of the page. Discuss the fact that whenever the measures of the angles are added, their sum is 180°. Then give triangles such as those below and work with students to find the number of degrees in the missing angle. Students may generalize that "You add the two angles you know and subtract this from 180 to find the missing angle."

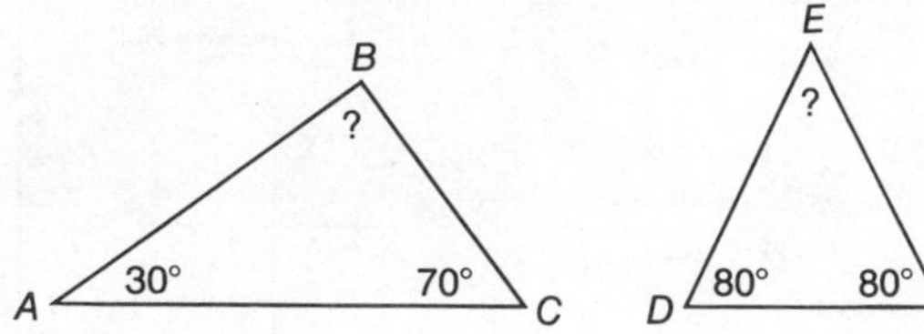


## Triangles

Here are some important kinds of triangles.

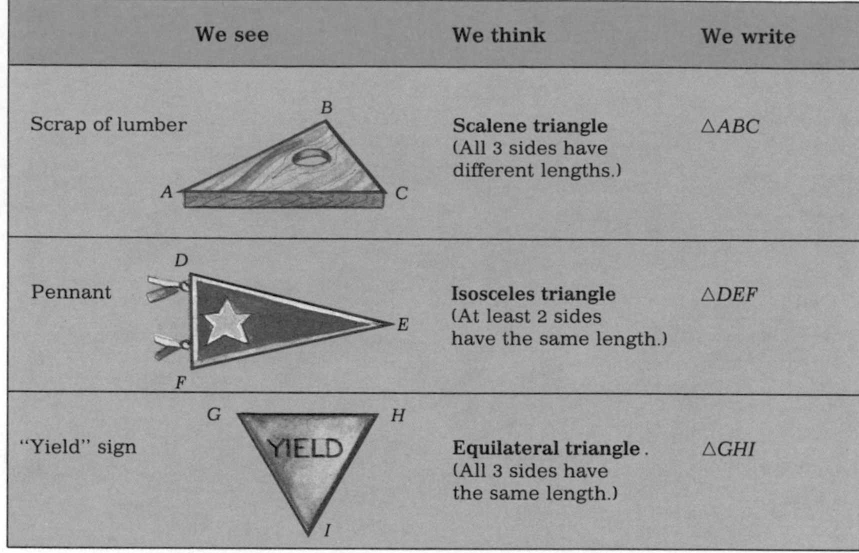

| | We see | We think | We write |
|---|---|---|---|
| Scrap of lumber | | **Scalene triangle** (All 3 sides have different lengths.) | $\triangle ABC$ |
| Pennant | | **Isosceles triangle** (At least 2 sides have the same length.) | $\triangle DEF$ |
| "Yield" sign | | **Equilateral triangle**. (All 3 sides have the same length.) | $\triangle GHI$ |



Triangles are also named according to the size of their angles.

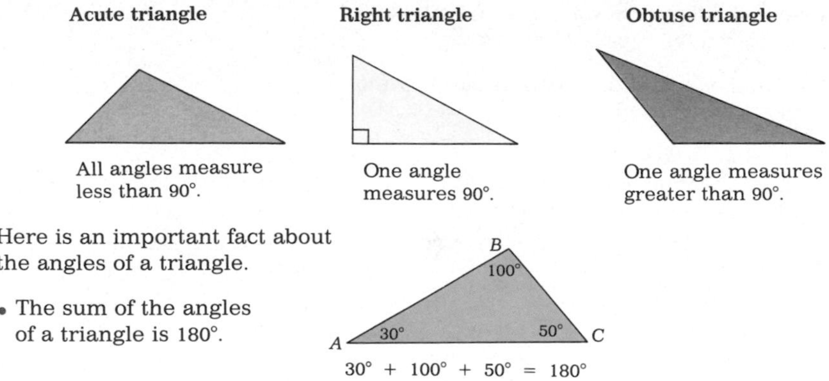


Here is an important fact about the angles of a triangle.

- The sum of the angles of a triangle is 180°.



## Follow Up

### Reteaching

Remind students that a triangle is a three-sided figure that can be described in two different ways—by the length of its sides and by the measure of its angles. A scalene triangle has sides of three different lengths; an isosceles triangle has two sides of the same length; an equilateral triangle has three sides of equal length. Remind students that a triangle has three angles whose sum is 180°. An acute triangle has three angles which each measure less than 90°; a right triangle has one angle measuring 90°; an obtuse triangle has one angle which measures greater than 90°. Help students show this information in a chart.

### Enrichment

Have students use their rulers to draw several triangles of different shapes. Then challenge them to measure all of the angles of each triangle to demonstrate that the sum of the angles of each triangle is 180°.

| Assignment Guide | | | |
|---|---|---|---|
| | Minimum | Average | Extended |
| page 259 | 1–11 | 1–11 | 1–13, TM |

Use letters to name each triangle. Tell whether the triangle is **scalene, isosceles,** or **equilateral.**

**1.**

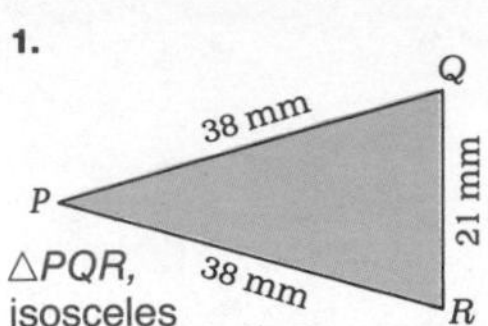


△PQR, isosceles

**2.**

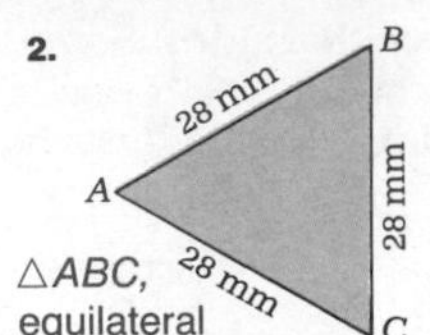


△ABC, equilateral

**3.**

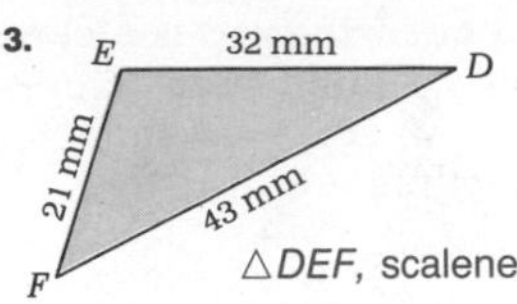


△DEF, scalene

Tell whether the triangle is **acute, right,** or **obtuse.**

**4.** obtuse

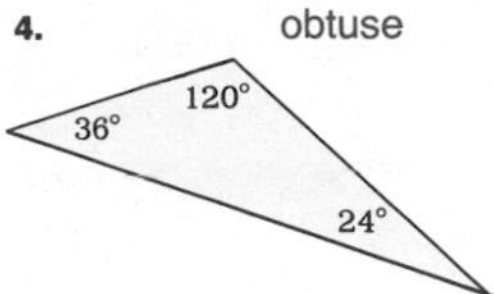


**5.** acute

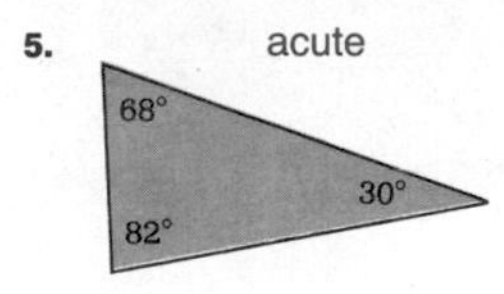


**6.** right

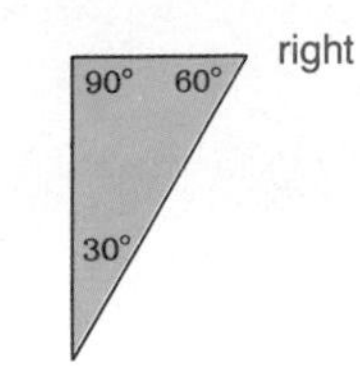


Give all possible names for each triangle (for example, **acute** and **scalene**).

**7.**

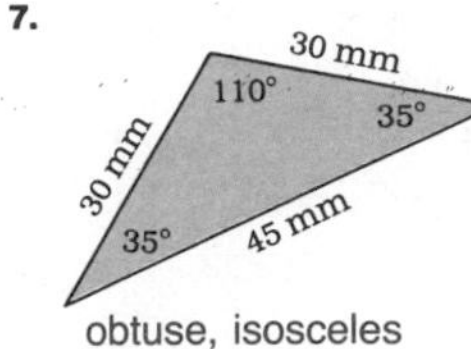


obtuse, isosceles

**8.**

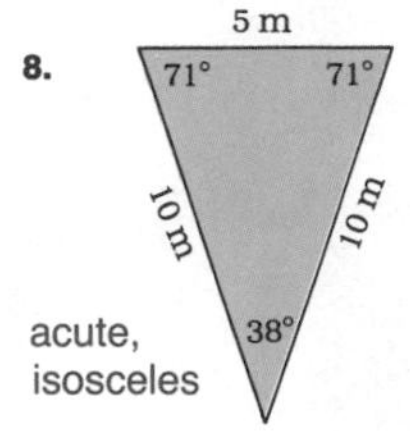


acute, isosceles

**9.** acute, equilateral

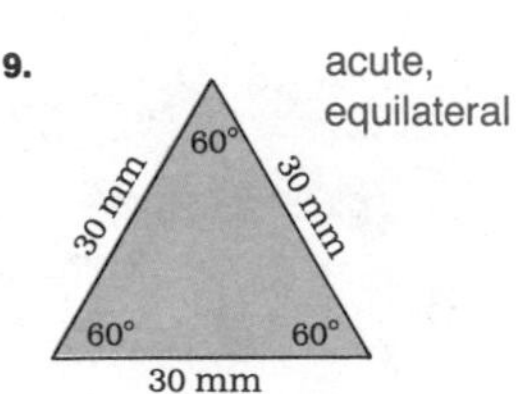


In each triangle find the angle measures that are not given.

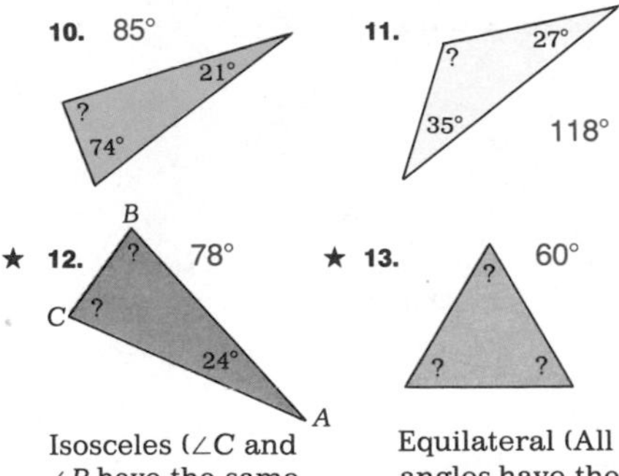


**10.** 85° **11.** 118° **★ 12.** 78° **★ 13.** 60°

12. Isosceles (∠C and ∠B have the same measure.)

13. Equilateral (All angles have the same measure.)

**Think Math**

**Triangle Puzzle**

Count the number of different triangles. There are 27 in all! How many can you find?

See teaching notes.

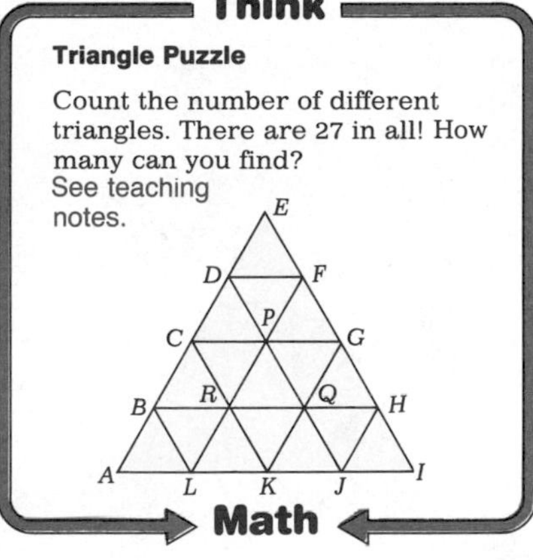




## Using Page 259

**Exercises 1–3** Note that the triangle in exercise 2 is isosceles because it has at least two sides that have the same length. However, it is also equilateral since all three sides have the same length. Students should understand that all equilateral triangles are also isosceles triangles, but not vice versa.

**Exercises 4–6** Encourage students to review the definitions of the three types of triangles before completing these exercises.

**Exercises 7–9** Note that in exercise 10 the triangle is isosceles, equilateral, and acute. Point out by calling students' attention to exercises 7 and 9 that an isosceles triangle can either be acute or obtuse.

**Exercises 10–11** In these exercises students subtract the sum of the two given angles from 180°.

**Exercises 12–13** For exercise 12 a student can reason that 180° − 24° is 156°; since the sum of equal angles is 156°, each angle must be 156° ÷ 2, or 78°. In exercise 13 students should recognize that because the triangle is equilateral, they can divide 180° by 3 to find the measure of each angle.

**Think Math** If students have difficulty counting the different triangles in the picture, they can trace a triangle of each different size, and then move them on the figure to count the triangles of a given size. Note that there are 16 triangles like △*DEF*, 7 like △*CEG*, 3 like △*BEH*, and 1 like △*AEI*.

## Ideas That Work

### Special Education

Give each student tongue depressors, straws, or three strips of tagboard that they can move around to form triangles. Then call out the name of the kind of triangle that you want them to create. For example:

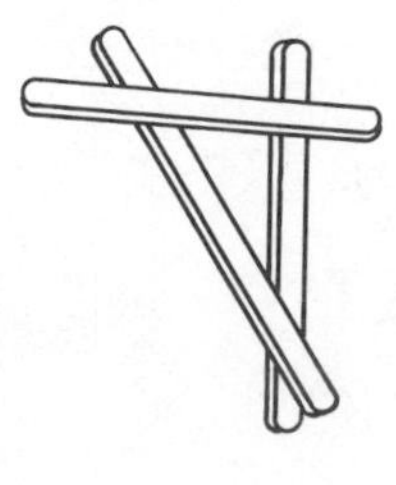

Acute

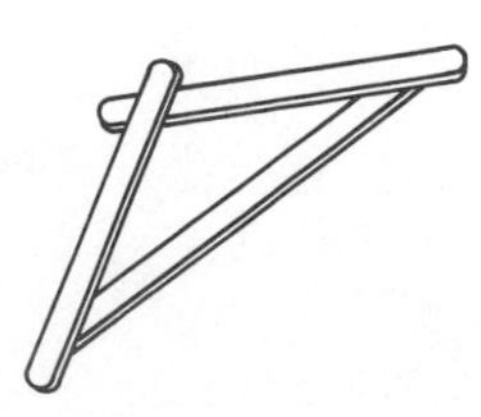

Obtuse

**Practice Supplement,** page 99

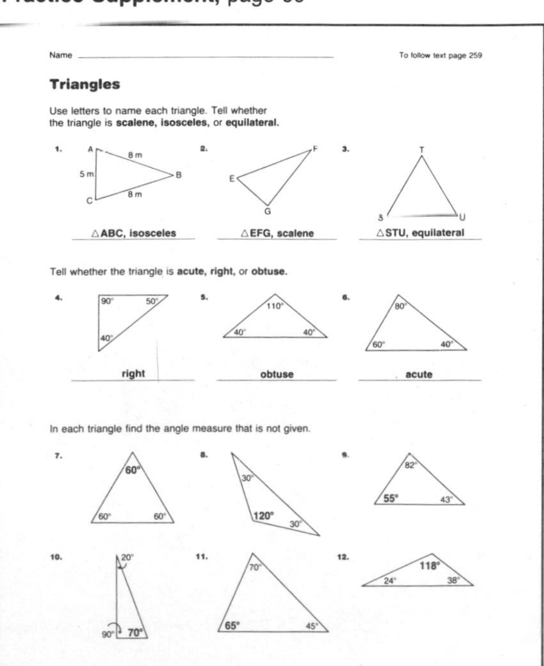

Name ______ To follow text page 259

**Triangles**

Use letters to name each triangle. Tell whether the triangle is **scalene, isosceles,** or **equilateral.**

1. △ABC, isosceles 2. △EFG, scalene 3. △STU, equilateral

Tell whether the triangle is **acute, right,** or **obtuse.**

4. right 5. obtuse 6. acute

In each triangle find the angle measure that is not given.

7. 60° 8. 120° 9. 55° 10. 70° 11. 65° 12. 118°

**Quick Review** Students draw clock faces with hands indicating the times below.

6:00 2:30 12:00 9:10 4:30 3:45 10:30 7:30

**Lesson Focus** To classify a quadrilateral as a square, rectangle, parallelogram, rhombus, or trapezoid

**Suggested Materials** Colored paper

## Ideas for Getting Started

Have each student cut out four right triangles with legs 4 cm and 8 cm. Draw pictures of a square, a rectangle, a parallelogram, and a trapezoid on the chalkboard. Then ask students to put the four triangles together to form each of the shapes below. Give help as necessary.

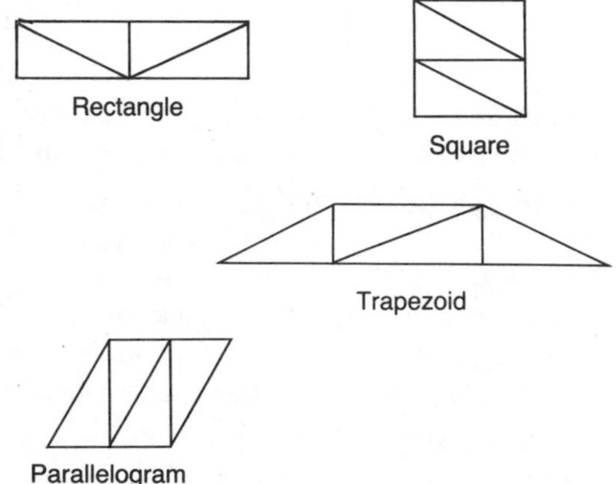


## Using Page 260

**Lesson Development** Draw a quadrilateral on the chalkboard, label the vertices, and have students name the sides and angles. Point out that any four-sided figure is a quadrilateral.

Then direct students' attention to the descriptions on the page. Draw a picture of a parallelogram, a square, a trapezoid, a rhombus, and a rectangle on the chalkboard. Ask students to name each of the figures. "Which two figures have four right angles?" (square and rectangle) "Which two figures have all sides the same length?" (square and rhombus) "Which two figures have two pairs of opposite sides parallel, but not all sides the same length?" (rectangle and parallelogram) "Which figure has only one pair of parallel sides?" (trapezoid)

## Quadrilaterals

A **quadrilateral** is a closed figure with 4 sides. Some information about different types of quadrilaterals is given below. For each picture give the letter of the description that fits it best.

| Pictures | Descriptions |
|---|---|
| **1.** C   | **A.** A **parallelogram** has two pairs of parallel sides. It also has two pairs of sides that have the same length. |
| **2.** A 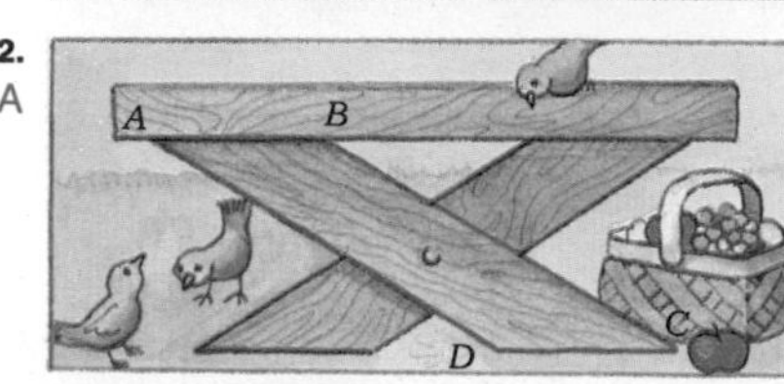  | **B.** A **square** has all sides the same length. All angles are right angles. |
| **3.** E   | **C.** A **trapezoid** has exactly one pair of parallel sides. |
| **4.** B 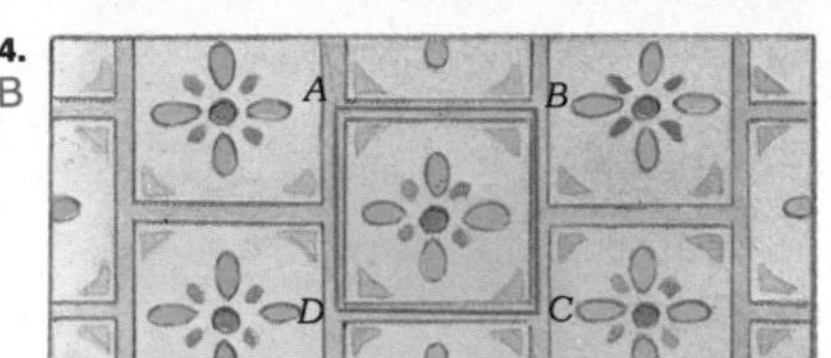  | **D.** A **rhombus** has all sides the same length and two pairs of parallel sides. |
| **5.** D   | **E.** A **rectangle** has two pairs of sides the same length and four right angles. |



## Follow Up

### Reteaching

Have students use dot arrays (TRB p. 272) to draw figures with four sides. Then discuss and have students draw the different kinds of quadrilaterals: squares, rectangles, parallelograms, rhombuses, and trapezoids. Show how one quadrilateral can be transformed into another by moving the sides.

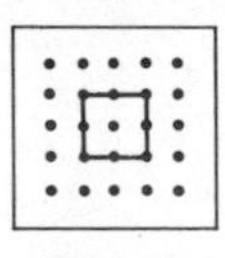
Square

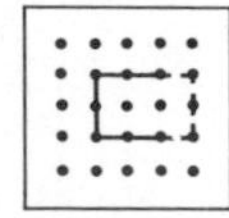
Rectangle

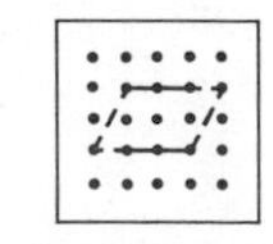
Parallelogram

Trapezoid

### Enrichment

Have students use all seven tangram pieces (TRB p. 280) to form a: **(1)** square, **(2)** rectangle, **(3)** parallelogram, and **(4)** trapezoid. For example:

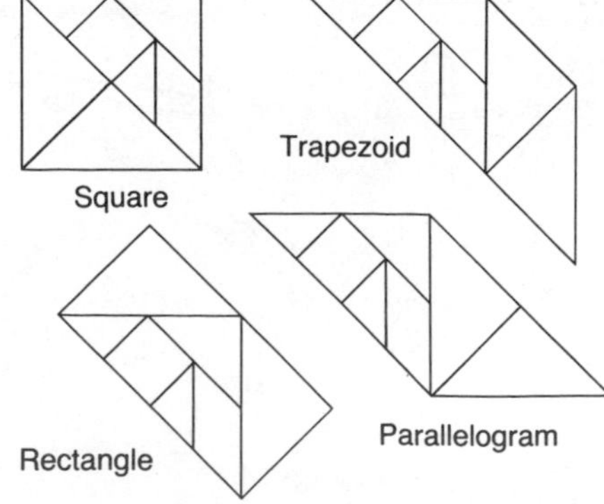

| Assignment Guide | | | |
|---|---|---|---|
| | Minimum | Average | Extended |
| page 261 | 1–9 | 1–9, TM | 1–9, TM |

Solve these problems about quadrilaterals.

1. Any figure with two pairs of parallel sides can be called a parallelogram. Which of these figures can also be called a parallelogram? A, C, D

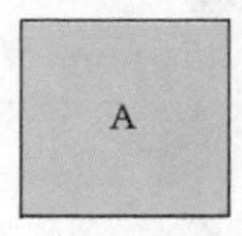

Square

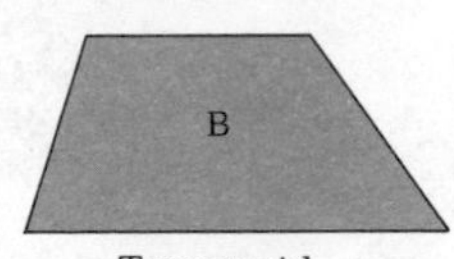

Trapezoid

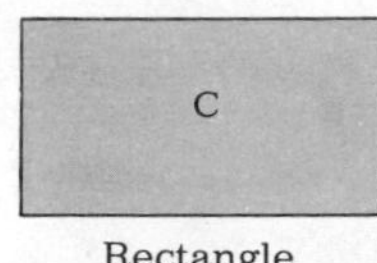

Rectangle

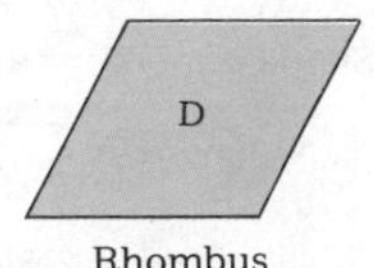

Rhombus

2. Any figure with four right angles can be called a rectangle. Which figure above (other than C) can also be called a rectangle? A

Find the sum of the angles of each quadrilateral below. Then complete the statement in exercise 7.

3. 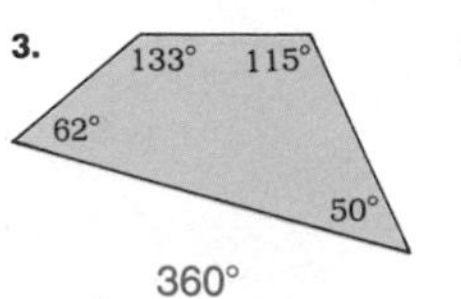

360°

4. 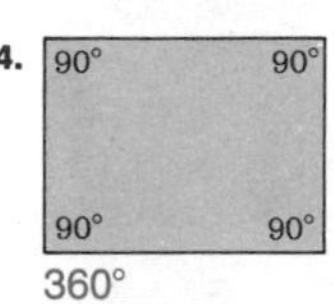

360°

5. 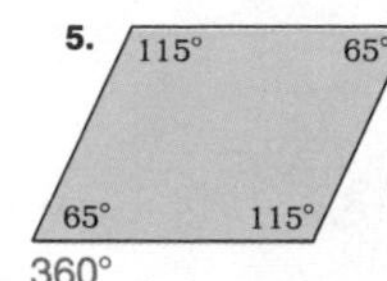

360°

6. 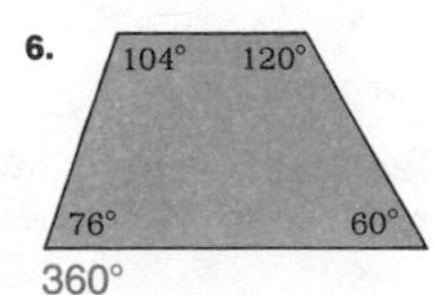

360°

7. The sum of the angles of any quadrilateral is <u>?</u>°. 360

8. Find the measure of $\angle A$ without using a protractor. 128°

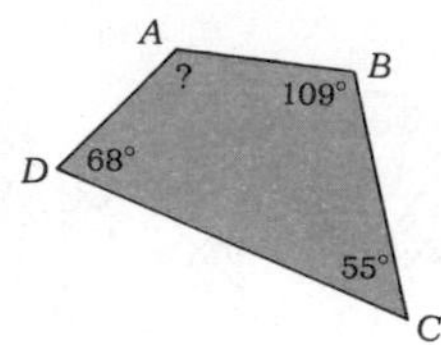


9. Which quadrilateral has four sides of equal length but is not a square? rhombus

**Think Math**

**Square Puzzle**

Try a little magic! Trace and cut out the square, cut along the dotted lines, and "change it into" the triangle.

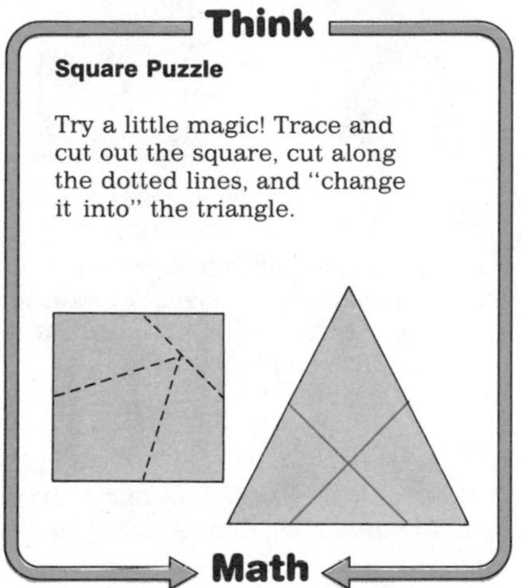



## Using Page 261

**Exercises 1–2** These exercises are designed to show the inclusion relationships with the quadrilaterals. For example, squares, rectangles, and rhombuses belong to the set of parallelograms. Exercise 2 emphasizes the idea that every square can also be called a rectangle.

**Exercises 3–7** These exercises are designed to help the students discover that the sum of the angles of a quadrilateral is 360°.

**Exercise 8** In this exercise students can subtract the sum of the angle measures given from 360 to find the missing number of degrees.

**Think Math** Remind students that patience and experimentation are often essential in solving puzzles like these. Encourage them to look for clues. If necessary, give hints like the following: "Which of the pieces in the square puzzle looks like it would fit in the top of the triangle?" (the middle piece)

**Reteaching Supplement,** page 61

Name ______ To follow text page 261

**Quadrilaterals**

All of the figures on this page are **quadrilaterals** because each is a closed figure with 4 sides.

Draw a line from each figure to the best description.

1. square
2. rectangle
3. rhombus
4. trapezoid
5. parallelogram

- all sides the same length
- 2 pairs of parallel sides

- 2 pairs of parallel sides
- 2 pairs of sides with the same length

- 2 pairs of sides with the same length
- 4 right angles

- exactly 1 pair of parallel sides

- all sides the same length
- 4 right angles

Write the name of each quadrilateral.

6. square
7. parallelogram
8. rectangle
9. trapezoid
10. rhombus
11. parallelogram

**Enrichment Supplement,** page 61

Name ______ To follow text page 261

**Quadrilaterals**

Figure $ABCD$ is a quadrilateral. Point $M$ is the midpoint of $\overline{AD}$. Mark the midpoints of $\overline{BC}$, $\overline{DC}$, and $\overline{AB}$. Label the midpoints $N$, $P$, and $R$.

1. Connect the midpoints to form another quadrilateral. The new quadrilateral should be a parallelogram. Its opposite sides are the same length. Which angles in the new quadrilateral have the same measures?
**$\angle MRP$ and $\angle MNP$, $\angle RMN$ and $\angle RPN$**

2. In the space below, draw a quadrilateral of your own. Construct the midpoints of the four sides. Connect them as you did above. What kind of figure do you have?
**a parallelogram**

**Practice Supplement,** page 100

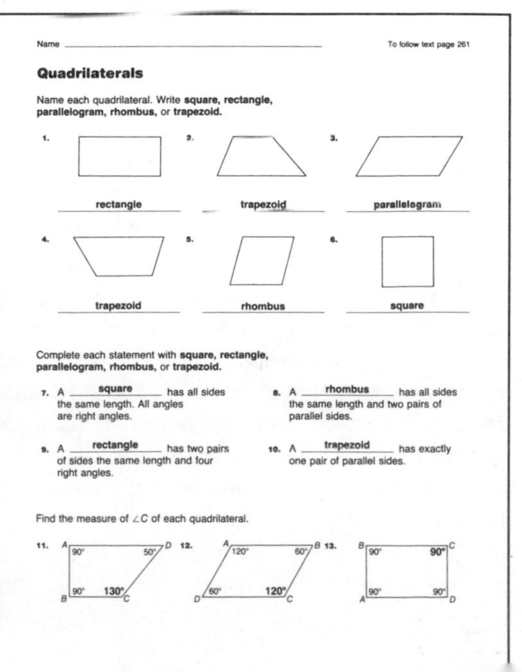
Name ______ To follow text page 261

**Quadrilaterals**

Name each quadrilateral. Write **square, rectangle, parallelogram, rhombus,** or **trapezoid.**

1. rectangle
2. trapezoid
3. parallelogram
4. trapezoid
5. rhombus
6. square

Complete each statement with **square, rectangle, parallelogram, rhombus,** or **trapezoid.**

7. A **square** has all sides the same length. All angles are right angles.
8. A **rhombus** has all sides the same length and two pairs of parallel sides.
9. A **rectangle** has two pairs of sides the same length and four right angles.
10. A **trapezoid** has exactly one pair of parallel sides.

Find the measure of $\angle C$ of each quadrilateral.

11. A 90°, D 50°, B 90°, C 130°
12. A 120°, B 60°, D 60°, C 120°
13. B 90°, C 90°, A 90°, D 90°

**Quick Review** Students tell how many pairs of parallel lines are in each figure.

| rectangle | circle | square | trapezoid | rhombus |
|---|---|---|---|---|
| 2 | 0 | 2 | 1 | 2 |

**Lesson Focus** To identify polygons including regular polygons; to draw a circle, given the radius or the diameter

**Suggested Materials** Geoboard or dot arrays (TRB p. 272)

## Ideas for Getting Started

Show an example of a polygon drawn on a dot array. Then ask students to draw or show polygons with 3, 4, 5, and 6 sides.

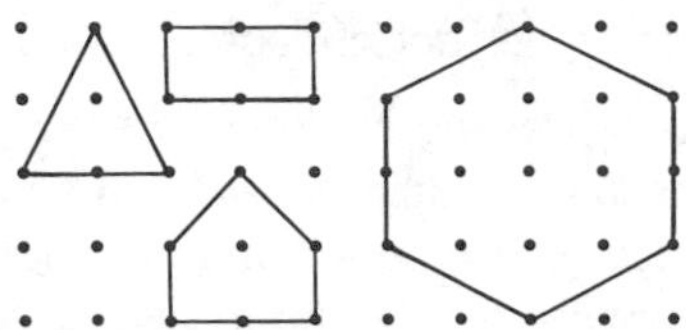

"Can you draw a polygon with more than 6 sides? What is the greatest number of sides you can show? Can you make a polygon that has all sides the same length?" (The square is the only one.)

## Using Page 262

**Lesson Development** If you used the Getting Started activity, relate the definition of a polygon given at the top of the page to that activity. Then direct students' attention to the figures at the top of the page. Point out that *penta* means "five," *hexa* means "six," *octa* means "eight," and *deca* means "ten." Ask students to identify other real-world objects that have the shape of these polygons. Emphasize that regular polygons have all sides the same length *and* all angles the same measure. Use three figures like the ones below to illustrate this idea.

All sides the same length, all angles the same measure.
**Regular polygon**

All sides the same, but not all angles the same.
**Not regular**

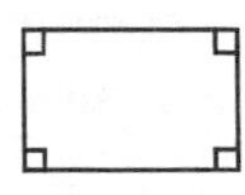

All angles the same, but not all sides the same.
**Not regular**

**Exercises 1–11** Note that the figure in exercise 6 is not a regular polygon because not all sides are the same length. The figure in exercise 8 is not a regular polygon because not all angles are the same measure. Exercises 9–10 are designed to introduce another notation for naming polygons. Encourage students to draw and then count the diagonals in exercise 11.

## Other Polygons

A **polygon** is a simple closed figure formed by line segments. Triangles and quadrilaterals are polygons. The pictures below suggest some other polygons.

Shape on soccer ball

Pentagon–5 sides

Commonly used nut

Hexagon–6 sides

Rug design

Octagon–8 sides

Costume jewelry

Decagon–10 sides

Name each of these polygons.

1. 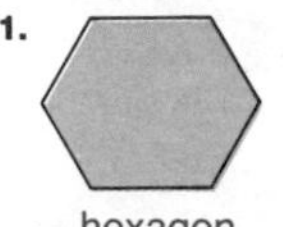 hexagon
2.  pentagon
3. 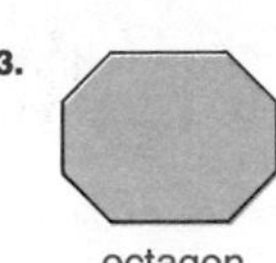 octagon
4. 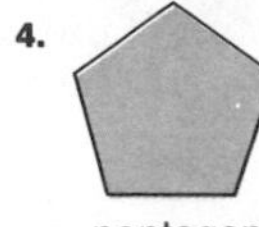 pentagon

**Regular polygons** have all sides the same length and all angles the same measure.

Are the figures below regular polygons? If not, why not?

5. 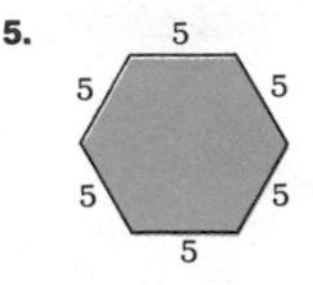

yes

6. 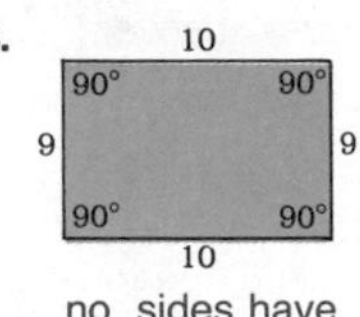

no, sides have different lengths

7. 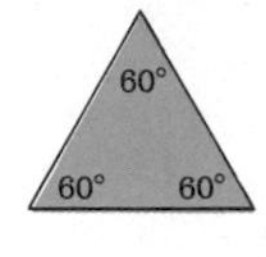

yes

8. 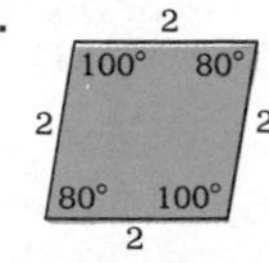

no, angles have different measures

Polygons are sometimes named by the number of sides they have. For example, a pentagon may be called a **5-gon.** Use this idea to name these two figures.

9. 12-gon
10. 10-gon

11. A **diagonal** is a segment (not a side) connecting two vertices of a polygon. How many diagonals does a hexagon have? 9

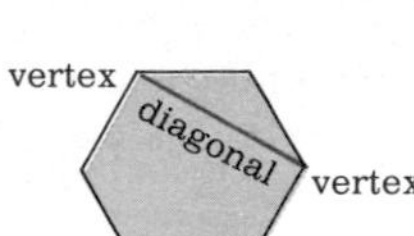


262

## Follow Up

### Reteaching

Show various polygons on a geoboard. Then illustrate regular polygons and explain what is meant by the term "regular polygon." Familiarize students with the names of polygons: square, pentagon, hexagon, and so on. Have students look for examples of various polygons in magazines, especially in the logos of companies in advertisements.

### Enrichment

Have students use polygons to form tiling patterns. The patterns might be used for placemats or for other decorative purposes. For example:

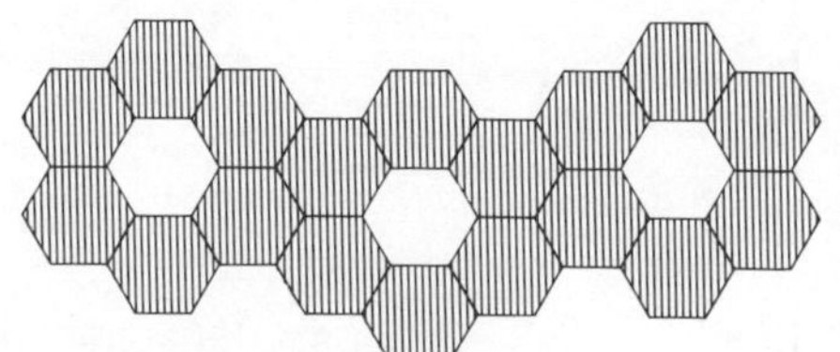

| Assignment Guide | | | |
|---|---|---|---|
| | Minimum | Average | Extended |
| page 262 | 1–10 | 1–10 | 1–11 |
| page 263 | 1–10 | 1–10 | 1–11 |

## Circles

A Ferris wheel suggests a **circle.** All the points on a circle are the same distance from the **center** (*O*).

Here are some more ideas about circles.

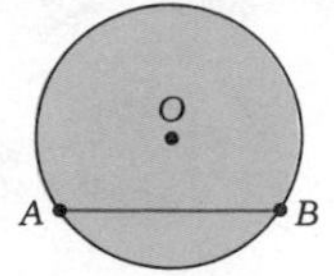


A **chord** is a segment with endpoints on the circle.

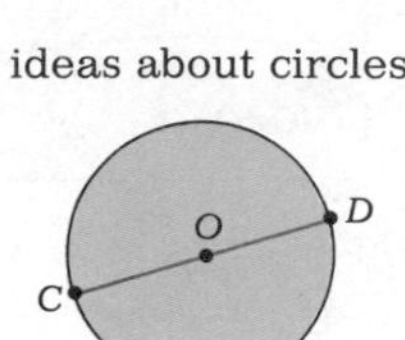


A **diameter** is a chord that contains the center.

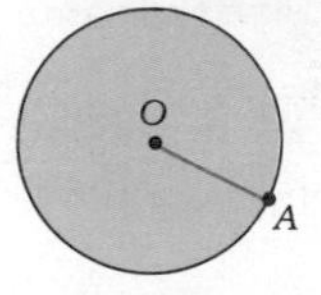


A **radius** is a segment with the center and a point on the circle as endpoints. It is half the length of the diameter.

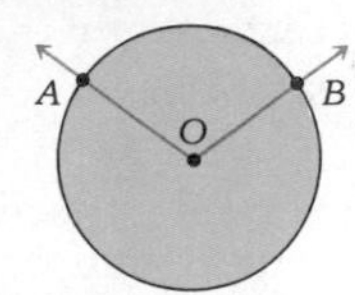


A **central angle** of a circle has the center as its vertex.

You can draw a circle using a compass.

O
center

Give the length of the radius or diameter of each circle.

**1.** 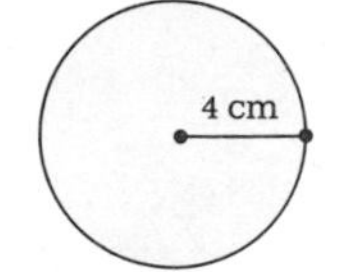


Diameter: ■ 8 cm

**2.** 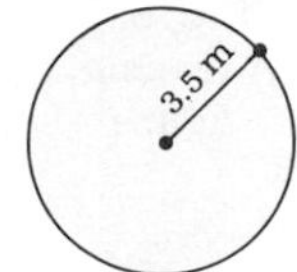


Diameter: ■ 7 m

**3.** 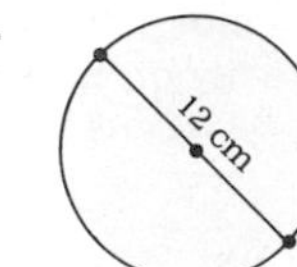


Radius: ■ 6 cm

**4.** 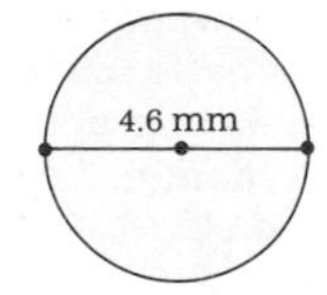


Radius: ■ 2.3 mm

Draw a circle with the given radius or diameter. student constructions

**5.** radius 4.5 cm **6.** diameter 10 cm **7.** radius 6 cm

Draw a circle with a central angle having the given measure. student constructions

**8.** 90° **9.** 35° **10.** 165°

**11.** Draw a 4-cm chord of a circle with a 3-cm radius. student construction



## Using Page 263

**Lesson Development** Direct students' attention to the picture of the Ferris wheel. Point out that the hub of the Ferris wheel represents the center of the circle and the seats represent points on the circle equidistant from the center. Draw large circles on the chalkboard and ask for volunteers to draw a chord, a diameter, and a radius. Encourage them to draw these segments in different positions in the circles.

**Exercises 1–11** Students should be able to distinguish a radius from a diameter. Remind them that the diameter is double the radius, and the radius is half the diameter. Note that students will need compasses for exercises 5–7 and 11 and protractors for exercises 8–10.

## Ideas That Work

### Special Education

Draw pictures of quadrilaterals on index cards, making sure to have a wide variety of examples for each type of quadrilateral. Where possible, vary the angle size, the distance between sides, the length of sides, and the orientation of the shape on the card (i.e., so that the sides of the shape are not parallel to the sides of the card).

Then have students sort these shape cards according to rules such as: all angles are right angles; all pairs of opposite sides are parallel; all pairs of opposite sides are the same length, and so on.

After each sorting, have students check to see which shapes turn up in the "yes" pile for each sorting rule. This provides a focus on the various properties each shape has.

After each sorting is completed and students have checked the shapes that have the various properties, have them add the property satisfied, or not satisfied, to the list for each shape. In the end, they will have developed a set of properties characterizing each of the shapes.

**Practice Supplement,** page 101

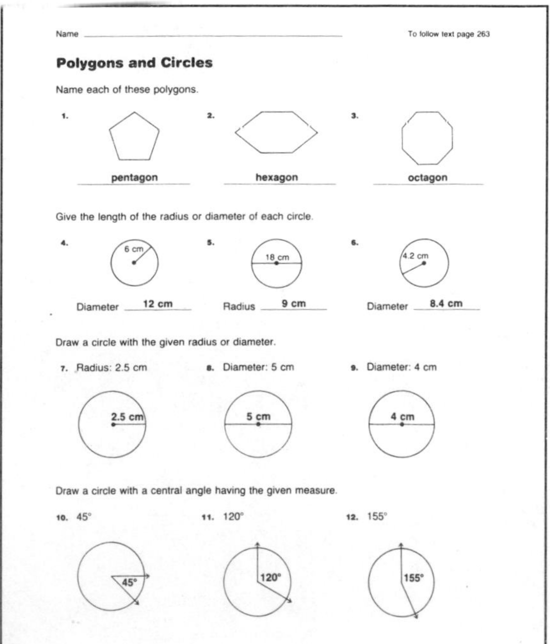

Name ______ To follow text page 263

**Polygons and Circles**

Name each of these polygons.

1. pentagon 2. hexagon 3. octagon

Give the length of the radius or diameter of each circle.

4. 6 cm — Diameter 12 cm
5. 18 cm — Radius 9 cm
6. 4.2 cm — Diameter 8.4 cm

Draw a circle with the given radius or diameter.

7. Radius: 2.5 cm 8. Diameter: 5 cm 9. Diameter: 4 cm

Draw a circle with a central angle having the given measure.

10. 45° 11. 120° 12. 155°

**Quick Review** Students give answers aloud, including the units of measure.

2 × 45 km   \$50.00 ÷ 10   6 L + 8 L   12 × 5 in.   5 cm − 4 cm
45 m ÷ 3   1.25 mL + 0.25 mL   12 × \$4.00   6 L × 9

**Lesson Focus** To identify congruent segments, angles, and polygons

**Suggested Materials** Tracing paper

## Ideas for Getting Started

Have students draw a line segment. Then ask them to draw a second segment with exactly the same length. They can accomplish this by measuring or using tracing paper. Similarly, have students draw an angle and then a second one with exactly the same measure. Finally have students draw a triangle. Then instruct them to draw an identical triangle using tracing paper. Have them draw congruent triangles in different locations by sliding the tracing paper, flipping the tracing paper, and rotating the tracing paper. Be sure to use words such as "same size and shape" in discussing these figures.

## Using Page 264

**Lesson Development** Discuss the two figures at the top of the page, pointing out that they have the same size and the same shape. Then have students read the definitions of congruent segments and congruent angles. On the chalkboard draw figures such as the ones below.

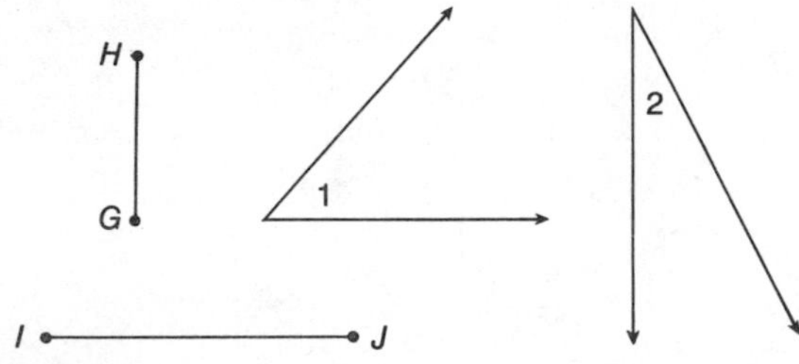


"Is segment $GH$ congruent to segment $IJ$? Is $\angle 1$ congruent to $\angle 2$?" Have students measure to decide.

Then draw two large congruent triangles on the chalkboard. Demonstrate by measuring that the matching angles and sides are congruent. List these congruent angles and sides on the chalkboard. Emphasize that whenever all the matching angles and all the matching sides of two polygons are congruent, the polygons are congruent.

## Congruent Figures

A figure and a copy of the figure that is the same size and shape as the original suggest the idea of **congruent figures.**

Two geometric figures are congruent to each other if they have the same size and shape.

Two segments are congruent if they have the same length.

We write: $\overline{AB} \cong \overline{CD}$

We say: "Segment $AB$ **is congruent to** segment $CD$."

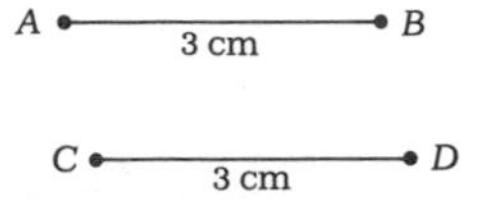


Two angles are congruent if they have the same measure.

We write: $\angle DEF \cong \angle GHI$

We say: "Angle $DEF$ **is congruent to** angle $GHI$."

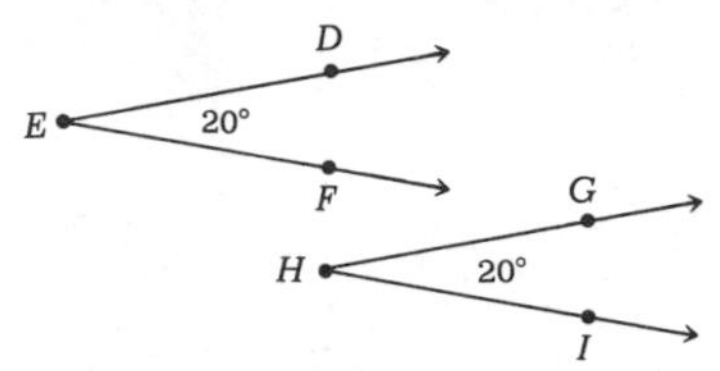


Two polygons are congruent if you can slide, flip, or turn one to make it fit exactly on the other. A tracing of one congruent figure will fit exactly on the figure congruent to it.

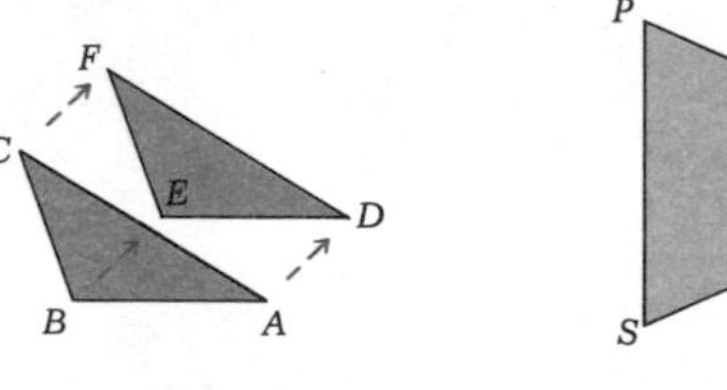


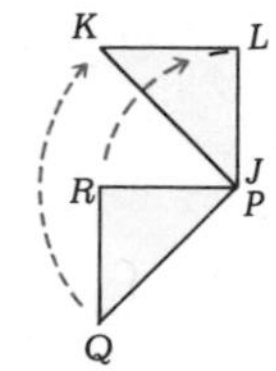


**Slide** $\triangle ABC \cong \triangle DEF$

**Flip** trapezoid $PQRS \cong$ trapezoid $ADCB$

**Turn** $\triangle JKL \cong \triangle PQR$

**Two congruent polygons,** such as $\triangle ABC$ and $\triangle DEF$, **have matching angles congruent and matching sides congruent.**
($\angle C \cong \angle F$, $\angle B \cong \angle E$, $\angle A \cong \angle D$ and $\overline{BC} \cong \overline{EF}$, $\overline{AB} \cong \overline{DE}$, $\overline{CA} \cong \overline{FD}$.)



## Follow Up

### Reteaching

Show students two congruent rectangles and ask them to decide if the rectangles are the same size. Focus on the sides and angles of the rectangles. Make a list of ways the rectangles are *equal,* and use it to discuss the idea of congruence.

1. Lengths of sides: Matching pairs of segments are *congruent.*
2. Measure of angles: Matching pairs of angles are *congruent.*
3. Size (area): The rectangles are *congruent* to one another.

### Enrichment

Give students the following sets of relations and ask them to construct and label pairs of triangles so that the statements are correct.

1. $\overline{RS} \cong \overline{UV}$, $\overline{ST} \cong \overline{VW}$, $\angle RST \cong \angle UVW$
2. $\overline{XY} \cong \overline{AB}$, $\overline{YZ} \cong \overline{BC}$, $\overline{ZX} \cong \overline{CA}$
3. $JK \cong MN$, $KL \cong NO$, $\angle JKL = 90°$, $\angle JKL \cong \angle MNO$
4. $\angle ABC \cong \angle DEF$, $\angle BCA \cong \angle EFD$, $\angle CAB \cong \angle FDE$

| Assignment Guide | | | |
|---|---|---|---|
| | Minimum | Average | Extended |
| page 265 | 1–6 | 1–6, TM | 1–6, TM |

1. Which pairs of segments are congruent? Measure or use a tracing to make sure. $\overline{AB} \cong \overline{MN}$, $\overline{CD} \cong \overline{KL}$, $\overline{EF} \cong \overline{GH}$, $\overline{IJ} \cong \overline{OP}$

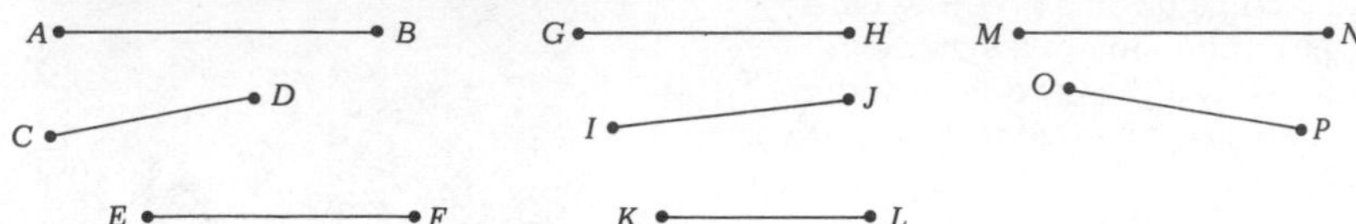

2. Which pairs of angles are congruent? Use your protractor or a tracing. $\angle GAI \cong \angle DEF$, $\angle RST \cong \angle PQZ$, $\angle MNT \cong \angle IJK$

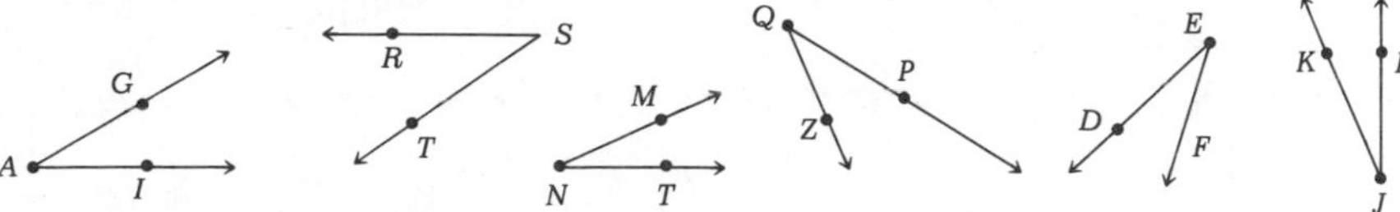

Make a tracing of one of each pair of figures and slide, turn, or flip it to try to make it fit on the other figure. Are the pairs of figures congruent? (Write **yes** or **no.**) Which motion did you use? (Write **slide, turn,** or **flip.**)

3. yes, turn
4. no, flip
5. yes, slide
6. no, turn

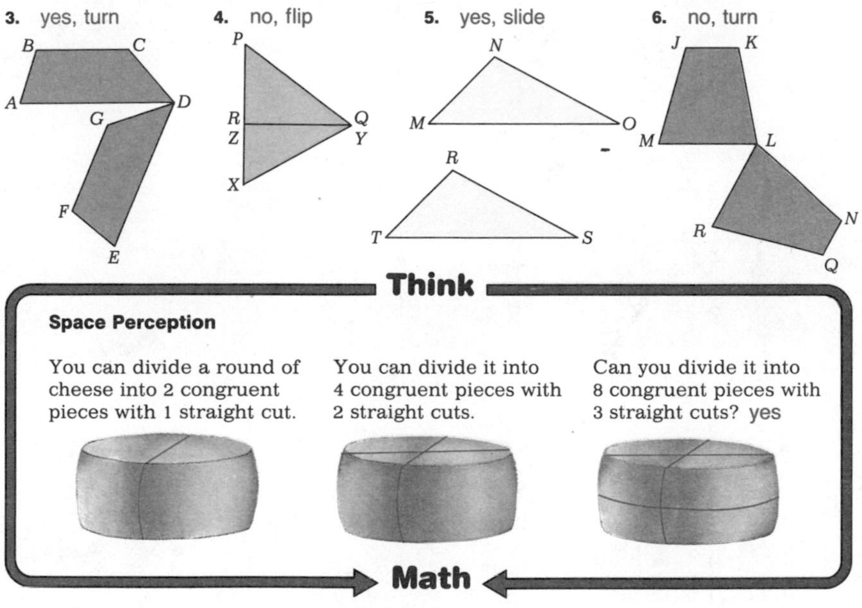

**Think Math**

**Space Perception**

You can divide a round of cheese into 2 congruent pieces with 1 straight cut.

You can divide it into 4 congruent pieces with 2 straight cuts.

Can you divide it into 8 congruent pieces with 3 straight cuts? yes



## Using Page 265

**Exercise 1** Advise students that they need to make accurate measurements to the nearest millimeter to make decisions about these segments. Be sure students use the congruent symbol: $\overline{AB} \approx \overline{MN}$, and so on. Have students use tracing paper to verify the congruent relationships.

**Exercise 2** Students may need to trace the angles shown and extend the sides in order to measure the angles accurately. Be sure to have them check the congruent relationships by tracing one angle and placing it over another angle.

**Exercises 3–6** After students have completed these exercises, select certain figures to emphasize the idea of matching congruent angles and matching congruent sides.

**Think Math** This exercise provides students with an opportunity to visualize congruent figures.

**Reteaching Supplement,** page 62

**Enrichment Supplement,** page 62

**Practice Supplement,** page 102

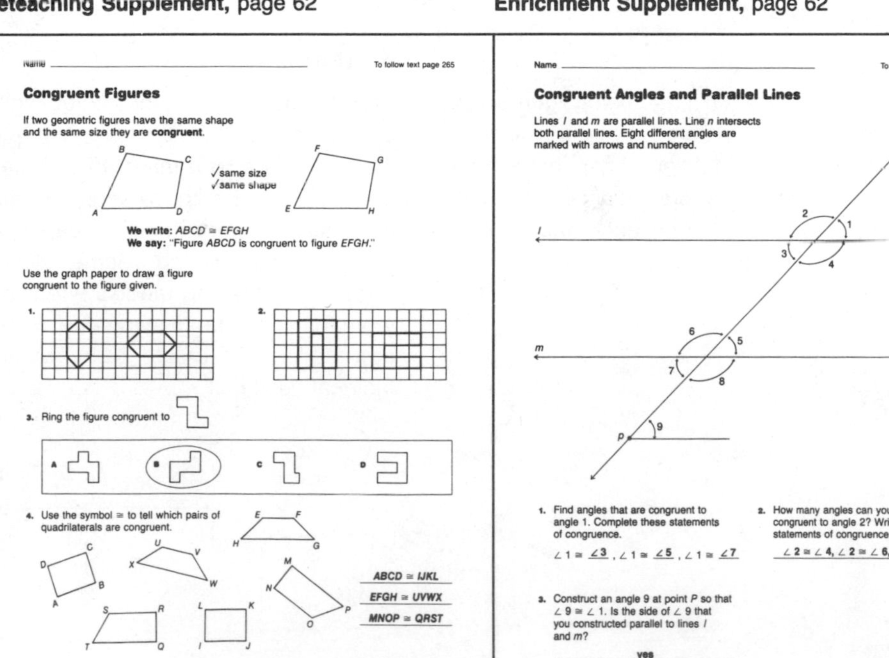

Name ______ To follow text page 265

**Congruent Figures**

If two geometric figures have the same shape and the same size they are **congruent.**

√same size
√same shape

**We write:** $ABCD \cong EFGH$
**We say:** "Figure $ABCD$ is congruent to figure $EFGH$."

Use the graph paper to draw a figure congruent to the figure given.

3. Ring the figure congruent to

4. Use the symbol ≅ to tell which pairs of quadrilaterals are congruent.

$ABCD \cong IJKL$
$EFGH \cong UVWX$
$MNOP \cong QRST$

Name ______ To follow text page 265

**Congruent Angles and Parallel Lines**

Lines $l$ and $m$ are parallel lines. Line $n$ intersects both parallel lines. Eight different angles are marked with arrows and numbered.

1. Find angles that are congruent to angle 1. Complete these statements of congruence.
$\angle 1 \cong \angle 3$, $\angle 1 \cong \angle 5$, $\angle 1 \cong \angle 7$

2. How many angles can you find that are congruent to angle 2? Write the statements of congruence.
$\angle 2 \cong \angle 4$, $\angle 2 \cong \angle 6$, $\angle 2 \cong \angle 8$

3. Construct an angle 9 at point $P$ so that $\angle 9 \cong \angle 1$. Is the side of $\angle 9$ that you constructed parallel to lines $l$ and $m$?
yes

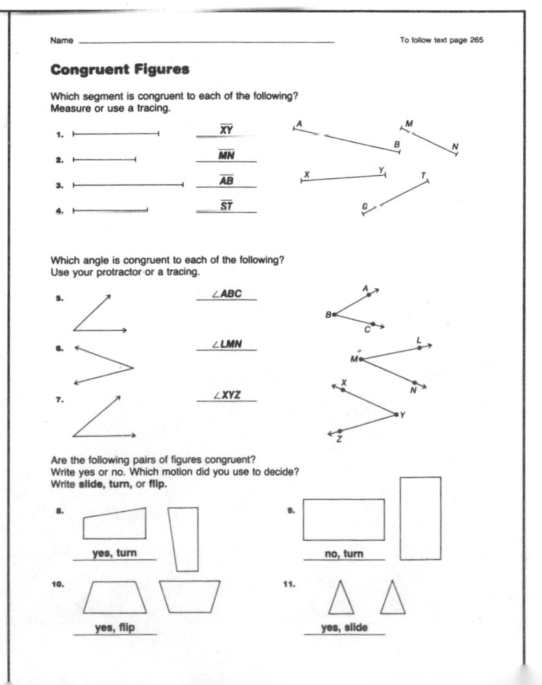

Name ______ To follow text page 265

**Congruent Figures**

Which segment is congruent to each of the following? Measure or use a tracing.

1. $\overline{XY}$
2. $\overline{MN}$
3. $\overline{AB}$
4. $\overline{ST}$

Which angle is congruent to each of the following? Use your protractor or a tracing.

5. $\angle ABC$
6. $\angle LMN$
7. $\angle XYZ$

Are the following pairs of figures congruent? Write yes or no. Which motion did you use to decide? Write **slide, turn,** or **flip.**

8. yes, turn
9. no, turn
10. yes, flip
11. yes, slide

**Quick Review** Students write standard numbers for these expanded numbers.
2 thousands, 3 tens, 5 ones 2,035 5 hundreds, 8 ones 508 six tens, 2 ones 62
4 thousands, 9 tens 4,090 8 ten thousands, 4 thousands, 5 tens 84,050
7 hundreds, 8 tens 780 6 thousands, 9 ones 6,009 seven tens, 2 ones 72

**Lesson Focus** To determine lines of symmetry in a geometric figure

**Suggested Materials** Paper for folding

## Ideas for Getting Started

Have students fold a sheet of paper, cut out a figure, and unfold it. "Can you use this method to make a square? a triangle? a pumpkin? the letter T? a trapezoid?" Have students fold the paper two or more times before cutting to produce figures with more than one line of symmetry.

## Using Page 266

**Lesson Development** Discuss the folded greeting card and the symmetric figure shown at the top of the page. Be sure students understand the idea of a symmetric figure and the line of symmetry.

Focus attention on the triangles in the center of the page. Point out that an equilateral triangle has three lines of symmetry, an isosceles (non-equilateral) triangle has only one line of symmetry, and that a scalene triangle has no lines of symmetry. "Can you name a quadrilateral that has two lines of symmetry?" (a rectangle or a rhombus) "Can you name a quadrilateral that has just one line of symmetry?" (an isosceles trapezoid or a kite-shaped quadrilateral) "How many lines of symmetry does a square have?" (four) Draw pictures or make cutouts as needed to illustrate these ideas.

**Exercises 1–6** Students often experience difficulty with figures such as exercise 5. If necessary, provide a model of a parallelogram that can be folded.

## Symmetric Figures

The picture on this greeting card suggests the idea of a **symmetric figure.** When the card is closed, the two halves of the figure fit exactly on each other. The fold line of the card is the **line of symmetry** of the figure.

Here are three familiar types of triangles and their lines of symmetry.

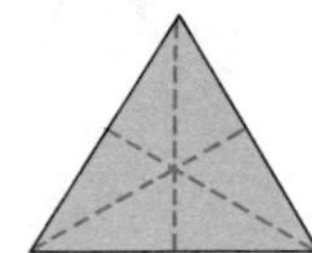

Equilateral triangle
3 lines of symmetry

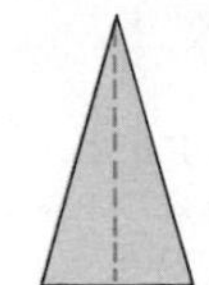

Isosceles triangle
1 line of symmetry

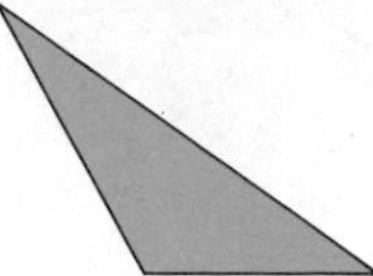

Scalene triangle
0 lines of symmetry

Is the dotted line a line of symmetry of the figure? Write **yes** or **no.**

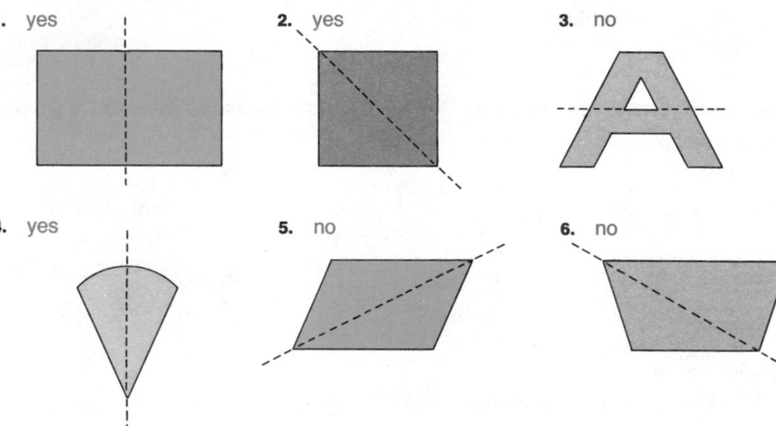




## Follow Up

### Reteaching

Have students cut geometric figures from colored paper and find all the lines of symmetry by folding. Then have them use a contrasting crayon or pencil to draw a dashed line along each line of symmetry for each figure.

### Enrichment

Provide students with incomplete figures such as shown below. Have them place the dotted line by a mirror to see the reflection. After they have seen the reflections, have students fold their papers and cut out each design. Some students might enjoy making models which have more than one line of symmetry. Encourage students to create their own symmetrical designs.

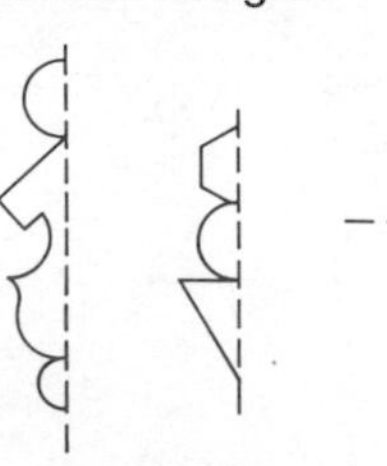

| Assignment Guide | | | |
|---|---|---|---|
| | Minimum | Average | Extended |
| page 266 | 1–6 | 1–6 | 1–6 |
| page 267 | 1–7, SK | 1–8, SK | 1–9, SK |

Give the numbers of lines of symmetry for each quadrilateral. Trace the figures, fold, and draw the lines if necessary.

1. 2

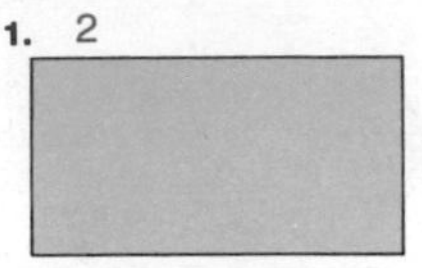

Rectangle

2. 0

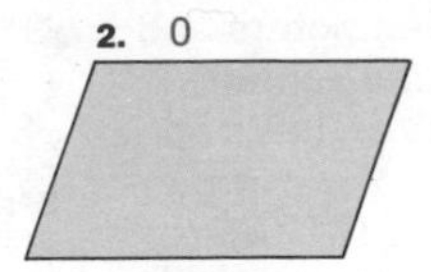

Parallelogram

3. 1

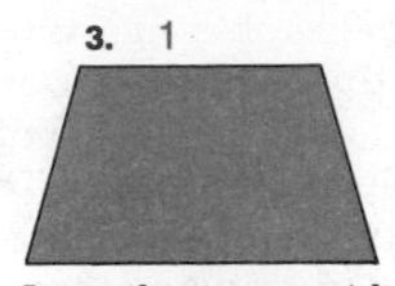

Isosceles trapezoid

4. 4

5. 1

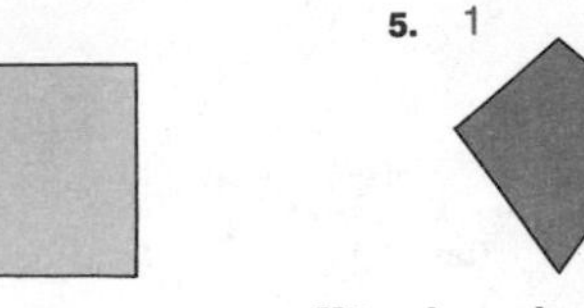

Square

Kite-shaped quadrilateral

6. 2

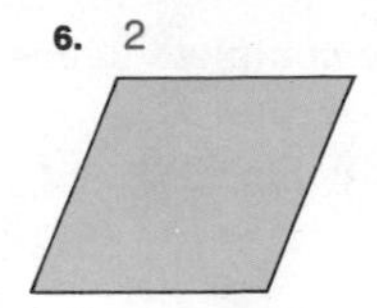

Rhombus

7. Which capital letters have just 1 line of symmetry? 2 lines of symmetry? more than 2 lines of symmetry? See teaching notes.

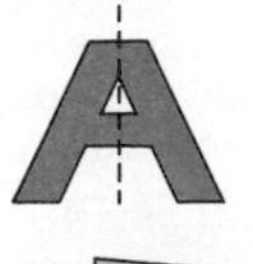

8. Fold a square sheet of paper once and make a cut so that the unfolded piece is
   A a heart  B a tree  C a pumpkin
   D the letter x  E another figure of your choice
   See teaching notes.

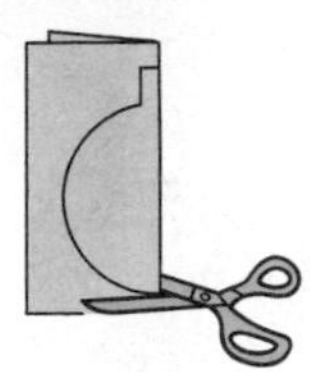

★ 9. Fold a square sheet of paper two times and cut off a corner. Unfold. How many lines of symmetry does the cut-out figure have? Experiment with a piece folded three times. See teaching notes.

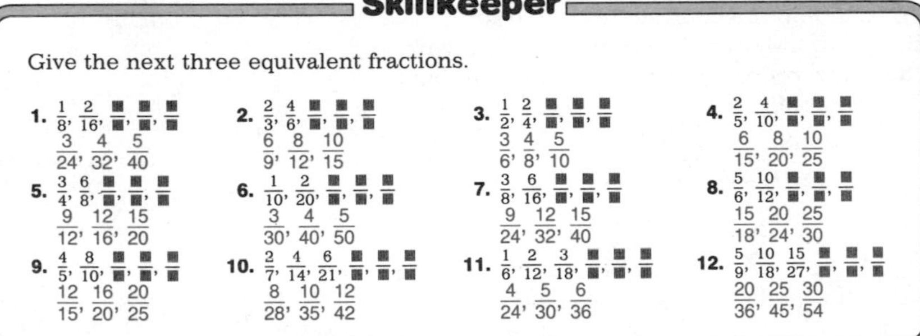

**Skillkeeper**

Give the next three equivalent fractions.

1. $\frac{1}{8}, \frac{2}{16}, \frac{\blacksquare}{\blacksquare}, \frac{\blacksquare}{\blacksquare}, \frac{\blacksquare}{\blacksquare}$ — $\frac{3}{24}, \frac{4}{32}, \frac{5}{40}$
2. $\frac{2}{3}, \frac{4}{6}, \frac{\blacksquare}{\blacksquare}, \frac{\blacksquare}{\blacksquare}, \frac{\blacksquare}{\blacksquare}$ — $\frac{6}{9}, \frac{8}{12}, \frac{10}{15}$
3. $\frac{1}{2}, \frac{2}{4}, \frac{\blacksquare}{\blacksquare}, \frac{\blacksquare}{\blacksquare}, \frac{\blacksquare}{\blacksquare}$ — $\frac{3}{6}, \frac{4}{8}, \frac{5}{10}$
4. $\frac{2}{5}, \frac{4}{10}, \frac{\blacksquare}{\blacksquare}, \frac{\blacksquare}{\blacksquare}, \frac{\blacksquare}{\blacksquare}$ — $\frac{6}{15}, \frac{8}{20}, \frac{10}{25}$
5. $\frac{3}{4}, \frac{6}{8}, \frac{\blacksquare}{\blacksquare}, \frac{\blacksquare}{\blacksquare}, \frac{\blacksquare}{\blacksquare}$ — $\frac{9}{12}, \frac{12}{16}, \frac{15}{20}$
6. $\frac{1}{10}, \frac{2}{20}, \frac{\blacksquare}{\blacksquare}, \frac{\blacksquare}{\blacksquare}, \frac{\blacksquare}{\blacksquare}$ — $\frac{3}{30}, \frac{4}{40}, \frac{5}{50}$
7. $\frac{3}{8}, \frac{6}{16}, \frac{\blacksquare}{\blacksquare}, \frac{\blacksquare}{\blacksquare}, \frac{\blacksquare}{\blacksquare}$ — $\frac{9}{24}, \frac{12}{32}, \frac{15}{40}$
8. $\frac{5}{6}, \frac{10}{12}, \frac{\blacksquare}{\blacksquare}, \frac{\blacksquare}{\blacksquare}, \frac{\blacksquare}{\blacksquare}$ — $\frac{15}{18}, \frac{20}{24}, \frac{25}{30}$
9. $\frac{4}{5}, \frac{8}{10}, \frac{\blacksquare}{\blacksquare}, \frac{\blacksquare}{\blacksquare}, \frac{\blacksquare}{\blacksquare}$ — $\frac{12}{15}, \frac{16}{20}, \frac{20}{25}$
10. $\frac{2}{7}, \frac{4}{14}, \frac{6}{21}, \frac{\blacksquare}{\blacksquare}, \frac{\blacksquare}{\blacksquare}, \frac{\blacksquare}{\blacksquare}$ — $\frac{8}{28}, \frac{10}{35}, \frac{12}{42}$
11. $\frac{1}{6}, \frac{2}{12}, \frac{3}{18}, \frac{\blacksquare}{\blacksquare}, \frac{\blacksquare}{\blacksquare}, \frac{\blacksquare}{\blacksquare}$ — $\frac{4}{24}, \frac{5}{30}, \frac{6}{36}$
12. $\frac{5}{9}, \frac{10}{18}, \frac{15}{27}, \frac{\blacksquare}{\blacksquare}, \frac{\blacksquare}{\blacksquare}, \frac{\blacksquare}{\blacksquare}$ — $\frac{20}{36}, \frac{25}{45}, \frac{30}{54}$



## Using Page 267

**Exercises 1–6** Encourage students to cut and fold figures to check their answers.

**Exercise 7** Before assigning this exercise, explain that lines of symmetry in capital letters may vary, according to the style of printing or type. In general, the following lines of symmetry can be observed:

1 line of symmetry: A, B, C, D, E, K, M, T, U, V
2 lines of symmetry: H, I
more than 2 lines of symmetry: 0

**Exercise 8** If students have difficulty with the figures in this exercise, let them use the figures below as guides.

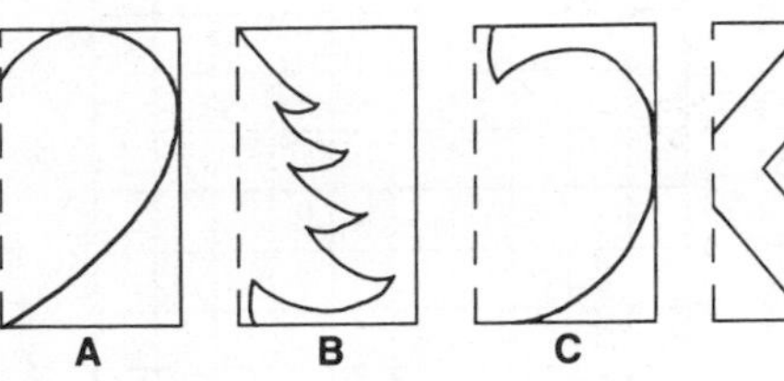


**Exercise 9** Encourage students to experiment making other creative figures by folding and cutting their papers in several different ways.

**Skillkeeper** This skill was originally taught in Chapter 8.

**Reteaching Supplement,** page 63

Name ______ To follow text page 267

**Symmetric Figures**

A figure that can be folded so that its two halves match exactly is a **symmetric figure.**

This letter has one **line of symmetry.** (The figure can be folded so the two sides match.)

This letter has two **lines of symmetry.**

Draw all the lines of symmetry for each figure.

1. (Find the other one.) 2. 3. 4. 5. 6.

Ring the figures that have at least one line of symmetry.

7. 8. 9. 10. 11. 12.

**Enrichment Supplement,** page 63

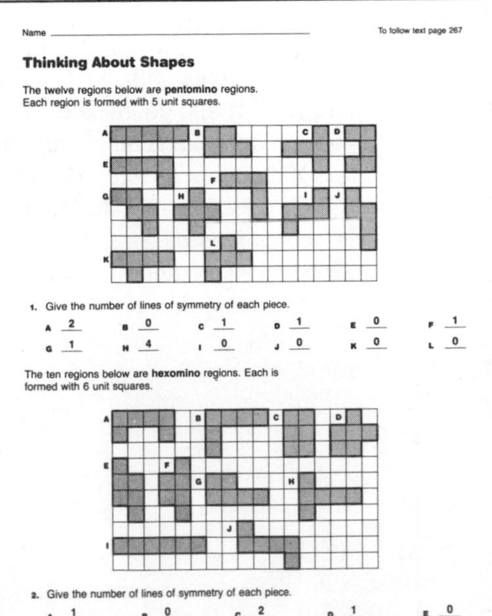

Name ______ To follow text page 267

**Thinking About Shapes**

The twelve regions below are **pentomino** regions. Each region is formed with 5 unit squares.

1. Give the number of lines of symmetry of each piece.

A 2  B 0  C 1  D 1  E 0  F 1
G 1  H 4  I 0  J 0  K 0  L 0

The ten regions below are **hexomino** regions. Each is formed with 6 unit squares.

2. Give the number of lines of symmetry of each piece.

A 1  B 0  C 2  D 1  E 0
F 1  G 0  H 1  I 2  J 0

**Practice Supplement,** page 103

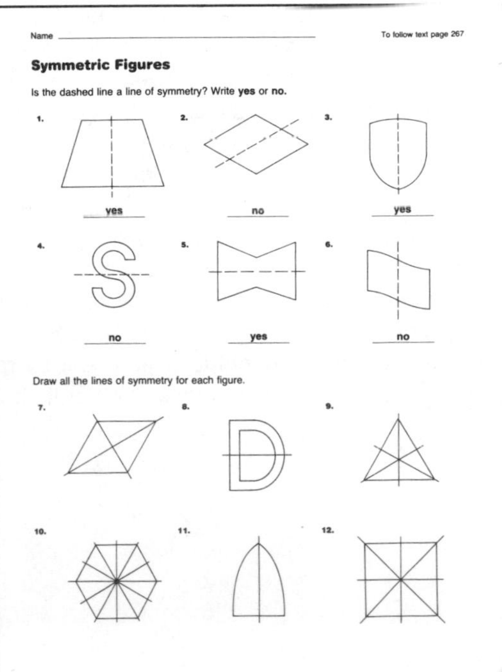

Name ______ To follow text page 267

**Symmetric Figures**

Is the dashed line a line of symmetry? Write **yes** or **no.**

1. yes  2. no  3. yes
4. no  5. yes  6. no

Draw all the lines of symmetry for each figure.

7. 8. 9. 10. 11. 12.

**Quick Review** Students give aloud numbers that are 10 greater and 10 less than the numbers listed below.

230 240, 220 | 90 100, 80 | 557 567, 547 | 11 21, 1 | 19 29, 9
1,982 1,992, 1,972 | 390 400, 380 | 14 24, 4 | 7,802 7,812, 7,792

**Lesson Focus** To graph figures, congruent figures, and similar figures

**Suggested Material** 10 by 10 grids (TRB p. 274)

## Ideas for Getting Started

Show the grid below on an overhead projector or on the chalkboard. Ask: "What did the triangle say to the rhombus after the rhombus straightened up?" Help students answer the riddle by matching the letters on the grid with the number pairs shown below.

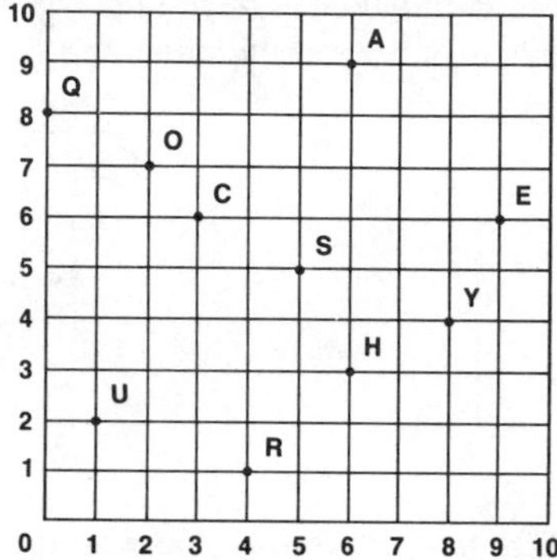


Answer:

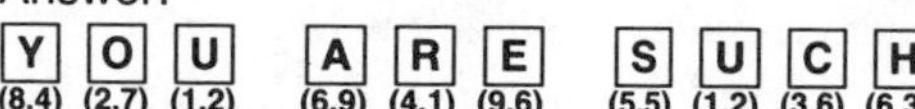


A S Q U A R E
(6,9) (5,5) (0,8) (1,2) (6,9) (4,1) (9,6)

## Using Page 268

**Lesson Development** Provide students with grids or graph paper and have them label the grids as shown in the first demonstration for graphing a figure. Emphasize that a figure is graphed by first plotting the points and then connecting them in the order given. Have students graph the figure shown. Then have them graph the following points: (2,5) (5,7) (8,5) (7,2) (3,2) (2,5).

Next direct students' attention to the section on graphing congruent figures. Instruct students to graph the original square and then graph the square with the coordinates produced by adding 4 to each number in the original coordinates. Point out that they could trace the first square and slide the tracing to fit on the second square. Ask students to guess and then check what would happen to the graph if 6 was added to each of the original coordinates.

Finally direct students' attention to the section on graphing similar figures. Have them graph the original triangle shown and the triangle resulting from multiplying each of the numbers in the coordinates by 3. Encourage students to experiment by multiplying the coordinates by numbers other than 3.

## Graphing Geometric Figures

### Graphing a Figure

You can graph a figure by graphing points and connecting them in order. The number pairs that tell us the location of a point on the graph are called **coordinates.** The graph of a common geometric figure is started for you. The figure is graphed by using these coordinates:

(3,5), (5,3), (5,0), (0,5), (3,5).

Show the complete figure on your graph. See graph.

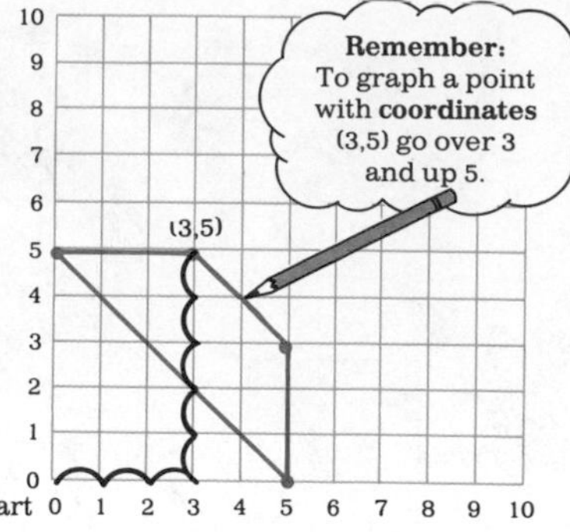


### Graphing Congruent Figures

You can find coordinates of a square congruent to the square shown by adding the same number to each of its coordinates. For example, try adding 4.

(1,2) → + 4 → (5,6)
(2,3) → + 4 → (6,7)
(3,2) → + 4 → (7,6)
(2,1) → + 4 → (6,5)

Graph the new coordinates on your paper to show the congruent square. See graph.

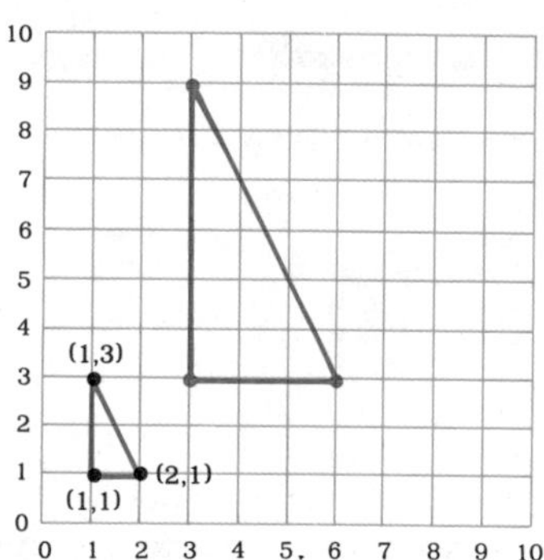


### Graphing Similar Figures

You can find the coordinates of a triangle similar to the triangle shown by multiplying each of its coordinates by the same number. For example, try multiplying by 3.

(1,3) → × 3 → (3,9)
(2,1) → × 3 → (6,3)
(1,1) → × 3 → (3,3)

Graph the new coordinates on your paper to show the similar triangle. See graph.

(1,3)
(2,1)
(1,1)



## Follow Up

### Reteaching

Provide students with a 10 by 10 grid (TRB p. 274) and coordinates for simple figures such as a rectangle and triangle. Have them mark and connect the points on their grids. Then help them multiply the coordinates by 2, 3, or 4, mark the new coordinates, and connect the points.

### Enrichment

Have students locate the coordinate points below and draw connecting line segments. Then have them draw a mirror image and name the coordinate points. Given coordinates: (5,5), (2,5), (5,2).

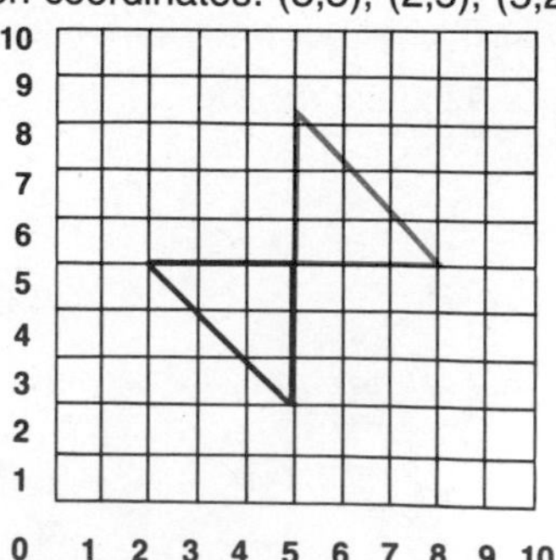

Mirror image: (5,8), (8,5), (5,5).

| Assignment Guide | | | |
|---|---|---|---|
| | Minimum | Average | Extended |
| page 269 | 1–12 | 1–12, TM | 1–12, TM |

Graph each of these figures. See teaching notes.

1. (1,1), (3,6), (6,3), (1,1)
2. (2,2), (2,6), (8,6), (8,2), (2,2)
3. (6,1), (4,3), (4,7), (6,9), (8,7), (8,3), (6,1)

Graph the figure for the coordinates given. Then graph a congruent figure by adding the number given to each of the coordinates. See teaching notes.

4. (1,1), (3,3), (3,1), (1,1) + 3
5. (1,1), (2,5), (2,1), (1,1) + 2
6. (1,4), (1,6), (3,6), (3,4), (2,3), (1,4) + 4
7. (1,2), (3,4), (7,4), (5,2), (1,2) + 3

Graph the figure for the coordinates given. Then graph a similar figure by multiplying each of the coordinates by the number given. See teaching notes.

8. (2,2), (1,3), (4,2), (2,2) × 2
9. (1,1), (2,2), (2,1), (1,1) × 3
10. (2,4), (6,6), (8,2), (4,0), (2,4) × $\frac{1}{2}$
11. (3,3), (3,6), (9,6), (9,3), (3,3) × $\frac{1}{3}$

12. Trace a favorite cartoon character on graph paper.

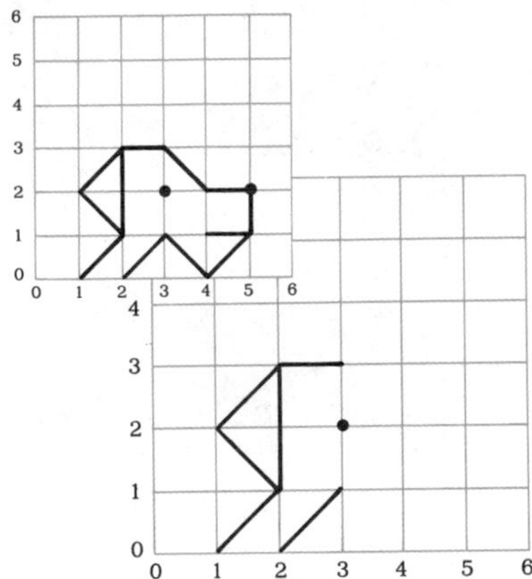

Use graph paper with larger squares or use a larger scale to make a similar but larger figure. student construction

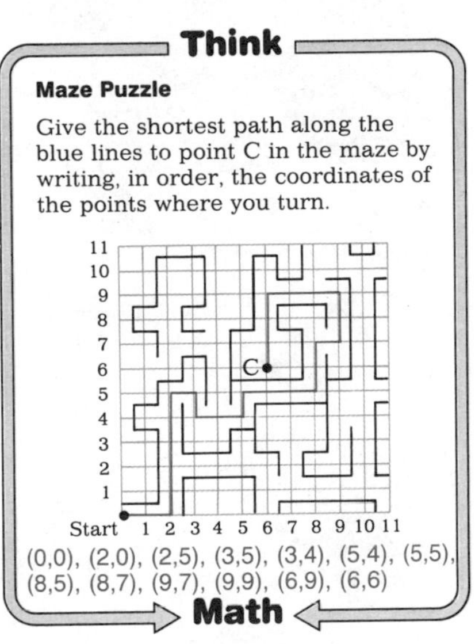

**Think**

**Maze Puzzle**

Give the shortest path along the blue lines to point C in the maze by writing, in order, the coordinates of the points where you turn.

(0,0), (2,0), (2,5), (3,5), (3,4), (5,4), (5,5), (8,5), (8,7), (9,7), (9,9), (6,9), (6,6)

**Math**



## Using Page 269

**Exercises 1–3** Graphing should show the following figures.

1. 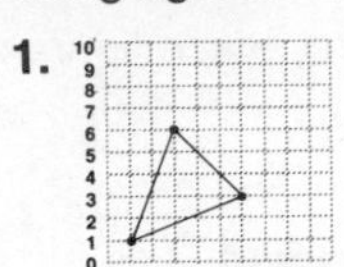
2. 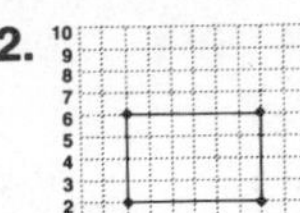
3. 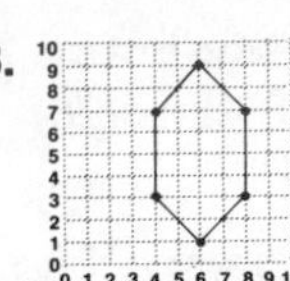

**Exercises 4–7** Graphing should show the following congruent figures.

4\.

5\.

6\. 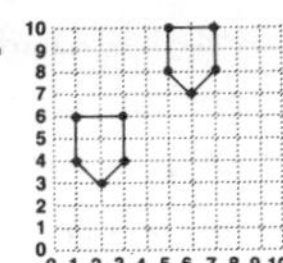

7\.

**Exercises 8–11** Graphing should show the following similar figures.

8\. 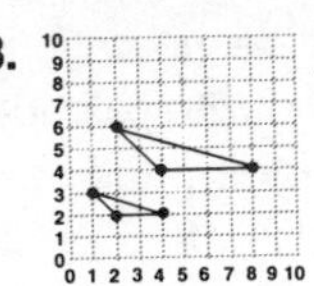

9\. 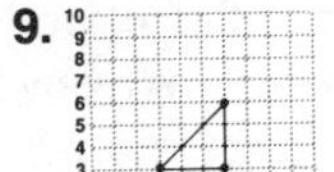

10\. 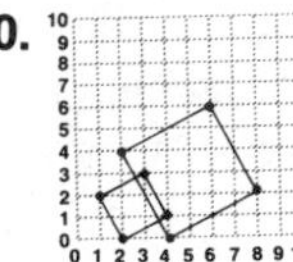

11\.

**Exercise 12** If necessary, help students with curved lines on a grid. Have students color their enlarged pictures and display them on the bulletin board.

**Think Math** Encourage students to solve the maze first and then look for the appropriate coordinates.

**Reteaching Supplement,** page 64

Name ______ To follow text page 269

**Graphing Geometric Figures**

Refer to the graph at the right for 1 through 4.

1. Write the coordinates of each point.
   A: (2, 1)
   B: (6, 6)
   C: (1, 5)
2. Add 5 to each coordinate of points A, B, and C.
   A': (7, 6)
   B': (11, 11)
   C': (6, 10)
3. Draw a triangle with new points A', B', and C' as vertices.
4. Are the two triangles congruent? yes

Refer to the graph at the right for 5 through 8.

5. Write the coordinates of each point.
   X: (7, 7)
   Y: (12, 9)
   Z: (6, 11)
6. Subtract 4 from each coordinate of points X, Y, and Z.
   X': (3, 3)
   Y': (8, 5)
   Z': (2, 7)
7. Draw a triangle with new points X', Y', and Z' as vertices.
8. Are the two triangles congruent? yes

**Enrichment Supplement,** page 64

Name ______ To follow text page 269

**An Amazing Graph**

Find a path along the lines to point C in the maze. Then write, in order, the coordinates of the points where you turned.

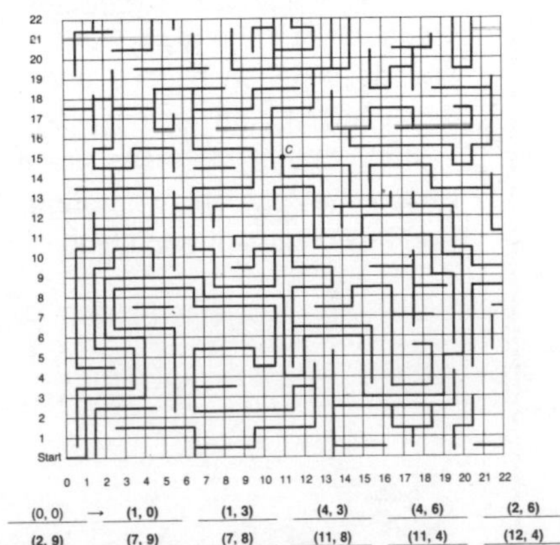

(0, 0) → (1, 0), (1, 3), (4, 3), (4, 6), (2, 6), (2, 9), (7, 9), (7, 8), (11, 8), (11, 4), (12, 4), (12, 6), (15, 6), (15, 3), (19, 3), (19, 5), (20, 5), (20, 10), (19, 10), (19, 12), (15, 12), (15, 11), (13, 11), (13, 14), (11, 14), (11, 15)

**Practice Supplement,** page 104

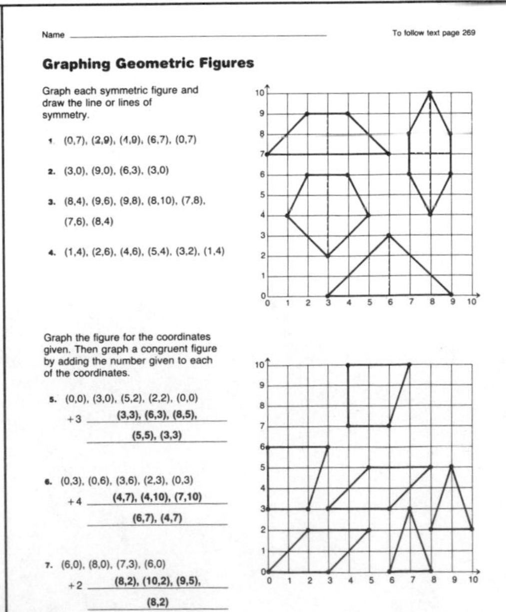

Name ______ To follow text page 269

**Graphing Geometric Figures**

Graph each symmetric figure and draw the line or lines of symmetry.

1. (0,7), (2,9), (4,9), (6,7), (0,7)
2. (3,0), (9,0), (6,3), (3,0)
3. (8,4), (9,6), (9,8), (8,10), (7,8), (7,6), (8,4)
4. (1,4), (2,6), (4,6), (5,4), (3,2), (1,4)

Graph the figure for the coordinates given. Then graph a congruent figure by adding the number given to each of the coordinates.

5. (0,0), (3,0), (5,2), (2,2), (0,0) +3 (3,3), (6,3), (8,5), (5,5), (3,3)
6. (0,3), (0,6), (3,6), (2,3), (0,3) +4 (4,7), (4,10), (7,10), (6,7), (4,7)
7. (6,0), (8,0), (7,3), (6,0) +2 (8,2), (10,2), (9,5), (8,2)

**Quick Review** Students give aloud numbers that are 100 greater and 100 less than the numbers listed below.

488 588, 388 | 100 200, 0 | 5,699 5,799, 5,599 | 459 559, 359
2,044 2,144, 1,944 | 990 1,090, 890 | 8,409 8,509, 8,309 | 129 229, 29

**Lesson Focus** To identify space figures; to find the number of faces, edges, and vertices of a polyhedron

**Suggested Materials** Tagboard, space figures (TRB p. 276)

## Ideas for Getting Started

Provide students with a copy of the space figure pattern for a cube. Have them cut out and fold the pattern and tape it together. Remind students that the faces of a cube are squares. "How many faces does a cube have?" (6) Point to a corner of the cube. "The corners of the cube are called vertices. How many vertices does a cube have?" (8) Run your finger along an edge of the cube. "How many edges does a cube have?" (12)

## Using Page 270

**Lesson Development** Discuss the 12-faced desk calendar pictured at the top of the page. Point out that the faces of this calendar are pentagons. Ask students to guess how many faces the calendar has (12). Introduce the term "polyhedron" and have students point to the figures in exercises 1–5 as you say the names. Then pick one of the figures and ask students to identify the polygons that make its faces. If possible, have models of these space figures available.

**Exercises 1–5** As students are matching the patterns with the space figures, encourage them to consider what types of polygons make up the faces of each polyhedron.

## Space Figures

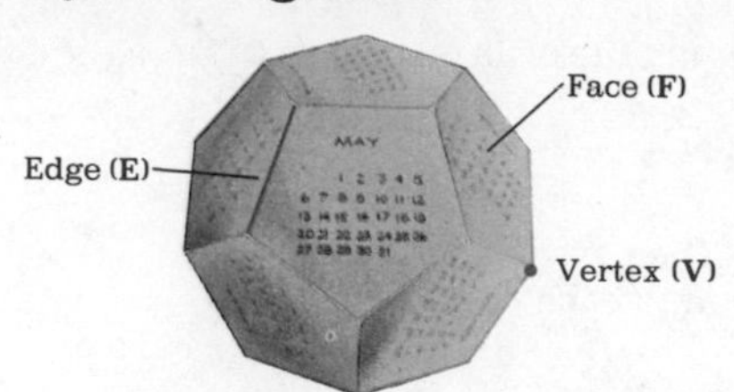


A 12-faced desk calendar suggests the idea of a **space figure.** It has **faces, edges,** and **vertices** as shown. Space figures whose faces are polygons are called **polyhedrons.**

Each polyhedron below can be made by folding one of the patterns on the right. Give the letter of the pattern for each polyhedron.

**Some Prisms** | **Polyhedron** | **Pattern**

1. D Triangular prism — A.
2. C Cube — B.
3. E Rectangular prism — C.

**Some Pyramids**

4. A Triangular pyramid — D.
5. B Square pyramid — E.

270

## Follow Up

### Reteaching

Show students geometric solids, especially cubes, pyramids, prisms, and other polyhedra. Allow students to feel and describe each solid and name its faces, edges, and vertices. Call attention to the fact that the faces are polygons. Encourage students to suggest real-world examples of each type of figure.

### Enrichment

Let students copy the polyhedron patterns below and construct tagboard models. Students then tell the number of faces, vertices, and edges for each polyhedron.

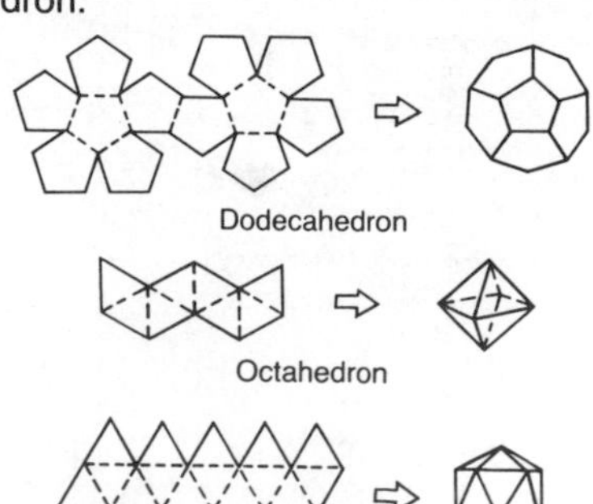
Dodecahedron
Octahedron
Icosahedron

| Assignment Guide | | | |
|---|---|---|---|
| | Minimum | Average | Extended |
| page 270 | 1–5 | 1–5 | 1–5 |
| page 271 | 1–10 | 1–10 | 1–10, TM |

None of the space figures below is a polyhedron, since none has a polygon as a face. Give an everyday object that suggests each figure. Sample answers are shown.

1. 
Cylinder can of food

2. 
Cone ice cream cone

3. 
Sphere baseball

Give the numbers needed to complete the table.

| | Space Figure | Number of Faces (F) | Number of Vertices (V) | Number of Edges (E) |
|---|---|---|---|---|
| 4. | Cube | 6 | ■ 8 | ■ 12 |
| 5. | Triangular pyramid | ■ 4 | 4 | ■ 6 |
| 6. | Pentagonal pyramid | ■ 6 | ■ 6 | 10 |
| 7. | Triangular prism | ■ 5 | ■ 6 | ■ 9 |
| 8. | Hexagonal prism | ■ 8 | ■ 12 | ■ 18 |

9. Use the table above to help you complete this formula.

$$E = F + V - ■ 2$$

10. Check the formula in exercise 9 to see if it works for a square pyramid. (See the picture on page 270.) $8 = 5 + 5 - 2$

**Think Math**

**Space Perception**

If you slice off each corner of a block of cheese, how many faces, edges, and vertices will the new figure have?
14, 36, 24

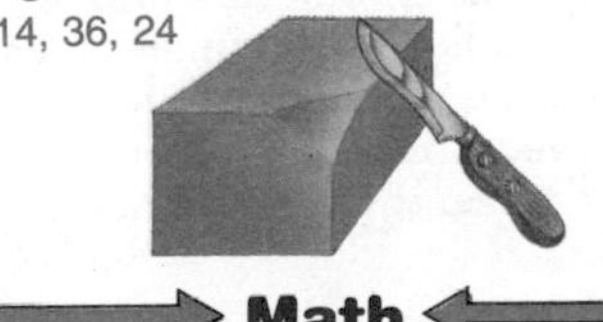



## Using Page 271

**Exercises 1–3** These exercises familiarize students with space figures that are not polyhedra, since these figures do not have polygons as faces.

**Exercises 4–8** If models of these figures are available, pass them around to help students complete the exercises.

**Exercises 9–10** Have students complete the formula for exercise 9 and test it on each figure to see that it works. Note that the formula works for all polyhedra.

**Think Math** If possible, use a clay model to complete the experiment. Many students will find the answer by imagining the corners cut off and counting the resulting vertices. Some students may simply decide that there are 3 vertices at each slashed-off "corner" so there are $8 \times 3$, or 24 vertices in the new figure. Other students might reason that there were 8 vertices on the cube, since each slice produces 2 additional vertices, in addition to the original 8, there would be a total of $8 + 2 \times 8$, or 24 vertices.

## Ideas That Work

### Math for the Gifted

Give students the following definitions for prisms and pyramids:

*A prism is a 3-dimensional figure whose bases are congruent polygons in parallel planes, and whose other faces are parallelograms.*

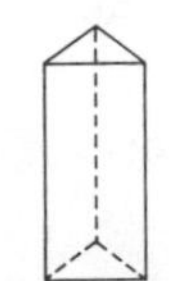
Triangular prism

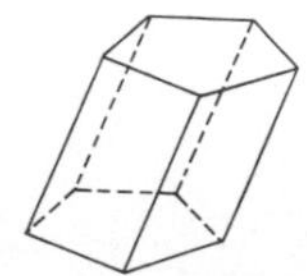
Pentagonal prism

Ask students to explain why the figure on the left is called a triangular prism and the figure on the right is called a pentagonal prism.

*A pyramid is a 3-dimensional figure with a polygonal base and triangular lateral faces. A tetrahedron is a triangular pyramid.*

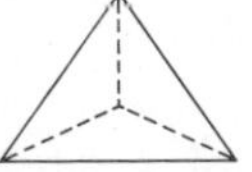
Triangular pyramid (tetrahedron)

Square pyramid

Ask students if they can suggest why one of the figures above is called a triangular pyramid, and the other is called a square pyramid.

**Practice Supplement,** page 105

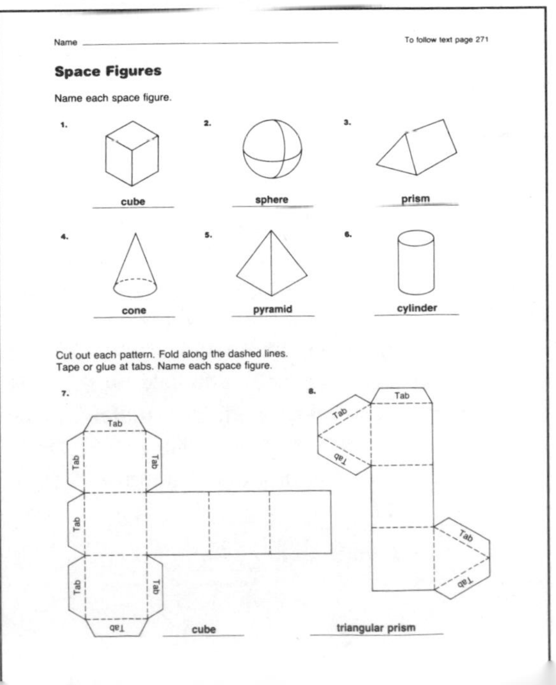
Name ______ To follow text page 271

**Space Figures**

Name each space figure.

1. cube
2. sphere
3. prism
4. cone
5. pyramid
6. cylinder

Cut out each pattern. Fold along the dashed lines. Tape or glue at tabs. Name each space figure.

7. cube
8. triangular prism

**Lesson Focus** To apply the strategies to solve nonroutine problems

## Ideas for Getting Started

Challenge students to name the nine problem-solving strategies. As students suggest a strategy, write it on the chalkboard. If you have made a problem-solving bulletin board, encourage students to use it as an aid to review.

## Using Page 272

**Lesson Development** Briefly review the 5-Point Checklist in the logo at the top of the page. Encourage students to refer to the list of problem-solving strategies to help them solve the problems on this page. Then use the hints and questions below to help students as necessary.

**Exercise 1** A possible strategy, Draw a Picture, was introduced on page 74. "What question do we want to answer about Arlene's fence?" (How many posts will she need?) "What shape is the fence she plans to make?" (rectangular) "How many posts will she need on each long side?" (7) "How many on the short sides?" (5) "Are there any posts on both the long and short sides?" (Yes, the four end posts.) Encourage students to draw a picture to show this.

**Exercise 2** A possible strategy, Find a Pattern, was introduced on page 246. "What do we want to find out about the house numbers?" (What is the fifteenth house number?) "What data is given in the problem?" (First house number is 3; second is 5; third is 7.) "What pattern can you find in these three numbers?" (House number is $2n + 1$.)

**Exercise 3** A possible strategy, Guess and Check, was introduced on page 48. "What do we want to find out about the boys' records?" (How many does each have?) "What information are we given?" (Jon has 3 times as many records as Lou; if each gets 4 more, Jon will have twice as many as Lou.) "If we guess that Lou has 5 records, how many would Jon have?" (15) "Does this check?" (No) Students may need to guess and check several combinations.

**Exercise 4** A possible strategy, Work Backward, was introduced on page 188. Elicit from students that the problem does not tell us the total number of friends who went to the movie, but that we can find this out by working backward. "How many people were left to play miniature golf?" (5) "How can we reverse the subtraction for the 4 who went home?" (Add 4.) "To find the number of people who went for a walk, what could we do?" (Multiply by 2.) "We could find out how many went to a restaurant by using what operation?" (Again, multiply by 2.) "How many of Graciela's friends went to a movie?" ($5 + 4 + 2 \times 2 = 36$)

## Problem Solving: Using the Strategies

Choose one or more of the strategies listed to help you solve each problem.

QUESTION
DATA
PLAN
ANSWER
CHECK
Choose the Operations
Guess and Check
Draw a Picture
Make a Table
Make an Organized List
Use Logical Reasoning
Work Backward
Solve a Simpler Problem
Find a Pattern


1. Arlene is building a fence around a rectangular garden 30 m long and 20 m wide. If she sets the posts 5 m apart, how many posts will she need for the fence? 20
2. The houses on one side of Gregory Street all have odd numbers. The first house number is 3, the second is 5, the third is 7, and so on. What is the fifteenth house number? 31
3. Jon now has 3 times as many records as Lou. If each of them gets 4 more records, Jon will have only twice as many as Lou. How many records does each have now? Jon, 12; Lou, 4
4. Some of Graciela's friends went to a movie. After the movie, half of them went to a restaurant. Of those who did not go to the restaurant, half went for a walk and 4 went home. This left 5 to play miniature golf. How many went to the movie? 36

## Chapter Review-Test

Give the name and symbol for each figure.

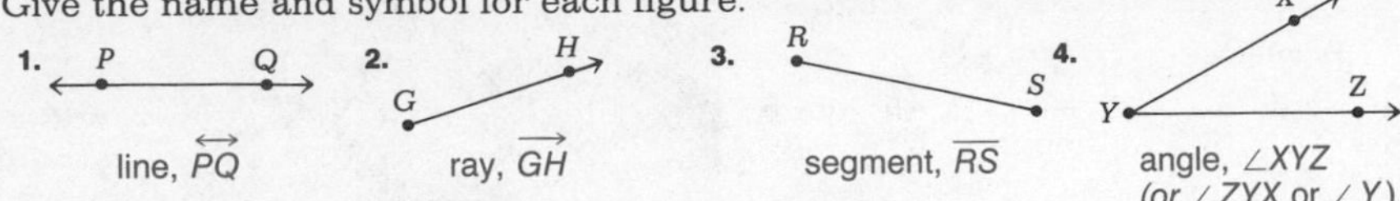


1. line, $\overleftrightarrow{PQ}$
2. ray, $\overrightarrow{GH}$
3. segment, $\overline{RS}$
4. angle, $\angle XYZ$ (or $\angle ZYX$ or $\angle Y$)

Give the measure of each angle and tell whether it is **acute, right,** or **obtuse.**

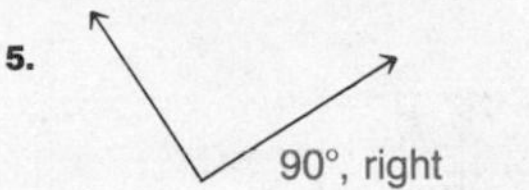
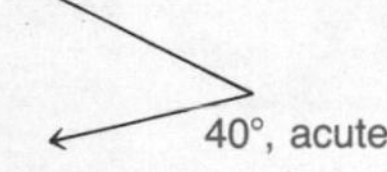

5. 90°, right
6. 40°, acute
7. 120°, obtuse

Use the figure on the right for items 8 and 9.

8. Use a symbol to name a pair of parallel lines.
   $\ell \parallel m$
9. Use a symbol to name a pair of perpendicular lines.
   $k \perp \ell$ or $k \perp m$

Give the name that best describes each polygon.

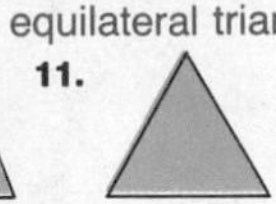

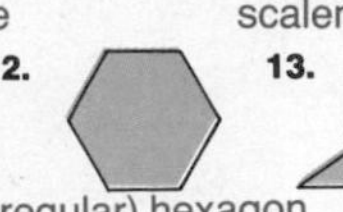
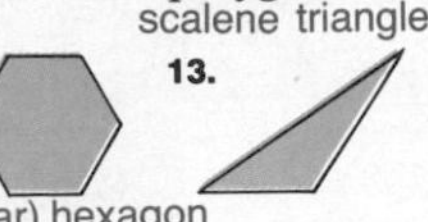
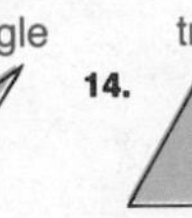
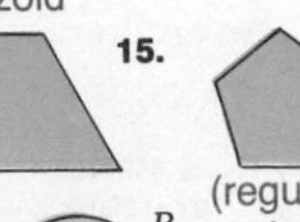
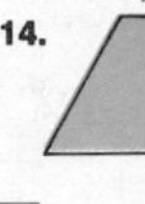

10. rhombus
11. equilateral triangle
12. (regular) hexagon
13. scalene triangle
14. trapezoid
15. (regular) pentagon

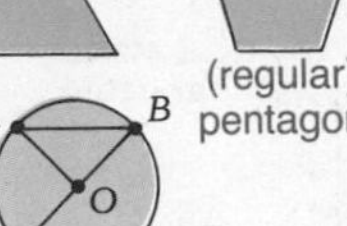


16. Which segment in circle O is a radius? $\overline{AO}$, $\overline{CO}$, or $\overline{BO}$
17. Which segment is a chord that is not a diameter? $\overline{AB}$

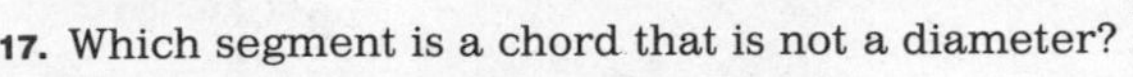

Use the figures in the graph for items 18–20.

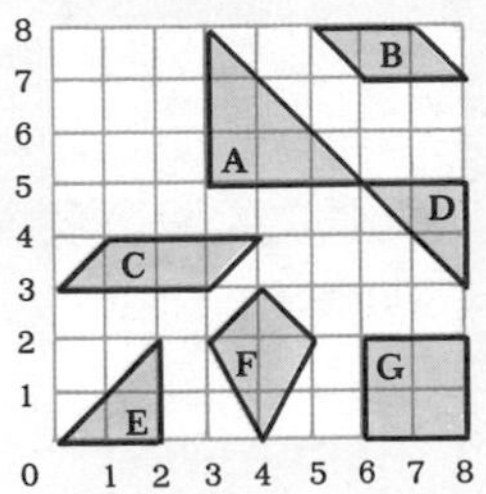


18. Give the coordinates of the figure that is similar but not congruent to the figure whose coordinates are (0,0), (2,0), (2,2). (3,5), (3,8), (6,5)
19. Name the figure that is congruent to figure D. E
20. How many lines of symmetry has figure G? 4

Use the figures at the right for items 21 and 22.

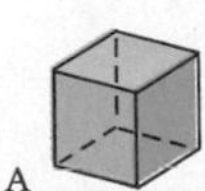
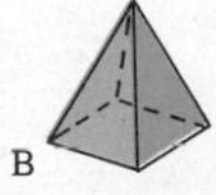


21. Give the name of each polyhedron.
    A—cube; B—square pyramid
22. Figure A has ■ faces, ■ edges, and ■ vertices.
    6, 12, 8



## Using Page 273

The exercises in the Chapter Review-Test emphasize the major concepts and skills presented in this chapter. These exercises may be used as a review assignment or as a test, depending upon your needs.

**Item Analysis** The table below correlates the Chapter Review-Test items with objectives and with the student text pages on which the concepts or skills were taught.

| Items | Objectives | Related text pages |
|---|---|---|
| 1–4 | 10.1 | 252–253 |
| 5–7 | 10.2 | 254–255 |
| 8–9 | 10.3 | 256–257 |
| 10–15 | 10.4 | 258–262 |
| 16–17 | 10.5 | 263 |
| 18–20 | 10.6 | 264–269 |
| 21–22 | 10.7 | 270–271 |

## Assessment Options

If you use the Chapter Review-Test as a review assignment, you may wish to use the multiple-choice test or the free-response test to evaluate mastery of the chapter objectives. The items on these tests have a one-to-one correspondence in terms of content and level of difficulty. A correlation of test items to objectives and student text pages is provided in the Management Guide for Chapter 10.

**Multiple-Choice Test,** TRB pages 10–12

**Free-Response Test,** TRB pages 67–68

## TRB Options

The following blackline masters are available for use with this chapter. If you have not already assigned these materials, you may wish to use them to close the chapter.

**Recreation,** TRB page 160

**Consumer Applications,** TRB page 178

**Calculator Technology,** TRB page 196

**Reading Math,** TRB page 228

**Family Involvement,** TRB pages 255–256

## Using Page 274

The exercises on this page are intended for those students who experienced difficulty with the Chapter Review-Test on page 273. Should students require reteaching of these key concepts and skills, please refer to the teaching notes below. Otherwise, the Another Look exercises can be assigned as independent work, with students using the accompanying sample problems and hints as guides.

**Exercises 1–5** Have students look at the box that shows the triangles. Say: "I'm thinking of a triangle that has exactly two sides congruent. What is its name?" (isosceles) "I'm thinking of a triangle that has one angle greater than 90°. What is its name?" (obtuse) Continue to ask questions such as these to review the ideas regarding these triangles. You may also want to ask questions such as, "I'm thinking of a triangle that has three lines of symmetry. Name it." (equilateral triangle) Remind the students that the sum of the angles of any triangle is 180°.

**Exercises 6–11** Direct students' attention to the box that describes quadrilaterals and other polygons. Ask questions such as, "A polygon has 4 congruent sides but no right angles. Name it." (rhombus) "One of the quadrilaterals shown has no lines of symmetry. Name it." (parallelogram) Review the idea that *penta* means "five," *hexa* means "six," and *octa* means "eight." Emphasize that these prefixes can help them name certain polygons.

**Exercises 12–15** Focus on the box that discusses circles. Ask: "How does the radius compare with the diameter?" (The radius is $\frac{1}{2}$ the diameter.) "How does the diameter compare with the radius?" (The diameter is twice the radius.) "What is the longest chord in a circle?" (the diameter) "Where is the vertex of a central angle of a circle?" (at the center of the circle) Emphasize these basic terms and use additional examples as necessary.

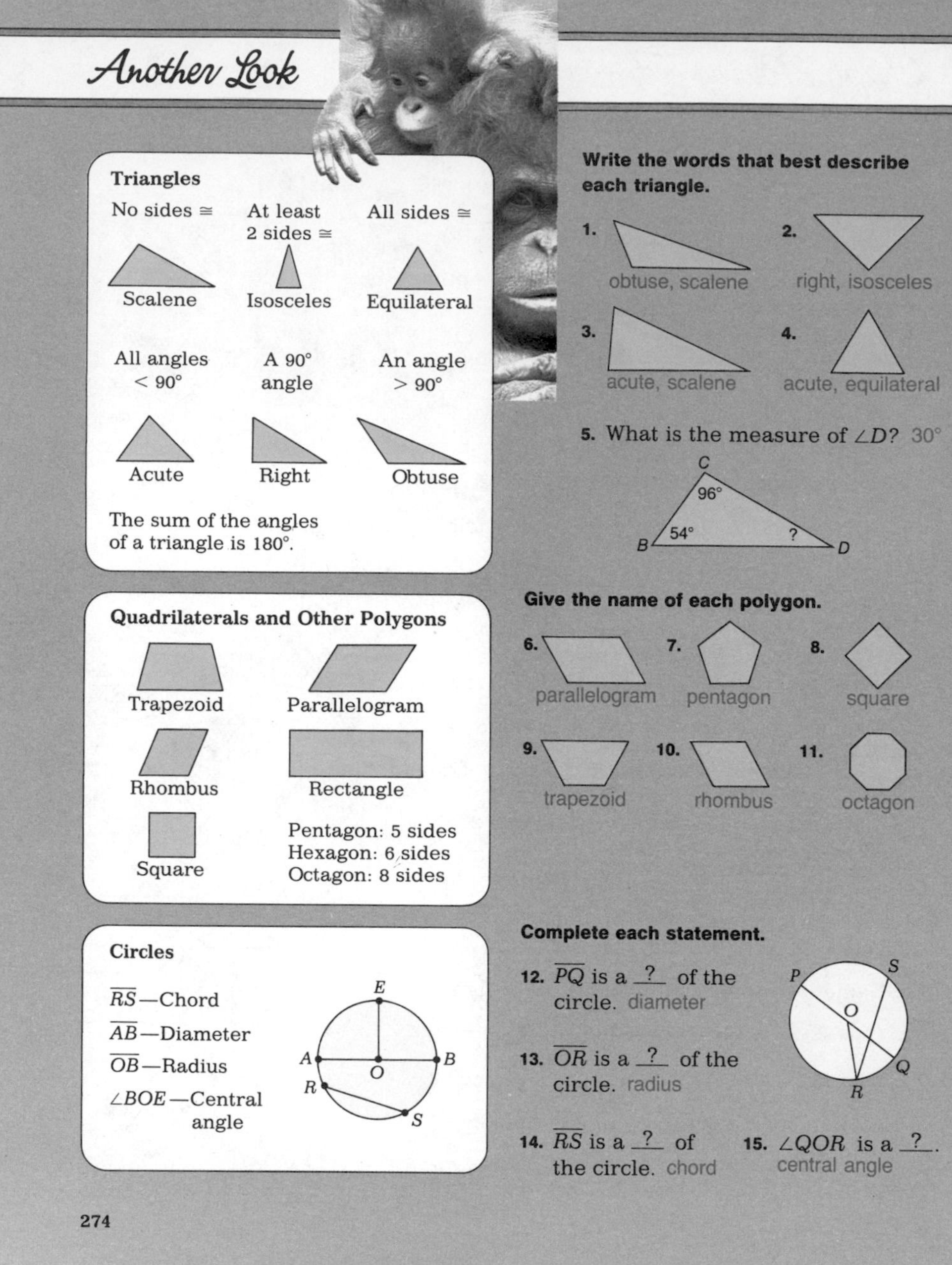


## Just for Teachers

### History of Math

Geometry is a branch of mathematics that originated more than twenty-five hundred years ago in the area around the Mediterranean. More of a philosophy than a practical explanation, Greek geometry eliminated the imperfections of measurement from the pure core of line, angle, and shape. In 300 B.C., Euclid compiled the essence of Greek geometry in the thirteen volumes of *Elements*. For more than two thousand years, *Elements* profoundly influenced other branches of mathematics.

As the nineteenth century began, certain mathematical discoveries challenged conventional explanations and philosophies in a number of branches. In geometry, debate over Euclid's parallel-lines axiom resulted in the formation of new geometries generally known as non-Euclidean. These new geometries explained some natural phenomena which Euclid's geometry could not. Perhaps the most widely known concept was the recognition that space is curved, i.e., the shortest distance between two points is not necessarily a straight line.

# Enrichment

### Geometric Constructions

To **construct** geometric figures, you use only a compass and the edge of a ruler. You do not use the ruler for measuring.

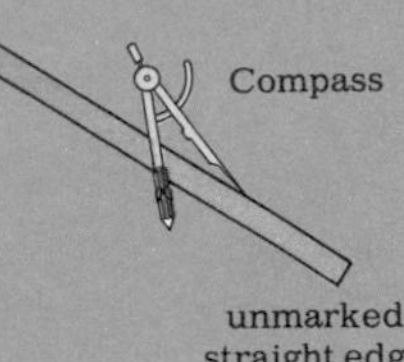


Here are some simple construction methods.

**Copying a Segment**

**Step 1**

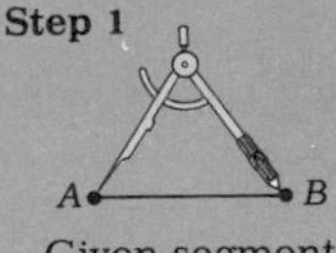


Given segment

Open your compass the length of the given segment.

**Step 2**

Draw a ray longer than the given segment. Use the opened compass to mark a copy of the segment on the ray.

**Copying an Angle**

**Step 1**

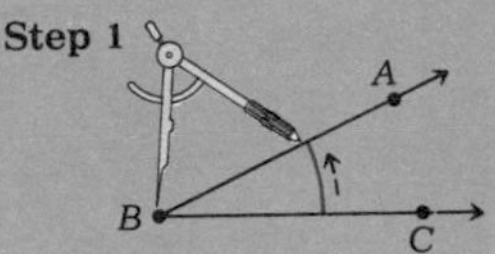


Given angle

Make an arc on the given angle.

**Step 2**

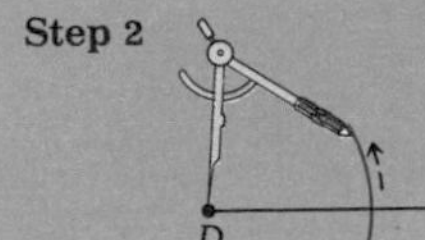


Draw a ray and draw an arc with the same radius on it.

**Step 3**

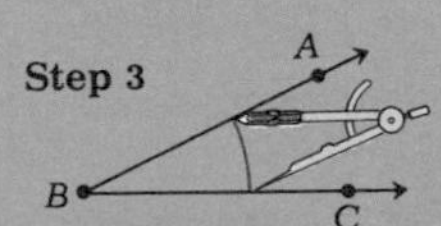


Measure the angle opening.

**Step 4**

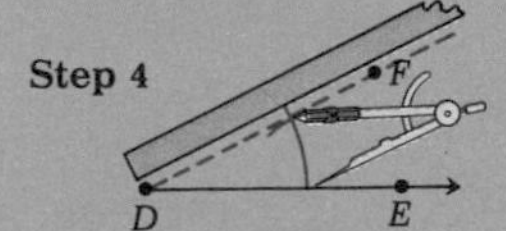


Mark the opening and draw the other side of the angle.

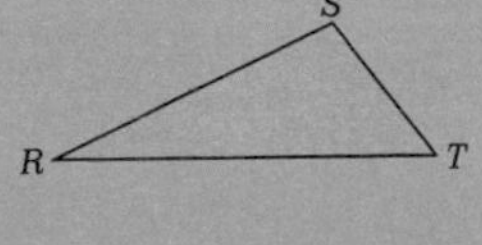


1. Use the idea of copying a segment to help you construct a triangle congruent to $\triangle RST$. student construction
2. Use the idea of copying an angle to help you start with this side and construct a triangle similar to $\triangle RST$. (Remember: the angles of similar triangles are congruent.) student construction

J ———————— K



The twentieth century has witnessed continued growth in geometry. One recently developed concept addresses the fact that both Euclidean and non-Euclidean geometries describe fairly regular shapes not usually occurring in nature. For example, Earth is considered a sphere, slightly flattened at the poles, when in actuality its surface is an irregular sphere. Fractal geometry—from the Latin word *fractus* meaning broken or fragmented—uses the computer to create irregular shapes resembling those found in nature. Developed and named in the 1970s by Benoit Mandelbrot of the Thomas J. Watson Research Center, fractal geometry has already been applied in such diverse fields as astronomy, seismology, meteorology, finance, and medicine. Shapes and curves drawn using fractal geometry accurately re-create and describe real-world phenomena such as shapes of clouds, stock market changes, and patterns of earthquake aftershocks.

## Using Page 275

This page is intended for those students who successfully completed the Chapter Review-Test on page 273. You may wish to assign this page as independent work while you use Another Look exercises to reteach the basic concepts and skills of the chapter. Or, you may decide that all students would benefit from exposure to this Enrichment activity.

**Lesson Development** Help familiarize students with the use of the compass and ruler by providing the tools for each student and by focusing on the discussion at the top of the page. Emphasize that the markings on the edge of the ruler are not to be used when completing a construction.

Then have students read the directions for copying a segment. Have students follow the directions to copy a given segment on their papers. If possible, use a chalkboard compass and straight edge to demonstrate this construction.

Next focus on the construction for copying an angle and have students complete the construction as you demonstrate it on the chalkboard. Use the word "congruent" to describe the results of each of these constructions.

**Exercises 1–2** Note in exercise 1 that the students must simply copy segment *RT,* then with compass point at *T* they must make an arc of a circle with radius the same as *ST.* With compass point at *R* they should make an arc of a circle with radius the same as *RS.* The intersection of these two arcs is the third vertice of the triangle which will be congruent to triangle *RST.* This construction involves the idea that if three sides of one triangle are congruent respectively to three matching sides of another triangle, the two triangles are congruent.

The construction in exercise 2 involves the idea that triangles are congruent if two sides and the included angle of one triangle are congruent respectively to matching sides and angle of the second triangle.

To extend this idea encourage students to make a triangle congruent to triangle *RST* by copying one side and two angles of the triangle.

# Review

## Using Page 276

The exercises on this page provide practice for maintaining cumulative skills. The emphasis in this Cumulative Review is on measurement with metric units (Chapter 7), multiplication and division of fractions (Chapter 9), and problem solving (Chapter 9).

**Item Analysis** The table below correlates the Cumulative Review items with objectives and with the student book pages on which the concepts or skills were taught.

| Items | Objectives | Related text pages |
|---|---|---|
| 1 | 7.1 | 170–175 |
| 2 | 7.2 | 178 |
| 3–5 | 9.2 | 236–238 |
| 6–8 | 9.1 | 226–233 |
| 9–11 | 9.3 | 239–243 |
| 12–13 | 9.4 | 234–235, 244–245 |

## *Cumulative Review*

Give the missing units.

1. 400 cm = 4 __?__
   A mm  B dm
   (C) m  D not given

2. 700 mL = 0.7 __?__
   A kg  (B) l
   C kl  D not given

3. Write a fraction for 0.25.
   A $\frac{2}{5}$  (B) $\frac{1}{4}$
   C $\frac{3}{4}$  D not given

4. Write a decimal for $\frac{4}{5}$.
   A 0.45  B 0.75
   (C) 0.8  D not given

5. Write a mixed decimal for $\frac{3}{8}$.
   A 0.375  B $0.62\frac{1}{2}$
   C $0.24\frac{1}{2}$  (D) not given

Multiply or divide.

6. $\frac{2}{5} \times \frac{3}{4}$
   A $\frac{5}{9}$  B $\frac{6}{9}$
   C $\frac{3}{20}$  (D) not given

7. $7 \times \frac{5}{14}$
   A $\frac{12}{14}$  B $5\frac{1}{2}$
   C $\frac{35}{98}$  (D) not given

8. $1\frac{1}{2} \times 1\frac{1}{2}$
   A 3  (B) $2\frac{1}{4}$
   C $1\frac{1}{4}$  D not given

9. $\frac{4}{9} \div \frac{4}{6}$
   A $\frac{8}{15}$  B $\frac{1}{3}$
   (C) $\frac{2}{3}$  D not given

10. $\frac{5}{9} \div 10$
    A 18  B $5\frac{5}{9}$
    (C) $\frac{1}{18}$  D not given

11. $6\frac{1}{4} \div \frac{5}{8}$
    A $\frac{32}{35}$  (B) 10
    C 18  D not given

12. Bud traveled for 4 h 16 min one day and 3 h 35 min the next day. What was his total traveling time?
    (A) 7 h 51 min  B 7 h 15 min
    C 8 h 1 min  D not given

13. Shelly wants to make 8 dog collars. She needs a piece of leather $\frac{3}{8}$ m long for each collar. How much leather does she need?
    (A) 3 m  B $3\frac{3}{8}$ m
    C $2\frac{3}{8}$ m  D not given

## Objectives

**11.1** Write a ratio as a fraction and use cross products to determine if the two ratios are equal.
**11.2** Write and solve proportions.
**11.3** Use proportions to solve problems involving similar figures or scale drawings.
**11.4** Use proportions to estimate distances on a map.
**11.5** Solve word problems using the 5-Point Checklist and cumulative computational skills.

## Summary

In this chapter students review and extend the concept of ratio and proportion. The idea of equal ratios is discussed, and equivalent fractions and cross products are then used to solve proportions. (A proportion is a statement that two ratios are equal.) Students then use the idea of similar triangles and proportion to solve problems involving height and scale drawings. A final lesson teaches students how to use a map scale to calculate distances.

## Mathematical Background

**Ratios** A ratio can be thought of as a comparison of two quantities. These comparisons are used in several different types of situations as listed below.

- To compare two different quantities of the same variable, e.g., amount of gas used yesterday to amount of gas used today, height last year compared to height this year.
- To compare part of a set to the whole set, e.g., season ticket holders to all ticket holders, apples to total pieces of fruit.
- To compare a part of a set to another part of the set, e.g., a set of people—compare males to females; a set of fruit—compare apples to oranges; a school class—compare boys to girls; a set of measurements—compare centimeters to meters (scale drawings).
- To compare two different variables measured in the same units, e.g., area of school playground to area of school building, quarts of lemon juice to quarts of water.
- To express a rate, e.g., kilometers per hour, meters per second, parts made per day. Note that some people differentiate between rates and ratios, since rates involve different variables and different units.

Ratios are expressed in various ways, for example: 3:4, 3 to 4, 3 out of 4, 3 per 4, and $\frac{3}{4}$.

To apply ratios to the solution of problems it is important to decide when two ratios are equal. If a specific pair of fractions has a common denominator, it is easy to tell by looking at the numerators whether or not the two fractions are equivalent and the ratios they represent are equal. Thus, for some ratios a look at the two fractions will tell if they are equivalent and the ratios are equal. For other ratios it is necessary either to reduce the fractions or to check cross products to make the decision.

**Solving Proportions** A proportion, an equation involving equal ratios in which one number is not known, can be solved using the idea of cross products. Listed below are four different types of proportions and their solutions with the variable in different positions.

$$\frac{3}{4} = \frac{n}{16}$$
$$3 \times 16 = 4 \times n$$
$$48 = 4 \times n$$
$$48 \div 4 = n$$
$$12 = n$$

$$\frac{3}{4} = \frac{12}{n}$$
$$3 \times n = 4 \times 12$$
$$3 \times n = 48$$
$$n = 48 \div 3$$
$$n = 16$$

$$\frac{3}{n} = \frac{12}{16}$$
$$3 \times 16 = n \times 12$$
$$48 = 12 \times n$$
$$48 \div 12 = n$$
$$4 = n$$

$$\frac{n}{4} = \frac{12}{16}$$
$$n \times 16 = 4 \times 12$$
$$16 \times n = 48$$
$$n = 48 \div 16$$
$$n = 3$$

Note that the first equation indicates that the cross products are equal since the equation was a proportion. In each case, it was necessary to multiply and then divide to find the missing number. After they have solved proportions, encourage students to substitute the number in the equation and use equivalent fractions or cross products to check to see if the solution is correct.

**Problem Solving** After students learn to solve proportions, it is important to provide a variety of situations in which ratios and proportions are used to solve problems. In this chapter, students are given the following types of problem-solving situations in which they can apply their skills in ratio and proportion.

- Problem solving using data from a story. In this lesson students look in a story for the ratio of heights or distances and then set up proportions to solve the problems.
- Using proportions to find heights. In these problems students use the idea that when two triangles are similar the ratios of the matching sides are equal. Students then write and solve proportions to find heights.
- Problem solving using data from a scale drawing or map. Using a scale for a drawing or map such as 2 cm = 3 m, we can form a scale ratio 2:3 and set up a proportion.

Finally, in this chapter the strategies developed for solving nonroutine problems are reviewed and applied.

### Vocabulary

| | | |
|---|---|---|
| ratio | equivalent fractions | proportion |
| equal ratio | cross product | scale ratio |

## Error Analysis

This chapter discusses the concepts of rate and proportion. A ratio is a comparison of two quantities or sets and can be expressed as a fraction. A proportion is an equation stating that two ratios are equal. These concepts provide a further dimension to students' basic mathematic skills.

The ideas of ratio and proportion, if not fully understood, provide potential for many errors. While some errors reflect misunderstanding of the concepts, others are the result of basic computational inaccuracies. Possible error patterns are given below.

**Error Pattern 1**

| | |
|---|---|
| $\frac{2}{3} = \frac{n}{12}$ | $\frac{4}{5} = \frac{n}{60}$ |
| $2n = 36$ | $4n = 300$ |
| $n = 18$ | $n = 75$ |

**Diagnosis** The student does not understand the idea of proportion as equivalent fractions and has multiplied numerators and then denominators as in multiplying fractions. The student has obviously not applied cross multiplication to check for equivalence.

**Remediation** First, review the idea of equivalent fractions. Use models to show that $\frac{1}{2}$ and $\frac{2}{4}$ are equivalent fractions. Then show that the cross products $1 \times 4$ and $2 \times 2$ are equal. Next show this relationship as a proportion $\frac{1}{2} = \frac{n}{4}$. Work through the equation to show how to use cross products to find the unknown factor.

**Error Pattern 2**

$\frac{3}{4} = \frac{6}{7}$ $\quad$ $\frac{5}{6} = \frac{7}{8}$ $\quad$ $\frac{6}{9} = \frac{8}{11}$ $\quad$ $\frac{1}{4} = \frac{5}{8}$

**Diagnosis** To create an equivalent fraction, the student has added an amount to both numerator and denominator instead of multiplying. This performance indicates a lack of understanding of the meaning of equivalent fractions.

**Remediation** Using one of the incorrect equations, for instance $\frac{3}{4} = \frac{6}{7}$, show $\frac{3}{4}$ and $\frac{6}{7}$ on a number line and elicit from students that these fractions are not equal.

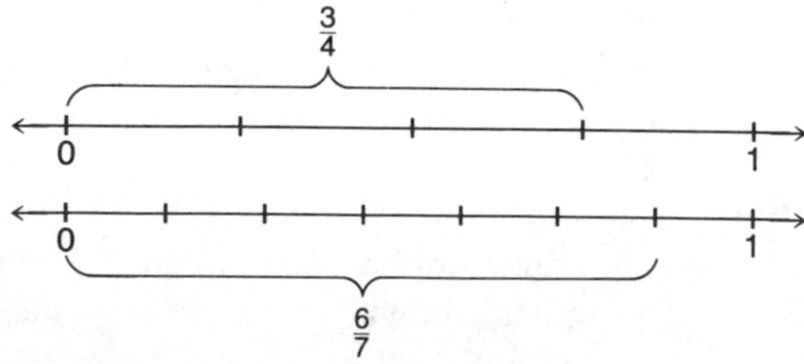


From this example, discuss how the error was made in the original equation. Then work through to find several equivalent fractions. Show how to use cross products to check accuracy, then illustrate these fractions on the number line.

## Problem Solving

### Teaching Students to Formulate Problems

The most important element in improving students' problem-solving performance is solving and discussing many problems. However, improving performance in problem solving involves more than simply doing a task over and over again. Formulating problems, a valuable component in an elementary school problem-solving program, focuses the student's attention on particular parts of the problem-solving process in isolation from actually solving problems. Some of the skills needed in formulating problems are:

- asking a question that makes sense,
- incorporating all relevant data in a story,
- incorporating action in a story appropriate for the operation(s) needed to find a solution.

The following two examples are situations in which students are asked to formulate a problem.

"Make up a story that you could solve using the equation $45 + 26 = ?$"

"Make up a story that this picture would help you to solve."

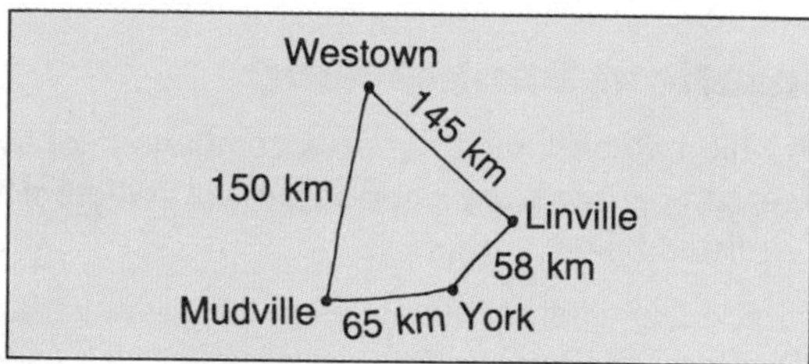


Numerous opportunities to formulate problems can facilitate the improvement of a student's problem-solving performance. Many such opportunities are included in this program. These experiences require very little teaching time, provide success experiences for most students, and are easy to generate. They should be given to students on a regular basis. For example, three days each week, the Quick Review in the Teacher's Edition could be followed by a "formulating-a-problem" activity. Providing frequent experiences in formulating problems can be a valuable addition to a problem-solving program.

## Special Education

The concepts of ratio and proportion can be difficult for special-needs students, depending on their developmental levels. Supplying numerous concrete examples of the ideas presented in the chapter and the teaching tips below will help special-needs students with this material.

### Seeing Ratios and Making Comparisons

The development of the ability to make comparisons requires that students be able to sort out the members of various groups according to some membership rule. An exercise to help build this skill is the following: Set a comparison rule such as the number of students present to number of students absent. Use student names on tagboard with small adhesive-backed magnets on the back of the cards to sort the names on the chalkboard. Then make the counts of the comparison as shown below.

This activity can be extended to compare other subsets of the class: boys to girls, boys to total class, girls to total class, and so on. With these exercises the comparison ideas and the directions of the comparisons will become familiar to the students. After the number of girls is compared to boys, turn the comparison around and compare the number of boys to girls. The fact that the order of the comparison is important should be stressed.

### Establishing Equal Ratios

Equal ratios can be modeled with colored game chips in the following manner: A given ratio such as 2 to 3 $\left(2{:}3 \text{ or } \frac{2}{3}\right)$ can be shown by placing 2 red chips on one side of a line and 3 white chips on the other side of the line. The number of chips on each side can then be doubled by placing another chip of the same color on top of the chips already in place. The total number of chips on each side can then be compared $\left(4 \text{ to } 6,\ 4{:}6, \text{ or } \frac{4}{6}\right)$. The two piles can be taken apart as shown below to illustrate that the original ratio of 2 to 3 is still true. Emphasize that the process of multiplying the chips by 2 only doubled the numbers in the comparison, not the ratio.

2 to 3 → 2 × 2 2 × 3 → 4 to 6

### Setting Up Proportions

Setting up equivalent ratios in problem-solving situations is often a difficult task for special-needs students. A game to help students deal with this difficulty is "Make a Proportion." For students to play this game have available index cards on which the numbers 1 through 15 are written. Students can be grouped into two or three teams. Six of the number cards are displayed, and students make as many proportions as they can from the six cards. For each correct proportion, a team scores 2 points. One such example of proportions is shown below.

| 1 | 7 | 8 |
|---|---|---|
| 2 | 4 | 14 |

$\frac{2}{14} = \frac{1}{7}$ $\frac{1}{2} = \frac{4}{8}$ $\frac{1}{2} = \frac{7}{14}$

$\frac{2}{8} = \frac{1}{4}$

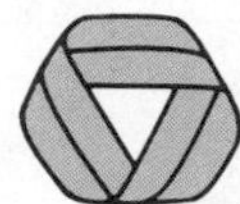

## Subject Integration

Subject matter related to other areas of the curriculum has been integrated into the following lessons. This provides an opportunity to highlight the interaction between mathematics and other subjects.

**Consumer Awareness** Visiting a bakery, pages 282–283

**Fine Arts** Reading classics, pages 284–285

**Science** Learning about dinosaurs, pages 290–291

**Social Studies** Visiting Yellowstone Park, pages 292–293

# Management Guide

| Teaching Chapter 11 | | | | Meeting Individual Needs | | | | | |
|---|---|---|---|---|---|---|---|---|---|
| Objectives | Chapter Content | Pages | TRB Test Items | Lesson Assignments | | | Follow Up | | |
| | | | | Minimum | Average | Extended | Reteaching | Enrichment | Practice |
| | Chapter Opener | 277 | | | | | | | |
| **11.1** Write a ratio as a fraction and use cross products to determine if the two ratios are equal. | Ratio | 278–279 | 1–4 | 1–6 / 1–16 | 1–6 / 1–16 | 1–6 / 1–16, TM | SE5 Ch 15 RS 65 | ES 65 | PS 106 |
| | Equal Ratios: Cross Products | 280–281 | 5–8 | 1–22, SK | 1–22, SK | 1–23, SK | SE 5 Ch 15 RS 66 | ES 66 | PS 107 |
| **11.2** Write and solve problems. | Solving Proportions | 282–283 | 9–12 | 1–26 | 1–28, TM | 1–28, TM | RS 67 | ES 67 | PS 108 |
| **11.3** Use proportions to solve problems involving similar figures or scale drawings. | Similar Figures | 286–287 | 13 | 1–6, SK | 1–7, SK | 1–8, SK | | | PS 110 |
| | Using Proportions to Find Heights | 288–289 | 14 | | 1–7 | 1–8, TM | RS 68 | ES 68 | PS 111 |
| | Using Scale Drawings | 290 | 15 | 1–3 | 1–3 | 1–3 | | | PS 112 |
| **11.4** Use proportions to estimate distances on a map. | Using a Map Scale to Estimate Distances | 292 | 16–19 | | 1–6 | 1–7 | RS 69 | ES 69 | PS 113 |
| **11.5** Solve word problems using the 5-Point Checklist and cumulative computational skills. | Problem Solving: Using Data from a Story | 284–285 | | 1–5, 7–9 | 1–10 | 1–11 | | | PS 109 |
| | Problem Solving: Using Data from Scale Drawings | 291 | 20–24 | 1–5 | 1–6 | 1–7 | | | |
| | Problem Solving: Practice | 293 | | 1–6 | 1–7 | 1–8 | | | |
| | Problem Solving: Using the Strategies | 294 | | | | | | | |
| | Chapter Review-Test | 295 | | | | | | | |
| | Another Look/Enrichment | 296–297 | | | | | | | |
| | Cumulative Review | 298 | | | | | | | |

**SE5** Student Edition, Book 5
**RS** Reteaching Supplement
**ES** Enrichment Supplement
**PS** Practice Supplement
**TM** Think Math
**SK** Skillkeeper
**TRB** Teacher's Resource Book

## Masters for Use

**. . . before Chapter 11**

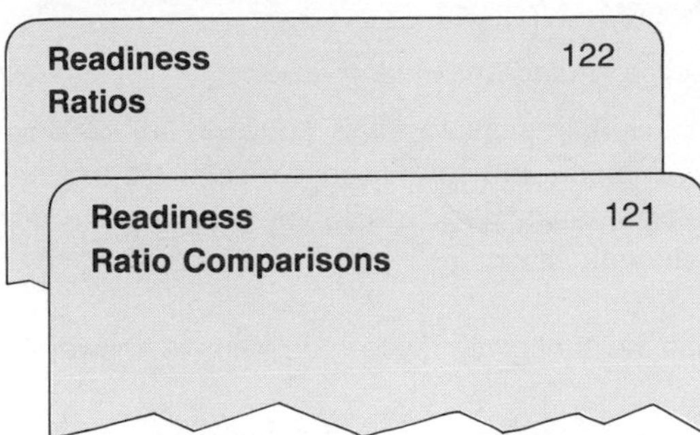


**. . . during Chapter 11**

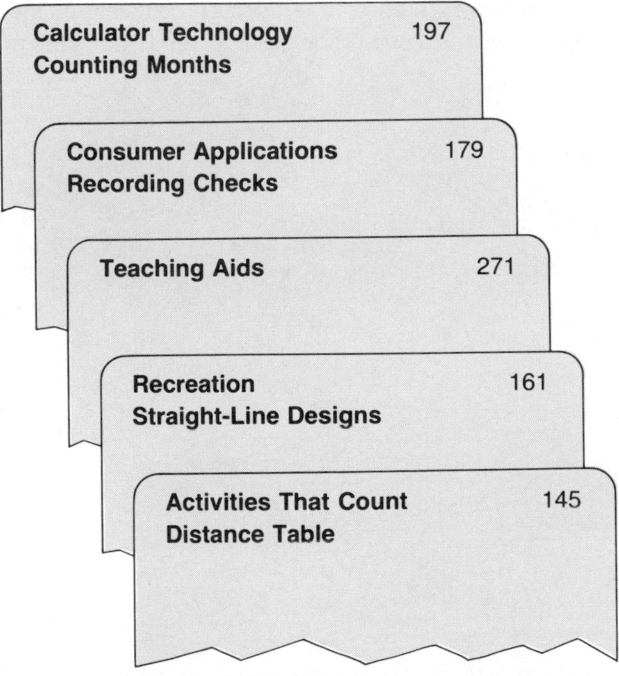


**. . . after Chapter 11**

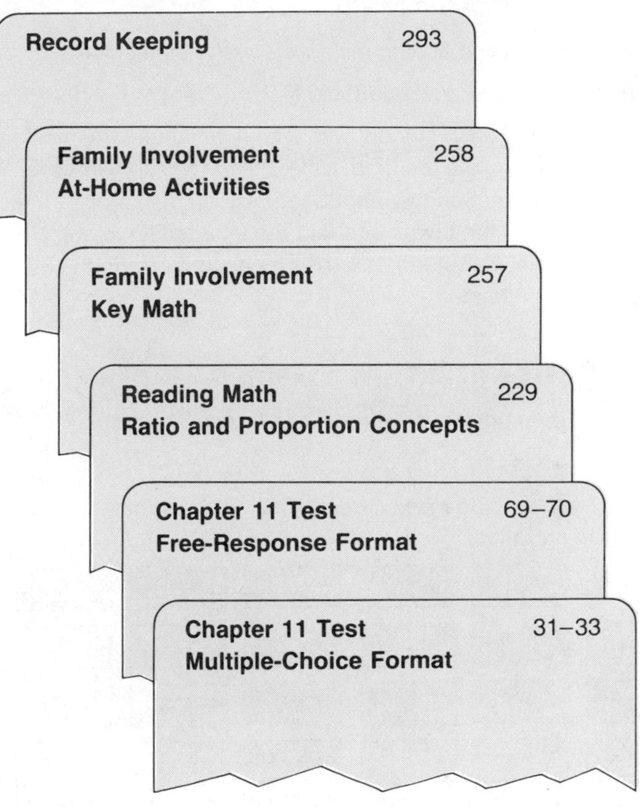


## Supplements

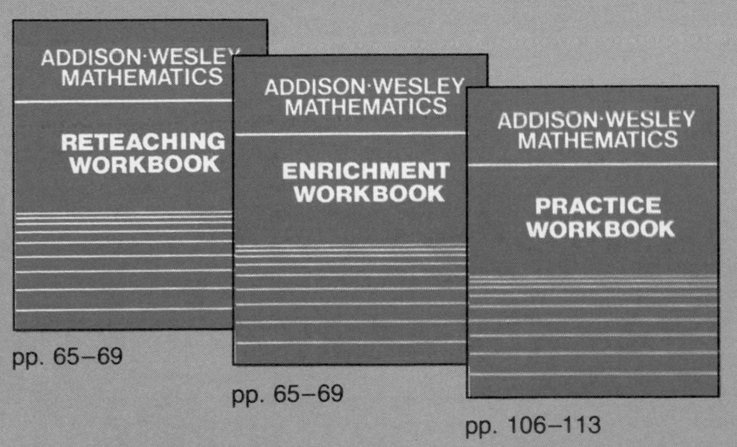


pp. 65–69

pp. 65–69

pp. 106–113

## Other Addison-Wesley Resources

**Books and Kits**

*The Arithmetic Primer* pp. 106–113

*Problem-Solving Experiences in Mathematics, Grade 6,* Problems 29, 30, 64, 65, 89, 104, 125, 144

# Activities That Count

Activities That Count are designed for use throughout this and subsequent chapters. Before beginning Chapter 11, you may wish to review these activities and select the ones you consider appropriate for your class.

## Distance Table  Math Lab

**Purpose** To practice finding distances with a map scale

**Materials** Map and distance table (TRB p. 145)

**Activity** Provide each student with a copy of the activity master. Have students complete the map scale, then make up names for 7 towns and place them on the map. Students can then measure the distances between the towns and use the information to complete the distance table. Tell students to use measurements to the nearest tenth of a centimeter.

## Ratio Concentration  Game

**Purpose** To recognize the three ways to express ratio

**Materials** 15 index cards

**Preparation** Cut the index cards in half. On each half, write one of the following ratios:

| | | | | | |
|---|---|---|---|---|---|
| 3 to 4 | 3:4 | $\frac{3}{4}$ | 1 to 10 | 1:10 | $\frac{1}{10}$ |
| 4 to 5 | 4:5 | $\frac{4}{5}$ | 10 to 1 | 10:1 | $\frac{10}{1}$ |
| 2 to 7 | 2:7 | $\frac{2}{7}$ | 3 to 10 | 3:10 | $\frac{3}{10}$ |
| 1 to 5 | 1:5 | $\frac{1}{5}$ | 8 to 15 | 8:15 | $\frac{8}{15}$ |
| 5 to 4 | 5:4 | $\frac{5}{4}$ | 9 to 25 | 9:25 | $\frac{9}{25}$ |

**Activity** Cards are mixed and placed facedown. Each player in turn selects two cards in an attempt to find two cards naming the same ratio. Player may continue to choose cards as long as the cards match. When the player fails to make a match, the cards are returned facedown to the playing surface and the next player takes a turn. The player who matches the most cards is the winner.

## School Survey  Project

**Purpose** To practice finding and writing ratios

**Activity** Students work in pairs or small groups to survey other sixth-grade students to see how many schools each student has attended while in elementary school. The survey could include fifth- or seventh-grade students, if necessary, to make a sampling of 35 to 40 students.

Students then use the survey results to write ratios to answer the questions below.

1. How many students had attended only 1 school?
2. How many students had attended only 2 schools?
3. How many students had attended 3 or more schools?
4. How many students had attended 4 or more schools?

When the survey of the sixth-grade students is complete, suggest that students survey a second-grade class to see if the ratios are the same.

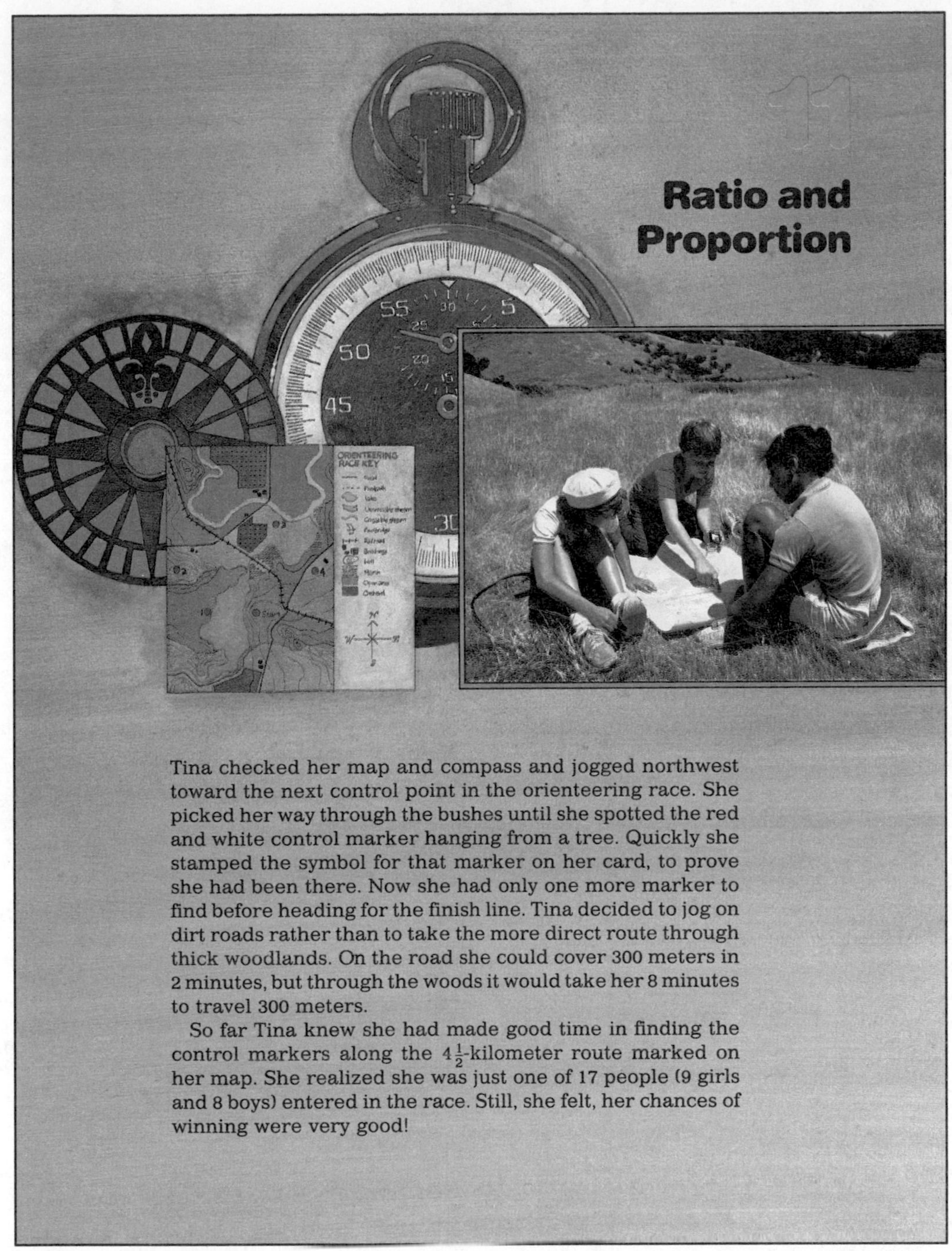
11

# Ratio and Proportion

Tina checked her map and compass and jogged northwest toward the next control point in the orienteering race. She picked her way through the bushes until she spotted the red and white control marker hanging from a tree. Quickly she stamped the symbol for that marker on her card, to prove she had been there. Now she had only one more marker to find before heading for the finish line. Tina decided to jog on dirt roads rather than to take the more direct route through thick woodlands. On the road she could cover 300 meters in 2 minutes, but through the woods it would take her 8 minutes to travel 300 meters.

So far Tina knew she had made good time in finding the control markers along the $4\frac{1}{2}$-kilometer route marked on her map. She realized she was just one of 17 people (9 girls and 8 boys) entered in the race. Still, she felt, her chances of winning were very good!

## Introducing the Chapter

**Discussion** Explain to students that in this chapter they will be learning about ratio and proportion. Then encourage students to discuss various kinds of footraces in which they or their friends may have participated. Point out that the story that opens this chapter concerns a special kind of race called *orienteering.* Explain that orienteering is different from most other races in that each contestant runs alone and, using a map and compass, selects his or her own route for the checkpoints that are indicated on the map. After students have had an opportunity to read the story and examine the art, encourage them to make up some questions based on the data in the story. As you teach the chapter, you may wish to refer back to this page and pose the questions suggested below.

## Follow-Up Questions

**After Page 279** Tina was one of 7 entrants in the orienteering race who were less than 14 years old. The other 10 entrants were older than 14. What is the ratio, in fraction form, of entrants older than 14 to entrants younger than 14? $\left(\frac{10}{7}\right)$

**After Page 281** For every 2 km Kyle traveled on the road during the race, he had to travel 3 km through fields and woods. Give this ratio in fraction form and three other ratios equal to it. $\left(\frac{2}{3}, \frac{4}{6}, \frac{6}{9}, \frac{8}{12}, \ldots\right)$

**After Page 292** Each centimeter on Tina's map represented an actual distance of 150 m. Tina found that the second checkpoint was 8 cm from the third checkpoint on her map. What was the actual distance between the second and the third checkpoint? (1,200 m)

# Ratio

**Quick Review** Students write answers in lowest terms.

$\frac{1}{4}+\frac{1}{3}=\frac{7}{12}$ $\frac{11}{12}+\frac{5}{6}=1\frac{3}{4}$ $\frac{9}{10}-\frac{1}{5}=\frac{7}{10}$ $\frac{4}{5}+\frac{8}{15}=1\frac{1}{3}$ $\frac{2}{3}+\frac{8}{9}=1\frac{5}{9}$

$\frac{5}{9}-\frac{1}{3}=\frac{2}{9}$ $\frac{15}{16}-\frac{1}{2}=\frac{7}{16}$ $\frac{2}{3}-\frac{1}{9}=\frac{5}{9}$ $\frac{13}{20}-\frac{2}{5}=\frac{1}{4}$

**Lesson Focus** To write ratios as fractions

## Ideas for Getting Started

Generate a discussion in which you name examples from the classroom using the language of ratio. It is not necessary to give a detailed explanation of what ratio means. For example, say: "The ratio of boys to girls is ____ to ____. The ratio of the number of windows to the number of doors is ____ to ____. The ratio of erasers to pieces of chalk is ____ to ____. The ratio of students absent to students present is ____ to ____."

## Using Page 278

**Lesson Development** Have students read the sentence that defines ratio and direct students' attention to the illustration. "We say that the ratio of blue bikes to red bikes is 3 to 4. What is the ratio of red bikes to blue bikes?" (4 to 3) Use this example to show how to write the ratio as 3:4, the phrase "3 to 4," or the fraction $\frac{3}{4}$. Elicit other ratio statements from students and ask volunteers to show the ratio using one of the methods discussed.

**Exercises 1–6** Before assigning the exercises, review the various meanings of ratio (see chapter overview, page 277A). These exercises are designed to illustrate some of the different types of ratios (or rates). In exercise 1 the language "3 out of every 5" is commonly used to express a ratio that compares a part of the set with the whole set. The ratio in exercise 2 could be described as 3 to 7. The language "2 for 7" could be used to describe the ratio in exercise 3. Exercise 4 uses a common way to describe scale on a map. In exercise 5 the ratio of kilometers to hours is used when describing a rate of speed. Such a ratio is sometimes called a unitary ratio, since it compares a certain number of kilometers with 1 hour.

Point out that each ratio, regardless of the language, can be written using a fraction. Be sure students understand that when the numerator and denominator of the fraction are interchanged, a different ratio has been established.

## Ratio

A **ratio** is used to compare two quantities. In the long-distance bike race, 3 of the bikes are blue and 4 of the bikes are red.

The ratio of blue bikes to red bikes is

**3 to 4**

We show this ratio by writing **3:4** or $\frac{3}{4}$.

Here are some other examples of how ratios are used. Write each ratio as a fraction.

1. In the long-distance bike race 3 out of every 5 riders are less than 18 years old. What is the ratio of **riders less than 18 to all riders?** $\frac{3}{5}$
2. When the pedal on a bike has turned 3 times in fourth gear, the rear wheel has turned 7 times. What is the ratio of **pedal turns to wheel turns?** $\frac{3}{7}$
3. Isabel bought 2 tickets for seats in the grandstand for $7. What is the ratio of **tickets to dollars?** $\frac{2}{7}$
4. A map showing the race course compares centimeters on the map to kilometers on the course by using the scale 1:5. What is the ratio of **centimeters to kilometers?** $\frac{1}{5}$
5. Kyle traveled an average of 20 km for every hour while bike riding. This average speed is written 20 km/h. What is the ratio of **kilometers to hours?** $\frac{20}{1}$
6. The refreshment stand sold 10 cases of beverages in 3 hours. What is the ratio of **cases to hours?** $\frac{10}{3}$



## Follow Up

### Reteaching

Place 5 red counters and 7 white counters in a cup. Shake the cup and roll the counters onto the table. Discuss how to compare the number of red counters to the number of white counters. If there are 5 red counters to 7 white counters, the ratio is 5 to 7. Discuss how this can be written—5 to 7, 5:7, or $\frac{5}{7}$. Then discuss what the ratio would be in comparing white counters to red counters. $\left(7 \text{ to } 5, 7{:}5, \text{ or } \frac{7}{5}\right)$ Make sure students understand this difference. Work through this procedure with several combinations of red and white counters.

### Enrichment

Have students go on a "Ratio Hunt" to find ratios that describe sets of objects inside or outside the classroom. For example, suggest that they find the ratio of the number of chairs to the number of tables, teachers to students, boys to girls, and so on.

| Assignment Guide | | | |
|---|---|---|---|
| | Minimum | Average | Extended |
| page 278 | 1–6 | 1–6 | 1–6 |
| page 279 | 1–16 | 1–16 | 1–16, TM |

Use the Bike Race Facts Sheet. Give each ratio as a fraction.

| Bike Race Facts Sheet | | |
|---|---|---|
| Number of riders entered | | 36 |
| Girls | 15 | |
| Boys | 12 | |
| Women | 4 | |
| Men | 5 | |
| Number of riders finishing | | 32 |
| Total kilometers | | 75 |
| Uphill | 20 | |
| Downhill | 15 | |
| Last year's winning time | | 3 h 20 min |
| This year's winning time | | 3 h 15 min |

1. number of riders finishing to number entered $\frac{32}{36}$
2. number of women entered to number of girls entered $\frac{4}{15}$
3. number of girls entered to number of women entered $\frac{15}{4}$
4. number of females entered to number of males entered $\frac{19}{17}$
5. number of uphill kilometers to total number of kilometers $\frac{20}{75}$
6. This year's winning time in minutes to last year's winning time in minutes. $\frac{195}{200}$

Write these ratios as fractions.

7. Bike flags: 2 for \$5. What is the ratio of flags to dollars? $\frac{2}{5}$
8. Arturo rode 47 km in 2 h. What is the ratio of kilometers to hours? $\frac{47}{2}$
9. Out of every 8 bikes in the race, 7 were 10-speed bikes. What is the ratio of all bikes to 10-speed bikes? $\frac{8}{7}$
10. A bike travels 29 m for every 14 times the wheel turns. What is the ratio of meters to wheel turns? $\frac{29}{14}$

11. 4 to 5 $\frac{4}{5}$
12. 7:10 $\frac{7}{10}$
13. 3 out of 7 $\frac{3}{7}$
14. 3 for every 2 $\frac{3}{2}$
15. 2 for 3 $\frac{2}{3}$
16. 1 of every 5 $\frac{1}{5}$

**Think Math**

**Discovering a Pattern**

Find the patterns in these ratios and give the next three ratios.

$\frac{1}{2}, \frac{3}{1}, \frac{3}{4}, \frac{7}{■}, \frac{■}{■}, \frac{■}{■}, \frac{■}{■}, \frac{11}{7}, \frac{18}{11}, \frac{29}{18}$

$\frac{3}{2}, \frac{7}{5}, \frac{17}{12}, \frac{41}{29}, \frac{■}{■}, \frac{■}{■}, \frac{■}{■}, \frac{99}{70}, \frac{239}{169}, \frac{577}{408}$



## Using Page 279

**Exercises 1–6** These exercises refer to the Bike Race Facts Sheet. Note that in exercises 4 and 6 students must use more than one operation to find the answers.

**Exercises 7–10** Encourage students to read these problems carefully. Continue to emphasize that the order makes a difference when giving the numbers in a ratio.

**Exercises 11–16** Each of these exercises illustrates different phrases or language used to express ratio. In each case, the ratio can be written as a fraction. After students have completed these exercises, have them reverse the numerator and denominator and give the phrase that would describe that ratio.

**Think Math** Encourage students to explore the pattern in these ratios. The first pattern can be described as follows: The sum of the numerator and denominator of one fraction is equal to the numerator of the following fraction. The denominator of each fraction is the numerator of the fraction that precedes it.

The second pattern is as follows: The sum of the numerator and denominator of one fraction is equal to the denominator of the fraction that follows it. Find the numerator of the following fraction by adding its denominator to the denominator of the preceding fraction.

**Reteaching Supplement,** page 65

**Enrichment Supplement,** page 65

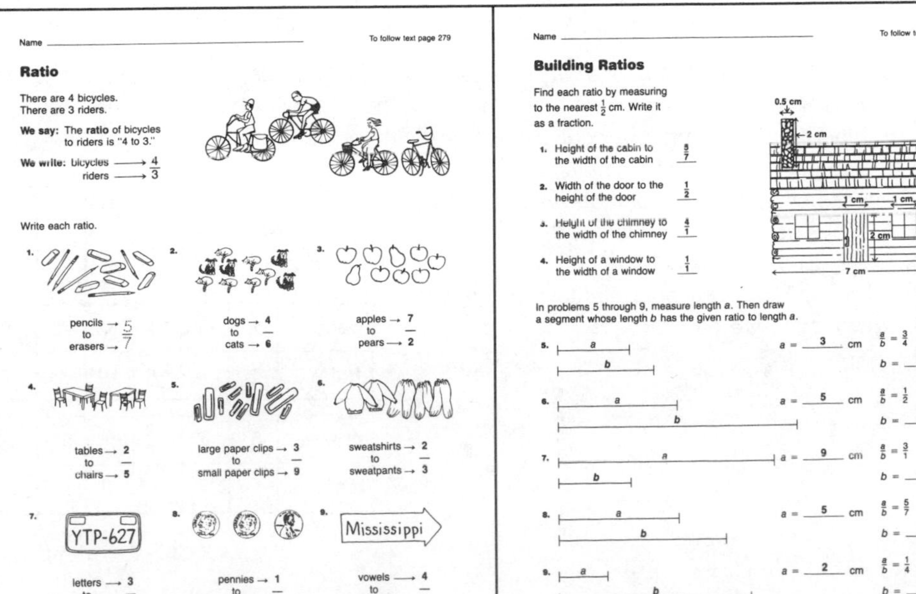

Name ______ To follow text page 279

**Ratio**

There are 4 bicycles.
There are 3 riders.

**We say:** The **ratio** of bicycles to riders is "4 to 3."

**We write:** bicycles → 4 / riders → 3

Write each ratio.

1. pencils → 5 to erasers → 7
2. dogs → 4 to cats → 6
3. apples → 7 to pears → 2
4. tables → 2 to chairs → 5
5. large paper clips → 3 to small paper clips → 9
6. sweatshirts → 2 to sweatpants → 3
7. YTP-627 — letters → 3 to numbers → 3
8. pennies → 1 to dimes → 2
9. Mississippi — vowels → 4 to consonants → 7

Name ______ To follow text page 279

**Building Ratios**

Find each ratio by measuring to the nearest $\frac{1}{2}$ cm. Write it as a fraction.



1. Height of the cabin to the width of the cabin $\frac{5}{7}$
2. Width of the door to the height of the door $\frac{1}{2}$
3. Height of the chimney to the width of the chimney $\frac{4}{1}$
4. Height of a window to the width of a window $\frac{1}{1}$

In problems 5 through 9, measure length $a$. Then draw a segment whose length $b$ has the given ratio to length $a$.

5. $a$ = 3 cm, $\frac{a}{b} = \frac{3}{4}$, $b$ = 4 cm
6. $a$ = 5 cm, $\frac{a}{b} = \frac{1}{2}$, $b$ = 10 cm
7. $a$ = 9 cm, $\frac{a}{b} = \frac{3}{1}$, $b$ = 3 cm
8. $a$ = 5 cm, $\frac{a}{b} = \frac{5}{7}$, $b$ = 7 cm
9. $a$ = 2 cm, $\frac{a}{b} = \frac{1}{4}$, $b$ = 8 cm

**Practice Supplement,** page 106

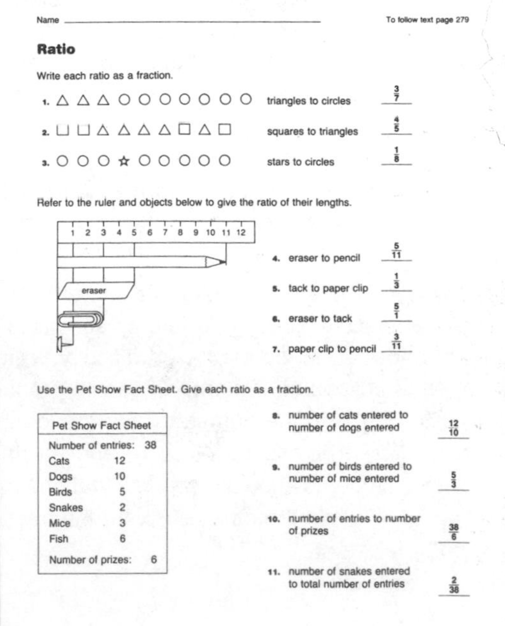

Name ______ To follow text page 279

**Ratio**

Write each ratio as a fraction.

1. △ △ △ ○ ○ ○ ○ ○ ○ ○ triangles to circles $\frac{3}{7}$
2. □ □ △ △ △ △ □ △ □ squares to triangles $\frac{4}{5}$
3. ○ ○ ○ ☆ ○ ○ ○ ○ ○ stars to circles $\frac{1}{8}$

Refer to the ruler and objects below to give the ratio of their lengths.



4. eraser to pencil $\frac{5}{11}$
5. tack to paper clip $\frac{1}{3}$
6. eraser to tack $\frac{5}{1}$
7. paper clip to pencil $\frac{3}{11}$

Use the Pet Show Fact Sheet. Give each ratio as a fraction.

| Pet Show Fact Sheet | |
|---|---|
| Number of entries: | 38 |
| Cats | 12 |
| Dogs | 10 |
| Birds | 5 |
| Snakes | 2 |
| Mice | 3 |
| Fish | 6 |
| Number of prizes: | 6 |

8. number of cats entered to number of dogs entered $\frac{12}{10}$
9. number of birds entered to number of mice entered $\frac{5}{3}$
10. number of entries to number of prizes $\frac{38}{6}$
11. number of snakes entered to total number of entries $\frac{2}{38}$

# Ratio

**Quick Review** Students tell whether each fraction is equal to $\frac{1}{2}$, $\frac{1}{3}$, or $\frac{1}{4}$.

$\frac{9}{27}$ $\frac{1}{3}$ $\frac{12}{24}$ $\frac{1}{2}$ $\frac{50}{150}$ $\frac{1}{3}$ $\frac{12}{36}$ $\frac{1}{3}$ $\frac{80}{160}$ $\frac{1}{2}$ $\frac{25}{100}$ $\frac{1}{4}$ $\frac{12}{48}$ $\frac{1}{4}$ $\frac{9}{18}$ $\frac{1}{2}$ $\frac{16}{64}$ $\frac{1}{4}$

**Lesson Focus** To use equivalent fractions and cross products to find equal ratios

## Ideas for Getting Started

Display this sign on the chalkboard.

**Amusement Park**
8 rides
for $5

"What is the ratio of rides to dollars?" $\left(\frac{8}{5}\right)$ "How many rides can you get for $10?" (16) "For $20?" (32) "For $25?" (40) As students answer these questions, fill in a table on the chalkboard as shown below.

| Rides | 8 | 16 | 24 | 32 | 40 | 48 | 56 | 64 |
|---|---|---|---|---|---|---|---|---|
| Dollars | 5 | 10 | 15 | 20 | 25 | 30 | 35 | 40 |

Tell students that the ratios $\frac{8}{5}, \frac{16}{10}, \frac{24}{15}, \frac{32}{20}, \frac{40}{25}$, and so on, from the table are called equal ratios.

## Using Page 280

**Lesson Development** Read and discuss the paragraph at the top of the page. Tell students that two ratios are equal if the fractions used to represent them are equivalent. Then have students read the two methods of deciding whether two fractions are equivalent. For method 1 ask: "What number can be multiplied by both the numerator and denominator of $\frac{5}{6}$ to give the fraction $\frac{10}{12}$?" (2) "Since $\frac{10}{12}$ can be built from $\frac{5}{6}$ by multiplying both numerator and denominator by the same number, we know the two fractions are equivalent." For method 2, ask: "What is the product of the numerator of the first fraction and the denominator of the second fraction?" (5 × 12, or 60) "What is the product of the denominator of the first fraction and the numerator of the second fraction?" (5 × 12, or 60) "What is the product of the denominator of the first fraction and the numerator of the second fraction?" (6 × 10, or 60) Remind students that the cross products are equal, the fractions are equivalent, thus the ratios are equivalent. Work through the example showing that we can use equivalent fractions to produce equal ratios.

**Warm Up** In exercise 1, observe students to see if they can use the idea of equivalent fractions to find equal ratios. If students have difficulty, remind them that fractions equivalent to $\frac{2}{3}$ can be produced by multiplying both the numerator and the denominator of $\frac{2}{3}$ by 2, by 3, by 4, by 5, and so on. In exercise 3 students should recognize that one cross product is 32 while the other is 35, so the fractions are not equivalent.

## Equal Ratios: Cross Products

At Madison School the ratio of students who walk to school to students who ride to school is $\frac{5}{6}$. In Sylvia's class the ratio is $\frac{10}{12}$. Are these ratios equal?

We can use either of these methods to decide.

**Method 1**
**Thinking About Equivalent Fractions**

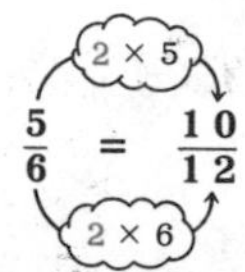


Since the fractions are equivalent, the ratios are equal.

**Method 2**
**Using Cross Products**

$\frac{5}{6}$ $\frac{10}{12}$ → 60
→ 60

Since these cross products are equal, the ratios are equal. When the cross products are not equal, the ratios are not equal.

We can find equal ratios the same way we find equivalent fractions.

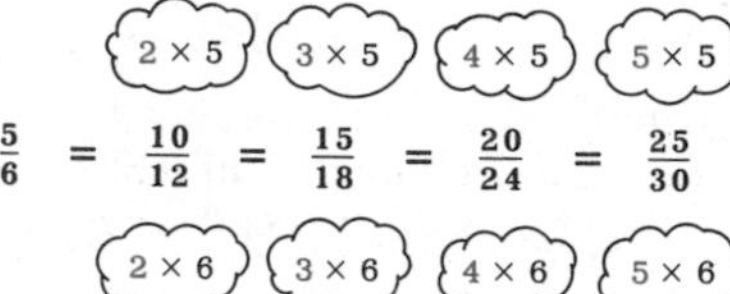


### Warm Up

1. Write four ratios equal to $\frac{2}{3}$. $\frac{4}{6}, \frac{6}{9}, \frac{8}{12}, \frac{10}{15}$
2. Use equivalent fractions to decide whether or not these ratios are equal: $\frac{3}{5}, \frac{12}{20}$ equal
3. Use the cross-products method to decide whether or not these ratios are equal: $\frac{4}{5}, \frac{7}{8}$ not equal

280

## Follow Up

**Reteaching**

Explain to students that one way to determine if two ratios are equal is to determine if the fractions are equivalent. For example, use 10 red counters and 14 white counters to model the ratio 10:14. "Is the fraction $\frac{5}{7}$ equivalent to the fraction $\frac{10}{14}$?" Show that because $\frac{2}{2} \times \frac{5}{7} = \frac{10}{14}$, the two fractions are equivalent. Thus, the two ratios are equal.

**Enrichment**

Provide students with the information in the charts below. Have them complete the table with equivalent ratios.

| pens | 2 | 4 | 8 | 12 | 16 | 18 |
|---|---|---|---|---|---|---|
| dollars | 5 | 10 | 20 | 30 | 40 | 45 |

| balls | 7 | 14 | 21 | 35 | 49 | 70 |
|---|---|---|---|---|---|---|
| bats | 2 | 4 | 6 | 10 | 14 | 20 |

| chairs | 6 | 12 | 42 | 48 | 60 | 120 |
|---|---|---|---|---|---|---|
| tables | 1 | 2 | 7 | 8 | 10 | 20 |

| Assignment Guide | | | |
|---|---|---|---|
| | Minimum | Average | Extended |
| page 281 | 1-22, SK | 1-22, SK | 1-23, SK |

Write four ratios in fraction form equal to each ratio given. Answers may vary; sample answers are given.

1. $\frac{1}{2}$ — $\frac{2}{4}, \frac{3}{6}, \frac{4}{8}, \frac{5}{10}$
2. $\frac{3}{4}$ — $\frac{6}{8}, \frac{9}{12}, \frac{12}{16}, \frac{15}{20}$
3. $\frac{5}{2}$ — $\frac{10}{4}, \frac{15}{6}, \frac{20}{8}, \frac{25}{10}$
4. $\frac{10}{3}$ — $\frac{20}{6}, \frac{30}{9}, \frac{40}{12}, \frac{50}{15}$
5. $\frac{3}{8}$ — $\frac{6}{16}, \frac{9}{24}, \frac{12}{32}, \frac{15}{40}$

Think about equivalent fractions to decide whether the ratios are equal. Write **equal** or **not equal.**

6. $\frac{4}{5}, \frac{8}{10}$ equal
7. $\frac{2}{5}, \frac{4}{9}$ not equal
8. $\frac{3}{2}, \frac{6}{4}$ equal
9. $\frac{1}{3}, \frac{3}{9}$ equal

Use cross products to decide whether the ratios are equal.

10. $\frac{3}{4}, \frac{5}{7}$ not equal
11. $\frac{2}{3}, \frac{6}{9}$ equal
12. $\frac{1}{4}, \frac{5}{20}$ equal
13. $\frac{2}{3}, \frac{7}{10}$ not equal
14. $\frac{5}{3}, \frac{7}{4}$ not equal
15. $\frac{3}{8}, \frac{12}{32}$ equal
16. $\frac{8}{20}, \frac{6}{15}$ equal
17. $\frac{3}{9}, \frac{5}{15}$ equal
18. $\frac{6}{4}, \frac{7}{5}$ not equal
19. $\frac{8}{12}, \frac{6}{9}$ equal
20. $\frac{7}{8}, \frac{4}{5}$ not equal
21. $\frac{5}{7}, \frac{4}{6}$ not equal

22. At Carver School 2 out of every 5 students walk to school. Is this ratio equal to 12 out of 30? yes

23. **DATA HUNT** Find the ratio of students in your school who take a bus to school to all students in your school. Is this ratio equal to the ratio for your class? Answers will vary.

## Skillkeeper

Give each product in lowest terms.

1. $\frac{3}{4} \times \frac{1}{2}$ $\frac{3}{8}$
2. $\frac{5}{6} \times \frac{2}{3}$ $\frac{5}{9}$
3. $\frac{3}{8} \times \frac{1}{4}$ $\frac{3}{32}$
4. $\frac{4}{9} \times \frac{2}{3}$ $\frac{8}{27}$
5. $\frac{1}{3} \times \frac{3}{10}$ $\frac{1}{10}$
6. $\frac{2}{5} \times \frac{2}{5}$ $\frac{4}{25}$
7. $\frac{4}{5} \times 15$ 12
8. $\frac{9}{10} \times 2$ $1\frac{4}{5}$
9. $1\frac{1}{2} \times 3$ $4\frac{1}{2}$
10. $2\frac{1}{4} \times 1\frac{1}{3}$ 3

Give each quotient in lowest terms.

11. $3 \div \frac{1}{2}$ 6
12. $\frac{3}{4} \div \frac{3}{8}$ 2
13. $\frac{2}{5} \div \frac{4}{9}$ $\frac{9}{10}$
14. $\frac{5}{12} \div 2$ $\frac{5}{24}$
15. $\frac{5}{6} \div \frac{1}{3}$ $2\frac{1}{2}$
16. $15 \div \frac{2}{3}$ $22\frac{1}{2}$
17. $\frac{7}{8} \div \frac{1}{4}$ $3\frac{1}{2}$
18. $\frac{2}{5} \div 4$ $\frac{1}{10}$
19. $2\frac{1}{2} \div 1\frac{1}{3}$ $1\frac{7}{8}$
20. $1\frac{1}{4} \div 1\frac{1}{2}$ $\frac{5}{6}$

281

## Using Page 281

**Exercises 6–9** Have students write the ratio in exercise 6 with common denominators and then test to see if the fractions are equivalent. In each of the other exercises students can simply observe multiples of the numerator and denominator to decide whether the fractions are equivalent.

**Exercises 10–21** In these exercises students must find cross products to see if the ratios are equivalent. Be sure students are multiplying the numerator of one fraction by the denominator of the other and are not multiplying the numerators times the denominators.

**Exercise 22** In this exercise students can choose either method from page 280 to decide if the ratios are equal.

**Data Hunt** This Data Hunt requires that students collect information to find the ratio of students who take the bus to school to all students in the school. If necessary, provide a systematic way for this information to be gathered collectively rather than individually.

**Skillkeeper** These skills were originally taught in Chapter 9.

### Reteaching Supplement, page 66

Name ______________________ To follow text page 281

**Equal Ratios: Cross Products**

**Equal Ratios**

$\frac{3}{4}, \frac{9}{12} \longrightarrow 3 \times 12 = 36$ and $4 \times 9 = 36$

$\frac{3}{4} = \frac{9}{12}$ The cross products are **equal.**

**NOT Equal Ratios**

$\frac{5}{6}, \frac{10}{15} \longrightarrow 5 \times 15 = 75$ and $6 \times 10 = 60$

$\frac{5}{6}$ does not equal $\frac{10}{15}$. The cross products are **not equal.**

Use cross products to decide whether the ratios are equal.

$1 \times 20 = 20$, $4 \times 5 = 20$ — $3 \times 30 = 90$, $10 \times 9 = 90$ — $3 \times 12 = 36$, $2 \times 9 = 18$

1. $\frac{1}{4}, \frac{5}{20}$ equal
2. $\frac{3}{10}, \frac{9}{30}$ equal
3. $\frac{3}{2}, \frac{9}{12}$ not equal
4. $\frac{4}{5}, \frac{32}{40}$ equal
5. $\frac{5}{1}, \frac{20}{10}$ not equal
6. $\frac{5}{12}, \frac{10}{24}$ equal
7. $\frac{6}{9}, \frac{18}{27}$ equal
8. $\frac{3}{8}, \frac{36}{96}$ equal
9. $\frac{16}{64}, \frac{2}{8}$ equal
10. $\frac{5}{12}, \frac{35}{60}$ not equal
11. $\frac{40}{48}, \frac{5}{6}$ equal
12. $\frac{5}{6}, \frac{60}{84}$ not equal
13. $\frac{4}{6}, \frac{18}{27}$ equal
14. $\frac{8}{6}, \frac{24}{20}$ not equal
15. $\frac{9}{24}, \frac{21}{56}$ equal
16. $\frac{8}{7}, \frac{5}{4}$ not equal
17. $\frac{12}{8}, \frac{14}{10}$ not equal
18. $\frac{8}{16}, \frac{12}{32}$ equal

### Enrichment Supplement, page 66

Name ______________________ To follow text page 281

**Ratios in Your World**

Collect the data needed to find each of the ratios below.
Hint: If one of the numbers of the ratio is a zero, substitute another number. Then write an equal ratio.
**Answers will vary.**

1. The number of letters in your first name to the number of letters in your last name
   □/□ Equal ratio → □/□
2. The number of letters in the name of your state to the number of letters in the name of your town or city
   □/□ Equal ratio → □/□
3. The number of vowels in the alphabet to all the letters in the alphabet
   □/□ Equal ratio → □/□
4. The number of girls in your class to the number of boys in your class
   □/□ Equal ratio → □/□
5. The number of windows in your classroom to the number of doors
   □/□ Equal ratio → □/□
6. The number of books in your desk to the number of subjects you study
   □/□ Equal ratio → □/□
7. The number of hours you watch television in a week to the number of hours you are in school in a week
   □/□ Equal ratio → □/□
8. The number of letters in the name of your school to the number of letters in the name of your town or city
   □/□ Equal ratio → □/□

### Practice Supplement, page 107

Name ______________________ To follow text page 281

**Equal Ratios: Cross Products**

Write four ratios in fraction form equal to each ratio.
**Answers will vary. Sample answers are given.**

1. $\frac{2}{5}$ — $\frac{4}{10}, \frac{6}{15}, \frac{8}{20}, \frac{10}{25}$
2. $\frac{5}{8}$ — $\frac{10}{16}, \frac{15}{24}, \frac{20}{32}, \frac{25}{40}$
3. $\frac{7}{3}$ — $\frac{14}{6}, \frac{21}{9}, \frac{28}{12}, \frac{35}{15}$
4. $\frac{4}{7}$ — $\frac{8}{14}, \frac{12}{21}, \frac{16}{28}, \frac{20}{35}$
5. $\frac{1}{6}$ — $\frac{2}{12}, \frac{3}{18}, \frac{4}{24}, \frac{5}{30}$
6. $\frac{4}{3}$ — $\frac{8}{6}, \frac{12}{9}, \frac{16}{12}, \frac{20}{15}$

Think about equivalent fractions to decide whether the ratios are equal.
Write **equal** or **not equal.**

7. $\frac{2}{9}, \frac{3}{6}$ not equal
8. $\frac{1}{2}, \frac{4}{8}$ equal
9. $\frac{4}{5}, \frac{6}{10}$ not equal
10. $\frac{2}{3}, \frac{6}{9}$ equal
11. $\frac{5}{8}, \frac{10}{12}$ not equal
12. $\frac{5}{6}, \frac{10}{12}$ equal
13. $\frac{3}{4}, \frac{12}{16}$ equal
14. $\frac{2}{9}, \frac{6}{18}$ not equal
15. $\frac{1}{4}, \frac{5}{16}$ not equal

Use cross products to decide whether the ratios are equal.
Write **equal** or **not equal.**

16. $\frac{5}{6}, \frac{42}{48}$ not equal
17. $\frac{2}{3}, \frac{4}{6}$ equal
18. $\frac{2}{5}, \frac{9}{25}$ not equal
19. $\frac{7}{8}, \frac{28}{32}$ equal
20. $\frac{2}{5}, \frac{6}{15}$ equal
21. $\frac{3}{8}, \frac{9}{24}$ equal
22. $\frac{2}{7}, \frac{3}{5}$ not equal
23. $\frac{4}{5}, \frac{16}{20}$ equal
24. $\frac{2}{3}, \frac{4}{9}$ not equal
25. $\frac{2}{3}, \frac{12}{16}$ not equal
26. $\frac{1}{2}, \frac{7}{15}$ not equal
27. $\frac{2}{4}, \frac{1}{2}$ equal
28. $\frac{7}{10}, \frac{21}{30}$ equal
29. $\frac{1}{4}, \frac{5}{12}$ not equal
30. $\frac{5}{8}, \frac{16}{15}$ not equal

# Ratio

**Quick Review** Students give the numbers to complete these equal ratios.

$\frac{7}{10} = \frac{\boxed{28}}{40}$ $\frac{12}{36} = \frac{1}{\boxed{3}}$ $\frac{7}{8} = \frac{\boxed{21}}{24}$ $\frac{\boxed{5}}{10} = \frac{1}{2}$ $\frac{1}{4} = \frac{\boxed{25}}{100}$ $\frac{3}{\boxed{4}} = \frac{75}{100}$

**Lesson Focus** To write and solve proportions

## Ideas for Getting Started

Write the following on the chalkboard: $3x = 15$; $4a = 28$; $6n = 30$; $9d = 36$. Ask: "How can we find the missing numbers in these equations?" Encourage students to suggest techniques for finding solutions. Possible suggestions may be: Since $3x = 15$, $x = 15 \div 3$. Write a division equation from the multiplication equations. Divide both sides of the equation by the same number. $3x = 15$, $\frac{3x}{3} = \frac{15}{3}$ or $x = 5$." Discuss the solution of each equation.

## Using Page 282

**Motivational Problem** Ask students to read the two paragraphs at the top of the page. Then as you discuss the problem and focus on the question, be sure students understand that we want to find the number of eggs for 42 dozen rolls. "How many eggs are needed for each 3 dozen rolls?" (2) "What is the ratio of eggs to dozens of rolls?" (2 to 3) "How can we find the number of eggs needed for 42 dozen rolls?" (We could find the missing number in a pair of equal ratios.)

**Lesson Development** Tell students that the ratio of the number of eggs needed for 42 rolls ($n$ to 42) is the same as the ratio 2 to 3. Remind them that a statement that two ratios are equal is called a proportion, and then write the proportion $\frac{2}{3} = \frac{n}{42}$ on the chalkboard. Use cross products to produce an equation and work through the procedure for solving the equation as shown with the instruction box. As you use cross products, remind students that because the two ratios are equal, the cross products are equal. Ask a volunteer to give the answer to the problem using a complete sentence.

**Other Examples** Note that in each example the missing number is in a different location in the proportion. Students should be aware that they may, if they like, always write the variable or letter on the left side of the equation as shown in the examples.

**Warm Up** Be sure students understand that if the ratios are equal, the cross products are equal, and an equation can be formed. If students have any difficulty solving an equation such as $2 \times n = 34$ in exercise 1, discuss these equations in terms of products and factors. Explain that two factors are multiplied together to give the product 34, so the product 34 can be divided by one of the factors, 2, to produce the other factor.

## Solving Proportions

A bakery uses 2 eggs for each 3 dozen rolls. How many eggs does the bakery need for 42 dozen rolls?

The ratio of eggs to dozens of rolls is 2 to 3. If we let the letter $n$ represent the number of eggs for 42 dozen, we can write a ratio equal to $\frac{2}{3}$.

$$\frac{2}{3} = \frac{n}{42}$$

A statement that two ratios are equal is called a **proportion.**

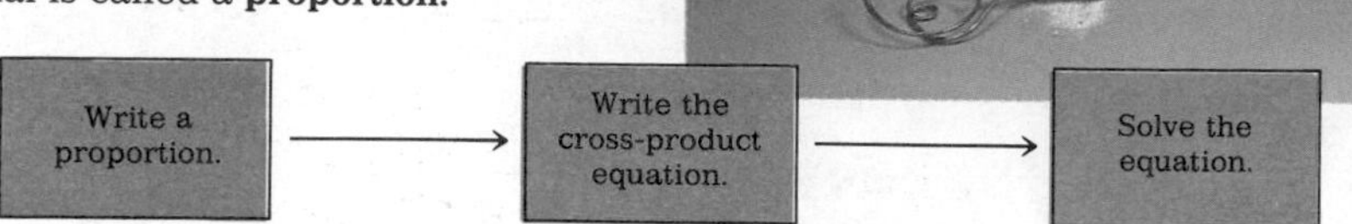


eggs → 2 / dozens of rolls → 3: $\frac{2}{3} = \frac{n}{42}$

$3 \times n = 2 \times 42$

$3 \times n = 84$
$n = 84 \div 3$
$n = 28$

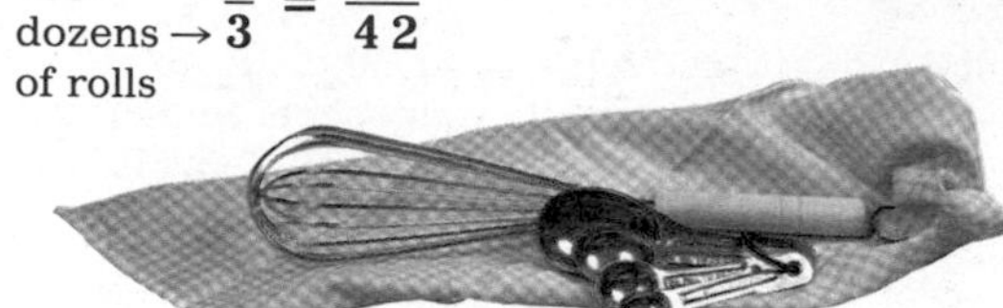

**Check:**

$\frac{2}{3} = \frac{28}{42}$ → 84, 84

Since the cross products are equal, the ratios are equal when $n = 28$.

The bakery needs 28 eggs for 42 dozen rolls.

**Other Examples**

$\frac{3}{4} = \frac{n}{52}$

$4 \times n = 3 \times 52$
$4 \times n = 156$
$n = 156 \div 4$, or 39

$\frac{3}{5} = \frac{42}{n}$

$3 \times n = 5 \times 42$
$3 \times n = 210$
$n = 210 \div 3$, or 70

$\frac{24}{n} = \frac{4}{3}$

$4 \times n = 24 \times 3$
$4 \times n = 72$
$n = 72 \div 4$, or 18

**Warm Up** Solve the proportions.

1. $\frac{1}{2} = \frac{n}{34}$ $n = 17$
2. $\frac{5}{4} = \frac{20}{n}$ $n = 16$
3. $\frac{3}{4} = \frac{48}{n}$ $n = 64$
4. $\frac{n}{64} = \frac{3}{4}$ $n = 48$



## Follow Up

### Reteaching

A proportion is an equation stating that two ratios are equal. Have students set up a proportion to compare 1 bicycle to the number of wheels: There is 1 bicycle to 2 wheels or $\frac{1 \text{ bicycle}}{2 \text{ wheels}}$. Help students set up the proportion to show $\frac{1 \text{ bicycle}}{2 \text{ wheels}} = \frac{n \text{ bicycle}}{8 \text{ wheels}}$, or $\frac{1}{2} = \frac{n}{8}$. Then work with students to cross multiply, $1 \times 8 = 2 \times n$; $8 = 2n$. Encourage students to suggest other examples, and help them set up and solve the suggested proportions.

### Enrichment

Challenge students to write and solve a proportion for each problem.

1. Casey's pulse beats 26 times in 20 seconds. How many times does it beat in one minute (60 seconds)?
$\frac{26}{20} = \frac{x}{60}$ **$x = 78$ beats in one minute**

2. After exercising, Edith breathes 8 times in 10 seconds. What is her breathing rate per minute?
$\frac{8}{10} = \frac{x}{60}$ **$x = 48$ breaths per minute**

3. Nathan breathes 9 times in 12 seconds after swimming. What is his breathing rate per minute after swimming?
$\frac{9}{12} = \frac{x}{60}$ **$x = 45$ breaths per minute**

| Assignment Guide | | | |
|---|---|---|---|
| | Minimum | Average | Extended |
| page 283 | 1–26 | 1–28, TM | 1–28, TM |

Solve the proportions.

1. $\frac{1}{4} = \frac{n}{48}$ $n = 12$
2. $\frac{4}{5} = \frac{n}{60}$ $n = 48$
3. $\frac{3}{8} = \frac{n}{96}$ $n = 36$
4. $\frac{2}{3} = \frac{n}{45}$ $n = 30$
5. $\frac{4}{7} = \frac{n}{28}$ $n = 16$
6. $\frac{3}{4} = \frac{24}{n}$ $n = 32$
7. $\frac{1}{3} = \frac{16}{n}$ $n = 48$
8. $\frac{3}{10} = \frac{30}{n}$ $n = 100$
9. $\frac{5}{6} = \frac{75}{n}$ $n = 90$
10. $\frac{6}{5} = \frac{72}{n}$ $n = 60$
11. $\frac{n}{42} = \frac{15}{18}$ $n = 35$
12. $\frac{n}{36} = \frac{45}{60}$ $n = 27$
13. $\frac{n}{35} = \frac{96}{60}$ $n = 56$
14. $\frac{n}{24} = \frac{65}{78}$ $n = 20$
15. $\frac{n}{7} = \frac{33}{21}$ $n = 11$
16. $\frac{16}{n} = \frac{24}{36}$ $n = 24$
17. $\frac{27}{n} = \frac{51}{34}$ $n = 18$
18. $\frac{18}{n} = \frac{21}{35}$ $n = 30$
19. $\frac{45}{n} = \frac{20}{36}$ $n = 81$
20. $\frac{57}{n} = \frac{19}{9}$ $n = 27$
21. $\frac{8}{15} = \frac{n}{75}$ $n = 40$
22. $\frac{11}{n} = \frac{110}{70}$ $n = 7$
23. $\frac{n}{13} = \frac{30}{78}$ $n = 5$
24. $\frac{7}{20} = \frac{56}{n}$ $n = 160$
25. $\frac{14}{n} = \frac{70}{85}$ $n = 17$

26. The bakery uses 3 apples for every 4 pieces of apple crisp. A club needs 72 pieces of apple crisp for a dinner party. How many apples will the bakery need to use? 54 apples

27. The bakery uses 5 cups of flour for every 2 loaves of bread. How much flour is needed for 3 dozen loaves of bread? (Be careful!) 90 cups

28. The ratio of the amount of wheat produced in China to the amount of wheat produced in the United States in a recent year was 3 to 4. If the United States produced 58,304 thousand tons that year, how many thousand tons were produced in China? 43,728 thousand tons

**Think Math**

**Estimation**

About how long would it take you to read a 400-page book? (Hint: Estimate the number of words you can read in 1 minute and the number of words on an average page.) Answers will vary.



## Using Page 283

**Exercises 1–25** Note in each of the first four rows of the exercises the variable is in a specific location in the proportion; in the last row the position of the variable changes. This should cause students little difficulty, but be alert to problems regarding which side of the equation to write the variable.

**Exercise 27** Note that in this exercise students must translate 3 dozen into 3 × 12 or 36 before setting up the proportion.

**Exercise 28** In this exercise students apply the idea of ratio and proportion to large numbers, which makes the use of the calculator appropriate.

**Think Math** The estimate for this problem will depend, of course, on the size of type and the reading level of the book involved. Encourage students to use a stopwatch or a watch with a second hand and conduct an experiment to find out how many words they can read in a minute. To estimate the number of words on a page, students may want to count the number of words in a random line and then multiply by the number of lines on the page. Challenge students to devise their own methods for these procedures.

**Reteaching Supplement,** page 67

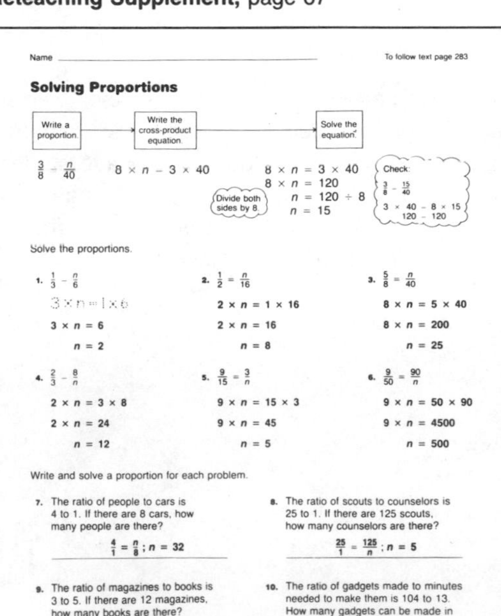

Name ______ To follow text page 283

**Solving Proportions**

Write a proportion. → Write the cross-product equation. → Solve the equation.

$\frac{3}{8} = \frac{n}{40}$   $8 \times n = 3 \times 40$   $8 \times n = 3 \times 40$; $8 \times n = 120$; $n = 120 \div 8$; $n = 15$ (Divide both sides by 8.)

Check: $\frac{3}{8} = \frac{15}{40}$; $3 \times 40 = 8 \times 15$; $120 = 120$

Solve the proportions.

1. $\frac{1}{3} = \frac{n}{6}$ — $3 \times n = 1 \times 6$; $3 \times n = 6$; $n = 2$
2. $\frac{1}{2} = \frac{n}{16}$ — $2 \times n = 1 \times 16$; $2 \times n = 16$; $n = 8$
3. $\frac{5}{8} = \frac{n}{40}$ — $8 \times n = 5 \times 40$; $8 \times n = 200$; $n = 25$
4. $\frac{2}{3} = \frac{8}{n}$ — $2 \times n = 3 \times 8$; $2 \times n = 24$; $n = 12$
5. $\frac{9}{15} = \frac{3}{n}$ — $9 \times n = 15 \times 3$; $9 \times n = 45$; $n = 5$
6. $\frac{9}{50} = \frac{90}{n}$ — $9 \times n = 50 \times 90$; $9 \times n = 4500$; $n = 500$

Write and solve a proportion for each problem.

7. The ratio of people to cars is 4 to 1. If there are 8 cars, how many people are there? $\frac{4}{1} = \frac{n}{8}$; $n = 32$
8. The ratio of scouts to counselors is 25 to 1. If there are 125 scouts, how many counselors are there? $\frac{25}{1} = \frac{125}{n}$; $n = 5$
9. The ratio of magazines to books is 3 to 5. If there are 12 magazines, how many books are there? $\frac{3}{5} = \frac{12}{n}$; $n = 20$
10. The ratio of gadgets made to minutes needed to make them is 104 to 13. How many gadgets can be made in 1 minute? $\frac{104}{13} = \frac{n}{1}$; $n = 8$

**Enrichment Supplement,** page 67

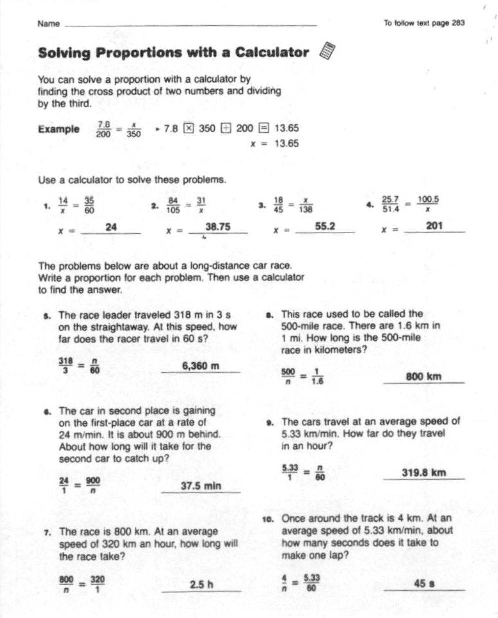

Name ______ To follow text page 283

**Solving Proportions with a Calculator**

You can solve a proportion with a calculator by finding the cross product of two numbers and dividing by the third.

**Example** $\frac{7.8}{200} = \frac{x}{350}$ ▸ 7.8 ⊠ 350 ⊞ 200 ⊟ 13.65; $x = 13.65$

Use a calculator to solve these problems.

1. $\frac{14}{x} = \frac{35}{60}$ $x =$ 24
2. $\frac{84}{105} = \frac{31}{x}$ $x =$ 38.75
3. $\frac{18}{45} = \frac{x}{138}$ $x =$ 55.2
4. $\frac{25.7}{51.4} = \frac{100.5}{x}$ $x =$ 201

The problems below are about a long-distance car race. Write a proportion for each problem. Then use a calculator to find the answer.

5. The race leader traveled 318 m in 3 s on the straightaway. At this speed, how far does the racer travel in 60 s? $\frac{318}{3} = \frac{n}{60}$ 6,360 m
6. The car in second place is gaining on the first-place car at a rate of 24 m/min. It is about 900 m behind. About how long will it take for the second car to catch up? $\frac{24}{1} = \frac{900}{n}$ 37.5 min
7. The race is 800 km. At an average speed of 320 km an hour, how long will the race take? $\frac{800}{n} = \frac{320}{1}$ 2.5 h
8. This race used to be called the 500-mile race. There are 1.6 km in 1 mi. How long is the 500-mile race in kilometers? $\frac{500}{n} = \frac{1}{1.6}$ 800 km
9. The cars travel at an average speed of 5.33 km/min. How far do they travel in an hour? $\frac{5.33}{1} = \frac{n}{60}$ 319.8 km
10. Once around the track is 4 km. At an average speed of 5.33 km/min, about how many seconds does it take to make one lap? $\frac{4}{n} = \frac{5.33}{60}$ 45 s

**Practice Supplement,** page 108

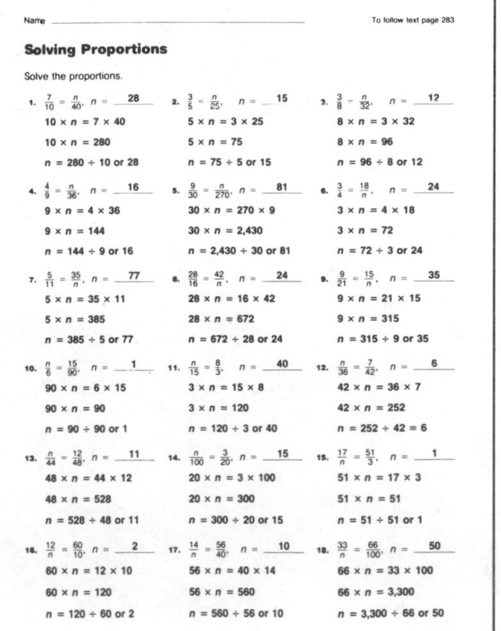

Name ______ To follow text page 283

**Solving Proportions**

Solve the proportions.

1. $\frac{7}{10} = \frac{n}{40}$, $n =$ 28 — $10 \times n = 7 \times 40$; $10 \times n = 280$; $n = 280 \div 10$ or 28
2. $\frac{3}{5} = \frac{n}{25}$, $n =$ 15 — $5 \times n = 3 \times 25$; $5 \times n = 75$; $n = 75 \div 5$ or 15
3. $\frac{3}{8} = \frac{n}{32}$, $n =$ 12 — $8 \times n = 3 \times 32$; $8 \times n = 96$; $n = 96 \div 8$ or 12
4. $\frac{4}{9} = \frac{n}{36}$, $n =$ 16 — $9 \times n = 4 \times 36$; $9 \times n = 144$; $n = 144 \div 9$ or 16
5. $\frac{9}{30} = \frac{n}{270}$, $n =$ 81 — $30 \times n = 270 \times 9$; $30 \times n = 2{,}430$; $n = 2{,}430 \div 30$ or 81
6. $\frac{3}{4} = \frac{18}{n}$, $n =$ 24 — $3 \times n = 4 \times 18$; $3 \times n = 72$; $n = 72 \div 3$ or 24
7. $\frac{5}{11} = \frac{35}{n}$, $n =$ 77 — $5 \times n = 35 \times 11$; $5 \times n = 385$; $n = 385 \div 5$ or 77
8. $\frac{28}{16} = \frac{42}{n}$, $n =$ 24 — $28 \times n = 16 \times 42$; $28 \times n = 672$; $n = 672 \div 28$ or 24
9. $\frac{9}{21} = \frac{15}{n}$, $n =$ 35 — $9 \times n = 21 \times 15$; $9 \times n = 315$; $n = 315 \div 9$ or 35
10. $\frac{n}{6} = \frac{15}{90}$, $n =$ 1 — $90 \times n = 6 \times 15$; $90 \times n = 90$; $n = 90 \div 90$ or 1
11. $\frac{n}{15} = \frac{8}{3}$, $n =$ 40 — $3 \times n = 15 \times 8$; $3 \times n = 120$; $n = 120 \div 3$ or 40
12. $\frac{n}{36} = \frac{7}{42}$, $n =$ 6 — $42 \times n = 36 \times 7$; $42 \times n = 252$; $n = 252 \div 42 = 6$
13. $\frac{n}{44} = \frac{12}{48}$, $n =$ 11 — $48 \times n = 44 \times 12$; $48 \times n = 528$; $n = 528 \div 48$ or 11
14. $\frac{n}{100} = \frac{3}{20}$, $n =$ 15 — $20 \times n = 3 \times 100$; $20 \times n = 300$; $n = 300 \div 20$ or 15
15. $\frac{17}{n} = \frac{51}{3}$, $n =$ 1 — $51 \times n = 17 \times 3$; $51 \times n = 51$; $n = 51 \div 51$ or 1
16. $\frac{12}{n} = \frac{60}{10}$, $n =$ 2 — $60 \times n = 12 \times 10$; $60 \times n = 120$; $n = 120 \div 60$ or 2
17. $\frac{14}{n} = \frac{56}{40}$, $n =$ 10 — $56 \times n = 40 \times 14$; $56 \times n = 560$; $n = 560 \div 56$ or 10
18. $\frac{33}{n} = \frac{66}{100}$, $n =$ 50 — $66 \times n = 33 \times 100$; $66 \times n = 3{,}300$; $n = 3{,}300 \div 66$ or 50

# Applications

**Quick Review** Students write answers in lowest terms.

$\frac{1}{4} \times \frac{2}{3} = \frac{1}{6}$ $\frac{3}{4} \div \frac{1}{2} = 1\frac{1}{2}$ $\frac{7}{8} \div \frac{2}{3} = 1\frac{5}{16}$ $\frac{5}{6} \times \frac{1}{5} = \frac{1}{6}$ $\frac{8}{11} \times \frac{1}{3} = \frac{8}{33}$

$\frac{7}{10} \times \frac{1}{4} = \frac{7}{40}$ $\frac{1}{2} \div \frac{1}{4} = 2$ $\frac{9}{10} \div \frac{4}{5} = 1\frac{1}{8}$ $\frac{1}{4} \times \frac{5}{7} = \frac{5}{28}$ $\frac{9}{2} \div \frac{2}{9} = 1$

**Lesson Focus** To use data from a story to solve word problems

## Ideas for Getting Started

To introduce this lesson, read excerpts from various parts of *Alice's Adventures in Wonderland* by Lewis Carroll. Tell students that Lewis Carroll, whose actual name was Charles Dodgson, was an accomplished mathematician as well as a writer, and that his writings frequently use mathematical ideas in a humorous manner. Then read other excerpts from *Gulliver's Travels* by Jonathan Swift and encourage comments from students.

## Using Page 284

**Lesson Development** Read and discuss the segment of the story shown at the top of the page. Be sure students understand that Alice can change her size by eating from a cake in her left hand or from a cake in her right hand. Remind students that she ate from her right hand and reduced her size to 9 inches high.

**Exercises 1–6** If necessary, in exercise 2 review the idea that 1 foot equals 12 inches. Note that exercise 3 uses the results of exercises 1 and 2. The ratio formed is 9 to 48 or 3 to 16. In exercises 5 and 6, help students set up proportions if necessary.

## Problem Solving: Using Data from a Story

Try these problems about story characters that either change sizes or are different size than usual!

Adapted from

**Alice's Adventures in Wonderland**

by Lewis Carroll

Alice came suddenly upon an open place, with a little house in it 4 feet high. "Whoever lives there," thought Alice, "it'll never do to come upon them in my normal size. Why, I should frighten them out of their wits!" So she began nibbling at the right-hand bit of wheatcake again and did not go near the house till she had brought herself down to 9 inches high.

1. What is Alice's reduced height in the story? 9 in.
2. What is the height of the little house in inches? 48 in.
3. What is the lowest-terms fraction for the ratio of Alice's reduced height to the height of the little house? (Use the answers to problems 1 and 2.) $\frac{3}{16}$

For problems 4–6, suppose that Alice's normal height is 4 feet 6 inches.

4. What is the lowest-terms fraction for the ratio of Alice's reduced height to her normal height? $\frac{1}{6}$
5. When Alice ate a small wheatcake from her left hand, she grew from her normal height to a height of 9 feet. If her normal shoe length was 6 inches and her shoes grew at the same rate as her height, how long would they be? 12 in.
6. Suppose the little house suddenly grew so that the ratio of its new height to Alice's normal height was equal to the ratio of its old height to Alice's reduced height. How many inches high would the house be? 288 in.

284

## Follow Up

### Reteaching

Generate a discussion about the two stories in this lesson. Then review the ideas of fraction, ratio, and proportion, using examples from the lesson to illustrate each point. For example:

- A Lilliputian ruler is $\frac{1}{12}$ the length of our customary ruler.
- The ratio of Alice's reduced height to her normal height was 1 to 6.
- If we use the fraction $\frac{3}{36}$ to compare the width of Lilliputian linen to our linen, we can find the amount of 6 widths of Lilliputian linen by writing a proportion $\frac{3}{36} = \frac{6}{n}$.

### Enrichment

Challenge students to write their own stories in which the characters are in proportion to the surroundings. Have students provide several questions based on the data in their stories to share with classmates.

| Assignment Guide | | | |
|---|---|---|---|
| | Minimum | Average | Extended |
| pages 284–285 | 1–5, 7–9 | 1–10 | 1–11 |

Adapted from

**Gulliver's Travels**

by Jonathan Swift

(Gulliver explains why he felt like a giant in the kingdom of the tiny Lilliputians!)

Two hundred seamstresses were employed to make me shirts. Their linen is usually 3 inches wide, while ours is 3 feet wide.

The seamstresses took my measure as I lay on the ground, with an inch-long ruler. Then they measured my thumb, and desired no more; for by a mathematical computation, twice round the thumb is once round the wrist.

7. Suppose the ratio of the width of Lilliputian linen to the width of our linen is equal to the ratio of a Lilliputian's height to a normal person's height. What is a Lilliputian's height? (Use 6 feet as "normal height.") 6 in.

8. What is the ratio of the length of the Lilliputian ruler to the length of our customary foot ruler? Is this the same as the ratio of Lilliputian height to normal height? (Use data from problem 7.) $\frac{1}{12}$; yes

9. The Lilliputian horses were $4\frac{1}{2}$ inches high. How high would a comparable normal horse be? (Use a 1 to 12 ratio.) 54 in.

10. **DATA HUNT** By how much does twice the distance around the base of your thumb differ from the distance around your wrist? Answers will vary.

11. **Try This** One morning a Lilliputian starts out to climb a steep mountain. The distance to the top is 10 yards. Each day he climbs 2 yards. Each night he slips back 1 yard. On what day—the eighth, the ninth, or the tenth—does he reach the top? the ninth day



## Using Page 285

**Exercises 7–9** Before assigning these exercises, read through the excerpt from *Gulliver's Travels.* In exercise 8 help students understand that since the Lilliputians used a rule 1 inch long, this would correspond to our rule which is 12 inches long, thus making a ratio of 1 to 12. For exercise 9 students might multiply $4\frac{1}{2}$ by 12 or set up the proportion 1:12 = $4\frac{1}{2}$ in.

**Data Hunt** This exercise allows students to measure to collect the data needed to solve the problem. If necessary, help students make a table to show the results and decide how accurate this "rule of thumb" is.

**Try This** A possible strategy, Draw a Picture, was taught on page 74.

**Discussion** Ask a student to read the problem carefully and express the question in his or her own words. "How tall is the mountain?" (10 yards) "How far does the Lilliputian climb each day?" (2 yards) "How far does he slip back each night?" (1 yard) "In planning a solution what strategy might you use?" Elicit from students that Draw A Picture would be a good strategy to use. If necessary, help students draw a picture to show each day's progress.

**Solution** The Lilliputian would reach the top of the mountain on the ninth day. Another way to look at the problem is that the Lilliputian gains 1 yard each day. On the eighth day he or she would be 8 yards up the mountain. During the ninth day the Lilliputian would gain 2 yards and reach the top.

## Ideas That Work

### Special Education

Use a sheet of graph paper (TRB p. 271) to show the ratio of two numbers such as 3 to 2 by marking the segments as shown. Have students draw the triangles, name the equivalent ratios, and then color the triangles formed.

To find other equivalent ratios, the sides of the triangle formed can be extended to find other points where the slanted line side of the triangle again crosses a point on the graph paper. Students can see that this happens again at 6 to 4 and at 9 to 6.

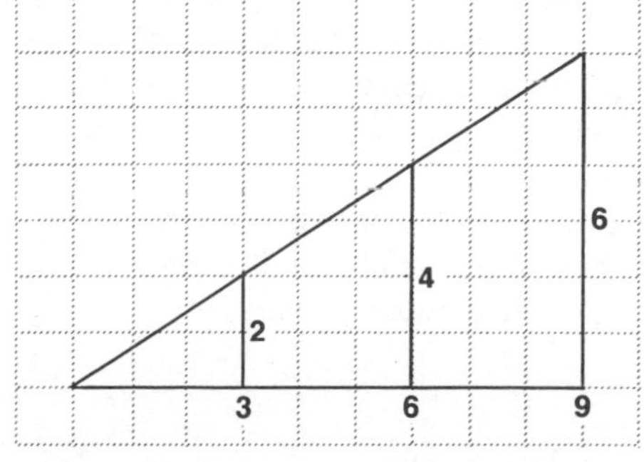


After students have observed the relationships in these triangles, encourage them to experiment with other ratios.

**Practice Supplement,** page 109

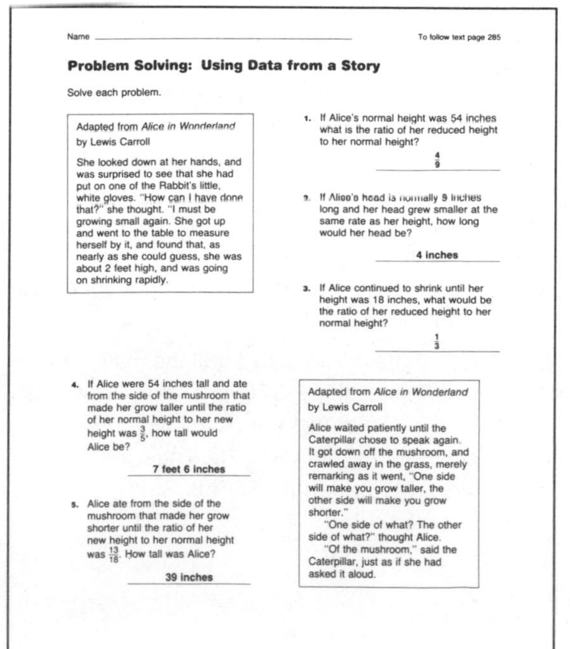

Name ______ To follow text page 285

**Problem Solving: Using Data from a Story**

Solve each problem.

Adapted from *Alice in Wonderland*
by Lewis Carroll

She looked down at her hands, and was surprised to see that she had put on one of the Rabbit's little, white gloves. "How can I have done that?" she thought. "I must be growing small again. She got up and went to the table to measure herself by it, and found that, as nearly as she could guess, she was about 2 feet high, and was going on shrinking rapidly.

1. If Alice's normal height was 54 inches what is the ratio of her reduced height to her normal height? **$\frac{4}{9}$**

2. If Alice's head is normally 9 inches long and her head grew smaller at the same rate as her height, how long would her head be? **4 inches**

3. If Alice continued to shrink until her height was 18 inches, what would be the ratio of her reduced height to her normal height? **$\frac{1}{3}$**

4. If Alice were 54 inches tall and ate from the side of the mushroom that made her grow taller until the ratio of her normal height to her new height was $\frac{3}{5}$, how tall would Alice be? **7 feet 6 inches**

5. Alice ate from the side of the mushroom that made her grow shorter until the ratio of her new height to her normal height was $\frac{13}{18}$. How tall was Alice? **39 inches**

Adapted from *Alice in Wonderland*
by Lewis Carroll

Alice waited patiently until the Caterpillar chose to speak again. It got down off the mushroom, and crawled away in the grass, merely remarking as it went, "One side will make you grow taller, the other side will make you grow shorter."

"One side of what? The other side of what?" thought Alice.

"Of the mushroom," said the Caterpillar, just as if she had asked it aloud.

**Quick Review** Write these abbreviations on the chalkboard. Students respond orally with the name for each.

cm kg L mL mg m g mm km dm

**Lesson Focus** To identify similar polygons and write proportions showing that matching sides have equal ratios

**Suggested Materials** Cutout triangles

## Ideas for Getting Started

Cut out three similar triangles as shown below from colored tagboard or heavy paper.

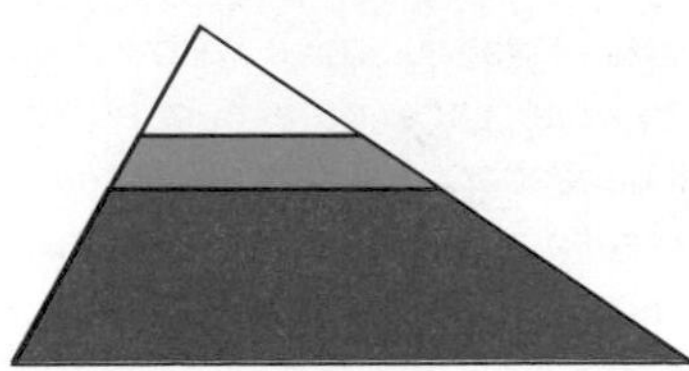

The sides of the white triangle should be $\frac{1}{3}$ the length of the sides of the red triangle and the sides of the blue triangle should be $\frac{1}{2}$ the length of the sides of the red triangle. Tell students that these triangles are the same shape because their angles are the same measure. (Place the triangles on top of each other as shown in the picture to illustrate the congruence of matching angles.) "How do you think the length of a selected side of the red triangle compares with the matching side of the blue triangle?" As you point to a certain side, have students guess the answer to the question. Then place the blue triangle on the red triangle and move the sides to show that the red triangle's side is twice the length of the blue triangle's side. "How do you think the length of a side of the red triangle compares with the length of a matching side of the white triangle?" (3 times as long)

## Using Page 286

**Lesson Development** Have students read the paragraph at the top of the page. Discuss the description of similar figures as it relates to the example of the original and enlarged copies. Have such a copy of the picture available, if possible.

Refer to the triangles pictured and emphasize that when two triangles are the same shape—not necessarily the same size—they are similar. Be sure students understand that congruent figures also can be called similar.

Use the triangle cutouts from the Getting Started activity or pictures of triangles to emphasize the two conditions for similarity of triangles. Provide several examples to illustrate these ideas. Continue to emphasize that similar figures are the same shape but not necessarily the same size.

**Warm Up** Note in exercise 4 that the multiple from triangle *PQR* to triangle *STU* is $\frac{1}{2}$, that is, we can multiply the sides of triangle *PQR* by $\frac{1}{2}$ to produce the matching side of triangle *STU*. Thus, the multiple for triangle *STU* to triangle *PQR* is 2.

## Similar Figures

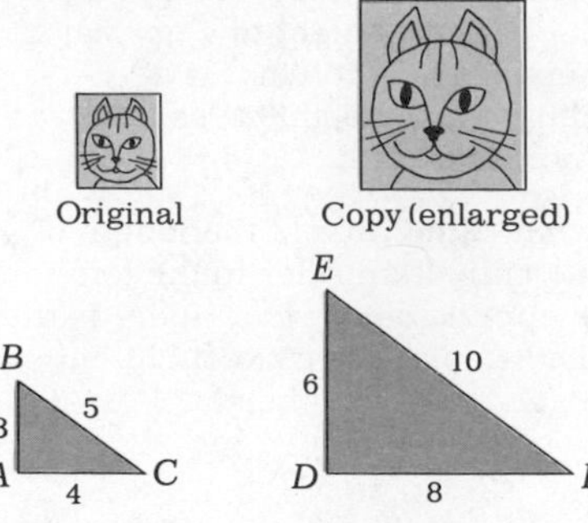


A figure and a copy of the figure that is the same shape as the original suggest the idea of **similar figures.** One similar figure may be larger or smaller than the other, or it may be the same size.

We write: $\triangle ABC \sim \triangle DEF$
We say: "$\triangle ABC$ is similar to $\triangle DEF$."

When triangles are similar:

- Matching angles are congruent. $\angle A \cong \angle D$, $\angle B \cong \angle E$, $\angle C \cong \angle F$
- The lengths of matching sides have equal ratios:

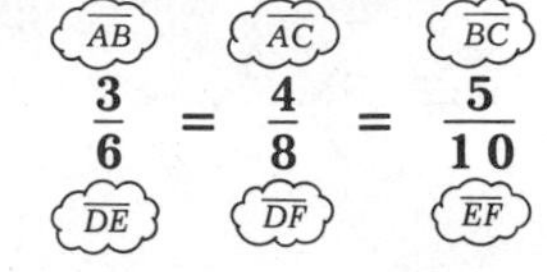


$$\frac{3}{6} = \frac{4}{8} = \frac{5}{10}$$

### Warm Up

Are the pairs of figures similar? Write **yes** or **no.**

**1.** yes **2.** no **3.** yes

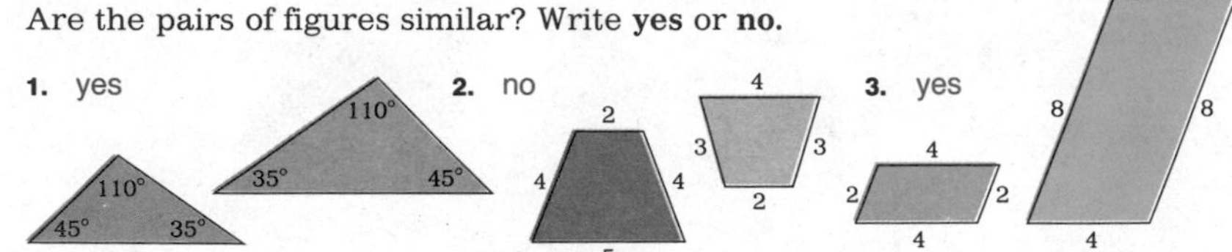


**4.** Which triangle is similar to $\triangle PQR$? Write proportions showing that matching sides have equal ratios. $\triangle STU$; $\frac{8}{4} = \frac{12}{6} = \frac{10}{5}$

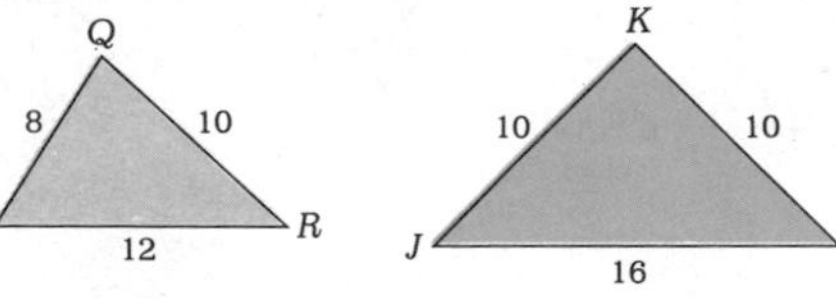


**5.** These two quadrilaterals are similar. Write proportions showing that matching sides have equal ratios. Include the length of the missing side. $\frac{1}{2} = \frac{2}{4} = \frac{3}{6} = \frac{4}{8}$

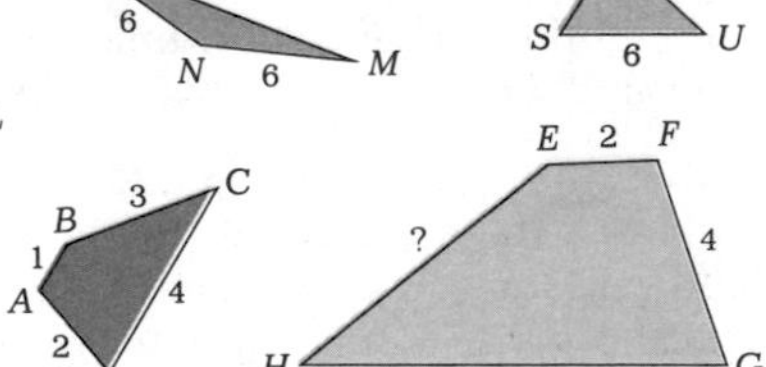


286

## Follow Up

### Reteaching

Make sets of similar triangles from colored paper and give a set to each small group of students. Help students use their protractors to measure each angle and their rulers to measure each side. Emphasize the fact that corresponding angles are equal and corresponding sides have equal ratios.

### Enrichment

Have students draw a small figure in the lower left corner of a large sheet of graph paper (TRB p. 271). Next have students place a series of points on the figure. Students then multiply the coordinates of each of the points by a given number. Finally, students graph the new coordinates and connect them to produce an enlargement of the original figure.

| Assignment Guide | | | |
|---|---|---|---|
| | Minimum | Average | Extended |
| page 287 | 1–6, SK | 1–7, SK | 1–8, SK |

Are the pairs of figures similar? Write **yes** or **no**.

**1.** yes **2.** yes **3.** no

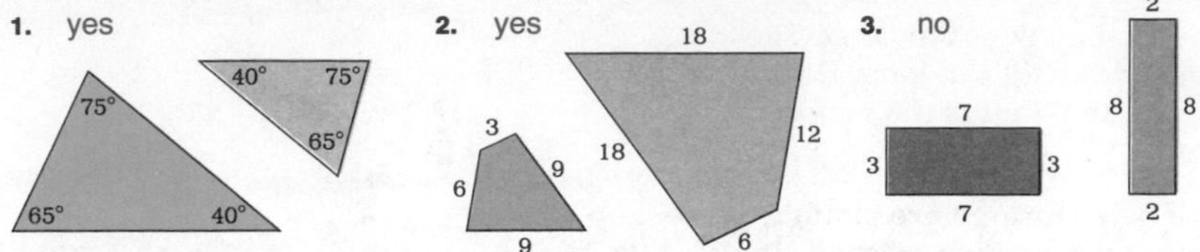


The figures in each exercise are similar. Write proportions showing that matching sides have equal ratios. Include the missing side length.

**4.** $\frac{5}{10} = \frac{7}{14} = \frac{10}{20}$

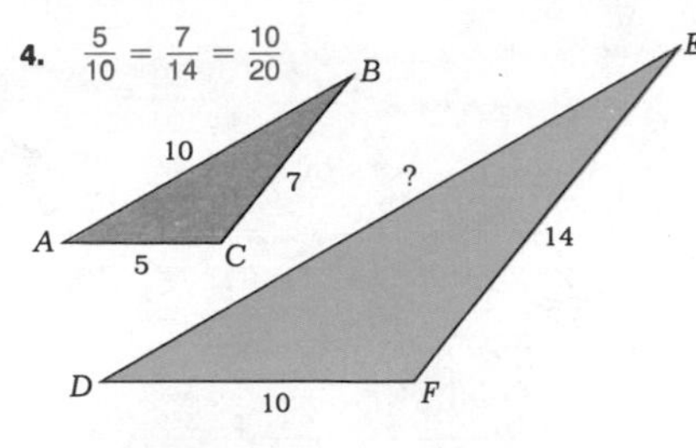


**5.** $\frac{8}{4} = \frac{8}{4} = \frac{8}{4}$

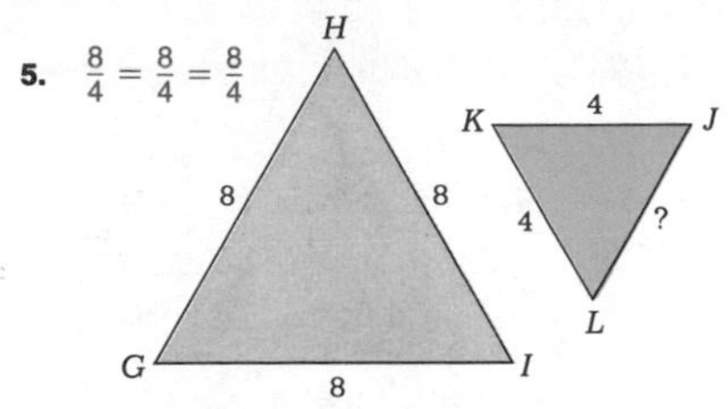


**6.**

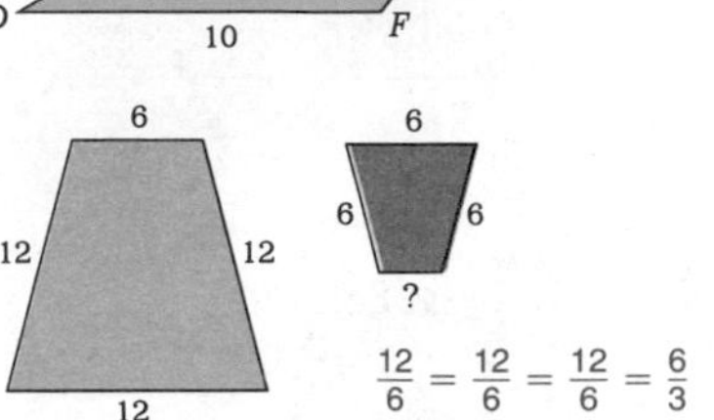
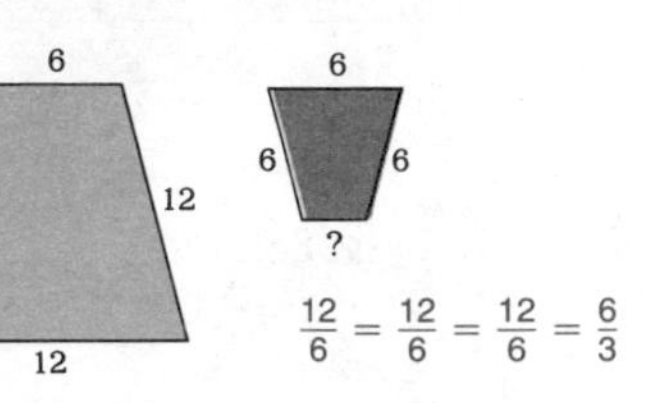


$\frac{12}{6} = \frac{12}{6} = \frac{12}{6} = \frac{6}{3}$

**7.**

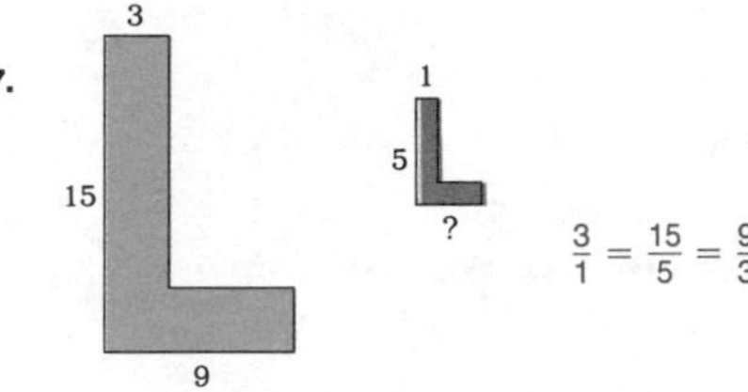


$\frac{3}{1} = \frac{15}{5} = \frac{9}{3}$

★ **8.** Copy this figure on a sheet of graph paper. Then draw a similar figure with sides twice as long on the graph paper. student construction

## Skillkeeper

Multiply or divide.

**1.** $2 \times 1\frac{1}{3}$ $\frac{8}{3} = 2\frac{2}{3}$ **2.** $3\frac{1}{2} \times 1\frac{1}{7}$ $\frac{8}{2} = 4$

**3.** $\frac{5}{8} \times 3\frac{1}{5}$ $\frac{2}{1} = 2$ **4.** $\frac{8}{9} \div \frac{2}{3}$ $\frac{4}{3} = 1\frac{1}{3}$

**5.** $4\frac{1}{2} \div \frac{3}{4}$ $\frac{6}{1} = 6$ **6.** $1\frac{2}{3} \div 1\frac{3}{7}$ $\frac{7}{6} = 1\frac{1}{6}$

Find the missing number.

**7.** $\frac{4}{5} = \frac{■}{100}$ 80 **8.** $\frac{3}{20} = \frac{15}{■}$ 100

**9.** $\frac{7}{10} = \frac{■}{100}$ 70 **10.** $\frac{41}{50} = \frac{82}{■}$ 100



## Using Page 287

**Exercises 1–3** Let students trace the smaller figure and move it into an appropriate position so that it may be checked against the larger figure to see if the figures appear to be similar.

**Exercises 4–7** If students have difficulty finding the missing side lengths in these exercises, suggest that they first identify the multiple that relates matching sides.

**Exercise 8** In this exercise, students apply the ideas of similarity and congruence to create a different kind of figure.

**Skillkeeper** These skills were originally taught in Chapters 8 and 9.

## Ideas That Work

### Math for the Gifted

Provide students with sheets of acetate to place over a centimeter grid. Tell students to trace a figure whose vertices (corners) fall at intersections of the lines on the grid. The transparency can then be projected onto tracing paper that has been mounted with masking tape on the wall or chalkboard. Students then use a colored marker or a crayon to outline the shapes on the tracing paper. The distance between the overhead and the wall should then be changed and another image of the figure traced on the same sheet. Finally, the transparency should be placed under the tracing paper and the original shape traced on the paper.

Students then measure the various corresponding sides and determine the multiple of the side lengths of each of the images when compared with the original drawing. Because a centimeter grid is used to draw the original shape, centimeters would be the best unit to use in the activity. If necessary, allow students to use the calculator to find the multiples.

**Practice Supplement,** page 110

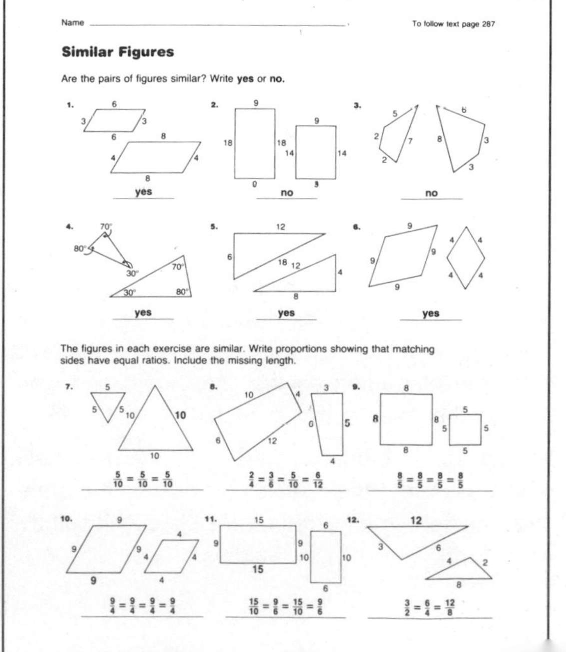
Name To follow text page 287

**Similar Figures**

Are the pairs of figures similar? Write **yes** or **no**.

1. yes 2. no 3. no

4. yes 5. yes 6. yes

The figures in each exercise are similar. Write proportions showing that matching sides have equal ratios. Include the missing length.

7. $\frac{5}{10} = \frac{5}{10} = \frac{5}{10}$ 8. $\frac{2}{4} = \frac{3}{6} = \frac{5}{10} = \frac{6}{12}$ 9. $\frac{8}{5} = \frac{8}{5} = \frac{8}{5} = \frac{8}{5}$

10. $\frac{9}{4} = \frac{9}{4} = \frac{9}{4} = \frac{9}{4}$ 11. $\frac{15}{10} = \frac{9}{6} = \frac{15}{10} = \frac{9}{6}$ 12. $\frac{3}{2} = \frac{6}{4} = \frac{12}{8}$

# Ratio

**Quick Review** Students write answers in lowest terms.

$5\frac{1}{4} - \frac{1}{4} = 5$  $8\frac{9}{10} + 2\frac{1}{10} = 11$  $3\frac{1}{2} - 1 = 2\frac{1}{2}$  $32\frac{4}{5} - 12\frac{2}{5} = 20\frac{2}{5}$

$5 + 2\frac{1}{3} = 7\frac{1}{3}$  $6\frac{3}{10} + 3\frac{3}{10} = 9\frac{3}{5}$  $12\frac{5}{8} + 4\frac{3}{4} = 17\frac{3}{8}$  $9\frac{2}{3} - 6\frac{1}{3} = 3\frac{1}{3}$

**Lesson Focus** To write and solve proportions using similar triangles to find heights

## Ideas for Getting Started

Briefly review the idea that similar triangles have the same shape, but not necessarily the same size. Help students to recall ideas about similar triangles they learned in the geometry chapter (matching angles of similar triangles are congruent, each side of one triangle is the same multiple of a matching side of a similar triangle). Then show the following triangle on the chalkboard and ask students to describe a triangle that is similar to it.

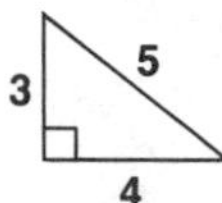


Students might describe the following triangles in which the sides have been multiplied by 2 and by 3.

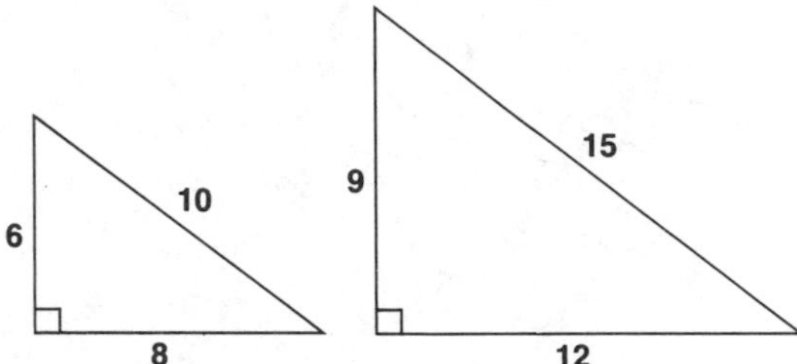


Emphasize the idea that the ratios of matching sides of these three triangles are equal, that is,

$$\frac{3}{6} = \frac{4}{8} = \frac{5}{10};\ \frac{3}{9} = \frac{4}{12} = \frac{5}{15};\ \frac{6}{9} = \frac{8}{12} = \frac{10}{15}.$$

## Using Page 288

**Motivational Problem** Have students read the first paragraph and then focus on the question. "What data do we know about the shadows?" (Heather's shadow is 2 m long; the tree's shadow is 9.4 m long.) "What other information do we know?" (Heather's height is 1 m.) "How can we find the height of the tree?" (Because the triangles are similar, we can use a proportion.)

**Lesson Development** Direct students' attention to the illustrations. Remind students that the triangles are similar and ask: "What is the ratio of Heather's shadow to the tree's shadow?" $\left(\frac{2}{9.4}\right)$ "If we let $h$ represent the tree's height, what is the ratio of Heather's height to the tree's height?" $\left(\frac{1}{h}\right)$ Tell students that because the triangles are similar, the ratios of the matching sides are equal. Emphasize that the ratio of the two shadows is equal to the ratio of the two heights. (The proportions might also be set up as height to shadow equal height to shadow.) Write the proportion on the chalkboard and work through the solution with students.

**Warm Up** If students have difficulty with these problems, direct their attention again to the statement that tells that the ratio of the shadow lengths is equal to the ratio of their heights.

## Using Proportions to Find Heights

Heather's shadow is 2 m long. The tree's shadow is 9.4 m long. Heather's height is 1 m. What is the height of the tree?

The triangles formed are similar. Since the ratios of matching sides of similar triangles are equal, we can write and solve a proportion for the problem.

1 m
2 m
? m
9.4 m

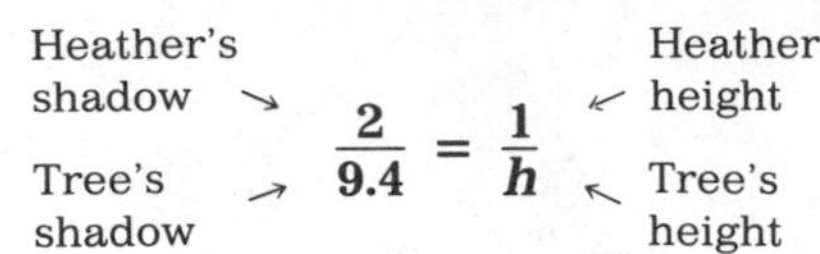


$2 \times h = 9.4 \times 1$

$h = 9.4 \div 2 = 4.7$

The ratio of the shadow lengths of two objects is equal to the ratio of their heights.

The height of the tree is 4.7 m.

**Warm Up** Write a proportion and solve it to find each height.
Proportions may vary.

1. ? m; 2 m; 4 m; 12 m
$\frac{12}{4} = \frac{h}{2}$; 6 m

2. 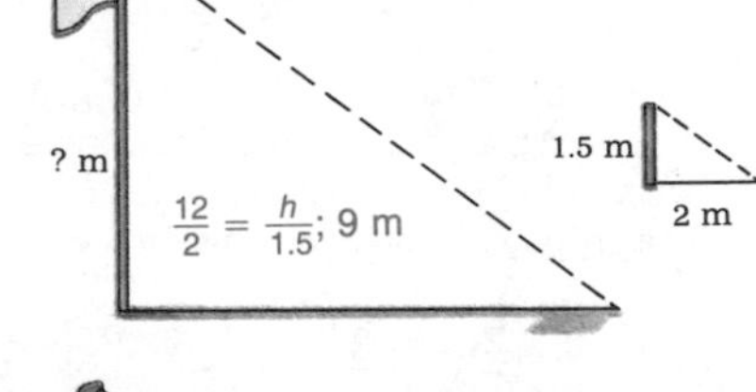

$\frac{12}{2} = \frac{h}{1.5}$; 9 m

3. 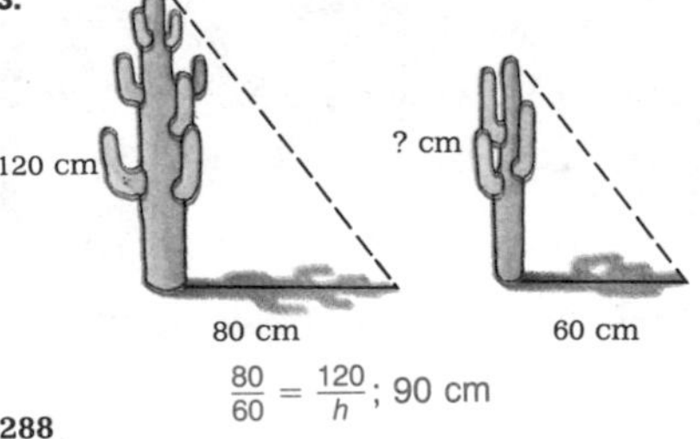

$\frac{80}{60} = \frac{120}{h}$; 90 cm

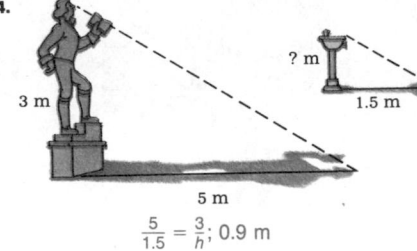

4. 3 m; ? m; 1.5 m; 5 m
$\frac{5}{1.5} = \frac{3}{h}$; 0.9 m



## Follow Up

### Reteaching

Demonstrate how a proportion is used to find heights by positioning an 8-inch pencil and a flashlight as shown below so that a shadow is formed.

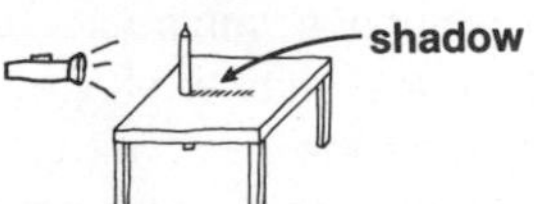


Measure the shadow and set up the ratio $\frac{\text{8 inches}}{\text{(length of shadow)}}$. Keeping the flashlight in the same position, replace the pencil with a longer stick. Set up the proportion below.

$$\frac{\text{8 inches}}{\text{length of shadow}} = \frac{\text{(length of stick)}}{\text{length of shadow } (n)}.$$

Then have students check the answer by measuring the stick.

### Enrichment

Challenge students to find the height of an object or structure by using equal ratios. Have them measure shadows and set up proportions to find the height of such objects as a tree, a telephone pole, the school building, and so on.

| Assignment Guide | | | |
|---|---|---|---|
| | Minimum | Average | Extended |
| page 289 | | 1–7 | 1–8, TM |



Write a proportion and solve it to find the height of each object.

1. The post is 1 m high and has a 2-m shadow. The airport traffic control tower has a 24-m shadow. How high is the tower? $\frac{1}{2} = \frac{h}{24}$; 12 m

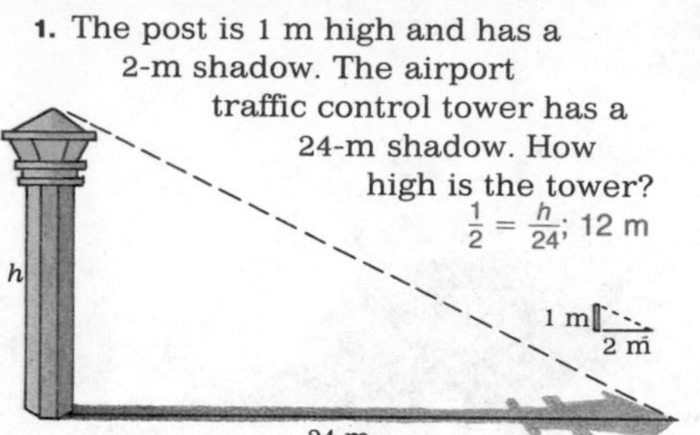


2. The meter stick has a 1.5-m shadow. The water tower has a 36-m shadow. How high is the water tower? $\frac{1}{1.5} = \frac{h}{90}$; 60 m

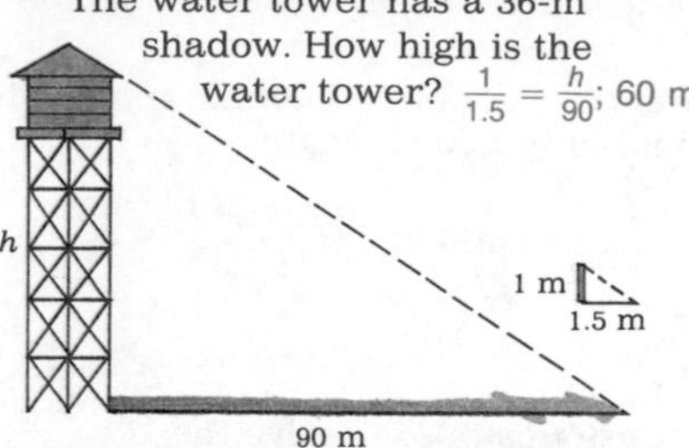


3. The person is 2 m tall and has a shadow 3 m long. The TV tower has a shadow 90 m long. How tall is the tower? $\frac{2}{3} = \frac{h}{36}$; 24 m

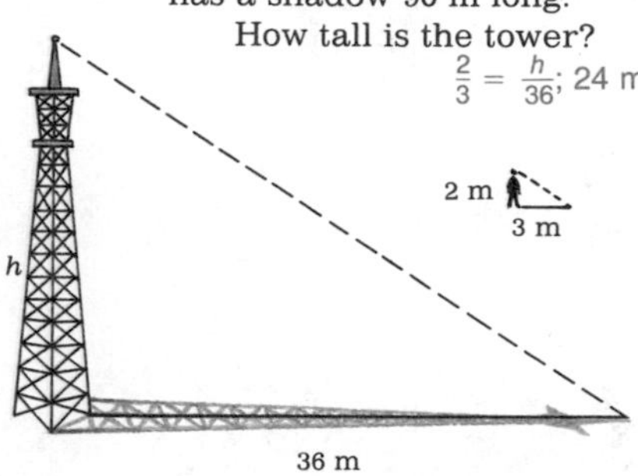


4. The balloon is directly above the tree. Its shadow is 24 m from the tree. The tree is 3 m tall and has a 4-m shadow. How high is the balloon? $\frac{h}{24} = \frac{3}{4}$; 18 m

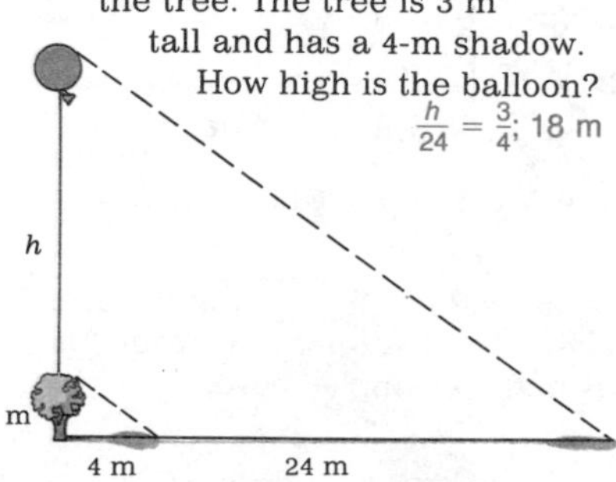


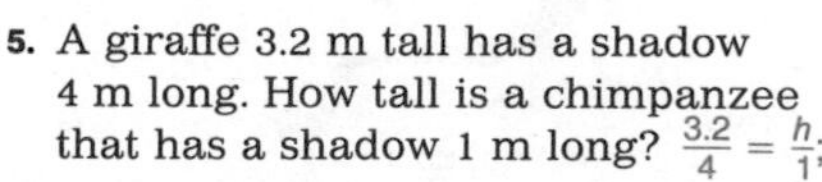

5. A giraffe 3.2 m tall has a shadow 4 m long. How tall is a chimpanzee that has a shadow 1 m long? $\frac{3.2}{4} = \frac{h}{1}$; 0.8 m

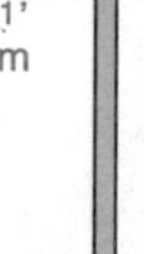

6. A street light 2.5 m tall has a shadow 3.5 m long. A building has a shadow 140 m long. How tall is the building? $\frac{2.5}{3.5} = \frac{h}{140}$; 100 m

7. **DATA HUNT** How high is the flagpole at your school? To find out, measure your height, your shadow, and the pole's shadow.
Answers will vary.

**Think**

**Logical Reasoning**

| Charges | |
|---|---|
| Cut a link | 15¢ |
| Weld a link | 35¢ |

Show how you can make one long chain from these 4 pieces for \$1.50. There is a cheaper way. What would it cost?
See teaching notes.

**Math**



## Using Page 289

**Exercises 1–4** In each of these exercises two similar triangles are given. Note that the problem restates the data that is shown in the picture. Observe students to see that they set up the proportions correctly. If necessary, repeat the statement on page 288 about ratios.

**Exercises 5–6** Encourage students to draw pictures to help them set up the proportion for these problems.

**Data Hunt** After students have measured their heights, their shadows' height, and the flagpole shadow, encourage them to draw a picture to help them find the solution to the problem. Students might work in small groups to solve this problem and then compare their results.

**Think Math** Encourage students to explore different ways the links could be cut and welded together to form a chain. The two methods discussed are shown below. If students have difficulty finding the second method, give a hint such as "Would it help to cut both links in one of the pairs shown?"

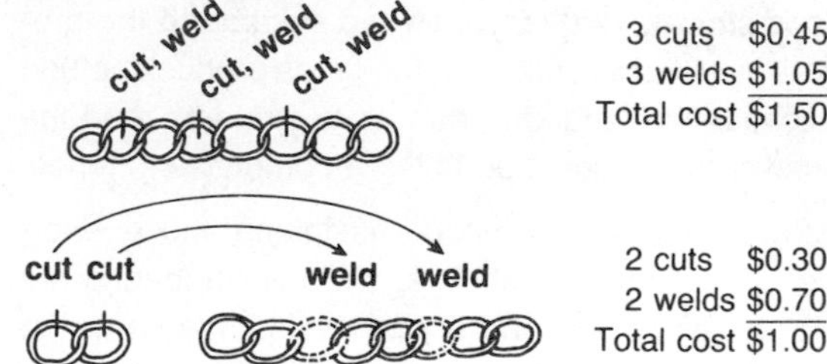

**Reteaching Supplement,** page 68

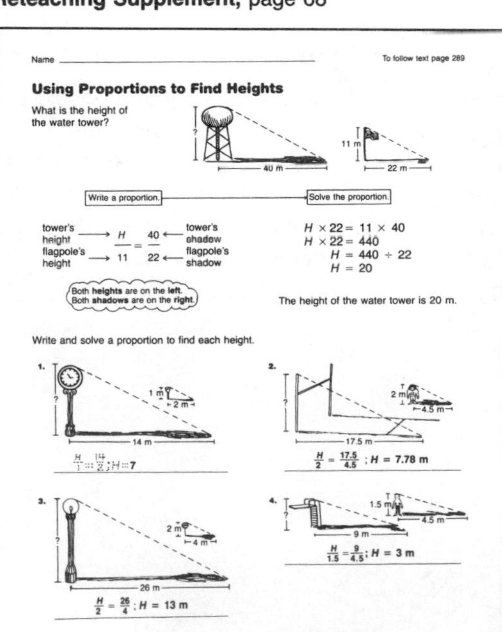

Name ____________ To follow text page 289

**Using Proportions to Find Heights**

What is the height of the water tower?

Write a proportion. → Solve the proportion.

tower's height → $\frac{H}{11} = \frac{40}{22}$ ← tower's shadow
flagpole's height → ← flagpole's shadow

Both **heights** are on the **left**. Both **shadows** are on the **right**.

$H \times 22 = 11 \times 40$
$H \times 22 = 440$
$H = 440 \div 22$
$H = 20$

The height of the water tower is 20 m.

Write and solve a proportion to find each height.

1. $\frac{H}{1} = \frac{14}{2}$; $H = 7$
2. $\frac{H}{2} = \frac{17.5}{4.5}$; $H = 7.78$ m
3. $\frac{H}{2} = \frac{26}{4}$; $H = 13$ m
4. $\frac{H}{1.5} = \frac{9}{4.5}$; $H = 3$ m

**Enrichment Supplement,** page 68

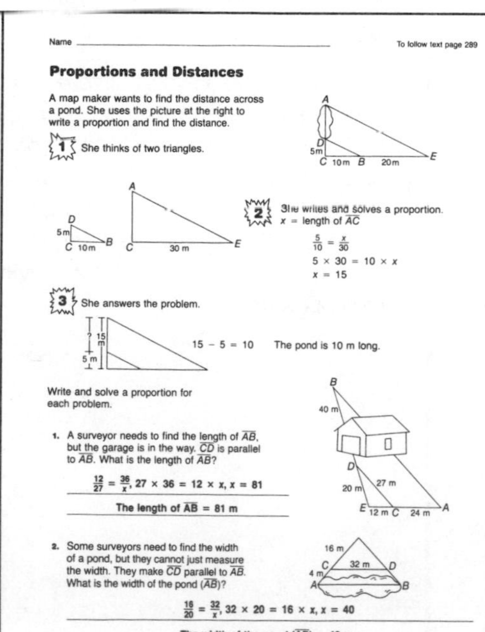

Name ____________ To follow text page 289

**Proportions and Distances**

A map maker wants to find the distance across a pond. She uses the picture at the right to write a proportion and find the distance.

1 She thinks of two triangles.

2 She writes and solves a proportion.
$x$ = length of $\overline{AC}$

$\frac{5}{10} = \frac{x}{30}$
$5 \times 30 = 10 \times x$
$x = 15$

3 She answers the problem.

$15 - 5 = 10$ The pond is 10 m long.

Write and solve a proportion for each problem.

1. A surveyor needs to find the length of $\overline{AB}$, but the garage is in the way. $\overline{CD}$ is parallel to $\overline{AB}$. What is the length of $\overline{AB}$?
$\frac{12}{27} = \frac{36}{x}$, $27 \times 36 = 12 \times x$, $x = 81$
The length of $\overline{AB}$ = 81 m

2. Some surveyors need to find the width of a pond, but they cannot just measure the width. They make $\overline{CD}$ parallel to $\overline{AB}$. What is the width of the pond ($\overline{AB}$)?
$\frac{16}{20} = \frac{32}{x}$, $32 \times 20 = 16 \times x$, $x = 40$
The width of the pond ($\overline{AB}$) = 40 m

**Practice Supplement,** page 111

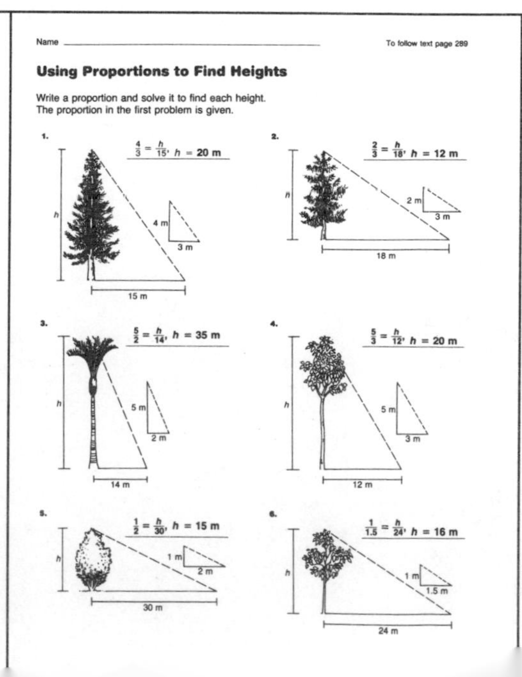

Name ____________ To follow text page 289

**Using Proportions to Find Heights**

Write a proportion and solve it to find each height. The proportion in the first problem is given.

1. $\frac{4}{3} = \frac{h}{15}$, $h = 20$ m
2. $\frac{2}{3} = \frac{h}{18}$, $h = 12$ m
3. $\frac{5}{2} = \frac{h}{14}$, $h = 35$ m
4. $\frac{5}{3} = \frac{h}{12}$, $h = 20$ m
5. $\frac{1}{2} = \frac{h}{30}$, $h = 15$ m
6. $\frac{1}{1.5} = \frac{h}{24}$, $h = 16$ m

**Quick Review** Students write answers in lowest terms.

$1\frac{1}{4} \div \frac{1}{4} = 5$ $5\frac{1}{4} \times 1\frac{1}{2} = 7\frac{7}{8}$ $\frac{2}{3} \times 3\frac{1}{2} = 2\frac{1}{3}$ $5\frac{1}{2} \div 1\frac{1}{3} = 4\frac{1}{8}$ $1\frac{3}{4} \times 3\frac{1}{2} = 6\frac{1}{8}$

$5\frac{2}{3} \div \frac{1}{2} = 11\frac{1}{3}$ $\frac{4}{5} \times 1\frac{1}{8} = \frac{9}{10}$

**Lesson Focus** To use scale drawings to find actual length; to use scale drawings to solve word problems

## Ideas for Getting Started

Generate a discussion in which students recall studies about prehistoric animals. If possible, have a book with pictures and information to supplement the discussion. Show a picture of the diplodocus and ask students to guess how the length of this animal compares with the length of the classroom. For example, the diplodocus was approximately 25 m long, about 3 times the length of a classroom. Discuss and compare student guesses.

## Using Page 290

**Lesson Development** Direct students' attention to the picture of the triceratops at the top of the page. Tell students that the scale is 2 cm to 3 m. This means that every 2 cm on the drawing represents 3 m of actual length. Put the scale ratio 2 to 3 on the chalkboard and use it to set up the proportions shown. Work through the solution to the proportion with students. Use the cross product method to check the solution, then have students read the answer to the question using a complete sentence.

**Exercises 1–3** Before assigning these exercises, remind students that we are comparing the picture length with the actual length. We know the scale ratio is 2 to 3, so we can set up a proportion to find the missing number—the actual length of the dinosaur. Note that exercises 1 and 3 involve decimal length. Some students may need help to solve these proportions. Other students may still need help setting up the proportions. Continue to focus on the scale ratio 2 to 3. Help students, if necessary, to use that ratio as a model in setting up the proportion.

## Using Scale Drawings

The picture is a scale drawing of a dinosaur scientists have named *triceratops*. How long was the triceratops?

Every **2 cm** of picture length represents **3 m** of the dinosaur's actual length.

The **scale ratio** is

$\frac{2}{3}$ ← cm / ← m

**Scale** 2 cm:3 m

We use this ratio to solve the problem.

$$\frac{2}{3} = \frac{6}{l} \begin{array}{l}\leftarrow \text{picture length (cm)}\\ \leftarrow \text{actual length (m)}\end{array}$$

$$2 \times l = 3 \times 6$$
$$2 \times l = 18$$
$$l = 18 \div 2, \text{ or } 9$$

The triceratops was 9 m long.

Measure the length of the picture. Then find the actual length of each dinosaur. Use the same scale as in the example above.

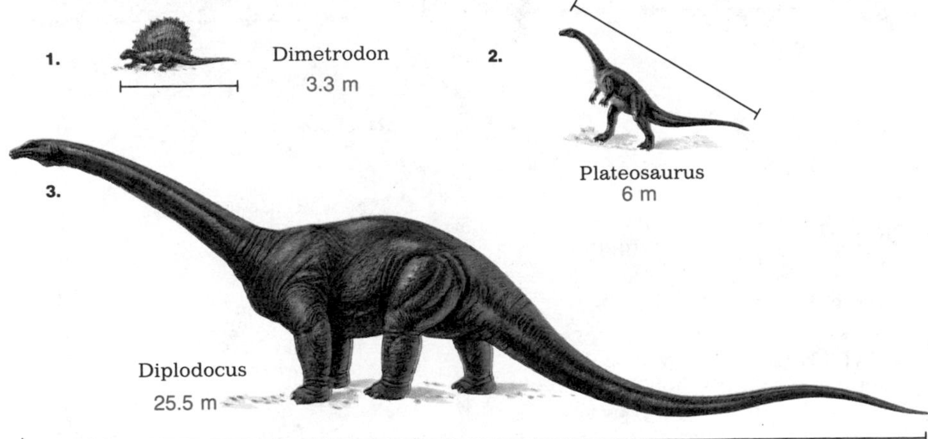


290

## Follow Up

### Reteaching

Have available several different examples of scale drawings from an encyclopedia or other reference book. Work with students to identify the scale ratio and then to find the actual length. Make sure students understand that equal ratio equations can be found by solving a cross-product equation.

### Enrichment

Provide students with graph paper (TRB p. 271) and challenge them to create a scale drawing of an imaginary animal. Tell students to include a scale ratio, and then to write a brief paragraph describing the creatures they have drawn.

| Assignment Guide | | | |
|---|---|---|---|
| | Minimum | Average | Extended |
| page 290 | 1–3 | 1–3 | 1–3 |
| page 291 | 1–5 | 1–6 | 1–7 |

## Problem Solving: Using Scale Drawings

Solve. Use the scale 2 cm:3 m.

Allosaurus

Tyrannosaurus

1. What was the actual length of the allosaurus? 10.5 m

2. An elephant is 3.5 m long. How many times that long was the allosaurus? (Use the answer from problem 1.) 3

3. What was the actual length of the tyrannosaurus? 15 m

4. A car might be $4\frac{1}{4}$ m long. How much more or less was the length of the tyrannosaurus than 4 car lengths? (Use the answer from problem 3.) 2 m less

Stegosaurus

5. A boxcar on a train might be 15.8 m long. How much more or less was the length of the stegosaurus than the length of a boxcar? 9.8 m less

6. **DATA BANK** Use the Data Bank on page 410 to find which prehistoric reptile was
   **A** closest in length to the allosaurus. mosasaur
   **B** 2.2 m shorter than the tyrannosaurus. ichthyosaur
   **C** about 2.1 times the length of the stegosaurus. plesiosaur

7. **Try This** The length of a brachiosaurus was 10 m greater than its height. The ratio of its height to its length was 3 to 5. How long and how tall was it? Hint: Guess and check. 25 m long, 15 m high



## Using Page 291

**Exercises 1–5** Note that exercises 1 and 3 are the same type of exercises as those on page 290. In exercises 2 and 4 students must use the answers for exercises 1 and 3 to solve the problems.

**Data Bank** This Data Bank includes three questions and requires students to analyze the table carefully. Remind students that they refer to the tables in the back of the book for the needed data.

**Try This** A possible strategy, Guess and Check, was taught on page 48.

**Discussion** "What is the question we want to answer about the brachiosaurus?" (How long and how tall was it?) "How much greater was its length than its height?" (10 m) "What is the ratio of its height to its length?" $\left(\frac{3}{5}\right)$ "Is there a way to use operations to find the answer?" (No, not enough information is given.) "What strategy might be helpful?" (Guess and Check) "Suppose we guess the height to be 20 m, what would the length be?" (20 + 10 or 30) "What would the ratio of height to length be?" (20 to 30, or 2 to 3) Encourage students to try another guess.

**Solution** The brachiosaurus is 15 m tall and 25 m long. If the height is 15 m, the length would be 15 + 10 or 25 m, and the ratio of height to length would be 15 to 25 or $\frac{3}{5}$. This length and height fit the conditions of the problem and seem reasonable.

## Ideas That Work

### Math for the Gifted

Place a mirror on the floor or ground between a volunteer and a tall object. Move the mirror along an imaginary line between the object and the person until the top of the object appears in the mirror. Then measure the distance from the person's feet to the top of the mirror image, the distance from the top of the mirror image to the base of the object, and from the mirror image to the person's eye. Write these measurements as a proportion as follows:

$$\frac{\text{eye height}}{\text{object height}} = \frac{\text{feet to image}}{\text{object to image}}$$

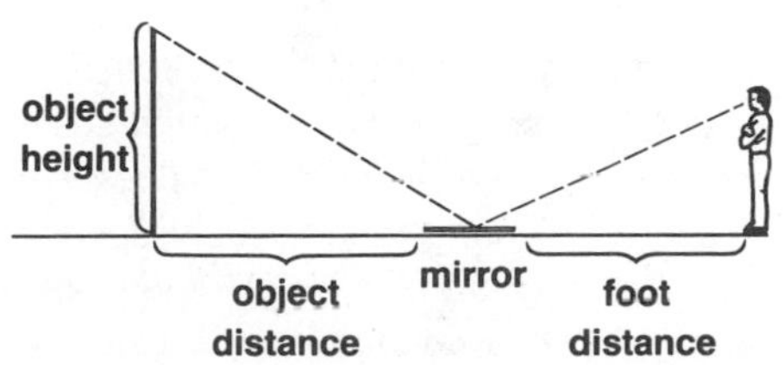


Challenge students to solve this proportion and then compare it to a measurement of the object. These measurements are best done in centimeters or meters. There may be some inaccuracy due to variations in measurement. Stress that this method can be used to get quick estimates; surveying instruments and more advanced mathematics are used to get accurate measurements.

**Practice Supplement,** page 112

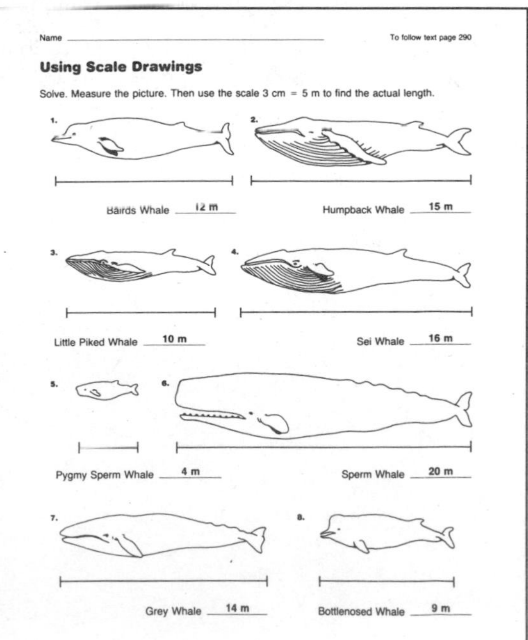

Name ________ To follow text page 290

**Using Scale Drawings**

Solve. Measure the picture. Then use the scale 3 cm = 5 m to find the actual length.

1. Bairds Whale 12 m
2. Humpback Whale 15 m
3. Little Piked Whale 10 m
4. Sei Whale 16 m
5. Pygmy Sperm Whale 4 m
6. Sperm Whale 20 m
7. Grey Whale 14 m
8. Bottlenosed Whale 9 m

**Quick Review** Students give answers in the appropriate units.

$\frac{1}{2} \times 60$ kg = 30 kg   6 mL $\div \frac{3}{4}$ = 8 mL   18 cm $\times \frac{1}{3}$ = 6 cm   $\frac{1}{3} \times 6$ km = 2 km

32 m $\times \frac{3}{4}$ = 24 m   16 L $\times \frac{3}{8}$ = 6 L   $\frac{1}{7} \times 56$ km = 8 km   $\frac{7}{8} \times \$40.00$ = \$35.00

**Lesson Focus** To use a map scale to estimate distances; to practice solving word problems involving all operations

## Ideas for Getting Started

Conduct a brief discussion about Yellowstone National Park. Tell students that the park was formed by an act of Congress in 1872 and is the largest national park. Also discuss the importance of maps and the fact that a map can be used to find the actual distance between two locations.

## Using Page 292

**Lesson Development** Direct students' attention to the map at the top of the page. Ask a volunteer to read the question. Point out that 1 cm on the map represents 10 km of actual distance. Tell students that we can use this fact to help us to find how many kilometers we must drive from West Thumb to the South Entrance. Observe with students that the map of Yellowstone Park is not an actual road map. Because of intervening mountains, bodies of water, and the like, the actual road distance between two points on a map such as this may be much greater than the distance "as the crow flies." However, the distances found by measuring line segments connecting points on this map do represent true distances. Then focus on the two steps shown. Emphasize that it is important to measure accurately. Encourage students to measure to the nearest tenth of a centimeter. Then write the proportion on the chalkboard and work through the solution with students. Emphasize that accurate measurement will assure an estimate close to the actual distance. Note that small variations in the students' rulers could cause some variation in their answers.

**Exercises 1–6** In each of these exercises students must first locate the places on the map. Continue to emphasize that careful measurement to the nearest tenth of a centimeter is needed. If necessary, help students set up proportions.

**Exercise 7** Note that this exercise requires that a decision be made. Students may wish to find the distance necessary to go through Norris and Canyon Village to Pahaska and compare it to their calculated trip through Old Faithful and West Thumb to Pahaska.

## Using a Map Scale to Estimate Distances

About how far must you drive to get from West Thumb to the South Entrance to Yellowstone National Park?

You can measure and use a scale for a map to estimate an actual driving or hiking distance.

Step 1
Measure the distance on the map.

Step 2
Solve a proportion to find the actual distance ($D$).

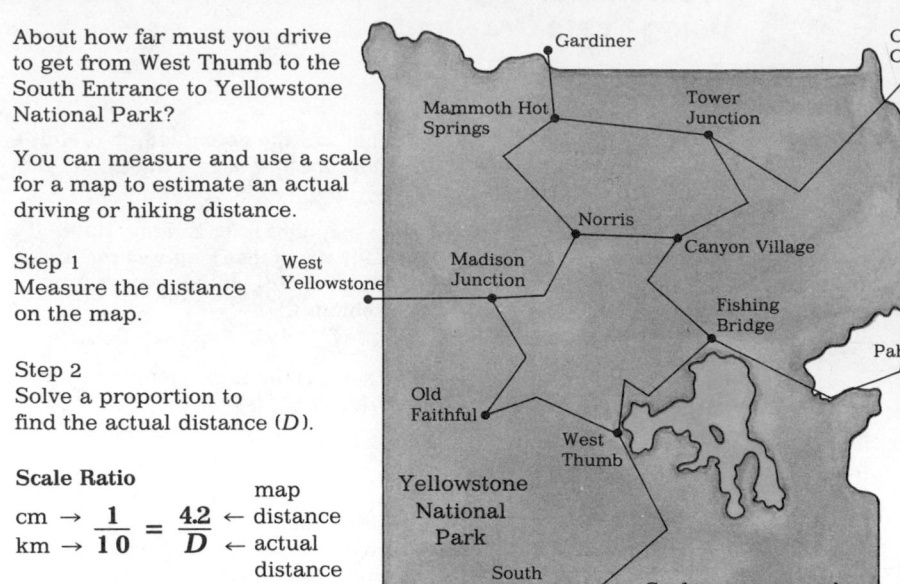

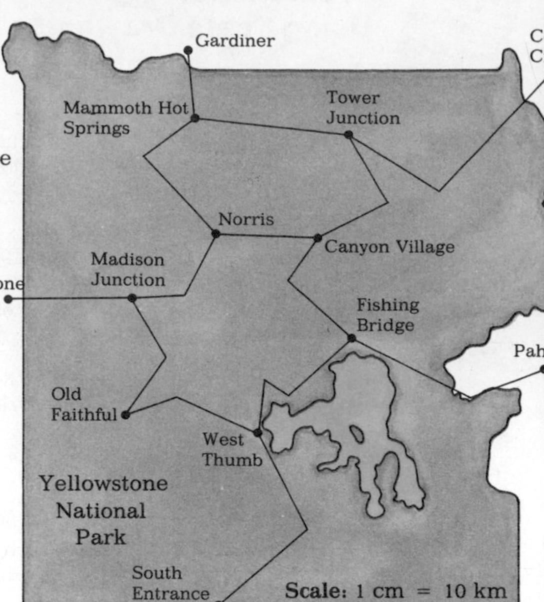


**Scale Ratio**

$$\begin{matrix} \text{cm} \rightarrow \\ \text{km} \rightarrow \end{matrix} \frac{1}{10} = \frac{4.2}{D} \begin{matrix} \leftarrow \text{map distance} \\ \leftarrow \text{actual distance} \end{matrix}$$

$D = 10 \times 4.2$, or $42$ km

Estimate these actual distances in Yellowstone National Park. Measure to the nearest tenth of a centimeter.

1. Cooke City to Tower Junction 30 km
2. Pahaska through Fishing Bridge to Canyon Village 66 km
3. Mammoth Hot Springs through Madison Junction to Old Faithful 81 km
4. Fishing Bridge through West Thumb to Old Faithful 58 km
5. South Entrance through Old Faithful to West Yellowstone 118 km
6. The shortest route from Gardiner through Canyon Village to Fishing Bridge 93 km
7. ★ The shortest route from West Yellowstone through the park to Pahaska 131 km



## Follow Up

### Reteaching

Help students find the distance from City A to City B on a map by using the scale and measuring as accurately as possible. A usual scale is 1 cm to 10 km. Suppose the distance from A to B measures 8.3 km. With students' help, set up the proportion, $\frac{1}{10} = \frac{8.3}{n}$. Work with students to find the distance from A to B. (83 km) Encourage students to try other examples.

### Enrichment

Suggest that students find the actual dimensions of the classroom, the playground, the school cafeteria, or a room in their home. Have them make a scale drawing of the floor plan for the area they have chosen. If necessary, help them plan the scale so that the drawing will fit on the size paper available. Encourage them to include in the drawing details such as furniture, windows, doors, landmarks, or trees.

| Assignment Guide | | | |
|---|---|---|---|
| | Minimum | Average | Extended |
| page 292 | | 1–6 | 1–7 |
| page 293 | 1–6 | 1–7 | 1–8 |

## Problem Solving: Practice

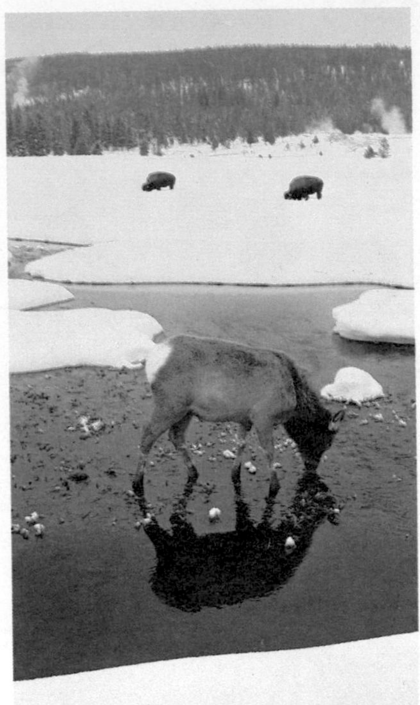

Solve.

1. A group of backpackers in Yellowstone hiked 402 km in 34 days. What was the average number of kilometers they hiked per day, to the nearest tenth of a kilometer? 11.8 km

2. The group started at Gardiner and hiked first to Old Faithful. They hiked 28 km farther than they would have if they had followed the road. Estimate how far they hiked. (Use the map and scale on page 292.) 122 km

3. One hiker weighed 56 kg. Her backpack weighed $\frac{1}{4}$ as much as she did. What was the total weight of the hiker and the backpack? 70 kg

4. Yellowstone National Park has $\frac{3}{4}$ million hectares of land. Forest covers $\frac{4}{5}$ of this land. How many million hectares is covered by forest? $\frac{3}{5}$ million hectares

5. Yellowstone Lake is 2,357 m above sea level. Mt. Holmes is 3,162 m above sea level. How much higher than the lake must a hiker climb to reach the top of the mountain? 805 m

6. It is estimated that if you travel through Yellowstone by car, you see only 0.05 of the park. The park has an area of 8,983 km$^2$. How much of this area do you see if you travel by car? 449 km$^2$

7. The hikers saw 3 bison and 8 elk. They had heard that there were about 600 bison in the park. If the animals they saw represent the ratio of bison to elk, how many elk would you expect to be in the park? 1,600

8. **Try This** Suppose you can run 8 m/s (meters per second) and a grizzly bear can run 16 m/s. You are 50 m ahead of the bear when it begins to chase you. It will take you 6 s to reach your cabin. Can you get to your cabin before the bear catches up to you? Yes, because after 6 s you will still be 2 m ahead of the bear.



## Using Page 293

**Lesson Development** Before assigning these exercises, briefly review with students the 5-Point Checklist in the logo at the top of the page.

**Exercises 1–7** Note that exercises 2 and 7 are probably best solved by setting up proportions. Exercises 3 and 4 involve multiplying fractions, and exercise 6 provides a review of multiplying by a small decimal.

**Try This** A possible strategy, Draw a Picture, was taught on page 74.

**Discussion** "What question do we want to answer about the grizzly bear?" (Can you get to your cabin before the bear catches up to you?) "How fast are we supposing that you can run?" (8 m/s) "How fast can the bear run?" (16 m/s) "How far ahead of the bear are you?" (50 m) "How many seconds will it take you to reach your cabin?" (6) "What strategy could you use to find the solution?" (It might help to draw a picture.)

**Solution** As shown below, if you run 6 s and the bear runs 6 s, the bear will still be 2 m behind you.

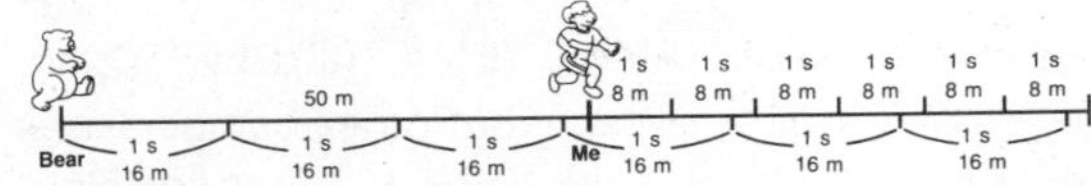


An alternate strategy could be Choose the Operations. If the bear runs for 6 s at 16 m/s, the bear will run 96 m. If you run 6 m at 8 m/s, you will run 48 m. 48 plus the 50 meters you were ahead of the bear makes 98 m. At the end of 6 s you will be 2 m ahead of the bear.

**Reteaching Supplement,** page 69

Name ____________ To follow text page 292

**Using a Map Scale To Estimate Distances**

Measure the distances between the cities on the map. Find the air distance between each pair of U.S. cities.
**Answers may vary depending on accuracy of measurement.**

San Francisco, Chicago, New York, Dallas
Scale: 1 mm = 86 km

1. San Francisco to New York 4,128 km

The distance on the map is 48 mm.

$\frac{48 \text{ mm}}{1 \text{ mm}} = \frac{D}{86 \text{ km}}$ (distances on the map; air distances)

$48 \times 86 = 1 \times D$
$4{,}128 = D$

2. San Francisco to Chicago 3,010 km
3. Chicago to New York 1,118 km
4. San Francisco to Dallas 2,408 km

Find the air distance between each pair of Canadian cities.

5. Halifax to Montreal 780 km
6. Montreal to Toronto 540 km
7. Toronto to Winnipeg 1,500 km
8. Winnipeg to Calgary 1,200 km
9. Calgary to Vancouver 600 km

Calgary, Vancouver, Winnipeg, Montreal, Halifax, Toronto
Scale: 1 mm = 60 km

**Enrichment Supplement,** page 69

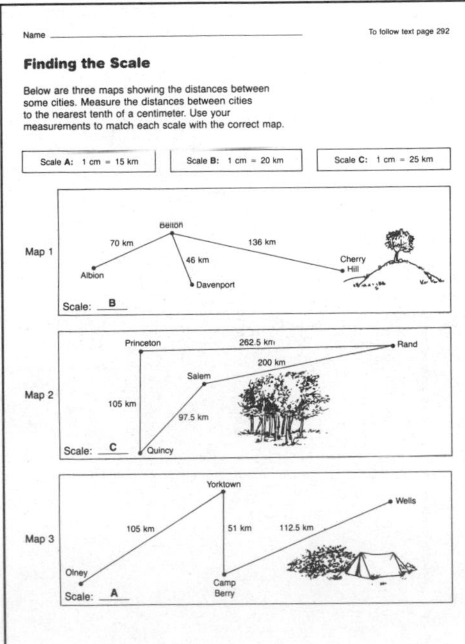
Name ____________ To follow text page 292

**Finding the Scale**

Below are three maps showing the distances between some cities. Measure the distances between cities to the nearest tenth of a centimeter. Use your measurements to match each scale with the correct map.

Scale **A**: 1 cm = 15 km
Scale **B**: 1 cm = 20 km
Scale **C**: 1 cm = 25 km



**Practice Supplement,** page 113

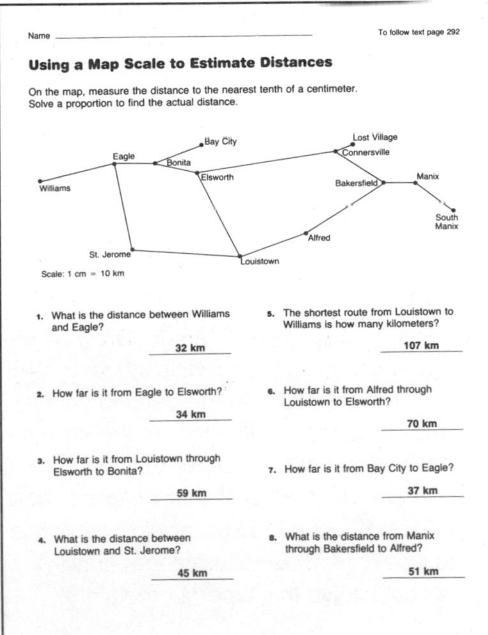
Name ____________ To follow text page 292

**Using a Map Scale to Estimate Distances**

On the map, measure the distance to the nearest tenth of a centimeter. Solve a proportion to find the actual distance.



1. What is the distance between Williams and Eagle? 32 km
2. How far is it from Eagle to Elsworth? 34 km
3. How far is it from Louistown through Elsworth to Bonita? 59 km
4. What is the distance between Louistown and St. Jerome? 45 km
5. The shortest route from Louistown to Williams is how many kilometers? 107 km
6. How far is it from Alfred through Louistown to Elsworth? 70 km
7. How far is it from Bay City to Eagle? 37 km
8. What is the distance from Manix through Bakersfield to Alfred? 51 km

**Lesson Focus** To apply the strategies to solve nonroutine word problems

## Ideas for Getting Started

Review the 5-Point Checklist by focusing on the logo in the upper left-hand corner of the page. Remind students that problem-solving strategies can help them plan how to solve a problem. If you have a problem-solving bulletin board, students could use it as an aid for review.

## Using Page 294

**Lesson Development** Have students read the list of strategies at the top of the page. Tell students that they will find one or more of the strategies useful in solving these problems. Encourage them to try different strategies if they have difficulty solving a problem.

**Exercise 1** A possible strategy, Make an Organized List, was introduced on page 132. "What do we want to know about the bike race?" (How many different orders for the finish of the race are possible?) "How many are in the race?" (4) "One possible order is (A)ndy, (B)ea, (C)athy, (D)ino. Keeping A in first place, what other combinations could there be?" (See list below.) "What combinations are possible with B, C, and D in first place?"

| ABCD | ABDC | ACDB | ACBD | ADBC | ADCB |
|---|---|---|---|---|---|
| BCAD | BCDA | BDAC | BDCA | BACD | BADC |
| CDAB | CDBA | CABD | CADB | CBAD | CBDA |
| DABC | DACB | DBCA | DBAC | DCAB | DCBA |

**Exercise 2** A possible strategy, Use Logical Reasoning, was taught on page 162. "What question is asked about the musical instruments?" (Who plays which instrument?) "What data is given?" Review the information about the four people and the four instruments. Point out that we cannot use the operations to solve this problem. Then help students use a chart to organize the information logically.

**Exercise 3** A possible strategy, Guess and Check, was taught on page 48. "What are we asked to find out about Lara's test points?" (How many of each type question did Lara answer correctly?) "How many questions did Lara answer correctly?" (22) "How many total points did she score?" (86) "If she answered 10 questions worth 3 points each, how many worth 5 points would she have answered correctly?" (12) "Does this check?" (no) "Try another guess."

**Exercise 4** A possible strategy, Draw a Picture, was introduced on page 74. Have students read the problem carefully and give the needed data as you draw an appropriate illustration on the chalkboard. "How far was it from the trapeze to the net?" (16 m) "If the clown bounced half that distance, how far would that be?" (8 m) "How far did he bounce the second time?" (4 m) Emphasize that drawing a picture can help solve this type of problem.

## Problem Solving: Using the Strategies

Choose one or more of the strategies listed to help you solve each problem below.

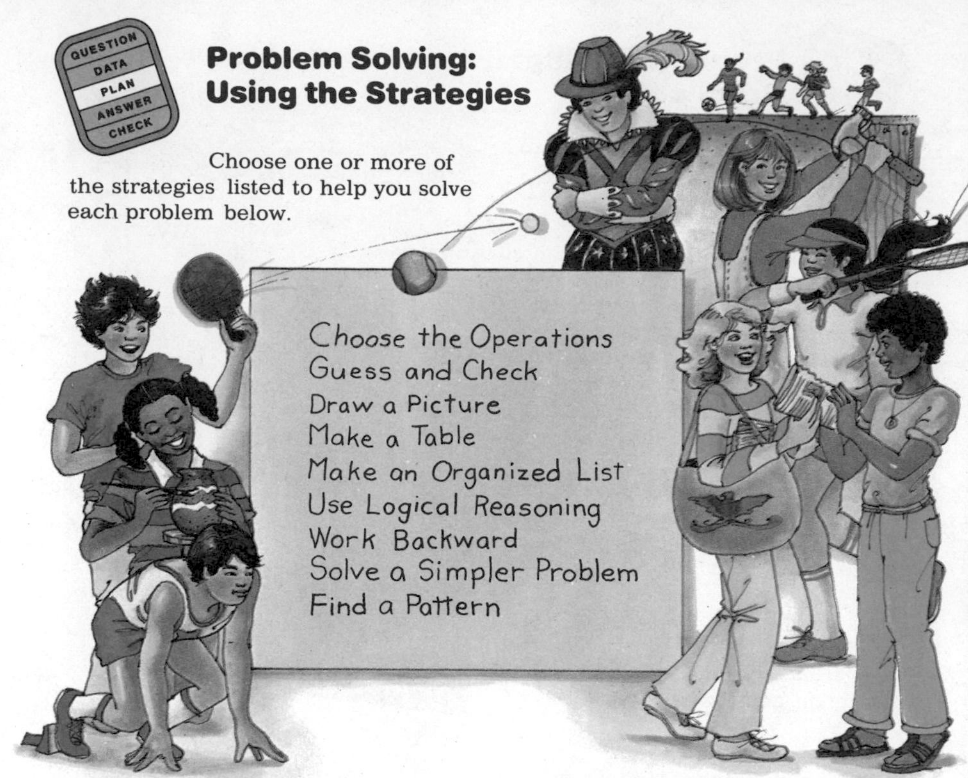

QUESTION
DATA
PLAN
ANSWER
CHECK
Choose the Operations
Guess and Check
Draw a Picture
Make a Table
Make an Organized List
Use Logical Reasoning
Work Backward
Solve a Simpler Problem
Find a Pattern


1. Andy, Bea, Cathy, and Dino are having a 1-km bike race. If there are no ties, how many different orders of finish for their bike race are possible? (One possible order is Andy first, Bea second, Cathy third, and Dino fourth.) 24 (See teaching notes.)

2. Jack, Kris, Lacey, and Milt each play one of these musical instruments: clarinet, flute, trumpet, guitar. Neither Kris nor Lacey has ever played the guitar. Milt plays the trumpet. Kris played the flute but no longer does. Who plays which instrument?
Jack, guitar; Kris, clarinet; Lacey, flute; Milt, trumpet

3. Mrs. Doyle gave a test. The test had 15 questions worth 3 points each and 15 questions worth 5 points each. Lara answered 22 questions correctly and scored 86 points. How many of each type questions did Lara answer correctly? 12 worth 3 points and 10 worth 5 points

4. A clown fell 16 m from a trapeze onto a special net. He bounced up $\frac{1}{2}$ as high as he fell each time until he bounced 1 m high and landed on the shoulders of another clown. Find the total distance the clown traveled. 45 m

## Chapter Review-Test

Write these ratios as fractions.

1. 3 to 4 $\frac{3}{4}$ 2. 9:10 $\frac{9}{10}$ 3. 2 out of 5 $\frac{2}{5}$ 4. 7 for 5 $\frac{7}{5}$ 5. 9 of every 10 $\frac{9}{10}$

Copy and complete to make equal ratios.

6. $\frac{2}{3} = \frac{4}{\blacksquare} = \frac{6}{\blacksquare} = \frac{8}{\blacksquare} = \frac{10}{\blacksquare}$ 6, 9, 12, 15
7. $\frac{5}{8} = \frac{\blacksquare}{16} = \frac{\blacksquare}{24} = \frac{\blacksquare}{32} = \frac{\blacksquare}{40}$ 10, 15, 20, 25
8. $\frac{5}{4} = \frac{10}{\blacksquare} = \frac{15}{\blacksquare} = \frac{20}{\blacksquare} = \frac{25}{\blacksquare}$ 8, 12, 16, 20

Write cross products to decide whether the ratios are equal.
Write **equal** or **not equal**.

9. $\frac{5}{12}, \frac{3}{8}$ not equal
10. $\frac{9}{12}, \frac{6}{8}$ equal
11. $\frac{7}{21}, \frac{3}{9}$ equal
12. $\frac{4}{5}, \frac{12}{20}$ not equal
13. $\frac{5}{3}, \frac{25}{15}$ equal
14. $\frac{3}{16}, \frac{9}{48}$ equal

Solve these proportions.

15. $\frac{3}{4} = \frac{n}{36}$ $n = 27$
16. $\frac{4}{5} = \frac{32}{n}$ $n = 40$
17. $\frac{n}{28} = \frac{15}{35}$ $n = 12$
18. $\frac{7}{n} = \frac{42}{60}$ $n = 10$
19. $\frac{27}{n} = \frac{15}{5}$ $n = 9$

20. Write a proportion and solve it to find the height of the tower. $\frac{1}{1.5} = \frac{h}{21}$; $h = 14$ m

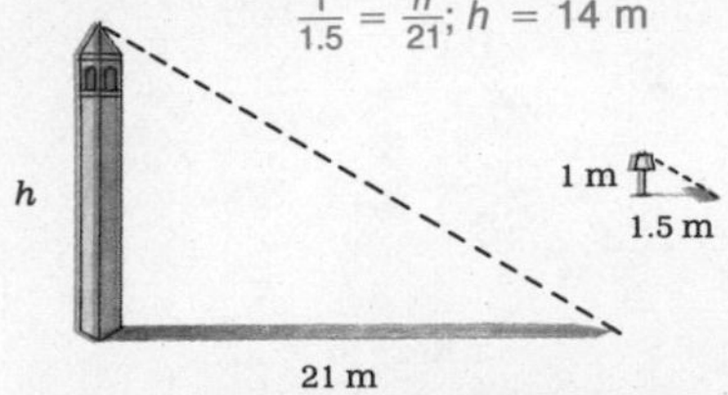
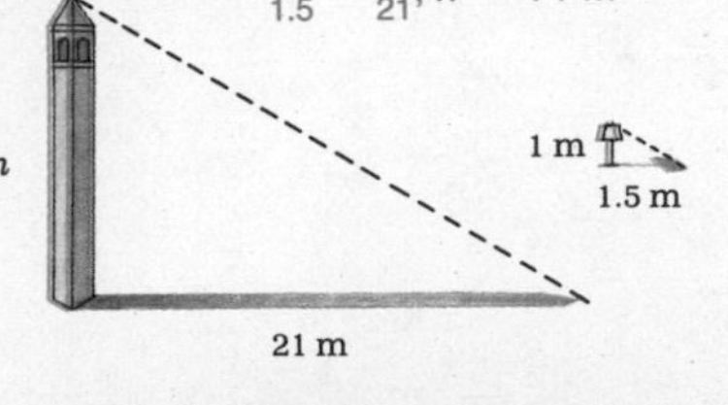


21. Measure the length of the picture. Then find the actual length of the camptosaurus. 4.2 m

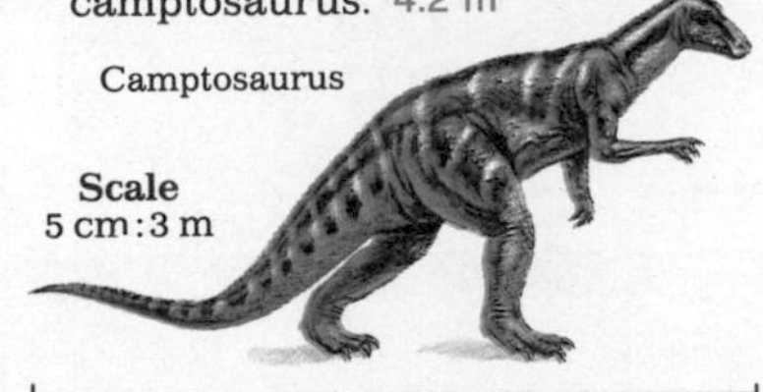


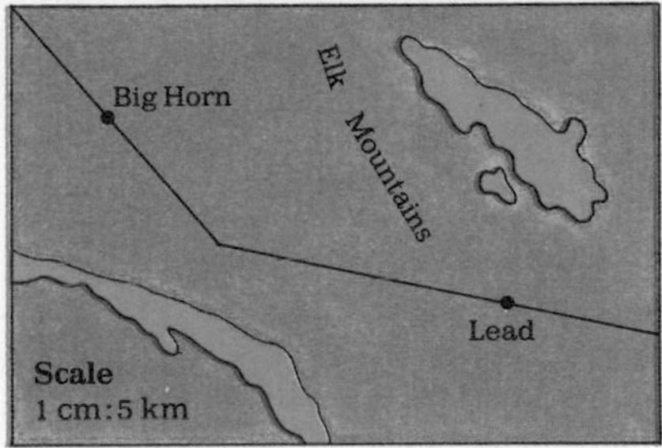


22. Use the map scale and measurement to estimate the actual distance from Big Horn to Lead. 27.5 km

23. In a recent year there were 3 grizzly bears for every 8 black bears in Yellowstone National Park. There were about 400 black bears in the park. About how many grizzly bears were there? 150

295

## Using Page 295

The exercises in the Chapter Review-Test emphasize the major concepts and skills presented in this chapter. These exercises may be used as a review assignment or as a test, depending upon your needs.

**Item Analysis** The table below correlates the Chapter Review-Test items with objectives and with the student text pages on which the concepts or skills were taught. Note that items 20 and 22 are derived from lessons for which no minimum assignment was suggested in the Assignment Guide.

| Items | Objectives | Related text pages |
|---|---|---|
| 1–14 | 11.1 | 278–281 |
| 15–19 | 11.2 | 282–283 |
| 20–21 | 11.3 | 286–290 |
| 22 | 11.4 | 292 |
| 23 | 11.5 | 284–285, 291, 293 |

## Assessment Options

If you use the Chapter Review-Test as a review assignment, you may wish to use the multiple-choice test or the free-response test to evaluate mastery of the chapter objectives. The items on these tests have a one-to-one correspondence in terms of content and level of difficulty. A correlation of test items to objectives and student text pages is provided in the Management Guide for Chapter 11. Note that items 14 and 16–19 are derived from lessons for which no minimum assignment was suggested in the Assignment Guide.

**Multiple-Choice Test,** TRB pages 31–33

**Free-Response Test,** TRB pages 69–70

## TRB Options

The following blackline masters are available for use with this chapter. If you have not already assigned these materials, you may wish to use them to close the chapter.

**Recreation,** TRB page 161

**Consumer Applications,** TRB page 179

**Calculator Technology,** TRB page 197

**Reading Math,** TRB page 229

**Family Involvement,** TRB pages 257–258

## Using Page 296

The exercises on this page are intended for those students who experienced difficulty with the Chapter Review-Test on page 295. Should students require reteaching of these key concepts and skills, please refer to the teaching notes below. Otherwise, the Another Look exercises can be assigned as independent work, with students using the accompanying sample problems and hints as guides.

**Exercises 1–7** This concept was originally taught on pages 278–279. Direct students' attention to the display box on the left. Have students review the three ways to indicate a ratio. Be sure students understand that the ratio 2 to 3 is different from the ratio 3 to 2.

**Exercises 8–11** This skill was originally taught on pages 280–281. Review the procedure for producing equal ratios as shown in the second display box. Emphasize that this is the same as the procedure used for producing equivalent fractions. Remind students that whenever they multiply the numerator and denominator by the same number, the result is an equivalent fraction. "In exercise 8 what number was the first numerator multiplied by to get the second numerator?" (2) "What should we multiply the denominator by to produce an equal ratio?" (2) "What number was the numerator multiplied by to get the third fraction?" (3) "What shall we multiply the denominator by to produce an equal ratio?" (3) Continue this type of questioning until you are confident that students understand this process.

**Exercises 12–21** This skill was originally taught on pages 282–283. Work through the example showing how to use cross products to solve a proportion. Remind students that if the ratios are equal, the cross products are equal, and vice versa. Point out that no matter where the variable is placed, the cross-product equation can be written with the variable on the left. Work through several examples to help students understand this procedure. Encourage them to check their solutions by finding the cross products.

## *Another Look*

Ratios compare quantities.

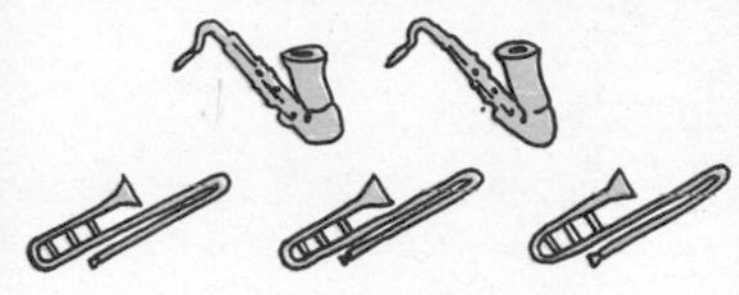

The ratio of saxophones to trombones is

2 to 3

We write: 2:3 or $\frac{2}{3}$

Equal ratios can be found by multiplying both numbers in the ratio by the same factor.

erasers

$$\frac{3}{10} = \frac{6}{20} = \frac{9}{30} = \frac{12}{40}$$

(×2) (×3) (×4)

cents

You can solve proportions by multiplying or dividing.

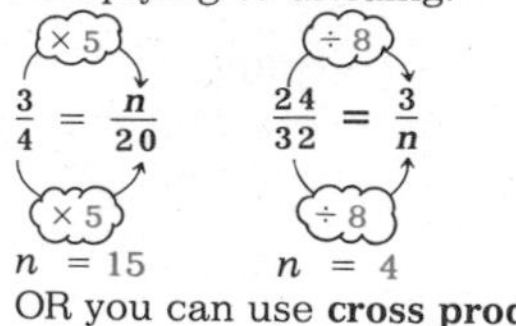

$\frac{3}{4} = \frac{n}{20}$ (×5) $n = 15$

$\frac{24}{32} = \frac{3}{n}$ (÷8) $n = 4$

OR you can use **cross products.**

$\frac{2}{3} = \frac{n}{36}$ ← These products are equal

$3 \times n = 2 \times 36$

$3 \times n = 72$

$n = 72 \div 3$, or 24

**Write each ratio as a fraction.**

1. The ratio of tubas to drums is 1 to 4. $\frac{1}{4}$
2. A map used the scale 2 cm = 5 m. $\frac{2}{5}$
3. At the meeting, 3 out of 4 people were adults. $\frac{3}{4}$
4. You can buy 3 tickets for \$5. $\frac{3}{5}$
5. A dinosaur traveled 3 km in 1 hour. $\frac{3}{1}$
6. Allison painted 4 chairs in 3 hours. $\frac{4}{3}$
7. The ratio of cats to dogs is 3:8. $\frac{3}{8}$

**Copy and complete to make equal ratios.**

8. $\frac{3}{8} = \frac{6}{■} = \frac{9}{■} = \frac{12}{■} = \frac{15}{■}$ 16, 24, 32, 40
9. $\frac{7}{10} = \frac{■}{20} = \frac{■}{30} = \frac{■}{40} = \frac{■}{50}$ 14, 21, 28, 35
10. $\frac{1}{4} = \frac{■}{8} = \frac{2}{■} = \frac{■}{16} = \frac{4}{■}$ 2, 8, 4, 16
11. $\frac{5}{6} = \frac{10}{■} = \frac{■}{18} = \frac{20}{■} = \frac{■}{30}$ 12, 15, 24, 25

**Solve the proportions.**

12. $\frac{n}{5} = \frac{8}{20}$ $n = 2$
13. $\frac{10}{4} = \frac{5}{n}$ $n = 2$
14. $\frac{15}{16} = \frac{n}{32}$ $n = 30$
15. $\frac{3}{25} = \frac{9}{n}$ $n = 75$
16. $\frac{45}{50} = \frac{n}{10}$ $n = 9$
17. $\frac{16}{n} = \frac{24}{30}$ $n = 20$
18. $\frac{1.5}{4.5} = \frac{n}{15}$ $n = 5$
19. $\frac{12}{5} = \frac{4.8}{n}$ $n = 2$
20. $\frac{n}{4} = \frac{6}{5}$ $n = 4.8$
21. $\frac{7}{n} = \frac{3.5}{14}$ $n = 28$



## Just for Teachers

### Mathematics in Art

Leonardo da Vinci wrote, "Let no one who is not a mathematician read my works." The relationship between art and mathematics was studied by many Renaissance painters who developed the technique of using perspective to convey three-dimensionality in their paintings. Perspective—from the Latin *pericere, per* meaning through, and *specere,* to look—is based upon the knowledge and application of mathematics and geometry.

Renaissance art reflected profound changes in European society. Medieval art had generally portrayed individuals according to their religious-political importance rather than how realistically proportional they were to their environment. Society was moving away from a religion-dominated life in which the Church was the central force in both intellectual and everyday life. The period witnessed a resurgence of the Greek idea that nature could be best understood by revealing its underlying mathematical structure. Science and mathematics began to explain the movements and positionings of the planets and the stars, and Earth was no longer considered the center of the universe. Artists began to represent this physical world accurately by incorporating perspective in their paintings.

## Enrichment

### The Number $\pi$—An Important Ratio

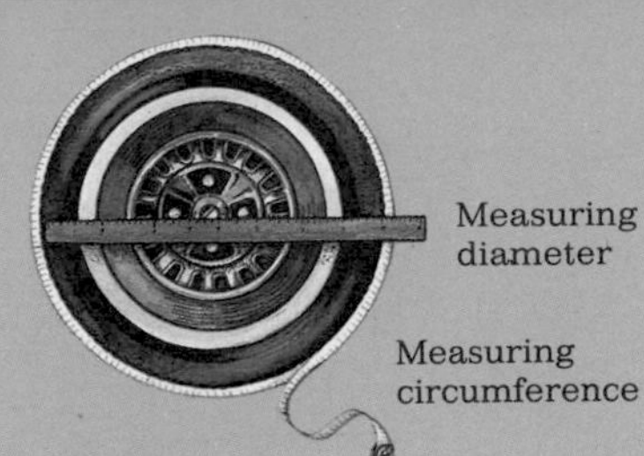


The **circumference** ($C$) of a circle is the distance around the circle. The **diameter** ($d$) of a circle is the distance across the circle (through the center).

The **ratio of $C$ to $d$** $\left(\frac{C}{d}\right)$ is a very important ratio!

The circumference of each circle is given. Measure the diameter to the nearest centimeter and find $\frac{C}{d}$ as a decimal to the nearest hundredth. See teaching notes.

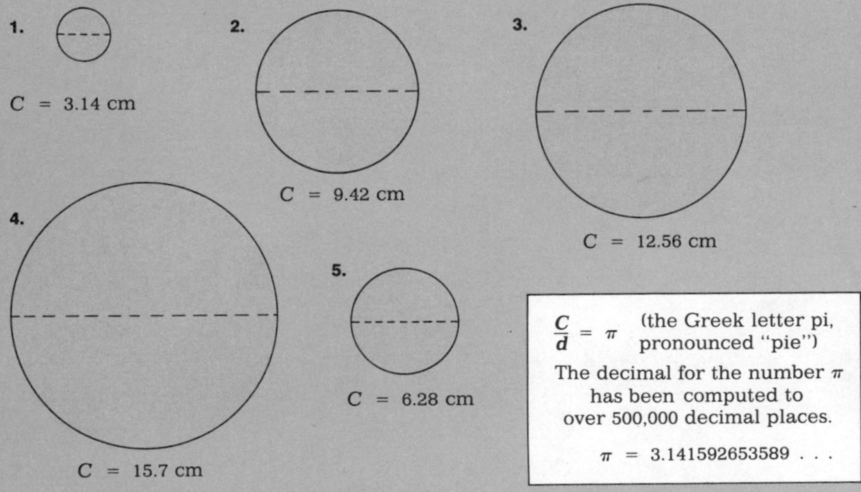


$\frac{C}{d} = \pi$ (the Greek letter pi, pronounced "pie")

The decimal for the number $\pi$ has been computed to over 500,000 decimal places.

$\pi = 3.141592653589\ldots$

6. Using string or a tape measure to find the circumference and diameter of several circular objects (food or drink containers, auto or bike tires, records, bracelet, pots or pans, and the like). Find the ratio $\frac{C}{d}$ as a decimal to the nearest hundredth. Is $\frac{C}{d}$ for your measurements close to $\pi$? Answers will vary.



One method artists used to achieve perspective was the use of parallel lines that appeared to converge at some vanishing point in the distance. Objects that were farther away from the eye appeared smaller than objects that were closer. By properly applying proportion and geometry, artists could convey three-dimensionality in their paintings.

Albrecht Durer (1471–1528), the German artist, devised a method for achieving perspective. He designed a glass grid through which the artist viewed the scene to be painted. Using an identical ruled paper or canvas, the artist represented section by section the subject or scene exactly as it appeared through the glass.

## Using Page 297

This page is intended for those students who successfully completed the Chapter Review-Test on page 295. You may wish to assign this page as independent work while you use the Another Look exercises to reteach the basic concepts and skills of the chapter. Or, you may decide that all students would benefit from exposure to this Enrichment activity.

**Lesson Development** Review the definitions given for circumference and diameter at the top of the page. Refer to the picture to help make these ideas clear. Remind students that we express a ratio as a fraction and that we can find a decimal for such a fraction by dividing. Thus a ratio can also be expressed as a decimal. The exercises in this lesson give students the opportunity to discover through their own calculations that the ratio of the circumference to the diameter of any circle is the same.

**Exercises 1–5** After students have completed these exercises, point out that the results for each problem should be very close to 3.14 depending on the accuracy of measurements and computations. Then call attention to the information in the display box. Make sure students understand that for any circle the ratio of the circumference to the diameter is a number called pi, represented by the symbol $\pi$.

**Exercise 6** Emphasize the importance of careful, accurate measurement in this exercise. To extend the idea, give students a problem such as the following: A rope 50 m long was needed to encircle one of the world's largest trees. What was the diameter of a cross section of the tree trunk? (15.92 m)

## Using Page 298

The exercises on this page provide practice for maintaining cumulative skills. The emphasis in this Cumulative Review is on addition and subtraction of fractions (Chapter 8), geometry (Chapter 10), and problem solving (Chapter 8).

**Item Analysis** The table below correlates the Cumulative Review items with objectives and with the student book pages on which the concepts or skills were taught.

| Items | Objectives | Related text pages |
|---|---|---|
| 1–4 | 8.4 | 207–215 |
| 5–8 | 10.4 | 258–262 |
| 9–10 | 10.5 | 263 |
| 11–12 | 10.7 | 270–271 |
| 13–14 | 8.5 | 203, 206, 216–217 |

## Cumulative Review

Add or subtract.

1. $\frac{3}{8} + \frac{3}{4}$
A $1\frac{1}{4}$ (B) $1\frac{1}{8}$ C $\frac{3}{8}$ D not given

2. $\frac{5}{9} - \frac{1}{3}$
(A) $\frac{2}{9}$ B $\frac{4}{6}$ C $\frac{4}{9}$ D not given

3. $3\frac{1}{2} + 4\frac{5}{6}$
A $7\frac{3}{4}$ (B) $8\frac{1}{3}$ C $8\frac{5}{6}$ D not given

4. $6\frac{1}{10} - 4\frac{1}{2}$
A $2\frac{3}{5}$ (B) $1\frac{3}{5}$ C $2\frac{1}{8}$ D not given

What kind of triangle is it?

5. 
A scalene
(B) isosceles
C equilateral
D not given

6. 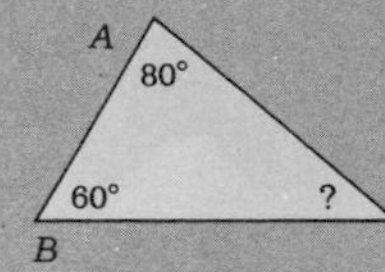
A acute
B right
(C) obtuse
D not given

7. What is the measure of $\angle C$?

A 80° 60° ? B C

A 90°
B 50°
(C) 40°
D not given

8. Name the polygon.
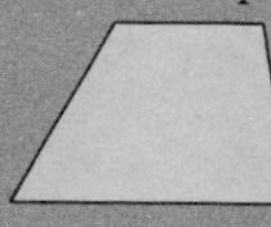
A parallelogram
B square
C rhombus
(D) not given

9. Name a diameter of circle O.
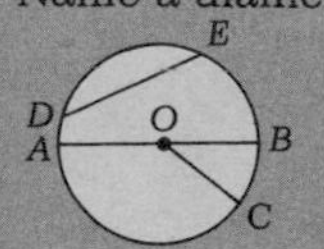

A $\overline{DE}$
B $\overline{OC}$
(C) $\overline{AB}$
D not given

10. Name a chord of circle O.
(A) $DE$ B $OC$
C $AO$ D not given

11. Name the space figure.

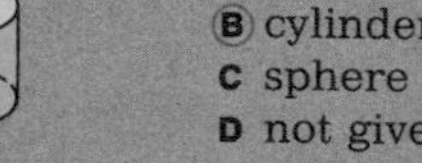
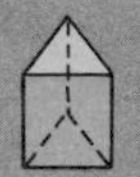
A cone
(B) cylinder
C sphere
D not given

12. Give the number of faces.
A 4
(B) 5
C 6
D not given

13. A recipe calls for $2\frac{1}{2}$ cups of apple juice and $1\frac{3}{4}$ cups of pineapple juice. What is the total amount of juice?
(A) $4\frac{1}{4}$ cups B $\frac{3}{4}$ cups
C $3\frac{1}{4}$ cups D not given

14. Ron has run $3\frac{4}{5}$ km. He wants to run a total of $6\frac{1}{2}$ km. How much farther must he run?
(A) $2\frac{7}{10}$ km B $10\frac{3}{10}$ km
C $3\frac{3}{10}$ km D not given

## Objectives

**12.1** Write comparisons as ratios, fractions, decimals, and percents.
**12.2** Find a percent of a number.
**12.3** Solve word problems using the 5-Point Checklist and cumulative computational skills.

## Summary

In this chapter students study the meaning of percent, the use of percent in describing real-world situations, and the relationships among ratios, fractions, decimals, and percents. Students learn procedures for writing a percent for a given decimal, a percent for a given fraction, a fraction for a given percent, and a decimal for a given percent. These techniques are extended to include percents that involve fractions and percents greater than 100 percent. Students then use these basic concepts and procedures to find the percent of a number and to solve word problems involving interest and discounts.

## Mathematical Background

**Percent** The word *percent* means literally "per one hundred." We can use percent when we want to compare numbers to 100. Thus, a percent can be thought of as a ratio in which the second number is always 100.

A hundred square outlined on graph paper can be used to illustrate the idea of percent. Note that 25%, $\frac{25}{100}$, and 0.25 represent the same number. That is, a given number can be written as a percent, a decimal, and a fraction.

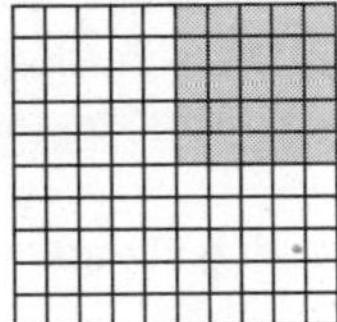

25 out of 100 squares are shaded
25% is shaded

**Fractions, Decimals, and Percents** Students should be able to write decimals and fractions as percents and vice versa. If they understand the concept of percent, translating from any column of row 1 in the table below to any other column should not be difficult.

| | Fraction | Decimal | Percent |
|---|---|---|---|
| 1. | $\frac{37}{100}$ | 0.37 | 37% |
| 2. | $\frac{25}{100}$ or $\frac{1}{4}$ | 0.25 | 25% |
| 3. | $\frac{375}{1,000}$ or $\frac{3}{8}$ | 0.375 | $37\frac{1}{2}$% |
| 4. | $\frac{125}{100}$ or $\frac{5}{4}$ | 1.25 | 125% |
| 5. | $\frac{2}{100}$ or $\frac{1}{50}$ | 0.02 | 2% |
| 6. | $\frac{\frac{1}{2}}{100}$ or $\frac{1}{200}$ or $\frac{5}{1,000}$ | 0.005 | $\frac{1}{2}$% |

In row 2, given the fraction $\frac{1}{4}$, a proportion can be used to find the decimal or percent, that is, $\frac{1}{4} = \frac{n}{100}$. After the proportion is solved, we can see that $n$ is 25 and we can write the decimal 0.25 or the percent 25%.

It is more difficult to write fractions such as the one in row 3 as a fraction with denominator 100. For example, $\frac{3}{8}$ can be written as $\frac{375}{1,000}$, which suggests the decimal 0.375. In the last row of the table we see that $\frac{1}{2}$% can be viewed as $\frac{\frac{1}{2}}{100}$, $\frac{1}{200}$, or $\frac{5}{1,000}$. Thus $\frac{1}{2}$% is the same as 0.005. After students understand this concept, they can write a decimal such as 0.375 as $37\frac{1}{2}$% and vice versa.

Row 4 of the table illustrates a percent greater than 100. To change such a percent to a fraction we can write the number over 100 and reduce. Thus 125% is $\frac{5}{4}$.

Row 5 of the table illustrates a single digit percent, and illustrates the point that the decimal place needed in this case is hundredths, not tenths.

The key skills emphasized here are that of (a) understanding the meaning of percent; (b) writing a fraction equivalent to a given fraction or to solve proportion; and (c) understanding decimal place value $\left(\text{e.g., to recognize that } 0.005 \text{ is } \frac{5}{1,000}\right)$.

Students should become familiar with the relationships involved among the three columns of the table. They also need to understand that division can be useful in writing a decimal or a percent for a given fraction; in fact, students should be encouraged to use the calculator to find a decimal for a given fraction. Note that for a fraction such as $\frac{2}{3}$, a mixed decimal could be used to show the percent or the percent could be approximated. For fractions such as $\frac{5}{8}$, the decimal produced is 0.625. If the students have a clear understanding about row 6 of the table, they will write this fraction as $62\frac{1}{2}$%.

**Finding Percents** After the skills of changing a percent to a decimal or a fraction are developed, students should have little trouble finding the percent of a number. For example, to find 25% of 64, students can change 25% to a fraction and then find $\frac{1}{4}$ of 64. Students could also change 25% to a decimal and find 0.25 × 64. Encourage students to use mental math as often as possible to find percents such as 25%, 50%, and perhaps 20% and 75%.

**Problem Solving** Problem-solving experiences in this chapter involve continued emphasis on the 5-Point Checklist and on the strategies developed. On page 307, Estimation with Percents, students think about a circle as 100%, half a circle as 50%, and one fourth a circle as 25%, and then use these percents as benchmarks to estimate other percents as described. Because interest is so important in real-world situations, there is a problem-solving lesson (Finding Interest, pages 310–311) to help students understand the role of interest in saving and borrowing. Using Data from an Advertisement on page 312 involves the idea of discount and sale price. On page 313, students practice problem-solving skills involving all operations. On page 314, the first of a series of five applied problems is introduced. These lessons provide real-world problems that might be encountered in an everyday setting. Students must carefully organize a large amount of data in order to decide on a solution to the problem.

### Vocabulary

| | | |
|---|---|---|
| percent | interest | sale price |
| mixed decimal | discount | |

## Error Analysis

This chapter presents the concept of percent and discusses the relationships among decimals, fractions, and percents. The material extends the use of fractions and how fractions are defined. In learning to write these comparisons, whole-number division skills and an understanding of multiples of 10 are essential prerequisite skills. Error patterns that might occur with the material in this chapter are discussed below.

**Error Pattern 1**

$33\frac{1}{3}\% = 3.3\frac{1}{3}$ $\qquad 37\frac{1}{2}\% = 3.7\frac{1}{2}$ $\qquad 83\frac{1}{2}\% = 8.3\frac{1}{2}$

**Diagnosis** The student has changed the percents to decimals by simply moving the decimal point two places to the left. The error has occurred because the student has counted the fraction as one decimal point, when in fact the counting should begin between the fraction and the whole numbers.

**Remediation** Start with a fraction such as $\frac{32}{100}$. Use a 10 by 10 grid to illustrate this comparison as 32 out of 100 or as 0.32. Then write this comparison as $0.32 = \frac{32}{100} = 32\%$. Have students look at the position of the decimal point and observe that when a decimal is changed to a percent the decimal point is moved two places to the right. Then show an example such as $0.33\frac{1}{2}$, and follow the same procedure. Move the decimal point two places to the right, placing it between the whole number and the fractional part. Explain to students that $0.33\frac{1}{2}\% = 33.\frac{1}{2}\%$. However, by convention, the decimal point is not written.

**Error Pattern 2**

```
     0.08 R4        0.37 R4        0.83 R2
  12)1.00         8)3.00         6)5.00
       96           2 4            4 8
        4            60             20
                     56             18
                      4              2
```

$\frac{1}{12} = 8\%$ $\qquad \frac{3}{8} = 37\%$ $\qquad \frac{5}{6} = 83\%$

**Diagnosis** The student has shown some insight into how to change a fraction to a decimal with the intent of changing to a percent. The problem arises when the student encounters a remainder; instead of writing the remainder as a ratio to the divisor, the student has placed a remainder in the quotient and then drops it when writing the decimal as a percent.

**Remediation** As students work through the division algorithm, help them focus on writing the remainder and the divisor as a ratio.

```
   0.83 2/6
 6)5.00
   4 8
    20
    18
    (2)
```

$\frac{5}{6} = 0.83\frac{2}{6} = 0.83\frac{1}{3}$

Remind students that they can find a decimal or a mixed decimal by dividing to two decimal places (or to hundredths) and then writing any remainder with the divisior as a ratio or a fraction. Use an example such as $\frac{3}{8}$ and show that the fraction can be written with the denominator 1,000 or as the decimal 0.375. Then help students see that $\frac{5}{1{,}000}$ is equivalent to $\frac{1}{200}$ or $\frac{\frac{1}{2}}{100}$, and thus $\frac{1}{2}\%$.

## Problem Solving

### Adjusting Instruction for Low Achievers

The problem-solving experiences in this program are appropriate for the wide range of achievement levels found in most classrooms. The types of experiences and the organization of these experiences, described in the teaching notes, provide the flexibility and the assistance necessary to meet the needs of a wide range of students. However, the instructional techniques used for teaching mathematics to low achievers must take into consideration their special needs. This is true for nearly every mathematics topic we teach, including problem solving. Below are some of the ways your problem-solving instruction can be adjusted to meet the needs of low achievers.

- Regular use of the tips for helping students understand problems. (See the Teaching Tips in Chapter 3.)
- Provide frequent opportunities to formulate problems. (See Chapter 11.)
- Discuss problems by relating students' work to each step in the 5-Point Checklist.
- Encourage students to act out problems.
- Encourage students to use objects to model a problem.
- Encourage students to draw pictures.
- Use hints that are problem-specific rather than general.
- Recognize and reinforce behaviors beyond getting correct answers, such as willingness, perseverance, or using the strategies, particularly at the beginning of the year.

All students, regardless of their achievement level, need to be competent problem solvers. The problem-solving experiences provided in this program, together with these teaching tips, will promote the improvement of problem-solving performance for all students.

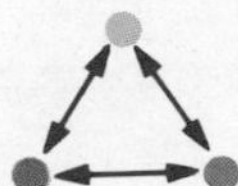

## Special Education

The development of the concepts of percent should follow closely the skills developed in ratio and proportion. Again, students must understand the importance of the order of the comparisons.

### Identifying the Comparisons

As percents are ratios whose denominator is 100, students must learn to recognize which number represents the part and which represents the comparison (whole) group in a given situation. These ideas can be developed and reinforced through the use of "Mark a Percent" cards. These cards are laminated index cards with a percent written on one side and a 10 by 10 grid with the given percent modeled on the other side. Students can use a set of 10 by 10 grids and a colored marker to make their own models of the written percents and then check their answers by turning over the cards. Reversing the process, students can look at the models on the cards, write the percents, and then turn the cards over to verify their answers.

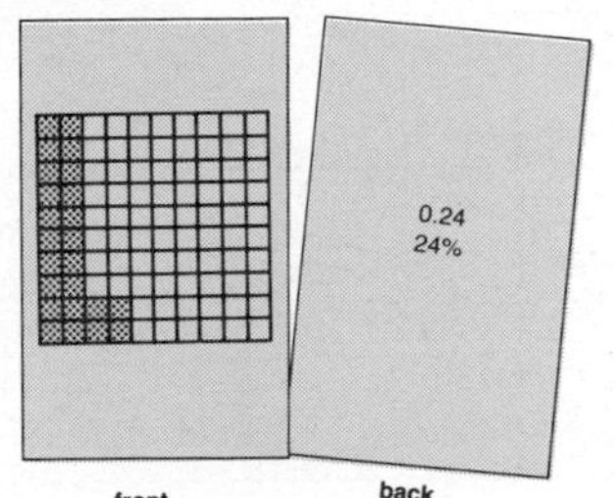


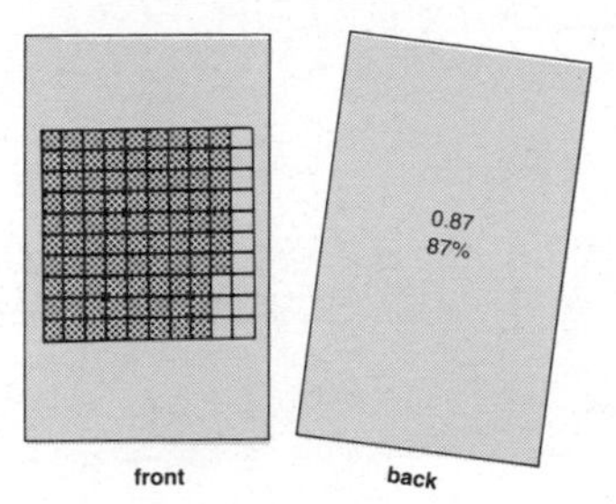


### Building Skills in Changing Comparisons

The development of the ability to change from one form representing percent to another can be aided by the use of "Percent Concentration." This game requires sets of cards for each percent used, such as the following shown for 25 percent: 2 cards labeled 1 to 4, and two each marked 0.25, 25%, and $\frac{1}{4}$. The cards (about 40 in number) are mixed and dealt out facedown. Players turn the cards over, a pair at a time, looking for different cards representing the same amount. If such a pair is found, players take it and try 2 more cards. If no match is found, the cards are turned back over and turn passes to the next player. The game continues until all cards have been picked up. The player with the most cards is the winner.

### Finding Percents Less Than 1 or Greater Than 100

Dealing with percents less than 1 or greater than 100 can be handled through the use of the 10 by 10 grid models and the idea of equivalent ratios. Show the percent 23.5% in fraction form on a grid. The percent can be modeled as shown below.

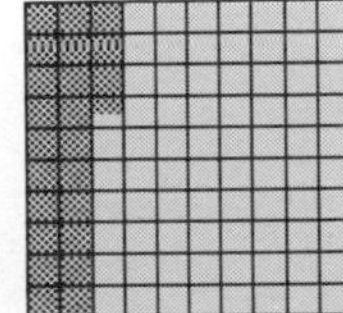

A ratio showing the number of shaded squares to total squares is 23.5 to 100. This ratio can be shown as a ratio without decimals by the comparison 235 to 1,000, or by a fraction $\frac{235}{1,000}$. This can be further analyzed by thinking of having each square of the model divided into 10 smaller units as shown below. The shaded area is then 235 out of the 1,000 small rectangles.

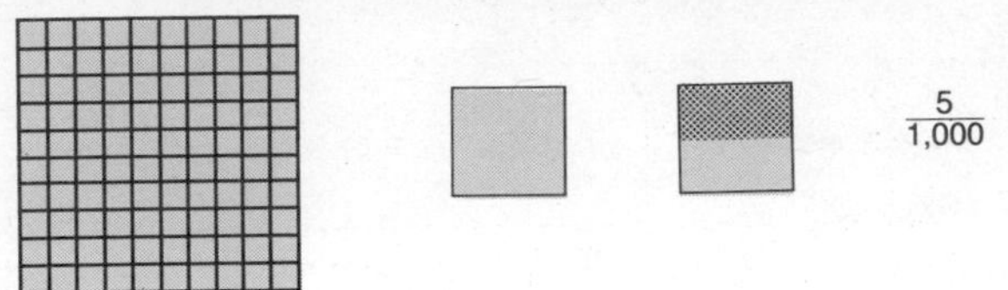


The same approach can be used to show percents greater than 100. A percent such as 346% can be rewritten as 3 and $\frac{46}{100}$ and shown as modeled below.

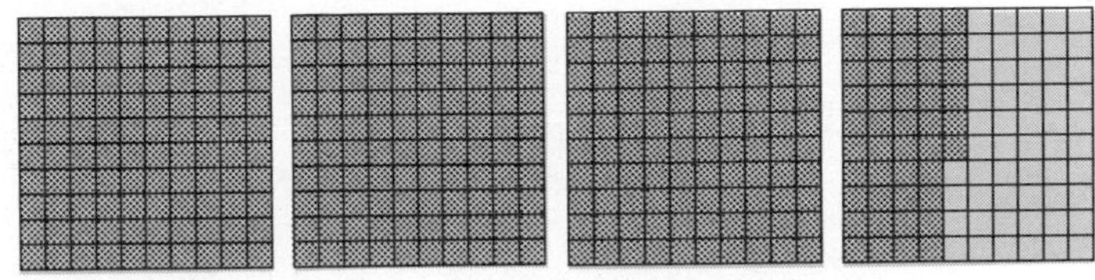

## Subject Integration

Subject matter related to other areas of the curriculum has been integrated into the following lessons. This provides an opportunity to highlight the interaction between mathematics and other subjects.

**Fine Arts** Making mosaics, page 301; using gold in jewelry, pages 304–305

**Science** Surveying breakfast habits, pages 302–303; studying bees, page 313

**Social Studies** Learning about fears, pages 308–309

**Consumer Awareness** Using interest, pages 310–311; finding discounts, page 312

**Career Awareness** Farming, page 299

# Management Guide

| Teaching Chapter 12 | | | | Meeting Individual Needs | | | | | |
|---|---|---|---|---|---|---|---|---|---|
| | | | | Lesson Assignments | | | Follow Up | | |
| Objectives | Chapter Content | Pages | TRB Test Items | Minimum | Average | Extended | Reteaching | Enrichment | Practice |
| | Chapter Opener | 299 | | | | | | | |
| **12.1** Write comparisons as ratios, fractions, decimals, and percents. | Percent | 300–301 | 1–3 | 8–13 / 1–4 | 8–13 / 1–4 | 8–13 / 1–4 | SE5 Ch 15 RS 70 | ES 70 | PS 114 |
| | Percents, Fractions, and Decimals | 302–303 | 4–11 | 1–44, SK | 1–45, SK | 1–45, SK | SE5 Ch 15 RS 71 | ES 71 | MP 426 PS 115 |
| | Writing Fractions and Decimals as Percents | 304–305 | 12–16 | 1–31 | 1–33 | 1–33, TM | SE5 Ch 15 | | MP 427 PS 116 |
| | More About Percents, Fractions, and Decimals | 306 | 17–18 | 1–20 | 1–20 | 1–20 | SE5 Ch 15 RS 72 | ES 72 | MP 427 PS 117 |
| **12.2** Find a percent of a number. | Finding a Percent of a Number | 308–309 | 19–24 | 1–33, SK | 1–34, SK | 1–35, SK | SE5 Ch 15 RS 73 | ES 73 | MP 427 PS 118 |
| **12.3** Solve word problems using the 5-Point Checklist and cumulative computational skills. | Problem Solving: Estimation with Percents | 307 | 25–30 | 1–8 | 1–8 | 1–9 | | | |
| | Problem Solving: Finding Interest | 310–311 | | 1–4 / 1–8 | 1–4 / 1–9 | 1–4 / 1–10 | RS 74 | ES 74 | PS 119 |
| | Problem Solving: Using Data from an Advertisement | 312 | | 1–4 | 1–4 | 1–5 | | | PS 120 |
| | Problem Solving: Practice | 313 | | 1–6 | 1–7 | 1–8 | | | |
| | Applied Problem Solving | 314 | | | | | | | |
| | Chapter Review-Test | 315 | | | | | | | |
| | Another Look/Enrichment | 316–317 | | | | | | | |
| | Technology | 318–319 | | | | | | | |
| | Cumulative Review | 320 | | | | | | | |

**SE5** Student Edition, Book 5
**RS** Reteaching Supplement
**ES** Enrichment Supplement
**PS** Practice Supplement
**MP** More Practice
**TM** Think Math
**SK** Skillkeeper
**TRB** Teacher's Resource Book

## Teacher's Resource Book

### Masters for Use

**. . . before Chapter 12**

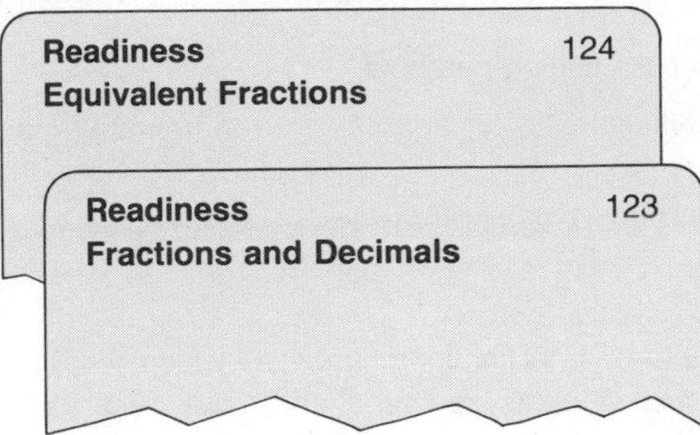


**. . . during Chapter 12**

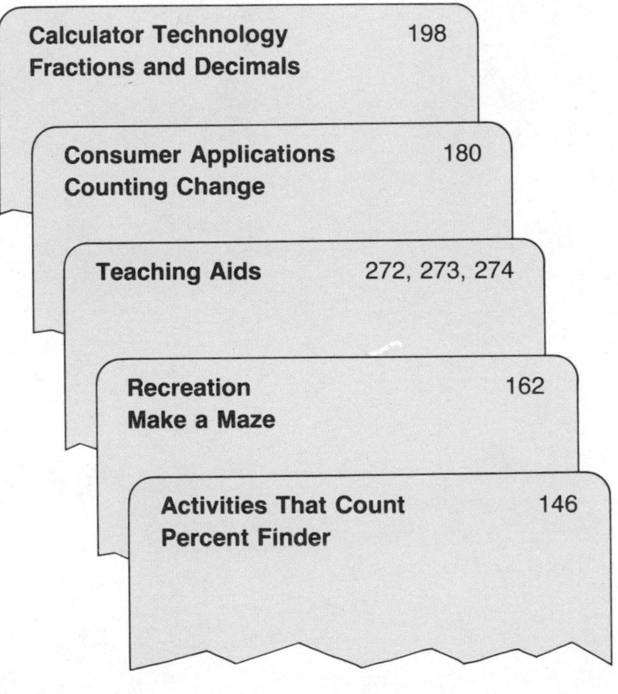


**. . . after Chapter 12**

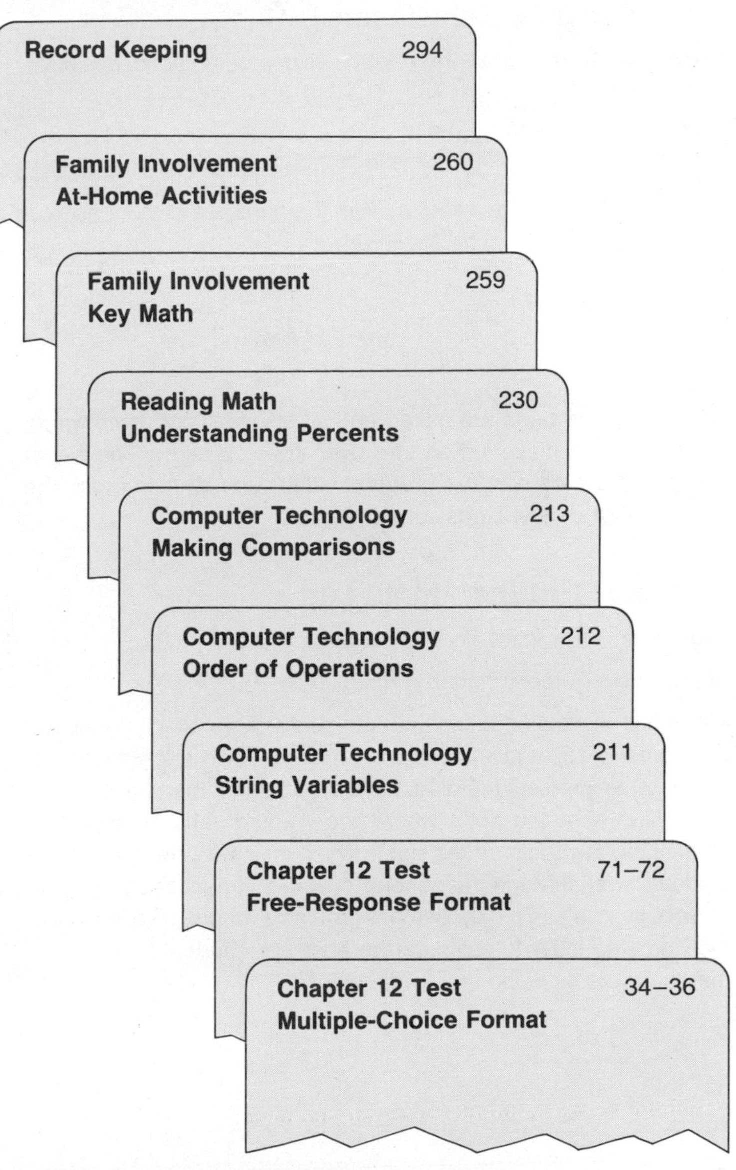


### Supplements

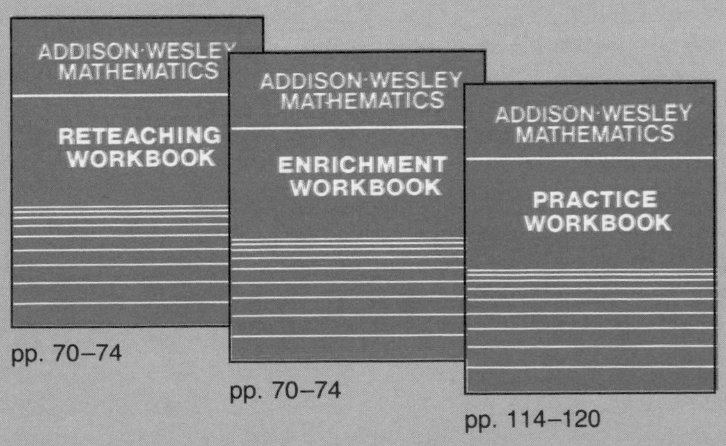


pp. 70–74

pp. 70–74

pp. 114–120

### Other Addison-Wesley Resources

**Books and Kits**

*The Mad Minute* pp. 176–190

*Skillseekers 3* (%) Lessons 1–2

*The Arithmetic Primer* pp. 248–252, 257–259

*Arithmetic Skill Cards* pp. D 11–14, AP 18, 20

*Problem-Solving Experiences in Mathematics, Grade 6,* Problems 29, 30, 64, 65, 89, 104, 125, 144

**Technology**

*Computer Math Activities* Volume 4

*Computer Math Games* Volume 1

# Activities That Count

Activities That Count are designed for use throughout this and subsequent chapters. Before beginning Chapter 12, you may wish to review these activities and select the ones you consider appropriate for your class.

## High Card Wins! Game

**Purpose** To recognize the relative values of fractions, decimals, and percents

**Materials** 50 index cards

**Preparation** On each card write a fraction, decimal, or percent as shown below. An answer key with the numbers in order according to value could also be prepared.

| $\frac{1}{2}$ | 30% | 0.75 | 65% | 0.42 |
|---|---|---|---|---|

**Activity** The cards are mixed and all are dealt out facedown to the players. All players then turn over their top cards. The player who has the card with the greatest value wins all the cards. The player with the most cards wins the game.

## Percent Finder Math Lab

**Purpose** To practice finding percents

**Materials** Percent Finder (TRB p. 146)

**Activity** Have students place one straightedge along the dotted line from 0 to 130 and another positioned vertically along the dotted line at 50 to intersect the diagonal line. Students then trace a horizontal line from the point where the diagonal and vertical lines intersect to the scale on the right, which indicates the answer. Let students work through the second example, if necessary.

Have students make up percent problems for one another, using the Percent Finder to estimate the answers. Students then check their answers by doing the computations.

## Using Percentages Project

**Purpose** To practice finding percents

**Materials** Advertisements or articles from newspapers and magazines

**Activity** Students find examples of the use of percent in the advertisements or articles and then use that data to generate several problems involving percent.

Set aside a table or bulletin board area on which to display the projects, so that students can read and solve each other's problems.

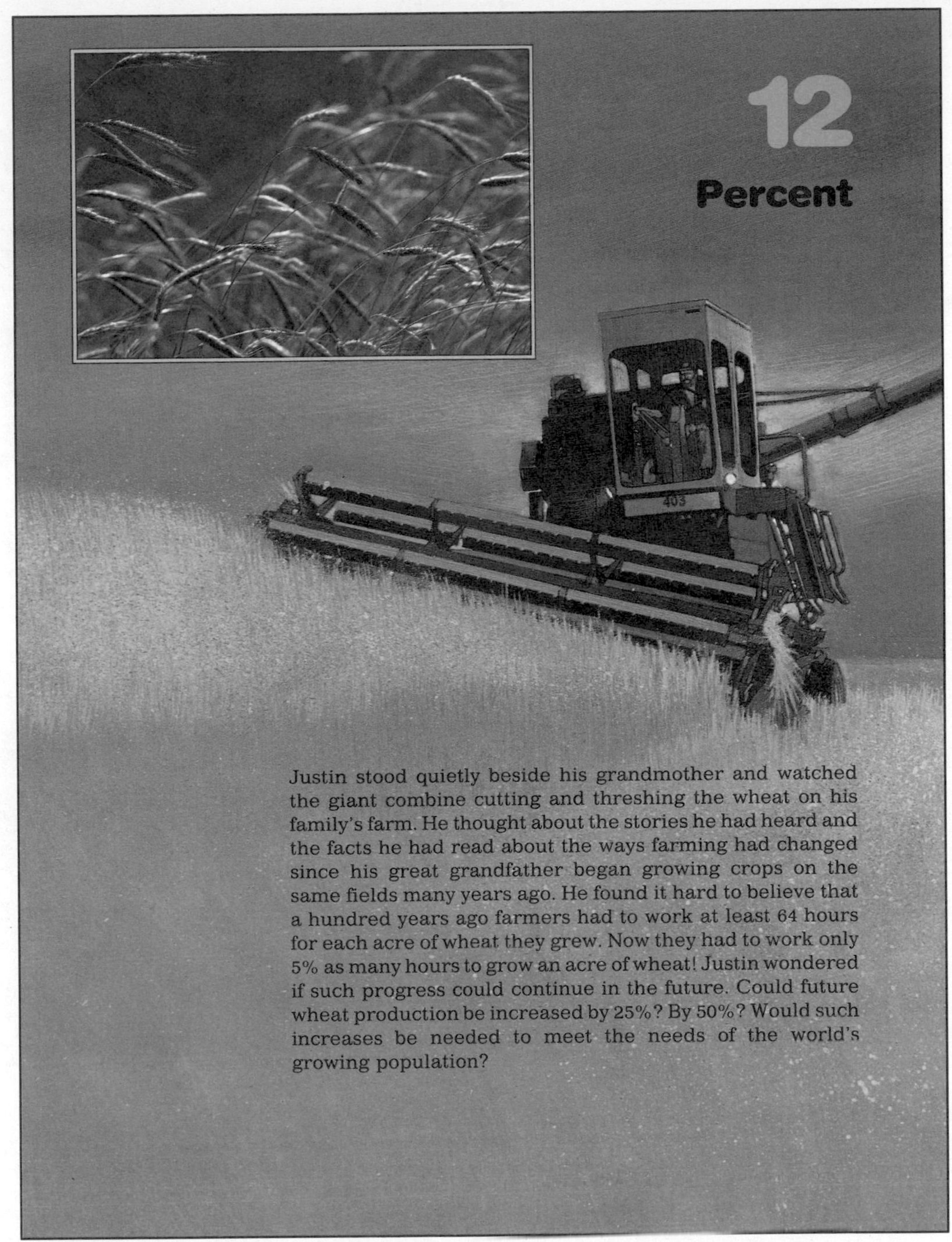

12
Percent
Justin stood quietly beside his grandmother and watched the giant combine cutting and threshing the wheat on his family's farm. He thought about the stories he had heard and the facts he had read about the ways farming had changed since his great grandfather began growing crops on the same fields many years ago. He found it hard to believe that a hundred years ago farmers had to work at least 64 hours for each acre of wheat they grew. Now they had to work only 5% as many hours to grow an acre of wheat! Justin wondered if such progress could continue in the future. Could future wheat production be increased by 25%? By 50%? Would such increases be needed to meet the needs of the world's growing population?


## Introducing the Chapter

**Discussion** Explain to students that in this chapter they will learn about percent and how it relates to decimals, fractions, and ratios. Then lead a brief discussion of the way improvements in farming methods and equipment have increased the productivity of farms in this country over the last hundred years. After students have had an opportunity to read the story and enjoy the art, encourage them to make up questions involving the data given in the story. As you teach the chapter, you may wish to refer to this page and present the problems suggested below.

## Follow-Up Questions

**After Page 301** The Jenkins have 0.74 of their land planted in wheat. What percent of their land is planted in wheat? (74%)

**After Page 303** The Grimaldis grow soybeans on 45% of their farmland. What is the lowest-terms fraction for this percent? $\left(\frac{9}{20}\right)$

**After Page 306** Belinda's family uses $37\frac{1}{2}\%$ of their land as pasture for grazing sheep. Give this percent as a decimal and as a lowest-terms fraction. $\left(0.375; \frac{3}{8}\right)$

**After Page 309** The Steiners sold their family farm for \$180,000. The buyers paid 30% cash on the purchase of the farm. How much cash did the buyers pay? (\$54,000)

# Percent

**Quick Review** Students say aloud the fraction that each ratio represents.

6 out of 7 | 5:8 | 12 to 20 | 1:7 | 28:2 | 1 to 3
14 of every 100 | 2 for 7 | 6:9 | 16 for every 25

**Lesson Focus** To use models to find percents, ratios, fractions, and decimals

**Suggested Materials** Graph paper (TRB p. 271)

## Ideas for Getting Started

Have students use the graph paper to cut out or outline a 10 by 10 array of squares. "How many rows of squares?" (10) "How many squares in each row?" (10) "How many squares altogether?" (100) Tell students to color any number of squares out of 100 that they wish. Then have them show the array to a classmate for about 5 seconds. Have the classmate estimate and verify the number of squares in the array that are colored. Students then change roles, and the second student in the partnership estimates the number of squares that have been colored by the first student. As you discuss these experiences, stress the phrase ". . . out of 100."

## Using Page 300

**Lesson Development** Read the information at the top of the page. "How many tiles are on the board?" (100) "How can we find out how many tiles are brown?" (Count the number of tiles.) "How many tiles out of 100 are brown?" (50 out of the 100 tiles are brown.) Discuss the meaning of the word "percent" and the symbol used for percent. Emphasize the expressions "per 100" or "out of 100" or "for each 100." Work through the first 7 exercises with students as they refer to the illustration. In each case, emphasize the number colored out of 100.

**Exercises 8–13** Encourage students to, first, estimate their answers and then count to check their estimates. Be sure they write their answers using the percent symbol for both the percent and the estimate. As you discuss these exercises, continue to refer to the concept of percent as per 100.

### Percent

Evita made this mosaic by gluing 100 colored tiles on a board.

How many tiles out of 100 are brown?

We use percent to compare a number with 100. The word **percent** means **per one hundred.** The symbol % is used for percent.

**50** out of **100** tiles are brown.
**50%** of the tiles are brown.

Find the percent of Evita's tiles that are the color named.

**1.** yellow 1% **2.** red 14% **3.** blue 4% **4.** green 6% **5.** purple 25%

**6.** not white 100% **7.** black 0%

For exercises 8–13, first estimate the percents. Then count to check your estimates.

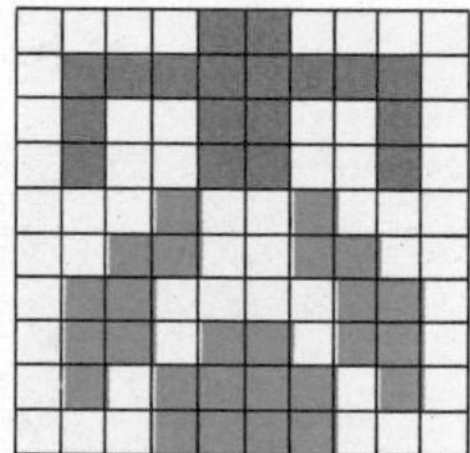

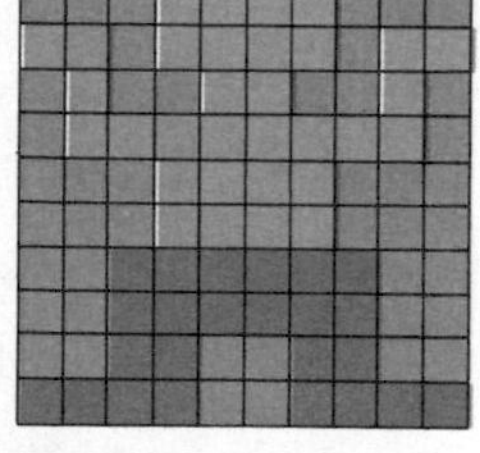

What percent of the tiles are

**8.** red? 18% **9.** yellow? 56% **10.** blue? 26%

What percent of the tiles are

**11.** green? 32% **12.** brown? 24% **13.** orange? 44%



## Follow Up

### Reteaching

Display a 10 by 10 grid (TRB p. 274) and elicit from students that the grid represents 1 whole, and that it contains 100 smaller squares. Use the grids to develop and discuss the following ideas:

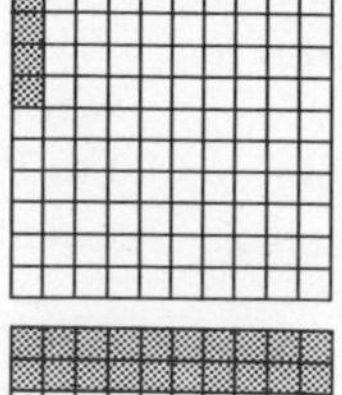

4 squares are shaded
4 of 100 are shaded
$\frac{4}{100}$ are shaded

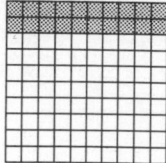

2 tenths are shaded
20 squares are shaded
$\frac{20}{100}$ or $\frac{2}{10}$ are shaded

### Enrichment

Have students cut out squares and triangles from different colored paper. Challenge them to make creative designs using the cutouts as mosaic tiles. After their designs are completed, students should indicate what percent of the tiles are in each design.

| Assignment Guide | | | |
|---|---|---|---|
| | Minimum | Average | Extended |
| page 300 | 8–13 | 8–13 | 8–13 |
| page 301 | 1–4 | 1–4 | 1–4 |

We can use **ratios, fractions, decimals,** and **percents** to describe the same situation.

Write the missing numbers to show what part is shaded.

Example:

| | ratio | fraction | decimal | percent |
|---|---|---|---|---|
| Example | 75 to 100 | $\frac{75}{100}$ | 0.75 | 75% |
| 1. | ■ to 100 (62) | ■ ($\frac{62}{100}$) | ■ (0.62) | ■ (62%) |
| 2. | ■ to 100 (8) | ■ ($\frac{8}{100}$) | ■ (0.08) | ■ (8%) |
| 3. | ■ to 100 (50) | ■ ($\frac{50}{100}$) | ■ (0.50) | ■ (50%) |
| 4. | ■ to 100 (100) | ■ ($\frac{100}{100}$) | ■ (1.00) | ■ (100%) |



## Using Page 301

**Exercises 1–4** Before assigning these exercises, discuss ways to refer to one dollar and parts of a dollar. Remind students that one-half dollar is 50 pennies out of 100 or $\frac{50}{100}$ of a dollar. It is also \$0.50 and 50% of a dollar. Then discuss the example if 75 squares out of 100 are shaded. Note how this can be represented as a ratio, a fraction, a decimal, and a percent. After students have completed the exercises, discuss each exercise emphasizing the relationships between these ways of representing rational numbers.

**Reteaching Supplement,** page 70

Name ______ To follow text page 301

**Percent**

20 of the 100 circles are solid. The ratio is **20 to 100.**
**We say:** "$\frac{20}{100}$ or 0.20 of the circles are solid."
**We also say:** "20 percent of the circles are solid."
**We write:** 20% of the circles are solid.

Write the ratio, fraction, decimal, and percent.

| | 1. | 2. (32 are solid.) | 3. (75 are solid.) | 4. | 5. | 6. |
|---|---|---|---|---|---|---|
| ratio: | 50 to 100 | 32 to 100 | 75 to 100 | 80 to 100 | 100 to 100 | 15 to 100 |
| fraction: | $\frac{50}{100}$ | $\frac{32}{100}$ | $\frac{75}{100}$ | $\frac{80}{100}$ | $\frac{100}{100}$ | $\frac{15}{100}$ |
| decimal: | 0.50 | 0.32 | 0.75 | 0.80 | 1.00 | 0.15 |
| percent: | 50% | 32% | 75% | 80% | 100% | 15% |

**Enrichment Supplement,** page 70

Name ______ To follow text page 301

**100% Correct**

First estimate the percent shaded in each picture. Then count to find the exact percent. **Estimates will vary.**

1. Estimate: ____ % Exact: 48 %
2. Estimate: ____ % Exact: 40 %
3. Estimate: ____ % Exact: 29 %
4. Estimate: ____ % Exact: 51 %

**Answers will vary for problems 5 and 6.**

5. Letters in the initials for your name (shade in your initials)
   Estimate: ____ % Exact: ____ %
6. Digits in the number for your age (shade in your age)
   Estimate: ____ % Exact: ____ %

**Practice Supplement,** page 114

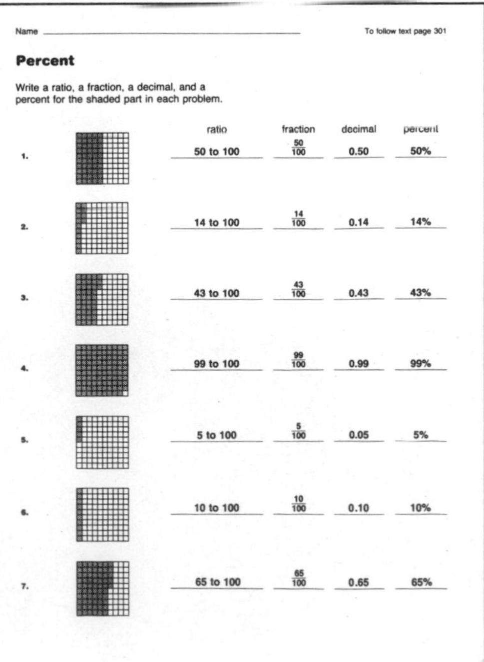

Name ______ To follow text page 301

**Percent**

Write a ratio, a fraction, a decimal, and a percent for the shaded part in each problem.

| | ratio | fraction | decimal | percent |
|---|---|---|---|---|
| 1. | 50 to 100 | $\frac{50}{100}$ | 0.50 | 50% |
| 2. | 14 to 100 | $\frac{14}{100}$ | 0.14 | 14% |
| 3. | 43 to 100 | $\frac{43}{100}$ | 0.43 | 43% |
| 4. | 99 to 100 | $\frac{99}{100}$ | 0.99 | 99% |
| 5. | 5 to 100 | $\frac{5}{100}$ | 0.05 | 5% |
| 6. | 10 to 100 | $\frac{10}{100}$ | 0.10 | 10% |
| 7. | 65 to 100 | $\frac{65}{100}$ | 0.65 | 65% |

**Quick Review** Students align the problems vertically and find the sums and differences.

0.9062 + 0.087 0.9932 4.559 + 122.7 127.259 8.45 − 6.7 1.75
16.22 − 12.78 3.44 4.367 + 28.807 33.174
30.09 + 0.233 + 12.2 42.523 7.03 − 6.39 0.64

**Lesson Focus** To express a decimal or a fraction with denominator 100 as a percent and to express a percent as a decimal or a fraction

**Suggested Materials** Graph paper (TRB p. 271)

## Ideas for Getting Started

Have students cut out or outline a 10 by 10 grid. Then give them instructions on cards such as shown below.

| Color | |
|---|---|
| 25% | red |
| 0.35 | blue |
| $\frac{40}{100\%}$ | green |

When students have completed the coloring of the grid ask: "What percent of the grid is colored blue?" (35%) "What decimal tells the part of the grid that is colored green?" (0.40) "What fraction tells the part of the grid that is colored red?" $\left(\frac{25}{100}\right)$ If students have difficulty with any one of these questions, encourage them to count the number of squares out of 100 and write the required percent, decimal, or fraction. "What percent of the grid is colored with some color?" (100%)

## Using Page 302

**Lesson Development** Direct students' attention to the chart at the top of the page describing breakfast habits. Tell students that usually all the data in a chart is given in either decimals, fractions, or percents. Ask them to think about how the data in this chart could be changed to show a percent for each statement. Then read through each of the examples and accompanying think clouds to show how each number can be written as a decimal, a percent, or a fraction.

**Warm Up** Note that in exercise 5 there is a single-digit number over 100, or 2%. If necessary, refer back to the 10 by 10 grids and the models to help students with the concept of percent.

## Percents, Fractions, and Decimals

A recent survey gave this data about breakfast habits of persons in the United States.

Write the decimal and the fraction as percents.

**Breakfast Habits**

**0.58** of the people surveyed eat breakfast daily.

$\frac{26}{100}$ of the people surveyed never eat breakfast.

**16%** of the people surveyed sometimes eat breakfast.

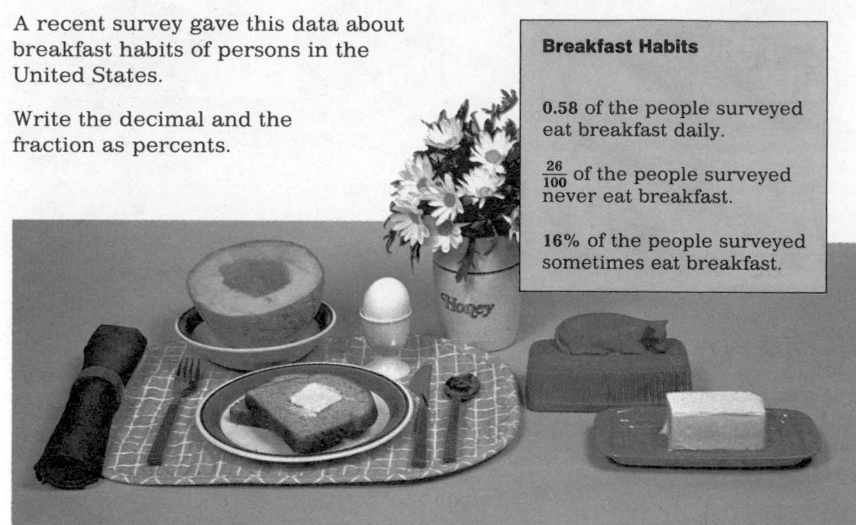


**Decimal** 0.58 ↓ **Percent** 58% (Think 58 **hundredths.**)

**Fraction** $\frac{26}{100}$ ↓ **Percent** 26% (% means **hundredths.**)

Write the percent in the box as a decimal and as a fraction.

**Percent** 16% ↓ **Decimal** 0.16 (Think 16 **hundredths.**)

**Percent** 16% ↓ **Fraction** $\frac{16}{100}$ (% means **hundredths.**)

or $\frac{4}{25}$, reduced to lowest terms.

**Warm Up** Write each decimal or fraction as a percent.

**1.** 0.35 35% **2.** $\frac{15}{100}$ 15% **3.** $\frac{68}{100}$ 68% **4.** 0.06 6% **5.** $\frac{2}{100}$ 2%

Write as lowest-terms fractions.

**6.** 25% $\frac{1}{4}$ **7.** 75% $\frac{3}{4}$ **8.** 6% $\frac{3}{50}$

Write as decimals.

**9.** 35% 0.35 **10.** 100% 1.00 **11.** 50% 0.50

302

## Follow Up

**Reteaching**

Place 32 red counters and 68 white counters in stacks on a table. Have students count to verify that there are 100 counters. Help students recall that percent means "per hundred." Use a chart as shown below to show each of the comparisons.

| Decimal | Fraction | Percent |
|---|---|---|
| 0.32 red | $\frac{32}{100}$ red | 32% red |
| 0.68 white | $\frac{68}{100}$ white | 68% white |

Use centimeter graph paper to mark off a 10 by 10 square. Help students model and write percents, decimals, and fractions as suggested by students.

**Enrichment**

Provide students with 10 by 10 dot arrays (TRB p. 273). Have them draw rings around a number of dots of their choosing and then write a percent to show what part of the dots is ringed.

| Assignment Guide | | | |
|---|---|---|---|
| | Minimum | Average | Extended |
| page 303 | 1–44, SK | 1–45, SK | 1–45, SK |

Write each decimal as a percent.

**1.** 0.25 25% **2.** 0.67 67% **3.** 0.40 40% **4.** 0.12 12% **5.** 0.10 10% **6.** 0.09 9%
**7.** 0.76 76% **8.** 0.50 50% **9.** 0.38 38% **10.** 0.19 19% **11.** 0.05 5% **12.** 0.98 98%

Write each fraction as a percent.

**13.** $\frac{24}{100}$ 24% **14.** $\frac{50}{100}$ 50% **15.** $\frac{10}{100}$ 10% **16.** $\frac{8}{100}$ 8% **17.** $\frac{1}{100}$ 1% **18.** $\frac{100}{100}$ 100%

Write each percent as a decimal.

**19.** 43% 0.43 **20.** 26% 0.26 **21.** 17% 0.17 **22.** 8% 0.08 **23.** 40% 0.40 **24.** 2% 0.02
**25.** 50% 0.50 **26.** 35% 0.35 **27.** 76% 0.76 **28.** 87% 0.87 **29.** 94% 0.94 **30.** 16% 0.16

Write each percent as a fraction in lowest terms.

**31.** 25% $\frac{1}{4}$ **32.** 35% $\frac{7}{20}$ **33.** 40% $\frac{2}{5}$ **34.** 17% $\frac{17}{100}$ **35.** 110% $\frac{11}{10}$ **36.** 4% $\frac{1}{25}$
**37.** 90% $\frac{9}{10}$ **38.** 2% $\frac{1}{50}$ **39.** 45% $\frac{9}{20}$ **40.** 30% $\frac{3}{10}$ **41.** 23% $\frac{23}{100}$ **42.** 65% $\frac{13}{20}$

**43.** In the survey of breakfast habits only 0.24 of the persons felt they weighed what they should. What percent is this? 24%

**44.** Write each fraction as a percent. Do the fractions add to $\frac{100}{100}$ (100%)? 38%, 27%, 35%; yes

| Eating Habits (fraction of people in the United States) | | |
|---|---|---|
| Snack daily | Sometimes snack | Never snack |
| $\frac{38}{100}$ | $\frac{27}{100}$ | $\frac{35}{100}$ |

**45.** In a different survey of eating habits, $\frac{4}{5}$ of the persons surveyed said they eat their biggest meal of the day in the evening. What percent of those surveyed eat their biggest meal at some time other than in the evening? 20%

## Skillkeeper

Write each ratio as a fraction.

**1.** 7 to 9 $\frac{7}{9}$ **2.** 5:11 $\frac{5}{11}$ **3.** 8 out of 12 $\frac{8}{12}$ **4.** 3 for 2 $\frac{3}{2}$ **5.** 3 of 10 $\frac{3}{10}$
**6.** 5 for every 3 $\frac{5}{3}$ **7.** 6 to 13 $\frac{6}{13}$ **8.** 9:14 $\frac{9}{14}$ **9.** 6 per 4 $\frac{6}{4}$ **10.** 15 to 7 $\frac{15}{7}$

Copy and complete to make equal ratios.

**11.** $\frac{4}{25} = \frac{■}{100}$ 16 **12.** $\frac{13}{50} = \frac{■}{100}$ 26 **13.** $\frac{17}{20} = \frac{■}{100}$ 85 **14.** $\frac{■}{100} = \frac{75}{50}$ 150 **15.** $\frac{■}{10} = \frac{70}{100}$ 7

More Practice, page 426, Set C



## Using Page 303

**Exercises 1–12** Be alert for confusion between decimals such as 0.40 and 0.04 or 0.09 and 0.90. These exercises should not cause any difficulty for students who understand decimal and percent concepts.

**Exercises 13–18** Note that each of these fractions has a denominator of 100. Continue to emphasize the idea that percent means hundredths, thus $\frac{8}{100}$, for example, can be written 8%.

**Exercises 19–30** These exercises should not be difficult for most students. However, with exercise 22 for example, students might look at 8% and think "8 hundredths." Be sure they write the decimal 0.08 and *not* the decimal 0.80 or *80* hundredths.

**Exercises 31–42** If necessary, briefly review the procedure for reducing a fraction to lowest terms before assigning these exercises.

**Exercises 43–45** These verbal exercises are further applications of the ideas developed in this lesson. In exercise 43 elicit from students that if all the persons are represented in the chart, the sum of the fractions should equal 100 hundredths or 100%.

**Skillkeeper** These skills were originally taught in Chapter 11.

**More Practice,** page 426, Set C

**Reteaching Supplement,** page 71

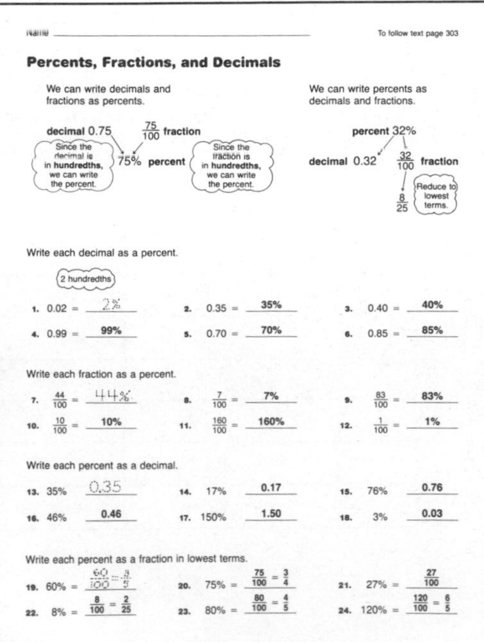

Name ______ To follow text page 303

**Percents, Fractions, and Decimals**

We can write decimals and fractions as percents.

decimal 0.75 — $\frac{75}{100}$ fraction — 75% percent

Since the decimal is in **hundredths**, we can write the percent.

Since the fraction is in **hundredths**, we can write the percent.

We can write percents as decimals and fractions.

percent 32% — decimal 0.32 — $\frac{32}{100}$ fraction — $\frac{8}{25}$ Reduce to lowest terms.

Write each decimal as a percent.

2 hundredths

1. 0.02 = 2% 2. 0.35 = 35% 3. 0.40 = 40%
4. 0.99 = 99% 5. 0.70 = 70% 6. 0.85 = 85%

Write each fraction as a percent.

7. $\frac{44}{100}$ = 44% 8. $\frac{7}{100}$ = 7% 9. $\frac{83}{100}$ = 83%
10. $\frac{10}{100}$ = 10% 11. $\frac{160}{100}$ = 160% 12. $\frac{1}{100}$ = 1%

Write each percent as a decimal.

13. 35% 0.35 14. 17% 0.17 15. 76% 0.76
16. 46% 0.46 17. 150% 1.50 18. 3% 0.03

Write each percent as a fraction in lowest terms.

19. 60% = $\frac{60}{100} = \frac{3}{5}$ 20. 75% = $\frac{75}{100} = \frac{3}{4}$ 21. 27% = $\frac{27}{100}$
22. 8% = $\frac{8}{100} = \frac{2}{25}$ 23. 80% = $\frac{80}{100} = \frac{4}{5}$ 24. 120% = $\frac{120}{100} = \frac{6}{5}$

**Enrichment Supplement,** page 71

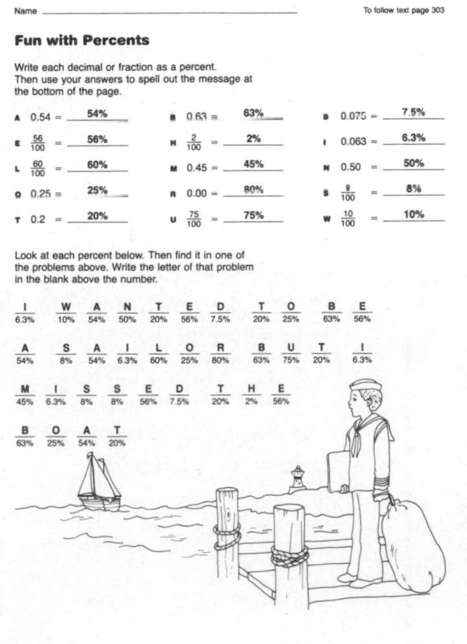

Name ______ To follow text page 303

**Fun with Percents**

Write each decimal or fraction as a percent. Then use your answers to spell out the message at the bottom of the page.

A 0.54 = 54% B 0.63 = 63% D 0.075 = 7.5%
E $\frac{56}{100}$ = 56% H $\frac{2}{100}$ = 2% I 0.063 = 6.3%
L $\frac{60}{100}$ = 60% M 0.45 = 45% N 0.50 = 50%
O 0.25 = 25% R 0.80 = 80% S $\frac{8}{100}$ = 8%
T 0.2 = 20% U $\frac{75}{100}$ = 75% W $\frac{10}{100}$ = 10%

Look at each percent below. Then find it in one of the problems above. Write the letter of that problem in the blank above the number.

I (6.3%) W (10%) A (54%) N (50%) T (20%) E (56%) D (7.5%) T (20%) O (25%) B (63%) E (56%)
A (54%) S (8%) A (54%) I (6.3%) L (60%) O (25%) R (80%) B (63%) U (75%) T (20%) I (6.3%)
M (45%) I (6.3%) S (8%) S (8%) E (56%) D (7.5%) T (20%) H (2%) E (56%)
B (63%) O (25%) A (54%) T (20%)

**Practice Supplement,** page 115

Name ______ To follow text page 303

**Percents, Fractions, and Decimals**

Write each decimal as a percent.

1. 0.75 75% 2. 0.59 59% 3. 0.03 3%
4. 0.11 11% 5. 0.70 70% 6. 0.97 97%
7. 0.08 8% 8. 0.28 28% 9. 0.20 20%

Write each fraction as a percent.

10. $\frac{36}{100}$ 36% 11. $\frac{40}{100}$ 40% 12. $\frac{6}{100}$ 6%
13. $\frac{90}{100}$ 90% 14. $\frac{17}{100}$ 17% 15. $\frac{65}{100}$ 65%
16. $\frac{5}{100}$ 5% 17. $\frac{110}{100}$ 110% 18. $\frac{160}{100}$ 160%

Write each percent as a decimal.

19. 77% 0.77 20. 15% 0.15 21. 8% 0.08
22. 60% 0.60 23. 48% 0.48 24. 100% 1.00
25. 4% 0.04 26. 22% 0.22 27. 112% 1.12

Write each percent as a fraction in lowest terms.

28. 4% $\frac{1}{25}$ 29. 55% $\frac{11}{20}$ 30. 75% $\frac{3}{4}$
31. 20% $\frac{1}{5}$ 32. 81% $\frac{81}{100}$ 33. 60% $\frac{3}{5}$
34. 5% $\frac{1}{20}$ 35. 140% $\frac{7}{5}$ 36. 6% $\frac{3}{50}$

# Percent

**Quick Review** Students give orally one equivalent fraction for each of the following fractions:

$\frac{1}{2}$ $\frac{1}{4}$ $\frac{5}{4}$ $\frac{3}{4}$ $\frac{1}{10}$ $\frac{2}{5}$ $\frac{3}{2}$ $\frac{7}{10}$ $\frac{4}{7}$ $\frac{100}{10}$

**Lesson Focus** To write fractions and decimals as percents

## Ideas for Getting Started

In preparation for writing a fraction with the denominator 100 that is equivalent to a given fraction, write equations such as these on the chalkboard and ask students to give the missing numbers.

| | |
|---|---|
| 2 × ___ = 100 | 20 × ___ = 100 |
| 4 × ___ = 100 | 25 × ___ = 100 |
| 5 × ___ = 100 | 40 × ___ = 100 |
| 10 × ___ = 100 | 50 × ___ = 100 |

Leave the completed equations on the chalkboard as you proceed with the lesson.

## Using Page 304

**Motivational Problem** Have students read the paragraph at the top of the page. Briefly explain that what we call "pure gold" is not actually *pure* because pure gold would be too soft to use in rings or other jewelry. "What question do we want to answer about the ring?" (What percent of the ring is gold?) "Pure gold is how many karats?" (24) "The ring in the problem is how many karats?" (18) "How can we find the percent of the ring that is gold?" (Change the fraction to a percent.)

**Lesson Development** Write the fraction $\frac{3}{4}$ on the chalkboard and ask for suggestions about how to write this fraction as a percent. Focus on each of the procedures in turn and ask: "What number must I use to multiply both the numerator and denominator of the fraction in order to produce an equivalent fraction with denominator 100?" If necessary, refer to the equation "4 × ___ = 100" on the chalkboard. Then write $\frac{3}{4} = \frac{75}{100} = 75\%$.

Remind students that they can also find percent by dividing the numerator of the fraction by the denominator. Then work through this division to show how to find the decimal 0.75, which can be written as 75%.

**Other Examples** Note that the first example involves an improper fraction. The procedure for changing the percent is the same as that used with the fraction $\frac{3}{4}$. In the second example, because there is no fraction equivalent to $\frac{2}{3}$ with the denominator 100, we find a mixed decimal by dividing the numerator by the denominator and write $66\frac{2}{3}\%$.

**Warm Up** In exercises 1–6 students must first find an equivalent fraction with denominator 100. Difficulties here might reflect a lack of understanding of percent as "per one hundred" and of the procedure for finding an equivalent fraction. In exercises 7 through 12 give students guidelines as to how far to carry out the division.

## Writing Fractions and Decimals as Percents

Since "pure" gold is 24 karats, 18 karat gold is $\frac{18}{24}$ or $\frac{3}{4}$ pure gold.

What percent of an 18 karat gold ring is gold?

SALE!
18 Karat Gold
Birthstone Rings

Here are two ways to find the percent.

**Finding an equivalent fraction with denominator 100**

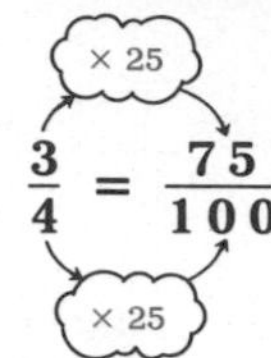

$$\frac{3}{4} \overset{\times 25}{=} \frac{75}{100}$$

**Finding a decimal or mixed decimal by dividing**

$$\begin{array}{r} 0.75 \\ 4\overline{)3.00} \\ \underline{28} \\ 20 \\ \underline{20} \\ 0 \end{array}$$

An 18 karat gold ring is 75% gold.

**Other Examples**

$\frac{5}{4} = \frac{125}{100} = 125\%$

$1.35 = 1\frac{35}{100} = \frac{135}{100} = 135\%$

Sometimes we must first reduce to lowest terms.

$\frac{6}{8} = \frac{3}{4} = \frac{75}{100} = 75\%$

$$\frac{2}{3} \rightarrow \begin{array}{r} 0.66\frac{2}{3} \\ 3\overline{)2.00} \\ \underline{18} \\ 20 \\ \underline{18} \\ 2 \end{array} \rightarrow 66\frac{2}{3}\%$$

**Warm Up** Find an equivalent fraction with denominator 100. Then write the fraction as a percent.

1. $\frac{1}{2}$ $\frac{50}{100}$, 50%
2. $\frac{1}{4}$ $\frac{25}{100}$, 25%
3. $\frac{3}{5}$ $\frac{60}{100}$, 60%
4. $\frac{7}{10}$ $\frac{70}{100}$, 70%
5. $\frac{5}{4}$ $\frac{125}{100}$, 125%
6. $\frac{13}{20}$ $\frac{65}{100}$, 65%

Divide to find a decimal or a mixed decimal for each fraction. Then write the decimal as a percent.

7. $\frac{2}{5}$ 0.40; 40%
8. $\frac{1}{3}$ $0.33\frac{1}{3}$; $33\frac{1}{3}\%$
9. $\frac{4}{3}$ $1.33\frac{1}{3}$; $133\frac{1}{3}\%$
10. $\frac{3}{8}$ $0.37\frac{1}{2}$; $37\frac{1}{2}\%$
11. $\frac{5}{6}$ $0.83\frac{1}{3}$; $83\frac{1}{3}\%$
12. $\frac{7}{4}$ 1.75; 175%

304

## Follow Up

### Reteaching

Review equivalent fractions by having students play a game in which they match equivalent fractions such as $\frac{1}{4}$ and $\frac{25}{100}$. Each fraction must be matched with one having a denominator of 100. Then remind students of the two ways to find percent.

1. Change a fraction to an equivalent fraction having 100 as the denominator and then rewrite as a percent.

   $\frac{1}{4} = \frac{25}{100} = 0.25 = 25\%$

2. Use division to find a decimal or mixed decimal for a fraction.

   $$\begin{array}{r} 0.25 \\ 4\overline{)1.00} \end{array} = 25\%$$

### Enrichment

Have students fill in the chart below.

| Fraction | Decimal | Percent |
|---|---|---|
| $\frac{1}{5}$ | 0.2 | 20% |
| $\frac{2}{5}$ | 0.4 | 40% |
| $\frac{3}{5}$ | 0.6 | 60% |
| $\frac{5}{5}$ | 1.0 | 100% |
| $\frac{1}{8}$ | $0.12\frac{1}{2}$ | $12\frac{1}{2}\%$ |
| $\frac{3}{8}$ | $0.37\frac{1}{2}$ | $37\frac{1}{2}\%$ |
| $\frac{7}{8}$ | $0.87\frac{1}{2}$ | $87\frac{1}{2}\%$ |
| $\frac{1}{3}$ | $0.33\frac{1}{3}$ | $33\frac{1}{3}\%$ |
| $\frac{2}{3}$ | $0.66\frac{2}{3}$ | $66\frac{2}{3}\%$ |

| Assignment Guide | | | |
|---|---|---|---|
| | Minimum | Average | Extended |
| page 305 | 1–31 | 1–33 | 1–33, TM |

Find an equivalent fraction with denominator 100. Then write a percent for each fraction.

**1.** $\frac{2}{5}$ $\frac{40}{100}$, 40% **2.** $\frac{3}{10}$ $\frac{30}{100}$, 30% **3.** $\frac{2}{4}$ $\frac{50}{100}$; 50% **4.** $\frac{1}{5}$ $\frac{20}{100}$; 20% **5.** $\frac{9}{20}$ $\frac{45}{100}$; 45% **6.** $\frac{12}{25}$ $\frac{48}{100}$; 48%

**7.** $\frac{3}{50}$ $\frac{6}{100}$; 6% **8.** $\frac{19}{20}$ $\frac{95}{100}$; 95% **9.** $\frac{17}{25}$ $\frac{68}{100}$; 68% **10.** $\frac{6}{5}$ $\frac{120}{100}$; 120% **11.** $\frac{24}{20}$ $\frac{120}{100}$; 120% **12.** $\frac{12}{10}$ $\frac{120}{100}$; 120%

Reduce the fraction to lowest terms. Then write a percent by first finding an equivalent fraction with denominator 100.

**13.** $\frac{6}{30}$ $\frac{1}{5}$, $\frac{20}{100}$; 20% **14.** $\frac{9}{12}$ $\frac{3}{4}$, $\frac{75}{100}$; 75% **15.** $\frac{8}{16}$ $\frac{1}{2}$, $\frac{50}{100}$; 50% **16.** $\frac{14}{20}$ $\frac{7}{10}$, $\frac{70}{100}$; 70% **17.** $\frac{6}{15}$ $\frac{2}{5}$, $\frac{40}{100}$; 40% **18.** $\frac{15}{12}$ $\frac{5}{4}$, $\frac{125}{100}$; 125%

Divide to find a decimal or mixed decimal for each fraction. Then write the decimal as a percent.

**19.** $\frac{5}{8}$ $0.62\frac{1}{2}$; $62\frac{1}{2}\%$ **20.** $\frac{3}{5}$ 0.60; 60% **21.** $\frac{1}{6}$ $0.16\frac{2}{3}$; $16\frac{2}{3}\%$ **22.** $\frac{6}{5}$ 1.20; 120% **23.** $\frac{7}{8}$ $0.87\frac{1}{2}$; $87\frac{1}{2}\%$ **24.** $\frac{5}{3}$ $1.66\frac{2}{3}$; $166\frac{2}{3}\%$

**25.** $\frac{3}{16}$ $0.18\frac{3}{4}$; $18\frac{3}{4}\%$ **26.** $\frac{7}{12}$ $0.58\frac{1}{3}$; $58\frac{1}{3}\%$ **27.** $\frac{3}{7}$ $0.42\frac{6}{7}$; $42\frac{6}{7}\%$ **28.** $\frac{7}{6}$ $1.16\frac{2}{3}$; $116\frac{2}{3}\%$ **29.** $\frac{7}{5}$ 1.40; 140% **30.** $\frac{7}{4}$ 1.75; 175%

**31.** White gold used to make jewelry is often $\frac{4}{5}$ pure gold. What percent of pure gold is this? 80%

**32.** If pure gold is 24 karats, what percent of a 10-karat ring is pure gold? $41\frac{2}{3}\%$

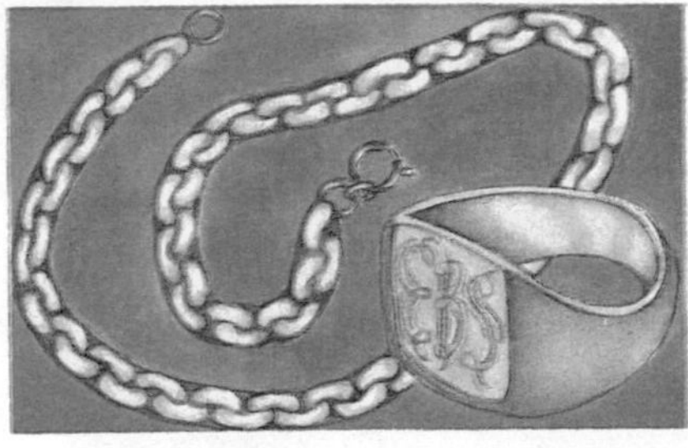

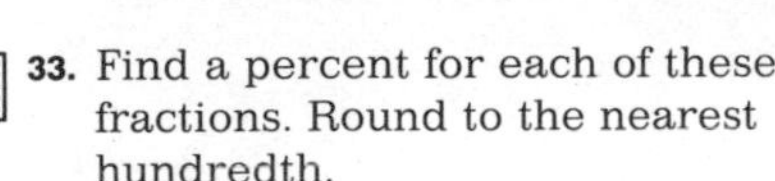

**33.** Find a percent for each of these fractions. Round to the nearest hundredth.

$\frac{57}{76}$, $\frac{147}{200}$, $\frac{51}{85}$, $\frac{51}{136}$, $\frac{95}{114}$, $\frac{347}{689}$
75%, 73.5%, 60%, 37.5%, 83.33%, 50.36%

**Think**

**Shape Perception**

What percent of the large square is shaded red? How could you show someone that your answer is correct? 50%; See teaching notes.

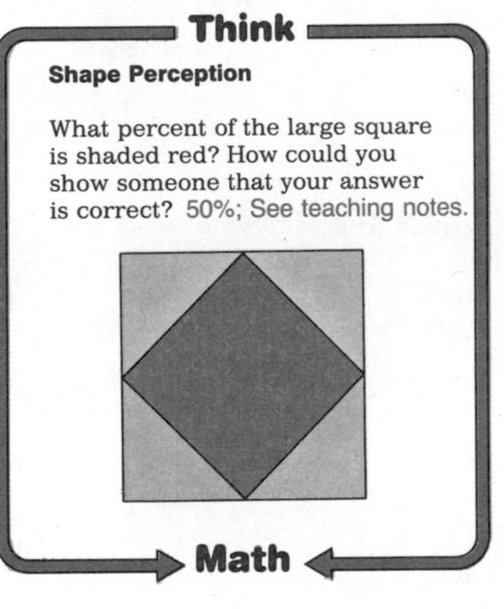

**Math**

More Practice, page 427, Set A



## Using Page 305

**Exercises 1–12** Point out to students that for each given fraction there is only one equivalent fraction with denominator 100. Learning to recognize these equivalent fractions and decimals will be helpful for students.

**Exercises 13–18** Point out that some fractions can be reduced so that they have denominators like the denominators in exercises 1–12. If necessary, briefly review the procedure for reducing a fraction to lowest terms.

**Exercises 19–30** Note that all these fractions, except exercises 20, 22, 29, and 30, use a mixed decimal to produce the correct percent. If necessary, work additional examples to review how to divide to find a mixed decimal.

**Exercise 33** This exercise provides an opportunity to use calculators to find percents. Here it is necessary to divide larger numbers to find the percent. Remind students that the division might not come out even and the percent will need to be rounded to the nearest hundredth.

**Think Math** If students have estimated that the area shaded is 50% of the square, use this method to convince them that this estimate is correct: Draw dotted lines to show that 4 of 8 congruent triangles have been shaded. $\frac{4}{8} = \frac{1}{2} = 50\%$.

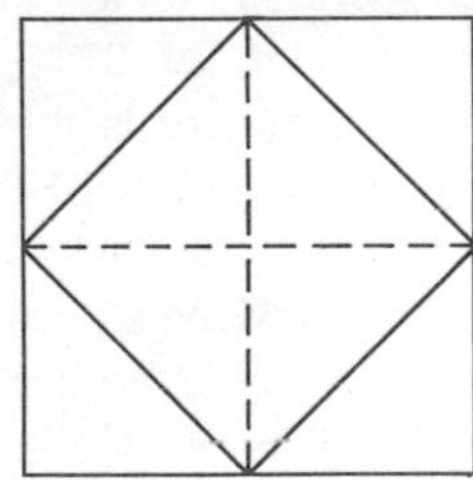

**More Practice,** page 427, Set A

## Ideas That Work

### Special Education

The following activity gives students practice in estimating percents and in making judgments about various information in a circle graph.

Make several overhead transparencies showing data represented by circle graphs. These transparencies can then be projected on the wall for a period of time (depending on the abilities of the students and the difficulty of the material).

Students can then be asked to respond to a series of questions designed to elicit the information given in the graphs. Appropriate questions might ask for a brief description of what data is given, discuss the percent of the total represented by a given part of the graph, or ask whether or not specific information was included in the graph.

This activity helps build comprehension skills, short-time memory skills, and estimation and approximation skills—all necessary for problem solving and applying mathematics to real-world situations.

**Practice Supplement,** page 116

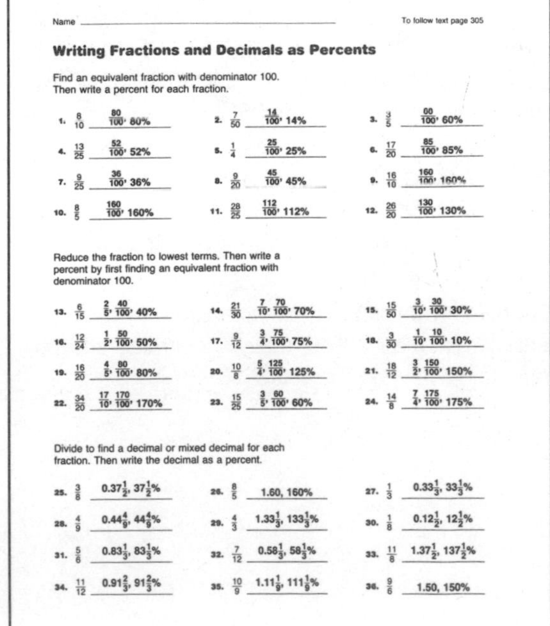

Name ______________________ To follow text page 305

**Writing Fractions and Decimals as Percents**

Find an equivalent fraction with denominator 100. Then write a percent for each fraction.

| | | |
|---|---|---|
| 1. $\frac{8}{10}$ $\frac{80}{100}$, 80% | 2. $\frac{7}{50}$ $\frac{14}{100}$, 14% | 3. $\frac{3}{5}$ $\frac{60}{100}$, 60% |
| 4. $\frac{13}{25}$ $\frac{52}{100}$, 52% | 5. $\frac{1}{4}$ $\frac{25}{100}$, 25% | 6. $\frac{17}{20}$ $\frac{85}{100}$, 85% |
| 7. $\frac{9}{25}$ $\frac{36}{100}$, 36% | 8. $\frac{9}{20}$ $\frac{45}{100}$, 45% | 9. $\frac{16}{10}$ $\frac{160}{100}$, 160% |
| 10. $\frac{8}{5}$ $\frac{160}{100}$, 160% | 11. $\frac{28}{25}$ $\frac{112}{100}$, 112% | 12. $\frac{26}{20}$ $\frac{130}{100}$, 130% |

Reduce the fraction to lowest terms. Then write a percent by first finding an equivalent fraction with denominator 100.

| | | |
|---|---|---|
| 13. $\frac{6}{15}$ $\frac{2}{5}$, $\frac{40}{100}$, 40% | 14. $\frac{21}{30}$ $\frac{7}{10}$, $\frac{70}{100}$, 70% | 15. $\frac{15}{50}$ $\frac{3}{10}$, $\frac{30}{100}$, 30% |
| 16. $\frac{12}{24}$ $\frac{1}{2}$, $\frac{50}{100}$, 50% | 17. $\frac{9}{12}$ $\frac{3}{4}$, $\frac{75}{100}$, 75% | 18. $\frac{3}{30}$ $\frac{1}{10}$, $\frac{10}{100}$, 10% |
| 19. $\frac{16}{20}$ $\frac{4}{5}$, $\frac{80}{100}$, 80% | 20. $\frac{10}{8}$ $\frac{5}{4}$, $\frac{125}{100}$, 125% | 21. $\frac{18}{12}$ $\frac{3}{2}$, $\frac{150}{100}$, 150% |
| 22. $\frac{34}{20}$ $\frac{17}{10}$, $\frac{170}{100}$, 170% | 23. $\frac{15}{25}$ $\frac{3}{5}$, $\frac{60}{100}$, 60% | 24. $\frac{14}{8}$ $\frac{7}{4}$, $\frac{175}{100}$, 175% |

Divide to find a decimal or mixed decimal for each fraction. Then write the decimal as a percent.

| | | |
|---|---|---|
| 25. $\frac{3}{8}$ $0.37\frac{1}{2}$, $37\frac{1}{2}\%$ | 26. $\frac{8}{5}$ 1.60, 160% | 27. $\frac{1}{3}$ $0.33\frac{1}{3}$, $33\frac{1}{3}\%$ |
| 28. $\frac{4}{9}$ $0.44\frac{4}{9}$, $44\frac{4}{9}\%$ | 29. $\frac{4}{3}$ $1.33\frac{1}{3}$, $133\frac{1}{3}\%$ | 30. $\frac{1}{8}$ $0.12\frac{1}{2}$, $12\frac{1}{2}\%$ |
| 31. $\frac{5}{6}$ $0.83\frac{1}{3}$, $83\frac{1}{3}\%$ | 32. $\frac{7}{12}$ $0.58\frac{1}{3}$, $58\frac{1}{3}\%$ | 33. $\frac{11}{8}$ $1.37\frac{1}{2}$, $137\frac{1}{2}\%$ |
| 34. $\frac{11}{12}$ $0.91\frac{2}{3}$, $91\frac{2}{3}\%$ | 35. $\frac{10}{9}$ $1.11\frac{1}{9}$, $111\frac{1}{9}\%$ | 36. $\frac{9}{6}$ 1.50, 150% |

**Quick Review** Students divide each number by 10 and 100.

0.75 0.8 750.06 25.67 14 26.2 805
0.55 1.25 0.314 0.01 4.8 68
85.35 0.28 90.03 4,509 907 12.357

**Lesson Focus** To write percents as decimals and fractions; to solve word problems involving percents as decimals and fractions

**Suggested Materials** Meter sticks

## Ideas for Getting Started

Show students a meter stick and say that the meter stick is to represent 1 or 1 whole. "How many centimeters in a meter?" (100) "What percent of the whole meter stick is 30 cm?" $\left(\frac{30}{100}\text{ or }30\%\right)$ "What percent is 75 cm?" (75%) "42 cm?" (42%) "$38\frac{1}{2}$ cm?" $\left(38\frac{1}{2}\%\right)$ "How many millimeters in a centimeter?" (10) "How many millimeters in a meter?" (100 × 10 or 1,000) "If 1 mm is $\frac{1}{1,000}$ of a meter, what part of a meter is 5 mm or $\frac{1}{2}$ cm?" $\left(\frac{1}{2}\text{ cm is }\frac{5}{1,000}\text{ of a meter}\right)$ Use other examples as needed to help students understand these relationships.

## Using Page 306

**Motivational Problem** Have students read the problem at the top of the page. "What question do we want to answer about the tennis games?" (What fraction of the games did the player win?) "What percent of the games did she win?" $\left(87\frac{1}{2}\%\right)$ "How can we write this percent as a fraction?" (First write it as a decimal with denominator of 100.)

**Lesson Development** Write $87\frac{1}{2}\%$ on the chalkboard. "I'm thinking of $87\frac{1}{2}\%$ of a meter stick. How many centimeters is this?" (87.5 cm) "How many millimeters is this?" (87.5 × 10 or 875 mm) "What part of the meter stick is this?" $\left(\frac{875}{1,000}\right)$ "What is this fraction reduced to lowest terms?" $\left(\frac{7}{8}\right)$ Write each of the steps on the chalkboard, using the meter stick as a model to illustrate. Then have students give the answer to the question using a complete sentence.

**Other Examples** In the first example a percent larger than 100% is given. Point out that this can be written as a fraction with the denominator 100 and reduced in the normal manner. One way to write this percent as a decimal would be to write it first as a mixed number with a denominator 100 rather than reducing first. The third example involves a fractional percent. Point out that this mixed decimal can be thought of in the same way as the number at the top of the page. Students should understand that in writing a mixed decimal such as $0.12\frac{1}{2}$ they can replace the $\frac{1}{2}$ with a 5 in the thousandths place and write 0.125.

**Exercises 1–20** These exercises include percents larger than 100%, mixed decimals, and percents for review and practice.

## More About Percents, Fractions, and Decimals

A tennis player won $87\frac{1}{2}\%$ of her games during a season. What fraction of the games did she win?

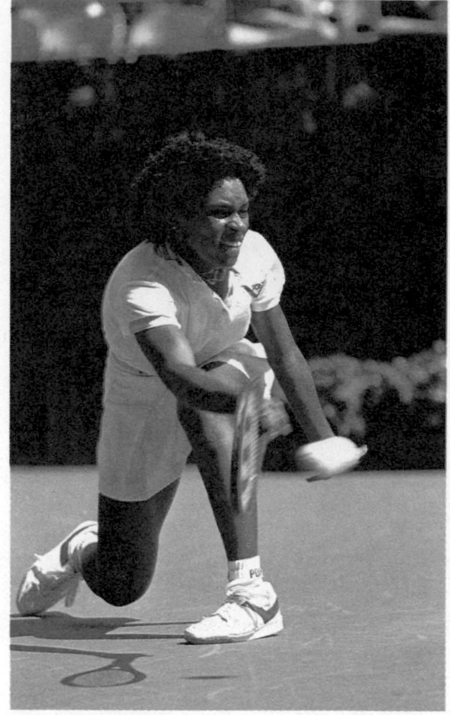

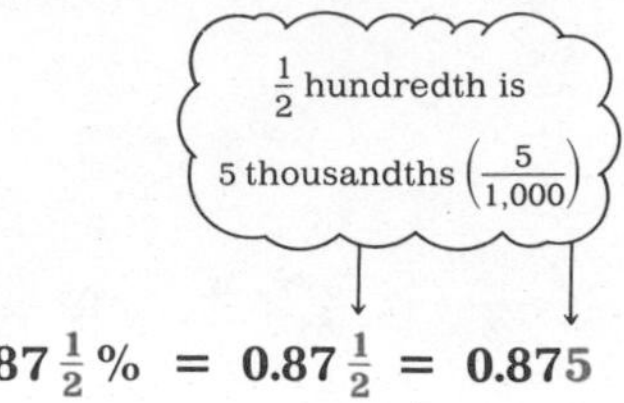


$$87\tfrac{1}{2}\% = 0.87\tfrac{1}{2} = 0.875$$

$$0.875 = \frac{875}{1,000} = \frac{7}{8}$$

The tennis player won $\frac{7}{8}$ of her games.

**Other Examples**

$$125\% = \frac{125}{100} = \frac{5}{4} = 1\tfrac{1}{4}$$

$$125\% = \frac{125}{100} = 1\tfrac{25}{100} = 1.25$$

$$12\tfrac{1}{2}\% = 0.12\tfrac{1}{2} = 0.125 = \frac{125}{1,000} = \frac{1}{8}$$

Write a decimal and a lowest-terms fraction for each percent.

| | | | | |
|---|---|---|---|---|
| **1.** $37\frac{1}{2}\%$ <br> 0.375; $\frac{3}{8}$ | **2.** 150% <br> 1.5; $1\frac{1}{2}$ | **3.** 10% <br> 0.10; $\frac{1}{10}$ | **4.** 5% <br> 0.05; $\frac{1}{20}$ | **5.** 120% <br> 1.20; $1\frac{1}{5}$ |
| **6.** $27\frac{1}{2}\%$ <br> 0.275; $\frac{11}{40}$ | **7.** 75% <br> 0.75; $\frac{3}{4}$ | **8.** $62\frac{1}{2}\%$ <br> 0.625; $\frac{5}{8}$ | **9.** 60% <br> 0.60; $\frac{3}{5}$ | **10.** 110% <br> 1.10; $1\frac{1}{10}$ |
| **11.** 175% <br> 1.75; $1\frac{3}{4}$ | **12.** $12\frac{1}{2}\%$ <br> 0.125; $\frac{1}{8}$ | **13.** 8% <br> 0.08; $\frac{2}{25}$ | **14.** $24\frac{1}{2}\%$ <br> 0.245; $\frac{49}{200}$ | **15.** 30% <br> 0.30; $\frac{3}{10}$ |
| **16.** $22\frac{1}{2}\%$ <br> 0.225; $\frac{9}{40}$ | **17.** 15% <br> 0.15; $\frac{3}{20}$ | **18.** $87\frac{1}{2}\%$ <br> 0.875; $\frac{7}{8}$ | **19.** 90% <br> 0.90; $\frac{9}{10}$ | **20.** 145% <br> 1.45; $1\frac{9}{20}$ |



More Practice, page 427, Set B

## Follow Up

### Reteaching

Begin a discussion by reviewing the percents shown below.

$$12\% = \frac{12}{100} = \frac{3}{25}$$
$$80\% = \frac{80}{100} = \frac{4}{5}$$
$$100\% = \frac{100}{100} = 1$$
$$120\% = \frac{120}{100} = 1\tfrac{1}{5}$$

Focus on the definition of percent as "per hundred"; thus, when a percent is given, we can rewrite it as a fraction with denominator of 100. Then show an example such as $22\frac{1}{2}\%$ and help students work through to find the percent.

$$22\tfrac{1}{2}\% = 0.22\tfrac{1}{2} = 0.225 = \frac{225}{1,000} = \frac{9}{40}$$

### Enrichment

Have students cross out the expressions that do not name the percent shown in the center of the circle. Then challenge them to create a percent circle to exchange with their classmates.

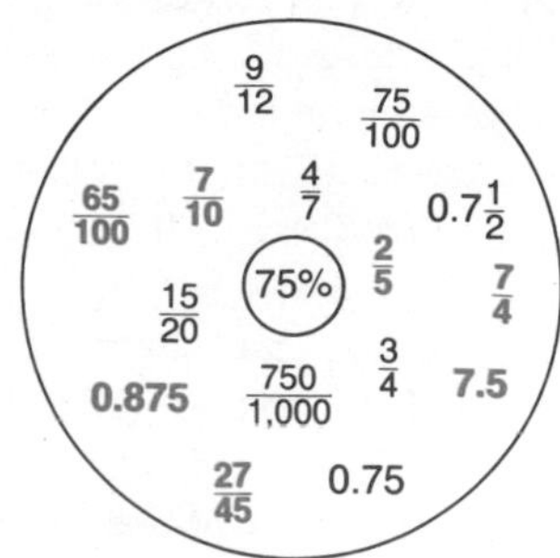

| Assignment Guide | | | |
|---|---|---|---|
| | Minimum | Average | Extended |
| page 306 | 1–20 | 1–20 | 1–20 |
| page 307 | 1–8 | 1–8 | 1–9 |

## Problem Solving: Estimation with Percents

The circle graphs show the results of a poll on students' TV preferences. The first graph shows that about $\frac{1}{4}$ of the students named Channel 5 as their favorite. For the problems below, choose the best estimate for the percent described.

**Favorite TV Channel**

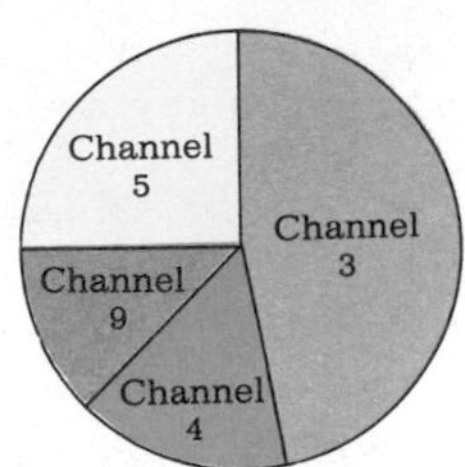


1. About what percent preferred Channel 3? A
   A 47%  B 55%  C 40%
2. About what percent named Channel 4? A
   A 15%  B $37\frac{1}{2}$%  C 25%

**Favorite Kind of TV Program**

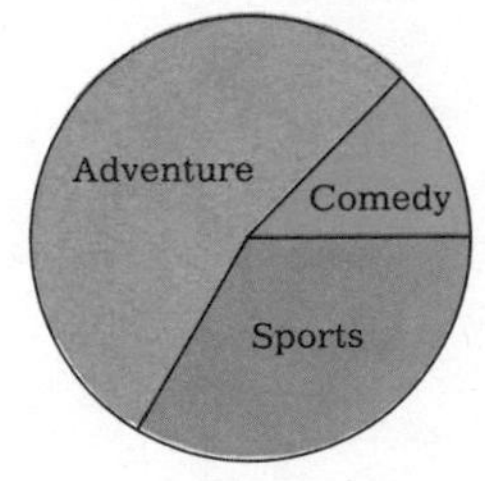


3. About what percent of the students liked sports programs best? C
   A 25%  B 40%  C $33\frac{1}{3}$%
4. About what percent chose adventure? B
   A 48%  B 55%  C 70%
5. About what percent like comedy best? C
   A 20%  B 5%  C $12\frac{1}{2}$%

**Favorite TV Sports Program**

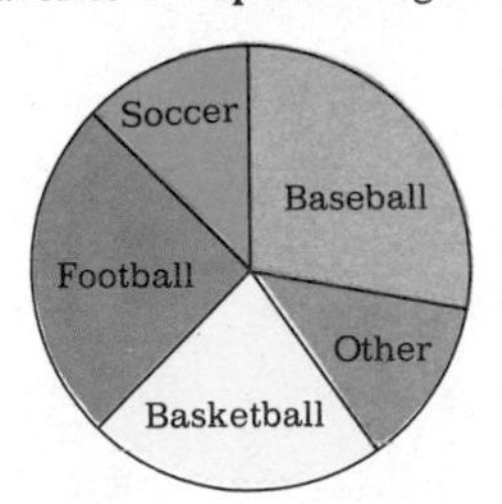


6. About what percent of the students like watching football best? B
   A 15%  B 25%  C $37\frac{1}{2}$%
7. About what percent prefer watching soccer? B
   A 28%  B $12\frac{1}{2}$%  C 5%
8. What is your estimate of the total percent for basketball and baseball? A
   A 50%  B 75%  C 36%
9. **Try This** A TV set was left on 6 hours longer on Monday than on Tuesday. It was on only $\frac{1}{3}$ as long on Tuesday as on Monday. How long was it on each day?
   9 hours on Monday, 3 hours on Tuesday



## Using Page 307

**Lesson Development** Direct students' attention to the section labeled "Channel 5" in the circle graph at the top of the page. "What part of the circle represents Channel 5?" $\left(\frac{1}{4}\right)$ "What percent is this?" (25%) "Is the part that represents Channel 3 more or less than 50%?" (less) Read through the instructions to make sure students understand they are to choose the best estimate for each percent.

**Exercises 1–8** In these exercises, students must evaluate each section and consider the percentage choices available. Note that students could subtract their estimates in exercises 3 and 4 from 100% to find the best estimate for comedy in exercise 5.

**Try This** A possible strategy, Guess and Check, was taught on page 48.

**Discussion** "What question is asked about the TV set in the problem?" (How many hours was the TV on Monday and on Tuesday?) "Was it on longer on Monday or on Tuesday?" (It was on 6 hours longer on Monday.) "How did the time the set was on Tuesday compare with the time it was on Monday?" (The set was on $\frac{1}{3}$ as long on Tuesday as on Monday.) "In planning the solution, could we choose one of the operations to solve the problem?" (No, there is not enough information given.) "What strategy could we use as a plan for solving the problem?" (Guess and Check)

**Solution** The TV was on 9 hours on Monday and 3 hours on Tuesday. If we guess that the TV was on 3 hours on Tuesday, then it would be on 3 + 6, or 9 hours on Monday. Since 3 is one third of 9, the solution checks.

**More Practice,** page 427, Set B

**Reteaching Supplement,** page 72

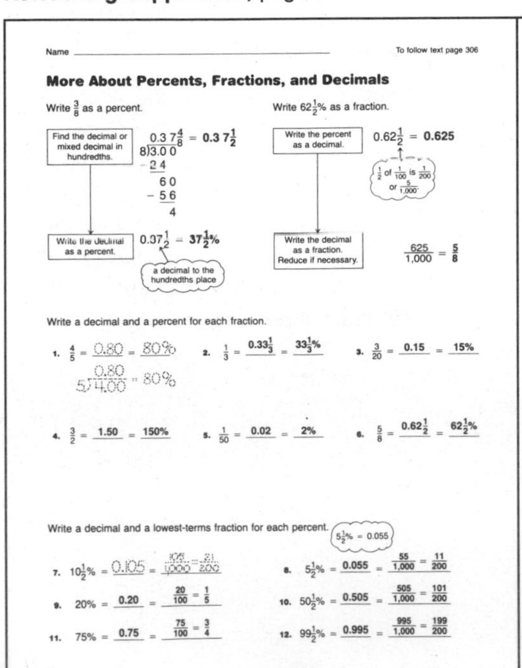
Name ______ To follow text page 306

**More About Percents, Fractions, and Decimals**

Write $\frac{3}{8}$ as a percent.

Find the decimal or mixed decimal in hundredths. $8\overline{)3.00}$ = $0.37\frac{4}{8}$ = $0.37\frac{1}{2}$ (− 24, 60, − 56, 4)

Write the decimal as a percent. $0.37\frac{1}{2}$ = $37\frac{1}{2}$% (a decimal to the hundredths place)

Write $62\frac{1}{2}$% as a fraction.

Write the percent as a decimal. $0.62\frac{1}{2}$ = **0.625** ($\frac{1}{2}$ of $\frac{1}{100}$ is $\frac{1}{200}$ or $\frac{5}{1,000}$.)

Write the decimal as a fraction. Reduce if necessary. $\frac{625}{1,000} = \frac{5}{8}$

Write a decimal and a percent for each fraction.

1. $\frac{4}{5}$ = 0.80 = 80% ($5\overline{)4.00}$ = 0.80 = 80%)
2. $\frac{1}{3}$ = $0.33\frac{1}{3}$ = $33\frac{1}{3}$%
3. $\frac{3}{20}$ = 0.15 = 15%
4. $\frac{3}{2}$ = 1.50 = 150%
5. $\frac{1}{50}$ = 0.02 = 2%
6. $\frac{5}{8}$ = $0.62\frac{1}{2}$ = $62\frac{1}{2}$%

Write a decimal and a lowest-terms fraction for each percent. ($5\frac{1}{2}$% = 0.055)

7. $10\frac{1}{2}$% = 0.105 = $\frac{105}{1000} = \frac{21}{200}$
8. $5\frac{1}{2}$% = 0.055 = $\frac{55}{1,000} = \frac{11}{200}$
9. 20% = 0.20 = $\frac{20}{100} = \frac{1}{5}$
10. $50\frac{1}{2}$% = 0.505 = $\frac{505}{1,000} = \frac{101}{200}$
11. 75% = 0.75 = $\frac{75}{100} = \frac{3}{4}$
12. $99\frac{1}{2}$% = 0.995 = $\frac{995}{1,000} = \frac{199}{200}$

**Enrichment Supplement,** page 72

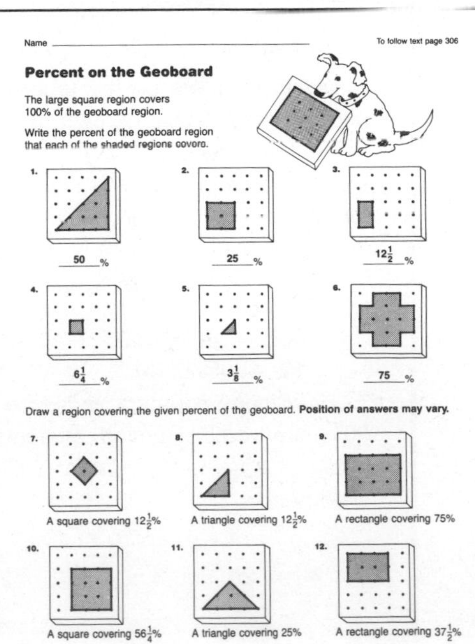
Name ______ To follow text page 306

**Percent on the Geoboard**

The large square region covers 100% of the geoboard region.

Write the percent of the geoboard region that each of the shaded regions covers.

1. 50 %
2. 25 %
3. $12\frac{1}{2}$ %
4. $6\frac{1}{4}$ %
5. $3\frac{1}{8}$ %
6. 75 %

Draw a region covering the given percent of the geoboard. **Position of answers may vary.**

7. A square covering $12\frac{1}{2}$%
8. A triangle covering $12\frac{1}{2}$%
9. A rectangle covering 75%
10. A square covering $56\frac{1}{4}$%
11. A triangle covering 25%
12. A rectangle covering $37\frac{1}{2}$%

**Practice Supplement,** page 117

Name ______ To follow text page 306

**More About Percents, Fractions, and Decimals**

Write a decimal and a lowest-terms fraction for each percent.

1. 95% $0.95, \frac{19}{20}$
2. 2% $0.02, \frac{1}{50}$
3. 60% $0.60, \frac{3}{5}$
4. 88% $0.88, \frac{22}{25}$
5. 160% $1.60, 1\frac{3}{5}$
6. 25% $0.25, \frac{1}{4}$
7. $17\frac{1}{2}$% $0.175, \frac{7}{40}$
8. 48% $0.48, \frac{12}{25}$
9. 150% $1.50, 1\frac{1}{2}$
10. 175% $1.75, 1\frac{3}{4}$
11. $12\frac{1}{2}$% $0.125, \frac{1}{8}$
12. 115% $1.15, 1\frac{3}{20}$
13. 35% $0.35, \frac{7}{20}$
14. 12% $0.12, \frac{3}{25}$
15. 3% $0.03, \frac{3}{100}$
16. $45\frac{1}{2}$% $0.455, \frac{91}{200}$
17. 55% $0.55, \frac{11}{20}$
18. $18\frac{3}{4}$% $0.1875, \frac{3}{16}$
19. 66% $0.66, \frac{33}{50}$
20. 140% $1.4, 1\frac{2}{5}$
21. 9% $0.09, \frac{9}{100}$
22. 68% $0.68, \frac{17}{25}$
23. 45% $0.45, \frac{9}{20}$
24. 185% $1.85, 1\frac{17}{20}$
25. $2\frac{1}{2}$% $0.025, \frac{1}{40}$
26. 112% $1.12, 1\frac{3}{25}$
27. $22\frac{1}{2}$% $0.225, \frac{9}{40}$
28. 65% $0.65, \frac{13}{20}$
29. 116% $1.16, 1\frac{4}{25}$
30. $87\frac{1}{2}$% $0.875, \frac{7}{8}$
31. 5% $0.05, \frac{1}{20}$
32. 28% $0.28, \frac{7}{25}$
33. 130% $1.30, 1\frac{3}{10}$
34. $10\frac{1}{2}$% $0.105, \frac{21}{200}$
35. 125% $1.25, 1\frac{1}{4}$
36. 4% $0.04, \frac{1}{25}$
37. 57% $0.57, \frac{57}{100}$
38. $57\frac{1}{2}$% $0.575, \frac{23}{40}$
39. 136% $1.36, 1\frac{9}{25}$
40. $43\frac{3}{4}$% $0.4375, \frac{7}{16}$
41. 156% $1.56, 1\frac{14}{25}$
42. 90% $0.90, \frac{9}{10}$
43. $33\frac{1}{3}$% $0.33\frac{1}{3}, \frac{1}{3}$
44. 46% $0.46, \frac{23}{50}$
45. 108% $1.08, 1\frac{2}{25}$

# Percent

**Quick Review** Put these exercises on the chalkboard. Students write answers as quickly and as accurately as possible.

| 350 | 458 | 265 | 0.125 | 0.60 | 560 |
|---|---|---|---|---|---|
| × 0.25 | × 0.36 | × 0.06 | × 45 | × 340 | × 1.5 |

**Lesson Focus** To find the percent of a number

## Ideas for Getting Started

If possible, have available examples of percent applications from magazines, newspapers, advertisements, and so on. As you discuss these applications, help students become aware of the many common uses of percent in everyday situations.

## Using Page 308

**Motivational Problem** Ask students to read the problem at the top of the page. "What do we want to know about the survey?" (How many children were afraid of thunder and lightning?) "How many children were in the class?" (32) "What percent of them are afraid of thunder?" (25%) "How can we find the number of students who are afraid of lightning?" (Find 25% of 32.)

**Lesson Development** Ask students to name the fraction that is equal to 25%. $\left(\frac{1}{4}\right)$ "What decimal is equal to 25%?" (0.25) Tell students that 25% of 32 is the same as $\frac{1}{4} \times 32$ or $0.25 \times 32$. Work with students to complete each of the examples to show that the answer in both cases is 8. Then have students read the sentence that gives the answer to the problem. Emphasize that we can often use "mental math" to find a percent such as 10%, 25%, or 50%.

**Other Examples** Note that the first example can be done mentally as a fraction. The second situation is done easiest with decimal multiplication. In the third example decimal multiplication involving thousandths is required.

**Warm Up** Exercises 1–4 involve changing a percent to a fraction and finding the product of a fraction times a whole number. As you observe students, check to see that they complete each of these steps correctly. Exercises 5–8 are similar except that they require decimal multiplication or changing a percent to a decimal.

## Finding a Percent of a Number

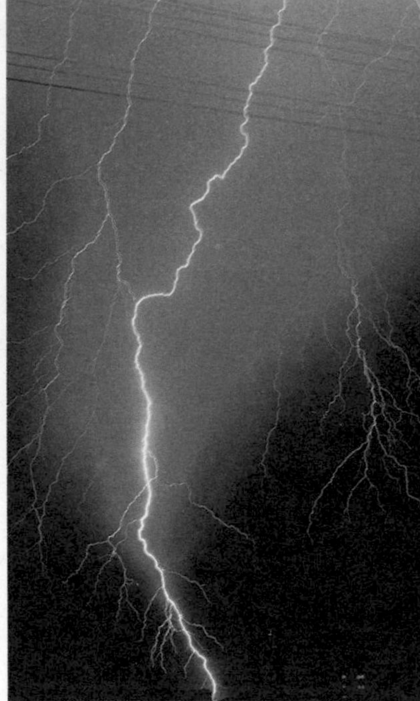

A survey of 32 children showed that 25% of them were afraid of thunder and lightning. How many of the children were afraid of thunder and lightning?

Here are two ways to find a percent of a number.

**Using a fraction**

$$25\% = \frac{25}{100} = \frac{1}{4}$$

$$\frac{1}{4} \times 32 = 8$$

We can use mental math for this since $\frac{1}{4}$ of 32 is the same as 32 ÷ 4!

**Using a decimal**

$$25\% = 0.25$$

```
   32
× 0.25
  160
  64
 8.00
```

8 of the 32 children were afraid of thunder and lightning.

**Other Examples**

50 % of 180
↓
$\frac{1}{2} \times 180 = 90$

14 % of 35

```
   35
× 0.14
  140
  35
 4.90
```

$37\frac{1}{2}$% of 24

```
    24
× 0.375
   120
  168
  72
 9.000
```

**Warm Up** Find the percent of each number.

Use a fraction: **1.** 25% of 28 — 7 **2.** 50% of 84 — 42 **3.** 75% of 12 — 9 **4.** 20% of 50 — 10

Use a decimal: **5.** 23% of 120 — 27.6 **6.** 13% of 240 — 31.2 **7.** 5% of 135 — 6.75 **8.** $12\frac{1}{2}$% of 64 — 8



## Follow Up

### Reteaching

Place 40 counters on the table: 12 red and 28 white. "What percent of the total amount are red?" Elicit from students that the fraction $\frac{12}{40}$ shows that 12 counters are red. Then work through the following process:

$$\frac{12}{40} = \frac{3}{10} = \frac{30}{100} = 30\%$$

$30\% \times 40 = 0.30 \times 40 = 12.00$
12 is 30% of 40

"How many counters would be red if 50% are red?" Remind students that $50\% = \frac{50}{100} = \frac{1}{2}$. Then write the statements:

$\frac{1}{2}$ of 40 = 50% of 40
$\frac{1}{2} \times 40 = 20$, and $0.50 \times 40 = 20$.

### Enrichment

Have students check the local newspapers to find out what the current interest rates are. Then challenge students to write word problems based on the information they have gathered involving interest paid or earned on savings or on loans. Students then exchange problems with classmates.

| Assignment Guide | | | |
|---|---|---|---|
| | Minimum | Average | Extended |
| page 309 | 1–33, SK | 1–34, SK | 1–35, SK |

Find the percent of each number. Use a fraction.

**1.** 50% of 120 60 **2.** 25% of 20 5 **3.** 75% of 40 30 **4.** 10% of 150 15

**5.** 20% of 35 7 **6.** 40% of 45 18 **7.** 5% of 80 4 **8.** 60% of 500 300

**9.** 90% of 100 90 **10.** 75% of 200 150 **11.** 30% of 60 18 **12.** 25% of 48 12

Find the percent of each number. Use a decimal.

**13.** 19% of 26 4.94 **14.** 43% of 85 36.55 **15.** 76% of 95 72.2 **16.** $12\frac{1}{2}$% of 72 9

**17.** 3% of 32 0.96 **18.** 87% of 24 20.88 **19.** 24% of 36 8.64 **20.** 11% of 20 2.2

**21.** $37\frac{1}{2}$% of 56 21 **22.** $7\frac{1}{2}$% of 18 1.35 **23.** $62\frac{1}{2}$% of 480 300 **24.** 98% of 324 317.52

Find the percent of each number.

**25.** 31% of 90 27.9 **26.** 78% of 100 78 **27.** 25% of 240 60 **28.** $12\frac{1}{2}$% of 64 8

**29.** 45% of 180 81 **30.** 67% of 250 167.5 **31.** 13% of 86 11.18 **32.** $62\frac{1}{2}$% of 720 450

**33.** Only 8% of a large group of children said they were afraid of heights. Using this percent, how many children in a class of 25 would you expect to be afraid of heights? 2

**34.** In a class of 25 students, 36% of them had a fear of deep water. In another class of 25 students, 40% of them had a fear of deep water. How many more children in the second class had this fear than in the first class? 1

**35. DATA BANK** What is the most common fear among adults in the United States? How many people out of 3,000 have this fear? (See the Data Bank, page 409.) Speaking in front of groups; 1,230

## Skillkeeper

Solve the proportions.

**1.** $\frac{5}{8} = \frac{15}{n}$ $n = 24$ **2.** $\frac{8}{6} = \frac{n}{3}$ $n = 4$ **3.** $\frac{20}{4} = \frac{n}{1}$ $n = 5$ **4.** $\frac{25}{30} = \frac{5}{n}$ $n = 6$ **5.** $\frac{n}{40} = \frac{7}{4}$ $n = 70$

**6.** $\frac{18}{21} = \frac{n}{7}$ $n = 6$ **7.** $\frac{14}{20} = \frac{7}{n}$ $n = 10$ **8.** $\frac{2}{3} = \frac{n}{30}$ $n = 20$ **9.** $\frac{12}{7} = \frac{24}{n}$ $n = 14$ **10.** $\frac{5}{n} = \frac{35}{21}$ $n = 3$

Find the products.

**11.** $25 \times 0.6$ 15.0 **12.** $80 \times 0.25$ 20 **13.** $72 \times 0.12$ 8.64 **14.** $14 \times 1.8$ 25.2 **15.** $5.7 \times 0.34$ 1.938



## Using Page 309

**Exercises 1–12** For students having difficulty with these exercises, provide a brief review with exercises such as $\frac{3}{4} \times 40$. Students can do these by dividing 40 by 4 and then multiplying by 3. Or, they can find the product by fraction multiplication $\left(\frac{3}{4} \times \frac{40}{1} = 30\right)$.

**Exercises 13–24** Check students' work in problems such as 16, 21, 22, and 23 to see that the appropriate decimal is used in the computation.

**Exercises 25–34** For these exercises students must decide whether to multiply using decimals or fractions. Note that exercise 27 is probably most easily done by finding $\frac{1}{4}$ of 240. Note that exercise 34 involves three separate operations.

**Data Bank** Remind students that the data needed to solve this problem can be found in the Data Bank in the back of the book. It is important for students to have experiences in which the data needed to solve a problem is not given in the problem itself.

**Skillkeeper** These skills were originally taught in Chapter 11 and in Chapter 6.

**More Practice,** page 427, Set C

**Reteaching Supplement,** page 73

Name ______ To follow text page 309

### Finding a Percent of a Number

Find 12% of 248 using a decimal.

Write the percent as a decimal. 12% = **0.12**

Multiply. $248 \times 0.12$: 496, 2480, 29.76

Find 15% of 50 using a fraction.

Write the percent as a fraction. $15\% = \frac{15}{100} = \frac{3}{20}$

Multiply. $\frac{3}{20} \times \frac{50}{1} = \frac{15}{2} = 7\frac{1}{2}$

Find the percent of each number. Use a decimal.

1. $8\frac{1}{2}$% of 24 2.04 ($8\frac{1}{2}\% = 0.085$; $24 \times 0.085$: 120, 192, 2.040) 2. 125% of 168 210 (125% = 1.25) 3. 27% of 90 24.3 (27% = 0.27)

4. 99% of 312 308.88 5. $26\frac{1}{2}$% of 180 47.7 6. 3% of 294 8.82

Find the percent of each number. Use a fraction.

7. 75% of 80 60 ($75\% = \frac{3}{4}$; $\frac{3}{4} \times \frac{80}{1} = 60$) 8. 60% of 20 12

9. 50% of 86 43 10. 18% of 400 72

11. 83% of 100 83 12. 5% of 2000 100

**Enrichment Supplement,** page 73

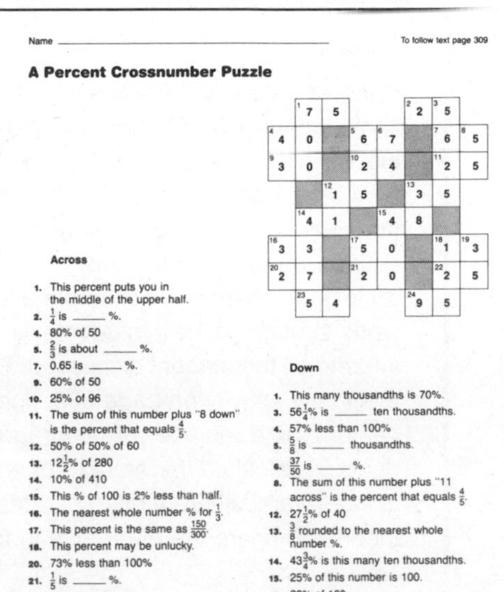
Name ______ To follow text page 309

### A Percent Crossnumber Puzzle

| | | | | | | | |
|---|---|---|---|---|---|---|---|
| | 7 | 5 | | | 2 | 5 | |
| 4 | 0 | ■ | 6 | 7 | ■ | 6 | 5 |
| 3 | 0 | ■ | 2 | 4 | ■ | 2 | 5 |
| | ■ | 1 | 5 | ■ | 3 | 5 | |
| | 4 | 1 | ■ | 4 | 8 | ■ | |
| 3 | 3 | ■ | 5 | 0 | ■ | 1 | 3 |
| 2 | 7 | ■ | 2 | 0 | ■ | 2 | 5 |
| | 5 | 4 | | | 9 | 5 | |

**Across**

1. This percent puts you in the middle of the upper half.
2. $\frac{1}{4}$ is ____ %.
4. 80% of 50
5. $\frac{2}{3}$ is about ____ %.
7. 0.65 is ____ %.
9. 60% of 50
10. 25% of 96
11. The sum of this number plus "8 down" is the percent that equals $\frac{4}{5}$.
12. 50% of 50% of 60
13. $12\frac{1}{2}$% of 280
14. 10% of 410
15. This % of 100 is 2% less than half.
16. The nearest whole number % for $\frac{1}{3}$.
17. This percent is the same as $\frac{150}{300}$.
18. This percent may be unlucky.
20. 73% less than 100%
21. $\frac{1}{5}$ is ____ %.
22. $\frac{1}{2}$ of $\frac{1}{2}$ would be ____ %.
23. 60% of 90
24. If you have this %, you have all but $\frac{1}{20}$ of it.

**Down**

1. This many thousandths is 70%.
3. $56\frac{1}{4}$% is ____ ten thousandths.
4. 57% less than 100%
5. $\frac{5}{8}$ is ____ thousandths.
6. $\frac{37}{50}$ is ____ %.
8. The sum of this number plus "11 across" is the percent that equals $\frac{4}{5}$.
12. $27\frac{1}{2}$% of 40
13. $\frac{3}{8}$ rounded to the nearest whole number %.
14. $43\frac{3}{4}$% is this many ten thousandths.
15. 25% of this number is 100.
16. 20% of 160
17. This many hundredths equals 52%.
18. $\frac{5}{4}$ is ____ %.
19. 25% of 140 is ____ .

**Practice Supplement,** page 118

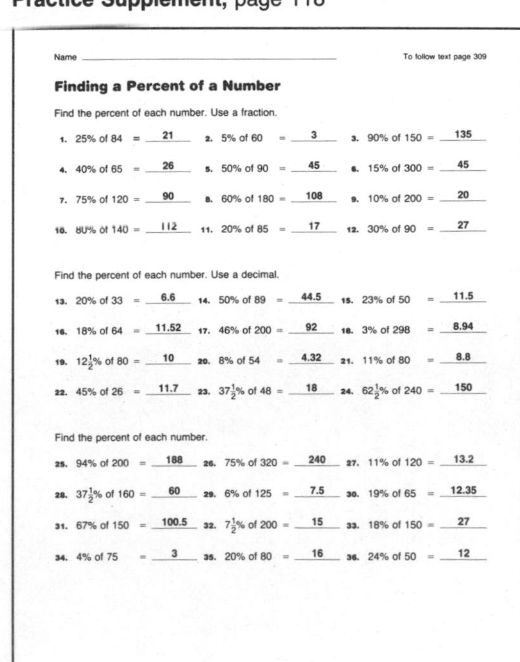
Name ______ To follow text page 309

### Finding a Percent of a Number

Find the percent of each number. Use a fraction.

1. 25% of 84 = 21 2. 5% of 60 = 3 3. 90% of 150 = 135
4. 40% of 65 = 26 5. 50% of 90 = 45 6. 15% of 300 = 45
7. 75% of 120 = 90 8. 60% of 180 = 108 9. 10% of 200 = 20
10. 80% of 140 = 112 11. 20% of 85 = 17 12. 30% of 90 = 27

Find the percent of each number. Use a decimal.

13. 20% of 33 = 6.6 14. 50% of 89 = 44.5 15. 23% of 50 = 11.5
16. 18% of 64 = 11.52 17. 46% of 200 = 92 18. 3% of 298 = 8.94
19. $12\frac{1}{2}$% of 80 = 10 20. 8% of 54 = 4.32 21. 11% of 80 = 8.8
22. 45% of 26 = 11.7 23. $37\frac{1}{2}$% of 48 = 18 24. $62\frac{1}{2}$% of 240 = 150

Find the percent of each number.

25. 94% of 200 = 188 26. 75% of 320 = 240 27. 11% of 120 = 13.2
28. $37\frac{1}{2}$% of 160 = 60 29. 6% of 125 = 7.5 30. 19% of 65 = 12.35
31. 67% of 150 = 100.5 32. $7\frac{1}{2}$% of 200 = 15 33. 18% of 150 = 27
34. 4% of 75 = 3 35. 20% of 80 = 16 36. 24% of 50 = 12

**Quick Review** Students give the number that makes each statement true.

$\frac{3}{4}$ of 80 = (80 ÷ 4) × □ $\frac{2}{5}$ of 5 = (5 ÷ □) × 2

$\frac{6}{10}$ of 40 = (40 ÷ □) × 6 $\frac{5}{7}$ of □ = (49 ÷ 7) × 5 $\frac{3}{4}$ of 8 = (□ ÷ 4) × 3

**Lesson Focus** To solve word problems that involve finding interest

## Ideas for Getting Started

Discuss experiences students might have had with a savings account from which interest is received or with an installment purchase on which interest is paid. Elicit a discussion about advertisements from local savings and loan companies or from local businesses that offer to finance purchases. If possible, show students a savings account book in which the interest payment has been posted and added to the previous balance.

## Using Page 310

**Lesson Development** Direct students' attention to the statement at the top of the page. Review the idea that interest is a fee paid for the use of someone else's money. Direct students' attention to the information showing rate of interest, amount deposited, and interest earned. "How much money was deposited?" ($125) "What was the rate of interest?" (8%) "How much was the interest?" ($10) Be sure students understand how the amount of interest was calculated and have them read the complete statement that tells about the amount of interest.

Direct students' attention to the promissory note in the middle of the page. "How much was borrowed from the stereo store?" ($450) "What is the rate of interest to be paid?" (12%) "How is the amount of interest calculated?" (by finding 12% of 450) Be sure students understand how the calculation was made. Then have them read the sentence that tells the amount of interest charged.

**Exercises 1–4** After students have completed the exercises, discuss the answers. Students might observe that the interest rate to borrow money is higher than the interest received on savings. Encourage them to discuss why this is usually true.

QUESTION / DATA / PLAN / ANSWER / CHECK

## Problem Solving: Finding Interest

**Interest** is a fee paid for the use of someone's money.

Banks and savings and loan companies pay you interest for using the money you deposit in a savings account.

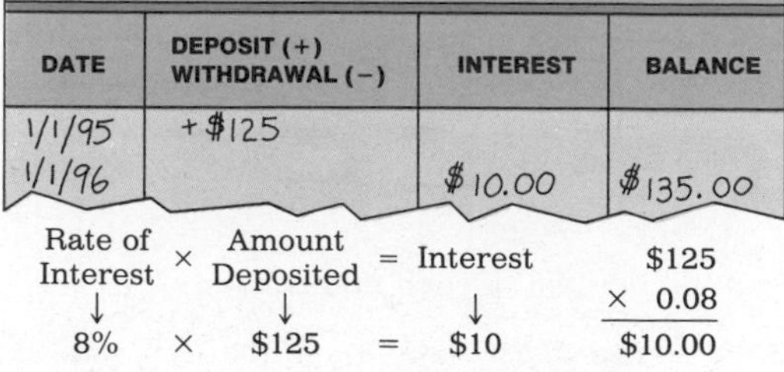

**Eversafe Savings and Loan Co.**

| DATE | DEPOSIT (+) WITHDRAWAL (−) | INTEREST | BALANCE |
|---|---|---|---|
| 1/1/95 | +$125 | | |
| 1/1/96 | | $10.00 | $135.00 |

Rate of Interest × Amount Deposited = Interest
8% × $125 = $10

$125
× 0.08
$10.00

The interest paid on $125 for 1 year at 8% per year is $10.

You pay interest when you borrow money to buy something.

STEREO—$450
Buy Now!
Pay next year.
Interest rate 12%

DATE 12/30/95

PROMISSORY NOTE

I, Will X. Pend, promise to pay
Stan's Stereo Store the amount of
$ 450 plus interest at a rate
of 12 % on 12/30/96.
signed Will X. Pend

Rate of Interest × Amount Borrowed = Interest
12% × $450 = $54

$450
× 0.12
900
450
$54.00

The interest charge for 1 year on a $450 loan at 12% per year is $54.

Find the interest for 1 year on the following amounts.

1. Amount Deposited: $50
   Interest Rate: 10%
   Interest: ▩ $5
2. Amount Borrowed: $300
   Interest Rate: 15%
   Interest: ▩ $45
3. Amount Deposited: $425
   Interest Rate: 9%
   Interest: ▩ $38.25
4. Amount Borrowed: $1,500
   Interest Rate: 12%
   Interest: ▩ $180

310

## Follow Up

### Reteaching

Bring to class an advertisement of an item students might be interested in buying, such as a stereo unit. Discuss that if they borrowed money to buy the stereo, they would have to pay interest—a fee paid for the use of the money. Establish an interest charge, for example 9%, and work through to help students find the interest on the amount discussed. Relate this to the activity on page 308, finding a percent of a number. Encourage students to calculate the amount of interest using several different interest rates, and then to compare the difference in totals.

### Enrichment

Have students complete the table below. Point out that they find not only the amount of interest but also the total amount they would have in the bank at the end of the year, which is the amount of savings plus interest earned.

| Savings | Interest Rate | Amount of Interest | Savings plus Interest |
|---|---|---|---|
| $100 | 6% | $6.00 | $106.00 |
| $40 | 8% | **$3.20** | **$43.20** |
| $300 | 11% | **$33.00** | **$333.00** |
| $75 | 10% | **$7.50** | $82.50 |
| $140 | $9\frac{1}{2}$% | **$13.30** | **$153.30** |
| $25 | 5% | **$1.25** | **$26.25** |

| Assignment Guide | | | |
|---|---|---|---|
| | Minimum | Average | Extended |
| page 310 | 1–4 | 1–4 | 1–4 |
| page 311 | 1–8 | 1–9 | 1–10 |

Solve these problems about interest on saving and loans.

1. Marcus deposited $50 in a savings account. The rate of interest was 8% per year. How much interest did he receive at the end of a year? $4

2. The bank paid Joan 10% interest on $280 she deposited in a savings account. How much money did the bank pay Joan for using her money for 1 year? $28

3. Sam borrowed $500 to buy a TV set. The interest rate was 12%. How much interest must Sam pay at the end of a year? $60

4. Mr. Cole borrowed $4,000 to help buy a new car. At a 9% rate, how much interest will he pay to borrow this money for 1 year? $360

5. Esperanza deposited $1000 in a savings account that paid interest at a 7% rate. How much money will be in the account after the interest is paid at the end of 1 year? $1,070

6. Joey borrowed $250 at 14% interest. How much interest will he owe at the end of a year? How much will he owe altogether? $35; $285

7. The Robinsons deposited $2,500 in a savings account that pays interest at the rate of 11%. If they leave the money in the account for a year, what will the total amount in their account be at the end of the year, after the interest has been paid? $2,775

8. Ms. Barents borrowed $9,500 to use for home improvements. The interest rate was 12%. How much did she have to pay altogether if she paid back the loan at the end of the year? $10,640

9. **DATA HUNT** How much interest would you receive if you deposited $500 in a local bank or savings and loan company for 1 year? Answers will vary.

10. **Try This** Pedro has 6 coins. One third of his coins are dimes. The dimes are $\frac{1}{4}$ of the total value of the coins. What coins does Pedro have? 2 dimes, 2 quarters, 2 nickels



## Using Page 311

**Exercises 1–8** Note that in the first four exercises, students are asked to find only the percent of a number. In exercises 5–8 they must first find the amount of interest, then add that amount to a previous amount.

**Data Hunt** This Data Hunt asks students to find what rate of interest they would be paid on a savings account. If the information is not readily available, select a student representative to call a local firm to collect the information for the class.

**Try This** A possible strategy, Choose the Operations, was taught on page 16.

**Discussion** "What do we want to know about Pedro's coins?" (What coins does Pedro have?) "What part of his coins are dimes?" $\left(\frac{1}{3}\right)$ "What part of the total value of his coins are the dimes?" $\left(\frac{1}{4}\right)$ "As you plan a solution, what is the first information you must find?" (How many of Pedro's coins are dimes? That is, $\frac{1}{3}$ of 6 is 2 coins.) "What is the value of these coins?" (20¢) "If this value is $\frac{1}{4}$ of the total value, what is the total value of the coins?" (4 × 20¢ or 80¢) "If 2 of the 6 coins are dimes, the other 4 coins total 80¢. What do you know about the remaining 4 coins?" (At least some of them must be quarters.)

**Solution** Pedro has 2 dimes, 2 nickels, and 2 quarters or 80¢. Because there cannot be three quarters and two dimes, there must be two quarters. Then 2 quarters and 2 dimes total 70¢, which means that the remaining 2 coins must be nickels.

### Reteaching Supplement, page 74

Name ____________ To follow text page 311

**Problem Solving: Finding Interest**

Matt deposited $85.00 in a savings account. The rate of interest was 6% per year. How much money will he have in his account at the end of one year?

Find the amount of savings and the interest rate. → Multiply the savings by the interest rate. → Add the amount of interest to the amount of savings.

Savings: $85
Interest rate: 6%

Write the percent as a decimal. 6% = 0.06

$85 × 0.06 = $5.10

$85.00 + 5.10 = $90.10

Matt will receive $5.10 interest at the end of one year, so he will then have $90.10 in his account.

Complete the table.

| | Savings | Interest rate (per year) | Amount of interest | Savings + interest |
|---|---|---|---|---|
| 1. | $ 25.00 | 6% | $1.50 | $26.50 |
| 2. | $130.00 | 8% | $10.40 | $140.40 |
| 3. | $575.00 | 12% | $69.00 | $644.00 |
| 4. | $137.50 | 10% | $13.75 | $151.25 |
| 5. | $850.00 | 7% | $59.50 | $909.50 |

Solve.

6. How much interest would Susan earn on $271 in one year if her savings account had an interest rate of 9% per year? **$24.39**

7. How much money will Mr. Remus have at the end of one year if he deposits $890 in a savings account which earns 6% interest per year? **$943.40**

8. Mr. Muncey has deposited $1450 in a savings account which earns 8% interest per year. How much money will he have in his account after one year? **$1566.00**

9. Ms. Karmon has deposited $750 in a savings account which earns 5% interest per year. How much money will she have after 6 months? **$768.75**

### Enrichment Supplement, page 74

Name ____________ To follow text page 311

**Story Time**

Make up the missing data in each advertisement. Then write a story problem that can be solved using data in the story. **Stories and answers will vary.**

1. ____ % off
FLASHLIGHT
ON SALE!
Reg. 5²⁵
Now ____

2. ____ % off
GOOD VALUE!
ON SALE!
TENNIS RACKET Reg. 24⁷⁵
Now ____

3. ____ % off
STAINLESS STEEL VACUUM BOTTLE
Reg. 22⁴⁵
Now ____

4. ____ % off
ELECTRIC CLASS TIME
Reg. 8¹⁵
Now ____

### Practice Supplement, page 119

Name ____________ To follow text page 311

**Problem Solving: Finding Interest**

Find the interest for one year on the following amounts.

1. Amount deposited: $70
Interest rate: 10%
Interest: **$7**

2. Amount borrowed: $650
Interest rate: 13%
Interest: **$84.50**

3. Amount deposited: $225
Interest rate: 8%
Interest: **$18**

4. Amount borrowed: $400
Interest rate: 14%
Interest: **$56**

5. Amount deposited: $700
Interest rate: 9%
Interest: **$63**

6. Amount borrowed: $550
Interest rate: 16%
Interest: **$88**

Solve each problem.

7. Susan deposited $150 in a savings account. The rate of interest was 8% per year. How much interest did she receive at the end of the year? **$12**

8. Judy borrowed $1,200 to buy a stereo. The interest rate was 14%. How much interest must Judy pay at the end of a year? **$168**

9. The bank paid Brad 8% interest on $300 in his savings account. How much money did the bank pay Brad for using his money for one year? **$24**

10. Vicky borrowed $5,000 to help buy a new car. At a 13% interest rate, how much interest will she pay to borrow this money for one year? **$650**

11. Danny borrowed $600 at 12% interest. How much interest will he owe at the end of a year? **$72**

12. Phillip deposited $450 in a savings account that paid interest at a 12% rate. How much money will be in the account after the interest is paid at the end of one year? **$504**

# Applications

**Quick Review** Students give the value of $n$ in each proportion.

$\frac{8}{2} = \frac{n}{1}$ $\frac{2}{100} = \frac{1}{n}$ $\frac{n}{250} = \frac{1}{5}$ $\frac{7}{n} = \frac{21}{300}$ $\frac{18}{n} = \frac{3}{1}$ $\frac{n}{12} = \frac{6}{36}$

**Lesson Focus** To use data from an advertisement to solve word problems involving discounts; to practice solving word problems involving all operations

## Ideas for Getting Started

Bring a variety of advertisements from newspapers, catalogs, or other sale brochures to class and discuss the meaning of sales and discounts. "Which is better, a 10% sale or a 20% sale?" (a 20% sale) "Why?" (There is more taken off the price in a 20% sale.) "Is there a difference between '20% off' and '20% discount' or 'reduced 20%'?" (No, these are just different ways of saying the same thing.)

## Using Page 312

**Lesson Development** Discuss the definitions of discount and sale price given at the top of the page. Then write the following on the chalkboard:

regular price − discount = sale price

Have students read the example, emphasizing the two steps: (1) Find the amount of discount; and (2) Subtract the discount from the regular price. Work through the problem to find 20% of $6.95. Then have students subtract the discount, $1.39, from the regular price of $6.95 to find the sale price. Have students use a complete sentence to give the answer to the question.

**Exercises 1–4** As students complete these exercises, continue to emphasize the two steps in finding the sale price. Remind students that "20% off" in exercise 1 means "20% discount," and in exercise 3 "reduced 25%" means "25% discount." Note that exercises 3 and 4 involve more than one operation.

**Try This** A possible strategy, Work Backward, was taught on page 188.

**Discussion** "What question are we asked about Narissa's money?" (How much money did she have before buying the records?) "How much money did Narissa spend on the record album?" (half of her money) "How much did she spend for the single record?" ($4.54) "How much did she have then?" ($8.32) "Since we know how much Narissa had after buying the records and we know how much she paid for the records, could we work backward to find the solution?" (yes)

**Solution** Narissa started with $25.72. Working backward, $8.32 + $4.54 = $12.86; 12.86 doubled is $25.72.

**Extension** Jason spent $\frac{1}{4}$ of his money on a book. Then he spent $6.75 on a record. After that, he had $5.34. With how much money did he start? ($48.36)

## Problem Solving: Using Data From an Advertisement

The **discount** is an amount subtracted from the regular price of an item.

The **sale price** is the cost of an item after the discount has been subtracted.

What is the sale price of the Super Group album?

**Step 1.** Find the amount of discount (20% of $6.95).

0.20 × $6.95 = **$1.39** ← **discount**

**Step 2.** Subtract the discount from the regular price.

$6.95 − $1.39 = **$5.56** ← **sale price**

Answer the questions about the ads below.

1. What is the sale price? $20

2. What is the sale price? $7.20

3. Which sale price is less? How much less? $35 watch; $2 less

4. What is the total sale price of the camera and case? $76.50

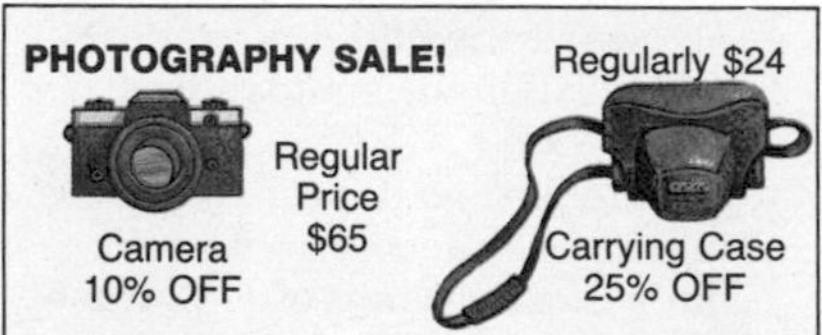


5. **Try This** Narissa spent half of her money to buy a record album. Then she spent $4.54 for a record cleaning kit. After that she still had $8.32. With how much money did she start? $25.72



## Follow Up

### Reteaching

Review writing a decimal as a percent, writing a percent as a decimal, and finding a percent of a number. Then give examples that suggest each idea. For example:

- Suppose a sale sign reads "$\frac{1}{2}$ off every item." What percent is this?
- A pair of jeans usually sells for $18.75. This month they are marked 30% off. What is the sale price?

Generate a discussion in which students identify real-world situations where they could find the discount and sale price.

### Enrichment

Challenge students with the following puzzle: A student had 100 coins totaling $5.00. He had no nickels. What coins did he have? Hint: 60% of the coins were of one kind. **60 pennies, 39 dimes, and 1 half dollar**

| Assignment Guide | Minimum | Average | Extended |
|---|---|---|---|
| page 312 | 1–4 | 1–4 | 1–5 |
| page 313 | 1–6 | 1–7 | 1–8 |

## Problem Solving: Practice

Solve these problems about bees and honey. Use the 5-Point Checklist (page 8).

1. A colony of bees collects 180 kg of nectar a year. The weight of the honey that can be made from this nectar is 25% of the weight of the nectar. How many kilograms of honey is this? 45 kg

2. The smallest honeybee is only 10 mm long. The largest is 190% as long as the smallest. How long is the largest honeybee? 19 mm

3. A recipe for honey-nut bread uses $\frac{1}{2}$ cup of honey. How much honey is used to make $2\frac{1}{2}$ times this recipe? $1\frac{1}{4}$ cups

4. There are about 80,000 bees in an average hive. About 2% of these bees are scouts who look for the sources of nectar in the area. How many scouts are in an average hive? 1,600

5. An average colony of bees produces about 45 kg of honey a year. The bees eat about 55% of this amount. How many kilograms of honey are left for human use? 20.25 kg

6. Some colonies of bees produce as much as 48 kg of honey a year. They fly 70,000 km to collect nectar for 1 kg of honey. How many kilometers do they fly to make an average month's supply of honey? 280,000 km

7. Beekeepers in the United States sell about 93,400,000 kg of honey and beeswax each year. Only 2% of this amount is beeswax. Find how much honey is sold each year. 91,532,000 kg 91,532,000 kg

8. **Try This** A bee starts at its hive and flies to a flower 100 m away. After each flight it returns to the hive and flies to a new flower half as far away as the one before. How far does it travel if the last flower is 12.5 m away? 375 m



## Using Page 313

**Lesson Development** Tell students that bees are very important because over 100,000 species of plants cannot form seeds without pollination by the bees. Then remind students that the 5-Point Checklist can be used as a guide in solving problems.

**Try This** A possible strategy, Draw a Picture, was taught on page 74.

**Discussion** "What question do we want to answer about the bee?" (What was the total distance it traveled?) "How far did the bee fly on the first trip to a flower?" (100 m) "How far away is the next flower?" (half as far, or 50 m) "How far away is the last flower?" (12.5 m) "What strategy might be useful in planning a solution?" (We could draw a picture.)

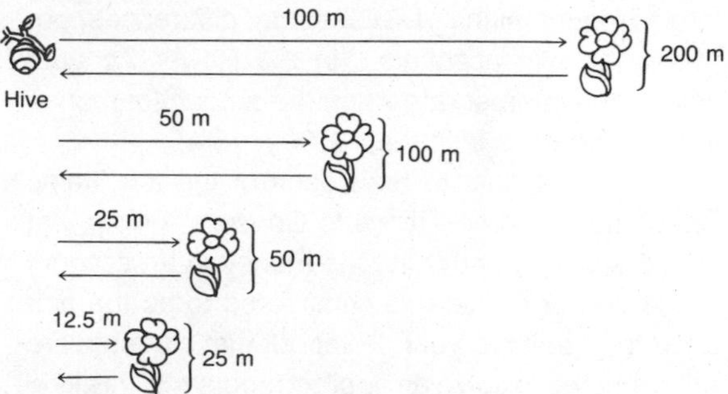


**Solution** The bee traveled a total of 375 m. The four round trips are: 200 + 100 + 50 + 25 or 375 m.

## Ideas That Work

### Math for the Gifted

Provide students with a sale catalog. Have them pretend to spend as much of \$670.00 as possible on any items they want. However, they cannot go even a penny over the \$670.00 or they are "out." For any item costing more than \$50.00, students may deduct 15%; any item costing from \$30.00 to \$49.99, deduct 12%; any item costing from \$10.00 to \$29.99, deduct 10%. To extend the activity, have students include sales tax, shipping, and insurance costs.

**Practice Supplement,** page 120

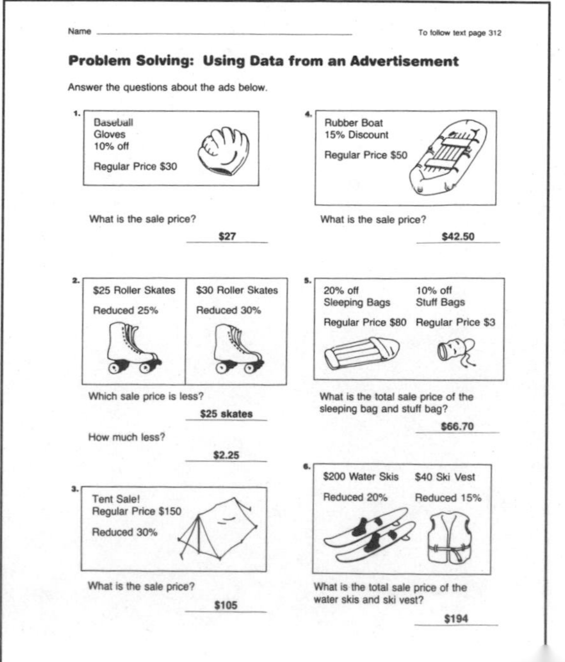
Name ____________ To follow text page 312

**Problem Solving: Using Data from an Advertisement**

Answer the questions about the ads below.

1. Baseball Gloves 10% off Regular Price \$30
What is the sale price? \$27

2. \$25 Roller Skates Reduced 25% | \$30 Roller Skates Reduced 30%
Which sale price is less? \$25 skates
How much less? \$2.25

3. Tent Sale! Regular Price \$150 Reduced 30%
What is the sale price? \$105

4. Rubber Boat 15% Discount Regular Price \$50
What is the sale price? \$42.50

5. 20% off Sleeping Bags Regular Price \$80 | 10% off Stuff Bags Regular Price \$3
What is the total sale price of the sleeping bag and stuff bag? \$66.70

6. \$200 Water Skis Reduced 20% | \$40 Ski Vest Reduced 15%
What is the total sale price of the water skis and ski vest? \$194

**Lesson Focus** To interpret, organize, and use data to make a decision about a real-world problem

## Ideas for Getting Started

Briefly review the procedure for finding the amount of interest paid at a given interest rate. "Suppose you have $300 in the bank for one year at an interest rate of 8%. How much interest would you earn? ($300 × 0.08 or $24) "In one year how much interest would $500 earn at an interest rate of 7%?" ($500 × 0.07 or $35)

## Using Page 314

**Lesson Development** Invite a student to read aloud the problem at the top of the page. Then ask the group to study the descriptions of the two savings account plans. Discuss the differences between the two accounts. "In the Power Account what is the interest rate when the amount of money in the account is less than $100?" (5%)

Call on students to read each of the four items listed under "Some Things to Consider." Note that item 3 simply means that the money in an account at the end of the year is considered to be the balance for the entire year. Point out that students are not expected to solve an applied problem of this kind quickly. Stress the importance of carefully organizing the important information. Advise students to read the facts several times before they answer the questions or make a decision.

### Applied Problem Solving

You are going to start a savings account at the Worthington Federal Bank. Which kind of savings account will you choose?

**Super Saver Account**
Interest Rate—6% per year

**Power Account**
Interest Rate—7% per year
$100 minimum balance
(Under $100—5%)

**Some Things to Consider**

- You have $150 to put in a savings account now.
- You may want to withdraw $60 next week for a pair of skates.
- If you withdraw $60 next week and deposit no more money the rest of the year, the interest is calculated as if you had $90 in the bank all year.
- You get a free blanket if you start a Super-Saver Account and a free calculator if you start a Power Account.

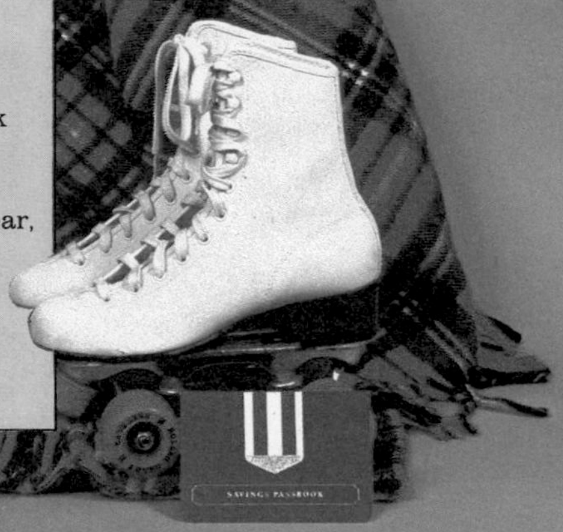

**Some Questions to Answer**

1. How much interest would you earn if you had $150 in the Power Account for the entire year? $10.50
2. How much interest would you earn if you had $150 in the Super-Saver Account for the entire year? $9.00
3. How much interest would you earn from each account if you withdrew $60 for skates and did not deposit more money? Power $4.50; Super $5.40

**What Is Your Decision?**

Will you start a Super-Saver Account or a Power Account? Answers will vary.



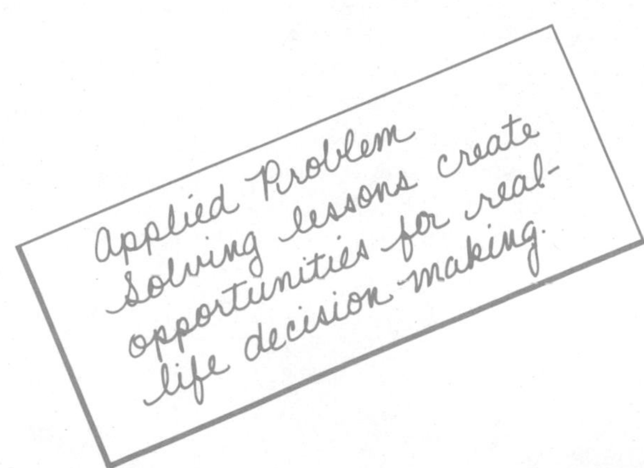

Applied Problem
Solving lessons create
opportunities for real-
life decision-making.

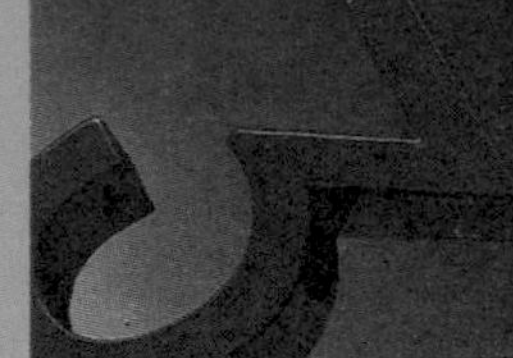

## Chapter Review-Test

Write the ratio, fraction, decimal, and percent to show how much is shaded.

1. ratio 37 to 100  2. fraction $\frac{37}{100}$  3. decimal 0.37  4. percent 37%

Write each decimal or fraction as a percent.

5. 0.34 34%  6. $\frac{74}{100}$ 74%  7. 0.08 8%  8. $\frac{9}{100}$ 9%  9. $\frac{36}{100}$ 36%

Write each percent as a decimal.

10. 43% 0.43  11. 99% 0.99  12. 50% 0.50  13. 5% 0.05  14. 24% 0.24

Write each percent as a fraction in lowest terms.

15. 25% $\frac{1}{4}$  16. 50% $\frac{1}{2}$  17. 75% $\frac{3}{4}$  18. 20% $\frac{1}{5}$  19. 80% $\frac{4}{5}$

Write a percent for each fraction by finding an equivalent fraction.

20. $\frac{3}{5}$ 60%  21. $\frac{1}{10}$ 10%  22. $\frac{7}{4}$ 175%  23. $\frac{9}{20}$ 45%  24. $\frac{6}{25}$ 24%

Write a percent for each fraction by dividing to find a decimal.

25. $\frac{1}{12}$ $8\frac{1}{3}$%  26. $\frac{3}{16}$ $18\frac{3}{4}$%  27. $\frac{2}{3}$ $66\frac{2}{3}$%  28. $\frac{5}{6}$ $83\frac{1}{3}$%  29. $\frac{3}{8}$ $37\frac{1}{2}$%

30. Write a decimal and a lowest-terms fraction for $62\frac{1}{2}$% and 120%. 0.625; $\frac{5}{8}$; 1.2; $1\frac{1}{5}$

Find the percent of each number.

31. 75% of 16 12  32. 23% of 95 21.85  33. 30% of 200 60  34. 80% of 650 520

35. How much interest will Tim receive from a deposit of $300 at a 9% interest rate for 1 year? $27

36. What is the sale price of a $44-pair of binoculars with a 25% discount? $33

37. Honey is 20% water. How many kilograms of water are in the 45 kg of honey a colony of bees might produce in a year? 9 kg



## Using Page 315

The exercises in the Chapter Review-Test emphasize the major concepts and skills presented in this chapter. These exercises may be used as a review assignment or as a test, depending upon your needs.

**Item Analysis** The table below correlates the Chapter Review-Test items with objectives and with the student text pages on which the concepts or skills were taught.

| Items | Objectives | Related Text Pages |
|---|---|---|
| 1–30 | 12.1 | 300–306 |
| 31–34 | 12.2 | 308–309 |
| 35–37 | 12.3 | 307, 310–313 |

## Assessment Options

If you use the Chapter Review-Test as a review assignment, you may wish to use the multiple-choice test or the free-response test to evaluate mastery of the chapter objectives. The items on these tests have a one-to-one correspondence in terms of content and level of difficulty. A correlation of test items to objectives and student text pages is provided in the Management Guide for Chapter 12.

**Multiple-Choice Test,** TRB pages 34–36

**Free-Response Test,** TRB pages 71–72

## TRB Options

The following blackline masters are available for use with this chapter. If you have not already assigned these materials, you may wish to use them to close the chapter.

**Recreation,** TRB page 162

**Consumer Applications,** TRB page 180

**Calculator Technology,** TRB page 198

**Computer Technology,** TRB pages 211–213

**Reading Math,** TRB page 230

**Family Involvement,** TRB pages 259–260

# Reteaching

## Using Page 316

The exercises on this page are intended for those students who experienced difficulty with the Chapter Review-Test on page 315. Should students require reteaching of these key concepts and skills, please refer to the teaching notes below. Otherwise, the Another Look exercises can be assigned as independent work, with students using the accompanying sample problems and hints as guides.

**Exercises 1–15** These ideas were originally taught on pages 300–305. Direct students' attention to the review of the meaning of percent in the display box at the left. Point out that to write a percent as a fraction, drop the percent sign, write the number with a denominator of 100, and reduce the fraction to lowest terms. To write a fraction as a percent, write an equivalent fraction with a denominator of 100 and use the numerator to write the percent; or divide the numerator by the denominator, round or use a mixed decimal. Remind students that 100% is 1 whole and that when there is more than a whole the percent will be greater than 100.

**Exercises 16–27** These ideas were originally taught on pages 302–306. Focus on the display box and emphasize again that percent means hundredth. Thus we can change a percent to a decimal by writing the number as a decimal in hundredths. When we see a percent such as $62\frac{1}{2}$, we can replace the one half by 5 and write a decimal 0.625. Remind students that 100% equal 1.00, 200% equal 2.00, 150% equal 1.50, and 175% equal 1.75. Encourage students to say the percents or the decimals aloud. For example, saying "72 hundredths" for 0.72 can make it easier for students to write 72%.

**Exercises 28–35** This skill was originally taught on pages 308–309. Review the two procedures for finding a percent of a number. When students use fractions to find a percent, encourage them to watch for places where they can use mental math to find the answer. When students use decimals, be sure they understand how to write a percent as a decimal and to place the decimal point in the decimal multiplication. In exercise 32 involving a single-digit percent, be sure students write 8% as 0.08. In exercise 34 help students recall that $12\frac{1}{2}\%$ is written as 0.125 and remind them in exercise 35 that 125% is written as the decimal 1.25.

## *Another Look*

Percent means **per hundred**.

$55\% = \frac{55}{100} = \frac{11}{20}$

$\frac{3}{5} = \frac{60}{100} = 60\%$

$\frac{5}{8} \rightarrow 8\overline{)5.000} = 0.625 \rightarrow 62\frac{1}{2}\%$

$175\% = \frac{175}{100} = \frac{7}{4} = 1\frac{3}{4}$

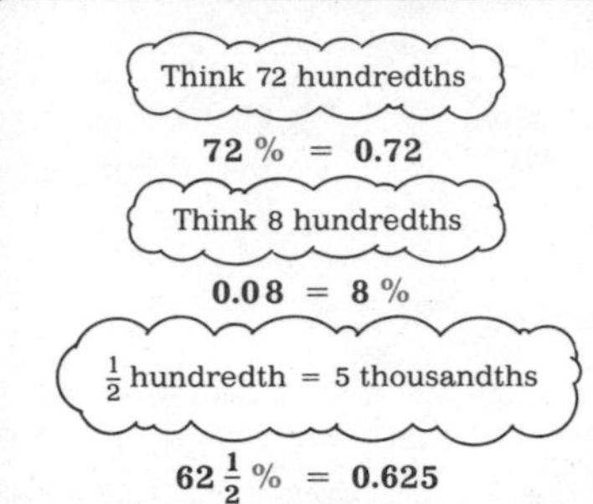


**Finding a percent of a number**

1. Using fractions
   $25\% \text{ of } 48 = \frac{1}{4} \times 48$, or 12
2. Using decimals
   24 % of 48 is 11.52

$$\begin{array}{r} 48 \\ \times\ 0.24 \\ \hline 192 \\ 96\phantom{0} \\ \hline 11.52 \end{array}$$

**Write a lowest-terms fraction for each percent.**

1. 23% $\frac{23}{100}$  2. 45% $\frac{9}{20}$  3. 50% $\frac{1}{2}$
4. 17% $\frac{17}{100}$  5. 6% $\frac{3}{50}$  6. 25% $\frac{1}{4}$
7. 150% $1\frac{1}{2}$  8. 75% $\frac{3}{4}$  9. $87\frac{1}{2}\%$ $\frac{7}{8}$

**Write a percent for each fraction.**

10. $\frac{1}{5}$ 20%  11. $\frac{1}{4}$ 25%  12. $\frac{2}{5}$ 40%
13. $\frac{3}{4}$ 75%  14. $\frac{5}{8}$ $62\frac{1}{2}\%$  15. $\frac{3}{25}$ 12%

**Write a decimal for each percent.**

16. 67% 0.67  17. 13% 0.13  18. 8% 0.08
19. 125% 1.25  20. 1% 0.01  21. $37\frac{1}{2}\%$ 0.37

**Write a percent for each decimal.**

22. 0.38 38%  23. 0.02 2%  24. 0.50 50%
25. 0.80 80%  26. 1.75 175%  27. 0.75 75%

**Find the percent of the number.**

28. 50% of 50 25
29. 25% of 100 25
30. 10% of 90 9
31. 27% of 58 15.66
32. 8% of 120 9
33. 75% of 24 1
34. $12\frac{1}{2}\%$ of 240 30
35. 125% of 500 625

316

## Just for Teachers

### History of Math

To understand the development of percent, it is useful to examine its relationship to fractions. Fractions have been a part of mathematics—both pure and applied—since antiquity. However, the treatment of fractions has varied from culture to culture. The Egyptians limited the numerator to a specific number. Others such as the Babylonians and the Romans limited the denominator to a particular number or powers of that number. The Babylonians, who used a base of 60 in their number system, devised notation symbols which eliminated the need to write the denominator. We see this in remnants of their system still in use today: 7′ means $\frac{7}{60}$; 7″ means $\frac{7}{3,600}$ ($60^2$). Once we devised the decimal point and the percent sign, our base 10 positional notation system drew upon the same principle—the implied constant denominator.

Like the concept of fractions, the basic idea of percent is ancient. To establish a standard for taxation, the Roman emperor Augustus (63 B.C.–A.D. 14) levied a tax at the rate of 1:100 on all goods sold at auction. Other Roman taxes were assessed in fractions that were easily reduced to hundredths.

As the decimal system became known in Europe during the Middle Ages, merchants and financiers recognized the usefulness of the new numbers in the marketplace and

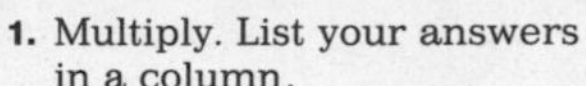

# Enrichment

### Using a Calculator to Explore Number Patterns

A calculator helps you make difficult calculations quickly. It can also help you discover number patterns. Try these. Use your calculator!

**1.** Multiply. List your answers in a column.

| 142,857 × 1 | 142,857 × 2 | 142,857 × 3 |
|---|---|---|
| 142,857 | 285,714 | 428,571 |
| 142,857 × 4 | 142,857 × 5 | 142,857 × 6 |
| 571,428 | 714,285 | 857,142 |

What did you discover?
See teaching notes.

**2.** Are these statements true? yes

15 × 15 = (10 × 20) + 25
25 × 25 = (20 × 30) + 25
35 × 35 = (30 × 40) + 25

Can you discover a pattern and complete these questions?

45 × 45 = ? (40 × 50) + 25
55 × 55 = ? (50 × 60) + 25
65 × 65 = ? (60 × 70) + 25

**3.** Guess the missing numbers. Then check your guesses.

6 × 7 = 42
66 × 67 = 4,422
666 × 667 = 444,222
6,666 × 6,667 = *n* 44,442,222
66,666 × 66,667 = *n* 4,444,422,222

**4.** Look for a pattern. Guess the missing numbers. Then check your guesses.

| | |
|---|---|
| 74 × 74 = 5,476 | 43 × 43 = 1,849 |
| 73 × 75 = 5,475 | 42 × 44 = 1,848 |
| 87 × 87 = 7,569 | 68 × 68 = *n* 4,624 |
| 86 × 88 = *n* 7,568 | 67 × 69 = 4,623 |

Try some others like this.

**5.** Guess the missing products. Then check your guesses.

(15,873 × 7) × 1 = 111,111
(15,873 × 7) × 2 = 222,222
(15,873 × 7) × 3 = 333,333
(15,873 × 7) × 4 = *n* 444,444
(15,873 × 7) × 5 = *n* 555,555
(15,873 × 7) × 6 = *n* 666,666

**6.** Find the answers. Is there a pattern?

(9 − 1) ÷ 8 = *n* 1
(98 − 2) ÷ 8 = *n* 12
(987 − 3) ÷ 8 = *n* 123
(9,876 − 4) ÷ 8 = *n* 1,234
(98,765 − 5) ÷ 8 = *n* 12,345
(987,654 − 6) ÷ 8 = *n* 123,456
(9,876,543 − 7) ÷ 8 = *n* 1,234,567
(98,765,432 − 8) ÷ 8 = *n* 12,345,678



began to carry out the computations involving money using 100 as a base. While the decimal evolved as efficient notation for money amounts, the term "per centum" (per hundred) was used to denote tax, interest, and other types of rates. Such expressions as "20p 100" and "Xp cento" denoted 20 percent and 10 percent respectively. Other expressions were "XX. per .c." for 20 percent, and "VIII in X percento" for 8 to 10 percent.

Our present symbol for percent appears to have originated in an anonymous Italian manuscript of 1425, when the common notation "p100" or "P cento" was replaced by "P $\mathcal{E}$." By 1650, the $\mathcal{E}$ had become $\frac{o}{o}$, and "per $\frac{o}{o}$" was commonly used. Later the "per" was dropped and it became simply $\frac{o}{o}$, and finally %. Its written form also evolved from the Latin *per centum,* to the Italian *per cento* and *per cent,* to our modern *percent.*

## Using Page 317

This page is intended for those students who successfully completed the Chapter Review-Test on page 315. You may wish to assign this page as independent work while you use the Another Look exercises to reteach the basic concepts and skills of the chapter. Or, you may decide that all students would benefit from exposure to this Enrichment activity.

**Lesson Development** Provide calculators for individual students or for small groups of students as necessary. Tell students that there are many interesting number patterns that can be investigated using the calculator. Then have students read the paragraph at the top of the page. Read through the instructions in each box as necessary to make sure that students understand what they are being asked to do.

**Exercise 1** The answers for each of the problems can be read from the circular array shown below. To find the first answer, start at 1 and read clockwise. To find the answer to 142,857 × 2, start at 2 and read clockwise, and so on. Challenge students to find other patterns in these answers.

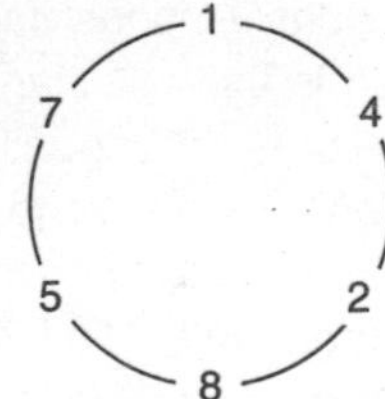


**Exercise 2** This exercise suggests a quick way to find the square of two numbers ending in 5. For example, to find 65 × 65 multiply 60 × 70 and then add 25.

**Exercise 3** Students should be able to make a reasonable guess after observing the pattern in the answers given.

**Exercise 4** This pattern is based on the following mathematical generalization:

$$(a - 1) \times (a + 1) = (a^2 - 1).$$

**Exercises 5–6** Encourage students to use their calculators to verify their guesses in these exercises.

**Lesson Focus** To use and adapt simple computer programs that involve string variables

## Ideas For Getting Started

Review the idea that we can use letters as variables to be replaced by numbers. Write $a \div b$ on the chalkboard. "What is the answer when $a$ is replaced by 56 and $b$ is replaced by 8?" (7) Then tell students that variables can be used to represent names or words as well as numbers. Choose four students from the class, for example, Ann, Bob, Carlos, and Dee. Write on the chalkboard: Let A$ = Ann, B$ = Bob, C$ = Carlos, and D$ = Dee. Then give these students directions using the variables. For example, "A$ should shake hands with C$. D$ should sharpen a pencil. D$ and A$ should change desks." Emphasize the idea that a letter or word followed by a dollar sign can be used as a variable to represent words in BASIC language.

## Using Page 318

**Lesson Development** Refer to the picture on the page and discuss how a microcomputer might be used in a police department. Read the paragraph at the top of the page emphasizing that a symbol such as A$, which is used to stand for a string of printed characters or words, is called a string variable. Direct students' attention to Computer Program A. "What string of letters does the variable A$ represent in this program?" (Ted Tarzan, 204 Oak St.) Point out that when a LET statement is used to tell what a string variable represents, the string of characters is shown inside quotes. Emphasize that quotes are not used around the string variable in a PRINT statement.

Discuss the RUN of this program and encourage students to suggest other simple programs that define a string variable. If a microcomputer is available, type in the suggested programs, have students predict the RUN, and verify their predictions.

Then direct students' attention to Computer Program B. Tell students that more than one string variable can be defined in a given program. Also point out that any number of letters can be included in the word that makes up the string variable, as long as it begins with a single letter and ends with a dollar sign. Be sure students understand that the letters inside the quotes are printed as shown when the program is run.

**Exercise 1** Students should correct lines 10 and 20 by putting quotes around the words "HI" and "THERE." Emphasize the need for quotes.

```
RUN: HI
     THERE
```

**Exercise 2** Students should give lines 30 and 40 without quotes.

```
RUN: BILL
     12 YEARS OLD
```

*Technology*

**Using Strings in Computer Programs**

For some computer programs it is useful to have a simple symbol to stand for a name, an address, a license plate number or a **string** of printed characters.

A symbol such as **A$**, called a **string variable**, is used for this purpose.

Police departments use computers to keep accurate records and find information quickly.

Study these examples.

**Computer Program A**

```
10 LET A$ = "TED TARZAN,
   204 OAK ST."
20 PRINT A$
30 END
```

(The quotes are important here.) (No quotes here)

When you type RUN and press RETURN, the computer shows

```
TED TARZAN, 204 OAK ST.
```

**Computer Program B**

```
10 LET NAME$ = "JO SPEEDY"
20 LET LI$ = "CN-135864"
30 PRINT NAME$
40 PRINT LI$
50 END
```

(String variables must begin with a letter and end with $.)

The RUN for this program is

```
JO SPEEDY
CN-135864
```

Each program below contains errors. Write the corrected lines for the program and give the RUN for each. See teaching notes.

1.
```
10 LET A$ = HI
20 LET B$ = THERE
30 PRINT A$
40 PRINT B$
50 END
```

2.
```
10 LET NAME$ = "BILL"
20 LET AGE$ = "12 YEARS OLD"
30 PRINT "NAME$"
40 PRINT "AGE$"
50 END
```

318

## Technology for Teachers

BASIC is only one of more than one hundred fifty computer languages now in existence. It was originally written in 1963 at Dartmouth College to help students with no background in programming to learn to use the computer. Today the language is used by professionals for a wide variety of applications.

PILOT and Logo are other languages you and your students may want to learn about. PILOT was first written as a language for teachers writing instructional material for use on computers. Rather than common English words, PILOT commands are initials representing English words. For example, T represents the command to type or print on the screen. A stands for Accept and is most like the Input statements in BASIC. M means to Match and is one of the commands that makes the language especially good for instructional material, since you can give the computer several possible answers that would be acceptable responses. J represents Jump and is somewhat like a GOTO in BASIC. Since the commands are single letters, some versions of PILOT are useful as introductory programming language for children.

Logo is best known for the part of the language called Turtle Graphics. The Logo language was developed in the Artificial Intelligence Department at MIT to study the

Give the RUN for each program. See teaching notes.

1.
```
10 LET N$ = "IKE"
20 LET PH$ = "452-5909"
30 PRINT N$
40 PRINT PH$
50 END
```

2.
```
10 PRINT "WHAT'S YOUR NAME?"
20 INPUT N$
30 PRINT "HI " N$        Use your name.
40 PRINT "IT'S NICE TO WORK
   FOR YOU."
50 END
```

3.
```
10 LET A$ = "ONE"
20 LET B$ = "TWO-"
30 LET C$ = "THREE-"
40 LET D$ = "FOUR-"
50 PRINT D$; C$; B$; A$
60 END
```

4.
```
10 LET T1$ = "SCALENE "
20 LET T2$ = "ISOSCELES "
30 LET T3$ = "EQUILATERAL"
40 PRINT "3 TYPES OF TRIANGLES"
50 PRINT T1$; T2$; T3$
60 END
```

5.
```
10 PRINT "LET'S ESTIMATE
   YOUR ADULT HEIGHT."
20 PRINT "HOW MANY CM TALL
   ARE YOU NOW?"
30 INPUT H
40 PRINT "ARE YOU A BOY OR
   A GIRL?"
50 INPUT X$
60 IF X$ = "GIRL" THEN 90
70 PRINT "YOUR ADULT HEIGHT
   (CM) WILL BE ABOUT ";
   (5 * H)/4
80 GOTO 100
90 PRINT "YOUR ADULT HEIGHT
   (CM) WILL BE ABOUT ";
   (10 * H)/9
100 END
```

6. A computer can "add words." What do you think the RUN for this program will be?

```
10 LET A$ = "MICKEY-"
20 LET B$ = "MOUSE"
30 PRINT A$ + B$
40 END
```

★ 7. Write a program of your own that uses a string variable.



actual learning process. Turtle Graphics provides students with an opportunity to explore the relationship between lines, angles, shapes, distance, and direction. Turtle Graphics can be especially useful in exploring many fundamental geometric concepts. Unlike most other computer languages, you can write your own language in Logo, naming your procedures as you develop them. In this way, students can "invent" their own version of the language. The Technology lesson in Chapter 16 gives students an opportunity to work with Logo.

## Using Page 319

**Exercise 1** Note that the use of the letters N and PH suggests that the RUN might be a person's telephone number.

```
RUN: IKE
     452-5909
```

**Exercise 2** Note that in line 30 the computer is asked to print a word that has been enclosed in quotes and a word that is the value of the string variable.

```
RUN: WHAT'S YOUR NAME?
     ? (STUDENT)
     HI (STUDENT)
     IT'S NICE TO WORK FOR YOU
```

**Exercise 3** If necessary, review the use of semicolons in a PRINT statement. Note that the use of semicolons allows the values for the variables to be printed closer together on the computer screen.

```
RUN: FOUR-THREE-TWO-ONE
```

**Exercise 4**

```
RUN: 3 TYPES OF TRIANGLES
SCALENE  ISOSCELES  EQUILATERAL
```

**Exercise 5** Note that this program asks for both a numerical input and a word input. Note the difference in the regular variable H and the string variable X$. Explain to students that the formulas in this exercise are sometimes used by physicians to predict adult height from a person's height at age 12. Stress that these formulas may or may not give accurate predictions and should be considered "just for fun."

**Exercise 6** This exercise illustrates the computer's capability of "adding" the values of string variables to create sentences.

```
RUN: MICKEY-MOUSE
```

**Exercise 7** Encourage students to be creative in writing their own programs.

## Using Page 320

The exercises on this page provide practice for maintaining cumulative skills. The emphasis in this Cumulative Review is on multiplication and division of fractions (Chapter 9), ratio and proportion (Chapter 11), and problem solving (Chapter 11).

**Item Analysis** The table below correlates the Cumulative Review items with objectives and with the student book pages on which the concepts or skills were taught.

| Items | Objectives | Related text pages |
|---|---|---|
| 1–4 | 9.1 | 226–233 |
| 5–7 | 9.2 | 236–238 |
| 8–9 | 9.3 | 239–243 |
| 10–11 | 11.1 | 278–281 |
| 12 | 11.2 | 282–283 |
| 13–14 | 11.5 | 284–285, 291, 293 |

## *Cumulative Review*

Multiply or divide.

**1.** $7 \times \frac{5}{8}$
A $2\frac{1}{2}$ (B) $4\frac{3}{8}$
C $9\frac{3}{8}$ D not given

**2.** $\frac{2}{3} \times \frac{3}{8}$
(A) $\frac{1}{4}$ B $\frac{5}{11}$
C $\frac{5}{24}$ D not given

**3.** $3\frac{3}{4} \times 1\frac{1}{3}$
A 9 B $\frac{1}{5}$
C $1\frac{1}{4}$ (D) not given

**4.** $8 \times 2\frac{1}{4}$
A $10\frac{1}{4}$ B $16\frac{1}{4}$
(C) 18 D not given

**5.** Write the lowest-terms fraction for 0.05.
A $\frac{1}{5}$ (B) $\frac{1}{20}$
C $\frac{5}{10}$ D not given

**6.** Write a decimal for $\frac{4}{25}$.
A 0.4 B 0.25
C 0.8 (D) not given

**7.** Write a mixed decimal for $\frac{5}{8}$.
A $6.2\frac{1}{2}$ (B) $0.62\frac{1}{2}$
C $0.625\frac{1}{2}$ D not given

Divide.

**8.** $\frac{3}{4} \div \frac{3}{7}$
A $1\frac{1}{4}$ (B) $1\frac{3}{4}$
C $\frac{9}{28}$ D not given

**9.** $2\frac{1}{2} \div 7\frac{1}{2}$
A 3 B $18\frac{3}{4}$
(C) $\frac{1}{3}$ D not given

**10.** Write the ratio as a fraction: 2 adults to 3 children.
A $\frac{3}{2}$ (B) $\frac{2}{3}$
C $\frac{2}{5}$ D not given

**11.** Give the missing number. $\frac{5}{8} = \frac{■}{40}$
A 20 (B) 25
C 32 D not given

**12.** Solve the proportion. $\frac{n}{18} = \frac{5}{6}$
A $n = 12$ (B) $n = 15$
C $n = 18$ D not given

**13.** A map scale is 2 cm:9 km. How many kilometers does 14 cm represent?
A 28 B 23
C 126 (D) not given

**14.** $\frac{3}{5}$ of the students in Antonia's class are in the chorus. If there are 25 people in her class, how many are in the chorus?
(A) 15 B 18
C 20 D not given

## Objectives

**13.1** Read and interpret graphs.

**13.2** Find the mean, median, and mode for a set of data.

**13.3** Identify possible outcomes and predict the probability of a given event.

**13.4** Solve word problems using the 5-Point Checklist and cumulative computational skills.

## Summary

In this chapter students read and interpret bar graphs, pictographs, circle graphs, and line graphs. Students learn to evaluate graphs according to title, label, and number scale. Then students are asked to complete graphs and use data from graphs to solve word problems. The concepts of mean, median, and mode are introduced and examined as students learn to find a measure of central location for a collection of data. The idea of the probability of a simple event is introduced and used in a variety of situations. The use of probability to predict outcomes and establish expectations is included. Opportunities to solve a variety of problems and cumulative practice of computational skills are provided throughout the chapter.

## Mathematical Background

**Graphing** Graphing is often thought of as a visual presentation of statistical data. Numerical data and relationships that are difficult to interpret are easily visualized and presented in the form of a bar graph, a pictograph, a circle graph, or a line graph. Graphs can help answer questions about data by showing the data in pictures.

The main components of the type of graphs discussed above are: (a) a title, (b) labels for all parts, and (c) numbers or a number scale. The two major goals of an instructional unit on graphs are to develop the ability to read and interpret graphs and to develop the ability to make a graph from a given set of data.

A careful study of the title of the graph is important in helping students learn to read a graph. Helping students understand the various parts of a graph also helps develop their reading ability. Graphing experience is not complete, however, until questions about the graph and interpretation of the pictorial data are formulated and answered. Throughout the chapter students are encouraged to discuss and interpret graphs in order to discover patterns and relationships. For example, a quick glance at the sections of a circle graph will show which category is the greatest and which is the least.

In working with bar graphs it is important to consider those with vertical bars, with horizontal bars, and with double bars. When working with pictographs, students need to recognize that a part of a symbol may be used to indicate half the value that the symbol represents.

In preparation for the time when they will make circle graphs on their own, students need to finish graphs that are partially completed. After students have mastered the skill in transferring data from a table to a graph on which the title, scale, and labels are given, they are ready to make graphs on their own. An important concept in making a circle graph is the idea that there are 360° in a circle. So to represent 25% of the circle for example, we would find 25% of 360° or 90°.

Of major importance in making a line graph is the number scale to use. In helping students make a line graph, encourage them to experiment with different number scales and to observe the results.

**Mean, Median, and Mode** One valuable bit of information that can be useful in analyzing a collection of data is called a *measure of central location.* One such number, the *arithemetic mean* (often referred to as the average), can be thought of as a single number that best represents the numbers in the collection of data. The arithmetic mean of a set of $n$ measurements is the sum of these measurements divided by $n$. One important note about the mean is that its value may be significantly affected by one or two extreme values in the set of numbers.

Another useful measure of central location is the *median.* The median is the value of the middle number when the data are ordered from smallest to largest. For example, if the numbers are 2, 7, 5, 1, 11, the data arranged in order are 1, 2, 5, 7, 11; the median or middle value is 5. In another example, if the numbers are 8, 13, 2, 6, 17, and 5, the data arranged in order are 2, 5, 6, 8, 13, and 17. Because there is an even number of items in the data, there are two middle values, 6 and 8. The median then is the value halfway between these values, or 7. Unlike the mean, the median is relatively unaffected by the extreme values in the set of data.

A third measure of central location is the *mode.* This is the value of the number that occurs most often in the set of data. For example, in the set of data 3, 8, 13, 12, 13, 6, 9, 12, and 13, the number 13 is the mode since it occurs with the greatest frequency.

**Probability** If you spin a spinner such as shown below, you perform a simple *experiment.* A set of all possible outcomes for an experiment is called a *sample space* or *outcome set.*

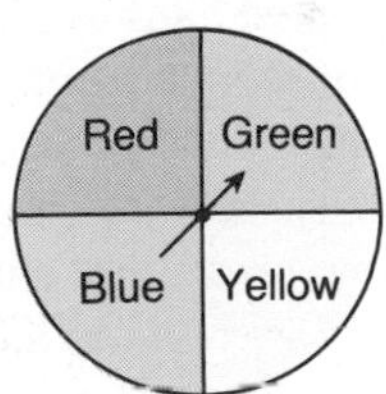


The outcome set for this experiment would be $S = \{\text{red, green, blue, yellow}\}$. Since each of the outcomes in this set is as likely to occur as another, the outcomes are said to be *equally likely.* Any subset of this outcome set is called an *event.* For example, if you spin the spinner and it lands on green, the outcome green would be an event. Similarly, the outcome red or yellow would also be an event. The probability of the spinner landing on green, $P(g)$, would be the number of outcomes green compared to the total number of outcomes or $\frac{1}{4}$. Note that the probability of a particular event can always be written as a fraction between 0 and 1 inclusive.

**Problem Solving** In the problem-solving lesson on page 333, students use data from a double bar graph to solve word problems. On page 335 students practice solving .word problems using all operations and cumulative computational skills. On page 340 students organize and interpret data to solve an applied problem involving a savings account.

**Vocabulary**

| | | |
|---|---|---|
| bar graph | line graph | mode |
| pictograph | mean | probability |
| circle graph | median | equally likely |

## Error Analysis

In this chapter on graphing and probability, students are introduced to two different ways to interpret data. Graphs represent data in ways that can be interpreted visually, while probability skills provide students with a way to use data to predict a given outcome.

Interpreting and making graphs requires competency in many prerequisite skills. If students cannot construct a graph, or if they make errors in reading a graph, the teacher should look for inadequate knowledge of these prerequisite skills. Several of these skills are discussed below.

**Bar Graphs** The prerequisite skills needed to understand bar graphs include the use of whole number sequencing to make and interpret number scales as well as whole number addition and subtraction skills to interpret data.

**Pictographs** The prerequisite skills needed in interpreting pictographs include the use of whole number operations to represent and interpret data.

**Line Graphs** The prerequisite skills necessary in dealing with line graphs include the following: whole number sequences necessary to make and interpret scales; whole number addition and subtraction skills needed to interpret data; geometry skills to find points that represent data; and an understanding of line segments that connect points.

**Circle Graphs** The prerequisite skills that are essential in the study of circle graphs include geometry skills to understand the concept of a circle; fraction skills to find part of a whole; an understanding of percent to represent parts of a circle; and whole number division necessary to interpret a circle graph.

If students have difficulties with graphing, they may need help with the above prerequisite skills. Perceptual difficulties and disabilities may also play a part in errors that students make.

Mean, median, and mode are number relationships that are used in the interpretation of sets of data. They represent basic statistical ideas and have many real-world applications. Computation of a mean involves basic mathematical skills and is a source of potential errors.

The development of probability skills builds on the concepts of ratio and proportion. Thus, an understanding of and skill in dealing with fractions are necessary skills in the study of probability.

## Problem Solving

### A Problem-of-the-Week Bulletin Board

One way to introduce problem-solving experiences in the classroom is through the use of a "problem-of-the-week" bulletin board. This approach to teaching problem solving allows you to provide students with challenging mathematics problems without impinging on your teaching time. Many students enjoy problems that they can work at for a time, leave, and then return to.

The bulletin board design below is useful for a problem-of-the-week. The bulletin board can be entitled "Have You Tried This?" and consists of four parts.

- *The Problem*—a statement of the problem
- *Will This Help?*—questions and ideas related to the problem
- *What Others Have Tried*—samples of possible methods for solving the problem
- *What I Have Tried*—a space for students to display their own attempts at solving the problem

The problem statement is always visible, but the other sections of the board are designed so that only one piece of information can be seen at a time. For example, each question for "Will This Help?" is printed on a separate sheet of paper so that to read more than one question it is necessary to flip to the next sheet. The lower edges of the pages are covered.

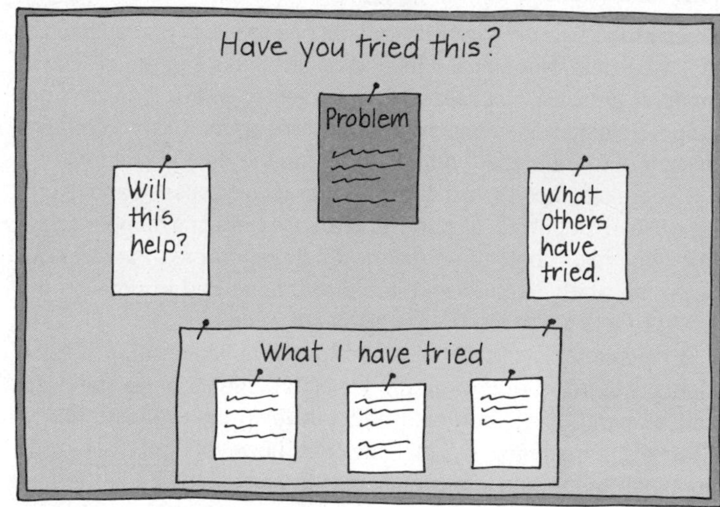

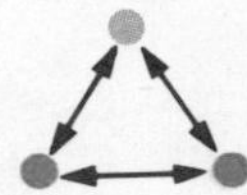

## Special Education

The development of skills involving graphing and probability are important daily living skills for the special-needs students. It is not so much the creation of such graphs or the carrying out of the probability experiments, but rather the interpretation of the data that is important. The following activities should be helpful in developing these skills with the special-needs students.

### Developing Graph-Reading Skills

In approaching the reading of a graph, students should learn to recognize the location of the title, the labels for the information, and the number scale. Use a sample graph such as the one below and ask the following kinds of questions: What is the title of the graph? What numbers are on the scale? What other labels are on the graph? Skills in locating the information are important and should be stressed in developing the interpretation of graphical information.

Eye Color of 30 Sixth-Grade Students

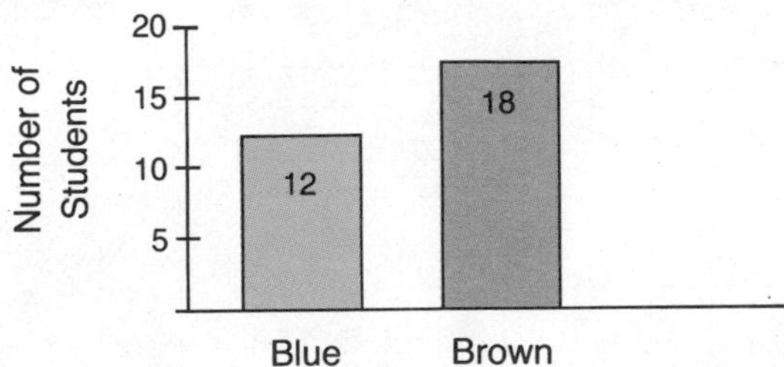


It is important also to help modify these skills as the focus moves from one form of graphing to another. The skills transfer easily from bar to line graphs, but pictographs and circle graphs often cause special problems.

### Writing Graph Stories

After students have developed skills for interpreting the titles, labels, and scales for a graph, they should be given simple graphs and asked to write stories that might accompany the graph in a magazine or newspaper. Allow some artistic license in order to build interpretation skills. Have students share their stories with the class, and then ask them to check on the interpretations the authors have made, if available.

### Setting Up and Checking Probabilities

After students have started to work with probability, have them make their own spinners using thumbtacks, paper clips, and heavy tagboard as shown below. Mark and color selected percents on several different circles. (See sample circle below.) Note the various percents on the circles, and then have students conduct spinning experiments, keeping tallies of the outcomes. Compare these outcomes with the comparison of the percents of a whole.

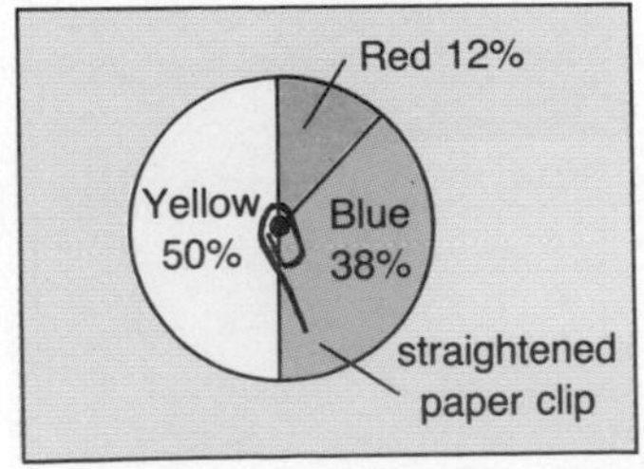


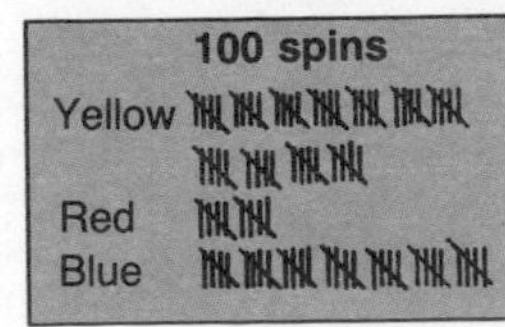


### Using "Graph and Guess" Bags

The concepts of graphing and probability can be tied together using experiments with bags of different colored counters or similar materials. Students open a bag, decide on categories, labels, and titles for a graph to describe the materials in the bag. They can then graph the information on graph paper. As an extension they could outline the expected results for ten random selections, replacing each drawn object before the next one is drawn. One such experiment is shown below.

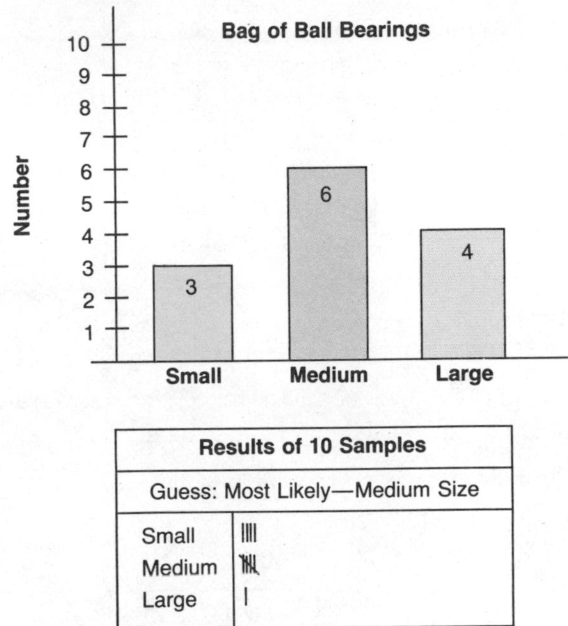


| Results of 10 Samples | |
|---|---|
| Guess: Most Likely—Medium Size | |
| Small | \|\|\|\| |
| Medium | 卌 |
| Large | \| |

Note: Have students "draw" by dumping out one bearing, because size could be felt.

## Subject Integration

Subject matter related to other areas of the curriculum has been integrated into the following lessons. This provides an opportunity to highlight the interaction between mathematics and other subjects.

**Social Studies** Comparing populations, pages 324–325
**Science** Whooping cranes, page 321; observing infant growth, pages 328–329; collecting weather data, pages 330–331; evaluating test scores, pages 334–335
**Consumer Awareness** Newspaper customers, page 333; fund raising, page 339

# Management Guide

| Teaching Chapter 13 | | | | Meeting Individual Needs | | | | | |
|---|---|---|---|---|---|---|---|---|---|
| Objectives | Chapter Content | Pages | TRB Test Items | Lesson Assignments: Minimum | Lesson Assignments: Average | Lesson Assignments: Extended | Follow Up: Reteaching | Follow Up: Enrichment | Follow Up: Practice |
| | Chapter Opener | 321 | | | | | | | |
| **13.1** Read and interpret graphs. | Bar Graphs | 322–323 | 1–3 | 1–4 | 1–5 | 1–5, TM | SE5 Ch 14 | | PS 121 |
| | Pictographs | 324–325 | 4–6 | 1–6 / 1–3, SK | 1–6 / 1–4, SK | 1–6 / 1–4, SK | SE5 Ch 14 RS 75 | ES 75 | PS 122 |
| | Circle Graphs | 326–327 | 7–9 | 1–7 / 1–5 | 1–7 / 1–5 | 1–7 / 1–5, TM | SE5 Ch 14 RS 76 | ES 76 | PS 123 |
| | Line Graphs | 328–329 | 10–12 | 1–5 / 1–3 | 1–5 / 1–4 | 1–5 / 1–4, TM | SE5 Ch 14 RS 77 | ES 77 | PS 124 |
| | Evaluating Graphs | 330–331 | | | 1–5 / 1–7 | 1–5 / 1–7, TM | | | PS 125 |
| **13.2** Find the mean, median, and mode for a set of data. | Mean | 332 | 13–14, 17 | 1–6 | 1–6 | 1–6 | | | PS 126 |
| | Median and Mode | 334 | | | 1–6 | 1–6 | RS 79 | ES 79 | PS 127 |
| **13.3** Identify possible outcomes and predict the probability of a given event. | Probability | 336–337 | 15–16, 18–19 | 1–3 / 1–7, SK | 1–3 / 1–11, SK | 1–3 / 1–11, SK | SE5 Ch 14 RS 80 | ES 80 | PS 128 |
| | Probability and Prediction | 338 | 20–21 | | 1–3 | 1–4 | SE5 Ch 14 | | |
| | Probability and Expected Numbers | 339 | 22 | | 1–4 | 1–6 | SE5 Ch 14 | | PS 129 |
| **13.4** Solve word problems using the 5-Point Checklist and cumulative computational skills. | Problem Solving: Using Data from a Double Bar Graph | 333 | 23–25 | 1–5 | 1–5 | 1–6 | RS 78 | ES 78 | |
| | Problem Solving: Practice | 335 | | 1–5 | 1–8 | 1–9 | | | |
| | Applied Problem Solving | 340 | | | | | | | |
| | Chapter Review-Test | 341 | | | | | | | |
| | Another Look/Enrichment | 342–343 | | | | | | | |
| | Cumulative Review | 344 | | | | | | | |

**SE5** Student Edition, Book 5
**RS** Reteaching Supplement
**ES** Enrichment Supplement
**PS** Practice Supplement
**MP** More Practice
**TM** Think Math
**SK** Skillkeeper
**TRB** Teacher's Resource Book

## Masters for Use

**. . . before Chapter 13**

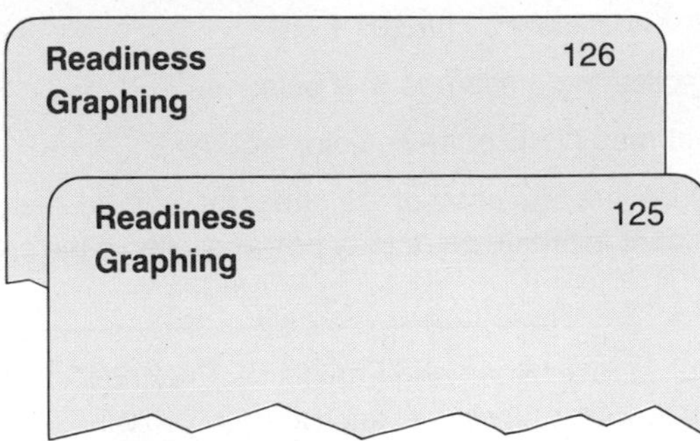


**. . . after Chapter 13**

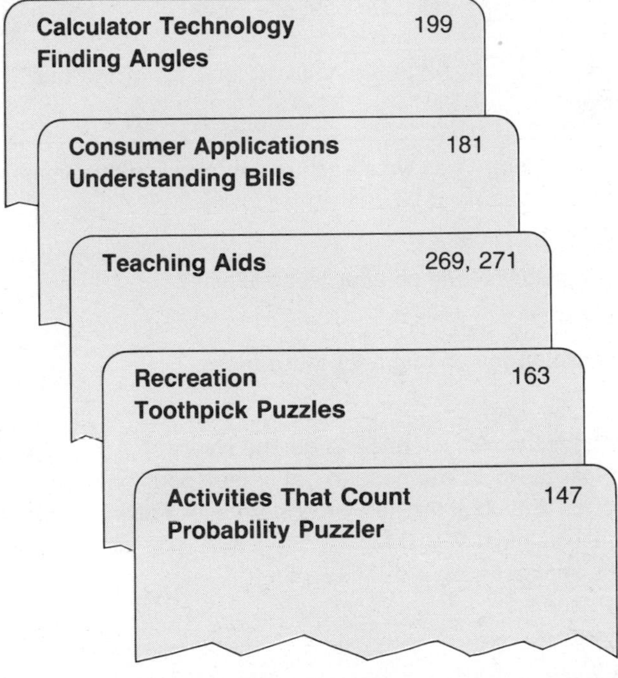


**. . . during Chapter 13**

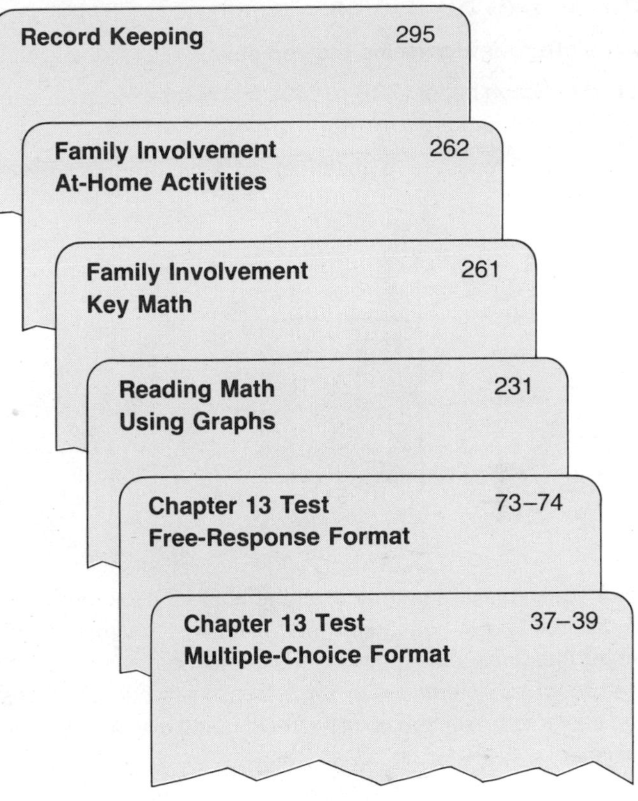


## Supplements

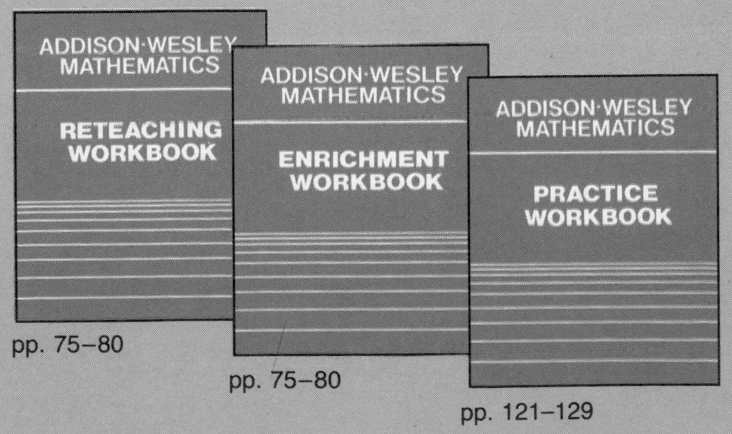


pp. 75–80

pp. 75–80

pp. 121–129

## Other Addison-Wesley Resources

**Books and Kits**

*Baseball, A Game of Numbers* pp. 142–167

*Problem-Solving Experiences in Mathematics, Grade 6,* Problems 29, 30, 64, 65, 89, 104, 125, 144, 145, 146, 147, 148, 149, 150

# Activities That Count

Activities That Count are designed for use throughout this chapter and subsequent chapters. Before beginning Chapter 13, you may wish to review these activities and select the ones you consider appropriate for your class.

## Number Darts Game

**Purpose** To review graphing ordered pairs

**Materials** Graph paper (TRB p. 269), two number cubes—each labeled 1 through 6

**Preparation** Prepare a gamesheet on inch graph paper as shown below.

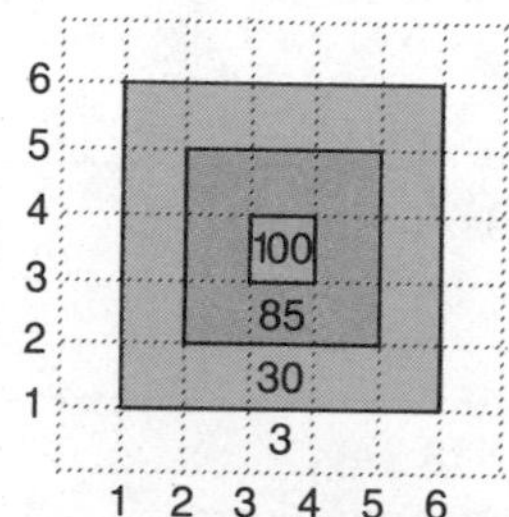


**Activity** Each player in turn tosses the number cubes and calls out the ordered pair to be marked. For example, "3 across, 4 up." The player then marks that point on the gamesheet and tallies the indicated score, as determined by the region in which the point lies. The first player to reach 300 points without going over that amount is the winner.

## Whose Birthday? Project

**Purpose** To check the accuracy of a probability statement

**Materials** Reference books such as encyclopedias, *Almanac,* or *Book of Lists*

**Preparation** Set aside a bulletin board area with the following caption: Mathematical calculations have shown that if you choose a group of 25 people, the chances are about 1 in 2 that two of the people will have the same birthday. If there are 35 people, the chances increase to 3 in 4 that there will be two people with the same birthday.

**Activity** Have students find the birthdays of people in one or more of the groups below. Students compare the number of same-day birthdays in each group to see if the probabilities appear to check.

- American presidents
- your class
- another class
- astronauts
- famous painters
- scientists
- sports figures
- family members

## Probability Puzzler Math Lab

**Purpose** To practice the outcomes of a coin toss

**Materials** Street map (TRB p. 147), coin, tagboard

**Preparation** Duplicate one copy of the street map for each student. Use the tagboard to create an activity poster similar to the one below.

> Start for a walk at River Road and Park Drive. Pretend that you are going to walk 4 blocks. At each corner, you will flip a coin to decide which way to go.
>
> (H) Heads: Go north one block.
>
> (T) Tails: Go east one block.
>
> If you toss (T) (H) (T) (T), you will end up at the bus station.

On individual index cards write each of the following questions:

1. Where would you end up after these tosses?
(H) (T) (H) (T)
2. Where would you end up after these tosses?
(H) (H) (T) (H)
3. Where would you end up after these tosses?
(H) (H) (H) (H)
4. What tosses would you need to get the library?
5. What tosses would you need to get to the sports shop?
6. Could you end up at the hardware store after walking 4 blocks, using the coin rules?

Prepare a separate card with answers.

1. sports shop
2. pet store
3. pizza parlor
4. (T) (T) (T) (T)
5. Four possible tosses:
(H) (H) (T) (T) or (T) (T) (H) (H)
(H) (T) (H) (T) or (T) (H) (T) (H)
6. no

**Activity** Students choose one or more of the activity cards, and work out the answers to the questions.

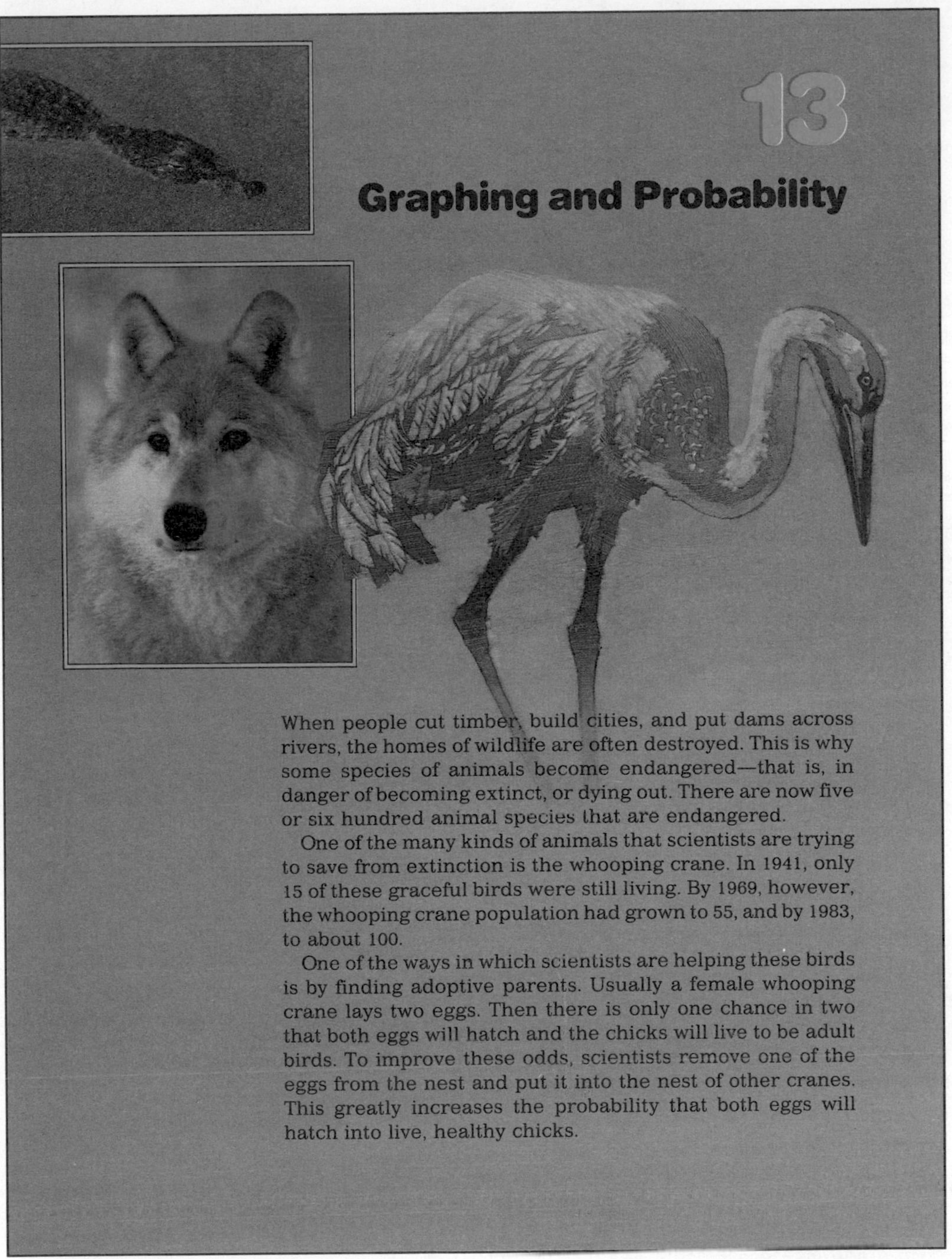

13

## Graphing and Probability

When people cut timber, build cities, and put dams across rivers, the homes of wildlife are often destroyed. This is why some species of animals become endangered—that is, in danger of becoming extinct, or dying out. There are now five or six hundred animal species that are endangered.

One of the many kinds of animals that scientists are trying to save from extinction is the whooping crane. In 1941, only 15 of these graceful birds were still living. By 1969, however, the whooping crane population had grown to 55, and by 1983, to about 100.

One of the ways in which scientists are helping these birds is by finding adoptive parents. Usually a female whooping crane lays two eggs. Then there is only one chance in two that both eggs will hatch and the chicks will live to be adult birds. To improve these odds, scientists remove one of the eggs from the nest and put it into the nest of other cranes. This greatly increases the probability that both eggs will hatch into live, healthy chicks.

## Introducing the Chapter

**Discussion** Explain to students that in this chapter they will be learning more about graphing and the concept of probability. Introduce a brief discussion of wildlife conservation and the reasons why many animal species in the world today are in danger of becoming extinct. Students may find it interesting to consult an almanac or other reference work that lists the species of animals that are endangered. After giving students time to read the story and examine the art, encourage them to create some questions based on data given in the story. As you teach the chapter, you may wish to refer back to this page, and present the questions suggested below.

## Follow-Up Questions

**After Page 325** If you were making a pictograph to show the growth of the whooping crane population from 1969 through 1983, what number of cranes would you have each symbol represent? (Answers may vary; 5 or 10 would be logical choices.)

**After Page 331** Suppose you made a bar graph to show the whooping crane population in each year from 1975 through 1985. On the graph's vertical scale you list numbers to show the whooping crane population. What would you show on the graph's horizontal scale? (the years 1975 through 1985)

**After Page 334** The estimated whooping crane populations in the years 1979 through 1983 were 85, 88, 91, 96, and 100. What are the mean and the median of those populations? (mean, 92; median, 91)

# Graphs

**Quick Review** Students respond orally with the number that is midway between each pair.

| | | | | |
|---|---|---|---|---|
| 6, 10 8 | 111, 113 112 | 15, 21 18 | 50, 100 75 | 12, 16 14 |
| 9, 27 18 | 150, 160 155 | 3, 9 6 | 600, 800 700 | 64, 68 66 |

**Lesson Focus** To read, interpret, and complete bar graphs

## Ideas for Getting Started

Conduct a brief discussion about the sports students like to watch. Then have students vote for their favorite sports. Record the results in a table like the one below.

| | |
|---|---|
| Soccer | 8 |
| Basketball | 6 |
| Tennis | 4 |
| Baseball | 3 |
| Other | 7 |

Ask how the same data could be shown in a graph. Lead the group to help you to make the graph shown here.

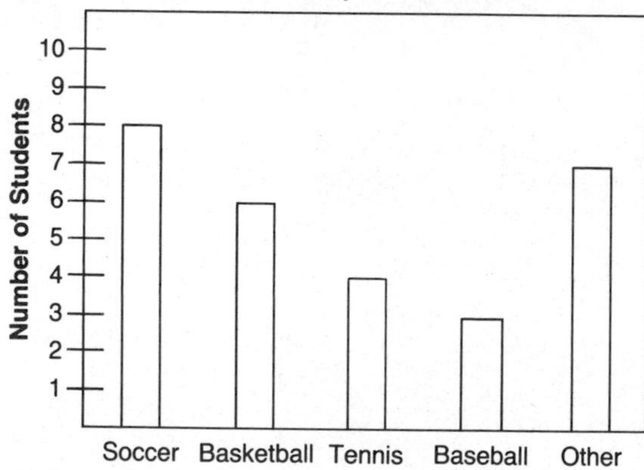


Point out that every graph should have a title, that every part of a graph should be labeled, and that all graphs should have appropriate number scales.

## Using Page 322

**Lesson Development** Ask students to read the paragraph about the sixth grade classes at Pond Run School and to study the graph. Refer to the *title* of the graph, the *labels* showing the picnic grounds and the number of votes, and the *number scale.* Emphasize that these three elements are found on every graph. Also point out that bar graphs can be made with either vertical bars or with horizontal bars.

Discuss the value of a graph. "Suppose you needed to know quickly how many students voted for a particular picnic ground. Would it be faster to read a couple of paragraphs about the votes or to look at a graph? If you wanted to compare the votes for different picnic grounds, would it be easier to read a report about the votes or to look at a graph?" Students should conclude that we can obtain information quickly and easily from graphs.

## Bar Graphs

The sixth grade classes at Pond Run School took a vote on where they would like to have their spring picnic. They used a bar graph to show the results of their vote.

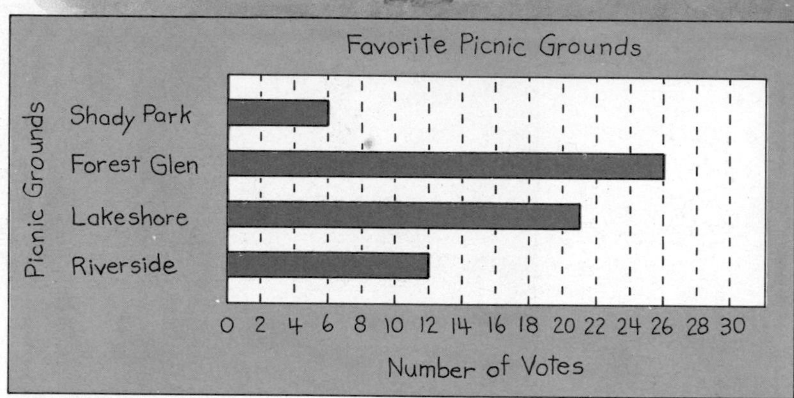


1. What is the title of the bar graph? Favorite Picnic Grounds
2. What do the numbers on the horizontal scale stand for? Number of votes
3. Which picnic ground received the most votes? How many? Forest Glen, 26
4. How many people voted for Lakeshore? 21
5. Which were the two least favored picnic grounds? How many students voted for each? Shady Park and Riverside; 6, 12
6. How many students voted in all? 65

322

## Follow Up

### Reteaching

Find a simple bar graph in a newspaper or magazine to use as a basis for discussion. Generate a discussion in which the following points are brought out:

- What is the title of the graph?
- What information do the number scales give?
- What are some of the relationships that are apparent on the graph?

### Enrichment

Have student conduct a survey to find the number of minutes it takes students to get to school. Have them show the data in a chart using tally marks. Then have students use the data from the tally to make a bar graph. For example:

| Time to Get to School | |
|---|---|
| Minutes | Number of Students |
| 30 or more | \|\| |
| 20–29 | 𝍸 |
| 10–19 | 𝍸 |
| 5–9 | 𝍸 |
| 4 or less | 𝍸 |

| Assignment Guide | | | |
|---|---|---|---|
| | Minimum | Average | Extended |
| page 323 | 1–4 | 1–5 | 1–5, TM |

The class also voted on which games they wanted to play. They recorded the results of their vote in the table at the right. Copy and complete the bar graph below using the data in the table.

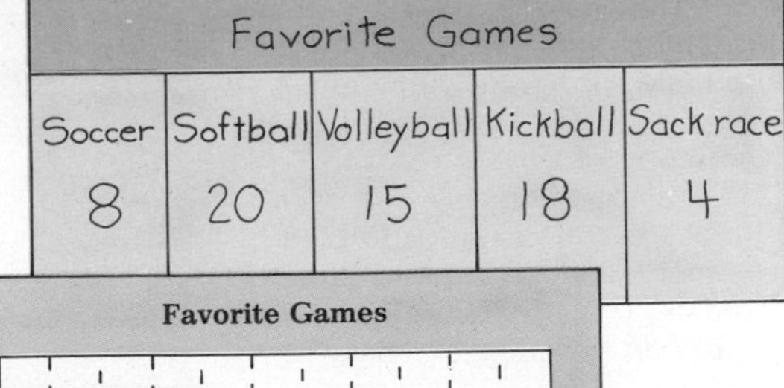

| Favorite Games | | | | |
|---|---|---|---|---|
| Soccer | Softball | Volleyball | Kickball | Sack race |
| 8 | 20 | 15 | 18 | 4 |

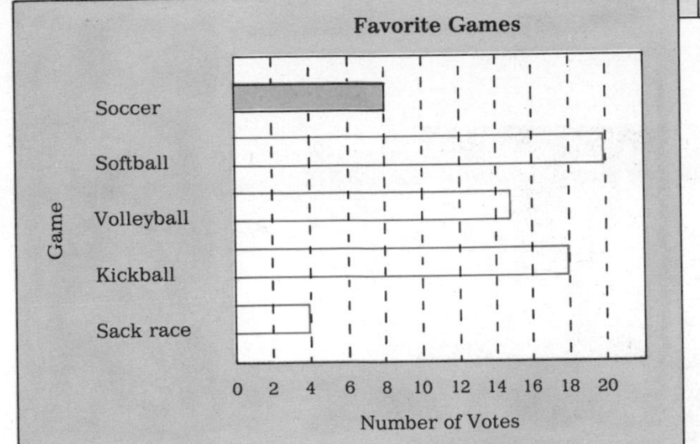


1. Which game received the most votes? softball
2. Which bar in your graph is the longest? softball
3. Which bar in your graph ends between the dotted lines? volleyball
4. The class decided to play the two most favored games. Which did they play? softball, kickball

★ 5. Survey your class on one of these ideas. Make a bar graph to show the results of your survey.
   A favorite food
   B favorite drink
   C favorite sport Answers will vary.

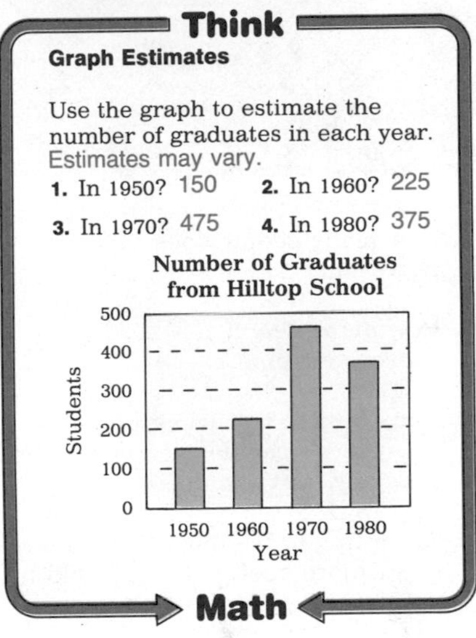

**Think Math**

**Graph Estimates**

Use the graph to estimate the number of graduates in each year.
Estimates may vary.

1. In 1950? 150
2. In 1960? 225
3. In 1970? 475
4. In 1980? 375





## Using Page 323

**Exercises 1–4** Before assigning these exercises, have students read the paragraph at the top of the page. Be sure they understand the source of the information in the table. Emphasize the importance of the title, the labels, and the number scale, and encourage students to be as accurate as possible.

**Exercise 5** Students are to collect data by taking a survey. Then they are to make a bar graph of the results. Remind students that every graph must have a title, labels, and a number scale.

**Think Math** Students are to make estimates as they interpret the bar graph. Point out that the estimate is easy when the bar ends about halfway between two numbers on the scale. Encourage students to think about "halfway between" when they are estimating the numbers for the years 1960, 1970, and 1980. Extend the activity by having students draw similar graphs with bars of different lengths. Students can then exchange graphs to estimate.

## Ideas That Work

### Special Education

To prepare special-needs students for work with pictographs, use the following activity. This activity can also help students review the idea of ratio.

Use index cards on which objects are attached or tallied as the graph is made. After the required number of objects is shown on the card, the card is turned over and one of the symbols from the pictograph is drawn on the back of the card. When all of the objects have been sorted or tallied, the cards can be removed from the graph and the symbols drawn, leaving a completed graph.

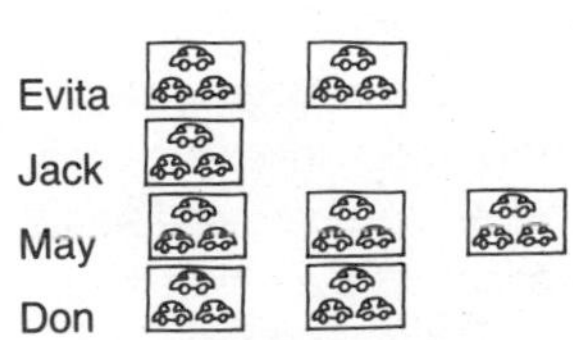

Each [car] represents 3 toy cars.

**Practice Supplement,** page 121

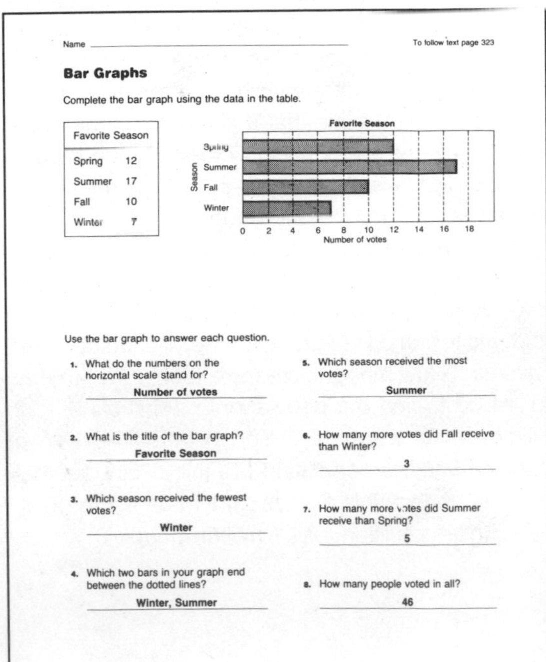

Name ____________ To follow text page 323

**Bar Graphs**

Complete the bar graph using the data in the table.

| Favorite Season | |
|---|---|
| Spring | 12 |
| Summer | 17 |
| Fall | 10 |
| Winter | 7 |



Use the bar graph to answer each question.

1. What do the numbers on the horizontal scale stand for? Number of votes
2. What is the title of the bar graph? Favorite Season
3. Which season received the fewest votes? Winter
4. Which two bars in your graph end between the dotted lines? Winter, Summer
5. Which season received the most votes? Summer
6. How many more votes did Fall receive than Winter? 3
7. How many more votes did Summer receive than Spring? 5
8. How many people voted in all? 46

# Graphs

**Quick Review** Students write the number that makes each number sentence true.

(6 × 10) + (3 × [6]) = 78    14 + 6 = ([10] × 2)    64 ÷ 8 = [1] × 8

45 + 9 = 9 × [6]    16 + 8 = 8 × [3]    (7 × 2) + ([2] × 6) = 14 + 12

**Lesson Focus** To read, interpret, and complete pictographs

## Ideas for Getting Started

On the chalkboard draw the following table and the ticket.

**Tickets Sold for the School Play**

| Day | Mon. | Tues. | Wed. | Thurs. | Fri. |
|---|---|---|---|---|---|
| Tickets Sold | 50 | 30 | 120 | 75 | 100 |

Ticket

Explain that the information in the table could be shown as a pictograph, or picture graph. Instead of writing numbers, we could draw tickets to represent the number of tickets sold. Point to the drawing of the ticket. "If this stands for 1 ticket sold, how many tickets would we draw to show the number of tickets sold on Monday?" (50) "Tuesday?" (30) Point out that drawing that many pictures would take a lot of time and that counting all those tickets would also take a lot of time.

Challenge the class to think of an easier way to show the number of tickets sold, other than using 1 ticket for each ticket sold. (Students may suggest that 1 ticket represent 5 or 10 tickets.) "Suppose 1 ticket stands for 10 tickets sold. How many tickets would we draw to show the number of tickets sold Monday?" (5 tickets) "Tuesday?" (3 tickets) "Wednesday?" (12 tickets)

On the chalkboard draw a half ticket beside the full ticket. "If 1 ticket stands for 10 tickets sold, what does a half ticket stand for?" (5) "How many tickets would we draw to show the number of tickets sold on Thursday?" $\left(7\frac{1}{2}\text{ tickets}\right)$

## Using Page 324

**Lesson Development** Have students read the paragraph at the top of the page. Point out that the exact population of each state in the table has been rounded to the nearest million. Call attention to the pictograph and explain that it gives the same information the table does. In this pictograph, the symbol of a stick figure is used to represent a certain number of people. "How many people does each stick figure represent?" (2 million) "How many people would one half of a stick figure represent?" (1 million) Identify the title of the pictograph. Then ask students to find on the graph the population of Pennsylvania. "How many figures are there?" (6) "What do we do to find the population?" (Multiply 6 × 2 million, which equal 12 million people.) Next have students find the population of Ohio. Point out that there are 5 complete figures and 1 half figure. (5 × 2 million + 1 million, or 11 million people)

## Pictographs

The table shows the populations of the six states with the greatest populations according to the 1980 census. Allan rounded each number to the nearest 1 million and made a **pictograph** to show the data. Use his pictograph to answer the questions below.

| State | Exact Population | Rounded Population |
|---|---|---|
| California | 23,668,562 | 24,000,000 |
| New York | 17,557,288 | 18,000,000 |
| Texas | 14,228,383 | 14,000,000 |
| Pennsylvania | 11,866,728 | 12,000,000 |
| Illinois | 11,418,461 | 11,000,000 |
| Ohio | 10,797,419 | 11,000,000 |

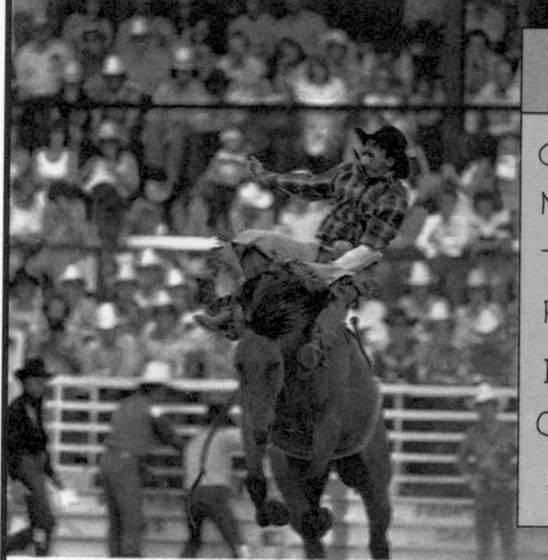

**Population of the Six Largest States (1980 Census)**

| | |
|---|---|
| California | ♀♀♀♀♀♀♀♀♀♀♀♀ |
| New York | ♀♀♀♀♀♀♀♀♀ |
| Texas | ♀♀♀♀♀♀♀ |
| Pennsylvania | ♀♀♀♀♀♀ |
| Illinois | ♀♀♀♀♀ʕ |
| Ohio | ♀♀♀♀♀ʕ |

♀ = 2 million people; ʕ = 1 million people

1. How many people does each ♀ represent? 2 million

2. How many people does each ʕ represent? 1 million

3. According to the pictograph, how many more people live in California than in New York? 6 million

4. According to the table, exactly how many more people live in California than in New York? 6,111,274

5. In the pictograph, which two states appear to have the same population? According to the exact populations given in the table, do these states actually have the same populations? Ohio and Illinois; no

6. Suppose a state has a population of 8,248,325. How would you show the state's population in a pictograph like the one above? ♀♀♀♀



## Follow Up

### Reteaching

Remind students that a pictograph is often used to show data involving very large numbers where a numerical scale would be impractical. Explain that a picture or symbol is used to indicate a larger value and that the symbol often suggests the topic being discussed. For instance, in a pictograph that discussed the numbers of cars in the United States, a drawing of a car might be used. Review that when only a part of the symbol is shown, it indicates that only part of the value of the symbol applies. For example, if [car] was used to represent 1 million cars, [half car] would represent $\frac{1}{2}$ million, or 500,000 cars.

### Enrichment

Provide students with the data below and graph paper (TRB p. 271). Challenge students to use the data to make pictographs. Let students suggest a symbol they could use to represent a specified number of votes.

| Favorite Playground Sport | |
|---|---|
| Soccer | 60 votes |
| Softball | 85 votes |
| Volleyball | 40 votes |
| Kickball | 75 votes |
| Others | 30 votes |

| Assignment Guide | | | |
|---|---|---|---|
| | Minimum | Average | Extended |
| page 324 | 1–6 | 1–6 | 1–6 |
| page 325 | 1–3, SK | 1–4, SK | 1–4, SK |

Copy the table at the right. Round the population of each city to the nearest million. Then copy and complete the pictograph below the table.

| Six Largest United States Cities* (1980 Census) | | |
|---|---|---|
| City | Exact Population | Rounded Population |
| New York | 9,080,777 | 9,000,000 |
| Los Angeles | 7,445,721 | 7 ■ |
| Chicago | 7,057,853 | 7 ■ |
| Philadelphia | 4,700,966 | 5 ■ |
| Detroit | 4,344,139 | 4 ■ |
| San Francisco | 3,226,867 | 3 ■ |

*Metropolitan Areas

Six Largest United States Cities* (1980 Census)

New York
Los Angeles
Chicago
Philadelphia
Detroit
San Francisco

= 2 million people  = 1 million people

*Metropolitan Areas

1. Which city has the greatest population? the least population? New York; San Francisco
2. According to the pictograph, which cities appear to have the same population? Do these cities actually have the same population? Los Angeles and Chicago; no
3. Using data from the graph, what is the total population for all 6 cities? 35 million
4. **DATA BANK** About how many more Cherokee than Pueblo Indians are in the United States? (See the Data Bank, page 410.) Round each population to the nearest ten thousand. Make a pictograph to show the data and use your graph to answer the question. about 40,000; see teaching notes.

**Skillkeeper**

Write a percent for each fraction.

1. $\frac{3}{4}$ 75%  2. $\frac{5}{8}$ $62\frac{1}{2}$%  3. $\frac{7}{10}$ 70%  4. $\frac{9}{25}$ 36%
5. $\frac{17}{20}$ 85%  6. $\frac{1}{2}$ 50%  7. $\frac{4}{5}$ 80%  8. $\frac{37}{50}$ 74%

Write a percent for each decimal.

9. 0.67 67%  10. 0.5 50%  11. 0.04 4%  12. 2.8 280%
13. 4.25 425%  14. 0.93 93%  15. 0.01 1%  16. 0.725 $72\frac{1}{2}$%



## Using Page 325

**Lesson Development** Have the class read the directions at the top of the page. Tell students that a metropolitan area is a central city and the surrounding communities. Then have each student complete the chart as directed. Next have students copy and complete the pictograph. Call on students to identify the title of the graph and the code that tells what the stick figures stand for. "How many stick figures are needed to show the population of Detroit?" (2 stick figures) "What is the population of Los Angeles?" (7 million) "How many *complete* stick figures will show a number less than or equal to the actual population of Los Angeles?" (3 stick figures would show 6 million) "How many more stick figures are needed?" (one half of a stick figure to show another 1 million)

**Exercises 1–3** Read through the exercises and tell students to use their pictographs to help them answer the questions.

**Data Bank** Students are to find the population figures in the Data Bank in the back of the book. Remind students to round each figure to the nearest ten thousand. "Suppose we use one stick figure to represent a certain number of Indians. How many people should each stick figure represent?" Discuss the advantages of various choices. The best choice is probably to have 1 stick figure represent 10,000 Indians. Help students as necessary to complete the pictograph.

**Skillkeeper** These skills were originally taught in Chapter 12.

**Retcaching Supplement,** page 75

Name ____________ To follow text page 325

**Bar Graphs and Pictographs**

Gina kept a record of her test scores for two weeks. Use the **bar graph** to answer the questions.

1. On which test did Gina score the highest? What was her score? English; 95
2. On which test did she score the lowest? What was her score? **Social Studies; 65**
3. Gina's score in math was 10 points higher than the score in which subject? **Science**
4. Gina's score was 15 points lower in which subject than in math? **Spelling**

Test Scores

about half way between 90 and 100

Score: 0, 10, 20, 30, 40, 50, 60, 70, 80, 90, 100

Subject: Math, Science, Social Studies, English, Spelling, Health

Carver School conducted a newspaper collection drive. Use the **pictograph** to answer the questions.

5. On which day was the largest amount of newspapers collected? **Thursday**
6. On which day were 55 kg of newspapers collected? **Friday**
7. How many more newspapers were collected on Wednesday than on Monday? **25 kg**
8. How many kilograms of newspapers were collected in all? **225**

Newspapers Collected for Recycling

= 5 kg

Monday
Tuesday
Wednesday
Thursday
Friday

Each represents 10 kg of newspapers

**Enrichment Supplement,** page 75

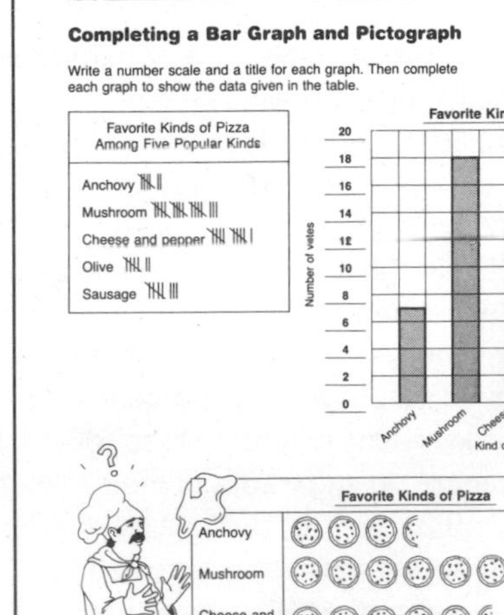

Name ____________ To follow text page 325

**Completing a Bar Graph and Pictograph**

Write a number scale and a title for each graph. Then complete each graph to show the data given in the table.

| Favorite Kinds of Pizza Among Five Popular Kinds |
|---|
| Anchovy 𝍸 II |
| Mushroom 𝍸 𝍸 𝍸 III |
| Cheese and pepper 𝍸 𝍸 I |
| Olive 𝍸 II |
| Sausage 𝍸 III |



Favorite Kinds of Pizza

Anchovy
Mushroom
Cheese and pepper
Olive
Sausage

= 2 votes

**Practice Supplement,** page 122

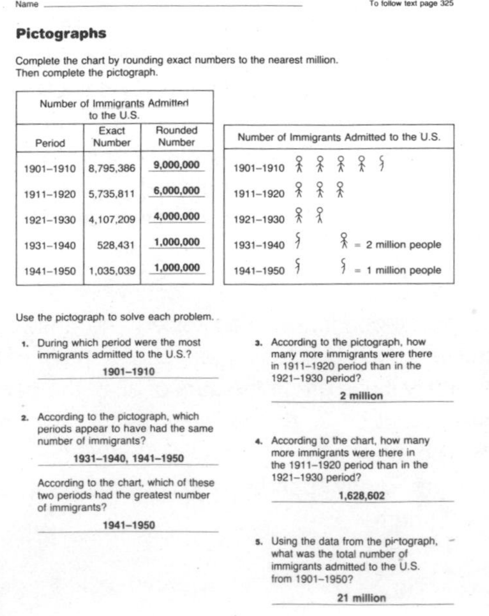

Name ____________ To follow text page 325

**Pictographs**

Complete the chart by rounding exact numbers to the nearest million. Then complete the pictograph.

| Number of Immigrants Admitted to the U.S. | | |
|---|---|---|
| Period | Exact Number | Rounded Number |
| 1901–1910 | 8,795,386 | 9,000,000 |
| 1911–1920 | 5,735,811 | 6,000,000 |
| 1921–1930 | 4,107,209 | 4,000,000 |
| 1931–1940 | 528,431 | 1,000,000 |
| 1941–1950 | 1,035,039 | 1,000,000 |

Number of Immigrants Admitted to the U.S.

1901–1910
1911–1920
1921–1930
1931–1940
1941–1950

= 2 million people
= 1 million people

Use the pictograph to solve each problem.

1. During which period were the most immigrants admitted to the U.S.? **1901–1910**
2. According to the pictograph, which periods appear to have had the same number of immigrants? **1931–1940, 1941–1950**
   According to the chart, which of these two periods had the greatest number of immigrants? **1941–1950**
3. According to the pictograph, how many more immigrants were there in 1911–1920 period than in the 1921–1930 period? **2 million**
4. According to the chart, how many more immigrants were there in the 1911–1920 period than in the 1921–1930 period? **1,628,602**
5. Using the data from the pictograph, what was the total number of immigrants admitted to the U.S. from 1901–1950? **21 million**

# Graphs

**Quick Review** Students write each percent as a lowest-terms fraction.

75% $\frac{3}{4}$ 60% $\frac{3}{5}$ 3% $\frac{3}{100}$ 19% $\frac{19}{100}$ 50% $\frac{1}{2}$ 80% $\frac{4}{5}$

5% $\frac{1}{20}$ 10% $\frac{1}{10}$ 40% $\frac{2}{5}$ 2% $\frac{1}{50}$ 49% $\frac{49}{100}$ 20% $\frac{1}{5}$ 15% $\frac{3}{20}$

**Lesson Focus** To read, interpret, and complete circle graphs

## Ideas for Getting Started

Draw the following circles on the chalkboard.

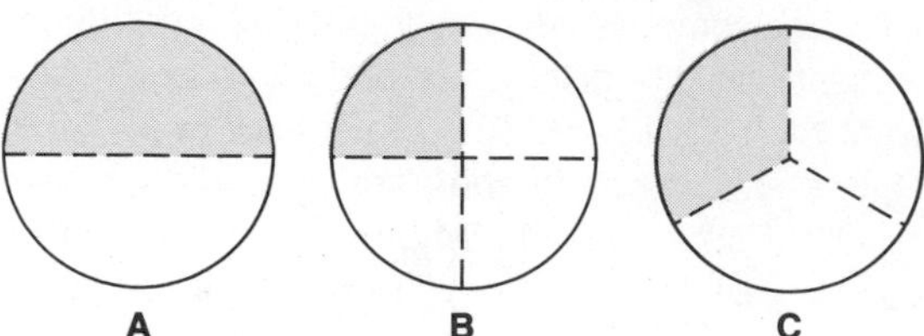


Explain that a whole circle represents 1 day, or 24 hours. "How many hours are represented by the shaded part of circle A?" ($\frac{1}{2}$ of 24, or 12 hours) "How many hours are represented by the shaded part of circle B?" ($\frac{1}{4}$ of 24, or 6 hours) "How many hours are represented by the shaded part of circle C?" ($\frac{1}{3}$ of 24, or 8 hours) Draw another circle on the chalkboard and ask for a volunteer to divide the circle so that the shaded part shows 3 hours. (The circle must be divided into 8 equal parts with one part shaded. Ask another student to divide a circle so that the shaded part shows 4 hours. (6 parts with one part shaded) Explain that these shaded circles are examples of circle graphs.

## Using Page 326

**Motivational Problem** Have students read the paragraph at the top of the page. "What are we asked to find out about Randy's day?" (How many hours is Randy in school?) "What data do we need in order to answer the question?" (hours in the day; percent of the day Randy is in school) Point out that we must refer to the circle graph of Randy's activities for the needed data. "What operation could we use to find the solution?" (We can multiply to find the number of hours.)

**Lesson Development** Ask students to identify the title of the graph. "How much time does a complete circle represent?" (1 day, or 24 hours) Then work through the example with the class. Emphasize that either decimals or fractions can be used to find the number of hours shown by a section of the circle. Work through a second example to find how many hours Randy spends sleeping. On the chalkboard show how this amount can be found by writing $37\frac{1}{2}\%$ as the decimal 0.375. Multiply $24 \times 0.375 = 9$. (Randy spends 9 hours sleeping.)

**Exercises 1–7** Have students work these exercises independently, then review the answers together. When discussing exercise 1, point out that for every circle graph the sum of all of the percents must equal 100, or the whole circle. When discussing exercise 4, ask students to find the number of hours Randy spends doing other things. ($\frac{1}{5}$ of 24, or $4\frac{4}{5}$ hours)

## Circle Graphs

Randy made a circle graph to show how he usually spends his time. About how many hours is Randy in school?

Randy's Activities for One Day (24 h)

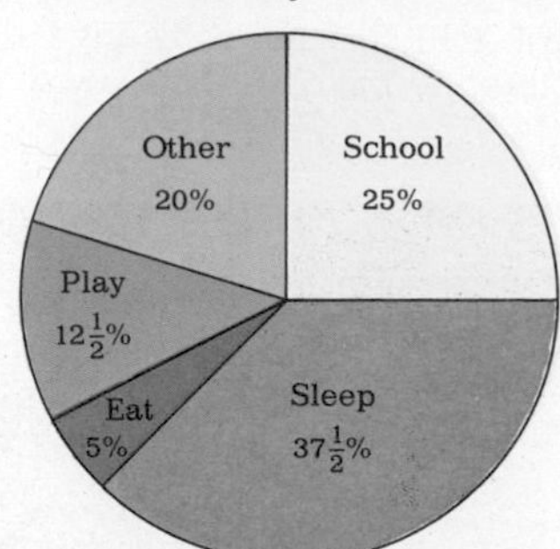


Since we want to find how many hours 25% of one day is, we should multiply.

25% of 24 →

$$\begin{array}{r} \overset{2}{24} \\ \times\ 0.25 \\ \hline 120 \\ 48 \\ \hline 6.00 \end{array}$$

25% = $\frac{1}{4}$
$\frac{1}{4}$ of 24 is
$\frac{1}{4} \times 24 = 6$

Randy spends about 6 hours in school.

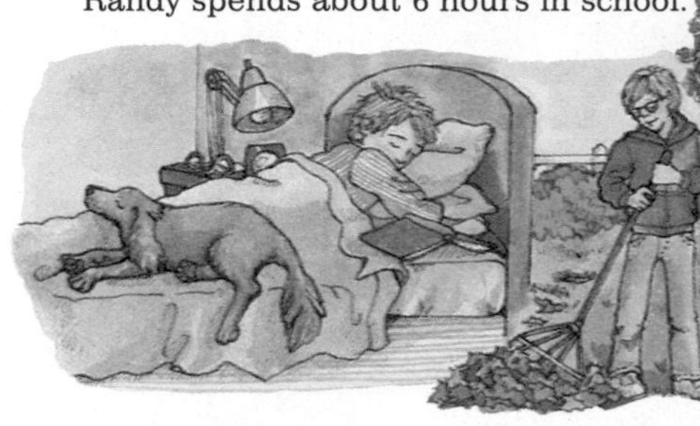

Use the circle graph above to answer these questions.

1. What is the sum of all the percents in the graph? 100%
2. How many hours each day does Randy spend eating? 1.2 h
3. How many hours each day does Randy spend playing? 3 h
4. List two activities that could be in the "other" category. Answers will vary.
5. Does Randy get more or less than 8 hours of sleep? more
6. What percent of the day does he spend sleeping and playing? 50%
7. How many hours of each day is Randy either in school or playing? 9 h



## Follow Up

### Reteaching

Work with students to construct a circle graph for the following problem. John had \$10.00 to spend last week. He spent 25% on a movie, 10% on food, 50% on clothes, and 15% on records.

Explain that a circle graph can be used to show the total amount of John's spending money. Find the part of the circle required to show each percent by multiplying each percent times 360°. For example, to show 25% of the circle, multiply $0.25 \times 360$. Discuss each step as you set up the graph, emphasizing that the total circle (360°) represents 100% of the money.

### Enrichment

Have students draw a circle with a compass. Direct them to cut the circle out and fold it in half three times. Students then label the eight divisions to show how they spend eight hours during the day when they are away from school. Each segment of the circle will represent one hour. Possible categories might be eating, homework, music lessons, play, or chores.

| Assignment Guide | | | |
|---|---|---|---|
| | Minimum | Average | Extended |
| page 326 | 1–7 | 1–7 | 1–7 |
| page 327 | 1–5 | 1–5 | 1–5, TM |

Use the circle graph about favorite main dishes for questions 1–4.

1. What is the total number of students in the survey? 120
2. Which main dish is liked by the most students? meat
3. How many students prefer chicken? 30
4. How many prefer spaghetti? 18

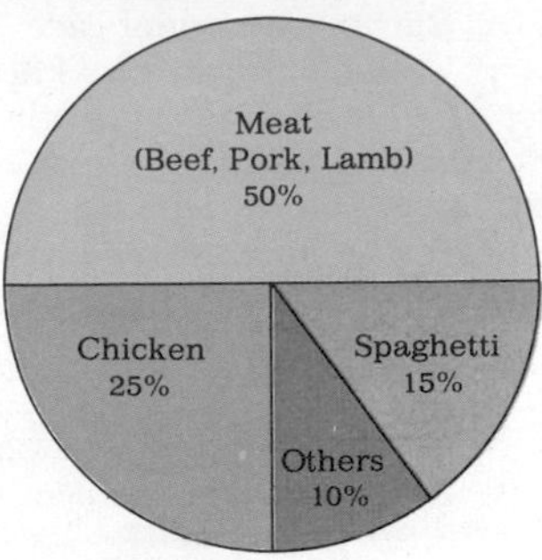


5. Each section in the circle graph shows 10%. Copy and complete the circle graph using the data in the table below. Use the dotted lines as a guide to show the approximate size of each section.

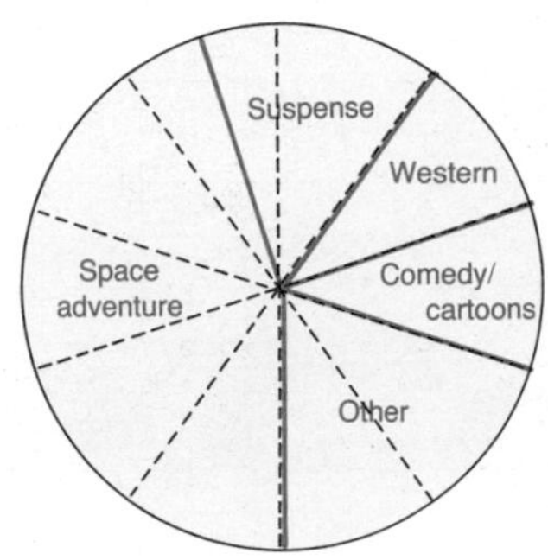


| Favorite Kinds of Movies for 100 Students | |
|---|---|
| Space adventure | 45% |
| Comedy/cartoons | 10% |
| Western | 10% |
| Suspense | 15% |
| Other | 20% |

**Think Math**

**Shape Perception**

**A** Fold a piece of paper in half.

**B** Fold it in half again.

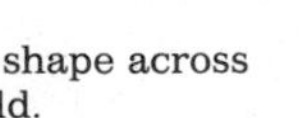

**C** Cut a shape across the fold.

Draw the shape you think will appear when you unfold the paper. How many lines of symmetry do you think the cut-out shape will have? Unfold the paper and compare the cut-out shape with your drawing.
See teaching notes.



## Using Page 327

**Exercises 1–4** Before assigning these exercises, direct students' attention to the circle graph. Remind students that the whole circle represents 100% of the students surveyed, or 120 students. When students have completed the exercises, ask: "How many students prefer something other than the main dishes listed here?" (12 students)

**Exercise 5** Point out that this circle has been divided into 10 equal sections. If necessary, review with students that each part of the circle is $\frac{1}{10}$ or 10%. Make sure students understand that in order to show 45% or 15%, it would be necessary to use $\frac{1}{2}$ of a section along with the required number of 10% sections. Then have students verify that the percents given add up to 100% and that the number of students represented in each category add up to 100.

**Think Math** In this exercise students are asked to predict the shape and the number of lines of symmetry they will find after following the directions. If students cut out a free-form shape like the one shown in the illustration, the figure will have 2 lines of symmetry.

**Reteaching Supplement,** page 76

Name ______ To follow text page 327

**Circle Graphs**

Use of 1,000 Tons of Coal in a Year: Industry 42%, Other uses 13%, Fuel 7%, Electric power 38%

Use of 10,000 Barrels of Oil in a Year: Gasoline 44%, Fuel oil 37%, Other uses 19%

This **circle graph** shows how 1,000 metric tons of coal were used in a recent year.

1. What percent of coal was used for electric power? 38%
2. For which purpose was the greatest amount of coal used? **industry**
3. How many metric tons of coal were used for electricity? (Multiply 1,000 by 0.38.) **380**
4. How many metric tons of coal were used for fuel *and* other uses? **200**
5. Which category consumed less than $\frac{1}{10}$ of the coal used in the year? **fuel**

This **circle graph** shows how 10,000 barrels of oil were used in a recent year.

6. What percent of oil was used for gasoline? **44%**
7. Which two categories used more than $\frac{3}{4}$ of the oil consumed in the year? **gasoline, fuel oil**
8. How many barrels of oil were used for gasoline? (Multiply 10,000 by 0.44.) **4,400**
9. How many barrels of oil were used for fuel oil? **3,700**

**Enrichment Supplement,** page 76

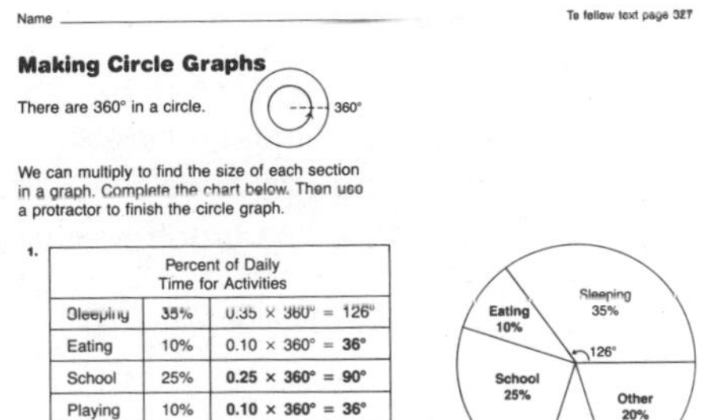

Name ______ To follow text page 327

**Making Circle Graphs**

There are 360° in a circle.

We can multiply to find the size of each section in a graph. Complete the chart below. Then use a protractor to finish the circle graph.

1.

| Percent of Daily Time for Activities | | |
|---|---|---|
| Sleeping | 35% | 0.35 × 360° = 126° |
| Eating | 10% | 0.10 × 360° = **36°** |
| School | 25% | **0.25 × 360° = 90°** |
| Playing | 10% | **0.10 × 360° = 36°** |
| Other | 20% | **0.20 × 360° = 72°** |

2.

| Percent of School Hours per Week | | |
|---|---|---|
| Math | 15% | 0.15 × 360° = 54° |
| Reading and language arts | 25% | **0.25 × 360° = 90°** |
| Social studies | 15% | **0.15 × 360° = 54°** |
| Science | 10% | **0.10 × 360° = 36°** |
| Music | 5% | **0.05 × 360° = 18°** |
| Art | 5% | **0.05 × 360° = 18°** |
| Recess | 5% | **0.05 × 360° = 18°** |
| Lunch | 20% | **0.20 × 360° = 72°** |

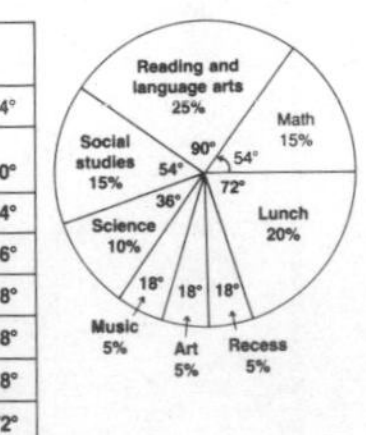


**Practice Supplement,** page 123

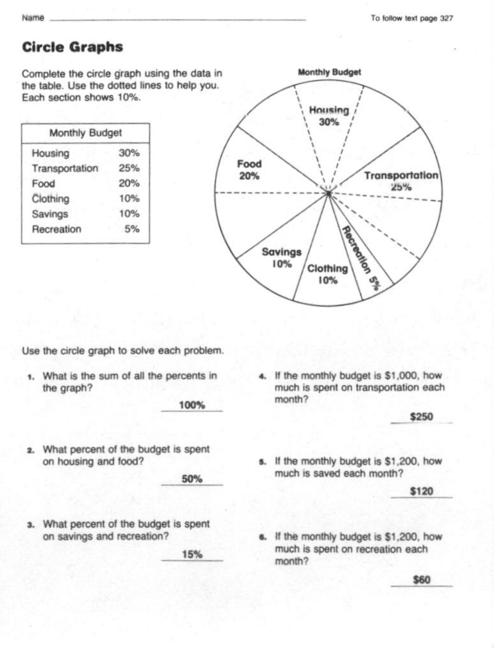

Name ______ To follow text page 327

**Circle Graphs**

Complete the circle graph using the data in the table. Use the dotted lines to help you. Each section shows 10%.

| Monthly Budget | |
|---|---|
| Housing | 30% |
| Transportation | 25% |
| Food | 20% |
| Clothing | 10% |
| Savings | 10% |
| Recreation | 5% |

Monthly Budget: Housing 30%, Food 20%, Transportation 25%, Savings 10%, Clothing 10%, Recreation 5%

Use the circle graph to solve each problem.

1. What is the sum of all the percents in the graph? **100%**
2. What percent of the budget is spent on housing and food? **50%**
3. What percent of the budget is spent on savings and recreation? **15%**
4. If the monthly budget is $1,000, how much is spent on transportation each month? **$250**
5. If the monthly budget is $1,200, how much is saved each month? **$120**
6. If the monthly budget is $1,200, how much is spent on recreation each month? **$60**

# Graphs

**Quick Review** As an oral drill, students give each number rounded to the place whose digit is underlined.

| 0.0866 | 23.455 | 9,555,203 | 423.275 | 0.3499 |
|---|---|---|---|---|
| 5,704 | 12.87 | 7.699 | 890,350 | 2,580,600 |

**Lesson Focus** To read, interpret, and complete line graphs

## Ideas for Getting Started

On the chalkboard copy the following table and graph.

| Age | 5 | 7 | 9 | 11 | 13 |
|---|---|---|---|---|---|
| Height (cm) | 110 | 122 | 132 | 143 | 157 |

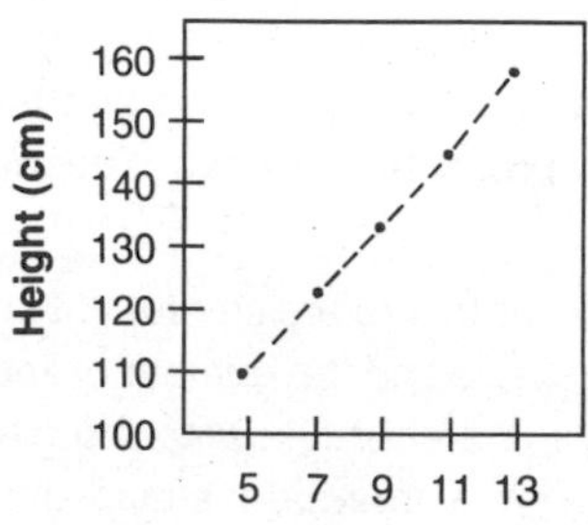


Explain that the table shows how a child's height changes from age 5 to age 13. Then say that the same information can be shown in a line graph. "At age 5, what was the child's height?" (110 cm) "Where shall we mark a point to show this on the graph?" Invite a volunteer to come to the chalkboard and mark a point opposite 110 and above age 5. Continue asking questions until all the coordinate age-height points are marked. Then draw a broken line to connect them. "Does the child's height increase or decrease between ages 5 and 13?" (It increases.) "When does the height seem to increase the most?" (between ages 11 and 13)

## Using Page 328

**Lesson Development** Ask students to read the opening paragraph and to study the line graph. Then have students identify the title, the labels, the scale of age in months, and the scale of height in centimeters. "What does the last point, or dot, on the graph tell us?" (At 12 months, Wendell's height was 75 cm.) Between 0 and 12 months does the line go up or down on the chart?" (up) "What does that show—even without reading the height scale?" (Wendell grew taller.)

**Exercises 1–5** These exercises can be done as a group activity, or have students work independently. After all the exercises have been completed, ask how many centimeters Wendell grew in 12 months.

## Line Graphs

All of Dr. Cardona's patients are babies or young children. She keeps records of their changes in height and weight from one visit to the next. The line graph shows how one of her patients grew in height from birth to 12 months of age.

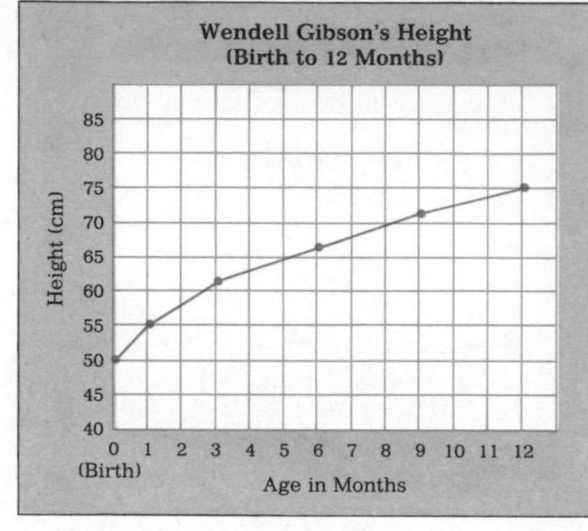


Answer these questions about the line graph.

1. What was Wendell's height at birth? 50 cm
2. How much did Wendell grow from birth to 1 month? 5 cm
3. During which 3-month period did Wendell grow the fastest: birth to 3 months or 3 months to 6 months? birth to 3 months
4. During which two 3-month periods did Wendell grow the same amount? 3 to 6 months and 6 to 9 months
5. Estimate Wendell's height at 10 months. 72 cm and 73 cm are good estimates.



## Follow Up

### Reteaching

Tell students that a line graph can show a change over time. Generate a discussion about the graph below. Elicit from students why a line graph was used.

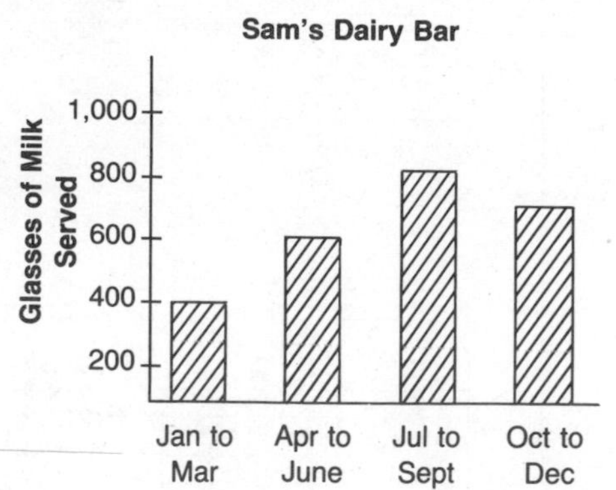


### Enrichment

Have students collect samples of line graphs from newspapers and magazines to create an instructional bulletin board. Encourage students to use colored paper to point out all of the features of the graphs, including the kind of data that is highlighted in the graphs.

| Assignment Guide | | | |
|---|---|---|---|
| | Minimum | Average | Extended |
| page 328 | 1–5 | 1–5 | 1–5 |
| page 329 | 1–3 | 1–4 | 1–4, TM |

Dr. Cardona recorded the weight changes for one of her patients from birth until the baby was 12 months old. Copy and complete the graph using the data about Joanne's weight. Then answer the questions.

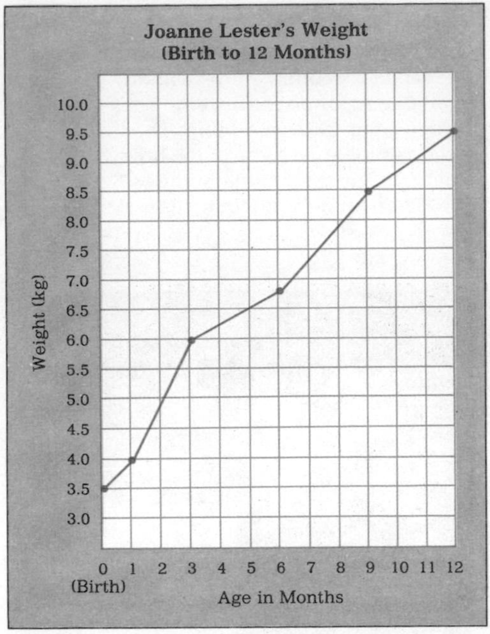


| Joanne Lester's Weight | |
|---|---|
| Age | Weight (kg) |
| Birth | 3.5 |
| 1 month | 4.0 |
| 3 months | 6.0 |
| 6 months | 6.8 |
| 9 months | 8.5 |
| 12 months | 9.5 |

1. Did Joanne's weight increase more from 1 to 3 months of age or from 6 to 9 months of age? How much more? from 1 to 3 months; 0.3 kg more
2. About how much do you think Joanne weighed when she was 2 months old? About 5 kg is a good estimate.
3. About how much do you think Joanne weighed when she was 13 months old? About 10 kg is a good estimate.

★ 4. Use the table below to make a line graph showing Joanne Lester's growth in weight from 2 to 6 years of age. Answers will vary.

| Age in years | 2 | 3 | 4 | 5 | 6 |
|---|---|---|---|---|---|
| Weight (kg) | 12 | 14 | 16 | 17.5 | 19.5 |

**Think**

**Discover a Pattern**

Look for a pattern in the products of the first three problems. Use your pattern to find the other products.

1. 15 × 15 = 225 (1×2)(5×5)
2. 25 × 25 = 625 (2×3)(5×5)
3. 35 × 35 = 1,225 (3×4)(5×5)
4. 45 × 45 = 2,025 (4×5)
5. 55 × 55 = 3,025 (5×6)
6. 65 × 65 = 4,225 (6×7)

**Math**



## Using Page 329

**Lesson Development** Ask students to read the first paragraph and make sure they understand the directions. Have students relate the title, labels, and number scales on the graph to the headings on the table. Be sure that students know how to mark a point for each age-weight coordinate. When the graphs are completed, have students use them to work the exercises.

**Exercise 1** To answer the first question in this exercise, students can compare the increase in weight by the steepness, or slope, of the line on the graph. To answer the second question, students must find the difference between the weight at 1 month and the weight at 3 months, and the difference between the weight at 6 months and the weight at 9 months. Then they must find the difference of these increases.

**Exercises 2–3** Students are asked to estimate what Joanne's weight was at two different ages.

**Exercise 4** Students must construct their own line graph, using data from a table. Remind students to choose a title, to include labels, and to choose a number scale.

**Think Math** Students are to look for a pattern that will provide a mental shortcut for finding certain products. Point out that each problem involves a product of a 2-digit number ending in 5 times itself. Give hints as necessary to help students to discover that the product always ends in $5^2$ or 25. Also help them to discover that the first digit of the 2-digit number times its successor gives the first two digits in the product.

**Reteaching Supplement,** page 77

Name ________ To follow text page 329

**Line Graphs**

Use the **line graph** about temperature to answer the questions.

Outside Temperature: April 1

Degrees Celsius: 2, 4, 6, 8, 10, 12, 14, 16

Hour of the morning: Midnight, 1, 2, 3, 4, 5, 6, 7, 8, 9, 10, 11, Noon

about 5°C

increase in temperature

Jay sold tickets for the school play. Use the **line graph** to answer the questions.

Jay's Ticket-Selling Record

Number of tickets sold: 1, 2, 3, 4, 5, 6, 7, 8

Day of the week: Mon, Tue, Wed, Thur, Fri, Sat

the highest point

1. At what time was the outside temperature 6°C? **6 a.m.**
2. What was the temperature at noon? **14°C**
3. At what three hours of the day did the temperature remain constant at 7°C? **7 a.m., 8 a.m., 9 a.m.**
4. What was the lowest outdoor temperature for April 1? **4°C**
5. What was the outside temperature between 7:00 and 9:00 a.m.? **7°C**
6. What was Jay's best day for sales? **Monday**
7. What was his poorest day for sales? **Friday**
8. On which days were the same number of tickets sold? **Wednesday, Thursday**
9. How many tickets were sold on Monday and Tuesday together? **9**
10. Between which two days did Jay have the greatest drop in sales? **Monday, Tuesday**

**Enrichment Supplement,** page 77

Name ________ To follow text page 329

**Follow the Bouncing Ball**

When a new tennis ball is dropped from 200 cm it bounces several times. This calculator code shows how to find the height of the next bounce.

first bounce, second bounce, third bounce

200 [×] 0.6 [×] 0.6 [×] 0.6 and so on

Each time you multiply by 0.6.

1. Copy the table. Use a calculator and follow the code to find the height for the first 10 bounces. Start with 200 cm. Round the heights to the nearest hundredth of a centimeter.

| Bounce | Height (cm) |
|---|---|
| 1 | **120 cm** |
| 2 | **72 cm** |
| 3 | **43.2 cm** |
| 4 | **25.92 cm** |
| 5 | **15.55 cm** |
| 6 | **9.33 cm** |
| 7 | **5.60 cm** |
| 8 | **3.36 cm** |
| 9 | **2.02 cm** |
| 10 | **1.21 cm** |

140 cm, 130 cm, 120 cm, 110 cm, 100 cm, 90 cm, 80 cm, 70 cm, 60 cm, 50 cm, 40 cm, 30 cm, 20 cm, 10 cm, 0

Bounce: 1, 2, 3, 4, 5, 6, 7, 8, 9, 10

2. Make a line graph to show the data from your table.
3. According to the code, how many bounces will the ball make before the number on the calculator rounded to the nearest hundredth is zero? **21**

**Practice Supplement,** page 124

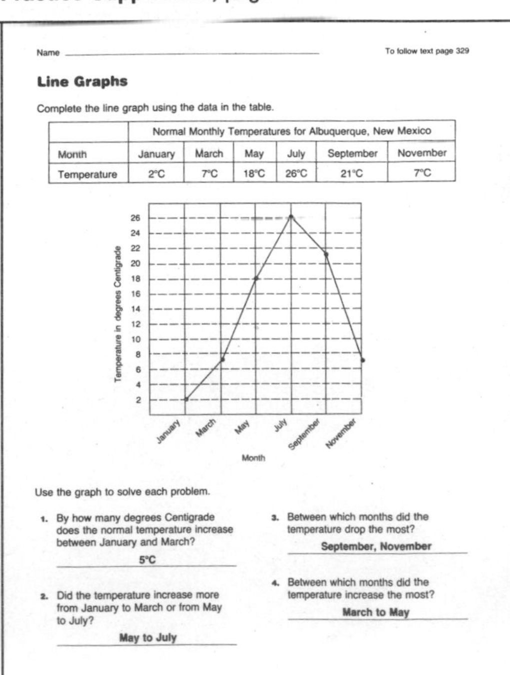

Name ________ To follow text page 329

**Line Graphs**

Complete the line graph using the data in the table.

| | Normal Monthly Temperatures for Albuquerque, New Mexico | | | | | |
|---|---|---|---|---|---|---|
| Month | January | March | May | July | September | November |
| Temperature | 2°C | 7°C | 18°C | 26°C | 21°C | 7°C |



Use the graph to solve each problem.

1. By how many degrees Centigrade does the normal temperature increase between January and March? **5°C**
2. Did the temperature increase more from January to March or from May to July? **May to July**
3. Between which months did the temperature drop the most? **September, November**
4. Between which months did the temperature increase the most? **March to May**

**Quick Review** Students find these decimal sums and differences.

| 0.89 | 0.46 | 5.27 | 25.62 | 7.65 | 0.087 | 9.18 |
|---|---|---|---|---|---|---|
| − 0.08 | + 0.42 | − 1.37 | + 0.38 | − 2.55 | + 0.143 | − 7.46 |
| 0.81 | 0.88 | 3.90 | 26.00 | 5.10 | 0.230 | 1.72 |

**Lesson Focus** To evaluate graphs by title, labels, and number scale

## Ideas for Getting Started

Have students bring to class graphs from newspapers or news magazines. Call on students to describe each graph, to tell what type of graph it is (bar, pictograph, circle, or line) and to identify the title and labels. Select several of the graphs and discuss how they would change if the number scales were changed. Invite students to display the graphs on the bulletin board.

## Using Page 330

**Lesson Development** Tell students that in this lesson they will analyze the parts of graphs. Have students read the paragraph at the top of the page. Ask a volunteer to describe the data in the table. Call attention to the graph. "What important parts are missing from the graph?" (title, label, number scale)

**Exercises 1–5** After students have completed these exercises, discuss the answers, emphasizing the importance of the components of a graph. In exercise 4, most students will probably suggest a line graph as the other type of graph that could be used to show the rainfall data. However, a pictograph (or even a circle graph) could also be used to depict this data. In discussing exercise 5, ask: "In which direction would the bars go if the months were on the vertical side and the rainfall amounts were on the horizontal side?" (The bars would be horizontal instead of vertical.)

## Evaluating Graphs

A science class collected data about rainfall during one school year. They recorded their data in a table. Then the class made a bar graph to show the data. Study their table and bar graph. Then answer the questions below.

Monthly Rainfall for One School Year

| Month | Amount (cm) |
|---|---|
| September | 5 |
| October | 25 |
| November | 20 |
| December | 18 |
| January | 4 |
| February | 7 |
| March | 16 |
| April | 18 |
| May | 10 |

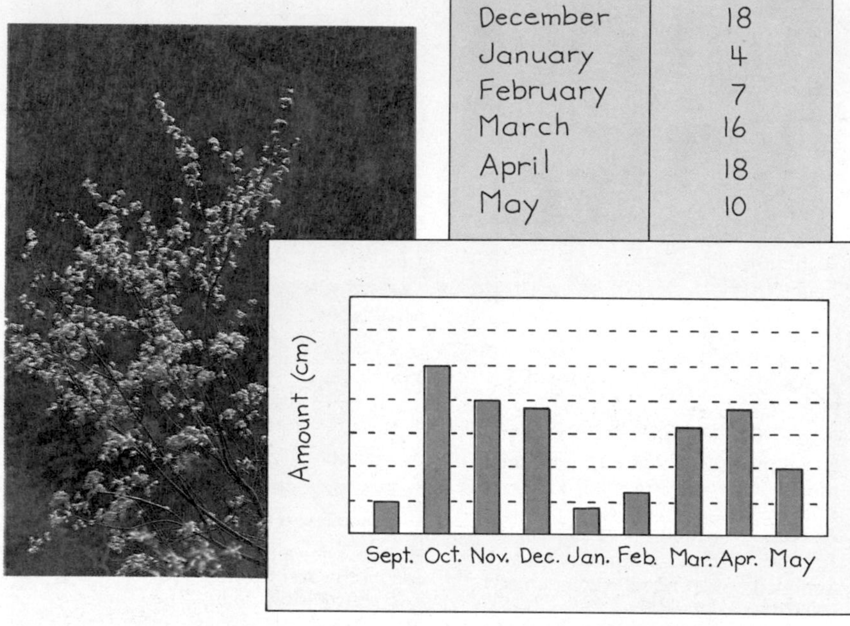


1. All graphs should have a **title.** Write an appropriate title for the bar graph. Monthly Rainfall During the School Year
2. All parts of a graph should be fully **labeled.** What other label should be on the horizontal scale? Month
3. Most graphs should have a **number scale.** What numbers should be written on this vertical scale? 0, 5, 10, 15, . . . (or 5, 10, 15, . . .)
4. What other type of graph (line graph, pictograph, or circle graph) could the class have used to show the data? See teaching notes.
5. Could the months have been placed on the vertical side and the amount of rainfall on the horizontal side? yes



## Follow Up

### Reteaching

Discuss the following common features of all graphs:

- Title: What information should be included in a title?
- Number scale: How is the number scale determined?
- Labels: What should the labels tell?

Have students name the types of graphs studied in this chapter. Then review some of the special features of each type of graph and name an example of the kind of data that might be shown in each.

### Enrichment

Have each student make a graph of their choosing and then write several questions that require interpreting the graph. Let students share their graphs and questions with other members of the class.

| Assignment Guide | | | |
|---|---|---|---|
| | Minimum | Average | Extended |
| page 330 | | 1–5 | 1–5 |
| page 331 | | 1–7 | 1–7, TM |

The number scale used for a graph may influence the conclusions you reach about the data shown. Study each pair of graphs. Then answer the questions.

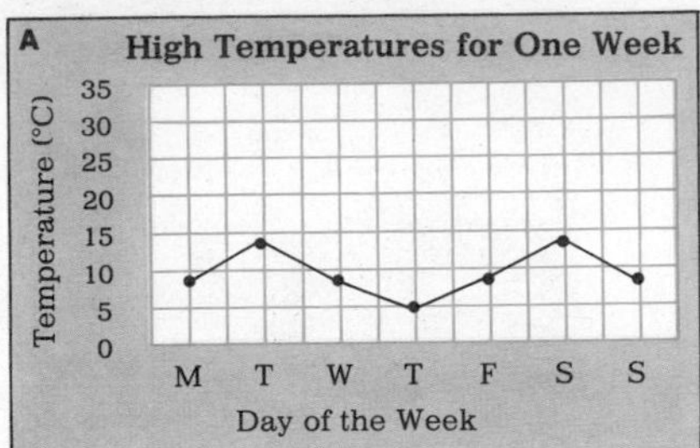


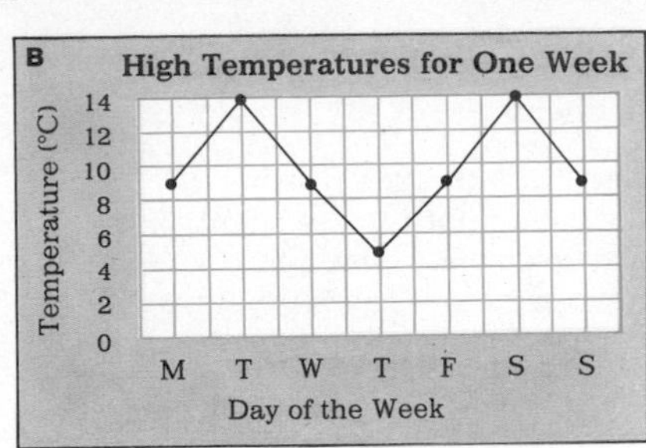


1. Are the temperatures for each day the same on both graphs? yes
2. How many degrees does each space between horizontal lines represent in graph A? in graph B? 5°; 2°
3. Which graph might be more likely to cause you to exclaim, "The daily high temperatures have certainly gone up and down this week!"? Why? graph B; slope of lines is steeper

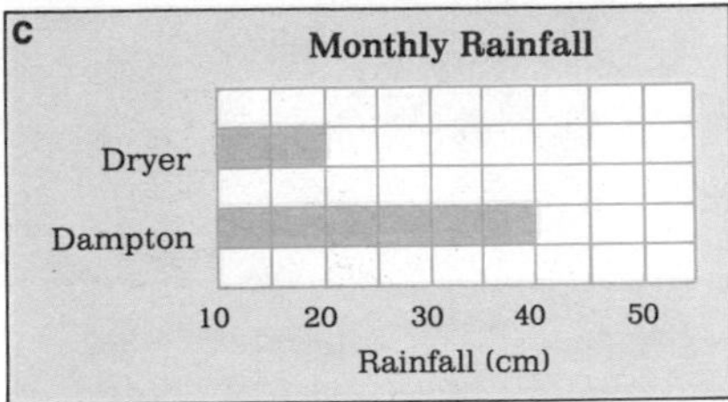


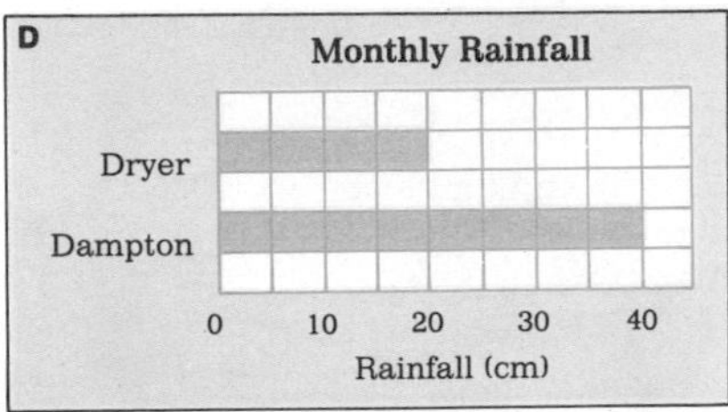


4. Do both graphs show the same total amount of rainfall for each city? yes
5. Is the length of the bar for Dampton twice as long as the length of the bar for Dryer in both graphs? no
6. Which graph, C or D, gives a clearer idea of the relationship between the amounts of rainfall in the two cities? graph D
7. How is the number scale on graph C different from the number scale on graph D? The scale on C begins with 10 rather than 0.

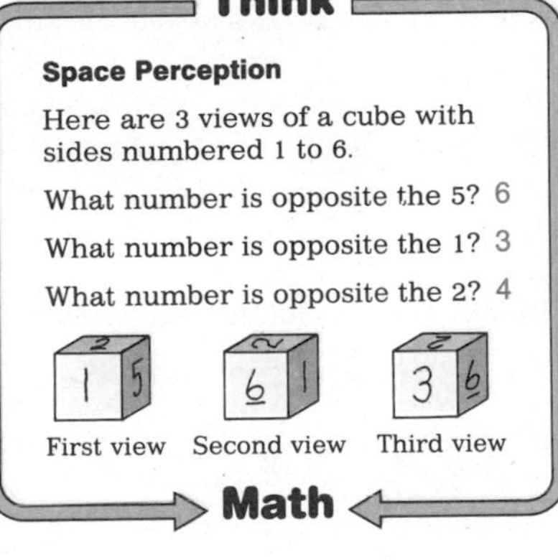

Think
Space Perception
Here are 3 views of a cube with sides numbered 1 to 6.
What number is opposite the 5? 6
What number is opposite the 1? 3
What number is opposite the 2? 4
First view
Second view
Third view
Math




## Using Page 331

**Exercises 1–3** Call attention to graphs A and B and discuss them. Stress how the differences in the vertical scales affect the look of the two graphs. "What scale might you use on this graph so that the temperatures would appear even less varied than those on graph A?" (The spaces between horizontal lines might represent 10°.) "How could you change the number scale so that the temperatures might seem to vary even more than those in graph B?" (The spaces between horizontal lines might represent 1°.)

**Exercises 4–7** Call attention to graphs C and D, which deal with monthly rainfall. Point out how a shortened number scale affects the appearance of the data.

**Think Math** Encourage students to study the cubes and to think about the relative positions of the numbers on the cubes.

## Ideas That Work

### Math for the Gifted

In this activity, graphing skills can be used to develop problem-solving skills, such as Find a Pattern. Experiences like these can also help build a tie between mathematics and science.

In the graph shown here, the amount of stretch in a given spring is shown for a given number of weights. By looking at the graph, students can see that the spring stretches 4 cm for each added weight. Using this information, students can write a prediction equation for this spring and these weights. Students can then be asked to generalize from the results of this experiment.

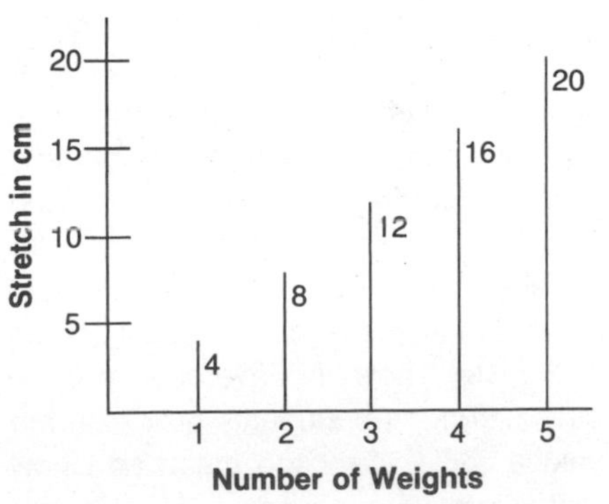


spring stretch = number of weights × 4 cm

**Practice Supplement,** page 125

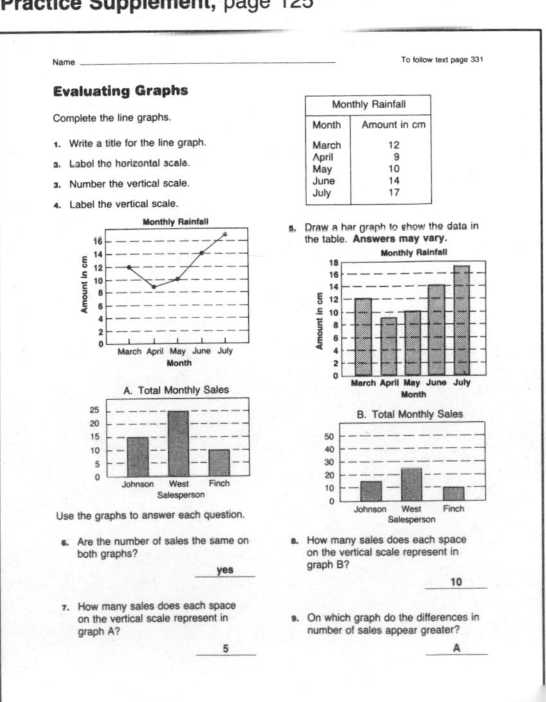

Name ______

To follow text page 331

**Evaluating Graphs**

Complete the line graphs.

1. Write a title for the line graph.
2. Label the horizontal scale.
3. Number the vertical scale.
4. Label the vertical scale.

| Monthly Rainfall | |
|---|---|
| Month | Amount in cm |
| March | 12 |
| April | 9 |
| May | 10 |
| June | 14 |
| July | 17 |



5. Draw a bar graph to show the data in the table. **Answers may vary.**







Use the graphs to answer each question.

6. Are the number of sales the same on both graphs? **yes**
7. How many sales does each space on the vertical scale represent in graph A? **5**
8. How many sales does each space on the vertical scale represent in graph B? **10**
9. On which graph do the differences in number of sales appear greater? **A**

**Quick Review** Students write the symbol (>, <, =) that makes each number sentence true.

$(2 \times 16) + (4 \times 16) \; = \; 6 \times 16$ $\quad 45 \div 5 \; = \; 54 \div 6$ $\quad 64 \div 8 \; < \; 6 + 3$

$100 - 35 \; > \; 8 \times 8$ $\quad 40 + 30 \; < \; 20 + 60$ $\quad (5 \times 4) + (6 \times 3) \; < \; 20 + 19$

**Lesson Focus** To find the mean, or average, of a set of numbers; to solve word problems using data from a double bar graph

## Ideas for Getting Started

On the chalkboard draw the following bar graph.

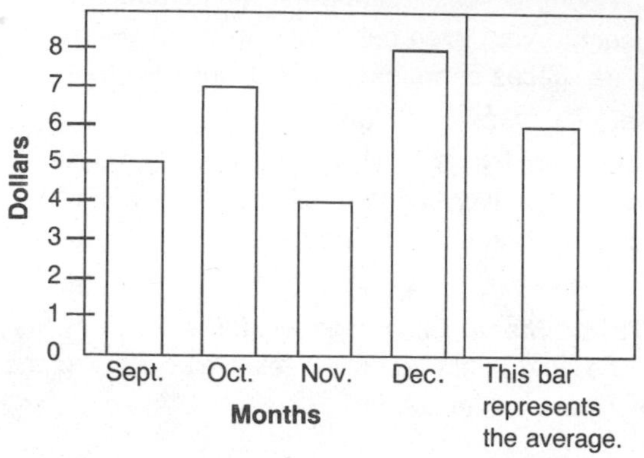


Using the information from the bar graph, students guess an average monthly income for the class. Students then cut strips of paper to represent their guesses. Next have students total the four monthly amounts and divide to find the actual mean and compare with their guesses.

## Using Page 332

**Lesson Development** Write *mean* on the chalkboard and explain that it is another term for *average.* Remind students that they have learned to find the average of a set of numbers. Call on a volunteer to read aloud the paragraphs at the top of the page. Have students identify the question and the data. Then use the first example to review finding the average, or mean, of a set of numbers. "What is the first step?" (Find the sum of the numbers.) "What is the second step?" (Divide the sum by the number of numbers involved.) Have students check the decimal answer by multiplying. "What does 149.2 tell us?" (the mean number of customers for the paper route)

**Other Example** Work this example with the class. Point out that the division is completed through the hundredths place and that the quotient is rounded to the nearest tenth.

**Exercises 1–6** Assign these exercises as independent work. Review as necessary how to divide by a single digit and how to round to the nearest tenth. Encourage students to check their answers by multiplying.

## Mean

Another name for the **average** of a set of numbers is the **mean.** Finding means sometimes involves decimal quotients.

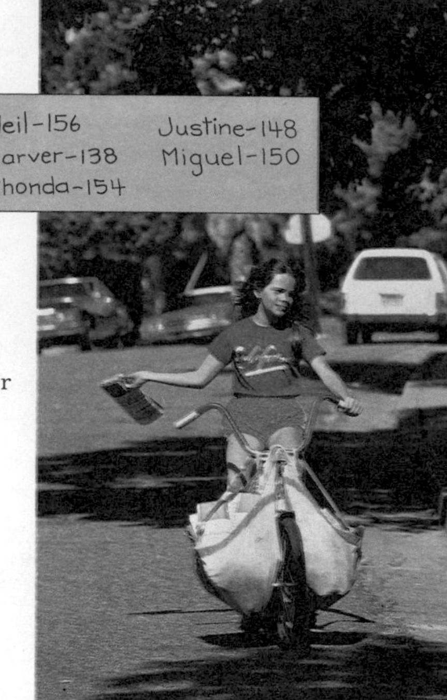


The list shows the number of customers for the 5 students in Mr. Hayden's class who deliver newspapers. What is the mean number of customers for the paper routes?

Find the total number of customers.

```
  156
  138
  154
  148
+ 150
  746
```

Divide by the number of delivery people.

```
   149.2
5)746.0
  5
  24
  20
   46
   45
    10
    10
     0
```

The mean number of customers for the paper route is 149.2.

**Another Example**

Find the mean (to the nearest tenth).

```
                     84
                     39        55.25
84, 39, 46, 52 →     46  →  4)221.00  →  The mean (rounded to
                   + 52                   the nearest tenth)
                    221                   is 55.3.
```

Find the mean. Round to the nearest tenth when necessary.

1. 148, 175, 164, 161 162
2. 46, 25, 31, 62, 26 38
3. 318, 262, 178 252.7
4. 16.2, 15.7, 15.4, 16.6, 14.8 15.7
5. 22, 34, 9, 62, 70, 80 46.2
6. 14.22, 17, 8.7, 6.56, 14.27 12.2

332

## Follow Up

### Reteaching

Encourage students to share ideas commonly associated with the term *average,* such as "average daily temperature," "average score," or "average height and weight." After a brief discussion, remind students that *mean* is another name for the average of a set of numbers. Present students with a sample set of test scores and review how the average is computed. Elicit from students how extreme values could affect the mean and how representative the mean is for a set of numbers.

### Enrichment

Challenge students to find data for which they can compute mean scores. Possible ideas might include: the mean for number of parents attending open house per class, the mean per class for money raised at the school fair; mean high and low temperatures for the past week.

| Assignment Guide | | | |
|---|---|---|---|
| | Minimum | Average | Extended |
| page 332 | 1–6 | 1–6 | 1–6 |
| page 333 | 1–5 | 1–5 | 1–6 |

## Problem Solving: Using Data from a Double Bar Graph

QUESTION / DATA / PLAN / ANSWER / CHECK

Estimate the number of customers shown by each bar. Use your estimates to solve the problems below.

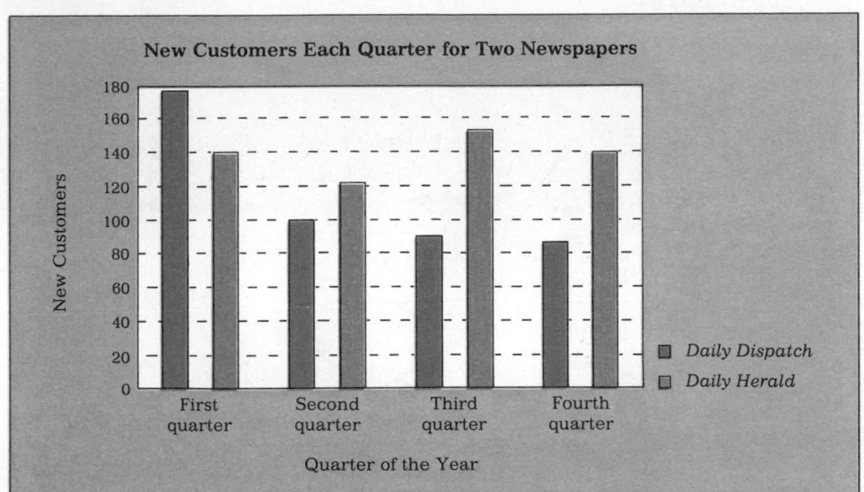


1. Which paper had the greatest number of new customers in any quarter? Daily Dispatch
2. About how many more new customers did the *Daily Herald* get in the third quarter than the *Daily Dispatch*? about 60
3. During which quarter was there the least difference in the numbers of new customers for the two papers? About how great was the difference that quarter? Second; about 20
4. How many new customers did the *Daily Dispatch* get during the second half of the year? during the first half of the year? about 174; about 278
5. List your estimates of the number of new customers for each paper for each quarter. What is the mean number of new customers for each paper? Dispatch–110-115; Herald–135-140
6. **Try This** Rosa started a new paper route. The first week she found 1 new customer. The second week, she found 4 new customers, the third week 7 new customers, the fourth week 10 new customers, and so on. If she continued getting customers in this way, during which week did she get 30 new customers? Hint: Make a table and look for a pattern. during the eleventh week



## Using Page 333

**Lesson Development** Call students' attention to the double bar graph. Point out that by using double bars, two sets of data can be shown on one graph. This kind of graph is especially useful to compare two sets of data. "About how many new customers did the *Daily Dispatch* have during the first quarter?" (almost 180) "How many customers did the *Daily Herald* have during the first quarter?" (140) "Which newspaper had more customers during this quarter?" *(Daily Dispatch)*

**Exercises 1–5** Be sure that students understand what is asked in each exercise. Give help as needed in estimating the number of new customers. Exercise 3 asks two questions. The first can be answered by simply looking for the quarter in which the two bars are closest in length.

**Try This** A possible strategy, Find a Pattern, was taught on page 246.

**Discussion** "What is the question about Rosa's paper route?" (During which week did Rosa get 30 new customers?) "How many new customers did Rosa get the first week?" (1) "The second week?" (4) "The third week?" (7) "How many more new customers did Rosa get each week than the week before?" (3) Have students find a pattern and extend it to find the answer to the problem.

**Solution** Rosa got 30 new customers during the eleventh week.

| Week | 1 | 2 | 3 | 4 | 5 | 6 | 7 | 8 | 9 | 10 | 11 |
|---|---|---|---|---|---|---|---|---|---|---|---|
| New Customers | 1 | 4 | 7 | 10 | 13 | 16 | 19 | 22 | 25 | 28 | 31 |

**Reteaching Supplement,** page 78

**Enrichment Supplement,** page 78

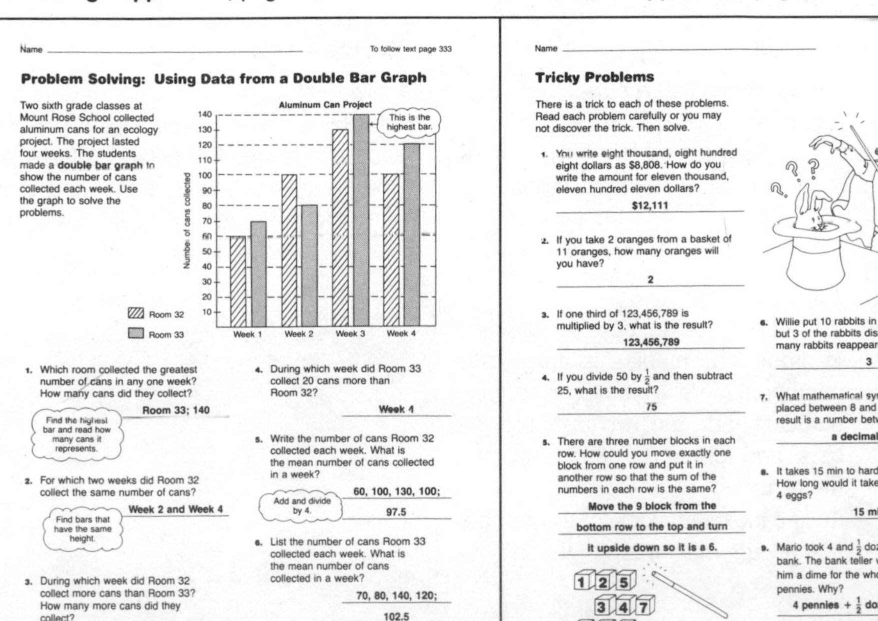
Name ______ To follow text page 333

**Problem Solving: Using Data from a Double Bar Graph**

Two sixth grade classes at Mount Rose School collected aluminum cans for an ecology project. The project lasted four weeks. The students made a **double bar graph** to show the number of cans collected each week. Use the graph to solve the problems.



1. Which room collected the greatest number of cans in any one week? How many cans did they collect? Room 33; 140
   (Find the highest bar and read how many cans it represents.)
2. For which two weeks did Room 32 collect the same number of cans? Week 2 and Week 4
   (Find bars that have the same height.)
3. During which week did Room 32 collect more cans than Room 33? How many more cans did they collect? Week 2; 20
4. During which week did Room 33 collect 20 cans more than Room 32? Week 4
5. Write the number of cans Room 32 collected each week. What is the mean number of cans collected in a week? 60, 100, 130, 100; 97.5
   (Add and divide by 4.)
6. List the number of cans Room 33 collected each week. What is the mean number of cans collected in a week? 70, 80, 140, 120; 102.5

Name ______ To follow text page 333

**Tricky Problems**

There is a trick to each of these problems. Read each problem carefully or you may not discover the trick. Then solve.

1. You write eight thousand, eight hundred eight dollars as $8,808. How do you write the amount for eleven thousand, eleven hundred eleven dollars? $12,111
2. If you take 2 oranges from a basket of 11 oranges, how many oranges will you have? 2
3. If one third of 123,456,789 is multiplied by 3, what is the result? 123,456,789
4. If you divide 50 by $\frac{1}{2}$ and then subtract 25, what is the result? 75
5. There are three number blocks in each row. How could you move exactly one block from one row and put it in another row so that the sum of the numbers in each row is the same? Move the 9 block from the bottom row to the top and turn it upside down so it is a 6.



6. Willie put 10 rabbits in his hat. All but 3 of the rabbits disappeared. How many rabbits reappeared? 3
7. What mathematical symbol can be placed between 8 and 9 so that the result is a number between 8 and 9? a decimal point
8. It takes 15 min to hard boil 1 egg. How long would it take to hard boil 4 eggs? 15 min
9. Mario took 4 and $\frac{1}{2}$ dozen pennies to a bank. The bank teller would only give him a dime for the whole lot of pennies. Why? 4 pennies + $\frac{1}{2}$ dozen pennies is 10 pennies

**Practice Supplement,** page 126

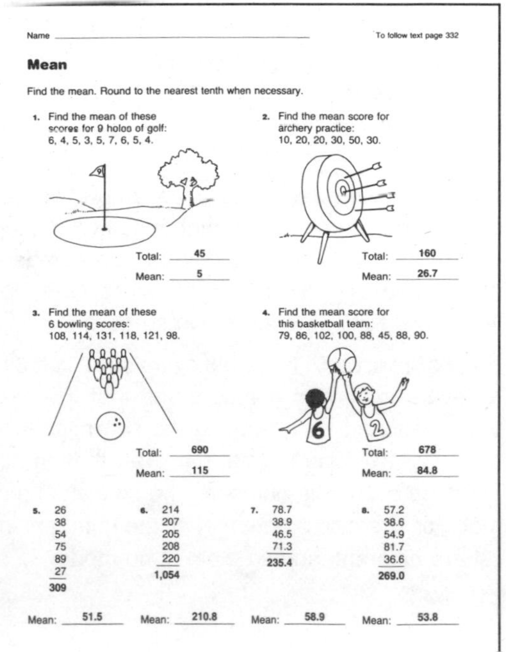
Name ______ To follow text page 332

**Mean**

Find the mean. Round to the nearest tenth when necessary.

1. Find the mean of these scores for 9 holes of golf: 6, 4, 5, 3, 5, 7, 6, 5, 4.
   Total: 45
   Mean: 5
2. Find the mean score for archery practice: 10, 20, 20, 30, 50, 30.
   Total: 160
   Mean: 26.7
3. Find the mean of these 6 bowling scores: 108, 114, 131, 118, 121, 98.
   Total: 690
   Mean: 115
4. Find the mean score for this basketball team: 79, 86, 102, 100, 88, 45, 88, 90.
   Total: 678
   Mean: 84.8

| 5. | 6. | 7. | 8. |
|---|---|---|---|
| 26 | 214 | 78.7 | 57.2 |
| 38 | 207 | 38.9 | 38.6 |
| 54 | 205 | 46.5 | 54.9 |
| 75 | 208 | 71.3 | 81.7 |
| 89 | 220 | 235.4 | 36.6 |
| 27 | 1,054 | | 269.0 |
| 309 | | | |
| Mean: 51.5 | Mean: 210.8 | Mean: 58.9 | Mean: 53.8 |

**Quick Review** Students write each fraction as a percent.

$\frac{3}{4}$ 75% | $\frac{7}{10}$ 70% | $\frac{1}{4}$ 25% | $\frac{2}{50}$ 4% | $\frac{1}{20}$ 5% | $\frac{97}{100}$ 97%
$\frac{4}{5}$ 80% | $\frac{1}{5}$ 20% | $\frac{1}{10}$ 10% | $\frac{3}{5}$ 60%

**Lesson Focus** To find the median and mode for a set of data; to solve word problems involving all operations

## Ideas for Getting Started

Have students write their height in centimeters on an index card. Collect the cards, draw one at random, and tack it on the bulletin board. Continue to draw cards and to place them before, after, or above the first card, depending on whether the number is greater than, less than, or equal to the number on the first card. The result will look something like this:

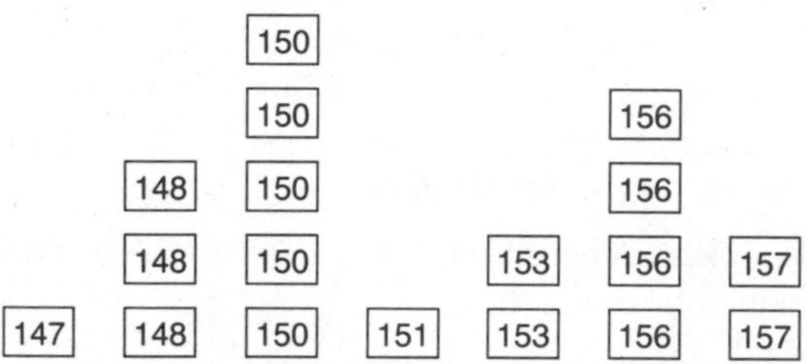


"Which height occurs most often?" (150) Tell students that they will learn a special name for this number. "Which height is right in the middle of all the heights?" Start removing simultaneously the cards with the highest and lowest heights. Then remove the next highest and lowest heights. Continue until only one height remains. (151) Tell students that the number on this card is the middle height and that the lesson will introduce a special name for it.

## Using Page 334

**Lesson Development** Have students read the first paragraph and the statements in the boxes. Call attention to the list of scores for the math test and invite a student to write the list on the chalkboard. "How many numbers are in the list?" (9) "What number has just as many numbers above it as below it?" (39) "What do we call the middle number in a list of numbers arranged in order?" (median) Call on a volunteer to write *median* on the chalkboard. "Which numbers appear more than once?" (46 and 38) "Which of these numbers appears more often?" (38) "What do we call the number that appears most often in the list?" (mode) Ask a student to write *mode* on the chalkboard.

**Other Examples** In the first example, stress that when there is an even amount of numbers, the median is the average of the two middle numbers. In the second example stress that since both 86 and 100 occur twice, there are two modes.

**Exercises 1–6** Note that exercises 2 and 6 have an even amount of numbers and that the median must be found by averaging the two middle numbers. For exercise 2 note that even though all the numbers are whole numbers, the median is a decimal. For exercise 5 note that all the numbers in the list are different, and so there is no mode.

## Median and Mode

The highest score a student could get on a particular math test was 50. The teacher placed the test scores on the chalkboard in order from highest to lowest. What is the **median** for the test scores? What is the **mode** for the test scores?

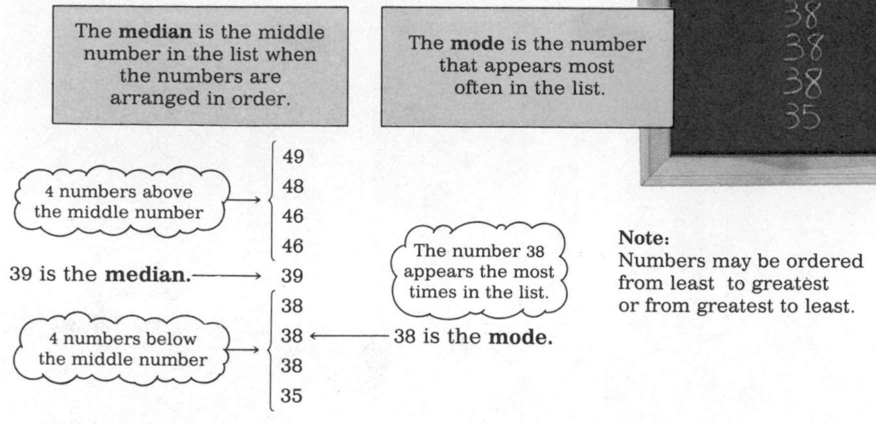

The **median** is the middle number in the list when the numbers are arranged in order.
The **mode** is the number that appears most often in the list.
49
48
46
46
39
38
38
38
35


4 numbers above the middle number

39 is the **median.**

4 numbers below the middle number

The number 38 appears the most times in the list.

38 is the **mode.**

49, 48, 46, 46, 39, 38, 38, 38, 35

**Note:** Numbers may be ordered from least to greatest or from greatest to least.

**Other Examples**

**25, 20, 20, 16, 14, 12**

Since there is no middle number, the median is the mean (or average) of 20 and 16.
(20 + 16) ÷ 2 = 18
**18** is the median.

**20** is the mode.

**86, 86, 90, 94, 110, 100, 100**

**94** is the median.

There are two modes.
**100** and **86** are the modes.

Arrange the numbers in order. Then find the median and the mode or modes.

**1.** 9, 8, 7, 6, 5, 8, 4, 2, 3 6; 8

**2.** 34, 38, 20, 35, 35, 19, 30, 36 34.5; 35

**3.** 46, 50, 29, 74, 46, 68, 50, 14 48; 50, 46

**4.** 58, 58, 70, 56, 54, 56, 59, 23 57; 56, 58

**5.** 9.9, 12.4, 10.8, 10.4, 7.4, 12.6, 7.5 10.4; no mode

**6.** 78, 110, 138, 50, 142, 130, 78, 61 94; 78



## Follow Up

### Reteaching

Remind students that median and mode are terms associated with sets of data. Help students find the median and the mode for the set of numbers below.

10, 12, 25, 10, 14, 16, 8

- To find the median, arrange numbers in order. The median is the middle number. If there is an even amount of numbers, add the two middle numbers and divide by 2 to find the median.
- To find the mode, look for the number that occurs most often in the list.

### Enrichment

Provide students with a set of data such as class test scores, sports events scores, and so on. Challenge students to use the given data to compute the median and the mode.

| Assignment Guide | | | |
|---|---|---|---|
| | Minimum | Average | Extended |
| page 334 | | 1–6 | 1–6 |
| page 335 | 1–5 | 1–8 | 1–9 |

## Problem Solving: Practice

Solve.

1. A perfect score on a certain science test is 280 points. There are 35 items on the test and each item is worth the same number of points. How many points is each test item worth? 8

2. A social studies test has 25 items. The first 24 items are worth 5 points each, and the last item is worth 20 points. If a student answers all items correctly, what will her score be? 140

Use the lists of Pat's spelling and science test scores for problems 3 through 8.

| Spelling test scores: 88, 75, 90, 62, 82, 95, 98 |
|---|
| Science test scores: 96, 90, 74, 70, 80, 86 |

3. How many points greater was Pat's highest spelling score than her lowest spelling score? 36 points

4. How much greater or less was Pat's mean score for spelling tests than her mean score for science tests? (Round each mean to the nearest tenth.) Mean for spelling tests was 1.6 points greater.

5. A mean score of 90 or more for her science tests would earn Pat an A in science. By how many points (to the nearest tenth) did Pat miss getting an A? 7.3 points

6. How much greater or less was Pat's median score for spelling tests than her median score for science tests? Median for spelling tests was 5 points greater.

7. Pat's score on her next spelling test was 98. What is the new median score for spelling tests? 89

8. If Pat's score on her next science test is 100, would her new mean score be high enough to earn her an A (a mean of 90 or more)? no

9. **Try This** Pat is having both a spelling and a science quiz today. She has a spelling quiz every 3 school days and a science quiz every 5 school days. How many school days will it be before she again has both quizzes on the same day? 15 days



## Using Page 335

**Lesson Development** Briefly review the 5-Point Checklist. Note that the problems on this page involve a variety of operations. Encourage students to read each problem carefully.

**Exercises 3–8** Note that students must refer to the list of scores for the data needed to solve these problems.

**Try This** A possible strategy, Make a Table, was introduced on page 100.

**Discussion** "What is the question we want to answer about Pat's spelling and science quizzes?" (In how many days will both be on the same day?) "How often does Pat have a spelling quiz?" (every 3 school days) "A science quiz?" (every 5 school days) "If Pat has a spelling quiz 3 days from now, when will she have another?" (6 days from now) "If Pat has a science quiz 5 days from now, when will she have another?" (10 days from now) Help students make a table to help answer the question.

**Solution** In 15 school days both quizzes will fall on the same day.

**Day**

| | 1 | 2 | 3 | 4 | 5 | 6 | 7 | 8 | 9 | 10 | 11 | 12 | 13 | 14 | 15 |
|---|---|---|---|---|---|---|---|---|---|---|---|---|---|---|---|
| **Spelling** | | | X | | | X | | | X | | | X | | | X |
| **Science** | | | | | X | | | | | X | | | | | X |

**Extension** Joe is having a math quiz and a social studies quiz today. He has a math quiz every 4 school days and a social studies quiz every 6 school days. How many school days will it be before Joe again has both quizzes on the same day? (12 days)

**Reteaching Supplement,** page 79

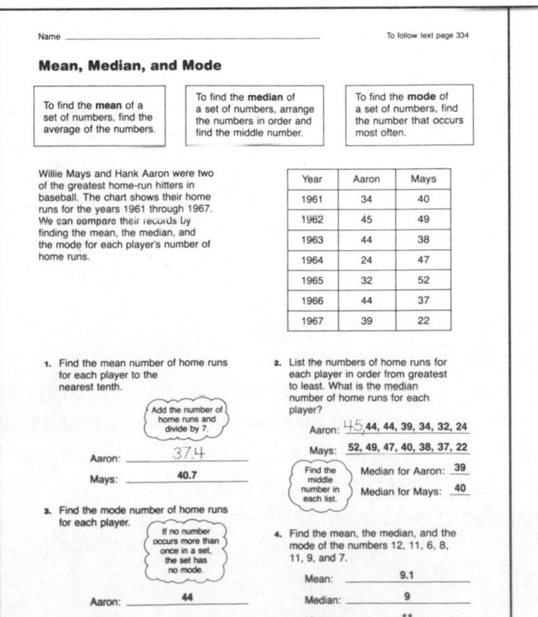

Name ________ To follow text page 334

### Mean, Median, and Mode

To find the **mean** of a set of numbers, find the average of the numbers.

To find the **median** of a set of numbers, arrange the numbers in order and find the middle number.

To find the **mode** of a set of numbers, find the number that occurs most often.

Willie Mays and Hank Aaron were two of the greatest home-run hitters in baseball. The chart shows their home runs for the years 1961 through 1967. We can compare their records by finding the mean, the median, and the mode for each player's number of home runs.

| Year | Aaron | Mays |
|---|---|---|
| 1961 | 34 | 40 |
| 1962 | 45 | 49 |
| 1963 | 44 | 38 |
| 1964 | 24 | 47 |
| 1965 | 32 | 52 |
| 1966 | 44 | 37 |
| 1967 | 39 | 22 |

1. Find the mean number of home runs for each player to the nearest tenth.
   (Add the number of home runs and divide by 7.)
   Aaron: 37.4
   Mays: 40.7

2. List the numbers of home runs for each player in order from greatest to least. What is the median number of home runs for each player?
   Aaron: 45, 44, 44, 39, 34, 32, 24
   Mays: 52, 49, 47, 40, 38, 37, 22
   (Find the middle number in each list.)
   Median for Aaron: 39
   Median for Mays: 40

3. Find the mode number of home runs for each player.
   (If no number occurs more than once in a set, the set has no mode.)
   Aaron: 44
   Mays: —

4. Find the mean, the median, and the mode of the numbers 12, 11, 6, 8, 11, 9, and 7.
   Mean: 9.1
   Median: 9
   Mode: 11

**Enrichment Supplement,** page 79

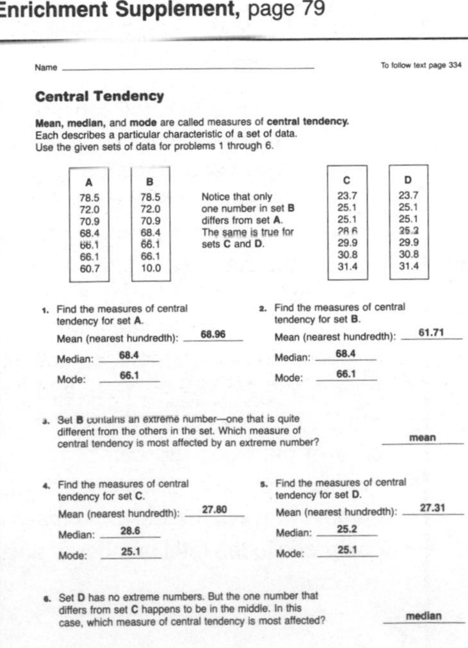

Name ________ To follow text page 334

### Central Tendency

**Mean, median,** and **mode** are called measures of **central tendency.** Each describes a particular characteristic of a set of data. Use the given sets of data for problems 1 through 6.

| A | B |
|---|---|
| 78.5 | 78.5 |
| 72.0 | 72.0 |
| 70.9 | 70.9 |
| 68.4 | 68.4 |
| 66.1 | 66.1 |
| 66.1 | 66.1 |
| 60.7 | 10.0 |

Notice that only one number in set **B** differs from set **A**. The same is true for sets **C** and **D**.

| C | D |
|---|---|
| 23.7 | 23.7 |
| 25.1 | 25.1 |
| 25.1 | 25.1 |
| 28.6 | 25.2 |
| 29.9 | 29.9 |
| 30.8 | 30.8 |
| 31.4 | 31.4 |

1. Find the measures of central tendency for set **A**.
   Mean (nearest hundredth): 68.96
   Median: 68.4
   Mode: 66.1

2. Find the measures of central tendency for set **B**.
   Mean (nearest hundredth): 61.71
   Median: 68.4
   Mode: 66.1

3. Set **B** contains an extreme number—one that is quite different from the others in the set. Which measure of central tendency is most affected by an extreme number? mean

4. Find the measures of central tendency for set **C**.
   Mean (nearest hundredth): 27.80
   Median: 28.6
   Mode: 25.1

5. Find the measures of central tendency for set **D**.
   Mean (nearest hundredth): 27.31
   Median: 25.2
   Mode: 25.1

6. Set **D** has no extreme numbers. But the one number that differs from set **C** happens to be in the middle. In this case, which measure of central tendency is most affected? median

**Practice Supplement,** page 127

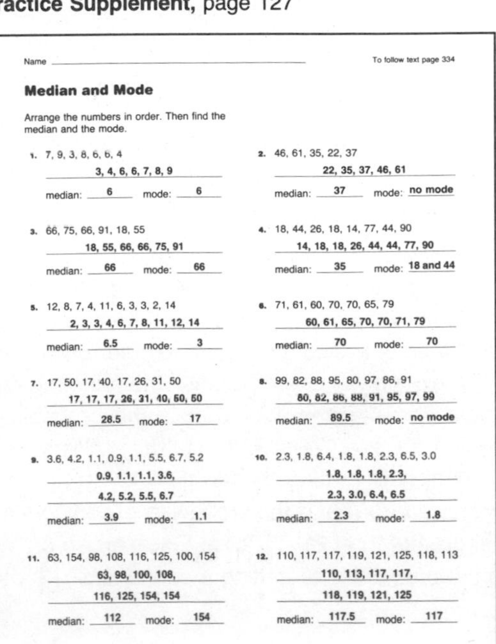

Name ________ To follow text page 334

### Median and Mode

Arrange the numbers in order. Then find the median and the mode.

1. 7, 9, 3, 8, 6, 6, 4
   3, 4, 6, 6, 7, 8, 9
   median: 6 mode: 6

2. 46, 61, 35, 22, 37
   22, 35, 37, 46, 61
   median: 37 mode: no mode

3. 66, 75, 66, 91, 18, 55
   18, 55, 66, 66, 75, 91
   median: 66 mode: 66

4. 18, 44, 26, 18, 14, 77, 44, 90
   14, 18, 18, 26, 44, 44, 77, 90
   median: 35 mode: 18 and 44

5. 12, 8, 7, 4, 11, 6, 3, 3, 2, 14
   2, 3, 3, 4, 6, 7, 8, 11, 12, 14
   median: 6.5 mode: 3

6. 71, 61, 60, 70, 70, 65, 79
   60, 61, 65, 70, 70, 71, 79
   median: 70 mode: 70

7. 17, 50, 17, 40, 17, 26, 31, 50
   17, 17, 17, 26, 31, 40, 50, 50
   median: 28.5 mode: 17

8. 99, 82, 88, 95, 80, 97, 86, 91
   80, 82, 86, 88, 91, 95, 97, 99
   median: 89.5 mode: no mode

9. 3.6, 4.2, 1.1, 0.9, 1.1, 5.5, 6.7, 5.2
   0.9, 1.1, 1.1, 3.6,
   4.2, 5.2, 5.5, 6.7
   median: 3.9 mode: 1.1

10. 2.3, 1.8, 6.4, 1.8, 1.8, 2.3, 6.5, 3.0
    1.8, 1.8, 1.8, 2.3,
    2.3, 3.0, 6.4, 6.5
    median: 2.3 mode: 1.8

11. 63, 154, 98, 108, 116, 125, 100, 154
    63, 98, 100, 108,
    116, 125, 154, 154
    median: 112 mode: 154

12. 110, 117, 117, 119, 121, 125, 118, 113
    110, 113, 117, 117,
    118, 119, 121, 125
    median: 117.5 mode: 117

# Probability

**Quick Review** Students write the number that makes each expression an equivalent fraction.

$\frac{\boxed{4}}{8} = \frac{1}{2}$ $\frac{3}{\boxed{9}} = \frac{1}{3}$ $\frac{1}{10} = \frac{10}{\boxed{100}}$ $\frac{10}{50} = \frac{100}{\boxed{500}}$ $\frac{3}{4} = \frac{\boxed{27}}{36}$ $\frac{8}{10} = \frac{\boxed{64}}{80}$

**Lesson Focus** To predict the probability of a given event

**Suggested Materials** Coins

## Ideas for Getting Started

Tell the class that you are going to toss a penny. "What are the possible outcomes? How many different ways can the coin land?" (2; heads or tails) "Are the outcomes equally likely? That is, are the chances as good for getting heads as for getting tails?" (yes)

On the chalkboard draw a target like the one shown below.

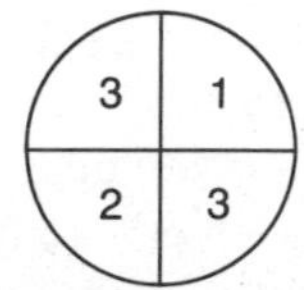

3
1
2
3

"If you toss a dart at the target, what are the possible outcomes?" (You could hit 1, 2, or 3.) "Are the outcomes equally likely?" Lead students to see that hitting 3 is most likely because there are 2 chances in 4 of hitting 3. There is only 1 chance in 4 of hitting either 1 or 2.

"Suppose you have 6 marbles in a bag; 4 are blue and 2 are red. If you draw a marble from the bag, what are the possible outcomes?" (You would get either a red marble or a blue one.) "Are the outcomes equally likely?" (No; there are 4 chances in 6 that you will draw a blue.)

## Using Page 336

**Lesson Development** Have students read the first paragraph and examine the spinner. "How many numbers are on the spinner?" (5) "How many of those numbers are odd numbers?" (3—1, 3, 5) Read aloud the statements in the three boxes. Explain how we arrive at the fractional number by comparing the number of odd-number outcomes to the total number of outcomes. Since there are 3 odd numbers and a total of 5 numbers altogether, the probability of getting an odd number is $\frac{3}{5}$.

Discuss examples A, B, and C with the class. For example, ask: "How many of the 5 outcomes are numbers less than 3?" (2) "How many outcomes altogether?" (5) "What is the probability of getting a number less than 3?" $\left(\frac{2}{5}\right)$

**Exercises 1–3** Call attention to the exercises and have the experiment read aloud. Be sure that students understand each experiment and how to read across to find the information for each one.

To extend the exercises, ask the following questions: For exercise 1, "What is the probability of getting an even number?" $\left(\frac{2}{4}, \text{ or } \frac{1}{2}\right)$ "What is the probability of getting an odd number? $\left(\frac{2}{4}, \text{ or } \frac{1}{2}\right)$ For exercise 2, "What is the probability of getting a number greater than 2?" $\left(\frac{4}{6}, \text{ or } \frac{2}{3}\right)$ For exercise 3, "What is the probability of getting a consonant? $\left(\frac{4}{6}, \text{ or } \frac{2}{3}\right)$

### Probability

The new board game Hector bought has a spinner like the one shown here. What is the **probability** of getting an odd number with one spin of the pointer?

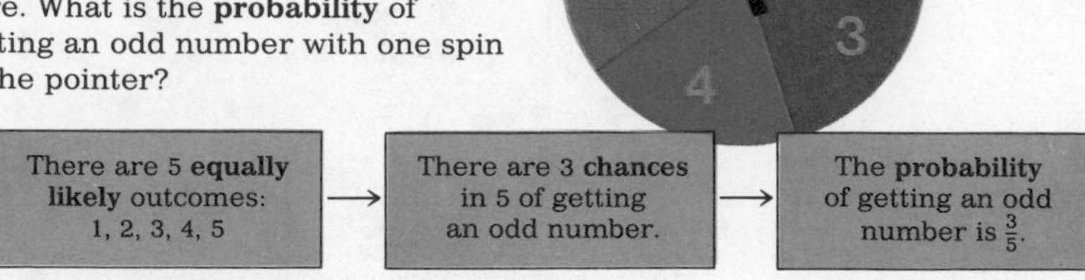

There are 5 **equally likely** outcomes: 1, 2, 3, 4, 5
There are 3 **chances** in 5 of getting an odd number.
The **probability** of getting an odd number is $\frac{3}{5}$.

Here are some other examples for the spinner.

A. There are 2 chances in 5 of getting an even number. → The probability of getting an even number is $\frac{2}{5}$.

B. There are 5 chances in 5 of getting a number less than 6. → The probability of getting a number less than 6 is $\frac{5}{5}$ or 1.

C. There are 0 chances in 5 of getting a number greater than 5. → The probability of getting a number greater than 5 is $\frac{0}{5}$ or 0.

Each outcome is equally likely in the following experiments. Give the missing information in each row.

| Experiment | Outcomes | Chances | Probability |
|---|---|---|---|
| **1.** Draw a card without looking. | 1 2 3 4 | There is 1 chance in ■ of getting a 3. 4 | The probability of getting a 3 is ■. $\frac{1}{4}$ |
| **2.** Toss a cube with sides numbered 1–6. | 1 2 3 4 5 6 | There are ■ chances in 6 of getting an odd number. 3 | The probability of getting an odd number is ■. $\frac{3}{6}$ or $\frac{1}{2}$ |
| **3.** Toss a cube that has one of the letters A, B, C, D, E, F on each face. | A B C D E F | There are 2 chances in ■ of getting a vowel (A or E). 6 | The probability of getting a vowel is ■. $\frac{2}{6}$ or $\frac{1}{3}$ |

## Follow Up

### Reteaching

While students watch, place a red, a blue, a white, and a green chip into a cup. Shake the cup and pull out a chip at random. Have students note the color. Replace the chip and repeat the procedure. After a few trials, ask: "How many chips are in the cup?" (4) "If I pull out 1 chip, what are the chances that it will be red?" $\left(\frac{1}{4}\right)$ Write this statement on the chalkboard: $\frac{\text{number of red chips}}{\text{number of chips}}$. Then add 2 more red chips to the cup. "What is the probability of getting a red chip?" $\left(\frac{3}{6}\right)$ Stress that the probability of an outcome is the number of ways the outcome may occur compared to the total number of possible outcomes.

### Enrichment

Have students make a spinner like the one below using a paper plate, paper clip, and fastener.

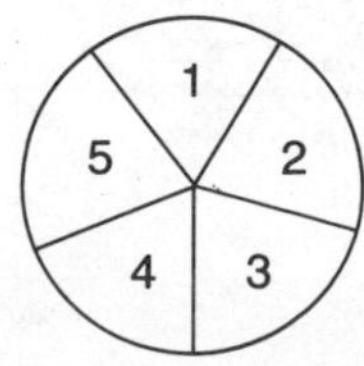

1
5
2
4
3

Students work in pairs, spinning the spinner 20 or 30 times to see if the probability of getting an odd or an even number is the same as the outcome predicted in the lesson on this page.

| Assignment Guide | | | |
|---|---|---|---|
| | Minimum | Average | Extended |
| page 336 | 1–3 | 1–3 | 1–3 |
| page 337 | 1–7, SK | 1–11, SK | 1–11, SK |

Suppose you draw one of these cards without looking.

1. What are the possible outcomes? 3, 6, 2, 8, 10
2. Are the outcomes equally likely? yes
3. What is the probability of getting an odd number? $\frac{1}{5}$
4. What is the probability of getting a red card? $\frac{4}{5}$

Suppose you draw a marble without looking.

5. What are the possible outcomes? green, yellow
6. Do you have a better chance of getting a green marble or a yellow marble? green
7. What is the probability of getting a green marble? $\frac{10}{12}$ or $\frac{5}{6}$

Suppose you spin the pointer.

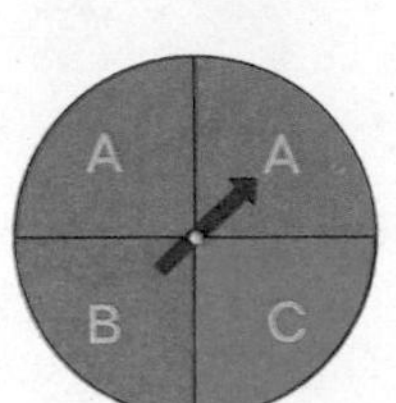


8. Which letter do you think you would get most often in 12 spins? A
9. Which color do you think you would get most often in 12 spins? about the same number of each
10. What is the probability that you will get an A? $\frac{2}{4}$ or $\frac{1}{2}$
11. What is the probability that the pointer will stop on a red space? $\frac{1}{4}$

## Skillkeeper

Find the percent of each number.

1. 20% of 20 4
2. 5% of 40 2
3. 15% of 300 45
4. 75% of 160 120
5. 30% of 50 15
6. 2% of 30 0.6
7. 150% of 72 108
8. 29% of 200 58

Find the products.

9. $3.6 \times 2.4 = 8.64$
10. $8.7 \times 6.3 = 54.81$
11. $5.15 \times 8.4 = 43.260$
12. $4.8 \times 0.25 = 1.200$
13. $4.12 \times 3.20 = 13.1840$



## Using Page 337

**Exercises 1–4** Suggest that students examine the illustration and read questions 1–4 before writing any answers. Point out that in item 3, students are to write a fraction to compare the number of outcomes involving an odd number with the total number of outcomes.

**Exercises 5–7** Call attention to the illustration. "How many green marbles are in the box?" (10) "How many yellow marbles are in the box?" (2)

**Exercises 8–11** Be sure that students examine the spinner and count the number of its sections. When discussing the answers, stress the meaning of probability. Follow up by asking students to suggest other probability questions for each illustration.

**Skillkeeper** This skill was taught in Chapter 12.

**Reteaching Supplement,** page 80

Name ______ To follow text page 337

### Probability

Suppose you draw one card from the hat without looking.

1. There is 1 **chance** in 5 of drawing an *A*. What is the **probability** of drawing an *A*? $\frac{1}{5}$

(5 equally likely outcomes. 1 outcome is an *A*.)

2. The chance of drawing a *C* is 1 in 5 What is the probability of drawing a *C*? $\frac{1}{5}$
3. The chance of drawing an *E* is 1 in 5. What is the probability of drawing an *E*? $\frac{1}{5}$

Suppose you draw one marble from the box without looking.

(6 equally likely outcomes.)

4. There are 4 **chances** in 6 of drawing a striped marble. What is the **probability** of drawing a striped marble? $\frac{4}{6}$ or $\frac{2}{3}$
5. There are 2 chances in 6 of drawing a white marble. What is the probability of drawing a white marble? $\frac{2}{6}$ or $\frac{1}{3}$
6. The chance of drawing a black marble is 0 in 6. What is the probability of drawing a black marble? $\frac{0}{6}$

Suppose you spin the pointer.

7. What is the probability of the arrow stopping on *A*? $\frac{1}{4}$
8. What is the probability of the arrow stopping on *B*? $\frac{2}{4}$ or $\frac{1}{2}$
9. What is the probability of the arrow stopping on *C*? $\frac{1}{4}$

**Enrichment Supplement,** page 80

Name ______ To follow text page 337

### Probability with Number Cubes

1. Suppose you have two number cubes. One is white, the other gray. There are 36 different possible outcomes when the two number cubes are tossed. Show these outcomes on the cube faces below.
2. How many outcomes above have a total of 8 dots on the two faces? 5
   The chances of getting 8 are 5 in 36.
   The probability of getting 8 is $\frac{5}{36}$
3. How many outcomes above result in a sum of 7? 6
   The chances of getting 7 are 6 in 36.
   The probability of getting 7 is $\frac{1}{6}$
   In 60 tosses of the two cubes, about how many 7s would you expect to get? 10
4. How many outcomes have a sum of 12? 1
   The probability of getting 12 is $\frac{1}{36}$
5. Which sum should occur more often—5 or 10? 5
6. How many outcomes result in "doubles" (both cubes having the same number of dots)? 6
   What is the probability of getting 6? $\frac{1}{36}$
7. Suppose two cubes are tossed 1,000 times. Predict the number of times the given sum (outcome) would occur in the 1,000 tosses. Round to the nearest whole number.
   2 28, 3 56, 4 83, 5 111, 6 139, 7 167, 8 139, 9 111, 10 83, 11 56, 12 28

**Practice Supplement,** page 128

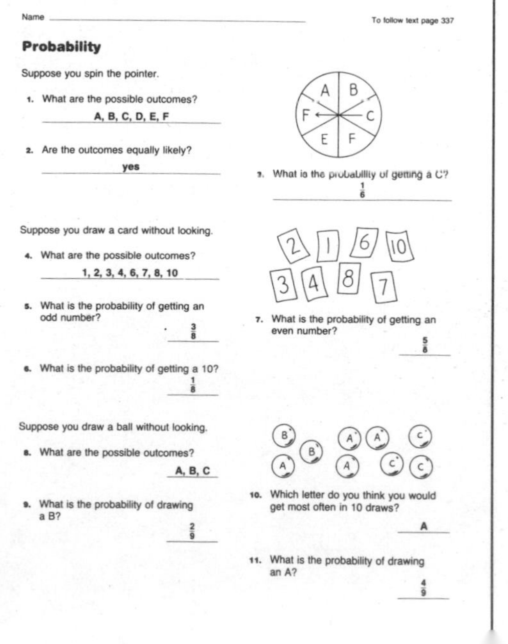

Name ______ To follow text page 337

### Probability

Suppose you spin the pointer.

1. What are the possible outcomes? A, B, C, D, E, F
2. Are the outcomes equally likely? yes
3. What is the probability of getting a C? $\frac{1}{6}$

Suppose you draw a card without looking.

4. What are the possible outcomes? 1, 2, 3, 4, 6, 7, 8, 10
5. What is the probability of getting an odd number? $\frac{3}{8}$
6. What is the probability of getting a 10? $\frac{1}{8}$
7. What is the probability of getting an even number? $\frac{5}{8}$

Suppose you draw a ball without looking.

8. What are the possible outcomes? A, B, C
9. What is the probability of drawing a B? $\frac{2}{9}$
10. Which letter do you think you would get most often in 10 draws? A
11. What is the probability of drawing an A? $\frac{4}{9}$

# Probability

**Quick Review** Students give answers to these problems in lowest terms.

$1 - \frac{6}{7} = \frac{1}{7}$ $\quad \frac{5}{8} + \frac{5}{8} = 1\frac{1}{4}$ $\quad \frac{9}{11} - \frac{5}{11} = \frac{4}{11}$ $\quad \frac{3}{10} - \frac{1}{5} = \frac{1}{10}$ $\quad 1\frac{1}{3} + \frac{2}{3} = 2$

$1\frac{3}{7} - \frac{4}{7} = \frac{6}{7}$ $\quad \frac{4}{5} + \frac{3}{5} = 1\frac{2}{5}$ $\quad \frac{7}{16} + \frac{9}{16} = 1$ $\quad 2 - \frac{1}{2} = 1\frac{1}{2}$ $\quad 1\frac{5}{8} + \frac{1}{4} = 1\frac{7}{8}$

**Lesson Focus** To find the probability and make a prediction about a given event; to use probability to identify possible outcomes

**Suggested Materials** 100 tongue depressors or similar items, colored pens

## Ideas for Getting Started

In a sack put 60 tongue depressors marked with a red dot, 30 marked with a blue dot, and 10 with a yellow dot. Tell the class that in the sack there are 100 sticks marked in red, blue, and yellow. Explain that there is a way to predict which color is on the greatest number of sticks without counting all 100 sticks. "We can take a sample of sticks from the sack and make a prediction based on the number of different colored sticks in the sample." Have students draw 20 sticks from the sack and count the different colored dots on the sticks. "Which color is on more sticks?"

## Using Page 338

**Motivational Problem** Ask students to read the first paragraph at the top of the page and to restate the question in their own words. "What data can be used to help answer this question?" (Kermit made 40 of 60 free throws during the season.) Tell students that they can use this data to predict whether Kermit will make the free throw.

**Lesson Development** Work through the solution to this problem on the chalkboard. "How many shots has Kermit made?" (40) "What is the total number of shots he has taken?" (60) "What is the probability of making the shot?" $\left(\frac{40}{60} \text{ or } \frac{2}{3}\right)$ Be sure students understand that the probability of making the shot plus the probability of missing it is equal to 1. That is, the probability of each of the outcomes together should equal 1. In this case the probability of missing the shot is $\frac{1}{3}$. Since the probability of making the shot is greater, we can predict that Kermit is more likely to make the shot than to miss it.

**Exercises 1–4** In exercise 2 be sure students understand that when a probability is given as a percent, they can write it as a fraction. Note in exercise 3 that when the probability is $\frac{1}{2}$, we cannot make a reasonable prediction. Be sure to emphasize that these exercises are only predictions. For example, in exercise 4 it is possible that Arnold could win the bicycle; however, it is reasonable to predict that he will not win.

## Probability and Prediction

Kermit Thompson has one free throw to shoot with the score tied and 1 second remaining in the game. This season Kermit has taken 60 free throws and has made 40 of them. What is the probability he will make the free throw?

Make a prediction. Is he more likely to make the shot or miss it?

**Probability**

$\frac{\text{shots made} \rightarrow 40}{\text{shots taken} \rightarrow 60} = \frac{2}{3}$

The probability of making the shot is $\frac{2}{3}$.

**Prediction**

The probability of making the shot is $\frac{2}{3}$.

The probability of missing it is $1 - \frac{2}{3}$ or $\frac{1}{3}$.

$\frac{2}{3} > \frac{1}{3}$

He is more likely to make the shot than to miss it.

Find the probability and make a prediction.

1. Hollie Wilson has taken 80 free throws this season and has made 50 of them. What is the probability that she will make her next free throw? Is she more likely to make it or miss it? $\frac{5}{8}$; make
2. According to the weather report, the chance of rain for the first World Series game is 70% (or 7 out of 10). What is the probability of rain? Do you think it is more likely to rain or not to rain? $\frac{7}{10}$; to rain
3. A baseball team has won 12 out of 24 games so far. What is the probability it will win its next game? Is the team more likely to win or to lose the next game? $\frac{1}{2}$; cannot predict
4. There were 50 tickets sold for a drawing for a free bicycle at a local sports store. Arnold bought 5 tickets. What is the probability he will win the bicycle? Is he more likely to win the bicycle or not win it? $\frac{1}{10}$; not win

## Follow Up

### Reteaching

Tell students that predictions can be made by studying data acquired over a period of time and determining a probability. Work through the example below with students.

Over the past year, there were 3,000 persons who tried to throw the hoop over the milk bottle at Cindy's ring toss booth at the circus. Of that number only 50 were successful. What is the probability that the next person will be successful?

probability of success $= \frac{50}{3{,}000} = \frac{5}{300} = \frac{1}{60}$

**We can predict that 1 out of 60 persons will make a successful toss.**

### Enrichment

Have students choose 50 telephone numbers at random from the telephone book and make a tally of the frequency with which the last digit of a number is the same as the first digit. Students then determine the probability that a given telephone number will have the same first and last digits. Have students check another 50 numbers and compare the outcome with their first predictions.

| Assignment Guide | | | |
|---|---|---|---|
| | Minimum | Average | Extended |
| page 338 | | 1–3 | 1–4 |
| page 339 | | 1–4 | 1–6 |

## Probability and Expected Numbers

Luella is helping the PTA raise money for new playground equipment. She plans to telephone 40 people and ask for donations. The probability of getting a donation on one telephone call is $\frac{1}{5}$. How many donations might she expect to get?

Since the probability of getting a donation on one phone call is $\frac{1}{5}$, we multiply to find the number of donations we might expect from 40 calls.

$$\frac{1}{5} \times 40 = \frac{1}{\not{5}_1} \times \frac{\not{40}^{8}}{1} = \frac{8}{1} = 8$$

Check $\frac{8}{40} = \frac{1}{5}$

Luella might expect to get 8 donations out of 40 phone calls.

Find the expected results.

1. Carlos is trying to get donations for playground equipment by making house-to-house visits. The probability of getting a donation this way is $\frac{2}{5}$. How many donations might Carlos expect if he talks with 40 people? 16

2. Based on last year's record, the probability of Brainard School's winning any one basketball game is $\frac{1}{3}$. How many games might Brainard expect to win this year out of 24 games? 8

3. Past experience shows that $\frac{3}{4}$ of Ella's customers for weekday newspapers also take the Sunday paper. Ella hopes to get 28 new customers this month. How many of the new customers might she expect to take the Sunday paper? 21

4. The records of Locosta's Market show that the probability that at least one egg will be broken in each carton they receive is $\frac{3}{20}$. If they receive a shipment of 160 cartons, how many of the cartons might they expect to contain broken eggs? 24

5. The probability of rain on any given day in September in Bay City is $\frac{1}{5}$. How many rainy days might Bay City expect in September? (Remember, September has 30 days.) 6 days

6. A farmer knows that 1 out of every 20 tomato plants will not live to produce tomatoes. This year the farmer planted 200 tomato plants. How many plants might the farmer expect to live to produce tomatoes? 190



## Using Page 339

**Lesson Development** Ask students to read the problem and to identify the question and the data. Point out that because the probability is $\frac{1}{5}$, we can expect 1 out of every 5 people to give a donation.

Read the second paragraph with the class. "How do we find $\frac{1}{5}$ of 40?" (We can multiply.) Work the problem on the chalkboard. "What does the answer 8 tell us?" (Luella might get 8 donations out of 40 calls.) Have students reread the problem to see whether the answer makes sense. Emphasize the usefulness of knowing how to use probability to make a prediction about a given situation.

**Exercises 1–6** Read through these problems with students as necessary. Point out in exercise 1 that the probability of $\frac{2}{5}$ means that $\frac{2}{5}$ of the people contacted could be expected to donate. Exercise 6 requires two steps. Students can use the information to arrive at the probability that $\frac{1}{20}$ of the plants will die. Students then must subtract to find how many plants will live.

## Ideas That Work

### Special Education

To illustrate the idea of mean (average), provide students with this measurement activity. Each of the measurements can be represented by a strip of colored paper a given number of centimeters long. After the strips of paper are labeled with the appropriate measurement, they are taped end to end. If there are six measures, for example, the strip should be folded into six equal lengths as shown. Then a separate strip of paper the length of the folded strip can be cut out to represent the average length of the six strips that were taped together. The original six pieces of paper can then be cut apart and mounted on a graph along with the piece that represents the mean (average) length. The accuracy of this experiment can be checked by adding and dividing to find the average.

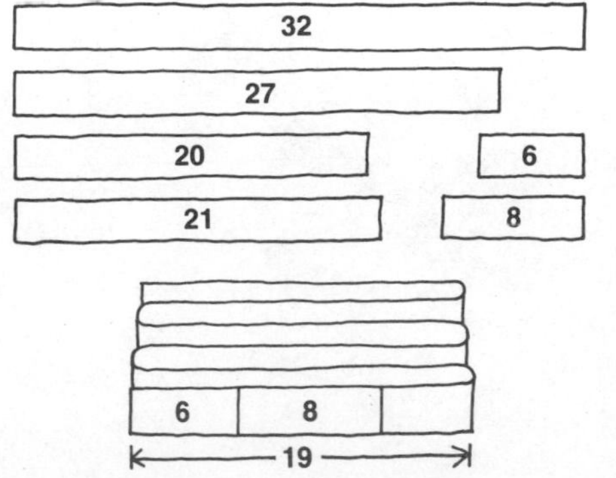


**Practice Supplement,** page 129

Name ____________ To follow text page 339

**Probability, Prediction, and Expected Numbers**

Find the probability and make a prediction.

1. Bob Temple has been at bat 40 times this season. He has made 8 hits. What is the probability that he will get a hit next time at bat? Is he more likely to get a hit or not get a hit? **$\frac{1}{5}$, not hit**

2. A soccer team has won 16 out of 20 games so far. What is the probability it will win its next game? Is the team more likely to win or lose the next game? **$\frac{4}{5}$, win**

3. 80 people attended the grand opening of a restaurant. There were 20 door prizes. What was the probability of winning a door prize? Were you more likely to win a prize or not win a prize? **$\frac{1}{4}$, not win**

4. 120 tickets were sold for a drawing for a television. Ms. Louis bought 2 tickets. What is the probability she will win the television? Is she more likely to win the television or not win? **$\frac{1}{60}$, not win**

Find the expected results.

5. Wendy Summer has been making 2 out of every 3 free throws in basketball. How many free throws might she expect to make out of 18 shots? **12**

6. The probability of snow on any given day in November in Wellsville is $\frac{1}{6}$. How many snowy days might Wellsville expect in November? (November has 30 days.) **5**

7. John Parks has won $\frac{1}{6}$ of the races he has run this year. If he runs in 12 races, how many might he expect to win? **2**

8. 1 out of every 3 people who come into Mr. Field's store buy something. If Mr. Field has 54 customers how many sales might he expect to make? **18**

**Lesson Focus** To interpret, organize, and use data to make a decision about a real-world problem

## Ideas for Getting Started

Briefly discuss any experiences students might have had playing or watching the game of golf. Share any information available on local golf courses and costs associated with playing on the courses. Remind students that we can apply problem-solving skills in making decisions about recreation as well as about jobs or other real-world situations.

## Using Page 340

**Lesson Development** Read through and discuss the problem at the top of the page. Be sure students understand the decision they are asked to make and the three options suggested. Remind students that they should take some time to think about and organize the data in order to make the decision.

Then have students work independently or in small groups. Note that the questions suggest things students might need to know in order to make the decision. They might, however, decide to find the answers to more questions before making their decision.

After students have completed the problem, provide ample time for discussion and for students to justify their decisions. As with other applied problems, there can be more than one reasonable decision possible. Note that questions 4 and 5 suggest that if there are between 6 games and 28 games played, the permit will be cheaper than either the regular fee or the season pass. Following are other considerations that students might want to make:

- A season pass is more convenient, and there is no need to worry about how many additional games you might want to play.
- One important consideration is the number of times the individuals will be able to play. Since this is not known, students will have to make some assumptions about the situation in order to arrive at their decision.

## Applied Problem Solving

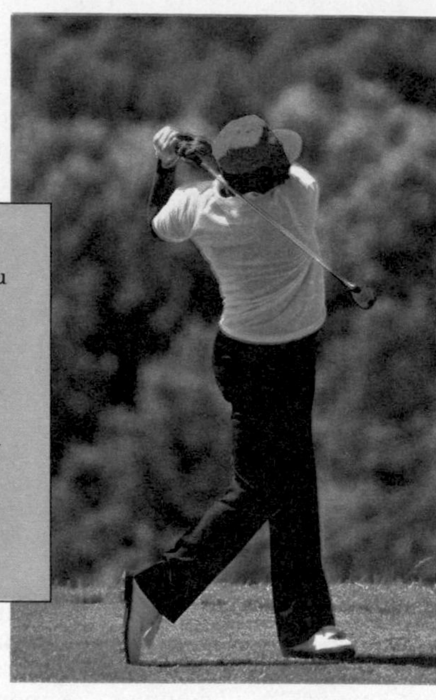

You want to play golf on a city course near you during the summer season. You must decide whether to pay regular fees, buy a permit, or buy a season pass.

**Some Things to Consider**

- You do not know for sure how many times you will play. You would like to play an average of once a week at least, possibly twice a week.
- You will be away on vacation 1 week.
- The regular fee is $6 per game.
- A permit costs $20 in advance. Every time you play, you pay an additional $2.50.
- A season pass costs $90 per season. You can then play anytime, with no other cost.
- Your summer season is 13 weeks long.

**Some Questions to Answer**

1. What would it cost to play an average of once a week during your summer season and pay regular fees? $72
2. What would it cost to play an average of twice a week and pay regular fees? $144
3. What would it cost to play an average of once a week with a permit? Twice a week? $50; $80
4. How many games could you play with a permit for a total cost equal to the cost of a season pass? 28
5. How many games can you play before paying regular fees costs more than the total cost with a permit? 6 games

**What Is Your Decision?**

Will you pay regular fees, buy a permit, or buy a season pass? Answers will vary.

## Chapter Review-Test

Use the bar graph for questions 1–3.

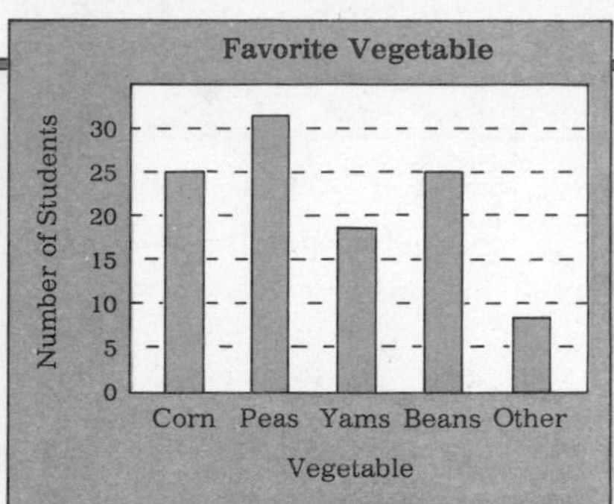


1. Which vegetable was selected by the most students? peas
2. About how many people picked yams? 18
3. Which two foods were picked by the same number of students? corn; beans

Use the circle graph for questions 4–6.

Favorite Music of 60 People

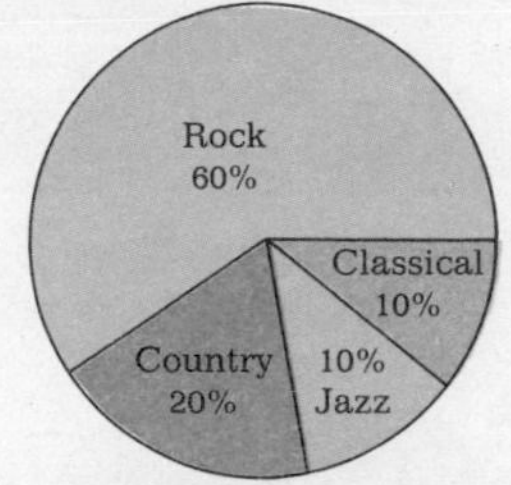


4. What is the sum of the percents? 100
5. How many people picked rock? 36
6. How many more people picked country music than picked jazz music? 6

Use these test scores for questions 7–9.

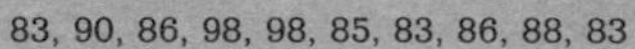


7. What is the mean of the scores? 88
8. What is the mode of the scores? 83
9. What is the median of the scores? 86

Use the cards for questions 10–12.

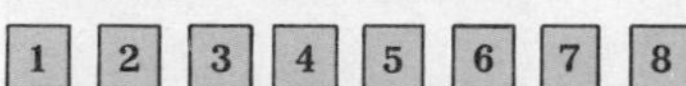


10. What is the probability of getting a 3 on one draw? $\frac{1}{8}$
11. What is the probability of getting an even number? $\frac{4}{8}$ or $\frac{1}{2}$
12. Suppose the cards were in a hat and you drew one card. If you did this 40 times, how many times might you expect to get a 5? 5
13. The first five days of the week had these amounts of rain:
    3 cm, 2 cm, 1 cm, 3 cm, 1 cm
    What was the mean amount of rain per day? 2 cm
14. Jodie made these scores on her first six health tests:
    68, 76, 87, 74, 96, 82
    What was Jodie's median score? 79



## Using Page 341

The exercises in the Chapter Review-Test emphasize the major concepts and skills presented in this chapter. These exercises may be used as a review assignment or as a test, depending upon your needs.

**Item Analysis** The table below correlates the Chapter Review-Test items with objectives and with the student text pages on which the concepts or skills were taught. Note that items 8, 9, and 14 are derived from a lesson for which no minimum assignment was suggested in the Assignment Guide. Only those students who were assigned this lesson should be expected to complete the corresponding Chapter Review-Test items.

| Items | Objectives | Related Text Pages |
|---|---|---|
| 1–6 | 13.1 | 322–331 |
| 7–9 | 13.2 | 332, 334 |
| 10–12 | 13.3 | 336–339 |
| 13–14 | 13.4 | 333, 335 |

## Assessment Options

If you use the Chapter Review-Test as a review assignment, you may wish to use the multiple-choice test or the free-response test to evaluate mastery of the chapter objects. The items on these tests have a one-to-one correspondence in terms of content and level of difficulty. A correlation of test items to objectives and student text pages is provided in the Management Guide for Chapter 13. Note: Items 18–19 and 22 are derived from a lesson for which no minimum assignment was suggested in the Assignment Guide.

**Multiple-Choice Test,** TRB pages 37–39

**Free-Response Test,** TRB pages 73–74

## TRB Options

The following blackline masters are available for use with this chapter. If you have not already assigned these materials, you may wish to use them to close the chapter.

**Recreation,** TRB page 163

**Consumer Applications,** TRB page 181

**Calculator Technology,** TRB page 199

**Reading Math,** TRB page 231

**Family Involvement,** TRB pages 261–262

## Using Page 342

The exercises on this page are intended for those students who experienced difficulty with the Chapter Review-Test on page 341. Should students require reteaching of these key concepts and skills, please refer to the teaching notes below. Otherwise, the Another Look exercises can be assigned as independent work, with students using the accompanying sample problems and hints as guides.

**Exercises 1–4** This skill was originally taught on pages 322–323 and 330–331. Review the parts of the bar graph—title, labels, number scale. Help students use the information in the think clouds to answer the questions.

**Exercises 5–8** This skill was originally taught on pages 326–327. Call attention to the title and labels of the circle graph. Review that the percents shown in the graph should equal 100%. Discuss how to find 30% of 10 hours in order to determine the number of hours spent reading.

**Exercises 9–11** This skill was originally taught on page 332. Call attention to the list of numbers in the display box. Review the steps for finding the mean of a set of numbers: Add the numbers and divide by the number of addends. Remind students that the *mean* is a representative number for the set of numbers listed.

## *Another Look*

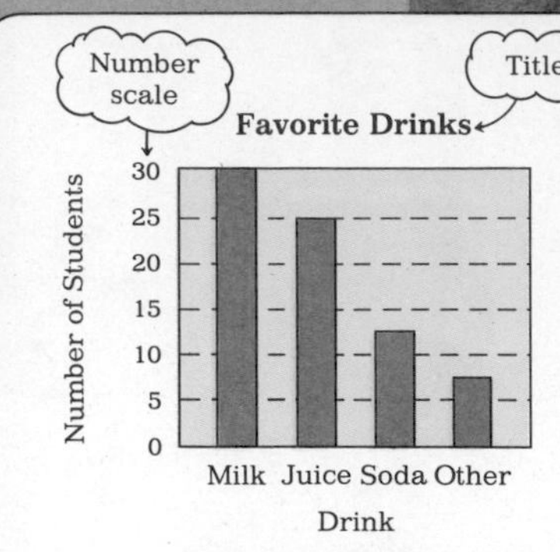


**Answer these questions about the bar graph.**

1. Which drink was selected by the most students? milk
2. About how many students picked soda? 12
3. How many more students picked milk than picked juice? 5
4. How many students does the space from one horizontal line to the next stand for? 5

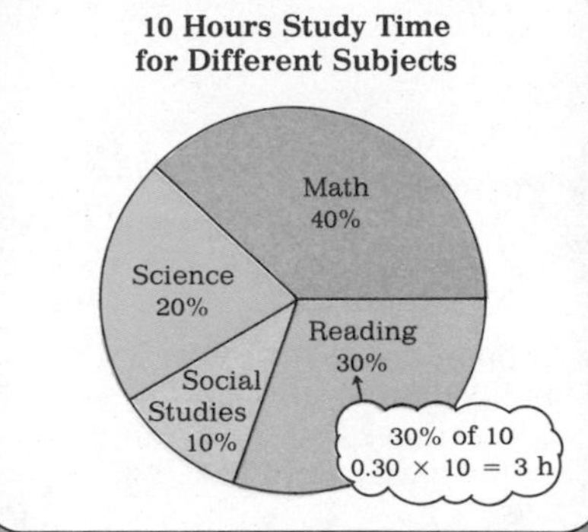


**Answer these questions about the circle graph.**

5. What was the total number of hours spent studying? 10 h
6. What is the sum of the percents? 100
7. How many hours were spent studying math? 4 h
8. How many hours were spent studying science? 2 h

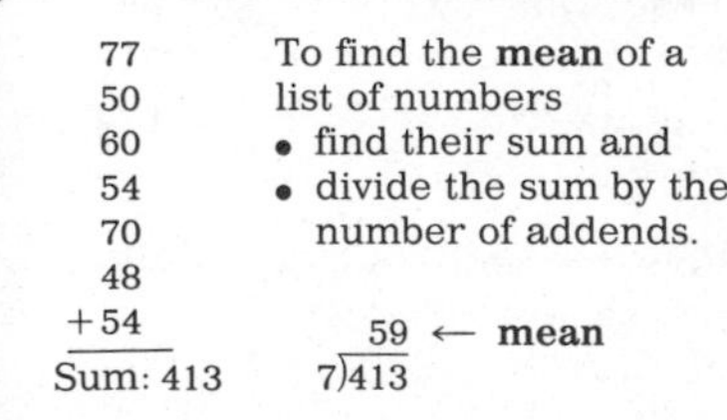


**Find the mean of each list of numbers. Round to the nearest tenth when necessary.**

9. 17, 14, 24, 19, 16 18
10. 48, 39, 42, 51, 63, 44 47.8
11. 129, 116, 133, 120, 106 120.8



## Just for Teachers

### Social Contribution to Mathematics

Card games became popular among the European aristocracy during the fourteenth century. Apparently brought to Europe from China, playing cards were at that time printed by another Chinese invention, block printing. A French nobleman, the Chevalier de Mere, anxious to minimize his gambling losses, approached a French philosopher, Blaise Pascal, with a problem. Was there any way to evaluate scientifically the possible results of chance events?

In correspondence with the jurist Pierre de Fermat, Pascal began to formulate what would become the mathematics of probability. Though their mutual work began on a less than profound problem, it resulted nonetheless in a significant new branch of mathematics.

Another type of European gambler who benefitted almost immediately from the principles articulated by Pascal and Fermat was the underwriter of major oceanic voyages of trade and discovery. Originally just a financial backer, the underwriter became an insurer, and was more interested in variables and risks.

## Enrichment

### Motion Geometry: Translations

Rectangle 2 is called a **slide image** or **translation image** of rectangle 1. Each point of the rectangle was moved **right 4, up 3.**

Copy each figure on graph paper. Make the moves as directed to draw a translation image of each figure.

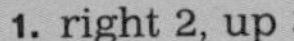

1. right 2, up 3

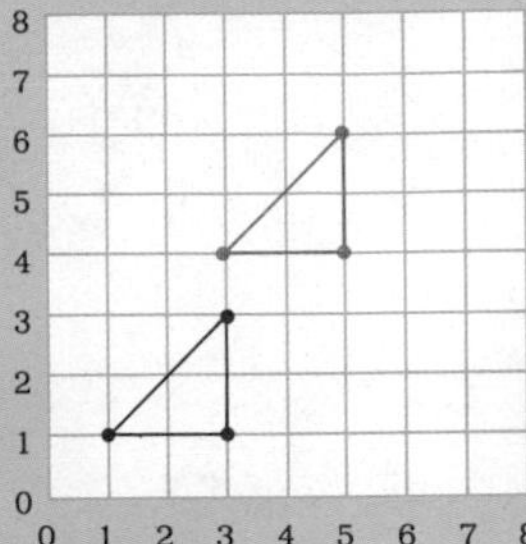

2. left 2, up 3

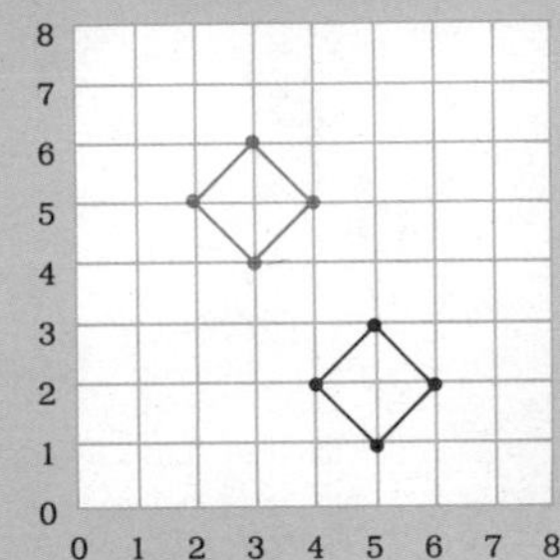

3. right 2, up 2

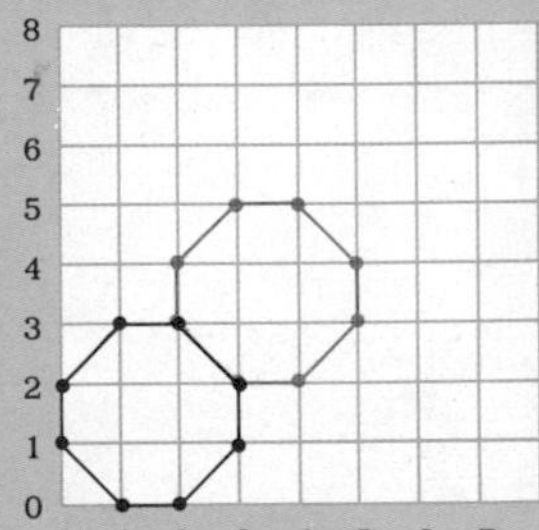

4. right 3

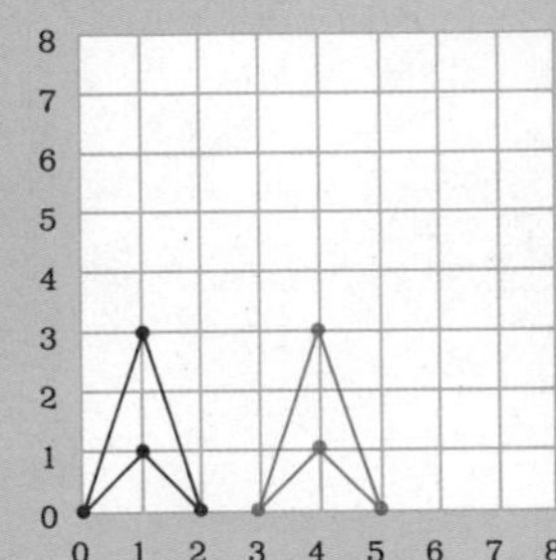

5. Draw a simple figure of your own choice on graph paper. Give instructions for making the moves for a translation image of the figure. Let a classmate try it!



## Using Page 343

This page is intended for those students who successfully completed the Chapter Review-Test on page 341. You may wish to assign this page as independent work while you use Another Look exercises to reteach the basic concepts and skills of the chapter. Or, you may decide that all students would benefit from this Enrichment activity.

**Lesson Development** Review the ideas of graphing ordered pairs by asking students to give the coordinates of the points that are the corners of rectangle 1. ((1, 2), (1, 4), (4, 2), (4, 4)) Tell students that each point of rectangle 1 was moved in the distance and the direction of the dotted arrow (right 4, up 3) to produce the slide image, or translation image, of rectangle 1—that is, rectangle 2. Then read and discuss the directions with students.

When students have completed the exercises, emphasize that translating a figure does not change either its size or its shape.

**Exercise 5** Students are to draw figures on graph paper. Encourage students to be creative, but not too complicated. To vary the activity, have students show a figure and its image to a classmate who then gives the directions for translating the figure.

About 30 years after Pascal and Fermat took on the Chevalier's gambling problem, Edward Lloyd opened a coffeehouse in London. By 1700, Lloyd's was a major meeting place for shipping underwriters, and the insurance industry had published its first actuarial tables. With respect to property and life insurance, probability required a great deal more development and refinement to be statistically accurate and economically viable for such institutions as Lloyd's of London. Nevertheless, the course of mathematics had again been altered and its content enriched by the interests and activities of society.

## Using Page 344

The exercises on this page provide practice for maintaining cumulative skills. The emphasis in this Cumulative Review is on geometry (Chapter 10), percents (Chapter 12), and problem solving (Chapter 12).

**Item Analysis** The table below correlates the Cumulative Review items with objectives and with the student book pages on which the concepts or skills were taught.

| Items | Objectives | Related text pages |
|---|---|---|
| 1–4 | 10.4 | 258–262 |
| 5–7 | 10.5 | 263 |
| 8–10 | 12.1 | 300–306 |
| 11–12 | 12.2 | 308–309 |
| 13–14 | 12.3 | 307, 310–313 |

## Cumulative Review

Which word describes each triangle?

1. 
   Ⓐ scalene
   B isosceles
   C equilateral
   D not given

2. 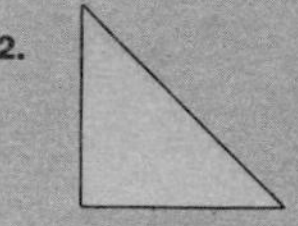
   A acute
   Ⓑ right
   C obtuse
   D not given

Name each polygon.

3. 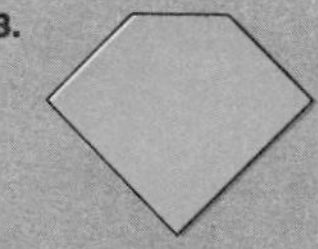
   Ⓐ pentagon
   B hexagon
   C octagon
   D not given

4. 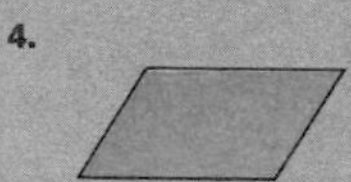
   Ⓐ parallelogram
   B rhombus
   C trapezoid
   D not given

Use circle $O$ for items 5–7.

5. Name a radius.
   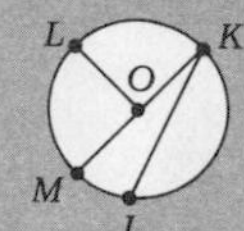
   
   Ⓐ $\overline{OL}$
   B $\overline{MK}$
   C $\overline{KJ}$
   D not given

6. Name a central angle.
   Ⓐ $\angle LOM$ B $\angle MKJ$
   C $\angle K$ D not given

7. Name a chord.
   A $\overline{LO}$ B $\overline{MO}$
   C $\overline{KO}$ Ⓓ not given

8. Give a fraction for 85%.
   A $\frac{19}{20}$ B $\frac{9}{10}$
   C $\frac{3}{4}$ Ⓓ not given

9. Give a percent for 0.67.
   A 76% B 6.7%
   Ⓒ 67% D not given

10. Give a decimal for 18%.
    A 1.8 B 8.1
    C 18.0 Ⓓ not given

11. Find 25% of 80.
    A 50 B 200
    Ⓒ 20 D not given

12. Find 65% of 240.
    A 1,560 Ⓑ 156
    C 305 D not given

13. Eldora's class wants to sell 70 tickets to the school carnival. They have already sold 70% of that number. How many have they sold?
    A 150 B 60
    C 56 Ⓓ not given

14. In a survey of 120 people 45% said that they watch the news on TV every day. How many people in the group watch the TV news daily?
    A 45 Ⓑ 54
    C 57 D not given

## Objectives

**14.1** Find the perimeter of a region.
**14.2** Find the circumference of a circle.
**14.3** Find the area of a rectangle or a triangle.
**14.4** Find the area of a circle.
**14.5** Find the surface area or volume of a box.
**14.6** Solve word problems using the 5-Point Checklist and cumulative computational skills.

## Summary

In this chapter students first find perimeter of polygons and circumference of circles. The concept of area is reviewed and extended, and formulas for finding the area of a rectangle and of a triangle are developed. Students first use models to make the formula for finding the area of a circle seem reasonable and then apply the formula to find the area of various size circles. Next, the formula for finding the area of a rectangle is used to find the surface area of a box. Then a formula for finding the volume of a box is developed and practiced. Throughout the chapter these procedures for finding perimeter, circumference, surface area, and volume are presented in problem-solving situations.

## Mathematical Background

**Perimeter and Circumference** The sum of the lengths of the sides of a polygon is called the perimeter of the polygon. Students often think of the perimeter of a figure as the distance around the figure. Since it is common to find the perimeter of a rectangle, a formula for this perimeter is introduced.

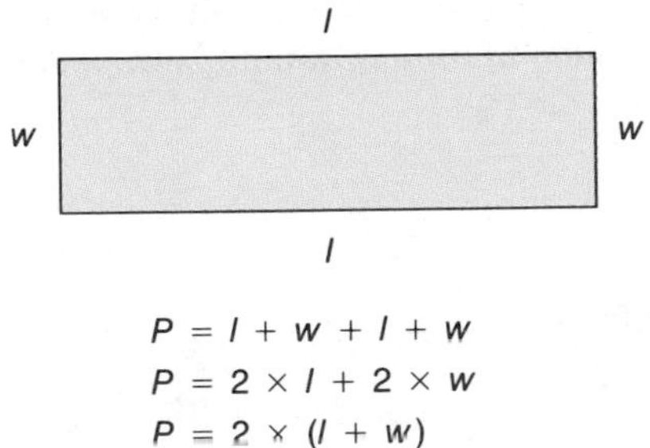


$$P = l + w + l + w$$
$$P = 2 \times l + 2 \times w$$
$$P = 2 \times (l + w)$$

Note that the three equations given above suggest that to find the perimeter of a rectangle, one can add the lengths of the sides; double the length, double the width, and add; or add the length and width and double this number.

The circumference of a circle can be thought of as the distance around the circle or as the "length" of the circle. It is interesting to note that for any circle, the circumference is a little more than 3 times the diameter. Stated another way, the ratio of the circumference of a circle to the diameter is a little more than 3. This ratio specifically is the number $\pi$. $\pi = 3.1415926$ (to 7 decimal places).

**Area** The area of a region is the number of unit squares it takes to completely cover the region. In a rectangle in which there are 3 rows with 6 squares in each row, the total number of squares can be found by multiplying $3 \times 6$. This reasoning suggests that for a rectangle, Area = length $\times$ width.

Using the figure below will help students understand why the area of a triangle is $\frac{1}{2}$ base $\times$ height. The area of the rectangle is $b \times h$. Since region A and region B are congruent and region C and region D are congruent, we can see that the triangle has half the area of the rectangle. Thus to find the area of a triangle, we can use the formula $\frac{1}{2} \times b \times h$.

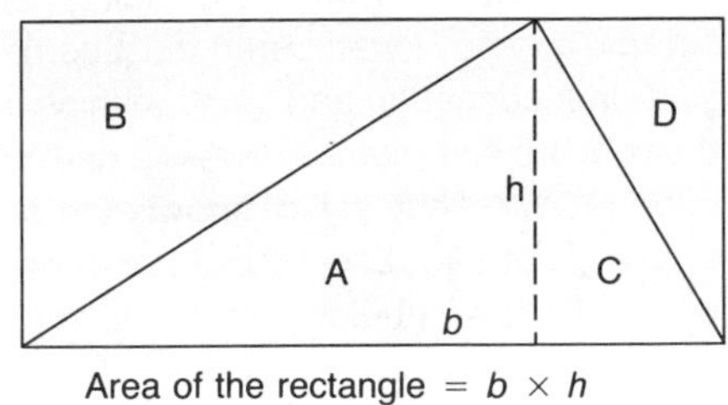


Area of the rectangle $= b \times h$
Area of the triangle $= \frac{1}{2} \times b \times h$

To help students understand the formula for finding the area of a circle, $A = r^2$, have them draw circles on graph paper, and then count squares and parts of squares to estimate the area of the circle. By using the radius of the circle, they can compare their estimates with the value for $\pi r^2$. This estimation provides a feeling that the formula is reasonable. Another way to show that the formula makes sense is explained in the text. When the sectors are rearranged to form a rectangular shape, we can see that the width of the figure is the radius of the circle and the length is $\frac{1}{2}$ the circumference of the circle. Thus, the area of the rectangle, $\frac{1}{2} C \times r$, approximates the area of the circle.

**Surface Area and Volume** The surface area of a box can be found by adding the areas of each of its surfaces. Thus the formula for the area of a rectangle is applied six times and these areas added together to find the surface area of a box with six rectangular faces.

The volume of a box can be thought of as the number of unit cubes the box will hold. In other words, the bottom layer in a box might have 3 rows of cubes with 4 cubes in each row or 12 cubes per layer. If the box is 2 units high, we can put 2 layers in the box. Thus, the volume of the box would be $4 \times 3 \times 2$ or 24 cubic units. This is generalized to the formula Volume = length $\times$ width $\times$ height.

**Problem Solving** Problems in this chapter are designed to help students apply the ideas of perimeter, surface area, and volume in solving everyday problems. The 5-Point Checklist continues to serve as a guide for solving problems. On page 347, Using Data from a Picture, students see that geometric figures can be useful in helping find solutions to certain problems. In a problem-solving practice lesson on page 351, the problems emphasize area, but include a variety of operations with whole numbers, fractions, and decimals. In Using Estimation, page 357, students are encouraged to use estimation to check the reasonableness of their calculated solutions. A variety of problems involve finding the volume of a figure. Applied Problem Solving, page 360, provides students with an opportunity to organize ideas, collect data, make several related calculations, and then to make a decision about a real-world situation.

### Vocabulary

| | | |
|---|---|---|
| perimeter | pi | surface area |
| circumference | area | volume |

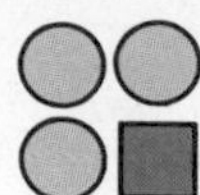

## Error Analysis

The ideas introduced in this chapter are basic to an understanding of geometric relationships. The content of this chapter is easily applied to real-world situations and problems encountered almost daily. The chapter introduces formulas for finding perimeter, area, and volume. A formula to be remembered must be based on a firm understanding of the concepts and relationships it represents. Computational errors are common as students deal with the formulas in this chapter. Many reflect lack of knowledge of the concepts and relationships while others reflect lack of arithmetic skill. Some common errors are discussed below.

**Error Pattern 1**

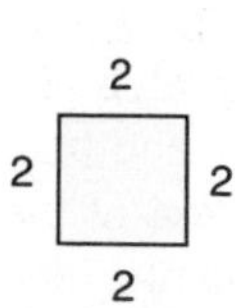


$p = 2(l + w)$
$= 2(4) = 8$

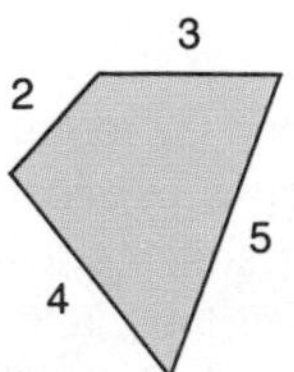


$p = 2(2 + 3 + 4 + 5)$
$= 2(14) = 28$

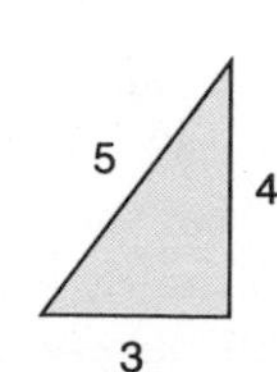


$p = 2(5 + 4 + 3)$
$= 2(12) = 24$

**Diagnosis** The student has learned that the formula for finding the perimeter of a square or a rectangle is $p = 2(l + w)$. The formula has been applied without careful attention to the type of figure.

**Remediation** Review the basic idea of perimeter as the distance around a figure. Observe and discuss the distance around each of the sample figures. Refer to this distance as the perimeter. Emphasize that there is a special way to simplify the procedure *if* the figure is a square or rectangle. Stress that this formula cannot be applied in every instance.

**Error Pattern 2**

$D = 12$

Find area of the circle.

Given $D = 12$, $\pi = 3.14$
$A = D\pi$
$A = \pi r^2 = 3.14 \times (12^2) = 3.14 \times 144 = 452.16$

**Diagnosis** The student has used the correct formula for finding area, but has failed to use the correct dimension in the formula. The student has not divided the diameter by 2 in order to find the radius. This is a common error made by students as they replace variables in formulas with values.

**Remediation** Discuss the definition of diameter and the radius of a circle. On the chalkboard, draw several circles on which you alternately identify diameter and then radius, pointing out the relationship: radius $= \frac{1}{2}$ diameter.

Next work through the sample problem, using the correct value in the formula.

Emphasize the following points as you help students identify and correct their errors in this chapter:

- Perimeter is expressed in a linear unit of measure.
- Area is expressed in terms of square units.
- Volume is expressed in terms of cubic units.
- Radius $= \frac{1}{2}$ diameter; diameter $= 2 \times$ radius.

## Problem Solving

### Starting a Problem-Solving Resource Center

In the previous chapter, a "problem-of-the-week" bulletin board was suggested as one way to provide your students with challenging mathematics problems. A problem-solving resource center is a second way. This resource center should be more than a collection of challenging problems. A good resource center is one where students can get assistance (without asking the teacher) when they become stymied on a problem and one where students can extend their work on a similar problem.

To set up a resource center with these characteristics, use three problem-solving file boxes labeled as shown below.

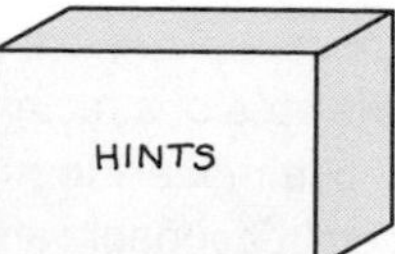


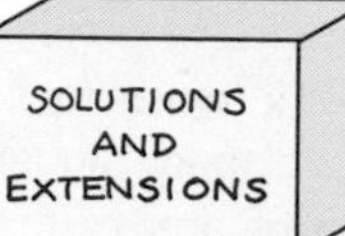


The "Problems" box contains a collection of problems. One problem should be on each numbered card. The cards could be grouped by levels of difficulty or by chapter to correspond with strategies developed in the student book. The "Hints" box contains cards numbered to correspond to the problem cards. One side of each card lists questions which, if answered correctly, would help students find a solution. On the other side of the card are answers to the questions.

In the "Solutions and Extensions" box, one side of each card shows one or two solutions to the problem. The other side has a problem that is an extension of the original problem. These cards can also be numbered to correspond to the numbers on the "Problems" and "Hints" cards.

The strategy lessons and Try This problems in the student book together with the teaching notes for these lessons can provide useful models for the types of problems, hints, and extensions to be used in the resource center.

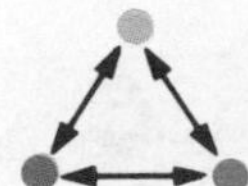

## Special Education

The following chapter on measurement provides a wealth of hands-on opportunities for the special-needs student. These opportunities allow students to make use of a variety of senses and skills. As much as possible, the activities used should encourage active student involvement.

### Developing Circumference Concepts

The development of the formula for the circumference of the circle can be accomplished in the classroom using some cardboard calipers made with metric rulers, flexible metric tape measures, and a calculator. The calipers can be made from cardboard and a metric ruler as shown below and then used to measure the diameters of circular objects in the classroom. The measurements can be noted on a worksheet as shown. The circumferences of the same objects can be measured with the metric tape measures and entered on the appropriate lines on the worksheet. The hand calculator is then used to calculate the ratio of the length of the circumference to the length of the diameter for each of the objects measured. The result of each of these calculations can then be entered on the chart. Comparisons of these values can help students accept the stated value of $\pi$.

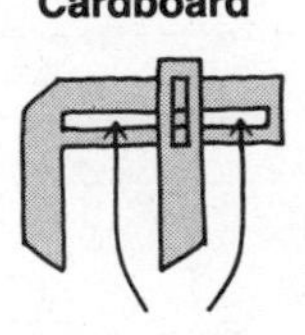

| Circumference | Diameter | C/d |
|---|---|---|
| 45 cm | 14 cm | 3.21 |
| 63 cm | 20 cm | 3.15 |

### Building Students' Understanding

Special-needs students might not have as good a recollection of earlier work with perimeter, area, and volume as other students in the class. Hence, they will need more review of these topics than other students. This review should involve physical reconstructions of the ideas of area and volume. In particular, students should have work that reviews the basic concepts of area and volume. In area they need to think of covering and in volume they need to think of filling. This suggests that students need to have experiences that slowly construct the ideas and provide a framework for the computation that follows.

In studying area, students should spend time covering rectangles with square units of paper, counting the rows and columns, and then determining the product that applies. This process should be related to the array model for multiplication. This sort of development will help provide students with a basic understanding of the process, as many may have difficulty remembering the actual formulas for calculating the answers.

For volume, students will need practice in stacking wooden blocks into open-topped boxes having the same dimensions in terms of whole numbers of the blocks. The various levels of the blocks can then be removed from the boxes, and the process of calculating the area of the base ($l \times w$) and multiplying this number by the height ($h$) can be related to finding the product $l \times w \times h$. These steps in the development of the problem are shown below.

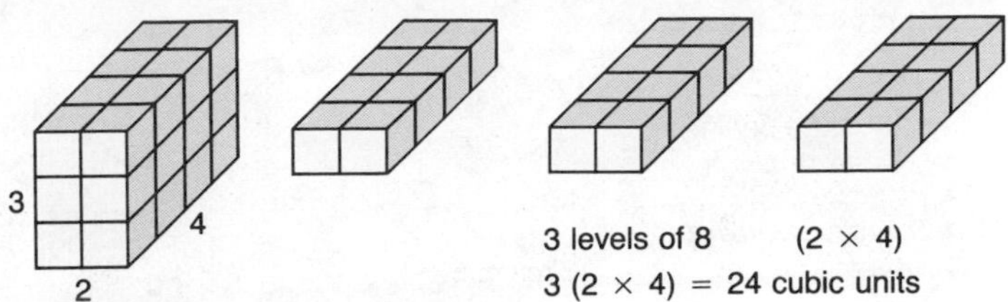


To help build the steps to the formula for area, use the sections of the circular model on page 354. These steps might be carried out as shown below. At each step of the process, review with students that the length of half of the circumference is $\pi r$ and that the length of the straight edge of the developing shape is $r$, the radius of the circle that was cut up to start the process.

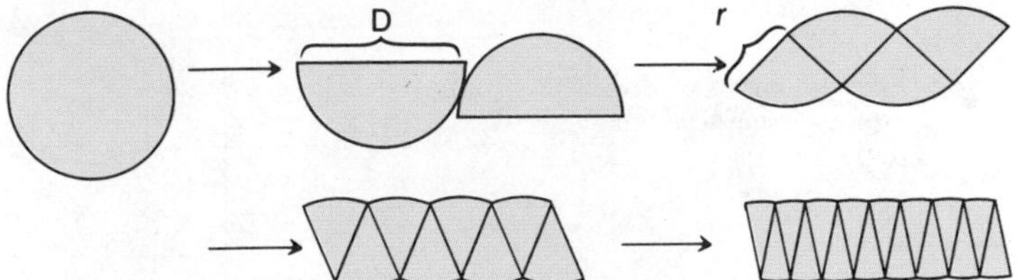


### Providing Organization for Calculating Surface Area

One of the most difficult topics in this chapter for the special-needs student is the calculation of surface area for a given rectangular solid. Many of these problems are related to students' inability to recognize all of the surfaces and then to combine the various area calculations. To ease this problem, have students assemble a box, then cut the box apart. Students can then sort out the pieces, measure and calculate the separate areas, and add to get the total surface area. The steps in this activity are illustrated below.

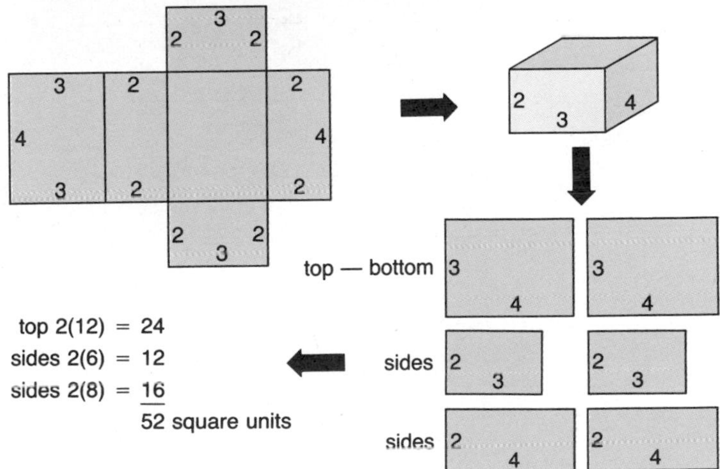

## Subject Integration

Subject matter related to other areas of the curriculum has been integrated into the following lessons. This provides an opportunity to highlight the interaction between mathematics and other subjects.

**Social Studies** Maya civilization, page 345

# Management Guide

| Teaching Chapter 14 | | | | Meeting Individual Needs | | | | | |
|---|---|---|---|---|---|---|---|---|---|
| | | | | Lesson Assignments | | | Follow Up | | |
| Objectives | Chapter Content | Pages | TRB Test Items | Minimum | Average | Extended | Reteaching | Enrichment | Practice |
| | Chapter Opener | 345 | | | | | | | |
| **14.1** Find the perimeter of a region. | Perimeter | 346 | 1–5 | 1–6 | 1–6 | 1–6 | | | PS 130 |
| **14.2** Find the circumference of a circle. | Circumference | 348–349 | 6–8 | 1–5, 7, SK | 1–9, SK | 1–10, SK | RS 81 | ES 81 | PS 131 |
| **14.3** Find the area of a rectangle or a triangle. | Area of a Rectangle | 350 | 9–10 | 1–9 | 1–9 | 1–9 | RS 82 | ES 82 | PS 132 |
| | Area of a Triangle | 352–353 | 11–13 | 1–11 | 1–12 | 1–12, TM | RS 83 | ES 83 | PS 133 |
| **14.4** Find the area of a circle. | Area of a Circle | 354–355 | 14–16 | 1–10 | 1–11 | 1–11, TM | RS 84 | ES 84 | PS 134 |
| **14.5** Find the surface area or volume of a box. | Surface Area | 356–357 | 17–20 | 1–6, SK | 1–7, SK | 1–8, SK | RS 85 | ES 85 | PS 135 |
| | Volume | 358 | | 1–9 | 1–9 | 1–9 | RS 86 | ES 86 | PS 136 |
| **14.6** Solve word problems using the 5-Point Checklist and cumulative computational skills. | Problem Solving: Using Data from a Picture | 347 | 21–25 | 1–6 | 1–7 | 1–8 | | | |
| | Problem Solving: Practice | 351 | | 1–6 | 1–7 | 1–8 | | | |
| | Problem Solving: Using Estimation | 359 | | 1–6 | 1–8 | 1–9 | | | |
| | Applied Problem Solving | 360 | | | | | | | |
| | Chapter Review-Test | 361 | | | | | | | |
| | Another Look/Enrichment | 362–363 | | | | | | | |
| | Cumulative Review | 364 | | | | | | | |

**SE5** Student Edition, Book 5
**RS** Reteaching Supplement
**ES** Enrichment Supplement
**PS** Practice Supplement
**TM** Think Math
**SK** Skillkeeper
**TRB** Teacher's Resource Book

## Masters for Use

**. . . before Chapter 14**

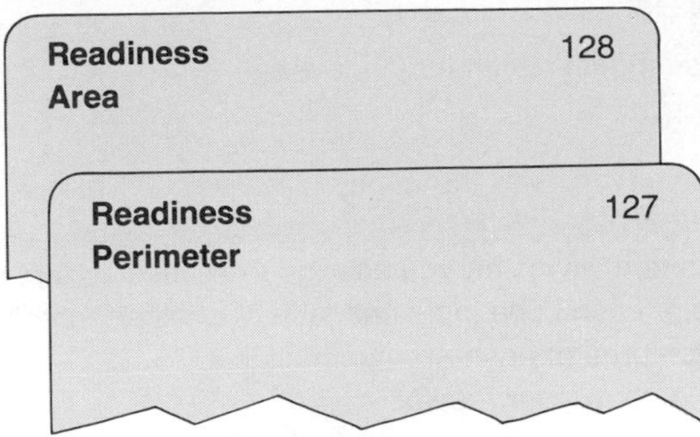


**. . . during Chapter 14**

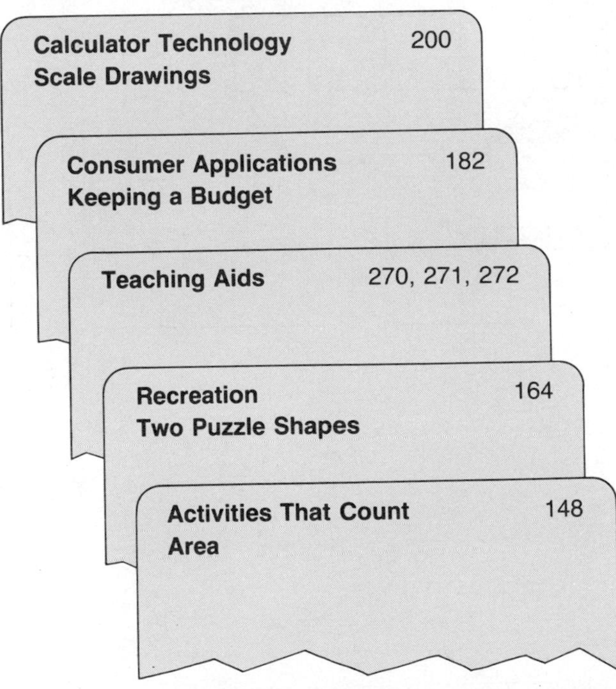

Calculator Technology
Scale Drawings
200
Consumer Applications
Keeping a Budget
182
Teaching Aids
270, 271, 272
Recreation
Two Puzzle Shapes
164
Activities That Count
Area
148


**. . . after Chapter 14**

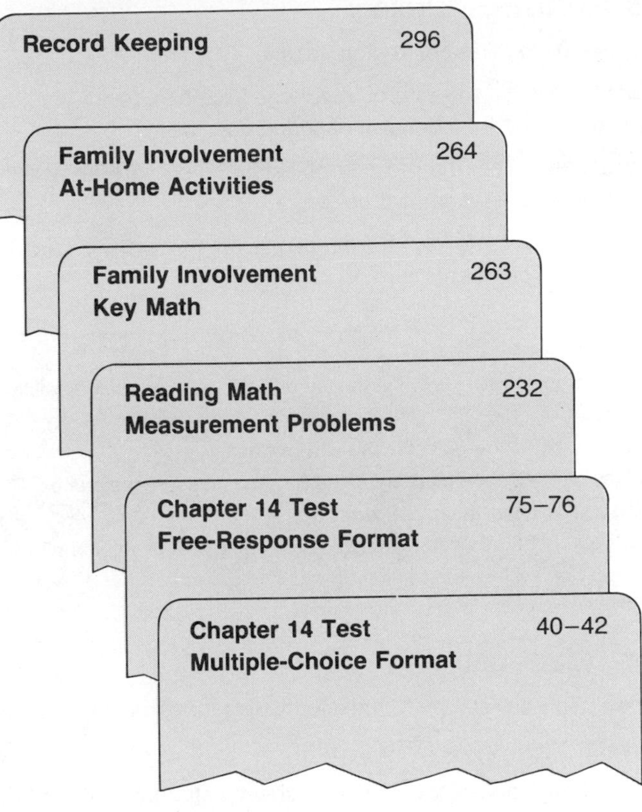


## Supplements

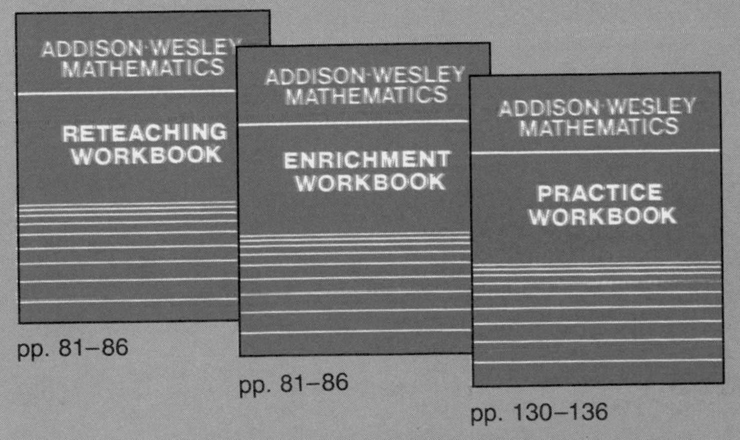


pp. 81–86

pp. 81–86

pp. 130–136

## Other Addison-Wesley Resources

**Books and Kits**

*The Metric System* pp. 31–49, 51–53

*Dice and Dots* Game 9

*Arithmetic Skill Cards* pp. AP 5–7, 9, 11–12

*Problem-Solving Experiences in Mathematics, Grade 6,* Problems 29, 30, 64, 65, 89, 104, 125, 144

# Activities That Count

Activities That Count are designed for use throughout this chapter and subsequent chapters. Before beginning Chapter 14, you may wish to review these activities and select the ones you consider appropriate for your class.

## Find Volume Project

**Purpose** To experiment finding volume

**Materials** Plastic waterproof tray, large juice can, rocks or other heavy objects, graduated liter measuring cup, water

**Preparation** Label the rocks or objects, and prepare an activity card with directions as shown below.

**Activity** Students follow the directions on the activity card to carry out the experiment.

For each object:

1. Put an empty juice can in the tray, and fill the can with water exactly even with the top.
2. Carefully place the object in the can of water.
3. Lift the can with the object out of the tray and measure the number of milliliters of water that overflowed.
4. The volume of the overflow water is the same as the volume of the object. Record this information on a chart.

## Area Math Lab

**Purpose** To illustrate the formula for finding the area of a triangle

**Materials** Work sheet (TRB p. 148)

**Activity** Using one of the TRB worksheets, students cut out the dashed-line triangles on the right and position them with the matching solid-line triangle on the left to make 3 rectangles. Students then use the formula for finding the area of a rectangle and the formula for finding the area of a triangle, and compare their results.

## Surface Area Math Lab

**Purpose** To use models to find surface area

**Materials** 6 cubes

**Activity** Students work with the cubes to answer the following questions:

1. How many different ways can you arrange the cubes so that at least one face of each cube joins one face of another cube?
2. Find the surface area of each arrangement.
3. Make a chart to show your results.
4. What is the smallest surface area?
5. What is the greatest surface area?

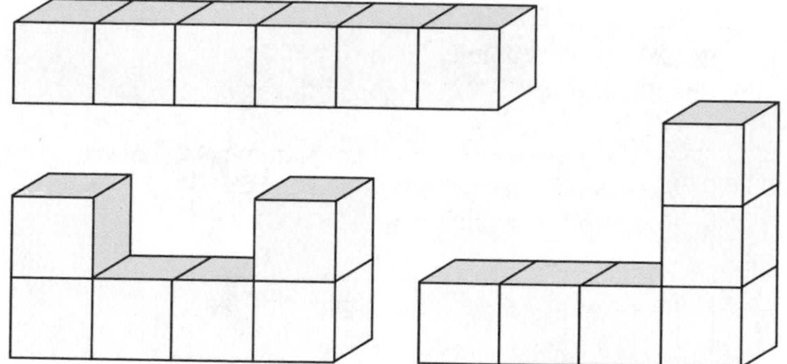

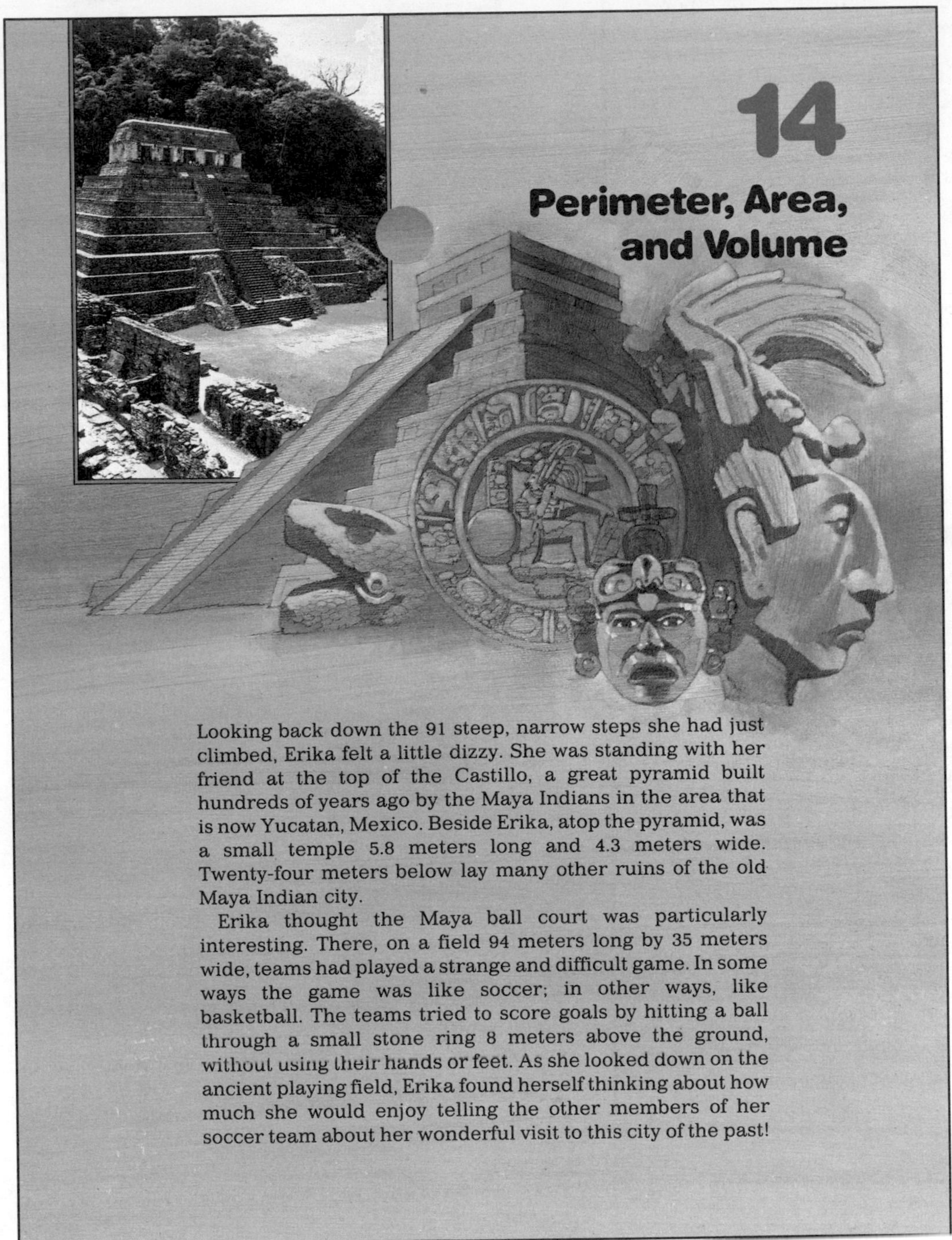

14

Perimeter, Area, and Volume

Looking back down the 91 steep, narrow steps she had just climbed, Erika felt a little dizzy. She was standing with her friend at the top of the Castillo, a great pyramid built hundreds of years ago by the Maya Indians in the area that is now Yucatan, Mexico. Beside Erika, atop the pyramid, was a small temple 5.8 meters long and 4.3 meters wide. Twenty-four meters below lay many other ruins of the old Maya Indian city.

Erika thought the Maya ball court was particularly interesting. There, on a field 94 meters long by 35 meters wide, teams had played a strange and difficult game. In some ways the game was like soccer; in other ways, like basketball. The teams tried to score goals by hitting a ball through a small stone ring 8 meters above the ground, without using their hands or feet. As she looked down on the ancient playing field, Erika found herself thinking about how much she would enjoy telling the other members of her soccer team about her wonderful visit to this city of the past!

## Introducing the Chapter

**Discussion** Explain to students that in this chapter they will be able to review and strengthen their understanding of the concepts of perimeter, area, and volume. Then encourage them to discuss briefly what they may know about ancient American Indian civilizations such as the Aztec and Maya of Mexico and Central America and the Inca of Peru. Afterward, allow time for students to read the story and examine the illustrations. Then have students make up questions of their own involving the data from the story. As you teach the chapter, you may wish to refer to this page and pose the questions suggested below.

## Follow-Up Questions

**After Page 347** The smallest ball court among the ruins Erika visited was a rectangular field 19.8 m long and 6.1 m wide. What was the perimeter of this field? (51.8 m)

**After Page 349** One of the natural water wells in the ancient Maya city has a diameter of 49 m. What is the circumference of the well? Use $3\frac{1}{7}$ for $\pi$. (154 m)

**After Page 351** Among some other Maya ruins is a palace that covers a rectangular area 97.5 m long and 12.2 m wide. What is the area in square meters? (1,189.5 $m^2$)

**After Page 357** A Maya building called "the House of Turtles" (because its walls are covered with carvings of turtles) is 27.4 m long, 9.4 m wide, and 6.1 m high. What is this building's volume? (1,571.116 $m^3$)

**Quick Review** Students respond orally with these products.
(8 + 4) × 2  2 × (30 + 10)  (6 + 5) × 2  2 × (10 + 15)
(2 × 3) + (2 × 4)  (20 + 30) × 2  (2 × 6) + (2 × 4)

**Lesson Focus** To find the perimeter of a polygon; to use data from a picture to solve problems

## Ideas for Getting Started

Have students walk along each wall of the classroom using steps they think are 1 meter long to estimate how many steps (meters) it takes to return to the starting point. Have students compare their estimates using the term "distance around the classroom."

Have students estimate another perimeter, such as the distance around the edge of a math book. Encourage students to suggest shortcuts for making estimates, such as doubling one length and one width, based on their insight into the idea of perimeter.

## Using Page 346

**Lesson Development** Read the problem at the top of the page and have students identify the data and the question. "How can we find the total distance around the state of Colorado?" (Add the lengths and widths of each side.)

Work through the problem on the chalkboard. Ask students to suggest shorter ways to find the perimeter (double the length, double the width, then add the two together; add the length and width, then double the answer). Discuss the formula shown in the cloud on the right.

**Exercises 1–6** Point out in exercise 1 that students are to find the perimeter of Kansas as if the state were a rectangle formed by the solid and dotted lines. In exercise 2, have students suggest shortcuts for finding the perimeters of geometric figures, such as regular pentagons. (Multiply the length of one side by 5.)

## Perimeter

The state of Colorado is one of the states that is nearly rectangular. It is approximately 589 km long and 456 km wide. If you could drive all the way around it, about how far would you drive?

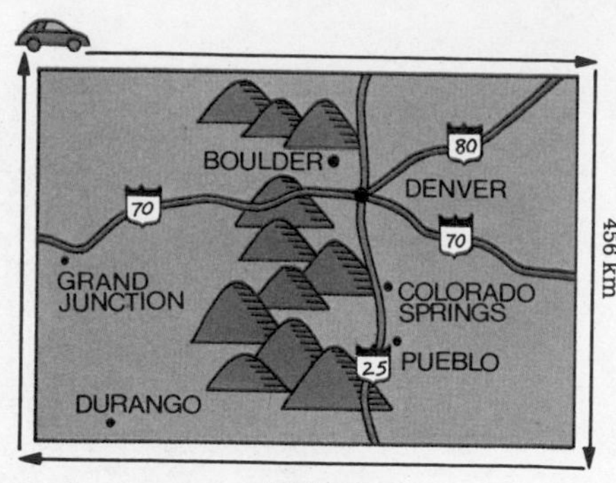


The distance around a figure is called the **perimeter** of the figure.

To find the perimeter, add the lengths of the sides.

$$\begin{array}{r} 589 \\ 456 \\ 589 \\ +\ 456 \\ \hline 2{,}090 \end{array}$$

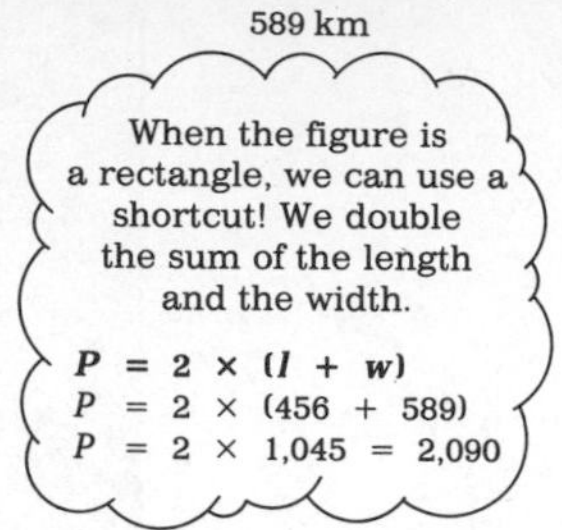

When the figure is a rectangle, we can use a shortcut! We double the sum of the length and the width.
P = 2 × (l + w)
P = 2 × (456 + 589)
P = 2 × 1,045 = 2,090


If you could drive around the perimeter of Colorado you would drive about 2,090 km.

Find the perimeter of each figure.

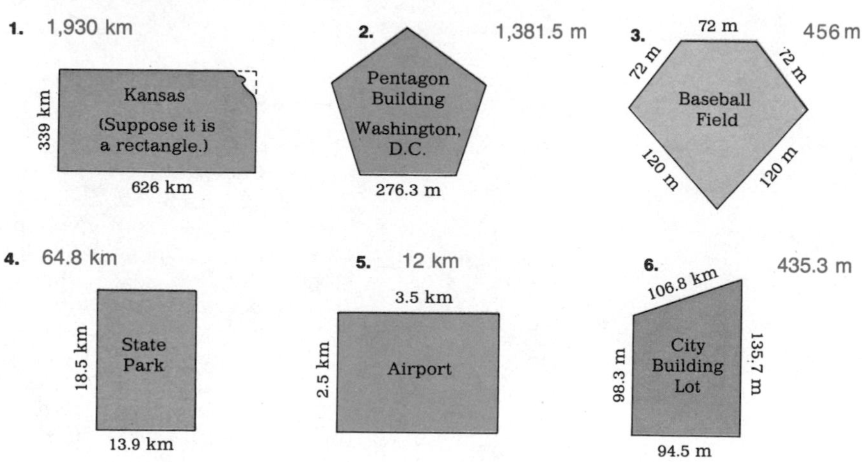




## Follow Up

### Reteaching

Show students the following illustration.

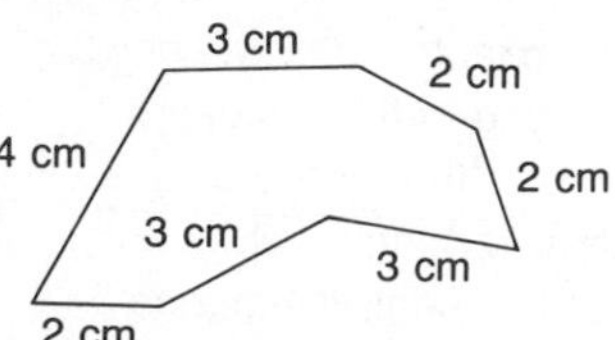


Make up a story situation such as "If an insect walks completely around the figure, how far will it walk?" As you trace the perimeter, record the distance covered—3 cm + 2 cm + 2 cm + 3 cm + 3 cm + 2 cm + 4 cm = 19 cm. Use the term *perimeter* as you refer to the distance around the figure.

### Enrichment

Provide students with a variety of geometric figures duplicated on graph paper (TRB p. 270). Have students measure, compute, and record the perimeter of each figure. Then challenge students to draw another figure with the same perimeter as each of the given figures.

| Assignment Guide | Minimum | Average | Extended |
|---|---|---|---|
| page 346 | 1–6 | 1–6 | 1–6 |
| page 347 | 1–6 | 1–7 | 1–8 |

QUESTION DATA PLAN ANSWER CHECK

## Problem Solving: Using Data from a Picture

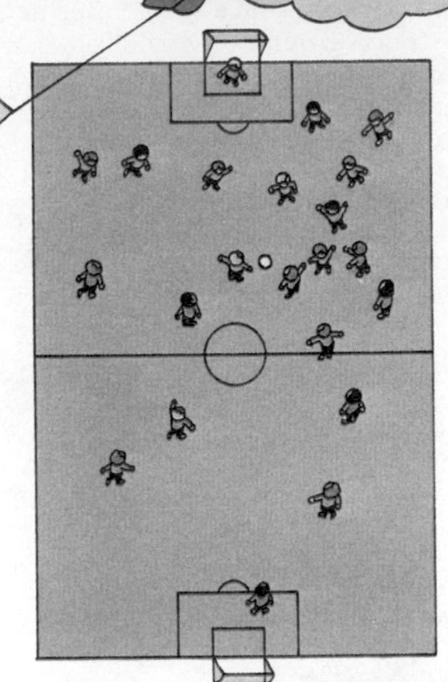

Pictures are given for some of these **perimeter problems.** For others, you may need to draw a picture of your own in order to solve the problem.

1. A bulletin board has the length and width shown. What is its perimeter? 550 cm (122 cm; 153 cm)
2. The width of a garden is 8.4 m. Its length is 16.8 m. What is the perimeter of the garden? 50.4 m
3. The width of a soccer field is 46 m. The length is 45 m greater than the width. What is the perimeter of the field? 274 m
4. A home is to be built on a lot shaped like a trapezoid. The parallel sides are 36.6 m and 27.8 m long. Each of the other sides is half as long as the longest side. What is the perimeter of the lot? 101 m (27.8 m; ?; ?; 36.6 m)
5. A sail for a sailboat is shaped like a right triangle. The longest side is 8.5 m. The next-longest side is 0.5 m shorter than the longest side. The third side is $\frac{1}{3}$ the sum of the lengths of the other two sides. What is the perimeter? 22 m
6. A pennant is shaped like an isosceles triangle. The short side is 24 cm and is half the length of a longer side. What is the perimeter of the pennant? 120 cm (24 cm)
7. A pen for a dog was made in the shape of a kite. Each of the two longer sides is 9.4 m long. Each of the two shorter sides is 2.8 m less than this. What is the perimeter of the pen? 32 m
8. **Try This** A picture frame is twice as long as it is wide. The perimeter of the frame is 228 cm. What are the length and the width of the picture frame? 76 cm, 38 cm

347

## Using Page 347

**Lesson Development** Direct student's attention to the 5-Point Checklist logo in the upper left corner. Point out that this lesson focuses on using data from pictures. Emphasize the importance of pictures in organizing given data and understanding the problem, and work through an example. Have students come to the chalkboard and draw a picture that illustrates the question.

**Exercises 1–8** In some of these exercises, the pictures are given; in others, students will need to draw their own. In exercises 4–7, point out that more than one operation is involved. Note the use of fractions in exercise 5.

**Try This** A possible strategy, Guess and Check, was taught on page 48.

**Discussion** "What two things are we asked to find about the picture?" (the length and the width of the frame) "What data are we given?" (The length of the frame is twice the width; the perimeter of the frame is 228 cm.) Point out that there is not enough information to use combinations of operations to find the answer. "What strategy could we use to solve the problem?" (Guess and Check) "Which distance is best to guess first?" (width) Have students suggest amounts for the width of the frame and check their estimates.

**Solution** The width of the frame is 38 cm and the length is 76 cm.

38 + 76 = 114
114 × 2 = 228 cm

## Ideas That Work

### Special Education

To review the concept of perimeter, let students determine the classroom perimeter using student arm span as the unit. The distance around the classroom walls can be measured in terms of student units as shown in the illustration. The total length of the chain of arm spans can be found. This total can then be used to calculate in student arm span length the perimeter of the schoolgrounds, a nearby park, or your state.

**Practice Supplement,** page 130

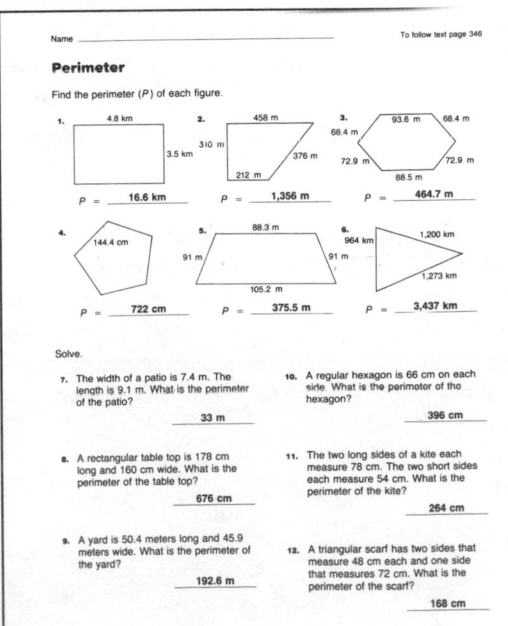

Name ______________________ To follow text page 346

**Perimeter**

Find the perimeter ($P$) of each figure.

1. 4.8 km; 3.5 km — $P$ = 16.6 km
2. 458 m; 310 m; 376 m; 212 m — $P$ = 1,356 m
3. 93.6 m; 68.4 m; 68.4 m; 72.9 m; 72.9 m; 88.5 m — $P$ = 464.7 m
4. 144.4 cm — $P$ = 722 cm
5. 88.3 m; 91 m; 91 m; 105.2 m — $P$ = 375.5 m
6. 964 km; 1,200 km; 1,273 km — $P$ = 3,437 km

Solve.

7. The width of a patio is 7.4 m. The length is 9.1 m. What is the perimeter of the patio? 33 m
8. A rectangular table top is 178 cm long and 160 cm wide. What is the perimeter of the table top? 676 cm
9. A yard is 50.4 meters long and 45.9 meters wide. What is the perimeter of the yard? 192.6 m
10. A regular hexagon is 66 cm on each side. What is the perimotor of tho hexagon? 396 cm
11. The two long sides of a kite each measure 78 cm. The two short sides each measure 54 cm. What is the perimeter of the kite? 264 cm
12. A triangular scarf has two sides that measure 48 cm each and one side that measures 72 cm. What is the perimeter of the scarf? 168 cm

**Quick Review** Students give the products, then check answers by dividing.

| 2.5 | 13.2 | 8.2 | 10.06 | 38.7 | 5.9 | 26.3 | 108.15 |
|---|---|---|---|---|---|---|---|
| × 5 | × 8 | × 6 | × 9 | × 4 | × 7 | × 8 | × 3 |
| 12.5 | 105.6 | 49.2 | 90.54 | 154.8 | 41.3 | 210.4 | 324.45 |

**Lesson Focus** To find the circumference of a circle by using the formula $C = \pi d$

**Suggested Materials** Circular objects, tape measure

## Ideas for Getting Started

Make a table like the one shown below.

| Object | Diameter ($d$) (cm) | Special Factor | Circumference ($C$) (cm) |
|---|---|---|---|
| cup | 8.4 | $\frac{26.4}{8.4}$ or 3.14 | 26.4 cm |

Have students use the tape measure to determine the diameter and the circumference of circular objects to the nearest millimeter (0.1 cm). Tell them to look for a special, or missing, factor that when multiplied by the diameter will give the circumference. To find the factor, students can divide the circumference by the diameter. In the example above, students could have used a calculator to divide 26.4 by 8.4 to arrive at 3.14 to the nearest hundredth. After the special factor is found, have students multiply the diameter by the special factor to check their results.

Have students make similar measurements and calculations with other circular objects. Emphasize the idea that the special factor is approximately the same, regardless of the size of the circular object.

## Using Page 348

**Lesson Development** Have students read the information at the top of the page describing pi. Point out that pi is an unending number that can be computed to any desired number of places. It is the ratio of the circumference of a circle to the diameter, or the special factor that multiplies by the diameter to give the circumference. Have students find the decimal for $\frac{1}{7}$ to verify that $3\frac{1}{7}$ is a close approximation of pi.

Consider each of the examples on the page in turn. "What is the diameter of the auto tire?" (52 cm) "What is the formula for finding the circumference?" ($C = \pi d$) "What approximation is used for pi?" (3.14) Discuss the other example in a similar manner.

**Warm Up** Encourage students to round their answers to the nearest hundredth. Difficulties may arise due to errors in computation or incorrect substitution in the formula. If necessary, present another example in which the radius of the object is given and point out that $C = \pi d$ or $C = 2\pi r$.

## Circumference

The **circumference** (perimeter or distance around) of any circle can be calculated by multiplying the diameter of the circle by the special number $\pi$ (pronounced "pie").

Study these examples.

**A Special Number**

$\pi$ = **3.1415926** (to 7 decimal places)

We use **3.14** or **$3\frac{1}{7}$** as an approximation for $\pi$.

Auto Tire

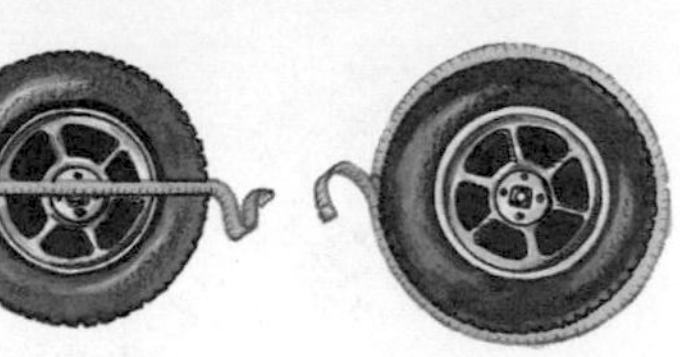

Diameter: 52 cm Circumference: ?

$$C = \pi \times d$$

$$C = 3.14 \times 52$$

$$C = 163.28 \text{ cm}$$

Bike Wheel

Diameter: 63 cm Circumference: ?

$$C = \pi \times d$$

$$C = 3\tfrac{1}{7} \times 63$$

$$C = \tfrac{22}{7} \times 63$$

$$C = 22 \times 9 = 198 \text{ cm}$$

**Warm Up** Find the circumference.

1. Use 3.14 for $\pi$.

Tractor tire

Diameter: 1.3 m Circumference: ■ 4.082 m

2. Use $3\frac{1}{7}$ for $\pi$.

Small moped tire

Diameter: 42 cm Circumference: ■ 132 cm



## Follow Up

**Reteaching**

Remind students that the distance around a circle is called the circumference. Show students how to use a string to lay around a circular object, then extend and measure the string. After students have measured several objects, make a chart to show the relationship between circumference and diameter. Use this relationship to help students understand the formula $\frac{C}{d} = \pi$, and the inverse $C = \pi \times d$.

**Enrichment**

Instruct students to use their compasses to draw a cartoon figure made of circles. The body of the figure should be three circles—each having a radius $\frac{1}{2}$ that of the circle below it. For each arm, students can use two circles that are $\frac{1}{2}$ the radius of the head of the figure. Challenge students to use other sizes of circles to decorate their cartoon figures.

| Assignment Guide | | | |
|---|---|---|---|
| | Minimum | Average | Extended |
| page 349 | 1–5, 7, SK | 1–9, SK | 1–10, SK |

Find the circumference of each object.

1. Record 95.77 cm

$d$ = 30.5 cm
Use 3.14 for $\pi$.

2. Bike gear 66 cm

$d$ = 21 cm
Use $3\frac{1}{7}$ for $\pi$.

3. Flower bed 7.85 m

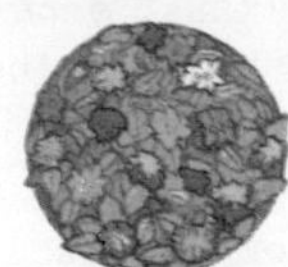

$d$ = 2.5 m
Use 3.14 for $\pi$.

4. Clock face 88 cm

$d$ = 28 cm
Use $3\frac{1}{7}$ for $\pi$.

5. Mower wheel 47.85 cm

$d$ = 15.24 cm
Use 3.14 for $\pi$.

6. Earth 20,042.62 km

$r$ = 6,383 km
Use 3.14 for $\pi$.

Find the circumference. Use 3.14 for $\pi$.

7. 109.9 mm

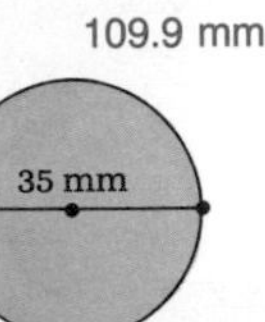


8. 76.93 mm

24.5 mm

9. 31.4 mm

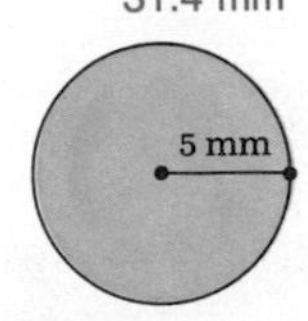


10. **DATA HUNT** About how much greater is the circumference of a 33 rpm phonograph record than that of a 78 rpm (or a 45 rpm) record? Measure the diameters. about 16 cm; about 40 cm

## Skillkeeper

Find the percent of each number.

| | | | |
|---|---|---|---|
| **1.** 12% of 50 6 | **2.** 20% of 50 10 | **3.** 16% of 50 8 | **4.** 25% of 60 15 |
| **5.** 10% of 60 6 | **6.** 15% of 60 9 | **7.** 80% of 20 16 | **8.** 35% of 20 7 |
| **9.** 95% of 20 19 | **10.** 40% of 80 32 | **11.** 25% of 80 20 | **12.** 60% of 80 48 |



## Using Page 349

**Exercises 1–9** Exercises 2 and 4 use $3\frac{1}{7}$ as the approximatioin for $\pi$; the remaining exercises use 3.14. In exercise 6, the radius of Earth is given. Students can double the radius to determine the diameter. In exercise 7, $3\frac{1}{7}$ could also be used because 35 is divisible by 7.

**Data Hunt** This exercise encourages students to collect data by measuring the diameters of different phonograph records. You may wish to provide an alternative to this exercise allowing students to choose between it and other exercises, such as "How much greater is the circumference of a large can of juice than a small can of juice?" or "How much greater is the circumference of a wheel on a ten-speed bike than a wheel on a dirt bike?"

**Skillkeeper** This skill was originally taught in Chapter 12.

**Reteaching Supplement,** page 81

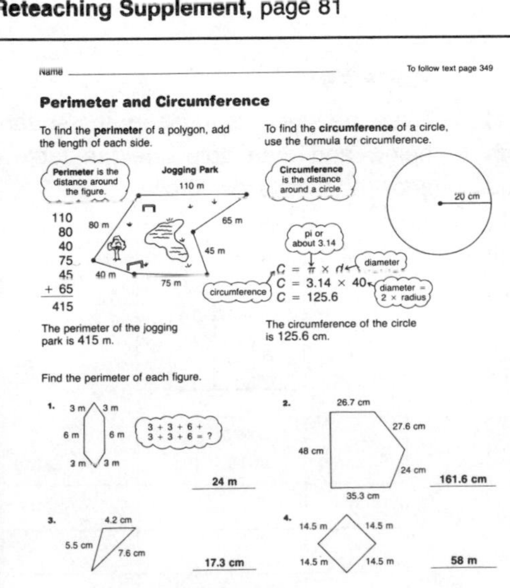

Name ______ To follow text page 349

**Perimeter and Circumference**

To find the **perimeter** of a polygon, add the length of each side.

**Perimeter** is the distance around the figure.

Jogging Park: 110 m, 65 m, 45 m, 75 m, 40 m, 80 m

110
80
40
75
45
+ 65
415

The perimeter of the jogging park is 415 m.

To find the **circumference** of a circle, use the formula for circumference.

**Circumference** is the distance around a circle.

20 cm

$C = \pi \times d$ (pi or about 3.14; diameter)
$C = 3.14 \times 40$ (diameter = 2 × radius)
$C = 125.6$ (circumference)

The circumference of the circle is 125.6 cm.

Find the perimeter of each figure.

1. 3 m, 3 m, 6 m, 6 m, 3 m, 3 m (3 + 3 + 6 + 3 + 3 + 6 = ?) **24 m**
2. 26.7 cm, 27.6 cm, 24 cm, 35.3 cm, 48 cm **161.6 cm**
3. 4.2 cm, 5.5 cm, 7.6 cm **17.3 cm**
4. 14.5 m, 14.5 m, 14.5 m, 14.5 m **58 m**

Find the circumference of each circle. Use 3.14 for $\pi$.

5. 12.5 cm (12.5 + 12.5 = 25.0 is the diameter.) **78.5 cm**
6. 78 mm **244.92 mm**

**Enrichment Supplement,** page 81

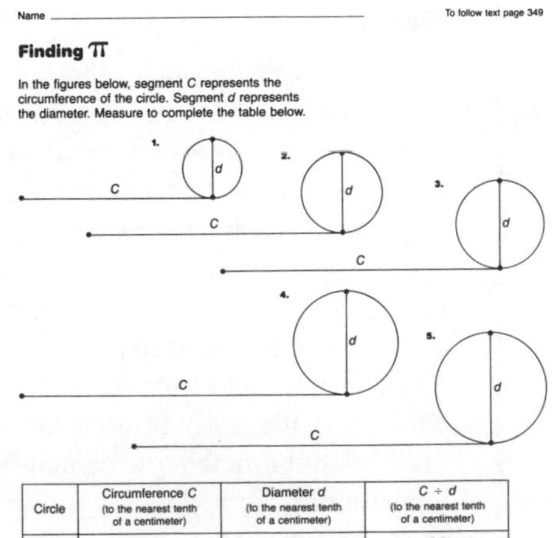

Name ______ To follow text page 349

**Finding π**

In the figures below, segment $C$ represents the circumference of the circle. Segment $d$ represents the diameter. Measure to complete the table below.

| Circle | Circumference $C$ (to the nearest tenth of a centimeter) | Diameter $d$ (to the nearest tenth of a centimeter) | $C \div d$ (to the nearest tenth of a centimeter) |
|---|---|---|---|
| 1 | **6.5** | **2** | **3.3** |
| 2 | **8.5** | **2.7** | **3.1** |
| 3 | **9.4** | **3** | **3.1** |
| 4 | **11** | **3.5** | **3.1** |
| 5 | **12.1** | **3.8** | **3.2** |

What is the average of the 5 numbers you found for $C \div d$ (to the nearest hundredth)? **3.16**
This average should be close to the number $\pi$ (3.14159 . . .).
What is the difference between your average and $\pi$ (use 3.14)? **0.02**

**Practice Supplement,** page 131

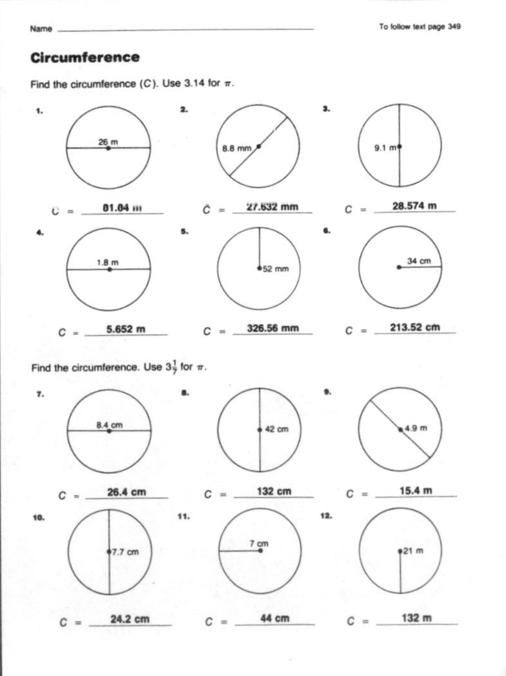

Name ______ To follow text page 349

**Circumference**

Find the circumference ($C$). Use 3.14 for $\pi$.

1. 26 m $C$ = **81.64 m**
2. 8.8 mm $C$ = **27.632 mm**
3. 9.1 m $C$ = **28.574 m**
4. 1.8 m $C$ = **5.652 m**
5. 52 mm $C$ = **326.56 mm**
6. 34 cm $C$ = **213.52 cm**

Find the circumference. Use $3\frac{1}{7}$ for $\pi$.

7. 8.4 cm $C$ = **26.4 cm**
8. 42 cm $C$ = **132 cm**
9. 4.9 m $C$ = **15.4 m**
10. 7.7 cm $C$ = **24.2 cm**
11. 7 cm $C$ = **44 cm**
12. 21 m $C$ = **132 m**

**Quick Review** Put these problems on the chalkboard. Students check their answers with the inverse operations.

| 46 + 82 | 40)3,600 | \$17.03 − 4.38 | 75 − 26 | \$43.72 + 14.99 | 62 × 3 | 4)7,360 | 314 × 9 |
|---|---|---|---|---|---|---|---|
| 128 | 90 | \$12.65 | 49 | \$58.71 | 186 | 1,840 | 2,826 |

**Lesson Focus** To find the area of a rectangle using the formula $A = l \times w$; to solve word problems involving area of a rectangle

**Suggested Materials** Graph paper (TRB p. 271)

## Ideas for Getting Started

Have students draw rectangles 6 units long and 4 units wide on graph paper. Tell them that the area of the rectangle is the number of square units it takes to fill or cover the rectangle. Have them count the squares. "What is the area of the rectangle?" (24 square units) "How many rows of squares are in the rectangle?" (4) "How many squares are in each of the rows?" (6) "How could you find the number of squares without counting each one?" (Multiply 4 × 6.) Have students draw rectangles with the dimensions 5 × 3, 8 × 6, and 9 × 4. Discuss these rectangles in a similar way, focusing on the shortcut for finding the area of each. Emphasize the difference between perimeter and area.

## Using Page 350

**Lesson Development** Have students read the problem, state the question in their own words, and identify the data. "How can we find how many tiles it would take to cover the wall area?" (Multiply 9 × 6.) Tell students that the area of a rectangular region is the number of square units needed to cover it. The number of square units can be found by multiplying the number of squares in a row by the number of rows. Write $A = l \times w$ on the chalkboard and demonstrate how the formula is used in the exercise. Have students give a complete statement to describe the solution to the problem. If necessary, review the meaning of the decimeter unit as you work the problem, and be sure students give the answer in square decimeters.

**Exercises 1–9** If necessary, work another exercise or two as examples. Assign the remaining exercises as independent work.

## Area of a Rectangle

How many tiles 1 decimeter square are needed to cover the wall area behind this kitchen stove?

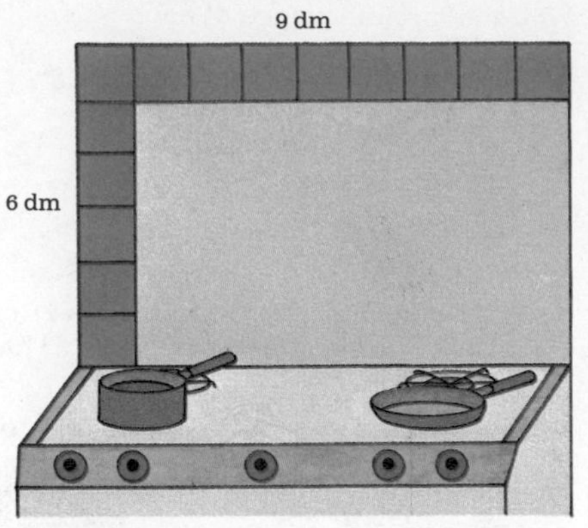


The **area** of a rectangular region is the number of unit squares needed to cover the region.

We can find the area in two different ways.

**Thinking About Squares**

There are 9 squares in each row.
There are 6 rows of squares.
There are 9 × 6, or 54 squares.

The area of the rectangle is 54 $dm^2$.
(Read **$dm^2$** as **"square decimeters."**)

**Using a Formula**

| Area | | length | | width |
|---|---|---|---|---|
| $A$ | = | $l$ | × | $w$ |
| ↓ | | ↓ | | ↓ |
| $A$ | = | 9 | × | 4 |
| $A$ | = | 54 $dm^2$ | | |

Find the area of each rectangular region.

1. 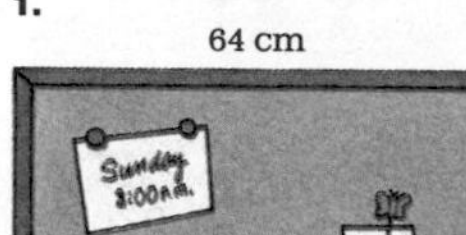


2,496 $cm^2$

2. 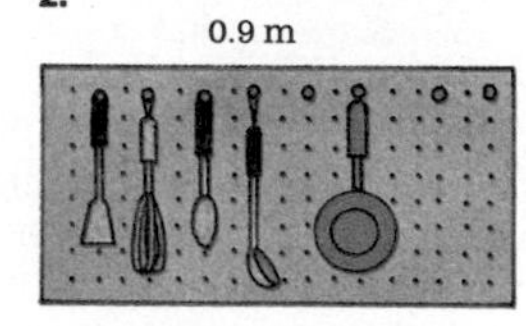


1.62 $m^2$

3. 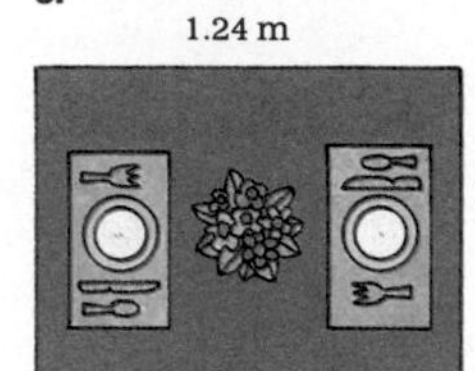


1.22 $m^2$

4. Kitchen floor
$l$ = 6.4 m
$w$ = 4.5 m
28.8 $m^2$

5. Lot for a house
$l$ = 45 m
$w$ = 36 m
1,620 $m^2$

6. Housing subdivision
$l$ = 2.5 km
$w$ = 4.5 km
11.25 $km^2$

7. City
$l$ = 15.5 km
$w$ = 9.5 km
147.3 $km^2$

8. Kitchen wall
$l$ = 4.8 m
$w$ = 2.5 m
12 $m^2$

9. Recipe card
$l$ = 120 mm
$w$ = 85 mm
10,200 $mm^2$



## Follow Up

### Reteaching

Use geoboards to review the concept of area. First, establish values for the length and the width of several rectangles, and set up a chart to highlight length, width, and area. Define area as the number of square units. Then show the rectangles on the geoboards and count the number of square units enclosed in the rectangle. Refer to the chart, and let students observe that the area of a rectangle can also be determined by multiplying the length times the width.

### Enrichment

Have the students measure the squares below and then complete the table to show how squares "grow."

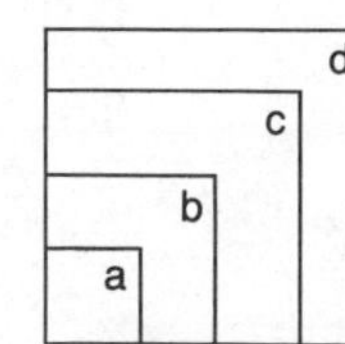


| Square | Length of side (cm) | Area ($cm^2$) |
|---|---|---|
| a | | |
| b | | |
| c | | |
| d | | |

# Applications

| Assignment Guide | | | |
|---|---|---|---|
| | Minimum | Average | Extended |
| page 350 | 1–9 | 1–9 | 1–9 |
| page 351 | 1–6 | 1–7 | 1–8 |

## Problem Solving: Practice

Use the 5-point checklist on page 8 to help you solve these **area problems.**

1. A rectangular room is 5.75 m long and 3.5 m wide. What is the area of the room's floor? 20.125 $m^2$

2. A rectangular mirror is 1.75 m long and 86 cm wide. What is its area? Note: When finding the area, be sure to use the same unit for the length and the width. 1.505 $m^2$ or 15,050 $cm^2$

3. A rectangular lot is 36 m long and 32 m wide. A house on the lot covers 25% of the lot's area. What is the area of the house? 288 $m^2$

4. What is the area of the floor of the room pictured below? 96 $m^2$

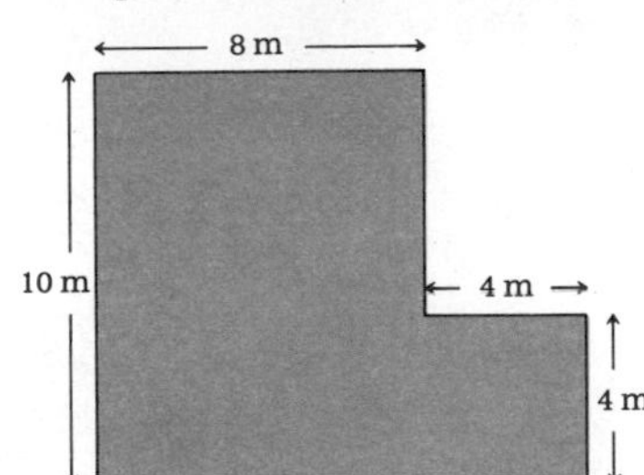


5. A rectangular room is 6.5 m long and 4.5 m wide and has 2.5 m high ceilings. What is the total area of the room's walls if the window and door use 2.75 $m^2$ of the wall space? 52.25 $m^2$

★ 6. The **square root** of a number, such as 1,024, is the number that when multiplied by itself gives that number as the product. The side of a square is the square root of the area of the square. Guess and check to find the length of the sides of a square whose area is 1,024 $mm^2$. 32 $mm^2$

7. **DATA HUNT** What is the area of your classroom floor in square meters? Measure to the nearest hundredth of a meter. Answers will vary.

8. **Try This** The Handys have 36 m of fence. What is the area of the largest rectangular pen they can make? Hint: Make a table. 81 $m^2$



## Using Page 351

**Lesson Development** Call attention to the 5-Point Checklist logo at the top of the page. Caution students to plan carefully when solving these problems dealing with area.

**Exercises 1–6** In exercise 2 students must convert to either centimeters or meters before calculating the area. In exercise 4 students can find the area of an irregular object by adding together the areas of regular objects.

**Data Hunt** Students might work in small groups to collect the data to solve this problem and then compare answers.

**Try This** A possible strategy, Make a Table, was taught on page 100.

**Discussion** Have students restate the question in their own words and identify the needed data. "What might you do to organize the information?" (Make a table.)

**Solution** The largest rectangular pen that the Handys can make is 81 $m^2$.

| w | l | Perimeter | Area |
|---|---|---|---|
| 3 m | 15 m | 36 m | 45 $m^2$ |
| 4 m | 14 m | 36 m | 56 $m^2$ |
| 5 m | 13 m | 36 m | 65 $m^2$ |
| 6 m | 12 m | 36 m | 72 $m^2$ |
| 7 m | 11 m | 36 m | 77 $m^2$ |
| 8 m | 10 m | 36 m | 80 $m^2$ |
| 9 m | 9 m | 36 m | 81 $m^2$ |
| 10 m | 8 m | 36 m | 80 $m^2$ |
| ⋮ | ⋮ | ⋮ | ⋮ |

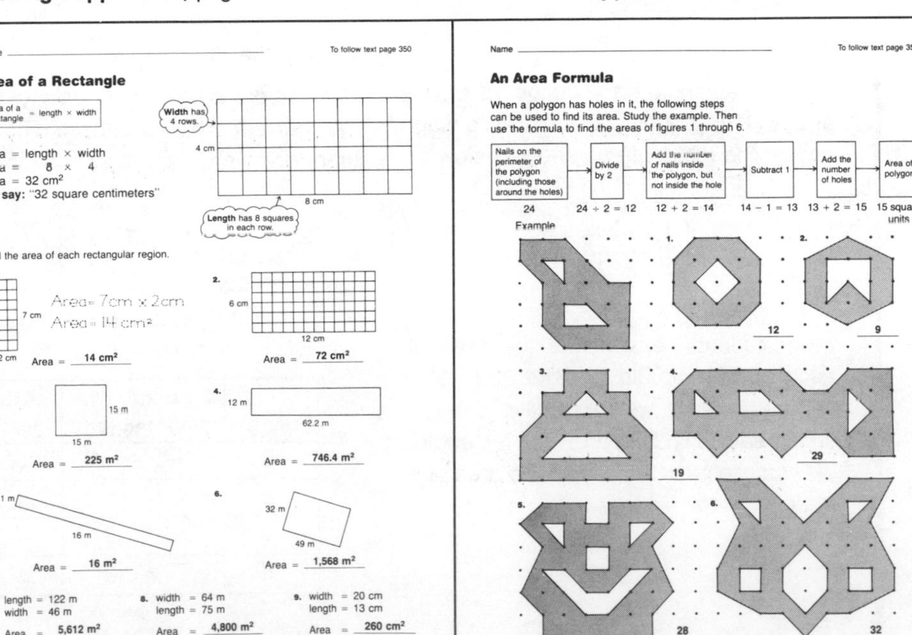

**Reteaching Supplement,** page 82

Name ______ To follow text page 350

### Area of a Rectangle

Area of a Rectangle = length × width

Area = length × width
Area = 8 × 4
Area = 32 $cm^2$
**We say:** "32 square centimeters"



Find the area of each rectangular region.

1. 7 cm, 2 cm. Area = 7cm × 2cm, Area = 14 $cm^2$. Area = 14 $cm^2$
2. 6 cm, 12 cm. Area = 72 $cm^2$
3. 15 m, 15 m. Area = 225 $m^2$
4. 12 m, 62.2 m. Area = 746.4 $m^2$
5. 1 m, 16 m. Area = 16 $m^2$
6. 32 m, 49 m. Area = 1,568 $m^2$
7. length = 122 m, width = 46 m. Area = 5,612 $m^2$
8. width = 64 m, length = 75 m. Area = 4,800 $m^2$
9. width = 20 cm, length = 13 cm. Area = 260 $cm^2$

**Enrichment Supplement,** page 82

Name ______ To follow text page 350

### An Area Formula

When a polygon has holes in it, the following steps can be used to find its area. Study the example. Then use the formula to find the areas of figures 1 through 6.

| Nails on the perimeter of the polygon (including those around the holes) | → Divide by 2 | → Add the number of nails inside the polygon, but not inside the hole | → Subtract 1 | → Add the number of holes | → Area of polygon |
|---|---|---|---|---|---|
| 24 | 24 ÷ 2 = 12 | 12 + 2 = 14 | 14 − 1 = 13 | 13 + 2 = 15 | 15 square units |

Example

1. 12
2. 9
3. 19
4. 29
5. 28
6. 32

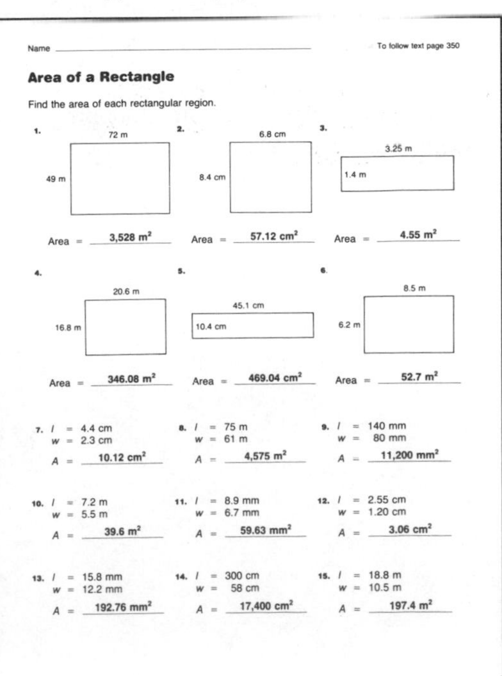

**Practice Supplement,** page 132

Name ______ To follow text page 350

### Area of a Rectangle

Find the area of each rectangular region.

1. 72 m, 49 m. Area = 3,528 $m^2$
2. 6.8 cm, 8.4 cm. Area = 57.12 $cm^2$
3. 3.25 m, 1.4 m. Area = 4.55 $m^2$
4. 20.6 m, 16.8 m. Area = 346.08 $m^2$
5. 45.1 cm, 10.4 cm. Area = 469.04 $cm^2$
6. 8.5 m, 6.2 m. Area = 52.7 $m^2$
7. $l$ = 4.4 cm, $w$ = 2.3 cm, $A$ = 10.12 $cm^2$
8. $l$ = 75 m, $w$ = 61 m, $A$ = 4,575 $m^2$
9. $l$ = 140 mm, $w$ = 80 mm, $A$ = 11,200 $mm^2$
10. $l$ = 7.2 m, $w$ = 5.5 m, $A$ = 39.6 $m^2$
11. $l$ = 8.9 mm, $w$ = 6.7 mm, $A$ = 59.63 $mm^2$
12. $l$ = 2.55 cm, $w$ = 1.20 cm, $A$ = 3.06 $cm^2$
13. $l$ = 15.8 mm, $w$ = 12.2 mm, $A$ = 192.76 $mm^2$
14. $l$ = 300 cm, $w$ = 58 cm, $A$ = 17,400 $cm^2$
15. $l$ = 18.8 m, $w$ = 10.5 m, $A$ = 197.4 $m^2$

**Quick Review** Students complete the number sentences and underline those from the same fact family.

$9 \times 7 = \square$    $60 + \square = 63$    $\square \div 7 = 9$    $\square \div 9 = 7$

$\square = 63 \div 9$    $\square \times 7 = 63$    $63 - \square = 50$

**Lesson Focus** To find the area of a triangle by using the formula $A = \frac{1}{2} \times b \times h$

**Suggested Materials** Puzzle boards or colored paper cutouts

## Ideas for Getting Started

Show students a large red triangle and a large blue triangle formed from the pieces shown below.

"How many ways can you rearrange the pieces of these triangles to form a rectangle?" Encourage students to find the following solutions.

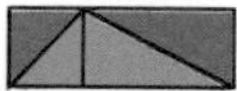

"Is the original large blue triangle congruent to the original large red triangle?" (yes) "How many large triangles does it take to form the rectangle?" (2) "How does the area of one of the large triangles compare with the area of the rectangle?" (It is $\frac{1}{2}$ the area of the rectangle.) Emphasize that the area of each of the triangles is $\frac{1}{2}$ the area of the rectangle. Point out that the height and length of the base of the original triangles is the same as the height and length of the base of the rectangle they form.

## Using Page 352

**Lesson Development** Point out the puzzle picture at the top of the page and emphasize the two points brought out in the demonstration: the height and base of the rectangle are the same as the height and base of the original triangles; it takes two congruent triangles to fit into one rectangle, so the area of one of the triangles is $\frac{1}{2}$ the area of the rectangle. Write the formula $A = \frac{1}{2} \times b \times h$ on the chalkboard and discuss it. Emphasize the formula for finding the area of a triangle as you work through the examples. Note that the height of the triangle in Example B is the same as the dashed line drawn from the top of the triangle perpendicular to the extended base.

**Warm Up** Have students use the formula to work through the exercises. Be sure students give their answers in square units.

## Area of a Triangle

Eric's teacher made puzzle boards to help the class learn about the area of a triangle.

**Puzzle:**
Can you make the puzzle pieces for the congruent triangles fit the rectangle?

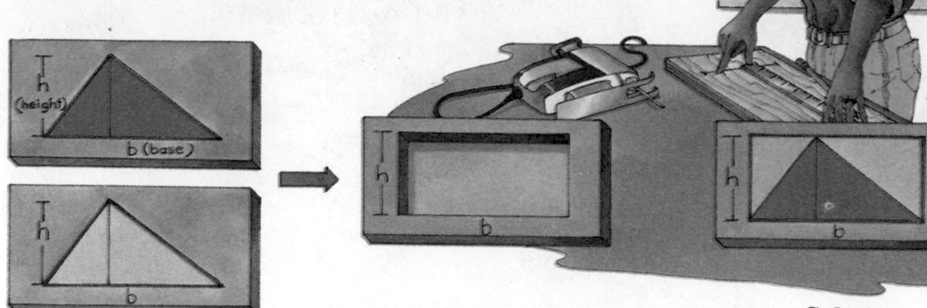


**Solution**

Since two congruent triangles fit into one rectangle with base and height the same as the triangles', the area of a triangle is one half the area of a rectangle.

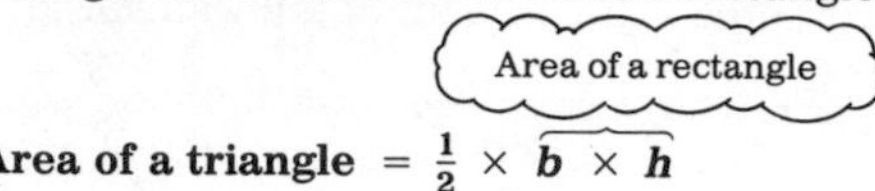


**Area of a triangle** $= \frac{1}{2} \times b \times h$

**Example A**

$A = \frac{1}{2} \times b \times h$

$A = \frac{1}{2} \times 8.6 \times 4.8$

$A = 4.3 \times 4.8 = 20.64 \text{ cm}^2$

height 4.8 cm, base: 8.6 cm

**Example B**

$A = \frac{1}{2} \times b \times h$

$A = \frac{1}{2} \times 12 \times 10$

$A = 6 \times 10 = 60 \text{ cm}^2$

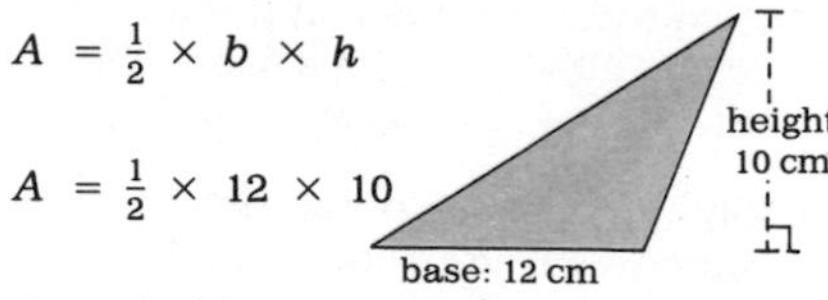


**Warm Up** Find the area.

**1.** 72 cm²

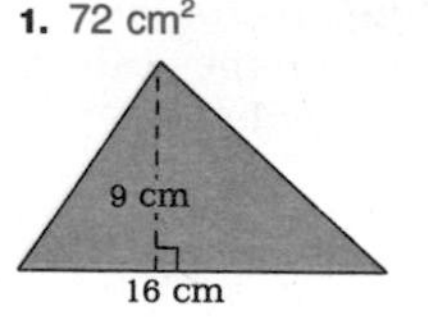


**2.** 24 m²

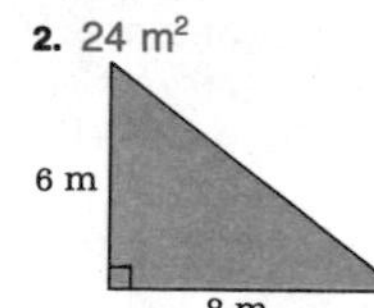


**3.** 65.1 mm²

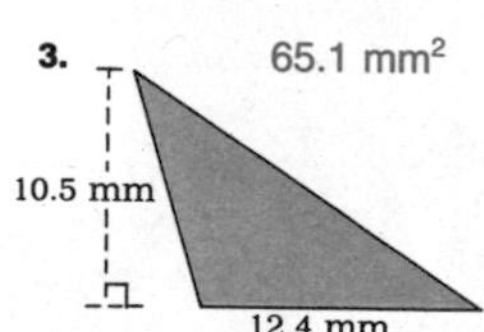


352

## Follow Up

### Reteaching

Make a rectangle on a geoboard or dot arrays (TRB p. 272) and construct a diagonal in the rectangle as shown below.

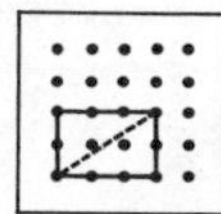

Help students reason that the area of each triangle should be $\frac{1}{2}$ the area of a rectangle. Since we can multiply length times width to find the area of a rectangle, we can use $\frac{1}{2}(l \times w)$ to find the area of a triangle.

### Enrichment

Have students draw diagonals for each of the four squares as shown. Then have them complete the table.

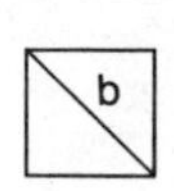

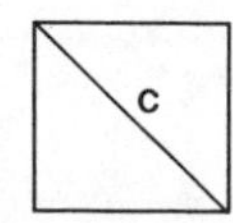

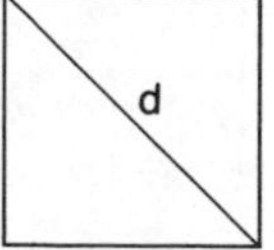


| Triangle | Length of diagonal (cm) | Area (cm²) |
|---|---|---|
| a | | |
| b | | |
| c | | |
| d | | |

| Assignment Guide | | | |
|---|---|---|---|
| | Minimum | Average | Extended |
| page 353 | 1–11 | 1–12 | 1–12, TM |

Find the area.

1. 48 cm²

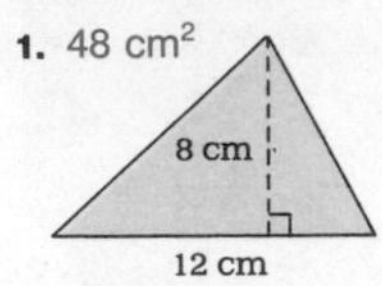


2. 36 m²

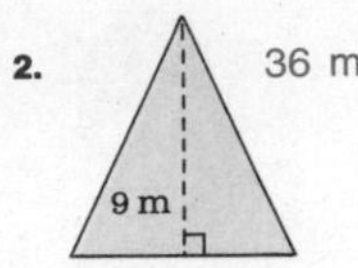


3. 701.5 cm²

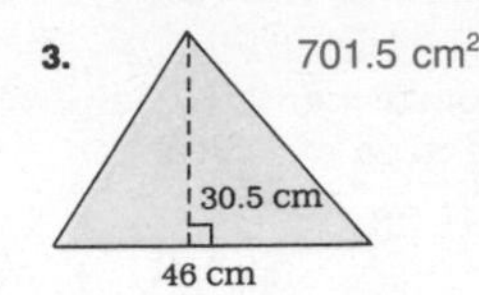


4. 30.1 cm²

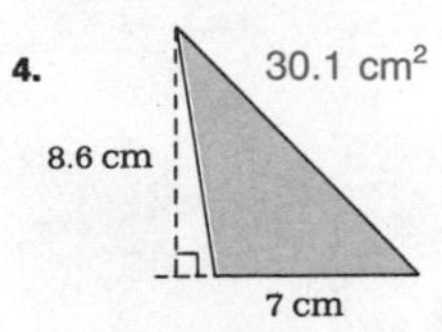


5. 234 mm²

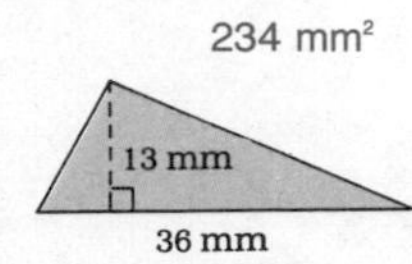


6. 8.4 mm²

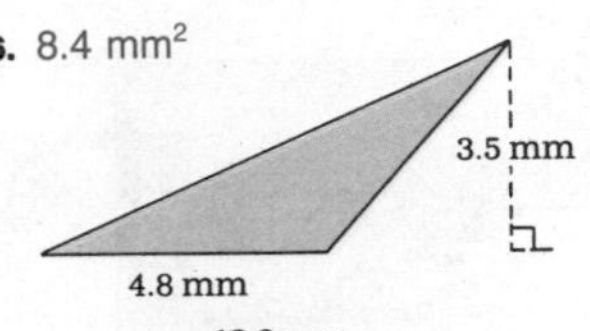


7. 20 cm²

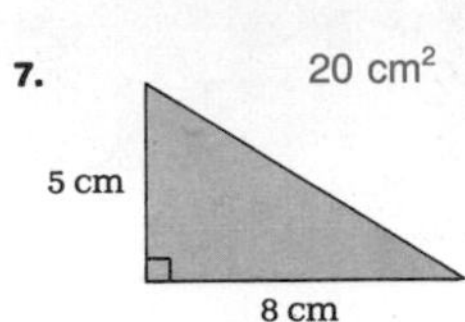


8. 38 cm²

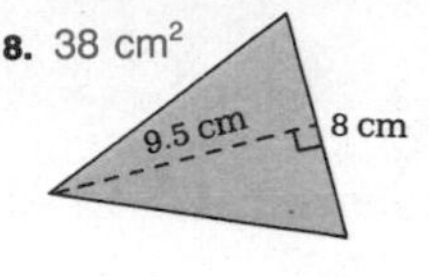


9.

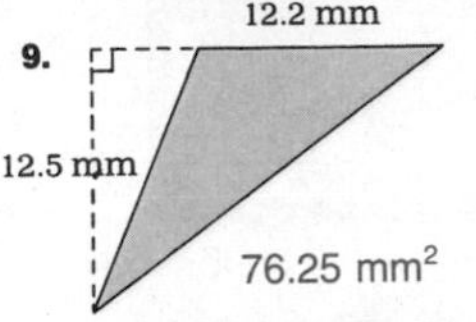


76.25 mm²

10. What is the area of this triangular corner lot? 643.56 m²

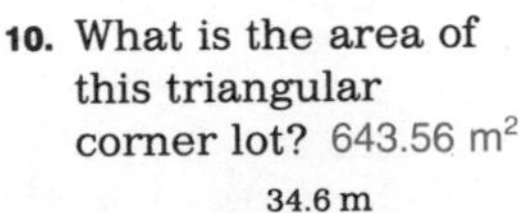
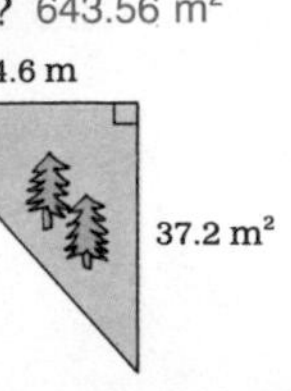


11. What is the total area of these sails? 17 m²

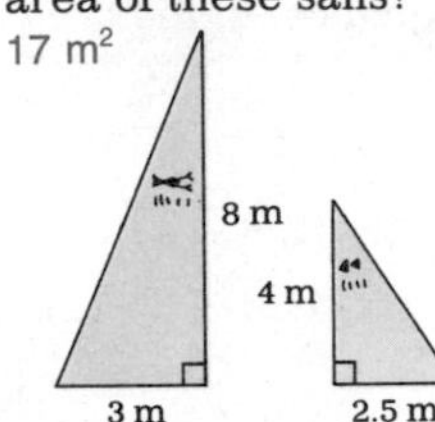


★ 12. What is the area of this four-sided field? 816 m²

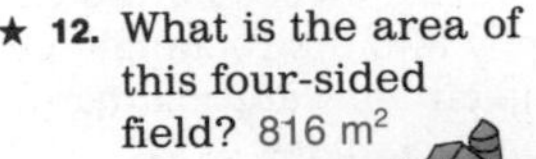
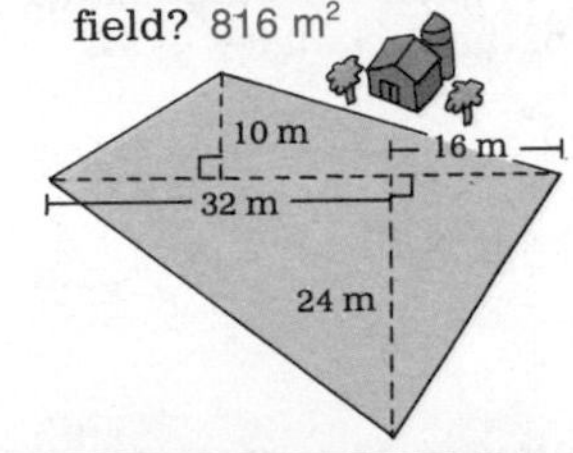


## Think Math

**Area of a Parallelogram**

The puzzle pieces for the parallelogram can be made to fit into the rectangle puzzle board. Write a formula for the area of a parallelogram. $A = b \times h$

Find the area of this parallelogram. 636 mm²

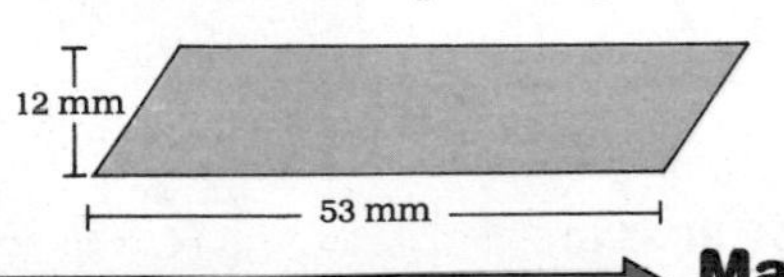


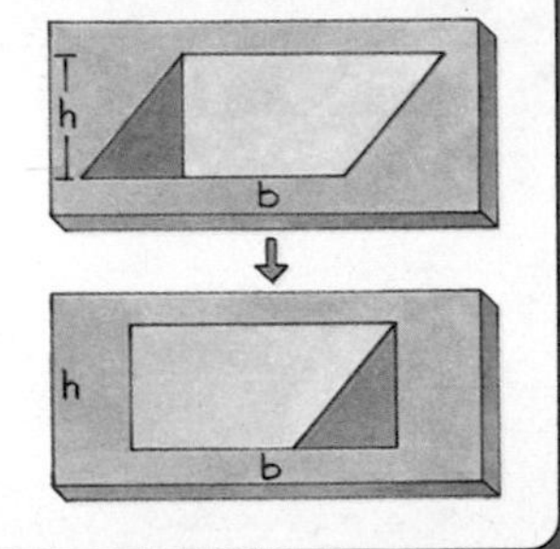




## Using Page 353

**Exercises 1–9** As students complete these exercises, pay particular attention to their work in exercises 4, 6, and 9. Be sure they substitute the correct numbers in the formula and understand that the numbers given represent the base and altitude.

**Exercises 10–11** These exercises suggest some real-world situations using the areas of triangles. In exercise 11, the areas of the two triangles must be added together.

**Exercise 12** This exercise shows how any quadrilateral area can be broken down into the sum of the areas of its triangles. This procedure is often used by surveyors to find the area of such regions.

**Think Math** Encourage students to cut construction paper into pieces similar to those shown in the puzzle. They can then manipulate the pieces to verify that pieces of a parallelogram can be rearranged to make a rectangle that has the same base and height as the parallelogram. Extend the lesson by having students find the areas of additional parallelograms in different positions and of different shapes.

**Reteaching Supplement**, page 83

Name ______ To follow text page 353

**Area of a Triangle**

Area (A) of a Triangle $= \frac{1}{2} \times$ base (b) $\times$ height (h)

$A = \frac{1}{2} \times b \times h$
$A = \frac{1}{2} \times 28 \times 14$
$A = 14 \times 14$
$A = 196$ cm²
square centimeters

$A = \frac{1}{2} \times b \times h$
$A = \frac{1}{2} \times 60 \times 36$
$A = 30 \times 36$
$A = 1{,}080$ m²
square meters

Find the area of each triangle.

1. $A = \frac{1}{2} \times 24.6 \times 14.2$ Area = 174.66 cm²

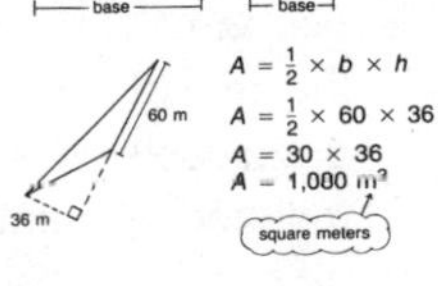
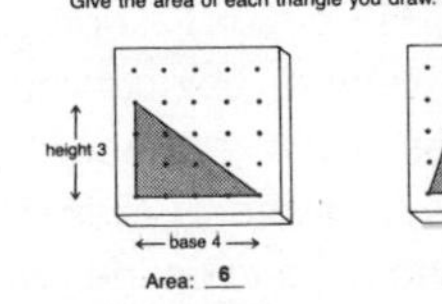

2. Area = 1,085 cm²

3. Area = 13.2 cm²
4. Area = 132 m²
5. Area = 54.72 mm²

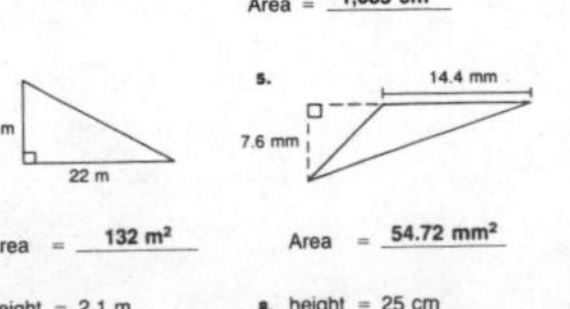
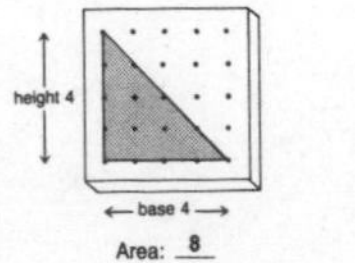

6. height = 11 m, base = 7 m, Area = 38.5 m²
7. height = 2.1 m, base = 3.2 m, Area = 3.36 m²
8. height = 25 cm, base = 5 cm, Area = 62.5 cm²

**Enrichment Supplement**, page 83

Name ______ To follow text page 353

**How Many Can You Find?**

1. Draw other triangles with different shapes that have base 4 and height 3. Give the area of each triangle you draw. **Drawings will vary.**

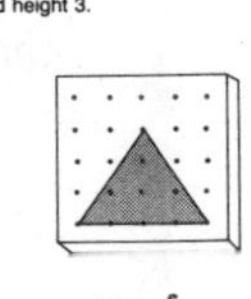
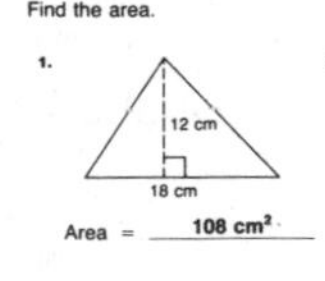

Area: 6 Area: 6 Area: 6

2. Draw triangles with different shapes that have base 4 and height 2. Give the area of each. **Drawings will vary.**

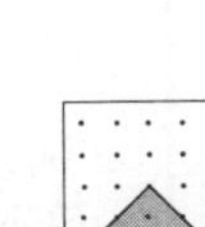

Area: 4 Area: 4 Area: 4

3. Draw triangles with different shapes that have base 4 and height 4. Give the area of each. **Drawings will vary.**

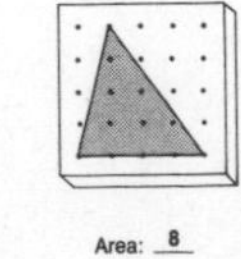
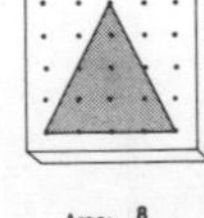

Area: 8 Area: 8 Area: 8

**Practice Supplement**, page 133

Name ______ To follow text page 353

**Area of a Triangle**

Find the area.

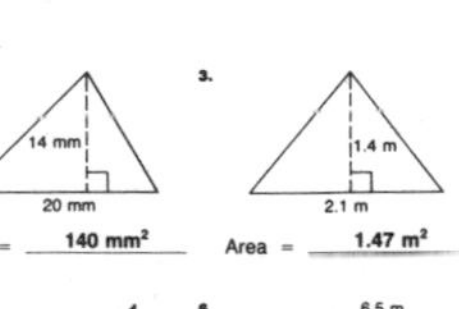

1. Area = 108 cm²
2. Area = 140 mm²
3. Area = 1.47 m²

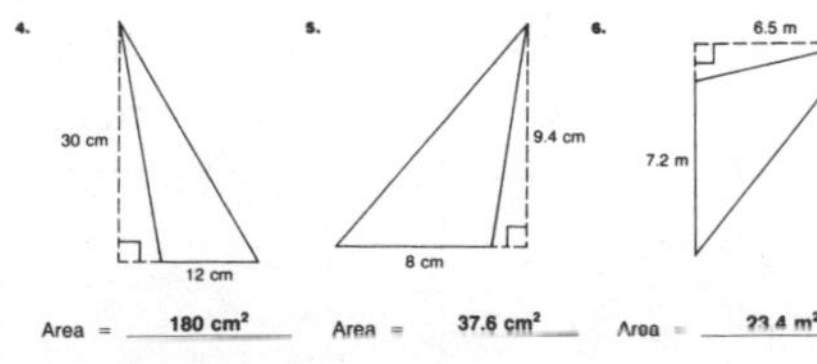

4. Area = 180 cm²
5. Area = 37.6 cm²
6. Area = 23.4 m²
7. Area = 160 mm²
8. Area = 8.96 m²
9. Area = 113.4 cm²
10. Area = 13.6 m²
11. Area = 1,488 cm²
12. Area = 61.74 mm²

**Quick Review** For each radius or diameter, students give aloud the other value.
$D$ = 12 cm $r$ = 6 cm  $r$ = 0.9 km $D$ = 1.8 km  $r$ = 24 m $D$ = 12 m
$D$ = 7 mm $r$ = 3.5 mm  $r$ = 0.5 cm $D$ = 1 cm
$D$ = 6 m $r$ = 3 m  $D$ = 18 mm $r$ = 9 mm

**Lesson Focus** To find the area of a circle by using the formula $A = \pi r^2$

**Suggested Materials** Graph paper (TRB p. 272), compass

## Ideas for Getting Started

Have students draw a circle on graph paper as shown below. Then draw the table on the chalkboard.

| radius $r$ | $r^2$ | $3 \times r^2$ | Estimated area |
|---|---|---|---|
| 3 | 9 | 27 | 28 |
| 4 | | | |
| 5 | | | |
| 6 | | | |

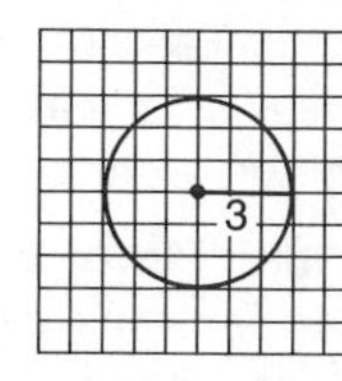


"What is the radius squared?" (9) "What is $3 \times r^2$?" (27) "Count the squares and parts of squares to estimate the area of the circle. What is the estimate?" (28) Point out that the area of the circle is a little more than $3 \times r^2$. Have students draw other circles to complete the table.

## Using Page 354

**Lesson Development** Point out the puzzle boards at the top of the page. "How many sections (sectors) are in each half of the circle as shown by the solid lines?" (5) "How many sectors have been placed in the rectangle on the puzzle board?" (10) "What is the length of one side of the rectangle?" $\left(\frac{1}{2} C\right)$ "What is the area of the rectangle?" $\left(\frac{1}{2} C \times r\right)$ Point out that the area of the circle is approximately equal to the area of the rectangle. Write $A = \frac{1}{2} C \times r$ on the chalkboard. Remind students that the circumference is $\pi \times$ diameter, and $\frac{1}{2}$ the circumference is $\pi \times$ radius because the radius is $\frac{1}{2}$ the diameter. Replace $\frac{1}{2}$ $C$ with $\pi \times r$ and write the equation $A = \pi \times r \times r$, or $A = \pi \times r^2$.

Some students might have difficulty understanding this explanation of the formula. However, they will have opportunities at later levels to understand it more thoroughly. The most important goal in this lesson is to enable students to use the formula correctly to find the area of the circle.

**Warm Up** Emphasize that $r^2$ is $r \times r$. Note in exercise 3 that students must realize that the radius is $\frac{1}{2}$ the diameter and find that measurement before using the formula. Remind students that area is given in square units.

## Area of a Circle

Puzzle boards can also help you learn about the area of a circle.

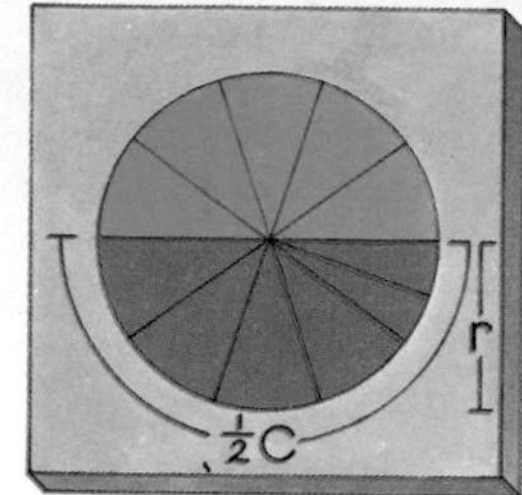

The puzzle pieces for the circle can be fitted almost exactly into the rectangle puzzle board. The area of the circle is approximately equal (≈) to the area of the rectangle!

We write:
$A = \frac{1}{2}C \times r$
$A = \pi \times r \times r$
$A = \pi \times \mathbf{r^2}$

$C = \pi \times$ diameter, so $\frac{1}{2}C = \pi \times$ radius.

**Warm Up** Find the area of each circle.

**1.** 78.5 cm²
radius 5 cm
$A = 3.14 \times r \times r$
$A = 3.14 \times 5 \times 5$
$A$ = ▩ cm²

**2.** 314 mm²
radius 10 mm
$A = 3.14 \times r \times r$
$A = 3.14 \times 10 \times 10$
$A$ = ▩ mm²

**3.** 200.96 mm²
diameter 16 mm
$D = 16$, so $r = 8$
$A = 3.14 \times 8 \times 8$
$A$ = ▩ mm²

354

## Follow Up

### Reteaching

Provide students with several sheets of graph paper (TRB p. 270). Then ask students to find several objects that have circular regions, such as paper cups or cans of various sizes. Students then trace around the objects on the graph paper and estimate the areas by counting squares. Next, work with students as they measure the diameter, find the radius, and use the formula to find the area of each circle.

### Enrichment

Ask students to go to a local pizza parlor and find out the prices and diameters of pizzas of various sizes. Have them find the area of each pizza and how much that pizza costs per square unit of area. In this manner, students can determine which pizza is the best buy.

| Assignment Guide | Minimum | Average | Extended |
|---|---|---|---|
| page 355 | 1–10 | 1–11 | 1–11, TM |

Find the area of each circle. Use 3.14 for $\pi$. Round to the nearest hundredth when necessary.

1. 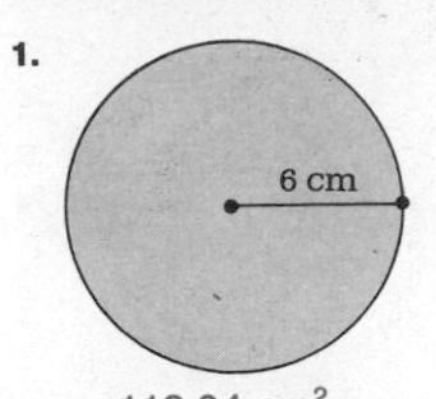

113.04 $cm^2$

2. 2.4 mm
18.09 $mm^2$

3. 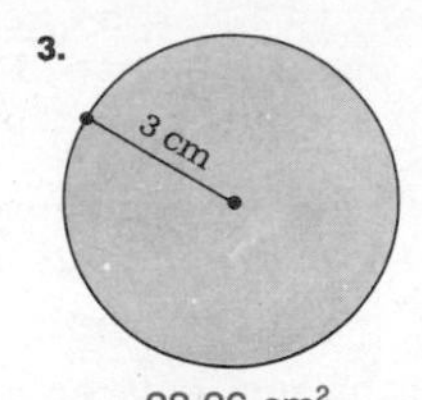

28.26 $cm^2$

4. 8 cm
50.24 $cm^2$

5. 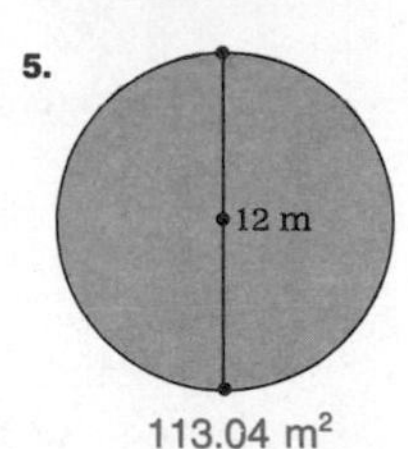

113.04 $m^2$

6. 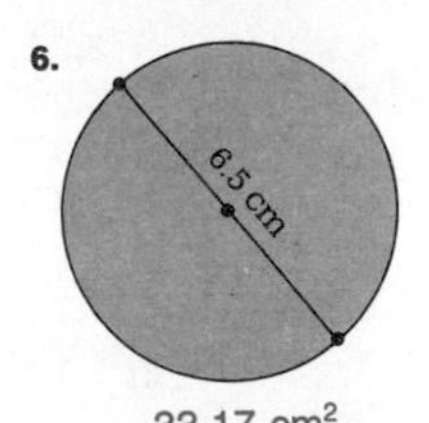

33.17 $cm^2$

7. 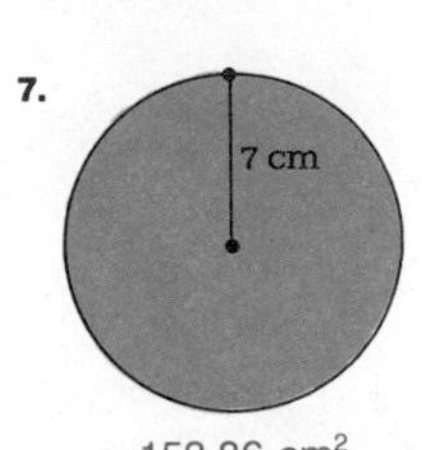

153.86 $cm^2$

8. 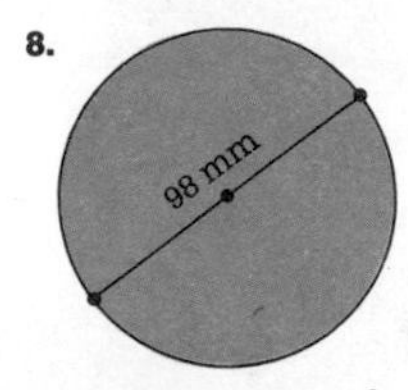

7,539.14 $mm^2$

9. 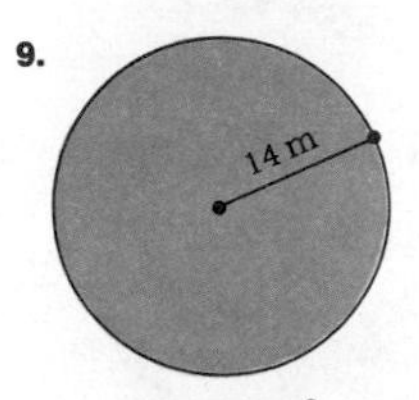

615.44 $m^2$

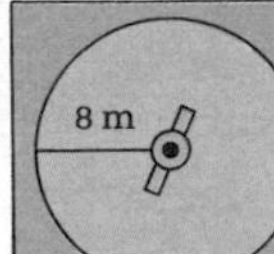


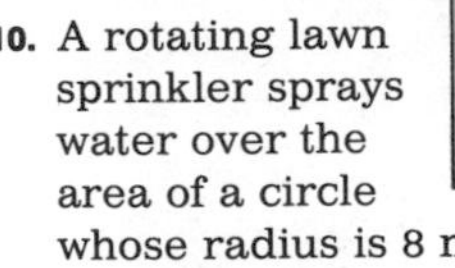

10. A rotating lawn sprinkler sprays water over the area of a circle whose radius is 8 m. What is the area of the lawn watered? 200.96 $m^2$

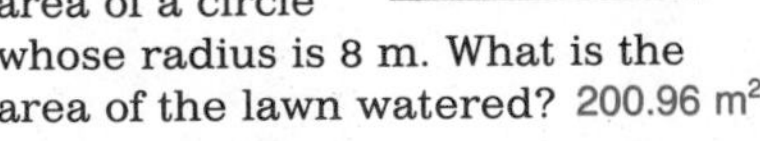

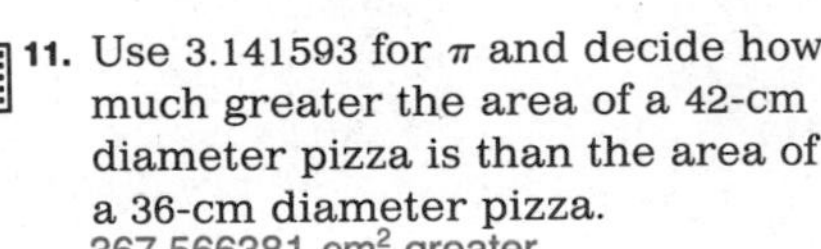

11. Use 3.141593 for $\pi$ and decide how much greater the area of a 42-cm diameter pizza is than the area of a 36-cm diameter pizza.
367.566381 $cm^2$ greater

**Think Math**

**Area Estimation**

Estimate the area of the circle as accurately as you can by counting square units and parts of square units.

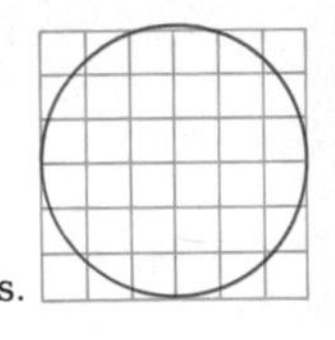

By how much does your estimate differ from the actual area? (Use 3.14 for $\pi$.) Estimates will vary. Actual area: $3.14 \times 3 \times 3 = 28.26$ square units



## Using Page 355

**Exercises 1–9** In exercises 4, 5, 6, 8, and 9 note that students must find the radius before using the area formula.

**Exercise 10** In this exercise students are given the radius and are asked to apply the formula to find the area of a circle.

**Exercise 11** In this calculator exercise, point out that the greater the number of decimal places students use in the approximation for $\pi$, the closer they will come to the exact area of a given circle. Have students see if their calculators have a symbol key that automatically produces the decimal for $\pi$. If not, they will have to enter the decimal given.

**Think Math** Encourage students to estimate the area of the circle by counting the squares and parts of squares as accurately as possible. The object is to come as close as possible to the actual area by estimating. Be sure students complete their estimates before using the formula to find the exact area. Extend the exercise by having students estimate the area of an ellipse or some other figure with curved sides.

**Reteaching Supplement,** page 84

Name ______ To follow text page 355

**Area of a Circle**

Count the squares and parts of squares to estimate the area of each circle. Then find the exact area using this formula:
Area = $\pi$ × (radius)² = $\pi$ × radius × radius

1. radius: 2 cm
Estimate: 12 cm²
Area = 3.14 × (2)²
Area = 3.14 × 2 × 2 (Use 3.14 for $\pi$.)
Area = 12.56 cm²

2. 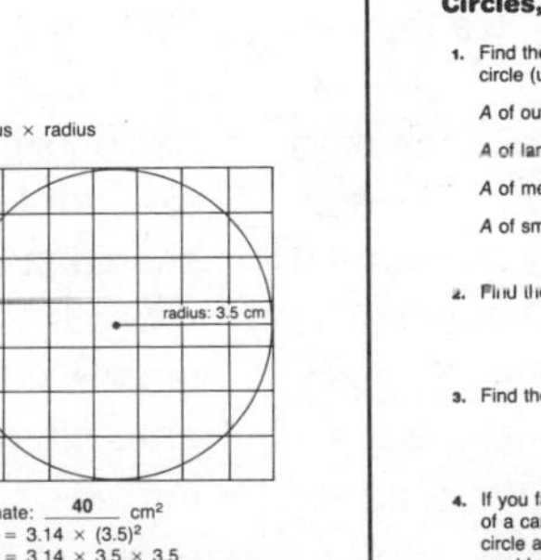
radius: 3.5 cm
Estimate: 40 cm²
Area = 3.14 × (3.5)²
Area = 3.14 × 3.5 × 3.5
Area = 38.465 cm²

Find the area of each circle. Use 3.14 for $\pi$. Round to the nearest hundredth when necessary.

3. 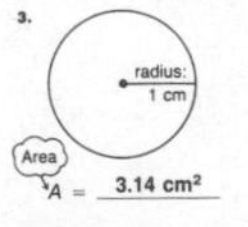 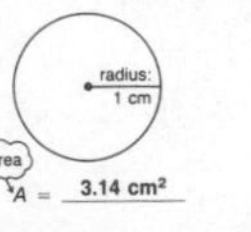
radius: 1 cm
(Area) A = 3.14 cm²

4. 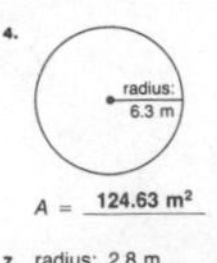 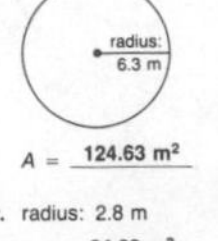
radius: 6.3 m
A = 124.63 m²

5. 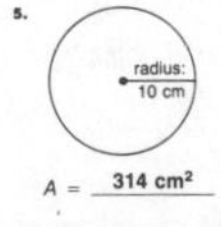
radius: 10 cm
A = 314 cm²

6. radius: 3 m A = 28.26 m²
7. radius: 2.8 m A = 24.62 m²
8. radius: 5.4 m A = 91.56 m²
9. radius: 8 cm A = 200.96 cm²
10. radius: 1.9 cm A = 11.34 cm²
11. radius: 6 m A = 113.04 m²

**Enrichment Supplement,** page 84

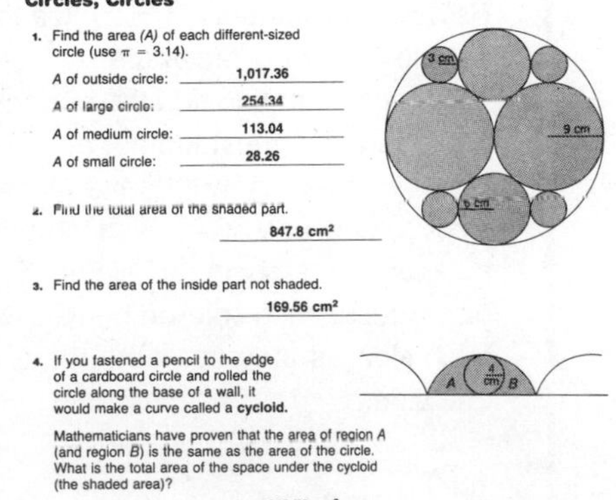

Name ______ To follow text page 355

**Circles, Circles**

1. Find the area (A) of each different-sized circle (use $\pi$ = 3.14).
A of outside circle: 1,017.36
A of large circle: 254.34
A of medium circle: 113.04
A of small circle: 28.26

2. Find the total area of the shaded part. 847.8 cm²

3. Find the area of the inside part not shaded. 169.56 cm²

4. If you fastened a pencil to the edge of a cardboard circle and rolled the circle along the base of a wall, it would make a curve called a **cycloid**.
Mathematicians have proven that the area of region A (and region B) is the same as the area of the circle. What is the total area of the space under the cycloid (the shaded area)? 150.72 cm²

5. Is the area of the outside ring less than, equal to, or greater than the area of the innermost circle? equal to

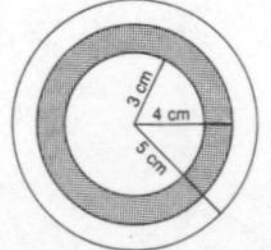


**Practice Supplement,** page 134

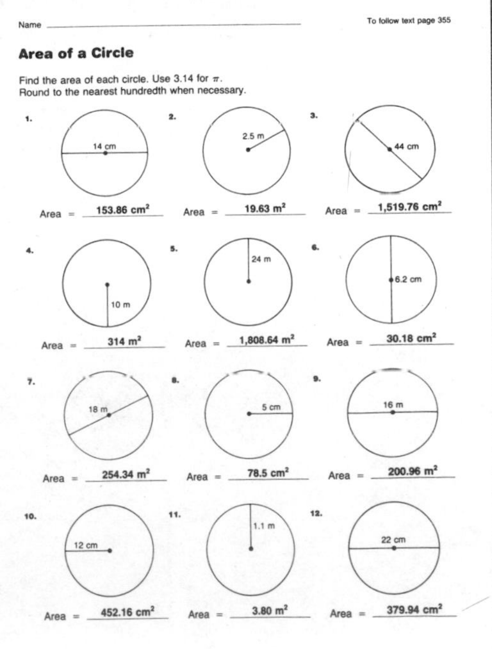

Name ______ To follow text page 355

**Area of a Circle**

Find the area of each circle. Use 3.14 for $\pi$. Round to the nearest hundredth when necessary.

1. 14 cm — Area = 153.86 cm²
2. 2.5 m — Area = 19.63 m²
3. 44 cm — Area = 1,519.76 cm²
4. 10 m — Area = 314 m²
5. 24 m — Area = 1,808.64 m²
6. 6.2 cm — Area = 30.18 cm²
7. 18 m — Area = 254.34 m²
8. 5 cm — Area = 78.5 cm²
9. 16 m — Area = 200.96 m²
10. 12 cm — Area = 452.16 cm²
11. 1.1 m — Area = 3.80 m²
12. 22 cm — Area = 379.94 cm²

**Quick Review** Students write the value of these amounts of money.
1 dollar, 6 pennies $1.06 3 quarters, 3 pennies 78¢ 4 dimes 2 pennies 42¢
2 dimes 15 pennies 35¢ 6 nickels 30¢ 1 quarter 2 dimes 45¢
1 dollar, 1 quarter, 1 dime $1.35 1 dollar, 4 nickels, 3 pennies $1.23

**Lesson Focus** To find the surface area of a rectangular figure

**Suggested Materials** Shoebox or similar box with a lid

## Ideas for Getting Started

Review the formula for finding the area of a rectangle. Hold up a shoebox and say: "The length of the lid is 32 cm. The width is 15 cm. What is the area of the lid?" (480 $cm^2$) Repeat the exercise with the side of the box and have students identify the formula. Hold up the box again and ask: "How many pairs of congruent rectangles can you find on the box?" (3 pairs: top and bottom, ends, sides) Be sure students understand that a box (a rectangular prism) has 6 faces.

## Using Page 356

**Lesson Development** Be sure students understand the question. Have them identify the data in the picture. (the length, width, and height of the box) "How can you find the total surface area of the box?" (Find the area of each face, then add the areas together.) Tell students that the *surface area* of a figure is the sum of the area of all the faces.

"How can you find the area of the top of the box?" (Multiply 65 by 32.) "What is the area of the bottom of the box?" (the same as the top) "How can you find the area of the end of the box?" (Multiply 32 by 36.) "What is the area of the other end?" (the same) "How can you find the area of the front side of the box?" (Multiply 65 by 36.) "What is the area of the back side?" (the same as the front) Have students calculate the area of each face. Add the areas on the chalkboard to find the total surface area. Be sure students understand that they could have added the areas of the top, one side, and one end and doubled that sum.

**Warm Up** Students may confuse finding surface area with finding volume. Work with students who seem to be multiplying length × width × height instead of length × width to find the area of each face. Be sure students give answers in square units rather than cubic units.

## Surface Area

How many square centimeters of colored paper are needed to cover the surface of the record storage box?

The **surface area** of a figure is the sum of the areas of all its faces.

We find the surface area of the box by adding the areas of six rectangles.

| | | |
|---|---|---|
| Top: | 65 × 32 = | 2,080 |
| Bottom: | 65 × 32 = | 2,080 |
| Front: | 65 × 36 = | 2,340 |
| Back: | 65 × 36 = | 2,340 |
| End: | 32 × 36 = | 1,152 |
| End: | 32 × 36 = | 1,152 |
| | | 11,144 |

The surface area of the box is 11,144 $cm^2$.

**Warm Up** Find the surface area of each object.

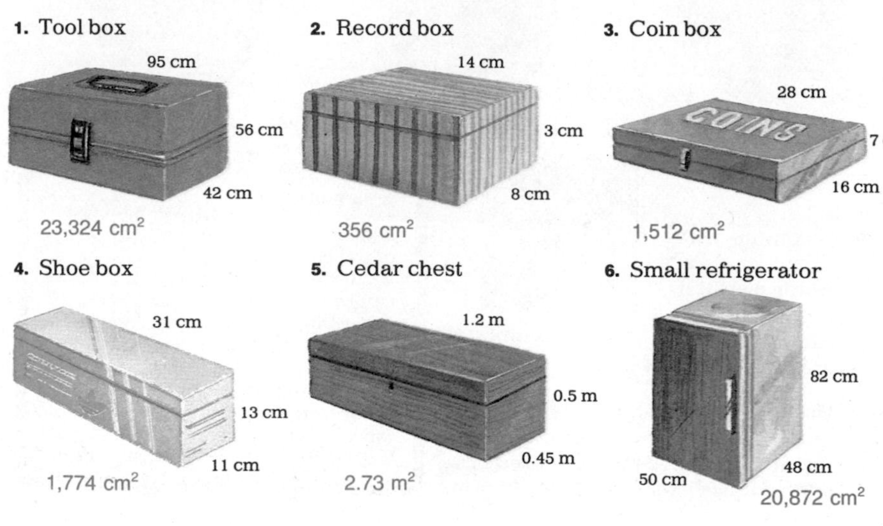


356

## Follow Up

### Reteaching

Review with students the formula for finding the area of a rectangle: $A = l \times w$. Tell students that to find the surface area of a figure, we must look at all the parts. Provide students with several different size boxes, and work with students to measure and count all sides. Suggest that students use colored pencils to mark each side as they compute the area for that side.

### Enrichment

Provide pairs of students or small groups of students with ten cubes each. Have students place the number cubes side by side to form rectangular prisms. They should start with one cube and continue until all ten cubes are included. Challenge students to find out how the surface area changes as the number of cubes increases.

**Solution: The pattern is $4n + 2$, where $n$ is the number of cubes.**

| Assignment Guide | | | |
|---|---|---|---|
| | Minimum | Average | Extended |
| page 357 | 1–6, SK | 1–7, SK | 1–8, SK |

Find the surface area of each box.

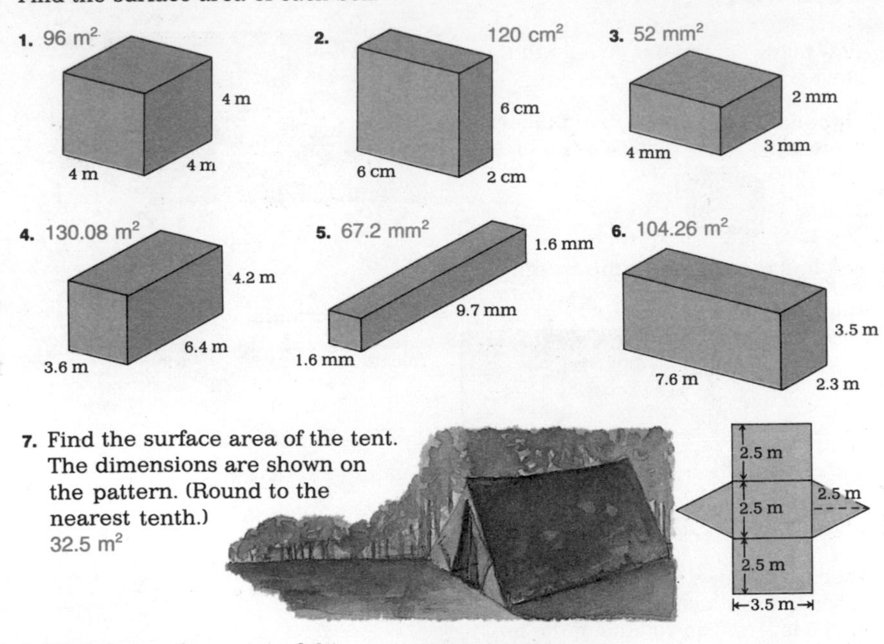


7. Find the surface area of the tent. The dimensions are shown on the pattern. (Round to the nearest tenth.)
32.5 m²

★ 8. Find the surface area of this can. The dimensions are shown on the pattern. Use 3.14 for $\pi$.
376.8 cm²

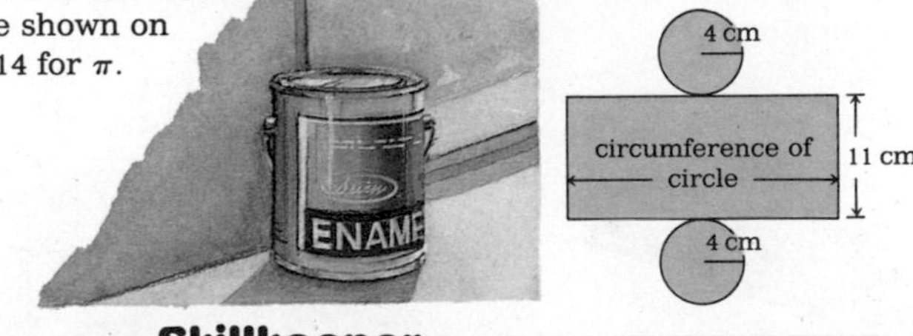


**Skillkeeper**

Find the mean of each list of numbers.
Round to the nearest tenth when necessary.

1. 2, 18, 13, 7 10
2. 22, 41, 10, 27 25
3. 67, 48, 53, 61, 70 59.8
4. 113, 128, 116, 132 122.3
5. 3, 8, 11, 5, 4 6.2
6. 17, 38, 51, 26, 28 32
7. 248, 273, 259, 263, 240 256.6
8. 74, 63, 82, 59, 91, 67 72.7
9. 298, 47, 93, 966 351



## Using Page 357

**Exercises 1–6** If students have difficulty finding the surface areas of the boxes, repeat the demonstration from the previous page, emphasizing that three pairs of congruent rectangles make up the surface area of each box.

**Exercise 7** To find the surface area of the tent, students must find the area of three rectangles and two triangles.

**Exercise 8** Students must find the circumference of the circle and use that measurement to find the area of the two circles, then add that amount to the area of the rectangle.

**Skillkeeper** This skill was originally taught in Chapter 13.

**Reteaching Supplement,** page 85

Name ______ To follow text page 357

**Surface Area**

We can find the **surface area** of a box by finding the sum of the areas of all its faces.

1. Area of face *A* is 15 cm². ($A$ = 5 cm × 3 cm = 15 cm²)
2. Area of the face opposite face *A* is 15 cm². (same area as for *A*)
3. Area of face *B* is 40 cm².
4. Area of the face opposite face *B* is 40 cm².
5. Area of face *C* is 24 cm².
6. Area of the face opposite face *C* is 24 cm².
7. Total surface area of the solid is 158 cm². (Add the areas of all 6 faces.)

Find the surface area of each box.

8. Surface area = 108 cm²
9. Surface area = 62 mm²
10. Surface area = 348 cm²
11. Surface area = 26 cm²
12. Surface area = 726 m²
13. Surface area = 192 cm²
14. Surface area = 88 m²
15. Surface area = 34 cm²
16. Surface area = 78 cm²

**Enrichment Supplement,** page 85

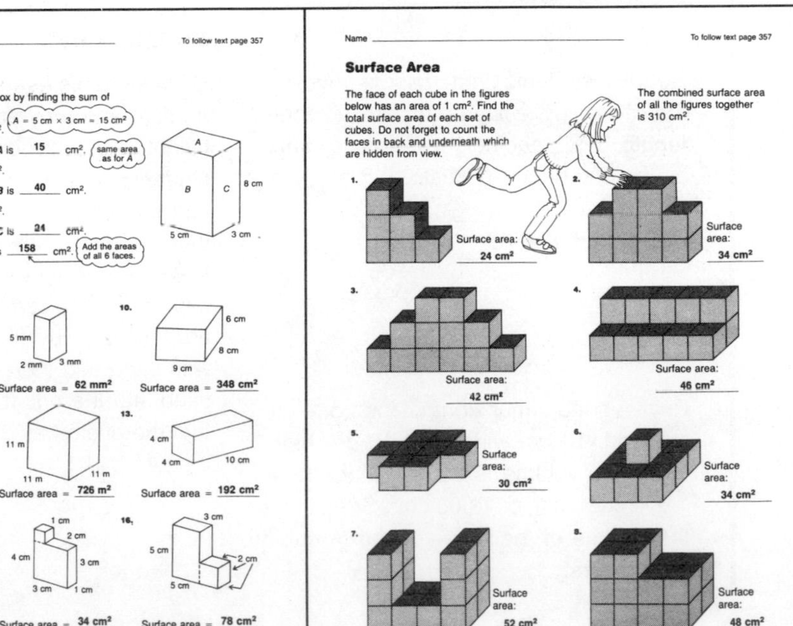

Name ______ To follow text page 357

**Surface Area**

The face of each cube in the figures below has an area of 1 cm². Find the total surface area of each set of cubes. Do not forget to count the faces in back and underneath which are hidden from view.

The combined surface area of all the figures together is 310 cm².

1. Surface area: 24 cm²
2. Surface area: 34 cm²
3. Surface area: 42 cm²
4. Surface area: 46 cm²
5. Surface area: 30 cm²
6. Surface area: 34 cm²
7. Surface area: 52 cm²
8. Surface area: 48 cm²

**Practice Supplement,** page 135

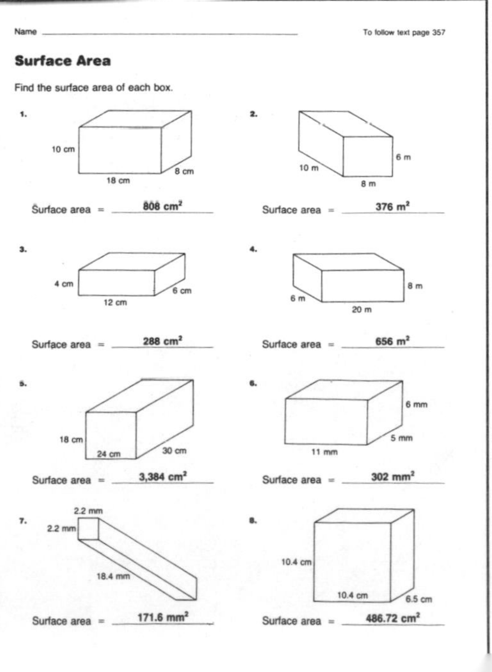

Name ______ To follow text page 357

**Surface Area**

Find the surface area of each box.

1. Surface area = 808 cm²
2. Surface area = 376 m²
3. Surface area = 288 cm²
4. Surface area = 656 m²
5. Surface area = 3,384 cm²
6. Surface area = 302 mm²
7. Surface area = 171.6 mm²
8. Surface area = 486.72 cm²

# Measurement

**Quick Review** Students give the number that makes each expression true.

$7 \times \boxed{5} \times 2 = 10 \times 7$ $8 \times 7 \times 5 = 40 \times \boxed{7}$ $\boxed{10} \times 2 \times 4 = 8 \times 10$

$4 \times 8 \times 5 = 20 \times \boxed{8}$ $5 \times \boxed{3} \times 4 = 3 \times 20$ $\boxed{3} \times 9 \times 10 = 27 \times 10$

**Lesson Focus** To find the volume of a prism using the formula $V = l \times w \times h$; to use estimation to solve word problems involving volume

**Suggested Materials** Cubes or blocks

## Ideas for Getting Started

If possible, show a box of cubes to students and say: "Look at one layer. How many cubes are in each row of the layer? How many rows are in the layer? How many cubes are in the layer? How many layers are there? How many cubes are there in all?" Repeat the exercise with different-sized boxes of cubes. If a box of cubes is not available, stack cubes to make a rectangular prism and use it to ask the questions.

## Using Page 358

**Lesson Development** Ask students to read the information at the top of the page and examine the art. "How many cubes are in each row of the bottom layer?" (5) "How many rows are in the bottom layer?" (4) "How many layers are in the box?" (3) "What procedure could you use to find the total number of cubes?" (Multiply the number of cubes in each row by the number of rows in each layer by the number of layers.) Tell students that the *volume* of a box is the number of cubic units it will hold.

Have students look at the second example and relate it to the illustration at the top of the page. Then write on the chalkboard the formula given and ask students to fill in the amounts for the length, width, and height of the box. After students have calculated the volume, remind them that volume is always given in cubic units.

**Exercises 1–9** Be sure students do not confuse the formula for finding volume with the formula for finding surface area.

## Volume

How many centimeter cubes will the box hold?

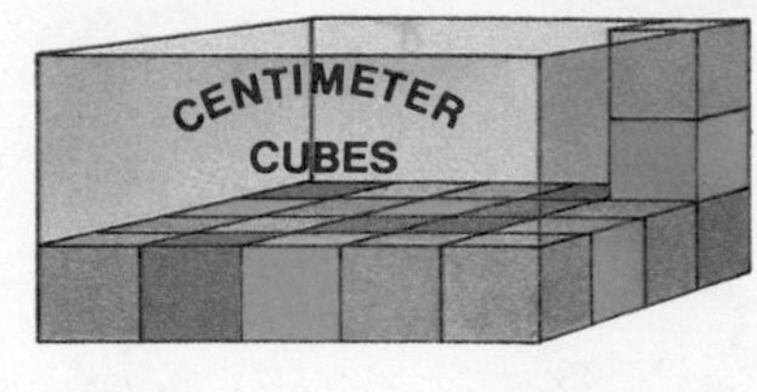


The **volume** of a box is the number of cubic units it will hold. We can use this unit

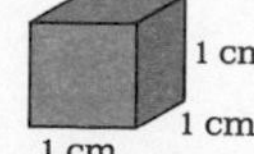


and find the volume of this box in two ways.

**Thinking About Cubes**

There are 5 rows of 4 cubes, or 20 cubes in each layer. The box will hold 3 layers. The volume of the box is 5 × 4 × 3, or 60 cm³ (cubic centimeters).

**Using a Formula**

| volume | | length | | width | | height |
|---|---|---|---|---|---|---|
| **V** | = | ***l*** | × | ***w*** | × | ***h*** |
| ↓ | | ↓ | | ↓ | | ↓ |
| *V* | = | 5 | × | 4 | × | 3 |
| *V* | = | 60 cm³ | | | | |

Find the volume of each box.

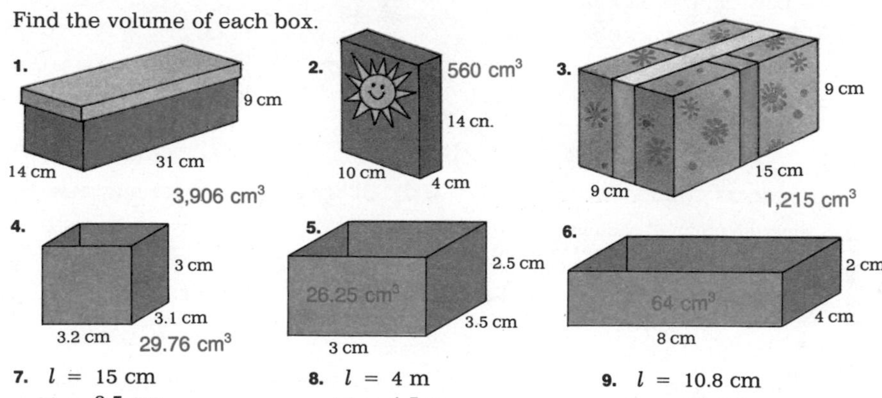


7. $l$ = 15 cm
   $w$ = 3.5 cm
   $h$ = 10 cm 525 cm³

8. $l$ = 4 m
   $w$ = 1.5 m
   $h$ = 2 m 12 m³

9. $l$ = 10.8 cm
   $w$ = 7.0 cm
   $h$ = 5.5 cm 415.8 cm³



## Follow Up

### Reteaching

Remind students that volume involves the three dimensions of an object—length, width, and height. Use a box such as the one below to illustrate this.

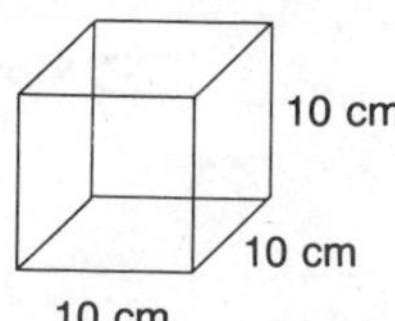


Point out the dimensions of the box—10 cm long, 10 cm wide, and 10 cm high. Thus, the volume is 10 × 10 × 10 = 1,000 cubic cm, or 1,000 cm³. Stress that the volume of the box is given in cubic centimeters.

### Enrichment

Have students use tagboard to construct a prism and a pyramid that are of equal height and have congruent bases. Ask students to predict which space figure has the greater volume and encourage them to guess how many times greater. Remove one face so that students can test their predictions regarding the figure's volume by first filling the pyramid with sand and then carefully pouring the sand into the prism. Elicit from students that the prism has 3 times the volume of the pyramid.

| Assignment Guide | Minimum | Average | Extended |
|---|---|---|---|
| page 358 | 1–9 | 1–9 | 1–9 |
| page 359 | 1–6 | 1–8 | 1–9 |

## Problem Solving: Using Estimation

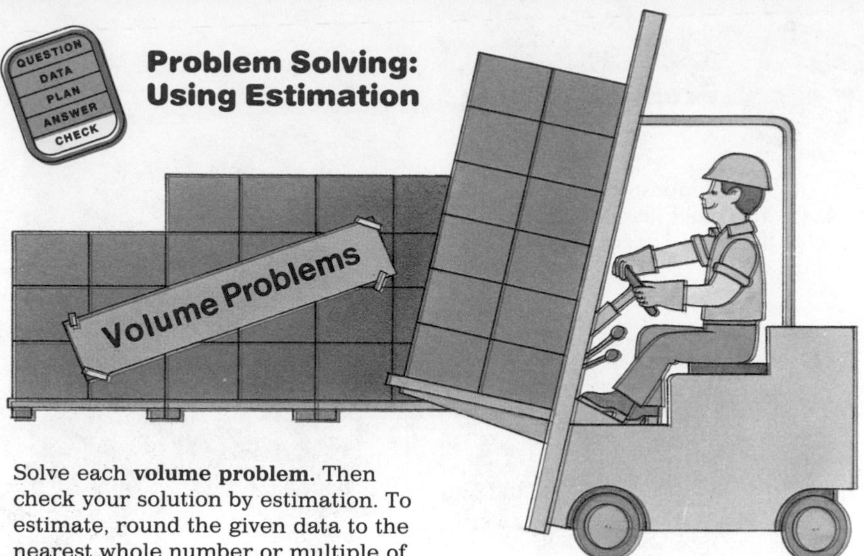


Solve each **volume problem.** Then check your solution by estimation. To estimate, round the given data to the nearest whole number or multiple of 10 before calculating the answer.

1. A room is 4.2 m long, 3 m wide, and 2.8 m high. What is the volume of the room in cubic meters ($m^3$)? 35.28 $m^3$; est. 36 $m^3$
2. A flower box is 61 cm long, 32 cm wide, and 38 cm high. How many cubic centimeters of soil are needed to fill it? 74,176 $cm^3$; est. 72,000 $cm^3$
3. What is the volume of a swimming pool that is 20.4 m long and 9.8 m wide, and has an average depth of 1.9 m? 379.848 $m^3$; est. 400 $m^3$
4. A storage locker is 3.7 m long, 2.8 m wide, and 2.3 m deep. How much space is left after 11.75 $m^3$ of luggage is placed in the locker? 12.078 $m^3$; est. 12 $m^3$
5. A food storage freezer is 1.4 m long, 1 m wide, and 0.9 m deep. How many cubic meters less is its volume than that of a freezer with a volume of 1.75 $m^3$? 0.49 $m^3$; est. 0.75 $m^3$
6. A large gift box is 24.2 cm long, 17.5 cm wide, and 4.3 cm high. How many more cubic centimeters will it hold than a box 18.2 cm long, 13.3 cm wide, and 3.5 cm high? 973.84 $cm^3$; est. 800 $cm^3$
7. **DATA BANK** A bar of soap might be 9 cm long, 6 cm wide, and 3 cm high. Suppose you have a bar of metal this size. How many grams would it weigh if it were iron? copper? silver? gold? lead? aluminum? (See Data Bank, page 407.) See teaching notes.
8. **DATA HUNT** A cubic meter of air weighs about 1.29 kg. About how much does the air in your classroom weigh? Answers will vary.
9. **Try This** A fish tank is 60 cm long, 25 cm wide, and 20 cm high. How many times as much water will a larger tank hold if each dimension is twice as great? 8

359

## Using Page 359

**Lesson Development** Point out the 5-Point Checklist logo at the top of the page. Tell students that this lesson will focus on the last of the five steps, the Check. Emphasize the usefulness of estimation in checking to see if the answer to a problem makes sense.

**Data Bank** Note that the table in the Data Bank gives the weight in grams of one cubic centimeter of these metals. Emphasize the idea that it is often necessary to measure or to experiment to find problem-solving data.

**Answers**
**Iron 1,279.8 g; copper 1,451.52 g; silver 1,701 g; gold 3,126.6 g; lead 1,830 g; aluminum 275.4 g**

**Data Hunt** In this exercise students must determine the dimensions of the classroom and find the volume before they can find the weight of the air. Remind students to give their answers in cubic kilograms.

**Try This** A possible strategy, Choose the Operations, was taught on page 16.

**Discussion** "Are we asked to find how much water a larger tank will hold? (No, we are asked how many times as much water a tank will hold whose dimensions are twice as great as the smaller tank.) "What are the dimensions of the smaller tank?" ($l$ = 60; $w$ = 25; $h$ = 20) "In planning the solution, what must you find in order to help you solve the problem?" (first, the volume of the smaller tank, then the volume of the tank with dimensions twice as great)

**Solution** The volume of the large tank is 8 times the volume of the smaller tank. The volume of the smaller tank is 60 × 25 × 20, or 30,000 $cm^3$. Thus, the larger tank has a volume of 120 × 50 × 40, or 240,000 $cm^3$.

**Reteaching Supplement,** page 86

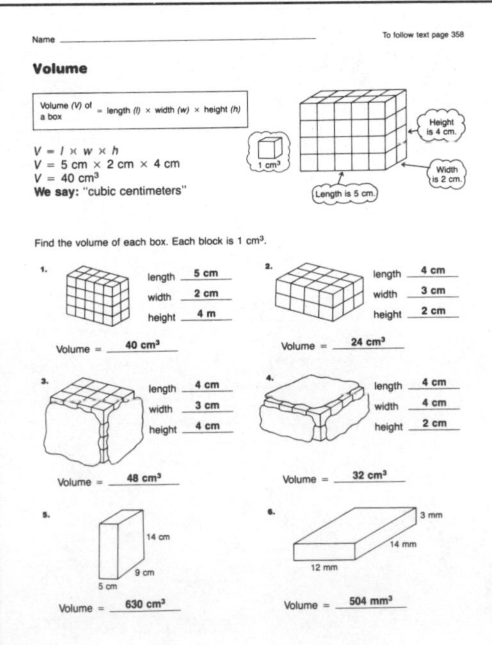
Name ______ To follow text page 358

**Volume**

Volume ($V$) of a box = length ($l$) × width ($w$) × height ($h$)

$V = l \times w \times h$
$V$ = 5 cm × 2 cm × 4 cm
$V$ = 40 $cm^3$
**We say:** "cubic centimeters"



Find the volume of each box. Each block is 1 $cm^3$.

1. length 5 cm, width 2 cm, height 4 m. Volume = 40 $cm^3$
2. length 4 cm, width 3 cm, height 2 cm. Volume = 24 $cm^3$
3. length 4 cm, width 3 cm, height 4 cm. Volume = 48 $cm^3$
4. length 4 cm, width 4 cm, height 2 cm. Volume = 32 $cm^3$
5. 14 cm, 9 cm, 5 cm. Volume = 630 $cm^3$
6. 3 mm, 14 mm, 12 mm. Volume = 504 $mm^3$

**Enrichment Supplement,** page 86

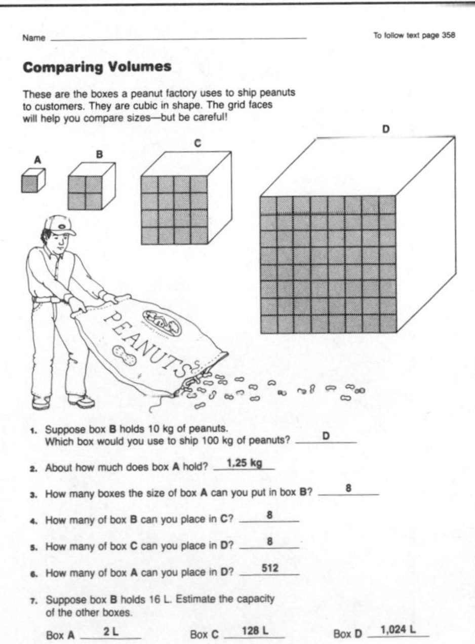
Name ______ To follow text page 358

**Comparing Volumes**

These are the boxes a peanut factory uses to ship peanuts to customers. They are cubic in shape. The grid faces will help you compare sizes—but be careful!



1. Suppose box **B** holds 10 kg of peanuts. Which box would you use to ship 100 kg of peanuts? D
2. About how much does box **A** hold? 1.25 kg
3. How many boxes the size of box **A** can you put in box **B**? 8
4. How many of box **B** can you place in **C**? 8
5. How many of box **C** can you place in **D**? 8
6. How many of box **A** can you place in **D**? 512
7. Suppose box **B** holds 16 L. Estimate the capacity of the other boxes.
   Box **A** 2 L  Box **C** 128 L  Box **D** 1,024 L

**Practice Supplement,** page 136

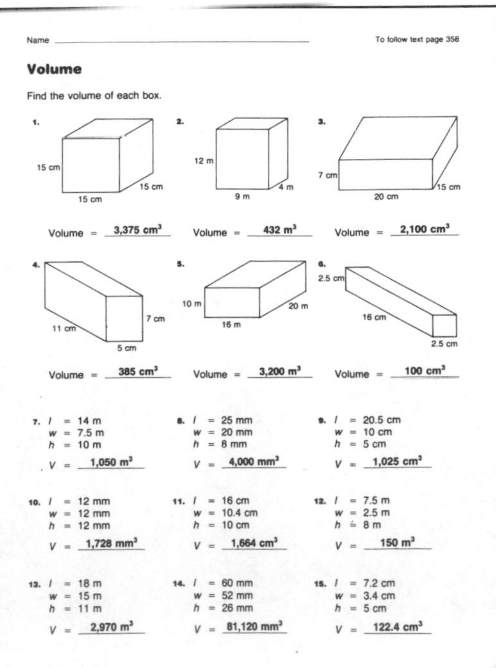
Name ______ To follow text page 358

**Volume**

Find the volume of each box.

1. 15 cm, 15 cm, 15 cm. Volume = 3,375 $cm^3$
2. 12 m, 9 m, 4 m. Volume = 432 $m^3$
3. 7 cm, 20 cm, 15 cm. Volume = 2,100 $cm^3$
4. 11 cm, 7 cm, 5 cm. Volume = 385 $cm^3$
5. 10 m, 16 m, 20 m. Volume = 3,200 $m^3$
6. 2.5 cm, 16 cm, 2.5 cm. Volume = 100 $cm^3$
7. $l$ = 14 m, $w$ = 7.5 m, $h$ = 10 m, $V$ = 1,050 $m^3$
8. $l$ = 25 mm, $w$ = 20 mm, $h$ = 8 mm, $V$ = 4,000 $mm^3$
9. $l$ = 20.5 cm, $w$ = 10 cm, $h$ = 5 cm, $V$ = 1,025 $cm^3$
10. $l$ = 12 mm, $w$ = 12 mm, $h$ = 12 mm, $V$ = 1,728 $mm^3$
11. $l$ = 16 cm, $w$ = 10.4 cm, $h$ = 10 cm, $V$ = 1,664 $cm^3$
12. $l$ = 7.5 m, $w$ = 2.5 m, $h$ = 8 m, $V$ = 150 $m^3$
13. $l$ = 18 m, $w$ = 15 m, $h$ = 11 m, $V$ = 2,970 $m^3$
14. $l$ = 60 mm, $w$ = 52 mm, $h$ = 26 mm, $V$ = 81,120 $mm^3$
15. $l$ = 7.2 cm, $w$ = 3.4 cm, $h$ = 5 cm, $V$ = 122.4 $cm^3$

**Lesson Focus** To interpret, organize, and use data to make a decision about a real-world problem

## Ideas for Getting Started

Discuss some of the procedures and things to consider when seeding a lawn. You might want to explain that grass seed is put on with a spreader, and that there are settings on the spreader that allow the seed to be put on at different rates. Remind students that applied problems such as these do not have a single answer. Answers will depend on how students evaluate and classify the data. Different people will make different decisions for equally good reasons.

## Using Page 360

**Lesson Development** Be sure students understand the situation and question. Discuss the information given. Encourage students to suggest a plan for processing the data to make a decision. Identify the major things that must be known to solve the problem (area of the lawn to be reseeded, number of kilograms of grass seed needed for desired coverage, cost considerations).

Have students classify the data, make the calculations, and make a decision either individually or in small groups. As a group, discuss the decisions and the factors that may have had an influence, for example, percentage of space taken up by walkways and flowerbeds, amount of money that can be budgeted, and so on.

## Applied Problem Solving

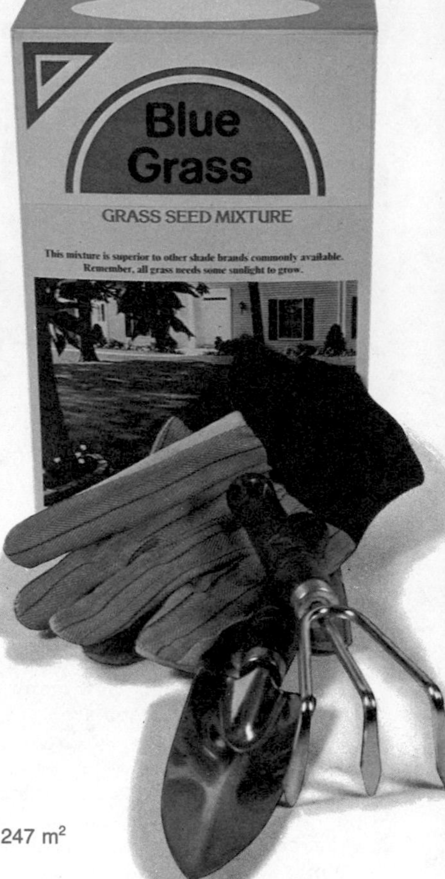


Suppose you are reseeding a lawn with bluegrass. You need to decide how many boxes of grass seed to buy.

**Some Things to Consider**

- The house takes up an area 19 m long and 13 m wide on a lot that is 36 m long and 34 m wide.
- For a light cover of grass, you need 1 kg of seed for every 100 $m^2$ of lawn. For a heavy cover, you need 1.5 kg of seed for every 100 $m^2$ of lawn.
- You can buy grass seed only in boxes of 2 kg of seed per box.
- A box of grass seed costs $10.95.

**Some Questions to Answer**

1. What is the area of the lot? 1,224 $m^2$
2. What is the area covered by the house? 247 $m^2$
3. What is the area of the lawn? 977 $m^2$
4. How many kilograms of seed do you need for a light cover of grass? for a heavy cover of grass? 9.77 kg; 14.655 kg
5. How many boxes of seed do you need for a light cover of grass? for a heavy cover? 5 (4.885); 8 (7.3275)

**What Is Your Decision?**

How many boxes of seed will you buy?
Answers will vary.

## Chapter Review-Test

1. Find the perimeter and area of this rectangle. 108 cm; 648 cm²

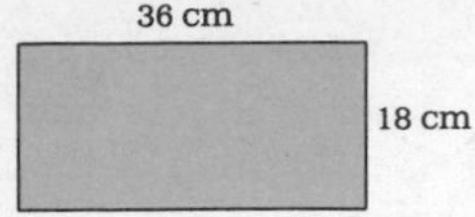


Find the perimeter and area of these triangles.

2. 24 cm; 240 cm²

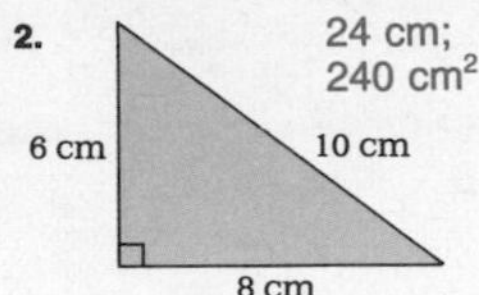


3. 58.4 cm; 144 cm²

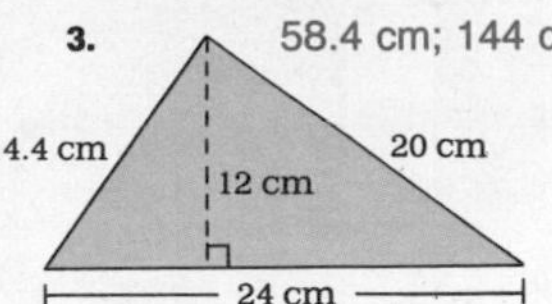


4. 37.5 cm; 36 cm²

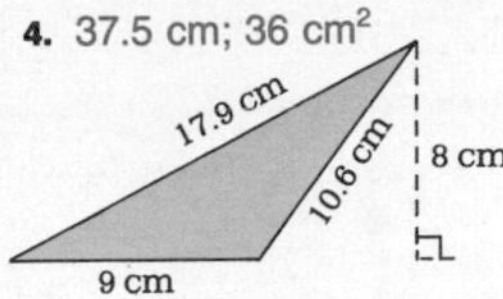


Find the circumference and area of these circles. Use 3.14 or $3\frac{1}{7}$ for $\pi$.

5. 

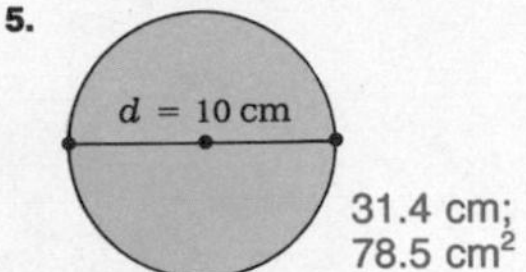


31.4 cm; 78.5 cm²

6. 

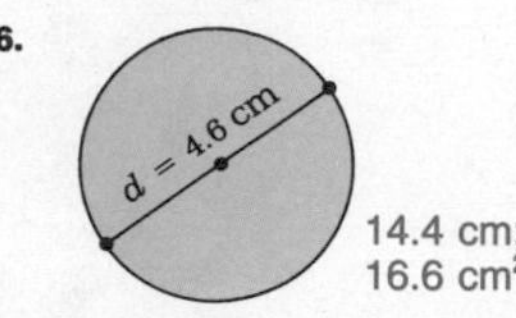


14.4 cm; 16.6 cm²

7. 

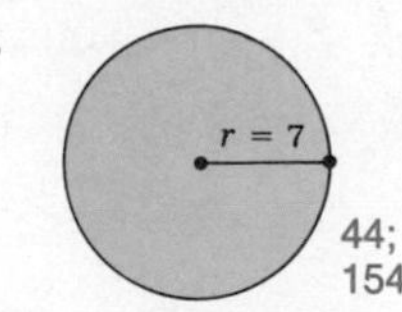


44; 154

Find the surface area and volume of these figures.

8. 

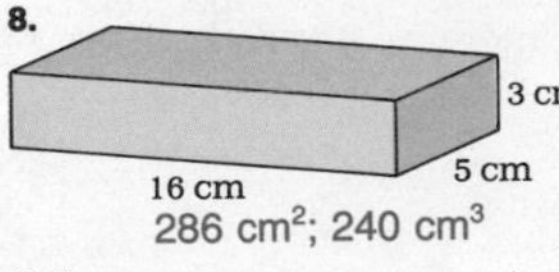


286 cm²; 240 cm³

9. 

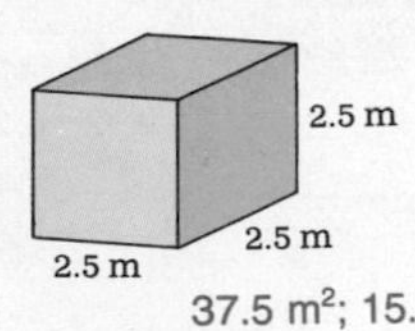


37.5 m²; 15.6 m³

10. 880 cm²; 1,344 cm³

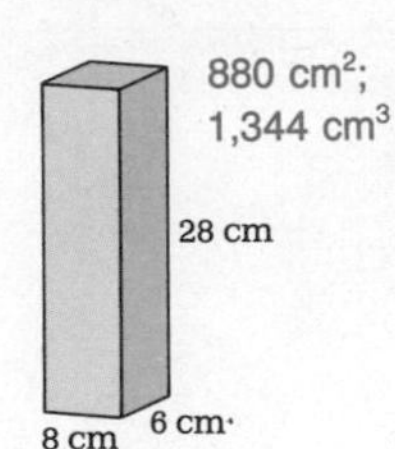


Solve.

11. A parking lot is 35 m longer than it is wide. It is 45 m wide. What is the perimeter of the lot? 250 m

12. A garden is 9.5 m long. Its width is 1.5 less than its length. What is the area of the garden? 76 m²

13. A storage chest has length 1.2 m, width 0.7 m, and height 0.8 m. What is the volume of the chest? What is the surface area? 0.672 m²; 4.72 m²



### Using Page 361

The exercises in the Chapter Review-Test emphasize the major concepts and skills presented in this chapter. These exercises may be used as a review assignment or as a test, depending upon your needs.

**Item Analysis** The table below correlates the Chapter Review-Test items with objectives and with the student text pages on which the concepts or skills were taught.

| Items | Objectives | Related text pages |
|---|---|---|
| 1–4 | 14.1, 14.3 | 346, 350, 352–353 |
| 5–7 | 14.2, 14.4 | 348–349, 354–355 |
| 8–10 | 14.5 | 356–358 |
| 11–13 | 14.6 | 347, 351, 359 |

### Assessment Options

If you use the Chapter Review-Test as a review assignment, you may wish to use the multiple-choice test or the free-response test to evaluate mastery of the chapter objectives. The items on these tests have a one-to-one correspondence in terms of content and level of difficulty. A correlation of test items to objectives and student text pages is provided in the Management Guide for Chapter 14.

**Multiple-Choice Test,** TRB pages 40–41

**Free-Response Test,** TRB pages 75–76

### TRB Options

The following blackline masters are available for use with this chapter. If you have not already assigned these materials, you may wish to use them to close the chapter.

**Recreation,** TRB page 164

**Consumer Applications,** TRB page 182

**Calculator Technology,** TRB page 200

**Reading Math,** TRB page 232

**Family Involvement,** TRB pages 263–264

## Using Page 362

The exercises on this page are intended for those students who experienced difficulty with the Chapter Review-Test on page 361. Should students require reteaching of these key concepts and skills, please refer to the teaching notes below. Otherwise, the Another Look exercises can be assigned as independent work, with students using the accompanying sample problems and hints as guides.

**Exercises 1–4** These skills were originally taught on pages 346, and 350. Have students review the formulas for finding the perimeter and area of a rectangle, focusing on one formula at a time. Remind students that when finding the perimeter, they must add the lengths of all four sides even though only two lengths are given. Review the idea that the area is the number of square units it takes to cover or fill a figure, and it can be found by multiplying the length times the width.

**Exercises 5–8** These skills were originally taught on pages 346, 352 and 353. Have students review the formula for finding the area of a triangle. Point out that students may find one half of the base and then multiply that number by the height. Point out that the height is always the perpendicular distance from a vertex to the base or the extension of the base. Have students identify the base and height in each diagram. Note that in exercise 7, the base is not at the bottom of the triangle.

**Exercises 9–12** These skills were originally taught on pages 348–349 and 354–355. Review the formulas in the last box on the left, starting with the formula for finding the circumference of a circle. Emphasize that the diameter of the circle must be known in order to apply the formula. If the radius is given, it must be doubled to find the diameter. Review the formula for finding the area of a circle. Remind students that in the formula they must multiply the radius by itself and then multiply the result times $\pi$. Note that in exercises 9 and 10 the diameter is given and students must divide by 2 to find the radius for each circle.

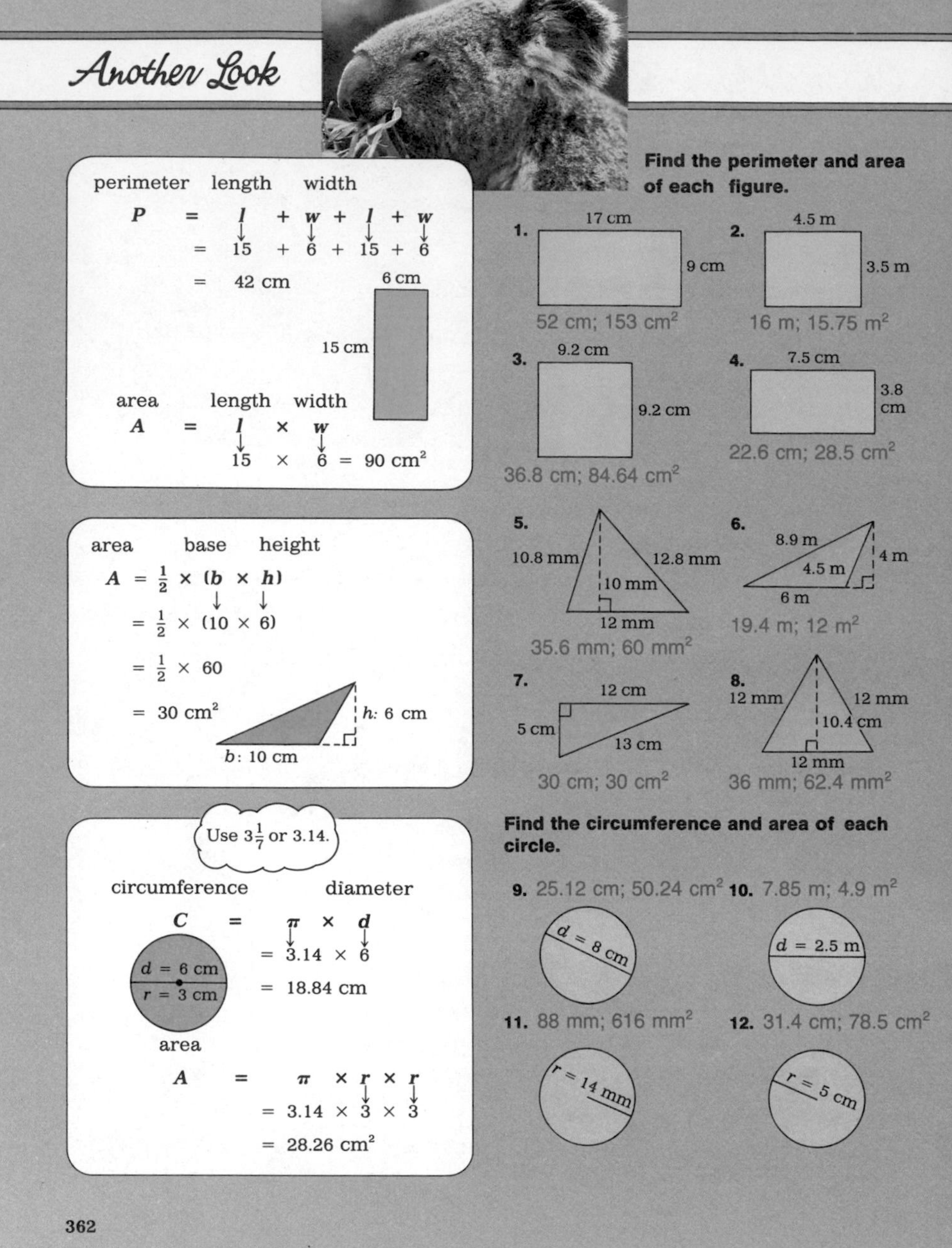

*Another Look*

perimeter length width

$P = l + w + l + w$

$= 15 + 6 + 15 + 6$

$= 42$ cm



area length width

$A = l \times w$

$15 \times 6 = 90 \text{ cm}^2$

area base height

$A = \frac{1}{2} \times (b \times h)$

$= \frac{1}{2} \times (10 \times 6)$

$= \frac{1}{2} \times 60$

$= 30 \text{ cm}^2$



Use $3\frac{1}{7}$ or 3.14.

circumference diameter

$C = \pi \times d$

$= 3.14 \times 6$

$= 18.84$ cm



area

$A = \pi \times r \times r$

$= 3.14 \times 3 \times 3$

$= 28.26 \text{ cm}^2$

**Find the perimeter and area of each figure.**

1.  52 cm; 153 $\text{cm}^2$
2.  16 m; 15.75 $\text{m}^2$
3.  36.8 cm; 84.64 $\text{cm}^2$
4.  22.6 cm; 28.5 $\text{cm}^2$
5.  35.6 mm; 60 $\text{mm}^2$
6.  19.4 m; 12 $\text{m}^2$
7.  30 cm; 30 $\text{cm}^2$
8.  36 mm; 62.4 $\text{mm}^2$

**Find the circumference and area of each circle.**

9. 25.12 cm; 50.24 $\text{cm}^2$ 
10. 7.85 m; 4.9 $\text{m}^2$ 
11. 88 mm; 616 $\text{mm}^2$ 
12. 31.4 cm; 78.5 $\text{cm}^2$ 

362

## Just for Teachers

### Mathematics in the Physical Sciences

Archimedes (287–212 B.C.) was a mathematician and inventor during the great Alexandrian period of intellectual inquiry and discovery. He was hired by the king of Syracuse, Hieron II, to discover a method for determining if the king's crown was pure gold or if, as the king suspected, silver had been substituted for part of the gold.

Archimedes' problem was one of physics, a science particularly fluent with mathematical language used to investigate, discover, and then to express ideas about the world and the universe. According to legend, Archimedes was taking a bath when he realized how to solve the king's problem.

The discovery was that of hydrostatic weighing. An object is first weighed under normal conditions. Then it is weighed again underwater where the water it displaces will buoy it up so that it weighs less. If the king's crown contained any silver, the difference would be less than if it were pure gold—i.e., a particular volume of gold will weigh more than the same volume of silver.

## Enrichment

**Geometry Geoboard Areas**

You can find the area of figures on a geoboard or dot paper by counting unit squares ☐ or by finding the area of a triangle that is half of some square or rectangle.

Geoboard

Give the number for each ■.

1. The area of square A is 1, so the area of triangle B is ■ square unit(s). $\frac{1}{2}$
2. The area of rectangle C is 2, so the area of triangle D is ■ square unit(s). 1
3. The area of the rectangular region is ■ square units. 12
4. The area of the yellow region is ■ square units. 6
5. The area of the brown region is ■ square units. 3
6. The area of the blue region is ■ square units. 3

You can also find the area of any figure on a geoboard or dot paper by using **Pick's formula.**

Number of nails on the boundary of the figure

Number of nails inside the figure

$$\text{Area} = \frac{b}{2} + i - 1$$

Use Pick's formula to find the area of these figures. Check by counting squares.

7. 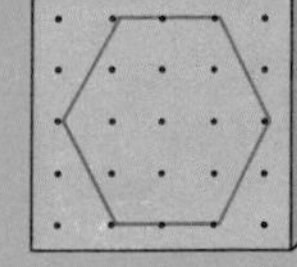
12 square units

8. 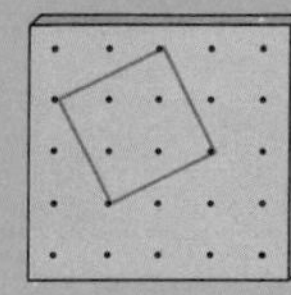
5 square units

9. 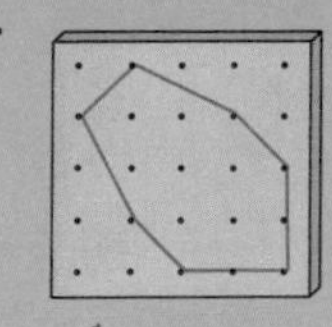
$10\frac{1}{2}$ square units

10. 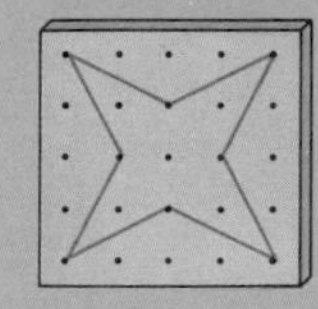
8 square units

11. Make some figures of your own on the geoboard or dot paper. Find their areas using Pick's formula. Check your answers by counting squares or parts of squares. Figures and areas will vary.



What about objects that float? By extension, one would assume that, volume for volume, the floating object weighs less than water and so is buoyed up completely. Ice, however, is water in a different state, and yet floats in water. This is because water occupies more volume in its solid state than it does in its liquid form and, therefore, per unit volume it weighs less and so it floats.

## Using Page 363

This page is intended for those students who successfully completed the Chapter Review-Test on page 361. You may wish to assign this page as independent work while you use the Another Look exercises to reteach the basic concepts and skills of the chapter. Or, you may decide that all students would benefit from exposure to this Enrichment activity.

**Lesson Development** Use the demonstration geoboard to show sequences such as the following.

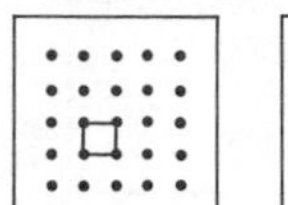
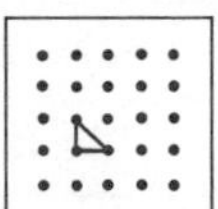
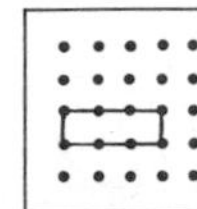
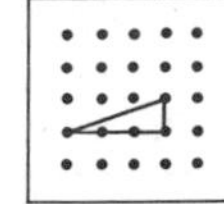

The general idea to be developed is that if you know the area of a square or rectangle, the area of the triangle produced when the square or rectangle is divided in half will be half that of the square or rectangle. Present students with problems such as the one shown below in which they are asked to find the area of triangle F.

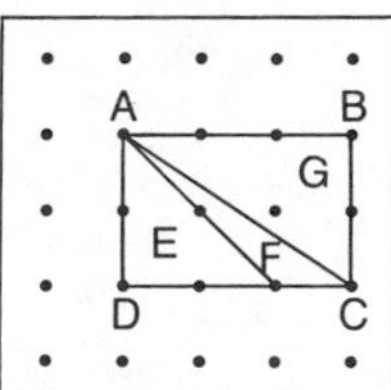


Help students see that they can find the area of rectangle ABCD and subtract from it the area of triangle E and the area of triangle G to find the area of triangle F. Note that the area of triangle E is half the area of a larger square and that the area of triangle G is half the area of rectangle ABCD.

Write Pick's formula on the chalkboard and tell students that *b* stands for the number of nails on the boundary of the figure, and *i* stands for the number of nails inside the figure. In exercise 7, *b* is 8, and *i* is 9. The area is $\frac{8}{2} + 9 - 1$, or 12. Students can verify the answer by counting the squares or using the formula.

## Using Page 364

The exercises on the page provide cumulative skill maintenance practice. The emphasis in this Cumulative Review is on graphing and probability (Chapter 13), ratio and proportion (Chapter 11), and problem solving (Chapter 11).

| Items | Objectives | Related text pages |
|---|---|---|
| 1–3 | 13.1 | 322–331 |
| 4–5 | 13.2 | 332 |
| 6–8 | 11.1 | 278–281 |
| 9–12 | 11.2 | 282–283 |
| 13–14 | 11.5 | 284–285, 291, 293 |

## *Cumulative Review*

For items 1–3 use the graph below.

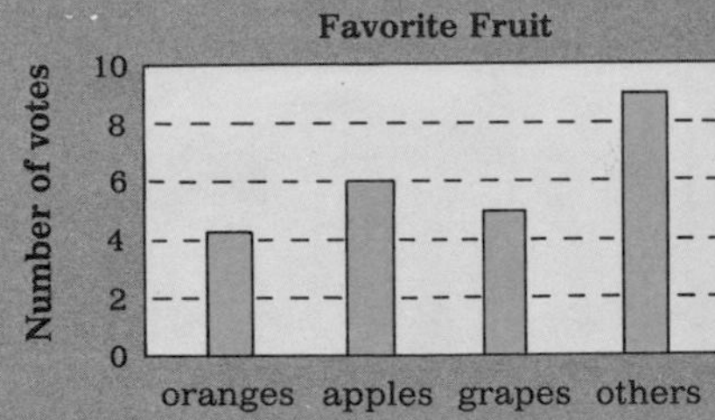


1. How many votes were for grapes?
   A 4 (B) 5
   C 6 D not given

2. Which fruit got the least votes?
   A apples B grapes
   (C) oranges D not given

3. How many more votes did "others" get than apples?
   A 2 B 6
   C 9 (D) not given

4. Give the mean of these numbers: 56, 24, 44, 87, 44
   A 44 (B) 51
   C 52 D not given

5. Give the mean of these numbers to the nearest tenth: 145, 126, 159, 138, 130
   A 138 B 140
   C 139 (D) not given

For items 6–8 choose the fraction for each ratio.

6. 4:7
   A 4 is to 7 B $\frac{7}{4}$
   (C) $\frac{4}{7}$ D not given

7. 6 tickets for $5
   A $\frac{6}{11}$ (B) $\frac{6}{5}$
   C 6 to 5 D not given

8. 3 dogs to every 4 cats
   A $\frac{3}{12}$ B $\frac{4}{3}$
   (C) $\frac{3}{4}$ D not given

Solve for $n$.

9. $\frac{3}{8} = \frac{n}{24}$
   A $n = 3$ (B) $n = 9$
   C $n = 12$ D not given

10. $\frac{5}{6} = \frac{25}{n}$
    A $n = 11$ (B) $n = 30$
    C $n = 25$ D not given

11. $\frac{20}{28} = \frac{4}{n}$
    A $n = 8$ B $n = 5$
    C $n = 6$ (D) not given

12. $\frac{35}{50} = \frac{n}{10}$
    (A) $n = 7$ B $n = 5$
    C $n = 15$ D not given

13. There are 3 red marbles and 5 yellow marbles in a bag. If you draw 1 marble, what is the probability of getting a yellow marble?
    A $\frac{3}{5}$ B $\frac{3}{8}$
    (C) $\frac{5}{8}$ D not given

14. Glen drew a map with the scale 2 cm = 5 km. If Aton is 12 cm from Beeton on the map, how many kilometers is Aton from Beeton?
    A 12 km (B) 30 km
    C $\frac{5}{12}$ D not given

## Objectives

**15.1** Find sums and differences of two integers.

**15.2** Compare two integers using the inequality symbols $>$ or $<$.

**15.3** Give integer coordinates of points in a coordinate plane.

**15.4** Solve word problems using the 5-Point Checklist and cumulative computational skills.

## Summary

In this chapter students develop an understanding of the concept of an integer. They learn to identify integers that are opposites of each other and to associate the integers with points on the number line. Students then use a number line to add two integers. After the idea of addition of integers is developed, the relationship between addition and subtraction is used to find the difference of two integers. Integer subtraction is presented as finding the missing addend in an addition equation.

As with other number concepts they have studied, students use the number line to compare integers. They also order a set of integers by comparing them two at a time. Graphing skills are extended to involve coordinate axes with both positive and negative integers. Students give either an ordered pair of integers for a point or a point for an ordered pair of integers.

## Mathematical Background

**Integers** As suggested on page 366, integers can be used to describe situations in the real world. Note that the set of integers consists of the set of negative integers, zero, and the set of positive integers. Students might think of starting with the zero and the numbers to the right of zero on the number line. These integers, which act exactly like the whole numbers, are called positive integers. For each positive integer there is an opposite, or negative, integer that is the same distance from 0 on a number line extended to the left. We can think of each negative integer as being the opposite of some positive integer and each positive integer as being the opposite of some negative integer. On pages 368 and 370 a number line is used to suggest procedures for adding integers. For students who have difficulty with the number line, the idea below can be useful.

> The sum of an integer and its opposite is zero.
> ${}^{+}3 + {}^{-}3 = 0,\ {}^{-}5 + {}^{+}5 = 0 \ldots$

This idea can be modeled using red and black checkers. Red represents "in the hole" and black, "to the good." Thus three red checkers and three black checkers nullify or cancel out each other. The checker model can also be used to find integer sums as shown.

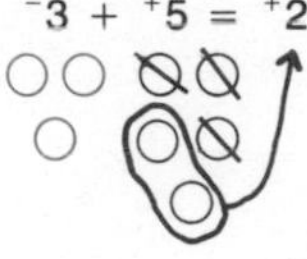


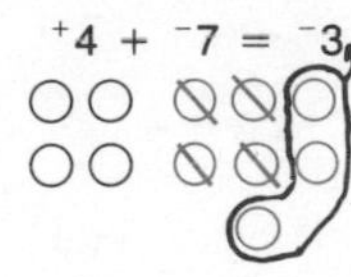


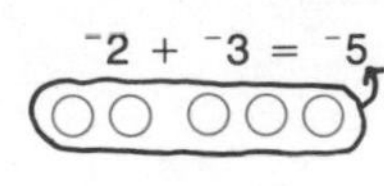


This idea can also be modeled using the following situation.

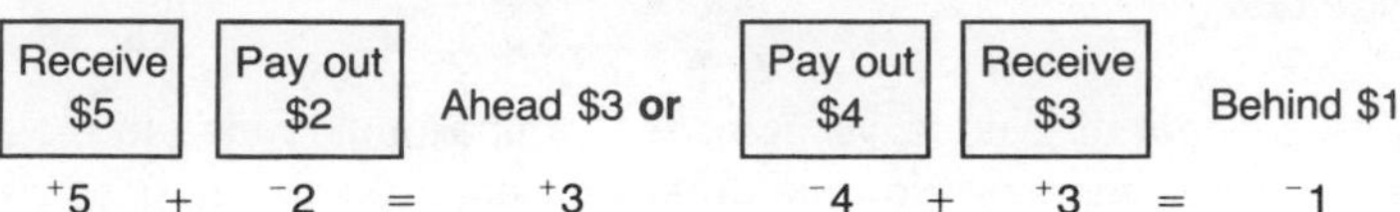


Since some students might grasp one model better than another, use the kind of model that makes the most sense to individual students.

Students should be aware that the basic properties (zero, commutative, associative) hold true for integers as for whole numbers.

To find differences between integers we emphasize the relationship between addition and subtraction. That is, students find differences by looking for missing addends as shown below.

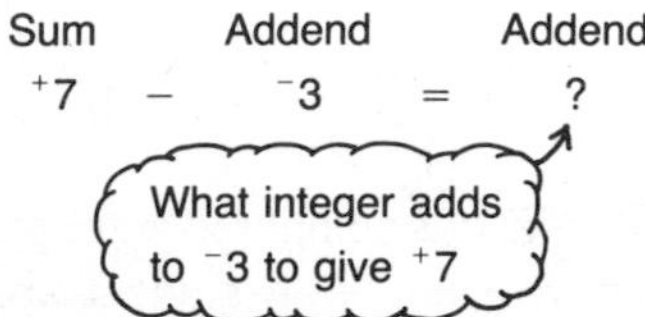


Since ${}^{+}10 + {}^{-}3 = {}^{+}7$, we see that the missing addend (difference) above is ${}^{+}10$. So ${}^{+}7 - {}^{-}3 = {}^{+}10$. Some students may discover the following rule: To subtract an integer, add its opposite. However, it is preferable that this rule not be taught initially as the procedure for finding differences of integers. After students understand the concept of opposites, the rule can be introduced and used.

**Comparing and Ordering Integers** Technically speaking, one integer is less than another integer if a positive number can be added to the first integer to give the second. For example, ${}^{-}2$ is less than ${}^{+}4$ because ${}^{+}6$ can be added to ${}^{-}2$ to get ${}^{+}4$. In practice, however, students would probably use a mental image of the number line to compare two integers.

As with whole numbers, fractions, and decimals, a list of integers can be ordered by comparing them two at a time and listing them from greatest to least or from least to greatest.

**Graphing Integers** When two integer number lines are placed perpendicularly, coordinate axes are formed, which allows the use of ordered pairs of integers to locate points. When students graphed whole numbers, they used only the quadrant in the upper right hand corner. In graphing integers, the number of quadrants is increased to four, and any point in the plane can be designated with an ordered pair of integers.

**Problem Solving** The problem-solving lesson on pages 374–375, Using Data from a Newspaper, applies the idea of integers in several real-world situations—under and over par golf strokes, temperatures below and above 0, land above and below sea level, stock gains or losses, seconds before and after blast-off, and football gains or losses. On page 397, problem-solving practice exercises involve several operations with decimals, ratios, percents, and integers. The applied problem-solving lesson, page 380, deals with a car rental. Students are asked to study the facts carefully, to select and organize the data, to make the necessary calculations, and then to make a decision.

## Vocabulary

| | | |
|---|---|---|
| integers | negative integers | origin |
| positive integers | opposites | |

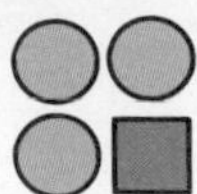

## Error Analysis

The concept of a negative number is a challenging idea to most sixth grade students. However, many misconceptions are possible as students confront the content of this chapter. Students frequently confuse signs for the operations with the signs that indicate a positive or negative integer. The distinction between the two uses of the signs should be a carefully developed part of the initial teaching of integers. The fact that addition and subtraction of integers requires a somewhat different approach than subtraction of whole numbers is another source of confusion. Some common error patterns are discussed below.

**Error Pattern 1**

$^-7 > {}^-2$ $\quad$ $^-5 > {}^-1$ $\quad$ $^+7 < {}^-15$ $\quad$ $^+6 < {}^-9$

**Diagnosis** The student has compared numbers without regard to the positive or negative signs. The student apparently has concluded that $^-7$ is greater than $^-2$ because 7 is greater than 2. This response indicates a lack of understanding of the basic concept of integers.

**Remediation** To develop a concept of opposites, generate a discussion asking students to respond with the opposite for the following terms:

| | |
|---|---|
| decrease (increase) | spend (earn) |
| lose (gain) | plus (minus) |

Next draw a number line on the chalkboard, but include only the zero. As you place each positive integer to the right of the zero, point out the positive sign that you have included. Then ask students to give the number they think should be placed in the corresponding place to the left of the zero. As you write that integer on the number line, be sure to point out the negative sign you have included. Stress that positive and negative integers are opposites as illustrated by the number line.

**Error Pattern 2**

| | |
|---|---|
| $^+4 + {}^-3 = {}^+7$ | $^-4 + {}^-5 = {}^-9$ |
| $^-6 + {}^-1 = {}^-7$ | $^+8 + {}^-3 = {}^+11$ |
| $^+6 + {}^-8 = {}^+14$ | $^-4 + {}^+13 = {}^-17$ |

**Diagnosis** The student has added the given digits and recorded the sums with the positive or negative sign of the first addend. Apart from affixing a sign in the answer, the student has disregarded the resulting value of the integers, indicating a lack of understanding of the concept of positive and negative integers.

**Remediation** Review the basic ideas of addition of whole numbers on the number line. Show an example such as $^+4 + {}^+5$, pointing out that we always begin to count at 0. Remind students that numbers to the right on a number line are called positive integers, and numbers to the left are called negative integers.

Then use an example such as $^-3 + {}^+4$. Start at 0 and show $^-3$ (move three spaces to the left). Tell students that we move to the left on the number line to count negative integers. Then show $^+4$ by counting four spaces to the right from the $^-3$ position on the number line. Thus, we can see that $^-3 + {}^+4 = {}^+1$

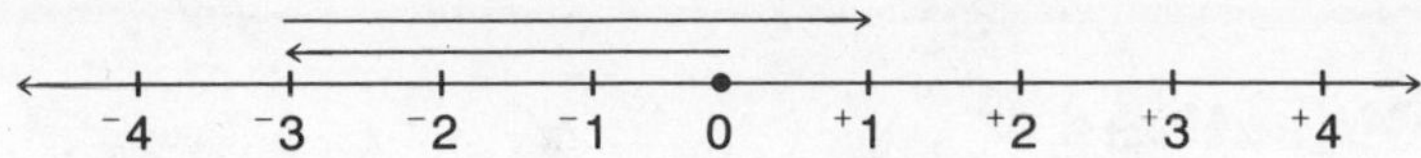


Work through several sample equations on the number line, particularly those that students have done incorrectly.

## Problem Solving

### Writing Problem Extensions

In Chapter 8, problem extensions (posing another problem similar to the original problem) were identified as an excellent way to help students better understand the problem-solving process in general and the use of specific problem-solving strategies in particular. In that chapter, it was suggested that the teacher provide students with extensions of the problem. Another technique for improving problem-solving performance is to encourage students to write their own problem extensions. There are many ways to extend a given problem. Below is a problem and three extensions of that problem.

> Some chickens and cows are in a barnyard. Altogether there are 10 animals and 28 legs. How many chickens and how many cows are in the barnyard?

Extension 1: *Change the numbers in the problem.*
Some chickens and cows are in a barnyard. Altogether there are 16 animals and 50 legs. How many chickens and how many cows are in the barnyard?

Extension 2: *Change the conditions of the problem.* (The condition that there were more than 10 chickens was added in this example.)
Some chickens and cows are in a barnyard. Altogether there are 28 legs and there are more than 10 chickens. How many chickens and how many cows are in the barnyard?

Extension 3: *Reverse the given and wanted in the problem.*
Some chickens and cows are in a barnyard. There are 7 chickens and 5 cows. Altogether how many animal legs are in the barnyard?

In your early work with students on writing problem extensions, tell them the particular way you want them to extend a given problem. Later, allow them to decide how to extend a problem. Also encourage students to find their own ways to extend problems. Following are additional ways in which students might extend problems: (a) add unnecessary data; (b) change the data source (e.g., place the data from a story in a chart or picture); (c) write another question that could be answered with the given data and (d) use combinations of all of the above ways.

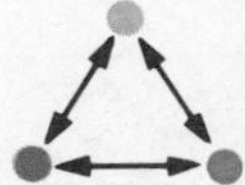

## Special Education

We use the idea of integers regularly in our everyday lives. We borrow money from a friend and then pay it back. The temperature rose 10° but then dropped 12° during the night. Even the learning disabled student has little difficulty comprehending these ideas in context. However, when the same ideas are expressed symbolically with positive and negative integers, many students become confused. Most can readily tell how much a friend owes them if $5 was borrowed, and they might even use the expression "I'm $5 in the hole." However, the mathematical representation $^{-}5$ is not so easily understood.

Many special-needs students have difficulty dealing with the written integer form. Students are now asked to interpret familiar ideas and signs (+ and −) in a new way and with new language. They must now decide whether a sign means "add" or "positive," "subtract" or "negative." Students with language problems have particular difficulty because it is hard for them to elicit or associate new meanings in unfamiliar contexts.

Suggestions for dealing with these difficulties during early concept development for integers are outlined below. These ideas can be used to supplement the work of this chapter. Ideas for modifying the presentation of subtraction as well as several additional comments to assist the special-needs student are also given below.

### Using a Body Number Line

Have students think of their bodies as number lines. Spreading both arms out, they can let the left arm represent the negative integers and the right arm the positive ones. Their body is zero. Students can use their body number lines for comparing or computing with integers. To add a negative 5 to a positive 4, for example, they must pass through 0 and on to negative 1. Doing this for several sample problems helps students internalize the action of integer addition.

An alternative to arm stretching is to tape a smaller number line from shoulder to shoulder across a student's back. The body midline, then, is the "zero." As the teacher dramatizes a simple addition problem by finger movement on the student's back, the student can, with eyes closed, repeat the problem as it is enacted, or with eyes open, mimic the teacher's movements by "finger walking" the addition on a personal number line placed on the desk in front of the student.

### Using Two Steps

If students have difficulty with the subtraction exercises of this chapter, try the idea suggested below, showing the subtraction in two steps: first to zero, and then on.

$$^{+}9 - {}^{-}2 = ?$$

"What integer added to $^{-}2$ gives $^{+}9$?"
Student thinks of (or uses) the number line:
Start at $^{-}2$, move to 0, then on to $^{+}9$.
That is a move of $^{+}11$.

Students are encouraged to picture moves to a target integer. But if the move crosses the midline (zero) point, it is calculated in two steps as illustrated.

### Using Colors to Cue

As students begin to plot points in all four quadrants, a color-coded grid can be helpful. Ordered pairs then are color-coded according to quadrant, as shown below.

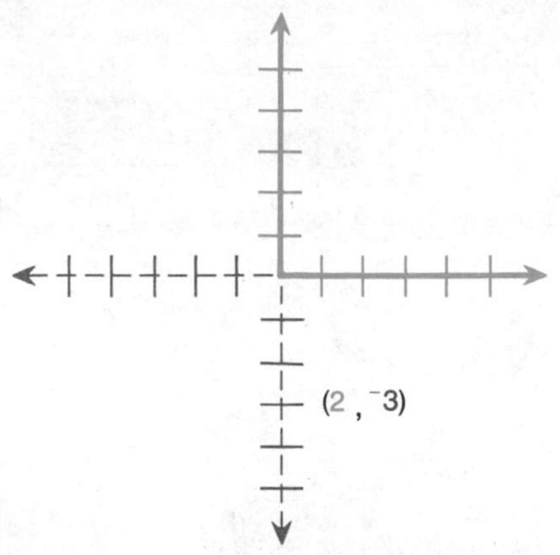


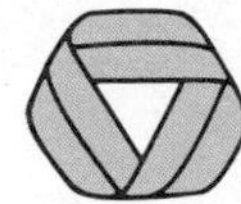

## Subject Integration

Subject matter related to other areas of the curriculum has been integrated into the following lessons. This provides an opportunity to highlight the interaction between mathematics and other subjects.

**Physical Education** Jogging, pages 368–369
**Social Studies** Elevation above and below sea level, pages 372–373, 374; geographic center of U.S. page 378
**Science** Weather on Mars, page 365; facts about Earth, page 377

# Management Guide

| Teaching Chapter 15 | | | | Meeting Individual Needs | | | | | |
|---|---|---|---|---|---|---|---|---|---|
| | | | | Lesson Assignments | | | Follow Up | | |
| Objectives | Chapter Content | Pages | TRB Test Items | Minimum | Average | Extended | Reteaching | Enrichment | Practice |
| | Chapter Opener | 365 | | | | | | | |
| **15.1** Find sums and differences of two integers. | Positive and Negative Integers | 366–367 | 1–4 | 1–22 | 1–26 | 1–26, TM | RS 87 | ES 87 | PS 137 |
| | Adding Integers | 368–369 | 5–7 | 1–23, SK | 1–23, SK | 1–23, SK | RS 88 | ES 88 | MP 428<br>PS 138 |
| | More Adding Integers | 370–371 | 8–12 | 1–24 | 1–28 | 1–28, TM | | | MP 428<br>PS 139 |
| | Subtracting Integers | 372–373 | 13–18 | 1–19, SK | 1–20, SK | 1–21, SK | RS 89 | ES 89 | MP 428<br>PS 140 |
| **15.2** Compare two integers using the inequality symbols > or <. | Comparing and Ordering Integers | 376 | 19–24 | 1–16, 17, 20 | 1–12, 17–22 | 1–22 | RS 90 | ES 90 | MP 428<br>PS 142 |
| **15.3** Give integer coordinates of points in a coordinate plane. | Graphing with Integers | 378–379 | 25–30 | | 1–30 | 1–33, TM | RS 91 | ES 91 | PS 143 |
| **15.4** Solve word problems using the 5-Point Checklist and cumulative computational skills. | Problem Solving: Using Data from a Newspaper | 374–375 | 31–35 | 1–12 | 1–12 | 1–13 | | | PS 141 |
| | Problem Solving: Practice | 377 | | 1–7 | 1–8 | 1–9 | | | |
| | Applied Problem Solving | 380 | | | | | | | |
| | Chapter Review-Test | 381 | | | | | | | |
| | Another Look/Enrichment | 382–383 | | | | | | | |
| | Cumulative Review | 384 | | | | | | | |

**SE5** Student Edition, Book 5
**RS** Reteaching Supplement
**ES** Enrichment Supplement
**PS** Practice Supplement
**MP** More Practice
**TM** Think Math
**SK** Skillkeeper
**TRB** Teacher's Resource Book

# Teacher's Resource Book

## Masters for Use

**. . . before Chapter 15**

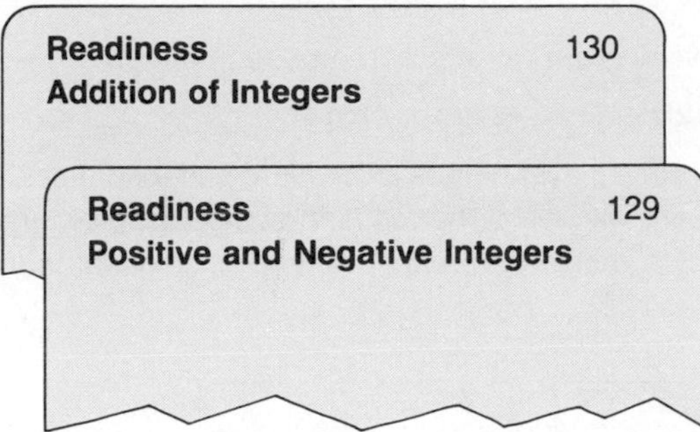


**. . . during Chapter 15**

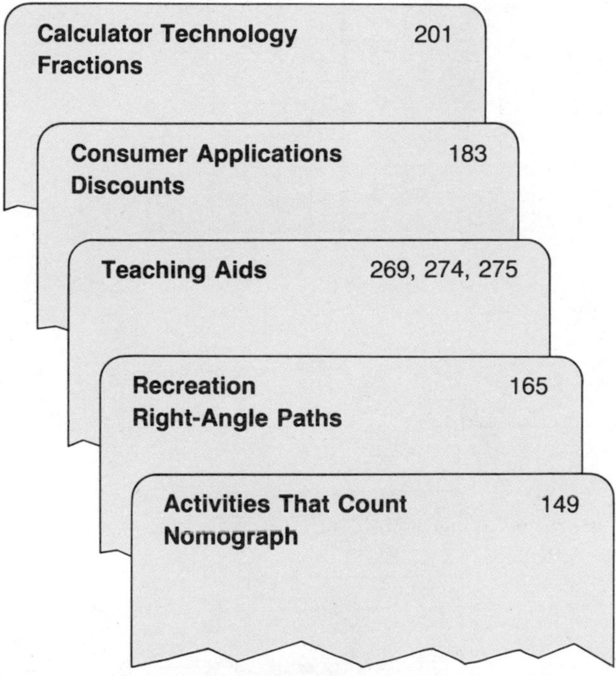


**. . . after Chapter 15**

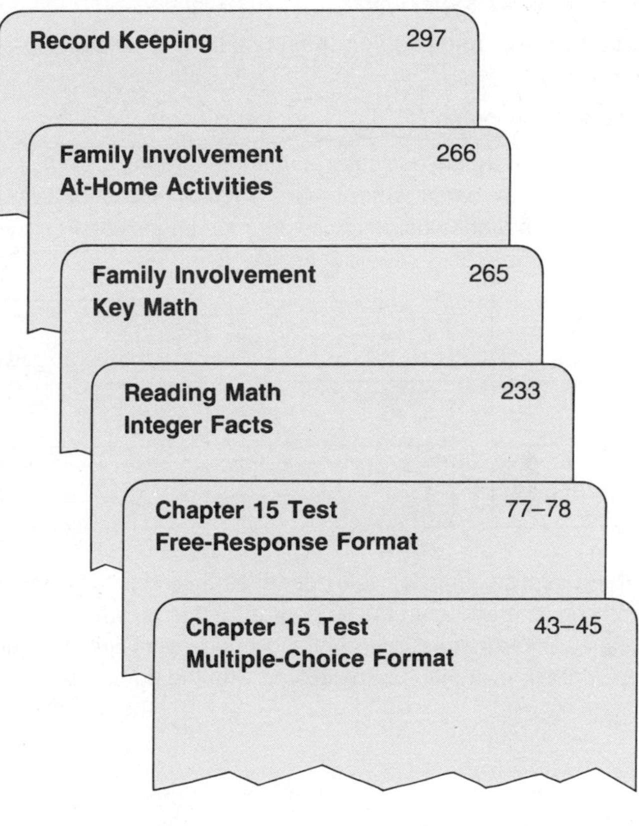


## Supplements

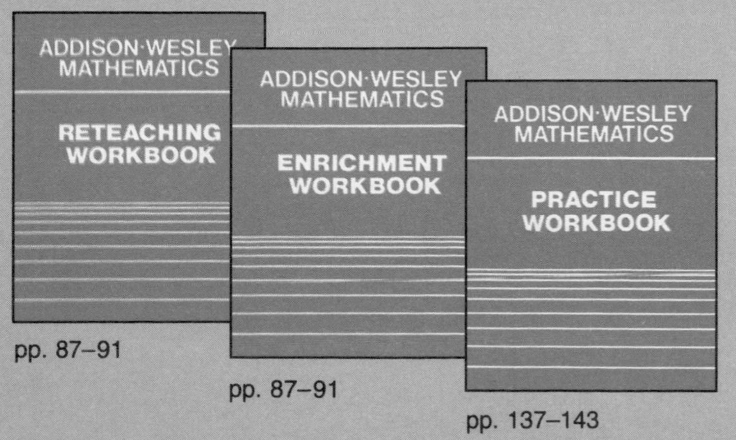


pp. 87–91

pp. 87–91

pp. 137–143

## Other Addison-Wesley Resources

### Books and Kits

*The Arithmetic Primer* pp. 282–288, 304–306

*Problem-Solving Experiences in Mathematics, Grade 6,* Problems 29, 30, 64, 65, 89, 104, 125, 144, 145, 146, 147, 148, 149, 150

### Technology

*Computer Math Activities* Volumes 1–5

*Computer Math Games* Volumes 1–3, 6

# Activities That Count

Activities That Count are designed for use throughout this and subsequent chapters. Before beginning Chapter 15, you may wish to review these activities and select the ones you consider appropriate for your class.

## Integers Nomograph Math Lab

**Purpose** To use a nomograph to find sums and differences of integers

**Materials** Nomograph (TRB p. 149), index cards

**Preparation** Duplicate one copy of the nomograph for each student. On the index cards write integer addition and subtraction equations such as those below. Answers may be included on the backs of the cards or in a separate answer key.

| | | |
|---|---|---|
| **1.** ${}^{-}7 - {}^{-}5$ **${}^{-}2$** | **2.** ${}^{+}8 - {}^{-}4$ **${}^{+}12$** | **3.** ${}^{-}3 - {}^{-}12$ **${}^{-}15$** |
| **4.** ${}^{-}12 + {}^{+}8$ **${}^{-}4$** | **5.** ${}^{+}3 + {}^{-}14$ **${}^{-}11$** | **6.** ${}^{-}8 + {}^{-}9$ **${}^{-}17$** |
| **7.** ${}^{+}6 + {}^{-}11$ **${}^{-}5$** | **8.** ${}^{-}7 + {}^{+}4$ **${}^{-}3$** | **9.** ${}^{+}10 - {}^{-}2$ **${}^{+}12$** |

**Activity** Direct students to use a ruler or straightedge to help find the sums and differences on the nomograph. After they have completed the available index cards, challenge students to write integer problems of their own that can be solved with the nomograph.

## Coordinate Tic-Tac-Toe Game

**Purpose** To review graphing of ordered pairs of integers

**Materials** Coordinate grid (TRB p. 275)

**Activity** In turn each player names an ordered pair (coordinates) and marks that point with his or her chosen symbol (X or 0). The player who gets 5 symbols in a row, column, or diagonal is the winner.

Example:

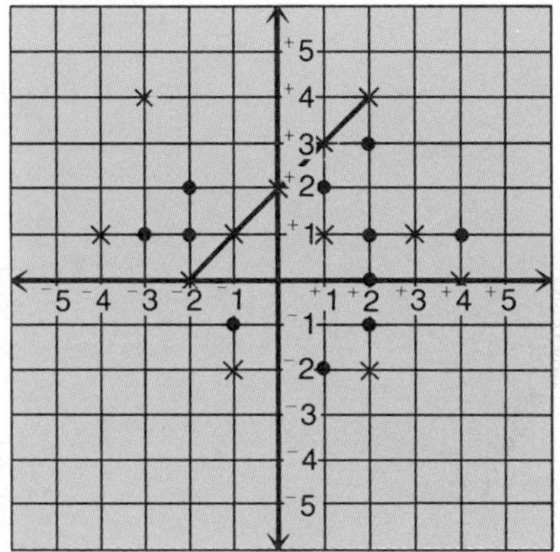


## Integer Roll Game

**Purpose** To practice addition of positive and negative integers

**Materials** Inch graph paper (TRB p. 269), 3 number cubes, colored markers

**Preparation** Label two of the number cubes ${}^{-}6$ through ${}^{-}1$ and the third cube ${}^{+}1$ and ${}^{+}6$. Prepare a gameboard cut from the graph paper as shown below.

| ⁻3 | 5 | ⁻2 | 4 | ⁻5 | 0 |
|---|---|---|---|---|---|
| ⁻1 | ⁻8 | ⁻6 | ⁻9 | 1 | ⁻3 |
| 2 | ⁻5 | ⁻9 | ⁻4 | 3 | ⁻7 |
| ⁻7 | 1 | 0 | 10 | ⁻8 | 10 |
| ⁻6 | 4 | 2 | 12 | 5 | ⁻1 |
| ⁻4 | 11 | ⁻2 | 3 | 12 | 11 |

**Activity** Each player chooses a set of markers. In turn, each player tosses any two of the cubes, adds the numbers shown, and covers the corresponding integer on the gameboard with a marker. A player who cannot find the number on the board must pass. The first player to cover four cells in a row, column, or diagonal is the winner.

To vary the game, include subtraction of integers. Before tossing the number cubes, a player may choose whether to add or subtract the resulting integers.

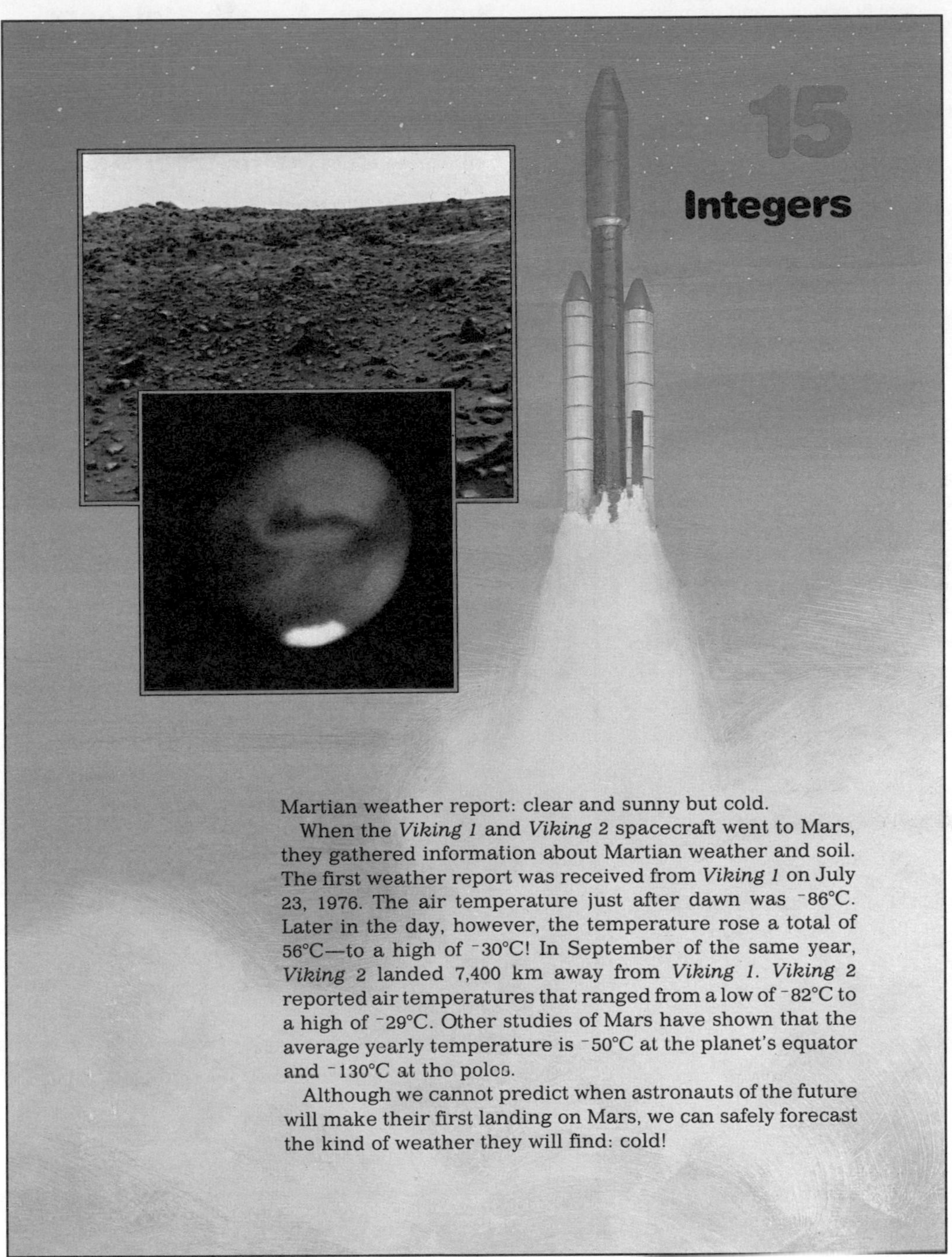

# 15 Integers

Martian weather report: clear and sunny but cold.

When the *Viking 1* and *Viking 2* spacecraft went to Mars, they gathered information about Martian weather and soil. The first weather report was received from *Viking 1* on July 23, 1976. The air temperature just after dawn was $^-86$°C. Later in the day, however, the temperature rose a total of 56°C—to a high of $^-30$°C! In September of the same year, *Viking 2* landed 7,400 km away from *Viking 1*. *Viking 2* reported air temperatures that ranged from a low of $^-82$°C to a high of $^-29$°C. Other studies of Mars have shown that the average yearly temperature is $^-50$°C at the planet's equator and $^-130$°C at the poles.

Although we cannot predict when astronauts of the future will make their first landing on Mars, we can safely forecast the kind of weather they will find: cold!

## Introducing the Chapter

**Discussion** After explaining to students that in this chapter they will be learning about the set of numbers called "integers," lead the class in a brief discussion of any space probes that may have been in the news in recent months. You might also let them discuss any facts about Mars that they may have learned in science studies or elsewhere. After the discussion, allow students time to read the story and enjoy the illustrations. Then encourage students to create some questions relating to the data in the story. As you teach the chapter, you may wish to refer back to this page and present the problems suggested below.

## Follow-Up Questions

**After Page 369** One day the temperature on Mars was 42°C at noon. Two hours later the temperature had dropped 19°. What was the temperature then? ($^-61$°C)

**After Page 371** At midmorning the temperature on Mars was $^-43$°C. By noon the temperature was 14° higher. What was the temperature on Mars at noon? ($^-29$°C)

**After Page 373** During one night on Mars the temperature reached a low of $^-124$°C. During the next day the temperature rose to a high of $^-56$°C. How many degrees greater than $^-124$°C is a temperature of $^-56$°C? (68°C greater)

# Integers

**Quick Review** Students give the number that makes each expression true.

14 − (7 + [7]) = 0 6 − ([4] + 2) = 0 11 − (4 + [7]) = 0

[15] − (7 + 8) = 0 18 − (9 + [9]) = 0 20 − (18 + [2]) = 0

**Lesson Focus** To identify positive and negative integers

## Ideas for Getting Started

On the chalkboard write a list of words such as those in the first column. Ask students to give a word that means the opposite of each of the words.

| | |
|---|---|
| decrease | (increase) |
| up | (down) |
| below | (above) |
| find | (lose) |
| plus | (minus) |
| negative | (positive) |

Tell students that numbers have opposites also. Then draw a number line on the chalkboard.

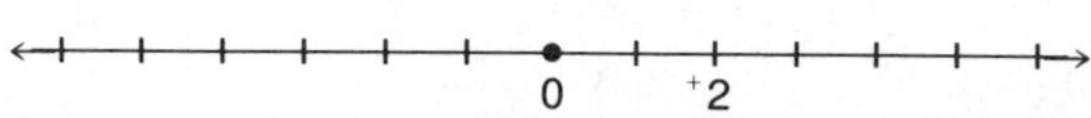


Write $^{+}2$ as shown on the number line. Next, write $^{-}2$ the same distance to the left of 0 on the number line. Then write another positive number with its corresponding negative number on the number line, using language such as "negative 2 is the opposite of positive 2" and "positive 2 is the opposite of negative 2."

## Using Page 366

**Lesson Development** Show the number line below on the chalkboard, using colored chalk, if available, to highlight the positive integers, the negative integers, and zero.

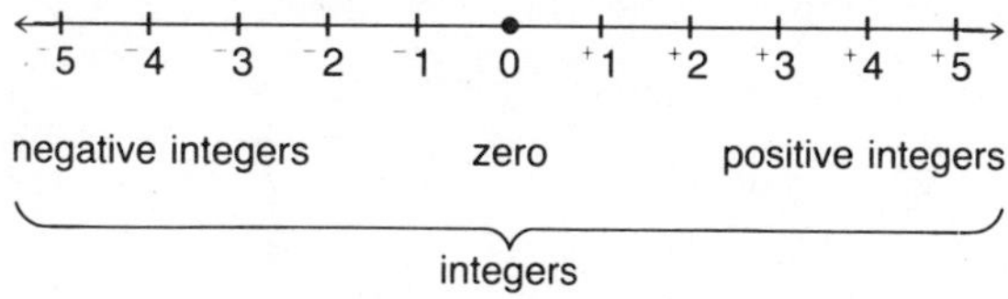


Tell students that the set of integers contains the positive integers, the negative integers, and the number 0. Use the term "opposites" to describe the positive and negative integers. Explain to students that positive integers can be written without the plus sign, but throughout this chapter plus signs are used for emphasis.

Then direct students' attention to the example number line at the top of the page. "What word is the opposite of the word gain?" (lose) "What integer is opposite the integer positive 4?" (negative 4) "What integer is opposite the integer negative 4?" (positive 4) Work through each of the example number lines by asking questions such as: "If $^{+}6$ represents 6 km above sea level, what integer represents 6 km below sea level?" "If $^{-}3$ represents 3 hours ago, what does $^{+}3$ represent?" "If $^{+}5$ represents 5 degrees above 0, what integer represents 5 degrees below 0?" "If $^{+}8$ represents pouring 8 L into a pail, what does the integer $^{-}8$ represent?"

## Positive and Negative Integers

**Integers** are numbers that are used to describe things that are opposites of each other. The integers include the **positive integers**, the **negative integers**, and **zero.** The number lines below suggest that every integer but zero has an opposite.

Give the missing integers.

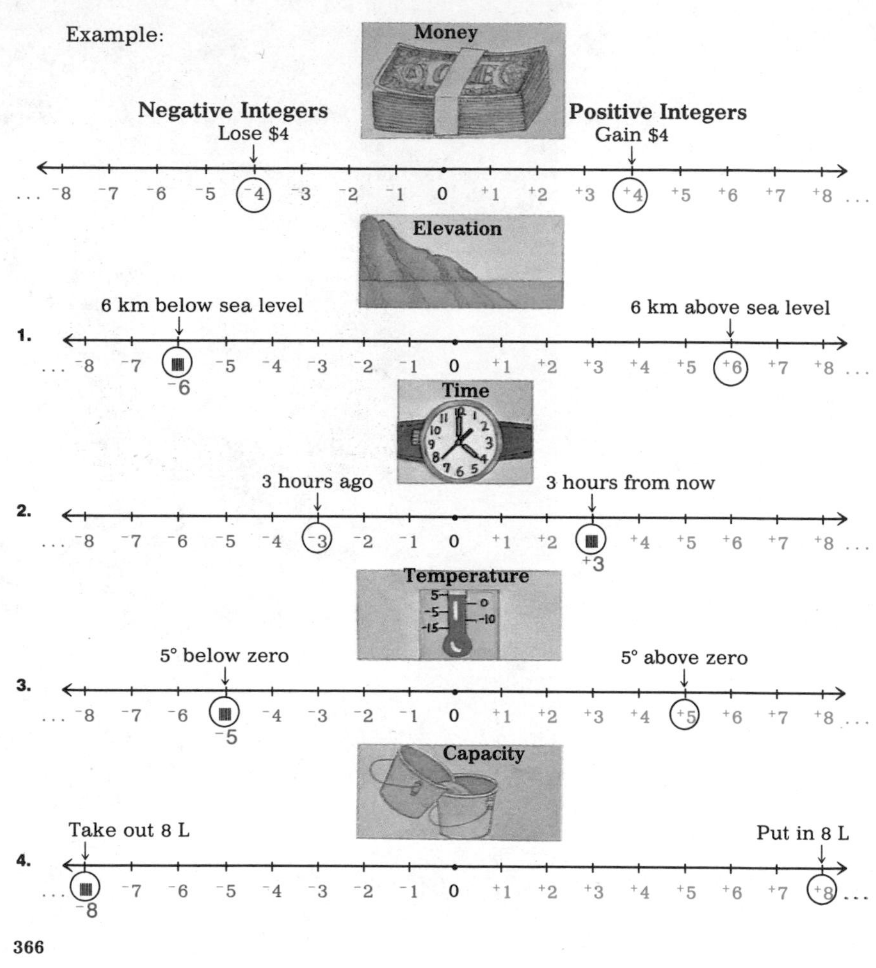


## Follow Up

### Reteaching

Ask students to give an example of a negative integer. A possible response could be the temperature outside when there is a negative 5 degrees, or 5 degrees below zero. Use the idea of temperatures and a thermometer to talk about negative numbers and show how $^{+}5$ and $^{-}5$ would be pictured on a number line. Focus on how to read the integer $^{-}5$ as "negative five." Have students identify $^{-}5$ as five spaces to the left on the number line. Then ask a volunteer where we could find $^{+}5$ on the number line.

### Enrichment

Ask students to make a list of as many pairs of opposite terms as they can. For example, lose 10 points, gain 10 points. Then challenge students to write integer equations for the opposites they have named.

**Assignment Guide**

| | Minimum | Average | Extended |
|---|---|---|---|
| page 367 | 1–22 | 1–26 | 1–26, TM |

Give the opposite idea and the opposite of the integer.

Example: Gain 3 kg, +3     Answer: Lose 3 kg, -3

1. Increase 7 kg, +7 — Decrease 7 kg, -7
2. 18 km east, +18 — 18 km west, -18
3. 4 flights up, +4 — 4 flights down, -4
4. 6 s before blastoff, -6 — 6 s after blastoff, +6
5. Spent $10, -10 — Earned $10, +10
6. 7 steps forward, +7 — 7 steps backward, -7
7. Lose 5 points, -5 — Gain 5 points, +5
8. Gain 6 yards, +6 — Lose 6 yards, -6
9. $2 profit, +2 — $2 loss, -2

Give the opposite of each integer.

10. 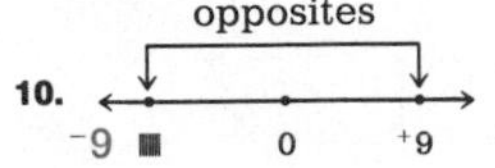


11. 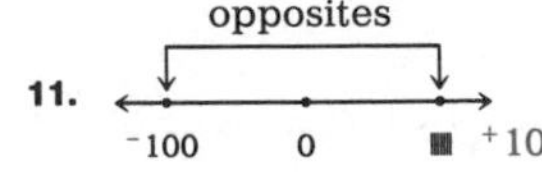


12. 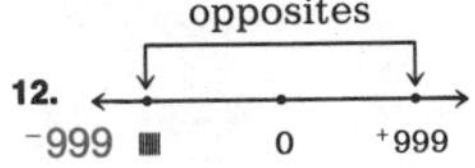


13. +4 -4  14. -6 +6  15. +56 -56  16. -89 +89  17. -167 +167  18. +732 -732

Complete the following statements.

19. If -8 means 8 km below sea level, then +8 means __?__. 8 km above sea level
20. If +4 means 4° above zero, then __?__ means 4° below zero. -4
21. The opposite of a negative integer is a __?__ integer. positive
22. The opposite of a positive integer is a __?__ integer. negative

Think of the number line as going on forever in both directions. Give the integer for the points described.

... -6 -5 -4 -3 -2 -1 0 +1 +2 +3 +4 +5 +6 ...

Example: 3 units to the right of 0.
Answer: +3

23. 4 units to the left of 0 -4
25. 35 units to the right of 0 +35
24. 6 units to the right of 0 +6
26. 128 units to the left of 0 -128

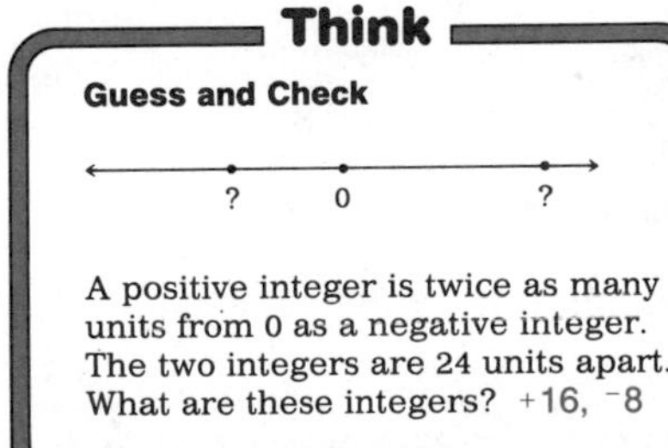

Think
Guess and Check
? 0 ?
A positive integer is twice as many units from 0 as a negative integer. The two integers are 24 units apart. What are these integers? +16, -8
Math


367

## Using Page 367

**Exercises 1–9** If students have difficulty with these exercises, refer to number lines similar to those on page 366; encourage students to think about opposites.

**Exercises 10–18** Students should have little difficulty with these exercises. Emphasize the idea that the opposite of any negative integer is a positive integer the same distance from zero, and the opposite of any positive integer is a negative integer the same distance from zero.

**Exercises 19–22** These exercises are planned to help students move from specific examples to a generalization about negative and positive integers. If necessary, tell students that zero can be thought of as the opposite of itself.

**Exercises 23–26** Having students think about how far an integer is from zero on the number line helps to broaden the concept of an integer. It also provides readiness for later work with absolute value. These exercises also provide a background for the question asked in the Think Math below.

**Think Math** Encourage students to apply the Guess and Check strategy to this problem. They can pick any negative integer, for example -6. Since -6 is 6 units from 0, they would choose a positive integer that was twice as far from 0, in this case +12. These two integers are 18 units apart. To find two integers that satisfy these conditions and are 24 units apart students would make a second guess. The problem is easily solved if guesses are refined until -8 and +16 are chosen.

### Reteaching Supplement, page 87

Name ________  To follow text page 367

**Positive and Negative Integers**

Each number has a number opposite it on the number line.
The whole numbers to the left of zero are **negative integers.**
The whole numbers to the right of zero are **positive integers.**

Opposites

-7 **-6** -5 -4 **-3** -2 **-1** 0 **+1** +2 **+3** +4 +5 **+6** +7

Write the missing integer.

1. opposites: -8, 0, +8
2. opposites: -9, 0, +9
3. opposites: -12, 0, +12
4. opposites: -14, 0, +14
5. opposites: -17, 0, +17
6. opposites: -40, 0, +40
7. opposites: -75, 0, +75
8. opposites: -100, 0, +100
9. opposites: -200, 0, +200

Write the opposite and the integer.
Example: Lose $3, -3   Answer: Find $3, +3

10. Spend $6, -6 **Earn $6, +6**
11. Earn $10, +10 **Spend $10, -10**
12. Decrease 7, -7 **Increase 7, +7**
13. 8° below zero, -8 **8° above zero, +8**
14. Forward 15, +15 **Backward 15, -15**
15. Gain 3 kg, +3 **Lose 3 kg, -3**
16. Win 12, +12 **Lose 12, -12**
17. 6° above zero, +6 **6° below zero, -6**
18. Lose 1 kg, -1 **Gain 1 kg, +1**
19. Find $5, +5 **Lose $5, -5**

### Enrichment Supplement, page 87

Name ________  To follow text page 367

**Temperature Problems**

Use what you know about integers to answer these questions.

Celsius Temperature

1. The temperature at noon was 3°C. By midnight the temperature had fallen 8°. What was the temperature at midnight? **-5°C**
2. One winter day the high temperature for the day was -10°C. The low temperature was 12° less than the high. What was the low temperature? **-22°C**
3. Normal body temperature is 37°C. Normal room temperature is 20°C. How much higher is body temperature? **17°C**
4. On a very hot summer day the temperature might be as high as 43°C. On a very cold winter day the temperature might be as low as -29°C. How many degrees warmer is the summer temperature? **72°C**
5. The temperature on a cool day was -2°C. The temperature fell 9°. What was the new temperature? **-11°C**
6. About 95% of the world's population live in parts of the world whose average temperature is between 4.5°C and 27°C. What is the difference in these average temperatures? **22.5°C**
7. Miami, Florida, had a temperature of 22°C. On the same day Bemidji, Minnesota, had a temperature of -23°C. How many degrees colder was it in Bemidji? **45°C**
8. The sunlit side of the planet Mercury has a temperature of 480°C. The dark side of the planet has a temperature 660° lower than the sunlit side. What is the temperature of the dark side of Mercury? **-180°C**
9. After a very cold low temperature of -21°, the temperature rose 12°. What was the new temperature? **-9°C**
10. The boiling point of water is 100°C. How many degrees lower is normal body temperature? (See problem 3.) **63°C**

### Practice Supplement, page 137

Name ________  To follow text page 367

**Positive and Negative Integers**

Give the opposite of each integer.

1. +6 **-6**  2. -2 **+2**  3. +1 **-1**  4. +27 **-27**  5. -97 **+97**
6. +10 **-10**  7. -5 **+5**  8. -8 **+8**  9. -21 **+21**  10. +1,001 **-1,001**
11. +9 **-9**  12. +56 **-56**  13. -268 **+268**  14. +786 **-786**  15. +100 **-100**

Give the opposite of each integer.

16. opposites: **-5**, 0, +5
17. opposites: **-27**, 0, +27
18. opposites: 12, 0, **+12**
19. opposites: 68, 0, **+68**
20. opposites: **-38**, 0, +38
21. opposites: **-800**, 0, +800

Give the opposite idea and the opposite integer.

22. Earned $5, +5 **Spent $5** **-5**
23. 4° below zero, -4 **4° above zero** **+4°**
24. Gained 3 kg, +3 **Lost 3 kg** **-3**
25. Won $17, +17 **Lost $17** **-17**
26. Up 6 flights of stairs, +6 **Down 6 flights of stairs** **-6**

# Integers

**Quick Review** Students give the symbol $(>, <, =)$ to make each expression true.

$2 + 9 > 9 + 1$ $\quad 6 + 9 = 5 + 10$ $\quad 13 - 8 < 12 - 6$

$17 - 8 > 16 - 9$ $\quad 12 - 9 = 10 - 7$ $\quad 15 - 5 > 14 - 5$

$14 - 7 > 15 - 10$ $\quad 5 + 10 < 6 + 11$

**Lesson Focus** To use a number line to find the sum of two negative or two positive integers

## Ideas for Getting Started

Ask several questions such as: "If you lost $5 and then lost $4 more, how many dollars would you have lost altogether?" ($9) "If you gained 4 pounds and gained 3 more pounds, how many pounds would you have gained altogether?" (7 lb) Then write these equations on the chalkboard.

$$^{-}5 + {}^{-}4 = ?$$
$$^{+}4 + {}^{+}3 = ?$$

"What do you think the sums would be?" (Students probably will give the correct sums.) Then ask students to use a number line to "prove" that the sums they have given are correct. Discuss the use of models in showing the sums of two negative or two positive integers.

## Using Page 368

**Motivational Problem** Read the problem at the top of the page. "What do we want to find out about Tim's jogging?" (How far did he jog; what direction from home did he jog?) "What data does the problem give?" (He first jogged 5 km west, then west 3 km more.) "Since we are combining two amounts, what operation should we use to solve the problem?" (addition)

**Lesson Development** On the chalkboard draw a number line like the one shown on the page. "How can we show Tim's 5 km jog?" (Draw an arrow from 0 to $^{-}5$.) "How can we show Tim's 3 km jog?" (Draw an arrow from $^{-}5$ to $^{-}8$.) "How can we show the combined results?" (a total of 8 km from home, or $^{-}8$) Direct students' attention to the addition equation showing $^{-}5 + {}^{-}3 = {}^{-}8$. Then ask for volunteers to show $^{-}6 + {}^{-}2$ and $^{-}1 + {}^{-}5$ on the number line.

Discuss the second example in the same manner. Emphasize that we can also use the number line to show addition of positive integers.

**Warm Up** Students will probably not need to use the number line to find these sums. However, the number line can be used to verify sums.

## Adding Integers

Tim jogged 5 km west from his home. Then he jogged 3 km further west. How far and in what direction was he from home?

To solve this problem, we can add negative integers.

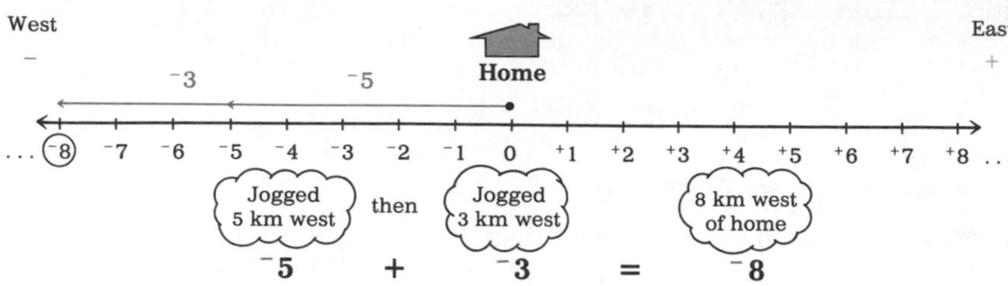


Tim was 8 km west of home.

In the situation below, we add positive integers.

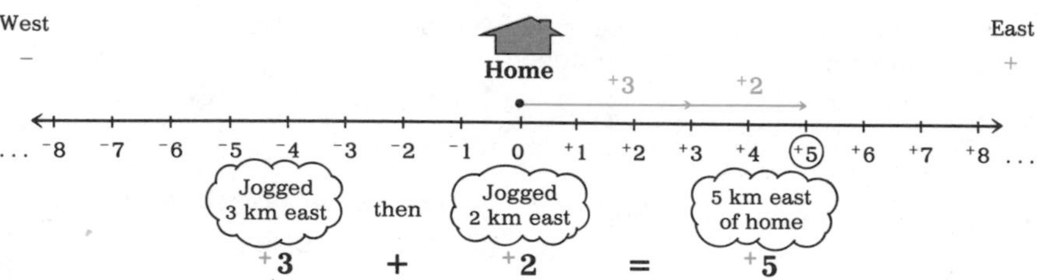


### Warm Up

Find the sum. Use the number line if needed.

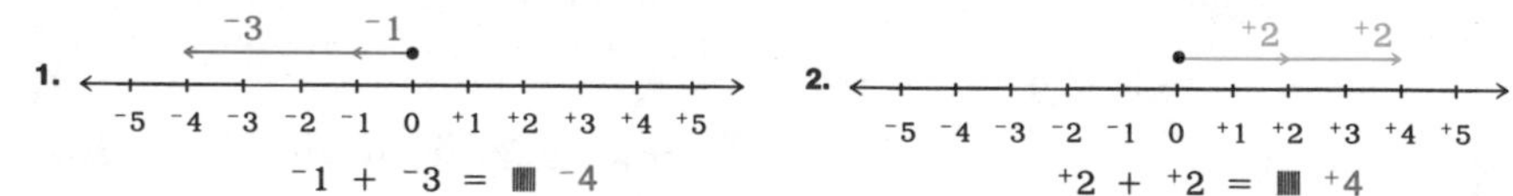


1. $^{-}1 + {}^{-}3 = ■$ $\quad ^{-}4$
2. $^{+}2 + {}^{+}2 = ■$ $\quad ^{+}4$



## Follow Up

### Reteaching

Draw a number line on the chalkboard. Tell students that you are at zero and are going to move back and forth on the number line. Explain that ($^{-}$) means move to the left, and ($^{+}$) means move to the right. That is, ($^{-}3$) means move 3 spaces to the left, and ($^{+}3$) means move 3 spaces to the right. Work with students to show the addition of several negative integer equations. Lead students to recognize the pattern:

negative + negative = negative.

Repeat the procedure with positive integers. Show each step on the number line and note the pattern:

positive + positive = positive.

### Enrichment

Write the following equations on the chalkboard for students to solve. If possible, let students use calculators to check their answers.

1. $^{+}6 + {}^{+}13 + {}^{+}23 = n$ $\quad ^{+}42$
2. $^{+}10 + {}^{+}20 + {}^{+}30 = n$ $\quad ^{+}60$
3. $^{-}5 + {}^{-}12 + {}^{-}35 = n$ $\quad ^{-}52$
4. $^{-}26 + {}^{-}18 + {}^{-}2 = n$ $\quad ^{-}46$
5. $^{+}14 + {}^{+}8 + 0 = n$ $\quad ^{+}22$
6. $^{-}3 + {}^{-}4 + {}^{-}5 = n$ $\quad ^{-}12$
7. $0 + {}^{-}6 + {}^{-}6 = n$ $\quad ^{-}12$
8. $^{+}1 + {}^{+}20 + {}^{+}1 = n$ $\quad ^{+}22$
9. $^{-}19 + {}^{-}1 + {}^{-}20 = n$ $\quad ^{-}40$
10. $^{+}35 + {}^{+}5 + {}^{+}5 = n$ $\quad ^{+}45$

| Assignment Guide | | | |
|---|---|---|---|
| | Minimum | Average | Extended |
| page 369 | 1–23, SK | 1–23, SK | 1–23, SK |

Write an addition equation for each number line picture.

1. $^{+}5 + ^{+}4 = ^{+}9$

2. $^{-}3 + ^{-}4 = ^{-}7$

3. $^{+}2 + ^{+}8 = ^{+}10$

4. $^{-}6 + ^{-}4 = ^{-}10$

Find the sums. Think about the number line if needed.

| | | | |
|---|---|---|---|
| **5.** $^{-}2 + ^{-}3$ $^{-}5$ | **6.** $^{+}4 + ^{+}3$ $^{+}7$ | **7.** $^{+}6 + ^{+}1$ $^{+}7$ | **8.** $^{-}5 + ^{-}4$ $^{-}9$ |
| **9.** $^{+}7 + ^{+}3$ $^{+}10$ | **10.** $^{-}8 + ^{-}1$ $^{-}9$ | **11.** $^{-}9 + ^{-}2$ $^{-}11$ | **12.** $^{+}6 + ^{+}6$ $^{+}12$ |
| **13.** $^{-}4 + ^{-}4$ $^{-}8$ | **14.** $^{-}8 + ^{-}4$ $^{-}12$ | **15.** $^{+}9 + ^{+}3$ $^{+}12$ | **16.** $^{-}6 + ^{-}5$ $^{-}11$ |
| **17.** $^{-}8 + ^{-}7$ $^{-}15$ | **18.** $^{-}9 + ^{-}8$ $^{-}17$ | **19.** $^{+}7 + ^{+}6$ $^{+}13$ | **20.** $^{+}4 + ^{+}9$ $^{+}13$ |

21. The sum of two positive integers is a __?__ integer. positive

22. The sum of two negative integers is a __?__ integer. negative

23. Kate jogged 4 km west, then rested and jogged 5 more km west. How far and in what direction was she from home? 9 km west

## Skillkeeper

Find each area.

| | | | |
|---|---|---|---|
| **1.** $l$ = 15 cm | **2.** $l$ = 52 m | **3.** $l$ = 9.4 m | **4.** $l$ = 2.8 cm |
| $w$ = 8 cm | $w$ = 10 m | $w$ = 6.3 m | $w$ = 4 cm |
| $A$ = ■ 120 $cm^2$ | $A$ = ■ 520 $m^2$ | $A$ = ■ 59.22 $m^2$ | $A$ = ■ 11.2 $cm^2$ |

Find each area. Use 3.14 for $\pi$ and the formula $A = \pi \times r \times r$.

| | | | |
|---|---|---|---|
| **5.** $r$ = 3 cm | **6.** $d$ = 4 m | **7.** $r$ = 1.5 m | **8.** $d$ = 8 cm |
| $A$ = ■ 28.26 $cm^2$ | $A$ = ■ 12.56 $m^2$ | $A$ = ■ 7.065 $m^2$ | $A$ = ■ 50.24 $cm^2$ |

More Practice, page 428, Set A



## Using Page 369

**Exercises 1–4** If students need help with these exercises, emphasize that each arrow represents an integer and that the sum is the "combination" of the two arrows. Since the first arrow starts at 0 it is easy to determine that integer. To find the integer for the second arrow, however, students must count units or spaces on the number line. In exercise 1, for example, the first integer is $^{+}5$. The second integer is found by counting the space between 5 and 6, between 6 and 7, between 7 and 8, and between 8 and 9. The arrow has moved to the right an additional 4 units, thus the integer represented is $^{+}4$.

**Exercises 5–20** Students should have little difficulty with these exercises. However, if difficulties do arise, refer to the number line to review the procedure.

**Exercises 21–23** Exercises 21 and 22 summarize the basic idea in this lesson. This is an appropriate time to emphasize that when 0 is added to any integer, the result is that integer.

**Skillkeeper** These skills were originally taught in Chapter 14.

**More Practice,** page 428, Set A

**Reteaching Supplement,** page 88

Name ______ To follow text page 369

### Adding Integers

Jumps to the **right** show **addition of positive integers.**
Jumps to the **left** show **addition of negative integers.**

$^{+}7 + ^{-}4 = ^{+}3$

$^{-}2 + ^{-}3 = ^{-}5$

$^{-}6 + ^{+}4 = ^{-}2$

Show the jumps and find the sums.

1. $^{+}5 + ^{-}2 =$ $^{+}3$
2. $^{-}1 + ^{-}3 =$ $^{-}4$
3. $^{-}5 + ^{+}3 =$ $^{-}2$

Find the sums. Think about the number line if necessary.

| | | |
|---|---|---|
| **4.** $^{+}9 + ^{-}5 =$ $^{+}4$ | **5.** $^{-}3 + ^{-}2 =$ $^{-}5$ | **6.** $^{+}4 + ^{+}8 =$ $^{+}12$ |
| **7.** $^{-}6 + ^{+}6 =$ 0 | **8.** $^{-}10 + ^{+}6 =$ $^{-}4$ | **9.** $^{+}15 + ^{-}7 =$ $^{+}8$ |
| **10.** $^{-}5 + ^{-}3 =$ $^{-}8$ | **11.** $^{-}14 + ^{+}8 =$ $^{-}6$ | **12.** $^{+}10 + ^{-}9 =$ $^{+}1$ |
| **13.** $^{-}6 + ^{-}1 =$ $^{-}7$ | **14.** $^{-}8 + ^{+}5 =$ $^{-}3$ | **15.** $^{+}7 + ^{-}16 =$ $^{-}9$ |

**Enrichment Supplement,** page 88

Name ______ To follow text page 369

### Patterns in Addition of Integers

Look for patterns to help you complete each set of equations.

**1.**

| | | |
|---|---|---|
| $6 + 4 =$ 10 | $6 + ^{-}1 =$ 5 | $6 + ^{-}6 =$ 0 |
| $6 + 3 =$ 9 | $6 + ^{-}2 =$ 4 | $6 + ^{-}7 =$ $^{-}1$ |
| $6 + 2 =$ 8 | $6 + ^{-}3 =$ 3 | $6 + ^{-}8 =$ $^{-}2$ |
| $6 + 1 =$ 7 | $6 + ^{-}4 =$ 2 | $6 + ^{-}9 =$ $^{-}3$ |
| $6 + 0 =$ 6 | $6 + ^{-}5 =$ 1 | $6 + ^{-}10 =$ $^{-}4$ |

**2.**

| | | |
|---|---|---|
| $^{-}5 + 5 =$ 0 | $^{-}5 + 0 =$ $^{-}5$ | $^{-}5 + ^{-}5 =$ $^{-}10$ |
| $^{-}5 + 4 =$ $^{-}1$ | $^{-}5 + ^{-}1 =$ $^{-}6$ | $^{-}5 + ^{-}6 =$ $^{-}11$ |
| $^{-}5 + 3 =$ $^{-}2$ | $^{-}5 + ^{-}2 =$ $^{-}7$ | $^{-}5 + ^{-}7 =$ $^{-}12$ |
| $^{-}5 + 2 =$ $^{-}3$ | $^{-}5 + ^{-}3 =$ $^{-}8$ | $^{-}5 + ^{-}8 =$ $^{-}13$ |
| $^{-}5 + 1 =$ $^{-}4$ | $^{-}5 + ^{-}4 =$ $^{-}9$ | $^{-}5 + ^{-}9 =$ $^{-}14$ |

**3.**

| | | |
|---|---|---|
| $0 +$ 7 $= 7$ | $5 +$ 2 $= 7$ | $10 +$ $^{-}3$ $= 7$ |
| $1 +$ 6 $= 7$ | $6 +$ 1 $= 7$ | $11 +$ $^{-}4$ $= 7$ |
| $2 +$ 5 $= 7$ | $7 +$ 0 $= 7$ | $12 +$ $^{-}5$ $= 7$ |
| $3 +$ 4 $= 7$ | $8 +$ $^{-}1$ $= 7$ | $13 +$ $^{-}6$ $= 7$ |
| $4 +$ 3 $= 7$ | $9 +$ $^{-}2$ $= 7$ | $14 +$ $^{-}7$ $= 7$ |

**4.**

| | | |
|---|---|---|
| $^{-}5 +$ 5 $= 0$ | $^{-}5 +$ 4 $= ^{-}1$ | $^{-}5 +$ 14 $= 9$ |
| $^{-}5 +$ 6 $= 1$ | $^{-}5 +$ 3 $= ^{-}2$ | $^{-}5 +$ 13 $= 8$ |
| $^{-}5 +$ 7 $= 2$ | $^{-}5 +$ 2 $= ^{-}3$ | $^{-}5 +$ 12 $= 7$ |
| $^{-}5 +$ 8 $= 3$ | $^{-}5 +$ 1 $= ^{-}4$ | $^{-}5 +$ 11 $= 6$ |
| $^{-}5 +$ 9 $= 4$ | $^{-}5 +$ 0 $= ^{-}5$ | $^{-}5 +$ 10 $= 5$ |

**Practice Supplement,** page 138

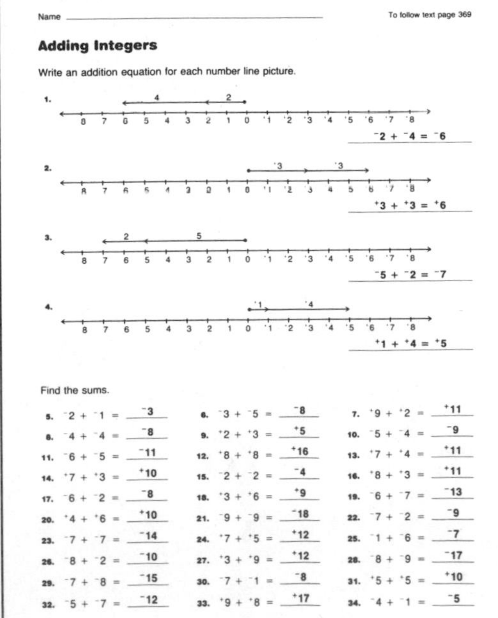

Name ______ To follow text page 369

### Adding Integers

Write an addition equation for each number line picture.

1. $^{-}2 + ^{-}4 = ^{-}6$
2. $^{+}3 + ^{+}3 = ^{+}6$
3. $^{-}5 + ^{-}2 = ^{-}7$
4. $^{+}1 + ^{+}4 = ^{+}5$

Find the sums.

| | | |
|---|---|---|
| **5.** $^{-}2 + ^{-}1 =$ $^{-}3$ | **6.** $^{-}3 + ^{-}5 =$ $^{-}8$ | **7.** $^{+}9 + ^{+}2 =$ $^{+}11$ |
| **8.** $^{-}4 + ^{-}4 =$ $^{-}8$ | **9.** $^{+}2 + ^{+}3 =$ $^{+}5$ | **10.** $^{-}5 + ^{-}4 =$ $^{-}9$ |
| **11.** $^{-}6 + ^{-}5 =$ $^{-}11$ | **12.** $^{+}8 + ^{+}8 =$ $^{+}16$ | **13.** $^{+}7 + ^{+}4 =$ $^{+}11$ |
| **14.** $^{+}7 + ^{+}3 =$ $^{+}10$ | **15.** $^{-}2 + ^{-}2 =$ $^{-}4$ | **16.** $^{+}8 + ^{+}3 =$ $^{+}11$ |
| **17.** $^{-}6 + ^{-}2 =$ $^{-}8$ | **18.** $^{+}3 + ^{+}6 =$ $^{+}9$ | **19.** $^{-}6 + ^{-}7 =$ $^{-}13$ |
| **20.** $^{+}4 + ^{+}6 =$ $^{+}10$ | **21.** $^{-}9 + ^{-}9 =$ $^{-}18$ | **22.** $^{-}7 + ^{-}2 =$ $^{-}9$ |
| **23.** $^{-}7 + ^{-}7 =$ $^{-}14$ | **24.** $^{+}7 + ^{+}5 =$ $^{+}12$ | **25.** $^{-}1 + ^{-}6 =$ $^{-}7$ |
| **26.** $^{-}8 + ^{-}2 =$ $^{-}10$ | **27.** $^{+}3 + ^{+}9 =$ $^{+}12$ | **28.** $^{-}8 + ^{-}9 =$ $^{-}17$ |
| **29.** $^{-}7 + ^{-}8 =$ $^{-}15$ | **30.** $^{-}7 + ^{-}1 =$ $^{-}8$ | **31.** $^{+}5 + ^{+}5 =$ $^{+}10$ |
| **32.** $^{-}5 + ^{-}7 =$ $^{-}12$ | **33.** $^{+}9 + ^{+}8 =$ $^{+}17$ | **34.** $^{-}4 + ^{-}1 =$ $^{-}5$ |

**Quick Review** Students write only the answers for these problems.

| | | | | |
|---|---|---|---|---|
| 76 × 5 = **380** | 2.01 − 1.88 = **0.13** | \$12.15 + 39.78 = **\$51.93** | 76 + 1,432 + 228 = **1,736**<br>873 − 346 = **527** | 35)167.3 = **4.78** |

**Lesson Focus** To use a number line to find the sum of two integers

## Ideas for Getting Started

Write the following problems on the chalkboard.

$^{+}6 + {}^{+}6 =$ ______ $^{+}6 - {}^{+}7 =$ ______

$^{+}6 - {}^{+}5 =$ ______

Then ask students the following questions: "If you earn \$6 and then spend \$6, have you gained, lost, or stayed the same?" (stayed the same) "If you earn \$6 and spend \$5, have you gained, lost, or stayed the same?" (gained) "How much have you gained?" (\$1) If you earn \$6 and spend \$7, have you gained, lost, or stayed the same?" (lost) "How much have you lost?" (\$1)

## Using Page 370

**Lesson Development** On the chalkboard draw a number line like those shown on this page. Tell students that bike trips to the east of home are represented by a positive integer and trips to the west of home are represented by a negative integer. Draw arrows showing the rides shown in the first example and tell students that the end point of the trip is 5 km west of home and therefore is represented by the integer $^{-}5$. Note that the idea behind these exercises is that the sum of an integer and its opposite is 0. For example, in example A, $^{+}3 + {}^{-}3$ is 0. This leaves $^{-}5$ more, so the answer is $^{-}5$.

Use the number line to show other examples on the chalkboard as necessary. Then work through examples B and C with students. Ask questions such as the following for each example: "Where do we start for the first trip?" (0) "How far and in what direction is the first trip?" (2 units to the west) "Since we follow the first trip with the second trip, we start at $^{-}2$ for the second trip. How far and in what direction is this trip?" (6 units to the right) "Are we now east or west of home?" (east of home) "How far to the east?" (4 units) "What integer represents this direction and distance?" ($^{+}4$) Use other examples as needed to be sure students understand how to use the number line to find the sum of two integers.

## More Adding Integers

Here are some examples of bike trips which suggest additions involving a positive and a negative number. Study each example. Give the missing sums.

**A.**

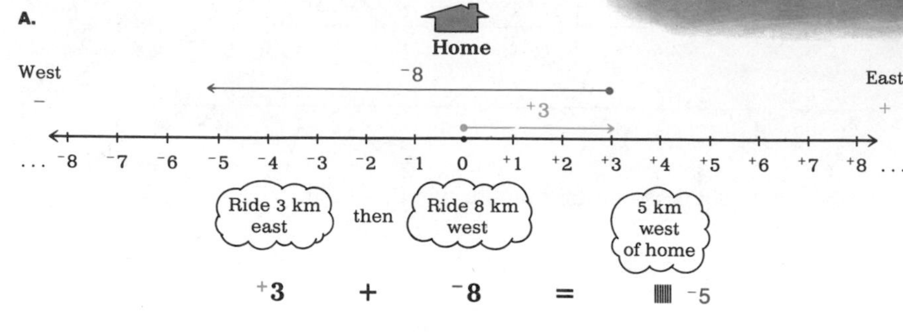


**B.**

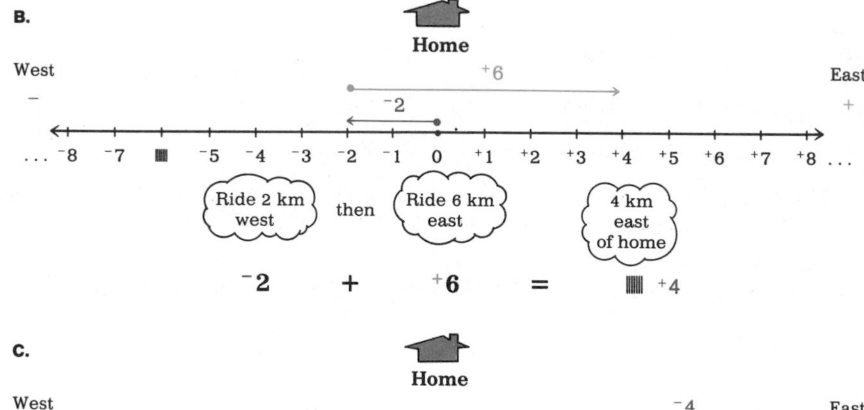


**C.**

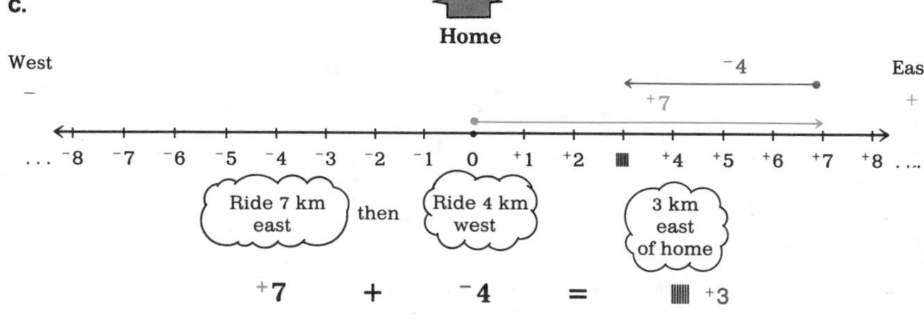




## Follow Up

### Reteaching

Use a number line to show combining two integers. Remind students that we always start at 0 on the number line. Then ask students to think about the equation $^{-}2 + {}^{+}3 = \square$. Show this on the number line. We start at 0, move two spaces to the left ($^{-}2$), then move three spaces to the right ($^{+}3$). The result is $^{+}1$. Next show the equation $^{+}2 + {}^{-}5 = \square$. Again, we begin at 0, move two spaces to the right ($^{+}2$), then move five spaces to the left ($^{-}5$). "What is the integer on the number line where we stop?" ($^{-}3$) Use several other examples to help students find the sums of integers on the number line.

### Enrichment

Write the following equations on the chalkboard and challenge students to find the sums.

1. $^{-}9 + {}^{+}6 = n$ **$^{-}3$**
2. $^{-}6 + {}^{-}12 = n$ **$^{-}18$**
3. $^{+}4 + {}^{-}6 = n$ **$^{-}2$**
4. $^{+}128 + {}^{-}128 = n$ **0**
5. $^{-}36 + {}^{+}49 = n$ **$^{+}13$**
6. $^{+}5 + {}^{-}12 + {}^{-}5 = n$ **$^{-}12$**
7. $^{-}18 + {}^{-}23 + {}^{+}38 = n$ **$^{-}3$**
8. $^{-}15 + {}^{-}39 = n$ **$^{-}54$**
9. $^{-}26 + {}^{+}26 + {}^{-}13 = n$ **$^{-}13$**
10. $^{+}8 + {}^{+}16 + {}^{-}3 = n$ **$^{+}21$**

| Assignment Guide | Minimum | Average | Extended |
|---|---|---|---|
| page 371 | 1–24 | 1–28 | 1–28, TM |

Write an addition equation for each number line picture.
Order of addends may vary.

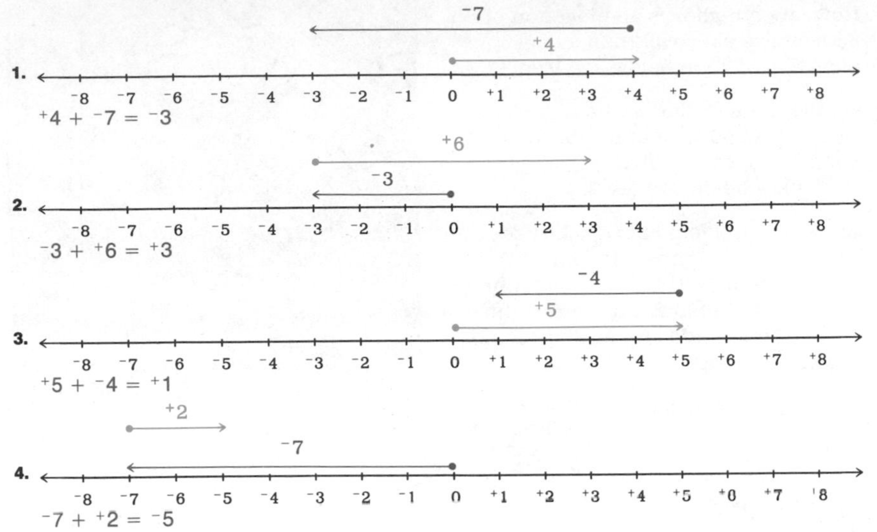

1. $^{+}4 + ^{-}7 = ^{-}3$
2. $^{-}3 + ^{+}6 = ^{+}3$
3. $^{+}5 + ^{-}4 = ^{+}1$
4. $^{-}7 + ^{+}2 = ^{-}5$

Find the sums. Use a number line when needed.

5. $^{+}7 + ^{-}3$ $^{+}4$
6. $^{+}6 + ^{+}8$ $^{+}14$
7. $^{+}4 + ^{-}3$ $^{+}1$
8. $^{+}6 + ^{-}6$ 0
9. $^{+}2 + ^{-}6$ $^{-}4$
10. $^{-}17 + ^{+}8$ $^{-}9$
11. $^{+}1 + ^{-}9$ $^{-}8$
12. $^{-}9 + ^{+}4$ $^{-}5$
13. $^{-}6 + ^{-}4$ $^{-}10$
14. $^{+}9 + ^{-}5$ $^{+}4$
15. $^{-}2 + ^{+}8$ $^{+}6$
16. $^{+}9 + ^{+}7$ $^{+}16$
17. $^{-}7 + ^{+}16$ $^{+}9$
18. $^{-}13 + ^{+}6$ $^{-}7$
19. $^{+}3 + ^{-}8$ $^{-}5$
20. $^{-}4 + ^{+}13$ $^{+}9$
21. $^{-}8 + ^{+}8$ 0
22. $^{+}13 + ^{-}7$ $^{+}6$
23. $^{-}14 + ^{+}8$ $^{-}6$
24. $^{+}7 + ^{-}2$ $^{+}5$

★ 25. $^{-}47 + ^{+}23$ $^{-}24$ ★ 26. $^{+}82 + ^{-}46$ $^{+}36$ ★ 27. $^{+}23 + ^{-}89$ $^{-}66$ ★ 28. $^{-}46 + ^{+}93$ $^{+}47$

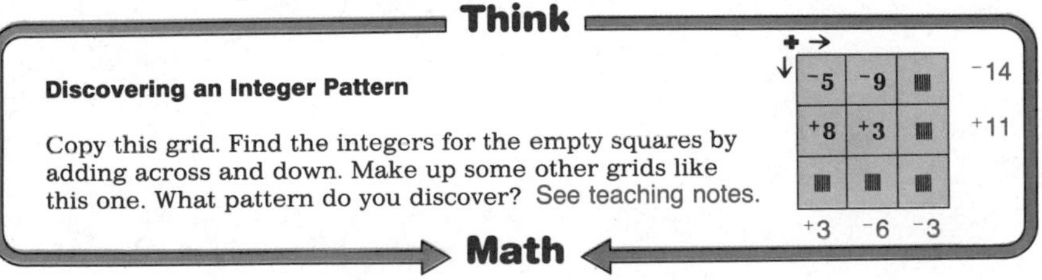

**Think Math**

**Discovering an Integer Pattern**

Copy this grid. Find the integers for the empty squares by adding across and down. Make up some other grids like this one. What pattern do you discover? See teaching notes.

| + | | | |
|---|---|---|---|
| $^{-}5$ | $^{-}9$ | ■ | $^{-}14$ |
| $^{+}8$ | $^{+}3$ | ■ | $^{+}11$ |
| ■ | ■ | ■ | |
| $^{+}3$ | $^{-}6$ | $^{-}3$ | |

More Practice, page 428, Set B



## Using Page 371

**Exercises 1–4** As with earlier exercises, the major difficulty for students comes in deciding the integer to be used for the second arrow. Be sure students count the spaces between numbers as units rather than the marks for the numbers. If students have difficulty, have them draw number lines and use a red pencil to mark each unit as they count.

**Exercises 5–24** If needed, provide students with number-line practice sheets so that they can draw arrows to show sums or to verify sums.

**Exercises 25–28** These larger sums might motivate the more able students to discover this shortcut for finding sums of integers: To find the sum of two integers, find the difference of the numbers, disregarding the positive or negative signs, and attach the sign of the larger of the two numbers to this difference.

**Think Math** As students complete these sums, they will find that the sum of the first two numbers in the third column is always the same as the sum of the first two numbers in the bottom row. The exercise illustrates the generalization shown below.

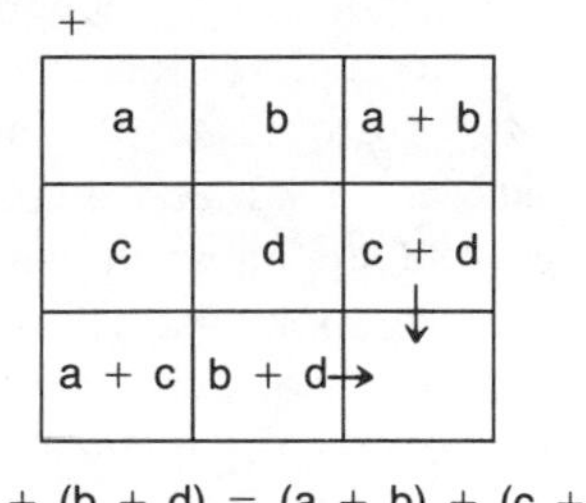

| + | | |
|---|---|---|
| a | b | a + b |
| c | d | c + d |
| a + c | b + d | |

$$(a + c) + (b + d) = (a + b) + (c + d)$$

**More Practice,** page 428, Set B

## Ideas That Work

### Special Education

To reinforce addition of integers, let students team with a partner to play "Add-O."

Prepare several game mats as shown, 3 markers per player, and 2 number cubes labeled 2, 4, 6, 7, 8, 9, and $^{-}1$, $^{-}3$, $^{-}5$, $^{-}7$, $^{-}8$, $^{-}9$.

Each player begins the game with all three markers in one of the empty end rows. The object of the game is to get all three markers to the spaces on the opposite side of the game mat. In turn, a player rolls the number cubes, selects one of the two integers, and adds it to an available integer on the game mat. If the addition is correct, a marker can be moved to that space. A number line can be used if needed, and a calculator can be used to check answers. The free spaces may be occupied at any turn. If no move is possible, player must pass.

| | | | | | |
|---|---|---|---|---|---|
| | $^{-}2$ | 5 | Free | 8 | |
| | 9 | 7 | $^{-}5$ | $^{-}3$ | |
| | $^{-}4$ | Free | 6 | $^{-}1$ | |

**Practice Supplement,** page 139

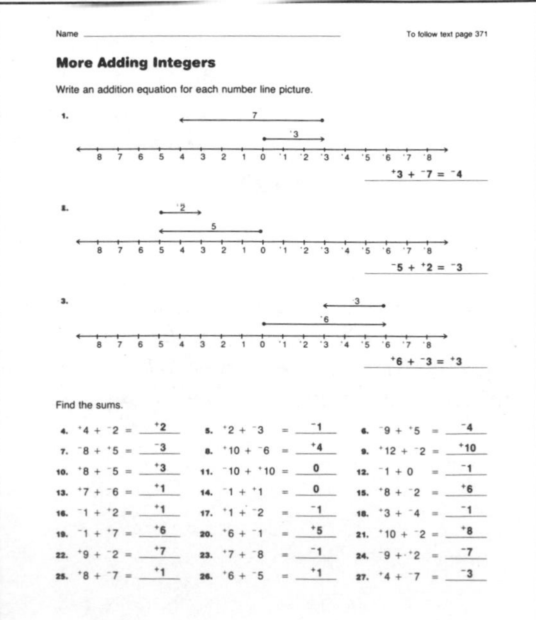

Name ______________ To follow text page 371

**More Adding Integers**

Write an addition equation for each number line picture.

1. $^{+}3 + ^{-}7 = ^{-}4$
2. $^{-}5 + ^{+}2 = ^{-}3$
3. $^{+}6 + ^{-}3 = ^{+}3$

Find the sums.

| | | |
|---|---|---|
| 4. $^{+}4 + ^{-}2 =$ $^{+}2$ | 5. $^{+}2 + ^{-}3 =$ $^{-}1$ | 6. $^{-}9 + ^{+}5 =$ $^{-}4$ |
| 7. $^{-}8 + ^{+}5 =$ $^{-}3$ | 8. $^{+}10 + ^{-}6 =$ $^{+}4$ | 9. $^{+}12 + ^{-}2 =$ $^{+}10$ |
| 10. $^{+}8 + ^{-}5 =$ $^{+}3$ | 11. $^{-}10 + ^{+}10 =$ 0 | 12. $^{-}1 + 0 =$ $^{-}1$ |
| 13. $^{+}7 + ^{-}6 =$ $^{+}1$ | 14. $^{-}1 + ^{+}1 =$ 0 | 15. $^{+}8 + ^{-}2 =$ $^{+}6$ |
| 16. $^{-}1 + ^{+}2 =$ $^{+}1$ | 17. $^{+}1 + ^{-}2 =$ $^{-}1$ | 18. $^{+}3 + ^{-}4 =$ $^{-}1$ |
| 19. $^{-}1 + ^{+}7 =$ $^{+}6$ | 20. $^{+}6 + ^{-}1 =$ $^{+}5$ | 21. $^{+}10 + ^{-}2 =$ $^{+}8$ |
| 22. $^{+}9 + ^{-}2 =$ $^{+}7$ | 23. $^{+}7 + ^{-}8 =$ $^{-}1$ | 24. $^{-}9 + ^{+}2 =$ $^{-}7$ |
| 25. $^{+}8 + ^{-}7 =$ $^{+}1$ | 26. $^{+}6 + ^{-}5 =$ $^{+}1$ | 27. $^{+}4 + ^{-}7 =$ $^{-}3$ |

# Integers

**Quick Review** Students estimate answers by rounding 2-digit numbers to the nearest ten and 3-digit numbers to the nearest hundred.

$46 - 19$ 30 $92 + 77$ 170 $960 - 889$ 100 $92 \times 18$ 180 $24\overline{)178}$ 10 $602 \div 28$ 20

**Lesson Focus** To use the inverse relationship between addition and subtraction to find the difference of two integers

## Ideas for Getting Started

Write these addition equations on the chalkboard:

$468 + 379 = 847$ $\frac{3}{8} + \frac{3}{5} = \frac{39}{40}$ $4.968 + 3.759 = 8.727$

Next write these subtraction equations:

$847 - 379$ $\frac{39}{40} - \frac{3}{5} = \_\_\_\_$ $8.727 - 3.759$

"How can you find these differences quickly without computing?" Without being prompted, students should be able to give the differences by looking at the addition equations. Ask them to explain why they know that the differences are correct. A typical response might be: I can subtract by finding a missing addend. Since I know that 468 + 379 = 847, I know that 847 − 379 = 468.

## Using Page 372

**Lesson Development** Read the first paragraph at the top of the page. Be sure students understand the question asked. "What are the two sea level measurements we are asked to compare?" (4 km below sea level and 6 km above sea level) "What integers represent the measurements?" ($^-4$ and $^+6$) "Since we are comparing two numbers, what operation should we use to find the answer?" (subtraction) Before proceeding, have students refer to the picture and count the units between $^-4$ and $^+6$ to verify that the difference between these integers is 10. Then write the equation $^+6 - {}^-4 = \_\_\_\_$ on the chalkboard. "What integer added to $^-4$ to give $^+6$?" ($^+10$) Have students verify that $^+10 + {}^-4 = {}^+6$. Remind students that subtraction can be thought of as finding the missing addend.

**Other Examples** Work through each of these examples, emphasizing the idea that if the sum and one addend is known, the difference is the other addend. Check each of the completed subtraction problems by verifying that the addition equation is correct.

**Warm Up** Be alert for students who are having difficulty with (a) the relationship between addition and subtraction, (b) techniques for adding integers, (c) thinking about a missing addend. Students who are having difficulty might benefit from writing fact families. For example, give students an addition equation such as $4 + {}^-9 = {}^-5$ and ask them to write another addition equation and two subtraction equations using the same sum and addends. ($^-9 + {}^+4 = {}^-5$, $^-5 - {}^+4 = {}^-9$, $^-5 - {}^-9 = {}^+4$)

## Subtracting Integers

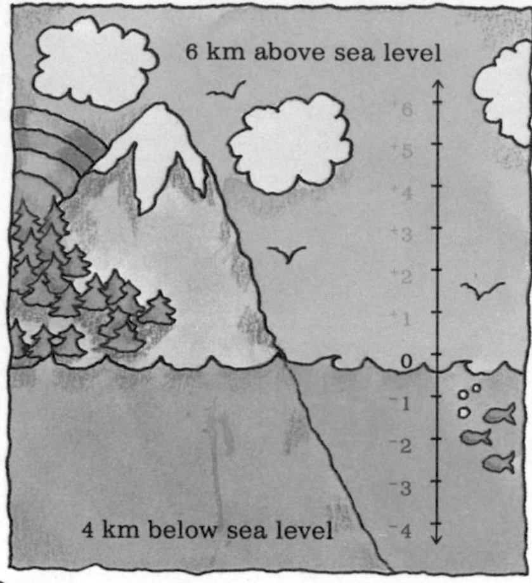


How much higher is an elevation of 6 km above sea level than an elevation of 4 km below sea level?

On the number line in the picture, we see that $^+6$ is 10 units above $^-4$, so 6 km above sea level is 10 km higher than 4 km below sea level.

Since the problem above asks us to compare two numbers ($^+6$ and $^-4$) we can also subtract to find the answer. As with whole numbers, we can think of subtracting integers as finding the missing addend.

sum addend addend

$^+6 - {}^-4 = ?$ ← What integer adds to $^-4$ to give $^+6$?

Since $^+10 + {}^-4 = {}^+6$, $^+6 - {}^-4 = {}^+10$

**Other Examples**

s a a a a s
$^-6 - {}^-4 = {}^-2$, because $^-2 + {}^-4 = {}^-6$

$^+4 - {}^-6 = {}^+10$, because $^+10 + {}^-6 = {}^+4$

s a a a a s
$^-6 - {}^+4 = {}^-10$, because $^-10 + {}^+4 = {}^-6$

$^-4 - {}^-6 = {}^+2$, because $^+2 + {}^-6 = {}^-4$

**Warm Up** Subtract. Check by adding.

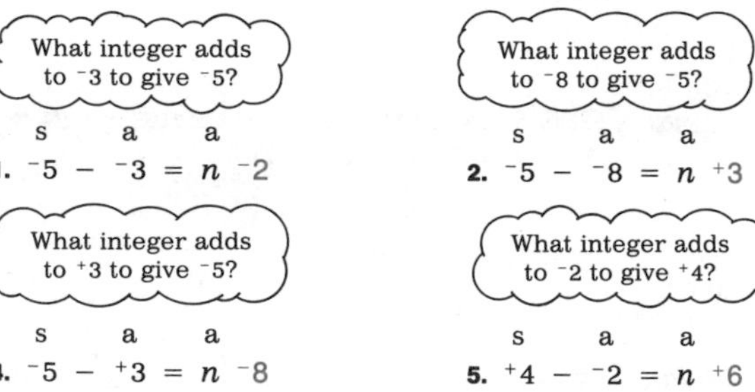

What integer adds to $^-3$ to give $^-5$?
1. $^-5 - {}^-3 = n$ $^-2$

What integer adds to $^-8$ to give $^-5$?
2. $^-5 - {}^-8 = n$ $^+3$

What integer adds to $^-3$ to give $^+1$?
3. $^+1 - {}^-3 = n$ $^+4$

What integer adds to $^+3$ to give $^-5$?
4. $^-5 - {}^+3 = n$ $^-8$

What integer adds to $^-2$ to give $^+4$?
5. $^+4 - {}^-2 = n$ $^+6$

What integer adds to $^+5$ to give $^-4$?
6. $^-4 - {}^+5 = n$ $^-9$

372

## Follow Up

### Reteaching

Review the relationship of addition and subtraction. Remind students about how they used addition facts to find a missing addend in subtraction. Then show an equation such as $^-3 + ? = {}^+2$. "What number added to $^-3$ would give $^+2$? Use a number line to illustrate.

$^-3 + ? = {}^+2$

$^-4$ $^-3$ $^-2$ $^-1$ 0 $^+1$ $^+2$ $^+3$ $^+4$

Encourage students to suggest other integer fact families to model on the number line.

### Enrichment

Use 2 different colored number cubes, both labeled 1 through 6. Designate one colored cube to represent positive integers and the other cube to represent negative integers. Students take turns tossing the number cubes and determining the resulting sum. Make the game more challenging by having students find the difference. (Students should agree before the round which color represents the sum and which the addend.)

| Assignment Guide | | | |
|---|---|---|---|
| | Minimum | Average | Extended |
| page 373 | 1–19, SK | 1–20, SK | 1–21, SK |

Find the differences.
Thinking of addends and a sum may help you.

(s a a)

1. $^{+}3 - ^{-}5 = n$  $^{+}8$
2. $^{-}2 - ^{+}6 = n$  $^{-}8$
3. $^{-}2 - ^{-}4 = n$  $^{+}2$
4. $^{+}5 - ^{-}3 = n$  $^{+}8$
5. $^{-}3 - ^{+}8 = n$  $^{-}11$
6. $^{+}8 - ^{-}6 = n$  $^{+}14$
7. $^{-}8 - ^{-}5 = n$  $^{-}3$
8. $^{+}2 - ^{+}9 = n$  $^{-}7$
9. $^{-}5 - ^{-}4 = n$  $^{-}1$
10. $^{+}5 - ^{-}1 = n$  $^{+}6$
11. $^{+}2 - ^{-}3 = n$  $^{+}5$
12. $^{+}6 - ^{-}1 = n$  $^{+}7$
13. $^{-}8 - ^{-}8 = n$  $0$
14. $6 - ^{-}3 = n$  $^{+}9$
15. $^{-}9 - ^{-}8 = n$  $^{-}1$
16. $^{-}5 - 0 = n$  $^{-}5$
17. $^{+}6 - ^{+}9 = n$  $^{-}3$
18. $^{+}2 - ^{-}4 = n$  $^{+}6$

19. How much higher is an elevation of 5 km above sea level ($^{+}5$) than an elevation of 3 km below sea level ($^{-}3$)? 8 km

20. Write and solve an integer equation for this problem. How much higher is an elevation of 2 km below sea level ($^{-}2$) than an elevation of 7 km below sea level ($^{-}7$)? $^{-}2 - ^{-}7 = n; n = ^{+}5$

★ 21. You may have discovered this rule:

> To subtract an integer, add its opposite.

Examples:

$^{-}1 - ^{+}6 = ^{-}1 + ^{-}6 = ^{-}7$

$^{+}6 - ^{-}4 = ^{+}6 + ^{+}4 = ^{+}10$

Use the rule to check the differences in exercises 1–10 above. Show your work.
See teaching notes.

## Skillkeeper

Find the volume. Use the formula $V = l \times w \times h$.

1. $l$ = 9 cm, $w$ = 3 cm, $h$ = 5 cm, $V$ = ■ 135 cm$^3$
2. $l$ = 7 m, $w$ = 4 m, $h$ = 2 m, $V$ = ■ 56 m$^3$
3. $l$ = 80 mm, $w$ = 70 mm, $h$ = 40 mm, $V$ = ■ 224,000 mm$^3$
4. $l$ = 35 m, $w$ = 2.4 m, $h$ = 3 m, $V$ = ■ 252 m$^3$
5. $l$ = 20 cm, $w$ = 8.6 cm, $h$ = 4.2 cm, $V$ = ■ 722.40 cm$^3$
6. $l$ = 18.4 mm, $w$ = 10.8 mm, $h$ = 6.5 mm, $V$ = ■ 1,291.680 mm$^3$

More Practice, page 428, Set C



## Using Page 373

**Exercises 1–18** If students have difficulty with any of these exercises, continue to stress the related addition equation and finding the missing addend. It may be more helpful for some students to think about first "making zero." For example, in exercise 1 they would think, "$^{+}5 + ^{-}5 = 0$." I need 3 more to make the sum $^{+}3$. So the missing addend is $^{+}8$. Use this technique only if it is helpful and seems to come easy for students.

**Exercises 19–20** Encourage students to solve these problems by comparing with subtraction and not by counting. In exercise 19 the subtraction equation would be $^{+}5 - ^{-}3 = n$. In exercise 20 the equation would be $^{-}2 - ^{-}7 = n$.

**Exercise 21** Students may have already discovered the rule given in this exercise, although the intent of the lesson is to emphasize subtraction as finding the missing addend. This exercise is designed for those students who have had little difficulty with the content of the lesson.

**Answers**

1. $^{+}3 + ^{+}5 = ^{+}8$
2. $^{-}2 + ^{-}6 = ^{-}8$
3. $^{-}2 + ^{+}4 = ^{+}2$
4. $^{+}5 + ^{+}3 = ^{+}8$
5. $^{-}3 + ^{-}8 = ^{-}11$
6. $^{+}8 + ^{+}6 = ^{+}14$
7. $^{-}8 + ^{+}5 = ^{-}3$
8. $^{+}2 + ^{-}9 = ^{-}7$
9. $^{-}5 + ^{+}4 = ^{-}1$
10. $^{+}5 + ^{+}1 = ^{+}6$

**Skillkeeper** These skills were originally taught in Chapter 14.

**More Practice,** page 428, Set C

**Reteaching Supplement,** page 89

Name ____________ To follow text page 373

### Subtracting Integers

To subtract integers, find the missing addend.

$^{+}2 - ^{-}3 = ?$ → Think: $? + ^{-}3 = ^{+}2$; $^{+}5 + ^{-}3 = ^{+}2$, so $^{+}2 - ^{-}3 = ^{+}5$
(sum) (addend) (missing addend)

$^{-}6 - ^{+}4 = ?$ → Think: $? + ^{+}4 = ^{-}6$; $^{-}10 + ^{+}4 = ^{-}6$, so $^{-}6 - ^{+}4 = ^{-}10$

Find the missing addends and differences.

1. $8 + ^{-}8 = 0$; $0 - ^{-}8 = 8$
2. $^{-}3 + ^{-}9 = ^{-}12$; $^{-}12 - ^{-}9 = ^{-}3$
3. $^{-}1 + ^{+}3 = ^{+}2$; $^{+}2 - ^{+}3 = ^{-}1$
4. $^{+}9 + ^{-}8 = ^{+}1$; $^{+}1 - ^{-}8 = ^{+}9$
5. $^{-}6 + ^{-}12 = ^{-}18$; $^{-}18 - ^{-}12 = ^{-}6$
6. $^{-}1 - ^{+}4 = 3$; $^{+}3 - ^{+}4 = ^{-}1$
7. $^{+}7 + ^{-}8 = ^{-}1$; $^{-}1 - ^{-}8 = ^{+}7$
8. $^{+}8 + ^{-}6 = ^{+}2$; $^{+}2 - ^{-}6 = ^{+}8$
9. $^{-}3 + ^{+}5 = ^{+}2$; $^{+}2 - 5 = ^{-}3$
10. $^{-}5 + ^{-}3 = ^{-}8$; $^{-}8 - ^{-}3 = ^{-}5$
11. $^{+}9 + ^{-}4 = ^{+}5$; $^{+}5 - ^{-}4 = ^{+}9$
12. $^{-}4 + ^{+}3 = ^{-}1$; $^{-}1 - ^{+}3 = ^{-}4$

Find the differences.

13. $^{-}8 - ^{-}8 = 0$
14. $^{+}3 - ^{-}5 = ^{+}8$
15. $^{-}4 - ^{+}2 = ^{-}6$
16. $^{-}10 - ^{-}5 = ^{-}5$
17. $^{+}4 - ^{-}3 = ^{+}7$
18. $^{-}2 - ^{+}6 = ^{-}8$
19. $^{-}2 - ^{+}5 = ^{-}7$
20. $^{+}9 - ^{+}18 = ^{-}9$
21. $^{-}7 - ^{-}3 = ^{-}4$

**Enrichment Supplement,** page 89

Name ____________ To follow text page 373

### Integer Magic Squares

Complete these integer magic squares.

1.

| | | |
|---|---|---|
| $^{-}3$ | 2 | 1 |
| 4 | 0 | $^{-}4$ |
| $^{-}1$ | $^{-}2$ | 3 |

Magic sum: 0

2.

| | | |
|---|---|---|
| $^{-}5$ | 0 | $^{-}1$ |
| 2 | $^{-}2$ | $^{-}6$ |
| $^{-}3$ | $^{-}4$ | 1 |

Magic sum: $^{-}6$

3.

| | | |
|---|---|---|
| $^{-}6$ | 4 | 2 |
| 8 | 0 | $^{-}8$ |
| $^{-}2$ | $^{-}4$ | 6 |

Magic sum: 0

4.

| | | |
|---|---|---|
| $^{-}4$ | $^{-}3$ | $^{-}8$ |
| $^{-}9$ | $^{-}5$ | $^{-}1$ |
| $^{-}2$ | $^{-}7$ | $^{-}6$ |

Magic sum: $^{-}15$

5. Start with any of the magic squares above. Subtract $^{-}3$ from each number in the square. Do you still have a magic square? yes

Squares will vary.

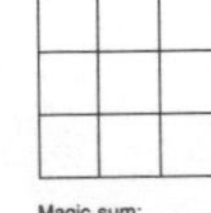

Magic sum: ____

**Practice Supplement,** page 140

Name ____________ To follow text page 373

### Subtracting Integers

Find the differences. Thinking of addends and a sum may help you.

(s a a)

1. $^{+}3 - ^{-}10 = ^{+}13$
2. $^{-}1 - ^{-}8 = ^{+}7$
3. $^{-}2 - ^{+}3 = ^{-}5$
4. $^{+}3 - ^{-}6 = ^{+}9$
5. $^{-}1 - ^{+}2 = ^{-}3$
6. $^{-}2 - ^{+}4 = ^{-}6$
7. $^{+}5 - ^{-}3 = ^{+}8$
8. $^{-}4 - ^{-}2 = ^{-}2$
9. $^{+}7 - ^{-}3 = ^{+}10$
10. $^{-}1 - ^{+}6 = ^{-}7$
11. $^{+}8 - ^{-}7 = ^{+}15$
12. $^{-}9 - ^{+}6 = ^{-}15$
13. $^{+}8 - ^{+}3 = ^{+}5$
14. $^{-}4 - ^{+}5 = ^{-}9$
15. $0 - ^{-}3 = ^{+}3$
16. $^{+}7 - ^{+}10 = ^{-}3$
17. $^{+}9 - ^{-}3 = ^{+}12$
18. $^{+}10 - ^{-}1 = ^{+}11$
19. $^{-}5 - ^{+}2 = ^{-}7$
20. $0 - ^{+}8 = ^{-}8$
21. $^{-}8 - ^{-}7 = ^{-}1$
22. $^{-}1 - ^{-}9 = ^{+}8$
23. $^{-}6 - ^{+}3 = ^{-}9$
24. $^{-}3 - ^{-}10 = ^{+}7$
25. $^{+}2 - ^{+}7 = ^{-}5$
26. $^{+}1 - ^{-}6 = ^{+}7$
27. $^{+}5 - ^{-}6 = ^{+}11$
28. $^{+}1 - ^{+}7 = ^{-}6$
29. $^{-}5 - ^{-}7 = ^{+}2$
30. $^{-}4 - ^{+}8 = ^{-}12$

# Applications

**Quick Review** Students give the standard number for these expanded numbers.

(5 × 100) + (4 × 10) + (6 × 1) 546 | 800 + 3 + 7,000 7,803
(3 × 100) + (7 × 10) + (8 × 1) 378 | 1 thousand + 5 tens 1,050

**Lesson Focus** To use data from a newspaper to solve word problems involving integers

**Suggested Materials** Newspapers

## Ideas for Getting Started

Divide the class into small groups and give a daily newspaper to each group. Ask them to find situations where integers are used or situations that could be interpreted using integers. Examples might include above and below par scores in golf, number of degrees above and below 0 in weather reports, or information from the stock market report page. Use this information to generate a discussion about the usefulness of integers.

## Using Page 374

**Lesson Development** Direct students' attention to each of the displays on the page. In the Sports News be sure students understand that ⁻8 means 8 strokes under par and ⁺4 means 4 strokes over par. Emphasize that just as with whole numbers, to compare scores we subtract. Thus, to find the difference between two scores, we would subtract either the over par or under par score.

In discussing the Travel Section, remind students that elevations can be represented using positive and negative integers, and that they also can be compared by subtraction.

Remind students that they can check the solution to any subtraction problem by adding.

## Problem Solving: Using Data from a Newspaper

Use the data from the "newspaper clippings" as needed to solve the problems.

1. How many more strokes did Lopez take than Nicols? (Hint: Find ⁻2 − ⁻8.) 6
2. How many more strokes did Gilper take than Lopez? 6
3. Suppose Beam had finished with 8 fewer strokes. What would Beam's score have been? ⁻2

**Sports News**

Nichols wins the holiday golf tournament by a big margin!

| | | |
|---|---|---|
| Nichols | ⁻8 | (8 strokes under par*) |
| Lopez | ⁻2 | |
| Gilper | ⁺4 | (4 strokes over par) |
| Beam | ⁺6 | |

*8 fewer strokes than the standard number of strokes for the course.

4. What was the difference between the nationwide high and low temperatures? 81°F
5. What was the difference between the nationwide low and the record local low? 36°F
6. The local low yesterday was 4°F higher than today's local low. What was yesterday's local low? 52°F

**Today's Weather**

| | | |
|---|---|---|
| Nationwide high | 75°F | (San Antonio, TX) |
| Nationwide low | ⁻6°F | (Bismark, N.D.) |
| Local high | 70°F | |
| Local low | 48°F | |
| Record local high | 82°F | |
| Record local low | 30°F | |

7. How much higher is the elevation of Mt. Whitney than the elevation of Death Valley? 14,776 ft

**Travel Section**

Many of the visitors to Death Valley, California, know that at 282 ft below sea level it is the lowest point in the United States. Not so many of them know that less than 125 mi away lies Mt. Whitney. This 14,494 ft high peak is the highest point in the United States south of Alas

374

## Follow Up

### Reteaching

To reinforce the ideas of negative and positive integers, generate a discussion to encourage students to offer their observations of real-world application of integers. Games in which points are gained and lost are useful in helping students understand this concept. Continue to use the terms positive and negative integers as you discuss these situations.

### Enrichment

Provide students with copies of several newspapers. Then challenge them to find examples of integers such as those suggested in this lesson. Tell students to copy the appropriate data, and then create several word problems using that data, to share with their classmates.

| Assignment Guide | | | |
|---|---|---|---|
| | Minimum | Average | Extended |
| pages 374–375 | 1–12 | 1–12 | 1–13 |

8. Antar stock had gained 5 points the day before. What was the total change for the two days? $^{+}8$

9. What is the difference between the greatest gain and the greatest loss for a local stock? $^{+}9$

10. Benco stock had lost 3 points the day before. What was its total change for the two days? $^{-}7$

**Stock Market Report**

| Local Stock | Points Gained or Lost* |
|---|---|
| Antar | $^{+}3$ |
| Benco | $^{-}4$ |
| Carbenz | $^{+}1$ |
| DRL | $^{-}2$ |
| Ensil | $^{+}5$ |

On Wall Street the jump in stock prices

*Dollars per share increase or decrease

11. How many seconds after liftoff did the rocket engines run? $^{+}315$ s

**National News**

The powerful engines on the space shuttle rocket were started 45 seconds before liftoff ($^{-}45$ s). They ran for a total of 360 seconds to

**Late Sports Report**

Football running back Tom Gallup carried the ball the last three plays to give the Eagles a 21–14 win over the Bearcats. He gained 5 yards, lost 7 yards, and gained 9 yards to cross the goal line on the final play. He

12. How many total yards did Tom Gallup gain on the last 3 plays? 7 yd

13. **Try This** On the back of a clipping cut from a newspaper, Steve saw this picture of the top 3 layers of a monument that was to be built in the city park. How many blocks do you think are needed in all if there are to be 10 layers? 220

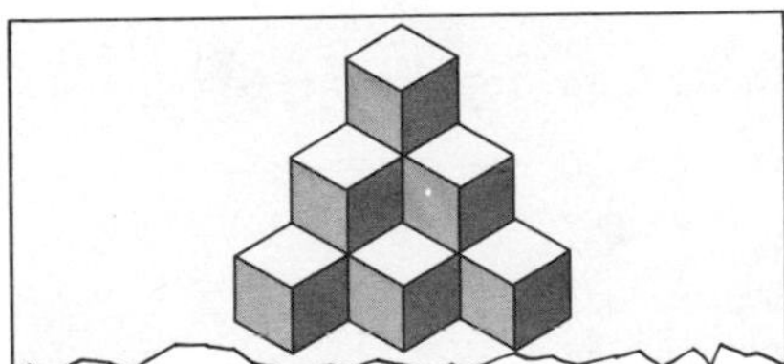



## Using Page 375

**Exercises 8–12** Before assigning these exercises, go over each of the displays to be sure students understand how integers are used to represent the ideas in each situation. Note that some of the exercises, for example exercises 8 and 10, can be solved simply by counting. Encourage students, however, to write equations to show how addition can be used to solve the problems. Note also that exercise 11 can be solved by finding 360 − 45, or it can be solved by finding 360 + $^{-}45$.

**Try This** A possible strategy, Find a Pattern, was taught on page 246.

**Discussion** "What question are we asked about the blocks in the monument?" (How many blocks are needed in 10 layers?) "How many blocks in the third layer?" (6) If necessary, help students draw a picture to show this. "How many blocks would there be in the fourth layer?" (10) "In planning a solution, what strategy might be helpful?" (Find a Pattern)

**Solution** For 10 layers there would be a total of 220 blocks required. The table below shows the pattern observed in adding 1 layer each time.

| Layer | Number of blocks | |
|---|---|---|
| 1 | 1 | |
| 2 | 3 | +2 |
| 3 | 6 | +3 |
| 4 | 10 | +4 |
| 5 | 15 | +5 |
| 6 | 21 | +6 |
| 7 | 28 | +7 |
| 8 | 36 | +8 |
| 9 | 45 | +9 |
| 10 | 55 | +10 |
| Total | 220 | |

## Ideas That Work

### Chalk It Up

Place the puzzles below on the chalkboard, and give students the following directions:

In Puzzle A, the sum of the integers along the path is equal to the sum at the end. Find such a path for Puzzle B. You can move only horizontally or vertically.

Start

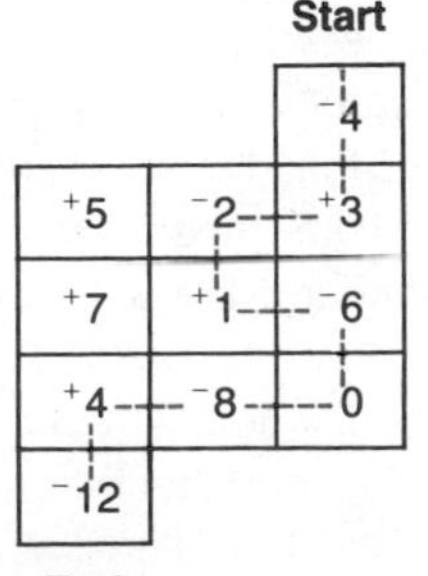

End

Start

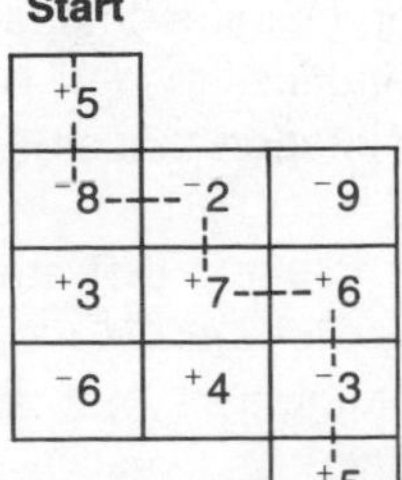

End

**Practice Supplement,** page 141

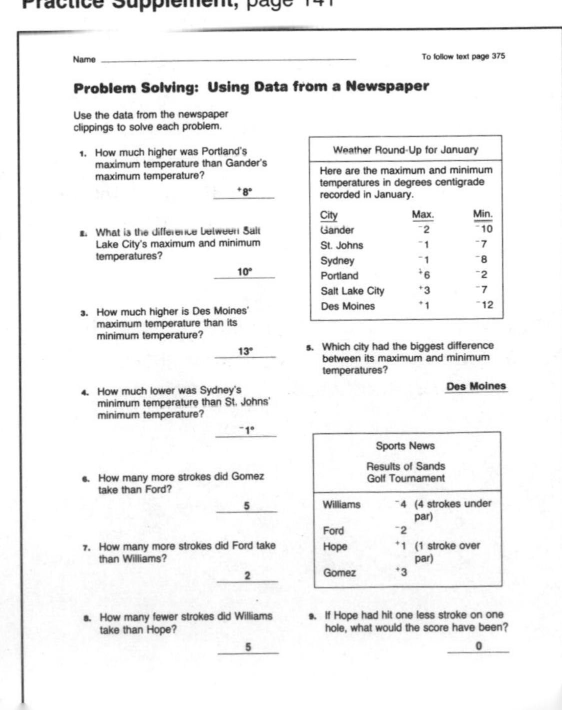

Name ________________ To follow text page 375

**Problem Solving: Using Data from a Newspaper**

Use the data from the newspaper clippings to solve each problem.

1. How much higher was Portland's maximum temperature than Gander's maximum temperature? $^{+}8°$

2. What is the difference between Salt Lake City's maximum and minimum temperatures? 10°

3. How much higher is Des Moines' maximum temperature than its minimum temperature? 13°

4. How much lower was Sydney's minimum temperature than St. Johns' minimum temperature? $^{-}1°$

Weather Round-Up for January

Here are the maximum and minimum temperatures in degrees centigrade recorded in January.

| City | Max. | Min. |
|---|---|---|
| Gander | $^{-}2$ | $^{-}10$ |
| St. Johns | $^{-}1$ | $^{-}7$ |
| Sydney | $^{-}1$ | $^{-}8$ |
| Portland | $^{+}6$ | $^{-}2$ |
| Salt Lake City | $^{+}3$ | $^{-}7$ |
| Des Moines | $^{+}1$ | $^{-}12$ |

5. Which city had the biggest difference between its maximum and minimum temperatures? **Des Moines**

6. How many more strokes did Gomez take than Ford? 5

7. How many more strokes did Ford take than Williams? 2

8. How many fewer strokes did Williams take than Hope? 5

Sports News

Results of Sands Golf Tournament

| | | |
|---|---|---|
| Williams | $^{-}4$ | (4 strokes under par) |
| Ford | $^{-}2$ | |
| Hope | $^{+}1$ | (1 stroke over par) |
| Gomez | $^{+}3$ | |

9. If Hope had hit one less stroke on one hole, what would the score have been? 0

# Integers

**Quick Review** Students write the symbol (>, <, =) that makes each expression true.

6 + 8 (=) 9 + 5 3 × 9 (<) 4 × 7 23 + 5 (<) 24 + 6 35 − 5 (>) 5 × 5
3 + 4 (<) 7 + 1 9 + 4 (>) 12 + 0 18 ÷ 6 (=) 5 − 2

**Lesson Focus** To compare two integers and order a list of integers; to solve word problems involving all operations

## Ideas for Getting Started

Draw a number line on the chalkboard. Point to one integer with your left hand and the other integer with your right hand and ask: "Which of these integers is greater? Why?" Elicit from students that whole numbers are positioned on the number line in the order in which they are counted. From this, help them generalize that the greater integer is the integer that is farther to the right on a number line.

## Using Page 376

**Lesson Development** Discuss the boys' game scores in the problem at the top of the page. Then have students read the information in the table, interpreting $^{+}5$ as a score "to the good" and $^{-}3$ as a score "in the hole." "What was Bart's score?" ($^{+}5$) "What was Jeral's score?" ($^{-}6$) "How can we decide which of these scores is greater?" (Think about the locations of the integers on the number line.) Direct students' attention to the number line shown in the text or to a similar number line drawn on the chalkboard. "Which integer, $^{+}5$ or $^{-}6$ is farther to the right on the number line?" ($^{+}5$) "Which integer is greater?" ($^{+}5$ is greater than $^{-}6$)

Use these ideas of comparing integers to order the integers in the table at the top of the page. "Is there an integer greater than $^{+}5$ in the table?" (no) "What integer is the next smaller number below $^{+}5$?" ($^{+}2$, since a positive integer is greater than either 0 or a negative integer.) Continue to compare the integers two at a time and help students list them from greatest to least.

**Other Examples** Discuss each of these examples by locating them on the number line. In each case verify the decision by having students give an integer that can add to the smaller integer to give the larger.

**Exercises 1–16** Encourage students to use or think about a number line if they are having difficulty comparing integers. Help students make the generalization that each positive integer is greater than 0 and is greater than any negative integer. Help them also see that the farther a negative integer is to the left of 0, the smaller the negative integer is.

**Exercises 17–22** Again allow students to use a number line if they have difficulty ordering the integers. After the integers are positioned on a number line, the ordering process is simple.

## Comparing and Ordering Integers

Here are scores for a game some students played. Negative integers show scores "in the hole," and positive integers show scores "to the good." Who had a higher score, Bart or Jeral? Can you list the scores in order from greatest to least?

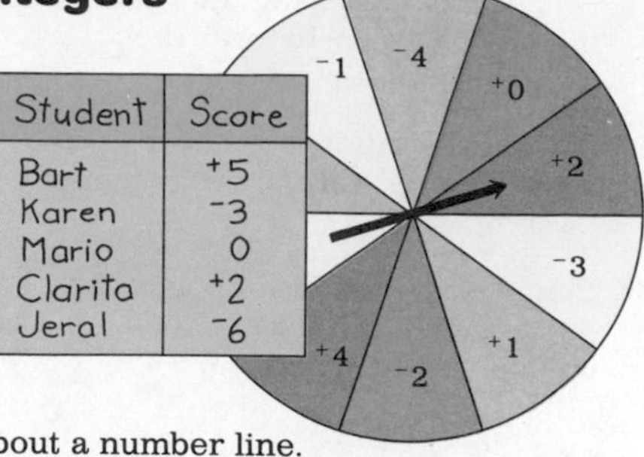


### Comparing Integers

We can compare integers by thinking about a number line. The integer that is farther to the right is the greater of two integers.

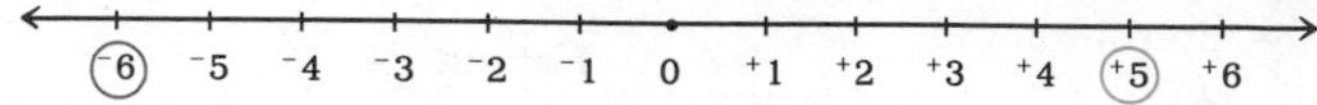


$^{+}5 > ^{-}6$ Bart's score was greater than Jeral's.

### Ordering Integers

We order a list of integers by comparing them two at a time.

| | | |
|---|---|---|
| Bart | $^{+}5$ | Scores ordered from greatest to least |
| Clarita | $^{+}2$ | |
| Mario | 0 | |
| Karen | $^{-}3$ | |
| Jeral | $^{-}6$ | |

**Other Examples**

$^{-}1 > ^{-}2$ $^{-}3 < ^{+}1$ $^{+}2 < ^{+}5$ $0 > ^{-}5$ $^{-}3 > ^{-}20$

Write > or < for each ●.

1. $^{+}4$ ● $^{-}3$ >
2. $^{+}7$ ● $^{+}9$ <
3. $^{-}1$ ● $^{+}2$ <
4. $^{+}4$ ● 0 >
5. $^{-}5$ ● $^{-}2$ <
6. $^{+}3$ ● $^{-}3$ >
7. $^{+}1$ ● $^{-}4$ >
8. $^{-}12$ ● $^{-}35$ >
9. 0 ● $^{-}6$ >
10. $^{+}2$ ● $^{-}4$ >
11. $^{-}8$ ● $^{+}3$ <
12. $^{-}5$ ● $^{+}5$ <
13. $^{-}6$ ● $^{-}5$ <
14. $^{-}1$ ● $^{-}9$ >
15. $^{+}3$ ● $^{-}5$ >
16. $^{+}6$ ● $^{-}15$ >

Order from greatest to least.

17. $^{-}4, ^{+}3, 0, ^{-}2, ^{-}6, ^{+}7$
$^{+}7, ^{+}3, 0, ^{-}2, ^{-}4, ^{-}6$
18. $^{-}2, ^{+}7, ^{-}1, ^{+}1, ^{-}4, ^{+}3$
$^{+}7, ^{+}3, ^{+}1, ^{-}1, ^{-}2, ^{-}4$
19. $^{+}16, ^{-}4, ^{+}3, ^{-}14, ^{-}17$
$^{+}16, ^{+}3, ^{-}4, ^{-}14, ^{-}17$

Order from least to greatest.

20. $^{-}15, ^{+}6, ^{+}10, 0, ^{-}8, ^{-}3$
$^{-}15, ^{-}8, ^{-}3, 0, ^{+}6, ^{+}10$
21. $^{+}8, 0, ^{-}1, ^{+}1, ^{-}4, ^{+}14$
$^{-}4, ^{-}1, 0, ^{+}1, ^{+}8, ^{+}14$
22. $^{-}89, ^{+}98, ^{-}99, ^{+}100, ^{-}86$
$^{-}99, ^{-}89, ^{-}86, ^{+}98, ^{+}100$

 More Practice, page 428, Set D

## Follow Up

### Reteaching

Refer to the idea of playing golf to discuss ordering integers. Remind students that a negative score—"under par"—means fewer strokes than the standard, and that a positive score means more strokes than the standard. Show this idea on a number line, focusing on the idea that as we move to the left, integers become smaller in value, and that they increase in value as we move to the right.

### Enrichment

Have students make a number line as shown, with letters corresponding to each point. Then have them give the letters for the points described.

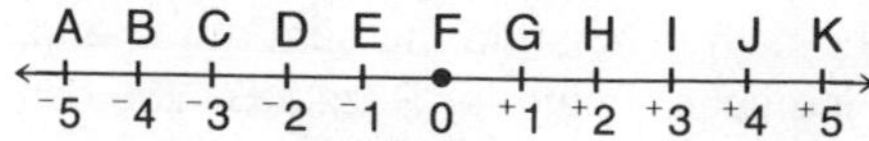


1. Points for integers that are greater than $^{-}5$ and less than 0. B, C, D, E
2. Points for integers that are less than or equal to $^{-}3$. A, B, C
3. Points for integers that are less than $^{-}2$ and greater than $^{-}5$. B, C
4. Points for integers that are greater than $^{-}2$ and less than $^{+}3$. E, F, G, H

| Assignment Guide | | | |
|---|---|---|---|
| | Minimum | Average | Extended |
| page 376 | 1–16, 17, 20 | 1–12, 17–22 | 1–22 |
| page 377 | 1–7 | 1–8 | 1–9 |

## Problem Solving: Practice

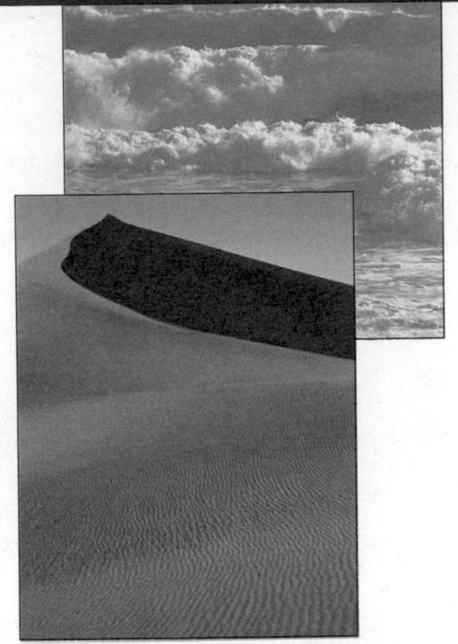

Solve.

1. Some scientists say that the earth is about 4.5 billion years old. The first life on earth may have appeared 3.54 billion years ago. For how long was the earth without life? 0.96 billion years
2. The oldest rock found so far on earth is 0.8 times as old as the earth. Use data from problem 1 to find the age of this rock. 3.6 billion years
3. The ratio of the average diameter of the moon to the average diameter of the earth is 3 to 11. The average diameter of the moon is about 3,450 km. About what is the average diameter of the earth? about 12,650 km
4. Water covers 71% of the earth's surface. What percent of the earth's surface does land cover? 29%
5. Mt. Everest, the earth's highest mountain, reaches a height of 8,543 m above sea level ($^{+}8{,}543$ m). The Mariana Trench in the Pacific Ocean, the deepest known part of any ocean, is 10,918 m below sea level ($^{-}10{,}918$ m). What is the difference of these two elevations? 19,461 m
6. The highest temperature recorded on earth (in Africa) was $^{+}58$°C. The lowest temperature recorded (in Antarctica) was $^{-}88$°C. What is the difference between these temperatures? 146°C
7. The lowest sea temperature is $^{-}2$°C (in the White Sea). The highest sea temperature is $^{+}38$°C warmer than this (in the Persian Gulf). What is the highest sea temperature? $^{+}36$°C
8. **DATA BANK** How many hours difference in time is there between Beijing (Peking), China, and Los Angeles, California? List the cities given from most hours earlier than GMT to most hours later than GMT. (See Data Bank, page 408.) 16 hours; see teaching notes.
9. **Try This** The Pacific Ocean (with nearby seas) makes up $\frac{1}{2}$ of the total ocean area. The Indian Ocean (with nearby seas) makes up $\frac{2}{10}$ of the total ocean area. The rest is the Atlantic Ocean (with nearby seas), which covers 72 million km$^2$. What is the total ocean area? 240 million km$^2$



## Using Page 377

**Lesson Development** Briefly review the 5-Point Checklist. If needed, review procedures for adding and multiplying decimals (exercises 1 and 2), solving proportions (exercise 3), finding the percent of a number (exercise 4).

**Exercises 1–7** In exercise 5 suggest that students subtract the negative integer from the positive integer ($^{+}8{,}543 - {}^{-}10{,}918$) to insure a positive integer for the difference. Encourage students to write equations for exercise 3.

**Data Bank** If necessary, explain that GMT (Greenwich Mean Time) is the meridian of longitude that passes through Greenwich, England, and is the starting point for the various world time zones.

**Answer: Los Angeles, Chicago, Ottawa, Caracas, Buenos Aires, London, Brussels, Cairo, Baghdad, Djakarta, Beijing, Tokyo**

**Try This** A possible strategy, Choose the Operations, was taught on page 16.

**Discussion** "What do we want to find out about the oceans?" (the total area for all oceans) "What part of the total ocean area is the Pacific Ocean?" $\left(\frac{1}{2}\right)$ "What part of the total is the Indian Ocean with nearby seas?" $\left(\frac{2}{10}\right)$ "What is the area of the remaining part?" (72 million km$^2$) "In planning a solution, is there other useful information we could find?" (the fraction of ocean area that is the Atlantic).

**Solution** The total ocean area is 240 million km$^2$. The Pacific Ocean and Indian Ocean areas together make up $\frac{7}{10}$ of the total ocean area; thus, the Atlantic Ocean is $\frac{3}{10}$ of the total area. Since $\frac{3}{10}$ of the area is 72 million km$^2$, then $\frac{1}{10}$ of the ocean area would be 72 million ÷ 3, or 24 million km$^2$.

**More Practice,** page 428, Set D

**Reteaching Supplement,** page 90

Name ______ To follow text page 376

**Comparing and Ordering Integers**

10 9 8 7 6 5 4 3 2 1 0 1 2 3 4 5 6 7 8 9 10

Write > or < for each ○.

Think about the number line to compare the two integers.

1. 0 (>) 1 — 0 is to the right of $^{-}1$ on the number line.
2. 3 (<) 1 — $^{-}3$ is to the left of 1 on the number line.
3. 5 (>) 9 — 5 is to the right of $^{-}9$ on the number line.
4. 9 (>) 4
5. 16 (<) 19
6. 11 (<) 2
7. 16 (>) 0
8. 16 (<) 12
9. 7 (>) 7
10. 46 (>) 37
11. 14 (>) 29
12. 0 (>) 19
13. 1 (>) 14
14. 26 (>) 31
15. 9 (>) 12

Write the integers of each group in order from least to greatest.

16. 7, 6, 2, 14, 8, 2 — Order the numbers less than 0. Order the numbers greater than 0. $^{-}14, {}^{-}7, {}^{-}2, {}^{+}2, {}^{+}6, {}^{+}8$
17. 24, 2, 16, 21, 9, 7, 0 — $^{-}21, {}^{-}16, {}^{-}7, 0, {}^{+}2, {}^{+}9, {}^{+}24$
18. 62, 4, 9, 120, 84, 132 — $^{-}132, {}^{-}84, {}^{-}62, {}^{-}4, {}^{+}9, {}^{+}120$
19. 0, $^{-}76$, 35, 30, 40, 39 — $^{-}40, {}^{-}39, 0, {}^{+}30, {}^{+}35, {}^{+}76$

**Enrichment Supplement,** page 90

Name ______ To follow text page 376

**More or Less**

Write in order from smallest to largest all of the integers **between** the two given ones.

1. $^{-}3$ and $^{+}3$ — $^{-}2, {}^{-}1, 0, {}^{+}1, {}^{+}2$
2. $^{-}2$ and $^{+}1$ — $^{-}1, 0$
3. 0 and $^{+}5$ — $^{+}1, {}^{+}2, {}^{+}3, {}^{+}4$
4. $^{-}7$ and $^{+}2$ — $^{-}6, {}^{-}5, {}^{-}4, {}^{-}3, {}^{-}2, {}^{-}1, 0, {}^{+}1$
5. $^{-}8$ and $^{-}6$ — $^{-}7$
6. $^{-}7$ and 0 — $^{-}6, {}^{-}5, {}^{-}4, {}^{-}3, {}^{-}2, {}^{-}1$
7. $^{-}12$ and $^{-}4$ — $^{-}11, {}^{-}10, {}^{-}9, {}^{-}8, {}^{-}7, {}^{-}6, {}^{-}5$
8. $^{-}18$ and $^{-}20$ — $^{-}19$
9. 0 and $^{-}9$ — $^{-}8, {}^{-}7, {}^{-}6, {}^{-}5, {}^{-}4, {}^{-}3, {}^{-}2, {}^{-}1$

Write the next 5 integers **less than** the given integer.

10. $^{+}8$ — $^{+}7, {}^{+}6, {}^{+}5, {}^{+}4, {}^{+}3$
11. $^{+}2$ — $^{+}1, 0, {}^{-}1, {}^{-}2, {}^{-}3$
12. 0 — $^{-}1, {}^{-}2, {}^{-}3, {}^{-}4, {}^{-}5$
13. $^{-}3$ — $^{-}4, {}^{-}5, {}^{-}6, {}^{-}7, {}^{-}8$
14. 5 — $^{-}6, {}^{-}7, {}^{-}8, {}^{-}9, {}^{-}10$
15. $^{-}99$ — $^{-}100, {}^{-}101, {}^{-}102, {}^{-}103, {}^{-}104$

Write "greater than" or "less than" in each blank to complete the sentence.

16. A positive integer is **greater than** a negative integer.
17. An integer is **greater than** an integer that is to the left of it on the number line.
18. If you add two negative integers, the sum will be **less than** zero.
19. If you subtract a negative integer from a positive integer the difference will be **greater than** zero.

**Practice Supplement,** page 142

Name ______ To follow text page 376

**Comparing and Ordering Integers**

Write > or < for each ○.

1. $^{-}5$ (<) $^{+}3$
2. $^{+}1$ (>) $^{-}2$
3. $^{+}4$ (>) $^{-}5$
4. $^{-}2$ (>) $^{-}4$
5. $^{-}6$ (<) $^{+}3$
6. $^{-}3$ (<) $^{+}1$
7. $^{-}4$ (<) $^{+}4$
8. $^{+}5$ (>) $^{-}1$
9. $^{+}1$ (>) $^{-}8$
10. 0 (>) $^{-}3$
11. $^{-}8$ (<) $^{+}5$
12. $^{+}7$ (>) 0
13. $^{-}9$ (>) $^{-}12$
14. $^{-}7$ (<) $^{+}5$
15. $^{-}4$ (>) $^{-}10$

Order from greatest to least.

16. $^{+}3, {}^{-}7, {}^{+}4, {}^{-}1, {}^{-}4$ — $^{+}4, {}^{+}3, {}^{-}1, {}^{-}4, {}^{-}7$
17. $0, {}^{+}9, {}^{-}5, {}^{+}3, {}^{-}11$ — $^{+}9, {}^{+}3, 0, {}^{-}5, {}^{-}11$
18. $^{-}2, {}^{+}2, {}^{-}6, {}^{+}4, {}^{+}6$ — $^{+}6, {}^{+}4, {}^{+}2, {}^{-}2, {}^{-}6$
19. $^{+}5, {}^{-}9, {}^{-}3, {}^{+}7, 0$ — $^{+}7, {}^{+}5, 0, {}^{-}3, {}^{-}9$
20. $^{-}10, {}^{+}15, {}^{-}13, {}^{-}12, {}^{+}9$ — $^{+}15, {}^{+}9, {}^{-}10, {}^{-}12, {}^{-}13$
21. $^{+}22, {}^{-}19, {}^{+}18, {}^{-}16, {}^{+}15$ — $^{+}22, {}^{+}18, {}^{+}15, {}^{-}16, {}^{-}19$

Order from least to greatest.

22. $^{+}7, {}^{-}6, {}^{+}4, {}^{-}7, {}^{+}2$ — $^{-}7, {}^{-}6, {}^{+}2, {}^{+}4, {}^{+}7$
23. $^{+}11, {}^{-}12, {}^{+}17, {}^{-}20, {}^{+}13$ — $^{-}20, {}^{-}12, {}^{+}11, {}^{+}13, {}^{+}17$
24. $^{-}1, 0, {}^{-}4, {}^{+}8, {}^{-}7$ — $^{-}7, {}^{-}4, {}^{-}1, 0, {}^{+}8$
25. $^{-}15, {}^{-}17, 0, {}^{+}19, {}^{-}12$ — $^{-}17, {}^{-}15, {}^{-}12, 0, {}^{+}19$
26. $^{+}46, {}^{-}33, {}^{+}21, {}^{-}57, {}^{-}66$ — $^{-}66, {}^{-}57, {}^{-}33, {}^{+}21, {}^{+}46$
27. $^{+}67, {}^{-}76, {}^{+}76, {}^{-}67, {}^{+}79$ — $^{-}76, {}^{-}67, {}^{+}67, {}^{+}76, {}^{+}79$

# Integers

**Quick Review** Put these numbers on the chalkboard. Students multiply aloud two of the numbers and add the third number to the product.

5, 6, 7 8, 3, 10 9, 0, 8 4, 3, 9 7, 6, 2 9, 7, 5
3, 4, 5 6, 4, 6 8, 9, 1 4, 9, 6 3, 7, 8

**Lesson Focus** To use ordered pairs of integers to graph a given point

**Suggested Materials** 10 by 10 grids (TRB p. 274)

## Ideas for Getting Started

On the chalkboard draw a 10 by 10 grid or provide each student with a copy of the grid. Use the grid to review graphing of whole number coordinates. "I am thinking of a point that has the coordinates (3,4). How do I graph this point?" (Over 3 and up 4 on the grid.) Then mark a point on the grid. "How can I describe the location of this point?" "What are the coordinates of the point?"

## Using Page 378

**Lesson Development** Have students read the paragraph that tells about the geographic center of the United States. Point out that we can use that center as the origin or the intersection of the two axes and then use integer coordinates to show the approximate locations of other cities. Refer to the map of the United States with the coordinate axes superimposed. Work through the four examples to be sure students understand how to use coordinates to find the city and how to name the coordinates of a given location.

Then use the grid below and ask questions such as: "Both numbers in the coordinates for a point are negative. In what quadrant is the point?" (Quadrant III) "Both numbers in the coordinates for a point are positive. In what quadrant is this point?" (Quadrant I) "Describe the coordinates of a point in Quadrant II." (The first number is negative, the second number positive.) "In Quadrant IV?" (The first number is positive, the second number is negative.)

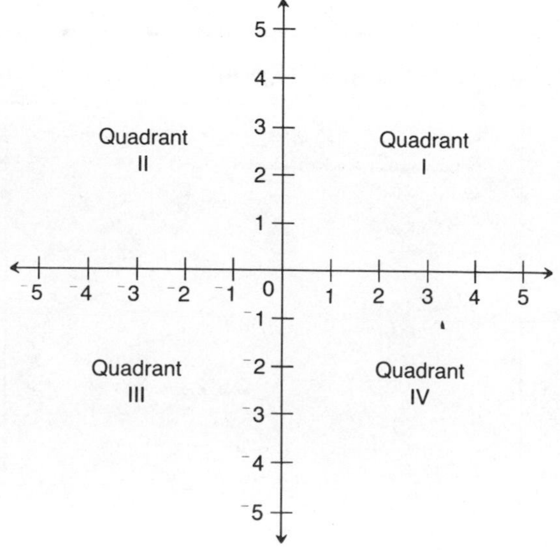


## Graphing with Integers

A spot near Lebanon, Kansas, is the geographic center of the United States (not including Alaska and Hawaii). We can use this center as the **origin** (0,0) and **ordered pairs** of integers (coordinates) to show the approximate locations of some other cities.

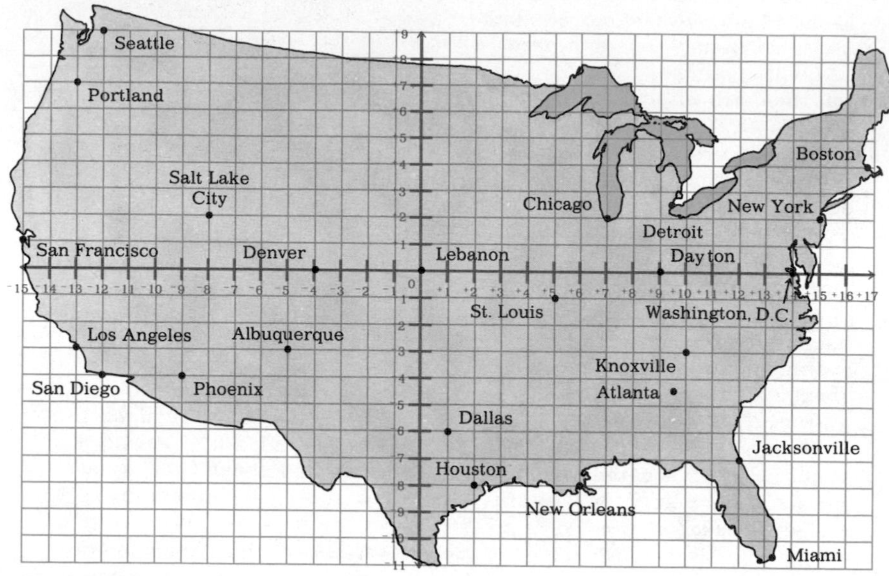


**Examples**

Chicago: right 7, up 2 **$(^{+}7,^{+}2)$**
Denver: left 4, up 0 **$(^{-}4,0)$**
Knoxville: right 10, down 3 **$(^{+}10,^{-}3)$**
Phoenix: left 9, down 4 **$(^{-}9,^{-}4)$**

Use ordered pairs of integers to give the locations of these cities.

**1.** New York $(^{+}15,^{+}2)$
**2.** Seattle $(^{-}12,^{+}9)$
**3.** Dayton $(^{+}9,0)$
**4.** Jacksonville $(^{+}12,^{-}7)$
**5.** Albuquerque $(^{-}5,^{-}3)$
**6.** New Orleans $(^{+}6,^{-}$

What cities are at these locations?

**7.** $(^{+}14,0)$ Washington, D.C.
**8.** $(^{-}13,^{+}7)$ Portland
**9.** $(^{-}12,^{-}4)$ San Diego
**10.** $(^{-}8,^{+}2)$ Salt Lake City
**11.** $(^{+}1,^{-}6)$ Dallas
**12.** $(^{-}15,^{+}1)$ San Francisco
**13.** $(^{+}2,^{-}8)$ Houston
**14.** $(^{+}5,^{-}1)$ St. Louis

378

## Follow Up

### Reteaching

Show a coordinate grid (TRB p. 275) on the chalkboard or an overhead projector. Discuss how we can use these number lines to identify points (ordered pairs) in any location on the grid. Begin to graph points and have students identify the coordinates. Name point A and show how it was graphed—for example, over 2, up 1—with ordered pair (2,1). Next graph point B, over 2, down 2 (2,2). Continue to locate points in each quadrant, pointing out to students when the ordered pairs are positive integers, negative integers, or both.

### Enrichment

Provide students with a 10 by 10 coordinate grid (TRB p. 275). Using the ordered pair (0,0) as the center or origin, students plot and record coordinate points for a symmetrical figure. Students then exchange grids, find and connect the ordered pairs with line segments to discover the figure plotted by their classmates.

| Assignment Guide | | | |
|---|---|---|---|
| | Minimum | Average | Extended |
| page 379 | | 1–30 | 1–33, TM |

Use the graphs below for exercises 1–30.

A

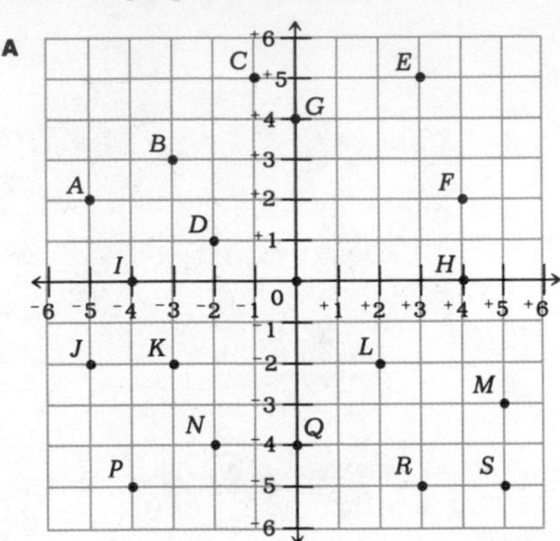

B

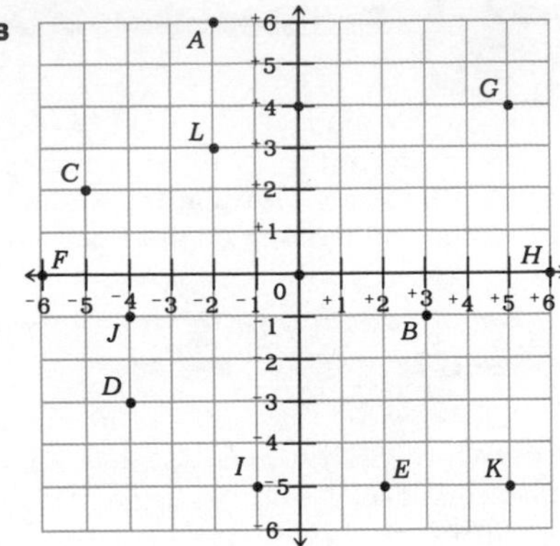

Give the ordered pair for each point on graph A.

**1.** $A\ (^-5,^+2)$ **2.** $D\ (^-2,^+1)$ **3.** $G\ (0,^+4)$ **4.** $F\ (^+4,^+2)$ **5.** $I\ (^-4,0)$ **6.** $K\ (^-3,^-2)$

**7.** $H\ (^+4,0)$ **8.** $B\ (^-3,^+3)$ **9.** $L\ (^+2,^-2)$ **10.** $R\ (^+3,^-5)$ **11.** $N\ (^-2,^-4)$ **12.** $P\ (^-4,^-5)$

**13.** $M\ (^+5,^-3)$ **14.** $S\ (^+5,^-5)$ **15.** $E\ (^+3,^+5)$ **16.** $C\ (^-1,^+5)$ **17.** $Q\ (0,^-4)$ **18.** $J\ (^-5,^-2)$

Give the point on graph B for each ordered pair.

**19.** $(^+5,^+4)$ G **20.** $(^-2,^+6)$ A **21.** $(^-4,^-3)$ D **22.** $(^-6,0)$ F

**23.** $(^+3,^-1)$ B **24.** $(^-5,^+2)$ C **25.** $(^+2,^-5)$ E **26.** $(^+6,0)$ H

**27.** $(^-1,^-5)$ I **28.** $(^-2,^+3)$ L

**29.** $(^+5,^-5)$ K **30.** $(^-4,^-1)$ J

Graph each figure on graph paper by graphing and connecting points.
See teaching notes.

**31.** A kite: $(^+4,^-3)$ $(^-3,0)$ $(^-4,^+5)$ $(^+1,^+4)$

**32.** A triangle: $(^+2,^-2)$ $(^-4,^+4)$ $(2,^+4)$

**33.** Just for fun: $(^-8,^-1)$ $(^-3,^+4)$ $(^-2,^+6)$ $(^-1,^+6)$ $(^-1,^+4)$ $(^+7,^-1)$ $(^+7,^-2)$ $(^+6,^-3)$ $(^+4,^-2)$ $(^+6,^-4)$ $(^+5,^-4)$ $(^-1,^-2)$ $(^-2,^-8)$ $(^-8,^-1)$. As extras, include $(^-1,^+2)$ and $(^+6,^-1)$.

**Think Math**

**Logical Reasoning**

Write >, <, or = for each ●.

1. $^+7 + ^-3$ ● $^+3 + ^-7$ >
2. $^-4 + ^+2$ ● $^+4 - ^-2$ <
3. $^-6 + ^-3$ ● $^-3 - ^+6$ =
4. $^+5 - ^-2$ ● $^-2 + ^+9$ =
5. $^+8 - ^+1$ ● $^+1 + ^-8$ >
6. $^-8 + ^-1$ ● $^+1 - ^+10$ =

379

## Using Page 379

**Exercises 1–30** Be sure students understand that to determine the point or the coordinates for a point, they must start at the origin and move horizontally as indicated by the first integer and vertically as indicated by the second integer. Note that exercises 3, 5, 7, and 17 are points on the axes in which one of the integers in the ordered pair is 0.

**Exercises 31–33** Be sure students start with the first point given and connect the points in order. If necessary, remind students to connect the last point with the first point in order to complete the picture.

**Answers:**

31. 32.

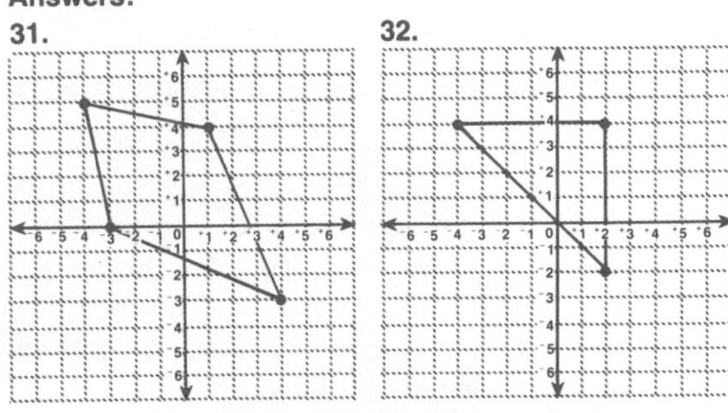

33.

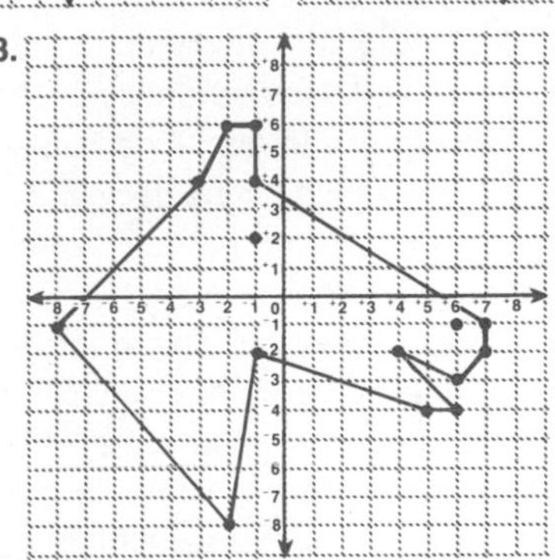

**Think Math** This activity gives students an opportunity to apply their skills in adding, subtracting, and comparing integers.

**Reteaching Supplement,** page 91

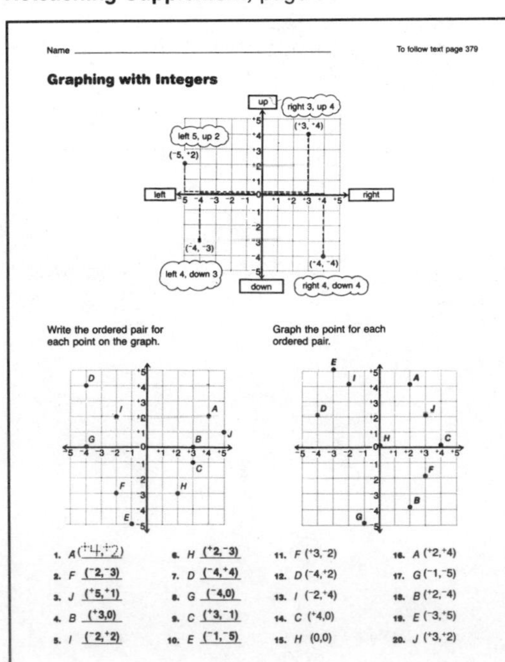

Name ______ To follow text page 379

**Graphing with Integers**



Write the ordered pair for each point on the graph.

Graph the point for each ordered pair.

1. A $(^+4,^+2)$ 6. H $(^+2,^-3)$ 11. F $(^+3,^-2)$ 16. A $(^+2,^+4)$
2. F $(^-2,^-3)$ 7. D $(^-4,^+4)$ 12. D $(^-4,^+2)$ 17. G $(^-1,^-5)$
3. J $(^+5,^+1)$ 8. G $(^-4,0)$ 13. I $(^-2,^+4)$ 18. B $(^+2,^-4)$
4. B $(^+3,0)$ 9. C $(^+3,^-1)$ 14. C $(^+4,0)$ 19. E $(^-3,^+5)$
5. I $(^-2,^+2)$ 10. E $(^-1,^-5)$ 15. H (0,0) 20. J $(^+3,^+2)$

**Enrichment Supplement,** page 91

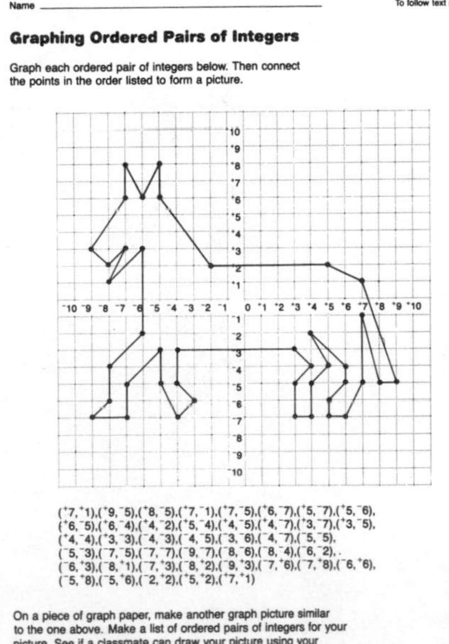

Name ______ To follow text page 379

**Graphing Ordered Pairs of Integers**

Graph each ordered pair of integers below. Then connect the points in the order listed to form a picture.

$(^+7,^+1),(^+9,^-5),(^+8,^-5),(^+7,^-1),(^+7,^-5),(^+6,^-7),(^+5,^-7),(^+5,^-6),(^+6,^-5),(^+6,^-4),(^+4,^-2),(^+5,^-4),(^+4,^-5),(^+4,^-7),(^+3,^-7),(^+3,^-5),(^+4,^-4),(^+3,^-3),(^-4,^-3),(^-4,^-5),(^-3,^-6),(^-4,^-7),(^-5,^-5),(^-5,^-3),(^-7,^-5),(^-7,^-7),(^-9,^-7),(^-8,^-6),(^-8,^-4),(^-6,^-2),(^-6,^+3),(^-8,^+1),(^-7,^+3),(^-8,^+2),(^-9,^+3),(^-7,^+6),(^-7,^+8),(^-6,^+6),(^-5,^+8),(^-5,^+6),(^-2,^+2),(^+5,^+2),(^+7,^+1)$

On a piece of graph paper, make another graph picture similar to the one above. Make a list of ordered pairs of integers for your picture. See if a classmate can draw your picture using your ordered pairs.

**Practice Supplement,** page 143

Name ______ To follow text page 379

**Graphing with Integers**

Give the ordered pair for each point.

1. A $(^-5,^+4)$ 2. B $(^+5,0)$
3. C $(^+2,^+3)$ 4. D $(^-2,^-2)$
5. E $(^-3,0)$ 6. F $(^-5,^-5)$
7. G $(^+2,^-5)$ 8. H $(^+4,^-4)$
9. I $(^+5,^+5)$ 10. J $(^-3,^+5)$
11. K $(^+1,^-3)$ 12. L $(^-4,^-2)$

Give the point on the graph for each ordered pair.

13. $(0,^+4)$ R 14. $(^+5,^-2)$ U
15. $(^-5,^+5)$ X 16. $(^-4,^+1)$ P
17. $(^-3,^+5)$ V 18. $(^-1,0)$ S
19. $(^+4,^+1)$ N 20. $(^+1,^+2)$ W
21. $(^-2,^-2)$ Y 22. $(^-3,^-5)$ M
23. $(^+3,^+3)$ Q 24. $(^+4,^-3)$ T

Graph each figure by graphing and connecting the points.

25. Diamond: $(0,^+1)$ $(^-3,^+3)$ $(^-1,^+4)$ $(^+1,^+4)$ $(^+3,^+3)$ $(0,^+1)$
26. Triangle: $(^-4,^+2)$ $(^-2,^-3)$ $(^-5,^-4)$ $(^-4,^+2)$
27. House: $(^+1,^+1)$ $(^+4,^+1)$ $(^+5,^-2)$ $(^+4,^-2)$ $(^+4,^-5)$ $(^+3,^-5)$ $(^+3,^-4)$ $(^+2,^-4)$ $(^+2,^-5)$ $(^+1,^-5)$ $(^+1,^-2)$ $(0,^-2)$ $(^+1,^+1)$

# Applications

**Lesson Focus** To interpret, organize, and use data to make a decision about a real-world problem.

## Ideas for Getting Started

Pass around to students brochures or advertisements for rental car services. Discuss differences in the charges and types of plans that are possible when renting a car. Discuss the fact that some of the rental companies provide discounts for employees of certain businesses or organizations. Ask students to share their ideas about the rental car company they think they would choose.

## Using Page 380

**Lesson Development** Be sure students understand the various considerations for this problem. Remind them that they should take ample time to understand the question, to read and select needed data, to plan a solution, and to do the necessary calculations to find the answer. Then go over the information with them and be sure they understand each of the statements. Ask for suggestions about things they should consider in making the decision. Allow students to work independently on the questions and to make their decision. Finally, discuss the decisions and the reasons for the decisions. Be sure students understand that there can be more than one possible solution.

As students consider this problem, be sure they are aware that there are other possible trips that could be taken. Also, encourage students to ask for additional data. For example, students might want to know if it is reasonable that each of these trips is a full one-day trip, or if they did take the trips, would they have additional time available for other trips. Another factor students might want to consider is how "carefree" they want to be. That is, with which of the plans would their time be the most restricted and how much would being "carefree" be worth to them?

QUESTION / DATA / PLAN / ANSWER / CHECK

## Applied Problem Solving

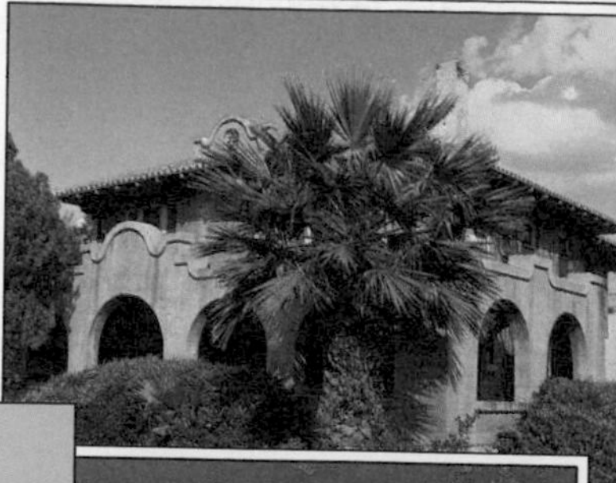

You are in Flagstaff, Arizona. You want to rent a car to do some weekday sightseeing while on vacation. Should you use the Unlimited Driving or the Per Kilometer rental plan?

**Some Things to Consider**

- The weekday rates for the Unlimited Driving Plan are \$48 per day.
- The weekday rates for the Per Kilometer rental plan are \$19 each day plus 12¢ for each kilometer.
- You are going to rent a car for 4 days.
- You may take trips from Flagstaff to these places:
  Petrified Forest, 176 km from Flagstaff
  Grand Canyon, 216 km from Flagstaff
  Meteor Crater, 64 km from Flagstaff
- You are also going to do some driving around Flagstaff.

**Some Questions to Answer**

1. What would be the total cost of the Unlimited Driving rate? \$48 × 4 = \$192
2. What would be the total cost, not including kilometers driven, at the Per Kilometer rate? \$19 × 4 = \$76
3. What would be the total cost at the Per Kilometer rate including round trips from Flagstaff to each of the other places listed? \$185.44

A-1 Rental

**What Is Your Decision?**

Will you use the Unlimited Driving Plan or the Per Kilometer rental plan? Answers will vary.

## *Chapter Review-Test*

Give the opposite of each integer.

**1.** $^+4$ $^-4$ **2.** $^-3$ $^+3$ **3.** $^-8$ $^+8$ **4.** $^+12$ $^-12$ **5.** $^-72$ $^+72$ **6.** $^+135$ $^-135$

Give the integer for the point on the number line that is

**7.** 6 units to the left of 0. $^-6$ **8.** 13 units to the right of 0. $^+13$

Find the sums.

**9.** $^+3 + {}^+7$ $^+10$ **10.** $^+2 + {}^-6$ $^-4$ **11.** $^-4 + {}^-10$ $^-14$ **12.** $^-3 + {}^+9$ $^+6$

**13.** $^-12 + {}^+5$ $^-7$ **14.** $^+7 + {}^-3$ $^+4$ **15.** $^-9 + {}^-6$ $^-15$ **16.** $^+8 + {}^-7$ $^+1$

Find the differences. Thinking of addends and a sum may help.

**17.** s a a: $^-5 - {}^-3 = n$ $^-2$ **18.** s a a: $^+4 - {}^-1 = n$ $^+5$ **19.** s a a: $^-3 - {}^+6 = n$ $^-9$

**20.** s a a: $^+2 - {}^+8 = n$ $^-6$ **21.** s a a: $^-7 - {}^-4 = n$ $^-3$ **22.** s a a: $^-3 - {}^-9 = n$ $^+6$

Write > or < for each ●.

**23.** $^+12$ ● $^+7$ > **24.** $^-1$ ● $^+3$ < **25.** $^-4$ ● $^-10$ > **26.** $^+9$ ● $^-10$ > **27.** 0 ● $^-5$ >

Give the ordered pairs for these points.

**28.** A ($^+3$,0) **29.** B ($^-3$,$^+2$)

**30.** C ($^-1$,$^-3$) **31.** D ($^+4$,$^-2$)

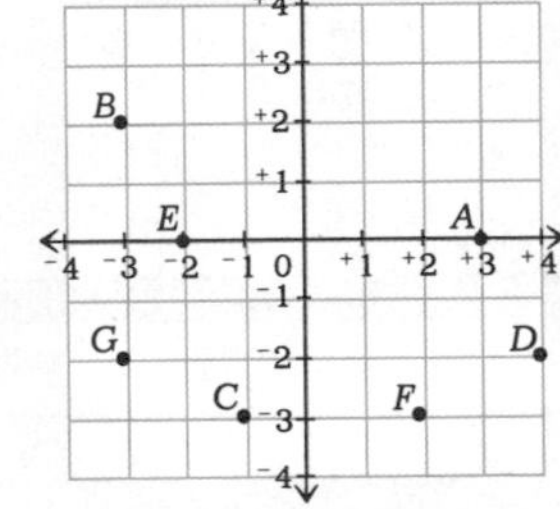


Give the points for these ordered pairs.

**32.** ($^-2$,0) E **33.** ($^-3$,$^-2$) G **34.** ($^+2$,$^-3$) F

Solve.

**35.** The temperature at 7:00 a.m. was $^-4$°C. It increased $^+7$°C by noon. What was the temperature at noon? $^+3$°C

**36.** Mountain City has an elevation of $^+4$ km. Valley City has an elevation of $^-1$ km. What is the difference of these elevations? $^+5$ km



## Using Page 381

The exercises in the Chapter Review-Test emphasize the major concepts and skills presented in this chapter. These exercises may be used as a review assignment or as a test, depending upon your needs.

**Item Analysis** The table below correlates the Chapter Review-Test items with objectives and with the student text pages on which the concepts or skills were taught. Note that items 28–34 are derived from a lesson for which no minimum assignment was suggested. Only those students who were assigned this lesson should be expected to complete the corresponding Chapter Review-Test items.

| Items | Objectives | Related Text Pages |
|---|---|---|
| 1–22 | 15.1 | 366–373 |
| 23–27 | 15.2 | 376 |
| 28–34 | 15.3 | 378–379 |
| 35–36 | 15.4 | 374–375, 377 |

## Assessment Options

If you use the Chapter Review-Test as a review assignment, you may wish to use the multiple-choice test or the free-response test to evaluate mastery of the chapter objectives. The items on these tests have a one-to-one correspondence in terms of content and level of difficulty. A correlation of test items to objectives and student text pages is provided in the Management Guide for Chapter 15. Note: Items 18–19 and 22 are derived from a lesson for which no minimum assignment was suggested in the Assignment Guide.

**Multiple-Choice Test,** TRB pages 43–44

**Free-Response Test,** TRB pages 77–78

## TRB Options

The following blackline masters are available for use with this chapter. If you have not already asigned these materials, you may wish to use them to close the chapter.

**Recreation,** TRB page 165

**Consumer Applications,** TRB page 183

**Calculator Technology,** TRB page 201

**Reading Math,** TRB page 233

**Family Involvement,** TRB pages 265–266

## Using Page 382

The exercises on this page are intended for those students who experienced difficulty with the Chapter Review-Test on page 381. Should students require reteaching of these key concepts and skills, please refer to the teaching notes below. Otherwise, the Another Look exercises can be assigned as independent work with students using the accompanying sample problems and hints as guides.

**Exercises 1–12** This concept was originally taught on pages 366–367. Direct students' attention to the number line at the left showing opposites. Remind students that each positive integer has an opposite that is negative and that each negative integer has an opposite that is positive. Note that some of the integers in the exercises are so large that students will not be able to use the number line.

**Exercises 13–26** This skill was originally taught on pages 368–371. Have students carefully examine the number line examples at the left. Remind them that they can show a sum on the number line by starting at 0 and drawing an arrow to show the first integer. From the tip of this arrow, they can draw a second arrow to indicate the second integer, counting the units or spaces on the number line. The tip of the second arrow indicates the sum of the two integers.

**Exercises 27–32** This skill was originally taught on pages 372–373. Direct students' attention to the display box at the left and focus on subtraction as finding the missing addend. Remind students that when subtracting, the sum and one addend is given. The missing addend is the difference.

**Exercises 33–40** This skill was originally taught on page 376. Have students focus on the number line and examples at the left. Be sure they understand that the positive direction on the number line is to the right and the negative direction is to the left. Emphasize the idea that integers to the right on a number line are greater than integers to the left. Encourage students to draw or think about number lines as necessary. Note that students sometimes make mistakes on problems such as exercise 40 because one negative integer seems larger than the other negative integer. Watch for errors involving these types of integers and use the number line to clarify.

Opposites

$\ldots {}^{-}5\ {}^{-}4\ {}^{-}3\ {}^{-}2\ {}^{-}1\ 0\ {}^{+}1\ {}^{+}2\ {}^{+}3\ {}^{+}4\ {}^{+}5 \ldots$

Negative Integers — Zero — Positive Integers

**Give the opposite of each integer.**

| | | |
|---|---|---|
| **1.** $^{-}1$ $^{+}1$ | **2.** $^{+}4$ $^{-}4$ | **3.** $^{-}8$ $^{+}8$ |
| **4.** $^{-}20$ $^{+}20$ | **5.** $^{+}56$ $^{-}56$ | **6.** $^{-}127$ $^{+}127$ |
| **7.** $^{+}14$ $^{-}14$ | **8.** $^{-}86$ $^{+}86$ | **9.** $^{+}675$ $^{-}675$ |
| **10.** $^{-}324$ $^{+}324$ | **11.** $^{+}189$ $^{-}189$ | **12.** $^{-}10$ $^{+}10$ |

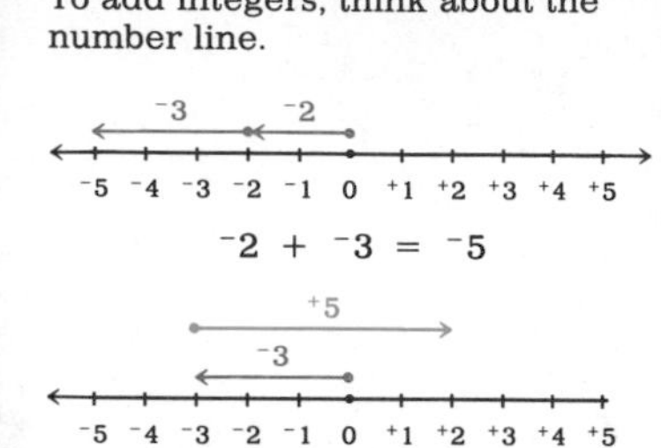


**Find the sums.**

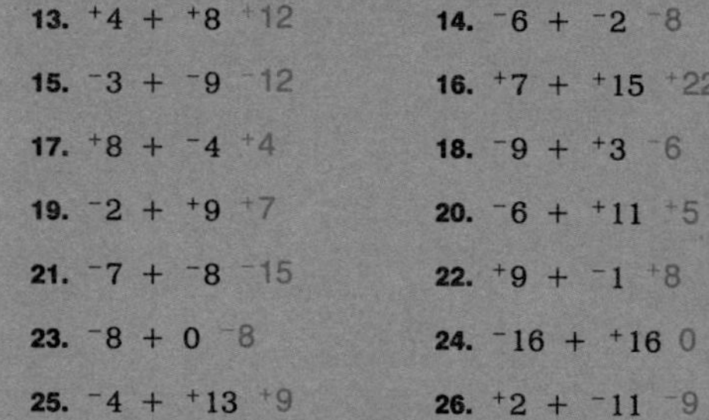

| | |
|---|---|
| **13.** $^{+}4 + {}^{+}8$ $^{+}12$ | **14.** $^{-}6 + {}^{-}2$ $^{-}8$ |
| **15.** $^{-}3 + {}^{-}9$ $^{-}12$ | **16.** $^{+}7 + {}^{+}15$ $^{+}22$ |
| **17.** $^{+}8 + {}^{-}4$ $^{+}4$ | **18.** $^{-}9 + {}^{+}3$ $^{-}6$ |
| **19.** $^{-}2 + {}^{+}9$ $^{+}7$ | **20.** $^{-}6 + {}^{+}11$ $^{+}5$ |
| **21.** $^{-}7 + {}^{-}8$ $^{-}15$ | **22.** $^{+}9 + {}^{-}1$ $^{+}8$ |
| **23.** $^{-}8 + 0$ $^{-}8$ | **24.** $^{-}16 + {}^{+}16$ 0 |
| **25.** $^{-}4 + {}^{+}13$ $^{+}9$ | **26.** $^{+}2 + {}^{-}11$ $^{-}9$ |

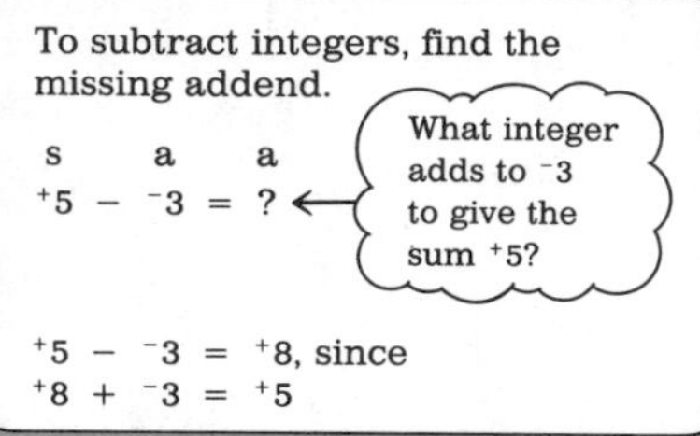


**Find the differences.**

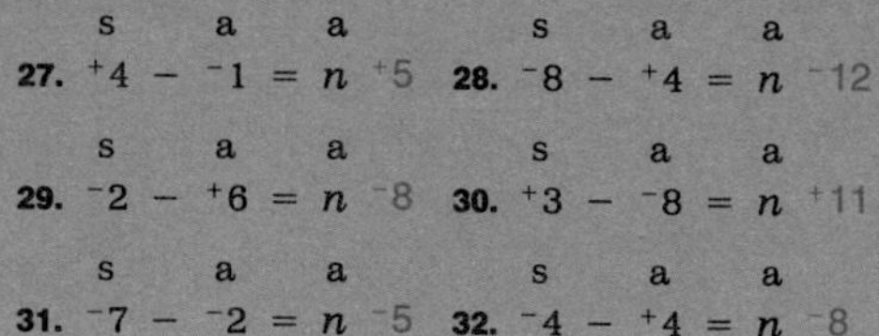

| | |
|---|---|
| **27.** $^{+}4 - {}^{-}1 = n$ $^{+}5$ (s a a) | **28.** $^{-}8 - {}^{+}4 = n$ $^{-}12$ (s a a) |
| **29.** $^{-}2 - {}^{+}6 = n$ $^{-}8$ (s a a) | **30.** $^{+}3 - {}^{-}8 = n$ $^{+}11$ (s a a) |
| **31.** $^{-}7 - {}^{-}2 = n$ $^{-}5$ (s a a) | **32.** $^{-}4 - {}^{+}4 = n$ $^{-}8$ (s a a) |

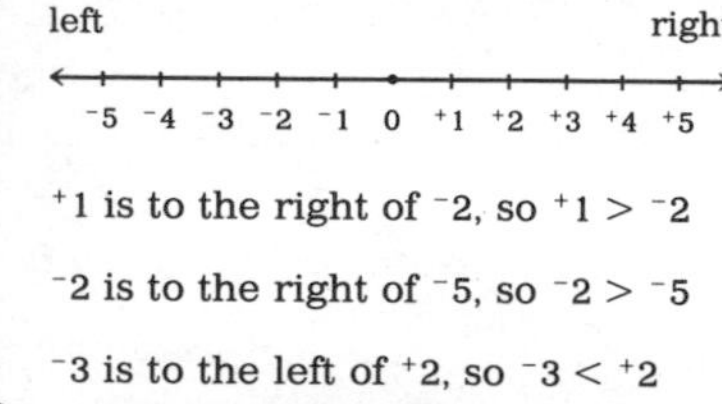


**Write > or < for each ●.**

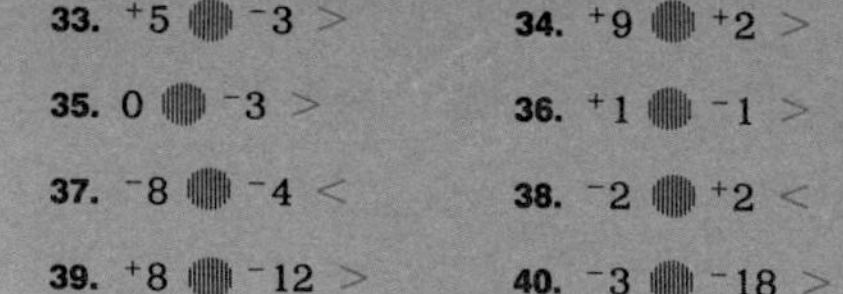

| | |
|---|---|
| **33.** $^{+}5$ ● $^{-}3$ > | **34.** $^{+}9$ ● $^{+}2$ > |
| **35.** 0 ● $^{-}3$ > | **36.** $^{+}1$ ● $^{-}1$ > |
| **37.** $^{-}8$ ● $^{-}4$ < | **38.** $^{-}2$ ● $^{+}2$ < |
| **39.** $^{+}8$ ● $^{-}12$ > | **40.** $^{-}3$ ● $^{-}18$ > |

382

## Just for Teachers

### History of Math

Our number system including the concept of zero appears to have originated in the Orient. However, number symbols found on the stone columns of a temple built in 250 B.C. in India resembled later Hindu numerals, and some mathematical records indicate that zero was an invention of the Hindus. There was, however, ample opportunity for each culture to influence the other. Exchanges of mathematical information began to take place between China and India after about A.D. 150. By about 400, Hindu mathematics included the nine numeric symbols and zero. Although the Hindu word for zero, *sunya*, indicated at first an empty column on the abacus, within the Hindu numeration system the concept became so well developed that it eliminated entirely the need for mechanical aids to computation. In time, zero evolved from place-holder to a fully recognized number.

The concept of the "negative number" also appears to have originated in the Orient. As early as 200 B.C., the Chinese used negative numbers as subtrahends, though they did not formulate rules for the use of negative numbers until the thirteenth century. Hindu mathematicians wrote of the "negative and affirmative qualities" of numbers

## Enrichment

### Using a Calculator to Check Integer Patterns

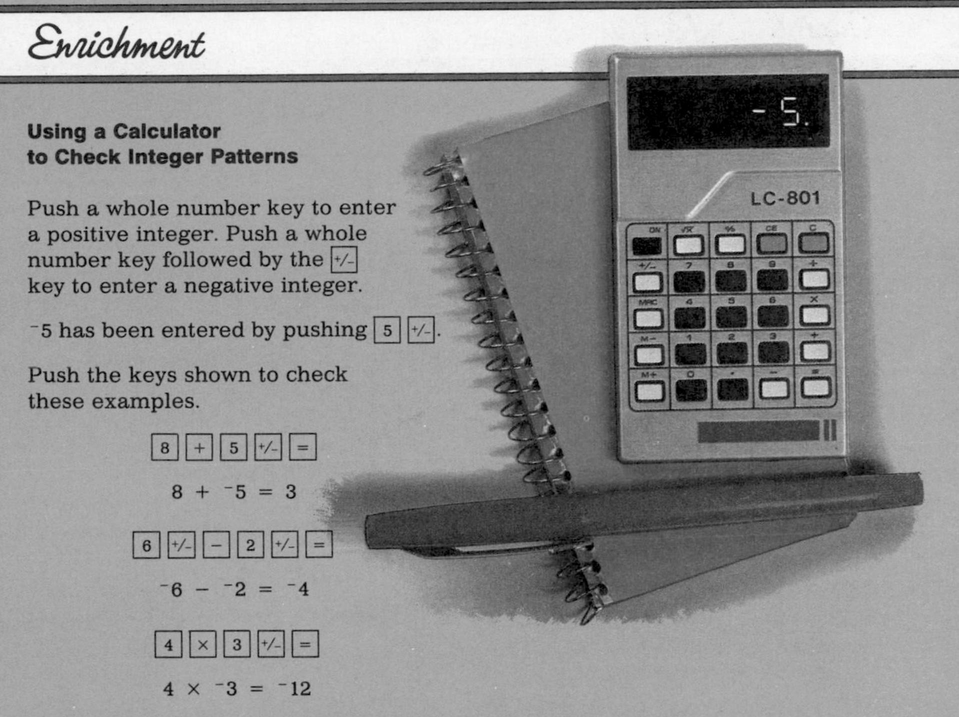


Push a whole number key to enter a positive integer. Push a whole number key followed by the [+/-] key to enter a negative integer.

$^{-}5$ has been entered by pushing [5] [+/-].

Push the keys shown to check these examples.

[8] [+] [5] [+/-] [=]

$8 + {}^{-}5 = 3$

[6] [+/-] [−] [2] [+/-] [=]

$^{-}6 - {}^{-}2 = {}^{-}4$

[4] [×] [3] [+/-] [=]

$4 \times {}^{-}3 = {}^{-}12$

Copy each column of equations. Use your calculator to solve each equation. What patterns do you see? See teaching notes.

| 1. | 2. | 3. | 4. |
|---|---|---|---|
| $5 + 4 = ?$ 9 | $4 - 4 = ?$ 0 | $4 \times 4 = ?$ 16 | $4 \times {}^{-}4 = ?$ $^{-}16$ |
| $5 + 3 = ?$ 8 | $4 - 3 = ?$ 1 | $4 \times 3 = ?$ 12 | $3 \times {}^{-}4 = ?$ $^{-}12$ |
| $5 + 2 = ?$ 7 | $4 - 2 = ?$ 2 | $4 \times 2 = ?$ 8 | $2 \times {}^{-}4 = ?$ $^{-}8$ |
| $5 + 1 = ?$ 6 | $4 - 1 = ?$ 3 | $4 \times 1 = ?$ 4 | $1 \times {}^{-}4 = ?$ $^{-}4$ |
| $5 + 0 = ?$ 5 | $4 - 0 = ?$ 4 | $4 \times 0 = ?$ 0 | $0 \times {}^{-}4 = ?$ 0 |
| $5 + {}^{-}1 = ?$ 4 | $4 - {}^{-}1 = ?$ 5 | $4 \times {}^{-}1 = ?$ $^{-}4$ | $^{-}1 \times {}^{-}4 = ?$ 4 |
| $5 + {}^{-}2 = ?$ 3 | $4 - {}^{-}2 = ?$ 6 | $4 \times {}^{-}2 = ?$ $^{-}8$ | $^{-}2 \times {}^{-}4 = ?$ 8 |
| $5 + {}^{-}3 = ?$ 2 | $4 - {}^{-}3 = ?$ 7 | $4 \times {}^{-}3 = ?$ $^{-}12$ | $^{-}3 \times {}^{-}4 = ?$ 12 |
| $5 + {}^{-}4 = ?$ 1 | $4 - {}^{-}4 = ?$ 8 | $4 \times {}^{-}4 = ?$ $^{-}16$ | $^{-}4 \times {}^{-}4 = ?$ 16 |

5. Use your calculator to help you make up some rules for multiplying and dividing integers. See teaching notes.



## Using Page 383

This page is intended for those students who successfully completed the Chapter Review-Test on page 381. You may wish to assign this page as independent work while you use Another Look exercises to reteach the basic concepts and skills of the chapter. Or, you may decide that all students would benefit from exposure to this Enrichment activity.

**Lesson Development** Have students work individually or in small groups with a calculator. Be sure they understand how to enter both positive and negative integers in the calculator. Then have students copy each column of equations, leaving a blank for the answer.

**Exercises 1–4** Students should quickly identify the patterns in these exercises. In columns three and four be sure students check each problem to verify the pattern.

**Exercise 5** Challenge students to form some rules for multiplying and dividing integers and to check these rules with specific examples on their calculators. If a hint is necessary, suggest that students refer to column four where they can observe that a negative integer times a negative integer produces a positive integer.

possibly because they worked with quadratic equations and recognized that negative numbers could be used to solve these equations. They also used negative numbers as subtrahends, marking them with a small dot or circle.

Western mathematicians were reluctant to accept the decimal system—particularly those numbers representing "less than nothing"—when it began to filter into Europe during the eleventh or twelfth century. In 1259, an official edict forbade the bankers of Florence to use Hindu numbers, positive or negative. It was, however, almost immediately popular with Medieval merchants, craftsmen, and bankers. Eventually the decimal system won out but the refusal of many mathematicians to accept negative numbers lasted into the fourteenth century.

## Using Page 384

The exercises on this page provide practice for maintaining cumulative skills. The emphasis in this Cumulative Review is on percents (Chapter 12); perimeter, area, and volume (Chapter 14); and problem solving (Chapter 14).

**Item Analysis** The table below correlates the Cumulative Review items with objectives and with the student book pages on which the concepts or skills were taught.

| Items | Objectives | Related text pages |
|---|---|---|
| 1–5 | 12.1 | 300–306 |
| 6–7 | 12.2 | 308–309 |
| 8 | 14.1 | 346 |
| 9 | 14.2 | 348–349 |
| 10 | 14.3 | 350–351 |
| 11 | 14.4 | 354–355 |
| 12 | 14.5 | 358 |
| 13–14 | 14.6 | 357, 351, 359 |

## *Cumulative Review*

**1.** Give a fraction for 8%.

**A** $\frac{1}{10}$ **B** $\frac{8}{25}$
**C** $\frac{1}{8}$ **(D)** not given

**2.** Give a fraction for 80%.

**(A)** $\frac{4}{5}$ **B** $\frac{2}{3}$
**C** $\frac{1}{8}$ **D** not given

**3.** Give a percent for $\frac{3}{5}$.

**A** 30% **B** 50%
**(C)** 60% **D** not given

**4.** Give a decimal for 135%.

**A** 0.135 **B** 13.5
**(C)** 1.35 **D** not given

**5.** Give a percent for 1.65.

**A** $16\frac{1}{2}$% **(B)** 165%
**C** $1\frac{13}{20}$% **D** not given

**6.** Find 25% of 36.

**A** 8 **B** 45
**C** 27 **(D)** not given

**7.** Find 5% of 140.

**(A)** 7 **B** 70
**C** 28 **D** not given

**8.** Find the perimeter.

1.6 cm
3.2 cm

**A** 5.12 $cm^2$
**B** 4.8 cm
**(C)** 9.6 cm
**D** not given

**9.** Find the area.

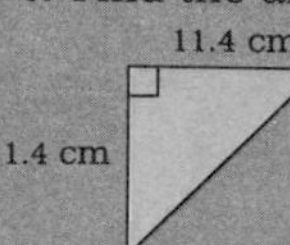


**(A)** 64.98 $cm^2$
**B** 129.96 $cm^2$
**C** 22.8 $cm^2$
**D** not given

**10.** Find the circumference.
Use 3.14 for $\pi$ and $C = \pi \times d$.

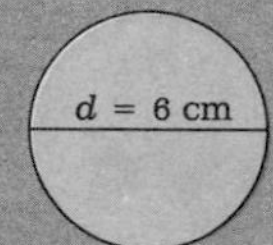


**A** 9.42 cm
**(B)** 18.84 cm
**C** 113.04 cm
**D** not given

**11.** Find the area.
Use 3.14 for $\pi$ and $A = \pi \times r \times r$.

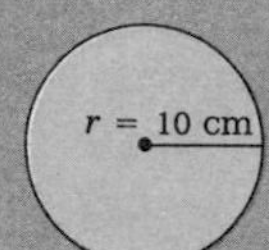


**A** 31.4 $cm^2$
**(B)** 314 $cm^2$
**C** 1,256 $cm^2$
**D** not given

**12.** Find the volume.

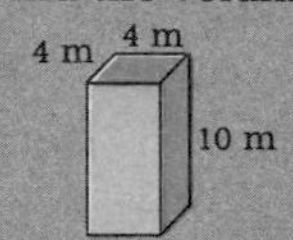


**(A)** 160 $m^3$
**B** 80 $m^3$
**C** 56 $m^3$
**D** not given

**13.** What is the area of a square garden if each side is 25 meters long?

**A** 125 $m^2$ **B** 500 $m^2$
**C** 100 $m^2$ **(D)** not given

**14.** 60% of the 125 members of a club voted for Mark for treasurer. How many members voted for Mark?

**(A)** 75 **B** 50
**C** 100 **D** not given

## Objectives

**16.1** Find and use appropriate units of length involving inches, feet, yards, and miles.
**16.2** Find and use appropriate units of capacity involving tablespoons, ounces, cups, pints, quarts, and gallons.
**16.3** Choose appropriate units to measure weight.
**16.4** Estimate and measure temperatures using degrees Fahrenheit.
**16.5** Solve word problems using the 5-Point Checklist and cumulative computational skills.

## Summary

In this chapter students become familiar with the basic customary units for measuring length, area, volume, capacity, weight, and temperature. They measure objects to the nearest inch, $\frac{1}{2}$ inch, $\frac{1}{4}$ inch, $\frac{1}{8}$ inch, and $\frac{1}{16}$ inch. As with metric units they add, subtract, and multiply given lengths using two units. Throughout the chapter students are asked to estimate measures using customary units in order to develop a feel for the size of that unit. Word problems, including those solved using a calculator and those solved using strategies from earlier lessons, are included.

## Mathematical Background

**Length** Length measurement, like other measurement, involves choosing an object to be measured, selecting an appropriate unit, and finding out how many units are needed to extend as far or as long or to cover the object to be measured.

While decimals play a major role when working with metric units, fractions are important when working with customary units. For example, the inch ruler below shows $\frac{1}{2}$, $\frac{1}{4}$, $\frac{1}{8}$, and $\frac{1}{16}$ inch units.

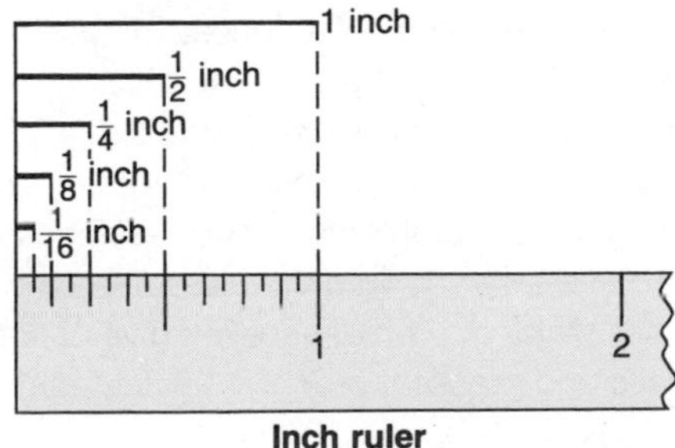

Inch ruler

Students learn to read these marks on the ruler. Later they will use the marks to measure to these units.

Students often need to combine lengths or to find the difference of lengths given using two different units. The example below shows that an understanding of the relationship between two units is important if appropriate trades are to be made.

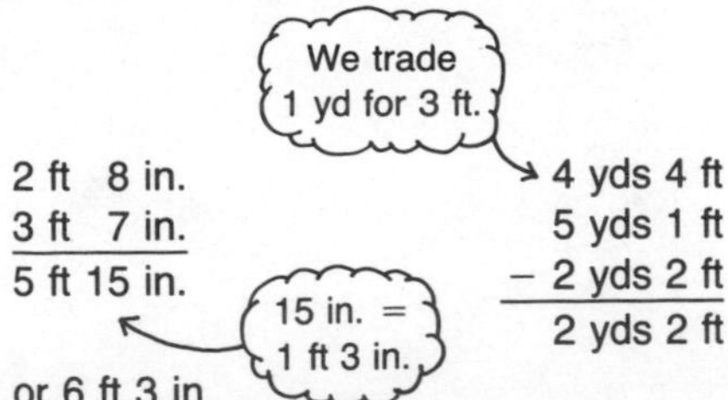


**Perimeter, Area, Volume, Surface Area** For a review of these ideas, refer to the overview for Chapter 14. The customary units used for area are square inch, square yard, square foot, and so on. The customary units for volume are cubic inch, cubic foot, cubic yard, and so on. If necessary, review these measurement ideas with students, using models for a square inch or cubic inch.

**Capacity, Weight, and Temperature** The customary units most often used for capacity and weight are shown in the tables below.

**Capacity: Customary Units**

| Unit | Relationships |
|---|---|
| fluid ounce (oz) | |
| cup (c) | 1 c = 8 oz |
| pint (pt) | 1 pt = 16 oz = 2 c |
| quart (qt) | 1 qt = 4 c = 2 pt |
| gallon (gal) | 1 gal = 8 pt = 4 qt |

**Weight: Customary Units**

| Unit | Relationships |
|---|---|
| ounce (oz) | |
| pound (lb) | 1 lb = 16 oz |
| ton (T) | 1 T = 2,000 lb |

For temperature the basic unit is degrees Fahrenheit (°F).

**Problem Solving** In this chapter most of the problem-solving experiences are applications of the basic ideas of measurement. Again, it is useful to emphasize the 5-Point Checklist shown in the logo in every problem-solving lesson, and to encourage students to use the Checklist as a guide. The problem-solving lessons in this chapter include: Using Data From a Picture, pages 392–393, which involves perimeter, area, volume, and surface area; Problem-Solving Practice, pages 395 and 397; and Using a Calculator, page 399.

In Applied Problem Solving on page 400, students must process data and organize it so that several calculations can be made in order to make a decision about a real-world problem. As students work this problem, emphasize the idea that it is not necessary to arrive at the answer quickly; it is important to take time to understand and organize the data needed to make the final decision.

### Vocabulary

| | | |
|---|---|---|
| inch | square mile | quart |
| foot | cubic inch | gallon |
| yard | cubic foot | ounce |
| mile | fluid ounce | pound |
| square inch | cup | ton |
| square foot | pint | degree Fahrenheit |

# Teaching Tips

## Error Analysis

The content in this chapter may be approached in two ways: by practical experiences in measuring and by studying the actual measurements in symbolic fashion. The former approach is recommended to help students understand relationships and to gain a meaning of units and of different sized units. The appropriateness of a unit for a given measure is determined by actually using units in a measurement setting and discussing the relative size of units. Real-world experiences can play a part in the knowledge students bring to measuring situations and how familiar they are already with a particular unit.

A further goal of this chapter is to make students aware of the role of measurement in everyday life and to help them develop facility with the more frequently used customary units. The computational work in this chapter involves converting from one unit to another as well as adding, subtracting, and multiplying units of measure. Be sensitive to any student experiencing difficulty, since this may be due to an inability to handle arithmetical computation.

## Problem Solving

### Using the Hand-Held Calculator

The solution to many problem-solving situations involves the use of computational skills. As a result, many problem-solving experiences are viewed as an opportunity for students to review computational skills. However, an overemphasis on computational skills during problem solving can shift attention away from what should be the major focus of problem solving—namely, understanding problems and selecting and carrying out appropriate solution strategies. There are many problem-solving situations where students could be allowed to use a hand-held calculator in order to reduce the time needed with paper and pencil calculations and to increase the time spent *thinking* about problems. In the following situations students could be allowed to use a calculator.

- The use of the Guess and Check strategy can be encouraged by the use of a calculator since the time required to check each guess is minimized.
- Possible number patterns can be tested rapidly with the aid of the calculator.
- Many problems involving the strategies Work Backward or Choose the Operations require several computational steps. The use of a calculator for these problems allows students to focus on how the action in the story suggests the operations needed to find a solution.
- Numerous problem-solving lessons in this program focus on estimation. In many of the lessons, the calculator can be used to find the exact answer after the student has completed the estimate.

Using a calculator during problem solving will instill enthusiasm in students. Many students will view the use of a calculator in school as a novelty and as a result will be enthusiastic about being allowed to use it. And, perhaps most important of all, the calculator may be the only vehicle by which students who are poor at computation can participate in problem-solving experiences. Problem-solving experiences for students with computational deficiencies should not be delayed until those deficiencies are remedied.

The calculator as a tool for problem-solving has strong support for the "real world" where problems in business, industry, and science, for example, are solved with the aid of the calculator. Thus, the use of the calculator in problem-solving gives students experience in a realistic and practical problem-solving mode.

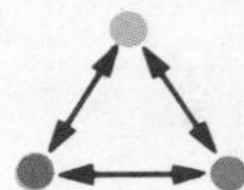

## Special Education

As skills are developed with customary units of measure, the special-needs students often encounter difficulties involving interference with other measurement skills, trading rules not based on ten, and confusion in the scales in measuring length.

### Converting Customary Units

The conversion of one customary unit to another can be aided through the use of conversion cards as illustrated below. In the example on the left, we want to convert the measure from feet to inches. The label of feet is covered with a card showing the conversion factor in inches (12) and the multiplication carried out. In the example on the right, we are converting from inches to feet, so we cover the label inches with a card labeled $\frac{1}{12}$ foot and carry out the indicated computation. As a further aid list the conversion facts both ways on a chart and display in the classroom.

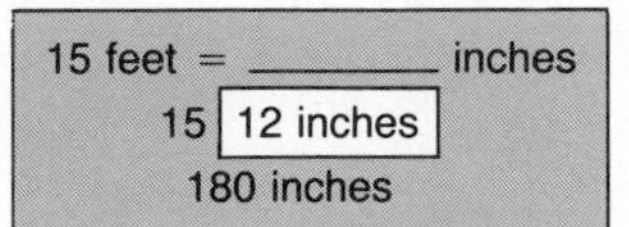


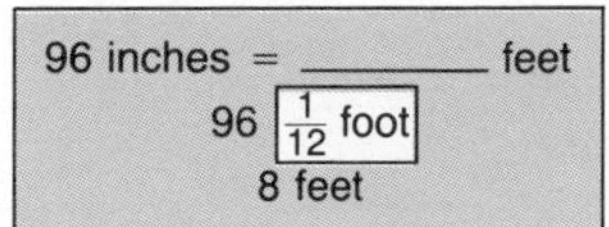


### Computing with Customary Units

The development of computational skills in customary units with the special-needs students requires an understanding of the above conversion factors. Then stress can be placed on the ideas of dealing with like units and making necessary trades, regardless of the operation involved. In general, these calculations should be restricted to linear measurements involving inches and feet and to capacity measures involving pints, quarts, and gallons.

The development of trading facts can be facilitated by using wooden rods having twelve cubes to the rod and containers representing pints, quarts, and gallons. Problems should be worked through with models before students are expected to work problems symbolically.

### Estimating and Measuring

Students must learn to estimate a reasonable answer, carry out the measurement, check against the estimate, remeasure if there is an unreasonable difference between the two, and then record the measurement. If possible, outside activities should be included, relating customary units to sports, careers, or school dimensions.

## Subject Integration

Subject matter related to other areas of the curriculum has been integrated into the following lessons. This provides an opportunity to highlight the interaction between mathematics and other subjects.

**Fine Arts** Making pottery, page 385
**Career Awareness** Carpentry, pages 388–389
**Consumer Awareness** Comparing container capacity, pages 394–395; shipping costs, page 397; building a tool shed, page 400

# Management Guide

| Teaching Chapter 16 | | | | Meeting Individual Needs | | | | | |
|---|---|---|---|---|---|---|---|---|---|
| Objectives | Chapter Content | Pages | TRB Test Items | Lesson Assignments | | | Follow Up | | |
| | | | | Minimum | Average | Extended | Reteaching | Enrichment | Practice |
| | Chapter Opener | 385 | | | | | | | |
| **16.1** Find and use appropriate units of length involving inches, feet, yards, and miles. | Length: Customary Units | 386–387 | 1–6 | 1–26 | 1–28 | 1–30, TM | SE5 Ch 16 | | PS 144 |
| | Inches and Fractions | 388–389 | 7–8 | 1–20, SK | 1–20, SK | 1–23, SK | SE5 Ch 16 RS 92 | ES 92 | PS 145 |
| | Computing with Lengths | 390 | 9–11 | 1–9 | 1–9 | 1–9 | SE5 Ch 16 RS 93 | ES 93 | PS 146 |
| | Estimating with Customary Units | 391 | 12–13 | 1–6 | 1–6 | 1–7 | SE5 Ch 16 | | |
| **16.2** Find and use appropriate units of capacity involving tablespoons, ounces, cups, pints, quarts, and gallons. | Capacity | 394 | 14–16 | 1–18 | 1–18 | 1–18 | SE5 Ch 16 RS 95 | ES 95 | PS 148 |
| **16.3** Choose appropriate units to measure weight. | Weight | 396 | 17–20 | 1–19 | 1–19 | 1–19 | SE5 Ch 16 RS 96 | ES 96 | PS 149 |
| **16.4** Estimate and measure temperatures using degrees Fahrenheit. | Temperature | 398 | 21–24 | 1–14 | 1–14 | 1–15 | SE5 Ch 16 | | PS 150 |
| **16.5** Solve word problems using the 5-Point Checklist and cumulative computational skills. | Problem Solving: Using Data from a Picture | 392–393 | 25–30 | 1–14 | 1–16 | 1–17 | RS 94 | ES 94 | PS 147 |
| | Problem Solving: Capacity | 395 | | 1–6 | 1–7 | 1–8 | | | |
| | Problem Solving: Weight | 397 | | 1–5 | 1–7 | 1–8 | | | |
| | Problem Solving: Using a Calculator | 399 | | 1–6 | 1–7 | 1–8 | | | |
| | Applied Problem Solving | 400 | | | | | | | |
| | Chapter Review-Test | 401 | | | | | | | |
| | Another Look/Enrichment | 402–403 | | | | | | | |
| | Technology | 404–405 | | | | | | | |
| | Cumulative Review | 406 | | | | | | | |

**SE5** Student Edition, Book 5
**RS** Reteaching Supplement
**ES** Enrichment Supplement
**PS** Practice Supplement
**MP** More Practice
**TM** Think Math
**SK** Skillkeeper
**TRB** Teacher's Resource Book

## Masters for Use

**. . . before Chapter 16**

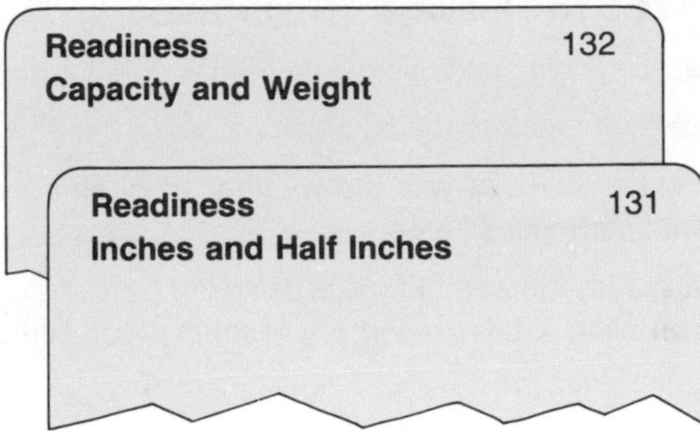


**. . . during Chapter 16**

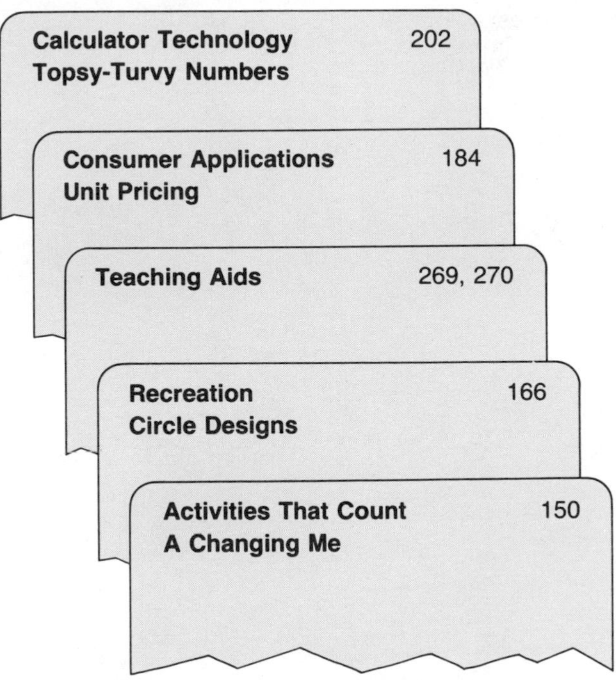


**. . . after Chapter 16**

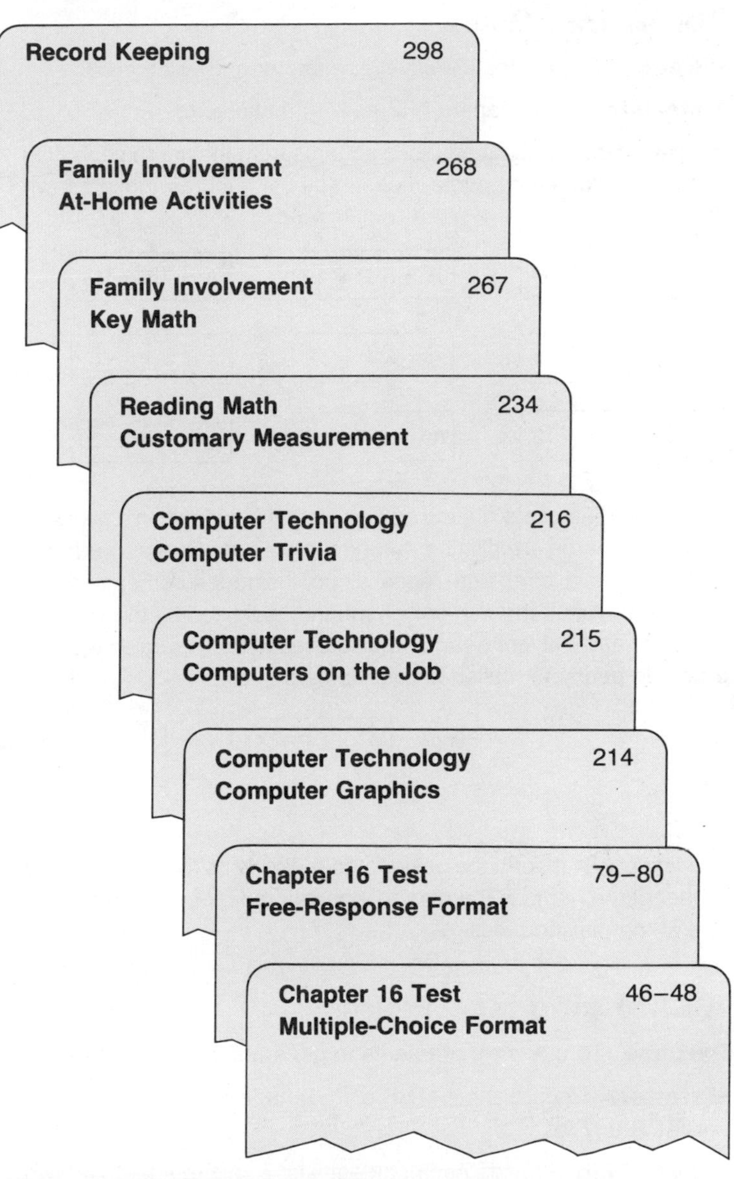


## Supplements

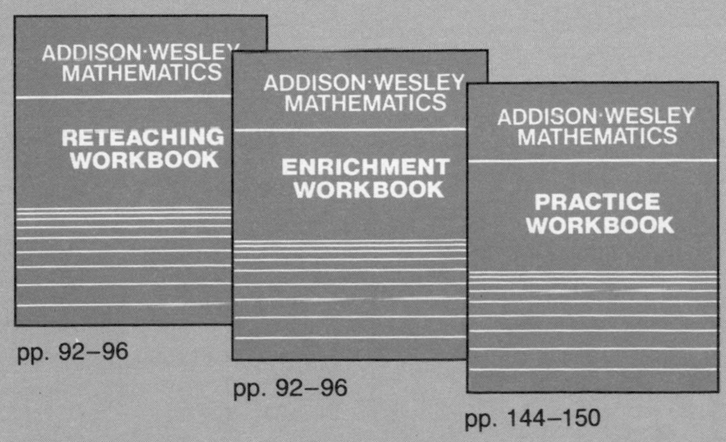


## Other Addison-Wesley Resources

**Books and Kits**

*The Arithmetic Primer* pp. 227–280

*Problem Solving Experiences in Mathematics,* Grade 6
Problems 3, 43, 58, 83

# Activities That Count

Activities That Count are designed for use throughout this chapter and subsequent chapters. Before beginning Chapter 16, you may wish to review these activities and select the ones you consider appropriate for your class.

## Peri-Area Game

**Purpose** To practice identifying perimeter and volume

**Materials** Graph paper (TRB p. 269), index cards

**Preparation** Cut out one-inch squares from the graph paper. On about 15 index cards, write measurements such as those shown below.

| A = 3 P = 8 | A = 5 P = 12 | A = 7 P = 16 |
|---|---|---|
| A = 8 P = 14 | A = 8 P = 16 | A = 6 P = 12 |
| A = 7 P = 12 | A = 10 P = 17 | A = 10 P = 20 |

**Activity** The cards are mixed and placed facedown in a pile, and the inch-squares are divided among the players. One player in the group draws a card and reads aloud the measurements. Each player then takes the number of squares indicated by the value of A on the card. Players arrange the squares to form a region with the area and perimeter called for on the card.

Example: 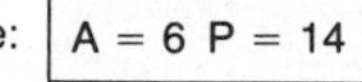

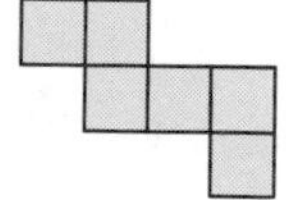

The first player to form the designated region wins the squares. The winner of the game is the person who has the most squares at the end of the playing time.

## A Changing Me Project

**Purpose** To use measurements to generate word problems

**Materials** Record sheet (TRB p. 150), tape measure, graph paper (TRB p. 270)

**Preparation** Provide each student with a record sheet and two pieces of graph paper.

**Activity** At scheduled times during the study of this chapter, students find the measurements indicated on the record sheet. Students then use the suggestions below to generate word problems about their measurements.

- Amount of change over time
- Measurement showing greatest change
- Measurement showing least change
- Ratios and percents describing change
- Averages

## Reading a Weather Map Math Lab

**Purpose** To practice finding and using data from a weather map

**Materials** Newspaper weather maps, index cards

**Preparation** Provide students with the weather maps and the following topics written on index cards.

**Activity** Students study the weather maps using the topics below as guides, and then write a brief report about their observations about the map.

Average temperature in the state capital

Rainfall in inches

Snowfall in inches

Barometric readings

Three highest temperatures

Three lowest temperatures

Cities between 80° and 90°

Cities above 90°

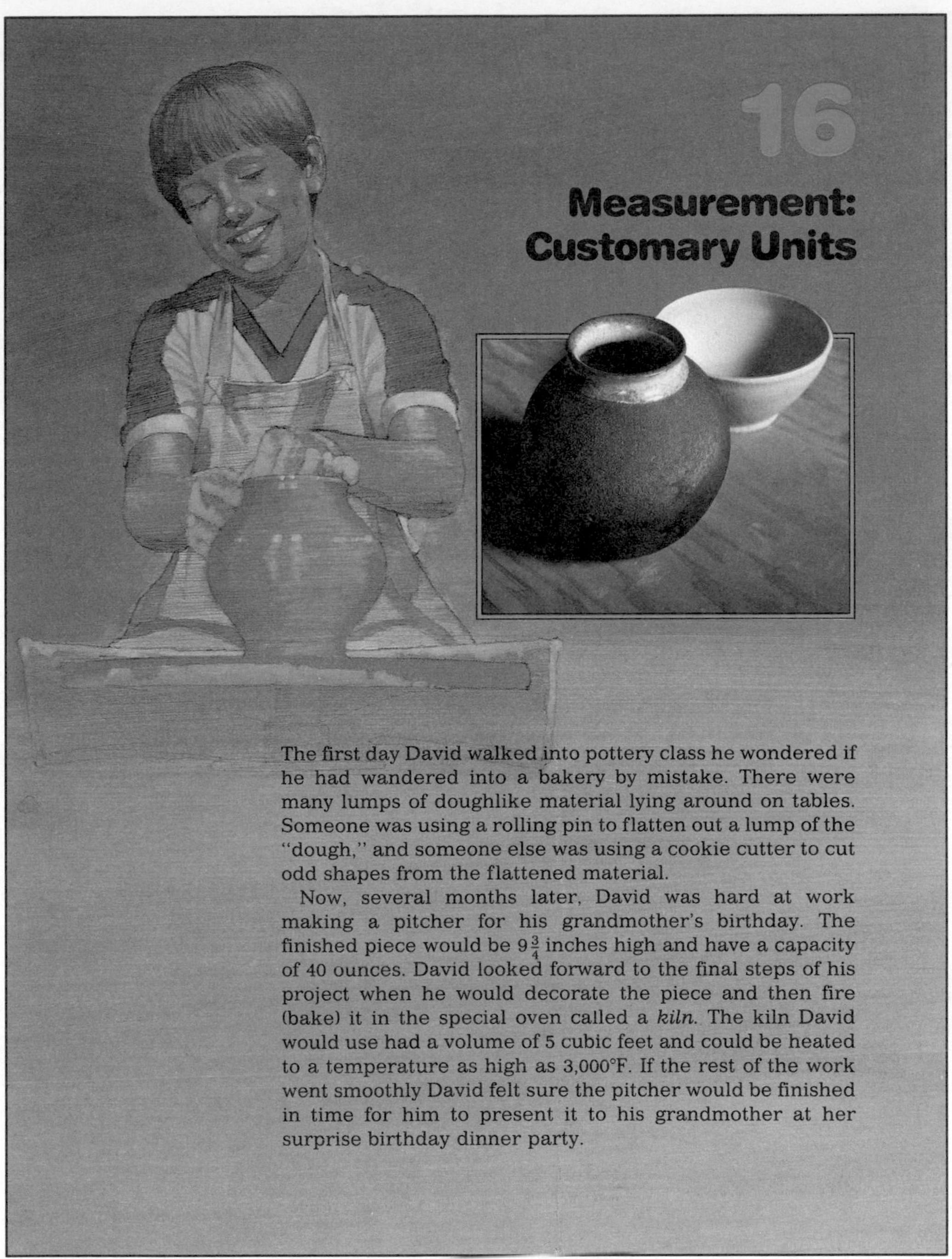

16
Measurement:
Customary Units
The first day David walked into pottery class he wondered if he had wandered into a bakery by mistake. There were many lumps of doughlike material lying around on tables. Someone was using a rolling pin to flatten out a lump of the "dough," and someone else was using a cookie cutter to cut odd shapes from the flattened material.
Now, several months later, David was hard at work making a pitcher for his grandmother's birthday. The finished piece would be $9\frac{3}{4}$ inches high and have a capacity of 40 ounces. David looked forward to the final steps of his project when he would decorate the piece and then fire (bake) it in the special oven called a *kiln*. The kiln David would use had a volume of 5 cubic feet and could be heated to a temperature as high as 3,000°F. If the rest of the work went smoothly David felt sure the pitcher would be finished in time for him to present it to his grandmother at her surprise birthday dinner party.


## Introducing the Chapter

**Discussion** Explain to students that in this chapter they will review and extend their skills in working with customary units of measure. Lead a discussion of handicrafts such as pottery making, leather tooling, and macramé. Give students time to talk about experiences they or their friends may have had with these crafts. After students have had an opportunity to read the story and enjoy the art, encourage them to make up questions based on the data in the story. As you teach the chapter, you may wish to refer to this page and pose the questions suggested below.

## Follow-Up Questions

**After Page 387** The work tables in David's pottery classroom are 78 in. long. How many feet long are the tables? ($6\frac{1}{2}$ ft)

**After Page 390** Amelia rolled out 3 ropes of clay. Each rope was 1 ft 9 in. long. What was the total length of the ropes of clay? (5 ft 3 in.)

**After Page 393** The gift box David used for his grandmother's pitcher was 8 in. long, 7 in. wide, and 12 in. high. What was the volume of the box? (672 in.$^3$)

**After Page 395** The pitcher David made had a capacity of 40 oz. What was the capacity of the pitcher in quarts? ($1\frac{1}{4}$ qt)

**Quick Review** Students round 3-place decimals to the nearest hundredth and 2-place decimals to the nearest tenth.

46.05 16.308 0.622 1.95 0.88 8.67 5.32 8.019
0.881 0.62 35.85 14.79 0.252 10.55

**Lesson Focus** To choose appropriate customary units of length and to change from one customary length unit to another

**Suggested Materials** Foot ruler, yardstick

## Ideas for Getting Started

Provide students with a foot ruler and a yardstick. Encourage them to look for distances that are about 1 yard, about 1 foot, and about 1 inch long. For an inch they might suggest the length of a joint on a finger, the width of an eraser, or the width of a knuckle on the thumb; for a foot, the distance from the elbow to the wrist or shoulder, the distance from bottom of knee to ankle bone, or two hands long; for a yard, the width of a door or from one side of a person's head to the tip of their outstretched finger on the other side.

## Using Page 386

**Lesson Development** Direct students' attention to the illustrations showing the basic units at the top of the page. If you used the Getting Started activity, relate each of the four units to distances or the estimations made earlier. Encourage students to suggest other examples of these units.

**Warm Up** As students give the answers orally to exercises 1 through 5, review the relationships between the units. Give students a few minutes to think about exercises 6 through 12. Then ask a student to read the sentence and give the correct unit for the statement. Discuss any difficulties students seem to have with the choices by selecting certain objects in the classroom and having students measure the object to get a sense of the appropriateness of the unit chosen.

## Length: Customary Units

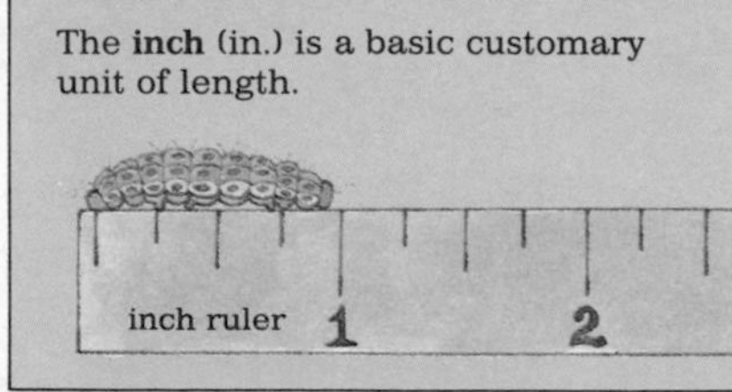

The **inch** (in.) is a basic customary unit of length.
inch ruler
1
2


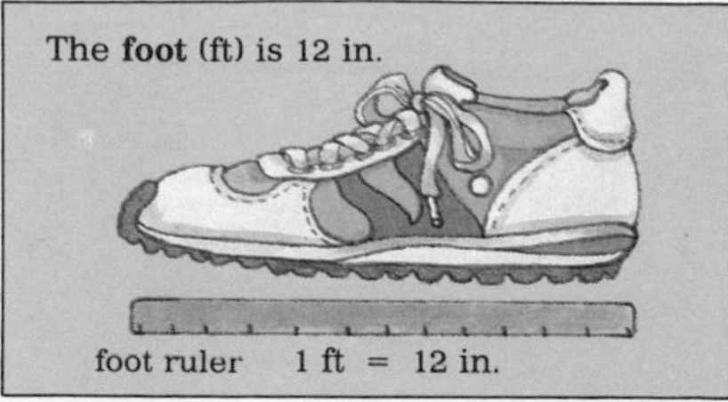


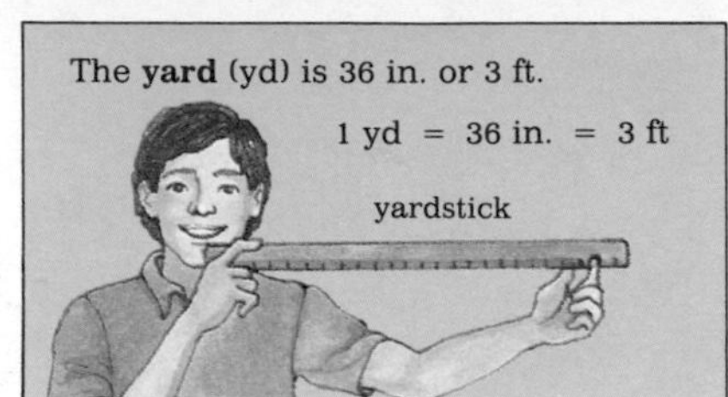

The **foot** (ft) is 12 in.
foot ruler 1 ft = 12 in.

The **yard** (yd) is 36 in. or 3 ft.
1 yd = 36 in. = 3 ft
yardstick


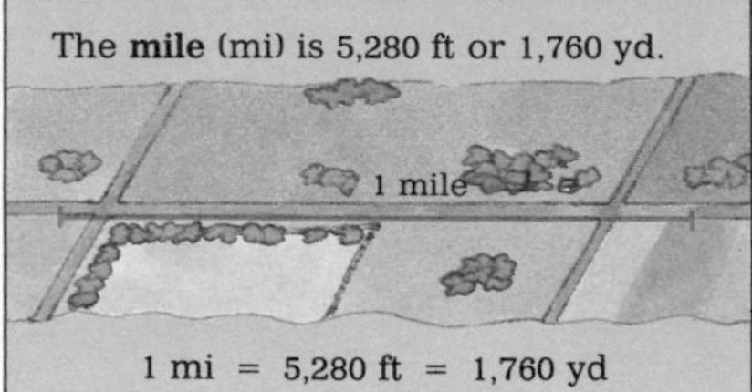

The **mile** (mi) is 5,280 ft or 1,760 yd.
1 mile
1 mi = 5,280 ft = 1,760 yd


### Warm Up

1. A mile is ■ yd long. 1,760
2. A mile is ■ ft long. 5,280
3. A yard is ■ ft long. 3
4. A yard is ■ in. long. 36
5. A foot is ■ in. long. 12

Which unit would you use? Write **in., ft, yd,** or **mi.**

6. The book is 10 __?__ long. in.
7. The length of a football field is 100 __?__. yd
8. The height of a mountain is 26,472 __?__. ft
9. The car is 14 __?__ long. ft
10. The nail is 3 __?__ long. in.
11. The distance from Dallas to Washington, D.C., is 1,372 __?__. mi
12. The football player is 73 __?__ tall. in.

386

## Follow Up

### Reteaching

Help students identify common objects to be measured in inches, feet, and yards, emphasizing the relationships between these common linear units: 12 in. = 1 ft, 3 ft = 1 yd, and 1,760 yd = 1 mi. Let students suggest other real-world examples of customary units. Then ask students to explain how to change each measurement to another unit; for example, from feet to inches (multiply by 12), from inches to feet (divide by 12), or from feet to yards (divide by 3).

### Enrichment

Encourage students to work in pairs or teams to play "What am I?" In turn students challenge a partner to name an object that is a given number of inches, feet, or yards away. The student says "I am thinking of an object that is about . . . ." The student then gives an estimated distance as a clue. If the partner guesses the object, he or she makes the next challenge with a similar measurement estimate.

| Assignment Guide | | | |
|---|---|---|---|
| | Minimum | Average | Extended |
| page 387 | 1–26 | 1–28 | 1–30, TM |

Give the number for each ■.

Example: 6 ft = ■ in.
There are 12 in. in 1 ft, so 6 ft = 6 × 12 = 72 in.

1. 4 ft = ■ in. 48
2. 3 yd = ■ ft 9
3. 4 yd = ■ in. 144
4. 2 mi = ■ ft 10,560
5. 3 mi = ■ yd 5,280
6. $2\frac{1}{2}$ ft = ■ in. 30
7. $\frac{3}{4}$ ft = ■ in. 9
8. $2\frac{1}{2}$ yd = ■ in. 90
9. $\frac{1}{2}$ mi = ■ ft 2,640
10. $\frac{3}{4}$ mi = ■ yd 1,320
11. $4\frac{1}{4}$ yd = ■ in. 153
12. $1\frac{3}{4}$ ft = ■ in. 21

Complete the following.

Example: 27 ft = ■ yd
3 ft = 1 yd, so 27 ft = 27 ÷ 3 = 9 yd

13. 36 in. = ■ ft 3
14. 12 ft = ■ yd 4
15. 72 in. = ■ yd 2
16. 10,560 ft = ■ mi 2
17. 1,760 yd = ■ mi 1
18. 60 in. = ■ ft 5
19. 48 in. = ■ ft 4
20. 180 in. = ■ yd 5
21. 18 in. = ■ ft $1\frac{1}{2}$
22. 54 in. = ■ yd $1\frac{1}{2}$
23. 6 in. = ■ ft $\frac{1}{2}$
24. 18 in. = ■ yd $\frac{1}{2}$
25. A football field is 100 yd long. How many feet is this? 300
26. One track event is the 880-yd race. How many feet is this? 2,640
27. How many miles do you run when you run two 880-yd races? 1 mi
28. How many yards is a $\frac{1}{4}$-mile horse race? 440 yd
29. A basketball player is 6 ft 10 in. tall. How many inches is this? 82 in.
30. On a baseball diamond, home plate is 66 ft 6 in. from the pitcher's mound. How many inches is this? 798 in.

**Think Math**

**Space Perception**

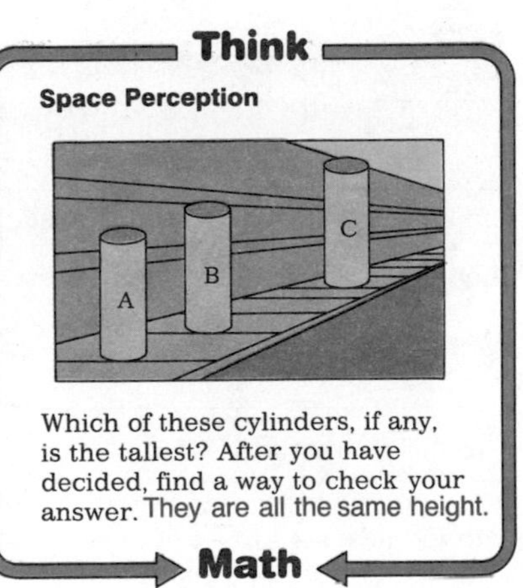


Which of these cylinders, if any, is the tallest? After you have decided, find a way to check your answer. They are all the same height.



## Using Page 387

**Exercises 1–12** Work at least two examples on the chalkboard before assigning these exercises. Note that since there are 12 in. in 1 ft, students can multiply to find the missing number in each exercise. For example, there are 6 × 12 or 72 in. in 6 ft. Note that exercises 6–12 involve multiplying by a fraction or mixed number.

**Exercises 13–24** In each of these exercises, students change a given measurement to a measurement in a larger unit. Thus they must divide to find the missing number. As you work examples like the one shown, emphasize that since each 3 ft make 1 yd, in 27 ft there are 27 ÷ 3 or 9 yd.

**Exercises 25–30** Encourage students to read these exercises carefully to decide the correct operation to find the resulting measurement.

**Think Math** This is an optical illusion. After students have made their guesses, encourage them to measure using an inch ruler to the nearest $\frac{1}{8}$ inch or make two marks on a sheet of paper to indicate the height of a given cylinder. Then compare these marks with the other cylinders.

## Ideas That Work

### Special Education

Modified rulers as shown below can be used to help students develop the skill of measuring to the nearest $\frac{1}{4}$ inch. These rulers can be made with red and blue ditto masters, positioning the rulers diagonally on an $8\frac{1}{2}''$ × 11″ paper.

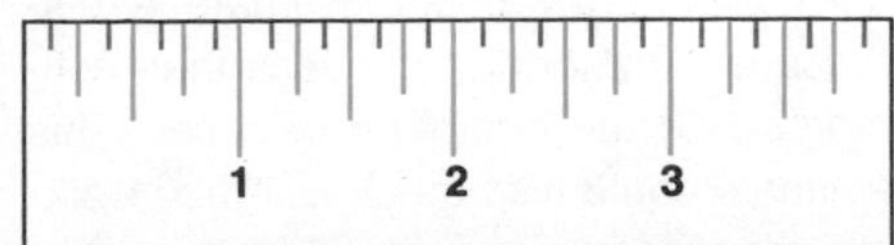


The inch, $\frac{1}{4}$, $\frac{1}{2}$, and $\frac{3}{4}$ inch marks are blue; the $\frac{1}{8}$, $\frac{3}{8}$, $\frac{5}{8}$, and $\frac{7}{8}$ inch marks are red. Students use the rulers to practice rounding to the nearest $\frac{1}{4}$ inch as follows: Have students identify each of the $\frac{1}{4}$ or $\frac{1}{8}$ inch marks on the ruler. Then review the rule for rounding up when the measure is half way or more to the next measure. These skills can then be translated to the modified rulers, using the red marks as judgment marks for the rounding process. After students have used the modified rulers for a few days, move back to regular rulers. Continue to stress the use of the $\frac{1}{8}$, $\frac{3}{8}$, $\frac{5}{8}$, and $\frac{7}{8}$ marks in making judgments. If necessary, have special-needs students use rulers having units no smaller than $\frac{1}{8}$ inch.

**Practice Supplement,** page 144

Name ______________________ To follow text page 387

**Length: Customary Units**

Which unit would you use? Write **in., ft, yd,** or **mi.**

1. A pen is 6 __in.__ long
2. The air distance between New York and Chicago is 1,859 __mi__.
3. A woman's ring finger is 3 __in.__ long.
4. A bed is 2 __yd__ long.
5. A table is 30 __in.__ high.
6. A door is 8 __ft__ tall.
7. The Empire State Building is 1,472 __ft__ tall.

Complete the following.

8. 1 ft = __12__ in.
9. 1 mi = __1,760__ yd
10. 1 yd = __3__ ft
11. 1 mi = __5,280__ ft
12. 1 yd = __36__ in.
13. 2 ft = __24__ in.
14. 4 yd = __12__ ft
15. 3 yd = __108__ in.
16. 15 ft = __5__ yd
17. 48 in. = __4__ ft
18. 2 mi = __10,560__ ft
19. 3 mi = __5,280__ yd
20. 18 in. = __$1\frac{1}{2}$__ ft
21. 9 ft = __3__ yd
22. 108 in. = __3__ yd
23. $\frac{1}{3}$ mi = __1,760__ ft
24. $1\frac{1}{2}$ yd = __54__ in.
25. $\frac{1}{4}$ mi = __440__ yd
26. 24 in. = __$\frac{2}{3}$__ yd
27. $\frac{3}{4}$ ft = __9__ in.
28. 2,640 ft = __$\frac{1}{2}$__ mi
29. 48 in. = __$1\frac{1}{3}$__ yd

# Measurement

**Quick Review** Students add the fractions below, giving answers in lowest terms.

$\frac{1}{2} + \frac{1}{4}$ $\frac{3}{4}$ $\qquad$ $\frac{3}{4} + \frac{3}{16}$ $\frac{9}{16}$ $\qquad$ $\frac{1}{16} + \frac{7}{8}$ $\frac{15}{16}$ $\qquad$ $\frac{2}{3} + \frac{1}{9}$ $\frac{7}{9}$

$\frac{5}{8} + \frac{3}{4}$ $1\frac{3}{8}$ $\qquad$ $\frac{3}{16} + \frac{1}{2}$ $\frac{11}{16}$ $\qquad$ $\frac{5}{6} + \frac{1}{3}$ $1\frac{1}{6}$ $\qquad$ $\frac{3}{4} + \frac{1}{2}$ $\frac{5}{6}$

**Lesson Focus** To measure objects to the nearest inch, $\frac{1}{2}$ inch, $\frac{1}{4}$ inch, $\frac{1}{8}$ inch, and $\frac{1}{16}$ inch

**Suggested Materials** Ruler marked in $\frac{1}{2}$, $\frac{1}{4}$, $\frac{1}{8}$, and $\frac{1}{16}$ inch divisions

## Ideas for Getting Started

Hand out a worksheet with finely-drawn lines on it. One line should be between $4\frac{3}{16}$ and $4\frac{4}{16}$ inches long. Another should be between $5\frac{9}{16}$ and $5\frac{10}{16}$ inches long. Other lines with lengths between two $\frac{1}{16}$ inch marks should be given. Tell students that the accuracy of a measurement depends on the unit of measure—the smaller the unit, the greater the accuracy. Ask them to use their inch rulers to measure a selected line as accurately as possible.

## Using Page 388

**Lesson Development** Direct students' attention to the ruler shown at the top of the page. "Think only about the inch marks on the ruler. Which mark is the length of the longest nail closest to?" (3 in.) "What is the length of this nail to the nearest inch?" (3 in.) Ask the same questions about the shorter nail. Next ask students to think about the marks that divide the ruler into half-inch segments. Note that those marks include the inch marks. Help students see that the length of the longer nail to the nearest $\frac{1}{2}$ in. is also 3 in., and the length of the shorter nail to the nearest $\frac{1}{2}$ in. is $2\frac{1}{2}$ in. Ask similar questions about each of the other pictures. Be sure students see that to measure to a given unit, they must find the mark that is closest to the tip of the object.

**Warm Up** Give students a few minutes to measure the segments given. Compare and discuss measurements. Draw an enlarged ruler on the chalkboard for students who are having difficulty, and discuss the meaning of each of the marks. As a review, draw the ruler on the chalkboard and have students tell you where to make each set of marks.

## Inches and Fractions

We can use fractions when measuring lengths more precisely than to the nearest inch.

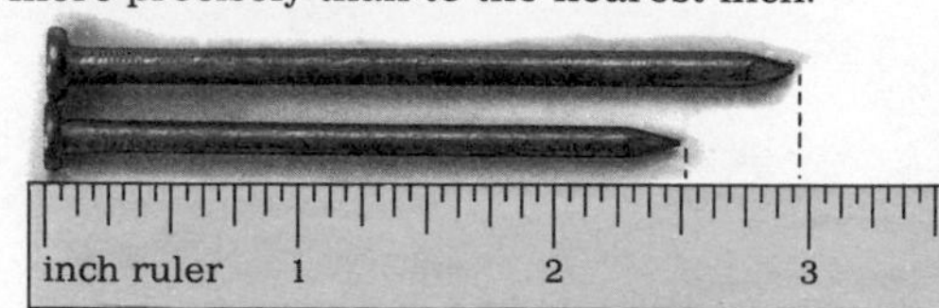


The length of each nail to the nearest inch is 3 in.
The length of the shorter nail to the nearest $\frac{1}{2}$ **inch** is $2\frac{1}{2}$ in.
The length of the longer nail to the nearest $\frac{1}{2}$ **inch** is 3 in.

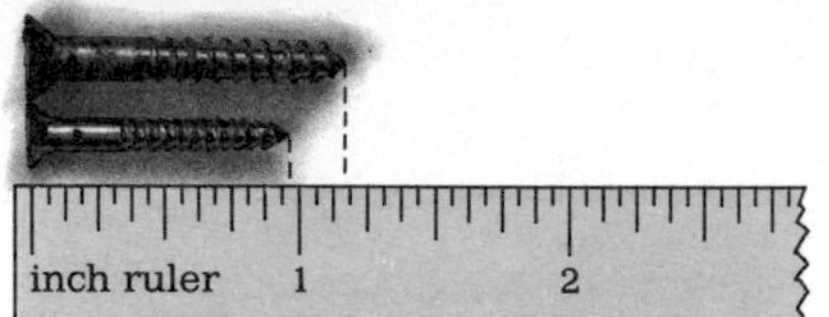


The length of each screw to the nearest $\frac{1}{2}$ inch is 1 in.

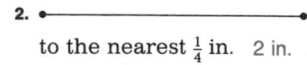

The length of the longer screw to the nearest $\frac{1}{4}$ **inch** is $1\frac{1}{4}$ in.

The length of the shorter screw to the nearest $\frac{1}{4}$ **inch** is 1 in.

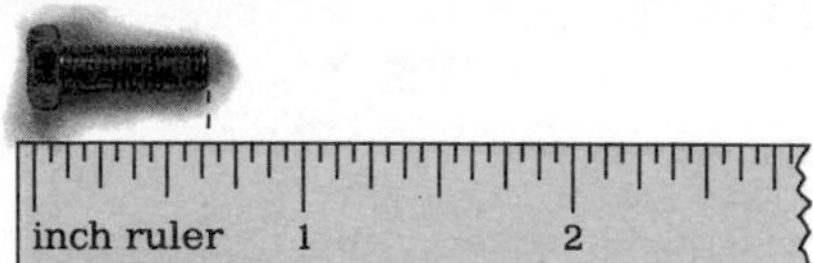


The length of the bolt to the nearest $\frac{1}{4}$ inch is $\frac{3}{4}$ in.

The length of the bolt to the nearest $\frac{1}{8}$ **inch** is $\frac{5}{8}$ in.

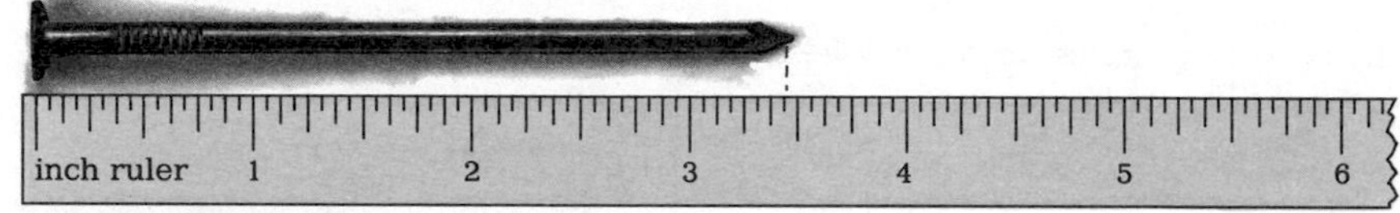


The length of the nail to the nearest $\frac{1}{8}$ inch is $3\frac{1}{2}$ in.

The length of the nail to the nearest $\frac{1}{16}$ **inch** is $3\frac{7}{16}$ in.

**Warm Up** Measure the segments.

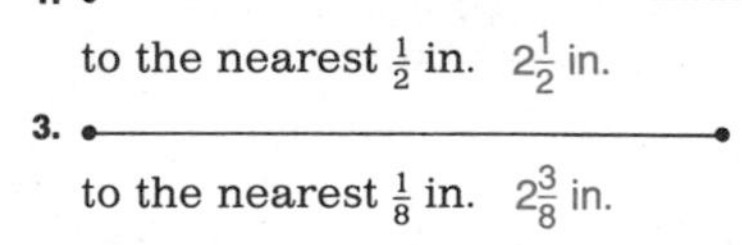

1. to the nearest $\frac{1}{2}$ in. $2\frac{1}{2}$ in.
2. to the nearest $\frac{1}{4}$ in. 2 in.
3. to the nearest $\frac{1}{8}$ in. $2\frac{3}{8}$ in.
4. to the nearest $\frac{1}{16}$ in. $2\frac{5}{16}$ in.



## Follow Up

### Reteaching

Draw a unit length on the chalkboard. Then, as you divide the unit into halves, then fourths, eighths, and sixteenths, discuss the relationship between each segment. Then have students look at a ruler and relate each of the subunits on the chalkboard with the subunits on the ruler. Use an overhead projector with a transparent ruler marked in $\frac{1}{16}$ in. segments and ask for volunteers to show how to measure to the nearest inch, $\frac{1}{2}$ in., $\frac{1}{4}$ in., and $\frac{1}{16}$ in.

### Enrichment

Have each student measure his or her normal walking step. Then have students use this measurement and the number of feet or inches in a mile to estimate the number of steps they would take in walking 1 mi. After students have made this calculation, they could estimate a distance of 1 mi, and then check their estimates with the odometer of a car. This estimate could also be checked by walking around the school track if the exact length is known.

| Assignment Guide | Minimum | Average | Extended |
|---|---|---|---|
| page 389 | 1–20, SK | 1–20, SK | 1–23, SK |

Measure each segment to the fraction of an inch named.

1. to the nearest $\frac{1}{2}$ in. $4\frac{1}{2}$ in.
2. to the nearest $\frac{1}{4}$ in. $3\frac{3}{4}$ in.
3. to the nearest $\frac{1}{8}$ in. $4\frac{5}{8}$ in.
4. to the nearest $\frac{1}{16}$ in. $4\frac{7}{16}$ in.

Draw a segment with the length given. Student constructions

| | | | |
|---|---|---|---|
| 5. 3 in. | 6. $2\frac{1}{2}$ in. | 7. 4 in. | 8. $5\frac{1}{2}$ in. |
| 9. $2\frac{1}{4}$ in. | 10. $4\frac{3}{4}$ in. | 11. $\frac{2}{4}$ in. | 12. $3\frac{1}{8}$ in. |
| 13. $2\frac{3}{8}$ in. | 14. $\frac{5}{8}$ in. | 15. $6\frac{7}{8}$ in. | 16. $\frac{6}{8}$ in. |
| 17. $4\frac{7}{16}$ in. | 18. $3\frac{3}{16}$ in. | 19. $4\frac{9}{16}$ in. | 20. $1\frac{15}{16}$ in. |

★ 21. A segment is midway between $4\frac{3}{4}$ in. and 5 in. long. What is the length of the segment? $4\frac{7}{8}$ in.

★ 22. A segment is midway between $3\frac{1}{8}$ in. and $3\frac{1}{4}$ in. long. What is the length of the segment? $3\frac{3}{16}$ in.

★ 23. A segment is midway between $2\frac{7}{16}$ in. and $2\frac{1}{2}$ in. long. What is the length of the segment? $2\frac{15}{32}$ in.

## Skillkeeper

Give the opposite of each integer.

1. $^-16$ $^+16$ 2. $^+12$ $^-12$ 3. $^-43$ $^+43$ 4. $^-2$ $^+2$ 5. $^+6$ $^-6$ 6. $^-10$ $^+10$

Write > or < for each ●.

7. $^+5$ ● $^+6$ < 8. $^-7$ ● $^+1$ < 9. 0 ● $^-3$ > 10. $^-2$ ● $^-6$ > 11. $^-5$ ● $^+4$ <

Find the sums and differences.

12. $^+3 + {}^-7$ $^-4$ 13. $^+4 + {}^-2$ $^+2$ 14. $^+4 - {}^+5$ $^-1$ 15. $^+6 - {}^-1$ $^+7$

16. $^-5 + {}^-3$ $^-8$ 17. $^+2 - {}^-6$ $^+8$ 18. $^-7 - {}^-1$ $^-6$ 19. $^+7 + {}^-6$ $^+1$



## Using Page 389

**Exercises 1–20** Caution students to be careful as they measure these segments and to be sure they are aligning their rulers correctly. Make sure they understand the meaning of the marks on the rulers. Emphasize the necessity for accurate placement of rulers and accurate reading of the measurements. Note that answers may vary slightly according to the rulers used.

**Exercises 21–23** If students seem to need a hint with these exercises, suggest that they think about the given measurements as fractions with a common denominator.

**Skillkeeper** These skills were originally taught in Chapter 15.

**Reteaching Supplement**, page 92

Name ______ To follow text page 389

**Inches and Fractions**

These show inches. This is $\frac{1}{4}$ inch. This is $\frac{1}{4}$ inch. This is $\frac{1}{4}$ inch. There are 2 $\frac{1}{2}$ inches in each inch. There are 4 $\frac{1}{4}$ inches in each inch. There are 8 $\frac{1}{8}$ inches in each inch.

Measure each segment to the fraction of an inch named.

1. Nearest $\frac{1}{2}$ inch $1\frac{1}{2}$ inches
2. Nearest $\frac{1}{4}$ inch $2\frac{1}{4}$ inches
3. Nearest $\frac{1}{8}$ inch $1\frac{3}{8}$ inches
4. Nearest $\frac{1}{4}$ inch $2\frac{3}{4}$ inches
5. Nearest inch 3 inches
6. Nearest $\frac{1}{2}$ inch $2\frac{1}{2}$ inches

Draw a line segment with the given length.

7. $1\frac{3}{4}$ in.
8. $2\frac{5}{8}$ in.
9. $\frac{1}{2}$ in.
10. $\frac{7}{8}$ in.
11. $5\frac{3}{8}$ in.

**Enrichment Supplement**, page 92

Name ______ To follow text page 389

**A Measurement Hunt**

Choose a friend and have a measurement hunt. Find objects you estimate to be the given length. Then measure to find the actual length. Measure the actual length to the nearest $\frac{1}{4}$ in. The winner is the one whose estimate is closest to the actual length. **Answers will vary.**

| Length | You: Object | You: Length (nearest $\frac{1}{4}$ in.) | Your Friend: Object | Your Friend: Length (nearest $\frac{1}{4}$ in.) |
|---|---|---|---|---|
| 1. 6 in. | | | | |
| 2. 12 in. | | | | |
| 3. $\frac{1}{2}$ in. | | | | |
| 4. 2 in. | | | | |
| 5. 18 in. | | | | |
| 6. $2\frac{1}{2}$ in. | | | | |

On another piece of paper, use a straightedge (*not* a ruler) to draw a line segment you estimate to be the length given. Then use a ruler to measure your line segment to the nearest $\frac{1}{8}$ in. Score one point if your segment is within $\frac{1}{8}$ in. of the given length. Compare your score to a friend's. **Answers will vary.**

| | Actual length | Score | | Actual length | Score |
|---|---|---|---|---|---|
| 7. 2 in. | | | 10. $5\frac{1}{8}$ in. | | |
| 8. $7\frac{1}{2}$ in. | | | 11. $10\frac{1}{4}$ in. | | |
| 9. $3\frac{3}{4}$ in. | | | 12. $12\frac{5}{8}$ in. | | |

Total points: ______

13. On another piece of paper, draw a rectangle with an area of 20 in.². Measure to find the actual area. If the area of your rectangle is not between 16 and 24 in.², try drawing another one.

**Practice Supplement**, page 145

Name ______ To follow text page 389

**Inches and Fractions**

Measure each line segment.

1. to the nearest $\frac{1}{2}$ in. $2\frac{1}{2}$ in.
2. to the nearest $\frac{1}{4}$ in. $3\frac{3}{4}$ in.
3. to the nearest $\frac{1}{8}$ in. $2\frac{3}{8}$ in.
4. to the nearest $\frac{1}{16}$ in. $3\frac{3}{16}$ in.

Draw a segment with the given length.

5. 5 in.
6. $6\frac{1}{4}$ in.
7. $5\frac{3}{4}$ in.
8. $4\frac{5}{16}$ in.
9. $1\frac{1}{8}$ in. 10. 2 in.
11. $\frac{1}{2}$ in. 12. $\frac{15}{16}$ in.
13. $2\frac{1}{4}$ in. 14. $\frac{7}{8}$ in.
15. $1\frac{5}{16}$ in. 16. $1\frac{1}{2}$ in.
17. $1\frac{5}{8}$ in. 18. $2\frac{1}{16}$ in.
19. $1\frac{3}{8}$ in. 20. 1 in.

**Quick Review** Students give the number that makes each equation true.

36 ÷ [3] = 12 12 × 6 = 60 + [12] 4 × 12 = 6 × [8] 2 × 12 = [20] + 4

5 × 12 = 50 + [10] 7 × 4 = 24 + [4] 24 − 12 = 12 × [1]

**Lesson Focus** To add, subtract, or multiply measures given in two customary units; to estimate length using customary units

## Ideas for Getting Started

Give students a few minutes to try to find the answer to this problem.

> A high school basketball player was 6 ft 2 in. tall. An elementary school basketball player was 4 ft 9 in. tall. How much taller was the high school basketball player?

Some students may try to change the measurements to inches, perform the operations, and then change back to feet and inches. Others may attempt to do the operations in feet and inches. Discuss the techniques students used in finding their answers or the difficulties they encountered in solving the problem.

## Using Page 390

**Motivational Problem** Discuss briefly any experiences students have had braiding plastic strips to make "ropes." Then have them focus on the questions that are asked in problems A, B, and C. For question A ask: "How long is Nancy's rope?" (1 ft 9 in. long) "How long is Beth's rope?" (3 ft 7 in. long) "What must we do to find the length of the two ropes together?" (add) For question B ask: "What must we do to compare and find how much longer Beth's rope is than Nancy's?" (subtract) For question C ask: "How many times as long as Nancy's rope is Carla's?" (3 times as long) "How can we find the length of Carla's rope if we know the length of Nancy's rope?" (Multiply the length of Nancy's rope by 3.)

**Lesson Development** Work each problem on the chalkboard and focus on the trading needed for each answer. Compare the solutions to these examples with students' work on the problem in the Getting Started activity. Discuss how computing units of length is similar to adding, subtracting, and multiplying whole numbers.

**Exercises 1–9** As you assign these exercises, tell students to write the answer in simplest form. If students have difficulties, review the relationship between feet and inches, yards and feet, and yards and inches. Also review the trading procedures if necessary.

## Computing with Lengths

At camp, Nancy braided plastic strips to make a colorful rope 1 ft 9 in. long. Beth made a rope 3 ft 7 in. long.

**A.** How long a rope will they have if they fasten their two ropes together?

```
   1 ft  9 in.
 + 3 ft  7 in.
   4 ft 16 in.
```

More than 1 foot. 16 in. = 1 ft 4 in.

The combined rope will be 5 ft 4 in. long.

**B.** How much longer is Beth's rope than Nancy's?

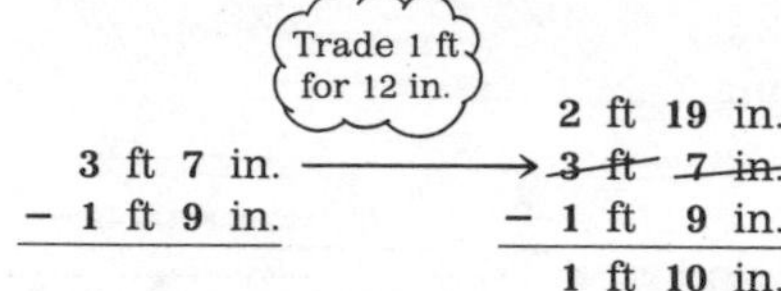

Trade 1 ft for 12 in.

```
   3 ft 7 in.   →     2 ft 19 in.
 − 1 ft 9 in.         3 ft  7 in. (crossed out)
                    − 1 ft  9 in.
                      1 ft 10 in.
```

Beth's rope is 1 ft 10 in. longer.

**C.** Carla made a rope 3 times as long as Nancy's. How long is it?

```
    1 ft  9 in.
 ×        3
    3 ft 27 in.
 or 5 ft  3 in.
```

27 in. is 2 ft 3 in.

Carla's rope is 5 ft 3 in. long.

Find the sum, difference, or product.

| | | |
|---|---|---|
| **1.** 4 ft 8 in. + 3 ft 7 in. = 8 ft 3 in. | **2.** 4 yd 2 ft + 7 yd 2 ft = 12 yd 1 ft | **3.** 3 ft 11 in. + 2 ft 10 in. = 6 ft 9 in. |
| **4.** 6 ft 3 in. − 2 ft 7 in. = 3 ft 8 in. | **5.** 3 ft 6 in. − 1 ft 9 in. = 1 ft 9 in. | **6.** 5 yd 1 ft − 2 yd 2 ft = 2 yd 2 ft |
| **7.** 3 ft 4 in. × 2 = 6 ft 8 in. | **8.** 6 ft 8 in. × 3 = 20 ft | **9.** 5 yd 2 ft × 4 = 22 yd 2 ft |

390

## Follow Up

### Reteaching

Have students find and measure the length of two sticks. "What is the total length of the two sticks? How much longer is one stick than the other?" Encourage students to find the answers first by adding or subtracting the two measures and then to check their answers by measuring. For students who have difficulty with the computations, review the conversion relationships and discuss how to carry out the trading.

### Enrichment

Provide students with the following measurements and have them match Column A to Column B.

| Column A | Column B |
|---|---|
| C 1. 3 ft 27 in. | A 2 ft 4 in. |
| F 2. 2 yd 2 ft | B 12 in. |
| A 3. 28 in. | C 1 yd 27 in. |
| G 4. 108 in. | D 3 ft 28 in. |
| E 5. 72 in. | E 2 yd |
| B 6. 1 ft | F 96 in. |
| D 7. 5 ft 4 in. | G 3 yd |

| Assignment Guide | Minimum | Average | Extended |
|---|---|---|---|
| page 390 | 1–9 | 1–9 | 1–9 |
| page 391 | 1–6 | 1–6 | 1–7 |

## Estimating with Customary Units

First estimate the length. Then measure the length of the object. Estimates will vary.

1\. Your estimate: ■ in.
Actual measure: ■ in. (to the nearest $\frac{1}{2}$ in.) $5\frac{1}{2}$

2\. Pencil Lead
Your estimate: ■ in.
Actual measure: ■ in. (to the nearest $\frac{1}{4}$ in.) 3

3\. Your estimate: ■ in.
Actual measure: ■ in. (to the nearest $\frac{1}{8}$ in.) $4\frac{2}{8}$ or $4\frac{1}{4}$

4\. Your estimate: ■ in.
Actual measure: ■ in. (to the nearest $\frac{1}{16}$ in.) 2

First estimate. Then measure the actual length. Answers will vary.

5\. Your arm span
Your estimate: ■ ft ■ in.
Actual measure: ■ ft ■ in.
(to the nearest $\frac{1}{2}$ in.)

6\. Length of your normal step
Your estimate: ■ ft ■ in.
Actual measure: ■ ft ■ in.
(to the nearest inch)

★ 7. Estimate a distance of 50 ft by stepping it off. Measure to see by how many feet or inches your estimate varies from the measured distance. Answers will vary.



## Using Page 391

**Lesson Development** Select an object such as a book and ask students to estimate the width in inches. After students have had an opportunity to make their estimates, measure the book and give its measurement to the nearest inch, to the nearest $\frac{1}{2}$ inch, and to the nearest $\frac{1}{4}$ inch. Have students estimate the length of the objects pictured on the page and then check the estimates by measuring to the nearest unit suggested.

**Exercises 1–4** Note that students are to make their estimates using illustrations of these objects. As an alternative, provide the actual objects for these exercises.

**Exercises 5–6** These exercises involve estimating and measuring lengths of actual distances or objects in the classroom. If possible, let students work in small groups to complete these exercises.

**Exercise 7** Encourage groups of students to try to step off a distance close to 50 ft. To extend this exercise, let students count steps and devise a way to find out the average length of one of their steps.

### Reteaching Supplement, page 93

Name ______ To follow text page 390

**Computing with Lengths**

12 inches = 1 foot
3 feet = 1 yard
36 inches = 1 yard

Example: (Trade.)
4 yd 1 ft
− 2 yd 2 ft

3 yd 4 ft (1 less yard, 3 more feet, 1 + 3 = 4)
− 2 yd 2 ft
1 yd 2 ft

Example:
6 ft 9 in.
+ 4 ft 6 in.
10 ft 15 in. (more than 12 in.) (Trade.)

(Add the inches. Then add the feet.)
6 ft 9 in.
+ 4 ft 6 in.
10 ft 15 in. =
11 ft 3 in.
(15 in. = 12 in. + 3 in. = 1 ft 3 in.)

Find the sum, difference, or product.

1\. 5 yd − 2 yd 1 ft → **2 yd 2 ft** (4 yd 3 ft − 2 yd 1 ft → 2 yd 2 ft)
2\. 2 yd 2 ft + 3 yd 2 ft → **6 yd 1 ft**
3\. 4 ft 8 in. + 6 ft 9 in. → **11 ft 5 in.**
4\. 3 yd 7 in. − 1 yd 4 in. → **2 yd 3 in.**
5\. 2 yd 1 ft + 6 yd 2 ft → **9 yd**
6\. 12 ft 6 in. − 8 ft 9 in. → **3 ft 9 in.**
7\. 4 yd 1 ft − 1 yd 2 ft → **2 yd 2 ft**
8\. 3 ft 9 in. − 1 ft 11 in. → **1 ft 10 in.**
9\. 8 ft 10 in. + 6 ft 11 in. → **15 ft 9 in.**
10\. 3 ft 6 in. × 3 → **10 ft 6 in.** (Multiply first, then change inches to feet.)
11\. 2 yd 2 ft × 6 → **16 yd**
12\. 5 ft 8 in. × 6 → **34 ft**

### Enrichment Supplement, page 93

Name ______ To follow text page 390

**More Length Problems**

| Riverside College Basketball Starting Lineup | |
|---|---|
| Player | Height |
| J. Wilkerson | 6 ft 4 in. |
| R. Washington | 6 ft 7 in. |
| T. Johnson | 6 ft 8 in. |
| F. Irving | 6 ft 10 in. |
| T. Gonzalez | 7 ft 1 in. |

1\. What is the average height (to the nearest $\frac{1}{2}$ in.) of the players in the starting lineup? **6 ft $8\frac{1}{2}$ in.**

2\. What is the difference in height between the tallest player and the shortest player? **9 in.**

3\. The rim of the basket is 10 ft from the ground. How high would T. Gonzalez have to jump for his head to hit the rim? **2 ft 11 in.**

4\. On another team 4 of the 5 players were the same height as 4 of the players on Riverside's team. Their tallest player was $2\frac{1}{2}$ in. shorter than the tallest player on Riverside's team. How much less is the average height of this other team than the average height of Riverside's team? **$\frac{1}{2}$ in.**

**Answers will vary for problems 5, 6, and 8.**

5\. Hundreds of years ago the average man was 5 ft 6 in. tall. Measure your height to the nearest inch. How much taller or shorter are you than 5 ft 6 in.? ______

6\. Tiny waists were once very fashionable. The smallest waist recorded in modern times was 13 in. Measure your waist to the nearest $\frac{1}{2}$ in. How much larger is your waist? ______

7\. The longest moustache ever grown was 102 in. long. The longest beard was $17\frac{1}{2}$ ft. How much longer was the beard than the moustache? **9 ft**

8\. The tallest man ever measured stood 8 ft 11 in. The length of his arm, shoulder to fingertip, was about 3 yd 1 in. Measure the length of your arm. How much shorter is your arm? ______

### Practice Supplement, page 146

Name ______ To follow text page 390

**Computing with Lengths**

Find the sum.

1\. 2 ft 9 in. + 3 ft 5 in. → **6 ft 2 in.**
2\. 5 ft 11 in. + 6 ft 9 in. → **12 ft 8 in.**
3\. 1 ft 6 in. + 4 ft 6 in. → **6 ft**
4\. 4 yd 2 ft + 3 yd 2 ft → **8 yd 1 ft**
5\. 1 yd 1 ft + 5 yd 2 ft → **7 yd**
6\. 7 ft 8 in. + 1 ft 5 in. → **9 ft 1 in.**

Find the difference.

7\. 9 ft 2 in. − 7 ft 6 in. → **1 ft 8 in.**
8\. 3 ft 7 in. − 2 ft 11 in. → **8 in.**
9\. 6 ft 4 in. − 4 ft 10 in. → **1 ft 6 in.**
10\. 6 yd 1 ft − 3 yd 2 ft → **2 yd 2 ft**
11\. 5 yd 5 in. − 1 yd 9 in. → **3 yd 32 in.**
12\. 7 yd 1 in. − 2 yd 2 in. → **4 yd 35 in.**

Find the product.

13\. 4 ft 4 in. × 4 → **17 ft 4 in.**
14\. 2 ft 3 in. × 3 → **6 ft 9 in.**
15\. 1 ft 9 in. × 2 → **3 ft 6 in.**
16\. 3 ft 2 in. × 7 → **22 ft 2 in.**
17\. 5 yd 1 ft × 3 → **16 yd**
18\. 3 yd 2 ft × 4 → **14 yd 2 ft**

**Quick Review** Students estimate answers by rounding to the nearest ten or hundred.

21 × 9 200 14 × 89 900 284 ÷ 7 40 499 ÷ 95 5 76 × 11 800
180 ÷ 22 10 25 × 16 600 58 × 27 180 877 ÷ 33 30

**Lesson Focus** To use data from a picture to solve word problems involving perimeter, area, volume, and surface area

**Suggested Materials** Graph paper (TRB p. 270)

## Ideas for Getting Started

Provide a sheet of graph paper for each student and present the following problem:

> A rectangular pen is to be made from 24 ft of fence. What is the largest area such a pen can have (if sides are whole number lengths)?

Ask for suggestions from students about ways to solve this problem. Encourage them to use the graph paper to draw a picture. As students make suggestions regarding the solution, use the opportunity to evaluate their understanding of perimeter and area. Have students count the squares to determine the area and then check by multiplying the length of the rectangle by the width. Remind them to add the length of each of the sides of the figures to find the perimeter.

## Using Page 392

**Lesson Development** Refer to the display box at the top of the page giving review information about perimeter and area. Ask a volunteer to read exercise 1. "What question is asked?" (What is the area of the garden?) "What data do we need?" (the length and the width of the garden) "Is the data stated in the problem?" (no) "Can we get the data from the picture?" (yes) Review the 5-Point Checklist and emphasize that the data needed for these problems can be found in the pictures.

**Exercises 1–8** Remind students that if the length and width is given in feet, the area should be given in square feet. If length and width are given in yards, the area will be square yards, and so on.

QUESTION
DATA
PLAN
ANSWER
CHECK

## Problem Solving: Using Data from a Picture

Solve. Use data from the pictures as needed.

**Perimeter and Area**

The **perimeter** of a rectangle is the distance around it.

$l$ = 7 ft

$w$ = 4 ft

$P = 2(l + w)$

$P = 7 + 4 + 7 + 4 = 22$ ft

The **area** of a rectangle is the number of square units it takes to cover it.

$A = l \times w$
$A = 7 \times 4$

Area = 28 ft² (square feet)

1. What is the area of the garden in square feet? 180 ft²

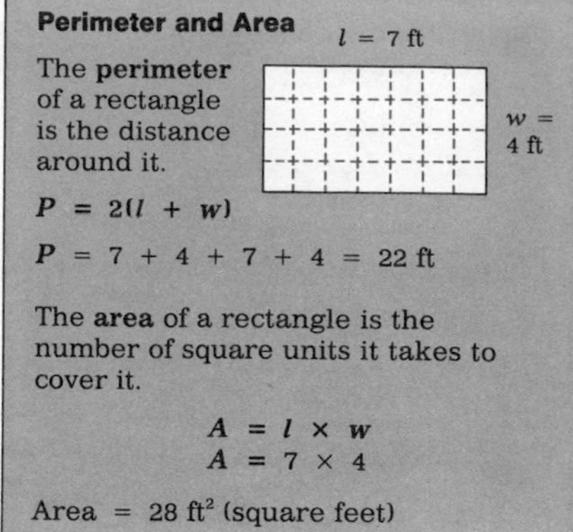

2. How many feet of fencing are needed to build a fence around the garden? 54 ft
3. What is the area of the picture in square inches? 384 in.²
4. How much framing board would be needed to go around the picture? Give the answer in feet and inches. 6 ft 8 in.

5. The furniture in the room pictured at the right uses about 39 yd² of floor area. How much open floor space is left in the room? 69 yd²
6. Baseboard is needed to go around all except the fireplace side of the room. How many yards will be needed? 33 yd

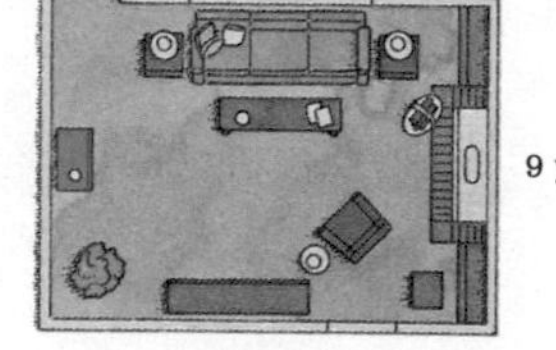


7. A bike path equal in total length to the perimeter of the park is to be made around the park. How long will the path be? 46 mi
8. The park has 8 mi² of lakes. What is the land area of the park? 118 mi²

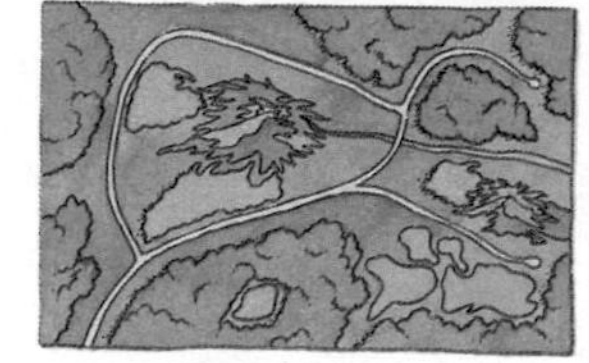


392

## Follow Up

### Reteaching

Duplicate the following figures on graph paper (TRB p. 270). Have students count the squares to find the perimeter and area of each figure.

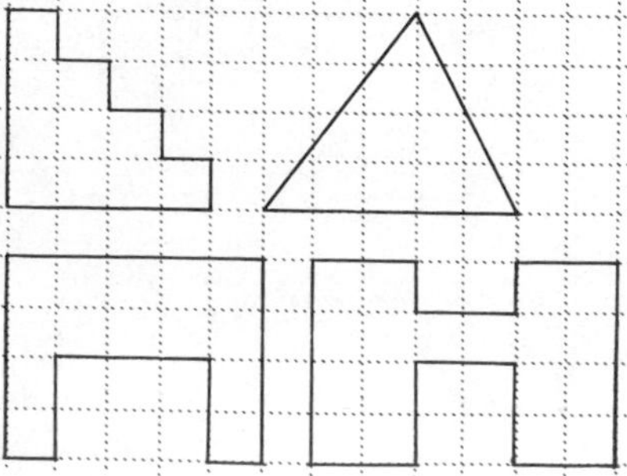

### Enrichment

Provide students with graph paper (TRB p. 270) and several irregular shapes such as the one below. Challenge them to determine the area and the perimeter.

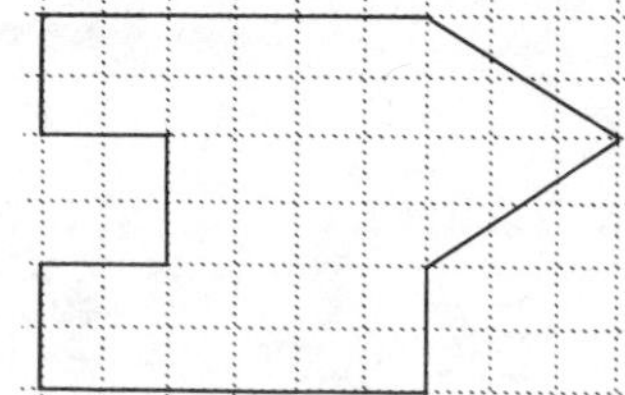

| Assignment Guide | | | |
|---|---|---|---|
| | Minimum | Average | Extended |
| pages 392–393 | 1–14 | 1–16 | 1–17 |

9. What is the volume of the storage chest? 24 ft³

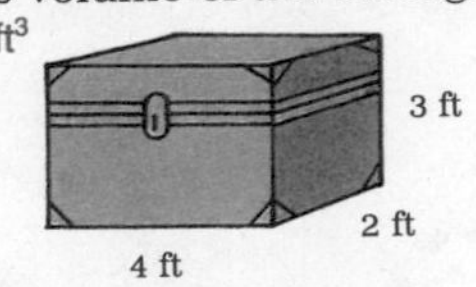


10. How many square feet of decorative paper will it take to cover it? 52 ft²

11. How much paper would it take to cover the surface of the shipping box?
784 in.²

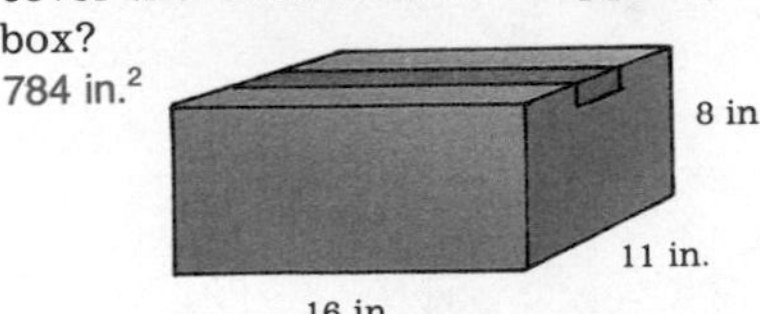


12. What is the volume of the shipping box above? 1,408 in.³

13. How many cubic inches of space will the stereo speaker use when it is packed for shipping? 3,696 in.³

14. All faces of the stereo speaker except the front and back are to be varnished. How many square inches is this? 864 in.²

★ 15. Concrete is often sold by the cubic yard. About how many cubic yards of concrete are needed for a sidewalk 40 ft long, 3 ft wide, and 4 in. thick (high)?
about $1\frac{1}{2}$ yd³

16. **DATA HUNT** How many cubic feet of air are in your classroom for each person in your class?
Answers will vary.

17. **Try This** A cord of wood is enough wood to make a stack 8 ft by 4 ft by 4 ft. Mr. Woodburner was charged \$120 per cord for a load of wood. The load of wood made a stack 12 ft long, 3 ft wide, and 4 ft high. How much should Mr. Woodburner have paid for this much wood? \$135

**Volume and Surface Area**

The **volume** of a box is the number of unit cubes it takes to fill it.

height: 3 ft
width: 2 ft
length: 4 ft

$V = l \times w \times h$

$V = 4 \times 2 \times 3$

Volume = 24 ft³ (cubic feet)

The **surface area** of a box is the sum of the areas of each of its faces.

s.a. = 12 + 12 + 6 + 6 + 8 + 8
s.a. = 52 ft²

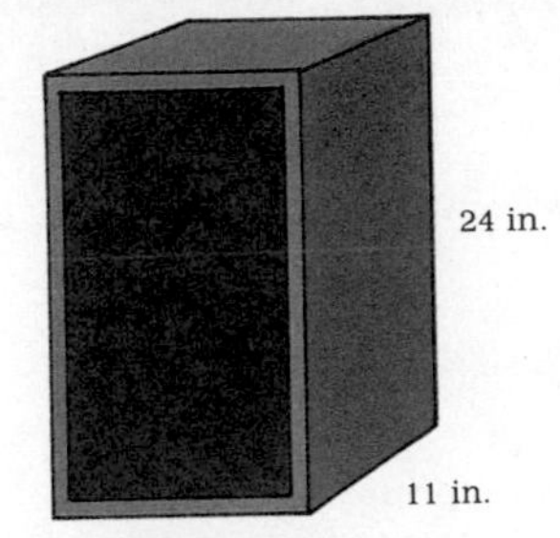

## Using Page 393

**Exercises 9–14** Remind students that volume should be given in cubic units.

**Exercise 15** Make sure that students understand that three dimensions are involved in the calculation for this problem, and that the answer should be given in cubic yards.

**Data Hunt** If necessary, explain that dividing the number of cubic feet by the number of students will give the number of cubic feet of air for each person.

**Try This** A possible strategy, Choose the Operations, was taught on page 16.

**Discussion** "What question is asked in the problem?" (How much should Mr. Woodburner have paid for his wood?) "What are the dimensions of a stacked cord of wood?" (8 ft × 4 ft × 4 ft) "What is the cost of a cord of wood?" (\$120) "What were the dimensions of the stack of wood Mr. Woodburner received?" (12 ft by 3 ft by 4 ft) "As you plan a solution, what do you need to know about Mr. Woodburner's wood?" (How many cords did he receive?) "How can you use volume to help find this answer?" (Compare the volume of Mr. Woodburner's wood with the volume of a cord of wood.)

**Solution** Mr. Woodburner should have paid \$135 for his wood. A cord of wood is 128 ft³; the volume of Mr. Woodburner's wood was 12 × 3 × 4 or 144 ft³. To find the number of cords, divide 144 by 128 = 1.125 cords. 1.125 × \$120 per cord = \$135.

**Reteaching Supplement,** page 94

Name ______ To follow text page 393

**Problem Solving: Using Data from a Picture**

Solve. Use data from the pictures as needed.

1. What is the total area covered by the garage? 2,000 ft²
(Find the length and the width. Use A = l × w.)
2. Each wall of the garage is 1 ft thick. What is the inside area of the garage? 1,824 ft²
(Subtract 2 ft from each outside length and width.)
3. A driveway is 35 ft long and as wide as the garage. What is the area of the driveway? 1,400 ft²
4. A furniture refinisher charges \$1.50 per square foot. What is the cost to refinish the chest? \$48
(Find the area of all 6 sides.)
5. What is the approximate volume of the chest? 12 ft³
6. What is the volume of the fish tank? 7,200 in.³

Garage Plans; Storage; Storage; 50 ft; 40 ft; 2 ft; 3 ft; 2 ft; 20 in.; 12 in.; 30 in.

**Enrichment Supplement,** page 94

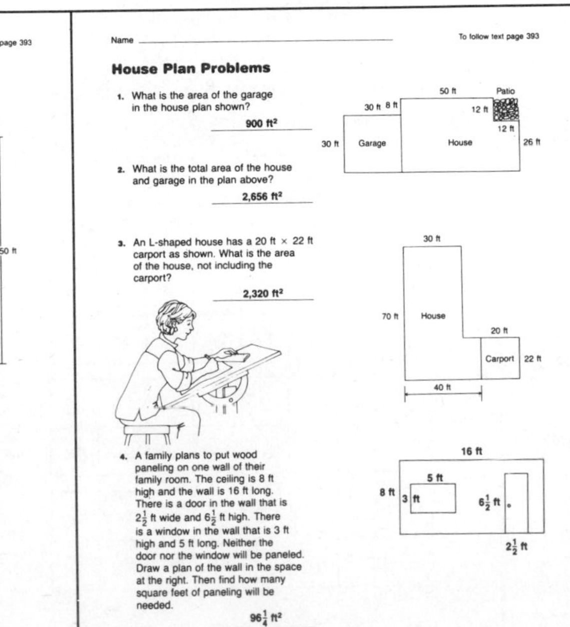
Name ______ To follow text page 393

**House Plan Problems**

1. What is the area of the garage in the house plan shown? 900 ft²
2. What is the total area of the house and garage in the plan above? 2,656 ft²
3. An L-shaped house has a 20 ft × 22 ft carport as shown. What is the area of the house, not including the carport? 2,320 ft²
4. A family plans to put wood paneling on one wall of their family room. The ceiling is 8 ft high and the wall is 16 ft long. There is a door in the wall that is $2\frac{1}{2}$ ft wide and $6\frac{1}{2}$ ft high. There is a window in the wall that is 3 ft high and 5 ft long. Neither the door nor the window will be paneled. Draw a plan of the wall in the space at the right. Then find how many square feet of paneling will be needed. $96\frac{1}{4}$ ft²



**Practice Supplement,** page 147

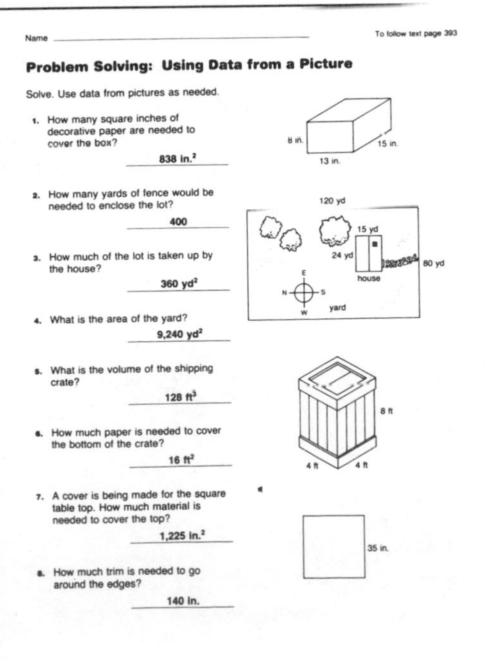
Name ______ To follow text page 393

**Problem Solving: Using Data from a Picture**

Solve. Use data from pictures as needed.

1. How many square inches of decorative paper are needed to cover the box? 838 in.²
2. How many yards of fence would be needed to enclose the lot? 400
3. How much of the lot is taken up by the house? 360 yd²
4. What is the area of the yard? 9,240 yd²
5. What is the volume of the shipping crate? 128 ft³
6. How much paper is needed to cover the bottom of the crate? 16 ft²
7. A cover is being made for the square table top. How much material is needed to cover the top? 1,225 in.²
8. How much trim is needed to go around the edges? 140 in.

**Quick Review** Students subtract the fractions below, giving answers in lowest terms.

$\frac{4}{5} - \frac{1}{3}$ $\mathbf{\frac{7}{15}}$ $\frac{3}{4} - \frac{1}{2}$ $\mathbf{\frac{1}{4}}$ $\frac{4}{9} - \frac{1}{9}$ $\mathbf{\frac{1}{3}}$ $\frac{1}{2} - \frac{1}{8}$ $\mathbf{\frac{3}{8}}$ $\frac{3}{10} - \frac{1}{5}$ $\mathbf{\frac{1}{10}}$
$\frac{9}{10} - \frac{1}{2}$ $\mathbf{\frac{2}{5}}$ $\frac{7}{8} - \frac{5}{16}$ $\mathbf{\frac{9}{16}}$ $\frac{1}{3} - \frac{2}{9}$ $\mathbf{\frac{1}{9}}$ $\frac{4}{5} - \frac{7}{10}$ $\mathbf{\frac{1}{10}}$

**Lesson Focus** To find liquid measure in customary units; to solve word problems involving customary units

**Suggested Materials** Cup, pint, quart, and gallon containers

## Ideas for Getting Started

Label the containers and put them on display in the classroom. Discuss with students situations in which these capacity containers are used. Possible uses might include: jars for canning, milk or juice cartons or bottles, containers for holding gasoline and oil for automobiles (quarts and gallons), and containers for measuring ingredients in recipes.

## Using Page 394

**Lesson Development** Direct students' attention to the display boxes at the top of the page. "How many tablespoons are in 1 fluid ounce?" (2) "A cup will fill how many 1-oz containers?" (8) "How many tablespoons would that be?" (16) "A pint will fill how many cups?" (2) "A quart will fill how many pints?" (2) "How many cups would that be?" (4) "A gallon will fill how many quarts?" (4) "How many pints are in a gallon?" (8) "How many cups are in a gallon?" (16) If students have difficulty with these units, illustrations like the ones below can be helpful.

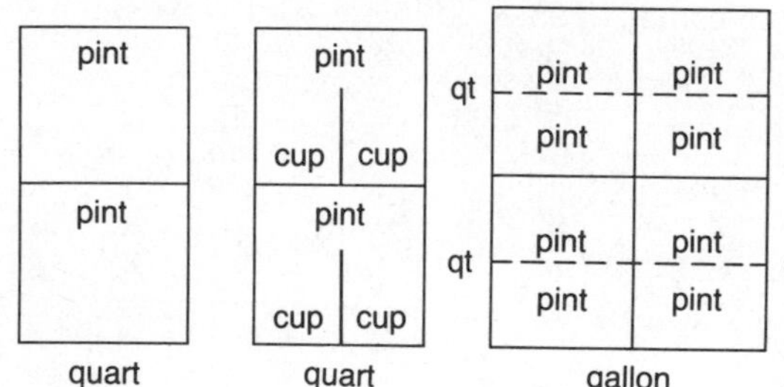


**Exercises 1–12** For these exercises students use the relationships pictured on the page. If necessary, help students reason as follows: Since 1 ounce equals 2 tablespoons, then 2 ounces would be 4 tablespoons.

**Exercises 13–18** These exercises extend the exercises above. Students often find it useful to think in terms of how many of one container another container can fill.

## Capacity

A **fluid ounce** (oz) is a basic customary unit of capacity.

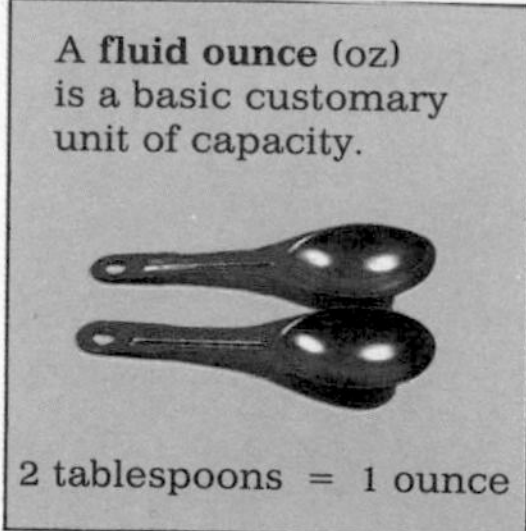

2 tablespoons = 1 ounce

A **cup** (c) holds 8 oz.

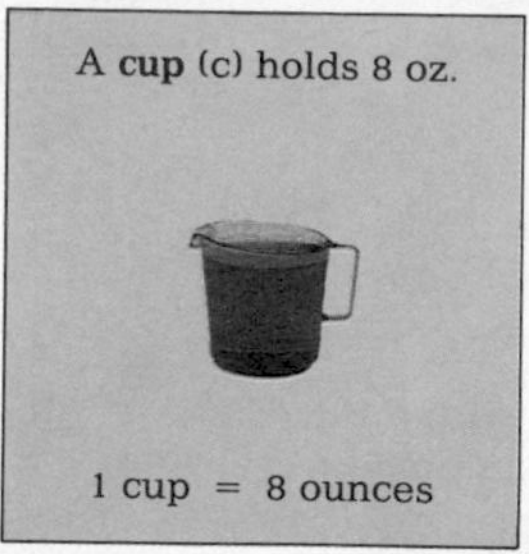

1 cup = 8 ounces

A **pint** (pt) holds 2 c.

1 pint = 2 cups

A **quart** (qt) holds 2 pt.

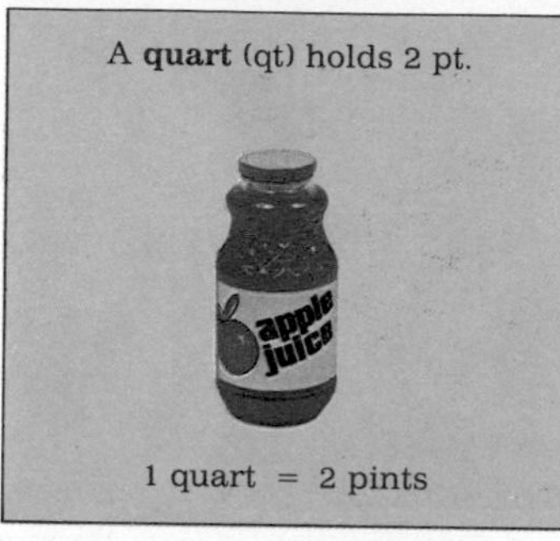


1 quart = 2 pints

A **gallon** (gal) holds 4 qt.

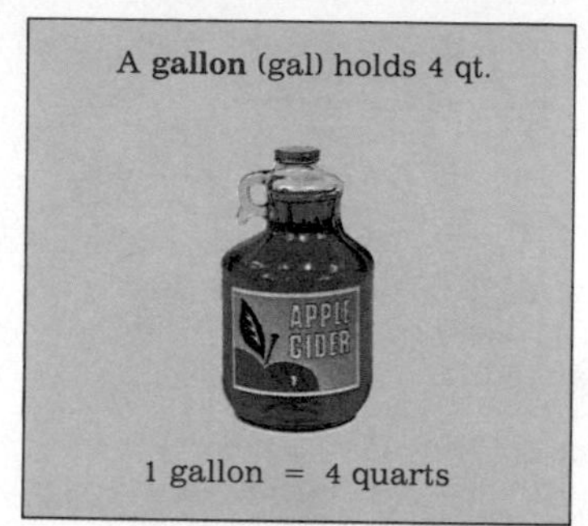


1 gallon = 4 quarts

Give the missing numbers.

**1.** 2 oz = ■ tablespoons 4
**2.** 2 c = ■ oz 16
**3.** 2 qt = ■ pt 4
**4.** 3 pt = ■ c 6
**5.** 2 gal = ■ qt 8
**6.** 1 qt = ■ c 4
**7.** 1 gal = ■ pt 8
**8.** 1 gal = ■ c 16
**9.** 8 qt = ■ gal 2
**10.** 4 c = ■ qt 1
**11.** $\frac{1}{2}$ pt = ■ c 1
**12.** $\frac{1}{2}$ gal = ■ qt 2
**13.** 1 cup of cooking oil fills ■ tablespoons. 16
**14.** A quart of milk fills ■ cups. 4
**15.** 1 gallon and 2 pints of limeade fill ■ cups. 20
**16.** 1 pint of cough syrup fills ■ tablespoons. 32
**17.** A gallon of honey fills ■ pint jars. 8
**18.** 2 pints and 2 cups of tomato juice fill ■ quarts. $1\frac{1}{2}$



## Follow Up

### Reteaching

Help students supply the missing numbers in the tables below.

| Pints | 1 | 2 | 3 | 4 | 5 | 6 |
|---|---|---|---|---|---|---|
| Cups | 2 | 4 | **6** | **8** | **10** | **12** |

| Cups | 1 | 2 | 3 | 4 | **5** | **6** |
|---|---|---|---|---|---|---|
| Ounces | 8 | 16 | **24** | **32** | 40 | 45 |

| Quarts | 1 | 2 | 3 | **4** | 5 | 6 |
|---|---|---|---|---|---|---|
| Cups | 4 | 8 | **12** | 16 | **20** | **24** |

| Gallons | 1 | **2** | 3 | 4 | 5 | 6 |
|---|---|---|---|---|---|---|
| Cups | 16 | 32 | **48** | **64** | **80** | **96** |

### Enrichment

Label several graduated containers for cups, pints, and quarts by a letter of the alphabet. Challenge students to estimate and record the estimated capacity for each container. Students then check their estimates by filling each container with water or sand to verify the capacity.

| | Assignment Guide | | |
|---|---|---|---|
| | Minimum | Average | Extended |
| page 394 | 1–18 | 1–18 | 1–18 |
| page 395 | 1–6 | 1–7 | 1–8 |

## Problem Solving: Practice

Solve.

1. Ned bought 6 pint bottles of grape juice. How many quarts of grape juice was this? 3 qt

2. How many cups of lemonade are in six 12-oz cans of lemonade? 9 c

3. Milk costs $2.24 a gallon. Is this more than or less than 49¢ per quart? How much more or less is it? 28¢ more

4. A container holds $1\frac{1}{2}$ gal of apple juice. How many quarts does it hold? 6 qt

5. A can holds 1 qt of orange juice. Another can holds 28 oz of juice. Which can holds more juice? How many ounces more does it hold? Quart can holds 4 oz more.

6. Estela paid 20¢ for $\frac{1}{2}$ pt of milk for her lunch. Her mother paid $1.12 for $\frac{1}{2}$ gal of milk. How much more or less per quart did Estela pay than her mother? Estela paid 24¢ a quart more.

7. A storage can measures 1 ft by 1 ft by 1 ft. If a gallon has a volume of 231 in.$^3$, how many gallons does the can hold? (Round the answer to the nearest tenth.) 7.5 gal

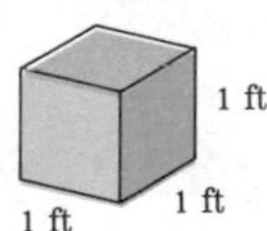

8. **Try This** Suppose you have a 4-qt jar and an 11-qt jar and a barrel of apple cider. There are no markings on either jar. How can you use these jars to get 5 qt of cider in the larger jar? See teaching notes.

395

## Using Page 395

**Lesson Development** Review the 5-Point Checklist in the logo at the top of the page. Tell students that these problems involve units of capacity and the relationships between them. After students have completed the problems, discuss each of the solutions.

**Try This** A possible strategy, Use Logical Reasoning, was taught on page 162.

**Discussion** Have students state the question in the problem in their own words. "What size jars do you have to work with?" (a 4-qt jar and an 11-qt jar) "Are there markings on the jars?" (no) "As you plan a solution, compare the jars you have with the amount you want to measure." (We have a 4-qt jar, but we want to measure 5 quarts.) "If you poured three 4-qt jars into the 11-qt jar, how much would be left in the 4-qt jar?"

**Solution** First, pour three 4-qt jars into the 11-qt jar. This leaves one quart in the 4-qt jar. Empty the 11-qt jar and pour the one quart into it. Then fill the 4-qt jar and pour this into the 11-qt jar, too. There will now be 5 quarts in the 11-qt jar.

### Reteaching Supplement, page 95

Name ______ To follow text page 394

**Capacity**

1 cup (c) 1 cup → 1 pint (pt) 1 pint → 1 quart (qt) 1 quart 1 quart 1 quart → 1 gallon (gal)

2 cups = 1 pint | 2 pints = 1 quart | 4 quarts = 1 gallon

Find the missing numbers.

1. 2 pt = **1** qt
2. 2 c = **1** pt
3. 4 qt = **1** gal
4. 12 qt = **3** gal
5. 6 pt = **3** qt
6. 8 c = **2** qt
7. 2 qt = **4** pt
8. 1 gal = **8** pt
9. 1 qt = **4** c
10. 2 gal = **8** qt
11. 10 pt = **5** qt
12. 8 pt = **16** c

Solve.

13. A cafeteria used 50 qt of milk one day. How many gallons were used? **$12\frac{1}{2}$**

14. A host served 20 cups of juice at a party. How many quarts were served? **5**

15. Mrs. Swanson made 3 gallons of tomato sauce. She froze the sauce in 1-pint containers. How many cartons did she use? **24**

16. Tanya estimates that each person at her party will drink 4 cups of punch. If 16 people are going to be at the party, how many quarts of punch are needed? **16**

### Enrichment Supplement, page 95

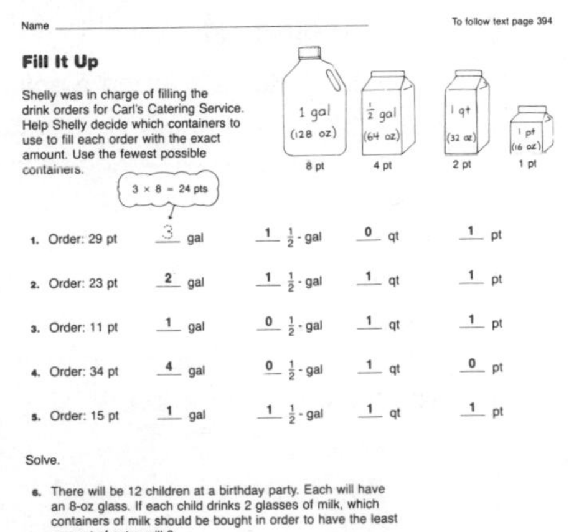
Name ______ To follow text page 394

**Fill It Up**

Shelly was in charge of filling the drink orders for Carl's Catering Service. Help Shelly decide which containers to use to fill each order with the exact amount. Use the fewest possible containers.



1. Order: 29 pt  3 gal  **1** $\frac{1}{2}$-gal  **0** qt  **1** pt
2. Order: 23 pt  **2** gal  **1** $\frac{1}{2}$-gal  **1** qt  **1** pt
3. Order: 11 pt  **1** gal  **0** $\frac{1}{2}$-gal  **1** qt  **1** pt
4. Order: 34 pt  **4** gal  **0** $\frac{1}{2}$-gal  **1** qt  **0** pt
5. Order: 15 pt  **1** gal  **1** $\frac{1}{2}$-gal  **1** qt  **1** pt

Solve.

6. There will be 12 children at a birthday party. Each will have an 8-oz glass. If each child drinks 2 glasses of milk, which containers of milk should be bought in order to have the least amount of extra milk? **1 gal, 1 $\frac{1}{2}$-gal**

7. Suppose the glasses in problem 6 only held 6 oz. Which milk containers should be bought? **1 gal, 1 pt**

8. A 1-gal container of milk regularly costs $2.24 but is on sale for $1.94. The $\frac{1}{2}$-gal size costs $1.25. How much less do you pay buying the 1-gal size on sale than buying two $\frac{1}{2}$-gal containers at the regular price? **$0.56**

### Practice Supplement, page 148

Name ______ To follow text page 395

**Capacity**

Give the missing numbers.

1. 2 tablespoons = **1** oz
2. 8 oz = **1** c
3. 1 pt = **2** c
4. 1 qt = **2** pt
5. 4 qt = **1** gal
6. 2 oz = **4** tablespoons
7. 2 c = **16** oz
8. 3 pt = **6** c
9. 8 pt = **4** qt
10. 2 gal = **8** qt
11. 4 c = **2** pt
12. 1 c = **$\frac{1}{2}$** pt
13. 3 qt = **6** pt
14. 12 qt = **3** gal
15. $\frac{1}{2}$ gal = **2** qt
16. A 2-gallon bucket of water will fill **16** pints.
17. 8 cups of tomato sauce fill **2** quarts.
18. 8 ounces of vanilla fill **16** tablespoons.
19. 1 quart and 1 pint of milk fill **6** cups.
20. 1 gallon and 1 quart of juice fill **10** pints.

Solve.

21. Andy used 1 gallon of apple juice and 2 quarts of grapefruit juice to make a fruit drink. How many cups of juice did he have? **24**

22. A pitcher holds 2 quarts of lemonade. How many cups does it hold? **8**

23. A quart of pear juice costs $2.19. How much more or less is this than 62¢ per 8-ounce bottle? **29¢ less**

24. Orange juice comes in 12-ounce cans and in 1-pint cans. Which holds more? How much more? **1-pint can, 4 oz more**

# Measurement

**Quick Review** Students write the numbers that complete each equation.

$125 - 25 = \boxed{80} + 20$ $(8 \times 10) + (2 \times 4) = \boxed{88}$ $(5 \times 7) + \boxed{5} = 40$

$(\boxed{10} \times 3) = (15 \times 2)$ $72 \div 8 = \boxed{1} \times 9$ $(\boxed{6} + 4) \times 3 = 30$

**Lesson Focus** To find weight using customary units; to solve word problems involving customary units of weight

**Suggested Materials** Scales for weighing ounces and pounds, objects to weigh

## Ideas for Getting Started

Pass around the classroom 1-oz and 1-lb weights or objects that weigh about 1 lb and about 1 oz. For example, four sheets of paper or an ordinary letter often weighs about an ounce; a large paperback almanac might weigh about a pound. Let students handle and compare these objects to help students become familiar with these units of weight.

## Using Page 396

**Lesson Development** Direct students' attention to the illustrations at the top of the page. Point out that the ounce is a basic customary unit of weight. Make sure students understand that the fluid ounce is a unit of liquid measure. Tell students that a package of 5 nickels weighs about an ounce and that a tennis ball weighs about 2 oz. Then ask: "A pound is how many ounces?" (16) "A ton is how many pounds?" (2,000)

**Exercises 1–12** Remind students to use the information at the top of the page to solve these problems. For example, in exercise 3 students might reason: Since 1 pound is 16 ounces, then 3 pounds is 48 ounces. Encourage students to check their answers to the exercises by working in the opposite direction. For example, in exercise 7 if they arrived at the answer "2 lb," they could multiply 16 by 2 to find the original 32 oz.

**Exercises 13–19** In these exercises involving estimation in various units of weight, students can use estimation and comparison to find answers.

## Weight

An **ounce** (oz) is a basic customary unit of weight.

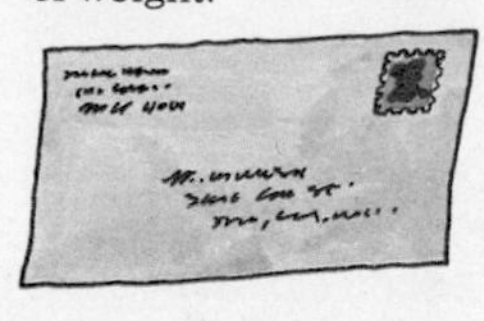

A letter might weigh 1 ounce.

A **pound** (lb) is 16 oz.

A football boxed for mailing

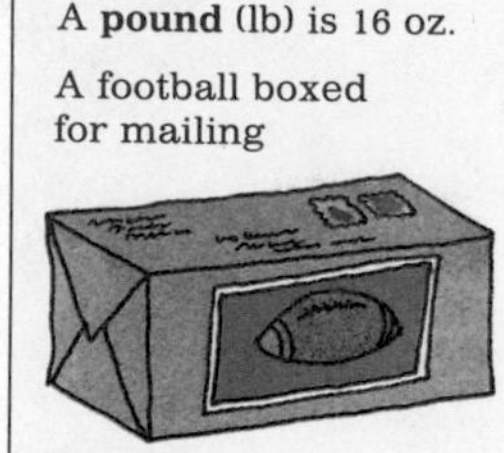

1 pound = 16 ounces

A **ton** (T) is 2,000 lb.

A small mail delivery truck

1 ton = 2,000 pounds

Give the missing numbers.

1. 1 lb = ■ oz 16
2. 1 T = ■ lb 2,000
3. 3 lb = ■ oz 48
4. 4 T = ■ lb 8,000
5. $\frac{3}{4}$ lb = ■ oz 12
6. $\frac{1}{2}$ T = ■ oz 16,000
7. 32 oz = ■ lb 2
8. 10,000 lb = ■ T 5
9. 18 oz = ■ lb $1\frac{1}{8}$
10. 5,000 lb = ■ T $2\frac{1}{2}$
11. 30 T = ■ lb 60,000
12. 256 oz = ■ lb 16

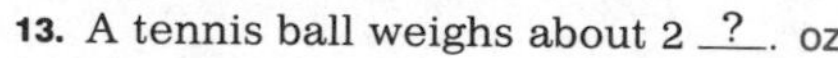

Complete each sentence. Write **oz, lb,** or **T.**

13. A tennis ball weighs about 2 _?_. oz
14. A person might weigh 140 _?_. lb
15. A large whale might weigh 160 _?_. T
16. An automobile might weigh $1\frac{1}{2}$ _?_. T
17. A book might weigh 28 _?_. oz
18. A loaf of bread might weigh 1 _?_. lb
19. A large elephant might weigh 5 _?_. T



## Follow Up

### Reteaching

To help students develop a solid understanding of the relative weights of objects, let them handle various objects that weigh about 1 oz, 8 oz, 16 oz (1 lb), and 10 lb. Work with students to identify the weight of each object. Then after discussing the smaller weights, tell students that a car or a large horse might weigh about 2,000 lb, or 1 ton.

### Enrichment

Have students find the rates for mailing letters, packages, or books through the U.S. or Canadian mail. Provide students with a list of items to be mailed and their weights. Have students use these rates to compute the cost for each item to be mailed to a specific destination in the state or province in which they live.

**Assignment Guide**

| | Minimum | Average | Extended |
|---|---|---|---|
| page 396 | 1–19 | 1–19 | 1–19 |
| page 397 | 1–5 | 1–7 | 1–8 |

## Problem Solving: Practice

Solve.

1. A package weighs 56 oz. How many pounds does it weigh? $3\frac{1}{2}$ lb

2. A wooden gift box containing 12 large apples was mailed to a friend. The empty box weighed 2 lb. When filled, the box weighed 8 lb. About how much did one of the apples weigh? $\frac{1}{2}$ lb

3. A company shipped 10,000 boxes of softballs weighing 8 oz per box. How many tons were shipped? $2\frac{1}{2}$ T

4. In a recent year the postal rate on first class letters was 20¢ for the first ounce and 17¢ for each additional ounce. How much did it cost to mail an 8-ounce letter? $1.39

5. To mail books in a recent year it cost 63¢ for the first pound, 23¢ for each additional pound through 7 lb, and 14¢ for each pound over 7 lb. What did it cost to mail a box of books that weighed 144 oz? $2.29

6. **DATA BANK** How many pounds does a basketball weigh? Give your answer as a mixed number. List the weights of other balls used for sports from lightest to heaviest. (See Data Bank, p. 410.) $1\frac{3}{8}$ lb; see teaching notes.

7. **DATA HUNT** Is the total weight of the students in your class more than or less than a ton? How many pounds more or less? Answers will vary.

8. **Try This** Jed weighs 3 times as much as Luis. Together the two boys weigh 180 lb. What is the weight of each boy? Luis, 45 lb; Jed 135 lb.



## Using Page 397

**Lesson Development** Encourage students to read the problems carefully and focus on the question. Except for exercises 6 and 7, the necessary data is given in each problem. Thus students can consider the data as they plan the solution.

**Data Bank** Remind students that they can find the needed data in the back of the book. **Answers: $\frac{1}{12}$ oz, $1\frac{1}{2}$ oz, 2 oz, 5 oz, $9\frac{1}{2}$ oz, 15 oz, 16 oz, 256 oz**

**Data Hunt** In this exercise students must decide how much data to collect and how much estimation to use. Be sure to discuss the technique students used to find their answers.

**Try This** A possible strategy, Guess and Check, was taught on page 48.

**Discussion** "What weights are we asked to find in the problem?" (Jed's weight, Luis's weight) "What do we know about the boys' weights?" (Jed weighs 3 times as much as Luis. Jed's weight plus Luis's weight equals 180 lb.) "Could we choose an operation to solve the problem?" (No, not enough information is given.) "To plan a solution, could we try Guess and Check? Suppose we guess Luis's weight to be 50 lb. How much would Jed weigh?" (3 × 50 or 150 lb) "What would the boys weigh together?" (200 lb) "Since a guess of 50 lb for Luis's weight is too large, what would be a better guess?" (Guess a smaller number for Luis's weight.)

**Solution** Luis weighs 45 lb; Jed weighs 135 lb. If Luis's weight is 45 lb, Jed weighs 3 times 45 or 135; 45 plus 135 is 180 lb.

**Reteaching Supplement,** page 96

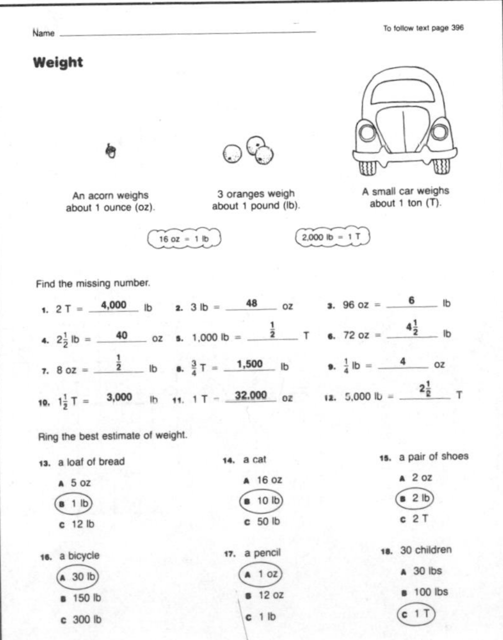
Name ________ To follow text page 396

**Weight**

An acorn weighs about 1 ounce (oz).
3 oranges weigh about 1 pound (lb).
A small car weighs about 1 ton (T).

16 oz = 1 lb
2,000 lb = 1 T

Find the missing number.

1. 2 T = **4,000** lb
2. 3 lb = **48** oz
3. 96 oz = **6** lb
4. $2\frac{1}{2}$ lb = **40** oz
5. 1,000 lb = **$\frac{1}{2}$** T
6. 72 oz = **$4\frac{1}{2}$** lb
7. 8 oz = **$\frac{1}{2}$** lb
8. $\frac{3}{4}$ T = **1,500** lb
9. $\frac{1}{4}$ lb = **4** oz
10. $1\frac{1}{2}$ T = **3,000** lb
11. 1 T = **32,000** oz
12. 5,000 lb = **$2\frac{1}{2}$** T

Ring the best estimate of weight.

13. a loaf of bread — A 5 oz; **(B 1 lb)**; C 12 lb
14. a cat — A 16 oz; **(B 10 lb)**; C 50 lb
15. a pair of shoes — A 2 oz; **(B 2 lb)**; C 2 T
16. a bicycle — **(A 30 lb)**; B 150 lb; C 300 lb
17. a pencil — **(A 1 oz)**; B 12 oz; C 1 lb
18. 30 children — A 30 lbs; B 100 lbs; **(C 1 T)**

**Enrichment Supplement,** page 96

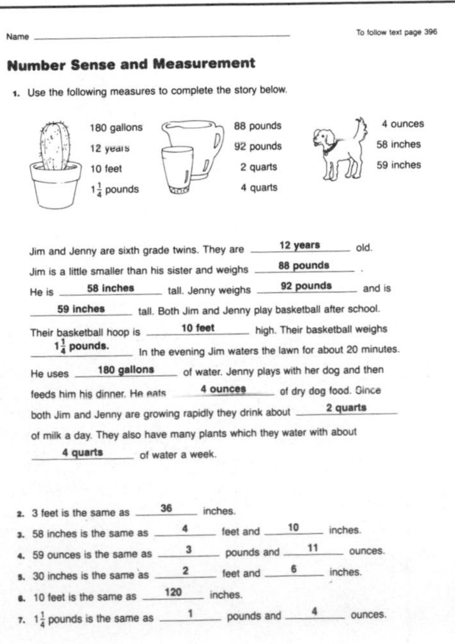
Name ________ To follow text page 396

**Number Sense and Measurement**

1. Use the following measures to complete the story below.

180 gallons, 12 years, 10 feet, $1\frac{1}{4}$ pounds
88 pounds, 92 pounds, 2 quarts, 4 quarts
4 ounces, 58 inches, 59 inches

Jim and Jenny are sixth grade twins. They are **12 years** old. Jim is a little smaller than his sister and weighs **88 pounds**. He is **58 inches** tall. Jenny weighs **92 pounds** and is **59 inches** tall. Both Jim and Jenny play basketball after school. Their basketball hoop is **10 feet** high. Their basketball weighs **$1\frac{1}{4}$ pounds.** In the evening Jim waters the lawn for about 20 minutes. He uses **180 gallons** of water. Jenny plays with her dog and then feeds him his dinner. He eats **4 ounces** of dry dog food. Since both Jim and Jenny are growing rapidly they drink about **2 quarts** of milk a day. They also have many plants which they water with about **4 quarts** of water a week.

2. 3 feet is the same as **36** inches.
3. 58 inches is the same as **4** feet and **10** inches.
4. 59 ounces is the same as **3** pounds and **11** ounces.
5. 30 inches is the same as **2** feet and **6** inches.
6. 10 feet is the same as **120** inches.
7. $1\frac{1}{4}$ pounds is the same as **1** pounds and **4** ounces.

**Practice Supplement,** page 149

Name ________ To follow text page 397

**Weight**

Write the missing numbers.

1. 1 T = **2,000** lb
2. 1 lb = **16** oz
3. $\frac{1}{2}$ lb = **8** oz
4. $\frac{1}{2}$ T = **1,000** lb
5. 3 T = **6,000** lb
6. 2 lb = **32** oz
7. 48 oz = **3** lb
8. 8,000 lb = **4** T
9. 24 oz = **$1\frac{1}{2}$** lb
10. 3,000 lb = **$1\frac{1}{2}$** T
11. 128 oz = **8** lb
12. $\frac{1}{4}$ lb = **4** oz

Complete each sentence. Write **oz, lb,** or **T.**

13. A pair of shoes might weigh 2 **lb**.
14. A bar of soap might weigh 3 **oz**.
15. A Grizzly bear might weigh $\frac{1}{2}$ **T**.
16. An orange might weigh 4 **oz**.

Solve.

17. A papaya weighs 20 oz. How many pounds does it weigh? **$1\frac{1}{4}$ lb**
18. An apple grower sold 2,000 bags of apples. Each bag weighed 10 lb. How many tons of apples did he sell? **10 T**
19. June bought 72 oz of cherries. They cost $1.10 per pound. How much did she pay? **$4.95**
20. A store bought 500 cartons of juice. Each carton contains 24 8-oz juice bottles. How many tons is this? **3 T**

**Quick Review** Students write answers only for these problems.

| 65 | 873 | $7.37 | $18.05 | 53 | 4.36 | 180 ÷ 6 30 |
|---|---|---|---|---|---|---|
| + 48 | − 346 | + 5.89 | − 8.63 | × 42 | × 0.2 | 132 R2 |
| 113 | 527 | $13.26 | $ 9.42 | 2,226 | 0.872 | 3)398 |

**Lesson Focus** To estimate temperatures in degrees Fahrenheit; to use a calculator to solve word problems

**Suggested Materials** Fahrenheit thermometer

## Ideas for Getting Started

Divide the class into groups of 3 or 4 students and have each group estimate various temperatures and then use a Fahrenheit thermometer to find these temperatures. For example, students might find today's outdoor temperature, today's room temperature, or the temperature of cold or hot water from a faucet. When students have completed these activities, discuss their estimates and the actual temperatures.

## Using Page 398

**Lesson Development** Direct students' attention to the Fahrenheit thermometer and the temperatures indicated by the letters A through F. Tell students they can use the pictures in exercises 1–6 to help them estimate the temperatures on the thermometer. Elicit from students their reasoning for matching a picture with a given letter. If students have difficulty with this, give hints with questions such as, "Is a high fever above or below normal body temperature?" (above) "Is it very far above or below?" (No, it should be fairly close.) "Is room temperature more or less than normal body temperature?" (less) "Is it more or less than freezing water?" (more) "Which is colder—ice cream or cold water?" (Ice cream: it is frozen.) "Which is hotter—hottest recorded temperature or hot soup?" (Hot soup; it is almost boiling.) Questions such as these should help students use a process of elimination to match the letters with the pictures.

**Exercises 7–10** Encourage students to use the temperatures they already know and the process of elimination to make a judgment about the best selection for each temperature. Discuss with students why they selected the answer they did.

**Data Hunt** Some students may have collected this information in the Getting Started activity. Have them check it again for the purposes of this exercise, and then find the difference between the two measurements.

## Temperature

The degree Fahrenheit (°F) is the basic customary unit of temperature.

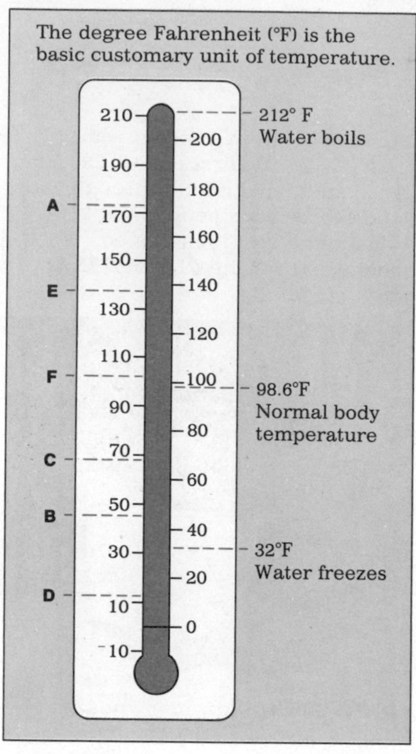


Give the letter on the thermometer that is the best estimate for the temperature suggested by each picture.

1. Hottest recorded U.S. temperature E

2. Hot cocoa (not quite boiling) A

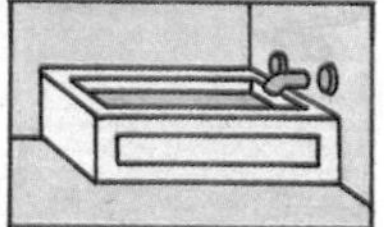

3. Warm bath water F

4. Cold water B

5. Room temperature C

6. Frozen custard D

Choose the most reasonable temperature for each.

7. Melting lead
   A 99°F C
   B 212°F
   C 621°F
8. Ice water
   A 60° B
   B 33°F
   C 0°F
9. Hot summer day
   A 95°F A
   B 55°F
   C 35°F
10. Inside a freezer
    A 125°F B
    B 25°F
    C 50°F
11. Slight fever
    A 100°F A
    B 95°F
    C 105°F
12. Hot soup
    A 180°F A
    B 100°F
    C 50°F
13. Cool fall day
    A 50°F A
    B 90°F
    C 10°F
14. Hot faucet water
    A 60°F C
    B 90°F
    C 150°F
15. **DATA HUNT** What is the difference between today's indoor temperature and today's outdoor temperature in °F? Answers will vary.



## Follow Up

### Reteaching

Give students the following Fahrenheit temperatures: 35°, 55°, 80°, and 145°. Have them make a chart as shown below. Tell them to list as many things as they can think of that might be about that temperature.

| | |
|---|---|
| 35° | a cold drink |
| 55° | a cool fall day |
| 80° | a pleasant summer day |
| 145° | warm faucet water |

### Enrichment

Let students use a Fahrenheit thermometer to check and record the outside temperature hourly. They then use the data to make a bar graph as shown below.

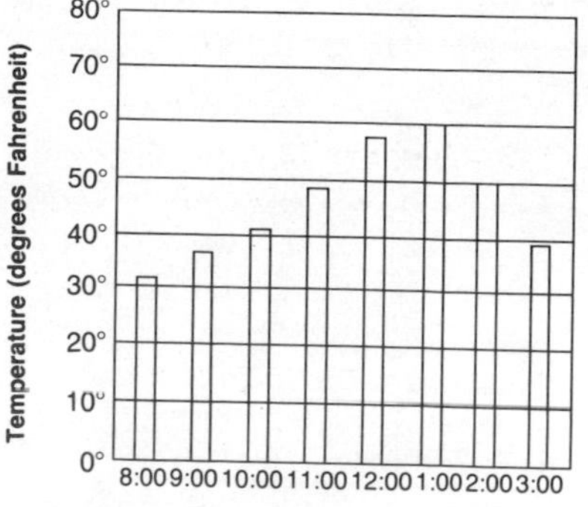

| Assignment Guide | | | |
|---|---|---|---|
| | Minimum | Average | Extended |
| page 398 | 1–14 | 1–14 | 1–15 |
| page 399 | 1–6 | 1–7 | 1–8 |

## Problem Solving: Using a Calculator

Use a calculator to solve each problem below.

1. A dollar bill is 6 in. long. How much money would you have if you had a string of dollar bills laid end to end for 1 mile? $10,560

2. A small car costs $5,695. The car weighs 2,654 lb. What is the cost for each pound of car? $2.15

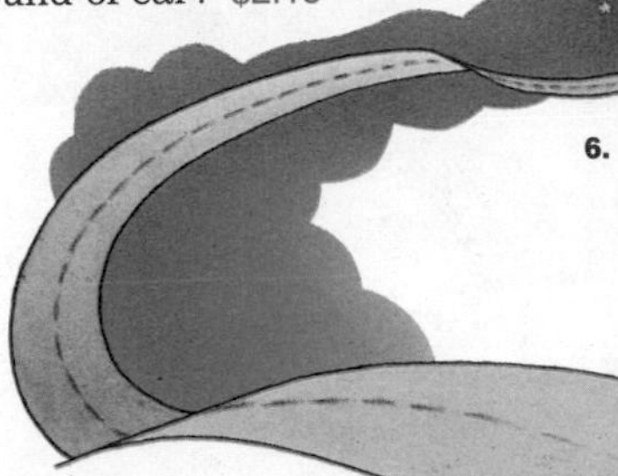

3. Suppose you could drive the 238,866 miles from the earth to the moon in an automobile at 55 miles per hour. How many hours, to the nearest whole number of hours, would it take you to drive there and back? How many days? 8,686 h; 361.9 days

4. How many years would it take you to walk the 24,901 miles around the earth if you walked at a rate of 12 miles a day? 5.7 years

5. An ounce of nickels contains 6 nickels. An 85-lb student has a bag of nickels that weighs the same as she does. What is the value of the money in the bag? $408

6. Each person in this country makes about 4.5 lb of trash a day. How many tons of trash does your family make in a year? How many tons does your town or city make? Answers will vary.

7. **DATA HUNT** Find your pulse rate. If your heart has beaten at this rate ever since you were born, about how many times had your heart beaten when you had your last birthday? Answers will vary.

8. **Try This** Suppose a rich king gave his favorite daughter 1 oz of gold the first day, 2 oz the second, 4 oz the third, 8 oz the fourth, and so on. If the gold was worth $489 an ounce, what was the value of all her gold after 10 days? $500,247



## Using Page 399

**Lesson Development** Tell students to use their calculators to do these problems. Remind them to focus on the questions, the data, and the plan for the solution of the problem as suggested by the 5-Point Checklist in the logo.

**Data Hunt** If necessary, show students how to check their pulse rates. One way is to count the pulse beats for 10 seconds and multiply by 6 to find the pulse rate per minute. Have students check their pulse rates two or three times to check the accuracy.

**Try This** A possible solution, Find a Pattern, was taught on page 246.

**Discussion** "What is the question asked about the king's daughter and the gold?" (What was the value of her gold after 10 days?) "How much gold did the king give his daughter the first day?" (1 oz) "The second day?" (2 oz) "The third day?" (4 oz) "How much is the gold worth per ounce?" ($489) "In planning the solution what do you need to find first?" (The total number of ounces of gold the king gave his daughter.) "Do you see a pattern?"

**Solution** After 10 days, the king would have given his daughter 1,023 oz of gold; at $489 an ounce, this would be 1,023 × $489, or $500,247.

| day | ounces given | total ounces |
|---|---|---|
| 1 | 1 | 1 |
| 2 | 2 | 3 |
| 3 | 4 | 7 |
| 4 | 8 | 15 |
| 5 | 16 | 31 |
| ⋮ | ⋮ | ⋮ |
| 10 | 512 | 1,023 |
| 11 | 1,024 | |

## Ideas That Work

### Special Education

Another important measurement skill is the ability to estimate measures (linear, perimeter, area, volume, capacity, weight, and temperature) using pictures of situations. This type of estimation activity requires students to use reasoning from context in making estimates.

Mount a picture of a given situation on one side of a piece of tagboard with estimation questions related to the objects shown in the picture. On the reverse side of the card, provide a range of possible estimates for each question, along with suggestions as to how the estimation range was established from the picture. These activity cards could be helpful for all students in the class.

**Practice Supplement,** page 150

Name ______________________ To follow text page 398

**Temperature**

Circle the most reasonable temperature.

1. hot tea — A 60°F, B 100°F, C 180°F (circled)
2. room temperature — A 30°F, B 70°F (circled), C 110°F
3. hot bath — A 100°F (circled), B 80°F, C 40°F
4. spring day — A 120°F, B 65°F (circled), C 35°F
5. hot oven — A 150°F, B 400°F (circled), C 70°F
6. ice tea — A 35°F (circled), B 0°F, C 50°F
7. water freezes — A 0°F, B 32°F (circled), C 45°F
8. inside a refrigerator — A 80°F, B 42°F (circled), C 0°F
9. water boils — A 100°F, B 150°F, C 212°F (circled)
10. hot summer day — A 100°F (circled), B 70°F, C 50°F
11. your temperature — A 125°F, B 99°F (circled), C 77°F
12. hot oatmeal — A 140°F (circled), B 90°F, C 60°F
13. inside a freezer — A 60°F, B 40°F, C 20°F (circled)
14. a cat's temperature — A 65°F, B 90°F, C 102°F (circled)
15. winter day — A 100°F, B 75°F, C 35°F (circled)

**Lesson Focus** To interpret, organize, and use data to make a decision about a real-world problem

## Ideas for Getting Started

Conduct a brief discussion on how a carpenter might use mathematics in his or her work. Elicit from students that before carpenters can determine the cost of a job, they must ascertain by measuring the kind of materials and the amount of materials needed. Once this has been determined, the carpenter can calculate the cost of building materials, tools, and labor to find the overall cost of the construction.

## Using Page 400

**Lesson Development** Briefly discuss experiences students might have had in building a tool shed. Then pose the problem at the top of the page about whether to build the floor from $\frac{3}{4}$-in. plywood or from 1 by 6 boards. Be sure students understand the major question or decision to which they must respond. Then point out that there is quite a lot of data given for the problem and that the data must be studied carefully before students can decide which is pertinent to the decision to be made. In planning the solution, ask students what the major considerations will be in making this decision. (cost of the two alternatives, time needed for each alternative, possible problems or difficulties associated with each of the alternatives) Then help students focus on the questions given for consideration relative to planning the solution. These questions should help students decide on the alternatives.

Finally, after students have answered the five questions, ask them to make a decision. Note in this particular case that the plywood costs $32 and the 1 by 6 boards cost $30.16. However, students should consider that it would take more time to build the floor using the 1 by 6 boards. It would also take more nails. On the other hand, the 1 by 6 board floor may be more sturdy than the $\frac{3}{4}$-in. plywood floor. As students give their choices, discuss the alternatives and rationale for the choices. Make sure students understand that there is no single correct answer for this applied problem.

QUESTION
DATA
PLAN
ANSWER
CHECK

## Applied Problem Solving

You are going to build a tool shed. You need to decide whether to build the floor from $\frac{3}{4}$-in. plywood or from 1 by 6 boards.

**Some Things to Consider**

$\frac{3}{4}$ in.
$5\frac{1}{2}$ in.

- The floor is to be a 6 ft by 8 ft rectangle.
- A 1 by 6 board is actually $\frac{3}{4}$ in. by $5\frac{1}{2}$ in. These boards come in 6, 8, 10, 12, 14, 16, 18, and 20 ft lengths. They cost 29¢ for each foot of length.
- The $\frac{3}{4}$ in. plywood comes in 4 ft by 8 ft pieces. Plywood of average quality costs 50¢ a square foot. You cannot buy just a part of a 4 by 8 ft piece.
- You want to build the tool shed as cheaply and as quickly as possible.

**Some Questions to Answer**

1. How many full sheets of plywood would it take to build the floor? How many square feet is that? What would the cost be? 2 sheets; 64 $ft^2$; $32
2. How many inches wide is the floor? 72 in.
3. How many 1 by 6 boards will be needed? 13
4. How long must each board be? How many ft of boards are needed? 8 ft; 104 ft
5. What would be the total cost for the boards? $30.16

**What Is Your Decision?**

Will you use plywood or will you use 1 by 6 boards?
Answers may vary.

## Chapter Review-Test

Give the missing numbers.

1. 6 ft = ■ in. 72
2. 5 yd = ■ ft 15
3. 3 yd = ■ in. 108
4. 3 mi = ■ ft 15,840
5. $1\frac{1}{2}$ mi = ■ yd 2,640
6. 24 in. = ■ ft 2
7. 21 ft = ■ yd 7
8. 36 in. = ■ yd 1
9. 72 in. = ■ yd 2
10. Estimate the length of this segment. Then give the length to the nearest $\frac{1}{2}$ in., $\frac{1}{4}$ in., and $\frac{1}{8}$ in. Estimates will vary; 3 in., $2\frac{3}{4}$ in., $2\frac{7}{8}$ in.

Add, subtract, or multiply.

11. 6 ft 9 in. + 3 ft 7 in. = 10 ft 4 in.
12. 8 yd 1 ft − 2 yd 2 ft = 5 yd 2 ft
13. 4 ft 5 in. × 3 = 13 ft 3 in.

Give the missing numbers.

14. 1 c = ■ oz 8
15. 1 pt = ■ c 2
16. 1 gal = ■ qt 4
17. 1 qt = ■ pt 2
18. 1 oz = ■ tablespoons 2
19. 12 qt = ■ gal 3
20. 1 T = ■ lb 2,000
21. 1 lb = ■ oz 16
22. 32 oz = ■ lb 2

Choose the best estimate for each.

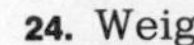

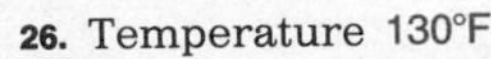

23. Weight 6 oz

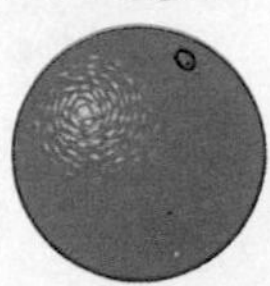

6 oz  4 lb  $\frac{1}{8}$ T

24. Weight 2 lb

4 oz  2 lb  $\frac{1}{4}$ T

25. Temperature 45°F

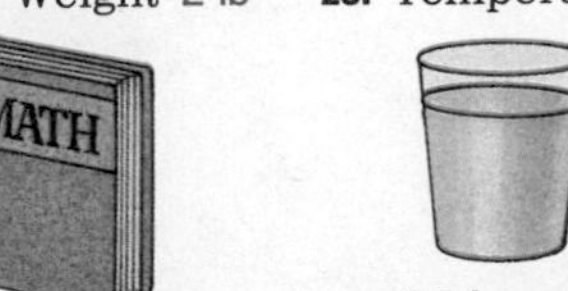

cold faucet water
10°F  45°F  90°F

26. Temperature 130°F

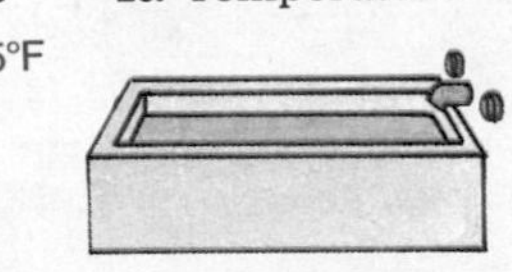

hot bath water
65°F  130°F  210°F

Solve.

27. How many cups are in six 12-oz cans of pineapple juice? 9 c
28. A house covers $\frac{1}{4}$ the area of a lot 42 yd long and 36 yd wide. How many square yards does it cover? How many feet of fencing are needed to put a fence around the lot? 378 $yd^2$; 468 ft

401

## Using Page 401

The exercises in the Chapter Review-Test emphasize the major concepts and skills presented in this chapter. These exercises may be used as a review assignment or as a test, depending upon your needs.

**Item Analysis** The table below correlates the Chapter Review-Test items with objectives and with the student text pages on which the concepts or skills were taught.

| Items | Objectives | Related text pages |
|---|---|---|
| 1–13 | 16.1 | 386–391 |
| 14–22 | 16.2 | 394 |
| 23–24 | 16.3 | 396 |
| 25–26 | 16.4 | 398 |
| 27–28 | 16.5 | 392–393, 395, 397, 399 |

## Assessment Options

If you use the Chapter Review-Test as a review assignment, you may wish to use the multiple-choice test or the free-response test to evaluate mastery of the chapter objectives. The items on these tests have a one-to-one correspondence in terms of content and level of difficulty. A correlation of test items to objectives and student text pages is provided in the Management Guide for Chapter 16.

**Multiple Choice Test,** TRB pages 46–48

**Free-Response Test,** TRB pages 79–80

**End-of-Year Test,** TRB pages 85–88

## TRB Options

The following blackline masters are available for use with this chapter. If you have not already assigned these materials, you may wish to use them to close the chapter.

**Recreation,** TRB page 166

**Consumer Applications,** TRB page 184

**Calculator Technology,** TRB page 202

**Computer Technology,** TRB pages 214–216

**Reading Math,** TRB page 234

**Family Involvement,** TRB pages 267–268

## Using Page 402

The exercises on this page are intended for those students who experienced difficulty with the chapter review test on page 401. Should students require reteaching of these key concepts and skills, please refer to the teaching notes below. Otherwise, the Another Look exercises can be assigned as independent work with students using the accompanying sample problems and hints as guides.

**Exercises 1–10** These skills were originally taught on pages 386–387. Have students review the relationships given in the display box on the left. Remind them that since 1 ft = 12 in., they can multiply the number of feet times 12 to find the number of inches. And since 1 yd = 3 ft, they can multiply the number of yards times 3 to find the number of feet. Also remind them that since there are 12 in. in 1 ft, they could find the number of feet by dividing 60 by 12. If students have difficulty, ask questions to bring out the relationships above.

**Exercises 11–13** These skills were originally taught on pages 388–389. Have students examine the examples in the display box at the left. Point out that the first ruler is divided into marks $\frac{1}{2}$ in. apart. "Which mark is closest to the tip of the pencil?" (the $\frac{1}{2}$ in. mark at 4) "What is the length to the nearest $\frac{1}{2}$ inch?" (4 inches) Point out that the second ruler has been divided using marks $\frac{1}{4}$ in. apart. "Which $\frac{1}{4}$ in. mark is closest to the tip of the pencil?" ($6\frac{1}{2}$) "What is the length to the nearest $\frac{1}{4}$ inch?" ($6\frac{1}{2}$) Point out that the third ruler has been divided by marks $\frac{1}{8}$ in. apart. "Which of the $\frac{1}{8}$ in. marks is closest to the tip of the nail?" ($1\frac{3}{8}$) "What is the length to the nearest $\frac{1}{8}$ in.?" ($1\frac{3}{8}$ in.)

**Exercises 14–17** This skill was originally taught on page 390. Point out that the numbers for each of the units are added and a trade is made whenever possible in the answer. In the example for instance, 15 in. are traded for 1 ft and 3 in. Point out that in exercise 16 we must trade 1 of the feet for 12 in.

**Exercises 18–27** These skills were originally taught on pages 394, 396, and 398. Ask students to review the relationships shown in the box at the left. "1 quart equals how many pints?" (2) "1 pound equals how many ounces?" (16) and so on. Help students see that we can multiply to change from a larger unit to a smaller one, and we can divide to change from a smaller unit to a larger one. If students have difficulty, ask questions such as "1 lb equals 16 oz so 3 lb equal how many ounces?" (3 × 16) "1 gal equals 4 qt so 12 qt equal how many gallons?" (12 ÷ 4 or 3 gal)

## Another Look

**Length**
12 inches (in.) = 1 foot (ft)
3 ft = 1 yard (yd)
36 in. = 1 yd
5,280 ft = 1 mile (mi)
1,760 yd = 1 mi

**Give the missing numbers.**

1. 4 ft = ■ in. 48
2. 6 yd = ■ ft 18
3. 5 yd = ■ in. 180
4. 3 mi = ■ ft 15,840
5. 2 mi = ■ yd 3,520
6. $3\frac{1}{2}$ ft = ■ in. 42
7. $1\frac{3}{4}$ yd = ■ in. 63
8. $2\frac{1}{3}$ yd = ■ ft 7
9. 72 in. = ■ ft 6
10. 24 ft = ■ yd 8

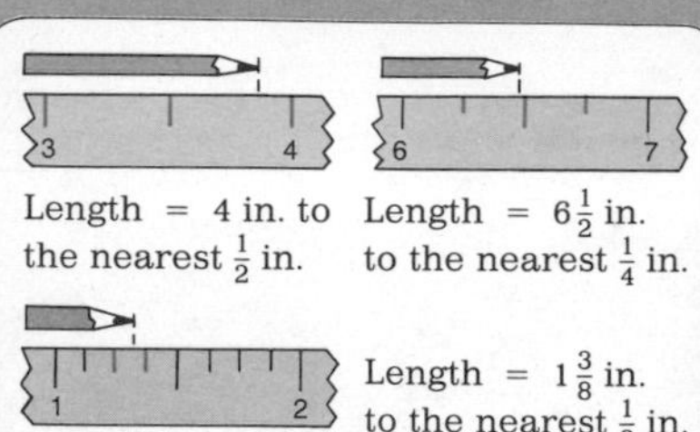

Length = 4 in. to the nearest $\frac{1}{2}$ in.

Length = $6\frac{1}{2}$ in. to the nearest $\frac{1}{4}$ in.

Length = $1\frac{3}{8}$ in. to the nearest $\frac{1}{8}$ in.

**Measure to the unit shown.**

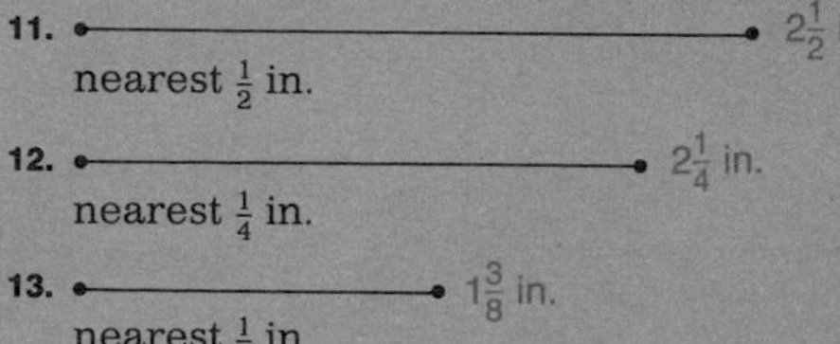

11. nearest $\frac{1}{2}$ in. $2\frac{1}{2}$ in.
12. nearest $\frac{1}{4}$ in. $2\frac{1}{4}$ in.
13. nearest $\frac{1}{8}$ in. $1\frac{3}{8}$ in.

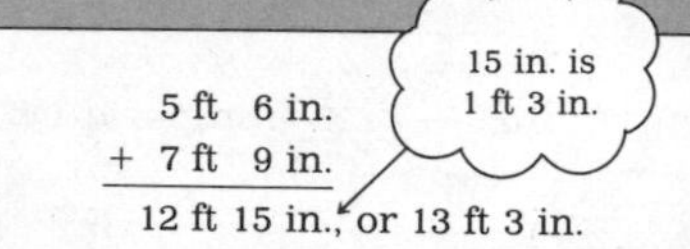

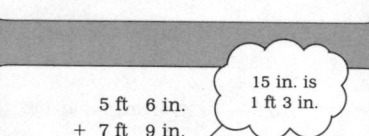

5 ft 6 in.
+ 7 ft 9 in.
12 ft 15 in., or 13 ft 3 in.

**Add, subtract, or multiply.**

14. 7 ft 10 in. + 3 ft 8 in. = 11 ft 6 in.
15. 6 yd 24 in. + 3 yd 30 in. = 10 yd 18 in.
16. 12 ft 3 in. − 4 ft 9 in. = 7 ft 6 in.
17. 6 yd 2 ft × 4 = 26 yd 2 ft

**Capacity**
8 fluid ounces (oz) = 1 cup (c)
2 cups = 1 pint (pt)
2 pt = 1 quart (qt)
4 qt = 1 gallon (gal)

**Weight**
16 ounces (oz) = 1 pound (lb)
2,000 lb = 1 ton (T)

**Temperature**
Water freezes at 32° Fahrenheit (32°F) and boils at 212°F.

**Give the missing numbers.**

18. 4 c = ■ oz 32
19. 3 pt = ■ c 6
20. 5 qt = ■ pt 10
21. 2 gal = ■ qt 8
22. 3 lb = ■ oz 48
23. 2 T = ■ lb 4,000
24. 2 qt = ■ c 8
25. 48 oz = ■ lb 3
26. 1 gal = ■ pt 8
27. 12 qt = ■ gal 3

402

## Just for Teachers

### History of Math

When we measure an object we must do three things:

1. Choose a *unit* of measure.
2. Divide the object we wish to measure into units.
3. Count the number of units.

The measure of an object is the number of units we count. Clearly, the measure of an object depends upon the choice of unit used. Furthermore, the choice of unit depends upon the system of measurement that we use.

In the United States today, we use two major different systems of measurement: the metric system of measurement and the customary system of measurement.

The units used in the customary system of measurement have a long and interesting history. Many of the units for length were originally parts of the human body. The unit called a *cubit* was the distance from the elbow to the tip of the middle finger. The unit of an *inch* comes from ancient Rome, where a uncia was a unit that was the width of a person's thumb. A *foot* was the length of a person's foot and was about 12 thumbs long, therefore 12 inches are equal to 1 foot. A *yard* was 3 feet and was the distance from a person's nose to the tip of the index finger of an outstretched arm.

## Enrichment

### Large Numbers and Scientific Notation

Try this quiz about large numbers!

Match the questions with the answers.

| ANSWERS | QUESTIONS |
|---|---|
| 1. 1,000 (or 10 hundreds) | A About how many seats are there in a large stadium? |
| 2. 10,000 (or 100 hundreds) | B About how many pages are there in a thick telephone book? |
| 3. 100,000 (or 1,000 hundreds) | C About how many grains of sand are there in a cup? |
| 4. 1,000,000 (or 1,000 thousands) | D About how many minutes are there in 2,000 years? |
| 5. 1,000,000,000 (or 1,000 millions) | E How many centimeters do you run in a 100 m dash? |

*See upside down answers to check your score.

Here are some period names to help you read a very large number.

| Sextillions | Quintillions | Quadrillions | Trillions | Billions | Millions | Thousands | Ones |
|---|---|---|---|---|---|---|---|
| ↓ | ↓ | ↓ | ↓ | ↓ | ↓ | ↓ | ↓ |
| 476 , | 587 , | 319 , | 608 , | 742 , | 871 , | 023 , | 964 |

**Scientific notation** is often used to write very large numbers. Here is an example.

Distance from the earth to the sun: 93,000,000 miles (to the nearest million)

Distance in scientific notation: $\underbrace{9.3}_{\text{a number between 1 and 10}} \times \underbrace{10^7}_{\text{a power of 10}}$

Can you read these numbers and write them in scientific notation?

1. Recent estimation of world's population: 4,000,000,000
   four billion; $4.0 \times 10^9$
2. Distance across the Milky Way Galaxy: 6,000,000,000,000,000,000 miles
   six quintillion; $6 \times 10^{18}$
3. Distance from the earth to the sun and back: 186,000,000 miles
   one hundred eighty-six million, $1.86 \times 10^8$

*Upside-down answers: A-3, E-2, D-5, B-1, C-4



## Using Page 403

This page is intended for those students who successfully completed the Chapter-Review test on page 401. You may wish to assign this page as independent work while you use Another Look exercises to reteach the basic concepts and skills of the chapter. Or, you may decide that all students would benefit from exposure to this Enrichment activity.

**Lesson Development** Have students write their answers to the quiz on their papers. After they have checked their answers, discuss each item. Some answers are best arrived at through a process of elimination, while some can be calculated. For question D, for example, note that there are 60 × 24 × 365 or approximately 60 × 20 × 400 or 500,000 minutes in a year. In 2,000 years there would be about 500,000 × 2,000 or 1,000,000,000 minutes. For question E, since there are 100 cm in 1 m there would be 100 × 100, or 10,000 cm in 100 m.

Then help students pronounce the name of the periods beyond billions. Write numbers such as 342,687,978,346,075,379 on the chalkboard and have students refer to the period names given to read these numbers.

Finally, describe the procedure for writing a number using scientific notation. Students should be aware that multiplying by a power of 10 such as $10^7$ moves the decimal point 7 places to the right. In each case, encourage students to read the numbers first and then to write each number using scientific notation.

In 1795 France adopted the metric system of measurement. In this decimal system of measurement each unit and subunit are related to the basic unit by a power of 10. About this same time the new United States was considering what measurement system to officially adopt. Following the lead of France, the United States adopted a decimal currency system, instead of the old English system. However, the United States retained the other old customary units of measure due to long social and commercial connections with England. Meanwhile the metric system of measurement spread from France to all the countries around the world. In 1866 metric units were made legally acceptable in the United States. Today the United States remains the last major nation in the world that has not made the metric system the official measurement for the country. Even though numerous educational and scientific professional organizations have endorsed the metric system and have urged that it be officially adopted, the dual systems—customary and metric—continue to be used.

**Lesson Focus** To use Logo commands to write Logo procedures

## Ideas for Getting Started

Write the following commands on the chalkboard: FORWARD, RIGHT, LEFT, BACK, CLEAR SCREEN, and HOME. Ask students to pretend that a square of the chalkboard is a computer screen. Then have them follow directions as the computer would do. Tell them that the command FORWARD tells them to go toward the top of the chalkboard; the command BACK tells them to go toward the bottom of the chalkboard; CLEAR SCREEN signals that the writing on the chalkboard is to be erased; HOME signals that the chalk is to be returned to the center of the chalkboard. Ask a volunteer to come to the chalkboard and follow the commands that you give. Have the student start in the middle of the chalkboard. If you give the command FORWARD, the student should draw a line toward the top of the chalkboard. If you give the command RIGHT 90, the student would then draw an appropriate line 90° to the right.

## Using Page 404

**Lesson Development** Have students read the paragraph at the top of the page. Point out that the Logo language is a complete language that deals with a number of commands involving numbers and words. In this lesson we will look at just the graphics part of the Logo language. Then direct students' attention to the table that gives some examples of Logo commands. If possible, allow students to work individually or in small groups on the microcomputer to experiment using the Logo commands. Point out that the command CLEAR SCREEN erases the lines the turtle has drawn on the screen. The command HOME returns the turtle to the starting position in the middle of the screen pointing up.

Describe the procedures for drawing a regular hexagon emphasizing the efficiency of the REPEAT command. Demonstrate this with the microcomputer, if possible. Then discuss the procedures used to draw an equilateral triangle. Students may not understand that after drawing one side of the triangle, the turtle must be turned 120° to the right in order to form an angle 60° with the original side.

## *Technology*

**Computer Graphics—Using Logo Commands**

A computer can draw geometric shapes on the computer screen. A special computer language, called **Logo,** can be used to give the computer the desired commands. A small triangle, called a **turtle,** moves around the screen to make the geometric drawings. Some examples of Logo commands are shown in the table.

| Logo Command | Turtle Movement | Picture |
|---|---|---|
| FD 40 | Draws a segment 40 units FORWARD. | |
| BK 30 | Draws a segment 30 units BACK. | |
| RT 60 | Turns to the RIGHT (clockwise) 60°. | 60° |
| LT 90 | Turns to the LEFT (counterclockwise) 90°. | 90° |
| REPEAT | Repeats a command, as: REPEAT 2 [FD 20 RT 90] | |

At the start the turtle is in the middle of the screen and points up. Turns (RT or LT) totaling 360° are needed to turn the turtle completely around.

To draw the regular hexagon at the right, the turtle must draw 6 segments each 30 units long. After drawing each segment, the turtle must turn right 60°. To make the turtle draw the hexagon, you can type this command 6 times:

```
FD 30 RT 60
```

or you can type this REPEAT command once:

```
REPEAT 6 [FD 30 RT 60]
```

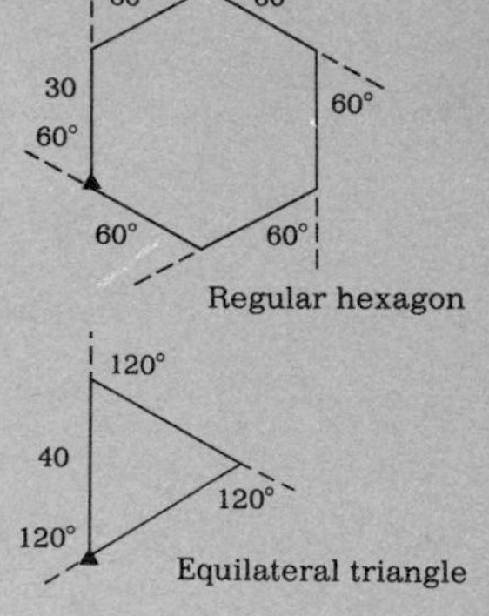

Regular hexagon

Equilateral triangle

What REPEAT command would you use to make the turtle draw an equilateral triangle with each side 40 units long? REPEAT 3 [FD 40 RT 120]



## Technology for Teachers

Logo was created in 1968 by Seymour Papert and a team of researchers whose major interest was the process of learning. Logo's designers saw the computer as an educational tool that could create new types of learning environments in which children could structure their own knowledge. The language can be learned through investigative activities, many of which are self-initiated. Logo lends itself to endless exploration and discovery.

Turtle graphics is the best known Logo feature. It is often used to introduce the basic ideas of Logo programming, as well as basic geometric concepts. Commands such as FORWARD, BACK, RIGHT, and LEFT are "built in" the language and called primitives. One special aspect of Logo is that the user can define new words and these words can become part of the computer's vocabulary. The definition of a new word is called a procedure.

The philosophy behind Logo and a detailed description of its development can be found in *Mindstorms: Children, Computers, and Powerful Ideas,* by Papert.

Copy and complete the Logo command for each picture.

1.

```
FD 40 RT 120
 ?  20 FD
```

2.

```
BK 30  ?  45 LT
FD 40
```

3.

```
 ?  45 FD 60 RT
```

4.

```
FD 20 RT 90
FD 20 RT 135
 ?  28.2 RT 135 FD
```

5.

```
FD 30 LT 90
FD 30  ?  90 RT
FD 30 RT 90
```

6.

```
REPEAT 2
[RT 60  ?  50] FD
```

7. 



Write a command using REPEAT that will make the turtle draw a square 50 units long on each side. REPEAT 4 [FD 50 RT 90]

8.



Write a command using REPEAT that will make the turtle draw a regular pentagon 40 units long on each side. REPEAT 5 [FD 40 RT 72]

9. Draw the figure that the turtle would draw in response to this Logo command:
REPEAT 8 [FD 30 RT 45]
Regular octagon with sides 30 units long

10. Write a Logo command of your own. Draw the picture that the turtle would draw for your command. Commands will vary.



## Using Page 405

**Exercises 1–3** Stress that the turtle starts out in the middle of the screen pointing up. In exercise 1, for example, point out that the turtle has to be turned 120° from its straight up position in order to form a 60° angle with the original line.

**Exercises 4–6** Draw the lines and the turtle triangle on the chalkboard to demonstrate these commands. Use a protractor as necessary to show the angle through which the turtle turns.

**Exercise 8** Point out that the turtle must turn 72° to go in the direction necessary to form a pentagon. Also point out that to form a pentagon the turtle must turn 72° five times before returning to the original location—a total of 360°.

**Exercise 9** If necessary, draw lines and show the angles on the chalkboard to help students see the effect of this command. If a microcomputer is available, have students experiment with these and other commands.

**Exercise 10** Provide ample time for students to explore the commands developed in this lesson. Encourage creativity and allow for a wide variety of procedures.

## Using Page 406

The exercises on this page provide practice for maintaining cumulative skills. The emphasis in this Cumulative Review is on perimeter and area (Chapter 14), integers (Chapter 15), measurement in customary units (Chapter 16), and problem solving (Chapter 16).

**Item Analysis** The table below correlates the Cumulative Review items with objectives and with the student book pages on which the concepts or skills were taught.

| Items | Objectives | Related text pages |
|---|---|---|
| 1 | 14.1 | 346 |
| 2 | 14.2 | 348–349 |
| 3 | 14.3 | 350 |
| 4 | 14.4 | 356–357 |
| 5–7 | 15.1 | 368–373 |
| 8–9 | 15.2 | 376 |
| 10 | 16.1 | 386–391 |
| 11 | 16.2 | 394 |
| 12 | 16.3 | 396 |
| 13–14 | 16.5 | 392–393, 395, 397, 399 |

## *Cumulative Review*

1. Find the perimeter.

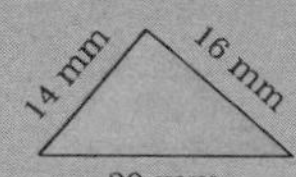


Ⓐ 50 mm
B 2,240 $mm^2$
C 25 mm
D not given

2. Find the circumference. Use 3.14 for $\pi$ and $C = \pi \times d$.

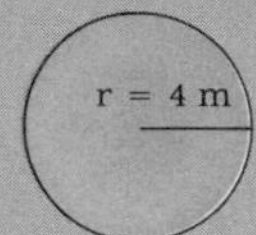


A 6.28 m
B 12.56 m
Ⓒ 25.12 m
D not given

3. Find the area.

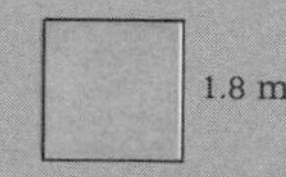


Ⓐ 3.24 $m^2$
B 1.62 $m^2$
C 3.6 $m^2$
D not given

4. Find the surface area.

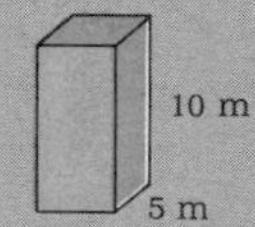


A 200 $m^2$
B 125 $m^2$
C 20 $m^2$
Ⓓ not given

Find the sum or difference.

5. $^+6 + {}^-4$
Ⓐ $^+2$ B $^-2$
C $^+10$ D not given

6. $^-9 + {}^+14$
Ⓐ $^+5$ B $^+23$
C $^-23$ D not given

7. $^-6 - {}^-3$
Ⓐ $^-3$ B $^-9$
C $^+3$ D not given

Which symbol (>, <, or =) goes in each ●?

8. $^+3$ ● $^-7$
Ⓐ > B < C =

9. $^-6$ ● $^+6$
A > Ⓑ < C =

Give the missing numbers.

10. 3 ft = ■ in.
A 4 B 24
Ⓒ 36 D not given

11. 4 pt = ■ c
A 2 Ⓑ 8
C 16 D not given

12. 2 lb = ■ oz
A 8 B 16
Ⓒ 32 D not given

13. Randy used 16 fluid ounces of milk in a recipe. How many cups of milk did he use?
A 8 B 4
Ⓒ 2 D not given

14. Indra needs 6 yd of rope. She has 3 yd 2 ft. How much more rope does she need?
A 3 yd 1 ft Ⓑ 2 yd 1 ft
C 2 yd 2 ft D not given

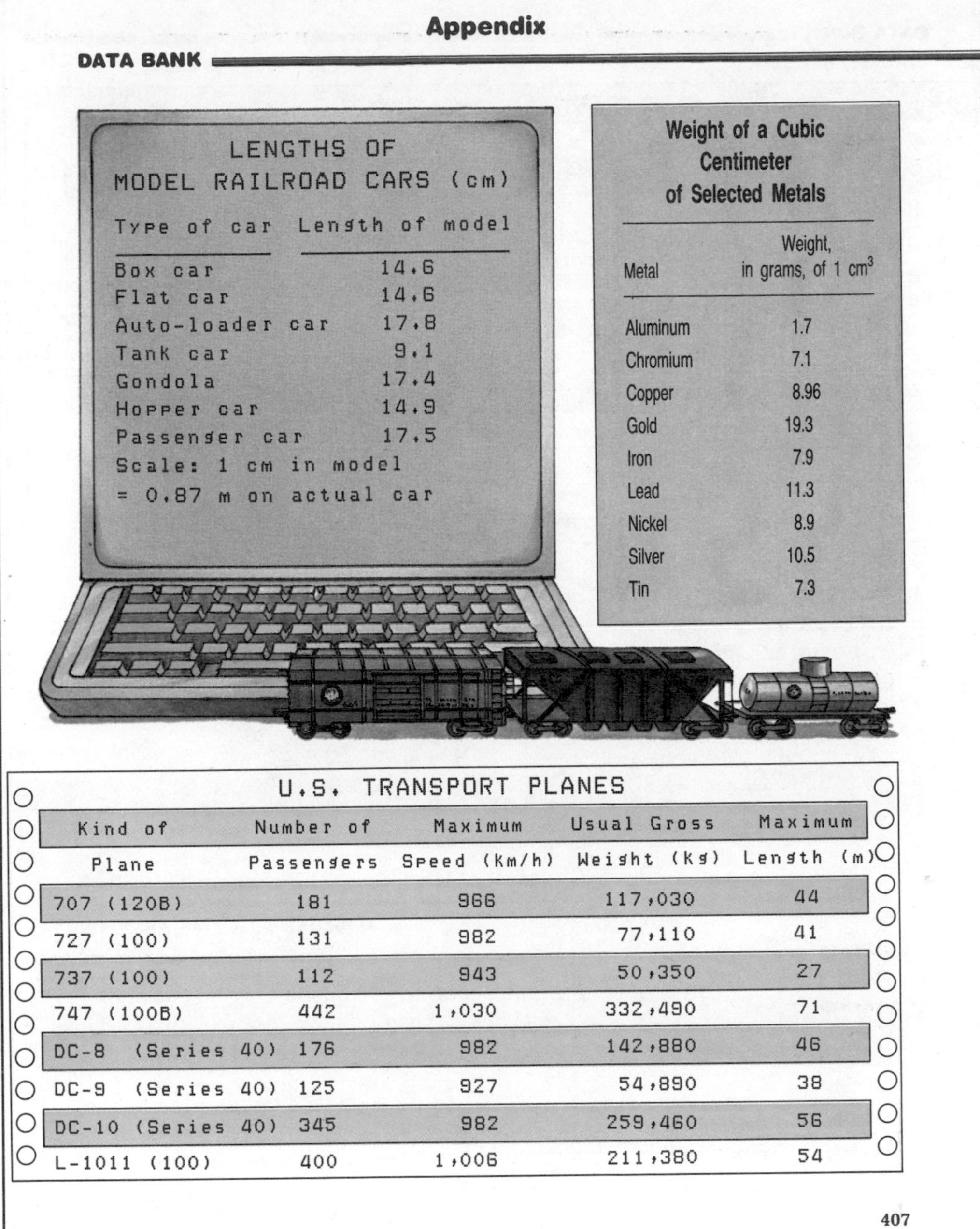

LENGTHS OF MODEL RAILROAD CARS (cm)

| Type of car | Length of model |
|---|---|
| Box car | 14.6 |
| Flat car | 14.6 |
| Auto-loader car | 17.8 |
| Tank car | 9.1 |
| Gondola | 17.4 |
| Hopper car | 14.9 |
| Passenger car | 17.5 |

Scale: 1 cm in model = 0.87 m on actual car

**Weight of a Cubic Centimeter of Selected Metals**

| Metal | Weight, in grams, of 1 $cm^3$ |
|---|---|
| Aluminum | 1.7 |
| Chromium | 7.1 |
| Copper | 8.96 |
| Gold | 19.3 |
| Iron | 7.9 |
| Lead | 11.3 |
| Nickel | 8.9 |
| Silver | 10.5 |
| Tin | 7.3 |

U.S. TRANSPORT PLANES

| Kind of Plane | Number of Passengers | Maximum Speed (km/h) | Usual Gross Weight (kg) | Maximum Length (m) |
|---|---|---|---|---|
| 707 (120B) | 181 | 966 | 117,030 | 44 |
| 727 (100) | 131 | 982 | 77,110 | 41 |
| 737 (100) | 112 | 943 | 50,350 | 27 |
| 747 (100B) | 442 | 1,030 | 332,490 | 71 |
| DC-8 (Series 40) | 176 | 982 | 142,880 | 46 |
| DC-9 (Series 40) | 125 | 927 | 54,890 | 38 |
| DC-10 (Series 40) | 345 | 982 | 259,460 | 56 |
| L-1011 (100) | 400 | 1,006 | 211,380 | 54 |

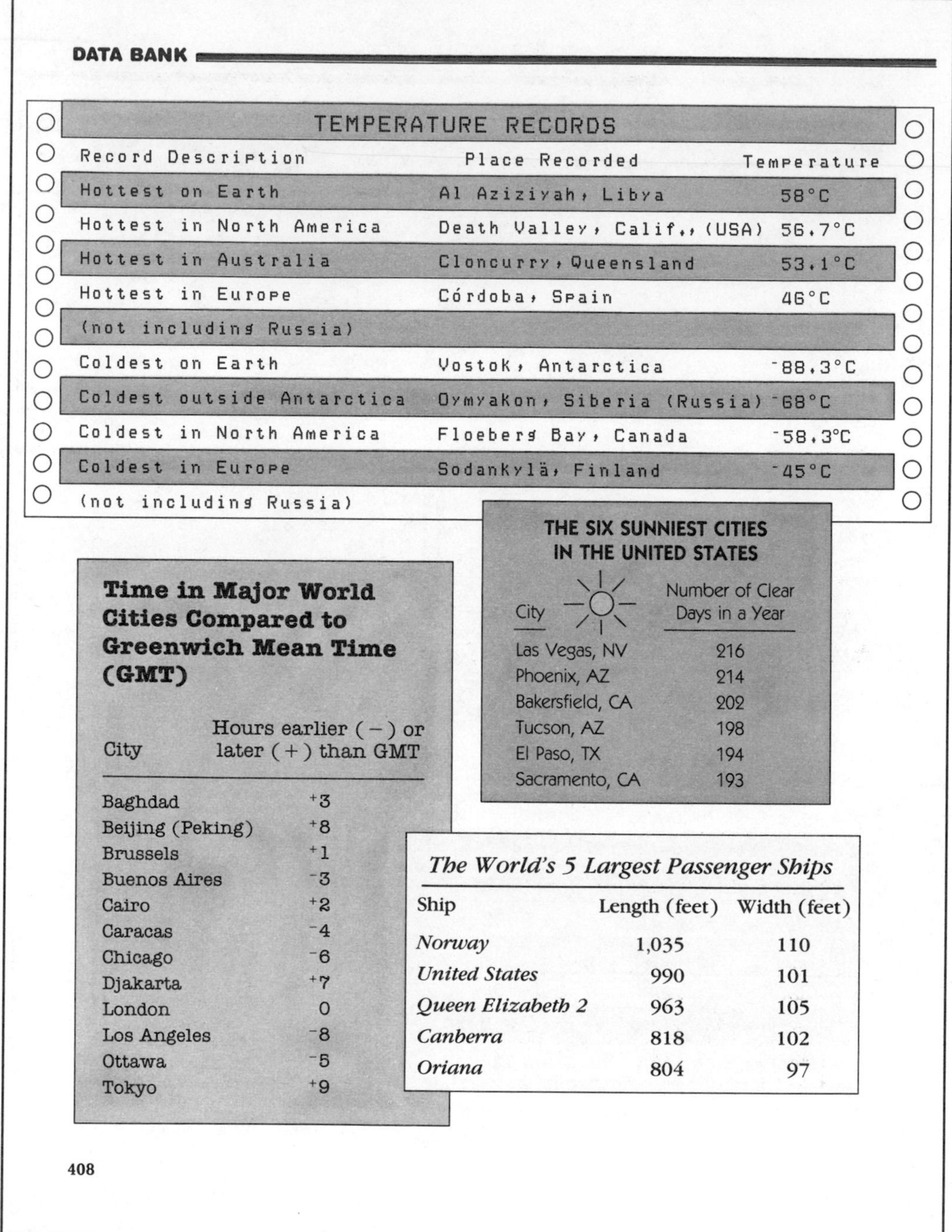

DATA BANK

| TEMPERATURE RECORDS | | |
|---|---|---|
| Record Description | Place Recorded | Temperature |
| Hottest on Earth | Al Aziziyah, Libya | 58°C |
| Hottest in North America | Death Valley, Calif., (USA) | 56.7°C |
| Hottest in Australia | Cloncurry, Queensland | 53.1°C |
| Hottest in Europe (not including Russia) | Córdoba, Spain | 46°C |
| Coldest on Earth | Vostok, Antarctica | $^{-}88.3$°C |
| Coldest outside Antarctica | Oymyakon, Siberia (Russia) | $^{-}68$°C |
| Coldest in North America | Floeberg Bay, Canada | $^{-}58.3$°C |
| Coldest in Europe (not including Russia) | Sodankylä, Finland | $^{-}45$°C |

**Time in Major World Cities Compared to Greenwich Mean Time (GMT)**

| City | Hours earlier (−) or later (+) than GMT |
|---|---|
| Baghdad | $^{+}3$ |
| Beijing (Peking) | $^{+}8$ |
| Brussels | $^{+}1$ |
| Buenos Aires | $^{-}3$ |
| Cairo | $^{+}2$ |
| Caracas | $^{-}4$ |
| Chicago | $^{-}6$ |
| Djakarta | $^{+}7$ |
| London | 0 |
| Los Angeles | $^{-}8$ |
| Ottawa | $^{-}5$ |
| Tokyo | $^{+}9$ |

THE SIX SUNNIEST CITIES IN THE UNITED STATES

| City | Number of Clear Days in a Year |
|---|---|
| Las Vegas, NV | 216 |
| Phoenix, AZ | 214 |
| Bakersfield, CA | 202 |
| Tucson, AZ | 198 |
| El Paso, TX | 194 |
| Sacramento, CA | 193 |

*The World's 5 Largest Passenger Ships*

| Ship | Length (feet) | Width (feet) |
|---|---|---|
| *Norway* | 1,035 | 110 |
| *United States* | 990 | 101 |
| *Queen Elizabeth 2* | 963 | 105 |
| *Canberra* | 818 | 102 |
| *Oriana* | 804 | 97 |

408

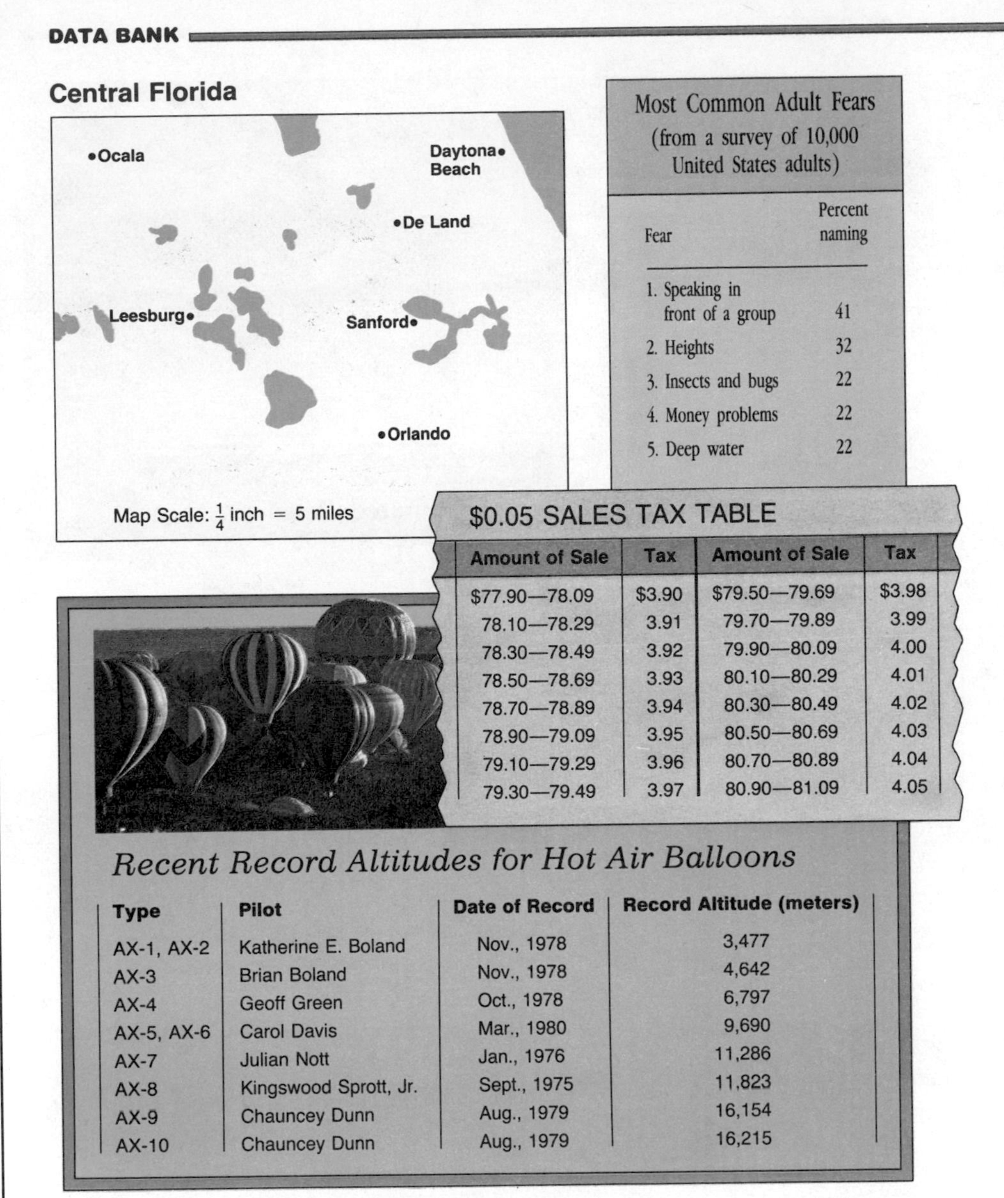

DATA BANK

## Central Florida



Most Common Adult Fears
(from a survey of 10,000 United States adults)

| Fear | Percent naming |
|---|---|
| 1. Speaking in front of a group | 41 |
| 2. Heights | 32 |
| 3. Insects and bugs | 22 |
| 4. Money problems | 22 |
| 5. Deep water | 22 |

$0.05 SALES TAX TABLE

| Amount of Sale | Tax | Amount of Sale | Tax |
|---|---|---|---|
| $77.90—78.09 | $3.90 | $79.50—79.69 | $3.98 |
| 78.10—78.29 | 3.91 | 79.70—79.89 | 3.99 |
| 78.30—78.49 | 3.92 | 79.90—80.09 | 4.00 |
| 78.50—78.69 | 3.93 | 80.10—80.29 | 4.01 |
| 78.70—78.89 | 3.94 | 80.30—80.49 | 4.02 |
| 78.90—79.09 | 3.95 | 80.50—80.69 | 4.03 |
| 79.10—79.29 | 3.96 | 80.70—80.89 | 4.04 |
| 79.30—79.49 | 3.97 | 80.90—81.09 | 4.05 |

*Recent Record Altitudes for Hot Air Balloons*

| Type | Pilot | Date of Record | Record Altitude (meters) |
|---|---|---|---|
| AX-1, AX-2 | Katherine E. Boland | Nov., 1978 | 3,477 |
| AX-3 | Brian Boland | Nov., 1978 | 4,642 |
| AX-4 | Geoff Green | Oct., 1978 | 6,797 |
| AX-5, AX-6 | Carol Davis | Mar., 1980 | 9,690 |
| AX-7 | Julian Nott | Jan., 1976 | 11,286 |
| AX-8 | Kingswood Sprott, Jr. | Sept., 1975 | 11,823 |
| AX-9 | Chauncey Dunn | Aug., 1979 | 16,154 |
| AX-10 | Chauncey Dunn | Aug., 1979 | 16,215 |

DATA BANK

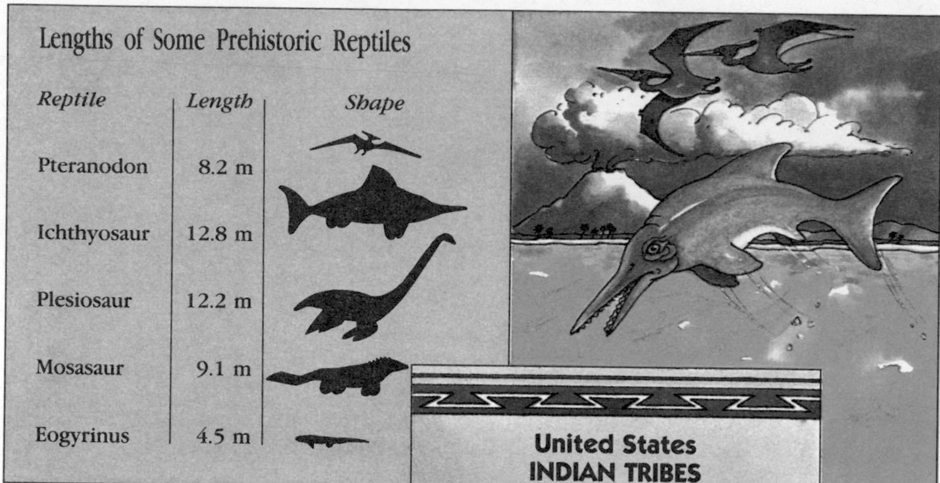

## Lengths of Some Prehistoric Reptiles

| *Reptile* | *Length* | *Shape* |
|---|---|---|
| Pteranodon | 8.2 m | |
| Ichthyosaur | 12.8 m | |
| Plesiosaur | 12.2 m | |
| Mosasaur | 9.1 m | |
| Eogyrinus | 4.5 m | |

## United States INDIAN TRIBES

| Tribe | Population |
|---|---|
| CHIPPEWA | 92,377 |
| CHEROKEE | 66,150 |
| NAVAHO | 96,743 |
| CREE | 72,572 |
| PUEBLO | 30,971 |

## Approximate Weights of Balls Used in Popular Sports

| Ball | Weight (oz) |
|---|---|
| Baseball | 5 |
| Basketball | 22 |
| Bowling ball | 256 |
| Football | 15 |
| Golf ball | $1\frac{1}{2}$ |
| Soccer ball | 16 |
| Table tennis ball | $\frac{1}{12}$ |
| Tennis ball | 2 |
| Volleyball | $9\frac{1}{2}$ |

## BOWLING ALLEY MEASUREMENTS

Length of lane.................19.17 m
Width of lane..................1.06 m
Length of approach area.................4.6 m
Width of gutter................0.23 m

## MORE PRACTICE

### Set A For use after page 3

Find the sums or differences.

| 1. | 2. | 3. | 4. | 5. | 6. | 7. |
|---|---|---|---|---|---|---|
| 3 | 5 | 3 | 4 | 0 | 6 | 8 |
| + 0 | + 3 | + 5 | + 6 | + 7 | + 8 | + 6 |
| 3 | 8 | 8 | 10 | 7 | 14 | 14 |

| 8. | 9. | 10. | 11. | 12. | 13. | 14. |
|---|---|---|---|---|---|---|
| 9 | 12 | 10 | 5 | 7 | 0 | 13 |
| − 9 | − 0 | − 1 | − 5 | − 0 | − 0 | − 3 |
| 0 | 12 | 9 | 0 | 7 | 0 | 10 |

| 15. | 16. | 17. | 18. | 19. | 20. | 21. |
|---|---|---|---|---|---|---|
| 3 | 6 | 3 | 5 | 3 | 1 | 4 |
| 2 | 1 | 8 | 7 | 3 | 5 | 2 |
| + 4 | + 2 | + 3 | + 4 | + 3 | + 9 | + 8 |
| 9 | 9 | 14 | 16 | 9 | 15 | 14 |

### Set B For use after page 5

Find the products.

| 1. | 2. | 3. | 4. | 5. | 6. | 7. |
|---|---|---|---|---|---|---|
| 3 | 0 | 2 | 3 | 9 | 1 | 4 |
| × 0 | × 7 | × 3 | × 2 | × 1 | × 9 | × 7 |
| 0 | 0 | 6 | 6 | 9 | 9 | 28 |

| 8. | 9. | 10. | 11. | 12. | 13. | 14. |
|---|---|---|---|---|---|---|
| 7 | 1 | 3 | 0 | 5 | 3 | 6 |
| × 4 | × 3 | × 1 | × 8 | × 3 | × 5 | × 1 |
| 28 | 3 | 3 | 0 | 15 | 15 | 6 |

15. (5 × 2) × 3 30 16. 5 × (2 × 3) 30 17. (3 × 2) × 5 30

### Set C For use after page 7

Divide. Check by multiplying.

| Problem | Quotient |
|---|---|
| 1. 8)8 | 1 |
| 2. 2)2 | 1 |
| 3. 1)2 | 2 |
| 4. 1)5 | 5 |
| 5. 3)3 | 1 |
| 6. 1)3 | 3 |
| 7. 3)6 | 2 |
| 8. 4)0 | 0 |
| 9. 1)6 | 6 |
| 10. 6)0 | 0 |
| 11. 1)1 | 1 |
| 12. 2)8 | 4 |
| 13. 6)24 | 4 |
| 14. 6)30 | 5 |
| 15. 7)21 | 3 |
| 16. 2)14 | 7 |
| 17. 5)25 | 5 |
| 18. 6)36 | 6 |

### Set D For use after page 11

Do the operations in the order shown by the parentheses.

1. (8 + 3) − 2 9 2. (21 ÷ 3) × 2 14 3. 5 + (8 − 4) 9

4. (9 ÷ 3) × 5 15 5. (9 − 1) × 4 32 6. 3 + (3 × 3) 12



### Set A For use after page 29

Write > (greater than) or < (less than) for each ⬤.

1. 251 ⬤ 261 < 2. 6,900 ⬤ 6,799 > 3. 5,055 ⬤ 5,505 <

4. 10,901 ⬤ 11,009 < 5. 32,018 ⬤ 31,801 > 6. 658,334 ⬤ 659,000 <

Order from least to greatest.

7. 3,191; 3,011; 3,121; 3,111
3,011; 3,111; 3,121; 3,191

8. 28,303; 29,003; 28,330; 28,033
28,033; 28,303; 28,330; 29,003

### Set B For use after page 31

Round to the nearest ten. Then round to the nearest hundred.

1. 841 — 840; 800
2. 513 — 510; 500
3. 1,458 — 1,460; 1,500
4. 8,325 — 8,330; 8,300
5. 5,899 — 5,900; 5,900
6. 9,431 — 9,430; 9,400
7. 15,235 — 15,240; 15,200
8. 11,129 — 11,130; 11,100
9. 32,623 — 32,620; 32,600
10. 51,174 — 51,170; 51,200

Round to the nearest thousand.

11. 2,542 — 3,000
12. 18,033 — 18,000
13. 10,501 — 11,000
14. 61,399 — 61,000
15. 120,760 — 121,000

Round to the nearest ten thousand.

16. 7,026 — 10,000
17. 23,360 — 20,000
18. 182,300 — 180,000
19. 909,090 — 910,000
20. 750,990 — 750,000

### Set C For use after page 33

Estimate by rounding to the nearest ten.

| 1. | 2. | 3. | 4. | 5. |
|---|---|---|---|---|
| 21 | 86 | 72 | 128 | 135 |
| + 54 | + 93 | − 47 | − 69 | − 91 |
| 70 | 180 | 20 | 60 | 50 |

Estimate by rounding to the nearest thousand.

| 6. | 7. | 8. | 9. | 10. |
|---|---|---|---|---|
| 11,873 | 3,866 | 23,788 | 5,870 | 18,625 |
| − 9,260 | + 2,149 | − 14,022 | + 4,366 | − 10,440 |
| 3,000 | 6,000 | 10,000 | 10,000 | 9,000 |

Estimate by rounding to the nearest dollar.

| 11. | 12. | 13. | 14. | 15. |
|---|---|---|---|---|
| $6.50 | $19.52 | $13.60 | $6.49 | $20.89 |
| + 3.25 | − 12.80 | + 5.80 | + 3.71 | + 3.90 |
| $10.00 | $ 7.00 | $20.00 | $10.00 | $25.00 |

**Set A** **For use after page 37**

Add.

| | | | | |
|---|---|---|---|---|
| **1.** 291<br>+ 439<br>730 | **2.** 875<br>+ 327<br>1,202 | **3.** 266<br>+ 478<br>744 | **4.** 893<br>+ 653<br>1,546 | **5.** 1,257<br>+ 3,669<br>4,926 |
| **6.** 8,575<br>+ 3,446<br>12,021 | **7.** 2,288<br>+ 623<br>2,911 | **8.** 3,497<br>+ 928<br>4,425 | **9.** 28,735<br>+ 16,884<br>45,619 | **10.** 67,343<br>+ 35,582<br>102,925 |
| **11.** \$3.92<br>+ 4.57<br>\$8.49 | **12.** \$27.93<br>+ 17.58<br>\$45.51 | **13.** \$32.65<br>+ 13.24<br>\$45.89 | **14.** \$542.18<br>+ 96.22<br>\$638.40 | **15.** \$789.79<br>+ 251.88<br>\$1,041.67 |

**Set B** **For use after page 39**

Add.

| | | | | |
|---|---|---|---|---|
| **1.** 239<br>87<br>+ 125<br>451 | **2.** 521<br>893<br>+ 326<br>1,740 | **3.** 1,297<br>793<br>+ 3,442<br>5,532 | **4.** 10,926<br>6,337<br>+ 15,488<br>32,751 | **5.** \$872.50<br>36.77<br>+ 96.48<br>\$1,005.75 |
| **6.** 1,175<br>228<br>312<br>+ 1,480<br>3,195 | **7.** 13,396<br>18,472<br>16,585<br>+ 21,929<br>70,382 | **8.** 28,194<br>61,462<br>31,221<br>+ 29,967<br>150,844 | **9.** \$125.79<br>89.62<br>105.37<br>+ 74.43<br>\$395.21 | **10.** \$312.99<br>287.43<br>364.31<br>+ 289.36<br>\$1,254.09 |

**Set C** **For use after page 41**

Subtract.

| | | | | |
|---|---|---|---|---|
| **1.** 611<br>− 329<br>282 | **2.** 471<br>− 393<br>78 | **3.** 1,952<br>− 1,899<br>53 | **4.** 3,926<br>− 477<br>3,449 | **5.** 5,855<br>− 3,286<br>2,569 |
| **6.** 11,966<br>− 3,429<br>8,537 | **7.** 13,341<br>− 9,755<br>3,586 | **8.** 23,113<br>− 14,754<br>8,359 | **9.** 15,282<br>− 9,336<br>5,946 | **10.** 88,753<br>− 87,995<br>758 |
| **11.** \$23.25<br>− 14.87<br>\$8.38 | **12.** \$34.17<br>− 12.93<br>\$21.24 | **13.** \$85.55<br>− 13.89<br>\$71.66 | **14.** \$251.14<br>− 147.92<br>\$103.22 | **15.** \$583.92<br>− 124.77<br>\$459.15 |



**Set A** **For use after page 43**

Subtract.

| | | | | |
|---|---|---|---|---|
| **1.** 803<br>− 125<br>678 | **2.** 980<br>− 297<br>683 | **3.** 1,208<br>− 543<br>665 | **4.** 2,004<br>− 1,885<br>119 | **5.** 3,080<br>− 1,762<br>1,318 |
| **6.** 3,000<br>− 1,793<br>1,207 | **7.** 4,080<br>− 1,296<br>2,784 | **8.** 13,031<br>− 8,542<br>4,489 | **9.** 5,008<br>− 4,397<br>611 | **10.** 6,093<br>− 4,399<br>1,694 |
| **11.** 26,000<br>− 13,345<br>12,655 | **12.** \$19.00<br>− 16.82<br>\$ 2.18 | **13.** \$33.00<br>− 25.87<br>\$ 7.13 | **14.** \$52.00<br>− 27.75<br>\$24.25 | **15.** \$40.00<br>− 23.12<br>\$16.88 |

**Set B** **For use after page 59**

Write >, <, or = for each ●.

**1.** 0.9 ● 0.09 > **2.** 3.2 ● 3.32 < **3.** 68.1 ● 68.11 < **4.** 0.303 ● 0.033 >

**5.** 4.51 ● 4.510 = **6.** 0.105 ● 0.099 > **7.** 0.999 ● 1 < **8.** 0.0009 ● 0.001 <

**9.** 2.0004 ● 1.999 > **10.** 0.0304 ● 0.340 < **11.** 8.891 ● 8.918 < **12.** 0.05103 ● 0.05310 <

Order the numbers from least to greatest.

**13.** 0.0312; 0.039; 0.0041; 0.0301; 0.0049
0.0041; 0.0049; 0.0301; 0.0312; 0.039

**14.** 0.1043; 0.0976; 0.0909; 0.1100; 0.1009
0.0909; 0.0976; 0.1009; 0.1043; 0.1100

**Set C** **For use after page 61**

Round to the nearest tenth.

**1.** 3.25 3.3 **2.** 0.064 0.1 **3.** 12.503 12.5 **4.** 0.882 0.9 **5.** 5.742 5.7

Round to the nearest hundredth.

**6.** 1.983 1.98 **7.** 6.0451 6.05 **8.** 0.057 0.06 **9.** 1.1192 1.12 **10.** 20.022 20.02

Round to the nearest whole number.

**11.** 8.5 9 **12.** 3.27 3 **13.** 16.0003 16 **14.** 54.587 55 **15.** 0.54 1

**Set A For use after page 65**

Add.

1. 5.8 + 3.2 = 9.0
2. 19.03 + 3.45 = 22.48
3. 0.88 + 0.93 = 1.81
4. 3.497 + 0.095 = 3.592
5. 0.53 + 3.877 = 4.407
6. 6.694 + 5.078 = 11.772
7. 68.35 + 18.29 = 86.64
8. $19.52 + 89.78 = $109.30
9. $355.85 + 576.92 = $932.77
10. 0.542 + 9.099 = 9.641
11. 6.2 + 3.3 + 4.8 = 14.3
12. 99.32 + 3.18 + 101.9 = 204.40
13. $33.25 + 9.85 + 62.15 = $105.25
14. $69.75 + 5.28 + 14.63 = $89.66
15. 0.30883 + 1.09203 + 0.35104 = 1.75190

**Set B For use after page 67**

Subtract.

1. 9.6 − 3.8 = 5.8
2. 80.71 − 16.25 = 64.46
3. 0.33 − 0.26 = 0.07
4. 1.511 − 0.367 = 1.144
5. 1.813 − 0.098 = 1.715
6. $0.92 − 0.87 = $0.05
7. $39.21 − 12.53 = $26.68
8. $100.05 − 87.66 = $ 12.39
9. $49.51 − 29.69 = $19.82
10. $13.22 − 11.09 = $ 2.13
11. 1.793 − 0.985 = 0.808
12. 30.226 − 5.908 = 24.318
13. 0.0185 − 0.0137 = 0.0048
14. $0.89 − 0.05 = $0.84
15. 5.3321 − 3.9874 = 1.3447

**Set C For use after page 85**

Multiply.

1. 42 × 2 = 84
2. 91 × 3 = 273
3. 27 × 7 = 189
4. 79 × 4 = 316
5. 57 × 8 = 456
6. 125 × 6 = 750
7. 723 × 4 = 2,892
8. 615 × 8 = 4,920
9. $2.59 × 7 = $18.13
10. 2,183 × 8 = 17,464
11. 4,619 × 3 = 13,857
12. $23.34 × 8 = $186.72
13. $87.95 × 7 = $615.65
14. 51,622 × 8 = 412,976
15. 31,409 × 4 = 125,636



**Set A For use after page 89**

Multiply.

1. 29 × 19 = 551
2. 35 × 27 = 945
3. 61 × 23 = 1,403
4. 127 × 17 = 2,159
5. 342 × 63 = 21,546
6. 1,205 × 21 = 25,305
7. 2,267 × 73 = 165,491
8. 4,967 × 44 = 218,548
9. 3,803 × 67 = 254,801
10. 4,571 × 89 = 406,819
11. $3.96 × 27 = $106.92
12. $7.82 × 37 = $289.34
13. $9.54 × 63 = $601.02
14. $17.84 × 76 = $1,355.84
15. $39.98 × 82 = $3,278.36

**Set B For use after page 95**

Multiply.

1. 205 × 124 = 25,420
2. 334 × 106 = 35,404
3. 218 × 292 = 63,656
4. 455 × 265 = 120,575
5. 807 × 700 = 564,900
6. 469 × 239 = 112,091
7. 625 × 304 = 190,000
8. 289 × 378 = 109,242
9. 567 × 899 = 509,733
10. 692 × 475 = 328,700
11. 711 × 243 = 172,773
12. 409 × 653 = 267,077
13. 788 × 526 = 414,488
14. 891 × 189 = 168,399
15. 322 × 486 = 156,492
16. 1,021 × 205 = 209,305
17. 2,416 × 315 = 761,040
18. 4,877 × 129 = 629,133
19. 6,697 × 872 = 5,839,784
20. 5,833 × 475 = 2,770,675

**Set C For use after page 110**

Estimate these quotients. Round so that you can use a basic fact.

1. 284 ÷ 7 40
2. 555 ÷ 8 70
3. 416 ÷ 7 60
4. 494 ÷ 7 70
5. 352 ÷ 68 5
6. 121 ÷ 32 4
7. 535 ÷ 61 9
8. 398 ÷ 84 5
9. 71)284 4
10. 54)295 6
11. 93)814 9
12. 63)1,781 30
13. 48)2,457 50
14. 587)4,217 7
15. 575)5,377 9
16. 921)8,079 9

**Set A For use after page 115**

Divide and check.

| | | | | |
|---|---|---|---|---|
| 1. 7)652 93 R1 | 2. 8)238 29 R6 | 3. 6)558 93 | 4. 5)3,182 636 R2 | 5. 7)6,118 874 |
| 6. 8)4,282 535 R2 | 7. 5)9,877 1,975 R2 | 8. 8)$36.48 $ 4.56 | 9. 7)$65.87 $ 9.41 | 10. 5)12,284 2,456 R4 |
| 11. 6)43,026 7,171 | 12. 9)61,911 6,879 | 13. 8)45,336 5,667 | 14. 7)31,283 4,469 | 15. 6)20,489 3,414 R5 |

**Set B For use after page 123**

Divide and check.

| | | | | |
|---|---|---|---|---|
| 1. 42)381 9 R3 | 2. 62)546 8 R50 | 3. 23)218 9 R11 | 4. 45)360 8 | 5. 72)655 9 R7 |
| 6. 95)760 8 | 7. 59)413 7 | 8. 61)317 5 R12 | 9. 75)450 6 | 10. 99)912 9 R21 |
| 11. 26)236 9 R2 | 12. 41)333 8 R5 | 13. 67)206 3 R5 | 14. 85)512 6 R2 | 15. 49)147 3 |

**Set C For use after page 124**

Divide. Watch for estimates that need to be changed.

| | | | | |
|---|---|---|---|---|
| 1. 52)315 6 R3 | 2. 58)563 9 R41 | 3. 26)210 8 R2 | 4. 53)368 6 R50 | 5. 84)589 7 R1 |
| 6. 36)183 5 R3 | 7. 68)333 4 R61 | 8. 43)426 9 R39 | 9. 73)442 6 R4 | 10. 56)506 9 R2 |
| 11. 23)206 8 R22 | 12. 38)267 7 R1 | 13. 69)278 4 R2 | 14. 93)553 5 R88 | 15. 54)436 8 R4 |

**Set D For use after page 127**

Divide and check.

| | | | | |
|---|---|---|---|---|
| 1. 23)1,035 45 | 2. 56)952 17 | 3. 61)1,586 26 | 4. 39)1,992 51 R3 | 5. 54)1,404 26 |
| 6. 57)3,881 68 R5 | 7. 35)4,486 128 R6 | 8. 53)21,889 413 | 9. 86)36,378 423 | 10. 87)49,245 566 R3 |
| 11. 69)24,702 358 | 12. 59)$316.24 $5.36 | 13. 48)$428.16 $8.92 | 14. 36)19,052 529 R8 | 15. 62)54,384 877 R10 |



**Set A For use after page 128**

Divide.

| | | | | |
|---|---|---|---|---|
| 1. 36)2,880 80 | 2. 56)2,270 40 R30 | 3. 25)777 31 R2 | 4. 23)2,392 104 | 5. 21)10,626 506 |
| 6. 57)11,630 204 R2 | 7. 41)21,735 530 R5 | 8. 13)1,380 106 R2 | 9. 26)13,026 501 | 10. 32)1,643 51 R11 |
| 11. 22)26,510 1,205 | 12. 28)58,912 2,104 | 13. 14)78,834 5,631 | 14. 41)43,043 1,049 R34 | 15. 35)105,160 3,004 R20 |

**Set B For use after page 129**

Divide.

| | | | |
|---|---|---|---|
| 1. 126)1,134 9 | 2. 523)4,184 8 | 3. 329)2,303 7 | 4. 488)2,932 6 R4 |
| 5. 255)2,300 9 R5 | 6. 417)3,344 8 R8 | 7. 536)2,687 5 R7 | 8. 369)2,796 7 R213 |
| 9. 584)3,237 5 R317 | 10. 214)7,490 35 | 11. 364)9,464 26 | 12. 599)38,935 65 |

**Set C For use after page 139**

Estimate the products by rounding so that you can use a basic fact.

| | | | | |
|---|---|---|---|---|
| 1. 4.8 × 3.2 = 15 | 2. 5.34 × 3 = 15 | 3. 9.26 × 3.44 = 27 | 4. 8.65 × 3.87 = 36 | 5. 2.042 × 3.24 = 6 |
| 6. 31.54 × 7.3 = 210 | 7. 83.64 × 4.12 = 320 | 8. 72.29 × 65.89 = 4,900 | 9. $26.67 × 4.9 = $150 | 10. $214.85 × 8.7 = $1,800 |

Estimate the quotients by rounding so that you can use a basic fact.

| | | | |
|---|---|---|---|
| 11. 6)289.41 50 | 12. 5.8)476.44 80 | 13. 8.7)541.92 60 | 14. 4.6)248.11 50 |
| 15. 5.4)$286.25 $60 | 16. 8.3)724.36 90 | 17. 8.8)814.46 90 | 18. 2.3)$136.42 $70 |

**Set A For use after page 141**

Multiply.

| | | | | |
|---|---|---|---|---|
| 1. 4.5 × 2.8<br>12.60 | 2. 7.9 × 8.4<br>66.36 | 3. 0.23 × 5<br>1.15 | 4. 3.79 × 4<br>15.16 | 5. 1.29 × 0.27<br>0.3483 |
| 6. 34.5 × 3.7<br>127.65 | 7. 9.24 × 5.8<br>53.592 | 8. 0.46 × 0.35<br>0.1610 | 9. $3.52 × 7.4<br>$26.048 | 10. $102.12 × 0.4<br>$40.848 |
| 11. 32.4 × 1.37<br>44.388 | 12. 1.334 × 0.9<br>1.2006 | 13. 91.45 × 8.1<br>740.745 | 14. 5.47 × 3.1<br>16.957 | 15. $209.25 × 1.13<br>$236.4525 |

**Set B For use after page 143**

Multiply.

| | | | | |
|---|---|---|---|---|
| 1. 0.2 × 0.9<br>0.18 | 2. 0.05 × 0.03<br>0.0015 | 3. 6.8 × 0.7<br>4.76 | 4. 3.08 × 0.07<br>0.2156 | 5. 12.26 × 0.005<br>0.06130 |
| 6. 25.03 × 0.2<br>5.006 | 7. $5.79 × 0.06<br>$0.3474 | 8. 89.22 × 0.13<br>11.5986 | 9. 0.062 × 0.07<br>0.00434 | 10. 124.3 × 0.006<br>0.7458 |
| 11. 324.7 × 0.09<br>29.223 | 12. 85.3 × 13.4<br>1,143.02 | 13. $17.69 × 0.08<br>$1.4152 | 14. 0.032 × 0.051<br>0.001632 | 15. 0.091 × 0.012<br>0.001092 |

**Set C For use after page 144**

Multiply. Write only the answers.

| | | | |
|---|---|---|---|
| 1. 8.51 × 10<br>85.1 | 2. 0.03 × 10<br>0.3 | 3. 10 × 5.921<br>59.21 | 4. 10 × 89.06<br>890.6 |
| 5. 0.029 × 10<br>0.29 | 6. 100 × 7.54<br>754 | 7. 12.3 × 100<br>1,230 | 8. 0.1 × 100<br>10 |
| 9. 100 × 5.003<br>500.3 | 10. 100 × 45.95<br>4,595 | 11. 1,000 × 0.07<br>70 | 12. 3.245 × 1,000<br>3,245 |
| 13. 0.29 × 1,000<br>290 | 14. 1,000 × 4.6<br>4,600 | 15. 1.000 × 0.79<br>790 | 16. 1,000 × 5.9<br>5,900 |



**Set A For use after page 149**

Divide. Check your answers.

| | | | | |
|---|---|---|---|---|
| 1. 7)5.81<br>0.83 | 2. 5)13.30<br>2.66 | 3. 9)27.45<br>3.05 | 4. 4)121.6<br>30.4 | 5. 7)36.61<br>5.23 |
| 6. 8)751.2<br>93.9 | 7. 5)0.310<br>0.062 | 8. 6)324.6<br>54.1 | 9. 7)65.87<br>9.41 | 10. 6)1.338<br>0.223 |
| 11. 23)94.53<br>4.11 | 12. 15)76.80<br>5.12 | 13. 24)77.28<br>3.22 | 14. 21)14.49<br>0.69 | 15. 54)46.98<br>0.87 |
| 16. 42)22.26<br>0.53 | 17. 36)122.76<br>3.41 | 18. 12)$63.72<br>$5.31 | 19. 14)$173.32<br>$ 12.38 | 20. 52)$117.52<br>$ 2.26 |

**Set B For use after page 151**

Find the quotients. Round to the nearest tenth.

| | | | | |
|---|---|---|---|---|
| 1. 4)13<br>3.3 | 2. 6)25<br>4.2 | 3. 7)62<br>8.9 | 4. 9)3.8<br>0.4 | 5. 14)72<br>5.1 |
| 6. 7)122<br>17.4 | 7. 23)89<br>3.9 | 8. 12)3.49<br>0.3 | 9. 15)61.2<br>4.1 | 10. 16)145<br>9.1 |

Find the quotients. Round to the nearest hundredth or cent.

| | | | | |
|---|---|---|---|---|
| 11. 8)3<br>0.38 | 12. 7)15<br>2.14 | 13. 13)20<br>1.54 | 14. 11)65<br>5.91 | 15. 15)25.3<br>1.69 |
| 16. 6)$2.98<br>$0.50 | 17. 6)$50.18<br>$ 8.36 | 18. 8)$12.85<br>$ 1.61 | 19. 14)$32.67<br>$ 2.33 | 20. 12)$27.44<br>$ 2.29 |

**Set C For use after page 152**

Divide. Write only the answers.

| | | | | |
|---|---|---|---|---|
| 1. 3.7 ÷ 10<br>0.37 | 2. 12.19 ÷ 10<br>1.219 | 3. 7.05 ÷ 10<br>0.705 | 4. 126 ÷ 10<br>12.6 | 5. 28.3 ÷ 10<br>2.83 |
| 6. 61.9 ÷ 100<br>0.619 | 7. 0.7 ÷ 100<br>0.007 | 8. 652.3 ÷ 100<br>6.523 | 9. 12 ÷ 100<br>0.12 | 10. 903 ÷ 100<br>9.03 |
| 11. 500 ÷ 1,000<br>0.5 | 12. 169 ÷ 1,000<br>0.169 | 13. 3.9 ÷ 1,000<br>0.0039 | 14. 38 ÷ 1,000<br>0.038 | 15. 457 ÷ 1,000<br>0.457 |

**Set A For use after page 157**

Divide. Round to the nearest hundredth when necessary.

1. 5.6)17.92 3.2 2. 2.1)8.61 4.1 3. 0.32)1.968 6.15 4. 0.04)0.2092 5.23

5. 4.7)2.444 0.52 6. 0.6)1.908 3.18 7. 4.6)8.694 1.89 8. 0.85)2.856 3.36

9. 0.05)1.237 24.74 10. 0.9)3.667 4.07 11. 0.004)0.014 3.5 12. 0.08)0.536 6.7

**Set B For use after page 159**

Divide. Check by multiplying.

1. 0.06)2.88 48 2. 0.003)0.078 26 3. 0.012)6.24 520 4. 0.09)86.4 960

5. 2.6)180 50 6. 6.1)244 40 7. 0.015)1.2 80 8. 0.28)140 500

9. 0.043)9.89 230 10. 1.5)8.4 5.6 11. 2.9)20.3 7 12. 0.044)35.2 800

**Set C For use after page 197**

Find the missing numerator or denominator.

1. $\frac{2}{3} = \frac{■}{18}$ 12 2. $\frac{1}{8} = \frac{■}{32}$ 4 3. $\frac{3}{5} = \frac{24}{■}$ 40 4. $\frac{4}{9} = \frac{■}{45}$ 20 5. $\frac{5}{6} = \frac{35}{■}$ 42

6. $\frac{2}{7} = \frac{12}{■}$ 42 7. $\frac{4}{5} = \frac{■}{20}$ 16 8. $\frac{3}{16} = \frac{■}{32}$ 6 9. $\frac{7}{10} = \frac{21}{■}$ 30 10. $\frac{11}{12} = \frac{55}{■}$ 60

Write one fraction equivalent to the given fraction. Sample answers are given.

11. $\frac{3}{10}$ $\frac{6}{20}$ 12. $\frac{4}{9}$ $\frac{8}{18}$ 13. $\frac{1}{6}$ $\frac{2}{12}$ 14. $\frac{4}{7}$ $\frac{8}{14}$ 15. $\frac{4}{11}$ $\frac{8}{22}$ 16. $\frac{3}{5}$ $\frac{6}{10}$ 17. $\frac{9}{10}$ $\frac{18}{20}$

**Set D For use after page 198**

Find the greatest common factor for each pair of numbers.

1. 8 20 4 2. 6 26 2 3. 20 16 4 4. 35 50 5 5. 16 48 16 6. 7 15 1

7. 21 28 7 8. 6 32 2 9. 8 52 4 10. 21 56 7 11. 24 60 12 12. 18 54 18



**Set A For use after page 199**

Write each fraction in lowest terms.

1. $\frac{6}{21}$ $\frac{2}{7}$ 2. $\frac{9}{30}$ $\frac{3}{10}$ 3. $\frac{8}{28}$ $\frac{2}{7}$ 4. $\frac{25}{40}$ $\frac{5}{8}$ 5. $\frac{15}{35}$ $\frac{3}{7}$ 6. $\frac{14}{42}$ $\frac{1}{3}$

7. $\frac{12}{32}$ $\frac{3}{8}$ 8. $\frac{18}{45}$ $\frac{2}{5}$ 9. $\frac{20}{42}$ $\frac{10}{21}$ 10. $\frac{36}{60}$ $\frac{3}{5}$ 11. $\frac{16}{20}$ $\frac{4}{5}$ 12. $\frac{24}{30}$ $\frac{4}{5}$

**Set B For use after page 200**

Write each improper fraction as a mixed number or whole number.

1. $\frac{10}{3}$ $3\frac{1}{3}$ 2. $\frac{22}{5}$ $4\frac{2}{5}$ 3. $\frac{22}{6}$ $3\frac{4}{6} = 3\frac{2}{3}$ 4. $\frac{33}{2}$ $16\frac{1}{2}$ 5. $\frac{56}{8}$ 7 6. $\frac{67}{10}$ $6\frac{7}{10}$

7. $\frac{37}{15}$ $2\frac{7}{15}$ 8. $\frac{29}{4}$ $7\frac{1}{4}$ 9. $\frac{28}{13}$ $2\frac{2}{13}$ 10. $\frac{44}{9}$ $4\frac{8}{9}$ 11. $\frac{95}{5}$ 19 12. $\frac{49}{6}$ $8\frac{1}{6}$

**Set C For use after page 201**

Write each mixed number as an improper fraction.

1. $2\frac{4}{5}$ $\frac{14}{5}$ 2. $1\frac{7}{10}$ $\frac{17}{10}$ 3. $5\frac{2}{9}$ $\frac{47}{9}$ 4. $3\frac{4}{7}$ $\frac{25}{7}$ 5. $5\frac{3}{8}$ $\frac{43}{8}$ 6. $4\frac{1}{10}$ $\frac{41}{10}$

7. $9\frac{5}{8}$ $\frac{77}{8}$ 8. $2\frac{7}{11}$ $\frac{29}{11}$ 9. $7\frac{3}{5}$ $\frac{38}{5}$ 10. $6\frac{5}{9}$ $\frac{59}{9}$ 11. $7\frac{2}{3}$ $\frac{23}{3}$ 12. $10\frac{1}{5}$ $\frac{51}{5}$

**Set D For use after page 202**

Write >, <, or = for each ●.

1. $\frac{5}{8}$ ● $\frac{7}{12}$ > 2. $\frac{2}{3}$ ● $\frac{4}{9}$ > 3. $\frac{4}{10}$ ● $\frac{6}{15}$ = 4. $\frac{2}{5}$ ● $\frac{3}{7}$ <

5. $2\frac{2}{3}$ ● $2\frac{3}{4}$ < 6. $1\frac{8}{10}$ ● $1\frac{12}{15}$ = 9. $5\frac{5}{9}$ ● $5\frac{4}{7}$ < 10. $3\frac{3}{5}$ ● $3\frac{4}{7}$ >

Compare the fractions or mixed numbers two at a time.
Then list them in order from least to greatest.

11. $\frac{3}{10}, \frac{2}{7}, \frac{2}{5}$ — $\frac{2}{7}, \frac{3}{10}, \frac{2}{5}$
12. $2\frac{4}{7}, 2\frac{1}{3}, 2\frac{9}{14}$ — $2\frac{1}{4}, 2\frac{4}{7}, 2\frac{9}{14}$
13. $\frac{2}{3}, \frac{5}{9}, \frac{4}{7}$ — $\frac{5}{9}, \frac{4}{7}, \frac{2}{3}$
14. $2\frac{1}{7}, \frac{7}{8}, 1\frac{1}{4}$ — $\frac{7}{8}, 1\frac{1}{4}, 2\frac{1}{7}$

**Set A For use after page 205**

Add or subtract.

1. $\frac{5}{6} + \frac{1}{6}$ $\quad \frac{6}{6} = 1$
2. $\frac{3}{11} + \frac{2}{11}$ $\quad \frac{5}{11}$
3. $\frac{4}{5} + \frac{3}{5}$ $\quad \frac{7}{5} = 1\frac{2}{5}$
4. $1\frac{4}{9} + 3\frac{2}{9}$ $\quad 4\frac{6}{9} = 4\frac{2}{3}$
5. $2\frac{3}{10} + 4\frac{1}{10}$ $\quad 6\frac{4}{10} = 6\frac{2}{5}$
6. $\frac{7}{8} - \frac{6}{8}$ $\quad \frac{1}{8}$
7. $\frac{9}{10} - \frac{3}{10}$ $\quad \frac{6}{10} = \frac{3}{5}$
8. $1\frac{7}{9} - 1\frac{5}{9}$ $\quad \frac{2}{9}$
9. $5\frac{4}{11} - 3\frac{2}{11}$ $\quad 2\frac{2}{11}$
10. $10\frac{4}{5} - 3\frac{1}{5}$ $\quad 7\frac{3}{5}$
11. $\frac{3}{8} - \frac{1}{8}$ $\quad \frac{2}{8} = \frac{1}{4}$
12. $\frac{4}{11} + \frac{3}{11}$ $\quad \frac{7}{11}$
13. $6\frac{5}{16} + 3$ $\quad 9\frac{5}{16}$
14. $2\frac{11}{16} - 1\frac{7}{16}$ $\quad 1\frac{4}{16} = 1\frac{1}{4}$
15. $3\frac{17}{30} + 4\frac{7}{30}$ $\quad 7\frac{24}{30} = 7\frac{4}{5}$

**Set B For use after page 207**

Find the least common denominator of these fractions.

1. $\frac{3}{8}, \frac{1}{16}$ 16
2. $\frac{5}{12}, \frac{1}{3}$ 12
3. $\frac{3}{4}, \frac{2}{7}$ 28
4. $\frac{1}{2}, \frac{3}{5}$ 10
5. $\frac{5}{8}, \frac{1}{6}, \frac{2}{3}$ 24
6. $\frac{3}{10}, \frac{3}{4}$ 20
7. $\frac{1}{2}, \frac{3}{20}$ 20
8. $\frac{5}{24}, \frac{7}{8}$ 24
9. $\frac{4}{5}, \frac{3}{7}$ 35
10. $\frac{2}{3}, \frac{7}{12}, \frac{4}{5}$ 60

**Set C For use after page 209**

Add.

1. $\frac{1}{8} + \frac{3}{4}$ $\quad \frac{7}{8}$
2. $\frac{2}{3} + \frac{1}{6}$ $\quad \frac{5}{6}$
3. $\frac{1}{10} + \frac{2}{5}$ $\quad \frac{5}{10} = \frac{1}{2}$
4. $\frac{5}{12} + \frac{1}{6}$ $\quad \frac{7}{12}$
5. $\frac{1}{4} + \frac{7}{8}$ $\quad \frac{9}{8} = 1\frac{1}{8}$
6. $\frac{1}{3} + \frac{2}{9}$ $\quad \frac{5}{9}$
7. $\frac{3}{8} + \frac{1}{10}$ $\quad \frac{19}{40}$
8. $\frac{2}{5} + \frac{3}{15}$ $\quad \frac{9}{15} = \frac{3}{5}$
9. $\frac{3}{20} + \frac{4}{5}$ $\quad \frac{19}{20}$
10. $\frac{3}{4} + \frac{4}{5}$ $\quad \frac{31}{20} = 1\frac{11}{20}$
11. $\frac{1}{8} + \frac{1}{6}$ $\quad \frac{7}{24}$
12. $\frac{3}{5} + \frac{2}{3}$ $\quad \frac{19}{15} = 1\frac{4}{15}$

Subtract.

13. $\frac{7}{12} - \frac{1}{2}$ $\quad \frac{1}{12}$
14. $\frac{9}{20} - \frac{2}{10}$ $\quad \frac{5}{20} = \frac{1}{4}$
15. $\frac{4}{9} - \frac{1}{3}$ $\quad \frac{1}{9}$
16. $\frac{3}{4} - \frac{7}{16}$ $\quad \frac{5}{16}$
17. $\frac{4}{5} - \frac{3}{4}$ $\quad \frac{1}{20}$
18. $\frac{5}{6} - \frac{5}{18}$ $\quad \frac{10}{18} = \frac{5}{9}$

423

**Set A For use after page 211**

Find the sums.

1. $3\frac{1}{2} + 2\frac{3}{8}$ $\quad 5\frac{7}{8}$
2. $10\frac{1}{6} + 3\frac{1}{12}$ $\quad 13\frac{3}{12} = 13\frac{1}{4}$
3. $1\frac{4}{5} + 3\frac{2}{15}$ $\quad 4\frac{14}{15}$
4. $10\frac{7}{9} + 25\frac{2}{3}$ $\quad 35\frac{13}{9} = 36\frac{4}{9}$
5. $16\frac{4}{5} + 17\frac{3}{20}$ $\quad 33\frac{19}{20}$
6. $1\frac{1}{2} + 3\frac{5}{8} + 7\frac{3}{16}$ $\quad 11\frac{21}{16} = 12\frac{5}{16}$
7. $24\frac{5}{9} + 14\frac{1}{3} + 6\frac{1}{6}$ $\quad 44\frac{19}{18} = 45\frac{1}{18}$
8. $33\frac{1}{5} + 2\frac{1}{2} + 17\frac{1}{6}$ $\quad 52\frac{26}{30} = 52\frac{13}{15}$
9. $15\frac{1}{3} + 41\frac{5}{6} + 29\frac{1}{6}$ $\quad 85\frac{8}{6} = 86\frac{1}{3}$
10. $68\frac{2}{3} + 9\frac{1}{4} + 10\frac{5}{12}$ $\quad 87\frac{16}{12} = 88\frac{1}{3}$

**Set B For use after page 213**

Subtract.

1. $6\frac{5}{6} - 5\frac{1}{3}$ $\quad 1\frac{3}{6} = 1\frac{1}{2}$
2. $10\frac{3}{4} - 7\frac{1}{8}$ $\quad 3\frac{5}{8}$
3. $13\frac{4}{5} - 5\frac{3}{10}$ $\quad 8\frac{5}{10} = 8\frac{1}{2}$
4. $11\frac{7}{8} - 6\frac{5}{16}$ $\quad 5\frac{9}{16}$
5. $5\frac{5}{9} - 4\frac{1}{3}$ $\quad 1\frac{2}{9}$
6. $20\frac{11}{12} - 15\frac{3}{4}$ $\quad 5\frac{2}{12} = 5\frac{1}{6}$
7. $16\frac{4}{9} - 7\frac{1}{6}$ $\quad 9\frac{5}{18}$
8. $12\frac{4}{5} - 12\frac{2}{3}$ $\quad \frac{2}{15}$
9. $8\frac{3}{4} - 3\frac{2}{5}$ $\quad 5\frac{7}{20}$
10. $9\frac{5}{6} - 7\frac{3}{4}$ $\quad 2\frac{1}{12}$
11. $27\frac{3}{5} - 17\frac{1}{7}$ $\quad 10\frac{16}{35}$
12. $19\frac{3}{10} - 17\frac{1}{5}$ $\quad 2\frac{1}{10}$
13. $27\frac{7}{8} - 15\frac{1}{3}$ $\quad 12\frac{13}{24}$
14. $11\frac{5}{6} - 10\frac{1}{12}$ $\quad 1\frac{9}{12} = 1\frac{3}{4}$
15. $9\frac{5}{6} - 8\frac{7}{9}$ $\quad 1\frac{1}{18}$

**Set C For use after page 215**

Subtract.

1. $3\frac{1}{7} - 1\frac{5}{7}$ $\quad 1\frac{3}{7}$
2. $4\frac{1}{5} - 2\frac{3}{10}$ $\quad 1\frac{9}{10}$
3. $7 - 3\frac{5}{6}$ $\quad 3\frac{1}{6}$
4. $10\frac{3}{8} - 9\frac{3}{4}$ $\quad \frac{5}{8}$
5. $15\frac{2}{9} - 8\frac{5}{6}$ $\quad 6\frac{7}{18}$
6. $11\frac{1}{4} - 8\frac{5}{6}$ $\quad 2\frac{5}{12}$
7. $10\frac{3}{10} - 7\frac{7}{10}$ $\quad 2\frac{6}{10} = 2\frac{3}{5}$
8. $20\frac{2}{5} - 9\frac{2}{3}$ $\quad 10\frac{11}{15}$
9. $17\frac{3}{5} - 13\frac{5}{6}$ $\quad 3\frac{23}{30}$
10. $30\frac{1}{12} - 2\frac{2}{9}$ $\quad 27\frac{31}{36}$

424

**Set A For use after page 231**

Find the product in lowest terms.

1. $\frac{9}{20} \times \frac{2}{9}$ $\frac{1}{10}$
2. $\frac{4}{5} \times \frac{1}{2}$ $\frac{2}{5}$
3. $\frac{2}{5} \times \frac{5}{6}$ $\frac{1}{3}$
4. $\frac{2}{3} \times \frac{5}{6}$ $\frac{5}{9}$
5. $\frac{10}{9} \times \frac{9}{10}$ $1$
6. $\frac{2}{3} \times \frac{12}{19}$ $\frac{8}{19}$
7. $\frac{4}{9} \times \frac{27}{28}$ $\frac{3}{7}$
8. $\frac{3}{5} \times \frac{10}{27}$ $\frac{2}{9}$
9. $\frac{3}{2} \times \frac{6}{7}$ $\frac{9}{7} = 1\frac{2}{7}$
10. $\frac{3}{14} \times 7$ $\frac{3}{2} = 1\frac{1}{2}$
11. $\frac{3}{7} \times \frac{14}{15}$ $\frac{2}{5}$
12. $\frac{2}{17} \times \frac{34}{35}$ $\frac{4}{35}$
13. $9 \times \frac{5}{81}$ $\frac{5}{9}$
14. $\frac{5}{3} \times \frac{33}{35}$ $\frac{11}{7} = 1\frac{4}{7}$
15. $\frac{39}{49} \times \frac{7}{13}$ $\frac{3}{7}$

**Set B For use after page 233**

Find the product in lowest terms.

1. $1\frac{1}{3} \times 4\frac{1}{2}$ $6$
2. $1\frac{3}{8} \times 1\frac{3}{5}$ $2\frac{1}{5}$
3. $2\frac{2}{3} \times 3$ $8$
4. $4\frac{2}{7} \times \frac{2}{5}$ $1\frac{5}{7}$
5. $1\frac{5}{9} \times 3\frac{6}{7}$ $6$
6. $12 \times 1\frac{5}{6}$ $22$
7. $3\frac{1}{3} \times 1\frac{3}{5}$ $5\frac{1}{3}$
8. $2\frac{2}{5} \times 20$ $48$
9. $3\frac{3}{7} \times 3\frac{1}{2}$ $12$
10. $2\frac{1}{3} \times 1\frac{5}{28}$ $2\frac{3}{4}$
11. $18 \times 2\frac{1}{9}$ $38$
12. $3\frac{3}{5} \times 5\frac{1}{2}$ $19\frac{4}{5}$

**Set C For use after page 236**

Write the lowest-terms fraction or mixed number for each decimal.

1. 0.2 $\frac{1}{5}$
2. 0.15 $\frac{3}{20}$
3. 3.65 $3\frac{13}{20}$
4. 0.01 $\frac{1}{100}$
5. 7.02 $7\frac{1}{50}$
6. 5.075 $5\frac{3}{40}$
7. 0.045 $\frac{9}{200}$
8. 8.062 $8\frac{31}{500}$
9. 9.55 $9\frac{11}{20}$
10. 2.6 $2\frac{3}{5}$
11. 75.085 $75\frac{17}{200}$
12. 0.001 $\frac{1}{1,000}$
13. 3.24 $3\frac{6}{25}$
14. 0.128 $\frac{16}{125}$
15. 0.012 $\frac{3}{250}$

**Set D For use after page 237**

Write a decimal for each fraction.

1. $\frac{3}{5}$ 0.6
2. $\frac{3}{10}$ 0.3
3. $\frac{37}{100}$ 0.37
4. $\frac{7}{4}$ 1.75
5. $\frac{9}{5}$ 1.8
6. $\frac{7}{10}$ 0.7
7. $\frac{1}{20}$ 0.05
8. $\frac{5}{2}$ 2.5
9. $\frac{9}{8}$ 1.125
10. $\frac{1}{5}$ 0.2
11. $\frac{91}{100}$ 0.91
12. $\frac{13}{8}$ 1.625
13. $\frac{9}{4}$ 2.25
14. $\frac{5}{16}$ 0.3125
15. $\frac{9}{20}$ 0.45
16. $\frac{9}{16}$ 0.5625
17. $\frac{23}{20}$ 1.15
18. $\frac{189}{100}$ 1.89



**Set A For use after page 241**

Find the quotients.

1. $\frac{1}{3} \div \frac{1}{6}$ $2$
2. $8 \div \frac{4}{5}$ $10$
3. $\frac{11}{12} \div \frac{11}{12}$ $1$
4. $\frac{4}{3} \div \frac{5}{12}$ $\frac{16}{5} = 3\frac{1}{5}$
5. $\frac{4}{5} \div 6$ $\frac{2}{15}$
6. $\frac{3}{8} \div \frac{3}{16}$ $2$
7. $\frac{2}{3} \div \frac{4}{15}$ $\frac{5}{2} = 2\frac{1}{2}$
8. $\frac{4}{5} \div 12$ $\frac{1}{15}$
9. $\frac{7}{20} \div \frac{14}{15}$ $\frac{3}{8}$
10. $\frac{5}{8} \div \frac{5}{6}$ $\frac{3}{4}$
11. $\frac{2}{7} \div \frac{3}{14}$ $\frac{4}{3} = 1\frac{1}{3}$
12. $3 \div \frac{9}{10}$ $\frac{10}{3} = 3\frac{1}{3}$
13. $\frac{4}{9} \div \frac{5}{12}$ $\frac{16}{15} = 1\frac{1}{15}$
14. $\frac{3}{10} \div \frac{9}{40}$ $\frac{4}{3} = 1\frac{1}{3}$
15. $\frac{9}{8} \div \frac{3}{16}$ $6$

**Set B For use after page 243**

Divide and check.

1. $1\frac{2}{3} \div 3\frac{3}{4}$ $\frac{4}{9}$
2. $6\frac{1}{8} \div 1\frac{3}{4}$ $3\frac{1}{2}$
3. $9 \div 3\frac{3}{8}$ $2\frac{2}{3}$
4. $2\frac{1}{3} \div 4\frac{2}{3}$ $\frac{1}{2}$
5. $4\frac{1}{6} \div 2\frac{1}{2}$ $1\frac{2}{3}$
6. $1\frac{3}{7} \div 2\frac{6}{7}$ $\frac{1}{2}$
7. $6\frac{3}{8} \div 5\frac{2}{3}$ $1\frac{1}{8}$
8. $\frac{9}{10} \div 3\frac{3}{5}$ $\frac{1}{4}$
9. $4\frac{4}{5} \div 12$ $\frac{2}{5}$
10. $4\frac{2}{7} \div 2\frac{1}{7}$ $2$
11. $9\frac{1}{7} \div 2\frac{2}{7}$ $4$
12. $3\frac{5}{9} \div 5\frac{1}{3}$ $\frac{2}{3}$
13. $7\frac{1}{2} \div 2\frac{2}{5}$ $3\frac{1}{8}$
14. $2\frac{1}{5} \div \frac{11}{15}$ $3$
15. $3\frac{3}{4} \div 1\frac{9}{16}$ $2\frac{2}{5}$

**Set C For use after page 303**

Write each decimal as a percent.

1. 0.36 36%
2. 0.28 28%
3. 0.02 2%
4. 0.17 17%
5. 0.07 7%
6. 0.92 92%

Write each fraction as a percent.

7. $\frac{13}{100}$ 13%
8. $\frac{79}{100}$ 79%
9. $\frac{85}{100}$ 85%
10. $\frac{1}{100}$ 1%
11. $\frac{25}{100}$ 25%
12. $\frac{112}{100}$ 112%

Write each percent as a decimal.

13. 89% 0.89
14. 54% 0.54
15. 12% 0.12
16. 60% 0.60
17. 39% 0.39
18. 99% 0.99

Write each percent as a fraction in lowest terms.

19. 80% $\frac{4}{5}$
20. 11% $\frac{11}{100}$
21. 24% $\frac{6}{25}$
22. 46% $\frac{23}{50}$
23. 75% $\frac{3}{4}$
24. 90% $\frac{9}{10}$

**Set A For use after page 305**

Find an equivalent fraction with denominator 100. Then write a percent for each fraction.

1. $\frac{9}{10}$ $\frac{90}{100}$, 90% 2. $\frac{3}{4}$ $\frac{75}{100}$, 75% 3. $\frac{11}{50}$ $\frac{22}{100}$, 22% 4. $\frac{4}{5}$ $\frac{80}{100}$, 80% 5. $\frac{17}{20}$ $\frac{85}{100}$, 85% 6. $\frac{4}{25}$ $\frac{16}{100}$, 16%

7. $\frac{4}{20}$ $\frac{20}{100}$, 20% 8. $\frac{15}{30}$ $\frac{50}{100}$, 50% 9. $\frac{9}{15}$ $\frac{60}{100}$, 60% 10. $\frac{42}{56}$ $\frac{75}{100}$, 75% 11. $\frac{12}{40}$ $\frac{30}{100}$, 30% 12. $\frac{20}{25}$ $\frac{80}{100}$, 80%

Divide to find a decimal or mixed decimal for each fraction. Then write the decimal as a percent.

13. $\frac{1}{3}$ $0.33\frac{1}{3}$, $33\frac{1}{3}$% 14. $\frac{3}{8}$ $0.37\frac{1}{2}$, $37\frac{1}{2}$% 15. $\frac{2}{5}$ 0.40, 40% 16. $\frac{3}{10}$ 0.30, 30% 17. $\frac{4}{7}$ $0.57\frac{1}{7}$, $57\frac{1}{7}$% 18. $\frac{4}{9}$ $0.44\frac{4}{9}$, $44\frac{4}{9}$%

19. $\frac{5}{6}$ $0.83\frac{1}{3}$, $83\frac{1}{3}$% 20. $\frac{9}{8}$ $1.12\frac{1}{2}$, $112\frac{1}{2}$% 21. $\frac{5}{16}$ $0.31\frac{1}{4}$, $31\frac{1}{4}$% 22. $\frac{4}{3}$ $1.33\frac{1}{3}$, $133\frac{1}{3}$% 23. $\frac{1}{11}$ $0.09\frac{1}{11}$, $9\frac{1}{11}$ 24. $\frac{1}{12}$ $0.08\frac{1}{3}$, $8\frac{1}{3}$%

**Set B For use after page 306**

Write a decimal and a lowest-terms fraction for each percent.

1. 25% 0.25, $\frac{1}{4}$ 2. 30% 0.30, $\frac{3}{10}$ 3. 14% 0.14, $\frac{7}{50}$ 4. 43% 0.43, $\frac{43}{100}$ 5. 32% 0.32, $\frac{8}{25}$

6. 85% 0.85, $\frac{17}{20}$ 7. $6\frac{1}{2}$% 0.065, $\frac{13}{200}$ 8. 48% 0.48, $\frac{12}{25}$ 9. 115% 1.15, $1\frac{3}{20}$ 10. $3\frac{2}{5}$% 0.034, $\frac{17}{500}$

11. $20\frac{1}{2}$% 0.205, $\frac{41}{200}$ 12. 64% 0.64, $\frac{16}{25}$ 13. $\frac{1}{2}$% 0.005, $\frac{1}{200}$ 14. $21\frac{1}{5}$% 0.212, $\frac{53}{250}$ 15. 144% 1.44, $1\frac{11}{25}$

**Set C For use after page 309**

Find the percent of each number.

1. 75% of 20 15 2. 21% of 13 2.73 3. $12\frac{1}{2}$% of 400 50 4. 67% of 35 23.45

5. 60% of 30 18 6. 72% of 150 108 7. $37\frac{1}{2}$% of 24 9 8. 25% of 160 40

9. 39% of 80 31.2 10. $87\frac{1}{2}$% of 480 420 11. 14% of 25 3.50 12. 71% of 55 39.05



**Set A For use after page 369**

Find the sums.

1. $^-4 + {}^-7$ $^-11$ 2. $^+3 + {}^+5$ $^+8$ 3. $^-2 + {}^-8$ $^-10$ 4. $^+8 + {}^+5$ $^+13$

5. $^-3 + {}^-8$ $^-11$ 6. $^-7 + {}^-9$ $^-16$ 7. $^+4 + {}^+10$ $^+14$ 8. $^+5 + {}^+1$ $^+6$

9. $^+6 + {}^+4$ $^+10$ 10. $^-3 + {}^-12$ $^-15$ 11. $^-1 + {}^-7$ $^-8$ 12. $^-10 + {}^-2$ $^-12$

**Set B For use after page 371**

Find the sums.

1. $^+8 + {}^-3$ $^+5$ 2. $^-3 + {}^-8$ $^-11$ 3. $^+11 + {}^+2$ $^+13$ 4. $^-9 + {}^+3$ $^-6$

5. $^+2 + {}^-4$ $^-2$ 6. $^-15 + {}^+8$ $^-7$ 7. $^-7 + {}^-2$ $^-9$ 8. $^+10 + {}^+5$ $^+15$

9. $^-7 + {}^-9$ $^-16$ 10. $^+5 + {}^+6$ $^+11$ 11. $^+3 + {}^-11$ $^-8$ 12. $^-5 + {}^-7$ $^-12$

**Set C For use after page 373**

Find the differences. Thinking of addends and a sum may help you.

1. $\overset{s}{^+3} - \overset{a}{^-9} = \overset{a}{n}$ $^+12$ 2. $\overset{s}{^-2} - \overset{a}{^+5} = \overset{a}{n}$ $^-7$ 3. $\overset{s}{^+2} - \overset{a}{^-5} = \overset{a}{n}$ $^+7$

4. $\overset{s}{^-1} + \overset{a}{^+7} = \overset{a}{n}$ $^+6$ 5. $\overset{s}{^+3} - \overset{a}{^+8} = \overset{a}{n}$ $^-5$ 6. $\overset{s}{^+6} - \overset{a}{^-8} = \overset{a}{n}$ $^+14$

7. $\overset{s}{^+2} - \overset{a}{^+7} = \overset{a}{n}$ $^-5$ 8. $\overset{s}{^+5} - \overset{a}{^-5} = \overset{a}{n}$ $^+10$ 9. $\overset{s}{^-5} + \overset{a}{^+6} = \overset{a}{n}$ $^+1$

**Set D For use after page 376**

Write > or < for each ●.

1. $^+5$ ● $^-3$ > 2. $^-8$ ● $^-7$ < 3. $^-2$ ● $^+4$ < 4. $^-5$ ● $^-9$ >

5. $^+3$ ● $^-4$ > 6. $^+6$ ● $^-5$ > 7. $^-7$ ● $^-20$ > 8. $^+1$ ● $^-12$ >

9. $^-10$ ● $^-2$ < 10. $^+2$ ● $^-1$ > 11. $^-4$ ● $^+3$ < 12. 0 ● $^-7$ >

Order from greatest to least.

13. $^-10$, $^-18$, $^+5$, $^+1$, $^+12$, 0
$^+12$, $^+5$, $^+1$, 0, $^-10$, $^-18$

14. $^+1$, $^-4$, $^+8$, $^+4$, $^-10$, $^+2$
$^+8$, $^+4$, $^+2$, $^+1$, $^-4$, $^-10$

15. $^-12$, $^-15$, $^-6$, $^-30$, $^-10$, $^-8$
$^-6$, $^-8$, $^-10$, $^-12$, $^-15$, $^-30$

## TABLE OF MEASURES

| Metric System | | Customary System | |
|---|---|---|---|
| **Length** | | | |
| 1 centimeter (cm) | 10 millimeters (mm) | 1 foot (ft) | 12 inches (in.) |
| 1 decimeter (dm) | 100 millimeters (mm)<br>10 centimeters (cm) | 1 yard (yd) | 36 inches (in.)<br>3 feet (ft) |
| 1 meter (m) | 1,000 millimeters (mm)<br>100 centimeters (cm)<br>10 decimeters (dm) | 1 mile (m) | 5,280 feet (ft)<br>1,760 yards (yd) |
| 1 kilometer (km) | 1,000 meters (m) | | |
| **Area** | | | |
| 1 square meter ($m^2$) | 100 square decimeters ($dm^2$)<br>10,000 square centimeters ($cm^2$) | 1 square foot ($ft^2$) | 144 square inches ($in.^2$) |
| **Volume** | | | |
| 1 cubic decimeter ($dm^3$) | 1,000 cubic centimeters ($cm^3$)<br>1 liter (L) | 1 cubic foot ($ft^3$) | 1,728 cubic inches ($in.^3$) |
| **Capacity** | | | |
| 1 teaspoon | 5 milliliters (mL) | 1 cup (c) | 8 fluid ounces (fl oz) |
| 1 tablespoon | 12.5 milliliters (mL) | 1 pint (pt) | 16 fluid ounces (fl oz)<br>2 cups (c) |
| 1 liter (L) | 1,000 milliliters (mL)<br>1,000 cubic centimeters ($cm^3$)<br>1 cubic decimeter ($dm^3$)<br>4 metric cups | 1 quart (qt) | 32 fluid ounces (fl oz)<br>4 cups (c)<br>2 pints (pt) |
| | | 1 gallon (gal) | 128 fluid ounces (fl oz)<br>16 cups (c)<br>8 pints (pt)<br>4 quarts (qt) |
| **Weight** | | | |
| 1 gram (g) | 1,000 milligrams (mg) | 1 pound (lb) | 16 ounces (oz) |
| 1 kilogram (kg) | 1,000 grams (g) | | |
| **Time** | | | |
| 1 minute (min) | 60 seconds (s) | 1 year (yr) | 365 days<br>52 weeks<br>12 months |
| 1 hour (h) | 60 minutes (min) | | |
| 1 day (d) | 24 hours (h) | | |
| 1 week (w) | 7 days (d) | 1 decade | 10 years |
| 1 month (mo) | about 4 weeks | 1 century | 100 years |

## GLOSSARY

**a.m.** A way to indicate time from 12:00 midnight to 12:00 noon.

**acute angle** An angle that has a measure less than 90°.

**acute triangle** A triangle in which each angle has a measure less than 90°.

**addend** One of the numbers to be added.

Example: 3 + 5 = 8 (3 and 5 are addends)

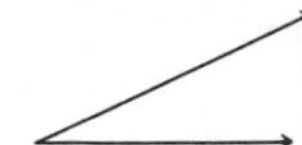

**addition** An operation that gives the total number when two or more numbers are put together.

**angle** Two rays from a single point.

**area** The measure of a region, expressed in square units.

**average** The quotient obtained when the sum of a set of numbers is divided by the number of addends.

**bit** Binary digit, 0 or 1.

**capacity** The volume of a space figure given in terms of liquid measurement.

**central angle** An angle whose vertex is the center of a circle.

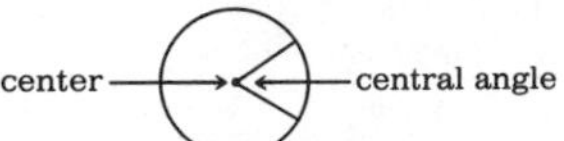


**chord** A segment containing any two points of a circle.

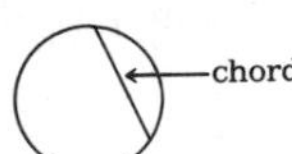


**circle** A plane figure in which all the points are the same distance from a point called the center.

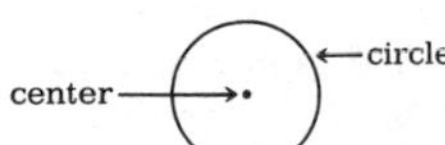


**circumference** The distance around a circle.

**common factor** A number that is a factor of two different numbers is a common factor of those two numbers.

**common multiple** A number that is a multiple of two different numbers is a common multiple of those two numbers.

**compass** An instrument used to make circles.

**composite number** A whole number greater than 1 that has more than two factors.

**cone** A space figure with one circular face and one vertex.

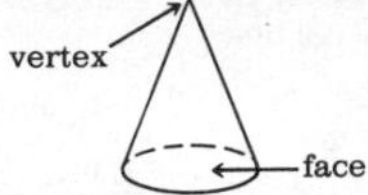


**congruent figures** Figures that have the same size and shape.

**coordinates** Number pair used in graphing.

**cross products** Products obtained by multiplying the numerator of one fraction by the denominator of a second fraction, and the denominator of the first fraction by the numerator of the second fraction.

**cube** A space figure whose faces are all squares.

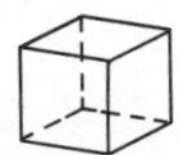

**customary units of measure** See Table of Measures, page 429.

**data** Information.

**data bank** A place where information is stored.

**decagon** A polygon with 10 sides.

**decimal** Any base-ten numeral written using a decimal point.

3.2 ← decimal
↑
decimal point

**degree** A unit of angle measure.

**degree Celsius** (°C) A metric unit for measuring temperature.

**degree Fahrenheit** (°F) A customary unit for measuring temperature.

**denominator** The number below the line in a fraction.

$\frac{3}{4}$ ← denominator

**diagonal** A segment, other than a side, connecting two vertices of a polygon.

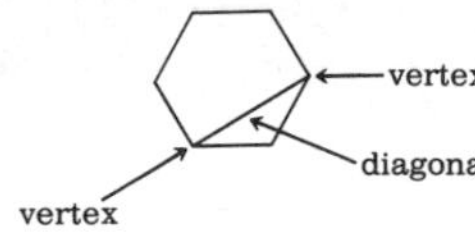

**diameter** A chord that passes through the center of a circle.

diameter

center

**difference** The number obtained by subtracting one number from another.

Example: $\begin{array}{r} 9 \\ -\ 4 \\ \hline 5 \end{array}$ ← difference

**digits** The symbols used to write numerals: 0, 1, 2, 3, 4, 5, 6, 7, 8, and 9.

**dividend** A number to be divided.

$7\overline{)28}$ with quotient 4 ← dividend

**division** An operation that tells how many sets or how many in each set.

**divisor** The number by which a dividend is divided.

divisor ⟶ $7\overline{)28}$ with quotient 4

**edge** One of the segments making up any of the faces of a space figure.

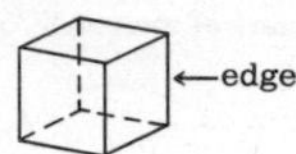


**END** An instruction in a computer program that tells the computer to stop.

**equality** (equals, or =) A mathematical relation of being exactly the same.

**equally likely outcomes** Outcomes that have the same chance of occurring.

**equal ratios** Ratios that give the same comparison. $\frac{9}{27}$ and $\frac{1}{3}$ are equal ratios.

**equation** A number sentence involving the use of the equality symbol.

Example: $9 + 2 = 11$

**equilateral triangle** A triangle with all 3 sides the same length and all angles the same measure.

**equivalent fractions** Fractions that name the same amount.

Example: $\frac{1}{2}$ and $\frac{2}{4}$

**estimate** To find an answer that is close to the exact answer.

**even number** A whole number that has 0, 2, 4, 6, or 8 in the ones place.

**expanded form** A way to write numbers that shows the place value of each digit.

Example: $9{,}000 + 300 + 20 + 5$

**exponent** A number that tells how many times another number is to be used as a factor

$5 \cdot 5 \cdot 5 = 5^3$ ← exponent ← base

**face** One of the plane figures (regions) making up a space figure.

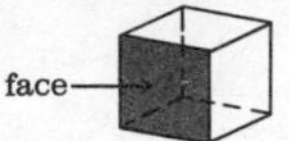


**factors** Numbers that are combined in the multiplication operation to give a number called the product.

$6 \times 7 = 42$
↖ ↗
factors

**flowchart** A chart that shows a step-by-step way of doing something.

**fraction** A number that expresses parts of a whole or a set.

Example: $\frac{3}{4}$

**GOTO** An instruction in a computer program that causes the computer to skip to a specified line in the program.

**graph** A picture that shows information in an organized way.

**greater than** (>) The relationship of one number being larger than another number.

Example: $6 > 5$, read "6 is greater than 5."

**greatest common factor (GCF)** The greatest number that is a factor of each of two numbers.

**grouping (associative) property** When adding (or multiplying) three or more numbers, the grouping of the addends (or factors) can be changed and the sum (or product) is the same.

Examples: $2 + (8 + 6) = (2 + 8) + 6$
$3 \times (4 \times 2) = (3 \times 4) \times 2$

**hexagon** A polygon with six sides.

**improper fraction** A fraction in which the numerator is greater than or equal to the denominator.

**INPUT** An instruction in a computer program that causes the computer to stop and request data while running a program.

**integers** The whole numbers together with their negatives.

Examples: $^-5$, 0, 23

**isosceles triangle** A triangle with at least 2 sides the same length and at least 2 angles the same measure.

**least common denominator (LCD)** The least common multiple of two denominators.

**least common multiple (LCM)** The smallest nonzero number that is a multiple of each of two given numbers.

**less than (<)** The relationship of one number being smaller than another number.

Example: $5 < 6$, read "5 is less than 6."

**line** A straight path that is endless in both directions.

**line of symmetry** A line on which a figure can be folded so that the two parts fit exactly.

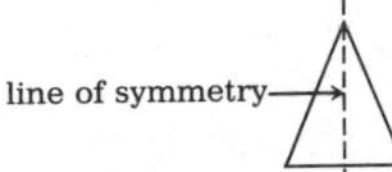


**LIST** A copy of a set of instructions that tells a computer what to do.

**Logo** A computer language that can be used for computer graphics.

**lowest terms** A fraction is in lowest terms if the numerator and denominator have no common factor greater than 1.

**mean** The quotient obtained when the sum of two or more numbers is divided by the number of addends.

**median** The middle number of a set of numbers that are arranged in order.

**metric units of measure** See Table of Measures, page 429.

**mixed decimal** A combination of a decimal and a fraction, such as $0.4\frac{1}{3}$.

**mixed number** A number that has a whole number part and a fraction part, such as $2\frac{3}{4}$.

**mode** In a list of data, the number or item that occurs most often. There may be more than one mode.

**multiple** A number that is the product of a given number and a whole number.

**multiplication** An operation that combines two numbers, called factors, to give one number, called the product.

**negative integer** Any number in the set $\{^-1, ^-2, ^-3, \ldots\}$

**number line** A line that shows numbers in order.

Example:

7 8 9 10

**numeral** A symbol for a number.

**numerator** The number above the line in a fraction.

$\frac{3}{4}$ ← numerator

**obtuse angle** An angle with a measure greater than 90° and less than 180°.

**obtuse triangle** A triangle with one angle measuring more than 90°.

**octagon** A polygon with 8 sides.

**odd number** A whole number that has 1, 3, 5, 7, or 9 in the ones place.

**one property** In multiplication, when either factor is 1, the product is the other factor.

**order (commutative) property** When adding (or multiplying) two or more numbers, the order of the addends (or factors) can be changed and the sum (or product) is the same.

Examples: $4 \times 5 = 5 \times 4$
$2 \times 3 = 3 \times 2$

**ordered pair** Two numbers that are used to give the location of a point on a graph.

**origin** The intersection of the coordinate axes; the point associated with the ordered pair (0,0).

**outcome** A possible result in a probability experiment.

**p.m.** A way to indicate time from 12:00 noon to 12:00 midnight.

**parallel lines** Two lines that lie in the same plane and do not intersect.

**parallelogram** A quadrilateral with two pairs of parallel sides.

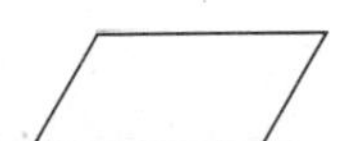

**pentagon** A polygon with five sides.

**percent (%)** Per 100; a way to compare a number with 100.

**perimeter** The distance around a figure.

**perpendicular lines** Two lines that intersect at right angles.

**pi** ($\pi$) The ratio of the circumference of a circle to its diameter. $\pi \approx 3.14$.

**place value** The value given to the place a digit occupies in a number.

Example: 3 5 6
hundreds place (3)
tens place (5)
ones place (6)

**plane figure** A figure that lies on a flat surface.

Examples: square triangle circle

**point** A single, exact location, often represented by a dot.

**polygon** A closed figure formed by line segments.

**polyhydron** A space figure whose faces are polygons.

**positive integer** Any number in the set {1, 2, 3, . . . }

**prime number** A number that has exactly 2 factors (the number itself and 1).

**PRINT** An instruction in a computer program that tells a computer to type something.

**prism** A space figure whose bases are congruent polygons in parallel planes and whose faces are parallelograms.

**probability** The probability that an event will occur in a set of equally likely outcomes is the number of ways the event can occur divided by the total number of possible outcomes.

**product** The result of the multiplication operation.

Example: $6 \times 7 = 42$ ← product

**program** A set of instructions that tells a computer what to do.

**proportion** A statement that two ratios are equal.

Example: $\frac{6}{9} = \frac{2}{3}$

**protractor** An instrument used for measuring angles.

**pyramid** A space figure whose base is a polygon and whose faces are triangles with a common vertex.

**quotient** The number (other than the remainder) that is the result of the division operation.

Examples: $45 \div 9 = 5$ (5 = quotient); $7\overline{)42}$ with 6 ← quotient

**radius** A segment from the center of a circle to a point on the circle.

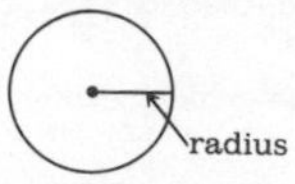

radius

**ratio** A pair of numbers used in making certain comparisons. The ratio of 3 to 4 can be written $\frac{3}{4}$.

**ray** A part of a line, having only one end point.

ray

**reciprocal** Two numbers are reciprocals if their product is 1. 5 and $\frac{1}{5}$ are reciprocals.

**rectangle** A quadrilateral that has four right angles.

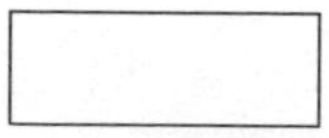

**regular polygon** A polygon with all sides the same length and all angles the same measure.

**remainder** The number less than the divisor that remains after the division process is completed.

Example: $7\overline{)47}$ = 6, 42, 5 ← remainder

**repeating decimal** A decimal with digits which from some point on repeat periodically. 6.2835835 . . . and 0.33333 . . . are repeating decimals. They may also be written $6.2\overline{835}$ and $0.\overline{3}$ respectively.

**rhombus** A quadrilateral with all sides the same length.

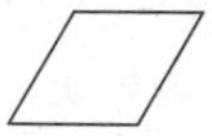

**right angle** An angle that has a measure of 90°.

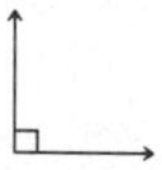

**right triangle** A triangle that has one right angle.

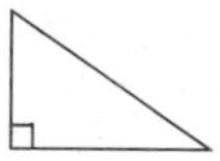

**Roman numerals** Numerals used by the Romans.

Examples: I = 1, V = 5, VI = 6

**rounding** Replacing specific numbers with numbers expressed in even units, such as tens, hundreds, or thousands.

Example: 23 rounded to the nearest 10 is 20.

**RUN** A command that tells the computer to execute a program.

**scale drawing** A drawing of an object made so that distances in the drawing are proportional to actual distances.

**scalene triangle** A triangle with no sides the same length and no angles the same measure.

**scientific notation** A system of writing a number as the product of a power of 10 and a number between 1 and 10.

Example: $2{,}300{,}000 = 2.3 \times 10^6$

**segment** A straight path from one point to another.

**similar figures** Two figures that have the same shape.

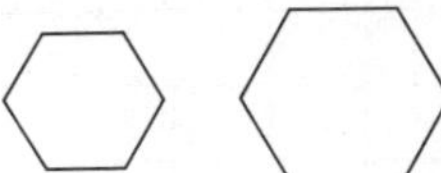

**space figure** A figure that has volume.

Examples:

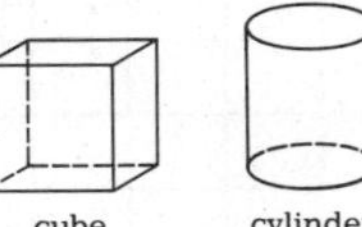


**sphere** A space figure in which all the points are the same distance from a center point.

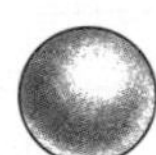

**square** A quadrilateral with four right angles and all sides the same length.

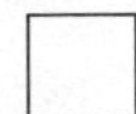

**subtraction** An operation that tells the difference between two numbers, or how many are left when some are taken away.

**sum** The number obtained by adding numbers.

Example:
$$\begin{array}{r} 3 \\ +\ 2 \\ \hline 5 \end{array} \leftarrow \text{sum}$$

**surface area** The sum of the areas of all the faces of a space figure.

**symmetric figure** A plane figure that can be folded in half so that the two halves match.

**trading** To make a group of ten from one of the next highest place value, or one from ten of the next lowest place value. Examples: one hundred can be traded for ten tens; ten ones can be traded for one ten.

**trapezoid** A quadrilateral with one pair of parallel sides.

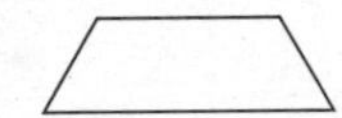

**triangle** A polygon with three sides.

**unit** An amount or quality used as a standard of measurement. See Table of Measures, page 429.

**vertex** (vertices) The point that the two rays of an angle have in common. Also, the common point of any two sides of a polygon.

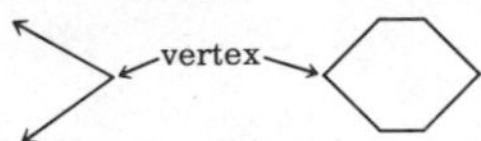


**volume** The number of cubic units of space that a space figure holds.

**whole number** Any number in the set {0, 1, 2, 3, . . .}.

**zero property** In addition, when one addend is 0, the sum is the other addend. In multiplication, when either factor is 0, the product is 0.

# Materials

This list is helpful in gathering and organizing materials that could be used for activities in each chapter.

| Useful Materials for Book 6 | Chapter 1 | 2 | 3 | 4 | 5 | 6 | 7 | 8 | 9 | 10 | 11 | 12 | 13 | 14 | 15 | 16 |
|---|---|---|---|---|---|---|---|---|---|---|---|---|---|---|---|---|
| abacus | | √ | | | | | | | | | | | | | | |
| cards, number* | √ | √ | √ | | | | | √ | | | | | | | | |
| compass | | | | | | | | | | | | | √ | √ | √ | |
| containers (cup, pint, quart, gallon) | | | | | | | √ | | √ | | | | | √ | | √ |
| containers (liter) | | | | | | | | √ | | | | | | | | |
| counters (beads, beans, buttons, chips, etc.) | | | | | | | | | | | √ | √ | √ | | | |
| cube, number | √ | √ | | √ | | | | | √ | | | | | √ | √ | |
| decimal models | | | √ | | | √ | | | √ | | | √ | | | | |
| dot arrays* | | | | | | √ | | | √ | | | √ | | √ | | |
| egg cartons | | | | | | | | | √ | | | | | | | |
| fraction models | | | | | | | | √ | √ | | √ | √ | | | | |
| geoboards | | | | | | | | | | √ | | | | √ | | |
| geometric models | | | | | | | | | | √ | √ | | | √ | | |
| grids, 10 by 10* | | | √ | | √ | | | | | √ | | √ | | | √ | |
| graph paper, centimeter* | | | √ | √ | √ | | √ | | √ | | √ | √ | √ | √ | | |
| graph, paper, fourth-inch* | | | | | | | | | √ | | | | | | | |
| graph paper inch* | √ | | | | | | | | √ | | | | √ | | | √ |
| hundred chart | √ | √ | | | | | | √ | √ | | √ | √ | | | | |
| interlocking cubes | √ | √ | √ | | | √ | | √ | √ | | √ | √ | | | | |
| meter sticks | | | | | | | √ | | | | | √ | | | | |
| number lines* | | √ | √ | | | √ | | √ | √ | | | | | | √ | |
| place-value models (base-20 blocks, counters etc.) | | √ | √ | √ | | √ | | | | | | | | | | |
| play money | | | √ | | | | | | | | | | | | | |
| probability devices | | | | | | | | | | | | | | √ | | |
| protractor | | | | | | | | | | √ | √ | | | | | |
| ruler, inch | | | | | | | | | √ | √ | | | | | | |
| ruler, metric | | | | | | | √ | | | | | | | | | |
| scale, metric | | | | | | | √ | | | | | | | | | |
| spinners | | √ | | √ | | | | | | | | | √ | | | |
| tangrams* | | | | | | | | | | √ | | | | | | |
| thermometer, Celsius | | | | | | | √ | | | | | | | | | √ |
| thermometer, Fahrenheit | | | | | | | √ | | | | | | | | | √ |
| yardsticks | | | | | | | | | | | | | | | | √ |

*A form of this material is available in the Teaching Aids section of the Teachers Resource Book.

Two courses of instruction help in pacing lessons throughout the school year.

## Long-Range Planning Chart

| Chapter | Minimum Course | Maximum Course |
|---|---|---|
| 1 Basic Facts | 8 days<br>pp. 1–15, 17–19, 22 | 6 days<br>pp. 1–22 |
| 2 Whole Numbers: Addition and Subtraction | 12 days<br>pp. 23–47, 49–52 | 9 days<br>pp. 23–52 |
| 3 Decimals: Addition and Subtraction | 10 days<br>pp. 53–67, 70–73, 75–78 | 8 days<br>pp. 53–78 |
| 4 Multiplication | 10 days<br>pp. 79–91, 94–99, 101–103, 106 | 11 days<br>pp. 79–106 |
| 5 Division | 12 days<br>pp. 107–131, 133–136 | 11 days<br>pp. 107–136 |
| 6 Decimals: Multiplication and Division | 13 days<br>pp. 137–161, 163–166 | 12 days<br>pp. 137–166 |
| 7 Measurement: Metric Units | 10 days<br>pp. 167–185, 187, 189–192 | 9 days<br>pp. 167–192 |
| 8 Addition and Subtraction of Fractions | 12 days<br>pp. 193–217, 219–221, 224 | 13 days<br>pp. 193–224 |
| **Mid-Year Review** | 3 days | 2 days |
| 9 Fractions: Multiplication and Division | 11 days<br>pp. 225–245, 247–250 | 12 days<br>pp. 225–250 |
| 10 Geometry | 10 days<br>pp. 251–271, 273–276 | 9 days<br>pp. 251–276 |
| 11 Ratio and Proportion | 8 days<br>pp. 277–287, 290–291, 293, 295–298 | 10 days<br>pp. 277–298 |
| 12 Percent | 8 days<br>pp. 299–313, 315–317, 320 | 10 days<br>pp. 299–320 |
| 13 Graphing and Probability | 8 days<br>pp. 321–329, 332–333, 335–337, 341–344 | 10 days<br>pp. 321–344 |
| 14 Perimeter, Area, Volume | 8 days<br>pp. 345–359, 361–364 | 9 days<br>pp. 345–364 |
| 15 Integers | 7 days<br>pp. 365–377, 381–384 | 9 days<br>pp. 365–384 |
| 16 Measurement: Customary Units | 7 days<br>pp. 385–399, 401–403, 406 | 8 days<br>pp. 385–406 |
| **End-of-Year Review** | 3 days | 2 days |
| **Total:** | 160 days | 160 days |

# Bibliography

## Books for the Teacher


Ashlock, Robert B. *Error Patterns in Computation: A Semi-Programmed Approach,* 3rd ed. Columbus, OH: Merrill, 1972.

Baratta-Lorton, Robert. *Mathematics—A Way of Thinking.* Menlo Park, CA: Addison-Wesley, 1977.

Barnett, Carne S., and Sharon Young. *Teaching Kids Math: Problem-Solving Activities to Help Young Children Learn and Enjoy Mathematics.* Englewood Cliffs, NJ: Prentice-Hall, 1982.

Biggs, Edith E., and James R. Maclean. *Freedom to Learn: An Active Learning Approach to Mathematics.* Don Mills, Ontario: Addison-Wesley Canada, 1969.

Billstein, Richard, Schlomo Libeskind, and Johnny W. Lott. *A Problem Solving Approach to Mathematics for Elementary School Teachers.* Menlo Park, CA: Benjamin/Cummings, 1981.

Bitter, Gary G., Jerald L. Mikesell, and Kathryn Maudeff. *Activities Handbook for Teaching the Metric System.* Boston: Allyn and Bacon, 1976.

Brandes, L. G. *Math Can Be Fun.* Portland, ME: J. Weston Walch, 1975.

Buxton, Laurie. *Do You Panic About Maths? Coping with Math Anxiety.* Exeter, NH: Heinemann Educational Books, 1981.

Caravella, Joseph R. *Minicalculators in the Classroom.* Reston, VA: National Council of Teachers of Mathematics, 1977.

Charles, R. I., et al. *Problem-Solving Experiences in Mathematics.* Menlo Park, CA: Addison-Wesley, 1984.

Charles, R. I., and F. K. Lester. *Problem Solving: What, Why, and How.* Palo Alto, CA: Dale Seymour, 1982.

Copeland, Richard W. *How Children Learn Mathematics.* New York: Macmillan, 1974.

Dumas, Enoch. *Math Activities for Child Involvement,* 2nd ed. Boston: Allyn and Bacon, 1977.

Jerman, Max, and Edward Beardslee. *Elementary Mathematical Methods.* New York: McGraw-Hill, 1978.

Johnson, D. A. *Games for Learning Mathematics.* Portland, ME: J. Weston Walch, 1978.

Kane, R. B., M. A. Byrne, and M. A. Hater. *Helping Children Read Mathematics.* New York: American Book, 1974.

Kennedy, Leonard, and Ruth Michon. *Games for Individualizing Mathematics Learning.* Columbus, OH: Merrill, 1973.

Kurtz, V. Ray. *Teaching Metric Awareness.* St. Louis: C. V. Mosby, 1976.

Litwiller, Bonnie H., and David R. Duncan. *Activities for the Maintenance of Computational Skills and Discovery of Patterns.* Reston, VA: National Council of Teachers of Mathematics, 1980.

*Metric System, The.* Menlo Park, CA: Addison-Wesley, 1974.

National Council of Teachers of Mathematics. *Applications in School Mathematics: 1979 Yearbook.* Reston, VA: National Council of Teachers of Mathematics, 1979.

________. *Developing Computational Skills: 1978 Yearbook.* Reston, VA: National Council of Teachers of Mathematics, 1978.

________. *Mathematics for the Middle Grades: 1982 Yearbook.* Reston, VA: National Council of Teachers of Mathematics, 1982.

________. *Problem Solving in School Mathematics: 1980 Yearbook.* Reston, VA: National Council of Teachers of Mathematics, 1980.

O'Daffer, P., and S. Clemens. *Geometry: An Investigative Approach.* Menlo Park, CA: Addison-Wesley, 1976.

________. *Metric Measurement for Teachers: An Activity Approach.* Menlo Park, CA: Addison-Wesley, 1976.

Papert, Seymour. *Mindstorms: Children, Computers, and Powerful Ideas.* New York: Basic Books, 1980.

Phillips, J. *Right Angles: Paper-Folding Geometry.* New York: Thomas Y. Crowell, 1972.

Piaget, Jean. *The Child's Conception of Number.* New York: Norton, 1965.

Pine, T. S., and J. Levine. *Measurements and How We Use Them.* New York: McGraw-Hill, 1974.

Rade, Lennart, and Burt A. Kaufman. *Adventures with Your Hand Calculator.* St. Louis: CERMEL, 1977.

Rudolph, W. B., and A. D. Claassen. *The Calculator Book.* Boston: Houghton Mifflin, 1976.

Ryan, W. T., and P. T. Vest. *Modern Metrics Made Easy.* Chicago: Clearvue, 1976.

Sentlowitz, Michael, and James M. Thelen. *Baseball: A Game of Numbers.* Menlo Park, CA: Addison-Wesley, 1977.

________, and Margaret Trivisone. *Dice and Dots.* Menlo Park, CA: Addison-Wesley, 1979.

Shoecraft, Paul Joseph, and Terry James Clukey. *The Mad Minute.* Menlo Park, CA: Addison-Wesley, 1981.

Skolnick, Joan, Carol Langbort, and Lucille Day. *How To Encourage girls in Math and Science: Strategies for Parents and Educators.* Englewood Cliffs, NJ: Prentice-Hall, 1982.

Smith, Seaton E., Jr., and Carl A. Backman. *Games and Puzzles for Elementary and Middle School Mathematics: Readings from the Arithmetic Teacher.* Reston, VA: National Council of Teachers of Mathematics, 1975.

Spencer, D. D. *The Story of Computers.* Ormond Beach, FL: Abacus Computer, 1975.

Suydam, Marilyn N., and Donald J. Desart. *Classroom Ideas from Research on Computational Skills.* Reston, VA: National Council of Teachers of Mathematics, 1976.

Thornburg, David D. *Picture This! An Introduction to Computer Graphics for Kids of All Ages.* Menlo Park, CA: Addison-Wesley, 1982.

________. *Picture This Too! An Introduction to Computer Graphics for Kids of All Ages.* Menlo Park, CA: Addison-Wesley, 1982.

Thornton, Carol A., et al. *Teaching Mathematics to Children with Special Needs.* Menlo Park, CA: Addison-Wesley, 1982.

Walls, F. *First Book of Puzzles and Brain Twisters.* New York: Franklin Watts, 1970.

Woodward, Dolores M. *Mainstreaming the Learning Disabled Adolescent: A Manual of Strategies and Materials.* Rockville, MD: Aspen Systems, 1981.


## Recommended Periodicals


*Arithmetic Teacher.* Reston, VA: National Council of Teachers of Mathematics.

*Instructor.* New York: Instructor Publications, Inc.

*Mathematics Teacher.* Reston, VA: National Council of Teachers of Mathematics.

## Books for the Student

Adler, David, and Byron Barton. *Roman Numerals.* New York: Thomas Y. Crowell, 1977.
Aho, Carolyn, et al. *Measure Matters* Level C. Palo Alto, CA: Creative Publications, 1976.
Armstrong, Louise. *How to Turn Lemons into Money.* New York: Harcourt Brace Jovanovich, 1976.
Ball, Marion J., and Sylvia Charp. *Be a Computer Literate.* Morristown, NJ: Creative Computing, 1977.
Barnett, Carne. *Metric Ease.* Palo Alto, CA: Creative Publications, 1975.
Barson, Alan. *Motivational Games for Mathematics.* Warrington, PA: Fabmath, 1981.
Bauman, Hans. *What Time Is It Around the World?* New York: Scroll Press, 1979.
Bitter, Gary G., and Thomas H. Metes. *Exploring with Pocket Calculators.* New York: Messner, 1977.
Brandes, L. G. *Math Can Be Fun.* Portland, ME: J. Weston Walch, 1975.
Branley, Franklyn M. *Weight and Weightlessness.* New York: Thomas Y. Crowell, 1972.
Charosh, Mannis. *Mathematical Games for One or Two.* New York: Thomas Y. Crowell, 1972.
_______. *Number Ideas Through Pictures.* New York: Thomas Y. Crowell, 1974.
D'Amato, Alex, and Janet D'Amato. *Galaxy Games.* New York: Doubleday, 1981.
D'Ignazio, Fred. *Creative Kids' Guide to Home Computers.* New York: Doubleday, 1981.
Doty, Roy, and Leonard Maar. *How Much Does America Cost?* New York: Doubleday, 1979.
Evans, Larry. *Three-Dimensional Mazes.* San Francisco: Troubador Press, 1976.
Fair, Jan. *Handy Math: Focus on Earning Money.* Palo Alto, CA: Creative Publications, 1981.
_______. *Handy Math: Focus on Managing Money.* Palo Alto, CA: Creative Publications, 1981.
Froman, Robert. *Angles Are Easy as Pie.* New York: Thomas Y. Crowell, 1976.
_______. *The Greatest Guessing Game.* New York: Thomas Y. Crowell, 1978.
Goeller, Lee. *How to Make an Adding Machine: That Even Adds Roman Numerals.* New York: Harcourt Brace Jovanovich, 1979.
Goodman, J. J. *The Maze Book.* Hayward, CA: Activity Resources, 1974.
Hahn, James, and Lynn Hahn. *The Metric System.* New York: Franklin Watts, 1975.
Heller, Ruth. *Designs for Coloring.* New York: Grosset & Dunlop, 1976.
Jacobs, Allan D., and Leland B. Jacobs, eds. *Arithmetic in Verse and Rhyme.* Champaigne, IL: Garrard, 1971.
James, Elizabeth, and Carol Barkin. *What Do You Mean by "Average"? Means, Medians, and Modes.* New York: Lothrop, 1978.
Jesperson, James, and Jane Fitz-Randolph. *Time and Clocks for the Space Age.* New York: Atheneum, 1979.
Leighton, Ralph, and Carl Feynman. *How to Count Sheep Without Falling Asleep.* New York: Prentice-Hall, 1976.
Levitin, Sonia. *The Mark of Conte.* New York: Atheneum, 1979.
Linn, Charles F. *Estimation.* New York: Thomas Y. Crowell, 1972.
Lowenstein, Dyno. *Graphs.* New York: Franklin Watts, 1976.
Madison, Arnold, and David L. Drotar. *Pocket Calculators: How to Use and Enjoy Them.* New York: Thomas Nelson, 1978.
Maher, John E. *Ideas About Measuring and Accounting.* New York: Franklin Watts, 1974.
Morgan, Tom. *Money, Money, Money: How to Get and Keep It.* New York: Putnam, 1978.
Murphy, Elaine C. *Developing Skills with Tables and Graphs.* Palo Alto, CA: Dale Seymour, 1981.
Nation, R. *Meters, Liters, and Grams: Understanding the Metric System.* New York: Hawthorn, 1974.
Phillips, J. *Right Angles: Paper-Folding Geometry.* New York: Thomas Y. Crowell, 1972.
Pine, T. S., and J. Levine. *Measurements and How We Use Them.* New York: McGraw-Hill, 1974.
Polis, A. Richard, Earl Beard, and Fred Donatucci. *Magic Squares and Arrays.* Warrington, PA: Fabmath, 1980.
Rice, Trevor. *Mathematical Games and Puzzles.* New York: St. Martin's, 1974.
Riedel, Manfred G. *Odds and Chances for Kids: A Look at Probability.* Englewood Cliffs, NJ: Prentice-Hall, 1979.
Spencer, Donald D. *Exploring the World of Computers.* Ormond Beach, FL: Camelot, 1982.
Srivastava, Jane Jonas. *Area.* New York: Thomas Y. Crowell, 1974.
Stern, David P. *Math Squared: Graph Paper Activities for Fun and Fundamentals.* New York: Teachers College Press, 1981.
Trivett, John V. *Building Tables on Tables: A Book About Multiplication.* New York: Thomas Y. Crowell, 1975.
Wallach, Paul J. *Meet the Metric System.* Belmont, CA: Pitman Learning, 1980.
Yeager, David Clark. *Mystery Story Problems: Division Facts.* Palo Alto, CA: Creative Publications, 1981.
_______. *Mystery Story Problems: Mixed Multiplication and Division Facts.* Palo Alto, CA: Creative Publications, 1981.
_______. *Mystery Story Problems: Multiplication Facts.* Palo Alto, CA: Creative Publications, 1981.

## Software

Battling Bugs/Concentration (Apple II Plus, Atari). St. Louis: Milliken.
Bumble Plot (Apple). Menlo Park, CA: The Learning Company.
Computer Math Activities (Apple). Menlo Park, CA: Addison-Wesley.
Computer Math Games (Apple). Menlo Park, CA: Addison-Wesley.
Delta Drawing (Apple, Atari, IBM). Cambridge, MA: Spinnaker.
Fractions (Apple II, TRS-80). Portland, OR: Quality Educational Designs.
Frenzy/Flip Flop (Apple II Plus, Atari). St. Louis: Milliken.
Milliken Math Fun! Series (Apple, Atari). St. Louis: Milliken.

# Index

*Teacher's Edition references are in italics.*

# Index

# Acknowledgments

## Photographs

**Craig Aurness/West Light:** 108 top
**Frank Balthis:** 293
**Tom Bean/Tom Stack & Associates:** 380 center
**Bill Benoit/Atoz Images:** 199
**Marc Bernheim/Woodfin Camp & Associates:** 345
**L. Blair/Woodfin Camp & Associates:** 164
**Elihu Blotnick*:** 380 top
**Sisse Brimberg/Woodfin Camp & Associates:** 64, 65
**Broderick/International Stock Photography Ltd.:** 58
**© Jerry Cooke/Earth Scenes:** 325
**Library of Congress:** 125
**Gerald A. Corsi/Tom Stack & Associates:** 377 center
**Culver Pictures:** 88
**J. DiMaggio/Focus On Sports:** 98
**Fawcett/Animals, Animals:** 342
**N. Flabi/Taurus Photos:** 241
**Focus On Sports:** 72, 120, 187, 193, 306
**Stephen Frisch:** 40, 41, 409
**Stephen Frisch*:** 1, 35, 47, 51, 79, 94, 109, 113, 170, 185, 210, 214, 215 top, 222, 225, 226, 244, 245, 251, 263, 279, 318, 332, 368, 374 top, 385, 388 top
**George Fry III*:** 105
**Mickey Gibson/Animals, Animals:** 316
**Stewart Green/Tom Stack & Associates,** 236 top
**Tom & Michele Grimm/International Stock Photography Ltd.:** 114
**Bob Hamburgh/Tom Stack & Associates:** 308
**Phil & Loretta Herman/Tom Stack & Associates:** 274
**Randall Hyman:** 53
**Jet Propulsion Lab:** 62
**Breck Kent/Animals, Animals,** 167
**Pierre Kopp/West Light:** 73 right
**Wayland Lee*/Addison-Wesley Publishing Company:** 6, 7, 11, 15, 28, 55, 56, 135, 144, 149 right, 181, 184, 196, 198, 203, 209, 215 bottom, 227, 266, 282, 283, 302, 314, 334, 336, 337, 360, 380 bottom, 383, 388 bottom, 394, 400
**Zig Leszczynski/Animals, Animals:** 248
**Willard Luce/Animals, Animals:** 102
**Steve Martin/Tom Stack & Associates:** 152
**Fred Mayer/Woodfin Camp & Associates:** 382
**David Mazonowicz/Monkmeyer Press Photo Service:** 36, 37
**Robert McClanahan/International Stock Photography Ltd.:** 84
**Dan McConnell/Atoz Images:** 23
**Dan McCoy/Rainbow:** 405
**R. Mendonca/Tom Stack & Associates:** 121
**Stephen Meyers/Animals, Animals:** 153
**Gary Milburn/Tom Stack & Associates:** 296
**Warren Morgan/Focus On Sports:** 159
**Kal Muller/Woodfin Camp & Associates:** 76
**Keith Murami/Tom Stack & Associates:** 149 left
**NASA:** 63, 142, 236 bottom, 365 top, 365 center, 375
**Mark Newman/Tom Stack & Associates:** 321 bottom
**Marvin Newman/Woodfin Camp & Associates:** 148
**Charles O'Rear/West Light:** 108 center
**Brian Parker/Tom Stack & Associates:** 190, 321 top, 377 top
**Stacy Pick/Stock, Boston:** 57
**Richard Pulling/Focus On Sports:** 29, 131
**Scott Ransom/Taurus Photos:** 362
**Ed Robinson/Tom Stack & Associates:** 2
**Ed Rooney/International Stock Photography:** 73 left
**Bill Ross/West Light:** 115
**L. L. Rue/Atoz Images:** 18, 220
**Kevin Schafer/Tom Stack & Associates:** 134
**Sepp Seitz/Woodfin Camp & Associates:** 299
**Sourciat/Animals, Animals:** 50
**Tom Stack/Tom Stack & Associates:** 10, 237 top
**Bill Stanton/International Stock Photography Ltd.:** 99
**Scott Thode/International Stock Photography Ltd.:** 96
**Jerry Wachter/Focus On Sports:** 340
**Bruce M. Willman/Tom Stack & Associates:** 137
**Rollie Wilson/Focus On Sports:** 324
**Ed Wolff/Earth Scenes:** 330
**Jim Yuskovitch/Tom Stack & Associates:** 21

Cover Photograph:
**© 1981 Jim Tuten/Black Star**

Special thanks to Mount Zion Hospital and Medical Center, San Francisco, for the use of their facilities for the photograph taken on page 185 and to the Federal Aviation Administration, San Francisco Airport Tower, for the use of their facilities for the photograph taken on page 222.

*Photographs provided expressly for the publisher.

# Acknowledgements


## Illustrations

**Robert Bausch** 392
**Elizabeth Callen** 138–139, 232–233, 338–339
**Dick Cole** 150–151, 212
**Betsy Day** 92
**Rae Ecklund** 128–129, 217, 230–231, 356–357
**Lisa French** 284–285
**Jon Goodell** 80–81
**John E. Hendrick** 322–323, 370
**Roberta Holmes** 328, 372
**Barbara Hoopes** 290–291, 295 upper right, 312–313
**Larry Hughston** 24–25, 90–91, 278–279
**Susan Jaekel** 4, 16, 32–33, 48, 74, 100, 122–123, 132, 140–141, 155, 162, 172–173, 188, 199, 218, 246, 272, 294, 300–301, 335, 352–353, 354, 390–391, 407, 410
**Heather King** 228, 252, 258, 260, 262
**Dennis Leatherman** 8–9
**Susan Lexa** 12–13, 68–69
**Marlene May** 174–175
**Jane McCreary** 168, 171, 182, 189, 194–195, 297, 326–327, 348–349, 386, 395
**Jim M'Guinness** 280–281
**Debby Morse** 70–71, 97, 180, 200–201, 256–257, 270–271
**Masami Miyamoto** 88, 254, 288–289, 295 upper left, 346–347, 350–351, 358–359, 393, 398–399, 401
**Dennis Nolan** 60–61, 116–117
**Bill Ogden** 86
**Sharron O'Neil** 242
**Kevin O'Shea** 82–83, 103, 124, 160, 179, 204, 206
**Ed Parker** 26–27
**Sandra Popovich** 191
**Blanche Sims** 110–111, 239, 311, 396–397
**Doug Smith** 1, 23, 30–31, 42–43, 45, 53, 79, 107, 137, 146–147, 167, 193, 225, 251, 277, 299, 321, 345, 365, 385
**Sandra Speidel** 38–39, 66–67
**Robert Steele** 14
**Michael G. Surles** 126–127
**Cynthia Swann-Brodie** 77, 112, 176–177, 178, 234–235, 265, 304–305, 366

## Editorial and Design Staff

**Project Manager** Rosalie Whitlock
**Student Edition Editors** Jerry Patterson, Susan Kimber
**Teacher's Edition Editors** Margaret Shanney, Katharine Fitch
**Project Designer** Don Taka
**Student Editions Designer** Ellen Schmutz
**Project Photo Editor** Margee Huntzicker